LESKO'S INFO-POWER

First Edition

by

MATTHEW LESKO

Editor: Andrew Naprawa

Research Director: Toni Murray

Researchers:

Claire Capretta
Patricia Dickey
Laura Hovenier
Kim Walker-Klarman
Judy Marcus
Mary Ann Martello
Shirley Massman
Roger Munter
Debbie Samson
Carol Sargent
Pam Schultz

LESKO'S INFO-POWER. Copyright 1990 by Matthew Lesko. All rights reserved. Printed in the United States of America.
Published by Information USA, Inc., P.O. Box E, Kensington, MD 20895

FIRST EDITION

Cover Design: Sally Whitehead

Photo: George Tames

Library of Congress Cataloging-in-Publication Data

Lesko, Matthew.

Lesko's Info-Power sourcebook.

ISBN #1-878346-02-4 (paperback)

Other books written by Matthew Lesko:

Getting Yours: The Complete Guide to Government Money

How to Get Free Tax Help

Information USA

The Computer Data and Database Source Book

The Maternity Sourcebook

Lesko's New Tech Sourcebook

The Investor's Information Sourcebook

The Federal Database Finder

The State Database Finder

Government Giveaways for Entrepreneurs

T O

all the federal and state bureaucrats who

eagerly share information that empowers us

to pursue our goals and dreams

Table of Contents

Introduction

Thank you for buying, borrowing, or stealing my book. I have spent over 15 years using and compiling government information. Even though I've written over 40 books on the subject, it is my hope that with every book, I get better at it. I believe that this is my best ever and I hope you can get good use out of *Info-Power*.

WARNING: THIS BOOK IS OUT OF DATE

You have to realize that the moment any book is printed, it is out of date. Especially this one with its 30,000 sources. A book of this size is sure to have some telephone numbers that have changed. But don't be discouraged. You can live with these small inconveniences. If you are calling a government office listed in the book and the telephone number gets you a local diner or some other wrong number, here's what you can do.

* Call the operator for the area and ask for the number of the office you're after. The directory assistance operator can be located by dialing the area code followed by 555-1212. To inquire about a toll-free number, call directory assistance at (800) 555-1212.

* Or, call us at (301) 369-1519. We will try and help you in anyway we can.

You can keep up to date with the information in this book by ordering our new editions when they become available. Each new edition will not only verify all the sources identified in the book but we plan on adding new information as well as new chapters and much more. We hope to be publishing updates every year.

You can also keep current by accessing this information online, via computer, through COMPUSERVE. We will be constantly updating this information on this computer service. For subscription information to COMPUSERVE call (800) 848-8199 in Columbus, Ohio. Thanks again for your interest in this book. I hope you will feel free to call with your comments and questions.

Happy Hunting,

Matthew Lesko

Information Is Power

Information is the key to opportunities. It's essential for all the important aspects of life:

* making the right investment,
* choosing the right career,
* seeking the latest medical cure, or
* buying at the best price.

But why, if we are living in an information society, do most of us base our decisions on hearsay, headlines, outdated or incomplete information? I think there are two reasons which explain this paradox:

* information overload, and
* poor information training.

Information overload is the more obvious of the two. We see it everywhere: the proliferation of magazines, newspapers, databases, and even television channels. I'll talk more about this later. What is an even more distressing problem is our inadequate information training.

Your Library Is Out Of Date

Today, most adults and even our children have been trained to believe that if you need information, you go to the library. That's fine for certain subjects, like literature and history, but inadequate for most of the important concerns that effect our lives everyday. Libraries are full of the traditional information resources but you will encounter major problems if you rely on these sources because:

* most books are out of date, and
* libraries represent only a fraction of the information available to us.

Books can tell you only about yesterdays, but the information needed to make critical decisions must reflect what is happening today and tomorrow, not the past. More than ever our world is changing at an ever increasing speed. What once took months, even years to change, now occurs in hours, even minutes.

Those who rely on yesterday's information are the ones who get hurt in our society. Take, for example, the steel workers who thought that they would make $25 per hour forever. What about those who believed all the hype a few years ago about how Individual Retirement Accounts (IRAs) would make their financial lives secure forever, but the rules have changed and the tax advantage isn't what it used to be. Books published in the traditional way are out of date before they hit the bookstores. How can you depend on a book offering investment advice when the manuscript was completed 18 to 24 months ago? It takes most New York publishers 9 to 12 months just to do the editing, proofing, and printing. With external events changing our landscape every day, like the stock market crash of 1987, or the fall of the Berlin Wall in 1989, we can no longer rely on such books.

Government Is World's Largest Source of Information

Traditional books represent only a fraction of the real powerful information that is available. Did you know that all of the major commercial publishers in our country generate approximately 50,000 books each year, but one little government publisher, the National Technical Information Service (NTIS), alone sells about 90,000 titles annually. And it's estimated that NTIS titles represent only a tiny portion of research that is actually published by federal agencies. And computers are not much of a help either. Most databases you access are bibliographies which fail to capture the latest information.

The government is the largest source of information in the world, and very little of it is available in any library. And, more important, the information you get from the government is going to be superior to most anything you can ever get commercially. If you purchase a book in the bookstore, you're likely to get the result of one to two years of some author's efforts. On the other hand, if you get a government study, often you are getting the results of hundreds of man years worth of work, along with the telephone number of the actual office that conducted the research. That's just how the government works and chances are the government study will be free.

Information Opportunities

By relying on traditional information sources, you are missing out on information opportunities. Such an opportunity occurs when you have intelligence that is current, comprehensive, reliable, and even cheaper than someone else's information. There is no unique opportunity for you when your stockbroker calls about a chance to invest in some biotechnology company, because the broker probably is sharing that tip with 5,000 other "special" clients. The real opportunity occurs when you have the information before the stockbroker. And you can get it, but not from conventional sources. How can you take advantage of a new cure for your medical ailment if your doctor is not aware of the latest therapies because the *New England Journal of Medicine* hasn't published a recent article on this disease. Or perhaps some scientific journal plans to run an article revealing a potential cure, but it is still in the editing process and won't be published for another three months. You need that information today, and you can get it but not from traditional sources.

Medicine is typical of the information overload when your doctor--the information provider--cannot possibly keep up on all the latest developments. That physician has got a practice to run, and the information changes too fast and constantly. But the best health information in the world *IS* available and *YOU* can get it.

Archives vs. Information

Libraries are great storehouses for literature and archival material. They handle traditional published materials very well, but do a relatively poor job in solving more current information problems. This is a pity since we are living in an information society, and information is the most important ingredient in our lives. Doesn't it make sense that libraries should be the most important building in the community, but they're not, mainly because information retrieval requires a different set of skills than the archival business. Archiving is more suited for passive, non-people oriented skills, the cloistered scholars. The communication skills needed in today's information society are action-oriented and people-oriented.

The Information Winners

The winners in this information age are those who learn how to tap into non-traditional sources, and use experts. Finding non-traditional sources of information, however, is no easy task. The government is the world's largest supplier of these non-traditional sources, but it does not advertise. The government spends billions collecting information and expertise but spends barely a nickel advertising its availability. Another problem is that much of the information is not collected for the reason for which you want to use it. Even people in the government who have the information often fail to realize that it can be used to solve your particular problem. Take, for example, the Census data. Every decade we spend over $1 billion dollars collecting information on all the noses and toilets in this country--the census of population and housing. The law which requires us to collect this information is, of course, the Constitution, which mandates that we count all Americans in order to figure out the number of Members of Congress. But the unintentional fallout of this law is a billion dollar market study which no one except the government can do. Not even a Fortune 500 company can afford to collect this amount of data. But when the results come out:

* companies can use the data to identify new markets;
* banks can decide where to locate branch offices;
* families can learn which are the best neighborhoods;
* inventors can determine the demand and need for their products.

Using Experts To Solve Information Overload

Knowing how to find and use experts is not only the solution to identifying the best in non-traditional information, but it is also the key in dealing with information overload. And what's ideal about this approach is that most all the best experts cost you nothing. The government, because it is the richest source for non-traditional information in the world, is also the richest source of experts. It is full of specialists who spend entire careers studying almost any topic from futures commodities to extraterrestrials. And they are available to anyone just for the price of a telephone call.

Find Out What Will Be In Books Tomorrow

If you access a computerized database and put in a term or keyword, you can get overwhelmed. Immediately it will be apparent that today anybody with a copier machine is a publisher, and once it is published, somebody with a database is indexing it. So a printout from your computer search might total 500 citations. If you want answers now, you are in worse shape than when you started. Why? Because the computer cannot distinguish the relevant articles from the bad ones, probably you need to retrieve all the articles cited. Also, as I mentioned earlier, much of what databases contain is from outdated published material.

My theory is that in an average of 7 telephone calls you can find an expert who has read all of those articles. This specialist can tell you which ones to read, or will know the answer on the spot so there will be no need to track down the articles. These experts also can tell you what will be in the database tomorrow because they are in the process of writing it or reviewing another expert's article. They are tracking developments minute by minute in their field of expertise.

And what's great about our society is that these experts are dying to talk to you. They devote their lives to studying a particular subject in a massive bureaucracy and most feel no one cares about what they do and know. I estimate that there are over 700,000 such experts in the federal government alone, and this does not count state governments, non-profit groups, and international organizations.

The real trick is in how you treat these experts. You must remember that these experts get the same paycheck regardless whether they help you for free for two weeks or if they hang up on you right after you say hello. You can't think of getting information in the terms we are taught in school. The best information is no longer in some impersonal book locked up in a dusty library. It's locked up in the heads of experts and other resource people, but now you have to learn a whole new set of skills to get at it. Once you do, you will have the power of information at your fingertips. Here are a few examples of what I am talking about.

* You want to know the best industries of the 1990s to invest in? The government has over 100 industry analysts at the Department of Commerce studying all the major industries in this country and forecasting what they will be doing in the next 5 years.

* Your teenager has run up a few hundred dollars on pornographic 900 numbers? The dial-a-porn expert the Federal Communications Commission can tell you about your legal position for not paying the bill.

* You want to know the market for polypropelene resin in 15 developing countries? There is a women at the Department of Commerce who collects all the official export and import statistics from every country in the world, and can provide you with latest available data.

The Care and Feeding of Bureaucrats

There is no magic in how you treat experts. Simply remember to treat them the way you want to be treated. But this is easy to forget when the bureaucratic runaround triggers instant frustration. While making your seven phone calls to find your expert--beware. These are common reactions.

* You get put on hold for what seems like hours.
* Everyone you talk with cannot understand your question and thinks you're off your rocker.
* After getting transferred and trying other numbers, you wind up talking with the same person twice.

What's important is not to lose your composure. Keep in mind that it will take an average of seven phone calls to find the person who can help. Otherwise, by the time you reach the expert you'll be angry and frustrated and that attitude will usually cause this information provider to end the conversation immediately. Remember that the expert wants to help you--if you give them a chance.

How High Priced Consultants Stop The World From Getting Ahead

I believe that most of us fail to pursue our dreams because we think that the information and resources needed are not available or that we are going to have to pay a lot to get it from some high-priced consultant. If more people learn the new information skills required, more of us will do what we feel is important to do. You don't have to hire a high-priced consultant to get the pertinent information you need to get started. And even if you do, these consultants usually have archaic information gathering skills and usually sell recycled information.

Let's say you have a crazy idea--selling bridal gowns through the mail and you wonder if there is a market for it. A consultant will charge you a minimum of $10,000 to do a market study. However, about $20 can translate into any State Government Data Center providing you with all the zip codes which have high concentrations of unmarried, eligible women, correlated with low concentrations of bridal gown

salons, or department stores with bridal salons.

Do you want to start your own non-profit organization to change the world? If you call a local attorney, they will charge you a few thousands dollars to fill out the IRS paperwork. Or you can call the Non-Profit Office at the IRS in Washington, D.C. that provides free help to anyone who runs into difficulty completing the tax-exempt forms.

Recently I even got trapped in this negative thinking when I had the idea of sponsoring "My Favorite Bureaucrat Award." I was worried about the rules and regulations for offering a cash prize. What does "Void Where Prohibited" really mean? I thought about hiring a lawyer to figure all this out until I realized that there must be someone in the government to call. And there was. I found a contest expert, an attorney at the Federal Trade Commission, who told me such a contest had the seal of approval so long as I didn't give away over $5,000. He informed me that two states require you to post a bond and complete tons of paperwork if the prize exceeds $5,000. Until I resolved all these questions I was reluctant to pursue my idea. (Incidentally, there is a lot more about the results of this contest in My Favorite Bureaucrat Chapter.)

In my 15 years of experience, most experts will outshine private consultants both in terms of the quality of information and the cost of it!

How To Find Mr. Potato

The techniques for locating an expert can best be illustrated by a classic story from the days when I was struggling to start my first information brokerage company in 1975.

At the time the business amounted only to a desk and telephone crowded in the bedroom of my apartment. As so often happens in a fledgling enterprise, my first client was a friend. His problem was this: "I must have the latest information on the basic supply and demand of Maine potatoes within 24 hours."

My client represented a syndicate of commodity investors which invests millions of dollars in Maine potatoes. When he called, these potatoes were selling at double their normal price and he wanted to know why. I knew absolutely nothing about potatoes, but figured I knew where to find out. The agreement with my client was that I would be paid only if I succeeded in getting the information (no doubt you guessed I no longer work this way).

Luck With The First Telephone Call

The first call I made was to the general information office of the U.S. Department of Agriculture USDA). I asked to speak to an expert on potatoes. The USDA operator referred me to Mr. Charlie Porter. At that point I wondered if this Mr. Porter was a department functionary with responsibility for handling crank calls, but the operator assured me that he was an agriculture economist specializing in potatoes. I telephoned Mr. Porter and explained how I was a struggling entrepreneur who knew nothing about potatoes and needed his help to answer a client's request. Charlie graciously gave me much of the information I needed, adding that he would be happy to talk at greater length either over the phone or in person at his office. I decided to go see him.

Only Problem Was Getting Out
Of Charlie's Office

For two and one half hours the next morning, the federal government's potato expert explained in intimate detail the supply and demand of Maine potatoes. Charlie Porter showed me computer printouts that reflected how the price had doubled in recent weeks. For any subject that arose during our conversation, Charlie had immediate access to a reference source. Rows of books in his office covered every conceivable aspect of the potato market. A strip of ticker tape that tracked the daily price of potatoes from all over the country lay across his desk.

Here in Charlie's office was everything anyone might ever want to know about potatoes. The problem, it turned out, was not in getting enough information, but how to leave his office gracefully. Once Charlie started talking, it was hard to stop him. It seemed that Charlie Porter had devoted his lifetime work studying the supply and demand of potatoes and finally someone with a genuine need sought his expertise.

One Potato...Two Potato...

When I was finally able to let Charlie know I had to leave, he pointed across the hall in the direction of a potato statistician whose primary responsibility was to produce a monthly report on potato production and consumption in the United States. From this statistician I learned about all the categories of potatoes that are tallied. It turns out the USDA counts all the potato chips sold every month, even how many Pringle potato chips are consumed. The statistician offered to place me on the mailing list to receive all this free monthly data.

The Art Of Getting An Expert To Talk

The information explosion requires greater reliance on experts in order to sift through the expanse of data. Cultivating an expert, however, demands an entirely different set of skills than old-fashioned library or archival research. You must know how to treat people so that they are ready, willing, and able to give you the information needed. It is human nature for most anyone to want to share their knowledge, but your approach will determine whether you ultimately get the expert to open up. So it is your job to create an environment that makes an individual want to share his or her expertise. Remember when dealing with both public and private sector experts, they will get the same paycheck whether they give you two weeks worth of free help or if they cut short the conversation.

Expectations: The 7-Phone Call Rule

There is no magic to finding an expert. It is simply a numbers game which takes an average of seven telephone calls. Dial up enough people and keep asking each for a lead. Patience and persistence are essential. This is why it is essential to remember "the 7-phone call rule".

If you make several calls and get upset because of being transferred from one person to another, you will be setting yourself up to fail once you locate the right expert. What is likely to happen is that when your "Charlie Porter" answers the telephone he is going to hear you complaining about how sick and tired you are of getting the runaround from his organization. Well, to Charlie, you don't sound like you are going to be the highlight of his day. He is going to figure out how to get rid of you.

This explains why some people are able to get information and others fail. Experienced researchers know it is going to take a number of telephone calls and they condition themselves to be patient. After all, the runaround is an unavoidable part of the information gathering process. Consequently, the first words that come out of your mouth are extremely important because they set the stage for engaging the expert on your behalf.

Ten Basic Telephone Tips

Here are a few pointers to keep in mind when you are casting about for an expert. These guidelines amount to basic common sense but are often forgotten by the time you get to that sixth or seventh phone call.

1) Introduce Yourself Cheerfully
The way you start the conversation will set the tone for the entire interview. Your greeting and initial comment should be cordial and cheerful. Your opening should give the feeling that this is not going to be just another telephone call, but a pleasant interlude in his or her day.

2) Be Open And Candid
You should be as candid as possible with your source since you are asking the same of him. If you are evasive or deceitful in explaining your needs or motives, your source will be reluctant to provide you with information. If there are certain facts you cannot reveal such as client confidentiality, explain just that. Most people will understand.

3) Be Optimistic
Throughout the entire conversation you should exude a sense of confidence. If you call and say "You probably aren't the right person" or "You don't have any information, do you?" it's easy for the person to respond, "You're right, I cannot help you." A positive attitude will encourage your source to stretch his mind to see how he might be able to help you.

4) Be Humble And Courteous
You can be optimistic and still be humble. Remember the adage that you can catch more flies with honey than you can with vinegar. People in general, and experts in particular, love to tell others what they know, as long as their position of authority is not questioned or threatened.

5) Be Concise
State your problem simply. Be direct. A long-winded explanation may bore your contact and reduce your chances for getting a thorough response.

6) Don't Be A "Gimme"
A "gimme" is someone who expects instant answers and displays a "give me that" attitude. It is important to be considerate and sensitive to the expert's time, feelings, and even his or her eccentricities.

7) Be Complimentary
This goes hand in hand with being humble. A well-placed compliment about your source's expertise or insight will serve you well. In searching for information in large organizations, you are apt to talk to many colleagues of your source, so it wouldn't hurt to convey the respect that your "Charlie Porter" commands. For example, "Everyone I spoke to said you are the person I must talk with." It is reassuring to know you have the respect of your peers.

8) Be Conversational
Avoid spending the entire time talking about the information you need. Briefly mention a few irrelevant topics such as the weather, the Washington Redskins, or the latest political campaign. The more social you are without being too chatty, the more likely that your source will open up.

9) Return The Favor
You might share with your source information or even gossip you have picked up elsewhere. However, be certain not to betray the trust of either your client or another source. If you do not have any relevant information to share at the moment, it would still be a good idea to call back when you are further along in your research.

10) Send Thank You Notes
A short note, typed or handwritten, will help ensure that your source will be just as cooperative in the future.

Coping With Misinformation

One of the major problems encountered by researchers is determining the accuracy of the information collected. If you are doing traditional market research and using primary sources, accuracy is not that complicated. Traditional market researchers are well aware of survey methods, sampling techniques, and computing errors using statistical standard deviation analysis. However, if you are a desk researcher, like Information USA, Inc. which relies on secondary sources and expert opinion, how do you compute the standard deviation for error? The answer is that you cannot use hard statistical techniques, but you can employ other soft forms of error checking.

Major Causes for Error and Prevention Tactics

Problem #1: Lost In The Jargon

It is not uncommon for researchers to be dealing frequently in areas of expertise where they do not have complete command of the industry jargon. In such situations it is easy to believe that you have found the exact information needed only to find out later that you missed the mark considerably. This is a common trap to fall into when fishing in unfamiliar waters. And if you have to do the job quickly, it is easy to believe that you know more than you really do or to avoid getting the complete explanation of specific jargon because you do not want to waste the time of the expert who is giving you the information. Here is an experience of a U.S. Department of Agriculture expert which illustrates this point.

This government expert received a call one day from an assistant at the White House. This hot shot, who acted pretty impressed with himself, said he was in a meeting with both the President and the head of the Meat Packers Association and needed to know right then the official number of cows in the United States. The livestock expert asked the presidential aide if that was exactly what he meant and then when he impatiently responded "Yes," the bureaucrat told him the figure. Within minutes the White House staffer called back and said the president of the Meat Packers Association laughed at him and claimed that there were twice as many cows. The assistant then realized he needed the number of all cows--all "male cows"--as well as all female ones.

The White House aide had a problem with semantics, probably a city slicker who never knew the difference between cows and cattle. This can happen to anyone, not only a self-assured Presidential aide. For example, if you want to know the market for computers, are you talking about free standing units or central processing units?

Solution #1: Act A Little Dumb

In order to prevent this type of embarrassment, you have to find an expert with whom you are comfortable. When I say comfortable, I mean someone you can go to and ask dumb questions. You will get the most help if you act very humble in your approach. If you request information with the arrogance of the over confident White House staffer, you may be given only the facts you ask for and nothing more. However, if you call up an expert and say something like "Oh God, can you please help me? I don't really know much about this, but my boss needs to know how many cows there are in the country." With more than a hint of indecision in your voice and honestly admitting you don't know much about the field, the expert is more likely to ask you some key questions that will ensure that you get the right figures.

Problem #2: Believing The Written Word Or A Computer

This is a more serious problem than the difficulties and confusion surrounding industry jargon. Mastering the terminology just requires a little homework. However, overcoming a deepseated belief that information either from a computer, in published sources, or from the government is always accurate can be like changing your religion. It took me years, as well as dozens of professional embarrassments, to overcome this problem.

Just because a figure is in print does not make it gospel. Remember the saying, "Figures don't lie, but liars can figure." Keep this in mind before betting the farm on anything you read in print, even if it comes out of a computer. A good illustration which follows pertains to Census Bureau information.

A few years ago we were doing a market study on stereo speakers and discovered that the figures the U.S. Bureau of the Census had for this market were off by over 50 percent. No one in the industry complained to the government because the industry was small and couldn't be bothered. But most of the companies involved knew that the figure was misleading and had no use for it. Another case is a Fortune 500 company which told us that for over 5 years it filled out the U.S. Census form under the wrong SIC code. An important caveat--this firm ranks as the number two manufacturer in the industry.

You have to remember that number crunchers at the Census Bureau and other such organizations are not always interested in the meaning behind the numbers. Much of their work is simply taking a number from block A, adding it to the number in block B, and placing the result in block C. Verifying where the numbers come from is not their job.

Published sources are an even a bigger problem than government data. Many believe that what you read in a magazine or a newspaper or hear on television or radio must be true. Nonsense, anyone and their brother can be interviewed by a magazine or newspaper, and usually what they say will get printed in a magazine or quoted on the air as long as it is not too outrageous. And, sometimes you are more likely to get it into print if it **is** outrageous. Afterall, most news stories are just accounts of what someone said as interpreted by a journalist.

The more general the media the less accurate it may be about an industry. In other words, an article in the ice cream industry trade magazine is more likely to be accurate than a similar story in the *New York Times*. The trade journal will have reporters who cover that particular industry and they will more than likely be able to flush out bad data. The newspaper, on the other hand, will do only one ice cream story a year, and will print almost anything it hears. So just because someone is quoted in an article does not mean that the information is correct.

I have seen much of this firsthand when on nationwide book promotion tours. In newspaper interviews or on radio and television talk shows, I can say almost anything and they will print or broadcast it, as is. I will give countless facts and figures based on my own biased research (remember that I am trying to sell books), and hardly ever will I be questioned or seriously challenged before, during or after the fact, about their authenticity. I don't know if it is laziness, apathy, or just plain lack of time that allows so much unchallenged information to be presented in the media. I have even blatantly lied to a reporter who thought of himself as a clone of CBS Mike Wallace of "60 Minutes." Before I started doing media interviews, I assumed that any good reporter worth his or her salt could find holes in what I presented and would expose me as some kind of fraud. I did not know how they would do it, but I guess my own insecurity prompted me to prepare for the worst. The reality is that most reporters spend little or no time studying the topic before they interview you, and if you become annoyed or angry, especially with this Mike Wallace type described above, you can blow them away with a exaggerated fact or half-truth that he will never be able to verify.

Solution #2: Find Another Industry Expert

Whether a figure comes from the Census Bureau, a trade magazine or off the tube, your best bet for determining whether the number is accurate and also the one you need is to track down an industry expert, other than the one quoted, and ask them to comment on the figure. What you are seeking is their biased opinion about the accuracy of the stated figure. If the expert believes the figure is correct but doesn't know why, find another expert.

Problem #3: Trusting An Expert

This may seem to contradict what I just said in the solution to problem #2, but stick with me and you will see the difference.

There are many times when you cannot start with published or printed data and all you can do is pick the brains of experts within the industry. This means that you will be getting facts and figures based on the best available guess from experts. Many times this is the only way to get the information you need.

Getting this type of soft data can be full of danger. After having worked for hours trying to find a friendly soul to share with you his innermost thoughts about the facts and figures of an industry or company, you do not want to turn him off with an antagonistic remark about the accuracy of his data.

Solution #3: Ask Why?

The best way to judge whether a source is knowledgeable about the fact or figure they gave you is to ask them how they arrived at the number. Such a question will likely initiate one of the following responses:

"I don't know. It's the best I can think of."
- A response like this will be a clue that the expert may not know what he is talking about and you should continue your search for a knowledgeable and willing expert.

"This is the figure I read from an industry association study."
- This should lead you to verify that such a study was conducted and to attempt to interview people involved with the report.

"The industry figure is XX because our sales are half that and we are number 2 in the industry."
- This is probably one of the best types of answers you can get. Any time an industry expert gives you a figure based on something he is positive about, you can almost take it to the bank. The best you can do after this is to find other industry analysts and ask them to comment on the figure you were given.

Misinformation can lead to a decision making disaster. Following the simple techniques described above can take you a long way down the road to making near excellent decisions based on near perfect information.

Case Study: Jelly Beans

In our information society, which produces thousands of databases and other resources every day, it seems that most decision makers rely primarily on traditional information sources. More often than not executives will spend lots of time and money trying to determine the size of a market or information about a competitor, and if the answer cannot be found through conventional sources, the corporate decision is made without the information. This does not have to be the case.

We believe that you can find solid information for most any problem, no matter how sensitive the issue may be if you use some unorthodox research techniques. To illustrate this point, here is a step-by-step account of how one of our researchers succeeded in gathering figures on the US market for jelly beans when a Fortune 500 firm came up empty-handed after exhausting all traditional sources. The prevailing view both inside and outside the industry was that this piece of the information puzzle could not be obtained.

It should be said at the outset that the estimates Information USA, Inc. finally obtained must not be regarded as 100% accurate, but they do represent the best available figures and, most likely, come within 10% to 15% of the actual number.

Opening Round

Faced with the problem of finding the US market for jelly beans, we already knew that our client had contacted the major market research firms, did some literature searches, and came up with practically no useful information. As is evident from 7this case study, this information hunt occurred when Ronald Reagan was President.

1) The first call was to the US Department of Commerce to locate the government's jelly bean expert. We were referred to Cornelius Kenny, the confectionary industry expert. Mr. Kenny was out that day and would call us back when he returned to the office.

2) A search of Gale's *Encyclopedia of Associations* identified four relevant trade associations. However, upon contacting them we were told that they provide information only to their members.

3) The White House seemed like a good bet because of Ronald Reagan's fondness for jelly beans and all the resulting publicity. The Public Affairs office at 1600 Pennsylvania Avenue said that it never obtained statistical information on the industry but could tell us tales about a life-size water buffalo and portraits of the President constructed of jelly beans. However, they suggested that we contact several lobbying organizations. Calls to these groups proved fruitless.

4) A call to the US Bureau of the Census uncovered John Streeter, an analyst who monitors the panned candy industry. He told us:

* jelly beans have never been counted and there would be no way to get the answer;

* non-Chocolate Panned Candy category within the Bureau's Annual Confectionary Survey contains jelly beans;

* the seasonal category of the Non-Chocolate Panned Candies, according to his estimates, contains 90% jelly beans because most jelly beans are sold during Easter and they are about the only non-chocolate panned manufactured candy sold on a seasonal basis;

* $37,804,000 worth of non-chocolate panned candy was shipped by US manufacturers in 1984, which represents about 48,354,000 pounds; the figures for total non-chocolate panned candy for 1984 totaled $251,525,000 and 237,308,000 pounds; and

* government regulations prohibited him from revealing the names of jelly bean manufacturers, but he did refer us to two trade associations he thought might help.

So this analyst at the Census Bureau, who tried to discourage us with warnings that no such figure for the jelly bean market exists, actually gave us quite concrete information as well as some valuable leads.

Armed and Dangerous With A Little Information

At this point we had a market estimate from one government expert based on a figure generated by the US Bureau of the Census. It may have sounded like the answer we were after, but taking that figure to our client at this juncture would be premature and possibly irresponsible. The main drawback was the estimate reflected only one person's opinion, and although he was an expert, he was not a true industry observer as one would be if they were actually in the business of selling jelly beans. At this stage our strategy was to find people in the industry who could give us their interpretation of these figures.

The Census expert referred us to one of the trade associations we already had contacted. However, when we called back saying that Mr. Streeter at the Census Bureau suggested we call them, the association promptly responded with a list of the 25 major jelly bean manufacturers. This is an example of how using the name of a government expert can get you in the door. When we phoned several manufacturers, they laughed when we told them of our effort to ascertain the market for jelly beans. Jelly beans had never been counted, they told us, and their advice was to give up.

At this point Mr. Kenny, the confectionary expert at the US Department of Commerce called us back and he, too, said that the market had never been measured. However, he did hazard a quess that the jelly bean market could be roughly 50% of the total Census figure for Non-Chocolate Panned Candy.

A separate call to a private research group which does trend analysis by surveying grocery stores shared its estimate that 90% of all jelly beans are sold at Easter.

Easier To Be A Critic Than A Source

Our lack of success in dealing with a few manufacturers caused us to change tactics. Instead of asking them to estimate the size of the jelly bean market, we began asking them what they thought of the figures we received from the industry analysts at the Commerce Department as well as the Census Bureau. We decided to try to find someone who actually filled out the Census survey and get a reaction to the Census figures. We spoke with the owner of Herbert Candies, a small candy company. He gave us his 1984 jelly bean production and cost statistics, told us he filled out the Census report, and readily explained what he thought the Census statistics meant in terms of jelly bean production and cost. Furthermore, using his calculator, he helped us arrive at national figures for 1984. He also told us which companies manufacture 80% of the jelly beans produced in the country.

Now, armed with actual figures for 1984 jelly bean production, average cost per pound, average number of jelly beans in a pound, and the percentage of jelly beans produced during Easter, we resumed calling manufacturers---this time to get their opinion of our figures. This was the real turning point in dealing with the manufacturers. Because everyone in the industry knew that there were no exact numbers on the size of the jelly bean market, as professionals, they were afraid to give a figure because anyone could say it was wrong. However, because they were experts in the business, they were not afraid to criticize someone else's information. Reactions from insiders were just what we needed to help hone a good working number. The manufacturers were able to tell us why our figures were good or not and they gave us sound reasons why the numbers should be adjusted, such as "Based on our sales figures your numbers sound a little low," or "Not all manufacturers report to the Bureau of the Census so that figure may be low."

To show how this tactic prompted many manufacturers to be candid about both the industry and their sales in particular, here are highlights of our conversations with nine companies. What is presented below may seem to be too detailed, but after reviewing them we hope that it proves our point about how open business executives can be about their company.

1) Owner, Herbert Candies (small manufacturer and retailer)

* 90% of jelly beans are sold at Easter
* 60% of Census seasonal category are jelly beans
* average cost of jelly beans is $1.00 per pound
* when President Reagan first got into office the jelly bean market shot up 150% but now it is back to normal
* 4 companies have 80% of the market with E.J. Brach the largest at 40%, Brock the second largest, followed by Herman Goelitz and Maillard
* his company sold 30,000 pounds this past year and 90% at Easter; 10,000 were gourmet beans at $3.20 per pound and 20,000 were regular jelly beans at $2.80 per pound

2) Marketing Department, Nabisco Confectionary

* suggested we call SAMI, a private market research firm
* estimated 90% of jelly beans are sold at Easter
* confirmed that E.J. Brach has 40% of the market

3) Vice President of Marketing and Sales, Herman Goelitz (producer of Bellies," Ronald Reagan's favorite)

* between 35% and 50% of his jelly beans are sold at Easter
* $1.00 per pound could be the average retail price
* a retailer can purchase jelly beans at $.60 per pound
* the retail price ranges between $1.25 and $5.00 per pound

4) General Manager, Burnell's Fine Candy (manufacturer of hanging bag jelly beans)

* 75% of jelly beans are sold at Easter
* $.60 to $.75 per pound is average manufacturer's price
* $1.59 is the average retail price
* 75% of Census seasonal category is probably jelly beans

5) Senior VP of Marketing and Sales, E.J. Brach (largest manufacturer)

* produces 24 million jelly beans annually at an average price of $.86 per pound
* there are approximately 100 beans per pound
* Brach's selling price is about industry average
* they have about 50% of the market
* 90% of the jelly beans sold at Easter sounds too high

6) Product Manager of Marketing Department, Brock Candy (second largest manufacturer)

* 85% to 95% of all jelly beans are sold at Easter
* average price paid by retailers is $.59 to $.99 per pound
* there are 130 to 140 jelly beans in a pound
* E.J. Brach has 40% to 50% of the jelly bean business - 32 to 45 million jelly beans sold in a year sounds correct given Brock's production figures; but probably it is closer to the high side
* Brock Candy is number 2 in the industry
* there are not many jelly bean manufacturers and basing total production on E.J. Brach's sales figures is a good way to arrive at an industry estimate

7) Traffic Manager, Powell Confectionary (medium size producer)

* 75% of jelly beans are sold at Easter judging from Powell's sales
* average retail price $.75 to $.80 perpound and the average manufacturer's price is $.65 to $.70 per pound
* 35 to 45 million jelly beans per year sounds reasonable
* it seems fair to double E.J.Brach production figures to get the total market because it has about 50% share of the market

8) President, Ferrara Panned Candy (largest panned candy producer)

* familiar with Census data and believes that jelly beans represent about 75% to 80% of the seasonal sales 80% to 90% of all jelly beans are sold at Easter
* 32 to 45 million pounds per year seems a bit low
* E.J. Brach has 50% of the packaged jelly bean market but has less than half of the bulk jelly bean market

9) New Product Development Manager, Farley Candy

* familiar with Census data and believes that the numbers are

understated because not all companies report their figures
* an industry estimate of 32 to 50 million pounds per year seems low

So much for all those who discouraged us from even tackling this issue of the market for jelly beans. All the data poured forth during these telephone conversations provided more information than our Fortune 500 client ever expected.

Deciding On An Estimate

As you can see from the interviews outlined above, traffic managers all the way up to company presidents were willing to give us their best estimate of the size of the market and even divulge their own company's sales figures.

After government experts, the figure seemed to cluster around the 45 to 50 million pound range. It may not be that obvious from just reading the highlights of our interviews, but that consensus became apparent after talking with about a dozen people.

Information Exchange Is A People Business

It is just surprising what company executives and government experts are willing to tell you if they are approached in the right way. You can find the answer to any question (or at least a good estimate) as long as you expect to make many phone calls and you treat each person on the other end of the telephone in a friendly, appreciative way.

The biggest difference between those who succeed in their information quest and those who fail boils down to whether or not they believe the information exists. If you persist in thinking the information can be found, nine times out of 10 you will get what you need.

My Favorite Bureaucrat Award

Each year Information USA will award $5,000 to the best story sent in on how some bureaucrat helped you. Two runner-up awards will also be given at $500 each. The first year of this contest ended on December 31, 1989 and was a resounding success. We received close to 1,000 entries and each one proved once again how important and powerful government resources can be. Listed below are a number of stories we received. The entry number at the end of the story reflects the number assigned to the entry at the time of submission. If you would like to know about the winner, contact our office. If you would like to submit an entry for next year send in a brief, verifiable story of 350 words or less about how some federal, state, or local government employee helped you. We prefer not to include elected officials, but if you must it's okay.

* Children's Book Writer Finds Success With Free Marketing, Legal and Tax Help

A man in Seattle Washington wrote a book called "Bill the Dog and Mr. TV Head," but didn't know what to do with his great idea until he contacted his local Small Business Development Center. He read about the center in Information USA's "Government Giveaways for Entrepreneurs." There he made an appointment to meet with a counselor, Bill Jacobs, the very next day. As the writer tells it, Bill Jacobs was great. He went over all the facts and asked twenty more questions that he hadn't ever thought about. Since the product was an educational book for children, Mr. Jacobs gathered a bundle of marketing information from the US Department of Education. He helped Matt settle on objectives and determined how to best meet the objectives. He also secured a government mailing list of those interested in the book, and arranged to get him lower mailing rates at the post office as well as help in filing his taxes. All of these services were free of charge. (Entry #3)

* Public Works Worker Passes Buck Quickly To Save Credit Manager's Job

A credit manager for the Sherwin-Williams company had trouble collecting on an old debt of $2,220 worth of paint sold to the Public Works Department of the City of Oakland, California. His boss said that if he didn't collect the check by the end of the month, he may have to suffer the consequences, both financially and emotionally. He kept calling Public Works and didn't receive any attention until a Ms. Perle Goins heard about his predicament. Perle processed the check immediately and called him to see if he would like to come down in person to pick it up. Although the San Francisco earthquake had recently occurred making travel difficult, he went down immediately to pick up the check. The credit manager says that Perle saved his job and possibly his career because "she cares and is willing to do what it takes to get the job done." (Entry #8)

* HUD Auditor Helps Co-Op Owners In Arizona

An auditor for HUD was sent to the Concord Village Co-Op in Tempe, Arizona to investigate a report of irregularities sent into HUD's Inspector General's Office. Since his initial visit he continues to return to investigate when aggravated co-op owners call on him. The owners feel that this auditor is their only recourse in dealing with management. (Entry #16)

* State Official Returns Kidnapped Son To Mom

In August, 1979, a separated woman living in Wisconsin came home one day to find her son had been kidnapped by his father. She contacted Christopher Foley, Wisconsin's Attorney General, and found that she had very little recourse because the father and boy had left the state. A year later Mr. Foley called the mother to tell her that the laws had changed so they had the right to go after the father and return the boy. By searching telephone records Mr. Foley was able to locate the father in Houston, Texas and had him arrested. Mom flew down to pick up her son. The mother feels she would never have had her child back if it were not for Mr. Foley's efforts to act above and beyond the call of duty by making that extra phone call one year later. (Entry #18)

* Inmate Says Welding Instructor Is Saving The World

An inmate at the Oregon State Penitentiary has a welding instructor named Joe Karvandi who is dedicated to helping inmates learn a trade or skill. Joe believes that inmates who respond to training are likely to be become productive members of society, because they've been given an example of a normal, responsible life style. The inmate feels that without this man's determination and concern for society, the percentage of repeat criminals would be much higher. He believes that Joe is reaching at least one in ten inmates and that his contribution is making our society a better and safer place to live. (Entry #30)

* County Official's House Call Is Highlight Of Plumber's Life

A woman named Sheri moved to rural Mississippi with her husband, 3 year old daughter, and 78 year old father. Within months of moving, her father was diagnosed with throat cancer. Her father's income came from a New York plumber's union pension which needed notarized documents so they could continue sending him checks to pay his medical bills. Sheri's father was bedridden so she couldn't leave the house to see a notary. Mr. Bobby Parker, a county beat supervisor, heard about the problem. He not only took the time to drive way out to their house to see her father and handle the paperwork, but he also visited with her father and made him feel like the most important appointment on his schedule--something much needed by a lonely, terminally ill, elderly man. Her father died a few months later taking with him the memory of his last and gratefully finest outside contact. (Entry #32)

* County Commissioner Is Last Hope For Dying Cancer Victim

A woman living on the East Coast traveled 1,100 miles to Oklahoma to care for her mother who was dying of stomach cancer. When she got there she found her mother in a messy situation. Her mother was living on $400 per month and the doctors and health care providers wanted to charge as much as $92 per visit. Everywhere she turned she was told that her mother was not eligible for any special medical programs. In desperation she called a friend who in turn called County Commissioner Elton Lamb. Within an hour Elton was at her house, took one look at her mother, and within minutes returned with the county nurse. The nurse proceeded to give her morphine, along with instructions on how to administer more when needed. Mr. Lamb took the woman's daughter aside and said "No widow-lady should have to suffer like this, just because she can't afford help. I am very sorry that happened and it is all taken care of now." That night her mother died in her arms. She will never - as long as she lives - forget the compassion of County Commissioner Elton Lamb. (Entry #41)

* State Librarian Saves Government Contractor Hundreds In Documents Costs

A contracts administrator in Utah works for a business that relies on government contracts. He relies on Ferne Kelso, Procurement Consultant at Utah's Military Specification Library, to deliver when he needs military specifications quickly and inexpensively. In recent months he has sent three different people over to her office to get documents. None had any prior knowledge about how to find the documents they needed, but by the end of their first library visit, they could easily find all of them. When they came across documents the library didn't have, Ferne directed them to the necessary sources and always recommended alternative sources with specific names and telephone numbers. Through her friendliness and wonderful, helpful attitude, she has saved his company hundreds of dollars in labor and documents costs. (Entry #44)

* Delinquent Taxpayer Finds A Helpful Hand At The IRS

A woman in Virginia Beach owed the IRS a lot of back taxes as well as penalties. Revenue Agent L.R. Phelps was assigned to find Mary and collect. When Ms. Phelps located Mary, she was very helpful in solving her problem and worked out a payment schedule. Ms. Phelps performed her job in a manner that was friendly but professional, understanding but firm, and patient but aggressive. Mary says she is embarrassed to admit she found a helpful bureaucrat and she's glad Ms. Phelps is in the position. (Entry #53)

* Iowa Governor Keeps Trucks Rolling For Small Businessman

My Favorite Bureaucrat

A dispatcher who works for Morgan Drive Away in Iowa, was trying to make sure one of the trucks loaded with gym equipment would make it in time to meet a ship in California. The ship would deliver the equipment to US servicemen overseas. Along the way the truck driver was stopped in a southern state and told by authorities that he couldn't travel that day because it was Columbus Day. If the driver didn't travel that day, he would miss the boat. The driver called the dispatcher. The dispatcher told management and somehow Governor Terry Brandstad called Sandy to tell him that he personally talked to the Governor of the southern state involved and everything was now on its way. (Entry #54)

* Local Agency Worker Gets Money In Hours to Save Family from Losing Home

A mortgage company in South Carolina had a client who was about to lose his house if he didn't make his payment the next day. The mortgage company took the client in to see Johnny Ruth Jenkins at the local Human Resource Center. She immediately sized up the situation and realized it was an emergency. She stopped what she was doing, skipped lunch, and within a few hours was able to get the funds from another government agency to pay the bill. Since the incident, the family has been back on their feet, but would have been homeless if it weren't for Ms. Jenkins. (Entry #70)

* Motor Vehicles Clerk Shows Driver How To Beat The System

A woman in Massachusetts and her husband moved and had to change their motor vehicle registrations. The woman took the necessary paperwork for her and her husband's car to Registry of Motor Vehicles to make the necessary changes. Changing the registration for her car was a snap. But when it came to her husband's car the clerk said, "We can't process this without your husband's signature." Her heart sank. She told the clerk it was going to take another day or two to get the signature because her husband worked a long way off. The clerk said, "Go outside, get your husband's signature and bring it back to me." The clerk kept repeating this phrase to her and she kept telling the clerk it was going to take two days. They kept going back and forth. She thought the clerk had no brains, and that there was a total breakdown in communication, so she left. On the way out the door she realized what the clerk was telling her to do. She went behind a tree and forged her husband's signature. When she came back into the office the clerk said, "you didn't have to go all the way outside." (Entry #72)

* State Tax Auditor Shows Small Business How To Reduce Tax

A woman was running a small business in New Jersey when the state tax auditor walked into her office one day and asked to see all of her records. After reviewing the documentation for several days, it was clear that she was due a heavy fine for not having the necessary paperwork to identify which customers were tax exempt, and a problem in her payroll records. However the agent was terrific. He was friendly and personable and told her exactly what to say in a letter to his supervisor to try and get the fine reduced. In a few weeks she received word that she would only have to pay a token fine. (Entry #77)

* Bureau of Mines Asbestos Researcher Saves the Day For Litigator

A legal researcher working on a class action asbestos case identified an important study at the National Archives that was 50 years old. The study concluded that asbestos is one of the most hazardous substances known to man. The study was signed, but the credentials of the author could not be found until the legal researcher contacted Bob Virta, staff asbestos researcher at the Bureau of Mines. Bob spent that afternoon in the Bureau's library and immediately faxed the researcher chapter and verse about the author in question. Bob sent articles with his comments on the side, information on his academic awards, the accession number of his correspondence file when he worked at the Bureau and even the location of the cemetery where he's buried. He also included a list of people who attended the funeral back in 1972. (Entry #78)

* Ex-Corporate Executive Saves Over $5,000 in Tax Accounting Charges by Using IRS Hotline

An ex-corporate executive in Delaware was used to having his taxes prepared by high priced tax consultants. When he retired he decided to try it himself, but ran into problem because he didn't know how to handle something called "passive activity losses". He called the IRS "800" number and found Mrs. Pat Phillips who researched his question and called him back within a day. She also followed up by sending him some sample worksheets explaining the solution in detail. The next tax season he called the IRS hotline again and continued to get excellent responses. He estimates that this free service has saved him at least $5,000 in tax consulting services. (Entry #83)

* Postal Service Consumer Affairs Gets Results for Lousy Delivery

A computer company in New Jersey moved their offices to a new location on the second floor of a building. The new postal carrier disliked having to climb up the flight of stairs and started harassing the company and obstructing mail delivery. The company called the carrier's supervisor, with no results. They contacted the regional office with no results. Then they called the US Postal Service's Office of Consumer Affairs in Washington, D.C. They wrote a letter as advised, and promptly got a visit from an official at the regional office, followed by an apology from the postal carrier. (Entry #84)

* New Jersey Chemical Company Succeeds In Business Thanks To Many Helpful Bureaucrats

A manager at Moeller Chemicals recalls Thomas Jefferson who said, "My God how little do my countrymen know what precious blessing they are in possession of and which no other people on earth enjoy." He believes helpful bureaucrats are one of these precious blessings Jefferson referred to. He has used Nina McGlone, a clerk at the US Department of Treasury, to help him through a tax problem which dates back to 1985. Special DEA Agent Leslie D. Hoppy at the US Department of Justice was a great help to him in showing their company how to fight against the illicit use of chemicals for the manufacture of narcotics. And, John Markus, Chief of Manufacturing and Quality Control for FDA's Center for Veterinary Medicine, has spent many valuable hours helping him through tedious animal drug applications both over the telephone and through the mail. (Entry #84)

* Young Woman Buys Condo With Help Of Little-Known Money Program

A woman living in the District of Columbia thought that at the age of 27 she would never be able to afford her own home--but she was wrong. A little-known local program allowed her to put down 5% on a one bedroom condo, gave her a loan at 3% for $16,000, and gave her a loan at 0% interest to cover the $4,000 closing costs. The rest was financed conventionally. (Entry #93)

* Customer Service Manager For Machinery Corporation Learns Real Customer Service From Government Trade Specialist

The customer service manager for a US subsidiary of a Japanese company was making calls all over the government trying to obtain the necessary forms for exporting and then reimporting repaired circuit boards from Japan. Someone eventually directed him to Mary at the US Department of Commerce. She listened to the problem and said she would find the answer. She got the answer, called him back immediately and volunteered to send him the necessary forms. She also volunteered to make the calls necessary to find out where he should send the forms. She was uncommonly courteous, polite and eager to help. She also called him back in a few days after he received the forms to see if everything had gone smoothly. This customer service manager said he "learned some principles about customer service" from her. (Entry #94)

* Congressional Assistant Helps Citizens Committee Turn NIKE Site Into Community Golf Course

Ed Murnane, while working as an assistant to Congressman Philip M. Crane, worked with the Citizens Committee of Arlington Heights, IL to convince the government to give up their plans to build a grandiose Army reserve center in the middle of their town and to instead deed the property over to the city to be used as a park. He went to bat for the community by helping to motivate, inspire and formulate a plan of action that was eventually effective. The city now has a 90 acre golf course that gets over 60,000 rounds of play a year. (Entry #97)

* Smiling INS Official Takes Pride In Helping Adopted Babies

A few years ago a couple living in New Jersey started the long, arduous and frustrating process of filing for a foreign adoption. It involved standing in lines for hours to pick up a single form and took them to city, state and federal offices. After one year of paperwork, they got a call from their adoption agency saying there was a baby girl waiting for them in Chile. They immediately went to work on the final paperwork because they were told it would take six weeks to process. After many telephone calls to the Newark INS Office, the woman finally reached a HUMAN who asked how she could help. When she heard about the baby she said, "How wonderful - you must be so excited. Come over to my office right away." When the woman arrived she was greeted by a smiling woman, Mrs. Pollard, who had an entire wall covered with pictures of "her babies" that she had helped get adopted in the US. What was supposed to take 6 weeks, this smiling bureaucrat did in only 30 minutes. On the way out the door, Mrs. Pollard wished her luck in her new role as a mother and said she expected a picture for her wall. (Entry #103)

* State Legislative Researcher Finds Money For Struggling Artists

Any time a researcher from the South Carolina Chamber of Commerce needs some information for one of her members, she calls Len Marini, researcher at the Joint Committee on Cultural Affairs. Although he has an amazing scope of professional and volunteer commitments, he always responds immediately to any of her needs. More astounding, is his dedication to the cultural community at a grass roots level. He devotes much of his time to help struggling artists, actors, photographers, et. al. He is creative in seeking ways to fund their projects, as well as providing moral support and guidance. He also participants in the arts. He serves on the boards of the local theatre and library, works the theatre concessions, and has had leading roles in productions such as A Streetcar Named Desire. (Entry #105)

* Call To County Consumer Office Gets Two Free T-Bones

A man in Nassau County, New York was walking into a local food market when he saw a sign on the window that read "Sirloin Steak $1.19 per pound" (this was a few years ago). When he walked over to the meat counter he saw only one badly cut steak in the case. He rang the bell and asked for another cut but was told there was nothing more to cut from. He asked to speak to the meat manager and got no results. He asked to see the store manager and got no results. He went home and called James Picken, Jr., Commissioner of Consumer Affairs. Later that night after he finished dinner, the doorbell rang and standing there was the store manager with two free 2-inch sirloins as a peace offering, thanks to the commissioner's phone call to the store. (Entry #111)

* Michigan Banker Gets The Law Changed In An Afternoon On The Hill

A Michigan banker visiting Capitol Hill with other bankers overheard talk about a piece of legislation which would effect his bank and a handful of other banks in the county. After talking to his Congressman's aide, who called other congressional aides, they were able to get the legislation changed within hours. (Entry #114)

* Government Helps Firearms Entrepreneur On Consulting Fees

An Air Force employee was very active in target shooting and decided to get into the business. He realized that he needed the proper licenses from the US Office of Alcohol, Tobacco and Firearms, when he saw advertisements in gun magazines for consultants who would charge big money to get this information. When he called the office directly he found that the government would send him the information for free, let him attend free seminars on the topic, and provide him with an 800 number to answer any special questions. (Entry #117)

* Bureaucrat Barred Thalidomide

During the early 1960's, thousands of pregnant women in Europe took a new sedative called thalidomide that resulted in the birth of babies without arms or legs or with other deformities. A low level GS-14 bureaucrat, Dr. Frances Lesey at the Food and Drug Administration, held off the pressures from the drug companies and even from within the FDA to approve the drug before she had finished testing it. (Entry 119)

* Coordinator of Vital Records Saves Families And Funeral Directors Valuable Time

Until recently it took 120 to 150 days to have either a major or minor correction made to a death certificate in New York City. When Mrs. Francine Benjamin went to work for the city Department of Health, she cut this time down to 10 days even though had been done the other way for 20 years. (Entry #121)

* US Attorney's Public Service Includes Towing Stranded Automobiles

Two women driving through Montana on the way to a wedding found themselves stranded in the middle of a Crow Indian Reservation. Along came a very kind man who stopped, drove them to the nearest town, got a tow chain, drove them back to their car, and towed them to a town 40 miles away where they could get help. He was the US Attorney for Billings. He wouldn't take money and said he hoped they would do the same if they found someone stranded.

* Social Security Administration Tracks Down Missing Father Of 20 Years

The parents of Mr. James divorced in 1943, while he was serving in the US Army Air Corps. Although he kept up with his mother, he could not find his father no matter how much searching he did through government organizations and public records. Twenty years later his congressman's office told him to write his father a letter explaining that he wanted to contact him, and they would have the Social Security Administration forward it to his last known address. In this way, confidentiality would be maintained. Within a week his father contacted him and arranged for an immediate two week visit. (Entry #124)

* Genealogy Researcher Gets A Surprise Bonanza From County Clerk

When a man in Illinois wrote to the County Clerk's office in Salem, Indiana, he was in for a pleasant surprise. His letter was a request for marriage records from the 1850's for some of his wife's ancestors. The clerk at the office not only sent him copies of the old marriage records, but gave him her home address and said that he could write her personally if he needed more information. He did write her and received so much family history information that it extended his wife's family line back to the pre-Revolutionary War era. Over the years he wrote to her a few more times and each time she responded quickly and efficiently. (Entry #135)

* State Geological Office Saves Residents From Collapsing Mines.

An area in Ohio was plagued by abandoned mines that were collapsing and seriously damaging houses. Property owners were descending on the local library to obtain precise information on the location of the mines. The library didn't have such information, but the head of reference services contacted the state Geological Survey Division and was put in touch with Mr. Rea. Mr. Rea saved the day. He patiently explained the terminology to the librarian in detail so that she could order the proper documents. There were different scale maps available and he advised her to first look at a small-scale map covering the whole county (which he sent free of charge), and then decided for which areas more detailed maps were needed. After the first phone call he even called back to explain that the maps were on light sensitive paper and should be kept away from light. Within days, and with his help, all the necessary maps were available for library patrons. (Entry #137)

* Local HUD Official Saves Mother Of Two From Living In The Streets

A young woman in Ohio living in HUD subsidized housing was about to be evicted because she was behind in rent. The woman had two children and also received aid for dependent children. Her sister called the local HUD office and asked to make arrangements for her the woman and her children to remain in their home if the rent was caught up and advance payments were made. The answer was a resounding no. The only immediate solution would have been to have her and her two children move into her mother's two bedroom apartment. Her mother had recently undergone a serious back operation and had no income, therefore the solution was not practical. Her sister called HUD again and had an opportunity to speak with Ms. Prince. Ms Prince superseded the system, allowed the woman to pay back rent, and gave her an extension on her lease pending an inspection. The woman was very grateful because she knew that once evicted from federal housing, she wouldn't be eligible to apply for subsidized rent again. If this had occurred, she would have been forced to live in a crowded situation or on the street. (Entry #138)

* Attorney General Retrieves $1,000 For Couple From Phantom Furniture Store

When a woman in Seattle got married she and her husband fell victim to a furniture scam. They paid $1,000 up front on $1,500 worth of furniture and waited for delivery. The furniture was never delivered. When they returned to the store a few days later the store was completely empty. They called the office of the state Attorney General and were told that there were many people ahead of them who had similar complaints against the company. They also told them that the owners had opened another store 20 miles away. They were given a choice of either waiting in line for legal action, or going to the new store and asking for a refund. They went to the new store, and were given a refund thanks to the information supplied by the Attorney General. (Entry #148)

* IRS Agent Shows Taxpayer How To Beat The System

A young man from Kansas who had recently married reworked his tax return dozens of times because he could not believe that he was going to owe the IRS $750. This was $750 he didn't have. He decided to go to the local IRS office and have them check it. The agent confirmed his worst fears, that he had computed his taxes correctly. But the agent also told him what to do if he couldn't pay the bill. "Do not send in your return until April 15th. Save every cent you can. Then on the 15th, go down to the post office just before midnight and mail your return. Enclose a check for as much as you have saved and a note stating that you cannot pay your tax liability in full at the present time, but you intend to as soon as possible. If you wait until the last minute to send in your return they won't get to it until July, and then it will go into a group of problem returns. They probably won't get to it until October. By then you should have saved enough to pay it off in full, plus interest on the late portion. It's all legal and you ought to come out fine." The man followed the agent's instructions, and just as the agent had predicted, it all worked out. (Entry #153)

* It Only Takes Hours For Newlyweds To Make Their First Move

A man from Detroit Michigan married a Canadian in Winnipeg, Manitoba. He had heard many horror stories about how long they would have to be separated until they could get the proper documentation allowing his wife to reside with

My Favorite Bureaucrat

him in the United States. When they went to the US Consulate in Winnipeg, they were met with long lines and were expecting the worst. Instead they met a consulate official named Jeffrey Baron. In less than an hour, he processed all the required paperwork to allow them to both enter the United States. He also explained everything they needed to cross the border into the United States. Instead of waiting weeks, they were able to go the US that same day. (Entry #168)

* State Senator Saves Beerman's Business

The state of Arizona passed a law which prevented a small beer business from ever doing business again. The owner thought he had lost everything until he contacted State Senator Pat Wright. She took the time to explain his rights to him and all the procedures required to change his situation. With her help and support he ended up in front of the State Senate Hearing Committee and had the law changed. (Entry #174)

* Local Official Pulls All The Stops To Help Woman Get Stop Light

A woman in Michigan wanted to get a traffic light at a dangerous corner near her home. She began collecting signatures, attending city council meetings, and writing city and state officials, but didn't get anywhere. She even collected accident data and understood the ins and out of the "Michigan Manual for Uniform Traffic Control Devices." Then state representative Alvin J. Hoekman got involved and gave her all the assistance he could. The light was installed shortly thereafter. (Entry #178)

* Consumer Utility Official Saves Customers Money, Returns Part Of Its Budget To The Treasury And Even Offers Free Meals

A report from the Attorney General of Colorado shows that in its first three years of operation, Colorado's Office of Consumer Counsel was solely responsible for $4.7 million in savings to utility customers, and was primarily responsible for $50 million in annual savings and $73 million more in one-time savings. During this same period of time their expenditures were $1.7 million and each year they returned part of their budget to the state treasury. After long meetings far away from home, the head of the office, Ron Binz, often invited committee members to stay at his home for dinner and a nights sleep. (Entry #180)

* IRS Agents Shows How Ignorance Does Not Have To Be Taxing

A taxpayer in New Jersey had a windfall in 1988, and in April of 1989 filed and paid a tax based primarily on his windfall. Then in August he received a notice of a penalty of $1,200 for not filing an Estimated Tax Payment. He knew nothing about such a filing and called the IRS 800 number for help. Mr. LeFleur answered the telephone and spent a good deal of time explaining the rules concerning Estimated Taxes. He also read and explained the categories under which he could claim an exception and not pay the penalty. It was obvious that his situation did not fit any of the exceptions. Mr. LeFleur suggested that he write a detailed letter asking to have the penalty removed. He felt that someone reading the letter might accept "Ignorance of the Law" as an excuse. The man wrote the letter and shortly thereafter was notified that his penalty had been lifted based on his explanation. (Entry #181)

* AID Official Helps US Company Get Turkish Contract

A US Company was bidding on a contract in Turkey to build a national radio transmission monitoring system. However, a Canadian company was about to get the contract because the Canadian government was going to throw in a $100,000 feasibility study to sweeten the deal. The US Agency for International Development (AID) decided to match the Canadian deal and, as a result the US company got the contract. (Entry #182)

* Generous Census Worker Helps Woman With Marketing Plan

A woman in Omaha needed to know the concentration of people between the ages of 40 and 60 in order to develop a marketing plan. She didn't know where to start so she called the clerk of her community for help. This call led to 4 additional calls. All of the kind and generous people she spoke to where willing to explain what data was available and the best place for her to obtain it. Within four hours, including lunch, she was back in her office with all the latest data she needed to solve her problem. (Entry #183)

* Third Grader Gets Help For Science Project From Senator's Office

A third grader in Louisiana had to do a project for science class on a famous astronaut. He and his mom went to the library and couldn't find anything very interesting to report on. When they got home they decided to call Senator John Glenn's Office in Washington, D.C. for help. Within one week the boy had a

wonderful autographed picture of the ex-astronaut along with a bunch of background articles to make him the envy of his class. (Entry #185)

* Transportation Secretary Gets Parachutist Out Of Jail

In October 1986 Michael Sergio showed his enthusiasm for the Mets baseball team by parachuting into the middle of Shea Stadium during the 6th game of the World Series, without permission. The criminal court of Queens treated it as a harmless venture and sentenced Sergio to 100 hours of community service and a $500 fine. However, the FAA held Sergio in contempt of court for not revealing the name of the pilot who flew his plane and sentenced him to 6 months in jail and a $100 a day fine for each day he continued his silence. As soon as Michael went to jail his parents wrote a letter of appeal to the Secretary of Transportation, Elizabeth Dole. Not only were his parents upset about the cruel and unusual punishment he was receiving, they were also very concerned because Michael's youngest brother was dying of cancer and his brother did not want Michael to be in jail when the end of his life came. Ms. Dole responded quickly and Michael was home with his brother within 3 weeks. (Entry #188)

* State Counselor Helps Vet When Congressman Fails

When a man from upstate New York received his military discharge, he had a service connected disability but was turned away by the Veterans Administration to receive financial compensation. He contacted his Congressman and even he couldn't help. Years later when a co-worker asked about his limping he told him his military disability story. The co-worker suggested that he see his brother-in-law who was a veteran's counselor for the state of New York. After a thorough medical exam, a review of the paperwork, and a hearing in front of the appeal board, the Veterans Administration approved him for compensation. (Entry #202)

* Postal Supervisor Bucks The System To Get A Company Its Money Sooner

When a small company moved their offices from Hillsdale to Lakewood New Jersey, they encountered a big problem. The business depended on the mail for its survival. All their orders and money came in by mail. But because of their move, for some reason their mail was taking up to 6 weeks to catch up to them. When they called their old post office to investigate the trouble the supervisor who answered the telephone took it upon himself to change the system and have their mail handled as first class mail each day and not as forwarded mail. This meant that they received the mail within one or two days instead of 6 weeks. (Entry #206)

• Senator Helps Flight Trainer Business Take Off

An entrepreneur in Milwaukee had been trying for 9 months to get federal, state and city agencies to look at his proposal for flight training, but no one would help him. As a last resort he sent a letter to Senator Proxmire detailing his proposal. Within a short period of time he received calls and letters of response from those agencies the Senator had contacted and his business was off and flying. (Entry #208)

* Commerce Official Bends The Rules To Refund $1,000 To Exporter

A management consultant in Chicago put down a $1,000 deposit to participate in an upcoming trade show in India sponsored by the US Department of Commerce. He hoped to represent a number of US companies at the show, but despite his best efforts he could not get a single company interested. When he called the Department of Commerce to cancel, he was told the registration dates had been extended and he still had time to solicit companies. The allotted time passed and he still didn't have a customer. He ask for a refund on his deposit but was informed that the 90 day stipulation had passed and that he was not entitled to the refund. He, however, argued that since they had extended the registration time he should be entitled to the refund. A letter to the supervisor of the person he had been dealing with got him his refund. (Entry #209)

* City Planner Shows Citizens How To Beat The System

A number of citizens in St. Petersburg were worried that the city ordinance requiring neighbor notification of the installation of satellite dishes might be overturned. When they contacted Bernice Darling, a planner at the City Planning Department she gave them great advice. She provided them with copies of the ordinance and the application for change. She also informed them of an upcoming city council meeting concerning the matter. With her help they were able to attend the meeting and stop the ordinance from being changed. (Entry #211)

* Federal Reserve Worker Finds Missing $10,000 For Lady From The Bronx

When a woman in the Bronx had a $20,000 Treasury Note ready to mature, she wrote to the Federal Reserve Board asking that the note be rolled over into two $10,000 notes maturing in 2 and 4 years respectively. She also instructed them to transfer all the interest into her account at Chase Manhattan Bank. When she got her statement from Chase she noticed that she only received interest on one note for $10,000. She called the New York Federal Reserve Bank thinking that all would be lost, but instead found Carol Hayes. Carol really understood the problem completely. She asked a few questions and took her number to call her back. And she did call back. Carol was able to follow the money through the Federal Reserve and into the computers of Chase. During the process Carol called to reassure her and called to give progress reports and kept saying that she hadn't forgotten and that the $10,000 was truly hers and she would find it. When she did find it the lady from the Bronx thanked her to no end and Carol simply said, "Just doing my job." (Entry #212)

* IRS Lets Delinquent Taxpayer Work Out A Deal

A fellow in Oklahoma City was making payments of $1,000 per month to the IRS to satisfy back taxes. However, before he had completed his payments he had back surgery and was laid up for two months unable to earn any money. When payments stopped, the IRS issued a "Notice to Levy" and had his checking and other accounts seized. Although he was truly in the wrong, he called the IRS and spoke to a Mrs. Petrie in the Dallas office. After she listened to his problem she rescinded the "Notice to Levy" and reinstated the repayment plan at half his original monthly payments. He says "this truly was an act of compassion by a caring woman, to whom I am grateful." (Entry #216)

* Woman With Special Title Problem Gets Special Help

A woman purchased a car in Vermont and took it to New York for registration. Due to special circumstances they said it would require 8 to 10 weeks to process the registration. The woman needed the car for local transportation to work as well as for medical reasons for her son, so she contacted her local assemblyman for assistance. His office said they could not help because they were Republican and the Commissioner of Motor Vehicles was a Democrat. She wrote to the local Department of State and they replied saying they could do nothing. At this time she called the main office of the Division of Motor Vehicles and after 5 or 6 transfers finally contacted Louise in the Titles Department. After explaining her situation, Louise contacted the Director of Titles and worked out a plan to personally walk her title through the bureaucracy. (Entry #217)

* Elderly Mugging Victim Gets Losses Back From State Program

While an elderly man was going through the turnstiles of the New York subway system a young man snatched his wallet and ran away. The man pursued the culprit but he was too fast to catch. He found two transit police and the three of them spent about a half an hour looking around, but with no luck. The transit police reported the crime to the local police station. A few days later the man read in the newspaper about a state program that compensates elderly residents who are victims of violent crimes. He applied thinking that nothing would happen. Low and behold, in a few weeks, he received a check in the mail for all the money he lost. (Entry #218)

* Labor Statistics Economist Contributes To Writer's Third Shift

A writer in Baltimore was struggling with a chapter on "How to Survive the Third Shift" for her new book about jobs. She wrote to a regional office of the Bureau of Labor Statistics and received a wonderful response from their office in Dallas. The person in charge of the office sent the writer two articles which served as the basis for the entire chapter in her book. The articles were titled "Late-Shift Employment in Manufacturing Industries" and "Workers on Late Shifts in a Changing Economy." (Entry #219)

* Balloonist Flying High With Help From FAA

When a fellow purchased a foreign registered hot air balloon he dreaded the inspection process required by the FAA. However, he was pleasantly surprised when he ran into Phil and Ernie who are specialists at the FAA. Although getting the balloon ready for inspection was a tedious process with many phone calls over a period of several months, he was very impressed by the two officials. They both had a "we want to help you get this done" attitude, and they always showed an interest in any questions or problems he had. Any forms he requested were sent out the same day and all of his phone calls were promptly returned. On the day of inspection, the balloonist was very late for his appointment, but Ernie stayed even though it put him behind schedule. Ernie also followed up the inspection to see if he was encountering any problems clearing up a few discrepancies. When he sent in his application for air worthiness, Ernie mailed back the necessary forms the following afternoon. (Entry #220)

* Management Consultant Gets The Business From Small Business Office

When a management consultant decided to try to get business from the federal government, he called over 50 small business offices in federal agencies who all but one simply sent him literature on how to do business with their agency. The one was Ila Burnell, Small Business Specialist at the Customs Service. She

immediately made a personal appointment to meet with him, and gave him other names to contact at Customs. In addition, she referred him to procurement people at NASA where she had formerly worked for many years. Using her name he contacted these people and was able to set up appointments immediately. Although it's too early to tell if business will come of this yet, he certainly has a running start thanks to Ila. (Entry #221)

* A Bureaucratic Belly Laugh Drops Homeowner's Taxes By $16,000

When a man in Mississippi found out that his property taxes had increased because his house was reassessed at a higher value, he called around asking how he could get his taxes reduced. The general consensus of opinion (and accompanying horselaughs) was that he talk to the county tax assessor. Not to be intimidated he called the county tax assessor, who answered his own telephone, and talked to him. When he explained that he might have been treated unfairly, the assessor asked if he was home during the day. He replied, "Hell no, I'm working two jobs to pay for my home." The tax man had an out and out belly laugh over the comment and said he would send someone out the next morning to reassess his house. The house was reassessed and the man's taxes were reduced by $16,000. (Entry #223)

* State Acts As Super Travel Agent

When a couple in Michigan wanted to travel to Niagara Falls and New York City last summer they called the 800 number for the New York State Department of Tourism. They could request packets of information by pressing numbers on their touch tone phone, and if they needed to talk to someone they were able to talk to an operator. The person answering the phone was friendly, courteous and to the point. They discussed some special subjects she wanted information on and the tourism official suggested other subjects they might find interesting. In a few weeks the couple had all the information they needed. They had brochures showing the places of interest, maps of everything, dining and lodging information bracketed by prices, as well as helpful tips on using mass transit. Based on all of this information, they made their plans and had an excellent vacation. (Entry #233)

* State Employee Gives Immediate Answers To Employer's Questions

A business owner in the state of Washington called the state capital several times for help in interpreting a new state law affecting him, but didn't get anywhere. Everyone was in a meeting and he was told that someone from a local office would call him back shortly. He thought to himself, "Oh Sure." The very next day, Candy Hansen, the Employment Standards Supervisor for the local agency called him. She listened to the question, but her initial perusal of the law did not identify the section pertaining to his question. She knew that the pertinent section was in the bill, she just had to find it. She apologized for not being able to cite chapter and verse immediately, and said that she didn't want to tie up his valuable time - could she call him back? Within a half hour she called him back with the answer and the next day he received a copy of the bill in the mail. (Entry #236)

* Labor Official Explains New Pension Law To Taxpayer

A man from Ohio called the US Department of Labor in Washington to get some information on a new pension law. The person he was directed to not only explained the law to him, but he also sent him literature about the law and then called him back and quizzed him on the particulars to ensure that he really understood the new law. (Entry #240)

* FAA Official Keeps Aircraft Company Flying High

A few years ago a small air craft company in Kentucky purchased the assets of another aircraft company that was going out of business. The one thing they were unable to purchase was the Type Certificate which is issued by the FAA and authorizes the company to manufacture new aircraft. They petitioned the FAA to revoke the original certificate on the grounds that it had been dormant for 25 years and to re-award it to their company. The official from the FAA assigned to the case could have easily recommended a denial of the petition on the grounds that the procedure was unprecedented, and could have saved himself a tremendous amount of work. Instead, he researched the case fully, visited the facility to see if they could support the responsibilities of a certificate, investigated the legal aspects of the case, contacted the State Corporate Commission to determine the bankruptcy status of the old company, and forwarded a detailed file to FAA headquarters with a recommendation that the petition be honored. An official from the Kentucky company told the FAA official that in 30 years of doing business he had never encountered a bureaucrat who went so far out of his way to help. The bureaucrat's response was, "the taxpayers pay me to do a service - I am just doing that." (Entry #242)

* Banking Commission Official Lowers Mortgage Rate Of Divorced Mother And Saves Her $20,000

A woman in Massachusetts had a "locked-in" deal with a bank to finance her new home at 8.75% interest. However, on the day before closing, a bank official

My Favorite Bureaucrat

called to tell her that because of current banking conditions they could not be held to the 8.75% rate and recalculated the rate to 11%. She had already paid the bank a non-refundable fee of $2,000. As a divorced mother of two, with no family in the area, and ready for settlement the following day, she felt helpless. A call to the State Banking Commission changed this. After she called, an official at the Commission made numerous calls to the bank as well as to the attorney handling the closing. The next day the woman went to the closing as advised by the Commission official, signed the mortgage, and immediately told the lawyers she wanted to cancel the mortgage she had just signed. The Commission official spent the next few days reprimanding the president of the bank. The bank president promptly sent the woman an apology along with a new mortgage at the 8.75% rate. The difference would have cost her $20,000 in extra interest.

* US Border Patrol Favors Canadian Student Who Doesn't Lie

A young Canadian couple was attending a college in Michigan on student visas. They were aware of the many difficulties others had encountered with proper papers and officials at the border. Once when they were returning from Canada, the wife discovered she had lost her official documents she needed to cross the border that day. They knew they could lie to the border officials and say that the she wasn't a student, so that she could enter on her husband's student visa. But they decided to be honest and explain the situation to the officials. They could have been sent back to Canada, but they weren't. The officials told them that many people lie to them and that they appreciated their honesty. The officials immediately found a way that they both could enter the country and get back to school. (Entry # 248)

* IRS Official Helps Woman In Illinois Turn $1,550 Loss Into $669 Gain

A woman in Illinois knew she would owe the IRS some money for the Self Employment Tax, but didn't expect to owe the $1,550 stated on a form she received from the IRS. After being unsuccessful trying to get someone at the IRS to explain why she owed that much money, she finally ran into Jean Doughty at the Kansas City IRS Office. Jean listened carefully and then offered to search out and actually look at the original document. She called back and they were going through the return together when Jean suddenly noticed that the woman had listed her income twice. She then offered to rework the whole return - all 8 pages, and check it out. About two weeks later the woman in Illinois got a corrected return and a refund check for $669. (Entry # 258)

* State Insulation Expert Offers Expert Advice To New Homeowner

A lady in Scottsdale is very grateful to Dennis Craston who works for the Arizona Risk Assessment Office. Thanks to his advice, she is living in a new home, secure in the knowledge that her children will be growing up surrounded by safe housing insulation. He made himself readily available by telephone to answer all of her environmental quality questions about Urea-Formaldehyde Form insulation and different ways to test for any dangerous toxins it released into the atmosphere. He was willing to listen and not pass the buck. "He offered realistic and helpful advice on testing, how to, where to, etc. He was like finding a lighthouse in a sea of indifference." (Entry #261)

Sam At The County Government Makes A Heroin Out Of Real Estate Consultant

A woman in Northern Virginia thanks Sam Demme at the County Department of Environmental Management for making her a success at her job. While working for a real estate management consulting firm, Sam turned her into an expert on the general procedure, forms, and processes involved in bonding and releasing commercial real estate projects. Over the four and one half years she dealt with Sam, each visit was met with a smile and each question, an answer. (Entry #269)

* Government Librarian Overwhelms Student Seeking Fellowship

When a student from Milwaukee decided she wanted to apply for a Fulbright grant to do research in Uruguay she was overwhelmed with the paperwork and turned to Mr. Dorn, the Hispanic Culture Specialist at the Library of Congress for help. This specialist was able to supply what she needed to complete the application including: 1) someone in Uruguay who would collaborate with her on the project, 2) the name, address, and telephone number for the National Library in Uruguay which she contacted directly for further information; and 3) a lengthy computer search, to verify that no publication existed which might have the same results as her intended research. (Entry #272)

* State Representative Shows That One Letter Can Make A Difference In Changing the Law

A man in North Carolina who usually felt insulated against politically related problems, was upset when he read in the paper that the North Carolina Legislature was about to change the requirements for children entering

elementary school. They were planning to move the cut-off date for 5 year olds from October 15th to July 1st so that the average age of children would be 3 and 1/2 months older and they would be likely to score better than other states who kept the later cut-off date. He became angry and decided to call his State representative at home. The representative came in from cutting the grass to answer the phone and told the concerned man that he just happened to be chairman of the education committee and would be discussing that proposal in the coming week. He suggested that he write a letter stating his opposition. The man was relieved to hear that shortly after writing his letter the proposal to change was dropped.

* Single Mom Realizes Dream Home Through Little-Known Government Program

A young single parent living in Pennsylvania thought she would never be able to afford her own home. She checked out the traditional, conventional, and FHA mortgages, and quickly realized that she would not be able to do it without some kind of miracle. But then she learned about a little known program aimed at low income people which made her dream come true. This program, at the Farmers Home Administration, subsidizes her mortgage payments, and the subsidy decreases as her mortgage increases until she is able to assume the full mortgage payment. Any interest the government paid on her behalf over the years is recaptured (based on a formula) when she sells the house. (Entry #282)

* Clerk Helps Couple Outfox Foxy Lawyer In Small Claims Court

A young couple, recently out of college, was moving to another town to start a new job. All was going along smoothly until the landlord decided not to refund their deposit of $100. The couple filed in small claims court and won, but were sent back when the landlord's attorney filed an evasive legal maneuver which stopped them from receiving their money. The couple had no attorney but with the help of Eileen, a clerk at the courthouse, they blocked the attorney's smart maneuver. She spent a lot of her time at the courthouse and on the telephone ensuring that the couple had correctly filled out the proper forms, enabling them to circumvent the landlord's action and collect the judgement. (Entry #282)

* Ohio Man Sends In $100 For Info - Gets A Bunch Back Along With His Check

A man in Ohio recently sent in a request for information concerning measuring instruments to the National Institutes of Standards and Technology along with a $100 check as payment for the information. He was quite surprised to discover his refunded check enclosed inside a massive packet of information relevant to his project, along with the assurance that more information was forthcoming. (Entry #296)

* City Clerk Shows Young Ice Cream Entrepreneur How To Fight City Hall

A young man in Colorado was trying to set up a business selling ice cream from bicycles fitted with freezers. When he inquired about getting the proper licenses from the city he was told that he would need to pay $50 for a license for each vendor he employed. Since the turnover among adolescent drivers is rapid, the cost would have been prohibitive. A woman in the city office explained the step-by-step process to try to change the law. He followed her procedures and after he presented his case to the city council, the ordinance was revised to allow his business to be licensed on a per vehicle basis. (Entry #297)

* Banker Finds A Friendly Banking Official When Starting A New Bank

When a banker in South Carolina submitted a charter for a new bank he was surprised when Mr. Fasbender, the government official assigned to handle the case, demonstrated a personal interest in the banker's efforts and took the time to explain the detailed procedures involved. He was not your "typical" government official. He maintained the high degree of professionalism required, and yet demonstrated that he truly was interested in the bank's success and that he cared. The banker says all this preceded his charter's approval. (Entry #300)

* City Clerk Helps Contest Winner Get $10,000 Prize

A man in Brooklyn was notified that he won $10,000 in a sweepstakes Money Magazine sponsored. But much to his surprise, a follow up letter a few months later informed him he was disqualified after an independent investigation into his application. The man didn't understand the disqualification and believed he was still a winner. He found help from a clerk at the New York City Office of Business Licensing who helped him compose a letter in response along with proper documentation to tell Money Magazine where they were mistaken. It worked, and he received the $10,000 prize. (Entry #305)

* Motor Vehicle Examiner's Advice Is Better Than The Doctor's

When a 70 year old woman in California went to have her drivers license renewed she knew she would have trouble passing the exam because she had just undergone cataract surgery in one eye. She passed the written exam but was unable to read the eye chart, even with her glasses on, and was told to go see a doctor and then return. After the doctor performed some minor corrective surgery she was sent back to motor vehicles with a note from the doctor recommending that she be given a license for two years. When she went back she again failed the eye test and was tested by a cold, impersonal driving examiner who scared the heck out of her. She tried to play on the examiner's sympathies but got nowhere. He was unbelievably nasty. After her driving test he said that he would test her vision again. When she started the eye test, the examiner told her to read from the upper or distance part of the bifocals (previous examiners never told her that). Then the nasty instructor said, "I don't care what your doctor says, I'm approving your license for another 4 years. You can see perfectly." (Entry #307)

* Customs Official Shows Trust To Free Man's $15,000 Dust Collector

A man in Utah unwittingly purchased a BMW that was improperly cleared through US Customs. As a result it sat in his garage because motor vehicles would not register it without the proper Customs form. Over the weeks he was shuffled unendingly through the Customs Offices at Terminal Island until someone finally told him what to send to obtain the form. He sent the required materials, then waited. Weeks passed and nothing happened. In a second series of calls he learned that he had been given poor advice and he was to send further materials. He sent them, and waited. Weeks passed and again, nothing happened. Finally he contacted Barbara Smith. The visits were formal at first, but soon they became chummy little talks. Then she did an amazing thing -- she decided to waive the most troubling of the paperwork, trusted in him, and sent the customs release form. Now his $15,000 dust collector is his daily transportation. (Entry #310)

* Helpful IRS Agent Shows Couple How To Appeal A Penalty

A couple in Michigan got a notice from the IRS to pay $2,583 in back taxes. After going through their paperwork, they determined that they did indeed owe the taxes, but did not think they had to pay the interest and penalty. They walked into their local IRS office and talked to Tim Whaley about the problem. He understood and explained how to write an appeal letter to get the interest and penalty removed. He worked with them over the weeks to ensure that all steps were taken properly by both the taxpayers and the IRS. The couple is now waiting for their answer. (Entry #311)

* Forest Service Ranger Helps Mountain Guide Find His Way Through The Paper Trail

When a mountain guide applied for a license in the Olympic National Forest in Washington, he knew he was in for trouble. The forest is made up of many autonomous ranger districts, creating inconsistencies in the application procedure and a monumental paper chase. Many of the districts seem most concerned with logging, and consider alternative uses of the forest an annoyance. Many districts don't even consider mountain guide applications in the same year they are submitted, and in some cases the permit fee costs more than a mountain guide can afford. This mountain guide was fortunate to have the help of Carol Both at the Quilcene Ranger Station. She discovered an obscure regulation that allowed her to create a master permit that would work in all districts of the forest. It not only saved the guide time and money, but streamlined the permit process as well. (Entry #317)

* Firehouse Gets Loan For Expansion After Being Denied

The Lawrence Township Fire Company waited years to be able to purchase a tract of land next to its firehouse. When opportunity finally knocked, they applied to the PA Emergency Management Volunteer Loan Assistance Program for a low-interest loan. The person who processed the application, for some unknown reason, by-passed normal procedure and stamped it "denied." After many calls, the fire company reached Ms. Sandra Lowan in the office of the loan program, who did some investigating. She discovered that the person who had denied the application had never even looked at it. Ms. Lowan took it upon herself to review the application again, found that it was in order, and set the necessary money aside in a special account awaiting the completion of further paperwork. (Entry #320)

* State Treasurer Sends Milwaukee Man $176 Surprise

In 1989 a man living in Wauwatosa received a letter from the State Treasurer of Wisconsin stating that if he could prove he once lived on 78th Street in Milwaukee they would send him $176. He did so, and they sent him the money. It seems that in 1959 he owned some stock in a company called Curtis Wright. They couldn't find him to send a dividend, so the state had been sitting on his money all that time. (Entry #322)

* Social Worker Goes Out Of Her Way To Keep Brothers In Foster Home Together

Two boys had to be placed in foster homes because their mother was entering drug rehabilitation. The two boys, 8 and 5 years old, were not able to be placed in the same house and their homes were 35 miles apart. The social worker who placed the boys tried to get them together, but when she couldn't she did the next best thing. She would personally take them together to visit their mom. She would also pick them up and take them to their grandparents for visits which would mean 5 or 6 hours on the road. The grandmother, who cares deeply for the boys, says they have responded wonderfully. (Entry # 327)

* Temporary Postmaster Didn't Give Up To Save Small Business Thousands On Postage

A small company in Wyoming was sending out their magazine to their customers at $1.05 a piece, and the postage was killing their business. They talked to their local postmaster about getting a lower rate, such as second class postage, but the local postmaster said there was no way they could ever qualify. Then one day a temporary postmaster took over and the businessman thought it couldn't hurt to ask a new person. When he asked, the temporary postmaster was excited about finding a way to get the small business to qualify for the second class postage rate. Although it took him 9 months, he finally found a way, and it saved the business thousands of dollars. (Entry #333)

* Damage To Beehive From Bear Is Reimbursed From Wild Bear Attack Grant Program

A man in Denver Colorado had his beehives broken into by a wild bear. He estimated the damage to be $8,000 and was surprised when he learned that he qualified for a grant from the Colorado Division of Wildlife which would reimburse him for the damage. In addition to immediately agreeing to repay him for his loses, they also placed traps, snares, and electric fences to prevent such an attack from happening again. (Entry # 341)

* State Attorney General Gets Retired School Teacher * Windfall After She's Stuck With 2 Timeshares

A retired school teacher in Texas was talked into a time share deal, even though she already owned one time share. The salesman told her if she purchased their property, they would take over responsibility for her old property. She purchased the new property, but, of course, the smooth talking salesman was wrong, and she was still responsible for the old property. She called the state Attorney General's office and they were terrific. They worked out a deal in which the company took back their property, and paid the woman's damages-- including all the payments she'd ever made on the first property plus an additional years maintenance fee and interest. When she continued to receive literature in the mail describing how she could win a new car or $5,000 if she purchased a time-share from this same company she'd just won a judgement from, she sent the literature to the Attorney General. A few months later she received a check for $50 from the US Department of Justice. The literature she, and others had received from the company was sent on to the Department of Justice to be used to win a case against them for false advertising. The judgement was distributed among all those who had complained, just as she had. (Entry #348)

* Newspaper Man Claims State Safety Official Saved 107 Traffic Deaths Last Year

A newspaper man who covers the Montana state capitol watched the Highway Traffic Safety Administrator cut the highway traffic death rate in the state from 300 to 193 last year. His research and steady advocacy were instrumental in winning stiffer anti-drunken driving laws and mandatory seat belt legislation in a climate where heavy drinking, heavier driving, and damn the torpedoes is practically a state motto. He reasoned that nothing educates better than a stern patrolman at the driver-side window, and aimed funding at boosting DWI arrests. He literally turned the DWI picture around in many communities. Many in the state's powerful tavern industry protested, but they couldn't argue with the result of his efforts--a major decrease in DWI crashes. (Entry #350)

* Government Researchers Help Student Get An A+ And Reach The Finals Of A Fulbright Scholarship

A 39 year old woman in Florida working on a paper in Irish Studies, contacted an Irish Studies expert at the Congressional Research Service on Capitol Hill. When she contacted him about a paper she was doing he spent close to an hour providing her with information which would have taken her months to locate, if she'd been able to locate it at all. He also gave her a number of other sources which proved to be invaluable. She got an A on her paper. Shortly thereafter, she contacted him again for some information she needed in order to apply for a Fulbright Scholarship. He didn't have the esoteric information she needed but he gave her the names of two contacts at the Irish Embassy who were able to provide her with the needed information. She didn't believe that she stood much of a chance of getting a Fulbright, but with this bureaucrat's help she is a finalist. (Entry #354)

My Favorite Bureaucrat

* Alaska Natural Resources Officer Saves Mining Entrepreneur from a $25,000 mistake.

A man in Alaska was about to purchase the rights to certain mines in Alaska for $25,000. He went to the State Office of Natural Resources where a Ms. Rosenau helped him do research to see if the person selling the mines actually owned them. In her thorough investigation of the documents, she found that the apparent owner did not own clear title and could not sell the mining claims. This could have easily been a $25,000 mistake.

* Single Parent Finishes College With Financial Assistance From State Pregnant Women's Program

A single woman in Michigan in her senior year of college, found out she was pregnant. Her baby was due shortly after the end of the semester in which she would receive her degree. As her due date approached, she felt great emotional, physical, academic, and most definitely financial pressures. At that point she heard about the Pregnant Woman's Program at the State Department of Social Services. This program provided financial assistance to pregnant women in need. She definitely felt she needed help. Her case worker was wonderful. She guided her step-by-step through the application process and made sure she got the financial help she needed to finish college and have her baby with as little stress as possible. (Entry #384)

* Birthday Greetings From President Reagan Bring Happiness to an 85 Year Old Man Who Deserved So Much

A woman arranged, through the White House, for her father to receive a greeting card from the President. Her father was so thrilled with it that he showed it to every visitor for months. (Entry #390)

* Office of Civil Rights Official Is The Only Person To Take Grandmother's Charge Of Sexual Harassment Seriously

Officials at the school where a grandmother was taking courses would not take her charges against a teacher for sexual harassment seriously. Everyone she turned to in the administration thought her charge was laughable. The college ignored their harassment policies. When she took her complaint to the Community College Board of Directors they stonewalled her. She finally contacted Bera Lee at the San Francisco Office of Civil Rights who took her complaint seriously. They investigated the case but could not officially find evidence for the grandmother as the case came down to her word against his. However, she found them to be very understanding and fair. (Entry #391)

* State Labor Official Is One Of The Best At Finding Jobs For Disabled Vets

He works 50 to 60 hours a week and spends his own money and time to get the job done. As a result he is one of the best in the country at getting jobs for disabled veterans. Each time Dan Bloodsworth negotiates with an employer to hire a disabled veteran, another man or woman is placed on the road to a new life and not one of them is accepting something for nothing from the government. (Entry #395)

* Apartment Manager Stuck Out His Can And Got Help From The Garbage Man

A man in California had trouble managing an apartment building. The donut shop next door continually littered the back of his property and used his dumpster. He called the police and the city sanitation departments, but didn't get any response. He finally got in touch with Gunter Moors, an Environmental Inspector with the city, who changed the situation around. In 15 minutes he was at the donut shop, established new rules for the shop to follow, and arranged for the dumpsters to be emptied twice a week. (Entry #397)

* When Local Government Gets Him $369 For Stolen Radio He Believes Paying Some Taxes May Be Worth It

Last year a man in Brooklyn had his radio and equalizer stolen while his car was parked in a commercial parking garage. He called the police to report the accident. He spent the next month trying to get his money back from the garage company. They wouldn't pay and he didn't have time to go to small claims court. He had filed a complaint with the Department of Consumer Affairs, but had never followed up on it. A few months later he got a call from a Consumer Affairs office asking if his problem had been settled. It seemed that the garage owner was standing in the office right at that moment seeking a renewal of his owner's license. The official was calling to see if his claim had been settled. Within a few days of the call the man received a check for $368. This makes it a little easier for him to pay taxes. (Entry #399)

* Soil Conservation Official A Friend To Farmers, Sportsmen And Environmentalists

Mr. Lloyd Wright a land-use planner for the US Soil Conservation Service, designed an agricultural Land Evaluation and Site Assessment (LESA) system which requires federal agencies to assess the negative reaction of any federal projects on farmers. He is also responsible for the wetlands program which helps wildlife, as well as fishermen, hunters, and environmentalists, through efforts to ensure that federal farm programs do not negatively impact wetlands. (Entry #400)

* City Tax Commissioner Gives Back More Taxes

The City Tax Commission of the City of Norfolk has expanded their program to ensure that more people are aware of the possible ways to reduce their real estate taxes. A certain commissioner helps his staff get the limelight for the work he has done. He is very active in the community. For instance, he throws birthday parties at senior citizen homes for those patients who turn 100 years old. (Entry #413)

* State Health Official Makes Life Easier For Parents Of Deaf Child

A couple in Pennsylvania finally decided they were ready for children after five years of marriage. When their first child was born, they were crushed to learn that their child was deaf. The woman quit her job to take care of the child's special needs. Shortly after this, the husband lost his job because of a plant closing. The woman turned to the state government for assistance and was happy to find Mr. Tornbloom who gave them a considerable amount of time, a wealth of information about programs and possibilities, and approved payment by the state for the child's hearing aid. The couple remarked, "He genuinely seemed to value his job." (Entry #416)

* Vital Records Supervisor Opens Express Lane For Woman In Need

A woman living near Chicago was concerned about her sister in Indianapolis whose 14 year old son had just died of cardiac arrest. Her sister's other son was in a hospital in Germany suffering from a collapsed lung. On the day after her son's funeral her sister decided to go immediately to Germany, but needed a passport. She called her sister and asked if she would be able to go to Chicago and pick up a copy of her birth certificate which she needed to get an emergency passport. She had to have the birth certificate in six hours so she could make her flight to Germany. The driving time alone took a good five hours, and when she arrived at Vital Records in Chicago, she was told the process of getting a copy of the certificate would take one hour, no matter what the circumstance. She then asked for the supervisor and explained her situation. The supervisor immediately took her hand and expressed his condolences, disappeared for a few minutes and returned with the certificate saying "you better get going." (Entry #418)

* Student In Wheel Chair Thanks Fast Moving Rehabilitation Counselor

A student at the University of Missouri was used to bureaucratic paperwork. With a post-polio handicap she often dealt with a state rehabilitation counsellor who drove her crazy with carbon copies in quadruplicate, his insistence that rules be followed in minute detail, and his insistence on having every scrap of paper pertaining to her existence dating back to the time of her birth. She got around campus in an electric wheel-chair she received from the state. One day when the batteries failed, she had to ask campus transportation to drive her around to her classes. To her surprise, when she called her counsellor about the problem he processed the paperwork immediately and in twenty hours she had her new batteries and was able to get herself to class. (Entry #420)

* IRS Auditor Finds Extra Bonus For Accountant

An accountant in a Texas company was worried when she heard that she would be responsible to work with an IRS auditor to audit the company's profit sharing plan. However, the experience changed her mind about IRS auditors. She found the auditor to be warm, friendly and extremely professional. More importantly, during the audit, a mistake in the vesting schedule was uncovered. When the company changed its year end a few years ago, the head of the company did not count the short year as a full year for vesting as required by law. This counting of the short year made the accountant completely vested in the plan, instead of 60% vested as she was told by her employer. An unexpected windfall thanks to the IRS. (Entry #421)

* IRS Problem Resolution Center Saves Home Over $65

The IRS wrote letters to a lady in Baltimore telling her they were going to seize her house if she didn't pay them $65. A few years before she and her husband had a cleaning woman once a week and erroneously filed the incorrect form when sending in her employment taxes. The poor lady tried for six months to straighten out the IRS computer with no success. Then came Mrs. Stapleton from the IRS Problem Resolution Center to the rescue. She straightened it all out for the grateful couple and they were able to save their house. (Entry #422)

* Lead Poisoning Expert Provides Worried Mother With Expert Advice

A woman in Maryland was frightened and confused when she learned that her daughter tested positive for lead poisoning. She called a number of different agencies attempting to discover the causes, treatments, and effects of lead poisoning. Although she found a number of offices which she thought might be able to help her, no one could give her any clear answers until she spoke with Dr. Susan Binder at the Centers For Disease Control in Atlanta. The doctor listened to her story in detail and outlined the possible causes of the poisoning. Together they arrived at the conclusion that recent house renovations were the likely culprit. She then discussed the potential long term effects, some of the basic steps she could take to help her daughter, current research and controversies on the subject, and sent current literature. But most importantly, Dr. Binder referred her to local experts and resources in her area where she could turn for further assistance. (Entry #423)

* State Worker Helps Couple Identify Little-Known Program To Pay For Baby's Skull Surgery

A couple in Illinois felt the financial pinch when they learned that their insurance coverage did not cover the C-section birth of their new daughter. They were also devastated to learn that their insurance would not cover the expenses associated with skull surgery which was needed immediately for their new baby. A case worker for the state Office of Crippled Children solved their problem by helping them through the maze of forms and questions needed to qualify for a program which would pay for their baby's operation. (Entry #525)

* Head Of State Surplus Property Helps With Computer Bargain

When a college professor went to Utah's Federal Surplus Division to investigate buying a used computer, the clerk was unable to provide him with enough technical information to make an educated purchase. He later called Bill Arseneau, head of the state's surplus division, who personally saw to it that the professor got all the information he needed to make his purchasing decision. (Entry #426)

* Education Secretary Meets With Unknown Professor And Gives Him Recommendation For Space Flight

A professor in Utah decided he wanted to try to apply for the NASA's Teacher in Space Program, but he needed a high powered recommendation to improve his chances of being accepted. Out of the blue, he called Secretary T.H. Bell, President Reagan's Education Secretary, and asked him to write a recommendation. Mr. Bell invited him to meet at his home. After a nice visit, Mr. Bell said that he would forward a recommendation. (Entry #427)

* Supercrat Writes Comic Strip For State Department As Well As Saving Cambodian Refugees From The Khmer Rouge

Chip Beck, a diplomat at the State Department, is an accomplished cartoonist who writes a Doonesbury type strip for a State Department magazine which makes fun of diplomats. During the Indochina War he also found himself responsible for 40,000 people fleeing communism in central Cambodia. They were encircled by 2 Khmer Rouge regiments and cut off from normal supply routes. He drove Ambassador John Gunther Dean around in an open air jeep during a torrential downpour to witness the plight of the unsheltered families in the midst of a war zone. He jokingly said to the Ambassador, "Sir, I wanted you to see what these people have to endure for the next six months if we don't provide shelter in a hurry."
(Entry #431)

* Social Services Official Provides Hotline For Inner-City Pastor

A Michigan pastor works closely with John Rosendall at the Michigan Department of Social Services. Over 60% of the pastor's people are on some form of public assistance. John gave the pastor a special number so that he can call him most any time of day to handle the problems of his parishioners. He will also check on many of the people who come to the church for help to see if they really need it. Once a family came to the church's food bank for free food and the pastor, questioning their story, contacted John about their background. John found out that the family was earning more money than many of the working families in the parish and most of their money was tax free. (Entry #434)

* Export Expert Provides Fast Info To Business

Bernadine at the Chicago office of the Department of Commerce goes well beyond the requirements of her job according to a researcher who regularly uses her services. Many times she has answered a critical request from an unknown caller to get export or import numbers on some esoteric data. Her expertise is a positive reflection on all US government workers and a godsend to researchers. (Entry #441)

* State Small Business Specialist Helps 20 Year Old Entrepreneur

A 20 year old entrepreneur in New Jersey didn't have money to hire consultants to get answers to all the questions he had about starting his own business. When he called the State Business Assistance Office all his questions were taken care of for free. The woman counselor informed him of the procedures for incorporation, how to protect the name of his business, as well as what forms and fees would be required. She also counselled him on the advantages of forming a partnership, and when he was unsure of taxes she helped him fill out the necessary forms. (Entry #442)

* Poultry Industry Expert Captures Consultant To Tell Him More Than He Ever Wanted To Know About Eggs.

A consultant from Silver Spring, Maryland was trying to get some information about the outlook and trends for chicken and eggs for a client who was in the business. After 6 telephone calls he made contact with Mr. Weimer, whom he was told from previous calls was the government's authority on the poultry industry. He made an appointment to meet with him and when he arrived, Mr. Weimer began a most in depth discussion with hand-outs, sheets and graphs that spelled everything out in a clear and concise manner. (Entry #444)

* Morton Downey Participant Gets Postal Official To Understand The Rules

While a postal worker from Brooklyn was sitting in the audience of the Morton Downey Jr. Show, he met an aging hippie from Colorado. The man in the audience said that he had difficulty cashing a $3,000 postal money order at the Lenox Hill, New York Post Office. The manager of the post office told him he needed two forms of identification when he only showed him one. The Brooklyn postal worker went home and researched the regulations and found that only one form of identification was required. He called the manager of the Lenox Hill office, and was assured that the station will now comply with regulations. (Entry #447)

* Dental Clinic Clerk Helps Homeless With Bad Teeth

A young man in Chicago who grew up in an upper middle class family found himself homeless for 6 years. When he finally began to get his life back together and had a full time job as a doorman he began to have problems with his teeth. His hard life had taken its toll on his teeth. They hurt so badly he couldn't sleep at night and he couldn't afford a dentist. He visited the dental clinic at Northwestern University whose prices were very reasonable but he still couldn't afford it. A young woman in the records office, who understood his situation, took it upon herself to call his brother and arrange payment. (Entry #451)

* FHA Official Helps Those With Late Payment Mortgages

A woman in Indiana is grateful to the woman who runs the local office of the Farmers Home Administration. Without the FHA she would not have been able to buy a home of her own. Soon after she moved in she was involved in an accident and was unable to work or pay her mortgage payments. The woman at the FHA Office was very understanding and arranged a repayment program for her once she started working again. (Entry 453)

* Postal Employee Fishes Out No Postage Birthday Cards From Mailbox - On A Sunday

A man in New Jersey waited until the last minute to get birthday cards from him and his one-year-old son for his wife. His wife's birthday was on Monday and it was Sunday. His wife only liked cards that arrived in the mail so he drove to the next town which had a Sunday pick-up hoping it would be delivered the next day. When he reached the mailbox and started writing out the cards, an impatient motorist pulled up behind him and started blowing his horn. Hurriedly he posted the cards. When he got home he realized that he didn't place stamps on his cards. It was Sunday, but he decided to call the post office. The man who answered the phone agreed to help. When he returned to the post office the man unlocked the door and came outside to the mailbox to retrieve the cards. He also advised him that if he wanted to have his wife receive her cards by the next day, he would have a better chance if he used another Sunday pickup box near by. He did, and his wife received both of the cards the next day on her birthday, thanks to the Sunday postal official. (Entry #455)

My Favorite Bureaucrat

* State Attorney General Gets Alimony Check For Retired Woman

A woman from New York was shocked when her ex-husband told her that he was no longer going to pay her alimony after he retired. He was due to retire soon and she knew she could not make it on her Social Security check alone. She contacted two lawyers to get copies of the laws regarding her situation but they never sent the right ones. When she ran out of money for lawyers she contacted the Assistant Attorney General of New York and he sent her copies of the laws which showed that her husband had to continue his alimony. She quickly sent him what she received from the state, and he agreed to live up to his responsibility. (Entry #457)

* Industry Expert Saves The Day For Consultant

A consultant in California received the book "Information USA" as a gift for his birthday last year and it sat collecting dust on his shelf because he believed "I am from the government and I'm here to help you" is one of the world's biggest lies. He changed his mind when a client walked in and wanted to buy something called Vanadium Slags. He couldn't find anyone who knew anything about them. But by chance he picked up Information USA and after 3 calls found Gordon Schmidt at the Department of Commerce. Gordon not only told him over the phone what it is, he also faxed him important information on the product within 15 minutes. The unexpected eagerness made him wonder if he was on Mars. He now believes that conscientious bureaucrats can make a big difference. (Entry #460)

* Opera Company Gets State Grant To Perform In Nursing Homes

A new opera company, wanting to perform in nursing homes, went to the state arts council for help. They weren't expecting much assistance, but to their surprise, they received moral support, encouragement, and $1,100 to get their opera going. (Entry #465)

* Official Makes State Day Center Happen With Her Own Time And Money

The Governor of Pennsylvania wanted a State Day Care Center quickly and wanted it to be a model program. Jane Snyder, who was given the project, first worried about how parents, already overburdened with jobs and child care, were going to form the Parents Association required by complex regulations. She helped start the association. She paid the application fees from her own pocket and never requested reimbursement. She didn't get overtime pay, but she felt the Day Care project was worth the many extra hours she worked. She got the center running on time and under budget. When the center opened, they needed to write a newsletter and no one could do it - no one except Jane who found time on Sunday afternoon. Gifts for the center's Christmas in July arrived compliments of Ms. Snyder as well as other incidentals which the budget didn't cover. At the grand opening, the Governor got all the attention and Jane was off camera consoling a crying youngster and helping a little boy fix his shoe laces. (Entry #476)

* State Program Provides Van For Wheelchair Dependent Man To Pursue His Dreams

A young man in Arizona had spinal surgery at the age of 12 and was confined to a wheelchair for the rest of his life. He dreamt of getting up and putting one foot in front of another and going where he wanted, like spreading wings to take flight. In high school he started to fly when he got an electric wheelchair. He started to do things like play drums in the school's marching band. In college he dreamt of being a sportscaster, but he realized at graduation he couldn't fly in his new life. He needed a van, so that he could start knocking on doors, meeting with people, and volunteering for internships--all the requirements for getting a job in broadcasting. Instead of sportscasting, he took a job telemarketing because it provided wheelchair transportation. Then he met Bill Butler at the state rehabilitation department who arranged for him to buy a $17,000 wheelchair equipped van so that he could pursue his dreams. He soon received the job of his life at a big local radio station and also found love for the first time in his life. (Entry #470)

* Bureaucrat Gives Human Response To Environmental Impact Statement

A federal official was working with a large Arizona utility company in preparing their environmental impact statement for their new coal-fired power plant. The statement had to pass muster from the state regulatory agencies. A letter of response from the state agency commented on the artist's rendering of the proposed power plant. The picture showed the main buildings, tall stacks, some landscaping, and a nondescript background with a few clouds drawn in. The letter asked if the sky would actually look like the picture. They guessed the state was trying to imply that the sky would fill up with black smoke even though the impact statement showed millions of dollars of state of the art air pollution control equipment. The federal official wrote back to the state saying the sky would look like the picture "Only on partly cloudy days." (Entry 476)

* Older Arizonian Writes Governor About Setting Up A Program To Help People Like Her, and Gets A Call To Set Up The Program

An unemployed, elderly American in Arizona had trouble finding work. In desperation, she wrote directly to the Governor about her problem. In her letter she also described, in some detail, a California program called Network Employment Unlimited that was successful in solving her kind of problem and told him that there should be something like this in Arizona. She also mentioned that she would be willing to help establish such a program. To her surprise, she got an immediate call from another state office wishing to meet with her and discuss setting up the program she had described in her letter. She met with the official and is currently involved in establishing the state program she suggested. (Entry #483)

* Writer Gets New and Old Help From IRS

When a freelance writer was working on an article about the first 1040 used 75 years ago, she got more help than she expected from Josie Downing at the IRS in Washington, D.C. Josie tracked down several internal publications unavailable outside the agency, and provided her with access to the IRS's vaults and files. She provided her with desk space when she came to town and complimentary photocopies. Josie also directed her to the right official at the National Archives for a copy of the first 1040. (Entry #486)

* A Call To The Interstate Commerce Commission Gets Goods Delivered

National Van Lines was holding the personal goods of a woman from Chicago while they disputed an apparent overcharge on the bill. The woman called the Interstate Commerce Commission in Washington, D.C., which in turn contacted the moving company and showed them where they were mistaken. They quickly delivered her goods. (Entry 487)

* Church Board Gets Census Demographics To Select New Pastor

A woman on a committee to select a new pastor for her church, took on the responsibility to find demographic information about the neighborhoods surrounding the church. She wrote to a regional office of the Bureau of the Census requesting the information. To her surprise, she received all the information she needed and more within five days. (Entry #489)

* Controller of Currency Clears Up Credit Rating for Credit Card Holder

A man living in Arizona didn't realize that he had a bad credit rating until he applied for credit at a local shopping center. He once had a credit card with the Bank of Boston and had tried to cancel the card but never got a response from the bank. The bank continued sending him a bill for the annual fee. When he didn't pay they also charged him interest on the fee and placed it in his credit report showing that he didn't pay his bills. The man then wrote to Senator Kennedy of Massachusetts who contacted the Controller of Currency in Washington, D.C. The Controller wrote to the bank, which cleared up the matter immediately. The bank sent a letter of apology to the man in Arizona. (Entry #490)

* City Code Official Helps Homeowner with Broken Bathroom

A man in Illinois accepted a $400 bid from a freelance repairman to have his bathroom retiled. It was considerably less than the $1,000 estimate he had received from a local store. When the freelancer started the job he kept asking for more money and he ended up charging $2,500. He later found out that the man was not a licensed plumber and was wanted in another county for writing bad checks. It cost the homeowner another $2,000 to have a reputable firm redo the job. A code enforcement officer for the city encouraged the homeowner to take the freelancer to court, and helped him through the legal paperwork. He also offered consumer tips on what he did wrong and how to avoid such an incident in the future. Now, the man contacts the code enforcement officer to have him check the credentials and reputation of a tradesman, before hiring. (Entry # 492)

* Election Commission Official Helps Biographer Over Five Year Period

Kent Cooper is a public servant in the disclosure unit of the Federal Election Commission. He believes that people who live in a democracy should be told clearly how their system of government can be used. When a young writer was living in Washington, D.C. Kent was always available to help him piece together campaign finance puzzles. Even after the writer moved thousands of miles away

Kent continued to help. For five years while the writer was working on a biography of Armand Hammer, Kent, almost always on his own initiative, informed the writer about Hammer's campaign contributions on the public record. He also sent printouts of PAC reports that Hammer had directed. (Entry #496)

* Forest Ranger Fulfills Dream In Life

A 47 year old woman with no job experience had always dreamed of working outdoors. When she applied to work as a Forest Technician at the Sierra National Forest it was a local forest ranger who renewed her faith in truth, justice and the American way by promoting equal opportunity and hiring her. She now spends her days planting aspens in beautiful green meadows, and building fences, bridges and gully plugs in an effort to save the environment. (Entry #507)

* State Licensing Official Cut Application Process From 12 Months To 5 Weeks

A woman from Michigan moved to Illinois to work as a nurse. It wasn't until after she got her job that she realized she needed an Illinois nursing certificate to work. The process to obtain a certificate took six to twelve months and she had to start work in six weeks. A call to Ms. Paoni at the Illinois Department of Professional Regulations made it all happen in just five weeks. Ms. Paoni personally walked every piece of paperwork through the system. (Entry #508)

* Conservation Officer Gets Rid Of Racoon Family For Sleepless Homeowner

A female racoon decided to deliver her babies in a crawl space under a woman's bedroom in Indiana. The woman tried everything to get rid of the mother racoon and her noisy children including traps, mothball fumes, recordings of barking dogs, and professional exterminators, but nothing worked. After six weeks of insomnia she called Phil, a friendly state conservation officer, who suggested she try rags dipped in ammonia. She did as he had recommended, and the noisy, pesky coons finally left. (Entry #509)

* Librarian Helps Visually Handicapped Want To Live

Recently a woman in Alabama discovered that she could neither read, watch television nor drive a car. She went to the local library and the woman in charge of services for the blind changed her life. She encouraged her to get a dog, and told her about the many free services available through the library, such as talking books. The dog and books helped to make her life full again. (Entry #514)

* State Insurance Commissioner Shows How A Cancerous Mole Is More Serious Than Breast Enlargements

A woman in North Carolina got a notice from her insurance company that they were not going to pay for her claim to have a cancerous mole removed from her back. She knew of a fellow worker who had just been paid by the same insurance company to have her breast enlarged and thought she was being treated unfairly. She contacted the state insurance commissioner and within the month received payment for her medical care. (Entry #527)

* FHA Official Shows Realtor How To Get Money For His Clients

A realtor in Montana gave up trying to take advantage of government programs to help his clients purchase homes. But he changed his mind fourteen months ago when John Walkup took over the FHA office. John holds monthly meetings to explain the programs that are available. He explains the need for each document, demystifies the process, and makes people feel good. He also holds educational meetings for realtors and streamlines their jobs. In just over a year he has managed to turn a clumsy, bumbling department into a thriving hub of loan activity.

* State Health Care Official Gets Money And Private Bill To Help Terminally Ill Boy

A Wisconsin couple's insurance company would not cover the medical expenses for their terminally ill son. They turned to a state counselor for help. An attorney who works for the service was able to get an insurance company to pay the $17,000 disputed bill and, also got the Governor to pass a law so that their son could be included in a program which provides special funds to allow him to come home from the hospital for visits three times a week when he is stable. (Entry #540)

* State Assemblyman Corrals Wild Steer With 4-Wheel Drive Bronco

A young girl watched as her prize steer, Boggie, bolted out of a California county fair gate. Several men attempted unsuccessfully to grab his rope. Boggie darted past the midway and out a gate onto Highway 86. He was on his way to becoming hamburger meat. As he ran down the highway, California highway patrolmen halted traffic and the chase continued. The steer sought refuge in an adjoining airport. Assemblyman Steve Peace was eating at a restaurant near the airport and saw the steer pursuit. He dashed from the restaurant and jumped into his Bronco to join the chase. Boggie loped down the runway with Steve in hot pursuit. The persuasive, gentle nudging of the Bronco against Boggie's hind quarters, soon coaxed him into submission against a fence. A livestock trailer was secured and Boggie returned safely to the fairgrounds. Despite the stressful event, Boggie did receive a gold ribbon. The assemblyman deserved one too. (Entry #542)

* State Director of Children Saves Money and Children's Welfare

The former Permanency Planning Director in the state of Michigan works in behalf of children who are developmentally disabled. She has a philosophy that all children have a right to a permanent home. As a result of her work, the federal government provided a small grant to establish a state-wide program in 1983 to support families as they care for their children with special needs at home. The program is now six years old, and has benefited hundreds of children and their families. The program has also enabled the state of Michigan to recover millions of dollars by averting the cost of placing children in institutions. (Entry #545)

* USDA Instructor Teaches Woman How To Give Out Federal Money and Not Succumb to Special Interest Groups

A woman in Washington, D.C. was placed in charge of giving out state grants for historic preservation. She took a grant managers course at the local US Department of Agriculture Extension Service. Her instructor instilled in her an attitude of fair play and honesty under pressure. On the job she quickly realized that when large amounts of public monies are at stake, there is great pressure to accommodate special interest groups. Those who do the accommodating rise rapidly on the pay scale until they are not needed anymore. She learned the valuable lesson that maintaining integrity is difficult to do, but possible. (Entry #568)

* Mayor Helps Couple Eliminate Flood Insurance

A young couple who could barely afford their Veterans Administration mortgage payments on their new house, learned that the VA required them to carry flood insurance in an area that had next to no chance of flooding. They wrote to the mayor of the town and in two weeks he sent engineers to designate the area as one that did not require flood insurance. (Entry #573)

* Free Trees Available From City Official

The head of the Tree Shade Commission of Paramus New Jersey promotes the planting, nurturing, and appreciation of trees in the borough. He has a tree nursery where baby trees, when they are big enough, are given to homeowners free of charge. He makes house-calls free of charge to check on the trees and to see if they are sick and whether or not they can be cured. If a tree dies, he'll replace it with a new one. On Community Health Day he man's a booth demonstrating how to maintain the good health of trees and plants. His staff organizes marathons through the park, allowing the runners to pass by and enjoy the trees. He provides wonderful Paramus Mulch free of charge for gardens or lawns. His mulch and his accomplishments are well known in surrounding towns, and he is often asked to speak to groups in the surrounding areas. (Entry #583)

* Chief Probation Official Saves Secretary's Life

In 1988 a woman in Michigan became painfully ill after finishing dinner in her apartment. The next morning she called her boss, the county's Chief Probation Official. He came over immediately and took her to the emergency room. After surgery it was learned that she had Chrohns Disease and would have died if the state official hadn't gone out of his way to get her to the hospital. (Entry #584)

* Hang Up Causes Attorney To Get Satisfaction

A woman in Illinois made a purchase by phone she was not satisfied with. She called the company and requested a refund but the company hung up on her. The Illinois state Attorney General's Office got her the refund in 90 days. (Entry #585)

My Favorite Bureaucrat

* Canadian Bureaucrat Helps New York

A businessman in New York praises a Canadian government official. Although the official was due to retire, he did not lose the desire to see the project he was responsible for through to the end. He was working with the state of New York to develop a new energy saving dry wall product. The dry wall absorbs heat when the room is too hot and discharges heat when the room is too cold. The project could have easily been lost in the cracks if he hadn't made it his duty to see it through to completion. (Entry #588)

* County Conservation Official Helps Homeowner Manage Runoff

When the county highway administration widened a road that ran through a woman's property in up state New York, she was troubled because they stripped thousands of feet of vegetation away and diverted run-off water into her pond. She called the county soil and water department and spoke with Fred Sinclair who arrived within days offering his knowledge and assistance. He gave her literature on water management and lent her his personal reference materials. He gave her his home telephone number, where she occasionally called him and each time he was extremely helpful, even after a long day at work. He gave her free government materials to help her re-seed the land and offered his know how to help with the planting. He has revisited the site many times and intends to do so until the problem is solved. (Entry #592)

* State Helps Single Mother Recover $55,000 In Child Support

A man left his wife and two year old daughter in 1977. Over time he accumulated a debt of $55,000 in child support payments. The state office of the Attorney General located him in another state through Department of Labor information files. They were also able to obtain his current salary, social security number, address, and the name of his employer. With this information they were able to serve him with a court summons and collect the money he owed for the child. (Entry #608)

* HUD Official Helps Couple Get House

The performance of Jim LaZott, a HUD official in Des Moines, Iowa was like a beacon of hope in a sea of chaos. When a young couple began working with the local HUD office to purchase a home, they found it nearly impossible to get even the basic information on HUD programs. That all changed when they met Jim. Everything was smooth sailing from there. (Entry #612)

* US Agriculture Official Gives Moscow Bears A Taste Of Freedom

When the Moscow Circus was visiting the United States last year an official from the Michigan Humane Society contacted the US Department of Agriculture concerning the circus's violation of the federal Animal Welfare Act. Together they tried to get the circus to voluntarily comply with the laws governing the cage sizes for wild animals in captivity. The circus's performing bears were transported and housed in cages that were so small they couldn't even turn around freely, let alone stand up and stretch. The animals were exhibiting stereotypical behavior characteristic of intensive confinement. But because federal laws do not specify exact cage dimensions, circus officials attempted to play a "catch 22" game to get around the law. Although the agriculture official realized that any moment he or his superiors could receive a call from the US State Department instructing them to leave the circus alone for political reasons, he pursued his mission. After many months of negotiations he was able to work out a compromise position in which the circus built a large exercise cage to the Department of Agriculture's specifications, and all the bears had four hours of daily access to this cage. (Entry #619)

* States Labor Official Cuts Insurance Rates For Small Business By 30%

The owners of a small foundry in Michigan site an official from the Michigan Department of Labor as the reason their workman's compensation insurance rates are 30% lower than their competitor's. This official showed up as soon as they opened their doors for business. He pointed out many areas that had to be addressed to eliminate potential OSSA and also set up a program where he made monthly visits to teach employees about safety. As a result the company has never had an OSSA, EPA or Michigan Department of Public Health violation, and received an award for going three years in a row without a lost time accident. This exemplary safety record caused their insurance rates to be 30% lower than their nearest competitor. (Entry #621)

* A Call To DC Results In Hand Delivered Tax Forms In AZ

A tax lawyer in Arizona had trouble getting a form from a local IRS office. He decided to contact the IRS Ombudsman's office in Washington, D.C. to complain about the problem. When he heard about the complaint, the Ombudsman called a local office and had an IRS agent hand deliver the form to the attorney. (Entry #626)

* Forest Service Helps Survival School Survive

A survival school located in Arizona has nothing but praise for the local forest service. They are a small business and whenever they can't meet the payments to obtain their necessary permits, the forest service allows them whatever time they need to make the payments, without penalizing them. Whenever they need to extend the range of their permit, the forest service will always accommodate them. Even when they failed to meet a deadline to sign some papers, a forest service official brought the papers to them, so they didn't have to pay a penalty. (Entry #627)

* State Nurse Helps Mothers Cope With Premature Babies

A woman in Delaware was devastated to learn that her baby would be born fourteen weeks early. She began working with a nurse from the state Early Intervention Program. After the birth of her son, the nurse visited him frequently throughout his four month hospital stay, and after the baby had returned to his home, she visited him many times to thoroughly evaluate his developmental progress. She was the first to spot his hearing loss and helped the couple obtain a state-funded hearing aid for him. She diagnosed his need for speech, physical, and occupational therapy, and helped enroll him in an excellent school. At this time the nurse was experiencing difficulties of her own at home. Her husband was dying of cancer. Despite this, she continued to be an extremely dedicated and compassionate person. (Entry #636)

* FDA Official Helps Inventor Get Clearance

The inventor of a medical device had to get clearance from the Food and Drug Administration before he could start selling his product to manufacturers. His initial call to the FDA resulted in pounds of booklets and forms. When he called back a second time, he not only got exact answers to his questions, but he also received the know how to achieve his dream. An FDA staffer sent him samples of successful applications to copy from, and told him exactly what was required of him to be accepted by the FDA. With this help, the inventor got his approval in record time. Most companies he spoke with were surprised at how quickly he had managed to cut through the bureaucratic red tape. (Entry #646)

* Student Gets Government Doctor To Help With Term Paper

In 1983, a student studying organizational psychology used the book "Information USA" to identify a physician at the National Institutes of Health to help him obtain information for a term paper. This doctor spoke to the student for over an hour helping him gain a basic understanding of the subject matter. The doctor's assistant sent the student an index of federally funded grants on the subject, a list of publications available from their office, and a thick annotated bibliography enabling him to do further research on the subject. All of this was free of charge. He also obtained the names of other researchers to contact and references to explore. (Entry #652)

* Counselor Takes 61 Year Old From Potential Suicide To Great Potential

A draftsman in Ohio was laid off at the age of 61. He couldn't find another job and became so depressed, he even considered suicide. By chance, he met a state vocational counselor and she changed his life. She helped him enroll in a computer aided drafting school to update his skills and found him a new job. (Entry #659)

* State Consultant Doubles Income For Small Business Owner For Free

A free consultant from Tennessee's Small Business Development Center helped a small metal products company on the verge of not making it. He helped double the company's income and gave the owner confidence in the future. The consultant suggested the business would benefit if it were to sell to the government. He showed them how to get on the state government's bidders list. Once they had been accepted he helped them figure out the cost of materials so that they could make a proper bid. The consultant also called the state to get answers to their many unanswered questions, and helped them locate materials and get credit extensions from suppliers. He taught the owner's wife how to do the payroll and other accounting functions. When the company was filling its biggest order, the owner hurt his leg and the doctors told him to stay off of it. Hearing this, the state consultant came by after he got off work, put on a pair of cover-alls and painted grills. One day the company was having trouble with their hydropic press. The owner was so frustrated he was about to scream, when the state official stopped by on his way home from work and fixed it himself, to the owner's amazement. The consultant has been checking up on the business for six months and has gotten them on three more bidders lists. (Entry #666)

* Unemployed Couple Learns About Program Where Employer Can Get Money If They Are Hired

In 1983 a couple moved to Tonawanda, New York to try to get jobs in their respective fields. However, when they couldn't find good jobs they were forced to live on their earnings from part time jobs and buy food stamps. Then they encountered an official with the local Jobs Training Partnership Act. He showed them how to make themselves more marketable by informing potential employers that they would be entitled to cash benefits if they hired them. This made the difference. The husband was hired and within the year he more than doubled his salary. The man realizes the Jobs Training Partnership Act was the main reason he was able to find employment. (Entry #679)

* Commerce Expert Helps Market Researcher

When a market researcher called the Material Handling Specialist at the Department of Commerce for some marketing data, he was told that the data he needed had not been collected by the government for the last three years. But the specialist, undaunted, said she would try to find some additional information and call him back. A couple of days later she called back and gave him a number of additional sources likely to provide the information he needed. She also went out of her way to apologize for not being able to help him directly and wished him luck. She encouraged him to call back if she could be of any further assistance.

* City Manager Pays For White Shirts Ruined In Washing Machine

A man in Elmhurst, Illinois got his first white collar job and purchased eight new white shirts. When his wife laundered his new shirts, to her surprise they all turned to a rust color. The called the city water department to see if there was anything wrong with the water and got a negative response. They then called the city manager trying to get a refund for his ruined shirts. After a couple of phone calls back and forth and a letter from the city attorney, his request was denied. He then showed up at the city manager's office and asked to see the water department's work sheets for the day in question. The city manager said it would take too much time to accommodate his request. After a few minutes of silence the man asked him if he would take a check for half the cost of the shirts now and the other half in about a week. (Entry #700)

* Judge Straightens Out Life Of Gambler

In 1987 a man from South Carolina found himself broke, out of a job, and in jail for writing bad checks to support his gambling habit. He was easily looking at spending the next five years in jail for his crimes. While in jail he wrote to a local judge for help. The judge called him to his office along with all the people he had written bad checks to. Together they worked out a payment plan and got him a job with the water department. Within a year he was made supervisor, paid off all his debts, got married again and is raising a family. (Entry #711)

* Fifty-Six Year Old Woman Thought She Was Unemployable

A 56 year old woman in Seattle suddenly found herself out of work and she thought she was unemployable. The Women's Bureau at the US Department of Labor made an appointment for her with the Mayor's Office for Senior Employment. There a counselor showed her the worth of her skills and got her a job as an editor. (Entry #712)

* Wife Who Works With County Crippled Children Teaches Husband Meaning Of Life

A man from Grand Rapids nominates his wife, who works for the Crippled Children Division of the Kent County Health Department, for the favorite bureaucrat award. She spends a considerable amount of time working out problems, expressing love, and offering understanding to parents who learn that their children will never be like other children. Many of the children die at a very young age. Her understanding of human needs has taught him compassion and tenderness which he would never have learned without her example. (Entry #715)

* Congressman Teaches Constituent How To Expect Good Things From People

A congressman from Michigan manages a summer vegetable stand in front of his house. He manages the stand by the honor system with a note asking patrons to place the money for the produce they purchase in an empty coffee can. A constituent recently learned while talking to the congressman, that he empties the can each night and in several years of operation he has never been cheated. The congressman said he believes that people respond to the expectations of others. If we assume others will betray us, people have nothing to lose by doing so; however, if we sincerely respect their potential for good, most people do not want to show themselves to be unworthy. (Entry #716)

* US Postal Service Employees Have Special Programs To Help The Needy At Christmas

During the Christmas season a committee at a local post office goes through hundreds of letters to Santa. The requests from children who ask for food, clothing, or blankets instead of toys, are granted from a special fund set up by postal workers. Fun letters from children asking for toys are also answered personally by postal workers. Mail carriers also submit names of families on their routes that are struggling. These families are adopted by groups of postal workers who donate money to purchase groceries, clothing, and toys for them. (Entry #720)

* Job Service Helps Homeless Ex-Marine And His Family

Last year a Vietnam Veteran and his family were homeless and broke. They were living in the back of their station wagon in West Virginia. They decided to go to Mesa, Arizona where they met a veterans affairs representative at the job service office who worked closely with the family to get them food, shelter, and work. By the end of the year, they had a Christmas tree in their own living room with presents under it. (Entry #722)

* EPA Makes Sure Woman Business Owner Gets Contract

A woman in Mississippi was running her husband's subcontracting business for some time while he was ill. When he died, a number of prime government contractors took away her business believing that she could not do the job alone. She contacted the EPA's Minority and Women's Business Representative who took up her case and made sure that the subcontracts were returned to her. She says that this official reaffirmed her belief that the compassion of an individual along with the power of a bureaucracy can protect small business in America. (Entry #714)

* Transportation Expert Puts Inventor Into Big Business

An inventor in New Jersey had a great idea for an automobile antitheft device. The product would enable the customer to permanently etch a federal number on car windows. This would cut down on thefts because a thief would have to replace the windows in the vehicle if he wanted to resell it. This would make car theft too expensive and time consuming. The inventor had trouble identifying insurance companies that offered premium discounts for such devices. Without this information the product would not have credibility or perceived value. He checked through Information USA newsletters for sources of assistance and came across the US Department of Transportation's Office of Motor Vehicle Theft Rulemaking Group. When he contacted the group, the woman he spoke with on the phone listed the insurance companies she thought might offer the discounts he was looking for. While on the line, she located a 52-page report that had been presented to Congress concerning motor vehicle theft, which added more states to the list that required insurance companies to provide a discount for this type of anti-theft device. She also gave him contacts to obtain further information and sent him a copy of the 52-page report, which arrived two days later. One of the contacts provided a free report from the state police agencies which demonstrated how such an antitheft device substantially increased the recovery rate of stolen vehicles from 20% to over 70%. This information was critical to the future growth and well being of this small business. (Entry #730)

* Government Expert On Paper Preservation Helps Comic Book Collector

A comic book collector in California was worried about the best way to preserve his rare, valuable comic book collection. Certain plastics used for comic storage are intensely destructive to paper, and he had no way of knowing which plastics were this type. Advertisements in trade magazines were deceptive and confusing. Using the copy of "Information USA" he'd received for Christmas, he contacted Carole Zimmermann, head of the Preservation Office at the Library of Congress. This cheerful public servant not only identified the plastic in question to be highly destructive, but also clarified confusing advertisements, explained the latest laboratory research, and suffered his ignorant questions with grace and an easy laugh. She shared her expansive knowledge in an unhurried, personable, and enjoyable conversation and saved him hundreds of dollars in potential damages. (Entry #736)

My Favorite Bureaucrat

---

* Rehabilitation Counselor Helps Woman in Illinois To See Again

As a result of a spinal tap, a woman in Illinois contracted Multiple Sclerosis. The effects of her disease caused her to lose her eyesight, lose her job, and have a car accident. In addition to the financial strains she already faced, the roof on her house also had to be replaced and there were a few other costly accidents that had to be taken care of. She went to the state's Office of Rehabilitation to see if they could help her find employment since she was blind. The counselor questioned the diagnosis of her eye condition and paid for another eye test. As a result of the test, she had eye surgery and regained her eyesight. (Entry #756)

Free Help in Finding Free Experts

* See also Experts Chapter

Not only is the world full of experts who are willing to help resolve your information problems for free, there are organizations whose mission it is to put you in touch with these experts. Here is a list of some of these clearinghouses arranged by subject area. Don't forget to use the Experts Chapter which includes the name and phone number of experts by keyword from aquaculture to zinc. Remember that these experts spend their lives studying specific areas and are waiting to help you for free as long as you treat them right.

* Agriculture and Commodities

Office of Information
U.S. Department of Agriculture
Room 402A
Washington, DC 20250 (202) 447-8005
A staff of research specialists are available to provide specific answers or direct you to an expert in any agricultural-related topic.
National Agricultural Library
10301 Baltimore Boulevard
Beltsville, MD 20705 (301) 344-3755
This library serves as an information clearinghouse.
National Agricultural Statistics Service
U.S. Department of Agriculture
14th & Independence Avenue SW
Washington, DC 20250 (202) 447-3896
ASS provides contacts for agricultural production, stocks, prices and other data.

* Arts and Entertainment

Performing Arts Library
John F. Kennedy Center
Washington, DC 20566 (202) 707-6245
This center which works jointly with the Library of Congress offers reference services on any aspect of the performing arts.

* Best and Worst Industries and Companies

U.S. Department of Commerce
Washington, DC 20230 (202) 377-1461
Over 100 analysts monitor all the major industries in the US and the companies within these industries ranging from athletic products to truck trailers.
Office of Industries
U.S. International Trade Commission
500 E Street SW, Room 504
Washington, DC 20436 (202) 252-1296
Experts analyze impact of world trade on U.S. industries ranging from audio components to x-ray apparatus.

* Business Advice

Roadmap Program
U.S. Department of Commerce
14th & Constitution Avenue NW
Washington, DC 20230 (202) 377-3176
Roadmap Program provides reference services on all aspects of commerce and business.
Library
U.S. Department of Commerce
14th & Constitution Avenue NW
Washington, DC 20230 (202) 377-5511
This library also provides reference services on all aspects of business.

* Country Experts

Country Officers
U.S. Department of State
2201 C Street NW
Washington, DC 20520 (202) 647-6575
Hundreds of experts are available to provide current political, economic, and other background information on the country they study.
U.S. Department of Commerce
International Trade Administration
Washington, D.C. 20230
Teams of experts from these regions can provide information on marketing and business practices for every country in the world.
Western Hemisphere Room 3826 (202) 377-5324
Europe Room 3863 (202) 377-5638

East Asia and Pacific, Room 3820 (202) 377-5251
Japan, Room 2318 (202) 377-4527
Africa, Near East, South Asia, Room 3872 (202) 377-4925
Agricultural and Trade Analysis Division
Economics Research Service
U.S. Department of Agriculture
1301 New York Ave., SW
Washington, DC 20005-4788 (202) 786-1700
This office provides information on agricultural-related aspects of foreign countries.
Foreign Agricultural Services
Information Division
U.S. Department of Agriculture
14th and Independence Avenue, NW
Washington, DC 20250 (202) 447-7115
FAS provides data on world crops, agricultural policies, and markets.
Division of International Minerals
Bureau of Mines
U.S. Department of Interior
2401 E Street, NW, Room W609
Washington, DC 20241 (202) 632-8970
Foreign country experts monitor all aspects of foreign mineral industries.

* Crime

National Criminal Justice Reference Service
National Institute of Justice
Box 6000
Rockville, MD 20850 (301) 251-5500
Database and reference service provide bibliographies and expertise free or sometimes for a nominal fee.
Uniform Crime Reporting Section
FBI
U.S. Department of Justice
7th and D Sts., NW
Washington, DC 20535 (202) 324-5038
Statistics are available on eight major crimes against person and property.

* Demographics, Economic and Industry Statistics

Data Users Service Division
Customer Service
Bureau of the Census
Washington, DC 20233 (301) 763-4100
Staff will guide you to the billions of dollars worth of taxpayer supported data.

* Economics: National, Regional and International

Bureau of Economic Analysis
U.S. Department of Commerce
Washington, DC 20230 (202) 523-0777
This is the first place to call for economic data.

* Education

Office of Educational Research and Improvement
U.S. Department of Education
555 New Jersey Ave., NW
Washington, DC 20208-1235 (202) 357-6289
A network of 16 information clearinghouses that identify literature, experts, audiovisuals, funding, etc.
Educational Information Branch
Office of Educational Research & Improvement
555 New Jersey Avenue
Washington, DC 20208-1235 (202) 626-9854 (800) 424-1616
Hotline provides referrals to other information sources on any aspect of education.

Information Starting Places

* Energy
National Energy Information Center
U.S. Department of Energy
1F048 Forrestal Building
Washington, DC 20585   (202) 586-8800
This office provides general reference services on Department of Energy data.
Conservation and Renewable Energy Inquiry and Referral Service
PO Box 8900
Silver Spring, MD 20907   (800) 523-2929
Free help on how to save energy as well as information on solar, wind, or any other aspect of renewable energy.
U.S. Department of Energy
Office of Scientific and Technical Information
PO Box 62
175 Oak Ridge Turnpike
Oak Ridge, TN 37831   (615) 576-1301
This office provides research and other information services on all energy related topics.

* Health
National Health Information Center
PO Box 1133
Washington, DC 20013-1133   (800) 336-4797 (301) 565-4167 in MD
For leads to both public and private sector health organizations, research centers and universities.
National Center for Health Statistics
U.S. Department of Health and Human Services
3700 East-West Highway, Room 1- 57
Hyattsville, MD 20782   (301) 436-8500
This clearinghouse can provide data on any aspect of health.

* Housing
Library and Information Services Center
U.S. Department of Housing and Urban Development
451 7th Street SW
Washington, DC 20410   (202) 755-6420
This library provides information on all aspects of housing and staff will direct you to a program which meets your needs.

* Import and Export Statistics
Foreign Trade Reference Room
U.S. Department of Commerce
Room 2233
Washington, DC 20230   (202) 377-2185
This library can provide data on many aspects of U.S. trade.

* Metals and Minerals
Division of Mineral Commodities (Domestic)
Bureau of Mines
U.S. Department of the Interior
Columbia Plaza
Washington, DC 20241   (202) 634-1187
Dozens of commodity specialists collect, analyze, and disseminate information on the adequacy and availability of the mineral base for the national economy.

Division of International Minerals
Bureau of Mines
U.S. Department of the Interior
Washington, DC 20241   (202) 632-8970
Dozens of country experts collect, analyze, and disseminate information on the adequacy and availability of the mineral base.

* Prices, Employment, Productivity And Living Conditions Statistics
Bureau of Labor Statistics
U.S. Department of Labor
441 G Street NW, Room 2822
Washington, DC 20212   (202) 523-1913
There are subject specialists in such areas as plant closings, labor force projections, producer price indexes, work stoppages.

* World Import and Export Statistics
World Trade Statistics
U.S. Department of Commerce
Room 1323
Washington, DC 20230   (202) 377-5242
This is place for numbers concerning most country's trade.

General Sources

These three offices are the places to get help in locating experts in government as well as the private sector and trade associations.

* Associations
Information Central
American Society of Association Executives
1575 Eye Street NW
Washington, DC 20005   (202) 626-2723
If you cannot find a relevant association after referring to *Gale's Encyclopedia of Associations* (which is available in most libraries) this organization will help find the right one.

* Government Experts
Federal Information Center
U.S. General Services Administration
18th & F Streets, NW
Washington, DC 20405   (202) 566-1937
Centers are located throughout the country and the staff will find you an expert in the government on most any topic.

* Technical Research
Science and Technology Division
Reference Section
Library of Congress
Washington, DC 20540   (202) 707-5639
This reference section offers both free and fee-based reference and bibliographic services.

State Information Starting Places

If you have trouble locating the exact office you need from the listing elsewhere in the book, this is the section for you. The first place you should start is with State Information Office listed below. The operators at these offices are normally trained to handle information requests from people who don't know where to go within the state bureaucracy. If you are not successful, try either or both of the other offices listed.

Governor's Office

Because the responsibilities of various state offices often overlap, it may be helpful to begin your data search by contacting the state governor's office. While every state has a central switchboard to field inquiries regarding state business, the number is usually helpful only if you already know which agency is responsible for gathering and interpreting the information you are after. If you are hazy in this regard, the state governor's office will certainly know the appropriate agency, department and, if you are lucky, even the name of the special contact person to call.

State Library

A vast amount of research information is available from the state library. After all, it is the official repository of state agency documents and the first place to start if you want to do all of the footwork yourself. In addition, most state libraries also shelve copies of federal government documents and publications.

State libraries are paid for with tax dollars and are open to the public. Collections usually include state legal codes, state historical documents, archival records, genealogy type information, business and economic records, statistical abstracts and annual reports.

In each library these is generally a government information person who can provide telephone and personal assistance to researchers. In addition, there is often a staff specialist to help with statistical questions.

The following is a list of state operators, librarians, and governor's offices.

State Information and Governor's Offices

Alabama
State Information: (205) 261-2500

Governor's Office: Office of the Governor, Statehouse, 11 South Union St., Montgomery, AL 36130 (205) 261-7100.

State Library: Alabama Public Library Service, 6030 Monticello Drive, Montgomery, AL 36130 (205) 277-7330.

Alaska
State Information: (907) 465-2111

Governor's Office: Office of the Governor, P.O. Box A, Juneau, AK 99811 (907) 465-3500.

State Library: Libraries and Museums, P.O. Box G, Juneau, AK 99811 (907) 465-2920.

Arizona
State Information: (602) 255-4900

Governor's Office: Office of Office of the Governor, 1700 West Washington St., Phoenix, AZ 85007 (602) 542-4900

State Library: Department of Library Archives and Public Records, State Capitol, Room 200, 1700 W. Washington, St., Phoenix, AZ 85007 (602) 542-4035

Arkansas
State Information: (501) 371-3000

Governor's Office: Office of the Governor, State Capitol Building, Room 250, Little Rock, AR 72201 (501) 682-2345.

State Library: Arkansas State Library, 1 Capitol Mall, Little Rock, AR 72201 (501) 682-2842.

California
State Information: (916) 322-9900

Governor's Office: Office of the Governor, State Capitol, Sacramento, CA 95814 (916) 445-2841.

State Library: California State Library, Library and Courts Building, P.O. Box 942837, Sacramento, CA 94237 (916) 322-4570.

Colorado
State Information: (303) 866-5000

Governor's Office: Office of the Governor, 136 State Capitol Building, Denver, CO 80203 (303) 866-2471.

State Library: Colorado State Library, 201 East Colfax Ave., Denver, CO 80203 (303) 866-6600.

Connecticut
State Information: (203) 240-0222

Governor's Office: Office of the Governor, 165 Capitol Ave., Hartford, CT 06106 (203) 566-2750.

State Library: Connecticut State Library, 231 Capitol Ave., Hartford, CT 06106 (203) 566-4777.

Delaware
State Information: (302) 736-4000

Governor's Office: Office of the Governor, Legislative Hall, Dover, DE 19901 (302) 736-4101.

State Library: Delaware State Library, 43 South DuPont Highway, Dover, DE 19903 (302) 736-4748.

District of Columbia
Information: (202) 727-1000

Mayor's Office: Executive Office of the Mayor, District Building, 1350 Pennsylvania Ave. N.W., Washington, D.C. 20004 (202) 727-6319.

Central Library: Martin Luther King, Jr. Memorial Library, 901 G. St. N.W., Washington, D.C. 20001 (202) 727-1126.

Florida
State Information: (904) 488-1234

Governor's Office: Office of the Governor, The Capitol, Tallahassee, FL 32399

Information Starting Places

(904) 488-4441.

State Library: Florida State Library, R.A. Gray Building, 500 Bruno St., Tallahassee, FL 32399 (904) 487-2651.

Georgia
State Information: (404) 656-2000

Governor's Office: Office of the Governor, 203 State Capitol, Atlanta, GA 30334 (404) 656-1776.

State Library: Georgia State Library, 301 Judicial Building, 40 Capitol Square, Atlanta, GA 30334 (404) 656-3468.

Hawaii
State Information: (808) 548-6222

Governor's Office: Office of the Governor, State Capitol, Honolulu, HI 96813 (808) 548-5420.

State Library: Hawaii State Library, 478 South King St., Honolulu, HI 96813 (808) 548-4775.

Idaho
State Information: (208) 334-2411

Governor's Office: Office of the Governor, State House, Boise, ID 83702 (208) 334-2100.

State Library: Idaho State Library, 325 West State St., Boise, ID 83702 (208) 334-2150.

Illinois
State Information: (217) 782-2000

Governor's Office: Office of the Governor, State Capitol, Springfield, IL 62701 (217) 782-6830.

State Library: Illinois State Library, 2nd and Edwards Sts., Springfield, IL 62756 (217) 782-7596.

Indiana
State Information: (317) 232-1000

Governor's Office: Office of the Governor, State House, Indianapolis, IN 46204 (317) 232-4567.

State Library: Indiana State Library, 140 North Senate, Indianapolis, IN 46204 (317) 232-3675.

Iowa
State Information: (515) 281-5011

Governor's Office: Office of the Governor, State Capitol, Des Moines, IA 50319 (515) 281-5211.

State Library: Iowa State Library, East 12th and Grand Sts., Des Moines, IA 50319 (515) 281-4118.

Kansas
State Information: (913) 296-0111

Governor's Office: Office of the Governor, State House, Topeka, KS 66612 (913) 296-3232.

State Library: Kansas State Library, State House, Topeka, KS 66612 (913) 296-3296.

Kentucky
State Information: (502) 564-3130

Governor's Office: Office of the Governor, State Capitol Building, Frankfort, KY 40601 (502) 564-2611.

State Library: Kentucky Department of Libraries and Archives, 300 Coffee Tree Road, P.O. Box 537, Frankfort, KY 40602 (502) 875-7000.

Louisiana
State Information: (504) 342-6600
Governor's Office: Office of the Governor, P.O. Box 94004, Baton Rouge, LA 70804 (504) 342-7015.

State Library: Louisiana State Library, P.O. Box 131, Baton Rouge, LA 70821 (504) 342-4923.

Maine
State Information: (207) 289-1110

Governor's Office: Office of the Governor, State House Station1, Augusta, ME 04333 (207) 289-3531.

State Library: Maine State Library, State House, Station 64, Augusta, ME 04333 (207) 289-5600.

Maryland
State Information: (301) 974-2000

Governor's Office: Office of the Governor, State House, Annapolis, MD 21404 (301) 974-3431.

State Library: Maryland State Archives, Hall of Records, 350 Rowe Boulevard, Annapolis, MD 21404.

Massachusetts
State Information: (617) 727-2121

Governor's Office: Office of the Governor, State House, Boston, MA 02133 (617) 727-9173.

Michigan
State Information: (517) 373-1837

Governor's Office: Office of the Governor, State Capitol Building, Lansing, MI 48913 (517) 373-3400.

State Library: Michigan State Library, 735 E. Michigan Ave., Lansing, MI 48909 (517) 373-1593.

Minnesota
State Information: (612) 296-6013

Governor's Office: Office of the Governor, 130 State Capitol, St. Paul, MN 55155 (612) 296-3391.

State Library: Legislative Reference Library, State Office Building, St. Paul, MN 55155 (612) 296-3398.

Mississippi
State Information: (601) 359-1000

Governor's Office: Office of the Governor, P.O. Box 139, Jackson, MS 39205 (601) 359-3100.

State Library: Department of Archives and History Library, P.O. Box 571, Jackson, MS 39205 (601) 359-1424.

Missouri
State Information: (314) 751-2000

Governor's Office: Office of the Governor, State Capitol, P.O. Box 720, Jefferson City, MO 65102 (314) 751-3222.

State Library: Missouri State Library, P.O. Box 387, Jefferson City, MO 65102 (314) 751-3615.

Montana
State Information: (406) 444-2511

Governor's Office: Office of the Governor, State Capitol, Helena, MT 59620 (406) 444-3111.

State Library: Montana State Library, 1515 East 6th Ave., Helena, MT 59620 (406) 444-3115.

Nebraska
State Information: (402) 471-2311

Governor's Office: Office of the Governor, State Capitol, P.O. Box 94848, Lincoln, NE 68509 (402) 471-2244.

State Library: Nebraska State Library, 1420 P. St., Lincoln, NE 68508 (402) 471-2045.

Nevada
State Information: (702) 885-5000

Governor's Office: Office of the Governor, State Capitol Bldg., Carson City, NV 89710 (702) 885-5130.

State Library: Nevada State Library, 401 North Carson St., Carson City, NV 89710 (702) 885-5130.

New Hampshire
State Information: (603) 271-1100

Governor's Office: Office of the Governor, State House, Concord, NH 03301 (603) 271-2121.

State Library: New Hampshire State Library, 20 Park St., Concord, NH 03301 (603) 271-2144.

New Jersey
State Information: (609) 292-2121

Governor's Office: Office of the Governor, 125 West State St., State House, Trenton, NJ 08625 (609) 292-6000.

State Library: New Jersey State Library, State House Annex, CN 520, Trenton, NJ (609) 292-6220.

New Mexico
State Information: (505) 827-4011

Governor's Office: Office of the Governor, State Capitol Building, Santa Fe, NM 87503 (505) 827-3800.

Governor's Office: State Library: New Mexico State Library, 325 Don Gaspar, Santa Fe, NM 87503 (505) 827-3800.

New York
State Information: (518) 474-2121

Governor's Office: Office of the Governor, State Capitol, Albany, NY 12224 (518) 474-8390.

State Library: New York State Library, Empire State Plaza, Madison Avenue, Albany, NY 12230 (518) 474-7646.

North Carolina
State Information: (919) 733-1110

Governor's Office: Office of the Governor, State Capitol, Raleigh, NC 27603 (919) 733-5811.

State Library: North Carolina State Library, 109 East Jones St., Raleigh, NC 27611 (919) 733-2570.

North Dakota
State Information: (701) 224-2000

Governor's Office: Office of the Governor, State Capitol, Bismark, ND 58505 (701) 224-2200.

State Library: North Dakota State Library, State Capitol, Bismark, ND 58505 (701) 224-2490.

Ohio
State Information: (614) 466-2000

Governor's Office: Office of the Governor, State House, Columbus, OH 43215 (614) 466-3555.

State Library: Ohio State Library, 65 South Front St., Columbus, OH 43266 (614) 644-7061.

Oklahoma
State Information: (405) 521-1601

Governor's Office: Office of the Governor, 212 State Capitol, Oklahoma City, OK 73105 (405) 521-2345.

State Library: Oklahoma State Library, 200 N.E. 18th St., Oklahoma City, OK 73105 (405) 521-2502.

Oregon
State Information: (503) 378-3131

Governor's Office: Office of the Governor, 254 State Capitol, Salem, OR 97310 (503) 378-3100.

State Library: Oregon State Library, State Library Building, Salem, OR 97310 (503) 378-4274.

Pennsylvania
State Information: (717) 787-2121

Governor's Office: Office of the Governor, 225 Main Capitol, Harrisburg, PA 17120 (717) 787-5962.

State Library: Pennsylvania State Library, P.O. Box 1601, Harrisburg, PA 17105 (717) 787-2646.

Rhode Island
State Information: (401) 277-2000

Governor's Office: Office of the Governor, 222 State House, Providence, RI 02903 (401) 277-2080.

State Library: Rhode Island State Library, State House, Providence, RI 02903 (401) 277-2473.

South Carolina
State Information: (803) 734-1000

Governor's Office: Office of the Governor, P.O. Box 11369, Columbia, SC 29211 (803) 734-9818.

State Library: South Carolina State Library, P.O. Box 11469, Columbia, SC 29225 (803) 734-8666.

South Dakota
State Information: (605) 773-3011

Governor's Office: Office of the Governor, State Capitol, Pierre, SD 57501 (605) 773-3212.

State Library: South Dakota State Library, 800 Governor's Dr., Pierre, SD 57501 (605) 773-3131.

Tennessee
State Information: (615) 741-3011

Governor's Office: Office of the the Governor, State Capitol, Nashville, TN 37219 (615) 741-2001.

State Library: Tennessee State Library, 403 7th Ave. North, Nashville, TN 37219 (615) 741-2764.

Texas
State Information: (512) 463-4630

Governor's Office: Office of the Governor, P.O. Box 12428, Austin, TX 78711 (512) 463-2000.

State Library: Texas State Library, P.O. Box 12927, Austin, TX 78711 (512) 463-5455.

Information Starting Places

Utah

State Information: (801) 533-4000

Governor's Office: Office of the Governor, State Capitol, Salt Lake City, UT 84114 (801) 538-1000.

State Library: Utah State Library, 2150 South 300 West, Salt Lake City, UT 84115 (801) 466-5888.

Vermont

State Information: (802) 828-1110

Governor's Office: Office of the Governor, Pavillion Office Building, Montpelier, VT 05602 (802) 828-3333.

State Library: Vermont State Library, State Office Building, Montpelier, VT 05602 (802) 828-3265.

Virginia

State Information: (804) 786-0000

Governor's Office: Office of the Governor, P.O. Box 1475, Richmond, VA 23212 (804) 367-1737.

State Library: Virginia State Library, 11th St and Capitol Square, Richmond, VA 23219 (804) 786-8929.

Washington

State Information: (206) 753-5000

Governor's Office: Office of the Governor, Legislative Building, Olympia, WA 98504 (206) 753-6780.

State Library: Washington State Library, Capitol Campus, Mail Stop AJ-11, Olympia, WA 98504 (206) 753-5590.

West Virginia

State Information: (304) 348-3456

Governor's Office: Office of the Governor, Main Capitol Complex, Charleston, WV 25305 (304) 348-2000.

State Library: West Virginia State Library, Cultural Center, Charleston, WV 25305 (304) 348-2041.

Wisconsin

State Information: (608) 266-2211

Governor's Office: Office of the Governor, P.O. Box 7863, Madison, WI 53707 (608) 266-1212.

State Library: State Historical Society, 816 State St., Madison, WI 53706 (608) 262-3338.

Wyoming

State Information: (307) 777-7011

Governor's Office: Office of the Governor, State Capitol, Cheyenne, WY 82002 (307) 777-7434.

State Library: Wyoming State Library, Supreme Court Building, 23rd and Capitol, Cheyenne, WY 82002 (307) 777-7283.

Federal Public Information Offices

Most every federal department, agency, and commission has a special staff to respond to inquiries from the public and the press. These public information offices are particularly helpful in providing details about new programs, proposed legislation, data, statistics, reports and other materials. Keep in mind that the public information office may not be aware or may not be in a position to share with you information that has not be officially released by the government agency. The policy of each office differs; some public information offices like many at the National Institutes of Health tend to offer to send photocopies of medical article abstracts and also provide the names and phone numbers of experts and NIH researchers. If others are reluctant to suggest whom you should talk with and, in this case, refer to the relevant chapter in *Info-Power* and place some calls to other offices within the agency or department.

Administrative Office of the U.S. Courts
811 Vermont Ave., NW
Washington, DC 20544
(202) 633-6040

Agricultural Cooperative Service
U.S. Department of Agriculture
P.O. Box 96576
Washington, DC 20090-6576
(202) 653-6973

Agricultural Marketing Service
U.S. Department of Agriculture
P.O. Box 96456
Washington, DC 20250
(202) 447-8999

Agricultural Research Service
U.S. Department of Agriculture
Agricultural Research Center
Bldg. 005
Beltsville, MD 20705
(301) 344-2264

Alaska Power Administration
U.S. Department of Energy
1000 Independence Ave., SW
Washington, DC 20585
(202) 586-2008

Alcohol, Drug Abuse, and Mental Health Administration
Department of Health and Human Services
5600 Fishers Lane
Rockville, MD 20857
(301) 443-4797

Alcohol, Tobacco, Firearms, Bureau of
Department of the Treasury
1200 Pennsylvania Ave., NW
Washington, DC 20226
(202) 566-7135

Animal and Plant Health Inspection Service
U.S. Department of Agriculture
14th and Independence, SW
Washington, DC 20250
(202) 447-2511

Antitrust Division
Department of Justice
10th St. and Constitution Ave., NW
Washington, DC 20530
(202) 633-6292

Architect of the Capitol
U.S. Capitol Building
Washington, DC 20515
(202) 225-1200

Aviation Administration
Department of Transportation
800 Independence Ave., SW
Washington, DC 20591
(202) 267-3484

Bilingual Education
Department of Education
330 C St., SW, Room 5086
Washington, DC 20202
(202) 732-5063

Bonneville Power Administration
U.S. Department of Energy
P.O. Box 3621
Portland, OR 97208
(503) 230-3474

Botanic Garden
Maryland and 1st Sts., SW
Washington, DC 20515
(202) 226-4082

Census, Bureau of the
Department of Commerce
Room 2705
Washington, DC 20233
(301) 763-4051

Centers for Disease Control
1600 Clifton Road NE
Atlanta, GA 30333
(404) 329-3311

Civil Rights Division
Department of Justice
P.O. Box 65310
Washington, DC 20035-5310
(202) 633-4224

Civil Rights, Office of
Department of Education
400 Maryland Ave., SW, Room 5000
Washington, DC 20202
(202) 732-1213

Civilian Radioactive Waste Management, Office of
U.S. Department of Energy
1000 Independence Ave., SW
Washington, DC 20585

(202) 586-2835

Coast Guard
Department of Tranportation
2100 2nd St., SW
Washington, DC 20593
(202) 267-1587

Commerce, Department of
14th and Constitution Ave. NW
Washington, DC 20230
(202) 377-4901
(202) 377-2000

Commodity Credit Corporation
U.S. Department of Agriculture
P.O. Box 2415
Washington, DC 20013
(202) 447-4785

Comptroller of the Currency
Department of the Treasury
490 L'Enfant Plaza East, SW
Washington, DC 20219
(202) 447-1800

Congressional Budget Office
Second and D Sts., SW
Washington, DC 20515
(202) 226-2600

Conservation and Renewable Energy
U.S. Department of Energy
1000 Independence Ave., SW
Washington, DC 20585
(202) 586-9346

Consumer Advisor Office
U.S. Department of Agriculture
14th and Independence, SW
Washington, DC 20250
(202) 382-9681

Cooperative State Research Service
U.S. Department of Agriculture
14th and Independence, SW
Washington, DC 20250
(202) 447-8268

Contract Compliance, Federal Office of
Department of Labor
200 Constitution Ave., NW, Room C-3325
Washington, DC 20210
(202) 523-9475
(202) 225-7000

Criminal Division
Department of Justice
10th and Constitution Ave., NW, Room 2107
Washington, DC 20530
(202) 633-2601

Crop Insurance Corporation, Federal
U.S. Department of Agriculture
14th and Independence, SW
Washington, DC 20250
(202) 447-3287

Customs Services
Department of the Treasury
1301 Constitution Ave., NW
Washington, DC 20229
(202) 566-8195

Deaf, National Technical Institute for the
One Lomb Memorial Drive
Rochester, NY 14623
(716) 475-6283

Defense Programs
U.S. Department of Energy
1000 Independence Ave., SW
Washington, DC 20585
(202) 586-5708

Drug Control Policy, National Office of
Executive Office of the President
Washington, DC 20500
(202) 673-2824

Drug Enforcement Administration
Department of Justice
Washington, DC 20537
(202) 633-7977

Economic Advisers, Council of
Old Executive Office Bldg.
Washington, DC 20500
(202) 395-5084

Economic Analysis, Bureau of
Department of Commerce
1401 K St., NW
Washington, DC 20230
(202) 523-0777

Economic Development Administration
Department of Commerce
14th and Constitution Ave., NW, Room 7808
Washington, DC 20230
(202) 377-5113

Economic Regulatory Administration
U.S. Department of Energy
1000 Independence Ave., SW
Washington, DC 20585
(202) 586-9563

Economic Research Service
U.S. Department of Agriculture
1301 New York Ave., NW
Room 228
Washington, DC 20005-4789
(202) 786-1504

Educational Research and Improvement, Office of
Department of Education
555 New Jersey Ave., NW, Room 600
Washington, DC 20203
(202) 357-6050

Education, Department of
400 Maryland Ave., SW
Washington, DC 20202
(202) 732-4576
(202) 377-2000 locator

Elementary and Secondary Education, Office of
Department of Education
400 Maryland Ave., SW, Room 2189
Washington, DC 20202
(202) 732-5113

Energy, Department of
1000 Independence Ave., SW
Washington, DC 20585
(202) 586-6827

Energy Information Administration
National Energy Information Center
U.S. Department of Energy
Room 1F048
1000 Independence Ave., SW
Washington, DC 20585
(202) 586-8800

Energy Regulatory Commission, Federal
U.S. Department of Energy
825 North Capitol St., NE
Washington, DC 20426
(202) 357-8118

Energy Research, Office of
U.S. Department of Energy
1000 Independence Ave., SW
Washington, DC 20585
(202) 586-5430

Engraving and Printing Bureau
Department of the Treasury
14th and C Sts., SW, Room 533M
Washington, DC 20228
(202) 447-0193

Environmental Quality, Council on
722 Jackson Pl., NW
Washington, DC 20503
(202) 395-5750

Extension Service
U.S. Department of Agriculture
14th and Independence, SW
Washington, DC 20250
(202) 447-4241

Family Support Administration
Department of Health and Human Services
370 L'Enfant Promenade, SW
Washington, DC 20447
(202) 252-4500

Farmers Home Administration
U.S. Department of Agriculture
14th and Independence, SW
Washington, DC 20250
(202) 447-4323

Federal Bureau of Investigation (FBI)
9th St. and Pennsylvania Ave., NW
Washington, DC 20535
(202) 324-3691

Financial Management Services
Department of the Treasury
401 14th St., SW, Room 554
Washington, DC 20227
(202) 287-0669

Fish and Wildlife Service
U.S. Department of the Interior
18th and C Sts., NW
Washington, DC 20240
(202) 343-5634

Food and Drug Administration
Department of Health and Human Services
5600 Fishers Lane
Rockville, MD 20857
(301) 443-1544

Food and Nutrition Service

U.S. Department of Agriculture
3101 Park Center Dr.
Alexandria, VA 22302
(703) 765-3276

Food, Safety and Inspection Service
U.S. Department of Agriculture
14th and Independence, SW
Washington, DC 20250
(202) 447-9351

Foreign Agricultural Service
U.S. Department of Agriculture
14th and Independence, SW
Washington, DC 20250
(202) 447-3448

Forest Service
U.S. Department of Agriculture
P.O. Box 96090
Washington, DC 20090
(202) 447-3760

Fossil Energy
U.S. Department of Energy
1000 Independence Ave., SW
Room 4G085; FE 5
Washington, DC 20585
(202) 586-6503

Gallaudet University
Department of Education
800 Florida Ave., NE
Washington, DC 20002-3625
(202) 651-5505

General Accounting Office
441 G St., NW
Washington, DC 20548
(202) 275-2812

Geological Survey
U.S. Department of the Interior
National Center
Reston, VA 22092
(703) 648-4460

Government Printing Office
North Capitol and H Sts., NW
Washington, DC 20401
(202) 275-3204

Grain Inspection Service, Federal
U.S. Department of Agriculture
14th and Independence, SW
Washington, DC 20250
(202) 475-3367

Health and Human Services, Department of
200 Independence Ave., SW
Washington, DC 20201
(202) 475-0257
(202) 245-6296 locator

Health Care Financing Administration
Department of Health and Human Services
200 Independence Ave., SW
Washington, DC 20201
(202) 245-6113

Health Resources and Services Administration
Department of Health and Human Services
5600 Fishers Lane

Information Starting Places

Rockville, ND 20857
(301) 443-2086

Highway Administration
Department of Transportation
499 7th St., SW
Washington, DC 20590
(202) 366-0660

House of Representatives
Clerk
The Capitol
Washington, DC 20515
(202) 224-3121

Housing and Urban Development, Department of
451 7th St., SW
Washington, DC 20410
(202) 755-6685

Howard University
Department of Education
2400 6th St., NW
Washington, DC 20059
(202) 686-5400

Human Development Services, Office of
Department of Health and Human Services
200 Independence Ave., SW
Washington, DC 20201
(202) 245-7246

Human Nutrition Information Service
U.S. Department of Agriculture
6505 Belcrest Rd.
Hyattsville, MD 20782
(301) 436-7725

Immigration and Naturalization Service
Department of Justice
425 I St., NW
Washington, DC 20536
(202) 633-4316

Immigration, Related Unfair Employment Practice, Special Counsel
Department of Justice
1100 Connecticut Ave., NW, Suite 800 or P.O. Box 65490
Washington, DC 20035
(202) 653-8480

Immigration Review, Executive Office of
5197 Leesburg Pike, Suite 2300
Falls Church, VA 22302
(202) 756-6171

Indian Affairs, Bureau of
U.S. Department of the Interior
18th and C Sts., NW
Washington, DC 20240
(202) 343-1711

Indian Health Service
Department of Health and Human Services
5600 Fishers Lane
Rockville, MD 20857
(301) 443-1083

Interior, Department of
18th and C Sts., NW
Washington, DC 20240
(202) 343-3171

Internal Revenue Service
Department of the Treasury
1111 Constitution Ave., NW
Washington, DC 20224
(202) 566-5000

International Cooperation and Development Office
U.S. Department of Agriculture
14th and Independence, SW
Washington, DC 20250
(202) 653-7589

International Trade Administration
Department of Commerce
500 E St., SW
Washington, DC 20436
(202) 252-1819

Justice, Department of
Constitution Ave. and 10th St., NW
Washington, DC 20530
(202) 633-2007
(202) 633-4000 locator

Justice, Office of
National Criminal Justice Reference
NCJRS
1600 Research Blvd. or P.O. Box 6000
Rockville, MD 20850
(202) 724-7782

Labor, Department of
200 Constitution Ave., NW, Room S-1032
Washington, DC 20210
(202) 523-7316
(202) 523-4000 Locator

Labor Management Relations, Bureau of
Department of Labor
200 Constitution Ave., NW
Washington, DC 20210
(202) 523-6045

Labor Statistics, Bureau of
Department of Labor
200 Constitution Ave., NW
Washington, DC 20210
(202) 523-1327

Land and Natural Resource Division
Department of Justice
9th and Pennsylvania Ave., NW
Washington, DC 20530
(202) 633-2701

Land Management, Bureau of
U.S. Department of the Interior
18th and C Sts., NW
Washington, DC 20240
(202) 343-5717

Law Enforcement Training Center
Department of the Treasury
Building 94
Glynco, GA 31524
(912) 267-2447

Library of Congress
101 Independence Ave., SE
Washington, DC 20540
(202) 707-2905

Maritime Administration

Department of Transportation
400 7th St., SW
Washington, DC 20590
(202) 266-5807

Marshals Service
Department of Justice
600 Army-Navy Drive
Arlington, VA 22202
(202) 307-9600

Mines, Bureau of
U.S. Department of the Interior
18th and C Sts., NW
Washington, DC 20240
(202) 343-5512

Minerals Management Service
U.S. Department of the Interior
18th and C Sts., NW
Washington, DC 20240
(202) 343-3983

Mine Safety and Health Administration
Department of Labor
4105 Wilson Boulevard, Room 601
Arlington, VA 22203
(703) 235-1452

Minority Business Development Agency
Department of Commerce
14th and Constitution Ave., NW, Room 6707
Washington, DC 20230
(202) 377-1936

National Institutes of Health (NIH)
Department of Health and Human Services
9000 Rockville Pike
Bethesda, MD 20892
(301) 496-4000

National Institute of Standards and Technology
Information Resources and Services Division
Department of Commerce
Building 101, Room A903
Gaithersburg, MD 20899
(301) 975-2758

National Security Council
Old Executive Office Bldg.
Washington, DC 20506
(202) 456-2930

National Technical Information Service (NTIS)
Department of Commerce
5285 Port Royal Road
Sills Building, Room 1000
Springfield, VA 22161
(703) 487-4802

Nuclear Energy
U.S. Department of Energy
1000 Independence Ave., SW
Washington, DC 20585
(202) 586-6823

Oceanic and Atmospheric Administration, National
Department of Commerce
14th and Constitution Ave., NW, Room 6013
Washington, DC 20230
(202) 377-8090

Occupational Safety and Health Administration

Department of Labor
200 Constitution Ave., NW
Washington, DC 20210
(202) 523-8017

Office of Management and Budget
Executive Office Bldg.
Washington, DC 20500
(202) 395-3080

Packers and Stockyards Administration
U.S. Department of Agriculture
14th and Independence, SW
Washington, DC 20250
(202) 382-9528

Park Service
U.S. Department of the Interior
18th and C Sts., NW
Washington, DC 20240
(202) 343-4747

Parole Commission
Department of Justice
5550 Friendship Blvd.
1 N. Park Bldg.
Bethesda, MD 20015
(301) 492-5990

Patent and Trademark Office
Department of Commerce
Washington, DC 20231
(703) 557-3341

Pension and Welfare Benefits Administration
Department of Labor
200 Constitution Ave., NW
Washington, DC 20210
(202) 523-8921

Policy Development, Office
Executive Office of the President
1600 Pennsylvania Ave., NW
Washington, DC 20500
(202) 456-1414

Postsecondary Education Office
Department of Education
400 Maryland Ave., SW
Washington, DC 20202
(202) 732-3547

President, Executive Office of
Presidential Comments Office
1600 Pennsylvania Ave., NW
Washington, DC 20500
(202) 456-7639

Prisons, Bureau of
Department of Justice
320 First St., NW
Washington, DC 20534
(202) 724-3198

Public Debt Bureau
Department of the Treasury
999 E St., NW, Room 553
Washington, DC 20239-001
(202) 376-4302

Railroad Administration
Department of Transportation
400 7th St., SW
Washington, DC 20590

(202) 366-0881

Reclamation, Bureau of
U.S. Department of the Interior
18th and C Sts., NW
Washington, DC 20240
(202) 343-4662

Research and Special Programs Administration
Department of Transportation
400 7th St., SW
Washington, DC 20590
(202) 366-4347

Rural Electric Administration
U.S. Department of Agriculture
14th and Independence, SW
Washington, DC 20250
(202) 382-1255

Saint Lawrence Seaway Development Corporation
Department of Transportation
400 7th St., SW
Washington, DC 20590
(202) 366-0091

Saving Bond Division
Department of the Treasury
1111 20th St., NW
Washington, DC 20226
(202) 634-5377

Science and Technology Policy, Office
New Executive Office Bldg.
Washington, DC 20506
(202) 395-6142

Secret Service
Department of the Treasury
1800 G St., NW, Room 895
Washington, DC 20223
(202) 535-5708

Senate
Secretary of the Senate
The Capitol
Washington, DC 20520
(202) 224-2115

Social Security Administration
Department of Health and Human Services
6401 Security Boulevard
Baltimore, MD 21235
(301) 965-1234

Soil Conservation Service
U.S. Department of Agriculture
P.O. Box 2890
Washington, DC 20013
(202) 447-4543

Southeastern Power Administration
U.S. Department of Energy
Samuel Elbert Bldg.
Elberton, GA 30635
(404) 283-9911

Southwestern Power Administration
U.S. Department of Energy
P.O. Box 1619
Tulsa, OK 74101
(918) 581-7474

Special Education and Rehabilitation Services, Office of
Department of Education
330 C St., SW, Room 3132
Washington, DC 20202
(202) 732-1723

State, Department of
Washington, DC 20520
(202) 647-6575
(202) 647-4000 locator

Surface Mining Reclamation and Enforcement, Office of
U.S. Department of the Interior
1951 Constitution Ave., NW
Washington, DC 20245
(202) 343-4953

Supreme Court of the United States
1 First St., NE
Washington, DC 20543
(202) 479-3211

Tax Division
Department of Justice
P.O. Box 45099
L'Enfant Plaza Bldg.
Washington, DC 20024
(202) 633-2901

Technology Assessment, Office of
U.S. Congress
600 Pennsylvania Ave., SE
Washington, DC 20510-8025
(202) 228-6204

Telecommunications and Information Administration, National
Department of Commerce
14th and Constitution Ave., NW, Room 4898
Washington, DC 20230
(202) 377-1551

Territorial and International Affairs
U.S. Department of the Interior
18th and C Sts., NW
Washington, DC 20240
(202) 343-3003

Thrift Supervision
Department of the Treasury
1700 G St., NW
Washington, DC 20552
(202) 906-6677

Toxic Substances and Disease Registry
Department of Health and Human Services
1600 Clifton Road NE
Atlanta, GA 30333
(404) 452-4111

Trade Representative, Office of U.S.
600 17th St., NW
Washington, DC 20506
(202) 395-3230

Traffic Safety Administration
Department of Tansportation
400 7th St., SW
Washington, DC 20590
(202) 366-9550

Transportation, Office of

U.S. Department of Agriculture
Washington, DC 20250
(202) 447-2511

Transportation, Department of
400 7th St., SW
Washington, DC 20590
(202) 366-5580
(202) 366-4000 locator

Travel and Tourism Administration, National
Department of Commerce
14th and Constitution Ave., NW, Room 1855
Washington, DC 20230
(202) 377-0137

Treasury, Department of
1500 Pennsylvania Ave., NW
Washington, DC 20220
(202) 566-2041
(202) 566-2000 locator

Urban Mass Transportation
Department of Transportation
400 7th St., SW
Washington, DC 20590
(202) 366-4043

U.S. Claims Court
717 Madison Pl., NW
Washington, DC 20005
(202) 633-7257

U.S. Court of Appeals for the Federal Circuit
717 Madison Pl., NW
Washington, DC 20439
(202) 633-6550

U.S. Mint
Department of the Treasury
633 3rd St., NW
Washington, DC 20220
(202) 376-0837

U.S. National Central Bureau
International Criminal Police Organization

Department of Justice
NCB/ICPO
Bicentennial Bldg, Room 600
Washington, DC 20530
(202) 272-8383

Veterans Affairs, Department of
810 Vermont Ave., NW
Washington, DC 20420
(202) 233-2741
(202) 233-2300 Locator

Veterans Employment and Training
Department of Labor
200 Constitution Ave., NW
Washington, DC 20210
(202) 523-9116

Vice President, Office of the
Old Executive Office Bldg.
Washington, DC 20501
(202) 456-7034

Vocational and Adult Education, Office of
Department of Education
330 C St., SW, Room 4090
Switzer Building
Washington, DC 20202
(202) 732-2251

Wage and Hour Division
Department of Labor
200 Constitution Ave., NW, Room S-3502
Washington, DC 20210
(202) 523-8305

Western Power Administration
U.S. Department of Energy
P.O. Box 3402
Golden, CO 80401-3398
(303) 231-1554

Worker's Compensation Programs, Office of
Department of Labor
200 Constitution Ave., NW, Room S-3524
Washington, DC 20210
(202) 523-7503

Information Starting Places

Hotlines

This list of hotlines reflects the range of information that is only a phone call away. The Department of Transportation's Auto Safety hotline can tell you about the safety features of a particular four-door compact. Another toll-free number will help you settle a complaint about a canceled flight. Details about a recall on canned tuna are readily available from the Food and Drug Administration hotline which operates on weekends and holidays. These hotlines, many of them toll-free numbers, can be terrific information starting places. Remember the seven-phone call rule, though, and dip into the relevant chapter of *Info-Power* for many other handy hotlines and information resources.

Agricultural Research Service	(202) 344-4296	**Flood Insurance**	(800) 638-6620 (301) 731-5300 in DC
Airline Consumer and Security	(800) FAA-SURE	**Food, OTC, RX: Complaints/Emergencies** (Food and Drug Administration)	(202) 443-1240 Weekends/Holidays (202) 857-8400
Airline Non-Safety Complaints	(202) 366-2220	**Food Safety and Inspection Service**	(800) 535-4555 (202) 447-3333 in DC
Animal and Plant Health Inspection Service	(202) 236-7279	**Foreign Agricultural News**	(202) 382-1728
Army Retirees' Pay	(800) 428-2290	**Forest Service**	(202) 447-3957
Auto Safety Hotline	(800) 424-9393 (202) 366-0123 in DC	**Former POW Hotline**	(800) 821-8139
Banks and S&L Complaints (Federal Deposit Insurance Corporation)	(800) 424-5488 (202) 898-3536 in DC	**Greetings Cards from the President**	(202) 456-2724
Blind Books Program (Library of Congress)	(800) 424-9100 (202) 727-2142 in MD	**Hazardous Waste & Superfund Information** (Environmental Protection Agency)	(800) 424-9346 (202) 382-3000
Child Abuse	(800) 621-4000 (800) 352-0386 in CA	**Home Equity Reverse Mortgages**	(800) 245-2691 (301) 251-5154 in MD
Children's Mail Section (White House)	(202) 456-7734	**Household Movers: Complaints**	(202) 275-7841
Commodity Brokers: Complaints	(202) 254-3067	**Housing Discrimination Hotline**	(800) 424-8590
Consumer Products and Toys: Recalls	(800) 638-2772 (800) 492-8104 in MD	**Housing Information**	(800) 245-2691 (301) 251-5154 in MD
Copyright Information	(202) 479-0700	**Internal Revenue Service**	(800) 424-1040
County Cooperative Extension Service	(202) 447-4111	**International Cooperation and Development**	(202) 653-9314
Crime Insurance: Homeowners/Business	(800) 638-8780 (301) 251-1660 in DC	**Justice Department Reference Service**	(800) 851-3420 (301) 251-5500 in MD
Criminal Justice	(800) 851-3420	**Justice Statistics**	(800) 732-3277
Crop Federal Insurance	(800) 222-3160	**Juvenile Justice Information**	(800) 638-8736
Energy Regulations: Complaints	(202) 357-9090	**Library of Congress Reference Desk**	(202) 707-5522
Energy Conservation and Renewable Resources	(800) 523-2929 (800) 462-4983 in PA (800) 233-3071 in AK & HI	**Medicare Recipient: Denial of Treatment**	(800) 638-0742 (800) 492-0353 in DC
Energy Conservation	(800) 428-2525 (800) 428-1718 in MT	**Medicaid Recipient: Denial of Treatment**	(800) 638-0742 (800) 492-0353 in DC
Executive Office of the President	(202) 456-7639		
Explosives: Thefts, Losses, Discoveries	(800) 424-9555 (202) 566-7777 in DC	**Navy Contractors: Complaints**	(800) 628-7732 (800) 897-6683 in PA
Exporters Service	(202) 377-4811	**Nuclear Energy Regulatory Commission**	(202) 492-0292
Export Licensing Conferences	(202) 377-8731	**Nuclear Tests Exposure**	(800) 336-3068
Federal Aviation Administration	(800) 255-1111	**Oil Spills Hotline**	(800) 424-8802 (202) 426-2675 in DC
Federal Budget and Debt (Congressional Budget Office)	(202) 226-2621	**Pesticides Information**	(800) 858-7378

Plants and Gardening; Botanic Gardens	(202) 226-4082
Political Elections and Fundraising (Federal Election Commission)	(800) 424-9530 (202) 376-3120 in DC
Public Housing and Drugs	(800) 245-2691 (301) 251-5154 in MD
Runaways: National Switchboard Messages from Runaways and Parents	(800) 972-3500 (800) 621-4000
Securities and Exchange Commission	(202) 272-3100
Selective Service Registration	(800) 621-5388
Sexually Transmitted Diseases	(800) 227-8922 (800) 982-5883 in MD
Small Business Administration Answer Desk	(800) 368-5855 (202) 653-7561 in DC
Small Business Export/Import Advisory Service	(800) 424-5201 (202) 566-8860 in DC

Small Business Roadmap Program	(202) 377-3176
Second Opinion Non-Emergency Surgery	(800) 638-6833 (800) 492-6603 in MD
Toxic Substances Control Act Information	(202) 554-1404
Trade Remedy Assistance and Complaints	(800) 343-9822
Transportation: Consumer Affairs	(202) 366-2220
US Congress Tours	(202) 225-6827
US Mint and Eagle Coins	(800) USA-GOLD
US Secret Service	(202) 535-5708
US Supreme Court	(202) 479-3011
US Trade Representative Section 301 Cases	(202) 395-3871
Veterans Insurance	(800) 422-8079
White House Switchboard	(202) 456-1414

Recorded Messages

You'll find many other recorded messages in every chapter, particularly in Health and Medicine as well as Federal Job Banks in the Careers and Workplace Chapter. Dozens of taped information spots prepared by the Immigration and Naturalization Service are included in the Law and Social Justice Chapter.

Agriculture Department News	(202) 488-8358
Army	(800) 446-9000
Bicentennial Gold Coins	(800) 822-6500 (202) 368-5500
Botanic Garden Upcoming Events	(202) 225-7099/8333
Commerce Department News	(202) 393-1847
Consumer Product Safety Commission Investigations	(301) 492-5709
Current Labor Statistics	(202) 523-9658
Economic Information	(202) 393-4100
Education Department Financial Aid	(800) 333-4636
Engraving and Printing	(202) 447-9702
Federal Communications Commission	(202) 632-0002
Federal Employees Special Benefits	(202) 632-5582
Federal Energy Regulatory Commission	(202) 357-8555
Federal Job Information Center	(202) 653-8468
Federal Trade Commission Meetings	(202) 326-2711
First Lady's Daily Schedule	(202) 456-6269
Former POW Benefits Hotline	(800) 821-8139
Gallaudet Library	TTY: (202) 651-5216 (202) 651-5217
Geological Survey Volunteers	(703) 648-7440
Gross National Product	(202) 898-2451
Immigration and Naturalization	(202) 633-4316
Interior Department News	(202) 343-3020
Labor Department News	(202) 523-6899
Leading Economic Indicators	(202) 898-2450
Merchandise, Trade, and Equipment Transactions	(202) 898-2453
Nation's Capital Events Hotline	(202) PA 4-0009

Naval Academy	(800) 638-9156
Naval Recruiting	(800) 327-NAVY
New Government Books	(202) 783-3238 ext.3
Nuclear Regulatory Commission Rules	(202) 492-7424
Pension Plans and Interest Rates	(202) 778-8899
Personal Income and Outlays	(202) 898-2452
President's Daily Schedule	(202) 456-2343
President's Voice on Current Issues	(800) 424-9090
Public Debt	(202) 287-4113
Public Health Corps Scholarships	(800) 638-0824
Savings Bonds	(800) USA-BOND
SBA Answer Desk	(800) 368-5855 (202) 653-7561 in DC
Small Business/SCORE Advice	(800) 621-5388
Smithsonian Dial-A-Museum	(202) 357-2020
Smithsonian Dial-A-Phenomenon	(202) 357-2000
Soil Conservation Service	(800) THE-SOIL
St. Lawrence Seaway Ship Arrival	(315) 769-2422
Time (within milliseconds)	(202) 653-1800
Thrift Supervision	(800) 424-5404 (202) 906-6988
Treasury Bills	(202) 287-4091
US House of Representatives Floor Votes	
Democratic Cloakroom	(202) 225-7400
Republican Cloakroom	(202) 225-7430
US International Transactions Weekend Preview	(202) 393-4102
US Senate Floor Votes	
Democratic Cloakroom	(202) 224-8541
Republican Cloakroom	(202) 224-8601
Veterans Insurance Hotline	(800) 422-8079
White House News	(800) 424-9090

Consumer Power
General Sources

* *See also Investments and Financial Services Chapter*
* *See also Agriculture and Farming Chapter*
* *See also Health and Medicine*

When you find yourself the victim of an unfair business practice, you don't have to sit there and do nothing. These sources are some of your major starting places for information on consumer issues, such as mail fraud, deceptive advertising, and warrantee enforcement. Here you'll find all kinds of information on consumer problems on everything from tanning salons and radon, to eye care and even funeral practices. You should also see the Expert Chapter for subject specific experts on all kinds of consumer issues.

* Advertising Practices
Federal Trade Commission
Advertising Practices
6th & Pennsylvania Ave., NW
Washington, DC 20580 (202) 326-3131
This division of the FTC promotes the distribution of truthful information to the public through law enforcement and oversight activities in the following areas: 1) General advertising for deceptive claims at the national and regional level. 2) Advertising claims for food and over-the-counter drugs, particularly claims relating to safety or effectiveness. 3) Tobacco advertising, which includes monitoring for unfair practices or deceptive claims, implementing cigarette and smokeless tobacco labeling laws, and reporting to Congress on cigarette and smokeless tobacco labeling, advertising, and promotion. 4) Performance and energy-savings claims for solar products, furnaces, window coverings, room heaters, wood burning products, gas-saving products and motor oils, and other products featuring energy conservation. for more information about any of these programs, contact this office.

* Advocacy Program
Federal Trade Commission
Bureau of Economics
6th & Pennsylvania Ave., NW
Washington, DC 20580 (202) 326-3430
Under the Advocacy Program, the FTC's three bureaus--Economics, Competition, and Consumer Protection--present comments to other Federal agencies concerning the effect of regulation on competition and consumers. Some recent studies have analyzed the effect of state entry regulation on retail automobile markets, certificate of need regulation in the health care field, and consumer information regulations in the insurance industry. For more information on these and other advocacy program studies, contact this bureau.

* Air Travelers' Rights and Complaints
Consumer Affairs Division
Intergovernmental and Consumer Affairs
Governmental Affairs
Office of the Secretary of Transportation
U.S. Department of Transportation
400 7th Street, SW
Washington, D.C. 20590 (202) 366-2220
If your problem cannot be resolved directly with the airline, contact this office for information on air travelers' rights and for assistance in resolving problems with airlines and charter flights. Complaints about delayed or canceled flights, reservations, lost baggage, smoking, refunds, and overbooking can also be handled here.

* Alcohol, Tobacco, and Firearms Information
Communications Center
Bureau of Alcohol, Tobacco, and Firearms
U.S. Department of the Treasury
1200 Pennsylvania Ave., NW
Washington, DC 20226 (202) 566-7777
This Center functions as a 24 hours a day, seven days a week clearinghouse for those seeking assistance from the Bureau of Alcohol, Tobacco, and Firearms.

* Alcohol, Tobacco, and Firearms: Laws and Regulations
Superintendent of Documents
Government Printing Office
Washington, DC 20402 (202) 783-3238
The *Alcohol, Tobacco, and Firearms Quarterly Bulletin* announces all new laws, regulations, codes, and rulings or changes related to alcohol, tobacco, and firearms. The subscription price is $13.00 per year (S/N 748-001-00000-0).

* Automobile Fuel Economy
Motor Vehicle Requirements Division
Office of Market Incentives
Rulemaking
National Highway Traffic Safety Administration
U.S. Department of Transportation
400 7th Street, SW, Room 5320
Washington, DC 20590 (202) 366-0486
NHTSA issues fuel economy standards and collects information on the technological and economic capabilities of automobile manufacturers to maximize fuel efficiency. Contact this office for information and referrals.

* Auto Safety Hotline
Office of Defects Investigation (NEF-10)
National Highway Traffic Safety Administration
U.S. Department of Transportation
400 7th Street, SW, Room 5326 (800) 424-9393
Washington, DC 20590 (202) 366-0123
This toll-free hotline is accessible in all 50 states, Puerto Rico, and the Virgin Islands. Consumers may call to report automobile safety problems or to request information on recalls, defects, investigations, child safety seats, tires, drunk driving, crash test results, seat belts, air bags, odometer tampering, and other related topics. Staff will also make referrals to state and other agencies. Also ask about the New Car Assessment Program (NCAP), which provides comparable data on the frontal crashworthiness of selected new vehicles.

* Buying By Phone
Federal Trade Commission
Enforcement Division
6th & Pennsylvania Ave., NW
Washington, DC 20580 (202) 326-3768
The FTC receives complaints indicating that businesses and other organizations have problems with some telephone solicitors who use illegal tactics to make sales or send unordered merchandise. For more information about these illegal solicitors, often called "WATS-line hustlers" because they use long-distance phone lines, contact your local FTC office, or the office above.

* Care Labeling
Federal Trade Commission
Marketing Practices
6th and Pennsylvania Ave., NW
Washington, DC 20580 (202) 326-3034
Under the FTC's Care Labeling Rule concerning textile clothing, a care label must be attached to most clothing--except articles that are used to primarily to cover or protect the head and hands--giving care instructions. For more information on the Care Labeling Rule and your rights, or to report clothing you have purchased that has no care label attached, contact the FTC.

* Consumer Affairs
Office of Consumer Affairs
U.S. Department of Health and Human Services

Consumer Power

Washington, DC 20201   (202) 634-4140

The OCA is responsible for providing the President and federal agencies with advice and information regarding the interests of American consumers. The OCA encourages and assists in developing new consumer programs; makes recommendations to improve federal consumer programs; cooperates with state agencies and voluntary organizations in advancing consumer interests; promotes improved consumer education; recommends legislation and regulations to help consumers; and encourages the exchange of ideas among industry, government, and consumers. The Consumer's Resource Handbook and Consumer Information Catalog are available free from Consumer Information Center, P.O. Box 100, Department 635H, Pueblo, CO 81009.

* Consumer Affairs - International

Commercial, Legislative and Business Affairs
Bureau of Economic and Business Affairs
Department of State
2201 C St., NW, Room 6822
Washington, DC 20520   (202) 647-1942

This office monitors developments in international consumer affairs and coordinates U.S. participation in international organizations dealing with consumer affairs policy.

* Consumer Complaint Letters to the FTC

Federal Trade Commission
Correspondence Branch
6th & Pennsylvania Ave., NW
Washington, DC 20580

Letters from consumers are very important to the work of the FTC. They are often the first indication of a problem in the marketplace and may provide the initial evidence to begin an investigation. Although the FTC is not authorized to resolve individual consumer complaints, it can act when it sees a pattern of possible law violations. If you have witnessed an incidence of unfair trade practice, write a letter to the FTC to help them determine if any federal action is warranted.

* Consumer Information Catalog

Catalog
Pueblo, CO 81009

Published quarterly, The *Consumer Information Catalog* includes a descriptive listing of approximately 200 booklets from a variety of federal agencies. The publications cover health, federal benefits, money management, housing, child care, employment, small business, education, food and nutrition, consumer protection, and more. Some booklets are free and some are available at cost. They include the following. The Center also has a list of over 100 booklets available free in Spanish. They include a variety of subjects such as health, money management, children, federal benefits, and more. To obtain a copy, write to LISTA, Pueblo, CO 81009.

* Consumer Information Center

Pueblo, CO 81009   (202) 566-1794

The Consumer Information Center was established in 1970 to help federal agencies and departments release consumer information they wish to bring to the public's attention and to help build public awareness and use of this information. CIC is a separately funded operation located in the General Services Administration, and it is under the policy guidance of the Special Adviser to the President for Consumer Affairs. CIC has a small staff of consumer information specialists available on a selected basis to speak at or participate in national conferences. CIC's exhibit, which includes free catalogs, is also available for major conferences.

* Consumer Information Media Hotline

Pueblo, CO 81009   (202) 566-1794

Members of the CIC media staff are ready to help reporters research consumer stories and can put reporters in touch with contacts who will answer questions directly.

* Consumer Publications

Federal Trade Commission
Public Reference Branch, Room 130
6th & Pennsylvania Ave., NW
Washington, DC 20580   (202) 326-2222

The following publications are available free of charge by visiting the FTC in person, but if that is not possible, the FTC will send you any of them free of charge except those marked with an asterisk (*), which are available for $.50 from the Consumer Information Center, Pueblo, CO 81009.

About Fine Jewelry*
Art Fraud
"Bargain" Jewelry
Buying By Phone

Buying Native American Jewelry
Care Labels: Caring For Your Clothes
Consumer Alert: Investing In Rare Coins
Consumer Guide to the FTC Funeral Rule
Consumer Quiz
Contest Cons
Dollars for Dancing
Door to Door Sales
Eye Care
Eyeglasses
Franchise and Business Opportunities
Generic Drugs
Health Claims: Separating Fact From Fiction
Health Questions: How To Talk To and Select Physicians, Pharmacists, Dentists, and Vision Care Specialists
Health Spas: Exercise Your Rights
How To Buy A Manufactured Home*
How To Write A Wrong: Complain Effectively And Get Results
Indoor Tanning*
Job-Hunting: Should You Pay?
Layaway Purchase Plans
Real Estate Brokers
Service Contracts
Shopping by Mail
Shopping by Phone and Mail
Telemarketing Travel Fraud*
Telephone Investment Fraud
Unordered Merchandise
Vacation Time Sharing Tips
Warranties
What's New About Care Labels
Work-At-Home Schemes
Your Home, Your Choice: A Workbook For Older People and Their Families*

Automobile

Automatic Transmission Repair*
Car Rental Guide
Car Ads: Low Interest Loans & Other Offers
Consumer Guide to Vehicle Leasing*
General Motors Consumer Mediation/Arbitration Program
New Car Buying Guide
Volkswagen Consumer Mediation/Arbitration Program

Consumer Financing

Escrow Accounts For Home Mortgages
Building A Better Credit Record: What To Do, What To Avoid*
Buying and Borrowing: Cash In On The Facts*
Consumer Handbook on Adjustable Rate Mortgages
Cosigning A Loan
Credit and Charge Card Fraud
Credit and Older Americans
Credit Billing Errors? Use FCBA
Credit Practices Rule
Electronic Banking
Equal Credit Opportunity
Fair Credit Reporting
Fair Credit Reporting Act
Fair Credit Billing
Fair Debt Collection
Fix Your Own Credit Problems and Save Money
Getting a Loan: Your Home As Security
Home Equity Credit Lines*
Income Tax Preparation Services
Lost or Stolen: Credit and ATM Cards
Money Matters: How To Talk To and Select Lawyers, Financial Planners, Tax Preparers, and Real Estate Brokers
Mortgage Money Guide*
Refinancing Your Home
Second Mortgage Financing
Scoring for Credit
Solving Credit Problems
Using Plastic: A Young Adult's Guide To Credit Cards
Women and Credit Histories

* Crashworthiness: Air Bags, Child Seats, Helmets, Seat Belts

Office of Crashworthiness Research (NRD-10)
Research and Development
National Highway Traffic Safety Administration
U.S. Department of Transportation
400 7th Street, SW
Washington, DC 20590   (202) 366-4862

Research is conducted on vehicle crashworthiness and crash avoidance. To determine how drivers and passengers fare in head-on collisions, information is collected on seat belts, air bags, child safety restraints, motorcycle helmets, fuel systems, rearview mirrors, tires, door locks, seats, bumpers, and school busses. The annual publication, *Federal Motor Vehicle Safety Standards and Regulations*, is available for $82.00 from the Government Printing Office. Superintendent of Documents, Washington, DC 20402; (202) 783-3238. New Car Assessment Program information on selected models is available from the Auto Safety Hotline: (800) 424-9393.

* Essential Air Service
Office of Aviation Analysis
Policy and International Affairs
Office of the Secretary of Transportation
U.S. Department of Transportation
400 7th Street, SW
Room 6401
Washington, DC 20590   (202) 366-5903
The Departments's Essential Air Service Program ensures that certain cities will be served by air transportation. The program establishes subsidy levels, selects carriers, processes applications to change service levels, and reviews fitness of carriers. Contact the office listed for information about this program.

* Explosives Hotline
Explosives Enforcement Branch
Bureau of Alcohol, Tobacco, and Firearms
U.S. Department of the Treasury
1200 Pennsylvania Ave., NW
Washington, DC 20226   (800) 424-9555, (202) 566-7395
Those with information on a major arson incident or bombing, or are aware of stolen explosives, may call the above hotline. One of four national response teams will be rushed to the scene within 24 hours. A report will be taken by those answering the phone, and the information will be transferred to the nearest agent in the area. Each of the four response teams is composed of 10 special agents, a forensic chemist, and an explosive specialist from ATF's Explosives Technology Branch. A state or local law enforcement or fire service official can request the services of a National Response Team by contacting an ATF Special Agent in charge at one of 22 strategic office locations throughout the United States:

Atlanta, GA: (404) 331-6146
Birmingham, AL: (205) 731-1209
Boston, MA: (617) 565-7042
Charlotte, NC: (704) 371-6125
Chicago, IL: (312) 620-7824
Cleveland, OH: (216) 522-7210
Dallas, TX: (214) 767-2250
Detroit, MI: (313) 226-7304
Houston, TX: (713) 229-3511
Kansas City, MO: (816) 374-3874
Los Angeles, CA: (213) 894-4812
Louisville, KY: (502) 582-5211
Miami, FL: (305) 536-4368
Nashville, TN: (615) 736-7879
New Orleans, LA: (504) 589-2048
New York, NY: (212) 264-4657
Philadelphia, PA: (215) 597-3050
San Francisco, CA: (415) 974-9589
Seattle, WA: (206) 442-4485
St. Louis, MO: (314) 425-5560
St. Paul, MN: (612) 290-3092
Washington, DC: (703) 285-2543

* Eye Care
Federal Trade Commission
Service Industry Practices
6th & Pennsylvania Ave., NW
Washington, DC 20580   (202) 326-3303
Under the FTC Rule, an eye care specialist is required to provide you with your eyeglass prescription, immediately after the examination, so that you can then comparison shop for eye glasses. The specialist, however, is not required to provide you with your contact lens fitting specifications. For more information on eye care products and services and your consumer rights, contact the FTC.

* Firefighting, Prevention, and Forest Fires Bibliography
Superintendent of Documents
Government Printing Office
Washington, DC 20402   (202) 783-3238
Fire safety publications are listed, including improving the fire safety of cigarettes and the effect of cigarettes on the ignition of furnishings. Free.

* Funeral Rule
Federal Trade Commission
Bureau of Consumer Protection
6th & Pennsylvania Ave., NW
Washington, DC 20580   (202) 326-3010
Each year Americans arrange more than two million funerals for family and friends, and the FTC has developed a trade regulation rule concerning funeral industry practices to enable consumers to obtain information about funeral arrangements. For a free brochure on the funeral rule, including price disclosures, embalming information, cremation, and contact this FTC office.

* General Motors Consumer Mediation Program
Federal Trade Commission
Enforcement Division
6th & Pennsylvania Ave., NW
Washington, DC 20580   (202) 326-3027
Under the terms of a 1983 FTC order, all owners of General Motors (GM) cars and light trucks with engine or transmission problems have an opportunity to get money back spent on repairs, or to get repairs by GM at no charge. For a free handbook about this mediation/arbitration program, call (800) 824-5109, or contact the FTC for a free fact sheet outlining your rights.

* Geologic Hazards
Geologic Inquiries
U.S. Geological Survey
911 National Center
Reston, VA 22092   (703) 648-4380
This division evaluates environmental hazards which are associated with earthquakes, volcanoes, floods, droughts, toxic materials, landslides, subsidence, and other ground failures. Methods of hazards prediction are developed through the study of the Earth's internal structure. Engineering problems are identified and solved, including problems in the selection of sites for power stations, highways, bridges, dams, and hazardous waste disposal.

* Grape Wine Label Information
Distribution Center
Bureau of Alcohol, Tobacco, and Firearms
U.S. Department of the Treasury
7943 Angus Ct.
Springfield, VA 22153   (703) 455-7801
The free brochure, *What You Should Know About Grape Wine Labels*, describes the elements written on a label for grape wine and what can be learned from the label. These include brand, vintage date, varietal designations, alcohol content, appellation of origin, viticultural area, name or trade name, and estate bottled.

* Health and the Environment
American Council on Science and Health
1995 Broadway
18th Floor
New York, NY 10023   (212) 362-7044
The American Council on Science and Health is a consumer education association providing the public with scientifically balanced evaluations of food, chemicals, the environment and health. Publications: *ASCH News and Views, Inside ACSH, ACSH Media Update*.

* Health Fraud
Federal Trade Commission
Bureau of Consumer Protection
6th & Pennsylvania Ave., NW
Washington, DC 20580   (202) 326-3128
Each year billions of consumer dollars are wasted on useless remedies and devices. This FTC office can provide you with information on how to spot worthless, fraudulent claims involving products which "cure" arthritis, cancer, weight loss, cellulite, baldness, and much more.

* Health Spa Complaints
Federal Trade Commission
Bureau of Consumer Protection
6th & Pennsylvania Ave., NW
Washington, DC 20580   (202) 326-3319
The most frequent complaints about health spas concern high pressure sales tactics, misrepresentations about facilities and services, and spas that go out of business. This office can provide you with more information about your rights or how to file a complaint.

* Interstate Bussing, Trucking, Railroad Complaints

The Interstate Commerce Commission has three regional offices which serve a variety of functions, one of which is to answer inquiries and assist the public with concerns regarding interstate bus, trucking, and railroad companies. The most frequent calls involve moving companies.

Consumer Power

Eastern

Interstate Commerce Commission, 3535 market St., Room 16400, Philadelphia, PA 19104; (215) 596-4040. States served: AL, CT, DE, D.C., FL, GA, KY, MA, MD, ME, MS, OH, PA, NC, NH, NJ, NY, RI, SC, TN, VA, VT, WV.

Central

Interstate Commerce Commission, Everett McKinley Dirken Building, 219 South Dearborn St., Room 1304, Chicago, IL 60604; (312) 353-6204. States served: AR, IA, IL, IN, KS, LA, MI, MO, MN, NE, ND, OK, SD, TX, WI.

Western

Interstate Commerce Commission, 211 Maine St., Suite 500, San Francisco, CA 94105; (415) 974-7125. States served: AK, AZ, CA, CO, ID, MT, NV, NM, OR, UT, WA, WY.

* Legal Action Against Companies

Federal Trade Commission
Office of the General Counsel
6th & Pennsylvania Ave., NW
Washington, DC 20580   (202) 326-2481

During an investigation, the FTC staff may find reason to believe that an individual company has violated the law. If the case is not settled by a formal agreement with the company (a consent order), the FTC may decide to sue the company. Depending on the circumstances, the case will be tried before an administrative law judge or in federal court. The FTC may seek a cease and desist order, a preliminary or permanent injunction, consumer redress, or other appropriate relief.

* Loss and Damage of Cargo Claims

Office of Compliance and Consumer Assistance
Interstate Commerce Commission
12th St. and Constitution Ave., NW, Room 4412
Washington, DC 20423   (202) 274-7452

While the Commission does not have specific binding authority to adjudicate a dispute claim, it will render all possible assistance. There are several publications available to inform the consumer of his or her rights. *Loss and Damage Claims! Can You Collect?* provides the basic information on cargo claim problems. *Administrative Ruling 120* deals with concealed loss or damage claims. For a copy of these publications and further assistance, contact the Office of Compliance and Consumer Assistance.

* Marketing Practices

Federal Trade Commission
Marketing Practices
6th & Pennsylvania Ave., NW
Washington, DC 20580   (202) 326-3128

This division of the FTC brings law enforcement actions with regard to unfair or deceptive marketing and warranty practices. Although the FTC is not authorized to resolve individual consumer complaints, it can act when it sees a pattern of possible law violations. Deceptive sales programs areas include the following: business opportunities, multi-level marketing plans, and pyramid sales schemes; business and office supply sales schemes; counterfeit goods; fraudulent health spa practices; health or safety risks or defects in major consumer products, such as cars; rebate coupon problems; travel clubs or coupons and vacation certificates; and vacation timesharing or campground plans. This division also enforces actions regarding warranties, franchising rules, and funeral rules. For more information on these or other advertising issues, contact this office.

* Maximum Speed Limit

Police Traffic Services Division
Office of Enforcement and Emergency Services
Traffic Safety Programs
National Highway Traffic Safety Administration
U.S. Department of Transportation
400 7th Street, SW, Room 6124
Washington, DC 20590   (202) 366-5440

The National Maximum Speed Limit is 65 miles per hour on certain interstate highways. This office processes annual certifications of maximum speed limit enforcement programs throughout the U.S. and assists states in developing and improving enforcement efforts.

* Meat and Poultry Hotline

Food Safety and Inspection Service
U.S. Department of Agriculture
Washington, DC 20250   (800) 535-4555

This service takes calls from consumers on cases of meat or poultry food poisoning or complaints about meat or poultry spoilage due to improper packaging or processing. They can also provide you with health-oriented information on safe handling and storage of meats and poultry.

* Moving

Office of the Secretary
Interstate Commerce Commission
12th St. and Constitution Ave., NW
Washington, DC 20423   (202) 275-7833

When You Move: Your Rights and Responsibilities is a pamphlet your mover gives you to provide information about your rights and responsibilities as a shipper of household goods. It includes information on estimates, contracts, weight of shipment, pick-up and delivery, notification of charges, and payments. Also included is a section on filing of loss or damage claims.

* Moving and Trucking Complaint and Performance Data

Office of Compliance and Consumer Assistance
Interstate Commerce Commission
12th St. and Constitution Ave., NW
Washington, DC 20423   (202) 275-7849

Among the many consumer-oriented services of the ICC is a series of advisory bulletins alerting the public and prospective transportation users of the existence of certain transportation problems, and of a regulation requiring household goods carriers to furnish an information bulletin to each prospective customer. You may obtain these advisories by calling or writing this office.

* News Releases From FTC

Federal Trade Commission
Office of Public Affairs
6th & Pennsylvania Ave., NW
Washington, DC 20580   (202) 326-2178

This office provides information to the public through the media. It issues news releases on all significant Commission actions, responds to reporters' inquiries and arranges television, radio, and print interviews for FTC officials. OPA also issues a weekly calendar of Commission events and a weekly summary of press releases, called News Notes, which are available to the public. To be placed on the mailing list for News Notes or Weekly Calendar, contact this office.

* Odometer Tampering

Odometer Fraud Staff
Office of Chief Counsel
National Highway Traffic Safety Administration
U.S. Department of Transportation
400 7th Street, SW, Room 5219
Washington, DC 20590   (202) 366-9511

Federal law requires that the seller of a car sign a disclosure statement that the mileage on the odometer is accurate and has not been rolled back. NHTSA enforces the odometer law via inspections and criminal charges. Information on odometer tampering is also available from the Auto Safety Hotline: (800) 424-9393.

* Postal Inspection Service

Inspection Service Department
U.S. Postal Service
475 L'Enfant Plaza, SW
Washington, DC 20260-2100   (202) 268-4267

As the law enforcement arm of the Postal Service, The Postal Inspection Service protects the mails, postal funds, and property; investigates internal conditions and needs that may affect postal security and effectiveness; apprehends those who violate the postal laws; and audits financial and nonfinancial operations. Information on past and present schemes used to defraud the public is available as well. Help is available if you experience difficulty with a company or suspect that you have been the victim of mail fraud. There is a Regional Chief Inspector in each of the five postal regions. Information and complaints of postal violations should be presented to the nearest Postal Inspector in charge.

Central Region

Chicago
Main Post Office Bldg., Chicago, IL 60607-5401; (312) 765-4605
433 W. Van Buren St., Chicago, IL 60669-2201; (312) 765-4500

Denver
P.O. Box 329, Denver, CO 80201-0329; (303) 297-6220

Des Moines
P.O. Box 566, Des Moines, IA 50302-0566; (515) 253-9060

Detroit
P.O. Box 119, Detroit, MI 48232-3201; (313) 226-8184

Indianapolis
Suite 300, 3750 Guion Rd., Indianapolis, IN 46222-1669; (317) 9923-1601

Kansas City
P.O. Box 411606, Kansas City, MO 64141-1606; (816) 932-0400

Milwaukee
P.O. Box 788, Milwaukee, WI 53201-0788; (414) 291-2475

St. Louis
10th Fl., 200 S. Hanley Rd., St. Louis, MO 63199-2201; (314) 854-4760

St. Paul
P.O. Box 64558, St. Paul, MN 55164-2201; (612) 293-3202

Eastern Region

Cynwyd
1 Bala Cynwyd Plaza, Bala Cynwyd, PA 19004-3509; (215) 5668-4784

Baltimore
P.O. Box 1856, Baltimore, MD 21203-1856; (301) 347-3480

Charlotte
2901 I-85 S., Charlotte, NC 28228-3000; (704) 393-4470

Cincinnati
P.O. Box 2057, Cincinnati, OH 45201-2057; (513) 684-5700

Cleveland
P.O. Box 5726, Cleveland, OH 44101-0726; (216) 443-4000

Harrisburg
P.O. Box 3535, Harrisburg, PA 17105-3535; (717) 257-2330

Philadelphia
P.O. Box 7500, Philadelphia, PA 19101-9000; (215) 895-8450

Pittsburgh
1001 California Ave., Pittsburgh, PA 15290-9000; (412) 359-7900

Richmond
P.O. Box 25009, Richmond, VA 23260-5009; (804) 775-6267

Washington, D.C
P.O. Box 96096, Washington, DC 20066-6096; (202) 636-2339

Northeast Region

Newark
Gateway No. 2, McCarter Hwy. & Market St., Newark, NJ 07175-0001; (201) 621-5500
P.O. Box 509, Newark, NJ 07101-5901; (201) 596-5450

Boston
P.O. Box 2217, Boston, MA 02202-2217; (617) 654-5825

Buffalo
685 Ellicott Sq., Buffalo, NY 14203-2545; (716) 856-3674

Hartford
P.O. Box 2169, Hartford, CT 06145-2169; (203) 646-6060

New York
P.O. Box 5555, James Farley Bldg., New York, NY 10116-0555; (212) 330-3844

San Juan
P.O. Box 3667, San Juan, PR 00936-9614; (809) 753-2856

Southern Region

Memphis
10th Fl., 1407 Union Ave., Memphis, TN 38161-0001; (901) 722-7700
P.O. Box 3180, Memphis, TN 38173-0180; (901) 576-2077

Atlanta
P.O. Box 16489, Atlanta, GA 30321-0489; (404) 765-7369

Birmingham
P.O. Box 2767, Birmingham, AL 35202-2767; (205) 521-0270

Fort Worth
P.O. Box 162929, Fort Worth, TX 76161-2929; (713) 236-7000

Houston
P.O. Box 1276, Houston, TX 77251-1276; (713) 236-7000

Miami
P.O. Box 520772, Miami, FL 33152-0772; (305) 591-0379

New Orleans
P.O. Box 51690, New Orleans, LA 70151-1690; (504) 589-1200

Tampa
P.O. Box 22526, Tampa, FL 33622-2526; (813) 228-2481

Western Region

San Bruno
850 Cherry Ave., San Bruno, CA 94098-0100; (415) 742-4411

Oakland
P.O. Box 24005, Oakland, CA 94623-1005; (415) 636-2600

Pasadena
P.O. Box 2000, Pasadena, CA 91102-2000; (818) 405-1200

Phoenix
P.O. Box 20666, Phoenix, AZ 85036-0666; (602) 223-3660

Portland
Suite 790, 921 SW Washington, Portland, OR 97205-2898; (503) 294-2263

San Diego
P.O. Box 2110, San Diego, CA 92112-2110; (619) 233-0610

San Francisco
P.O. Box 882000, San Francisco, CA 94188-2000; (415) 550-5602

Seattle
P.O. Box 400, Seattle, WA 98111-4000; (206) 442-6300

* Radon

Public Information Center
Environmental Protection Agency
401 M St., SW, PM-211 B
Washington DC 20460   (202) 475-7751

A Citizen's Guide to Radon helps readers understand the radon problem and decide if they need to take action to reduce radon levels in their homes. It explains what radon is, how it is detected, and what the results mean. Contact this office for your free copy.

* Reference Guides on Consumer Concerns

Science and Technology Division
Reference Section
Library of Congress
Washington, DC 20540   (202 707-5580

Informal series of reference guides are issued free from the Science and Technology Division under the general title, *LC Science Tracer Bullet*. These guides are designed to help readers locate published material on subjects about which they have only general knowledge. New titles in the series are announced in the weekly Library of Congress *Information Bulletin* that is distributed to many libraries including:

80-14 Automotive Maintenance & Repair
80-18 Health Foods
81-6 Pets and Pet Care
81-9 Cable Television (Cable TV)

* Service Industry Practices

Federal Trade Commission
Service Industry Practices
6th & Pennsylvania Ave., NW
Washington, DC 20580   (202) 326-3303

This FTC division focuses on deception and misrepresentation in the advertising of professional services. Law enforcement activities are directed toward restrictions on advertising and other business practices of professional that may impede competition and consumer choice. Other activities include investigating investment schemes; monitoring industry standards and certification programs and the Retail Food Advertising and Marketing Practices Rule. Program areas include advertising, eyeglasses, employment counseling services, health care services, and legal services. This division's current investment fraud investigations focus on gemstones, cellular phone lotteries, rare coins, and art. Contact this division for more information on any of these programs or investigations.

* Shopping By Mail

Federal Trade Commission
Marketing Practices
6th & Pennsylvania Ave., NW
Washington, DC 20580   (202) 326-3128

Ordering merchandise by mail can be a convenient way to save time, energy, and sometimes money, but if your merchandise arrives late or not at all, you need to know your rights. The FTC can furnish you with information concerning the Mail Order Merchandise Rule, but to resolve a complaint against a company, contact your local Postmaster, your local consumer protection agency, or the Direct Marketing Association at 6 East 43rd St., New York, NY 10017.

* State Motor Vehicle Inspections

Records and Motor Vehicle Services Division (NTS-43)
National Highway Traffic Safety Administration
U.S. Department of Transportation
400 7th Street, SW
Washington, DC 20590   (202) 366-2676

NHTSA's Motor Vehicle Inspection Program is aimed at providing car owners with preventative information on what repairs are needed to achieve greater safety, lower pollution, and better mileage. The annual *Study of the State Motor Vehicle Inspection Program* is available from this office.

* Telemarketing Travel Fraud

Federal Trade Commission
Marketing Practices
6th & Pennsylvania Ave., NW
Washington, DC 20580   (202) 326-3128

Have you ever been tempted to buy one of those bargain-priced travel packages sold over the telephone? Be careful. Your dream vacation may turn into a misadventure if you fall victim to one of the many travel scams being sold over the phone which are defrauding consumers out of millions of dollars each month. If you feel you are a victim of just such a scam, or you want information on how to avoid them, contact this office for their free brochure.

* Trade Regulation Enforcement

Federal Trade Commission
Enforcement Division
6th & Pennsylvania Ave., NW
Washington, DC 20580   (202) 326-2996

This division of the FTC monitors compliance with Commission orders and, along with the Regional Offices, enforces a number of trade regulations and specific laws. What follows is a brief listing of some of the FTC laws and regulations, along with the respective FTC expert in that area:

Appliance Labeling Rule, which requires the disclosure of energy costs of home appliances. James Mills, (202) 326-3035.

Cooling-Off Rule, which requires sellers to five consumers notice of their three-day cancellation rights for sales may away from the seller's place of business. Joyce Plyler, (202) 326-3021.

Games of Chance in the Food Retailing and Gasoline Industries Rule, which requires disclosure of the odds of winning prizes, the random distribution of the winning prize pieces, and the publication of the winners' names. John Mendenhall, Cleveland Regional Office, (216) 522-4210.

Negative Option Rule, which requires sellers who use negative option purchase plans, such as book and record clubs, to give members at least 10 days to reject the monthly selection. Elaine Kolish, (202) 326-3042.

Octane Posting and Certification Rule, which requires the posting of octane ratings on gasoline dispensers. Neil Blickman, (202) 326-3038.

R-value Rule, which requires sellers to disclose the thermal efficiency of home insulation. Kent Howerton, (202) 326-3013.

Used Car Rule, which requires dealers to post on each used car a "Buyers Guide" that gives information about the warranty coverage, tells the meaning of an "as is" sale, and suggests that consumers ask about getting an independent inspection before buying the car. Joyce Plyler, (202) 326-3021.

Fair Packaging and Labeling Act, which requires consumer commodities to be accurately labeled to describe the product's identity and net quantity. Bret Smart, Los Angeles Regional Office, (213) 209-7890.

Hobby Protection Act, which requires imitation coins, medals, and other monetary items to be marked "copy," and imitation political items to be marked with the year of manufacture. Robert Easton, (202) 326-3029.

Textile, Wool, and Fur Acts, which protect consumers against mislabeling, false advertising, and false invoicing of textile, wool, and fur products. Bret Smart, Los Angeles Regional Office, (213) 209-7890.

Amended Wool Products Labeling and Textile Fiber Products Identification Acts, which require all wool and textile items, domestic or imported, to be labeled with the country of origin. Steve Ecklund, (202) 326-3034.

Unordered Merchandise Statute, which permits consumers to keep, as a free gift, merchandise they received through the U.S. mail but did not order. Vada Martin, (202) 326-3002.

* Transportation Issues

Office of Public Interest Groups
Intergovernmental and Consumer Affairs
Governmental Affairs
Office of the Secretary of Transportation
U.S. Department of Transportation
400 7th Street, SW
Washington, D.C. 20590   (202) 366-1524

This office acts as a liaison between Congress, state and local governments, business and industry, and public interest groups to ensure that their needs are considered when Department policy decisions are made. Public and private organizations can contact this office to communicate needs and comment on DOT programs and regulations.

* Transportation Safety Institute

Transportation Safety Institute (DMA-60)
Research and Special Programs Administration
U.S. Department of Transportation
6500 South MacArthur Blvd.
Oklahoma City, OK 73125   (405) 680-3153

The Institute supports the Department's efforts to reduce transportation accidents. It develops and conducts training programs for Federal, state, and local governments; industry; and foreign personnel. Courses are offered in aviation, highway, marine, pipeline, and railroad safety; materials analysis; transportation security; and other subjects.

* Vehicle Importation

Public Information Division
U.S. Customs Service
Department of the Treasury
P.O. Box 7407
Washington, DC 20044   (202) 566-8195

The pamphlet, *Importing a Car*, outlines the provisions for dutiable entry or free entry of automobiles, trucks, and motorcycles. Prior arrangements, documentation, safety and emissions standards, and federal tax guidelines are also discussed.

* Vehicle Manufacturer Safety Compliance

Vehicle Manufacturer Safety Compliance (NEF-30)
Enforcement
National Highway Traffic Safety Administration
U.S. Department of Transportation
400 7th Street, SW
Washington, DC 20590   (202) 366-2832

To ensure that foreign and domestic vehicle and equipment manufacturers comply with federal motor vehicle safety standards, this office performs compliance testing, inspections, and investigations involving about 150 performance requirements and nearly 3000 equipment items.

* Vehicle Research and Testing

Vehicle Research and Test Center
Research and Development
National Highway Traffic Safety Administration
U.S. Department of Transportation
P.O. BOX 37
East Liberty, OH 43319   (513) 366-4521

NHTSA evaluates the effectiveness of Federal Motor Vehicle Safety Standards. This engineering facility performs tests to obtain basic data used to establish standards for safety and fuel efficiency of motor vehicles.

* Volkswagen Consumer Mediation Program

Federal Trade Commission
Bureau of Consumer Protection
6th & Pennsylvania Ave., NW
Washington, DC 20580   (202) 326-3022

Under the terms of a 1988 FTC order, Volkswagen has established a mediation program for all owners of Volkswagen of America or Audi cars and light trucks with engine problems. To find out more about whether you qualify to receive a settlement for reimbursement for repairs, contact either the FTC, your local Better Business Bureau, or Volkswagen of America, Inc.

* Warranties

Federal Trade Commission
Division of Marketing Practices
6th & Pennsylvania Ave., NW
Washington, DC 20580   (202) 326-3128

Although the FTC cannot intervene in individual disputes and does not handle private cases, the FTC does want to know if companies are meeting their warranty obligations. To report violations of the Warranty Act or warranty-related problems, or to request information concerning warranties in general, contact this office.

* Work-At-Home Schemes

Division of Marketing Practices
Federal Trade Commission
6th & Pennsylvania Ave., NW
Washington, DC 20580   (202) 326-3128

Be careful about work-at-home ads--stuffing envelopes, assembling work, and others--especially ones that promise you large profits in a short period of time. While some of these plans are legitimate, many are not, and if you feel you've been taking advantage of, or if you'd like to know precautions to take against fraudulent schemes, contact the Better Business Bureau, your local Postmaster, your state's Attorney General's office, or the FTC.

State Consumer Protection Offices

You are interested in investing in a company that sells educational courses to the public, but you want to know if they are getting any complaints about their sales practices. How can you find out? Or perhaps you are the manufacturer of a potato peeler which is sold with a warning against using the product on anything other than potatoes. Are you protected from a law suit brought against you by a consumer who cut his finger while using your potato peeler on an orange? On the consumer side, you may have a problem with a product or service, and the retailer has ignored your complaints or given you the run around. What are your rights? In any of these cases, you will probably need consumer protection advice, and quickly. Instead of hiring a high-priced consumer lawyer to solve your problems, contact your state Consumer Affairs Office, which can give you as much, if not more, of the information and advice you may need as the lawyer can give you, but for free.

The kinds of information available from these offices varies from state-to-state; however, most of them can help you with your inquiry or complaint. Aside from just handling complaints, many states publish valuable consumer information on their in-state companies. For example, Alabama will provide you with a listing of all companies that have gone out of business; Arkansas publishes a Buyer Beware List of companies that have been brought to court; New York and Iowa publish yearly reports naming companies that have had complaints filed against them; and Oklahoma and New Mexico release periodic press releases to warn the public of companies that have had court actions taken against them.

If you have yet to purchase a product and want to make sure that you don't get a lemon, state Consumer Offices can help you, too. Most states will provide some information by phone about companies that have had complaints filed against them in the state. Some states, however, require that you speak directly with the investigator assigned to the case, while in others your request must be in writing. Currently, the following states will provide listings of all companies that have had complaints filed against them: Alabama, Arkansas, Delaware, Maine, Maryland, Michigan, Vermont. And 18 states have toll free numbers for in-state consumers to file complaints or to search out information about whether a company has had complaints filed against it. Only five states--Colorado, Illinois, Nevada, Missouri, and West Virginia--do not provide any consumer protection information at all.

Most offices will advise you to take the following steps when lodging a complaint of your own. First, contact the retailer in person or by phone and let them know the nature of the problem. If that doesn't yield the proper response, take step two: write an angry letter that clearly states the problem, the date of purchase, a copy of the receipt, cancelled check, or itemized charge bill, and what you would consider a fair and equitable settlement. If you still get no satisfactory response, contact the Consumer Affairs Office.

If you purchased an offending product in another state, start with that state's Consumer Affairs Office. Most offices offer a wide selection of information and educational materials, and most will be glad to answer your questions or direct you toward someone who can. But before you even start, it is very important that you have copies of any relevant sales receipts, other sales documents, and all correspondence between yourself and the retailer and/or manufacturer.

State Consumer Protection Offices

Alabama
Office of Attorney General, Consumer Protection Division, 11 South Union St., Montgomery, AL 36130; (205) 261-7334, 800-392-5658. Information on a specific company can be obtained by writing to this office. A listing of complaints filed against a company as well as a listing of companies that have gone out of business can be obtained.

Alaska
Consumer Protection Section, Office of Attorney General 1031 W. Fourth Ave. Suite 110, Anchorage, AK 99501; (907) 279-0428. Printed information is available on the types of businesses this office investigates. A listing of companies filed in this office is available including the company name, address and zip code.

Arizona
Financial Fraud Division, Office of Attorney General, 1275 W. Washington St., Phoenix, AZ 85007; (602) 255-3702, 800-352-8431. Information on complaints on a specific company can be given over the phone. A listing of companies in their files with complete name, address and zip code is also available.

Arkansas
Consumer Protection Division, Office of Attorney General 201 E. Markham St., Little Rock, AR 72201; (501) 371-2341, 800-482-8982. Information can be given over the phone on current lawsuits pending, or the names of companies who have failed to respond to a complaint after it has been issued. A Buyer Beware List is distributed which informs consumers which companies have been brought to court.

California
State Department of Consumer Protection, 1020 N. St., Sacramento, CA 95814; (916) 445-1254. Data is computerized and available on computer readable formats. A disclosure policy prohibits the release of company information. This office will refer consumers to appropriate licensing boards if necessary.

Colorado
Consumer Protection Unit, Office of Attorney General, 1525 Sherman St., Denver, CO 80203; (303) 866-3561. A disclosure policy prohibits the release of any company information. No publications available.

Connecticut
Department of Consumer Protection, State Office Building, 165 Capitol Ave., Hartford, CT 06106; (203) 566-4999, 800-842-2649, 800-538-2277. Requests for specific information on a company must be made in writing. Information given on the company's license, and complaint record over the last 2 years.

Delaware
Division of Consumer Affairs, Department of Community Affairs, 820 North French St., Wilmington, DE 19801; (302) 571-3250, 800-443-2179, 800-736-4000. A list of companies with registered complaints can be obtained from this office.

District of Columbia
Department of Consumer and Regulatory Affairs, 614 H. St., NW, Washington, DC 20001; (202) 727-7170. Specific information on some companies may be given over the phone, including the name of the company president or officer. For detailed information a request must be made in writing.

Florida
Department of Agriculture and Consumer Services, Division of Consumer Services, 508 Mayo Building, Tallahassee, FL 32399; (904) 488-2226, 800-342-2176, 800-342-2175, 800-327-3382. Information on complaints of a specific company can be given over the phone. Some information available on computer readable formats.

Georgia
Office of Consumer Affairs, 2 Martin Luther King, Jr. Dr., Plaza Level, East Tower, GA 30334; (404) 656-3790.

Hawaii

Office of Consumer Protection, Department of Commerce and Consumer Affairs, P.O. Box 3767, Honolulu, HI 96812; (808) 548-2560. Information on the number of complaints filed, date of complaints and a public review of a specific company can be given over the phone.

Idaho

Office of Consumer Protection, State House, Room 210, Boise, ID 83720. Consumer brochures available. Data is computerized but business status reports are not given to the general public.

Illinois

Consumer Protection Division, Office of Attorney General, 500 S. Second St., Springfield, IL 62706; (217) 782-0244, 800-252-8666. Information on a specific company not given over the phone. Data is computerized but not released. Mediation consumer brochures are available.

Indiana

Consumer Protection Division, Office of Attorney General, 219 State House, Indianapolis, IN 46204; (317) 232-6330, 800-382-5516. All company information is available for public record but must have the permission of the specific company before it can be released to the public. Data files are computerized and available on computer readable formats with company consent.

Iowa

Consumer Protection Division, Office of Attorney General, 1300 E. Walnut, Cooper Building, Des Moines, IA 50319; (515) 281-5926. Information on the number of complaints filed on a specific company can be given over the phone by an assigned investigator. A yearly report is published and available to the public. No computer listings available.

Kansas

Consumer Protection Division, Office of Attorney General, Kansas Judicial Center, 2nd Floor, Topeka, KS 66612; (913) 296-3751, 800-432-2310. Complaint or information on a lawsuit for a specific company can be given over the phone by talking with the case attorney. Data files are computerized but a complete listing of companies in the file is considered confidential.

Kentucky

Consumer Protection Division, Office of Attorney General, 209 Saint Clair St., Frankfort, KY 40601; (502) 564-2200, 800-432-9257. Information on complaints of a specific company can be given over the phone. Various consumer brochures published.

Louisiana

Department of Urban and Community Affairs, P.O. Box 94453, Baton Rouge, LA 70804; (504) 342-7013. Litigation information on a specific company can be given over the phone.

Maine

Bureau of Consumer Credit Protection, State House Station # 35, Augusta, ME *** (207) 289-3721. Investigation results of a specific company can be given over the phone. Staff will also advise you on registration or license information for a specific company. Consumer purchasing brochures available. Data is in the process of becoming computerized. A listing of all companies in their file including name, address and zip code is available in hand written form.

Maryland

Consumer Protection Division, Office of Attorney General, 7 North Calvert St., Baltimore, MD 21202; (301) 528-8662. Information on the number of complaints within a 3 year period a company has received can be obtained over the phone. Data files are computerized, and available on computer readable formats. A listing of all companies in their file is available to the public.

Massachusetts

Consumer Protection Division, Department of Attorney General, 131 Tremont St., 1st floor, Boston, MA 02111; (617) 727-2200. Information on complaints and specific fees charged by a specific company can be obtained over the phone. Data files are computerized. For specific company requests, the name, address and zip code is provided.

Michigan

Consumer Protection Division, Office of Attorney General, 525 West Ottawa, Lansing, MI 48913; (517) 373-1140. Information on the number of complaints or written inquiries of a specific company can be given over the phone (limited to 2 requests at a time). Computer listings of companies and their addresses available for a fee of $.20 per page.

Minnesota

Office of Consumer Services, Office of Attorney General, 117 University Avenue, St. Paul, MN 55155; (612) 296-2331. The status of legal action and information on complaints of a specific company can be given over the phone. No computer listings available.

Mississippi

Consumer Protection Division, Office of Attorney General, P.O. Box 220, Jackson, MS 39205; (601) 354-6018. Information on complaints filed for a specific company can be given over the phone. Data files are not computerized.

Missouri

Department of Economic Development, P.O. Box 1157, Jefferson City, MO 65102; (314) 751-4962. There is no Consumer Protection Agency is Missouri, for specific information contact this office.

Montana

Consumer Affairs Unit, Department of Commerce, 1424 Ninth Ave., Helena, MT 59620; (406) 444-4312, 800-332-2272. Information on complaints on a specific company can be given over the phone. All investigative information is confidential. Data files are not computerized.

Nebraska

Consumer Protection Division, Department of Justice, P.O. Box 94906, Lincoln, NE 68509. A computer check detailing the nature of a complaint for a specific company, and if the complaint was resolved is available from this office. Data files are computerized.

Nevada

Consumer Affairs Office, 2601 E. Sahara, Suite 247, Las Vegas, NV 89158; (702) 486-4150. A disclosure policy prohibits the release of any company information.

New Hampshire

Consumer Protection Bureau, Office of Attorney General, State House Annex, Concord, NH 03301; (603) 271-3641. Information on court actions for a specific company can be given over the phone. Some data is computerized, entire files not available to the public.

New Jersey

Division of Consumer Affairs, 1100 Raymond Blvd, Room 504, Newark, NJ 07102; (201) 648-4010, 800-242-5846. Information on the nature of complaints filed for a specific company can be given over the phone. Data files are computerized but an entire listing of all companies not available.

New Mexico

Consumer and Economic Crime Division, Office of Attorney General, P.O. Drawer 508, Santa Fe, NM 87504; (505) 872-6060, 800-432- 2070. Information on complaints on a specific company can be given over the phone. A press release is published every two weeks warning consumers of current scams. Data files are not computerized.

New York

New York State Consumer Protection Board, 99 Washington Ave., Albany, NY 12210; (518) 474-8583. An annual report is available to the public. Data files are computerized in the complaint unit located in Buffalo and Rochester. Call this office for referral.

North Carolina

Consumer Protection Section, Office of Attorney General, Department of Justice Building, P.O. Box 629, Raleigh, NC 27602; (919) 733-7741. Information on the number of complaints filed for a specific company can be obtained from the specialist who handled the case. Published information is available on complaint laws. Data files are computerized, but a listing of all companies on file is not released.

North Dakota

Consumer Fraud Division, Office of Attorney General, State Capitol Building, Bismarck, ND 58505; (701) 224-2210. Information on the complaint record of a specific company can be given over the phone. Various consumer brochures are published. Data files are not computerized.

Ohio

Consumer Frauds and Crimes Section, Office of Attorney General, 30 East Broad St., State Office Tower, Columbus, OH 43266; (614) 466-4986, 800-282-0515. Only information concerning a law suit against a specific company can be given over the phone. Various consumer brochures are published. Names of businesses with complaints filed against them are released with a written request.

Oklahoma

Consumer Affairs, Office of Attorney General, State Capitol Building, Room 105, Oklahoma City, OK 73105; (405) 521-3921. Information on the number of complaints, and legal action taken against a specific company can be given over the phone. Consumer brochures and press releases are available. Data files are not computerized.

Oregon

Financial Fraud Section, Department of Justice, Justice Building, Salem, OR 97310; (503) 378-4320. Information on the number of complaints and a brief summary of the complaints against a specific company can be given over the phone. Various consumer brochures are available including the Unlawful Trade Practices Act. Data files are computerized, but no listings available.

Pennsylvania

Bureau of Consumer Protection, Office of Attorney General, Strawberry Square, 14th Floor, Harrisburg, PA 17120; (717) 787-9707, 800-441-2555. Only information concerning a court case of a specific company can be given over the phone. Data files are computerized, no listings available.

Rhode Island

Consumer Protection Division, Department of Attorney General, 72 Pine St., Providence, RI 02903; (401) 277-2104. Information concerning cases of consumer fraud are available. Data is computerized and available on computer readable formats. A complete listing of all companies in their files with the name, address, zip code of each company is available.

South Carolina

Consumer Protection Office, Office of Attorney General, P.O. Box 5757, Columbia, SC 29250; (803) 734-3970, 800-922-1594. Information on complaints and the closing of a specific company can be obtained over the phone. Information is also available on the company's credit rating and certification (if it applies).

South Dakota

Division of Consumer Affairs, Office of Attorney General, Anderson Building, Pierre, SD 57501; (605) 773-4400. Information on complaints on a specific company can be given over the phone include the firm's name and address. Data files are computerized but a complete listing of all businesses in the file is not available. A consumer handbook is published.

Tennessee

Antitrust and Consumer Protection Division, Office of Attorney General, 450 James Robertson Parkway, Nashville, TN 37219; (615) 741-2672. Information on whether or not a complaint has been filed against a specific company is available over the phone. For more detailed information the investigator on the case must be contacted. A Consumer Survival Kit is distributed as well as various consumer brochures.

Texas

Consumer Protection Division, Office of Attorney General, 714 Jackson, Suite 700, Dallas, TX 75202; (214) 742-8944. Information on complaints on a specific company can be given over the phone. Some data is computerized. No lists available.

Utah

Division of Consumer Protection, Department of Business Regulation, 160 E. 300 South, Salt Lake City, UT 84111; (801) 530-6601. Information on complaints taken to court are available over the phone. Various consumer information publications are available including the Unfair Practice Act, Lemon Law, and other brochures on fraud and pyramid schemes. Data files are not computerized.

Vermont

Consumer Assistance Program, PERILL HALL, UVM, Burlington, VT 05405; (802) 656-3183. A listing of complaints made, how many, a brief summary and how and if the complaint was resolved is available for a specific company. Data files are computerized a computer listing can be generated. Various consumer brochures available on housing, credit, mail order, auto, health, and money matters.

Virginia

Office of Consumer Affairs, P.O. Box 1163, Richmond, VA 23209; (804) 786-2042. Information on if a complaint exists, if it was resolved and how is available for a specific company over the phone. Various brochures concerning Virginia consumer laws are published. Data files are computerized from 1986 to the present. No listings available.

Washington

Attorney General's Office, Consumer Protection and Anti-trust Division, 710 Second Ave., Room 1300, Seattle, WA 98104; (206) 464-7744. To have access to complaint files, a public disclosure agreement form must be filled out. The only information given out over the phone is if a company has been sued.

West Virginia

Consumer Protection Division, Office of Attorney General, 812 Quarrier St., Charleston, WV 25301; (304) 348-8986, 800-368-8808. A disclosure policy prohibits the release of any information on a specific company.

Wisconsin

Office of Consumer Protection, Department of Justice, P.O. Box 7856, Madison, WI 53707; (608) 266-9836, 800-362-3020. Information on complaints filed on a specific company can be given over the phone. Various consumer brochures are published. Some data are computerized.

Wyoming

Consumer Protection Office, Office of Attorney General, 123 State Capitol Building, Cheyenne, WY 82002; (307) 777-7841. Information on complaints on a specific company can be given over the phone. Some data are computerized. No listings available.

Money, Banking, and Credit

* Banking and Credit Problem Hotline

Office of Consumer Affairs
Federal Deposit Insurance Corporation
550 17th St., NW, Room F-130   (800) 424-5488
Washington, DC 20429   (202) 898-3535

This office answers questions and addresses complaints regarding FDIC-insured banks. A computerized system helps to track complaints from their initial filing to their resolution. A follow-up complaint satisfaction survey is also conducted periodically. Banking questions may be directed to the nearest regional FDIC office, or call the FDIC's toll-free customer service hotline between 9 a.m. and 4 p.m. EST, Monday through Friday.

* Consumer Banking and Finance Publications

What follows is a list of the Federal Reserve Banks across the U.S., along with their free consumer publications available:

Board of Governors of the Federal Reserve System
Publications Services, MS-138
20th St. & Constitution Ave., NW
Washington, DC 20551   (202) 452-3244

Consumer Handbook on Adjustable Rate Mortgages. Explains adjustable rate mortgages and some of the risks and advantages.
Consumer Handbook to Credit Protection Laws. Tells how consumer credit laws can help in shopping for and applying for credit and in keeping a good credit record.
Consumer's Guide to Mortgage Closings. Explains the mortgage closing process.
Consumer's Guide to Mortgage Lock-Ins. Describes various aspects of mortgage lock-ins.
Consumer's Guide to Mortgage Refinancing. Discusses the process and some of the risks and advantages to mortgage refinancing.
Federal Reserve Glossary. Defines many of the terms used in monetary policy and in bank supervision.
Guide to Business Credit and the Equal Credit Opportunity Act. Advises consumers of their rights under the Act when applying for a business loans and helps consumers prepare effective loan presentations.
Guide to Federal Reserve Regulations. Explains the goals and scope of Federal Reserve regulations.
How to File a Consumer Credit Complaint. Tells how to file a complaint against a bank.
If You Use a Credit Card. Explains federal law safeguards against lost cards, what to do about unsatisfactory goods purchased with credit cards, and how to compute and compare credit card charges.

Federal Reserve Bank of Atlanta
Public Information Department
104 Marietta St. NW
Atlanta, GA 30303-2713   (404) 521-8788

Economic Review. A bimonthly publication presenting new research and articles on the economy of the Southeast.

Federal Reserve Bank of Boston
Bank and Public Services Department
600 Atlantic Ave.
Boston, MA 02106   (617) 973-3459

Checkpoints. Explains how to write, deposit, and cash checks; also available in Spanish and Portuguese.
Consumer Education Catalog. Lists consumer education materials published by the System.
New England Economic Indicators. Quarterly report of statistical data for the nation and New England states.
New England Economic Review. Publishes articles of broad economic interest six times a year.

Federal Reserve Bank of Chicago
Public Information Center
230 S. LaSalle St.
Chicago, IL 60690   (312) 322-5111

Economic Perspectives. Bimonthly publication on banking, business, and agriculture.
Seventh District Economic Data. Provides statistical data on population, business, agriculture, foreign trade, and finance for the five states of the 7th Federal Reserve District.

Federal Reserve Bank of Cleveland
Public Information Department
P.O. Box 6387

Cleveland, OH 44101   (216) 579-2047

Economic Review. Quarterly publication featuring monetary, economic, and banking topics of district and national interest.
Economic Trends (Chartbook). Charts latest economic statistics and briefly discusses the current economy.

Federal Reserve Bank of Dallas
Public Affairs Department
Station K
Dallas, TX 75222   (214) 651-6289 or 6266

Agricultural Highlights. Discusses regional agricultural developments.
District Highlights. Quarterly analysis of district economic and financial developments.
Economic Review. Bimonthly publication of articles on economic and financial topics.
Energy Highlights. Summarizes developments in the energy industry; four times a year.

Federal Reserve Bank of Kansas City
Public Affairs Department
925 Grand Ave.
Kansas City, MO 64198   (816) 881-2402

Economic Review. Discusses a variety of economic and financial topics; 10 issues per year.

Federal Reserve Bank of Minneapolis
Public Affairs
250 Marquette Ave.
Minneapolis, MN 55480   (612) 340-2446.

Agricultural Credit Conditions. Quarterly survey of district farm economy.
Consumer Credit Protection: Do You Know Your Rights? Easy-to-understand summary of consumers' credit protection rights.
District Economic Conditions. Analyzes nonfarm economic activity of the district and each state; quarterly.
Quarterly Review. Includes feature articles on the district economy.
Your Credit Rights. Contains learning activities on establishing and using credit; intended for consumer groups and teachers.

Federal Reserve Bank of New York
Public Information Department
33 Liberty Street
New York, NY 10045   (212) 720-6134

Consumer Credit Regulators (Fedpoints 17). Reviews the responsibilities of the 12 federal organizations charged with administering consumer regulations.
Quarterly Review. Reports on business activities and the money and bond markets.

Federal Reserve Bank of Philadelphia
Public Information Department
P.O. Box 66
Philadelphia, PA 19105   (215) 574-6115

Business Outlook Survey. Reports on manufacturing in the district and provides forecasts for the next six months; monthly.
Business Review. Bimonthly articles for readers with a general interest in economics.
Buying Treasury Securities. Provides basic information on investing in Treasury bills, notes, and bonds.
Electronic Banking for Today's Consumer. Explains electronic services such as ATMs, direct deposit, bill-paying services, and point-of-sale terminals, as well as consumer protections of Regulation E.
Fair Debt Collection Practices Act. Summarizes the main provisions of the Act.
Give Yourself Credit. Guides consumers through various credit protection laws.
How the New Equal Credit Opportunity Act Affects You. Outlines the Act's main provisions for consumers.
Plastic Fraud: Getting a Handle on Debit and Credit Cards. Discusses consumer awareness concerning credit and debit card fraud and the regulations protecting consumers.
Quarterly Regional Economic Report. Analyzes the economy of the district.
Your Credit Rating. Describes the importance of credit histories and consumers' rights when using credit, including ways to correct records.

Federal Reserve Bank of Richmond
Public Services Department
P.O. Box 27622
Richmond, VA 23261   (804) 697-8000

Black Banks. Profiles operating revenue and distribution by profit/loss size of black banks.

Consumer Power

Community Affairs Officers at Federal Reserve Banks. Outlines the Community Affairs Officer's role, duties, and responsibilities, particularly those related to the Community Reinvestment Act.
Cross Sections. Quarterly reviews of business and economic developments.

Federal Reserve Bank of St. Louis
Public Information Office
P.O. Box 442
St. Louis, MO 63166   (314) 444-8421
Agriculture: an Eighth District Perspective. Quarterly summary of national and district agricultural developments.
Annual U.S. Economic Data. Provides selected economic statistics.
Business: An Eighth District Perspective. Summarizes national and district business developments.
Review. Examines national and international economic developments; analyzes various sectors of the district; ten issues per year.

Federal Reserve Bank of San Francisco
Public Information Department
P.O. Box 7702
San Francisco, CA 94120   (415) 974-2163
Give Yourself Credit. Guides the consumer through various credit protection laws.
Review. Discusses selected economic, banking, and financial topics; quarterly.

* Consumer Expenditure and Family Budgets
Consumer Expenditure Surveys Division
Office of Prices and Living Conditions
Bureau of Labor Statistics
Department of Labor
600 E St., NW, Room 4216
Washington, DC 20212   (202) 272-5156
The *Consumer Expenditure Studies*, a continuing annual survey of consumer expenditures and income, is the basic source of data for the revision of items and weights in the market basket of consumer purchases to be priced for the Consumer Price Index. Selected data is classified by income class, family size, and other demographic and economic characteristics of consumer units. Coverage includes the urban population of the U.S. through 1983, and the total population in 1984 and after.

* Consumer's Financial Guide
Publications Section
Printing Branch, Stop C-11
U.S. Securities and Exchange Commission
Washington, DC 20549   (202) 272-7040
The free publication, *Consumer's Financial Guide*, contains basic information on choosing investments and keeping them safe, trading securities, and the different protections guaranteed by law. To obtain this publication contact this office.

* Consumer Price Index Within 24 hours
National Technical Information Service
U.S. Department of Commerce
5285 Port Royal Road
Springfield, VA 22151   (703) 487-4630
A Consumer Price Index data summary is available by mailgram within 24 hours of the CPI release. It provides unadjusted and seasonally adjusted U.S. City Average data for All Urban Consumers and for Urban Wage Earners and Clerical Workers. The cost of this service is $145.00 per year.

* Consumer Prices
Office of Prices and Living Conditions
Bureau of Labor Statistics
Department of Labor
600 E St., NW, Room 3216
Washington, DC 20212   (202) 272-5160
The Labor Department measures consumer price changes for a predetermined market basket of consumer goods and services for two population groups: all urban consumers, and urban wage earners and clerical workers. The fixed market basket includes 382 entry level items representing all goods and services purchased for everyday living by all urban residents. Monthly and bimonthly indexes are available for various geographic regions.

* Consumer Purchasing Power Index
Superintendent of Documents
Government Printing Office
Washington, DC 20402   (202) 783-3238
Each monthly issue of the *Consumer Price Index Detailed Report* provides a comprehensive summary of price movements for the month, plus statistical tables, charts, and technical notes. The report covers two indexes, the Consumer Price Index for All Urban Consumers, and the Consumer Price Index for Wage Earners and Clerical Workers. The indexes reflect data for the U.S. city average and selected areas. An annual subscription is available for $21.00.

* Credit and ATM Cards
Federal Trade Commission
Credit Practices
6th & Pennsylvania Ave., NW
Washington, DC 20580   (202) 326-3175
Loss or theft of credit and ATM cards is a serious consumer problem; however, there are laws which establish procedures for you and your creditors to follow to resolve problems with these cards. This office investigates credit card fraud and can give you information on what to do if any of your cards are missing or stolen.

* Credit Card and Computer Fraud
Fraud Division
Office of Investigations
U.S. Secret Service
Department of the Treasury
1800 G St., NW
Washington, DC 20223   (202) 535-5850
The fraudulent use of credit and debit cards is a federal violation. Investigations are conducted by the Secret Service, including stolen or lost credit cards, the misuse of credit card account numbers, automated teller machine fraud, telephone fraud involving long distance calls, and other types of access device fraud.
Computer fraud is a recent concern of the Secret Service. New law enforcement techniques are being pioneered in an effort to identify computer criminals.

* Credit Pamphlets
Office of Consumer Affairs
Federal Deposit Insurance Corporation
550 17th St., NW, Room F-130
Washington, DC 20429   (202) 898-3535
The following FDIC pamphlets are free and are available in English and Spanish. Consumer Information. Provides an overview of the FDIC, its regional offices, and the major consumer and civil rights laws and regulations that protect bank customers. Equal Credit Opportunity and Age. Describes Credit Law and age discrimination. Equal Credit Opportunity and Women. Describes Credit Law and issues of sex and marital status. Fair Credit Billing. Offers consumers advice on handling disputes regarding billing errors and defective merchandise in ways designed to protect their credit rating. Fair Credit Reporting Act. Details consumers' rights to know what credit and personal information has been obtained about them by "Consumer Reporting Agencies" and what their rights are to challenge inaccurate information. Truth in Lending. Explains how the Truth in Lending Law protects consumers from hidden finance charges when obtaining credit.

* Credit Practices
Federal Trade Commission
Credit Practices Division
6th & Pennsylvania Ave., NW
Washington, DC 20580   (202) 326-3175
This division of the FTC works to ensure that creditors, credit counselors, certain mortgage lenders, and others who grant credit do not engage in unfair or deceptive acts or practices in providing credit or credit-related services. It also enforces the specific consumer protection statutes and rules listed below. Contact this division for more information about these topics. Consumer Leasing Act, which requires lessors to give consumers specific information on lease costs and terms. Electronic Fund Transfer Act, which requires institutions to disclose in writing important terms, such as charges for electronic fund transfers. Equal Credit Opportunity Act, which prohibits any creditor from denying credit to a consumer on the basis of sex, marital status, color, race, religion, national origin, age, or receipt of public assistance. Truth in Lending Act, which requires creditors to disclose in writing certain cost information, such as the annual percentage rate (APR), before consumers enter into credit transactions. Credit Practices Rule, which prohibits certain security interests and collection remedies in consumer credit contracts--namely, confessions of judgment, wage assignments, waivers of exemption, and security interests in certain household goods. Holder-in-Due Course Rule, which preserves consumers'claims and defenses involving performance of merchandise bought on credit against a non-seller owner of the credit contract.

* Credit Problems
Federal Trade Commission
Bureau of Consumer Protection
Credit Practices Division
6th & Pennsylvania Ave., NW
Washington, DC 20580   (202) 326-3175
Before you pay a credit repair clinic to "fix" your credit record, learn what the law says and consider saving your money by making some phone calls yourself. This office can give you more information on how to "fix" your own credit rating, along their free brochure.

* Credit Protection Laws

Publication Services
MS-138, Board of Governors
Federal Reserve System
Washington, DC 20551   (202) 452-3244

The *Consumer Handbook to Credit Protection Laws*, which can help you better understand how the credit protection laws can help you, is available free from this office.

* Damaged Currency Redemption

Office of Currency Standards
Bureau of Engraving and Printing
U.S. Department of the Treasury
Room 344A, BEPA
P.O. Box 37048
Washington, DC 20013   (202) 447-0545

All mutilated currency may be sent to the above address where trained personnel will determine if it can be exchanged at face value. All final decisions for redemption of this currency are made by the Treasurer of the United States. Currency should be sent by registered mail to the P.O. box address above.

* Direct Deposit of Social Security Payments

Office of the Assistant Commissioner Field Operations
Financial Management Service
U.S. Department of the Treasury
401 14th St., SW
Washington, DC 20227   (202) 287-0311

Presumed Direct Deposit is an approach of establishing Direct Deposit as the "normal" way to receive Social Security benefit payments. Sign-up techniques are simplified. Customer Service is being increased in over-the-counter and over-the-phone contacts. Beneficiaries may still choose to receive a check if they prefer or if they do not have a banking relationship.

* Donations to the Public Debt

Office of the Commissioner
Bureau of the Public Debt
U.S. Department of the Treasury
999-E St., NW
Washington, DC 20239   (202) 376-4300

Since the U.S. Government maintains a public debt of more than $1.9 trillion dollars, and is currently paying $176 billion in interest to pay off this debt, they are asking for donations from the general public to pay off the debt. The Treasury has an account into which money received as gifts is deposited. The money is used to pay at maturity, or to redeem or buy before maturity, an obligation of the Government included in the public debt. You can send donations to: Bureau of the Public Debt, Department G, Washington, D.C. 20239-0601.

* Fair Credit Billing

Federal Trade Commission
Division of Credit Practices
6th & Pennsylvania Ave., NW
Washington, DC 20580   (202) 326-3175

Credit card billing errors do occur, but they are simple to resolve if you know how to use the Fair Credit Billing Act, which protects your rights as a card user. For a free brochure on this Act or on credit billing laws in general, contact the FTC.

* Fair Credit Reporting

Federal Trade Commission
Credit Practices
6th & Pennsylvania Ave., NW
Washington, DC 20580   (202) 326-3175

If you've ever applied for a charge account, a personal loan, insurance, or a job, someone is probably keeping a file on you. This file might contain information on how you pay your bills, or whether you've been sued, arrested, or have filed for bankruptcy. Credit bureaus gather and sell this information as "consumer reports" to creditors, employers, and other businesses, but the Fair Credit Reporting Act protects you by requiring credit bureaus to furnish correct and complete information. This office can give you more information on your rights.

* Fair Debt Collection

Federal Trade Commission
Credit Practices
6th & Pennsylvania Ave., NW
Washington, DC 20580   (202) 326-3175

If you use credit cards, owe money on a loan, or are paying off a home mortgage, you are a "debtor." And although you may never come in contact with a debt collector, if you do, you should know the law to make sure you are treated fairly. This office can provide you with information about your rights as a debtor.

* Women and Credit Histories

Federal Trade Commission
Bureau of Consumer Protection
6th & Pennsylvania Ave., NW
Washington, DC 20580   (202) 326-3175

Each year many women are denied credit because they cannot show how they have used it, but two federal laws, the Equal Credit Opportunity Act and the Fair Credit Reporting Act, give you specific rights that help protect your credit history and make it easier for you to obtain credit. For more information, including a brochure on how to establish your credit, contact the FTC.

Product Safety

* Accident Investigations Data Base

National Injury Information Clearinghouse
U.S. Consumer Product Safety Commission
5401 Westbard Avenue, Room 625
Washington, DC 20207   (301) 492-6424

CPSC accident investigation reports provide information about an accident's sequence, human behavior, and role of the consumer product in the accident. Following is a description of the information in the CPSC's Accident Investigations database, which includes accidents occurring after mid-1972: the state in which the accident occurred; the victim's background, including age, race sex, education, and number of days incapacitated; the injury diagnosis; the consumer product involved; the product manufacturer; and more. Most information requests are answered without charge within 10 working days, but there is a charge for costs in excess of $25.

* Consumer Commission Meetings and Reports

Office of the Secretary
U.S. Consumer Product Safety Commission
Washington, DC 20207   (202) 492-6800

Commission meetings and meetings of the commissioners or Commission staff with persons outside of government are generally open to the public. In addition, records of what was discussed at those meetings are available for public inspection. Notices of meetings are generally published in the Commission's Public Calendar at least seven days before the meetings take place. Contact this office for a free copy of the Public Calendar.

* Consumer Deputy Program

Consumer Product Safety Commission
5401 Westbard Avenue
Washington, DC 20207   (202) 492-5788

As an unpaid volunteer, you can work with district and regional Commission offices to visit retail stores to make sure that the stores are complying with CPSC guidelines. Volunteers identify themselves to the store, check the inventory, and then report their findings back to the CPSC. The most recent Deputy program involves monitoring stores for the illegal sale of lawn darts.

* Consumer Injury Surveillance System

National Injury Information Clearinghouse
U.S. Consumer Product Safety Commission
5401 Westbard Avenue, NW
Washington, DC 20207   (202) 492-6424

The National Electronic Injury Surveillance System (NEISS) collects injury data from a sample of hospitals with emergency rooms across the U.S. and its territories. This data provides national estimates of the number and severity of injuries associated with but not necessarily caused by consumer products and treated in hospital emergency rooms. Information gathered from these and other sources, such as death certificates and reported incidents, guides the Commission in setting priorities for selecting types of products for further investigation and action. NEISS data are available in various computer formats. Any of the standard reports may be requested from this office, while custom reports are available at variable rates.

* Consumer Outreach Programs

Consumer Product Safety Commission
5401 Westbard Avenue
Washington, DC 20207   (202) 492-6580

By contacting the Commission's main office in Washington, D.C., or your local CPSC regional office, you can arrange to have a consumer education specialist visit your business, school, community group, or organization for a presentation on consumer product hazards and safety strategies.

* Consumer Product/Product-Related Injury Hotline

Office of Information and Public Affairs
Consumer Product Safety Commission
Washington, DC 20207   (800) 638-2772

To report a hazardous product or product-related injury, call this toll-free number. This hotline handles more than 200,000 calls each year. Operators are on duty from 10:30 a.m. to 4:00 p.m. Eastern Standard Time, Monday through Friday.

* Consumer Product Safety Commission Library

Consumer Product Safety Commission
5401 Westbard Avenue, NW, Room 546
Washington, DC 20207   (301) 492-6544

The CPSC library's collection includes reference materials on engineering, economics, and health sciences, which CPSC staff and other researchers may use for background on product safety issues. The library does not include CPSC documents and publications.

* Consumer Safety Databases

Consumer Product Safety Commission
5401 Westbard Avenue
Washington, DC 20207   (202) 492-6424

Although the Commission does not maintain databases which are accessible to outside users, specific requests for data are handled by the Commission's National Injury Information Clearinghouse or the Division of Automated Data Processing. Data may be provided to the requestor in the form of printouts, 9 track tapes, or 5 1/4 inch floppy diskettes. All information disclosed must first meet the disclosure requirements of the Consumer Product Safety Act. What follows is sampling of the Commission's databases, along with phone numbers:

American Association of Poison Centers: Information on childhood poisoning incidents received annually and prepared on various substance categories. (202) 492-6477

All Terrain Vehicle (ATV) Deaths: Information on ATV-related deaths, including investigation and injury reports, and death certificates. (202) 492-6470

Chemicals in Products: Contains complete chemical and biological information on consumer products. (202) 492-6962

Childhood Drowning Study: Contains information of swimming pool-related deaths of children. (202) 492-6470

Death Certificates: Information on death certificates involving product-related deaths in the U.S. (202) 492-6539

Establishment Inventory System: Maintains information on businesses which CPSC monitors or otherwise contacts, including data on firms, products, inspections, samples, and violations. (202) 492-6400

Fire Incident Reporting System: Contains information on electrical and range/oven fires collected from fire departments throughout the U.S. (202) 492-6539

Lawn Mower Special Survey: Maintains reports of lawn mower-related injuries over the last four years. (202) 492-6470

PCAT Data Collection: Contains children poisoning information, including records of ingestion by product categories for children under 5 years of age. (202) 492-6539

Product Defect Identification: contains manufacturer and retail reports to CPSC of product defects with injury risks, along with complaints and injuries of which the companies are aware (202) 492-6608

* Consumer's Resource Handbook

Office of Information and Public Affairs
U.S. Consumer Product Safety Commission
Washington, DC 20207   (800) 638-2772

This free Consumer's Resource Handbook shows you how to communicate more effectively with manufacturers, retailers, and service providers. The first section features tips on avoiding purchasing problems and getting the most for your money by giving steps for handling your own complaint and writing an effective complaint letter. The second section, the Consumer Assistance Directory, lists consumer offices in both public and private sectors that provide assistance for consumer complaints.

* Explosives Hotline

Explosives Enforcement Branch
Bureau of Alcohol, Tobacco, and Firearms
U.S. Department of the Treasury
1200 Pennsylvania Ave., NW   (800) 424-9555
Washington, DC 20226   (202) 566-7395

Those with information on a major arson incident or bombing, or are aware of stolen explosives, may call the above hotline. One of four national response teams will be rushed to the scene within 24 hours. A report will be taken by those answering the phone, and the information will be transferred to the nearest agent in the area. Each of the four response teams is composed of 10 special agents, a forensic chemist, and an explosive specialist from ATF's Explosives Technology Branch. A state or local law enforcement or fire service official can request the services of a National Response Team by contacting an ATF Special Agent in charge at one of 22 strategic office locations throughout the United States:

Atlanta, GA: (404) 331-6146
Birmingham, AL: (205) 731-1209
Boston, MA: (617) 565-7042
Charlotte, NC (704) 371-6125
Chicago, IL: (312) 620-7824
Cleveland, OH: ((216) 522-7210
Dallas, TX: (214) 767-2250
Detroit, MI: (313) 226-7304
Houston, TX: (713) 229-3511
Kansas City, MO: (816) 374-3874
Los Angeles, CA: (213) 894-4812
Louisville, KY: (502) 582-5211
Miami, FL: (305) 536-4368
Nashville, TN: (615) 736-7879
New Orleans, LA: (504) 589-2048
New York, NY: (212) 264-4657
Philadelphia, PA: (215) 597-3050
San Francisco, CA: (415) 974-9589
Seattle, WA: (206) 442-4485
St. Louis, MO: (314) 425-5560
St. Paul, MN: (612) 290-3092
Washington, DC: (703) 285-2543

* Explosives Incidents Statistics

Explosives Division
Office of Law Enforcement
Bureau of Alcohol, Tobacco, and Firearms
U.S. Department of the Treasury
1200 Pennsylvania Ave., NW, Room 2209
Washington, DC 20226   (202) 566-7159

The annual *Explosives Incidents Report* highlights statistics of explosive incidents and stolen explosives and recoveries. Tables include incidents by state, by target, and by types of explosives used. Significant explosives incidents during the year are also described. To obtain a copy of the report, contact Distribution Center, Bureau of Alcohol, Tobacco, and Firearms, U.S. Department of the Treasury, 7943 Angus Ct., Springfield, VA 22153.

*Firearms: Federal Regulations

Distribution Center
Bureau of Alcohol, Tobacco, and Firearms
U.S. Department of the Treasury
7943 Angus Ct.
Springfield, VA 22153   (703) 455-7801

Federal firearms laws are outlined in the free book, *Your Guide to Federal Firearms Regulation: 1988-1989.* Regulations concerning state firearms control assistance; machine guns, destructive devices, and certain other firearms; certain firearms administered by other federal agencies; commerce in firearms and ammunition, and the importation of arms, ammunition and implements of war are included.

* Firearms Identification

Distribution Center
Bureau of Alcohol, Tobacco, and Firearms
U.S. Department of the Treasury
7943 Angus Ct.
Springfield, VA 22153   (703) 455-7801

The free publication, *Identification of Firearms,* helps individuals in identifying weapons classified as firearms, including destructive devices. Pictures and descriptions are included of machine guns and machine pistols, shotguns, rifles, silencers, and other weapons and destructive devices.

* Fishery Products Grading and Inspection

Utilization Research and Services
National Marine Fisheries Service
National Oceanic and Atmospheric Administration
Department of Commerce
1335 East-West Hwy., Room 6142
Silver Spring, MD 20910   (301) 427-2355

The National Marine Fisheries Service conducts a voluntary seafood inspection program on a fee-for-service bases. A wide range of inspection services are available to any interested party, including harvesters, processors, food-service distributors, and importers and exporters. These services include vessel and plant sanitation inspection, product evaluation (in-plant and warehouse lot), product specification review, label review, laboratory analyses (microbiological tests,

chemical contaminant/indices of decomposition, species identification), training, and education and information. This office has a great deal of information concerning inspections, grading of products, and regulations. They also publish a document listing fishery products that have been produced in fish establishments approved by the National Marine Fisheries Service.

* National Injury Information Clearinghouse

Consumer Protection Safety Commission
5401 Westbard Avenue, Room 625
Washington, DC 20207   (301) 492-6424

This clearinghouse collects, investigates, analyzes, and distributes injury data and information relating to the causes and prevention of death, injury, and illness associated with consumer products. Its maintains thousands of detailed investigative reports of injuries associated with consumer products and has access to automated databases with several million incidents of injuries that have been reported by a nationwide network of hospital emergency departments. Technical analysts prepare publications, such as hazard analyses, special studies, and data summaries, a catalog of which is available by contacting the clearinghouse.

* Publications

Office of Information and Public Affairs
U.S. Consumer Product Safety Commission
Washington, DC 20207   (800) 638-2772

The following consumer publications describe some of the common hazards associated with the use of consumer products and recommend ways to avoid these hazards. They come in the form of fact sheets (F.S.), brochures, and materials developed especially for use by classroom teachers. Some of the publications listed here can also be requested from the Commission' Regional Offices.

General Information
Who We Are and What We Do
Compilation of Laws
Consumer Resource Handbook (1988)
CPSC Hotline Brochure
Some Federal Consumer Oriented Agencies (F.S. 52)

Annual Reports
Annual Report 1987
Annual Report 1986
Annual Report 1984 Part II
Annual Report 1983 Part II
Annual Report 1982
Annual Report 1981 Parts I,II

Bicycle Safety
Sprocketman (a comic book for high
   school age students)
Mini Bikes (F.S. 38)

Children's Furniture
Cribs (F.S. 43)
High Chairs (F.S. 70)
Bunk Beds (F.S. 71)
Tips for Your Baby's Safety - Nursery Equipment
   Checklist (English and Spanish)
The Safe Nursery - A Buyer's Guide to Nursery
   Equipment (English and Spanish)
Be Sure It's Safe For Your Baby

Children's Safety
Skateboards (F.S. 93)
Protect Your Child
Bumps Teachers Guide
Super Sitter

Compliance Publications
Retailers Guide (1/86)
Guide for Manufacturers, Distributors,
   and Retailers
Guide for Retailers (9/84)

Curriculum Guides and Lessons for Use By Educators
It's no Accident - Consumer Product Safety
   Guide for Teachers of Grades 3-6
Flammable Products: A Guide for Teachers of
   Secondary Grades
Flammable Products: A Guide for Teachers of
   Elementary Grades (Spanish)
Flammable Fabrics: Teacher's Guide (4T)
Flammable Fabrics: Student Readings (4-S)
Halloween Safety Teacher's Guide (9T)
Holiday Safety Teacher's Guide (7T)
Poison Prevention Teacher's Guide (6T)

Electric Safety

Consumer Power

Ranges and Ovens (F.S. 9)
TV Fire and Shock (F.S. 11)
Electric Blenders (F.S. 50)
Clothes Dryers (F.S. 73)
Ground Fault Circuit Interrupters (F.S. 99)
CPSC Guide to Electrical Safety
Consumer Product Safety Alert on Antennas
Electrical Safety Room by Room Audit
 Checklist (English and Spanish)
 (This is also available on "slow play disc"
 for the blind.)

Final Reports
Final Report of the National Conference on
 Product Safety (1982)
Final Report of the National Conference on
 Product Safety (1984)
Final Report of the National Consumer Product
 Safety Conference for Retailers
Final Report of the National Conference on
 Fire Toxicity

Fire Safety
Fireworks (F.S. 12)
Upholstered Furniture (F.S. 53)
Halloween Safety (F.S. 100)
What You Should Know About Smoke
 Detectors
Give a Gift--Give a Smoke Detector (poster)
Home Fire Safety Checklist

Hazardous Substances
School Science Laboratories: A Guide to Some
 Hazardous Products
Asbestos in the Home
List of Asbestos in Hair Dryers
Methylene Chloride Safety Alert

Holiday Safety
Merry Christmas With Safety

Home Heating Equipment
Space Heaters (F.S. 34)
Fireplaces (F.S. 44)
Furnaces (F.S. 79)
Wood Burning Stoves (F.S. 92)
Kerosene Heaters (F.S. 97)
Electric Space Heaters (F.S. 98)
464 Chimneys Safety Alert (1984)
Caution: Choosing and Using Gas
 Space Heaters
What You Should Know About Kerosene
 Heaters
What You Should Know About Space
 Heaters

Home Insulation
Installing Insulation Safety
Insulation Installers Guide
Q&A Urea Formaldehyde Foam
 Insulation

Indoor Air Quality
The Inside Story: A Guide to Indoor Air
 Quality

Outdoor Power Equipment
Power Mowers (F.S. 1)
Chain Saws (F.S. 51)
Chain Saw Safety Guide
Consumer Product Safety Alert on Chain Saws

Mower Hazards and Safe Practices (poster)
Power Mower and Maintenance Storage Tips
Safety, Sales, and Services
Power Lawn Mower Safety Kit--Teachers Manual
Power Mower Hazards and Safety Features (poster)

Older Consumers Safety
Home Safety Checklist for Older Consumers
 (English and Spanish)

Playground Equipment
Play Happy, Play Safely: Little Big Kids
 (4-6 years)
Handbook for Playground Safety, Volume I,
 General Guidelines
Handbook for Playground Safety, Volume II,
 Technical Guidelines

Poison Prevention
First Aid Brochure
Locked-up Poisons (English and Spanish)
Poison Lookout Checklist
Poison Prevention Packaging: A Text for
 Pharmacies and Physicians

Pool Safety
Children and Pool Safety Checklist
Backyard Pool--CPSC Safety Alert (5/87)

Spanish Fact Sheets
Power Mowers (F.S. 1)
Kitchen Ranges (F.S. 61)
Carbon Monoxide (F.S. 13)
Infant Falls (F.S. 20)
Mobile Homes (F.S. 39)
Older Consumers and Stairway Accidents (F.S. 48)
Kitchen Knives (F.S. 83)
Trampolines (F.S. 85)

Toys Safety
Toys (F.S. 47)
Electric Toys (F.S. 61)
Toy Chests (F.S. 74)
Baby Rattles (F.S. 86)
For Kids Sake, Think Toy Safety Pamphlet
 (English and Spanish)
Toy Safety Coloring Book (English and
 Spanish)
Which Toy For Which Child 0-5 Years
Which Toy For Which Child 6-12

Miscellaneous
All Terrain Vehicle (ATV) Safety Alert
How to Plan and Conduct Consumer Product
 Safety Information Programs
Ladders (F.S. 56)
Clothes Dryers (F.S. 73)
Publications Catalog
Refuse Bins (F.S. 81)

* Safety Standard Changes
Consumer Product Safety Commission
5401 Westbard Avenue
Washington, DC 20207   (202) 492-6580

If you think that the current safety specifications on a certain product, such as
a toy or a kitchen appliance, aren't tough enough, you can petition the CPSC to
make the changes and possibly have your recommendations used in the new
specifications. Contact this office for more details.

Post Office and Mailing

* Administrative Support Manual

Communications Department
U.S. Postal Service
475 L'Enfant Plaza, SW
Washington, DC 20260-3121   (202) 268-2143

This subscription service consists of a basic manual and supplementary material for an indeterminate period. This manual describes matters of internal administration in the Postal Service. It includes functional statements as well as policies and requirements regarding security, communications (printing directives, forms, records, newsletters), government relations, procurement and supply, data processing systems, maintenance, and engineering. A subscription is available for $22 domestic, $27.50 foreign from: Superintendent of Documents, Government Printing Office, Washington, D.C. 20402-0001; (202) 783-3238.

* Aerogrammes

International Postal Affairs Department
U.S. Postal Service
475 L'Enfant Plaza, SW
Washington, DC 20260   (202) 268-2445

Aerogrammes are flat sheets of paper that serve as both letters and envelopes. They are specially stamped, marked for folding, and already gummed. Meant for foreign airmail only, aerogrammes can be mailed anywhere in the world at a lower postage rate than regular airmail.

* A Consumer's Guide to Postal Crime Prevention

Public Affairs Branch
The Postal Inspection Service
US Postal Service
475 L'Enfant Plaza, SW
Washington, DC 20260   (202) 268-4293

The free booklet, A Consumer's Guide to Postal Crime Prevention, is full of tips and ideas on how to discourage mail thieves and how to help put mail fraud con artists out of business. Consumers who believe they are victims of mail fraud should write the nearest office of the Postal Inspection Service or refer the information through their local postmaster.

* A Guide to Business Mail Preparation

Marketing Department
Regular Mail Services Division
U.S. Postal Service
475 L'Enfant Plaza, SW, Room 5541
Washington, DC 20260-6336   (202) 268-2222

This free guide provides voluntary guidelines for postal customers and their suppliers regarding the preparation of letter mail for successful processing on the latest in high-speed automated mail sorting equipment. Computerized mail processing is faster, more efficient, economical, and accurate than older manual or mechanized sorting and mailing methods. Information on addressing for automation, postnet bar codes, and FIM patterns is covered.

* Business Guide to Postal Crime Prevention

Public Affairs Branch
The Postal Inspection Service
US Postal Service
475 L'Enfant Plaza, SW
Washington, DC 20260   (202) 268-4293

The booklet, Postal Crime Prevention: A Business Guide, shows business owners how to protect themselves from con artists and thieves whose business is mail fraud and mail theft. It includes information on different types of mail fraud to watch for, check cashing precautions, guidelines for mailroom security, bombs in the mail, and additional information.

* Business Mailer Information

Communications Department
U.S. Postal Service
475 L'Enfant Plaza, SW
Washington, DC 20260   (202) 268-2158

The free monthly publication, Memo to Mailers, advises business mailers of all rate and classification changes as well as other postal news. It is available from "Memo to Mailers," Post Office Box 999, Springfield, VA 22150-0999.

* Business Reply Mail

Rates and Classification Department
U.S. Postal Service
475 L'Enfant Plaza, SW
Washington, DC 20260   (202) 268-5311

Businesses and others who want to encourage responses to their mailings by paying the postage for those responses might consider using business reply mail. Under this service, all responses are returned to the sender from any U.S. post office to any valid address in the United States. Business reply mail must be prepaid according to a specified format, and a small annual fee is charged for each permit issued. The mailer guarantees to pay the postage for all replies returned to him or her at the regular first class rate plus a business reply fee. For additional information, contact this office.

* Business Reply Mailgram

Rates and Classification Department
U.S. Postal Service
475 L'Enfant Plaza, SW
Washington, DC 20260   (202) 268-5311

A Business Reply Mailgram is now available for customers who require a quick turnaround response. This mailgram provides all of the features of a regular Mailgram with the addition of a built-in response device using a Business Reply envelope. Contact this office for more information.

* Carrier Alert Program

Communications Department
U.S. Postal Service
475 L'Enfant Plaza, SW
Washington, DC 20260   (202) 268-2158

Pioneered by the Postal Service and the National Association of Letter Carriers, the Carrier Alert Program encourages letter carriers to watch participants' mailboxes for mail accumulations that might signal illness or injury. Accumulations of mail are reported by carriers to their supervisors who then notify a sponsoring agency through locally developed procedures, for follow-up action. Since its founding in 1982, this lifeline has been cited for saving dozens of lives.

* Consumer Advocate

The Consumer Advocate
U.S. Postal Service
475 L'Enfant Plaza, SW, Room 5821
Washington, DC 20260-2202   (202) 268-2281

The Consumer Advocate, a postal ombudsman, represents the interest of the individual mail customer in matters involving the Postal Service by bringing complaints and suggestions to the attention of top postal management and solving the problems of individual customers. Contact your postmaster and if your problem cannot be solved by your local post office.

* Consumer's Directory of Postal Services and Products

Consumer Advocate
U.S. Postal Service
475 L'Enfant Plaza West, SW
Washington, DC 20260-2202

This directory, which discusses the various services and products the Postal Service offers, will help you choose the right service to meet your individual needs and save time and money. Included is information on mail services, addressing and packaging, special services, stamp collecting and mail fraud. To obtain a copy contact this office or your local post office.

* Current Mail Rates, Fees and Services

Rates and Classification Department
U.S. Postal Service
475 L'Enfant Plaza, SW
Washington, DC 20260   (202) 268-5169

This department can give you information on current mail rates, fees, and services.

* Customer Service Representatives

Marketing and Communications Group
U.S. Postal Service
475 L'Enfant Plaza, SW
Washington, DC 20260   (202) 268-2267

Consumer Power

The U.S. Postal Service has a local sales staff of Customer Service Representatives found in main post offices. Their services include helping you get the most for your postage dollar; showing you how to set up a mail room; resolving your business mail problems and selling services. Contact this office for more information on getting these services.

* Customs

United States Customs Service
Treasury Department
PO Box 7407
Washington, DC 20229-7407   (202) 566-2957

All mail originating in foreign countries and most United States territories is subject to U.S. Customs Service examination upon entering the United States. Many imported goods are subject to U.S. customs duty. When goods enter by mail, the duty assessed by Customs is collected by the Postal Service, as is a customs clearance and delivery fee on each mail piece on which customs duty is paid.

* Design Licenses

Law Department
U.S. Postal Service
475 L'Enfant Plaza, SW
Washington, DC 20260   (202) 268-2329

Designs of postage stamps issued after January 1, 1978, are copyrighted and may not be reproduced except under license granted by the U.S. Postal Service. Earlier designs are in the public domain and may be reproduced without permission for philatelic, educational, historical, and newsworthy purposes.

* Directives and Forms Catalog

Document Control Division
Office of Information Services
Information Resource Management Department
U.S. Postal Service
Washington, DC 20260-1571

This document is a catalog of all national directives and forms currently used in the Postal Service. A complete edition of this publication is published three times a year. Interim changes appear regularly in the "Directives Update" and "Forms Update" in the "Postal Bulletin." Also included is a list of directives which the public may obtain free of charge at main post offices.

* Domestic Mail Manual

Consumer Affairs Department
U.S. Postal Service
475 L'Enfant Plaza, SW, Room
Washington, DC 20260-6300   (202) 268-2281

The manual is designed to assist customers in obtaining maximum benefits from domestic postal services. It includes applicable regulations and information about rates and postage, classes of mail, special services, wrapping and mailing requirements, and collection and delivery services. The subscription service consists of four cumulative issues a year and is available for $19 domestic, $23.75 foreign from: Superintendent of Documents,
Government Printing Office, Washington, DC 20402-0001; (202) 783-3238.

* Freedom of Information Requests

General Counsel
Postal Rate Commission
1333 H St., NW, Suite 300
Washington, DC 20268-0001   (202) 789-6820

For information requests under the Freedom of Information Act, contact the office above.

* Hazardous and Illegal Items

Postal Inspection Service
U.S. Postal Service
475 L'Enfant Plaza, SW
Washington, DC 20260-2186

It is illegal to send through the U.S. Mail any article, composition, or material which may kill or injure another person, or obstruct mail service or damage property. Harmful matter includes, but is not limited to poisons, poisonous animals, insects, and reptiles, including all types of snakes and spiders; all disease germs or scabs, and all explosives, flammable material, dangerous machines, and mechanical, chemical or other devices or compositions which may catch fire or explode. Contact this office for more information on the guidelines.

* History of Rural Post Offices

Administrative Office
Postal Rate Commission
1333 H St., NW, Suite 300
Washington, DC 20268-0001   (202) 789-6840

At the Crossroads: An Inquiry into Rural Post Offices and the Communities They Serve investigates the sociological implications and community effects resulting from the closing of a post office in a small rural community. The study shows the history and development of postal delivery and the Postal Service as it affects rural areas. Write or call for a free copy.

* International Mail Manual

International Postal Affairs Department
U.S. Postal Service
475 L'Enfant Plaza, SW
Washington, DC 20260   (202) 268-2445

This manual sets forth the policies, regulations, and procedures governing international mail services offered to the public by the Postal Service. It includes the postage rates, fees, and mail preparation information for Postal Union mail, parcel post, and International Express Mail, as they apply to each individual country. A subscription is available for $14 domestic, and $17.50 foreign from: Superintendent of Documents, Government Printing Office, Washington, DC 20402-0001; (202) 783-3238.

* International Surface Airlift

International Postal Affairs
U.S. Postal Service
475 L'Enfant Plaza, SW
Washington, DC 20260   (202) 268-2445

International Surface Air Lift service provides fast delivery, at a cost lower than airmail, for publications and printed matter sent overseas a that surface rate. The postage rate is a per pound rate.

* Legal Restrictions

Postal Inspection Service
U.S. Postal Service
475 L'Enfant Plaza, SW
Washington, DC 20260-2186   (202) 268-4293

There are legal restrictions on the mailing of radioactive material, firearms, knives, and sharp instruments, drugs and narcotics, and other controlled substances as defined by Federal law and related Federal regulations. Certain potentially harmful or dangerous articles and substances may be mailed if special packaging and labeling requirements are met. Your local postmaster or account representative can provide more details.

* Library

Library
U.S. Postal Service
475 L'Enfant Plaza SW, Room 11800
Washington, DC 20260-1641   (202) 268-2904

Along with a working collection of materials in law, the social sciences, and technology, the Postal Library contains a unique collection of postal materials, legislative files from the 71st Congress to date, reports, pamphlets, clippings, photographs, general postal histories, periodicals of the national postal employee organizations, Universal Postal Union studies, and Postal laws and regulations handbooks and manuals. The library is open to the public weekdays from 9 a.m. to 4 p.m. Reading Rooms are located on the 11th Floor North.

* Mail Fraud

Postal Inspection Service
U.S. Postal Service
475 L'Enfant Plaza, SW
Washington, DC 20260-2186   (202) 268-4293

Mail Fraud is a scheme to get money or anything of value from the public by offering a product, service, or investment opportunity that does not live up to its claims. Prosecutors must prove the claims were intentionally misrepresented and that the mails were used to carry out the scheme. The Postal Inspection Service investigates violations of the mail fraud law. Consumer complaints are the primary basis for investigation by Postal Inspectors. Some of the more common mail fraud schemes include medical fraud, work-at-home-schemes, land fraud, charity fraud, insurance fraud, investment fraud, and home improvement fraud.

* Mailing Free Matter For Blind

and Visually Handicapped Persons
Office of Consumer Affairs
US Postal Service
475 L'Enfant Plaza, SW
Washington, DC 20260   (202) 268-2281

The free pamphlet, Mailing Free Matter For Blind and Visually Handicapped Persons, is designed to answer the most often asked questions about mailing free matter for the visually handicapped. It discusses qualifying, eligibility, conditions and restrictions on mailings, and the steps to make special arrangements for delivery.

* Mailing Services for the Blind and Handicapped

Office of the Consumer Advocate
U.S. Postal Service
L'Enfant Plaza, SW
Washington, DC 20260-6320   (202) 268-2281

Persons who are blind or who cannot use or read conventionally-printed material due to a physical handicap may qualify to mail items free of postage. To be eligible, a competent authority must submit a statement to the post office where postage-free mailings will be made or received, certifying that the individual is unable to read conventional reading material. Certain conditions and restrictions apply. The same general rules apply to both domestic and international mail service. Special arrangements for delivery or pickup of free mail for eligible persons may be arranged through local post offices depending on the circumstances. Contact this office for more information.

* Mailing to the Soviet Union

International Postal Affairs Department
U.S. Postal Service
475 L'Enfant Plaza, SW
Washington, DC 20260-6500   (202) 245-4575

Of all countries of the world with which the U.S. Postal Service exchanges mail, none has created more problems for U.S. mailers than the Soviet Union. U.S. mailers can reduced many of their frustrations by getting clear information on how to send mail to the Soviet Union, and how to seek redress if problems are encountered. Contact this office for more information on prohibited items, restricted articles, and size and weight limits.

* National ZIP Code and Post Office Directory

Delivery Distribution Department
U.S. Postal Service
475 L'Enfant Plaza, SW
Washington, DC 20260   (202) 268-6990

Proper ZIP Code information is essential for speedy and economic delivery of your mail. The "ZIP Code Directory" is an up-to-date and comprehensive listing of ZIP Code information by state and post office. It includes instructions for quickly finding a ZIP Code number when an address is known. The ZIP Code Directory also includes official lists of post offices, named stations, named branches, and community post offices in the United States. The volume includes a wealth of handy information about ZIP Codes, postal abbreviations, and basic postal procedures and is an indispensable aid that is worth its price many times over. Available for $15.00 from: Superintendent of Documents, Government Printing Office, Washington, DC 20402-0001; (202) 783-3238.

* Pornography

Postal Inspection Service
U.S. Postal Service
475 L'Enfant Plaza, SW
Washington, DC 20260-2186   (202) 636-2339

To stop the mailing of unsolicited sexually-oriented advertisements to yourself or your minor children, fill out "Application for Listing Pursuant of 39 USC 3010," at your local post office. Thirty days after your name has been added to the Postal Service reference list, any mailer who sends you sexually oriented advertisements is subject to legal action by the U.S. Government. To stop the mailing of any further advertisements to yourself which you consider "erotically arousing or sexually provocative," fill out *Notice for Prohibitory Order Against Sender of Pandering Advertisement in the Mails*, at your local post office.

* Postal Bulletin

Communications Department
U.S. Postal Service
475 L'Enfant Plaza, SW
Washington, DC 20260   (202) 268-2143

This weekly publication contains current orders, instructions and information relating to the Postal Service, including philatelic, airmail, money order, parcel post, etc. The subscription is available for $64.00 domestic, and $80.00 foreign per year from: Superintendent of Documents, Government Printing Office, Washington, DC 20402-0001; (202) 783-3238.

* Postal Commission Procedures

Administrative Office
Postal Rate Commission
1333 H St., NW, Suite 300
Washington, DC 20268-0001   (202) 789-6840

The publication, *The Postal Rate Commission in Brief*, outlines the steps of various cases and decisions for which the Commission is responsible. The steps in a postal rate case and the decision procedure are outlined, as well as those of a mail classification case. Change in nationwide service, the appeal process for closing or consolidating a small post office, and the way in which rate or service complaints are handled are also described. Contact this office to receive a copy.

* Postal Financial Management Manual

Superintendent of Documents
Government Printing Office
Washington, DC 20402-0001   (202) 783-3238

The Financial Management Manual presents an overview of the financial activities of the Postal Service. It summarizes the following topics: general accounting, post office accounting, accounts receivable and accounts payable, budget and planning, payroll accounting and control of assets. The subscription costs $27.00 domestic, and $33.75 foreign.

* Postal Inspection Service

Inspection Service Department
U.S. Postal Service
475 L'Enfant Plaza, SW
Washington, DC 20260-2100   (202) 268-4267

As the law enforcement arm of the Postal Service, The Postal Inspection Service protects the mails, postal funds, and property; investigates internal conditions and needs that may affect postal security and effectiveness; apprehends those who violate the postal laws; and audits financial and nonfinancial operations. Information on past and present schemes used to defraud the public is available as well. Help is available if you experience difficulty with a company or suspect that you have been the victim of mail fraud. There is a Regional Chief Inspector in each of the five postal regions. Information and complaints of postal violations should be presented to the nearest Postal Inspector in charge.

Central Region

Chicago
Main Post Office Bldg., Chicago, IL 60607-5401; (312) 765-4605
433 W. Van Buren St., Chicago, IL 60669-2201; (312) 765-4500

Denver
P.O. Box 329, Denver, CO 80201-0329; (303) 297-6220

Des Moines
P.O. Box 566, Des Moines, IA 50302-0566; (515) 253-9060

Detroit
P.O. Box 119, Detroit, MI 48232-3201; (313) 226-8184

Indianapolis
Suite 300, 3750 Guion Rd., Indianapolis, IN 46222-1669; (317) 9923-1601

Kansas City
P.O. Box 411606, Kansas City, MO 64141-1606; (816) 932-0400

Milwaukee
P.O. Box 788, Milwaukee, WI 53201-0788; (414) 291-2475

St. Louis
10th Fl., 200 S. Hanley Rd., St. Louis, MO 63199-2201; (314) 854-4760

St. Paul
P.O. Box 64558, St. Paul, MN 55164-2201; (612) 293-3202

Eastern Region

Cynwud
1 Bala Cynwyd Plaza, Bala Cynwyd, PA 19004-3509; (215) 5668-4784

Baltimore
P.O. Box 1856, Baltimore, MD 21203-1856; (301) 347-3480

Charlotte
2901 I-85 S., Charlotte, NC 28228-3000; (704) 393-4470

Cincinnati
P.O. Box 2057, Cincinnati, OH 45201-2057; (513) 684-5700

Cleveland
P.O. Box 5726, Cleveland, OH 44101-0726; (216) 443-4000

Harrisburg
P.O. Box 3535, Harrisburg, PA 17105-3535; (717) 257-2330

Philadelphia
P.O. Box 7500, Philadelphia, PA 19101-9000; (215) 895-8450

Pittsburgh
1001 California Ave., Pittsburgh, PA 15290-9000; (412) 359-7900

Richmond
P.O. Box 25009, Richmond, VA 23260-5009; (804) 775-6267

Washington, D.C.
P.O. Box 96096, Washington, DC 20066-6096; (202) 636-2339

Consumer Power

Northeast Region

Newark
Gateway No. 2, McCarter Hwy. & Market St., Newark, NJ 07175-0001; (201) 621-5500
P.O. Box 509, Newark, NJ 07101-5901; (201) 596-5450

Boston
P.O. Box 2217, Boston, MA 02202-2217; (617) 654-5825

Buffalo
685 Ellicott Sq., Buffalo, NY 14203-2545; (716) 856-3674

Hartford
P.O. Box 2169, Hartford, CT 06145-2169; (203) 646-6060

New York
P.O. Box 5555, James Farley Bldg., New York, NY 10116-0555; (212) 330-3844

San Juan
P.O. Box 3667, San Juan, PR 00936-9614; (809) 753-2856

Southern Region

Memphis
10th Fl., 1407 Union Ave., Memphis, TN 38161-0001; (901) 722-7700
P.O. Box 3180, Memphis, TN 38173-0180; (901) 576-2077

Atlanta
P.O. Box 16489, Atlanta, GA 30321-0489; (404) 765-7369

Birmingham
P.O. Box 2767, Birmingham, AL 35202-2767; (205) 521-0270

Fort Worth
P.O. Box 162929, Fort Worth, TX 76161-2929; (713) 236-7000

Houston
P.O. Box 1276, Houston, TX 77251-1276; (713) 236-7000

Miami
P.O. Box 520772, Miami, FL 33152-0772; (305) 591-0379

New Orleans
P.O. Box 51690, New Orleans, LA 70151-1690; (504) 589-1200

Tampa
P.O. Box 22526, Tampa, FL 33622-2526; (813) 228-2481

Western Region

San Bruno
850 Cherry Ave., San Bruno, CA 94098-0100; (415) 742-4411

Oakland
P.O. Box 24005, Oakland, CA 94623-1005; (415) 636-2600

Pasadena
P.O. Box 2000, Pasadena, CA 91102-2000; (818) 405-1200

Phoenix
P.O. Box 20666, Phoenix, AZ 85036-0666; (602) 223-3660

Portland
Suite 790, 921 SW Washington, Portland, OR 97205-2898; (503) 294-2263

San Diego
P.O. Box 2110, San Diego, CA 92112-2110; (619) 233-0610

San Fransisco
P.O. Box 882000, San Francisco, CA 94188-2000; (415) 550-5602

Seattle
P.O. Box 400, Seattle, WA 98111-4000; (206) 442-6300

* Postal Life: The Magazine for Postal Employees
Communications Department
U.S. Postal Service
475 L'Enfant Plaza, SW
Washington, DC 20260   (202) 268-2143
This bimonthly periodical contains articles, with illustrations, about new methods, techniques and programs of the U.S. Postal Service. Its purpose is to keep postal employees informed and abreast of developments in the U.S. Postal Service. The subscription is available for $5.50 domestic, and $6.90 foreign per year from: Superintendent of Documents, Government Printing Office, Washington, DC 20402-0001; (202) 783-3238.

* Postal Operations Manual
Communications Department
U.S. Postal Service
475 L'Enfant Plaza, SW
Washington, DC 20260   (202) 268-2143
This manual sets forth policies for the internal operations of post offices. It includes retail services, mail processing, transportation, delivery services, and fleet management. The subscription costs $37.00 domestic, and $46.25 foreign from: Superintendent of Documents, Government Printing Office, Washington, DC 20402-0001; (202) 783-3238.

* Postal Publications
Contact your local post office.
Introduction To Stamp Collecting. Offers advice on starting a collection, ideas for various types of collections, how to obtain and care for stamps, and philatelic resources, organizations, and publications.
INTELPOST EMS Express Mail. This brochure provides information on service, rates and benefits, and service destinations. Pick one up at your local post office.
How to Pack and Wrap Parcels for Mailing and How to Prepare and Wrap Packages. Contain helpful tips and guidelines for mailing packages, including minimum size standards, mailing nonstandard-size parcels, and selecting the proper container. They are available at your local post office.
Acceptance of Hazardous, Restricted or Perishable Matter. Contains detailed information on hazardous material. Your local postmaster or account representative can provide you with a copy of this publication.
Express Mail Corporate Account & Express Mail General Information. Provides information on service options, preparing your package, rates and making payments, and how to protect your packages.
Selling to the Postal Service. Offers details on Postal Service procurement including specific supplies and services.
Customer Guide to Filing Indemnity Claims on Domestic Mail. Explains the specific procedures that must be followed when filing a claim for compensation including who can file, when to file, where to file, how to file, and information on claim forms. Copies are available at your local post office.

* Postal Publications and Handbooks
Data Information Center
Document Control Division
U.S. Postal Service
475 L'Enfant Plaza, SW
Washington, DC 20260   (202) 268-2852
Postal Service Publication No. 223 lists all technical publications available, including titles of publications and their supply source.

* Postal Rate Commission
Postal Rate Commission
1333 H St., NW, Suite 300
Washington, DC 20268-0001   (202) 789-6800
The Postal Rate Commission considers proposed changes in postal rates, fees, and mail classifications and to issue recommendations to the Governors of the Postal Service. It also considers changes in the nature of available postal service. Postal Service decisions to close or consolidate post offices are also reviewed. The Commission also investigates complaints concerning postal rates and service on the national level. Five Commissioners serve a six-year term of office and are appointed by the President.

* Postal Rate Commission Open Meetings
General Counsel
Postal Rate Commission
1333 H St., NW, Suite 300
Washington, DC 20268-0001   (202) 789-6820
The Commission meetings are the forums where postal rates, fees, mail classifications, service changes, and post office closings and consolidations are discussed. They are open to the public, except in special circumstances, but public participation is not permitted. Documents from these meetings are also available to the public at the headquarters offices.

* Postal Rate Complaints
General Counsel
Postal Rate Commission
1333 H St., NW, Suite 300
Washington, DC 20268-0001   (202) 789-6820
Written complaints may be addressed to the above office if you feel changes are needed in the rate and classification structure of mail or if you believe the nationwide system of the Postal Service can be improved. Local problems must be addressed to the U.S. Postal Service directly.

60

* Postal Rate Consumer Information

Consumer Advocate
Postal Rate Commission
1333 H St., NW, Suite 300
Washington, DC 20268-0001 (202) 789-6830

Information on the activities of the Postal Rate Commission is distributed by the Consumer Advocate. If a postal rate case is pending, the newspapers and other media are alerted. Consumer groups are also notified.

* Postal Service Changes

Postal Rate Commission
1333 H St., NW, Suite 300
Washington, DC 20268-0001 (202) 789-6800

The Postal Service asks the Postal Commission for their advisory opinion on proposed changes in nationwide postal services, rates, and classifications. These formal requests are then published in the *Federal Register*.

* Postal Service Films

Communications Department
The U.S. Postal Service
475 L'Enfant Plaza, SW
Washington, DC 20260 (202) 268-2156

A few general films are available for loan to the public. One film, for example, traces the route of a letter as it goes through the postal service system, and another film demonstrates the importance of letters in people's lives.

* Postal Speakers Network

Assistant Postmaster General
Communications Department
U.S. Postal Service
475 L'Enfant Plaza, SW, Room 5300
Washington, DC 20260 (202) 268-2143

Speakers may be scheduled free of charge provided two to three months notice is given and provided those interested give preliminary information. It is also possible to coordinate Postal Service participation in meetings of national organizations and associations. Speakers for meetings that are regional or local in nature are scheduled by the appropriate Regional Postmaster General's office or the Regional Chief Inspector's office.

* Practice and Procedures

Administrative Office
Postal Rate Commission
1333 H St., NW, Suite 300
Washington, DC 20268-0001 (202) 789-6840

Rules of Practice and Procedure describes in detail the methods for handling the Postal Rate Commission's responsibilities. First is a listing of rules that apply to general business matters, including term definitions, the docket and hearing calendar, inquiries, and public attendance at Commission meetings. Rules are also written for rates or fees changes, for changing the mail classification schedule, for postal service changes, and for rate and service complaints. The method for filing testimony by those who wish to intervene in rate and classification proceedings is also included, as well as the procedure for an appeal to a decision to close or consolidate small post offices.

* Products and Services

The Marketing Department
The U.S. Postal Service
475 L'Enfant Plaza, SW, Room 5014
Washington, DC 20260 (202) 268-2222

For information on specific U.S. Postal Service products and services, contact this office.

* Regional and Field Division Offices

U.S. Postal Service
475 L'Enfant Plaza, SW
Washington, DC 20260-0010

In addition to the national headquarters, regional and field division offices supervise more than 40,000 post offices, branches, stations, and community post offices throughout the United States. Each of the five Regional Postmasters General manage postal activities in a geographical area as indicated below.

Central Region
433 W. Van Buren St., Chicago, IL 60699-0100; (312) 765-5000. Areas served: CO, IL, IN (except ZIP Codes 420, 423, 424, 470, 476, 477), IA, KS, MI, MN, MO, NE, ND, SD, WI, WY.

Eastern Region
P.O. Box 8601, Philadelphia, PA 19197-0100; (215) 496-6001. Areas served: DC, DE, IN (ZIP Codes 420, 423, 424, 470, 476, 477), KY, MD, NJ (ZIP Codes 080-084), NC, OH, PA, SC, VA, WV.

Northeast Region
6 Griffin Park Rd., North Windsor, CT 06006-0100; (203) 285-7001. Areas served: CT, MA, ME, NH, NJ (ZIP Codes 070-079, 085-089), NY, Puerto Rico, RI, VT, Virgin Islands.

Southern Region
1407 Union Ave., Memphis, TN 38166-0100; (901) 722-7333. Areas served: AL, AR, FL, GA, LA, MS, OK, TN, TX (except ZIP Codes 797-799).

Western Region
850 Cherry Ave., San Bruno, CA 94099-0100; (415) 742-4922. Areas served: AK, AZ, CA, HI, ID, MT, NV, NM, OR, TX (ZIP Codes 797-799), UT, WA, Pacific Possessions and Trust Territories.

* Public Hearings on the Postal System

Docket Section
Postal Rate Commission
1333 H St., NW, Suite 300
Washington, DC 20268-0001 (202) 789-6845

When a proposed change in the national Postal Service is recommended before the Postal Rate Commission, public hearings are held. Testimony is given on the program, and those in attendance are given an opportunity to address questions. The records of these public hearings are used in making the final decisions on postal system changes. To be placed on the mailing list to receive notices of these hearings, contact the office above. A hearing calendar and a docket of all proceedings from the hearings is also available for public inspection. Office hours are 8 a.m. to 5 p.m., Monday through Friday. You must have the docket number of the proceeding you wish to examine.

* Rural or Highway Contract Route

Rural Delivery Division
Delivery and Distribution and Transportation Department
U.S. Postal Service
Washington, DC 20260 (202) 268-6990

General distribution of third class mail to each boxholder on a rural or highway contract route, or for each family on a rural route, or for all boxholders at a post office that does not have city or village carrier service, may have the mail addressed omitting the names of individuals and box or route numbers if the mailer uses this form of address: "Postal Customer," or, to be more specific: "Rural (or Highway Contract Route) Boxholder, City (or town), State." On request, a Postmaster will furnish mailers with the number of families and boxes served on each route.

* Small Post Office Closings

Delivery Distribution and Transportation Department
U.S. Postal Service
475 L'Enfant Plaza, SW
Washington, DC 20260 (202) 268-6990

Contact this office for information on small post office closings or consolidations.

* Third-Class Mail Preparation

Communications Department
U.S. Postal Service
475 L'Enfant Plaza, SW
Washington, DC 20260-3121 (202) 268-2143

If you're planning to mail at the third-class bulk rates, this publication explains what bulk business mail is, and how to get the most out of it. If you already have the necessary permits to mail at the bulk third-class rates, this publication will serve as a valuable reference.

Housing and Real Estate
General Sources

See also Your Community Chapter

This chapter provides good starting places for finding information in the housing and real estate industry. You'll find sources on such topics as surplus property, urban homesteading, construction standards, and even historic preservation. There's information here for anyone interested in housing and real estate, including first time home buyers, urban planners, and real estate speculators. Whether you're looking for mortgage counseling, foreclosed properties, or information on housing discrimination, you should be able to find what you're looking for.

* Affordable Housing: Joint Venture For (JVAH)

Single Family Development Division
Office of Insured Single Family Housing
Department of Housing and Urban Development
Washington, DC 20410-8000   (202) 755-6700

The goal of the JVAH is affordable home ownership for middle-income Americans. By involving builders, developers, local governments, and others connected with the housing industry concerned with housing affordability, the JVAH creates affordable home ownership opportunities through regulatory reform, elimination of red tape, and the use of innovative construction and land planning techniques. It focuses on controllable factors contributing to housing costs, including deregulation and building code modification. The JVAH enlists community organizations to work for affordable housing by helping them launch their own affordable housing campaigns and functioning as a clearinghouse for resource materials and ideas. The information kit, Affordable Housing, available through this office, includes information on the following: Planning for Affordable Single-Family Housing, How Local Regulatory Improvements Can Help, What States Can Do, and Streamlining Local Regulations, as well as a bibliography of general affordable housing publications and checklists for single-family and multi-family objectives.

* Accessible Housing Reports for the Handicapped

HUD USER
P.O. Box 6091   (800) 245-2691
Rockville, MD 20850   (301) 251-5154

HUD USER makes the following series of reports available on research performed to make buildings accessible to and usable by all Americans:

Access to the Built Environment: A Review of Literature (#660, $13.00). Describes the history of efforts to achieve a barrier-free environment and pertinent Federal, State, and municipal laws and regulations.
Accessible Buildings for People With Walking and Reaching Limitations (#661, $13.00). Discusses the research conducted in such areas as wheelchair maneuvers, ramps, toilet stalls, bathrooms, kitchens, doorways, elevators, and public phones and mailboxes.
Accessible Buildings for People With Severe Visual Impairments (#662, $13.00). Reports the results of a study of orientation and mobility problems that occur in visually impaired individuals in architectural settings, and solutions for dwellings to conform to American National Standards Institute specifications.
A Cost-Benefit Analysis of Accessibility (#664, $8.00). Presents a cost-benefit analysis for removing architectural barriers from residential and nonresidential buildings.
Adaptable Dwellings (#665, $8.00). Reviews the research completed to determine what parts of a dwelling should be designed for accessibility and to what extent special features are needed from a disabled person's viewpoint.
Adaptable Housing: Marketing Accessible Housing for Everyone ($3.00). A primer of adaptable housing for designers and builders, as well as developers, managers, architects, product manufacturers, and government and building code officials.

* American Housing Survey for the United States

HUD User
P.O. Box 6091
Rockville, MD 20850   (800) 245-2691; or (301) 251-5154

This survey is the result of personal and telephone interviews of approximately 190,000 households in 44 selected metropolitan areas conducted by the Census Bureau for HUD. Information is provided on the size and composition of the U.S. housing inventory, occupant characteristics, changes in the stock due to new construction, indicators of housing and neighborhood quality, and the characteristics of recent movers. The study contains hundreds of different kinds of information on such housing-related topics as age, race sex, and income of households; source of income--wages, pensions, dividends, welfare, Social Security; reasons for moving from last home; type and condition of housing; amount of rent or mortgage payment, value of property, purchase price,

downpayment; number of rooms, bedrooms, baths; repairs, alterations, additions; plumbing, heating, cooling equipment, and other appliances; cost of fuel and utilities, type of fuel used; neighborhood quality--police protection, hospitals; neighborhood problems--crime, pollution, street noise.

The information from this survey can be used in many ways. Mortgage lenders, developers, marketing analysts, and demographers can use the survey information to examine economic and social trends for planning and decisionmaking. Manufacturers, housing analysts, financial institutions, and planners may study particular markets, which builders and real estate brokers can rely on to help them better understand their housing markets. Data is also available on magnetic tape or compact disc. If you need microdata, the survey is now available in CD-ROM (compact disc-read only memory)in two formats: ASCII and SAS internal format. The cost is $3.00 for the information in hard copy, and $125 for the data on CD-ROM.

* Builder and Developer Publications

HUD USER
P.O. Box 6091   (800) 245-2691
Rockville, MD 20850   (301) 251-5154

The following is a sampling of publications of interest to real estate developers, builders, and others in the housing construction industry. $3.00 is charged per document for handling.

Adaptable Housing: A Technical Manual for Implementing Adaptable Dwelling Unit Specifications (PDR-1124)
Affordable Housing Challenge and Response, Vol.1: Affordable Residential Land Development (PDR-1128 (v1)
Affordable Housing Challenge and Response, Vol.2: Affordable Residential Construction (PDR-1128(v2)
*Home Builder's Guide for Earthquake Design (** Earthquake Design)*
Home Building Cost Cuts: Construction Methods and Materials for Affordable Housing (looseleaf bulletins) (PDR-628)
Noise Assessment Guidelines (PDR-735)
Rehabilitation Guidelines 1986: Nos. 1-11 (PDR-613-1(3) through 8(3), PDR-632, PDR-631, PDR-935). Includes guidelines on setting and adopting standards for building rehabilitation, approval of building rehabilitation, managing official liability associated with building rehabilitation, egress, electrical, plumbing, fire ratings, archaic materials and assemblies, structural assessment, walls, windows, roofs, and building systems.
EER-2 Energy Efficient Residence: Research Results (PDR-904)
Reducing Energy Costs in Multifamily Housing (PDR-1055(1)
Regional Guidelines for Building Passive Energy Conserving Homes (PDR-355(2))
Site Planning for Solar Access: A Guidebook for Residential Developers and Site Planners (PDR-481(2))
Building Housing for the Low-Income Elderly (PDR-929)
Cost of Lead Based Paint Abatement in Public Housing (PDR-708)
*Fourth Report to Congress on Mobile Homes (**Fourth Report)*
*Planning for Affordable Single-Family Housing (**Planning Single-Family Housing)*
Survey of Passive Solar Homes (PDR-589)
Housing Special Populations: A Resource Guide - 1987 ($3.00). Provides the housing specialist with resources on housing the elderly, disabled persons, and the homeless. Annotated references to reports, books, and articles provide access to pertinent up-to-date information. Photographs help illustrate the unique circumstances and real life situations faced by these special groups. Also included in the guide is a list of organizations - with names, addresses, and phone numbers - to allow networking opportunities with colleagues.
Environmental Hazards in Residential Construction - 1987 ($2.50). Indoor pollutants are an increasingly alarming health hazard. This is a guide to reports, articles, pamphlets, and books addressing four indoor environmental hazards: asbestos, radon gas, lead-based paint, and formaldehyde. A resource section lists organizations, government resources, and periodicals that can provide additional information.

Blueprint Catalog. Describes 48 full size working drawings of affordable and energy-efficient housing designs available from HUD USER (Free)(** Blue Cat).
Designing Affordable Houses (S/N 023-000-00702-9, $1.75). Various plans for building moderate cost homes.
House Construction: How to Reduce Costs (S/N 001-000-03729-3, $2.50).
Finishing Wood Exteriors (S/N 001-000-04450-8, $3.25). Provides information on the characteristics and proper application of finishes to solid and reconstituted wood products. Also discusses the different kinds of wood, the selection, application, and maintenance practices that affect surfaces to be finished.

* Community and Urban Planning Publications

HUD USER
P.O. Box 6091
Rockville, MD 20850 (800)   245-2691 or (301) 251-5154

The following is a sampling a publications of interest to community and urban planners available for a $3 handling charge.

Local Property Urban Homesteading Demonstration (PDR-1134)
Rental Housing: Condition and Outlook (PDR-685)
Affordable Housing: How Local Regulatory Improvements Can Help (PDR-714(3)
Affordable Housing: What States Can Do (PDR-713(3)
Housing Rehabilitation for Small Cities, Second Edition: The Community Development Approach (CPD-1062)
How to Design a Rental Rehabilitation Program: Training Exercises for Program Operators (CPD-1062)
Case Study of Local Control Over Housing Development: The Neighborhood Strategy Area (PDR-732)
Final Report of the Evaluation of the Urban Initiatives Anti-Crime Demonstration (PDR-969)
Impact Evaluation of the Urban Development Action Grant Program (PDR-694)
Implementing Community Development: A Study of the Community Development Block Grant Program (PDR-989)
Working Partners: 100 Success Stories of Local Community Development (CPD-630(3))
*Helping the Homeless: A Resource Guide (** Homeless Guide)*
Insider's Guide to Managing Public Housing, Vol. 1, Diagnosing Management Problems (PDR-638)
Insider's Guide to Managing Public Housing, Vol. 2, Analysis Guide (PDR-639)
*Tools and Techniques for Housing Development: A Guidebook for Local Officials (**Tools and Techniques)*
American Housing Survey, 1983
Effects of Tax Reform on Housing and Urban Development - 1987 ($2.50). The articles and reports in this resource guide will help builders, architects, planners, local government officials, and other housing and urban development professionals analyze the effects of the new law on homebuilding and financing, real estate investment, municipal capital spending, and low-income housing construction and financing.
Housing Rehabilitation: Programs, Techniques, and Resources - 1987 ($5.00). This guide to publications offers an overview of housing rehabilitation in central cities in the U. S., covering rehabilitation technology, local approaches, Federal programs, and historic preservation. A list of relevant organizations, journal titles, and other resources is included.
Enterprise Zones in America: A Selected Resource Guide - 1986 ($2.50). The goal of enterprise zones is the stimulation of business--especially small enterprises--in depressed areas through the provision of tax and other incentives and through deregulation. This reference guide includes summaries and bibliographic information on 31 publications which focus in the historical background of the concept, discuss key issues involved in creating zones, and summarize reports based on State and local experiences with enterprise zones. *Affordable Housing: A Selected Resource Guide--1985* ($2.50). This guide, with more than 50 annotated listings, is divided into five sections: Cost-Saving Design and Technology, Local Actions to Promote Affordable Housing, Financing, Case Studies, and Outreach Materials.
Homeless Assistance Information Kit (Free). This gives an overview of HUD homeless assistance programs and other recent materials on the subject. (Free)(** Homeless Kit).
Multi-Family Homesteading: A Guide for Local Governments (S/N023-000-00754-1, $6.00). Explains how conversion of underutilized or abandoned multi-family property to shared ownership by long-term residents can help a community. Discusses selection of developers, property selection, project planning and design, financing, marketing, and management of these developments.

* Counseling for Homebuyers, Homeowners, and Tenants

Single Family Servicing Branch
Secretary-Held and Counseling Services
Office of Insured Single Family Housing
Department of Housing and Urban Development
Washington, DC 20410-8000   (202) 755-6664

To help reduce delinquencies, defaults, and foreclosures, HUD provides free counseling to homeowners and tenants under its programs through HUD-approved counseling agencies. The counselors advise and assist homeowners with budgeting, money management, and buying and maintaining their homes. Contact this office or your local HUD office of information on the counseling agency nearest you.

* Consumer Housing Publications

Consumer Information Center
Pueblo, CO 81002

Write to the above address to order any of the following publications:

Consumer Handbook on Adjustable Rate Mortgages. Basic features, advantages and risks, and terminology associated with adjustable rate mortgages. (1984, Federal Reserve Board, Federal Home Loan Bank Board, 428V, $.50).
A Consumer's Guide to Mortgage Lockins. What they are and how you can lock-in interest rates and points when applying for a mortgage. (1988, Federal Reserve Board, 426V, $.50).
A Consumer's Guide to Mortgage Refinancing. What the costs are and how to tell if the time is right to refinance your home. (1988, Federal Reserve Board, 427V, $.50).
Home to Buy a Manufactured (Mobile) Home. What to consider when buying a manufactured home, such as selection, placement, warranties, installation, and inspection. (1985, Federal Trade Commission, 429V, $.50).
The Mortgage Money Guide. Handy guide to different types of mortgages and loan financing options. Includes a table of monthly mortgage costs at various rates. (1988, Federal Trade Commission, 137V. $1.00).
U.S. Real Property Sales List. Quarterly listing of when, where, and how federal surplus real estate will be sold. Where to go for more information on specific places of property. (Revised quarterly, General Services Administration, 565V, Free).
Urban Homesteading. This program transfers federally-owned residences to communities for sale to qualified individuals. Gives general qualifications and state HUD offices and Urban Homesteading Coordinators in cities where you can apply. (1987, HUD, 430V, $.50).
Your Home, Your Choice. Discusses housing options for the elderly, such as homesharing, home adaptations, and nursing homes - with a checklist to help you decide. (1985, Federal Trade Commission 466V, $.50).
Simple Home Repairs Inside. How to repair or replace faucets, plugs, screens, tiles, and more. (1986, Department of Agriculture, 141V, $1.50).
Are There Any Public Lands For Sale? Describes the federal program to sell excess undeveloped public land and why there are no more lands available for homesteading. (1988, Dept. of the Interior, 136V $1.00).

* Country Homes

USDA
Farmers Home Administration, Single Family Housing Division
14th and Independence Ave., SW
Washington, DC 20250   (202) 382-1474

The Farmers Home Administration makes low-interest loans to qualified applicants to purchase homes or farms in rural areas. They are also charged with disposing of properties that are foreclosed. First, they Farmers Home Administration makes any necessary repairs to the property, then offers them for sale to people who have the same qualifications as those applying for loans. Eligible applicants also qualify to purchase at special low interest rates (as low as 1%). If no eligible applicants purchase a property, it is then put up for sale to the general public at competitive prices. If the property is not sold within 10 days, it is reduced by 10%.

* Directory of Information Resources in Housing and Urban Development

HUD USER
P.O. Box 6091   (800) 245-2691
Rockville, MD 20850   (301) 251-5154

The most recent edition of this directory lists 150 trade and professional organizations, public agencies, advocacy groups, and research and educational institutes in housing and urban development. Each entry describes the organization's purpose and services and includes an address and telephone number. These contacts can provide current relevant information on today's key housing issues. The Directory also describes 54 online databases available in the field. This publication is available for $25.00.

* Earth Sheltered Buildings

Science and Technology Division
Reference Section
Library of Congress
Washington, DC 20540   (202) 707-5580

Informal series of reference guides are issued free from the Science and Technology Division under the general title, *LC Science Tracer Bullet.* These guides are designed to help readers locate published material on subjects about which they have only general knowledge. New titles in the series are announced in the weekly Library of Congress *Information Bulletin* that is distributed to many libraries. The relevant study is No. *82-3Earth Sheltered Buildings.*

* Escrow Accounts For Home Mortgages

Federal Trade Commission
Division of Credit Practices
6th & Pennsylvania Ave., NW

Housing and Real Estate

Washington, DC 20580 (202) 326-3175

Each month millions of homeowners pay money into escrow accounts to cover property taxes and hazard insurance through their lending institutions, but many don't even know what these escrow accounts really are. If you have questions about escrow practices, rates, and laws, contact your bank, your state banking agency, or the FTC.

* Equal Opportunity in HUD-Assisted Programs (Title VI)

Office of Fair Housing and Equal Opportunity
Department of Housing and Urban Development
Washington, DC 20410-2000 (202) 755-5904

HUD determines the extent to which its programs comply with Federal laws forbidding discrimination in all federally funded activities. This office investigates complaints and reviews HUD programs to eliminate discrimination. Activities are made more responsive to minorities and promote their participation in HUD programs. Technical assistance is available to state and local agencies with civil rights problems.

* Fair Housing Complaints

Fair Housing Enforcement Division
Office of Fair Housing and Equal Opportunity
Department of Housing and Urban Development
Washington, DC 20410-2000 (202) 755-7252
For filing complaints: (800) 424-8590; or (202) 426-3500

HUD administers the law that prohibits discrimination in housing on the basis of race, color, religion, sex, and national origin; investigates complaints of housing discrimination; and attempts to resolve them through conciliation. Two common forms of discrimination are redlining and steering. Redlining is the illegal practice of refusing to originate mortgage loans in certain neighborhoods on the basis of race or ethnic origin. Steering is the illegal act of limiting the housing shown by a real estate agent to a certain ethnic group. If you have experienced housing discrimination, you should file a complaint with any HUD office in person, by mail, or by telephone at the numbers listed here. HUD refers complaints to state and local fair housing agencies.

* Fair Housing: Voluntary Compliance

Office of Voluntary Compliance
Office of Fair Housing and Equal Opportunity
Department of Housing and Urban Development
Washington, DC 20410-2000 (202) 755-7007

HUD promotes voluntary compliance in the private sector and with other Federal agencies in the area of fair housing activities nationwide. HUD executes Voluntary Affirmative Marketing Agreements with housing industry groups, both locally and nationwide. Comprehensive fair housing plans are also developed with local units of government. HUD also organizes volunteer citizen groups to work with these plans and agreements. Trade and professional organizations in housing and related fields, including homebuilders, real estate brokers, mortgage lenders, and rental property managers are asked to comply.

* Federal National Mortgage Association (Fannie Mae)

Federal National Mortgage Association
3900 Wisconsin Ave., NW
Washington, DC 20016 (202) 752-7000

This governmental financial institution has been created to serve as a secondary source of mortgage funds. By purchasing loans from lenders, it serves as a conduit for funds from investors into the loan industry. Even though it is a privately-owned, profit-motivated corporation, the Secretary of HUD has regulatory authority over Fannie Mae's operations.

* Foreign Investment in the U.S.

Land Branch, ERS
U.S. Department of Agriculture
1301 New York Ave., NW
Washington, DC 20005-4788 (202) 786-1425

Foreign investment in U.S. agricultural land has been reported for 12.5 million acres in 1,859 of the 3,041 counties in the U.S. Foreign Ownership of U.S. Agricultural Land through December 31 1988 lists data for each county to show the number of acres, its value, country of origin, and use of the land. This publication is also available on tape from AFIDA Database (1-800-999-6779).

* Ginnie Mae Mortgage-Backed Securities

Government National Mortgage Association
Department of Housing and Urban Development
Washington, DC 20410-9000 (202) 755-5926

The Government National Mortgage Association guarantees the timely payment of principal and interest on securities issued by lenders and backed by pools of Government-underwritten residential mortgages. The program's purpose is to attract non-traditional investors into the residential mortgage market by offering them a high-yield, risk-free, Government-guaranteed security which has none of the servicing obligation associated with a mortgage loan portfolio. GNMA II,

which supplements the original program, has a central paying agent, Chemical Bank, which makes consolidated payments to investors. Larger, geographically-dispersed, multiple-issuer mortgage pools, as well as custom pools, are offered. A mix of interest rates is also provided among the mortgages within the pool. Securities under this program are privately issued and backed by pools of FHA or Veteran's Administration mortgages. Included in the mortgage pools are single-family level payment, graduated payment, growing equity, and manufactured housing loans. Lending institutions under this program must be in good standing and have adequate net worth, staffing, and experience.

* Handicapped Access to Buildings

Architectural and Transportation Barriers
Compliance Board
1111 18th St., NW, 5th Floor
Washington, DC 20036-3894 (202) 653-7834

This organization, affiliated with the U.S. Department of Education, provides information in compliance with standards for access to and use of buildings by handicapped persons. Below is a listing of free publications available:

Uniform Federal Accessibility Standards: Architectural requirements for access to federally funded facilities. Based on the ATBCB Minimum Guidelines and Requirements for Accessible Design. *Access America: The Architectural Barriers Act and You:* Describes the ATBCB and how to file complaints about accessible federally funded buildings. About Barriers. Describes barrier removal nationally and contains suggestions for action locally. *Access Travel: Airports: A Guide to Accessibility of Terminals:* Describes 519 airports in 62 countries. *Resource Guide to Literature on a Barrier Free Environment:* A state-of-the-art guide to barrier-related literature, research studies and legislation. *You'll Do It Every Time:* A cartoon parking "ticket" to remind people that handicapped parking signs are no joke. Available in pads of 50.

* Handicapped Housing Information for Developers

Office of Elderly and Assisted Housing
Department of Housing and Urban Development
Washington, DC 20410-8000 (202) 755-3287

This office can provide you with complete information on the procedure to obtain Section 202 funding for handicapped housing projects. An information packet, which outlines the program requirements and the specifications for the construction of the project to be funded, is available.

* Historic Preservation

Superintendent of Documents
Government Printing Office
Washington, DC 20402 (202) 783-3238

The following publications on historic preservation are available from the GPO for $1 unless otherwise noted:

Aluminum and Vinyl Siding on Historic Buildings: The Appropriateness of Substitute Materials for Resurfacing Historic Wood Frame Buildings
Architectural Character: Identifying the Visual Aspects of Historic Buildings as an Aid to Preserving Their Character Cleaning and Waterproof Coating of Masonry Buildings
Conserving Energy in Historic Buildings
Dangers of Abrasive Cleaning to Historic Buildings
Exterior Paint Problems on Historic Woodwork
Historic America: Buildings, Structures, and Sites ($29)
Interior Building: Its Architecture and Its Art ($8.50)
Keeping It Clean: Removing Exterior Dirt, Paint, Stains, and Graffiti From Historic Masonry Buildings ($2.50)
Metals in America's Historic Buildings: Uses and Preservation Treatment ($6)
National Register of Historic Places
New Exterior Additions to Historic Buildings: Preservation Concerns
Preservation Briefs: Recognizing and Resolving Common Preservation Problems ($9)
Preservation of Historic Adobe Buildings
Preservation of Historic Concrete Problems and General Approaches
Preservation of Historic Glazed Architectural Terra-Cotta
Preservation of Historic Pigmented Structural Glass, Vitrolite and Carrara Glass
Preservation Tax Incentives for Historic Buildings
Rehabilitating Historic Storefronts
Rehabilitating Interiors in Historic Buildings: Identifying and Preserving Character, Defining Elements
Repair and Thermal Upgrading of Historic Steel Windows ($1.25)
Repair of Historic Wooden Windows
Repointing Mortar Joints in Historic Brick Buildings
Roofing for Historic Buildings
Secretary of the Interior's Standards for Rehabilitation and Guidelines for Rehabilitating Historic Buildings ($2)
Interpreting the Secretary of the Interior's Standards for Rehabilitation, Volume 3 ($9)
Technologies for Prehistoric and Historic Preservation ($10)
Use of Substitute Materials in Historic Buildings: Exterior Applications

* Home Ownership Publications

Veterans Assistance Office
Department of Veterans Affairs
810 Vermont Ave., NW
Washington, DC 20420   (202) 233-2044
The following publications are available to veterans from their VA regional office:

Pointers for the Veteran Homeowner. A guide for veterans whose home mortgage is guaranteed or insured under the GI Bill.
To the Home-Buying Veteran. A guide for veterans planning to buy or build homes with a VA loan.
VA-Guaranteed Home Loans for Veterans. To help you understand what the VA can and cannot do for the home purchaser.

* Houses From Failed Saving and Loans Companies

Resolution Trust Corporation   (800) 431-0600
Washington, DC 20429   (202) 789-6316
As a result of the hundreds of failed US Savings and Loan institutions the US Government has on had over 30,000 real property assets is it attempting to auction off at the best available price. The inventory contains approximately 12,000 single family homes, 2,500 commercial properties and 800 parcels of undeveloped land.

* Housing Consumer Publications

Superintendent of Documents
Government Printing Office
Washington, DC 20402   (202) 783-3238
The following publications are geared toward home buyers, and prospective home buyers, who may not be familiar with such issues as consumer rights, mortgages, financing, and much more. Each publication is followed by the GPO order number and price.

Buying Lots From Developers (S/N 023-000-00694-4, $2.50). Includes information on the facts the buyer should obtain before buying, his consumer rights, dishonest sales practices to watch for, and where to make complaints.
Settlement Costs: A HUD Guide (S/N 023-000-00721-5, $1.50)
Wise Home Buying (S/N 023-000-00752-5, $1.00). Instructs the first-time home buyer in selecting and financing a house. Discusses the relation of housing costs to income, new versus old houses, mortgage loans, real estate brokers, and more.
Home Buyer's Vocabulary (S/N 023-000-00751-7, $1.00). Provides general, nontechnical definitions of terms the potential home buyer will encounter in buying and financing a home.
Homeowner's Glossary of Building Terms (S/N 023-000-00750-9, $1.00). Provides an alphabetical list of terms used in home construction, repair, and maintenance as a quick reference for homeowners not familiar with building terminology.

* Housing Discrimination

Fair Housing Enforcement Division
Office of Fair Housing and Equal Opportunity
Department of Housing and Urban Development
Washington, DC 20410-2000   (202) 755-7252
Technical assistance is available to state and local agencies, private and public groups, and profit or nonprofit organizations to help them prevent or eliminate discriminatory housing practices.

* Housing Finance Statistics

Financial Policy Division
Office of Housing
Department of Housing and Urban Development
Washington, DC 20410   (202) 755-7270
Studies are conducted by the Financial Policy Division of HUD in areas relating to the mortgage market, securities, taxation, market trends, interest rates, among others. If you are interested in receiving information about these subjects or want to be placed on the mailing list, contact this office.

* Housing Research and Policy

Assistant Secretary for Policy
Development and Research
Department of Housing and Urban Development
Washington, DC 20410-6000   (202) 755-6996
This office is responsible for economic and policy analyses, research, demonstrations, and evaluations of national housing and community development. All policy development data generated by HUD are made available to interested parties, such as state and local governments, financial institutions, builders, developers, neighborhood groups, and universities and colleges. The research addresses many issues, including the management, operation, and maintenance of the insured and assisted multi-family housing inventory; the stability of the nation's housing finance system; the design of sound mortgage instruments and improvements in FHA programs; the increase of housing affordability through technological and regulatory improvements; the improvement of public housing; the assurance of a supply of affordable rental housing units; the promotion of fair and nondiscriminatory housing; and the study of housing-related health problems.

* HUD Counseling Agency Program

Single Family Servicing Branch
Secretary-Held and Counseling Services
Office of Insured Single Family Housing
Department of Housing and Urban Development
Washington, DC 20410-8000   (202) 755-6664
Housing counseling grants are awarded on a competitive basis to HUD-approved counseling agencies to reimburse them partially for costs. These agencies and private and public organizations must be competent and have knowledge and experience in housing counseling. The maximum grant available is $40,000 per agency.

* HUD's Major Publication Sources

HUD USER
P.O. Box 6091   (800) 245-2691
Rockville, MD 20850   (301) 251-5154
HUD USER, the research information service sponsored by HUD's Office of Policy Development and Research, distributes the latest research in the fields of housing and urban development in a variety of formats tailored to your needs. These include

HUD USER ONLINE - Bibliographic database dedicated to housing and urban development, available on BRS/SEARCH Service.
Document delivery - Printed copies of recently published reports and photocopies of unpublished and out-of-print materials.
Resource guides - illustrated collections of abstracts on topics of special interest, such as housing rehabilitation, enterprise zones, public housing, alternative housing arrangements, affordable housing, fair housing, elderly housing, homelessness, and accessible environments for the disabled.
Directory of Information Resources in Housing and Urban Development - a valuable reference tool providing descriptions of 114 organizations and 37 online databases in the housing, construction, and planning fields.
Searches on HUD USER ONLINE - performed by HUD USER reference specialists to help you locate documents containing information in your area of interest.
Blueprints - full-sized working drawings that can help both the professional builder and the do-it-yourself homeowner apply the newest in energy-efficient and cost-effective housing design.
Microfiche - copies of any non-copyrighted documents in HUD USER ONLINE in an economical and space-saving format.
Audiovisual programs - to stimulate discussion at group meetings on improving housing and neighborhoods.

* HUD Public Information Clearinghouse

Program Information Center
Department of Housing and Urban Development
Washington, DC 20410   (202) 755-6420
If you need additional assistance and direction to particular programs within HUD, or have questions about how HUD can work for you, contact the Program Information Center, and they will gladly assist you.

* Land Sale Fraud

Federal Trade Commission
Marketing Practices
6th & Pennsylvania Ave., NW
Washington, DC 20580   (202) 326-3128
This office investigates fraud as it relates to the sale of land to the public, and can provide you with information about your rights and how to avoid fraudulent practices.

* Land Sales

Interstate Land Sales Registration
Department of Housing and Urban Development
Washington, DC 20410-8000   (202) 755-0502
The registration of interstate land sales protects subdivision lot purchasers by prohibiting fraudulent practices requiring land developers and promoters full financial disclosure. Before a lot can be sold or leased two conditions must be met by developers: 1) A Statement of Record must be filed with HUD, containing full and current disclosure about the ownership of the land, the state of title, planned physical characteristics, planned availability of roads, services, utilities, and other matters; and 2) A printed Property Report must be delivered to each purchaser or lessee in advance of signing the contract or agreement. Anti-fraud provisions apply to subdivisions containing 25 or more lots. HUD may seek an injunction against any developer whom it can show is violating or about to violate the law, and may suspend the registration of a developer whose Statement of Record or Property Report contains misrepresentation or omits material facts.

Housing and Real Estate

* Lenders Offering FHA-Insured Mortgages

Office of Insured Single Family Housing
Department of Housing and Urban Development
Washington, DC 20410-8000　　　　　　　(202) 755-0316

This HUD office maintains a listing of lenders who participate in FHA-insured mortgage programs. You can also get this information by contacting your local Field Office.

* Mobile Home Construction and Safety Standards

Office of Single Family Housing
Office of Manufactured Housing and Regulatory Functions
Manufactured Housing and Construction Standards Division
Department of Housing and Urban Development
Washington, DC 20410-8000　　　　　　　(202) 755-6290

HUD issues Federal manufactured home construction and safety standards to reduce the number of personal injuries and deaths, and the amount of insurance costs and property damage resulting from manufactured home accidents. The program also strives to improve the quality and durability of manufactured homes. Standards are enforced by HUD directly or by various States which have established State administrative agencies that participate in the program. HUD inspects factories and obtains records needed to enforce the standards, and if standards are not met, the manufacturer is forced to notify the consumer and to correct any defects found.

* Multifamily Property Disposition

Multifamily Sales Division
Office of Multifamily Housing
Department of Housing and Urban Development
Washington, DC 20410　　　　　　　　　(202) 755-7220

Multifamily properties are sold through sealed-bid auctions across the country. This office maintains a listing of the current available properties. To be placed on the mailing list for current and new properties that become available, contact this office.

* Multifamily Property Standards

Government Printing Office
Superintendent of Documents
Washington, DC 20402　　　　　　　　　(202) 783-3238

HUD publishes a subscription service entitled *Minimum Property Standards, Volume II, Multifamily Housing*. The services consist of a basic manual and quarterly revisions in looseleaf form. Standards in the areas of health and safety, durability, energy, the elderly, and the handicapped are included. The subscription price is $35.00/year. (S/N 923-001-00000-0).

* Native American Indians and Housing

Office of Public Affairs
Bureau of Indian Affairs
U.S. Department of the Interior
18th and C Sts., NW
Washington, DC 20240　　　　　　　　　(202) 343-1711

The free booklet, *American Indians Today: Answers to Your Questions, 1988*, contains useful information on the Native American Indians and their relationship to the Bureau of Indian Affairs. Programs within the Bureau, including education, health services, and housing are briefly outlined and contain recent statistics. Many questions are answered within the booklet, including the rights of the Indians to own land and have their own governments. A map locates the Indian lands and communities, showing Federal and State Indian Reservations and other Indian groups. An excellent bibliography, prepared by the Smithsonian Institution, is included.

* Real Estate Settlements

Real Estate Settlement Procedures Act (RESPA)
Office of Insured Single Family Housing
Department of Housing and Urban Development
Washington, DC 20410-8000　　　　　　　(202) 755-5676

RESPA requires that lenders give all borrowers of federally-insured mortgage loans a HUD-prepared booklet with information about real estate transactions, settlement services, cost comparisons, and relevant consumer protection laws. When applying for a loan, borrowers must receive the booklet along with the lender's good faith estimate of the settlement costs they are likely to incur. One day before settlement, the borrower may request that the person conducting the settlement provide information on the actual settlement costs. At settlement, both the buyer and seller are entitled to a settlement statement that itemizes the costs they paid in connection with the transaction.

* Recent Research Results (RRR)

HUD USER
P.O. Box 6091
Rockville, MD 20850　　　　　　(800) 245-2691 (301) 251-5154

This newsletter contains short summaries of reports recently published under the auspices of the HUD Office of Policy Development and Research. To be put on the mailing list, contact this office.

* Rental Rates

Technical Support Division
Office of Multifamily Housing
Department of Housing and Urban Development
Washington, DC 20410　　　　　　　　　(202) 426-0035

The Federal Register contains a yearly listing of the fair market rental rates in 450 market areas around the country. The data show the rental rates for various types of dwellings.

* Research in Assisted Housing

Assistant Secretary for Policy
Development and Research
Department of Housing and Urban Development
Washington, DC 20410-6000　　　　　　　(202) 755-5600

This office conducts research and evaluations to develop more efficient, effective, and equitable ways to assist low-income households. HUD's assisted housing programs are monitored and evaluated, and alternatives are investigated. Data is collected and analyzed by the Department's staff and made available to interested parties, to federal agencies, and to Congress. Assisted housing research conducted includes the following areas: administrative costs of operating assisted housing programs, development costs of assisted housing programs, alternative assisted housing demonstrations, efficient, effective management of public housing projects, benefits to participants in assisted housing programs, and environmental hazards in assisted housing.

* Single Family Property Auctions

Sales Promotion Branch
Office of Single Family Housing
Department of Housing and Urban Development
Washington, DC 20410　　　　　　　　　(202) 755-5832

Single-family homes are sold by sealed-bid auction in every city in the country. These properties are advertised in local newspapers.

* Surplus Property

Public Benefit Program
Division of Health Facilities Planning
PHS, Room 17A10
5600 Fishers Lane
Rockville, MD 20857　　　　　　　　　(301) 443-2265

The Public Health Service has real estate property available for use under two programs. The first program allows the property to be used for a public health purpose by local and state governments and private nonprofit organizations certified under the IRS code. The property can be used for such projects as nursing homes, clinics, or mental health centers. You are deeded the property with a thirty year period of restriction. The second program allows the property to be used by local government or private nonprofit organizations for homeless shelters.

* Surplus Veterans Homes

Department of Veterans Affairs
810 Vermont Ave, NW
Washington, DC 20420　　　　　　　　　202-233-4000

The Department of Veterans Affairs sells foreclosed properties through private real estate brokers. Properties are frequently advertised in local newspapers. Almost any real estate agent can show you the property. Local Veterans offices are the best sources of information on the procedures involved in purchasing these properties.

Prices drop on those homes that are not soled in a certain period of time. Veterans financing is possible, but you get a 10% discount if you pay cash. See the Section on Computerized Electronic Bulletin Boards for getting this information on-line with your modem.

* Urban Homesteading

Urban Homesteading Office
Office of Urban Rehabilitation
Community Planning and Development
Department of Housing and Urban Development
Washington, DC 20410-7000　　　　　　　(202) 755-5324

Urban homesteading is designed to revitalize declining neighborhoods and reduce the amount of federally-owned properties by transferring vacant and unrepaired single-family properties to new homeowners for rehabilitation. Federally-owned properties are transferred to local governments that have developed homesteading programs approved by HUD. Local governments then transfer the properties for a nominal sum to eligible individuals or families called homesteaders. Priority is given to lower-income persons. The homesteaders must occupy the property as a principal residence for at least five years, and must bring it up to local code standards within three years. Rehabilitation may be carried out by a contractor or by the homesteader.

* Urban Policy Report to Congress
Assistant Secretary for Policy
Development and Research
Department of Housing and Urban Development
Washington, DC 20410-6000   (202) 755-5600

Under the Urban Growth and New Community Development Act of 1970, Congress is required to develop a national urban growth policy report every two years. This report summarizes trends, identifies significant problems, evaluates the effectiveness of federal efforts to deal with the problems, and makes recommendations for legislative and administrative actions.

* Urban Trees Money
Cooperative Forestry, FS
U.S. Department of Agriculture
P.O. Box 96090
Washington, DC 20090-6090
OR: Your regional Forest Service Office   (703) 235-1376

The USDA will provide financial, technical, and related assistance in order to plant and protect trees, maintain and use wood from trees in open spaces, green belts, roadside screens, parks woodlands, curb areas, and residential developments in urban areas.

* Veterans Foreclosed Homes
Department of Veterans Affairs
810 Vermont Ave, NW
Washington, DC 20420   (202) 233-4000

The Department of Veterans Affairs sells foreclosed properties through private real estate brokers. Properties are frequently advertised in local newspapers, giving information such as address, number of bedrooms and bathrooms, particular defects in the property and price. Almost any real estate can show you the property. Local Veterans offices are the best source of information on the procedures involved in purchasing these properties. Many local offices maintain the information on local on-line bulletin boards. See the Chapter on Electronic Bulletin Boards.

Federal Money for Housing and Real Estate

The following is a description of the federal funds available to renters, homeowners, developers, and real estate investors for housing in urban and rural areas. This information is derived from the *Catalog of Federal Domestic Assistance* which is published by the U.S. Government Printing Office in Washington, D.C. The number next to the title description is the official reference for this federal program. Contact the office listed below the caption for further details.

* Water Bank Program   10.062
Agricultural Stabilization and Conservation Service
Department of Agriculture
P.O. 2415
Washington, DC   20013   (202) 447-6221
To conserve surface waters; preserve and improve the nation's wetlands; increase migratory waterfowl habitat in nesting, breeding, and feeding areas in the U.S.; and secure environmental benefits for the nation. Types of assistance: direct payment. Estimate of annual funds available: $ 10,409,000.

* Rural Clean Water Program (RWCP)   10.068
Conservation and Environmental Protection Division
Agricultural Stabilization and Conservation Service
Department of Agriculture
P.O. Box 2415
Washington, DC   20013   (202) 447-6221
To achieve improved water quality in the most cost-effective manner possible in keeping with the provisions of adequate supplies of food, fiber, and a quality environment. Types of assistance: direct payment. Estimate of annual funds available: $ 316,000.

* Emergency Loans   10.404
Administrator, Farmers Home Administration
Department of Agriculture
Washington, DC   (202) 382-1632
To assist family farmers, ranchers and aquaculture operators with loans to cover losses resulting from major and/or natural disasters. Types of assistance: loan guarantee. Estimate of annual funds available: $ 600,000,000.

* Farm Operating Loans   10.406
Director, Farmer Programs Loan Making Division
Farmers Home Administration
Department of Agriculture
Washington, DC   20250   (202) 382-1632
To enable operators of not larger than family farms through the extension of credit and supervisory assistance, to make efficient use of their land, labor, and other resources. Types of assistance: loan guarantee. Estimate of annual funds available: $ 3,498,109,000.

* Farm Ownership Loans   10.407
Administrator, Farmers Home Administration
Department of Agriculture
Washington, DC   20250   (202) 382-1632
To assist eligible farmers, ranchers, and aquaculture operators, including farming cooperatives, corporations, partnerships, and joint operations through the extension of credit to become owner-operators of not larger than family farms. Types of assistance: loan guarantee. Estimate of annual funds available: $ 819,000,000.

* Very Low and Low Income Housing Loans (Section 502 Rural Housing Loans)   10.410
Administrator, Farmers Home Administration
Department of Agriculture
Washington, DC   20250   (202) 447-7967
To assist lower-income rural families to obtain decent, safe, and sanitary dwellings and related facilities. Subsidized funds are available only for low- and very low-income applicants. The funds are loans for new or existing construction not currently financed or owned by FMHA. Types of assistance: direct loans. Estimate of annual funds available: $ 1,761,700,000.

* Rural Housing Site Loans

(Section 532 and 524 Site Loans)   10.411
Administrator, Farmers Home Administration
Department of Agriculture
Washington, DC   20250   (202) 382-1474
To assist public or private nonprofit organizations interested in providing sites for housing, to acquire and develop land in rural areas to be subdivided as adequate building sites. Types of assistance: direct loans. Estimate of annual funds available: $ 1,070,000.

* Rural Rental Housing Loans   10.415
Administrator, Farmers Home Administration
Department of Agriculture
Washington, DC   20250   (202) 382-1604
To provide economically designed and constructed rental and cooperative housing and related facilities suited for independent living for rural residents. Types of assistance: loan guarantee. Estimate of annual funds available: $ 554,900,000.

* Very Low-Income Housing Repair Loans and Grants (Section 504 Rural Housing Loans and Grants)   10.417
Administrator, Farmers Home Administration
Department of Agriculture
Washington, DC   20250   (202) 447-7967
To give very low-income rural homeowners an opportunity to make essential repairs to their homes to make them safe and to remove health hazards to the family or community. Types of assistance: loans, grants. Estimate of annual funds available: $ 11,330,000.

* Rural Rental Assistance Payments (Rental Assistance)   10.427
Administrator, Farmers Home Administration
Department of Agriculture
Washington, DC   20250   (202) 382-1604
To reduce the rents paid by low-income families occupying eligible Rural Rental Housing (RRH) Rural Cooperative Housing (RCH), and Farm Labor Housing (LH) projects financed by the Farmers Home Administration through its Sections 515, 514, and 516 loans and grants. Types of assistance: direct payment. Estimate of annual funds available: $ 275,310,000.

* Guaranteed Rural Housing Loans - Demonstration Program   10.429
Administrator, FMHA, USDA
Washington, DC   20250   (202) 382-1474
To assist rural families with incomes not exceeding 100 percent of median in obtaining decent, safe, and sanitary dwellings and related facilities. Types of assistance: loan guarantee. Estimate of annual funds available: $ 90,000,000.

* Rural Housing Preservation Grants   10.433
Multiple Family Housing Loan Division
Farmers Home Administration
Department of Agriculture
Washington, DC   20250   (202) 382-1606
To assist very low and low-income rural homeowners in obtaining adequate housing to meet their needs by providing the necessary assistance to repair or rehabilitate their housing. Types of assistance: grants. Estimate of annual funds available: $ 19,140,000.

* Interest Reduction Payments-Rental and Cooperative Housing for Lower Income Families (236)   14.103

Director, Office of Multifamily Housing Management
Department of Housing and Urban Development
Washington, DC 20410 (202) 426-3968
To provide good quality rental and cooperative housing for persons of low- and moderate-income by providing interest reduction payments in order to lower their housing costs. Types of assistance: direct payments. Estimate of annual funds available: $ 625,651,000.

* Rehabilitation Mortgage Insurance 203(k) 14.108

Director, Single Family Development Division
Department of Housing and Urban Development
Washington, DC 20410 (202) 755-6720
To help families repair or improve, purchase and improve, or refinance and improve existing residential structures more than one year old. Types of assistance: loan guarantee. Estimate of annual funds available: $ 21,365,000.

* Manufactured Home Loan Insurance-Financing Purchase of Manufactured Homes as Principal Residences of Borrowers (Title I) 14.110

Director, Title I Insurance Division
Department of Housing and Urban Development
Washington, DC 20410 (202) 755-6880
To make possible reasonable financing of manufactured home purchases. Types of assistance: loan guarantee. Estimate of annual funds available: $ 0.

* Mortgage Insurance-Construction or Substantial Rehabilitation of Condominium Projects 234 (d) 14.112

Insurance Division
Office of Insured Multifamily Housing Development
HUD
Washington, DC 20410 (202) 755-6223
To enable sponsors to develop condominium projects in which individual units will be sold to home buyers. Types of assistance: loan guarantee. Estimate of annual funds available: $ 0.

* Mortgage Insurance - Homes 203(b) 14.117

Director, Insured Family Development Division
Office of Single Family Housing, HUD
Washington, DC 20410 (202) 755-6700
To help families undertake home ownership. Types of assistance: loan guarantee. Estimate of annual funds available: $ .3672E+11.

* Mortgage Insurance 203(h): Homes for Disaster Victims 14.119

Director, Single Family Development Division
Office of Insured Single Family Housing, HUD
Washington, DC 20410 (202) 755-6700
To help victims of a major disaster undertake home ownership on a sound basis. Types of assistance: loan guarantee. Estimate of annual funds available: $ 0.

* Mortgage Insurance-Homes for Low and Moderate Income Families 221(d)(2) 14.120

Director, Single Family Development Division
Office of Insured Family Housing, HUD
Washington, DC 20410 (202) 755-6700
To make homeownership more readily available to families displaced by a natural disaster, urban renewal, or other government actions and to increase homeownership opportunities for low-income and moderate-income families. Types of assistance: loan guarantee. Estimate of annual funds available: $ 149,598,354.

* Mortgage Insurance: Homes in Outlying Areas 203(i) 14.121

Director, Insured Single Family Development Division
Office of Single Family Housing
HUD
Washington, DC 20410 (202) 755-6700
To help families purchase homes in outlying areas. Types of assistance: loan guarantee. Estimate of annual funds available: $ 0.

* Mortgage Insurance: Homes in Urban Renewal Areas (22 Homes) 14.122

Director, Insured Single Family Development Division
Office of Single Family Housing
HUD
Washington, DC 20410 (202) 755-6700
To help families purchase or rehabilitate homes in urban renewal areas. Types of assistance: loan guarantee. Estimate of annual funds available: $ 2,032,000.

* Mortgage Insurance-Housing in Older, Declining Areas 223(e) 14.123

Single Family Development Division
Office of Insured Single Family Housing
Washington, DC 20410 (202) 755-6700
To assist in the purchase or rehabilitation of housing in older, declining urban areas. Types of assistance: loan guarantee. Estimate of annual funds available: $ 43,698,000.

* Mortgage Insurance-Land Development (Title X) 14.125

Director, Single Family Development Division
Office of Insured Single Family Housing, HUD
Washington, DC 20410 (202) 755-6700
To assist the development of subdivisions on a sound economical basis. Types of assistance: loan guarantee. Estimate of annual funds available: $ 73,080,930.

* Mortgage Insurance-Cooperative Projects (213 Cooperatives) 14.126

Insurance Division
Office of Insured Multifamily Housing Development
HUD
Washington, DC 20410 (202) 755-6223
To make it possible for nonprofit cooperative ownership housing corporations or trusts to develop or sponsor the development of housing projects to be operated as cooperatives. Types of assistance: loan guarantee. Estimate of annual funds available: $ 0.

* Mortgage Insurance-Manufactured Home Parks (207(m) Manufactured Home Parks) 14.127

Insurance Division
Office of Insured Multifamily Housing Development
Department of Housing and Urban Development
Washington, DC 20410 (202) 755-6223
To make possible the financing of construction or rehabilitation of manufactured home parks. Types of assistance: loan guarantee. Estimate of annual funds available: $ 0.

* Mortgage Insurance - Purchase by Homeowners of Fee Simple Title from Lessors (240) 14.130

Director, Single Family Development Division
Office of Insured Single Family Housing, HUD
Washington, DC 20410 (202) 755-6700
To help homeowners obtain fee-simple title to the property which they hold under long-term leases and on which their homes are located. Types of assistance: loan guarantee. Estimate of annual funds available: $ 0.

* Mortgage Insurance: Purchase of Sales-Type Cooperative Housing Units (213 Sales) 14.132

Director, Single Family Development Division
Office of Insured Family Housing, HUD
Washington, DC 20410 (202) 755-6700
To make available good quality, new housing for purchase by individual members of a housing cooperative. Types of assistance: loan guarantee. Estimate of annual funds available: $ 0.

* Mortgage Insurance: Purchase of Units in Condominiums (234(c)) 14.133

Director, Single Family Development Division
Office of Insured Single Family Housing, HUD
Washington, DC 20410 (202) 755-6700
To enable families to purchase units in condominium projects. Types of assistance: loan guarantee. Estimate of annual funds available: $ 2,716,191,000.

* Mortgage Insurance: Rental Housing (207) 14.134

Insurance Division
Office of Insured Multifamily Housing Development
HUD
Washington, DC 20410 (202) 755-6223
To provide good quality rental housing for middle income families. Types of assistance: loan guarantee. Estimate of annual funds available: $ 9,337,000.

Housing and Real Estate

* **Mortgage Insurance: Rental Housing for Moderate Income Families and Elderly Market Interest Rate 221(d)(3) and (4) Multifamily 14.135**
Insurance Division
Office of Insured Multifamily Housing Development
HUD
Washington, DC 20410 (202) 755-6223
To provide good quality rental or cooperative housing for moderate income families and the elderly. Types of assistance: loan guarantee. Estimate of annual funds available: $ 233,419,000.

* **Mortgage Insurance-Rental Housing for the Elderly (231) 14.138**
Insurance Division
Office of Insured Multifamily Housing Development
HUD
Washington, DC 20410 (202) 755-6223
To provide good quality rental housing for the elderly. Types of assistance: loan guarantee. Estimate of annual funds available: $ 15,561,000.

* **Mortgage Insurance-Rental Housing in Urban Renewal Areas (220 Multifamily) 14.139**
Insurance Division
Office of Insured Multifamily Housing Development
HUD
Washington, DC 20410 (202) 755-6223
To provide good quality rental housing in urban renewal areas, code enforcement areas, and other areas designated for overall revitalization. Types of assistance: loan guarantee. Estimate of annual funds available: $ 24,898,000.

* **Section 106(b) Nonprofit Sponsor Assistance Program (Nonprofit Sponsor Loan Fund) 14.141**
Director
Assisted Elderly and Handicapped Housing Division
Office of Elderly and Assisted Housing, HUD
Washington, DC 20410 (202) 426-8730
To assist and stimulate prospective private nonprofit sponsors/borrowers of Section 202 housing to develop sound housing projects for the elderly or handicapped. Types of assistance: loan. Estimate of annual funds available: $ 960,000.

* **Property Improvement Loan Insurance for Improving All Existing Structures and Building of New Nonresidential Structures (Title I) 14.142**
Director, Title I Insurance Division
HUD
Washington, DC 20410 (202) 755-6880
To facilitate the financing of improvements to homes and other existing structures and the building of new nonresidential structures. Types of assistance: loan guarantee. Estimate of annual funds available: $ 1,138,000,000.

* **Supplemental Loan Insurance-Multifamily Rental Housing 14.151**
Insurance Division
Office of Insured Multifamily Housing Development
HUD
Washington, DC 20411 (202) 755-6223
To finance repairs, additions and improvements to multifamily projects, group practice facilities, hospitals, or nursing homes already insured by HUD or held by HUD. Types of assistance: loan guarantee. Estimate of annual funds available: $ 31,123,000.

* **Mortgage Insurance for the Purchase or Refinancing of Existing Multifamily Housing Projects (Section 223(f) Insured Under Section 207) 14.155**
Office of Insured Multifamily Housing Development
Insurance Division, HUD
Washington, DC 20410 (202) 755-6223
To provide mortgage insurance to lenders for the purchase or refinancing of existing multifamily housing projects, whether conventionally financed or subject to federally insured mortgages. Types of assistance: loan guarantee. Estimate of annual funds available: $ 11,719,000.

* **Lower Income and Very Low Income**

Housing Assistance Program (Existing Housing/Moderate Rehabilitation) 14.156
Office of Elderly and Assisted Housing
Existing Housing Division
HUD
Washington, DC 20410 (202) 755-6887
To aid very low income families in obtaining decent, safe and sanitary rental housing. Types of assistance: direct payment. Estimate of annual funds available: $ 9,769,198,000.

* **Housing for the Elderly or Handicapped (202) 14.157 Assisted Elderly and Handicapped Housing Division**
Office of Elderly and Assisted Housing, HUD
Washington, DC 20410 (202) 426-8730
To provide for rental or cooperative housing and related facilities (such as central dining) for the elderly or handicapped. Types of assistance: loan. Estimate of annual funds available: $ 480,106,000.

* **Section 245 Graduated Payment Mortgage Program 14.159**
Director, Single Family Development Division
Office of Insured Single Family Housing, HUD
Washington, DC 20410 (202) 755-6720
To facilitate early home ownership for households that expect their incomes to rise. Types of assistance: loan guarantee. Estimate of annual funds available: $ 487,713,000.

* **Single-Family Home Mortgage Coinsurance (Single-Family Coinsurance Program) 14.161**
Director, Single Family Development Division
Office of Insured Single Family Housing, HUD
Washington, DC 20410 (202) 755-6700
To improve quality and timeliness of service to mortgagors by streamlining HUD mortgage insurance processing. Types of assistance: loan guarantee. Estimate of annual funds available: $ 159,312,000.

* **Mortgage Insurance-Combination and Manufactured Home Lot Loans (Title I) 14.162**
Director, Title I Insurance Division, HUD
Washington, DC 20410 (202) 755-6880
To make possible reasonable financing of manufactured home purchases and lot to place it on. Types of assistance: loan guarantee. Estimate of annual funds available: $ 1,138,000,000.

* **Mortgage Insurance-Cooperative Financing (203(n)) 14.163**
Director, Single Family Development Division
Office of Insured Single Family Housing, HUD
Washington, DC 20410 (202) 755-6700
To provide insured financing for the purchase of the Corporate Certificate and Occupancy Certificate. Types of assistance: loan guarantee. Estimate of annual funds available: $ .3672E+11.

* **Operating Assistance for Troubled Multifamily Housing Projects (Flexible Subsidy Fund) (Troubled Projects) 14.164**
Chief, Program Support Branch
Management Operations Division
Office of Multifamily Housing Management, HUD
Washington, DC 20410 (202) 755-5654
To provide assistance to restore or maintain the physical and financial soundness of certain projects assisted or approved for assistance under the National Housing Act or under the Housing and Urban Development Act of 1965. Types of assistance: grants, direct payments. Estimate of annual funds available: $ 38,150,000.

* **Mortgage Insurance-Homes-Military Impacted Areas (238(c)) 14.165**
Director, Single Family Development Division
Office of Insured Single Family Housing, HUD
Washington, DC 20410 (202) 755-6700
To help families undertake home ownership in military impacted areas. Types of assistance: loan guarantee. Estimate of annual funds available: $ 7,462,000.

* **Mortgage Insurance-Homes for Members of the Armed**

Services (Section 222)   14.166
Director, Single Family Development Division
Office of Insured Single Family Housing, HUD
Washington, DC   20410   (202) 755-6700
To help members of the armed services on active duty to purchase a home.
Types of assistance: loan guarantee. Estimate of annual funds available:
$ 4,384,000.

* Mortgage Insurance-Two Year Operating Loss Loans, Section 223(d)   14.167
Office of Insured Multifamily Housing Development
Insurance Division Housing, HUD
Washington, DC   20410   (202) 755-6223
To insure a separate loan covering operating losses incurred during the first two
years following the date of completion of a multifamily project with a HUD
insured first mortgage. Types of assistance: loan guarantee. Estimate of annual
funds available: $ 49,796,000.

* Mortgage Insurance-Growing Equity Mortgages (GEMs)   14.172
Director, Single Family Development Division
Office of Insured Single Family Housing, HUD
Washington, DC   20410   (202) 755-6700
To provide a rapid principal reduction and shorter mortgage term by increasing
payments over a 10 year period, thereby expanding housing opportunities to the
homebuying public. Types of assistance: loan guarantee. Estimate of annual
funds available: $ 487,713,000.

* Multifamily Coinsurance (Section 223(f); Section 221(d); Section 232)   14.173
Office of Insured Multifamily Housing Development
Coinsurance Division, HUD
Washington, DC   20410   (202) 426-7113
Under the coinsurance programs, HUD authorizes approved lenders to coinsure
mortgage loans. In exchange for the authority to perform the required
underwriting, servicing, management and property disposition functions,
approved lenders assume responsibility for a portion of any insurance loss on the
coinsured mortgage. Types of assistance: loan guarantee. Estimate of annual
funds available: $ 855,870,000.

* Housing Development Grants   14.174
Director, Development Grants Division
Rm. 6110, Office of Elderly and Assisted Housing
HUD
451 7th St., SW
Washington, DC   20410   (202) 755-6142
To support the construction or substantial rehabilitation of rental housing in
areas experiencing severe shortages of decent rental housing opportunities for
families and individuals without other reasonable and affordable housing
alternatives in the private market. Types of assistance: grants. Estimate of
annual funds available: $ 20,000,000.

* Adjustable Rate Mortgages (ARMS)   14.175
Director, Single Family Development Division
Office of Insured Single Family Housing, HUD
Washington, DC   20410   (202) 755-6700
To provide mortgage insurance for an adjustable rate mortgage which offers
lenders more assurance of long term profitability than a fixed rate mortgage,
while offering consumer protection. Types of assistance: loan guarantee.
Estimate of annual funds available: $ .3672E+11.

* Housing Voucher Program   14.177
Office of Elderly and Assisted Housing
Housing Voucher Division, Housing, HUD
Washington, DC   20410   (202) 755-6477
To aid very low income families in obtaining safe and sanitary rental housing.
Types of assistance: direct payment. Estimate of annual funds available:
$ 9,769,198,000.

* Supporting Housing Demonstration Program (Transitional Housing; Permanent Housing for Handicapped Homeless Persons)   14.178
Morris Bourne, Director
Transitional Housing Staff, Office of Housing, HUD
451 7th St., SW
Washington, DC   20410   (202) 755-9075
To develop innovative approaches for providing housing and supporting services
to facilitate the transition to independent living for homeless persons who are
capable of making the transition with in 24 months, and to provide permanent
housing for handicapped persons. Types of assistance: grants, direct payments.
Estimate of annual funds available: $ 80,000,000.

* Nehemiah Housing Opportunity Grant Program (Nehemiah Housing)   14.179
Morris E. Carter, Director
Single Family Housing Development Division, HUD
451 7th St, SW
Washington, DC   20410   (202) 755-6700
To provide an opportunity for those families who otherwise would not be
financially able to realize their dream of owning a home. Types of assistance:
grant. Estimate of annual funds available: $ 20,000,000.

* Community Development Block Grants/Entitlement Grants   14.218
Entitlement Cities Division
Office of Block Grant Assistance
Community Planning and Development
451 7th St., SW
Washington, DC   20410   (202) 755-5977
To develop viable urban communities, by providing decent housing and a
suitable living environment. Types of assistance: grants. Estimate of annual
funds available: $ 2,053,100,000.

* Community Development Block Grants/Small Cities Program (Small Cities)   14.219
State and Small Cities Division
Office of Block Grant Assistance, Community
Planning and Development, HUD
451 7th St., SW
Washington, DC   20410   (202) 755-0367
The primary objective of this program is the development of viable urban
communities by providing decent housing, a suitable living environment, and
expanding economic opportunities. Types of assistance: grants. Estimate of
annual funds available: $ 38,395,000.

* Section 312 Rehabilitation Loans   14.220
Community Planning and Development
Office of Urban Rehabilitation, HUD
451 7th St., SW
Washington, DC   20410   (202) 755-0367
To promote the revitalization of neighborhoods by providing funds for
rehabilitation of residential, non-residential and mixed use property in areas
determined to be eligible by local governments for activities under either the
Community Development block grant, Urban Development Action Grant, or
Section 810 Urban Homesteading areas. Types of assistance: loans. Estimate
of annual funds available: $ 19,510,000.

* Urban Homesteading   14.222
Director, Urban Homesteading Program
Office of Urban Rehabilitation, HUD
Washington, DC   20410   (202) 755-5324
To provide homeownership opportunities to credit-worthy individuals and
families primarily of lower income, utilizing federally-owned housing stock.
Types of assistance: other. Estimate of annual funds available: $ 13,831,000.

* Rental Housing Rehabilitation (Rental Rehabilitation)   14.230
David M. Cohen, Office of Urban Rehabilitation
Community Planning and Development, HUD
451 7th St., SW
Washington, DC   20410   (202) 755-5685
To increase the supply of standard rental housing units affordable to lower
income families. Types of assistance: grants. Estimate of annual funds
available: $ 177,418,000.

* Specially Adapted Housing for Disabled Veterans (Paraplegic Housing)   64.106
Department of Veterans Affairs
Washington, DC   20420
To assist certain severely disabled veterans in acquiring suitable housing units,
with special fixtures and facilities made necessary by the nature of the veterans
disabilities. Types of assistance: direct payment. Estimate of annual funds
available: $ 13,750,000.

* Veterans Housing-Guaranteed and Insured Loans (VA

Housing and Real Estate

Home Loans) 64.114
Department of Veterans Affairs
Washington, DC 20420

To assist veterans, certain service personnel, and certain unmarried surviving spouses of veterans, in obtaining credit for the purchase, construction or improvement of homes on more liberal terms than are generally available to non-veterans. Types of assistance: loan guarantee. Estimate of annual funds available: $36,000.

* Veterans Housing-Direct Loans for Disabled Veterans 64.118
Department of Veterans Affairs
Washington, DC 20420

To provide certain severely disabled veterans with direct housing credit in connection with grants for specially adaptable housing with special features or movable facilities made necessary by the nature of their disabilities. Types of assistance: direct loans. Estimate of annual funds available: $ 33,000.

* Veterans Housing-Manufactured Home Loans 64.119
Department of Veterans Affairs
Washington, DC 20420

To assist veterans, servicepersons, and certain unmarried surviving spouses of veterans in obtaining credit for the purchase of a manufactured home on more liberal terms than are available to non-veterans. Types of assistance: loan guarantee. Estimate of annual funds available: $ 36,714,000.

* Weatherization Assistance for Low-Income Persons 81.042
Mary E. Fowler, Chief
Weatherization Assistance Programs, Branch 232
Conservation and Renewable Energy, DOE
Forrestal Bldg.
Washington, DC 20585　　　　　　　　　　　(202) 586-2204

To insulate the dwellings of low income persons particularly the elderly and handicapped low income in order to conserve needed energy and to aid those persons least able to afford higher utility costs. Types of assistance: grants. Estimate of annual funds available: $ 161,357,000.

* Flood Insurance 83.100
David L. Cobb, Federal Insurance Administration
FEMA
Washington, DC 20472　　　　　　　　　　　(202) 646-2774

To enable persons to purchase insurance against losses from physical damage to or loss of buildings and or contents therein caused by floods, mudflow, or flood related erosion in the U.S. Types of assistance: Insurance. Estimate of annual funds available: $ 511,961,000.

State Money For Housing and Real Estate

State Initiatives

While affordable housing has long held an important place on the federal government's policy agenda, budget cutbacks in recent years have forced the government to turn over many housing responsibilities to the states. Housing finance agencies (HFAs) have been created by states to issue tax-exempt bonds to finance mortgages for lower-income first-time home buyers and to build multi-family housing.

States are involved in a host of initiatives throughout the broad spectrum of housing finance and development. Interim construction financing programs which can reduce the basic costs of lower-income housing projects have been initiated in a number of states, together with innovative homeownership programs and programs directed toward rehabilitation improvement energy conservation.

States are also venturing into areas which have not received as much public sector attention until recently. By encouraging non-traditional types of housing, such as accessory units, shelters, and single room occupancy housing, states are addressing important elements of the housing market.

In Colorado, the state Housing and Finance Authority (CHFA) has issued more than $1.75 billions of bonds and notes since its establishment in 1973, providing housing for more than 31,000 families and individuals of low and moderate income; 15,800 first-time homebuyers and 15,570 rental housing units. In recent years the state has broadened CHFA's authority to allow it to develop finance programs to assist the growth of small business, help exports with insurance on goods sold overseas, and similar projects.

Colorado has done more than simply help its citizens find housing: the programs have resulted in construction employment of more than 20,000 jobs, with wages estimated at almost $20 million in new local real estate taxes and an indirect gain of $1.6 billion for the state.

West Virginia is the only state lacking a housing finance program, while Wisconsin has 15 different programs, including special programs for minorities and women. Maryland operates 14 programs, including those to help people with closing costs and settlement expenses. It also has special funds available for the elderly and is developing an emergency mortgage fund to help people who have fallen behind in their payments. Nonprofit developers can also tap the state for money to build low-cost rental units.

Funds are also available for persons who take steps to make their homes more energy efficient, for homeowners and landlords who remove lead paint from dwelling units, for houses without plumbing or those with plumbing that is disfunctional, for handicapped persons, and to help landlords defray the costs of bringing low-income housing into compliance with state and local housing codes. There are also funds for nonprofit organizations to acquire or renovate existing houses and apartments for use as group homes for special needs such as mentally retarded. The following is a complete listing of state housing programs.

Housing Offices

Alabama
Alabama Housing Finance Authority, 614 Adams Avenue, Montgomery, AL 36130, (205) 261-4310.
1) Homeowners: below-market interest rate home loans to low- and moderate-income families.
2) Developers: tax-exempt funds to multi-family developers, who build housing projects in which a significant number of apartments must be rented to low- and moderate-income persons.

Alaska
Alaska Housing Finance Corp., P.O. Box 101020, 235 East 8th Avenue, Anchorage, AK 99510, (907) 276-5599.
1) Home Ownership Assistance Program (interest subsidy to as low as 6%).
2) Mobile Home Loan Program.
3) Taxable Mortgage Program (for others than first time homebuyers and veterans).
4) Triplex/Fourplex Mortgage Program (up to $400,000 with 10% down).
5) Tax Exempt Mortgage Program (loans up to $157,190 for single family and $176,996 for duplexes).
6) Pledged Account Mortgage Program (graduated payment mortgage program).
7) Second Mortgage Program (up to $99,900 for single family homes and $127,800 for duplexes can be used for home purchase or home improvement).
8) Veterans Mortgage Program (low interest loans to veterans and members of the reserve and National Guard).
9) Refinance Program (reduce monthly payments on existing loans).
10) Rental Program (loans for rental property).
11) Non-Conforming Property Program (homes which cannot be financial through traditional financing).
12) Condominium Projects (loans for condominium owners).
13) Mobile Home Park Loans.

Arizona
Arizona Department of Commerce, 1700 West Washington, Phoenix, AZ 85007, (602) 255-5705.
1) Low-Income Housing Tax Credits: federal income tax credits for owners of low-income housing units.

Arkansas
Arkansas Development Finance Authority, P.O. Box 8023, 100 Main St., Suite 200, Little Rock, AR 72203, (501) 682-5900.
1) Affordable Housing Program: loans to developers to build houses less than $45,000.
2) Single-Family: 8.35% loans to first time homebuyers for the purchase of a single-family home.

California
California Housing Finance Agency, 1121 I Street, 7th Floor, Sacramento, CA 95814, (916) 322-3991.
1) Single-Family Programs: loans to first time homeowners with 5% down and 7.5% interest.
2) Multifamily Program: permanent financing for builders and developers of multi-unit family, elderly and congregate rental housing.
3) 80/20 Rental Housing Mortgage Loans: below-market mortgages for projects where at least 20% of the units are set aside for very low-income tenants at affordable rates.
4) Development Loan Program: 7% loans to small and minority developers.
5) Self-Help Housing Program: funds to non-profit developers in order to produce self-help housing.
6) Low-Income Rental Allowance Pilot Program: subsidies to low income renter who are not eligible for other available federal housing assistance.

Colorado
Colorado Housing Finance Authority, 777 Pearl Street, Denver, CO 80203-3716, 303-861-8962.
1) Single-Family Program: Lower-than-market-interest rates available to first-time homeowners.
2) Multi-family: a variety of sponsoring entities available to address special housing needs. Programs available for developers to construct multi-family housing.
3) Small Business Owners: Commercial Financing Programs financial assistance provided to assist small businesses with expansion of their facilities.

Connecticut

Housing and Real Estate

Connecticut Housing Finance Authority, 40 Cold Spring Road, Rocky Hill, CT 06067, (203) 721-9501.
1) Home Mortgage Program: low-interest mortgages for low-and moderate-income persons and families.
2) Rehabilitation Mortgages: loans to protect or improve livability or energy efficiency of a home.
3) Single-Family Construction Loans: low-interest (4-8%) construction financing to profit and non-profit building with resultant savings reflected in lower home sales price.
4) Construction/Rehabilitation Financing for Affordable Rental Housing: permanent low-interest mortgages to develop small rental properties that will retain low and moderate housing in older city neighborhoods.
5) Reverse Annuity Mortgages (RAM): allows senior citizens to convert their home's equity into monthly tax-free cash payments.

Delaware
Delaware State Housing Authority, Division of Housing and Community Development, 10 the Green, P.O. Box 1401, Dover, DE 19903, (302) 736- 4263.
1) Single-Family Mortgage Program: low-interest loans to first-time home buyers.
2) Housing Development Funds: loans to developers of housing for low- and moderate-income persons and families.
3) Housing Rehabilitation Loan Program: $15,000 for ten years at 3% to fix up single-family homes.
4) Rent Subsidy Programs: money to provide subsidies for low- and moderate-income rental housing.
5) Transitional Living Facility for Women: a program to provide affordable housing and support services to low-income mothers.

District of Columbia
DC Housing Finance Agency, 1401 New York Avenue, NW Suite 540, Washington, DC 20005, (202) 628-0311.
1) Single-Family Forward Commitment Mortgage Purchase Program: loans to first-time home buyers with 5% down and 8.5% interest.
2) Home Purchase Assistance Program: interest-free second trust loans up to $16,000 to low-income households for the purchase of single- family homes.
3) Tenant Assistance Program (TAP): money to provide subsidies for elderly or handicapped housing.
4) Distressed Properties Improvement Program: tax moratorium and/or deferral or forgiveness of indebtedness to the District of Columbia for distressed occupied rental properties.

Florida
Florida Housing Finance Agency, 2571 Executive Center Circle East, Tallahassee, FL 32399, (904) 488-4197.
1) Single-Family Mortgage: first-time home buyers can receive mortgage as low as 7.9%.
2) Multi-family Insured Mortgage Loans: below market loans to developers of rental housing.
3) Loan-to-Lender Construction Loan Program: Construction financing to developers of low-income public housing.

Georgia
Georgia Residential Finance Authority, 1190 West Druid Hills Drive, Suite 270, Atlanta, GA 30329, (404) 984-3334.
1) Single-Family Homeownership Loan Program: 1.5% below prevailing interest rates for first-time homeowners.
2) Mortgage Credit Certificate Program: 20% of mortgage interest can be used as a federal tax credit.
3) Payment of some or all of rental costs for low income families or singles who are elderly, handicapped or disabled.
4) Multi-family Bond Program: below-market interest rate loans to develop or rehabilitate multifamily rental housing.
5) Low-Income Housing Credit Program: federal income tax credits to construct or rehabilitate low-income rental housing.
6) Section 8 Existing Housing Assistance: rental assistance subsidy payments to landlords of low-income individuals or families.
7) Rental Rehabilitation Program: loans and grants up to $5,000 per unit to rehabilitate rental housing.
8) Appalachian: grants and loans for site development, technical assistance and others for low-and moderate-income housing projects.
9) Development Advances for Nonprofit Sponsors: financial and technical assistance to qualified nonprofit organizations engaged in the development of low- and moderate-income rental housing.
10) Georgia Energy Fund: loans and grants up to $3,00 for energy saving home improvements.
11) Homeless Shelter Programs: grants to shelter facilities for building improvements and renovation.

Hawaii
Hawaii Housing Authority, 1002 North School Street, P.O. Box 17907, Honolulu, HI 96817, (808) 848-3230.
1) Hula Mae Single-Family Program: low-interest loans to first-time homebuyers.
2) Rental Assistance Program: rent subsidies to tenants in approved projects.
3) Tax Reform: Multi-Family Program: tax credits to investors in qualified low-income rental housing projects.
4) Modernization and Maintenance: funds for the preservation and maintenance of existing housing.

5) Housing Finance Revolving Fund: long-term mortgage financing in geographic areas or for projects where private mortgage insurers will not insure.

Idaho
Idaho Housing Agency, 760 W. Myrtle, Boise, ID 83702, (208) 336-0161.
1) Mortgage Credit Certificates: homes buyers who have not owned a home in the last three years can claim 20% of their mortgage interest as a tax credit.

Illinois
Illinois Housing Development Authority, 401 N. Michigan Ave., Suite 900, Chicago, IL 60611, (312) 836-5100.
1) Single-Family Mortgage Purchase Program: below-market rate loans to first-time homebuyers.
2) Multi-family Program: loans to developers of low- and moderate- income housing.
3) Moderate Rehabilitation Program: low-interest loans to rehabilitate low-income housing.
4) Chicago Local Initiatives Support Corporation: aid to community- based developers to provide low-income housing.
5) Rehabilitation: low-interest loans to individuals for home improvements.
6) Home Builder Program: financing for the construction of new housing throughout Illinois.
7) Congregate Housing Finance Program: loans for congregate housing for the elderly.
8) Training Program: training programs for resident managers of elderly housing developments.

Indiana
Indiana Housing Finance Authority, One North Capitol, Suite 515, Indianapolis, IN 46204, (317) 232-7777.
1) Single-family Program: loans to homebuyers at 1 to 2 percentage points below the market rate.
2) Multi-Family Program: loans for developers of low- and moderate- income housing.
3) Mortgage Credit Certificate Program: tax credits to families purchasing mobile homes.

Iowa
Iowa Finance Authority, 200 East Grand Avenue, Suite 222, Des Moines, IA 50309, (515) 281-4058.
1) Single-Family Mortgage Loans: low-interest loans to homebuyers
2) Mortgage Credit Certificate Program: tax credits of up to 20% of the interest paid annually on home loans.
3) Apartment Loan Programs: new construction and rehabilitation loans for low- and moderate-income apartment developers.
4) Group Home Loan Program: loans for the construction or rehabilitation of living units for the physically handicapped, mentally disabled or youth.
5) Small Business Loan Program: loans for small business.
6) Title Guaranty Program: to guaranty (insure) titles to Iowa real estate.

Kansas
State of Kansas, Department of Commerce, 400 S.W. 8th, 5th Floor, Topeka, KS 66603, (913) 296-3481.
1) Tax Credits for Low-Income Housing: tax credits for developers who rent to low-income families.
2) Topeka Energy Program: up to $300 for homeowners, renters and landlords who make energy improvements.
3) Housing Energy Assistance Program: storm windows, insulation and caulking for low-income homeowners and renters.
4) Low-Cost/No-Cost Program: up to $50 worth of low-cost energy conservation materials to low-income homeowners and renters.
5) Kansas Conservation Bank: low-interest loans for improvements for low- and moderate-income homeowners and landlords.
6) KPL/Gas Service Customer Financing Program: loans to all incomes to purchase insulation or heating and cooling appliances which are more energy efficient.
7) Emergency Program: up to $2,000 grant for repaired of serious emergency problems for low-income homeowners.
8) People Matching People Program: up to $1,000 grant for material to make basic repairs for low-income homeowners.
9) Major Rehabilitation: up to $15,000 grant for making major repairs to bring a home up to city code standards.
10) North Topeka East NIA Repair Program: free home improvement materials earned proportional to labor donated in work.
11) Rental Rehabilitation Loan Program: loans up to $5,000 per rental unit to bring unit up to city code standard.
12) 312 Home Improvement Loan Program: loans as low as 4% for moderate-income homeowners for home improvements.
13) Home Improvement Loans: loans for moderate- and upper-income homeowners and landlords.
14) Home Maintenance and Repair Service: quality home repairs and home improvements at modest costs for elderly and handicapped, all incomes.

Kentucky
Kentucky Housing Corporation, 1231 Louisville Road, Frankfort, KY 40601, (502) 564-7630.

1) Single-Family Mortgage Loans: low-interest loans to homebuyers who currently do not own property.
2) Small City Infill Lot Construction: funds to builders for permanent financing of houses to be constructed in eligible areas.
3) Cluster Loan Program: below-market interest rate financing to specified distressed urban neighborhoods.
4) Elderly Rural Rehabilitation Program: grants to elderly in rural areas for the installment of indoor plumbing facilities.
5) Grants to the Elderly for Energy Repairs (GEER): grants to elderly for home energy repairs.
6) Senior Homeownership Program: low-interest rates loans to homebuyers aged 62 and over.
7) Training for Affordable Construction (TAC): grants to builders and developers willing to hire and train unemployed Vietnam Veterans.
8) Housing Trust: single-family loans for eligible low-income families.
9) One-Parent Family Facility Program: housing provided for one-parent families.

Louisiana

Louisiana Housing Finance Agency, 5615 Corporate, Suite 61, Baton Rouge, LA 70808-2515, (504) 925-3675.
1) Single-Family - lower-interest rate (8.8%) 30 yr. FHA/VA financing for first-time homebuyers.
2) Multi-family - financing available for developers of low-moderate income housing development.
3) Tax Credit Program - federal income tax credit provisions provided to developers of low-to-moderate multi-family development.
4) Housing Assistance - rental assistance to low-income families.

Maine

Maine State Housing Authority, P.O. Box 2669, 295 Water Street, Augusta, ME 04330, 207-623-2981, (800) 452-4668.
1) Home Start Purchase Program: low-income loans for first-time homebuyers.
2) Rural Housing Program: financing to developers for the development of low-income rental housing in rural areas.
3) Small Projects Initiatives Program: funding to new developers for the development of new small rental units.
4) Fuel Oil Conservation Loan Program: 3% loans for energy-related improvements to homeowners and apartment owners.
5) Home Preservation Grant Program: grants for home improvements for very-low-income homeowners.
6) Home Shelter Financing: 1% mortgage loans for development or repairs to homeless shelters.
7) Boarding Care Facility Demonstration Mortgage Purchase Program: permanent financing at below-market mortgage rates for a limited number of boarding care facilities.
8) New Housing Initiatives Program: loans, grants, revolving funds or administrative fees for developing non-traditional single- family and rental housing initiatives to persons of low-income.
9) Enterprise Foundation Partnership: financial and technical assistance to community based housing groups for people living at or below the poverty level.
10) Housing Opportunities for Maine (HOME) Trust Fund.

Maryland

Department of Housing and Community Development, 45 Calvert St., Annapolis, MD 21401, (301) 974-2176.
1) Rental Housing Production Program: loans to developers or non-profit organizations to cover the costs of construction, rehabilitation, acquisition or related development costs through interest rate writedowns or rent subsidies.
2) Market-Rate Rental Housing: below-market rate construction and permanent financing for the construction and rehabilitation of multi-family rental housing for persons with limited incomes.
3) Mortgage Purchase Program: below-market interest rate mortgage financing for low- and moderate-income homebuyers.
4) Homeownership Development Program: reduced interest mortgage loans to first-time homebuyers for new homes in approved housing developments.
5) Home and Energy Loan Program: below-market interest rate loans for home and energy conservation improvements for single-family homes.
6) Multi-Family Home & Energy Loan Program: rehabilitation and energy conservation loans for multi-family rental projects and single scattered-site rental properties.
7) Homeownership Incentive Program: low-interest loans to eligible low-income buyers.
8) Housing Rehabilitation Program: loans to limited income homeowners, owners of multi-unit residential buildings and owners of small nonresidential properties.
9) Rental Housing Program: construction loans and permanent financing for constructing, rehabilitating, acquiring and operating rental housing developments.
10) Group Home Financing Program: low-interest, no interest deferred payment loans to non-profit organizations to purchase and modify housing for use as group homes and shelters.
11) Livability Code Rehabilitation Program: low interest, no interest and deferred payments to finance improvements needed to bring properties into compliance with local housing codes.
12) Residential Lead Paint Abatement Program: loans to finance the abatement of lead paint in rental properties.

13) Elderly Rental Housing Program: new construction financing for rental housing for elderly citizens.
14) Rental Housing Allowance Pilot Program: subsidies to very-low-income individuals with emergency needs.

Massachusetts

Massachusetts Housing Finance Agency, 50 Milk Street, Boston, MA 02190, (617) 451-3840.
1) Rental Housing: below-market rate financing to rental unit developers.
2) Homeownership Opportunity Program: housing for purchase by first- time low- and moderate-income homebuyers at 30 to 40 percent below market rates.
3) General Lending: special loans for Vietnam Era Veterans, low- income and minority borrowers and physically handicapped.
4) Neighborhood Rehabilitation Programs: funds for people who buy and/or rehabilitate homes in locally designated neighborhoods.
5) New Construction Set-Aside: funds for purchasers of new homes and condominiums built by specific developers.
6) Home Improvement Program: loans for owner-occupied, one- to four-family homes.
7) State Housing Assistance for Rental Productions (SHARP): interest rate subsidies to developers for production of rental housing where at least 25% are available to low-income households.
8) Project TAP (Tenant Assistance Program): training for project residents for drug- and alcohol-related problems.

Michigan

Michigan State Housing Development Authority, Plaza One, Fourth Floor, 401 South Washington Square, P.O. Box 30044, Lansing, MI 48909, (517) 373-8370.
1) Rental Housing for Families and Senior Citizens: loans and tax exempt financing for the construction, rehabilitation, and purchase of rental housing.
2) Single-Family Home Mortgage: low-interest loans for single-family homes and condominiums.
3) Michigan Mortgage Credit Certificates: federal income tax credits that give homebuyers more income to qualify for a mortgage.
4) Home and Neighborhood Improvement Loans: home improvement loans for homes over 20 years old at interest rate from 1 to 9 percent.
5) Section 8 Existing Rental Allowance Program: rent subsidies for low-income persons who find their own housing in private homes and apartment buildings.
6) Moderate Rehabilitation Loans to Landlords: loans to landlords for rehabilitation of units.
7) Housing for the Handicapped: financing for group homes for the handicapped.
8) Michigan Energy Bank: low-interest rehabilitation loans for homeowners.
9) Grants to Neighborhood and Nonprofit Housing Organizations: grants for home improvement, urban homesteading, and other local housing programs.
10) Housing for the Homeless: grants to organizations to operate shelters for the homeless.
11) Up to $27,000 in prizes for new ideas, products, design solution to cut cost of housing construction.
12) High Risk Home Improvement Program: interest-free home repair loans to high-risk and low-income household in the City of Grand Rapids.

Minnesota

Minnesota Housing Finance Agency, 400 Sibley Street, St. Paul, MN 55101, (612) 296-9951, (800) 652-9747).
1) Single-Family Mortgage Loan Program: low-interest loans as well as downpayment and monthly payment assistance for first-time homebuyers.
2) Indian Housing Programs: mortgage and home improvement financing for tribal housing as well as homeownership loans at below-market interest rates.
3) Innovative Housing Loan Program: no-interest and low-interest loans to develop housing that is innovative in design, construction, marketing and/or financing.
4) Home Improvement Loan Program: low-interest loans for home improvement.
5) Rehabilitation Loan Program: rehabilitation loans to low-income homeowners.
6) Accessibility Deferred Loan Program: interest-free loans to households with a disabled member.
7) Rental Rehabilitation Grant Program: dollar-for-dollar grants to rental property owners.
8) Rental Rehabilitation Loan Program: low-interest loans to rental property owners.
9) Energy Improvement Loan Insurance Program: loan insurance for rental property owners to improve energy conservation.
10) Multifamily Housing Development Program: financing and other incentives for multifamily developers.
11) Section 8 Housing Assistance: rents subsidies for low-income renters.
12) Elderly Home Sharing Program: grants to nonprofits who assist elderly in sharing homes.

Mississippi

Mississippi Housing Finance Corporation, 510 George Street, Suite 204 Dickson Building, Jackson, MS 39201, (601) 961-4514.
1) Targeted and Non-Targeted New Mortgage Loans: low-interest loans to low- or moderate-income homebuyers.

Missouri

Missouri Housing Development Commission, 3770 Broadway, Kansas City, MO 64111, (816) 756-3790.

1) Multifamily Program: low-interest rate mortgages to developers of multi-family developments.
2) Single-Family Housing: below-market interest rate mortgages for first-time homebuyers.
3) Neighborhood Loan Program: loans to neighborhood organizations and/or developers for acquiring and rehabilitating residential properties.
4) Home Improvements/Weatherization Loan Program: low-interest loans to assist qualified homeowners in home improvements that will increase energy efficiency.
5) Blended Rate Financing: low-interest rates to developers to stimulate production of housing for low-and moderate-families and individuals.
6) Housing for the Homeless: loans to assist the placement of homeless individuals and families.

Montana

Montana Board of Housing, 2001 Eleventh Avenue, Helena, MT 59620, (406) 444-3040.
1) Single-Family Programs: low-interest loans to low-income families.
2) Multi-family Program: construction loans to developers of multi-family units for persons and families of lower income.

Nebraska

Nebraska Investment Finance Authority, 1033 O Street, Suite 304, Lincoln, NE 68508, (402) 477-4406.
1) Single-Family Recycling Loan Program: low-cost loans for single family homes, townhomes, condominiums, mobile homes, and up to 4-unit dwellings.
2) Floating-Rate Monthly Demand Multifamily Loan Program: attractive interest rates for developers of rental housing for low- and moderate-income households.
3) Home Improvement Loan Program: low-interest loans to homeowners to make needed home improvements.
4) Agricultural Finance Programs:
First-Time Farmer Loan: loans to purchase agricultural real estate.
FmHA: loans to refinance existing agricultural loans.

Nevada

Department of Commerce, Housing Division, 1050 E. William, Suite 435, Carson City, NV 89710, (702) 885-4258.
1) Homeowners: loans to moderate-income families with no previous homeownership interest within the last 3 years.
2) Industrial Development Bonds: low financing costs for new construction or expansion manufacturing projects.
3) Rural Area Housing Program: low-interest mortgage loans to developers to develop affordable rental units outside metropolitan areas.

New Hampshire

Housing Finance Authority, P.O. Box 5087, Manchester, NH 03108, (603) 472-8623.
1) Rental Assistance: rental subsidies to eligible families, elderly, disabled or handicapped.
2) Single-Family Mortgage Program: low-interest mortgage funds to qualifying individuals and households.
3) Affordable Mortgage Program: a pilot program for low-income households, mortgage rates are based on the incomes of eligible borrowers in rural areas.
4) 80/20: low-interest financing to produce rental units with a portion made available to moderate-income households.
5) Multi Family Housing Program: construction loans for small rental projects for private for-profit developers and non-profit organizations.
6) Public Lands Program: financing for new construction on surplus state land.
7) Special Needs Fund: funding for housing for individuals with special needs.

New Jersey

New Jersey Housing Agency, 3625 Quakerbridge Road, Lawrenceville, NJ 08640, (609) 292-6055.
1) Home Mortgage Program: low-interest loans to urban area first-time buyers with a 5% downpayment.
2) Buy and Fix It: low-interest, fixed-rate mortgage to homebuyers to purchase a house in need of repair and fix it.
3) Home Improvement Loan Program: below-market interest rates for home improvements for qualified homeowners.
4) Radon Remediation Loans: up to $15,000 for radon contamination remediation procedure. No income restrictions.
5) Multi-family Loan Process: financing to developers for rental units in which a minimum of 18% of units will be reserved for low- and moderate-income families.
6) Energy: 0% interest loans on energy-related rehabilitation.
7) Small Project Financing: financing for small rental housing developments.
8) The Repair Loan Program: loans to finance the rehabilitation of occupied rental developments.
9) Continuing Care Retirement Communities: construction loans and lower-than-market mortgage interest rates for residential communities for senior citizens.

New Mexico

Mortgage Finance Authority, 344 Fourth St. S.W., Albuquerque, NM 87102, (505) 843-6880.
1) Single-Family Program: below-market loans to first-time homebuyers.

2) Rehabilitation Loans: loans to rehabilitate existing homes.
3) Multi-Family Programs: financing of multi-family housing for low- and moderate-income tenants.

New York

State of New York, Executive Department, Division of Housing and Community Renewal, One Fordham Plaza, Bronx, NY 10458, (212) 519-5800.
1) Nehemiah Plan: financing for the development of new 3 bedroom houses in East Brooklyn for purchasers with the incomes of $20,000--$40,000.
2) Special Needs Housing Demonstration Program: grants to non-profit sponsors for single room occupancy dwellings units for low-income individuals.
3) Low-Income Housing Trust Fund: funds to non profit sponsors to rehabilitate existing properties into affordable low-income housing.
4) Multi-Family Housing Funds: funds to maintain the physical and financial soundness of multi-family housing developments
5) Public Housing Modernization Program: grants to public housing projects to make needed repairs and improvements.
6) Housing Development Fund: interest-free advances to non-profit sponsors developing housing with private- or government-aided mortgages
7) Rental Rehabilitation Program: up to $5,000 per unit to subsidize up to 50% of the cost of moderate rehabilitation of residential units in lower-income neighborhoods.
8) Rural Preservation Companies Program: funds to local not-for- profit organizations engaging in a variety of activities for the benefit of low- and moderate-income persons.
9) Rural Rental Assistance Program: monthly rent subsidy payments to owners of multi-family projects on behalf of low-income tenants.

North Carolina

North Carolina Housing Finance Agency, 3300 Drake Circle, Suite 200, Raleigh, NC 27607, 919-781-6115.
1) Single-Family Mortgage Loan Program: below-market, fixed-rate loans for first-time homebuyers.
2) Multi-family Unsubsidized Program: below-market financing to developers of multi-unit apartments for moderate-income families.
3) Multi-family Subsidized Loan Program: below-market, fixed-rate financing for developers of multi-unit projects located outside major metropolitan areas.
4) Home Improvement Loan Program: rehabilitation loans of up to $15,000 at rates as low as 1% to improve owner occupied housing.
5) Homeownership Assistance Program: cash contribution as a recapturable second note/deed of trust to families earning below $20,000.
6) Governor's NCHFA/FmHA Elderly Subsidy Program: rental subsidy of up to $100 per month based on occupant's income.

North Dakota

Housing Assistance Program, 1600 East Interstate Avenue, Bismark, ND 58501, (701) 224-2323.
1) Housing Assistance: rental assistance program for low-income renter households and mobile home space renters.
2) First-Time Homebuyers: low interest loans for low- to moderate-income first-time homebuyers.

Ohio

Ohio Housing Finance Agency, 65 East State St., Columbus, OH 43266, (614) 466-7970.
1) Mortgage Program: first-time homebuyers can claim 20% of their mortgage interest as a tax credit.
2) Seed Money Loan Program: no-interest loans to non-profit, public and limited profit entities to arrange financing for low- and moderate income rental housing developments.
3) Cuyahoga County Bonus Mortgage Program: 25% bonus program loans at below-market rate interest to eligible borrowers to purchase homes in neighborhoods that are racially segregated.

Oklahoma

Oklahoma Housing Finance Agency, 1140 Northwest 63rd St, Suite 200, Oklahoma City, OK 73116, (405) 848-1144.
1) Rental Assistance: subsidized monthly payments to low-income renters.
2) Homebuyers: low-interest loans to first-time homebuyers.

Oregon

Oregon Housing Agency, Housing Division, 110 Labor & Industries Building, Salem, OR 97310, (503) 378-4343.
1) Elderly and Disabled Housing Program: below-market interest rate mortgage loans for multi-family housing for elderly and disabled.
2) Multi-Unit Program: long-term financing for multi-unit rental housing for low-income families and families.
3) Seed Money Advance Program: no-interest advances to nonprofits to cover preconstruction costs.
4) Construction Loan Program: funds for construction of multi-unit developments.
5) Low-Income Housing Tax Credit: federal income tax credits to developers who construct, rehabilitate, or acquire qualified low-income rental housing.
6) Loans to Lenders: low-interest loans to home buyers through lenders
7) Single-Family Mortgage Program: below-market interest rate loans to low- and moderate-income Oregon home buyers.

8) Mortgage Credit Certificate Program: federal tax credit for low- and moderate-income Oregonians to purchase, improve or rehabilitate a single-family residence.

9) Technical Assistance: provide information, planning, educational services and technical assistance to individuals, government agencies, and public or private housing sponsors.

Pennsylvania

Pennsylvania Housing Finance Agency, 2101 North Front St. Harrisburg, PA 17105, (717) 780-3800.

1) Rental Housing Program: tax-exempt, below-market interest financing for multi-family rental housing projects which reserve 2% of the units for lower-income tenants.

2) Single-Family Homeownership Program: attractive fixed-interest rate loans to qualified homebuyers with 5% down.

3) Emergency Mortgage Assistance Program: loans to eligible homeowners suffering financial hardship.

4) Multi-Family Housing: permanent or short-term construction financing for developers of multi-unit rental projects.

5) Homeowners Emergency Mortgage Assistance Program: loans to keep delinquent homeowners from losing their homes to foreclosure.

Rhode Island

Rhode Island Housing and Mortgage Finance Corporation, 60 Eddy St., Providence, RI 02903, (401) 751-5566.

1) New Homes Program: below-market, fixed-rate mortgages for first-time homebuyers purchasing newly-built, single-family homes or condominiums.

2) Homeownership Opportunity: 8% loans for low and moderate income first-time buyers with 5% down.

3) New Homes: 8.75% loans to middle-income, first-time buyers with a 5% downpayment.

4) Elderly Home Equity: tax-free monthly income to qualified elderly homeowners. Loans to be repaid solely from the sale of the home upon death.

5) Home Repair: 3% fixed rate-loans to make needed repairs on 1 to 6 unit dwellings owned or occupied by low- and moderate-income persons.

6) Access Independence Loans: 3% fixed rate, interest-deferred loans to make homes more accessible for people with handicapping conditions.

7) Rental Housing Production and Rehabilitation: tax-exempt and/or taxable bond financing for developers for projects where a minimum of 20% of the units are rented to low-income tenants.

8) Affordable Housing Partnership Program: low interest loans for locally-developed housing initiatives to rehab or build rental housing and single-family homes for low- and moderate-income persons.

9) Emergency Housing and Shelter Trust Fund: grants to provide immediate physical improvements to existing shelters and a permanent fund for non-profit groups that provide emergency housing assistance.

South Carolina

South Carolina State Housing Authority, 1710 Gervais St., Suite 300, Columbia, SC 29201, (803) 758-2844.

1) Single-Family Programs: below-market interest rate mortgages for low- and moderate-to-low income persons and families.

2) Rental Housing Programs: construction loans to construct houses for rental property for low and moderate-to-low income persons

3) Existing Rental Housing Program: financial assistance to low- income tenants.

4) Moderate Rehabilitation Program: mortgage financing for the upgrade of substandard rental housing.

5) Rental Rehabilitation Program: grant, deferred payment loan or a below-market interest rate loan to improve rental housing acquired by local government.

6) Basic Homes Demonstration Program: permanent mortgage financing for newly-constructed homes in the price range of $20,000-- $40,000.

South Dakota

South Dakota Housing Development Authority, P.O. Box 1237, Pierre, SD 57501, (605) 773-3181.

1) Existing Housing Assistance Payments Program: money to assist lower-income families pay for modest rental housing.

2) Homeownership Program: low-interest loans to eligible homebuyers.

3) Energy Efficiency Program - New Construction: new construction loans for homes complying with super-insulation standards.

Tennessee

Tennessee Housing Development Agency, 700 Landmark Center, 401 Church St., Nashville, TN 37219, (615) 741-4979.

1) Homeownership Program: reduced-interest-rate loans to low- and moderate-income families.

2) Veterans: permanent mortgage financing available for disabled Veterans who need specially designed homes.

3) Rental Rehabilitation: lower-than-market loans to owners of rental property to rehabilitate units. This program also offers a grant of up to $5000 per unit to keep the cost of rehabilitation down.

4) Owner-built Homes: permanent mortgage financing for homes built by the owners. Sweat equity serves as the downpayment.

5) Turnkey III: subsidized rent to bring economically viable residents into personal home ownership.

6) Urban Development Action Grant: loans to homebuyers at a very reduced-or zero-interest rate to be used as a downpayment on a home.

7) Rental Housing: subsidy funds to low-income households.

8) Technical Assistance Program: technical assistance to public and private sponsors of low- and moderate-income housing.

Texas

Texas Housing Agency, PO Box 13941 Capitol Station, Austin, TX 78711, (512) 472-7500.

1) Single-Family Home Purchase Program: 7.99% with 3 to 5% down mortgages for first-time homebuyers.

2) Mortgage Credit Certificate Program: up to $2,000 of federal tax credits for first-time homeowners.

3) Multi-Family Loan Program: below-market interest rate loans for apartment developers.

4) Low-Income Rental Housing Tax Credit: federal tax credits for those who wish to acquire, construct, or rehabilitate rental housing for low-income families.

Utah

Utah Housing Finance Agency, 177 East 100 South, Salt Lake City, UT 84111, (801) 521-6950.

1) Single-Family Mortgage Program: money to first-time homebuyers in targeted areas with required downpayment.

Vermont

Vermont Housing Finance Agency, One Burlington Sq., PO Box 408, Burlington, VT 05402, (802) 864-5743, (800) 222-VFHA.

1) Mortgage Plus: federal income tax credit for up to 20% of interest on a home loan.

2) Mortgages for Vermonters: low-interest mortgages.

3) New Home Program: 7.75% to 8.25% mortgages for new homes that are energy efficient.

4) Single-Family Mortgage Purchase Program Interfacing with the Burlington Community Land Trust: below-market financing to qualified individuals.

5) Energy-Rated Homes of Vermont Mortgage Program: money to modify homes to make them energy efficient.

Virginia

Virginia Housing Development Authority, 13 South 13th St. Richmond, VA 23219, (804) 782-1986.

1) Home Mortgage Loan Program: below-market loans to eligible homebuyers with required down payment.

2) Virginia Housing Fund: deferred loan payments, below-market rate loans for lower-income people.

Washington

Washington State Housing Finance Commission, 710 Second Avenue, Suite 1090, Seattle, WA 98104, (206) 464-7139.

1) Mortgage Credit Certificate Program: tax credits to prospective first-time home buyers purchasing manufactured, newly-constructed or existing homes.

2) Single-Family Home Ownership Program: below-market loans to first- time home buyers with a 5% downpayment.

3) Multi-family Program: financing to developers of multi-family projects where at least 20% or more units will be rented to lower- to mid-income persons, the elderly or the handicapped.

4) Congregate Housing/Retirement Service Center Program: construction financing for developers to produce housing for the elderly.

5) Insured Home Improvement Program: loans to make home improvements in the City of Seattle.

West Virginia

West Virginia Housing Development Fund, 814 Virginia St., East, Charleston, WV 25301, (304) 345-6475.

Wisconsin

Wisconsin Housing and Economic Development Authority, PO Box 1728, Madison, WI 53701, (608) 267-2308.

1) Home Ownership Mortgage Loan Program: low interest, fixed rate, 30-year loans.

2) Housing and Neighborhood Conservation Program: low interest loans to repair properties and install energy-conserving improvements.

3) Home Energy Loan Program: low-interest loans to make energy conserving improvements on homes.

4) DEER Program: money to nonprofits to acquire and rehabilitate older single-family and two-family homes with special emphasis on energy conservation, restored homes are then sold.

5) Rental Housing Programs: financing of rental housing for low-and moderate-income individuals and families, elderly and disabled.

6) Community Housing Alternatives Program: loans for construction, purchase or rehabilitation of projects to house those who are chronically disabled due to mental illness, development disability, physical disability, or alcohol- or other drug-related dependence, or those over 60 years of age.

7) Market-Rate Rental Housing Program: construction and permanent financing for multi-family housing.

8) Rental Rehabilitation Program: money for rehabilitation of rental units.

9) Low-Income Housing Tax Credits: federal tax credits for low-income rental housing in Wisconsin.

10) WHEDA Foundation Grants: grants to non-profit housing project sponsors.

11) Business Development Bond Program: financing for small- and medium-sized businesses.

12) Linked Deposit Loan Program: loans to businesses that are more than 50% owned by women or minorities.

13) Commercial and Industrial Energy Loan Program: low-cost financing to small businesses for energy conservation improvements.

14) Credit Relief Outreach Program: agricultural related families can receive interest rate reduction and loan guarantees of up to $20,000

15) News Start Loan Programs: provides farmers with lower-cost, fixed- rate funds.

Wyoming

Wyoming Community Development Authority, 139 W 2nd Street, Suite-1C, P.O. Box 634, Casper, WY 82602, (307) 265-0603.

Funding for single-family homes, multi-family projects, and economic development.

Gardening

* Alternative Farming Systems

Alternative Farming Systems
U.S. Department of Agriculture
10301 Baltimore Blvd.
Beltsville, MD 20705 (301) 344-3704

This center covers organized farming or gardening that includes low-input, sustainable, or regenerative agriculture. Conservation tillage and other cultivation practices, such as intercropping, crop rotation, and use of green manures, are also covered.

* Botanic Garden: 10,000 Plant Species

U.S. Botanic Garden
Office of Director
2245 First St., SW
Washington, DC 20024 (202) 225-8333

The Botanic Garden is a living museum open daily, free of charge, containing noteworthy collections, including Economic Plants, Cycads, Orchids, Begonias, Cacti and Succulents, Carnivorous Plants, Bromeliads, Ferns, Roses, Palms, and other miscellaneous tropical and subtropical plants, many of which are rare species. There are special displays during most of the year, and in their proper seasons banana, papaya, orange, lemon, tangerine, kumquat, averrhoa, coffee, and surinam cherry are displayed in luxuriant fruiting. Included in its glasshouse collections are many of the plants brought to the U.S. Botanic Garden from the Wilkes Expedition to the South Seas in 1842. The entire collection of the Garden includes over 10,000 species and varieties of plant growth. The collection attracts many visitors annually, including botanists, horticulturists, students, and garden club members. The horticultural and botanical library is available by appointment only.

* Botanical Garden Tours

Public Programs Office
U.S. Botanic Garden
245 1st St., SW
Washington, DC 20024 (202) 226-4082

The Botanic Garden is open to the public from 9 a.m. to 9 p.m. daily June through August, and from 9 a.m. to 5 p.m. the rest of the year. Tours are given to interested groups, including garden clubs, professional organizations, and school children.

* Botanical Specimens for Plant Breeders

U.S. Botanic Garden
Office of Director
2245 First St., SW
Washington, DC 20024 (202) 225-8333

Though not operated as a scientific institution, the Botanic Garden does make educational facilities available for study to students, botanists, and floriculturists on many rare and interesting botanical specimens. Working with scientists, the Garden grows, displays, and keeps records on significant botanical collections for study and for exchange with other institutions. The Garden is a gene pool resource for plant breeders. It is also involved in the preservation of rare or endangered plants and is actively building and displaying economic plants. Every year botanical specimens are received from all over the world with requests for identification, and one of the services offered by the Garden to the public is the identification of such specimens and the furnishing of information relating to the proper care for them, and methods of growing them.

* Christmas Tree Diseases

Superintendent of Documents
Government Printing Office
Washington, DC 20402 (202) 783-3238

Tree publications are listed, including those of interest to tree growers and the lumber industry. Also featured is a guide to Christmas Tree diseases and books listing the tropical timbers of the world. Free.

* Compost and Improved Soil

Soil Microbial Systems
U.S. Department of Agriculture
Building 318, Room 108 BARC-E
Beltsville, MD 20705 (301) 344-3163

This office provides technical assistance on the production and use of compost, soil, and microbes.

* Desert and Tropical Plants Museum

The Conservatory
Maryland Avenue
1st to 2nd Sts., SW
Washington, DC 20024 (202) 255-6646

The Conservatory houses permanent collections of tropical, subtropical, and desert plants in an exhibition area of 38,000 square feet. Just across from the Conservatory on Independence Avenue, the Frederic Auguste Bartholdi Park features displays of bulbs, annuals, and perennials.

* Environmental Impact on Plant Species

U.S. Botanic Garden
Office of Director
2245 First St., SW
Washington, DC 20024 (202) 225-8333

In these times of global changes, with climate changes, the greenhouse effect, and the need for species diversity, having the Strategically placed at the foot of our nation's Capitol, the Botanic Garden's spectacular displays of significant plant collections can have a strong impact on people's awareness of the environment.

* Gardening and Plant Propagation Workshops

Poplar Point
700 Howard Road, SE
Anacostia, DC 20020 (202) 225-6420

The Poplar Point Production Facility is a nursery and greenhouse range responsible for plant production for the U.S. Botanic Garden and the entire Capitol Hill Complex. The facility is open by appointment and occasionally tours of the facility are conducted for the public. Next year a new nursery will be built and many hands-on classes and workshops on gardening and plant propagation will be held there.

* Gypsy Moth Control

Printing and Distribution Management Branch, APHIS
U.S. Department of Agriculture
Federal Building, Room G-100
6505 Belcrest Rd.
Hyattsville, MD 20782 (301) 436-7176

The following publication is available free of charge from APHIS: *Don't Move the Gypsy Moth* (July 1985). This tells how to make sure outdoor household articles don't spread gypsy moths.

* Horticulture

Horticulture
U.S. Department of Agriculture
10301 Baltimore Blvd.
Beltsville, MD 20705 (301) 344-3704

This center covers technical horticultural or botanical question, economic botany, wild plants of possible use, herbs, bonsai, and floriculture.

* Horticultural Classes: Medicinal Plants to Lawn Care

Public Programs Office
U.S. Botanic Garden
245 1st St., SW
Washington, DC 20024 (202) 226-4082

Horticultural classes are held throughout the year on timely subjects related to botanical, horticultural, and environmental interests. Many leading scientists are featured as lecturers and all classes are free of charge. Classes consist of a lecture incorporating slides or demonstrations, tours or workshops. Some examples of recent classes include Fall Lawn Care, Decorating With Exotics, Native Medicinal Plants, and The Dynamics of Horticultural Therapy. A calendar of all classes is available.

* Horticulture Clearinghouse

Horticulture
U.S. Department of Agriculture
10301 Baltimore Blvd.
Beltsville, MD 20705 (301) 344-3704

This center covers technical horticultural or botanical question, economic botany, wild plants of possible use, herbs, bonsai, and floriculture.

Housing and Real Estate

* Indoor and Outdoor Insects Identification

Contact your local USDA
Extension Service Agent

Technical assistance is available to help you identify and eliminate any problems you may have caused by insects and bugs. You are encouraged to catch one of the insects which are causing the problem and send it in for analysis. Contact your local Extension Service for more information.

* Landscaping

Landscape Architect
Engineering Division
Soil Conservation Service
U.S. Department of Agriculture
6129 South Building
Washington, DC 20250   (202) 447-9155

Assistance is available to help anyone with landscaping-related problem from your local USDA Extension Service agents. Help is also available to those having problems with larger projects involving conservation can contact the above office.

* National Arboretum

U.S. National Arboretum
3501 New York Ave.
Educational Department
Washington, DC 20002   (202) 475-4815

Various woody ornamental and outdoor plants are grown and cared for on the 444 acres comprising the U.S. National Arboretum. Admission and parking are free, and guided tours for 10 or more are available with 3 weeks advance notice. Many free classes are offered, along with many special events and functions associated with gardening and growing plants. A free monthly newsletter lists the monthly calendar.

* Patents on Seeds

Plant Variety Protection Office
Commodities Scientific Support Division
AMS, NAL, Room 500
Beltsville, MD 20705   (301) 344-2518

Unique seeds, with few exceptions, that are sexually reproduced can be protected by patents, The protection, which extents for 18 years, provides owners with exclusive rights to sell, reproduce, export, and produce the seed.

* Plant and Flower Shows

Office of the Director
U.S. Botanic Garden
245 1st St., SW
Washington, DC 20024   (202) 225-8333

Spectacular seasonal plant and flower shows are scheduled throughout the year. The Annual Spring Flower Show features spring flowering plants and is held from Palm Sunday through Easter Sunday. The Summer Terrace Display is held on the patio in front of the Conservatory from late May through September. Hundreds of flowering and foliage plants in hanging baskets highlight this event. Mid-November through Thanksgiving Day features The Annual Chrysanthemum Show. The Annual Poinsettia Show takes place from mid-December through the Christmas holidays. The Garden also hosts various plant and flower shows sponsored by area garden clubs and plant societies each year. Each show has a theme and offers excellent ideas for new plants, innovative garden designs, and uses state-of-the-art gardening techniques. Special exhibits are being prepared for The U.S. Botanic Garden's 150th Anniversary in 1992. Call (202) 225-7099 for more information about shows.

* Plant Care and Botanical Garden Calendar

Public Programs Office
U.S. Botanic Garden
245 1st St., SW
Washington, DC 20024   (202) 226-4082

Handouts are provided on plant culture, sources for plants and care for certain plants. A pamphlet offers a self-guided tour of the Garden. Brochures including schedules for shows and horticultural classes, and historical information about the Garden are also available.

* Plant Care Telephone Line and Information Service

Plant Information Service
U.S. Botanic Garden
245 1st St., SW
Washington, DC 20024   (202) 225-8333

The Garden serves as a center for plant information offering a telephone information service as well as responding to written inquiries Monday through Friday from 9:00 a.m. to 11:30 a.m.

* Plant Protection and Rescue Center

U.S. Botanic Garden
Office of Director
2245 First St., SW
Washington, DC 20024   (202) 225-8333

Serving as a Plant Rescue Center for the USDA's Animal and Plant Health Inspection Service, the Botanic Garden is legally obligated to care for and preserve the multitude of protected plants it receives that are illegally shipped into the U.S. Through this program, the Garden helps visitors recognize the value of preservation and protection of plants.

* Plants: Research and Reference

National Arboretum Library
3501 New York Ave., NE
Washington, DC 2000   (202) 475-4815

This library will provide information on many aspects of indoor plants and gardening.

* Seed Quality and Inspection Labs

Federal Seed Lab
U.S. Department of Agriculture
Beltsville, MD 20705   (301) 344-2089

The federal government can test seeds to determine their quality and whether they are free from contamination. They will also prosecute any agent that transfers contaminated or mislabled seed from state to state. Seeds are examined by or at a state agent's request, and there may be some fee involved.

* Sick House Plants, Pets, Trees, and Lawns

Contact your local USDA
Extension Service Agent

Free technical assistance is available to help diagnose and cure diseases of plants and animals. Services range from telephone consultations and free literature, to analyzing your pets' stools or your plants' leaves for disease.

* Tracer Bulletins to Gardening References

Science and Technology Division
Reference Section
Library of Congress
Washington, DC 20540   (202) 707-5580

Informal series of reference guides are issued free from the Science and Technology Division under the general title, *LC Science Tracer Bullet.* These guides are designed to help readers locate published material on subjects about which they have only general knowledge. New titles in the series are announced in the weekly Library of Congress *Information Bulletin* that is distributed to many libraries. The following is a list of *Tracer Bullets* currently available:

80-1 Green Revolution
81-2 Medicinal Plants
81-15 History of American Agriculture
82-2 Gardening
82-6 Biological Control of Insects
83-5 Plant Exploration & Introduction
85-1 Herbs and Herb Gardening
85-2 Landscape Gardening
85-10 Rose Culture
86-3 Jojoba & Other Oilseed Plants
86-4 Composite Materials
88-5 Soil Erosion

* Wood Pests

Forest Insect and Disease Research
U.S. Department of Agriculture
FS, Room 609 RP-E
Arlington, VA 22209   (703) 235-8065
OR: Your local Forest Service or Extension Office

The USDA provides technical assistance for insect and diseases to wood, whether it is in use, stored, wood products, or urban trees. All insect and disease suppression projects must meet specific criteria for federal participation.

Education
School: Grades K-12

* See also Careers and Workplace Chapter
* See also Drugs and Chemical Enforcement Chapter
* See also Current Events and Homework Chapter
* See also Weather and Maps Chapter

Studies and new assessments of American education abound. Take advantage of the numerous clearinghouses which are excellent starting points for information. Resources on pre-school and early childhood development are sprinkled here. Vocational education is included in the next section on postsecondary education. Students and teachers alike will find very relevant information in the Current Events and Homework Chapter toward the end of the book. And, of course, additional classroom materials and lesson plans are identified throughout the book.

* Academic Affairs

Academic Affairs
Veterans Health Services and Research Administration
Department of Veterans Affairs
810 Vermont Ave., NW, Room 876
Washington, DC 20420   (202) 233-5094
The DVA conducts the largest coordinated health professions education and training efforts of its kind in the U.S. Its purpose is to assure high quality health care for veterans and to develop a sufficient number of all categories of professional and other health personnel. For more information contact the office above.

* Alternative versus Traditional Schools

ERIC Clearinghouse on Educational Management
University of Oregon
1787 Agate St.
Eugene, OR 97403-5207   (503) 686-5043
Subject areas include all aspects of the administration, leadership, finance, governance, and structure of public and private education organizations at the elementary, middle, and secondary levels, including facility planning, design, construction, equipment and furnishing, and maintenance; and pre-service and in-service preparation of administrators. Topics covered include the social, technological, political, and legal contexts of education organizations, and of State and Federal programs and policies, and traditional and alternative schools.

* American Educators Teaching Abroad

Superintendent of Documents
Government Printing Office
Washington, DC 20402   (202) 783-3238
The United States Information Agency publishes many teaching materials, including books, maps, complete teaching modules, and 14 magazines in 20 languages. By law most USIA publications may be distributed only in foreign countries. However, by congressional action, two magazines are available in the United States. *English Teaching Forum*, a quarterly for English teachers worldwide, is published by USIA's English Language Programs Division. *Problems of Communism* is a bi-monthly forum for American and foreign scholars discussing communist and socialist affairs. It is published in English and Spanish. Both these magazines are available through the GPO.

* American Studies for Foreigners

Division of Study of the U.S.
United States Information Agency
301 Fourth St., SW, Rom 256
Washington, DC 20547   (202) 485-2557
The Division for the Study of the U.S. promotes foreign education through conferences, seminars, exchange programs for foreign educators, grants, and development of school resource materials. The Academic Specialist Branch provides grants for American teachers to instruct their peers at foreign educational institutions. Contact this office for more information.

* Army Reserve Community Projects: From Baseball to Language Training

Chief of U.S. Army Reserve
Public Affairs, The Pentagon
Washington, DC 20310   (202) 697-7369
The Army Reserve provides a variety of community services through their special programs. Requests are handled on a case by case basis based on their current ability to help. Projects might involve building a community playground or a baseball field. Through the Adopt-a-School Program, Corps people with special skills or training teach special courses, such as a foreign language or communications, or may be involved in extra-curricular activities. Contact your local Army Reserve headquarters or the above office for further information.

* Arts Education

National Arts Education Research Center
New York University School of Education, Health,
Nursing and Arts Profession
32 Washington Place, #31
New York, NY 10003   (212) 998-5050
Major research areas include the processes of successful teaching and curriculum in arts education; videotape documentation of successful teaching in arts education; and educational relationships among the schools and cultural institutions.

* Arts in Education Initiatives

Arts-In-Education
National Endowment for the Arts
1100 Pennsylvania Ave., NW, Room 602
Washington, DC 20506   (220) 682-5426
The Arts-In-Education Program is a partnership program through cooperative efforts of the Arts Endowment, state arts and education agencies, local communities, and other organizations. The Program's overall goal is to advance the arts as part of basic education. Grants are awarded to place practicing artists in a variety of educational settings and to support other projects designed to enhance arts education in schools. Arts in Schools Basic Education Grants encourage plans and projects that promote the arts in schools as a basic component of the curriculum in kindergarten through high school.

* Art Slides, Films, Video Loan Program

Art Extension Programs
National Gallery of Art
Extension Services
Constitution & 6th St., NW
Washington, DC 20565   (202) 842-6273
Color slide programs, films, and videocassette are loaned at no cost to schools, libraries, community organizations, and individuals across the nation. The programs deal with a wide range of subjects drawn from the Gallery's permanent collections and special exhibitions. A free catalog listing all free-loan Extension Programs is available.

* Bilingual and Minority Languages Affairs Multifunctional Resource Centers

Office of Bilingual Education and Minority
Languages Affairs
330 C St., SW
Washington, DC 20202   (202) 732-5063
These resource centers provide inservice training and technical assistance to parents and educational personnel participating in, or preparing to participate in, instructional programs for limited English proficient children. The centers work closely with state and federal programs in their regions to coordinate program improvement for language minority children. Their efforts include training in the theory and practice of second language acquisition; techniques for developing

English language skills; methods for improving content area instruction for language minority children; increasing parent involvement; the use of paraprofessionals in the classroom; dropout prevention; and the integration of multicultural materials in instructional programs. MRCs conduct local and regional workshops, participate in state, regional and federal training programs, and provide inservice and consultation support to individual schools and districts.

Brown University, New England Multifunctional Resource Center, 345 Blackstone Blvd., Weld Building, Providence, RI 02906, (401) 274-9548. Serving: Maine, New Hampshire, Vermont, Massachusetts, Connecticut, and Rhode Island.

Hunter College and the Research Foundation of the City University of New York, 695 Park Ave., Box 367, New York, NY 10021, (212) 772-4762. Serving: New York.

Georgetown University, 1916 Wilson Blvd., Suite 302, Arlington, VA 22201, (703) 875-0900. Serving: Pennsylvania, Ohio, West Virginia, Virginia, Kentucky, New Jersey, Delaware, Maryland, and District of Columbia.

Florida International University School of Education, Tamiami Campus, TRM03, Miami, FL 33199, (305) 554-2962. Serving: Alabama, Florida, Georgia, Mississippi, North Carolina, South Carolina, and Tennessee.

InterAmerica Research Associates, Midwest Bilingual Education
MRC 2360 East Devon Ave., Suite 3011, Des Plaines, IL 60018, (312) 269-6070. Serving: Arkansas, Illinois, Indiana, Louisiana, and Missouri.

Upper Great Lakes MRC, Wisconsin Center for Education Research, University of Wisconsin, Madison, 1025 West Johnson St., Madison, WI 53706, (608) 263-4216. Serving: Iowa, Michigan, Minnesota, and Wisconsin.

Southwest Education Development Laboratory, 211 East 7th St., Austin, TX 78701, (512) 476-6861. Serving: Texas.

University of Oklahoma, Division of Continuing Education and Public Affairs, 555 Constitution Ave., Norman, OK 73037, (405) 325-1711. Serving: Oklahoma, Kansas, Nebraska, South Dakota, and North Dakota.

Interface Network, Inc., 4800 S.W. Griffith Drive, Suite 202, Beaverton, OR 97005, (503) 644-5741. Serving: Idaho, Oregon, Montana, Washington, and Wyoming.

Arizona State University, College of Education, Tempe, AZ 85287, (602) 965-5688. Serving: Arizona, New Mexico, Utah, Colorado, and Nevada.

San Diego State University Foundation, 6363 Alvarado Court, Suite 200, San Diego, CA 92120, (619) 594-5193. Serving: Southern California.

ARC Associates, Inc., 310 Eighth St., Suite 311, Oakland, CA 94607, (415) 834-9455. Serving: Northern California.

Metropolitan University, Apartado 21150, Rio Piedras, PR 00928, (809) 766-1717. Serving: Puerto Rico and Virgin Islands.

ARC Associates, Inc., 1314 South King St. Suite 1456, Honolulu, HI 96814, (808) 536-4494. Serving: Hawaii and America Samoa.

University of Guam, Project BEAM, College of Education, UOG Station, Mangilao, Guam 96913, Telex: 721-6275. Serving: Guam, Wake Island, the Commonwealth of the Northern Marianas, the Republic of Palau, the Republic of the Marshall Islands, and the Federated States of Micronesia.

Interface Network, Inc., 3650 Lake Otis Parkway Suite 102 Anchorage, AK 99501, (907) 563-7787. Serving: Alaska.

* Bilingual and Minority Languages
Evaluation Assistance Centers
Office of Bilingual Education and Minority
Languages Affairs
330 C St., SW
Washington, DC 20202   (202) 732-5063
These evaluation assistance centers provide training and technical assistance, on request, to state and local education agencies serving limited English proficient students. The EAC-East and EAC-West present workshops and seminars at regional meetings, state education agency events, multi-local education agency conferences, and sponsored meetings under the office. In addition, they provide direct, on-site training and consultations to individual projects and respond to written and telephone requests for information and assistance.

Evaluation Assistance Centers - East:
Georgetown University, 1916 Wilson Boulevard, Suite 302, Arlington, VA 22201, (800) 626-5443; or (703) 875-0900.

RMC Research Corporation, 400 Lafayette Rd., Hampton, NH 03842, (800) 258-0802; or (603) 926-8888.

Evaluation Assistance Center - West:
University of New Mexico, College of Education, Albuquerque, NM 87131, (505) 277-7281.

* Bilingual Education Clearinghouse
National Clearinghouse for Bilingual Education
8737 Colesville Rd., Suite 900
Silver Spring, MD 20910   (800) 647-0123
NCBE provides information to practitioners in the field on curriculum materials, program models, methodologies, and research findings on the education of limited English proficient (LEP) individuals. They also offer an electronic information system, free to users, where you may access a database of curriculum materials and literature related to the education of LEP persons. An electronic bulletin board is also available which contains news from federal, state, and local education agencies, conference announcements, and other current information. NCBE also develops and publishes three types of publications: a bimonthly newsletter, occasional papers, and program information guides. Their newsletter, FORUM, is available free of charge. Below is a sampling of other publications available through this organization:

Assessment and Placement of Language Minority Students: Procedures for Mainstreaming ($1.50)
Meeting the Needs of Gifted anmd Talented Minority Language Students: Issues and Practices ($1.50)
Using Computer Concepts as Problem Solving Tools in the Language Learning Classroom ($2.50)
Parent Involvement: A Resource for the Education of Limited English Students ($2.50)
Affective Considerations in Bilingual Education: Problems and Solutions ($4.00)
Program Development to Meet the Educational Needs of Limited English Proficient Students: A Bibliography of Capacity Building ($5.00)
Review of the State-of-the-Art of Educational Technologies Implemented in Programs Serving LEP Students ($10.50)
Application of Immersion Education in the United States ($2.25)

* Books and Reading
Center for the Book
Library of Congress
Washington, DC 20540(202) 707-5221
A partnership between the federal government and private industry, the Center for the Book works closely with other organizations to explore important issues dealing with books and educational communities. The Center encourages reading and research about books and reading and serves as a catalyst by bringing together authors, publishers, librarians, booksellers, educators, scholars, and readers to discuss common concerns. Four primary concerns are: television and the printed word, reading development, international role of the book, and publishing. The center is funded by tax-deductible contributions.

* Braille U.S. Constitution
National Braille Press, Inc.
88 St. Stephen St.
Boston, MA 02115
Individuals may request free copies of the U.S. Constitution in Braille at the above address.

* Captioned Movies and Videos for the Hearing Impaired
Modern Talking Pictures
500 Park St., North
St. Petersburg, FL 33709   (813) 541-7571
This company's captioned film/video program provides a free loan service of educational and theatrical films and videos for various groups to assist deaf/hearing impaired persons in educational and recreational pursuits. Comprehensive, free catalogs list over 3,500 films and videocassettes. Language controlled open-captions (subtitles) appear on each film and video.

* Children's Literature
Children's Literature Center
National Programs
Library of Congress
Washington, DC 20540(202) 707-5535
The Center prepares lists and scholarly bibliographies and provides other reference services for individuals who serve children, including scholars, writers, teachers, librarians, and illustrators. The center also has many publishers' catalogs that list titles to be published in the upcoming year, a wide range of periodicals about children's literature, and lists from rare and used book sellers. *Books for Children*, a guide to reference sources for children's literature published annually for $1 per issue, is available from the Superintendent of Documents, Government Printing Office, Washington, D.C. 20402; (202) 783-3238.

* Constitution Bicentennial Commission
Publication Division
Commission on the Bicentennial of the U.S. Constitution
8080 17th St., NW, Suite 800
Washington, DC 20006   (202) 653-9800
A monthly newsletter, *We the People*, is published by the Commission. The newsletter highlights activities of the Commission nationwide. Subscriptions are free upon request.

* Constitution Week Activities
Education Division
Commission on the Bicentennial of the U.S. Constitution
808 17th St., NW, Suite 800
Washington, DC 20006   (202) 653-5109
September 17-23 is Constitution Week, and the Commission has designed an educational poster graphically representing "We the People" through the faces of children. The back of the poster features teaching suggestions on the Constitution and citizenship, appropriate for elementary, middle, and high school levels. Also available is a forty-page booklet, *Constitution Week: An American Legacy*, with ideas and suggestions for planning and implementing Constitution Week activities. Contact this office for more information.

* Consumer Publications for Students and Teachers
Office of Information and Public Affairs
U.S. Consumer Product Safety Commission
Washington, DC 20207   (800) 638-2772
The following consumer publications describe some of the common hazards associated with the use of consumer products and recommend ways to avoid these hazards. They come in the form of fact sheets (F.S.), brochures, and materials developed especially for use by classroom teachers. Some of the publications listed here can also be requested from the Commission' Regional Offices.
It's No Accident: A Guide for Teachers of Grades 3-6
Flammable Products: A Guide for Teachers of Secondary Grades
Flammable Products: A Guide for Teachers of Elementary Grades (Spanish)
Flammable Fabrics: Teacher's Guide (4T)
Flammable Fabrics: Student Readings (4-S)
Halloween Safety Teacher's Guide (9T)
Holiday Safety Teacher's Guide (7T)
Poison Prevention Teacher's Guide (6T)

* Curriculum and Student Standards
Center for Policy Research in Education
The Eagleton Institute of Politics Rutgers
The State University of New Jersey
Wood Lawn--Neilson Campus
New Brunswick, NJ 08901   (201) 828-3872
Major research areas include curriculum and student standards, teacher policies, indicators and monitoring, new roles and responsibilities; and evolution of reform.

* Counseling and Personnel Services Information
ERIC Clearinghouse on Counseling and Personnel Services University of Michigan School of Education
Room 2108 610 East University St.
Ann Arbor, MI 48109-1259   (313) 764-9492
Subject areas cover the preparation, practice, and supervision of counselors at all educational levels and in all settings; theoretical development of counseling and guidance; personnel procedures such as testing and interviewing and the analysis and distribution of the resulting information; group work and case work; nature of pupil, student, and adult characteristics; personnel workers and their relation to career planning, family consultations, and student orientation activities.

* Creative and Analytical Thinking Skills
Commissioner of Patents and Trademarks
Patent and Trademark Office
Department of Commerce
2121 Crystal Dr., Room 1101C
Arlington, VA 22202   (703) 557-1610
Project XL is a PTO outreach program designed to encourage the development of analytical and creative thinking and problem-solving skills among America's youth. The principal focus of this effort is on the promotion of educational programs that teach critical and creative thinking. They present national and regional conferences, and established an Education Roundtable, an open forum and nation discussion network. This office distributes an information guide called the Inventive Thinking Project, designed to channel students in grades K-12 into the inventive thinking process through the creation of their own unique inventions or innovations. They are also in the process of developing an educator's resource guide and a special curriculum. Contact this office for more information about Project XL and the assistance and products they have

available.

* Current Education Information On-Line
OERI Electronic Bulletin Board
Office of Educational Research and Development
Department of Education   (800)-222-4922 (202)- 626-9853
This free service offers a means of obtaining current tables of education data, bulletins, and announcements of data tapes and reports. In operation 24 hours a day, this bulletin board can be accessed by toll-free, using a modem and almost any type of microcomputer with communications software.

* Disabilities Information Clearinghouse
Clearinghouse on Disability Information Program
Information and Coordination Staff
U.S Department of Education
Room 3132, Mary Switzer Building
Washington, DC 20202-2524   (202) 732-1723 or (202) 732-1241
This clearinghouse will provide you with a free bibliography of disability publications which are available through other Federal agencies and departments. What follows is a sampling of those publications:

Adult Basic Education Programs for Disabled Adults.
Educating Students with Learning Problems: A Shared Responsibility.
Free Appropriate Public Education for Students with Handicaps: Requirements under Section 504 of the Rehabilitation Act of 1973.
EEO and Affirmative Action for Employment of Handicapped Persons by Federal Contractors.
Employers are Asking about Accommodating Workers with Disabilities. Identifies common barriers in the workplace and provides suggestions for accommodation.

Fact Sheet No. 7, Handicapped Assistance Loans. Explains the qualifications and conditions for loan approval to small business owners with physical handicaps.

Hiring the Mentally Restored Makes Dollars and Sense. Includes the following publications: Affirmative Action to Employ Mentally Restored People; Eight Questions Employers Ask about Hiring the Mentally Restored; and The Mentally Restored & Work: A Successful Partnership.
A Summary Guide to Social Security and Supplemental Income with Incentives for the Disabled and Blind. This booklet was designed to assist professionals who need to know the work incentive provisions for working with potential or actual SSI or SSDI beneficiaries.
Your Medicare Handbook: A Comprehensive Guide to Your Medicare Hospital and Medical Insurance Benefits.
Facts about Down Syndrome.
Caring about Kids: Helping the Hyperactive Child. Discusses the causes, diagnosis, and treatment of hyperactivity in children.
Periodontal Disease and Diabetes: A Guide for Patients.
Housing and Disabled People--Q and A's for the Disabled.
Statistics Related: SSA Research and Statistics Publications Catalog. Bibliography listing studies conducted or funded by the Social Security Administration. A number of the studies deal with disability related topics.

* Drug Prevention Videos
Office of Public Affairs
US Department of Education
400 Maryland Ave., SW
Washington, DC 20202   (202) 732-4637
Eight productions, close-captioned for the hearing impaired, have been designed to inform students, attending kingergarten through 12th grade, about the dangers of drug use in an engaging and entertaining manner. Contact this office for further information on borrowing or purchasing these videos.

* Educational Materials on the U.S. Constitution
Education Division
Commission on the Bicentennial of the U.S. Constitution
808 17th St., NW , Suite 800
Washington, DC 20006   (202) 653-5109
Educational kits and skills handbooks on the Presidency, Congress, and the Judiciary are available to teachers. Scholastic, Inc. is producing and distributing these materials in two editions; Elementary (grades 3-6) and Junior/Senior high (grades 7-12). A video documentary on the founding of the U.S. government has been developed as a supplement to the kit and handbooks. A classroom wall chart of the Presidents is also available. Contact this office for further information.

* Education Grant Programs Guide
1989 Guide to Department of Education Programs
Superintendent of Documents
U.S. Government Printing Office
Washington, DC 20402
Published annually, the *Guide* gives a brief description of the financial assistance

programs available through the U.S. Department of Education. The cost of this publication is $3.50.

* Education Information and Assistance

Office of Public Affairs
U.S. Department of Education
400 Maryland Ave., SW
Washington, DC 20202   (202) 732-4576

If you need information about a particular educational issue, this is a useful starting place.

* Education Information Processing and Reference

ERIC Processing and Reference Facility
ORI, Inc. Information Systems
2440 Research Boulevard, Suite 550
Rockville, MD 20850-3238   (301) 590-1420

This centralized information processing unit serves all components that contribute to the ERIC system: Central ERIC, 16 clearinghouses, the ERIC Document Reproduction Service, Oryx Press (publisher of the *Current Index to Journals in Education*), and the Government Printing Office (publisher of Resources in Education). Their services include facility management and support; facility operations; reference and user services; and technical support for systems maintenance. From the ERIC database, this facility produces a variety of products and publications, including *Resources in Education* and its semi-annual indexes, ERIC Thesaurus and other system publications, and copies of the ERIC database tape that it provides to subscribers around the world.

* Education Publications

Superintendent of Documents
U.S. Government Printing Office
Washington, DC 20402-9371   (202) 783-3238

Becoming a Nation of Readers: Implications for Teachers. ($1.50 - S/N 065-000-00260-4).

Dealing with Dropouts: The Urban Superintendent's Call to Action. ($3.25 - S/N 065-000-00321-0).

Class Size and Public Policy: Politics and Panaceas ($2.75 S/N 065-000-00326-1). Describes the issues surrounding reduction in class size in the public schools.

Places Where Children Succeed: A Profile of Outstanding Public Elementary Schools. ($3.50, S/N 065-000-00323-6). Describes the national recognition program, the criteria, and processes that led to the selection of the schools and basic background information about the characteristics of the schools.

What Works: Research About Teaching and Learning, second edition ($3.00 - S/N 065-000-00304-0). Update of the original What Works, it contains 59 practical findings of ways to help educate children. A Spanish version is also available from ERIC in microfiche.

Alliance for Excellence: Librarians Respond to 'A Nation at Risk'. ($2.50, S/N 065-000-00207-8).

Assessment of Readiness for School: Implications for a Statistical Program, Report of a Planning Conference, 1/31/87. ($4.50, S/N 065-000-00316-3). Assesses readiness of students for kindergarten or the first grade.

Basic Educational Skills Project: Your Child and Language ($2.25 - S/N 017-092-00089-8). Describes how infants and young children learn to talk.

Your Child and Math ($3.00 - S/N 017-092-00081-2)

Your Child and Problem Solving ($2.25 - S/N 017-092-00085-5)

Beautiful Junk ($2.50 - S/N 017-092-0004-9). Consists of a list of 'found materials' or equipment and supplies which can be acquired at relatively low cost to supplement purchased program aids considered necessary for a preschool program.

Elementary School Aerospace Activities: A Resource for Teachers ($6.50, S/N 033-000-00693-4). Contains many suggestions for teaching children about space exploration which have been field tested in elementary schools.

Experiences in School Improvement: Story of 16 American Districts ($4.50, S/N 065-000-00343-1).

Good Secondary Schools: What Makes Them Tick? ($1.00, S/N 065-000-00273-6).

How to Help Your Child Achieve in School ($3.75, S/N 065-000-00176-4).

Living in Space: Books I and II ($4.75 each, S/Ns 033-000-01000-1 and 033-000-01001-0). Contains classroom and home activities designed to encourage student interest in space.

Safety in the Air: A Curriculum About Flight and Air Traffic Control Designed for Middle School Students ($3.50, S/N 050-007-00661-6).

Soozie and Katy: We're Teaming Up for Your Good Health: President's Drug Awareness Campaign ($1.25, S/N 027-004-00036-9). Study guide which promotes home and classroom discussions of medicine and use and misuse of drugs. Intended for very young children.

Watch Out, Storms Ahead! Owlie Skywarn's Weather Book ($1.50, S/N 003-017-00513-5). Prepared especially for elementary school children, this informational comic book tells what to do during hurricanes, tornados, flash floods, and lightning storms. Includes quizzes.

Directory of Academic Institutions and Organizations: Drug, Alcohol, and Employee Assistance Program Educational Resources (1988) ($4.50, S/N 017-024-01355-2).

Involvement in Learning: Realizing the Potential of American Higher Education ($4.50, S/N 065-000-00353-8).

Pocket Guide to Federal Help for Individuals With Disabilities ($1.00, S/N 065-000-00314-7).

Check This Out: Highlights of Model Library Programs ($2.00, S/N 065-000-00346).

Digest of Education Statistics, 1988 ($19.00, S/N 065-000-00351). Includes statistics on institutions, resources, faculty and students, outcomes, and public and private support.

* Education Savings Bonds

U.S. Savings Bonds Division
Department of the Treasury
1111 20th St., NW
Washington, DC 20226   (202) 634-5353

The new education savings bond program permits qualified taxpayers to exclude from their gross income all or a portion of the interest earned on eligible Series EE savings bonds issued after 1989. To qualify for this exclusion, tuition and other post-secondary educational expenses must be incurred by the taxpayer, the taxpayer's spouse, or the taxpayer's dependent at postsecondary educational institutions. These institutions are those that meet federal financial aid program standards. In addition, there are income limitations on participation in the program. Contact this office for more information on the program.

* Elementary and Early Childhood Education Information

ERIC Clearinghouse on Elementary and Early
Childhood Education
University of Illinois
805 West Pennsylvania Ave.
Urbana, IL 61801-4897   (217) 333-1386

Subject areas cover all aspects of the cognitive, emotional, social, and physical development and education of children from birth through early adolescence, excluding specific elementary school curriculum areas. Among the topics covered are prenatal and infant development and care; child care programs and community services for children at local, state, and federal levels; parent, child, and family relationships; home and school relationships; technology and children; preparation of early childhood teachers and caregivers; foster care and adoption; theoretical and philosophical issues related to children's development and education.

* Elementary and Middle Schools

Center for Research on Elementary and Middle Schools
Johns Hopkins University
3505 North Charles St.
Baltimore, MD 21218   (301) 338-7570

Major research areas include effective elementary and middle schools, and school improvement.

* Elementary Education

Center for the Learning and Teaching of
Elementary Subjects
Michigan State University
College of Education
East Lansing, MI 48824   (517) 353-6470

Major research areas include ideal curriculum, instruction, and assessment practices in elementary content areas; integrated studies of current practice; and improvement of existing practice.

* Environmental Education Materials

Public Information Center
Environmental Protection Agency
401 M St., SW, PM-211 B
Washington, DC 20460   (202) 475-7751

Environmental Education Materials For Teachers and Young People is a free annotated list of educational materials on environmental issues. Entries include diverse materials ranging from workbooks and lesson plans to newsletters, films, and computer software intended for young people. Educational materials available from sources other than EPA are listed alphabetically following the name of their sponsoring organization or group. A separate listing of selected EPA publications and other material available from EPA's Public Information Center is included in this pamphlet, as well as a short descriptive list of environmental education resource facilities. Contact this office to order your free copy.

* Evaluation, Standards, and Testing

Center for Research on Evaluation, Standards and Student Testing
Regents of the University of California
Center for the Study of Evaluation
University of California at Los Angeles
Los Angeles, CA 90025   (213) 825-4711

Major research areas include testing for the improvement of learning; systems for evaluating and improving educational quality; the impact of testing and evaluation on educational standards, policy, and practice; and school reform.

* Gifted and Talented National Clearinghouse

ERIC Clearinghouse on Handicapped and Gifted
Children Council for Exceptional Children
1920 Association Dr.
Reston, VA 22091-1589   (703) 620-3660

Subject areas include all aspects of the education and development of handicapped persons, including prevention of handicaps, identification and assessment of handicaps, and intervention and enrichment programs for the handicapped both in special settings and within the mainstream. All aspects of the education and development of gifted persons are also covered.

* Grants for Constitution Curricula

Education Division
Commission on the Bicentennial of the U.S. Constitution
808 17th St., NW, Suite 800
Washington, DC 20006   (202) 653-5110

Two competitions are held annually, in November and May, for educational grants to be awarded for the further study of the U.S. Constitution. The Commission invites proposals for projects designed to provide elementary and secondary school students with a strengthened understanding of the Constitution and Bill of Rights. Proposals should demonstrate how students will benefit and should result in instructional ideas, methods, and materials that teachers can share with others. For May, 1990 projects proposals, the focus should center on the study of the judicial branch and its historical development. In the 1990-1991 school year, the focus should be on the Bill of Rights and the subsequent amendments. The Commission accepts applications from and awards grants to local educational agencies, private elementary and secondary schools, private organizations, individuals, and state and local public agencies in the United States. Colleges, universities, and adult education programs within the above categories are eligible to apply provided that the proposed project or program is designed principally to benefit elementary and secondary students. Educational organizations concerned with ethnic and minority interests and special groups, such as learning disabled and hearing impaired, are encouraged to apply. Awards will not be given to profit-making organizations. Grants have ranged from $6,500 to $164,000. Contact the office above for a program announcement.

* Head Start Schooling for Low-Income 3-5 Year Olds

Head Start Bureau
U.S. Department of Health and Human Services
P.O. Box 1182
Washington, DC 20013

Project Head Start, a comprehensive child development program, was launched by the Federal Government in 1965 to help young children from low-income families get a better start in life. The education program is administered by the Administration for Children, Youth and Families, Grants are awarded by Health and Human Services Regional Offices to local public agencies and private non-profit organizations for the purpose of operating a Head Start program at the community level. There are special programs for Indian and migrant farmworker children.

* High School and Intercollegiate Debate Topics

Your Congressman's Office

A series of free reports are prepared by the Congressional Research Service of the Library of Congress that contain pertinent excerpts, bibliographic references, and other materials related to debate topics for that year. For high school debate teams, the topics are selected by the National University Extension Service Association, and for college, the topics are selected by the American Speech Association.

* High School Student Pages at U.S. Congress

Page Board
Room H-154, The Capitol
Washington, DC 20515   (202) 225-3505

Being a Page is an opportunity to live in the nation's capitol and see Congress at work. Pages are selected by Representatives and Senators whose seniority permits this privilege. Pages must be at least juniors in high school. They serve principally as messengers carrying documents, letters, and messages between the House and Senate, Members' offices, committees, and the Library of Congress. They also prepare the House and Senate Chambers for each day's business. Pages serve one or two terms of an academic year and also during the summer months. Their tenure depends on ability, conduct, academic performance, and their sponsor's term in office.

* High School Training

Veterans Assistance Office
Department of Veterans Affairs
810 Vermont Ave., NW
Washington, DC 20420   (202) 233-2044

A veteran may pursue high school training or training to pass the GED examination and may receive educational assistance allowance without a charge against basic entitlement. Additional secondary school training, such as refresher courses or deficiency courses, are permitted if needed to qualify for admission to an appropriate educational institution. Contact your VA regional office for more information.

* Historical Pictorial Map Contest

Education Division
Commission on the Bicentennial of the U.S. Constitution
808 17th St., NW
Suite 800
Washington, DC 20006   (202) 653-5109

In this national competition, students are asked to depict, on outline maps, key events significant to the development of early American history from 1607 to 1803. Competitions are held at upper elementary, middle, and high school levels within each congressional district, with winning entries advancing to State and national competition. All entries receive certificates of recognition, and winning schools at each level receive cash awards for the purchase of educational materials. National winners receive a free trip to Washington, D.C., for a special awards ceremony. Contact this office for more information.

* How Our Laws Are Made

Superintendent of Documents
Government Printing Office
Washington, DC 20402   (202) 275-3030

The booklet, How Our Laws Are Made, is prepared by the House of Representatives and provides a plain language explanation of how a legislative idea travels the complex passageways of the federal lawmaking process to become a statute. It is available for $2.50 from the Superintendent of Documents.

* Indian Education

Office of Indian Education
Bureau of Indian Affairs
U.S. Department of the Interior
18th and C Sts., NW
Washington, DC 20240   (202) 343-2175

The Office of Indian Education provides funding for both public and private Indian schools. Also sponsored are adult education classes and college scholarships. To receive information regarding Indian Education statistics and various programs sponsored by the Bureau of Indian Affairs, contact the office above.

* International Youth Exchange

The Bureau of Educational and Cultural Affairs
United States Information Agency
301 Fourth St., SW, Room 357
Washington, DC 20547   (202) 485-7299

This office administers grants to non-profit organizations for international educational and cultural exchanges for youths 15 to 25 years of age. Organizations wishing to become sponsors, or individuals wishing to be put in contact with sponsoring organizations, can receive free information from this office.

* Languages and Linguistics Education Information

ERIC Clearinghouse on Languages and Linguistics
Center for Applied Linguistics
1118 22nd St., NW
Washington, DC 20037-0037   (202) 429-9551

Subject areas cover languages and language sciences; theoretical and applied linguistics; all areas of foreign language, second language and linguistics pedagogy, or methodology; psycholinguistics and the psychology of language learning; cultural and intercultural context of languages; application of linguistics in language teaching; bilingualism and bilingual education; sociolinguistics; study abroad and international exchanges; teacher training and qualifications specific to the teaching of a foreign language and second language; commonly and uncommonly taught languages, including English as a second language; related curriculum developments and problems.

* Literature Education

Center for Learning and Teaching of Literature
State University of New York at Albany
School of Education
1400 Washington Ave.
Albany, NY 12222   (518) 442-5026

Major research areas include current emphases in curriculum and instruction; teaching and learning processes; and assessment.

* NASA Education Workshops for Elementary School Teachers (NEWEST)

Elementary and Secondary Programs Branch

Educational Affairs Division
Mail Code XEE
NASA Headquarters
Washington, DC 20546 (202) 453-8386

NEWEST is for elementary school teachers (grades 1-6) in all disciplines. Selected teachers are awarded a two-week, expense- paid workshop at a NASA field center, with each center hosting about 20 teachers. The workshops vary from center to center. Although all focus on current NASA programs, each center conducts activities unique to its work. During their stay, teachers meet with scientists, technicians, and educational specialists. Teachers are instructed how to apply their experiences to their elementary curriculum.

* NASA Minority Summer High School Apprentice Research Program (SHARP)

Elementary and Secondary Programs Branch
Educational Affairs Division
National Aeronautics and Space Administration
Mail Code XEE
Washington, DC 20546 (202) 453-8386

SHARP provides an opportunity for targeted underrepresented minority students in grades 10-12 who live within commuting distance of a participating NASA field center to take part in an eight-week, paid apprenticeship, where they work directly with NASA scientists or engineers. Interested students submit an application and references from a school administrator, teacher, or guidance counselor. Chosen students work with scientists or engineers whose work is related to his or her career aspirations, which may include computers, research, navigation, or guidance systems.

* Native American Indians

Office of Public Affairs
Bureau of Indian Affairs
U.S. Department of the Interior
18th and C Sts., NW
Washington, DC 20240 (202) 343-1711

The free booklet, *American Indians Today: Answers to Your Questions, 1988*, contains useful information on the Native American Indians and their relationship to the Bureau of Indian Affairs. Programs within the Bureau, including education, health services, and housing are briefly outlined and contain recent statistics. Many questions are answered within the booklet, including the rights of the Indians to own land and have their own governments. A map locates the Indian lands and communities, showing Federal and State Indian Reservations and other Indian groups. An excellent bibliography, prepared by the Smithsonian Institution, is included.

* Natural History Museum Education Program

National Museum of Natural History
Office of Education
Room 212, Mail Stop 158
Washington, D.C. 20560 202-357-2747

The museum has an extensive educational school program with film and workshops available at your school or the museum, including museum lesson tours, the Discovery Room, the Naturalist Center, and instructional kits. A catalog of services can be sent to you. The Office also publishes a quarterly calendar of films and events at the Museum.

* Parent Pamphlets on Student Performance

Consumer Information Center
P.O. Box 100
Pueblo, Colorado 81002

AIDS and the Education of Our Children: A Guide for Parents and Teachers (Free; 507V).
Schools That Work: What Works in Educating Disadvantaged Children (Free, 509V).
Schools Without Drugs (Free:, 510V).
Help Your Child Become a Good Reader ($.50, 411V).
Help Your Child Do Better in School ($.50, 412V).
Help Your Child Improve in Test-Taking ($.50, 413V).
Help Your Child Learn to Write Well ($.50, 415V).

* Plant a Tree for the Bicentennial

Publication Division
Commission on the Bicentennial of the U.S. Constitution
8080 17th St., NW, Suite 800
Washington, DC 20006 (202) 653-9800

The Commission, in cooperation with the United States Department of Agriculture, is encouraging us to plant a tree to commemorate the Bicentennial. The guide, *Plant a Tree for the Bicentennial of the Constitution*, answers many questions concerning where to plant a tree, what type of tree to plant, how the tree should be planted, and the care of the tree. Contact this office for your free copy.

* Presidential Honor Students

White House Commission on Presidential Scholars
U.S Department of Education
Room 2079
400 Maryland Ave., SW
Washington, DC 20202 (202) 732-5113

This annual program honors 141 students chosen among the nation's most outstanding graduating high school seniors. Those students who become Presidential Scholars are chosen on the basis of their accomplishments in many areas--academic and artistic success, demonstrated leadership, and involvement in school and community. The Scholars are given a medallion and are invited to Washington, D.C. where they are honored. There is no monetary award.

* Reading and Communication Skills Information

ERIC Clearinghouse on Reading and Communication Skills
Indiana University
Smith Research Center
2805 East 10th St., Suite 150
Bloomington, IN 47405-2373 (812) 335-5847

Subject areas include reading, English and communication skills (verbal and nonverbal) preschool through college; education research and development in reading, writing, speaking, and listening; identification, diagnosis, and remediation of reading problems; speech communication, mass communication, interpersonal and small group interaction, interpretation, rhetorical and communication theory, instructional development, speech sciences, and theater. Preparation of instructional staff and related personnel in these areas are also covered.

* Reading Is Fundamental

Reading Is Fundamental
600 Maryland Ave., SW, Suite 500
Washington, DC 20024 (202) 287-3220

The RIF Guide to Encouraging Young Readers ($8.95) Hundreds of kid-tested activities designed to engage children from infancy to age 11 in the fun of reading; an annotated reading list of 200 children's books; resource listing of book clubs and magazines, parent's books and concerned organizations.
Children's Bookshelf ($1.00). Annotated list of 106 books organized for four age ranges.
Reading is Fun! ($1.00). Tips for parents to prepare young children for reading.
Books to Grow On ($2.00) Magazine for parents including reading tips and games and puzzles for young readers.
Children Who Can Read, But Don't ($.50) How to help readers aged 9-12 discover the fun of reading.
Choosing Good Books for Children ($.50). Information and resources to help parents find appropriate books for children to age 12.
Encouraging Soon-to-Be Readers ($.50) How to excite preschoolers about books and help them to develop skills that lead to reading.
Magazines and Family Reading ($.50) Ways that magazines can get the whole family turning pages.
Reading Aloud to Your Children ($.50) The why's, when's, where's, what's and how's of reading aloud.
Reading: What's In It for Teenagers/Teenagers and Reading ($.50). Two brochures in one, perforated for parents to keep their half and give the other half to their teenager. *TV and Reading* ($.50). Suggestions to help parents help their children achieve a healthy balance.
Upbeat and Offbeat Activities to Encourage Reading ($.50). Playful projects and activities to help preschoolers and beginning readers build skills.

* Reading Research Center

Reading Research and Education Center
University of Illinois
174 Children's Research Center
51 Gerty Drive Champaign, IL 61820 (217) 333-2552

Major research areas include acquisition of knowledge and skills, instruction in reading, text characteristics, and reading proficiency.

* Rural Education and Small Schools Clearinghouse

ERIC Clearinghouse on Rural Education and Small Schools Appalachia Educational Laboratory, Inc.
1031 Quarrier St.
P.O. Box 1348
Charleston, WV 25325-1348
(304) 347-0400

Subject areas cover economic, cultural, social, or other factors related to education programs and practices for rural residents; American Indians/Alaska Natives, Mexican Americans, and migrants; education practices and programs in all small schools; and outdoor education. This includes programs, practices, and materials that provide learning experiences designed to meet the special needs of rural populations and schools where conditions of smallness are a factor.

* School Administrators and Management Clearinghouse

ERIC Clearinghouse on Educational Management
University of Oregon
1787 Agate St.
Eugene, OR 97403-5207   (503) 686-5043
Subject areas include all aspects of the administration, leadership, finance, governance, and structure of public and private education organizations at the elementary, middle, and secondary levels, including facility planning, design, construction, equipment and furnishing, and maintenance; and pre-service and in-service preparation of administrators. Topics covered include the social, technological, political, and legal contexts of education organizations, and of State and Federal programs and policies, and traditional and alternative schools.

* School Discipline, Phonics and Other Publications

U.S. Department of Education
Office of Educational Research and Improvement
555 New Jersey Ave., NW
Washington, DC 20208-5641
Elementary School Recognition Program (brochure) (PIP 88-821): Describes the program, requirements, characteristics of successful schools and information on how to apply. *Improving School Discipline (IS 88-161).*
Students at Risk (IS 89-540).
Ten Steps to a Successful Magnet Program (OR 88-510).
Ten Ways to Help Your Children Become Better Readers.
What We Know About Phonics (IS 88-163).
Employment Outcomes of Recent Master's and Bachelor's Degree Recipients (CS 88-251).
Students Report Job Success More Important Than Making Money (CS 88-436).
Check This Out Fact Sheet: Literacy for Every Adult Project (LP89-732).
Check This Out Fact Sheet: Read-Aloud Programs for the Elderly (LP 89-731).
Helping Your Child Use the Library (LP 89-712).
Approaches to Drug and Alcohol Abuse (PIP 89-857).
Drug Prevention Curricula: A Guide to Selection and Implementation (PIP 88-835).
Five Tips to Improving Teaching (IS 87-127).
The Impact on Children's Education: TV's Influence on Cognitive Development (OR 88-507).
School Climate and Reading Performance (CS 88-605).
Education Statistics - 1988 Pocket Digest (OERI # 88611, Series: PD-88). Selected key statistics from the Digest of Education.
Pocket Projections, 1977-78 to 1997-98. (OERI No. 88612, Series: PP-88). Pocket-sized pamphlet of projections of key elementary/secondary and higher education statistics.
American Education at a Glance (OERI No. 89618, Series: NA). A variety of charts and tables providing an overview of American education.
Young Adult Literacy and Schooling (OERI No. 88604).
Teacher Incentive Programs in Public Schools (OERI No. 89063, Series: PUP-85).

* Secondary Schools

National Center on Effective Secondary Schools
University of Wisconsin - Madison
1025 West Johnson St.
Madison, WI 53706   (608) 263-7575
Major research areas include a clearinghouse on academic achievement; non-instructional influences on adolescent engagement and achievement; the stratification of learning opportunities in middle and high schools; higher-order thinking in the high school curriculum; programs and policies to serve at risk students; and alternative structures and the quality of teacher worklife.

* Secondary School Teaching

Center for Research on the Context of
Secondary School Teaching
Stanford University - School of Education
CERAS Building
Stanford, CA 94305   (415) 723-4972
Major research areas include conceptualization and development; the relationship of context to school workplace conditions, teaching and student outcomes; state reform and teacher contexts; inner city, high poverty schools; and alternative schools.

* Social Studies and Curriculum Kits

Sir S Documents
Education Branch
National Archives and Records Administration
8th St. & Pennsylvania Ave., NW, Room 505
Washington, DC 20408   (202) 523-3298
A catalog is available which contains supplemental teaching units with primary sources from the National Archives. Each unit is a package of materials that serves as a complete classroom set. A unit contains about 50 reproductions of documents, with some also including cassette tapes. The materials deal with certain key issues of the period, with governmental and political responses to these issues, and with public attitudes. Each unit includes a detailed teachers'

guide containing developmental exercises to help students examine the documents. Each unit costs $35.

* Social Studies/Social Science Education Information

ERIC Clearinghouse on Social Studies/Social
Science Education
Social Studies Development Center
Indiana University
Smith Research Center
2805 East Tenth St., Suite 120
Bloomington, IN 47405-2373   (812) 335-3838
Subject areas include all levels of social science education (history, geography, anthropology, economics, sociology, social psychology, and political science); applications of theory and research to social science education; values education; contribution of social science disciplines; comparative education (K-12); social studies content and curriculum materials on such subjects as law-related education, bias and discrimination, and aging. Subjects also include the humanities (music and art).

* Speakers on the Constitution

Speakers Bureau
Commission on the Bicentennial of the U.S. Constitution
808 17th St., NW, Suite 800
Washington, DC 20006   (202) 653-5331
The Speakers Bureau is a referral service which has over 500 speakers nationwide with expertise on a wide range of topics. Bibliographies, speeches, quotations, and articles on Constitution-related subjects are also available through the Bureau. Contact this office for more information.

* Student Curriculum on the Constitution and Bill of Rights

Education Division
Commission on the Bicentennial of the U.S. Constitution
808 17th St., NW, Suite 800
Washington, DC 20006   (202) 653-5109
Upper elementary, middle, and high school students may participate in an in-depth six-week program that improves their knowledge of the U.S. Constitution, either on a competitive basis or not. In the competitive program, classes participate in congressional hearings and respond to specific questions before panels of actual judges. Competition is held at the congressional district, State, and national levels. In the non-competitive program, entire classes work together, prepare and present statements, and answer questions on constitutional topics before a panel of community representatives acting as congressional committee members. Contact this office for more information on the program.

* Student Essay Contest on the Constitution

Education Division
Commission on the Bicentennial of the U.S. Constitution
808 17th St., NW, Suite 800
Washington, DC 20006   (202) 653-5109
In cooperation with the Daughters of the American Revolution, an essay contest is held during Constitution Week of each year. Eleventh and twelfth graders can participate at the state and national levels. The deadline is mid-January. Winners are given a trip to Washington, D.C. For information on essay contest entry and qualifications, contact your local chapter of the DAR.

* Students with Handicaps National Clearinghouse

ERIC Clearinghouse on Handicapped and Gifted
Children Council for Exceptional Children
1920 Association Dr.
Reston, VA 22091-1589   (703) 620-3660
Subject areas include all aspects of the education and development of handicapped persons, including prevention of handicaps, identification and assessment of handicaps, and intervention and enrichment programs for the handicapped both in special settings and within the mainstream. All aspects of the education and development of gifted persons are also covered.

* Teacher Education Clearinghouse

ERIC Clearinghouse on Teacher Education
American Association of Colleges for Teacher
Education (AACTE)
One Dupont Circle, NW, Suite 610
Washington, DC 20036-2412   (202) 293-2450
Subject areas cover school personnel at all levels; teacher selection and training; pre-service and in-service preparation and retirement; the theory, philosophy, and practice of teaching; curricula and general education not specifically covered by other clearinghouses. Also included are all aspects of physical education, health, dance, and recreation education.

* Teacher Education Research

National Center for Research on Teacher Education
College of Education
Michigan State University
Erickson Hall
East Lansing, MI 48824-1034   (517) 355-9302

Major research areas include program purposes, character, and quality; teacher learning; instrument development; and information distribution.

* Teaching Materials on the Constitution

Center for Research and Development
in Law-Related Education (CRADLE)
Wake Forest University School of Law
P.O. Box 7206, Reynolds Station
Winston-Salem, NC 27109   (919) 761-5872

The Commission on the Bicentennial of the U.S. Constitution, in conjunction with Wake Forest University, makes available a national repository of teaching materials about the Constitution. Primarily on the Law and the Constitution, the resources are written for use by teachers from pre-kindergarten through 12th grades. Write for a free catalog.

* Teacher's Guide to Selective Service Registration

Public Affairs
Selective Service System
1023 31st St., NW
Washington, DC 20435   (202) 724-0790

A Teacher's Guide to Selective Service Registration is designed to assist teachers in their preparation of lessons covering the Selective Service System and describes the purpose, history, organization, and function of the System. With a summary of important teaching points, and questions and answers at the end of each chapter, this guide assists teachers in teaching their students about the Selective Service System. For additional information, contact this office.

* Testing Educational Achievement

National Assessment of Educational Progress
Educational Testing Service
P.O. Box 2923
Princeton, NJ 08541   (800) 223-0267

NAEP surveys the educational achievement of 9-year-olds, 13-year-olds, 17-year-olds, and at grades 4, 8, and 12, and periodically, young adults. The surveys are conducted in such areas as art, career and occupational development, citizenship, literature, mathematics, music, reading, science, social studies, and writing. Different learning areas are assessed every two years, and all areas are periodically reassessed to measure changes in educational achievement. A publications brochure is available through this office, and surveys may be purchased. Below is a sampling of other publications available through NAEP:

Reading Objectives: 1986 and 1988 ($5.00)
Writing Objectives: 1988 ($5.00)
Literature and U.S. History: The Instructional Experience and Factual Knowledge of High School Juniors ($8.50)
Who Reads Best? Factors Relating to Reading Achievements: Grades 3, 7 and 11. ($11.00)
Computer Competence: The First National Assessment ($12.50)
The Mathematics Report: Are We Measuring Up? (12.50)
The Science Report Card: Elements of Risk and Recovery ($14.00) An Executive

Summary to the Math Report Card (Free)
Science Learning Matters: An Interpretive Overview to the Science Report Card (Free)

* Tests, Measurement, and Evaluation Clearinghouse

ERIC Clearinghouse on Tests, Measurement, and Evaluation
American Institutes for Research
Washington Research Center
3333 K St., NW
Washington, DC 20007-3893   (202) 342-5060

Subject areas include the assessment and evaluation of education projects or programs; tests and other measurement devices; methodology of measurement and evaluation; research design and methodology; human development; and learning theory in general.

* Urban Community Enrichment Program

Elementary and Secondary Programs Branch
Educational Affairs Division
Mail Code XEE
NASA Headquarters
Washington, DC 20546   (202) 453-8386

UCEP is specifically targeted toward middle-school students in urban areas with high percentages of minorities. NASA specialists will meet with school representatives to formulate a custom-tailored program to fit the school's needs. Typically a program begins with teacher orientation workshops followed by assemblies, a series of student workshops, and classroom visits. In the classroom, NASA specialists work with students on various hands-on activities, such as building rockets or airplanes or learning about how information is transmitted from space back to Earth.

* Urban Education Clearinghouse

ERIC Clearinghouse on Urban Education
Teachers College
Columbia University Institute for Urban
and Minority Education
Main Hall, Room 303, Box 40
525 West 120th St.
New York, NY 10027-9998   (212) 678-3433

Subject areas include programs and practices in schools in urban areas and the education of racial/ethnic minority children and youth in various settings--local, national, and international; the theory and practice of education equity; urban and minority experiences; and urban and minority social institutions and services.

* Writing Skills: Students and Instructors

Center for the Study of Writing
School of Education
University of California at Berkeley
Berkeley, CA 94720   (415) 643-7022

Major research areas include writing and the writer; writing and instruction; interactions: writing and reading, writing and speaking, and writing and computers.

College and Continuing Education

* Adult and Vocational Curriculum National Network

National Network for Curriculum Coordination
in Vocational and Technical Education
Office of Vocational and Adult Education

The six coordination centers provide leadership in curriculum coordination activities and offer a variety of curriculum-related activities, which include collecting and distributing curriculum information and products and assisting individuals, schools, and groups in addressing and resolving problems.

Western Curriculum Coordination Center, College of Education, University of Hawaii, 1776 University Ave., Wist. 216 Honolulu, HI 96822, (808) 948-7834. Serving: American Samoa, Arizona, California, Guam, Hawaii, Nevada, and Trust Territory Government of Northern Marianas.

East Central Curriculum Coordination Center, Sangamon State, University, F-2, Springfield, IL 62708, (217) 786-6375. Serving: Delaware, District of Columbia, Indiana, Illinois, Maryland, Michigan, Minnesota, Ohio, Pennsylvania, Virginia, West Virginia, and Wisconsin.

Southeast Curriculum Coordination Center, Mississippi State University, Research and Curriculum Unit, P.O. Drawer DX, Mississippi State, MS 39762, (601) 325-2510. Serving: Alabama, Florida, Georgia, Kentucky, Mississippi, North Carolina, South Carolina, and Tennessee.

Northeast Curriculum Coordination Center, New Jersey Vocational Education Resource Center, Rutgers University, Crest Way, Aberdeen, NJ 07747, (201) 290-1900. Serving: Connecticut, Maine, Massachusetts, New Hampshire, New Jersey, New York, Puerto Rico, Rhode Island, Vermont, and Virgin Islands.

Mideast Curriculum Coordination Center, State Department of Vocational and Technical Education, 1500 West Seventh Ave., Stillwater, OK 74074-4364, (405) 377-2000, Ext.252. Serving: Arkansas, Iowa, Kansas, Louisiana, Missouri, Nebraska, New Mexico, Oklahoma, and Texas.

Northwestern Curriculum Coordination Center, St. Martin's College Old Main, Room 478, Lacey, WA 98503, (206) 438-4456. Serving: Alaska, Colorado, Idaho, Montana, North Dakota, Oregon, South Dakota, Utah, Washington, and Wyoming.

* Adult Continuing Education Clearinghouse

ERIC Clearinghouse on Adult, Career and
and Vocational Education
Ohio State University Center on Education and
Training for Employment
1960 Kenny Rd.
Columbus, OH 43210-1090   (800) 848-4815 (614) 292-4353

Subject areas cover all levels of adult and continuing education from basic literacy training through professional skill upgrading; vocational and technical education covering all service areas for secondary, postsecondary, and adult education populations; career education and career development programs for all ages and populations in educational, institutional, business, and industrial settings.

* Adult Education on the Constitution

Education Division
Commission on the Bicentennial of the U.S. Constitution
808 17th St., NW, Suite 800
Washington, DC 20006   (202) 653-5109

The Commission is funding the development of specially designed and easily read adult education materials on the U.S. Constitution. These materials consist of four discussion-based modules on aspects of the Constitution, a *Discussion Leader's Guide and Handbook*, a *Supplementary Guide for Tutors of the Functionally Illiterate*, and an introductory video. Contact this office for more information.

* Adult Educators

Clearinghouse on Adult Education
U.S. Department of Education
Office of Vocational and Adult Education
330 C St., SW
Washington, DC 20202   (202) 732-2396

This clearinghouse links the adult education community with existing resources in adult education. The Bibliography of Resource Materials provides a complete list of materials available from the clearinghouse. Examples include a directory of adult education-related programs, fact sheets on such topics as literacy and disabled adults, and materials concerning English as a second language.

* American and Foreign Teachers Exchange Program

Office of Academic Programs
United States Information Agency
301 Fourth St., SW, Room 353
Washington, DC 20547   (202) 485-2555

The Advising, Teaching, and Specialized Programs Division serves overseas education advising centers, foreign exchange students in the U.S., and administers the International Student Exchange Program for one-to-one exchange of university students. Its Teacher Exchange Branch arranges one and two way exchanges of U.S. and foreign teachers, and summer seminars for U.S. teachers to study abroad. Free brochures and applications are available.

* American Educators Teaching Abroad

Superintendent of Documents
Government Printing Office
Washington, DC 20402   (202) 783-3238

The United States Information Agency publishes many teaching materials, including books, maps, complete teaching modules, and 14 magazines in 20 languages. By law most USIA publications may be distributed only in foreign countries. However, by congressional action, two magazines are available in the United States. *English Teaching Forum*, a quarterly for English teachers worldwide, is published by USIA's English Language Programs Division. *Problems of Communism* is a bi-monthly forum for American and foreign scholars discussing communist and socialist affairs. It is published in English and Spanish. Both these magazines are available through the GPO.

* Bicentennial Campus Program

Education Division
Commission on the Bicentennial of the U.S. Constitution
808 17th St., NW, Suite 800
Washington, DC 20006   (202) 653-5109

All post-secondary institutions are eligible for this campus program. To participate, an institution must establish a Bicentennial Committee broadly representative of the campus community. It must also sponsor Bicentennial activities through 1991 and be approved, in some cases, by its state Bicentennial Commission. Among the wide range of activities sponsored on campuses are seminars, conferences, film series, lecture series, speakers, and essay contests. Through these activities, a campus is designated a Bicentennial Campus. Contact this office for more information.

* Black Universities and Agricultural Sciences

Special Advisor to the Deputy Secretary
Agricultural Stabilization and Conservation Service
P.O. Box 2415
Washington, DC 20013   (202) 447-4797

The USDA has a unique relationship with 17 historically black universities that began in 1890 when these schools were designated by Congress as Land-Grant Institutions. In 1988 a symposium was sponsored by USDA at one of these institutions to re-examine the partnership between USDA and the universities. Work is underway on a number of recommendations that came from this conference:

- Programs of financial assistance are being developed to help minorities through college.
- Liaison officers are working at each school to recruit students into the agricultural sciences and from there into careers at USDA.
- A marketing program is being developed for careers in agriculture and home economics and for educational opportunities at the 1990's.
- A K-12 career awareness initiative program is underway in food and agricultural sciences.
- More than 400 summer jobs were created around the country in the agricultural sciences for students.
- Partnerships between predominantly white land-grant institutions and the historically black schools.
- A program is being developed to work with the agricultural high schools in areas of higher education and career development.

* Career Education

ERIC Clearinghouse on Adult, Career and
and Vocational Education

Ohio State University Center on Education and
Training for Employment
1960 Kenny Rd.
Columbus, OH 43210-1090   (800) 848-4815 (614) 292-4353
Subject areas cover all levels of adult and continuing education from basic literacy training through professional skill upgrading; vocational and technical education covering all service areas for secondary, postsecondary, and adult education populations; career education and career development programs for all ages and populations in educational, institutional, business, and industrial settings.

* College-Community Forums

Education Division
Commission on the Bicentennial of the U.S. Constitution
808 17th St., NW, Suite 800
Washington, DC 20006   (202) 653-5109
Community-college forums are designed to engage college faculty, community leaders, and citizens in public discussion of constitutional issues and provide them with a better understanding of the history and principles of the U.S. Constitution. Forum programs take place on college campuses, in town libraries, civic centers, or other public places and are supported in part by Commission funding. Participants are supplied booklets discussing the topics with background information to provide a focus for discussion. The Commission also provides a handbook offering suggestions for the arrangements at such events.

* Community-College Environmental Curricula Grants

National Workforce Development Staff
Office of Research and Development
Environmental Protection Agency
401 M St., SW, Room NE312
Washington DC 20460   (202) 382-2573
The National Workforce Development Staff awards money to community colleges to support the development of environment-related curriculum, allowing these colleges to then train State employees. The office also awards fellowships to State employees to continue their education concerning the environment. The fellowship applications are given out through the individual States. Contact this office for more information.

* College Courses

Information Office
U.S. Department of Agriculture Graduate School
Capital Gallery Building
600 Maryland Ave. S.W., Room 129
Washington, DC 20024   (202) 447-4419
The USDA Graduate School, which is open to the public, offers college courses on nonagricultural subjects at reasonable prices.
Although the school does not grant degrees, college credits are awarded and can be transferred to other universities. Some lectures are available on film, videotape, and in manuscript form.

* Cooperative Education Program

Personnel Policy and Work Force
Effectiveness Division
Mail Code NPM
NASA Headquarters
Washington, DC 20546   (202) 453-2603
CEP gives high school, college, and graduate students an opportunity to work at a NASA field center while completing their education. Participating students usually alternate working one semester with studying one semester. In addition to job experience, the program also serves as a recruitment tool. Interested students must be attending school, be enrolled in their school's coop program, maintain at least a 2.0 overall grade point average, and be recommended by the school. Each NASA field center negotiates its own cooperative agreements with school in its geographic area, and it is usually the responsibility of a school to initiate the venture.

* Cultural and Educational International Exchange

Office of Public Liaison
United States Information Agency
301 Fourth St., SW, Room 602
Washington, DC 20547   (202) 485-2355
The USIA distributes the free *Directory of Resources for Cultural and Educational Exchanges and U.S. Information*, a treasure trove of information on cultural and educational exchange programs in the U.S. The directory provides contacts and background information of government agencies and non-profit and private organizations which sponsor exchange programs.

* Fellowships: Latin America

Inter-American Fellowship Programs
P.O. Box 9486

Arlington, VA 22209-0486   (703) 841-3800
This grant program stresses practical solutions to obstacles in grassroots development by fostering increased attention within the academic community on micro-level development in Latin America and the Caribbean. Part of the fellowships go to scholars and professionals from research and development institutions in Latin America and the Caribbean whose work would benefit from graduate-level study at U.S. universities, while other fellowships go to doctoral candidates and master's-level students enrolled in U.S. universities to conduct field research in Latin America or the Caribbean.

* Foreign Exchange Students and Agriculture

Office of International Cooperation,
International Training Division
U.S. Department of Agriculture
2121 K St., NW, Room 201
Washington, DC 20250-4300   (202) 653-8320
Students from developing countries can obtain assistance in identifying where to train in agriculture in the U.S. and in other countries.

* Foreign Language Training

Defense Language Institute
Foreign Language Center
Non-Resident Division
Presidio of Monterey, CA 93944   (408) 647-5000
The Defense Language Institute is one of the world's largest language training centers. The holdings of its library--over 100,000 books in 50 languages--are available through a national inter-library loan program. The non-resident division offers foreign language courses for sale. A catalog of the languages available may be obtained for $5.25. Write or call for brochures on the Institute and information regarding inter-library loans.

* Foreign Student Support Services

Advising, Teaching, and Specialized Programs Division
Office of Academic Programs
Bureau of Educational and Cultural Affairs
United States Information Agency
301 Fourth St., SW, Room 349
Washington, DC 20547   (202) 485-7434
USIA develops a variety of programs to aid foreign students in the United States. Free information is available.

* Foreign Training for Veterans, Inservice Students and Eligible Dependents

Veterans Assistance Office
Department of Veterans Affairs
810 Vermont Ave., NW
Washington, DC 20420   (202) 233-2044
The pamphlet, *Foreign Training for Veterans, Inservice Students and Eligible Dependents*, provides general information about the approval of courses at foreign schools. It also provides specific information for veterans, inservice students and dependents planning to pursue training at a foreign school. This pamphlet lists those foreign schools which offer at least one course approved for training. Note, however, that not all the courses at a listed school are necessarily approved for training. Please read the pamphlet carefully. It is available from your regional VA office.

* Fulbright Foreign Studies Scholarships

Office of Academic Programs
The Bureau of Educational and Cultural Affairs
United States Information Agency
301 Fourth St., SW, Room 234
Washington, DC 20547   (202) 485-7360
This office develops and runs all academic programs of USIA, including the best-known educational exchange, the Fulbright Scholarship program. About 5,000 Fulbright grants are awarded each year to American students, teachers, and scholars to work abroad and to foreign citizens to teach, study, and conduct research in the U.S. In addition to the Fulbright program, the Academic Exchange Programs Division of this office administers grants to private agencies conducting complementary programs to the Fulbright academic exchanges, and has responsibilities for foreign research centers, Fulbright commissions, and seminars for foreign Fulbright students. Contact this office for more information and application forms for the Fulbright program.

* Health Care Training Programs

Academic Affairs
Veterans Health Services and Research Administration
Department of Veterans Affairs
810 Vermont Ave., NW, Room 876
Washington, DC 20420   (202) 233-5094

The DVA has over 2,000 training relationships between VA health care facilities and schools of medicines, dentistry, nursing, pharmacy, social work, and other allied health professions and occupations at the graduate and undergraduate levels. For more information contact the office above.

* Health Professional Scholarship Program

Associated Health Professions
Education Programs Services
Veterans Health Services and Research Administration
Department of Veterans Affairs
810 Vermont Ave., NW, Room 878
Washington, DC 20420   (202) 233-3588

The VA Health Professional Scholarship Program assists in the recruitment of health professionals in the VA health care system. In return for scholarship support while in college, participants agree to serve a minimum of one year in VA medical centers in the discipline for which degree was awarded. For more information, contact the office above.

* Higher Education Clearinghouse

ERIC Clearinghouse on Higher Education
George Washington University
One Dupont Circle
Washington, DC 20036-1183   (202) 296-2597

Subject areas cover education beyond the secondary level that leads to a four-year, masters, doctoral, or professional degree and includes courses and programs designed to enhance or update skills obtained in these degree programs. Also included are student programs, conditions, and problems at colleges and universities. Other areas include academic advising, university and college faculty; graduate and professional education; professional continuing education; governance and management of higher education institutions; legal issues and legislation; financing; planning and evaluation; facilities--their structural design, management implications, curriculum and instructional problems, programs, and development; and business or industry education programs leading to a degree.

* Higher Education Partnerships

Higher Education Programs
Room 350 A, Administration Building
U.S. Department of Agriculture
Washington, DC 20250   (202) 447-7854

In order to maintain superior scientific and professional expertise in the food and agricultural sciences, higher education must make major shifts in such areas as instructional emphasis, faculty competencies, and scientific instrumentation. Working with colleges and universities, business, and industry, USDA's Higher Education Program (HEP) has initiated several national projects aimed at federal-state and public-private partnerships;
assessing competencies needed by scientists; revitalizing curricula; improving faculty development programs; strengthening industry-academia networks to stimulate outstanding students; developing student recruitment programs; and gathering manpower supply-demand statistics and career information.

* Higher Education Programs

Higher Education Programs
Room 350 A Administration Building
U.S. Department of Agriculture
Washington, DC 20250   (202) 447-7854

Although the USDA does not make individual loans or scholarships to students, it does makes grants to universities to carry out various programs. For information on individual monetary awards, contact your local cooperative extension agent. The USDA administers the following programs:

Morrill-Nelson Formula Grants: Land-grant institutions use Morrill-Nelson funds to support faculty salaries, curriculum development, and other instructional operating costs. All food and agricultural sciences resident instruction programs at land-grant institutions are eligible for this support. The current annual appropriation is $2.8 million--$50,000 per school.

Food and Agricultural Sciences National Needs Graduate Fellowship Grants: This program consists of competitive institutional grants to recruit and support new graduate students in areas with shortages of expertise in biotechnology, agricultural engineering, food and agricultural marketing, food science, and human nutrition. The fellowship program is a national investment strategy to attract outstanding students to pursue advanced degrees in food and agricultural sciences. Institutions with Master's or doctoral programs in these fields are eligible to participate.

* International Auditor Fellowship Program

Director
Office of International Audit Organization Liaison
General Accounting Office
441 G St., NW, Room 7806

Washington, DC 20548   (202) 275-4707

GAO attempts to share its knowledge and experience with other nations, particularly from the developing world. The most visible effort is the Comptroller General's International Auditor Fellowship Program, established in 1979, through which a small number of auditors from developing countries are selected annually to spend three to six months in an academic and on-the-job experience program in the U.S. Although GAO cannot pay travel and subsistence for the Fellows, it provides the training itself at no cost, and assists many participants in obtaining financial aid from the U.S. Agency for International Development, and the United Nations Development Program, and Fellows are increasingly receiving aid from their own governments. This is GAO's lead office in dealing with representatives of international audit organizations, and those of individual foreign governments.

* Junior Colleges Clearinghouse

ERIC Clearinghouse on Junior Colleges
University of California at Los Angeles
Mathematical Sciences Building, Room 8118
405 Hilgard Ave.
Los Angeles, CA 90024-1564   (213) 825-3931

Subject areas include the development, administration, and evaluation of two-year public and private community and junior colleges, technical institutes, and two-year branch university campuses. This covers the organization, administration, finance, governance, role and mission, and futures of such institutions; staff preparation, development, and evaluation; curricula and program; teaching methods; student services; libraries and learning resource centers; and methodologies of research applied to two-year colleges.

* Land-Grant Colleges

Extension Service Information Office
U.S. Department of Agriculture
Room 3328 S
Washington, DC 20250   (202) 447-3029

Congress originally mandated that federal funds be used to support a college or university in each state in 1862, which established the land-grant college network. In 1890 additional legislation was passed to include 17 traditionally black institutions. Today, a large variety of initiatives are taking place at these institutions aimed at building and improving programs to educate students in the agricultural sciences. Cooperative Extension Offices, which provide practical education and information to scientists, researchers, farmers, as well as the general public, are located at each land-grant institution. Liaison work with educational, research, government, business, and public and private organizations is conducted. The state agricultural experiment stations--located at the land grant institutions--conduct agricultural research geared at critical state, regional, and national issues.

* Lunar Samples for University Educators

Johnson Space Center
Curator's Office, Code SN2
Houston, TX 77058

Under the Thin Section Program a set of lunar thin sections is available for instructive and study purposes by college and university science instructors. The materials consist of twelve samples of lunar soils and rocks and a description booklet. Contact this office for information on participating in this program.

* NASA University Programs Branch

Educational Affairs Division
Mail Code XEU
NASA Headquarters
Washington, DC 20546   (202) 453-8344

This program awards grants to graduate students on a competitive basis whose research interests are compatible with NASA research programs. Fellowships are for one year and are renewable, based on progress reports, of up to three years. The fellowships also allow students to carry out a plan of study or research at their home university, but those awarded by NASA field centers require fellows to spend some time at the center, usually from a few weeks to a summer each year.

* Postsecondary Education National Center

National Center for Research to
Improve Postsecondary Teaching and Learning
School of Education
University of Michigan
Ann Arbor, MI 48198-1259   (313) 936-2741

Major research areas include classroom teaching and learning strategies; curricular design: influences and impact; faculty as a key resource; organizational context for teaching and learning; learning, teaching and technology; research leadership, and design and integration.

* Postsecondary School Administration

Center for Postsecondary Governance and Finance
University of Maryland
College of Education, Room 4114
CSS Building
College Park, MD 20742-2435
Major research areas cover the examination of postsecondary education finance and governance.

* Resident Research Associate Program

University Programs Branch
Educational Affairs Division
Mail Code XEU
NASA Headquarters
Washington, DC 20546   (202) 453-8344

This program gives postdoctoral scientists and engineers an opportunity to perform research at specified NASA field centers, working full time on the research that their award is based on and must be in residence at the sponsoring field center during the entire associateship. Awardees must hold a PhD, ScD, or other earned research doctoral degree recognized in U.S. academic circles as equivalent to the PhD, and must also demonstrate superior ability for creative research.

* Sea-Grant Colleges

Office of Oceanic Research Programs
National Oceanic and Atmospheric Administration
Department of Commerce
1335 East-West Hwy.
Silver Spring, MD 20910   (202) 377-8090

The National Sea Grant College Program is a national network of over 300 colleges, universities, research institutions, and consortia working in partnership with industry and the federal government to support Great Lakes and marine research, education, and extension services. This program provides support for institutions engaged in comprehensive marine research, education, and advisory service programs, supports individual projects in marine research and development, and sponsors education of ocean scientists and engineers, marine technicians, and other specialists at selected colleges and universities.

* Service Academy Appointments

For those seeking appointments to the service academies, it is necessary to write your U.S. Senator or Representative for a recommendation. Call the Capitol switchboard to reach your Member of Congress at (202) 224-3121.

* State Clearinghouses for Adult Education

The following are sources of adult information at the state level:
Comprehensive Adult Student Assessment System, 2725 Congress St., Suite 1-M, San Diego, CA 92110 (619) 230-2975

Dissemination Network for Adult Educators, 1575 Old Bayshore Highway, Burlingame, CA 94010, (800) 672-2494 (in CA), (415) 692-2956 This network provides information, in-service training, and technical assistance to adult educators. A bi-monthly publication, Network News, is available free of charge.

Connecticut Adult Education Staff Development Center, 64 St. James St., West Hartford, CT 06119, (203) 233-8001 The center provides adult educators with comprehensive professional development services, access to the Adult Education Resource Library collection of over 8,500 materials, technical assistance, and information distribution.

ACE Staff Development Network of Delaware, International Reading Association, 800 Barksdale Rd., P.O. Box 8139, Newark, DE 19714-8139, (302) 731-1600.

Northern Area Adult Education Service Center, Northern Illinois University, Gabel Hall, Room 200, DeKalb, IL 60115, (815) 753-1441.

Central Illinois Adult Education Service Center, Regional Office of Education, 200 South Frederick St., Rantoul, IL 61866, (217) 893-9696.

Southern Illinois Adult Education Service Center, Southern Illinois University, Building 3, 0147, Edwardsville, IL 62026, (618) 692-2254.

Indiana Adult Education Resource Center, 3725 N. Mitthoeffer Rd., Indianapolis, IN 46236, (317) 899-0822.

Adult Resource Center, Independence Community College, 217 West Main, Independence, KS 67301, (316) 331-4420.

Central Kansas Resource Center, USD #373, 725 Main, Newton, KS 67114, (316) 283-0957.

Adult Education Center, 422 South Main, Ottawa, KS 66067, (913) 242-6719.

Adult Resource Center, 1201 First Ave., Dodge City, KS 67801, (316) 225-0186.

Kentucky Heartland Adult Resource Center, 110 South Main St., Elizabethtown, KY 42701, (502) 737-0452.

Adult Education Program Resource Center, Worcester State College, 486 Chandler St., Worcester, MA 01602, (617) 793-8157.

The Center for Adult Learning and Literacy, Ronan Hall, 251 Central, Michigan University, Mount Pleasant, MI 48859, (517) 774-6793.

University of Southern Mississippi, Adult Education Clearinghouse, Southern Station 5154, Hattiesburg, MS 39406, (601) 266-4621

Lifelong Learning Resource Network, College of Education, Montana State University, Bozeman, MT 59717, (406) 994-4731.

Adult Education Resource Center, Glassboro State College, 307 Girard Rd., Glassboro, NJ 08028, (609) 863-7131.

Adult Education Resource Center, Jersey City State College, Jersey City, NJ 07305, (201) 547-3101.

Community and Continuing Education Information Service, The New York State Education Department, Albany, NY 12234, (518) 474-3639.

Literacy Assistance Center, Inc., 15 Dutch St., 4th Floor, New York, NY 10038, (212) 267-5309.

Statewide Adult Education Resource Center, 222 West Bowen, Bismarck, ND 58504, (701) 221-3790.

Advance Pennsylvania Department of Education, Resource Center, 333 Market St., 11th Floor, Harrisburg, PA 17126-0333, (717) 783-9192.

Trends Austin Community College, P.O. Box 2285, Austin, TX 78768, (512) 472-1387.

Vermont Educational Resource Center, Department of Education, 120 State St., Montpelier, VT 05602, (802) 828-3352.

Virginia Adult Basic Education Resource Center, Room 4065, Oliver Hall, 1015 W. Main St., Box 2020, Richmond, VA 23284-2020, (800) 237-0178; or (804) 367-6521.

West Virginia Vocational Curriculum Laboratory, Cedar Lakes Conference Center, Ripley, WV 25271, (800) 982-5627.

* Veterans Continuing Education

Continuing Education Service
Academic Affairs
Veterans Health Services and Research Administration
Department of Veterans Affairs
810 Vermont Ave., NW, Room 875E
Washington, DC 20420   (202) 233-5183

The DVA conducts system-wide continuing education programs to bring the latest in scientific, medical and management knowledge to VHS&RA employees. These programs include workshops, seminars and individual training, and all forms of audiovisual, print, and transmission media. Contact the office above for more information.

* Vocational Education Clearinghouse

ERIC Clearinghouse on Adult, Career and
and Vocational Education
Ohio State University Center on Education and
Training for Employment
1960 Kenny Rd.
Columbus, OH 43210-1090   (800) 848-4815 (614) 292-4353

Subject areas cover all levels of adult and continuing education from basic literacy training through professional skill upgrading; vocational and technical education covering all service areas for secondary, postsecondary, and adult education populations; career education and career development programs for all ages and populations in educational, institutional, business, and industrial settings.

* Vocational Education Research

National Center Clearinghouse
National Center for Research in Vocational Education
Graduate School of Education, Tolman Hall
University of California
Berkeley, CA 94720   (415) 642-4004

This clearinghouse identifies all vocational education improvement projects and maintains a database listing the projects. They also maintain a database describing vocational education curriculum materials and monitor the development of military technical training materials and determine their transferability to civilian technical training institutions.

* White House Fellowship Program
President's Commission on White House Fellowships
712 Jackson Place, NW
Washington, DC 20503   (202) 395-4522

The White House Fellowship program is a highly competitive opportunity to participate in and learn about the Federal government from a unique perspective. For one year, 11 to 19 Fellows are selected to work in the Executive Office of the President or in an Executive Branch department or agency. The qualities being sought are high levels of achievement, demonstrated leadership, commitment to serve others, and the skill which would make one a good special assistant in the

short run and a national leader in the long run. Although there is no age limit, the program is designed to encourage future leaders rather than reward established leaders. For further information, contact the above office.

* Workplace Safety and Health Courses
Division of Training and Manpower Development
National Institute for Occupational Safety and health
4676 Columbia Parkway
Cincinnati, OH 45226   (513) 533-8221

This division offers courses for industry and health care professional on such topics as occupational safety, industrial hygiene, and safety in the laboratory. For a course listing and description, contact this office.

Science Teachers and Students

* Aerospace Education

National Headquarters
Civil Air Patrol
Maxwell AFB, AL 36112-5572   (205) 293-5463

The Civil Air Patrol (CAP), the civilian auxiliary of the U.S. Air Force, offers workshops, materials, and programs for all grade levels, from kindergarten through the postgraduate level. Resources include activity books, posters, guides to aerospace education and careers, textbooks for one-year high school elective courses in aerospace, and a guide to additional educational resources available from the Department of Defense that includes resources available from military installations, the Air National Guard, Air Force Recruiting Services, military museums, and other sites.

* Aerospace Education Services Program

Elementary and Secondary Programs Branch
Educational Affairs Division
Mail Code XEE
NASA Headquarters
Washington, DC 20546   (202) 453-8386

Under AESP, previously known as Spacemobile, specialists, all former teachers themselves, reach millions of students each year as they cross the county from September to June each year, assisting school so students and teachers can see first-hand what NASA is all about. Visits are scheduled by NASA field centers, and all cover the principles of rocketry, living and working in space, aeronautics, space science, and NASA's history and accomplishments. Schools are encouraged to arrange for an in- service workshop for teachers, which will be conducted at the school by an AESP specialist prior to the visit.

* Aerospace Software Directory

Educational Technology Branch
Educational Affairs Division
Mail Code XE
NASA Headquarters
Washington, DC 20546   (202) 453-8388

The Aerospace Software Directory, a survey of all commercially available aerospace-related software, is available for download via Spacelink and at NASA Teacher Resource Centers. The current directory contains information on more than 75 software packages and how to obtain them. An updated directory containing more than 200 packages will soon be available and updated regularly.

* Aviation and Space Science Instruction

Aviation Education Officer
Federal Aviation Administration
Department of Transportation
800 Independence Ave., SW
Washington, DC 20591

The FAA's Aviation Education Program offers volunteer assistance to the nation's schools through the following programs: career guidance; tours of airports, control towers, and other facilities; classroom lectures and demonstrations; aviation safety information; aviation education resource materials; computerized clearinghouse of aviation and space information; aviation science instruction programs for home/school computers; "Partnerships-in-Education" activities; and teachers' workshops. Write to the above office for more information.

* Aviation Materials for Educators

Office of Public Affairs
Federal Aviation Administration
Aviation Education Program
800 Independence Ave., SW
Washington, DC 20591   (202) 366-4000

The Federal Aviation Administration (FAA), as part of its effort to promote better understanding of aviation and air transportation, offers educational materials and publications to both teachers and students. These include instructional materials, films, aviation career information, historical publications, and a guide to additional materials from other sources.

* Challenger Center for Space Science Education

Challenger Center for Space Science Education
1101 King Street, Suite 190
Alexandria, VA 22314   (703) 683-9740

The Challenger Center is a privately funded, nonprofit organization founded as a living memorial to the Challenger crew by stimulating space-related education. The center plans to construct a series of simulated space environment centers linked to museums, science centers, and school districts throughout the world through a comprehensive, international endowment campaign. The first center, the Challenger Center Space-Life Station, will be built in the Washington, D.C., area, and will serve as headquarters for the network. An educator membership is available that includes a journal, newsletter, updates, and conference information.

* Community Involvement Program

Elementary and Secondary Programs Branch
Educational AFfairs Division
Mail Code XEE
NASA Headquarters
Washington, DC 20546   (202) 453-8386

Through a series of meetings, NASA staff members and community educators custom-tailor each Community Involvement Program to match the community where it is held. A typical CIP might include school assemblies, teacher workshops, a visit by an astronaut, exhibits in shopping centers and schools, presentations by NASA scientists, competitions for students, and public events.

* Cooperative Education Program

Personnel Policy and Work Force
Effectiveness Division
Mail Code NPM
NASA Headquarters
Washington, DC 20546   (202) 453-2603

CEP gives high school, college, and graduate students an opportunity to work at a NASA field center while completing their education. Participating students usually alternate working one semester with studying one semester. In addition to job experience, the program also serves as a recruitment tool. Interested students must be attending school, be enrolled in their school's coop program, maintain at least a 2.0 overall grade point average, and be recommended by the school. Each NASA field center negotiates its own cooperative agreements with school in its geographic area, and it is usually the responsibility of a school to initiate the venture.

* Educational Publications Directory

U.S. Government Printing Office
Washington, DC 20401   (202) 783-3238

The Educational Affairs Division of NASA produces an annual directory of educational and technical publications that can be purchased through the GPO. It contains ordering information and order forms, but does not include publications available from NASA field centers, a listing of which is available from the Teacher Resource Center serving your geographic area.

* Environmental/Energy Education

Environmental/Energy Education
Land Resources Division
Resource Development
Tennessee Valley Authority
Norris, TN 37828   (615) 632-1640

Much of TVA's environmental education effort is accomplished through university-based environmental education centers. The TVA has worked with several universities and colleges across the Valley and seven states to develop environmental education teaching aids and programs for schools, along with workshops for teachers. At the national level, the TVA has been involved in coordinating programs with the Environmental Protection Agency. In addition, TVA offers teacher workshops and interpretive programs for groups at Land Between the Lakes, an experimental area for schools and the public to study total resource management. Contact this office of more information on the TVA's environmental education programs.

* Graduate Student Researchers Program

University Programs Branch
Educational Affairs Division
Mail Code XEU
NASA Headquarters
Washington, DC 20546   (202) 453-8344

This program awards grants to graduate students on a competitive basis whose research interests are compatible with NASA research programs. Fellowships are for one year and are renewable, based on progress reports, of up to three years. The fellowships also allow students to carry out a plan of study or research at their home university, but those awarded by NASA field centers require fellows to spend some time at the center, usually from a few weeks to a summer each year.

* Lunar Rocks On Loan

Johnson Space Center
Educational Coordinator
Houston, TX 77058

Under the Educational Disk Program, NASA will loan teachers six samples of lunar material (three lunar soils and three lunar rocks) encapsulated in a six-inch diameter clear lucite disk, accompanied by written and graphic descriptions of each sample in the disk; a film; a sound and slide presentation; a teacher workbook; and additional printed material. Science teachers may qualify for the use of the disk by attending one of the many workshops sponsored by NASA's Space Science Education Specialists scheduled during the year at different locations throughout the U.S.

* Math Competition: MATHCOUNTS

Elementary and Secondary Programs Branch
Educational Affairs Division
Mail Code XEE
NASA Headquarters
Washington, DC 20546   (202) 453-8388

MATHCOUNTS is an annual math competition for 7th and 8th grade students that brings a number of organizations together, including NASA and the U.S. Department of Education to promote and reward excellence in mathematics. Competition begins each September with a qualifying test, and those who qualify are then coached by their teachers for the regional competition in February, the State competition in April, and the national competition in May in Washington, D.C.

* Mathematics Education

Center for the Learning and Teaching of Mathematics
Wisconsin Center for Education Research
University of Wisconsin at Madison
1025 West Johnson St.
Madison, WI 53706   (608) 263-4285

Major research areas include cognitively guided instruction in mathematics education; learning and instruction of algebra, early arithmetic, geometry, and rational numbers; mathematics curriculum study; and the assessment of mathematics.

* NASA Education Workshops for Elementary

School Teachers (NEWEST)
Elementary and Secondary Programs Branch
Educational Affairs Division
Mail Code XEE
NASA Headquarters
Washington, DC 20546   (202) 453-8386

NEWEST is for elementary school teachers (grades 1-6) in all disciplines. Selected teachers are awarded a two-week, expense- paid workshop at a NASA field center, with each center hosting about 20 teachers. The workshops vary from center to center. Although all focus on current NASA programs, each center conducts activities unique to its work. During their stay, teachers meet with scientists, technicians, and educational specialists. Teachers are instructed how to apply their experiences to their elementary curriculum.

* NASA Education Workshop for Math and

Science Teachers (NEWMAST)
Elementary and Secondary Programs Branch
Educational Affairs Division
Mail Code XEE
NASA Headquarters
Washington, DC 20546   (202) 453-8386

NEWMAST makes awards to math, science, and technology teachers in grades 7-12 with a two week, expense-paid workshop at a NASA field center each year. Applications must be submitted in the winter, and the winners are announced in the spring. Teachers are chosen on the basis of educational background, teaching experience, recommendations, personal and professional goals, and an essay explaining how selection for NEWMAST will benefit the applicant's students, colleagues, and community.

* NASA Report To Educators

Distribution Officer
Mail Code XEP
NASA Headquarters
Washington, DC 20546   (202) 453-8380

This report, a free quarterly prepared for more than 100,000 members of the educational community, contains educational information, including information on technology spinoffs, new publications and resource materials, conferences, and ongoing programs and competitions.

* Resident Environmental Education

Environmental/Energy Education
Land Between The Lakes
Resource and Development
Tennessee Valley Authority
Golden Pond, KY 42231   (502) 924-1606

The Youth Station and Brandon Spring at Land Between The Lakes operates the residential education program to promote better environmental understanding, aesthetic appreciation, and man's place in nature. These dorm-style activity areas are open year-round and accommodate kindergarten through college-level groups. Groups are welcome to carry out their own programs, or the staff can help in developing them. Activities include canoeing, pond studies, and nature walks. With Murray (Kentucky) State University Center for Environmental Education, the staff provides additional workshops for area teachers and in-service students.

* Resident Research Associate Program

University Programs Branch
Educational Affairs Division
Mail Code XEU
NASA Headquarters
Washington, DC 20546   (202) 453-8344

This program gives postdoctoral scientists and engineers an opportunity to perform research at specified NASA field centers, working full time on the research that their award is based on and must be in residence at the sponsoring field center during the entire associateship. Awardees must hold a PhD, ScD, or other earned research doctoral degree recognized in U.S. academic circles as equivalent to the PhD, and must also demonstrate superior ability for creative research.

* Science and Engineering Fairs

Elementary and Secondary Programs Branch
Educational Affairs Division
Mail Code XEE
NASA Headquarters
Washington, DC 20546   (202)453-8386

NASA takes part in the International Science and Engineering Fair for high school students by awarding certificates of merit at the regional and state levels of competition, and sending a team of judges to the international fair, where they select up to 12 students to receive an expense-paid trip with their teachers to a NASA field center. Local science fairs that are not affiliated with the international fair can take part in NASA's award system by requesting information from the field center serving their geographical area.

* Science Education

National Center for Improving Science Education
The Network, Inc.
290 South Main St.
Andover, MA 01810   (508) 470-1080
or
Washington D.C. Office
1920 L St., NW, Suite 202
Washington, DC 20036   (202) 467-0652

Major research areas include the assessment of science; science curriculum study; and science instruction study.

* Science, Mathematics, and Environmental Education Information

ERIC Clearinghouse on Science, Mathematics,
and Environmental Education
Ohio State University
1200 Chambers Rd., Room 310
Columbus, OH 43212-1792   (614) 292-6717

Subject areas cover science, mathematics, environmental, and engineering education at all levels, and within these broad subject areas, the following topics: development of curriculum and instructional materials; teachers and teacher education; learning theory/outcomes (including the impact of such factors as interest level, intelligence, values, and concept development upon learning in these fields); education programs; research and evaluative studies; media applications; and computer applications.

* Science, Technology, and Social Science Data Base

General Reading Rooms
Library of Congress
Washington, DC 20540   (202) 707-5522

The *Science, Technology, and Social Science Database* is a computerized directory

Education

of more than 14,000 organizations or individuals who will provide information to the general public on topics primarily in science, technology, and the social sciences. Citations generally contain the name of the organization or person, mailing address, telephone number, areas of interest, special collections, publications, and special services.

* Space Camp

Space and Rocket Center
One Tranquility Base
Huntsville, AL 35807-0680   (800) 63-SPACE (205) 837-3400
Space Camp and Space Academy, sponsored by the Space and Rocket Center, give both children and adults an opportunity to take part in mission-oriented programs similar to an actual space mission. Participants spend from three to ten days learning about the principles of rocketry and living in space, and then go through a simulated mission. Prices range from $400 to $800, depending on the program and age of the participant.

* Space Education Resource Center

U.S. Space Foundation
1525 Vapor Trail
Colorado Springs, CO 80916   (719) 550-1000
The U.S. Space Foundation serves as a national resource for research and educational information on all aspects of space. The foundation has developed or assisted other organizations and individuals in developing space-related educational materials and offering teacher workshops. The staff is also available for classroom visits.

* Space-Exposed Experiment Developed for Students (SEEDS)

Elementary and Secondary Programs
Educational Affairs Division
Mail Code XEO
NASA Headquarters
Washington, DC 20546   (202) 453-2995
In 1984, 65 pounds of tomato seeds were put aboard a passive satellite launched aboard the Space Shuttle. The plan calls for the seeds to be retrieved in November 1989 and then made available, along with control seeds, to teachers who requested participation in the program. The students will then germinate the two groups of seeds and determine the effects, if any, of long-term exposure to radiation and other conditions in space. As the retrieval date nears, NASA plans to contact those on the list to receive seeds to verify that they still want to participate. But because of cancellations, teachers not on the original list are encouraged to continue to request the seeds.

* Spacelink

Spacelink Administrator
Marshall Space Flight Center
Mail Code CA-20
Huntsville, AL 35807   (205) 544-6527
Spacelink is an information access system that allows individuals to log on and receive news about current NASA programs and activities and other space-related information, including historical and astronaut data, lesson plans and classroom activities, and even entire publications, such as the "Aerospace Software Directory" and "Educational Publications Directory." Although primarily intended as a resource for teachers, anyone with a personal computer and modem can access the network. The only charge is the cost of the long distance phone call. The first time you access the network, you identify yourself as a new user and are then given a hands-on guide to the use of the network. Spacelink is menu-driven and self-explanatory, so even novice computer users should experience no major difficulties.

* Space Science Student Involvement Program

Elementary and Secondary Programs Branch
Educational Affairs Division
Mail Code XEE
NASA Headquarters
Washington, DC 20546 (202) 453-8386
The Space Science Student Involvement Program, an annual program that involves students in creating experiments, art, and newspaper articles in areas of interest to NASA, honors outstanding student work through awarding various prizes, but the awards are secondary to participation in classroom activities. Students complete in five categories, some of which are broken down into separate competitions for different grade levels. Depending on the category, winners receive expense-paid trips to NASA field centers or national science symposia, and cash awards. What follows is a listing of the different categories for competition:

Space Station Proposal: for students in grades 6-8 and 9-12. The entry must be a proposal for an experiment that theoretically can be performed on the Space Station. Although experiments do not have to be constructed or performed, they should demonstrate their value and applicability to space.

National Aerospace Internship: Zero-Gravity Research Facility Proposal: Open to students in grades 9-12. Students propose experiments that theoretically can be tested in the Zero-Gravity Research Facility at Lewis Research Center.
National Aerospace Internship: Wind Tunnel Proposal: Open to students in grades 10-12. Students propose experiments that theoretically can be tested in the Wind Tunnel at Langley Research Center.
School Newspaper Competition: Open to students in grades 6-8 and 9-12. Students submit a promotional advertisement or article about SSIP that was published in their school newspaper.
National Juried Art Competition: Mars Settlement: Open to students in grades 6-8 and 9-12. Students research and illustrate their concept of the first settlement on Mars which can accommodate 10 people, illustrate life support and transportation, and be accompanied by an explanatory paragraph.

* Satellite Videoconferences

Video Conference Coordinator
NASA Aerospace Education Services Program
Oklahoma State University
300 N. Cordell
Stillwater, OK 74078   (405) 744-7015

Educational Technology Branch
Educational Affairs Division
Mail Code XE
NASA Headquarters
Washington, DC 20546   (202) 453-8388
During the school year, a series of educational programs is delivered by satellite to teachers across the country. The content of each videoconference varies, but all cover aeronautics or space science topics of interest to the educational community. Past topics have included the Hubble Space Telescope, the Freedom Space Station, and the Space Shuttle program. The broadcasts are interactive; a number is flashed across the bottom of the screen, and viewers can call collect to ask questions or take part in a discussion.

* Space Museum Education Programs

Office of Education, P-700
National Air and Space Museum
Smithsonian Institution
Washington, DC 20560   (202) 786-2106
The National Air and Space Museum offers a wide variety of educational activities, including making personnel available for teacher workshops, assistance in preparing resource materials, and making many of its resource materials available in the museum's Education Resource Center. The museum also offers teacher workshops year-round and produces classroom activities and materials for use in conjunction with a planned trip to the museum or as enrichment materials.

* Space Orientation Course for Educators

Space and Rocket Center
One Tranquility Base
Huntsville, AL 35807-0680   (800) 63-SPACE,(205) 837-3400
This orientation course for educators is a five-day program that introduces educators to space-related topics and shows them how to incorporate what they learn there into classroom activities.

* Space Science Student Involvement Program

Elementary and Secondary Programs Branch
Educational Affairs Division
Mail Code XEE
NASA Headquarters
Washington, DC 20546   (202) 453-8386
The Space Science Student Involvement Program, an annual program that involves students in creating experiments, art, and newspaper articles in areas of interest to NASA, honors outstanding student work through awarding various prizes, but the awards are secondary to participation in classroom activities. Students complete in five categories, some of which are broken down into separate competitions for different grade levels. Depending on the category, winners receive expense-paid trips to NASA field centers or national science symposia, and cash awards. What follows is a listing of the different categories for competition:

Space Station Proposal: for students in grades 6-8 and 9-12. The entry must be a proposal for an experiment that theoretically can be performed on the Space Station. Although experiments do not have to be constructed or performed, they should demonstrate their value and applicability to space.

National Aerospace Internship: Zero-Gravity Research Facility Proposal: Open to students in grades 9-12. Students propose experiments that theoretically can be tested in the Zero-Gravity Research Facility at Lewis Research Center.

National Aerospace Internship: Wind Tunnel Proposal: Open to students in grades 10-12. Students propose experiments that theoretically can be tested in the Wind Tunnel at Langley Research Center.

School Newspaper Competition: Open to students in grades 6-8 and 9-12. Students submit a promotional advertisement or article about SSIP that was published in their school newspaper.

National Juried Art Competition: Mars Settlement: Open to students in grades 6-8 and 9-12. Students research and illustrate their concept of the first settlement on Mars which can accommodate 10 people, illustrate life support and transportation, and be accompanied by an explanatory paragraph.

* Summer Faculty Fellowship Program

University Programs Branch
Educational Affairs Division
Mail Code XEU
NASA Headquarters
Washington, DC 20546   (202) 453-8344

This fellowship program gives faculty fellows in various academic disciplines the opportunity to use NASA field centers to perform research. Those selected spend 10 weeks at a field center and received a stipend. The program is open to U.S. citizens with teaching or research appointments in universities or colleges; priority is given to applicants with two years of experience, and most have doctorate degrees and carry an academic title of assistant, associate, or full professor. About 200 fellowships are awarded each year.

* Summer High School Apprentice Research Program (SHARP)

Elementary and Secondary Programs Branch
Educational Affairs Division
National Aeronautics and Space Administration
Mail Code XEE
Washington, DC 20546   (202) 453-8386

SHARP provides an opportunity for targeted underrepresented minority students in grades 10-12 who live within commuting distance of a participating NASA field center to take part in an eight-week, paid apprenticeship, where they work directly with NASA scientists or engineers. Interested students submit an application and references from a school administrator, teacher, or guidance counselor. Chosen students work with scientists or engineers whose work is related to his or her career aspirations, which may include computers, research, navigation, or guidance systems.

* Teacher-In-Space Program

Elementary and Secondary Programs Branch
Educational Affairs Division
Mail Code XEE
NASA Headquarters
Washington, DC 20546   (202) 453-8386

As part of the Challenger Center for Space Science Education, 100 education ambassadors from the NASA space program travel across the country, spreading the word about the education opportunities and programs from NASA. This program does not, however, take applications from teachers who wish to travel in space. For more information on NASA ambassadors, contact this office.

* Teacher Resource Centers

Educational Affairs Division
Office of External Relations
National Aeronautics and Space Administration
Washington, DC 20546   (202) 453-1110

These resource centers contain a wealth of information for educators interested in space- and science-related material: publications, reference books, slides, audio cassettes, video cassettes, telelecture programs, computer programs, lesson plans and activities, and lists of publications available from government and nongovernment sources. Much of the material is free. In the case of media such as video cassettes, however, educators are asked to supply their own media; copying facilities are available at all field centers. What follows is a list of the TRCs and the regions they serve:

Ames Research Center, Teacher Resource Center, Mail Stop 204-7, Moffett Field, CA 94035; (415) 694-6077. Areas served: Alaska, Arizona, California, Hawaii, Idaho, Montana, Nevada, Oregon, Utah, Washington, and Wyoming.

Jet Propulsion Laboratory, Teacher Resource Center, JPL Educational Outreach, Mail Stop CS-530, Pasadena, CA 91109; (818) 354-6916. Areas served: Same as Ames Research Center above.

John F. Kennedy Space Center, Educator Resource Library, Mail Stop ERL, Kennedy Space Center, FL 32899; (305) 867-4090. Areas served: Florida, Georgia, Puerto Rico, and Virgin Islands.

Langley Research Center, Teacher Resource Center, Mail Stop 146, Hampton, VA 23665-5225; (804) 865-4468/3017. Areas served: Kentucky, North Carolina, South Carolina, Virginia, and West Virginia.

Lyndon B. Johnson Space Center, Teacher Resource Center, Mail Stop AP-4, Houston, TX 77058; (513) 483-8696. Areas served: Colorado, Kansas, Nebraska, New Mexico, North Dakota, Oklahoma, South Dakota, and Texas.

John C. Stennis Space Center, Teacher Resource Center, Building 1200, Stennis Space Center, MS 39529; (601) 688-3338. Area served: Mississippi.

Goddard Space Flight Center, Teacher Resource Laboratory, Mail Stop 130.3, Greenbelt, MD 20771; (301) 286-8570. Area served: Connecticut, Delaware,, District of Columbia, Maine, Maryland, Massachusetts, New Hampshire, New Jersey, New York, Pennsylvania, Rhode Island, and Vermont.

Lewis Research Center, Teacher Resource Center, Mail Stop 8-1, Cleveland, OH 44135; (216) 433-2016/2017. Areas served: Illinois, Indiana, Michigan, Minnesota, Ohio, and Wisconsin.

Marshall Space Flight Center, Alabama Space and Rocket Center, NASA Teacher Resource Center, Huntsville, AL 35807; (205) 544-5812. Areas served: Alabama, Arkansas, Iowa, Louisiana, Missouri, and Tennessee.

* Teacher Resource Network

Educational Affairs Division
Office of External Relations
National Aeronautics and Space Administration
Washington, DC 20546   (202) 453-1110

To make information available to the educational community, NASA has created the Teacher Resource Network made up of Teacher Resource Centers, Regional Teacher Resource Centers, and the Central Operation of Resources for Educators.

* Teacher Workshops

Elementary and Secondary Programs Branch
Educational Affairs Division
Mail Code XEE
NASA Headquarters
Washington, DC 20546   (202) 453-8386

Aerospace Education Services Program (AESP) specialists conduct workshops for teachers each summer at NASA field centers, elementary and secondary schools, and on college campuses. Workshops cover astronomy, aeronautics, life in space, principles of rocketry, Earth sciences, and remote sensing. A typical workshop includes how-to and hands-on activities to help teachers incorporate what they learn into classroom activities and programs to supplement existing curricula.

* Teaching Materials for Geology

Geologic Inquiries Group
U.S. Geological Survey
907 National Center
Reston, VA 22092   (703) 648-4383

Packets of geological teaching aids for different grade levels and geographic location are available from the Geologic Inquiries Group and from the Earth Science Information Centers listed elsewhere in this book. These packets include lists of reference materials, various maps and map indexes, and a selection of general interest publications. Requests for teachers packets should be sent on school letterhead, indicating the grade level and subject of interest.

* Urban Community Enrichment Program

Elementary and Secondary Programs Branch
Educational Affairs Division
Mail Code XEE
NASA Headquarters
Washington, DC 20546   (202) 453-8386

UCEP is specifically targeted toward middle-school students in urban areas with high percentages of minorities. NASA specialists will meet with school representatives to formulate a custom-tailored program to fit the school's needs. Typically a program begins with teacher orientation workshops followed by assemblies, a series of student workshops, and classroom visits. In the classroom, NASA specialists work with students on various hands-on activities, such as building rockets or airplanes or learning about how information is transmitted from space back to Earth.

Innovation and Trends

* Appalachia Education Research Center

Appalachia Educational Laboratory, Inc.
1030 Quarrier St. P.O. Box 1348
Charleston, WV 25325   (304) 347-0400
Major activity areas include classroom instruction, school governance and administration, policy and planning, professional preparation and research, regional liaison center, school service center, and rural and small schools. States served: Kentucky, Tennessee, Virginia, and West Virginia.

* Arts Education Research and Testing

University of Illinois at Urbana - Champaign
College of Applied and Fine Arts
105 Davenport House
809 South Wright St.
Champaign, IL 61820-6219   (217) 333-2186
Major research areas include the development and validation of standardized achievement tests in the area of artistic processes and techniques in art history; national study on literacy and art education; role of music in general education; status surveys in art, visual, dance and drama in the elementary and secondary schools; drama/theatre, visual and dance; influence on culture condition on the learning of arts; development of computer assisted testing (music education); design of studies in dance; designs of studies in theatre; status survey of music education in elementary and secondary schools; and arts education field work: observational studies.

* Congressional Technology Assessment Fellowships

Congressional Fellowships
Personnel Office
Office of Technology Assessment
Congress of the United States
Washington, DC 20510
OTA awards up to six fellowships each year, providing an opportunity for individuals of demonstrated outstanding ability to gain a better understanding of science and technology issues facing Congress, along with the ways in which Congress establishes national policy related to these issues. Applications must be received by January 31. Stipends range from $28,000 to $55,000, depending upon background and experience. For further information, write this office.

* Document Reproduction of Education Research

ERIC Document Reproduction Service
Computer Mirofilm Corporation
3900 Wheeler Ave.
Alexandria, VA 22304-5110   (703) 823-0500 (800) 227-3742
This service is responsible for microfilming the ERIC documents announced in Resources in Education. Once microfilmed the RIE documents can be purchased as either microfiche or paper reproductions by simply calling EDRS. You can expect to receive your requests within 3 to 5 working days. EDRS supplies more than 1 million microfiche each month to over 750 locations around the world.

* Educational Abstracts Journal

Resources in Education (RIE)
Superintendent of Documents
U.S. Government Printing Office
Washington, DC 20402-9371   (202) 783-3238
Published for the U.S. Department of Education in twelve monthly issues, Resources in Education, a monthly abstract journal of ERIC, covers the document literature of education. It is indexed by subject institution, personal author, and publication type. A year's subscription to the journal is $66.00, and the semi-annual index is $20.00 per year.

* Education and Employment

National Center on Education and Employment
Teachers College
Columbia University
Box 174
New York, NY 10027   (212) 678-3091
Major research areas include education and the labor market; the role of family background, school characteristics, and school curriculum in the link between education and labor market outcomes; youth participation in job training and labor market outcomes; knowledge acquisition at work; and community-based planning for work-related education.

* Educational Institutions Providing the ERIC System

ERIC Processing and Reference Facility
2440 Research Blvd., Suite 550
Rockville, MD 20850   (301) 590-1420
The free Directory of ERIC Information Service Providers lists all of the service providers, primarily colleges and universities, within the ERIC system according to geographical region. It includes organizations that provide computerized searches of the ERIC database, that have sizeable collections of ERIC microfiche, and that subscribe to and collect the various ERIC publications.

* Education Reform and Policy Research

Center for Policy Research in Education
The Eagleton Institute of Politics Rutgers
The State University of New Jersey
Wood Lawn--Neilson Campus
New Brunswick, NJ 08901   (201) 828-3872
Major research areas include curriculum and student standards, teacher policies, indicators and monitoring, new roles and responsibilities; and evolution of reform.

* Educational Research and Databases

Center for Electronic Records
National Archives and Records Administration
8th St. & Pennsylvania Ave., NW, Room 20E
Washington, DC 20408   (202) 523-3267
This center holds a variety of records pertaining to educational research, including data from the U.S. Department of Education, Office of Education, Department of Health, Education, and Welfare, as well as other government agencies. Some of the data consists of basic skills test scores, teacher questionnaires, and principal questionnaires.

* Educational Resources Information Center (ERIC) Clearinghouses

Office of Educational Research and Improvement
555 New Jersey Ave., NW
Washington, DC 20208   (202) 357-6088
The Educational Resources Information Center (ERIC) is a national education information system responsible for developing, maintaining, and providing access to the world's largest education research database. The ERIC system includes a network of clearinghouses, each of which acquires and reviews documents and prepared indexes and abstracts, which are then entered into the ERIC database, which contains over 650,000 abstracts. ERIC is made available to a wide variety of users through multiple means, including microfiche collections (available in over 700 libraries around the world) and through vendor-provided online and compact disk-read only memory (CD-ROM) searching. Periodic reports, digests, and other documents are prepared by the clearinghouses, each of which covers education research and practice in an assigned topic area. Each clearinghouse also provides a variety of user services, including training, and responds to numerous requests for information. A Pocket Guide to ERIC and All About ERIC are available free of charge from this office to clarify the activities of the ERIC system.

* Educational Technology

Educational Technology Center
Harvard Graduate School of Education
337 Gutman Library
6 Appian Way
Cambridge, MA 02138   (617) 495-9373
Major research areas include mathematics, science, computer education, and new technologies.

* Education Technologies

Office of Technology Assessment
600 Pennsylvania Ave., SE
Washington, DC 20510   (202) 228-6936
New curriculum requirements, shortages of qualified teachers in some subjects, sparse student enrollment in some regions, and rising costs for educational services contribute to an increasing need for effective methods for providing instruction. OTA is currently studying these problems and the various technological options, their costs, effectiveness, and tradeoffs, in the K-12 school setting. Contact Linda Roberts, the project director, for more information.

* Far West Educational Research and Development

Far West Laboratory for Educational Research and Development
1855 Folsom St.
San Francisco, CA 94103 (415) 565-3000
Major activity areas include teaching and learning, improving organizational effectiveness, professional preparation and development, students at risk, Center for Educational Policy, Southern Service Center, rural and small schools, planning and evaluation, and publication services. States served: Arizona, California, Nevada, and Utah.

* Grants and Contracts Service

Office of Management
U.S. Department of Education
400 Maryland Ave.
Washington, DC 20202 (202) 732-2804
This office publishes the pamphlet, *GCMS: Grants and Contracts Management System*, which gives you over-all information about the on-line information system which monitors the educational grant and procurement contract awards of the U.S. Department of Education. It also contains a telephone list of contacts within the system to call for information and inquiries on the status of your application. For information concerning GCMS, contact the Director, Management Support Division, Grants and Contracts Service, (202) 732-2773.

* Guidelines for Publishing Educational Material with ERIC

ERIC Educational Resources Information Center
2440 Research Boulevard, Suite 550
Rockville, MD 20850-3238
This free pamphlet outlines the types of documents suitable for ERIC publication and the procedure for submitting the documents to ERIC.

* Guide to the Department of Education Office of Educational Research and Improvement

America's Education Fact Finder
Office of Educational Research and Improvement
Department of Education
555 New Jersey Ave., NW
Washington, DC 20208
The *Guide* is free pamphlet is an overview of the functions of the Office of Educational Research and Development. It also contains important phone numbers to call for specific projects within the department, including Research, Library Programs, and Information Services.

* Information Resources Clearinghouse

ERIC Clearinghouse on Information Resources
Syracuse University School of Education
030 Huntington Hall
150 Marshall St.
Syracuse, NY 13244-2340 (315) 443-3640
Subject areas cover educational technology and library and information science at all levels. This includes instructional design, development and evaluation with emphasis on educational technology, along with the media of educational communication; computers and microcomputers, telecommunications (cable, broadcast, satellite); audio and video recordings, film and other audiovisual materials, as they pertain to teaching and learning. Within library and information science, the focus is on the operation and management of information services for education-related organizations. All aspects of information technology related to education are considered within this scope.

* Language Education and Research

Center for Language Education and Research
University of California
1100 Glendon Ave., Suite 1740
Los Angeles, CA 90024 (213) 206-1486
Major research areas include academic knowledge base; professional development of the language educator; improvement of content of curricula and programs; linguistic and metalinguistic underpinnings of academic learning; second language instructional programs; language attrition; relations across linguistic minority programs; and second language programs.

* Languages and Linguistics Education Information

ERIC Clearinghouse on Languages and Linguistics
Center for Applied Linguistics
1118 22nd St., NW
Washington, DC 20037-0037 (202) 429-9551
Subject areas cover languages and language sciences; theoretical and applied linguistics; all areas of foreign language, second language and linguistics pedagogy, or methodology; psycholinguistics and the psychology of language learning; cultural and intercultural context of languages; application of linguistics in language teaching; bilingualism and bilingual education; sociolinguistics; study abroad and international exchanges; teacher training and qualifications specific to the teaching of a foreign language and second language; commonly and uncommonly taught languages, including English as a second language; related curriculum developments and problems.

* Leadership in Education

Center for School Leadership
Graduate School of Education
Harvard University
Monroe C. Guttman Library
Appian Way
Cambridge, MA 02138-3704 (617) 495-3575
Major research areas ask the following: What is good school leadership? How does good school leadership come about? What will good school leadership mean in the future?

* Learning Skills

Center for the Study of Learning
Learning, Research and Development Center
University of Pittsburgh
3939 O'Hara St.
Pittsburgh, PA 15260 (412) 624-7485
Major research areas include mathematics, science, social studies learning, and learning skills.

* Midwest Regional Education Research Lab

Mid-Continent Regional Educational Laboratory
Denver Office: 12500 East Iliff, Suite 201
Aurora, CO 80014 (303) 337-0990

Kansas City Office: 4709 Belleview Ave.
Kansas City, MO 64112 (816) 756-2401
Their major activities are to foster regional communication and networks; distribute information, and provide technical assistance to improve educational practice; strengthen the region's capacity to design and implement policies that support school improvement; develop databases on economic, social, political, and educational trends in the region; develop new resources aimed at improving education for students most in need; and rural and small schools. States served: Colorado, Kansas, Nebraska, Missouri, Wyoming, North Dakota, and South Dakota.

* National Longitudinal Study

National Educational Longitudinal Study of 1988 (NELS:88)
National Opinion Research Center
1155 East 60th St.
Chicago, IL 60637 (312) 702-8998
NELS:88 is a longitudinal study that begins with a survey in 1988 of eighth grade students, their schools, teachers, and their parents. This study will track the critical transitions experienced by young adults as they progress through junior high school, high school, and postsecondary education into the world of work. This study will yield policy-relevant information about such topics as high school effectiveness, discipline, homework, coursetaking patterns, cognitive ability, dropouts, private schools, vocational education, special education, instruction for limited-English-speaking students, postsecondary access and choice, student financial assistance, employment during high school and college, transfer behaviors, vocational training, on-the-job training, labor force participation, employment stability, family formation, and graduate/professional training. Conducted every two years, published information concerning the survey is available in June of the year following the actual survey. For information on how to obtain the results of the survey, contact the Center for Education Statistics, Elementary/Secondary Outcomes Division, (202) 357-6777.

* North Central Region Lab

North Central Regional Educational Laboratory
295 Emroy Ave.
Elmhurst, IL 60126 (312) 941-7677
Major activity areas include improving student performance, strengthening the quality of instruction, developing the education professions, and rural and small schools. States served: Illinois, Indiana, Iowa, Michigan, Minnesota, Ohio, and Wisconsin.

* Northeast Education Research Lab

Regional Laboratory for Educational Improvement
of the Northeast and Islands
290 South Main St.
Andover, MA 01810 (508) 470-0098
Major activity areas include leadership for school improvement, teacher development, public policy for school improvement, at-risk youth, rural and small

schools, and program governance and support. Areas served: Connecticut, Maine, Massachusetts, New Hampshire, New York, Rhode Island, Vermont, Puerto Rico, and the Virgin Islands.

* Northwest Regional Lab

Northwest Regional Educational Laboratory
101 S.W. Main St., Suite 500
Portland, OR 97204   (503) 275-9500

Major activity areas include evaluation assessment, cultural understanding, and equity; business and human resource agencies; professional development, rural and small schools, school improvement; and technology. Other Laboratory Programs include education and work; evaluation and assessment; institutional development and communication; literacy and language; planning and service coordination; R&D for Indian education; school improvement program; technology program; and the Western Center for Drug-Free Schools and Communities. Areas served: Alaska, Idaho, Montana, Oregon, Washington, American Samoa, Guam, Hawaii, and the Northern Mariana Islands.

* Regional Educational Laboratories Programs for the Improvement of Practice

Educational Networks Division
Office of Educational Research and Improvement
555 New Jersey Ave., NW
Washington, DC 20208   (202) 357-6186

This office funds nine regional laboratories which carry out applied research, development, and technical assistance for educators, parents, and decisionmakers in the 50 states, the District of Columbia, Puerto Rico, the Virgin Islands, and the Pacific Basin Region. Each laboratory serves a geographic region and is governed by an independent board of directors. Those listed here are under a five-year contract through November 30, 1990. These laboratories plan programs through an ongoing assessment of regional needs, a knowledge of the current trends in research practice, and interaction with the many other agencies and institutions that assist communities and schools with educational improvement. Improving schools and classrooms is the goal of the laboratories, a goal they carry out through a common set of five tasks or functions:

* Working with other regional organizations to apply research and improve schools. Partner organizations include state departments of education, intermediate school districts and intradistrict collaboratives, universities, colleges, and state associations of educators and parents;

* Assisting state-level policymakers on the implications of educational research and practice for policies and programs;

* Conducting applied research and developing materials, programs, and publications that support the mission of school and classroom improvement;

* Collaborating with other laboratories, research centers, and national associations to extend and enhance related research and development;

* Developing effective internal management, governance, planning, and self-evaluation, as well as reviewing regional needs and developments.

* Research and Development Centers Nationwide

National Research and Development Centers
Office of Educational Research and Development
555 New Jersey Ave., NW
Washington, DC 20208   (202) 357-6079

These university-based centers focus research on topics of national significance to educational policy and practice. Each center works in a defined field on a multi-year (and usually multi-disciplinary) program of research and development. Each center's role is to: 1) exercise leadership in its mission area; 2) conduct programmatic research and development; 3) attract the sustained attention of the best researchers to education problems; 4) create a long-term interaction between researchers and educators; 5) participate in a network for collaborative exchange in the education community; and 6) engage in an information distribution program.

* Research for Better Schools

Research for Better Schools
444 North Third St.
Philadelphia, PA 19123   (215) 574-9300

Major activity areas include institutional development, cooperative school improvement, state leadership assistance, applied research, products for special populations, national networking, and rural and small schools. Areas served: Delaware, District of Columbia, Maryland, Pennsylvania, and New Jersey.

* Southeastern Education Research Lab

Southeastern Educational Improvement Laboratory
P.O. Box 12746
200 Park Offices, Suite 204
Research Triangle Park, NC 27709-2746   (919) 549-8216

Major activity areas include improving writing, math, and leadership skills; making effective use of technology; state policy and educational reform; the teaching profession; dropout prevention; and rural and small schools. States served: Alabama, Florida, Georgia, Mississippi, North Carolina and South Carolina.

* Southwest Regional Education Research Lab

Southwest Educational Development Laboratory
211 East Seventh St.
Austin, TX 78701   (512) 476-6861

Major activity areas include improving teacher and administrator performance, improving school and classroom productivity, facilitating student achievement, information services for education decisionmakers, and rural and small schools. States served: Arkansas, Louisiana, New Mexico, Oklahoma, and Texas.

* Statistics and Information

Office of Educational Research and
Improvement Information Services
555 New Jersey Ave., NW
Washington, DC 20208   (800) 424-1616 (202) 626-9854

This office is staffed with statisticians and education information specialists who can answer your questions about education statistics, research, technology, and practice, particularly as they related to programs in OERI. Information Services sells education data on tape and runs special tabulations against OERI databases. A free pamphlet, *America's Education Fact Finder: Office of Educational Research and Improvement*, lists important phone numbers and describes the major areas of OERI services.

* Technology in Education

Center for Technology in Education
Bank St. College of Education
610 West 112th St.
New York, NY 10025   (212) 663-7200

Major research areas include integrating technology into learning and instruction; assessing learning; linking reform and restructuring to learning and technology; and adapting and designing advanced technologies.

Money for Teachers and Schools

Grants from the federal government are available not only to educators and faculty but to universities and other educational institutions. In addition to the money programs identified here for medical school and other fields, more grants are listed in the Careers and Workplace Chapter. The information is taken from the *Catalog of Federal Domestic Assistance* which is published by the U.S. Government Printing Office in Washington, D.C. The number next to the title description is the official reference number listed in this catalog. Contact the office listed below the title for details.

* Post-Baccalaureate Facility Fellowships (Faculty Fellowships)   13.147
Anastasia Buchanan, Division of Nursing
Health Resources and Services Administration, PHS
Room 5C-13, 5600 Fishers Lane
Rockville, MD   20857   (301) 443-5763
To provide grants to eligible schools of nursing to: investigate cost-effective alternatives to traditional health care modalities; examine nursing interventions that result in positive outcomes in health status; address other ares of nursing practice. Types of assistance: grants. Estimate of annual funds available: $ 1,079,000.

* Grants for Two Year Programs of Schools of Medicine or Osteopathy (Two Year Schools)   13.149
Dr. Donald Weaver, Director, Division of Medicine
Health Resources and Services Administration, PHS
Room 4C-25, 5600 Fishers Lane
Rockville, MD   20857   (301) 443-6190
To maintain and improve schools which provide the first or last two years of education leading to the degree of Doctor of Medicine or Osteopathy. Types of assistance: grants. Estimate of annual funds available: $ 211,600.

* Grants for Faculty Training Projects in Geriatric Medicine and Dentistry (Geriatric Fellowships)   13.156
Dr. Donald Weaver, Director, Division of Medicine
Health Resources and Services Administration, PHS
Room 4C-25, 5600 Fishers Lane
Rockville, MD   20857   (301) 443-6190
To assist in the operation of postdoctoral training preparing current and future faculty for leadership roles in geriatric medicine and dentistry. Types of assistance: grant. Estimate of annual funds available: $ 3,491,000.

* Excellence in Minority Health Education and Care (Centers for Excellence)   13.157
Grants Management Officer
Health Resources and Services Administration
Room 8C-22, 5600 Fishers Lane
Rockville, MD   20857   (301) 443-2100
To strengthen the national capacity to train minority students in the health professions; and to support the health professions schools which have trained a significant number of the nation's minority health professionals. Types of assistance: grants. Estimate of annual funds available: $ 9,459,000.

* Capitation Grants for Schools of Public Health (Capitation Grants)   13.339
John R. Westcott, Grants Management Officer
Health Resources and Services Administration
5600 Fishers Lane, Room 8C-22
Rockville, MD   20857   (301) 443-6880
To provide financial assistance to accredited schools of public health which meed requirements for sustaining total full-time equivalent student enrollment levels. Types of assistance: grants. Estimate of annual funds available: $ 4,698,000.

* Nurse Training Improvement - Special Projects (Special Projects, Grants and Contracts for Improvement in Nurse Training)   13.359
Dr. Mary Hill, Division of Nursing
Health Resources and Services Administration, PHS
5600 Fishers Lane
Rockville, MD   20857   (301) 443-6193

To help schools of nursing and other institutions improve the quality and availability of nursing education through projects for specified purposes such as providing continuing education for nurses, demonstrating improved geriatric training, increasing nursing personnel in rural areas. Types of assistance: grants. Estimate of annual funds available: $ 11,970,000.

* Minority Biomedical Research Support (MBRS)   13.375
Director, Minority Biomedical Research Support
Program Branch
Division of Research Resources
National Institutes of Health
Bethesda, MD   20892   (301) 496-6745
To address the lack of representation of minorities in biomedical research by increasing the pool of minorities pursing research careers. Types of assistance: grants. Estimate of annual funds available: $ 28,147,000.

* Cancer Research Manpower   13.398
Dr. Vincent J. Cairoli, Chief
Cancer Training Branch
Division of Cancer Prevention and Control
National Cancer Institute EPN/232B
Bethesda, MD   20892   (301) 496-8580
To make available support for nonprofit institutions interested in providing biomedical training opportunities for individuals interested in careers in basic and clinical research to support important areas of the National Cancer Program. Types of assistance: grants. Estimate of annual funds available: $ 41,781,000.

* Administration on Developmental Disabilities - University Affiliated Programs   13.632
Program Development Division
Office of Human Development Services
Department of Health and Human Services
Washington, DC   20201   (301) 245-1961
To defray the cost of administration and operation of programs that: (1) provide interdisciplinary training for personnel concerned with developmental disabilities. Types of assistance: grants. Estimate of annual funds available: $ 12,570,000.

* Child Welfare Services Training Grants   13.648
Director, Program Support Division
Children's Bureau, Administration for Children,
Youth, and Families
P.O. Box 1182
Washington, DC   20013   (202) 755-7820
To develop and maintain an adequate supply of qualified and trained personnel for the field of services to children and their families, and to improve educational programs and resources for preparing personnel for this field. Types of assistance: grant. Estimate of annual funds available: $ 3,696,000.

* Special Programs for the Aging - Title IV - Training Research and Discretionary Projects and Programs   13.668
Mike Suzuki, Associate Commissioner
Office of Program Development
Administration on Aging, DHHS
Washington, DC   2021   (202) 245-0442
To provide adequately trained personnel in the field of aging, improve knowledge of the problems and needs of the elderly, and to demonstrate better ways of improving the quality of life for elderly. Types of assistance: grants. Estimate of annual funds available: $ 24,173,000.

Education

---

* Health Careers Opportunity Program 13.822

Grants Management Officer
Health Resources and Services Administration
Room 8C-22, 5600 Fishers Lane
Rockville, MD 20857   (301) 443-6857
To identify, recruit, and select individuals from disadvantaged backgrounds for education and training in a health or allied health professions school. Types of assistance: grant. Estimate of annual funds available: $ 18,692,037.

* Area Health Education Centers (AHEC) 13.824

Dr. Donald Weaver, Director
Division of Medicine HRSA, PHS
5600 Fishers Lane
Rockville, MD 20857   (301) 443-6190
To improve the distribution, supply, quality, utilization, and efficiency of health personnel in the health service delivery system and for the purpose of increasing the regionalization of educational responsibilities of health professions schools. Types of assistance: grants. Estimate of annual funds available: $ 12,527,000.

* Medical Library Assistance 13.879

Dr. Jeanne Brand, Extramural Programs
National Library of Medicine
Bethesda, MD 20894   (301) 496-6131
To improve health information services by providing funds to train professional personnel, strengthen library and information services, support biomedical publication, and conduct research in information science and in medical information. Types of assistance: grants. Estimate of annual funds available: $ 13,551,000.

* Minority Access to Research Careers (MARC) 13.880

Edward Blynum, Program Director (MARC Program)
National Institute of General Medical Sciences, NIH
Bethesda, MD 20892   (301) 496-7941
To assist minority institutions to train greater numbers of scientist and teachers in health related fields. Types of assistance: grants. Estimate of annual funds available: $ 9,053,000.

* Grants for Physician Assistant Training Program (Physical Assistant Training Program) 13.886

Dr.Donald Weaver, Director, Division of Medicine
Bureau of Health Professions, HRSA, PHS, DHHS
Parklawn Bldg., Room 4C-25
5600 Fishers Lane
Rockville, MD 20857   (301) 443-6190
To enable public or nonprofit private health or educational entities to meet the cost of projects to plan, develop and operate programs for the training of physicians assistants. Types of assistance: grants. Estimate of annual funds available: $ 452,000.

* Resource and Manpower Development in the Environmental Health Sciences (Core Centers and Research Training Program) 13.894

Director, Division of Extramural Research
and Training
National Institute of Environmental Health Sciences
P.O. Box 12233
Research Triangle Park, NC 27709   (919) 541-7723
To provide long-term, stable support for broadly based multidisciplinary research and training on environmental health problems in Environmental Health Sciences Center. Types of assistance: grant. Estimate of annual funds available: $ 25,303,000.

* Grants for Faculty Development in Family Medicine 13.895

Dr. Donald Weaver, Director
Division of Medicine, HRSA, PHS
Room 4C-25, 5600 Fishers Lane
Rockville, MD 20857   (301) 443-6190
To increase the supply of physician faculty available to teach in family medicine programs and to enhance the pedagogical skills of faculty presently teaching in family medicine. Types of assistance: grants. Estimate of annual funds available: $ 4,757,000.

* Residency Training and Advanced Education in the General Practice of Dentistry 13.897

Richard G. Weaver, Dental Health Branch
Division of Assoc. & Dental Health Professions

HRSA, PHS, 5600 Fishers Lane
Rockville, MD 20857   (301) 443-6837
To assist schools of dentistry and institutions conducting post-graduate dental training in defraying the costs of projects to plan, develop, and operate an approved residency or advanced educational program in the general practice of dentistry. Types of assistance: grants. Estimate of annual funds available: $ 1,691,000.

* National Health Promotion 13.900

Deputy Director, Office of Disease Prevention
and Health Promotion, DHHS
Room 2132, 330 C Street, SW
Washington, DC 20201   (202) 245-7611
To engage national membership organizations from various sectors as a means of expanding and coordinating health promotion efforts. Types of assistance: grants. Estimate of annual funds available: $ 363,080.

* Grants for Faculty Development in General Internal Medicine and/or General Pediatrics (GIM/GP Faculty Development) 13.900

Dr. Donald Weaver, Director
Division of Medicine, HRSA, PHS
Room 4C-25, 5600 Fishers Lane
Rockville, MD 20857   (301) 443-6190
To promote the development of faculty skills in physicians (full-time, part-time, volunteer, fellows and/or residents) who are currently teaching or who plan teaching careers in general internal medicine and/or general pediatrics training programs. Types of assistance: grants. Estimate of annual funds available: $ 3,633,703.

* Grants for the Training of Health Professions in Geriatrics 13.969

Mr. William Koenig
HRSA, PHS, Department of Health and Human Services
5600 Fishers Lane
Rockville, MD 20857   (301) 443-6887
To develop regional resource centers focused on strengthening multidisciplinary training of health professionals in geriatric health care. Types of assistance: grants. Estimate of annual funds available: $ 9,382,000.

* Health Professions Recruitment Program for Indians (Recruitment Program) 13.970

Division of Grants and Contracts
Grants Management Branch
Indian Health Service, PHS, DHHS
Room 6A-33, 5600 Fishers Lane
Rockville, MD 20857   (301) 4443-5204
To identify Indians with a potential for education or training in the health professions and to encourage and assist them to enroll in health or allied health professional schools. Types of assistance: grants. Estimate of annual funds available: $ 600,000.

* Grants for Establishment of Departments of Family Medicine (Family Medicine Departments) 13.984

Dr. Donald Weaver, Director
Division of Medicine, BHPR, HRSA, PHS
Room 4C-25, 5600 Fishers Lane
Rockville, MD 20857   (301) 443-6190
To assist in establishing, maintaining or improving family medicine academic administrative units to provide clinical instruction in family medicine in order that these units are comparable in status, faculty and curriculum to those other clinical units at the applying school. Types of assistance: grants. Estimate of annual funds available: $ 2,235,000.

* Airway Science (AWS) 20.107

Office of Training and Higher Education, ANT 30
Federal Aviation Administration
400 7th St., SW, Plaza Room PL-10
Washington, DC 20591   (202) 366-7003
To assist recognized colleges and/or universities in the need for facilities and equipment for Airway Science (AWS) curriculum students. Types of assistance: grants. Estimate of annual funds available: $ 1,000,000.

* State Marine Schools 20.806

Bruce J. Carlton, Director
Office of Maritime Labor and Training
Maritime Administration
Department of Transportation

Washington, DC 20590   (202) 366-5755
To train merchant marine officers in state marine schools. Types of assistance: direct payment. Estimate of annual funds available: $ 27,576,000.

* Promotion of the Arts - Arts in Education 45.003
Dr. Warren Newman
Arts in Education Program
Room 602, National Endowment for the Arts
The Nancy Hanks Center
1100 Penn. Ave., NW
Washington, DC 20506   (202) 682-5797
To encourage state and local arts agencies to develop long-term strategies in assisting appropriate state and local education authorities to establish the arts as basic in education. Types of assistance: grants. Estimate of annual funds available: $ 5,600,000.

* Promotion of the Humanities - Summer Seminars for College Teachers 45.116
Summer Seminars for College Teachers
Division of Fellowships and Seminars
National Endowment for the Humanities, Room 316
Washington, DC 20506   (202) 786-0463
To provide opportunities for teachers in five, four, and two-year colleges; for scholars employed in libraries, museums, historical associations, and other humanities institution to work during the summer in their areas of interest under the direction of distinguished scholars at institutions with library resources suitable for advanced study and research. Types of assistance: grants. Estimate of annual funds available: $ 3,780,000.

* Promotion of the Humanities - Summer Stipends 45.121
Division of Fellowships and Seminars, Summer Stipends
National Endowment for the Humanities, Room 316
Washington, DC 20506   (202) 786-0466
To provide support for individual faculty and staff members at universities and two-year and four-year colleges and for others who have made or have demonstrated promise of making significant contributions to the humanities. Types of assistance: grants. Estimate of annual funds available: $ 800,000.

* Promotion of the Humanities-Elementary and Secondary Education in the Humanities 45.127
Elementary and Secondary Education in the Humanities
National Endowment for the Humanities
Room 302
Washington, DC 20506   (202) 786-0377
To increase the effectiveness of humanities teaching in our nation's elementary, middle, and secondary schools. Types of assistance: grants. Estimate of annual funds available: $ 7,344,000.

* Promotion of the Humanities-Fellowships for University Teachers 45.142
Fellowships for University Teachers
Division of Fellowships and Seminars
National Endowment for the Humanities, Room 316
Washington, DC 20506   (202) 786-0466
To provide time for uninterrupted study and research to university teachers, and faculty members of postgraduate professional schools who can make significant contributions to thought and knowledge in the humanities. Types of assistance: grant. Estimate of annual funds available: $ 3,165,000.

* Promotion of the Humanities - Fellowships for College Teachers and Independent Scholars 45.143
Fellowships for College Teachers and Independent Scholars
Division of Fellowships and Seminars, Rm 316
National Endowment for the Humanities
Washington, DC 20506   (202) 786-0466
To provide opportunities for college teachers and independent scholars to pursue independent study and research that will enhance their capacities as teachers, scholars, or interpreters of the humanities. Types of assistance: grants. Estimate of annual funds available: $ 3,390,000.

* Promotion of the Humanities-Reference Materials/Tools 45.145
Division of Research Programs, Reference
Materials/Tools
Room 318

National Endowment for the Humanities
Washington, DC 20506   (202) 786-0358
To fund, wholly or partially projects which create research tools important for scholarly research. Types of assistance: grants. Estimate of annual funds available: $ 2,615,000.

* Promotion of the Humanities-Higher Education in the Humanities 45.150
Higher Education in the Humanities
National Endowment for the Humanities, Room 302
Washington, DC 20506.   (202) 786-0380
To assist institutions of higher education in their efforts to improve the teaching of the humanities. Types of assistance: grants. Estimate of annual funds available: $ 7,344,000.

* Promotion of the Humanities-Summer Seminars for School Teachers 45.151
Summer Seminars for School Teachers
Division of Fellowships and Seminars
National Endowment for the Humanities, Room 316
Washington, DC 20506   (202) 786-0463
To provide opportunities for school teachers to work during the summer under the direction of a distinguished teacher and active scholar at colleges and universities throughout the country, studying seminal works in the humanities in a systematic and thorough way. Types of assistance: grant. Estimate of annual funds available: $ 3,725,000.

* Promotion of the Humanities - Travel to Collections (Travel to Collections) 45.152
Division of Fellowships and Seminars/Travel to Collections, Room 316
National Endowment for the Humanities
Washington, DC 20506   (202) 786-0463
To advance basic research in the humanities by enabling American scholars to travel to use the research collections of libraries, archives, museums or other research repositories to consult research materials which are of fundamental importance for the progress of scholarly work. Types of assistance: grants. Estimate of annual funds available: $ 300,000.

* NEH/Reader's Digest Teacher Scholar Program 45.154
Elementary and Secondary Education in the Humanities
National Endowment for the Humanities, Room 302
Washington, DC 20506   (202) 786-0377
To increase the effectiveness of humanities teaching in our nation's elementary, middle, and secondary schools. Types of assistance: grants. Estimate of annual funds available: $ 1,500,000.

* Teacher Preparation and Enhancement 47.066
Division of Teacher Preparation and Enhancement
National Science Foundation
1800 G. St., NW
Washington, DC 20550   (202) 573-7073
To attract highly talented men and women to elementary, middle/junior high and secondary school science and mathematics teaching careers, to improve preservice teacher preparation programs to develop teachers capabilities in these critical areas. Types of assistance: grants. Estimate of annual funds available: $ 63,525,000.

* Materials Development, Research, and Informal Science Education 47.067
Materials Development, Research, and Informal Science Education
National Science Foundation
1800 G St., NW
Washington, DC 20550   (202) 357-7452
To expand the knowledge base and to provide new and improved models and materials resources needed to increase the quality of and continuously renew, the Nation's precollege education system in mathematics, science and technology. Types of assistance: grants. Estimate of annual funds available: $ 44,002,000.

* Studies and Program Assessment 47.068
Office of Studies and Program Assessment
National Science Foundation
1800 G. St., NW
Washington, DC 20500   (202) 357-7425
To serve a major role in policy formulation to improve and strengthen science

and engineering education in the U.S. and to provide support for leadership efforts of the Foundation in science in engineering education activities. Types of assistance: grants. Estimate of annual funds available: $ 4,500,000.

* Research Initiation and Improvement   47.069
Division of Research Initiation and Improvement
National Science Foundation
1800 G St., NW
Washington, DC   20550   (202) 357-7552
Types of assistance: grant. Estimate of annual funds available: $ 23,043,000.

* Undergraduate Science, Engineering and Mathematics Education   47.071
Division of Undergraduate Science
Engineering and Mathematics Education
National Science Foundation, Rm 6739
2800 G. St., NW
Washington, DC   20500   (202) 357-7051
To assist college and universities to achieve and maintain strong, high quality undergraduate science, engineering and mathematics instructional programs for all of their students. Types of assistance: grants. Estimate of annual funds available: $ 28,000,000.

* Air Pollution Control Manpower Training   66.003
EPA, Grants Administration Division, PM 216
Washington, DC   20460
To develop career-oriented personnel qualified to work in pollution abatement and control. Types of assistance: grants. Estimate of annual funds available: $ 400,000.

* Air Pollution Control - Technical Training   66.006
Betsy Dodson
Air Pollution Training Institute, EPA
Research Triangle Park, NC   27711   (919) 541-2401
To provide technical training to personnel from state and local air pollution control agencies. Types of assistance: training. Estimate of annual funds available: $ 241,000.

* National Gallery of Art Extension Services   68.001
Department of Extension Programs
National Gallery of Art
Washington, DC   20565   (202) 737-4215
To provide educational material on the Gallery's collections and exhibitions free of charge except for transportation costs, to schools, colleges, and libraries across the Nation. Types of assistance: other. Estimate of annual funds available: $ 698,000.

* University-Laboratory Cooperative Program   81.004
Larry L. Barker
Division of University and Industry Programs
Office of Energy Research, DOE
Washington, DC   20585   (202) 586-8947
To provide college and university science and engineering faculty and students with energy-related training and research experience in areas of energy research at DOE facilities. Types of assistance: grants, other. Estimate of annual funds available: $ 8,000,000.

* Energy Policy, Planning and Development   81.080
Stephen F. Durbin
Resource Management Office
Policy Planning and Analysis
Forrestal Bldg., 1000 Independence Ave., SW
Washington, DC   20585   (202) 586-5325
To provide financial assistance for gathering outside experts for seminars, conferences and work groups to discuss specific energy policy issues and write recommendations and reports. Types of assistance: grants. Estimate of annual funds available: $ 150,000.

* Minority Educational Institution Research Travel Fund (MIRT)   81.083
Isiah O. Sewell
Office of Minority Economic Impact MI-2.2, DOE
Forrestal Bldg., Rm 5B-110
Washington, DC   20585   (202) 586-1953
To provide travel funds to faculty members and graduate students of minority postsecondary educational institutions to encourage and assist in initiating and improving energy related research. Types of assistance: direct payment.

Estimate of annual funds available: $ 50,000.

* Minority Educational Institution Assistance   81.094
Isiah O. Sewell
Office of Minority Economic Impact, DOE
1000 Independence Ave., SW
Washington, DC   20585   (202) 586-1593
Types of assistance: grants. Estimate of annual funds available: $ 1,000,000.

* Educational Exchange - University Lecturers (Professors) and Research Scholars (Fulbright-Hays Program)   82.002
Council for International Exchange of Scholars
11 Dupont Circle, Suite 300
Washington, DC   20036
To improve and strengthen the international relations of the U.S. by promoting mutual understanding among the peoples of the world through educational exchanges. Types of assistance: grants. Estimate of annual funds available: $ 20,138,170.

* Adult Education-State Administered Basic Grant Program   84.002
D. Kay Wright
Division of Adult Education
Office of Assistant Secretary for Vocational and
 Adult Education
Department of Education
Washington, DC   20202-7320   (202) 732-2270
To improve educational opportunities for adults and to encourage the establishment of adult education programs. Types of assistance: grants. Estimate of annual funds available: $ 136,344,000.

* Bilingual Education   84.003
Rudolph Munis
Office of Bilingual Education and Minority
 Languages Affairs
Department of Education
330 C St., SW, Room 1086
Washington, DC   20202   (202) 732-5700
To develop and carry out programs of bilingual education in elementary and secondary schools. Types of assistance: grant, direct payment. Estimate of annual funds available: $ 151,946,000.

* Civil Rights Technical Assistance and Training   84.004
Division of Discretionary Grants
Steven L. Brockhouse
Office of Elementary and Secondary Education
400 Maryland Ave., SW
Washington, DC   20202-6438.   (202) 732-4360
To provide technical assistance and training services to school districts to cope with educational problems occasioned by discrimination from race, sex, and national origin. Types of assistance: grants. Estimate of annual funds available: $ 23,443,000.

* Education of Handicapped Children in State-Operated or Supported Schools (Chapter 1, ESEA Handicapped)   84.009
Division of Assistance to States
Office of the Asst. Secretary for Special Education
 and Rehabilitative Services
Department of Education
Washington, DC   20202   (202) 732-1025
To extend and improve comprehensive educational programs for handicapped children enrolled in state-operated or state-supported schools. Types of assistance: grants. Estimate of annual funds available: $ 148,200,000.

* Educationally Deprived Children - Local Educational Agencies (Chapter 1, of Title I, ESEA)   84.010
Compensatory Education Programs
Office of Elementary and Secondary Education
Department of Education
400 Maryland Ave., SW, Rm 2043
Washington, DC   20202   (202) 732-4682
To provide financial assistance to local educational agencies to meet the special needs of educationally deprived children selected in accordance with Section 1014 of Chapter 1. Types of assistance: grants. Estimate of annual funds

available: $4,026,100,000.

* Migrant Education-Basic State Formula Grant Program (State Migrant Education Program) 84.011
Office of Migrant Education
Office of Elementary and Secondary Education
Department of Education
400 Maryland Ave., SW
Washington, DC 20202   (202) 732-4746
To establish and improve programs to meet the special educational needs of migratory children of migratory agricultural workers or migratory fishers. Types of assistance: grants. Estimate of annual funds available: $ 263,436,000.

* Educationally Deprived Children - State Administration (Chapter 1, ESEA; State Administration) 84.012
Compensatory Education Programs
Office of Elementary and Secondary Education
Department of Education
400 Maryland Ave. SW, Rm 2043
Washington, DC 20202   (202) 732-4682
To provide financial assistance to enable state educational agencies to meet their administrative responsibilities under the Chapter 1 program. Types of assistance: grant. Estimate of annual funds available: $ 40,508,000.

* Neglected and Delinquent Children (Chapter 1 ESEA; Neglected and Delinquent) 84.013
Compensatory Education Programs
Office of Elementary and Secondary Education
Department of Education
400 Maryland Ave., SW, Room 2043
Washington, DC 20202   (202) 732-4682
To provide financial assistance to State agencies to meet the special needs of institutionalized neglected or delinquent children and children in community day programs for whom they have an educational responsibility. Types of assistance: grants. Estimate of annual funds available: $ 31,616,000.

* Follow Through 84.014
Compensatory Education Programs
Office of Elementary and Secondary Education
Department of Education
400 Maryland Ave., SW, Room 2043
Washington, DC 20202   (202) 732-4682
To sustain and augment in primary grades the gains that children from low income families make in Head Start and other quality preschool programs. Types of assistance: grants. Estimate of annual funds available: $ 7,262,000.

* National Resource Centers and Fellowships Program for Language and Area or Language and International Studies 84.015
Joseph F. Belmonte
Advanced Training and Research Branch
Center for International Education
7th and D St., SW
Washington, DC 20202   (202) 732-3283
To promote instruction in those modern foreign languages area and international studies critical to national needs by supporting the establishment, strengthening and operation of such programs at colleges and universities. Types of assistance: grant. Estimate of annual funds available: $ 11,234,000.

* Undergraduate International Studies and Foreign Language Programs 84.016
International Studies Branch
Center for International Education
Office of Postsecondary Education
Department of Education
7 and S St., SW
Washington, DC 20220   (202) 732-3290
The Undergraduate International Studies and Foreign Language program issues awards to institutions of higher education an public and nonprofit private agencies and organizations. Types of assistance: grants. Estimate of annual funds available: $ 2,725,000.

* International Research and Studies (HEA Title VI Research and Studies) 84.017
Division of Advanced Training and Research
International Education Programs

Department of Education
7 and D St., SW
Washington, DC 20202   (202) 732-3297
To improve foreign language and area studies training through support of research and studies, experimentation and development of specialized instructional materials. Types of assistance: grant. Estimate of annual funds available: $ 1,480,000.

* Fulbright-Hays Seminars Abroad - Special Bilateral Projects (Fulbright Exchange) 84.018
International Studies Branch
Center for International Education
Department of Education
Room 3053
7 and D Sts., SW
Washington, DC 20202   (202) 732-3292
To increase mutual understanding and knowledge between the people of the U.S. and those in other countries by offering qualified U.S. educators opportunities to participate in short-term study seminars. Types of assistance: grants. Estimate of annual funds available: $ 775,000.

* Fulbright-Hays Training Grants - Faculty Research Abroad 84.019
Merian Kane
Center for International Education
Department of Education
Room 3053, 7 and D Sts.
Washington, DC 20202   (202) 732-3301
To help universities and colleges strengthen their language and area studies programs by enabling faculty members to conduct research abroad in order to improve their skill in languages. Types of assistance: grants. Estimate of annual funds available: $ 692,000.

* Fulbright-Hays Training Grants - Group Projects Abroad 84.021
Office of Asst Secretary for Postsecondary Education
Department of Education
7 and D Sts., SW
Washington, DC 20202   (202) 732-3294
To help educational institutions improve their programs in modern foreign language and area studies. Types of assistance: grants. Estimate of annual funds available: $ 2,013,000.

* Handicapped-Innovation and Development (Research in Education for the Handicapped) 84.023
Division of Innovation and Development
Office of Asst. Secretary for Special Education and
  Rehabilitative Services
Department of Education
400 Maryland Ave., SW
Washington, DC 20202
To improve the education of handicapped children through research and development projects and model programs (demonstrations). Types of assistance: grant. Estimate of annual funds available: $ 17,026,000.

* Handicapped Early Childhood Education (Early Education Program) 84.024
Nancy Safer
Division of Educational Services
Special Education Programs
Department of Education
400 Maryland Ave., SW
Washington, DC 20202   (202) 732-1109
To support demonstrations, dissemination and implementation of effective approaches to preschool and early childhood education handicapped children. Types of assistance: grants. Estimate of annual funds available: $ 23,147,000.

* Handicapped Education-Deaf-Blind Centers (Services for Deaf-Blind Children and Youth) 84.025
Nancy Safer
Division of Educational Services
Special Education Service, Department of Education
400 Maryland Ave., SW
Washington, DC 20202   (202) 723-1109
To provide technical assistance to state education agencies and to improve services to deaf-blind children and youth. Types of assistance: grants. Estimate of annual funds available: $ 14,189,000.

Education

* Handicapped Media Services and Captioned Films (Media Materials; Technology for the Handicapped) 84.026

Nancy Safer
Division of Educational Services
Special Education Programs, Department of Education
Washington, DC 20202   (202) 732-1109
To maintain a free loan service of captioned films for the deaf and instruction media for the educational, cultural, and vocational enrichment of the handicapped. Types of assistance: direct payment. Estimate of annual funds available: $ 13,403,000.

* Handicapped-State Grants (Part B, Education of the Handicapped Act) 84.027

Division of Assistance to States
Office of Special Education, Department of Education
400 Maryland Ave., SW
Washington, DC 20202   (202) 732-1025
To provide grants to states to assist them in providing a free appropriate public education to all handicapped children. Types of assistance: grants. Estimate of annual funds available: $1,475,449,000.

* Handicapped Regional Resource and Federal Centers 84.028

Mary Gardner
Division of Assistance to States
Office of Special Education, Department of Education
400 Maryland Ave., SW
Washington, DC 20202   (202) 732-1026
To establish regional resource centers which provide advice and technical services to educators for improving education of handicapped children. Types of assistance: grants. Estimate of annual funds available: $ 6,338,000.

* Handicapped Education-Special Education Personnel Development (Training Personnel for the Education of the Handicapped) 84.029

Norm How
Division of Personnel Preparation
Special Education Programs, Department of Education
Washington, DC 20202   (202) 732-1070
To address identified shortages of special education teachers and related service personnel. Types of assistance: grants. Estimate of annual funds available: $ 67,095,000.

* Clearinghouses for the Handicapped Program 84.030

Division of Educational Services
Office of Asst. Secretary for Special Education
  and Rehabilitative Services
Department of Education
400 Maryland Ave, SW
Washington, DC 20202
To disseminate information regarding education programs and services for handicapped children. Types of assistance: grants. Estimate of annual funds available: $ 1,135,000.

* Higher Education-Institutional Aid Special Needs Program 84.031

Institutional Aid Programs Office of
  Postsecondary Education, Department of Education
400 Maryland Ave., SW
Washington, DC 20202   (202) 732-3308
To help eligible colleges and universities to strengthen their management and fiscal operations. Types of assistance: grants. Estimate of annual funds available: $ 77,459,000.

* Library Services (LSCA-Title I) 84.034

Robert Klaassen
Public Library Support Staff
Library Programs, Department of Education
Washington, DC 20208   (202) 357-6303
To assist in extending public library services to areas without service or with inadequate service. Types of assistance: grants. Estimate of annual funds available: $ 79,388,820.

* Interlibrary Cooperation and Resource Sharing (LSCA-Title III) 84.035

Robert Klaassen
Public Library Support Staff
Library Programs
Office of Educational Research and Improvement
Department of Education
Washington, DC 20208   (202) 357-6303
To plan and take steps leading to the development of cooperative networks. Types of assistance: grants. Estimate of annual funds available: $ 18,719,960.

* Library Career Training (HEA Title II-B) 84.036

Yvonne Carter
Library Development Staff, Library Programs
Department of Education
55 New Jersey Avenue, NW
Washington, DC 20208   (202) 357-6320
To assist institutions of higher education and library organizations and agencies in training or retraining persons in areas of library specialization where there are shortages. Types of assistance: grants. Estimate of annual funds available: $ 400,000.

* Library Research and Demonstration (HEA Title II-B) 84.039

Yvonne Carter
Library Development Staff
Department of Education
55 New Jersey Ave., NW
Washington, DC 20208-1430   (202) 357-6320
To award grants and contracts for research and/or demonstration projects in areas of specialized services intended to improve library and information science practices. Types of assistance: grants. Estimate of annual funds available: $ 308,000.

* Student Support Services 84.042

Division of Student Services
Office of Postsecondary Education
Department of Education
400 Maryland Ave., SW
Washington, DC 20202   (202) 732-4804
To provide supportive services to disadvantaged college students to enhance their potential for successfully completing the postsecondary education program in which they are enrolled. Types of assistance: grants. Estimate of annual funds available: $ 86,599,000.

* Vocational Education-Basic Grants to States 84.048
Division of Vocational Education

Winifred I. Warnat
Department of Education
400 Maryland Ave., SW
Washington, DC 20202   (202) 732-2441
To assist states in expanding, improving, modernizing, and developing quality vocational education programs. Types of assistance: grants. Estimate of annual funds available: $ 715,600,000.

* Vocational Education - Consumer and Homemaking Education 84.049

Winifred I. Warnat
Director, Division of Vocational Education
Department of Education
400 Maryland Ave., SW
Washington, DC 20202   (202) 732-2441
To assist states in conducting programs in consumer and homemaking education. Types of assistance: grants. Estimate of annual funds available: $ 33,118,000.

* National Vocational Education Research 84.051

Glenn C. Boerrigter
Department of Education
Division of National Programs
400 Maryland Ave., SW
Washington, DC 20202   (202) 732-2367
To provide support for the National Center for Research in Vocational Education and six curriculum coordination centers and special research projects. Types of assistance: grants. Estimate of annual funds available: $ 7,102,963.

* Higher Education-Cooperative Education (Cooperative Education Program) 84.055

Division of Higher Education Incentive Programs
Office of Postsecondary Education
Department of Education

Washington, DC 20202   (202) 732-4861
To provide federal support for planning establishing expanding and carrying out of projects of cooperative education in institutions of higher education. Types of assistance: grants. Estimate of annual funds available: $ 13,622,000.

* Indian Education-Special Programs and Projects (Indian Education Act-Subpart 2) 84.061
Indian Education Programs
Office of Elementary and Secondary Education
Department of Education
400 Maryland Ave., SW
Washington, DC 20202   (202) 732-1887
To plan, develop and implement programs and projects for the improvement of educational opportunities for Indian children, to prepare and improve the qualifications of persons serving Indian students in educational personnel positions. Types of assistance: grants. Estimate of annual funds available: $ 12,307,000.

* Indian Education-Adult Indian Education (Indian Education Act-Subpart 3) 84.062
Indian Education Programs
Office of Elementary and Secondary Education
Department of Education
400 Maryland Ave., SW
Washington, DC 20202   (202) 732-1887
To plan develop and implement programs for Indian adults to decrease the rate of illiteracy, increase the mastery of basic skills, increase the number who earn high school equivalency diplomas. Types of assistance: grants. Estimate of annual funds available: $ 4,000,000.

* Higher Education-Veterans Education Outreach Program (VEOP) 84.064
Neil McArthur
Division of Higher Education Incentive Programs
Office of Postsecondary Education
Department of Education
Washington, DC 20202   (202) 732-4406
To encourage colleges and universities to service the special needs of veterans, especially the physically disabled or educationally disadvantaged veterans. Types of assistance: direct payments. Estimate of annual funds available: $ 2,838,000.

* Educational Opportunity Centers 84.066
Division of Student Services
Education Outreach Branch
Department of Education
400 Maryland Ave., SW
Washington, DC 20202   (202) 732-4804
To provide information on financial and academic assistance available for qualified adults desiring to pursue a program of postsecondary education and to assist them in applying for admission to institution of postsecondary education. Types of assistance: grants. Estimate of annual funds available: $ 11,665,000.

* Indian Education-Grants to Indian Controlled Schools (Indian Education-Part A Set-Aside, NonLEAs) 84.072
Indian Education Programs
Department of Education
Office of Elementary and Secondary Education
400 Maryland Ave., SW
Washington, DC 20202   (202) 732-1887
To provide financial assistance to Indian controlled schools to develop and implement elementary and secondary school programs designed to meet the special educational needs of Indian children. Types of assistance: grants. Estimate of annual funds available: $ 3,500,000.

* National Diffusion Network (NDN: National Diffusion Network) 84.073
Lee Wickline
National Diffusion Network, Recognition Division
55 New Jersey Ave., NW
Washington, DC 20208   (202) 357-6134
To promote and accelerate the systematic, rapid dissemination and adopting by public and nonpublic educational institutions nationwide. Types of assistance: grants. Estimate of annual funds available: $ 11,066,000.

* Postsecondary Education Programs for Handicapped Persons (Postsecondary Programs) 84.078

Joseph Rosenstein
Division of Educational Services
Special Education Programs
Department of Education
400 Maryland Ave., SW
Washington, DC 20202   (202) 732-1176
To develop and operate specially designed model programs of vocational, technical, postsecondary or adult education for deaf or other handicapped persons. Types of assistance: grants. Estimate of annual funds available: $ 5,770,000.

* Womens Educational Equity (Women's Educational Equity Act Program) 84.083
Director, Division of Discretionary Grants
Office of Elementary and Secondary Education
Department of Education
400 Maryland Ave., SW
Washington, DC 20202   (202) 732-4351
To promote educational equity for women and girls at all levels of education and to provide financial assistance to local educational institutions to help them meet the requirements Title IX. Types of assistance: grants. Estimate of annual funds available: $ 2,949,000.

* Handicapped Education-Severely Handicapped Program (Programs for Severely Handicapped Children and Youth) 84.086
Nancy Safer
Division of Educational Services
Department of Education
400 Maryland Ave., SW
Washington, DC 20202   (202) 732-1109
To improve and expand innovative educational/training services for severely handicapped children and youth; Types of assistance: grants. Estimate of annual funds available: $ 5,297,000.

* Strengthening Research Library Resources (HEA Title II-C) 84.091
Louise Sutherland
Library Development Staff
Library Programs, Department of Education
Washington, DC 20208-5571   (202) 357-6322
To promote research and education of high quality throughout the U.S by providing financial assistance. Types of assistance: grants. Estimate of annual funds available: $ 5,675,000.

* Bilingual Vocational Instructor Training 84.099
Division of National Programs
Office of Vocational and Adult Education
Department of Education
400 Maryland Ave., SW
Washington, DC 20202   (202) 732-2365
To provide training for instructors and other ancillary personnel in bilingual vocational training programs. Types of assistance: grants, direct payment. Estimate of annual funds available: $ 565,650.

* Bilingual Vocational Materials, Methods, and Techniques 84.100
Laura Kar
Division of National Programs
Office of Vocational and Adult Education
Department of Education
400 Maryland Ave., SW
Washington, DC 20202   (202) 732-2365
To develop instructional materials, methods, techniques, to encourage research programs and demonstration projects and to overcome the shortage of instructional materials available for bilingual vocational training programs. Types of assistance: grants. Estimate of annual funds available: $ 377,100.

* Training for Special Programs Staff and Leadership Personnel 84.103
May Weaver
Division of Student Services
Office of Postsecondary Education
Department of Education
400 Maryland Ave., SW
Washington, DC 20202   (202) 732-4804
To provide training for staff and leadership personnel unemployed in, or preparing for employment in, projects funded under the Special Programs for Students from Disadvantaged Backgrounds. Types of assistance: grants.

Estimate of annual funds available: $ 1,281,000.

* Fund for the Improvement of Postsecondary Education (FIPSE) 84.116

Fund for the Improvement of Postsecondary Education
Office of the Asst. Secretary for Postsecondary
Education
7 and D Sts., SW, Rm 3100
Washington, DC 20202   (202) 732-5750

To provide assistance for innovative programs which improve the access to and the quality of postsecondary education. Types of assistance: grants. Estimate of annual funds available: $ 11,856,000.

* Educational Research and Development 84.117

Department of Education
Office of Educational Research and Improvement
55 New Jersey Ave., NW
Washington, DC 20208   (202) 357-6079

To provide grants, contracts and cooperative agreements to individuals and institutions seeking to advance knowledge about education policy and practice. Types of assistance: grants. Estimate of annual funds available: $ 18,794,000.

* Minority Science Improvement (MSIP) 84.120

Argelia Velez-Rodriguez
Division of Higher Education Incentive Programs
Department of Education
Washington, DC 20202   (202) 732-4396

To assist institutions to improve the quality of preparation of their students for graduate work or careers in science. Types of assistance: grants. Estimate of annual funds available: $ 5,307,000.

* Secretary's Discretionary 84.122

Department of Education, FIRST
Office of Educational, Research and Improvements
Washington, DC 20202   (202) 357-6496

To assist in research, dissemination, demonstration, improvement of training, and technical assistance activities, which address some national education priority as authorized by Section 583 of the Education Consolidation and Improvement Act. Types of assistance: grants. Estimate of annual funds available: $ 4,691,000.

* Law-Related Education 84.123

School Improvement Programs
Office of Elementary and Secondary Education
400 Maryland Ave., SW
Washington, DC 20202   (202) 732-4357

To support programs at the elementary and secondary school levels by developing and implementing model projects designed to institutionalize law-related. Types of assistance: grants. Estimate of annual funds available: $ 3,952,000.

* Territorial Teacher Training Assistance Program 84.124

Education Networks Division
Program for the Improvement of Practice
Department of Education
Washington, DC 20208   (202) 357-6616

To provide assistance for the training of teachers in elementary and secondary public and private schools in Guam, etc. Types of assistance: grants. Estimate of annual funds available: $ 1,976,000.

* Rehabilitation Services - Basic Support (Basic Support) 84.126

Office of Program Operations
Rehabilitation Services Administration
Department of Education
Washington, DC 20202   (202) 732-1406

To provide vocational rehabilitation services to persons with mental and/or physical handicaps. Types of assistance: grants. Estimate of annual funds available: $ 1,437,973,057.

* Rehabilitation Training 84.129

Rehabilitation Services Administration
Office of Special Education and Rehabilitative Services
Department of Education
Washington, DC 20202   (202) 732-1400

To support projects to increase the numbers and improve the skills of personnel trained in providing vocational rehabilitation services to handicapped individuals

in areas targeted as having personnel shortages. Types of assistance: grants. Estimate of annual funds available: $ 30,134,000.

* Migrant Education-High School Equivalency Program (HEP) 84.141

Office of Migrant Education
Office of Elementary and Secondary Education
U.S. Department of Education
400 Maryland Ave., SW
Washington, DC 20202   (202) 732-4746

To assist students who are engaged or who whose families are engaged in migrant and other seasonal farm work to obtain the equivalent of a secondary school diploma. Types of assistance: grant. Estimate of annual funds available: $ 7,410,000.

* Federal State and Local Partnerships for Educational Improvement (Chapter 2, State Block Grants) 84.151

Division of Educational Support
State and Local Educational Programs
Office of Elementary and Secondary Education
Department of Education
Washington, DC   (202) 732-4156

To assist state and local educational agencies to improve elementary and secondary education. Types of assistance: grants. Estimate of annual funds available: $ 462,977,000.

* Business and International Education 84.153

International Studies Branch
Center for International Education
Department of Education
Rm 3053
Washington, DC 20202   (202) 732-3302

To promote innovation and improvement in international business education curricula at institution of higher education and serve the needs of business community. Types of assistance: grants. Estimate of annual funds available: $ 2,125,000.

* Secondary Education and Transitional Services for Handicapped Youth 84.158

Division of Educational Services
Office of Special Education Program
400 Maryland Ave., SW
Washington, DC 20202   (202) 732-1109

To strengthen and coordinate education, training, and related services for handicapped youth. Types of assistance: grant. Estimate of annual funds available: $ 7,284,000.

* Training Interpreters for Deaf Individuals 84.160

Office of Special Education and Rehabilitative
Services
Department of Education
Washington, DC 20202   (202) 732-1322

To support projects, increase the numbers and improve the skills of manual and oral interpretive who provide services to deaf individuals. Types of assistance: grants. Estimate of annual funds available: $ 900,000.

* State Grants for Strengthening the Skills of Teachers and Instruction in Mathematics and Science 84.164

Dr. Allen A. Schmieder, Suite 2040
School Improvement Programs
400 Maryland Ave., SW
Washington, DC 20202   (202) 732-4336

To improve the skills of teachers and instruction in the areas of mathematics and science, also to increase the accessibility of such instruction to all students. Types of assistance: grants. Estimate of annual funds available: $ 128,440,000.

* National Programs For Strengthening, Teaching, and Administration in Mathematics and Science Programs 84.168

Department of Education, FIRST
Office of Educational Research and Improvement
Washington, DC 20208   (202) 357-6496

To provide support for projects designed to improve the quality of instruction in mathematics and science. Types of assistance: grants. Estimate of annual funds available: $ 8,892,000.

* Construction, Reconstruction, and Renovation of Academic Facilities (Academic Facilities Program) 84.172

Division of Higher Education Incentive Programs
Office of Postsecondary Education
Department of Education
Washington, DC 20202 (202) 732-4389
To provide assistance to institutions of postsecondary education in order to construct reconstruct or renovate academic facilities. Types of assistance: grants. Estimate of annual funds available: $ 6,366,000.

* Leadership in Educational Administration Development (LEAD) 84.178

Hunter Moorman
Office of Educational Research and Improvement
Department of Education
Washington, DC 20208 (202) 357-6116
To provide assistance for eligible parties to establish and operate technical assistance centers that promote the development of leadership skills in school administrators. Types of assistance: grants. Estimate of annual funds available: $ 8,222,000.

* Technology, Educational Media and Materials for the Handicapped (Technical Development) 84.180

Division of Innovation and Development
Office of Asst. Secretary for Special Education and
Rehabilitative Services
Department of Education
400 Maryland Ave., NW
Washington, DC 20202
To provide contracts, grants, or cooperative agreements for the purpose of advancing the use of new technology. Types of assistance: grants. Estimate of annual funds available: $ 4,730,000.

* Handicapped Infants and Toddlers (Early Intervention Grants) 84.181

Nancy Safer
Division of Educational Services
Office of Special Education Program
Department of Education
400 Maryland Ave., SW
Washington, DC 20202 (202) 732-1109
To assist each state and territory to develop a state-wide comprehensive, coordinated multidisciplinary, interagency, system to provide early intervention services for handicapped infants and toddlers and their families. Types of assistance: grants. Estimate of annual funds available: $ 69,831,000.

* National Programs for Drug-Free Schools and Communities 84.184

Department of Education
Office of Elementary and Secondary Education
Room 4132
400 Maryland Ave., SW
Washington, DC 20202 (202) 732-4579
To assist in drug and alcohol abuse education and prevention, personnel training and curriculum demonstration activities, as authorized by the Drug Free Schools and Communities Act of 1986. Types of assistance: grants. Estimate of annual funds available: $ 59,770,000.

* Drug-Free Schools and Communities - State Grants (Drug-Free Schools and Communities) 84.186

Allen King
Department of Education
Office of Elementary and Secondary Education
400 Maryland Ave., SW
Washington, DC 20202 (202) 732-4599
To provide financial assistance to establish programs of alcohol and drug abuse education and prevention coordinated with related community efforts and resources. Types of assistance: grants. Estimate of annual funds available: $ 287,730,000.

* Supported Employment Services for Individuals with Severe Handicaps (Supported Employment Services Program) 84.187

Mark E. Shob
Office of Program Operations
Rehabilitation Services Administration
Department of Education
Washington, DC 20202-2574 (202) 732-1406
To provide grants for training and traditionally time limited post employment services leading to supported employment for individuals with severe handicaps. Types of assistance: grants. Estimate of annual funds available: $ 26,900,000.

* Christa McAuliffe Fellowships (CMFP) 84.190

Department of Education
Office of the Asst. Secretary for Elementary and
Secondary Education
400 Maryland Ave., SW
Washington, DC 20202 (202) 732-4342
To reward excellence in teaching by providing financial assistance to outstanding teachers to continue their education. Types of assistance: grants. Estimate of annual funds available: $ 1,892,000.

* National Adult Education Research 84.191

Richard F. DiColar
Division of National Programs
Office of Vocational and Adult Education
Department of Education
400 Maryland Ave., SW
Washington, DC 20202 (202)732-2362
Types of assistance: grant. Estimate of annual funds available: $ 412,000.

* Adult Education for the Homeless 84.192

Division of Adult Education
Office of Vocational and Adult Education
Department of Education
400 Maryland Ave., SW
Washington, DC 20202 (202) 732-2390
To provide literacy training and basic skills remediation for adult homeless individuals, including a program of outreach activities. Types of assistance: grants. Estimate of annual funds available: $ 7,094,000.

* Bilingual Education Support Services 84.194

Office of Bilingual Education and Minority
Languages Affairs
Edward Fuentes
330 C St., SW, Room 5086
Washington, DC 20202 (202) 732-5972
To provide in-service training and technical assistance to parents and educational personnel participating in, or preparing to participate in bilingual education programs. Types of assistance: grants. Estimate of annual funds available: $ 20,772,000.

* Bilingual Education Training Grants 84.195

Division of National Programs
Office of Bilingual Education and Minority
Languages Affairs
Dr. Mary T. Mahony
330 C St., SW, Room 50861
Washington, DC 20202 (202) 732-5722
To provide financial support for programs designed to meet the training needs for additional or better trained education personnel in Bilingual Education. Types of assistance: grants. Estimate of annual funds available: $ 30,413,000.

* College Library Technology and Cooperation Grants (HEA Title II-D) 84.197

Linda Loeb, Program Officer
Library Development Staff, Library Programs
Department of Education
Washington, DC 20202 (202) 357-6902
To encourage resource sharing activities among the libraries in institutions of higher education through the use of technology and networking. Types of assistance: grants. Estimate of annual funds available: $ 3,651,000.

* Workplace Literacy 84.198

Nancy Brooks
Division of National Programs
Office of Vocational and Adult Education
Department of Education
400 Maryland Ave., SW
Washington, DC 20202 (202) 732-2269
The Adult Education Act was amended to establish workplace literacy partnerships. Types of assistance: grants. Estimate of annual funds available: $ 11,856,000.

Education

* Vocational Education-Cooperative Demonstration 84.199

Richard DiCola
Division of National Programs
Office of Vocational and Adult Education
Department of Education
400 Maryland Ave., SW
Washington, DC 20202 (202) 732-2362
To support exemplary cooperative demonstration programs for high technology training pertaining to vocational education. Types of assistance: grants. Estimate of annual funds available: $ 14,361,000.

* School Dropout Demonstration Assistance (Dropout Prevention Program) 84.201

John Fiegel
Department of Education
Division of Educational Support
Office of Elementary and Secondary Education
400 Maryland Ave., SW
Washington, DC 20202 (202) 732-4342
To provide financial assistance to local educational agencies, educational partnerships and community based organizations to establish and demonstrate effective dropout prevention and reentry programs. Types of assistance: grants. Estimate of annual funds available: $ 21,736,000.

* STAR Schools Program (Star Schools) 84.203

Frank Withrow
Office of Educational Research and Improvement
Department of Education
Washington, DC 20208-5644 (202) 357-6200
To provide demonstration grants to eligible telecommunications partnerships to develop, construct and acquire audio and visual facilities and equipment. Types of assistance: grants. Estimate of annual funds available: $ 14,399,000.

* School, College, and University Partnership (SCUP) 84.204

May J. Weaver
Department of Education
Division of Student Services
400 Maryland Ave., SW
Washington, DC 20202 (202) 732-4804
To encourage partnerships between institutions of higher education and secondary schools serving low-income students to support programs that improve the academic skills of public and private nonprofit secondary school students. Types of assistance: grants. Estimate of annual funds available: $ 2,760,000.

* Educational Personnel Training 84.207

Allen King, Director
Drug-Free Schools and Communities Program
Department of Education
400 Maryland Ave., SW
Washington, DC 20202 (202) 732-4599
To provide financial assistance to State Education Agencies and Institutions of Higher Education to establish, expand or enhance programs and activities for the training of teachers in drug abuse programs. Types of assistance: grants. Estimate of annual funds available: $ 7,000,000.

* Native Hawaiian Model Curriculum Implementation Project (Kamehameha Elementary Education Program (KEEP)) 84.208

Ramon Ruiz
Department of Education
400 Maryland Ave., SW
Washington, DC 20202 (202) 732-4153
To implement and increase the impact of the Kamehameha Elementary Education Program Model Demonstration Curriculum. Types of assistance: direct payment. Estimate of annual funds available: $ 395,200.

* Native Hawaiian Family Based Education Centers 84.209

Mr. Ramon Ruiz
Department of Education, School Improvement Programs
400 Maryland Ave., SW
Washington, DC 20202 (202) 732-4153
To develop and operate a minimum of eleven family based education centers throughout the Hawaiian Islands. Types of assistance: direct payment. Estimate of annual funds available: $ 1,778,400.

* First Schools and Teachers 84.211

Daniel Schecter
Department of Education, FIRST
Office of Educational Research and Improvement
Washington, DC 20208 (202) 357-6496
To support projects to improve educational opportunities for the performance of elementary and secondary school students and teachers. Types of assistance: grants. Estimate of annual funds available: $ 3,952,000.

* First Family School Partnerships 84.212

Daniel Schecter
Department of Education, FIRST
Office of Educational Research and Improvement
Washington, DC 20208 (202) 357-6496
To increase the involvement of families in improving the educational achievement of their children in preschool, elementary and secondary schools. Types of assistance: grants. Estimate of annual funds available: $ 1,976,000.

* Even Start - Local Education Agencies 84.213

Mary Jean LeTendre
Department of Education
Compensatory Education Programs
Office of Elementary and Secondary Education
400 Maryland Ave., SW
Washington, DC 20202 (202) 732-4682
To provide family centered education projects to help parents become full partners in the education of their children. Types of assistance: grants. Estimate of annual funds available: $ 14,375,400.

* Even Start - Migrant Education 84.214

John Staehle
Office of Elementary and Secondary Education
Migrant Education, Department of Education
400 Maryland Ave., SW, Room 2145
Washington, DC 20202 (202) 732-4746
To establish and improve programs to meet the special educational needs of the children of migratory agricultural worker. Types of assistance: grants. Estimate of annual funds available: $ 444,600.

* The Secretary's Fund for Innovation in Education 84.215

Daniel Schecter
Department of Education, FIE
Office of Educational Research and Improvement
Washington, DC 20208 (202) 357-6496
To conduct projects that offer the promise of identifying and disseminating innovative educational approaches at the preschool, elementary and secondary level. Types of assistance: grants. Estimate of annual funds available: $ 15,678,000.

* Student Literacy Corps 84.219

Department of Education
Office of the Deputy Asst. Secretary for Higher Education Programs
400 Maryland Ave., SW
Washington, DC 20202
To promote student literary corps projects operated by institutions of higher education where volunteer undergraduates will serve as unpaid literacy tutors in public community agencies. Types of assistance: grants. Estimate of annual funds available: $ 4,940,000.

* Center for International Business Education 84.220

Susanna Easton
International Studies Branch
Center for International Education
Department of Education, Room 3052
400 Maryland Ave., SW
Washington, DC 20202 (202) 732-3302
To serve the international needs of the business community by promoting improved business strategies in international trade. Types of assistance: grants. Estimate of annual funds available: $ 741,000.

* Native Hawaiian Special Education 84.221

Dr. Martin J. Kaufman (202) 732-1107
To operate projects addressing the special education needs of Native Hawaiian Students. Types of assistance: grants. Estimate of annual funds available: $ 494,000.

* National School Volunteer Program   84.222

Daniel Schecter
FIRST Program
Office of Educational Research and Improvement
Department of Education
55 New Jersey Ave., NW
Washington, DC 20208   (202) 357-6496
To conduct volunteer programs nationally in schools.   Types of assistance:
grants. Estimate of annual funds available: $ 988,000.

* State-Administered English Literacy   84.223

Ronald Pugsley
Division of Adult Education
Office of Vocational and Adult Education
Department of Education
400 Maryland Ave., SW
Washington, DC 20202   (202) 732-2272
To provide grants to states to conduct English literacy projects for individuals of
limited English proficiency.   Types of assistance: grants. Estimate of annual

* Bicentennial Educational Grant Program   90.001

Commission on the Bicentennial of the U.S.
Constitution
Attn: Educational Programs
808 17th St., NW
Washington, DC 20006   (202) 653-5110
To help elementary and secondary school teachers develop a better
understanding of the history and development of the U.S. Constitution and Bill
of Rights so that they will become more able to teach the Constitution to young
learners. Types of assistance: grants. Estimate of annual funds available:
$ 3,600,000.

Federal Money for Students

Both the federal government and state governments have student loan programs and other financial assistance to pursue higher education. And these programs are not limited to young adults but the elderly as well. The federal programs identified here are taken from the *Catalog of Federal Domestic Assistance* which is published by the US Government Printing Office in Washington, D.C. The number next to the title is the official reference. In the case of either the federal agency, contact the office listed below the title for more details. Refer to the next section for a state-by-state listing of financial aid and scholarships for students.

* Minority Research and Teaching Grants (MRTP Small Grants Program) 10.140
Dr. Ezra Naughton
Minority Research and teaching Programs
Office of Advocacy and Enterprise
Department of Agriculture
14th & Independence Ave., SW
Washington, DC 20250   (202) 447-2019
Types of assistance: grants. Estimate of annual funds available: $ 100,000.

* Minority Research and Teaching Grants (MRTP Small Grants Program) 10.140
Dr. Ezra Naughton
Minority Research and Teaching Programs
Office of Advocacy and Enterprise
Dept. of Agriculture
14th & Independence Ave., SW
Washington, DC 20250   (202) 447-2019
Types of assistance: grants. Estimate of annual funds available: $ 100,000.

* Food and Agricultural Sciences National Needs Graduate Fellowship Grants 10.210
Director, Higher Education Programs
Department of Agriculture
Administration Bldg., Room 350-A
14th & Independence Ave., SW
Washington, DC 20250   (202) 447-7854
To award grants to colleges and universities that have superior teaching and research competencies in the food and agricultural sciences to encourage outstanding students to pursue and complete a graduate degree in an area of food and agricultural sciences. Types of assistance: grants. Estimate of annual funds available: $ 2,766,440.

* Selected Reserve Educational Assistance Program (Montgomery GI Bill Act of 1984) 12.609
Assistant Secretary of Defense (Reserve Affairs)
Pentagon, Room 3E325
Washington, DC 20301-1500   (202) 695-7459/7429
To encourage and sustain membership in the National Guard and Reserves. Types of assistance: direct payment. Estimate of annual funds available: $ 116,000,000.

* Health Education Assistance Loans (HEAL) 13.108
Michael Heninburg
Division of Student Assistance
Bureau of Health Professions
HRSA, PHS, Rm 8-39, 5600 Fishers Lane
Rockville, MD 20857   (302) 443-1173
To authorize Health Education Assistance Loans (HEAL) for educational expenses available from eligible lenders such as banks, credit unions, savings and loan associations, etc. Types of assistance: loan guarantee. Estimate of annual funds available: $ 200,000,000.

* Grants for Preventive Medicine Residency Training (Preventive Medicine Residency) 13.117
Donald Weaver
Director, Division of Medicine
Health Resources and Services Administration
5600 Fishers Lane
Rockville, MD 20857   (301) 443-6190

To promote the post-graduate education of physicians in preventive medicine Types of assistance: grants. Estimate of annual funds available: $ 1,503,000.

* Grants for Podiatric Medicine Training (Podiatric Medicine) 13.119
Dr. Donald Weaver, Director, Division of Medicine
Health Resources and Services Administration
5600 Fishers Lane
Rockville, MD 20857   (301) 443-6190
To provide clinical training for podiatry students recruited from areas that are currently under-served. Types of assistance: grants. Estimate of annual funds available: $ 350,000.

* Health Professions Pregraduate Scholarship Program for Indians 13.123
IHS Scholarship Program, Indian Health Services
Public Health Service, DHHS
5600 Fishers Lane, Room 6-12
Rockville, MD 20857   (301) 443-6197
Types of assistance: grants. Estimate of annual funds available: $ 1,451,440.

* Nurse Anesthetist Traineeships 13.124
Division of Nursing
Bureau of Health Professions
Health Resources and Services Administration, PHS
Rm 5C-13, 5600 Fishers Lane
Rockville, MD 20857   (301) 443-6880
To provide traineeships for full-time study in accredited training programs for registered nurses who have completed 12 months of study in nurse anesthetist training programs. Types of assistance: grants. Estimate of annual funds available: $ 784,000.

* Financial Assistance for Disadvantaged Health Professions Students (FADHPS) 13.139
Division of Student Assistance
Health Resources and Services Administration, PHS
Parklawn Bldg. Room 8-23
5600 Fishers Lane
Rockville, MD 20857   (301) 443-1173
To assist disadvantaged health professions students who are of exceptional financial need to obtain a degree in medicine, osteopathic medicine, or dentistry by providing financial support to help pay for their costs of eduction. Types of assistance: grant. Estimate of annual funds available: $ 4,849,000.

* Post-Baccalaureate Facility Fellowships (Faculty Fellowships) 13.147
Anastasia Buchanan, Division of Nursing
Health Resources and Services Administration, PHS
Room 5C-13, 5600 Fishers Lane
Rockville, MD 20857   (301) 443-5763
To provide grants to eligible schools of nursing to: investigate cost-effective alternatives to traditional health care modalities, examine nursing interventions that result in positive outcomes in health status, address other ares of nursing practice. Types of assistance: grants. Estimate of annual funds available: $ 1,079,000.

* Special International Postdoctoral Research Program in Acquired Immunodeficiency Syndrome 13.154
Chief, International Research and Awards Branch

Fogarty International Center
Bethesda, MD 20892 (301) 496-6688
To support collaborative research between the U.S. and foreign scientists who wish to enhance their knowledge and skills in the epidemiology, diagnosis, prevention, and treatment of acquired immunodeficiency syndrome (AIDS). Types of assistance: grants. Estimate of annual funds available: $ 700,000.

* National Health Service Corps Loan Repayment (NHSC Loan Repayment Program) 13.162
Director, Division of Health Services Scholarships
Health Resources and Services Administration
Room 7-34, 5600 Fishers Lane
Rockville, MD 20857 (301) 443-3744
To help assure an adequate supply of trained health professionals for the National Health Service Corps by providing for the repayment of educational loans for participants who agree to serve an applicable period of time in a health manpower shortage. Types of assistance: grants. Estimate of annual funds available: $ 4,501,000.

* Indian Health Service Educational Loan Repayment (IHS Loan Repayment Program) 13.164
Hazel Black, Health Manpower Support Branch, IHS
Room 9A-22, Parklawn Bldg.
5600 Fishers Lane
Rockville, MD 20857 (301) 443-4242
To help insure an adequate supply of trained health professionals for Indian Health Service facilities by providing for the repayment of educational loans for participants who agree to serve an applicable period of time at a facility. Types of assistance: grants. Estimate of annual funds available: $ 2,000,000.

* Grants for State Loan Repayment (State Loan Repayment Program) 13.165
Director
Division of National Health Service Corps
Health Resources and Services Administration
Room 7A-39, 5600 Fishers Lane
Rockville, MD 20857 (301) 443-2900
To assist states in establishing loan repayment programs that will help to assure an adequate supply of trained health professionals in states by providing for the repayment of health professions educational loans for participants who agree to serve an applicable period of time in a health manpower shortage area in the state. Types of assistance: grant. Estimate of annual funds available: $ 4,501,000.

* National Research Service Awards - Health Services Research Training 13.225
National Center for Health Services Research and
 Health Care Technology Assessment, PHS
Department of Health and Human Services
Rm 18A-10, Parklawn Bldg.
Rockville, MD (301) 443-4033
To provide predoctoral and postdoctoral training opportunities in health services research. Types of assistance: grant. Estimate of annual funds available: $ 1,322,975.

* Occupational Safety and Health-Training Grants (ERC; Educational Resource Centers) 13.263
Procurement and Grants Office, CDC, DHHS
1600 Clifton Road, NE, Mail Stop E14
Atlanta, GA 30333 (404) 842-6575
To develop specialized professional personnel in occupational safety and health problems with training in occupational medicine. Types of assistance: grants. Estimate of annual funds available: $ 10,095,000.

* Alcohol and Drug Abuse Clinical or Service-Related Trainingships for Registered Nurses) 13.274
Frances Cotter
Division of Clinical and Prevention Research
National Institute on Alcohol Abuse and Alcoholism
5600 Fishers Lane
Rockville, MD 20857 (301) 443-1207
To provide specialized training of heath and allied health professions personnel to assure that the alcohol and drug abuse knowledge and skills of such personnel are appropriate to the needs of those they serve. Types of assistance: grants. Estimate of annual funds available: $ 1,100,000.

* Mental Health National Research Service Awards

for Research Training (NRSA Program) 13.282
Dr. Lyle Bivens, Director
Division of Basix Sciences
Room 11-803, 5600 Fishers Lane
Rockville, MD 20857 (301) 443-3563
To assure a continuing and adequate supply of well-trained personnel who are able to conduct research on mental health problems. Types of assistance: grant. Estimate of annual funds available: $ 19,710,000.

* National Health Service Corps Scholarship Program (NHSC Scholarship Program) 13.288
National Health Service Corps Scholarship Program
Health Resources and Services Administration
PHS, DHHS, Parklawn Bldg., Room 7-16
5600 Fishers Lane
Rockville, MD (301) 443-1646
To support training of physicians, dentists, and other health professionals as requested for professional service as members of the National Health Service Corps in Health Manpower Shortage Areas of the United States. Types of assistance: grants. Estimate of annual funds available: $ 0.

* Nurse Practitioner and Nurse Midwife Education and Traineeships 13.298
Dr. Thomas P. Phillips
Division of Nursing
Health Resources and Services Administration, PHS
Room 5C-26, 5600 Fishers Lane
Rockville, MD 20857 (302) 443-6333
To educate registered nurses who will be qualified to provide primary health care. Types of assistance: grants. Estimate of annual funds available: $ 11,773,000.

* Health Professions Student Loans (HPSL) 13.342
Division of Student Assistance
Health Resources and Services Administration, PHS
Room 823, 5600 Fishers Lane
Rockville, MD 20857 (301) 443-1173
To increase educational opportunities for students in need of financial assistance to pursue a course of study in specified health professions by providing long term low interest loans. Types of assistance: loans. Estimate of annual funds available: $ 4,300,000.

* Professional Nurse Traineeships (Nurse Traineeships; Trainee) 13.358
Anastasia Buchanan, Division of Nursing
Health Resources and Services Administration
PHS, DHHS, 5600 Fishers Lane
Room 5C-13
Rockville, MD 20857 (301) 443-5768
To prepare registered nurses as administrators, researchers, teachers, nursing specialist, nurse midwives, and nurse practitioners for positions in hospitals and related institutions in public health agencies. Types of assistance: grants. Estimate of annual funds available: $ 1,275,200.

* Nursing Student Loans (NSL) 13.364
Division of Student Assistance
Health Resources and Services Administration
PHS, DHHS, Parklawn Bldg. Rm 8-23
5600 Fishers Lane
Rockville, MD 20857 (301) 443-1173
To assist students in need of financial assistance to pursue a course of study in professional nursing education by providing long-term, low interest loans, currently at the rate of 5 percent. Types of assistance: loans. Estimate of annual funds available: $ 6,000,000.

* Minority Biomedical Research Support (MBRS) 13375
Director, Minority Biomedical Research Support
 Program Branch
Division of Research Resources
National Institutes of Health
Bethesda, MD 20892 (301) 496-6745
To address the lack of representation of minorities in biomedical research by increasing the pool of minorities pursing research careers. Types of assistance: grants. Estimate of annual funds available: $ 28,147,000.

* Grants for Graduate Training in Family Medicine (Family Medicine Residency) 13.379
Dr. Donald Weaver

Director, Division of Medicine
Health Resources and Services Administration
Room 4C25, 5600 Fishers Lane
Rockville, MD 20857 (301) 443-6190
To increase the number of physicians practicing family medicine. Types of assistance: grants. Estimate of annual funds available: $ 11,827,000.

* Cancer Research Manpower 13.398
Dr. Vincent J. Cairoli, Chief
Cancer Training Branch
Division of Cancer Prevention and Control
National Cancer Institute EPN/232B
Bethesda, MD 20892 (301) 496-8580
To make available support for nonprofit institutions interested in providing biomedical training opportunities for individuals interested in careers in basic and clinical research to support important areas of the National Cancer Program. Types of assistance: grants. Estimate of annual funds available: $ 41,781,000.

* Child Development Associate Scholarships 13.614
Mrs. Dollie Wolverton, Head Start Bureau
400 6th St., SW
Washington, DC 20024 (202) 755-7710
To support the cost of assessing and providing credentials to candidates for certification as Child Development Associates (CDA). Types of assistance: grants. Estimate of annual funds available: $ 1,450,000.

* Child Welfare Services Training Grants 13.648
Director, Program Support Division
Children's Bureau, Administration for Children
Youth and Families
P.O. Box 1182
Washington, DC 20013 (202) 755-7820
To develop and maintain an adequate supply of qualified and trained personnel for the field of services to children and their families, and to improve educational programs and resources for preparing personnel for this field. Types of assistance: grant. Estimate of annual funds available: $ 3,696,000.

* Special Programs for the Aging-Title IV-Training, Research and Discretionary Projects and Programs 13.668
Mike Suzuki, Associate Commissioner
Office of Program Development
Administration on Aging, DHHS
Washington, DC 2021 (202) 245-0442
To provide adequately trained personnel in the field of aging, improve knowledge of the problems and needs of the elderly, and to demonstrate better ways of improving the quality of life for elderly. Types of assistance: grants. Estimate of annual funds available: $ 24,173,000.

* Scholarships for Students of Exceptional Financial Need (EFN Scholarship) 13.820
Michael Heninburg
Division of Student Assistance, Health Resources
and Services Administration, PHS
Room 8-23, 5600 Fishers Lane
Rockville, MD 20857 (301) 443-1173
To make funds available to authorized health professions schools to award scholarships to health professions students of exceptional financial need. Types of assistance: grant. Estimate of annual funds available: $ 6,578,000.

* Health Careers Opportunity Program 13.822
Grants Management Officer
Health Resources and Services Administration
Room 8C-22, 5600 Fishers Lane
Rockville, MD 20857 (301) 443-6857
To identify recruit, and select individuals from disadvantaged backgrounds for education and training in a health or allied health professions school. Types of assistance: grant. Estimate of annual funds available: $ 18,692,037.

* Medical Library Assistance 13.879
Dr. Jeanne Brand
Extramural Programs
National Library of Medicine
Bethesda, MD 20894 (301) 496-6131
To improve health information services by providing funds to train professional personnel, strengthen library and information services, support biomedical publication, and conduct research in information science and in medical information. Types of assistance: grants. Estimate of annual funds available:

$ 13,551,000.

* Minority Access to Research Careers (MARC) 13.880
Edward Blynum
Program Director (MARC Program)
National Institute of General Medical Sciences, NIH
Bethesda, MD 20892 (301) 496-7941
To assist minority institutions to train greater numbers of scientists and teachers in health related fields. Types of assistance: grants. Estimate of annual funds available: $ 9,053,000.

* Grants for Residency Training in General Internal Medicine and/or General Pediatrics (Primary Care Training) 13.884
Dr. Donald Weaver, Director
Division of Medicine, HRSA, PHS
Room 4C25, 5600 Fishers Lane
Rockville, MD 20857 (301) 443-6190
To promote the graduate education of physicians who plan to enter the practice of general internal medicine or general pediatrics. Types of assistance: grants. Estimate of annual funds available: $ 13,749,297.

* Grants for Physician Assistant Training Program (Physical Assistant Training Program) 13.886
Dr. Donald Weaver, Director
Division of Medicine
Bureau of Health Professions, HRSA, PHS, DHHS
Parklawn Bldg., Room 4C-25
5600 Fishers Lane
Rockville, MD 20857. (301) 443-6190
To enable public or nonprofit private health or educational entities to meet the cost of projects to plan, develop and operate programs for the training of physicians assistants. Types of assistance: grants. Estimate of annual funds available: $ 452,000.

* Resource and Manpower Development in the Environmental Health Sciences (Core Centers and Research Training Program) 13.894
Director, Division of Extramural Research and
Training
National Institute of Environmental Health Sciences
P.O. Box 12233
Research Triangle Park, NC 27709 (919) 541-7723
To provide long-term, stable support for broadly based multidisciplinary research and training on environmental health problems in Environmental Health Sciences Center. Types of assistance: grant. Estimate of annual funds available: $ 25,303,000.

* Grants for Predoctoral Training in Family Medicine (Predoctoral Training) 13.896
Dr. Donald Weaver, Director
Division of Medicine, HRSA, PHS
Room 4C-25, 5600 Fishers Lane
Rockville, MD 20857 (301) 443-6190
To assist schools of medicine and osteopathy in meeting the cost of projects to plan, develop, and operate professional predoctoral training programs in the field of family medicine. Types of assistance: grant. Estimate of annual funds available: $ 4,178,000.

* Residency Training and Advanced Education in the General Practice of Dentistry 13.897
Richard G. Weaver, Dental Health Branch
Division of Assoc. & Dental Health Professions
HRSA, PHS, 5600 Fishers Lane
Rockville, MD 20857 (301) 443-6837
To assist schools of dentistry and institutions conducting post-graduate dental training in defraying the costs of projects to plan, develop, and operate an approved residency or advanced educational program in the general practice of dentistry. Types of assistance: grants. Estimate of annual funds available: $ 1,691,000.

* Health Administration Graduate Traineeships 13.962
John R. Westcott, Grants Management Officer
Bureau of Health Professions, HRSA
Room 8C-22, 5600 Fishers Lane
Rockville, MD 20857 (301) 443-6880
To support eligible students enrolled in accredited graduate programs in health

administration, hospital administration of health policy analysis and planning. Types of assistance: grants. Estimate of annual funds available: $ 470,000.

* Traineeships for Students in Schools of Public Health and Other Graduate Public Health Programs (Public Health Traineeships)   13.964

John R. Westcott, Grants Management Officer, HRSA
Room 8C-22, 5600 Fishers Lane
Rockville, MD   20857   (301) 443-6880
To support traineeships for students in graduate educational programs in accredited schools of public health or other public or nonprofit educational entities (excluding programs eligible for support under Section 791A which offer graduate programs for training. Types of assistance: grants. Estimate of annual funds available: $ 2,819,000.

* Grants for the Training of Health Professions in Geriatrics   13.969

Mr. William Koenig
HRSA, PHS, Department of Health and Human Services
5600 Fishers Lane
Rockville, MD   20857   (301) 443-6887
To develop regional resource centers focused on strengthening multidisciplinary training of health professionals in geriatric health care. Types of assistance: grants. Estimate of annual funds available: $ 9,382,000.

* Health Professions Scholarship Program   13.972

Larry Thomas
IHS Scholarship Program
Indian Health Service, PHS, DHHS
Room 6-12, 5600 Fishers Lane
Rockville, MD   20857   (301) 443-6197
To provide scholarships to Indians and other students at health professions schools in order to obtain health professionals to serve Indians. Types of assistance: grants. Estimate of annual funds available: $ 4,058,000.

* Senior International Fellowships   13.989

Bettie J. Graham, Ph.D., Chief
International Research Awards Branch
Fogarty International Center
Bethesda, MD   20892   (301) 496-6688
To promote the exchange of ideas and information about the latest advances in the biomedical and behavioral sciences between U.S. biomedical scientists and those of other nations of the world and to bring to the foreign and U.S. institutions the knowledge and professional scientific background which will lead to improvement in the biomedical research potential of both institutions. Types of assistance: grants. Estimate of annual funds available: $ 922,000.

* Community Development Work-Study Program   14.234

Department of Housing and Urban Development
Community Planning and Development
Office of Program Policy Development
Technical Assistance Div.
451 7th St., SW
Washington, DC   (202) 755-6092
Under the Community Development Work-Study Program (CSWSP), HUD will make grants to institutions of higher education, either directly or through area-wide planning organizations or states, for the purpose of providing assistance to economically disadvantaged and minority students who participate in community development work-study programs and are enrolled full-time graduate or undergraduate programs in community management. Types of assistance: grants. Estimate of annual funds available: $ 3,000,000.

* Urban Mass Transportation Managerial Training Grants (Mass Transit Technology and Technical Assistance Program)   20.503

Office of Technical Assistance and Safety
Urban Mass Transportation Administration
Department of Transportation
400 Seventh St., SW
Washington, DC   20590   (202) 366-0080
To provide fellowships for training of managerial, technical and professional personnel employed in the urban mass transportation field. Types of assistance: grants. Estimate of annual funds available: $ 1,953,000.

* U.S. Merchant Marine Academy (Kings Point)   20.807

Bruce J. Carlton, Director
Office of Maritime Labor and Training
Maritime Administration

Department of Transportation
Washington, DC   20590   (202) 366-5755
To train merchant marine officers. Types of assistance: training. Estimate of annual funds available: $ 20,587,000.

* Federal Employment for Disadvantaged Youth - Part Time (Stay-in-School Program)   27.003

Yolanda Wilson, Programs Division
Office of Affirmative Recruiting and Employment
Office of Personnel Management
1900 E St., NW
Washington, DC   20415   (202) 632-0601
To give disadvantaged young people, 16 years of age and older, an opportunity for part-time employment with federal agencies in order to allow them to continue their education without interruptions caused by financial pressures. Types of assistance: federal employment. Estimate of annual funds available: $ 0.

* Federal Employment for Disadvantaged Youth - Summer (Summer Aids)   27.004

Office of Affirmative Recruiting and Employment
Office of Personnel Management
1900 E St., NW
Washington, DC   20415   (202) 632-0601
To give disadvantaged young people, 16 years of age or older, meaningful summer employment with the federal Government. Types of assistance: federal employment. Estimate of annual funds available: $ 0.

* Federal Summer Employment (Summer Jobs in Federal Agencies)   27.006

Staffing Policy Division
Career Entry and Employee Development Group
Office of Personnel Management
1900 E St., NW
Washington, DC   20415   (202) 632-0728
To provide summer employment primarily for college students and high schools students with special skills. Types of assistance: federal employment. Estimate of annual funds available: $ 0.

* Promotion of the Arts - Arts Administration Fellows Program (Fellowship Program)   45.021

Arts Administration Fellows Program
National Endowment for the Arts
1100 Penn Ave., NW
Washington, DC   20506   (202) 682-5786
To provide a limited number of 13 week fellowships for professionals in arts management and related fields. Types of assistance: grants. Estimate of annual funds available: $ 200,000.

* Promotion of the Humanities - Younger Scholars (High School and College Students) 45.115

Division of Fellowships and Seminars
Younger Scholars Program
Room 316, National Endowment for the Humanities
Washington, DC   20506   (202) 786-0643
To support non-credit humanities projects during the summer by college students and advanced high school students. Types of assistance: grants. Estimate of annual funds available: $ 400,000.

* Promotion of the Humanities-Fellowships for University Teachers   45.142

Fellowships for University Teachers
Division of Fellowships and Seminars
National Endowment for the Humanities, Room 316
Washington, DC   20506   (202) 786-0466
To provide time for uninterrupted study and research to university teachers, and faculty members of postgraduate professional schools who can make significant contributions to thought and knowledge in the humanities. Types of assistance: grant. Estimate of annual funds available: $ 3,165,000.

* Promotion of the Humanities - Fellowships for College Teachers and Independent Scholars 45.143

Fellowships for College Teachers and Independent
Scholars
Division of Fellowships and Seminars, Rm 316

Education

National Endowment for the Humanities
Washington, DC 20506 (202) 786-0466
To provide opportunities for college teachers and independent scholars to pursue independent study and research that will enhance their capacities as teachers, scholars, or interpreters of the humanities. Types of assistance: grants. Estimate of annual funds available: $ 3,390,000.

* Promotion of the Humanities-Regrants Program/ Selected Areas 45.153

National Endowment for the Humanities
Regrants Program/International Research
Room 318
Washington, DC 20506 (202) 786-0204
To award funds that will be regranted through fellowships and grants-in-aid to support individual American scholars pursuing research in all fields of the humanities. Types of assistance: grants. Estimate of annual funds available: $ 145,000.

* Graduate Research Fellowships 47.009

Dr. Douglas S. Chapin
Graduate Fellowships, Division of Research Career
Development
National Science Foundation
1800 G. Street, NW
Washington, DC 20550 (202) 357-7856
To provide tangible federal encouragement to highly talented graduate students for advanced study in the sciences, mathematics and engineering. Types of assistance: grants. Estimate of annual funds available: $ 24,016,000.

* Young Scholars (National Science Foundtion) 47.072

Dr. Elmina D. Johnson
Division of Research Career Development
National Science Foundation, Room 6730
1800 G. St., NW
Washington, DC 20500 (202) 357-7538
To identify secondary school students with high potential, high ability in science mathematics and/or engineering and to facilitate their making of informed career choices. Types of assistance: grants. Estimate of annual funds available: $ 7,000,000.

* Veterans Educational Assistance (Noncontributory GI Bill) 64.111

Department of Veterans Affairs
Washington, DC 20420
To make service in the Armed Forces more attractive by extending benefits of a higher education to qualified persons who might not otherwise be able to afford such an education. Types of assistance: direct payment. Estimate of annual funds available: $ 333,026,000.

* Post-Vietnam Era Veterans' Educational Assistance (Voluntary-Contributory Matching Program) 64.120

Department of Veterans Affairs
Central Office
Washington, DC 20420
To provide educational assistance to persons entering the Armed Forces after December 31, 1976 and before July 1, 1985, to assist persons in obtaining an education they might otherwise not be able to afford. Types of assistance: direct payment. Estimate of annual funds available: $ 208,120,000.

* All Volunteer Force Educational Assistance (Montgomery GI Bill Active Duty) 64.124

Department of Veterans Affairs
Central Office
Washington, DC 20420
To help service persons readjust to civilian life after their separation from military service. Types of assistance: direct payment. Estimate of annual funds available: $ 46,091,000.

* University-Laboratory Cooperative Program 81.004

Larry L. Barker
Division of University and Industry Programs
Office of Energy Research, DOE
Washington, DC 20585 (202) 586-8947
To provide college and university science and engineering faculty and students with energy-related training and research experience in areas of energy research at DOE facilities. Types of assistance: grants, other. Estimate of annual funds available: $ 8,000,000.

* Pre-Freshman Engineering (PREP) 81.047

Division of University and Industry Programs
Office of Energy Research, DOE
Forrestal Bldg., 1000 Independence Ave., SW
Washington, DC 20585 (202) 586-1634
To alleviate manpower shortages in engineering by preparing and guiding minority and women high school students in the selection of college preparatory courses in science and mathematics. Types of assistance: grants. Estimate of annual funds available: $ 300,000.

* Minority Educational Institution Research Travel Fund (MIRT) 81.083

Isiah O. Sewell
Office of Minority Economic Impact MI-2.2, DOE
Forrestal Bldg., Rm 5B-110
Washington, DC 20585 (202) 586-1953
To provide travel funds to faculty members and graduate students of minority postsecondary educational institutions to encourage and assist in initiating and improving energy related research. Types of assistance: direct payment. Estimate of annual funds available: $ 50,000.

* Minority Honors Training and Industrial Assistance Program (Minority Honors Program) 81.084

Isiah O. Sewell
Office of Minority Economic Impact, DOE
Forrestal Bldg., Room 5B-110
Washington, DC 20585. (202) 586-1593
To provide scholarship funding to financially needy minority honor students pursuing training in energy related technologies and to develop linkages with energy industries. Types of assistance: grants. Estimate of annual funds available: $ 402,000.

* Science and Engineering Research Semester 81.097

Donna J. Prokop
Division of University and Industry Programs
Office of Energy Research, DOE
Washington, DC 20585 (202) 586-8949
To give college juniors and seniors the opportunity to participate in hands-on research at the cutting edge of science at the DOE National laboratories. Types of assistance: training, direct payment. Estimate of annual funds available: $ 1,500,000.

* Educational Exchange-Graduate Students (Fulbright Program) 82.001

Institute of International Educational
809 United Nations Plaza
New York, NY 10017
To improve and strengthen international relations of the U.S. by promoting better mutual understanding among the peoples of the world through educational exchanges. Types of assistance: grants. Estimate of annual funds available: $ 5,518,581.

* Educational Exchange-University Lecturers (Professors) and Research Scholars (Fulbright-Hays Program) 82.002

Council for International Exchange of Scholars
11 Dupont Circle, Suite 300
Washington, DC 20036
To improve and strengthen the international relations of the U.S. by promoting mutual understanding among the peoples of the world through educational exchanges. Types of assistance: grants. Estimate of annual funds available: $ 20,138,170.

* Adult Education-State Administered Basic Grant Program 84.002

D. Kay Wright
Division of Adult Education
Office of Assistant Secretary for Vocational and
Adult Education
Department of Education
Washington, DC 20202-7320 (202) 732-2270
To improve educational opportunities for adults and to encourage the establishment of adult education programs. Types of assistance: grants. Estimate of annual funds available: $ 136,344,000.

* Supplemental Educational Opportunity Grants

(SEOG) 84.007
Division of Policy and Program Development
Student Financial Assistance Programs
Department of Education
400 Maryland Ave., SW
Washington, DC 20202 (202) 732-4490
To provide eligible undergraduate postsecondary students with demonstrated financial need with grant assistance to help meet educational expenses. Types of assistance: direct payments. Estimate of annual funds available: $ 440,739,000.

* National Resource Centers and Fellowships Program for Language and Area or Language and International Studies 84.015
Joseph F. Belmonte
Advanced Training and Research Branch
Center for International Education
7th and D St., SW
Washington, DC 20202 (202) 732-3283
To promote instruction in those modern foreign languages area and international studies critical to national needs by supporting the establishment, strengthening and operation of such programs at colleges and universities. Types of assistance: grant. Estimate of annual funds available: $ 11,234,000.

* Fulbright-Hays Training Grants-Doctoral Dissertation Research Abroad 84.022
Center for International Education
Office of Asst Secretary for Postsecondary Education
Department of Education, Room 3928
7 and D Sts., SW
Washington, DC 20202 (202) 732-3298
To provide opportunities for graduate students to engage in full-time dissertation research abroad in modern foreign language and area studies. Types of assistance: grants. Estimate of annual funds available: $ 1,680,000.

* Handicapped Education - Special Education Personnel Development (Training Personnel for the Education of the Handicapped) 84.029
Norm How
Division of Personnel Preparation
Special Education Programs
Department of Education
Washington, DC 20202 (202) 732-1070
To address identified shortages of special education teachers and related service personnel. Types of assistance: grants. Estimate of annual funds available: $ 67,095,000.

* Guaranteed Student Loans (Stafford Loans, PLUS Loans, Supplemental Loans for Students (SLS) and Consolidation Loans 84.032
Division of Policy and Program Development
Student Financial Assistance Programs
Department of Education
Washington, DC 20202 (202) 732-4242
To authorize guaranteed loans for education expenses available from eligible lenders such as banks, credit unions, savings and loan associations, pension funds, insurance companies, and schools to vocational undergraduate and graduate students enrolled at eligible postsecondary institutions. Types of assistance: loan guarantee. Estimate of annual funds available: $ 12,591,000.00.

* College Work-Study Program (CWS) 84.033
G. Oren, Division of Policy and Program Development Student Financial Assistance Programs
Department of Education
400 Maryland Ave., SW
Washington, DC 20202 (202) 732-4490
To provide part-time employment to eligible postsecondary students to help meet educational expenses. Types of assistance: direct payment. Estimate of annual funds available: $ 612,142,000.

* Library Career Training (HEA Title II-B) 84.036
Yvonne Carter
Library Development Staff
Library Programs, Department of Education
55 New Jersey Avenue, NW
Washington, DC 20208 (202) 357-6320
To assist institutions of higher education and library organizations and agencies in training or retraining persons in areas of library specialization where there are

shortages. Types of assistance: grants. Estimate of annual funds available: $ 400,000.

* Perkins Loans 84.038
G. Orem, Division of Program and Policy Development
Department of Energy
400 Maryland Ave., SW
Washington, DC 20202 (202) 732-4490
To provide eligible postsecondary students with demonstrated financial need with low-interest loan funds to help meet educational expenses. Types of assistance: direct payment. Estimate of annual funds available: $ 184,956,000.

* Talent Search 84.044
Division of Student Services
Education Outreach Branch, Department of Education
400 Maryland Ave., SW, Room 3030
Regional Office Bldg. 3
Washington, DC 20202 (202) 732-4804
To identify disadvantaged youths with potential for postsecondary education to encourage them in continuing in and graduating from secondary school and in enrolling programs of postsecondary education. Types of assistance: grants. Estimate of annual funds available: $ 26,240,000.

* Upward Bound 84.047
Division of Student Services
Education Outreach Branch, Department of Education
400 Maryland Ave., SW
Room 3060, Regional Office Bldg. 3
Washington, DC 20202 (202) 732-4804
To generate skills and motivation necessary for success in education beyond high school among low income and potential first generation college students and veterans. Types of assistance: grants. Estimate of annual funds available: $ 91,990,000.

* Vocational Education-Basic Grants to States 84.048
Winifred I. Warnat
Division of Vocational Education
Department of Education
400 Maryland Ave., SW
Washington, DC 20202 (202) 732-2441
To assist states in expanding, improving, modernizing and developing quality vocational education programs. Types of assistance: grants. Estimate of annual funds available: $ 715,600,000.

* Pell Grant Program 84.063
Division of Policy and Program Development
Office of Postsecondary Education
Department of Education
400 Maryland Ave., SW
Washington, DC 20202 (800) 353-INFO
To provide eligible undergraduate postsecondary students with demonstrated financial need with grant assistance to help meed educational expenses. Types of assistance: direct payment. Estimate of annual funds available: $ 4,574,325,000.

* Educational Opportunity Centers 84.066
Division of Student Services
Education Outreach Branch, Department of Education
400 Maryland Ave., SW
Washington, DC 20202 (202) 732-4804
To provide information on financial and academic assistance available for qualified adults desiring to pursue a program of postsecondary education and to assist them in applying for admission to institution of postsecondary education. Types of assistance: grants. Estimate of annual funds available: $ 11,665,000.

* Grants to States for State Student Incentives (State Student Incentive Grants; SSIG) 84.069
Fred H. Sellers
Division of Policy and Program Development
Office of Student Financial Assistance
Department of Education
Washington, DC 20202 (202) 732-4507
To provide grants to the states for use in programs of financial assistance to eligible postsecondary students. Types of assistance: grants. Estimate of annual funds available: $ 71,895,000.

* Indian Education - Fellowships for Indian Students (Section 423 Fellowships) 84.087

Education

Indian Education Programs
Office of Elementary and Secondary Education
Department of Education
400 Maryland Ave., SW
Washington, DC 20202 (202) 732-1887
To enable Indian students to pursue a course of study leading to a post-baccalaureate degree in medicine, psychology, clinical psychology, law, education and related fields. Types of assistance: grants. Estimate of annual funds available: $ 1,600,000.

* Patricia Roberts Harris Fellowships (Graduate Programs) 84.094
Charles H. Miller
Division of Higher Education Incentive Programs
Office of Postsecondary Education
Department of Education
Washington, DC 20202 (202) 732-4395
Provide grants to institutions of higher education to support fellowships for graduate and professional education to students demonstrating financial need. Types of assistance: grants. Estimate of annual funds available: $ 15,711,000.

* Law School Clinical Experience Program 84.097
Division of Higher Education Incentive Programs
Office of Postsecondary Education
Department of Education
Washington, DC 2022 (202) 732-4395
Establish and expand programs in law schools to provide clinical experience to students in the practice of law. Types of assistance: grants. Estimate of annual funds available: $ 3,952,000.

* Fund for the Improvement of Postsecondary Education (FIPSE) 84.116
Fund for the Improvement of Postsecondary Education
Office of the Asst. Secretary for Postsecondary
 Education
7 and D Sts., SW, Rm 3100
Washington, DC 20202 (202) 732-5750
To provide assistance for innovative programs which improve the access to and the quality of postsecondary education. Types of assistance: grants. Estimate of annual funds available: $ 11,856,000.

* Law-Related Education 84.123
School Improvement Programs
Office of Elementary and Secondary Education
400 Maryland Ave., SW
Washington, DC 20202 (202) 732-4357
To support programs at the elementary and secondary school levels by developing and implementing model projects designed to institutionalize law-related education. Types of assistance: grants. Estimate of annual funds available: $ 3,952,000.

* Rehabilitation Training 84.129
Rehabilitation Services Administration
Office of Special Education and Rehabilitative Services
Department of Education
Washington, DC 20202 (202) 732-1400
To support projects to increase the numbers and improve the skills of personnel trained in providing vocational rehabilitation services to handicapped individuals in areas targeted as having personnel shortages. Types of assistance: grants. Estimate of annual funds available: $ 30,134,000.

* Legal Training for the Disadvantaged (The American Bar Association Fund for Public Education) 84.136
Division of Higher Education Incentive Programs
Office of Postsecondary Education
Department of Education
Washington, DC 20202 (202) 732-4393
To provide educationally and economically disadvantaged students many with marginal or less than traditional admissions credentials. Types of assistance: grants. Estimate of annual funds available: $ 1,892,000.

* Migrant Education-High School Equivalency Program (HEP) 84.141
Office of Migrant Education
Office of Elementary and Secondary Education
U.S. Department of Education
400 Maryland Ave., SW
Washington, DC 20202 (202) 732-4746
To assist students who are engaged or who whose families are engaged in migrant and other seasonal farm work to obtain the equivalent of a secondary school diploma. Types of assistance: grant. Estimate of annual funds available: $ 7,410,000.

* Migrant Education - College Assistance Migrant Program (CAMP) 84.149
Office of Migrant Education
Office of Elementary and Secondary Education
Department of Education
400 Maryland Ave., SW, Rm 2145
Washington, DC 20202 (202) 732-4746
To assist students who are engaged, or whose families are engaged, in migrant and other seasonal farmwork who are enrolled or are admitted for enrollment on a full-time basis in the first academic year at an institution of higher education. Types of assistance: grants. Estimate of annual funds available: $ 1,482,000.

* Business and International Education 84.153
International Studies Branch
Center for International Education
Department of Education, Rm 3053
Washington, DC 20202 (202) 732-3302
To promote innovation and improvement in international business education curricula at institution of higher education and serve the needs of business community. Types of assistance: grants. Estimate of annual funds available: $ 2,125,000.

* Training Interpreters for Deaf Individuals 84.160
Office of Special Education and Rehabilitative
 Services
Department of Education
Washington, DC 20202 (202) 732-1322
To support projects, increase the numbers and improve the skills of manual and oral interpretive who provide services to deaf individuals. Types of assistance: grants. Estimate of annual funds available: $ 900,000.

* State Grants for Strengthening the Skills of Teachers and Instruction in Mathematics and Science 84.164
Dr. Allen A. Schmieder, Suite 2040
School Improvement Programs
400 Maryland Ave., SW
Washington, DC 20202 (202) 732-4336
To improve the skills of teachers and instruction in the areas of mathematics and science, also to increase the accessibility of such instruction to all students. Types of assistance: grants. Estimate of annual funds available: $ 128,440,000.

* Jacob K. Javits Fellowships 84.170
Division of Higher Education Incentive Programs
Office of Postsecondary Education
Department of Education
Washington, DC 20202 (202) 732-4415
To provide fellowships to individuals for graduate study in the arts, humanities and social sciences to individuals of superior ability. Types of assistance: grants. Estimate of annual funds available: $ 7,904,000.

* Paul Douglas Teacher Scholarships 84.176
Department of Education
Office of Asst. Secretary for Postsecondary
 Education
Division of Policy and Program Development
Washington, DC 20202 (202) 732-4507
To provide scholarships through the states that enable and encourage outstanding high school graduates who demonstrate an interest in teaching. Types of assistance: grants. Estimate of annual funds available: $ 15,235,297.

* Robert C. Byrd Honors Scholarships (Byrd Scholarship Program) 84.185
Fred H. Sellers
Department of Education
Office of Student Financial Assistance
Division of Policy and Program Development
Washington, DC 20202 (202) 732-4507
To provide scholarships to promote student excellence and achievement to recognize exceptionally able students who show promise of continued academic achievement. Types of assistance: grants. Estimate of annual funds available: $ 8,200,000.

*** Christa McAuliffe Fellowships (CMFP)   84.190
Department of Education**
Office of the Asst Secretary for Elementary and
 Secondary Education
400 Maryland Ave., SW
Washington, DC   20202   (202) 732-4342
To reward excellence in teaching by providing financial assistance to outstanding teachers to continue their education. Types of assistance: grants. Estimate of annual funds available: $ 1,892,000.

*** Graduate Assistance in Areas of National Need
(GAANN)   84.200**
Allen P. Cissell
Division of Higher Education Incentive Programs
Office of Postsecondary Education
Department of Education
Washington, DC   20202   (202) 732-4415
To provide federal support to graduate academic departments, programs, and units of institutions of higher education for the purpose of sustaining and enhancing the capacity for teaching and research in academic areas of national need. Types of assistance: grants. Estimate of annual funds available: $ 12,844,000.

*** Grants to Institutions to Encourage Minority
Participation in Graduate Education (Minority
Participation in Graduate Education)   84.202**
Walter T. Lewis
Division of Higher Education Incentive Programs
Office of Postsecondary Education
Department of Education
Washington, DC   20202   (202) 732-4393
To provide grants to institutions of higher education to enable them to identify talented undergraduate students that demonstrate financial need and are from minority groups under-represented in graduate education. Types of assistance: grants. Estimate of annual funds available: $ 3,476,000.

*** Jacob K. Javits Gifted and Talented Students
(Gifted and Talented)   84.206**
L. Ann Benjamin
Research Applications Division

Programs for the Improvement of Practice
Department of Education
55 New Jersey Ave., NW
Washington, DC   20202   (202) 357-6187
To provide financial assistance to state and local educational agencies, institutions of higher education and other public and private agencies and organizations to stimulate research, development training and similar activities designed to ensure that needs of elementary and secondary schools meet the special educational needs of gifted and talented students. Types of assistance: grants. Estimate of annual funds available: $ 7,904,000.

* Native Hawaiian Gifted and Talented   84.210
Ramon Ruiz
Department of Education
School Improvement Programs
400 Maryland Ave., SW
Washington, DC   20202   (202) 732-4153
To provide financial assistance to the University of Hawaii at Hilo to establish a native Hawaiian Gifted and Talented Center. Types of assistance: direct payment. Estimate of annual funds available: $ 790,400.

*** Ronald E. McNair Post-Baccalaureate Achievement
(McNair Programs)   84.217**
May J. Weaver
Department of Education
Division of Student Services
400 Maryland Ave., SW
Washington, DC   20202   (202) 732-4804
To provide grants for higher education institutions to prepare low-income first generation college students for doctoral study. Types of assistance: grants. Estimate of annual funds available: $ 1,482,000.

* Harry S. Truman Scholarship Program   85.001
Malcolm C. McCormack, Executive Secretary
712 Jackson Place, NW
Washington, DC   20006   (202) 395-4831
To honor former President Harry S. Truman through the operation of an education scholarship program, financed by a permanent trust fund endowment to develop increased opportunities for young Americans to prepare for and pursue careers in public service. Types of assistance: direct payment. Estimate of annual funds available: $ 2,431,000.

State Money for Students

Alabama
Alabama Commission on Higher Education, One Court Square, Suite 221, Montgomery, Alabama 36197, (205) 269-2700. Alabama's programs are to encourage Alabama residents to attend in-state schools. The programs include the Student Assistance Program; the Student Grant Program; the Emergency Secondary Education Scholarship Program for Math & Science; and grants for children of deceased policemen/firefighters.

Alaska
Alaska Commission on Postsecondary Education, Pouch FP, Juneau, AK 99811; (907) 465-2854. Alaska's programs include the Alaska Teacher Scholarship Loan Program.

Arizona
Arizona Commission for Postsecondary Education, 1937 West Jefferson Street, Phoenix, AZ 85009; (602) 255-3109. Scholarships are offered by many of Arizona's universities.

Arkansas
Arkansas Department of Higher Education, 1220 West Third Street, Little Rock, AR 72201; (501) 371-1441. Arkansas' programs include the Loan Emergency Program awarded to students from areas with poor education systems, and the Governor's Scholar Program awarded to the top students in the state.

California
California Student Aid Commission, P.O. Box 942845, Sacramento, CA 94245-0845; (916) 445-0880. California's programs include grants, loans, and scholarships. A workbook with information on these programs is available.

Colorado
Colorado Commission on Higher Education, 1300 Broadway, 2nd Floor, Denver, CO 80203; (303) 866-2723. Colorado administers eight programs in the areas of grants, scholarships, and work-study. It also offers a Diversity Grant Program for students from underrepresented groups.

Connecticut
Connecticut Board of Higher Education, 61 Woodland Street, Hartford, CT 06105-2391; (203) 566-2618. Need-based grants are one of the programs administered by the state of Connecticut.

Delaware
Delaware Postsecondary Education Commission, 820 French Street, Wilmington, DE 19801; (302) 571-3240. Delaware's programs include need- and merit-based scholarship programs. Scholarship loans can be repaid by one-year of service for each year of support.

District of Columbia
Office of State Education Affairs, 2100 Martin Luther King, Jr., Ave., SE, Suite 401, Washington, DC 20020; (202) 727-3688. The District of Columbia's programs include need-based grants for residents.

Florida
Florida Office of Student Financial Aid, State Programs Unit, Florida Education Center, Tallahassee, FL 32399; (904) 488- 1034. Florida offers approximately twenty-six scholarships, grants, and loans. Some of its programs include A Critical Teacher Shortage Loan Program, the "Chappie" James Scholarship awarded to the most promising student, and the Challenger Astronauts Memorial Scholarships. Fellowships and loans are also offered to graduate students.

Georgia
Georgia Department of Education, Division of General Instruction, 1952 Twin Towers East, Atlanta, GA 30334-5040; (404) 656-5812. Georgia's programs include scholarships and grants. A merit-based program includes the Georgia Scholar Program.

Hawaii
Hawaii Department of Education, Student Personnel Services, 1302 Queen Emma Street, Room A-207, Honolulu, HI 96813; (808) 548-4394. Hawaii's programs include scholarships and grants. *Bulletin 15* describes Hawaii's programs and includes other pertinent information.

Idaho
Office of the State Board of Education, 307 Len B. Jordan Building, 650 West State Street, Boise, ID 83720; (208) 334- 2270. Idaho administers programs which include the Idaho Scholarship Program, the Education Incentive Program in Education and Nursing, and a Work-Study Program.

Illinois
Illinois Student Aid Commission, 106 Wilmont Road, Deerfield, IL 60015; (708) 948-8550. Illinois' programs include scholarships based on merit and need and are offered to Illinois residents attending a college or university within the state.

Indiana
State Student Assistance Commission of Indiana, 964 North Pennsylvania St., Indianapolis, IN 46204; (317) 232-2350. Indiana's programs include a need-based grant program and a merit-based Hoosier Scholar Program.

Iowa
Iowa College Aid Commission, 201 Jewett Building, Ninth and Grant Avenue, Des Moines, IA 50309; (515) 282-3501. Some of the programs Iowa offers include an Iowa Tuition Grant, a State of Iowa Scholarship, a Loan Reimbursement in Nursing, and Technical Grants to a two-year community college.

Kansas
Kansas Board of Regents, Capital Tower, 400 8th St., SW, Suite 609, Topeka, KS 66603; (913) 296-3517. Kansas administers approximately sixteen programs in grants and scholarships, including a Scholarship Program which awards a maximum of $1,000 per year. Nursing scholarships which meet certain criteria and graduate scholarships are also administered.

Kentucky
Kentucky Higher Education Assistance Authority, 1050 US 127 South, Frankfort, KY 40601; (502) 564-3553. Kentucky strives to keep its tuition at state colleges and universities affordable by using state monies. Scholarships and grants are offered to students.

Louisiana
Special Commission on Education Services, P.O. Box 91202, Baton Rouge, LA 70821-9202; (504) 922-1011. Louisiana's programs include grants and scholarships.

Maine
Maine Department of Higher Education, State House Station 119, Augusta, ME 04333; (207) 289-2183. Maine administers various scholarships, grants, and loans, including the Maine Student Incentive Program offered to a resident attending a college in Maine or in any other of the five New England states. Post-graduate scholarships in the medical field are also available.

Maryland
Maryland Higher Education Commission, The Jeffrey Building, 16 Francis Street, Suite 209, Annapolis, MD 21401; (301) 974- 5370. Maryland offers scholarships, loans, and grants, in addition to Senatorial and House of Delegate scholarships which are awarded annually.

Massachusetts
Board of Regents of Higher Education, Scholarship Office, 330 Stuart Street, Boston, MA 02116; (617) 727-9420. Massachusetts administers approximately twelve scholarships programs and a Graduate Grant Program.

Michigan
Michigan Department of Education, Student Financial Assistance Services, P.O. Box 3008, Lansing, MI 48909; (517) 373-3394. Michigan administers scholarships, grants, and loans.

Minnesota
Minnesota Higher Education Coordinating Board, Capitol Square Building, Suite 400, 550 Cedar Street, St. Paul, MN 55101, (612) 296-3974. Minnesota's programs include grants, loans, a State Grant Program, and a Child-Care Program.

Mississippi
Board of Trustees of State Institutions of Higher Learning, 3825 Ridgewood Rd., Jackson, MS 39211-6453; (601) 982-6570. Mississippi administers approximately fifteen programs, including scholarships, grants, and loans, all of which are need-and/or merit-based.

Missouri

Missouri Coordinating Board of Higher Education, P.O. Box 1438, Jefferson City, MO 65102; (314) 751-3940. Missouri's programs include the need-based Missouri Student Grant and the Missouri Higher Education Academic Scholarship awarded to those students who scores on the SAT or ACT fall within the top three percent (this award is revised annually).

Montana

Office of the Commissioner of Higher Education, 35 South Last Chance Gulch, Helena, MT 59620; (406) 444-6570. Montana's programs include need- and merit-based scholarships.

Nebraska

Nebraska Coordinating Commission for Postsecondary Education, 301 Centennial Mall, South, P.O. Box 95005, Lincoln, NE 68509-5505; (402) 471-2847. Nebraska administers a "decentralized" form of student aid in higher education. Monies are allocated based on a formula to postsecondary schools. Students should contact the financial aid office at the college they plan to attend for scholarship, grant, and loan information.

Nevada

Nevada Department of Education, 400 West King Street, Carson City, NV 89710; (702) 885-3104. Nevada administers financial programs through their colleges.

New Hampshire

New Hampshire Postsecondary Education Commission, 2 Industrial Park Drive, Concord, NH 03301; (603) 271-255). New Hampshire administers approximately six programs in state scholarships and grants. Students must meet residency requirements.

New Jersey

New Jersey Department of Higher Education, Office of Student Assistance, 4 Quakerbridge Plaza, CN 540, Trenton, NJ 08625; (609) 588-3228. New Jersey administers approximately five programs in state scholarships and grants. Included in these five are the Distinguished State Scholar Program and the Tuition Aid Grant. Recipients must be New Jersey residents attending a college within the state.

New Mexico

New Mexico Education Assistance Foundation, P.O. Box 27020, Albuquerque, NM 81725; (505) 345-3391. New Mexico administers scholarships, grants, and loans.

New York

New York Higher Education Services Corporation, Student Information, Albany, NY 12255; (518) 474-5592. New York administers approximately twenty-one state programs, including two general Grant Programs for full- and part-time students and undergraduate Scholarship and Fellowship awards. New York also administers an Empire State Excellence Scholarship.

North Carolina

North Carolina State Education Assistance Authority, P.O. Box 2688, Chapel Hill, NC 27514; (919) 549-8614. North Carolina administers scholarship, grant, and loan programs.

North Dakota

North Dakota Student Financial Assistance Program, State Capitol, 600 East Boulevard, Bismarck, ND 58505; (701) 224-4114. North Dakota administers approximately three programs, including the merit-based North Dakota Scholars Program.

Ohio

Ohio Board of Regents, 30 East Broad Street, Columbus, OH 43215; (614) 466-7420. Ohio administers approximately five need- and merit-based program, plus an Instructional Grant Program. All of these programs are restricted to Ohio residents only.

Oklahoma

Oklahoma State Regents for Higher Education, 500 Education Building, State Capitol Complex, Oklahoma City, OK 73105; (405) 521-2444. Oklahoma administers approximately six programs, including the merit-based Chancellors Scholarship Program. These programs are restricted to Oklahoma residents attending a college in-state.

Oregon

Oregon State Scholarship Commission
1445 Willamette Street, Eugene, OR 97401; (503) 686-4166. Oregon administers

programs for need-based grants, academic- and need-based cash awards, and private awards. These are available to Oregon residents only.

Pennsylvania

Pennsylvania Higher Education Assistance Agency, 660 Boas Street, Harrisburg, PA 17102; (717) 257-2550. Pennsylvania administers programs in the areas of grants, loans, and scholarships.

Rhode Island

Rhode Island Higher Education Assistance Authority, 560 Jefferson Boulevard, Warwick, RI 02886; (401) 277-2050. Rhode Island administers one Grant Program and three Scholarship Programs, including a Teacher Scholarship for "the best and the brightest." These programs are awarded on the basis of need and/or merit.

South Carolina

South Carolina Commission on Higher Education, 1333 Main Street, Suite 300, Columbia, SC 29201; (803) 253-6260. South Carolina administers scholarship and grant programs to approximately eighteen private colleges.

South Dakota

South Dakota Department of Education and Culturan Affairs, Office of the Secretary, 700 Governors Drive, Pierre, SD 57501; (605) 773-3134. South Dakota administers approximately five need- and merit-based programs in the areas of scholarships and grants.

Tennessee

Tennessee Student Assistance Corporation, 404 James Robertson Parkway, Suite 1250, Parkway Towers, Nashville, TN 37243-0820; (615) 741-1346. Tennessee administers state grants, loans, and scholarships.

Texas

Texas Coordinating Board on Higher Education, Box 12788, Capitol Station, Austin, TX 78711; (512) 462-6400. Texas is a decentralized state for programs. Students should contact the Financial Aid office at the college they plan to attend for grant, scholarship, and loan information

Utah

Utah System for Higher Education, 355 West North Temple, 3 Triad, Suite 550, Salt Lake City, UT 84180-1205; (801) 538-5247. Utah administers state funds using a decentralized system. Students should contact the Financial Aid Office at the college they plan to attend.

Vermont

Vermont Student Assistance Corporation, P.O. Box 2000, Champlain Mill, Winooski, VT 05404; (802) 655-9602. Vermont's programs include the need-based Vermont Incentive Program Grant and non-degree Grant Programs and Honors Scholarships.

Virginia

Virginia State Council of Higher Education, Office of Financial Aid, James Monroe Building, 101 North 14th Street, Richmond, VA 23219; (804) 225-3146. Virginia administers need- and merit-based programs for scholarships, grants, and work-study.

Washington

Council for Postsecondary Education, 917 Lakeridge Way, GV 11, Olympia, WA 98504; (206) 753-3571. Washington administers approximately five programs including the Washington State Need Grant and the Washington Scholars Program.

West Virginia

West Virginia Higher Education Program, P.O. Box 4007, Charleston, WV 25364-4007; (304) 347-1266. West Virginia's programs include scholarships (including a Teacher's Scholarship), grants, and college work-study.

Wisconsin

State of Wisconsin Higher Educational Aids Board, P.O. Box 7885, Madison, WI 53707-7885; (608) 267-2206. Wisconsin administers approximately eight need- and merit-based scholarships and grants. Programs are also available for Indians, minorities, and the handicap.

Wyoming

Wyoming Department of Higher Education, Hathaway Building, Cheyenne, WY 82002; (307) 777-6213. Wyoming administers scholarships and grants, including a First Generation American Scholarship to a qualifying high school senior in Wyoming.

State Education Information

A friend recently had the idea of marketing "Class of 2001" T-shirts to the parents of the kindergarten class of '88. Faced with the problem of estimating the size of the market, he did what any sharp young entrepreneur would do -- he turned to his state department of education for all of the little details...and a mailing list to boot.

It would probably take some effort to come up with a service or product that a school district doesn't buy short of military hardware (but that too might be changing). Like the federal government, schools purchase just about everything under the sun. Each state has a department of education or public instruction which collects and disseminates information on students, staff, school finances, and other related matters. And this data can help you sell a lot more than just T-shirts.

You can use the data to find the names and addresses of science teachers if you've got a great new product for demonstrating chemical reactions or cell osmosis; of math teachers if you've got 3-D geometry models or a novel new software idea; or PE teachers if you're designing football gear for the next century. Remember, teachers are usually the first to lobby for specific new textbooks and learning tools.

Information on the student population of a given school district can yield a pretty accurate picture of who lives where, what their parents earn and how they spend it -- priceless marketing information available at no or little cost to you. If you sell real estate or insurance, having accurate school district information may be essential in closing a sale or targeting new clients.

In addition, there is plenty of money to be made with accurate information on high school seniors. From yearbooks to class rings, prom gowns to SAT tutorials, the senior class is an industry unto itself. So, rather than wait for the "Class of 2001" to grow up, many businesses are already using state education information to get a edge over the competition.

Each state has a Department of Education or Public Instruction which collects and disseminates information pertaining to students, staff, finances and general matters. A representation of types of data collected and maintained is as follows:

Students:
- by grade
- by sex
- by ethnicity
- by special programs (special education, vocational education, bilingual and English as a second language, compensatory education, gifted and talented, migrant)
- by curriculum enrollment, graduates, dropouts, accidents, immunizations, projected enrollment and attendance, test scores.

Educators and Staff:
- Professional job assignments (teachers, administrators, support staff and aides, secretaries)
- sex
- ethnicity
- salaries
- program areas

- highest college degree attained
- months of contract
- days employed
- certification/permits granted
- tenure
- experience.

School District Finances:
- district budgeting and audited accounting data on revenues
- expenditures
- assets
- liabilities
- fund balances
- bond/loan requirements
- local school tax information
- district detailed state aid calculations
- total receipts and disbursements
- taxable property values.

General:
- number of districts
- demographic data
- address and telephone numbers of school campuses within district
- maps
- census.

By observing trends in statistical data, a school system can monitor school programs, improve data management, and address changing economic perspectives in education. In each state a statistical service department is responsible for the identification, implementation, and operation of data collection procedures. Within each state, various offices are responsible for:

* Analyzing, interpreting, and disseminating data relating to public and private elementary and secondary schools. Some offices also include data on colleges and universities of the state;
* Coordinating data collection procedures within the department;
* Recommending policies and procedures for processing statistics;
* Conducting special statistical studies; and
* Preparing projections and estimates.

The information each education department needs is collected annually, and by using machine-readable forms and electronic data processing, various outputs are produced.

Descriptive Reports

These are the major source of information that states regarding their school programs. Data include enrollment by grade and race, daily session data, distribution of graduating class, number of dropouts, special programs, availability of resources (videos, computers etc.), and a faculty listing.

Statistical Reports

A wide variety of statistical analyses of characteristics of public school professional staff are produced, including such factors as salary, degree status, certification status, experience, sex, and age. Summaries of various factors are usually available by school, school district, county, geographic region and for the total state. Also, a number of student statistics can be easily generated including: enrollment by grade, racial/ethnic characteristics, course registrations, student staff ratios, class size, and teacher load.

Special Requests

Requests for special data are handled in a variety of ways. Simple requests can be resolved by referencing a publication. Other more complex requests require custom searching of the databases and may require computer programming. From our survey of services offered by educational departments, we found that 73% offer their statistics on computer magnetic tapes or diskettes, 87% are willing to do customer searches and provide a printout of selected statistics, 51% will provide teacher's names with school addresses either as a printout or on mailing labels, and all states have a listing of their schools with addresses, phone numbers and other important information. In some cases there is a cost recovery fee, and in most cases a written request is preferred and will receive a higher priority.

List of State Department of Education Offices

Alabama
Alabama Department of Education, Montgomery, AL 36130; (205) 261-5156. Services: computer searches, printouts and magnetic tapes. Publications: *Annual Report.*

Alaska
Alaska Department of Education, P.O.F, Juneau, AK; (907) 465-2910. Services: computer searches, printouts and magnetic tapes. Teachers names and addresses are released. Publications: *Annual Report.*

Arizona
Arizona Department of Education, 1535 West Jefferson, Phoenix, AZ 85007; (602) 255-3652. Services: computer searches, printouts and magnetic tapes. Publications: *Annual Report.*

Arkansas
Arkansas Department of Education, 4 State Capitol Mall, Little Rock, AR 72201; (501) 371-1667. Services: computer searches, printouts and magnetic tapes. Publications: *Affecting Basic Skills Achievement Through Technology - A Research Report, Arkansas Policy Statements, Federal Focus, Needs Assessment: Education for Economic Security Act - Title II, EESA, Networking Strategies: Community Education Proven Practice II, Private Schools in Arkansas, Statistical Summary for the Public Schools of Arkansas.*

California
California Department of Education, 721 Capitol Mall, P.O. Box 944272, Sacramento, CA 94244; (916) 322-7373. Services: computer searches, printouts and magnetic tapes. Publications: *Enrollment Data, Racial or Ethnic Distribution of Staff and Students in California Public Schools, Language Census Report.*

Colorado
Colorado Department of Education, 201 E. Colfax, Denver, CO 80203 303-866-6837. Services: computer searches if data readily available. Teachers names and addresses released. Publications: *Status of K-12 Public Education in Colorado.*

Connecticut
Connecticut Department of Education, Office of Research and Evaluation, Box 2219, Hartford, CT 06145; (203) 566-5497. Services: computer searches, printouts and magnetic tapes. Publications: *Annual Report.*

Delaware
Delaware Department of Public Instruction, John Townsend Building P.O. Box 1402, Dover, DE 19903; (302) 736-4583. Services: computer searches and printouts on current data only. No sexual data released. Publications: *Report*

of Educational Statistics.

Florida
Florida Department of Education, 275 Knott Building, Tallahassee, FL 32399; (904) 487-2280. Services: computer searches and printouts as long as data exists. Publications: *MIS Statistical Brief (monthly), Profiles of Florida School Districts.*

Georgia
Georgia Department of Education, Twin Towers East, Atlanta, GA 30334; (404) 656-2400. Services: computer searches and printouts of existing data. Publications: *Annual Report.*

Hawaii
Hawaii Department of Education, P.O. Box 2360, Honolulu, HI 96804; (808) 548-2362. Services: not available to the public. Publications: *Education Today in Hawaii, Annual Financial Report.*

Idaho
Idaho Department of Education, Len B. Jordan Office Building, 650 West State Street, Boise, ID 83720; (208) 334-3301. Services: computer searches, printouts if data exists. Publications: *Financial Summaries, Annual Statistical Report Public School Certified Personnel and Employees in Noncertified Positions.*

Illinois
Illinois State Board of Education, 100 North First St., Springfield, IL 62777; (217) 782-2221. Services: computer searches, printouts and magnetic tapes. Publications: *Annual Statistical Report, Illinois Public School Districts and Schools.*

Indiana
Indiana Department of Education, Education Information Systems, Room 229, State House, Indianapolis, IN 46204; (317) 232-6610. Services: computer searches, printouts and magnetic tapes. Teachers names and addresses released. Publications: *Fall Enrollment Report, Non-English Language Background, Indiana Public School Professional Personnel Data, Noncertified Personnel Data, Annual Fall School Report, School Transportation Report.*

Iowa
Iowa Department of Education, Grimes State Office Building, Des Moines, IA 50319; (515) 281-4738. Services: computer searches, printouts and magnetic tapes. Teachers names and addresses released. Publications: *Annual Report.*

Kansas
Kansas State Department of Education, 120 East 10th St., Topeka, KS 66612; (913) 296-4961. Services: computer searches, printouts and magnetic tapes. Publications: *A Strategic Plan for Kansas Public Education for the Year 2005, Annual Report, State-wide Goals for Education in Kansas, Profile of Kansas Schools, Profiles of Kansas Education Personnel: Superintendents, Teachers, Elementary Principals, Principals, AVTS Directors, and Community College Presidents, 125 Years of Kansas History: How Should Educators Approach It?*

Kentucky
Kentucky Department of Education, Frankfort, KY 40601; (502) 564-4813. Services: computer searches and printouts. Teachers names and home addresses released. Publications: *Profiles of Kentucky Public Schools, Public School Financial Analysis, Local District Annual Financial Reports, Receipts and Expenditures, Public School Salaries.*

Louisiana
Louisiana Department of Education, P.O. Box 94064, Baton Rouge, LA 70804; (504) 342-1803. Services: computer searches, printouts and magnetic tapes. Publications: *Annual Financial and Statistical Report.*

Maine
Maine Department of Educational and Cultural Services Educational Building, Station No. 23, Augusta, ME 04333; (207) 289-5944-- Services: computer searches, printouts and magnetic tapes upon special request. Teachers names and addresses released. Publications: *Maine School Statistics, Students Educated at Public Expense, Resident Per Pupil Operating Costs, Maine Educational Facts.*

Maryland
Maryland Department of Education, Office of Management and Information Systems, 200 West Baltimore St., Baltimore, MD 21201; (301) 333-2659. Services: computer searches and printouts from large databases only (enrollment, finance, staff). Publications: *Annual Report.*

Massachusetts
Massachusetts Department of Education, 1385 Hancock St., Quincy, MA 02169; (617) 770-7203. Services: one magnetic tape is available containing attendance data. Publications: *Distribution of High School Graduates, Per Pupil Expenditure.*

Michigan
Michigan Department of Education, Information Center Data Services, P.O. Box 30008, Lansing, MI 48909; (517) 373-4333. Services: computer searches,

printouts, magnetic tapes and diskettes available. Teachers names and addresses are released. Publications: *Financial Data Statistics, Fingertip Facts.*

Minnesota

Minnesota Department of Education, Data Management Information, 550 Cedar St., Capitol Square Bldg., St. Paul, MN 55101; (612) 296-6104. Services: computer searches, printouts and magnetic tapes. Teachers' names and addresses available on labels from the Documents Division. Publications: *Annual Report.*

Mississippi

Mississippi Department of Education, P.O. Box 771, Jackson, MS 39205; (601) 359-3527. Services: computer searches, printouts and magnetic tapes. Teachers' names and addresses are available. Publications: *Annual Report, Statistical Report, School Dropouts by Reasons.*

Missouri

Missouri Department of Education School Data Section P.O. Box 480 Jefferson City, MO 65102; (314) 751-2569. Services: Computer searches and printout requests are evaluated individually. Publications: *Report of the Public Schools of Missouri.*

Montana

Montana Office of Public Instruction, State Capitol, Helena, MT 59620; (406) 444-3656. Services: computer searches, printouts and magnetic tapes. Publications: *Public Education in Montana.*

Nebraska

Nebraska Department of Education Management Information Systems, Box 94987, 301 Centennial Mall, South Lincoln, NE 68509; (402) 471-2367. Services: computer searches, printouts and magnetic tapes. Teachers' names and addresses are released. Publications: *Annual Report.*

Nevada

Nevada Department of Education, 400 W. King St., Carson City, NV 89710; (702) 885-3100. Services: computer searches, printouts done upon special request for a fee. Teachers' names and addresses are released. Publications: *Status Report.*

New Hampshire

New Hampshire Department of Education, State Office Park South 101 Pleasant St., Concord, NH 03301; (603) 271-3494. Services: computer searches, printouts and magnetic tapes for a fee. Teachers' names and addresses are released under certain circumstances. Publications: *Biennial Report.*

New Jersey

New Jersey Department of Education, 225 West State St., Trenton, NJ 08625; (609) 292-7629. Services: computer searches, printouts and magnetic tapes. Publications: *Annual Report.*

New Mexico

New Mexico Department of Education, Education Building, Santa Fe, NM 87501; (505) 827-6524. Services: computer searches, printouts and magnetic tapes available after July 1988. Teachers' names and addresses released under certain circumstances. Publications: *New Mexico School District Profile.*

New York

New York Department of Education, Information Center on Education, Albany, NY 12234; (518) 474-8716. Services: computer searches, printouts and magnetic tapes available with special requests. Teachers' names and addresses released to professional organizations. Publications: *Projections of Public and Nonpublic School Enrollment and High School Graduates, Public School Professional Personnel Report, Nonpublic School Enrollment and Staff, Distribution of High School Graduates and College-Going Rate, Racial/Ethnic Distribution of Public School Students and Staff, Education Statistics.*

North Carolina

North Carolina Department of Public Education, 116 W. Edenton St., Raleigh, NC 27603; (919) 733-9722. Services: computer searches, printouts and magnetic tapes. Teachers' names and addresses are released. Publications: *Annual Data Plan, Selected Financial Data.*

North Dakota

North Dakota Department of Public Instruction, Bismark, ND 58505; (701) 224-2268. Services: computer searches, printouts and magnetic tapes for a fee. Teachers' names and addresses are released. Publications: *Finance Facts, Statewide Summary on Personnel.*

Ohio

Ohio Department of Education, Computer Services, Room 808, 65 Front St., Columbus, OH 43215; (614) 466-2329. Services: computer searches, printouts and magnetic tapes. Publications: Nothing available until December 1988.

Oklahoma

Oklahoma State Department of Education, 2500 N. Lincoln Blvd., Oklahoma City, OK 73105; (405) 521-3354. Services: computer searches, printouts and

magnetic tapes. Publications: *Annual Report* (3 volumes).

Oregon

Oregon Department of Education, Data Processing, 700 Pringle Parkway S.E., Salem, OR 97310; (503) 378-3581. Services: computer searches, printouts and magnetic tapes. Publications: *Oregon School District Census by ESD Lines, School District Budget Summary, Status of School District Tax Bases, Oregon School Districts - Organization, Location and Size, Oregon Public and Private High School Graduates - Actual and Projected.*

Pennsylvania

Pennsylvania Department of Education Office of Data Services 333 Market St., Harrisburg, PA 17126; (717) 787-2644. Services: computer searches, printouts and magnetic tapes. Teachers' names and addresses are released. Publications: *Status Report On Education In Pennsylvania.*

Rhode Island

Rhode Island Department of Education, 22 Hayes St., Providence, RI 02908; (401) 277-2841. Services: computer searches, printouts under special circumstances, limited availability. Publications: *Statistical Tables.*

South Carolina

South Carolina Department of Education, Rutledge, Management Information Section, Office of Research, Room 605, Rutledge Building, Columbia, SC 29201; (803) 734-8262. Services: computer searches, printouts and magnetic tapes. Teachers' names and address available upon written request. Publications: *Pupils in South Carolina Schools, Supplemental Salary Study Selected School, District, and County Personnel; Preliminary Report of the 1987 Statewide Testing Program, Teacher Salary Study, Annual Salary Study, Superintendents and Principals 1986-1987.*

South Dakota

South Dakota Department of Education & Cultural Affairs, Richard F. Kneip Building, 700 Governors Dr., Pierre, SD 57501; (605) 773-3447. Services: omputer search, printouts and magnetic tapes. Teachers' names and addresses available on mailing labels. Publications: *Educational Statistics Digest.*

Tennessee

Tennessee Department of Education, Office of the Commissioner, Cordell Hull Building Nashville, TN 37219; (615) 741-0728. Services: computer searches normally not available. Publications: *Annual Statistics Report.*

Texas

Texas Department of Education, 1701 N. Congress, Austin, TX 78701; (512) 463-9093. Services: computer searches, printouts and magnetic tapes. Publications: *Texas Public Education and You.*

Utah

Utah Department of Public Instruction, 250 East 500 South, Salt Lake City, UT 84111; (801) 533-5866. Services: computer searches, printouts and magnetic tapes. Teachers' names and addresses are released. Publications: *Annual Report.*

Vermont

Vermont Department of Education, Statistics and Information Unit State Office Building, 120 State St., Montpelier, VT 05602; (802) 828-3151. Services: Not set up to provide printouts or tapes at this time. Publications: *Annual Statistical Report of Schools.*

Virginia

Virginia Department of Education, 101 N. 14th St., Richmond, VA 23219; (804) 225-2099. Services: computer searches, printouts if data is readily available.

Washington

Washington Superintendent of Public Instruction, Old Capitol Building, FG-11, Olympia, WA 98504; (206) 753-1700. Services: computer searches, printouts and magnetic tapes. Teachers' names and addresses available upon special request.

West Virginia

West Virginia Department of Education, Capitol Complex, Charleston, WV 25305; (304) 348-8830. Services: there is no centralized computer center. Databases are maintained in various bureaus. Publications: *Annual Report.*

Wisconsin

Wisconsin Department of Public Instruction 125 S. Webster P.O. Box 7841 Madison, WI 53707; (608) 266-3390. Services: computer searches if data exists. Teachers' names and addresses available on mailing labels. Publications: *Annual Report.*

Wyoming

Wyoming Department of Education, Statistical Department, Hathaway Building, 2nd Floor, Cheyenne, WY 82002; (307) 777-7673. Services: a computer searches, printouts and magnetic tapes.

Careers and Workplace
General Sources

* See also Business & Industry Chapter
* See also Economics, Statistics and Demographics Chapter
* See also Your Community: Money for Communities and Non-Profits Chapter

Each month, several federal and state agencies collect, analyze, and publish data which reflect the current employment and unemployment situation around the country. This information often reveals changing profiles of the U.S. work force, future trends, and even the impact technological innovations on the work force. Besides employment statistics, you'll also find information on such hot topics as child care, foreign labor trends, genetic testing, and literacy in the workplace.

* 800 Labor Publications

Office of Information and Public Affairs
Department of Labor
200 Constitution Ave., NW
Room S1032
Washington, DC 20210   (202) 523-7316

This office can provide you with a free catalog of publications of the U.S. Department of Labor. It contains over 800 title listings in 26 labor categories, and provides ordering information.

* Affirmative Action: Successful Strategies

Superintendent of Documents
Government Printing Office
Washington, DC 20402   (202) 783-3238

Opportunity 2000: Creative Affirmative Action Strategies for a Changing Workforce is a study which profiles the strategies that companies use to ease the conflict between work and family responsibilities and to recruit, develop, and retain minority and economically disadvantaged workers, disabled workers, older workers, and veterans. This publication is available for $5.00. For more information contact: Information Office, Employment Standards Administration, Department of Labor, 200 Constitution Ave., NW, Room C4331, Washington, D.C. 20210; (202) 523-8743.

* American Workforce in the Year 2000

Superintendent of Documents
Government Printing Office
Washington, DC 20402   (202) 783-3238

Workforce 2000, a Department of Labor funded study that looks into the workplace and workforce changes that will take place by the year 2000. The department is using this study to rethink their policies and programs in order to prepare the country for the changes ahead. The study looks at the forces shaping the American economy, scenarios for the year 2000, work and workers in the year 2000 and six challenges the country will face. This publication is available for $5.00.

* Caribbean Basin Employment and Trade

Bureau of International Economic Affairs
Department of Labor
200 Constitution Ave., NW, Room S5355
Washington, DC 20210   (202) 523-7597

The annual report, *Trade and Employment Effects of the Caribbean Basin Economic Recovery Act*, describes the provisions included in the CBERA, along with the benefits they provide to beneficiary countries. It also analyzes changes in U.S. trade with CBERA countries, and looks at trends in U.S. employment in those industries which have undergone the most significant changes in trade flows. Contact this office for more information on the report.

* Changing Workplace and Labor Force

Industry Injuries and Illnesses Data
Superintendent of Documents
Government Printing Office
Washington, DC 20402   (202) 783-3238

Many of the Bureau of Labor Statistics' major surveys and research studies are available in the BLS bulletin series, which include more than 100 area and industry wage studies each year and about 40 volumes dealing with a wide range of economic subjects. Here are examples of publications in this series. *New Worklife Estimates* contains detailed working life tables and is widely used in

liability litigations ($3.25). *Women at Work: A Chartbook* focuses on women's economic activity: labor force trends; occupational and industrial employment patterns; and market work of women in a family context ($4.00). *Children of Working Mothers*, part of the Special Labor Force Report series, discusses the increases in the number of children with working mothers and the two major reasons for this growth ($3.00). *Occupational Projections and Training Data* serves as a statistical and research supplement to the *Occupational Outlook Handbook*, provides detailed data on careers and projected occupational employment, replacement needs, and education and training program completions ($5.50).

* Child Care Survey and Trends

Information Office
Department of Labor
200 Constitution Ave., NW, Room S1032
Washington, DC 20210   (202) 523-9711

The free report, *Child Care: A Workforce Issue*, is a product of a Department of Labor internal task force on child care, and is the first step toward understanding child care as a workforce issue. It includes a survey of current activities on the government and private level, examines work-related trends and needs, and analyzes potential problems.

* Child Labor Laws

Child Labor Programs
Employment Standards Administration
200 Constitution Ave., NW, Room S3510
Washington, DC 20210   (202) 523-7640

The Fair Labor Standards Act protects young workers from employment that might interfere with their educational opportunities or be hazardous to their health or well-being. There are different standards for work allowed, depending upon the age of the child. Contact the Child Labor Programs office for more information.

* Commissions on Women

Women's Bureau
Department of Labor
200 Constitution Ave., NW, Room S3315
Washington, DC 20210   (202) 523-6631

This Bureau provides funds and other assistance to support regional conferences of women's commissions and the annual convention of The National Association of Commissions for Women, an umbrella organization. The women's commission movement continues to grow, and now 247 state, regional, and local commissions for women are reported.

* Competitiveness in the Workplace

Office of Technology Assessment
600 Pennsylvania Ave., SE
Washington, DC 20510   (202) 228-6352

Currently, OTA is exploring the connections between new workplace technologies, employee training, and competitiveness. The study will examine such topics as national investment in training; demographic changes in the work force; employee training in countries that are major industrial competitors of the U.S.; and policy questions concerning existing Federal programs. Contact Wendell Fletcher, the project director, for more information.

Careers and Workplace

* Consumer Price Index and Labor Data on Computer Diskette

BLS Office of Publications
Department of Labor
441 G St., NW, Room 2831A
Washington, DC 20212 (202) 523-7827

Computer diskettes offer an easy-to-use way to manipulate data for economists, other social scientists, researchers, managers, and policymakers with an interest in measuring employment, prices, productivity, injuries and illnesses, and wages. BLS diskette users need an IBM-compatible microcomputer and Lotus 1-2-3 Version 1A or Version 2. Each diskette contains the named data series and a brief technical description that highlights regular revisions, if any, and typical uses for statistics. A flyer is available which describes the diskettes available and their cost.

* Current Employment Analyses

Office of Employment and Unemployment Statistics
Bureau of Labor Statistics
Department of Labor
441 G St., NW, Room 2486
Washington, DC 20212 (202) 523-1944

Labor force statistics from the *Current Population Survey* provide a comprehensive body of information on the employment and unemployment experience of the nation's population, classified by age, sex, race, and a variety of other characteristics. The data is published in a variety of sources, including the monthly news release, *The Employment Situation*, and the monthly periodical, *Employment and Earnings*. Data uses include economic indicators, measure of potential labor supply, and evaluation of wage rates and earnings trends for specific demographic groups.

* Current Wage Developments

Superintendent of Documents
Government Printing Office
Washington, DC 20402 (202) 783-3238

Each monthly issue of *Current Wage Developments* includes selected wage and benefit changes, work stoppages, major agreements that expire during the next month, calendar of features, and statistics on compensation changes. The cost is $15.00 per year. For more information on this data, contact Office of Compensation and Working Conditions, Bureau of Labor Statistics, Department of Labor, 441 G St., NW, Room 2021, Washington, D.C. 20212; (202) 523-1382.

* Employer Resource Kit on Employees' Family Needs

Work and Family Clearinghouse
Women's Bureau
Department of Labor
200 Constitution Ave., NW, Room S3306
Washington, DC 20210 (800) 827-5335

The *Work and Family Resource Kit* is designed to help employers understand the range of family needs emerging in the workplace and the numerous ways a company can respond. It provides a state-of-the-art review of these options as well as advantages and disadvantages. Also listed are references and resources to help employers select the most appropriate response for their employees' family needs.

* Employment and Earnings: Monthly Publication

Editors
Bureau of Labor Statistics
Department of Labor
441 G St., NW, Room 2089
Washington, DC 20212 (202) 523-1959

Employment and Earnings is a monthly publication prepared by the Office of Employment and Unemployment Statistics, with data collected by the Bureau of the Census and state employment security agencies. Detailed information is given according to employment status and characteristics of the employed and unemployed. The data are also categorized into employment setting, hours and earnings, and state and labor force data. Subscriptions can be ordered for $25.00 per year by contacting: Superintendent of Documents, Government Printing Office, Washington, D.C. 20402; (202) 783-3238.

* Employment and Unemployment: Monthly Data and Estimates

Office of Employment and Unemployment Statistics
Bureau of Labor Statistics
441 G St., NW, Room 2919
Washington, DC 20212 (202) 523-1694

This office collects, analyzes, and publishes detailed industry data on employment, wages, hours, and earnings of workers on payrolls of non-agricultural business establishments. It also publishes monthly estimates of state and local area unemployment for use by federal agencies in allocating funds as required by various federal laws. In addition, the office provides current data on occupational employment for most industries for economic analysis and for vocational guidance and education planning.

* Employment Policy and Goals

National Commission for Employment Policy
1522 K St., NW, Suite 300
Washington, DC 20005 (202) 724-1545

This Commission is an independent federal agency with responsibility for examining broad issues of development, coordination, and administration of employment and training programs, as well as advising the President on national employment and training issues. Some of the major responsibilities of the Commission include identifying and examining the employment goals and needs of the nation, examining and evaluating the effectiveness of federally-assisted employment and training programs, and evaluating the impact of tax policies on needs of the nation. The Commission conducts and sponsors research, analyzes the findings, holds public hearings, and publishes an annual report of its findings and recommendations. A current listing of Commission publications is available.

* Employment Projections: 650 Occupations and 300 Industries

Office of Economic Growth and Employment Projections
Department of Labor
601 D St., NW, Room 4414
Washington, DC 20212 (202) 272-5278

This office produces national occupational employment projections for over 650 detailed occupations for all industries combined and within over 300 detailed industries.

* Employment Research and Evaluation Studies

Office of Policy-Research and
Evaluation Projects
Department of Labor
200 Constitution Ave., NW, Room S2006
Washington, DC 20210 (202) 523-6181

A free listing is available of all the employment research and evaluation projects completed since 1970 by the Department of Labor, along with information on how to obtain copies of the reports. The inventory is broken down into major topic areas and the reports are listed chronologically.

* Employment Statistics for 800 Occupations and 400 Industries

Office of Employment and Unemployment
Bureau of Labor Statistics
Department of Labor
441 G St., NW, Room 2913
Washington, DC 20212 (202) 523-1949

Available occupational employment statistics include data on employment by occupation and industry for about 800 occupations and 400 industries. Published in bulletins, such as *Occupational Employment* in (industries), data are used for evaluation of current and historical employment by industry and occupation and vocational planning.

* Foreign Economic Impact on U.S. Employment

Office of International Economic Affairs
Bureau of International Labor Affairs
200 Constitution Ave., NW, Room S5325
Washington, DC 20210 (202) 523-7610

The Labor Department's foreign economic research program evaluates the effects of foreign economic developments on the earnings and employment of U.S. workers. This includes quantitative analysis of the impact of policies on international trade, investment, and technology transfer. Often undertaken in response to congressionally-mandated studies or to requests from other executive branch agencies, research is conducted by staff economists and supplemented by outside research contractors. A complete list of the research is available by contacting this office.

* Foreign Labor Trends

Office of Foreign Relations
Bureau of International Labor Affairs
Department of Labor
200 Constitution Ave., NW, Room S5006
Washington, DC 20210 (202) 523-6257

The Department of State has 47 labor foreign service attaches placed in embassies all over the world. They monitor and report foreign labor developments, as well as educate other countries on U.S. labor developments. They submit annual reports, including an additional 70 embassy reports, to the U.S. Department of Labor, which then publishes the *Foreign Labor Trends Series*. Available through Superintendent of Documents, Government Printing Office, Washington D.C. 20402; (202) 783-3238.

* Foreign Visitor Program

Special Mediation Services
Federal Mediation and Conciliation Service (FMCS)
2100 K St., NW, Room 709
Washington, DC 20427   (202) 653-6271

Representatives of labor, management, and governments from around the world can see how arbitration, mediation, collective bargaining, and employee involvement programs function in the U.S. by participation in this visitor program. Industrial labor relations are targeted. For more information, contact the Special Mediation Services office listed.

* Future Jobs in 250 Industries

Office of Economic Growth
Bureau of Labor Statistics
Department of Labor
601 D St., NW, Room 4000
Washington, DC 20212   (202) 272-5381

This office has information on 250 industries regarding employment requirements, specifically on the demand for employment in the future. Industries covered follow the 1972 Standard Industrial Classification Manual. The November, 1989, issue of the *Monthly Labor Review* provides an overview of the data available.

* Genetic Testing in the Workplace

Office of Technology Assessment
600 Pennsylvania Ave., SE
Washington, DC 20510   (202) 228-6690

OTA is now studying the state-of-the-art technologies used by employers for genetic screening and monitoring, which includes a survey of the 500 largest U.S. industries, to largest utilities, and 11 major unions to determine the current nature and extent of employer testing. Also being examined is the impact of genetic testing; relevant ethical issues; and legal issues, including employment discrimination. Contact Robyn Nishimi, the project director, for more information.

* Government Contractors Employment Standards

Office of Federal Contract Compliance Program
Employment Standards Administration
Department of Labor
200 Constitution Ave., NW, Room C3325
Washington, DC 20210   (202) 523-9475

This office ensures that federal contractors and subcontractors or contractors with federally-assisted construction contracts do not discriminate against any employee or applicant for employment because of race, color, religion, or national origin, and that these contractors take affirmative action to hire and promote qualified handicapped people, Vietnam-era veterans, and disabled veterans of all wars. This office also investigates complaints to determine whether federal contractors are meeting these obligations.

* Government Labor Statistics Programs

Office of Publications
Bureau of Labor Statistics
Department of Labor
441 G St., NW, Room 2421
Washington, DC 20212   (202) 523-1221

The free publication, *Major Programs of the Bureau of Labor Statistics*, presents in concentrated form the scope of the Bureau's major statistical programs, the data available, the form of publication, some of the uses of the data, and selected publications and data tapes.

* Handicapped Persons Affirmative Action

Office of Federal Compliance Programs
Employment Standards Administration
Department of Labor
200 Constitution Ave., NW, Room C3325
Washington, DC 20210   (202) 523-9475

The Rehabilitation Act of 1973 prohibits most employers doing business with the federal government from discriminating in employment against handicapped persons. Employers with contracts in excess of $2,500 must take affirmative action to hire and promote qualified handicapped persons.

* History of Labor in the U.S.

Assistant Secretary for Policy
Department of Labor
200 Constitution Ave., NW, Room S2109
Washington, DC 20210   (202) 523-6461

The Labor Historian can answer any historical inquiries regarding the Department. Questions usually coming from Congressional offices, newspapers, and students. As well as conducting his own research on various aspects of Department history, the historian also assists those researching the Department of Labor. The Historian maintains a large photo collection which is open to the public.

* Home-Based Manufacturing Operations

Wage and Hour Division
Employment Standards Administration
Department of Labor
200 Constitution Ave., NW, Room S3516
Washington, DC 20210   (202) 523-7043

Home-based industry work has always been permitted except in seven industries: knitted outerwear, women's apparel, jewelry manufacturing, gloves and mittens, button and buckle manufacturing, handkerchief manufacturing, and embroidery. In 1984, the U.S. Labor Department lifted the total ban on home work in knitted outerwear, and is now considering a proposal to lift the ban on all industries except women's apparel and those jewelry manufacturing operations in the home that may be hazardous. Contact this office for more information on homework and FLSA enforcement.

* Hours and Earnings Monthly Survey

Office of Employment and
Unemployment Statistics
Bureau of Labor Statistics
Department of Labor
441 G St., NW, Room 2919
Washington, DC 20212   (202) 523-1694

A monthly survey provides hours and earnings data collected from payroll records of business establishments. The data available includes gross hours and earnings of production or nonsupervisory workers in 454 industries, and overtime hours in 323 manufacturing industries. The data are published in a variety of sources, and are used as economic indicators, wage negotiations, and economic research and planning.

* Industry and Employment Projections

Office of Economic Growth and
Employment Projections
Bureau of Labor Statistics
Department of Labor
601 D St., NW, Room 4414
Washington, DC 20212   (202) 272-5278

State and area employment data classified by industry division, and gross weekly hours and earnings for production and related workers in manufacturing is available, as is other data, including demographic employment/unemployment, monthly labor force and unemployment, occupational employment, and area wage surveys.

* Industry-Occupation Employment Matrix

Office of Economic Growth and Employment Projections
Bureau of Labor Statistics
Department of Labor
601 D St., NW, Room 4000
Washington, DC 20212   (202) 272-5283

The National Industry-Occupation Employment Matrix provides detailed information on the distribution of occupational employment by industry. Coverage is for over 650 detailed occupations--wage and salary, self-employed, and unpaid family workers, and wage and salary workers only for over 300 detailed industries.

* Industry Technological Trends

Industry Productivity Studies Division
Office of Productivity and Technology
Department of Labor
200 Constitution Ave., NW, Room S4320
Washington, DC 20210   (202) 523-9219

This office looks at a variety of technological trends. One study analyzes major impending changes in products, materials, and production methods in selected industries; their present and future applications; and their effect on output, productivity, employment, skill levels, training, and occupational requirements. Another study analyzes technological changes that have major effects on more than one industry. Coverage includes selected innovations such as computers and numerical control of machine tools, with an emphasis on innovations that will be important in the next five to 10 years.

* International Labor Affairs

International Labor Organization
Bureau of International Organization Affairs
Department of State
2201 C St., NW, Room 5336
Washington, DC 20520   (202) 647-4196

Careers and Workplace

As a United Nations affiliate, the International Labor Organization is comprised of three parts: government, worker, and employee delegations from 150 countries. Headquartered in Geneva, the ILO meets three times a year and holds an annual conference. The ILO serves as a multilateral technical assistance agency designed to promote free labor in a free market system, along with investigating international human rights complaints. They also take a major role in workers rights, such as the right to bargain collectively, and protection from discrimination.

* Job Counseling and Placement Fraud

Federal Trade Commission
Bureau of Consumer Protection
6th & Pennsylvania Ave., NW
Washington, DC 20580   (202) 326-3650

The FTC often receives complaint letters about job counseling and placement services which charge large fees and misrepresent their services. For information on how to select a legitimate employment service or to complain about one which you feel has misrepresented itself, contact your local FTC office.

* Job Corps Statistics

Office of Job Corps
Employment and Training Administration
Department of Labor
200 Constitution Ave., NW, Room N4510
Washington, DC 20210   (202) 535-0550

Job Corps statistics are available, including cost statistics, enrollee demographics, and enrollee outcomes. Contact this office for further information.

* Labor Force: A National Profile

Office of Employment and Unemployment Statistics
Bureau of Labor Statistics
Department of Labor
441 G St., NW, Room 2486
Washington, DC 20212   (202) 523-1944

The labor force statistics available include employment status of the U.S. population 16 years and over by age, sex, race, hispanic ethnicity, martial status, family relationships, Vietnam-era Vietnam status, educational attainment, school enrollment, and residence in metropolitan/nonmetropolitan areas and poverty/nonpoverty areas. Also included is information concerning employed and unemployed persons by occupation, industry, and class of worker, as well as characteristics, work history, and job seeking intentions of persons not in the labor force. Special topics, such as the labor force status of particular groups of the population, occupational mobility and work experience, are also available.

* Labor Force Population Trends

Office of Employment and Unemployment Statistics
Bureau of Labor Statistics
Department of Labor
441 G St., NW, Room 2486
Washington, DC 20212   (202) 523-1944

This office analyzes and publishes data from the *Current Population Survey* on the labor force, employment, unemployment, as well as on persons not in the labor force. Studies based on the CPS data cover a broad range of topics, including annual analyses of labor market developments, occupational analyses, characteristics of special worker groups (such as minorities and women maintaining families), and employment-related economic hardship.

* Labor Statistics Availability

Division of Information Services
Bureau of Labor Statistics
Department of Labor
441 G St., NW, Room 2831A
Washington, DC 20212   (202) 523-1221

The Bureau of Labor Statistics can provide you with a tentative release schedule for BLS major economic indicators. The schedule lists the information available (i.e., employment situation, consumer price index, productivity and costs, etc.), as well as the date and time of the information release. The *BLS Update* also contains the release dates for the quarter.

* Labor Statistics Catalog

Office of Publications
Bureau of Labor Statistics
441 G St., NW
Washington, DC 20212   (202) 523-1239

The free quarterly publication, *BLS Update*, contains a complete list of new BLS publications, including a brief description and ordering information. Also included are BLS summaries, data services, telephone numbers for recorded summaries of BLS data, as well as general information concerning BLS.

* Labor Statistics Handbook

Publications
Bureau of Labor Statistics
Department of Labor
441 G St., NW
Washington, DC 20212   (202) 523-1221

The annual *Handbook of Labor Statistics* contains historical data for the major statistical series produced by the Bureau and is available for $9.50.

* Labor Statistics Monthly Review

Superintendent of Documents
Government Printing Office
Washington, DC 20402   (202) 783-3238

Each issue of the *Monthly Labor Review* includes analytical articles, 47 pages of current statistics, reports on industrial relations, book reviews, and other features for a cost of $20 per year.

* Labor Surplus Areas and Government Contracts

Superintendent of Documents
Government Printing Office
Washington, DC 20402   (202) 783-3238

Area Trends in Employment and Unemployment is a list of labor surplus areas, which are designated as such by the Department of Labor. This list is used to give priority in awarding government contracts. Once an area has been placed on the list, it remains there for one year. This monthly publication is available for $25. For more information on the labor surplus issues, contact: Employment Service, Employment and Training Administration, U.S. Department of Labor, 200 Constitution Ave., NW, Room N4456, Washington, D.C. 20210; (202) 535-0189.

* Library on Labor Movement and Occupational Evolution

Department of Labor
200 Constitution Ave., NW, Room N2439
Washington, DC 20210   (202) 523-6992

This library has a wealth of historical labor material, as well as collections of state labor department reports, documents, and trade union journals. The library is open to the public and staffed by reference librarians, who will assist you in locating materials.

* Local Area Employment and Unemployment

Office of Employment and Unemployment Statistics
Bureau of Labor Statistics
Department of Labor
441 G St., NW, Room 2083
Washington, DC 20212   (202) 523-1038

This office provides laborforce, employment, and unemployment data estimated by state employment security agencies. These data are used primarily to allocate federal funds to local jurisdiction. The coverage includes annual average data with demographic detail for 50 states, the District of Columbia, 30 large metropolitan areas, and 11 of their central cities, and monthly data to include 50 states, 330 areas, 3,100 counties, and 500 cities of 50,000 or more. The data are published in a variety of sources, including the annual bulletin, *Geographic Profile of Employment and Unemployment*, and the monthly periodical, *Employment and Earnings*.

* Longitudinal Employment Surveys

Office of Economic Research
Bureau of Labor Statistics
Department of Labor
441 G St., NW, Room 2026
Washington, DC 20212   (202) 523-1347

Every couple of years, this office updates *The National Longitudinal Surveys*, which study employment profiles of certain age groups . The groups include: young women who were 14-24 in 1968; mature women who were 30-44 in 1967; and youth who were 14-21 in 1979. Information available includes labor market activities, characteristics of jobs, earnings, unemployment, social and demographic characteristics, education, and training.

* Minimum Wage and Overtime Pay Standards

Office of Information and Consumer Affairs
Employment Standards Administration
Department of Labor
200 Constitution Ave., NW, Room C4331
Washington, DC 20210   (202) 523-8743

The Fair Labor Standards Act establishes minimum wages, overtime pay, recordkeeping, and child labor standards which affect some 73 million employees. It requires employers to pay at least the federally-standardized minimum wage per hour to all covered and nonexempt employees, and to pay one and one-half times their regular pay for all hours worked over 40 in the work week.

* Minimum Wage Exemptions
Special Employment Branch
Wage and Hour Division
Employment Standards Administration
Department of Labor
200 Constitution Ave., NW, Room S3516
Washington, DC 20210 (202) 523-8727
This office issues certificates allowing employers to pay subminimum wages to full-time students, trainees, and handicapped workers. Contact this office for more information regarding these certificates.

* Necessary Job Skills in Today's and Tomorrow's Labor Force
Information Office
Employment Training Administration
Department of Labor
200 Constitution Ave., NW, Room S2322
Washington, DC 20210 (202) 523-6871
Building A Quality Workforce is a joint initiative of the U.S. Departments of Labor, Education and Commerce. The first part of this free report describes research about entry level skills, business needs, current and projected skills gaps, and how well education is responding to the challenge. The second contains descriptive profiles of several communities working on closing the gap between workplace needs and workforce capabilities.

* Occupational Titles and Classifications Dictionary
Superintendent of Documents
Government Printing Office
Washington, DC 20402 (202) 783-3238
A compendium of approximately 20,000 occupations, the *Dictionary of Occupational Titles* defines each occupation and provides a classification structure that groups them in terms of related duties and activities. It also includes sections on the purpose of the dictionary and how to use the data bank for job placement. All occupational titles are arranged alphabetically and by industry for easy reference. The cost is $32.00. A 1986 supplement is available for $5.50. A magnetic tape of the dictionary is available for $210.00 from: National Technical Information Service, 5285 Port Royal Rd., Springfield, VA 22161; (703) 487-4650.

* On-site Child Care
Women's Bureau
Department of Labor
200 Constitution Ave., NW, Room S3309
Washington, DC 20210 (202) 523-6652
The free publication, *Employers and Child Care: Benefiting Work and Family*, is designed for employers and employees concerned with developing programs and policies to assist in quality and cost-efficient child care programs while parents are at work. Created to help in a vast array of situations, it provides guidance to those who wish to improve employee productivity and business' ability to recruit and retain the best workers. It is designed for people who are concerned about fulfilling two essential and often conflicting responsibilities--working and caring for their families.

* Pension Benefit Guaranty Corporation
Public Affairs
Pension Benefit Guaranty Corporation
2020 K St., NW, Room 7100
Washington, DC 20006-1860 (202) 778-8840
This office is a good starting place for hunting down information on pensions.

* Plant Closings and Permanent Layoffs
Office of Labor-Management Programs
Bureau of Labor-Management Relations
Department of Labor
200 Constitution Ave., NW, Room N5416
Washington, DC 20210 (202) 357-0473
The Industrial Adjustment Service was created to help address the problems of workers affected by plant closings or major lay-offs. IAS provides a broad array of services and information to help lessen the impact of dislocation and speed up the transfer of dislocated workers to new jobs. IAS works directly with a particular enterprise, with a particular industry, and/or with state and local government officials and private sector representatives to help them develop the knowledge and skills necessary to deal with plant closings and lay-offs, and to assist dislocated workers. Available information includes workshops, technical assistance, publications, and information regarding the Canadian response to permanent lay-offs.

* Plant Closings Notifications

Notification (WARN)
Office of Employment and Training Programs
Employment and Training Administration
Department of Labor
200 Constitution Ave., NW, Room N4703
Washington, DC 20210 (202) 535-0577
WARN requires that employers with 100 or more employees provide 60 days advance notice of a plant closing or mass layoff. A plant closing is a permanent or temporary shutdown of a single site of employment or one or more facilities or operating unit within a single site or employment, resulting in an employment loss at the site during any 30-day period for 50 or more employees. A mass layoff is a reduction in force at a single site during and 30 day period which results in the employment loss of at least 1/3 of the employees and at least 50 employees or at least 500 employees.

* Productivity and Technology Statistics
Office of Productivity and
Technology Studies
Bureau of Labor Statistics
Department of Labor
200 Constitution Ave., NW, Room S4320
Washington, DC 20210 (202) 523-9244
This office is responsible for three major research programs. The productivity program compiles and analyzes productivity and related statistics on the U.S. business economy and its major sectors, and on individual industries and government. The technological studies program investigates trends in technology and their impact on employment and productivity. And the international labor statistics program compiles and analyzes data on productivity and related factors in foreign countries for comparison with the U.S. experience. The free directory, *BLS Publications on Productivity and Technology*, lists all the publications of each program.

* Roadmap to All Labor Data
Superintendent of Documents
Government Printing Office
Washington, DC 20402 (202) 783-3238
The *BLS Handbook of Methods* provides comprehensive information for each major program of the Bureau of Labor Statistics on sources of data, statistical procedures, where the data are published, and their uses and limitations. It includes descriptions for labor force statistics, occupational pay surveys, Employment Cost Index, productivity measures, Consumer Price Index, and for much more. The cost is $11.00.

* Trade-Related Employment Issues
Bureau of International Labor Affairs
Department of Labor
200 Constitution Ave., NW, Room S2235
Washington, DC 20210 (202) 523-6043
The Bureau of International Labor Affairs represents the Department of Labor in the development of international economic and trade policies that affect the welfare of U.S. workers. This role includes conducting research on trade-related employment issues, coordinating advice received from Labor Advisory Committees on Trade authorized by the Trade Agreements Act of 1979, and acting as a liaison between other federal departments, agencies, and organized labor. The Bureau is also a member of various interagency committees charged with trade policy functions, and continues to participate in the formulation of U.S. immigration policy.

* Unemployment Insurance for Lost Wages
Office of Employment and Unemployment Statistics
Bureau of Labor Statistics
Department of Labor
441 G St., NW, Room 2919
Washington, DC 20212 (202) 523-1694
Insured Employment and Wages data are collected quarterly by state employment security agencies in cooperation with BLS. The data available include monthly employment, total quarterly wages, taxable wages, employer contributions, and reporting units, by industry, county, and state, for workers covered by state unemployment insurance laws and by the Unemployment Compensation for Federal Employees program.

* Union Contracts Database
Legal Services Office
Federal Mediation and Conciliation Service (FMCS)
2100 K St., NW, Room 712
Washington, DC 20427 (202) 653-5305
The office also maintains a database of union contracts searchable by company name and dating back one year. Information can be obtained by written request.

* Veterans and Federal Contracts

Veterans Employment and Training
Department of Labor
200 Constitution Ave., NW, Room S1313
Washington, DC 20210 (202) 523-9116

Federal government contractors and subcontractors (with government contracts of $10,000 or more) are required by law to take affirmative action to employ and to advance in employment qualified special disabled and Vietnam-era Veterans. All suitable employment openings must be given to the nearest local State Employment Office. A Veterans Employment and Training Representative is located in each office to provide employment advice and assistance to veterans. Contact the Office of Federal Contract Compliance Programs if it appears that a contractor has failed to comply. Complaints can be made to: Office of Federal Contract Compliance Programs, Department of Labor, 200 Constitution Ave., NW, Room C3325, Washington, DC 20210; (202) 523-9475.

* Veterans Employment Program

Assistant Secretary for Veterans
Employment and Training
Department of Labor
200 Constitution Ave., NW, Room S1313
Washington, DC 20210 (202) 523-9116

Employment-related services designed to aid veterans include counseling, testing, and skills training; unemployment compensation for newly separated ex-service members while they look for civilian employment; tax credits for private employers who hire certain target groups of veterans; placement in private and public sector jobs; and reemployment rights assistance. For more information, contact the Veterans' Employment and Training Office.

* Wage and Hour Investigations

Employment Standards Administration
Department of Labor
200 Constitution Ave., NW, Room S3028
Washington, DC 20210 (202) 523-8353

This division administers the Fair Labor Standards Act, which includes minimum wage, overtime pay, and child labor provisions. Its responsibilities also have grown to include other laws and regulations which protect worker's wages and working conditions. Wage and Hour Division compliance officers across the country conduct investigations of employers covered by the various laws which the division administers, to determine whether workers are being paid in compliance with the laws. They are also responsible for investigating complaints filed by employees who allege that their employers discriminated against them for actions they took to further the purposes of various environmental protection laws, and for improving conditions for migrant farm workers.

* Wage and Industrial Relations Information

Office of Compensation and Working Conditions
Bureau of Labor Statistics
Department of Labor
441 G St., NW, Room 2021
Washington, DC 20210 (202) 523-1763

The Bureau of Labor Statistics conducts three major types of occupational wage surveys: 1) area surveys, 2) industry surveys, and 3) a national white-collar salary survey. Non-wage compensation is covered in a comprehensive survey of the incidence and characteristics of employee benefit plans. They also develop measures of trends in employee compensation. The office's program of studies in labor-management relations includes analyses of wage and benefit changes in major collective bargaining agreements, statistics on work stop pages, and reports on pending labor-management negotiations in major bargaining units.

* Wage and Price Indexes on Computer Tape

Bureau of Labor Statistics
Department of Labor
441 G St., NW, Room 1077
Washington, DC 20212 (202) 523-7827

BLS major data series are available on magnetic tape. The standard format is 9-track, 6250 BPI. In addition to the data files listed, BLS makes some microdata tapes and also prepares customized data files on a cost-for-service basis. Available data files include consumer expenditures, consumer price index, export-import price indexes, and labor force, as well as many others. A brochure is available which describes the tapes, ordering information, and the cost of each tape.

* Wage Surveys: Area, Industry and White Collar Earnings

Office of Compensation and Working Conditions
Bureau of Labor Statistics
Department of Labor
441 G St. NW, Room 2021
Washington, DC 20210 (202) 523-1763

This office conducts three different types of wage surveys. The area and industry surveys provide annual data on averages and distributions of earnings for selected occupations in major industry groups in metropolitan areas. The white-collar salary survey is the annual *Professional, Administrative, Technical, and Clerical Survey* which is used in the Federal pay-setting process and provides data on salaries in white-collar occupations from a national sample of establishments.

* White-Collar Salaries

Benefit Levels Division
Office of Compensation Levels and Trends
Bureau of Labor Statistics
Department of Labor
441 G St., NW, Room 2025
Washington, DC 20210 (202) 523-1246

The annual white-collar salary survey provides data on salaries in white-collar occupations from a national sample of establishments. The data available includes averages and distributions of salary rates for about 100 professional, administrative, technical, and clerical work levels. The results are published in the annual news release, *White-Collar Salaries*, and the annual bulletin, *National Survey of Professional, Administrative, Technical, and Clerical Pay*.

* Women and Office Automation

Women's Bureau
Department of Labor
200 Constitution Ave., NW, Room S3309
Washington, DC 20210 (202) 523-6652

The impact of automation on the quality of worklife as well as on the economic well-being of clerical workers and their families is a matter of priority for the Women's Bureau. The free publication, *Women and Office Automation: Issues for the Decade Ahead*, discusses the quality of work, training and retraining, home-based clerical work, and health and safety issues.

* Women in the Workforce Clearinghouse

Women's Bureau
Department of Labor
200 Constitution Ave., NW, Room S3315
Washington, DC 20210 (202) 523-6665

The Women's Bureau offers a free listing of publications they have available. They have eighteen fact sheets on women workers, as well as information on women in technology, careers/job options, child care, and standards and legislation affecting women. The Bureau has a variety of program models available dealing with employment of women and several conference models. Currently, the staff is focusing on identifying the characteristics of cities presently experiencing labor shortages and other economic stresses expected to be more wide spread by the year 2000, the impact of trade competition on women's jobs, child care for women workers, and many other women's issues. *There's No Such Thing As Women's Work* is a video which reviews the history of women in the workforce and provides information about meeting present day work and family challenges.

* Women Worker Data

Office of Publications
Bureau of Labor Statistics
Department of Labor
441 G St., NW, Room 2421
Washington, DC 20212 (202) 523-1221

This office publishes a wide array of information about women in the labor force. This information is presented to the public through a variety of publications, including news releases, periodicals, bulletins, reports, tapes, and diskettes. The pamphlet, *Where to Find BLS Statistics on Women*, identifies the particular publications in which specific data services may be found, along with information on how to obtain BLS publications. The data includes information labor force status, employment, and unemployment, earnings and hours of work, education, occupational injuries and illness, and unpublished data.

* Work and Family Clearinghouse

Women's Bureau
Department of Labor
200 Constitution Ave., NW, Room S3306
Washington, DC 20210 (800) 827-5335

The Work and Family Clearinghouse was designed and established to assist employers in identifying the most appropriate policies for responding to the dependent care (child and/or elder care) needs of employees who are seeking to balance their dual responsibilities. Information and guidance are available in five broad areas: direct services, information services, financial assistance, flexible policies, and public-private partnership. Technical assistance includes national and state information sources, bibliographic references, conference information, research and statistics. *Program Profiles* are available which describe employer-related child and elder care systems already in place.

* Work Permits for Foreigners

Labor Certification Division

Employment Service
Employment and Training Administration
Department of Labor
200 Constitution Ave., NW, Room N4456
Washington, DC   20210   (202) 535-0163

If an employer wishes to hire foreign workers, he must first obtain a foreign labor certificate, which is a statement from the U.S. Department of Labor stating that there is no U.S. citizen available to fill the job. The Department investigates to make sure that the wages and working conditions of the foreign workers will not seriously affect the wages and working conditions of U.S. workers. An employer applies for a foreign labor certificate through the local state employment service office, which then conducts a job hunt before sending the application form to the area regional office for approval or disapproval.

* Workplace Literacy, Youth Training and Other Projects

Office of Strategic Planning and Policy Development
Employment and Training Administration
Department of Labor
200 Constitution Ave., NW, Room N5637
Washington, DC   20210   (202) 535-0677

Research, Demonstration, and Evaluation Projects summarizes the projects funded by the Employment and Training Administration. The most recent focus has been on workplace literacy, youth, worker adjustment, women-families-welfare, and improving employment and training programs. This free catalog provides several indexes and ordering information.

* Work Stoppages and Strikes

Office of Compensation and
Working Conditions

Bureau of Labor Statistics
Department of Labor
441 G St., NW, Room 2032
Washington, DC   20212   (202) 523-1320

This office generates monthly and annual data on major strikes and lock outs. The coverage includes all strikes and lock outs involving 1,000 workers or more and lasting more than one shift. This information measures collective bargaining and economic effects of work stoppages.

* Youth 2000

Information Office
Employment and Training Administration
Department of Labor
200 Constitution Ave., NW, Room S2322
Washington, DC   20210   (202) 523-6871

Youth 2000, a nationwide "call to action" between now and the year 2000, is designed to enlist the involvement of all sectors of society in helping vulnerable youth to achieve social and economic self-sufficiency and fulfill their potential as contributing members of society. Youth 2000 brings the Departments of Labor and Health and Human Services together to focus state and local attention on opportunities and challenges facing the nation and its young people. ETA regional offices work with state and community leaders during the year to promote public awareness of youth-related issues and continues efforts to stimulate new dialogue, an important step in mobilizing resources to address issues associated with at-risk youth, including illiteracy, failure to complete high school, teen pregnancy, and alcohol and other drug abuse.

Career and Job Training

For anyone looking for help choosing a career, changing jobs, or finding a job, there is plenty of help at little or no cost. Not only can you find where the job opportunities are, you can also see what the job market will be for any profession next year, or even five years from now. If you want to know what part of the country is the best market for, say nurses or engineers, you can find out in one phone call. If you want to choose a major in college that will be marketable when you graduate, that's available too. There are even national computerized job banks and job matching programs listed here that will help match your background and abilities with available jobs. Besides help finding a job, you'll also find job training and retraining vocational programs, along with plenty of assistance for such special groups as the disabled, displaced homemakers, the elderly, veterans, and those layed off from large industries.

* Airline Jobs Bank
Office of Labor-Management Programs
Bureau of Labor-Management Relations
U.S. Department of Labor
200 Constitution Ave., NW, Room N5416
Washington, DC 20210   (202) 357-0473
The Airline Rehire Program gives displaced airline workers first-right-of-hire preference for jobs with pre-deregulation air carriers if the displaced workers had at least four years service prior to October 24, 1978. One of the key features of this program is a national listing of airline vacancies compiled through the Interstate Job Bank, a national center for job information maintained by the U.S. U.S. Department of Labor. The list is updated weekly and distributed to the 2400 local Job Service offices run by state employment security agencies. All carriers are required to list openings with the Job Bank, and anyone may use the list to obtain information about airline vacancies.

* Art Conservation and Museum Careers
Office of Museum Programs
Smithsonian Institution
900 Jefferson Dr. S.W.
Washington, DC 20560   (202) 357-3101
The Audiovisual department of the Office of Museum Programs has forty slide and video programs, covering topics such as museum careers, museum environments, and conservation and preservation. You can view the slides and videotapes at the Office of Museum Programs.

* At-Risk Youth and Employment
Information Office
Employment and Training Administration
U.S. Department of Labor
200 Constitution Ave., NW, Room S2322
Washington, DC 20210   (202) 523-6871
Youth 2000, a nationwide "call to action" between now and the year 2000, is designed to enlist the involvement of all sectors of society in helping vulnerable youth to achieve social and economic self-sufficiency and fulfill their potential as contributing members of society. Youth 2000 brings the Departments of Labor and Health and Human Services together to focus state and local attention on opportunities and challenges facing the nation and its young people. ETA regional offices work with state and community leaders during the year to promote public awareness of youth-related issues and continues efforts to stimulate new dialogue, an important step in mobilizing resources to address issues associated with at-risk youth, including illiteracy, failure to complete high school, teen pregnancy, and alcohol and other drug abuse.

* Aviation Careers
Aviation Education Officer
Federal Aviation Administration
U.S. Department of Transportation
800 Independence Ave., SW
Washington, DC 20591   (202) 267-3469
The FAA's Aviation Education Program offers volunteer assistance to the nation's schools through the following programs: career guidance; tours of airports, control towers, and other facilities; classroom lectures and demonstrations; aviation safety information; aviation education resource materials; computerized clearinghouse of aviation and space information; aviation science instruction programs for home/school computers; "Partnerships-in-Education" activities; and teachers' workshops. Write to the above office for more information.

* Career Encyclopedia and Prospects
Office of Information
Bureau of Labor Statistics
U.S. Department of Labor
441 G St., NW
Washington, DC 20212   (202) 523-1221
The *Occupational Outlook Handbook* is an encyclopedia of careers covering 225 occupations. For each of these, information is included on what the work is like, 1986 employment figures, educational and training requirements, advancement possibilities, job prospects through the year 2000, earnings-related occupations, and where to find additional information. The cost of the handbook is $22.00. The *Occupational Outlook Quarterly* can help students, guidance counselors, and employment counselors keep abreast of current occupational and employment developments between editions of the *Occupational Outlook Handbook*. The quarterly supplement provides you with advice on how to get a job, articles on new occupations, addresses and phone numbers for more information on apprenticeships and training, and information on special scholarships for talented students. The cost of the *Quarterly* is $5 per year. Both books can be ordered by contacting: Superintendent of Document, Government Printing Office, Washington, DC 20402; (202) 783-3238. Both of these books are available at public libraries.

* Careers in Dozens of Fields
Superintendent of Documents
Government Printing Office
Washington, DC 20402   (202) 783-3238
The following reprints are available from the *Occupational Outlook Handbook*:

Business, Managerial, and Legal Occupations. $2.50
Clerical and Other Administrative Support Occupations. $1.75
Communications, Design, Performing Arts, and Related Occupations. $1.50
Computer and Mathematics-Related Occupations. $1.50
Construction and Extractive Occupations. $1.75
Dietetics, Nursing, Pharmacy and Therapy Occupations. $1.50
Education, Social Service, and Related Occupations. $2.00
Engineering, Scientific, and Related Occupations. $1.75
Health Technologists and Technicians. $1.50
Mechanics, Equipment Installers, and Repairers. $2.00
Medical and Dental Practitioners and Assistants. $1.25
Metalworking and Woodworking Occupations. $1.50
Production and Transportation Occupations. $2.00
Protective Service Occupations and Compliance Inspectors. $1.00
Sales Occupations. $1.25
Service Occupations: Food, Cleaning, Health and Personal. $1.50
Technologists and Technicians, Except Health. $1.25
Tomorrow's Jobs: Overview. $1.25

* Career Options: Art Museums to Zoos
Superintendent of Documents
Government Printing Office
Washington, DC 20402   (202) 783-3238
The U.S. Department of Labor publishes a $7.00 book titled *Career Opportunities in Art Museums, Zoos and Other Interesting Places.*

* Coast Guard Training
Coast Guard Training
U.S. Coast Guard
U.S. Department of Transportation
Aeronautical Center
MPB 237, P.O. Substation 18
Oklahoma City, OK 73169-6999   (405) 680-4265

Coast Guard personnel are trained for advancement through a nonresident course program developed by this Institute. For more information about Guard training or for referral to Institute staff members, contact the number listed.

* Creative Writers Publishing Grants

Literature Program
National Endowment for the Arts
1100 Pennsylvania Ave., NW, Room 723
Washington, DC 20506   (202) 682-5451

The Literature Program assists individual creative writers and literature translators, encourages wider audiences for contemporary literature, and assists non-profit literary organizations. Fellowships enable writers and translators to set aside time for writing and research. Publishing grants provide assistance to literary magazines, small presses, and various distribution projects. Grants are also available to support residencies for writers to allow them to interact with their public. Literary centers may request funds but must offer a regular format of readings, workshops, and technical assistance for writers. Grants can be made to individuals or to non-profit organizations if such donations qualify as charitable deductions under Section 170(c) of the Internal Revenue Code of 1954. Grants range from $2,000 to $50,000.

* Criminal Justice Career Opportunities

Superintendent of Documents
Government Printing Office
Washington, DC 20402   (202) 783-3238

The *Criminal Justice Careers Guidebook* provides detailed information on criminal justice occupations in the areas of law enforcement, corrections and rehabilitation, and the judiciary. Duties, job requirements, and opportunities are described for each occupation and sources of further information are identified. It can be purchased from GPO for $7.00.

* Dictionary of 20,000 Occupational Titles

Superintendent of Documents
Government Printing Office
Washington, DC 20402   (202) 783-3238

A compendium of approximately 20,000 occupations, the *Dictionary of Occupational Titles* defines each occupation and provides a classification structure that groups them in terms of related duties and activities. It also includes sections on the purpose of the dictionary and how to use the data bank for job placement. All occupational titles are arranged alphabetically and by industry for easy reference. The cost is $32.00. A 1986 supplement is available for $5.50. A magnetic tape of the dictionary is available for $210.00 from: National Technical Information Service, 5285 Port Royal Rd., Springfield, VA 22161; (703) 487-4650.

* Disabled Veterans: Job Matching Service

Veterans Employment and Training
U.S. Department of Labor
200 Constitution Ave., NW, Room S1313
Washington, DC 20210   (202) 523-9116

Located in most employment service offices, the Disabled Veterans' Outreach Program is staffed by veterans who provide special assistance to other veterans and help them obtain employment and training services. The DVOP staff develop networks of employer contacts and work with community groups and veterans organizations in their effort to find jobs for their clients. Unique to this program is the emphasis to seek out and help disabled and Vietnam-era veterans.

* Dental Health Professions

Division of Associated and Dental Health Professions
Health Resources and Services Administration
5600 Fishers Lane, Room 8-101
Rockville, MD 20857   (301) 443-6854

This division serves as a principle focus with regard to health professions education, practice, and service research, in the fields of dentistry, optometry, pharmacy, veterinary medicine, public health, and allied health professions. It supports and conducts programs, surveys, and studies to analyze and improve the quality, development, organization, utilization, and credentialing of personnel in these fields. It also supports and conducts special educational initiatives. A publications list for professionals is available.

* Disease Control and Environmental Health Training

Training and Laboratory Program Office
Centers for Disease Control
1600 Clifton Rd.
Atlanta, GA 30333   (404) 639-2142

The Centers for Disease Control offers course work on such topics as environmental health sciences, communicable disease control, and vector-born disease control. Anyone can take these courses; however, they are designed for hospital personnel and health care providers. These classes are offered at a variety of locations, as well as many being available as self-study training courses.

* Displaced Homemakers Job Network

Job Network for Displaced Homemakers
1411 K St., NW
Suite 930
Washington, DC 20005   (202) 628-6767

Supported by the Women's Bureau at the U.S. Department of Labor, the Displaced Homemakers Network is the only national organization which addresses the specific concerns of displaced homemakers. Through its Washington, D.C., office, it works to increase displaced homemakers' options for economic self-sufficiency, to provide information about the public policy issues which affect displaced homemakers, to provide technical assistance resources for service providers, and to help program staff around the country locate the information and expertise they need to develop programs that work for displaced homemakers. There are many publications and newsletters available, and the staff can assist you in locating a displaced homemakers program near you.

*Employment in Transportation

Central Employment Office
Office of Personnel
U.S. Department of Transportation
400 7th St., SW, Room 9113
Washington, DC 20590   (202) 366-9394

Employment inquiries for positions in Washington, D.C., should be submitted to this office. Regional and district offices handle employment in their areas. Civil Service positions include air traffic controller; electronics maintenance technicians; civil, aeronautical, automotive, electronic, and highway engineers; and administrative, management, and clerical positions.

* Employee Training Technologies and Competitiveness

Office of Technology Assessment
600 Pennsylvania Ave., SE
Washington, DC 20510   (202) 228-6352

Currently, OTA is exploring the connections between new workplace technologies, employee training, and competitiveness. The study will examine such topics as national investment in training; demographic changes in the work force; employee training in countries that are major industrial competitors of the U.S.; and policy questions concerning existing Federal programs. Contact Wendell Fletcher, the project director, for more information.

* Environmental Protection Job Opportunities

Superintendent of Documents
Government Printing Office
Washington, DC 20402   (202) 783-3238

The U.S. Department of Labor publishes the *Environmental Protection Careers Guidebook* which is sold by the Government Printing Office for $7.50.

* Epidemic Intelligence Service

Epidemiology Program Office
Centers for Disease Control
Atlanta, GA 30333   (404) 639-3588

The Epidemic Intelligence Service is a two-year program of service and on-the-job training for health professionals, most of whom are physicians, in the practice of epidemiology. The officers have opportunities to investigate disease outbreaks, conduct epidemiologic studies, teach, travel, and present and publish their work. The class begins with a training course, and then the class responds to inquiries, monitors reports of disease, investigates outbreaks, and analyzes epidemiologic data.

* Experimental Job Training Opportunities

Office of Strategic Planning and
 Policy Development
Employment and Training Administration
U.S. Department of Labor
200 Constitution Ave., NW, Room N5637
Washington, DC 20210   (202) 535-0659

This office plans and implements Pilot and Demonstration Programs to provide job training, employment opportunities, and related services for individuals with specific disadvantages. These programs address industry-wide skill shortages and offer technical expertise to particular client groups. They also develop information networks among organizations with similar Job Training Partnership Act-related objectives. Administered at the National level and operated at the state and local level, these programs cover disadvantaged groups in the labor market, including offenders, individuals with limited English language proficiency, handicapped person, women, single parents, displaced homemakers, youth, older workers, those who lack educational credentials and public assistance recipients.

Careers and Workplace

* Federal Aviation Administration Academy

Federal Aviation Administration
Department of Transportation
P.O. Box 25082, AAC-900
Oklahoma, OK 73125 (405) 680-6900

The Academy is the principal source of technical information on U.S. civil aviation. It conducts training for FAA personnel through resident or correspondence courses and occasional on-site training. Air traffic training is available for specialists who man the FAA airport traffic control towers, air route traffic control center, and flight service stations. Electronic training is also available for engineers and technicians who install and maintain navigation and traffic control communications facilities. Initial and recurrent training is also conducted for air carrier and general operations inspectors. The Academy provides air navigation facilities and flight procedures analysis to flight inspection personnel.

* Financial and Other Service Sector Jobs

Superintendent of Documents
Government Printing Office
Washington, DC 20402 (202) 783-3238

The U.S. Department of Labor publishes a book for $7.00 titled *Occupational Employment in Mining, Construction, Finance, and Services* which can be purchased from the Government Printing Office.

* Fish Husbandry Training Academy

National Fisheries Center
U.S. Fish and Wildlife Service
Box 700
Kearneysville, WV 25430 (304) 725-8461 x5333

The National Fisheries Center and its five field stations are world-renowned as a focal point for fish health research and fisheries development. Studies include nutrition, genetics, diseases, management technology, and technical services. The facility contains a training academy of fish husbandry.

* Foreign Service Career Counseling

Personnel Office
Special Services Branch
United States Information Agency
301 Fourth St., SW, Room 525
Washington, DC 20547 (202) 485-2628

Information on career opportunities in the Foreign Service is available from this office.

* Future Job Trends by Occupation

Superintendent of Documents
Government Printing Office
Washington, DC 20402 (202) 783-3238

A supplement to the latest edition of the *Occupational Outlook Handbook, Occupational Projections and Training Data* provides detailed, comprehensive statistics and technical data supporting the information presented in the *Handbook*. It also presents a broad overview of expected trends in employment in the mid 1990's and provides employment data for approximately 200 occupations profiled in the *Handbook*. This supplement is a key reference source for training officials, education planners, and vocational and employment counselors. The cost is $5.50.

* Health Careers

Superintendent of Documents
Government Printing Office
Washington, DC 20402 (202) 783-3238

The Labor Department publishes a reference book on employment opportunities and trends titled *Health Careers Guidebook* which can be purchased for $7.50 from the Government Printing Office.

* Highly Skilled Jobs Apprenticeship

Bureau of Apprenticeship and Training
Employment and Training Administration
U.S. Department of Labor
200 Constitution Ave., NW, Room N4649
Washington, DC 20210 (202) 523-0540

Apprenticeship is a combination of on-the-job training and related classroom instruction in which workers learn the practical and theoretical aspects of a highly skilled occupation. Apprenticeship programs are operated on a voluntary basis by employers, employer associations, or management and labor groups. The role of the federal government is to encourage and promote the establishment of apprenticeship programs and provide technical assistance to program sponsors. The related classroom instruction is given in the program sponsor's training facility or a local technical school or junior college.

* Indians and Job Training

Office of Tribal Services
Bureau of Indian Affairs
U.S. Department of the Interior
18th and C Sts., NW
Washington, DC 20240 (202) 343-2111

This office serves as a cross between the Health and Human Services, Labor, Justice, and Housing and Urban Development Departments for the Indian population. The needy are paid welfare subsidies and provided job training. This office also operates 19 special federal courts and funds 127 tribal courts, along with administering the police force for Indian reservations, and a rehabilitation program for Indian homes.

* Information and Records Management Training

Records Administration Information Center
National Archives and Records Administration
8th St. & Pennsylvania Ave., NW
Washington, DC 20408 (202) 724-1471

The Directory of Records Administration Training Programs in the Washington, D.C. Area lists classes available from government, academic, and private sources in such subject areas as records management, Information Resource Management, micrographics, and optical disks. Contact this office for a copy.

* International Trade Commission Jobs

Office of Personnel
U.S. International Trade Commission
500 E St., SW, Room 314
Washington, DC 20436 (202) 252-1653

Information on employment can be obtained from the Personnel Director. Personnel employed include international economists, attorneys, accountants, commodity and industry specialists and analysts, and clerical and other support personnel.

* Job Corps Conservation Centers

Office of Historically Black College
  and University Programs and Job Corps
U.S. Department of the Interior
18th and C Sts., NW
Washington, DC 20240 (202) 343-2403

This residential program provides job training for disadvantaged youth throughout the country. You must be between the ages of 16 and 22 to participate. Twelve conservation centers are located throughout the country for training purposes.

* Job Corps for Youths

Office of Job Corps
Employment and Training Administration
U.S. Department of Labor
200 Constitution Ave., NW, Room N4510
Washington, DC 20210 (202) 535-0550

The Job Corps, a Federally administered national employment and training program, is designed to serve severely disadvantaged youth 16-21 years old. Enrollees are provided food, housing, education, vocational training, medical care, counseling, and other support services. The program prepares youth for stable, productive employment and entrance into vocational/technical schools or other institutions for further education or training. Job Corps centers range in capacity from 175 to 2,600 enrollees. Some of the centers are operated by the U.S. Departments of Interior and Agriculture (civilian conservation centers), while the remaining centers are operated under contracts with the U.S. U.S. Department of Labor primarily by major corporations. Vocational training is given in such occupations as auto repair, carpentry, painting, nursing, business and clerical skills, as well as preparation for the General Education Development (GED) high school equivalency examination. To apply, contact and Job Service office, or call the Job Corps Alumni Association's toll-free number: (800) 424-2866.

* Jobs For Seniors 55 Years and Up

Office of Special Targeted Programs
Employment and Training Administration
U.S. Department of Labor
200 Constitution Ave., NW, Room N4643
Washington, DC 20210 (202) 535-0521

Sponsored by state and territorial governments and eight national organizations, the Senior Community Service Employment Program promotes the creation of part-time jobs in community service activities for jobless, low-income persons who are at least 55 years of age and have poor employment prospects. Individuals work in part-time jobs at senior citizens centers, in schools or hospitals, in programs for the handicapped, in fire prevention programs, and on beautification and restoration projects. This program makes possible and array of community services to the elderly. SCSEP participants must be at least 55 years of age, have family income of not more than 25% above the Federal poverty level, and be capable of performing the tasks to which they are assigned. For more information, contact state offices for the aging, area agencies on aging, or local job service offices.

* Job Training and Employment Services

Office of the Assistant Secretary
for Employment and Training
U.S. Department of Labor
200 Constitution Ave., NW, Room S2321
Washington, DC 20210   (202) 523-6191

The Job Training Partnership Act provides job training and employment services for economically disadvantaged adults and youth, dislocated workers, and others who face significant employment barriers. The goal of this Act is to move the jobless into permanent, unsubsidized, self-sustaining employment. State and local governments have primary responsibility for the management and administration of job training programs. In addition, a new public/private partnership has been created to plan and design training programs as well as to deliver training and other services.

* Job Training and Workplace Research and Development

Office of Strategic Planning and Policy Development
Employment and Training Administration
U.S. Department of Labor
200 Constitution Ave., NW, Room N5637
Washington, DC 20210   (202) 535-0677

Research, Demonstration, and Evaluation Projects summarizes the projects funded by the Employment and Training Administration. The most recent focus has been on workplace literacy, youth, worker adjustment, women-families-welfare, and improving employment and training programs. This free catalog provides several indexes and ordering information.

* Junior Foreign Service Officer Trainee Program

Personnel Office
Special Services Branch
United States Information Agency
301 Fourth St., SW, Room 525
Washington, DC 20547   (202) 485-2628

Each December the Foreign Service Officer Examination is held at many locations in this country and overseas to screen candidates for the Junior Officer Trainee Program. Date, locations, and other information is available from this office.

* Literature Translators Opportunities

Literature Program
National Endowment for the Arts
1100 Pennsylvania Ave., NW, Room 723
Washington, DC 20506   (202) 682-5451

The Literature Program assists individual creative writers and literature translators, encourages wider audiences for contemporary literature, and assists non-profit literary organizations. Fellowships enable writers and translators to set aside time for writing and research. Publishing grants provide assistance to literary magazines, small presses, and various distribution projects. Grants are also available to support residencies for writers to allow them to interact with their public. Literary centers may request funds but must offer a regular format of readings, workshops, and technical assistance for writers.

Grants can be made to individuals or to non-profit organizations if such donations qualify as charitable deductions under Section 170(c) of the Internal Revenue Code of 1954. Grants range from $2,000 to $50,000.

* Local Help for Job Seekers

Employment and Training Administration
U.S. Department of Labor
200 Constitution Ave., NW, Room N4470
Washington, DC 20210   (202) 523-0157

The U.S. Employment Service, through affiliated state employment agencies, operates almost 2,000 local employment service (job service) offices. They assist job seekers in finding employment and assist employers in filling job vacancies. They administer occupational aptitude tests and circulate information about jobs and training opportunities.

* Marketing Your Job Talents

Superintendent of Documents
Government Printing Office
Washington, DC 20402   (202) 783-3238

The best selling book, *Merchandising Your Job Talents*, shows job hunters how to sell their knowledge, skills, and experience effectively in today's competitive marketplace. It covers everything from self-appraisal and resume preparation to testing and interviewing. Sample resumes and a sample letter of application are included as guidelines in this $2.75 publication.

* Matching Yourself with the Workworld

Superintendent of Documents
Government Printing Office
Washington, DC 20402   (202) 783-3238

Designed to assist you in comparing job characteristics with your skills and interests, the publication, *Matching Yourself with the World of Work*, lists and defines 17 occupational characteristics and requirements, and matches these characteristics with 200 occupations chosen from the 1988-89 *Occupational Outlook Handbook*. It is available for $1.00.

* Medical/Scientist Training

Medical Scientist Training Program
National Institute of General Medical Sciences
Westwood Building, Room 905
Bethesda, MD 20892   (301) 496-7301

The MSTP provides assistance to students attempting to receive the dual degree of MD-PHD. Candidates must show evidence of high academic performance and significant prior research experience. Up to six years of support is given, and candidates must attend MSTP support institutions.

* Migrant and Seasonal Farmworker Opportunities

Employment and Training Administration
U.S. Department of Labor
200 Constitution Ave., NW, Room N4641
Washington, DC 20210   (202) 535- 0500

This office administers a national program to help combat chronic unemployment, underemployment, and substandard living conditions among migrant and seasonal farm workers and their families. Supportive services are available to farm workers who seek alternative job opportunities that will enable them to secure stable employment at an income above the poverty level, and improve the living standard of those who remain in the agricultural labor market. Through grants to public and private non-profit institutions, economically disadvantaged farmworker families are furnished training and other employment--related services, including classroom training, on-the-job training, work experience, and supportive services. Supportive services include day care, health care, legal aid, transportation assistance and food and housing in emergency situations. You can contact this office for help in finding a local sponsor.

* Mining and Construction Jobs

Superintendent of Documents
Government Printing Office
Washington, DC 20402   (202) 783-3238

The U.S. Department of Labor publishes a book for $7.00 titled *Occupational Employment in Mining, Construction, Finance, and Services*.

* Minority Access to Biomedical Research Careers

Minority Access to Research Careers Program
National Institute of General Medical Sciences
Westwood Buildings, Room 9A18
Bethesda, MD 20892   (301) 496-7301

This program provides special training opportunities in biomedical science for students and faculty at institutions with substantial minority enrollments. There are four types of support: 1) Honors Undergraduate Research Training Program, which provides support to institutions to teach and provide research training to honors students in their junior or senior year who plan biomedical research careers. 2) The Predoctoral Fellowship provides support for graduates of the MARC honors undergraduate program to pursue a graduate degree in the biomedical sciences (not medical school). 3) The Faculty Fellowship Program provides opportunities for research training for faculty members of colleges with high minority enrollment. 4) The Visiting Scientist Fellowship provides support for outstanding scientists-teachers to serve as visiting scientists at colleges with substantial minority enrollments.

* Modern Archives Management Training

Office of Public Programs
National Archives and Records Administration
8th St. & Pennsylvania Ave., NW, Room 505
Washington, DC 20408   (202) 523-3298

The "Modern Archives Institute: Introduction to Modern Archives Administration," is a two-week archival training course that offers an introduction to archival theory and practice for participants. It is sponsored by the National Archives Trust Fund Board, and includes lectures, discussions, workshops, and visits to the Manuscript Division of the Library of Congress and various units of the National Archives. The Institute is offered twice a year.

* National Computerized Job Bank

United States Employment Service
Employment and Training Administration

135

Careers and Workplace

U.S. Department of Labor
200 Constitution Ave., NW, Room N4456
Washington, DC 20210 (202) 535-0189
A computerized network connecting more than 2,000 Job Service (Employment Service) Offices, the Interstate Job Bank is your opportunity to explore available jobs listed in all 50 states. When an employer cannot fill a job with local talent, the job than gets listed with the Interstate Job Bank. Jobs are listed three ways; as a detailed job description, and on two indexes, one listed by State and one by occupation. You may have access to any one of these listings through the Job Service Office. After you have selected the jobs you are interested in, a review with your local Job Service representative is in order. A proper plan is developed which may include sending your resume directly to an employer or to a Job Service office in another State. The Interstate Job Bank is a free service.

* Native Americans and Museum Professions

Office of Museum Programs
Smithsonian Institution
900 Jefferson Dr. S.W.
Washington, DC 20560 (202) 357-3101
The Native American Museums Program provides information services and educational opportunities for employees of tribal and urban native American museums and cultural centers. The Program offers workshops, short-term residencies, technical assistance, publications, and audio-visual materials on museums.

* Native Americans: Job Training

Office of Special Targeted Programs
Employment and Training Administration
U.S. Department of Labor
200 Constitution Ave., NW, Room N4643
Washington, DC 20210 (202) 535-0502
The U.S. U.S. Department of Labor sponsors special employment and training programs designed to help jobless Native Americans. Those eligible include Indians, Eskimos, Aleuts, Hawaiians, and other persons of native American descent who are economically disadvantaged, unemployed, or underemployed. In addition to job referrals, these programs offer job training, counseling, and other employment-related services to help Native Americans prepare for and hold productive jobs. To make participation easier, child care, transportation, and training allowances are included as part of the programs. You can apply by contacting tribal or other grantees representing the reservations or villages who receive Labor Department grants, or you can get further information by contacting the office above.

* Non-manufacturing Industries Job Outlook

Superintendent of Documents
Government Printing Office
Washington, DC 20402 (202) 783-3238
The Labor Department publishes a book titled *Occupational Employment in Selected Nonmanufacturing Industries* which can be purchased for $5.00 from the Government Printing Office.

* Nursing Research Training

National Center for Nursing Research
National Institutes of Health
Building 31, Room 5B25
9000 Rockville Pike
Bethesda, MD 20892 (301) 496-0207
The National Center for Nursing Research supports nursing research and research training related to patient care, the promotion of health, and the prevention of disease. NCNR also supports studies of nursing interventions, procedures, and delivery methods, as well as the ethics of patient care. Publications are available regarding NCNR and its research grant process.

* Occupational Exploration Encyclopedia

Superintendent of Documents
Government Printing Office
Washington, DC 20402 (202) 783-3238
The *Guide For Occupational Exploration* is an invaluable reference source which provides detailed occupational and labor market information you can use to assist job seekers in getting and keeping a job. The *Guide* groups thousands of occupations in the world of work by the interests, traits, and abilities required for successful performance. It also gives descriptive summaries for each work group and assists individuals in reviewing, understanding, and evaluating their own interests and relating them to pertinent career fields. It is available at many public libraries. Another complementary resource is *Selection Workbook for Use with Guide for Occupational Exploration* is available for $4.25.

* Occupational Safety and Health Courses

Division of Training and Manpower Development
National Institute for Occupational Safety and Health

4676 Columbia Parkway
Cincinnati, OH 45226 (513) 533-8221
This division offers courses for industry and health care professionals on such topics as occupational safety, industrial hygiene, and safety in the laboratory. For a course listing and description, contact this office.

* Oceanographic Corps Jobs

Commission Personnel Division
NOAA Corps
National Oceanic and Atmospheric Administration
Department of Commerce
11400 Rockville Pike
Rockville, MD 20852 (301) 443-8616
The NOAA Corps is the uniformed service of the Department of Commerce responsible for operating and managing NOAA's fleet of hydrographic, oceanographic, and fisheries-research ships and for supporting NOAA scientific programs. Engineering, computer science, mathematics, and science baccalaureate or higher degree graduates are sought for positions in the Corps.

* Office Automation Impact on Women

Women's Bureau
U.S. Department of Labor
200 Constitution Ave., NW, Room S3309
Washington, DC 20210 (202) 523-6652
The impact of automation on the quality of worklife as well as on the economic well-being of clerical workers and their families is a matter of priority for the Women's Bureau. The free publication, *Women and Office Automation: Issues for the Decade Ahead*, discusses the quality of work, training and retraining, home-based clerical work, and health and safety issues.

* Pilot Schools

U.S. Government Printing Office
Superintendent of Documents
Washington DC 20402 (202) 783-3238
The *List of Certified Pilot Schools* is an up-to-date directory of pilot training schools in the U.S. It is available for $1.75 from the GPO (#050-007-00763-9).

* Reemployment Help for the Jobless

Office of Employment and Training Programs
Employment and Training Administration
U.S. Department of Labor
200 Constitution Ave., NW, Room N4703
Washington, DC 20210 (202) 535-0577
The Economic Dislocation and Worker Adjustment Assistance Act (EDWAA) provides assistance to dislocated workers whose employment loss means they are unlikely to return to their previous industries or occupations. This includes workers who lose their jobs because of plant closings or mass lay-offs; long-term unemployed persons with limited local opportunities; and farmers, ranchers, and other self-employed persons who become jobless due to general economic conditions or national disasters. EDWAA has a local service-delivery system through which sub-state areas and grantees provide assistance to workers. Major activities and services under EDWAA include: 1) rapid response: the state's Dislocated Worker Unit (DWU) must be alerted to plant closings and mass lay-offs, and responds with on-site services to assist workers facing job losses; 2) retraining services, including basic education, occupational skills and/or on-the-job training; 3) needs-related payments: dislocated workers may receive payments to complete their training once their unemployment insurance is exhausted; and 4) reemployment services, such as job search and placement, and relocation assistance. Contact this office for further information.

* Securities and Exchange Commission Jobs

The Director of Personnel
U.S. Securities and Exchange Commission
450 5th St., NW
Washington, DC 20549 (202) 272-2519
With the exception of the attorney category, positions are in the competitive civil service and are filled generally by selection from lists of eligibles who have taken civil service examinations. The Commission operates a college and law school recruitment program, including on-campus visitations for interview purposes. Inquiries should be directed to this office.

* Skills Needed For Specific Jobs

Superintendent of Documents
Government Printing Office
Washington, DC 20402 (202) 783-3238
Selected Characteristics of Occupations Defined in the Dictionary of Occupational Titles is a supplement to the *Dictionary of Occupational Titles* which can save you time in matching individual skills and qualifications to available positions. It provides information on the training time, the physical demands, and environmental conditions for particular jobs. For more information regarding

this publication and other career and occupation publications contact: Office of Public Affairs, Employment and Training Administration, 200 Constitution Ave., NW, Room S2322, Washington, D.C. 20210; (202) 523-6871.

* Special Help To Workers Laid Off
Office of Trade Adjustment Assistance
Employment and Training Administration
U.S. Department of Labor
601 D St., NW, Room 6434
Washington, DC 20210 (202) 376-2646

The Trade Act of 1974 provides assistance to workers who become totally or partially separated from employment because of increased import competition. Such assistance may consist of training, job search and relocation allowances, special help in finding a new job, and weekly cash benefits equal to the level of regular unemployment compensation payable in the separated worker's state (A worker must exhaust all unemployment insurance benefits available in his state before collecting weekly cash benefits under the Trade Act). Petitioning worker groups may be certified eligible to apply for worker adjustment assistance if the department determines that increased imports of articles like or directly competitive with those produce by the petitioning worker's firm contributed importantly to decreased sales or production and to worker separations.

* State Employment Services for the Unemployed
Employment and Training Administration
U.S. Department of Labor
200 Constitution Ave., NW, Room S2307
Washington, DC 20210 (202) 523-6050

This administration's threefold responsibilities cover: 1) training programs, including the Job Training Partnership Act (JTPA), which prepares unskilled and dislocated workers for productive employment; 2) the network of state employment service offices, which helps place people in jobs; and 3) income maintenance for those who lose their jobs through no fault of their own. Under JTPA alone, more than two million persons are provided employment and training services each year. Federal funds are apportioned to the states, which provide the training and other services, working with local governments, business and industry, labor, education, and nonprofit groups. About 2,200 state employment service offices across the country make over three million job placements annually. For those out of work, state unemployment insurance offices, operating under federal guidelines, provide weekly cash benefits which become an important revenue source in local communities.

* Tomorrow's Jobs in 250 Industries
Office of Economic Growth
Bureau of Labor Statistics
U.S. Department of Labor
601 D St., NW, Room 4000
Washington, DC 20212 (202) 272-5381

This office has information on 250 industries regarding employment requirements, specifically on the demand for employment in the future. Industries covered follow the 1972 Standard Industrial Classification Manual. The November, 1989, issue of the *Monthly Labor Review* provides an overview of the data available.

* U.S. Merchant Marine Academy
U.S. Merchant Marine Academy
Maritime Administration
U.S. Department of Transportation-Kings Point
Long Island, NY 11024 (516) 773-5000

Future merchant marine officers are trained here in navigation instrumentation, ship maneuvering, ship management, and communications. The Academy also administers a Federal assistance program for maritime academies in California, Maine, Massachusetts, Michigan, New York, and Texas.

* Veterans' Employment and Training Help
Veterans' Employment and Training Service (VETS)
U.S. Department of Labor
200 Constitution Ave., NW, Room S1315
Washington, DC 20210 (202) 523-9116

The Veterans' Employment and Training Service is responsible for administering veterans' employment and training programs and activities through VETS to ensure that legislative and regulatory mandates are accomplished. The field staff of VETS works closely with and provides technical assistance to State Employment Security Agencies and Job Training Partnership Act grant recipients to ensure that veterans are provided the priority services required by law. They also coordinate with employers, labor unions, veterans, service organizations, and community organizations through planned public information and outreach activities.

* Veterans' Reemployment Rights
Veterans' Employment and Training

U.S. Department of Labor
200 Constitution Ave., NW, Room S1313
Washington, DC 20210 (202) 523-9116

The law provides that any employee enlisting in or inducted into the Armed Services, who leaves a position in order to perform military service, will be given back his or her position that he or she otherwise would have achieved had it not been for his or her military service. For more information on qualifications and eligibility, or if you need to register a complaint, contact this office.

* Vocational Job Preparation and Opportunities
Superintendent of Documents
Government Printing Office
Washington, DC 20402 (202) 783-3238

The book, *Vocational Preparation and Occupations*, can help job seekers to apply what they've learned in the classroom to office practices in the workplace. It provides comprehensive and reliable information for approximately 570 vocational programs, describing the physical demands, environmental conditions, and preparation and study time required for a wide variety of occupations. The cost is $21.00. For more information on career publications contact: Office of Public Affairs, Employment and Training Administration, 200 Constitution Ave., NW, Room S2322, Washington, DC 20210; (202) 523-6871.

* Welfare Recipients: Job Training Programs
Employment and Training Administration
U.S. Department of Labor
200 Constitution Ave., NW, Room N4470
Washington, DC 20210 (202) 535-0174

Under the Work Incentive Program, employment, training, and social supportive services such as child care, housing assistance, medical services, etc., are available to public welfare applicants and recipients in order to enable them to become self-supporting and independent of welfare assistance. All welfare applicants and recipients must register with the WIN program.

* Women in Non-traditional Careers
Superintendent of Documents
Government Printing Office
Washington, DC 20402 (202) 783-3238

For use by career counselors and educators, *Women in Non-traditional Careers: Journal and Curriculum Guide*, contains a comprehensive selection of ideas, activities, and resources. It can help women to learn more about careers in carpentry, mechanics, printing, engineering, architecture, and other non-traditional fields. Included with the *Guide* is a sample journal which can be used in the classroom to allow women to record their thoughts in diary format. The journal contains questions, facts, and quotes intended to enhance self-understanding with regard to non-traditional roles. The cost is $47.00.

* Women's Jobs in Highway Construction
Women's Bureau
U.S. Department of Labor
200 Constitution Ave., NW, Room S3309
Washington, DC 20210 (202) 523-6652

Women in Highway Construction, a jointly-funded project of the Women's Bureau, the Employment and Training Administration, and the Federal Highway Administration, will identify the barriers women face in the construction trades and develop a model program to be used by State Highway Departments and highway construction contractors in recruiting and hiring women.

* Youth Conservation Corps: Conservation
United States Youth Conservation Corps
U.S. Fish and Wildlife Service
National Park Service
Washington, DC 20240 (202) 343-5951

The Park Service's Youth Conservation Corps is a summer employment program for young men and women, ages 15 through 18, who work, learn, and earn wages accomplishing needed conservation work on public lands. The program is also administered by the Forest Service of the U.S. Department of Agriculture. Projects include constructing trails, building campground facilities, planting trees, collecting litter, clearing streams, improving wildlife habitats, and office work. Limited positions are available.

* Youth Conservation Corps: Health Professions
National Health Service Corps Scholarship Program
5600 Fishers Lane, Room 637
Rockville, MD 20857 (301) 443-6354

The National Health Service Corps helps alleviate the shortage of health professionals in geographically isolated or rural areas by offering a loan repayment program. The program pays the participants' lenders up to $20,000 a year toward their qualified health professions education loans during their contracted service periods.

Careers and Workplace

* Youth Conservation Corps Regional Offices

Youth Program Officer
National Park Service
U.S. Department of the Interior
Room 4415, P.O. Box 37127
1100 L St., NW
Washington, DC 20013-7127 (202) 343-5514

Alaska
National Park Service, 2525 Gambell St., Room 107, Anchorage, AK 99503; (907) 257-2698. Serving: Alaska

Mid-Atlantic Region
National Park Service, 143 S. Third St., Philadelphia, PA 19106; (215) 597-5375. Serving: Delaware, Maryland, Pennsylvania, Virginia, and West Virginia

Midwest Region
National Park Service, 1709 Jackson St., Omaha, NE 68102; (402) 221-3995. Serving: Illinois, Indiana, Iowa, Kansas, Minnesota, Michigan, Missouri, Nebraska, Ohio, and Wisconsin

Washington, D.C.
National Park Service, 1100 Ohio Dr., SW, Washington, DC 20242; (202) 485-9855. Serving: D.C., Maryland, and Virginia

North Atlantic Region
National Park Service, 15 State St., Boston, MA 02109; (617) 565-8860. Serving: Maine, Massachusetts, New Hampshire, New Jersey, New York, Rhode Island, Vermont, and Connecticut

Pacific Northwest Region
National Park Service, 83 S. King St., Suite 212, Seattle, WA 98104; (206) 442-1006. Serving: Washington, Oregon, and Idaho

Rocky Mountain Region
National Park Service, 12795 West Alameda Parkway, P.O. Box 25287, Lakewood, CO 80225; (303) 969-2605. Serving: Colorado, Montana, North Dakota, South Dakota, Utah, and Wyoming

Southeast Region
National Park Service, 75 Spring St., SW, Atlanta, GA 30303; (404) 331-4290. Serving: Alabama, Florida, Georgia, Tennessee, Mississippi, Kentucky, North Carolina, South Carolina, Puerto Rico, and the Virgin Islands

Southwest Region
National Park Service, P.O. Box 728, Santa Fe, NM 87504; (505) 988-6371. Serving: Arkansas, Louisiana, New Mexico, Oklahoma, and Texas

Western Region
National Park Service, 450 Golden Gate Ave., Box 3603, San Francisco, CA 94102; (415) 556-1866. Serving: Arizona, California, Nevada, and Guam

Employee Benefits and Rights

Pension plans, lie detector tests, affirmative action, and many other issues of worker protection are covered here. With these sources you'll be able to find out how your employee benefits compare with thousands of others across the country, how to protect your pension, or even how to contest the findings of a lie detector test. Additional sources on union grievance procedures and rights are included in the next section on Labor-Management Cooperation.

* Affirmative Action of Handicapped Persons
Office of Federal Compliance Programs
Employment Standards Administration
Department of Labor
200 Constitution Ave., NW, Room C3325
Washington, DC 20210   (202) 523-9475

The Rehabilitation Act of 1973 prohibits most employers doing business with the federal government from discriminating in employment against handicapped persons. Employers with contracts in excess of $2,500 must take affirmative action to hire and promote qualified handicapped persons.

* Child Labor Laws
Child Labor Programs
Employment Standards Administration
200 Constitution Ave., NW, Room S3510
Washington, DC 20210   (202) 523-7640

The Fair Labor Standards Act protects young workers from employment that might interfere with their educational opportunities or be hazardous to their health or well-being. There are different standards for work allowed, depending upon the age of the child. Contact the Child Labor Programs office for more information.

* Coal Miners' Benefits
Coal Mine Workers' Compensation Division
Employment Standards Administration
Department of Labor
200 Constitution Ave., NW
Room C3526
Washington, DC 20210   (202) 523-6795

Benefits are available for medical treatment and monthly payments to coal miners totally disabled from pneumoconiosis (black lung) arising from employment in the nation's coal mines. There are also benefits for the miner's dependents and to certain survivors of miners who died while totally disabled from pneumoconiosis. A copy of the Black Lung Benefits Act is available by contacting this office.

* Employee Benefits National Survey
Office of Compensation Levels and Trends
Bureau of Labor Statistics
Department of Labor
441 G St., NW, Room 2021
Washington, DC 20212   (202) 523-1382

This office conducts an annual survey of employers in the private sector and sample data on the incidence and characteristics of employee benefit plans. Data available include incidence and detailed characteristics of 11 private sector employee benefits paid for, at least in part, by the employer. The data are presented separately for three occupational groups: professional-administrative; technical-clerical; and production workers.

* Employee Pay and Benefits Cost Index
Office of Compensation and Working Conditions
Bureau of Labor Statistics
Department of Labor
441 G St., NW, Room 2026
Washington, DC 20212   (202) 523-1160

The quarterly *Employment Cost Index* measures changes in total compensation (wages, salaries, and employer costs for employee benefits) in wages and salaries only. Coverage includes all private industry and state and local government workers, but excludes Federal government, farm, household, self-employed, proprietors, and unpaid family workers.

* Employee Protection on Garnishing Wages
Wage-Hour Division

Employment Standards Administration
Department of Labor
200 Constitution Ave., NW, Room 3502
Washington, DC 20210   (202) 523-8305

The Federal Wage Garnishment Law limits the amount of an employee's disposable earnings which may be withheld in any one week by an employer to satisfy creditors. "Disposable Earnings" means that part of an employee's earnings remaining after deduction of any amount required by law. This law does not apply to bankruptcy court orders and debts for state and federal taxes. This law also prohibits an employer from discharging an employee whose earnings have been subjected to garnishment for any one indebtedness. Contact this office for more information on wage garnishments.

* Employee Whistleblower Abuse and Waste Hotline
Inspector General's Office
Department of Commerce
14th St. and Constitution Ave., NW
Room 7898C   (800) 424-5197
Washington DC 20230   (202) 377-2495

This hotline was established so that consumers and employees could report fraud, abuse, or waste within any office in the Department of Commerce. All reports are investigated and reports can be made anonymously. The Pentagon, HUD, and other government departments also have whistleblower hotlines.

* Employer's and Employee's Pension Guides
Public Affairs
Pension Benefit Guaranty Corporation
2020 K St., NW, Room 7100
Washington, DC 20006-1860   (202) 778-8840

This office will provide you with the following publications free of charge:

Employer's Pension Guide. This is a cooperative project of the Pension and Welfare Benefits Administration of the U.S. Department of Labor, the Internal Revenue Service, and the Pension Benefit Guaranty Corporation to provide a general overview of the responsibilities under federal law of employers who sponsor single-employer defined benefit pension plans. It describes federal pension law effective as of 1989. However, it is not intended to be, nor is it, all-inclusive; for specific legal or technical information, consult these federal agencies or a private sector employee benefits specialist.

Your Guaranteed Pension. This booklet answers some of the most frequently asked questions about the Pension Benefit Guaranty Corporation and its termination insurance program for single-employer defined benefit pension plans. The answers in it apply to pension plan terminations taking place in 1989. For terminations that occurred in previous years, different rules may apply.

Your Pension: Things You Should Know About Your Pension Plan. This publication is intended to serve as a handy explanation of pension plans; what they are, how they operate, and the rights and options of participants. It should not be relied upon for information about your specific pension plan. That information should be obtained from your Plan Administrator or the Summary Plan Description of your pension plan.

* Farm Worker Protection and Rights
Farm Labor Programs
Employment Standards Administration
Department of Labor
200 Constitution Ave., NW, Room S3510
Washington, DC 20210   (202) 523-7605

The Migrant and Seasonal Agricultural Workers Protection Act requires agricultural employers, agricultural associations, and farm labor contractors to observe certain labor standards when employing migrant and seasonal agricultural workers, unless exemptions apply. Certain persons and organizations, such as family businesses, small businesses, some seed and tobacco operations, labor unions, and their employees, are exempt. MSPA requires farm labor contractors to register with the U.S. Department of Labor. Contact this office for more information about the Act and for a list of workers' rights.

* Federal Wage-Hour Standards

Program Development and Research Division
Employment Standards Administration
Department of Labor
200 Constitution Ave., NW, Room 3319
Washington, DC 20210 (202) 523-8288

This division conducts research on the major programs within the Employment Standards Administration. Within the Wage-Hour Division, research is conducted on the provisions of the Fair Labor Standards Act and the Davis-Bacon Act. Within the Workers' Compensation Programs, they look into the provisions of the Federal Employees' Compensation Act, and publish annual reports concerning the Longshoremen and Black Lung Benefits Acts. They also conduct research on federal contract compliance.

* Foreigners and Work Permits

Labor Certification Division
Employment Service
Employment and Training Administration
Department of Labor
200 Constitution Ave., NW, Room N4456
Washington, DC 20210 (202) 535-0163

If an employer wishes to hire foreign workers, he must first obtain a foreign labor certificate, which is a statement from the U.S. Department of Labor stating that there is no U.S. citizen available to fill the job. The Department investigates to make sure that the wages and working conditions of the foreign workers will not seriously affect the wages and working conditions of U.S. workers. An employer applies for a foreign labor certificate through the local state employment service office, which then conducts a job hunt before sending the application form to the area regional office for approval or disapproval.

* Formal Labor Complaints

Office of the General Counsel
National Labor Relations Board
1717 Pennsylvania Ave., NW, Room 1001
Washington, DC 20570 (202) 254-9150

The General Counsel issues and prosecutes formal complaints before the National Labor Relations Board.

* Freedom on Information Act Requests

Disclosure Officer
Pension Benefit Guaranty Corporation
2020 K St., NW
Washington, DC 20006-1860 (202) 778-8839

Contact the office above for Freedom of Information Act requests.

* Job Counseling and Placement Fraud

Federal Trade Commission
Bureau of Consumer Protection
6th & Pennsylvania Ave., NW
Washington, DC 20580 (202) 326-3650

The FTC often receives complaint letters about job counseling and placement services which charge large fees and misrepresent their services. For information on how to select a legitimate employment service or to complain about one which you feel has misrepresented itself, contact your local FTC office.

* Lie Detector Testing

Wage and Hour Division
Employment Standards Administration
Department of Labor
200 Constitution Ave., NW, Room S3502
Washington, DC 20210 (202) 523-8305

The Employee Polygraph Protection Act prohibits most private employers from using lie detector tests either for pre-employment screening or during the course of employment. Federal, State, and local government employers are exempted for the Act. The law provides several limited exemptions which permit the use of polygraph tests. For more information on the law and the use of polygraphs, contact this office.

* Longshore and Harbor Workers Benefits

Longshore and Harbor Worker's
Compensation Division
Department of Labor
200 Constitution Ave., NW, Room C4315
Washington, DC 20210 (202) 523-8572

The Longshore and Harbor Worker's Compensation Act covers all maritime workers for job-related injury, illness, or death on the navigable waters of the U.S., as well as employees working on adjoining piers, docks, and terminals. Compensation is paid by insurance carriers or by employers who are self-insured.

* Pension and Retirement Audits

Office of the Chief Accountant
Pension and Welfare Benefits Administration
Department of Labor
200 Constitution Ave., NW, Room N5677
Washington, DC 20210 (202) 523-8951

This office serves as the U.S. Department of Labor's primary advisor on accounting, auditing, and actuarial issues stemming from its responsibilities under the Employee Retirement Income Security Act and the Federal Employees' Retirement System Act. It serves as the primary agency contact with accounting and actuarial organizations, as well as with federal and state agencies on accounting matters. It also administers a comprehensive system of compliance audits under FERSA and reviews annual financial reports.

* Pension Benefit Annual Report

Public Affairs
Pension Benefit Guaranty Corporation
2020 K St., NW, Room 7100
Washington, DC 20006-1860 (202) 778-8840

This publication contains information on PBGC, including financial statements and an actuarial report. To obtain a copy contact the office above.

* Pension Benefits

Office of Research and Economic Analysis
Pension and Welfare Benefits Administration
Department of Labor
200 Constitution Ave., NW, Room N5647
Washington, DC 20210 (202) 523-9421

This office can provide you with a list of reports prepared under contract to the U.S. Department of Labor concerning pensions. Some of the more recent studies include pension plan terminations with asset reversions, study of the investment performance of ERISA plans, and the effect of job mobility on pension plans.

* Pension Failure Early Warning

Coverage and Inquiries Branch
Insurance Operations Department
Pension Benefit Guaranty Corporation
2020 K St., NW
Washington, DC 20006-1860 (202) 778-8800

An "early warning system" is provided under the Employee Retirement Income Security Act (ERISA) of 1974, which requires that PBGC be notified within 30 days if an insured pension plan or plan sponsor is experiencing certain problems. Contact this office for more information. This notice is intended to provide PBGC with an opportunity to determine whether action is necessary to protect the interests of either the plan participants or the pension insurance program. PBGC may assess a penalty of up to $1,000 a day for failure to provide such required information. Contact the office above for more information including information on filing reportable events.

* Pension Insurance Premiums

Coverage and Inquiries Branch
Insurance Operations Department
Pension Benefit Guaranty Corporation
2020 K St., NW
Washington, DC 20006-1860 (202) 778-8800

PBGC's insurance is financed by premiums paid by covered plans or employers sponsoring these plans, and employer liability owed to PBGC when underfunded plans terminate. The PBGC administers two pension insurance programs: the single-employer program and the multiemployer program. Under the single-employer program, a company can voluntarily terminate its plan using either a standard termination procedure or a distress termination procedure. In addition, the PBGC may seek termination of a plan when necessary to protect the interests of the plan participants, of the plan, or of the PBGC. The PBGC must seek plan termination when a plan cannot pay current benefits. Multiemployer pension plans are maintained under collectively-bargained agreements between employee representatives and two or more unrelated employers. If a PBGC-insured multiemployer plan becomes insolvent, it receives financial assistance from the PBGC, thus enabling the plan to pay participants their guaranteed benefits. Contact the office above for more information.

* Pension Plan Financial Statements

Financial Operations Department
Pension Benefit Guaranty Corporation
2020 K St., NW, Room 6000
Washington, DC 20006-1860 (202) 778-8801

Contact the office above to obtain information on the PBGC combined financial statements which include the assets and liabilities of all defined benefit pension plans for which the Corporation is trustee.

* Pension Plan Insurance Coverage
Coverage and Inquiries Branch
Insurance Operations Department
Pension Benefit Guaranty Corporation
2020 K St., NW
Washington, DC 20006-1860 (202) 778-8800
For additional information or assistance on the single-employer defined benefit pension plan insurance program, or on defined benefit plan terminations, contact the office above.

* Pension Plans: Disclosure Requirements
Public Disclosure Room
Pension and Welfare Benefits Administration
Department of Labor
200 Constitution Ave., NW, Room N5507
Washington, DC 20210 (202) 523-8771
If you are covered by a pension plan and/or a welfare benefit plan, the administrator of your plan must give you a summary plan description (SPD), written in a manner easily understood, which provides information about eligibility, benefits, and procedures. Plan administrators also are required to provide you with a summary of any important changes in the SPD; a summary of the annual report that is filed with the Internal Revenue Service; a statement of accrued and vested benefits when you leave employment or have a break in service; and a written explanation if your claim for benefits has been denied. Administrators file copies of the SPD and certain other reports with the U.S. Department of Labor and are available to the public.

* Pension Plans Publications
Division of Public Information
Pension and Welfare Benefits Administration
Department of Labor
200 Constitution Ave., NW, Room N5666
Washington, DC 20210 (202) 523-8921
The publications listed below are available free of charge from this office:

What You Should Know About the Pension Law
How to File a Claim for Your Benefit
Your Pension
Often-Asked Questions About Employee Retirement Benefits
Trouble-Shooter's Guide to Filing the ERISA Annual Reports
Know Your Pension Plan
How to Obtain Employee Benefit Documents From the Labor Department
Reporting and Disclosure Guide for Employee Benefit Plans
Summary Plan Description Requirements Under ERISA
The Prudence Rule and Pension Plan Investments Under ERISA
Fiduciary Standards: Employee Retirement Income Security Act
Exemptions From ERISA Prohibited Transactions Provision
ERISA Reports to Congress
U.S. Department of Labor Highlights
PWBA Fact Sheets
PWBA: Administering The Pension and Welfare Law
A Brief Look at Pension Plan Chargers Under the Tax Reform Act of 1986

* Pension Protection and Retirement Equity
Pension and Welfare Administration
Department of Labor
200 Constitution Ave., NW, Room N5666
Washington, DC 20210 (202) 523-8921
The Retirement Equity Act of 1984 was designed to provide greater pension equity for women and for all workers and their spouses by taking into account changes in work patterns and marriage as an economic partnership. The new provisions lower the age for earning pension credits, provides for leaves of absences from work, and allow for greater benefits relating to marriage. Contact this office for further information.

* Pension Public Records
Disclosure Officer
Pension Benefit Guaranty Corporation
2020 K St., NW, Room 7100
Washington, DC 20006-1860 (202) 778-8839
Trusteeship plans, opinion letters, opinion manuals, litigation, termination case data sheets, and case log terminating plans updated quarterly are available for inspection from the office above. Also, *Annual Premium Reports* on microfilm filed by pension plans may be inspected. Contact the office above.

* Pension Terminations

Coverage and Inquiries Branch
Insurance Operations Department
Pension Benefit Guaranty Corporation
2020 K St., NW
Washington, DC 20006-1860 (202) 778-8800
Employers may end ("terminate") a defined benefit pension plan, but only if they meet safeguards designed to protect the plan participants. This can be accomplished either through a standard termination or a distress termination. In addition, PBGC may take action to terminate a plan if certain statutory criteria are met. PBGC encourages employers who are considering plan termination to explore alternatives that may enable them to preserve the plan and avoid benefit losses for their employees. Such alternatives may include "freezing" a plan or continuing to maintain and fund a plan although the facility has been shut down and its employees laid off. Employers should consult with private employee benefit specialists, the IRS, or PBGC for more information on these and other alternatives.

* Pension Trusteeships
Coverage and Inquiries Branch
Insurance Operations Department
Pension Benefit Guaranty Corporation
2020 K St., NW
Washington, DC 20006-1860 (202) 778-8800
If a plan qualifies for distress termination and can pay all of its benefit liabilities, PBGC will authorize the plan administrator to distribute the assets and complete the termination as in a standard termination. If the plan cannot pay all of its benefit liabilities, the plan administrator may be authorized to distribute the assets or PBGC may become trustee of the plan, either by agreement with the plan administrator or by order of a U.S. District Court. As trustee, PBGC will acquire the plan's records and assets, if any, as well as responsibility for benefit payments. PBGC will use its insurance funds to the extent necessary to pay the plan participants their guaranteed benefits. The plan's sponsor and its controlled group then become liable to PBGC for unpaid contributions and for unfunded benefit liabilities. Contact the office above for further information.

* Private Pension and Welfare Protection
Pension and Welfare Benefits Administration
Department of Labor
200 Constitution Ave., NW, Room N5666
Washington, DC 20210 (202) 523-8921
The Retirement Equity Act (1984) is designed to provide greater pension equity for women and for all workers and their spouses. It liberalizes such rules as those affecting participation, vesting, break in service, joint-and-survivor annuity, and alienation and assignment of benefits. This new law also protects the benefits of millions of workers and their beneficiaries in private pension plans and sets minimum standards to protect the interest of participant and their beneficiaries. Contact this office for more information.

* Statistical History of Pension Claims
Corporate Policy and Research Department
Pension Benefit Guaranty Corporation
2020 K St., NW, Room 7300
Washington, DC 20006-1860 (202) 778-8851
Contact the office above to obtain information on pension liabilities guaranteed by the PBGC which includes assets of terminated plans, statutory employer liability, and the resulting net claims.

* Transit System Employee Protection
Office of Labor-Management Programs
Bureau of Labor-Management Relations
Department of Labor
200 Constitution Ave., NW, Room N5416
Washington, DC 20210 (202) 357-0473
Federal law requires that arrangements be made to protect the rights of transit system employees when a state or local body uses federal funds to acquire or improve that system. This requirement is one of several laws administered by the U.S. Department of Labor to protect specific employees who might be adversely affected by a federal program. The protective arrangements must include preservation of rights, privileges, and benefits under existing collective bargaining agreements, continuation of collective bargaining rights, protection of individual employees against a worsening of their positions, assurances of employment and priority of reemployment, and paid training or retraining programs. An employee who believes he or she has been adversely affected as a result of federal transit assistance can make a claim with the U.S. Department of Labor.

* Unemployment Insurance and Reemployment
Demonstration Project
Unemployment Insurance Service
Employment and Training Administration
Department of Labor
200 Constitution Ave., NW, Room S4231

Washington, DC 20210   (202) 523-7831

The Employment and Training Administration has begun to review a number of nontraditional approaches to the Unemployment Insurance system. These alternative approaches involve several demonstration projects and include the following reemployment services: job search assistance, referral to training, relocation assistance, monetary incentives to search for work faster, and grants for self-employment. For more information about these projects, contact this office.

* Unemployment Insurance Help

Employment and Training Administration
Department of Labor
200 Constitution Ave., NW, Room S4231
Washington, DC 20210   (202) 523-7831

Unemployment Insurance programs provide limited compensation to workers who lose their jobs through no fault of their own. The Federal government establishes guidelines and pays state administrative costs from funds collected under the Federal Unemployment Tax Act, and the states operate the program under these guidelines. Claimants must be able to work, available to work, and seeking work.

* Unemployment Insurance Laws: State Comparisons

Superintendent of Documents
Government Printing Office
Washington, DC 20402   (202) 783-3238

The Comparison of State Unemployment Insurance Laws analyzes State unemployment insurance statutes. It provides text and tables on coverage, taxation, benefits, eligibility, administration of program, and temporary disability benefits. A three year subscription is available for $32.00. For more information on the laws contact: Unemployment Insurance, Employment and Training Administration, Department of Labor, 200 Constitution Ave., NW, Room C4512, Washington, D.C. 20210; (202) 535-0200.

* Unemployment Insurance Surveys

Office of Legislation and Actuarial Services
Employment and Training Administration
Department of Labor
200 Constitution Ave., NW, Room S4519
Washington, DC 20210   (202) 535-0630

The *UI Data Summary* is produced quarterly from state-reported data contained in the Unemployment Insurance Data Base, as well as UI-related data from outside sources. This report is intended to provide the user with a quick overview of the status of the unemployment insurance system at the national and state levels. Tables are provided for each state, and many data items are repeated on summary tables.

* Veteran Reemployment Rights

Veterans Employment and Training
Department of Labor
200 Constitution Ave., NW, Room S1313
Washington, DC 20210   (202) 523-9116

The law provides that any employee enlisting in or inducted into the Armed Services, who leaves a position in order to perform military service, will be given back his or her position that he or she otherwise would have achieved had it not been for his or her military service. For more information on qualifications and eligibility, or if you need to register a complaint, contact this office.

* Veteran Job Training Program

Assistant Secretary For Veterans
Employment and Training
Department of Labor
200 Constitution Ave., NW, Room S1313
Washington, DC 20210   (202) 523-9116

Employment-related services designed to aid veterans include counseling, testing, and skills training; unemployment compensation for newly separated ex-service members while they look for civilian employment; tax credits for private employers who hire certain target groups of veterans; placement in private and public sector jobs; and reemployment rights assistance. For more information, contact the Veterans Employment and Training Office.

* Vietnam and Disabled Vets Job Placement

Veterans Employment and Training
Department of Labor
200 Constitution Ave., NW, Room S1313
Washington, DC 20210   (202) 523-9116

Federal government contractors and subcontractors (with government contracts of $10,000 or more) are required by law to take affirmative action to employ and to advance in employment qualified special disabled and Vietnam-era Veterans. All suitable employment openings must be given to the nearest local State Employment Office. A Veterans Employment and Training Representative is located in each office to provide employment advice and assistance to veterans. Contact the Office of Federal Contract Compliance Programs if it appears that a contractor has failed to comply. Complaints can be made to: Office of Federal Contract Compliance Programs, Department of Labor, 200 Constitution Ave., NW, Room C3325, Washington, D.C. 20210; (202) 523-9475.

* Workers' Compensation for Federal Employees

Federal Employees' Compensation Division
Office of Workers' Compensation Programs
Employment Standards Administration
Department of Labor
200 Constitution Ave., NW, Room S3229
Washington, DC 20210   (202) 523-7552

This office can provide you with a variety of free publications which explain the Federal Employees' Compensation Act, claim forms for work-related disabilities or deaths, as well as checklists for evidence required in support of claims for occupational diseases, such as work-related coronary illness, pulmonary disease, and hearing loss. *Federal Injury Compensation* is a free publication which lists questions and answers regarding the Federal Employees' Compensation Act. Contact this office for a list of publications, and further information.

Labor-Management Relations

Reducing tensions between management and workers and improving the quality of worklife are emerging issues for companies nationwide. Here you will find all kinds of information on such issues as collective bargaining agreements, union contracts, cooperative workshops, and pending legislation. You can find additional sources on productivity, one of the underlying goals of labor-management cooperation, in the Business & Industry chapter.

* Arbitrators and Mediators

Federal Mediation and Conciliation Service (FMCS)
2100 K St., NW
Washington, DC 20427 (202) 653-5300
Through its regional offices and suboffices, FMCS assists federal agencies, private sector employers, and labor organizations in resolving labor-management disputes. When there is no local or state resource available, the parties involved may contact the regional FMCS office to be assigned a qualified mediator or arbitrator, on call 24 hours a day. Upon request, mediators will assist the parties in resolving disputes, and arbitrators will make a final decision. Technical assistance includes training for one or both parties in developing constructive methods of dispute resolution, help in forming committees, and collective bargaining workshops. Contact your local FMCS office for any of these services.

* Case Processing of Worker Grievances

Management and Information Systems Branch
National Labor Relations Board
1717 Pennsylvania Ave., NW, Room 393
Washington, DC 20570 (202) 634-4124
This service monitors all NLRB cases from their initial filing to their final resolution. Information regarding regional cases is tabulated and detailed in reports issued periodically to Board members for their use only. Summaries and statistical tables regarding these cases are published in the Annual Report available from the U.S. Government Printing Office.

* Collective Bargaining Agreements and Case Files

Office of Research and Information Management
National Mediation Board
1425 K St., NW, Room 910
Washington, DC 20572 (202) 357-0466
The public may inspect copies of collective bargaining agreements between labor and management of rail and air carriers at this office. Copies of awards and interpretations issued by the National Railroad Adjustment Board are also available. Write or visit the office listed above to access copies of collective bargaining agreements. Some National Railroad Adjustment Board documents may require a Freedom of Information Act request. Submit FOIA requests to the National Mediation Board at above address, telephone (202) 523-5996.

* Collective Bargaining Annual Report

Office of Public Affairs
Federal Mediation and Conciliation Service (FMCS)
2100 K St., NW, Room 909
Washington, DC 20427 (202) 653-5290
Booklets about collective bargaining, arbitration, and mediation in the private, federal, State, and local sectors are available from this office. The *FMCS Annual Report* summarizes major negotiations and important developments of the year. To obtain these publications and for further information, contact Public Affairs.

* Collective Bargaining Units

Division of Information
National Labor Relations Board
1717 Pennsylvania Ave., NW, Room 710
Washington, DC 20570 (202) 632-4950
A bargaining unit, in general, is a group of two or more employees whose mutual interests form a reasonable basis for collective bargaining. The National Labor Relations Board is responsible for determining units appropriate for collective bargaining purposes. Questions concerning bargaining units should be directed to this office, or to the regional office in the area where the employee unit is located.

* Cooperative and Employee Involvement Programs

Information Office
Bureau of Labor-Management Relations
Department of Labor

200 Constitution Ave., NW, Room N5419
Washington, DC 20210 (202) 523-6098
Film/Video Sourcebook for Cooperative and Employee Involvement Programs covers films and videotapes which deal directly with cooperative and employee involvement programs. It does not include films on motivation, behavior, supervision, or self-training. Description and distribution information accompanies each listing. Contact this office for your free copy.

* Cooperative Labor-Management Clearinghouse

Information Office
Bureau of Labor-Management Relations
Department of Labor
200 Constitution Ave., NW, Room N5402
Washington, DC 20210 (202) 523-6481
The Bureau has developed a national information clearinghouse to help with the exchange of information among employers, unions, and others interested to joint labor-management programs, and innovative workplace practices. A computerized database contains basic information on programs operating in a variety of firms and organizations in the private and public sectors, including the names of individuals in these organizations who can provide additional information. Listings from the clearinghouse are available to all interested parties upon request. Database information can be accessed easily according to type of industry and employer size, geographic area, program type/features, program scope and workplace issues addressed, union involvement and year program began.

* Employer/Union Cooperative Efforts

Superintendent of Documents
Government Printing Office
Washington, DC 20402 (202) 783-3238
The Bureau of Labor Statistics publishes *Labor-Management Cooperation: Recent Efforts and Results* describes the kinds of problems employers and unions face and illustrates some of the cooperative strategies adopted in seeking solutions ($6.00).

* Federal Labor Relations Documents

Office of Case Control
Federal Labor Relations Authority (FLRA)
500 C St., SW
Washington, DC 20424 (202) 382-0748
Case file information is maintained on FLRA hearings and cases prosecuted to ensure compliance with the rights and obligations of federal employees to organize, bargain collectively, and participate in labor organizations. To view FLRA case dockets and decisions, call ahead to this office to arrange for a visit.

* Federal Labor Relations Freedom of Information

Public Information Office
Federal Labor Relations Authority (FLRA)
500 C St., SW
Washington, DC 20424 (202) 382-0711
The Public Information Office listed above is the Freedom of Information Act contact for the Authority.

* Federal Labor Relations Library

Library
Federal Labor Relations Authority (FLRA)
500 C St., SW, Room 235
Washington, DC 20424 (202) 382-0765
A small specialized collection is housed here. Material covers federal service labor-management relations and the Federal Labor Relations Authority. The library is open to the public, but due to tight security in the building, you are advised to call ahead for an appointment.

Careers and Workplace

* Foreign Visitor Program

Special Mediation Services
Federal Mediation and Conciliation Service (FMCS)
2100 K St., NW, Room 709
Washington, DC 20427   (202) 653-6271

Representatives of labor, management, and governments from around the world can see how arbitration, mediation, collective bargaining, and employee involvement programs function in the U.S. by participation in this visitor program. Industrial labor relations are targeted. For more information, contact the Special Mediation Services office listed.

* Labor-Management Developments

Information Office
Bureau of Labor-Management Relations
Department of Labor
200 Constitution Ave., NW, Room N5419
Washington, DC 20210   (202) 523-6098

Labor-Management Cooperation Briefs is a free monthly publication which include reports on significant literature and events of current interest related to labor-management issues.

* Labor Practices in Federal Service

Public Information Office
Federal Labor Relations Authority (FLRA)
500 C St., SW
Washington, DC 20424   (202) 382-0711

Contact this office to obtain a copy of the *FLRA Annual Report*, which describes significant decisions of the FLRA and case processing statistics of the General Counsel of the Authority. Cases of alleged unfair labor practices in federal service are investigated and prosecuted by the General Counsel and are heard by the FLRA's Office of Administrative Law Judges.

* Labor Union Regulations

Office of Labor-Management Standards
Department of Labor
200 Constitution Ave., NW, Room S1032
Washington, DC 20210   (202) 523-7343

Labor-Management Standard is a newsletter sent to approximately 200 international unions, informing the union presidents about OLMS compliance assistance and enforcement programs. As part of the publication, OLMS includes *Labor-Management Reporting and Disclosure Act Compliance Tips*, which are detachable sheets that can be distributed to affiliated locals to assist them in complying with various LMRDA provisions.

* Mediation Board Publications

Office of Executive Secretary
National Mediation Board
1425 K St., NW, Room 910
Washington, DC 20572   (202) 523-5920

There are three annual subscription mailing lists available from the Board. Costs may be reduced or waived when it is in the public interest to do so.
Subscription List #1, $175: *Annual Reports of the NMB; Certifications and Dismissals; Determination of Craft or Class; Findings Upon Investigation; Emergency Board Reports*
Subscription List #2, $ 50: *Annual Reports of the NMB; Emergency Board Reports; Determination of Craft or Class*
Subscription List #3, $ 35: *The Representation Manual* and amendments

* Mediation Cases

Legal Services Office
Federal Mediation and Conciliation Service (FMCS)
2100 K St., NW, Room 712
Washington, DC 20427   (202) 653-5305

This office represents FMCS in legal cases. In unusually complex and technical mediation efforts, Legal Services staff participate as part of the mediation team. Contact this office for more information on labor-management conciliation cases.

* Mediation National Board Freedom of Information

National Mediation Board
1425 K St., NW,
Washington, DC 20572   (202) 523-5996

This office handles Freedom of Information Act requests regarding the National Mediation Board.

* Mediation Service Freedom of Information

Legal Services Office
Federal Mediation and Conciliation Service (FMCS)
2100 K St., NW, Room 712
Washington, DC 20427   (202) 653-5305

This office handles FMCS Freedom on Information Act requests.

* Negotiation Impasses

Federal Services Impasses Board
Federal Labor Relations Authority (FLRA)
500 C St., SW, Room 215
Washington, DC 20424   (202) 382-0981

When negotiation impasses develop between Federal agencies and employee representatives, this panel provides assistance in resolving the stalemate. The following publications are available: *Guide to Hearing Procedures of the Federal Services; Impasses Panel; Subject Matter Index; Table of Cases; and the Annual Report*.

* Newsletter

Information office
Bureau of Labor-Management Relations
Department of Labor
200 Constitution Ave., NW, Room N5419
Washington, DC 20210   (202) 523-6098

Labor Relations Today is a free bimonthly newsletter which contains articles, labor-management profiles and resources relative to labor-management relations.

* NLRB Annual Report

Division of Information
National Labor Relations Board
1717 Pennsylvania Ave., NW, Room 710
Washington, DC 20570   (202) 632-4950

The National Labor Relations Board's activities and its significant case decisions for the previous fiscal year are highlighted in its Annual Report. Included are summaries of unique and/or precedent setting unfair labor practice decisions and representation elections. Statistical tables break down case information into such categories as geographic location, type of industry involved, actions taken, and final case disposition. Questions regarding the report should be directed to this office, and to purchase the report, contact the Superintendent of Documents, Government Printing Office, Washington, DC 20402; (202) 783-3238.

* NLRB Cases

Office of the Executive Secretary
National Labor Relations Board
1717 Pennsylvania Ave., NW, Room 701
Washington, DC 20570   (202) 254-9118

All pertinent information regarding current cases before the NLRB is tracked by this service. Summaries include such information as the type of allegation, industries involved, location of the incident, and actions already taken. This document is for internal National Labor Relations Board use only.

* NLRB Elections

Division of Information
National Labor Relations Board
1717 Pennsylvania Ave., NW, Room 710
Washington, DC 20570   (202) 632-4950

Secret ballot elections, conducted by the National Labor Relations Board, are held by employees to determine whether union representation is desired for the purpose of collective bargaining. The Board publishes a monthly update, *National Labor Relations Board Monthly Election Report*, available for $17 per year from Superintendent of Documents, Government Printing Office, Washington, DC 20402; (202) 783-3238. Contact this office for more information regarding petitioning for an election as well as Certification of Representative, Decertification, Withdrawal of Union-Shop Authority, Employer Petition, Unit Clarification, and Amendment of Certification.

* NLRB Meetings

Division of Information
National Labor Relations Board
1717 Pennsylvania Ave., NW, Room 710
Washington, DC 20570   (202) 632-4950

The public is usually allowed to attend National Labor Relations Board meetings. Information regarding upcoming meetings is published in the "Federal Register" or can be attained through this office.

* NLRB Publications

Division of Information
National Labor Relations Board
1717 Pennsylvania Ave., NW, Room 710
Washington, DC 20570   (202) 632-4950

Contact this office to obtain a free list of the National Labor Relations Board publications. The list includes information regarding the documents' frequency of publication, stock numbers, and cost.

* NLRB Public Information Room

Records Management
National Labor Relations Board
1717 Pennsylvania Ave., NW, Room 260
Washington, DC 20570   (202) 254-9488
This facility provides for public inspection of the Board's decisions, appeals, and advice papers.

* NLRB Speakers

Division of Information
National Labor Relations Board
1717 Pennsylvania Ave., NW, Room 710
Washington, DC 20570   (202) 632-4950
Personnel from Washington headquarters and the regional offices serve as speakers and panelists before bar associations, labor and management organizations, as well as education and civic groups. For more information regarding the speaker program, contact this office or your nearest National Labor Relations Board regional office.

* NLRB Weekly Summary

Superintendent of Documents
Government Printing Office
Washington, DC 20402   (202) 783-3238
The NLRB's publication, "Weekly Summary of National Labor Relations Board Cases," is available through the Government Printing Office for $84 per year.

* Partnership Workshops

Information Office
Bureau of Labor-Management Relations
Department of Labor
200 Constitution Ave., NW, Room N5419
Washington, DC 20210   (202) 523-6098
The Bureau of Labor-Management Relations and Cooperative Programs offer two technical assistance workshops to help explore new labor-management directions. These workshops aid teams of decision makers as they weigh the pros and cons of becoming involved partners. They offer organizations--both large and small, in the public and private sectors--the chance to discover new strategies that can bring them higher productivity, and involved and committed workforce, and a better workplace. *Orientation to Labor-Management Initiatives* is a one-day workshop which highlights the core concepts that drive cooperative labor-management relationships. *Partners in Change* is a 2 1/2 day seminar for organizations that have moved toward cooperative labor-management relationships. Contact this office to have either of these programs conducted at your work site.

* Publications Catalog

Information Office
Bureau of Labor-Management Relations
Department of Labor
200 Constitution Ave., NW, Room 5419
Washington, DC 20210   (202) 523-6098
This office can provide you with a free catalog of publications on labor-management cooperation and relations, along with information on the Bureau and the Cooperative Information Clearinghouse.

* Quality-of-Worklife

National Audiovisual Center
8700 Edgeworth Dr.
Capitol Heights, MD 20743   (301) 763-1891
Work Worth Doing is a two-part news documentary which describes how six progressive companies and their unions are using a variety of cooperative labor relations practices and quality-of-work-life programs not only to survive in the market place, but to thrive. *Part I* is an overview of several types of programs instituted in various organizations, and *Part II* provides more detailed information about how these programs were implemented and are maintained. Each part costs $110.00.

* Railroad Carrier Employee Grievances

National Railroad Adjustment Board
National Mediation Board
175 W. Jackson Blvd., Room A931
Chicago, IL 60604   (312) 886-7303
The Railroad Adjustment Board handles carrier employee grievances and disputes related to the interpretation and application of existing contracts which cannot be resolved in the usual manner. Disputes may concern rates of pay or working conditions, for example. Disputes are referred by petition of either or both parties to the appropriate Adjustment Board division.
-First Division: Train and yard service employees including engineers, firemen, hostlers, conductors, and trainmen

-Second Division: Machinists, boilermakers, blacksmiths, sheetmetal workers, carmen, coach cleaners, powerhouse employees, and railroad shop laborers
-Third Division: Clerical employees, station and tower employees, telegraph employees, dispatchers, maintenance of way men, freight handlers, store employees, signalmen, sleeping car conductors, porters, maids, and dining car employees
-Fourth Division: Employees of carriers directly or indirectly engaged in transportation of passengers or cargo by water and employees not coming under the jurisdiction of the other three divisions
For further information, contact the office listed.

* Resource Center

Information Office
Bureau of Labor-Management Relations
200 Constitution Ave., NW, Room N5419
Washington, DC 20210   (202) 523-6098
This bureau conducts national and regional conferences and symposia for labor, management, and other audiences to examine emerging industrial relations issues and trends. The Bureau also conducts research on industrial relations policies and practices, with particular emphasis on factors which help or hinder the conduct of labor-management relations. The research results are published and available through the Bureau, as is a bibliographic listing of recent books, articles, and special reports. A free publications catalog is also available, as is *Labor Relations Today*, a free bimonthly newsletter dealing with labor-management relations issues.

* Unfair Labor Practice Charges

Office of Appeals
National Labor Relations Board
1717 Pennsylvania Ave., NW, Room 1154
Washington, DC 20570   (202) 254-9316
Unfair labor practice charges may be filed by employees, employers, and unions against businesses and\or labor organizations at the nearest National Labor Relations Board regional office. If the regional office refuses to issue a complaint, contact this main office..

* Unfair Labor Practice Hearings

Division of Administrative Law Judges
National Labor Relations Board
1375 K St., NW, Room 1121
Washington, DC 20005   (202) 633-0500
Administrative law judges conduct formal hearings regarding unfair labor practices. In addition to ruling on these cases, the judges assign hearing dates and maintain the calendar of upcoming cases.

* Union Bylaws and Public Information

Disclosure Room
Office of Labor-Management Standards
Department of Labor
200 Constitution Ave., NW, Room N5620
Washington, DC 20210   (202) 523-8861
Unions must file information reports, constitutions and bylaws, and annual financial reports with the Secretary of Labor. Officers and employees of labor unions must report any loans and gifts received from, or certain financial interests in, employers whose employees the union represents. Employers who engage in certain financial dealings with their employees, unions, and labor-relations consultants must file reports, as well as labor-relations consultants who enter into agreements with employers to persuade employees as to the manner of exercising their rights. All reports are public information, and may be examined at the OLMS national and regional offices. The publication, *Reports Required*, gives detailed information on who needs to file reports, and general rules relating to these reports.

* Union Contracts Bargaining Calendar

Superintendent of Documents
Government Printing Office
Washington, DC 20402   (202) 783-3238
The Bureau of Labor Statistics' publishes *Bargaining Calendar*, a yearly schedule of information on anticipated contract adjustments between labor and management negotiators. Major situations in which contracts will terminate, deferred wage increases will become due, changes in the Consumer Price Indexes will be reviewed, and contracts will be renewed ($5.00).

* Union Contracts Clearinghouse

Public File of Collective Bargaining Agreements
Labor-Management Relations
Bureau of Labor Statistics
Department of Labor
441 G St., NW, Room 2032

Washington, DC 20212   (202) 523-1597

The Bureau of Labor Statistics maintains for public examination and use a file of collective bargaining agreements, including an annual and monthly calendar of contract expirations. The file covers 5,000 agreements in private industry and government, including virtually all those covering bargaining units with 1,000 employees or more, exclusive of railroads and airlines. Negotiators for both labor and management use this data.

* Union Contracts Database

Legal Services Office
Federal Mediation and Conciliation Service (FMCS)
2100 K St., NW, Room 712
Washington, DC 20427   (202) 653-5305

The office also maintains a database of union contracts searchable by company name and dating back one year. Information can be obtained by written request.

* Union Contracts: Help Getting Copies

Office of Labor-Management Standards
Department of Labor
200 Constitution Ave., NW, Room S2203
Washington, DC 20210   (202) 523-9674

Every employee (whether or not a union member) is entitled, on request, to receive from a local union a copy of each collective bargaining agreement made by the local which directly affects that person's rights as an employee. OLMS should be notified if the union fails to furnish copies of the agreements.

* Union Investigations

Office of Labor-Management Standards
Department of Labor
200 Constitution Ave., NW, Room S2203
Washington, DC 20210   (202) 523-9674

The Labor-Management Reporting and Disclosure Act authorizes the Secretary of Labor to investigate any union to determine whether a violation has occurred. The investigation can be prompted by an analysis of reports a union files or in response to specific complaints. If the investigation is based on a complaint, information such as the complainant's name and the specific details of the complaint will not be disclosed, and the union will not be allowed to review the complaint or obtain a copy of it. Criminal violations will be referred to the Justice Department.

* Union Members' Bill of Rights

Office of Labor-Management Standards
Department of Labor
200 Constitution Ave., NW, Room S2203
Washington, DC 20210   (202) 523-9674

The Labor-Management Reporting and Disclosure Act grants certain rights to union members and protects their interests by promoting democratic procedures within labor organizations. The Act establishes a Bill of Rights for union members; reporting requirements for labor organizations, union officers, and employees, employers, labor-relations consultants, and surety companies; standards for the regular election of union officers; and certain safe guards for labor organization funds. Copies of the law and additional information are available from this office.

* Worker Adjustment Efforts

Information Office
Bureau of Labor-Management Relations
Department of Labor
200 Constitution Ave., NW, Room N5419
Washington, DC 20210   (202) 523-6098

Cooperative Labor-Management Worker Adjustment Programs is a free study of companies and unions using techniques and procedures which provide invaluable lessons for management, unions, state and local officials, and others involved in plant closing and dislocated worker issues.

* Workers and Managers Collaborative Strategies

Office of Labor-Management Relations
Department of Labor
200 Constitution Ave., NW, Room N5419
Washington, DC 20210   (202) 523-6098

This office assists workers and managers who are interested in creating labor-management cooperation programs, which are joint efforts by labor and management to further their interests by working together. Their aim is to satisfy and involve more employees, along with creating more effective, adaptive, and productive organizations. This office assists these efforts by providing information and technical assistance; sharing reports and case-studies on current programs, issues, and practices; and supporting conferences, symposia, demonstration projects, and research in the field.

Occupational Health and Safety

* See also Drug and Chemical Dependence Chapter

All sorts of work-related health and safety issues are covered here, including radiation from computer screens, high blood pressure, smoking restrictions, and exposure to hazardous materials. These sources can tell you whom to contact for the latest scientific data on work-related injuries and safety, along with assistance to businesses to help them follow federal and state safety guidelines. You'll find additional sources mentioned in the Health and Medicine Chapter in the section on Chemicals, Toxics and other Health Hazards.

* Accident Reporting Network
Office of Field Programs
Occupational Safety and Health Administration
Department of Labor
200 Constitution Ave., NW, Room N3603
Washington, DC 20210 (202) 523-7725

All employers are required to report all accidents which result in a work-related death or five or more hospitalizations to the nearest OSHA office within 48 hours. You can not be discriminated against, fired, demoted, or otherwise penalized for complaining about a hazard to your employer, requesting an OSHA inspection, or participating in union safety and health activities. OSHA can take action, including going to court if necessary, to force your employer to restore your job, earnings, and benefits. You will not have to pay and legal fees.

* Airline Pilots Medical Certification
Civil Aeromedical Institute
Federal Aviation Administration
Department of Transportation
Mike Monroney Aeronautical Center
P.O. Box 25082
Oklahoma, OK 73125 (405) 680-4806

CAMI operates a program for the medical certification of airmen, and educates pilots and physicians in matters related to aviation safety. It is also responsible for developing and producing brochures, slides, and training films for distribution to aviation groups and organizations. Contact CAMI for more information on certification or these education programs.

* Appealing an OSHA Standard
Office of the Assistant Secretary
Occupational Safety and Health Administration
Department of Labor
200 Constitution Ave., NW, Room S2315
Washington, DC 20210 (202) 523-7162

No decision on a permanent standard is ever reached without due consideration of the arguments and data received from the public in written submissions and at hearings. However, any person who may be adversely affected by a final or emergency standard may file a petition within 60 days for judicial review of the standard with the U.S. Court of Appeals for the circuit in which the objector lives or has his business.

* Appealing OSHA Citations
Office of Information
Occupational Safety and Health Review Commission
1825 K St., 4th Floor
Washington, DC 20006-1246 (202) 634-7943

If an employer disagrees with any aspect of an Occupational Safety and Health Administration citation, issued by an inspector in the workplace, the employer must notify OSHA of that disagreement within 15 working days of receiving the citation. The employer is then entitled to have its dispute resolved by this Commission. A case that comes before the Commission is first heard and decided by an Administrative Law Judge. The judge's decision may be reviewed at the discretion of the Commission members, who have the authority to change that decision. Commission decisions and Judges' decisions not reviewed by the Commission can be appealed to the United States Court of Appeals.

* Audiovisuals on Occupational Safety and Health
Audiovisual Training Programs
National Audiovisual Center
Customer Services Section
8700 Edgeworth Dr.
Capitol Heights, MD 20743 (301) 763-1896

The *Occupational Safety and Health Audiovisual Training Programs* catalog lists over 65 high quality, low-cost hazard training programs from the safety experts at OSHA, NIOSH, and other federal agencies. It features OSHA's popular *Hazard Recognition Series* that teaches people what they need to know to work safety in a variety of situations. Contact this office for your free catalog.

* Aviation Medicine
Biomedical and Behavioral Science Division
Office of Aviation Administration
Federal Aviation Administration
Department of Transportation
800 Independence Ave., SW, Room 325
Washington, DC 20591 (202) 267-3535

The FAA conducts aeromedical research on in the following areas:
-Psychology: evaluates spatial disorientation and visual perception in the aviation environment;
-Physiology: performance and health of aircrew and air traffic controllers under diverse environmental conditions;
-Toxicology: toxic hazards such as pesticides used in aerial application, products of combustion and ionizing radiation from air shipment of radioactive cargo in the high-altitude environment;
-Protection and survival: studies of techniques for lessening or preventing crash injuries, developing concepts and evaluating survival equipment used under adverse physical conditions, establishing human physical limitations of civil aviation operations, and evaluating emergency procedures for downed aircraft.

* Businesses Promoting Health
National Health Information Clearinghouse
P.O. Box 1133 (800) 336-4797
Washington, DC 20013 (301) 565-4167 (MD and DC)

Health Promotion and Business Coalitions: Current Activities and Prospects for the Future provides an overview of the health education and promotion activities of 105 business health coalitions and includes five detailed case studies. This 78 page manual (Order No. W0003) is available for $2.00.

* Chemical Hazards
Clearinghouse for Occupational Safety and Health Information
NIOSH
4676 Columbia Parkway
Cincinnati, OH 45226 (513) 533-8287

This clearinghouse can answer a wide range of questions regarding chemical hazards in the workplace and occupational safety by using their databases (National Occupational Hazard Survey and NIOSH Technical Information Center) to research your questions. They have many publications, such as Prevention of Leading Work-Related Diseases and NIOSH Recommendations for Occupational Safety, including a free catalog.

* College Courses
Division of Training and Manpower Development
National Institute for Occupational Safety and Health
4676 Columbia Parkway
Cincinnati, OH 45226 (513) 533-8221

This division offers courses for industry and health care professionals on such topics as occupational safety, industrial hygiene, and safety in the laboratory. For a course listing and description, contact this office.

* Companies Inspected by OSHA
Office of Management Data Systems
Directorate of Administrative Programs
Occupational Safety and Health Administration
Department of Labor

Careers and Workplace

200 Constitution Ave., NW, Room N3661
Washington, DC 20210   (202) 523-7008
This office can provide you with the entire range of inspection data, including who, what, when, where, and why companies were inspected, and the violations that were found.

* Employee Health Promotion Efforts

National Health Information Clearinghouse
P.O. Box 1133   (800) 336-4797
Washington, DC 20013   (301) 565-4167 (MD and DC)
Worksite Health Promotion: A Bibliography of Selected Books and Resources lists and describes resources for employee health promotion programs. This 22 page pamphlet (Order No. W0005) is available for $2.00.

* Employee Safety Program

Consumer Product Safety Commission
5401 Westbard Avenue
Washington, DC 20207   (202) 492-6580
Through one of its regional offices, the Commission will arrange for a consumer safety specialist to visit your business or workplace at no charge for a presentation of safety hazards and accident prevention on-the-job.

* Equipment for Determining Hazards in the Workplace

Occupational Safety and Health Administration
Department of Labor
U.S. Post Office Bldg.
Fifth and Walnut Sts.
Cincinnati, OH 45202   (513) 684-3721
The OSHA Cincinnati Laboratory develops, evaluates, calibrates, and repairs hazard measurement instrumentation and equipment. They can provide you with information on all aspects of this equipment.

* Environmental and Occupational Health

Society for Occupational and Environmental Health (SOEH)
P.O. Box 42360
Washington, DC 20015-0360   (202) 762-9319
This society's members include physicians, hygienists, economists, laboratory scientists, academics, and labor and industry representatives.

* Hazards Detection

National Institute for Occupational Safety and Health
4676 Columbia Parkway
Cincinnati, OH 45226   (800) 356-4674
NIOSH is responsible for conducting research to make the nation's workplaces healthier and safer by responding to urgent requests for assistance from employers, employees, and their representatives where imminent hazards are suspected. They conduct inspections, laboratory and epidemiologic research, publish their findings, and make recommendations for improved working conditions to regulatory agencies. NIOSH trains occupational health and safety workers and communicates research results to those concerned.

* Hazards Outreach Program

Office of Field Programs
Department of Labor
200 Constitution Ave., NW, Room N3603
Washington, DC 20210   (202) 523-7725
Local offices of the Occupational Safety and Health Administration carry out many different programs: enforcement, standard setting, state programs, voluntary compliance programs, and training and education. OSHA personnel are available to speak at civic clubs, union meetings, and trade association gatherings to explain new OSHA standards, encourage participation in OSHA rule makings, and answer questions about the agency's approach to workplace safety and health. OSHA also demonstrates, to the extent possible, technical equipment and materials. Prepackaged training programs are available to unions or trade groups. Contact you local OSHA office for more information.

* Health Hazard Evaluation

                                         (800) 35-NIOSH
Employers, employees, or their representatives who suspect a health problem in the workplace can request a National Institute of Occupation Safety and Health (NIOSH) Health Hazard Evaluation to assess the problem.

* Health Initiatives in the Workplace

Office of Workplace Initiatives
National Institute on Drug Abuse, Room 10A53
5600 Fishers Lane
Rockville, MD 20857   (301) 443-6780

This office develops policies and provides leadership for the implementation and administration of a national program to eliminate illegal drug use in the workplace. Its programs include research, treatment, training, and prevention activities as well as projects related to the development of a comprehensive Drug-Free Workplace program. OWI has developed mandatory guidelines for federal workplace drug testing programs, which include scientific and technical requirements and certification standards for laboratories engaged in urine drug testing for federal agencies. OWI analyzes and recommends Employee Assistance Programs and distributes a four-part videotape series on drugs at work.

* Health On-the-Job and Future Strategies

National Health Information Clearinghouse
P.O. Box 1133   (800) 336-4797
Washington, DC 20013   (301) 565-4167 (MD and DC)
The Future of Work and Health: Implications for Health Strategies summarizes emerging trends in work and health and explores issues concerning the development of health care strategies for worksites in the future. Copies of this 46-page booklet (Order No. W0013) is available for $2 to cover postage/handling.

* Health Promotion in the Workplace

Office of Disease Prevention and Health Promotion
Public Health Service
330 C St., SW, Room 2132
Washington, DC 20201   (202) 472-5660
This office works on developing policies for the Year 2000 objectives for health promotion. Their Preventive Services Task Force is developing recommendations for clinical practice, in addition to a worksite Health Promotion Task Force and a Nutrition Branch. This office also operates the Health Promotion Clearinghouse which offers many publications.

* High Blood Pressure Screening

High Blood Pressure Information Center
4733 Bethesda Ave., Suite 530
Bethesda, MD 20814   (301) 951-3260
The High Blood Pressure Information Center can send you information on setting up a screening program in the workplace.

* Industrial Hygiene

National Institute for Occupational Safety and Health
4676 Columbia Parkway
Cincinnati, OH 45226   (800) 356-4674
NIOSH is responsible for conducting research to make the nation's workplaces healthier and safer by responding to urgent requests for assistance from employers, employees, and their representatives where imminent hazards are suspected. They conduct inspections, laboratory and epidemiologic research, publish their findings, and make recommendations for improved working conditions to regulatory agencies. NIOSH trains occupational health and safety workers and communicates research results to those concerned.

* Industry Health Studies

Division of Surveillance
Hazard Evaluation and Field Studies
National Institute for Occupational Safety and Health
4676 Columbia Parkway
Cincinnati, OH 46226   (800) 356-4674
NIOSH conducts a wide range of studies regarding occupational health. They look at exposure to chemicals, PCB, and asbestos in the workplace, as well as other occupational health hazards. This information is made public to companies, unions, and private citizens.

* Industry Injuries and Illnesses Data

Superintendent of Documents
Government Printing Office
Washington, DC 20402   (202) 783-3238
Many of the Bureau of Labor Statistics' major surveys and research studies are available in the BLS *Bulletin Series*, which include more than 100 area and industry wage studies each year and about 40 volumes dealing with a wide range of economic subjects. For example, *Occupational Injuries and Illnesses in the United States by Industry* is an annual report with detailed tables showing the job-related injury and illness experience of employees in a wide range of industries. Contact this office for more information on available publications on occupational injury and illness statistics.

* Information Clearinghouse

Information Office
Occupational Safety and Health Administration
Department of Labor

200 Constitution Ave., NW, Room S2315
Washington, DC 20210 (202) 523-8151
This office can provide you with information regarding the various OSHA programs, and can direct your inquiries to the appropriate office. The staff also schedules and coordinates public hearings and supports advisory committees in their development of recommendations to the Assistant Secretary of OSHA.

* Injured Workers Statistics
   Office of Safety, Health and Working Conditions
   Bureau of Labor Statistics
   Department of Labor
   601 D St., NW, Room 4014
   Washington, DC 20210 (202) 272-3467
This office maintains the nationwide employer record keeping system on job-related injuries and illnesses, conducts the annual survey based on these records and analyzes the results, and compiles supplementary statistics from other sources. States provide additional information on occupational accidents and exposures from workers' compensation records which give a sharper definition of occupational safety and health problems, associated characteristics, and possible action indicators. The *Work Injury Report* examines selected types of work injures to develop a detailed profile of characteristics associated with the injuries data from questionnaires completed by injured workers.

* Injuries and Illnesses On-the-Job
   Office of Safety, Health and Working Conditions
   Bureau of Labor Statistics
   Department of Labor
   601 D St., NW
   Washington, DC 20210 (202) 272-3467
An annual survey, conducted by State employment security agencies on a cooperative basis with Bureau of Labor Statistics, provides data on the incidence of occupational injuries and illnesses by industry and State. Data available include incidence votes by private industry for injuries and illnesses, with estimates of numbers of fatal and nonfatal cases, and lost workday cases. *Work Injury Report Surveys* provide data collected from employees on characteristics of selected types of injuries. Data available include type of equipment involved, availability and use of protective devices, worker activity at time of accident, amount of training worker received, and presence of hazardous conditions.

* Job Safety and Health Information Clearinghouse
   Technical Data Center
   Occupational Safety and Health Administration
   Department of Labor
   200 Constitution Ave., NW, Room N2634
   Washington, DC 20210 (202) 523-9700
This center houses technical information on all industries covered by OSHA. They maintain a library of 8,000 volumes and 250 journals, as well as an extensive microform collection of industry standards and OSHA rule making records. They have access to a wide variety of databases, including Dialog and two of their own. The Center is also the docket office and holds the hearing records on standards, the comments, and final rules, and can provide certified copies. The center is open to the public 8:15 a.m. to 4:45 p.m., Monday through Friday.

* Manufacturing Plants and Chemical Registry
   National Institute of Occupational Safety and Health
   Division of Surveillance Hazard Evaluation
   4676 Columbia Parkway
   Cincinnati, OH 45226 (513) 841-4491
NIOSH maintains two databases, the National Occupational Hazard Survey Databases I & II, which contain surveys of 5,000 manufacturing plants each. NIOSH administers a questionnaire, investigates health and safety programs, and conducts an inventory of chemicals. Through the databases, NIOSH can identify potential exposure agents, describe health and safety programs, and by chemical can develop estimates of number of people exposed.

* Mine Accident Prevention Training
   Division of Policy and Program Coordination
   Education and Training
   Mine Safety and Health Administration
   Department of Labor
   4015 Wilson Blvd., Room 576
   Arlington, VA 22203 (703) 235-1400
Training is an important tool for preventing accidents and avoiding unsafe and unhealthful working conditions. Training specialists coordinate their districts various training and miners to tailer programs specifically to individual needs. Training specialists conduct examinations to certify miners for certain specialized work, review training plans submitted by the mine operators, conduct various accident prevention programs, and assist at regional mine rescue contests.

* Miner Health and Safety Training Academy

Continuing Education Department
P.O. Box 1166
Beckley, WV 25801 (304) 255-6451
The National Mine Health and Safety Academy is the world's largest educational institution devoted solely to safety and health in mining. The academy serves as the central training facility for federal mine inspectors and mine safety professionals from other government agencies, the mining industry, and labor. Courses are offered on safety and inspection procedures, accident prevention, investigations, industrial hygiene, mine emergency procedures, mining technology, and management theory and techniques. The academy also provides field training and serves as a technical resource to help meet the mining community's instructional needs.

* Mine Safety and Health Case Files
   Docket Office
   Federal Mine Safety and Health Review Commission
   1730 K St., NW, 6th Floor
   Washington, DC 20006 (202) 653-5629
Transcripts of hearings and written decisions on mine safety and health cases brought before the Commission are housed here. Cases may involve mine closure orders, citations, or violations of mandatory safety and health standards, for example. Records may be freely accessed on a walk-in basis, but if a case is not recent, call ahead as old files are archived and may require a couple of weeks to retrieve.

* Mine Safety and Robotics
   Health, Safety, and Mining Technology
   Bureau of Mines
   U.S. Department of the Interior
   2401 E St., NW
   Washington, DC 20241 (292) 634-1251
The Bureau is studying ways to improve mine safety and to eliminate the health risks of mining. One of the areas of emphasis is finding ways to reduce a miner's exposure to respirable dust, which causes black lung and other respiratory diseases. Studies in safety precautions help companies build more stable mines with better roof support systems and more efficiently detect flammable gases and ignition sources. Research on automation and robotics to do the more hazardous jobs is also being done.

* Mine Safety Clearinghouse
   Office of Information and Public Affairs
   Mine Safety and Health Administration
   Department of Labor
   4015 Wilson Blvd.
   Arlington, VA 22203 (703) 235-1452
This office can provide you with general information regarding the Mine Safety and Health Administration, as well as brochures, manuals, and other publications regarding mine safety and health.

* Mine Safety Reviews
   Acting Chairman
   Federal Mine Safety and Health Review Commission
   1730 K St., NW, 6th Floor
   Washington, DC 20006 (202) 653-5644
Cases are brought before this commission and its Administrative Law Judges by the Mine Safety and Health Administration, mine operators, and miners or their representatives. Cases reviewed usually revolve around actions of the Mine Safety and Health Administration, which enforces occupational safety standards in U.S. surface and underground mines. Hearings are held as close as practical to locations of the mines involved. The Office of Administrative Law Judges operates from the following locations: 2 Skyline Plaza, 5203 Leesburg Pike, Falls Church, VA 22041, (703) 756-6200; and at the Colonnade Center, Room 280, 1244 Speer Blvd., Denver, CO 80204; (303) 844-5266. For further information on Commission activities, contact the Chairman's office listed above.

* Mining Hazards: Safety and Prevention Assistance
   Office of Information
   Mine Safety and Health Administration
   Department of Labor
   4015 Wilson Blvd
   Arlington, VA 22203 (703) 234-1452
Specialists from MSHA's technical support facilities can provide technical and engineering assistance in helping to reduce hazards in their operations' mining systems. MSHA's engineers, scientists, and industrial hygienists often suggest possible solutions to difficult problems dealing with the safe design or maintenance of mining equipment and machinery, roof support or ventilation systems and mine waste facilities, and with the regular measurement and control of miners' exposure to health hazards such as nose, radiation, or harmful dust.

* Mining Industry Training Products

National Mine Health and Safety Academy
Attention: Business Office
P.O. Box 1166
Beckley, WV 25802   (304) 256-3257

The free catalog, *Training Products for the Mining Industry*, is divided into three major sections: films and videotapes; training materials such as instructional programs and safety manuals; and a complete listing of available MSHA informational reports. Each item includes a brief description, ordering information, and cost.

* Mining Injury and Illness Registry

MSHA Safety and Health Technology Center
Mine Safety and Health Administration
Department of Labor
P.O. Box 25367
Denver, CO 80225   (303) 236-2716

MSHA specialists collect, analyze, and publish data obtained from mine operators on the prevalence of work-related injuries and illnesses in the mining industry. This information helps MSHA's own staff, mining companies, and labor organizations gauge the effectiveness of their safety programs and to make needed improvements. MSHA specialists also publish a number of analytical studies and reports each year for use by the mining industry and the general public.

* Occupational Health and Safety TVA Investigations

Human Resources
Tennessee Valley Authority
MPB 1E 215B-M
Muscle Shoals, AL 35660

This office formulate and oversees the implementation of TVA's occupational health and safety policies and plans. It develops and issues standards for control of hazards in the workplace, supports the investigation of serious accidents, and ensures appropriate follow-through. The staff coordinates TVA review of regulatory requirements and industry trends relating to safety practices, and develops agency comments on proposed regulations. Staff develops and delivers management and employee safety orientation and training in health and safety. The program provides industrial hygiene services for the agency, including surveys to measure employee exposure to toxic chemicals and physical agents, and recommends appropriate administrative and engineering control methods. It is responsible for handling workplace and community noise prevention programs, and by-product material licensing support and radiation safety services.

* Occupational Safety and Health Review Regional Offices

Atlanta
1365 Peachtree St., NE, Rm. 240, Atlanta, GA 30309-3119; (404) 347-4197

Boston
McCormack Post Office and Court House, Rm., 420, Boston, MA 02109-4501; (617) 223-9746

Dallas
Federal Bldg., Rm. 7B11, 1100 Commerce St., Dallas, TX 75242-0791; (214) 767-5271

Denver
1244 N. Speer Blvd., Rm. 250, Denver, CO 80204-3582; (303) 844-2281

* OSHA Certificate of Service

Executive Secretary
Occupational Safety and Health Review Commission
1825 K St., 4th Floor
Washington, DC 20006-1246   (202) 634-7943

Documents that have been filed with the Commission or an Administrative Law Judge of the Commission must be copied and given to all parties in a case, either by first-class mail or by hand. A statement must also be submitted showing the date and manner of the delivery and the names of the persons receiving copies of the documents.

* OSHA Commission Decisions Index

Executive Secretary
Occupational Safety and Health Review Commission
1825 K St., 4th Floor
Washington, DC 20006-1246   (202) 634-7943

The *Index to Decisions of the OSHRC*, which lists company names and OSHRC docket numbers, is sold based on the number of pages and the years requested. For a price quote, contact the above office. Subscriptions to microfiche copies of OSHRC decisions, called *OSHRC Reports*, are available from the Superintendent of Documents, Government Printing Office, Washington, D.C.

* OSHA Commission Docket

Office of Information
Occupational Safety and Health Review Commission
1825 K St., NW, 4th Floor
Washington, DC 20006-1246   (202) 634-7943

Copies of the proceedings of any of the cases decided by the Commission and Administrative Law Judges are available for public inspection. An appointment in advance is needed with the office above.

* OSHA Commission Publications

Office of Information
Occupational Safety and Health Review Commission
1825 K St., NW, 4th Floor
Washington, DC 20006-1246   (202) 634-7943

The following information booklets are free upon request describing the function of the Commission: *Simplified Proceedings, Rules of Procedure, A Guide to Procedures of the OSHRC*, and the *Annual Report to the President*.

* OSHA Complaint and Response

Executive Secretary
Occupational Safety and Health Review Commission
1825 K St., 4th Floor
Washington, DC 20006-1246   (202) 634-7943

Within 30 calendar days of the date on which the Commission receives an employer's Notice of Contest, the Secretary of Labor must file a written complaint with the Commission. A copy must be sent to the employer and any other parties in the case. The complaint sets forth in detail the alleged violation for which the employer received the citation. The employer must then file a written answer to the complaint with the Commission within 30 calendar days after receipt of the complaint. This answer must admit or deny each paragraph and subparagraph of the complaint. The answer is filed by mailing it to the address above.

* OSHA Employer Notice of Contest

Office of Information
Occupational Safety and Health Review Commission
1825 K St., 4th Floor
Washington, DC 20006-1246   (202) 634-7943

There are two steps that must be taken by an employer who wishes to contest all or part of a citation received from the Occupational Safety and Health Administration. Within 15 working days from receipt of the proposed penalty, the employer must notify the Labor Department of the employer's intent to contest all or part of the citation, the penalty proposed, or the time allowed for the correction of the alleged violation. This notification is called a *Notice of Contest*. After the Department of Labor notifies the Review Commission that the citation has been contested, the employer will receive a notice from the Review Commission that the case has been filed. Forms will also be supplied to notify affected employees and their union that a notice of contest has been filed.

* OSHA Freedom of Information Act Requests

Freedom of Information Act Officer
Occupational Safety and Health Review Commission
1825 K St., NW, 4th Floor
Washington, DC 20006-1246   (202) 634-7943

Freedom of Information requests should be sent to the officer above.

* OSHA Simplified Appeals Process

Executive Secretary
Occupational Safety and Health Review Commission
1825 K St., 4th Floor
Washington, DC 20006-1246   (202) 634-7943

Simplified proceedings are designed to expedite the resolution of cases, to make it easier for those appearing before the Commission to proceed without an attorney, to reduce paperwork, and to reduce the expense of litigation. This process is used in cases where the issues are less involved and a formal procedure is not needed for a fair hearing. Contact this office for more information.

* Petition for Modification of Abatement

Executive Secretary
Occupational Safety and Health Review Commission
1825 K St., 4th Floor
Washington, DC 20006-1246   (202) 634-7943

If an employer has made a good faith effort to correct an OSHA violation within the given abatement period but has not been able to do so because of reasons beyond his/her control, he/she may file a petition for modification of abatement. This petition is filed with the Occupational Safety and Health Administration

Area Director no later than the end of the next working day following the day on which abatement was to have been completed.

* Petitioning the Government on Safe Working Conditions
Office of the Assistant Secretary
Occupational Health and Safety Administration
Department of Labor
200 Constitution Ave., NW, Room S2315
Washington, DC 20210 (202) 523-7162
OSHA can begin standards-setting procedures on its own initiative, or in response to petitions from other parties, including the Secretary of Health and Human Services, the National Institute for Occupational Safety and Health, State and local governments, any nationally-recognized standards-producing organization, employer or labor representative, or any other interested party. Contact this office for more information on the standard setting procedure.

* Publications and Training Materials
OSHA Publications
Occupational Safety and Health Administration
Department of Labor
200 Constitution Ave., NW, Room N4101
Washington, DC 20210 (202) 523-9667
Contact this office for a list of OSHA free publications and *Federal Register* reprints pertaining to OSHA. These publications are available at no charge.

* Regulations
Subscription Service
Superintendent of Documents
Government Printing Office
Washington, DC 20402 (202) 783-3238
The OSHA subscription service was developed to assist the public in keeping current with OSHA standards. This service provides all standards, interpretations, regulations, and procedures in easy to use loose-leaf form, punched for use in a three-ring binder. All changes and additions are issued for and indefinite period of time. The following volumes are available:

General Standards and Interpretations (includes agriculture)
Maritime Standards and Interpretations
Construction Standards and Interpretations
Other Regulations and Procedures
Field Operations Manual
Industrial Hygiene Field Operations Manual

* Review Commission
Occupational Safety and Health Review Commission
1825 K St., 4th Floor
Washington, DC 20006-1246 (202) 634-7960
The Occupational Safety and Health Review Commission serves as a court to resolve disputes that arise under the Occupational Safety and Health Act of 1970, which involves workplace inspections. The Commission is not connected in any way with the Department of Labor or the Occupational Safety and Health Administration.

* Safety and Health Training Institute
Occupational Safety and Health Administration
Department of Labor
1555 Times Dr.
Des Plaines, IL 60018 (312) 297-4810
The OSHA Training Institute in DesPlaines, Illinois, provides basic and advanced training and education in safety and health for federal and state compliance officers; state consultants; other federal agency personnel; private sector employers; and employees and their representatives. Institute courses cover such areas as electrical hazards, machine guarding, ventilation, and ergonomics. Many courses are available for personnel in the private sector dealing with such subjects as safety and health in the construction industry and methods of voluntary compliance with OSHA standards.

* Safety and the Workplace: Onsite Consultation
OSHA Publications
Occupational Safety and Health Administration
Department of Labor
200 Constitution Ave., NW, Room N4101
Washington, DC 20210 (202) 523-9667
Using a free consultation service, employers can find out about potential hazards at their worksites, improve their safety management systems, and even qualify for a one-year exemption from routine OSHA inspections. Primarily targeted for smaller businesses, this safety and health consultation program is completely separate from the OSHA inspection effort. In addition, no citations are issued or penalties proposed. These consultations are carried out through State OSHA

consultation programs. Contact this OSHA office for a listing of these state programs.

* Scientific and Medical Issues
Directorate of Technical Support
Department of Labor
200 Constitution Ave., NW, Room N3653
Washington, DC 20210 (202) 523-7031
This office serves as the principal source of agency expertise with respect to scientific, engineering, and medical issues involved in the overall occupational safety and health field. The Directorate manages a centralized program to provide technical interpretations and clarifications of OSHA standards, rule making and related matters.

* Small Business and Employee Health
National Health Information Clearinghouse
P.O. Box 1133 (800) 336-4797
Washington, DC 20013 (301) 565-4167 (MD and DC)
Small Business and Health Promotion: The Prospects Look Good. A Guide for Providers of Health Promotion Programs presents small business owners' views on health promotion, suggesting ways that community-based programs can work effectively with small businesses. This 35-page booklet (Order No. W0004) is available for $2.00.

* Small Business Health and Safety
National Institute for Occupational Safety and Health
4676 Columbia Parkway
Cincinnati, OH 45226 (513) 533-8287
Many publications are available through this office regarding safety, occupational hazards, and occupational safety and health programs for a variety of business settings. Contact this office for a free catalog of publications.

* Smoking Restrictions and Bans
Office of Smoking and Health
5600 Fishers Lane, Room 1-10
Rockville, MD 20857 (301) 443-1690
No Smoking: A Decision Maker's Guide to Reducing Smoking at the Workplace discusses the impact of smoking on employees and businesses and describes programs companies have used to restrict or ban smoking at work. This 42-page manual (Order No. W0001) is available, $2 handling fee.

* Speakers from OSHA
Occupational Safety and Health Review Commission
1825 K St., NW, 4th Floor
Washington, DC 20006-1246 (202) 634-7943
The Chairman, General Counsel, and members of the Commission have participated as speakers for various industry and civic organizations. A written request to the individual is necessary for a confirmation of availability and attendance.

* Standards on Occupational Safety and Health
Superintendent of Documents
Government Printing Office
Washington, DC 20402 (202) 783-3238
The *Federal Register* is one of the best sources of information on standards, since all OSHA standards are published there when adopted, as are all amendments, corrections, insertions, or deletions. Annual subscriptions are available from the Government Printing Office. Each year the office of the *Federal Register* publishes all current regulations and standards in the *Code of Federal Regulations*, available at many libraries and from the Government Printing Office. OSHA's regulations are collected in Title 29 of the CFR, Part 1900-1999.

* Toxic Hazards in the Workplace
Salt Lake City Laboratory
Occupational Safety and Health Administration
Department of Labor
P.O. Box 15200
Salt Lake City, UT 84115 (801) 524-5287
The OSHA Analytical Laboratory conducts extensive analyses, tests, and studies of all samples submitted by safety and health compliance officers and others to evaluate toxicity and the existence of health hazards.

* Worker Health and Safety Standards
Directorate of Health Standards Programs
Occupational Safety and Health Administration
Department of Labor
200 Constitution Ave., NW, Room N3718

Washington, DC 20210   (202) 523-7075

OSHA develops mandatory health standards for such varied fields as manufacturing, construction, longshoring, agriculture, law and medicine, charity and disaster relief, organized labor, and private education. Contact this office about these standards.

* Workplace Safety and Health Awards

Occupational Safety and Health Administration
Department of Labor
200 Constitution Ave., NW, Room N3700
Washington, DC 20210   (202) 523-7266

Designed to augment OSHA's enforcement efforts, the Star, Merit, and Demonstration Programs encourage and recognize excellence in occupational safety and health. Only those companies which demonstrate commitments to workplace safety and health beyond the requirements of the OSHA standards are eligible. Participation in the programs exempts a worksite from OSHA's programmed inspections. Companies must have strong safety and health programs, along with employee participation. Contact this office for an application, information, and complete details regarding the various programs.

* Worksite Health Promotion Survey

National Health Information Clearinghouse
P.O. Box 1133   (800) 336-4797
Washington, DC 20013-1133   (301) 565-4167 (MD and DC)

National Survey of Worksite Health Promotion Activities: A Summary provides the findings of this 1985 telephone survey of a representative sampling of worksites with 50 or more employees. This monograph (Order No. M0005) is available for $2.00.

* Worksite Health Programs

National Health Information Clearinghouse
P.O. Box 1133   (800) 336-4797
Washington, DC 20013-1133   (301) 565-4167 (MD and DC)

Worksite Wellness Media Reports illustrate examples of worksite health promotion programs and also present comprehensive reports on health facts. These reports are designed for the media covering the business community. The latest report totaling 318 pages (Order No.W0015) is available for $3.00.

Federal Employment

As the largest single employer in the country, the federal government has plenty of benefits, programs, and services for its employees, many of whom may not know all that's available to them. Here federal employees will find information sources on pensions, compensation, new job opportunities, health benefits, merit pay, and countless other programs.

* Affirmative Employment
Office of Affirmative Employment Programs
Office of Personnel Management
1900 E St., NW, Room 7353
Washington, DC 20415   (202) 632-4420
The Office of Personnel Management (OPM) seeks to eliminate nonmerit considerations such as race, color, religion, sex, national origin, or age from all aspects of federal employment through its affirmative employment efforts. OPM also operates selective placement programs for physically and mentally handicapped persons, and programs for other groups including veterans, youths, and women. Contact this office for more information.

* Alcoholic and Drug Treatment Programs
Employee Health Services Branch
Personnel Systems and Oversight Group
Office of Personnel Management
1900 E St., NW, Room 7412
Washington, DC 20415   (202) 632-5558
All government employee health and alcoholism/drug abuse programs are overseen by this office. Contact this office for more information.

* Annuities
Retirement and Insurance Group
Annuitant Services Division
Office of Retirement Programs
Office of Personnel Management
1900 E St., NW, Room 3321
Washington, DC 20415   (202) 632-4610
This office has free pamphlets describing annuity benefits under the civil service retirement system. Contact this office for more information.

* Appeals Process
Office of the Appeals Counsel
Merit Systems Protection Board
1120 Vermont Ave., NW, Room 864
Washington, DC 20419   (202) 653-8888
The Office of Appeals Counsel assists the Board in judicially settling petitions for review from initial decisions issued by administrative judges in the regional offices. The office receives and analyzes the petitions, researches applicable laws, rules, and precedents, and submits proposed opinions to the board members for their final settlement. When an agency issues a decision notice to an employee on a matter that is appealable to the Board, the agency must provide the employee with a notice of the time limits for the appeal and the address for filing the appeal, a copy of or access to a copy of the Board's regulations, a copy of the appeal form, and a notice of any right the employee has to file a grievance.

* Appeals Regional Offices
Office of the Executive Director
Merit Systems Protection Board
1120 Vermont Ave., NW, Room 800
Washington, DC 20419   (202) 653-7980
The MSPB Regional Offices are located in 11 major metropolitan areas throughout the United States: Atlanta, Boston, Chicago, Dallas, Denver, New York, Philadelphia, St. Louis, San Francisco, Seattle, and Washington, DC. These offices receive and process the initial appeals filed with the Board. Administrative judges in the regional offices have the primary function of issuing fair, timely, and well-reasoned decisions on all appeals. Contact this office for a listing of these offices and more information.

* Aviation Careers
Aviation Education Officer
Federal Aviation Administration
U.S. Department of Transportation
800 Independence Ave., SW
Washington, DC 20591   (202) 267-3469
The FAA's Aviation Education Program offers volunteer assistance to the nation's schools through the following programs: career guidance; tours of airports, control towers, and other facilities; classroom lectures and demonstrations; aviation safety information; aviation education resource materials; computerized clearinghouse of aviation and space information; aviation science instruction programs for home/school computers; "Partnerships-in-Education" activities; and teachers' workshops. Write to the above office for more information.

* Civil Service Exams
Federal Job Information Center
General Information
Office of Personnel Management
1900 E St., NW, Room 1416
Washington, DC 20415   (202) 737-9616
Information on Civil Service Exams is contained in the pamphlet, *Current Federal Examination Announcements* (AN-2279). This free pamphlet is available from any Federal Job Information Center.

* Compensation Benefits
Office of Worker's Compensation Programs
Employment Standards Administration
Department of Labor
200 Constitution Ave., NW, Room S3524
Washington, DC 20210   (202) 523-7503
The Federal Employees' Compensation Act provides compensation benefits to civilian employees of the U.S. for disability due to personal injury sustained while in the performance of duty. The Act also provides compensation for employment-related disease. Benefits also available to injured employees include rehabilitation, medical, surgical, and hospital services and supplies, and necessary transportation expenses. FECA provides compensation to dependents if the injury or disease causes the employees's death.

* Employee and Annuitant Information Center
Retirement Information Branch
Retirement Programs
Retirement and Insurance Group
Office of Personnel Management
1900 E St., NW, Room 1323B
Washington, DC 20415   (202) 632-7700
This clearinghouse offers guidance on federal retirees' annuities.

* Employee Conduct Regulations
Office of Government Ethics
Office of Personnel Management
1201 New York Ave., Suite 500
Washington, DC 20005   (202) 523-5757
Ethics in Government, federal regulations, and a digest of opinions since 1979 is outlined in the *Agency Relations Packet*, which is available free from the above office.

* Environmental Protection Agency Job Hotline
Recruitment
Environmental Protection Agency
401 M Street SW
Washington, DC 20460   (800) 338-1350
This EPA National Recruitment Program Number enables potential hires to contact the Agency for employment information and assists EPA managers in locating and hiring qualified employees to fill vacant positions. The number operates Monday through Friday, 8:30 a.m. to 4:30 p.m. (EST).

Careers and Workplace

* Ethics in Federal Workplace

Office of Government Ethics
Office of Personnel Management
1201 New York Ave., Suite 500
Washington, DC 20005   (202) 523-5757

To prevent conflicts of interest on the part of officers and employees of any executive agency, overall direction of executive branch policies is provided by this office. Rules and regulations are developed here pertaining to employee conduct and post-employment conflicts of interest, and public financial disclosure is monitored. Contact this office for more information.

* Executive Development Center

Federal Executive Institute
Office of Personnel Management
Route 29
North Charlottesville, VA 22903   (804) 942-6200

The Federal Executive Institute (FEI) is an interagency executive development center which responds to the training and development needs of federal executives. FEI programs schedule courses that are designed to facilitate executive improvement. Programs in four categories are conducted: The Executive leadership and Management Program, the Senior Executive Education program, FEI alumni Follow-up Conferences, and Special Programs.

* Executive Management Training

Washington Management Institute
Executive Personnel and Management Development
Office of Personnel Management
1121 Vermont Ave., NW, Room 308
Washington, DC 20415   (202) 632-5671

Executive and managerial training and development services to support government agencies in their efforts to achieve greater efficiency and effectiveness in managing federal programs is provided by the Institute. Send mail to P.O. Box 988, Washington, D.C. 20044.

* Exemption from Competitive Service

Examination Services Division
Office of Personnel Management
1900 E St., NW, Room 6303
Washington, DC 20415   (202) 632-6000

Information and advice on "exemption" from competitive service is available from this office.

* Ex-Railroad Workers Placement Service

Unemployment and Sickness Insurance
Railroad Retirement Board
844 Rush St.
Chicago, IL 60611   (312) 751-4800

The Board operates a free job placement service for experienced railroad workers who have lost their jobs. It is available to those claiming unemployment benefits. Contact this office or the nearest Railroad Retirement Board Office for more information.

* Federal Contracts

Acquisitions Division
Administrative Group
Office of Personnel Management
1900 E St., NW, Room 1452
Washington, DC 20415   (202) 632-5476

Information on contracts can be obtained by contacting one of the regional offices listed below.

Atlanta Region
Richard B. Russell Federal Building, 75 Spring Street, SW, Atlanta, GA 30303-3019; (404) 331-3459. Serving: Alabama, Florida, North Carolina, South Carolina, Georgia, Mississippi, Tennessee, and Virginia

Chicago Region
John C. Kluczynski Federal Building, 230 South Dearborn Street, Chicago, IL 60604; (312) 353-2901. Serving: Illinois, Indiana, Iowa, Kansas, Kentucky, Michigan, Minnesota, Missouri, Nebraska, North Dakota, Ohio, South Dakota, West Virginia, and Wisconsin

Dallas Region
1100 Commerce Street, Dallas, TX 75242; (214) 767-8235. Serving: Arkansas, Arizona, Colorado, Louisiana, Montana, New Mexico, Oklahoma, Texas, Utah, and Wyoming

Philadelphia Region
William J. Green, Jr., Federal Building, 600 Arch Street, Philadelphia, PA 19106-1596; (215) 597-4431. Serving: Connecticut, Delaware, Maine, Maryland, Massachusetts, New Hampshire, New Jersey, New York, Pennsylvania, Puerto Rico, Rhode Island, Vermont, and Virgin Islands

San Francisco Region
211 Main Street, 7th Floor, San Francisco, CA 94105; (415) 974-9662. Serving: Alaska, California, Hawaii, Idaho, Nevada, Oregon, Pacific Ocean Area, and Washington

* Federal Employees' Attitudes Surveys

Center for Electronic Records
National Archives and Records Administration
8th St. & Pennsylvania Ave., NW, Room 20E
Washington, DC 20408   (202) 523-3267

This center has data pertaining to federal employees' attitudes on a variety of topics, and can provide you with a complete list of the survey samples.

* Federal Employees Current Attitudes

Office of Planning and Evaluation
Office of Personnel Management
1900 E St., NW
Washington, DC 20415   (202) 632-4468

A government-wide attitude survey of federal employees was administered to establish a baseline of employee attitudes about their jobs and work environment. Groupings include federal agencies, pay levels, pay systems, and supervisory and non-supervisory personnel. Federal Employee Attitudes: Phase 2--Follow Up, a report, can be purchased from the Superintendent of Documents, Government Printing Office, Washington, D.C. 20402; (202) 783-3238.

* Federal Job Information Centers

Federal Job Information Center
General Information
Office of Personnel management
1900 E St., NW, Room 1416
Washington, DC 20415   (202) 737-9616

Federal Job Information Centers are located in major metropolitan areas. This network of centers provides information on summer employment, necessary application forms, exams, and all other aspects pertaining to federal employment. Federal Job Information Centers, a free directory, is available from the above office. By using the government pages of your local phone directory, you will be able to locate the center nearest you.

* Federal Labor Relations Authority
Freedom of Information

Public Information Office
Federal Labor Relations Authority (FLRA)
500 C St., SW
Washington, DC 20424   (202) 382-0711

The Public Information Office listed above is the Freedom of Information Act contact for the Authority.

* FED Fact Pamphlets

Office of Public Affairs
Office of Personnel Management
1900 E St., NW, Room 5F12
Washington, DC 20415   (202) 632-1213

Pamphlets that cover a variety of subjects related to government employees are issued by the Office of Personnel Management. Single copies are available free, and multiple copies of FED Facts must be purchased from the Superintendent of Documents, Government Printing Office, Washington, D.C. 20402; (202) 783-3238.

Incentive Awards Program
Political Activity of Federal Employees
The Federal Retirement System
Financial Protection for Federal Employees
The Federal Merit Promotion Policy
Serving the Public: The extra Step
The Federal Wage System
Meeting Your Financial Obligations
Maternity Leave
Employee Appeals from Actions
The Displaced Employee Program
Reductions in Force in Federal Agencies
Reemployment Rights of Federal Employees Who Perform Duty in the Armed Forces
Federal Labor Relations
Pay Under the General Schedule
The Cost of Living Allowance for Federal Employees
The intergovernmental Mobility Program
How Your GS Job is Classified
Merit System Principles and Prohibited Personnel Practices

Furlough

* Forest Ranger Jobs

Forest Service
U.S. Department of Agriculture
Recruitment
P.O. Box 2417
Washington, DC 20013   (703) 235-2730
Contact this office for information on a career as a forest ranger.

* General Schedule Classification

Office of Public Affairs
Office of Personnel Management
1900 E St., NW, Room 5F12
Washington, DC 20415   (202) 632-2433
A variety of publications on government service classifications are available. Single copies are free, including *A Report on Study of Position Classification Accuracy in Executive Branch on Occupation Under the General Schedule* and *FED Facts on How Your GS Job is Classified*. The *Handbook of Occupational Groups and Series of Classes ($120.00)* is sold by the Superintendent of Documents, Government Printing Office, Washington, D.C. 20402; (202) 783-3238.

* Government Affairs Institute

Government Affairs Institute
Executive Personnel and Management
  Development Division
Office of Personnel Management
1121 Vermont Ave., NW, Room 200
Washington, DC 20415   (202) 632-5662
This office offers the following services: interagency seminars, conducted on Capitol Hill to provide on-site experience with Congress; single-agency or single-program projects, tailored to meet the specific needs of an agency or clusters of agencies with related missions; courses offered by the Government Affairs Institute designed to meet developmental needs of current and future executives and managers. Seminars for support staff personnel are also offered. Contact this office for more information.

* Health Benefits

Insurance Programs
Retirement and Insurance Programs
Office of Personnel Management
1900 E St., NW, Room 3415
Washington, DC 20415   (202) 632-4670
This office oversees the federal employees health benefits program which includes various types of hospital, surgical and medical benefits for federal employees. Numerous free publications are available on this subject: *Federal Employee health Benefits Program* (biweekly and monthly health benefits rates), and *Information to Consider in Choosing a Health Plan*. Contact this office for more information.

* Health Professions in U.S. Public Health Corps

Office of Data Analyses and Management
Bureau of Health Professions
5600 Fishers Lane, Room 8-43
Rockville, MD 20857   (301) 443-6936
The Bureau of Health Professions supports the development of human resources needed to staff the U.S. health care system. It is concerned with health professions education, credentialing of health care personnel, and analysis of data to project needs for health care personnel. They also support student assistance and analyze current and future personnel supply, requirements and distribution. This office can supply you with data regarding health profession supply distribution on the level of nursing training in any area of the country. This information is often used by consultants, corporations involved with medical technology, and other government agencies.

* Incentive Awards

Personnel Systems and Oversight Group
Office of Personnel Management
1900 E St., NW, Room 5468
Washington, DC 20415   (202) 632-8950
Cash and honor awards are available under the incentive award program to employees for effecting improvements in government operations or services through their suggestions, inventions, and superior performance. The following publications are available for free: *Federal Incentive Awards Program-Annual Report*; and *Limited Resources-Unlimited Ideas*. Contact this office for more information.

* Index To OPM Information

Publishing Management Branch
Administration Group
Internal Distribution
Office of Personnel Management
1900 E St., NW, Room B430
Washington, DC 20415   (202) 632-4677
The annual OPM index with quarterly supplements is available at no cost from this office. This index lists all Office of Personnel Management publications, including information required to be available under the Freedom of Information Act. Requests must be submitted in writing.

* Insurance Programs

Insurance Programs
Retirement and Insurance Group
Office of Personnel Management
1717 H St., NW, Room 3415
Washington, DC 20415   (202) 632-4670
The free pamphlet, *Federal Employees Group Life Insurance Program*, provides information on regular and optional life insurance programs. Contact this office for more information.

* Interagency Training Courses

Office of Washington Training and Development Services
Washington Area Service Center
Office od Personnel Management
1121 Vermont Ave., NW, Room 1216TC
Washington, DC 20415   (202) 632-4410
The *Interagency Training Catalog of Courses* contains a variety of training programs offered by various federal agencies. These courses are available to federal, State, and local government employees. The following is a sample listing of courses: automated data processing, communications and office skills, general management, labor relations, management sciences, personnel management, and records management. Contact this office for more information.

* Job Grading System

Standard Development Staff
Office of Classifications
Personnel Systems and Oversight Group
Office of Personnel Management
1900 E St., NW, Room 7H29
Washington, DC 20415   (202) 653-9382
The publication, *Job Grading System for Trades and Labor Occupations*, is available on a subscription basis ($100) from the Superintendent of Documents, Government Printing Office, Washington, D.C. 20402; (202) 783-3238. For additional information contact the office above.

* Labor Agreement Information Retrieval System (LAIRS)

Labor Agreement Information Retrieval System
Office of Employee and Labor Relations
Personnel Systems and Oversight Group
Office of Personnel Management
1900 E St., NW, Room 7431
Washington, DC 20415   (202) 632-5406
The LAIRS system provides current and historic information about the federal labor relations program. The information is provided in the form of computer searches, microfiche of full text decisions, published analytic reports, current periodicals, and variety of audio-visual training aids. The file contains negotiated agreements, arbitration awards, and significant Federal labor relations decisions. A fee schedule is included. This system publishes labor-management reports, surveys, digests, and other related publications. A publications list and additional information can be obtained from the above office.

* Labor Management Information

Labor Agreement Information Retrieval Systems
Office of Personnel Management
1900 E St., NW, Room 7429
Washington, DC 20415   (202) 632-5406
This public reference room has labor-management reports, surveys, and analyses available for public viewing. An appointment is suggested.

* Labor-Management Relations

Employee Labor and Agency Relations
Personnel Systems and Oversight Group
Office of Personnel Management
1900 E St., NW, Room 7412
Washington, DC 20415   (202) 632-8047
This office provides information, guidance, and assistance to agencies, unions, and the public on federal labor-management relations. Eligible labor organizations are consulted in the development and revision of government-wide personnel policies.

Careers and Workplace

* Labor Management Surveys
Labor Agreement Information Retrieval System
Office of Personnel Management
1900 E St., NW, Room 7431
Washington, DC 20415   (202) 632-5406
The LAIRS (Labor Agreement Information Retrieval System) generates numerous surveys and analytical studies, including:

A Survey of Unfair Labor Practice Complaints in The Federal Government
Maternity/Sick Leave Provisions in Federal Agreements
Productivity Clauses in Federal Agreements
Single copies of these publications are available free of charge.

* Labor Practices in Federal Service
Public Information Office
Federal Labor Relations Authority (FLRA)
500 C St., SW
Washington, DC 20424   (202) 382-0711
Contact this office to obtain a copy of the *FLRA Annual Report*, which describes significant decisions of the FLRA and case processing statistics of the General Counsel of the Authority. Cases of alleged unfair labor practices in federal service are investigated and prosecuted by the General Counsel and are heard by the FLRA's Office of Administrative Law Judges.

* Labor Relations Documents
Office of Case Control
Federal Labor Relations Authority (FLRA)
500 C St., SW
Washington, DC 20424   (202) 382-0748
Case file information is maintained on FLRA hearings and cases prosecuted to ensure compliance with the rights and obligations of federal employees to organize, bargain collectively, and participate in labor organizations. To view FLRA case dockets and decisions, call ahead to this office to arrange for a visit.

* Labor Relations Reading
Library
Federal Labor Relations Authority (FLRA)
500 C St., SW, Room 235
Washington, DC 20424   (202) 382-0765
A small specialized collection is housed here. Material covers federal service labor-management relations and the Federal Labor Relations Authority. The library is open to the public, but due to tight security in the building, you are advised to call ahead for an appointment.

* Loans Available to Federal Retirees
External Affairs
Federal Retirement Thrift Investment Board
805 Fifteenth St., NW
Washington, DC 20005   (202) 523-5660
Federal Employee's Retirement System and Civil Service Retirement System employees may borrow their own contributions and earnings from the Thrift Savings Plan account for the purchase of a primary residence, medical expenses, educational expenses, and financial hardships. The minimum loan is $1,000, and the loan is repaid through regular payroll allotments. For more information about loans, federal employees should ask their employing agency for copies of the *Thrift Savings Plan* loan program materials.

* Merit Systems Protection Personnel Practices
Office of Policy and Evaluation
Merit Systems Protection Board
1120 Vermont Ave., NW, Room 884
Washington, DC 20419   (202) 653-8900
The Merit Systems Protection Board conducts special studies on the civil service and other executive branch merit systems and reports to the President and the Congress on whether the federal work force is being adequately protected against political abuses and prohibited personnel practices. You can receive a list and free copies of MSPB reports by contacting the office. Some recently released reports include *First-Line Supervisory Selection in the Federal Government*, and *U.S. Office of Personnel Management and the Merit System: A Retrospective Assessment*.

* Occupational Health Facilities
Employee Health Services Branch
Employee and Labor Relations
Personnel Oversight
Office of Personnel Management
1900 E St., NW
Washington, DC 20415   (202) 632-5558

A directory of Federal Occupational health Facilities is available from this office for free.

* OPM Library
Finance and Administrative Services
Administration Group
Office of Personnel Management
1900 E St., NW, Room 5L44
Washington, DC 20415   (202) 632-4432
The OPM Library contains a comprehensive collection of materials on personnel management and the federal civil service. The library also issues *Personnel Literature*, a monthly with an annual index ($18.00) which is available from the Superintendent of Documents, Government Printing Office, Washington, D.C. 20402; (202) 783-3238.

* Merit Pay
Office of Public Affairs
Office of Personnel Management
1900 E St., NW,
Washington, DC 20415   (202) 632-7433
Information on the merit pay system for supervisors and management officials in grades below Senior Executive Schedules is available in the publication, *FED Facts on Merit System Principles and Prohibited Personnel Practices*, which are available from the above office.

* Negotiation Impasses
Federal Services Impasses Board
Federal Labor Relations Authority (FLRA)
500 C St., SW, Room 215
Washington, DC 20424   (202) 382-0981
When negotiation impasses develop between Federal agencies and employee representatives, this panel provides assistance in resolving the stalemate. The following publications are available: *Guide to Hearing Procedures of the Federal Services; Impasses Panel; Subject Matter Index; Table of Cases; and the Annual Report*.

* Pay and Benefits Inquiries
Office of Retirement and Insurance Policy
Office of Personnel Management
1900 E St., NW, Room 4330
Washington, DC 20415   (202) 632-3772
Questions about federal holidays, salary schedules, group life insurance, health benefits, occupational health insurance, sick leave, retirement, and so on, can be answered by this office.

* Pension and Retirement Audits
Office of the Chief Accountant
Pension and Welfare Benefits Administration
Department of Labor
200 Constitution Ave., NW, Room N5677
Washington, DC 20210   (202) 523-8951
This office serves as the U.S. Department of Labor's primary advisor on accounting, auditing, and actuarial issues stemming from its responsibilities under the Employee Retirement Income Security Act and the Federal Employees' Retirement System Act. It serves as the primary agency contact with accounting and actuarial organizations, as well as with federal and state agencies on accounting matters. It also administers a comprehensive system of compliance audits under FERSA and reviews annual financial reports filed under ERISA.

* Personnel Investigations
Office of Federal Investigations
Investigation Group
Office of Personnel Management
600 E St., NW, Room 800
Washington, DC 20004   (202) 376-3800
Used in support of the selection and appointment processes, these investigations serve several purposes: to determine the suitability of applicants under consideration for appointment; to check on applicants or employees under consideration for appointment to positions having either national security or special professional or administrative qualifications requirements, or both; and to enforce civil service regulations. The Office of Personnel Management also makes loyalty determinations of United States citizens employed or under consideration for employment by international organizations of which the United States is a member.
Contact this office for more information.

* Personnel Investigator
Office of the Special Counsel
1120 Vermont Ave   (202) 653-7188

156

Washington, DC 20419   (800) 872-9855

The Office of the Special Counsel is an independent investigative and prosecuting agency that litigates before the Merit Systems Protection Board. The office is responsible for investigating allegations of prohibited personnel practices, prohibited political activities by federal and certain state and local employees, arbitrary or capricious withholding of information in violation of the Freedom of Information Act, prohibited discrimination when found by appropriate authority, and other activities prohibited by any civil service law, rule, or regulation. The office is also responsible for receiving and referring to the appropriate agency information that indicates a violation of any law, rule, or regulation, mismanagement, a gross waste of funds, an abuse of authority, or a substantial and specific danger to public health or safety. The Special Counsel may request the Merit Systems Protection Board to order disciplinary action against any employee who violates civil service laws, rules, and regulations. Any federal employee may file a complaint with the office.

* Personnel Management

Personnel and EEO Division
Office of Personnel Management
1900 E St., NW, Room 1469
Washington, DC 20415   (202) 632-6118

This office manages the following personnel management responsibilities: government-wide classification system, administration of government pay systems; development and operation of information systems to support and improve federal personnel management decisionmaking; and independent evaluation of agency personnel management systems. Contact this office for more information.

* Personnel Management Manual

Inventory Management
Office of Personnel Management
1900 E St., NW, Room E453
Washington, DC 20415   (202) 632-4677

The *Federal Personnel Manual* covers all aspects of personnel management and includes letters, bulletins, and supplements. This publication is prepared by the various units within the Office of Personnel Management and is available on a subscription basis from the Superintendent of Documents, Government Printing Office, Washington, D.C. 20402; (202) 783-3238.

* Personnel Publications

Library
Finance and Administrative Services
Administration Group
1900 E St., NW, Room 5L44
Washington, DC 20415   (202) 632-4432

Personnel Literature is a monthly publication that includes about 200 or so personnel management subjects, such as performance evaluation, productivity, executives, employee training and development, and labor management relations. It includes federal, State, and local governments, foreign governments, and private organizations. It is sold for $18.00 per year by the Superintendent of Documents, Government Printing Office, Washington, D.C. 20402; (202) 783-3238.

* Personnel Records Archives

National Personnel Records Center
National Archives and Records Administration
111 Winnebago Street
St. Louis, MO 63118   (314) 425-5722

Federal employees' personnel records are transferred and stored in the National Personnel Records Center. The Center can answer questions regarding the information available, and can provide copies of documents. Contact the Center for more information.

* Personnel Records Archives Center

National Personnel Records Center
National Archives and Records Administration
9700 Page Blvd.
St. Louis, MO 63132   (314) 263-7247

The National Personnel Records Center stores the personnel records of former federal civilian employees. The Center can answer requests for information, most of which are inquiries relating to claims for benefits.

* Personnel Records System

Agency Relations Group
Office of Personnel Management
1900 E St., NW, Room 5305
Washington, DC 20415   (202) 632-7714

Basic Personnel Records and Files System describes the personnel records system of the Office of Personnel Management. This publication is available by subscription for $65.00 from the Superintendent of Documents, Government Printing Office, Washington, D.C. 20402; (202) 783-3238.

* Postal Career Executive Service

Employee Relations Department
The U.S. Postal Service
475 L'Enfant Plaza, SW
Washington, DC 20260   (202) 268-3643

The postal career executive program develops qualified managers and supervisors through training, educational and work experiences. Contact this office for more information about this program.

* Postal Inspector Jobs

Chief Postal Inspector
U.S. Postal Service
475 L'Enfant Plaza, SW
Washington, DC 20260   (202) 268-4267

Information about Inspection Service employment may be obtained from the Chief Postal Inspector.

* Postal Service Employee/Labor Relations Manual

Employee Relations Department
U.S. Postal Service
475 L'Enfant Plaza, SW
Washington, DC 20260   (202) 268-3643

This subscription service consists of a basic manual and updated transmittal letters for an indeterminate period. This manual sets forth the personnel policies and regulations governing employment with the Postal Service. Topics covered include organization management, job evaluation, employment and placement, pay administration, employee benefits, employee relations, training, safety and health, and labor relations. The subscription is available for $29.00 domestic, and $36.25 foreign per year from: Superintendent of Documents, Government Printing Office, Washington, D.C. 20402-0001; (202) 783-3238

* Postal Service Employment

Employee Relations Department
U.S. Postal Service
475 L'Enfant Plaza, SW
Washington, DC 20260   (202) 268-3643

General information about jobs such as clerk, letter carrier, etc., including information about programs for veterans, may be obtained by contacting the nearest post office. Individuals, generally college graduates interested in engineering, management, finance, personnel work, or in employment as physicists, mathematicians, and operations research analysts, may obtain information by contacting the above office.

* Postal Service Handicapped Employment

Employee Relations Department
U.S. Postal Service
475 L'Enfant Plaza, SW
Washington, DC 20260   (202) 268-3643

The Postal Service created a noncompetitive hiring process for severely handicapped applicants. This program allows the Veterans Administration and State agencies for the disabled (once certified by the Postal Service as having appropriate screening and development capabilities) to refer severely handicapped individuals for direct career appointments.

* Postal Service Union Negotiations

Human Resources Group
U.S. Postal Service
475 L'Enfant Plaza, SW Room 9021
Washington, DC 20260   (202) 268-3619

The Postal Service is the only Federal agency whose employment policies are governed by a process of collective bargaining. Labor contract negotiations, affecting all bargaining unit personnel, as well as personnel matters involving employees not covered by collective bargaining agreements, are administered by the Human Resources Group.

* Presidential and Vice-Presidential Financial Reporting

Office of Government Ethics
Office of Personnel Management
1201 New York Ave., NW, Suite 500
Washington, DC 20005   (202) 523-5757

This office is responsible for the financial statements of top personnel in the Executive Branch, including the President, Vice President, and anyone with a basic rate of pay equal to or above a General Schedule-16. All appointees file with the agency in which they are employed. The financial statements of the U.S. President and the Vice President are available.

* Presidential Management Intern Programs

Careers and Workplace

Presidential Management Intern Programs
Office of Personnel Management
1900 E St., NW, Room 7H34
Washington, DC 20415

Two-year internships in the federal service are available for recipients of graduate degrees in general management with a public sector focus. Contact this office for more information about the Presidential Management Intern Program.

* Productivity Among Civil Servants

Industry Productivity Studies Division
Office of Productivity and Technology
Bureau of Labor Statistics
Department of Labor
200 Constitution Ave., NW, Room S4320
Washington, DC 20210 (202) 523-9244

Productivity measures are developed annually for various functional levels within the Federal government. The information available includes annual indexes of output per employee year, unit labor costs, compensation per employee year, and out put and employee years. Data come from 455 organizations within 48 Federal departments and agencies.

* Public Policy Training

Executive Seminar Center
Office of Training
Office of Personnel Management
1121 Vermont Ave., NW, Room 1200
Washington, DC 20044 (202) 632-6802

The following Centers are residential interagency training facilities to aid government agencies in meeting programmatic and managerial training needs. Federal, State, and local governments may take advantage of the programs. The curriculum includes seminars on administration of public policy; public program management; science, technology and public policy; national economy and public policy; intergovernmental relations; domestic policies and programs; management and executive development; energy policies and programs. Locations of the centers are as follows:

Eastern Executive Seminar Center, c/o U.S. Merchant Marine Academy, Kings Point, NY 11024; (516) 487-4500 or 482-8200, ext 343
Central Executive Seminar Center, Broadway and Kentucky Ave., Oak Ridge, TN 37831-3515; (615) 576-1730
Western Executive Seminar Center, 1405 Curtis, Denver, CO 80202

* Railroad Certificate of Service Months and Compensation

Research and Employment Accounts
Railroad Retirement Board
844 Rush St.
Chicago, IL 60611 (312) 751-4968

Each year railroad employees receive a Certificate of Service Months and Compensation (Form BA-6) from their employers or from the Board, which provides a current record of service and compensation. Contact the above listed office to report incorrect information.

* Railroad Employees Benefit Statistics

Office of Public Affairs
Railroad Retirement Board
844 Rush St.
Chicago, IL 60611 (312) 751-4777

Information on Board operations and on the laws it administers is available. Publications include *Annual Report, Statistical Supplement, Monthly Benefit Statistics*, and several informational pamphlets. The *Annual Report* can be ordered from the Superintendent of Documents, Government Printing Office, Washington, D.C. 20402; (202) 783-3238.

* Railroad Retirement and Survivor Benefits

Bureau of Retirement Claims
Railroad Retirement Board
844 Rush St.
Chicago, IL 60611 (312) 751-4600

Railroad retirement benefits include regular employee retirement annuities after 10 year of service, supplemental annuities, spouse annuities, cost-of-living increases in employee and spouse retirement benefits, and other survivor benefits. *Railroad Retirement and Survivor Benefits* describes these benefits and provides practical information on how to claim them. It also includes relevant tax information.

* Railroad Retirement Appeals Process

Bureau of Hearings and Appeal
Railroad Retirement Board
844 Rush St.

Chicago, IL 60611 (312) 751-4790
Railroad employees can demand an official review of any determination to deny their benefits. If the review still denies the benefits, the employee can appeal.

* Railroad Retirement Benefit Conferences

Labor Member
Railroad Retirement Board
844 Rush St.
Chicago, IL 60611 (312) 751-4905

The Board conducts conferences to describe the benefits available under its retirement-survivor, unemployment-sickness, and Medicare programs. Attendants receive a copy of the *Informational Conference Handbook*--a comprehensive source of information on Board programs--plus pamphlets and other materials highlighting Board programs.

* Railroad Retirement Board Field Offices

Railroad Retirement Board
844 Rush St.
Chicago, IL 60611 (312) 751-4777

Railroad Retirement Board offices are located across the country in localities accessible to large numbers of railroad workers. Personnel are on hand to explain benefit rights and responsibilities, assist employees in applying for benefits, and to answer questions related to the Board's programs. To locate the nearest Board office check the telephone directory under "United States Government", your Post Office, or a Federal Information Center. If there is no Board office nearby, call the nearest district office to set up an appointment to meet with a traveling Board representative.

* Railroad Retirement Board Freedom of Information

Office of Information Resources Management
Railroad Retirement Board
844 Rush St.
Chicago, IL 60611 (312) 751-4692

For Freedom of Information Act requests, contact the above office.

* Railroad Employee Service and Earnings Records

Research and Employment Accounts
Railroad Retirement Board
844 Rush St.
Chicago, IL 60611 (312) 751-4968

Records of service and earnings are kept on all railroad employees since 1936. The records are kept under the employee's Social Security number. Businesses covered by this program include railroads engaged in interstate commerce and some of their subsidiaries, railroad associations, and national railway labor organizations. Contact this office for more information on the records and how to access them.

* Railroad Workers Sickness and Unemployment Benefits

Bureau of Unemployment and Sickness Insurance
Railroad Retirement Board
844 Rush St.
Chicago, IL 60611 (312) 751-4800

Railroad unemployment insurance provides cash benefits in the form of unemployment benefits and sickness benefits. Under the Railroad Unemployment Insurance Act, an employee's eligibility is generally based on railroad service and earnings in the previous calendar year. Contact this office or your nearest Railroad Retirement Board regional office for more information on benefits.

* Retiree Interfund Transfers

External Affairs
Federal Retirement Thrift Investment Board
805 Fifteenth St., NW
Washington, DC 20005 (202) 523-5660

Open seasons for Federal employees provide the opportunity for Federal Employees' Retirement System employees to transfer a portion of their previously invested contributions and all earnings on their own contributions among three investment Plans: the Government Securities Investment Fund, the Common Stock Index Investment Fund, and the Fixed Income Index Investment Fund. Contact the above office or your employing Federal agency for further information.

* Retirees Health and Life Insurance

Office of Personnel Management
1900 E St., NW, Room 3H37
Washington, DC 20415 (202) 632-7700

Comparisons of various types of medical benefits and life insurance for retired federal employees are available from this office.

* Retirement Benefits

Office of Retirement Programs
Retirement and Insurance Group
Adjudication Division
Retirement Information Office
Office of Personnel Management
1900 E St., NW, Room 1323
Washington, DC 20415 (202) 632-7700

All claims for benefits under the retirement system must be adjudicated. Benefits are not paid automatically. Information on how to apply for retirement benefits, death benefits, and refunds is available from this office.

* Retirement Programs

Retirement Information Office
Office of Retirement Programs
Retirement and Insurance Group
Office of Personnel Management
1900 E St., NW, Room 1323
Washington, DC 20415 (202) 632-7700

You can get a variety of free publications on government retirement programs from this office. Some of these include *Federal Retirement Facts*; *Your Retirement System* (questions and answers on the federal civil service retirement law; *Information for Annuitants*; *Retirement Benefits When You Leave the Government Early*; and *Federal Fringe Benefits Facts*.

* Retirement Thrift Personnel Training Program

Federal Retirement Thrift Investment Board
805 Fifteenth St., NW
Washington, DC 20005 (202) 523-4511

The Board annually trains personnel in Federal agencies, particularly benefits officers, on the summary of the Thrift Benefits Plan. These persons are then prepared to explain the plan to other Federal employees and to answer questions concerning the options under the plan.

* Retirement Thrift Savings Plan

External Affairs
Federal Retirement Thrift Investment Board
805 Fifteenth St., NW
Washington, DC 20005 (202) 523-5660

Federal employees may benefit from this retirement savings and investment plan, which provides tax deferral on up to 5 percent for Civil Service Retirement System employees and 10 percent for Federal Employees' Retirement System employees from their basic pay. It also provides secure investments in the Government Securities Investment Fund, immediate vesting in one's own contributions and their earnings, a loan program, portability if leaving Government service, and a choice of withdrawal options. For further information, contact the above office for the brochure, *Thrift Savings Plan for Federal Employees*.

* Salary Schedules

Advisory Services Division
Office of Pay and Benefits
Office of Personnel Management
1900 E St., NW, Room 4330
Washington, DC 20415 (202) 632-5582

Salary and grade rates are available for General Schedule, Executive Schedule, and Senior Executive Schedule employees. Contact this office for more information.

* Senior Executive Candidates

Executive Personnel and Management Development
Office of Personnel Management
P.O. 7230
Washington, DC 20044 (202) 632-5443

This program prepares senior federal managers and other employees at a certain level to enter the Senior Executive Service by providing opportunities to improve upon and/or acquire the management and executive competencies required for the SES. Details about the program are available from the office listed above.

* Senior Executive Service

Senior Executive Service Division (SES)
Office of Personnel Management
1900 E St., NW, Room 6R48
Washington, DC 20415 (202) 632-4486

SES provides every eligible senior manager the chance to shift top career managers around to meet the senior executive's needs. Additional information on the service is available from this office.

* Speakers About Public Service

Office of Public Affairs
Office of Personnel Management
1900 E St., NW
Washington, DC 20415 (202) 632-7433

Professional societies, business and labor groups, and other organizations can contact this office to arrange for representatives of the Office of Personnel Management to speak on federal personnel policies and changes.

* Special Benefits

Advisory Service
Office of Pay and Benefits Division
Retirement and Insurance Group
Office of Personnel Management
1900 E St., NW, Room 4330
Washington, DC 20415 (202) 632-5582

Information on special civil service benefits is available from the Advisory Service. This is a recorded message.

* Standards for Federal Employment

Office of Classifications
Qualification Standards Branch
Career Entry and Employee Development Group
Office of Personnel Management
199 E St., NW, Room 6515
Washington, DC 20415 (202) 632-0557

Standards for evaluating employment requirements for most government occupations are developed by this office. Minimum qualification standards are provided to individual agencies, and they can then add more qualifications of their own if necessary. Contact this office for more information.

* Summer Job Announcements

Federal Job Information Center
General Information
Office of Personnel Management
1900 E St., NW, Room 1416
Washington, DC 20415 (202) 653-9264

Announcements and information on summer employment opportunities with federal agencies is available.

* Tax Savings and the Retirement Thrift Savings Plan

External Affairs
Federal Retirement Thrift Investment Board
805 Fifteenth St., NW
Washington, DC 20005 (202) 523-5660

Thrift Savings Plan contributions are deducted from Federal pay before Federal and, in most cases, State income taxes are calculated. Until you withdraw your TSP account, you pay no income tax on the money you contribute, the money your agency contributes (if you are a Federal Employees' Retirement System employee), or the earnings on your account. For further information, contact your Federal employing agency or the above office for a copy of *Summary of the Thrift Savings Plan for Federal Employees*.

* Thrift Plan Investment Options

External Affairs
Federal Retirement Thrift Investment Board
805 Fifteenth St., NW
Washington, DC 20005 (202) 523-5660

Under present law, most Plan assets in the early years of investing, including some contributions (all of them if you are a Civil Service Retirement System employee) and all agency contributions, must be invested in a fund consisting of short-term, nonmarketable U.S. Treasury securities specially issued to the Thrift Savings Plan. This is the Government Securities Investment Fund or the G Fund. Federal Employee' Retirement System employees may make some of their own contributions, and beginning in 1993, may allocate some of their agency's contributions, to either the Common Stock Index Investment Fund or the Fixed Income Index Investment Fund or both. For a description of the advantages and risks of these investment options, contact your federal agency or the office above for a copy of *Summary of the Thrift Savings Plan for Federal Employees*.

* Thrift Savings Annuities

External Affairs
Federal Retirement Thrift Investment Board
805 Fifteenth St., NW
Washington, DC 20005 (202) 523-5660

The Thrift Savings Plan provides a number of life annuity choices for Federal employees. A life annuity is a monthly benefit paid to you for life. You may choose to receive equal monthly payments or choose initially lower payments that increase each year. Some choices also provide your surviving spouse or other

Careers and Workplace

designated survivor with a monthly benefit for life after you die. The joint life annuities provide either a 100 percent or 50 percent survivor benefit. Contact the benefit officer at your employing Federal agency for more details.

* Thrift Savings Plan Investment Management

External Affairs
Federal Retirement Thrift Investment Board
805 Fifteenth St., NW
Washington, DC 20005   (202) 523-5660

The five member Board of the Federal Retirement Thrift Investment Board establishes the Plan's investment policies. The actual management of the money in the Plan is handled differently for each of the three investment funds. The Government Securities Investment Fund is managed directly by experienced financial/investment analysts on the Board staff following the policies adopted by the Board. The other two funds, the Common Stock Index Investment Fund and the Fixed Income Index Investment Fund, are handled by private sector investment managers. The firms are selected by the Executive Director of the Board through the competitive procurement process.

* Whistleblower Abuse and Waste Hotlines

Inspector General's Office
Department of Commerce
14th St. and Constitution Ave., NW
Room 7898C   (800) 424-5197
Washington DC 20230   (202) 377-2495

This hotline was established so that consumers and employees could report fraud, abuse, or waste within any office in the Department of Commerce. All reports are investigated and reports can be made anonymously. The Pentagon, HUD, and other government departments also have whistleblower hotlines.

* Withdrawing Money under the Thrift Savings Plan

External Affairs
Federal Retirement Thrift Investment Board
805 Fifteenth St., NW
Washington, DC 20005   (202) 523-5660

You cannot withdraw any portion of your Thrift Savings Plan account while you are still employed by the Federal government. The basic purpose of the plan is to provide a retirement income. For further information, contact the above office.

* Work Force Analysis and Statistics

Superintendent of Documents
Government Printing Office
Washington, DC 20402   (202) 783-3238

Statistics and analyses are available on the Federal Civilian Work Force. A bi-monthly publication, *Federal Civilian Work Force Statistics*, contains information on current employment by branch, agency, and area; trends of employment and payroll, and accessions and separations. Summary tables and narrative analyses are given. This can be purchased for $8.00 a year from GPO.

* Working for the U.S.A.

Federal Job Information Center
General Information
Office of Personnel Management
1900 E St., NW, Room 1416
Washington, DC 20415   (202) 737-9616

This free pamphlet is available from any Federal Job Information Center.

Federal Job Banks

Here you will find the offices within each of the government agencies and departments which have responsibility for personnel. Dial-a-Job recorded messages inform callers about immediate job openings. Future employment prospects, the interview process, and other questions about the civil service can be directed to these offices which are staffed with knowledgeable federal employees. In the cases of those agencies which are not listed here or only have a recorded message, refer to the Federal Public Information Offices section in Information Starting Places Chapter. If you run into any difficulties with a particular federal office, contact either of your U.S. Senator or Representative.

ACTION
Room 5101
1100 Vermont Avenue, N.W.
Washington, D.C. 20525
(202) 634-9263
(202) 634-1000 recorded message

Administrative Conference of the U.S.
2120 L St., NW, Suite 500
Washington, DC 20037
(202) 254-7020

African Development Foundation
1625 Massachusetts Ave., NW
Suite 600
Washington, DC 20036
(202) 673-3916

Agency for International Development
320 21st Street, N.W.
Washington, D.C. 20523
(202) 632-1850
(202) 632-3942

Agriculture, Department of
14th St. & Independence Ave., S.W.
Washington, D.C. 20250
(202) 447-5625
(202) 447-2436
(202) 447-2108

Agricultural Research Job Line
Beltsville, Maryland
(301) 344-1124
(301) 344-2288 recorded message

Air Force, Department of the
The Pentagon
Civilian Personnel
Washington, DC 20310
(202) 695-4389
(202) 695-9028 DIAL-A-JOB recorded message

Alcohol Tobacco & Firearms Bureau
Employment Branch 1216
Department of the Treasury
1200 Pennsylvania Avenue, N.W.
Washington, D.C. 20226
(202) 566-7321

American Battle Monument Commission
Pulaski Building
20 Massachusetts Ave., NW, Room 5124
Washington, DC 20314
(202) 272-0534

Appalachian Regional Commission
1666 Connecticut Ave., Suite 721 NW
Washington, DC 20235
(202) 673-7896

Arms Control & Disarmament Agency
320 21st Street, N.W.
Washington, D.C. 20418

(202) 647-2034

Army, Department of
Personnel & Employment Service
The Pentagon
Washington, D.C. 20310-6800
(202) 695-0010

Board for International Broadcasting
Administrative Management Assistant
1201 Connecticut Ave., NW
Washington, DC 20036,
(202) 254-8040

Bureau of Public Debt
Department of the Treasury
999 E Street, N.W.
Washington, D.C. 20239
(202) 447-1407 recorded message

Census Bureau
14th St. & Constitution Ave., N.W.
Washington, D.C. 20230
(301) 763-5537

Central Intelligence Agency
Washington, D.C. 20505
(202) 351-2028

Civil Rights Commission
5401 Westbard Avenue
Bethesda, Maryland 20207
(301) 492-6660

Commission of Fine Arts
708 Jackson Place, NW
Washington, DC 20006
(202) 566-1066

Commission on the Bicentennial of the U.S. Constitution
808 17th St., Room 864, NW
Washington, DC 20006
(202) 653-5351.

Commodity Futures Trading Commission
2033 K St., Suite 202, NW
Washington, DC 20581
(202) 254-3275
(202) 254-3346 recorded message

Consumer Product Safety Commission
5401 Westbard Ave.
Bethesda, MD
(301) 492-6500

Defense, Department of
The Pentagon
Civilian Personnel
Washington, D.C. 2031
(202) 697-9336
(202) 697-9335

Defense Logistics Agency
C.P.O. 13C 666 Cameron Station

Alexandria, VA 22304-6100
(703) 274-7087
(703) 274-7372 recorded message

Education, Department of
400 Maryland Avenue, S.W.
Washington, D.C. 20202
(202) 732-5553
(202) 732-5559
(202) 732-5499 recorded message

Equal Employment Opportunity Commission
1801 L St., NW
Washington, DC 20507
(202) 663-4337
(202) 663-4306

Employment Standards Administration
Bureau of Labor Statistics
Department of Labor
441 G Street N.W.
Washington, D.C. 20212
(202) 523-7545

Energy, Department of
1000 Independence Ave., S.W.
Washington, D.C. 20585
(202) 586-4333 recorded message
(202) 586-8839

Environmental Protection Agency
401 M Street, S.W.
Washington, D.C.
(202) 382-3144
(202) 655-4000
(202) 755-5055 recorded message

Executive Office of the President
725 17th Street, N.W.
Washington, D.C. 20503
(202) 395-3766

Export-Import Bank of the U.S.
811 Vermont Avenue, N.W.
Washington, D.C. 20571
(202) 566-8834

Farm Credit Administration
Human Resources Division
Room 3400
1501 Farm Credit Drive
Mclean, VA 22102
(703) 883-4135
(703) 883-4139 recorded message.

Federal Aviation Administration
800 Independence Avenue, N.W.
Washington, D.C. 20591
(202) 267-3229

Federal Bureau of Investigation
J. Edgar Hoover Building
9th St. & Pennsylvania Ave., N.W.
Washington, D.C. 20535
(202) 324-6164 recorded message
(202) 324-6171 recorded message

Federal Communications Commission
1919 M Street, N.W.
Washington, D.C.20554
(202) 632-7120

Federal Deposit Insurance Corporation
Personnel Officer
999 E St., NW
Washington, DC 20463
(202) 376-5290

Federal Election Commission
Personnel Officer
999 E St., NW
Washington, DC 20463
(202) 376-5290

Federal Emergency Management Agency
Office of Personnel
500 C St., SW, Room 810
Washington, DC 20472
(202) 646-4041 vacancy hotline number.

Federal Home Loan Bank Board
1700 G Street, N.W.
Washington, D.C. 20552
(202) 906-6060

Federal Labor Relations Authority
500 C Street, S.W.
Washington, D.C. 20573
(202) 382-0751

Federal Maritime Commission
1100 L St., NW, Room 10103
Washington, DC 20573
(202) 523-5773

Federal Mediation and Conciliation Service
2100 K St., NW, Room 718
Washington, DC 20427
(202) 653-5260

Federal Mine Safety and Health Review Commission
Administrative Officer
1730 K St., NW
Washington, DC 20006
(202) 653-5615

Federal Reserve System
Human Resources Management
20th St. and Constitution Ave., NW,
Washington, DC 20551
(202) 452-3880
(202) 452-3038 recorded message

Federal Retirement Thrift Investment Board
Personnel Officer
805 16th St., NW,
Washington, DC 20005
(202) 523-8028

Federal Trade Commission
Pennsylvania Ave. at 6th Street, N.W.
Washington, D.C. 20591
(202) 326-2020

Forest Service
General Employment
Room 913 RP-E
Rosslyn, Virginia 22209
(703) 235-2730

General Accounting Office
Office of Recruitment
441 G Street, N.W.
Washington, D.C. 20536
(202) 275-6361 GS 2-12
(202) 275-6017 GS 13 & Up

General Services Administration
Office of Personnel
General Services Building
18th and F St, NW, Room 1100
Washington, DC 20405
(202) 566-0370

Government Printing Office
North Capitol & H Street, N.W.
Washington, D.C. 20401
(202) 275-2951

Health and Human Services, Department of
200 Independence Ave., S.W.
Washington, D.C. 20201
(301) 443-6900

Health and Human Services, Department of
Alcohol Drug Abuse & Mental Health
Administration PHS-HHE
5600 Fishers Lane

Rockville, Maryland
(301) 443-5407
(301) 443-2282

Health and Human Services, Department of
Health Resources & Services Administration
5600 Fishers Lane
Rockville, Maryland 20857
(301) 443-1230 recorded message

Health and Human Services, Department of
National Institute of Health
9000 Rockville Pike
Bethesda, MD 20205
(301) 496-1209 recorded message

House of Representative
U.S. Capitol Placement Office
House Office Building
Room 219
Washington, D.C. 20515
(202) 226-6731

Housing and Urban Development, Department of
451 7th Street, S.W.
Washington, D.C. 20410
(202) 755-5408
(202) 755-0381
(202) 755-3203 recorded message

Immigration & Naturalization Service
425 Eye Street, N.W.
Washington, D.C. 20536
(202) 633-4330

Inter-American Foundation
1515 Wilson Blvd.
Rosslyn, Virginia 22209
(703) 841-3866

Interior, Department of
18th & C Streets, N.W.
Washington, D.C. 20240
(202) 343-6702
(202) 634-4719 Bureau of Mines
(202) 358-1743 Fish & Wildlife
(202) 343-7581 Indian Affairs
(202) 343-4649 Park Service
(202) 343-8093 Park Service

Internal Revenue Service (IRS)
Department of the Treasury
1111 Constitution Ave., N.W.
Washington, D.C. 20224
(202) 566-3617

International Development Cooperation Agency
320 21st Street, N.W.
Washington, D.C. 20523
(202) 663-1491 Foreign Service
(202) 663-1400 Civil Service

International Trade Commission
701 E Street, N.W.
Washington, D.C. 20436
(202) 252-1653

Interstate Commerce Commission
12th & Constitution Ave.,N.W.
Washington, D.C. 20423
(202) 275-7288

Justice, Department of
10th St. & Constitution Ave., N.W.
Washington, D.C. 20530
(202) 272-8271 recorded message

Labor, Department of
200 Constitution Avenue, N.W.
Washington, D.C.
(202) 523-6666
(202) 523-6646 recorded message
(800) 637-9774 toll-free job info

Library of Congress
101 Independence Avenue, N.W.
Washington, D.C. 20594
(202) 707-5295 recorded message

Merit Systems Protection Board
Personnel Division
1120 Vermont Ave., NW,
Washington, DC 20419
(202) 653-5916

National Aeronautics and Space Administration
Human Resources Management Division
Code DP, 400 Maryland Ave., SW
Washington, DC 20546
(202) 453-8478

National Archives and Records Administration
Personnel Services Division
7th and Pennsylvania Ave., NW,
Washington, DC 20408
(202) 724-1525
(800) 634-4898 hotline number

National Art Gallery
Washington, D.C. 20594
(202) 842-6282
(202) 842-6298 recorded message

National Capitol Planning Commission
Office of Administration
1325 G. St., NW
Washington, DC 20576
(202) 724-0170

National Credit Union Administration
Office of Personnel
1776 G St., NW, 7th Floor
Washington, DC 20045
(202) 682-9720

National Endowment for the Arts
100 Pennsylvania Ave., NW, Room 208
Washington, DC 20506
(202) 682-5405

National Endowment for the Humanities
100 Pennsylvania Ave., NW, Room 417
Washington, DC 20506
(202) 786-0415

National Labor Relations Board
1717 Pennsylvania Ave., NW
Washington, DC 20750
(202) 254-9168

National Mediation Board
1425 K St., Suite 910, NW
Washington, DC 20572
(202) 523-5950

National Oceanic and Atmospheric Administration
Department of Commerce
Washington, DC 20230
(301) 443-8373

National Science Foundation
1800 G St., Room 208, NW
Washington, DC 20550
(202) 357-5000

National Security Agency
ATT: M 232
Fort Meade, MD 20755-6000
(301) 859-6444

National Technical Information Service
Washington, D.C.
(201) 487-4468

National Transportation Safety Board
800 Independence Ave., Suite 801, SW
Washington, DC 20594

(202) 382-6717
(202) 382-6542 recorded message

Navy, Department of
Civilian Personnel
CCPO-CC, Room 424
Washington, D.C. 20376-5006
(202) 692-4139
(202) 691-4133 recorded message

Nuclear Regulatory Commission
Office of Personnel
Washington, DC 20555
(301) 492-4661

Occupational Safety and Health Administration
200 Constitution Ave., NW
Washington, DC 20210
(202) 523-8015
(202) 523-1590

Occupational Safety and Health Review Commission
1825 K St., NW, Room 413
Washington, DC 20006
(202) 634-7991

Office of Personnel Management
Congressional Liaison Of OPM
Rayburn House Office Building
Washington, D.C. 20515
(202) 225-4955 recorded message

Overseas Private Investment Corporation
1615 M Street, N.W.
Washington, D.C.
(202) 457-7013

Panama Canal Commission
2000 L St., Room 550, NW
Washington, DC 20036
(202) 634-6441

Peace Corps
806 Connecticut Avenue, N.W.
Washington, D.C.
(202) 254-8336
(800) 424-8580 x214 toll-free job info
(202) 254-3400 recorded message

Pennsylvania Avenue Development Corporation
1331 Pennsylvania Ave., NW, Suite 1220 North
Washington, DC 20004-1703
(202) 724-9091.

Pension Benefit Guaranty Corporation
2020 K St., NW, Room 3700
Washington, DC 20006
(202) 778-8808

Postal Rate Commission
Administrative Office
1333 H St., Suite 300, NW
Washington, DC 20268-0001
(202) 789-6840

Railroad Retirement Board
Director of Personnel
844 Rush St,
Chicago, IL 60611
(312) 751-4580

Securities and Exchange Commission
450 5th Street, N.W.
Washington, D.C. 20549
(202) 272-2519

Selective Service System
1023 31st Street, N.W.
Washington, D.C. 20435
(202) 724-0430

Senate
Hart Senate Office Building
Room S H 142 B
Washington, D.C. 20510
(202) 224-9164

Small Business Administration
1441 L Street, N.W.
Washington, D.C. 20416
(202) 653-6600

Smithsonian Institution
1000 Jefferson Drive, S.W.
Washington, D.C. 20560
(202) 287-3100 recorded message

State, Department of
2201 C Street, N.W.
Washington, D.C. 20520
(202) 647-6132
(202) 647-7284 recorded message
(703) 875-7211 Foreign Service
(202) 647-7290 Civil Service

Tennessee Valley Authority
400 West Summit Hill Drive
ET 5C50P- K
Knoxville, TN 37902
(615) 632-7746

Treasury, Department of
15th St. & Pennsylvania Ave.,N.W.
Washington, D.C. 20220
(202) 566-2540 recorded message

U.S. Information Agency
301 4th St, SW, Room 518
Washington, DC 20547
(202) 485-2659
(202) 485-2539 recorded message

U.S. International Development Cooperative Agency,
2401 E St., Room 1430, NW
Washington, DC 20523
(202) 663-1423
(202) 663-1299

U.S. International Trade Commission
Office of Personnel
500 E St., Room 314, SW
Washington, DC 20436
(202) 252-1653

U.S. Postal Service
475 L'Enfant Plaza
Room 1813, SW
Washington, DC 20260-0010
(202) 268-3646
(202) 268-3218 reorded message.

U.S. Tax Court
400 2nd St., NW, Room 146
Washington, DC 20217
(202) 376-2724

U.S. Trade and Development Program
Agency for International Development
2401 E. St., NW, Room 1127
Washington, DC 20523
(202) 663-1431

Veterans Affairs, Department of
810 Vermont Avenue, N.W.
Washington, D.C. 20420
(202) 233-4000

Research Grants in Every Field

You'll discover from this list of federal grants that research opportunities exist in almost every occupational field from forestry to injury prevention to library development. The following is a description of the federal dollars available to researchers, organizations, and universities. Grants to teachers and those involved in education are listed separately in the Education Chapter. This information is taken from the *Catalog of Federal Domestic Assistance* which is published by the U.S. Government Printing Office in Washington, D.C. The number next to the title description is the official reference number listed in this catalog. Contact the office listed below the title for more details.

* **Minority Research and Teaching Grants (MRTP Small Grants Program) 10.140**
Dr. Ezra Naughton, Minority Research and
 Teaching Programs
Office of Advocacy and Enterprise
Department of Agriculture
14th & Independence Ave., SW
Washington, DC 20250 (202) 447-2019

* **Minority Research and Teaching Grants (MRTP Small Grants Program) 10.140**
Dr. Ezra Naughton, Minority Research and
 Teaching Programs
Office of Advocacy and Enterprise
Dept. of Agriculture
14th & Independence Ave., SW
Washington, DC 20250 (202) 447-2019

* **Grants for Agricultural Research, Special Research Grants (Special Research Grants) 10.200**
Administrator, Cooperative State Research Service
Department of Agriculture
Washington, DC 20250 (202) 447-4423

* **Cooperative Forestry Research (McIntire-Stennis Act) 10.202**
Administrator, Cooperative State Research Service
Department of Agriculture
Washington, DC 20250 (202) 447-4423

* **Payments to 1890 Land-Grant Colleges and**
Tuskegee University 10.205
Administrator, Cooperative State Research Service
Department of Agriculture
Washington, DC 20250 (202) 447-4423

* **Grants for Agricultural Research-Competitive**
Research Grants 10.206
Chief Scientist, Competitive Research Grants Office
Department of Agriculture, Aerospace Bldg.
Room 323, 14th & Independence Ave, SW
Washington, DC 20250 (202) 457-5022

* **Animal Health and Disease Research 10.207**
Administrator, Cooperative State Research Service
Department of Agriculture
Washington, DC 20250 (202) 447-4423

* **Higher Education Strengthening Grants 10.211**
Administrator, Cooperative State Research Service
Department of Agriculture
Washington, DC 20250 (202) 447-4423

* **Competitive Research Grants for Forest and Rangeland Renewable Resources (Forestry**

Competitive Grants) 10.213
Director, Competitive Research Grants, OGPS, CSRS
Department of Agriculture, Room 323
Aerospace Bldg, 14th & Independence Ave., SW
Washington, DC 20250 (202) 475-5022

* **Morrill-Nelson Funds for Food and Agricultural Higher Education 10.214**
Dr. K. Jane Coulter or Mr. Patrick J. Casula
Higher Education Programs
Office of Grants & Program Systems
Dept. of Agriculture
Washington, DC 20250 (202) 447-7854

* **Low Input Farming Systems-Research and Education 10.215**
Administrator
Cooperative State Research Service
Department of Agriculture
Washington, DC 20250 (202) 447-4423

* **Technical Agricultural Assistance 10.960**
Mr. Harry Mattox
Office of International Cooperation and Development
Technical Assistance Division
Department of Agriculture
Washington, DC 20250 (202) 653-7320

* **International Agricultural Research - Collaborative Program (International Research) 10.961**
Mr. Jim Butcher
Office of International Cooperation and Development
International Research Division
Department of Agriculture
Washington, DC 20250 (202) 653-7462

* **International Training-Foreign Participant 10.962**
Mr. Richard Affleck
Office of International Cooperation and Development
International Training Division
Department of Agriculture
Washington, DC 20250 (202) 653-8320

* **Research and Evaluation Program 11.312**
David H. Geddes, Room H-7319
EDA, Department of Commerce
Washington, DC 20230 (202) 377-4085

* **Anadromous and Great Lakes Fisheries Conservation 11.405**
Director, Office of Fisheries Conservation
 and Management
National Marine Fisheries Service
1335 East-West Highway
Silver Spring, MD 29010 (202) 673-5272

* Interjurisdictional Fisheries Act of 1986 11.407
Director, Office of Fisheries Conservation
and Management
National Marine Fisheries Service
1335 East-West Hwy
Silver Spring, MD 20910   (301) 427-2347

* Sea Grant Support 11.417
Director, National Sea Grant College Program
National Oceanic and Atmospheric Administration
Silver Spring Metro Ctr
No. 1, East West Hwy
Silver Spring, MD 20920   (301) 427-2448

*** Financial Assistance for Marine Pollution
Research 11.426**
NOAA, National Ocean Service
Office of Oceanography and Marine Assessment
N/OMA3 Ocean Assessments Division
Rockville, MD 20852

*** Fisheries Development and Utilization
Research and Development Grants and
Cooperative Agreements Program 11.427**
Office of Trade and Industry Services
National Marine Fisheries Service
NOAA, Department of Commerce
Silver Spring, MD 20910   (301) 427-2358

* Marine Sanctuary Program 11.429
Chief, Marine and Estuarine Management Division
Office of Ocean and Coastal Resource Management
National Ocean Service, NOAA
1825 Conn. Ave, N.W.
Washington, DC   (202) 673-5126

* Undersea Research 11.430
Director, Office of Undersea Research
National Oceanic and Atmospheric Administration
1335 East-West Hwy
Silver Spring, MD 20910   (302) 427-2426

* Climate and Atmospheric Research 11.431
Director, Office of Global Programs
National Oceanic and Atmospheric Administration
1335 East-West Hwy
Silver Spring, MD 20910   (303) 427-2474

*** Public Telecommunications Facilities-Construction and
Planning (PTFP) 11.550**
Dennis R. Connors, Acting Director
Public Telecommunications Facilities Program
NTIA, Room 4625, Department of Commerce
14th & Constitution Ave., NW
Washington, DC   (202) 377-5802

*** Measurement and Engineering Research
and Standards 11.609**
National Bureau of Standards
Gaithersburg, MD 20899

*** Regional Centers for the Transfer of
Manufacturing Technology 11.611**
Dr. Philip N. Nanzetta, Director
NIST MTC Program, Rm B112
Metrology Bldg, NIST
Gaithersburg, MD 20899   (301) 975-3414

*** Minority Business Development Centers
(MBDC) 11.800**

Assistant Director, Office of Program Development
Rm 5096, Minority Business Agency
Department of Commerce
14th & Constitution Ave., NW
Washington, DC 20230   (202) 377-5770

* American Indian Program (AIP) 11.801
Assistant Director, Office of Program Development
Room 5096, Minority Business Development Agency
Department of Commerce
14th & Constitution Ave., NW
Washington, DC 20230   (202) 377-5770

*** Procurement Technical Assistance for Business Firms
(Procurement Technical Assistance (PTA)) 12.002**
Defense Logistics Agency, Cameron Station
Office of Small and Disadvantaged Business
Utilization (DLA-U), Room 4C112
Alexandria, VA 22304-6100   (202) 274-6471

* Food and Drug Administration-Research 13.103
Robert L. Robins, Chief
Grants and Assistance Agreements Section
Div. of Contracts and Grants, FDA
HFA-520, Rm 3-20, Parklawn Bldg.
5600 Fishers Lane
Rockville, MD   (301) 443-6170

*** Maternal and Child Health Federal Consolidated
Programs (Special Projects of Regional and
National Significance (SPRANS) 13.110**
Office of Maternal and Child Health
Bur. of Maternal and Child Health and Resource Dev.
HRSA, PHS, Rm 9-11, 5600 Fishers Lane
Rockville, MD 20852   (301) 443-2170

* Adolescent Family Life Research Grants 13.111
Office of Adolescent Pregnancy Programs, DHHS
Eugenia Eckard
Room 736E, Hubert Humphrey Bldg.
200 Independence Ave., SW
Washington, DC 20201 Telephone   (202) 245-1181

*** Characterization of Environmental
Health Hazards 13.112**
Director, Division of Extramural Research and Training
National Institute of Environmental Health Sciences
P.O. Box 12233
Research Triangle Park, NC 27709   (919) 541-7723

*** Biological Response to Environmental Health
Hazards 13.113**
Director, Division of Extramural Research
and Training
National Institute of Environmental Health Sciences
P.O. Box 12233
Research Triangle Park, NC 27709   (919) 541-7723

*** Applied Toxicological Research and Testing
(Bioassay of Chemicals and Test Development) 13.114**
Director, Division of Extramural Research
and Training
National Institute of Environmental Health Sciences
P.O. Box 12233
Research Triangle Park, NC 27709   (919) 541-7723

*** Biometry and Risk Estimation-Health Risks
From Environmental Exposures 13.115**
Director, Division of Extramural Research and
Training, National Institute of Environmental
Health Sciences
P.O. Box 12233
Research Triangle Park, NC 27709   (919) 541-7723

* Project Grants and Cooperative Agreements for Tuberculosis Control Programs 13.116
Chief, Grants Management Branch, CDC, PHS, DHHS
1600 Clifton Road, NE
Atlanta, GA   30333
(404) 842-6575

* Acquired Immunodeficiency Syndrome (AIDS) Activity (AIDS) 13.118
Procurement and Grants Office, Centers for
Disease Control, DHHS
1600 Clifton Road NE
Atlanta, GA   30333
(404) 842-6575

* Diseases of the Teeth and Supporting Tissues 13.121
Extramural Program, National Institute of Dental
Research, National Institutes of Health
Bethesda, MD   20892
(301) 496-7884

* Disorders of Craniofacial Structure and Function, and Behavioral Aspects of Dentistry 13.122
Extramural Program, National Institute of Dental
Research, National Institutes of Health
Bethesda, MD   20892
(301) 496-7807

* Centers for Research and Demonstration for Health Promotion and Disease Prevention (Prevention Centers) 13.135
S. Price Connor
Field Coordinator, CDC
Atlanta, GA   30333
(404) 639-1986

* Injury Prevention and Control Research Projects Injury Prevention Research Centers Applied Methods in Surveillance Projects and State and Community-Based Injury Control Projects 13.136
Division of Injury Epidemiology and Control
Center for Environmental Health and Insury Control
Center for Disease Control
Atlanta, GA   30333
(404) 488-4690

* Intramural Research Training Award (IRTA Program) 13.140
Associate Director for Intramural Affairs
National Institutes of Health
Shannon Bldg. Room 140
9000 Rockville Pike
Rockville, MD   20892
(301) 496-4920

* NIEHS Hazardous Waste Worker Health and Safety Training (Superfund Worker Training Program) 13.142
Director, Division of Extramural Research
and Training
National Institute of Environmental Health Sciences
P.O. Box 12233
Research Triangle Park, NC   27709
(919) 541-7723

* NIEHS Superfund Hazardous Substances-Basic Research and Education (NIEHS Superfund Research Program) 13.143
Director, Division of Extramural Research
and Training
National Institutes of Environmental Health Sciences
P.O. Box 12233
Research Triangle Park, NC   27709
(919) 541-7723

* AIDS Education and Training Centers 13.145
Dir, Division of Medicine
Bur. of Health Professions
Health Resources and Services Admin, Rm 4C03
5600 Fishers Lane
Rockville, MD   20857
(301) 443-6190

* Research Facilities Improvement (AIDS Infrastructure Projects) 13.167
Research Facilities Improvement Program
Division of Research Resources
National Institutes of Health
Bldg. 31, Room 3B13
Bethesda, MD   20892
(301) 496-8482

* Human Genome Research 13.172
Dr. Judith Greenberg
National Institute of General Medical Sciences
National Institutes of Health
Bethesda, MD   20892
(301) 496-7175

* Biological Research Related to Deafness and Communicative Disorders 13.173
Dr. Ralph F. Naunton, National Institute of
Deafness and Other Communicative Disorders
NIH, Federal Bldg. Room 1C11
Bethesda, MD   20892
(301) 496-1804

* Conference Grant (Substance Abuse) 13.174
Office for Substance Abuse Prevention (OSAP)
Alcohol, Drug Abuse and Mental Health Administration
Rm. 9A-54, 5600 Fishers Lane
Rockville, MD   20857
(301) 443-0365

* ADAMHA Small Instrumentation Program Grants (ASIP) 13.176
Dr. Louis Hus, Mr. James Moynihan
Division of Basic Science
NIMH, 5600 Fishers Lane, Room 11-95
Rockville, MD   20857
(301) 443-3107

* Health Services Research and Development Grants 13.226
National Center for Health Services Research
and Health Care Technology Assessment, PHS
DHHS, Rm 18A-10, Parklawn Bldg.
5600 Fishers Lane
Rockville, MD   20857
(301) 443-4033

* Mental Health Research Grants 13.242
Dr. Lyle Bivens, Director
Division of Basic Sciences
(Neurosciences research; behavioral sciences research; health and behavior research)
National Institute of Mental Health
5600 Fishers Lane
Rockville, MD 20857
(301) 443-3563

* Occupational Safety and Health Research Grants 13.262
Mr. Henry Casse, Procurement and Grants Office, DCD
DHHS, 1600 Clifton Road NE
Atlanta, GA   30333
(404) 842-6575

* Alcohol Scientist Development Award and Research Scientist Development Award for Clinicians (Research Center ("K") Awards) 13.271
Dr. Sue Shafer, Acting Director
Division of Basic Research
National Institute on Alcohol Abuse and Alcoholism
PHS, 5600 Fishers Lane
Rockville, MD
(301) 443-2530

* Alcohol National Research Service Awards for Research Training (NRSA Program) 13.272
Dr. Sue Shafer, Acting Director
Division of Basic Research
National Institute on Alcohol Abuse and Alcoholism

PHS, 5600 Fishers Lane
Rockville, MD   (301) 443-2530

* Alcohol Research Programs 13.273
Dr. Sue Shafer, Acting Director, Division of
Basic Research
National Institute on Alcohol Abuse and Alcoholism
PHS, 5600 Fishers Lane
Rockville, MD   (301) 443-2530

*** Drug Abuse National Research Service Awards
for Research Training (NRSA Program) 13.278**
Dr. Marvin Snyder, Director
Division of Preclinical Research Technology
National Institute on Drug Abuse
5600 Fishers Lane
Rockville, MD 20857   (301) 443-1887

* Drug Abuse Research Programs 13.279
Dr. Marvin Snyder, Director
Division of Preclinical Research
National Institute on Drug Abuse
5600 Fishers Lane
Rockville, MD 20857   (301) 443-1887

*** Mental Research Scientist Development Award and
Research Scientist Development Award for
Clinicians (Career Development ("K") Awards)
13.281**
Dr. Lyle Bivens, Director
Division of Basic Sciences
National Institute of Mental Health
Parklawn Bldg. 5600 Fishers Lane
Rockville, MD 20857   (301) 443-3563

*** Laboratory Animal Sciences and Primate Research
13.306**
Animal Resources Branch
Division of Research Resources
National Institutes of Health
Bethesda, MD 20892   (301) 496-5175

* General Clinical Research Centers 13.333
General Clinical Research Centers Program Branch
Division of Research Resources
National Institutes of Health
Bethesda, MD 20892   (301) 496-6595

* Biomedical Research Support 13.337
Biomedical Research Support Program
Division of Research Resources
National Institutes of Health
Bethesda, MD 20892   (301) 496-6743

*** Nursing Research - Health Promotion and
Disease Prevention 13.361**
Dr. Moira Shannon
National Center for Nursing Research, NIH, PHS
Bldg. 31, Room B1C02
Bethesda, MD 20892   (301) 496-0237

* Biomedical Research Technology 13.371
Biomedical Research, Technology Resources Branch
Dr. Suzanne Stimler
Division of Research Resources
National Institutes of Health
Bethesda, MD 20892   (301) 496-5411

*** Research Centers in Minority Institutions
(RCMI) 13.389**
Dr. Sidney A. McNairy, Jr. Program Director
RCMI, Division of Research Resources, NIH
Bethesda, MD 20205   (301) 496-6341

*** Academic Research Enhancement Award (AREA)
13.390**
Office of Special Programs and Initiatives
Office of Extramural Research
National Institutes of Health
Bethesda, MD 20892   (301) 496-1968

* Cancer Cause and Prevention Research 13.393
Dr. Richard H. Adamson, Director
Division of Cancer Etiology
National Cancer Institute
Bethesda, MD 20892   (301) 496-6618

* Cancer Detection and Diagnosis Research 13.394
Dr. Brian Kimes, Associate Director
Extramural Research Program
National Cancer Institute
Bethesda, MD 20892   (301) 496-8636

* Cancer Treatment Research 13.395
Dr. Mace Rothenberg, Special Assistant to the Director, National Cancer
Institute
Bethesda, MD 20892   (301) 496-6711

* Cancer Biology Research 13.396
Dr. Brian Kimes, Associate Director
Extramural Research Program
National Cancer Institute
Bethesda, MD 20892   (301) 496-8636

* Cancer Centers Support 13.397
Dr. Lucius Sinks, Chief
Cancer Center Branch
Division of Cancer Prevention and Control
National Cancer Institute, EPN/308C
Bethesda, MD 20892   (301) 496-7753

* Cancer Control 13.399
Dr. Joseph W. Cullen, Deputy Director
Division of Cancer Prevention and Control
National Cancer Institute
Bethesda, MD 20892   (301) 496-9569

*** Administration for Children, Youth and
Families - Head Start 13.600**
Administration for Children, Youth and Families
Head Start, Office of Human Development Services
Department of Health and Human Services
P.O. Box 1182
Washington, DC 20013   (202) 755-7782

*** Administration for Children, Youth and Families
- Child Welfare Research and Demonstration 13.608**
Chief, Discretionary Program Branch
Administration for Children, Youth and Families
Office of Human Development Services, OS
P.O. Box 1182
Washington, DC 20013   (202) 755-7420

* Social Services Research and Demonstration 13.647
Ann Queen, Director, Division of Research and
Demonstration
Department of Health and Human Services
Room 334-F, Hubert Humphrey Bldg
200 Independence Ave., SW
Washington, DC   (202) 472-3026

*** Administration for Children, Youth and
Families - Adoption Opportunities 13.652**
Delmar Weathers, Children's Bureau
Administration for Children, Youth and Families
P.O. Box 1182
Washington, DC 20013   (202) 426-2822

* Native American Programs - Research, Demonstration, and Evaluation 13.661
Martin Koenig
Administration for Native Americans
Department of Health and Human Services
Rm 334-F, 200 Independence Ave., SW
Washington, DC 20201   (202) 245-7730

* Administration for Children, Youth and Families - Child Abuse and Neglect Discretionary Activities (Child Abuse and Neglect Discretionary Activities) 13.670
Director, National Center on Child Abuse and
 Neglect (NCCAN)
Children's Bureau
P.O. Box 1182
Washington, DC 20013   (202) 245-2056

* Health Care Financing Research Demonstrations and Evaluations (HCFA Research) 13.766
George J. Schieber, Acting Director
Health Care Financing Administration, DHHS
6325 Security Blvd
Baltimore, MD 21207   (301) 966-6507

* Assistance Payments-Research 13.782
Gary Ashcraft, Director
Division of Program Evaluation
Family Support Administration
370 L'enfant Promenade, SW
Washington, DC 20447   (202) 252-5034

* Social Security-Research and Demonstration (SSA Research and Demonstration) 13.812
Lawrence H. Pullen, Chief, Grants Management Staff
Office of Acquisition and Grants, ODCM
Social Security Administration, 1-E-4
1710 Gwynn Oak Ave.
Baltimore, MD   (301) 965-9502

* Biophysics and Physiological Sciences 13.821
Dr. Marvin Cassman, Director
Biophysics and Physiological Sciences, NIH
Bethesda, MD 20892   (301) 496-7463

* Heart and Vascular Diseases Research 13.837
Director, Division of Heart and Vascular Diseases
National Heart, Lung, and Blood Institute
Bethesda, MD 20892   (301) 496-2553

* Lung Diseases Research 13.838
Director, Division of Lung Diseases
National Heart, Lung, and Blood Institute
Bethesda, MD 20892   (301) 496-7208

* Blood Diseases and Resources Research 13.839
Director, Division of Blood, Diseases, and Resources
National Heart, Lung, and Blood Institute
Bethesda, MD 20892   (301) 496-4868

* Dental Research Institutes-Research Centers in Oral Biology 13.845
Grants, Extramural Programs
National Institute of Dental Research, NIH
Bethesda, MD 20892   (301) 496-7748

* Arthritis, Musculoskeletal and Skin Diseases Research 13.846
Dr. S. Hausman, Deputy Director
Extramural Activities Program
National Institute of Arthritis and
 Musculoskeletal and Skin Diseases
Westwood Bldg., Rm 403, NIH
Bethesda, MD

* Diabetes, Endocrinology and Metabolism Research 13.847
Dr. E. Johnson, Director, Division of Diabetes,
 Endocrinology and Metabolic Diseases
Room 9A16, Bldg. 31, National Institute of
 Diabetes and Kidney Diseases, NIH
Bethesda, MD   (301) 496-7348

* Digestive Diseases and Nutrition Research 13.848
Dr. Jay Hoofnagle, Director
Division of Digestive Diseases and Nutrition
Room 9A23, Bldg. 31, NIH
Bethesda, MD 20892   (301) 496-1333

* Kidney Diseases, Urology and Hematology Research 13.849
Dr. G. Striker, Director
Division of Kidney, Urologic and
 Hematologic Diseases
Room 9A17, Bldg. 31, NIH
Bethesda, MD 20892   (301) 496-6325

* Biological Basis Research in the Neurosciences 13.854
Dr. John C. Dalton
Division of Extramural Activities, NINDS, NIH
Federal Bldg. Room 1016
Bethesda, MD 20892   (301) 496-9248

* Allergy, Immunology and Transplantation Research 13.855
Gary Thompson, Grants Management Branch
National Institute of Allergy and Infectious
 Diseases, NIH
Bethesda, MD 20892   (301) 496-7075

* Microbiology and Infectious Diseases Research 13.856
Gary Thompson, Grants Management Branch
National Institute of Allergy and
 Infectious Diseases, NIH
Bethesda, MD 20892   (301) 496-7075

* Pharmacological Sciences 13.859
Dr. Christine Carrico
Program Director (Pharmacological Sciences)
National Institute of General Medical Sciences, NIH
Bethesda, MD 20892   (301) 496-7707

* Genetics Research 13.862
Dr. Judith H. Greenberg
Program Director (Genetics)
National Institute of General Medical Sciences, NIH
Bethesda, MD 20892   (301) 496-7175

* Cellular and Molecular Basis of Disease Research 13.863
Dr. Charles Miller, Program Director
(Cellular and Molecular Basis of Disease)
National Institute of General Medical Sciences, NIH
Bethesda, MD 20892   (301) 496-7021

* Population Research 13.864
Donald E. Clark, Chief, Office of
 Grants and Contracts
National Institute of Child Health and Human Development, NIH
Bethesda, MD 20892   (301) 496-5001

Careers and Workplace

* **Research for Mothers and Children 13.865**
Donald E. Clark, Chief
Office of Grants and Contracts
National Institute of Child Health and Human
Development, NIH
Bethesda, MD 20892 (301) 496-5001

* **Aging Research 13.866**
Dr. Richard L. Sprott
National Institute of Aging, NIH
Bethesda, MD 20892 (301) 496-4996

* **Retinal and Choroidal Diseases Research 13.867**
Associate Director for Extramural and
Collaborative Programs
National Eye Institute, NIH
Bethesda, MD 20892 (301) 496-4903

* **Anterior Segment Diseases Research 13.868**
Associate Director for Extramural and Collaborative
Programs
National Eye Institute, NIH
Bethesda, MD 20892 (301) 496-4903

* **Strabismus, Amblyopia and Visual Processing 13.871**
Associate Director for Extramural and
Collaborative Programs
National Eye Institute, NIH
Bethesda, MD 20892 (301) 496-4903

* **Alcohol Research Center Grants 13.891**
Dr. Sue Shafer, Acting Director
Division of Basic Research
National Institute on Alcohol Abuse and Alcoholism
PHS, 5600 Fishers Lane
Rockville, MD 20857 (301) 443-2530

* **Resource and Manpower Development in the Environmental Health Sciences (Core Centers and Research Training Program) 13.894**
Director, Division of Extramural Research and Training
National Institute of Environmental Health Sciences
P.O. Box 12233
Research Triangle Park, NC 27709 (919) 541-7723

* **Family Planning-Services Delivery Improvement Research Grants (SDI) 13.974**
Patricia Thompson
Office of Population Affairs
Office of the Asst Secretary for Health, DHHS
Room 736E, Hubert Humphrey Bldg.
200 Independence Ave, SW
Washington, DC (202) 245-1181

* **Preventive Health Services - Sexually Transmitted Diseases Research, Demonstrations, and Public Information and Education Grants 13.978**
Chief, Grants Management Branch, Procurement and Grants Office
CDC, PHS, DHHS
2600 Clifton Road NE
Atlanta, GA 30333 (404) 842-6575

* **Corrections-Research and Evaluation and Policy Formulation 16.602**
Chief, Community Services Division
National Institute of Corrections
320 First St., NW, Room 200
Washington, DC 20534 (202) 724-3106

* **Employment and Training Research and Development Projects 17.248**
Lafayette Grisby, Chief
Division of Research and Demonstration
Employment and Training Administration
Department of Labor
Washington, DC 20210 (202) 535-0677

* **Occupational Safety and Health (OSHA) 17.500**
Chuck Welborn, Assistant Secretary
Occupational Safety and Health Administration
Department of Labor
Washington, DC 20210 (202) 523-9361

* **Urban Mass Transportation Grants for University Research and Training (Mass Transit Technology and Technical Assistance Program) 20.502**
Office of Technical Assistance and Safety
Office of Training
Research and Rural Transportation (UTS-31)
Urban Mass Trans. Admin.
400 7th St., SW, Rm 6100
Washington, DC (202) 366-0080

* **Urban Mass Transportation Technical Studies Grants (Technical Planning Studies) 20.505**
Director, Office of Planning Assistance
Office of Grants Management
Urban Mass Transportation Administration, DOT
400 7th St., SW
Washington, DC 20590 (202) 366-1662

* **University Transportation Centers Program 20.902**
Office of the Assistant Secretary for Policy and
International Affairs
Univ. Transportation Centers Program
Department of Transportation, Rm 20309
Washington, DC 20590 (202) 366-5442

* **Labor-Management Cooperation 34.002**
Division of Labor Management Grant Programs
Federal Mediation and Conciliation Service
2100 K St., NW
Washington, DC 20247 (202) 653-5320

* **Promotion of the Humanities-Regrants/Centers for Advanced Study 45.122**
Division of Research Programs,
Regrants/Centers for Advanced Study, Room 318
National Endowment for the Humanities
Washington, DC 20506 (202) 786-0204

* **Promotion of the Humanities-Reference Materials/Access 45.124**
Reference Materials/Access
Division of Research Programs, Room 318
National Endowment for the Humanities
Washington, DC 20506 (202) 786-0358

* **Promotion of the Humanities-Interpretive Research/ Humanities, Science and Technology 45.133**
Humanities, Science and Technology
Division of Research Programs
National Endowment for the Humanities
Room 318
Washington, DC 20506. (202) 786-0120

* **Promotion of the Humanities - Regrants Program/ International Research 45.148**
National Endowment for the Humanities
Regrants Program/International Research, Room 318
Washington, DC 20506 (202) 786-0204

* **Promotion of the Humanities-Office of Preservation 45.149**
Office of Preservation
National Endowment for the Humanities, Room 802

Washington, DC 20506   (202) 786-0570

* Promotion of the Humanities-Travel to Collections (Travel to Collections) 45.152
Division of Fellowships and Seminars/Travel
to Collections, Room 316
National Endowment for the Humanities
Washington, DC 20506   (202) 786-0463

* Promotion of the Humanities-Regrants Program/Selected Areas 45.153
National Endowment for the Humanities
Regrants Program/International Research
Room 318
Washington, DC 20506   (202) 786-0204

* Engineering Grants 47.041
Paul Herer, Planning and Resources Officer
Directorate for Engineering
National Science Foundation, Rm 1126C
1800 G St., NW
Washington, DC 20500   (202) 357-9774

* Mathematical and Physical Sciences 47.049
Asst. Director
Mathematical and Physical Sciences
National Science Foundation
1800 G. St, NW
Washington, DC 20550   (202) 357-9742

* Geosciences 47.050
Dr. Eugene W. Bierly, Atmospheric Sciences
National Science Foundation
1800 G. St., NW
Washington, DC 20550   (202) 357-9874

* Biological Behavioral and Social Sciences 47.051
Asst. Director, Biological, Behavioral and
Social Sciences
National Science Foundation
1800 G St., NW
Washington, DC 20550   (202) 357-9854

* Scientific, Technological and International Affairs (STIA) 47.053
Asst. Director, Directorate for Scientific,
Technological and International Affairs
National Science Foundation
1800 G. St., NW
Washington, DC 20550   (202) 357-7631

* Studies and Program Assessment 47.068
Office of Studies and Program Assessment
National Science Foundation
1800 G. St., NW
Washington, DC 20500   (202) 357-7425

* Research Initiation and Improvement 47.069
Division of Research Initiation and Improvement
National Science Foundation
1800 G St., N.W.
Washington, DC 20550   (202) 357-7552

* Computer and Information Science and Engineering (SISE) 47.070
Asst Director, Computer and Information
Science and Engineering
National Science Foundation
1800 G St., NW, Rm 306
Washington, DC 20550   (202) 357-7936

* Science and Technology Centers 47.073
Director, Office of Science and Technology

Research Centers Development
National Science Foundation
1800 G St., NW
Washington, DC 20550   (202) 357-9808

* Environmental Protection-Consolidated Research 66.500
Director, Research Grants Staff
RD-675, EPA
Washington, DC 20460   (202) 382-7473

* Pesticides Control Research 66.502
EPA, Grants Administration Division
PM 216
Washington, DC 20460

* Solid Waste Disposal Research 66.504
Director, Research Grants Staff
RD-675, EPA
Washington, DC 20460.   (202) 382-7473

* Water Pollution Control-Research, Development, and Demonstration 66.505
Director, Research Grants Staff, RD 675, EPA,
Washington, DC 20460   (202) 382-7473

* Safe Drinking Water Research and Demonstration 66.506
Director, Office of Research Grants
RD-675, EPA
Washington, DC 20460   (202) 382-7473

* Toxic Substances Research 66.507
Director, Research Grants Staff, RD-675, EPA
Washington, DC 20460   (202) 382-7473

* Superfund Innovative Technology Evaluation Program (SITE) 66.806
Richard Valentinetti, Chief
Hazardous Waste/Superfund Staff, EPA
401 M St., SW
Washington, DC 204670   (202) 382-2611

* University-Laboratory Cooperative Program 81.004
Larry L. Barker, Division of University and
Industry Programs
Office of Energy Research, DOW
Washington, DC 20585   (202) 586-8947

* Energy-Related Inventions 81.036
George Lewitt, Director
Office of Energy Related Inventions
National Institute of Standards and Technology
Gaithersburg, MD 20899   (301) 975-5500

* Basic Energy Sciences, High Energy and Nuclear Physics, Magnetic Fusion Energy, Health and Environmental Research, Program Analysis and Field Operations Management 81.049
William Burrier, Division of Acquisition and
Assistance Management Office of Energy Research, DOW
Mail Stop G-236
Washington, DC 20545   (301) 353-4946

* Energy Conservation for Institutional Buildings 81.052
Elmer Lee
Institutional Conservation Programs Division
Office of Conservation and Renewable Energy
CE-231, DOE
Washington, DC 20585 Telephone   (202) 586-8034

* University Coal Research 81.057
Mr. Jack Jennings
Office of Technical Coordination
Assistant Secretary of Fossil Energy
Washington, DC 20545   (202) 353-4251

* University Research Instrumentation 81.077
Donna J. Prokop, Division of University
and Industry Program
Office of Energy Research, DOE
Washington, DC 20585   (202) 586-8910

* Industrial Energy Conservation 81.078
James Demetrops, Office of Industrial Programs
CE-14, DOE
Washington, DC 20585   (202) 586-9495

*** Biofuels and Municipal Waste Technology and
Regional Programs 81.079**
Nicholas Lailas
Biofuels, and Municipal Waste Technology
Division, DOE
Washington, DC 20585   (202) 586-8021

* Energy Policy, Planning and Development 81.080
Stephen F. Durbin, Resource Management Office
Policy Planning and Analysis
Forrestal Bldg
1000 Independence Ave., SW
Washington, DC 20585   (202) 586-5325

*** Minority Educational Institution Research
Travel Fund (MIRT) 81.083**
Isiah O. Sewell, Office of Minority Economic Impact
MI-2.2, DOE
Forrestal Bldg. Rm 5B-110
Washington, DC 20585   (202) 586-1953

*** Conservation Research and Development
(Conservation) 81.086**
Noel K. Cole, Office of Deputy Assistant
Secretary for Conservation
Conservation and Renewable Energy
Washington, DC 20585   (202) 586-9232

*** Renewable Energy Research and Development
(Renewable Energy) 81.087**
Judy Florance
Renewable Energy-Research and Technology
Integration, DOE
Washington, DC 20585   (202) 586-9282

* International Affairs and Energy Emergencies 81.088
Dorothy Hawkins, Management Services Staff
International Affairs and Energy Emergencies
Forrestal Bldg.
1000 Independence Ave., SW
Washington, DC 20585   (202) 586-2995

* Fossil Energy Research and Development 81.089
Mr. Dwight Mottet
DOE, Fossil Energy Program
Germantown, MD 20545   (202) 353-2621

*** Socioeconomic and Demographic Research, Data
and Other Information 81.091**
Georgia R. Johnson
DOE, Forrestal Bldg. Room 5B-110
Washington, DC 20585   (202) 586-1593

* Remedial Action and Waste Technology 81.092
Office of Remedial Action and Waste Technology

Assist Secretary for Nuclear Energy, DOE
Washington, DC 20545   (301) 353-5006

*** Nuclear Energy Policy Planning and Development
81.093**
A.S. Lyman
Office of Nuclear Energy
Germantown Bldg.
Washington, DC 20545   (301) 353-4380

* Minority Educational Institution Assistance 81.094
Isiah O. Sewell
Office of Minority Economic Impact, DOE
1000 Independence Ave., SW
Washington, DC 20585   (202) 586-1593

*** Nuclear Energy, Reactor Systems, Development,
and Technology 81.095**
J. Colsh
Office of Nuclear Energy
Germantown Bldg.
Washington, DC 20545   (301) 353-3795

* Innovative Clean Coal Technology 81.096
C. Lowell Miller
DOE, Fossil Energy Program
Clean Coal Technology/Innovative Control Technology
Washington, DC 20585   (202) 586-7150

*** International Research and Studies (HEA
Title VI Research and Studies) 84.017**
Division of Advanced Training and Research
International Education Programs
Department of Education
7 and D St., SW
Washington, DC 20202   (202) 732-3297

*** Handicapped-Innovation and Development (Research
in Education for the Handicapped) 84.023**
Division of Innovation and Development
Office of Asst. Secretary for Special Education
and Rehabilitative Services
Department of Education
400 Maryland Ave., SW
Washington, DC 20202

*** Library Research and Demonstration (HEA
Title II-B) 84.039**
Yvonne Carter
Library Development Staff
Department of Education
555 New Jersey Ave., NW
Washington, DC 20208-1430   (202) 357-6320

* National Vocational Education Research 84.051
Glenn C. Boerrigter
Department of Education, Division of National
Programs
400 Maryland Ave., SW
Washington, DC 20202   (202) 732-2367

* Educational Research and Development 84.117
Department of Education
Office of Educational Research and Improvement
555 New Jersey Ave., NW
Washington, DC 20208   (202) 357-6079

* Secretary's Discretionary 84.122
Department of Education, FIRST
Office of Educational, Research and Improvements
Washington, DC 20202   (202) 357-6496

* National Institute on Disability and Rehabilitation Research 84.133

Director, National Institute on Disability
and Rehabilitation Research
Department of Education
400 Maryland Ave., SW
Washington, DC 20202   (202) 732-4532

* Handicapped-Special Studies 84.159

Division of Innovation and Development

Office of Special Education Programs
400 Maryland Ave., SW
Washington, DC 20202   (202) 732-1119

* National Adult Education Research 84.191

Richard F. DiColar
Division of National Programs
Office of Vocational and Adult Education
Department of Education
400 Maryland Ave., SW
Washington, DC 20202   (202) 732-2362

Artists, Designers, Performers

* See also Careers and Workplace; Research Grants in Every Field Chapter

Here is a sampling of the opportunities for dancers, fashion designers, sculptors, theater companies, musicians, and other artists but a complete list of federal grants for artists is outlined in "Money for the Arts" in this chapter. The Performing Arts Library listed below serves as a clearinghouse for information and reference assistance on dance, theater, opera, music as well as film and broadcasting.

* Actors, Mimes, and Playwrights Grants

Theater Program
National Endowment for the Arts
1100 Pennsylvania Ave., NW, Room 608
Washington, DC 20506   (202) 682-5425
The Theater Program provides financial assistance for the creation and presentation of work by professional artists, primarily in companies, and to bring the work to locales where theater is generally not available. There are fellowships for mimes and solo performance artists, as well as for playwrights. The Professional Theater Training category is designed to encourage efforts to raise professional standards by assisting professional training of theater artists. Grants are also available to organizations and publishers for projects and services that address the needs of the theater. Grants can be made to individuals and non-profit organizations if such donations qualify as charitable deductions under Section 170(c) of the Internal Revenue Code of 1954.

* American Culture and Folk Art Grants

Folk Arts Program
National Endowment for the Arts
1100 Pennsylvania Ave., NW, Room 725
Washington, DC 20506   (202) 682-5449
The Folk Arts Program supports the traditional arts that have grown through time within the many groups that make up the United States. The Program's objectives are to present and enhance this multi-cultural artistic heritage and to make it more available to a wider public audience. The Program offers grants for the presentation and documentation of traditional arts and artists, as well as for supporting the development of state- or regionally-based folk arts programs. Fellowships are given to master folk artists to provide national recognition.

* Art Grant Application Guide

Public Information Offices
National Endowment for the Arts
1100 Pennsylvania Ave., NW, Room 617
Washington, DC 20506   (202) 682-5400
The National Endowment for the Arts offers a free publication, the *Guide to the National Endowment for the Arts*, which outlines its various programs and grants, and provides a calendar of deadlines, as well as application information for the grants. Regional offices and other related agencies are also listed.

* Arts Education and Successful Teaching

National Arts Education Research Center
New York University School of Education, Health,
  Nursing and Arts Profession
32 Washington Place, #31
New York, NY 10003   (212) 998-5050
Major research areas include the processes of successful teaching and curriculum in arts education; videotape documentation of successful teaching in arts education; and educational relationships among the schools and cultural institutions.

* Artists as Teachers Grants

Arts-In-Education
National Endowment for the Arts
1100 Pennsylvania Ave., NW, Room 602
Washington, DC 20506   (220) 682-5426
The Arts-In-Education Program is a partnership program through cooperative efforts of the Arts Endowment, state arts and education agencies, local communities, and other organizations. The Program's overall goal is to advance the arts as part of basic education. Grants are awarded to place practicing artists in a variety of educational settings and to support other projects designed to enhance arts education in schools. Arts in Schools Basic Education Grants encourage plans and projects that promote the arts in schools as a basic component of the curriculum in kindergarten through high school.

* Classical Music Concerts

Information Office, LM103
Library of Congress
Washington, DC 20540   (202) 707-2905
A variety of cultural programs takes place each year in the Library, including poetry and other literary readings, lectures, and musical presentations. Among the most popular musical events are the Julliard String Quartet concerts featuring five Stradivari instruments given to the Library in the 1930s. Other gifts have brought the Library a variety of musical pieces including two Bach cantatas and sketches for portions of two Beethoven quartets. Recordings of Julliard concerts and many other programs are played on radio stations across the country, and lectures are often published for distribution. Also prints and photographs, maps and musical scores, rare books, and manuscripts are drawn from the collections and displayed in the Library in continually changing exhibitions. Many exhibits are sent on tour to libraries and museums across the nation. A free monthly calendar of events is available by written request.

* Dance and Choreography Grants

Dance Program
National Endowment for the Arts
1100 Pennsylvania Ave., NW, Room 621
Washington, DC 20506   (202) 682-5435
The Dance Program focuses on American dance, and offers grants to dance companies, choreographers, and dance organizations to allow for the improvement of their staffs, as well as supporting performers and performances and the commissioning of new work. The program also offers grants to organizations and individuals who provide services to dancers, choreographers and companies, such as those that provide performance space or communication within the dance world. A Choreographers Fellowship has been established which provides financial assistance for an individual's artistic growth, and the funds can be used for any project which aids in creative development. Grants can be made to individuals or to non-profit organizations if such donations qualify as charitable deductions under Section 170(c) of the Internal Revenue Code of 1954.

* Distinguished Designer Fellowships

Design Arts Program
National Endowment for the Arts
1100 Pennsylvania Ave., NW, Room 625
Washington, DC 20506   (202) 682-5437
Distinguished Designer Fellowships are awarded to people who have made lifetime contributions to the field of design, so as to allow them time to explore new concepts and ideas in design. Grants are also made to organizations that award design fellowships to broaden the base of support for the field. The Design Arts Program supports projects in the fields of architecture, landscape architecture, urban design, historic preservation, urban planning, interior design, industrial design, graphic design, and fashion design. Grants can be made to individual, or to non-profit organizations, including arts groups and local and state governments if such donations qualify as charitable deductions under Section 170(c) of the Internal Revenue Code of 1954. Grants can range from $5,000 to $40,000.

* Duck Stamp Design Competition

Federal Duck Stamp Office
U.S. Fish and Wildlife Service
4401 N. Fairfax Drive
Arlington, VA 22203   (703) 358-2020
Each year, a Duck Stamp Design Competition is held, with the winning design chosen by a panel of waterfowl and art experts. Any artist can enter the contest by submitting a 7 X 10 inch waterfowl design and paying an entry fee. The winner receives a pane of stamps bearing his or her design. Winning artists also sell prints of their prize entries which are eagerly sought by collectors.

* Fashion, Graphic, Industrial Designers Grants

Design Arts Program
National Endowment for the Arts
1100 Pennsylvania Ave., NW, Room 625
Washington, DC 20506   (202) 682-5437

The Design Arts Program supports projects in the fields of architecture, landscape architecture, urban design, historic preservation, urban planning, interior design, industrial design, graphic design, and fashion design. Grants are given to projects that advance design through practice, theory and research, media, and education concerning design. Some examples may be to produce a new graphic system, to study the theory of landscape architecture, or to produce a film on design issues. Grants are also made to organizations that award design fellowships to broaden the base of support for the field.

Grants can be made to individual, or to non-profit organizations, including arts groups and local and state governments if such donations qualify as charitable deductions under Section 170(c) of the Internal Revenue Code of 1954. Grants can range from $5,000 to $40,000.

* Folklife Crafts and American Traditions

Office of Folklife Programs
Smithsonian Institution
955 L'Enfant Plaza
Washington, DC 20590   (202) 287-3424

Through its annual Festival of American Folklife, the Smithsonian created a program of folklife presentations for the general public for two weeks each summer. The Office also carries on research in folklife traditions, publishes documentary and analytical studies, develops and organizes exhibitions with folklife themes, and cooperates with Universities and other institutions in presentation projects involving traditional craftsman and performing artists.

* Free National Gallery Concerts

National Gallery of Art
Constitution & 6th St., NW
Washington, DC 20565   (202) 842-6353

Free concerts are presented in the East Garden Court every Sunday evening, September to June. The National Gallery Orchestra performs and features guest musicians as well. Concerts are announced in the Calendar of Events.

* Jazz Performers, Choruses and Grants for Other Musicians

Music Program
National Endowment for the Arts
1100 Pennsylvania Ave., NW, Room 702
Washington, DC 20506   (202) 682-5445

The Music Program provides support for the creation and performance of music, with an emphasis on assisting the growth of American music and musicians. Fellowships for composers and collaborators, jazz performers and composers are designed to help create or complete new work. Jazz study apprenticeships are available to aspiring performers and professionals. Grants are awarded to solo recitalists to assist with study, rehearsal, and preparation costs. Support is available for single-music and multi-music presenters and for music festivals. Grants help jazz organizations hire professional management personnel and assist organizations with innovative projects that benefit the field of jazz. Music ensembles, choruses, and orchestras can receive grants to help pay a variety of expenses, such as salaries, touring, or collaboration with other groups. Music professional training supports music and advanced training on programs leading to professional careers in music. Grants also assist non-profit organizations and individuals in recording and distributing American music, and to establish a variety of residencies for composers or ensembles.

* Museum Artistic Initiative Grants

Museum Program
National Endowment for the Arts
1100 Pennsylvania Ave., NW, Room 624
Washington, DC 20506   (202) 682-5442

The Museum Program is designed to meet the needs of the museum field by providing funding for a variety of projects. The first is Professional Development, where they award grants for formal museum training programs, internships, and apprenticeships, as well as providing fellowships to museum professionals for independent study. The second category is Utilization of Museum Resources, which is designed to help organizations make greater use of museum collections and other resources. Grants help with reinstallation, exhibitions, and collection sharing. Grants can be used to develop related programs and events that enrich these presentations, including the preparation and publication of exhibition catalogs. The Education category provides for educational programs for the community, which can include outside specialists, and the Catalog category supports the cataloging of a permanent museum collection and the publication of materials related to the collection. Special Artistic Initiatives is designed to encourage long-term programming by museums and should include a unifying, thematic framework. The Museum Program helps museums conserve collections by providing grants for planning, conservation, and training. Grants also aid in collection maintenance through solving problems in

climate control, security, and storage. Museums are encouraged to purchase works by living American artists, as well as to mount or participate in special exhibitions.

* Musicians Overseas Concert Tours

Artistic Ambassador Program
Office of Private Sector Programs
Bureau of Educational and Cultural Affairs
United States Information Agency
301 Fourth St., SW, Room 100
Washington, DC 20547   (202) 485-7338

This program, begun in 1983, sends gifted American musicians who are not under professional management on overseas tours, where they give public concerts and work with music students and faculties. The program began with pianists, and now also includes piano-violin-cello trios. Contact this office for information on the selection process and tour itineraries.

* Opera and Musical Theater Funding

Opera-Musical Theater Program
National Endowment for the Arts
1100 Pennsylvania Ave., NW, Room 703
Washington, DC 20506   (202) 682-5447

The Opera-Musical Theater Program assists all forms of music theater generally involving voice. Grants support professional opera and musical theater production organizations, and the creation, development, rehearsal, and production of new American or seldom-produced works. Funds are available to bring performances to areas where they generally do not take place. Independent producers can also receive support for the development of new works. National service organizations and special projects. Individual and non-profit organizations can apply for grants, if such donations qualify as charitable deduction under Section 170(c) of the Internal Revenue Code of 1954.

* Overseas Speaking Opportunities for Artists

American Participants (AmParts)
Office of Program Coordination and Development
United States Information Agency
301 Fourth St., SW, Room 550
Washington, DC 20547   (202) 485-2764

AmParts are experts in a field--usually economics, international affairs, literature, the arts, U.S. political and social processes, sports, science, or technology--sent abroad by USIA to meet with groups or individual professional counterparts. Recruited on the basis of requests of USIA staff in other countries, AmParts often engage in informal lecture/discussions with small groups, grant media interviews, or speak before larger audiences. Those interested in the American Participant program are invited to submit a brief letter indicating times of availablity, along with a curriculum vitae and at least two lecture topics with brief talking points.

* Performing Artists International Tours

National Endowment for the Arts
1100 Pennsylvania Ave., NW, Room 517
Washington, DC 20506   (202) 682-5562

The Rockefeller Foundation, the United States Information Agency, and the Arts Endowment jointly fund performing artists invited to international festivals abroad and fund U.S. representation at major international exhibitions of visual art. Fellowships are also available to artists in various disciplines to work and study in Japan and France.

* Performing Arts and Visual Arts Copyright

Entries Catalogs
Superintendent of Documents
Government Printing Office
Washington, DC 20402   (202) 783-3238

The following copyright catalogs, which list materials registered only during the period covered by each issue, are available on microfiche only and are sold as individual subscriptions:

Part 1: Nondramatic Literary Works (quarterly) $11.00 per year.
Part 2: Serials and Periodicals (semi-annually) $5.00 per year.
Part 3: Performing Arts (quarterly) $11.00 per year.
Part 4: Motion Pictures and Filmstrips (semi-annually) $5 per year.
Part 5: Visual Arts (excluding maps) (semi-annually) $5 per year.

* Performing Arts Clearinghouse

John F. Kennedy Center for the Performing Arts
2700 F St. N.W.
Washington, DC 20566   (202) 872-0466

The Performing Arts Library is a joint project of the Library of Congress and the Kennedy Center, and offers information and reference assistance on dance, theater, opera, music, film, and broadcasting.

Arts and Humanities

Performing Arts Resource Center

Performing Arts Reading Room
Room LM113
Library of Congress
Washington, DC 20540 (202) 707-5504

The Performing Arts Reading Room houses the Library of Congress's non-book collections in the performing arts area: music, dance, sound recordings, motion pictures, and television. The collection includes more than 4,000,000 pieces of music and manuscripts, some 300,000 books and pamphlets, and about 350,000 sound recordings reflecting the development of music in Western civilization from earliest times to the present. Reference services are available. Adjacent to the reading room is the Recorded Sound Reference Center for users primarily interested in sound recordings and radio materials. Listening facilities are available in the reading room, but their use is limited of those doing research of a specific nature leading to publication or production. Musicians who wish to play music drawn from the Library's collection may use the piano available in an adjacant sound proof room.

* Polar Expeditions for Artists and Photographers

Ice Operations Division
Office of Navigation Safety and Waterways Services
U.S. Coast Guard
U.S. Department of Transportation
2100 2nd St., SW, Room 1202 A
Washington, DC 20593-0001 (202) 267-1450

The Coast Guard furnishes vessels to other agencies, such as the National Science Foundation, U.S. Geological Survey, and the Navy, to conduct research and ice operations in Arctic and Antarctic waters. The agencies sponsoring the missions select scientists, researchers, students, and in some cases, journalists, photographers, and artists to accompany the mission when space is available. This office is a good starting point for obtaining information on the pertinence of a mission to your field, to be directed to the appropriate agency sponsors, and for information about the data collected during missions.

* Surveys of Educational Schooling

University of Illinois at Urbana - Champaign
College of Applied and Fine Arts
105 Davenport House
809 South Wright St.
Champaign, IL 61820-6219 (217) 333-2186

Major research areas include the development and validation of standardized achievement tests in the area of artistic processes and techniques in art history; national study on literacy and art education; role of music in general education; status surveys in art, visual, dance and drama in the elementary and secondary schools; drama/theatre, visual and dance; influence on culture condition on the learning of arts; development of computer assisted testing (music education); design of studies in dance; designs of studies in theatre; status survey of music education in elementary and secondary schools; and arts education field work: observational studies.

* Studios, Exhibits, and Funding for Artists

Inter-Arts Program
National Endowment for the Arts
1100 Pennsylvania Ave., NW, Room 710
Washington, DC 20506 (202) 682-5444

The Inter-Arts Program supports projects which emphasize the creation, production, and exhibition of new works that cross the lines of individual disciplines of arts. The program funds presenting organizations, artists' colonies, and service organizations, as well as interdisciplinary projects involving original work by artists in a variety of disciplines. Grants help professional presenters improve their ability to present diverse arts programming in their community, and assist arts agencies that help presenters strengthen their skills in presenting artists. Grants can also be made to artists' colonies that provide studios, living space, and uninterrupted time to creative artists.

* Theater Company Funding

Theater Program
National Endowment for the Arts
1100 Pennsylvania Ave., NW, Room 608
Washington, DC 20506 (202) 682-5425

The Theater Program provides financial assistance for the creation and presentation of work by professional artists, primarily in companies, and to bring the work to locales where theater is generally not available. There are fellowships for mimes and solo performance artists, as well as for playwrights. The Professional Theater Training category is designed to encourage efforts to raise professional standards by assisting professional training of theater artists. Grants are also available to organizations and publishers for projects and services that address the needs of the theater. Grants can be made to individuals and non-profit organizations if such donations qualify as charitable deductions under Section 170(c) of the Internal Revenue Code of 1954.

* Theater Playbills and Rare Books Collection

Rare Book and Special Collections Division
Library of Congress, LJ 256
Washington, DC 20540 (202) 707-5434

The Rare Books Division contains about 300,000 volumes and 200,000 pamphlets, broadsides, theater playbills, title pages, manuscripts, posters, and photographs. The collection includes documents of the first fourteen congresses of the United States, the personal libraries of Thomas Jefferson and Harry Houdini, incunabula; miniature books and dime novels, and the Russian Imperial collection. The division has its own central card catalog plus special card files that describe individual collections or special aspects of books from many collections.

* Transportation Architecture and Beautification

Environment Division
Policy and International Affairs
Office of the Secretary of Transportation
U.S. Department of Transportation
400 7th Street, SW, Room 9217
Washington, D.C. 20590 (202) 366-4366

This is the DOT contact point for environmental issues. Staff can provide you with information and referrals on such subjects as highway beautification, transportation architecture, bicycle paths, historic preservation activities, and environmental impact statements.

* Travel Abroad for Artists and Performers

Office of Arts America
The Bureau of Educational and Cultural Affairs
United States Information Agency
301 Fourth St., SW, Room 567
Washington, DC 20547 (202) 485-2779

Arts America recruits artists and performers to visit other countries and provides some assistance to artists traveling privately. The USIA sends some 15 large fine arts exhibitions and 25 performing arts groups overseas annually. Panels set up by the National Endowment for the Arts recommends a group of candidates, from which the USIA selects the programs participants. A Speakers Program recruits artists from the fields of literature, film, and the plastic and performing arts, on the basis of requests from overseas posts. AculSpecs are American specialists, in one of the plastic or performing arts, who visit a foreign country for two weeks with a local host institution for a program of master classes, workshops, and demonstrations. Arts America sponsors about 30 of these programs a year. This office also provides support materials for major fine and performing arts projects; publishes a quarterly list of privately traveling artists; and tries to assist overseas posts in programming these performers.

* Visual Media Grants to Artists

Visual Arts Program
National Endowment for the Arts
1100 Pennsylvania Ave., NW, Room 729
Washington, DC 20506 (202) 682-5448

The Visual Arts Program awards fellowships to artists in a wide variety of visual media, enabling them to set aside time to pursue their work. It also awards grants to organizations that assist visual artists and support public art projects, such as art in parks, plazas, and airports. Funding is available for a variety of projects that enable visual artists to communicate with their peers and the public, and for a variety of on-going visual arts programs, including exhibitions and access to working facilities. Grants can be made to individuals or to non-profit organizations if such donations qualify as a charitable deduction under Section 170(c) of the Internal Revenue Code of 1954.

Film, Photography, and Media Arts

Numerous archives on broadcast and film are readily available not only to researchers but to the public at large. The government produces new audiovisuals every year on virtually every field of interest. These films, slide shows, video and audio tapes can be purchased and often rented. Grants available to the media arts community are listed in "Money for the Arts" in this chapter.

* 8,000 Government Films, Videos and Other Audiovisuals
National Audiovisual Center
National Archives and Records Administration
Customer Services Section P2
8700 Edgeworth Dr.
Capitol Heights, MD   20742   (301) 763-1896
The National Audiovisual Center was established to serve as the central source for all federally-produced audiovisual materials and to make them available to the public through information and distribution services. Through the Center's distribution programs, the public has access to more than 8,000 titles covering a wide range of subjects. Major subject concentrations in the Center's collection include history, medicine, dentistry and the allied health sciences, safety, aviation and space technology, vocational and management training, and the environmental sciences. The audiovisual materials are available for sale, rental, or preview. A *Media Resources Catalog* is available at no charge and lists the materials by subject and title.

* Aerial Photographs and Surveys
Cartographic and Architectural Branch
Special Archives Division
National Archives and Records Administration
8th St. & Pennsylvania Ave., NW
Washington, DC 20408   (703) 756-6700
The Cartographic and Architectural Branch has over 11 million maps, charts, aerial photographs, architectural drawings, patents, and ship plans, which constitute one of the world's largest accumulations of such documents. Some of the holdings are grouped under subject areas such as Mapping, which contains exploration and scientific surveys (Lewis and Clark Expedition), public land surveys, Indian affairs, topography and natural resources, navigation, census mapping, and maps of foreign countries. All the holdings can be examined in the research room at 841 South Pickett St., Alexandria, VA, from 8:00 a.m. to 4:30 p.m., Monday through Friday. Reproductions can be furnished for a fee.

* African Art and Culture Photographic Archives
National Museum of African Art
950 Independence Ave. S.W.
Washington, D. C. 20560   (202) 357-4654
The Eliot Elisofon Photographic Archives is devoted to the collection, preservation, and management of visual resources of sub-Saharan African Art. It conducts picture research and collaborates with art historians, anthropologists, filmmakers, and other interested specialists in the publication and exhibition of its images. In addition, it serves as an international clearinghouse for information about African art and cultural history. The collection is divided into two major categories: art, which includes photographs of art objects in the permanent collection, as well as in public and private collections; and field, which contains images of African life. An overall guide to the collection and a price list are available upon request.

* Air and Space Archival Videodiscs
National Air and Space Museum
Smithsonian Institution Press
Dept. 900
Blue Ridge Summit, PA 17214   (717) 794-2148
The National Air and Space Museum is reproducing its entire photo archives on videodiscs. Ten discs are planned, featuring color and black and white photographs of U.S. and foreign aircraft, as well as of the artifacts and people associated with the development of aviation and space flight.

* American Slides and Photographs Databases
Office of Research Support
National Museum of American Art
9th & G Sts. N.W.
Washington, D.C. 20560   (202) 357-1626
The Office of Research Support maintains seven research projects totaling over 530,000 art data records and over 250,000 photographic images. Each of the projects uses automation in cataloging information and images, thus providing the user with access to art information and reproductions in a variety of ways. The Peter A. Juley and Son Collection of more than 127,000 photographic negatives documenting American art and artists photographed between 1896 and 1975 by this New York City firm; and the Slide and Photograph Archives, a collection of over 90,000 slides and 200,000 photographs available for study and 20,000 slides available for loan. Please call in advance for an appointment.

* Art Slides, Films, Video Loan Program
Art Extension Programs
National Gallery of Art
Extension Services
Constitution & 6th St., NW
Washington, DC 20565   (202) 842-6273
Color slide programs, films, and videocassettes are loaned at no cost to schools, libraries, community organizations, and individuals across the nation. The programs deal with a wide range of subjects drawn from the Gallery's permanent collections and special exhibitions. A free catalog listing all free-loan Extension Programs is available.

* Film and Broadcast Resource Center
John F. Kennedy Center for the Performing Arts
2700 F St. N.W.
Washington, DC 20566   (202) 872-0466
The Performing Arts Library is a joint project of the Library of Congress and the Kennedy Center, and offers information and reference assistance on dance, theater, opera, music, film, and broadcasting.

* Film and Sound Recordings Archives
Motion Picture and Video and Sound Branch
National Archives and Records Administration
8th St. & Pennsylvania Ave., NW, Room 2W
Washington, DC 20408   (202) 523-3063
The Motion Picture, Sound, and Video Branch has 150,000 reels of motion picture film and several thousand videotapes from government sources and from private individuals and organizations. The films consist of edited and nonedited footage, documentaries, newsreels, news films, combat films, and research and development test films. The collection generally covers 1914 to the present. The Archives also holds a collection of more than 115,000 sound recordings received from federal and private agencies, and commercial and foreign sources. There are several card catalogs to assist you in research, and copies can be made upon request. It is best to call ahead for an appointment to reserve a viewing room.

* Filming on Public Lands
Land and Renewable Resources
Bureau of Land Management
U.S. Department of the Interior
18th and C Sts., NW
Washington, DC 20240   (202) 343-4896
The Bureau of Land Management issues leases, rights-of-way, and use permits for a wide variety of public lands including parks; power transmission and distribution lines; petroleum products collection and transmission systems; advertising and motion picture filming; and recreational events.

Arts and Humanities

* Fish and Wildlife Photographs

Audio Visuals
U.S. Fish and Wildlife Service
18th and C Sts., NW
Washington, DC 20240 (202) 343-5611

The Audio Visual Department of the U.S. Fish and Wildlife Service has an extensive collection of both black and white pictures and color slides of fish and wildlife. There is no charge for their lending service, which extends 30 or 90 days. If the photographs or slides are used in publications, the photographer and the U.S. Fish and Wildlife Service must be given credit.

* Folkways Musical Recordings Archive

Office of Folklife Programs
955 L'Enfant Plaza, SW, Suite 2600
Washington, DC 20560 (202) 287-3251

The Folkways Records Archive, comprising the Moses and Frances Asch Collection, contains material related to the 2,200 published recordings of Folkways Records. The Folkways collection documents world-wide musical traditions, the spoken words of significant American figures, historical events, and nonmusical sounds of technology and nature. A catalog of the archives holdings is available which includes information on how to purchase recordings of the music.

* Government Videotapes and Film Archives

Motion Picture and Video and Sound Branch
National Archives and Records Administration
8th St. & Pennsylvania Ave., NW, Room 2W
Washington, DC 20408 (202) 523-3063

The Motion Picture, Sound, and Video Branch has 150,000 reels of motion picture film and several thousand videotapes from government sources and from private individuals and organizations. The films consist of edited and nonedited footage, documentaries, newsreels, news films, combat films, and research and development test films. The collection generally covers 1914 to the present. The Archives also holds a collection of more than 115,000 sound recordings received from federal and private agencies, and commercial and foreign sources. There are several card catalogs to assist you in research, and copies can be made upon request. It is best to call ahead for an appointment to reserve a viewing room.

* Historical Sound Recordings

Motion Picture, Broadcasting,
and Recorded Sound Division
Library of Congress
Washington, DC 20540 (202) 707-5840

The sound recording collection reflects the entire spectrum of history of sound from wax cylinders to quadraphonic discs and includes such diverse media as wire recordings, aluminum discs, zinc discs, acetate-covered glass discs, rubber compound discs, and translucent plastic discs. The division has also recently made all of its materials recorded prior to 1909 available on 8-inch compressed audio discs for individual users in the Recorded Sound Reading Room using a micro computer. Included are the Berliner collection, from the company which invented and introduced disc recording, radio news commentaries from 1944 to 1946, eyewitness descriptions of marine combat and House of Representatives debates. For purchase by reaearchers, the Division's laboratory is prepared to make taped copies of recordings in good physical condition, when not restricted by copyright, performance rights, or provisions of gift or transfer. The requester is responsible for any necessary search--by mail or in person--of Copyright Office records to determine the copyright status of specific recordings. The Division also offers copies of some of its holdings for sale in disc form. These include a number of LP records of folk music, poetry, and other literature.

* Interactive Video Project

National Demonstration Laboratory for Interactive
Educational Technologies
Arts & Industries Building, Room 1130
Smithsonian Institution
Washington, D.C. 20560 (202) 357-4749

The National Demonstration Laboratory is a testing center for educational applications of interactive technologies and a clearinghouse of information about the technologies. It was established as a joint effort of the Smithsonian Institution and the Interactive Video Consortium, a group of public television stations actively involved with interactive technologies. The NDL clearinghouse database eventually will be accessible electronically. This online database will be available free of charge to all NDL Affiliates and to the public through paid subscription. The database will include information about basic attributes of interactive technologies, specific educational applications, bibliographic references, and equipment and software options. The coupling of interactive computer programs with multimedia materials offers educators the ability to maximize scarce resources, to address curriculum problems, and to reach new groups of learners. NDL conducts seminars and workshops which bring together educators, public broadcasters, and developers of software and hardware. They also identify elements of educational curricula that would be suitable for interactive video applications and distributes an assessment of interactive video user training and funding needs. Call or write for more information.

* Media Arts and Filmmaker Grants

National Endowment for the Arts
1100 Pennsylvania Ave., NW, Room 720
Washington, DC 20506 (202) 682-5452

This program provides support to individual artists working in these media and to non-profit organizations that help artists carry out their projects. The program also offers funding for a limited number of major public television and radio series that bring other art forms to a wide public. Grants are available to support productions in film and video that emphasize the use of these media as art forms. The American Film Institute Independent Filmmaker Program supports media artists working in animated, documentary, experimental, and narrative film and video. Fellowships are available through regional media arts centers, with funds also available to these centers to help make the arts of film and video more widely appreciated and practice. Grants assist organizations that distribute significant films and videotapes, and sponsor conferences, workshops, and publications. Grants can be made to individuals, or non-profit organizations, including arts centers, if such donations qualify as charitable deductions under Section 170(c) of the Internal Revenue Code of 1954.

* Motion Picture and Broadcasting Collection

Motion Picture, Broadcasting, and Recorded
Sound Division, LM 336
Library of Congress
Washington, DC 20540 (202) 287-5840

The Library's film and television collections contain more than 100,000 titles and more than 1,000 titles are added each month through copyright deposit, purchase, gift, or exchange. Items selected from copyright deposits include feature films and short works of all sorts, fiction and documentary, exemplifying the range of current film and video production. The collections also include some 90,000 stills. The film and television collections are maintained for research purposes. Limited viewing and listening facilities for individual users are provided in the reading rooms.

* Motion Picture and Sound Recordings Copyright Entries Catalogs

Superintendent of Documents
Government Printing Office
Washington, DC 20402 (202) 783-3238

The following copyright catalogs, which list materials registered only during the period covered by each issue, are available on microfiche only and are sold as individual subscriptions:

Part 4: Motion Pictures and Filmstrips (semi-annually) $5 per year.
Part 5: Visual Arts (excluding maps) (semi-annually) $5 per year.
Part 6: Maps (semi-annually) $5 per year.
Part 7: Sound Recordings (semi-annually) $7.50 per year.
Part 8: Renewals (semi-annually) $5.00 per year.

* Motion Picture Archives

National Museum of Natural History
10th St. & Constitution Ave., N.W.
Washington, D.C. 20560 (202) 357-3349

This Archives was established to collect and preserve Motion picture film and video recordings of Western and nonwestern cultures. The growing collection consists of over three million feet of ethnographic film and video records of diverse cultures from every major geographical region in the world. Access to the holdings is available though SIBIS. The HSFA performs a full range of archival functions, including locating and collecting ethnographic footage, conducting film preservation work, refining techniques for storing and maintaining archival film collections, and developing a system for cataloging ethnographic film and video materials. The HSFA sponsors public screenings and lectures, and serves as a national clearinghouse for information about ethnographic film. Researchers must make appointments forty-eight hours in advance.

* Panama Canal Photographs

Office of Public Affairs
Panama Canal Commission
APO Miami, FL 34011-5000 (507) 52-3165

8 x 10 glossy, black and white photographs are available free of charge showing the Locks towing locomotives helping ease container ships into locks of the Panama Canal. Contact this office for more information.

* Park System Photographs

Photo Library
Office of Public Affairs
National Park Service
U.S. Department of the Interior
18th and C Sts., NW
Washington, DC 20240 (202) 343-7394

This library contains photos and transparencies of the National Park Service that can be borrowed free of charge. Geologic features, living history, and natural history subjects are available.

* Photographic and Microform Archives
National Gallery of Art
Constitution & 6th St., NW
Washington, DC 20565 (202) 842-6039
The Photographic Archives is a study and research collection of black-and-white photographs, negatives, microforms and reproductive prints, which documents works of art and architecture and consists of over 1,232,000 photographs and negatives and 4,183,000 microform images. A summary listing of the current holdings is available. The Archives is open to all Gallery library users.

* Photographs from the U.S. Geological Survey
Photographic Library, MS 914
U.S. Geological Survey
Box 25046, Federal Center
Denver, CO 80225 (303) 236-1010
The Photographic Library of the U.S. Geological Survey contains a special collection of approximately 250,000 photographs. The Library may be used by the public as well as by personnel of other government agencies. Persons who wish to obtain prints, copy negatives, and duplicate transparencies from the collection are encouraged to visit the library. If this is not possible, the staff will prepare lists of specific photographs in response to requests. Many photographs are selected by searching U.S. Geological Survey publications and are identified by title and number of the publication as well as the number of the page and plate of the figure found. To obtain information on purchasing prints, negatives, or transparencies, contact the library directly.

* Photographs of Masterpieces
National Gallery of Art
Office of Photographic Services
Constitution & 6th St., NW
Washington, DC 20565 (202) 842-6231
Black and white, 8 x 10 photographs of works from the National Gallery of Art's permanent collections are available for purchase, either by visiting the Office of Photographic Services or by mail. Color transparencies of works from the Gallery, to be used for publication, are available for rental only and must be requested in writing.

* Photographic Views of the U.S. Capitol
The Curator's Office
Architect of the Capitol
The Capitol Building
Room SB15
Washington, DC 20515 (202) 225-1222
Views of the U.S. Capitol, a collection of seven popular views of the United States Capitol, are compiled from the Capitol collection maintained by the Architect of the Capitol. Reproductions may be purchased from the follwing office, but no photographs from this collection may be used for commercial purposes: Photoduplication Service, Library of Congress, Washington, DC 20540.

* Prints and Photographs Archives
Prints and Photographs Division
Library of Congress, LM 337
Washington, DC 20540 (202) 707-6394
More than 10 million items in the Library of Congress chronicle American life and society from its earliest days to the present through its prints and photographs. Items include auchitectural plans, posters, cartoons, drawings, and advertising labels. Reference librarians will assist those doing their own research, and they can furnish names of freelance picture researchers for individuals who cannot get to the Library.

* Public Lands Photos
Office of Public Affairs
Bureau of Land Management
U.S. Department of the Interior
18th and C Sts., NW
Washington, DC 20240 (202) 343-5717
Thousands of black and white photographs and color slides are available, including forestry, realty, minerals, and range subjects.

* Smithsonian Collection Slides and Photographs
Photographic Services
Smithsonian Institution
14th & Constitution Ave.
Washington, DC 20560 (202) 357-1487

Slides, transparencies, and prints (black and white and color) are available of photographs in the Smithsonian's collections. You can also order their seven slide series on a variety of topics, and most include a booklet and cassette tape. For a slide series catalog or ordering information, contact Photographic Services.

* Slide Lending Series on Art
National Gallery of Art
Constitution & 6th St., NW
Washington, DC 20565 (202) 842-6100
The National Gallery maintains a lending slide collection of over 50,000 images, which are loaned to the public free of charge. There is no list of the slide lending collection, but selections for National Gallery objects can be made from Gallery catalogs. Up to 50 slides can be borrowed at one time and may be kept for a period of two weeks. The slide library is open to the public.

* Six Million Still Pictures
Still Pictures Branch
National Archives and Records Administration
8th St. & Pennsylvania Ave., NW, Room 18N
Washington, DC 20408 (202) 523-3236
There are approximately six million still pictures in the Archives, including posters and photographs of artwork. Among the photographers represented in the Archives holdings are Matthew Brady, Carleton Watkins, William Henry Jackson, and Ansel Adams. There are leaflets which describe available selected photographs and slides in a variety of areas. Copies of still photographs are available as copy negatives and color and black-and-white prints and slides. Contact the office for information about photographs and a current price list.

* Sound Recordings of Poetry and Other Literature
Motion Picture, Broadcasting,
and Recorded Sound Division
Library of Congress
Washington, DC 20540 (202) 707-5840
The Library of Congress offers copies of some of its poetry and literature holdings for sale in disc form. Contact this office for information on what's available, along with prices.

* Space Photographs
Customer Services
Earth Resources Observation System Data Center (EROS)
U.S. Geological Survey
Sioux Falls, SD 57198 (605) 594-6511
The EROS Data Center maintains photographs from many of the space missions, including those of the space shuttle, Apollo, and Gemini. Contact the center directly for information concerning specific topics.

* TV and Radio Production Funding
Humanities Projects in Media
Division of General Programs
National Endowment for the Humanities
1100 Pennsylvania Ave., NW, Room 420
Washington, DC 20506 (202) 786-0278
The Humanities Projects in Media supports the planning, writing, or production of television and radio programs in the humanities, which are intended for general audiences. Awards are made for both adult and children's programming. The collaboration of scholars in the humanities with experienced writers, producers, and directors is required.Non-profit institutions, organizations and groups, including public television and radio stations may apply for grants.

* Washington Architecture Photographs
Commission of Fine Arts
708 Jackson Place, NW
Washington, DC 20006 (202) 566-1066
CFA maintains a file of photographs of past and present Washington, D.C., architectural projects which involve the CFA. Reproductions are available to the public for a processing fee upon written request. Call this office for information on what photographs are available in their files.

* Worldwide Film and Video Collection
Human Studies Film Archives
National Museum of Natural History
10th St. & Constitution Ave., N.W.
Washington, DC 20560 (202) 357-3349
This Archives was established to collect and preserve motion picture film and video recordings of Western and nonwestern cultures. The growing collection consists of over three million feet of ethnographic film and video records of

diverse cultures from every major geographical region in the world. Access to the holdings is available though SIBIS. The HSFA performs a full range of archival functions, including locating and collecting ethnographic footage, conducting film preservation work, refining techniques for storing and maintaining archival film collections, and developing a system for cataloging ethnographic film and video materials. The HSFA sponsors public screenings and lectures, and serves as a national clearinghouse for information about ethnographic film. Researchers must make appointments forty-eight hours in advance.

Money for the Arts

The following is a description of money programs available to artists and other interested parties from the Federal government. The information is taken from the *Catalog of Federal Domestic Assistance* which is published by the U S Government Printing Office in Washington, DC. The number next to the title description is the reference number listed in this *Catalog*. Contact the office listed below the title for more information about any of these programs.

* Promotion of the Arts-Design Arts 45.001

Director, Design Arts Program
National Endowment for the Arts
1100 Pennsylvania Ave., NW
Washington, DC 20506   (202) 682-5437
To promote excellence in design by funding activities in architecture, landscape architecture, urban design, historic preservation, planning, interior design, graphic design, industrial design and fashion design. Types of assistance: grants, direct payment. Estimate of annual funds available: $ 4,200,000.

* Promotion of the Arts-Dance 45.002

Dance Program
National Endowment for the Arts
1100 Pennsylvania Ave., NW.
Washington, DC 20506   (202) 682-5435
The Dance Program provides support for professional choreographers, dance companies, and organizations that present or serve dance. Types of assistance: grants, direct payments. Estimate of annual funds available: $ 9,152,000.

* Promotion of the Arts - Arts in Education 45.003

Dr. Warren Newman, Arts in Education Program
Room 602, National Endowment for the Arts
The Nancy Hanks Center
1100 Penn. Ave., NW
Washington, DC 20506   (202) 682-5797
To encourage state and local arts agencies to develop long-term strategies in assisting appropriate state and local education authorities to establish the arts as basic in education. Types of assistance: grants. Estimate of annual funds available: $ 600,000.

* Promotion of the Arts - Literature 45.004

Director, Literature Program
National Endowment for the Arts
1100 Penn. Ave., NW
Washington, DC 20506   (202) 682-5451
To aid creative writers of fiction and non-fiction, poets, and translators of literary works through fellowships, funding of residencies for writers and support for noncommercial literary magazines and small presses. Types of assistance: grants. Estimate of annual funds available: $ 5,000,000.

* Promotion of the Arts - Music 45.005

Director, Music Program
National Endowment for the Arts
1100 Penn. Ave., NW
Washington, DC 20506   (202) 682-5445
To support excellence in music performance and creativity and to develop informed audiences for music; throughout the country. Types of assistance: grants. Estimate of annual funds available: $ 15,650,000.

* Promotion of the Arts - Media Arts: Film/ Radio/Television 45.006

Clara Welsh, Media Arts Program
National Endowment for the Arts
1100 Penn. Ave., NW
Washington, DC 20506   (202) 682-5452
To provide grants in support of projects designed to assist individuals and groups to produce films, radio and video of high aesthetic quality, to exhibit and disseminate media arts. Types of assistance: grants. Estimate of annual funds available: $ 13,100,000.

* Promotion of the Arts - State Programs 45.007

Director, State Program
National Endowment for the Arts
100 Penn Ave., NW
Washington, DC 20506   (202) 682-5429
To assist state and regional public arts agencies in the development of programs for the encouragement of the arts and artists, and to assist organizations providing services at a national level to state or local arts agencies. Types of assistance: grants. Estimate of annual funds available: $ 25,526,000.

* Promotion of the Arts - Theater 45.008

Director, Theater Program
National Endowment for the Arts
1100 Penn. Ave., NW
Washington, DC 20506   (202) 682-5425
To provide grants to aid professional theater companies and theater artists, national theater service, organizations, professional theater training institutions, and professional theater presenters, including festivals. Types of assistance: grants. Estimate of annual funds available: $ 10,750,000.

* Promotion of the Arts - Visual Arts 45.009

Director, Visual Arts Program
National Endowment for the Arts
1100 Penn. Ave., NW
Washington, DC 20506   (202) 682-5448
To provide grants to assist visual artists including painters, sculptors, photographers, crafts artists, printmakers, artists specializing in drawing, artists creating books, video artists, performance artists, conceptual artists. Types of assistance: grants. Estimate of annual funds available: $ 6,100,000.

* Promotion of the Arts-Expansion Arts 45.010

E'Vonne C. Rorie
Expansion Arts Program
National Endowment for the Arts
1100 Penn. Ave., NW
Washington, DC 20560   (202) 682-5443
To provide grants to professionally directed arts organizations of high artistic quality which are deeply rooted in and reflective of the culture of a minority. Types of assistance: grants. Estimate of annual funds available: $ 6,700,000.

* Promotion of the Arts - Inter-Arts 45.011

Director, Inter-Arts Program
National Endowment for the Arts
1100 Penn. Ave., NW
Washington, DC 20506   (202) 682-5444
To provide grants for projects that potentially have national or regional impact. Types of assistance: grants. Estimate of annual funds available: $ 4,300,000.

* Promotion of the Arts - Museum 45.012

Director, Museum Program
National Endowment for the Arts
1100 Penn. Ave., NW
Washington, DC 20506   (202) 682-5444
To provide grants in support of American museum's essential activities and the evolving needs of the museum field. Types of assistance: grants. Estimate of annual funds available: $ 12,740,000.

* Promotion of the Arts - Challenge Grants 45.013

Challenge and Advancement Grant Programs
Room 617
National Endowment for the Arts
1100 Penn. Ave., NW
Washington, DC 20506   (202) 682-5436

Arts and Humanities

To assist on a one-time basis projects designed to have a lasting impact that can help move the nation forward in achieving excellence in the arts, access to, and/or appreciation of such excellence. Types of assistance: grants. Estimate of annual funds available: $ 18,500,000.

* Promotion of the Arts - Opera-Musical Theater 45.014
Director, Opera-Musical Theater Program
National Endowment for the Arts
1100 Penn Ave., NW
Washington, DC 20506   (202) 682-5447
To support excellence in the performance and creation of professional opera and musical theater throughout the Nation. Types of assistance: grants. Estimate of annual funds available: $ 6,517,000.

* Promotion of the Arts - Folk Arts 45.015
Director, Folk Arts Program
National Endowment for the Arts
1100 Penn Ave., NW
Washington, DC 20506   (202) 682-5449
To provide grants to assist, foster, and make publicly available the diverse traditional American folk arts throughout the country. Types of assistance: grants. Estimate of annual funds available: $ 3,100,000.

* Promotion of the Arts - Arts Administration Fellows
Program (Fellowship Program) 45.021
Arts Administration Fellows Program
National Endowment for the Arts
1100 Penn Ave., NW
Washington, DC 20506   (202) 682-5786
To provide a limited number of 13 week fellowships for professionals in arts management and related fields.Types of assistance: grants. Estimate of annual funds available: $ 200,000.

* Promotion of the Arts - Advancement Grants 45.022
Challenge and Advancement Grant Programs
Room 617
National Endowment for the Arts
1100 Penn. Ave., NW
Washington, DC 20506   (202) 682-5436
To assist arts organizations develop specific strategies to eliminate deficiencies in organizational management practice and to take carefully planned steps toward achievement of long range goals. Types of assistance: grants. Estimate of annual funds available: $ 1,300,000.

* Promotion of the Arts - Local Programs (Local Programs) 45.023
Local Programs, National Endowment for the Arts
Nancy Hawks Center
1100 Penn Ave., NW
Washington, DC 20506   (202) 682-5431
To enhance to the quality and availability of the arts by fostering expansion of public support for the arts at the local level and to strengthen the local arts agency as a mechanism for arts planning, financial support and development and to encourage joint planning for the arts by federal, state, and local art agencies, community leaders, public officials, art organizations, and artists. Types of assistance: grants. Estimate of annual funds available: $ 2,566,000.

* Promotion of the Humanities - Humanities Projects in Media 45.104
Division of General Programs
Humanities Projects in Media
National Endowment for the Humanities, Room 420
Washington, DC 20506   (202) 786-0278
To encourage and support radio and television production that advances public understanding and appreciation of the humanities by adults and young people of junior high and high school age. Types of assistance: grants. Estimate of annual funds available: $ 9,400,000.

* Arts and Artifacts Indemnity 45.201
Alice M. Wheliham, Indemnity Administrator
Museum Program, National Endowment for the Arts
Washington, DC 20506   (202) 682-5442
To provide for indemnification against loss or damage for eligible art works, artifacts and objects. Types of assistance: Insurance. Estimate of annual funds available: $ 0.

* National Gallery of Art Extension Services 68.001
Department of Extension Programs
National Gallery of Art
Washington, DC 20565   (202) 737-4215
To provide educational material on the Gallery's collections and exhibitions free of charge except for transportation costs, to schools, colleges, and libraries across the nation. Types of assistance: other. Estimate of annual funds available: $ 698,000.

Money for the Humanities

The following is a description of the money programs available to those interested in the humanities. The information is taken from the *Catalog of Federal Domestic Assistance* which is published by the U S Government Printing Office in Washington, DC. The number next to the title description is the reference number listed in this *Catalog*. Contact the office listed below the title for more information about any of the programs listed.

* Promotion of the Humanities - Humanities Projects in Media 45.104
Division of General Programs
Humanities Projects in Media
National Endowment for the Humanities, Room 420
Washington, DC 20506   (202) 786-0278
To encourage and support radio and television production that advances public understanding and appreciation of the humanities by adults and young people of junior high and high school age. Types of assistance: grants. Estimate of annual funds available: $ 9,400,000.

* Promotion of the Humanities - Public Humanities Projects 45.113
Public Humanities Projects
Division of General Programs
National Endowment for the Humanities, Room 426
Washington, DC 20506   (202) 786-0271
To support humanities projects addressed to out-of-school audiences. All projects must draw upon resources and scholars in the fields of the humanities. Types of assistance: grants. Estimate of annual funds available: $ 2,000,000.

* Promotion of the Humanities - Younger Scholars 45.115
Division of Fellowships and Seminars
Younger Scholars Program, Room 316
National Endowment for the Humanities
Washington, DC 20506   (202) 786-0643
To support non-credit humanities projects during the summer by college students and advanced high school students. Types of assistance: grants. Estimate of annual funds available: $ 400,000.

* Promotion of the Humanities - Summer Seminars for College Teachers 45.116
Summer Seminars for College Teachers
Division of Fellowships and Seminars
National Endowment for the Humanities, Room 316
Washington, DC 20506   (202) 786-0463
To provide opportunities for teachers in five, four, and two-year colleges; for scholars employed in libraries, museums, historical associations, and other humanities institution to work during the summer in their areas of interest under the direction of distinguished scholars at institutions with library resources suitable for advanced study and research. Types of assistance: grants. Estimate of annual funds available: $ 3,780,000.

* Promotion of the Humanities - Summer Stipends 45.121
Division of Fellowships and Seminars, Summer Stipends
National Endowment for the Humanities, Room 316
Washington, DC 20506   (202) 786-0466
To provide support for individual faculty and staff members at universities and two-year and four-year colleges and for others who have made or have demonstrated promise of making significant contributions to the humanities. Types of assistance: grants. Estimate of annual funds available: $ 800,000.

* Promotion of the Humanities - Regrants/Centers for Advanced Study 45.122
Division of Research Programs
Regrants/Centers for Advanced Study, Room 318
National Endowment for the Humanities
Washington, DC 20506   (202) 786-0204
To support interrelated research in well-defined subject areas at independent centers for advanced study, American research centers overseas, and independent research libraries and museums. Types of assistance: grants. Estimate of annual funds available: $ 925,000.

* Promotion of the Humanities - Reference Materials/ Access 45.124
Reference Materials/Access
Division of Research Programs, Room 318
National Endowment for the Humanities
Washington, DC 25006   (202) 786-0358
To fund, wholly or partially, projects which will improve and facilitate scholarly access to significant research resources in order to contribute to greater knowledge and understanding of the humanities. Types of assistance: grants. Estimate of annual funds available: $ 2,565,000.

* Promotion of the Humanities - Humanities Projects in Museums and Historical Organizations 45.125
Humanities Projects in Museums and Historical
Organizations
Division of General Programs, Room 419
National Endowment for the Humanities
Washington, DC 20506   (202) 786-0284
To assist museums, historical organizations, and other similar cultural institutions to plan and implement effective and imaginative programs which use material culture to convey and interpret the humanities to the general public. Types of assistance: grants. Estimate of annual funds available: $ 8,640,000.

* Promotion of the Humanities - Elementary and Secondary Education in the Humanities 45.127
Elementary and Secondary Education in the Humanities
National Endowment for the Humanities, Room 302
Washington, DC 20506   (202) 786-0377
To increase the effectiveness of humanities teaching in our Nation's elementary, middle, and secondary schools. Types of assistance: grants. Estimate of annual funds available: $ 7,344,000.

* Promotion of the Humanities - State Programs 45.129
Division of State Programs
National Endowment for the Humanities, Room 411
Washington, DC 20506   (202) 786-0254
To promote local humanities programming through renewable program grants to humanities councils within each of the 50 states, the District of Columbia, Puerto Rico, and the U.S. Virgin Islands for the purpose of regranting funds to local non-profit organizations. Types of assistance: grants. Estimate of annual funds available: $ 25,000,000.

* Promotion of the Humanities - Challenge Grants 45.130
Office of Challenge Grants, Room 429
National Endowment for the Humanities
Washington, DC 20506   (202) 786-0361
To support educational and cultural institutions and organizations in order to increase their financial stability and to sustain or improve the quality of humanities programs. Types of assistance: grants. Estimate of annual funds available: $ 16,700,000.

* Promotion of the Humanities - Texts/Publication Subvention 45.132
Division of Research Programs Texts/Publication
Subvention, Room 318
National Endowment for the Humanities
Washington, DC 20506   (202) 786-0207

Arts and Humanities

To ensure through grants to publishing entities the dissemination of works of scholarly distinction in the humanities. Types of assistance: grants. Estimate of annual funds available: $ 350,000.

* Promotion of the Humanities - Interpretive Research/ Humanities, Science and Technology 45.133

Humanities, Science and Technology
Division of Research Programs
National Endowment for the Humanities, Room 318
Washington, DC 20506 (202) 786-0120

To support humanities research designed to deepen our understanding of science and technology and its role in our culture. Types of assistance: grants. Estimate of annual funds available: $ 850,000.

* Promotion of the Humanities - Regrants/Conferences 45.134

Division of Research Programs
Regrants, Room 318
National Endowment for the Humanities
Washington, DC 20506 (202) 786-0204

To support conferences, symposia and workshops which enable scholars to discuss and advance the current state of research on a particular topic or to consider directions in which research in a given field should move. Types of assistance: grants. Estimate of annual funds available: $ 400,000.

* Promotion of the Humanities - Humanities Projects in Libraries and Archives 45.137

Division of General Programs
Humanities Projects in Libraries
National Endowment for the Humanities, Room 429
Washington, DC 20506 (202) 786-0271

To encourage public understanding o the humanities and an interest in academic and public libraries' humanities resources through thematic programs, exhibitions, publications, and other library activities to stimulate use of the resources. Types of assistance: grants. Estimate of annual funds available: $ 2,800,000.

* Promotion of the Humanities - Interpretive Research/ Projects 45.140

Interpretive Research/Projects
Division of Research Programs, Room 318
National Endowment for the Humanities
Washington, DC 20506 (202) 786-0210

To advance important original researching all fields of the humanities. Types of assistance: grants. Estimate of annual funds available: $ 2,800,000.

* Promotion of the Humanities - Fellowships for University Teachers 45.142

Fellowships for University Teachers, Division of
Fellowships and Seminars
National Endowment for the Humanities, Room 316
Washington, DC 20506 (202) 786-0466

To provide time for uninterrupted study and research to university teachers, and faculty members of postgraduate professional schools who can make significant contributions to thought and knowledge in the humanities. Types of assistance: grant. Estimate of annual funds available: $ 3,165,000.

* Promotion of the Humanities - Fellowships for College Teachers and Independent Scholars 45.143

Fellowships for College Teachers and Independent
Scholars
Division of Fellowships and Seminars, Rm 316
National Endowment for the Humanities
Washington, DC 20506 (202) 786-0466

To provide opportunities for college teachers and independent scholars to pursue independent study and research that will enhance their capacities as teachers, scholars, or interpreters of the humanities. Types of assistance: grants. Estimate of annual funds available: $ 3,390,000.

* Promotion of the Humanities - Reference Materials/ Tools 45.145

Division of Research Programs
Reference Materials/Tools, Room 318
National Endowment for the Humanities
Washington, DC 20506 (202) 786-0358

To fund, wholly or partially projects which create research tools important for scholarly research. Types of assistance: grants. Estimate of annual funds available: $ 2,615,000.

* Promotion of the Humanities - Texts/Editions 45.146

Division of Research Programs
Texts/Editions, Room 318
National Endowment for the Humanities
Washington, DC 20506 (202) 786-0207

To fund, wholly or partially, projects that create editions of materials important for scholarly research in the humanities and of interest to general audiences. Types of assistance: grants. Estimate of annual funds available: $ 2,700,000.

* Promotion of the Humanities - Texts Translations 45.147

Division of Research Programs
Texts/Translations, Room 318
National Endowment for the Humanities
Washington, DC 20506 (202) 786-0207

To support translations into English of texts and documents that will make major contributions to research in the humanities and lead to greater public awareness of the traditions and achievements of other cultures. Types of assistance: grants. Estimate of annual funds available: $ 1,100,000.

* Promotion of the Humanities - Regrants Program/ International Research 45.148

National Endowment for the Humanities
Regrants Program/International Research, Room 318
Washington, DC 20506 (202) 786-0204

To foster understanding by Americans of the history, culture and traditions of other nations. Types of assistance: grants. Estimate of annual funds available: $ 1,950,000.

* Promotion of the Humanities - Office of Preservation 45.149

Office of Preservation
National Endowment for the Humanities, Room 802
Washington, DC 20506 (202) 786-0570

To fund, wholly or partially, projects which will promote the preservation of research resources (library, archival, and other collections) relating to the humanities in the U.S. Types of assistance: grants. Estimate of annual funds available: $ 12,330,000.

* Promotion of the Humanities - Higher Education in the Humanities 45.150

Higher Education in the Humanities
National Endowment for the Humanities, Room 302
Washington, DC 20506 (202) 786-0380

To assist institutions of higher education in their efforts to improve the teaching of the humanities. Types of assistance: grants. Estimate of annual funds available: $ 7,344,000.

* Promotion of the Humanities - Summer Seminars for School Teachers 45.151

Summer Seminars for School Teachers
Division of Fellowships and Seminars
National Endowment for the Humanities, Room 316
Washington, DC 20506 (202) 786-0463

To provide opportunities for school teachers to work during the summer under the direction of a distinguished teacher and active scholar at colleges and universities throughout the country, studying seminal works in the humanities in a systematic and thorough way. Types of assistance: grant. Estimate of annual funds available: $ 3,725,000.

* Promotion of the Humanities - Travel to Collections (Travel to Collections) 45.152

Division of Fellowships and Seminars/Travel
to Collections, Room 316
National Endowment for the Humanities
Washington, DC 20506 (202) 786-0463

To advance basic research in the humanities by enabling American scholars to travel to use the research collections of librariarchives, museums, or other research repositories to consult research materials which are of fundamental importance for the progress of scholarly work. Types of assistance: grants. Estimate of annual funds available: $ 300,000.

* Promotion of the Humanities - Regrants Program/ Selected Areas   45.153

National Endowment for the Humanities
Regrants Program/International Research, Room 318
Washington, DC   20506   (202) 786-0204

To award funds that will be regranted through fellowships and grants-in-aid to support individual American scholars pursuing research in all fields of the humanities. Types of assistance: grants. Estimate of annual funds available: $ 145,000.

* NEH/Reader's Digest Teacher Scholar Program 45.154

Elementary and Secondary Education in the Humanities
National Endowment for the Humanities, Room 302
Washington, DC   20506   (202) 786-0377

To increase the effectiveness of humanities teaching in our nation's elementary, middle, and secondary schools. Types of assistance: grants. Estimate of annual funds available: $ 1,500,000.

* Institute of Museum Services   45.301

Institute of Museum Services
1000 Pennsylvania Ave, NW, Room 510
Washington, DC   20202   (202) 786-0536

To support the efforts of museums to conserve the nation's historic, scientific and cultural heritage. Types of assistance: grants, direct payments. Estimate of annual funds available: $ 211,500,000.

* National Historical Publications and Records Grants   89.003

National Archives and Records Administration
National Historical Publications and Records
 Commission
National Archives Bldg.
Washington, DC   20408   (202) 523-5384

To carry out the National Historical Documents Program which will help preserve important historical documents. Types of assistance: grants. Estimate of annual funds available: $ 4,339,000.

Historians, Scholars and Writers

In addition to source documents and other archives available to researchers, courses in historical editing and the work of an achivist are included. The section, "Money for the Humanities," in this chapter identifies additional funding and scholarship opportunities.

* Advertising Labels, Cartoons, Posters, Prints Archives

Prints and Photographs Division
Library of Congress, LM 337
Washington, DC 20540   (202) 707-6394

More than 10 million items in the Library of Congress chronicle American life and society from its earliest days to the present through its prints and photographs. Items include auchitectural plans, posters, cartoons, drawings, and advertising labels. Reference librarians will assist those doing their own research, and they can furnish names of freelance picture researchers for individuals who cannot get to the Library.

* Air and Space History Archives

Information Management Division
National Air and Space Museum
7th St. & Independence Ave. S.W.
Washington, D.C. 20590   202-357-3133

The National Air and Space Archives assembles and preserves documentary materials that chronicle the history and development of aerospace technology and exploration. Collection-level descriptions are available to researchers through SIBIS and will also be available soon in a published preliminary guide. The Archives also includes the U.S. Air Force Pre-1954 Still Photograph Collection and videodisc viewing facilities.

* Alexander Graham Bell and History of American Science

Joseph Henry Papers
Arts and Industries Building, 2188
900 Jefferson Dr. S.W.
Washington, D.C. 20560   (202) 357-2787

The Joseph Henry Papers conducts research on the life of Joseph Henry (1797-1878), first secretary of the Smithsonian Institution, the early history of the Smithsonian, and the development of American science during the mid-nineteenth century. It has over ninety thousand manuscripts, as well as research aids and reference guides. In addition, the Joseph Henry Papers curates the Bell-Henry Library, which contains the scientific library of Alexander Graham Bell and the personal library of Henry. Appointments should be made in advance.

* American Civilization Studies

Smithsonian Institution
Office of American Studies
2306 Massachusetts Ave. N.W.
Washington, DC 29590   (202) 673-4872

This office conducts a program in the material aspects of American civilization for graduate students enrolled in cooperating Universities. Interested students should apply to the American Studies department of the George Washington University or the University of Maryland, or the Office of American Studies.

* American Ethnology Archive of Historical Manuscripts

National Museum of Natural History
10th St. & Constitution Ave. N.W.
Washington, DC 20560   (202) 357-1986

The NAA holds the Bureau of American Ethnology's collection of historical manuscripts that relates to the linguistics, ethnology, archeology, physical anthropology, and history of North American Natives. It also has the administrative records of the Department of Anthropology. The photograph collection incorporates 150,000 original negatives and prints made by photographers who worked with American Indian subjects. Other pictorial materials are available through SIBIS.

* American History and Advertising History Archives

National Museum of American History
12th St. & Constitution Ave. N.W.
Washington, DC 20560   (202) 357-3270

The Archives Center provides research materials for museum staff, scholars, students, writers and other researchers. The collections are organized in four areas: Manuscripts (personal papers and records of businesses and other organizations); Advertising history; Historical photographs; and Films, audiotapes, and videotapes covering a number of subject areas. Holdings are described through SIBIS. Researchers are urged to call in advance.

* American History Branch Library

National Museum of American History
Room 5016
12th & Constitution Ave. N.W.
Washington, DC 20560   (202) 357-2414

The Library houses a collection of 165,000 volumes of book and bound journals on engineering, transportation, military history, science, applied science, decorative arts, and domestic and community life in addition to American history and the history of science and technology. They have special collections of trade literature and materials about world fairs. The Library is open to the public by appointment.

* American Portraits Research Center

National Portrait Gallery
8th & F Sts. N.W.
Washington, DC 20560   (202) 357-2578

The Catalog of American Portraits, administered by the National Portrait Gallery, is a national reference center whose files contain photographs and documentation for more than eighty thousand likenesses of historically important Americans. Arranged alphabetically by subject, the files are extensively cross-referenced by artist. A continuing Automated National Portrait Survey has made its holdings more readily accessible to researchers. Computerized indices by subject, artist, occupation, location, and medium make the catalog a valuable resource.

* Anthropology, Archeology, Bibliography and Other Interpretative Research Funding

Division of Research Programs
National Endowment for the Humanities
1100 Pennsylvania Ave., NW, Room 318
Washington, DC 20506   (202) 786-0201

The purpose of this Program is to support scholarly research and interpretation that will advance knowledge and deepen or broaden understanding of major topics in the humanities. Projects supported in this program include biographies, research in various humanities disciplines, cultural anthropology, and archeology.

* Archeological Assistance

Archeological Assistance Division
National Park Service
U.S. Department of the Interior
1100 L St., NW
Washington, DC 20005   (202) 343-4101

This division of NPS provides technical assistance to federal and state agencies on the identification, evaluation, and preservation of archeological properties. AAD is developing a series of technical publications, including *Archeological Assistance Program Technical Briefs*. The National Archeological Database is maintained, along with other archeological clearinghouses.

* Architectural Drawings and Cartographic Archives

Cartographic and Architectural Branch
Special Archives Division
National Archives and Records Administration
8th St. & Pennsylvania Ave., NW
Washington, DC 20408   (703) 756-6700

The Cartographic and Architectural Branch has over 11 million maps, charts, aerial photographs, architectural drawings, patents, and ship plans, which constitute one of the world's largest accumulations of such documents. The

Branch holds architectural and engineering drawings created by civilian and military agencies. All the holdings can be examined in the research room at 841 South Pickett St., Alexandria, VA, from 8:00 a.m. to 4:30 p.m., Monday through Friday. Reproductions can be furnished for a fee.

* Architecture in the National Parks

Park Historic Architecture Division
National Park Service
U.S. Department of the Interior
1100 L St., NW
Washington, DC 20005 (202) 343-8146

Activities related to the preservation of historic and prehistoric structures and cultural landscapes within the National Park System are administered by this office. *A List of Classified Structures* is maintained, which is an inventory of all historic and prehistoric structures in the System. A bibliography of Cultural Resources Management is also administered, listing all reports that address cultural resources in the Park System.

* Archives Center

National Museum of American History
12th St. & Constitution Ave. N.W.
Washington, D.C. 20560 (202) 357-3270

The Archives Center provides research materials for museum staff, scholars, students, writers and other researchers. The collections are organized in four areas: Manuscripts (personal papers and records of businesses and other organizations); Advertising history; Historical photographs; and Films, audiotapes, and videotapes covering a number of subject areas. Holdings are described through SIBIS. Researchers are urged to call in advance.

* Book Promotion Overseas of American Authors

Book Programs Division
Office of Cultural Centers and Resources
Bureau of Educational and Cultural Affairs
United States Information Agency
301 Fourth St., SW, Room 320
Washington, DC 20547 (202) 485-2896

USIA helps in the translation, publication, and promotion of American books overseas. The Promotion Branch organizes traveling book exhibits and supports an American presence at international book fairs. The Field Operations Branch supports the translation and publication of a broad range of titles, mostly in the social sciences and humanities.

* Comic Books and Cartoon History

Smithsonian Books and Recordings
P.O. Box 10229
Des Moines, IA 50381 (800) 678-2677

A *Smithsonian Book of Comic-Book Comics* ($21.96) is the definitive collection from the Golden Age of 1938-1955. A *Smithsonian Collection of Newspaper Comics* ($29.97) brings you more than 750 comic sequences from 1896 to the present day.

* Continental Congress and Other Diplomatic Papers

Civil Reference Branch
National Archives and Records Administration
8th St. & Pennsylvania Ave., NW, Room
Washington, DC 20408 (202) 523-3238

The Civil Reference Branch holds the records of all government civilian agencies, including records of the Continental Congress and other diplomatic records.

* Creative Writers Publishing Grants

Literature Program
National Endowment for the Arts
1100 Pennsylvania Ave., NW, Room 723
Washington, DC 20506 (202) 682-5451

The Literature Program assists individual creative writers and literature translators, encourages wider audiences for contemporary literature, and assists non-profit literary organizations. Fellowships enable writers and translators to set aside time for writing and research. Publishing grants provide assistance to literary magazines, small presses, and various distribution projects. Grants are also available to support residencies for writers to allow them to interact with their public. Literary centers may request funds but must offer a regular format of readings, workshops, and technical assistance for writers. Grants can be made to individuals or to non-profit organizations if such donations qualify as charitable deductions under Section 170(c) of the Internal Revenue Code of 1954. Grants range from $2,000 to $50,000.

* Declassified Government Documents

Records Declassification Division
Office of the National Archives

National Archives and Records Administration
8th St. & Pennsylvania Ave., NW, Room 18W
Washington, DC 20408 (202) 523-3165

This office performs systematic review and research-initiated review of security-classified records using guidelines prepared by federal agencies having jurisdiction over the information. These guidelines provide the National Archives with the authority to systematically review and declassify most records more than 30 years old. With research-initiated review, requests are submitted under the provisions of the Freedom of Information Act. The Archives then refers the classified document to the responsible agency for possible release.

* Decorative and Interior Arts Research Center

Doris and Henry Dreyfuss Study Center and Library
Cooper-Hewitt Museum
Smithsonian Institution's National Museum of Design
2 East 91st St.
New York, NY 10128 (212) 860-6887

The Study Center and Library serve as a resource for scholars, researchers, designers, and students for the study of design. The library contains fifty thousand volumes, with specialized holdings in decorative arts, textiles, and needlework, wallcoverings, architecture, pattern and ornament, landscape design, industrial design, interior design, theater design, and graphic design. Researchers are asked to call or write in advance. Photographs may be ordered through the museum's Photographic Services Department.

* Every Book Published Since 1454

Catalog Management and Publications Division
LA 2004
Library of Congress
Washington, DC 20540 (202) 707-5965

The *National Union Catalog* lists the world's books published since 1454 and held in approximately 1,100 North American libraries and other union catalogs that record the location of books in Slavic, Hebraic, Japanese, and Chinese languages (if Romanizad). The catalog is produced on microfiche, and many libraries have it.

* Federal Government's Watchdog History

Information Handling and Support Facilities
General Accounting Office
P.O. Box 6015
Gaithersburg, MD 20877 (202) 275-6241

The free book, *GAO: An Administrative History 1966-1981*, describes the role and operations of the GAO, and its evolution over the past fifteen years. The activities of the GAO offices and divisions are detailed, and their functions and accomplishments are described.

* Fellowship Program for Researchers and Scholars

Woodrow Wilson International Center for Scholars
Smithsonian Institution
1000 Jefferson Dr. S.W.
Washington, DC 20560 (202) 357-2763

The Center conducts a fellowship program for advanced research, and awards 40 residential fellowships annually in an international competition to individuals with outstanding project proposals representing the entire range of scholarship, with strong emphasis on the humanities and social sciences. Where appropriate, Fellows may be associated with one of the Center's eight programs: the American Society and Politics Program; the Asia Program; the East European Program; the History, Culture, and Society Program; the International Security Studies Program; the Kennan Institute for Advanced Russian Studies; the Latin American Program; or the West European Program. The Center sponsors an extensive series of meetings, information discussions, and formal colloquia on special topics. They also publish the *Wilson Quarterly*.

* Folk Culture Archive

American Folklife Center
Library of Congress
Washington, DC 20540 (202) 707-6590

This Center collects and maintains archives, conducts scholarly research, and coordinates the development of field projects, performances, exhibitions, festivals, workshops, publications, and audiovisual programs on American folklife. *Folk Life Center News* is a free quarterly newsletter on folklife activities and programs. The Center maintains and administers an extensive collection of folk music, folk culture, ethnomusicology, and grass-roots oral history--both American and international--in published and unpublished forms. The Archive houses more than 30,000 hours of folk-related recordings, manuscripts, and raw materials. The Archive Reading Room contains more than 4,000 books and periodicals, plus unpublished theses, and dissertations, field notes, and many textual and some musical transcriptions and recordings. A free listing of the Archive's publications is available.

Arts and Humanities

* Folklife Studies Worldwide

Office of Folklife Programs Archive/
Folkways Records Archive
Office of Folklife Programs
955 L'Enfant Plaza S.W., Suite 2600
Washington, DC 20560   (202) 287-3251

The Office of Folklife Programs Archive contains folkloristic materials generated through research for and documentation of the Festival of American Folklife Studies Monograph/Film Series. These materials document hundreds of folk culture traditions from the United States and forty-five other countries. Researchers should call for an appointment.

* Fulbright Foreign Exchange Scholarships

Office of Academic Programs
Bureau of Educational and Cultural Affairs
United States Information Agency
301 Fourth St., SW, Room 234
Washington, DC 20547   (202) 485-7360

This office develops and runs all academic programs of USIA, including the best-known educational exchange, the Fulbright Scholarship program. About 5,000 Fulbright grants are awarded each year to American students, teachers, and scholars to work abroad and to foreign citizens to teach, study, and conduct research in the U.S. In addition to the Fulbright program, the Academic Exchange Programs Division of this office administers grants to private agencies conducting complementary programs to the Fulbright academic exchanges, and has responsibilities for foreign research centers, Fulbright commissions, and seminars for foreign Fulbright students. Contact this office for more information and application forms for the Fulbright program.

* Gettysburg Address and Other Manuscripts

Manuscript Division
Special Collections, LM 102
Library of Congress
Washington, DC 20540   (202) 707-5387

More than 40 million pieces of manuscript material are housed in the Manuscript Division, including the letters, diaries, speech drafts (including the copy of the Gettysburg Address), scrapbooks, telegrams, and so forth of influential people. For instance, the Library owns the papers of 23 of the presidents from George Washington to Calvin Coolidge, as well as materials of Clara Barton, Signmnd Freud, and Benjamin Franklin. The Manuscript is open to persons engaged in serious research who present proper identification. Hours of operation are 8:30 a.m. to 5:00 p.m., Monday through Saturday (except national holidays).

* Government Agencies' Significant Records

Office of the National Archives
National Archives and Records Administration
8th St. & Pennsylvania Ave., NW, Room 20E
Washington, DC 20408   (202) 523-3267

The Center for Electronic Records administers computer files having enduring value that have been transferred to the National Archives from other federal agencies. A free copy of the *Center for Electronic Records Title List (A Partial and Preliminary List of the Datasets in Custody of the National Archives)* is available, as is information regarding their reference services and charges.

* Government Humanities Grants News

Public Affairs Office
National Endowment for the Humanities
1100 Pennsylvania Ave., NW, Room 410
Washington, DC 20506   (202) 786-0435

Humanities is a bimonthly magazine published by NEH features articles by nationally known scholars and writers on current humanities topics, listings of recent grants by discipline, calendars of grant application deadlines, guide sections for those who are thinking of applying for an NEH grant, and essays about noteworthy NEH-supported projects. A subscription for $9 per year is available from the Superintendent of Documents, Government Printing Office, Washington, D.C. 20402; (202) 783-3238.

* Government Record Management News

Records Administration Information Center
Agency Services Division
National Archives and Records Administration
8th St. & Pennsylvania Ave., NW
Washington, DC 20408   (202) 724-1471

The Records Administration Information Center is a valuable resource for all records managers. This Center can answer your specific records management questions and direct you to useful publications and other sources of assistance, along with arranging for individual assistance with planning for training, electronic records systems, developing records schedules, and other projects. *Recordfacts Update* is published by the Records Administration Information Center to share news about records administration throughout the federal records community. The newsletter provides information on National Archives

programs and initiatives, agency records management programs, and available resources. This free publication is directed mostly to federal records managers, but is an excellent resource for any records managers.

* Grants for Archival History and Preservation

National Archives and Records Administration
8th St. & Pennsylvania Ave., NW, Room 300
Washington, DC 20408   (202) 523-3092

The Commission awards grants to promote a variety of historically-oriented projects, such as archival programs, documentary publications projects, and archival and editorial education. The Publications Program provides grant money for printed and microfilm publications of the papers of famous American diplomats, politicians, reformers, scientists, labor figures, as well as corporate and organizational records. A subsidy program provides grants to non-profit presses to help support publication costs of sponsored editions. The Records Program makes grants to state and local governments, historical societies, archives, libraries, and associations for the preservation, arrangement, and description of historical records. Education programs include an institute to train scholars in documentary editing and fellowships in the fields of documentary editing and archival administration.

* Guides to Scholarly Sources

Smithsonian Institution Press
Dept. 900
Blue Ridge Summit, PA 17214   (717) 794-2148

Produced by the Woodrow Wilson International Center for Scholars, these guides are designed to be descriptive, evaluative surveys of source materials. Each guide is divided into two parts. Part I examines area collections - libraries; archives and manuscript depositories; art, film, music, and map collections; and data banks. Part II focuses on pertinent activities of Washington-based organizations, public and private. Given for each are its related functions, materials and products. The series includes:

     Cartography and Remote Sensing
     African Studies
     East Asian Studies
     South Asian Studies
     Southeast Asian Studies
     Central and East European Studies
     Northwest European Studies
     Latin American and Caribbean Studies
     Middle Eastern Studies
     Russian/Soviet Studies
     Film and Video Collections
     Audio Resources

* Handbook of North American Indians

Smithsonian Institution Press
Dept 900
Blue Ridge Summit, PA 17214   (717) 794-2148

This twenty-volume encyclopedia summarizes knowledge about all Native peoples north of Mesoamerica, including cultures, languages, history, prehistory, and human biology. This bound series is a standard reference work for anthropologists, historians, students, and the general public. It contains chapters by authorities on each topic, including one on each tribe.

* Historical Documents Editing Classes

National Historical Publications and
    Records Commission
National Archives and Records Administration
8th St. & Pennsylvania Ave., NW, Room 607
Washington, DC 20408   (202) 523-5384

The NHPRC Institute for the Editing of Historical Documents is held for two weeks each summer at the University of Wisconsin, Madison. Admission is competitive and applicants should hold a Masters degree in American History or American Studies or have equivalent training. Tuition is $250.

* Historical Grants for Humanities Disciplines Study

Division of Research Programs
National Endowment for the Humanities
1100 Pennsylvania Ave., NW, Room 318
Washington, DC 20506   (202) 786-0201

In this category, the Endowment supports research that employs the theories and methods of humanities disciplines to study science, technology, and medicine. Historical studies and studies of the fundamental concerns that lie behind current issues are eligible for funding. An example would be an historian studying the history of the Islamic hospital to better understand the development of Western medicine.

* Historical Handbook Series Bibliography

Superintendent of Documents

Government Printing Office
Washington, DC 20402   (202) 783-3238
Historical landmarks are described in the historical handbooks featured in this listing. Sites include Antietam Battlefield, Devil's Tower in Wyoming, Ford's Theatre, Glacier Bay, Lincoln Memorial, and Nez Perce National Historical Park in Idaho, among others. Free.

* Historic American Buildings Survey

Historic American Buildings Survey
National Park Service
U.S. Department of the Interior
P.O. Box 37127
Washington, DC 20013-7127   (202) 343-9625
The *Historic American Buildings Survey* has led the approach of preservation through the documentation of historic buildings, and landscape architectural and streetscape recording. Priority is given to those buildings administered by the National Park Service, to nationally significant structures (including National Historic Landmarks), and to historic buildings that are threatened by demolition. Collections of the *Survey* are accessible to the public in the Library of Congress' Prints and Photographs Division in Room 339 of the James Madison Building, First and Independence, SE, Washington, D.C. All records can be reproduced.

* Historic American Engineering Record

Historic American Engineering Record
National Park Service
U.S. Department of the Interior
P.O. Box 37127
Washington, DC 20013-7127   (202) 343-9625
Historic American Engineering Record was established to document historic engineering, industrial, and technological works throughout the country. It is conducted by the Park Service in cooperation with the American Society of Civil Engineers and the Library of Congress. The records take the form of measured drawings, professional photographs, historical reports, technical analyses, and motion pictures. This collection, like the *Historic American Building Survey*, is also accessible to the public at the Library of Congress' Prints and Photographs Division, Room 339, James Madison Building, First and Independence Ave., SE, Washington, DC.

* Historic Landmarks

The National Historic Landmarks Program
National Park Service
U.S. Department of the Interior
1100 L St., NW
Washington, DC 20005   (202) 343-8167
Under the National Historic Landmarks Program, historic sites are identified for their national significance. Sites and structures found nationally significant by the Secretary are eligible for designation as National Historic Landmarks and are included in the *National Register* and listed monthly in the *Federal Register*. Upon the owner's agreement to adhere to accepted preservation precepts, landmark designation is recognized by the award of a bronze plaque and a certificate.

* Historic Preservation Assistance

Preservation Assistance Division
National Park Service
U.S. Department of the Interior
1100 L St., NW
Washington, DC 20005   (202) 343-9573
The Preservation Assistance Division guides Federal and state agencies and the general public in historic preservation project work. Standards and guidelines are established, information on technical prservation is distributed, and training is given on technical preservation approaches and treatments. This office also administers the Preservation Tax Incentives program, the status of National Historic Landmarks, and the Historic Preservation Fund grant-in-aid program.

* Historic Preservation Council

Advisory Council on Historic Preservation
1100 Pennsylvania Ave., NW
Washington, DC 20004   (202) 786-0503
Affiliated with the U.S. Department of the Interior, this council advises Congress and the President on matters of historic preservation. The Council is composed of the Secretaries of the Interior, Housing and Urban Development, Commerce, Treasury, Transportation, and Agriculture; the Attorney General; the Administrator of the General Services Administration; the Chairman of the National Trust for Historic Preservation; the Secretary of the Smithsonian Institution; and 10 non-federal members appointed by the President.

* Historic Preservation Publications

Cultural Resources Programs
National Park Service

U.S. Department of the Interior
1100 L St., NW, Room 6321
Washington, DC 20240   (202) 343-7625
The *Catalog of Historic Preservation Publications* is a valuable listing of books on the subject of historic preservation. Books on the actual preservation of old buildings are included, as well as the procedures to follow to register buildings in the National Register. Archeological research, architecture, historic landmarks, and anthropology are also featured subjects.

* Historic Sites of the United States

Superintendent of Documents
Government Printing Office
Washington, DC 20402   (202) 783-3238
The GPO bibliography of public buildings, landmarks, and historic sites of the United States is divided into the categories of historic sites, posters, preservation methods for historic buildings, and descriptions of public buildings. Highlights include a poster of the Statue of Liberty and an historic guide to the White House. Free.

* History of the U.S. Capitol

Superintendent of Documents
Government Printing Office
Washington, DC 20402   (202) 275-3030
The Capitol provides a pictorial and narrative history of the U.S. Capitol building and the Congresses that have served there. Included are sections devoted to the Architects of the Capitol, the Speaker of the House, House and Senate Leadership, pages of the U.S. Congress, Congress in international affairs, elected officers of the Senate, a profile of the 100th Congress, women in American politics, and related information. The cost is $10.00 from the Government Printing office, but if you contact your congressman's office, you can get a complimentary copy.

* Humanities Publication Funding

Division of Research Programs
National Endowment for the Humanities
1100 Pennsylvania Ave., NW, Room 318
Washington, DC 20506   (202) 786-0201
This Program provides support for the preparation for publication of texts that promise to make major contributions to the study of the humanities. Support is available for editions of works and documents, for translation of works into English, and for the publication and distribution of scholarly books in all fields of the humanities.

* Indian Ancestry

Branch of Tribal Enrollment
Bureau of Indian Affairs
U.S. Department of the Interior
18th and C Sts., NW
Washington, DC 20240   (202) 343-1702
Tracing your Indian ancestry requires that you first do basic genealogical research to obtain following information: the names of your Indian ancestors; dates of birth, marriages, and death; where they lived; their brothers and sisters; and very importantly, their tribal affiliations. To verify that your ancestors are on official tribal rolls or censuses, contact the National Archives and Records Administration, Civil Resources Division, 8th and Pennsylvania Ave., NW, Washington, D.C. 20408, (please do not call). You may also receive assistance from the office above. The requirements of the particular tribe of your Indian ancestors will determine whether you are eligible for membership.

* Information On Demand

General Reading Rooms Division
Library of Congress, LJ 144
Washington, DC 20540   (202) 707-5543
If you need information that is contained in the material in the Library of Congress collections, the reference staff will find it for you and relay it over the phone. If the information you require is too extensive, however, the reference staff will refer you to private researchers who work on a fee basis.

* International Scholars Exchange Programs

International Activities
3123 S. Dillon Ripley Center
1100 Jefferson Dr. S.W.
Smithsonian Institution
Washington, D.C. 20560   (202) 357-2763
Handbook on International Research and Exchanges serves as a basic reference document for Smithsonian staff who travel abroad on official business or who engage in international scholarly or museum exchanges. Although directed toward Smithsonian staff, this publication can give others helpful tips for conducting research and exchanges abroad, including visas, research permits and

money concerns, and also covers issues surrounding immigration and international visitors.

* International Peace Fellowships

Jennings Randolph Program for International Peace
United States Institute of Peace
1550 M St. N.W.
Washington, D.C. 20005 (202) 457-1700
This Program provides fellowships to scholars and leaders in peace to undertake research and other appropriate forms of communication on issues of international peace and the management of international conflict. The Fellowship Program has three levels: Jennings Randolph Distinguished Fellows are individuals whose careers show extraordinary accomplishment concerning questions of international peace; United States Institute of Peace Fellows are individuals also of accomplishment, but of somewhat less eminence; and United States Institute of Peace Scholars are individuals working on doctoral dissertations in the field.

* International Research and Advanced Study Grants

Division of Research Programs
National Endowment for the Humanities
1100 Pennsylvania Ave., NW, Room 318
Washington, DC 20506 (202) 786-0201
Grants in the Centers for Advanced Study category support interrelated research efforts at independent research libraries and museums, American research centers overseas, and centers for advanced study. Grants awarded by the centers enable individual scholars to pursue their own research and to participate in the interchange of ideas among the Centers' scholars. Grants in the International Research category provide funds to national organizations and learned societies to enable scholars to pursue research abroad, to attend or participate in international conferences, and to engage in collaborative work with foreign colleagues.

* Korean War Data Files

Center for Electronic Records
National Archives and Records Administration
8th St. & Pennsylvania Ave., NW, Room 20E
Washington, DC 20408 (202) 523-3267
The Center for Electronic Records maintains military data files for all branches of the military and a variety of records on Korean War.

* Laws and How They Are Made

Superintendent of Documents
U.S. Government Printing Office
Washington, DC 20402 (202) 783-3238
The handbook, *How Our Laws Are Made*, is designed to enable every citizen to gain a greater understanding of the Federal legislative process. It discusses the various steps of the Federal lawmaking process from the origin of an idea for a legislative proposal through its publication as a statute. It is $2.50 from GPO.

* Library of Congress Reading Rooms

Main Reading Room
Library of Congress
Washington, DC 20540 (202) 707-5521
Located on the first floor of the Thomas Jefferson Building, the main reading room contains material on American history, economics, fiction, language and literature, political science, government documents, and sociology. A reference collection for these materials is also housed there. These reading rooms are not equipped to answer reference questions over the telephone, but will provide information on their collections, hours of operation, and the like.
Social Science/(202) 707-5538
Microform/(202) 707-5471
Local History and Genealogy/(202) 707-5537
Newspapers and Current Periodicals/(202) 707-5690
Science/(202) 707-5639
Law Library/(202) 707-5079
Performing Arts/(202) 707-5507
Performing Arts Library at the Kennedy
 Center/(202) 707-6245
Motion Picture, Broadcasting, and Recorded Sound/(202) 707-5840
Archive of Folk Culture/(202) 707-6590
Prints and Photographs/(202) 707-6394
Manuscripts/(202) 707-5383
Rare Book and Special Collections/(202) 707-5434
Geography and Map/(202) 707-6277
Hispanic/(202) 707-5400
European/(202) 707-5415
Asian/(202) 707-5420
African and Middle Eastern Division/(202) 707-5528

* Literary Works Copyright Entries Catalogs

Superintendent of Documents
Government Printing Office
Washington, DC 20402 (202) 783-3238
The following copyright catalogs, which list materials registered only during the period covered by each issue, are available on microfiche only and are sold as individual subscriptions:
Part 1: Nondramatic Literary Works (quarterly) $11.00 per year.
Part 2: Serials and Periodicals (semi-annually) $5.00 per year.

* Literature Translators Funding

Literature Program
National Endowment for the Arts
1100 Pennsylvania Ave., NW, Room 723
Washington, DC 20506 (202) 682-5451
The Literature Program assists individual creative writers and literature translators, encourages wider audiences for contemporary literature, and assists non-profit literary organizations. Fellowships enable writers and translators to set aside time for writing and research. Publishing grants provide assistance to literary magazines, small presses, and various distribution projects. Grants are also available to support residencies for writers to allow them to interact with their public. Literary centers may request funds but must offer a regular format of readings, workshops, and technical assistance for writers.
Grants can be made to individuals or to non-profit organizations if such donations qualify as charitable deductions under Section 170(c) of the Internal Revenue Code of 1954. Grants range from $2,000 to $50,000.

* Manuscript and Archives Repositories

Repositories in the United States
National Historical Publications
 and Records Commission
Oryx Press
2214 North Central at Encanto
Phoenix, AZ 85004 (800) 457-ORYX
The Directory of Archives and Manuscripts provides in-depth information on over 4,500 archives and manuscript repositories. Each entry describes contents of holdings, physical size of the collection, dates covered by materials, materials solicited, and bibliographic references to selected guides. This *Directory* is available for $55.

* Manuscript Preservation Archive

National Endowment for the Humanities
1100 Pennsylvania Ave., NW, Room 802
Washington, DC 20506 (202) 786-0570
Vast numbers of source documents are in danger of destruction due to the disintegration of the paper on which they are written. This program provides support to projects that deal with this problem, such as those that save informational content, improve collection maintenance, and develop preventive care practices. Non-profit institutions and organizations may apply.

* Minority Research Grants

Fellowships and Grants
Smithsonian Institution
Washington, D.C. 20560 (202) 357-3271
The Smithsonian offers fellowships and internships for research and study in fields which are actively pursued by the museums and research organizations of the Institution. Both predoctoral and postdoctoral fellowships are available, as well as Minority Faculty Fellowships. The length of the term and size of the stipend vary. The Minority and Native American Internship Programs are performed under direct supervision of Smithsonian staff, as tutorial situations.

* Modern Archives Management Training Course

Office of Public Programs
National Archives and Records Administration
8th St. & Pennsylvania Ave., NW, Room 505
Washington, DC 20408 (202) 523-3298
The "Modern Archives Institute: Introduction to Modern Archives Administration," is a two-week archival training course that offers an introduction to archival theory and practice for participants. It is sponsored by the National Archives Trust Fund Board, and includes lectures, discussions, workshops, and visits to the Manuscript Division of the Library of Congress and various units of the National Archives. The Institute is offered twice a year.

* National Air and Space Museum Branch Library

National Air and Space Museum
7th & Independence Ave. S.W.
Room 3100
Washington, D.C. 20590 (202) 357-3133
This library houses more than 30,000 books, 4700 periodical titles, 6,000,000 technical reports, and is enriched by a documentary archival collection which

includes 900,000 photographs, drawings, and other documents. The scope of the collection covers history of aviation and space, flight technology, aerospace industry, biography, lighter-than-air technology and history, rocketry, earth and planetary sciences, and astronomy. The Library is open to the public by appointment.

* National Anthropological Archives
National Museum of Natural History
10th St. & Constitution Ave. N.W.
Washington, D.C. 20560   (202) 357-1986
The NAA holds the Bureau of American Ethnology's collection of historical manuscripts that relates to the linguistics, ethnology, archeology, physical anthropology, and history of North American Natives. It also has the administrative records of the Department of Anthropology. The photograph collection incorporates 150,000 original negatives and prints made by photographers who worked with American Indian subjects. Other pictorial materials are available through SIBIS.

* National Archives Conferences and Workshops
Office of Public Affairs
National Archives and Records Administration
8th St. & Pennsylvania Ave., NW
Washington, DC 20408   (202) 523-3099
A free, monthly Calendar of Events is available which includes information on free films and lectures, as well as information on workshops, exhibitions, and tours.

* National Archives Posters and Publications
Publications Sales
National Archives and Records Administration
8th St. & Pennsylvania Ave., NW
Washington, DC 20408   (202) 523-3164
There are several brochures which list publications available from the National Archives and Records Administration. *Select List of Publications of the National Archives and Records Administration* includes publications of several finding aids to records held by NARA that are currently in print. Also included are professional archival papers and books, and other materials of interest to researchers. *Publications from the National Archives* includes guide and indices to collections in specific areas and publications that will be useful to archivists, historians and researchers, as well as general-interest books concerning U.S. history of the National Archives. *Celebrating the Constitution* booklet describes more than 50 publications, gifts, and audiovisual programs that relate to the Constitution. *Full-Color High Quality Posters from Your National Archives* illustrates 29 popular historical and contemporary posters and postcards.

* National Register of Historic Places
Interagency Resources Division
National Park Service
U.S. Department of the Interior
1100 L St., NW
Washington, DC 20005   (202) 343-9500
The National Register of Historic Places is administered by the Interagency Resources Division of NPS. Along with the Preservation Assistance Division, this office administers the Historic Prservation Fund grants-in-aid to states and the National Trust for Historic Preservation. Technical workshops and other assistance is provided on preservation planning, and a database of historic information is maintained.

* Native Americans and Other Minorities Bibliography
Superintendent of Documents
Government Printing Office
Washington, DC 20402   (202) 783-3238
The publications describing the Native American Indian are listed in this bibliography. Also included are a selection of books discussing the Black, Hispanic, and other minority populations. Free.

* Native American Indian Publications
Office of Public Affairs
Bureau of Indian Affairs
U.S. Department of the Interior
18th and C Sts., NW
Washington, DC 20240   (202) 343-1711
The following is a listing of free publications from the Bureau of Indian Affairs Public Affairs office. Due to the limited supply and small staff only one copy of each publication may be requested.

Booklists:
Book List for Young Readers
General Reading List for Adults
Languages

Legends and Myths
Music
Religions and Ceremonials
Wars and Local Disturbances
Origin

* Natural History Library
Natural History Library
10th and Constitution Ave. N.W.
Washington, DC 20560   (202) 357-4696
This library houses 330,000 books and bound journals and receives 1,963 journal subscriptions. The library consists of a main location and several subject-based locations. Topics covered include biology, geology, paleontology, ecology, anthropology, botany, entomology, and mineral sciences. Call to make an appointment or for information on the location of the subject-based libraries.

* National Registry of Natural Landmarks
National Registry Branch
National Park Service
U.S. Department of the Interior
1100 L St., NW
Washington, DC 20005   (202) 343-9536
The Park Service conducts natural region studies to identify areas that are of potential national significance. These areas are then studied in the field by scientists. Natural areas considered of national significance are cited by the Secretary of the Interior as eligible for recognition as Registered Natural Landmarks. The owner may apply for a certificate and bronze plaque designating the site.

* Newspapers and Periodicals From Around the World
Library of Congress
Washington, DC 20540   (202) 707-5650
Hundreds of different newspapers and periodicals from all fifty states and countries around the world are available on microfilm for $24 for domestic and $27 for foreign publications. Subscriptions are available or single issues can be ordered. Orders must be prepaid or charged to a standing account at the Library of Congress.

* North American Indian Handbook
Superintendent of Documents
Government Printing Office
Washington, DC 20402   (202) 783-3238
Handbook of North American Indians is the first to be published of a set of volumes that will give a summary of the prehistory, history, and cultures of the native peoples of America who lived north of central Mexico.
Arctic. Vol.5, 1984 (S/N 047-000-00398-9, $29.00)
Subarctic. Vol. 6, 1981 (S/N 047-000-00374-1, $25.00)
California. Vol. 8, 1981. (S/N 047-000-00347-4, $25.00)
Southwest. Vol. 9, 1979. Covers Puebloan peoples and general Southwest prehistory and history. (S/N 047-000-00361-0, $23.00)
Southwest. Vol. 10, 1983. Contains 56 articles about the non-Puebloan peoples of the Southwest and some surveys on the entire Southwest. (S/N 047-000-00390-3, $25.00)
Great Basin. Vol. 11, 1986. Surveys the Shoshone, Bannock, Ute, Paiute, Washoe, and Kawaiisu peoples who once inhabited the entire Great Basin region of western North America.(S/N 047-000-00401-2, $27.00)
Northeast. Vol. 15, 1978. (S/N 047-000-00351-2, $27.00)

* Overseas Research Grants
Fellowships and Grants
Smithsonian Institution
Washington, D.C. 20560   (202) 357-3271
The office also administers a Special Foreign Currency Program, a nationally competitive grants program for research carried out by U.S. institutions in countries where the United States owns local currencies deemed by the Treasury Department to be in excess of normal U.S. needs. Write or call for more information or applications.

* Overseas Tour for Scholars
American Participants (AmParts)
Office of Program Coordination and Development
United States Information Agency
301 Fourth St., SW, Room 550
Washington, DC 20547   (202) 485-2764
AmParts are experts in a field--usually economics, international affairs, literature, the arts, U.S. political and social processes, sports, science, or technology--sent abroad by USIA to meet with groups or individual professional counterparts. Recruited on the basis of requests of USIA staff in other countries, AmParts often engage in informal lecture/discussions with small groups, grant media interviews, or speak before larger audiences. Those interested in the American Participant program are invited to submit a brief letter indicating times of

availablity, along with a curriculum vitae and at least two lecture topics with brief talking points. A free brochure on the program is available from this office.

* Peace and International Relations Research Studies

United States Institute of Peace
1550 M St. N.W.
Washington, D.C. 20005　　　　　　　　　　　(202) 457-1700

The Institute of Peace designs and directs research and studies projects carried out through a process which includes the production of working papers on selected topics and their discussion by experts in public session. Working-group projects proceed through four or more public sessions involving a core group of experts. Studies are conceived on the same scale, but with a changing cast of experts. Public workshops are three-hour, monthly events designed for group discussion around a discrete topic of current concern.

* Peale Family Papers (1735-1885)

Peale Family Papers
National Portrait Gallery
8th & F Sts. N.W.
Washington, DC 20560　　　　　　　　　　　(202) 357-2565

The Peale Family Papers is a project that carries on research in eighteenth and early nineteenth century art and cultural history, with particular attention to Maryland and Philadelphia from 1735 to 1885. The project's files contain documents, correspondence, diaries, manuscripts, writings, secondary literature and some photographs of Charles Wilson Peale, his children and his relatives. The files may be consulted by appointment.

* Political Science Fellowships

United States Institute of Peace
1550 M St. N.W.
Washington, D.C. 20005　　　　　　　　　　　(202) 457-1700

The Grants Program provides financial support to nonprofit organizations, official public institutions, and individuals to fund projects on various themes and topics of interest. Past projects have included the role of third-party negotiators in the resolution of regional conflicts, religious and ethical questions in war and peace, and the use of non-violent sanctions in confronting political violence. Call or write for more information regarding grant application procedures.

* Preservation of Library Materials

National Preservation Program Office
Library of Congress, LMG 21
Washington, DC 20540　　　　　　　　　　　(202) 707-1840

The Preservation Office is involved in a constant race against time to preserve its millions of items from disintegration. Newspapers are immediately microfilmed, motion pictures are rushed to refrigerated vaults, manuscripts are put in fumigating vaults, and maps are encased in polyester envelopes. But the main problem for preservationists is acid and its affect on paper. Recently the Library's chemists developed a technique whereby wood pulp books are placed in huge vacuum tanks which are flooded with diethyl zinc gas, thus deacidifying them for another hundred years. Research continues on longstanding preservation problems. A series of leaflets on various preservation and conservation topics is available from the office.

* Presidential Documents and Public Papers

Office of the Federal Register
National Archives and Records Administration
8th St. & Pennsylvania Ave., NW, Room 8401
Washington, DC 20408　　　　　　　　　　　(202) 523-5230

The *Weekly Compilation of Presidential Documents* is published each week and contains all of the President's statements, nominations, acts he approves, weekly schedules, transcripts of speeches; basically all of his actions. A subscription is available by contacting the Superintendent of Documents, Government Printing Office, Washington, DC, 20402; (202) 783-3238.

* Presidential Papers

Superintendent of Documents
U.S. Government Printing Office
Washington, DC 20402　　　　　　　　　　　(202) 783-3238

The following volumes are part of *Public Papers of the Presidents*, a series containing documents from certain periods of the Presidency. Public messages, nominations, appointments, Executive orders, speeches, and statements of the President as issued by the Press Secretary can be found within these volumes. The volumes available from GPO include the following:

Gerald R. Ford, Book I, 1975, $22.00
Jimmy Carter, 1978, Book I, $24.00
Jimmy Carter, 1979, Book I, $24.00
Jimmy Carter, 1979, Book II, $24.00
Jimmy Carter, 1980-81, Book I, $21.00
Jimmy Carter, 1980-81, Book II, $22.00

Jimmy Carter, 1980-81, Book III, $24.00
Ronald Reagan, 1981, $25.00
Ronald Reagan, 1982, Book II, $25.00
Ronald Reagan, 1983, Book I, $31.00
Ronald Reagan, 1983, Book II, $32.00
Ronald Reagan, 1984, Book I, $36.00
Ronald Reagan, 1984, Book II, $36.00
Ronald Reagan, 1985, Book I, $34.00
Ronald Reagan, 1985, Book II, $30.00
Ronald Reagan, 1986, Book I, $37.00
Ronald Reagan, 1986, Book II, $35.00

* Presidential Libraries

National Archives and Records Administration
8th St. & Pennsylvania Ave., NW, Room 104
Washington, DC 20408　　　　　　　　　　　(202) 523-3212

Through the Presidential Libraries, which are located on sites selected by the presidents and built with private funds, the National Archives preserves and makes available for use the Presidential records and personal papers that document the actions of a particular president's administration. In addition to providing reference services on Presidential documents, each library prepares documentary and descriptive publications and operates a museum to exhibit documents, historic objects, and other memorabilia of interest to the public. Each library provides research grants to scholars and graduate students for the encouragement of research in Presidential libraries' holdings and of publication or works based on such research. Public programs of the libraries include conferences, lectures, films, tours, commemorative events, and seminars. For further information, contact the Presidential library of your choice.

Herbert Hoover Library, West Branch, IA, 52358, (319) 643-5301
Franklin D. Roosevelt Library, Hyde Park, NY, 12538, (914) 229-8114
Harry S. Truman Library, Independence, MO, 64050; (816) 374-6719
Dwight D. Eisenhower Library, Abilene, KS, 67410; (913) 263-4751
John F. Kennedy Library, Boston, MA, 02125; (617) 929-4500
Lyndon B. Johnson Library, Austin, TX, 78705; (512) 482-5137
Gerald R. Ford Library, Ann Arbor, MI, 48109; (313) 668-2218
Gerald R. Ford Museum, Grand Rapids, MI, 49504; (616) 456-2675
Nixon Presidential Materials Staff, Washington, DC, 20408; (703) 756-6498
Jimmy Carter Library, Atlanta, GA, 30307; (404) 331-3942

* Private Library Space for Researchers

Research Facilities Section
General Reading Rooms
Library of Congress
Washington, DC 20540　　　　　　　　　　　(202) 707-5211

For increased convenience, full-time scholars and researchers may apply for study desks in semi-private areas within the Library of Congress.

* Reproductions and Help for Researchers

National Archives and Records Administration
8th St. & Pennsylvania Ave., NW, Room 205
Washington, DC 20408　　　　　　　　　　　(202) 523-3218

Staff members provide reference service on records by responding in person, over the telephone, and in writing to requests for information from or about records, making original records available to researchers in research rooms, providing researchers with copies of records for a fee, and preparing microform publications of heavily used series of records. The Reference Services Branch refers requests to the branch in the National Archives that has custody of the relevant records. *Ordering Reproductions From the National Archives* is a helpful brochure which outlines the information needed to fill your request. Contact the References Services Branch for more information.

* Regional Archive Centers Nationwide

Regional Archives System
National Archives and Records Administration
8th St. & Pennsylvania Ave., NW
Washington, DC 20408　　　　　　　　　　　(202) 523-3032

This periodic newsletter includes information regarding activities at the various regional archives centers, including workshops, exhibits, publications, and networking information.

* Smithsonian Archives Guide

Smithsonian Archives
Smithsonian Institution
900 Jefferson Dr. S.W.
Washington, DC 20560　　　　　　　　　　　(202) 357-1420

This free *Guide to Smithsonian Archives* is a reference resource to the holdings of the Archives, giving a detailed listing of the records, papers, and projects the Archives has, as well as information regarding their use.

* Smithsonian Institution Library Services

Smithsonian Institution Libraries
10th St. & Constitution Ave. N.W.
Washington, DC 20560   (202) 357-2139

The libraries of the Smithsonian Institution include approximately 950,000 volumes, with strengths in natural history, museology, history of science, and the humanities. Inquiries on special subjects or special collections should be addressed to the appropriate branch library or to the Central Reference and Loan.

* State Historical Records

National Historical Publications and Records Commission
National Archives and Records Administration
8th St. & Pennsylvania Ave., NW, Room 607
Washington, DC 20408   (202) 523-5386

The governor of each state appoints a State Historical Records Coordinator, who is in charge of either the state archival agency of the state-funded historical agency. The governor also appoints a State Historical Records Advisory Board, which is the central advisory body for state projects and records planning. The Board makes funding recommendations to the National Historical Publications and Records Commission concerning records grant applications from institutions and organizations in the state. The Board may also undertake projects and studies of its own, solicit or develop proposals for Commission-funded projects, and review the progress of State Category Grants funded by the Commission. The grants fund projects for the preservation, arrangement, and description of historical records.

* Status of Presidential Documents

Executive Clerks Office
The White House
Washington, DC 20500   (202) 456-2226

The Executive Clerks Office reviews, processes, and records all documents signed by the President. To find out the status of any official Presidential proclamation, Executive order, nomination, appointment or legislation, contact the office above.

* Telephone Reference Service at

Library of Congress
Library of Congress
Washington, DC 20540   (202) 707-5522

This service provides information to callers about the collections within the Library of Congress and how they can be used. In planning your research, remember that the Library of Congress is the library of last resort--all other inter-library loan avenues must be exhausted before you may borrow a book from the Library of Congress. Always begin your research with your local library.

* Thomas Jefferson's Library and Other Rare Books Collection

Rare Book and Special Collections Division
Library of Congress, LJ 256
Washington, DC 20540   (202) 707-5434

The Rare Books Division contains about 300,000 volumes and 200,000 pamphlets, broadsides, theater playbills, title pages, manuscripts, posters, and photographs. The collection includes documents of the first fourteen congresses of the United States, the personal libraries of Thomas Jefferson and Harry Houdini, incunabula; miniature books and dime novels, and the Russian Imperial collection. The division has its own central card catalog plus special card files that describe individual collections or special aspects of books from many collections.

* Vice-Presidential Papers

Office of Presidential Libraries
National Archives and Records Administration
8th St. & Pennsylvania Ave., NW, Room 104
Washington, DC 20408   (202) 523-3312

Vice-Presidential records are subject to the same provisions as Presidential records and become property of the United States Government.

* Vietnam War Records

Center for Electronic Records
National Archives and Records Administration
8th St. & Pennsylvania Ave., NW, Room 20E
Washington, DC 20408   (202) 523-3267

The Center has records created between 1954 and 1975 by U.S. Army- Vietnam, U.S. Military Assistance Command-Thailand, and U.S. Military Assistance Command-Vietnam. Together they constitute the central documentary record on the war in Southeast Asia. They have divisional and brigade records, as well as records of combat units, which include those performing infantry, armor, aviation, artillery, and calvary functions, and those support units performing engineering signal, maintenance, and medical functions.

* Visual Arts Fellowships

National Gallery of Art
Center for Advanced Study in the Visual Arts
Constitution & 6th St., NW
Washington, DC 20565   (202) 842-6480

The Center has a four-part program of fellowships, meetings, publications, and research in the field of visual arts. The Center offers a series of discussions, symposia, and lectures. Nine pre-doctoral fellowships are available for productive scholarly work in the history of art, architecture, and urban form, as well as senior fellowships and visiting senior fellowships for post-doctoral studies. Center 8 is a publication which contains research reports by members of the Center, as well as a record of the activities of the Center. The Center also publishes an annual listing of research in the history of art sponsored by a number of granting institutions.

* Washington D.C. Historic Street Plans

Public Information Office
Pennsylvania Avenue Development Corporation
1311 Pennsylvania Ave., NW
Suite 1220 North
Washington, DC 20004   (202) 724-9059

The following publications are available:

Pennsylvania Avenue Development Corporation, Annual Report, 1988
The Pennsylvania Avenue Plan, 1974
Amendments to the Pennsylvania Avenue Plan
The Avenue Report (a quarterly newsletter)

* Weekly Presidential Documents

Superintendent of Documents
U.S. Government Printing Office
Washington, DC 20402   (202) 783-3238

The *Weekly Compilation of Presidential Documents*, compiles transcripts of the President's news conferences, messages to Congress, public speeches and statements, and other presidential materials released by the White House. The *Compilation* carries a *Monthly Dateline* and covers materials released during the preceding week. Each issue carries an index of contents and a cumulative index to prior issues. Separate indexes are published quarterly, semiannually, and annually. Other finding aids include lists of laws approved by the President and of nominations submitted to the Senate, and a checklist of White House releases. Subscriptions are $96.00 per year, and single copies are $2.00.

* White House Publications Listing

Publications Services
Executive Office of the President
725 17th St., NW
Washington, DC 20500   (202) 395-7332

Publications of the Executive Office of the President is listing of the documents issued from EOP, including where to obtain them. Contact the office above to get your free copy.

* White House Watergate Tapes and Transcripts

Nixon Presidential Materials Project
Office of Presidential Libraries
National Archives and Records Administration
8th St. & Pennsylvania Ave., NW
Washington, DC 20408   (703) 756-6498

The White House Watergate tapes are available for public listening and consist of 31 conversations that were played to the juries as evidence in *United States v. John B. Connally* and *United States v. John D. Ehrlichman, Harry R. Haldeman, Robert Mardian, John N. Mitchell, and Kenneth W. Parkinson*. This is a total of 12½ hours of conversation. You can order transcripts of the conversations for a small fee, and can make an appointment to listen to the tapes at the Archives Annex at 845 South Pickett Street, Alexandria, Virginia. The remaining White House tapes are currently undergoing archival processing.

* World War II Military Data Files

Center for Electronic Records
National Archives and Records Administration
8th St. & Pennsylvania Ave., NW, Room 20E
Washington, DC 20408   (202) 523-3267

The Center for Electronic Records maintains military data files for all branches of the military and a variety of records from World War II.

* World War II Nazi Records

National Archives and Records Administration
8th St. & Pennsylvania Ave., NW, Room 8N
Washington, DC 20408   (202) 523-7191

This office holds all the records of the German Army that were captured during World War II, and can direct you to guides to the collection.

Museums and Cultural Resources

The national museums and libraries span geographical and cultural boundaries to allow anyone to tap into arts, ethnography, anthropology, craft, architecture, archeology, history, oral tradition and folklore as well as natural history. The Museological Clearinghouse may serve as a good point of departure to locate the collections and experts in a particular time in history as well as to learn about trends in the museum world. Also refer to the section on Money for the Arts in this chapter which includes federal funding for exhibits and promotion of the arts.

* African Art National Museum
National Museum of African Art
Smithsonian Institution
950 Independence Ave. S.W.
Washington, DC 20590 (202) 357-4600

The National Museum of African Art is dedicated to the collection, exhibition, and study of traditional arts of sub-Saharan Africa. Included in the collection are sculptures, textiles, jewelry, architectural elements, decorative arts, and utilitarian objects. They have an extensive education program, in addition to gallery lectures, programs for families and films for children. A free calendar of exhibitions and programs is available.

* African Art and Culture Photographic Archives
National Museum of African Art
950 Independence Ave. S.W.
Washington, D. C. 20560 (202) 357-4654

The Eliot Elisofon Photographic Archives is devoted to the collection, preservation, and management of visual resources of sub-Saharan African Art. It conducts picture research and collaborates with art historians, anthropologists, filmmakers, and other interested specialists in the publication and exhibition of its images. In addition, it serves as an international clearinghouse for information about African art and cultural history. The collection is divided into two major categories: art, which includes photographs of art objects in the permanent collection, as well as in public and private collections; and field, which contains images of African life. An overall guide to the collection and a price list are available upon request.

* African Art Library
Smithsonian Institution
950 Independence Ave. S.W.
Washington, DC 20560 (202) 357-4875

The Library maintains a collection of 15,000 books and 280 periodical titles on traditional and contemporary arts of Africa, including sculptural and decorative arts, ethnography, anthropology, craft, architecture, archeology, history, oral tradition and folklore, and African retentions in the New World. The Library is open to the public by appointment.

* Afro-American History and Cultures Exhibit
Anacostia Neighborhood Museum
Smithsonian Institution
1901 Fort Place S.E.
Washington, DC 20020 (202) 287-3306

This museum presents exhibitions on the history and cultures of Afro-Americans. The Research Department, open for use by scholars, conducts independent studies in the areas of Afro-American history, minority and ethnic studies, and history of Washington, D.C. The Education Department develops independent programs and activities to serve the needs and interests of the local school community. These activities include a traveling puppet troupe, teacher workshops and seminars, and a circulating library of children's books for use by teachers.

* Air Force Art Collection
Secretary of the Air Force
Art and Museum Branch
The Pentagon, Room 5C941
Washington, DC 20330 (202) 697-6629

The Air Force Museum has available 8 x 10 reproduction photographs of the Air Force art collection. They will accept written requests.

* Alpine's Northwest
Superintendent of Documents
Government Printing Office
Washington, DC 20402 (202) 783-3238

The Alpine's Northwest (Large Poster). This is a poster of an artist's rendition of Washington State's mountains as the snows begin to melt, bursting with an abundance of wildflowers, mammals, and birds. Measures 30 by 40 inches. 1989. (S/N 024-005-01047-5, $4.25)

* American Art Collections Nationwide
Archives of American Art
Smithsonian Institution
8th & F Sts. N.W.
Washington, DC 20560 (202) 357-2781

The Archives of American Art publishes a quarterly *Journal* that contains articles based on its collections and features reports from the regional centers. Separate publications include: *The Card Catalog of the Manuscript Collections of the Archives of American Art; Archives of American Art Collection of Exhibition Catalogs; Archives of American Art, A Directory of Resources*; and *Archives of American Art, A Checklist of the Collection.*

* American Art Museum
Barney Studio House
National Museum of American History
Smithsonian Institution
2306 Massachusetts Ave. N.W.
Washington, DC (202) 357-2700

The house, a curatorial department of the National Museum of American Art, was built by artist Alice Pike Barney in 1902 to be her home, studio and salon. Now renovated, this unique showplace is filled with paintings by Mrs. Barney and her friends, ornate furniture, oriental rugs and decorative bibelots. It is open by reservation for guided visits, and an annual series of programs is presented in the spirit of the salons given by Mrs. Barney.

* American Arts and Industries Museum
Discovery Theater
Smithsonian Institution
Arts and Industries Building
900 Jefferson Dr. S.W.
Washington, DC 20560 (202) 357-1500

Currently, the Arts and Industries Building houses "1876: A Centennial Exhibition", which recalls the ambiance of the Victorian era by recreating the United States Centennial Exhibition held in Philadelphia in 1876. The building also houses the Smithsonian's Discovery Theater, which, from October to June, offers a changing series of live performances designed for young people and their families, including presentations by puppeteers, dancers, actors, mimes, and singers.

* American Crafts and Designers
Renwick Gallery
17th & Pennsylvania Ave. N.W.
Washington, DC 20560 (202) 357-2531

The Renwick Gallery of the National Museum of American Art exhibits the creative achievements of designers and craftspeople in the United States. The programs include lunchtime films, concerts, and other musical events, lectures and craft demonstrations, and children's programs related to current exhibitions. A free monthly calendar is available.

* American Culture and Folk Art Grants
Folk Arts Program
National Endowment for the Arts
1100 Pennsylvania Ave., NW, Room 725
Washington, DC 20506 (202) 682-5449

The Folk Arts Program supports the traditional arts that have grown through time within the many groups that make up the United States. The Program's objectives are to present and enhance this multi-cultural artistic heritage and to make it more available to a wider public audience. The Program offers grants for the presentation and documentation of traditional arts and artists, as well as for supporting the development of state- or regionally-based folk arts programs. Fellowships are given to master folk artists to provide national recognition.

* American History Branch Library

National Museum of American History
Room 5016
12th & Constitution Ave. N.W.
Washington, DC 20560   (202) 357-2414

The Library houses a collection of 165,000 volumes of book and bound journals on engineering, transportation, military history, science, applied science, decorative arts, and domestic and community life in addition to American history and the history of science and technology. They have special collections of trade literature and materials about world fairs. The Library is open to the public by appointment.

* American History National Museum

National Museum of American History
Smithsonian Institution
12th Sts. & Constitution Ave. N.W.
Washington, DC 20560   (202) 357-2510

The museum's mission is to illuminate through collections, exhibitions, research, publications, and educational programs, the entire history of the United States, including the external influences that have helped to shape the national character. From the patent model Eli Whitney's cotton gin to a Ford Model T, objects on display at the Museum embody the nation's scientific, technological, and cultural heritage. Recent major reinstallations treat everyday life in America just after the Revolutionary War, the American Industrial Revolution, and the diverse origins of the American people. You will find exhibits on agriculture, medicine, armed forces history, graphic arts, ceramics, glass, political history, and many other areas. Educational activities are directed toward both children and adults. Musical programs are offered regularly. Demonstration Centers offer participatory educational experiences where visitors may touch and handle objects.

* American Painting and Sculpture Databases

Office of Research Support
National Museum of American Art
9th & G Sts. N.W.
Washington, D.C. 20560   (202) 357-1626

The Office of Research Support maintains seven research projects totaling over 530,000 art data records and over 250,000 photographic images. Each of the projects uses automation in cataloging information and images, thus providing the user with access to art information and reproductions in a variety of ways. The research databases are: the Inventory of American Paintings Executed before 1914, a computerized index to over 250,000 paintings; the Inventory of American Sculpture, an on-line interactive database accessible through SIBIS, containing information on sculpture and outdoor monuments; the Pre-1877 Art Exhibition Catalog Index, recording works of art listed in catalogs of art exhibitions held in the U.S. and Canada; the Smithsonian Art Index, which lists drawings, prints, paintings, and sculptures located in Smithsonian scientific, technical, and historical collections; the Permanent Collection Database, comprising over 32,000 objects in the museum's collection; the Peter A. Juley and Son Collection of more than 127,000 photographic negatives documenting American art and artists photographed between 1896 and 1975 by this New York City firm; and the Slide and Photograph Archives, a collection of over 90,000 slides and 200,000 photographs available for study and 20,000 slides available for loan. Please call in advance for an appointment.

* American Portraits Research Center

National Portrait Gallery
8th & F Sts. N.W.
Washington, DC 20560   (202) 357-2578

The Catalog of American Portraits, administered by the National Portrait Gallery, is a national reference center whose files contain photographs and documentation for more than eighty thousand likenesses of historically important Americans. Arranged alphabetically by subject, the files are extensively cross-referenced by artist. A continuing Automated National Portrait Survey has made its holdings more readily accessible to researchers. Computerized indices by subject, artist, occupation, location, and medium make the catalog a valuable resource.

* Antiques amd Historical Design

National Cooper-Hewitt Museum of Design
Smithsonian Institution
2 E. 91st St.
New York, NY 10128   (212) 860-6868

The Cooper-Hewitt Museum is the only museum in the United States devoted exclusively the study and exhibition of historical and contemporary design. The collection contains textiles, wallpaper, furniture, ceramics, glass, architectural ornaments, metalwork, woodwork, drawings and prints. A joint venture with the Book-of-the-Month Club offers a 15-page series entitled *The Smithsonian Illustrated Library of Antiques*. A continuing series of handbooks surveying each

of the collections now numbers 20 titles. Educational programs offered include lectures, craft workshops, repair clinics, seminars, young people's classes, and performing arts demonstrations.

* Archeological Policies for National Parks

Anthropology Division
National Park Service
U.S. Department of the Interior
1100 L St., NW
Washington, DC 20005   (202) 343-8161

The Anthropology Division of NPS is responsible for developing service-wide archeological and ethnographic program policies, guidelines, and standards. This function is concerned with preservation, protection, and visitor use activities related to the archeological aspects of the cultural resources of the Park System.

* Architectural and Engineering Drawings

Cartographic and Architectural Branch
Special Archives Division
National Archives and Records Administration
8th St. & Pennsylvania Ave., NW
Washington, DC 20408   (703) 756-6700

The Cartographic and Architectural Branch has over 11 million maps, charts, aerial photographs, architectural drawings, patents, and ship plans, which constitute one of the world's largest accumulations of such documents. The Branch holds architectural and engineering drawings created by civilian and military agencies. All the holdings can be examined in the research room at 841 South Pickett St., Alexandria, VA, from 8:00 a.m. to 4:30 p.m., Monday through Friday. Reproductions can be furnished for a fee.

* Architecture of the U.S. Capitol

The Curator's Office
Architect of the Capitol
The Capitol Building
Room SB15
Washington, DC 20515   (202) 225-1222

A packet of fact sheets on the various features and artifacts of the Capitol is available free of charge. It includes information on the Statue of Freedom; the tile floor of the Capitol; the history of the old subway transportation system connecting the Capitol and the Russell Office Building; the Rotunda Frieze; the "cornstalk" or "corncob" columns and capitals; the dome; the historic catafalque; Washington's tomb; those who have lain in state in the rotunda; the flags over the east and west central fronts; and the architects and architecture of the Capitol.

* Army and Air Force 1.2 Million Photographs

U.S. Department of Defense
Still Media Records Center
Code SSRC
Washington, DC 20374   (202) 433-2166

This center maintains a collection of over 1.2 million photographs and views on the Air Force and Army from 1954 to the present, and on the Navy and Marine Corps from 1959 to the present. Reprints can be purchased for a nominal fee. Write or call for a general information sheet and current price list.

* Army Art and Photograph Archive

U.S. Army Center of Military History
Attn: DAMH-HSA
20 Massachusetts Ave., NW
Washington, DC 20314   (703) 274-8292

The Center maintains a photographic library and archives of all paintings in the Army art collection. They have a catalog of negatives, and you can order prints for a small fee. Write or call for their free brochure describing their collection.

* Art Donations and Bequests

Development Department
National Gallery of Art
Constitution & 6th St., NW
Washington, DC 20565   (202) 842-6372

The Gallery seeks gifts-in-kind of American and Western European works of art. All donations should be discussed with the Development Department.

* Art Exhibits for American Embassies

Bureau of Administration
Department of State
21st & Virginia Ave., NW
Room B-258
Washington, DC 20520   (202) 647-5723

The State Department is responsible for placing original American art in U.S. Embassies. Based on cooperation between the government and the private

Arts and Humanities

sector, Museums, corporate and private collectors, commercial galleries, and artists donate or lend American art representing all styles, periods, and media. Currently, more than 3,000 works of art valued at more than $35.2 million are being circulated in 123 countries. Write for an information brochure.

* Art Exhibits Insurance Coverage
Arts and Artifacts Indemnity Museum
National Endowment for the Arts
1100 Pennsylvania Ave., NW, Room 624
Washington, DC 20506   (202) 682-5442
This program provides grants for insurance against loss or damage for art works borrowed for international exhibitions. Individuals, non-profit institutions, and government agencies may apply. The art works can be insured for up to $50 million.

* Art Exhibits in the Halls of Congress
Secretary of the Senate
U.S. Capitol
Washington, DC 20510   (202) 224-3121
Most people tour the Capitol and admire its art work, but miss the works of art throughout all the buildings in the Capitol complex. The Rayburn House Office Building displays a statue of Sam Rayburn. The basement rotunda in the Cannon House Office Building displays a large model of the Capitol. The Hart Senate Office Building has an impressive Alexander Calder sculpture which fills the entire atrium courtyard space. Large, stately, richly detailed caucus rooms are historic places where major public hearings over the past three quarters of a century have taken place. The subway tunnel between the Cannon House Office Building and the Capitol is the site for a display of paintings done by high school artists who enter their works in congressional district competitions sponsored by the Congressional Arts Caucus.

* Art Exhibits Overseas
Office of Arts America
The Bureau of Educational and Cultural Affairs
United States Information Agency
301 Fourth St., SW, Room 567
Washington, DC 20547   (202) 485-2779
Arts America recruits artists and performers to visit other countries and provides some assistance to artists traveling privately. The USIA sends some 15 large fine arts exhibitions and 25 performing arts groups overseas annually. Panels set up by the National Endowment for the Arts recommeds a group of candidates, from which the USIA selects the programs participants. A Speakers Program recruits artists from the fields of literature, film, and the performing arts, on the basis of requests from overseas posts. AcuISpecs are American specialists, in one of the plastic or performing arts, who visit a foreign country for two to six weeks with a local host institution for a program of master classes, workshops, and demonstrations. Arts America sponsors about 30 of these programs a year. This office also provides support materials for major fine and performing arts projects; publishes a quarterly list of privately traveling artists; and tries to assist overseas posts in programming these performers.

* Art History Archive from 18th Century On
Archives of American Art
AmericaArt and Portrait Gallery
8th & F Sts. N.W.
Washington, DC 20560   (202) 357-2781
The Archives of American Art is dedicated to the collection, preservation, and study of papers and other primary records of the history of the visual arts in America. Its collections, comprising more than eight million items, are the world's largest single source for such information. The collections include correspondence, journals, business papers, and other documentation of artists, dealers, critics, art historians, and art institutions from the eighteenth century to the present. Microfilm copies of many of the collections are available through interlibrary loan. Holdings of the Archives are described in a published card catalog (1980 -) and on SIBIS. In addition to its headquarters in Washington DC, the Archives of American Art maintains offices in five cities: Boston: (617) 565-8444; Detroit: (313) 226-7544; New York City: (212) 662-5015; San Francisco: (415) 556-2530; and Los Angeles: (818) 405-7847, all of which serve as regional collecting and research centers, and provide microfilm of the collections to researchers. The Archives publishes the Archives of American Art Journal and sponsors symposia and lectures on art history subjects.

* Art in the Capitol
The Curator's Office
Architect of the Capitol
The Capitol Building
Room SB15
Washington, DC 20515   (202) 225-1222
The U.S. Capitol is a recognized work of art. The classical architecture and the interior embellishments set the backdrop for the variety and scope of American history and culture. Much of the Capitol's art collection is catalogued in *Art in the Capitol*, published by the Architect of the Capitol under the direction of the Joint Committee on the Library.

* Arts in Education Initiatives
Arts-In-Education
National Endowment for the Arts
1100 Pennsylvania Ave., NW, Room 602
Washington, DC 20506   (220) 682-5426
The Arts-In-Education Program is a partnership program through cooperative efforts of the Arts Endowment, state arts and education agencies, local communities, and other organizations. The Program's overall goal is to advance the arts as part of basic education. Grants are awarded to place practicing artists in a variety of educational settings and to support other projects designed to enhance arts education in schools. Arts in Schools Basic Education Grants encourage plans and projects that promote the arts in schools as a basic component of the curriculum in kindergarten through high school.

* Art Slides, Films, Video Loan Program
Art Extension Programs
National Gallery of Art
Extension Services
Constitution & 6th St., NW
Washington, DC 20565   (202) 842-6273
Color slide programs, films, and videocassettes are loaned at no cost to schools, libraries, community organizations, and individuals across the nation. The programs deal with a wide range of subjects drawn from the Gallery's permanent collections and special exhibitions. A free catalog listing all free-loan Extension Programs is available.

* Asia and Near East Art National Collection
Sackler Gallery
Smithsonian Institution
Washington Institution
Washington, DC 20560   (202) 357-1924
Opened in 1987, the Sackler Gallery has over 1000 art objects from China, South and Southeast Asia, and the ancient Near East given to the museum by the late Arthur M. Sackler. Future programs at the gallery include major international shows offering both surveys of distinctive traditions and comparative exhibitions showing the art of different centuries, geographic areas, and types of patronage. Most exhibitions will be accompanied by public programs and scholarly symposia. The Sackler has a library and a slide study room which are open to the public. *Asian Art* is a quarterly journal published by Oxford University Press in association with the Sackler Gallery *Scholar's Guides to Washington D.C.*.

* Asian and Near Eastern Art Museum
Freer Gallery of Art
Smithsonian Institution
Twelfth St. & Jefferson Dr. S.W.
Washington, DC 20560   (202) 357-2103
The Freer Gallery of Art is a museum of Asian and Near Eastern Art from the third millennium B.C. to the early 20th century. It also houses a group of works by late 19th and early 20th century American artists. The building, the original collection, and an endowment fund were the gift of Charles Lang Freer. The 26,800 Art works now in the Freer's Asian and Near Eastern collections include paintings, ceramics, manuscripts, metalwork, and sculpture. The Freer and the Sackler Gallery have joined together to share staff and research facilities, as well as a library housed at the Sackler. The Technical Laboratory conducts research and conservation of objects from the Freer and Sackler collections. It undertakes technical analyses of Asian art, investigates and rectifies conservation problems, and ensures that art works are in stable condition for exhibition. A free public lecture series is held where scholars present illustrated lectures on Asian and Near Eastern Art. The Freer is currently undergoing a major construction and renovation project and will be closed until 1992.

* Attracting Wider Audience to Smithsonian Museums
Office of the Committee for a Wider Audience
Arts & Industries Building
Room 3101
Smithsonian Institution
Washington, DC 20560   (202) 357-4569
The role of this Office is to extend the reach of Smithsonian programs to segments of the public that traditionally have been under-represented in the institution's audience. The office helps museums, offices, and bureaus throughout the institution in their outreach efforts. The OCWA systematically ensures participation in minority groups at receptions and special events.

* Audiovisual Materials for Art Exhibits
National Gallery of Art
Audiovisual Department
Constitution & 6th St., NW
Washington, DC 20565   (202) 842-6565

This office produces multi-image programs which accompany major exhibitions, as well as archival videotaping of exhibitions, special events, and lectures.

* Central Museological Clearinghouse

Office of Museum Programs
A and I Building 2235
900 Jefferson Dr. S.W.
Washington, DC 20560   (202) 357-3101

This information center and library has a working collection of resources on all aspects of museum operations. The Center, as the only central source of museological information in the United States, also contains evaluation studies, visitor surveys, volunteer manuals, long-range development plans, sample by-laws, and characters and museum collection management records. The Center is open to the public by appointment.

* Color Reproductions of National Collection

National Gallery of Art
Constitution & 6th St., NW
Washington, DC 20565   (202) 842-6353

The Publications Sales Department offers a large selection of color reproductions and scholarly publications related to the collections, exhibits, and other activities of the Gallery. Additional offerings include books and videocassettes on fine art and architecture, slide sets from the permanent collection, framed and matted reproductions and games. A free color reproductions mail order catalog is available.

* Conservators and Archacometry Training

Conservation-Analytical Laboratory
Smithsonian Institution
Museum Support Center
4210 Silver Hill Rd.
Suitland, MD 20560   (202) 287-3700

The Conservation-Analytical Laboratory engages in research in the conservation, technical study, and analysis of museum objects and related materials. Conservation-related information is made available to museum professionals nationwide and to the general public. In the archacometry program, physical scientists engage in analytical and technical studies of artifacts. The laboratory performs conservation treatments on objects from the Smithsonian collections that present special problems. The conservation training program provides internship training for conservation students and organizes advanced specialist training courses for practicing conservators.

* Conservation and Preservation Survey

National Institute for the Conservation
of Cultural Property, Inc (NIC)
Arts and Industries Building
900 Jefferson Dr. S.W.
Smithsonian Institution
Washington, DC 20560   (202) 357-2295

This clearinghouse for museums and conservationists is currently undertaking several projects, including the Conservation Assessment Survey Program, which is designed to help museums organize and weed out their collections; and the Save Outdoor Sculpture (SOS) project, which catalogs, inventories, and ensures that outdoor sculptures are treated properly.

* Contemporary and Historical Design

National Cooper-Hewitt Museum of Design
Smithsonian Institution
2 E. 91st St.
New York, NY 10128   (212) 860-6868

The Cooper-Hewitt Museum is the only museum in the United States devoted exclusively the study and exhibition of historical and contemporary design. The collection contains textiles, wallpaper, furniture, ceramics, glass, architectural ornaments, metalwork, woodwork, drawings and prints. A continuing series of handbooks surveying each of the collections now numbers 20 titles. Educational programs offered include lectures, craft workshops, repair clinics, seminars, young people's classes, and performing arts demonstrations.

* Dial-A-Museum

Visitor Information Center
Smithsonian Institution
1000 Jefferson Dr., SW
Washington, DC 20560   (202) 357-2020

By calling this number, you will hear a taped telephone message with daily announcements on new exhibits and special events.

* Disabled Smithsonian Visitors

Visitor Information and Associates' Reception Center

Smithsonian Institution
1000 Jefferson Dr. S.W.
Washington, DC 20560   (202) 357-2700

A free guide book to the Smithsonian is available for disabled visitors, which includes information on parking, transportation, wheelchair access, bathrooms, and telephones. Sign language and oral interpreter services may be arranged three days in advance. Several museums have large-print brochures available.

* Elderly and Disabled Access to the Arts

Office for Special Constituencies
National Endowment for the Arts
1100 Pennsylvania Ave., NW
Room 605
Washington, DC 20506   (202) 682-5532 (202) 682-5496 TDD

The Office for Special Constituencies assists individuals and organizations in making arts activities accessible to older adults, disabled people, and those in institutions. Contact this Office for assistance and materials, including examples of how other arts groups have made their programs available to special groups, along with model project guidelines.

* Endowment for the Arts Grant Application Guide

Public Information Offices
National Endowment for the Arts
1100 Pennsylvania Ave., NW, Room 617
Washington, DC 20506   (202) 682-5400

The National Endowment for the Arts offers a free publication, the *Guide to the National Endowment for the Arts*, which outlines its various programs and grants, and provides a calendar of deadlines, as well as application information for the grants. Regional offices and other related agencies are also listed.

* Family Art Programs in Washington

National Gallery of Art
Education Division
Constitution & 6th St., NW
Washington, DC 20565   (202) 842-6246

Family programs are offered on Saturday mornings for families with children ages 6 to 12. These events usually include a film or special activity and a tour and lasts about 1 1/2 hours. Advance registration is required.

* Famous American Portraits

National Portrait Gallery
Smithsonian Institution
8th & G Sts. N.W.
Washington, D. C. 20560   (202) 357-2995

The National Portrait Gallery's collection consists of paintings, sculpture, prints, drawings, and photographs of figures significant to the history of the United States. At any given time, any number of research projects may be in progress on topics in American history, biography, and portraiture. This unique reference facility contains documentation on nearly 70,000 portraits of noted Americans. The Gallery provides a full range of educational services both within the museum and out in the community, including a Speakers' Bureau, a Lunchtime Lectures Series, and "Portraits in Motion" performance series, which presents actors and musicians in readings, concerts, and plays.

* Films and Lectures on Art

National Gallery of Art
Constitution & 6th St., NW
Washington, DC 20565   (202) 842-6353

Free films on art, along with feature films, are presented at the Gallery. The *Calendar of Events* lists the titles and times of the showings. Free lectures are given by distinguished scholars on Sundays. No reservations are needed, but seating is limited. Andrew W. Mellon Lectures in the Fine Arts, a six-lecture series given at the Gallery, encompasses the history, criticisms, and theory of the visual and performing arts. All lectures also are announced in the Gallery's *Calendar*.

* Folklife Crafts and American Traditions

Office of Folklife Programs
Smithsonian Institution
955 L'Enfant Plaza
Washington, DC 20590   (202) 287-3424

Through its annual Festival of American Folklife, the Smithsonian created a program of folklife presentations for the general public for two weeks each summer. The Office also carries on research in folklife traditions, publishes documentary and analytical studies, develops and organizes exhibitions with folklife themes, and cooperates with Universities and other institutions in presentation projects involving traditional craftsman and performing artists.

* Folklife Studies Worldwide

Arts and Humanities

Office of Folklife Programs Archive/
Folkways Records Archive
Office of Folklife Programs
955 L'Enfant Plaza S.W., Suite 2600
Washington, DC 20560   (202) 287-3251

The Office of Folklife Programs Archive contains folkloristic materials generated through research for and documentation of the Festival of American Folklife Studies Monograph/Film Series. These materials document hundreds of folk culture traditions from the United States and forty-five other countries. Researchers should call for an appointment.

* Folkways Musical Recordings Archive

Office of Folklife Programs
955 L'Enfant Plaza, SW, Suite 2600
Washington, DC 20560   (202) 287-3251

The Folkways Records Archive, comprising the Moses and Frances Asch Collection, contains material related to the 2,200 published recordings of Folkways Records. The Folkways collection documents world-wide musical traditions, the spoken words of significant American figures, historical events, and nonmusical sounds of technology and nature. A catalog of the archives holdings is available which includes information on how to purchase recordings of the music.

* Hirshhorn Museum and Sculpture Garden

Smithsonian Institution
8th St. & Independence Ave. S.W.
Washington, D. C. 20560   (202) 357-3091

The Hirshhorn Museum and Sculpture Garden is devoted to the exhibition, interpretation, and study of modern and contemporary art. The Collection consists of 19th and 20th century sculpture, paintings, prints and drawings. Children's events and a supplementary program of lectures, documentary films, art films, and performing arts are offered. Outreach programs provide on-site classroom preparation, lecture services for adult community groups, and a teachers' workshop course.

* Historic Architecture in the National Parks

Park Historic Architecture Division
National Park Service
U.S. Department of the Interior
1100 L St., NW
Washington, DC 20005   (202) 343-8146

Activities related to the preservation of historic and prehistoric structures and cultural landscapes within the National Park System are administered by this office. *A List of Classified Structures* is maintained, which is an inventory of all historic and prehistoric structures in the System. A bibliography of Cultural Resources Management is also administered, listing all reports that address cultural resources in the Park System.

* Humanities Exhibits at Museums and Historical Organizations Grants

Division of General Programs
National Endowment for the Humanities
1100 Pennsylvania Ave., NW, Room 420
Washington, DC 20506   (202) 786-0284

This Program provides support for the planning and implementation of temporary and permanent exhibitions, historic site interpretations, publications, lectures and other educational programs, which engage the public in a greater appreciation and understanding of the humanities. Grants allow institutions to plan projects that interpret collections and to carry out permanent or temporary projects. Grants can support the cataloguing of a collection to make possible their use in programs on the humanities, as well as allowing for planning of computerized documentation. Self-study grants allow an organization to evaluate its humanities resources and develop long-range plans. Grants can be made to non-profit organizations, including local and state governments, if such donations qualify as charitable deductions under Section 170(c) of the Internal Revenue Code of 1954.

* Import Controls on Cultural Property

Cultural Property Advisory Committee
Bureau of Educational and Cultural Affairs
United States Information Agency
301 Fourth St., SW, Room 247
Washington, DC 20547   (202) 485-6612

This Presidential committee, comprised private citizens who are archaeologists, art dealers, representatives of the museum community, or the general public, advises the deputy USIA director, who determines whether the U.S. should impose import controls on endangered archaeological and ethnological materials at the request of foreign countries. The Cultural Property staff investigates and reports to the committee, and serves as liaison to federal agencies and to the archaeological, art dealer, museum, and preservation communities affected by U.S. actions under the 1983 Cultural Property Act.

* Indian Arts and Crafts Development

Indian Arts and Crafts Board
Bureau of Indian Affairs
U.S. Department of the Interior
18th and C Sts., NW
Washington, DC 20240   (202) 343-2773

The Indian Arts and Crafts Board promotes the development of Native Indian arts and crafts so that the artists will achieve economic stability. Three museums are operated by the Board: the Sioux Indian Museum in Rapid City, South Dakota; the Museum of the Plains Indian in Browning, Montana; and the Southern Plains Indian Museum in Anadarko, Oklahoma. These museums contain historic artifacts of these Indian tribes, but primarily function as contemporary showcases of Indian art. The Board also provides advisory services for Indian artists and craftsmen. To obtain a free *Source Directory* listing some 250 locations where Indian art can be seen and purchased, contact the office above.

* Indian Arts and Crafts Directory

Indian Arts and Crafts Board
Bureau of Indian Affairs, Room 4004
U.S. Department of the Interior
Washington, DC 20240   (202) 343-2773

The Indian Arts and Crafts Board has compiled a source directory of arts and crafts businesses owned and operated by Indians, Eskimos and Aleuts. The free directory lists the name, address, and phone number of each business and the types of products sold. The Indian Arts and Crafts Board's goal is to make the Indian populations more economically independent through their native arts and crafts.

* Indian Craft Shops

Indian Craft Shop
Bureau of Indian Affairs
U.S. Department of the Interior
18th and C Sts., NW
Washington, DC 20240   (202) 343-4056

Indian Craft Shop
Bureau of Indian Affairs
U.S. Department of the Interior
1050 Wisconsin Ave., NW
Washington, DC 20007   (202) 342-3918

These shops contain Indian crafts that can be purchased by the public. The hours at the Main Building location are 8:30 a.m. to 4:30 p.m., Monday through Friday. At the Wisconsin Avenue location, the hours are 10:00 a.m. to 7:00 p.m., Monday through Saturday, and 12:00 noon to 6:00 p.m., Sunday.

* Indian Museums

Southern Plains Indian Museum
P.O. Box 749
Anadarko, OK 73005   (405) 247-6221

Museum of the Plains Indian
P.O. Box 400
Browning, MT 59417   (406) 338-2230

Sioux Indian Museum
P.O. Box 1504
Rapid City, SD 57709   (605) 348-0557

These three Indian museums are administered by the Indian Arts and Crafts Board of the Bureau of Indian Affairs, U.S. Department of the Interior. The museums issue free informational pamphlets and brochures about their respective programs and exhibition activities. Contact the museums directly to be placed on their mailing lists.

* Indian Publications and Audiovisuals

Indian Arts and Crafts Board
Bureau of Indian Affairs, Room 4004
U.S. Department of the Interior
Washington, DC 20240   (202) 343-2773

The Indian Arts and Crafts Board has compiled a listing of their publications and audiovisuals available to the public. Titles include *Comtemporary Southern Plains Indian Metalwork, Painted Tipis by Contemporary Plains Indian Artists, Coyote Tales of the Montana Salish, Contemporary Indian Artists - Montana/Wyoming,* and *Contemporary Southern Plains Indian Painting.* Two slide lecture kits are available for purchase at $50.00 each: *Contemporary Indian and Eskimo Crafts of the United States* and *Contemporary Sioux Painting.*

* International Museum Scholars Exchange

International Activities

3123 S. Dillon Ripley Center
1100 Jefferson Dr. S.W.
Smithsonian Institution
Washington, D.C. 20560 (202) 357-2763
Handbook on International Research and Exchanges serves as a basic reference document for Smithsonian staff who travel abroad on official business or who engage in international scholarly or museum exchanges. Although directed toward Smithsonian staff, this publication can give others helpful tips for conducting research and exchanges abroad, including visas, research permits and money concerns, and also covers issues surrounding immigration and international visitors.

* Military Photographic Archives

Still Picture Branch (NNSP)
National Archives Records Administration
Eighth and Pennsylvania Ave., NW, Room 18N
Washington, DC 20408 (202) 523-3236
The archives holds the official photographic collection for the Army, Navy, and Marine Corps dating 1955 back to the founding of the country. Patrons can order photographic reproductions and posters for a small fee. Write or call for a price sheet, a "Select List" of period topics--including The Civil War, World War II, the Old West, the American Revolution, and American Cities--and a catalog entitled *War and Conflict*.

* Museum Artistic Initiative Grants

Museum Program
National Endowment for the Arts
1100 Pennsylvania Ave., NW, Room 624
Washington, DC 20506 (202) 682-5442
The Museum Program is designed to meet the needs of the museum field by providing funding for a variety of projects. The first is Professional Development, where they award grants for formal museum training programs, internships, and apprenticeships, as well as providing fellowships to museum professionals for independent study. The second category is Utilization of Museum Resources, which is designed to help organizations make greater use of museum collections and other resources. Grants help with reinstallation, exhibitions, and collection sharing. Grants can be used to develop related programs and events that enrich these presentations, including the preparation and publication of exhibition catalogs. The Education category provides for educational programs for the community, which can include outside specialists, and the Catalog category supports the cataloging of a permanent museum collection and the publication of materials related to the collection. Special Artistic Initiatives is designed to encourage long-term programming by museums and should include a unifying, thematic framework. The Museum Program helps museums conserve collections by providing grants for planning, conservation, and training. Grants also aid in collection maintenance through solving problems in climate control, security, and storage. Museums are encouraged to purchase works by living American artists, as well as to mount or participate in special exhibitions. Grants can be made to non-profit institutions if such donations qualify as charitable deductions under Section 170(c) of the Internal Revenue Code of 1954. Some of the grants are matching grants, and the range goes up to $125,000.

* Museum Careers and Conservators Audiovisuals

Office of Museum Programs
Smithsonian Institution
900 Jefferson Dr. S.W.
Washington, DC 20560 (202) 357-3101
The Audiovisual department of the Office of Museum Programs has forty slide and video programs, covering topics such as museum careers, museum environments, and conservation and preservation. You can view the slides and videotapes at the Office of Museum Programs.

* Museum Career Training Grants

National Museum Act
Smithsonian Institution
Arts and Industries Building
900 Jefferson Dr. S.W.
Washington, DC 20560 (202) 357-2257
The National Museum Act authorizes the Smithsonian to make grants that would enhance professionalism in museums. Awards are made for training career employees in museum practices, for research on museum-related problems and for projects involving the distribution of technical information. Grants are made to museums, museum-related organizations, academic institutions, and sponsored individuals pursuing careers in conservation practices.

* Museum Collections in National Parks

Curatorial Services Division
National Park Service
U.S. Department of the Interior
1100 L St., NW
Washington, DC 20005 (202) 343-8138

National Park Service museum collections are managed by this branch of NPS. The office's *NPS Museum Handbook* provides guidelines on the acquisition, documentation, cataloging, conservation, storage, use, and disposition of museum objects. The Automated National Catalog System maintains the centralized records of museum pieces belonging to the Park System.

* Museum Conservation Science Center

Museum Support Center Library
Smithsonian Institution
42210 Silver Hill Rd.
Suitland, MD 20746 (202) 287-3666
This library provides information about conservation of materials and museum objects, conservation science, which includes archaeometry, the study of museum environments, and the analysis of materials by such means as X-ray, diffraction, and gas chromatography. This library is open to the public by appointment.

* Museum Contracts and Small Business

Office of Procurement Property Management
Smithsonian Institution
Washington, D.C. 20560 (202) 287-3238
This office provides information regarding contract application for services such as supplies, construction, equipment, and research. They can answer questions regarding the application process, and can direct you to offices possibly in need of your services.

* Museum of the U.S. Department of the Interior

Departmental Museum
U.S. Department of the Interior
18th and C Sts., NW, Room 1240
Washington, DC 20240 (202) 343-2743
The highlights of this museum's exhibit include Native American artifacts and dioramas depicting the history of each of DOI's Bureaus. Of particular interest to children is a collection of fossils and a display of fragments from the moon's surface. The display is oriented to children in the fourth grade and older, but younger children are welcome. The hours of operation are 8 a.m. to 4 p.m., Monday through Friday.

* Museum Programs Clearinghouse

Smithsonian Institution
Office of Museum Programs
900 Jefferson Dr. S.W.
Washington, DC 20560 (202) 357-3101
The Office of Museum Programs provides professional development training, advisory assistance, and research services to the national and international museum community and the Smithsonian staff through sponsorship of workshops, internships, and professional visitor programs, an audiovisual production and loan program, a museum reference center, a native American training program, and publications. The Audio-visual Program distributes slide-cassette and video-tape programs on conservation, exhibitions, museum education, security, museum careers, and folklife. The Native American Museums Program provides information services and educational opportunities for employees of tribal and urban native American museums and cultural Centers. The Program offers workshops, short-term residencies, technical assistance, publications, and audio-visual materials on museums.

* National Air and Space Museum

Smithsonian Institution
7th St. & Independence Ave. S.W.
Washington, D.C. 20560 (202) 357-1552
The National Air and Space Museum was established to memorialize the development of air and space flight, and to collect, display, and preserve aeronautical and space flight artifacts. The 23 galleries contain items ranging from the Wright 1903 Flyer to Apollo 11. The Langley Theater, with a giant screen presentation, shows a variety of films every half hour, as does the Albert Einstein Planetarium. Both charge a small fee. There are live, free presentations concerning the current night sky, and there are monthly sky lectures by staff and guest speakers. A summer concert series is presented on the terrace. The Museum's Education Resource Center provides air-and-space-related materials for teachers. The Office of Education produces three new publications: *Discovery*, a curriculum package for kindergarten through third grade; 5, 4, 3, 2, 1, a guide for the very young visitor; and *Skylines*, a quarterly newsletter for educators.

* National American Art Collection

National Museum of American Art
Smithsonian Institution
8th & 9th Sts. N.W.
Washington, DC 20560 (202) 357-3095
The National Museum of American Art's collections of American paintings, sculptures, graphics, folk art, and photographs exhibit a broad range of artistic

Arts and Humanities

achievement in America from the 18th century to the present. The museum holds extensive public programs which include lectures, symposia, concerts, poetry readings, and other special events. A free calendar of events is available. NMAA conducts extensive research on American Art and has implemented seven discrete research databases totalling over 530,000 records (see Office of Research Support). They also publish a scholarly journal, *Smithsonian Studies in American Art*, with articles ranging from interviews with artists to discussions of artistry in films.

* National Gallery Collection Catalogs
Division of Records and Loans
National Gallery of Art
Constitution & 6th St., NW
Washington, DC 20565 (202) 842-6234
The Gallery is publishing a systematic catalog of its entire collection of paintings, sculpture, decorative arts, and Steiglitz photographs. Twenty-five volumes are planned, and the first volume, *Early Netherlandish Paintings*, is available now at the Museum for $14.95.

* National Gallery's Permanent Collection Catalog Museum Shop
National Portrait Gallery
Smithsonian Institution
8th & F Sts. N.W.
Washington, DC 20560 (202) 357-1447
This book contains photographs of the entire collection of the National Portrait Gallery, including the sculptures. The cost is $24.95 ($3.95 for shipping and handling).

* Native American Internship Opportunities
Fellowships and Grants
Smithsonian Institution
Washington, D.C. 20560 (202) 357-3271
The Smithsonian offers fellowships and internships for research and study in fields which are actively pursued by the museums and research organizations of the Institution. Both predoctoral and postdoctoral fellowships are available, as well as Minority Faculty Fellowships. The length of the term and size of the stipend vary. The Minority and Native American Internship Programs are performed under direct supervision of Smithsonian staff, as tutorial situations.

* Natural History Collection: Anthropology to Zoology
Museum of Natural History
Smithsonian Institution
10th & Constitution Ave. N.W.
Washington, DC 20008 (202) 357-2664
The Museum of Natural History is responsible for the largest natural history collections in the world. The collections are organized into eight major research and curatorial units: the departments of Anthropology, Botany, Entomology, Invertebrate Zoology, Mineral Sciences, Paleobiology, and Vertebrate Zoology and the Smithsonian Oceanographic Sorting Center. Some of the objects and specimens include minerals and gems, meteoritic geology, sea life, insects, ice age mammals, origins and traditions of Western Civilization, and the splendors of nature. The size of the collection increases by up to a million new specimens annually. The museum conducts research on a wide variety of topics, and more than 2,000 scholars visit the museum each year. A free calendar of events is available outlining programs, symposia, lectures, and films available.

* Natural History Library
Natural History Library
10th and Constitution Ave. N.W.
Washington, DC 20560 (202) 357-4696
This library houses 330,000 books and bound journals and receives 1,963 journal subscriptions. The library consists of a main location and several subject-based locations. Topics covered include biology, geology, paleontology, ecology, anthropology, botany, entomology, and mineral sciences. Call to make an appointment or for information on the location of the subject-based libraries.

* Natural History Museum Education Program
National Museum of Natural History
Office of Education
Room 212, Mail Stop 158
Washington, D.C. 20560 (202) 357-2747
The museum has an extensive educational school program with film and workshops available at your school or the museum, including museum lesson tours, the Discovery Room, the Naturalist Center, and instructional kits. A catalog of services can be sent to you. The Office also publishes a quarterly calendar of films and events at the Museum.

* Numismatic Collection: Coins, Medals, Paper Money
National Museum of American History
Smithsonian Institution
12th & Constitution Ave. N.W.
Washington, DC 20560 (202) 357-1798
The Numismatic Collection contains 900,000 coins, medals, and paper money from ancient times to the present day.

* Outdoor Sculpture (SOS) Project
National Institute for the Conservation
of Cultural Property, Inc (NIC)
Arts and Industries Building
900 Jefferson Dr. S.W.
Smithsonian Institution
Washington, DC 20565 (202) 357-2295
This clearinghouse for museums and conservationists is currently undertaking several projects, including the Conservation Assessment Survey Program, which is designed to help museums organize and weed out their collections; and the Save Outdoor Sculpture (SOS) project, which catalogs, inventories, and ensures that outdoor sculptures are treated properly.

* Post-Byzantine Art to Present Library
National Gallery of Art
Constitution & 6th St., NW
Washington, DC 20565 (202) 842-6511
The Gallery's library has over 150,000 volumes with a specialty in Renaissance and Baroque art. The collection covers the period from Post-Byzantine to the present, focusing on the history and criticism of art. The stacks themselves are closed; however, the library is open to the public, but you should call for the hours and to make an appointment.

* Philatelic Collection: Stamps and Postal Memorabilia
National Museum of American History
12th & Constitution Ave. N.W.
Washington, DC 20560 (202) 357-1796
This is the largest and most extensive collection of postage stamps and postal memorabilia in the world, and is the third most valuable collection in the Smithsonian. It comprises 16 million objects, including a pair of confederate stamps, Amelia Earhardt's flight jacket, and the mail wrapper the Hope Diamond was sent in when it was donated to the Smithsonian. The museum has slide programs available free of charge to civic groups, postal unions, and philatelic organizations.

* Photographs of Masterpieces
National Gallery of Art
Office of Photographic Services
Constitution & 6th St., NW
Washington, DC 20565 (202) 842-6231
Black and white, 8 x 10 photographs of works from the National Gallery of Art's permanent collections are available for purchase, either by visiting the Office of Photographic Services or by mail. Color transparencies of works from the Gallery, to be used for publication, are available for rental only and must be requested in writing.

* Slide Lending Series on Art
National Gallery of Art
Constitution & 6th St., NW
Washington, DC 20565 (202) 842-6100
The National Gallery maintains a lending slide collection of over 50,000 images, which are loaned to the public free of charge. There is no list of the slide lending collection, but selections for National Gallery objects can be made from Gallery catalogs. Up to 50 slides can be borrowed at one time and may be kept for a period of two weeks. The slide library is open to the public.

* Smithsonian Archives Guide
Smithsonian Archives
Smithsonian Institution
900 Jefferson Dr. S.W.
Washington, DC 20560 (202) 357-1420
This free *Guide to Smithsonian Archives* is a reference resource to the holdings of the Archives, giving a detailed listing of the records, papers, and projects the Archives has, as well as information regarding their use.

* Smithsonian Central Exhibits Office
Smithsonian Institution
1111 N. Capitol St.
Washington, D.C. 20560 (202) 357-3118
The Office provides design, editorial production, installation and other specialized exhibition services for a variety of Smithsonian programs. For instance, they recently completed a life-size model of the jaw of a prehistoric

shark, and also provided texts, graphic panels, maps, and time lines for a traveling exhibit on Ancient Syria.

* Smithsonian Institution Library Services

Smithsonian Institution Libraries
10th St. & Constitution Ave. N.W.
Washington, DC 20560   (202) 357-2139

The libraries of the Smithsonian Institution include approximately 950,000 volumes, with strengths in natural history, museology, history of science, and the humanities. Inquiries on special subjects or special collections should be addressed to the appropriate branch library or to the Central Reference and Loan.

* Smithsonian Institution Press

Smithsonian Institution
1111 North Capitol St.
Washington, DC 20560   (202) 287-3738

The Smithsonian has been publishing books since its foundation and functions like a university press. It publishes 70 scholarly books each year, in addition to several hundred popular books on topics such as science, art, American history and architecture. Call for a free catalog.

* Smithsonian Museum Internships

Office of Museum Programs
Arts & Industries Building
Room 2235
Smithsonian Institution
Washington, D. C. 20560   (202) 357-3101

Three publications are available for interns: *Internships and Fellowships* describes the majority of internship and fellowship programs at the Smithsonian. The *Handbook for Smithsonian Interns* provides information about Smithsonian procedures, facilities, services and activities available to interns. *Housing Information for Interns and Fellows* is a guide to short-term housing in the Washington metropolitan area. A new publication, *Internship Opportunities at the Smithsonian 1989 - 1991*, is a comprehensive listing of all the internships available at each of the museums.

* Smithsonian Museum Merchandise

Capital Gallery Building
600 Maryland Ave. S.W   (202) 287-3563 .
Washington, DC 20560   mail order catalog (202) 357-1826

Many of the Smithsonian museums run shops which sell books, crafts, games, toys, posters, and cards. They also have a mail-order service which publishes three merchandise catalogs each year.

* Smithsonian Slides and Photographs

Photographic Services
Smithsonian Institution
14th & Constitution Ave.
Washington, DC 20560   (202) 357-1487

Slides, transparencies, and prints (black and white and color) are available of photographs in the Smithsonian's collections. You can also order their seven slide series on a variety of topics, and most include a booklet and cassette tape. For a slide series catalog or ordering information, contact Photographic Services.

* Smithsonian Records and Books

Smithsonian Institution
P.O. Box 10229
Des Moines, IA 50381   (800) 247-5072

The Smithsonian Institution produces and markets recordings of both modern and classical works, illustrating research in music history developed by Smithsonian staff and, in many cases, performed on instruments from the Institute's extensive collection. The Recordings include a wide range of music from country and western, to jazz to Bach. The Smithsonian also publishes quality illustrated books and a free catalog.

* Statue of Liberty

Superintendent of Documents
Government Printing Office
Washington, DC 20402   (202) 783-3238

The Statue of Liberty Exhibit is a full-color pamphlet describing the museum of the Statue of Liberty. It recounts the history of the Statue, describes the intricacies of its architecture and design, and provides information on its French designers and its massive refurbishing. 1988 (S/N 024-005-01025-4, $2.50).

* Traveling National Gallery Exhibits

Exhibit Lending Service
National Gallery of Art
Constitution & 6th St., NW
Washington, DC 20565   (202) 842-6083

The National Lending Service was established to make the collections of the Gallery accessible to musums throughout the U.S. This is accomplished through two programs: the Extended Loan Program which allows a museum to borrow up to five works of art for a year; and the Special Exhibition Program which provides exhibitions of up to 50 works in groups of 10, for periods of 4 to 6 weeks. Call or write for information on qualifications and costs.

* Visual Arts Fellowships

National Gallery of Art
Center for Advanced Study in the Visual Arts
Constitution & 6th St., NW
Washington, DC 20565   (202) 842-6480

The Center has a four-part program of fellowships, meetings, publications, and research in the field of visual arts. The Center offers a series of discussions, symposia, and lectures. Nine pre-doctoral fellowships are available for productive scholarly work in the history of art, architecture, and urban form, as well as senior fellowships and visiting senior fellowships for post-doctoral studies. *Center 8* is a publication which contains research reports by members of the Center, as well as a record of the activities of the Center. The Center also publishes an annual listing of research in the history of art sponsored by a number of granting institutions.

State Arts Programs

Alabama

Alabama Arts Council, 1 Dexter Ave., Montgomery, AL 36130; (205) 242-4075. Alabama administers twelve Fellowship Programs in the Arts. These Fellowships are in increments of $2,500 and $5,000.

Alaska

Alaska Arts Council, Juneau, AK 99811; (907) 279-1558. Alaska administers several grant Programs and Project grants for artists. Monetary grant monies range from $800 for Project Grants to approximately $24,000 to a non-profit organization in 1989. The Artists in Schools program employs visual artists, dancers, musicians, actors, puppeteers, poets, writers, and traditional Native artists to conduct in-depth residencies, workshops and performances in schools throughout the state.

Arizona

Arizona Arts Commission, 417 W Roosevelt St. Phoenix, AZ 85003; (602) 279-1558. Arizona administers Arts Programs to individual Artists and non-profit organizations within the state. They have the Artists in Education Program, Artists Fellowship Programs, and general grant fund monies.

Arkansas

Arkansas Arts Council, 225 East Markeham St., Little Rock, AR 72201; (501) 371-2539. Arkansas administers Fellowships to individuals ranging from $5,000 to $10,000. Grants are given to organizations ranging from $500 to $60,000. Program support grants are also given to organizations. Monies are given yearly in visual arts and literature and every third year in music and dance.

California

California Arts Council, Public Information Council, 1901 Broadway Suite A, Sacramento, CA 95818; (916) 322-9900. California administers Grants to individuals and organizations ranging from $1,000 to $100,000. Fellowships are given to individuals only in increments of $5,000.

Colorado

Colorado Council on the arts, 750 Pennsylvania, Denver, CO 80203; (303) 894-2517. Colorado administered one million dollars in grants to approximately two hundred Arts organizations and individuals in 1989. Grants are in increments from $1,000 to $5,000 and are given to Colorado residents only. Creative Fellowships are given in such areas as visual arts, poetry, and folk art. These are administered on a rotating schedule.

Connecticut

Connecticut Commission on Arts, 227 Lawrence St., Hartford, CT 06106; (203) 566-4770. Connecticut administers Grant Programs to increase the quality of Art to the public. The maximum grants given are $25,000. Recipients must meet certain criteria along with meeting residency requirements.

Delaware

Delaware Division of the Arts, 820 North French St., Wilmington, DE 19801; (302) 736-5304. Delaware administers Fellowships in the Arts including poets and writers. Project Support Grants are offered for non-profit organizations as well as Operating Support Grants. Project Grants range from $500 to $3,000.

District of Columbia

District of Columbia Council of Arts, 410 8th St., nw, 5th Floor, Stables Art Center, Washington, DC 20004; (202) 724-5613. The District of Columbia administers approximately eight programs in the Arts. Training Projects for Professional Artists along with Project Support for groups and individuals are given. These projects range from $5,000 to $40,000 for major institutions.

Florida

Florida Arts Council, Division of Cultural Affairs, Department of State, Tallahassee, FL 32399-0250; (904) 487-2980. Florida administers Artists Fellowships and Grants to non-profit organizations. Awards in amounts of $5,000 are given to professional artists. They also sponsor the Arts in Education Program.

Georgia

Georgia Council for Arts, 2982 East Exchange Pl., Suite 100, Tucker, GA 30084; (404) 493-5780. Georgia administers Grants to non-profit organizations and Grants to individuals to complete projects. The maximum award that can be requested for individuals ia $5,000 and $150,000 for organizations.

Hawaii

Hawaii State Foundation On Culture and Arts, 335 Merchant St., Room 202, Honolulu, HI 96813; (808) 548-4145. Hawaii administers programs in the areas of Grants to it's residents. They have a Purchases of Services Program. Funding is divided among eight different categories in the Arts.

Idaho

Idaho Commission on Arts, 304 West State St., Boise, ID 83720; (206) 334-2119. Idaho administers Grants and Fellowships to artists and organizations within the State ranging from $3,000 to $25,000 for organizations and $3,000 for individuals. Also available are Apprenticeship Programs. Idaho has grants available for Folk Art and Arts in Rural Towns Program.

Illinois

Illinois Arts Commission, State Of Illinois Center, 100 West Randolph Suite 10-500, Chicago, IL 60601; (312) 814-6750. Illinois administers Grant Programs to non-profit organizations and Fellowships to individuals only. Special Assistance Grants are also available to non-profit organizations.

Indiana

Indiana Arts Commission, 46 South Pennsylvania, 6th Floor, Indianapolis, IN 46204; (317) 232-1288. Indiana administers Grants and Fellowships to Artists and non-profit organizations within the State.

Iowa

Iowa Council On Arts, Capitol Complex, Des Moines, IA 50319; (515) 281-4451. Iowa administers approximately sixty programs to Artists and non-profit organizations. Grants range from $70 to $25,000. A Directory of Programs and Services can be obtained from the above address.

Kansas

Kansas Arts Commission, Jayhawk Tower, 700 Jackson, Suite 1004, Topeka, KS 66603; (913) 296-3335. Kansas administers the Artists Fellowship Program. Four awards are given yearly by application based on need and talent. Professional Development Grant Workshops are also held. Grants are given to developing professionals, as well as students. These programs are for Kansas residents only.

Kentucky

Kentucky Arts Council, Berryhill, Frankfort, KY 40601; (502) 564-3757. Kentucky administers The Artists Fellowship Program with ten awards being given in the amount of $5,000 each on a yearly basis. Awards are given to working professional artists meeting residency requirements.

Louisiana

Louisiana State Division Of Arts, PO Box 44247, Baton Rouge, LA 70804; (504) 342-8180. Louisiana administers Grants to organizations and Fellowships to individuals. Grant amounts are up to $350,000 or 5% of the organization's budget, whichever is less. Fellowship amounts are $5,000.

Maine

Maine Arts Commission, State House, Station 25, Augusta, ME 04333; (207) 289-2724. Maine administers Grants and Fellowships to organizations and individuals in the amount of $2,000. An Artist in Residence Program is also awarded.

Maryland

Maryland Arts Council, 15 W Mulberry St., Baltimore, MD 21202; (301) 333-8232. Maryland administers Grants to individuals and organizations under nine different disciplines. For fiscal year 1990, individuals can be awarded amounts ranging from $2,500 to $6,000.

Massachusetts

Massachusetts Cultural Council, 80 Boylston St., Boston, MA 02116; (617) 727-3668. This 24 year old agency traditionally funds individuals and non-profit groups incorporated in Massachusetts in 20 different programs. Areas of funding include fellowships, education, community art, minority artists, and contemporary arts. Guidelines for this state's programs will soon be available from the Council.

Michigan

Michigan Council for the Arts, 1200 Sixth St., Detroit, MI 48226-2461; (313) 256-3731. Grant programs are arranged in three general funding programs: Arts Organizations, Arts Projects, and Individual Artists. To request program guidelines, contact the specific Client Service Unit listed for each category. Any nonprofit organization or institution , artist, local government, school or community group in Michigan is eligible to apply for MCA grant funds. All funded activities must take place within the state and comply with equal opportunity standards.

Minnesota

Minnesota State Arts Board, 432 Summit Ave, St. Paul, MN 55102; (612) 297-4211. Minnesota administers several grants to individuals and organizations. Grants to individuals include Artist Assistance Fellowships ($6,00 for time, materials, and living expenses), Career Opportunity Grants, the Headlands Project Residency Project, and the Folk Arts Apprenticeships ($100 to $4,000 for the study of traditional artform with master fold artist).

Mississippi

Mississippi Arts Commission, 239 North Lanar St., Suite 207, Jackson, MS 39201; (601) 359-1000. Mississippi administers six Granting Programs and General Operating support grants for Arts in Cultural Organizations that fund up to 10& of the organization's income. Local arts organizations are funded up to 25% of their income. Project Support Grants range up to $5,000. Arts in Education Special Projects and Artists in Residence Program range up to $7,000. There are $5,000 Grants for Artist Fellowships that are on a three year rotating cycle for each discipline. Fifty percent of an Artist's fees are covered from the Touring Arts Roasters program.

Missouri

Missouri State Council on the Arts, Wainwright Office Complex, 111 N. 7th St., Suite 105, St. Louis, MO; (314) 444-6845. Missouri's State Council on the Arts is intended to increase the arts. It funds art programs and individuals (individuals must be a resident and must have 50% matching funds).

Montana

Montana Arts Council, 48 N. Last Chance Gulch, Helena, MT 59620; (406) 444-6430. This state agency promotes the state's diverse arts, artists, and cultural organizations. Programs which are administered include grants to organizations, fellowships for individuals, artists in schools programs, and a writers program (to help get first book published). A free newsletter for artists is available.

Nebraska

Nebraska Arts Council, 1313 Farman On The Mall, Omaha, NE 69102-1873; (402) 471-2211. Nebraska Arts Council is funded by the state of Nebraska and the National Endowment of the Arts. Funds are provided for non-profit Arts and non-Art organizations incorporated into the state. Grant categories for Arts organizations include: Year-Long Program, Projects, Artists in School-Communities, Learning through the Arts, Community challenge, Local partnership Incentive Program, Mini-grants, Dance on Tour, Professional Development Grants, and the Nebraska Touring Program, Depending upon the category, grants range from $500 to a maximum of $50,000. Non-Arts organizations include: Artists in Schools/Communities, Learning through the Arts, Mini grants, Nebraska Touring Program, and Project Grants. Most grants require a cash match.

Nevada

Nevada State Council on the Arts, 329 Flint St., Reno, NV 89501; (702) 789-0225. Nevada provides a variety of grant and fellowship programs for artists and non-profit organizations in the state and for those bringing their artistic talents to Nevada. The Artist in Residence program provides an opportunity for artists around the country to spend one month in a work/instruction arrangement within elementary and high schools, community centers, and other organizations. Direct assistance grants are available for Nevada residents up to $1,000 for organizational projects and for individual artists for their work or travel. Grants of up to $7,500 are given to organizations in Nevada for performing arts and visual arts productions brought into the state from outside the area. Artist fellowships are available for Nevada residents that provide living expenses during the artist's career. Fellowships from $2,000 to $8,000 are offered. Slide or documentation of the artist's work must be submitted, and exhibition records must be shown as evidence of artistic activity and contributions to the community. Folk arts apprenticeships, with grants totaling $2,000, are also provided where folk artists have the opportunity to work with master craftsmen in order to learn skills to be passed down through generations.

New Hampshire

New Hampshire Division of Arts, Council of the Arts, 40 North Main St., Concord, NH 03301; (603) 271-2789. New Hampshire administers Grants in four categories: 1) Umbrella Grants, 2) Touring Program, 3) Arts in Education, and 4) Percent for Art Program. Monies vary depending upon the individual category, ranging from $50 to $15,000. The Percent for Art Program is a slide registry for commissioning for new pieces of art for new State buildings being built.

New Jersey

New Jersey State Council on the Arts, 4 n Broad St., CN 306, Trenton, NJ 08625; (609) 292-6130. The New Jersey State Council on the Arts awards matching grants to organizations incorporated in New Jersey in the following funding categories: general operating support, special project support, state/county partnership block grants, challenge and endowment grants, and Arts Basic to Education grants. Challenge grants are offered to leverage increased contributions from corporate, foundation, and other private and public sources. Arts Basic to Education Grants provide funds to those groups whose mission is to provide art education to children in grades k-12. Non-profit organizations in the state may also apply for non-matching grants in the areas of technical assistance, development. artistic focus, and fellowship support. Technical assistance grants, awarded to strengthen the effectiveness of arts management skills, have ranged from $5,000 to $15,000. Emerging and developing New Jersey arts organizations may apply for development grants, traditionally between $5,000 and $40,000. Fellowship support is available for individual artists of New Jersey traditionally in amounts from $5,000 to $15,000. Applications must be received by February of each year. Areas of artistic talent that are eligible include literature, dance, music, composition, opera/music theater composition, interdisciplinary work, visual arts, such as sculpture, painting, graphics, and experimental design arts, crafts, photography, and media arts.

New Mexico

New Mexico Cultural Affairs Arts Division, 224 East Palace Ave, Sante Fe, NM 87506; (505) 827-6490. New Mexico administers Grants to non-profit organizations in the areas of Arts in Education, Teacher training and Artists Residencies, and Public Art Programs. One percent of the cost of the project for Art in public places is granted to eligible candidates.

New York

New York State Council on the Arts, 915 Broadway, New York, NY 10010; (212) 614-2904. Non-profit arts organizations in New York may receive grants from the Council. Arts and education, dance groups, museums, theater, and folk arts are among the categories eligible. Individual artists are funded through sponsoring organizations. These individual grants are available in five areas; film production, media production, visual artist sponsored projects, theater commissions, and music commissions. The amount of funding available is dependent of the project being proposed.

North Carolina

North Carolina Cultural Resources Arts Council, 109 East Jones St., Raleigh, NC 27611; (919) 733-2821. North Carolina administers Grants and Awards to Artist and non-profit organizations, as well as operating support to eligible major institutions. Program and salary assistance, Fellowships and Project Grants, and Summer Intern Programs are available to residents of the state.

North Dakota

North Dakota Council On Arts, Black Building #606, 118 Broad Way, Fargo, ND 58102; (701) 237-8959. North Dakota administers Grants and Scholarships in various categories: Institutional Grants, Artists in Resident by duration , Training Arts, In ACCESS Program, and Fellowship Programs. Monies vary depending upon the individual program awarded. These monies range from $100 up $20,000. In the training Arts, sponsors apply for up to 40% of the Artist fee.

Ohio

Ohio Council on Arts, 727 East Main St., Columbus, OH 43205; (614) 466-2613. Individual Fellowships are granted to residents with at least one year residency prior to the January 15 deadline imposed. No student may apply. These Fellowships range from $5,000 to $10,000. Work may have been previously created. No project proposals are considered, nor are the awards based upon need. Awards are given also for good work. There is a Peer Panel review. Ohio has Artist in Public Institutions and Artist in Public Education Awards. Funding varies. There are numerous other services available to the residents of Ohio.

Oklahoma

State Arts Council of Oklahoma, 640 Jim Thorpe Bldg., Oklahoma City, OK 73105; (405) 521-2931. Projects undertaken by non-profit art organizations within Oklahoma can receive matching grants from this Council for individual projects. There is no limit to the amount of the grants; however, they are dependent on the appropriations available. Applications must be filed 18 months prior to funding. Grants of over $2,000 and under $2,000 are offered for arts projects making a request within a shorter time frame. Those grants for under $2,000 are usually given to smaller organizations or towns sponsoring special performances or exhibits. A matching grant program whereby identified artists tour and perform on behalf of the Council is sponsored in cooperation with interested organizations. Minority grants of up to $5,000, particularly focused on the Indian population of Oklahoma, are offered to promote artistic efforts. Sixty grants of $500 each are being given to interested cities, towns, and schools who participate in Oklahoma's Homecoming '90 program. An artist in residence matching grant program is also available for elementary and high schools.

Oregon

Oregon Arts Commission, 835 Summer St., NE, Salem, OR 97301; (503) 378-3131. Oregon administers Grants and Fellowships to non-profit organizations within the state of Oregon. There is one dead line per year. Some of the categories are: Program Grants-Operating, Special Project-one of a kind, Oregon Arts Challenge-major institutions receiving a percent of the groups budget, Arts in Education Project Grants, Presenting Grants, Development of Cultural facilities, and Professional Development Grants. Monies range from $500 to $225,000, depending upon the individual program. Eight individual artists fellowships of $3,000 are awarded per year. There are two $10,000 Masters fellowship awards for film video awarded per year.

Pennsylvania

Pennsylvania Council on the Arts, Room 216, Finance Bldg., Harrisburg, PA 17120; (717) 787-6883. Fellowships are provided to qualified artists in Pennsylvania from this state Council. Non-profit organizations in the state may receive general operating and specific support grants. Funding is given to some organizations requesting assistance with summer programs, including music, presenting organizations, cross disciplinary programs, and theater. Local arts festivals may also receive financial aid. Bussing grants are provided to non-profit organizations if they are transporting groups to art activities. Consultant fees of $1,000 can be obtained by organizations requiring outside technical assistance.

Rhode Island

Rhode Island State Council On The Arts, 95 Cedar ST., Suite 103, Providence, RI 02903; (401) 277-3880. Grants are available from this organization to non-profit organizations and artists in Rhode Island. Organizational grants fall into three categories; access, arts programs, and residencies in elementary and high schools. The amount of money granted varies, depending on the operating budget of the organization applying for the funding. Individual fellowships are available for artists in 12 areas of practice. Artist project grants and folk art apprenticeships are also sponsored. An artist development fund has also been established to enhance artistic experience and to provide contingency funding.

South Carolina

South Carolina Art Commission, 1800 Gervais St., Columbia, SC 29201; (803) 734-8696. South Carolina offers Artist Development, Community Arts Development , Arts Education Grants, Fellowships, and a variety of direct programs for state residents. These categories require matching funds. At the same time Teacher
incentive Programs are offered which do not require matching funds.

South Dakota

South Dakota Arts Council, 108 W 11th St., Sioux Falls, SD 57102-0788; (605) 339-6646. Organization grants are offered by this Council whereby 10 percent of the operating expenses are funded to state and community arts councils in South Dakota. Matching project grants are available for state arts organizations and for other organizations with work related to South Dakota. The Arts Bank underwrites performances in South Dakota up to $500. Technical assistance, with a maximum amount of $500, is provided to State arts organizations. An excursion program offers up to $500 for an individual artist to participate in a learning experience through the Council's professional development program. Touring groups may receive a grant of up to 50% of tour costs that provides additional opportunities for performances. Schools may apply for the Artists in Schools residence program for grades K-12 in order to benefit from working with well-known artists from both in and out of state. South Dakota artists may apply for fellowships of $5,000 each. Emerging artists are also offered fellowships in the amount of $1,000, and projects of artists can be funded for up to 50% of the total cost. Artists from around the country interested in the Artists in Schools residency may apply to be a participant. Awards are $700 for one week, $2,800 for one month, and $9,600 for one semester. Individual artists matching grants are also available for state residents wishing to tour additional locations. South Dakota teachers may also apply for art educator grants of up to $1,000.

Tennessee

Tennessee Art Commission, 320-6th Ave North, Suite 100, Nashville, TN 37243-0780; (615) 741-1701. Tennessee administers Grants to residents which are members of non-profit organizations and individuals ranging from $500 to $50,000 depending on the size of the organization or the program which the individual applies for. Special opportunities are available for the residents of the state of Tennessee.

Texas

Texas Commission on the Arts,Box 13406, Capitol Station, Austin, TX 78711-3406; (512) 463-5535. Texas administers Grants in three categories: Organization, Project, and Touring. There are fourteen separate programs such as Arts in Education, Rural Arts Programming, Exhibits Support, Special Events, Planning Grants, and many others. Texas supports non-profit organizational arts and does Arts related Programming.

Utah

Utah Council of Arts, 617 E S Temple, Salt Lake City, UT 84102; (801) 538-3000. The Utah Arts Council administers several grants to non-profit organizations. Grants range from $300 to $140,000 and includes general support grants, Challenger grants (to $2,500), and Community Arts Development grants (to $3,000). The Arts Council also administers community-state partnerships, performing art tours, an arts-in-education program, folk arts apprenticeships, and design arts programs.

Vermont

Vermont Council on Arts, 136 State St., Montpelier, VT 05602; (802) 828-3291. The mission of the Vermont Council on Arts is to foster a vital Artistic Community and Excellence in the Arts, and to make available the richness and diversity of the arts to all. Grants and fellowships for non-profit organizations range from $3,500 for individual artists fellowships, $40 for touring programs, to $10,000 for organizations. The Vermont Council on Arts is not part of the State Government. They are an independent non-profit organization and therefore offer memberships to its residents, produces a publication, and elects its Board of Trustees from its membership.

Virginia

Virginia Commission for the Arts, James Monroe Bldg. 17th Floor, 101 N 14th St., Richmond, VA 23219-3683; (804) 225-3132. Virginia Commission for the Arts is the State Agency which supports the arts through distributing grants annually to Artists and Arts organizations. It provides technical assistance and arts management. Through various programs monies are distributed totaling up to $5,000,000 at times. Grants are awarded to individuals in such areas as play-writing and literature.

Washington

Washington State Arts Commission, 110 9th and Columbia Bldg., MS-GH11, Olympia, WA 98504-4111; (206) 753-3860. Five fellowships of $5,000 each are given annually to Washington artists. Grants are also provided to non-profit organizations for program projects and operating support. These matching grants range from $1,000 to $79,000. The Artist in Residence is sponsored in public schools and institutions with grants totaling $1,500. Cultural enrichment programs are supported within the school systems. The Arts in Public Places Program provides that 1/2 of 1% of the money for each government financed building is to be allocated for the purchase of art.

West Virginia

Department of Culture and History, Arts and Humanities Division, Capital Complex Cultural Center, Charleston, WV 25305; (304) 348-0240. This department supports and promotes the arts of West Virginia. Grants are administered to artists, craft people, and organizations. They range from $250 to $80,00 and usually fund 50% of projects. The department has approximately $1 million a year to grant.

Wisconsin

Wisconsin Arts Board, 131 w Wilson St., Suite 301, Madison, WI 53703; (608) 266-0190. Wisconsin administers approximately fifteen programs in the Arts. Programs are awarded in apprenticeships, development, fellowships, new work awards, and Educational Opportunity Grants. An Arts in Education Residency Program is also awarded to schools and community agencies. Preference is given to Wisconsin residents, but these programs are open to all US residents.

Wyoming

Wyoming Arts Council, 2320 Capitol Ave., Cheyenne, WY 82002; (307) 777-7742. Wyoming administers such programs in Individual Artists Grants for specific projects. Arts and Education programs to fund school or community non-profit organizations and to provide project or technical support to non-profit organizations.

Your Community
Urban and Rural Resources

* See also Auctions and Surplus Property Chapter
* See also Careers and Workplace Chapter
* See also Drugs and Chemical Dependence Chapter
* See also Education Chapter
* See also Government Financial Aid to Individuals Chapter
* See also Housing and Real Estate Chapter

On nearly every page of this book there are numerous resources mentioned that can benefit your community. Non-profit and service organizations are eligible to apply for federal loans and grants which are intended for education, job training, housing and economic development. The most relevant money programs for cities and towns are identified in this chapter but others appear throughout this book. Regional offices which dot the country bring the resources and experts of the federal government closer as well. Also browse through the index and discover thousands of films and other audiovisuals which are available for community groups.

* Arson Prevention Traveling Exhibit
Office of Fire Prevention and Arson Control
Federal Emergency Management Agency
16825 South Seton Ave.
Emmitsburg, MD 21727 (301) 447-1200
Arson Trailers tour the country to provide technical and educational assistance to State, local, and national fire service and community groups. Their public educations demonstrations include fire safety issues, local fire problems, and smoke detector usage and maintenance.

* Appalachian Communities Aid
Appalachian Regional Commission
News and Public Affairs
1666 Connecticut Avenue, NW
Room 328
Washington, DC 20235 (202) 673-7968
The Commission provides various grants and loans for economic, physical, and social development of the 13-state Appalachian region, which includes parts of Alabama, Georgia, Kentucky, Maryland, Mississippi, New York, North Carolina, Ohio, Pennsylvania, South Carolina, Tennessee, Virginia, and all of West Virginia. The Commission publishes the *Appalachian Regional Commission Annual Report* which provides financial statistics, activities and programs over the past year.

* Communications Networks and New Technologies
Office of Technology Assessment
600 Pennsylvania Ave., SE
Washington, DC 20510 (202) 228-6774
Recent advances in information storage and transmission technologies, occurring in a new deregulated and intensely competitive economic climate, are rapidly changing the Nation's communication networks. OTA is studying the role of the Federal government in this area, along with how to coordinate them, resolve potential conflicts between them, and examine new communication systems abroad and their potential relationships to the U.S. systems. Contact Linda Garcia, the project director, for more information.

* County Cooperative Extension Service
Executive Officer
U.S. Department of Agriculture
Room 340A Administration Building
Washington, DC 20250 (202) 447-4111
The USDA operates an extension program in 3,165 counties located in all of the 50 states and the U.S. territories. Federal, state, and local governments share in financing and conducting cooperative extension educational programs to help farmers, processors, handlers, farm families, communities, and consumers apply the results of food and agricultural research. The Extension Service has targeted 9 national initiatives to provide a new focus for educational efforts.

1) Alternative Agricultural Opportunities: Helps farmers use a distinctive approach to alternative crop and livestock enterprises to integrate marketing, management, and production factors into a total business plan.

2) Building Human Capital: Helps people develop marketable job skills, make informed career decisions, and expand available opportunities.

3) Competitiveness and Profitability of American Agriculture:
To enhance farmers' competitiveness and profitability, Extension helps farmers improve production, finance, and management skills; develop new technology; adjust profitability to global market changes; and strengthen business and support systems.

4) Conservation and Management of Natural Resources: Helps people benefit from natural ecosystems without destroying them, sustain a productive natural resource base, market natural resource goods and services, and formulate and implement sound public policies.

5) Family and Economic Well-Being: Helps families manage finances and make sound financial decisions; confront and deal with such problems as alcohol and drug abuse, teenage pregnancy, and unemployment; and develop strategies for retirement.

6) Improving Nutrition, Diet, and Health: Extension offers up-to-date information about the relationship of dietary practices to lifestyle factors; the safety, quality, and composition of foods; and consumers' needs and perceptions about the food industry.

7) Revitalizing Rural America: In cooperation with local governments, Extension programs emphasize how to increase competitiveness and efficiency of rural programs, explore methods to diversify local economies and attract new business, adjust to impact of change, develop ways to finance and deliver services, and train leaders to make sound policy decisions for rural communities.

8) Water Quality: Work with consumers, producers and local government to learn more about the importance of high-quality ground water and the conservation of water resources. Emphasis is also on the effects of agricultural chemicals and contaminants on water quality.

9) Youth at Risk: Extension is helping expand youth outreach resources to meet the needs of youth, develop programs for the most susceptible youth populations, provide leadership and job skills, and increase training of professionals and volunteers to work in communities to prevent and treat problems.

* Community and Rural Economic Development
Valley Resource Center
Resource Development
Tennessee Valley Authority
600 Summit Hill Dr.
Knoxville, TN 37902-2801 (615) 632-4400
The Valley Resource Center can be contacted for information on community and rural economic development programs.

* Community Health Services Grants
Bureau of Health Care Delivery and Assistance
Health Resources and Services Administration
5600 Fishers Lane, Room 7-05
Rockville, MD 20857 (301) 443-2320
The Bureau of Health Care Delivery and Assistance Services focuses nationally on efforts to ensure the availability and delivery of health care services in health manpower shortage areas, to medically undeserved populations, and to special

services populations, such as migrants or the homeless. The Bureau provides project grants to community-based organizations to meet the health needs of the undeserved or special needs populations.

* County Governments Environmental Activities
National Association of Counties (NACo)
440 1st St., NW
8th Floor
Washington, DC 20001 (202) 393-6226
NACo serves as a forum for improving the nation's county governments and to communicate the county viewpoint to national officials. NACo acts as a liaison with other levels of government, serves as a national advocate for counties, and achieves a public understanding of the role of counties in the intergovernmental system.

* Dredging Permits
Regulatory Branch
U.S. Army Corps of Engineers
20 Massachusetts Ave., NW, Room 6235
Washington, DC 20314 (202) 272-0199
You must obtain a Corps permit if you plan to locate a structure, excavate, or discharge dredged or fill material in waters of the United States, including wetlands, or if you plan to transport dredged material for the purpose of dumping it into ocean waters. Contact the appropriate District Engineer office for current information and to apply for a permit. You may contact the above office for addresses and telephone numbers of the District offices.

* Economic Research Studies
Public Affairs
Economic Development Administration
Department of Commerce
14th St. and Constitution Ave., NW
Washington, DC 20230 (202) 377-5113
Economic Research Studies of the Economic Development Administration is an annotated bibliography listing economic research reports published by the Economic Development Administration. Each of the 210 entries includes an abstract and ordering information. The reports cover a broad range of topics and concentrate on the causes of economic distress and of economic growth, the basic remedy for distress. Contact EDA for your free copy.

* Election Assistance
Federal Election Commission
Information Services
999 E Street, NW
Washington, DC 20463 (202) 376-3120
In an effort to promote voluntary compliance with the law, this office provides technical assistance to candidates and committees and others involved in elections. Staff will research and answer questions on the Federal Election Campaign Act and FEC regulations, procedures, and advisory opinions; direct workshops on the law; and publish a wide range of materials.

* Fair Lending Practices
Fair Lending Analyst
Office of Consumer Affairs
Federal Deposit Insurance Corporation
550 17th St., NW, Room F-130
Washington, DC 20429 (202) 898-3535
The Community Reinvestment Act of 1977 empowers the FDIC to monitor FDIC-insured, state-chartered banks to make sure that the banks are meeting the credit needs of the communities they serve, including low- and middle-income areas. Questions regarding community reinvestment should be directed to the nearest FDIC regional office or to the Fair Lending Analyst at the above office.

* Free Experts on Loan
to Community Organizations
Pearson Program
Bureau of Personnel
Department of State
2201 C St NW, Room 2807
Washington, DC 20520 (202) 647-3308
The two objectives of this program are to allow State and local governments and related organizations to utilize the experience and expertise of Foreign Service Officers and to permit Foreign Service Officers to be assigned to positions with substantial program management responsibilities. Frequently officers are assigned to serve as special assistants to governors, mayors, city managers, and county commissioners. They have been assigned to a State department of social services, a regional local government innovation group, and to the Pan American Games organizing group. Interested organizations should discuss requests with the Office of Training and Liaison, and then submit a proposal. The Department of State will then identify an interested officer for the position.

* Free Food For Non-Profit Institutions
Food Distribution Program
Food and Nutrition Service
3101 Park Center Dr., Room 502
Alexandria, VA 22302 (703) 756-3680
Charitable and rehabilitation institutions are usually eligible to receive surplus commodities stored by USDA. The commodities available are dairy products, grain oil, and peanuts.

* Geographic Names Information
Branch of Geographic Names
U.S. Geological Survey
National Center, MS 523
Reston, VA 22092 (703) 648-4547
The USGS Branch of Geographic Names maintains a national research, coordinating, and information center to which all problems and inquiries concerning domestic geographic names can be directed. This office compiles name information, manages a names data repository, maintains information files, and publishes materials on domestic geographic names. The USGS, in cooperation with the Board on Geographic Names, maintains the *National Geographic Names Data Base* and compiles *The National Gazetteer of the United States of America* on a state-by-state basis.

* Health Services for Indigents
Bureau of Health Care Delivery and Assistance
Health Resources and Services Administration
5600 Fishers Lane, Room 7-05
Rockville, MD 20857 (301) 443-2320
The Bureau of Health Care Delivery and Assistance Services focuses nationally on efforts to ensure the availability and delivery of health care services in health manpower shortage areas, to medically underserved populations, and to special services populations, such as migrants or the homeless. It also administers the National Health Service Corps Program which recruits health care practitioners and places them in areas having shortages of people trained in health-related fields.

* Historic Places National Register
Interagency Resources Division
National Park Service
U.S. Department of the Interior
1100 L St., NW
Washington, DC 20005 (202) 343-9500
The National Register of Historic Places is administered by the Interagency Resources Division of NPS. Along with the Preservation Assistance Division, this office administers the Historic Preservation Fund grants-in-aid to states and the National Trust for Historic Preservation. Technical workshops and other assistance is provided on preservation planning, and a database of historic information is maintained.

* Local Environmental Health Managers
National Conference of Local
Environmental Health Administrators (NCLEHA)
Summit County Health Department
1100 Graham Circle
Cuyahoga Falls, OH 44224 (216) 923-4891
The National Conference of Local Environmental Health Administrators promotes efficient and effective local environmental health programs. NCLEHA is affiliated with the National Environmental Health Association.

* Local Government Environmental Activities
International City Managers Association (ICMA)
1120 6th St., NW
Suite 300
Washington, DC 20005 (202) 626-4600
The purposes of ICMA are to enhance the quality of local government and to nurture and assist professional local government administrators in the U.S. and other countries.

* Mayors of Large Cities
U.S. Conference of Mayors
1620 I St., NW
4th Floor
Washington, DC 20006 (202) 293-7330
The United States Conference of Mayors is the official nonpartisan organization of cities with populations of 30,000 or more. It has taken the lead in calling national attention to the problems and the potential of urban America.

* Medical Services and Personnel Shortages Survey

National Clearinghouse for Primary Care Information
8201 Greensboro Dr., Suite 600
McLean, VA 22102   (703) 821-8955

This clearinghouse provides information services to support the planning, development, and delivery of ambulatory health care to urban and rural areas where shortages of medical personnel and services exist. Its primary audience is health care providers who work in community health centers. They have a list of publications and can make referrals to other health-related organizations. This clearinghouse also publishes a newsletter, "Primary Care Perspectives."

* Military Base Closures: Community Adjustment

Office of Economic Adjustment
U.S. Department of Defense
The Pentagon, Room 4C767
Washington, DC 20301-4000

The Office of Economic Adjustment assists local communities, areas or states affected by U.S. Department of Defense actions, such as base closures, establishment of new installations, and cutbacks or expansion of activities. It publishes a number of free publications on these issues, including *Communities in Transition, Economic Recovery,* and *Twenty-five Years of Civilian Re-use.* Write or call for more information.

* National Governor's Association

National Governor's Association (NGA)
444 North Capitol St., NW
Suite 250
Washington, DC 20001   (202) 624-5300

NGA serves as a vehicle through which governors influence the development and implementation of national policy and apply creative leadership to state problems.

* National League of Cities

National League of Cities (NLC)
1301 Pennsylvania Ave., NW
Suite 600
Washington, DC 20004   (202) 626-3000

NLC is dedicated to making cities efficient and improving the delivery of municipal services by providing answers to questions about the day-to-day realities of running a city or town including refuse collection, employment practices, police management, cable television, hazardous waste management and international trade.

* Non-Profits and Foreign Exchange Programs

Office of Private Sector Programs
Bureau of Education and Cultural Affairs
United States Information Agency
301 Fourth St., SW, Room 216
Washington, DC 20547   (202) 485-7348

Grants and assistance are given to private non-profit organizations for exchange programs which further USIA goals of promoting mutual understanding between Americans and others. Any non-profit organization can submit proposals for partial funding.

* Place and Feature Names: State-by-State Dictionary

Books and Open File Reports
U.S. Geological Survey
Box 25425, Federal Center
Denver, CO 80225   (303) 236-7476

The National Gazetteer of the United States of America is a geographic dictionary of place and feature names, published on a state-by-state basis. It includes a glossary of terms and abbreviations, a map of counties in a state, and an alphabetical listing of USGS topographic quadrangle maps of the state, in addition to the information contained in the *National Geographic Names Data Base.* Also listed are names of features from other historical sources. Variant names are listed and cross-referenced to their official names. A variant name is any other known name or spelling applied to a feature other than the official name.

* Planned Approach to Community Health (PATCH)

Centers for Chronic Disease Prevention
and Health Promotion
Centers for Disease Control
1600 Clifton Rd., NE
Bldg 3, Room 117
Atlanta, GA 30333   (404) 639-2838

CCDPHP staff work with State and local health departments and community members to organize local intervention programs. The center provides materials and technical assistance, and the communities invest their time and resources and make the program work. Programs have focused on cholesterol screening and nutrition, smoking cessation, alcohol misuse, and prevention of injuries from falls. The PATCH program also conducts international training conferences.

* Public Works Engineering

American Public Works Association (APWA)
1313 East 60th St.
Chicago, IL 60637   (312) 667-2200

The American Public Works Association consists of government officials, engineers, administrators and others engaged in the various aspects of public works and published *APWA Reporter and APWA Directory.*

* Resource Development

Resource Development
Tennessee Valley Authority
Muscle Shoals, AL 35660   (615) 632-4636

The TVA plans to fund several future development programs. These include the stewardship of TVA facilities and landholdings; the improvement of water resources; the development of the Land Between the Lakes to reach its potential as a national demonstration model; and the production of fertilizer technology that supports a profitable and competitive agriculture. Group economic and rural development programs will also be funded in the Valley Resource Center to expand the Valley's service sector, upgrade literacy and job skills, promote a competitive manufacturing section, and expand employment in natural resource-based industries.

* Rural Agricultural Processing Industries

Science and Education
U.S. Department of Agriculture
Washington, DC 20250   (202) 447-5923

If your community wants to establish and operate an agricultural processing plant, the USDA can help you assess the project's potential. USDA will act as liaison to help find needed services, know-how, financial support, and any other assistance needed for such an enterprise.

* Rural Communities Clearinghouse

Rural Information Center
U.S. Department of Agriculture
10301 Baltimore Blvd.
Beltsville, MD 20705   (301) 344-3719

This center handles matters of economic competitiveness, economic development, local government, rural communities, community leadership, and natural resources. This center is a joint project of USDA's Extension Service and NAL.

* Rural Communities Financial Assistance

Farmers Home Administration (FmHA)
U.S. Department of Agriculture
Washington, DC 20250   (202) 447-4323

FmHA provides financial assistance to rural people and communities that cannot obtain commercial credit at affordable terms. Applicants must be unable to obtain credit from usual commercial sources. Examples of the types of loans available are Emergency Loans, Youth Project Loans, Housing Repair Loans and Grants, and Business and Industry Loan Guarantees.

* State Legislatures Coordination

National Conference of State Legislatures (NCSL)
444 North Capitol St., NW
Suite 500
Washington, DC 20001   (202) 624-5400

NCSL is a national organization of state legislators and legislative staff whose aims are to improve the quality and effectiveness of state legislators, to ensure states a strong, cohesive voice in the federal decision-making process and to foster interstate communication and cooperation.

* Telecommunications Expertise for Libraries, Schools, Fire Departments

Public Telecommunications Facilities Program
National Telecommunications and
Information Administration
Department of Commerce
14th St. and Constitution Ave. NW Room 4625
Washington, DC 20230   (202) 377-5802

By identifying public service telecommunications needs, NTIA assists schools, hospitals, libraries, policy, fire departments, and government agencies in using advanced telecommunications systems and technology to achieve their goals.

* Towns and Townships Advocacy

Your Community

National Association of Towns and Townships (NATT)
1522 K St., NW
Suite 730
Washington, DC 20005   (202) 737-5200
NATT is a federation of state organizations and individual communities which
provide technical assistance, educational services and public policy support to
local government officials of small communities across the country.

Neighborhood Improvements

* Aerial Photographs of Your Neighborhood
Customer User Services
Earth Resources Observation System Data Center (EROS)
U.S. Geological Survey
Sioux Falls, SD 57198   (605) 594-6511
Aerial photographs are available from this center for most geographical regions of the country. Prices range from $6 to $65, depending on whether they are black and white or color photographs. Contact this office for ordering information.

* Afro-American and Minority Health Projects
Office of Minority Health
Department of Health and Human Services
200 Independence Ave., SW
Room 118F
Washington, DC 20201   (202) 245-0020
This office serves as the focal point for the implementation of the recommendations and findings from the Report of the Secretary's Task Force on Black and Minority Health. Community-based projects are being designed to reduce the more than 60,000 excess deaths each year among minority Americans. Major activities include conferences, grants for innovative community health strategies developed by minority coalitions, and research on risk factors affecting minority health. The Report may be obtained from OMH.

* Aircraft Noise
Noise Abatement Division
Office of Environment and Energy
Federal Aviation Administration
Department of Transportation
800 Independence Ave., SW, Room 432
Washington, DC 20591   (202) 267-3553
This FAA division conducts research on reducing noise levels of new aircraft, and retrofitting older aircraft to reduce noise levels.

* Air Force Bands
U.S. Air Force
Bands and Music Branch
The Pentagon, SAF/PAG
Washington, DC 20330-1000   (202) 695-0019
If there is an Air Force band stationed near you, you can request a public performance in your town. For information on where the bands are located and who to contact to schedule a performance, call the above coordinating office.

* Air Shows
Headquarters, U.S. Marine Corps
Code OLAC
Washington, DC 20380   (202) 694-1034
The Marine Corps can provide aviation demonstrations for community events. Contact your local Marine Corps headquarters or the above office for a referral.

* Anti-Drug Abuse Community Grants
Drug Abuse Prevention Oversight Staff
Office of the Secretary
U.S. Department of Education
400 Maryland Ave., SW, Room 4145
Washington, DC 20202-0100   (202) 732-4599
State and Local Grants Program: This is a formula grant program which allocates funds to States based on school-age enrollment. Funds are to be used for anti-drug abuse efforts in schools and community-based organizations. Contact Allen King, (202) 732-4599.

* Army Band and Chorus
Community Relations Division
U.S. Army Public Affairs
The Pentagon, Room 2E631
Washington, DC 20310   (202) 697-2707
To arrange for a performance in your community by the Army Field Band and Soldiers Chorus, the Golden Knights paratrooper unit, color guards, and other marching units, contact your nearest Army installation, or the above office for a referral.

* Army Paratroopers and Color Guards
Community Relations Division
U.S. Army Public Affairs
The Pentagon, Room 2E631
Washington, DC 20310   (202) 697-2707
To arrange for a performance in your community by the Golden Knights paratrooper unit, color guards, and other marching units, contact your nearest Army installation, or the above office for a referral.

* Army Reserve Band and Color Guard
Chief of U.S. Army Reserve
Public Affairs
The Pentagon
Washington, D.C. 20310   (202) 697-7369
To request an Army Reserve band performance in your town, or to arrange for a color guard at a former military person's funeral,
contact your local Army Reserve headquarters or the above office for a referral.

* Army Reserve Community Projects: Baseball to Language Training
Chief of U.S. Army Reserve
Public Affairs, The Pentagon
Washington, DC 20310   (202) 697-7369
The Army Reserve provides a variety of community services through their special programs. Requests are handled on a case by case basis based on their current ability to help. Projects might involve building a community playground or a baseball field. Through the Adopt-a-School Program, Corps people with special skills or training teach special courses, such as a foreign language or communications, or may be involved in extra-curricular activities. Contact your local Army Reserve headquarters or the above office for further information.

* Art Exhibits: Parks, Plazas, Airports
Visual Arts Program
National Endowment for the Arts
1100 Pennsylvania Ave., NW, Room 729
Washington, DC 20506   (202) 682-5448
The Visual Arts Program awards fellowships to artists in a wide variety of visual media, enabling them to set aside time to pursue their work. It also awards grants to organizations that assist visual artists and support public art projects, such as art in parks, plazas, and airports. Funding is available for a variety of projects that enable visual artists to communicate with their peers and the public, and for a variety of on-going visual arts programs, including exhibitions and access to working facilities.

* Bank Loans and Community Reinvestment
Community Affairs Officer
Federal Reserve System
20th St. & Constitution Ave., NW
Washington, DC 20551   (202) 452-3000
The Community Reinvestment Act encourages banks and other institutions to help meet the credit needs for housing and other purposes in their communities. In accordance with this Act, the Community Affairs Officer and staff at each of the 12 Federal Reserve Banks are responsible for advising depository institutions of private and public resources for community development. The officers also facilitate communications between borrowers, lending institutions, local government agencies, and others involved with community development financing. A pamphlet outlining the Community Reinvestment Act responsibilities of the Community Affairs Officers may be requested from the Federal Reserve Bank of Richmond, or the Community Affairs Officer at any Federal Reserve Bank.

* Cities in Schools: Truancy, Dropouts, Violence
Office of Juvenile Justice
and Delinquency Prevention
U.S. Department of Justice
633 Indiana Ave., NW
Washington, DC 20531   (202) 724-5911
Cities in Schools, a public-private partnership that addresses the problems of dropouts and school violence, is designed to reduce school absenteeism and

dropout rates by coordinating services for at-risk youngsters. Five regional offices help serve the 26 operating programs throughout the country and assist other local communities to initiate new Cities in Schools programs.

* Community Action Against Alcohol and Drug Addiction

National Clearinghouse on Alcohol and Drug Information
PO Box 2345
Rockville, MD 20892 (301) 468-2600
Communities: What You Can Do About Drug and Alcohol Abuse discusses various strategies for parent groups, schools, and workplaces and details various educational materials available. Single copies of this booklet (No.84-1310) are available free.

* Community Anti-Drug Alliance

ACTION
Drug Alliance Office
806 Connecticut Ave., NW
Washington, DC 20525 (202) 634-9757
ACTION supports community-based prevention and education efforts with grants, contracts, conferences, and technical assistance.
Nonprofit organizations and state and local governments are eligible to receive grants from ACTION. An announcement is made in the Federal Register regarding the type of activities that the ACTION grant is available for and organizations are encouraged to apply. ACTION also maintains a mailing list which sends copies of the notices appearing in the Federal Register directly to those on the list. To get the name of your organization on this list, call the number above.

* Community Business Development

Public Affairs
Economic Development Administration
Department of Commerce
14th St. and Constitution Ave., NW
Room 7824
Washington, DC 20230 (202) 377-3081
The Economic Development Administration provides loan guarantees to industrial and commercial firms, and technical assistance and grants to enable communities and firms to find solutions to problems that stifle economic growth. Contact this office for more information.

* Community Drug Abuse Situation

Information Systems Unit
Office of Diversion Control
Drug Enforcement Administration
U.S. Department of Justice
1405 Eye St. NW, Room 719
Washington, DC 20537 (202) 633-1316
For those who want to understand and evaluate the scope and magnitude of drug abuse in the United States, this network is an invaluable information source. Whether you are a local public administrator considering programs, a reporter on the heels of a story, or just a concerned parent, the Drug Abuse Warning Network can provide you with needed information. More than 900 hospital emergency rooms and medical examiner facilities supply data to the program. DAWN identifies drugs currently in vogue, determines existing patterns and profiles of abuse/abuser in Standard Metropolitan Statistical Areas, monitors systemwide abuse trends, detects new abuse entities and polydrug combinations, and provides data needed for rational control and scheduling of drugs being abused. It is the full-information source on the drug problem in America.

* Community Involvement with Workplace Drug Abuse

National Audiovisual Center
Customer Service Section
8700 Edgeworth Drive
Capitol Heights, MD 20743-3701 (301) 763-1896
National Clearinghouse for Alcohol and Drug Information
P.O. Box 2345
Rockville, MD 20852 (301) 468-8200
"Finding Solutions" portrays drug abuse in the workplace as a community-wide problem; thus the solutions offered through education and prevention are presented as personal, workplace, and community responsibilities. Specific emphasis is placed on the need to effectively deliver accurate and credible information to the workforce, to promote workplace peer involvement and build community partnerships. It is available for sale and rental.

* Crime Insurance for Homeowners and Business

Federal Crime Insurance
P.O. Box 6301
Rockville, MD 20850 (800) 638-8780 (301) 251-1660 in DC
The Federal Crime Insurance Program is a federally subsidized program

sponsored by the Federal Emergency Management Adminstration for homeowners and commercial businesses to insure against burglary and robbery. To find out if your state is eligible and for further information, contact the office above. Those living in Maryland outside D.C. should call collect: (301) 251-1660.

* Ethnic or Racial Tensions Resolution

Community Relations Service
U.S. Department of Justice
5550 Friendship Blvd., Suite 300
Chevy Chase, MD 20815 (301) 492-5929
If your community is being torn apart by ethnic disputes or police-citizen conflicts, you may need help from this special service, set up by the Civil Rights Act of 1964. The Community Relations Service exists to resolve such disputes. The agency provides direct conciliation and mediation assistance to communities to facilitate the peaceful, voluntary resolution of racial and ethnic disputes or conflicts, and the peaceful co-existence of police and citizens' groups in the rapidly changing neighborhoods of today's cities. The CRS regularly provides conferences, training workshops, and publications to any and all communities in an attempt to forestall such disputes. However, when tensions do break out, the CRS will initiate whatever steps are necessary to begin making progress toward bringing about a resolution. They normally begin with extensive informal discussions with public or police officials and local community leaders, but if the agency and the parties determine that formal negotiations offer the best hope for a settlement, the agency arranges and mediates the negotiations.

* Fire Prevention and Education

Office of Fire Prevention and Arson Control
U.S. Fire Administration
16825 South Seton Ave.
Emmitsburg, MD 21727 (301) 447-1122
For information on technical and educational assistance to State, local, and national fire services and community groups, contact the office above. Information on fire safety, residential sprinkler trailers and smoke detector usage and maintenance can be obtained from this office. Various forms of educational assistance (pamphlets, books, tapes) can be obtained. Call the office above to receive the following publications, and to find out how to receive the monthly newsletter, *Operation Life Safety.*
After the Fire: Returning (#5-0027)
America's Burning (#5-0078)
Check Your Hotspots Kit (#5-0101)
Home Fire Protection Fire Sprinkler (#5-0007)
It's Alarming (#5-0035)
Fire in the U.S. (#5-0035)
Mini-Computers (#5-0012)
Organizing Your Community (#5-0068)
Public Fire Education Today (#5-0049)
Safety and Your Christmas Tree (#5-0029)
Smoke Detector and Fire Safety Guide (#5-0039)
Smoke Detector Kit (#5-0079)
Smoke Detectors: Don't Stay at Home (#5-0104)
Urban Fire Education (#5-0006)
U.S. Fire Administration Brochure (#5-0067)
Winter Fires (#5-0031)

* Fire Safety for Children

U.S. Fire Administration
16825 South Seton Ave.
Emmitsburg, MD 21727 (301) 447-1122
Contact the office above to obtain materials on fire safety for children. The following materials are available, in addition to Sesame Street education materials on fire safety education:
Adolescent Firesetter Handbook, ages 14 - 18 (#5-0091)
Child Firesetter Handbook, ages 7 - 13 (#5-0107)
Child Firesetter Handbook, ages 0 - 7 (#5-0106)
Curious Kids Kit (#5-0121)
Juvenile Firesetter Handbook - Dealing with Children Ages 7-14 (FA-63)

* Free Christmas Trees

Division of Forestry
Bureau of Land Management
U.S. Department of the Interior
Washington, DC 20240 (202) 653-8864
The BLM officials issue permits to cut Christmas trees for a nominal fee on Bureau of Land Management-administered lands in the 11 Western states and Alaska. Free-use permits are available from the Bureau to non-profit organizations for timber and trees to be used exclusively by that organization. This excludes the resale of any free timber or trees by those organizations.

* Historic Preservation Assistance

Preservation Assistance Division
National Park Service
U.S. Department of the Interior

1100 L St., NW
Washington, DC 20005 (202) 343-9573
The Preservation Assistance Division guides Federal and state agencies and the general public in historic preservation project work. Standards and guidelines are established, information on technical preservation is distributed, and training is given on technical preservation approaches and treatments. This office also administers the Preservation Tax Incentives program, the status of National Historic Landmarks, and the Historic Preservation Fund grant-in-aid program.

* Homeless, Migrants, Refugees: Health Services

Bureau of Health Care Delivery and Assistance
Health Resources and Services Administration
5600 Fishers Lane, Room 7-05
Rockville, MD 20857 (301) 443-2320
The Bureau of Health Care Delivery and Assistance Services focuses nationally on efforts to ensure the availability and delivery of health care services in health manpower shortage areas, to medically underserved populations, and to special services populations, such as migrants or the homeless. It also administers the National Health Service Corps Program which recruits health care practitioners and places them in areas having shortages of people trained in health-related fields.

* Job Creation Assistance

Technical Assistance Division
Economic Development Administration
Department of Commerce
14th St. and Constitution Ave., NW
Washington, DC 20230 (202) 377-2127
The Technical Assistance Division of EDA sponsors programs of technical assistance to local communities which are designed to discover new ways to generate jobs. Local governments, non-profit organizations, and private firms can apply. Contact this office for more information.

* Marine Corps Air Show

Commandant of the Marine Corps (OLAC)
Headquarters Marine Corps
Washington, DC 20380 (202) 694-1034
Watch the AV8 Harrier jump jet (it shoots straight up and turns around in mid-air), the Drum and Bugle Corps, and Marine bands perform. You may write to the above address or your nearest Corp installation for their brochure explaining Marine Corps programs and how to complete the forms to arrange for these units' performance in your community. They can also provide you with a patriotic speaker for Veterans Day and Memorial Day events.

* Marine Corps Bands and Color Guards

Headquarters, U.S. Marine Corps
Code OLAC
Washington, DC 20380 (202) 694-1034
The Marine Corps can provide bands and color guards for community events. The Corps sponsors the Devil Pup program. Contact your local Marine Corps headquarters or the above office for a referral.

* Marine Corps Summer Camp

Headquarters, U.S. Marine Corps
Code OLAC
Washington, DC 20380 (202) 694-1034
The Marine Corps sponsor a summer camp for high school youth. Contact your local Marine Corps headquarters or the above office for a referral.

* National Guard Community Participation

National Guard Bureau
Attn: NGB-PAC
4501 Ford Ave.
Alexandria, VA 22301-1457 (202) 756-1923
Local National Guard units provide bands, color guards, and flight demonstrations for community events upon request of civic groups. The Guard also sponsors annual open houses and conducts tours of the local bases. A Speakers Bureau will provide experts to speak on defense and local issues, and the Guard sponsors orientation trips for civic leaders. Call or write for more information on the Guard's varied community assistance programs, including the loan of equipment to civic groups.

* Navy Bands and Concerts

U.S. Navy Band
Public Affairs Office
Washington Navy Yard
Washington, DC 20374-1052 (202) 433-2394
The U.S. Navy Concert Band and its specialty units--including the Commander's Trio, Windjammers, Tuba-Euphonium Quartet, Sea Chanters, Country Current,

and the Commodores--are available to perform at community events nationwide. Units of the band perform a wide range of musical styles, from jazz, folk, and blue grass to classical chamber and cocktail music. Write or call for information on how to request the Band.

* Neighborhood Crime Comparison Information

Uniform Crime Reporting Section
Federal Bureau of Investigation
U.S. Department of Justice
9th & Pennsylvania Ave., NW, GRB
Washington, DC 20535 (202) 324-2614
If you'd like to know how safe your prospective new neighborhood is, contact the Uniform Crime Reporting Section. This annual report, Crime In the United States contains an exact reading of the crime rates of any city in America (down to the types of crimes committed most frequently in which neighborhoods). Also, local police departments of most major cities have neighborhood crime reports available and will actually rate the safety factor of your new address for you.

* Neighborhood Safety Videos and Publications

National Institute of Justice
NCJRS, Box 6000
Dept. AID
Rockville, MD 20850 (800) 851-3420 (301) 251-5500 in DC
NIJ has these and other publications and videos on crime prevention and the law. Many of the documents are free of charge, while others are available for a modest fee. When ordering or inquiring about an NIJ publication, refer to its NCJ number.
Crime Stoppers: A National Evaluation (RIB). 1986, 5 pp. (NCJ 102292).
The Growing Role of Private Security (RIB). 1984, 5 pp. (NCJ 94703).
Guardian Angels: An Assessment of Citizen Response to Crime: Executive Summary. 1986, 31 pp. (NCJ 1009111).
Improving the Use and Effectiveness of Neighborhood Watch Programs (RIA). 1988, 4 pp. (NCJ 108618).
Neighborhood Safety (Crime file videotape). 1985 (NCJ 97227). VHS, Beta, or 3/4-inch.
Taking a Bite Out of Crime: The Impact of a Mass Media Crime Prevention Campaign. 1984, 78 pp. (NCJ 93350).

* Neighborhood Watch Programs

Office of Crime Prevention
National Institute of Justice
U.S. Department of Justice
633 Indiana Ave. NW
Washington, DC 20531 (202) 724-7684
If you're interested in starting a Neighborhood Watch Program in your town, or want to know how you can make yours better, contact the Neighborhood Watch Specialists at the National Institute of Justice. They will be glad to help you make your neighborhood a safer place.

* Recycling Efforts

Public Information Center
Environmental Protection Agency
401 M St., SW, PM-211 B
Washington DC 20460 (202) 4475-7751
Recycling Works! is a free booklet that provides information about successful recycling programs initiated by state and local agencies. It also describes private recycling efforts and joint recycling ventures of government and businesses.

* Residential Fire Sprinklers

Federal Emergency Management Agency
16825 South Seton Ave.
Emmitsburg, MD 21727 (301) 447-1021
Through its regional offices, FEMA conducts demonstrations of how residential fire sprinklers operate. Contact your regional FEMA office or the office above for more information.

* Telecommunications Expertise for Libraries, Schools, Fire Departments

Public Telecommunications Facilities Program
National Telecommunications and
Information Administration
Department of Commerce
14th St. and Constitution Ave., NW
Room 4625
Washington, DC 20230 (202) 377-5802
By identifying public service telecommunications needs, NTIA assists schools, hospitals, libraries, policy, fire departments, and government agencies in using advanced telecommunications systems and technology to achieve their goals.

* ## Toys for Tots
    Commanding General (PAO)
    4th Marine Division (Rein.), FMF
    U.S. Marine Corps Reserve
    4400 Dauphine St.
    New Orleans, LA 70146-5400

The Marine Corps Reserve sponsors an annual Christmas "Toys for Tots" project, which collects toys for needy children. To learn how to donate or provide a collection point at your place of business, contact your local Marine Corps Reserve office or the above office for more information.

* ## Waste Management Policy
    Association of Metropolitan Sewerage Agencies (AMSA)
    1015 18th St., NW
    Suite 1002
    Washington, DC 20036   (202) 659-9161

The Association of Metropolitan Sewerage Agencies consists of sewerage agencies in areas with more than 250,000 people. It serves to exchange technical data and deals with the federal government on environmental and regulatory matters.

* ## Woodsy Owl: Litter Cleanup
    U.S. Department of Agriculture
    Forest Service, P.O. Box 96090
    Washington, DC 20090-6090 (202) 475-3785

To increase children's awareness of our delicate environment, the Forest Service's Woodsy Owl campaign has a variety of free materials available, including coloring sheets, detective sheets, song sheets, patches, "Woodsy Owl on Camping" (brochure), and stickers. A Woodsy Owl costume is available to some community groups to compliment "Give A Hoot! Don't Pollute" campaign.

Traffic and Transportation

* Commuter and Air Taxi Services

Commuter and Air Taxi Branch
Transportation Division
Office of Flight Operations
Federal Aviation Administration
Department of Transportation
800 Independence Ave., SW, Room 303
Washington, DC 20591   (202) 267-8086

Contact this office for information regarding policy, regulations, and directives for commuter and air taxi aircraft. A list is available of air taxi operators and commercial operators of small aircraft.

* Essential Air Passenger Service

Aviation Analysis
Federal Aviation Administration
Department of Transportation
800 Independence Ave., SW, Room 5100
Washington, DC 20591   (202) 267-5903

This office guarantees that certain cities will be served by airlines. It also represents community views. Contact this office for more information on airport service.

* Funded Traffic Safety Projects

Evaluation Staff (NTS-02.1)
Traffic Safety Programs
National Highway Traffic Safety Administration
U.S. Department of Transportation
400 7th Street, SW
Washington, DC 20590   (202) 366-2759

Once known as the National Project Reporting System, funded project information collected by this office from each state is stored in a database. Projects are funded in areas such as occupant safety and alcohol. Findings are assembled annually in a published report providing an overview of the projects, their status, and how funding is apportioned, such as amounts to each project and within each project, amount to education, to enforcement, and to other areas. Contact the Evaluation Staff for details.

* Handicapped Assistance and Mass Transit

Office of Research, Training,
and Rural Transportation
Urban Mass Transit Administration
400 7th St., SW, Room 6102
Washington, DC 20590   (202) 366-4995

UMTA is involved in a Congressionally-mandated project with the National Easter Seals Committee to study accessibility problems faced by the handicapped who use mass transit. The office runs a series of demonstrations on improved arrangements to help the handicapped.

* Highway Safety Accident Prevention

Office of Highway Safety (HHS-21)
Associate Administrator for Safety and Operations
Federal Highway Administration
U.S. Department of Transportation
400 7th St., SW
Washington, DC 20590   (202) 366-1153

Highway construction safety programs are funded to remove, relocate, or shield roadside obstacles; to identify and correct hazards at railroad crossings; and to improve signing, pavement markings, and signalization. For information and referral, contact the Office of Highway Safety. The following publications are also available:

Highway Safety Improvement Programs, Annual Report
Status Report of Federal Funds Used for Highway Safety Programs.
Several other reports prepared by this office are available from National Technical Information Service, 5285 Port Royal Road, Springfield, VA 22161; (703) 487-4650. A sampling of titles follows:
Inexpensive Accident Countermeasures at Narrow Bridges
Legibility and Driver Response to Selected Lane and Road Closure Barricades
Re-Evaluation of Traffic Control at Non-Signalized Intersections
Rollover Potential of Vehicles on Embankments, Sideslopes, and Other Roadside Features; *Railroad-Highway Grade Crossing Signal Visibility Improvement Program, Final Report*
Constant Warning Time Devices for Railroad-Highway Crossings: Technical Summary

Studies of the Road Marking Code

* Highway Traffic Safety Records

Technical Reference Division (NAD-52)
Office of Administrative Operations
National Highway Traffic Safety Administration
U.S. Department of Transportation
400 7th Street, SW
Washington, DC 20590   (202) 366-2768

NHTSA reports and records are available for public inspection at this location, and database searches can be requested for a fee. Holdings include vehicle research and test reports; investigation reports on accidents and defects; recall information; compliance reports; consumer complaints; consumer advisories; filmed records of research and tests; NHTSA *Technical Reports*; engineering specifications; and certification information. Both light and heavy highway vehicles are covered. Call ahead to ensure that the records you need will be on hand.

* Mass Transit Program Evaluation

Program Evaluation Division
Urban Mass Transit Administration
Department of Transportation
400 7th St., SW, Room 9306
Washington, DC 20590   (202) 366-1727

This office can provide you with information on its recent and on-going evaluations of projects and programs implemented by UMTA. For information on earlier evaluations regarding bus, subway, and other modes of urban transit.

* Maximum Speed Limit

Police Traffic Services Division
Office of Enforcement and Emergency Services
Traffic Safety Programs
National Highway Traffic Safety Administration
U.S. Department of Transportation
400 7th Street, SW, Room 6124
Washington, DC 20590   (202) 366-5440

The National Maximum Speed Limit is 65 miles per hour on certain interstate highways. This office processes annual certifications of maximum speed limit enforcement programs throughout the U.S. and assists states in developing and improving enforcement efforts.

* National Driver Register

National Driver Register (NTS-24)
Traffic Safety Programs
National Highway Traffic Safety Administration
U.S. Department of Transportation
400 7th Street, SW, Room 5119
Washington, DC 20590   (202) 366-4800

The *National Driver Register* is a central, computerized index of state records on drivers whose operator licenses have been revoked, denied, or suspended for more than 6 months. Data includes name, birthdate, height, weight, eye color, date and reason for action, and date of reinstatement. Applications for driver licenses are routinely checked against the register, and states exchange information via an electronic system.

* Occupants Displaced by Highway Construction

Office of Right-of-Way (HRW-22)
Office of Right-of-Way and Environment
Federal Highway Administration
U.S. Department of Transportation
400 7th St., SW, Room 3219
Washington, DC 20590   (202) 366-0342

This office administers FHWA's lead role in implementing the Uniform Relocation Assistance and Real Property Acquisition Policies Act. When Federally funded highway construction projects involve displacing residents from acquired property, this Act sets policies for purchase of the land and relocating the people on it. The publication, *Your Rights and Benefits as Displaced Under the Federal Relocation Assistance Program*, is available from this office.

Your Community

* Pedestrian and Driver Research

Office of Driver and Pedestrian Research (NRD-40)
Research and Development
National Highway Traffic Safety Administration
U.S. Department of Transportation
400 7th Street, SW
Washington, DC 20590   (202) 366-9591

This office studies factors affecting the safety of drivers and pedestrians. Research areas include determining the causes of unsafe driving and developing countermeasures; the effectiveness of vehicle occupant safety restraints; the effect of alcohol and drugs; the safety concerns of bicycles, motorcycles, and mopeds; driver license standards; and young drivers. This office can refer you to staff researching the topic of your interest.

* Pedestrian Safety

Geometric and Roadside Design Branch
Engineering Division
Office of Engineering Program Development
Federal Highway Administration
U.S. Department of Transportation
400 7th St., SW, Room 3128
Washington, DC 20590   (202) 366-1315

Highway design and roadside facilities are studied by this office to determine their impact on pedestrians and bicyclists. The publication, *Pedestrian and Bicycle Facilities*, provides you with information about the roadside designs and structures used in safety-related applications.

* Private Sector Initiatives in Mass Transit

Office of Private Sector Initiatives
Office of Budget and Policy
Urban Mass Transit Administration
Department of Transportation
400 7th St., SW, Room 9300
Washington, DC 20590   (202) 366-1666

This office encourages private sector involvement in mass transit throughout the United States. Specifically, they work through the following four areas:

1) Competitive Contracting: Local transit authorities are encouraged to open the provisioning of services up to private sector competition.
2) Entrepreneurial Services: Groups in the private sector are encouraged to start self-sustaining transit services (such as taxi and bus) in cooperation with local transit authorities.
3) Joint Development: Federal assistance is available to help plan public/private sector joint ventures at transit facilities.
4) Demand Management Program: Federal funds are available to encourage local employers and merchants to develop techniques to help manage transportation and mobility problems in their areas.

* Public Private Transportation Network

(800) 522-7786

This technical support and information system draws on the expertise of private sector operators and other experts in the transportation field. In addition to these speakers, the Network also arranges seminars.

* Road Signs

Traffic Control Development Applications Division (HTO-21)
Traffic Control Systems
Traffic Operations Division
Office of Safety and Operations
Federal Highway Administration
U.S. Department of Transportation

400 7th St., SW
Washington, DC 20590   (202) 366-2184

Efforts by this division improve the effectiveness and uniformity of such traffic control devices as road signs, signal lamps, and highway markings throughout the country. Standards are developed for designing signs and using other traffic control devices. The meanings of road signs and markings are described in *Road Symbol Signs*, which can be obtained by contacting the office listed above. Two other publications on the subject, listed below, are available from the Superintendent of Documents, U.S. Government Printing Office, Washington, D.C. 20402; (202) 783-3238: *Manual on Uniform Traffic Control Devices*, ($22.00) *Standard Highway Signs Book*, ($30.00)

* Roadway Beautification

Special Programs and Evaluation Branch (HRW-12)
Program Requirements Division
Office of Right-of-Way and Environment
Federal Highway Administration
U.S. Department of Transportation
400 7th St., SW
Washington, DC 20590   (202) 366-2017

Junkyards and outdoor advertising along federally aided and interstate highways are regulated under a program conducted through this office. The publication, *Junkyards, the Highway, and Visual Quality*, offers information on this program. To obtain a copy, or to request further details on highway beautification programs, contact the branch listed.

* Traffic Accident Data

Performance Evaluation Branch
Office of Highway Safety
Federal Highway Administration
U.S. Department of Transportation
400 7th St., SW
Washington, DC 20590   (202) 366-2159

Statistics are kept here on fatal and injury accident rates for the Nation's highways. An extensive list of publications related to accidents and highway safety is also maintained. Call or write this office to request the data you need.

* Urban Mass Transportation Research

Manager, UMTRIS
Transportation Research Board
National Research Council
2101 Constitution Ave., NW
Washington, DC 20418   (202) 334-2995

The Urban Mass Transportation Research Information Service is a computerized database on worldwide transportation research. Administered by the Transportation Research Board (TRB), it covers all phases of conventional, new, and automated public transportation. UMTRIS features database storage/retrieval of abstracts of technical papers, journal articles, research reports, computer program descriptions, and statistical sources, as well as state-of-the-art bibliographies. Descriptions of ongoing research, especially that sponsored by UMTA, are also included. UMTRIS offers the public nearly 20,000 information references to ongoing and completed research activities, and adds 2,000 new references annually to the database. In addition to serving as the central source of technical information to the public and private sectors, UMTRIS also serves as an institutional memory for UMTA projects and project reports. The database can be searched online by any computer with a modem through DIALOG Information Services File 63. UMTRIS is supported by a National Network of Transportation Libraries (18), and they serve both as repositories that house and make UMTA documents available to the general public, as well as document delivery centers that provide UMTRIS users with full text copies of citations retrieved from the database.

Fires, Floods, and Disaster Relief

* Arson Control and Clearinghouse

U.S. Fire Administration
16825 South Seton Ave.
Emmitsburg, MD 21727 (301) 447-1122

The Arson Resource Center is available to help answer your questions and locate resources related to arson. It was established several years ago by the U.S. Fire Administration, and has developed an impressive collection of arson-related materials. FEMA personnel and NETC students can borrow materials from the Center, and books and research reports are available to the general public through area libraries (interlibrary loan). Audio-visual and general references are stored in the Center for in-house use. The following publications and source materials on arson are available from the USFA free of charge:

Arson Bibliography (#5-0001)
Arson Lab (#5-0003)
Arson Overview Report ($5-0024)
Arson Victims: Suggestions (#5-0034)
Arson Resource Directory (#5-0087)
Arson Prosecution Issues (#5-0086)
Rural Arson Control (#5-0110)
Establishing an Arson Strike Force (#5-0111)

* Bomb Shelters Designs

Federal Emergency Management Agency
P.O. Box 70274
Washington, DC 20024 (202) 646-3484

The following free publications will show you the ins and outs of bomb shelters and their construction:

Shelters in New Homes (TR-60). Shows how any home builder or owner can provide an area that protects against fallout radiation and windstorm without sacrificing its day-to-day usefulness. It includes examples of multi-purpose areas, shelter designs and details, and radiation shielding principles.
Cost Benefits in Shelters (TR-69). Explores various areas of cost savings resulting from the incorporation of basic fallout shelter design techniques in new buildings.
Home Fallout Shelter--Snack Bar--Basement Location Plan D (H-12D). A snack bar built of brick and concrete block can be converted into shelter.
Home Fallout Shelter: Outside Concrete Shelter (H-12-1).
Home Fallout Shelter: Aboveground Home Shelter (H-12-2).
Home Blast Shelter: Underground Concrete Shelter (H-12-3).
Technical Standards for Fallout Shelter Designs (TM 72-1). Shows the technical architectural and environmental standards for fallout shelter design.

* Dam Safety and Hazards

Federal Emergency Management Agency
P.O. Box 70274
Washington, DC 20024 (202) 646-3484

The following publications are available from the office above and contain information on dam safety:

Civil Preparedness Guide: National Dam Safety Program for S & L (CPG 1-39)
Dam Safety: An Owner's Guidance Manual (FEMA 145)
Dam Safety: Know the Potential Hazard (L-152)
Federal Guidelines for Dam Safety (FEMA-93)
Financing Dam Safety Projects (FEMA-61)
Glossary of Terms for Dam Safety (FEMA-148)

* Disaster Relief Grants and Loans

Federal Emergency Management Agency
P.O. Box 70274
Washington, DC 20024 (202) 646-3484

The following free publications will help you through the application process for Federal disaster relief grants and loans:

Handbook for Applicants (DR&R-1). Prescribes policy and procedures for requesting, obtaining, and administering FEMA grants for public assistance under the Disaster Relief Act of 1974.
Community Disaster Loan Handbook (DR&R-5). For local governments outlying FEMA Community Disaster Loan Program.
Documenting Disaster Damage (DR&R-7). Concerned with the need to maintain proper records so that you can fill out, update, maintain and submit various papers, in order to receive FEMA funds.
Your Disaster Assistance Center: Federal, State, and Local Aid (DR&R- 10). Handbook on how to apply for assistance after a disaster.

* Disaster Relief and Recovery Help

Federal Emergency Management Agency
P.O. Box 70274
Washington, DC 20024 (202) 646-3484

The *Digest of Federal Assistance Programs* (DR&R-21) is designed to serve as an initial source of information for private citizens and public officials who need disaster assistance. It is a compendium of Federal programs specifically designed to supplement State and local relief and recovery efforts, as well as programs that may serve to lessen the effects of civil disasters or emergencies. It includes programs that either require a Presidential declaration of a major disaster or emergency and those which do not.

* Earthquakes and Small Businesses

Federal Emergency Management Agency
P.O. Box 70247
Washington, DC 20024 (202) 646-3484

Guidelines for Local Small Businesses in Meeting the Earthquake Threat is a booklet designed to help small businesses prepare for and respond to a catastrophic earthquake. It contains information on assessing earthquake risks and provides a planning framework for preparation, response, and long-term recovery for a small business.

* Earthquake Hazard Reduction Program

Federal Emergency Management Agency
P.O. Box 70274
Washington, DC 20024 (202) 646-3484

The publication, *National Earthquake Hazard Reduction Program Five Year Plan*, presents an overview of FY 1985-89 program plans for the National Earthquake Hazard Reduction Program (HEHRP). It emphasizes the goals, objectives, and funding requirements for each of the participating major program elements. It also provides a comprehensive and coherent presentation of the activities projected by each participating agency for 5 fiscal years. It is available from the office above.

* Earthquake Safety Checklist

Federal Emergency Management Agency
P.O. Box 70274
Washington, DC 20024 (202) 646-3484

The following publications provide information on earthquake preparedness and safety:

Family Earthquake Safety Home Hazard Hunt and Drill (FEMA-113). Discusses how to identify and correct hazards in the home and practice what to do if an earthquake occurs.
Coping With Children's Reactions to Earthquakes and Other Disasters (FEMA-48). Deals with children's fears and anxieties following a disaster.
Earthquake Safety Checklist (FEMA-46). Safety tips for preparation, response to, and immediate aftermath of an earthquake.
Earthquakes (L-111). Offers safety tips for potential victims of earthquakes.

* Emergency and Fire Professionals Protection

Federal Emergency Management Agency
P.O. Box 700274
Washington, DC 20024 (202) 646-3484

The *U.S. Fire Administration Brochure* (L-160) describes the programs offered by the U.S. Fire Administration, including those that help fire service professionals manage fire data that gets the public involved, educates fire and emergency professionals, helps protect firefighters, promotes life-saving technology.

* Emergency Broadcast System

Federal Emergency Management Agency
P.O. Box 70274
Washington, DC 20024 (202) 646-3484

The leaflet, *Emergency Broadcast System* (L-93), cites the EBS as a method of communicating with the American public in the event of war, threat of war, or grave national crisis.

* Emergency Education Network

Emergency Education Network (EENET)
National Emergency Training Center
16825 South Seton Ave.
Emmitsburg, MD 21727 (301) 447-1068

EENET is owned and operated by FEMA to provide State and local emergency management personnel with quality education and training. Fourteen shows per year are produced to be shown to live audiences via satellite or by cable. Contact the office above for further information.

* Emergency Management Institute

Emergency Management Institute
National Emergency Training Center
16825 South Seton Ave,
Emmitsburg, MD 21727   (301) 447-1000
This Institute provides courses on several different topics in emergency management and civil defense. For more information contact the office above.

* Emergency Management Materials

Federal Emergency Management Agency
P.O. Box 70274
Washington, DC 20024   (202) 646-3484
Publications on emergency management are listed below:
Emergency Management in Public Administration Education (FEMA- 106)
Emergency Management the Human Factor (FEMA-108)
Emergency Management, U.S.A. Home Study Course (HS-2)
Emergency Management, USA (L-124)
In Time of Emergency - A Citizen's Handbook on Emergency Management (H-14)

* Emergency Medical Services

Federal Emergency Management Agency
P.O. Box 70274
Washington, DC 20024   (202) 646-3484
Introduction to Emergency Medical Services (SM 220) is a student manual which includes lectures, discussions, slide/tape presentations, case studies, and an optional workshop. Lessons cover topics on the historical perspective, system design, resources, medical control, EMS councils, legal and medical issues, communications, and mutual aid.

* Emergency Planning Educational Teleconferences

U.S. Fire Administration
Federal Emergency Management Agency
16825 South Seton Ave.
Emmitsburg, MD 21727   (301) 447-1122
FEMA holds an annual series of educational teleconferences for fire service and emergency management audiences on such topics as stress management, public affairs, residential sprinklers, flammable gases and liquids, AIDS, and radiation transportation accidents, and hazardous materials training. Copies of previous 52 shows are available for a charge, or could be borrowed from the State Emergency Management Offices, or one of the 10 FEMA Regional Offices.

* Emergency Plans for Acutely Toxic Chemicals

Emergency Planning & Community Right(800)535-0202 (202) 479-2449
This EPA hotline provides communities with help in preparing for accidental releases of toxic chemicals. Communities can call to obtain interim guidelines regarding *Acutely Toxic Chemicals*. These guidelines cover Organizing a Community, Developing a Chemical Contingency Plan, and gathering site-specific information. The hotline also provides a list of more than 400 acutely toxic chemicals.

* Emergency Preparedness Offices Nationwide

The Federal Emergency Management Administration has regional offices throughout the country.
Region I
FEMA, J.W. McCormack Post Office and Courthouse Building, Room 442, Boston, MA 02109; (617) 223-9540. Serving: Connecticut, Maine, Massachusetts, New Hampshire, Rhode Island, and Vermont.

Region II
FEMA, 26 Federal Plaza, Room 1349, New York, NY 10278; (212) 238-8208. Serving: New Jersey, New York, Puerto Rico, and Virgin Islands.

Region III
FEMA, Liberty Square Building (Second Floor), 105 South Seventh St., Philadelphia, PA 19106; (215)931-5500. Serving: Delaware, District of Columbia, Maryland, Pennsylvania, Virginia, and West Virginia.

Region IV
FEMA, 1371 Peachtree Street, NE, Suite 700, Atlanta, GA 30309; (404) 853-4200. Serving: Alabama, Florida, Georgia, Kentucky, Mississippi, North Carolina, South Carolina, and Tennessee.

Region V
FEMA, 175 Jackson Blvd, 4th Floor, Chicago, IL 60604; (312) 408-5500. Serving: Illinois, Michigan, Minnesota, Ohio, and Wisconsin

Region VI
FEMA, Federal Regional Center 206, 800 North Loop 288, Denton, TX 76201; (817) 898-9399. Serving: Arkansas, Louisiana, New Mexico, Oklahoma, and

Texas.

Region VI
FEMA, Federal Official Building, 911 Walnut Street, Room 200, Kansas City, MO 64106; (816)283-7061. Iowa, Kansas, Missouri, and Nebraska.

Region VII
FEMA, Denver Federal Center Building 710, PO Box 25267, Denver, CO 80225; (303) 235-4811. Serving: Colorado, Montana, North Dakota, South Dakota, Utah, and Wyoming.

Region IX
FEMA, Presidio of San Francisco, Building 105, San Francisco, CA 94129; (415)923-7100. Serving: Arizona, California, Hawaii, and Nevada.

Region X
FEMA, Federal Regional Center, 130 228th Street, SW, Bothell, WA 98021-9796; (206) 481-8800. Serving: Alaska, Idaho, Oregon, and Washington.

* Emergency Preparedness Publications

Federal Emergency Management Agency
P.O. Box 70274
Washington, DC 20024   (202) 646-3484
The *FEMA Publications Catalog* (FEMA-20) lists FEMA publications which are available to help meet the needs of citizens in emergency management matters. These publications are on subjects such as civil defense, earthquakes, floods, hurricanes, tornadoes, fire, nuclear accidents, acts of terrorism, dam safety, and hazardous materials incidents.

* Emergency Preparedness Responsibilities

Federal Emergency Management Agency
P.O. Box 70274
Washington, DC 20024   (202) 646-3484
The *Data Base Guide* (FPG 47.101) is a complete inventory of the automated data files used in support of the FEMA program offices. Included are data files which are the result of a cooperative effort between FEMA and other federal departments and agencies having delegated emergency preparedness responsibilities. These files have detailed information on virtually all of the resources important to the defense of, or--in the event of enemy attack--the survival and recovery of, the United States.

* Emergency Relief and Excess Food

Commodity Operations Division
U.S. Department of Agriculture
ASCS, Room 5755 South Building
Washington, DC 20250   (202) 477-5074
The Commodity Credit Corporation buys, stores, and distributes such commodities as dry milk, wheat, rice, and corn, which are acquired through price support programs. The commodities are sent overseas as donations, distributed to domestic food programs, or given to relief agencies in times of emergencies.

* Emergency Training National Center

National Emergency Training Center
Federal Emergency Management Agency
16825 South Seton Ave.
Emmitsburg, MD 21727   (800) 638-1821 (301) 447-1032
The Learning Resource Center is the NETC campus library for students in all areas of training at the National Emergency Training Center, and for the U.S. Fire Administration. Services include all types of reference work and interlibrary loans. Contact the office above for further information.

* Firefighters Safety and Health

Office of Firefighter Health and Safety
U.S. Fire Administration
16825 South seton Ave.
Emmitsburg, MD 21727   (301) 477-1185
This office develops national standards for firefighter's health and safety and also researches and analyzes data concerning the well-being of firefighters while exposed to such hazards as fire, heat, toxic chemicals. Research on firefighters protective clothing and equipment and a hazardous chemical materials response suit is also being studied. Contact the office above for more information.

* Fire Incident Reporting System

Office of National Fire Data and Analysis
U.S. Fire Administration
16825 South Seton Ave.

Emmitsburg, MD 21727   (301) 447-1272
This office quantifies and analyzes fire loss experienced at the local, State, and federal levels. Data are available on standard fire incidents. This office offers participants both mainframe and microcomputer applications for data collection and analysis. For more information and information on the Management Application Project (MAP) and the National Fire Incident Reporting System (NFIRS), contact the office above.

* Films on Emergency Management
Federal Emergency Management Agency
P.O. Box 70274
Washington, DC 20024   (202) 646-3484
The *Motion Picture Catalog* (FEMA-2) contains a current list of motion pictures of the Federal Emergency Management Agency. This catalog will be updated periodically as new films come out. These films are public information films, in 16mm color or black & white. They are cleared for television use and public nonprofit exhibition.

* Flood Damage Prevention
Flood Protection Branch
Air and Water Resources
River Basin Operations
Resource Development
Liberty Bldg. Rm 2N200A
Knoxville, TN 37902   (615) 632-4455
TVA's local flood damage prevention program helps communities avoid flood damages through a variety of measures, including floodplain zoning, flood proofing, and flood insurance. To assess flood risks, a field staff of engineers gathers data which is used when considering community development proposals. The TVA promotes the wise use of flood hazard areas with information, guidance, and assistance for individuals and businesses to avoid and adjust to flood areas. Staff works with local officials to assess community flood situations, and evaluate and install prevention and warning programs. A great emphasis is placed on environmental aspects as the program tries to maintain the natural benefits of flood plains and meet community needs through use and management of river corridors.

* Flood Insurance
for Property Owners
Federal Emergency Management Agency
Federal Insurance Administration
500 C Street, SW
Washington, DC 20472   (800) 638-6620
The National Flood Insurance Program (NFIP) helps property owners to purchase flood insurance. This insurance is designed to provide an insurance alternative to disaster assistance to meet the escalating costs of repairing damage. Contact the office above for information about the laws, regulations, or administrative policies related to the NFIP. Maryland residents outside of D.C. should call: (800) 492-6605, and those in Alaska, Guam, Hawaii, Puerto Rico, and Virgin Islands residents should call: (800) 638-6831.
Questions and Answers on the National Flood Insurance Program (FIA-2) contains 59 questions and answers about the National Flood Insurance Program.

* Flood Plain Management Assistance
U.S. Army Corps of Engineers
Attn: CECW-PF
20 Massachusetts Ave., NW
Washington, DC 20314   (202) 272-0169
The Army Corps of Engineers provides information, guidance, and technical assistance to civic groups and organizations in developing regulations for flood plain use. These services help communities understand the extent and magnitude of flood hazards in their areas. For information, contact the above office.

* Flood Preparedness Publications
Federal Emergency Management Agency
P.O. Box 70274
Washington, DC 20024   (202) 646-3484
The Flood Insurance Administration series of publications provide information on specific topics within the National Flood Insurance Program. The following publications can be obtained from the office above:
Flood Emergency and Residential Repair Handbook (FIA-13). Provides homeowners, residential contractors, and local government officials with procedures for dealing with flood hazards and damages to homes and their contents.

* Flood-Prone Areas
Federal Emergency Management Agency
P.O. Box 700274
Washington, DC 20024   (202) 646-3484 (800) 333-1363
The Federal Emergency Management Agency publishes the *Flood Hazard*

Boundary Map which shows the flood-prone areas within the community. Each map consists of one Map Index Page and one or more map sheets for all of the areas within the community's corporate limits subject to flooding. Call the number above for more information and map requests. *How to Read a Flood Insurance Rate Map* (FIA-10) is a guide to help identify and understand key features of the Flood Insurance Rate Map.

* General Hazard Insurance
Federal Emergency Management Agency
P.O. Box 70274
Washington, DC 20024   (202) 646-3484
The *Insurance Handbook for Public Assistance* (DR&R-3) is a policy and procedural handbook for local, State, and Federal officials concerned with administering general hazard insurance and flood insurance requirements under the Disaster Relief Act of 1974.

* Hazardous Materials and Emergency Response
Toxicology Information Program (TIP)
National Library of Medicine
8600 Rockville Pike
Bethesda, MD 20894   (301) 496-6308
TIP was established to provide national access to information on toxicology. The program is charged with setting up computerized databases of information from the literature of toxicology and from the files of both governmental and non-governmental organizations. Among the databases are TOXLINE (Toxicology Information Online) and CHEMLINE, a chemical dictionary file. TIP implemented the TOXNET (Toxicology Data Network) system of toxicologically-oriented data banks, including the HSDB (Hazardous Substances Data Bank), which is useful in chemical emergency response. TIP also supports the Toxicology Information Response Center, which provides reference services to the scientific community.

* Hazardous Material Transportation Accidents
Information Systems Division (DHM-63)
Office of Hazardous Materials Transportation
Research and Special Programs Administration
U.S. Department of Transportation
400 7th Street, SW, Room 8112
Washington, DC 20590   (202) 366-4555
This division collects and analyzes accident data from transporters of hazardous materials by highway, rail, air, and water and from container manufacturers. Information stored in the database includes the hazardous material involved, transporter name and mode, packaging used, cause of accident, and results. Contact the above office for searches. There may be a charge.

* Hurricane Safety for Kids
Children's Television Workshop
Dept. CES/NH
One Lincoln Plaza
New York, NY 10023
FEMA funded the creation of the *Big Bird Gets Ready for Hurricanes* kit, which is intended to help teachers and parents teach kids about hurricanes in a non-frightening way. The kit contains a 16-page booklet, a record of "The Hurricane Blues," and a board game. The cost is $2.25 per kit, and the *Big Bird Get Ready Videotape* is $19.95. Both can be ordered from the above address.

* Integrated Emergency Management System (IEMS)
Federal Emergency Management Agency
P.O. Box 70274
Washington, DC 20024   (202) 646-3484
The publication, *The Integrated Emergency Management System (IEMS) Multi-Year Development Plan (MYDP)* (CPC 84-1), clarifies the intent and purpose of the multi-year development planning process to be implemented in FY84 by FEMA Regions and the States and by local areas at the discretion of the States.

* Legal Services for Disaster Victims
Federal Emergency Management Agency
P.O. Box 70274
Washington, DC 20024   (202) 646-3484
The *Manual for Disaster Legal Services* has been prepared by FEMA and the Young Lawyers Division (YLD) of the American Bar Association. Its purpose is to orient new and potential volunteers to the FEMA-YLD Program for offering legal services to victims following major disasters. In order to facilitate this orientation, the *Manual* emphasizes schematic diagram, paraphases statutes and regulations, and simplifies many issues relating to the program.

* Mental Health Services Response to
Emergencies, Disasters and Crises

Emergency Services Branch
National Institutes of Health

National Institute of Mental Health
5600 Fishers Lane, Room 11C25
Rockville, MD 20857 (301) 443-4735

The Emergency Services Branch oversees three programs: 1) The Emergency Research Program studies the psychosocial response to mass emergencies; 2) The Crisis Counseling Program administers crisis counseling grants to states in which there has been a Presidentially-declared disaster; 3) The Emergency Preparedness Program plans for alcohol, drug abuse, and mental health disaster-related services nationwide. The program provides technical assistance and public education materials to states and local agencies in times of emergencies, and has three publications designed for non-mental health emergency workers (police, fire, emergency medical personnel) which focus on mental health issues.

* Natural Disaster and Nuclear Attack Planning for Families

Federal Emergency Management Agency
P.O. Box 70274
Washington, DC 20024 (202) 646-3484

In Time of Emergency: A Citizen's Handbook on Emergency Management (H-14) is addressed directly to the individual and the family to provide information and guidance on what can and should be done to prepare for a major natural disaster or nuclear attack.

* Natural Disaster Relief

Office of Government and Public Affairs
U.S. Department of Agriculture
Washington, DC 20250 (202) 447-3298

This free publication provides an overview of USDA's disaster assistance programs. It describes types of assistance available and where to apply for assistance. Local extension agents in each county can approve disaster applications for the following: conservation structures (when located on eligible lands); rehabilitation of farm lands destroyed by disaster; crop payment subsidies for disruption caused by disaster to regular crop schedules; sale of animal feed at below market price in emergency situations; animal grazing on reserve or conservation lands in emergency situations; donation of animal feed to Indian reservations when needed; and donation of grain to migratory wildfowl domains. The federal government will also remove debris from a major disaster from publicly- or privately-owned lands or waters.

* Nuclear Crisis Planning

Federal Emergency Management Agency
P.O. Box 70274
Washington, DC 20024 (202) 646-3484

Preparedness Planning for a Nuclear Crisis (HS-4) is a FEMA home-study course that will help your better prepare for a nuclear attack by providing information on the following: the effects of nuclear weapons; evacuation and sheltering; preparation of stocking of fallout shelters; and development of emergency plans to improve the chance of survival for individuals and families.

* Nuclear Fallout Shelters

Federal Emergency Management Agency
P.O. Box 70274
Washington, DC 20024 (202) 646-3484

The free booklet, *HUD Aids for Fallout Shelter Development (TR-58)*, describes the principal programs of the Department of Housing and Urban Development which can be used to promote and develop fallout shelters when the requirements of the specific programs are met.

* Posters: Natural and Civil Disasters

Federal Emergency Management Agency
P.O. Box 70274
Washington, DC 20024 (202) 646-3484

The following natural disaster informational posters are from FEMA:
Flood Insurance
Hurricane
Outdoor Warning Systems
Winter Watch for Kids
Earthquake
Tornadoes
Emergency Poster
Accidental Launch Warning Message Threat Areas

* Temporary Housing

Federal Emergency Management Agency
P.O. Box 70274
Washington, DC 20024 (202) 646-3484

The Mobile Home Sales Handbook (DAP-20) establishes the Federal Emergency Management Agency policy regarding the sale of mobile homes, under Section 404 of the Disaster Relief Act of 1974, to eligible temporary housing occupants. It prescribes the methods, techniques, and procedures utilized in the sales transaction.

* Tornadoes, Hurricanes, and Flash Floods

Federal Emergency Management Agency
P.O. Box 70274
Washington, DC 20024 (202) 646-3484

The following FEMA publications will better help you prepare for severe weather disasters:
Hurricane Safety: Tips for Hurricanes (L-105)
Tornado Safety Tips (L-148)
Survival in a Hurricane Wallet Card
Tips for Tornado Safety Wallet Card
Big Bird Gets Ready for Hurricane Kit

* Winter Storm Safety

Federal Emergency Management Agency
P.O. Box 70274
Washington, DC 20024 (202) 646-3484

These FEMA publications will help you prepare for the winter storm season:
Safety Tips for Winter Storms (L-96).
Winter Survival Coloring Book (FEMA-26). Includes safety tips on winter for children.
Winter Survival Test. A test about safety precautions to be taken around the home before winter storms strike, including heating systems, room heaters and fireplaces, kitchen pipes, and emergency supplies.

Money For Communities and Non-Profits

The federal money programs outlined here are designed to help communities solve many of today's difficult problems. Economic development such as job training funds are identified. Community improvements such as emergency shelters, rural housing, senior centers, mass transit, and airport modernization loans and grants are also described. You will discover various services such as school lunch and nutrition programs, runaway halfway houses and health clinics. This information is derived from the *Catalog of Federal Domestic Assistance* which is published by the US Government Printing Office in Washington, D.C. The number next to the title description is the reference number listed in this *Catalog*. Contact the office listed below the title for more details.

* Resource Conservation and Development Loans 10.414
Director, Community Facilities Division
Farmers Home Administration
Department of Agriculture
Washington, DC 20250 (202) 382-1490
To provide loan assistance to local sponsoring agencies in authorized areas where acceleration of program of resource conservation, development, and utilization will increase economic opportunities for local people. Types of assistance: direct loan. Estimate of annual funds available: $ 1,207,000.

* Water and Waste Disposal Systems for Rural Communities 10.418
Administrator, Farmers Home Administration
Department of Agriculture
Washington, DC 20250 (202) 447-7967
To provide basic human amenities, alleviate health hazards and promote the orderly growth of the rural areas of the nation by meeting the need for new and improved rural water and waste disposal facilities. Types of assistance: loans, grants. Estimate of annual funds available: $ 330,380,000.

* Watershed Protection and Flood Prevention Loans 10.419
Director, Community Facilities Division
Farmers Home Administration
Department of Agriculture
Washington, DC 20250 (202) 382-1490
To provide loan assistance to sponsoring local organizations in authorized watershed areas for share of costs for works of improvements. Types of assistance: loan. Estimate of annual funds available: $ 7,949,000.

* Rural Self-Help Housing Technical Assistance (Section 523 Technical Assistance) 10.420
Administrator, Farmers Home Administration
Department of Agriculture
Washington, DC 20250 (202) 382-1474
To provide financial support for the promotion of a program of technical and supervisory assistance that will aid needy very low and low-income individuals and their families in carrying out mutual self-help housing efforts in rural areas. Types of assistance: grants. Estimate of annual funds available: $ 16,542,509.

* Community Facilities Loans 10.423
Director, Community Facilities Division
Farmers Home Administration
Department of Agriculture
Washington, DC 20250 (202) 382-1490
To construct, enlarge, extend, or otherwise improve community facilities providing essential services to rural residents. Types of assistance: loans. Estimate of annual funds available: $ 95,700,000.

* Technical Assistance and Training Grants 10.436
Administrator, Farmers Home Administration
Department of Agriculture
Washington, DC 20250 (202) 447-7967
To identify and evaluate solutions; to assist applicants in preparing applications made in accordance with Subparts A and H of 1942; and to improve operation and maintenance of water and waste disposal facilities in rural areas. Types of assistance: grants. Estimate of annual funds available: $ 1,094,000.

* Intermediary Relending Program 10.439
Farmers Home Administration
Room 6321, South Agriculture Building
Washington, DC 20250 (202) 475-4100
To finance business facilities and community development. Types of assistance: loans. Estimate of annual funds available: $ 14,000,000.

* Cooperative Extension Service 10.500
Extension Service
Department of Agriculture
Washington, DC 20250 (202) 447-3377
To help people and communities identify and solve their farm, home, and community problems through the practical application of research findings of USDA and the Land-Grant Colleges and Universities. Types of assistance: grants. Estimate of annual funds available: $ 346,465,000.

* Child Nutrition: State Administrative Expenses 10.560
Director, Child Nutrition Division
Food and Nutrition Service
Department of Agriculture
Alexandria, VA 22302 (703)756-3590
To provide each state agency with funds for its administrative expenses in supervising and giving technical assistance to local schools, school districts and institutions in their conduct of child nutrition programs. Types of assistance: grants. Estimate of annual funds available: $ 56,754,000.

* Nutrition Education and Training Program (NET Program) 10.564
Nutrition and Technical Services Division
Food and Nutrition Service
Department of Agriculture
Alexandria, VA 22302 (703)756-3554
To help subsidize State and local programs that encourage the dissemination of nutrition information to children participating, or eligible to participate in the school lunch and related child nutrition programs. Types of assistance: grants. Estimate of annual funds available: $ 5,000,000.

* Temporary Emergency Food Assistance (Administrative Costs) 10.568
Food Distribution Division, FNS, USDA
Room 502, Park Office Center
3101 Park Center Drive
Alexandria, VA 22302 (703)756-3680
To make funds available to States for storage and distribution costs incurred by nonprofit eligible recipient agencies in providing food assistance to needy persons. Types of assistance: grants. Estimate of annual funds available: $ 50,000,000.

* Temporary Emergency Food Assistance (Food Commodities) 10.569
Food Distribution Division, FNS, USDA
Room 502, Park Office Center
3101 Park Center Drive
Alexandria, VA 22302 (703)756-3680
To make food commodities available to States for distribution to the needy. Types of assistance: grants. Estimate of annual funds available: $ 120,000,000.

* Food Commodities for Soup Kitchens 10.571

Food Distribution Division, Food and
Nutrition Service
Department of Agriculture
Alexandria, VA 22302   (703)756-3680
To improve the diets of the homeless. Types of assistance: grants. Estimate of annual funds available: $ 40,000,000.

* Cooperative Forestry Assistance 10.664

Deputy Chief, State and Private Forestry
Forest Service, Department of Agriculture
P.O. Box 96090
Washington, DC 20090-6090   (202) 447-3332
With respect to nonfederal forest and other rural lands to assist in the advancement of forest resources management; the encouragement of the production of timber; the control of insects and diseases affecting trees and forests. Types of assistance: grants. Estimate of annual funds available: $ 43,731,000.

* Schools and Roads - Grants to States (25 Percent Payments to States 10.665

James Turner, Acting Director of Fiscal
and Public Safety
Forest Service, USDA, Room 701 RPE
P.O. Box 96090
Washington, DC 20090-6090   (703) 235-8159
To share receipts from the National Forests with the States in which the National Forests are situated. To be used for the benefit of the public schools and public roads of the county or counties in which the National Forest is situated. Types of assistance: grants. Estimate of annual funds available: $ 338,825,000.

* Schools and Roads - Grants to Counties (Payments to Counties) 10.666

James Turner, Acting Director of Fiscal
and Public Safety
Forest Service, USDA, Room 701 RPE
P.O. Box 96090
Washington, DC 20090-6090   (703) 235-8159
To share receipts from National Grasslands and Land Utilization Projects with the counties in which the National Grasslands and Land Utilization Projects are situated. To be used for school or road purposes or both. Types of assistance: grants. Estimate of annual funds available: $ 16,413,000.

* Additional Lands - Grants to Minnesota (Minnesota Special) 10.668

James Turner, Acting Director of Fiscal
and Public Safety
Forest Service, USDA, Room 701 RPE
P.O. Box 96090
Washington, DC 20090-6090   (703) 235-8159
To share National Forest receipts with the State of Minnesota in connection with lands situated in the counties of Cook, Lake, and St. Louis which are withdrawn from entry and appropriation under the public land laws of the United States. Types of assistance: grants. Estimate of annual funds available: $ 716,000.

* Accelerated Cooperative Assistance for Forest Programs on Certain Lands Adjacent to the Boundary Waters Canoe Area (BWCA) 10.669

Christopher Holmes, Deputy Chief
State and Private Forestry
Forest Service, Department of Agriculture
P.O. Box 2417
Washington, DC 20013   (703) 235-1537
To provide a system of grants in cooperation with the State of Minnesota, Division of Forestry, for the intensive management of forest resources on state, county, and private lands adjacent to the Boundary Waters Canoe Area Wilderness. Types of assistance: grants. Estimate of annual funds available: $ 2,800,000.

* Great Plains Conservation 10.900

Deputy Chief for Programs
Soil Conservation Service
Department of Agriculture
P.O. Box 2890
Washington, DC 20013   (202) 447-4527
To conserve and develop the Great Plains soil and water resources by providing technical and financial assistance to farmers, ranchers, and others in planning and implementing conservation practices. Types of assistance: direct payment. Estimate of annual funds available: $ 12,286,000.

* Resource Conservation and Development 10.901

Deputy Chief for Programs
Soil Conservation Service
Department of Agriculture
P.O. Box 2890
Washington, DC 20013   (202) 447-4527
To encourage and improve the capability of state and local units of government and local nonprofit organizations in rural areas to plan, develop and carry out programs for resource conservation and development. Types of assistance: grants. Estimate of annual funds available: $ 7,500,000.

* Watershed Protection and Flood Prevention (Small Watershed Program; PL-566 Program) 10.904

Deputy Chief for Programs
Soil Conservation Service
Department of Agriculture
P.O. Box 2890
Washington, DC 20013   (202) 447-4527
To provide technical and financial assistance in planning and carrying out works of improvement to protect, develop, and utilize the land and water resources in small watersheds. Types of assistance: grants. Estimate of annual funds available: $ 92,703,000.

* Rural Abandoned Mine Program (RAMP) 10.910

Deputy Chief for Programs
Soil Conservation Service
Department of Agriculture
P.O. Box 2890
Washington, DC 20013   (202) 447-4527
To protect people and the environment from the adverse effects of past coal mining practices, and to promote the development of soil and water resources of unreclaimed mined lands. Types of assistance: direct payments. Estimate of annual funds available: $ 4,594,000.

* Economic Development - Grants for Public Works and Development Facilities 11.300

David L. McIlwain, Director, Public Works Division
Economic Development Administration
Room H7326, Herbert Hoover Bldg.
Department of Commerce
Washington, DC   (202) 377-5265
To promote long-term economic development and assist in the construction of public works and development facilities needed to initiate and encourage the creation or retention of permanent jobs in the private sector in areas experiencing severe economic distress. Types of assistance: grants. Estimate of annual funds available: $ 139,266,000.

* Economic Development - Business Development Assistance 11.301

Deputy Assistant Secretary for Loan Programs
Economic Development Administration
Room H7844, Herbert Hoover Bldg.
Department of Commerce
Washington, DC   (202) 377-5067
To sustain industrial and commercial viability in designated areas by providing financial assistance to businesses that create or retain permanent jobs, expand or establish plants in redevelopment areas for projects where financial assistance is not available from other sources on terms and conditions that would permit accomplishment of the project and further economic development in the area. Types of assistance: loan guarantee, grants. Estimate of annual funds available: $ 20,000,000.

* Economic Development-Support for Planning Organizations (Development District Program; Redevelopment Area Program; and Indian Program) 11.302

Luis F. Bueso, Director Planning Division
Economic Development Administration
Rm H7023, Herbert Hoover Bldg.
Washington, DC 20230   (202) 377-2873
To assist in providing administrative aid to multi-county district and redevelopment area (primarily Indian reservations and lands) economic development planning and implementation capability and thereby promote effective utilization of resources in the creation of full-time permanent jobs for the unemployed and the underemployed in high distress areas. Types of assistance: grants. Estimate of annual funds available: $ 18,205,000.

* Economic Development-Technical Assistance 11.303

Richard E. Hage, Technical Assistance Programs
Economic Development Administration
Room H7319, Herbert Hoover Bldg.
Department of Commerce
Washington, DC   (202) 377-2127

To promote economic development and alleviate under-employment and unemployment in distressed areas, EDA operates a technical assistance program. Types of assistance: grants. Estimate of annual funds available: $ 6,706,000.

* Economic Development-Public Works Impact Projects 11.304

David L. McIlwain, Director, Public Works Division
Economic Development Administration
Room H7326, Herbert Hoover Bldg.
Washington, DC   (202) 377-5265

To promote long-term economic development and assist in providing immediate useful work (i.e., construction jobs) to unemployed and underemployed persons in designated project areas. Types of assistance: grants. Estimate of annual funds available: $ 139,266,000.

* Economic Development-State and Local Economic Development Planning (302(a) Grants-State and Urban Planning Programs) 11.305

Luis F. Bueso, Director Planning Division
Economic Development Administration
Room H7023, Herbert Hoover Bldg.
Department of Commerce
Washington, DC   20230   (202) 377-3027

To help state and/or local governments formulate and implement economic development plans designed to reduce unemployment and increase incomes. Types of assistance: grants. Estimate of annual funds available: $ 4,790,000.

* Special Economic Development and Adjustment Assistance Program-Sudden and Severe Economic Dislocation and Long-term Economic Deterioration (SSED and LTED) 11.307

Paul J. Dempsey, Director
Economic Adjustment Division
Economic Development Administration
Rm H7327, Herbert Hoover Bldg.
Department of Commerce
Washington, DC   (202) 377-2659

To assist state and local areas develop and/or implement strategies designed to address adjustment problems resulting from sudden and severe economic dislocation such as plant closings (SSED), or from long-term economic deterioration in the area's economy (LTED). Types of assistance: grants. Estimate of annual funds available: $ 24,657,000.

* Research and Evaluation Program 11.312

David H. Geddes
Room H-7319, EDA
Department of Commerce
Washington, DC   20230   (202) 377-4085

To assist in the determination of causes of unemployment, under-employment, underdevelopment, and chronic depression in various areas and regions of the nation. Types of assistance: grants. Estimate of annual funds available: $ 1,210,000.

* Anadromous and Great Lakes Fisheries Conservation 11.405

Director, Office of Fisheries Conservation
and Management
National Marine Fisheries Service
1335 East-West Hwy
Silver Spring, MD   29010   (202) 673-5272

To cooperate with the states and other nonfederal interests in the conservation, development, and enhancement of the nation's anadromous fish and the fish in the Great Lakes and Lake Champlain that ascent streams to spawn, and for the control of sea lamprey. Types of assistance: grants. Estimate of annual funds available: $ 2,343,000.

* Interjurisdictional Fisheries Act of 1986 11.407

Director, Office of Fisheries Conservation
and Management
National Marine Fisheries Service
1335 East-West Hwy
Silver Spring, MD   20910   (301) 427-2347

To assist states in managing interjurisdictional fisheries resources. Types of assistance: grants. Estimate of annual funds available: $ 0.

* Coastal Zone Management Program Administration Grants 11.419

Chief, Coastal Programs Division
Office of Ocean Coastal Resource Management
National Ocean Service, NOAA
Department of Commerce
1825 Connecticut Ave., NW
Washington, DC   673-2515

To assist states in implementing and administering Coastal Zone Management programs that have been approved by the Secretary of Commerce. Types of assistance: grants. Estimate of annual funds available: $ 33,000,000.

* Coastal Zone Management Estuarine Research Reserves 11.420

Chief, Marine and Estuarine Management
 Division
Office of Ocean and Coastal Resource Management
National Ocean Service, NOAA
Department of Commerce
1825 Connecticut, Ave., NW
Washington, DC   (202) 673-5126

To assist states in the acquisition, research, development and operation of national estuarine research reserves for the purpose of creating natural field laboratories to gather data and make studies of the natural and human processes occurring within the estuaries of the coastal zone. Types of assistance: grants. Estimate of annual funds available: $ 2,790,000.

* Fisheries Development and Utilization Research and Development grants and Cooperative Agreements Program 11.427

Office of Trade and Industry Services
National Marine Fisheries Service, NOAA
Department of Commerce
Silver Spring, MD   20910   (301) 427-2358

To foster the development and strengthening of the fishing industry of the United States and increase the supply of wholesome, nutritious fish and fish products available to consumers. Types of assistance: grants. Estimate of annual funds available: $ 5,000,000.

* Intergovernmental Climate-Programs 11.428

National Climate Program Office, NOAA
Department of Commerce
11400 Rockville Pike
Rockville, MD   20852   (301) 443-8981

To aid states in the initiation of regional climate centers which will supply guidance, information and climate data to users in the private and public sectors. Types of assistance: grants. Estimate of annual funds available: $ 1,500,000.

* Marine Sanctuary Program 11.429

Chief, Marine and Estuarine Management Division
Office of Ocean and Coastal Resource Management
National Ocean Service, NOAA,
Department of Commerce
1825 Connecticut Ave., NW
Washington, DC   (202) 673-5126

To identify areas of the marine environment of special national significance due to their resource or human-use values; to provide authority for comprehensive and coordinated conservation and management of these marine areas that will complement existing regulatory authorities. Types of assistance: grants. Estimate of annual funds available: $ 766,000.

* Regional Centers for the Transfer of Manufacturing Technology 11.611

Dr. Philip N. Nanzetta, Director, NIST MTC Program
Rm B112, Metrology Bldg, NIST
Gaithersburg, MD   20899   (301) 975-3414

To establish regional centers, the functions of which are to accelerate the transfer of advanced manufacturing technology from the NIST automated manufacturing research facility and similar research and development laboratories to small and medium sized U.S. based manufacturing firms. Types of assistance: grants. Estimate of annual funds available: $ 1,000,000.

* Minority Business and Industry Association - Minority Chambers 11.802

Asst. Director, Office of Program Development
Rm 5096, Minority Business Development Agency
Department of Commerce (MB and IA/C of C)
14th & Constitution Ave, NW
Washington, DC 20230 (202) 377-5770
To provide financial assistance for Minority Business and Industry
Association/Minority Chambers of Commerce (MB and IA/C of C) which act
as advocates for their members and the minority community. Types of
assistance: grants. Estimate of annual funds available: $ 1,420,000.

* Payments to States in Lieu of Real Estate Taxes 12.112

HQ, U.S. Army Corps of Engineers, Attn: CERM-F
20 Massachusetts Ave., NW
Washington, DC 20314-1000(202) 2721925
To compensate local taxing units for the loss of taxes from federally acquired
lands, 75 percent of all monies received or deposited in the Treasury during any
fiscal year for the account of leasing of lands acquired by the United States for
flood control, navigation and allied purposes. Types of assistance: grants.
Estimate of annual funds available: $ 5000000.

* Military Construction, Army National Guard 12.400

Chief, Army Installations Division
National Guard Bureau, Pentagon
Washington, DC 20310 (202) 697-1732
To provide a combat-ready reserve force and facilities for training and
administering the Army National Guard units in the 50 states, District of
Columbia, Commonwealth of Puerto Rico, Virgin Islands, and Guam. Types of
assistance: grants. Estimate of annual funds available: $ 113,867,000.

* Impact Assistance for Areas Affected by the East Coast Trident Program (Community Impact Assistance) 12.608

Director, Office of Economic Adjustment, OASD
(FM&P), Pentagon, Rm. 4C767
Washington, DC 20301-4000 (202) 697-9155
To assist communities located near the Naval Submarine Base in Kings Bay,
Georgia. Types of assistance: grants. Estimate of annual funds available:
$ 5,000,000.

* Joint Military/Community Comprehensive Land Use Plans 12.610

Director, Office of Economic Adjustment, OASD
(FM&P), Pentagon, Room 4C767
Washington, DC 20301-4000 (202) 697-9155
To enable the Army, Navy, Air Force, and Marine Corps to participate in
development and implementation of "Joint Military/Community Comprehensive
Land Use Plans." Types of assistance: grants. Estimate of annual funds
available: $ 350,000.

* Mental Health Planning and Demonstration Projects 13.125

Mr. James Stockdill, Director
Division of Education and Service Systems Liaison
NIMH, Parklawn Bldg., Room 11C-26
5600 Fishers Lane
Rockville, MD 20857 (301) 443-3606
To promote the development of community support systems for the long-term
mentally ill, including inappropriately institutionalized individuals, mentally
disturbed children and youth, and homeless individuals in communities. Types
of assistance: grants. Estimate of annual funds available: $ 25,920,000.

* Emergency Medical Services Children (EMS for Children) 13.127

Div. of Maternal, Child and Infant Health
Bureau of Health Care Delivery and Assistance
Health Resources and Services Admin.
Rm 9-11, 5600 Fishers Lane
Rockville, MD 20857 (301) 443-2170
To support demonstration projects for the expansion and improvement of
emergency medical services for children who need treatment for trauma or
critical care. Types of assistance: grants. Estimate of annual funds available:
$ 2,964,000.

* Technical and Non-Financial Assistance to Community and Migrant Health Centers 13.129

Director, Division of Primary Care Services

Bureau of Health Care Delivery and Assistance
Health Resources and Services Admin., Rm 7A-55
5600 Fishers Lane
Rockville, MD 20857 (301) 443-2260
To provide assistance to community health centers (CHCs) in the following
areas: the initiation of new shared services activities involving specific CHCs
within a state or region; and the enhancement of the clinical capability of centers
within a state or region including assistance in retention and recruitment of
providers. Types of assistance: grants. Estimate of annual funds available:
$ 3,000,000.

* Primary Care Services-Resource Coordination and Development Cooperative Agreements (Primary Care Services Cooperative Agreements) 13.130

Director, Div. of Primary Care Services
Bureau of Health Care Delivery and Assistance
Health Resources and Services Admin., Rm 7A-55
5600 Fishers Lane
Rockville, MD 20857 (301) 443-3476
To coordinate local, state, and federal resources contributing to primary care
service delivery in the state to meet the needs of medically under-served
populations through community and migrant health centers, and the retention,
recruitment and oversight of the National Health Service Corps and other health
professions. Types of assistance: grants. Estimate of annual funds available:
$ 4,140,000.

* Health Services Delivery to Persons with AIDS - Demonstration Grants (AIDS Service Demonstration Projects) 13.133

Office of AIDS Program
Bureau of Maternal and Child Health
and Resources Development
Health Resources and Services Admin., Rm 9A-05
5600 Fishers Lane
Rockville, MD 20857 (301) 443-0652
To observe demonstration projects in Standard Metropolitan Statistical Areas
(SMSAs) for the development and improvement of ambulatory and
community-based medical and social services for persons with acquired immune
deficiency syndrome (AIDS) and AIDS-related conditions. Types of assistance:
grants. Estimate of annual funds available: $ 10,756,000.

* Assistance for Organ Procurement Organizations 13.134

Director, Division of Organ Transplantation
BMCH & RD, Health Resources and Services
Admin., Rm 9-31
5600 Fishers Lane
Rockville, MD 20857 (301) 443-7577
To provide for the planning, establishment, initial operation, and expansion of
qualified organ procurement organizations. Types of assistance: grants.
Estimate of annual funds available: $ 1,314,373.

* Minority Community Health Coalition Demonstration 13.137

Betty Lee Hawks, Rm 118F
Hubert Humphrey Bldg.
200 Independence Ave., SW
Washington, DC 20201 (202) 245-0020
To demonstrate that coalitions of local community agencies can be formed to
effectively impact on the disease risk factors and related health problems of
minority groups, through unique and innovative methods of modifying behavioral
and environmental factors involved. Types of assistance: grants. Estimate of
annual funds available: $ 1,400,000.

* Protection and Advocacy for Mentally Ill Individuals (Mentally Ill P and A Services) 13.138

Mr. James Stockdill, Director
Division of Education and Service System Liaison
NIMH, Parklawn Bldg., Rm 11C-26
5600 Fishers Lane
Rockville, MD 20857 (301) 443-3606
To enable the establishment and administration of a new system in each state to:
protect and advocate the rights of mentally ill individuals and investigate
incidents of abuse and neglect of mentally ill individuals. Types of assistance:
grants. Estimate of annual funds available: $ 8,000,000.

* Drug and Alcohol Abuse Prevention - High-Risk Youth Demonstration Grants 13.144

Dr. Stephen Gardner, Chief
Demonstration Operations Branch
Div. of Demonstrations and Eval., Alcohol, Drug
Abuse and Mental Health Admin., Rm 13A45
Rockville, MD   (301) 468-2600
To support prevention demonstration programs that will develop client and/or
service systems targeted toward: decreasing the incidence and prevalence of drug
and alcohol use among high-risk youth. Types of assistance: grant. Estimate of
annual funds available: $ 24,540,000.

* AIDS Education and Training Centers 13.145

Director, Division of Medicine
Bureau of Health Professions, Health Resources and
  Services Admin., Rm 4C03
5600 Fishers Lane
Rockville, MD 20857   (301) 443-6190
To provide education and training to primary care providers and others on the
treatment and prevention of acquired immune deficiency syndrome (AIDS) in
collaboration with health professions schools, local hospitals and health
departments. Types of assistance: grants. Estimate of annual funds available:
$ 13,751,000.

AIDS Drug Reimbursements 13.146

Director, Bureau of Maternal and Child Health
  Health Resources and Services Admin., Room 9-03
Parklawn Bldg.
5600 Fishers Lane
Rockville, MD 20857   (301) 443-0652
To cover the cost of the drug azidothymidine (AZT) and any other drug which
proves to prolong the life of a person with AIDS who is a low-income individual
no covered under the state Medicaid program or third party payors. Types of
assistance: grants. Estimate of annual funds available: $ 15,000,000.

* Mental Health Services for the Homeless Block Grant (MHSH) 13.150

Mr. Thomas Reynolds, Grants Management Officer
Block Grant Programs, ADAMHA, Rm 13C-20
Parklawn Bldg.
5600 Fishers Lane
Rockville, MD 20857   (301) 443-3334
To provide financial assistance to states to support services to chronically
mentally ill individuals who are homeless or who are subject to a significant
probability of becoming homeless. Types of assistance: grants. Estimate of
annual funds available: $ 14,128,000.

* Project Grants for Health Services to the Homeless (Homeless Assistance Program) 13.151

Harold Dame, Director, Health Care Services for
the Homeless Program, Health Resources and
Services Admin., Rm 7-15
Parklawn Bldg.
5600 Fishers Lane
Rockville, MD 20857   (301) 443-8134
To provide health care services to homeless persons. Types of assistance: grants.
Estimate of annual funds available: $ 14,820,000.

* Community Demonstration Grant Projects for Alcohol and Drug Abuse Treatment of Homeless Individuals (NIAAA Homeless Demonstration Grants) 13.152

Barbara Lubran, Homeless Initiative
NIAAA, Rm 16C-02
5600 Fishers Lane
Rockville, MD 20857   (301) 443-0786
To provide, document and evaluate successful and replicable approaches to
community-based alcohol and/or drug abuse treatment and rehabilitation
services for individuals with alcohol or drug-related problems who are homeless
or at imminent risk of becoming homeless. Types of assistance: grants.
Estimate of annual funds available: $ 4,545,000.

* Pediatric AIDS Health Care Demonstration Program 13.153

Div. of Services for Children with Special Health
  Needs, Health Resources and Services Admin
Room 9A-11, Parklawn Bldg.
5600 Fishers Lane
Rockville, MD 20857   (301) 443-2170
To support demonstration projects for strategies and innovative models for
intervention in pediatric AIDS and coordination of services for childbearing
women and children with AIDS. Types of assistance: grants. Estimate of

annual funds available: $ 7,901,000.

* Rural Health Research Centers 13.155

Ms. Arlene Granderson, Office of Rural Health
  Policy, Health Resources and Services Admin.
Parklawn Bldg., Rm 14-22
5600 Fishers Lane
Rockville, MD 20857   (301) 443-2720
To support the development of rural health research centers to provide an
information base and policy analysis capacity on the full range of rural health
issues. Types of assistance: grants. Estimate of annual funds available:
$ 1,500,000.

* State Comprehensive Mental Health Service Planning Development Grants 13.158

Maury Lieberman, Director, State Comprehensive
  Mental Health Planning Program
NIMH, Room 7-103
5600 Fishers Lane
Rockville, MD 20857   (301) 443-4257
To initiate or enhance a planning process at the state level that will lead to the
design and implementation of a community-based system of comprehensive
mental health services for adults with severe and persistent mental illness and
child and adolescent populations with severe emotional disorders. Types of
assistance: grants. Estimate of annual funds available: $ 4,787,000.

* Health Care Services in the Home 13.159

Bureau of Health Care Delivery and Assistance
Health Resources and Services Admin., Rm 8A-17
Parklawn Bldg.
5600 Fishers Lane
Rockville, MD 20857   (301) 443-3476
To provide grants to the states for assisting grantees in carrying out
demonstrations projects; to identify low-income individuals who can avoid
institutionalized or prolonged hospitalization if skilled medical services or related
health services are provided in the home. Types of assistance: grants. Estimate
of annual funds available: $ 2,470,000.

* Minority AIDS Education/Prevention Grants 13.160

Jacqueline Bowles, M.D., Rm 118F
Hubert Humphrey Bldg.
200 Independence Ave., SW
Washington, DC 20201   (202) 245-0020
To demonstrate that minority community-based organizations and national
organizations can effectively develop and implement human HIV infection
education and prevention strategies, using innovative approaches to prevent and
reduce HIV transmission among minority populations. Types of assistance:
grants. Estimate of annual funds available: $ 1,400,000.

* Health Program for Toxic Substances and Disease Registry 13.161

Dr. Barry Johnson, Assoc. Administrator, CDC, PHS
1600 Clifton Rd., NE
Atlanta, GA 30333   (404) 488-4590
To work closely with state, local, and other federal agencies to reduce or
eliminate illness, disability and death resulting from exposure to the public and
workers to toxic substances at spill and waste disposal sites. Types of assistance:
grants. Estimate of annual funds available: $ 32,243,000.

* Health Services in the Pacific Basin 13.163

Howard Lerner
Bureau of Health Care Delivery and Assistance, PHS
Rm. 7A-55, 5600 Fishers Lane
Rockville, MD 20857   (301) 443-8134
To develop projects to build capacity and improve health services and systems,
particularly preventive health services in the Commonwealth of the Northern
Mariana Islands, American Samoa, Guam, Federated States of Micronesia, and
Republic of Palau, and to provide technical assistance in support of such
projects. Types of assistance: grants. Estimate of annual funds available:
$ 741,000.

* Indian Health Service Health Promotion and Disease Prevention Demonstration Projects (HP/DP Demonstration Projects) 13.166

Kay Carpenter, Grants Management Branch
Indian Health Service, PHS, Room 6A-33
5600 Fishers Lane
Rockville, MD 20857   (301) 443-5204

Your Community

To develop demonstration projects to determine the most effective and cost-efficient means of: providing health promotion and disease prevention services, encouraging Indians to adopt good health habits, and reducing health risks to Indians, particularly the risks of heart disease, cancer, stroke, diabetes, depression and lifestyle-related accidents. Types of assistance: grants. Estimate of annual funds available: $ 500,000.

* Human Immunodeficiency Virus (HIV) Services

Planning Program Grants (HIV Services
 Planning Program) 13.168
Office of Special Projects
Health Resources and Services Admin., Room 9-13
5600 Fishers Lane
Rockville, MD 20857 (301) 443-6775
To assist cities and states which have not been affected by the human immunodeficiency virus (HIV) epidemic to the same extent as high incidence cities in developing a coordinated strategy for the delivery of services to persons with HIV infection. Types of assistance: grants. Estimate of annual funds available: $ 3,600,000.

* Model Projects for Pregnant and Postpartum Women and Their Infants (Substance Abuse) 13.169

Bernard McColgan, Director, Division of
 Demonstrations and Evaluation, Alcohol, Drug
 Abuse and Mental Health Admin., Rm. 13A-54
5600 Fishers Lane
Rockville, MD (301) 443-4564
To promote the involvement and coordinated participation of multiple organizations in the delivery of comprehensive services for substance-abusing pregnant and postpartum women. Types of assistance: grants. Estimate of annual funds available: $ 4,000,000.

* Community Youth Activity Demonstration Grants 13.170

Office for Substance Abuse, Alcohol, Drug Abuse
and Mental Health Administration, Rm 9A-40
5600 Fishers Lane
Rockville, MD 20857 (301) 443-0369
To provide assistance to states for the purpose of establishing and evaluating innovative alcohol and other drug abuse prevention services for youth and to encourage organizations in contact with these youth-at-risk to form partnerships for the purpose of carrying out activities and projects to prevent alcohol and other drug use among this population. Types of assistance: grants. Estimate of annual funds available: $ 1,061,600.

* Community Youth Activity Program Block Grants (CYAP) 13.171

Mr. Thomas Reynolds, Grants Management Officer
Alcohol, Drug Abuse and Mental Health Administration
Rm. 13C-20, Parklawn Bldg.
5600 Fishers Lane
Rockville, MD 20857 (301) 443-3334
To provide financial assistance for the support of prevention services and partnerships designed to develop community activities targeted toward alcohol and other drug abuse prevention through education, training and recreation projects. Types of assistance: grants. Estimate of annual funds available: $ 3,633,750.

* Drug Abuse Treatment Waiting List Reduction Grants 13.175

Mr. Glenn Kamber, Office of Communications
 and External Affairs
Alcohol, Drug Abuse and Mental Health Admin., PHS
Rm. 12-C-15, 5600 Fishers Lane
Rockville, MD 20857 (301) 443-3783
To make one-time grants available to public and non-profit private entities to reduce drug abuse treatment waiting lists by expanding the capacity of existing programs. Types of assistance: grants. Estimate of annual funds available: $ 75,000,000.

* Family Planning-Services (Umbrella Councils) 13.217

Deputy Asst. Secretary for Population Affairs
Department of Health and Human Services
Room 736E, Hubert Humphrey Bldg.
200 Independence Ave., SW
Washington, DC (202) 245-0151
To provide educational, counseling, comprehensive medical and social services necessary to enable individuals to freely determine the number and spacing of their children, and by doing so helping to reduce maternal and infant mortality and promote the health of mothers and children. Types of assistance: grants. Estimate of annual funds available: $ 128,440,000.

* Community Health Centers 13.224

Director, Division Primary Care Services
Health Resources and Services Admin., Room 7A-55
Parklawn Bldg.
5600 Fishers Lane
Rockville, MD 20857 (301) 443-2260
To support the development and operation of community health centers which provide primary health services, supplemental health services and environmental health services to medically under-served populations. Types of assistance: grants. Estimate of annual funds available: $ 411,812,000.

* Indian Health Service-Health Management Development Program Indian Health) 13.228

Division of Grants and Contracts
Indian Health Service, PHS, Room 6A-33
5600 Fishers Lane
Rockville, MD 20857 (301) 443-5204
To improve the quality of the health of American Indians and Native Alaskans by providing a full range of curative, preventative and rehabilitative health services. Types of assistance: grants. Estimate of annual funds available: $ 12,500,000.

* Mental Health Clinical or Service Related Training Grants 13.244

Mr. James Stockdill, Director
Division of Education and Service Systems Liaison
NIMH, Parklawn Bldg., Rm 11C-26
5600 Fishers Lane
Rockville, MD 20857 (301) 443-3606
To encourage mental health specialists to work in areas and settings where severe shortages exist; to increase the number of qualified minority personnel in the mental health professions. Types of assistance: grants. Estimate of annual funds available: $ 12,844,000.

* Migrant Health Centers Grants 13.246

Director, Migrant Health Program
Health Resources and Services Admin., Room 7A55
5600 Fishers Lane
Rockville, MD 20857 (301) 443-1153
To support the development and operation of migrant health centers and projects which provide primary health care services, supplemental health services and environmental health services which are accessible to migrant and seasonal agricultural farm workers and their families. Types of assistance: grants. Estimate of annual funds available: $45,646,000.

* National Health Service Corps 13.258

Dr. Audrey Manley, Director
National Health Service Corps
Health Resources and Services Admin., Rm 7A-39
Parklawn Bldg.
5600 Fishers Lane
Rockville, MD 20857 (301) 443-2900
To improve the delivery of health care services to residents in areas critically short of health personnel by the assignment of additional medical personnel. Types of assistance: loans. Estimate of annual funds available: $ 39,866,000.

* Family Planning-Personnel Training 13.260

Office of the Assistant Secretary for Health
Department of Health and Human Services, Rm 736E
Hubert Humphrey Bldg.
200 Independence Ave., SW
Washington, DC 20201 (202) 245-0151
To provide job specific training for personnel to improve the delivery of family planning services. Types of assistance: grants. Estimate of annual funds available: $ 3,232,000.

* Childhood Immunization Grants (Section 317, Public Health Service Act; Immunization Program) 13.268

Dr. Walter Dowdle, Acting Director, CDC
PHS, DHHS, 1600 Clifton Rd., NE
Atlanta, GA 30333 (404) 639-3291
To assist states and communities in establishing and maintaining preventive health service programs to immunize individuals against vaccine-preventable diseases. Types of assistance: grants. Estimate of annual funds available: $ 126,797,000.

* Centers for Disease Control - Investigations and Technical Assistance   13.283

Dr. Walter Dowdle, Acting Director, CDC
PHS, DHHS, 1600 Clifton Rd., NE
Atlanta, GA   30333   (404) 639-3291
To assist state and local health authorities and other health related organizations in controlling communicable disease, chronic diseases, and other preventable health conditions. Types of assistance: grants. Estimate of annual funds available: $ 270,743,179.

* Native American Programs - Financial Assistance Grants   13.612

Administration for Native Americans
Department of Health and Human Services, Rm 344-F
200 Independence Ave., SW
Washington, DC   20201   (301) 245-7730
To provide financial assistance to public and private nonprofit organizations including Indian Tribes, urban Indian centers, Native Alaskan villages, Native Hawaiian organizations, rural off-reservation groups, and Native American Pacific Island groups for the development and implementation of social and economic development strategies that promote self-sufficiency. Types of assistance: grants. Estimate of annual funds available: $ 27,351,000.

* Administration for Children, Youth and Families - Runaway and Homeless Youth   13.623

Associate Commissioner
Family and Youth Services Bureau
Department of Health and Human Services
P.O. Box 1182
Washington, DC   20013   (202) 755-7800
To develop local facilities to address the immediate needs of runaway and homeless youth and their families. Types of assistance: grants. Estimate of annual funds available: $ 26,923,000.

* Administration on Developmental Disabilities - Basic Support and Advocacy Grants   13.630

Director, Program Operations Division
Department of Health and Human Services
Washington, DC   20201   (202) 245-2897
To assist states in the development of a comprehensive system and a coordinated array of services in order to support the developmentally disabled to achieve their maximum potential and ensure the protection of their legal and human rights. Types of assistance: grants. Estimate of annual funds available: $ 79,534,000.

* Administration on Developmental Disabilities - Projects of National Significance   13.631

Program Development Division
Administration on Developmental Disabilities
Department of Health and Human Services
Washington, DC   20201   (202) 245-1961
To provide grants and contracts for projects of national significance to increase and support the independence, productivity, and integration into the community of persons with developmental disabilities. Types of assistance: grants. Estimate of annual funds available: $ 2,901,000.

* Special Programs for the Aging - Title III, Part B Grants for Supportive Services and Senior Centers   13.633

Dr. Joyce Berry, Associate Commissioner
Office of Human Development Services
Department of Health and Human Services
Washington, DC   20201   (202) 245-0011
To assist state agencies on aging and their area agencies to foster the development of community-based systems of service for older persons via statewide planning and area planning and provision of supportive services, including multi-purpose senior centers. Types of assistance: grants. Estimate of annual funds available: $ 276,640,000.

* Children's Justice Grants to States   13.643

Josephine Reisnyder
National Center on Child Abuse and Neglect
Administration for Children, Youth and Families
P.O. Box 1182, SW
Washington, DC   20013   (202) 245-2860
To encourage states to enact child protective reforms which are designed to improve the handling of child abuse cases and the investigation and prosecution of cases of child abuse. Types of assistance: grants. Estimate of annual funds available: $ 6,297,873.

* Child Welfare Services - State Grants   13.645

Betty Stewart, Associate Commissioner
Children's Bureau
Administration for Children, Youth and Families
P.O. Box 1182
Washington, DC   20013   (202) 755-7600
To establish, extend, and strengthen child welfare services provided by state and local public welfare agencies to enable children to remain in their own homes. Types of assistance: grants. Estimate of annual funds available: $ 246,679,000.

* Social Services Research and Demonstration   13.647

Ann Queen, Director
Division of Research and Demonstration
Department of Health and Human Services
Room 334-F, Hubert Humphrey Bldg.
200 Independence Ave., SW
Washington, DC   (202) 472-3026
To promote effective social services for dependent and vulnerable populations such as the poor, the aged, children and youth, Native Americans, and the handicapped. Types of assistance: grants. Estimate of annual funds available: $ 3,550,000.

* Adoption Opportunities: Administration for Children, Youth and Families   13.652

Delmar Weathers
Children's Bureau
Administration for Children, Youth and Families
P.O. Box 1182
Washington, DC   20013   (202) 426-2822
To provide financial support for demonstration projects to improve adoption practices; to gather information on adoptions; and to provide training and technical assistance to improve adoption services. Types of assistance: grants. Estimate of annual funds available: $ 6,027,000.

* Grants to Indian Tribes: Special Programs for the Aging (Title VI, Part A Indian Programs)   13.655

Dr. Joyce Berry, Associate Commissioner
Office of State and Tribal Programs
Administration on Aging
Department of Health and Human Services
Washington, DC   20201   (202) 245-0011
To promote the delivery of supportive services, including nutrition services to older Indians and Alaskan Natives. Types of assistance: grants. Estimate of annual funds available: $ 7,410,000.

* Drug Abuse Prevention and Education for Runaway and Homeless Youth (Runaway Youth Drug Abuse Prevention and Education)   13.657

Frank Fuentes, Family and Youth Services Bureau
Administration for Children, Youth and Families
330 C St., SW
Washington, DC   20201   (202) 755-8888
To expand and improve existing drug abuse and prevention services to runaway and homeless youth and their families. Types of assistance: grants. Estimate of annual funds available: $ 12,000,000.

* Foster Care - Title IV-E   13.658

Betty Stewart, Associate Commissioner
Children's Bureau
P.O. Box 1182
Washington, DC   20013   (202) 755-7600
To provide Federal Financial Participation (FFP) in assistance on behalf of eligible children needing care away from their families (in foster care) who are in the placement and care of the state agency administering the program. Types of assistance: grant. Estimate of annual funds available: $ 1,363,971,000.

* Adoption Assistance   13.659

Betty Stewart, Associate Commissioner
Children's Bureau
P.O. Box 1182
Washington, DC   20013   (202) 755-7600
To provide Federal Financial Participation (FFP) to states which meet certain eligibility tests, in the adoption subsidy costs for the adoption of children with special needs. Types of assistance: grants. Estimate of annual funds available:

$ 133,936,000.

* Drug Abuse Prevention and Education Relating to Youth and Gangs 13.660

Frank Fuentes, Family and Youth Services Bureau
Administration for Children, Youth and Families
330 C St., SW
Washington, DC 20201 (202) 755-7800
To prevent and reduce the participation of youth in gangs that engage in illicit drug-related activities. Types of assistance: grants. Estimate of annual funds available: $ 12,500,000.

* Native American Programs - Training and Technical Assistance 13.662

Administration for Native Americans
Department of Health and Human Services, Room 344-F
200 Independence Ave., SW
Washington, DC 20201 (202) 245-7714
To promote the goal of economic and social self-sufficiency for American Indians, Native Hawaiians, Native Alaskans, and Native American Pacific Island groups. Types of assistance: grants. Estimate of annual funds available: $ 1,000,000.

* Comprehensive Child Development Centers 13.666

Allen Smith
Administration for Children, Youth and Families
P.O. Box 1182
Washington, DC 20013 (202) 755-7782
To plan for and carry out projects for intensive, comprehensive, integrated and continuous supportive services for infants, toddlers, and pre-schoolers from low-income families to enhance their intellectual, social, emotional and physical development. Types of assistance: grants. Estimate of annual funds available: $ 19,160,000.

* Social Services Block Grant (Social Services) 13.667

Director, Office of Policy, Planning and Legislation
Office of Human Dev. Services
200 Independence Ave., SW
Washington, DC 20201 (202) 245-2892
To enable each State to furnish social services best suited to the needs of the individuals residing in the State. Types of assistance: grant. Estimate of annual funds available: $ 2,700,000,000.

* Administration for Children, Youth and Families - Child Abuse and Neglect State Grants 13.669

Mary McKeough
National Center on Child Abuse and Neglect
Children's Bureau
P.O. Box 1182
Washington, DC 20013 (202) 245-2856
To assist states in improving and increasing activities for the prevention and treatment of child abuse, and to develop, strengthen, and carry out the program objectives through State grants. Types of assistance: grants. Estimate of annual funds available: $ 11,647,500.

* Family Violence Prevention and Services 13.671

Office of Policy, Planning and Legislation
Office of Human Development Services
200 Independence Ave., SW
Washington, DC 20201 (202) 245-2892
To demonstrate the effectiveness of assisting states and Indian Tribes in the prevention of family violence and to provide immediate shelter and related assistance for victims of family violence and their dependents. Types of assistance: grants. Estimate of annual funds available: $ 8,219,000.

* Child Abuse Challenge Grants 13.672

Josephine Reifsnyder
Administration for Children, Youth and Families
P.O. Box 1182
Washington, DC 20013 (202) 245-2860
To encourage states to establish and maintain trust funds or other funding mechanisms, including direct state appropriations to support child abuse and neglect prevention activities. Types of assistance: grants. Estimate of annual funds available: $ 4,834,000.

* Grants to States for Planning and Development of Dependent Care Programs (Dependent Care Planning and Development) 13.673

Family and Youth Services Bureau
Administration for Children, Youth and Families
400 6th St., SW
Washington, DC 20201 (202) 755-8888
To assist states in the planning, development, establishment, expansion or improvement of services related to dependent care resource and referral and services related to school age child care before and after school. Types of assistance: grants. Estimate of annual funds available: $ 11,856,000.

* Independent Living 13.674

Beverly Stubber, Director
Program Operation Division, Children's Bureau
Administration for Children, Youth and Families
P.O. Box 1182
Washington, DC 20014 (202) 755-7447
To assist states and localities in establishing and carrying out programs designed to assist children, with respect to whom foster care maintenance payments are being made by the state and who have attained age 16, in making the transition from foster care to independent living. Types of assistance: grants. Estimate of annual funds available: $ 45,000,000.

* State Medicaid Fraud Control Units 13.775

Jim Shields, Director
State Fraud Branch, Office of the Secretary, DHHS
Rm 5449, North Bldg.
330 Independence Ave., SW
Washington, DC 20201 (202) 475-6520
To control provider fraud in the states Medicaid program. Types of assistance: grants. Estimate of annual funds available: $ 48,455,000.

* State Survey and Certification of Health Care Providers and Suppliers 13.777

Wayne Smith, Ph.D., Director
Office of Survey and Certification
Health Standards and Quality Bureau
Health Care Financing Administration
6325 Security Blvd.
Baltimore, MD 21207 (301) 966-6763
To provide financial assistance to any state which is able and willing to determine through its state health agency or other appropriate state agency that providers and suppliers of health care services are in compliance with federal regulatory health and safety standards. Types of assistance: grants. Estimate of annual funds available: $ 121,538,000.

* Child Support Enforcement (Title IV-D) 13.783

Wayne Stanton, Director
Office of Child Support Enforcement
Family Support Administration, 6th Floor
370 L'Enfant Promenade, SW
Washington, DC 20447 (202) 252-4500
To enforce the support obligations owed by absent parents to their children, locate absent parents, establish paternity and obtain child, spousal and medical support. Types of assistance: grants. Estimate of annual funds available: $ 941,000,000.

* Child Support Enforcement Research (OCSE Research) 13.784

David Arnaudo, Acting Chief
Planning and Evaluation Branch
Office of Child Support Enforcement, 4th Floor
370 L'Enfant Promenade, SW
Washington, DC 20447 (202) 252-5364
To discover, test, demonstrate, and promote utilization of new concepts which will increase cost effectiveness, reduce welfare dependency, and increase child support collections form absent parents. Types of assistance: grants. Estimate of annual funds available: $ 250,000.

* Refugee and Entrant Assistance-State Administered Programs 13.787

Bill F. Gee, Director
Office of Refugee Resettlement
Family Support Administration, 6th Floor
370 L'Enfant Promenade, SW
Washington, DC 20447 (202) 252-4545
To subsidize states for assistance provided to refugees, including Cuban and Haitian entrants for resettlement throughout the country, by funding maintenance and medical assistance, social services, and targeted assistance for eligible refugees and Cuban and Haitian entrants. Types of assistance: direct payment.

Money For Communities and Non-Profits

Estimate of annual funds available: $ 326,726,000.

* Refugee Assistance-Voluntary Agency Programs 13.788
Bill F. Gee, Director
Office of Refugee Resettlement
Family Support Administration, 6th Floor
370 L'Enfant Promenade, SW
Washington, DC 20447   (202) 252-4545
To assist refugees in becoming self-supporting and independent members of American society, by providing grant funds to voluntary resettlement agencies currently resettling these refugees in the United States. Types of assistance: grants. Estimate of annual funds available: $ 15,808,000.

* Community Services Block Grant 13.792
James C. Checkan, Chief, Division of Block Grants
Office of Community Services
Family Support Administration, DHHS
370 L'Enfant Promenade, SW
Washington, DC 20447   (202) 252-5255
To provide services and activities having a measurable and potential major impact on causes of poverty in the community or those areas of the community where poverty is a particularly acute problem. Types of assistance: grant. Estimate of annual funds available: $ 318,630,000.

* Community Services Block Grant-Discretionary Awards 13.793
Ms. Jacqueline G. Lemire, Acting Director
Office of State and Project Assistance
Family Support Administration
370 L'Enfant Promenade, SW
Washington, DC 20447   (202) 252-5248
To support program activities of national or regional significance to alleviate the causes of poverty in distressed communities which promote full-time permanent jobs for poverty level project area residents. Types of assistance: direct payment. Estimate of annual funds available: $ 37,120,000.

* Community Services Block Grant Discretionary Awards-Community Food and Nutrition 13.795
Mr. Jim Hearn, Chief
Community Food and Nutrition Program (CFNP)
Family Support Administration
370 L'Enfant Promenade, SW
Washington, DC 20447   (202) 252-5252
To provide for community-based, local, and stateside programs which: coordinate existing private and public food assistance resources to better serve low-income populations and to assist low-income communities to identify potential sponsors of child nutrition programs and initiate new programs in under-served areas. Types of assistance: grants, direct payment. Estimate of annual funds available: $ 2,418,000.

* Emergency Community Services for the Homeless 13.796
Janet Fox, Office of Community Services
Family Support Administration
370 L'Enfant Promenade, SW
Washington, DC 20447   (202) 252-5254
To use public resources and programs in a coordinated manner to meet the critically urgent needs of the homeless of the nation; and to provide funds for programs to assist the homeless with special emphasis on elderly persons, handicapped persons, families with children, Native Americans and veterans. Types of assistance: grants. Estimate of annual funds available: $ 18,918,000.

* Community Services Block Grant Discretionary Awards-Demonstration Partnerships 13.797
Marshall Borman, Office of the Director
Office of Community Services
370 L'Enfant Promenade, SW
Washington, DC 20447   (202) 252-5251
To stimulate eligible entities to develop new approaches to provide for greater self-sufficiency of the poor; test and evaluate the new approaches, disseminate project results and strengthen the ability of eligible entities to integrate, coordinate and redirect activities to promote maximum self-sufficiency. Types of assistance: grant. Estimate of annual funds available: $ 3,512,000.

* Project Grants for Non-Acute Care, Intermediate and Long-Term Care Facilities (1610(b) Program)

13.887
Ms. Katharine Buckner, Office of Health Facilities
Bureau of Maternal and Child Health and
 Resources Development, Rm 11A-10
5600 Fishers Lane
Rockville, MD 20857   (301) 443-0271
To renovate, expand, repair, equip, or modernize non-acute care intermediate and long-term care facilities for patients with AIDS. Types of assistance: grants. Estimate of annual funds available: $ 3,952,000.

* National Health Promotion 13.900
Deputy Director, Office of Disease Prevention
 and Health Promotion, DHHS, Room 2132
330 C Street, SW
Washington, DC 20201   (202) 245-7611
To engage national membership organizations from various sectors as a means of expanding and coordinating health promotion efforts. Types of assistance: grants. Estimate of annual funds available: $ 363,080.

* Graduate Programs In Health Administration 13.963
Mr. John Westcott, Grants Management Officer
Bureau of Health Professions
Health Resources and Services Administration
Rm. 8C-22, 5600 Fishers Lane
Rockville, MD 20857   (301) 443-6880
To support accredited graduate education programs in health administration, hospital administration, and health planning Types of assistance: grants. Estimate of annual funds available: $ 1,410,000.

* Coal Miners Respiratory Impairment Treatment Clinics and Services (Black Lung Clinics) 13.965
Director, Div. of Primary Care Services
Health Resources and Services Administration
Room 7A-55, 5600 Fishers Lane
Rockville, MD 20857   (301) 443-2260
To develop high quality, patient oriented, integrated systems of care which assure access to and continuity of appropriate primary, secondary and tertiary care with maximum use of existing resources. Types of assistance: grants. Estimate of annual funds available: $ 3,216,000.

* Preventive Health Services - Sexually Transmitted Diseases Control Grants 13.977
Dr. Walter R. Dowdle, Acting Director, CDC
PHS, DHHS
1600 Clifton Road, NE
Atlanta, GA 30333   (404) 639-3291
To reduce morbidity and mortality by preventing cases and complications of sexually transmitted diseases (STD). Types of assistance: grants. Estimate of annual funds available: $ 61,354,800.

* Mental Health Disaster Assistance and Emergency Mental Health 13.982
Dr. Mary Lystad, Chief
Disaster Assistance and Emergency Mental Health
 Section, NIHMH
5600 Fishers Lane
Rockville, MD 20857   (301) 443-4735
Provision of supplemental emergency mental health counseling to individuals affected by major disasters, including the training of volunteers to provide such counseling. Types of assistance: grants. Estimate of annual funds available: $ 397,614.

* Health Programs for Refugees (Immigration and Nationality Act) 13.987
Dr. Walter R. Dowdle, Acting Director, CDC
PHS, DHHS
Atlanta, GA 30333   (404) 639-1286
To assist states and localities in providing health assessment and follow-up activities to new refugees and in addressing refugee health problems of public health concern. Types of assistance: grants. Estimate of annual funds available: $ 4,138,000.

* Cooperative Agreements for State-Based Diabetes Control Programs 13.988
Chief, Grants Management Office
Procurement and Grants Office, CDC, PHS, DHHS
Atlanta, GA 30333   (404) 842-6575
To implement comprehensive programs which will ensure that persons with

diabetes who are at high risk for certain complications of diabetes are identified, entered into the health are system and receive on going state-of-the-art preventive care and treatment. Types of assistance: grants. Estimate of annual funds available: $ 4,861,000.

* National Health Promotion 13.990
Deputy Director, Office of Disease Prevention
and Health Promotion, DHHS, Room 2132
330 C St, SW
Washington, DC 20201   (202) 245-7611
To engage national membership organizations from various sectors as a means of expanding and coordinating health promotion efforts. Types of assistance: grants. Estimate of annual funds available: $ 1,325,000.

* Preventive Health and Health Services Block Grant (PHS Block Grants) 13.991
Chief, Grants Management Branch, CDC
Atlanta, GA 30333   (404) 842-6575
To provide states with resources for comprehensive preventive health services including: emergency medical services, health incentive activities, hypertension programs, rodent control, etc. Types of assistance: grant. Estimate of annual funds available: $ 85,259,000.

* Alcohol and Drug Abuse and Mental Health Services Block Grant (ADMS Block Grant) 13.992
Mr. Thomas Reynolds, Grants Management Officer
Block Grant Programs, ADAMHA, Rm 13C-20
Parklawn Bldg.
5600 Fishers Lane
Rockville, MD 20857   (301) 443-3334
To provide financial assistance to States and Territories to support projects for the development of more effective prevention, treatment and rehabilitating programs and activities to deal with alcohol and drug abuse. Types of assistance: grants. Estimate of annual funds available: $ 765,314,000.

* Maternal and Child Health Services Block Grant 13.994
Office of Maternal and Child Health
Health Resources and Services Administration, PHS
Rm 9A-11, 5600 Fishers Lane
Rockville, MD 20857   (301) 443-2170
To enable states to maintain and strengthen their leadership in planning, promoting, coordinating and evaluating health care for mothers and children and in providing health services for mothers and children who do not have access to adequate health care. Types of assistance: grants. Estimate of annual funds available: $ 46,293,300.

* Adolescent Family Life-Demonstration Projects 13.995
Office of Adolescent Pregnancy Programs
Office of the Assistant Secretary for Health, DHHS
Rm. 736E, HHH Bldg.
200 Independence Ave., SW
Washington, DC   (301)245-6335
To promote adoption as an alternative for adolescent parents. Types of assistance: grants. Estimate of annual funds available: $ 6,114,000.

* Mortgage Insurance-Hospitals (242 Hospitals) 14.128
Insurance Division
Office of Insured Multifamily Housing Development
HUD
Washington, DC 20410   (202) 755-6223
To make possible the financing of hospitals. Types of assistance: loan guarantee. Estimate of annual funds available: $ 217,858,000.

* Mortgage Insurance-Nursing Homes, Intermediate Care Facilities and Board and Care Homes (232 Nursing Homes) 14.129
Insurance Division, Office of Insured Multifamily
Housing Development, HUD
Washington, DC 20412   (202) 755-6223
Types of assistance: loan guarantee. Estimate of annual funds available: $ 233,419,000.

* Section 106(b) Nonprofit Sponsor Assistance Program (Nonprofit Sponsor Loan Fund) 14.141
Director, Assisted Elderly and Handicapped Housing

Division, Office of Elderly and Assisted
Housing, HUD
Washington, DC 20410   (202) 426-8730
To assist and stimulate prospective private nonprofit sponsors/borrowers of Section 202 housing to develop sound housing projects for the elderly or handicapped. Types of assistance: loan. Estimate of annual funds available: $ 960,000.

* Congregate Housing Services Program (CHSP) 14.170
Assisted Elderly and Handicapped Housing Division
Office of Elderly and Assisted Housing
Department of Housing and Urban Development
Washington, DC 20410   (202) 755-5866
To prevent premature or unnecessary institutionalization of elderly-handicapped, non-elderly handicapped, and temporarily disabled, to provide a variety of innovative approaches for the delivery of meals and non-medical supportive services while utilizing existing service programs and to fill gaps existing service systems. Types of assistance: grants. Estimate of annual funds available: $ 6,400,000.

* Housing Development Grants 14.174
Director, Development Grants Division, Rm. 6110
Office of Elderly and Assisted Housing, HUD
451 7th St., SW
Washington, DC 20410   (202) 755-6142
To support the construction or substantial rehabilitation of rental housing in areas experiencing severe shortages of decent rental housing opportunities for families and individuals without other reasonable and affordable housing alternatives in the private market. Types of assistance: grants. Estimate of annual funds available: $ 20,000,000.

* Nehemiah Housing Opportunity Grant Program (Nehemiah Housing) 14.179
Morris E. Carter, Director
Single Family Housing Development Division, HUD
451 7th St., SW
Washington, DC 20410   (202) 755-6700
To provide an opportunity for those families who otherwise would not be financially able to realize their dream of owning a home. Types of assistance: grant. Estimate of annual funds available: $ 20,000,000.

* Community Development Block Grants/Entitlement Grants 14.218
Entitlement Cities Division
Office of Block Grant Assistance
Community Planning and Development
451 7th St., SW
Washington, DC 20410   (202) 755-5977
To develop viable urban communities, by providing decent housing and a suitable living environment. Types of assistance: grants. Estimate of annual funds available: $ 2,053,100,000.

* Community Development Block Grants/Small Cities Program (Small Cities) 14.219
State and Small Cities Division
Office of Block Grant Assistance Community Planning
and Development, HUD
451 7th St., SW
Washington, DC 20410   (202) 755-6223
The primary objective of this program is the development of viable urban communities by providing decent housing, a suitable living environment, and expanding economic opportunities. Types of assistance: grants. Estimate of annual funds available: $ 38,395,000.

* Section 312 Rehabilitation Loans 14.220
Community Planning and Development
Office of Urban Rehabilitation, HUD
451 7th St., SW
Washington, DC 20410   (202) 755-0367
To promote the revitalization of neighborhoods by providing funds for rehabilitation of residential, non-residential and mixed use property in areas determined to be eligible by local governments for activities under either the Community Development Block Grant, Urban Development Action Grant, or Section 810 Urban Homesteading areas. Types of assistance: loans. Estimate of annual funds available: $ 19,510,000.

* Urban Development Action Grants 14.221

Office of Urban Development Action Grants
Community Planning and Development, HUD
451 7th St., SW
Washington, DC 20410 (202) 755-6290
To assist severely distressed large and small cities, urban counties, Guam, the Virgin Islands, Indian Tribes and non-distressed cities containing pockets of poverty in alleviating economic deterioration by means of increased public and private investment in order to aid in economic recovery. Types of assistance: grants. Estimate of annual funds available: $ 49,337,000.

* Urban Homesteading 14.222
Director, Urban Homesteading Program
Office of Urban Rehabilitation, HUD
Washington, DC 20410 (202) 755-5324
To provide homeownership opportunities to credit-worthy individuals and families primarily of lower income, utilizing federally-owned housing stock. Types of assistance: other. Estimate of annual funds available: $ 13,831,000.

* Indian Community Development Block Grant Program 14.223
Office of Program Policy Development
Community Planning and Development, HUD
451 7th St., SW
Washington, DC 20410 (202) 755-6092
To provide assistance to Indian Tribes and Alaska Native Villages in the development of viable Indian Communities. Types of assistance: grants. Estimate of annual funds available: $ 27,000,000.

* Community Development Block Grants/Secretary's Discretionary Fund/Insular Area 14.225
Office of Program Policy Development
Community Planning and Development, HUD
451 7th St., SW
Washington, DC 20410 (202) 755-6092
To provide community development assistance to American Samoa, Guam, the Northern Mariana Islands, Palau and the Virgin Islands. Types of assistance: grants. Estimate of annual funds available: $ 7,000,000.

* Community Development Block Grants/Secretary's Discretionary Fund/Technical Assistance Program 14.227
Office of Program Policy Development
Community Planning and Development, HUD
451 7th St., SW
Washington, DC 20410 (202) 755-6876
To help states, units of general local government, Indian tribes and area wide planing organizations to plan, develop and administer local Community Development Block Grant and Urban Development Action Grant programs. Types of assistance: grants, direct payments. Estimate of annual funds available: $ 10,750,000.

* Community Development Block Grants/State's Program 14.228
State and Small Cities Division
Office of Block Grant Assistance
Community Planning and Development, HUD
451 7th St., SW
Washington, DC 20410 (202) 755-6876
The primary objective of this program is the development of viable urban communities by providing decent housing, a suitable living environment and expanding economic opportunities principally for persons of low and moderate income. Types of assistance: grants. Estimate of annual funds available: $ 841,505,000.

* Rental Housing Rehabilitation (Rental Rehabilitation) 14.230
David M. Cohen, Office of Urban Rehabilitation
Community Planning and Development, HUD
451 7th St., SW
Washington, DC 20410 (202) 755-5685
To increase the supply of standard rental housing units affordable to lower income families. Types of assistance: grants. Estimate of annual funds available: $ 177,418,000.

* Emergency Shelter Grants Program (ESGP) 14.231
James Broughman, Director
Entitlement Cities Division, Rm. 7282, HUD
451 7th St., SW

Washington, DC 20410 (202) 755-5977
The program is designed to help improve the quality of existing emergency shelters for the homeless, to help make available additional emergency shelters, and to help pay the costs of operating emergency shelters. Types of assistance: grants. Estimate of annual funds available: $ 47,302,000.

* Community Development Block Grant/Secretary's Discretionary Fund Special Projects (Special Projects Program) 14.232
Office of Program Policy Development
Community Planning and Development, HUD
451 7th St., SW
Washington, DC 20410 (202) 755-6090
To award grants to states and units of general local government for special projects that address community development activities. Types of assistance: grants. Estimate of annual funds available: $ 12,250,000.

* Fair Housing Assistance Program-State and Local (FHAP) 14.401
Assistant Secretary for Fair Housing and
Equal Opportunity, HUD
451 7th St., SW
Washington, DC 20410 (202) 755-0455
To provide to those agencies to whom HUD must refer Title VIII complaints both the incentives and resources required to develop an effective work force to handle complaints and provide technical assistance and training. Types of assistance: grants. Estimate of annual funds available: $ 4,300,000.

* Community Housing Resource Board Program (CHRB) 14.403
Florence L. Maultsby, Director
HUD, Office of Fair Housing and Equal Opportunity
Office of Voluntary Compliance
Washington, DC 20410 (202) 755-7007
To provide funding to Community Housing Resource Boards (CHRBs) that have the responsibility of providing program implementation assistance to housing industry groups that have signed Voluntary Affirmative Marketing Agreements (VAMAs) with HUD. Types of assistance: grants. Estimate of annual funds available: $ 1,000,000.

* Mariel-Cubans 16.572
Louise Lucas, Bureau of Justice Assistance
Office of Justice Programs
633 Indiana Avenue, NW
Washington, DC 20531 (202) 724-8374
To provide financial reimbursements to states for their expenses by reason of Mariel-Cubans having to be incarcerated in state facilities for terms requiring incarceration for the period of October 1, 1988 through September 30, 1989, following their conviction of a felony committed after having been paroled into the U.S. by the Attorney General during the 1980 influx of Mariel-Cubans. Types of assistance: grant. Estimate of annual funds available: $ 5,000,000.

* Criminal Justice Block Grants 16.573
Office of Justice Program
Bureau of Justice Assistance
Department of Justice
Washington, DC 20531 (202) 272-6838
To provide financial assistance to states and units of local government in carrying out programs to improve the criminal justice system with emphasis on projects to assist in the drug control problem. Types of assistance: grants. Estimate of annual funds available: $ 2,463,000.

* Emergency Federal Law Enforcement Assistance 16.577
Louise Lucas, Bureau of Justice Assistance
Office of Justice Programs
Department of Justice
633 Indiana Ave., NW
Washington, DC 20531 (202) 724-8374
To provide necessary assistance to and through a state government to provide an adequate response to an uncommon situation which requires law enforcement, which is or threatens to become of serious or epidemic proportions and with respect to which state and local resources are inadequate to protect the lives and property of citizens or to enforce the criminal law. Types of assistance: grants. Estimate of annual funds available: $ 1,148,000.

* Narcotics Control Discretionary Grant Program (Discretionary Program) 16.580

Office of Justice Programs
Bureau of Justice Assistance
Department of Justice
633 Indiana Ave., NW
Washington, DC 20531 (202) 272-4606
To enhance the capacity of each state to define the drug problem and to focus on program development on areas of greatest need. Types of assistance: grant. Estimate of annual funds available: $ 30,071,000.

* Drug Law Enforcement Program-Prison Capacity (Prison Capacity Program) 16.581
Nicholas L. Demos, Office of Justice Programs
Bureau of Justice Assistance
Department of Justice
Washington, DC 20531 (202) 272-4605
To provide technical assistance, training and financial support to state, local and private nonprofit organizations dealing with state prison capacities and their alternatives. Types of assistance: grants. Estimate of annual funds available: $ 3,000.

* Crime Victim Assistance/Discretionary Grants 16.582
Marti Speights, Division Director
Office for Victims of Crime
Office of Justice Programs
Department of Justice
633 Indiana Ave., NW
Washington, DC 20531 (202) 272-6500
One percent of the Crime Victims Fund is statutorily reserved by the Office for Victims of Crime for grants to provide training and technical assistance services to eligible crime victims assistance programs and for financial support of services to victims of federal crime by eligible crime victims assistance programs. Types of assistance: grants, direct payments. Estimate of annual funds available: $ 935,000.

* Children's Justice Act Discretionary Grants for Native American Indian Tribes (Children's Justice Act for Native American Indian Tribes) 16.583
Marti Speights, Division Director
Office for Victims of Crime
Office of Justice Programs
Department of Justice
633 Indiana Ave., NW
Washington, DC 20531 (202) 272-6500
Fifteen percent of the funds from the Crime Victims Services that are transferred to the Department of Health and Human Services as part of the Children's Justice Act are to be statutorily reserved by the Office for Victims of Crime to make grants for the purpose of assisting native American Indian tribes in developing, establishing and operating programs. Types of assistance: grants, direct payments. Estimate of annual funds available: $ 631,000.

* Corrections-Training and Staff Development 16.601
National Institute of Corrections
320 Fist St., NW, Room 200
Washington, DC 20534 (202) 724-3106
To devise and conduct in various geographical locations, seminars, workshops and training programs for law enforcement officers, judges and judicial personnel, probation and parole personnel, correctional personnel, welfare workers and other personnel, including lay ex-offenders and paraprofessionals, connected with the treatment and rehabilitation of criminal and juvenile offenders. Types of assistance: grants. Estimate of annual funds available: $ 2,273,544.

* Corrections-Technical Assistance/Clearinghouse 16.603
Technical Assistance Coordinator
National Institute of Corrections
320 First St., NW, Room 200
Washington, DC 20534 (202) 724-3106
To encourage and assist federal, state, and local government programs and services, and programs and services of other public and private agencies, institutions, in their efforts to develop and implement improved corrections programs. Types of assistance: grants. Estimate of annual funds available: $ 2,895,000.

* Labor Force Statistics 17.002
Thomas J. Plewes
Bureau of Labor Statistics
Department of Labor

Washington, DC 20212 (202) 523-1180
To provide statistical data on labor force activities. Types of assistance: grants. Estimate of annual funds available: $ 110,264,000.

* Employment Service 17.207
Robert A. Schaerfl
Director, United States Employment Service
Employment and Training Administration
Department of Labor
Washington, DC 20210 (202) 535-0157
To place persons in employment by providing a variety of placement-related services without charge to job seekers and to employers seeking qualified individuals to fill job openings. Types of assistance: grants. Estimate of annual funds available: $ 763,752,000.

* Dislocated Workers: Employment and Training Assistance 17.246
Robert N. Columbo
Employment and Training Administration
Department of Labor
200 Constitution Ave., NW
Washington, DC 20210 (202) 535-0577
To assist dislocated workers obtain unsubsidized employment through training and related employment services using a decentralized system of state programs. Types of assistance: grants. Estimate of annual funds available: $ 284,626,000.

* Migrant and Seasonal Farmworkers (Migrant and Other Seasonally Employed Farmworker Programs) 17.247
Office of Special Targeted Programs
Division of Seasonal Farmworker Programs
Employment and Training Administration
Dept. of Labor, Rm 4641
200 Constitution Ave., NW
Washington, DC (202) 535-0500
To provide job training, job search assistance, and other supportive services for those individuals who suffer chronic seasonal unemployment and underemployment in the agricultural industry. Types of assistance: grants. Estimate of annual funds available: $ 68,522,000.

* Employment Services and Job Training-Pilot and Demonstration Programs 17.249
Administrator, Office of Strategic Planning and Policy Development
Employment and Training Administration
Department of Labor
200 Constitution Ave., NW
Washington, DC (202) 535-0677
To provide, foster, and promote job training and other services which are most appropriately administered at the national level and which are operated in more than one state to groups with particular disadvantage in the labor market. Types of assistance: grants. Estimate of annual funds available: $ 38,964,000.

* Job Training Partnership Act (JTPA) 17.250
Robert N. Colombo
Employment and Training Administration
Department of Labor
200 Constitution Ave., NW
Washington, DC 20210 (202) 535-0577
To provide job training and related assistance to economically disadvantaged individuals and others who face significant employment barriers. Types of assistance: grants. Estimate of annual funds available: $ 1,788,772,000.

* Native American Employment and Training Programs 17.251
Division of Indian and Native American Programs
Employment and Training Administration
Department of Labor, Room N4641
200 Constitution Ave., NW
Washington, DC (202) 535-0502
To afford job training to Native Americans facing serious barriers to employment, who are in special need of such training to obtain productive employment. Types of assistance: grants. Estimate of annual funds available: $ 59,713,000.

* Mine Health and Safety Grants 17.600
Assistant Secretary of Labor for Mine Safety and Health
Mine Safety and Health Administration

Dept. of Labor,
Ballston Towers No. 3
Arlington, VA 22203 (703) 235-8264
To assist states in developing and enforcing effective mine health and safety laws and regulations. Types of assistance: grants. Estimate of annual funds available: $ 4,988,000.

* Disabled Veterans Outreach Program 17.801
Veterans Employment and Training Service
Office of the Assistant Secretary for Veterans
Employment and Training
Dept. of Labor, Rm S-1316
200 Constitution Ave., NW
Washington, DC (202) 523-9110
To provide funds to states to provide job and job training opportunities for disabled and other veterans through contacts with employers. Types of assistance: grants. Estimate of annual funds available: $ 72,962,000.

* Local Veterans Employment Representative Program (LVER Program) 17.804
Veterans Employment and Training Service
Office of the Asst. Secretary for Veterans
Employment and Training
Dept. of Labor, Rm S1316
200 Constitution Ave., NW
Washington, DC 20210 (202) 523-9110
To provide funds to State Employment Service/Job Service Agencies to ensure that there is local supervision of compliance with federal regulations, performance standards, and grant agreement provisions in carrying out requirements of 38 USC 2004 in providing veterans with maximum employment and training opportunities. Types of assistance: grants. Estimate of annual funds available: $ 66,998,000.

* Boating Safety Financial Assistance 20.005
Commandant, U.S. Coast Guard
Washington, DC 20593-0001 (202) 267-0978
To encourage greater state participation and uniformity in boating safety, particularly to permit the states to assume the greater share of boating safety education , assistance, and enforcement activities. Types of assistance: grants. Estimate of annual funds available: $ 60,000,000.

* Airport Improvement Program (AIP) 20.106
FAA, Office of Airport Planning and Programming
Grants-in-Aid Division, APP-500
800 Independence Ave., SW
Washington, DC 20591 (202) 267-3831
To assist sponsors, owners, or operators of public-use airports in the development of a nationwide system of airports adequate to meet the needs of civil aeronautics. Types of assistance: grants. Estimate of annual funds available: $ 1,400,000,000.

* Highway Planning and Construction (Federal-Aid Highway Program) 20.205
Thomas O. Willete, Director
Office of Engineering, FHA
400 7th St., SW
Washington, DC 20590 (202) 366-4853
To assist state highway agencies (SHA) in the development of an integrated, interconnected network of highways by constructing and rehabilitating the interstate highway system and building or improving primary, secondary and urban systems roads, and streets. Types of assistance: grants. Estimate of annual funds available: $ 1,371,300.

* Motor Carrier Safety Assistance Program (MCSAP) 20.218
Associate Administrator for Motor Carriers
FHA
Washington, DC 20590 (202) 366-2519
To reduce the number and severity of accidents and hazardous materials incidents involving commercial motor vehicles by substantially increasing the level of enforcement activity and the likelihood that safety defects, driver deficiencies, and unsafe carrier practices will be detected and corrected. Types of assistance: grants. Estimate of annual funds available: $ 46,700,000.

* Grants-In-Aid for Railroad Safety-State Participation (State Participation in Railroad Safety) 20.303
Associate Administrator for Safety
Federal Railroad Administration, Room 8320A

400 7th St., SW
Washington, DC 20590 (202) 366-0895
To promote safety in all areas of railroad operations; reduce railroad related accidents and casualties; and to reduce damage to property caused by accidents involving any carrier of hazardous materials by providing State participation in the enforcement and promotion of safety practices. Types of assistance: grants. Estimate of annual funds available: $ 950,000.

* Local Rail Service Assistance (National Rail Service Continuation Grants) 20.308
Office of Passenger and Freight Services
Federal Railroad Administration, Rm 5410
400 7th St., SW
Washington, DC 20590 (202) 366-1677
To maintain efficient local rail freight services. Types of assistance: Grant. Estimate of annual funds available: $ 10,996,000.

* Urban Mass Transportation Capital Improvement Grants (Capital Grants) 20.500
Urban Mass Transportation Administration
Department of Transportation
400 7th St., SW
Washington, DC 20590
To assist in financing the acquisition, construction, reconstruction and improvement of facilities and equipment for use, by operation, lease, or otherwise in mass transportation service in urban areas. Types of assistance: grants. Estimate of annual funds available: $ 825,208,000.

* Urban Mass Transportation Managerial Training Grants (Mass Transit Technology and Technical Assistance Program) 20.503
Office of Technical Assistance and Safety
Urban Mass Transportation Administration
Department of Transportation
400 Seventh St., SW
Washington, DC 20590 (202) 366-0080
To provide fellowships for training of managerial, technical and professional personnel employed in the urban mass transportation field. Types of assistance: grants. Estimate of annual funds available: $ 1,953,000.

* Urban Mass Transportation Technical Studies Grants (Technical Planning Studies) 20.505
Director, Office of Planning Assistance
Office of Grants Management
Urban Mass Transportation Administration, DOT
400 7th St., SW
Washington, DC 20590 (202) 366-1662
To assist in planning, engineering and designing of urban mass transportation projects, and other technical studies in a program for a united or officially coordinated urban transportation system. Types of assistance: grants. Estimate of annual funds available: $ 47,687,000.

* Urban Mass Transportation Capital and Operating Assistance Formula Grants 20.507
Director, Office of Planning Assistance
Office of Grants Management
Urban Mass Transportation Administration, DOT
400 7th St., SW
Washington, DC 20590 (202) 366-1662
To assist in financing the acquisition, construction, cost effective leasing, planning and improvement of facilities and equipment for use by operation or lease or otherwise in mass transportation service. Types of assistance: grants. Estimate of annual funds available: $ 1,904,730,000.

* Public Transportation for Nonurbanized Areas (Section 18) 20.509
Urban Mass Transportation Administration
Office of Grants Management
Office of Capital and Formula Assistance
400 7th St., SW
Washington, DC 20590 (202) 366-2053
To improve, initiate, or continue public transportation services in nonurbanized areas by providing financial assistance for the acquisition, construction and improvement of facilities and equipment and the payment of operating expenses by operating contract, lease or otherwise. Types of assistance: grants. Estimate of annual funds available: $ 87,318,000.

Your Community

* Urban Mass Transportation Technical Assistance   20.512

Associate Administrator for Technical
Assistance and Safety (UTS-1)
Urban Mass Transportation Administration, DOT
400 7th St., SW, Rm. 6431
Washington, DC   20590   (202) 366-4052
To improve mass transportation service, to contribute toward meeting total urban transportation needs at a minimum cost, and to assist in the reduction of urban transportation needs by improving the ability of transit industry operating officials to plan, manage, and operate their systems more effectively and safely. Types of assistance: grants. Estimate of annual funds available: $ 7,133,000.

* Capital Assistance Program for Elderly and Handicapped Persons (Section (b)(2))   20.513

Urban Mass Transportation Administration
Office of Grants Management
Office of Capital and Formula Assistance
400 7th St., SW
Washington, DC   20590   (202) 366-2053
To provide financial assistance in meeting the transportation needs of elderly and handicapped persons where public transportation services are unavailable. Types of assistance: grants. Estimate of annual funds available: $ 35,057,000.

* State and Community Highway Safety   20.600

Brian McLaughlin, Coordinator of Regional
Operations
National Highway Traffic Safety Administration
Washington, DC   20590   (202) 366-2121
To provide a coordinated national highway safety program to reduce traffic accidents, deaths, injuries, and property damage. Types of assistance: grants. Estimate of annual funds available: $ 124,400,000.

* Pipeline Safety   20.700

William Gute
Research and Special Programs Administration, DOT
400 7th St., SW
Washington, DC   20590   (202) 366-4046
To develop and maintain state natural gas, liquified natural gas, and hazardous liquid pipeline safety programs. Types of assistance: grants. Estimate of annual funds available: $ 4,400,000.

* Tax Counseling for the Elderly   21.006

Marion L. Butler, Tax Counseling for the Elderly
Taxpayer Service Division, IRS
1111 Constitution Ave., NW
Washington, DC   20224   (202) 566-4904
To authorize the Internal Revenue Service to enter into agreement with private or public nonprofit agencies or organizations to establish a network of trained volunteers to provide free income tax information and return preparation assistance to elderly taxpayers. Types of assistance: direct payment. Estimate of annual funds available: $ 2,789,000.

* Appalachian Supplements to Federal Grant-In-Aid Community Development   23.002

Executive Director, Appalachian Regional Commission
1666 Connecticut Avenue, NW
Washington DC   20235   (202) 673-7874
To meet the basic needs of local areas and assist in improving creation of jobs and private sector involvement and investment by funding development facilities such as water and sewage systems, sewage treatment plants, industrial sites and providing basic water and sewer facilities. Types of assistance: grants. Estimate of annual funds available: $ 17500.

* Appalachian Development Highway System (Appalachian Corridor)   23.003

Executive Director, Appalachian Regional Commission
1666 Connecticut Ave., NW
Washington, DC   20235   (202) 673-7874
To provide a highway system which, in conjunction with other federally-aided highways, will open u areas with development potential within the Appalachian region where commerce an d communication have been inhibited by lack of adequate access. Types of assistance: grants. Estimate of annual funds available: $ 52,924,000.

* Appalachian Health Programs (Appalachian 202 Health Programs)   23.004

Executive Director, Appalachian Regional Commission
1666 Connecticut Avenue, NW
Washington DC   20235   (202) 673-7874
To make primary health care accessible, reduce infant mortality and recruit needed health manpower in designed "health-shortage" areas. Types of assistance: grants. Estimate of annual funds available: $ 763,100.

* Appalachian Housing Project Planning Loan, Technical Assistance Grant and Site Development and Off-Site Improvement Grant   23.005

Executive Director, Appalachian Regional Commission
1666 Connecticut Ave.,NW
Washington, DC   20235   (202) 673-7874
To stimulate the creation of jobs and private sector investment through low and moderate income housing construction and rehabilitation, and to assist in developing site and off-site improvements for low and moderate income housing in the Appalachian Region. Types of assistance: grant. Estimate of annual funds available: $ 1,500,000.

* Appalachian Local Access Roads   23.008

Executive Director
Appalachian Regional Commission
1666 Connecticut Ave., NW
Washington, DC   20235   (202) 673-7874
To provide access to industrial, commercial, educational, recreational, residential and related transportation facilities which directly or indirectly relate to the improvement of the areas determined by the states to have significant development potential. Types of assistance: grant. Estimate of annual funds available: $ 5,000,000.

* Appalachian Local Development District Assistance (LDD)   23.009

Executive Director
Appalachian Regional Commission
1666 Connecticut Ave., NW
Washington, DC   20235   (202) 673-7874
To provide planning and development resources in multicounty areas; to help develop the technical competence essential to sound development assistance. Types of assistance: grant. Estimate of annual funds available: $ 3,200,000.

* Appalachian Mine Area Restoration   23.010

Executive Director, Appalachian Regional Commission
1666 Connecticut Ave., NW
Washington, DC   20235   (202) 673-7874
To further the creation of jobs by rehabilitating areas presently damaged by deleterious mining practices and by controlling or abating mine drainage pollution. Types of assistance: Grant. Estimate of annual funds available: $ 0.

* Appalachian State Research, Technical Assistance, and Demonstration Projects (State Research)   23.011

Executive Director, Appalachian Regional Commission
1666 Connecticut Ave., NW
Washington, DC   20235   (202) 673-7874
To expand the knowledge of the region to the fullest extent possible by means of state-sponsored research studies, technical assistance and demonstration projects in order to assist the Commission in accomplishing the objectives of the Act. Types of assistance: grant. Estimate of annual funds available: $ 1,000,000.

* Appalachian Vocational and Other Education Facilities and Operations   23.012

Executive Director
Appalachian Regional Commission
1666 Connecticut Ave., NW
Washington DC   20235   (202) 673-7874
To provide the people of the region with the equipment, renovation and operating funds for training and education necessary to obtain employment at their best capability for available job opportunities. Types of assistance: grants. Estimate of annual funds available: $ 3,000,000.

* Appalachian Child Development   23.013

Executive Director, Appalachian Regional Commission
1666 connecticut Ave., NW
Washington, DC   20235   (202) 673-7874
To provide child development services throughout the region which meet the needs of industry and its employees. Types of assistance: grants. Estimate of annual funds available: $ 318,635.

* Training Assistance to State and Local Government 27.009

Assistant Director, Office of Employee and
 Executive Development
Office of Personnel Management
P.O. Box 7230
Washington, DC 20044   (202) 632-6802
To assist state and local governments and Indian tribal governments in training professional, administrative, and technical personnel to increase their capability for mission accomplishment. Types of assistance: training. Estimate of annual funds available: $ 0.

* Presidential Management Intern Program 27.013

Programs Division, Office of Affirmative
 Recruiting and Employment
Career Entry and Employee Development Group
Office of Personnel Management
1900 E St., NW
Washington, DC   (202) 632-0496
To attract to the federal service graduate students of exceptional potential who are receiving advanced degrees in a variety of academic disciplines and who have a clear interest in and commitment to a career in the analysis and management of public programs and policies. Types of assistance: federal employment. Estimate of annual funds available: $ 203000.

* Employment Discrimination-State and Local Anti-Discrimination Agency Contracts 30.002

Robert L. Walker, Program Development and
 Coordination Division, Systemic Investigation
 and Individual Compliance Programs
EEOC, Rm 433
2403 E St., NW
Washington, DC   (202) 634-6806
To assist EEOC in the enforcement of Title VII of the Civil Rights Act of 1964, as amended and of the age discrimination in employment act of 1967 by investigating and resolving charges of employment discrimination based on race, color, religion, sex, national origin, etc. Types of assistance: direct payment. Estimate of annual funds available: $ 20,000,000.

* Employment Discrimination Project Contracts - Indian Tribes 30.009

Robert L. Walker, Director, Program Development
 and Coordination Division, Systemic Investigation
 and Individual Compliance Program
EEOC, 2403 E St., NW
Washington, DC   (202) 634-6806
To insure the protection of employment rights of Indians working on reservation. Types of assistance: grants. Estimate of annual funds available: $ 20,000,000.

* Labor-Management Cooperation 34.002

Division of Labor Management Grant Programs
Federal Mediation and Conciliation Service
2100 K St., NW
Washington, DC 20247   (202) 653-5320
Types of assistance: grants. Estimate of annual funds available: $ 11,900,000.

* Community Development Revolving Loan Program for Credit Unions (CDCU) 44.002

Mr. Floyd Lancaster, Community Development
 Revolving Loan Program for Credit Unions
National Credit Union Administration
1776 G St., NW
Washington, DC 20456   (202) 682-9780
To support community based credit unions in their efforts to stimulate economic development activities which result in increased income, ownership and employment opportunities for low-income residents and to provide basic financial and related services to residents of their communities. Types of assistance: direct loans. Estimate of annual funds available: $ 0.

* Promotion of the Arts-State Programs 45.007

Directors, State Program
National Endowment for the Arts
100 Penn Ave., NW
Washington, DC 20506   (202) 682-5429
To assist state and regional public arts agencies in the development of programs for the encouragement of the arts and artists, and to assist organizations providing services at a national level to state or local arts agencies. Types of assistance: grants. Estimate of annual funds available: $ 25,526,000.

* Promotion of the Arts-Expansion Arts 45.010

E'Vonne C. Rorie
Expansion Arts Program
National Endowment for the Arts
1100 Penn Ave., NW
Washington, DC 20560   (202) 682-5443
To provide grants to professionally directed arts organizations of high artistic quality which are deeply rooted in and reflective of the culture of a minority. Types of assistance: grants. Estimate of annual funds available: $ 6,700,000.

* Promotion of the Arts: Inter-Arts 45.011

Director, Inter-Arts Program
National Endowment for the Arts
1100 Penn Ave., NW
Washington, DC 20506   (202) 682-5444
To provide grants for projects that potentially have national or regional impact. Types of assistance: grants. Estimate of annual funds available: $ 4,300,000.

* Promotion of the Arts - Challenge Grants 45.013

Challenge and Advancement Grant Programs
Room 617, National Endowment for the Arts
1100 Pennsylvania Ave., NW
Washington, DC 20506   (202) 682-5436
To assist on a one-time basis, projects designed to have a lasting impact that can help move the National forward in achieving excellence in the arts, access to, and/or appreciation of such excellence. Types of assistance: grants. Estimate of annual funds available: $ 18,500,000.

* Promotion of the Arts-Folk Arts 45.015

Director, Folk Arts Program
National Endowment for the Arts
1100 Pennsylvania Ave., NW
Washington, DC 20506   (202) 682-5449
To provide grants to assist, foster, and make publicly available the diverse traditional American folk arts throughout the country. Types of assistance: grants. Estimate of annual funds available: $ 3,100,000.

* Promotion of the Arts (Local Programs) 45.023

Local Programs, National Endowment for the Arts
Nancy Hawks Center
1100 Pennsylvania Ave., NW
Washington, DC 20506   (202) 682-5431
To enhance to the quality and availability of the arts by fostering expansion of public support for the arts at the local level and to strengthen the local arts agency as a mechanism for arts planning, financial support and development and to encourage joint planning for the arts by Federal, state, and local art agencies, community leaders, public officials, art organizations, and artists. Types of assistance: grants. Estimate of annual funds available: $ 2,566,000.

* Management and Technical Assistance for Socially and Economically Disadvantaged Businesses: 7(j) Development Assistance Program 59.007

Associate Administrator for Minority Small Business
1441 L St., NW, Room 602
Washington, DC 20416   (202) 653-6475
To provide management and technical assistance through qualified individuals, public or private organizations to existing or potential businesses which are economically and socially disadvantaged or which are located in areas of high concentration of unemployment. Types of assistance: grants. Estimate of annual funds available: $ 8,080,000.

* Physical Disaster Loans (7(b) Loans (DL)) 59.008

Disaster Assistance Division, SBA
1441 L St., NW
Washington, DC 20416   (202) 653-6879
To provide loans to the victims of designated physical-type disasters for uninsured loans. Types of assistance: loans, loan guarantee. Estimate of annual funds available: $ 280,000,000.

* Service Corps of Retired Executives Association (SCORE) 59.026

National SCORE Office
1129 20th St., NW
Washington, DC 20036   (202) 653-6279
To utilize the management experience of retired and active business executives to counsel and train potential in existing small businesses. Types of assistance: grants, other. Estimate of annual funds available: $ 900,000.

* Small Business Development Center (SBDC) 59.037

Small Business Administration
Office of Small Business Development Center
1441 L St., NW, Room 317
Washington, DC 20416 (202) 653-6768
To provide management counseling, training and technical assistance to the small business community through Small Business Development Centers (SBDCs). Types of assistance: grants. Estimate of annual funds available: $ 45,000,000.

* Veterans State Domiciliary Care 64.014

Asst. Chief, Medical Director for Geriatrics
and Extended Care
Department of Veterans Affairs
Washington, DC 20420 (202) 233-3679
To provide financial assistance to states furnishing domiciliary care to eligible veterans in State Veterans Homes which meet the standards prescribed by the Secretary of Veterans Affairs. Types of assistance: grants. Estimate of annual funds available: $ 13,188,000.

* Veterans State Nursing Home Care 64.015

Asst. Chief, Medical Director for Geriatrics
and Extended Care
Department of Veterans Affairs
Washington, DC 20420 (202) 233-3679
To provide financial assistance to states furnishing nursing home care to eligible veterans in State Veterans Homes which meet the standards prescribed by the Secretary of Veterans Affairs. Types of assistance: grants. Estimate of annual funds available: $ 69,100,000.

* Veterans State Hospital Care 64.016

Asst. Chief Medical Director for Geriatrics
and Extended Care
Department of Veterans Affairs
Washington, DC 20420 (202) 233-3679
To provide financial assistance to states furnishing hospital care to eligible veterans in State Veterans Homes which meet the standards prescribed by the Secretary of Veterans Affairs. Types of assistance: grants. Estimate of annual funds available: $ 3,669,000.

* State Cemetery Grants 64.203

Director, State Cemetery Grant Program
National Cemetery System
Department of Veterans Affairs
810 Vermont Ave., NW
Washington, DC 20420 (202) 233-2313
To assist states in the establishment, expansion and improvement of veterans cemeteries. Types of assistance: grants. Estimate of annual funds available: $ 9,000,000.

* Air Pollution Control Program Support 66.001

Steve Hitte, Air Quality Management Division
Office of Air and Radiation, EPA
Research Triangle Park, NC 27711 (919) 541-0886
To assist state, municipal, intermunicipal, and interstate agencies in planning developing, establishing, improving and maintaining adequate programs for prevention and control of air quality standards. Types of assistance: grants. Estimate of annual funds available: $ 101,500,000.

* Air Pollution Control-Technical Training 66.006

Betsy Dodson
Air Pollution Training Institute, EPA
Research Triangle Park, NC 27711 (919) 541-2401
To provide technical training to personnel from state and local air pollution control agencies. Types of assistance: training. Estimate of annual funds available: $ 241,000.

* Construction Grants for Wastewater Treatment Works 66.418

James Hanlon, Director, Municipal Construction
Division, WH-547
Office of Municipal Pollution Control, EPA
Washington, DC 20460 (202) 382-5859
To assist and serve as an incentive in construction of municipal wastewater treatment works which are required to meet state and/or federal water quality standards. Types of assistance: grants. Estimate of annual funds available: $ 1,166,000,000.

* Water Pollution Control-State and Interstate Program Support (106 Grants) 66.419

Edmund M. Notzon, Director
Analysis and Evaluation Division
Office of Water Regulations and Standards
Office of Water, EPA
Washington, DC 20460 (202) 382-5389
To assist states, territorial Indian Tribes and interstate agencies in establishing and maintaining adequate measures for prevention and control of surface and ground water pollution. Types of assistance: grants. Estimate of annual funds available: $ 67,100,000.

* Water Quality Control Training Seminars, Data and Monitoring Publications (STORET-Storage and Retrieval System) 66.423

Phillip H. Lindenstruth, Chief
Client Services Branch
Office of Information Resources Management
Washington, DC 20460 (202) 382-7220
To provide state, interstate and other water pollution control and water resource management agencies orientation and where requested training in the use of the storage and retrieval system used by EPA. Types of assistance: Training. Estimate of annual funds available: $ 0.

* State Public Water System Supervision 66.432

Ray Enyeart, Office of Drinking Water
Office of Water, EPA
Washington, DC 20460 (202) 382-5551
To foster development and maintenance of state programs which implement the Safe Drinking Water Act. Types of assistance: Grant. Estimate of annual funds available: $ 33,450,000.

* State Underground Water Source Protection 66.433

Francoise Brasier, Chief
Underground Injection Control Branch
Office of Drinking Water
Office of Water, EPA
401 M St., SW
Washington, DC 20460 (202) 382-5530
To foster development and implementation of underground injection control (UIC) programs under the Safe Drinking Water Act. Types of assistance: grants. Estimate of annual funds available: $ 10,500,000.

* Water Pollution Control-Lake Restoration Cooperative Agreements (Clean Lakes Program) 66.435

Environmental Protection Agency
Grants Administration Division (PM-216)
Washington, DC 20460
To provide financial assistance to states for assessing the water quality of publicly-owned freshwater lakes, diagnosing the causes of degradation in publicly owned lakes, developing lake restoration and protection plans. Types of assistance: grants. Estimate of annual funds available: $ 12,500,000.

* Construction Management Assistance (Construction Grants Delegation to States) 66.438

Robert Lee, Delegation Management Branch
Municipal Construction Division, WH-547
Environmental Protection Agency
Washington, DC 20460 (202) 382-7359
To assist and serve as an incentive in the process of delegating the states a maximum amount of authority for conducting day-to-day matters related the management of the construction grant program. Types of assistance: Grant. Estimate of annual funds available: $ 60,531,000.

* Water Quality Management Planning (205(j)) 66.454

Edmund M. Notzon, Director
Analysis and Evaluation Division
Office of Water Regulations and Standards, EPA
401 M St., SW
Washington, DC 20460 (202) 382-5389
To assist states (including territories and the District), public comprehensive planning organizations, and interstate organizations in carrying out water quality management planning. Types of assistance: grants. Estimate of annual funds available: $ 23,000,000.

* Construction Grants for Abatement of Combined

Sewer Overflow Pollution in Marine Bays and Estuaries (Marine CSO Reserve) 66.455

Municipal Facilities Division
Office of Municipal Pollution Control
Office of Water
Environmental Protection Agency
Washington, DC 20460

To award grants to Combined Sewer Overflow projects which are designed to restore uses of the receiving waters in Bays and Estuaries which have been impaired by the impact of CSOs. Types of assistance: grants. Estimate of annual funds available: $ 10,000,000.

* National Estuary Program 66.456

Louise Wise, Chief
Technical Support Division
Office of Marine and Estuarine Protection, EPA
Washington, DC 20460 (202) 475-7102

To authorize the Agency to convene Management Conferences with participants from states, legislatures, etc., to develop programs to protect and restore coastal resources in estuaries of national significance. Types of assistance: grants. Estimate of annual funds available: $ 9,677,837.

* Capitalization Grants for State Revolving Funds (State Revolving Fund) 66.458

Robert Lee, Delegation Management Branch
Municipal Construction Division
Office of Municipal Control, EPA
Washington, DC 20460 (202) 382-7359

To create State Revolving Funds through a program of capitalization grants to states which will provide a feasible transition to state and local financing of municipal wastewater treatment facilities. Types of assistance: grants. Estimate of annual funds available: $ 1,361,000,000.

* Nonpoint Source Reservation (205(j)(5)) 66.459

James Meck, Chief, Nonpoint Sources Branch
Criteria and Standards Division
Office of Water Regulations and Standards, EPA
401 M St., SW
Washington, DC 20460 (202) 382-7100

To assist states in developing and implementing non-point source management programs. Types of assistance: grants. Estimate of annual funds available: $ 12,500,000.

* Air Pollution Control Research 66.501

Environmental Protection Agency
Grants Administration, PM 216
Washington, DC 20460

Types of assistance: grants. Estimate of annual funds available: $ 15,469,300.

* Environmental Protection Consolidated Grants - Program Support (Consolidated Program Support Grants) 66.600

Richard Mitchell, Grants Administration Division
PM 216f, Environmental Protection Agency
Washington, DC 20460 (202) 382-5297

The consolidated program support grant is an alternative assistance delivery mechanism which allows a state or local agency responsible for continuing pollution control programs to develop an integrated approach to pollution control. Types of assistance: grants. Estimate of annual funds available: $ 30,000,000.

* Pesticides Enforcement Program 66.700

A.E. Conroy II, Director
Office of Compliance Monitoring
Office of Pesticides and Toxic Substances, EPA
Washington, DC 20460 (202) 382-7003

To assist states in developing and maintaining comprehensive pesticide enforcement programs. Types of assistance: grants. Estimate of annual funds available: $ 8,803,400.

* Toxic Substances Compliance Monitoring Cooperative Agreements 66.701

A.E. Conroy II, Director
Office of Compliance Monitoring
Office of Pesticides and Toxic Substances, EPA
Washington, DC 20460 (202) 382-3807

To assist states in developing and maintaining comprehensive Toxic Substance enforcement programs. Types of assistance: grants. Estimate of annual funds

available: $ 2,200,000.

* Asbestos Hazards Abatement (Schools) Assistance (Hazard Abatement Assistance Branch HAAB) 66.702

Regina Busong
Environmental Protection Agency
401 M St., SW
Washington, DC 20460 (202) 382-3949

To create a program information distribution, technical and scientific assistance and financial support Local Education Agencies. Types of assistance: grants, direct loans. Estimate of annual funds available: $ 13,005,000.

* Pesticides Certification Program 66.704

Stephen Johnson
Field Operations Division, OPP
Office of Pesticides and Toxic Substances, EPA
Washington, DC 20460 (703) 557-7410

To assist states, territories and possessions of the U.S., including the District of Columbia and Indian Tribes, in developing and maintaining comprehensive programs to certify applicators to apply restricted use pesticides. Types of assistance: grants. Estimate of annual funds available: $ 1,680,000.

* Hazardous Waste Management State Program Support 66.801

Grants Administration Division, EPA
Washington, DC 20460

To assist state governments in the development and implementation of an authorized hazardous waste management program for the purpose of controlling the generation, transportation, treatment, storage and disposal of hazardous waste. Types of assistance: grants. Estimate of annual funds available: $ 66,000,000.

* Hazardous Substance Response Trust Fund (Superfund) 66.802

Jon Baker Wine, Chief
State Involvement Section
Office of Emergency and Remedial Response, EPA
Washington, DC 20460 (202) 382-2443

To determine level of hazard at sites listed in the CERCLA Information System. Types of assistance: grants. Estimate of annual funds available: $ 195,529,167.

* State Underground Storage Tanks Program (UST Program) 66.804

Joseph Retzer, Director
Implementation Division
Underground Storage Tank Program (OSWER), EPA
401 M St., SW
Washington, DC 20460 (202) 382-7601

To assist states in Development and implementation of their own underground storage tank programs to operate in lieu of the federal Program. Types of assistance: grants. Estimate of annual funds available: $ 9,000,000.

* Underground Storage Tank Trust Fund Program 66.805

Joseph Retzer, Director
Implementation Division
Office of the Underground Storage Tanks, EPA
Waterside Mall, 401 M St., SW
Washington, DC 20460 (202) 382-7601

To support the development of state corrective action and enforcement programs that address releases from underground storage tanks containing petroleum. Types of assistance: grants. Estimate of annual funds available: $ 42,500,000.

* Superfund Technical Assistance Grants for Citizen Groups at Priority Sites 66.806

Murray Newton
Office of Emergency and Remedial Response, EPA
401 M St., SW
Washington, DC 20460 (202) 382-2443

To provide resources for community groups to hire technical advisors who can assist them in interpreting technical information concerning the assessment of potential hazards and the selection and design of appropriate remedies. Types of assistance: grants. Estimate of annual funds available: $ 5,540,000.

* Foster Grandparent Program (FGP) 72.001

Program Officer, Foster Grandparent Program

Senior Companion Program, ACTION
806 Connecticut Ave., NW
Washington, DC 20525 (202) 634-9349
To provide part-time volunteer service opportunities for low income persons age 60 and over and to give supportive person-to-person service in health, education welfare and related settings to help alleviate the physical mental and emotional problems of infants, children or youth having special or exceptional needs. Types of assistance: grants. Estimate of annual funds available: $ 58,928,000.

* Retired Senior Volunteer Program (RSVP) 72.002

Program Officer
Retired Senior Volunteer Program, ACTION
1100 Vermont Ave., NW
Washington, DC 20525 (202) 634-9353
To provide a variety of opportunities for retired persons, aged 60 or over to serve their community through significant volunteer service. Types of assistance: grants. Estimate of annual funds available: $ 30,862,000.

* Service-Learning Programs 72.005

ACTION, Student Community Service Programs
1100 Vermont Ave., NW
Washington, DC 20525 (202) 634-9424
To encourage and enable students in secondary, vocational and post-secondary schools to participate in community service projects addressing poverty related problems. Types of assistance: grants. Estimate of annual funds available: $ 1,352,000.

* Senior Companion Program 72.008

Program Officer
Foster Grandparent Senior Companion Program
Development and Planning Branch, ACTION
1100 Vermont Ave., NW
Washington, DC 20525 (202) 634-9351
To provide volunteer opportunities for low income people aged 60 and older which enhance their ability to remain active and provide critically needed community services. Types of assistance: grants. Estimate of annual funds available: $ 25,135,000.

* Volunteerism: Minigrants Program 72.010

Technical Assistance Officer
Program Demonstration and Development Division
Room M513, ACTION
1100 Vermont Ave., NW
Washington, DC 20525 (202) 634-975
To initiate, strengthen and/or supplement volunteer efforts and to encourage broad-based volunteer citizen participation. Types of assistance: grants. Estimate of annual funds available: $ 150,000.

* State Office of Voluntarism (SOV) 72.011

National SOV Program Manager
Program Development and Demonstration Division
ACTION, Room M 513
1100 Vermont Ave., NW
Washington, DC 20525 (202) 634-9749
To promote and coordinate voluntary participation in state and local government and public and private nonprofit organizations by fostering developing creating and/or supporting Offices of Voluntarism at the state level to stimulate new active citizen initiatives. Types of assistance: grants. Estimate of annual funds available: $ 100,000.

* Volunteer Demonstration Program (Demonstration Grants) 72.012

Asst. Director
Program Demonstration and Development Division
ACTION, 1100 Vermont Ave., NW
Washington, DC 20525 (202) 634-9757
To explore areas of human and social concern where citizens, as volunteers can contribute toward individual self-reliance and community self-sufficiency. Types of assistance: grants. Estimate of annual funds available: $ 754,000.

* Technical Assistance Program (TAP) 72.013

Technical Assistance Officer
Technical Assistance Program, ACTION
1100 Vermont Ave., NW
Washington, DC 20525 (202) 634-9757
To help voluntary and nonprofit organizations respond to the training, technical assistance and management needs of volunteers and organizations undertaking voluntary efforts. Types of assistance: grants. Estimate of annual funds available: $ 46,000.

* Drug Alliance 72.014

Director, Drug Alliance
Program Demonstration and Development Division
ACTION
1100 Vermont Ave., NW
Washington, DC 20525 (202) 634-9759
To strengthen and expand the efforts of community-based volunteer groups working to prevent drug abuse. Types of assistance: grants. Estimate of annual funds available: $ 313,000.

* Energy Extension Service 81.050

Ronald W. Bowes, Chief
Energy Management and Extension Branch, DOE
(CE-221), Forrestal Bldg.
1000 Independence Ave., SW
Washington, DC 20585 (202) 586-8288
To encourage individuals and small establishments to reduce energy consumption and convert to alternative energy sources. Types of assistance: grants. Estimate of annual funds available: $ 3,844,000.

* Energy Conservation for Institutional Buildings 81.052

Elmer Lee
Institutional Conservation Programs Division
Office of Conservation and Renewable Energy, CE-231
Department of Energy
Washington, DC 20585 (202) 586-8034
Types of assistance: grants. Estimate of annual funds available: $ 36,600,000.

* Nuclear Waste Disposal Siting (Consultation and Cooperation Financial Assistance) 81.065

James C. Bresee
Office of Civilian Radioactive Waste Management
Washington, DC (202) 586-9173
To provide for the development of a repository for the disposal of high level radioactive waste and spent nuclear fuel. Types of assistance: direct payment. Estimate of annual funds available: $ 16,000,000.

* Energy Task Force for the Urban Consortium 81.081

Linda J. DelaCroix, Project Manager
Building Services Division
Office of Conservation and Renewable Energy, DOE
1000 Independence Ave., SW
Washington, DC 20585 (202) 586-1851
To develop the capability to address energy related problems and to evaluate and test community energy supply and conservation techniques. Types of assistance: grants. Estimate of annual funds available: $ 1,960,000.

* Reimbursement for Firefighting on Federal Property 83.007

Clyde A. Bragdon, Jr., Administrator,
U.S. Fire Administration
500 C St., SW, Federal Center Plaza
Washington, DC 20472 (301) 447-1080
To provide that each fire service organization which engages in firefighting operations on Federal property may be reimbursed for their direct expenses and direct losses incurred in firefighting Types of assistance: direct payment. Estimate of annual funds available: $ 0.

* Community-Based Anti-Arson Program 83.008

Office of Acquisition Management
Attn: Cathy Green, Room 732
500 C St., SW
Washington, DC 20472
To assist local community based anti-arson organizations increase and intensify arson mitigation efforts. Types of assistance: grants. Estimate of annual funds available: $ 300,000.

* Emergency Management Institute-Training Assistance (Student Stipend Reimbursement Program (SEP)) 83.400

National Emergency Training Center
Student Services Branch
16825 S. Seton Ave.
Emmitsburg, MD 21727 (301) 447-1000
To defray travel and per diem expenses of state and local emergency

management personnel who attend training courses conducted by the Emergency Management Institute. Types of assistance: direct payment. Estimate of annual funds available: $ 700,000.

* Emergency Management Institute-Architect/Engineer Student Program 83.401

Linda Whitaker
Engineering and Survey Branch, FEMA
Washington, DC 20472 (202) 646-3061
To train architectural or engineering students to survey buildings to determine the degree to which they provide protection against nuclear disaster effects. Types of assistance: Training. Estimate of annual funds available: $ 0.

* Emergency Management Institute-Field Training Program (Comprehensive Cooperative Agreements (CCA)) 83.403

Emergency Management Institute
16825 S. Seton Ave.
Emmittsburg, MD 21227 (301) 447-1000
To provide FEMA support to state-based training programs. Types of assistance: grants, Training. Estimate of annual funds available: $ 4,500,000.

* National Fire Academy-Training Assistance (State Stipend Reimbursement Program) 83.405

National Emergency Training Center
Student Services Branch
16825 S. Seton Ave.
Emmitsburg, MD 21727 (301) 447-1000
To provide travel stipends to students attending Academy courses, train the trainer, and in-service instructor training. Types of assistance: direct payment. Estimate of annual funds available: $ 1,102,163.

* Civil Defense - State and Local Emergency Management Assistance (Emergency Management Assistance) 83.503

Marilyn Barton, Office of Civil Defense
State and Local Programs and Support Directorate
FEMA
Washington, DC 20472 (202) 646-3510
To develop civil defense organizations in the states and their political subdivisions in order to plan for and coordinate emergency activities in the event of attack or natural disaster. Types of assistance: grants. Estimate of annual funds available: $ 58,123,000.

* Other State and Local Direction, Control and Warning 83.504

Earl Tildon
Direction and Control Branch, FEMA
Washington, DC 20472 (202) 646-3094
To assist state and local governments in preventive maintenance and corrective maintenance management planning and repair and replacement costs of emergency communications and warning systems and emergency operating center equipment and facilities. Types of assistance: grants. Estimate of annual funds available: $ 1,543,000.

* State Disaster Preparedness Grants (Disaster Preparedness Improvement Grant) 83.505

Gregory Jones
Office of Disaster Assistance Programs
State and Local Programs and Support, FEMA
Washington, DC 20472 (202) 646-3668
To assist states in developing and improving state and local plans, programs, and capabilities for disaster preparedness and prevention. Types of assistance: grants. Estimate of annual funds available: $ 2,800,000.

* State and Local Emergency Operating Centers (EOC) 83.512

Earl T. Tildon, Direction and Control Branch
Emergency Management Systems Support Division, FEMA Washington,
DC 20472 (202) 646-3094
To enhance effective, reliable and survivable direction and control capabilities of state and local government. Types of assistance: grant. Estimate of annual funds available: $ 5,000,000.

* State and Local Warning and Communications

Systems 83.513

Joseph H. Massa
Communications Management Officer, FEMA
Washington, DC 20472 (202) 646-3083
To maintain the civil defense readiness of state and local governments by furnishing matching funds for the purchase of equipment and supporting materials for state and local direction and control. Types of assistance: grants. Estimate of annual funds available: $ 500,000.

* Population Protection Planning 83.514

C. Dwight Poe
State and Local Programs and Support Directorate
FEMA
Washington, DC 20472 (202) 646-3492
To assist states and localities to develop multi-hazard emergency operations plans that detail the planning provisions that are necessary to ensure the protection of people from the effects of nuclear attack. Types of assistance: grants. Estimate of annual funds available: $ 8,400,000.

* Disaster Assistance 83.516

Deborah Hard, FEMA
Office of Disaster Assistance Programs
Washington, DC 20472 (202) 646-3612
To provide supplemental assistance to states, local government, certain private nonprofit organizations and individuals in alleviating suffering and hardship resulting from major disasters or emergencies declared by the President. Types of assistance: grants, direct payment. Estimate of annual funds available: $ 220,000,000.

* Hazard Mitigation Assistance 83.519

Karen Helbrecht, Hazard Mitigation Branch
Disaster Assistance Programs, FEMA
500 C St., SW
Washington, DC 20472 (202) 646-3358
To assist states or local units of government in preparing a hazard mitigation plan. Types of assistance: grants. Estimate of annual funds available: $ 200,000.

* Hurricane Preparedness Grants (Hurricane Preparedness) 83.520

Frederick H. Sharrocks, Jr.
Earthquakes and Natural Hazards Programs Division
State and Local Programs and Support, FEMA
Washington, DC 20472 (202) 646-2796
Major objectives of the Hurricane Preparedness Program are to provide technical and financial assistance to state and local governments to conduct a Hurricane Preparedness Study that addresses the unique consequences of hurricanes in high-risk, high-population areas, reduce hurricane-caused injuries and save lives by assisting in the preparation of a hurricane evacuation plan, and reduce property damage caused by hurricanes. Types of assistance: grants. Estimate of annual funds available: $ 50,000.

* Earthquake Hazards Reduction Grants (Earthquake Hazards Reduction) 83.521

Gary D. Johnson
Earthquakes and Natural Hazards Programs Division
State and Local Programs and Support, FEMA
Washington, DC 20472 (202) 646-2799
To reduce, abate and mitigate the potential loss of life and property as the result of the occurrence of an earthquake by fostering the increase in public awareness. Types of assistance: Grant. Estimate of annual funds available: $ 1,565,000.

* Radiological Defense (Radiological Defense (RADEF)) 83.522

Michael S. Pawlowski, Chief
Radiological Defense Branch
Office of Civil Defense
Systems Support Division, FEMA
Washington, DC 20472 (202) 646-3080
To develop and implement Radiological Defense capabilities to minimize the effects of war-related radiological hazards. Types of assistance: grants. Estimate of annual funds available: $ 8,122,000.

* Federal Emergency Management Food and Shelter Program (Emergency food and Shelter) 83.523

Fran McCarthy, FEMA
Office of Disaster Assistance Programs
Washington, DC 20472 (202) 646-3648
To supplement and expand on-going efforts to provide shelter, food and

supportive services for needy families and individuals. Types of assistance: grants. Estimate of annual funds available: $ 114,000,000.

* National Defense/National Direct/Perkins Loan Cancellations (formerly National Direct Student Loan (NDSL) 84.037

Robert R. Coates
Division of Program Operations
Student Financial Assistance Programs
400 Maryland Ave., SW
Washington, DC 20202 (202) 732-3715

To reimburse institutions for their share of loans cancelled for National Defense Student Loan recipients who become teachers or who perform active military service in the U.S. Armed Forces. Types of assistance: direct payment. Estimate of annual funds available: $ 32,306,000.

* Impact Aid-Construction (Impact Aid; Construction) 84.040

Charles E. Hansen
Program Operations, Impact Aid Program
Department of Education
400 Maryland Ave., SW
Washington, DC 20202-6244 (202) 732-4651

To provide assistance for the construction of urgently needed minimum school facilities in school districts which have had substantial increases in school membership as a result of new or increased Federal Activities. Types of assistance: grants. Estimate of annual funds available: $ 24,700,000.

* Impact Aid-Maintenance and Operation (Impact Aid/Disaster Aid) 84.041

Charles Hansen
Impact Aid Program
Office of Elementary and Secondary Education
Department of Education
400 Maryland Ave., SW
Washington, DC 20202 (202) 732-4651

To provide financial assistance to local educational agencies when enrollments or availability of revenue are adversely affected by federal activities. Types of assistance: direct payment. Estimate of annual funds available: $ 708,396,000.

* Vocational Education-State Councils 84.053

Division of Vocational Education
Office of Asst Secretary for Vocational
and Adult Education
Dept. of Education
400 Maryland Ave., SW
Washington, DC 20202 (202) 732-2441

To advise the State Board for Vocational Education on the development and administration of the State Plan. Types of assistance: grants. Estimate of annual funds available: $ 7,904,000.

* Indian Education-Formula Grants to Local Educational Agencies (Indian Education Act - Subpart 1) 84.060

Office of Indian Educations
Department of Education
400 Maryland Ave., SW
Washington, DC 20202 (202) 732-1887

To develop and carry out elementary and secondary school programs designed to meet the special educational and culturally related academic needs of Indian children. Types of assistance: grants. Estimate of annual funds available: $ 49,248,000.

* Rehabilitation Services-Basic Support (Basic Support) 84.126

Office of Program Operations
Rehabilitation Services Administration
Department of Education
Washington, DC 20202 (202) 732-1406

To provide vocational rehabilitation services to persons with mental and/or physical handicaps. Types of assistance: grants. Estimate of annual funds available: $ 1,437,973,057.

* Rehabilitation Services-Service Projects (Rehabilitation Service Projects) 84.128

Rehabilitation Services Administration
Office of Asst. Secretary for Special Education
and Rehabilitative Services
Department of Education
Washington, DC 20202 (202) 732-1347

To provide funds to state vocational rehabilitation agencies and public nonprofit organizations for projects and demonstration which hold promise of expanding and otherwise improving services for groups of mentally and physically handicapped individuals over and above those provided by the Basic Support Program. Types of assistance: grants. Estimate of annual funds available: $ 47,687,000.

* Migrant Education - Interstate and Intrastate Coordination Program 84.144

Office of Migrant Education
Office of Elementary and Secondary Education
Debarment of Education
400 Maryland Ave., SW, Room 2145
Washington, DC 20202 (202) 732-4746

To carry out activities to improve the interstate and intrastate coordination of migrant education between state and local education agencies. Types of assistance: grants. Estimate of annual funds available: $ 8,264,000.

* Transition Program for Refugee Children 84.146

Office of Bilingual Education and Minority
Languages Affairs
Department of Education
330 C St., SW, Rm 5086
Washington DC 20202 (202) 732-5708

To provide financial assistance to state and local educational agencies to meet the special educational needs of eligible refugee children enrolled in elementary and secondary schools. Types of assistance: grants. Estimate of annual funds available: $ 15,808,000.

* Public Library Construction (LSCA Title II) 84.154

Public Library Support Staff
Library Programs
Department of Education
Washington, DC 20208 (202) 357-6303

To assist with public library construction. Types of assistance: grants. Estimate of annual funds available: $ 21,877,520.

* Removal of Architectural Barriers to the Handicapped 84.155

Special Education Programs
Department of Education
400 Maryland Ave., SW
Washington, DC 20202 (202) 732-1025

To provide financial assistance to state educational agencies an through them local educational agencies and intermediate educational units to pay all or part of the costs of altering existing buildings and equipment to remove architectural barriers to the handicapped. Types of assistance: grants. Estimate of annual funds available: $ 0.

* Client Assistance For Handicapped Individuals (CAP) 84.161

Department of Education
Associate Commissioner for Program Operations
Office of Special Education and Rehabilitative
Services
Washington, DC 20202 (202) 732-1406

To provide assistance in informing and advising clients and client applicants of available benefits under the Rehabilitation Act. Types of assistance: grants. Estimate of annual funds available: $ 7,682,000.

* Library Services for Indian Tribes and Hawaiian Natives 84.163

Library Development Staff, Library Programs
Office of Educational Research and Improvement
Department of Education
Washington, DC 20208 (202) 357-6323

To promote the extension of public library services to Indian people living on or near reservations; for Indian tribes and Indian in Oklahoma. Types of assistance: grants. Estimate of annual funds available: $ 2,448,700.

* Magnet Schools Assistance 84.165

Division of Discretionary Grants, Room 2040
400 Maryland Ave., SW
Washington, DC 20202 (202) 732-4360

To provide grants to eligible local educational agencies for use in magnet schools that are part of approved desegregation plans. Types of assistance: grants. Estimate of annual funds available: $ 113,620,000.

* Library Literacy (LSCA Title VI) 84.167

Library Development Staff, Library Programs
Office of Educational Research and Improvement
Department of Education
Washington, DC 20208 (202) 357-6321

To provide support to state public libraries for coordinating and planning library literacy programs and making arrangements for training librarians and volunteers to carry out such programs. Types of assistance: grants. Estimate of annual funds available: $ 4,730,000.

* Handicapped-Preschool Grants 84.173

Division of Educational Services
Office of the Asst. Secretary for Special Education
and Rehabilitative Services
Department of Education
Washington, DC 20202 (202) 732-1109

To provide grants to states to assist them in providing a free appropriate public education to preschool age handicapped children. Types of assistance: grants. Estimate of annual funds available: $ 247,000,000.

* Vocational Education-Community Based Organizations 84.174

Department of Education
Office of Asst. Secretary for Vocational
and Adult Education
400 Maryland Ave., SW
Washington, DC 20202 (202) 732-2441

To provide educational assistance to severely disadvantaged youth, through the collaboration of public agencies, community based organizations and business concerns to enable them to succeed in vocational education. Types of assistance: grant. Estimate of annual funds available: $ 8,892,000.

* Leadership in Educational Administration Development (LEAD) 84.178

Hunter Moorman
Office of Educational Research and Improvement
Department of Education
Washington, DC 20208 (202) 357-6116

To provide assistance for eligible parties to establish and operate technical assistance centers that promote the development of leadership skills in school administrators. Types of assistance: grants. Estimate of annual funds available: $ 8,222,000.

* Drug Free Schools and Communities-Regional Centers 84.188

Alan King
Drug-Free Schools and Communities Staff
Office of Elementary and Secondary Education
400 Maryland Ave., SW
Washington, DC 20202 (202) 732-4599

To provide financial assistance to maintain five regional centers to train school teams and assist local education agencies in developing and strengthening programs of alcohol and drug abuse education and prevention. Types of assistance: grants. Estimate of annual funds available: $ 15,638,000.

* Demonstration Centers for the Retraining of Dislocated Workers 84.193

Paul Geib
Division of National Programs
Office of Vocational and Adult Education
Department of Education
400 Maryland Ave., SW
Washington, DC 20202 (202) 732-2364

To establish one or more demonstration centers for the retraining of dislocated workers in order to demonstrate the application of general theories of vocational education to the specific problems of retraining displaced workers. Types of assistance: grants. Estimate of annual funds available: $ 212,420.

* State Activities - Education of Homeless Children and Youth 84.196

Compensatory Education Programs
Office of Elementary and Secondary Education
Department of Education
400 Maryland Ave., SW, Room 2043
Washington, DC 20202 (202) 732-4682

To establish or designate an office in each state educational agency and Outlying Area for the coordination of education for homeless children and youth. Types of assistance: grants. Estimate of annual funds available: $ 4,834,000.

* Native Hawaiian Family Based Education Centers 84.209

Department of Education
Mr. Ramon Ruiz
School Improvement Programs
400 Maryland Ave., SW
Washington, DC 20202 (202) 732-4153

To develop and operate a minimum of eleven family based education centers throughout the Hawaiian Islands. Types of assistance: direct payment. Estimate of annual funds available: $ 1,778,400.

* Capital Expenses (Chapter 1 - Capital Expenses) 84.216

Department of Education
Mary Jean LeTendre
Compensatory Education Programs
400 Maryland Ave., SW, Room 2043
Washington, DC 20202 (202) 732-4682

To provide payments to local educational agencies for increases in capital expenses paid from Chapter 1 funds for the purpose of regaining levels of instructional services to eligible private school children. Types of assistance: grants. Estimate of annual funds available: $ 19,760,000.

* State Improvement (Chapter 1 State Improvement Program Grants) 84.218

Department of Education
Compensatory Education Programs
Office of Elementary and Secondary Education
400 Maryland Ave., SW
Washington, DC 20202 (202) 732-4682

To provide payments to state and local educational agencies to operate Chapter 1 program improvement plans. Types of assistance: grants. Estimate of annual funds available: $ 5,686,000.

* Native Hawaiian Special Education 84.221

Dr. Martin J. Kaufman

(202) 732-1107

To operate projects addressing the special education needs of Native Hawaiian Students. Types of assistance: grants. Estimate of annual funds available: $ 494,000.

Volunteerism

* ACTION/VISTA Activities
ACTION
1100 Vermont Ave., NW
Room 1100
Washington, DC 20525   (202) 634-9108

ACTION Update contains articles on the latest ACTION programs and projects, along with notices of upcoming volunteer-related events and publications of interest.

* Anti-Drug Programs in Your Community
ACTION
Drug Alliance Office
1100 Vermont Ave., NW
Washington, DC 20525   (202) 634-9282

Created in response to the Anti-Drug Act of 1986, ACTION's anti-drug effort encourages and promotes volunteer, community-based programs for the nation's at-risk youth and the elderly. The free booklet, "Take Action Against Drug Abuse: How to Start a Volunteer Anti-Drug Program in Your Community," outlines the "how to" strategies of getting started, fundraising, grantsmanship, long-term fundraising, volunteer recruitment and management, and publicity. Contact this office to receive a free booklet and for more information on setting up an anti-drug program in your community.

* Community Volunteer Service Programs
ACTION
Drug Alliance Office
806 Connecticut Ave., NW
Washington, DC 20525   (202) 634-9757

ACTION is the principal agency in the Federal Government for administering volunteer service programs. Many of the various components of ACTION, such as Foster Grandparents and VISTA, are involved in community drug abuse education, prevention or treatment programs. The Drug Alliance Office coordinates the agency's drug abuse activities, awards grants that strengthen and expand local volunteer activities combatting illegal drug use among youth and the misuse of prescription and over-the-counter drugs by the elderly, provides training and technical assistance, and conducts public awareness and education efforts.

* Consumer Watchdogs
Consumer Deputy Program
Consumer Product Safety Commission
5401 Westbard Avenue
Washington, DC 20207   (202) 492-5788

As an unpaid volunteer, you can work with district and regional Commission offices to visit retail stores to make sure that the stores are complying with CPSC guidelines. Volunteers identify themselves to the store, check the inventory, and then report their findings back to the CPSC. The most recent Deputy program involves monitoring stores for the illegal sale of lawn darts.

* Fish and Wildlife Service
U.S. Fish and Wildlife Service
4401 N. Fairfax Dr.
Arlington, VA 22203   (703) 343-5333

Would you like to spend some time banding birds at a national wildlife refuge, feeding fish at a national fish hatchery, or doing research in a laboratory? Then consider volunteering with the U.S. Fish and Wildlife Service. There are no age requirements; however, anyone under 18 must have written parental approval. Young people under 16 years of age are encouraged to volunteer as part of a supervised group, such as a Boy Scout troop, Girl Scout troop, or 4H Club. Contact one of the U.S. Fish and Wildlife regional offices for possible volunteer programs in your area.

* Forest Service Volunteers
Public Affairs Office
U.S. Department of Agriculture
P.O. Box 96090
Washington, DC 20090-6090   (202) 475-3777

The Forest Service has a volunteer program for almost everyone--retirees, professionals, housewives, students, teenagers, and youngsters. Typical jobs include working with specialists in resource protection and management, cooperative forestry, or research. You may also work at a Visitor Information Center by conducting interpretive natural history walks.

* Foster Grandparents Volunteers
Foster Grandparent Program
ACTION
1100 Vermont Ave., NW
Washington, DC 20525   (202) 634-9349

As Foster Grandparents, low-income persons 60 and over provide companionship and guidance to mentally, physically, or emotionally handicapped children who are abused, neglected, in the juvenile justice system, or who have other special needs. Foster Grandparents are assigned to individual children on a one- to-one basis. Most Grandparents serve in "volunteer stations" such as public schools, day care centers, residential facilities and hospitals for mentally retarded, emotionally disturbed and physically handicapped children; in correctional facilities and in homes of abused/neglected children. Typically, Foster Grandparents devote two hours daily to each of two children during a 20-hour service week. Volunteers receive a modest tax-free stipend to cover the cost of volunteering; transportation, a meal while in service, accident and liability insurance, and an annual physical examination. For more information on becoming a foster grandparent, or on having a foster grandparent program in your community, contact this office.

* Health Research Volunteers
Normal Volunteer Program
Clinical Center
Building 10, Room 1N226
Bethesda, MD 20892   (301) 496-4763

Many of the research programs at National Institutes of Health require normal volunteers who can provide clinicians with indices of normal body functions. There is a small compensation for their participation.

* National Archives and Geneaology
National Archives and Records Administration
8th St. & Pennsylvania Ave., NW, Room G-8
Washington, DC 20408   (202) 523-3183

Volunteers are needed to lead tours, welcome visitors at the information desk, assist staff with information and administrative services, and to become genealogical staff aides to assist new genealogical researchers.

* National Park Service
Office of Public Affairs
National Park Service
U.S. Department of the Interior
18th and C Sts., NW
Washington, DC 20240   (202) 343-4747

The National Park Service provides many opportunities for volunteers to help at their many parks and historic sites. Contact the National Park nearest you for more information.

* National Volunteer Week
Office of National Service
Old Executive Office Building, Room 100
The White House
Washington, DC 20500   (202) 456-6266

Each spring, the President sets aside a week for the special recognition of volunteers and their achievements. ACTION promotes National Volunteer Week among federal agencies, state and local governments, and private organizations that use volunteers nationwide.

* Retired Business Executives
Service Corps of Retired Executives (SCORE)
National SCORE Office
U.S. Small Business Administration
1129 20th Street, NW
Room 410
Washington, DC 20416   (800)368-5855   (202) 653-6279)

Retired business executives volunteer their time and services to help small business solve their operating and management problems. Assigned SCORE counselors visit the owners in their places of business to analyze the problems and offer guidance. In addition to learning more about the SCORE program by calling the toll-free SBA Answer Desk, also refer to your local telephone directory to contact the community-based SCORE center.

* Retired Peace Corps Volunteers

Office of Private Sector Development
Peace Corps
806 Connecticut Avenue, NW
Room M-1210
Washington, DC 20526   (202) 254-6360

This office serves as the link between the corporate community and the Peace Corps' Office of Returned Volunteer Services.

* Retired Senior Volunteers (RSVP)

ACTION
1100 Vermont Ave., NW
Washington, DC 20525   (202) 634-9353

RSVP offers opportunities for older citizens to use their talents and experience in community service, ranging from first aid to tutoring. RSVP operates through grants to public and private non-profit organizations in local communities. Anyone retired and aged 60 or over is eligible to be an RSVP volunteer. Volunteers services include adult basic education, guardians ad litum, tax aides, consultancy services, Meals on Wheels, museum tour guides, low-cost weatherization and home repair, classroom aides, health care and substance abuse counseling, home visitation and long term care, telephone reassurance and many others.   Contact this office for more information on becoming a retired senior volunteer, or if you would like to set up a program in your community.

* Senior Companions

ACTION
1100 Vermont Ave., NW
Washington, DC 20525   (202) 634-9351

Senior Companions, all low-income persons 60 or over, provide care and companionship to other adults, especially the elderly, in an effort to help them maintain their highest level of independent living. The supportive services given by Senior Companions helps prevent the inappropriate institutionalization of homebound persons.   Special emphasis areas include acute care discharge planning, mental health, substance abuse, and care of the terminally ill. Applicants must be at least 60 years old, physically able, and willing to serve 20 hours per week and meet income eligibility guidelines, which vary from state to state.

Contact this office for more information on becoming a senior companion, or if you would like to set up a program in your community.

* Smithsonian Curatorial-Aides

Visitor Information and Associates' Reception Center
Smithsonian Institute
1000 Jefferson Drive S.W.
Washington, DC 20560   (202) 357-2700

Volunteers can participate in an independent program in which their educational and professional backgrounds are matched with curatorial or research requests from within the Smithsonian Institution.

* Smithsonian Museums Tour Guides

Visitor Information and Associates' Reception Center
Smithsonian Institute
1000 Jefferson Drive S.W.
Washington, DC 20560   (202) 357-2700

Volunteers are needed and welcomed at the Smithsonian Institution to serves as information volunteers or tour guides at many of the museums and Smithsonian programs and activities.

* Smithsonian Research Expeditions

Smithsonian National Associates
Smithsonian Institution
490 L'Enfant Plaza S.W.
Washington, D.C. 20560   (202) 357-1350

The Smithsonian Research Expeditions Program gives volunteers an opportunity to provide assistance to Smithsonian researchers and scholars. Expedition participants contribute their labor and financial support to projects led by Smithsonian scientists, curators, and research associates that result in exhibitions, publications, and collections for the Smithsonian Institution. Collaborating with staff, expedition volunteers work in field settings, laboratories, and archives to collect, organize, and interpret data. Expeditions cover a range of topics from archaeological digs to photographing radios. Financial Support contributed by participants is used for direct project expenses and follow-up work related to these projects.

* Speakers for Community Groups

See all other Chapters.

Every federal department and many government agencies have a speakers bureau to inform interested organizations and citizen groups about many of the major community concerns. Many resources are available on medical issues such as health fairs and cholesterol screening. Public education, space programs, housing programs, weapons systems are some of the other areas where federal experts might be available to come to speak.

* Student Community Service

Student Service Learning Program
ACTION
1100 Vermont Ave., NW
Washington, DC 20525

Student Community Service projects are designed to encourage students to undertake volunteer service in their communities to enhance the educational value of the service experience and to serve the needs of the low-income community. Volunteers are non-stipended and must be enrolled in secondary, secondary vocational, or post-secondary schools on an in-school or out-of-school basis. Contact this office for more information on becoming a student volunteer, or if you would like student volunteers assigned to your community.

* Veterans Voluntary Service

Chief of Voluntary Services
Veterans Administration Medical Center

Refer to your local telephone directory for the nearest VA hospital or medical center. Many opportunities exist for volunteers to help veterans.

* Volunteers In Service To America (VISTA)

ACTION
1100 Vermont Ave., NW
Washington, DC 20525   (800) 424-8580 (202) 634-9410

VISTA volunteers work to alleviate poverty in the United States. They are assigned to serve on a full-time, full-year basis at the request of public or private non-profit organizations. Volunteers live and work among the poor, serving in urban areas, rural areas, or on Indian reservations, and share their skills and experience in such fields as literacy, employment training, food distribution, shelter for the homeless, and neighborhood revitalization. Volunteers must be citizens or permanent residents of the U.S. and at least 18 years of age. They receive a basic subsistence allowance covering housing, food and incidentals. An additional $75 a month is paid as a stipend upon completion of service. Also, while in service, VISTA volunteers may be eligible for deferment of repayment of certain types of student loans, or under certain circumstances cancellation of a portion of National Direct Student loans. Contact this office for more information on becoming a VISTA volunteer or getting VISTA volunteers to help out in your community.

* Volunteer Resource Center

ACTION Resource Center
1100 Vermont Ave., NW
Room 1100
Washington, DC 20525   (202) 634-9108

By consulting their computerized catalog which includes thousands of volunteer-related sources, the Resource Center can provide you with information on   publications, audiovisual materials, technical assistance programs, and resource people throughout the country.

Government Financial Help To Individuals
Poor, Elderly, Disabled, and Unemployed

* See also Your Community Chapter
* See also Housing and Real Estate Chapter

Besides the well-known federal programs like food stamps and job training for dislocated workers, there are many other financial assistance plans such as compensation to crime victims, health benefits for refugees, temporary child care and crisis nurseries. The following is a description of these money programs available along with community organizations which in turn distribute government assistance to needy Americans. The information is taken from the *Catalog of Federal Domestic Assistance* which is published by the US Government Printing Office in Washington, D.C. The number next to the title description is a reference number listed in this *Catalog*. Contact the office listed below the title for more details.

* Food Stamps 10.551
Scott Dunn, Deputy Administrator
Food Stamp Programs
Food and Nutrition Service
Department of Agriculture
Alexandria, VA 22302   (703) 756-3026
To improve diets of low-income households by increasing their food purchasing ability. Types of assistance: direct payment. Estimate of annual funds available: $ 11,430,000

* School Breakfast Program 10.553
Director, Child Nutrition Division
Food and Nutrition Service
Department of Agriculture
Alexandria, VA 22302   (703) 756-3590
To assist states in providing a nutritious nonprofit breakfast service for school students, through cash grants and food donations. Types of assistance: grants. Estimate of annual funds available: $ 509,723,000.

* National School Lunch Program 10.555
Director, Child Nutrition Division
Food and Nutrition Service
Department of Agriculture
Alexandria, VA 22302   (703) 756-3590
To assist states, through cash grants and food donations, in making the school lunch program available to school students of all incomes and to encourage the domestic consumption of nutrition agricultural commodities. Types of assistance: grants. Estimate of annual funds available: $3,097,825,000.

* Special Milk Program for Children 10.556
Samuel P. Bauer, Director
Child Nutrition Division
Food and Nutrition Service
Department of Agriculture
Alexandria, VA 22302   (703) 756-3590
To provide subsidies to schools and institutions to encourage the consumption of fluid milk by children of high school grade and under. Types of assistance: grants. Estimate of annual funds available: $ 15,748,000.

* Special Supplemental Food Program for Women, Infants, and Children (WIC Program) 10.557
Ronald Vogel, Director
Supplemental Food Programs Division
Food and Nutrition Service
Department of Agriculture
Alexandria, VA 22302.   (703) 756-3746
To supply, at no cost, supplemental nutrition foods and nutrition eduction as an adjunct to good health care to low-income pregnant and postpartum women, infants and children identified to be at nutritional risk. Types of assistance: grants. Estimate of annual funds available: $ 1,541,092,838.

* Child Care Food Program 10.558
Sam P. Bauer, Director
Director, Child Nutrition Division

Food and Nutrition Service
Department of Agriculture
Alexandria, VA 22302   (703) 756-3590
To assist states, through grants-in-aid and other means, to maintain nonprofit food service programs for children in public and private nonprofit non-residential institutions providing child care; family day care homes and private for-profit centers that receive compensation under title XX for at least 25 persons. Types of assistance: grants. Estimate of annual funds available: $ 15,274,000.

* Summer Food Service Program for Children 10.559
Samuel P. Bauer, Director
Director, Child Nutrition Division
Food and Nutrition Service
Department of Agriculture
Alexandria, VA 22302   (703) 756-3590
To assist states, through grants-in-aid and other means, to conduct nonprofit food service programs for needy children during the summer months. Types of assistance: grants. Estimate of annual funds available: $ 149,245,000.

* State Administrative Matching Grants for Food
Stamp Program   10.561
Scott Dunn
Deputy Administrator for Food Stamp Programs
Food and Nutrition Service
Department of Agriculture
Alexandria, VA 22302   (703) 756-3026
To provide federal financial aid to state agencies for costs incurred to operate the Food Stamp Program. Types of assistance: grants. Estimate of annual funds available: $1,193,221,000.

* Nutrition Assistance for Puerto Rico (NAP) 10.566
G. Scott Dunn, Deputy Administrator
Food Stamp Programs
Food and Nutrition Service
Department of Agriculture
Alexandria, VA 22303   (703) 756-3026
A cash grant alternative to the food stamp program to improve diets of needy persons residing in the Commonwealth of Puerto Rico. Types of assistance: direct payment. Estimate of annual funds available: $ 908,250,000.

* Food Distribution Program on Indian Reservations
10.567
Alberta C. Frost, Director
Food Distribution Division
Food and Nutrition Service
Department of Agriculture
Alexandria, VA 22302   (703) 756-3660
To improve the diets of needy persons in households on or near Indian reservations and to increase the market for domestically produced foods acquired under surplus removal or price support operations. Types of assistance: grants. Estimate of annual funds available: $ 16,095,957.

* Nutrition Program for the Elderly (Commodities) (NPE)   10.570

Food Distribution Division
Food and Nutrition Service
Department of Agriculture
Alexandria, VA   22302   (703) 756-3680
To improve the diets of the elderly and to increase the market for domestically produced foods acquired under surplus removal or price support operations. Types of assistance: grants. Estimate of annual funds available: $ 141,293,000.

* Mental Health Services for Cuban Entrants   13.120

Dr. Thomas Bornemann
Refugee Mental Health Program, NIMH
Room 18-49, Parklawn Bldg.
5600 Fishers Lane
Rockville, MD   20857   (301) 443-2130
To support a complete range of treatment settings which are needed for mentally ill and/or developmentally disabled Cuban entrants currently in federal custody. Types of assistance: grants. Estimate of annual funds available: $ 5,000,000.

* Nutrition Services; Special Programs for the Aging Title III, Part C-Nutrition Services   13.635

Dr. Joyce Berry, Associate Commissioner
Department of Health and Human Services
Washington, DC   20201   (202) 245-0011
To provide grants to states to support nutritious meals, nutrition education, and other appropriate nutrition services for older Americans. Types of assistance: grants. Estimate of annual funds available: $ 356,668,000.

* Special Programs for the Aging-title III, Part D - In-Home Services for Frail Older Individuals   13.641

Associate Commissioner for State and Tribal
 Programs
Administration on Aging
Department of Health and Human Services
Washington, DC   20201   (202) 245-0011
To provide grants to states for in-home services to frail older individuals, including in-home supportive services for older individuals who are victims of Alzheimer's disease and related disorders. Types of assistance: grants. Estimate of annual funds available: $ 4,834,000.

* Temporary Child Care and Crisis Nurseries   13.656

Joan Goffney
Children's Bureau
Program Support Division
400 6th St., SW
Washington, DC   20201   (202) 755-7730
To provide temporary, non-medical care for handicapped children and children with chronic or terminal illnesses to alleviate social, emotional and financial stress among the families of such children. Types of assistance: grants. Estimate of annual funds available: $ 4,949,000.

* Adoption Assistance   13.659

Betty Stewart, Associate Commissioner
Children's Bureau
P.O. Box 1182
Washington, DC   20013   (202) 755-7600
To provide Federal Financial Participation (FFP) to states which meet certain eligibility tests, in the adoption subsidy costs for the adoption of children with special needs. Types of assistance: grants. Estimate of annual funds available: $ 133,936,000.

* Medical Assistance Program (Medicaid; Title XIX)   13.714

Fred Schutzman, Director
Health Care Financing Admin.
Department of Health and Human Services
Rm 233, E. High Rise Bldg.
6325 Security Blvd.
Baltimore, MD   21207   (301) 966-3229
To provide financial assistance to states for payments of medical assistance on behalf of cash assistance recipients, children, pregnant women, and the aged who meet income and resource requirements, and other categorically eligible groups. Types of assistance: grants. Estimate of annual funds available: $ 34,290,000.

* Medicare-Hospital Insurance (Medicare)   13.773

Barbara Gagel, Director
Bureau of Program Operations, Rm 300
Meadows East Building Health Care
 Financing Administration
Baltimore, MD   21207   (301) 966-5874
To provide hospital insurance protection for covered services to persons age 65 or above, to certain disabled persons and to individuals with chronic renal disease. Types of assistance: direct payment. Estimate of annual funds available: $ 57,100,000

* Medicare-Supplemental Medical Insurance (Medicare)   13.774

Barbara Gagel, Director
Bureau of Program Operation, Room 300
Meadows East Bldg.
Health Care Financing Administration
Baltimore, MD   21207   (301) 966-5874
To provide medical insurance protection for covered services to persons age 65 or over, to certain disabled persons and to individuals with chronic renal disease who elect this coverage. Types of assistance: direct payment. Estimate of annual funds available: $ 46,145,000,000.

* Family Support Payments to States Assistance Payments   13.780

Office of the Director
Office of Family Assistance
Department of Health and Human Services
5th Flr, Aerospace Bldg
370 L'Enfant Promenade, SW
Washington, DC   20447   (202) 252-4950
To set general standards for state administration; provide the federal financial share to states for Aid to Families with Dependent Children (AFDC). Types of assistance: grants. Estimate of annual funds available: $ .1016E + 11.

* Job Opportunities and Basic Skills Training (JOBS)   13.781

Office of the Director
Family Support Administration
5th Floor, Aerospace Bldg.
370 L'Enfant Promenade, SW
Washington, DC   20447   (202) 252-4950
To assure that needy families with children obtain the education, training, and employment that will help them avoid long-term welfare dependence. Types of assistance: grants. Estimate of annual funds available: $ 39,000,000.

* State Legalization Impact Assistance Grants (SLIAG)   13.786

Norman Thompson, Director
Division of State Legalization Assistance
Family Support Administration
370 L'Enfant Promenade, SW
Washington, DC   20447   (202) 252-4571
To offset part of the costs state and local governments incur in providing public subsistence assistance, public health assistance, and educational services to eligible legalized aliens. Types of assistance: grants. Estimate of annual funds available: $ 643,500,000.

* Low-Income Home Energy Assistance   13.789

Floyd D. Brandon, Director
Office of Energy Assistance
Family Support Administration
370 L'Enfant Promenade, SW
Washington, DC   20447   (202) 252-5296
To make grants available to states and other jurisdictions to assist eligible households to meet the costs of home energy. Types of assistance: grants. Estimate of annual funds available: $1,383,200,000.

* Work Incentive Program/Win Demonstration Program (WIN/WIN Demo)   13.790

Ronald E. Putz, Exec. Director
National Coordination Committee, WIN
Department of Labor
Washington, DC   20210   (202) 535-0174
To move men, women, and out-of-school youth, age 16 or older from dependency on Aid to Families with Dependent Children (AFDC) grants to economic independence through permanent, productive employment by providing appropriate education, job training, job placement and other related

services. Types of assistance: grants. Estimate of annual funds available: $ 91,440,000.

* Social Security-Disability Insurance 13.802

Office of Public Inquiries
Room 4100, Annex
Social Security Administration
Baltimore, MD 21235   (301) 965-2736
To replace part of the earning lost because of a physical or mental impairment severe enough to prevent a person from working. Types of assistance: direct payment. Estimate of annual funds available: $ .2232E+11.

* Social Security - Retirement Insurance 13.803

Office of Public Inquiries
Room 4100, Annex
Social Security Administration
Baltimore, MD 21235   (301) 965-2736
To replace part of the earnings lost due to retirement. Types of assistance: direct payment. Estimate of annual funds available: $ .1577E+12.

* Social Security - Special Benefits for Persons Aged 72 and Over 13.804

Office of Public Inquiries
Room 4100, Annex
Social Security Administration
Baltimore, MD 21235   (301) 965-2736
To assure some regular income to certain persons age 72 and over who had little or no opportunity to earn Social Security protection during their working years. Types of assistance: direct payment. Estimate of annual funds available: $ 24,000,000.

* Social Security - Survivors Insurance 13.805

Office of Public Inquiries
Room 4100, Annex
Social Security Administration
Baltimore, MD 21235   (301) 965-2736
To replace part of the earnings lost to dependents because of the worker's death. Types of assistance: direct payment. Estimate of annual funds available: Not specified.

* Special Benefits for Disabled Coal Miners (Black Lung) 13.806

Office of Public Inquiries
Room 4100, Annex
Social Security Administration
6401 Security Blvd.
Baltimore, MD 21235   (301) 965-2736
To pay benefits to coal miners who have become disabled due to pneumoconiosis (black lung disease) or other chronic lung disease arising from coal mine employment and their dependents or survivors. Types of assistance: direct payment. Estimate of annual funds available: $ 892,000,000.

* Supplemental Security Income 13.807

Office of Public Inquiries
Room 4100, Annex
Social Security Administration
Baltimore, MD 21235   (301) 965-2736
To assure a minimum level of income to persons who have attained age 65 or are blind or disabled, whose income and resources are below specified levels. Types of assistance: direct payment. Estimate of annual funds available: $ .1134E+11.

* Health Programs for Refugees (Immigration and Nationality Act) 13.987

Dr. Walter R. Dowdle, Acting Director
CDC, PHS, DHHS
Atlanta, GA 30333   (404) 639-1286
To assist states and localities in providing health assessment and follow-up activities to new refugees and in addressing refugee health problems of public health concern. Types of assistance: grants. Estimate of annual funds available: $ 4,138,000.

* Cooperative Agreements for State-Based Diabetes Control Programs 13.988

Chief, Grants Management Office
Procurement and Grants Office

CDC, PHS, DHHS
Atlanta, GA 30333   (404) 842-6575
To implement comprehensive programs which will ensure that persons with diabetes who are at high risk for certain complications of diabetes are identified, entered into the health are system and receive on going state-of the-art preventive care and treatment. Types of assistance: grants. Estimate of annual funds available: $ 4,861,000.

* Congregate Housing Services Program (CHSP) 14.170

Assisted Elderly and Handicapped Housing Division
Office of Elderly and Assisted Housing
Department of Housing and Urban Development
Washington, DC 20410   (202) 755-5866
To prevent premature or unnecessary institutionalization of elderly-handicapped, non-elderly handicapped, and temporarily disabled, to provide a variety of innovative approaches for the delivery of meals and non-medical supportive services while utilizing existing service programs and to fill gaps in existing service systems. Types of assistance: grants. Estimate of annual funds available: $ 6,400,000.

* Housing Voucher Program 14.177

Office of Elderly and Assisted Housing
Housing Voucher Division
Housing, HUD
Washington, DC 20410   (202) 755-6477
To aid very low income families in obtaining safe and sanitary rental housing. Types of assistance: direct payment. Estimate of annual funds available: $ 9,769,198,000.

* Supporting Housing Demonstration Program (Transitional Housing; Permanent Housing for Handicapped Homeless Persons) 14.178

Morris Bourne, Director
Transitional Housing Staff
Office of Housing, HUD
451 7th St., SW
Washington, DC 20410   (202) 755-9075
To develop innovative approaches for providing housing and supporting services to facilitate the transition to independent living for homeless persons who are capable of making the transition with in 24 months, and to provide permanent housing for handicapped persons. Types of assistance: grants, Direct payments. Estimate of annual funds available: $ 80,000,000.

* Public Safety Officers Death Benefits Program 16.571

William F. Powers, Director
or Richard J. Condon
Public Safety Officers Benefits Program
Bureau of Justice Assistance
Washington, DC 20531   (202) 724-7620
To provide a $100,000 death benefit to the eligible survivors of federal, state or local public safety officers whose death is the direct and proximate result of a personal injury sustained in the line of duty. Types of assistance: direct payment. Estimate of annual funds available: $ 24,279,000.

* Crime Victim Assistance 16.575

Duane Ragan, Division Director
Office for Victims of Crime
Office of Justice Programs
Department of Justice
633 Indiana Ave., NW
Washington, DC   (202) 724-5947
Each year provide up to 45 percent of the Crime Victims Fund generated through federal criminal fines, penalty assessments, forfeited appearance bonds to be distributed to the states to support crime victim assistance programs. Types of assistance: grants. Estimate of annual funds available: $ 43,560,000.

* Crime Victim Compensation 16.576

Duane Ragan, Division Director
Office for Victims of Crime
Office of Justice Programs
Department of Justice
Washington, DC 20531   (202) 724-5947
To provide up to 49.5 percent per year of the Crime Victims fund generated through federal criminal fines, penalty assessment, forfeited appearance bonds, bail bonds, etc., to be distributed among the states to the direct benefit derived by victims from the program. Types of assistance: grants. Estimate of annual funds available: $ 61,613,000.

* Unemployment Insurance 17.225
Jeanette Rozzero, Director
Unemployment Insurance Service
Employment and Training Administration
Department of Labor,
Washington, DC 20210   (202) 523-7831

To administer program of unemployment insurance for eligible workers through federal and state cooperation; to administer payment of Trade Adjustment Assistance Types of assistance: grant, direct payment. Estimate of annual funds available: $ 1,654,998,000.

* Senior Community Service Employment Program (SCSEP) (Older Worker Program) 17.235
Office of Special Targeted Programs
Employment and Training Administration
Department of Labor, Room N4641
200 Constitution Ave., NW
Washington, DC 20210   (202) 535-0500

To provide foster and promote useful part-time work opportunities in community service activities for low income persons who are 55 years old and older. Types of assistance: grant. Estimate of annual funds available: $ 343,824,000.

* Trade Adjustment Assistance - Workers 17.245
Marvin Fooks, Director
Office of Trade Adjustment Assistance
Employment and Training Administration
Department of Labor
601 D St., NW, Room 6434
Washington, DC   (202) 376-2646

To provide adjustment assistance to workers adversely affected by increased imports of articles like or directly competitive with articles produced by such workers firm. Types of assistance: direct payment. Estimate of annual funds available: $ 276,000,000.

* Dislocated Workers: Employment and Training Assistance 17.246
Robert N. Columbo
Employment and Training Administration
Department of Labor
200 Constitution Ave., NW
Washington, DC 20210   (202) 535-0577

To assist dislocated workers obtain unsubsidized employment through training and related employment services using a decentralized system of State programs. Types of assistance: grants. Estimate of annual funds available: $ 284,626,000.

* Migrant and Seasonal Farmworkers (and Other Seasonally Employed Farmworkers) 17.247
Office of Special Targeted Programs
Division of Seasonal Farmworker Programs
Employment and Training Administration
Dept. of Labor, Rm 4641
200 Constitution Ave., NW
Washington, DC   (202) 535-0500

To provide job training, job search assistance, and other supportive services for those individuals who suffer chronic seasonal unemployment and underemployment in the agricultural industry. Types of assistance: grants. Estimate of annual funds available: $ 68,522,000.

* Employment Services and Job Training - Pilot and Demonstration Programs 17.249
Administrator, Office of Strategic Planning
  and Policy Development
Employment and Training Administration
Department of Labor
200 Constitution Ave., NW
Washington, DC   (202) 535-0677

To provide foster, and promote job training and other services which are most appropriately administered at the national level and which are operated in more than one State to groups with particular disadvantage in the labor market. Types of assistance: grants. Estimate of annual funds available: $ 38,964,000.

* Job Training Partnership Act (JTPA) 17.250
Robert N. Colombo
Employment and Training Administration
Department of Labor

200 Constitution Ave., NW
Washington, DC 20210   (202) 535-0577

To provide job training and related assistance to economically disadvantaged individuals and others who face significant employment barriers. Types of assistance: grants. Estimate of annual funds available: $ 1,788,772,000.

* Native American Employment and Training Programs 17.251
Division of Indian and Native American Programs
Employment and Training Administration
Department of Labor, Room N4641
200 Constitution Ave., NW
Washington, DC   (202) 535-0502

To afford job training to Native Americans facing serious barriers to employment, who are in special need of such training to obtain productive employment. Types of assistance: grants. Estimate of annual funds available: $ 59,713,000.

* Longshore and Harbor Workers' Compensation 17.302
Office of Workers's Compensation Programs
Division of Longshore and Harbor Workers'
  Compensation
Washington, DC 20210   (202) 523-8721

To provide compensation for disability or death resulting from injury, including occupational disease, to eligible private employees. Types of assistance: direct payment. Estimate of annual funds available: $ 4,000,000.

* Coal Mine Workers Compensation (Black Lung) 17.307
Division of Coal Mine Workers Compensation
Office of Workers Compensation Programs
Employment Standards Administration
Dept. of Labor
Washington, DC 20210   (202) 523-6692

To provide benefits to coal miners who have become totally disabled due to coal workers pneumoconiosis (CWP) and to widows and other surviving dependents of miners who have died of this disease, or who were totally disabled from the disease at the time of death. Types of assistance: direct payment. Estimate of annual funds available: $ 625,687,000.

* Claims Against Foreign Missions (Foreign Missions Act) 19.203
Mr. Ralph Chiocco
Office of Foreign Missions
Department of State
Washington, DC 20520   (202) 673-5312

To assure that all persons in the United States who are damaged in motor vehicle, vessel or aircraft accidents through the fault of a member of a foreign mission will have an opportunity to recover compensation for their damages. Types of assistance: Insurance. Estimate of annual funds available: $ 0.

* Tax Counseling for the Elderly 21.006
Marion L. Butler
Tax Counseling for the Elderly
Taxpayer Service Division, IRS
1111 Constitution Ave., NW
Washington, DC 20224   (202) 566-4904

To authorize the Internal Revenue Service to enter into agreement with private or public nonprofit agencies or organizations to establish a network of trained volunteers to provide free income tax information and return preparation assistance to elderly taxpayers. Types of assistance: direct payment. Estimate of annual funds available: $ 2,789,000.

* Appalachian Vocational and Other Education Facilities and Operations 23.012
Executive Director
Appalachian Regional Commission
1666 Connecticut Ave., NW
Washington, DC 20235   (202) 673-7874

To provide the people of the region with the equipment, renovation and operating funds for training and education necessary to obtain employment at their best capability for available job opportunities. Types of assistance: grants. Estimate of annual funds available: $ 3,000,000.

Government Financial Help to Individuals

* Federal Employment Assistance For Veterans 27.002

Robert Carbonneau
Office of Affirmative Recruiting and Employment
Office of Personnel Management
1900 E St., NW, Rm 6332
Washington, DC 20415   (202) 632-0643
To provide assistance to veterans in obtaining federal employment. Types of assistance: employment. Estimate of annual funds available: $ 230,000.

* Federal Employment for Individuals with Disabilities (Selective Placement Program) 27.005

Office of Affirmative Recruiting and Employment
Office of Personnel Management
1900 E St., NW
Washington, DC 20414   (202) 632-0643
To encourage federal agencies to provide assistance to persons with disabilities in obtaining and retaining federal employment. Types of assistance: federal employment. Estimate of annual funds available: $ 120,000.

* Social Insurance for Railroad Workers 57.001

Public Affairs Railroad Retirement Board
844 Rush St.
Chicago, IL 60611   (312) 751-4777
To pay rail social security, rail industry pensions, special windfalls, supplemental annuities, permanent and occupational disability and sickness and unemployment benefits to workers and their families. Types of assistance: direct payment. Estimate of annual funds available: $7,111,000,000.

* Pension to Veterans' Surviving Spouse and Children (Death Pension) 64.105

Department of Veterans Affairs
Washington, DC 20420
To assist needy surviving spouses, and children of deceased war-time veterans whose deaths were not due to service. Types of assistance: direct payment. Estimate of annual funds available: $ 1,337,333,000.

* Senior Environmental Employment Program (SEE) 66.508

EPA, Office of Research and Development
of Exploratory Research
Washington, DC 20460
To use the talents of older Americans to provide technical assistance to federal, state and local environment agencies for projects of pollution prevention abatement and control. Types of assistance: grants. Estimate of annual funds available: $ 13,000,000.

* Weatherization Assistance for Low-Income Persons 81.042

Mary E. Fowler, Chief
Weatherization Assistance Programs, Branch 232
Conservation and Renewable Energy, DOE
Forrestal Bldg.
Washington, DC 20585   (202) 586-2204
To insulate the dwellings of low income persons, particularly the elderly and handicapped low income, in order to conserve needed energy and to aid those persons least able to afford higher utility costs. Types of assistance: grants. Estimate of annual funds available: $ 161,357,000.

* Centers for Independent Living 84.132

Office of Developmental Programs
Rehabilitation Services Administration, OSERS
Department of Education
400 Maryland Ave., SW
Washington, DC 20202   (202) 732-1326
To provide independent living services to individuals with severe handicaps to assist them to function more independent in family and community settings or

secure and maintain appropriate employment. Types of assistance: grants. Estimate of annual funds available: $ 25,688,000.

* Comprehensive Services for Independent Living (Comprehensive Services Part A) 84.169

Dr. Susan Daniels
Office of Asst. Secretary for Special Education
and Rehabilitative Services
Department of Education
Washington, DC 20202   (202) 732-1347
To provide independent living services for individuals with severe handicaps in assisting them to function independently in family and community settings or to secure and maintain appropriate employment. Types of assistance: grants. Estimate of annual funds available: $ 12,526,000.

* Rehabilitation Services - Independent Living Services for Older Blind Individuals 84.177

Yvonne Neal, Rehabilitation Services Administration
OSERS, Department of Education
MES Bldg., Rm 3328
330 C St., NW
Washington, DC 20202   (202) 732-1410
To provide independent living services to older blind individuals. Types of assistance: grants. Estimate of annual funds available: $ 5,632,000.

* Supported Employment Services for Individuals with Severe Handicaps (Supported Employment Services Program) 84.187

Mark E. Shob
Office of Program Operations
Rehabilitation Services Administration
Department of Education
Washington, DC 20202-2574   (202) 732-1406
To provide grants for training and traditionally time limited post employment services leading to supported employment for individuals with severe handicaps. Types of assistance: grants. Estimate of annual funds available: $ 26,900,000.

* Demonstration Centers for the Retraining of Dislocated Workers 84.193

Paul Geib
Division of National Programs
Office of Vocational and Adult Education
Department of Eduction
400 Maryland Ave., SW
Washington, DC 20202   (202) 732-2364
To establish one or more demonstration centers for the retraining of dislocated workers in order to demonstrate the application of general theories of vocational education to the specific problems of retraining displaced workers. Types of assistance: grants. Estimate of annual funds available: $ 212,420.

* State Grants for Technology and Related Assistance to Individuals with Disabilities (Technology Assistance Program) 84.224

Dr. James Rewick, NIDRR
400 Maryland Ave., SW
Washington, DC 20202   (202) 732-1134
To provide grants to states to assist them in developing and implementing comprehensive consumer responsive state-wide programs of technology related assistance for individuals with disabilities. Types of assistance: grants. Estimate of annual funds available: $5,100,000.

* Pension Plan Termination Insurance (ERISA) 86.001

Pension Benefit Guaranty Corporation
2020 K St., NW
Washington, DC 20006   (202) 778-8800
To encourage the continuation and maintenance of voluntary private pension plans for the benefit of their participants. Types of assistance: Insurance of annual funds available: $ 744,962,000.

Veterans and Dependents

* See also International Relations and Defense

This section identifies the offices, mostly at the U.S. Department of Veterans Affairs, which compensates Americans who have served in the U.S. Armed Forces and their dependents. By some of the caption headings a number appears which is the official reference from the U.S. Government Printing Office's *Catalog of Federal Domestic Assistance*. Contact the office listed below the title for more details.

* Agent Orange or Nuclear Radiation Exposure

Veterans Assistance Office
Department of Veterans Affairs
810 Vermont Ave., NW
Washington, DC 20420 (202) 233-2044

The Department of Veteran Affairs is authorized by law to provide certain health care services to any veteran of the Vietnam Ear (August 5, 1964 through May 7, 1975) who, while serving in Vietnam, may have been exposed to dioxin or to a toxic substance in a herbicide or defoliant used for military purposes. VA has an onging program for examining veterans concerned about the possible health effects of Agent Orange exposure. Vietnam veterans are encouraged to request an examination at their nearest VA healthcare facility. A veteran who participates will receive a comprehensive physical examination and be asked to complete a questionnaire about service experience in Vietnam. The veteran is advised, through personal consultation, of the results of that examination. The examination determines the current health status of the veteran and assists in detecting any illnes or injury the veteran may have, regardless of origin, which may serve as the basis for follow-up. The finding of these examinations are entered into a registry. The same process is available for any veteran who exposed while serving on active duty to ionizing radiation from the detonation of a nuclear device in connection with the veteran's participation in the test of a nuclear device or with the American occupation of Hiroshima and Nagasaki, Japan during the period beginning on September 11, 1945, and ending on July 1, 1946. The veteran should contact the nearest VA medical center for an examination.

* Alcohol and Drug Dependence Treatment

Veterans Assistance Office
Department of Veterans Affairs
810 Vermont Ave., NW
Washington, DC 20420 (202) 233-2044

After hospitalization for alcohol or drug treatment, veterans may be eligible for outpatient care, or may be authorized to continue treatment or rehabilitation in facilities such as halfway houses or therapeutic communities at VA expense. For more information contact your VA medical center.

* Appealing Veterans Benfit Claims

Veterans Assistance Office
Department of Veterans Affairs
810 Vermont Ave., NW
Washington, DC 20420 (202) 233-2044

Veterans who believe they have VA benefits coming to them but have been denied those benefits have the right to appeal. Not all VA findings are appealable, but those dealing with compensation or pension benefits, education benefits, waiver of recovery of overpayments, and reimbursement of unauthorized medical services are typical issues which may be appealed to the Board of Veterans Appeals. Additional information on appeals may be found in VA pamphlet 1-1, *Board of Veterans Appeals, Appeals Regulations and Rules of Practice*, available from the office above.

* Automobiles and Adaptive Equipment for Certain Disabled Veterans and Members of the Armed Forces 64.100

Department of Veterans Affairs
Washington, DC 20420

To provide financial assistance to certain disabled servicepersons and veterans toward the purchase price of an automobile or other conveyance and an additional amount for adaptive equipment. Types of assistance: direct payment. Estimate of annual funds available: $ 16,007,000.

* Benefits Assistance Service

Veterans Assistance Office
Department of Veterans Affairs

810 Vermont Ave., NW
Washington, DC 20420 (202) 233-2044

This office provides veterans on their first visit with information about and assistance is applying for various federal benefits. The information provided can also be found in the VA regional offices.

* Benefits Information

Veterans Assistance Office
Department of Veterans Affairs
810 Vermont Ave., NW
Washington, DC 20420 (202) 233-2044

The Department of Veterans Affairs provides a full range of benefits for eligible veterans and dependents. Toll-free benefits information is available to all veterans at VA regional offices. Check your local telephone directory under United States Government, Department of Veterans Affairs, for the benefits information in your area--or ask your directory assistance operator. Other sources that provide information about benefits are service organizations and state and local offices of veterans affairs.

* Board of Veterans Appeals Decisions

Board of Veterans Appeals
Department of Veterans Affairs
Washington, DC 20420 (202) 233-3336

The appellate decisions of the Board of Veterans Appeals have been indexed to facilitate access to the contents of decisions (BVA Index 1-01-1). The index is published quaterly in microfiche form with an annual cumulation. It is organized to provide citations to BVA decisions under subject terms chosen to describe the issues adjudicated in the appeals. For information on obtaining the index or purchasing a microfiche copy, contact your regional VA office or the office above.

* Burial Expenses

Veterans Assistance Office
Department of Veterans Affairs
810 Vermont Ave., NW
Washington, DC 20420 (202) 233-2044

Benefits are available to help with the burial expensies of veterans and certain dependents or survivors. Assistance for burial of dependents and survivors is limited to interment in a national cemetery. For more information contact your regional VA office.

* Burial Expenses Allowance for Veterans 64.101

Department of Veterans Affairs
Washington, DC 20420

To provide a monetary allowance not to exceed $150 toward the plot or interment expense for certain veterans not buried in a national cemetery. Types of assistance: direct payment. Estimate of annual funds available: $ 148,771,000.

* Burial Flags

Veterans Assistance Office
Department of Veterans Affairs
810 Vermont Ave., NW
Washington, DC 20420 (202) 233-2044

An American flag is available to drape the casket of an eligible veteran, after which it may be given to the next of kin, a close friend, or an associate of the deceased. The VA may also issue a flag for a veteran who is missing in action and is later presumed dead. Apply at any VA regional office or most local post offices.

* Burial in Arlington National Cemetery

Superintendent

Arlington National Cemetery
Arlington, VA 22211   (202) 695-3252/3250
The Arlington National Cemetery is under the jurisdiction of the Department of the Army, and burial is limited to specific categories of military personnel and veterans except in the case of cremated remains to be placed in the columbarium. For more information contact the office above.

* Burial in National Cemeteries

Veterans Assistance Office
Department of Veterans Affairs
810 Vermont Ave., NW
Washington, DC 20420   (202) 233-2044
Burial in a VA national cemetery is available to any eligible veteran, spouse, unremarried widow/widower, minor children, and under certain conditions, unmarried adult children. Detailed information regarding eligibility and interments is contained in the VA pamphlet, *Interments in National Cemeteries*. Contact your regional VA office for this pamphlet and for more information and assistance in filing burial benefit claims.

* Chaplain Service

Chaplain Service (125)
Department of Veterans Affairs
810 Vermont Ave., NW
Washington, DC 20420   (202) 233-5137
The Chaplain Service provides for the spiritual welfare of the patients at VA facilities. The program includes opportunities for religious worship in the appropriate setting, pastoral ministry to individual patients and administration in crises situations, opportunities for sacramental ministry and pastoral counseling and other supportive suervices to aid in the total care and treatment of veteran patients. For more information, contact the office above.

* Compensation

Veterans Assistance Office
Department of Veterans Affairs
810 Vermont Ave., NW
Washington, DC 20420   (202) 233-2044
Veterans who are disabled by injury or disease incurred or aggravated during active service in the line of duty during wartime or peacetime service and discharged or separated under other than dishonorable conditions are eligible for VA compensation. Eligible veterans are entitled to monthly disability payments. For more information on eligibility and benefits, contact your regional VA office.

* Compensation for Service-Connected Deaths for Veterans Dependents (Death Compensation) 64.102

Department of Veterans Affairs
Washington, DC 20420
To compensate surviving spouses, children, and dependent parents for the death of any veteran who died before January 1, 1957, because of a service-connected disability. Types of assistance: direct payment. Estimate of annual funds available: $ 19,888,000.

* Dental Treatment

Veterans Assistance Office
Department of Veterans Affairs
810 Vermont Ave., NW
Washington, DC 20420   (202) 233-2044
The VA provides dental services to eligible veterans on an outpatient basis. Outpatient dental treatment begins with an intraoral examinations and may include the full spectrum of modern diagnostic, surgical, restorative, and preventive techniques. In some instances, the dental care may be comprehensive in nature, while in other cases, the type and extent of treatment may be limited. The measure of treatment is determined by specific eligiblities, service-connection, and/or correlation of the dental conditions with the veteran's medical problems. For more information, including eligibility, contact the nearest VA medical center.

* Dietetic Service

Dietetic Service
Veterans Health Services and Research Administration
Department of Veterans Affairs
810 Vermont Ave., NW, Room 927
Washington, DC 20420   (202) 233-3389
VA dietitians direct nutritional care veterans in all settings by providing active programs which encompass the entire range of nutrition services. There are 13 VA sponsored Dietetic Internships which graduate registration eligible dietitians each year. For more information, contact the office above.

* Disabled Veterans Outreach Program 17.801

Veterans Employment and Training Service
Office of the Assistant Secretary for
Veterans Employment and Training
Dept. of Labor, Rm S-1316
200 Constitution Ave., NW
Washington, DC   (202) 523-9110
To provide funds to states to provide job and job training opportunities for disabled and other veterans through contacts with employers.Types of assistance: grants. Estimate of annual funds available: $ 72,962,000.

* Domiciliary Care

Veterans Assistance Office
Department of Veterans Affairs
810 Vermont Ave., NW
Washington, DC 20420   (202) 233-2044
The VA provides care on an ambulatory self-care basis for veterans disabled by age or disease who are not in need of acute hospitalization and who do not need the skilled nursing services provided in nursing homes. For information on eligibility and general information, contact any VA office.

* Domiciliary Care (VA Domiciliary Care) 64.008

Asst. Chief, Medical Director for Geriatrics
and Extended Care (181)
Department of Veterans Affairs
Washington, DC 20420   (202) 233-3692
To provide the least intensive level of VA inpatient care for ambulatory veterans disabled by age or illness who are not in need of more acute hospitalization and who do not need the skilled nursing provided in nursing homes. Types of assistance: other. Estimate of annual funds available: $ 143,920,000.

* Driver Training for the Handicapped

Rehabilitation Medicine Service
Department of Veterans Affairs
810 Vermont Ave., NW
Washington, DC 20420   (202) 233-2373
The VA provides driver education and training for all eligible handicapped veterans and certain military personnel. The DVA has established 40 driver training centers for the handicapped throughout the U.S. For more information, contact the office above.

* Education and Training

Veterans Assistance Office
Department of Veterans Affairs
810 Vermont Ave., NW
Washington, DC 20420   (202) 233-2044
VA administers basic programs for veterans and servicepersons seeking assistance for education and training. For eligible persons with service between February 1, 1955, and December 31, 1976, such assistance is available under the noncontributory GI Bill. Veterans and servicepersons who entered the military from January 1, 1977, through June 30, 1985, may receive educational assistance under a contributory plan. Individuals entering on active duty after June 30, 1985, may receive benefits under the Montgomery GI Bill. Contact your regional VA office for specific information on eligibility and benefits.

* Employment and Training Program 17.802

Veterans Employment and Training Service
Office of the Assistant Secretary for
Veterans Employment and Training
Rm. S1316
200 Constitution Ave., NW
Washington, DC 20210   (202) 523-9110
To develop programs to meet the employment and training needs of service-connected disabled veterans, veterans of the Vietnam era and veterans who were recently separated from the military service. Types of assistance: grants. Estimate of annual funds available: $ 9,517,000.

* Fee-Basis Medical Program

Veterans Assistance Office
Department of Veterans Affairs
810 Vermont Ave., NW
Washington, DC 20420   (202) 233-2044
The VA authorizes veterans to receive medical services from other individuals or organizations by compensating participating members for services performed and paying the veteran for travel expenses incurred for the visit. For more information, contact the nearest VA Medical Center or regional VA office.

* Federal Benefits for Veterans and Dependents

Superintendent of Documents
U.S. Government Printing Office
Washington, DC 20402   (202) 783-3238

The booklet, *Federal Benefits for Veterans and Dependents*, provides information on the many benefits made available to veterans and dependents. It is available from GPO for $2.75.

* Fiduciary and Field Examinations

Veterans Assistance Office
Department of Veterans Affairs
810 Vermont Ave., NW
Washington, DC 20420   (202) 233-2044

For information on payment of VA benefits on behalf of adult beneficiaries who are incompetent or under some other legal disability, contact the VA regional office. Information on payments of benefits to minor beneficiaries who are not in care of a natural or adoptive parent can also be obtained from the VA regional office.

* Headstone or Grave Marker

Director
Monument Service (42)
National Cemetery System
Department of Veterans Affairs
Washington, DC 20420   (202) 275-1494 or 1495

Headstones and markers are provided for the gravesites of eligible veterans buried in private or national cemeteries. Eligibility is the same as for burial in a national cemetery. The headstone or grave marker is provided without charge and shipped at government expense to the consignee designated. The cost of placing the marker in a private cemetery must be borne by the applicant. Forward applications (VA Form 40-1330) to the address above. VA regional offices will provide information and other assistance. For more information contact the office above.

* Health Care Product Support

Director
Department of Veterans Affairs
Marketing Center
P.O. Box 76
Hines, IL 60141   (312) 216-2479

The Marketing Center (MKC) is the largest combined contracting activity within the Department of Veterans Affairs. It is responsible for supporting the health care delivery systems of the DVA and other government agencies by providing and validating a centralized acquisition program for health care products in a cost effective manner. The primary responsiblity of the MKC is assuring contracts are in place to support the DVA's Central Distribution System. Contact the office above for more information.

* Health Care System

Veterans Assistance Office
Department of Veterans Affairs
810 Vermont Ave., NW
Washington, DC 20420   (202) 233-2044

Perhaps the most visible of all VA benefits and services are its hospitals and medical care services, which make up the largest health care system in the free world. More than 90 percent of VA employees are associated with medical care. Of VA's 172 medical centers, some 140 are affiliated with 104 medical schools. More than half of America's practicing physicians receive training in VA medical centers. In addition to medical centers, the health care system includes nursing homes, domiciliaries, and readjustment counseling Vet centers. Contact the nearest VA medical center for specific information.

* High School Training

Veterans Assistance Office
Department of Veterans Affairs
810 Vermont Ave., NW
Washington, DC 20420   (202) 233-2044

A veteran may pursue high school training or training to pass the GED examination and may receive educational assistance allowance without a charge against basic entitlement. Additional secondary school training, such as refresher courses or deficiency courses, are permitted if needed to qualify for admission to an appropriate educational institution. Contact your VA regional office for more information.

* Home Ownership Publications

Veterans Assistance Office
Department of Veterans Affairs
810 Vermont Ave., NW
Washington, DC 20420   (202) 233-2044

The following publications are available to veterans from their VA regional office:

Pointers for the Veteran Homeowner. A guide for veterans whose home mortgage is guaranteed or insured under the GI Bill.
To the Home-Buying Veteran. A guide for veterans planning to buy or build homes with a VA loan.
VA-Guaranteed Home Loans for Veterans. To help you understand what the VA can and cannot do for the home purchaser.

* Insurance

Veterans Assistance Office
Department of Veterans Affairs
810 Vermont Ave., NW
Washington, DC 20420   (202) 233-2044

Low cost insurance is available for veterans with service-connected disabilities. Veterans who are totally disabled may apply for a waiver of premiums on these policies. For more information on GI life insurance and Servicemen's Group Life Insurance (SGLI), Veterans Group Life Insurance (VGLI), and Veterans Mortgage Life Insurance (VMLI), contact the nearest VA office. The Insurance Information Toll-Free Number, (800) 422-8079, is a nationwide source for insurance inquiries and requests for service. It is also useful for policyholders and beneficiaries who are covered by a VA administered life insurance policy. Calls can be made to the number above from 8:00 a.m. to 5:30 p.m. EST.

* Job-Finding Assistance

Veterans Assistance Office
Department of Veterans Affairs
810 Vermont Ave., NW
Washington, DC 20420   (202) 233-2044

Assistance in finding jobs is provided to veterans through state employment/job service local offices throughout the country. The Local Veterans Employment Representatives provide functional supervision of job counseling, testing, and employment referral and placement services provided to veterans. Priority in referral to job openings and training opportunities is given to eligible veterans, with preferential treatment for disabled veterans. In addition, the job service assists veterans who are seeking employment by providing information about job markets on-the-job and apprenticeship training opportunities in cooperation with VA Regional Offices and Vet Centers. Veterans should apply for this kind of help at their nearest local state employment service/job service office, not VA.

* Life Insurance (GI Insurance 64.103)

Department of Veterans Affairs
Regional Office and Insurance Center
P.O. Box 8079
Philadelphia PA 29101   1-800-422-8079

To provide life insurance protection for veterans of World War I, World War II, Korean conflict and service-disabled veterans separated from active duty on or after April 25, 1951, and to provide mortgage protection life insurance for those disabled veterans who are given a VA grant to secure specially adapted housing under Chapter 21, Title 38, USC. Types of assistance: direct loan, insurance. Estimate of annual funds available: $ 55,116,000.

* Loans

Veterans Assistance Office
Department of Veterans Affairs
810 Vermont Ave., NW
Washington, DC 20420   (202) 233-2044

Certain veterans and dependents are eligible for GI loans for homes, condiminiums, and manufactured homes. Also, certain disabled veterans of military service may be entitled under certain conditions to a grant from VA for a home specially adapted to their needs. For more information on these loans and grants, contact the nearest VA regional office.

* Medical Care for Dependents or Survivors

CHAMPVA Registration Center
Department of Veterans Affairs Medical Center
1055 Clermont St.
Denver, Colorado 80220   (800) 331-9935

The Civilian Health and Medical Program is a medical benefits program through which VA helps pay for medical services and supplies that eligible dependents and survivors of certain veterans obtain from civilian, non-VA sources. Normally, care under this program will be provided in non-VA facilities. VA facilities may be utilized for treatment when (1 they are equipped to provide the care, and (2 use of these facilities does not interfere with care and treatment of veterans. For more information, including eligibility, contact the office above, or call (800) 843-5710 in Colorado.

* Medical Service

Medical Service
Veterans Health Services and Research Administration
Department of Veterans Affairs

Government Financial Help to Individuals

810 Vermont Ave., NW
Washington, DC 20420 (202) 233-3097
This office is the representative, advocate, and monitoring office of Internal Medicine which constitutes the major bed and clinic service in the VA. It includes Cardiology, Pulmonary Disease, Gastroenterology, Hematology, Oncology, Endocrinology, Infectious Disease, Nephrology, Rheumatology, Dermatology, General Internal Medicine, Nutrition, Geriatrics, and Clinical Pharmacology. As such, this Service is responsible for a variety of important functions designed to maintain high standards of patient care, education, research, and administration. Contact the office above for further information.

* Memorial Markers and Memorial Plots

Veterans Assistance Office
Department of Veterans Affairs
810 Vermont Ave., NW
Washington, DC 20420 (202) 233-2044
A memorial headstone or marker may be furnished on application by a close relative recognized as the next of kin to commemorate any eligible veteran, including a person who died in active military service, whose remains have not been recovered or identified; who was buried at sea; who was donated to science; or who who cremated and the ashes scattered without interment of any portion of the ashes. The memorial may be erected in a private cemetery in a plot provided by the applicant or in a memorial section of a national cemetery. Contact the nearest VA regional office for more information.

* National Cemeteries 64.201

Director, Field Operations
National Cemetery System
Department of Veterans Affairs
Washington, DC 20420 (202) 275-1486
To provide for interment in national cemeteries of veterans and members of the Armed Forces of the United States whose service terminated other than dishonorably and certain eligible dependents. Types of assistance: other. Estimate of annual funds available: $ 45,978,000.

* Nursing Home Care

Veterans Assistance Office
Department of Veterans Affairs
810 Vermont Ave., NW
Washington, DC 20420 (202) 233-2044
For admission or transfer to VA Nursing Home Care Units, it is essentially the same as for hospitalization. Direct admission to private nursing homes at VA expense is limited to (1 veterans who require nursing care for a service-connected disability after medical determination by VA; (2 any person in an Armed Forces hospital who required a protracted period of nursing care and who will become a veteran upon discharge from the Armed Forces; and (3 a veteran who had been discharged from a VA medical center and is receiving VA medical center based home health services. VA may transfer veterans who need nursing home care to private nursing homes at VA expense from VA medical centers, nuring homes or domiciliaries. For more information, contact and VA medical facility.

* Office of Systems Planning, Policy, and Acquisition Control (004M)

Department of Veterans Affairs
810 Vermont Ave., NW
Washington, DC 20420 (202) 233-5167
Contact the office above to obtain a copy of *Veterans Affairs Information Systems Plan: Fiscal year 1987-1993.*

* Overseas Medical Benefits

Veterans Assistance Office
Department of Veterans Affairs
810 Vermont Ave., NW
Washington, DC 20420 (202) 233-2044
Reimbursed fee-basis medical care is available outside of the U.S. to veterans for treatment of service-connected disabilities and conditions adjunct to the rated disabilities. Prior to treatment, an authorization must be obtained from the nearest American embassy or consulate. In Canada, veterans should contact the local office of the Canadian Department of Veterans Affairs. In emergency situations, treatment should be reported within 72 hours. Nursing care is not available in foreign jurisdiction.

* Patient Treatment File

Reports and Statistics (10A4Z)
Veterans Health Services and Research Administration
Department of Veterans Affairs
810 Vermont Ave., NW
Washington, DC 20420 (202) 233-6920
The *Patient Treatment File* is a discharge oriented database which contains medical and administrative data for the following types of care provided or paid

for by the Department of Veterans Affairs: VA and non-VA hospitals, VA and non-VA nursing homes, and VA domiciliaries. The file is maintained in fiscal year segments so that complete data for a particular year is not available until some months after the end of the fiscal year. For more information, including the types of data collected, contact the office above.

* Paraplegic Housing - Specially Adapted Housing for Disabled Veterans 64.106

Department of Veterans Affairs
Washington, DC 20420
To assist certain severely disabled veterans in acquiring suitable housing units, with special fixtures and facilities made necessary by the nature of the veterans disabilities. Types of assistance: direct payment. Estimate of annual funds available: $ 13,750,000.

* Pensions

Veterans Assistance Office
Department of Veterans Affairs
810 Vermont Ave., NW
Washington, DC 20420 (202) 233-2044
Those eligibile for VA pensions include wartime veterans with limited income discharged under other than dishonorable conditions after 90 or more days service who are permanently and totally disabled for reasons not traceable to service, nor due to willful misconduct or vicious habits. Veterans 65 years of age or older and not working are considered permanently and totally disabled. A pension is not payable to those who have estates that can provide adequated maintenance. For more information on eligibility and benefits, contact your regional VA office.

* Pension for Non-Service-Connected Disability for Veterans (Pension) 64.104

Department of Veterans Affairs
Washington, DC 20420
To assist wartime veterans in need whose non-service connected disabilities are permanent and total, preventing them from following a substantially gainful occupation. Types of assistance: direct payment. Estimate of annual funds available: $ 2,592,917,000.

* Pension to Veterans, Surviving Spouses, and Children (Death Pension) 64.105

Department of Veterans Affairs
Washington, DC 20420
To assist needy surviving spouses, and children of deceased war-time veterans whose deaths were not due to service. Types of assistance: direct payment. Estimate of annual funds available: $ 1,337,333,000.

* Presidential Memorial Certificates

Veterans Assistance Office
Department of Veterans Affairs
810 Vermont Ave., NW
Washington, DC 20420 (202) 233-2044
Presidential Memorial Certificates expressing the country's grateful recognition of the person's service in the armed forces and bearing the signature of the President are made available to the next of kin of deceased eligible veterans or of persons who were members of the Armed Forces at time of death. Eligible recipients include the next of kin, a relative or friend upon request, or an authorized representative acting on behalf of such relative or friend. Notice of a veteran's death is normally received in one of VA's regional offices, and that facility identifies the next of kin from the veteran's records and requests the certificates from Washington, D.C. Next of kin of veterans
need not apply. Others should apply to a VA regional office.

* Prisoners of War (POW) Hotline

POW Hotline (800) 821-8139
The above national 24-hour toll-free number offers specialized assistance for former prisoners of war. Calls received in Washington, D.C., after normal office hours are recorded for response the next business day. The POW information line supplements the toll-free service for all veterans at regional offices and complements assistance provided by POW coordinations at all VA medical centers.

* Procurement of Headstones and Markers 64.202

Director, Monument Service
Department of Veterans Affairs
Washington, DC 20420 (202) 275-1495
To provide headstones or markers for all unmarked graves in national, post and state Veterans cemeteries and upon receipt of application for the unmarked graves of eligible veterans interred in private cemeteries. Types of assistance:

direct payments. Estimate of annual funds available: $ 21,303,000.

* Prosthetic Devices

Veterans Assistance Office
Department of Veterans Affairs
810 Vermont Ave., NW
Washington, DC 20420   (202) 233-2044

Veterans may be provided prosthetic appliances necessary for treatment of any condition when receiving hospital, domiciliary, or nursing home care in a facility under the direct jurisdiction of the VA. For more information, contact the Prosthetic Activity at VA medical center.

* Readjustment Counseling Service

Readjustment Counseling Service (10B/RC)
Department of Veterans Affairs
810 Vermont Ave., NW, Room 851
Washington, DC 20420   (202) 233-3317

The Readjustment Counseling Service Vietnam Era Veterans Outreach Centers (Vet Centers) are community-based, Department of Veterans Affairs (VA) services which were established following a recognition of the special readjustment needs of veterans who served during the Vietnam War, and from a desire to provide needed reajustment assistance to both top combat veterans and to support personnel of the Vietnam Era. The mission of the Readjustment Counseling Service (RCS) is to provide a wide range of outreach and direct psychosocial counseling services through storefront operations to veterans of the Vietnam era in order to help them make a satisfactory post-war readjustment to civilian life. For more information, including obtaining the address of your nearest Vet Center, contact the office above.

* Recreation Service

Recreation Service (11K)
Veterans Health Services and Research Administration
Department of Veterans Affairs
Washington, DC 20420   (202) 233-5389

The VA's recreational programs attempt to improve the quality of patient's lives and facilitate their reentry into the community. For more information, contact the office above.

* Rehabilitation Research

Rehabilitation Research and Development (110)
Department of Veterans Affairs
810 Vermont Ave., NW
Washington, DC 20420   (202) 233-5177

This program focuses directly on the needs of the veteran who is functionally impaired as a result of amputation, paralysis, or the loss or impairment of his or her vision, hearing, or speech. The latest computer and other technological advances are used to develop devices, techniques, and concepts in rehabilitation that will minimize the disability and promote functional independence among disabled veterans. Information and technology transfer is distributed through interagency agreements and collaborative efforts with the private sector. Contact the office above for more information.

* Social Work

Social Work Service (122)
Department of Veterans Affairs
810 Vermont Ave., NW
Washington, DC 20420   (202) 233-2614

Social Work Service is an integral part of the overall VA health-care program and operates in close concert with all medical services. Its purpose is to provide help to veterans and their families in resolving the psychosocial, emotional, and economic problems in dealing with the stresses of illness and disability. Social workers furnish psychosocial, diagnostic, and treatment services to the comprehensive treatment of veteran patients moving through admission, hospitalization, and post-hospital care back into the community. Social workers are also actively involved in outreach, readmission, and aftercare phases of the Department of Veterans Affairs' health care programs. For further information, contact the office above.

* Survivors and Dependents Educational Assistance 64.117

Department of Veterans Affairs
Central Office
Washington, DC 20420

To provide partial support to those seeking to advance their education who are qualifying spouses, surviving spouses, or children of deceased or disabled veterans, or of service personnel who have been listed for a total of more than 90 days as missing in action, or as prisoners of war. Types of assistance: direct payment. Estimate of annual funds available: $ 99,416,000.

* Veterans' Court of Appeals

Court of Veterans Appeals
1625 K St., NW, Suite 400
Washington DC 20006   (202) 254-6600

A Court of Veterans Appeals reviews benefit claims that are appealed on or after November 18, 1988. The Court has exclusive jurisdiction to review decisions of the Board of Veterans Appeals.

* Veterans Compensation for Service-Connected Disability (Compensation) 64.109

Department of Veterans Affairs
Washington, DC 20420

To compensate veterans for disabilities incurred or aggraved during military service according to the average impairment in earning capacity such disability would case in civilian occupations. Types of assistance: direct payment. Estimate of annual funds available: $ 8,523,517,000.

* Veterans Dependency and Indemnity Compensation for Service-Connected Death (SIC) 64.110

Department of Veterans Affairs
Washington, DC 20420

To compensate surviving spouses, children, and parents for the death of any veteran who died on or after January 1, 1957, because of a service-connected disability, or while in the active military, naval or air service. Types of assistance: direct payment. Estimate of annual funds available: $ 2,138,646,000.

* Veterans Hospital Based Home Care 64.022

Asst. Chief, Medical Director for Geriatrics and
Extended Care
Department of Veterans Affairs
Washington DC 20420   (202) 233-3692

To provide individual medical, nursing, social and rehabilitative services to eligible veterans in their home environment by VA hospital staff. Types of assistance: other. Estimate of annual funds available: $ 22,829,000.

* Veterans Nursing Home Care (VA Nursing Home Care) 64.010

Asst. Chief Medical Director for Geriatrics
and Extended Care
Department of Veterans
Washington, DC 20402   (202) 233-3692

To accommodate eligible veterans who are not acutely ill and not in need of hospital care, but who require skilled nursing care, related medical services, supportive personal care and individual adjustment services. Types of assistance: other. Estimate of annual funds available: $ 60,708,000.

* Veterans Outpatient Care 64.011

Director for Administration
Department of Veterans Affairs
Washington, DC 20420   (202) 233-2504

To provide medical and dental services, medicines and medical supplies to eligible veterans on an outpatient basis. Types of assistance: other. Estimate of annual funds available: $ 2,363,895,000.

* Veterans Prescription Service (Medicine for Veterans) 64.012

Asst. Chief, Medical Director for Clinical Affairs
Department of Veterans Affairs
Washington, DC 20420   (202) 233-3277

To provide eligible veterans and certain dependents and survivors of veterans with prescription drugs and expendable prosthetic medical supplies from VA pharmacies upon presentation of prescriptions from a licensed physician. Types of assistance: Other. Estimate of annual funds available: $ 497,121,000.

* Veterans Prosthetic Appliances (Prosthetics Services) 64.013

Asst. Chief, Medical Director for Clinical Affairs
Department of Veterans Affairs
Washington, DC 20420   (202) 233-2011

To provide through purchase and/or fabrication, prosthetic and related appliances, equipment and services to disabled veterans so that they may live and work as productive citizens. Types of assistance: other. Estimate of annual funds available: $ 104,780,000.

* Veterans Rehabilitation - Alcohol and Drug Dependence (Alcohol and Drug Dependence Treatment Program, Mental Health and Behavioral Sciences Service) 64.019

Director, Mental Health and Behavioral Sciences
 Services
Department of Veterans Affairs
Washington, DC 20420   (202) 233-5193

To provide medical, social and vocational rehabilitation to eligible alcohol and drug dependent veterans. Types of assistance: other. Estimate of annual funds available: $ 340,481,000.

* Vocational Rehabilitation for Disabled Veterans (Vocational Rehabilitation) 64.116

Department of Veterans Affairs
Central Office
Washington, DC 20420

To provide all services and assistance necessary to enable service-disabled veterans and service persons hospitalized pending discharge to achieve maximum independence in daily living and, to the maximum extent feasible to become employable and to obtain and maintain suitable employment. Types of assistance: direct payment. Estimate of annual funds available: $ 107,010,000.

* Vocational Rehabilitation for Service-Disabled Veterans Receiving Unemployability VA Compensation 64.122

Department of Veterans Affairs
Central Office
Washington, DC 20420

To enable eligible veterans to become employable and to obtain and maintain employment consistent with their abilities, aptitudes and interest. Types of assistance: direct payment. Estimate of annual funds available: $ 0.

* Vocational Training for Certain Veterans Receiving VA Pension   64.123

Department of Veterans Affairs
Central Office
Washington, DC 20420

To assist new pension recipients to resume and maintain gainful employment by providing vocational training and other services. Types of assistance: direct payment. Estimate of annual funds available: $ 650,000.

* Voluntary Service

Veterans Assistance Office -
Department of Veterans Affairs
810 Vermont Ave., NW
Washington, DC 20420   (202) 233-2044

The Department of Veterans Affairs encourages and trains volunteers to work at VA facilities in a variety of assignments beneficial to veterans and rewarding to volunteers. For complete information on voluntary service, contact the Chief of Voluntary Service at the nearest VA Medical Center.

* Work-Study Program

Veterans Assistance Office
Department of Veterans Affairs
810 Vermont Ave., NW
Washington, DC 20420   (202) 233-2044

Veteran-students enrolled as full-time students may agree to perform VA-related services and receive an additional allowance. The veterans who are 30 percent or more disabledfrom service-connected disabilities will be given preference. Contact your regional VA office for more information.

Tourist Adventures

* See also Arts and Humanities; Museums and Cultural Centers Chapter
* See also Weather and Maps Chapter
* See also International Trade Chapter

Here you'll find new ideas for your vacations that you'll probably never get from a travel agent. What about a polar expedition on an icebreaker? If you plan to travel to Europe, what about seeing if the U.S. Information Agency has any interest in paying you to give a lecture? Even if you don't have the energy to visit campgrounds or glaciers, you can still travel to those places simply by writing away for brochures, posters, and other publications available from the National Park Service. Boaters will find all sorts of information about rules, regulations, and safety, including coloring books for the youngsters. You'll also find handy tips for airborne travelers, on both domestic and international flights. We've also compiled a complete listing of each state's travel and tourism hotlines, which can help you map out any trip you want to take in the country.

* Agricultural Research Center Tours
Tour Coordinator
Agricultural Research Center
U.S. Department of Agriculture
Building 302
Beltsville, MD   (301) 344-2483
Visitors to the Beltsville Agricultural Research Center can arrange for guided tours. The center is closed to the public on Saturdays, Sundays, and holidays to see a computerized milking parlor and dwarf fruit tree orchard.

* Air Force Base Tours
Secretary of the Air Force
Office of Public Affairs
The Pentagon, Room 4A120
Washington, DC 20330   (202) 697-9079
Attend an annual open house on your local Air Force base, where you will tour the base, view aircraft on display, and watch an air show. Contact the Air Force installation nearest you, or the above office for a referral.

* Air Force Test Flight Center Tours
Air Force Flight Test Center
Public Affairs Office
Edwards Air Force Base, CA 93523-5000   (805) 277-3510
The Test Center sponsors an annual open house, usually in October, when the public is invited on a six-hour tour of the base. You can view the aircraft up close, watch a demonstration of the military "working" dogs, and view historical films of the base. Write or call the Public Affairs Office for more information.

* Airport and Control Tower Tours
Aviation Education Officer
Federal Aviation Administration
Department of Transportation
800 Independence Ave., SW
Washington, DC 20591   (202) 267-3469
The FAA's Aviation Education Program offers volunteer assistance to the nation's schools through the following programs: career guidance; tours of airports, control towers, and other facilities; classroom lectures and demonstrations; aviation safety information; aviation education resource materials; computerized clearinghouse of aviation and space information; aviation science instruction programs for home/school computers; "Partnerships-in-Education" activities; and teachers' workshops. Write to the above office for more information.

* American War Memorials
The American Battle Monuments Commission
Casimir Pulaski Building
20 Massachusetts Avenue, NW
Washington, DC 20314-0300   (202) 272-0533
Presently 124,921 U.S. War Dead are interred in U.S. administered cemeteries around the world, including 24 military burial grounds on foreign soil, and 15 separate monuments, 4 memorials, and 2 tablets in the United States. Each year the Commission publishes attractive, free pamphlets which highlight individual memorials, and include locations, site descriptions and photographs, brief histories of the battles in which the deceased fought, and directions from the nearest major airports. Back issues covering specific memorials are also available at no charge.

* Army Facilities Tours
Community Relations Division
U.S. Army Public Affairs
The Pentagon, Room 2E631
Washington, DC 20310   (202) 697-2707
The Army arranges tours of its facilities and special exhibits for the public. You may watch paratroopers jump, rangers train, tanks and artillery fire, and personally talk to soldiers about their jobs. Contact your nearest army installation for more information, or the above office which will refer you to the appropriate contact.

* Botanical Garden Tours
Public Programs Office
U.S. Botanic Garden
245 1st St., SW
Washington, DC 20024   (202) 226-4082
The Botanic Garden is open to the public from 9 a.m. to 9 p.m. daily June through August, and from 9 a.m. to 5 p.m. the rest of the year. Tours are given to interested groups, including garden clubs, professional organizations, and school children

* Buffalo and Cattle Refuges
Division of Refuges
U.S. Fish and Wildlife Service
4401 N. Fairfax Dr.
Arlington, VA 22203   (703) 358-1744
Buffalo and Texas longhorn cattle, as well as deer and elk, can be enjoyed at wildlife refuges maintained by the U.S. Department of the Interior. Wichita Mountains in Oklahoma and Fort Niobrara in Nebraska preserve these animals in their natural habitat. The government periodically auctions these animals to the public at these locations. For more information, contact the refuge managers directly: Fort Niobrara National Wildlife Refuge, Hidden Timber Route, HC 14, Box 67, Valentine, NE 69201; (402) 376-3789. Witchita Mountains Wildlife Refuge, Rt. 1, Box 448, Indiahoma, OK 73552; (405) 429-3222. You can see Buffalo also at the National Bison Range in Moiese, Montana. For more information on this refuge, contact National Bison Range, Moiese, MT 59824; (406) 644-2211.

* Capitol Hill Guided Tours
Capitol Guide Service
The Capitol
Washington, DC 20515   (202) 225-6827
Before leaving home for vacation, write your Representative and/or Senator-- as far in advance as possible--for tickets to the morning congressional tour specifying the date you wish to visit. Tickets are limited, but it's worth a try. Also request a Visitor's Pass for each member of your party to view a session of the House and/or Senate. House and Senate passes are not interchangeable, and they do not admit the bearer to special events and to a joint session of the Congress. House Gallery passes are good for both sessions of Congress. Senate Gallery passes are good for only one session. Sometimes visitors get a chance to speak with their elected representatives or their staff. Foreigners wishing to enter need only to door.

Vacations and Business Travel

The Capitol is located between Constitution and Independence Avenues at First Street. The East Front entrance at East Capitol Street is open daily, 9:00-4:30, except Thanksgiving, Christmas, and New Year's. Free 35-minute guided tours leave from the Rotunda every 10 minutes (more frequently in the summer) between 9 a.m. and 3:45 p.m. You'll view the National Statuary Hall, the House and Senate Chambers, and the Rotunda. The Capitol Rotunda and Statuary Hall are open in the summer until 10 p.m. The House and Senate Wings are also open when either of those legislative bodies is in night session.

* Currency Engraving and Printing Tours

Bureau of Engraving and Printing
U.S. Department of the Treasury
14th and C Streets, SW   (202) 447-9916
Washington, DC 20228   (202) 447-9709

A continuous self-guided tour at the Bureau features actual currency production. Visitors are able to view the various production steps, and tour guides are available to answer questions and assist visitors. Visitors may purchase uncut sheets of currency, engraved prints, small bags of shredded currency, and souvenir cards at the Visitor's Center. Tours may be taken Monday through Friday from 9 a.m. to 2 a.m., and admission is free.

* Diplomatic Reception Rooms

Tour Office
Department of State
2201 C St., NW
Washington, DC 20520   (202) 647-3241

Diplomatic reception rooms, which showcase American cultural heritage of the 18th and 29th centuries, are furnished with priceless antiques that have been donated or loaned to the State Department. These rooms are used for official functions by the President, the Vice President, the Secretary of State, and other governmental officials. The tour office can arrange public tours upon request.

* Engineering Inventions and Tours

Tours
National Institute of Standards and Technology
Gaithersburg, MD 20899   (301) 975-3585

Free tours of the various facilities at NIST are given on Thursdays at 9:30 a.m. They generally last for two hours, and the public is welcome, but should schedule reservations in advance through Jan Hauber at the office above.

* Federal Reserve Visitors

Office of Protocol
Federal Reserve System
Room B2217-B
20th St. & Constitution Ave., NW
Washington, DC 20551   (202) 452-3149

Those interested in visiting the Federal Reserve Board in Washington, D.C., should contact this office. At least one tour is conducted weekly and special arrangements may be made to accommodate groups of 10 or more.

* Glacier Bay and Other Historical Landmarks

Superintendent of Documents
Government Printing Office
Washington, DC 20402   (202) 783-3238

Historical landmarks are described in the historical handbooks featured in this listing. Sites include Antietam Battlefield, Devil's Tower in Wyoming, Ford's Theatre, Glacier Bay, Lincoln Memorial, and Nez Perce National Historical Park in Idaho, among others. Free.

* House of Representatives Passes

Your Member of Congress
U.S. Capitol
Washington, DC 20515   (202) 224-3121

The U.S. House of Representatives meets in the House Chamber in the south wing of the Capitol. The public is seated in the side and rear galleries; seats are available to those who secure passes from their Representative on a first come, first served basis.

* Indian Museums

Southern Plains Indian Museum
P.O. Box 749
Anadarko, OK 73005   (405) 247-6221

Museum of the Plains Indian
P.O. Box 400
Browning, MT 59417   (406) 338-2230

Sioux Indian Museum
P.O. Box 1504

Rapid City, SD 57709   (605) 348-0557

These three Indian museums are administered by the Indian Arts and Crafts Board of the Bureau of Indian Affairs, U.S. Department of the Interior. The museums issue free informational pamphlets and brochures about their respective programs and exhibition activities. Contact the museums directly to be placed on their mailing lists.

* Indian Reservations

If you are interested in visiting an Indian reservation on your vacation, or even if you are just interested in finding out more firsthand information about a particular tribe or reservation, you should contact any of the following offices listed below. Since not every Indian reservation allows public tours, you'll have to contact each individually to find out any tourism programs.

Anadarko Agency
P.O. Box 309, Anadarko, OK 73005; (405) 247-6673

Anchorage Agency
1675 C Street, Anchorage, AK 99501; (907) 271-4088

Ardmore Agency
P.O. Box 997, Ardmore, OK 73402; (405) 223-6767

Bethel Agency
P.O. Box 347, Bethel, AK 99559; (907) 543-2726

Blackfeet Agency
Browning, MT 59417; (406) 338-7534

Cherokee Agency
Cherokee, NC 28719; (704) 497-9131

Cheyenne River Agency
P.O. Box 325, Eagle Butte, SD 57625; (605) 964-6611

Chinle Agency
P.O. Box 7, Chinle, AZ 86503; (602) 674-5211

Choctaw Agency
421 Powell, Philadelphia, MS 39350; (601) 656-1521

Colorado River Agency
Rt. 1, Box 9-C, Parker, AZ 85344; (602) 669-6121

Colville Agency
P.O. Box 111, Nespelem, WA 99155; (509) 634-4901

Concho Agency
P.O. Box 96, Concho, OK 73022; (405) 262-7481

Crow Agency
Crow Agency, MT 59022; (406) 638-2827

Crow Creek Agency
P.O. Box 616, Ft. Thompson, SD 57339; (605) 245-2311

Eastern Navajo Agency
P.O. Box 32, Crownpoint, NM 87313; (505) 786-5228

Flathead Agency
Box A, Pablo, MT 59855; (406) 675-2700

Fort Apache Agency
P.O. Box 560, Whiteriver, AZ 85941; (602) 338-4364

Fort Belknap Agency
P.O. Box 98, Harlem, MT 59526; (406) 353-2901 ext. 23

Fort Berthold Agency
P.O. Box 370, New Town, ND 58763; (701) 627-4707

Fort Defiance Agency
P.O. Box 619, Fort Defiance, AZ 86504; (602) 729-5041

Fort Hall Agency
Fort Hall, ID 83203; (208) 238-3710

Fort Peck Agency
P.O. Box 637, Poplar, MT 59255; (406) 768-5312

Fort Totten Agency
P.O. Box 270, Fort Totten, ND 58335; (701) 766-4545

Fort Yuma Agency
P.O. Box 1591, Yuma, AZ 85364; (602) 572-0248

Great Lakes Agency

Ashland, WI 54806; (715) 682-4527/8

Hopi Agency
P.O. Box 158, Keams Canyon, AZ 86034; (602) 738-2228

Horton Agency
P.O. Box 31, Horton, KS 66439; (913) 486-2161

Jicarilla Agency
P.O. Box 167, Dulce, NM 87528; (505) 759-3651

Laguna Agency
P.O. Box 1448, Laguna, NM 87026; (505) 243-4467

Lower Brule Agency
P.O. Box 190, Lower Brule, SD 57548; (605) 473-5512

Menominee Area Rep
Minneapolis Area Office, 15 South 5th St., 10th Floor, Minneapolis, MN 55402; (612) 349-3597

Mescalero Agency
P.O. Box 189, Mescalero, NM 88340; (505) 671-4421

Metlakatla Field Station
P.O. Box 458, Metlakatla Field Station, Metlakatla, AK 99926; (907) 886-3791

Miami Agency
P.O. Box 391, Miami, OK 74355; (918) 542-3396

Michigan Agency
Federal Square Office Plaza, P.O. Box 884, Sault Ste. Marie, MI 49783; (906) 632-6809

Minnesota Sioux Field Rep
Minneapolis Area Office, 15 South 5th St., 6th Floor, Minneapolis, MN 55402; (612) 349-3607

Muskogee Area Office
Old Federal Bldg., Muskogee, OK 74401; (918) 687-2296

Nome Agency
P.O. Box 1108, Nome, AK 99762; (907) 443-2284

Northern Cheyenne Agency
Lame Deer, MT 59043; (406) 477-8242

Northern Idaho Agency
P.O. Box 277, Lapwai, ID 83540; (208) 843-2267

Northern Pueblos Agency
1570 Pachaco Street, Building D6, Santa Fe, NM 87501; (505) 988-6431

Okmulgee Agency
P.O. Box 370, Okmulgee, OK 74447; (918) 756-3950

Olympic Peninsula Agency
P.O. Box 120, Office Building, Hoquiam, WA 98550; (206) 533-9100

Osage Agency
Pawhuska, OK 74056; (918) 287-2495

Papago Agency
P.O. Box 578, Sells, AZ 85634; (602) 383-7286

Pawnee Agency
P.O. Box 440, Pawnee, OK 74058; (918) 762-2585

Pima Agency
P.O. Box 8, Sacaton, AZ 85247; (602) 562-3326

Pine Ridge Agency
P.O. Box 1203, Pine Ridge, SD 57770; (605) 867-5121

Puget Sound Agency
3006 Colby St., Federal Bldg., Everett, WA 98201; (206) 258-2651

Ramah-Navajo Agency
Ramah, NM 87321; (505) 775-3235

Red Lake Agency
Red Lake, MN 56671; (218) 679-3361

Rocky Boy's Agency
Box Elder, MT 59521; (406) 395-4476

Rosebud Agency
P.O. Box 550, Rosebud, SD 57570; (605) 747-2224

Sac & Fox
Tama, IA 56671; (515) 484-4041

Salt River Agency
Rt. 1, P.O. Box 117, Scottsdale, AZ 85256; (602) 241-2842

San Carlos Agency
P.O. Box 209, San Carlos, AZ 85550; (602) 475-2321

Seminole Agency
6075 Stirling Rd., Hollywood, FL 33024; (305) 581-7050, Extension 820-7288

Shawnee Agency
Route 5, Box 148, Shawnee, OK 74801; (405) 273-0317

Shiprock Agency
P.O. Box 966, Shiprock, NM 87420; (505) 368-4427

Siletz Agency
P.O. Box 539, Siletz, OR 97380; (503) 444-2679

Sisseton Agency
P.O. Box 688, Agency Village, SD 57262; (605) 698-7676

Southern Paiute Field Station
Box 986, Cedar City, UT 84720; (801) 586-1121

Southern Pueblos Agency
P.O. Box 1667, Albuquerque, NM 87103; (505) 766-3021

Southern Ute Agency
P.O. Box 315, Ignacio, CO 81137; (303) 563-4511

Spokane Agency
P.O. Box 389, Wellpinit, WA 99040; (509) 258-4561

Standing Rock Agency
P.O. Box E, Ft. Yates, ND 58538; (701) 854-3431

Tahlequah Agency
P.O. Box 828, Tahlequah, OK 74465; (918) 456-6146

Talihina Agency
P.O. Drawer H, Talihina, OK 74571; (918) 567-2207

Truxton Canon Agency
Valentine, AZ 86437

Turtle Mountain Agency
P.O. Box 60, Belcourt, ND 58316; (701) 477-3191

Uintah & Ouray Agency
Fort Duchesne, UT 84026; (801) 722-2406

Umatilla Agency
P.O. Box 520, Pendleton, OR 97801; (503) 276-3811

Ute Mountain Agency
General Delivery, Towaoc, CO 81334; (303) 565-8471

Wahpeton Indian School
Wahpeton Indian School, Wahpeton, ND 58075; (701) 642-3796

Wapato Irrigation Project
P.O. Box 220, Wapato, WA 98951; (509) 877-3155

Warm Springs Agency
P.O. Box 1239, Warm Springs, OR 97761; (503) 553-1121

Western Navajo Agency
P.O. Box 127, Tuba City, AZ 86045; (602) 762-4251

Wewoka Agency
P.O. Box 1060, Wewoka, OK 74884; (405) 257-6257

Wind River Agency
Ft. Washakie, WY 82514; (307) 332-7812

Winnebago Agency
Winnebago, NE, 68071; (402) 878-2201

Yakima Agency
P.O. Box 632, Toppenish, WA 98948; (509) 865-2255

Yankton Agency
Wagner, SD 57380; (605) 384-3651

Vacations and Business Travel

Zuni Agency
P.O. Box 369, Zuni, NM 87327; (505) 782-4453

* Korean War Veterans Memorial

The American Battle Monuments Commission
Casimir Pulaski Building
20 Massachusetts Avenue, NW
Washington, DC 20314-0300　　　　　(202) 272-0533

In 1986 a new law authorized the ABMC to erect a memorial in the Washington, D.C., area to honor all servicemen and women of the Armed Forces of the United States who served during the Korean War, particularly those who were killed in action, are still listed as Missing in Action, or were held as prisoners of war. For information on its concept, construction, and fund raising efforts, contact the ABMC.

* Lawrence Livermore Computer Facility Tours

Visitors Center
Lawrence Livermore National Laboratory
Greenville Road
Livermore, CA 94550　　　　　(415) 422-9797

The National Laboratory conducts public tours of its computing center. You must, however, be 18 years of age or older. For information, contact the Visitors Center.

* Missile Testing Center Tours

U.S. Department of the Army
Public Affairs Office
Building 122
White Sands Missile Range, NM 88002-5047　　　　　(505) 678-1134

This research and missile testing center invites the public to an open house twice a year, which includes a visit to the "Trinity Site" where the first atomic detonation took place. The center publishes a brochure and fact sheets on its history, mission, and wide range of programs. The test range also functions as a wildlife preserve. Write or call for their free publications and information on open house days.

* Museum of the U.S. Department of the Interior

Departmental Museum
U.S. Department of the Interior
18th and C Sts., NW, Room 1240
Washington, DC 20240　　　　　(202) 343-2743

The highlights of this museum's exhibit include Native American artifacts and dioramas depicting the history of each of DOI's Bureaus. Of particular interest o children is a collection of fossils and a display of fragments from the moon's surface. The display is oriented to children in the fourth grade and older, but younger children are welcome. The hours of operation are 8 a.m. to 4 p.m., Monday through Friday.

* Music at the Capitol

Architect's Office
Room SB-15
Washington, DC 20515　　　　　(202) 225-1200

The Capitol and the House and Senate office buildings resound, especially during the spring and summer months, with all types of music. The American Festival/Concerts at the Capitol are sponsored by the Congress and the Secretary of the Interior. They are performed by the National Symphony and have been conducted by various maestros. The Service bands and choral groups of the Air Force, Army, Marine Corps, and Navy provide summer night entertainment for the public in concerts that have become a Capitol tradition. Concerts are free and seating on the lawn and picnics are in order. In addition, the Capitol and its various office buildings are filled throughout the year, but especially during the winter holiday season, with the joyous voices of choral groups. These appearances are arranged well in advance by the Senators or Representatives through the Architect of the Capitol.

* National Aquarium

Main Commerce Building
U.S. Fish and Wildlife Service
14th St. and Constitution Ave., NW
Washington, DC 20240　　　　　(202) 377-2826

This public aquarium houses both fresh water and marine animals. Exhibits are representations of our natural environment and demonstrate basic biological concepts and principles. The admission fee is $1.50 for adults and $.75 for senior citizens and children under 12.

* National Arboretum Tours

U.S. National Arboretum
3501 New York Ave.
Educational Department
Washington, DC 20002　　　　　(202) 475-4815

Various woody ornamental and outdoor plants are grown and cared for on the 444 acres comprising the U.S. National Arboretum. Admission and parking are free, and guided tours for 10 or more are available with 3 weeks advance notice. Many free classes are offered, along with many special events and functions associated with gardening and growing plants. A free monthly newsletter lists the monthly calendar.

* National Park Service Folders Bibliography

Superintendent of Documents
Government Printing Office
Washington, DC 20402　　　　　(202) 783-3238

National Park Service brochures are featured, including the lesser-known areas of the national parks and a Washington, D.C., guide. Also included are books on the preservation of historic structures. Free.

* Nation's Capitol Walker's Guide

Public Information Office
Pennsylvania Avenue Development Corporation
1311 Pennsylvania Ave., NW
Suite 1220 North
Washington, DC 20004　　　　　(202) 724-9091

A Walker's Guide to Pennsylvania Avenue provides the locations and architects of the PADC projects on Pennsylvania Avenue. This guide is free.

* Natural Landmarks Registry

National Registry of Natural Landmarks
National Registry Branch
National Park Service
U.S. Department of the Interior
1100 L St., NW
Washington, DC 20005　　　　　(202) 343-9536

The Park Service conducts natural region studies to identify areas that are of potential national significance. These areas are then studied in the field by scientists. Natural areas considered of national significance are cited by the Secretary of the Interior as eligible for recognition as Registered Natural Landmarks. The owner may apply for a certificate and bronze plaque designating the site.

* Panama Canal Tours

Orientation Services
The Office of Public Affairs
c/o Panama Canal Commission
APO Miami 34011-5000　　　　　(507) 52-3187

The Canal Guide Service, operated by the Panama Canal Commission, offers free tours of the Panama Canal to the public. Tours are given seven days a week from 9:00 a.m. to 5:00 p.m. The tour takes less than an hour and include a slight briefing, a topographical model of the Canal to view, and a film. Visitors are welcome at the Miraflores Locks on the Pacific side of the Isthmus where a pavilion provides a vantage point for viewing transiting ships. Interested members of the public should call two days in advance to make a reservation. Another attraction is the high doomed ceiling, the dramatic murals, and the marble columns and floor make the rotunda the main attraction of the Administration Building at Balboa Heights. The murals depict the digging of Gaillard Cut at Gold Hill, the erection of a lock gate, and the construction of the Gatun Dam spillway and Miraflores Locks. For more information, contact this office.

* Pentagon Art Tours

Director, Pentagon Tours
OASK-PA(DCR)
The Pentagon, Room 1E776
Washington, DC 20301　　　　　(202) 695-1776

Free tours of the Pentagon art collection are conducted Monday through Friday, except holidays, every half hour from 9:30 a.m. to 3:30 p.m. All you need is a valid I.D. to sign up; children under 10 must be accompanied by an adult. Go to the ticket window at the main concourse by the Metro entrance. Only if you have a group of 30 or more do you need to write for a reservation; otherwise, just come, first come, first served.

* Polar Expeditions with Civilians

Ice Operations Division
Office of Navigation Safety and Waterways Services
U.S. Coast Guard
U.S. Department of Transportation
2100 2nd St., SW, Room 1202 A
Washington, DC 20593-0001　　　　　(202) 267-1450

The Coast Guard furnishes vessels to other agencies, such as the National Science Foundation, U.S. Geological Survey, and the Navy, to conduct research and ice operations in Arctic and Antarctic waters. The agencies sponsoring the missions select scientists, researchers, students, and in some cases, journalists, photographers, and artists to accompany the mission when space is available. This office is a good starting point for obtaining information on the pertinence of a mission to your field, to be directed to the appropriate agency sponsors, and for information about the data collected during missions.

* Public Buildings and Historic Sites of the United States
Superintendent of Documents
Government Printing Office
Washington, DC 20402   (202) 783-3238
The GPO bibliography of public buildings, landmarks, and historic sites of the United States is divided into the categories of historic sites, posters, preservation methods for historic buildings, and descriptions of public buildings. Highlights include a poster of the Statue of Liberty and an historic guide to the White House. Free.

* Robots Engineering Lab Tour
Center for Manufacturing Engineering
National Engineering Laboratory
National Institute of Standards and Technology
Gaithersburg, MD 20899   (301) 975-3414
Demonstrations of robot-tended machining workstations, and inspection machines, as well as demonstrations of optical measurement of surface finish are presented for the public. To schedule a tour, contact this Center.

* Statue of Liberty
Superintendent of Documents
Government Printing Office
Washington, DC 20402   (202) 783-3238
The Statue of Liberty Exhibit is a full-color pamphlet describing the museum of the Statue of Liberty. It recounts the history of the Statue, describes the intricacies of its architecture and design, and provides information on its French designers and its massive refurbishing. 1988 (S/N 024-005-01025-4, $2.50).

* U.S. Congress Memorial and Historic Trees
Architect of the Capitol
U.S. Capitol Building
Washington, DC 20515   (202) 225-1200
Since the early 1900s, ninety-four memorial and historic trees have been planted. Seventy-three are still living on the Capitol grounds. Trees have been planted to memorialize different senators and congressman as well as such people as mothers of America and Vietnam veterans. To obtain a chart which will help you locate various dedicatory trees, contact the Architect's office.

* Voice of America Radio Public Tours
Office of External Affairs
Voice of America
United States Information Agency
330 Independence Ave., SW
Washington, DC 20547   (202) 485-6231
Tours of the main headquarters of the VOA, which produces radio programming in 43 languages heard all over the world, are given each weekday except legal holidays. A guide shows visitors the technical operations center, the newsroom, several studios, where either live broadcasts or recordings are being sent out, and a film on the VOA. The 45 minute free tours are scheduled for 8:40, 9:40 and 10:40 a.m., and 1:40 and 2:40 p.m. Reservations are preferred.

* Washington D.C. Art Museums

For tour information, contact the appropriate office listed below:

Anacostia Museum
Education, Anacostia Museum, 1901 Fort Place S.E., Washington, DC 20020; (202) 287-3369.

Cooper-Hewitt Museum
Membership Department, Cooper-Hewitt Museum, 2 East 91st St., New York, NY 10028; (212) 860-6868.

Freer Gallery of Art
Tour Information, Freer Gallery of Art, 12th St.& Independence Ave. S.W., Washington, DC 20560; (202) 357-2104.

Hirshorn Museum and Sculpture Garden
Office of Education, Hirshorn Museum and Sculpture Garden, 8th St. & Independence Ave. S.W., Washington, DC 20560; (202) 357-3235.

Kennedy Center
Tour Information, Friends of the Kennedy Center, Washington, DC 20566; (202) 254-3643.

National Air and Space Museum
Office of Volunteer Service, National Air and Space Museum, 7th St. & Independence Ave., S.W., Washington, DC 20560; (202) 357-1400.

National Gallery of Art
Education Office, National Gallery of Art, Washington, DC 20565; (202) 846-2646.

National Museum of African Art
Department of Education, National Museum of African Art, 950 Independence Ave., S.W., Washington, DC 20560; (202) 357-4600.

National Museum of American Art
Division of Museum Programs, National Museum of American Art, Smithsonian Institution, Washington, DC 20560; (202) 357-3095.

National Museum of American History
Office of Public Programs, National Museum of American History, 14th St. & Constitution Ave. N.W., Washington, D. C. 20560; (202) 357-1481; 357-1563 TDD.

National Museum of Natural History
Office of Education, National Museum of Natural History, 10th St. & Constitution Ave. N.W., Washington, DC 20560; (202) 357-2810.

National Portrait Gallery
Curator of Education, National Portrait Gallery, Eighth and F Sts. N.W., Washington, DC 20560; (202) 357-2920.

National Zoological Park
Friends of the National Zoo, National Zoological Park, 3000 Connecticut Ave., N.W., Washington, DC 20008; (202) 673-4960.

Smithsonian Environmental Research Center
Department of Education, Smithsonian Environmental Research Center, RR4, Box 28, Edgewater, MD 21037; (202) 261-4190, Ext 42.

* Washington, D.C. Landmarks and Points of Interest
Superintendent of Documents
Government Printing Office
Washington, DC 20402   (202) 783-3238
Washington, D.C.: Official National Park Guidebook is a colorful descriptive handbook of the Nation's Capitol and nearly Maryland, Virginia and West Virginia. It includes full-color photographs of Washington's landmarks, guide maps, and descriptive histories of all points of interest. 1989 (S/N 024-005-01034-3, $5.00).

* Washington, D.C. Pennsylvania Avenue Events
Public Information Office
Pennsylvania Avenue Development Corporation
1311 Pennsylvania Ave., NW
Suite 1220 North
Washington, DC 20004   (202) 724-9059
Throughout the year, various events are held on Pennsylvania Avenue. Dial (202) 724-0009 to hear a recorded message providing daily information about events on Pennsylvania Avenue.

* White House Tours
The White House Office
1600 Pennsylvania Ave., NW   (202) 456-1414
Washington, DC 20500   (202) 456-7041
Tours of the White House are held every Tuesday through Saturday from 10:00 a.m. to 12:00 noon, unless the White House is closed due to an official function. No tickets or reservations are required. For more information call the number above.

* Witness Congressional Committee Hearings and Meetings
Contact your Congressman or Senator, or
Senate or House Press Galleries   (202) 224-3121
Most House and Senate committee hearings and meetings are open to the public. Your Representative or Senator's office should be able to brief you on the subject matter of the hearing and give you a copy of the bill which will be discussed, or a summary of the previous testimony they have heard. By attending committee meetings, you can gain an understanding of the issues gaining the attention of lawmakers and see the legislative process at work. Another type of committee hearing is an "oversight" or investigative session. Members examine

Vacations and Business Travel

---

the operations of a government agency or search some area of public life that may require future legislation. Hearings are conducted for a variety of reasons; principal among them are to gather information, generate publicity, and assess the level of support. Informed and interested witnesses may appear before the committee, including Federal officials, interest group representatives, academic experts, and private citizens. A civics lesson in action, the committee "mark-up session" occurs after all the testimony has been received and when the drafting of the legislation and voting on provisions actually takes place. This is the heart of the legislative process, where all the political pressures collide with policy questions. It is at this stage when the language of the bill is determined by the committee. Contact your Senator and Representative or call the Senate or House Press Galleries at (202) 224-3121 for news about the schedule for committee activities.

Parks and Camping

* Architecture in the Parks

Historic Architectural Division
National Park Service
U.S. Department of the Interior
1100 L St., NW
Washington, DC 20005   (202) 343-8146

Activities related to the preservation of historic and prehistoric structures and cultural landscapes within the National Park System are administered by this office. *A List of Classified Structures* is maintained, which is an inventory of all historic and prehistoric structures in the System. A bibliography of Cultural Resources Management is also administered, listing all reports that address cultural resources in the Park System.

* Apostle Islands

Superintendent of Documents
Government Printing Office
Washington, DC 20402   (202) 783-3238

Apostle Islands: A Guide to Apostle Islands Lakeshore, Wisconsin recounts the history of these islands, describes the geographical features, and looks at the inland sea. It provides tips on where to visit, wild animal life, and plant life. Full-color photographs are included. (S/N 024-005-01023-8, $2.25).

* Bicycle Paths and Other Transit Environments

Environment Division
Policy and International Affairs
Office of the Secretary of Transportation
U.S. Department of Transportation
400 7th Street, SW, Room 9217
Washington, DC 20590   (202) 366-4366

This is the DOT contact point for environmental issues. Staff can provide you with information and referrals on such subjects as highway beautification, transportation architecture, bicycle paths, historic preservation activities, and environmental impact statements.

* Campgrounds on Public Lands

Office of Public Affairs
Bureau of Land Management
U.S. Department of the Interior
18th and C Sts., NW
Washington, DC 20240   (202) 343-5717

The *Recreation Guide to BLM Public Lands* features a map outlining all of the public lands used as recreational areas. Designations on the map include campgrounds, visitors centers, national wild and scenic rivers, national wilderness areas, and national historic and scenic trails. Also included are the states that contain public lands, and state and district offices to contact for additional information. Alaska, Arizona, California, Colorado, Idaho, Montana, Nevada, New Mexico, Oregon, Utah, Washington, and Wyoming are the key states described.

* Camping and Hiking East of the Mississippi

Land Between the Lakes
Resource and Development
Tennessee Valley Authority
Golden Pond, KY 42231   (502) 924-5602

Land Between the Lakes offers recreation for tourists on over 300 miles of undeveloped shoreline. The Woodlands Nature Center offers animal exhibits both animals and special programs for the public, including over 200 miles of hiking trails. Wrangler's Camp offers horseback riding on its 26 miles of trails, along with barns, tethers, and posts for riders. Turkey Bay offers an area reserved for off-road vehicle recreation. Three primary campgrounds offer over 1,000 sites and numerous informal shoreline campgrounds. Land Between the Lakes also boasts their own resident buffalo herd--the largest publicly-owned herd east of the Mississippi River. For more information on recreation opportunities at Land Between the Lakes, contact this office.

* Camping Guide to the National Parks

Superintendent of Documents
Government Printing Office
Washington, DC 20402   (202) 783-3238

The National Parks: Camping Guide 1988-89 contains basic information about the facilities and recreational opportunities available to users of the National Park System camping areas. It also provides an alphabetical list of camping areas by state. 1988 (S/N 024-005-01028-9, $3.50).

* Camping Reservations

Campsite reservations   (800) 283-CAMP

Call Ahead for Happy Camping is a Forest Service program that makes it easier for you to use the 156 National Forests, where you can hike, fish, camp, ski, or just relax. There are over 100,000 miles of trails and 10,000 recreation sites. Call this toll-free number to make reservations at any of the National Forests across the U.S.

* Lesser-Known Parks

Superintendent of Documents
Government Printing Office
Washington, DC 20402   (202) 783-3238

This publication of the National Park Service available is *The National Parks: Lesser-Known Areas* (024-005-0091106, $1.50).

* National and Historical Parks and Preserves

Alabama
Horseshoe Bend National Military Park, Rt. 1, Box 103, Daviston, AL 36256

Alaska
Bering Land Bridge National Preserve, P.O. Box 220, Nome, AK 99762
Denali National Park and Preserve, P.O. Box 9, McKinley Park, AK 99755
Gates of the Arctic National Park and Preserve, P.O. Box 74680, Fairbanks, AK 99707
Glacier Bay National Park and Preserve, Gustavus, AK 99826
Katmai National Park and Preserve, P.O. Box 7, King Salmon, AK 99613
Kenai Fjords National Park, P.O. Box 1727, Seward, AK 99664
Klondike Gold Rush National Historical Park, P.O. Box 517, Skagway, AK 99840
Kobuk Valley National Park, P.O. Box 1029, Kotzebue, AK 99752
Lake Clark National Park and Preserve, 701 C St., P.O. Box 61, Anchorage, AK 99513
Noatak National Preserve, P.O. Box 1029, Kotzebue, AK 99752
Sitka National Historical Park, P.O. Box 738, Sitka, AK 99835
Wrangell-St. Elias National, Park and Preserve, P.O. Box 29, Glenallen, AK 99588
Yukon-Charley Rivers, National Preserve, P.O. Box 64, Eagle, AK 99738

Arizona
Coronado National Memorial, Rural Route 2, P.O. Box 126, Hereford, AZ 85615
Grand Canyon National Park, P.O. Box 129, Grand Canyon, AZ 86023
Petrified Forest National Park, Petrified Forest National Park, AZ 86028

Arkansas
Arkansas Post National Memorial, Rt. 1, P.O. Box 16, Gillett, AR 72055
Buffalo National River, P.O. Box 1173, Harrison, AR 72601
Hot Springs National Park, P.O. Box 1860, Hot Springs, AR 71902
Pea Ridge National Military Park, Pea Ridge, AR 72751

California
Channel Islands National Park, 1901 Spinnaker Dr., Ventura, CA 93001
Golden Gate National Recreation Area, Fort Mason, Bldg. 201, San Francisco, CA 94123
Kings Canyon National Park, Three Rivers, CA 93271
Lassen Volcanic National Park, P.O. Box 100, Mineral, CA 96063
Point Reyes National, Seashore, Point Reyes, CA 94956
Redwood National Park, 1111 Second St., Crescent City, CA 95531
Santa Monica Mountains, National Recreation Area, 22900 Ventura Blvd, Suite 140, Woodland Hills, CA 91364
Sequoia National Park, Three Rivers, CA 93271
Whiskeytown-Shasta-Trinity, National Recreation Area, P.O. Box 188, Whiskeytown, CA 96095
Yosemite National Park, P.O. Box 577, Yosemite National Park, CA 95389

Colorado
Curecanti National Recreation Area, 102 Elk Creek, Gunnison, CO 81230
Mesa Verde National Park, Mesa Verde National Park, CO 81330
Rocky Mountain National Park, Estes Park, CO 80517

District of Columbia

Vacations and Business Travel

Constitution Gardens, 900 Ohio Dr., SW, Washington, DC 20242

John F.Kennedy Center for the Performing Arts, National Park Service, 2700 F St., NW, Washington, DC 20566

Lyndon B.Johnson Memorial, Grove on the Potomac, c/o NCP - George Washington Memorial Pkwy, Turkey Run Park, McLean, VA 22101

Rock Creek Park, 5000 Glover Rd., NW, Washington, DC 20015

Theodore Roosevelt Island, c/o George Washington Memorial Pkwy, Turkey Run Park, McLean, VA 22101

Thomas Jefferson Memorial and Tidal Basin, c/o NCP - Central, 900 Ohio Dr., SW, Washington, DC 20242

Florida

Big Cypress National Preserve, Star Route, P.O. Box 110, Ochopee, FL 33943

Biscayne National Park, P.O. Box 1369, Homestead, FL 33090

Canaveral National Seashore, P.O. Box 6447, Titusville, FL 32782

DeSoto National Memorial, 75th St., NW, Bradenton, FL 33529

Everglades National Park, P.O. Box 279, Homestead, FL 33030

Fort Caroline National Memorial, 12713 Fort Caroline Rd., Jacksonville, FL 32225

Gulf Islands National Seashore, 1801 Gulf Breeze Pkwy, Gulf Breeze, FL 32561

Georgia

Chattahoochee River National Recreation Area, 1978 Island Ford Pkwy, Dunwoody, GA 30350

Chickamauga and Chattanooga National Military Park, P.O. Box 2128, Fort Oglethorpe, GA 30742

Cumberland Island National Seashore, P.O. Box 806, St. Marys, GA 31558

Kennesaw Mountain National, Battlefield Park, P.O. Box 1167, Marietta, GA 30061

Guam

War in the Pacific National Historic Park, P.O. Box FA, Agana, GU 96910

Hawaii

Haleakala National Park, P.O. Box 369, Makawao, HI 96768

Hawaii Volcanoes National Park, Hawaii National Park, HI 96718

Kalaupapa National Historical Park, Kalaupapa, HI 96742

Pu'uhonua o Honaunau National Historical Park, P.O. Box 128, Honaunau Kona, HI 96726

Indiana

George Rogers Clark National Historical Park, 401 S. Second St., Vincennes, IN 47591

Indiana Dunes National Lakeshore, 1100 N. Mineral Springs Rd., Porter, IN 46304

Kentucky

Cumberland Gap National Historical Park, P.O. Box 1848, Middlesboro, KY 40965

Mammoth Cave National Park, Mammoth Cave, KY 42259

Louisiana

Jean Lafitte National Historical Park and Preserve, 423 Canal St., Room 210, New Orleans, LA 70130-2341

Maine

Acadia National Park, P.O. Box 177, Bar Harbor, MED 04609

Maryland

Antietam National Battlefield, P.O. Box 158, Sharpsburg, MD 21782

Assateague Island National Seashore, Rt. 2, P.O. Box 294, Berlin, MD 21811

Catoctin Mountain Park, 6602 Foxville Rd., Thurmont, MD 21788

Chesapeake and Ohio Canal Historical Park, P.O. Box 4, Sharpsburg, Md. 21782

Fort Washington Park, NCP - East, 1900 Anacostia Dr., SE, Washington, DC 20020

Greenbelt Park, 6565 Greenbelt Rd., Greenbelt, MD 20770

Piscataway Park, c/o NCP - East, 1900 Anacostia Dr. SE, Washington, DC 20019

Massachusetts

Boston National Historical Park, Charlestown Navy Yard, Boston, MA 02129

Cape Cod National Seashore, South Wellfleet, MA 02663

Lowell National Historical Park, 169 Merrimack St., Lowell, MA 01852

Minute Man National Historical Park, P.O. Box 160, 174 Liberty St., Concord, MA 01742

Michigan

Isle Royale National Park, 87 N. Ripley St., Houghton, MI 49931

Pictured Rocks National Lakeshore, P.O. Box 40, Munising, MI 49862

Sleeping Bear Dunes National Lakeshore, P.O. Box 277, 9922 Front St., Empire, MI 49630

Minnesota

Voyageurs National Park, P.O. Box 50, International Falls, MN 56649

Mississippi

Brices Cross Roads National Battlefield Site, c/o Natchez Trace Pkwy, Rural Route 1, NT-143, Tupelo, MS 38801

Gulf Islands National Seashore, 3500 Park Rd., Ocean Springs, MS 39564

Natchez Trace Parkway, Rural Route 1, NT-143, Tupelo, MS 38801

Tupelo National Battlefield, c/o Natchez Trace Pkwy, Rural Route 1, NT-143, Tupelo, MS 38801

Vicksburg National Military Park, 3201 Clay St., Vicksburg, MS 39180

Missouri

Jefferson National Expansion Memorial, 11 North 4th St., St. Louis, MO 63102

Ozark National Scenic Riverways, P.O. Box 490, Van Buren, MO 63965

Wilson's Creek National Battlefield, Postal Drawer C, Republic, MO 65738

Montana

Big Hole National Battlefield, P.O. Box 237, Wisdom, MT 59761

Bighorn Canyon National Recreation Area, P.O. Box 458, Fort Smith, MT 59035

Glacier National Park, West Glacier, MT 59936

Nevada

Great Basin National Park, Baker, NV 89311

Lake Mead National Recreation Area, 601 Nevada Hwy, Boulder City, NV 89005-2426

New Jersey

Morristown National Historical Park, Washington Place, Morristown, NJ 07960

New Mexico

Carlsbad Caverns National Park, 3225 National Parks Hwy, Carlsbad, NM 88220

Chaco Culture National Historical Park, Star Route 4, P.O. Box 6500, Bloomfield, NM 87413

New York

Federal Hall National Memorial, Manhattan Sites, 26 Wall St., New York, NY 10005

Fire Island National Seashore, 120 Laurel St., Patchogue, NY 11772

Gateway National Recreation Area, Floyd Bennett Field, Bldg. 69, Brooklyn, NY 11234

General Grant National Memorial, 122nd St. and Riverside Dr., New York, NY 10027

Hamilton Grange National Memorial, 287 Convent Ave., New York, NY 10031

Saratoga National Historical Park, R.D. 2, P.O. Box 33, Stillwater, NY 12170

Women's Rights National Historical Park, P.O. Box 70, Seneca Falls, NY 13148

North Carolina

Blue Ridge Parkway, 700 Northwestern Plaza, Asheville, NC 28801

Cape Hatteras National Seashore, Rt. 1, P.O. Box 675, Manteo, NC 27954

Cape Lookout National Seashore, P.O. Box 690, Beaufort, NC 28516

Guilford Courthouse National Military Park, P.O. Box 9806, Greensboro, NC 27429

Moores Creek National Battlefield, P.O. Box 69, Currie, NC 28435

Wright Brothers National Memorial, Cape Hatteras Group, Rt. 1, P.O. Box 675, Manteo, NC 27954

North Dakota

Theodore Roosevelt National Park, P.O. Box 7, Medora, ND 58645

Ohio

Cuyahoga Valley National Recreation Area, 15610 Vaughn Rd., Brecksville, OH 44141

Perry's Victory and International Peace Memorial, P.O. Box 549, 93 Delaware Ave., Put-in-Bay, OH 43456

Oklahoma

Chicksaw National Recreation Area, P.O. Box 201, Sulphur, OK 73086

Oregon

Crater Lake National Park, P.O. Box 7, Crater Lake, OR 97604

Fort Clatsop National Memorial, Rt. 3, P.O. Box 604-FC, Astoria, OR 97103

Pennsylvania

Delaware Water Gap National Recreation Area, Bushkill, PA 18324

Fort Necessity National Battlefield, The National Pike, R.D. 2, P.O. Box 528, Farmington, PA 51437

Gettysburg National Military Park, Gettysburg, PA 17325

Independence National Historical Park, 313 Walnut St., Philadelphia, PA 19106

Johnstown Flood National Memorial, c/o Allegheny Portage Railroad NHS, P.O. Box 247, Cresson, PA 16630

Thaddeus Kosciuszko National Memorial, c/o Independence NHP, 313 Walnut St., Philadelphia, PA 19106

Upper Delaware Scenic and Recreational River, P.O. Box C, Narrowsburg, NY 12764

Valley Forge National Historical Park, Valley Forge, PA 19481

Rhode Island

Roger Williams National Memorial, P.O. Box 367, Annex Station, Providence, RI 02901

South Carolina

Cowpens National Battlefield, P.O. Box 308, Chesnee, SC 29323

Kings Mountain National Military Park, P.O. Box 40, Kings Mountain, NC 28086

South Dakota
Badlands National Park, P.O. Box 6, Interior, SD 57750
Mount Rushmore National Memorial, P.O. Box 268, Keystone, SD 57751
Wind Cave National Park, Hot Springs, SD 57747

Tennessee
Big South Fork National River and Recreation Area, P.O. Drawer 630, Oneida, TN 37841
Fort Donelson National Battlefield, P.O. Box 434, Dover, TN 37058-0434
Great Smoky Mountains National Park, Gatlinburg, TN 37738
Obed Wild and Scenic River, P.O. Box 429, Wartburg, TN 37887
Shiloh National Military Park, P.O. Box 61, Shiloh, TN 38376
Stones River National Battlefield, Rt. 10, P.O. Box 495, Old Nashville Hwy, Murfreesboro, TN 37130

Texas
Amistad Recreation Area, P.O. Box 420367, Del Rio, TX 78842-0367
Big Bend National Park, Big Bend National Park, TX 79834
Big Thicket National Preserve, 3785 Milam, Beaumont, TX 77701
Chamizal National Memorial, c/o Federal Bldg., 700 E. San Antonio, Suite D-301, El Paso, TX 79901
Guadalupe Mountains National Park, H.C. 60, P.O. Box 400, Salt Flat, TX 79847-9400
Lake Meredith Recreation Area, P.O. Box 1438, Fritch, TX 79036
Lyndon B. Johnson National Historical Park, P.O. Box 329, Johnson City, TX 78636
Padre Island National Seashore, 9405 S. Padre Island Dr., Corpus Christi, TX 78482-5597
San Antonio Missions National Historical Park, 2202 Roosevelt Ave., San Antonio, TX 78210-4919

Utah
Arches National Park, P.O. Box 907, Moab, UT 84532
Bryce Canyon National Park, Bryce Canyon, UT 84717
Canyonlands National Park, 125 W. 200 South, Moab, UT 84532
Capital Reef National Park, Torrey, UT 84775
Glen Canyon National Recreation Area, P.O. Box 1507, Page, UT 86040
Zion National Park, Springdale, UT 84767-1099

Virginia
Appomattox Court House National Historical Park, P.O. Box 218, Appomattox, VA 24522
Arlington House, The Robert E. Lee Memorial, c/o George Washington Memorial Pkwy, Turkey Run Park, McLean, VA 22101
Colonial National Historical Park, P.O. Box 210, Yorktown, VA 23690
Fredericksburg and Spotsylvania National Military Park, P.O. Box 679, Fredericksburg, VA 22404
George Washington Memorial Parkway, Turkey Run Prk, McLean, VA 22101
Great Falls Park, 9200 Old Dominion Dr., Great Falls, VA 22066
Manassas National Battlefield Park, P.O. Box 1830, Manassas, VA 22110
Petersburg National Battlefield, P.O. Box 549, Rt. 36 East, Petersburg, VA 23804
Prince William Forest Park, P.O. Box 209, Triangle, VA 22172
Richmond National Battlefield Park, 3215 E. Broad St., Richmond, VA 23223
Shenandoah National Park, Rt. 4, P.O. Box 348, Luray, VA 22835
Wolf Trap Farm Park for the Performing Arts, 1551 Trap Rd., Vienna, VA 22180

Virgin Islands
Virgin Islands National Park, P.O. Box 7789, Charlotte Amalie, St. Thomas, VI 00801

Washington
Coulee Dam National Recreation Area, P.O. Box 37, Coulee Dam, WA 99116
Ebey's Landing National Historical Reserve, P.O. Box 774, 23 Front St., Coupeville, WA 98239
Klondike Gold Rush National Historical Park, 117 S. Main St., Seattle, WA 98104
Lake Chelan National Recreation Area, 2105 Hwy 20, Sedro Woolley, WA 98284
Mount Ranier National Park, Tahoma Woods Star Route, Ashord, WA 98304
North Cascades National Park, 2105 Hwy 20, Sedro Woolley, WA 98284
Olympic National Park, 600 E. Park Ave., Port Angeles, WA 98362
Ross Lake National Recreation Area, 2105 Hwy 20, Sedro Woolley, WA 98284
San Juan Island National Historical Park, P.O. Box 429, Friday Harbor, WA 98250

West Virginia
Appalachian National Scenic Trail, P.O. Box 807, Harpers Ferry, WV 25425
Harpers Ferry National Historical Park, P.O. Box 65, Harpers Ferry, WV 25425
New River Gorge National River, P.O. Box 2289, Oak Hill WV 25901

Wisconsin
Apostle Islands National Lakeshore, Rt. 1, P.O. Box 4, Bayfield, WI 54814
St. Croix and Lower St. Croix, National Scenic Riverways, P.O. Box 708, St. Croix Falls, WI 54024

Wyoming
Grand Teton National Park, P.O. Drawer 170, Moose, WY 83012
John D. Rockefeller Memorial Parkway, c/o Grand Teton National Park, P.O. Drawer 170, Moose, WY 83012
Yellowstone National Park, P.O. Box 168, Yellowstone National Park, WY 82190

* National Parks Exhibits and Programs
Division of Interpretation
National Park Service
U.S. Department of the Interior
1100 L St., NW, Room 2101
Washington, DC 20240 (202) 523-5270
The National Park Service assists its facilities in planning and carrying out their exhibits and visitor programs. Their future plans include more involvement in environmental education programs to be offered at the Park Service sites.

* National Park Service Clearinghouse
Technical Information Center
National Park Service
Denver Service Center
12795 W. Alameda Parkway
P.O. Box 25287
Denver, CO 80225-0287 (303) 969-2130
The Technical Information Center has been designated by the National Park Service as the central repository for all National Park Service-generated planning, design, and construction maps, drawings, and reports as well as related cultural, environmental, and other technical documents. Bibliographic data on aerial photography is also maintained. The Center reproduces and delivers copies of the available materials for the Service, other agencies, and the public, both here and abroad. Today, the system has a holding of 100,000 data records, which represent about 500,000 microfilm aperture cards of maps, plans, and drawings; 1,000 records of resource and site aerial photography; and 25,000 planning, design, environmental, cultural resource, and natural resource documents.

* National Park Service Films
National Audiovisual Center
8700 Edgeworth Dr.
Capitol Heights, MD 20743-3701 (800) 638-1300
The National Audiovisual Center contains more than 2,700 titles of videocassettes, films and slide/sound programs. Among them are some wonderful presentations produced by the National Park Service and the U.S. Fish and Wildlife Service. Materials may be rented or purchased. Contact the AV Center for specific information. Some titles include:

Everglades: Seeking a Balance
Gulf Island Beaches, Bays, Sands, and Bayous
California Gray Whale
Environmental Awareness
Giant Sequoia
One Man's Alaska
Sanctuary: The Great Smoky Mountains
Crater Lake
Yellowstone
Washington, DC: Fancy Free
Glacier Bay
Bighorn Canyon Experience
Cape Cod
What is a Mountain?
Living Waters of the Big Cypress
National Parks: Our Treasured Lands
Mt. McKinley
America's Wetlands
Parrots of Luquillo
Where the Fish Will Be
Patuxent Wildlife Research Center
Minnesota Valley National Wildlife Refuge

* National Park Service Management and Programming
Park Practice Program
National Park Service
U.S. Department of the Interior
P.O. Box 37127
Washington, DC 20013-7127 (202) 343-7067
The Park Practice Program is a cooperative effort between the National Park Service and the National Recreation and Park Association. Three publications are produced quarterly in an effort to instruct recreational and park directors on the latest information in the field:
TRENDS. Discusses topics of general interest in park and recreation management and programming.
GRIST. Contains practical solutions to everyday problems in park and recreation operations including energy conservation, cost reduction, safety, and maintenance and designs for small structures.

Vacations and Business Travel

DESIGN. Offers plans for park and recreation structures which demonstrate quality design and intelligent use of materials.

These publications are available as a set in an annual subscription of $45. *GRIST* is also available separately for a yearly price of $20 initially and $12 thereafter. Subscription inquiries should be addressed to: National Recreation and Park Association, 3101 Park Center Dr., Alexandria, VA 22302; (703) 820-4940.

* National Park Service Police

National Capital Region
National Park Service
U.S. Department of the Interior
1100 Ohio Dr., SW
Washington, DC 20242   (202) 426-6650

The U.S. Park Police have the same authority and powers as the Washington, D.C. metropolitan police. They also act as hosts to park visitors.

* National Parks Service Posters and Charts

Superintendent of Documents
Government Printing Office
Washington, DC 20402   (202) 783-3238

The following National Park Service posters and charts are available from GPO. Several titles can be purchased at special discounts when buying 100-count lots.

The Alpine Northwest
The Atlantic Barrier
The Desert
Edgar Allan Poe
Everglades
Glacier Bay
Hawaii Volcanoes
North Cascades Panorama
The Rocky Mountains
Statue of Liberty
Yosemite Panorama
National Park Service
American/British Charts

* National Park Service Regional Offices

Alaska
2525 Gambell St., Room 107, Anchorage, AK 99503; (907) 261-2690

Mid-Atlantic
Second and Chestnut Sts., Philadelphia, PA 19106; (215) 597-2284. Serving: PA, VA, WV, DE, MD

Midwest
1709 Jackson St., Omaha, NE 68102; (402) 221-3431. Serving: NE, MO, KS, IA, IL, IN, WI, MI, MN, OH

Washington, D.C.
1100 Ohio Dr., SW, Washington, DC 20242; (202) 485-9813

North-Atlantic
15 State St., Boston, MA 02109-3572; (617) 565-8841. Serving: NY, NJ, CT, RI, MA, NH, VT, ME

Pacific Northwest
83 South King St., Suite 212, Seattle, WA 98104; (206) 442-5565. Serving: WA, OR, ID

Rocky Mountain
12795 W. Alameda Pkwy, P.O. Box 25287, Denver, CO 80225; (303) 969-2875. Serving: MT, ND, SD, WY, UT, CO

Southeast
75 Spring St., Atlanta, GA 30303; (404) 331-5185. Serving: MS, TN, AL, GA, FL, SC, NC, KY, Virgin Is., PR

Southwest
P.O. Box 728, Santa FE, NM 87504-0728; (505) 988-6388. Serving: NM, TX, LA, OK, AR

Western
450 Golden Gate Ave., P.O. Box 36063, San Francisco, CA 94102; (415) 556-4196. Serving: CA, AZ, NV, HI, Guam, Northern Marianas Is., Am Samoa, Micronesia, Marshall Is., Palau

* National Park Service Reservations

Ticketron
Department R
401 Hackensack Ave.

Hackensack, NJ 07601

Reservations to the following national park sites are available from the agent listed above. Advanced notice of eights weeks is needed for individual campsites. Phone reservations must be made directly with those parks accepting them; this information is listed in the Ticketron brochure. The parks include: Acadia National Park, Maine; Assateague Island National Seashore, Maryland/Virginia; Cape Hatteras National Seashore, North Carolina; Grand Canyon National Park, Arizona; Great Smoky Mountains National Park, North Carolina/Tennessee; Joshua Tree National Monument, California; Rocky Mountain National Park, Colorado; Sequoia-Kings Canyon National Park, California; Shenandoah National Park, Virginia; Whiskeytown National Recreation Area, California; Yellowstone National Park, Idaho/Montana/Wyoming; Yosemite National Park, California.

* National Park Service Statistical Abstract

Statistical Office
Denver Service Center - TNT
National Park Service
U.S. Department of the Interior
P.O. Box 25287
Denver, CO 80225   (303) 969-2060

National Park Service statistics from 1982-1988 are included in the *Park Service Statistical Abstract*. Recreation visits in the Service are summarized in information tables, such as visitor use, total visits, visits by region and state, visits by urban-rural location, overnight stays, and number of tour buses.

* National Park Service Videos and Literature

Harpers Ferry Historical Association, Inc.
P.O. Box 197, High St.
Harpers Ferry, WV 25425   (304) 535-6881

This historical society serves as a distributing agency for the sale and rental of materials produced for the National Park Service. A catalog is available listing videos and handbooks, and another 80 historic films are available from the Association for purchase or three-day rental. Some video titles include: *Challenge of Yellowstone, Great Sand Dunes, Shenandoah: The Gift, Cape Cod Treasury, Gulf Islands, Antietam Visit, Civil War Artillery, A Lasting Victory (Robert E. Lee)*, and *Blessings of Liberty* (produced for the 200th birthday of the U.S. Constitution). The handbooks describe historical events and different locations within the Park Service. Inquire about a current listing of materials.

* National Parks Index

Superintendent of Documents
Government Printing Office
Washington, DC 20402   (202) 783-3238

Published yearly, *The National Parks: Index* describes the National Park System and provides information on the available facilities. The cost is $3.00.

* National Parks Visitor Facilities and Services

Conference of National Park Concessioners
Manmmoth Cave, KY 42259   (502) 773-2191

The publication, *National Park Visitor Facilities and Services*, lists all concessioner lodging and service information for the National Parks. To obtain a copy, send $4.15 to the office above.

* National Wildlife Refuges Guide

Superintendent of Documents
Government Printing Office
Washington, DC 20402   (202) 783-3238

National Wildlife Refuges: A Visitor's Guide is a foldout map of the United States including locations of all national wildlife refuges, a list of their names and addresses, and a description of available activities. 1988 (S/N 024-010-00680-2, $1.00).

* Recreation and Outdoor Activities Bibliography

Superintendent of Documents
Government Printing Office
Washington, DC 20402   (202) 783-3238

This bibliography is divided into the categories of boating and water activities, camping and hiking, fishing and hunting, national recreation areas, winter activities, and general information. Free.

* Recreation Guide to BLM Public Lands

Office of Public Affairs
Bureau of Land Management
U.S. Department of the Interior
18th and C Sts., NW
Washington, DC 20240   (202) 343-5717

The *Recreation Guide to BLM Public Lands* features a map outlining all of the public lands used as recreational areas. Designations on the map include campgrounds, visitors centers, national wild and scenic rivers, national wilderness areas, and national historic and scenic trails. Also included are the states that contain public lands, and state and district offices to contact for additional information. Alaska, Arizona, California, Colorado, Idaho, Montana, Nevada, New Mexico, Oregon, Utah, Washington, and Wyoming are the key states described.

* Recreation Market Study

Recreation Resources Assistance Division
National Park Service
U.S. Department of the Interior
1100 L St., NW
Washington, DC 20005   (202) 343-3780

The *National Recreation Survey* provides current information on what Americans do for recreation in the outdoors and their expectations of recreational opportunities. The survey contains valuable market data on such topics as favorite activities, importance of recreation areas and their distance from home, characteristics of trips and outings, characteristics of respondents who spend money on outdoor recreation, and reasons for discontinuing a recreation activity. Various tables that relate to the National Park System and its participants are included.

* State Parks, Forest Camping Areas and Other Recreation Areas

Community Relations
Governmental and Public Affairs
Tennessee Valley Authority
400 W. Summit Hill Dr.
Knoxville, TN 37902   (615) 632-8000

This office can provide you with a free pamphlet which describes recreation areas on the Tennessee Valley Authority lakeshores, including boat docks, resorts, state parks, U.S. Forest Service camp areas, and those county and municipal parks which have docks or camping areas.

* Summer Jobs in the Wild

United States Youth Conservation Corps
U.S. Fish and Wildlife Service
National Park Service
Washington, DC 20240   (202) 343-5951

The Youth Conservation Corps is a summer employment program for young men and women, ages 15 through 18, who work, learn, and earn wages accomplishing needed conservation work on public lands. The program is also administered by the Forest Service of the U.S. Department of Agriculture. Projects include constructing trails, building campground facilities, planting trees, collecting litter, clearing streams, improving wildlife habitats, and office work. Limited positions are available.

* Tourism Programs on Public Lands

Office of Public Affairs
Bureau of Land Management
U.S. Department of the Interior
18th and C Sts., NW
Washington, DC 20240   (202) 343-5717

In recognition of the importance of outdoor recreation to Americans, *Recreation 2000 Executive Summary* sets forth the commitment of the Bureau of Land Management to the management of outdoor recreation resources in the public lands. The plan highlights the areas in which the Bureau intends to concentrate future efforts, such as visitor information, resource protection, land ownerships, partnerships, volunteers, tourism programs, facilities, and permits, fees, and concessions. This publication also features a map outlining all of the public lands used as recreational areas. Designations on the map include campgrounds, visitors centers, national wild and scenic rivers, national wilderness areas, and national historic and scenic trails. Also included are the states that contain public lands, and state and district offices to contact for additional information. Alaska, Arizona, California, Colorado, Idaho, Montana, Nevada, New Mexico, Oregon, Utah, Washington, and Wyoming are the key states described.

* Whale Watching

Office of Protected Resources
National Marine Fisheries Service
National Oceanic and Atmospheric Administration
Department of Commerce
1335 East-West Hwy.
Silver Spring, MD 20910   (301) 427-2322

The Marine Mammal Protection Act commits the United States to long-term management and research programs to conserve and protect these animals. The National Marine Fisheries Service grants or denies requests for exemptions, issues permits, carries out research and management programs, enforces the Act, participates in international programs, and issues rules and regulations to carry out its mission to conserve and protect marine mammals. An annual report is available for the Office of Protected Resources, which gives detailed information regarding the activities of the Office. This office can also provide you with copies of the Act, and two publications: *First Aid For Stranded Marine Mammals*, and *Proceedings of the Workshop to Review and Evaluate Whale Watching Programs and Management Needs*.

* Wild and Scenic Rivers

Land and Renewable Resources
Bureau of Land Management
U.S. Department of the Interior
18th and C Sts., NW
Washington, DC 20240   (202) 343-4896

The Bureau of Land Management manages about 2,200 miles of the Wild and Scenic River System, primarily in the western United States. These areas are located in the directory, *Recreation Guide to BLM Public Lands*, available from the Office of Public Affairs, Bureau of Land Management, U.S. Department of the Interior, Washington, D.C. 20240.

* Woodsy Owl and Children's Materials

U.S. Department of Agriculture
Forest Service, P.O. Box 96090
Washington, DC 20090-6090   (202) 475-3785

To increase children's awareness of our delicate environment, the Forest Service's Woodsy Owl campaign has a variety of free materials available, including coloring sheets, detective sheets, song sheets, patches, "Woodsy Owl on Camping" (brochure), and stickers.

Boating and Fishing

* Advanced Marine Vehicles
Planning Branch
Research and Development Staff
Office of Engineering and Development
U.S. Coast Guard
U.S. Department of Transportation
2100 2nd St., SW, Room 6208
Washington, DC 20593-0001   (202) 267-1030
Information can be obtained here about research conducted by the Coast Guard in support of its operations and responsibilities. Areas of study include ice operations, ocean dumping, law enforcement, environmental protection, port safety and security, navigation aids, search and rescue procedures, recreational boating, energy, and advanced marine vehicles. For referral to specific personnel working in these areas, contact the Planning Branch.

* Aids to Navigation
Office of Navigation Safety and Waterways Services
U.S. Coast Guard
U.S. Department of Transportation
2100 2nd St., SW, Room 1116
Washington, DC 20593-0001   (202) 267-1965
The Coast Guard maintains aids to navigation such as lighthouses and lights, buoys, beacons, fog signals, and long-range radionavigation aids like LORAN-C and OMEGA. The aids are established to assist navigators in plotting safe courses on waters under U.S. jurisdiction and in certain international areas. The seven volumes of *Light Lists*, which detail the navigation aids in seven geographic areas, are available at varying cost from the Superintendent of Documents, Government Printing Office, Washington, D.C. 20402; (202) 783-3238. The *LORAN-C User Handbook*, which explains the radionavigation system and how to use it, is also available from GPO for $4.75.

* Army Corps of Engineers Recreational Facilities Films
U.S. Army Corps of Engineers
Directorate of Information Management
Visual Information Branch
20 Massachusetts Ave., NW
Washington, DC 20314
This office maintains a still photographic library and offers a free film loan and video distribution program. The Corps has educational and public relations films on their recreational facilities, navigation, flood control, hydro-electric power, and environmental systems. Write for information on the how to participate in the program.

* Boating Correspondence Course
U.S. Government Bookstore
World Savings Building
720 N. Main St.
Pueblo, CO 81003   (719) 544-3142
Designed for boaters who can't attend a boating class, *The Skipper's Course* covers basic navigation, legal requirements, anchoring, weather, emergency procedures, boat handling, and safety. A certificate of completion is awarded. Stock No: 050012002258. Price: $6.50.

* Coast Guard Courses and Textbooks
Coast Guard Auxiliary National Board, Inc.
9949 Watson Industrial Park
St. Louis, MO 63126
The following are textbooks used in Coast Guard Auxiliary public education courses. They can be ordered by writing to the above address, or you can get each textbook by taking the course of the same title through the Coast Guard. To find out where courses are offered near you, call the Courseline at (800) 336-BOAT; or (800) 245-BOAT in VA.

Boating Skills and Seamanship. Boating laws and regulations, boat handling, and navigation ($8.00).
Sailing and Seamanship. Same basic text as above, geared to sailboats ($8.00).
Advanced Coastal Piloting. How to read charts, plot courses, predict tides, and use navigation aids ($8.00).

* Coast Guard Rescue Service
SAR Database Manager
Search and Rescue Division

Office of Navigation Safety and Waterways Services
U.S. Coast Guard
U.S. Department of Transportation
2100 2nd St., SW, Room 1422
Washington, DC 20593-0001   (202) 267-1579
The Search and Rescue (SAR) program maintains a comprehensive system of resources to save lives and prevent personal injury and property damage on the navigable waters of the U.S. This system includes rescue vessels, aircraft, and communication facilities. A cooperative international distress response system is also maintained for incidents on the high seas. For more information about the Guard's SAR program, contact the branch listed above.

* Free Boat Inspection
Courtesy Marine Examination (CME)
BOAT/U.S. Foundation
880 S. Pickett St.   (800) 336-BOAT
Alexandria, VA 22304   (800) 245-BOAT (in VA)
The U.S. Coast Guard Auxiliary offers a free safety inspection called a Courtesy Marine Examination. A specially trained Coast Guard Auxiliarist will examine your craft to determine if it has all the necessary and recommended equipment. If properly equipped, you'll be awarded a CME decal. To arrange for your CME, call the toll-free number or contact your local Coast Guard Auxiliary.

* Land Between the Lakes
Land Between The Lakes
Natural Resources
Resource and Development
Tennessee Valley Authority
Golden Pond, KY 42231   (502) 924-5602
Land Between The Lakes is a 40-mile-long peninsula located between Kentucky and Barkley Lakes in west Kentucky and Tennessee. In its 25th year of operation, Land Between The Lakes is managed by TVA to provide an outstanding outdoor recreation experience. A living history farm exhibit called "Homeplace-1850," recreates life as it existed on a typical farmstead in the area before the Civil War. Exhibitors tend crops and animals, prepare meals, and perform hundreds of other farm chores in the same manner as their forebears did. Recreation programs at Land Between the Lakes are for everyone, but many programs are tailored to groups with special needs.

* Marine Advisory Service
National Sea-Grant College Program
National Oceanic and Atmospheric Administration
Department of Commerce
1335 East-West Hwy.
Silver Spring, MD 20910   (202) 377-8090
Operated through the Sea-Grant Colleges, the marine advisory service consists of agents and specialists who are experts in areas such as seafood technology, marine economics, coastal engineering, commercial fishing, recreation, and communications. These specialists provide a link between the people who live and work in coastal areas and researchers in the universities. They sponsor workshops, conferences, and seminars on marine issues for the public and representatives of industry and government agencies. They talk to high school science classes, as well as publish bulletins, fact sheets, newsletters, technical papers, and audio-visual materials concerning marine affairs. The following is a list of Sea-Grant Colleges, and people you can contact for more information.

* Marine Environmental Information
Pollution Response Branch
Marine Environmental Response Division
Office of Marine Safety, Security,
  and Environmental Protection
U.S. Coast Guard
U.S. Department of Transportation
2100 2nd St., SW, Room 2104   (202) 267-0518
Washington, DC 20593-0001   (202) 267-2611
This office responds to requests for marine environmental protection information from Congress and other federal agencies, state agencies, schools, industries, and the general public. Data is available on laws relating to the protection of the marine environment, incidents involving releases of oil or other hazardous substances, and federally funded spill response operations.

* Marine Fire and Rescue Technology

Library
Coast Guard Research and Development Center
U.S. Coast Guard
U.S. Department of Transportation
Avery Point
Groton, CT 06340-6096   (203) 441-2648

Marine research is conducted here in areas such as ice technology, navigation instrumentation technology, ocean dumping surveillance, pollution, search and rescue techniques, and marine fire and safety technology. This library is a good starting point for obtaining specific information about what research is done by the Center and for referrals to appropriate experts.

* Mariners Weather Log

National Oceanographic Data Center
National Oceanic and Atmospheric Administration
Universal Building Room 412
Washington, DC 20235   (202) 673-5549

The Mariners Weather Log is a unique source of information on marine weather and climate and their effects on operations at sea. Published quarterly by the National Oceanographic Data Center, the Mariners Weather Log provides comprehensive coverage of major storms of the North Atlantic and North Pacific, reports and annual summaries on tropical cyclones, information on the National Weather Service's Marine Observation Program, selected shipboard gale and wave observations, and general articles about weather and climate, hazards and safety precautions, and related marine lore. An annual subscription is available for $6 from the Superintendent of Documents, Government Printing Office, Washington, D.C. 20402; (202)783-3238.

* Navigation Regulations

Navigation Rules and Information Branch
Short-Range Aids to Navigation Division
Office of Navigation and Waterways Services
U.S. Coast Guard
U.S. Department of Transportation
2100 2nd St., SW, Room 1416E
Washington, DC 20593-0001   (202) 267-0357

The Coast Guard establishes regulations for waterways safety that must be followed by U.S. vessels on the high seas and inland waters. These include rules on maneuvering and requirements for lights, sound signals, and radio telephones. For information on the rules, contact the above office or obtain a copy of Navigation Rules, International and Inland, available for $6.00 from the Superintendent of Documents, Government Printing Office, Washington, D.C. 20402; (202) 783-3238. This rulebook is required by law to be carried on all vessels 39.4 feet or more in length.

* Pleasure Boating on the St. Lawrence Seaway

Public Affairs Office
Saint Lawrence Seaway Development Corporation
U.S. Department of Transportation
180 Andrews Street
Massena, NY 13662-1763   (315) 764-3232

The publication, Pleasure Craft Guide: The Seaway, provides you with information on boating in the St. Lawrence River. Contact this office to obtain your free copy.

* Recreational Fishing

Public Affairs
National Marine Fisheries Service
National Oceanic and Atmospheric Administration
Department of Commerce
1335 East-West Hwy.
Silver Spring, MD 20910   (202) 427-2370

The National Marine Fisheries Service manages the country's stocks of saltwater fish and shellfish for both commercial and recreational interests. NMFS administers and enforces the Magnuson Fishery Conservation and Management Act to assure that fishing stays within sound biological limits, and that U.S. commercial and recreational fishermen have the opportunity to harvest all the available fish within these limits. Several hundred Fisheries Service scientists conduct research relating to these management responsibilities in science and research centers in 15 states and the District of Columbia. Many of these laboratories have evolved a major field of interest, and have special knowledge of the fish in their geographical area that leads to predictions of abundance, economic forecasts, and direct assistance to sport fishermen and commercial fishing businesses.

* Recreational Maps and Navigational Charts

TVA Maps and Surveys
Tennessee Valley Authority
Chattanooga, TN 37402-2801   (615) 751-MAPS

Many recreational maps and navigational charts of TVA lakes are available to the public for a small fee. Detailed routes to shoreline recreation areas. The maps show water depths, the location of and detailed routes to the public recreation areas, boat docks, resorts, and roads. The navigational charts for the main lakes show navigation channels, buoys, lights, and other navigational aids, while maps for tributary lakes show the numbered signs TVA has installed at strategic locations on shore to aid fishermen and recreation boaters in locating their position. A map showing TVA dams and steam plants, including important facts about each of them, is available, along with cadastral and topographic maps, aerial photographs, and survey control data. Each request should specify the lake(s) of interest.

* Recreation Market Study

Recreation Resources Assistance Division
National Park Service
U.S. Department of the Interior
1100 L St., NW
Washington, DC 20005   (202) 343-3780

The National Recreation Survey provides current information on what Americans do for recreation in the outdoors and their expectations of recreational opportunities. The survey contains valuable market data on such topics as favorite activities, importance of recreation areas and their distance from home, characteristics of trips and outings, characteristics of respondents who spend money on outdoor recreation, and reasons for discontinuing a recreation activity. Various tables that relate to the National Park System and its participants are included.

* Recreation on Public Lands

Office of Public Affairs
Bureau of Land Management
U.S. Department of the Interior
18th and C Sts., NW
Washington, DC 20240   (202) 343-5717

In recognition of the importance of outdoor recreation to Americans, Recreation 2000 Executive Summary sets forth the commitment of the Bureau of Land Management to the management of outdoor recreation resources in the public lands. The plan highlights the areas in which the Bureau intends to concentrate future efforts, such as visitor information, resource protection, land ownerships, partnerships, volunteers, tourism programs, facilities, and permits, fees, and concessions.

* Resort Guides

National Oceanographic Data Center
National Environmental Satellite, Data, and Information Service
National Oceanic And Atmospheric Administration
Department of Commerce
Washington, DC 20235   (202) 673-5546

The National Oceanographic Data Center and the Sea Grant Programs in various coastal states have produced a series of climate guides to coastal recreation areas. The guides include useful information about winds, waves, and air and water temperatures, as well as tips on sportfish species, tourist attractions, weather hazards, and safety precautions. Single copies of these publications are available for a $3.00 mailing/handling charge per order (not per publication). The following is a list of the resort guides available:

Hawaii: The Big Island
Recreation and Weather Guide to the Minnesota Shore of Lake Superior
Western Lake Erie Recreational Climate Guide
Central Lake Erie Recreational Climate Guide
Lake Huron Recreation and Weather
Massachusetts Saltwater Fishing and Weather Guide
Nassau County (Long, Island, NY) Recreation and Climate Guide

* Safety Information for Marine Dealers

Marine Dealer Visitation Program
Office of Navigation Safety and Waterway Services
U.S. Coast Guard
U.S. Department of Transportation
2100 2nd St., SW   (800) 368-5647
Washington, DC 20593-0001   (202) 267-0780 (in DC)

Through the Marine Dealer Visitation Program, boating equipment dealers can receive updates on regulations, information on Courtesy Marine Examinations, and details about boating safety education courses. Participating dealers will be visited quarterly by a local Coast Guard Auxiliarist, be given a literature rack with boating brochures and pamphlets for customers, and will receive a "Cooperating Marine Dealer" decal for shop door or window. Marine dealers can participate by calling the Boating Safety Hotline listed above.

* Safety on Small Passenger Vessels

Marine Inspection Office
Your Local Coast Guard Office

Most small passenger vessels (less than 100 tons and carrying more than 6 people) are required to adhere to certain Coast Guard safety regulations. These include having a safety orientation procedure for passengers (announcement or placard), posting of emergency instructions, a life preserver for every person on board, and a Coast Guard safety certification. Marine Inspection Offices around the country issue the certificates. To find an Inspection Office near you, or to report a violation or complaint, call the Boating Safety Hotline (800) 368-5647; or (202) 267-0780 in D.C.

* Scenic River Study

Recreation Program
Lands
River Basin Operations
Tennessee Valley Authority
Norris, TN 37828   (615) 632-1606

The recreation staff completed a TVA river system evaluation, which identifies streams with recreation and aesthetic values, such as the French Broad River in western North Carolina, the eastern Tennessee River, and the Bear Creek streams in northern Alabama. This study also addresses one of the major problems which inhibits full enjoyment of these resources by Valley residents: a lack of easy access to the rivers. Contact this office for more information on this study and its findings.

* Swimming Areas and Aquatic Plants

Aquatic Biology Department
Resource Development
River Basin Operations
Water Resources
Tennessee Valley Authority
311 Broad St.
Chattanooga, TN 37402-2801   (615) 751-7324

TVA's two major weapons for controlling the spread of pesky aquatic plants, such as Eurasian watermilfoil, spiney-leaf naiad, and hydrilla in its reservoirs, is the winter and summer draw downs and the selective spraying of herbicides. Reservoir levels may be lowered several feet in the late summer to dry out and kill the roots of these plants embedded in shallow areas of the reservoirs; while at other times, lake levels may be held higher than normal to prevent sunshine from penetrating to the bottom and thus prevent germination and growth of new colonies. Selective use of approved herbicides in high priority use areas, such as swimming beaches, developed shoreline, and marinas, is another effective control method. Several experimental control strategies also are being tested on TVA lakes. One of the most promising is a cooperative effort between TVA and the U.S. Army Corps of Engineers. TVA proposes to conduct large scale demonstrations on Guntersville reservoir on the use of Grass Carp, hydrilla fly, a fungus to control watermilfoil, and other methods being currently tested on a smaller scale by the Corps Waterways Experiment Station.

* Toll-Free Help for Boaters

Boating Safety Hotline
Consumer and Regulatory Affairs Branch (G-NAB-5)
Auxiliary, Boating, and Consumer Affairs Division
Office of Navigation Safety and Waterways Services
U.S. Coast Guard
U.S. Department of Transportation
2100 2nd St., SW, Room 1109   (800) 368-5647
Washington, DC 20593-0001   (202) 267-0780 (in DC)

This service is toll-free throughout the U.S., including Alaska, Hawaii, Puerto Rico, and the Virgin Islands. Staff can provide you with information on such topics of interest to boaters as safety recalls, publications, Coast Guard department contacts and addresses, public education courses, and free Coast Guard services. If hotline operators cannot answer your question directly, you'll get a call back from someone who can. Ask for a consumer information packet, and you'll receive a group of publications and consumer *Fact Sheets* on topics like safe boating, getting help on the water, floatation devices, federal regulations, sanitation devices, and sources of boating education. The *Boater's Source Directory*, included in the packet, is a guide to a wide variety of federal, state, private, and non-profit agencies that provide literature, technical information, free services, and other assistance to recreational boaters. Among the freebies you can request is the *Water 'N Kids* coloring book for 4-8 year olds, which explains basic concepts of water safety. The hotline also takes consumer complaints about safety defects and violations. Operators answer between 8 a.m. and 4 p.m. Eastern Time, and an answering machine takes messages after hours.

* Updates for Mariners

Local Notice to Mariners
District Commander
Your local Coast Guard Office   (800) 368-5647

The free *Local Notice to Mariners* is issued weekly by each Coast Guard District. Intended for small craft owners, it advises you of changes in the status of aids to navigation (buoys, radiobeacons, etc.); chart updates; drawbridge operations; and safety warnings for particular areas. This *Local Notice* often includes temporary changes not included in the Defense Mapping Agency's *Notice to Mariners*. To order a subscription for the *Local Notice*, send a written request to the District Commander of your local Coast Guard office. For referral to the correct address, call the Boating Safety Hotline (800) 368-5647; or (202) 267-0780 in D.C.

* Water Recreation Areas

U.S. Army Corps of Engineers
Directorate of Civil Works
Natural Resources Management Branch
20 Massachusetts Ave., NW
Washington, DC 20314   (202) 272-0247

The Corps has a brochure and map showing the extensive recreational facilities available at U.S. Army Corps of Engineers lakes throughout the country. They offer camp sites, picnic areas, swimming beaches, hiking trails, boating, canoeing, fishing, ice fishing, hunting, and snowmobiling. The Corps also offers safety training classes in water-related sports. To arrange for a speaker to come to your school or to order the brochure entitled *Lakeside Recreation*, write or call the above office.

* Wild Rivers and Other Public Lands

Office of Public Affairs
Bureau of Land Management
U.S. Department of the Interior
18th and C Sts., NW
Washington, DC 20240   (202) 343-5717

The *Recreation Guide to BLM Public Lands* features a map outlining all of the public lands used as recreational areas. Designations on the map include campgrounds, visitors centers, national wild and scenic rivers, national wilderness areas, and national historic and scenic trails. Also included are the states that contain public lands, and state and district offices to contact for additional information. Alaska, Arizona, California, Colorado, Idaho, Montana, Nevada, New Mexico, Oregon, Utah, Washington, and Wyoming are the key states described.

International Travel

* American Experts Overseas Lecture Tour

Office of Program Coordination and Development
United States Information Agency
301 Fourth St., SW, Room 550
Washington, DC 20547   (202) 485-2764

AmParts are experts in a field--usually economics, international affairs, literature, the arts, U.S. political and social processes, sports, science, or technology--sent abroad by USIA to meet with groups or individual professional counterparts. Recruited on the basis of requests of USIA staff in other countries, AmParts often engage in informal lecture/discussions with small groups, grant media interviews, or speak before larger audiences. Those interested in the American Participant program are invited to submit a brief letter indicating times of availability, along with a curriculum vitae and at least two lecture topics with brief talking points. A free brochure on the program is available from this office.

* Animals and Plants Quarantine

APHIS
U.S. Department of Agriculture
Room G-110 Federal Building
6505 Belcrest Rd.
Hyattsville, MD 20782   (301) 436-8413

This office will advise travelers about what agriculture and related products may be brought into the U.S. from foreign countries.

* Arctic and Antarctic Polar Expeditions with Civilians

Ice Operations Division
Office of Navigation Safety and Waterways Services
U.S. Coast Guard
U.S. Department of Transportation
2100 2nd St., SW, Room 1202 A
Washington, DC 20593-0001   (202) 267-1450

The Coast Guard furnishes vessels to other agencies, such as the National Science Foundation, U.S. Geological Survey, and the Navy, to conduct research and ice operations in Arctic and Antarctic waters. The agencies sponsoring the missions select scientists, researchers, students, and in some cases, journalists, photographers, and artists to accompany the mission when space is available. This office is a good starting point for obtaining information on the pertinence of a mission to your field, to be directed to the appropriate agency sponsors, and for information about the data collected during missions.

* Binational Libraries and Cultural Centers Worldwide

Library Programs Division
Bureau of Educational and Cultural Affairs
United States Information Agency
301 Fourth St., SW, Room 314
Washington, DC 20547   (202) 485-2915

USIA maintains or supports 156 libraries and reading rooms in 95 countries, as well as library programs at 111 binational centers in 24 countries. Collections focus on fostering foreign understanding of U.S. people, history, and culture. A bi-weekly bibliography, listing 80-100 titles on international relations and developments in the U.S., is one of many library services provided for the overseas posts, including reference and research assistance.

* Booklets for Travelers

Government Printing Office
Superintendent of Documents
Washington, DC 20402   (202) 783-3238

The Department of State offers several brochures and pamphlets regarding traveling abroad ($1.00 each):

A Safe Trip Abroad. Provides suggestions for avoiding and coping with potential problems and crises abroad.
Tips for Americans Residing Abroad. Includes basic travel information and suggestions, as well as health, insurance, and assistance information of interest to senior citizens traveling abroad.
Your Trip Abroad. Provides basic information on such matters as passport applications, visas, and other documents; obtaining services and help overseas from U.S. consuls; and foreign legal requirements.
Tips for Travelers to the Caribbean.
Tips for Travelers to the People's Republic of China.
Tips for Travelers to Eastern Europe and Yugoslavia.
Tips for Travelers to the USSR.
Tips for Travelers to South Africa.

* Certification for Travel Abroad

Authentications
Foreign Affairs Center
Bureau of Administration
2201 C St., NW, Room 2815
Washington, DC 20520   (202) 647-7735

Several steps are necessary in order to get a document authenticated for a use by a foreign government. For legal papers to do business in a foreign government (such as a power of attorney), the papers must be notarized, signed by the Clerk of Court, and then sent to the Secretary of State for the State seal. This Office authenticates the State seal, verifying that it is a legal document. Foreign governments often require that any legal document, whether personal, educational or business related, be authenticated. This includes birth certificates, marriage licenses, divorce papers, or school transcripts.

* CIA World and Country Maps

National Technical Information Service
U.S. Department of Commerce
5285 Port Royal Road
Springfield, VA 22151   (703) 487-4650

Hundreds of maps generated by the Central Intelligence Agency are sold through NTIS. There are country maps as well as maps of continents are available. smaller geographical areas and city maps such as Moscow and Vicinity; Middle East Area Oilfields and Facilities; Israeli Settlement in the Gaza Strip; South Africa: Industrial Activity and Production; Africa Ethnolinguistic Groups; and street maps for Moscow, Shanghai and many other cities.

* Citizens Arrested Overseas

Citizens Emergency Center
Overseas Citizens Service
Bureau of Consular Affairs
2201 C St., NW, Room 48700
Washington, DC 20520   (202) 647-5225

The Citizens Emergency Center monitors the cases of Americans arrested abroad and acts as a liaison between the prisoner's family and consular officers overseas. A consular officer visits the American as soon as possible, provides information regarding the foreign legal system and a list of attorneys, and offers other assistance such as contacting family or friends. The consular officer's role in arrest cases is one of observation and support, regularly visiting the prisoner and checking his or her welfare, monitoring human rights, and the status of the case. The Center assists in transferring of funds, and when a prisoner's health or life is endangered by inadequate diet or medical care provided by the local prison, dietary food supplements and/or medical care may be arranged through a U.S. Government loan authorized under the Emergency Medical and Dietary Assistance Program.

* Citizens Emergency Center

Overseas Citizens Service
Bureau of Consular Affairs
2201 C St., NW, Room 4800
Washington, DC 20520   (202) 647-5225

This center provides assistance to and protects the welfare of U.S. citizens abroad in the following Ways:

Arrests - See "Citizens Arrested Overseas"

Financial Assistance - Assists Americans overseas who find themselves in financial trouble. They first attempt to locate private sources of funds from family or friends, and then assist with the transfer of funds to the individual. If none can be found, the Center will approve a repatriation loan which will pay for the individual's direct return to the nearest port of entry in the U.S.

Medical Assistance - Assists with handling the problems of Americans who become physically or mentally ill while traveling or living abroad. Locates and notifies family or friends, and transmits private funds. When necessary they will assist in the return of the ill or injured person to the U.S. with appropriate medical escort. Full expenses must be borne by citizen.

Deaths - The consular officer reports the death of a U.S. citizen to the next of kin, and will assist in making arrangements for local burial or for return of the body to the U.S. Cost must be borne by family members.

Welfare/Whereabouts - The Center relays the request for assistance and all pertinent data available on the individual to the U.S. Embassy or consulate responsible for the area where the individual is believed to be traveling or residing, and the consular officer then attempts to locate these individuals. In cases of disasters such as earthquakes, or plane crashes, the Center ascertains the names of U.S. citizens involved and informs their families.

Travel advisories - The Center gives advice to the public and U.S. Foreign Service posts on the advisability of travel to certain countries or areas.

Search and Rescue - The Center monitors the search and rescue efforts outside the U.S., such as attempting to locate missing planes or boats that might be carrying Americans.

* Commercial Library Program Publications List
Foreign Affairs Information Management Center
2201 C St., NW, Room 3239
Department of State
Washington, DC 20520   (202) 647-1062
This list provides a wide-ranging selection of publications useful to commercial reference facilities. It contains annotated bibliographies of directories, buyers' guides, yearbooks, atlases, etc., in general and in special product areas. State manufacturing and industrial directories are included, as are telex directories.

* Cost of Living Overseas
Office of Productivity and Technology
Bureau of Labor Statistics
Department of Labor
200 Constitution Ave., NW, Room S4214
Washington, DC 20212   (202) 523-9291
The quarterly *U.S. Department of State Indexes of Living Costs Abroad, Quarters Allowances, and Hardship Differentials* contains statistics computed by the Allowances Staff of the Department of State for use in establishing allowances to compensate American civilian government employees for costs and hardships related to assignments abroad. This information is also used by many business firms and other private organizations to assist in establishing private compensation systems. Detailed explanations of the methods of compiling the indexes, quarters allowances, and hardship differentials are published in *U.S. Department of State Indexes of Living Costs Abroad and Quarters Allowances: A Technical Description.*

* Country and Territory Info Pamphlets
Superintendent of Documents
Government Printing Office
Washington, DC 20402   (202) 783-3238
Background Notes, a series of short, factual pamphlets about various countries and territories of the world, plus selected international organizations, contain up-to-date information on each country's people, culture, geography, history, government, political conditions, economy, defense, and foreign relations with other countries, including the United States. A reading list provides additional sources of information about the country, and travel notes, maps, and occasional photographs are often included. A complete set can be purchased from the Government Printing Office for $32.00.

* Cruise the Panama Canal
The Panama Canal Commission
2000 L St, NW, Suite 550
Washington, DC 20036-4996   (202) 634-1212

Office of Public Affairs
Panama Canal Commission
APO Miami, FL 34011-5000   (507) 52-3165
Information on cruises of the Panama Canal is available through the above offices. At the Panama Canal you don't have to leave the ship to see the sights. Passengers can watch as their northbound cruise ship enters Pedro Miguel Locks on a northbound transit. In the distance they can see Gaillard Cut where the Canal passes through the Continental Divide. For more information, contact either of the above offices.

* Customs Information for Travelers
Public Information Office
U.S. Customs Service
Department of the Treasury
P.O. Box 7407
Washington, DC 20044   (202) 566-8195
Know Before You Go contains Customs hints for residents returning to the U.S. from abroad. Topics include declaration of articles acquired abroad, Customs exemptions, gifts, dutiable articles and those free of duty, rates of duty, prohibited and restricted articles, and other pointers.

* Customs Rules for Government Personnel:
Civilian and Military
Public Information Office

U.S. Customs Service
Department of the Treasury
P.O. Box 7407
Washington, DC 20044   (202) 566-8195
The free leaflet, *U.S. Customs Highlights for Government Personnel*, provides customs information for civilian employees and military personnel of the U.S. Government when returning to the States with personal and household effects after an extended tour of duty abroad and when returning on leave or TDY. Subjects include customs declarations and limitations, gifts, automobiles, and prohibited and restricted importations.

* Customs Rules for Private Flyers
Smuggling Investigations Division
Office of Enforcement Regulations
U.S. Customs Service
Department of the Treasury
1301 Constitution Ave., NW
Washington, DC 20229   (202) 566-8005
Private, corporate, and charter pilots on business or pleasure flights to and from foreign countries should become acquainted with the booklet, *Customs Rules for Private Flyers*, available from the Public Information Office, U.S. Customs Service, P.O. Box 7407, Washington, D.C. 20044. It sets forth basic Customs requirements, provides a list of airports at which Customs processing may be obtained, and explains overtime charges.

* Customs Tips for Visitors
Information Services Division
Office of Logistics Management
U.S. Customs Service
Department of the Treasury
1301 Constitution Ave., NW
Washington, DC 20229   (202) 566-3962
The free flyer, *Customs Tips for Visitors*, briefly describes the customs regulations for foreign visitors to the United States. Personal exemptions and a list of items that must meet certain requirements are featured. For further information on customs requirements for foreign visitors, the free pamphlet, *Customs Hints for Visitors*, is also helpful in outlining declarations, exemptions, gifts, duty, and prohibited and restricted articles. To obtain a copies of these publications, write to Public Information Office, U.S. Customs Service, P.O. Box 7407, Washington, D.C. 20044.

* Executive-Diplomat Seminars
Office of Public Programs
Department of State
Bureau of Public Affairs
2201 C St., NW, Room 5831
Washington, DC 20520   (202) 647-1433
The State Department holds seminars designed for corporate vice-presidents who do business abroad. These two day seminars, offered twice yearly, begin with a discussion of global foreign policy objectives, and then focus on economic topics and business opportunities. Contact this office for information on scheduling.

* Hostage Taking: Preparation, Avoidance and Survival
Superintendent of Documents
Government Printing Office
Washington, DC 20402   (202) 783-3238
The State Department' Bureau of Diplomatic Security publishes this pamphlet which explains what you can do to make yourself less susceptible to terrorist violence and how to improve your chances of survival should your efforts fail. Information includes personal preparations, security measures, and tips on hostage survival.

* Importing of Articles from Developing Countries
Public Information Office
U.S. Customs Service
Department of the Treasury
P.O. Box 7407
Washington, DC 20044   (202) 566-8195
Generalized System of Preferences (GSP) is a system used by many developed countries to help developing nations improve their financial or economic condition through export trade. It provides for the duty-free importation of a wide range of products from certain countries which would otherwise be subject to customs duty. The free pamphlet, *GSP and the Traveler*, lists popular tourist items eligible for duty-free treatment under GSP and the beneficiary countries.

* Importing Pleasure Boats
Carrier Rulings Branch
Office of Regulations and Rulings
U.S. Customs Service

Department of the Treasury
1301 Constitution Ave., NW, Room 2137
Washington, DC 20229 (202) 566-5706
When a pleasure boat or yacht arrives in the United States, the first landing must be at a Customs port or designated place where Customs service is available. The pamphlet, *Pleasure Boats*, explains the Customs formalities involving pleasure boats to help you plan your importation and reporting requirements, overtime charges, and provides other information relating strictly to pleasure boats. You can get a copy of *Pleasure Boats* from the Public Information Office, U.S. Customs Service, P.O. Box 7407, Washington, D.C. 20044.

* Overseas Citizens Services
Department of State
2201 C St., NW, Room 4800
Washington, DC 20520 (202) 647-3816
Overseas Citizens Services is responsible for administering laws, formulating regulations, and implementing policies relating to the broad range of consular services provided to U.S. citizens abroad. These services include providing assistance to and protecting the welfare of U.S. citizens abroad, overseeing the payment of Federal benefits overseas, documenting U.S. citizens born abroad, and making determinations concerning acquisition and nationality abroad. Overseas Citizens Services serves as a liaison between concerned family members, friends, and members of Congress in the United States and consular posts and citizens abroad.

* Overseas Security Advisory Council
Bureau of Diplomatic Security
Department of State
2201 C St., NW
Washington, DC 20520 (202) 647-2762
Overseas Security Advisory Council was established to promote security for American business interests abroad. In 1987, OSAC was extended overseas through the establishment of "mini-councils" in some of the world's most important business centers. Business representatives in these areas meet locally with Diplomatic Security Officers to promote security for Americans and American interests. Besides regular meetings to plan and exchange information, OSAC also produced a number of well-received publications, such as Security Guidelines for American Families Living Abroad and distributed the Diplomatic Security-produced children's security video, Are You A-OK. OSAC also sends threat advisories and general security information to more than 700 companies, and is now providing this information through a computer information database.

* Panama Canal Tours
Orientation Services
The Office of Public Affairs
c/o Panama Canal Commission
APO Miami 34011-5000 (507) 52-3187
The Canal Guide Service, operated by the Panama Canal Commission, offers free tours of the Panama Canal to the public. Tours are given seven days a week from 9:00 a.m. to 5:00 p.m. The tour takes less than an hour and include a slight briefing, a topographical model of the Canal to view, and a film. Visitors are welcome at the Miraflores Locks on the Pacific side of the Isthmus where a pavilion provides a vantage point for viewing transiting ships. Interested members of the public should call two days in advance to make a reservation. Another attraction is the high doomed ceiling, the dramatic murals, and the marble columns and floor make the rotunda the main attraction of the Administration Building at Balboa Heights. The murals depict the digging of Gaillard Cut at Gold Hill, the erection of a lock gate, and the construction of the Gatun Dam spillway and Miraflores Locks. For more information, contact this office. The history of the Panama Railroad has been closely linked with that of the Panama Canal since long before the waterway was opened to traffic. The first railroad built through the tropical jungles of the New World served for almost 60 years as the only means of transportation across the narrow Isthmus of Panama. Before the Canal was opened in 1914, the Panama Railroad was reported to have the heaviest traffic per mile of all the railroads in the world. The railroad makes five trips per day across the Isthmus, Monday through Friday, and three trips per day on Saturday and Sunday. The train takes an hour and a half to cross the Isthmus. For more information, contact this office.

* Passport Agent's Manual
Passport Services
Bureau of Consular Affairs
Department of State
2201 C St., NW, Room 5813
Washington, DC 20520 (202) 647-6633
The material in this manual is furnished for the passport agent's guidance and is intended to cover the most frequently encountered situations. It has information on evidence of citizenship, names allowed on passports, evidence of identity, and application procedures. A list of travel-related forms and brochures is also included.

* Passport Information

Passport Services
Bureau of Consular Affairs
Department of State
2201 C St., NW, Room 5813
Washington, DC 20520 (202) 326-6020
Passport Services provides a recorded message at (202) 647-0518 which explains the documents you need and application process for obtaining a passport, as well as reporting the loss or theft of your passport. It also explains how you can obtain a copy of the report of a birth or death of a U.S. citizen abroad. The message will direct you to the proper agencies for information regarding naturalization, travel advisories, customs regulations, and shots required by various countries.

* Passport Offices Throughout America

You may apply for a passport at any passport agency and at many Clerks of Court Offices or Post Offices designated to accept passport applications. The regional offices are as follows:

Boston
John F. Kennedy Building, Government Center, Room E123, Boston, MA 02203/(617) 935-3950.

Chicago
Kluczynski Office Building, 230 S. Dearborn St., Room 380, Chicago, IL 60604/(312) 353-7164.

Honolulu
New Federal Building, 300 Ala Moana Blvd., Room C-106, P.O. Box 50185, Honolulu, HI 96850/(808) 54-1922.

Houston
One Allen Center, 500 Dallas St., Houston, TX 77002/(713) 526-7832.

Los Angeles
Federal Building, 11000 Wilshire Blvd., Los Angeles, CA 92061/(213) 793-7080.

Miami
Federal Office Building, 51 Southwest 1st Ave., Room 1616, Miami, FL 33130/(305) 350-7348.

New Orleans
701 Loyal Ave., Postal Services Bldg., T-12005, New Orleans, LA 70113/(504) 682-2335.

New York
Rockefeller Center, International Bldg., 630 5th Ave., Room 270, New York, NY 10020/(212) 662-5430

Philadelphia
Federal Building, 600 Arch St., Room 4426, Philadelphia, PA 19106/(215) 660-2501.

San Francisco
525 Market St., Room 200, San Francisco, CA 94105/(415) 454-7980.

Seattle
Federal Building, 915 2nd Ave., Room 906, Seattle, WA 98174/(206) 399-7963.

Stamford
One Landmark Square, Broad and Atlantic Sts., Stamford, CT 06901/(2030 325-1803.

Washington, D.C.
Room G62, 1425 K St., NW, Washington, DC 20524/(202) 326-6020.

* Pet and Wildlife Importation
Public Information Office
U.S. Customs Service
Department of the Treasury
P.O. Box 7407
Washington, DC 20044 (202) 566-8195
The Public Health Service, U.S. Department of Agriculture, U.S. Fish and Wildlife Service, and the U.S. Department of the Treasury have combined efforts to describe the regulations on the importing of pets and wildlife into the United States. Pets, particularly dogs, cats, and turtles, brought into this country must be examined for possible evidence of disease that can be transmitted to humans. Certain animals are prohibited from entry that have been exposed to foot and mouth disease. Endangered species, both plant and animal, may not be imported without special permits. *Pets, Wildlife* explains these regulations in further detail.

* Returning U.S. Residents and Customs
Public Information Office

Vacations and Business Travel

U.S. Customs Service
Department of the Treasury
P.O. Box 7407
Washington, DC 20044 (202) 566-8195

Pocket Hints is a brief outline of customs responsibilities of returning residents. Duty free exemptions, restricted or prohibited articles, and customs declarations are summarized.

* Security Guidelines for American Enterprises

Bureau of Diplomatic Security
Overseas Security Advisory Council
Department of State, SA-10
Washington, DC 20520 (202) 647-2762

This publication provides security guidelines for American private sector and personnel abroad. This is the third OSAC publication printed and distributed by the State Department. The implementation of security guidelines contained in this publication could reduce the vulnerability of American private sector enterprises abroad to criminal or terrorist acts, and emphasize site selection and operational security. Previous publications include Crisis Management Guidelines and Security Guidelines for American Families Living Abroad.

* Terrorism and Diplomatic Security

Public Information
Bureau of Diplomatic Security
Department of State
2121 Virginia Ave., NW
Washington, DC 20520 (202) 647-2762

The Bureau of Diplomatic Security was created in 1985 in an effort to deal with terrorist attacks against overseas missions. All but the smallest of American overseas missions have a Regional Security Officer (RSO) on staff to manage security and keep employees safe on the job and at home. The bureau is responsible for the physical security of the mission, as well as construction and information security. Diplomatic Security Analysts study and analyze intelligence information from a variety of sources, including specific terrorist groups to better understand their tactics and anticipate their actions. They have also developed public service announcements and related security awareness materials for the American tourist, business traveler, and Foreign Service family. DS has produced educational videotapes and instructional materials that teach the basics of security to Americans living and working abroad. Other videos focus on professional conduct in foreign cultures. The pamphlet, Countering Terrorism, lists several suggestions for security measures for your home, family, and business, as well as what to do in the event of a kidnapping.

* Travel Advisories on Civil Unrest Around-the-World

Citizens Emergency Center
Overseas Citizens Services
Department of State
2201 C St., NW, Room 4800
Washington, DC 20520 (202) 647-5225

CEC is responsible for issuing travel advisories when events abroad are likely to adversely affect traveling Americans. Travel advisories often concern international conflict, civil unrest within individual countries, natural disasters, or disease outbreaks. Many of the advisories refer to temporary conditions and are cancelled when the problem no longer poses a threat to travelers.

* Travel Tips for Senior Citizens

Overseas Citizens Services
Department of State
2201 C St., NW, Room 4800
Washington, DC 20520 (202) 647-5226

This publication includes information on insurance, medication, travel advisories, and passports. They include a list of relevant publications, some practical travel tips, as well as the assistance you can expect from U.S. Embassies and consulates.

* Vessel Owners and Masters: Customs Rules

Public Information Office
U.S. Customs Service

Department of the Treasury
P.O. Box 7407
Washington, DC 20044 (202) 566-8195

Masters or vessel owners may incur penalties for violations of United States Customs laws, including violations committed by members of their crews. The brochure, *Notice to Masters of Vessels*, notifies the masters of proper precautions in the areas of arrival and entry, and merchandise in order to avoid penalties for violations.

* Visa Information for U.S. Citizens Wishing to Travel to Foreign Countries

Overseas Citizens Services
Department of State
2201 C St., NW, Room 4800
Washington, DC 20520 (202) 647-5225

This office can provide you with visa requirements for U.S. citizens wishing to travel to foreign countries. They stress that this information is subject to change and that the definitive information regarding visas can come only from the foreign embassies. This taped message lists all the countries, their current visa requirements, travel advisories for the countries, as well as the embassies' phone numbers.

* Visiting and Living Abroad

Office of Citizens Consular Services
Bureau of Consular Affairs
Department of State
2201 C St., NW, Room 4817
Washington, DC 20520 (202) 647-9018

This office provides services to U.S. citizens abroad in a variety of ways:

Acquisition and Loss of Citizenship: Determination of an individual's citizenship status is a function of the office if the person is not in the United States.

Passport and Registration Services Abroad: Issues passports, as well as Cards of Identity and Registration as proof of U.S. citizenship. This office officially records a person's U.S. citizenship and/or makes his/her residence a matter of record.

Consular Report of Birth: This official record is considered a basic citizenship document setting forth detailed information regarding the facts of birth and parentage, as basis for child's claim to citizenship.

Child Custody Disputes: Helps parents locate children abroad, monitors their welfare upon request, and provides general information about child custody laws and procedures.

Federal Benefits: Assists in processing claims and distributing checks.

International Adoption: Provides general information on adoptions, makes inquiries regarding status of cases, and assists in clarifying documentary requirements.

Judicial Services: Provides advice on the assistance which consular officers can render to U.S. citizens overseas engaged in private legal suits and maintains lists of attorneys. They also administer notarial and authentication functions.

Estates and Property Claims: Consular Officer has statutory responsibility for the personal estates of U.S. citizens who die abroad if the deceased has no legal representative in the country where the death occurred. The Office gives general information regarding property claims and provides a list of attorneys.

Selective Service Registration: Registers people for selective service.

Shipping and Seamen: This office has statutory responsibility to protect the interests of American seamen, vessels, and shipping firms abroad.

Voting: Provides non-partisan voting information and assists in requesting absentee ballots.

State Travel Hotlines

If you are interested in travel related industries, planning a dramatic coast-to-coast sightseeing trip, or scouting out possible areas for relocation, your efforts can be made somewhat easier with the help of state offices of tourism. These offices will provide you with maps, brochures, and other valuable information. If you are planning to visit a particular city--say Sioux Falls--someone in the South Dakota state tourist office might send you a booklet of fascinating historical attractions in the areas. If you want to know where to find the hotels, motels or restaurants, cafes, diners, movie theaters, supermarkets, drug stores or churches, this is the place to start.

If you are interested in a specific activity, not just travel advice and information on tourist attractions, these offices can help you as well. Say you want to pan for gold or visit an authentic western ghost town. Check with the state tourism office, and not you can get information on these sites, but maybe also the name of a good book to prepare you for your visit, or the name of a special guide or tour once you are in the area.

Other information from state tourism offices might include highway conditions, weather advice, local hotel/motel rates, and the best places to eat. In general, each state will provide information packages containing a travel guide, a calendar of events, state maps, and brochures from private, state, and regional tourist attractions.

State Travel and Tourism Hotlines

Alabama
(800) 832-5510 (205) 261-4169

Alaska
(907) 465-2010

Arizona
(602) 255-3618 (602) 542-3618

Arkansas
(501) 682-1219

California
(916) 322-1396

Colorado
(303) 866-2205

Connecticut
(800) 243-1685 (203) 566-3385

Delaware
(800) 441-8846 (302) 736-4254

District of Columbia
(202) 789-7000

Florida
(904) 488-5606

Georgia
(404) 656-3590

Hawaii
(808) 923-1811 (808) 548-2540

Idaho
(800) 635-7820 (208) 334-2470

Illinois
(800) 637-8560 (217) 782-7139

Indiana
(317) 232-8870

Iowa
(515) 281-3100

Kansas
(913) 296-2009

Kentucky
(502) 564-4930

Louisiana
(800) 23-GUMBO (504) 242-8119

Maine
(207) 289-2423

Maryland
(800) 381-1750 extension 250 (301) 333-6611

Massachusetts
(617) 727-3201

Michigan
(517) 373-0670

Minnesota
(612) 296-5029

Mississippi
(800) 647-2290 (601) 354-7011

Missouri
(314) 751-4133

Montana
(406) 449-2654 (406) 444-2654

Nebraska
(402) 471-3111

Nevada
(702) 885-4322

New Hampshire
(603) 271-2665

New Jersey
(609) 292-2470

New Mexico
(800) 545-2040 (505) 827-0291

New York
(212) 827-6100

North Carolina
(919) 733-4171

North Dakota
(800) 437-2077 (701) 224-2525

Ohio
(614) 466-8844

Vacations and Business Travel

Oklahoma
(405) 521-2406

Oregon
(800) 547-7842 (503) 378-6309

Pennsylvania
(717) 787-5453

Rhode Island
(800) 556-2484 (401) 277-2601

South Carolina
(803) 734-0127

South Dakota
(800) 843-1930 (605) 773-3301

Tennessee
(615) 741-2158

Texas
(512) 320-9692

Utah
(801) 533-5681 (801) 538-1030

Vermont
(802) 828-3236

Virginia
(804) 786-2051

Washington
(206) 753-5600

West Virginia
(800) 624-9110 (304) 348-2286

Wisconsin
(608) 266-2147

Wyoming
(800) 443-2784 (307) 777-7777

Domestic Tourism and Trends

* Airline Passenger Safety
Community and Consumer Liaison Division
Office of Public Affairs
Federal Aviation Administration
Department of Transportation
800 Independence Ave., SW
Washington, DC 20591   (202) 267-3481
Airline passengers who have inquiries or complaints regarding airplane safety should contact this office.

* Air Travelers' Rights and Complaints
Consumer Affairs Division
Intergovernmental and Consumer Affairs
Governmental Affairs
Office of the Secretary of Transportation
U.S. Department of Transportation
400 7th Street, SW
Washington, DC 20590   (202) 366-2220
If your problem cannot be resolved directly with the airline, contact this office for information on air travelers' rights and for assistance in resolving problems with airlines and charter flights. Complaints about delayed or canceled flights, reservations, lost baggage, smoking, refunds, and overbooking can also be handled here.

* AMTRAK Passenger Services
AMTRAK
60 Massachusetts Ave., N.E.
Washington, D.C. 20002   202-906-2733
The Passenger Services Department handles all of the onboard service aspects of AMTRAK, including all of its employees across the country.

* AMTRAK Customer Relations
AMTRAK
Customer Relations
60 Massachusetts Ave. N.E.
Washington, D.C. 20002   292-906-2121
You may call or write the Customer Relations Office concerning any comments or problems with AMTRAK service. Please include your ticket receipt and dates of travel to help with the resolution of your problem.

* Auto Safety Hotline
Office of Defects Investigation (NEF-10)
National Highway Traffic Safety Administration
U.S. Department of Transportation
400 7th Street, SW, Room 5326
Washington, DC 20590   (202) 366-0123 (800) 424-9393
This toll-free hotline is accessible in all 50 states, Puerto Rico, and the Virgin Islands. Consumers may call to report automobile safety problems or to request information on recalls, defects, investigations, child safety seats, tires, drunk driving, crash test results, seat belts, air bags, odometer tampering, and other related topics. Staff will also make referrals to state and other agencies. Also ask about the New Car Assessment Program (NCAP), which provides comparable data on the frontal crashworthiness of selected new vehicles.

* Consumer Rights on Airlines
Government Printing Office
Superintendent of Documents
Washington DC 20402   (202) 783-3238
Fly Rights is an easy-to-read booklet that explains the rights and responsibilities of air travellers. It is available at nominal cost from the GPO.

* Handicapped Visitors
Office of Research
United States Travel and Tourism Administration
Department of Commerce
114th St. and Constitution Ave., NW
Room 1516
Washington DC 20230   (202) 377-4028
The United States Welcomes Handicapped Visitors is a publication designed to give advice and guidance to handicapped visitors wishing to travel to and within the United States. It explains Federal regulations and policies of the various modes of transportation, as well as offering information regarding destinations, resources, publications, organizations, and some practical advice. Contact this office for your free copy.

* Multilingual Receptionists
United States Travel and Tourism Administration
Department of Commerce
14th St. and Constitution Ave., NW
Room 1865
Washington, DC 20230   (202) 377-0137
To ensure that international visitors enter the U.S. with minimal difficulty, USTTA sponsors a uniformed corps of multilingual receptionists at 12 gateway airports who provide interpreter and allied services required for U.S. entry formalities. International gateways offering this service include New York (Kennedy); Seattle; San Juan; Philadelphia; Miami; Boston; Los Angeles; Honolulu; Bangor; Atlanta; New Orleans and Baltimore-Washington International.

* Rail Tickets or Travel Information
AMTRAK
60 Massachusetts Ave., N.E.
Washington, D.C. 20002   1-800-USA-RAIL
For information regarding tickets or travel on AMTRAK, call 1-800-USA-RAIL. AMTRAK also publishes a travel planner which provides travel tips and services, as well as a listing AMTRAK's vacation packages.

* Tourism in the U.S.A.
United States Travel and Tourism Administration
Department of Commerce
14th St. and Constitution Ave. NW
Room 1865
Washington, DC 20230   (202) 377-0137
Tourism USA is a book produced as an aid to communities interested in initiating or developing tourism as a part of their economic development plan, and has been revised and expanded to also include international marketing and visitor services for special populations. Statistical data has been revised to reflect the most current facts available. This publication covers guidelines for tourism development, including appraising tourism potential, planning for tourism, assessing product and market, marketing tourism, visitor services, and sources of assistance.

* Tourism Offices
United States Travel and Tourism Administration
Department of Commerce
14th St. and Constitution Ave., NW
Room 1865
Washington, DC 20230   (202) 377-0140
The following is a complete listing of addresses and phone numbers for all state and territorial tourism offices. Contact the office listed above for your free copy.

* Tourism Revenue
Office for Tourism Marketing
United States Travel and Tourism Administration
Department of Commerce
14th St. And Constitution Ave. NW
Room 1862
Washington, DC 20230   (202) 377-4752
This office's goal is to increase the U.S. share of international visitors. This is accomplished through several means, one of which is cooperative marketing and advertising overseas. This office often puts together special advertising sections designed for foreign countries. A free publication, Marketing U.S. Tourism Abroad: A Manual of Cooperative Marketing Programs In USTTA Markets, lists cooperative advertising opportunities, travel shows, seminars, and travel missions. The Manual includes costs, formats, and deadlines. This Office also assists State and local travel organizations, and private industry around issues such as marketing tourism and visitor services.

* Travel Industry Market Research
Office of Research
United States Travel and Tourism Administration

Vacations and Business Travel

Department of Commerce
14th St. and Constitution Ave., NW
Room 1516
Washington, DC 20230   (202) 377-4028

USTTA gathers, analyzes and published international travel statistics, which define the direction and impact of foreign trends, determine foreign market potential, and guide marketing efforts. USTTA's *Inflight Survey* gathers essential marketing information on international travelers to and within the United States, as well as Americans traveling abroad. Conducted with public and private sector tourism organizations and 35 major international air carriers, the *Survey* provides data on travel patterns and preference of foreign visitors. The *Bibliography of Selected USTTA Research Publications & Marketing Manuals* is available at no charge, and includes a description and ordering information for the following USTTA publications:

Recap of International Travel To and From the United States. Summarizes annual developments in inbound/outbound tourism (free).

Summary and Analysis of International Travel to the United States. Provides monthly foreign visitor arrival statistics by region and for 90 different countries. Tables include a variety of travel data (price varies depending on year).
Outlook for International Travel To and From the United States. Provides one-year forecast of international travel to/from the U.S. (free).
Canadian Travel to the United States: 1988. Details Canadian tourism to the U.S. (free).

Impact of Foreign Visitors' Spending on State Economies 1985-1986. ($50.00)
In-Flight Survey of International Air Travelers. Overseas and Mexican Visitors to the United States and (2) U.S. Travelers to Mexico and Overseas Countries. Provides survey data on travel characteristics and spending patterns of international air travelers to and from the U.S. Free inbound and outbound profile sheets are available, along with an informational brochure and order form (prices range from $100 to $750).

Analysis of International Air Travel To and From the United States on U.S./Foreign Flag Carriers (free).

Pleasure Travel Markets to North America. The studies of travel behavior provide information on past travel characteristics, trip planning information, attitudes toward overseas travel, the image of the U.S., and travel market segments. An information packet and free *Highlights* publication for each years study is available (prices range from $30 to $525).

Sectorial Analyses Reports on International Travel. Reports commissioned on four key sectors of the travel industry: Lodging; Air Travel; Inter-City Bus; and Rental Car. The analyses look at the economic impact of international travel on each sector of the U.S. economy, as well as at other issues ($10.00 for each report).
USTTA Country Travel Market Surveys. Consumer Surveys of Eight Individual Country Markets. Surveys of potential international travelers in the United Kingdom, Germany, France, Japan, Australia, Italy, Netherlands, and Mexico ($14.95 for each report).

Marketing Tourism Abroad: USTTA's International Cooperative Marketing Manual. Provides information concerning the cooperative marketing programs offered by USTTA (free).

Developing A U.S. Regional Approach for Promoting Travel from Foreign Markets. Provides guidelines for developing regional organizational structures for planning and operating international tourism promotional programs ($15.00).
The United States Welcomes Handicapped Visitors- Designed to give advice and guidance to handicapped visitors wishing to travel to and within the United States (free).

* Traveling to the United States

Tourism Marketing
United States Travel and Tourism Administration
Department of Commerce
14th St. and Constitution Ave., NW
Washington, DC 20230   (202) 377-4752

Headquartered in Washington, D.C., USTTA has six regional tourism offices in Toronto, Mexico City, Tokyo, London, Paris, and Frankfurt. These offices deal with foreign travel agents and tour operators and facilitate familiarization programs for foreign travel writers and tour operators seeking information on American travel destinations.

Investments and Financial Services
General Sources

* See also Experts Chapter
* See also Information on People, Companies, and Mailing Lists Chapter

This section contains more information about those companies which offer investments than with investments themselves. More information about specific investments can be found in Information on People, Companies and Mailing Lists Chapter as well as the Experts Chapter. A great starting place for any information is the Consumer Information Hotline in this chapter's Banking section. Elsewhere in this chapter are roadmaps for numerous other questions about financial institutions such as the viability of your savings and loan or guides to establishing a credit union. You'll find the appropriate offices which can help you with such nightmares as lost government bonds or stolen government checks. And, what about that $20 bill that barely survived getting washed with your pants; probably you can redeem the damaged money by sending it to the federal office identified in the Money section.

* Credit Card and Computer Fraud

Fraud Division
Office of Investigations
U.S. Secret Service
Department of the Treasury
1800 G St., NW
Washington, DC 20223   (202) 535-5850

The fraudulent use of credit and debit cards is a federal violation. Investigations are conducted by the Secret Service, including stolen or lost credit cards, the misuse of credit card account numbers, automated teller machine fraud, telephone fraud involving long distance calls, and other types of access device fraud. Computer fraud is a recent concern of the Secret Service. New law enforcement techniques are being pioneered in an effort to identify computer criminals.

* Credit Card Collections

Office of the Assistant Commissioner Federal Finance
Financial Management Service
U.S. Department of the Treasury
401 14th St., SW
Washington, DC 20227   (202) 287-0719

Under the Credit Card Collection Network, Federal agencies are able to accept MasterCard and VISA from the public for payments of sales, services, fees, fines, and certain types of debts. By 1991, the annual volume via credit cards is expected to reach $6.5 billion.

* Direct Deposit of Federal Payments

Office of the Assistant Commissioner Field Operations
Financial Management Service
U.S. Department of the Treasury
401 14th St., SW
Washington, DC 20227   (202) 287-0311

This system electronically deposits Federal payments into the beneficiary's checking or savings account. It does away with the costs associated with checks, reducing the cost to 4 cents versus 30 cents for check processing.

* Electronic Benefit Services

Office of the Assistant Commissioner Federal Finance
Financial Management Service
U.S. Department of the Treasury
401 14th St., SW
Washington, DC 20227   (202) 287-0719

The Financial Management Service is developing a coordinated government-wide plan to electronically deliver benefits to recipients, such as Social Security, welfare payments, disability payments, through automated teller machines and point-of-sale terminals. The recipient will not need to have an account with the bank that operates the ATM or point-of-sale terminal.

* Electronic Data Interchange

Office of the Assistant Commissioner Field Operations
Financial Management Service
U.S. Department of the Treasury
401 14th St., SW
Washington, DC 20227   (202) 287-0311

The Financial Management Service is establishing an electronic funds transfer system, which would fully automate purchase, delivery, and payment cycles with agencies and businesses. As the Federal agencies expand, the number of automated trading partnerships would increase, and reductions in paperwork and delays in processing should significantly decrease.

* Electronic Federal Tax Deposit System

Office of the Assistant Commissioner Federal Finance
Financial Management Service
U.S. Department of the Treasury
401 14th St., SW
Washington, DC 20227   (202) 287-0719

Plans have been initiated by FMS for the design, development, and implementation of a new electronic-oriented system to replace the outmoded, paper-based, error-prone Federal Tax Deposit System. Employers would use this system to remit withholding and other payroll payments to the government.

* Federal Reserve System Resource Materials

Publication Services
MS-138, Board of Governors
Federal Reserve System
Washington, DC 20551   (202) 452-3244

The free guide, *Public Information Materials of the Federal Reserve System*, describes publications and audiovisual materials available from the Federal Reserve System. It lists materials appropriate for students, consumer groups, economists, bankers, and the general public. Copies of the booklet may be obtained from any Federal Reserve Bank or from the office above.

* Fedwire Deposit System

Office of the Assistant Commissioner Federal Finance
Financial Management Service
U.S. Department of the Treasury
401 14th St., SW
Washington, DC 20227   (202) 287-0719

This system electronically processes 200,000 transactions and $100 billion in receipts annually, providing same-day information to Treasury and the agencies about these deposits. Continuous access to the system is available through terminals linked to the computer.

* Thrift Institutions Supervision

Office of Thrift Supervision
U.S. Department of the Treasury
1700 G St., NW
Washington, DC 20552   (202) 906-6677

OTS is the regulatory successor to the Federal Home Loan Bank Board. It oversees the supervision of savings institutions by regulatory staff in its district offices. Regulations, directives, and policies are developed for the safe and sound operation of savings institutions and their compliance with federal law and regulations.

Banking

* Automated Clearinghouse Returns Compliance

Office of the Assistant Commissioner Field Operations
Financial Management Service
U.S. Department of the Treasury
401 14th St., SW
Washington, DC 20227   (202) 287-0311

The Automated Clearinghouse program was developed to assure the return of Direct Deposit funds if they cannot be properly posted to the accounts of recipients by financial institutions. This could involve the funds of either the Federal Government and its agencies or the public, depending on the Direct Deposit program being used.

* Bank Customer and Financial Industry Affairs

Customer and Industry Affairs
Comptroller of the Currency
U.S. Department of the Treasury
490 L'Enfant Plaza East, SW
Washington, DC 20219   (202) 287-4169

Consumer banking groups and other industries involved in the financial market are assisted by this office. It acts as a liaison as well as a provider of technical expertise in an effort to inform these groups of OCC policies and to foster a working relationship.

* Bank Education Programs

Consumer Activities
Bank Supervision
Comptroller of the Currency
U.S. Department of the Treasury
490 L'Enfant Plaza East, SW
Washington, DC 20219   (202) 287-4265

This office coordinates educational activities with banks, trade associations within the banking industry, and local consumer groups. Training professionals address issues relevant to the banking industry and OCC guidelines and assist in the development of compliance programs.

* Bank Examiners District Offices

Legislative and Public Affairs
Comptroller of the Currency
U.S. Department of the Treasury
490 L'Enfant Plaza East, SW
Washington, DC 20219   (202) 447-1820

Northeastern District: 1114 Avenue of the Americas, Suite 3900, New York, NY 10036; (212) 819-9860

Southeastern: 245 Peachtree Center Ave., Marquis One Tower, Suite 600, Atlanta, GA 30303; (404) 659-8855

Central: 440 S. LaSalle St., One Financial Place, Suite 2700, Chicago, IL 60605; (312) 663-8000

Midwestern: 2345 Grand Ave., Suite 700, Kansas City, MO 64108; 816-556-1800

Southwestern: 1600 Lincoln Plaza, 500 N. Akard, Dallas, TX 75201-3394; (214) 720-0656

Western: 50 Fremont St., Suite 3900, San Francisco, CA 94105; (415) 545-5900

* Bank Holding Companies

Division of Bank Supervision and Regulation
Federal Reserve System
Room 3172 , MS-174
20th St. & Constitution Ave., NW
Washington, DC 20551   (202) 452-2638

Bank holding companies must register with and report to the Federal Reserve System. A registered bank holding company must obtain the approval of the Board of Governors before acquiring more than 5% of the shares of either additional banks or permissible nonbanking companies. For more information on bank holding companies, contact this office.

* Banking Industry Research

Division of Research and Statistics
Federal Deposit Insurance Corporation
550 17th St., NW, Room 2024I
Washington, DC 20429   (202) 898-3741

The FDIC continually researches and monitors trends in the economy and banking industry. Existing and proposed legislation is studied, as are banking reforms and the effect of interest and inflation rates. The research staff recently completed "Mandate for Change: Restructuring the Banking Industry", a paperback book that examines the history of banking power, the changing marketplace, and the powers available to banks. For a copy of this book, or for a list of FDIC research papers by titles and authors, contact this office.

* Banking Law Library

Federal Reserve System
Room B1066
20th St. & Constitution Ave. NW
Washington, DC 20551   (202) 452-3284

For information on specific banking laws, contact the FRS Banking Law Library.

* Bank Liquidation

Division of Liquidation
Federal Deposit Insurance Corporation
1776 F St., NW, 8th Floor
Washington, DC 20429   (202) 898-7371

This office oversees the liquidation of failed banks which are insured by the FDIC, and cases are documented and maintained on file. For more information on accessing these files, contact this office.

* Bank Mergers

Division of Bank Supervision and Regulation
Federal Reserve System
Room 3172, MS-174
20th St. & Constitution Ave., NW
Washington, DC 20551   (202) 452-2638

The Federal Reserve Board must give prior approval to all proposed bank mergers between insured state-chartered member banks. Contact this office for more information on bank mergers.

* Banks in Developing Countries

Deputy Assistant Secretary for Developing Nations
Office of the Assistant Secretary of the Treasury
  for International Affairs
U.S. Department of the Treasury
1500 Pennsylvania Ave., NW, Room 3221
Washington, DC 20220   (202) 566-8243

This office assists in the development and operation of multinational banks in developing countries. These include the World Bank, Inter-American Development Bank, Asian Development Bank, and the African Development Bank.

* Bank Supervision and Regulation

Federal Reserve System
20th St. & Constitution Ave., NW
Washington, DC 20551   (202) 452-2773

The Federal Reserve Board supervises and regulates member banks and holding companies. Under the Depository Institutions Deregulation and Monetary Control Act of 1980, the FRS sets reserve requirements for and provides services to all U.S. depository institutions, not to just national banks and state-chartered member banks. The Board authorizes the acquisition of banks and closely related nonbanking activities by bank holding companies and other changes of control and mergers of banks and bank holding companies. Its responsibilities extend to many foreign activities of U.S. banking institutions and to foreign banking organizations operating in this country.

* Board of Governors

Federal Reserve System
20th St. & Constitution Ave., NW
Washington, DC 20551   (202) 452-2773

The responsibilities of the Board of Governors include supervising state member banks and all bank holding companies, overseeing Reserve Bank activities, writing consumer credit regulations, approving changes in the discount rate, setting reserve requirements, and establishing margin requirements. The seven members of the Board are appointed for 14-year terms by the U.S. President with the advice and consent of the Senate.

* Call Reports

Financial Disclosure Group
Federal Deposit Insurance Corporation
550 17th St., NW, Room F-518
Washington, DC 20429   1-800-843-1669

Prepared quarterly by all FDIC-insured banks and mutual savings banks, Report of Condition and Income Statements of Banks, or Call Reports, include balance sheets, income statements, and supporting statements. Banks can call the toll free number listed above for assistance in filling out Call Reports. When requesting a previously filed call report (currently available from March 1984 to June 1989), include the name of the bank and the quarter desired. Send requests to this office.

* Community Reinvestment

Fair Lending Analyst
Office of Consumer Affairs
Federal Deposit Insurance Corporation
550 17th St., NW, Room F-130
Washington, DC 20429   (202) 898-3535

The Community Reinvestment Act of 1977 empowers the FDIC to monitor FDIC-insured, state-chartered banks to make sure that the banks are meeting the credit needs of the communities they serve, including low- and middle-income areas. Questions regarding community reinvestment should be directed to the nearest FDIC regional office or to the Fair Lending Analyst at the above office.

* Compliance Information

Office of Consumer Affairs
Federal Deposit Insurance Corporation
550 17th St., NW, Room F-130
Washington, DC 20429   (202) 898-3535

For information regarding FDIC-insured, state-chartered banks complying with consumer laws and the Truth-in-Lending Act, contact any FDIC-insured bank, FDIC regional office, or the office above.

* Consumer Information

Office of Consumer Affairs
Federal Deposit Insurance Corporation
550 17th St., NW, Room F-130
Washington, DC 20429   (202) 898-3535,(800) 424-5488

This office answers questions and addresses complaints regarding FDIC-insured banks. A computerized system helps to track complaints from their initial filing to their resolution. A follow-up complaint satisfaction survey is also conducted periodically. Banking questions may be directed to the nearest regional FDIC office, or call the FDIC's toll-free customer service hotline between 9 a.m. and 4 p.m. EST, Monday through Friday.

* Comptroller of the Currency Publications

Information Office
Comptroller of the Currency
U.S. Department of the Treasury
490 L'Enfant Plaza East, SW
Washington, DC 20219   (202) 447-1800

Comptroller of the Currency
U.S. Department of the Treasury
P.O. Box 70004
Chicago, IL 60673-0004

The Comptroller of the Currency's Information Office requires that all requests for a publications listing or other information be in writing to the Washington address above. The *Banking Circulars* and *Bulletins* and the free publications must be ordered from the Washington address. All other manuals may be ordered directly from the Chicago address. Selected publications include the following:

Comptroller's Manual for Corporate Activities. This book makes available, in one place, OCC policies and procedures for processing applications for forming a new national bank. The manual can also be used by other institutions entering the national banking system, and by existing national banks expanding and restructuring. ($90.00)

Comptroller's Manual for National Banks. This looseleaf legal reference contains laws applicable to national banks with sections dealing with regulations and interpretive rulings issued by the OCC. ($90.00)

Comptroller's Manual for Consumer Examinations. This looseleaf publication is intended to assist the examiner in understanding consumer laws and regulations pertinent to national bank examinations. Examinations procedures are also

included. ($90.00)

Comptroller's Handbook for National Bank Examiners. Policies and procedures for the commercial examination of national banks are included in this looseleaf publication. ($90.00)

Comptroller's Handbook for National Trust Examiners. Policies and procedures are outlined for the examination of fiduciary activities of national banks. The handbook also assists the examiner in the preparation of examination reports of national bank trust departments, subsidiaries, and affiliates of national banks and their holding companies engaging in fiduciary activities. ($90.00)

Comptroller's Handbook for Compliance. For compliance examinations, this handbook is intended for use by examiners as a supervisory tool in performing compliance examinations and by bankers as a self-assessment tool for analyzing bank compliance systems. ($25.00)

Fair Housing Home Loan Data System. This booklet is published for mortgage lending departments and officials of national banks, containing the final regulation for the system, instruction forms, and examples. ($1.50)

The Director's Book. Provides guidance to directors of national banks, outlining the responsibilities of the board, highlighting areas of particular concern, and addressing in broad terms the duties and liabilities of the individual director. ($2.00)

Banking Bulletins and Circulars. Circulars provide information of continuing concern to national banks regarding OCC or OCC supported policies and guidelines. Bulletins inform readers of pending regulation changes and other general information. ($100.00 each)

Microcomputer Applications for Consumer Activities. A guide to calculating Annual Percentage Rates. The package includes instructions and a 5 1/4" diskette (MS-DOS) for use in IBM-compatible microcomputers. ($20.00)

Interpretations. This subscription provides legal staff interpretations, trust interpretive letters, and investment securities letters. This monthly package represents the informal views of the Comptroller's staff concerning the applications of banking law to contemplated activities or transactions. ($85.00)

Weekly Bulletin. Contains all corporate decisions made by the Comptroller's office nationwide each week. Applications, approvals or denials, and consummations are noted for new banks, mergers, consolidations, and purchases and assumptions that result in national banks. This publication also carries branch and title changes, changes in controlling ownership, and other corporate changes for national banks. ($250.00)

Quarterly Journal. Serves as a journal of record for the most significant actions and policies of the OCC. It is published in March, June, September, and December. The journal includes policy statements, decisions on banking structure, selected speeches, testimony, material released in the interpretive letter series, summaries of enforcement actions, statistical data, and other information of interest to the administration of national banks. ($60.00 annually)

Banking Competition and the Banking Structure. Reprints from the *National Banking Review.* ($1.50)

* Deposit Data

Financial Disclosure Group
Federal Deposit Insurance Corporation
550 17th St., NW, Room F-518
Washington, DC 20429   (800) 843-1669

Summary of Deposits is an survey conducted among all FDIC-insured banks every June 30, the results of which are published annually. The *Annual Report of Trust Assets*, a similar survey, is conducted every December 31, among all financial institutions with trust departments. Computer printouts of both surveys are available for all banking offices within a given county, Metropolitan Statistical Area (MSA), or state. Magnetic tapes of *Summary of Deposit* data and the *Annual Report of Trust Assets* data for all U.S. banks for a given year are available for $75 each. Requests for computer printouts and magnetic tapes are handled by this office, which offers a toll-free number for customer assistance.

* Enforcement and Supervision

Office of Supervision and Applications
Division of Bank Supervision
Federal Deposit Insurance Corporation
550 17th St., NW, Room 5008
Washington, DC 20429   (202) 898-6915

This office monitors insured banks for compliance with FDIC regulations and has authority to approve bank applications for deposit insurance and branch formation. This office also initiates cease-and-desist orders against insured banks in the event they fail to correct violations of laws, regulations, or agreements with the FDIC.

Investments and Financial Services

* Farm Credit Publications

Office of Congressional and Public Affairs
Farm Credit Administration
1501 Farm Credit Drive
McLean, VA 22102 (703) 883-4056

Information on obtaining publications and documents can be obtained from the office above. Some of the documents it has which are available include the following:

New releases issued since January 1, 1972
Biographies of Farm Credit Administration officials
Speeches by FCA officials
FCA Handbook - Statutes & Regulations (Set fee charged)
FCA Examination Manual (Set fee Charged)
FCA Bulletin (Published 10 days after FCA Board meetings)
FCA Report (Published on an as-needed basis)
FCA Orders
FCA Money and Credit Market Report
FCA Organization Chart
FCA Board Policies
FCA Annual Report

* Farm Credit System

Office of Congressional and Public Affairs
Farm Credit Administration
1501 Farm Credit Drive
McLean, VA 22102 (703) 883-4056

The Farm Credit System is a network of farmer-owned lending institutions and specialized service organizations. More than 70 years ago Congress created the System to provide American agriculture with a dependable source of credit at competitive rates. Today the System provides about one-third of the total credit used by America's farmers, ranchers, and their cooperatives. The *Farm Credit System 1989 Information Guide*, which provides information on the Farm Credit System, including a list of the System's banks, is available free from the office above.

* Federal Cash Concentration System

Office of the Assistant Commissioner Federal Finance
Financial Management Service
U.S. Department of the Treasury
401 14th St., SW
Washington, DC 20227 (202) 287-0719

CASH-LINK is FMS's effort to transform the Government's worldwide banking and cash operations. Through the resources of the banking community, the new system will electronically capture and report activity for government-wide collections. The new system will encompass seven collection systems: Treasury General Account Cash Concentration System; Financial Management Service Lockbox Network; Credit Card Collection Network; Fedwire Deposit System; Federal Reserve System; Farmers Home Administration Cash Concentration System; and Commodity Credit Corporation Cash Concentration System.

* Federal Information Change Notification

Office of the Assistant Commissioner Field Operations
Financial Management Service
U.S. Department of the Treasury
401 14th St., SW
Washington, DC 20227 (202) 287-0311

This is an automated procedure that financial institutions can use to notify Federal agencies that an error or change has occurred in the depositor's account number, the routing/transit number of the financial institution (small numbers on the bottom of checks), or the type of account (checking or savings) of an Automated Clearinghouse Payment.

* Federal Lockbox Network

Office of the Assistant Commissioner Federal Finance
Financial Management Service
U.S. Department of the Treasury
401 14th St., SW
Washington, DC 20227 (202) 287-0719

Office of the Assistant Commissioner Field Operations
Financial Management Service
U.S. Department of the Treasury
401 14th St., SW
Washington, DC 20227 (202) 287-0311

The above offices oversee the Lockbox Network which consists of seven banks in nine cities: Atlanta, Chicago, Dallas, Los Angeles, Newark, Philadelphia, Pittsburgh, San Francisco, and St. Louis. Lockboxes, actually post office boxes, are used to collect and deposit mailed payments. More than 200 agency accounts are involved, and $26 billion is collected and processed annually. All 10 Internal Revenue Service centers will utilize the lockbox network in 1989.

* Federal Reserve Banks and Treasury Servicing Offices

This is a list of every Treasury Direct servicing office in the U.S. Contact the servicing office closest to you to make transactions on your account, or to receive information about your Treasury security investments.

Federal Reserve Bank Atlanta, 104 Marietta St., NW, Atlanta, GA 30303; (404) 521-8657 (Recording)/(404) 521-8653

Federal Reserve Bank Baltimore, 502 S. Sharp St., P.O. Box 1378, Baltimore, MD 20203; (301) 576-3300

Federal Reserve Bank Birmingham, 1801 Fifth Ave., N., P.O. Box 10447, Birmingham, AL 35283; (205) 252-3141, Ext. 215 (Recording)/(205) 252-3141 (Ext 264)

Federal Reserve Bank Boston, 600 Atlantic Ave., P.O. Box 2076, Boston, MA 02106; (617) 973-3805 (Recording)/(617) 973-3810

Federal Reserve Bank Buffalo, 160 Delaware Ave., P.O. Box 961, Buffalo, NY 14240-0961; (716) 849-5046 (Recording)/(716) 849-5030

Federal Reserve Bank Charlotte, 401 South Tryon St., P.O. Box 30248, Charlotte, NC 28230; (704) 336-7100

Federal Reserve Bank Chicago, 230 South LaSalle St., P.O. Box 834, Chicago, IL 60690; (312) 786-1110 (Recording)/(312) 322-5369

Federal Reserve Bank Cincinnati, 150 East Fourth St., P.O. Box 999, Cincinnati, OH 45201; (513) 721-4787, Ext. 334)

Federal Reserve Bank Cleveland, 1455 East Sixth St., P.O. Box 6387, Cleveland, OH 44101; (216) 579-2490

Federal Reserve Bank Dallas, 400 South Akard St., Dallas, TX 75222; (214) 651-6362

Federal Reserve Bank Denver, 1020 16th St., P.O. Box 5228, Terminal Annex, Denver, CO 80217; (303) 572-2475 (Recording)/(303) 572-2470

Federal Reserve Bank Detroit, 160 W. Fort St., P.O. Box 1059, Detroit, MI 48231; (313) 964-6153 (Recording)/ (313) 964-6157

Federal Reserve Bank Houston, 1701 San Jacinto St., P.O. Box 2578, Houston, TX 77001; (713) 659-4433

Federal Reserve Bank Jacksonville, 800 West Water St., P.O. Box 2499, Jacksonville, FL 32231-2499; (904) 632-1179

Federal Reserve Bank Kansas City, 925 Grand Ave., P.O. Box 440, Kansas City, MO 64198; (816) 881-2767 (Recording)/(816) 881-2409

Federal Reserve Bank Little Rock, 325 West Capitol Ave., P.O. Box 1261, Little Rock, AR 72203; (501) 372-5451, ext. 273

Federal Reserve Bank Los Angeles, 950 Grand Ave., P.O. Box 2077, Terminal Annex, Los Angeles, CA 90051; (213) 624-7398

Federal Reserve Bank Louisville, 410 South Fifth St., P.O. Box 32710, Louisville, KY 40232; (502) 568-9232 (Recording)/(502) 568-9236

Federal Reserve Bank Memphis, 200 N. Main St., P.O. Box 407, Memphis, TN 38101; (901) 523-7171 Ext. 225 or 641

Federal Reserve Bank Miami, 9100 NW Thirty-Sixth St., P.O. Box 520847, Miami, FL 33152; (305) 593-9923 (Recording)/(305) 591-2065

Federal Reserve Bank Minneapolis, 250 Marquette Ave., Minneapolis, MN 55480; (612) 340-2075

Federal Reserve Bank Nashville, 301 Eighth Ave., N., Nashville, TN 37203; (615) 259-4006

Federal Reserve Bank New Orleans, 525 St. Charles Ave., P.O. Box 61630, New Orleans, LA 70161; (504) 522-1659 (Recording)/(504) 586-1505 ext. 293

Federal Reserve Bank New York, 33 Liberty St., Federal Reserve P.O. Station, New York, NY 10045; (212) 720-5823 (Recording)/(212) 720-6619

Federal Reserve Bank Oklahoma City, 226 Dean A. McGee Ave., P.O. Box 25129, Oklahoma City, OK 73125; (405) 270-8660 (Recording)/(405) 270-8652

Federal Reserve Bank Omaha, 2201 Farnam St., Omaha, NE 68102; (402) 221-5638 (Recording)/(402) 221-5633

Federal Reserve Bank Philadelphia, Ten Independence Mall, P.O. Box 90, Philadelphia, PA 19105; (215) 574-6580 (Recording)/(215) 574-6680

Federal Reserve Bank Pittsburgh, 717 Grant St., P.O. Box 867, Pittsburgh, PA 15230-0867; (412) 261-7988 (Recording)/(412) 261-7863

Federal Reserve Bank Portland, 915 SW Stark St., P.O. Box 3436, Portland, OR 97208; (503) 221-5931 (Recording)/(503) 221-5932

Federal Reserve Bank Richmond, 701 East Byrd St., P.O. Box 27622, Richmond, VA 23261; (804) 697-8000

Federal Reserve Bank Salt Lake City, 120 South State St.,P.O. Box 30780, Salt Lake City, UT 84130; (801) 322-7911 (Recording); (801) 355-3131

Federal Reserve Bank San Antonio, 126 E. Nueva St.,P.O. Box 1471, San Antonio, TX 78295, (512) 224-2141, Ext. 311 (Recording)/(512) 224-2141 ext. 303 or 305

Federal Reserve Bank San Francisco, 101 Market St., P.O. Box 7702, San Francisco, CA 94120; (415) 882-9798 (Recording)/ (415) 974-2330

Federal Reserve Bank Seattle, 1015 Second Ave., P.O. Box 3567, Terminal Annex, Seattle, WA 98124; (206) 442-1650 (Recording)/(206) 442-1652

Federal Reserve Bank St. Louis, 411 Locust St., P.O. Box 14915, St. Louis, MO 63178; (314) 444-8602 (Recording)/(314) 444-8665

* FDIC Publications

Office of Corporate Communications
Federal Deposit Insurance Corporation
550 17th St., NW, Room 6058
Washington, DC 20429   (202) 898-6996
This office distributes the following free publications:

Annual Report. Summarizes the FDIC's operations, regulatory activities, and financial statements. Also included are statistical tables summarizing FDIC assistance to problem and failed banks.

Data Book. This six-volume set contains deposit information for all commercial and mutual savings banks, including U.S.-based branches of foreign banks. Each volume focuses on a different geographic area and includes a national summary with tables on bank structure, class, and size.

Merger Decisions. An annual summary of the FDIC's approvals and denials of bank mergers.

Statistics on Banking. This annual report details bank statistical data, including the total number of banks and branches and information on incomes, assets, and liabilities of insured banks.

Symbol of Confidence. Provides an overview of the FDIC's history, responsibilities, and operations.

Trust Assets of Financial Institutions. Summarizes trust department data collected from all insured commercial banks. Data is presented by type of account, asset distribution, and size of account.

Your Insured Deposit. Provides examples of the FDIC's insurance coverage for common types of bank accounts.

* Finance Publications

Comptroller of the Currency
U.S. Department of the Treasury
P.O. Box 70004
Chicago, IL 60673-0004
A Partnership Approach to Neighborhood Commercial Reinvestment
Studies in Small Business Finance (pamphlet)
The Changing Shape of Retail Banking: Responding to Customer Needs

* International Banking

Analysis Section
Division of Bank Supervision
Federal Deposit Insurance Corporation
550 17th St., NW, Room 5050
Washington, DC 20429   (202) 898-6821
FDIC-insured banks must first obtain FDIC approval before they establish, operate, or relocate a branch in a foreign country. FDIC approval is also needed before these banks acquire any ownership interest in a foreign bank. Insured branches of foreign banks located in the U.S. are also monitored by the FDIC. For more information, contact the nearest regional FDIC office or the office above.

* International Finance

Office of Development Finance
Bureau of Economic and Business Affairs

Department of State
2201 C St., NW, Room 2529
Washington, DC 20520   (202) 647-9426
As the liaison with multilateral development banks, such as the World Bank, African Development Bank, Asian Development Bank, and InterAmerican Bank, this office works on such development issues as coordinating official U.S. Government assistance to promote economic security in developing countries. This office also coordinates with the Export-Import Bank on trade issues.

* Law, Regulations, and Related Acts

Office of Corporate Communications
Federal Deposit Insurance Corporation
550 17th St., NW, Room 6058
Washington, DC 20429   (202) 898-6996
FDIC Law, Regulations, and Related Acts is a three-volume, loose-leaf bound publication containing the FDI Act, FDIC rules and regulations, advisory opinions, pertinent statutes, and consumer protection material, among other information. Revisions and updates are published bimonthly. For $175 subscribers receive the three-volume set and updates through December of that year, and they are billed $175 each December to renew the update service.

* Legislation on Financial Institutions

Office of Financial Institutions
Office of the Assistant Secretary of the Treasury
for Domestic Finance
U.S. Department of the Treasury
1500 Pennsylvania Ave., NW
Washington, DC 20220   (202) 343-5337
Policy and legislation on the development and administration of banks and other financial institutions is handled by this office. A recent effort involved the study of the ailing thrift institutions, resulting in the formation of the Office of Thrift Supervision.

* Liquidation Litigation

Office of Corporate Communications
Federal Deposit Insurance Corporation
550 17th St., NW, Room 6058
Washington, DC 20429   (202) 898-6996
This office oversees liquidation litigation among FDIC-insured banks, as well as liquidation and insurance activities for the Federal Savings and Loan Insurance Corporation (FSLIC). Outside counsel is hired to help litigate an estimated 40,000 cases annually. Contact this office for more information on liquidation litigation issues.

* Office of Thrift Supervision District Offices

P.O. Box 9106 GMF, Boston, MA 02205-9106; (617) 542-0150

One World Trade Center, FL 103, New York, NY 10048; (212) 912-4600

One Riverfront Center, 20 Stanwix St., Pittsburgh, PA 15222-4893;
(412) 288-3400

P.O. Box 105217, Atlanta, GA 30348-5217; (404) 888-8000

P.O. Box 598, Cincinnati, OH 45201-0598; (513) 852-7500

P.O. Box 60, Indianapolis, IN 46206-0060; (317) 631-0130

111 E. Wacker Dr., Suite 800, Chicago, IL 60601-4360; (312) 565-5700

907 Walnut St., Des Moines, IA 50309; (515) 281-1100

P.O. Box 619027, Dallas/Fort Worth, TX 75261-9027; (214) 541-8500

P.O. Box 828, Topeka, KS 66601-0828; (913) 233-5300

P.O. Box 7165, San Francisco, CA 94120; (415) 393-1000

1501 Fourth Ave., FL 19, Seattle, WA 98101-1693; (206) 340-2300

* Office of Thrift Supervision Publications

Office of Thrift Supervision
U.S. Department of the Treasury
1700 G. St., NW
Washington, DC 20552   (202) 785-5485
Thrift Activities Regulatory Handbook. Addresses all of the major areas of concern to examiners and supervisors regarding the safety and soundness of regulated institutions. (Price: members - $50; non-members - $75)

Compliance Activities Regulatory Handbook. Addresses compliance examination matters related to consumer protection laws and regulations, such as the Truth in Lending Act, and those related to the public interest, such as the Community Reinvestment and Bank Secrecy Acts. (Price: members - $50; non-members - $75)

Service Corporations Regulatory Handbook. Addresses issues that primarily arise in dealing with service corporations and discusses relationships between those entities and the parent thrift. (Price: $50 - members; $75 - non-members)

Holding Companies Regulatory Handbook. Addresses areas of particular interest when reviewing holding company operations. (Price: $50 - members; $75 - non-members)

Trust Activities Regulatory Handbook. Designed to assist in the examination of those thrift institutions and their subsidiaries that engage in trust activities. (Price: $50 - members; $75 - non-members)

Application Processing Regulatory Handbook. Contains guidance on how to process and analyze thrift and holding company applications. (Price: $50 - members; $75 - non-members)

Federal Financial Institutions Examination Council (FFIEC) EDP Handbook. This handbook is published by the FFIEC and is currently used by all financial regulatory agencies as a guide for conducting EDP examinations. (Price: $75)

Office of Thrift Supervision Journal. Covers topics of importance to the thrift industry, such as home ownership; deposit insurance; strategic planning; capital adequacy; accounting; demographics; taxes; mortgage organizations, sales, and purchases; savings activity; director's responsibilities; and economic trends. For information on obtaining a subscription, call (202) 906-6600. The annual price is $45.

Membership Directory of Institutions. Published during the first quarter of each year, this free directory lists all savings institutions insured by the Savings Association Insurance Fund (SAIF) and the Federal Deposit Insurance Corporation (FDIC), as well as those institutions that are members of the Federal Home Finance Board but are not federally insured. For a copy, call (202) 416-2751.

Compliance: A Self-Assessment Guide. This guide will help thrift institutions develop or improve internal policies and programs to ensure compliance with consumer and public interest laws. $28

CEBA Guide: Questions and Answers. The questions answered in this guide are those most commonly asked by examination and supervisory staff during the Comprehensive Equality Banking Act of 1987 (CEBA) training programs. $3

Bulletin Subscription Series. Thrift Bulletins provide national guidance to alert regulated institutions to practices or events of concern to the thrift industry. The annual subscription price is $125.

* Problem Banks

Office of Corporate Communications
Federal Deposit Insurance Corporation
550 17th St., NW, Room 6058
Washington, DC 20429 (202) 898-6996

The FDIC uses the Uniform Interagency Bank Rating System to evaluate a bank's performance with respect to capital adequacy, asset quality, management/administration, earnings, and liquidity (known by the acronym CAMEL). Banks are rated on a scale from 1 to 5, with 1 indicating a very sound banking institution. Banks with ratings of 4 or 5 are considered to be problem banks, possibly requiring FDIC intervention and payoff. Individual bank ratings are not available to the public. Contact this office for more information about the rating system.

* Registration and Reporting

Public Files Suite
1776 G St., NW, 4th Floor
Washington, DC 20006 (202) 898-8909

The FDIC enforces the registration and reporting provisions of the 1934 Securities Exchange Act among FDIC-insured, nonmember banks. Banks with assets totalling more than $1 million and 500 or more security holders are required to file an initial registration statement which summarizes the bank's history, business operations, and overall financial condition. These banks are also required to file periodic reports which include Reports of Condition and Income Statements. The registration statements and periodic reports are filed and maintained in this office.

Money

* Congressional Coins
Customer Service Center
U.S. Mint
Department of the Treasury
10001 Aerospace Dr.
Landover, MD 20706 (301) 436-7400
The following Congressional coins can be purchased from the U.S. Mint:

Gold Five Dollar Congressional Coin. Features a rendition of the U.S. Capitol Dome and the spread eagle design from the Old Senate Chamber. Available as a proof for $215 and uncirculated for $200.

Silver Dollar Congressional Coin. Depicts the Statue of Freedom and the mace carried by the House's Sergeant at Arms. A proof is $29, and an uncirculated coin is $26.

Half Dollar Coins. $8 and $6

Congressional Commemorative Coin Sets Susan B. Anthony Dollar Coin. Available in an uncirculated souvenir set and in coin bags.

U.S. Mint proof coin sets and uncirculated sets can also be purchased. Contact this Center for more information.

* Counterfeit and Forgery Statistics
Public Affairs
U.S. Secret Service
Department of the Treasury
1800 G St., NW
Washington, DC 20223 (202) 535-5708
A statistical summary of activity within the Secret Service investigative area is available, including information on counterfeiting, check forgery, bond forgery, fraud, protective intelligence, and other criminal and noncriminal acts. Data includes investigative activity by fiscal year; counterfeiting trends of notes and coins; trends of counterfeit plant operations, including the production of counterfeit notes, office machine copies, food coupons, false IDs, and domestic and foreign currency; counterfeit notes received by major city and dollar amount; arrests; and forged checks and bonds received.

* Counterfeiting Investigations
Counterfeit Division
Office of Investigations
U.S. Secret Service
Department of the Treasury
1800 G St., NW
Washington, DC 20223 (202) 535-5756
Information may be obtained concerning facts about paper currency and recognizing counterfeit bills and coins. Guidelines are also available on what to do when you receive a counterfeit bill. For additional information, contact Public Affairs at (202) 535-5708.

* Counterfeit Money and Forged Checks
Superintendent of Documents
Government Printing Office
Washington, DC 20402 (202) 783-3238
Know Your Money describes and illustrates ways to recognize counterfeit bills and forged U.S. government checks. The price is $3.25 and the order number is S/N 048-006-00010-8).

* Currency and Stamp Production
Office of the Assistant Director, Operations
Bureau of Engraving and Printing
U.S. Department of the Treasury
14th and C Sts., SW
Washington, DC 20228 (202) 447-0229
The Bureau of Engraving and Printing designs, engraves, and prints United States paper currency; United States postage and revenue stamps; and miscellaneous engraved items for approximately 75 departments and independent agencies of the Federal Government. White house invitations, commissions, diplomas, certificates, identification cards, and liquor strip stamps are some of the approximately 700 miscellaneous products printed by the Bureau.

* Daily Treasury Statement
Superintendent of Documents
Government Printing Office
Washington, DC 20402 (202) 783-3238
Published daily except Saturdays, Sundays, and holidays, the subscription service, *Daily Treasury Statement*, outlines the cash and debt operations of the United States Treasury. The annual price is $174.00. (S/N 748-003-00000-2)

* Damaged Money Redemption
Office of Currency Standards
Bureau of Engraving and Printing
U.S. Department of the Treasury
Room 344A, BEPA
P.O. Box 37048
Washington, DC 20013 (202) 447-0545
All mutilated currency may be sent to the above address where trained personnel will determine if it can be exchanged at face value. All final decisions for redemption of this currency are made by the Treasurer of the United States. Currency should be sent by registered mail to the P.O. box address above.

* Federal Check Cashing Period
Office of the Assistant Commissioner Headquarters Operations
Financial Management Service
U.S. Department of the Treasury
3700 East West Highway
Hyattsville, MD 20782 (301) 436-6349
Effective October 1, 1989, all Treasury checks must be cashed or deposited within 12 months of issuance for payment to be valid. If this time lapses, the holder of the check must contact the agency from where the check was drawn and ask to have another check issued. Entitlement of the funds never ceases. This program within the FMS is called Limited Payability.

* Federal Collections
Office of the Assistant Commissioner Federal Finance
Financial Management Service
U.S. Department of the Treasury
401 14th St., SW
Washington, DC 20227 (202) 287-0719
The Financial Management Service is responsible for the largest collection system in the world--approximately $1 trillion annually. These collections include tax deposits, custom duties, loan repayments, fines, services, and proceeds from leases. FMS provides transaction processing to Federal agencies, manages the systems by which Government collections are made, and sets policy for the use of the collection systems.

* Federal Open Market Committee
Division of Monetary Affairs
Federal Reserve System, Room B3022
20th St. & Constitution Ave., NW
Washington, DC 20551 (202) 452-3761
The Federal Open Market Committee exercises broad control over the growth of the nation's money supply and is in charge of the System's operations in both domestic securities markets and in foreign exchange markets. The Committee is composed of the seven members of the Board of Governors and five Reserve Bank presidents, including the president of the New York Reserve Bank, which conducts foreign and domestic operations for the Committee. For information on the nation's money supply and securities markets, contact this office.

* Federal Payments
Office of the Assistant Commissioner Field Operations
Financial Management Service
U.S. Department of the Treasury
401 14th St., SW
Washington, DC 20227 (202) 287-0311
The issuance of payments is a central financial operation of the Financial Management Service. The Service disburses approximately 750 million payments annually, and issues payments for virtually all Federal civilian agencies, or approximately 85 percent of total Government payments. Payments are issued from seven Regional Financial Center locations on the basis of payment vouchers certified by Federal agencies.

Investments and Financial Institutions

* Forgery Investigations

Forgery Division
Office of Investigations
U.S. Secret Service
Department of the Treasury
1800 G St., NW
Washington, DC 20223   (202) 343-0412

Since there are more than 800 million U.S. Government checks issued each year, they are attractive to criminals who specialize in stealing and forging them. Retail merchants often unknowingly aid the forger by failing to request proper identification. For additional information on precautions to take, contact Public Affairs at (202) 535-5708.

* Gold and Silver Bullion Coins

Public Information Office
U.S. Mint
Department of the Treasury
633-3rd St., NW
Washington, DC 20220   (202) 376-0436

The American Eagle Gold and Silver Bullion Coins are being minted to purchase as investments. The gold coins are available in one ounce, half-ounce, quarter-ounce and tenth-ounce weights. The silver coins are minted only in the one ounce size. To determine their worth, simply check listings in your daily newspaper. The coins may be purchased from various brokerage companies, participating banks, coin dealers, and precious metal dealers. To obtain a listing of sales locations in your area, contact the office above.

* Lost Government Checks

Office of the Assistant Commissioner
Headquarters Operations
Financial Management Service
U.S. Department of the Treasury
3700 East West Highway
Hyattsville, MD 20782   (301) 436-6349

To make a claim against Treasury for a lost check or one you believe has been cashed with a forged endorsement, you first must contact the agency that issued the check and obtain a copy of it along with a claim form. The agency will then contact Treasury to handle your claim. The office above ultimately handles the claim, but requests that it be contacted only when all else fails.

* Monetary Policy

Division of Monetary Affairs
Federal Reserve System
Room B3022
20th St. & Constitution Ave., NW
Washington, DC 20551   (202) 452-3761

This FRS division analyzes issues in monetary policy, including open market operations, member bank discount borrowing at Federal Reserve Banks, and changes in reserve requirements.

* U.S. Mint Annual Report, 1988

Superintendent of Documents
Government Printing Office
Washington, DC 20402   (202) 783-3238

The *U.S. Mint Annual Report, 1988* is an interesting summary of all activities for 1988 within the U.S. Mint. In addition to the mint operations summary, including coinage activities and special events, there are tables featured with coinage statistics, gold and silver transactions, and internal operating funds. They are sold for $1.75 (S/N 048-005-00036-5).

* World Coinage Report

Superintendent of Documents
Government Printing Office
Washington, DC 20402   (202) 783-3238

The booklet, World Coinage Report, provides statistics on coinage for various nations of the world. Features listed include denomination, metallic composition, gross weight, diameter, thickness, edge, and number of pieces minted. It is sold for $2.75. (S/N 048-005-00034-9)

Credit Unions

* CAMEL Rating System

Office of Examination and Insurance
National Credit Union Administration
1776 G St., NW, Room 6601C
Washington, DC 20456   (202) 682-9640

Assigned following an examination of a credit union's safety and soundness, a CAMEL rating is a reliable indicator of future success or failure. The CAMEL rating looks at the key areas of a credit union's operations--capital adequacy, asset quality, management, earnings, and liquidity. Ratings range from Code 1, which is good, to Code 5, which is poor. For more information, contact the Office of Examination and Insurance.

* Central Liquidity Facility

National Credit Union Administration
1776 G St., NW, Room 818
Washington, DC 20456   (202) 682-9780

The Central Liquidity Facility is a mixed-ownership government corporation governed by the NCUA Board. CLF is a central source of short-term funds for the credit union system. It has a loan portfolio of $120.4 million and provided lines of credit totalling $13.5 million. To become a CLF member, a credit union or its designated agent must purchase stocks equal to one-half of one percent of the credit union's unimpaired capital and surplus.

* Chartering

Department of Insurance
National Credit Union Administration
1776 G St., NW, Room 6601C
Washington, DC 20456   (202) 682-9640

The NCUA Board grants Federal Credit Union charters to groups sharing a common bond of occupation or association, or to groups within a well-defined neighborhood, community, or rural district. A preliminary investigation is made to determine if certain minimum standards are met before granting a federal charter. Call or write to the office listed above for more information on the chartering process.

* Consumer Complaints

National Credit Union Administration
1776 G St., NW
Washington, DC 20456   (202) 682-9650

The Administration investigates the complaints of members who are unable to resolve problems with their federal credit union where these problems relate to a possible violation of the Federal Credit Union Act or to consumer protection regulations. Complaints should be sent directly to the appropriate office.

* Credit Union Information

Public Information
National Credit Union Administration
1776 G St., NW
Washington, DC 20456   (202) 682-9650

Several publications are available to assist you in starting a federal credit union. *Chartering and Organizing of Federal Credit Unions* provides basic information about credit unions and their membership policies. The *Federal Credit Union Handbook* is intended to assist the board of directors in conducting the credit union's affairs. Contact the regional NCUA office near you for further information.

* Credit Union Supervision

Department of Supervision
National Credit Union Administration
1776 G St., NW, Room 6611
Washington, DC 20456   (202) 682-9640

Supervisory activities are carried out through annual examiner contacts and through periodic policy and regulatory releases from the Administration. The Administration also maintains a warning system designed to identify emerging problems as well as to monitor operations between examinations.

* Examiner Training Programs

National Credit Union Administration
1776 G St., NW
Washington, DC 20456   (202) 682-9640

This office offers classroom, as well as on-the-job, training for new examiners, and offers technical seminars for senior examiners. These seminars cover such topics as consumer lending, investments, and dealing with problem case credit unions. The training programs are open to state supervisory personnel without charge.

* Liquidation

Department of Insurance
National Credit Union Administration
1776 G St., NW, Room 6601C
Washington, DC 20456   (202) 682-9640

Liquidation of federal credit unions is conducted according to the manual *Voluntary Liquidation Procedure for Insured Federal Credit Unions*. The major responsibility of the board is to conduct the liquidations in such a manner that the interest of the members, the insurance fund, and the creditors of the credit union are safeguarded. For information regarding liquidations, contact the Department of Insurance.

* Financial Performance Report

Public Information
National Credit Union Administration
1776 G St., NW
Washington, DC 20456   (202) 682-9650

The *Financial Performance Report*, an analytical tool created for management and supervisory purposes, is designed to provide a long-term picture of the financial trends and operating results of the credit union. The *FPR* is updated twice a year, with the December *FPR* providing percentile rankings that show where the credit union stands in relation to **all** other credit unions in key areas of financial performance. This publication breaks down the *FPR* and explains what each category means. A member has the right to inspect a federal credit union's books and records, including the board of directors' minutes.

* Insured Funds

Department of Insurance
National Credit Union Administration
1776 G St., NW, Room 6601C
Washington, DC 20456   (202) 682-9640

Share insurance is mandatory for federal credit unions and for state-chartered credit unions in many states, while optional for other state-chartered credit unions that meet NCUA standards. Credit union members' accounts are insured up to $100,000. The National Credit Union Share Insurance Fund requires each insured credit union to place and maintain a one-percent deposit of its insured savings with the NCUSIF. The publication *Your Insured Funds* offers further explanation concerning insurance.

* Listing of Federal Credit Unions

Freedom of Information Officer
National Credit Union Administration
1776 G St., NW, Room 7355
Washington, DC 20456   (202) 682-9700

A master list of the names and addresses of all federally insured credit unions is available for public inspection in the Washington and regional offices. Copies of the list may be obtained at a nominal cost by writing to the Freedom of Information Officer. You may also receive a free list of NCUA regional offices.

* Publications

National Credit Union Administration
1776 G St., NW, Room 7261
Washington, DC 20456   (202) 682-9700

A listing of NCUA publications is available from the Administrative office. These publications include the annual report, the credit union directory, as well as technical reports, such as *Chartering and Organizing of a Federal Credit Union*. There is a nominal charge for each publication.

Stocks and Bonds

* Accounting

Office of the Chief Accountant
U.S. Securities and Exchange Commission
450 5th St., NW
Washington, DC 20549   (202) 272-2050

The SEC's Chief Accountant consults with representatives of the accounting profession and other standard-setting bodies that promote new or revised accounting and auditing standards. One of the Securities and Exchange Commission's major objectives is to improve accounting and auditing standards and to maintain high standards of professional conduct by the independent accountants. This office also drafts rules and regulations that dictate the requirements for financial statements, and rules which require that accountants examining financial statements filed with the SEC be independent of their clients. For more information accounting procedures, contact this office.

* American Depository Receipts

Office of International Corporate Finance
U.S. Securities and Exchange Commission
450 5th St., NW
Washington, DC 20549   (202) 272-3246

U.S. investors who are interested in foreign securities may purchase American Depository Receipts. These are negotiable receipts, registered in the name of a U.S. citizen, which represent a specific number of shares of a foreign corporation. For more information about American Depository Receipts, contact this office.

* Annual Reports to Shareholders

Public Reference Branch
Securities and Exchange Commission
450 5th St., NW, Room 1024
Washington, DC 20549-1002   (202) 272-7450, (202) 272-7459 (TTD)

Although not a required SEC filing, the *Annual Report to Shareholders* is the main document most public companies use to give information about corporations to shareholders. It is usually a state-of-the-company report which includes an opening letter from the Chief Executive Officer, financial data, results of continuing operations, market segment information, new product plans, subsidiary activities and research and development activities on future programs. Some filings are available in printed form, but all are available on microfiche.

* Annual (10-K) Reports: Investment Information

Public Reference Room
U.S. Securities and Exchange Commission
450 5th St., NW
Washington, DC 20549   (202) 272-7450

Many companies whose stock is traded over the counter or on a stock exchange must file "full disclosure" reports on a regular basis with the SEC. The annual report, or *Form 10-K*, is the most comprehensive of these. It describes and contains statistical information on the company's business operations, properties, parents, and subsidiaries; its management, including their salaries and their security ownership in the company; any matters which have been submitted to a vote of shareholders; and significant legal proceedings which involve the company. *Form 10-K* also contains the audited financial statements of the company, including a balance sheet, an income statement, and a statement of where funds come from and how they are used. The public may obtain copies for a small fee by visiting or writing the office above.

* Arbitration Procedures

Publications Section
Printing Branch, Stop C-11
U.S. Securities and Exchange Commission
Washington, DC 20549   (202) 272-7040

Arbitration Procedures is a free publication available from this office which discusses procedures for disputes with brokerage firms involving financial claims.

* Broker/Dealer Registration

Registration
U.S. Securities and Exchange Commission
450 5th St., NW
Washington, DC 20549   (202) 272-7250

The registration of brokers and dealers who solicit and execute securities transactions is an important part of the work of the SEC. Broker-dealers must abide by the securities laws, the rules of the self-regulatory organization of which they are members, and SEC rules. Registrations must be kept up to date and must reflect any changes in financial conditions over time. The registration form shows: form of organization; if it is a corporation, the date and state of incorporation, and class of equity security; if it is a sole proprietorship, the person's residence and Social Security number; if it is a successor to a previous broker or dealer, the SEC file number of the predecessor; persons with controlling interests; how the business is financed; the firm's or person's standing with the SEC and other regulatory agencies, including disclosure of having made false statements to the SEC in the past, been convicted in the last 10 years of a related felony, been prohibited in the last 10 years from financial activities, aided anyone in violating related laws or rules, been barred or suspended as a broker-dealer, been the subject of a cease and desist order, been associated with a similar firm that went bankrupt, information about the person or business that maintains the applicant's records and holds funds of the applicant or its customers; details about companies which control or are controlled by the applicant; whether the applicant is an investment adviser; types of business done (such as floor activity, underwriting or mutual fund retailing); descriptions of any nonsecurity business; and information about principals, including positions, securities held, Social Security numbers, education and background. Customers have the right to expect that trades will be executed promptly and that the broker will try to secure the best price, for example. They should expect to receive written confirmation of trading, with information including the date of the transaction, the identity of the security bought or sold, and the number of shares, units, or principal amount of the security. Customers can expect information on the cost of the transaction, including commissions charged, from the broker.

* Broker-Dealer Revocations

Office of Chief Counsel
Division of Market Regulation
U.S. Securities and Exchange Commission
450 5th St., NW
Washington, DC 20549   (202) 272-3000

In the case members of an exchange or association, registered brokers or dealers, or individuals associated with any such firm, the Commission can issue an order specifying alleged illegal acts or practices and can direct that a hearing take place. If the Commission finds that the law has been violated, it may impose sanctions or bar a firm from conducting a securities business in interstate commerce or on exchanges, or an individual from association with a registered firm.

* Capital Formation for Small Businesses

The Office of Small Business Policy
Division of Corporation Finance
U.S. Securities and Exchange Commission
450 5th St., NW
Washington, DC 20549   (202) 272-2644

The Securities and Exchange Commission's main responsibility under the securities laws is to protect investors and to make sure the capital markets operate fairly and orderly. However, the Commission is careful not to let its regulations impair capital formation by small businesses. Therefore, the SEC has taken a number of steps to help small businesses raise capital and to ease the burden of undue regulations under the federal securities laws. The Commission is continually examining other ways to meet these goals. For more information, contact this office.

* Commission Meetings

Office of the Secretary
U.S. Securities and Exchange Commission
450 5th St., NW
Washington, DC 20549   (202) 272-2600

The Commission meets several times each month to debate and decide on regulatory issues. Like other regulatory agencies, the Commission has two types of meetings. Under the Government in the Sunshine Act, meetings may be open to the public and to members of the press; however, if it is necessary to protect the Commission's ability to conduct investigations and/or protect the rights of individuals and entities which may be the subject of Commission inquiries, meetings may be closed. Commission meetings are generally held to discuss and resolve issues the staff brings before the Commissioners. Issues may be interpretations of federal securities laws, amendments to existing rules under the laws, new rules (often to reflect changed conditions in the marketplace), actions to enforce the laws or to discipline those subject to direct regulation, legislation to be proposed by the Commission, and matters concerning administration of the Commission itself. Issues may be resolved in the form of new rules or amendments to existing ones, enforcement actions, or disciplinary actions.

Notices of open and closed Commission meetings and the agendas of open meetings are published the preceding week in the *SEC News Digest*. For more information on weekly meetings, contact this office.

* Confirmation of Transaction
Office of Consumer Affairs
U.S. Securities and Exchange Commission
450 5th St., NW
Washington, DC 20549   (202) 272-7440
Consumer Telecommunications for the deaf (TTY-Voice)
       (202) 272-7065

There is a fundamental distinction between a broker and a dealer. The broker is the customers' agent who buys or sells securities for them. The broker owes the customer the highest fiduciary responsibility and can charge only the agency commission that the customer agreed to. On the other hand, a dealer acts as a principal and buys securities from or sells securities to customers. The dealer's profit is the difference between the prices for which the securities are bought and sold. The dealer normally will not disclose the fee or commission charged for services rendered. The law requires that the customer receive a written "confirmation" of each securities transaction. This confirmation discloses whether the securities firm is acting as a dealer (a principal for its own account) or as a broker (an agent for the customer). If the firm is acting as a broker, the confirmation must also disclose the broker's compensation from all sources, as well as other information about the transaction.
For more information contact your regional office or contact the above SEC office.

* Consumer Complaints
Office of Consumer Affairs and Information Services
Investor Services Branch
U.S. Securities and Exchange Commission
450 5th St., NW
Washington, DC 20549   (202) 272-7440
Consumer Telecommunications for the deaf (TTY-Voice) (202) 272-7065

The Investor Services Branch reviews complaints from the investing public nationwide concerning their dealings with the securities industry and typically obtains written responses from firms mentioned in the complaint. Complaints regarding banks, broker-dealers, investors, junk bonds, investment advisers, and so on are all available for review by the general public. This office strives to improve and upgrade the SEC's complaint processing effort, analyze trends that surface as a result of complaints received, and increase the Commissions' activities in consumer education. Information suggesting a possible violation of federal securities laws is referred to appropriate Commission staff. When complaints entail private disputes between parties, Commission staff attempt informally to assist the parties in resolving the problem. The SEC also welcomes inquiries and reports about questionable securities practices. Investors should remember, however, that the SEC cannot function as a collection agency or directly represent them in a dispute. Direct investor complaints and grievances to the office above.

* Consumer's Financial Guide
Publications Section
Printing Branch, Stop C-11
U.S. Securities and Exchange Commission
Washington, DC 20549   (202) 272-7040

The free publication, *Consumer's Financial Guide*, contains basic information on choosing investments and keeping them safe, trading securities, and the different protections guaranteed by law. To obtain this publication contact this office.

* Corporate Finance Policy
Office of Corporate Finance
Office of the Assistant Secretary of the Treasury
for Domestic Finance
U.S. Department of the Treasury
1500 Pennsylvania Ave., NW
Washington, DC 20220   (202) 535-6334

This office is the Department of the Treasury's effort to influence the financial policy directives of corporations. The staff can help answer questions on the Treasury's guidelines on anything from leverage buyouts to junk bonds.

* Corporate Reorganization
Division of Corporation Finance
U.S. Securities and Exchange Commission
450 5th St., NW
Washington, DC 20549   (202) 272-2801

Reorganization proceedings in the U.S. Courts are begun by a debtor, voluntarily, or by its creditors. Federal bankruptcy law allows a debtor in reorganization to continue operating under the court's protection while it attempts to rehabilitate its business and work out a plan to pay its debts. If a debtor corporation has publicly issued securities outstanding, the reorganization process may raise many issues that will directly affect the rights of public investors. The SEC is authorized to appear in any reorganization case and to present its views on any issue. However, the Commission gets involved only in proceedings which involve significant public investor interest--protecting public investors holding the debtor's securities, and participating in legal and policy issues concerning public investors. The SEC also continues to address matters of traditional Commission expertise and interest relating to securities. Where appropriate, it reviews reorganization plan disclosure statements and participates in some aspects of law enforcement. The court can confirm a reorganization plan if it is accepted by creditors for at least two-thirds of the amounts of allowed claims, more than one-half the number of allowed claims, and at least two-thirds in amount of the allowed shareholder interest. The biggest protection for public investors is the required disclosure statement issued by the debtor to seek votes on the reorganization plan. In addition, plans involving publicly held debtors usually provide for issuing new securities to creditors and shareholders which may be exempt from registration. For more information on reorganization, contact this office.

* Corporate Reporting
Public Reference Room
U.S. Securities and Exchange Commission
450 5th St., NW
Washington, DC 20549   (202) 272-7450

Companies that want their securities registered and listed for public trading on an exchange have to file a registration application with both the exchange and the SEC. Companies that meet a specific size test, whose equity securities are traded over-the-counter, must file a similar registration form. Commission rules dictate the content and nature of these registration statements and require certified financial statements. Once their securities are registered, companies must file annual and other periodic reports to keep the file updated. Also, issuers must send certain reports to shareholders if they request them. Reports may be read at the public reference rooms, and copied there for a small fee, or obtained at reasonable rates from a copying service under contract to the Commission. For more information on registration, contact this office.

* Decisions and Reports
Superintendent of Documents
Government Printing office
Washington, DC 20402   (202) 783-3238

The Securities and Exchange Commission's decisions, as well as initial decisions which have become final and are very important, are printed in the SEC's *Decisions and Reports*. The latest volume, *Volume 48* (July 4, 1984-June 30, 1988), is available for $25.00 from the GPO.

* Directory of Companies
Public Reference Branch
Securities and Exchange Commission
450 5th St., NW, Room 1024
Washington, DC 20549-1002   (202) 272-7450, (202) 272-7459 (TTD)

The annual *Directory of Companies* is a compendium of all companies which are required to file annual reports with the Securities and Exchange Commission under the Securities Exchange Act of 1934. It lists companies alphabetically and classifies them by industry group according to the *Standard Industrial Classification Manual of the Budget (1988)*. It is available for $25.00 from: Superintendent of Documents, Government Printing Office, Washington, DC 20402; (202) 783-3238.

* EDGAR User Manual
The Office of EDGAR Management
U.S. Securities and Exchange Commission
450 5th St., NW
Washington, DC 20549-1101

Investors, securities analysts, and other members of the public have access to EDGAR information through a variety of subscriptions and services. A copy of the *EDGAR Instruction Manual*, which explains how to access and use the features of the EDGAR System is available. A copy of the *User Manual*, which provides detailed information and directions for making filings on EDGAR, is available as well by contacting this office.

* Electronic Security Processing
The Office of EDGAR Management
U.S. Securities and Exchange Commission
450 5th St., NW
Washington, DC 20549   (202) 272-3806

The EDGAR management system permits corporations to make their required filings electronically via direct transmission, diskettes, or tapes to the Commission. EDGAR will help to speed up the processing and handling of the 11 million pages of disclosure information that are currently filed with the SEC each year. Private companies are encouraged to offer filer training and support on a competitive basis. The public portions of these filings are available in hardcopy printouts and on microfiche. For more information on the EDGAR Management system, contact this office.

Investments and Financial Services

* Enforcement Activities

Division of Enforcement
U.S. Securities and Exchange Commission
450 5th St., NW
Washington, DC 20549   (202) 272-2900

The SEC's enforcement activities are designed to make sure that the Federal securities laws administered by the Commission are obeyed. These activities include measures to:

-Compel obedience to the disclosure requirements of the registration and other conditions of the act;
-Stop fraud and dishonesty in buying and selling securities;
-Obtain court orders prohibiting acts and practices that operate as a fraud upon investors or otherwise violate the laws;
-Suspend or revoke the registrations of brokers, dealers, and investment companies and investment advisers who willingly engage in fraudulent acts and practices;
-Suspend or bar from association persons associated with brokers, dealers, investment companies, and investment advisers who have violated any conditions of the Federal securities laws; and
-Prosecute persons who have engaged in fraudulent activities or other willful violations of those laws.

In addition, attorneys, accountants, and other professionals who violate the securities laws can loose their right to practice before the Commission. To this end, private investigations are conducted into complaints or other suspected securities violations. Evidence of law violations is used to revoke registration or used in Federal courts to control dishonest activities. If the evidence points to criminal fraud or some other type of intentional violation of the securities laws, the facts are referred to the Attorney General for criminal prosecution of the offenders. The Commission may assist in such prosecutions. For more information on enforcement contact this office.

* Exchange Registration

Registration
U.S. Securities and Exchange Commission
450 5th St., NW
Washington, DC 20549   (202) 272-7250

Registration with the Commission is required of National securities exchanges with a substantial securities trading volume, brokers and dealers who conduct securities business in interstate commerce, transfer agents, clearing agencies, government and municipal brokers and dealers, and securities information processors. To register, exchanges must show that they are organized to comply with the provisions of the statute as well as the rules and regulations of the Commission. The registering exchanges must also show that their rules ensure fair dealing and protect investors. Each exchange is a self-regulatory organization. Its rules must provide for the expulsion, suspension, or other disciplining of member broker-dealers for unjust and unfair trading conduct. Exchanges shall have full opportunity to establish self-regulatory measures ensuring fair dealing and investor protection. However, the SEC approves--by order, rule, or regulation--any rule changes of exchanges concerning various activities and trading practices if necessary. Exchange rules and revisions, proposed by exchanges or by the Commission, generally reach their final form after discussions between representatives of both bodies. For more information, contact this office.

* Fair and Orderly Markets

Division of Market Regulation
U.S. Securities and Exchange Commission
450 5th St., NW
Washington, DC 20549
(202) 272-3000

The SEC supervises the securities markets and the conduct of securities professionals. It also serves as a watchdog to protect against fraud in the sale of securities, illegal sales practices, market manipulation, and other violations of investors' trust by broker/dealers. Generally, individuals who buy and sell securities professionally must register with a self-regulatory organization (SRO), meet certain qualifications requirements, and obey the rules of conduct adopted by the SRO. The broker/dealer firms for which they work must in turn register with the SEC and obey its rules relating to financial conditions and sales practices. They also must obey the rules of the exchange they belong to, and the rules of the National Association of Securities Dealers.

* Foreign Securities

Office of International Corporate Finance
U.S. Securities and Exchange Commission
450 5th St., NW
Washington, DC 20549   (202) 272-3246

Foreign corporations that want to sell securities in the U.S. must register those securities with the SEC. They are generally subject to the same rules and regulations that apply to securities of U.S. companies, although the nature of information which foreign companies make available to investors may be somewhat different.

* Form 10-Q: Financial Background on Companies

Public Reference Room
U.S. Securities and Exchange Commission
450 5th St., NW
Washington, DC 20549   (202) 272-7450

The *Form 10-Q* is a report filed quarterly by most registered companies, containing information that is important for investors to know. It includes unaudited financial statements and provides a continuing view of the company's financial position during the year. The information includes the income statement; balance sheet; description of important changes since the previous quarter; legal processing; changes in securities; default upon senior securities; and other important events. The report must be filed for each of the first three fiscal quarters and is due within 45 days of the close of the quarter. For more information on these reports, contact this office.

* Fraudulent Securities Schemes

Publications Section
Printing Branch, Stop C-11
U.S. Securities and Exchange Commission
Washington, DC 20549   (202) 272-7040

Several free publications are available through the Securities and Exchange Commission that warn investors against various fraudulent schemes. These include *How to Avoid Ponzi and Pyramid Schemes, Applicability of Securities Laws to Pyramid Schemes*, and *Warning to Investors About Get-Rich-Quick Schemes*. To obtain copies of these publications contact the above office.

* Help in Choosing an Investment

Office of Public Affairs
U.S. Securities and Exchange Commission
450 5th St., NW
Washington, DC 20549   (202) 272-2650

If you are thinking about investing your money, you might need assistance in making the most suitable choices for your needs. The SEC is a good source of information on securities with many publications, a public reference room, disclosure reports, and ready information on how to protect yourself.

* Holding Companies Acquisitions

Division of Investment Management
Office of Public Utility Regulation
U.S. Securities and Exchange Commission
450 5th St., NW
Washington, DC 20549   (202) 272-3018

To be authorized by the SEC, holding companies and their subsidiaries that acquire securities and utility assets must meet the following standards: 1) The acquisition must not tend toward interlocking relations or concentrating control to the point that it is harmful to investors or the public interest; 2) Any fees, commissions, or other payments for the acquisition must be reasonable; 3) The acquisition must not complicate the capital structure of the holding company system or harm system functions; and 4) The acquisition must help develop an integrated public utility system that is economical and efficient. Contact this office for more information on these standards.

* Holding Companies Issuance and Sales of Securities

Division of Investment Management
Office of Public Utility Regulation
U.S. Securities and Exchange Commission
450 5th St., NW
Washington, DC 20549   (202) 272-3018

Proposed security issues by any holding company must be analyzed, evaluated, and approved by the SEC staff to make sure that the security issues meet the following tests: 1) They conform to the security structure of the issuer and of other companies in the same holding company system; 2) They be proportionate to the earning power of the company; 3) They must be fitting and needed to help the company's business operate economically and efficiently; 4) The fees, commissions, and other payments in connection with the issue must be reasonable; and 5) The terms and conditions of the issue or sale of the security must not damage public or investor interest.

Other regulatory provisions regulate dividend payments (in circumstances where payments might result in corporate abuses); inter-company loans; solicitation of proxies, consents, and other authorizations; and insider trading. "Upstream" loans from subsidiaries to their parents and "upstream" or "cross-stream" loans from public utility companies to any holding company in the same holding company system require Commission approval. All services performed for any company in a holding company system by a service company in that system must be rendered at a fair cost. Contact this office for more information.

* Inquiry Processing

Office of Consumer Affairs and Information Services
Investor Services Branch
U.S. Securities and Exchange Commission

450 5th St., NW
Washington, DC 20549 (202) 272-7440
Consumer Telecommunications for the deaf (TTY-Voice) (202) 272-7065
The Commission's consumer affairs staff received approximately 49,000 investor complaints and inquiries last year. These written or telephone complaints and inquiries are routinely tracked and analyzed through a computer program. In addition to tracking basic information about the specific entity named, investor information, and dates of correspondence, special codes are used to identify the type of entity and the nature of the complaint. Consumer affairs specialists research reference materials and/or databases in order to respond to inquiries. An investor must submit a complaint in writing if he or she wants Commission assistance in obtaining an explanation or resolution. In processing the majority of written complaints, the consumer affairs specialist requests a review of the complaint by the compliance or legal department of the appropriate broker-dealer, mutual fund, or issuer, along with a report of that department's findings. This report is then reviewed to determine whether it responds to the issues raised in the complainant's letter. In many cases, the firm will take action to resolve the problem. In others, the investor's claims or allegations are disputed. Since the Commission is not authorized to serve as a judge or arbitrator, the specialist advises the investor of his or her general rights of private recourse.

* Insider Securities Trading
Superintendent of Documents
Government Printing office
Washington, DC 20402 (202) 783-3238
The *Official Summary* is a monthly report of securities transactions and holdings reported by "insiders" (officers, directors, and certain others) under clauses and agreements in the Federal securities laws. The *Summary* sells for $10.00 a copy, or $67.00 per year for a subscription in the U.S.; and $12.50 a copy, or $87.75 per year subscription foreign.

* Insider Trading
Office of Disclosure Policy
Division of Corporation Finance
450 5th St., NW
Washington, DC 20549 (202) 272-2589
Insider trading controls curb misuse of important confidential information which is not available to the general public. Examples of such misuse are buying or selling securities to make a profit or to avoid losses based on nonpublic information--or by telling others of the information so that they may buy or sell securities--before such information is generally available to all shareholders. Fines are imposed up to three times the profit gained, or loss avoided, through the use of nonpublic information. To further control the misuse of nonpublic information, the SEC requires all company officers and directors to file an initial report with them, and with the exchange on which the stock may be listed, which shows their holdings. Thereafter, they must file reports for any month during which there was any change in those holdings. Also, profits gained from purchases and sales (or sales and purchases) of such equity securities within any six-month period may be recovered by the company or by any security holder on its behalf in U.S. District Court. Such "insiders" are also not allowed to make short sales of their company's equity securities.

* Internationalization of Capital Markets
Office of International Corporate Finance
U.S. Securities and Exchange Commission
450 5th St., NW
Washington, DC 20549 (202) 272-3246
The SEC has made special efforts to get a wide range of viewpoints on issues that affect investors and the securities industry. One of the issues Commissioners and industry and investor representatives discuss is internationalization. The Commission has worked out agreements with several nations and is in the process of discussing the need for greater coordination among the international capital markets. For more information, contact this office.

* Interstate Holding Companies
Division of Investment Management
Office of Public Utility Regulation
U.S. Securities and Exchange Commission
450 5th St., NW
Washington, DC 20549 (202) 272-3018
Interstate holding companies engaged, through subsidiaries, in the electric utility business or those that sell natural or manufactured gas are subject to SEC regulations on matters such as structure of the system, acquisitions, combinations, and issue and sales of securities. These systems must register with the Commission and file initial and periodic reports containing detailed information about their organization, financial structure, and operations. For more information on these reports, contact this office.

* Investment Advisers Registration
Division of Investment Management
Office of Disclosure and Investment Adviser Regulation
U.S. Securities and Exchange Commission

Washington, DC 20549 (202) 272-2107
Persons or firms who make money advising others about securities investment must register with the SEC and conform to standards designed to protect investors. The Commission may deny, suspend, or revoke investment adviser registrations if, after notice and hearing, it finds that a statutory disqualification exists and that the action is in the public interest. Persons or firms can be disqualified if they are convicted for financial crimes or securities violations, mail fraud, knowingly filing false reports with the Commission, and willfully violating the Advisers Act, the Securities Act, the Securities Exchange Act, the Investment Company Act, or the rules of the Municipal Securities Rulemaking Board. In these cases, registrations are denied, suspended, or revoked. The Commission may obtain injunctions to prevent these violations of the law from happening again in the future. The SEC may also recommend prosecution by the Department of Justice for fraudulent misconduct or willful violation of the law or Commission rules. The Commission has adopted rules that define fraudulent, deceptive, or manipulative acts and practices. Investment advisers are required to:

-Make known the reason they are selling securities to their clients;
-Maintain books and records according to Commission rules, and
-Make books and records available to the Commission for inspections.

* Investment Company Registration
Public Reference Room
Securities and Exchange Commission
450 5th St., NW
Washington, DC 20549 (202) 272-7450
Activities of companies who invest, reinvest, and trade in securities, and who offer their securities to the public, are subject to the following SEC regulations: 1) They must disclose their financial condition and investment policies to provide investors complete information about their activities; 2) They cannot substantially change the nature of their business or investment policies without stockholder approval; 3) They may not have officers or directors who are guilty of securities fraud; 4) Underwriters, investment bankers, or brokers must constitute only a minority of the directors; 5) They must submit management contracts (and any material changes) to security holders for their approval; 6) They may not perform transactions with their directors, officers, or affiliated companies or persons without SEC approval; 7) They are forbidden to issue senior securities except under specified conditions and terms; and 8) They are prohibited from pyramiding and cross-ownership of their securities. Other provisions involve the following: advisory fees that don't conform to an adviser's fiduciary duty; sales and repurchases of securities issued by investment companies; exchange offers; and other activities of investment companies, including special provisions for periodic payment plans and face-amount certificate companies. Investment companies must not only be registered, but must also file periodic reports and are subject to the SEC's proxy and "insider" trading rules. For more information, contact this office.

* Investor Brochure
Superintendent of Documents
Government Printing office
Washington, DC 20402 (202) 783-3238
The *Investor Brochure* contains helpful information every investor should know, including information on securities markets, how investors are protected, types of investments, how to choose an investment, getting started, trading stocks and bonds, investment companies, steps to take once you've made your investment, and more. It is available for $1.25 from the GPO.

* Legal Interpretation and Guidance
Office of the Chief Counsel
Division of Corporation Finance
U.S. Securities and Exchange Commission
450 5th St., NW
Washington, DC 20549 (202) 272-2573
The Securities and Exchange Commission is willing to help the public, prospective registrants, and others, interpret the securities laws and regulations. In this way they can help answer legal questions about how laws apply and are regulated in certain situations, and to aid them in following the laws. For example, this advice might include an informal opinion about whether the offering of a particular security is subject to registration requirements and, if it is, advice on the type of information that must go on the registration form. By interpreting the rules and laws, the SEC makes sure registrants conform to them. For help with interpreting laws, or guidance, contact this office.

* Lost and Stolen Securities
Securities Information Center, Inc.
P.O. Box 9121
Wellesley Hills, MA 02181 (617) 235-8270
Every insured bank, broker, and registered transfer agent must be registered with the Securities Information Center. The Center maintains a computerized reporting and inquiry system for lost, stolen, counterfeit, and forged securities. All FDIC-insured banks are required to contact the Securities Information Center when they take custody of stocks or bonds valued in excess of $10,000 in

order to verify their validity.

* Lost and Stolen Securities Database

Division of Market Regulation
U.S. Securities and Exchange Commission
450 5th St., NW
Washington, DC 20549   (202) 272-7393

The SEC has a computer-assisted reporting and inquiry system for lost, stolen, counterfeit, and forged securities. All insured banks and brokers, members of the federal reserve, dealers, and other securities firms are required to register with the Securities Information Center, Inc., P.O. Box 421, Wellesley Hills, MA 02181; (617) 235-8270, where a central database records reported thefts and losses. Contact this office for more information.

* Margin Trading

Office of Legal Policy and Trading Practices
Division of Market Regulation
U.S. Securities and Exchange Commission
450 5th St., NW
Washington, DC 20549   (202) 272-2836

The Board of Governors of the Federal Reserve System sets limits on the amount of credit available to purchase or carry securities, and then periodically reviews them. This is to make sure that to much of the nation's credit isn't used in the securities markets. While the credit restrictions are set by the Board, the SEC handles investigations and enforcement.

* Market Investigations

Division of Market Regulation
Office of Inspections and Financial Responsibility
U.S. Security and Exchange Commission
450 5th St., NW
Washington, DC 20549   (202) 272-2830

SEC regional offices and its Division of Market Regulation conduct surprise investigations to check the books and records of regulated people and organizations to make sure their business practices are legal. Inquiries are also conducted into changes in the market, especially stocks which don't appear to result from general market trends or from known developments affecting the issuing company. For more information, contact your regional office or contact or the office above.

* Market Surveillance

Market Surveillance
Division of Enforcement
U.S. Securities and Exchange Commission
450 5th St., NW
Washington, DC 20549   (202) 272-2230

Securities and Exchange Commission regulates securities trading practices in the exchange and the over-the-counter markets, and it has adopted regulations which, among other things, 1) define acts or practices which constitute a "manipulative or deceptive device or contrivance" prohibited by the statute; 2) regulate short selling, stabilizing transactions, and similar matters; 3) regulate the hypothecation of customers' securities; and 4) provide safeguards with respect to the financial responsibility of brokers and dealers. For more information on market surveillance, contact this office.

* Meeting Notes

Office of the Secretary
U.S. Securities and Exchange Commission
450 5th St., NW
Washington, DC 20549

For audiovisual tapes of the open meeting minutes, send your request in writing to this office.

* New Rules: Securities

Publications Section
U.S. Securities and Exchange Commission
450 5th St., NW, Stop 1-2
Washington, DC 20549   (202) 272-7460

For copies of recently adopted rules contact this office.

* Opening An Account

Public Reference Room
Securities and Exchange Commission
450 5th St., NW
Washington, DC 20549   (202) 272-7450

Before opening an account with a broker, talk with registered representatives at several firms to find the person who best suits your needs. It is added protection to know that most broker/dealers registered with the SEC are members of the Securities Investor Protection Corporation, a nonprofit membership corporation

which administers laws to help protect investors securities and funds held in brokerage accounts. Also, before choosing a broker, to get more factual information about the firm itself, you may order a copy of the firm's registration statement (Form BD) from the office above.

* Opinions and Orders

The Office of Administrative Law Judges
U.S. Securities and Exchange Commission
450 5th St., NW
Washington, DC 20549   (202) 272-7636

The Office of Opinions and Review
U.S. Securities and Exchange Commission
450 5th St., NW
Washington, DC 20549   (202) 272-7400

The administrative law judges are responsible for scheduling and conducting hearings on administrative proceedings instituted by others. Opinions and orders resulting from these hearings are prepared by the Office of Opinions and Review. For more information on these hearings contact either of the offices above.

* Ponzi or Pyramid Schemes

Office of Consumer Affairs and Information Services
Investor Services Branch
U.S. Securities and Exchange Commission
450 5th St., NW
Washington, DC 20549   (202) 272-7440
Consumer Telecommunications for the deaf (TTY-Voice)
                                        (202) 272-7065

The Securities and Exchange Commission will provide warnings against investing in a Ponzi or pyramid scheme. These schemes are varied, but usually promise very high yield, quick return, a "once in a lifetime" opportunity, and the chance to "get in on the ground floor." To notify the Securities and Exchange Commission of a fraudulent scheme and for further information, contact this office.

* Proxy Filings

Public Reference Branch
Securities and Exchange Commission
450 5th St., NW, Room 1024
Washington, DC 20549-1002   (202) 272-7450,(202) 272-7459 (TTD)

A proxy statement is a document which lets people know who holds stock in a company so they can cast educated votes on matters which are brought up at company meetings. Typically, a security holder is also given a "proxy" who can vote his or her securities if the holder does not attend the meeting. Definitive (final) copies of proxy statements and proxies are filed with the Commission at the time they are sent to security holders. Preliminary proxy filings are nonpublic upon filing, but may be obtained under FOIA once the definitive proxy has been filed and released. Some definitive filings are available in printed copy and on microfiche.

* Proxy Solicitations

Office of Chief Counsel
Division of Corporation Finance
U.S. Securities and Exchange Commission
Washington, DC 20549   (202) 272-2573

The SEC administers laws which check the votes from holders of registered securities, both listed and over-the-counter, to elect directors and/or to approve corporate action. Solicitations, whether by management or minority groups, must give all important information needed for holders to vote. Holders also must be given an opportunity to vote "yes" or "no" on each matter. In a contest for control of corporate management, the rules require the names and interests of all "participants" in the proxy contest be made known so that holders can vote intelligently on corporate actions that require their approval. The Commission's rules require that proposed proxy material be filed early so the Commission can examine it to be sure all the information needed is given. In addition, the rules allow shareholders vote at the annual meetings. For more information on proxy solicitations, contact this office.

* Publications Listing

Publications
U.S. Securities and Exchange Commission
450 5th St., NW, Mail Stop C-11
Washington, DC 20549   (202) 272-7460

You can obtain a listing of current SEC publications by visiting Publications in Room 3C48 or writing to the office above.

* Reference Microfiche

Public Reference Branch
Securities and Exchange Commission
450 5th St., NW, Room 1024

Washington, DC 20549-1002   (202) 272-7450,(202) 272-7459 (TTD)
The public may use the following reference microfiche in the Public Reference Room:

Workload List by File Name. Includes cumulative history and a quarterly supplement.
Workload List by File Number. Includes a cumulative history and a quarterly supplement.
SEC Public Reference. An alphabetical list of all registrants since 1934, including numbers of all files for each named registrant.
Ownership Report System: Cumulative. Contains the cumulative data in the *Official Summary of Security Transactions and Holdings* of corporate affiliates and "insiders."

* Registered Company Disclosure Statements (Prospectus)

Public Reference Room
U.S. Securities and Exchange Commission
450 5th St., NW
Washington, DC 20549   (202) 272-7450

Before any company offers its securities for sale to the general public, (with certain exceptions) it must file with the SEC a registration statement known as a "prospectus." The prospectus contains the basic business and financial information on an issuer dealing with a particular security that's being offered to help investors evaluate an investment and thereby helps them make an educated investment decision. In its registration statement, the company must provide information on the nature of its business, the company's management, the type of security it offers and its relation to other securities the company may have on the market, and the company's financial statements as certified by independent public accountants. Many companies must continue to update this information periodically, even if no new securities are being offered, and copies of the prospectus must be provided to investors. The SEC reviews registration statements for accuracy and completeness. Investors who purchase securities and suffer losses have important recovery rights under the law if they can prove that there was incomplete or inaccurate disclosure of important facts in the registration statement or prospectus. Investors may sue to recover losses through the courts if false or misleading statements were made in the prospectus. Some filings are available in paper form, and all filings are available on microfiche from the above office.

* Registration Exemptions for Securities

Registration
U.S. Securities and Exchange Commission
450 5th St., NW
Washington, DC 20549   (202) 272-7250

In general, registration requirements apply to securities of both domestic and foreign issuers, and to securities of foreign governments (or their instrumentalities) sold in domestic securities markets. However, some securities and transactions are exempt from registration provisions. Among these are:

-Private offerings to a limited number of persons or institutions who already have access to the information that registration would disclose and who do not propose to redistribute the securities;

-Offerings restricted to residents of the state in which the issuing company is organized and doing business;

-Securities of municipal, state, federal, and other governmental instrumentalities as well as charitable institutions, banks, and carriers subject to the Interstate Commerce Act;

-Offerings not exceeding certain specified amounts according to regulations of the Commission; and

-Offerings of "small business investment companies" made in accordance with rules and regulations of the Commission.

Whether or not the securities are exempt from registration, antifraud provisions apply to all sales of securities involving interstate commerce or the mails. For more information, contact this office.

* Regulations: Securities, Public Holding Companies

Publications Section
Printing Branch, Stop C-11
U.S. Securities and Exchange Commission
Washington, DC 20549   (202) 272-7040

Regulation S-X is a basic accounting regulation which along with a number of opinions issued as *Accounting Series Releases,* governs the form and content of most of the financial statements filed with the Commission. *Regulation S-X* contains a form and requirements for financial statements of the Securities Act of 1933, the Securities Exchange Act of 1934, the Public Utility Holding Company Act of 1935, the Investment Company Act, and the Energy Policy and Conservation Act. There is no charge for copies of these statutes, but a 9" x 12" self-addressed envelope with $1.58 postage must be enclosed with each order.

* Reviewing a Prospectus

Public Reference Room
Securities and Exchange Commission
450 5th St., NW
Washington, DC 20549   (202) 272-7450

If you are considering an investment in an open-end investment company, unit investment trust, or variable annuity, you should obtain and read a current prospectus before looking at other sales literature. Do not hesitate to seek advice if there is anything in the prospectus you do not understand. And if you do buy shares in the company, save the prospectus to refer to in the future. Some of the things the prospectus will tell you are the company's investment objectives--in other words, how it is designed to provide income, protect capital, minimize taxes, and so forth, the amount of any sales charges and the procedures for redeeming shares, and what risks may be involved in placing your money in that particular company. Registration is there to give you the facts about the company you're dealing with, and to thereby help you to make an informed decision. Keep in mind, however, that the Commission does not supervise the investment activities of these companies and that regulation by the Commission does not imply safety of investment. To obtain a current prospectus, contact this office.

* Revocations of Securities Registration

Office of Chief Counsel
Division of Market Regulation
U.S. Securities and Exchange Commission
450 5th St., NW
Washington, DC 20549   (202) 272-3000

The SEC can deny registration to securities firms and, in some cases, may impose sanctions against a firm and/or individual in a firm for violation of Federal securities laws (such as manipulation of the market price of a stock, misappropriation of customer funds or securities, or other abuse of customer trust). The Commission polices the securities industry through its own inspections and by working with other securities groups. Brokers and dealers who violate regulations risk suspension or loss of registration with the Commission (and thus the right to continue conducting an interstate securities business) or suspension or expulsion from a self-regulatory organization. For more information, contact this SEC office.

* Rulemaking

Office of Public Affairs
Securities and Exchange Commission
450 Fifth Street NW
Washington, DC 20549   (202) 272-2650

Rulemaking is one of the most common activities the divisions perform. The rules and registration forms that the SEC uses must constantly be evaluated and reviewed to make sure they are as practical and efficient as possible. If a particular rule appears to be burdensome or isn't achieving its objective, a staff members can recommend changes to the Commissioners. Many suggestions for rule changes follow consultation with industry representatives and others who are affected. The Commission normally gives advance public notice when they are planning to adopt new rules or registration forms, or to amend forms so that interested members of the public can comment on them. For information on rulemaking contact the individual divisions at the SEC.

* Schedule of Fees for Records Services

Public Reference Branch
Securities and Exchange Commission
450 5th St., NW
Washington, DC 20549-1002   (202) 272-7450

The *Schedule of Fees for Records Services* is a printed handout summarizing charges for search, review, and copy services for SEC records. To obtain your free copy contact this office.

* Section 13F Securities

Public Reference Branch
Securities and Exchange Commission
450 5th St., NW, Room 1024
Washington, DC 20549-1002   (202) 272-7450,(202) 272-7459 (TTD)

The quarterly publication, *13F Securities,* is a list of all current Section 13(f) securities, that is, securities of a class described in Section 13(d)(1) of the Exchange Act.

* Securities and Exchange Docket

The Commerce Clearing House, Inc.
4025 West Peterson Avenue
Chicago, IL 60646   (312) 583-8500

Sorg Inc.
Appeals Handbook Department

Investments and Financial Services

11 Eighth Ave.
New York, NY 10011   (212) 741-6600
The *SEC Docket* is a weekly collection of the full text of SEC releases, including the full texts of *Accounting Series* releases, corporate reorganization releases, and litigation releases. It is sold for $200 per year or $180 per year for two years. Subscriptions may be ordered from either of the companies listed above.

* Securities and Exchange Annual Reports
Superintendent of Documents
Government Printing office
Washington, DC 20402   (202) 783-3238
The First through Fiftieth SEC annual reports to Congress are out of print and available only for reference purposes in the SEC and Regional Offices. *The Fifty-First Annual Report (1985)* sells for $3.50, the *Fifty-Second (1986)* sells for $4.75, the *Fifty-Third (1987)* sells for $4.50, and the *Fifty-Fourth (1988)* sells for $5.00. These most recent annual reports are available at from the GPO.

* Securities and Exchange: How It Works
Publications Section
Printing Branch, Stop C-11
U.S. Securities and Exchange Commission
Washington, DC 20549   (202) 272-7040
The Work of the SEC discusses the laws administered by the Commission, its organization, and public information about it. To obtain a copy contact this office.

* Securities and Exchange Information Line
SEC Information Line
U.S. Securities and Exchange Commission
450 5th St., NW
Washington, DC 20549   (202) 272-5624
The Security and Exchange Commission's Information Line provides general information about the SEC 24 hours a day, 7 days a week. Different digit codes correspond to messages that callers might be interested in. The directory of messages and digit codes is as follows:

General Information
SEC Information Line Directory (10)
SEC Address and Business Hours (15)
SEC Organizational Structure (20)
Public Affairs (25)
Public Reference Room (30)
Publications (33)

Office of Consumer Affairs and Information Services
Investor Inquiries (35)
Investor Complaints (40)
Freedom of Information Act Requests (45)
Privacy Act Requests (50)

Division of Corporation Finance
Small Business Filers (55)
International Corporate Finance (60)

Division of Investment Management
Investment Adviser Registration (65)
Investment Company Registration (70)
Applications for Exemptive Relief (75)
Electronic Filing of Form N-SAR (80)

Division of Market Regulation
Broker-Dealer Registration (85)
Lost and Stolen Securities (90)
Trading Suspensions (95)

For operator assistance, press zero. Note that callers using rotary dial telephones cannot access messages in the system. These callers will automatically be switched to an operator for assistance.

* Securities and Exchange Monthly Statistical Review
The Office of Economic Analysis
U.S. Securities and Exchange Commission
450 5th St., NW
Washington, DC 20549   (202) 272-7104

Superintendent of Documents
Government Printing Office
Washington, DC 20402
The *SEC Monthly Statistical Review* contains data on odd lot and round lot transactions, block distributions, working capital of U.S. corporations, assets of noninsured pension funds, Rule 144 filings, and 8K reports. The Office of Economic Analysis collects, processes, and publishes data on the financial condition of the securities industry, registered securities issues, and the trading

volume and value of exchange-listed securities in its SEC Monthly Statistical Review. It is available for $19 per year from the Superintendent of Documents, Government Printing Office, Washington, D.C. 20402, and for more information on its contents, contact the SEC Public Reference Room.

* Securities and Exchange News Digest
Washington Service Bureau
1225 Connecticut Ave., NW
Washington, DC 20036   (202) 833-9200

Mead Data Central - LEXIS
1050 Connecticut Ave., NW
Suite 1090
Washington, DC 20036   (202) 785-3550
The *News Digest* is a daily summary of important SEC developments, including listings of registration, acquisition, and 8-K filings received by the Commission. It also lists certain no-action letters issued by the Commission, and time, date, place, and subject of Commission Open Meetings. The private firms listed above offer subscriptions to the *SEC News Digest*.

* Securities and Exchange Publications on Audio Cassettes
Publications Section
Printing Branch, Stop C-11
U.S. Securities & Exchange Commission
Washington, DC 20549   (202) 272-7040
SEC publications may be taped on audio cassette at the request of individuals with handicaps. Orders should allow time for taping and processing.

* Securities and Exchange Public Reference Room
Public Reference Branch
Securities and Exchange Commission
450 5th St., NW, Room 1024
Washington, DC 20549-1002   (202) 272-7450,(202) 272-7459 (TTD)
The SEC ordinarily makes public most of the information filed with it, including registration statements, proxy material, quarterly and annual reports, applications, and similar documents filed by corporations, mutual funds, or broker-dealers. Public Reference Rooms are located in Chicago, New York, and Washington, D.C., regional offices where individuals can review and copy all public documents. In addition, copies may be ordered by writing or phoning the Commission. This information filed with the Commission is available for inspection weekdays from 9:00 a.m. to 5:00 p.m., and copies of the text of this material can be obtained from a private contractor. For a cost estimate or to order materials, contact this office.

* Securities and Public Offerings
Center for Electronic Records
National Archives and Records Administration
8th St. & Pennsylvania Ave., NW, Room 20E
Washington, DC 20408   (202) 523-3267
The National Archives maintains wide variety of archival information regarding the Securities and Exchange Commission, such as a broker-dealer directory, a corporation index system, and an investment company datafile. These datafiles, which are often continuously updated, are for sale on 9 track computer tape on a cost recovery basis. For a complete list of the data available, along with a current price list, contact the Center for Electronic Records.

* Securities Databases
Public Reference Branch
Securities and Exchange Commission
450 5th St., NW, Room 1024
Washington, DC 20549-1002   (202) 272-7450,(202) 272-7459 (TTD)
Computer terminals which access certain SEC databases are located in the Reference Room for use by the public. You are welcome to use the terminals at any time during the business hours of the Public Reference Room. The databases are as follows:

Workload Teleprocessing Display System (WRKD). Provides an up-to-date listing of filings made by registrants. Filings are maintained on this index for approximately 40 months. Information on earlier filings may be found by using the history microfiche.
Securities Reporting System (SIRS). Provides information on securities transactions by company officers, directors, and beneficial owners. For each transaction, SIRS will list the trading date, name of the owner, number of shares involved, price per share, SEC received date, and the type of transaction (stock dividend, acquisition by gift, private purchase, open market purchase, stock split, etc.).
Proposed Sale of Securities Inquiry System (PSSI). An online retrieval system which lets the public access information filed on Forms 144. The system contains six months of historical data. Monthly updates are done around the 10th of each month. Searching by either the Issuer's Name or the Seller's Name or both, you

will receive information such as the name of the issuer, the seller, the class of security being sold, date acquired and acquisition codes, number of securities to be sold, market value, shares outstanding, and more.

Proceedings & Litigation Action Display System (PLAD). An online, public system capable of reviewing public litigation data. The data displayed includes the type of action, name, address, jurisdiction, action date, violation, and disposition. The types of actions are federal, state and Canadian, National Association of Securities Dealers, and Stock Exchange.

* Securities Laws: Legal Assistance
The Office of Small Business Policy
Division of Corporation Finance
U.S. Securities and Exchange Commission
450 5th St., NW
Washington, DC 20549   (202) 272-2644
The staff of the Office of Small Business Policy, as well as the personnel of the SEC Regional Offices, will assist you with any questions you may have regarding federal securities laws. For information about state securities laws, contact the appropriate state securities commissioner, whose office is usually located in the capital city.

* Securities Markets and Information Technology
Office of Technology Assessment
600 Pennsylvania Ave., SE
Washington, DC 20510   (202) 228-6772
Fundamental changes are taking place in the securities and related financial markets that will affect the structure and operations of the exchanges, the links between markets, the nature of the products traded, and the strategies by which they are traded. OTA is currently studying the role that new information technologies--computers and telecommunications--play in these accelerating changes. Contact Vary Coates, the project director, for more information.

* Securities Rules and Regulations
Superintendent of Documents
Government Printing office
Washington, DC 20402-9325   (202) 783-3238
The entire text of the Commissions's rules and regulations is available from several private publishers of legal information, and many books on this subject are available at public libraries. Volumes of *Title 17 of the Code of Federal Regulations of April 1988* are available to the public. Rules (forms & interpretive releases also) under the securities laws are available as follows:

Chapter I - Parts 1 to 199. These regulations administered by the Commodity Futures Trading Commission are $14.00.
Chapter II - Parts 200 to 239. This includes the SEC organization, conduct and ethics, information and requests, rules of practice, Regulation S-X and S-K and the Securities Exchange Act of 1933 for $14.00.
Chapter III - Parts 240 to End. This includes the Securities Exchange Act of 1934, the Public Utility Holding Company, and the Trust Indenture Investor Protection Corporation Acts for $21.00.

* Securities Violations: Litigation, Actions, and Proceedings
Public Reference Branch
Securities and Exchange Commission
450 5th St., NW, Room 1024
Washington, DC 20549-1002   (202) 272-7450,(202) 272-7459 (TTD)
The quarterly *Litigation, Actions and Proceedings Bulletin* contains information of official actions with respect to securities violations reported to the Commission. In addition, the *Bulletin* contains a supplement which lists the names of individuals reported as being wanted on charges of violations of law in connection with securities transactions. Contact this office for more information on obtaining copies.

* Small Business and the SEC
Publications Section
Printing Branch, Stop C-11
U.S. Securities and Exchange Commission
Washington, DC 20549   (202) 272-7040
The free booklet, *Q&A: Small Business and the SEC,* discusses capital formation and the federal securities laws and is designed to help you understand some of the basis, necessary requirements that apply when you wish to raise capital by selling securities. It answers such questions as:

What are the federal securities laws?
Is any special help available for a small business that wants to sell its securities?
Should my company "go public"?
How does my small business "go public"?
If my company becomes "public," what are its disclosure obligations?
Are there legal ways to sell securities without registering with the SEC?

Are there state law requirements in addition to those under the federal securities laws?
Where can I go for more information?

* Small Business Policy
The Office of Small Business Policy
Division of Corporation Finance
U.S. Securities and Exchange Commission
450 5th St., NW
Washington, DC 20549   (202) 272-2644
This office directs the SEC's small business rulemaking goals, reviews and comments on the impact the SEC rule proposals have on small issuers, and serves as a liaison with Congressional committees, government agencies, and other groups concerned with small business. Information on security laws that pertain to small business offerings may be obtained from this office.

* Standards for Securities Registration
Registration
U.S. Securities and Exchange Commission
450 5th St., NW
Washington, DC 20549   (202) 272-7250
Registering securities with the SEC does not stop the sale of stock in risky, poorly managed, or unprofitable companies. Nor does the Commission approve or disapprove securities on their merits. The only standard which must be met when registering securities is adequate and accurate disclosure of required information on the company and its securities it wants to sell. The fairness of the terms, the issuing company's chances of successful operation, and other factors affecting the merits of investing in the securities have no bearing on the question of whether or not securities may be registered. Contact this office for more information on SEC securities standards.

* Statutes
Publications Section
Printing Branch, Stop C-11
U.S. Securities and Exchange Commission
Washington, DC 20549   (202) 272-7040
The U.S. Securities and Exchange Commissions's mission is to administer federal securities laws to try to protect investors. The purpose of these laws is to make sure that the securities markets are fair and honest and to provide the means to enforce the securities laws through sanctions where necessary. Free copies of the following laws administered by the Commission are available from the above office:

Securities Act of 1933
Securities Exchange Act of 1934
Public Utility Holding Company Act of 1935
Trust Indenture Act of 1939
Investment Company Act of 1940
Investment Advisers Act of 1940

* Statutory Sanctions
Division of Enforcement
U.S. Securities and Exchange Commission
450 5th St., NW
Washington, DC 20549   (202) 272-2900
Commission investigations are conducted privately to determine whether there is valid evidence of a law violation; whether action should begin to determine if a violation actually occurred; and, if so, whether some sanction should be imposed. The following provisions of the law, along with disclosure requirements, tend to inhibit fraudulent stock promotions and operations to help build the public's confidence in securities investments. When facts show possible fraud or other law violations, the laws provide several courses of action the Commission may take:

-Civil injunction: where the SEC may apply to a U.S. District Court for an order forbidding the acts or practices claimed to violate the law or Commission rules.
-Administrative remedy, where the Commission may take specific action after hearings. It may issue orders to suspend or expel members from exchanges or over-the-counter dealers association; deny, suspend, or revoke broker-dealer registrations; or censure for misconduct or bar individuals from employment with a registered firm temporarily or permanently.

* Stop Orders
Office of Chief Counsel
Division of Corporation Finance
U.S Securities and Exchange Commission
450 5th St., NW
Washington, DC 20549   (202) 272-2573
The SEC may conclude that the lack of important information in some registration statements appears to be deliberate attempts to conceal or mislead. They may also conclude there is an attempt to conceal or mislead if the deficiencies are not corrected through the informal letter process. In these cases,

the Commission may decide that it is in the public interest to conduct a hearing to develop the facts by evidence which determines if a "stop order" should be issued to refuse or suspend the statement. Although losses which may have been suffered in the purchase of securities are not restored to investors by the stop order, the Commissions's order stops future public sales. Also, the decision and the evidence on which it is based may help notify investors of their rights and aid them in their own recovery suits. For more information on stop orders, contact this SEC office.

* Tender Offer Solicitations

Office of Tender Offers
Division of Corporation Finance
U.S. Securities and Exchange Commission
450 5th St., NW
Washington, DC 20549   (202) 272-3097

The Commission requires that important information be made known by anyone seeking to acquire over five percent of a company's securities by direct purchase or by tender offer. This information must also be given by anyone seeking shareholders to accept or reject a tender offer. Thus, as with the proxy rules, public investors holding stock in these corporations may make more informed decisions on takeover bids. These disclosure provisions are supported by certain other controls which help ensure investor protection in tender offers.

* The October 1987 Market Break

The Office of Consumer Affairs
U.S. Securities and Exchange Commission
450 5th St., NW
Washington, DC 20549   (202) 272-7440

The Office of Consumer Affairs participated with other SEC organizations in developing the staff report on the October 1987 market break. The office analyzed the "market break complaints" that the SEC and Self-regulatory organizations received from October 14th through the 30th in 1987. Over 1,500 written complaints resulted from the market break. An additional 9,300 telephone complaints and questions were received during a six-week period, beginning October 19. Findings resulting from the consumer complaint analysis are contained in Chapter 12 of the staff report entitled, *The October 1987 Market Break*. The report is available for $38.00 from the Superintendent of Documents, Government Printing Office, Washington, D.C. 20402; (202) 783-3238.

* Transaction Complaint Investigations

Division of Enforcement
U.S. Securities and Exchange Commission
450 5th St., NW
Washington, DC 20549   (202) 272-2900

Under the laws it administers, the SEC investigates complaints and other suspected law violations in securities transactions. Most of the Commission's investigations are private and are often about selling securities without registration or distorting facts about securities for sale are distorted or left out. Other types of inquiries relate to manipulating market prices of securities, misappropriating or illegally hypothecating customers' funds, conducting a securities business while bankrupt, broker-dealers buying or selling securities from or to customers at unfair prices, and broker-dealers who don't treat customers fairly. Inquiries and complaints by investors and the general public are the main sources of leads for detecting law violations in securities transactions. For more information on securities violations, contact this office.

* Treasury Securities

Federal Reserve Bank of Richmond
Public Services Department
P.O. Box 27622
Richmond, VA 23261   (804) 697-8000

On behalf of the U.S. Treasury, the Federal Reserve Banks handle public sales, transfers, and redemptions of U.S. government securities. *Investing In Government Securities* outlines procedures for purchasing marketable U.S. government securities and is available free from the Federal Reserve Bank of Richmond, or by contacting any Federal Reserve Bank for additional information.

* Treasury Securities Booklet

Federal Reserve Bank of Richmond
Public Services Department
P.O. Box 27622
Richmond, VA 23261   (804) 697-8000.

The booklet, Buying Treasury Securities at Federal Reserve Banks, which provides detailed information on buying treasury bills, notes, and bonds, can be purchased for $2.00 from this office.

* Trust Indentures

Division of Corporation Finance
U.S. Securities and Exchange Commission
450 5th St., NW
Washington, DC 20549   (202) 272-2800

The SEC ensures that bonds, debentures, notes, and similar debt securities offered for public sale and issued under trust indentures with more than $7.5 million of securities outstanding at any one time, conform to certain statutory standards. In an effort to protect the rights and interests of purchasers, the SEC works to:

-Prohibit the indenture trustee from conflicting interests which might affect its duties on behalf of the securities purchasers,
-Require the trustee to be a corporation with as little combined capital and surplus as possible,
-Impose high standards of conduct and responsibility on the trustee,
-Stop special collection of certain claims the issuer owes the trustee if there is default,
-Assure that the issuer supply the trustee with evidence of following indenture terms and conditions (such as those relating to the release or substitution of mortgaged property, issue of new securities, or satisfaction of the indenture), and
-Require the trustee to provide reports and notices to security holders.

They also work to make sure that the security holder's have a right to sue individually for principal and interest, except under certain circumstances. To help security holders communicate with each other on their rights as security holders, a list must be maintained. The SEC examines applications to qualify for trust indenture for compliance with the law and the Commission's rules. For more information on trust indentures, contact this office.

Government Bonds, Bills and Notes

* Education Savings Bonds

U.S. Savings Bonds Division
Department of the Treasury
1111 20th St., NW
Washington, DC 20226   (202) 634-5353

The new education savings bond program permits qualified taxpayers to exclude from their gross income all or a portion of the interest earned on eligible Series EE savings bonds issued after 1989. To qualify for this exclusion, tuition and other post-secondary educational expenses must be incurred by the taxpayer, the taxpayer's spouse, or the taxpayer's dependent at postsecondary educational institutions. These institutions are those that meet federal financial aid program standards. In addition, there are income limitations on participation in the program. Contact this office for more information on the program.

* Federal Debt Management

Federal Finance
Office of the Assistant Secretary of the Treasury
for Domestic Finance
U.S. Department of the Treasury
1500 Pennsylvania Ave., NW, Room 2334
Washington, DC 20220   (202) 566-5806

Federal debt instruments are administered by this office, including public debt securities, nonmarketable public issues, federal agency securities, and government-sponsored agency securities.

* Government Securities Claims

Claims Section
Office of Securities and Accounting Services
Bureau of the Public Debt
U.S. Department of the Treasury
300 13th St., SW
Washington, DC 20239   (202) 447-1339

This office handles claims for lost, stolen, mutilated, or destroyed government securities.

* Retirement Bonds

Bureau of the Public Debt
U.S. Department of the Treasury
200 Third St.
Parkersburg, WV 26106-1328   (304) 420-6516

Retirement plan bonds and individual retirement bonds are no longer being issued. Redemption tables with the current value of the bonds, beginning with those issued in 1963, are available.

* Savings Bond Buyer's Guide

Office of Public Affairs
Marketing and Communications Branch
U.S. Savings Bonds Division
Department of the Treasury
1111 20th St., NW
Washington, DC 20226   (202) 634-5377

Building Security, Fulfilling Dreams: U.S. Savings Bonds Buyer's Guide describes the information you need to purchase savings bonds, such as available series and denominations, interest rates, where to buy, registration, annual limitation on purchases, redemption, tax status, exchange of series HH bonds, and safety features.

* Savings Bonds Information Guide

Consumer Information Center
P.O. Box 100
Pueblo, CO 81002

The *Savings Bonds Question and Answer Book* explains everything about the savings bond program, including information on purchase, interest, maturity, replacement, redemption, exchange, and taxes. (451V - $.50)

* Savings Bonds: Lost, Stolen or Destroyed

Bond Consultant Branch
Bureau of the Public Debt
U.S. Department of the Treasury
200 Third St.
Parkersburg, WV 26106-1328   (304) 420-6112

If your Savings Bonds are lost, stolen, or destroyed, you can apply for free replacement to the address above.

* Savings Bonds Rate Information

U.S. Savings Bonds Division
Department of the Treasury
1111 20th St., NW
Washington, DC 20226   (800) US-BONDS

For the current market rate of U.S. Savings Bonds, call the above number 24 hours a day, seven days a week.

* Savings Bonds Statistics

Market Analysis Office
Planning and Product Development Branch
U.S. Savings Bonds Division
Department of the Treasury
1111 20th St., NW, Room 302
Washington, DC 20226   (202) 634-5360

To obtain statistics on sales, redemption, and retention of U.S. Savings Bonds, contact the office above.

* Savings Bonds Volunteer Activities

Office of Banking and Volunteer Activities
U.S. Savings Bonds Division
Department of the Treasury
1111 20th St., NW, Room 323
Washington, DC 20226   (202) 634-2062

Volunteers within the Savings Bond marketing effort are the chief executive officers within industry who promote the purchase of bonds through payroll deductions. Contact the above office for additional information.

* Savings Bonds: Where to Buy

Savings Bonds Operations
Bureau of the Public Debt
U.S. Department of the Treasury
200 Third St.
Parkersburg, WV 26106-1328   (304) 420-6112

Series EE Bonds may be purchased over the counter from or through most commercial banks, as well as many savings and loans and other financial institutions qualified as issuing agents. They may also be purchased in person or by mail from Federal Reserve Banks and the Treasury Department, Bureau of the Public Debt. EE Bonds may also be purchased through payroll savings plans offered by employers and through Bond-a-Month plans offered by some financial institutions. Series HH Bonds are available only on exchange for eligible Series EE/E Bonds, and U.S. Savings Notes, with total redemption values of $500 or more, and through the authorized reinvestment of the redemption proceeds of matured Series H Bonds. They are issued only by Federal Reserve Banks and the Bureau of the Public Debt.

* Savings Notes

Bureau of the Public Debt
U.S. Department of the Treasury
200 Third St.
Parkersburg, WV 26106-1328   (304) 420-6516

If you are a holder of savings notes, you may obtain information concerning their value and redemption from the office above.

* Treasury Direct

Securities Transactions Branch
Bureau of Public Debt
U.S. Department of the Treasury
300 13th St.
Washington, DC 20239-0001   (202) 287-4113
Hearing Impaired TTD Line: (202) 287-4097

Treasury Direct is the book-entry system within the Bureau of the Public Debt whereby new issues of bills, notes, and bonds are maintained as accounting records in a nationwide computer system with the Treasury and Federal Reserve, rather than in definitive form as engraved certificates. This involves only securities issued since July, 1986. The entire investment portfolio is maintained in a single master account. Direct access to your account is available nationwide from Federal Reserve Banks. Direct deposit of the refund, interest, and principal interest payments is also available. Multiple automatic reinvestment options can be used, enabling you to request reinvestment for up to two years after the first maturity date without having to complete and mail a reinvestment request. To mail tenders, address to: Bureau of the Public Debt, Department N, Washington, DC 20239-1500.

* Treasury Information Line

Customer Services
Bureau of Public Debt
U.S. Department of the Treasury
300 13th St.
Washington, DC 20239-0001   (202) 287-4113

This phone number is the path to discovering all the information you need to know concerning Treasury bills, notes, bonds, securities, savings Bonds, and other related topics. The following is a guide to finding the information you need on this electronic recorded message system:

  3 - Securities Analyst Assistance
  4 - Savings Bond Information
211 - Treasury Bill Offerings
212 - Treasury Note and Bond Offerings
221 - Treasury Bill Auction Results
222 - Treasury Note and Bond Auction Results
231 - Treasury Bill General Information
232 - Treasury Notes and Bonds General Information
233 - Treasury Direct System General Information
241 - Forms, Statement of Account, or IRS Form 1099 (Interest Earned)
251 - Treasury Securities Information
252 - Non-Receipt of Payment: Discount, Semi-Annual Interest, or Principal
253 - How to Report Change of Address
254 - Redeem Matured Registered and Bearer Treasury Securities
255 - Claim for Relief: Lost, Stolen, or Destroyed Registered and Bearer
        Treasury Securities
260 - Mail Gift to Reduce Public Debt

State Banking Information

With bank failures increasing and a major savings and loan crisis in progress, it makes good sense to know as much as possible about your bank and its officers. If the security of your hard-earned nest egg concerns you, it might not be a bad idea to investigate your bank through the state banking department. Each state maintains records on banks under its jurisdiction, and often this information is available to the public so long as you know how to go about getting it.

State banking offices are the best source of information on the financial status of all state chartered banks, providing information on the number and location of banks in your state, their assets, recent corporate changes (new board members, new branches). In addition, requesting a fiduciary statement can provide you with a full list of bank officers and stockholders. States also maintain information on other lending institutions--such as savings and loans and credit unions.

For whatever reasons, not all states are as forthcoming as others when it comes to providing information on specific banks and lenders. Georgia is the only state that does not provide any information on banks within its borders, while the District of Columbia began doing so in mid-1989. Colorado, North Dakota, and Washington state will only answer written requests for banking data.

The following are examples of the types of information state banking departments provide.

Reports

Most state banking departments provide some type of financial information on the institutions that they regulate. Alaska and Maine will provide performance and status reports on specific institutions, while twenty-one states provide annual reports to the public. Louisiana and Missouri provide quarterly reports containing the names and addresses of all regulated banks and savings and loan institutions. Only Alaska provides daily earnings statements on its banks.

Connecticut's annual report contains the following information:

-- consolidated Call Reports for all financial institutions.
-- comparative, consolidated report of conditions of financial institutions.
-- listing of all banks with the names of officers and directors
-- addresses of all financial institutions, including motor vehicle finance companies, licensed dealers, sale of check companies, transportation of money and valuables companies, and pre-need funeral contract companies
-- number and location of branch offices.

Phone Information

Information on regulated financial institutions is available by phone in fifteen states (see specific state).

Audits

In most states, bank audits are performed every 12 to 18 months. Louisiana, Oklahoma, Oregon and Vermont perform audits every two years; Maine and Tennessee every three years; and South Dakota and Vermont vary their audits between six months and five years. Texas is the only state that performs audits every six months. Audit information is confidential in most states, but Washington and Delaware will provide such information to the public. North Dakota, California, and Maryland provide limited audit information.

Directories

The following states have directories of financial institutions for a fee: Alaska, California, Iowa, Kansas, Missouri, and Texas.

Call Reports

Sixteen states allow public review of banking call reports -- simply a balance sheet and an income statement. Institutions must submit this information on a quarterly basis. Some states will give you this information over the telephone.

Mailing Lists

Twenty-four states provide mailing lists -- the following states at no charge: Florida, Idaho, Nevada, New Hampshire, New Jersey, North Carolina, and West Virginia.

List Of State Banking Departments

Alabama
Zack Thompson, Superintendent of Banks, State Banking Department, 166 Commerce St., Montgomery, AL 36130 (205) 261-3452. Regulates: 170 banks, state chartered and national banks; 1 savings and loan. An audit of each institution is done once a year. All information is sent to the Federal Reserve in Atlanta and not made public through this agency. General information on a specific institution can be given over the phone. Information is sent to the Federal Reserve in Atlanta. A mailing list of chartered banks is available for a fee.

Alaska
Willis F. Kirkpatrick, State Banking Department, P.O. Box 0, Juneau, AK 99811 (907) 465-2521. Regulates: 12 banks, 1 savings and loan, 1 small loan company, 12 premium financing companies and 2 credit unions. An audit of each institution is done once a year. All information is confidential. Only daily earnings statements are available. All information is sent to FDIC. A directory of all financial institutions is available for $10.00.

Arizona
State Banking Department, 3225 N. Central Ave., Suite 815, Phoenix, AZ 85012 (602) 255-4421. Regulates: 50 banks, 10 savings and loans, 1000 mortgage brokers, 150 credit unions, 700 used car dealers. An audit of each institution is done once a year. All information on the audit is confidential. Call Reports can be reviewed in the office. All information is sent to FDIC, Federal Bank Board, National Credit Union Administration. A mailing list of financial institutions is available for a fee.

Investments and Financial Services

Arkansas

Don Clark, Assistant Bank Commissioner, State Banking Department, Tower Bldg., 323 Center St., Suite 500, Little Rock, AR 72201 (501) 371-1117. Regulates 179 state chartered banks. Each institution is audited every 2 years, information is confidential. Performance reports of each bank are available for $25.00. Annual reports are available as well as a mailing list of financial institutions. Some data available on magnetic tape.

California

Howard Gould, Superintendent of Banks, State Banking Department, 235 Montgomery St., Suite 750, San Francisco, CA 94104; (415) 557-3535. Regulates: 280 state chartered banks, 42 trust companies, 102 foreign bank departments. Each institution is audited every 18 months. Information concerning a bank's assets can be given over the phone. A statistical table is available for $3.50, as well as a directory of financial institutions for a small fee.

Colorado

Richard B. Dobby, State Banking Commission, First W. Plaza, Suite 700, 303 W. Colfax, Denver, CO 80204; (303) 620-4358. Regulates: 189 state chartered banks, 5 trust companies, 79 industrial banks and 103 credit unions. Most information is confidential. For specific information on a bank, a written request is required.

Connecticut

Howard Brown, Jr., Banking Commissioner, Department of Banking, 44 Capitol Ave., Hartford, CT 06106; (203) 566-4560. Regulates: state banks, and savings and loans. Each institution is audited once a year, all information is confidential. Information from Call Reports is available over the phone, or can be inspected at the office. A mailing list of all financial institutions is available.

Delaware

John Malarkey, State Bank Commissioner, State Banking Commission, P.O. Box 1401, Dover, DE 19903; (302) 736-4235. Regulates: state chartered commercial banks. Audits are done annually and information is made available to the public. Annual Reports are available from this office, as well as a free mailing list of all financial institutions.

District of Columbia

Office of Banking and Financial Institutions, 1250 I. St., N.W., Washington, DC 20005; (202) 727-1566. Regulates: all depository institutions. No information available to the public until Spring, 1989.

Florida

Department of Banking and Finance, Division of Banking, Capitol Building, Suite 1401, Tallahassee, FL 32301; (904) 488-0370. Regulates: banks, savings and loans, credit unions and international agencies. Institutions are audited once every 18 months and data is kept confidential. Information is sent to FDIC. Call Report information can be given over the phone. A mailing list of all financial institutions is available at no charge.

Georgia

Department of Banking and Finance, 2990 Brandywine Rd., Suite 200, Atlanta, GA 30341; (404) 393-7330. Regulates: state chartered banks, sellers holding companies, credit unions and international banking offices. Institutions are audited between 12 and 18 months depending on size and age. Data files are kept confidential. For specific information on a bank, you must contact the bank individually. Data files are computerized but not available to the public.

Hawaii

Clifford Hisa, Commissioner, Department of Commerce and Consumer Affairs, Division of Financial Institutions, P.O. Box 2054, Honolulu, HI 96805; (808) 548-5855. Regulates: 7 banks, 2 saving and loans, 3 trust companies and 2 escrow companies. Each institution is audited once a year and data files are kept confidential. General comparative information on banks can be given over the phone. Information is sent to FDIC. A mailing list of financial institutions is available for $.25 per page.

Idaho

Director, Department of Finance, 700 West State St., Boise, ID 83720; (208) 334-3319. Regulates: 17 banks with 40 branches, 50 finance companies, and 60 credit unions. Audits are done between 18 months and 2 years depending on type of institution. All data files are kept confidential. Information is sent to FDIC, Federal Reserve, Federal Home Loan Bank, and the National Credit Union Administration. Annual Reports are available to the public as well as a mailing list of all financial institutions. There is no charge for the list.

Illinois

Commission of Bank and Trust Companies, 117 South 5th St., Reische Building, Room 100, Springfield, IL 62701; (217) 785-2837. Regulates: 825 state chartered banks, 400 national banks. Banks are audited once a year and data files are kept confidential. Data files are sent to FDIC. A mailing list of financial institutions is available in alphabetical order, or by county order for a fee of $10.00.

Indiana

Ruth Harrison, Director of Financial Institutions, Indiana State Office Building, Room 1024, Indianapolis, IN 46204; (317) 232-3956. Regulates: 280 banks, 100 credit unions, 50 savings and loans and 294 consumer credit loan companies. Each institution is audited once a year, all data files are kept confidential. Data files are sent to FDIC. Annual reports are made public as well as a mailing list of all the financial institutions. The mailing list is $100.00. Computerized data files includes banks opened, closed, or those with a new credit license. Data files are available to the public.

Iowa

Department of Banking, 200 E. Grand St., Suite 300, Des Moines, IA 50309; (515) 281-4014. Regulates: 490 state chartered banks, 340 loan companies, and 320 holding companies. Institutions are audited every 18 months. Data files are not made public; it is sent to FDIC in Kansas City. Information from Call Reports can be obtained for a fee of $.20 per page. Corporate files and stockholder lists are available for public inspection at the office. An Iowa Bank Directory is available for $12.50.

Kansas

J. Newton Mele, State Bank Commissioner, State Banking Department, 700 Jackson St., Topeka, KS 66603; (913) 296-2266. Regulates: 400 state banks. Each bank is audited every 18 months. Call Report information is available over the phone. A Kansas Bank Directory is available for a fee.

Kentucky

Thomas B. Miller, Commissioner of Banking and Securities, Department of Financial Institutions, 911 Leawood Dr., Frankfort, KY 40601; (502) 564-3390. Regulates: state chartered banks, credit unions, mortgage companies. Financial institutions are audited once a year. All information is kept confidential. An annual report which gives bank locations and licenses received is available for free. Some financial information and mailing list information is available in computer readable formats.

Louisiana

Fred C. Dent, Jr., Commissioner of Financial Institutions, Office of Financial Institutions, P.O. Box 94095, Baton Rouge, LA 70804; (504) 925-4660. Regulates: 208 state chartered banks, 50 savings and loans, 85 credit unions, and 1200 consumer loan companies. Institutions are audited every two years, all data files are kept confidential. A quarterly report is available for $10.00.

Maine

H. Donald DeMatteis, Bureau of Banking, Department of Business Regulation, State House Station #36, Augusta, ME 04333; (207) 289-3231. Regulates: 19 state chartered banks, 7 savings and loans and 17 credit unions. Institutions are audited every 3 years, all data files are kept confidential. Data files are sent to FDIC. Call Report and balance sheet information is available over the phone. A status report is done on an annual basis for the state legislature and is available to the public. A mailing list of all financial institutions is available as well as information in computer readable formats.

Maryland

Margie Muller, State Bank Commissioner, Department of Licensing and Regulation, The Brokerage, Suite 800, 34 Market Place, Baltimore, MD 21202; (301) 333-6808. Regulates: 70 state chartered banks, and credit unions. Institutions are audited once a year. All data files are kept confidential. Call Report information and balance sheet data can be obtained over the phone. A list of banks and their ratings can be obtained by visiting the office.

Massachusetts

Andrew Calamar, Commissioner, Division of Banks and Loan Agencies, 100 Cambridge St., 20th Floor, Boston, MA 02202; (617) 727-3120. Regulates: state chartered trust companies and credit unions. Audits are done once a year and all data files are kept confidential. Call reports are available for a fee of $8.00 per report. A mailing list of executives is available for a fee.

Michigan

Eugene Kuthy, Commissioner, Financial Institutions Bureau, Bank and Trust

Division, P.O. Box 30224, Lansing, MI 48909; (517) 373-3460. Regulates: 238 banks, 465 credit unions and 6 savings and loans. Institutions are audited annually and data files are kept confidential. An annual report is available to the public as well as a mailing list and computer readable formats of the financial institutions they regulate.

Minnesota

James G. Miller, Deputy Commissioner of Commerce, Financial Examinations Division, Department of Commerce, 500 Metro Square Bldg., 5th Floor, St. Paul, MN 55101; (601) 296-2135. Regulates: state chartered banks, mortgage companies, small loan companies and loan and thrifts (total of 5000). Each institution is audited every 18 months and data files are kept confidential. Data files are sent to FDIC. An annual report is available as well as Call Reports for $.50 per copy.

Mississippi

Department of Banking and Consumer Finance, P.O. Box 731, Jackson, MS 39205; (601) 359-1031. Regulates: 100 banks, 750 small loan companies, 1 trust company, 80 credit unions. Institutions are audited once a year and data files are kept confidential. Information from a branch application can be inspected at this office.

Missouri

Thomas Fitzsimmons, Commissioner's Office, Division of Finance, Department of Consumer Affairs, Regulation and Licensing, P.O. Box 716, Jefferson City, MO 65102; (314) 751-3397. Regulates: 500 banks and 500 small loan companies. Quarterly reports are available to the public. A bank directory is available for $14.00.

Montana

Bank Examiner, Department of Commerce, Lee Metcalf Bldg., 1520 E. 6th Ave., Room 50, Helena, MT 59620; (406) 444-2091. Regulates: 113 state banks. Each bank is audited once a year, data files are reported to FDIC. Call Report information, assets,and liability statements can be given over the phone. A mailing list is available from the Montana Bankers Association for $15.00, (406) 443-4121.

Nebraska

Director, Department of Banking and Finance, 301 Centennial Mall South, Lincoln, NE 68509; (402) 471-2171. Regulates: 309 commercial banks and 6 industrial banks. Each bank is audited once a year. All data files are confidential. Information is sent to FDIC. Financial information from Call Reports is available over the phone.

Nevada

L. Scott Walshaw, Department of Commerce, Financial Institutions Division, 406 E. 2nd St., Carson City, NV 89710; (702) 885-4260. Regulates: banks, savings and loans, credit unions, thrift and loan companies, consumer finance companies and debt collection organizations. Institutions are audited once a year, data files are sent to FDIC. Some financial information is available over the phone. A mailing list of all financial institutions is available for free. Some data files are available in computer readable formats.

New Hampshire

Mr. A. Roberge, Bank Commissioner, Department of Banking, 45 S. Main St., Concord, NH 03301; (603) 271-3561. Regulates: state chartered banks, trust companies and savings and loans. Institutions are audited every 18 months. All data files are kept confidential. An annual report and monthly bulletin is available to the public, as well as a list of pending applications. A mailing list of financial institutions is available at no cost.

New Jersey

Mary Parell, Commissioner, Department of Banking, 36 W. State St., P.O. Box CN-040, Trenton, NJ 08625; (609) 292-3420. Regulates: commercial and savings banks, credit unions, mortgage companies and small loan companies (6,000 total). Institutions are audited once a year and data files are kept confidential. An annual report and press releases are available. A mailing list of all financial institutions can be obtained at no charge. Some data may be available on computer magnetic tape.

New Mexico

Ray Adamer, Chief Examiner, Financial Institution Division, Battaan Memorial Building, Room 137, Santa Fe, NM 87503; (505) 827-7740. Regulates: 52 state banks, 35 state credit unions, 2 savings and loans, 24 escrow companies, 63 small loan companies and 10 mortgage companies. Institutions are audited once a year, data files are kept confidential. Information regarding the total asset of an institution can be given over the phone. An annual report is available to the public.

New York

Superintendent of Banks, State Banking Department, 2 Rector St., New York, NY 10006; (212) 618-6642. Regulates: state chartered banks, commercial banks, savings and loans, credit unions, and branches of foreign banks. Audits are done on an annual basis. Most data files are confidential. Brochures are available from the consumer division.

North Carolina

William T. Graham, Commissioner of Banks, Banking Commission, Department of Commerce, P.O. Box 29512, Raleigh, NC 27626; (919) 733-3016. Regulates: 54 state chartered banks, and finance companies. Institutions are audited once a year. Data files are kept confidential and sent to FDIC. Profit/loss statements are public information. A mailing list of all financial institutions is available at no charge.

North Dakota

Gary D. Preszler, Commissioner of Banking, State Capitol, Room 1301, Bismarck, ND 58505; (701) 224-2256. Regulates: 132 state chartered banks, 65 credit unions and money brokers. Institutions are audited every 3 years. Some data files are available to the public with a written request to the Commissioner. Data files are sent to FDIC. Information from a bank's Call Report is available over the phone. A mailing list of all financial institutions is available for a fee.

Ohio

John Burns, Deputy Superintendent of Banks, Division of Banks, Department of Commerce, Two Nationwide Plaza, 4th Floor, Columbus, OH 43215; (614) 466-2932. Regulates: state chartered banks. Banks are audited every 18 months. All data files are kept confidential. A copy of data is sent to FDIC. No mailing lists available.

Oklahoma

Banking Department, Oklahoma Banking Association, 4100 N. Lincoln Blvd., Oklahoma City, OK 73105; (405) 521-2783. Regulates: state chartered banks, credit unions, savings and loans, and trust companies (total 296). Institutions are audited every 2 years, all data files are kept confidential. Financial information and letters of correspondence can be reviewed by the public.

Oregon

Cecil R. Monroe, Deputy Administrator, Department of Insurance and Finance, Division of Finance and Capital Securities, 21 Labor and Industry Building, Salem, OR 97310; (503) 378-4140. Regulates: banks, trust companies, pawn brokers. Audits are performed every 2 years or when needed. All data files are confidential and sent to FDIC. Annual reports are available to the public. A mailing list of all financial institutions is available.

Pennsylvania

Sarah W. Hargrove, Secretary of Banking, 333 Market St., 16th Floor, Harrisburg, PA 17101; (717) 787-6991. Regulates: state chartered savings and loans, commercial banks, and foreign banks. Audits are done on a yearly basis, all data files are confidential. Data files are sent to FDIC. An annual report is available to the public.

Rhode Island

Susan D. Hayes, Assistant Director, Banking and Securities, Banking Insurance and Securities Administration, Department of Business Regulation, 100 N. Main St., Providence, RI 02903; (401) 277-2405. Regulates: 14 bank and trust companies, 3 savings and loans, 64 credit unions, and 320 finance companies. Audits are done once a year. All data files are kept confidential. Data files are sent to FDIC. An annual report is available for $15.00. Information from a Call Report is available from the office. Balance sheet data is computerized and available in various reports.

South Carolina

Robert C. Cleveland, Commissioner of Banking, Bank Examining Division, 1026 Sumter St., Room 217, Columbia, SC 29201; (803) 734-1050. Regulates: 53 state chartered banks, 1 trust company, 36 credit unions, and 9 savings and loans. Institutions are audited once a year. All data files are confidential and sent to FDIC. Information from a Call Report is available over the phone. An annual report is available which contains a list of all financial institutions and their addresses.

South Dakota

Richard A. Duncan, Director, Banking and Finance, State Capitol Building,

Pierre, SD 57501; (605) 773-3212. Regulates: 116 banks, 5 savings and loans, 10 mortgage companies, 2 loan companies, 16 finance companies. Audits are done periodically, between 1 to 5 years. All data files are confidential. An annual report is available to the public.

Tennessee
Dennis R. Phillips, Commissioner, Department of Financial Institutions, John Sevier Bldg., 4th Floor, Nashville, TN 37219 (615) 741-2236. Regulates: state banks, credit unions, savings and loans and money orders. Audits are done every 3 years. All data files are confidential. An annual report and information on a bank's total assets are available by visiting the office.

Texas
Kenney W. Littlefield, Banking Commissioner, Department of Banking, 2601 N. Lamar Ave., Austin, TX 78705 (512) 479-1200. Regulates: 870 banks, 3 private banks (uninsured). Audits are done every 6 months. All data files are confidential. Information is sent to the Federal Reserve and FDIC. Information on a Call Report is available by visiting the office. A directory of all financial institutions is available for a fee of $15.00.

Utah
George Sutton, Commissioner, Department of Financial Institutions, P.O. Box 89, Salt Lake City, UT 84110 (801) 530-6502. Regulates: 37 banks. Audits are done between 6 months and 5 years. All data files are kept confidential. Data files are sent to FDIC and the Federal Reserve. Information on a report of condition can be given over the phone. Annual reports are available to the public.

Vermont
Gretchen Babcosk, Department of Banking and Insurance, 120 State Street, Montpelier, VT 05602 (802) 828-3301. Regulates: 20 banks, 3 savings and loans, 59 credit unions, 62 license lenders. Audits are done every 2 years and data files are available to the public. Information is sent to FDIC. An annual report is available to the public.

Virginia
Sidney A. Bailey, Commissioner, Bureau of Financial Institutions, State Corporation Commission, P.O. Box 2AE, Richmond, VA 23205 Regulates: state chartered banks, credit unions, industrial loans, savings and loans, and mortgage brokers. (total of 500). Audits are done once a year. Data files are kept confidential. An annual report is available containing a list of financial institutions and the proper addresses.

Washington
Thomas H. Oldfield, Supervisor of Banking, Division of Banking, Department of General Administration, General Administration Bldg, Room 219, Olympia, WA 98504 (206) 753-6520. Regulates: 93 state banks. Audits are done once a year. Data can be obtained with a written request. Data files are sent to FDIC. An annual report is available to the public.

West Virginia
David Modie, Deputy Commissioner, Department of Banking, State Office Building #3, Suite 311, Charleston, WV 25305 (304) 348-2294. Regulates: 219 banks, 75 industrial loans, 24 credit unions, 55 small loan companies, 12 mortgage companies. Audits are done once a year. All data files are confidential. Information from Call Reports and correspondence is available for public inspection at this office. A mailing list of all financial institutions is available for free. Some financial information and Call Reports are computerized and information is released upon request.

Wisconsin
Richard E. Galecki, Office of the Commissioner of Banking, P.O. Box 7876, Madison, WI 53707 (608) 266-1621. Regulates: finance companies, loan companies, insurance companies, adjustment services, savings and loans and banks licensed as finance companies. All data files from an audit are confidential. Information available to the public includes complaints registered, rate charges and an annual report. A mailing list of all financial institutions is available for $10.50. Some data is available in computer readable formats.

Wyoming
Stanley R. Hunt, State Examiner, Herschler Bldg. 4th Floor, Cheyenne, WY 82002 (307) 777-6600. Regulates: 65 state chartered banks, 2 savings and loans and 2 trust companies. Audits are done annually and data files are kept confidential. Information is sent to regulatory agencies. An annual report and balance sheet information is available for public inspection at this office. A mailing list of all state and national banks is available.

Commodities

See also Agriculture and Farming Chapter.

* Commission-Registered Traders
Registration Unit
Commodity Futures Trading Commission
2033 K St., NW, Room 701
Washington, DC 20581 (202) 254-9703
Futures Commission brokers, commodity trading advisors, commodity pool operators, and other companies and individuals involved in futures trading register with the CFTC. To determine is a specific company or individual is registered call the Registration Unit. For a directory listing all firms involved in futures trading contact the National Futures Association, P.O. Box 98383, Chicago, IL 60693-0001, Attention: Business Systems Group, (312) 781-1300. Send check or money order for $25.00 and include your telephone number on the payment.

* Commodities Futures Trading Reference Books
Library
Commodity Futures Trading Commission
2033 K St., NW, 5th Floor
Washington, DC 20581 (202) 254-5901
A collection of commodity futures trading-related materials emphasizing law, economics, business, and commodities is maintained at the library. With approval and by pre-arranged appointment, limited public use of the facility is permitted. Contact the Library for details.

* Commodity Exchange Regulation
Division of Trading and Markets
Commodity Futures Trading Commission
2033 K St., NW, Room 640
Washington, DC 20581 (202) 254-8955
Regulation of the exchanges on which commodities futures are traded is the responsibility of this division. Approval of all futures contracts traded or exchanged must also be obtained from this office. For further information, contact the Division of Trading and Markets.

* Commodity Trading Complaints
Office of Proceedings
Complaint Section
Commodity Futures Trading Commission
2033 K St., NW
Washington, DC 20581 (202) 254-3067
This unit directs proceedings to determine if reparations are to be made to persons who claim damages as a result of violations of the Commodity Exchange Act. If you believe you may have been cheated or defrauded in trading transactions, the Commission should be advised. Staff here can also confirm if there are any pending or prior legal actions involving an individual or firm registered with the Commission.

* Company Information: FOIA Requests
Freedom of Information Office
Commodity Futures Trading Commission
2033 K St., NW, Room 211
Washington, DC 20581 (202) 254-3382
Information is collected by the Commission on futures commissions brokers, dealers, commodity futures exchanges, commodities trading advisors, and other individuals and companies involved in futures trading of commodities such as agricultural products, metals, and lumber. A FOIA request must be filed to obtain information that may be disclosed from registration applications, hearing and appeal transcripts, and other records on specific individuals and firms. Contact the FOIA office listed for details.

* Futures Markets Publications and Reports
Office of Communication and Education Services
Commodity Futures Trading Commission (CFTC)
2033 K St., NW
Washington, DC 20581 (202) 254-8630
Information from the Commission's studies of the functioning of futures markets can be obtained from this office. Reports and publications about the Commission and explaining commodities futures trading include:
CFTC Annual Report
Economic Purposes of Futures Trading
Farmers, Futures, and Grain Prices
Reading Commodity Futures Price Tables
CFTC Fact Sheets:
No. 1 - CFTC Reports and Offices
No. 2 - CFTC Publications and General Bibliography
No. 3 - Commodities Traded and Exchange Addresses
No. 4 - Visual Aids (Films and Slides)
No. 5 - Reporting Levels and Speculative Limits
Grain Pricing
Contact the office listed to obtain reports, publications, and information.

* International Mineral Data
Superintendent of Documents
Government Printing Office
Washington, DC 20402 (202) 783-3238
The *Minerals Yearbook, 1985: Volume 111 (Area Reports: International)* contains the latest available mineral data from more than 150 foreign countries and discusses the importance of minerals to the economies of these nations. It reviews the international minerals industry in general and its relationship to the world economy (S/N 024-004-02179-9, 1987: $36.00).

* Mineral Commodity Summaries 1989
Minerals Information Office
Bureau of Mines/U.S. Geological Survey
U.S. Department of the Interior
18th and C Sts., MS 2647-MIB
Room 2647
Washington, DC 20240 (202) 343-5520
Mineral Commodity Summaries 1989 lists the statistics available for 82 commodities, including domestic production and uses; salient statistics - United States; recycling; import sources; tariff; depletion allowance; government stockpile; events and trends; world mine production, reserves and reserve base; world resources; and substitutes. The expert's name and phone number of each report is also listed.

* Mineral Commodity Information
Minerals Information Office
Bureau of Mines/U.S. Geological Survey
U.S. Department of the Interior
18th and C Sts., MS 2647-MIB
Room 2647
Washington, DC 20240 (202) 343-5520
The Minerals Information Office is staffed by mineral experts who distribute a wide variety of mineral-related information and publications to meet and support the needs of the public, as well as government agencies and the scientific and industrial sectors. The staff provides information on the most current as well as past published reports pertaining to minerals, mining, processing, and research, as well as updated listings of current reports.

* Mineral Deposits Database
Minerals Information Office
Bureau of Mines/U.S. Geological Survey
U.S. Department of the Interior
18th and C Sts., MS 2647-MIB
Room 2647
Washington, DC 20240 (202) 343-5520
The *Personal Computer Advanced Deposit Information Tracking System Mineral Deposit Data Base* contains information on 3,000 domestic and foreign (market economy countries) mining operations, including operation data (name, company, locations, etc.) and operation status (operation type, processing and milling methods, capacity, etc.). The database covers 34 critical and strategic commodities, representing those deposits most significant in terms of value and tonnage.

* Mineral Production and Consumption
Information and Analysis Division
Bureau of Mines
U.S. Department of the Interior
2401 E St., NW
Washington, DC 20241 (202) 634-7131
The Bureau of Mines collects information about minerals from U.S. mining companies and mineral processing plants. Mineral production and consumption is monitored throughout the world through contacts with foreign governments, U.S. embassies, international publications, and visits to mines overseas. The

Investments and Financial Services

Bureau employs 11 state mineral specialists through cooperative data collection agreements with the states. Three regional field offices and nine research centers also gather information. The data is then made available to the public via reports, books, and computer disks.

* Minerals: Data, Industries, and Technology

Publication Distribution
Bureau of Mines
U.S. Department of the Interior
Cochrans Mills Rd.
P.O. Box 18070
Pittsburgh, PA 15236　　　　　　　　　　　　(412) 892-4338

The Bureau of Mines publishes several reports of investigations and information circulars that are free of charge to those interested in mineral research. *Mineral Industry Surveys* are published monthly, quarterly, and annually, presenting data on various minerals and metals. Reprints from *Minerals Yearbook 1987* are available and report on the mineral industry in the United States and abroad. *Minerals Facts and Problems* covers the technology used in the extraction and processing of minerals.

* Minerals Yearbooks Bibliography

Superintendent of Documents
Government Printing Office
Washington, DC 20402　　　　　　　　　　　(202) 783-3238

Yearbooks on metals and minerals are listed, as well as reports on the domestic and international industry. Free.

* Monitoring Commodity Trading

Division of Economics and Analysis
Commodity Futures Trading Commission
2033 K St., NW
Washington, DC 20581　　　　　　　　　　　(202) 254-3310

Proposed futures trading contracts are reviewed for validity by this division. It also analyzes the economic implications of CFTC regulations and policies and watchdogs trading to detect manipulations, price distortions, and congestion in the markets. For further details, contact the division listed.

Federal Tax Help

Why pay money to expensive tax preparers, tax accountants, and tax attorneys when you can get most of what they offer better and most likely free? Did you know the government has dozens of free tax help programs very few people know about. There is a special section at the end of this chapter for state tax assistance.

* Actuaries Enrollment Board

Joint Board for the Enrollment of
Actuaries
Internal Revenue Service
U.S. Department of the Treasury
1111 Constitution Ave., NW
Washington, DC 20220   (202) 535-6787

Individuals who wish to perform actuarial services must enroll with this Board within the IRS. The Board is also responsible for the supervision of actuaries and their enrollment revocation after fair hearings.

* Amending Your Tax Return

Service Center Directors
Deputy Commissioner, Operations
Internal Revenue Service
U.S. Department of the Treasury
1111 Constitution Ave, NW
Washington, DC 20224   (202) 566-4386

If you find that you did not report income on your tax form, did not claim deductions or credit you could have claimed, or you claimed deductions or credits that you should not have claimed, you can correct your return by filing a Form 1040X, Amended U.S. Individual Income Tax Return. Generally, this form must be filed within three years from the date of your original return or within two years from the date you paid your taxes, whichever is later. File Form 1040X with the IRS Service Center in your area, listed elsewhere in this book.

* Corporation Tax Statistics

Statistics of Income Division
Internal Revenue Service
U.S. Department of the Treasury
Attn: R:S:P
1111 Constitution Ave., NW, Attn; R:S:P
Washington, DC 20224   (202) 376-3900

Corporation Source Book, 1986 is a 480-page document that presents detailed income statement, balance sheet, tax and investment credit items by major and minor industries and size of total assets. It is part of an annual series and can be purchased for $175. A magnetic tape containing the tabular statistics is available for $1,500.

* Electronic Tax Filing

Electronic Filing Division
Internal Revenue Service
U.S. Department of the Treasury
1111 Constitution Ave., NW
Washington, DC 20224   (202) 535-4480

Electronic filing eliminates most of the manual processing of traditional paper returns and shortens the time of issuing a refund check by three weeks. Taxpayers in 50 states and the District of Columbia can file electronically. Only those showing a refund can be filed in this manner. Refunds may also be directly deposited to their checking or savings account. There is no charge for this service. You must file your taxes electronically through a qualified electronic filer.

* Estate and Gift Tax

Office of Passthroughs and
Special Industries
Internal Revenue Service
U.S. Department of the Treasury
1111 Constitution Ave., NW, Room 5427
Washington, DC 20224   (202) 535-9509

This office will help you on matters pertaining to the regulations of estate and gift tax.

* Federal Tax Guide for Older Americans

Committee on Aging
U.S. House of Representatives
Washington, DC 20515   (202) 226-3375

Congressional committees also publish useful, FREE publications to assist older Americans in preparing their tax returns. Contact this office to receive a copy.

* Foreign Language Assistance in Tax Preparation

Taxpayer Services, International
Internal Revenue Service
U.S. Department of the Treasury
950 L'Enfant Plaza
Washington, DC 20024   (202) 287-4311

Interpreters are available at the IRS in the major foreign languages to assist taxpayers who do not speak English. Written requests for help may be sent to the above office, and IRs interpreters will respond to the questions, but only in English. Sometimes the State Department assists in the interpretation of letters. Requests are received only for obtaining solutions to specific tax problems and not for the preparation of tax returns.

VITA centers in local area often have foreign interpreters if the population in that area warrants them. Contact your local IRS office in the white pages of your phone directory or your area's Taxpayer Education Coordinator, listed elsewhere in this book, for information.

Many of the IRS forms are also available in Spanish. They are:

1S Derechos del contribuyente (Your Rights as a Taxpayer), 179 Circular PR, Guia Contributiva Federal Para Patronos Puertoriquenos (Federal Tax Guide for Employers in Puerto Rico)

556S Revision de las Declaraciones de Impuesto, Derecho de Apelacion y Reclamaciones de Reembolsos (Examination of Returns, Appeal Rights, and Claims for Refund)

579S Como Preparar la Declaracion de Impuesto Federal (How to Prepare the Federal Income Tax Return)

586S Proceso de cobro (Deudas del impuesto sobre ingreso) (The collection Process: Income Tax Accounts)

594S Proceso de cobro (Deudas del impuesto por razon del empleo) (The Collection Process: Employment Tax Accounts)

850 English-spanish Glossary of Words and Phrases Used in Publications Issued by the Internal Revenue Service.

* Foreign Tax Credits

Assistant Commissioner (International)
Internal Revenue Service
U.S. Department of the Treasury
950 L'Enfant Plaza South, SW,
Attn: IN:C:TPS
Washington, DC 20024   (202) 287-4301

If you need information or assistance in the guidelines for foreign tax credit allowed for income taxes paid to foreign governments, contact this office. Income in this situation is taxed by both the United States and the foreign country. *Publication 514* from the IRS describes in detail the tax credit, who is eligible, and how to calculate the credit.

* Free Courses on How To Prepare Taxes

Volunteer and Education Branch
Taxpayer Service Division
Internal Revenue Service
U.S. Department of the Treasury
1111 Constitution Ave., NW, Room 1315
Washington, DC 20224   (202) 566-4904

Taxes

Those who want to be trained to prepare tax returns can do so through the VITA program. In return for the training you must volunteer some of your time to prepare taxes for others during the tax season. Contact one of the IRS Taxpayer Education Coordinators listed below or the toll-free number 1 (800) 424-1040, which is automatically routed to the district office in your area.

550 22d St., S, Stop 117, Birmingham, AL 35233; (205) 731-0403
P.O. Box 101500, Anchorage, AK 99510; (907) 261-4458
2120 N. Central Ave., Stop 6610-PX, Phoenix, AZ 85004; (602) 261-3861
P.O. Box 3778, Stop 25, Little Rock, AR 72203; (501) 378-5685
P.O. Box C-10, Laguna Niguel, CA 92677-1000; (714) 643-4060
300 N. Los Angeles St., Room 5205, Los Angeles, CA 90012; (213) 894-4574
P.O. Box 2900, Stop SA5650, Sacramento, CA 95812; (916) 978-4083
1221 Broadway, 4th Fl. Oakland, CA 94612; (415) 273-4233
55 S. Market St., Stop 77-01-6400, San Jose, CA 95113; (408) 291-7114
600 17th St.,Stop 6610-DEN, Denver, CO 80202-2490; (303) 844-3340
135 High St., Stop 115, Hartford, CT 06103; (203) 240-4154
P.O. Box 28, Wilmington, DE 19899; (302) 573-6411
(DC Office) P.O. Box 1076, Baltimore, MD 21203; (202) 488-3100, x. 2222
P.O. Box 292590, Stop 6030, Fort Lauderdale, FL 33329-2590; (305) 472-5124
400 W. Bay St.,Stop 6250, Jacksonville, FL 32202 (904) 791-2514
P.O. Box 1037, Room 110, Atlanta, GA 30370; (404) 331-3808
PJKK Building, P.O. Box 50089, Honolulu, HI 96850; (808) 541-3300
550 W. Fort St., Box 041, Boise, ID 83724; (208) 334-1307
P.O. Box 1193, Stop 32-1, Chicago, IL 60690; (312) 886-4609
P.O. Box 19201, Stop 8, Springfield, IL 62701; (217) 492-4386
P.O. Box 44211, Stop 60, Indianapolis, IN 46244; (317) 269-6216
P.O. Box 1337, Stop 30, Des Moines, IA 50305; (515) 284-4870
412 S. Main, Stop 6610-WIC, Wichita, KS 67202; (316) 291-6610
P.O. Box 1216, Stop 531, Louisville, KY 40201; (502) 582-6259
500 Camp St., Stop 21, New Orleans, LA 70130; (504) 589-2801
P.O. Box 1020, Augusta, ME 04330; (207) 622-8328
31 Hopkins Plaza, Room 615A, Baltimore, MD 21201; (301) 962-2222
JFK Federal Bldg., P.O. Box 9088, Boston, MA 02203; (617) 565-1645
P.O. Box 330500, Room 2442, Detroit, MI 48232-6500; (313) 226-3674
316 Robert St., Stop 26, St. Paul, MN 55101; (612) 290-3320
100 W. Capitol St.,Suite 504, Stop 30, Jackson, MS 39269; (601) 965-4142
P.O. Box 1147, H.W. Wheeler Station, St. Louis, MO 63188; (314) 539-5660
301 S. Park Ave., Drawer 10016, Helena, MT 59626-0016; (406) 449-5375
106 S. 15th St., Stop 27, Omaha, NE 68102; (402) 221-3501
300 Las Vegas Blvd., Las Vegas, NV 89101; (702) 388-6937
80 Daniel St. Portsmouth, NH 03801; (603) 436-7386
P.O. Box 476, Room 104, Newark, NJ 07101; (201) 645-6478
517 Gold Ave, SW, Stop 6610-ALB, P.O. Box 1967, Albuquerque, NM 87101; (505) 766-2537
Clinton Ave., and N. Pearl St., Room 614, Albany, NY 12207; (518) 472-2886
P.O. Box 606, RM G-5D, Brooklyn, NY 11202; (718) 780-6020
P.O. Box 1040, Niagara Sq. Station, Buffalo, NY 14201; (716) 846-4007
P.O. Box 34036, Church St. Station, New York, NY 10008; (212) 264-3310
320 Federal Pl., Room 128, Greensboro, NC 27401; (919) 333-5620
P.O. Box 2461, Fargo, ND 58108; (701) 239-5213
P.O. Box 3459, Cincinnati, OH 45201; (513) 684-2828
P.O. Box 99184, Cleveland, OH 44199; (216) 522-3414
200 NW 4th St., Stop 6610, Oklahoma City, OK 73102; (405) 231-4989
P.O. Box 2709, Portland, OR 97208; (503) 221-6565
600 Arch St., Room 6424, Philadelphia, PA 19106; (215) 597-0512
P.O. Box 2488, Room 123, Pittsburgh, PA 15230; (412) 644-6504
Mercantil Plaza Bldg., 10th Fl., Ave. Ponce de Leon, Stop 27 1/2, Hato Rey, PR 00917; (809) 498-5946
P.O. Box 6627, Providence, RI 02940; (401) 528-4276
1835 Assembly St., Columbia, SC 29201; (803) 253-3031
P.O. Box 370, Aberdeen, SD 57402-0370; (605) 226-7230
P.O. Box 1107, MDP 46, Nashville, TN 37202; (615) 736-2247
300 E. 8th St., Stop 6610-AUS, Austin, TX 78701; (512) 499-5439
1100 Commerce St., Stop 6610-DAL, Dallas, TX 75242; (214) 767-1428
4100 Westheimer, Stop 6610-SW, Suite 280, Houston, TX 77027; (713) 954-6878
465 S. 400 East, Stop 6610, SLC, Salt Lake City, UT 84111; (801) 524-6095
199 Main St., Burlington, VT 05401:(802) 951-6473
P.O. Box 10049, Room 5223, Richmond, VA 23240; (804) 771-2289
915 Second Ave., Seattle, WA 98174; (206) 442-4230
P.O. Box 1138, Stop 2108, Parkersburg, WV 26102; (304) 420-6612
P.O. Box 493, Milwaukee, WI 53201; (414) 291-3302
308 W 21st St., Stop 6610-CHE, Cheyenne, WY 82001; (307) 772-2325

* Free Legal Help If You Get Audited

Volunteer and Education Branch
Taxpayer Service Division
Internal Revenue Service
U.S. Department of the Treasury
1111 Constitution Ave., NW, Room 1315
Washington, DC 20224 (202) 566-4904

Under this program, law and graduate accounting school students are given special permission to practice before the IRS on behalf of taxpayers who cannot afford professional help. Volunteers are needed to help with the clinic operations or to serve as Student Tax Clinic Directors. Students work under the direction of their professors to handle legal and technical problems. Your local taxpayer education coordinator will inform you of tax clinics in your area.

* Free Tax Forms At Your Library

Volunteer and Education Branch
Taxpayer Service Division
Internal Revenue Service
U.S. Department of the Treasury
1111 Constitution Ave., NW, Room 1315
Washington, DC 20224 (202) 566-4904

The IRS supplies over 18,000 libraries, technical schools, prisons, and other facilities with free tax forms, audiovisual aids, and reference materials. These facilities are in need of volunteers to assist in distribution and use of these aids. Contact your local library or center and volunteer to help.

* Future Tax Legislation

Director, Legislative Affairs
Internal Revenue Service
U.S. Department of the Treasury
1111 Constitution Ave., NW
Washington, DC 20224 (202) 566-6070

The Legislative Affairs Division is responsible for developing IRS legislative proposals, tracking pending legislation, analyzing and implementing new legislation, and preparing responses to General Accounting Office reports.

For further information regarding taw laws that have introduced or for an assessment of future laws, you may wish to contact the following offices. Ask to speak with the person monitoring changes in the tax provision you are calling about.

U.S. Department of the Treasury, Legislative Affairs, 1500 Pennsylvania, Ave., Room 3134, Washington, DC 20224; (202) 566-2037
Senate Committee on Finance, 205 Dirksen Senate Office Building, Washington, DC 20510; (202) 224-4515
House Committee on Ways and Means, 1102 Longworth House Office Building, Washington, DC 20515; (202) 225-3625
Joint Committee on Taxation, 1015 Longworth House Office Building, Washington, DC 20515; (202) 225-3621

* Hotline for Tax Aspects of Retirement Plans

Employee Plans Technical and Actuarial Division
Internal Revenue Service
U.S. Department of the Treasury
1111 Constitution Ave., NW
Washington, DC 20224 (202) 566-6783/6784

The above numbers are hotlines to attorneys within this division that are there to discuss tax questions relating to retirement and pension plans, such as 401 (k) and 501 (c3). The hours are 1:30 to 4:00 p.m., Monday through Friday.

* How to Protect Older Americans From Overpayment

Special Committee on Aging
U.S. Senate
Washington, DC 20510 (202) 224-5364.

This FREE booklet is available by contacting this office directly.

* Individual Income Tax Statistics

Statistics of Income Division
Internal Revenue Service
U.S. Department of the Treasury
1111 Constitution Ave., NW, Attn:R:S:P
Washington, DC 20224 (202) 376-3900

Individual income data and tables for 1985 are available in the publication, *Individual Income Tax Returns*. Statistics include sources of income, exemptions, itemized deductions, and tax computations. Data is presented by size of adjusted gross income and marital status. This publication is $11 and is available from the Government Printing Office, Washington, D.C. 20402 (S/N 048-004-02285-1).

* Individual Tax Model

Statistics of Income Division
Internal Revenue Service
U.S. Department of the Treasury
1111 Constitution Ave., NW, Attn: R:S:P
Washington, DC 20224 (202) 376-3900

State tax officials determine rate structure and revenue yields through the use of Individual Tax Model. Public use tape files are available from the office above that include this tax model.

* Information for Tax Practitioners

Forms Distribution Centers
Internal revenue Service
U.S. Department of the Treasury
P.O. Box 25866, Richmond, VA 23289
P.O. Box 9903, Bloomington, IN 61799
Rancho Cordova, CA 95743-0001

1 (800) 424-3676

Tax practitioners can benefit from the following information made available to them from the IRS. Publication 1045, Information for Tax Practitioners, contains orders blanks for ordering bulk supplies of federal income tax forms. Also within the publication is a form that allows one to be placed on a mailing list in his IRS district to receive a tax practitioner's newsletter. Package X is also available to practitioners with the most popular tax forms and instructions on how to prepare them.

* In-House IRS Audit Manuals

Freedom of Information Reading Room
Internal Revenue Service
U.S. Department of the Treasury
1111 Constitution Ave., NW, Room 1569
Washington, DC 20224   (202) 566-3770

Tax audit manuals use by IRS staff and other in-house manuals are available to the public. Contact the office above for arrangements to use particular materials. For copies of manuals and written requests, write to: Internal Revenue Service, c/o Ben Franklin Station, P.O. Box 388, Washington, D.C. 20044, Attn: Freedom of Information Request.

Available IRS Technical Manuals:

Organization and Staffing (1100), $36.45
Policies of the Internal Revenue Service (1218), $14.55
Delegation Orders (1229), $17.10
Internal Management Document System (1230), $21.90
Disclosure of Official Information (1272), $63.15
Travel (1763), $29.85
General (4000), $20.10
Income Tax Examinations (4200), $74.85
Tax Audit Guidelines for Internal Revenue Examiners (4231), $27.20
Techniques Handbook for Specialized Industries (4232)
  1. Insurance, $15.45
  2. Auto Dealers, $2.55
  3. Textiles, $4.80
  4. Timber, $6.15
  5. Brokerage Firms, $11.90
  6. Railroads, $13.65
  7. Construction, $4.65
  8. Oil and Gas, $47.85
  9. Financial Institution, $6.45
  10. Public Utilities, $10.05
  11. Barter Exchanges, -0-
Tax Audit Guidelines, Partnerships, Estates and Trusts, and Corporations (4233), $22.55
Techniques Handbook for In-Depth Examinations (4235), $25.65
Examination Tax Shelters (4236), $10.65
Report Writing Guide for Income Tax Examiners (4237), $21.30
Examination Techniques Handbook for Estate Tax Examiners (4350), $27.15
Handbook for Quality Review (4419), $11.40
Employment Tax Procedures (4600), $12.90
Excise Tax Procedure (4700), $17.55
Handbook for Examination Group Managers (4(10)20), $15.75
Classification (41(12)0), $8.10
General Procedural Guides (5100), $24.45
Collection Quality Review System (CQRS) (5190), $4.05
Delinquent Return Procedures (5200), $10.05
Balance Due Account Procedures (5300), $23.55
Service Center Collection Branch Procedures (5400), $93.90
Service Center Collection Branch Managers (5415), $9.90
Automated Collection Function Procedures (5500), $18.60
Automated Collection System Managers (5512), $21.30
Collection Field Function Techniques and Other Assignments (5600), $32.25
Employment Tax Examinations (5(10)00), $12.60
Collection Technical Review Handbook for Employment Tax Examination (5(10)(20)), $2.25
Group Managers Handbook (56(20)0), $8.40
Field Branch Chief's Handbook (56(30)0), $3.75
Special Procedures (5700), $57.00
Special Procedures Function Managers (57(15)0), $3.90
Legal Reference Guide for Revenue Officers (57(16)0), $37.50
Records and Reports (5800), $9.60
Collection Reports for Field Managers (5890), $4.35
Collection Support Function (5900), $19.50
Taxpayer Service (6810), $51.45
Exempt Organizations (7751), $60.90
Private Foundations (7752), $40.05

Employee Plans Master File (7810), $10.50
Exempt Organizations Business Master File (7820), $26.70
Examination Procedures (7(10)00), $49.95
Employee Plans Examination Guidelines (7(10)54), $15.00
Exempt Organizations Exam. Guides Handbook (7(10)(69)), $13.80
Actuarial Guidelines (7(10)5(10)), $5.70
Appeals (Part VIII), $51.00
Handbook for Special Agents (9781), $84.15
Criminal Investigation (Part IX) $67.50
Technical (Part XI), $49.35
Employee Plans Training Program Phase I, Revised 10/87 (4210-01), $60.45
Employee Plans EP/EO CPE Operational Topics for 1989, Revised 12/88 (4213-002), $12.15
Employee Plans EP/EO CPE Technical Topics for 1989, Revised 12/88 (4213-003), $18.75
Employee Plans EP/EO CPE Technical Topics for 1989, Revised 3/89 (4213-005), $4.05
Employee Plans Training Program Phase II, Revised 01/87 (4220-01), $51.60
Exempt Organizations Continuing Professional Education Technical Instruction Program for 1986, Revised 01/86 (4277-20), $43.80
Exempt Organizations Continuing Professional Education Technical Instruction Program for 1987, Revised 01/87 (4277-25), $44.70
Exempt Organizations Continuing Professional Education Technical Instruction Program for 1988, Revised 01/88 (4277-28), $37.65
Exempt Organizations EP/EO CPE Operational Topics for 1989, Revised 01/89 (4277-31), $10.05
Exempt Organizations Continuing Professional Education Technical Instruction Program for 1989, Revised 01/89 (4277-32), $43.35
Exempt Organization Continuing Professional Education Technical Instruction Program for 1989 Index, Revised 01/89 (4277-33), $9.00

* Internal Revenue Bulletin

Superintendent of Documents
Government Printing Office
Washington, DC 20402 (202) 783-3238

The *Internal Revenue Bulletin* announces official Internal Revenue Service rulings, Treasury decisions, Executive Orders, legislation, and court decisions pertaining to Internal Revenue matters. The price is $104 per year (S/N 748-004-00000-9). Twice yearly, the weekly issues of the *Internal Revenue Bulletin* are consolidated into the *Cumulative Bulletins* (Jan-June and July-Dec). These *Bulletins* are not included as part of this subscription, but are sold as separate subscriptions. The subject bibliography, *Internal Revenue Cumulative Bulletins*, lists the bulletins available, dating back to 1940. Prices range from $8 to $42, depending on the year.

* International Income and Tax Studies

Statistics of Income Division
Internal Revenue Service
U.S. Department of the Treasury
1111 Constitution Ave., NW, Attn: R:S:P
Washington, DC 20224   (202) 376-3900

International income and tax information from 1979-1983 is provided in the publication, *Studies of International Income and Taxes*. Information includes foreign activity of U.S. corporations; activity of foreign corporations in the U.S.; foreign interests in U.S. corporations; and statistics related to individuals, trusts, and estates. Data is presented by geographical area or industrial activity, as well as other classifiers. The price is $45.

Purchasers will also be provided with additional information for one year as it becomes available. The one year period for receiving additional information can be extended at a cost of $35 per year. A long-term subscription is $150, covering data through August 1990. A new edition is scheduled for release in September 1990.

* International Tax Assistance

Office of the Associate Chief Counsel, International
Internal Revenue Service
U.S. Department of the Treasury
1111 Constitution Ave., NW
Washington, DC 20224   (202) 566-9053

International tax regulations and related materials are written by this office. The specialists will also offer technical assistance concerning questions relating to foreign taxes and tax credits. Refer also to Publications *54*, *Tax Guide for US Citizens and Resident Aliens Abroad*, and *514*, *Foreign Tax Credits for Individuals*, free from the IRS distribution centers.

* IRS Annual Statistics and Summary

Superintendent of Documents
Government Printing Office
Washington, DC 20402   (202) 783-3238

The *Internal Revenue Service Highlights* contains a wealth of information concerning the Internal Revenue Service. Program achievements within the IRS are discussed, and future goals are projected. Statistics for each year are included, such as collections and returns, refunds issued, examination of returns, civil penalties, appeals filed, exempt organizations statistics, and costs incurred by the IRS by activity and office. The price is $3.50 (S/N 048-004-02280-9).

* IRS Assistance Through the Media

Audio/Visual Branch
Public Affairs Division
Internal Revenue Service
U.S. Department of the Treasury
1111 Constitution Ave., NW
Washington, DC 20224   (202) 535-6585

Special programming promoted by the IRS for tax assistance includes radio and TV shows that allow viewers to phone in their tax questions. Watch for these in your local listings. For example, the IRS provides tax clinics for broadcast on public television stations which highlight the various tax forms and schedules, address changes in the tax law, and give helpful hints and information on where to get free assistance.

* IRS Collection of Delinquent Child Support Payments

District Directors
Deputy Commissioner, Operations
Internal Revenue Service
U.S. Department of the Treasury
1111 Constitution Ave, NW
Washington, DC 20224   (202) 566-4386

The Internal Revenue Service acts as a collection agent for a number of government agencies to collect money that taxpayers owe on delinquent child support payments and other delinquent government debts. Congress instructs the IRS to withhold all or part of the taxpayer's income tax refund to offset the amount of the delinquent payments. IRS acts as collection agent for the state welfare agencies in all child or spouse support cases. The refund amounts are used to reimburse the agencies for the support they furnish through aid to families with dependent children. The state agencies turn the funds over to the parents having custody of the children in nonwelfare cases.

* IRS Collections and Returns

Returns Processing and Accounting
Office of the Assistant Commissioner,
Taxpayer Service and Returns Processing
Internal Revenue Service
U.S. Department of the Treasury
1111 Constitution Ave., NW
Washington, DC 20224   (202) 566-6881

This office is responsible for the processing of collection and returns within the IRS tax system. Statistics generated from this office are available in the *Commissioner's Annual Report*, available from the Government Printing Office, Washington, D.C. 20402, for $3.50 (S/N 048-004-02280-9).

* IRS Community Outreach Assistance

Volunteer and Education Branch
Taxpayer Service Division
Internal Revenue Service
U.S. Department of the Treasury
1111 Constitution Ave., NW, Room 1315
Washington, DC 20224   (202) 566-4904

IRS employees and volunteers provide free tax help in coordination with local groups. The help is offered at places of business, community or neighborhood centers, libraries, colleges, and other popular locations. Within the Community Outreach program, line-by-line help with your income tax forms is provided. Tax information seminars are also held, including discussions, films or videotapes, and a question and answer period. The programs are aimed at particular interest groups, such as low-to-middle income people interested in preparing their own returns, or small business owners needing free tax assistance. Contact the taxpayer education coordinator in your area for additional information.

* IRS Criminal Investigation

Assistant Commissioner, Criminal Investigation
Internal Revenue Service
U.S. Department of the Treasury
1111 Constitution Ave., NW
Washington, DC 20224   (202) 566-6723

The mission of criminal investigation within the IRS is to encourage and achieve the highest possible level of voluntary compliance with the law by conducting investigations and recommending criminal prosecutions when warranted. Special agents target their efforts in the areas such as organized crime, narcotics trafficking, money laundering, questionable refund schemes, and tax shelters, of both domestic and international scope.

* IRS Private Letter Rulings and Information Letters

Technical Branch, Communications
Internal Revenue Service
U.S. Department of the Treasury
1111 Constitution Ave., NW
Washington, DC 20224   (202) 566-4780

If your tax situation warrants special interpretation on a particular tax deduction you would like to take, you can ask the IRS for a private letter ruling. The tax laws are applied to your case which can make this procedure time-consuming. To apply for a private-letter ruling, pertinent information must be sent, including names, addresses, taxpayer identification numbers, your IRS district office, a statement on why you qualify for the deduction, and legal documents pertaining to the case. Contact the above office on the procedure to follow. Someone from the IRS will be assigned to your case, and a notification will be sent to you on how to check the status of your ruling.

Determination letters are also issued by the IRS to businesses and organizations concerning questions related to employee pension plans and tax-exempt status. The procedure for submitting information for a determination letter is similar to filing for a private-letter ruling; however, both the IRS district offices and the national office receive these requests and make the determinations.

General information letters are frequently issued by the IRS, and the request for the information is not as formal as the above mentioned letters. Simply write a letter or postcard to either the IRS district office in your area or to the national office with your question or situation on which you would like advice.

If making an inquiry to the national office, all of the above letters should be addressed to: Internal Revenue Service (Attn: CC:CORP:T:U), P.O. Box 7604, Ben Franklin Station, Washington, DC 20224.

* IRS Research Efforts

Research Division
Assistant Commissioner, Planning,
Finance, and Research
Internal Revenue Service
U.S. Department of the Treasury
1111 Constitution Ave., NW
Washington, DC 20224   (202) 376-0356

IRS research efforts emphasize voluntary compliance, trend identification, and analysis. The IRS published estimates and projections of gross income owed but not voluntarily paid for individuals and corporations for selected years from 1973 through 1992. An analysis is also being completed on the net tax gap, the amount of income tax owed but not paid either voluntarily or involuntarily.

One of the primary objectives is to provide high quality service to taxpayers. IRS began conducting taxpayer opinion surveys in its functions that have direct contact with taxpayers to get initial or baseline measurements of taxpayer perceptions about the quality level of IRS service. A report has also been released on a new method for estimating taxpayer paperwork burden associated with preparation, recordkeeping, obtaining and learning materials, and filing forms associated with tax preparation.

* IRS Service Centers

Service Center Directors
Deputy Commissioner, Operations
Internal Revenue Service
U.S. Department of the Treasury
1111 Constitution Ave, NW
Washington, DC 20224   (202) 566-4386

The following is a listing of the Internal Revenue Service Centers where taxpayers must mail their tax forms. If an addressed envelope comes with your return, the IRS asks that you use it. If you do not have one, or if you have moved during the year, mail your return to the Internal Revenue Service Center for the place where you live. No street address is needed.

Service Center Offices:

Andover, MA: (617) 474-5549
Atlanta, GA: (404) 455-2049
Austin, TX: (512) 462-7025
Austin Compliance Center: (512) 326-0816
Brookhaven (Holtsville), NY: (516) 654-6886
Cincinnati, OH: (606) 292-5316
Fresno, CA: (209) 488-6437
Kansas City, MO: (816) 926-6828
Memphis, TN: (901) 365-5419
Ogden, UT: (801) 625-6374
Philadelphia, PA: (215) 969-2499

Regional Offices:
North Atlantic: (212) 264-0839
Mid-Atlantic: (215) 597-3991
Southeast: (404) 331-4506

Central: (513) 684-2587
Midwest: (312) 886-4291
Southwest: (214) 767-5762
Western: (415) 556-3035

* IRS Speakers and Customized Seminars

District Offices
Internal Revenue Service
U.S. Department of the Treasury
1111 Constitution Ave., NW
Washington, DC 20224 (800) 424-1040

The Internal Revenue Service provides trained speakers for area civic organizations and other interested groups. Tax clinics are often organized for special interest groups. The IRS has also sponsored call-in radio programs where you may inquire about specific tax information. Contact the district offices of the IRS listed in this publication and inquire through the Public Affairs Director if these programs are of interest to you.

*IRS Special Enrollment Agents

Office of the Director of Practice
Internal Revenue Service
U.S. Department of the Treasury
1111 Constitution Ave, NW
Washington, DC 20224 (202) 535-6787

IRS has designed a special enrollment of persons, other than attorneys and certified public accountants, who wish to represent clients before the IRS. This includes all matters connected with presentations to the Service, relating to a client's rights, privileges, and liabilities under laws or regulations administered by the Service. Such presentations include the preparation and filing of documents, all communications with the Service, and the representation of a client at conferences, hearings, and meetings. Candidates should be able to answer income tax accounting questions on the intermediate college course level. The following IRS publications, listed elsewhere in this book, will assist you in preparing for the examination:

17 Your Federal Income Tax
216 Conference and Practice Requirements
334 Tax Guide for Small Business
541 Tax Information on Partnerships
542 Tax Information on Corporations
553 Highlights of the 1989 Changes
560 Self-Employed Retirement Plans
589 Tax Information on S Corporations
590 Individual retirement Arrangements (IRAs)

Answers to the previous year's examination may be obtained from the above address to assist you in preparing for the exam.

* IRS Tax Compliance Program

Assistant Commissioner, Collection
Internal Revenue Service
U.S. Department of the Treasury
1111 Constitution Ave., NW
Washington, DC 20224 (202) 566-4033

The Information Returns Program (IRP) is a largely computerized compliance program used by the IRS to match third party information on items, such as wages, interest, dividends, and certain deductions, with the amounts reported by taxpayers on their income tax returns. The IRS also uses the information to identify people who are reported to have received income, but did not file returns. In 1988, the IRS sent out 3.8 million notices reflecting discrepancies, and 3 million notices were sent to taxpayers for failure to file a tax return based upon information returns filed.

* IRS Technical-Advice Memorandums

Technical Branch, Communications
Internal Revenue Service
U.S. Department of the Treasury
1111 Constitution Ave., NW
Washington, DC 20224 (202) 566-4780

If you are audited by the IRS and are in disagreement with the IRS agent over interpretation of a tax law, you can ask the agent to request a technical-advice memorandum for you. These memorandums must be requested through the IRS district offices. The national office then makes the final determination. Dollar amounts cannot be disputed through these memorandums, only the interpretation of the tax laws and procedures.

* IRS Walk-In Service Centers

Taxpayer Services
Internal Revenue Service
U.S. Department of the Treasury
1111 Constitution Ave., NW, Room 2422

Washington, DC 20224 (202) 377-6058

Although the IRS will not prepare your tax return for you, assistors are available throughout the country in local offices to help you as you prepare your own individual federal tax form. You are given the opportunity to learn how to research and prepare your own tax return. An assistor will walk you through the form. Often the instruction is presented in a group setting. These local offices are listed in the white pages of your phone directory under Internal Revenue Service. You may also find out about additional locations by calling your local Taxpayer Education Coordinator, listed elsewhere in this book.

* Learn What's New In Taxes

Volunteer and Education Branch
Taxpayer Service Division
Internal Revenue Service
U.S. Department of the Treasury
1111 Constitution Ave., NW, Room 1315
Washington, DC 20224 (202) 566-4904

Tax professionals (Tax Practitioners) are able to learn recent tax law changes at special institutes sponsored by qualified institutions, state and local governments, and professional and non-profit organizations. Volunteers for this program are qualified tax practitioners who might enjoy sharing their knowledge with fellow professionals in the field. Contact the taxpayer education coordinator in your area for additional information.

* Let the IRS Compute Your Taxes

District Offices
Internal Revenue Service
U.S. Department of the Treasury
1111 Constitution Ave., NW
Washington, DC 20224 (800) 424-1040

If you use Form 1040A to compute your taxes, the IRS will complete the calculation for your taxes. You must complete the tax return through Line 20. All income must be from wages and interest. Other minor stipulations also apply. Contact the above number for specific details on completing your taxes in this way.

* Money Waiting for You: Unclaimed Refunds

Accounting Branch
Internal Revenue Service
500 N. Capital Street
Washington, DC 20001 202-233-1002

This office processes returned refund checks. After an attempt has been made by the Post Office to track the taxpayer fails, the IRS computer checks names against W2 forms, employer records and Social Security records for a correct address. Regional Offices use the media to advertise names of taxpayers who are due refunds. If after three years the IRS has been unsuccessful in finding the taxpayer, the money is deposited into an unclaimed refund account where it remains until it is claimed. Should a taxpayer discover at any time that they did not receive their refund they should contact the Internal Revenue Service Center where they filed their claim, or the office listed above.

* Obtaining Prior Year Tax Returns

Service Center Directors
Deputy Commissioner, Operations
Internal Revenue Service
U.S. Department of the Treasury
1111 Constitution Ave, NW
Washington, DC 20224 (202) 566-4386

It is possible to obtain a copy of your prior year tax return by completing Form 4506, Request for Copy of Tax Form, and mailing it to the Service Center where you filed the return. The charge is $4.25 for each year's return and must accompany the request. If a taxpayer's authorized representative wishes to request a copy of a taxpayer's prior year return, he or she must attach a signed copy of Form 2848, Power of Attorney and Declaration of Representative, or other document authorizing him or her to act for the taxpayer. In lieu of Form 4506, you can send a written request to the Service Center including the following information: your name, your social security number, and if you filed a joint return, the name and social security number of your spouse, the form number, the tax period, and your current address. You must sign this request, and if a joint return was filed, only one signature is needed. Allow 45 days to process the request.

* Partnership Tax Data

Statistics of Income Division
Internal Revenue Service
U.S. Department of the Treasury
1111 Constitution Ave., NW, Attn: R:S:P
Washington, DC 20224 (202) 376-3900

The document, Partnership Source Book, is a 290-page document showing key partnership data for 1957 to 1983 at the minor, major and division industry level. It includes an historical definition of terms section and a summary of legislative changes affecting partnerships during that period. Tables feature number of partnerships and partners, business receipts, depreciation, taxes paid deduction, interest paid, payroll, payments to partners, and net income. Purchasers of this service will also be advised of the release of subsequent years' data. The price is $30.00. A magnetic tape containing the tabular statistics can be purchased for an additional $200.

* Small Business Tax Education Course

Volunteer and Education Branch
Taxpayer Service Division
Internal Revenue Service
U.S. Department of the Treasury
1111 Constitution Ave., NW, Room 1315
Washington, DC 20224   (202) 566-4904

Approximately 1,000 junior colleges and universities are now offering a new course designed by the IRS for tax education of those in small businesses. Course materials are designed by the IRS, and the college may present the material as either a credit or non-credit course. Nine areas are covered in the course, including business assets; use of the home for business; employment taxes; excise taxes; starting a business and recordkeeping; *Schedules C (Profit or Loss from a Business)*, *SE (Social Security Self-Employment Tax)*, *and 1040-ES (Estimated Tax for Individuals)*; self-employment retirement plans; partnerships; and tip reporting and allocation rules. contact a taxpayer education coordinator in your area, listed in this publication, for information on courses in your area.

* Sole Proprietorship Tax Statistics

Statistics of Income Division
Internal Revenue Service
U.S. Department of the Treasury
1111 Constitution Ave., NW, Attn: R:S:P
Washington, DC 20224   (202) 376-3900

The 244-page publication, *Sole Proprietorship Source Book*, shows key proprietorship data for 1957 through 1984, including number of businesses, business receipts, interest paid, depreciation, taxes paid deduction, payroll, and net income. The price is $95, and a magnetic tape of tabular statistics can be purchased for $245.

* Statistics of Income Bulletin

Statistics of Income Division
Internal Revenue Service
U.S. Department of the Treasury
Attn: R:S:P
1111 Constitution Ave., NW, Attn: R:S:P
Washington, DC 20224   (202) 376-3900

The *Statistics of Income Bulletin* provides the earliest published annual financial statistics from the various types of tax and information returns filed with the IRS. The *Bulletin* also includes information from periodic or special analytical studies of particular interest to tax administrators. Historical data is provided on selected types of taxpayers, including State data and gross internal revenue collections. This publication serves as an update to income statistics in the areas of corporate tax, partnership and sole proprietorship tax, and international and individual income tax. The quarterly subscription service is $20 annually and can be obtained through the Government Printing Office, Washington, D.C. 20402. The single copy price is $7.50.

* Tax Analysis

Office of Tax Analysis
Office of the Assistant Secretary
of the Treasury for Tax Policy
U.S. Department of the Treasury
1500 Pennsylvania Ave., NW
Washington, DC 20220   (202) 566-5374

This departmental office within Treasury analyzes tax programs and legislation and looks for alternative programs depending on the current economic climate. Advisors are available in many areas, such as economic modeling, revenue estimating, international taxation, individual taxation, business taxation, and depreciation analysis.

* Tax Assistance for the Military

Taxpayer Services, International
Internal Revenue Service
U.S. Department of the Treasury
950 L'Enfant Plaza
Washington, DC 20024   (202) 287-4311

The IRS sends trained instructors to military bases here and overseas to train personnel on tax procedures. Through the VITA program, these military personnel then organize internal training sessions to assist others in the preparation of their tax returns. Those chosen to be instructors often have experience in taxation or accounting. If your tax situation is complex, the Legal Assistance offices at military bases can assist you. United States embassies and consulates are also accessible for those in need of their services.

The following international telephone numbers are the local numbers of the 14 U.S. Embassies and consulates with full-time permanent staff from the IRS. Please check with your telephone company for any country or city codes required if you are outside the local dialing area. The Nassau and Ottawa numbers include the United States area codes.

Bonn, West Germany: 339-2119
Caracas, Venezuela: 285-21111, ext. 333
London, England: 408-8076 or 408-8077
Manila, Philippines: 521-7116, ext. 613 or 644
Mexico City, Mexico: (525) 211-0042, ext. 3559
Nassau, Bahamas: (809) 322-1181
Ottawa, Canada: (613) 238-5335
Paris, France: 4296-1202
Riyadh, Saudi Arabia: 488-3800, ext. 206
rome, Italy: 4674-2560
Sao Paulo, Brazil: 881-6511, ext. 287
Singapore: 338-0251, ext. 245
Sydney, Australia: 261-9275
Tokyo, Japan: 224-5466

Publication 3, Tax Information for Military Personnel, may also be useful to you. Write to your area's IRS forms and publications distribution center, listed elsewhere, for a copy or call (800) 424-3676.

* Tax Audits

Appeals Division
Office of Compliance
Internal Revenue Service
U.S. Department of the Treasury
1111 Constitution Ave., NW
Washington, DC 20224   (202) 566-6481

The IRS examines or audits federal tax returns to verify correctness of income, expenses, and credits. The Discriminant Function System selects most returns. This method scores each return for potential error based upon past experience. IRS personnel then screen the returns and select those most likely to have mistakes. Some returns are selected at random under the Taxpayer Compliance Measurement Program, and others are chosen by an income document matching program. Examinations are handled entirely by mail or take place in your home, place of business, an IRS office, or in the office of your attorney, accountant, or enrolled agent.

You may appeal an IRS decision to a regional Appeals Office, listed elsewhere in this book. The regional Appeals office is the only level of appeal within the IRS. Obtain *Form #556, Examination of Returns, Appeal Rights, and Claims for Refund*, from your regional distribution center.

Internal Revenue Service Regional Offices

Central: 550 Main St., Cincinnati, OH 45202. Serving: IN, KY, MI, OH, WV

Mid-Atlantic: 841 Chestnut St., Philadelphia, PA 19107. Serving: DE, MD, NJ, PA, VA.

Midwest: One N. Wacker St., Chicago, IL 60606. Serving: IL, IA, MN, MO, MT, NE, ND, SD, WI.

North-Atlantic: 90 Church St., New York, NY 10007. Serving: CT, ME, MA, NH, NY, RI, VT.

Southeast: 275 Peachtree St., NE, Atlanta, GA 30043. Serving: AL, AR, GA, FL, LA, MS, NC, SC, TN.

Southwest: LB-70 Stop 1000 SWRO, 7839 Churchill Way, Dallas, TX 75251. Serving: AZ, CO, KS, NM, OK, TX, UT, WY.

Western: 1650 Mission St., 5th Fl., San Francisco, CA 94103. Serving: AK, CA, HI, ID, NV, OR, WA.

IRS Regional Directors of Appeals

Room 7514, 550 Main St., Cincinnati, OH 45202

841 Chestnut St., Philadelphia, PA 19107

230 N. Dearborn, 29th Fl., Room 2972, Chicago, IL 60604

90 Church St., New York, NY 10007

Room 625, 275 Peachtree St., NE, Atlanta, GA 30043

LB-70, Stop 8000 SWRO, 7839 Churchill Way, Dallas, TX 75251

1650 Mission St., 5th Fl., SAn Francisco, CA 94103

* Tax Counseling for the Elderly

Volunteer and Education Branch
Taxpayer Service Division
Internal Revenue Service
U.S. Department of the Treasury
1111 Constitution Ave., NW, Room 1315
Washington, DC 20224   (202) 566-4904

TCE offers free tax help to people who are 60 years and older. Many of the volunteers within the program are also retired and are affiliated with non-profit groups that have received grants to operate a local TCE program. Funds are used so that volunteers may travel to wherever the assistance is needed: to retirement homes, neighborhood sites, or privates homes of the homebound. Contact your local taxpayer education coordinator for programs in your area.

The following IRS Publications are particularly useful for the elderly and are available FREE from your local IRS office or 1-800-424-3676.

*Publication 524, Credit for the Elderly and Disabled; and
Publication 554, Tax Benefits for Older Americans.*

* Tax Court

United States Tax Court
400 Second St., NW
Washington, DC 20217   (202) 376-2751

If your taxes are delinquent, the Internal Revenue Service will issue you a delinquency notice, whether you are a consumer or a corporation. If you wish to contest the delinquency, a petition for a hearing can be filed with the U.S. Tax Court. This court is an independent court and not part of the IRS. The court's decision is final and cannot be appealed.

* Tax Education for High School Students

Volunteer and Education Branch
Taxpayer Service Division
Internal Revenue Service
U.S. Department of the Treasury
1111 Constitution Ave., NW, Room 1315
Washington, DC 20224   (202) 566-4904

The IRS sponsors an introductory tax education program, *Understanding Taxes*, for high school students. Since many of the students have part-time jobs, the material that is learned can be practiced immediately. Instructional materials include computer software and video programs. Volunteer instructors are those who enjoy teaching and helping others, and who are knowledgeable about taxation. Your local taxpayer education coordinator will assist you in organizing these courses.

* Tax Exempt Organizations

Exempt Organizations Technical Division
Internal Revenue Service
U.S. Department of the Treasury
1111 Constitution Ave., NW, Room 6411
Washington, DC 20224   (202) 566-6208

This office within the IRS sets the qualifications of organizations seeking a tax exempt status. Compliance with the law is also monitored. For a listing of the names of exempt organizations through October 31, 1988, subscribe to *Cumulative List of Organizations*, as legislated through Section 170(c) of the Internal Revenue Code of 1954. The subscription is $38 annually and includes three cumulative quarterly supplements. Available from : Superintendent of Documents, Government Printing Office, Washington, DC 20402, (202) 783-3238.

* Tax Help for the Hearing Impaired

Taxpayer Services Division
Internal Revenue Service
U.S. Department of the Treasury
1111 Constitution Ave, NW
Washington, DC 20224   (202) 566-4825
Teletypewriter Number 1 (800) 428-4732

Telephone tax service by way of a teletypewriter is available from the IRS to assist hearing impaired taxpayers. During the IRS filing season, the hours of operation are 8 a.m. to 6:45 p.m. EST. In the non-filing season, the hours are 8 a.m. to 4:30 p.m. EST. The toll-free teletypewriter number in Indiana is 1 (800) 382-4059.

* Tax Help on Audio and Video Cassettes

Audio/Visual Branch
Public Affairs Division
Internal Revenue Service

U.S. Department of the Treasury
1111 Constitution Ave., NW
Washington, DC 20224   (202) 535-6585

The IRS provides local libraries with audio cassettes and videocassettes, for loan to the public, on how to fill out Forms 1040EZ, 1040A, 1040, and Schedules A and B. These tax tapes contain simple, step-by-step instructions to the forms and tax tips. Contact this office or your local library for more information.

* Tax Information in Braille

National Library Service for the Blind
and Physically Handicapped
1291 Taylor St.
Washington, DC 20542   (202) 707-5100

IRS materials are available in braille. They include *Publications 17, Your Federal Income Tax*, and *334, Tax Guide for Small Business*, and *Forms 1040, 1040A*, and *1040EZ* and instructions. They may be obtained at Regional Libraries for the Blind and Physically Handicapped. For a regional library in your area, contact the National Library Service for a listing.

* Tax Matters Digest System

Superintendent of Documents
Government Printing Office
Washington, DC 20402   (202) 783-3238

The *Bulletin Index - Digest System* contains the *Finding List* and *Digests* of all permanent tax matters published in the Internal Revenue System. Each subscription service consists of a basic manual and cumulative supplements for an indefinite period.

Service No. 1 - Income Taxes, 1953-1987. ($42) (S/N 948-001-00000-4)
Service No. 2 - Estate and Gift Taxes, 1953-1986. ($17) (S/N 948-002-00000-1)
Service No. 3 - Employment Taxes, 1953-1986. ($17) (S/N 948-003-00000-7)
Service No. 4 - Excise Taxes, 1953-1986. ($17) (S/N 948-004-00000-3)

* Tax Returns Prepared Free for Low Income, Elderly and Handicapped

Volunteer and Education Branch
Taxpayer Service Division
Internal Revenue Service
U.S. Department of the Treasury
1111 Constitution Ave., NW, Room 1315
Washington, DC 20224   (202) 566-4904

The Volunteer Income Tax Assistance (VITA) Program offers free tax help to people who cannot afford professional assistance. Volunteers help prepare basic tax returns for older, handicapped, and non-English-speaking taxpayers. Assistance is provided in the community at libraries, schools, shopping malls, and at other convenient locations.

Volunteers may take part in various VITA program activities, such as directly preparing returns, teaching taxpayers to prepare their own returns, managing a VITA site, or arranging publicity. Volunteers generally include college students, law students, members of professional business and accounting organizations, and members of retirement, religious, military, and community groups. The IRS provides VITA training materials and instructors. Training is conducted at a time and location convenient to volunteers and instructors. Generally, these sessions are offered in December through January each year.

The emphasis in VITA is to teach taxpayers to complete their own tax returns. A volunteer's role becomes that of an instructor rather than a preparer. VITA volunteers will teach taxpayers to prepare their own Forms 1040EZ, 1040A, 1040, and W-4. Assistance with state and local returns can also be provided. If complicated questions or returns are introduced, professional assistance will be provided or the taxpayer will be referred to one of the IRS publications for guidance. Contact your local taxpayer education coordinator for additional information on programs in your district.

Contact your local library or IRS office for locations near you.

* Tax Workshops for Small Businesses

Volunteer and Education Branch
Taxpayer Service Division
Internal Revenue Service
U.S. Department of the Treasury
1111 Constitution Ave., NW, Room 1315
Washington, DC 20224   (202) 566-4904

Small business tax workshops are organized to assist small business owners in understanding their tax obligations. Free workshops explain withholding tax responsibilities and the completion of employment tax returns. This is an excellent opportunity for experienced business persons to volunteer their time and show the "ropes" to someone just starting out. Contact the taxpayer education coordinator in your area for locations of these workshops.

The following IRS Publications are particularly useful to small business and are

Taxes

available FREE from your local IRS office or 1-800-424-3676.

Publication 334, Tax Guide for Small Business
Publication 583, Taxpayers Starting a Business.

* The Buck Stops Here

Problem Resolution Staff
Assistant to the Commissioner,
Taxpayer Ombudsman
Internal Revenue Service
U.S. Department of the Treasury
1111 Constitution Ave., NW
Washington, DC 20224   (202) 566-4948

Taxpayers who have been unable to resolve their problems after going through the normal IRS channels may use the Problem Resolution Program. The program's personnel are taxpayer advocates who have the authority to cut through red tape. Contact the IRS toll-free information numbers regarding tax questions, and ask for Problem Resolution assistance.

The following is a listing of Problem Resolution Officers' telephone numbers:

District Offices:

Aberdeen, SD: (605) 226-7278, ext. 215
Albany, NY: (518) 472-4482
Albuquerque, NM: (505) 766-3760
Anchorage, AK: (907) 261-4228/4230
Atlanta, GA: (404) 331-5232
Augusta, ME: (307) 780-3309
Austin, TX: (512) 499-5875
Baltimore, MD: (301) 962-3324
Birmingham, AL (205) 731-1177
Boise, ID: (208) 334-1324
Boston, MA: (617) 565-1857
Brooklyn, NY: (718) 780-6511/6111
Buffalo, NY: (716) 846-4574
Burlington, VT (802)951-6354
Cheyenne, WY: (307) 772-2489
Chicago, IL (312) 886-9183
Cincinnati, OH: (513) 684-3094
Cleveland, OH: (216) 522-7134
Columbia, SC: (803) 765-5939
Dallas, TX: (214) 767-1289
Denver, CO: (303) 844-3178
Des Moines, IA: (515) 284-4780
Detroit, MI: (313) 226-4380
Fargo, ND: (701) 237-5771, ext. 141
Ft. Lauderdale, FL (304) 527-7359
Greensboro, NC: (919) 333-5497
Hartford, CT: (203) 240-4179
Helena, MT: (406) 449-5244
Honolulu, HI: (808) 551-3300
Houston, TX: (713) 953-6436
Indianapolis, IN: (317) 269-6332
Jackson, MS: (601) 690-4800
Jacksonville, FL: (904) 791-3440
Laguana Niguel, CA: (714) 643-4182
Las Vegas, NV: (702) 388-6281
Little Rock, AR: (501) 378-6260
Los Angeles, CA: (213) 894-6953
Louisville, KY: (502) 582-6030
Manhattan, NY: (212) 264-2850
Milwaukee, WI (414) 291-3046
Nashville, TN: (615) 736-5219
New Orleans, LA: (504) 589-3001
Newark, NJ: (201) 645-6698/6263
Oklahoma City, OK: (405) 231-4150
Omaha, NE: (402) 221-4181
Parkersburg, WV: (304) 420-6616
Philadelphia, PA: (215) 597-3377
Phoenix, AZ: (602) 261-3604
Pittsburgh, PA: (412) 644-5987
Portland, OR: (503) 221-2333
Portsmouth, NH: (603) 433-0571
Providence, RI: (401) 528-4288
Richmond, VA: (804) 771-2643
Sacramento, CA: (916) 978-4079
Salt Lake City, UT: (801) 524-6287
San Francisco, CA (415) 556-5046
San Jose, CA: (408) 291-7132
Seattle, WA: (206) 442-7393
Springfield, IL: (217) 492-4517
St.Louis, MO: (314) 425-6770
St. Paul, MN: (612) 290-3077
Wichita, KS: (316) 291-6056
Wilmington, DE: (302) 573-6052

* Videos and Films on IRS Topics

Audio/Visual Branch
Public Affairs Division
Internal Revenue Service
U.S. Department of the Treasury
1111 Constitution Ave., NW
Washington, DC 20224   (202) 535-6585

IRS-produced films and videotapes are available directly from the IRS, without charge, to groups and interested organizations. To order one of the following films, call your local IRS office or call toll free 1-800-424-1040 and ask for Public Affairs.

Taxes and the Single Parent. The situations of three single parents and how taxes affect them are portrayed in this film. One parent is an accountant who explains the tax laws that relate to dependents, alimony, child care expenses, working students, etc. This is available on 3/4" and VHS videocassettes.

The IRS Guide to Retirement. Older Americans' pressing tax concerns are addressed in a question and answer format. An IRS representative answers tax questions about pensions, social security benefits, IRAs, and the sale of a home. Special tax benefits and sources of free IRS tax help are also discussed. This is available on 3/4" and VHS videocassettes.

Tax Forms '89. This is a line-by-line guide on how to fill out Forms 1040EZ, 1040A, 1040, and Schedules A and B. It explains how to choose the right tax return and discusses filing status, deductions, credits, tax computations, and other topics. This is available in 3/4" and VHS videocassettes, and in English and Spanish versions. Updated versions are available by January of each year.

Why Us, the Lakens?. This film, narrated by Lyle Waggoner, highlights taxpayers' rights during an IRS audit and their appeal rights. It follows the Laken family through their appeal, and the viewer learns how the audit procedure and the appeals system work. This is available on 16mm film and 3/4" videocassettes.

Por Que Nosotros, Los Garcia?. This is a Spanish version of the explanation of taxpayers' examination of returns and appeal rights. It is similar to *Why Us, The Lakens?* This is available on 16mm film and 3/4" videocassettes.

Por Que Los Impuestos? A reporter of a Spanish weekly newspaper covers the history of taxation, how taxes are used, the rights and responsibilities of taxpayers, and the different kinds of IRS assistance available. The film is especially suitable for social studies and history courses at adult education and community centers. Available on 16mm film and 3/4" videocassettes.

A Trip Down the Pipeline. Narrated by actor Terry Carter, this film shows how a tax return is processed at an IRS Service Center. The film depicts the various steps that occur in the processing cycle. It is available on 16m film.

A Vital Service. Aims at enlisting groups and organizations into the Volunteer Income Tax Assistance Program in which IRS trains volunteers to help the low-income, elderly non-English speaking and the handicapped complete their tax returns. It is available on 16mm film and 3/4" videocassettes.

Helping to Recover. Focuses on how to file claims for disaster, casualty and theft losses.

Hey, We're in Business. Stresses the IRS free assistance program for small business owners in such areas as good records, obligations to employees, and depreciation. It is available in English and Spanish.

* Voicing Opinions of IRS Tax Laws

Office of Chief Counsel, Corporate
Internal Revenue Service
U.S. Department of the Treasury
1111 Constitution Ave., NW, Attn: CC:CORP:T:R
Washington, DC 20224   (202) 566-3935

If you have a personal recommendation for changing a federal tax law, you may send written comments to the address above. The letter must include the section within the Internal Revenue Code in which the portion of the law appears. Please send an original and eight copies of the correspondence.

If you wish to comment on how to improve a tax form or instruction booklet, you may address correspondence to the Tax Forms Coordinating Committee, Internal Revenue Service, 1111 Constitution Ave., NW, Washington, DC 20224.

Senators and members of the House of Representatives can also be contacted if you wish to voice your opinions of tax laws and procedures. Write to: The Honorable (the senator's name), U.S. Senate, Washington, DC 20510; or The Honorable (your representative's name), U.S. House of Representatives, Washington, DC 20515.

* Wage Reporting

Returns, Processing, and Accounting
Internal Revenue Service

U.S. Department of the Treasury
1111 Constitution Ave., NW, Room 7009
Washington, DC 20224   (202) 566-6881
The combined annual wage reporting system was designed to assist employers in the reporting of taxes. For more assistance in this area, contact your local field office listed in your phone directory or the office above.

* Where To File: Mailing Address

If an addressed envelope came with your return, please use it. If you do not have one, or if you moved during the year, mail your return to the Internal Revenue Service Center for the place where you live. No street address is needed.

Florida, Georgia, South Carolina
Use this address: Atlanta, GA 39901

New Jersey, New York (New York City and counties of Nassau, Rockland, Suffolk, and Westchester)
Use this address: Holtsville, NY 00501

New York (all other counties), Connecticut, Maine, Massachusetts, New Hampshire, Rhode Island, Vermont
Use this address: Andover, MA 05501

Illinois, Iowa, Minnesota, Missouri, Wisconsin
Use this address: Kansas City, MO 64999

Delaware, District of Columbia, Maryland, Pennsylvania, Virginia
Use this address: Philadelphia, PA 19255

Indiana, Kentucky, Michigan, Ohio, West Virginia
Use this address: Cincinnati, OH 45999

Kansas, New Mexico, Oklahoma, Texas
Use this address: Austin, TX 73301

Alaska, Arizona, California (counties of Alpine, Amador, Butte, Calaveras, Colusa, Contra Costa, Del Norte, El Dorado, Glenn, Humboldt, Lake, Lassen, Mendocino, Modoc, Napa, Nevada, Placer, Plumas, Sacramento, San Joaquin, Shasta, Sierra, Siskiyou, Solano, Sonoma, Sutter, Tehama, Trinity, Yolo, and Yuba), Colorado, Idaho, Montana, Nebraska, Nevada, North Dakota, Oregon, South Dakota, Utah, Washington, Wyoming
Use this address: Ogden, UT 84201

California (all other counties), Hawaii
Use this address: Fresno, CA 93888

Alabama, Arkansas, Louisiana, Mississippi, North Carolina, Tennessee
Use this address: Memphis, TN 37501

American Samoa
Use this address: Philadelphia, PA 19255

Guam
Use This address: Commissioner of Revenue and Taxation
                                              855 West Marine Dr
                                              Agana, GU 96910

Puerto Rico (or if excluding income under section 933), Virgin Islands (Nonpermanent residents)
Use this address: Philadelphia, PA 19255

Virgin Islands (Permanent residents)
Use this address: V.I. Bureau of Internal Revenue
                                              Lockharts Garden No. 1A
                                              Charlotte Amalie,
                                              St. Thomas, VI 00802

Foreign country: U.S. citizens and those filing Form 2555 or Form 4563
Use this address: Philadelphia, PA 19255

All A.P.O. or F.P.O. addresses
Use this address: Philadelphia, PA 19255

Tax Hotlines

Toll-free telephone tax assistance is available in all 50 states, the District of Columbia, Puerto Rico, and the Virgin Islands. There is no long distance charge for your call. It is best to call early in the morning or later in the week for prompt service. The IRS offers these suggestions for using its services.

Call IRS With Your Tax Question:
If the instructions to the tax forms and our free tax publications have not answered your question, please call us Toll-Free. Toll-Free is a telephone call for which you pay only local charges.

Choosing the Right Number:
Use only the number listed below for your area. Use a local city number only if it is not a long distance call for you. Please do not dial 1-800 when using a local city number.

Before You Call:
Remember that good communication is a two-way process. IRS representatives care about the quality of the service we provide to you, our customer. You can help us provide accurate, complete answers to your tax questions by having the following information available.
  * The tax form, schedule, or notice to which your question relates.
  * The facts about your particular situation (the answer to the same question often varies from one taxpayer to another because of differences in their age, income, whether they can be claimed as a dependent, etc.).
  * The name of any IRS publication or other source of information that you used to look for the answer.

Before You Hang Up:
If you do not fully understand the answer you receive, or you feel our representative may not fully understand your question, our representative needs to know this. He or she will be happy to take the additional time required to be sure we have answered your question fully and in the manner which is most helpful to you.

According to the government, if the IRS makes an error in answering your question, you still will be held responsible for the payment of the correct tax. Should this occur, however, you will not be charged any penalty. To make sure that IRS representatives give accurate and courteous answers, a second IRS representative sometimes listens in on telephone calls. No record is kept of any taxpayer's identity.

Alabama
1-800-424-1040

Alaska
Anchorage, 561-7484
Elsewhere, 1-800-424-1040

Arizona
Phoenix, 257-1233
Elsewhere, 1-800-424-1040

Arkansas
1-800-424-1040

California

Refer to your local telephone directory under U.S. Government, Internal Revenue Service, Federal Tax Assistance.

Colorado
Denver, 825-7041
Elsewhere, 1-800-424-1040

Connecticut
1-800-424-1040

Delaware
1-800-424-1040

District of Columbia
488-3100

Florida
Jacksonville, 354-1760
Elsewhere, 1-800-424-1040

Georgia
Atlanta, 522-0050
Elsewhere, 1-800-424-1040

Hawaii
Oahu, 541-1040
Elsewhere, 1-800-424-1040

Idaho
1-800-424-1040

Illinois
Chicago, 435-1040
Elsewhere, 1-800-424-1040

Indiana
Indianapolis, 226-5477
Elsewhere, 1-800-424-1040

Iowa
Des Moines, 283-0523
Elsewhere, 1-800-424-1040

Kansas
1-800-424-1040

Kentucky
1-800-424-1040

Louisiana
1-800-424-1040

Maine
1-800-424-1040

Maryland
Baltimore, 962-2590
Montgomery County, 488-3100
Prince George's County, 488-3100
Elsewhere, 1-800-424-1040

Massachusetts
Boston, 523-1040
Elsewhere, 1-800-424-1040

Michigan
Detroit, 237-0800
Elsewhere, 1-800-424-1040

Minnesota
Minneapolis, 291-1422

St. Paul, 291-1422
Elsewhere, 1-800-424-1040

Mississippi
1-800-424-1040

Missouri
St. Louis, 342-1040
Elsewhere, 1-800-424-1040

Montana
1-800-424-1040

Nebraska
Omaha, 422-1500
Elsewhere, 1-800-424-1040

Nevada
1-800-424-1040

New Hampshire
1-800-424-1040

New Jersey
Newark, 622-0600
Elsewhere, 1-800-424-1040

New Mexico
1-800-424-1040

New York
Bronx, 732-0100
Brooklyn, 596-3770
Buffalo, 855-3955
Manhattan, 732-0100
Nassau, 222-1131
Queens, 596-3770
Rockland County, 997-1510
Staten Island, 596-3770
Suffolk, 724-5000
Westchester County, 997-1510
Elsewhere, 1-800-424-1040

North Carolina
1-800-424-1040

North Dakota
1-800-424-1040

Ohio
Cincinnati, 621-6281
Cleveland, 522-3000
Elsewhere, 1-800-424-1040

Oklahoma
1-800-424-1040

Oregon
Portland, 221-3960
Elsewhere, 1-800-424-1040

Pennsylvania
Philadelphia, 574-9900
Pittsburgh, 281-0112
Elsewhere, 1-800-424-1040

Puerto Rico
San Juan Metro area, 766-5040
Isla DDD, 766-5549

Rhode Island
1-800-424-1040

South Carolina
1-800-424-1040

South Dakota
1-800-424-1040

Tennessee
Nashville, 259-4601
Elsewhere, 1-800-424-1040

Texas
Dallas, 742-2440
Ft. Worth, 263-9229
Houston, 965-0440
Elsewhere, 1-800-424-1040

Utah
1-800-424-1040

Vermont
1-800-424-1040

Virginia
Bailey's Crossroads, 557-9230
Richmond, 649-2361
Elsewhere, 1-800-424-1040

Washington
Seattle, 442-1040
Elsewhere, 1-800-424-1040

West Virginia
1-800-424-1040

Wisconsin
Milwaukee, 271-3780
Elsewhere, 1-800-424-1040

Wyoming
1-800-424-1040

* Telephone Assistance Services for Deaf Taxpayers With TV/Telephone-TTY Equipment
Indiana residents (800) 382-4059
Elsewhere in U.S., including Alaska,
Hawaii, Virgin Islands, and Puerto Rico (800) 428-4732
Hours of Operation
8:00 A.M. to 6:45 P.M. EST (Jan. 1 - April 17)
8:00 A.M. to 4:30 P.M. EST (April 18 - Dec. 31)

* Toll-Free Taxpayer Assistance for International Residents
Taxpayer Services
Internal Revenue Service
U.S. Department of the Treasury
1111 Constitution Ave., NW, Room 2422
Washington, DC 20224 (202) 377-6058

The Internal Revenue Service has full-time permanent staff at 14 U.S. Embassies and Consulates around the world. Taxpayer service representatives travel during the filing season to many cities worldwide to offer help with tax returns. You may call your nearest U.S. Embassy, Consulate, or IRS office listed below to find out when and where assistance will be available in your area. All IRS offices are open Monday through Friday, except Riyadh, Saudi Arabia, which is open Saturday through Wednesday.

The following IRS telephone numbers are local numbers. Please check with your telephone company for any country or city codes required if you are outside the local dialing area. The Nassau and Ottawa numbers include the United States area Codes.

Bonn, West Germany: 339-2119
Caracas, Venezuela: 285-21111, ext. 333
London, England: 408-8076 or 408-8077
Manila, Philippines: 521-7116, ext. 613 or 644
Mexico City, Mexico: (525) 211-0042, ext. 3559
Nassau, Bahamas: (809) 322-1181
Ottawa, Canada: (613) 238-5335
Paris, France: 4296-1202
Riyadh, Saudi Arabia: 488-3800, ext. 206
Rome, Italy: 4674-2560
Sao Paulo, Brazil: 881-6511, ext. 287
Singapore: 338-0251, ext. 245
Sydney, Australia: 261-9275
Tokyo, Japan: 224-5466

Recorded Messages

Tele-Tax is an IRS toll-free telephone service which provides both automated refund information and recorded tax information. Recorded tax information is available on about 140 topics. It is accessible 24 hours a days, 7 days a week to taxpayers with push-button (tone-signaling) phones. Those with rotary or push-button (pulse dial) phone must call during normal office hours.

If eight weeks have lapsed since you mailed your tax return, you may check the status of your refund. When you call, have a copy of your tax return available because the operator will ask for the first social security number shown on the form, the filing status, and the exact amount of the refund. This service is available after March 15 of each year. If you are using a push-button (tone-signaling) phone, the hours are Monday through Friday, 6:30 AM to 6:00 PM. Hours may vary slightly in each area. If you are using a rotary or push-button (pulse dial) phone, the service is only available during normal office hours.

Below is a listing of the Tele-Tax phone numbers in each area. In major cities, a phone number is listed which is not toll-free. Do not add 1-800 to this number.

Alabama
1-800-554-4477

Alaska
1-800-554-4477

Arizona
Phoenix, 252-4909
Elsewhere, 1-800-554-4477

Arkansas
1-800-554-4477

California
Counties of Amador, Calaveras, Contra Costa, Marin, and San Joaquin, 1-800-428-4032
Los Angeles, 617-3177
Oakland, 839-4245
Elsewhere, 1-800-554-4477

Colorado
Denver, 825-7041
Elsewhere, 1-800-424-1040

Connecticut
1-800-554-4477

Delaware
1-800-554-4477

District of Columbia
628-2929

Florida
Jacksonville, 353-9579
Elsewhere, 1-800-554-4477

Georgia
Atlanta, 331-6572
Elsewhere, 1-800-554-4477

Hawaii
1-800-554-4477

Idaho
1-800-554-4477

Illinois
Chicago, 829-6397
Springfield, 789-0489
Elsewhere, 1-800-554-4477

Indiana
Indianapolis, 631-1010
Elsewhere, 1-800-554-4477

Iowa
1-800-554-4477

Kansas
1-800-554-4477

Kentucky
1-800-554-4477

Louisiana
1-800-554-4477

Maine
1-800-554-4477

Maryland
Baltimore, 244-7306
Elsewhere, 1-800-554-4477

Massachusetts
Boston, 523-8602
Elsewhere, 1-800-554-4477

Michigan
Detroit, 961-4282
Elsewhere, 1-800-554-4477

Minnesota
St. Paul, 224-4288
Elsewhere, 1-800-554-4477

Mississippi
1-800-554-4477

Missouri
St. Louis, 241-4700
Elsewhere, 1-800-554-4477

Montana
1-800-554-4477

Nebraska
Omaha, 221-3324
Elsewhere, 1-800-554-4477

Nevada
1-800-554-4477

New Hampshire
1-800-554-4477

New Jersey
Newark, 624-1223
Elsewhere, 1-800-554-4477

New Mexico
1-800-554-4477

New York

Brooklyn, 858-4461
Buffalo, 856-9320
Manhattan, 406-4080
Queens, 858-4461
Staten Island, 858-4461
Elsewhere, 1-800-554-4477

North Carolina
1-800-554-4477

North Dakota
1-800-554-4477

Ohio
Cincinnati, 421-0329
Cleveland, 522-3037
Elsewhere, 1-800-554-4477

Oklahoma
1-800-554-4477

Oregon
Portland, 294-5363
Elsewhere, 1-800-554-4477

Pennsylvania
Philadelphia, 592-8946
Pittsburgh, 261-1040
Elsewhere, 1-800-554-4477

Puerto Rico
1-800-554-4477

Rhode Island
1-800-554-4477

South Carolina
1-800-554-4477

South Dakota
1-800-554-4477

Tennessee
Nashville, 242-1541
Elsewhere, 1-800-554-4477

Texas
Dallas, 767-1792
Houston, 850-8801
Elsewhere, 1-800-554-4477

Utah
1-800-554-4477

Vermont
1-800-554-4477

Virginia
Richmond, 829-6397
Elsewhere, 1-800-554-4477

Washington
Seattle, 343-7221
Elsewhere, 1-800-554-4477

West Virginia
1-800-554-4477

Wisconsin
Milwaukee, 291-1783
Elsewhere, 1-800-554-4477

Wyoming
1-800-554-4477

* Tele-Tax Topic Numbers and Subjects
For your convenience, here is a listing of the tele-tax information subjects. The recording will ask you to enter the number of the subject you wish to hear. Have a paper and pencil handy to take notes. Push * then #2 to access the directory, and push 323 to hear a listing of titles within the directory.

IRS Procedures and Services
101 IRS help available: Volunteer tax assistance programs, toll-free telephone.
102 Tax assistance for handicapped individuals and the deaf
103 Small business tax workshops: Tax help for new businesses
104 Problem resolution program: Special help for problem situations
105 Public libraries: Tax information tapes and reproducible tax forms.
106 Examination procedures and how to prepare for an audit
107 The collection process
108 Tax fraud: How to report
109 Special enrollment examination to practice before IRS
110 Organizations: How to apply for exempt status
111 Audit appeal rights
112 Electronic filing
999 Local information

Filing Requirements, Filing Status, Exemptions
151 Who must file?
152 Which form: 1040, 1040A, or 1040EZ?
153 When, where, and how to file
154 What is your filing status?
155 Dependents
156 Estimated tax
157 Amended returns
158 Decedents

Types of Income
201 Wages and salaries
202 Tips
203 Interest received
204 Dividends
205 Refund of state and local taxes
206 Alimony received
207 Business income
208 Sole proprietorship
209 Capital gains and losses
210 Pensions and annuities
211 Pensions: The general rule
212 Lump-sum distributions: Profit-sharing plans
213 Rental income and expenses
214 Renting vacation property/Renting to relatives
215 Royalties
216 Farming and fishing income
217 Earnings for clergy
218 Unemployment compensation
219 Gambling income and expenses
220 Bartering income
221 Scholarships, fellowships and grants
222 Nontaxable income
223 Social security, tier 1, and catastrophic coverage
224 401(K) plans
225 Passive activities: Losses/Credits

Adjustments to Income
251 Employee business expenses
252 Individual retirement arrangements (IRAs)
253 Alimony paid
254 Bad debt reduction
255 Tax shelters

Itemized Deductions
301 Should I itemize?
302 Medical and dental expenses
303 Taxes
304 Moving expenses
305 Interest expense
306 Contributions
307 Casualty losses
308 Miscellaneous expenses
309 Business use of home
310 Business use of car
311 Business travel expenses
312 Business entertainment expenses
313 Educational expenses

Tax computation
351 Tax and credits figured by IRS
352 Self-employment tax
353 Five-year averaging for lump-sum distributions
354 Alternative minimum tax
355 Gift tax
356 Estate tax
357 Standard deduction

Tax Credits
401 Child care credit

Taxes

IRS Tax Forms

All Federal Income Tax Forms are listed in numerical order after this state-by-state roster to order these forms. To order any of the IRS forms, publications and instruction packets which are listed in the next section, call the toll-free IRS hotline at (800) 424-3676. To send for forms through the mail, write to the approriate state address below. Two copies of each form and one copy of each set of instructions will be sent.

Forms Distribution Centers

Alabama
P.O. Box 9903
Bloomington, IL 61799

Alaska
Rancho Cordova, CA 95743-0001

Arizona
Rancho Cordova, CA 95743-0001

Arkansas
P.O. Box 9903
Bloomington, IL 61799

California
Rancho Cordova, CA 95743-0001

Colorado
Rancho Cordova, CA 95743-0001

Connecticut
P.O. Box 25866
Richmond, VA 23289

Delaware
P.O. Box 25866
Richmond, VA 23289

District of Columbia
P.O. Box 25866
Richmond, VA 23289

Florida
P.O. Box 25866
Richmond, VA 23289

Georgia
P.O. Box 25866
Richmond, VA 23289

Hawaii
Rancho Cordova, CA 95743-0001

Idaho
Rancho Cordova, CA 95743-0001

Illinois
P.O. Box 9903
Bloomington, IL 61799

Indiana
P.O. Box 9903
Bloomington, IL 61799

Iowa
P.O. Box 9903
Bloomington, IL 61799

Kansas
P.O. Box 9903
Bloomington, IL 61799

Kentucky
P.O. Box 9903
Bloomington, IL 61799

Louisiana
P.O. Box 9903
Bloomington, IL 61799

Maine
P.O. Box 25866
Richmond, VA 23289

Maryland
P.O. Box 25866
Richmond, VA 23289

Massachusetts
P.O. Box 25866
Richmond, VA 23289

Michigan
P.O. Box 9903
Bloomington, IL 61799

Minnesota
P.O. Box 9903
Bloomington, IL 61799

Mississippi
P.O. Box 9903
Bloomington, IL 61799

Missouri
P.O. Box 9903
Bloomington, IL 61799

Montana
Rancho Cordova, CA 95743-0001

Nebraska
P.O. Box 9903
Bloomington, IL 61799

Nevada
Rancho Cordova, CA 95743-0001

New Hampshire
P.O. Box 25866
Richmond, VA 23289

New Jersey
P.O. Box 25866
Richmond, VA 23289

New Mexico
Rancho Cordova, CA 95743-0001

New York
P.O. Box 25866
Richmond, VA 23289

North Carolina
P.O. Box 25866
Richmond, VA 23289

North Dakota
P.O. Box 9903
Bloomington, IL 61799

Taxes

Ohio
P.O. Box 9903
Bloomington, IL 61799

Oklahoma
P.O. Box 9903
Bloomington, IL 61799

Oregon
Rancho Cordova, CA 95743-0001

Pennsylvania
P.O. Box 25866
Richmond, VA 23289

Puerto Rico
P.O. Box 25866
Richmond, VA 23289

Rhode Island
P.O. Box 25866
Richmond, VA 23289

South Carolina
P.O. Box 25866
Richmond, VA 23289

South Dakota
P.O. Box 9903
Bloomington, IL 61799

Tennessee
P.O. Box 9903
Bloomington, IL 61799

Texas
P.O. Box 9903
Bloomington, IL 61799

Utah
Rancho Cordova, CA 95743-0001

Vermont
P.O. Box 25866
Richmond, VA 23289

Virgin Islands
V.I. Bureau of Internal Revenue
Lockharts Garden No. 1A
Charlotte Amalie
St. Thomas, VI 00802

Virginia
P.O. Box 25866
Richmond, VA 23289

Washington
Rancho Cordova, CA 95743-0001

West Virginia
P.O. Box 25866
Richmond, VA 23289

Wisconsin
P.O. Box 9903
Bloomington, IL 61799

Wyoming
Rancho Cordova, CA 95743-0001

* Foreign Addresses

Forms Distribution Center
P.O. Box 25866
Richmond, VA 23289

Forms Distribution Center
Rancho Cordova, CA 95743-0001

Taxpayers with mailing addresses in foreign countries should send the order blank to either address. Send letter requests for other forms and publications to: Forms Distribution Center, P.O. Box 25866, Richmond, VA 23289.

* Numerical List of Federal Tax Return Forms and Related Forms

Timber/Forest Industries Schedules
Supplement to income tax return for taxpayers claiming a deduction for depletion of timber and for depreciation of plant and other timber improvements.
IT-IRC sec. 631; Regs. sec. 1.611-3
IT-IRC sec. 6012; Pub. 17

Tax Forms Package 1
Federal Income Tax Forms
A package of income tax forms for nonbusiness and nonfarm taxpayers. Contains one copy of instructions for Form 1040 and two copies of the following: Form 1040, Schedule A, and Schedule B.
IT-IRC sec. 6012; Pub. 17

Tax Forms Package 1-X
Federal Income Tax Forms
A package of income tax forms for nonbusiness and nonfarm taxpayers. Contains one copy of instructions for Form 1040 and two copies of the following: Form 1040, Schedule A, Schedule B, Form 2106 and instructions, and Form 2441 and instructions.
IT-IRC sec. 6012; Pub. 17

Tax Forms Package 2
Federal Income Tax Forms
A package of income tax forms for nonbusiness and nonfarm taxpayers. Contains one copy of instructions for Form 1040 and two copies of the following: Form 1040, Schedule A, Schedule B, Schedule D, Schedule E, Form 2441 and instructions, and Form 4562 and instructions.
IT-IRC sec. 6012; Pub. 17

Tax Forms Package 2-R
Federal Income Tax Forms
A package of income tax forms for nonbusiness and nonfarm taxpayers. Contains one copy of instructions for Form 1040 and two copies of the following: Form 1040, Schedule A, Schedule B, Schedule D, Schedule E, Schedule R and instructions, and Form 4562 and instructions.
IT-IRC sec. 6012; Pub. 17

Tax Forms Package 3
Federal Income Tax Forms
A package of income tax forms for business taxpayers. Contains one copy of instructions for Form 1040 and two copies of the following: Form 1040, Schedule A, Schedule B, Schedule C, Schedule D, Schedule E, Schedule SE, Form 2441 and instructions, and Form 4562 and instructions.
IT-IRC sec. 6012; Pub. 17

Tax Forms Package 3-E
Federal Income Tax Forms
A package of income tax forms for business taxpayers. Contains one copy of instructions for Form 1040 and two copies of the following: Forms 1040, Schedule A, Schedule B, Schedule C, Schedule D, Schedule E, Schedule SE, and Form 4562 and instructions.
IT-IRC sec. 6012; Pub. 17

Tax Forms Package 4
Federal Income Tax Forms
A package of income tax forms for farm taxpayers. Contains one copy of instructions for Form 1040 and two copies of the following: Form 1040, Schedule A, Schedule B, Schedule C, Schedule D, Schedule E, Schedule F, Schedule SE, Form 2441 and instructions, Form 4136, and Form 4562 and instructions.
IT-IRC sec. 6012; Pub. 17

Tax Forms Package 5
Federal Income Tax Forms
A package of income tax forms for individual taxpayers. Contains one copy of instructions for Form 1040A and two copies each of Form 1040EZ, Form 1040A, and Schedule 1 (Form 1040A).

Package X
Informational Copies of Federal Tax Forms
A two-volume set of income tax and information return forms, substitute forms information, and other information needed by tax practitioners to service their clients.

CT-1

Employer's Annual Railroad Retirement and Unemployment Repayment Tax Return

Used to report employees' and employers' taxes under the RRTA and RURT. Emp-IRC secs. 3201, 3202, 3221, 3321, 3322, and 6011; Regs. secs. 31.6011(a)-2, 31.6011(a)-3AT, and 31.6302(c)-2; Separate instructions

CT-2
Employee Representative's Quarterly Railroad Tax Return

Used to report employee representative's tax under the RRTA and RURT. Emp-IRC secs. 3211, 3321, and 6011; Regs. secs. 31.6011(a)-2 and 31.6011(a)-3AT

W-2
Wage and Tax Statement (For Use in Cities and States Authorizing Combined Form)

Used to report wages, tips and other compensation, allocated tips, employee social security tax, income tax, state or city income tax withheld; and to support credit shown on individual income tax return.
Emp-IRC sec. 6051; Regs. secs. 1.6041-2 and 31.6051-1; Circular E; Separate instructions

W-2AS
American Samoa Wage and Tax Statement

Used to report wages, tips, and other compensation, employee social security tax, Samoan income tax withheld, and to support credit shown on American Samoa individual income tax return.
Emp-IRC sec. 6051; Regs. sec. 31.6051-1, Circular SS

W-2c
Statement of Corrected Income and Tax Amounts

Used to correct previously filed Forms W-2, W-2P, W-2AS, W-2CNMI, W-2GU, and W-2VI.
Emp-IRC sec. 6051; Reg. sec. 1.6041-2 and 31.6051-1

499R-2/W-2PR
Puerto Rico Withholding Statement

Used to report social security wages, tips, and social security tax withheld for employees in Puerto Rico.
Emp-IRC sec. 6051; Regs. sec. 31.6051-1; Circular PR

W-2G
Statement for Recipients of Certain Gambling Winnings

Used to report gambling winnings and any taxes withheld.
IT-IRC sec. 3402(q) and 6041; Temp. Regs. sec. 7.6041-1 and Regs. sec. 31.3402(q)-1(f); See the separate Instructions for Forms 1099, 1098, 5498, 1096, and W-2G.

W-2GU
Guam Wage and Tax Statement

Used to report wages, tips and other compensation, employee social security tax, Guam income tax withheld, and to support credit shown on individual income tax return.
Emp-IRC sec. 6051; Regs. sec. 31.6051-1; Circular SS

W-2CNMI
Commonwealth of Northern Mariana Islands Wage and Tax Statement

Used to report wages, tips and other compensation, employee social security tax, CNMI income tax withheld, and to support credit shown on individual income tax return.
Emp-IRC sec. 6051; Regs. sec. 31.6050-1; Circular SS

W-2VI
U.S. Virgin Islands Wage and Tax Statement

Used to report wages, tips and other compensation, employee social security tax, VI income tax withheld, and to support credit shown on individual income tax return.
Emp-IRC sec. 6051; Regs. secs. 1.6041-2 and 31.6051-1; Circular SS

W-2P
Statement For Recipients of Annuities, Pensions, Retired Pay, or IRA Payments

Used to report periodic distributions from annuities, pensions, retirement pay, and payments from an IRA; Federal and state income tax withheld.
Emp-IRC sec. 3402(o); Regs. sec. 32.1-1; Circular E; Separate instructions

W-3
Transmittal of Income and Tax Statements

Used by employers and other payers to transmit Forms W-2 and W-2P to the Social Security Administration.
Emp-IRC sec. 6011; Reg. sec. 31.6051-2

W-3c
Transmittal of Corrected Income and Tax Statements

Used by employers and other payers to transmit corrected income and tax statements (Forms W-2c).
Emp-IRC sec. 6011; Reg. 31.6051-2

W-3PR
Transmittal of Withholding Statements

Used by employers to transmit Forms 499R-2/W-2PR.
Emp-IRC sec. 6011; Reg. sec. 31.6051-2; Circular PR

W-3SS
Transmittal of Wage and Tax Statements

Used by employers to transmit Forms W-2AS, W-2CNMI, W-2GU, and W-2VI.
Emp-IRC sec. 6011; Reg. sec. 31.6051-2; Circular SS

W-4
Employee's Withholding Allowance Certificate

Completed by employee and given to employer so that proper amount of income tax can be withheld from wages. Also used by employee to claim exemption from withholding by certifying that he or she had no liability for income tax for preceding tax year and anticipates that no liability will be incurred for current tax year.
Emp-IRC secs. 3402(f), 3402(m) and 3402(n); Regs. secs. 31.3402(f)(5)-1 and 31.3402(n)-1; Circular E

W-4P
Withholding Certificate for Pension or Annuity Payments

Used to figure amount of Federal income tax to withhold from periodic pension or annuity payments or to claim additional withholding or exemption from withholding for periodic or nonperiodic payments.
Emp-IRC sec. 3405

W-4S
Request for Federal Income Tax Withholding from Sick Pay

Filed with a third party payer of sick pay to request Federal income tax withholding.
Emp-IRC sec. 3402(o); Regs. sec. 31.3402(o)-3

W-5
Earned Income Credit Advance Payment Certificate

Used by employee to request employer to furnish advance payment of earned income credit with the employee's pay.
IRC sec. 3507

W-8
Certificate of Foreign Status

Used by foreign persons to notify payers of interest, mortgage interest recipients, or middlemen, brokers, or barter exchanges not to withhold or report on payments of interest, or on broker transactions or barter exchanges.
IRC secs. 3406, 6042, 6044, 6045, and 6049

W-9
Request for Taxpayer Identification Number and Certification

Used by a person required to file certain information returns with IRS to obtain the correct taxpayer identification number (TIN) of the person for whom a return is filed. Also used to claim exemption from backup withholding and to certify that the person whose TIN is provided is not subject to backup withholding because of failure to report interest and dividends as income.

W-10
Dependent Care Provider's Identification and Certification

Used by taxpayers to certify that the name, address, and taxpayer identification number of their dependent care provider is correct.
IRS secs. 21, 129, 501(c)(3)

SS-4
Application for Employer Identification Number

Used by employers and other entities to apply for an identification number.
Emp-IRC Regs. sec. 31.6011(b)-1; Circulars A and E

SS-4 PR
Solicitud de Numero de Identificacion Patronal

Used by employers and other entities in Puerto Rico to apply for an identification number. A variation of Form SS-4.
Emp-IR Regs. sec. 31.6011(b)-1; Circular PR

Taxes

SS-5
Application for a Social Security Card
Used by an individual to obtain a social security number and card.
Emp-IR Regs. sec. 31.6011(b)-2; Circulars A and E

SS-8
Information for Use in Determining Whether a Worker Is an Employee for Federal Employment Taxes and Income Tax Withholding
Used to furnish information about services of an individual, generally selected as representative of a class of workers, to get written determination on status.
Emp-IRC sec. 3121; Regs. sec. 31.3121(d)-1

SS-16
Certificate of Election of Coverage Under the Federal Insurance Contributions Act
Used by religious orders, whose members are required to take a vow of poverty, to elect social security coverage.
Emp-IRC sec. 3121(r); Regs. sec. 31.3121(r)-1

11-C
Stamp Tax and Registration Return for Wagering
Used to report taxes due under IRC sections 4401 and 4411, and as an application for registry and wagering activity. Upon approval of the return, the Service will issue a Special Tax Stamp.
Ex-IRC secs. 4411 and 4412; Regs. secs. 44.4412 and 44.4901

56
Notice Concerning Fiduciary Relationship
Used by persons to notify IRS that they are acting in fiduciary capacity for other persons.
IT-IRC sec. 6903; Regs. sec. 301.6903-1

637
Registration for Tax-Free Transactions Under Chapters 31, 32, and 38 of the Internal Revenue Code
Used as an application and certificate; by manufacturers, refiners or importers who buy taxable articles tax-free for further manufacture of taxable articles, or for resale direct to a manufacturer for such purpose. The original of the application is validated and returned as the Certificate of Registry by the District Director.
Ex-IRC secs. 4052, 4064(b)(1)(c), 4101, 4221, and 4661; Regs. secs. 48.4101-1, 48.4222(a)-1, and 48.4222(d)-1

637A
Registration for Tax-Free Sales and Purchases of Fuel Used in Aircraft
Used to register for tax-free sales under IRC section 4041(c). Filed by a seller who is a manufacturer, producer, importer, wholesaler, Jobber, or retailer; or by a seller that is a commercial airline, nonprofit educational organization, or other exempt user that wishes to sell or purchase tax-free fuel for use in aircraft. The original of the application is validated by the District Director and returned as the Certificate of Registry.
Ex-IRC sec. 4041(c); Regs. sec. 48.4041-11

706
United States Estate (and Generation-Skipping Transfer) Tax Return
Used for the estate of a deceased United States resident or citizen.
E&G-IRC sec. 6018; Regs. sec. 20.6018-1; Separate instructions

706-A
United States Additional Estate Tax Return
Used to report recapture tax under special use valuation.
E&G-IRC sec. 2032A; Separate instructions

706CE
Certificate of Payment of Foreign Death Tax
Used to report credit against United States estate tax for estate inheritance, legacy, or succession tax paid to a foreign government.
E&G-IRC sec. 2014; Regs. sec. 20.2014-5

706GS(D)
Generation-Skipping Transfer Tax Return for Distributions
Used by distributees to report generation-skipping transfer tax on taxable distributions from trusts subject to the tax.
E&G-IRC sec. 2601; Temp Regs. sec. 26.2662-1(b)(1); Separate instructions

706GS(D-1)

Notification of Distribution from a Generation-Skipping Trust
Used by trustees to report certain information to distributees regarding taxable distributions from a trust subject to the generation-skipping transfer tax.
E&G-IRC sec. 2601; Temp. Regs. sec. 26.2662-1(b)(1)

706GS(T)
Generation-Skipping Transfer Tax Return for Terminations
Used by trustees to report generation-skipping transfer tax on taxable terminations of trusts subject to the tax.
E&G-IRC sec. 2601; Temp. Regs. sec. 26.2662-1(b)(2); Separate instructions

706NA
United States Estate (and Generation-Skipping Transfer) Tax Return, Estate of nonresident not a citizen of the United States
Used for United States nonresident alien decedent's estate to be filed within 9 months after date of death.
E&G-IRC sec. 6018; Regs. sec. 20.6018-1(b); Separate instructions

Schedule S (Form 706)
Increased Estate Tax on Excess Retirement Accumulations
Used to pay the section 4980A increased estate tax on excess retirement accumulations.
E&G-IRC sec. 4980A(d)

709
United States Gift (and Generation-Skipping Transfer) Tax Return
Used to report gifts of more than $10,000 (or, regardless of value, gifts of a future interest in property).
E&G-IRC sec. 6019; Regs. sec. 25.6019-1; Separate instructions

709-A
United States Short Form Gift Tax Return
Used to report gifts of more than $10,000 but less than $20,000 if the gifts are nontaxable by reason of gift splitting.
E&G-IRC secs. 6019, 6075; Regs. sec. 25.6019-1

712
Life Insurance Statement
Used with Form 706 or Form 709.
E&G-IRC secs. 6001 and 6018; Regs. secs. 20.6001-1, 20.6018-4(d), and 25.6001-1(b)

720
Quarterly Federal Excise Tax Return
Used to report excise taxes due from retailers and manufacturers on sale or manufacture of various articles; taxes on facilities and services; taxes on certain products and commodities (gasoline, coal, etc); windfall profits and Inland waterways taxes.
Ex-IRC sec. 6011; Separate instructions

730
Tax on Wagering
Used to report taxes due under IRC section 4401.
Ex-IRC sec. 4401; Regs. sec. 44.6011(a)-1

843
Claim
Used to claim refund of taxes (other than income taxes) which were illegally, erroneously or excessively collected; or to claim amount paid for stamps unused or used in error or excess; and for a refund or abatement of interest or penalties assessed.
Misc-IRC secs. 6402, 6404, 6511, 6404(e), and 6404(f); Regs. secs. 31.6413(c)-1, 301.6402-2, and 301.6404-1

851
Affiliations Schedule
Used with Form 1120 by parent corporation for affiliated corporations included in consolidated tax return.
IT-IRC sec. 1502; Regs. sec. 1.1502-75(h)

872-C
Consent Fixing Period of Limitation Upon Assessment of Tax Under Section 4940 of the Internal Revenue Code
Used only with Form 1023, Application for Recognition of Exemption, by an organization described in Internal Revenue Code section 170(b)(1)(A)(vi) or

section 509(a)(2), to request the organization be treated as a publicly supported organization during an advance ruling period.
IT-IRC sec. 6501(c)(4)

926
Return by a Transferor of Property to a Foreign Corporation, Foreign Trust or Estate, or Foreign Partnership

Used to report transfers of property by a U.S. person to a foreign partnership, trust or estate, or corporation, and pay any excise tax due on the transfer.
IT-IRC sec. 1491; Regs. sec. 1.1491-2

928
Gasoline Bond

Used to post bond for excise tax on fuel.
Ex-IRC sec. 4101

940
Employer's Annual Federal Unemployment (FUTA) Tax Return

Used by employers to report Federal unemployment (FUTA) tax.
Emp-IRC sec. 6011; IRC Chapter 23; Regs. sec. 31.6011(a)-3; Circular E, Circular SS

940-EZ
Employer's Annual Federal Unemployment (FUTA) Tax Return

Used by employers to report Federal unemployment (FUTA) tax. This form is a simplified version of Form 940.
EMP-IRC sec. 6011; IRC Chapter 23; Regs. sec. 31.6011(a)-3; Circular E, Circular SS

940PR
Planilla Para La Declaracion Anual Del Patrono-La Contribucion Federal Para el Desempleo (FUTA)

Used by employers in Puerto Rico. A variation of Form 940.
Emp-IRC sec. 6011; IRC Chapter 23; Regs. sec. 31.6011(a)-3; Circular PR

941
Employer's Quarterly Federal Tax Return

Used by employer to report social security taxes and income taxes withheld, advance earned income credit (EIC), and back up withholding.
Emp-IRC secs. 3101, 3111, 3402, 3405 and 3406; Regs. secs. 31.6011(a)-1 and 31.6011(a)-4; Circular E

Sch. A (Form 941)
Record of Federal Backup Withholding Tax Liability

Used to report backup withholding liability when treated as a separate tax for depositing purposes.
Emp-IRC secs. 3406, 6302; Regs. secs. 31.6302 and 35a.9999-3

941c
Statement to Correct Information Previously Reported on the Employer's Federal Tax Return

Used by employers to correct wages, tips, and tax previously reported.
Emp-IRC secs. 6205 and 6402; Regs. secs. 31.6011(a)-1, 31.6205-1, and 31.6402(a)-2; Circulars A, E, and SS

941c PR
Planilla Para La Correccion De Informacion Facilitada Anteriormente En Complimiento Con La Ley Del Seguro Social

Used by employers in Puerto Rico. A variation of Form 941c.
Emp-IRC Chapter 21; Regs. secs. 31.6011(a)-1, 31.6205-1, and 31.6402(a)-2; Circular PR

941E
Quarterly Return of Withheld Federal Income Tax and Hospital Insurance (Medicare) Tax

Used by State and local government employers and by other organizations that are not liable for social security taxes. A variation of Form 941.
Emp-IRC secs. 3121(u) and 3402

941-M
Employer's Monthly Federal Tax Return

Used by employers to report withheld income tax and social security taxes (because they have not complied with the requirements for filing quarterly returns, or for paying or depositing taxes reported on quarterly returns).
Emp-IRC sec. 7512; Regs. sec. 31.6011(a)-5

941 PR
Planilla Para La Declaracion Trimestral Del Patrono-La Contribucion Federal al Seguro Social

Used by employers in Puerto Rico. A variation of Form 941.
Emp-IRC secs. 3101 and 3111; Regs. sec. 31.6011(a)-1; Circular PR

941SS
Employer's Quarterly Federal Tax Return

Used by employers in Virgin Islands, Guam, the Northern Marianne Islands, and American Samoa. A variation of Form 941.
Emp-IRC secs. 3101 and 3111; Regs. sec. 31.6011(a)-1; Circular SS

942
Employer's Quarterly Tax Return for Household Employees

Used by household employers quarterly to report social security and income taxes withheld from wages of household employees.
Emp-IRC secs. 3101 and 3111; Regs. sec. 31.6011(a)-1(a)(3)

942PR
Planilla Para La Declaracion Trimestral Del Patrono De Empleados Domesticos

Used by household employers in Puerto Rico to report social security taxes withheld from wages of household employees. A variation of Form 942.
Emp-IRC secs. 3101 and 3111; Regs. sec. 31.6011(a)-1(a)(3)

943
Employer's Annual Tax Return for Agricultural Employees

Used by Agricultural employers to report social security and income taxes withheld.
Emp-IRC secs. 3101, 3111 and 3402; Regs. sec. 31.6011(a)-1 and 31.6011(a)-4; Circular A

943A
Agricultrual Employer's Record of Federal Tax Liability

Used by agricultural employers who have a tax liability of $3,000 or more during any month.
Emp-IRC sec. 6302; Regs. sec. 6302(c)-1; Circular A

943 PR
Planilla Para La Declaracion Anual De La Contribucion Del Patrono De Empleados Agricolas

Used by agricultural employers in Puerto Rico. A variation of Form 943.
Emp-IRC secs. 3101 and 3111; Regs. sec. 31.6011(a)-1 and 31.6011(a)-4; Circular PR

943A-PR
Registro De La Obligacion Contributiva Del Patrono Agricola

Used by agricultural employers in Puerto Rico. A variation of Form 943A.
Emp-IRC sec. 6302; Regs. sec. 31.6302(c)-1; Circular PR

952
Consent to Fix Period of Limitation on Assessment of Income Taxes

Used when complete liquidation of a subsidiary is not accomplished within the tax year in which the first liquidating distribution is made. The receiving corporation is required to file this consent with its return for each tax year which falls wholly or partly within the period of liquidation.
IT-IRC sec. 332; Regs. sec. 1.332-4

966
Corporate Dissolution or Liquidation

Used (under IRC section 6043(a)) by corporations within 30 days after adoption of resolution or plan of dissolution, or complete or partial liquidation. (An information return.) IT-IRC sec. 6043(a)

970
Application to Use LIFO Inventory Method

Used to change to the LIFO inventory method provided by section 472.
IT-IRC sec. 472; Regs. sec. 1.472-3

972
Consent of Shareholder to Include Specific Amount in Gross Income

Used by shareholders of a corporation who agree to include in their gross income for their taxable year a specific amount as a tax dividend.
IT-IRC sec. 565

973
Corporation Claim for Deduction for Consent Dividends
Used by corporations that claim a consent dividends deduction. Accompanied by filed consents of shareholders on Form 972.
IT-IRC sec. 561

976
Claim for Deficiency Dividends Deduction by a Personal Holding Company, Regulated Investment Company, or Real Estate Investment Trust
Used by a personal holding company, regulated investment company, or real estate investment trust to claim a deficiency dividends deduction.
IT-IRC sec. 547 and 860; Regs. sec. 1.547-2(b)(2) and 1.860-2(b)(2)

982
Reduction of Tax Attributes Due to Discharge of Indebtedness
Used by a taxpayer who excludes from gross income under section 108 any amount of income attributable to discharge of indebtedness, in whole or in part, in the tax year, for which it is liable or subject. Also used as a consent of a corporation to adjustment of basis of its property under regulations prescribed under IRC section 1082(a)(2). IT-IRC secs. 108, 1017, and 1082

990
Return of Organization Exempt From Income Tax (Except Private Foundation)
Used by organizations exempt under IRC section 501(a) and described in Code section 501(c), other than private foundations. (An information return.)
IT-IRC sec. 6033; Regs. sec. 1.6033-1(a)(2); Separate instructions

Package 990-1
Organizations Exempt from Income Tax under section 501(c) (other than sections 501(c)(3), (c)(4), (c)(6), and (c)(7), of the Internal Revenue Code)
A package of information forms for exempt organizations. Contains one copy each of Instructions for Forms 990, 990-EZ, and 990-T; two copies each of Forms 990, 990-EZ, and 990-T. IT-IRC sec. 6033, one copy of Form 990-W, Form 1120-W, and instructions.

Package 990-2
Organizations Exempt from Income Tax under section 501(c)(3) (other than Private Foundations as defined in section 509(a), of the Internal Revenue Code)
A package of information forms for exempt organizations. Contains one copy each of Instructions for Forms 990, Schedule A (Form 990), 990-EZ, and 990-T; two copies each of Forms 990, Schedule A (Form 990), 990-EZ, and 990-T, one copy of Form 990-W, Form 1120-W, and instructions; one copy of Supplemental Instructions, and a sample filled-in Form 990 and Schedule A (Form 990). IT-IRC sec. 6033

Package 990-3
Organizations Exempt from Income Tax under section 501(c)(4) of the Internal Revenue Code
A package of information forms for exempt organizations. Contains one copy each of Instructions for Forms 990, 990-EX, and 990-T; two copies each of Forms 990, 990-EX, and 990-T, one copy of Form 990-W, Form 1120-W, and instructions; one copy of Supplemental Instructions, and sample filled-in Forms 990-EZ and 990-T.
IT-IRC sec. 6033

Sch. A (Form 990)
Organization Exempt Under 501 (c)(3) (Supplementary Information)
Used by organizations described in IRC section 501(c)(3) (other than private foundations filing Form 990-PF).
IT-IRC sec. 6033; Separate instructions

990-BL
Information and Initial Excise Tax Return for Black Lung Benefit Trusts and Certain Related Persons
Used by Black Lung Benefit Trusts exempt under Section 501(c)(21) as an information return. Also used by these trusts and certain related persons for attaching Schedule A (Form 990-BL) when taxes under sections 4951 or 4952 are due.
IT/EX-IRC sec. 501 (c)(21); Chapter 42; Separate instructions

990-C
Farmers' Cooperative Association Income Tax Return
Used by Farmers' Cooperative Marketing and Purchasing Association.
IT-IRC secs. 521, 1381, 1382, 1383, 1385, 1388, and 6012; Regs. secs. 1.522-1,

1.1381-1, 2, 1.1382-1, 2, 3, 4, 5, 6, 7, 1.1383-1, 1.1385-1, 1.388-1, and 1.6012-2(f); Separate instructions

990-EZ
Short Form Return of Organization Exempt Form Income Tax
Used by organizations of gross receipts less than $100,000 and total assets of less than $250,000 at end of year.
IT-IRC sec. 6033; Regs. sec. 1.6033-1(a)(2); Separate instructions

990-PF
Return of Private Foundation or Section 4947(a)(1) Trust Treated as a Private Foundation
Used by private foundations and Section 4947(a)(1) trusts. (An information return.)
IT/Ex-IRC sec. 6033; IRC Chapter 42; Separate instructions

Package 990-PF
Returns for Private Foundations or Section 4947(a)(1) Trusts Treated as Private Foundations
A package of information forms used by private foundations and Sections 4947(a)(1) trusts. In addition to Form 990-PF, this package includes Form 990-T and Form 4720, Form 990-W, Form 1120-W and instructions for each form, and filled-in samples of Form 990-PF.
IT-IRC sec. 6033

990-T
Exempt Organization Business Income Tax Return
Used by exempt organization with unrelated business income (under IRC section 511)
IT-IRC secs. 511 and 6012; Regs. secs. 1.6012-2(e) and 1.6012-3(a)(5); Separate instructions

990-W
Estimated Tax on Unrelated Business Taxable Income for Tax-Exempt Organization
Used as a worksheet by tax-exempt trusts and tax-exempt corporations to figure their estimated tax liability. Tax-exempt trusts and corporations should keep it for their records. IT-IRC sec. 6154

1000
Ownership Certificate
Used by a citizen, resident individual, fiduciary, partnership, or nonresident partnership all of whose members are citizens or residents who have interest in bonds of a domestic or resident corporation (containing a tax-free covenant and issued before January 1, 1934).
IT-IRC sec. 1461; Regs. sec. 1.1461-1(h)

1001
Ownership, Exemption, or Reduced Rate Certificate
Used by a nonresident alien individual or fiduciary, foreign partnership, foreign corporation or other foreign entity, nonresident foreign partnership composed in whole or in part of nonresident aliens (applies to IRC section 1451 only), or nonresident foreign corporation (applies to Code section 1451 only), receiving income subject to withholding under Code section 1441, 1442, or 1451. IT-IRC sec. 1461; Regs. sec. 1.1461-1(i)

Package 1023
Application for Recognition of Exemption Under Section 501(c)(3) of the Internal Revenue Code
Used to apply for exemption under section 501(a) IRC as organizations described in section 501(c)(3) (also sections 501(e) and (f)). Includes 3 copies of Form 872-C.
IT-IRC sec. 501; Regs. sec. 1.501(a)-1(a)(3)

Package 1024
Application for Recognition of Exemption Under Section 501(a) or Determination Under Section 120
Used by organizations to apply for exemption under IRC section 501(a) (as described in Code sections 501(c)(2), (4), (5), (6), (7), (8), (9), (10), (12), (13), (15), (17), (19), (20) and (25). (Also used to apply for a determination as a qualified plan under section 120.)
IT-IRC secs. 501, 120; Regs. sec. 1.501(a)-1(a)(3)

1028
Application for Recognition of Exemption Under Section 521 of the Internal Revenue Code
Used by farmers, fruit growers, or similar associations to claim exemption under IRC section 521.
IT-IRC sec. 521; Regs. sec. 1.521-1, Separate instructions

1040
U.S. Individual Income Tax Return
Used by citizens or residents of the United States to report income tax. (Also see Form 1040A, and 1040EZ.)
IT-IRC secs. 6012 and 6017; Regs. secs. 1.6012-1 and 1.6017-1; Pub. 17; Separate instructions

Sch. A (Form 1040)
Itemized Deductions
Used to report itemized deductions (medical and dental expense, taxes, contributions, interest, casualty and theft losses, moving expenses, miscellaneous deductions subject to the 2% AGI limit, and other miscellaneous deductions).
IT-IRC secs. 67, 163, 164, 165, 166, 170, 211, 212, 213, and 217; Pub. 17; See the separate instructions for Form 1040.

Sch. B (Form 1040)
Interest and Dividend Income
Used to list gross dividends received (if more than $400) and interest income (if more than $400), and to ask questions about foreign accounts and foreign trusts.
IT-IRC secs. 6012, 61, and 116; Pub. 17; See the separate Instructions for Form 1040.

Sch. C (Form 1040)
Profit or Loss From Business
Used to figure profit or (loss) from business or professions.
IT-IRC sec. 6017; Regs. sec. 1.6017-1; Pubs. 17 and 334; See the separate Instructions for Form 1040.

Sch. D (Form 1040)
Capital Gains and Losses
Used to report details of gain (or loss) from sales or exchanges of capital assets; to figure capital loss carry-overs from 1989 to 1990, and to reconcile Forms 1099-B with tax return. IT-IRC secs. 1202-1223, 6045; Pubs. 17 and 334; See the separate Instructions for Form 1040.

Sch. D-1 (Form 1040)
Continuation Sheet for Schedule D (Form 1040)
Used to attach to Schedule D (Form 1040) to list additional transactions in Parts 2a and 9a.

Sch. E (Form 1040)
Supplemental Income and Loss
Used to report income from rents, royalties, partnerships, S corporations, estates, trusts, REMICs, etc.
IT-IRC secs. 6012 and 6017; Regs. secs. 1.6012-1 and 1.6017-1; Pub. 17; See the separate Instructions for Form 1040.

Sch. F (Form 1040)
Farm Income and Expenses
Used to figure profit or (loss) from farming.
IT-IRC sec. 6012; Regs. sec. 1.61-4; Pub. 225; See the separate Instructions for Form 1040.

Sch. R (Form 1040)
Credit for the Elderly or the Disabled
Used to figure credit for the elderly and for persons under 65 who retired on permanent and total disability and received taxable disability benefits.
IT-IRC sec. 22; Pub. 17 and 524; Separate instructions

Sch. SE (Form 1040)
Social Security Self-Employment Tax
Used to figure self-employment income and self-employment tax.
IT-IRC secs. 1401 and 1402; See the separate Instructions for Form 1040.

1040A
U.S. Individual Income Tax Return
Used by citizens and residents of the United States to report income tax. (Also see Form 1040 and 1040EZ.)
IT-IRC sec. 6012; Regs. sec. 1.6012-1; Pub. 17; Separate instructions

1040C
U.S. Departing Alien Income Tax Return
Used by aliens who intend to depart from the U.S., to report income received, or expected to be received for the entire taxable year, determined as nearly as possible by the date of intended departure. (Also see Form 2063.)
IT-IRC sec. 6851; Regs. sec. 1.6851-2; Pub. 519; Separate instructions

1040-ES
Estimated Tax for Individuals
Used to pay income tax (including self-employment tax and alternative minimum tax) due (the tax that is more than the tax withheld from wages, salaries, and other payments for personal services). It is not required unless the total tax is more than withholding (if any) by $500 or more.
IT-IRC sec. 6654

1040-ES (Espanol)
Contribucion Federal Estimada Del Trabajo Por Cuenta Propia-Puerto Rico
Used in Puerto Rico. The payment vouchers are provided for payment of self-employment tax on a current basis.
IT-IRC sec. 6654

1040-ES (NR)
U.S. Estimated Tax for Nonresident Alien Individuals
Used by nonresident aliens to pay any income tax due in excess of the tax withheld. It is not required unless the total tax exceeds withholding (if any) by $500 or more.
IT-IRC sec. 6654

1040EZ
Income Tax Return for Single Filers With No Dependents
Used by citizens & residents of the United States to report income tax. (Also see Form 1040 and Form 1040A.)
IT-IRC sec. 6012; Reg. sec. 1.6012-1; Pub. 17; Separate instructions

1040NR
U.S. Nonresident Alien Income Tax Return
Used by all nonresident alien individuals, whether or not engaged in a trade or business within the United States, who file a U.S. tax return. Also used as required for filing nonresident alien fiduciary (estate and trusts) returns.
IT-IRC secs. 871 and 6012; Pub. 519; Separate instructions

1040 PR
Planilla Para La Declaracion De La Contribucion Federal Sobre El Trabajo Por Cuenta Propia-Puerto Rico
Used in Puerto Rico to compute self-employment tax in accordance with IRC Chapter 2 of Subtitle A, and to provide proper credit to taxpayer's social security account. IT-IRC secs. 6017 and 7651; Regs. sec. 1.6017-1; Circular PR

1040SS
U.S. Self-Employment Tax Return-Virgin Islands, Guam, and American Samoa
Used to compute self-employment tax in accordance with IRC Chapter 2 of Subtitle A, and to provide proper credit to taxpayer's social security account.
IT-IRC secs. 6017 and 7651; Regs. sec. 1.6017-1; Circular SS

1040X
Amended U.S. Individual Income Tax Return
Used to claim refund of income taxes, pay additional income taxes, or designate dollar(s) to a Presidential election campaign fund.
IT-IRC secs. 6402, 6404, 6511, and 6096; Separate instructions

1041
U.S. Fiduciary Income Tax Return
Used by a fiduciary of a domestic estate or domestic trust to report income tax.
IT-IRC sec. 6012; Regs. secs. 1.671-4, 1.6012-3(a), and 1.6041-1; Separate instructions

Sch. D (Form 1041)
Capital Gains and Losses
Used to report details of gain (or loss) from sales or exchanges of capital assets.
IT-IRC sec. 6012; Regs. sec. 1.6012-3(a); Separate instructions

Sch. J. (Form 1041)
Information Return Trust Allocation of an Accumulation Distribution (IRC section 665)
Used by domestic complex trusts to report accumulation distributions. IT-IRC secs. 665, 666, and 667

Sch. K-1 (Form 1041)
Beneficiary's Share of Income, Deductions, Credits, etc.
Used to report each beneficiary's share of the income, deductions, credits, and distributable net alternative minimum taxable income form the estate or trust.
IT-IRC sec. 6012; Regs. secs. 1.6012-3(a)

1041-A
U.S. Information Return-Trust Accumulation of Charitable Amounts
Used by a trust that claims a contribution deduction under IRC section 642(c), or by a trust described in Code section 4947(a)(2). (An information return.)
IT-IRC secs. 6034 and 6104; Regs. sec. 1.6034-1

Taxes

1041-ES
Estimated Income Tax for Fiduciaries
Used to figure and pay estimated tax for fiduciaries. IT-IRC sec. 6654

1041-T
Transmittal of Estimated Taxes Credited to Beneficiaries
Used by a trust to make an election under section 643(g) to credit an overpayment of estimated tax to beneficiaries.
IT-IRC sec. 643(g)

1042
Annual Withholding Tax Return for U.S. Source Income of Foreign Persons
Used by withholding agents to report tax withheld at source on certain income paid to nonresident aliens, foreign partnerships, or foreign corporations not engaged in a trade or business in the U.S. IT-IRC secs. 1441, 1442, and 1461; Regs. secs. 1.1441-1 and 1.1461-2(b); Separate instructions

1042S
Foreign Person's U.S. Source Income Subject to Withholding
Used by a withholding agent to report certain income and tax withheld at source for foreign payees. (An information return.)
IT-IRC sec. 1461; Regs. sec. 1.1461-2(c); Separate instructions

1045
Application for Tentative Refund
Used by taxpayers (other than corporations) to apply for a tentative refund from the carryback of a net operating loss, unused general business credit, or overpayment of tax due to a claim of right adjustment under section 1341(b)(1). T-IRC sec. 6411; Regs. sec. 1.6411-1

1065
U.S. Partnership Return of Income
Used by partnerships as an information return.
IT-IRC sec. 6031 and 6698; Regs. secs. 1.761-1(a), 1.6031-1, and 1.6033-1(a)(5); Separate instructions

Package 1065
Federal Income Tax Forms
A package of income tax forms for partnerships. Contains one copy of instructions for Form 1065, two copies of Form 1065, six copies of Schedule K-1 (Form 1065) and two copies of instructions, two copies of Form 4562 and one copy of instructions. T-IRC sec. 6031

Sch. D (Form 1065)
Capital Gains and Losses
Used to show partnership's capital gains and losses. IT-IRC 6031

Sch. K-1 (Form 1065)
Partner's Share of Income, Credits, Deductions, Etc.
Used to show partner's share of income, credits, deductions, etc.
IT-IRC secs. 702 and 703; Separate instructions

1066
U.S. Real Estate Mortgage Investment Conduit Income Tax Return
Used to report income, deductions, gains and losses, and the tax on net income from prohibited transactions, of a real estate mortgage investment conduit.
IT-IRC secs. 860D and 860F(e); Separate instructions

Sch. Q (Form 1066)
Quarterly Notice to Residual Interest Holder of REMIC Taxable Income or Net Loss Allocation
Used to show residual interest holder's share of taxable income (or net loss), excess inclusion, and section 212 expenses.
IT-IRC sec. 860G(c)

1078
Certificate of Alien Claiming Residence in the United States
Used by an alien claiming residence in the U.S., for income tax purposes. Filed with the withholding agent.
IT-IRC secs. 871 and 1441; Regs. secs. 1.1441-5 anc 1.871-3,4

1090
Statement of Income, and Profit and Loss Accounts
Used by a railroad company with Form 1120. IT-Instruction for Form 1120

1096
Annual Summary and Transmittal of U.S. Information Returns
Used to summarize and transmit Forms W-2G, 1098, 1099-A, 1099-B, 1099-DIV, 1099-G, 1099-INT, 1099-MISC, 1099-OID, 1099-PATR, 1099-R, 1099-S, and 5498. IT-IRC secs. 408(i), 6041, 6041A, 6042, 6043, 6044, 6045, 6047, 6049, 6050A, 6050B, 6050D, 6050E, 6050H, and 6050J

1098
Mortgage Interest Statement
Used to report $600 or more of mortgage interest from an individual in the course of a trade or business.
IT-IRC sec. 6050H; Regs. sec. 1.6050H-2; See the separate Instructions for Forms 1099, 1098, 5498, 1096, and W-2G

1099-A
Information Return for Acquisition or Abandonment of Secured Property
Used by lenders to report acquisitions by such lenders or abandonments of property that secures a loan.
IT-IRC sec. 6050J; Temp. Regs. sec. 1.6050J-1T; See the separate Instructions for Forms 1099, 1098, 5498, 1096, and W-2G

1099-B
Statement for Recipients of Proceeds From Broker and Barter Exchange Transactions
Used by a broker to report gross proceeds from the sale or redemption of securities, commodities or regulated futures contracts, or by a barter exchange to report the exchange of goods or services. IT-IRC sec. 6045; Regs. sec. 1.6045-1; See the separate instructions for Forms 1099, 1098, 5498, 1096, and W-2G

1099-DIV
Statement for Recipients of Dividends and Distributions
Used to report dividends and distributions. IT-IRC secs. 6042 and 6043; Regs. secs. 1.6042-2 and 1.6043-2; See the separate instructions for Forms 1099, 1098, 5498, 1096, and W-2G

1099-G
Statement for Recipients of Certain Government Payments
Used to report government payments such as unemployment compensation, state and local income tax refunds, credits, or offsets, discharges of indebtedness by the Federal Government, taxable grants, and subsidy payments form the Department of Agriculture.
IT-IRC secs. 6041, 6050B, 6050D, and 6050E; Regs. secs. 1.6041-1, 1.6050B-1, 1.6050D-1, and 1.6050E-1; See the separate Instructions for Forms 1099, 1098, 5498, 1096, and W-2G

1099-INT
Statement for Recipients of Interest Income
Used to report interest income. IT-IRC secs. 6041 and 6049; Regs. secs. 1.6041-1, 1.6049-4, and Temp. Regs. sec. 1.6049-7T; See the separate Instructions for Forms 1099, 1098, 5498, 1096, and W-2G

1099-MISC
Statement for Recipients of Miscellaneous Income
Used to report rents, royalties, prizes and awards, fishing boat proceeds, payments by health, accident and sickness insurers to physicians or other health service providers, fees, commissions or other compensation for services rendered in the course of the payer's business when the recipient is not treated as an employee, direct sales of $5,000 or more of consumer products for resale, substitute payments by brokers in lieu of dividends or tax-exempt interest, and crop insurance proceeds.
IT-IRC secs. 6041, 6041A, 6045(d), and 6050A; Regs. secs. 1.6041-1, 1.6045-2, and 1.6050A-1; See the separate Instructions for Forms 1099, 1098, 5498, 1096, and W-2G

1099-OID
Statement for Recipients of Original Issue Discount
Used to report original issue discount.
IT-IRC sec. 6049; Regs. sec. 1.6049-4; Temp. Regs. secs. 1.6049-4, 1.6049-5T, and 1.6049-7T; See the separate Instructions for Forms 1099, 1098, 5498, 1096, and W-2G

1099-PATR
Statement for Recipients (Patrons) of Taxable Distributions Received From Cooperatives
Used to report patronage dividends.
IT-IRC sec. 6044; Regs. sec. 1.6044-2; See the separate instructions for Forms 1099, 1098, 5498, 1096, and W-2G

1099-R
Statement for Recipients of Total Distributions From Profit-Sharing, Retirement Plans, Individual Retirement Arrangements, Insurance Contracts, Etc.
Used to report total distributions from profit-sharing, retirement plans and individual retirement arrangements, and certain surrenders of insurance contracts.
IT-IRC sec. 402, 408, and 6047; Temp Regs. sec. 35.3405-1; Regs. secs. 1.408-7 and 1.6047-1; See the separate Instructions for Forms 1099, 1098, 5498, 1096, and W-2G

1099-S
Statement for Recipients of Proceeds From Real Estate Transactions
Used by the person required to report gross proceeds from real estate transactions.
IT-IRC sec. 6045(e); Temp Regs. sec. 1.6045-3T; See the separate Instructions for Forms 1099, 1098, 5498, 1096, and W-2G

1116
Computation of Foreign Tax Credit (Individual, Fiduciary, or Nonresident Alien Individual)
Used to figure the foreign tax credit claimed for the amount of any income, war profits, and excess profits tax paid or accrued during the taxable year to any foreign country or U.S. possession. IT-IRC secs. 27, 901, and 904; Pub. 514; Separate instructions

1118
Computation of Foreign Tax Credit-Corporations
Used to support the amount of foreign tax credit claimed on corporation income tax returns.
IT-IRC secs. 901 through 906; Separate instructions

I (Form 1118)
Computation of Reduction of Oil and Gas Extraction Taxes
Used to compute the section 907(a) reduction for a corporation that is claiming a foreign tax credit with respect to any income taxes paid, accrued, or deemed to have been paid during the tax year with respect to foreign oil and gas extraction income.
IT-IRC sec. 907

Sch. J (Form 1118)
Separate Limitation Loss Allocations and Other Adjustments Necessary to Determine Numerators of Limitation Fractions, Year-End Recharacterization Balances and Overall Foreign Loss Account Balances
Used to show the adjustments to separate limitation income or losses in determining the numerators of the limitation fractions for each separate limitation; the year-end balances of separate limitation losses that were allocated among other separate limitations (in the current year or in prior years) that have yet to be recharacterized; and the balances in the overall foreign loss accounts at the beginning of the tax year, any adjustments to the account balances, and the balances, in the overall foreign loss accounts at the end of the tax year. IT-IRC sec. 904(f)

1120
U.S. Corporation Income Tax Return
Used by a corporation to report income tax. (Also see Form 1120-A.)
IT-IRC sec. 6012; Regs. secs. 1.1502-75(h), and 1.6012-2; Separate instructions

Package 1120
Federal Income Tax Forms
A package of income tax forms for corporations. Contains one copy of instructions for Forms 1120 and 1120-A, two copies of Form 1120, two copies of Form 1120-A, two copies of Schedule D, one copy of Form 1120-W, two copies of Form 3468, two copies of Form 7004, and two copies of Form 4562.
IT-IRC sec. 6012

Sch. D (Form 1120)
Capital Gains and Losses
Used with Forms 1120, 1120-A, 1120-DF, 1120-IC-DISC, 1120-F, 1120-FSC, 1120-H, 1120L, 1120-ND, 1120-PC, 1120-POL, 1120-REIT, 1120-RIC, 990-C and certain Forms 990-T to report details of gain (or loss) from sales or exchanges of capital assets, and to figure alternative tax.
IT-IRC secs. 1201 and 1231

Sch. PH (Form 1120)
Computation of U.S. Personal Holding Company Tax
Used to figure personal holding company tax; filed with the income tax return of every personal holding company.
IT-IRC secs. 541, 6012, and 6501(f); Separate instructions

1120-A
U.S. Corporation Short-Form Income Tax Return
Used by a corporation to report income tax.
IT-IRC sec. 6012; Regs. sec. 1.6012-2; Separate instructions

1120-DF
U.S. Income Tax Return for Designated Settlement Funds (Under section 468B)
Used by designated settlement funds to report contributions received, income earned, the administration expenses of operating the fund, and the tax on its investment income. IT-IRC secs. 468B and 6012; Separate instructions

1120F
U.S. Income Tax Return of a Foreign Corporation
Used by foreign corporations to report income tax.
IT-IRC secs. 881, 882, 884, 887, and 6012; Separate instructions

1120-FSC
U.S. Income Tax Return of a Foreign Sales Corporation
Used by foreign sales corporations to report income tax.
IT-IRC secs. 922, 6011(c), and 6012; Separate instructions

Sch. P (Form 1120-FSC)
Computation of Transfer Price or Commission
Used to compute transfer price or commission under IRC sections 925(a)(1) and (2).
IT-IRC sec. 6011(c)

1120-H
U.S. Income Tax Return for Homeowners Associations
Used by homeowner associations to report income tax. (An annual return.)
IT-IRC sec. 528 and Reg. sec. 1.528-8

1120-IC-DISC
Interest Charge Domestic International Sales Corporation Return
Used by domestic corporations that make the election under IRC section 992(b) to be a domestic international sales corporation.
IT-IRC secs. 6011(c) and 6072(b); Separate instructions

Sch. K (Form 1120-IC-DISC)
Shareholder's Statement of IC-DISC Distributions
Used to report deemed and actual distributions from an IC-DISC to shareholders and to report deferred DISC income and certain other information to shareholders.
IT-IRC secs. 6011(c)

Sch. P (Form 1120-IC-DISC)
Computation of Inter-company Transfer Price or Commission
Used to compute inter-company transfer prices or commissions under IRC sections 994(a)(1) and (2).
IT-IRC secs. 6011(c)

Sch. Q (Form 1120-IC-DISC)
Borrower's Certificate of Compliance with the Rules for Producer's Loans
Used by an IC-DISC to establish that the borrower is in compliance with the rules for producer's loans.
IT-Regs. sec. 1.993-4(d)

1120L
U.S. Life Insurance Company Income Tax Return
Used by life insurance companies to report income tax.
IT-IRC secs. 801 and 6012; Reg. sec. 1.6012-2; Separate instructions

1120-ND
Return for Nuclear Decommissioning Funds and Certain Related Persons
Used by nuclear decommissioning funds to report income, expenses, transfers of funds to the public utility that created it and to figure the taxes on income plus penalty taxes on trustees and certain disqualified persons. IT-IRC sec. 468A; Separate instructions

1120-PC
U.S. Property and Casualty Insurance Company Income

Taxes

Tax Return
Used by nonlife insurance companies to report income tax.
IT-IRC secs. 831 and 6012; Separate instructions

1120-POL
U.S. Income Tax Return for Certain Political Organizations
Used by certain political organizations to report income tax.
IT-IRC secs. 856 and 6012; Separate instructions

1120-REIT
U.S. Income Tax Return for Real Estate Investment Trusts
Used by real estate investment trusts to report income tax.
IT-IRC secs. 856 and 6012; Separate instructions

1120-RIC
U.S. Income Tax Return for Regulated Investment Companies
Used by regulated investment companies to report income tax.
IT-IRC secs. 851 and 6012; Separate instructions

1120S
U.S. Income Tax Return for an S Corporation
Used by S corporations that have made the election prescribed by IRC section 1362.
IT-IRC sec. 6037; IRC Subchapter S; Regs. sec. 1.6037-1; Separate instructions

Package 1120S
Federal Income Tax Forms
A package of income tax forms for S Corporations. Contains one copy of instructions for Form 1120S, two copies of Form 1120S, two copies of Schedule D (Form 1120S), two copies of Schedule K-1 (Form 1120S), two copies of shareholder's instructions for Schedule K-1 (Form 1120S), and two copies of Form 4562.
IT-IRC sec. 6037

Sch. D (Form 1120S)
Capital Gains and Losses and Built-in Gains
Used by S corporations that have made the election prescribed by IRC section 1362. Sch. D is used to report details of gains (and losses) from sales, exchanges or distribution of capital assets and to figure the tax imposed on certain capital gains and certain built-in gains.
IT-IRC secs. 1201 and 1231; and IRC Subchapter S; Separate instructions

Sch. K-1 (Form 1120S)
Shareholder's Share of Income, Credits, Deductions, Etc.
Used to show shareholder's share of income, credits, deductions, etc. A four-part assembly: A copy is filed with Form 1120S, a copy is for S corporation records, and a copy is given to each shareholder along with the separate instructions.
IT-IRC sec. 6037

1120-W
Corporation Estimated Tax
Used as a worksheet by corporations to figure estimated tax liability; not to be filed. Corporations should keep it for their records.
IT-IRC sec. 6655

1120X
Amended U.S. Corporation Income Tax Return
Used by corporations to amend a previously filed Form 1120 or Form 1120-A.
IT-Regs. sec. 301.6402-3

1122
Authorization and Consent of Subsidiary Corporation to be Included in a Consolidated Income Tax Return
Used as the authorization and consent of a subsidiary corporation to be included in a consolidated income tax return.
IT-IRC sec. 1502; Regs. sec. 1.1502-75(h)

1128
Application for Change in Accounting Period
Used to obtain approval of a change, adoption or retention of an accounting period.
IT-IRC sec. 442; Regs. secs. 1.442-1(b) and 1.1502-76; Separate instructions

1138
Extension of Time for Payment of Taxes by a Corporation Expecting a Net Operating Loss Carryback
Used by a corporation expecting a net operating loss carryback to request an extension of time for payment of taxes.
IT-IRC sec. 6164

1139
Corporation Application for Tentative Refund
Used by corporations to apply for a tentative refund from the carryback of a net operating loss, net capital loss, unused general business credit, or overpayment of tax due to a claim or right adjustment under section 1341(b)(1).
IT-IRC sec. 6411

1310
Statement of Person Claiming Refund Due a Deceased Taxpayer
Used by claimant to secure payment of refund on behalf of a deceased taxpayer.
IT-IRC sec. 6402; Regs. sec. 301.6402-2(e); Pubs. 17 and 559

1363
Export Exemption Certificate
Used by shipper or other person to suspend liability for the payment of the tax for a period of 6 months from the date of shipment from the point of origin. The original is filed with the carrier at time of payment of the transportation charges and the duplicate is retained with the shipping papers for a period of 3 years from the last day of the month during which the shipment was made from the point of origin. May also be used as a blanket exemption certificate, with approval of District Director.
Ex-IRC secs. 4271 and 4272; temp Regs. Part 154.2-1

2032
Contract Coverage Under Title II of the Social Security Act
Used to make an agreement pursuant to IRC section 3121(l).
Emp-IRC sec. 3121(l); Regs. sec. 36.3121(l)(1)-1

2063
U.S. Departing Alien Income Tax Statement
Used by a resident alien who has not received a termination assessment, or a nonresident alien who has no taxable income from United States sources.
IT-IRC sec. 6851(d); Regs. sec. 1.6851-2; Rev. Rul. 55-468; C.B.1955-2, 501; Pub. 519

2106
Employee Business Expenses
Used by employees to support deductions for business expenses.
IT-IRC secs. 62, 162, and 274; Instructions for Form 1040, Pub. 463; Separate instructions

2119
Sale of Your Home
Used by individuals who sold their principal residence whether or not they bought another one. Also used by individuals 55 or over who elect to exclude gain on the sale of their principal residence.
IT-IRC secs. 121 and 1034; Pub. 17; Separate instructions

2120
Multiple Support Declaration
Used as a statement disclaiming as an income tax exemption an individual to whose support the taxpayer and others have contributed.
IT-IRC sec. 152(c); Regs. sec. 1.152-3(c); Pub. 17

2210
Underpayment of Estimated Tax by Individuals and Fiduciaries
Used by individuals and fiduciaries to determine if they paid enough estimated tax. The form is also used to compute the penalty for underpayment of estimated tax.
IT-IRC sec. 6654; Regs. secs. 1.6654-1 and 1.6654-2; Separate instructions

2210F
Underpayment of Estimated Tax by Farmers and Fishermen
Used by qualified farmers and fishermen to determine if they paid enough estimated tax. Used only by individuals whose gross income from farming or fishing is at least two-thirds of their gross annual income. (All other individuals should use Form 2210.) The form is also used to compute the penalty for underpayment of estimated tax.
IT-IRC sec. 6654; Reg. secs. 1.6654-1 and 1.6654-2

2220
Underpayment of Estimated Tax by Corporations
Used by corporations to determine if they paid enough estimated tax. The form

IRS Tax Forms

is also used to compute the penalty for underpayment of estimated tax.
IT-IRC sec. 6655; Separate instructions

2290
Heavy Vehicle Use Tax Return
Used to report tax due on use of any highway motor vehicle which falls within one of the categories shown in the tax computation schedule on the form or meets certain weight limitations.
Ex-IRC sec. 4481; Regs. sec. 41.6011(a)-1(a)

2350
Application for Extension of Time to File U.S. Income Tax Return
Used by U.S. citizens and certain resident aliens abroad, who expect to qualify for special tax treatment to obtain an extension of time for filing an income tax return.
IT-IRC secs. 911 and 6081; Regs. sec. temporary 5b.911-6(b), 1.911-7(c), and 1.6081-2; Pub. 54

2438
Regulated Investment Company Undistributed Capital Gains Tax Return
Used to report tax payable on or before 30th day after close of company's taxable year. A copy is filed with Form 1120-RIC. (An annual return.)
IT-IRC sec. 852(b)(3); Regs. sec. 1.852-9

2439
Notice to Shareholder of Undistributed Long-Term Capital Gains
Used as an annual statement to be distributed to shareholders of a regulated investment company. (Copy to be attached to Form 1120-RIC.)
IT-IRC sec. 852(b)(3)(D)(i); Regs. sec. 1.852-9

2441
Child and Dependent Care Expenses
Used to figure the credit for child and dependent care expenses and/or the exclusion of employer-provided dependent care benefits. (To be attached to Form 1040.)
IT-IRC sec. 21 & 129; Regs. sec. 1.44A-1; Pubs. 17 and 503

2553
Election by A Small Business Corporation
Used by qualifying small business corporations to make the election prescribed by IRC section 1362.
IT-IRC sec. 1362; Separate instructions

2555
Foreign Earned Income
Used by U.S. citizens and resident aliens who qualify for the foreign earned income exclusion and/or the housing exclusion or deduction. (To be filed with Form 1040.)
IT-IRC secs. 911 and 6012(c); Regs. secs. 1.911-1 and 1.6012-1; Pub. 54; Separate instructions

2670
Credit or Refund-Exemption Certificate for Use by a Nonprofit
Educational Organization
Used by certain nonprofit educational organizations to support a claim for credit or refund to the person who paid the manufacturers excise tax, or the exemption of these sales from the special fuels tax under IRC Chapter 31.
Ex-IRC secs. 4041, 4221, and 4416; Regs. sec. 48.4221-6

2688
Application for Additional Extension of Time To File U.S. Individual Income Tax Return
Used to apply for an extension of time to file Form 1040.
IT-IRC sec. 6081; Regs. sec. 1.6081-1(b)(5); T.D.6436

2758
Application for Extension of Time To File Certain Excise, Income, Information, and Other Returns
Used to apply for an extension of time to file Form 1041 and certain other returns. A separate Form 2758 must be filed for each return.
IT-IRC sec. 6081; Regs. sec. 1.6081-1(b)

2848
Power of Attorney and Declaration of Representative
Used as an authorization for one person to act for another in any tax matter (except alcohol & tobacco taxes and firearms activities).

IT-Title 26, CFR, Part 601; Separate instructions

2848-D
Tax Information Authorization and Declaration of Representative
Used by one person to authorize another to receive or inspect confidential tax information (except alcohol and tobacco taxes and firearms activities) when power of attorney is not filed.
IT-Title 26, CFR, Part 601; Separate instructions

3115
Application for Change in Accounting Method
Used to secure approval for change in accounting method.
IT-IRC sec. 446(e); Regs. sec. 1.446-1(e); Separate instructions

3206
Information Statement by United Kingdom Withholding Agents Paying Dividends From United States Corporations to Residents of the U.S. and Certain Treaty Countries
Used to report dividends paid by U.S. corporations to beneficial owners of dividends paid through United Kingdom Nominees. Used when the beneficial owners are residents of countries other than United Kingdom with which the U.S. has a tax treaty providing for reduced withholding rates on dividends.
IT secs. 7.507 and 7.508 of T.D. 5532

3468
Computation of Investment Credit
Used by individuals, estates, trusts, and corporations claiming an investment credit or business energy investment credit. Also see Form 3800.
IT-IRC secs. 38, 46, 47, 48, and 49; Separate instructions

3491
Consumer Cooperative Exemption Application
Used by certain consumer cooperatives that are primarily engaged in retail sales of goods or services generally for personal, living or family use to apply for exemption from filing Forms 1096 and 1099-PATR.
IT-IRC sec. 6044(c); Regs. sec. 1.6044-4

3520
U.S. Information Return-Creation of or Transfers to Certain Foreign Trusts
Used by a grantor in the case of an inter vivos trust, a fiduciary of an estate in the case of a testamentary trust, or a transferor to report the creation of any foreign trust by a U.S. person or the transfer of any money or property to a foreign trust by a U.S. person.
IT-IRC sec. 6048; Regs. secs. 16.3-1 and 301.6048-1

3520-A
Annual Return of Foreign Trust with U.S. Beneficiaries
Used to report the operation of foreign trust that has U.S. beneficiaries.
IT-IRC sec. 6048

3800
General Business Credit
Used to summarize investment credit (Form 3468), jobs credit (Form 5884), credit for alcohol used as fuel (Form 6478), credit for increasing research activities (Form 6765), and low-income housing credit (Form 8586).
IT-IRC secs. 38 and 39; Separate instructions

3903
Moving Expenses
Used to support itemized deductions for expenses of travel, transportation and certain expenses attributable to disposition of an old residence and acquisition of a new residence for employees and self-employed individuals moving to a new job location.
IT-IRC sec. 217; Regs. sec. 1.217; Pub. 521; Separate instructions

3903F
Foreign Moving Expenses
Used by U.S. citizens or resident aliens moving to a new principal workplace outside the United States or its possessions.
IT-IRC 217(h); Pub. 521; Separate instructions

4029
Application for Exemption from Social Security Taxes and Waiver of Benefits
Used by members of qualified religious groups to claim exemption from social security taxes.
IT-IRC sec. 1402(g)

325

Taxes

4070
Employee's Report of Tips to Employer
Used by employees to report tips to employers.
Emp-IRC sec. 3102(c); Regs. sec. 31.6053-1(b)(2)

4070-A
Employee's Daily Record of Tips
Used by employees to keep a daily record of tips received.
Emp-IRC sec. 3102(c); Regs. sec. 31.6053-4

4070PR
Informe al Patrono de Propinas Recibidas por el Empleado
Used by employees in Puerto Rico. A variation of Form 4070.
Emp-IRC sec. 3102(c); Regs sec. 31.6053-1(b)(2)

4070A-PR
Registro Diario de Propinas Recibidas por el Empleado
Used by employees in Puerto Rico. A variation of Form 4070-A.
Emp-IRC sec. 3102(c); Regs. sec. 31.6053-4

4136
Computation of Credit for Federal Tax on Gasoline and Special Fuels
Used by individuals, estates, trusts, or corporations, including S corporations and domestic international sales corporations, to claim credit for Federal excise tax on the number of gallons of gasoline and special fuels used for business. Also used to claim the one-time credit allowed owners of qualified diesel-powered highway vehicles.
Ex-IRC secs. 34, 4041, 4081, 4091, 6420, 6421, and 6427

4137
Computation of Social Security Tax on Unreported Tip Income
Used by an employee who received tips subject to FICA tax but failed to report them to his or her employer.
IT/Emp-IRC sec. 3102; Regs. sec. 31.3102-3(d) and 31.6011(a)-1(d)

4224
Exemption From Withholding of Tax on Income Effectively Connected With the Conduct of a Trade or Business in the United States
Used to secure, at the time of payment, the benefit of exemption from withholding of the tax on certain income for nonresident alien individuals and fiduciaries, foreign partnerships, and foreign corporations.
IT-IRC secs. 1441 and 1442; Regs. sec. 1.1441-4

4255
Recapture of Investment Credit
Used by individuals, estates, trusts, or corporations to figure the increase in tax if regular or energy property was disposed of or ceased to qualify before the end of the proeprty class life or life years used to figure the credit.
IT-IRC sec. 47

4361
Application for Exemption from Self-Employment Tax for Use by Ministers, Members of Religious Orders and Christian Science Practitioners
Used by members of qualified religious groups to claim exemption from tax on self-employment income.
IT-IRC sec. 1402(e)

4461
Application for Approval of Master or Prototype Defined Contribution Plan
Used by employers who want an opinion letter for approval of form of a master or prototype plan.
IT-IRC secs. 401(a), and 501(a)

4461-A
Application for Approval of Master or Prototype Defined Benefit Plan
Used by employers who want an opinion letter for approval of form of a master or prototype plan.
IT-IRC secs. 401(a) and 501(a)

4461-B
Application of Master or Prototype Plan, or Regional Prototype Plan Mass Submitter Adopting Sponsor
Used by mass submitters who want approval on a plan of adopting sponsoring organization or sponsor.
IT-IRC secs. 401(a) and 501(a)

4466
Corporation Application for Quick Refund of Overpayment of Estimated Tax
Used to apply for a "quick" refund of overpaid estimated tax. (Must be filed before the regular tax return is filed.)
IT-IRC sec. 6425; Regs. sec. 1.6425-1(b)

4469
Computation of Excess Medicare Tax Credit
Used by railraod employee representatives and medicare qualified Government employees to figure their credit of excess medicare (hospital insurance benefits) tax.
IT-IRC sec. 6413(c)(3); P.L.80-248

4506
Request for Copy of Tax Form
Used by a taxpayer or authorized representative to request a copy of a tax return or Forms W-2 that were filed with the return.
IT-Regs. sec. 601.702

4506-A
Request for Public-Inspection Copy of Exempt Organization Tax Form
Used by a third-party for a copy of an exempt organization tax form which may be inspected at an IRS office.
IT-IRC sec. 6104(b)

4562
Depreciation and Amortization
Used by individuals, estates, trusts, partnerships, and corporations claiming depreciation and amortization. Also used to substantiate depreciation deductions for automobiles and other listed property.
IT-IRC secs. 167, 168, 179 and 280F; Separate instructions

4563
Exclusion of Income for Bona Fide Residents of American Samoa
Used by bona fide residents of American Samoa to exclude income from sources in American Samoa, Guam, and the Commonwealth of the Northern Mariana Islands, to the extent specified in IRC section 931.
IT-IRC sec. 931; Regs. sec. 1.931-1; Pub. 570

4626
Alternative Minimum Tax-Corporations
Used by corporations to figure their alternative minimum tax and their environmental tax.
IT-IRC secs. 55, 56, 57, 58, 59, and 291; Separate instructions

4684
Casualties and Thefts
Used by all taxpayers to figure gains (or losses) resulting from casualties and thefts.
IT-IRC sec. 165; Separate instructions

4720
Return of Certain Excise Taxes on Charities and Other Persons Under Chapters 41 and 42 of the Internal Revenue Code
Used by charities and other persons to compute certain excise taxes which may be due under IRC Chapters 41 and 42.
Ex-IRC secs. 4911, 4912, 4941, 4942, 4943, 4944, 4945, and 4955; Separate instructions

4768
Application for Extension of Time To File U.S. Estate (and Generation-Skipping Transfer) Tax Return and/or Pay Estate (and Generation-Skipping Transfer) Tax(es)
Used to apply for estate tax extensions in certain cases.
E&G-IRC secs. 6081 and 6161; Regs. sec. 20.6081-1 and 20.6161-1

4782
Employee Moving Expense Information
Used by employers to show the amount of any reimbursement or payment made to an employee, a third party for the employee's benefit, or the value of services furnished in-kind, for moving expenses during the calendar year.

IT-IRC secs. 82 and 217; Regs. sec. 31.6051-1(e)

4789
Currency Transaction Report
Used by financial institutions to report deposit, withdrawal, exchange of currency, or other payment or transfer, by, through, or to such financial institution which involves currency transactions of more than $10,000.
P.L.92-508; Treasury Regs. (31CFR103)

4797
Sales of Business Property
Used to report details of gain (or loss) from sales, exchanges, or involuntary conversions (from other than casualty and theft) of noncapital assets and involuntary conversions (other than casualty and theft) of capital assets, held in connection with a trade or business or a transaction entered into for profit. Also used to compute recapture amounts under sections 179 and 280F when the business use of section 179 or 280F property drops to 50% or less.
IT-IRC secs. 1231, 1245, 1250, 1252, 1254, and 1255; IT-IRC secs. 1202, 1211, and 1212; Separate instructions

4835
Farm Rental Income and Expenses
Used by landowner (or sublessor) to report farm rental income based on crops or livestock produced by the tenant where the landowner (or sublessor) does not materially participate in the operation or management of the farm. (Also see Schedule F (Form 1040).)
IT-IRC sec. 61

4868
Application for Automatic Extension of Time to File U.S. Individual Income Tax Return
Used to apply for an automatic 4-month extension of time to file Form 1040.
IT-IRC sec. 6081; Regs. sec. 1.6081-4; TD 7885

4876-A
Election To Be Treated as an Interest Charge DISC
Used by a qualifying corporation that wishes to be treated as an Interest Charge Domestic International Sales Corporation (Interest Charge DISC).
IT-Regs. sec. 1.921

4952
Investment Interest Expense Deduction
Used by an individual, estate, or trust to figure the deduction limitation for interest expense on funds borrowed that is allocable to property held for investment.
IT-IRC sec. 163(d)

4970
Tax on Accumulation Distribution of Trusts
Used by a beneficiary of a domestic or foreign trust to figure the tax attributable to an accumulation distribution.
IT-IRC sec. 667

4972
Tax on Lump-Sum Distributions
Used to determine the income tax on the income portion of lump-sum distributions.
IT-IRC sec. 402(e); Separate instructions

5074
Allocation of Individual Income Tax to Guam or the Commonwealth of the Northern Mariana Islands (CNMI)
Used as an attachment to Form 1040 filed by an individual who reports adjusted gross income of $50,000 or more, with gross income of $5,000 or more from Guam or CNMI sources.
IT-IRC sec. 935; Regs. sec. 301.7654-1(d)

5213
Election to Postpone Determination as to whether the Presumption that an Activity is Engaged in for Profit Applies
Used by individuals, trusts, estates, and S corporations to postpone a determination as to whether an activity is engaged in for profit.
IT-IRC sec. 183(e)

5227
Split-Interest Trust Information Return
Used by section 4947(a)(2) trusts treated as private foundations.
Ex-IRC sec. 6011; Separate instructions

5300

Application for Determination for Defined Benefit Plan
Used to request a determination letter as to the qualification of a defined benefit plan (other than a collectively-bargained plan).
IT-IRC sec. 401(a); Separate instructions

Sch. T (Form 5300)
Supplemental Application for Approval of Employee Benefit Plans
Used as an attachment to Forms 5300, 5301, 5303, 5307, and 6406 to provide information on how the applicant meets the requirements of the Tax Equity and Fiscal Responsibility Act of 1982, the Tax Reform Act of 1984, and the Retirement Equity Act of 1984, and the Tax Reform Act of 1986.
IT-IRC 401(a); Separate instructions

5301
Application for Determination for Defined Contribution Plan
Used to request a determination letter as to the qualification of a defined contribution plan (other than a collectively-bargained plan).
IT-IRC sec. 401(a); Separate instructions

5302
Employee Census
Used as a schedule of the 25 highest paid participants of a deferred compensation plan, which is attached to Forms 5300, 5301, 5303, and 5307 (where applicable).
IT-IRC sec. 401(a)

5303
Application for Determination for Collectively-Bargained Plan
Used to request a determination letter as to the qualification of a collectively-bargained plan. Also used by multiemployer plans covered by PBGC insurance to request a determination letter regarding termination.
IT-IRC sec. 401(a); Separate instructions

5305
Individual Retirement Trust Account
Used as an agreement between an individual and the individual's trustee for the establishment of an individual retirement account.
IT-IRC sec. 408(a)

5305-A
Individual Retirement Custodial Account
Used as an agreement between an individual and the individual's custodian for the establishment of an individual retirement account.
IT-IRC sec. 408(a)

5305-SEP
Simplified Employee Pension-Individual Retirement Accounts Contribution Agreement
Used as an agreement between an employer and his or her employees to establish a Simplified Employee Pension.
IT-IRC 408(k)

5305-A-SEP
Salary Reduction and Other Elective Simplified Employee Pension - Individual Retirement Accounts Contribution Agreement
Used as an agreement between an employer and his or her employees to establish a Simplified Employee Pension with an elective deferral.
IT-IRC sec. 408(k)(6)

5306
Application for Approval of Prototype or Employer Sponsored Individual Retirement Account
Used by banks, savings and loan associations, federally insured credit unions, and such other persons approved by the Internal Revenue Service to act as trustee or custodian, insurance companies, regulated investment companies and trade or professional societies or associations, to get the approval as to form of a trust or annuity contract which is to be used for individual retirement accounts or annuities. Also to be used by employees, labor unions and other employee associations that want approval of a trust which is to be used for individual retirement accounts.
IT-IRC sec. 408(a), (b), or (c)

5306-SEP
Application for Approval of Prototype Simplified Employee Pension-SEP
Used by program sponsors who want to get IRS approval of their prototype

Taxes

simplified employee pension (SEP) agreements.
IT-IRC sec. 408

5307
Application for Determination for Adopters of Master or Prototype, Regional Prototype or Volume Submitter Plans
Used to request a determination letter as to the qualification of any defined benefit or defined contribution plan (the form of which has been previously approved) other than a collectively bargained plan.
IT-IRC sec. 401(a); Separate instructions

5308
Request for Change in Plan/Trust Year
Used by employer or plan administrators to request approval of change in a plan year or a trust year.
IT-IRC sec. 412(c)(5), sec. 442

5309
Application for Determination of Employee Stock Ownership Plan
Used by corporate employers who wish to get a determination letter regarding the qualification of an Employee Stock Ownership Plan under IRC 409 or 4975(e)(7).
IT-IRC 409-4975(e)(7)

5310
Application for Determination Upon Termination; Notice of Merger, Consolidation or Transfer of Plan Assets or Liabilities; Notice of Intent to Terminate
Used by an employer who wishes a determination letter as to the effect of termination of a plan on its prior qualification under IRC section 401(a); by every employer or plan administrator (if designated) for any plan merger or consolidation; or to give notice to PBGC of intent, for any transfer of plan assets or liabilities to another plan to terminate a defined benefit pension plan.
IT-IRC secs. 401(a), 6058(b), ERISA sec. 4041(a); Separate instructions

5329
Return for Additional Taxes Attributable to Qualified Retirement Plans (Including IRAs), Annuities, and Modified Endowment Contracts
Used to report excise taxes or additional income tax owed in connection with individual retirement arrangements, annuities, and qualified retirement plans.
IT-IRC secs. 72, 4973, 4974, and 4980A; Separate instructions

5330
Return of Excise Taxes Related to Employee Benefits Plans
Used to report and pay the excise tax imposed by IRC section 4791 on a minimum funding deficiency, by Code section 4973(a)(2) on excess contributions to a section 403(b)(7)(A) custodial account, by section 4975 on prohibited transactions, by section 4976 on disqualified benefits from welfare plans, by 4977 on certain fringe benefits, and by 4978 on certain ESOP transactions.
Ex-IRC sec. 6011; Separate instructions

5452
Corporate Report of Nondividend Distributions
Used by corporations to report their nontaxable distributions.
IT-CFR 1.301-1, 1.316-1, 1.333-1, and 1.6042-2

5471
Information Return With Respect to a Foreign Corporation
Used by U.S. persons to report their activities with related foreign corporations.
IT-IRC secs. 951-972, 6035, 6038 and 6046; Separate instructions

Sch. M (Form 5471)
Foreign Corporation Controlled by a U.S. Person
Used by a U.S. person who controls a foreign corporation to report the activities between the U.S. person and the foreign corporation.
IT-IRC sec. 6038

Sch. N (Form 5471)
Foreign Personal Holding Company
Used by officers, directors, and shareholders of foreign personal holding companies to report information concerning the foreign personal holding company.
IT-IRC sec. 6035

Sch. O (Form 5471)
Organization or Reorganization of Foreign Corporation, and Acquisitions and Dispositions of its Stock
Used by U.S. persons to report acquisitions or dispositions of interests in foreign corporations.
IT-IRC sec. 6046

5472
Information Return of a Foreign Owned Corporation
Used for reporting the activities between foreign owned corporations and persons related to transactions made by the corporations.
IT-IRC sec. 6038A

5498
Individual Retirement Arrangement Information
Used to report contributions to individual retirement arrangements (IRAs) and the value of the account.
IT-IRC sec. 408(i)(o); Prop. Regs. sec. 1.408-5; See the separate Instructions for Forms 1099, 1098, 5498, 1096, and W-2G

5500
Annual Return/Report of Employee Benefit Plan (with 100 or more participants)
Used to report on deferred compensation plans and welfare plans that have at least 100 participants.
IT-IRC sec. 6058(a); ERISA section 103; Separate instructions

Sch. A (Form 5500)
Insurance Information
Used as an attachment to Forms 5500, 5500-C, or 5500-R to report information about insurance contracts that are part of a qualified deferred compensation plan.
ERISA section 103(e)

Sch. B (Form 5500)
Actuarial Information
Used to report actuarial information for a defined benefit plan. (Attached to Forms 5500, 5500-C, or 5500-R.)
IT-IRC sec. 6059; ERISA section 103(a); Separate instructions

Sch. C (Form 5500)
Service Provider Information
Used as an attachment to Form 5500 to report information about service providers and trustees of qualified deferred compensation plans. ERISA section 103.

Sch. P (Form 5500)
Annual Return of Fiduciary of Employee Benefit Trust
Used as an annual return for employee benefit trusts which qualify under section 401(a) and are exempt from tax under section 501(a). (Attach to Forms 5500, 5500-C or 5500-R.)
IT-IRC secs. 6033(a) and 6501(a)

Sch. SSA (Form 5500)
Annual Registration Statement Identifying Separated Participants with Deferred Vested Benefits
Used to list employees who separated from employment and have a deferred vested benefit in the employer's plan of deferred compensation. (Attached to Forms 5500, 5500-C, or 5500-R.)
IT-IRC sec. 6057

5500-C/R
Return/Report of Employee Benefit Plan (with fewer than 100 participants)
Used to report on deferred compensation plans and welfare plans that have fewer than 100 participants.
IT-IRC sec. 6058(a); ERISA section 103; Separate instructions

5500EZ
Annual Return of One-Participant Owners and Their Spouses Pension Benefit Plan
Used to report on pension profit-sharing, etc. plans that cover only an individual or an individual and the individual's spouse who wholely own a business.
IT-IRC sec. 6058(a); Separate instructions

5558
Application for Extension of Time to File Certain Employee Plan Returns
Used to provide a means by which a person may request an extension of time to file Forms 5500, 5500-C, 5500-R, or 5330.

5578

Annual Certification of Racial Nondiscrimination for a Private School Exempt from Federal Income Tax

Used by certain organizations exempt or claiming to be exempt under IRC section 501(c)(3) and operating, supervising, or controlling a private school (or schools) to certify to a policy of racial nondiscrimination.
IT-IRC sec. 6001; Rev. Proc. 75-50, 1975-2; C.B.587

5712
Election to be Treated as a Possessions Corporation Under Section 936

Used by a corporation to elect to be treated as a possessions corporation for the tax credit allowed under IRC section 936.
IT-IRC sec. 936(e)

5712-A
Cost Sharing or Profit Split Method Under Section 936(h)(5): Election and Verification

Used by a domestic corporation if ti elects to compute its taxable income under either the cost sharing method or the profit split method.
IT-IRC sec. 936(h)(5)

5713
International Boycott Report

Used by persons with operations in or related to any country associated in carrying out an international boycott.
IT-IRC sec. 999; Separate instructions

Sch. A (Form 5713)
Computation of the International Boycott Factor

Used by taxpayers in computing the loss of tax benefits under the international boycott factor method.
IT-IRC sec. 999

Sch. B (Form 5713)
Specifically Attributable Taxes and Income

Used by taxpayers in computing the loss of tax benefits under the specifically attributable taxes and income method.
IT-IRC sec. 999

Sch. C (Form 5713)
Tax Effect of the International Boycott Provisions

Used to summarize the loss of tax benefits resulting from the application of the international boycott provisions.
IT-IRC sec. 999

5735
Computation of Possessions Corporation Tax Credit Under Section 936

Used by qualified possessions corporations to compute credit allowed by IRC section 936.
IT-IRC sec. 936

Sch. P (Form 5735)
Allocation of Income and Expenses Under Section 936(h)(5)

Used by corporations that have elected the cost sharing or profit split method of computing taxable income. The form is attached to Form 5735.
IT-IRC sec. 935(h)(5)

5754
Statement By Person(s) Receiving Gambling Winnings

Used to list multiple winners of certain gambling proceeds.
IT-IRC sec. 3402(q); Regs. secs. 31.3402(q)-1(e) and 1.6011-3; See the separate Instructions for Forms 1099, 1098, 5498, 1096, and W-2G

5768
Election/Revocation of Election by an Eligible Section 501(c)(3) Organization to Make Expenditures to Influence Legislation

Used by certain eligible IRC section 501(c)(3) organizations to elect or revoke election to apply the lobbying expenditures provisions of code section 501(h).
IT-IRC secs. 501 and 4911

5884
Jobs Credit

Used by individuals, estates, trusts, and corporations claiming a jobs credit and any S corporation, partnership, estate or trust which apportion the jobs credit among their shareholders, partners, or beneficiaries. See also Form 3800.
IT-IRC secs. 38, 51, 52, and 53

6008
Fee Deposit for Outer Continental Shelf Oil

Used to deposit fees on oil that is produced on the Outer Continental Shelf.
IRC sec. 7805, sec. 302(d) of P.L.95-372

6009
Quarterly Report of Fees Due on Oil Production

Used to compute fees due on oil that is produced on the Outer Continental Shelf.
IRC sec. 7805, sec. 302(d) of P.L.95-372

6069
Return of Excise Tax on Excess Contributions to Black Lung Benefit Trust Under Section 4953 and Computation of Section 192 Deduction

Used by exempt Black Lung Benefit Trusts as a worksheet to determine deduction under section 192 and to report tax under section 4953.
IT/Ex-IRC secs. 192 and 4953

6088
Distributable Benefits from Employee Pension Benefit Plans

Used to report the 25 highest paid participants of a deferred compensation plan, which is attached to Form 5310.
IT-IRC sec. 401(a)

6118
Credit for Income Tax Return Preparers

Used by income tax return preparers to file for refund of penalties paid.
IT-IRC sec. 6696

6177
General Assistance Program Determination

Used by a General Assistance Program of a state or political subdivision of a state in order to be designated as a Qualified General Assistance Program for purposes of certifying individual recipients of the program for the jobs credit.
IT-IRC sec. 51(d)(6)(B)

6197
Gas Guzzler Tax

Used by automobile manufacturers and importers to report the tax on "gas guzzler" types of automobiles. The form is filed as an attachment to Form 720.
Ex-IRC sec. 4064

6198
At-Risk Limitations

Used by individuals, partners, S corporation shareholders, and certain closely-held corporations to figure the overall profit (loss) from an at-risk activity for the tax year, the amount at-risk, and the deductible loss for the tax year.
IT-IRC sec. 465; Separate instructions

6199
Certification of Youth Participating in a Qualified Cooperative Education Program

Used by a qualified school to certify that a student meets the requirements of Sec. 51(d)(8) as a member of a targeted group eligible for the jobs credit.
IT-IRC sec. 51

6251
Alternative Minimum Tax-Individuals

Used by individuals to figure their alternative minimum tax.
IT-IRC secs. 55, 56, 57, 58, and 59; Separate instructions

6252
Installment Sale Income

Used by taxpayers other than dealers, who sell real or personal property, and receive a payment in a tax year after the year of sale.
IT-IRC sec. 453; Pub. 537; Separate instructions

6406
Short Form Application for Determination for Amendment of Employee Benefit Plan

Used for amending a plan on which a favorable determination letter has been issued under ERISA.
IRC secs. 401(a) and 501(a); Separate instructions

6478
Credit for Alcohol Used as Fuel

Used by taxpayers to figure their credit for alcohol used as fuel. The credit is allowed for alcohol mixed with other fuels and for straight alcohol fuel. See also

Form 3800.
IT-IRC sec. 38 and 40

6497
Information Return of Nontaxable Energy Grants or Subsidized Energy Financing
Used by every person who administers a government program for a Federal, state, or local governmental entity or agent thereof, that provides grants or subsidized financing under programs a principal purpose of which is energy production or conservation if the grant or financing is not taxable to the recipient.
IT-IRC sec. 6050D; Regs. sec. 1.6050D-1

6627
Environmental Taxes
Used to report environmental taxes on petroleum and certain chemicals.
Ex-IRC secs. 4611, 4661, and 4671

6765
Credit for Increasing Research Activities (or for claiming the orphan drug credit)
Used by individuals, estates, trusts, and corporations claiming a research credit for increasing the research activities of a trade or business. Also used to claim the orphan drug credit. See also Form 3800.
IT-IRC secs. 28 and 41; Separate instructions

6781
Gains and Losses From Section 1256 Contracts and Straddles
Used by all taxpayers that held section 1256 contracts or straddles during the tax year.
IT-IRC secs. 1092 and 1256

7004
Application for Automatic Extension of Time to File Corporation Income Tax Return
Used by corporations and certain exempt organizations to request an automatic extension of 6 months to file corporate income tax return.
IT-IRC sec. 6081(b); Regs. sec. 1.6081-3

8023
Corporate Qualified Stock Purchase Election
Used by a purchasing corporation to elect section 338 treatment for the purchase of another corporation.
IT-IRC sec. 338(g); Temp. Regs. sec. sf 338-1

8027
Employer's Annual Information Return of Tip Income and Allocated Tips
Used by large food or beverage employers to report each establishment's gross receipts, charge receipts and charge tips, and allocated tips of employees.
IT-IRC sec. 6053(c); Regs. sec. 31.6053-3; Separate instructions

8027-T
Transmittal of Employer's Annual Information Return of Tip Income and Allocated Tips
Used by large food or beverage employers with more than one establishment to transmit Forms 8027.
IT-IRC sec. 6053(c); Regs. sec. 31.6053-3

8038
Information Return for Tax-Exempt Private Activity Bond Issues
Used by issuers of tax-exempt private activity bonds to provide IRS with information required by section 149(e).
IT-IRC sec. 149(e); Temp. Regs. sec. 1.149(e)-1T; Separate instructions

8038-G
Information Return for Tax-Exempt Governmental Bond Issues
Used by the issuers of tax-exempt governmental bonds (with issue prices of $100,000 or more) to provide IRS with information required by section 149(e).
IT-IRC sec. 149(e); Temp. Regs. sec. 1.149(e)-1T; Separate instructions

8038-GC
Consolidated Information Return for Small Tax-Exempt Governmental Bond Issues, Leases and Installment Sales
Used by the issuers of tax-exempt governmental bonds (with issue prices of less

than $100,000) to provide IRS with information required by section 149(e).
IT-IRC sec. 149(e); Temp. Regs. sec. 1.149(e)-1T

8082
Notice of Inconsistent Treatment or Amended Return
Used by partners, S corporation shareholders and residual holders of an interest in a REMIC to report inconsistent treatment of partnership, S corporation or REMIC items or to report amendment of partnership, S corporation or REMIC items. Form 8082 is also used by the TMP (tax matters partner or tax matters person) to make an administrative adjustment request (AAR) on behalf of the partnership, S corporation, or REMIC>
IT-IRC sec. 6222 and 6227(c); Separate instructions

8109
Federal Tax Deposit Coupon
Twenty-three preprinted deposit coupons for making deposits of Federal taxes (such as social security, Federal unemployment, and excise taxes) are contained in a coupon book. Instructions are in the coupon book, along with a reorder form (Form 8109A, FTD Reorder Form).
IT/Emp/Ex-IRC sec. 6302; Regs. secs. 1.6302-1, 1.6302-2, 31.6302(c)-1, 31.6302(c)-2, 31.6302(c)-3, 46.6302(c)-1, 48.6302(c)-1, 49.6302(c)-1, 51.4995-3, and 52.6302-1

8109-B
Federal Tax Deposit Coupon
An over-the-counter Federal tax deposit coupon for making Federal tax deposits when Form 8109 deposit coupons have been reordered but not yet received or when a new entity has received its employer identification number but has not yet received its initial order of Forms 8109.
IT/Emp/Ex-IRC sec. 6302; Regs. secs. 1.6302-1, 1.6302-2, 31.6302(c)-1, 31.6302(c)-2, 31.6302(c)-3, 46.6302(c)-1, 48.6302(c)-1, 49.6302(c)-1, 51.4995-3 and 52.6302-1

8210
Self-Assessed Penalties Return
Used by payers of certain interest and dividends to figure and pay penalties imposed with regard to the filing of certain information returns and the furnishing of certain payee statements.
PA-IRC secs. 6676(b), 6721, 6722, 6723, and 6724; Temp. Regs. sec. 301.6723-1T

8233
Exemption From Withholding on Compensation for Independent Personal Services of a Nonresident Alien Individual
Used by nonresident alien individuals to claim exemption from withholding on compensation for independent personal services because of an income tax treaty or the personal exemption amount. Also used by nonresident alien students, teachers, and researchers to claim exemption from withholding under a U.S. tax treaty on compensation for services.
IT-IRC sec. 1441; Reg. sec. 1.1441-4

8264
Application for Registration of a Tax Shelter
Used by tax shelter organizers to register certain tax shelters with the IRS, for purposes of receiving a tax shelter registration number.
IT-IRC sec. 6111; Regs. secs. 301.6111-1T; Separate instructions

8271
Investor Reporting of Tax Shelter Registration Number
Used by persons who have purchased or otherwise acquired an interest in a tax shelter required to be registered to report the tax shelter registration number. Form is attached to any tax return on which a deduction, credit, loss, or other tax benefit is claimed, or any income reported, from a tax shelter required to be registered.
IT-IRC sec. 6111; Regs. secs. 301.6111-1T

8274
Certification by Churches and Qualified Church-Controlled Organizations Electing Exemption from Employer Social Security Taxes
Used by churches and certain church-controlled organizations to elect exemption from social security taxes by certifying the organization is opposed to these taxes for religious purposes.
Emp-IRC sec. 3121(w)

8275
Disclosure Statement Under Section 6661
Used to disclose items which could cause a substantial understatement of income and is filed to avoid the penalty imposed by section 6661; Separate instructions
PA-IRC sec. 6661; Regs. sec. 1.6661; Separate instructions

8279

Election To Be Treated as a FSC or as a Small FSC

Used by qualifying corporations that wish to be treated as a Foreign Sales Corporation (FSC) or Small Foreign Sales Corporation (Small FSC).
IT-IRC sec. 927

8281

Information Return for Publicly Offered Original Issue Discount Instruments

Used by issuers of publicly offered debt instruments having OID to provide the information required by section 1275(c).
IT-IRC sec. 1275(c); Temp. Resg. sec. 1.1275-3T

8282

Donee Information Return

Used by exempt organizations who sells, exchanges, transfers, or otherwise disposes of the charitable property within 2 years after the date of the receipt of the contribution. The return is filed with the IRS and a copy is given to the donor.
IT-IRC sec. 6050L

8283

Noncash Charitable Contributions

Used by individuals, closely held corporations, personal service corporations, partnerships, and S corporations to report contributions of property other than cash in which the total claimed value of all property exceeds $500.
IT-IRC secs. 170; 1.170A-13 and 1.170A-13T; Separate instructions

8288

U.S. Withholding Tax Return for Dispositions by Foreign Persons of U.S. Real Property Interests

Used to transmit the withholding on the sale of U.S. real property by foreign persons.
IT-IRC sec. 1445; Regs. secs. 1.1445-1 through 1.1445-7; Temp. Regs. secs. 1.1445-9T through 1.1445-11T

8288-A

Statement of Withholding on Dispositions by Foreign Persons of U.S. Real Property Interests

Anyone filing Form 8288 must attach copies A and B of Form 8288-A for each person subject to withholding.
IT-IRC sec. 1445; Regs. secs. 1.1445-1 through 1.1445-7, Temp. Regs. secs. 1.1445-9T through 1.1445-11T

8288-B

Application for Withholding Certificate for Dispositions by Foreign Persons of U.S. Real Property Interests

Used to apply for a withholding certificate based upon certain criteria to reduce or eliminate withholding under section 1445.
IT-IRC sec. 1445; Regs. secs. 1.1445-3 and 1.1445-6 and Rev. Proc. 88-23

8300

Report of Cash Payments Over $10,000 Received in a Trade or Business

Used by a trade or business to report receipt of more than $10,000 cash in a transaction in the course of such trade or business.
IT-IRC sec. 6050I; Regs. 1.6050I-1

8308

Report of a Sale or Exchange of Certain Partnership Interests

Used by partnerships to report the sale or exchange of a partnership interest where a portion of any money or other property given in exchange for the interest is attributable to unrealized receivables or substantially appreciated inventory items (section 751(a) exchange).
IT-IRC sec. 6050K

8328

Carryforward Election of Unused Private Activity Bond Volume Cap

Used by the issuing authority of tax-exempt private activity bonds to elect under section 146(f) to carryforward the unused volume cap for specific projects.
IT-IRC sec. 146(f)

8329

Lender's Information Return for Mortgage Credit Certificates

Used by lenders of certified indebtedness amounts to report information regarding the issuance of mortgage credit certificates under section 25.
IT-IRC sec. 25; Regs. sec. 1.25-8T

8330

Issuer's Quarterly Information Return for Mortgage Credit Certificates

Used by issuers of mortgage credit certificates to report information required under section 25.
IT-IRC sec. 25; Regs. secs. 1.25-8T

8332

Release of Claim to Exemption for Child of Divorced or Separated Parents

Used to release claim to a child's exemption by a parent who has custody of his or her child and is given to the parent who will claim the exemption. The parent who claims the child's exemption attaches this form to his or her tax return.
IT-IRC sec. 152(e)(2); Temp. Regs. sec. 1.152-4T; Pub. 504

8362

Currency Transaction Reported by Casinos

Used by casinos licensed by a state or local government having annual gaming revenues in excess of $1 million to report each deposit, withdrawal, exchange of currency or gambling tokens or chips or other payment or transfer, by, through, or to such casino, involving currency of more than $10,000.
P.L.91-508; Treasury Regs. secs. 31 CFR 103.22; 31 CFR 103.26; and 31 CFR 103.36

8390

Information Return for Determination of Life Insurance Company Earnings Rate Under Section 809

Used by certain life insurance companies to gather information to compute various earnings rates required by section 809.
IT-IRC sec. 809; Separate instructions

8396

Mortgage Interest Credit

Used by qualified mortgage credit certificate holders to figure their mortgage interest credit and any carryover to a subsequent year.
IT-IRC sec. 25

8404

Computation of Interest Charge on DISC-Related Deferred Tax Liability

Used by shareholders of Interest Charge Domestic International Sales Corporations (IC-DISCs) to figure and report their interest on DISC-related deferred tax liability.
ITC 995(f); Treasury Regs. 1.995(f)

8453

U.S. Individual Income Tax Declaration for Electronic Filing

Used by qualified filers who file Forms 1040 and certain related schedules, 1040A and 1040EZ via electronic transmission on magnetic media. These filers must file Form 8453 to transmit the individual taxpayer's and return preparer's signature(s) for the return.
IT-IRC secs. 6012 and 6017

8453-E

Annual Return/Report of Employee Benefit Plan Magnetic Media/Electronic Filing

Used by qualified filers who file Forms 5500, 5500-C or 5500-R via electronic transmission.
IT-IRC sec. 6058

8453-F

U.S. Fiduciary Income Tax Declaration for Magnetic Tape/Electronic Filing

Used by qualified filers who file Form 1041 and related schedules via electronic transmission.
IT-IRC sec. 6012

8453-P

U.S. Partnership Declaration for Magnetic Tape/Electronic Filing

Used by qualified filers who file Form 1065 and related schedules via electronic transmission.
IT-IRC sec. 6031

8582

Passive Activity Loss Limitations

Used by individuals, estates, and trusts to figure the amount of any passive activity loss for the current tax year for all activities and the amount of the passive activity loss allowed on their tax returns.

Taxes

IT-IRC sec. 469; Separate instructions

8582-CR
Passive Activity Credit Limitations
Used by individuals, estates, and trusts to figure the amount of any passive activity credit for the current year and the amount allowed on their tax returns.
IT-IRC sec. 469; Separate instructions

8586
Low-Income Housing Credit
Used by owners of residential rental projects providing low-income housing to claim the low-income housing credit.
IT-IRC sec. 42

8594
Asset Acquisition Statement
Used by the buyer and seller of assets used in a trade or business involving goodwill or a going concern value.
IT-IRC 1060, Temp. Regs. sec. 1.1060-1T

8606
Nondeductible IRA Contributions, IRA Basis, and Nontaxable IRA Distributions
Used by individuals to report the amount of IRA contributions they choose to be nondeductible and to figure their basis in their IRA(s) at the end of the calendar year and the nontaxable part of any distributions they received.
IT-IRC sec. 408(o)

8609
Low-Income Housing Credit Allocation Certification
Used by housing credit agencies to allocate a low-income housing credit dollar amount. Also, used by low-income housing building owners to make elections and certify certain necessary information.
IT-IRC sec. 42

8610
Annual Low-Income Housing Credit Agencies Report
Used by housing credit agencies to transmit Forms 8609 and to report the dollar amount of housing credit allocations issued during the calendar year.
IT-IRC sec. 42

8611
Recapture of Low-Income Housing Credit
Used by taxpayers to recapture low-income housing credit taken in a prior year because there is a decrease in the qualified basis of a residential low-income housing building from one year to the next.
IT-IRC sec. 42(j)

8612
Return of Excise Tax on Undistributed Income of Real Estate Investment Trusts
Used by real estate investment trusts to report the excise tax on undistributed income.
EX-IRC sec. 4981

8613
Return of Excise Tax on Undistributed Income of Regulated Investment Companies
Used by regulated investment companies to report the excise tax on undistributed income.
EX-IRC sec. 4982

8615
Computation of Tax for Children Under Age 14 Who Have Investment Income of More Than $1,000
Used to see if any of a child's investment income in excess of $1,000 is taxed at his or her parent's rate and, if so, to figure the child's tax.

8621
Return by a Shareholder of a Passive Foreign Investment Company or Qualified Electing Fund
Used by U.S. persons who own an interest in a foreign investment company to report elections, terminations of elections, and amounts to be included in gross income.
IT-IRC secs. 1291, 1293, and 1294

8645
Soil and Water Conservation Plan Certification
Used by taxpayers to certify that the plan under which they are claiming conservation expenses is an approved plan.

IT-IRC sec. 175(c)(3)

8656
Alternative Minimum Tax-Fiduciaries
Used by a fiduciary of an estate or trust to compute the alternative minimum taxable income, distributable net alternative minimum taxable income, and to report any alternative minimum tax due.
IT-IRC secs. 55 - 59; Separate instructions

8689
Allocation of Individual Income Tax to the Virgin Islands
Used as an attachment to Form 1040 filed by an individual who reports adjusted gross income from Virgin Islands sources.
IT-IRC sec. 932

8693
Low-Income Housing Credit Disposition Bond
Used to post a bond to avoid recapture of the low-income housing credit under section 42(j)(6).
IT-IRC secs. 42 and 42(j)(6)

8697
Interest Computation Under the Look-Back Method for Completed Long-Term Contracts
Used by taxpayers to figure the interest due or to be refunded under the look-back method of section 460(b)(3) on certain long-term contracts entered into after February 28, 1986, that are accounted for under either the percentage of completion-capitalized cost method or the percentage of completion method.
IT-IRC secs. 460(a) and 460(b)(2)(B); Separate instructions

8703
Annual Certification by Operator of a Residential Rental Project
Used by operators of residential rental projects to provide annual information the IRS will use to determine whether the projects continue to meet the requirements of section 142(d). Operators indicate on the form the specific test the bond issuer elected for the project period and also indicate the percentage of low-income units in the residential rental project.
IT-IRC secs. 142

8709
Exemption From Withholding on Investment Income of Foreign Governments
Used by foreign governments or international organizations to claim exemption from withholding under sections 1441 and 1442 on items of income qualifying for tax exemption under section 892.
IT-IRC secs. 892

8716
Election To Have a Tax Year Other Than a Required Tax Year
Used by partnerships, S corporations, and personal service corporations to elect to have a tax year other than a required tax year.
IT-IRC sec. 444

Sch. H (Form 8716)
Section 280H Limitations for a Personal Service Corporation (PSC)
Used by personal service corporations to determine their compliance with the distribution requirements of Section 280H.
IRC secs. 280H and 444

8717
User Fee for Employee Plan Determination Letter Request
Used by applicants for Employee Plan determination letters to transmit the appropriate user fee.
Rev. Proc. 89-4, 1983-3 I.R.B. 18

8718
User Fee for Exempt Organization Determination Letter Request
Used by applicants for Exempt Organization determination letters to transmit the appropriate user fee.
Rev. Proc. 89-4. 1989-3 I.R.B. 18

8736
Application for Automatic Extension of Time to File Returns for a Partnership, a REMIC, or for Certain Trusts
Used to apply for an automatic three-month extension of time to file Form

1041(trust), Form 1041S, or Form 1065.
IT-IRC sec. 6081; Regs. secs. 1.6081-2T and 1.6081-3T

8743
Information on Fuel Inventories and Sales
Used by refiners and importers to report information on fuel inventories and sales. The form is filed as an attachment to Form 720.
EX-IRC secs. 4041, 4081, and 4091

8800
Application for Additional Extension of Time to File Return for a U.S. Partnership, REMIC, or for Certain Trusts
Used to apply for an additional extension of up to three months of time to file Form 1041 (trust), Forms 1041S, or Form 1065. A separate Form 8800 must be filed for each return.
IT-IRC sec. 6081; Regs. secs. 1.6081-2T and 1.6081-3T

8801
Credit for Prior Year Minimum Tax
Used by taxpayers to figure the minimum tax credit allowed for tax year.
IT-IRC sec. 53; Separate instructions

8802
Annual Summary of Capital Construction Fund Activity
Used by taxpayers who maintain a capital construction fund under section 607 of the Merchant Marine Act of 1936, to report deposits to and withdrawals from the fund and to report the balances of the memorandum accounts required by Internal Revenue Code section 7518(d).
IT-IRC sec. 7518; Separate instructions

8803
Limit on Alternative Minimum Tax For Children Under Age 14
Used by children under age 14 to see if the alternative minimum tax figured on Form 6251 can be reduced.
IT-IRC sec. 59(j)

8804
Annual Return for Partnership Withholding Tax (Section 1446)
Used to report the total liability under section 1446 for the partnership's tax year. Form 8804 is also a transmittal form for Form 8805.
IT-IRC sec. 1446; Rev. Proc. 89-31; Separate instructions

8805
Foreign Partner's Information Statement of Section 1446 Withholding Tax
Used to show the amount of effectively connected taxable income and the tax payments allocable to the foreign partner for the partnership's tax year.
IT-IRC sec. 1446; Rev. Proc. 89-31; Separate instructions

8807
Computation of Certain Manufacturers and Retailers Excise Taxes
Used by manufacturers, producers, and importers to figure the tax on the sale of fishing equipment, bows and arrows, pistols and revolvers, firearms, and shells and cartridges. And, used by retailers to figure the excise tax on the sale of truck, trailer, and semitrailer chassis and bodies, and tractors.
EX-IRC secs. 4161, 4181, and 4051

8809
Request for Extension of Time To File Information Returns
Used to request an extension of time to file Forms W-2, W-2G, W-2P, 1098, 1099, or 5498.
PA-IRC sec. 6081; Regs. sec. 1.6081-1

8810
Corporate Passive Activity Loss and Credit Limitations
Used by closely held C corporations and personal service corporations that have passive activity losses and/or credits.
IT-IRC sec. 469; Separate instructions

8811
Information Return for Real Estate Mortgage Investment Conduits (REMICs) and Issuers of Collateralized Debt Obligations
Used by REMICs and issuers of Collateralized Debt Obligations to report entity information needed to compile Publication 938, *Real Estate Mortgage Investment Conduit (REMIC) Reporting Information*.
IT-IRC secs. 860A-G and 1272(a))6)(C)(ii)

8813
Partnership Withholding Tax Payment (Section 1446)
Used to make payment to the Internal Revenue Service of withholding tax under section 1446. Each payment of section 1446 taxes made during the partnership's tax year must be accompanied by Form 8813.
IT-IRC sec. 1446; Rev. Proc. 89-31; Separate instructions

8814
Parent's Election to Report Child's Interest and Dividends
Used by parents who elect to report the interest and dividends of their child under age 14 on their own tax return. The form is used to figure the amount of the child's income to report on the parent's return and the amount of additional tax that must be added to the parent's tax.
IT-IRC 1(i)(7)

8816
Special Loss Discount Account and Special Estimated Tax Payments for Insurance Companies
Used by insurance companies that elect to take an additional deduction under section 847.
IT-IRC sec. 847

8817
Allocation of Patronage and Nonpatronage Income and Dividends
Used by taxable farmers cooperatives to show income and deductions by patronage and nonpatronage sources.

TD F 90-22.1
Report of Foreign Bank and Financial Accounts
Used by individuals, trusts, partnerships or corporations having a financial interest in, or signature authority or other authority over, bank, securities, or other financial accounts in a foreign country, when the accounts were more than $10,000 in aggregate value at any time during the calendar year.
P.L.91-508; Treasury Regs. (31CFR103)

Free Tax Publications

The Internal Revenue Service publishes many free publications to help you "make your taxes less taxing." The publications listed in this section give general information about taxes for individuals, small businesses, farming, fishing, and recent tax law changes. (Forms and schedules related to the subject matter of each publication are indicated after each listing.) You may want to order one of these publications, and then, if you need more detailed information on any subject, order the specific publication about it.

* IRS Forms and Publications Distribution
Taxpayer Services
Internal Revenue Service
U.S. Department of the Treasury
1111 Constitution Ave., NW, Room 2422
Washington, DC 20224   1 (800) 424-3676
Tax forms and publications can be obtained by calling the toll-free number. To send for forms through the mail, write to the state IRS address listed below. Two copies of each form and one copy of each set of instructions will be sent.

Alabama
P.O. Box 9903
Bloomington, IL 61799

Alaska
Rancho Cordova, CA 95743-0001

Arizona
Rancho Cordova, CA 95743-0001

Arkansas
P.O. Box 9903
Bloomington, IL 61799

California
Rancho Cordova, CA 95743-0001

Colorado
Rancho Cordova, CA 95743-0001

Connecticut
P.O. Box 25866
Richmond, VA 23289

Delaware
P.O. Box 25866
Richmond, VA 23289

District of Columbia
P.O. Box 25866
Richmond, VA 23289

Florida
P.O. Box 25866
Richmond, VA 23289

Georgia
P.O. Box 25866
Richmond, VA 23289

Hawaii
Rancho Cordova, CA 95743-0001

Idaho
Rancho Cordova, CA 95743-0001

Illinois
P.O. Box 9903
Bloomington, IL 61799

Indiana
P.O. Box 9903
Bloomington, IL 61799

Iowa

P.O. Box 9903
Bloomington, IL 61799

Kansas
P.O. Box 9903
Bloomington, IL 61799

Kentucky
P.O. Box 9903
Bloomington, IL 61799

Louisiana
P.O. Box 9903
Bloomington, IL 61799

Maine
P.O. Box 25866
Richmond, VA 23289

Maryland
P.O. Box 25866
Richmond, VA 23289

Massachusetts
P.O. Box 25866
Richmond, VA 23289

Michigan
P.O. Box 9903
Bloomington, IL 61799

Minnesota
P.O. Box 9903
Bloomington, IL 61799

Mississippi
P.O. Box 9903
Bloomington, IL 61799

Missouri
P.O. Box 9903
Bloomington, IL 61799

Montana
Rancho Cordova, CA 95743-0001

Nebraska
P.O. Box 9903
Bloomington, IL 61799

Nevada
Rancho Cordova, CA 95743-0001

New Hampshire
P.O. Box 25866
Richmond, VA 23289

New Jersey
P.O. Box 25866
Richmond, VA 23289

New Mexico
Rancho Cordova, CA 95743-0001

New York
P.O. Box 25866

Richmond, VA 23289

North Carolina
P.O. Box 25866
Richmond, VA 23289

North Dakota
P.O. Box 9903
Bloomington, IL 61799

Ohio
P.O. Box 9903
Bloomington, IL 61799

Oklahoma
P.O. Box 9903
Bloomington, IL 61799

Oregon
Rancho Cordova, CA 95743-0001

Pennsylvania
P.O. Box 25866
Richmond, VA 23289

Puerto Rico
P.O. Box 25866
Richmond, VA 23289

Rhode Island
P.O. Box 25866
Richmond, VA 23289

South Carolina
P.O. Box 25866
Richmond, VA 23289

South Dakota
P.O. Box 9903
Bloomington, IL 61799

Tennessee
P.O. Box 9903
Bloomington, IL 61799

Texas
P.O. Box 9903
Bloomington, IL 61799

Utah
Rancho Cordova, CA 95743-0001

Vermont
P.O. Box 25866
Richmond, VA 23289

Virgin Islands
V.I. Bureau of Internal Revenue
Lockharts Garden No. 1A
Charlotte Amalie
St. Thomas, VI 00802

Virginia
P.O. Box 25866
Richmond, VA 23289

Washington
Rancho Cordova, CA 95743-0001

West Virginia
P.O. Box 25866
Richmond, VA 23289

Wisconsin
P.O. Box 9903
Bloomington, IL 61799

Wyoming
Rancho Cordova, CA 95743-0001

* Foreign Addresses
Forms Distribution Center

P.O. Box 25866
Richmond, VA 23289

Forms Distribution Center
Rancho Cordova, CA 95743-0001
Taxpayers with mailing addresses in foreign countries should send requests or the order blank to whichever address is closer. Send letter requests for other forms and publications to: Forms Distribution Center, P.O. Box 25866, Richmond, VA 23289.

* Free IRS Publications and Forms
The forms and schedules related to the subject matter of each publication are indicated after each listing.

1 Your Rights as a Taxpayer
To ensure that you always receive fair treatment in tax matters, you should know what your rights are. This publication clarifies your rights at each step in the tax process.

1S Derechos del Contribuyente (Your Rights as a Taxpayer)
Spanish version of Publication 1.

2 The ABC's of Income Tax
This publication gives the basic tax rules that can help you prepare your individual tax return. It explains who must file a return, which tax form to use, when the return is due, and other general information. It will help you decide which filing status you qualify for, whether you can claim any dependents, and whether the income you are receiving is taxable. The publication goes on to explain the kinds of expenses you may be able to deduct and the various kinds of credits you may be able to take to reduce your tax.
Forms 1040, 1040A, 1040EZ, Schedules A, B, D, E, R, SE, Forms W-2. 2106. 2119, 2441, and 3903.

3 Tax Information for Military Personnel
This publication gives information about the special tax situations of active members of the Armed Forces. It includes information on items that are includible in and excludable from gross income, alien status, dependency exemptions, sale of residence, itemized deductions, tax liability, and filing returns.
Forms 1040, 1040A, 1040EZ, 1040NR, 1040X, 1310, 2106, 2688, 2848, 3903, 3903F, 4868 and W-2.

4 Student's Guide to Federal Income Tax
This publication explains the federal tax laws that apply to high school and college students. It describes the student's responsibilities to file and pay taxes, how to file, and how to get help.
Forms 1040EZ, W-2 and W-4.

17 Your Federal Income Tax
This publication can help you prepare your individual tax return. It takes you through the individual tax return and explains the tax laws that cover salaries and wages, interest and dividends, rental income, gains and losses, adjustments to income (such as alimony, and IRA contributions,) and itemized deductions.
Forms 1040, 1040A, 1040EZ, Schedules A, B, D, E, R, SE, Forms W-2, 2106, 2119, 2441, 3903.

225 Farmer's Tax Guide
This publication explains the federal tax laws that apply to farming. It gives examples of typical farming situations and discusses the kinds of farm income you must report and the different deductions you can take.
Schedules A, D, F, SE (Form 1040), and Forms 1040, 4136, 4255, 4562, 4684, 4797, 6251.

334 Tax Guide for Small Business
This book explains some federal tax laws that apply to businesses. It describes the four major forms of business organizations: sole proprietorship, partnership, corporation, and S corporation: and explains the tax responsibilities of each.
Schedule C (Form 1040), Schedule K-1 (Form 1065 and 1120S), Forms 1065, 1120, 1120-A, 1120S, 4562.

595 Tax Guide for Commercial Fishermen
This publication will familiarize you with the federal tax laws as they apply to the fishing industry. It is intended for sole proprietors who use Schedule C (Form 1040) to report profit or loss from fishing. This guide does not cover corporations or partnerships.
Schedule C (Form 1040), Forms 1099-MISC, 4562, 4797.

15 Circular E, Employer's Tax Guide
Every employer automatically receives this publication on its revision and every person who applies for an employer identification number receives a copy.
Forms 940, 941, and 941E.

51 Circular A, Agricultural Employer's Tax Guide

Taxes

Form 943.

54 Tax Guide for U.S. Citizens and Resident Aliens Abroad

This publication discusses the tax situations of U.S. citizens and resident aliens who live and work abroad. In particular, it explains the rules for excluding income and excluding or deducting certain housing costs. Answers are provided to questions that taxpayers abroad most often ask.
Forms 2555, 1116, and 1040, Schedule SE (Form 1040).

80 Circular SS, Federal Tax Guide for Employers in the Virgin Islands, Guam, American Samoa, and the Commonwealth of the Northern Mariana Islands

Forms 940, 941SS, and 943.

179 Circular PR, Guia Contributiva Federal Para Patronos Puertorriquenos (Federal Tax Guide for Employers in Puerto Rico)

Forms W-3PR, 940PR, 941PR, 942PR, and 943PR.

349 Federal Highway Use Tax on Heavy Vehicles

This publication explains which trucks, truck-tractors, and buses are subject to the federal use tax on heavy highway motor vehicles, which is one source of funds for the national highway construction program. The tax is due from the person in whose name the vehicle is either registered or required to be registered. The publication tells how to figure and pay the tax due.
Form 2290.

378 Fuel Tax Credits and Refunds

This publication explains the credit or refund allowed for the federal excise taxes paid on certain fuels, and the income tax credit available when alcohol is used as a fuel.
Forms 843, 4136 and 6478.

448 Federal Estate and Gift Taxes

This publication explains federal estate and gift taxes.
Forms 706 and 709.

463 Travel, Entertainment, and Gift Expenses

This publication explains what expenses you may deduct for business-related travel, meals, entertainment, and gifts and it discusses the reporting and recordkeeping requirements for these expenses. The publication also summarizes the deduction and substantiation rules for employees, self-employed persons (including independent contractors), and employers (including corporations and partnerships).
Form 2106.

501 Exemptions, Standard Deduction, and Filing Information

This publication provides answers to some basic tax questions: who must file; what filing status to choose; how many exemptions to claim; and how to figure the amount of the standard deduction. It also covers rules for foster care providers.
Form 2120 and 8332.

502 Medical and Dental Expenses

This publication tells you how to figure your deduction for medical and dental expenses. You may take this deduction only if you itemize your deductions on Schedule A (Form 1040).
Schedule A (Form 1040).

503 Child and Dependent Care Expenses

This publication explains the credit you may be able to take if you pay someone to care for your dependent who is under 13, your disabled dependent, or your disabled spouse. For purposes of the credit, "disabled" refers to a person physically or mentally unable to care for himself or herself.
Schedule 1 (Form 1040A), and Form 2441.

504 Tax Information for Divorced or Separated Individuals

This publication explains tax rules of interest to divorced or separated individuals. It covers filing status, dependency exemptions, and the treatment of alimony and property settlements.

505 Tax Withholding and Estimated Tax

This publication explains the two methods of paying tax under our pay-as-you-go system. They are (1) Withholding. Your employer will withhold income tax from your pay. Tax is also withheld from certain other types of income. You can have more or less withheld, depending on your circumstances. (2) Estimated tax. If you do not pay your tax through withholding, or do not pay enough tax that way, you might have to pay estimated tax.
Forms W-4, W-4P, W-4S, 1040-ES, 2210, and 2210F.

508 Educational Expenses

This publication explains what work-related educational expenses qualify for deduction, how to report your expenses and any reimbursement you receive, and which forms and schedules to use.
Form 2106 and Schedule A (Form 1040).

509 Tax Calendars for 1990

510 Excise Taxes for 1990

This publication covers in detail the various federal excise taxes reported on Form 720. These include the following groupings: environmental taxes; facilities and service taxes on communication and air transportation; fuel taxes; manufacturers taxes; vaccines; and heavy trucks, trailers and tractors. In addition, it briefly describes other excise taxes and tells which forms to use in reporting and paying the taxes.
Forms 720, 8743, and 8807.

513 Tax Information for Visitors to the United States

This publication briefly reviews the general requirements of U.S. income tax laws for foreign visitors. You may have to file a U.S. income tax return during your visit. Most visitors who come to the United States are not allowed to work in this country. Please check with the Immigration and Naturalization Service before you take a job.
Forms 1040C, 1040NR, 2063, and 1040-ES (NR).

514 Foreign Tax Credit for Individuals

This publication may help you if you paid foreign income tax. You may be able to take a foreign tax credit or deduction to avoid the burden of double taxation. The publication explains which foreign taxes qualify and how to figure your credit or deduction.
Form 1116.

515 Withholding of Tax on Nonresident Aliens and Foreign Corporations

This publication provides information for withholding agents who are required to withhold and report tax on payments to nonresident aliens and foreign corporations. Included are three tables listing U.S. tax treaties and some of the treaty provisions that provide for reduction of or exemption from withholding for certain types of income.
Forms 1042 and 1042S, 1001, 4224, 8233, 1078, 8288, 8288-B, 8804, 8805, 8288-A and W-8, 8813, and 8709.

516 Tax Information for U.S. Government Civilian Employees Stationed Abroad

This publication covers the tax treatment of allowances, reimbursements, and business expenses that U.S. government employees, including foreign service employees, are likely to receive or incur.

517 Social Security for Members of the Clergy and Religious Workers

This publication discusses social security coverage and the self-employment tax for the clergy. It also tells you how, as a member of the clergy (minister, member of a religious order, or Christian Science practitioner), you may apply for an exemption from the self-employment tax that would otherwise be due for the services you perform in the exercise of your ministry. Net earnings from self-employment are explained and sample forms are shown.
Form 2106, Form 1040, Schedule SE (Form 1040), and Schedule C (Form 1040).

519 U.S. Tax Guide for Aliens

This comprehensive publication gives guidelines on how to determine your U.S. tax status and figure your U.S. tax.
Forms 1040, 1040C, 1040NR, 2063, and Schedule A (Form 1040).

520 Scholarships and Fellowships

This publication explains the tax laws that apply to U.S. citizens and resident aliens who study, teach or conduct research in the United States or abroad under scholarships and fellowship grants.

521 Moving Expenses

This publication explains how, if you changed job locations last year or started a new job, you may be able to deduct your moving expenses. You may qualify for a deduction whether you are self-employed or an employee. The expenses must be connected with starting work at your new job location. You must meet a distance test and a time test. You also may be able to deduct expenses of moving to the United States if you retire while living and working overseas or if you are a survivor or dependent of a person who died while living and working overseas.
Forms 3903, 3903F, 4782.

523 Tax Information on Selling Your Home

This publication explains how you report gain from selling your home, how you may postpone the tax on part or all of the gain, and how you may exclude part or all of the gain from your gross income if you are 55 or older.
Form 2119.

524 Credit for the Elderly or the Disabled

This publication explains how to figure the credit for the elderly or the disabled. You may be able to claim this credit if you are 65 or older, or if you are retired on disability and were permanently and totally disabled when you retired. Figure the credit on Schedule R (Form 1040), Credit for the Elderly or the Disabled. To take the credit you must file a Form 1040.
Schedule R (Form 1040).

525 Taxable and Nontaxable Income

This publication discusses wages, salaries, fringe benefits, and other compensation received for services as an employee. In addition, it discusses items of miscellaneous taxable income as well as items that are exempt from tax.

526 Charitable Contributions

If you make a charitable contribution or gift to, or for the use of, a qualified organization, you may be able to claim a deduction on your tax return. This publication explains how the deduction is claimed, and the limits that apply.
Schedule A (Form 1040), Form 2106.

527 Residential Rental Property

This publication defines rental income, discusses rental expenses, and explains how to report them on your return. It also discusses casualty losses on rental property, passive activity limits, at-risk rules pertaining to rental property, and the sale of rental property.
Schedule E (Form 1040), and Forms 4562 and 4797.

529 Miscellaneous Deductions

This publication discusses expenses you generally may take as miscellaneous deductions on Schedule A (Form 1040), such as unreimbursed employee expenses and expenses of producing income. It does not discuss other itemized deductions, such as the ones for charitable contributions, moving expenses, interest, taxes, or medical and dental expenses.
Schedule A (Form 1040), Form 2106.

530 Tax Information for Homeowners (Including Owners of Condominiums and Cooperative Apartments)

This publication gives information about home ownership and federal taxes. It explains how to determine basis, how to treat settlement and closing costs, and how to treat repairs and improvements you make. The publication discusses itemized deductions for mortgage interest, real estate taxes, and casualty and theft losses. It also explains the mortgage interest credit.

531 Reporting Income From Tips

This publication gives advice about keeping track of cash and charge tips and explains that all tips received are subject to federal income tax. The publication also explains the rules about the information that employers must report to the Internal Revenue Service about their employees' tip income.
Forms 4070 and 4070A.

533 Self-Employment Tax

This publication explains the self-employment tax, which is a social security tax for people who work for themselves. It is similar to the social security tax withheld from the pay of wage earners.
Schedule SE (Form 1040).

534 Depreciation

This publication discusses the various methods of depreciation, including the modified accelerated cost recovery system (MACRS).
Form 4562.

535 Business Expenses

This publication discusses business expenses such as: fringe benefits; rent; interest; taxes; insurance; and employee benefit plans. It also outlines the choice to capitalize certain business expenses; discusses amortization and depletion; covers some business expenses that may be deductible in some circumstances and not deductible in others; and points out some expenses that are not deductible.

536 Net Operating Losses

537 Installment Sales

This publication discusses sales arrangements that provide for part or all of the selling price to be paid in a later year. These arrangements are "installment sales." If you finance the buyer's purchase of your property, instead of having the buyer get a loan or mortgage from a bank, you probably have an installment sale.
Form 6252.

538 Accounting Periods and Methods

This publication explains which accounting periods and methods can be used for figuring federal taxes, and how to apply for approval to change from one period or method to another. Most individual taxpayers use the calendar year for their accounting period and the cash method of accounting.
Forms 1128 and 3115.

541 Tax Information on Partnerships

Forms 1065 and Schedules D, K, and K-1 (Form 1065).

542 Tax Information on Corporations

Forms 1120 and 1120-A

544 Sales and Other Dispositions of Assets

This publication explains how to figure gain and loss on various transactions, such as trading or selling an asset used in a trade or business, and it explains the tax results of different types of gains and losses. Not all transactions result in taxable gains or deductible losses, and not all gains are taxed the same way.
Schedule D (Form 1040) and Form 4797.

545 Interest Expense

This publication explains what items may and may not be deducted as interest. (Interest is an amount paid for the use of borrowed money.) This publication also explains how much interest you may deduct and how to figure this amount. Where you deduct interest expense depends on why you borrowed the money.
Schedule A (Form 1040).

547 Nonbusiness Disasters, Casualties, and Thefts

This publication explains when you can deduct a disaster, casualty, or theft loss. Casualties are events such as hurricanes, earthquakes, tornadoes, fire, floods, vandalism, loss of deposits in a bankrupt or insolvent financial institution, and car accidents. The publication also explains how to treat the reimbursement you receive from insurance or other sources.
Form 4684.

549 Condemnations and Business Casualties and Thefts

This publication will help you figure your gain or loss if you have property that is condemned, or if you are forced to sell your property under threat of condemnation. Condemnation is the process by which private property is legally taken, for public use, in exchange for money or property, by the federal government, a state government, or a political subdivision. The publication also explains the deduction for casualties and thefts to business property. Casualties are events such as hurricanes, earthquakes, tornadoes, fires, floods, vandalism, and car accidents.
Forms 4797 and 4684.

550 Investment Income and Expenses

This publication explains which types of investment income are and are not taxable, when the income is taxed, and how to report it on your tax return. The publication discusses the treatment of tax shelters and investment-related expenses. The publication also explains how to figure your gain and loss when you sell or trade your investment property.
Forms 1099-INT and 1099-DIV, Schedules B and D (Form 1040).

551 Basis of Assets

This publication explains how to determine the basis of property. The basis of property you buy is usually its cost. If you received property in some other way, such as by gift or inheritance, you normally must use a basis other than cost.

552 Recordkeeping for Individuals

This publication can help you decide what records to keep and how long to keep them for tax purposes. These records will help you prepare your income tax returns so that you will pay only your correct tax. If you keep a record of your expenses during the year, you may find that you can reduce your taxes by itemizing your deductions. Deductible expenses include medical and dental bills, interest, contributions, and taxes.

553 Highlights of 1989 Tax Changes

This publication discusses the more important changes in the tax rules brought about by recent legislation, rulings, and administrative decisions. It does not discuss all new tax rules or detail all changes. It highlights the important recent changes that taxpayers should know about when filing their 1989 tax forms and when planning for 1990.

554 Tax Information for Older Americans

This publication gives tax information of special interest to older Americans. An example takes you through completing a tax return and explains such items as the sale of a home, the credit for the elderly or the disabled, the supplemental Medicare premium, and pension and annuity income. The publication includes filled-in forms and schedules that show how these and other items are reported.
Schedules B, D, and R (Form 1040), and Forms 1040 and 2119.

555 Community Property and the Federal Income Tax

This publication may help married taxpayers who are domiciled in one of the following community property states: Arizona, California, Idaho, Louisiana, Nevada, New Mexico, Texas, Washington or Wisconsin. If you wish to file a separate tax return, you should understand how community property laws affect the way you figure your tax before completing your federal income tax return.

Taxes

556 Examination of Returns, Appeal Rights, and Claims for Refund

This publication may be helpful if your return is examined by the Internal Revenue Service. It explains that returns are normally examined to verify the correctness of reported income, exemptions, or deductions, and it describes what appeal rights you have if you disagree with the results of the examination.

This publication also explains the procedures for the examination of items of partnership income, deduction, gain, loss, and credit. Information is given on how to file a claim for refund, the time for filing a claim for refund, and any limit on the amount of refund.

Forms 1040X and 1120X

556S Revision de las Declaraciones de Impuesto, Derecho de Apelacion y Reclamaciones de Reembolsos (Examination of Returns, Appeal Rights, and Claims for Refund)

(Spanish version of Publication 556)

Forms 1040X and 1120X

557 Tax-Exempt Status for Your Organization

This publication discusses how organizations become recognized as exempt from federal income tax under section 501(a) of the Internal Revenue Code. (These include organizations described in Code section 501(c).) The publication explains how to get a ruling or determination letter recognizing the exemption, and it gives other information that applies generally to all exempt organizations.

Forms 990, 990PF, 1023, and 1024.

559 Tax Information for Survivors, Executors, and Administrators

This publication can help you report and pay the proper federal income and estate taxes if you are responsible for settling a decedent's estate. The publication also answers many questions that a spouse or other survivor faces when a person dies.

Form 1040, Form 1041, Form 706, and Form 4810.

560 Self-Employed Retirement Plans

This publication discusses retirement plans for self-employed persons and certain partners in partnerships. These retirement plans are sometimes called Keogh plans or HR-10 plans.

561 Determining the Value of Donated Property

This publication can help donors and appraisers determine the value of property (other than cash) that is given to qualified organizations. It explains what kind of information you need to support a charitable deduction you claim on your return.

Form 8283.

564 Mutual Fund Distributions

This publication discusses the federal income tax treatment of distributions paid or allocated to you as an individual shareholder of a mutual fund. A comprehensive example shows distributions made by a mutual fund and an illustration of Form 1040.

Forms 1040, Schedule B (Form 1040), and Form 1099-DIV.

570 Tax Guide for Individuals in U.S. Possessions

This publication is for individuals with income from American Samoa, Guam, the Commonwealth of the Northern Mariana Islands, Puerto Rico, and the U.S. Virgin Islands.

Forms 4563, 5074, and 8689.

571 Tax-Sheltered Annuity Programs for Employees of Public Schools and Certain Tax-Exempt Organizations

This publication explains the rules concerning employers qualified to buy tax-sheltered annuities, eligible employees who may participate in the program, and the amounts that may be excluded from income.

Form 5330.

572 General Business Credit

This publication explains the general business credit which includes the investment credit, the low-income housing credit, the jobs credit, and the research credit. It also describes transition property qualifying for the investment credit, which was repealed for most property placed in service after 1985.

Forms 3800, 4255, and 5884.

575 Pension and Annuity Income (Including Simplified General Rule)

This publication explains how to report pension and annuity income on your federal income tax return. It also explains the special tax treatment for lump-sum distributions from pension, stock bonus, or profit-sharing plans.

Forms 1040, 1099-R and 4972.

578 Tax Information for Private Foundations and Foundation Managers

This publication covers tax matters of interest to private foundations and their managers, including the tax classification of the foundations, filing requirements, the tax on net investment income, and various excise taxes on transactions that violate the foundation rules.

Form 990-F

579S Como Preparar la Declaracion de Impuesto Federal (How to Prepare the Federal Income Tax Return)

Forms 1040, 1040A, 1040EZ.

583 Taxpayers Starting a Business

This publication shows sample records that a small business can use if it operates as a sole proprietorship. Records like these will help you prepare complete and accurate tax returns and make sure you pay only the tax you owe. This publication also discusses the taxpayer identification number businesses must use, information returns businesses may have to file, and the kinds of business taxes businesses may have to pay.

Schedule C (Form 1040), and Form 4562.

584 Nonbusiness Disaster, Casualty, and Theft Loss Workbook

This workbook can help you to figure your loss from a disaster, casualty or theft. It will help you most if you list your possessions before any losses occur. The workbook has schedules to help you figure the loss on your home and its contents. There is also a schedule to help you figure the loss on your car, truck, or motorcycle.

586A The Collection Process (Income Tax Accounts)

This publication explains your rights and duties as a taxpayer who owes tax. It also explains the legal obligation of the Internal Revenue Service to collect overdue taxes, and the way we fulfill this obligation. It is not intended to be a precise and technical analysis of the law in this area.

586S Proceso de cobro (Deudas del impuesto sobre ingreso)

(Spanish version of Publication 586A)

587 Business Use of Your Home

This publication can help you decide if you qualify to deduct certain expenses for using part of your home in your business. You must meet specific tests and your deduction is limited. Deductions for the business use of a home computer are also discussed.

Schedule C (Form 1040), and Form 4562.

588 Tax Information for Homeowners Associations

This publication gives tax information for homeowners associations. There are discussions about what associations can elect to be tax-exempt homeowners associations, how to make the election, and what tax obligations there are for organizations that are not exempt. There is also an example with a filled-in return for homeowners associations.

Form 1120-H

589 Tax Information on S Corporations

This publication discusses the way corporations are taxed under subchapter S of the Internal Revenue Code. In general, an "S" corporation does not pay tax on its income. Instead, it passes through its income and expenses to its shareholders, who then report them on their own tax returns.

Forms 1120S and Schedule K-1 (Form 1120S)

590 Individual Retirement Arrangements (IRAs)

This publication explains the rules for and the tax benefits of having an individual retirement arrangement (IRA). An IRA is a savings plan that lets you set aside money for your retirement. Generally, your contributions to an IRA are tax deductible in part or in full and the earnings in your IRA are not taxed until they are distributed to you.

Forms 1040, 5329 and 8606.

593 Tax Highlights for U.S. Citizens and Residents Going Abroad

This publication briefly reviews various U.S. tax provisions that apply to U.S. citizens or resident aliens who live or work abroad and expect to receive income from foreign sources.

594 The Collection Process (Employment Tax Accounts)

This booklet explains your rights and duties as a taxpayer who owes employer's quarterly federal taxes. It also explains how we fulfill the legal obligation of the Internal Revenue Service to collect these taxes. It is not intended as a precise and technical analysis of the law.

594S Proceso de cobro (Deudas del impuesto por razon del empleo)

(Spanish version of Publication 594.)

596 Earned Income Credit

This publication discusses who may receive the earned income credit, and how to figure and claim the credit. It also discusses how to receive advance payments of the earned income credit.
Forms W-5, 1040, and 1040A.

597 Information on the United States-Canada Income Tax Treaty

This publication reproduces the entire text of the U.S.-Canada income tax treaty, and also gives an explanation of provisions that often apply to U.S. citizens or residents who have Canadian source income. There is also a discussion that deals with certain tax problems that may be encountered by Canadian residents who temporarily work in the United States.

598 Tax on Unrelated Business Income of Exempt Organizations

This publication explains the unrelated business income tax provisions that apply to most tax-exempt organizations. An organization that regularly operates a trade or business that is not substantially related to its exempt purpose may be taxed on the income from this business. Generally, a tax-exempt organization with gross income of $1,000 or more from an unrelated trade or business must file a return.
Form 990-T.

686 Certification for Reduced Tax Rates in Tax Treaty Countries

This publication explains how U.S. citizens, residents, and domestic corporations may certify to a foreign treaty country that they are entitled to treaty benefits.

721 Tax Guide to U.S. Civil Service Retirement Benefits

This publication explains how the federal income tax rules apply to the benefits that retired federal employees or their survivors receive under the U.S. Civil Service Retirement System or Federal Employees Retirement System. There is also information on estate taxes.
Form 1040.

850 English-Spanish Glossary of Words and Phrases Used in Publications Issued by the Internal Revenue Service

901 U.S. Tax Treaties

This publication includes information about the reduced tax rates and exemptions from U.S. taxes provided under U.S. tax treaties with other countries. This publication is intended for residents of those countries who receive income from U.S. sources. Information for foreign workers and students is emphasized.
Form 1040NR

904 Interrelated Computations for Estate and Gift Taxes

Forms 706 and 709.

907 Tax Information for Handicapped and Disabled Individuals

This publication explains tax rules of interest to handicapped and disabled people and to taxpayers with disabled dependents. For example, you may be able to take a tax credit for certain disability payments, you may be able to deduct medical expenses, and you may be able to take a credit for expenses of care for disabled dependents.
Schedule A (Form 1040), Schedule R (1040), and Form 2441.

908 Bankruptcy and Other Debt Cancellation

This publication explains the income tax aspects of bankruptcy and discharge of debt for individuals and small businesses.
Forms 982, 1040, 1041, 1120.

909 Alternative Minimum Tax for Individuals

This publication discusses the alternative minimum tax, which applies to individuals.
Forms 6251, 8801, and 8803.

911 Tax Information for Direct Sellers

This publication may help you if you are a "direct seller," a person who sells consumer products to others on a person-to-person basis. Many direct sellers sell door-to-door, at sales parties, or by appointment in someone's home. Information on figuring your income from direct sales as well as the kinds of expenses you may be entitled to deduct is also provided.
Schedules C and SE (Form 1040).

915 Social Security Benefits and Equivalent Railroad Retirement Benefits

This publication explains when you have to include part of your social security or equivalent railroad retirement benefits in income on Form 1040. It also explains how to figure the amount to include.
Forms SSA-1099 and RRB-1099, Social Security Benefits Worksheet, Notice 703, Forms SSA-1042S and RRB-1042S.

917 Business Use of a Car

This publication explains the expenses that you may deduct for the business use of your car. Car expenses that are deductible do not include the cost of commuting expenses (driving from your home to your workplace). The publication also discusses the taxability of the use of a car provided by an employer and rules on leasing a car for business.
Form 2106

919 Is My Withholding Correct for 1990?

To help employees check their withholding, this publication has worksheets that will help them estimate both their 1990 tax and their total 1990 withholding. The employees can then compare the two amounts. The publication tells employees what to do if too much or too little tax is being withheld.
Form W-4.

924 Reporting of Real Estate Transactions to IRS

This publication informs sellers of certain real estate about the information they must provide to the real estate reporting person in order that the reporting person can complete the Form 1099-S that must be filed with the IRS.

925 Passive Activity and At-Risk Rules

This publication covers the rules that limit passive activity losses and credits and the at-risk limits.
Form 8582.

926 Employment Taxes for Household Employers

This publication shows how a household employer reports federal income tax withholding, social security (FICA), and unemployment taxes (FUTA). You may be a household employer if you have a babysitter, maid, or other employee who works in your house. The publication also shows what records you must keep.
Forms W-2, W-3, 940, 940EZ, and 942.

929 Tax Rules for Children and Dependents

This publication describes the tax law affecting certain children and dependents. No personal exemption is allowed to a taxpayer who can be claimed as a dependent by another taxpayer. The standard deduction for dependents may be limited. Minor children may have to pay tax at their parent's tax rate.
Form 8615, Form 8814, and Form 8803.

936 Limits on Home Mortgage Interest Deduction

This publication covers the rules governing the deduction of home mortgage interest if your acquisition cost exceeds $1 million ($500,000 if you are married filing separately) or your home equity debt exceeds $100,000 ($50,000 if you are married filing separately). Worksheets are provided to determine what interest expenses qualify as home mortgage interest.

937 Business Reporting

The first part of this publication explains your responsibilities, if you have employees, to withhold federal income taxes and social security taxes (FICA) from their wages, and to pay social security taxes and federal unemployment taxes (FUTA). It also discusses the rules for advance payment of the earned income credit, and for reporting and allocating tips.
The second part provides general information about the rules for reporting payments to nonemployees and transactions with other persons. It also provides information on taxpayer identification numbers, backup withholding, and penalties relating to information returns.
Forms W-2, W-2G, W-4, 940, 941, 1098, 1099 series, 4789, 5498, 8300, and 8308.

938 Real Estate Mortgage Investment Conduits (REMICS) Reporting Information (And Other Collateralized Debt Obligations (CDOs))

This new publication discusses reporting requirements for issuers of real estate mortgage investment conduits (REMICS) and collateralized debt obligations (CDOs). This publication also contains a directory of REMICS and CDOs to assist brokers and middlemen in fulfilling reporting requirements.

939 Pension General Rule (Nonsimplified Method)

This publication covers the nonsimplified General Rule for the taxation of pensions or annuities, which must be used if the Simplified General Rule is not applicable or is not chosen. For example, the nonsimplified method must be used for payments under commercial annuities. The publication also contains the necessary actuarial tables for this method.

1004 Identification Numbers Under ERISA

1045 Information for Tax Practitioners

1048 Filing Requirements for Employee Benefit Plans

Forms 5500, 5500-C/R, 5500-R, and 5500EZ.

1212 List of Original Discount Instruments

This publication explains the tax treatment of original issue discount (OID). It describes how (1) Brokers and other middlemen, who may hold the debt instruments as nominees for the owners, should report OID to IRS and to the owners on Forms 1099-OID or 1099-INT, and (2) Owners of OID debt instruments should report OID on their income tax returns. The publication gives rules for figuring the discount amount to report each year, if required. It also gives tables showing OID amounts for certain publicly-traded OID debt instruments, including short-term U.S. Government securities.

Schedule B (Form 1040) and Forms 1099-OID and 1099-INT.

1244 Employee's Daily Record of Tips (Form 4070-A) and Employee's Report of Tips to Employer (Form 4070)

This publication explains how you must report tips if you are an employee who receives tips. Copies of the monthly tip report you must give your employer are included, as well as a daily list you can use for your own records.

Forms 4070 and 4070-A.

State Tax Assistance

These state taxpayer service departments are the basic starting place for free assistance and guidance pertaining to your state taxes.

Alabama

Taxpayer Assistance
Alabama Income Tax Division
P.O. Box 327465
Montgomery, AL 36132-7465
(205) 242-1000

Alaska   (No individual income tax; corporation tax only)

Alaska Department of Revenue
Income and Excise Audit Division
Attn: Corporations Unit
P.O. Box SA
Juneau, AK 99801
(907) 465-2370

Arizona

Personal Income Tax
Arizona Department of Revenue
P.O. Box 29002
Phoenix, AZ 85038

Corporation Tax
Arizona Department of Revenue
P.O. Box 29079
Phoenix, AZ 85038

(602) 255-3381 (Information and fewer than 6 forms)
(602) 542-4260 (6 or more forms)

Arkansas

Arkansas Department of Finance Administration
Attn: Income Tax
P.O. Box 3628
Little Rock, AR 72203
(501) 682-7250 General Information
(501) 682-7280 Refund Information
(501) 682-7255 Forms

California

Personal
Franchise Tax Board
P.O. Box 942840
Sacramento, CA 942857-0000

Corporate
Franchise Tax Board
P.O. Box 942857
Sacramento, CA 94257-0500

(916) 369-0500

Colorado

Taxpayer Services
Department of Revenue
1375 Sherman Street
Denver, CO 80261

(303) 534-1209 (Personal)
(303) 534-1209 (Corporate)

Connecticut

Department of Revenue Services
92 Farmington Avenue
Hartford, CT 06105

(800) 321-7829 (Information and Forms)
(203) 566-8520 (Information)
(203) 297-5773 (Forms)

Delaware

Delaware Division of Revenue
820 North French Street
Wilmington, DE 19899

(800) 292-7826
(302) 571-3302

Florida

Florida Taxpayer Assistance
P.O. Box 5139
Tallahassee, FL 32314-5139

(800) 872-9909
(904) 488-6800
(904) 488-8422 (Bulk form orders)

Georgia

Income Tax Division
P.O. Box 38007
Atlanta, GA 30334

(404) 656-4071 (Personal)
(404) 656-4165 (Corporate)

Hawaii

Taxpayer Services Branch
Hawaii State Tax Collector
P.O. Box 259
Honolulu, HA 96809-02559

(800) 222-3229 (Information
(800) 222-7572 (Forms)
(808) 548-4242

Idaho

Idaho Department of Revenue and Taxation
P.O. Box 36
Boise, ID 83722

(208) 334-7660

Illinois

Illinois Department of Revenue
P.O. Box 19015
Springfield, IL 62794-9015

(800) 732-8866 (Information all year, Forms July - December)
(800) 624-2449 (Forms January - June)
(217) 782-3336

Indiana

Indiana Department of Revenue
Taxpayer Services Division
Room 104-B
100 North Senate Street
Indianapolis, IN 46204
(317) 232-2240

Iowa

Iowa Department of Revenue and Finance
Hoover State Office Building
Des Moines, IA 50319

(515) 218-3114 (Information and forms)
(515) 281-5370 (Bulk form orders)

Taxes

Kansas

Kansas Department of Revenue
Box 12001
Topeka, KS 66612-2001

(913) 296-3051 (Personal)
(913) 296-1711 (Business)

Kentucky

Kentucky Revenue Cabinet
Frankfort, KY 40618

(502) 564-4580 (Information)
(502) 564-3658 (Forms)

Louisiana

Louisiana Department of Revenue
and Taxation
P.O. Box 201
Baton Rouge, LA 70821

(504) 925-4611 (Information)
(504) 925-7352 (Forms)
(504) 925-4611 (Refund information)

Maine

State of Maine
Department of Taxation
Station 24
Augusta, ME 04333

(800) 452-1983 (Information)
(800) 338-5811 (Forms)
(207) 289-3695

Maryland

Comptroller of the Treasury
Income Tax Information
301 W. Preston St.
Baltimore, MD 21201

301-225-1995

Massachusetts

Massachusetts Department of Revenue
100 Cambridge Street
Boston, MA 02204
Attention: Correspondence Unit

(617) 727-4545

Michigan

Department of Treasury
430 West Allegan Street
Lansing, MI 48922

(800) 877-MICH (Information)
(517) 373-2910 (Information)
(517) 373-3386 (Information)
(800) FORM-2-ME (Forms)
(517) 373-6598 (Forms)
(517) 335-1144 (Forms)

Minnesota

Minnesota Taxpayer Assistance
10 River Park Plaza
St. Paul, MN 55146

(800) 652-9094 (Personal)
(612) 296-3781 (Personal)
(800) 657-3777 (Corporate)
(612) 296-6181 (corporate)

Mississippi

Mississippi State Tax Commission
P.O. Box 1033
Jackson, MS 39215
(601) 359-1141

Missouri

Taxpayer Assistance
Missouri Department of Revenue
P.O. Box 2200

Jefferson City, MO 65105-2200

(314) 751-3503 (Information)
(314) 751-5337 (Forms)

Montana

Montana Department of Revenue
Income Tax Division
P.O. Box 5803
Helena, MT 59604

(404) 444-2837 (Personal)
(404) 444-3388 (Corporate)

Nebraska

Nebraska Department of Revenue
Taxpayer Assistance
P.O. Box 94818
Lincoln, NE 68509

(800) 422-4618 (Personal Income Tax information, in season)
(402) 471-5729 (Personal Information, all year)
(800) 742-7474 (Corporate Information, all year)

Nevada

No Income Tax

New Hampshire

No Income Tax

New Jersey

New Jersey Division of Taxation
50 Barrack Street
CN 269
Trenton, NJ 08646

(800) 323-4400
(609) 292-6400

New Mexico

New Mexico Taxation and Revenue
P.O. Box 630
Santa Fe, NM 87509-0630
(505) 827-0700

New York

New York State Department of Taxation and Finance
Taxpayer Assistance Bureau
W. A. Harriman Campus
Albany, NY 12227

(800) 225-5829 (General Information)
(800) 443-3200 (Refund Information)
(800) 462-8100 (Forms)
(518) 438-6777 (All)

North Carolina

Information:
North Carolina Department of Revenue
P.O. Box 25000
Raleigh, NC 27640

Refund Information:
North Carolina Department of
Revenue
P.O. Box R
Raleigh, NC 27634

(800) 222-9965 (Information)
(800) 451-1404 (Forms)
(919) 733-4682 (All)

North Dakota

Office of State Tax Commissioner
600 East Boulevard Avenue
Bismarck, ND 58505-0599
(701) 224-3450

Ohio

Taxpayer Services
Ohio Department of Taxation
P.O. Box 2476

Columbus, Ohio 43266-0076
(800) 282-1780
(614) 846-6712

Oklahoma

Oklahoma Tax Commission
2501 Lincoln Boulevard
Oklahoma City, OK 73194

(800) 522-8165
(405) 521-3125

Oregon

Oregon Department of Revenue
Tax Help Section
955 Center Street, NE
Salem, OR 97310
(503) 371-2244

Pennsylvania

Personal:
Pennsylvania Department of Revenue
Taxpayer Services
Department 280101
Harrisburg, PA 17128-0101
(717) 787-8201

Corporate:
Pennsylvania Department of Revenue
Business Trust Fund Taxes
Department 280904
Harrisburg, PA 17128-0904
(717) 787-2416

Rhode Island

Rhode Island Division of Taxation
1 Capitol Hill
Providence, RI 02908

(401) 277-2905 (Information)
(401) 277-3934 (Forms)

South Carolina

South Carolina Department of Revenue
P.O. Box 125
Columbia, SC 29214

(803) 737-4709 (Information)
(803) 737-5080 (Forms)

South Dakota

No Income Tax

Tennessee

Tennessee Taxpayer Services
504 Andrew Jackson Building
Nashville, TN 37242

(615) 741-3581 (Information)
(615) 741-2481 (Forms)

Texas

No Income Tax

Utah

Utah State Tax Commission
160 East 3rd South
Salt Lake City, UT 84134
(801) 530-4848

Vermont

Personal:
Vermont Department of Taxes
Pavillion Office Building
Montpelier, VT 05602
(802) 828-2865

Corporate:
Vermont Department of Taxes
P.O. Box 547
Montpelier, VT 05602
(802) 828-2865

Virginia

Virginia Department of Taxation
P.O. Box 6L
Richmond, VA 23282

(804) 367-8031 (Personal)
(804) 367-8038 (Corporate)
(804) 367-8055 (Forms)

Washington

No Income Tax

West Virginia

West Virginia Department of Revenue
P.O. Box 3784
Charleston, WV 25337-3784

(800) 642-9016
(304) 348-3333

Wisconsin

Taxpayer Services
Wisconsin Department of Revenue
P.O. Box 8906
Madison, WI 53708

(608) 266-2486 (Personal, information and forms)
(608) 266-2772 (Corporate, information and forms)
(608) 267-2025 (Bulk form orders)

Wyoming

No Income Tax

Health and Medicine
Clearinghouses and Starting Points

* See also Experts Chapter
* See also Drugs and Chemical Dependence Chapter
* See also Careers and Workplace Chapter
* See also Economics, Demographics, and Statistics Chapter
* See also Environment and Nature Chapter
* See also Consumer Power Chapter

Unlike any other chapter in this book, you will discover one information clearinghouse after another. Some of these national resource centers provide telephone help on many concerns, for example, the Family Life Information Exchange and Project Share. Other offices like the Diabetic Information Clearinghouse have a more concentrated focus. The Public Health Service of the U.S. Department of Health and Human Services is the primary arm of the federal government which disseminates information about promoting health and preventing disease. It sponsors the National Health Information Center which is accessible by a toll-free number. The Center will answer questions, send out medical journal abstracts, fact sheets and other materials, and refer callers to more specialized clearinghouses, government offices, city and county health departments, national associations, health advocacy groups, private organizations and foundations that focus on your health concern. Other government agencies including the U.S. Department of Agriculture, the U.S. Environmental Protection Agency, and the Food and Drug Administration also serve both as watchdogs and information providers on the safety of pharmaceuticals, drinking water, hazardous wastes, and food inspection.

Suppose your doctor has recommended a CAT scan or you've just gotten worrisome lab test results, start by calling the National Health Information Center which can refer you to numerous organizations and one of the National Institutes of Health specializing in this type of health problem. Do you have an appointment with a surgeon in a few weeks and want to be prepared to discuss the pros and cons of the operation? Look through this section for published resources, databases, medical libraries, and information clearinghouses that will give you powerful research tools. But don't stop there. Consider contacting those universities and research centers identified in both the Medical Research section as well as the Careers and Workplace Chapter, specifically the section titled Research Grants in Any Field, to learn about new experimental medical procedures, tests, and treatments. And don't forget the hundreds of medical specialists whose phone numbers are listed in the Experts Chapter.

* Access to All Medical and Scientific Studies

National Library of Medicine
8600 Rockville Pike
Bethesda, MD 20894   (301) 496-6095

The National Library of Medicine (NLM) is the world's largest research library in a single scientific and professional field. The collection today stands at 4 million books, journals, technical reports, manuscripts, microfilms, and pictorial materials. The Library may be used by health professionals and health science students, and books and journals may also be requested on interlibrary loan (fee for loan transactions). The Library's computer-based Medical Literature Analysis and Retrieval System (MEDLARS) has bibliographic access to NLM's vast store of biomedical information. All of the MEDLARS databases are available through NLM's online network of more than 20,000 institutions and individuals. NLM charges a user fee for access to the system. The Regional Medical Library Program is intended to provide health science practitioners, investigators, and educators convenient access to health care and biomedical information resources. The Regional Libraries provide reference service, referral service, and online access to MEDLARS.

* AIDS National Information Clearinghouse

National AIDS Information Clearinghouse
P.O. Box 6003
Rockville, MD 20850   (301) 762-5111 (800) 458-5231 (bulk orders)

A Centers for Disease Control service, this clearinghouse has publications, posters, and videos dealing with AIDS which are free of charge. The publications include a fact sheet, guidelines for the prevention of the spread of AIDS in schools and the workplace, and the Surgeon General's report on AIDS. They have two online databases; one dealing with organization, and the other lists unpublished educational materials (no journals).

* Alcohol and Drug Information Center

National Clearinghouse for Alcohol and Drug Information
P.O. Box 2345
Rockville, MD 20852   (301) 468-2600

This clearinghouse makes referrals to local AA chapters and other self-help organizations as well as national associations as well as providing callers with materials about preventing or curing substance abuse.

* Almanac to National Institutes of Health

Division of Public Information
National Institutes of Health
Building 31, Room 2B03
Bethesda, MD 20892   (301) 496-4143

Published annually, the NIH Almanac presents pertinent facts about the National Institutes of Health. All the various institutes are listed, including information about their respective research and staffs. Historical data about NIH, as well as tables describing appropriations, staff and facilities, are also included. Information regarding lectures, Nobel Laureates, and the field units can also be found in this free sourcebook.

* America's Health Advisor: Surgeon General

Surgeon General
200 Independence Ave., SW
Room 716-G
Washington, DC 20201   (202) 245-6867

The Surgeon General provides leadership and direction for the Public Health Service Commissioned Corps. He serves as principal federal health advisor to the nation on public health matters and serves as the focal point for dialogue with professional societies, representing PHS at national and international meetings. The Surgeon General releases many reports such as Smoking and Health and Healthy People, and issues warnings to the public on health hazards. The Surgeon General also reviews plans for transportation, open testing, and disposal of lethal chemicals and biological agents.

* Arthritis Clearinghouse

National Arthritis and Musculoskeletal and Skin Diseases
Box AMS

Bethesda, MD 20892   (301) 468-3235
This clearinghouse responds to requests for information on arthritis, and musculoskeletal and skin diseases from health professionals and the general public. AMS uses the online database CHID (Combined Health Information Database) from which they can reference health information. Their bulletin, *MEMO*, published on an as-needed basis, contains current topics of interest. They can provide you with many brochures, reports, and other publications, along with a free publications listing.

* Cancer Hotline

Cancer Information Service
National Cancer Institute
Building 31, Room 10A18   (800) 4-CANCER   (800) 638-6070 Alaska
9000 Rockville Pike   (800) 524-1234 Hawaii
Bethesda, MD 20892   (301) 427-8656 Maryland
The Cancer Information Service assists cancer patients, families, and medical personnel on all aspects of cancer. They have information on treatment, rehab, and detection, as well as on financial assistance. Through their databases (see Automated Information Systems-Cancer), they have access to current research and physician referrals. Pamphlets, reports, and assistance in locating community resources is also available.

* Cancer Information Regional Offices

Cancer Information Service
National Cancer Institute
Building 31, Room 10A2A   (800) 4-CANCER
9000 Rockville Pike   (800) 524-1234 in Oahu, HI
Bethesda, MD 20892   (800) 638-6070 in AK
The National Cancer Institute has set up offices across the U.S. through which they route the Cancer Information Service calls for those particular areas. These offices offer the same services as the Cancer Information Service (see above). Contact this office for a list of offices and more information.

* Child Health and Development

Office of Research Reporting
National Institute of Child Health and Human Development
Building 31, Room 2A-32
9000 Rockville Pike
Bethesda, MD 20892   (301) 496-5133
This Institute disseminates information on fetal, maternal and child development, as well as materials on reproductive biology, contraception, mental retardation, and a host of other related fields.

* Child, Spouse, and Elder Abuse Clearinghouse

Clearinghouse on Family Violence Information
P.O. Box 1182
Washington, DC 20013   (703) 821-2086
This clearinghouse has information on spouse and elder abuse including brochures, audiovisual materials, and an in-house database from which they can retrieve reference materials and organizations involved with family violence.

* Communicative and Learning Disabilities

Office of Deafness and Communicative Disorders
Rehabilitation Services Administration
330 C St., SW, Room 3033
Washington, DC 20201   (202) 732-1401   (202) 732-1298 TDD
This office promotes improved and expanded rehabilitation services for deaf, hard of hearing, speech impaired, and language disordered individuals. As the liaison to national organizations and agencies concerned with deafness and communicative disorders, this office provides the following services: 1) they develop policies and standards for state rehabilitation agencies' work with these clients; 2) they review services to these clients by the agencies; and 3) they provide technical assistance to Rehabilitation Services Administration staff.

* Consumer Affairs Center

Director of Information
Office of Consumer Affairs
Department of Health and Human Services
Washington, DC 20201   (202) 634-4140
This bureau coordinates new consumer programs, promotes improved consumer education, and serves as the catalyst for new laws and regulations protecting the interests of American health care consumers. It publishes a useful catalog titled *Consumer's Resource Handbook* which is available free from the Consumer Information Center, P.O. Box 100, Dept. 635H, Pueblo, CO 81009.

* Deafness Resource Center

National Institute on Deafness and
    Other Communicative Disorders

NIH, Building 31, Room 1B62,
9000 Rockville Pike
Bethesda, MD 20892   (301) 496-7243
This--the newest Institute at NIH--funds intramural and extramural research on deafness and communicative disorders. Brochures and reports are available for professionals and the general public, covering a wide range of related topics.

* Diabetes Information Clearinghouse

National Diabetes Information Clearinghouse
Box NDIC
Bethesda, MD 20892   (301) 468-2162
NDIC responds to requests for information about diabetes and its complications and distributes information appropriate to health professionals, people with diabetes and their families, and the general public. They have many publications and bibliographies, as well as *Diabetes Dateline*, a free quarterly current awareness newsletter that features news about diabetes research, upcoming meetings and events, and new publications. NDIC uses the online database CHID (Combined Health Information Database) from which they can reference health information. Contact this office for a free listing of their publications or further information.

* Digestive Diseases Information Clearinghouse

National Digestive Diseases Information Clearinghouse
Box NDDIC
Bethesda, MD 20892   (301) 468-6344
NDDIC responds to requests for information about digestive diseases and distributes information to health professionals, people with digestive diseases, and the general public. They have many publications, as well as a news bulletin. NDDIC uses the online database CHID (Combined Health Information Database) from which they can access health information and organizations. Contact this office for a free listing of publications.

* Eye and Vision Clearinghouse

National Institute of Health
Building 31, Room 6A32
9000 Rockville Pike
Bethesda, MD 20892   (301) 496-5248
NEI conducts, fosters and supports basic and applied research, including clinical trials, related to the cause, natural history, prevention, diagnosis, and treatment of disorders of the eye and visual system. Several brochures and reports are available for the general public and health professionals on a wide variety of related topics.

* Family Information Center

Family Information Center
Department of Agriculture
National Agricultural Library Building, Room 304
Beltsville, MD 20705   (301) 344-3719
This center offers expertise and materials beyond home economics with a focus on family adjustment to change and the management of stress, family and individual adjustment to midlife, and the aging process.

* Food Additives, RX and Medical Devices Consumer Info

Office of Public Affairs
Food and Drug Administration
5600 Fishers Lane, HFE88
Rockville, MD 20857   (301) 443-3170
The FDA distributes many brochures and publications which cover a variety of topics, such as cosmetics, drugs, and foods. This office will gladly send you publications on topics that interest you. The *FDA Consumer*, which contains the latest developments at FDA, can be ordered for $12 per year from the Superintendent of Documents, Government Printing Office, Washington DC 20402, (202) 783-3238.

* Geochemistry and Health

Society for Environmental Geochemistry and Health (SEGH)
Life Science Dept.
University of Missouri
Rolla, MO 65401   (314) 341-4831
SEGH is comprised by individuals who are interested in the relationship between geochemistry and health.

* Health and Science Journals: Computerized Databases

National Library of Medicine
8600 Rockville Pike
Bethesda, MD 20894   (301) 496-6095
MEDLARS is the computerized system of databases at the National Library of

Health and Medicine

Medicine (NLM). The databases may be accessed by more than 20,000 universities, medical schools, commercial and non-profit organizations, and private individuals. MEDLARS contains 11,500,000 references to journal articles and books in the health sciences published after 1965. Some of the databases are:

MEDLINE: 700,000 references to biomedical journal articles published in the current and two preceding years.

CATLINE: 630,000 references to books and serials cataloged at NLM.

SERLINE: Bibliographic and preservation information for 70,000 serials titles.

AVLINE: Citations to 17,000 audiovisual teaching packages covering subject areas in the health sciences.

AIDSLINE: Bibliographic file of published literature on AIDS, focusing on the clinical and research aspects of the disease.

HISTLINE: 83,000 citations to monographs, journal articles, symposia, congresses, and similar composite publications as published annually in the Bibliography of the History of Medicine.

TOXLINE: Bibliographic references covering pharmacological, biochemical, physiological, environmental, and toxicological effects of drugs and other chemicals.

CHEMLINE: An online chemical dictionary with over 790,000 records.

HEALTH: Contains 400,000 references to literature on health planning, organization, financing, management, and manpower.

CANCERLIT: 580,000 references dealing with various aspects of cancer.

CLINPROT: Contains summaries of clinical investigations of new anti-cancer agents and treatment modalities.

PDQ: Provides state-of-the-art cancer treatment and referral information.

DIRLINE: A directory of organizations providing information in specific subject areas.

SIDILINE: Contains current month's input to MEDLINE.

BIOETHICSLINE: Contains citations to documents which discuss ethical and related public policy questions arising in health care or biomedical research.

POPLINE: Provides bibliographic citations to literature on population and family planning.

DOCUSER: Contains descriptive information about libraries and other organizations which use NLM's interlibrary loan services.

NAME AUTHORITY FILE: List of 300,000 personal names, corporate names, and decisions on how monographic series are classed.

MeSH VOCABULARY FILE: Information on 15,000 medical subject headings and 50,000 chemical substances used for indexing and retrieving references.

TOXNET: Provides information on potentially toxic or otherwise hazardous chemicals.

HSDB: Contains toxicological information strengthened with additional data related to the environment, emergency situations, and regulatory issues.

CCRIS: Contains evaluated data and information derived from both short- and long-term bioassays on 1200 chemical substances.

RTECS: Contains basic acute and chronic toxicity data on more than 92,000 potentially toxic chemicals.

* Health Data and Indexes

Clearinghouse on Health Indexes
Division of Analysis
National Center for Health Statistics
3700 East-West Highway, Room 2-27
Hyattsville, MD 20782
(301) 436-7035
This clearinghouse maintains a database which purports to reflect the health status of an individual or defined group. This data are designed to help planners, researchers, and administrators develop and improve health programs and strategies.

* Healthfinder Series:
Child Health to Long-term Care

ODPHP National Health Information Center

P.O. Box 1133
(800) 336-4797
Washington, DC 20013
(301) 565-4167 (in Maryland)
Healthfinder is a series of publications, each on a specific health topic. Each issue includes some general information, a list of publications available, and resources relevant to the topic. Health topics include Adolescent Health, Family Care, Online Health Information, Women's Health, and Long-term care.

* Health Services Publications Catalog

Office of Public Affairs
Health Resources and Services Administration
5600 Fishers Lane, Room 1443
Rockville, MD 20857
(301) 443-2086
The Health Resources and Services Administration offers a free catalog, Current Publications, which lists all the publications films, and videos produced by HRSA's three bureaus: Bureau of Health Care Delivery and Assistance, Bureau of Maternal and Child Health and Resources Development and Bureau of Health Professions.

* Heart, Lung, and Blood Disease Clearinghouse

National Heart, Lung and Blood Institute
Building 31, Room 4A-21
9000 Rockville Pike
Bethesda, MD 20892
(301) 496-4236
The Institute oversees the scientific investigation, prevention, and control of heart, blood vessel, lung, and blood diseases. The program emphasizes education concerning these diseases through a more rapid transfer of information into the mainstream of clinical medicine and personal health practices. Many publications are available for professionals and the general public on a wide variety of topics.

* Home Health Care and Hospice Resources

National Health Information Center
P.O. Box 1133
Washington, DC 20013
(800) 336-4797 (301) 565-4167 in MD
In its series called "Healthfinder", the center publishes a 6-page bulletin titled Family Care which lists organizations, self-help and support groups, as well as books about home care for the chronically or terminally ill or the disabled child or aging parent. Suggested resources for preparing for death such as living wills and organ or tissue donation are included in this "Healthfinder."

* Injury Information Clearinghouse

National Injury Information Clearinghouse
Consumer Product Safety Commission
5401 Westbard Avenue, Room 625
Washington, DC 20207
(301) 492-6424
This clearinghouse gathers, investigates, analyzes, and disseminates injury data relating to the causes and prevention of death, injury, and illness associated with consumer products. Use this information center to tap into the National Electronic Injury Surveillance System (NEISS) which selected hospital emergency rooms contribute case reports on product-related injuries.

* Laser Surgery Referral Network

National Health Information Center
P.O. Box 1133
Washington, DC 20013
(202) 429-9091 in DC (800) 336-4797
This center can provide you with names of organizations and agencies involved with laser surgery, which can then refer you to experts in the field.

* Medical Books for the Consumer

National Health Information Center
P.O. Box 1133
Washington, DC 20013
(301) 565-4167 in MD (800) 336-4797
In its "Healthfinder" series, the center publishes The Home Medical Library which lists numerous health books and medical guide available at libraries and bookstores in such subject areas as sports medicine, medications, child care, aging, and home health records.

* Mental Health Clearinghouse

National Institute of Mental Health
Alcohol, Drug Abuse and Mental Health Administration
5600 Fishers Lane, Room 15C05
Rockville, MD 20857
(301) 443-4515
NIMH conducts research on mental disorders and mental health services, distributes information, conducts demonstration programs for the prevention, treatment, and rehabilitation of the mentally ill. Research focuses on the biological, psychological, epidemiological, and social science aspects of mental health and illness. NIMH collaborates with other organizations to promote effective mental health programs and provides technical assistance.

* Minorities and Blacks Health Coordinator

Office of Minority Health
Department of Health and Human Services
200 Independence Avenue SW, Room 118F
Washington, DC 20201   (202) 245-0020

This office monitors community-based projects designed to reduce over 60,000 excess deaths each year among minority Americans and develops recommendations for health strategies and research on risk factors affecting these populations.

* National Health Information Center

National Health Information Center
P.O. Box 1133
Washington, DC 20013   (301) 565-4167 in MD (800) 336-4797

This center should be the initial phone call because it can direct you to more specialized clearinghouses as well as health organizations and foundations. The National Health Information Center, through its resource files and database (DIRLINE), responds to questions regarding health concerns and can send publications, bibliographies, and other material. A library focusing on health topics is open to the public, and the Center also produces many different directories, and resource guides, which are available for a minimal cost. A publications catalog is free of charge.

* Native Americans Health Services

Indian Health Service
Office of Communications
5600 Fishers Lane, Room 5A-54
Rockville, MD 20857   (301) 443-1118

The goal of the Indian Health Service is to raise the health level of American Indians and Alaskan Natives to the highest possible level. IHS accomplishes this by providing a comprehensive health services delivery system, which includes hospital and ambulatory medical care, preventive and rehabilitative services, and community environmental health programs, among them the construction of water and sanitation facilities for more than one million American Indians and Alaskan Natives. The program offers maximum opportunity for tribal involvement in developing these and other programs to meet their health needs. IHS operates 43 hospitals, 71 health centers, and more than 100 smaller health stations and satellite clinics. Indian tribes may contract with IHS to operate their own health care facilities and programs.

* Neighborhood Medical Libraries throughout the U.S.

Greater Northeastern Regional Medical Library Program, The New York Academy of Medicine, 2 East 103rd Street New York, NY 10029; (212) 876-8763. States served: Connecticut, Delaware, Maine, Massachusetts, New Hampshire, New Jersey, New York, Pennsylvania, Rhode Island, Vermont, and Puerto Rico.

Southeastern Regional Medical Library Service, University of Maryland Health Sciences Library, 111 South Greene St., Baltimore, MD 21201; (301) 328-2855 or (800) 638-6093. States served: Alabama, Florida, Georgia, Maryland, Mississippi, North Carolina, South Carolina, Tennessee, Virginia, West Virginia, District of Columbia, and Virgin Islands.

Greater Midwest Regional Medical Library Network, University of Chicago, Library of Health Sciences, P.O. Box 7509, Chicago, IL 60680; (312) 996-2464. States served: Iowa, Illinois, Indiana, Kentucky, Michigan, Minnesota, North Dakota, Ohio, South Dakota, and Wisconsin.

Midcontinental Regional Medical Library Program, University of Nebraska, Medical Center Library, 42nd & Dewey Avenue, Omaha, NE 68105; (402) 559-4326 or (800) MED-RML4. States served: Colorado, Kansas, Missouri, Nebraska, Utah, and Wyoming.

South Central Regional Medical Library Program, University of Texas, Southwestern Medical Center at Dallas, 5323 Harry Hines Blvd., Dallas, TX 75235; (214) 688-2085. States served: Arkansas, Louisiana, New Mexico, Oklahoma, and Texas.

Pacific Northwest Regional Health Sciences Library Service, Health Sciences Library and Information Center, University of Washington Seattle, WA 98195; (206) 543-8262. States served: Alaska, Idaho, Montana, Oregon, and Washington.

Pacific Southwest Regional Medical Library Service, Louise Darling Biomedical Library, University of California, 10833 Le Conte Ave., Los Angeles, CA 90024; (213) 825-1200. States served: Arizona, California, Hawaii, Nevada, and U.S. Territories in the Pacific Basin.

* Occupational Health Clearinghouse

Technical Information Branch
National Institute for Occupational Safety and Health Information
4676 Columbia Parkway
Cincinnati, OH 45226
Technical Info: (800) 35-NIOSH (513) 533-8328
Publications: (513) 841-4287
Library: (513) 533-8321

This center serves as a clearinghouse on occupational health, hazardous substances, and safety. Much of their information is available through interlibrary loans and online databases.

* Online Health Information

National Health Information Center
P.O. Box 1133
Washington, DC 20013   (301) 565-4167 in MD (800) 336-4797

In its series called "Healthfinder", the center publishes *Online Health Information* which lists databases which contain citations to the literature of medicine and health ranging from the National Library of Medicine MELINE to the American Association of Retired Persons database called AGELINE. This 12-page "Healthfinder" also highlights user-friendly software and computerized services, and contact information for vendors.

* Primary Care Information

Project Director
National Clearinghouse for Primary Care Information
8201 Greensboro Drive, Suite 600
McLean, VA 22102   (703) 821-8955

This center distributes materials on ambulatory care, financial management, primary health care, medical personnel and services primarily to health professionals as well as publications on community health centers, migrant health centers, childhood injury prevention efforts, clinical care and many other health concerns.

* Publications and Resource Catalog

National Health Information Center
P.O. Box 1133
Washington, DC 20013   (800) 336-4797 (301) 565-4167 in MD

This government clearinghouse publishes a 51-page catalog titled *Staying Healthy: A Bibliography of Health Promotion Materials*, which lists various Department of Health and Human Services clearinghouses and information centers as well as numerous health promotion and disease prevention booklets, fact sheets, program guides, films, videotapes, slides, and posters. The Office of Disease Prevention and Health Promotion of the U.S. Public Health Service also makes available single copies free of *Publications List* with an order form which describes publications under nine broad categories: Federal Programs and Policies; ODPHP Monograph Series; Community Health Promotion Programs; School Health Programs; Worksite Health Promotion Programs; Nutrition; Professional Education; Educational Materials; and Miscellaneous.

* Publications from all NIH Institutes

Public Information Division
National Institute of Health, Room 305
Bethesda, MD 20892   (301) 496-4143

The NIH Publications List (#89-7) is a free catalog which lists the publications available from each of the Institutes, as well as their addresses and phone numbers.

* Public Health Foundation

Public Health Foundation (PHF)
1220 L St., NW
Suite 350
Washington, DC 20005   (202) 898-5600

The Public Health Foundation represents the directors of public health agencies in each of the 50 states, the District of Columbia, and four U.S. territories. The purpose of the Public Health Foundation is to enhance national public health policy discussions, improve public health practice, foster professional development in public health and promote understanding about public health issues.

* Rehabilitation Resource Center

National Rehabilitation Information Center
8455 Colesville Road, Suite 935   (301) 588-9284 (MD only)
Silver Spring, MD 20910   (800) 346-2742 (voice and TDD)

This clearinghouse provides information on disability-related research, resources, and products for independent living as well as facts sheets, resource guides, and research and technical publications.

* Second Opinion Hotline

National Second Surgical Opinion Program
Health Care Financing Administration
330 Independence Ave., SW   (800) 492-6603 in Maryland only
Washington, DC 20201   (800) 638-6833

Health and Medicine

The National Second Surgical Opinion Program is an information resource for people faced with the possibility of non-emergency surgery. By calling its toll-free number, the staff will help you locate a surgeon or other specialist enrolled in the program who can offer you a second opinion. Pamphlets are available containing questions that patients looking for second opinions should ask.

* Speech and Language Disorders Clearinghouse

National Institute on Deafness and
Other Communicative Disorders
NIH, Building 31, Room 1B62,
9000 Rockville Pike
Bethesda, MD 20892   (301) 496-7243

This--the newest Institute at NIH--funds intramural and extramural research on communicative disorders. Brochures and reports are available for professionals and the general public, covering a wide range of related topics.

* Sports Medicine and Orthopedics Clearinghouse

Musculoskeletal Diseases Program
National Institute of Arthritis and Musculoskeletal
and Skin Diseases
Westwood Building, Room 407
Bethesda, MD 20205   (301) 468-3235

This program focuses on orthopedic research, which includes sports medicine, growth and development of bone and bone cells, as well as head injury. Staff can answer questions regarding current research and treatment issues. Brochures and pamphlets are available through the National Institute of Arthritis and Musculoskeletal and Skin Diseases.

* Statistical Sources Clearinghouse

National Health Information Center
P.O. Box 1133
Washington, DC 20013   (301) 565-4167 in MD (800) 336-4797

Healthfinder: Health Statistics lists government and private sources for gathering data about such health issues accidents and injuries; dental care; disability; diseases; disorders; environmental health; health care delivery; health care expenditures; personnel; insurance; minorities; nutrition; pharmaceuticals; and surgery. This "Healthfinder" bulletin also identifies data files and general reference guides such as the *Health Data Inventory* which is available from the National Technical Information Service.

* Stroke and Brain Disorders Resource Center

National Institute of Neurological Disorders and Stroke
National Institutes of Health
9000 Rockville Pike
Building 31, Room 8A06
Bethesda, MD 20892   (301) 496-4697

NINDS conducts and guides research on the causes, prevention, diagnosis, and treatment of fundamental neurological disorders and stroke and trauma. The Institute gives grants for extramural research, as well as providing fellowships. Other areas of research include cerebral palsy, autism, dyslexia, multiple sclerosis, Parkinson's and Huntington's diseases, and epilepsy. Brochures and pamphlets are available.

* Toll-Free Health Hotlines

Public Health Service AIDS Information Hotline
(800) 342-AIDS
(800) 342-SIDA for information in Spanish

National AIDS Information Clearinghouse
(800) 458-5231

National Gay Lesbian Crisisline
(800) 221-7044
(212) 529-1604 in NY, AK, and HI

Al-Anon Family Group Headquarters
(800) 356-9996
(212) 245-3151 in NY and Canada

Alcoholism and Drug Addiction Treatment Center
(800) 382-4357

National Council on Alcoholism
(800) NCA-CALL

Alzheimer's Disease and Related Disorders Association
(800) 621-0379
(800) 572-6037 in IL

Brookdale Center on Aging Alzheimer's Respite Line
(800) 648-COPE for placing orders

AMC Cancer Information
(800) 525-3777

Cancer Information Service (CIS)
(800) 4-CANCER
(808) 524-1234 in Oahu, HI (Neighbor Islands call collect)
(800) 638-6070 in AK

Y-Me Breast Cancer Support Group
(800) 221-2141
(312) 799-8228 in IL

Chemical Referral Center
(800) CMA-8200 in continental US and Hawaii
(202) 887-1315 in DC and for collect calls from AK

National Pesticide Telecommunications Network
(800) 858-7378

National Child Abuse Hotline
(800) 422-4453

Parents Anonymous Hotline
(800) 421-0353
(800) 352-0386 in CA

National Child Safety Council Childwatch
(800) 222-1464

National Hotline for Missing Children
(800) 843-5678
(202) 644-9836 in DC

National Runaway Switchboard
(800) 621-4000

Cystic Fibrosis Foundation
(800) 344-4823
(301) 951-4422 in MD

American Diabetes Association
(800) ADA-DISC
(703) 549-1500 in VA and DC metro area

Juvenile Diabetes Foundation International Hotline
(800) 223-1138
(212) 889-7575 in NY

National Down Syndrome Congress
(800) 232-6372
(312) 823-7550 in IL

National Down Syndrome Society Hotline
(800) 221-4602
(212) 460-9330 in NY

Safe Drinking Water Hotline
(800) 426-4791
(202) 382-5533 in DC

Just Say No Kids Club
(800) 258-2766
(415) 939-6666 in CA

National Cocaine Hotline
(800) COC-AINE

National Federation of Parents for Drug-Free Youth
(800) 554-KIDS
(301) 585-5437 in MD

Anorexia Bulimia Treatment and Education Center
(800) 33-ABTEC
(301) 332-9800 in MD

Bulimia Anorexia Self-Help
(800) 227-4785

Aerobics and Fitness Foundation

(800) BE FIT 86

ODPHP National Health Information Center
(800) 336-4797
(301) 565-4167 in MD

The Epilepsy Foundation of America
(800) EFA-1000
(301) 459-1000 in MD
(800) 492-2523 Baltimore affiliate

HEATH Resource Center
(800) 544-3284
(202) 939-9320 in DC

Job Accommodation Network
(800) 526-7234
(800) 526-4698 in WV

Library of Congress National Library Services for the Blind and Physically Handicapped
(800) 424-8567
(202) 287-5100 in DC

National Information System for Health Related Services (NIS)
(800) 922-9234
(800) 922-1107 in SC

National Rehabilitation Information Center
(800) 34-NARIC
(301) 588-9284 in MD

National Headache Foundation
(800) 843-2256
(800) 523-8858 in IL

American Cleft Palate Association
(800) 24-CLEFT
(800) 23-CLEFT in PA

Dial a Hearing Test
(800) 222-EARS
(800) 345-EARS in PA

Grapevine
(800) 352-8888 Voice and TDD
(800) 346-8888 in CA, Voice and TDD

Hearing Helpline
(800) 424-8576
(800) EAR-WELL
(703) 642-0580 in VA

National Association for Hearing and Speech Action Line
(800) 638-8255
(301) 897-0039 in HI, AK, and MD call collect

National Hearing Aid Helpline
(800) 521-5247
(313) 478-2610 in MI

Children's Hospice International
(800) 242-4453
(703) 684-0330 in VA

Hospice Education Institute Hospicelink
(800) 331-1620
(203) 767-1620 in CT

Hill Burton Hospital Free Care
(800) 638-0742
(800) 492-0359 in MD

Shriners Hospital Referral Line
(800) 237-5055
(800) 282-9161 in FL

Project Share
(800) 537-3788
(301) 231-9539 in MD

Huntington's Disease Society of America
(800) 345-4372
(212) 242-1968 in NY

Recovery of Male Potency
(800) 835-7667
(313) 966-3219 in MI

Federal Internal Revenue Service for TDD Users
(800) 428-4732 TDD
(800) 382-4059 in IN; TDD
(800) 424-1040 Voice

The Orton Dyslexia Society
(800) ABCD-123
(301) 296-0232 in MD

American Liver Foundation
(800) 223-0179
(201) 857-2626 in NJ

Asthma Information Line
(800) 822-ASMA

Lung Line National Asthma Center
(800) 222-5864
(303) 355-LUNG in Denver

Lupus Foundation of America
(800) 558-0121
(202) 328-4550 in DC

Terri Gotthelf Lupus Research Institute
(800) 82-LUPUS
(203) 852-0120 in CT

DHHS Inspector General's Hotline
(800) 368-5779
(301) 597-0724 in MD

American Mental Health Fund
(800) 433-5959
(800) 826-2336 in IL

National Foundation for Depressive Illness
(800) 248-4344

Office of Minority Health Resource Center
(800) 444-6472

National Multiple Sclerosis Society
(800) 624-8236

The Living Bank
(800) 528-2971
(713) 528-2971 in TX

Organ Donor Hotline
(800) 24-DONOR

American Paralysis Association
(800) 225-0292
(201) 379-2690 in NJ

APA Spinal Cord Injury Hotline
(800) 526-3456
(800) 638-1733 in MD

National Spinal Cord Injury Association
(800) 962-9629
(617) 935-2722 in MA

National Parkinson Foundation
(800) 327-4545
(800) 433-7022 in FL
(305) 547-6666 in Miami

Parkinson's Education Program
(800) 344-7872
(714) 640-0218 in CA

American Society of Plastic and Reconstructive

Health and Medicine

Surgeons
(800) 635-0635

Practitioner Reporting System
(800) 638-6725
(301) 881-0256 in MD (call collect)

ASPO/Lamaze (American Society for Psychoprophylaxis in Obstetrics)
(800) 368-4404
(703) 524-7802 in VA

Birth Control Information Line
(800) 468-3637

National Pregnancy Hotline
(800) 852-5683
(800) 831-5881 in CA
(213) 380-8750 in Los Angeles

Pregnancy Counseling Services
(800) 368-3336
(804) 847-6828 in VA

American Leprosy Missions (Hansen's Disease)
(800) 543-3131
(201) 794-8650 in NJ

Cooley's Anemia Foundation
(800) 221-3571
(212) 522-7222 in NY

Cornelia de Lange Syndrome Foundation
(800) 223-8355
(203) 693-0159 in CT

National Information Center for Orphan Drugs and Rare Diseases
(800) 336-4797
(301) 565-4167 in MD

National Lymphedema Network
(800) 541-3259

National Neurofibromatosis Foundation
(800) 323-7938
(212) 460-8980 in NY

National Organization for Rare Disorders
(800) 447-NORD
(203) 746-6518 in CT

National Tuberous Sclerosis Association
(800) 225-6872
(301) 459-9888 in MD

Tourette Syndrome Association
(800) 237-0717
(718) 224-2999 in NY

United Scleroderma Foundation
(800) 722-HOPE
(408) 728-2202 in CA

National Retinitis Pigmentosa Foundation
(800) 638-2300
(301) 225-9400 in MD

National Reye's Syndrome Foundation
(800) 233-7393
(800) 231-7393 in OH

Consumer Product Safety Commission
(800) 638-CPSC
(800) 638-8270 TDD
(800) 492-8104 TDD in MD

National Highway Traffic Safety Administration
(800) 424-9393
(202) 366-0123 in DC

National Safety Council

(800) 621-7619 for placing orders
(312) 527-4800 in IL

National Association for Sickle Cell Disease
(800) 421-8453
(213) 936-7205 in CA

Spina Bifida Information and Referral
(800) 621-3141
(301) 770-7222 in MD

American SIDS Institute
(800) 232-SIDS
(800) 847-7437 in GA

National SIDS Foundation
(800) 221-SIDS
(301) 459-3388 or 3389 in MD

Second Surgical Opinion Hotline
(800) 638-6833
(800) 492-6603 in MD

American Trauma Society (ATS)
(800) 556-7890
(301) 925-8811 in MD

American Kidney Fund
(800) 638-8299
(800) 492-8361 in MD

Peyronie's Society of America, Inc.
(800) 346-4875
(316) 283-2456 in KS

Simon Foundation
(800) 23-SIMON

VD Hotline (Operation Venus)
(800) 227-8922

American Council of the Blind
(800) 424-8666
(202) 393-3666 in DC

American Foundation for the Blind (AFB)
(800) 232-5463
(212) 620-2147

National Eye Care Project Helpline
(800) 222-EYES

Endometriosis Association
(800) 992-ENDO
(414) 962-8972 in WI

PMS Access
(800) 222-4767
(608) 833-4767 in WI

Women's Sports Foundation
(800) 227-3988
(212) 972-9170 in AK, HI, and CA

* Technology Assessment Reports
Office of Technology Assessment
Publications Order
U.S. Congress
Washington, DC 20510-8025   (202) 224-8996
These OTA publications are available through the office above, the Government Printing Office, and the National Technical Information Service. To find out correct ordering information and prices, along with brief summaries of the following studies, contact the OTA office above and request their current publications catalog.
Drugs in Livestock Feed (F-91)
Emerging Food Marketing Technologies (F-79)
Environmental Contaminants in Food (F-103)
Food Information Systems (F-35)
Impacts of Applied Genetics: Micro-Organisms, Plants, and Animals (HR-132)
Impacts of Technology on U.S. Cropland and Rangeland Productivity (F-166)
Nutrition Research Alternatives (F-74)
Open Shelf-Life Dating of Food (F-94)

Pesticide Residues in Food (F-398)

Biological Applications

Alternatives to Animal Use In Research, Testing, and Education (BA-273)
Artificial Insemination: Practice in the United States (BP-BA-48)
Assessment of Technologies for Determining Cancer Risk From the Environment (H-138)
Commercial Development of Tests for Human Genetic Disorders (Staff Paper)
Commercial Biotechnology: An International Analysis (BA-218)
Federal Policies and the Medical Devices Industry (H-229)
Federal Regulation and Animal Patents (Staff Paper)
Hearing Impairment and Elderly People (BP-BA-30)
Humane Gene Therapy (BP-BA-32)
Impacts of Applied Genetics: Micro-Organisms, Plants, and Animals (HR-132)
Impacts of Neuroscience (BP-BA-24)
Infertility: Medical and Social Choices (BA-358)
Innovative Biological Technologies for Lesser Developed Countries (BP-F-29)
Institutional Protocols for Decisions About Life-Sustaining Treatments (BA-389)
Life-Sustaining Technologies and the Elderly (BA-306)
Loosing a Million Minds: Confronting the Tragedy of Alzheimer's Disease a n d Other Dementias (BA-323)
Mapping Our Genes: Genome Projects - How Big, How Fast? (BA-373)
Methods for Locating and Arranging Health and Long-Term Care for Persons With Dementia (BA-403)
New Developments in Biotechnology: Field-Testing Engineered Organisms: Genetic and Ecological Issues (BA-350)
New Developments in Biotechnology: Ownership of Human Tissue and Cells (BA-337)
New Developments in Biotechnology: Patenting Life (BA-370)
New Developments in Biotechnology: Public Perceptions in Biotechnology (BP-BA-45)
New Developments in Biotechnology: U.S. Investment in Biotechnology (BA-360)
Preventing Illness and Injury in the Workplace (H-256)
Reproductive Health Hazards in the Workplace (BA-266)
The Role of Genetic Testing in the Prevention of Occupational Disease (BA-194)
Status of Biomedical Research and Related Technology for Tropical Diseases (H-258)
Technologies for Detecting Heritable Mutations in Human Beings (H-298)
Technologies for Managing Urinary Incontinence (HCS-33)
Technology and Aging in America (BA-264)
Transgenic Animals (Staff Paper)
World Population and Fertility Planning Technologies: The Next 20 Years (HR-157)

* Tracer Bulletins: Asthma to Edible Wild Plants

Science and Technology Division
Reference Section
Library of Congress
Washington, DC 20540   (202) 707-5580

Informal series of reference guides are issued free from the Science and Technology Division under the general title, *LC Science Tracer Bullet*. These guides are designed to help readers locate published material on subjects about which they have only general knowledge. New titles in the series are announced in the weekly Library of Congress *Information Bulletin* that is distributed to many libraries including the following health-related Tracer Bulletins:

80-4 *Aging*
80-5 *Low-Level Ionizing Radiation: Health Effects*
80-6 *Lasers and Their Applications*
80-9 *Terminal Care*
80-11 *Drug Research on Human Subjects*
80-18 *Health Foods*
81-2 *Medicinal Plants*
81-3 *Alcoholism*
81-17 *Epilepsy*
82-1 *Food Additives*
82-9 *Sickle Cell Anemia*
83-1 *Biofeedback*
83-6 *Mental Retardation*
83-8 *Women in the Sciences*
85-5 *Black Scientists*
85-6 *Acupuncture*
85-8 *Anorexia Nervosa/Bulimia*
85-10 *Rose Culture*
85-11 *Acquired Immune Deficiency Syndrome (AIDS)*
86-6 *Diabetes Mellitus*
86-8 *Indoor Air Pollution*
87-1 *Asbestos*
87-2 *Alzheimer's Disease*
87-6 *Stress: Physiological and Psychological Aspects*
87-7 *Osteoporosis*
89-5 *Human Diet & Nutrition*
89-7 *Allergy and Asthma*

* Women's Health Resources

National Health Information Center
P.O. Box 1133
Washington, DC 20013   (800) 336-4797 (301) 565-4167 in MD

In its series, *Healthfinder*, the center publishes *Women's Health* which lists many organizations that provide information on a broad range of topics including pregnancy, gynecological, domestic violence, sports and fitness, and occupational health. This 6-page reference also lists books of particular relevance to women and their health.

Healthy Lifestyle and Physical Fitness

Health professionals, community health centers, organizations, businesses, and individuals all can take advantage of the multitude of resources available to promote good health and prevent disease. Several federal agencies and departments as well as numerous national organizations offer bulletins, reference manuals, publications and expertise to encourage healthy lifestyle and medical care. The National Health Information Center, a clearinghouse sponsored by the U.S. government, can direct you to the proper agency such as the President's Council on Physical Fitness as well as private organizations.

* Adolescent Health Risk Assessment

Office of Technology Assessment
600 Pennsylvania Ave., SE
Washington, DC 20510   (202) 228-6590
OTA is working on a project to assess the health status of adolescents 10 to 18 years old and identify factors that put adolescents at risk for health problems, including racial and ethnic backgrounds, socioeconomic status, gender, and developmental stage. Particular attention will be paid to the availability, effectiveness, and accessibility of health services for adolescents. Contact Denise Dougherty, the project director, for more information.

* Aging and Lifestyle Changes

ODPHP National Health Information Center
P.O. Box 1133
Washington, DC 20013   (800) 336-4797 (301) 565-4167 (in MD)
A 30-page study titled *Aging and Health Promotion: Market Research for Public Health* proposes lifestyle changes for older adults and the executive summary is available for $2.00 and the full report can be purchased for $24.95 from the National Technical Information Center, 5285 Port Royal Road, Springfield, VA 22161 (No. PB84-211150).

* Behavior Patterns and Health

Office of Clinical Center Communications
Warren G. Magnuson Clinical Center
NIH, Building 10, Room 5C-305
9000 Rockville Pike
Bethesda, MD 20892   (301) 496-2563
A 36-page report titled *Behavior Patterns and Health* (No. 85-2682) discusses the scientific evidence linking behavior to disease and suggests ways to reduce the risks of heart attack, lung cancer, and stroke by changing our lifestyle.

* Cancer Prevention Awareness

Office of Cancer Communications
National Cancer Institute
Building 31, Room 10A-24
9000 Rockville Pike
Bethesda, MD 20892   (800) 4-CANCER (800) 492-6000 in MD
Over 100 programs are described in this free *Cancer Prevention Resource Directory* which gives names, addresses, and telephone numbers of many national associations and health departments which encourage cancer prevention activities. Single copies of this manual are available free.

* Cancer: Testicular Self-Exam

Office of Communications
National Cancer Institute
Building 31, Room 10A18
9000 Rockville Pike
Bethesda, MD 20892   (301) 496-5583
A free pamphlet, *Testicular Self-Examination* (No. 86-2636), provides information about risks and symptoms of testicular cancer and suggestions effective self-examinations.

* Childhood Injury Prevention

National Clearinghouse for Primary Care Information
8201 Greensboro Drive #600
McLean, VA 22102   (703) 821-8955
A 197-page guide titled *Developing Childhood Injury Prevention Programs: An Administrative Guide for State Maternal and Child Health (Title V) Programs* describes several demonstration projects and contains how-to information. Single copies of this manual are available free.

* Children: Risk Factors

National Center for Health Services Research
and Health Care Technology Assessment
Parklawn Building, Rm 18-12
5600 Fishers Lane
Rockville, MD 20857   (301) 443-4100
This Center offers research findings including *Determinants of Children's Health* (No. 81-3309) which summarizes six closely related studies on the determinants of child health, with particular emphasis on home and local environmental factors, parents' schooling, and family income.

* Community-Based Health Promotion

ODPHP National Health Information Center
P.O. Box 1133
Washington, DC 20013   (800) 336-4797 (301) 565-4167 (in Maryland)
In its series of "Healthfinders", this central clearinghouse publishes *Community Health Promotion Programs* which identifies resources and handbooks that can guide preventive health programs based in the local community, school, and worksite. It describes resources in various categories including Aging, AIDS Education, Substance Abuse, Cardiovascular Health, Cancer, Highway Safety, and Maternal and Child Health. This "Healthfinder" is available for $1.00 handling charge.

* Community Screening and Health Fairs

ODPHP National Health Information Center
P.O. Box 1133
Washington, DC 20013   (800) 336-4797 (301) 565-4167 (in Maryland)
In its series of "Healthfinders", the Center publishes *Health Fairs and Community Screening* which lists articles, publications, and professional organizations which offer information and assistance in running community screening and health fairs such as hosting high blood pressure clinics and testing for glaucoma. The cost of this "Healthfinder" is $1.00. *Screening in Health Fairs: A Critical Review of Benefits, Risks, and Costs* emphasizes that screening tests should be targeted to high-risk groups is available for a $2.00 handling fee.

* Elderly and Exercise

National Institute on Aging Information Center
2209 Distribution Circle
Silver Spring, MD 20910   (301) 495-3455
Don't Take It Easy - Exercise! is a free two-page fact sheet which suggests ways for older Americans to remain active and healthy.

* Exercise and Arthritis

National Arthritis and Musculoskeletal
and Skin Diseases Information Clearinghouse
P.O. Box 9782
Arlington, VA 22209   (703) 558-4999
A 20-page resource catalog titled *Exercise and Arthritis: An Annotated Bibliography, 1986* contains 37 references with abstracts, books, reports, and audiovisuals along with resources for developing an aquatic exercise regime, a home maintenance program, and exercises specifically for children.

* Exercise and Physical Fitness Programs

President's Council on Physical Fitness and Sports
450 5th St., NW, Suite 7103
Washington, DC 20001   (202) 272-3421
This executive branch office provides free single copies of many of its publications which range from swimming to walking: *Fitness Fundamentals, Fitness in the Workplace, One Step At A Time (An Introduction to Running); Physical Education: A Performance Checklist*. Several other pamphlets including *An Introduction to Physical Fitness* and *Aqua Dynamics: Physical Conditioning*

Through Water Exercises can be purchased from the Government Printing Office.

* Exercising Your Heart

National Heart, Lung, and Blood Institute
NIH, Building 31, Room 4A-21
9000 Rockville Pike
Bethesda, MD 20892   (301) 496-4236
Single copies are available at no charge on the following publications: *Exercise and Your Heart* (No. 81-1677), *NHLBI Facts About Exercise: How To Get Started, NHLBI Facts About Exercise: Sample Exercise Programs; NHLBI Facts About Exercise: What Is Fact and What Is Fiction?*

* Family Relationships and Lifecycles

Family Branch
U.S. Department of Agriculture
10301 Baltimore Blvd.
Beltsville, MD 20705   (301) 344-3719
This center answers questions about families throughout the lifecycle, from marital relationships and childbearing families to empty nest families and retirement, and deals with matters concerning social environment and family economics education.

* Federal Health Information Catalog

ODPHP National Health Information Center
P.O. Box 1133
Washington, DC 20013   (800) 336-4797 (301) 565-4167 (in Maryland)
Health Information Resources in the Federal Government identifies Federal agencies and projects that can provide information to health professionals and the general public. It includes major services and activities, publications and databases. Check with the Center to learn about the latest edition. A $2 fee covers the handling for this catalog.

* Genetic Screening in the Workplace

Office of Technology Assessment
600 Pennsylvania Ave., SE
Washington, DC 20510   (202) 228-6690
OTA is now studying the state-of-the-art technologies used by employers for genetic screening and monitoring, which includes a survey of the 500 largest U.S. industries, to largest utilities, and 11 major unions to determine the current nature and extent of employer testing. Also being examined is the impact of genetic testing; relevant ethical issues; and legal issues, including employment discrimination. Contact Robyn Nishimi, the project director, for more information.

* Health Promotion in the Workplace

Office of Disease Prevention and Health Promotion
Public Health Service
330 C St., SW, Room 2132
Washington, DC 20201   (202) 472-5660
As a policy arm of the Public Health Service, this office works on developing policies for the Year 2000 objectives for health promotion. Their Preventive Services Task Force is developing recommendations for clinical practice, in addition to a worksite Health Promotion Task Force and a Nutrition Branch. This office also operates the Health Promotion Clearinghouse which offers many publications.

* Health Promotion Project Funding

ODPHP National Health Information Center
P.O. Box 1133
Washington, DC 20013   (800) 336-4797 (301) 565-4167 (in Maryland)
The guide, *Locating Funds for Health Promotion Projects*, is designed to assist newcomers on their search for health promotion funding by introducing them to the major tasks involved and information services available. This publication is divided into four major sections. Section I discusses basic principles of fundseeking. Sections II and III discuss where and how to look for health promotion funds, focusing on both private and public sectors. Major foundations and Federal agencies interested in health promotion, as well as local sources are listed. Section IV lists resources--organizations, foundations, publications, and databases--that can be useful to those seeking funds. Also included is an appendix, which includes a glossary, a list of acronyms, a bibliography, and a sample grant application form.

* Health Risk Appraisal Tests

ODPHP National Health Information Center
P.O. Box 1133
Washington, DC 20013   (800) 336-4797 (301) 565-4167 (in Maryland)
In its "Healthfinder" series, the Center publishes a resource list on *Health Risk Appraisals* which identifies computer-scored, microcomputer-based, and self-

scored tests that analyze an individual's health history and current lifestyle to determine his or her risk for preventable death or chronic illness. This "Healthfinder" contains a vendor list of many corporate health promotion center, medical research institutions, and private organizations that offer such tests and the costs of each. *Health Risk Appraisals* is available for a $1.00 handling fee.

* Healthy Mothers, Healthy Babies

National Maternal and Child Health Clearinghouse
38th and R Streets, NW
Washington, DC 20057   (202) 625-8410
A joint effort by the federal government, state agencies, health organizations and the private sector called Healthy Mothers, Healthy Babies has been underway to prevent teenage pregnancy, premature babies, and improve prenatal services. Several resources guides are available free including *Healthy Mothers/Healthy Babies: The Community Connection and Health Mothers/Healthy Babies: A Compendium of Program Ideas for Serving Low-Income Women.*

* Healthy Teeth

National Institute of Dental Research
NIH, Building 31, Room 2C35
9000 Rockville Pike
Bethesda, MD 20892   (301) 496-4261
The mission of the National Institute of Dental Research (NIDR) is to support studies to establish the causes, develop better treatments, and ultimately find ways to prevent or substantially lower the risk of developing oral disease. NIDR has extramural and intramural research programs, and supports the Epidemiology and Oral Disease Prevention Program, which sponsors studies of oral disease and engages in controlled clinical trials of potential preventive agents. NIDR grants fellowships and career development awards and sponsors many conferences and workshops. They distribute a wide range of brochures, reports, and posters for both the general public and professionals (many of which are also in Spanish). Some of the topics covered are tooth decay, fluoride use, and the oral health of U.S. adults.

* Immunizations and Disease Prevention

Office of Consumer Affairs
Public Inquiries
Food and Drug Administration
5600 Fishers Lane (HFE-88)
Rockville, MD 20857   (301) 443-3170
This office has many free publications pertaining to vaccinations including *New Vaccine Protects Against Serious "Day Care" Disease, Shots Adults Shouldn't Do Without, Vaccines: Precious Ounces of Prevention,* and *Whooping Cough Still threatens U.S. Children.*

* Individual Wellness Self Test

ODPHP Health Information Center
P. O. Box 1133
Washington, DC 20013   (800) 336-4797 (301) 565-4167 in MD
This two-page questionnaire titled *HealthStyle: A Self Test* (No. H0012) is designed to help determine how healthful one's habits and lifestyle are and to identify areas in which change could be helpful. The Health Information Center encourages duplication of this camera-ready version. A single copy may be purchased for a $1.00 handling fee.

* Learning Disabilities Prevention

Public Inquiries Branch
National Institute of Mental Health
Parklawn building, Room 15C-05,
5600 Fishers Lane
Rockville, MD 20857   (301) 443-4513
Detection and Prevention of Learning Disorders (No. 77-337) discusses research findings of the most prevalent affliction of childhood. Experts at the institute are available and there are other free publications available.

* Lifestyle and Occupational Health Risk Scorecard

Health Risk Appraisal Activity
Centers for Disease Control
1600 Clifton Rd., NE
Building 3, A-11
Atlanta, GA 30333   (404) 329-3177
The Health Risk Appraisal Activity program works to develop computerized health risk appraisals (HRS); to provide technical assistance in their use through state and regional contacts; and to distribute general background information on HRA's. Current activities include supporting the development of a state-of-the-art, public domain HRA at the Carter Center, Emory University; integrating occupational risk appraisal with lifestyle risk appraisal; evaluating the effect on communities of HRA use; and supporting the development of HRA programs for specific populations.

* Mental Retardation Prevention

President's Committee on Mental Retardation
330 Independence Avenue SW
Room 4061
Washington, DC 20201   (202) 245-7634

A Guide for State Planning for the *Prevention of Mental Retardation and Related Developmental Disabilities* is a resource tool not intended solely for state-level health planners but also for city and county health departments, advocacy groups, organizations and others. Single copies of this 20-page manual are available free.

* Physical Fitness Awards for Adults

President's Council on Physical Fitness and Sports
450 5th St., NW, Suite 7103
Washington, DC 20001   (202) 272-3421

The Presidential Sports Award recognizes adult participation in a regular program of exercise. Men and women 15 years of age and older can qualify for the award in one or more of 43 different sports and fitness activities. Specific requirements for each activity have been established for a four-month period. Upon meeting the qualifying standards, participants receive a personalized Presidential certificate of achievement and a sports award lapel pin. The Amateur Athletic Union administers the program.

* Physical Fitness Awards for Youngsters

President's Council on Physical Fitness and Sports
450 5th St., NW, Suite 7103
Washington, DC 20001   (202) 272-3421

The President's Council on Physical Fitness and Sports conducts two award programs for young people ages 6-17 which are offered through the school system. The Presidential Physical Fitness Award is given for scoring at or above the 85th percentile on all five physical fitness tests. The Council also awards other award programs and fitness clinics. Contact this office for more information and a list of their publications.

* Preventive Health Goals

ODPHP National Health Information Center
P.O. Box 1133
Washington, DC 20013   (800) 336-4797 (301) 565-4167 (in Maryland)

The proceedings of an international symposium on preventive services in primary care held in 1987 are available which address recommendations and goals in a variety of fields ranging from dentistry, medicine, public health, and behavioral sciences. *Implementing Preventive Services* (No. F0022) discusses specific services such as immunizations, screening tests such as Pap Smears and mammography, and patient education. It is available for $3.00 handling fee.

* Preventive Health National Programs

Centers for Disease Control
1600 Clifton Rd., NE, E06
Atlanta, GA 30333   (404) 639-1819

This center plans, directs, and coordinates national programs of assistance involving preventive health services to State and local health agencies. CDC provides leadership to the health community, especially State and local agencies, in the development and implementation of improved preventive health services programs. It assists States and localities in specifying major health problems in the community and formulating intervention strategies, and through grants, assists them in establishing and maintaining prevention and control programs directed toward health problems. Some of the preventive health services covered include aa

dental disease, immunizations, sexually transmitted diseases and tuberculosis.

* Rural Health Care

Office of Technology Assessment
600 Pennsylvania Ave., SE
Washington, DC 20510   (202) 228-6590

OTA is currently reviewing and evaluating past and current rural health care efforts; examining how medical technologies have been and might be diffused into rural areas; and identifying policies that might improve the quality, affordability, and accessibility of rural health care. Contact Elaine Power, the project director, for more information.

* Safe Exercise, Nutrition, Medicines for Seniors

ODPHP Health Information Center
P. O. Box 1133
Washington, DC 20013   (800) 336-4797 (301) 565-4167 in MD

Healthy Older People, a public education program on health promotion and aging conducted by the Office of Disease Prevention and Health Promotion (ODPHP), encourages older people to adopt good health habits, concentrating on such areas as exercise, nutrition, injury prevention, smoking, and medicines. A list of broadcast and print materials is available to State and local groups, along with a list of State contacts, who are responsible for coordinating statewide activities. The program includes consumer education, professional education, and technical assistance. A Program Memo maintains information on activities and regional workshops.

* Surgeon General's Reports on Health Promotion

ODPHP Health Information Center
P. O. Box 1133
Washington, DC 20013   (800) 336-4797 (301) 565-4167 in MD

The nation's priorities are outlined in a 177-page report titled *Healthy People: The Surgeon General's Report on Health Promotion and Disease Prevention* (No. F0005) which identifies specific goals in five stages of human development. Single copy is available for $1.00 handling fee.

A companion version titled *Promoting Health/Preventing Disease: Objectives for the Nation* (No. F0009) discusses 15 priority areas. This 102-page report is available for $3.00 handling fee. The *1990 Health Objectives for the Nation: A Midcourse Review* (No. F0013) is available for $3.00.

* Walking and Fitness

President's Council on Physical Fitness and Sports
450 5th St., NW, Suite 7103
Washington, DC 20001   (202) 272-3421

The President's Council serves as a clearinghouse for information on all types of exercise programs including making available free a 16-page manual titled *Everybody's Walking For Fitness* and *Walking for Exercise and Pleasure*.

* Worksite Health Promotion

ODPHP Health Information Center
P. O. Box 1133
Washington, DC 20013   (800) 336-4797 (301) 565-4167 in MD

A 22-page catalog titled *Worksite Health Promotion: A Bibliography of Selected Books and Resources* (No. W0005) lists resources for employee health promotion programs including books, publications, and newsletters for employees and organizations.

Food Facts, Nutrition, and Diets

* See also Consumer Chapter
* See also Agriculture and Farming; Food Quality and Distribution Chapter

There are menu plans and recipes as well as very technical information about the nutritional value of every conceivable food product. Surplus commodities and donations to non-profits are contained here as well as in the Government Auctions and Surplus Property Chapter. Surveys of food expenditures and eating habits as well as eating disorders are just a phone call away.

* Agricola Database
Family Information Center
National Agricultural Library
U.S. Department of Agriculture
Room 304
Beltsville, MD 20705   (301) 344-3719
A computerized database called AGRICOLA contains information primarily on the agricultural sciences but includes a substantial number of citations to nutrition literature such as journal articles, government reports, serials, monographs, and pamphlets. The print counterpart to this online database is titled *Food and Nutrition Bibiography*. The database is accessible through two commercial vendors, BRS and DIALOG.

* Allergies: Special Recipes
Superintendent of Documents
U.S. Government Printing Office
Washington, DC 20402   (202) 783-3238
Cooking for People with Food Allergies is a 39-page booklet that provides information for those who need help managing food allergies or intolerances. It provides help selecting and preparing foods containing no wheat, milk, eggs, corn, or gluten. Recipes are included. $1.50 (001-000-04512-1).

* American Diet Surveys
Superintendent of Documents
U.S. Government Printing Office
Washington, DC 20402   (202) 782-3238
A survey to measure the food intake of individuals, the quality of the diet, and the response of American diets to short-term changes in food supplies is being conducted. This survey and other HNIS findings support research in agricultural planning, the formation of agricultural and food policy, food quality and regulation, and nutrition education. The survey is published in several parts:

Women 19-50 and Their Children 1-5, 1 Day 1985 (85-1) $4.25
Low Income Women 19-50 and Their Children 1-5, 1 Day 1985 (85-2) $18.95
Men 19-50 Years, 1 Day, 1985 (85-3) $4.75
Women 19-50 and Their Children 1-5, 1 Day, 1986 (86-1) $4.75

* Anorexia Nervosa and Bulimia
National Institute of Child Health
and Human Development
NIH, Building 31, Room 2A-32
Bethesda, MD 20892   (301) 496-5133
Facts About Anorexia Nervosa explains the causes, symptoms and treatments for anorexia and bulimia as well as ongoing research efforts at NIH. This 8-page pamphlet is available free.

* Basic Four Food Groups: Dietary Guidelines
ODPHP Health Information Center
PO Box 1133
Washington, DC 20013-1133   (800) 336-4797 (301) 565-4167 in MD
The recent edition of the government's recommendations about starch, fiber, fat, sodium, sugar, alcohol and food intake titled *Nutrition and Your Health Dietary Guidelines for Americans* is available for $2.00. The Government Printing Office also sells this 20-page pamphlet in bulk (100 copies for $27.00).

* Budget to Stretch Food Dollars or Food Stamps
Food and Nutrition Information Center
National Agricultural Library Building, Room 304
Beltsville, MD 20705   (301) 436-8617

A manual titled *Making Your Food Dollars Count: A Project Guide*, suggests ways to spend money and food stamps on nutritious foods and explains how to setup such a education campaign within a community. This reference is available on loan or can be borrowed through an interlibrary loan.

* Calcium and Other Special Needs of Women
Office of Public Affairs
Food and Drug Administration
5600 Fishers Lane, HFE88
Rockville, MD 20857   (301) 443-3170
Several publications are available free which address the special nutrition needs of females including *Please Pass That Woman Some More Calcium and Iron* (No. 85-2198), *Osteoporosis: Calcium, and Estrogens* (No. 85-1117), and *The Nutritional Gender Gap at the Dinner Table* (No. 84-2197).

* Cancer Prevention and Nutrition
Office of Cancer Communications
National Cancer Institute
Building 31, Room 10A-24
9000 Rockville Pike
Bethesda, MD 20892   (800) 4-CANCER (800) 492-6000 in MD
This institute offers the latest findings and scientific studies about nutrition and cancer including a free 51-page pamphlet titled *Diet, Nutrition and Cancer Prevention: A Guide to Food Choices* (No. 85-2711) which describes what is known about the interrelationships of diet and certain cancers.

* Cellulite Removal Gimmicks
Office of Public Affairs
Food and Drug Administration
5600 Fishers Lane, HFE88
Rockville, MD 20857   (301) 443-3170
The FDA monitors many weight loss related-products and warns consumers about gimmicks sold which promise to get rid of fat on the hips and thighs.

* Cholesterol Facts
National Cholesterol Education Program Information Center
4733 Bethesda Ave., Room 530
Bethesda, MD 20814   (301) 951-3260
The Cholesterol Information Center has specialists on staff and provides printed information on cholesterol, diet, and high blood pressure to the public and health professionals. Some of the brochures which they distribute includes *NHLBI Facts About Blood Cholesterol*.

* Community Nutrition Services
National Clearinghouse for Primary Care Information
8201 Greensboro Drive #600
McLean, VA 22102   (703) 821-8955
This center offers manuals for community health centers, primary care providers, home health services, HMOs, and outpatient clinics on approaches for a nutrition program, such as counseling and referral. Single copies of a 96-page *Guide for Developing Nutrition Services in Community Health Programs* is available free.

* Diabetes, Digestive and Kidney Diseases
Clinical Nutrition Research Units (CNRU)
National Institute of Diabetes and
Digestive and Kidney Diseases, NIH
Building 31, Room 9A04
9000 Rockville Pike
Bethesda, MD 20892   (301) 496-3583

Health and Medicine

The CNRU is an integrated array of research, educational, and service activities focused on human nutrition in health and disease. It serves as the focal point for an interdisciplinary approach to clinical nutrition research. The findings are published in journals.

* Dietary Analysis for the Individual

National Technical Information Service
5285 Port Royal Rd.
Springfield, VA 22261 (703) 487-4650
NTIS sells a simple software program for IBM PC-compatible computers which will give you a dietary analysis of the foods you eat in a meal or for each day. Just by entering the names of the foods you have eaten, this program, developed by the USDA's Human Nutrition Information Service, will give you nutrient data information, calories, and recommended daily allowances on over 850 foods. The Dietary Analysis Program software is available for $60.

* Dietary Essentials

Grand Forks Human Nutrition
Research Center
P.O. Box 7166
University Station
Grand Forks, ND 58202-7166 (701) 795-8456
This center focuses on defining human requirements for trace elements and the physiological and biochemical factors which influence those requirements.

* Drugs and Food Interactions

Office of Public Affairs
Food and Drug Administration
5600 Fishers Lane, HFE88
Rockville, MD 20857 (301) 443-3170
A free report titled *Food and Drug Interactions* (No. 94-3070) explains why some foods and medicines may interfere with each other, and suggests whys to avoid the problem.

* Eating Disorders

Office of Public Affairs
Food and Drug Administration
5600 Fishers Lane, HFE88
Rockville, MD 20857 (301) 443-3170
Bulimia and anorexia nervosa are discussed in a short pamphlet titled *Eating Disorders: When Thinness Becomes an Obsession* (No. 86-2211) which is available free.

* Eating Habits National Survey

Division of Health Examination Statistics
National Center for Health Statistics
3700 East-West Hwy., Room 2-58
Hyattsville, MD 20782 (301) 436-7068
This division collects data on health-related matters and administers the National Health and Nutrition Survey, which assesses the health and nutritional status of the general population through direct physical examination.

* Elderly and Menu Ideas

National Institute on Aging Information Center
2209 Distribution Circle
Silver Spring, MD 20910 (301) 495-3455
The Institute makes available free several "Age Pages" which offer tips for seniors including *Food: Staying Healthy After 65, Be Sensible About Salt, Hints for Shopping, Cooking and Enjoying Meals,* and *Dietary Supplements: More Is Not Always Better.*

* Fad Diets and Diet Books

Office of Public Affairs
Food and Drug Administration
5600 Fishers Lane, HFE88
Rockville, MD 20857 (301) 443-3170
How to Take Weight Off Without Getting Ripped Off (No. 85-1116) discusses weight reduction products, fad diets, and other diet aids. Another free publication titled *Diet Books Sell Well But....*(No. 84-1093) reviews and evaluates some of the popular diet plans.

* Fast Foods and Nutrition

Office of Public Affairs
Food and Drug Administration
5600 Fishers Lane, HFE88
Rockville, MD 20857 (301) 443-3170
A free pamphlet titled *What About Nutrients In Fast Foods?* examines the pros and cons of "fast foods" and analyses the nutritional value of various menus.

* Fiber and Roughage

Office of Public Affairs
Food and Drug Administration
5600 Fishers Lane, HFE88
Rockville, MD 20857 (301) 443-3170
Single copies of the booklet, *Fiber: Something Healthy to Chew On* (No. 85-2206) discusses the role of fiber in nutrition.

* Food and Nutrition Service Publications

Food and Nutrition Service
U.S. Department of Agriculture
Public Affairs Staff
3101 Park Center Dr.
Alexandria, VA 22302 (703) 756-3276
FNIS publishes a variety of brochures explaining the various food assistance programs it operates both for those eligible for the programs and for those who administer them. Programs include the Child Nutrition Program; Food Distribution Program; Women, Infants, and Children (WIC) Program; Food Stamp Program; and various nutrition education materials. Requests for the Publications List are available from the above office, or from the Food and Nutrition Service Regional Offices listed below. Most publications are available free; those for sale are sold through the Government Printing Office.

* Food and Nutrition Services Regional Offices

Contact the regional office nearest you for getting answers to questions over the phone as well as data and information materials.

Northeast Region, 10 Causeway St., Room 501, Boston, MA 02222-1068

Southeast Region, 1100 Spring St., N.W., Suite 250, Atlanta, GA 30367

Southwest Region, 1100 Commerce St., Room 5-C-30, Dallas, TX 75242

Western Region, 550 Kearny St., Room 400, San Francisco, CA 94108

Mid-Atlantic Region, Mercer Corporate Park, Corporate Blvd., Trenton, NJ 08650

Midwest Region, 50 E. Washington St., 4th Floor, Chicago, IL 60602

Northwest Region, 2420 W. 26th Ave., Suite 430-D, Denver, CO 80211

* Food Assistance to the Poor

Food and Nutrition Service (FNS)
Public Information Office
3101 Park Center Dr.
Park Office Center Bldg.
Alexandria, VA 22302 (703) 756-3276
FNS administers many federal-state programs to provide food assistance to those in need. The agency cooperates with state and local welfare agencies to administer the Food Stamp Program, which enables low-income families to purchase a greater variety of food to improve their diets. Additional agency programs help reduce agricultural surpluses by providing commodities and other foodstuffs to schools and other institutions for their use in special nutrition programs. These programs are designed to help needy children achieve nutritionally balanced diets. The Special Supplemental Food Program for Women, Infants, and Children (WIC) provides specific nutritious food supplements to pregnant and nursing women, as well as to children up to 5 years of age who are found to be "at nutritional risk" because of poor diet or low income. The Food Distribution Program donates food to various outlets: schools, charitable institutions, nutrition programs for the elderly, summer camps, disaster relief agencies, and programs for needy families on some Indian reservations.

* Food Consumption Research

U.S. Department of Agriculture
6505 Belcrest Rd., Room 368
Hyattsville, MD 20782 (301) 436-8457
Data have been collected and is being compiled for the 1987-88 Nationwide Food Consumption Survey (NFCS 1987-88). This survey, conducted every 10 years, provides comprehensive information on the consumption of foods and nutrients and on the dietary status of U.S. households and individuals. For a summary of survey results, contact the above office.

* Food Contamination Inspection

Center for Food Safety and
Applied Nutrition
Food and Drug Administration
200 C St., SW, Room 6815

Washington, DC 20204 (202) 245-1144
The Center for Food Safety and Applied Nutrition conducts research and develops standards on the composition, quality, nutrition, and safety of food, food additives, colors, and cosmetics. The Center has cooperative arrangements with industries, such as milk and shellfish, where representatives from FDA, the state, and the industry meet to develop model codes and standards for the food product. The Center is responsible for food labeling, requiring ingredients to be listed in order of composition, as well as other nutritional information, such as fat and sodium content. They regulate the infant formula industry, ensuring that basic nutrients be included in the formula. The Center also administers a program of sampling food for possible contamination. Radiation from the Chernobyl accident and the Chilean Grape embargo are two recent examples studied under this program.

* Food Expenditures and Consumer Attitudes
Food Marketing and Economics Branch
Economics Research Service
1301 New York Ave., NW
Washington, DC 20005-4788 (202) 786-1862
Studies and expertise on such topics as the convenience food market, food purchases away from home, the fast food industry, the relationship between consumer attitudes about nutrition and actual food expenditures, and the economic effects of food safety regulations are available from this office.

* Food Preparation and Refrigeration
Office of Public Affairs
Food and Drug Administration
5600 Fishers Lane, HFE88
Rockville, MD 20857 (301) 443-3170
Enfermedades Causadas Por Alimentos Contaminados (No. 80-2044S) is available only in Spanish and recommends proper food preparation and refrigeration of various types of foods and also discusses some common foodborne organisms.

* Food Safety and Additives Info
Office of Public Affairs
Food and Drug Administration
5600 Fishers Lane, HFE88
Rockville, MD 20857 (301) 443-3170
The FDA distributes many brochures and publications including *More Than You Ever Thought You Would Know About Food Additives* (No. 82-2160), *Consumer's Guide to Food Labels* (No. 85-2083), and *Sweetness Minus Calories = Controversy* (No. 85-2205). The *FDA Consumer*, which contains the latest developments at FDA, can be ordered for $12 per year from the Superintendent of Documents, Government Printing Office, Washington DC 20402, (202) 783-3238.

* Food Safety and Inspection
Office of Public Awareness
Food Safety and Inspection Service
Department of Agriculture
Room 1165-S (202) 447-9351 (202) 447-3333 in DC
Washington, DC 20205 (800) 535-4555 Meat and Poultry Hotline
This office inspects and analyzes domestic and imported meat and poultry and establishes standards for processed meat and poultry products. Questions can be answered about the proper handling, preparation, and refrigeration, food poisoning, food additives, food labeling, sodium, and herbs.

* Food Tampering and Foreign Objects
Emergency Services
Food and Drug Administration
5600 Fishers Lane
HFC-162, Room 1362
Rockville, MD 20857 (301) 443-1240
FDA has a 24-hour answering service at (202) 737-0448. If you find foreign objects or evidence of tampering with any food, drug (both human and animal), or cosmetic, you should report it to the Food and Drug Administration. This office deals with consumer complaints and recalls. You can also report the tampering to any of the FDA regional offices.

* Free Food For Non-Profit Institutions
Food Distribution Program
Food and Nutrition Service
3101 Park Center Dr., Room 502
Alexandria, VA 22302 (703) 756-3680
Charitable and rehabilitation institutions are usually eligible to receive surplus commodities stored by USDA. The commodities available are dairy products, grain oil, and peanuts.

* Government Dietary Guidelines
Human Nutrition Information Service (HNIS)

U.S. Department of Agriculture
Room 325 A, Federal Building
Hyattsville, MD 20782 (301) 436-5724
HNIS has developed seven basic eating principals, the Dietary Guidelines, that encourage variety, balance, moderation in food consumption. The first two guidelines recommend people eat a variety of foods that provide enough essential nutrients and calories to maintain a desirable weight; the other five suggest eating an adequate amount of starch and fiber and avoiding too much fat, sugar, sodium, and alcohol. Contact HNIS for a series of seven bulletins outlining the program.

* Healthy Menus
Food and Nutrition Information Center
U.S. Department of Agriculture
National Agricultural Library, Room 304
Beltsville, MD 20705 (301) 344-3719
Cartoons fill the pages of this booklet titled *Eating For Better Health* which contains nutrition and weight loss information as well as inexpensive recipes and menus. Other information and scientific findings are available from this agency.

* Health Promotion and Nutrition
Nutrition Branch
Office of Disease Prevention and Health Promotion
Public Health Service
330 C St., SW, Room 2132
Washington, DC 20201 (202) 472-5660
As a policy arm of the Public Health Service, this office works on developing policies for the Year 2000 objectives for health promotion. Their Preventive Services Task Force is developing recommendations for clinical practice, in addition to a worksite Health Promotion Task Force and a Nutrition Branch. This office also operates the Health Promotion Clearinghouse which offers many publications.

* Healthy Heart Menus
National Heart, Lung, and Blood Institute
NIH, Building 31, Room 42-21
9000 Rockville Pike
Bethesda, MD 20892 (301) 496-4236
The relationship between diet and heart disease is studied by this institute so it is an excellent place to learn the latest findings about reducing cholesterol and other risk factors. A lengthy 224-page report titled *Foods For Health: Report of the Pilot Program* (No. 83-2036) shares the results of a one-year experiment to increase consumer awareness and knowledge about nutrition as it relates to cardiovascular risk factors. Single copies of this report are available free as well as other pilot projects.

* Low-Income Families and Nutrition Awareness
Food and Nutrition Information Center
National Agricultural Library Building, Room 304
Beltsville, MD 20705 (301) 344-3719
The Idea Book: Sharing Nutrition Education Experiences is designed for WIC (Women, Infants, and Children) nutrition educators and contains chapters covering motivation, planning, lesson plans, etc. This 89-page resource is available on loan from the Center and also is available through interlibrary loan.

* Malnutrition and Nutrition Research
Western Human Nutrition Research Center
P.O. Box 29997
Presidio of San Francisco
San Francisco, CA 94129 (415) 556-9699
This center develops improved methods for monitoring and evaluating nutritional status and investigates factors that lead to malnutrition. It also conducts studies on human nutritional requirements.

* Nutrient Data Tapes
National Technical Information Service
5285 Port Royal Rd.
Springfield, VA 22261 (703) 487-4650
The Human Nutrition Information Service collects and publishes information on disc and magnetic tape on the nutritive composition of foods. The agency gathers data from the scientific literature and from government, university, and food industry laboratories and directs laboratory studies to produce information. HNIS also compiles information on yield and nutrient retention of food items at different stages in production. Complete ordering information is available from the above address. See Human Nutrition Information Service Reports to order print versions of this information.

Health and Medicine

* Nutrient Values and Food Groups

Public Information Officer
Human Nutrition Information Service
U.S. Department of Agriculture
Federal Building
6505 Belcrest Road, Room 363
Hyattsville, MD 20782   (301) 436-8617

This office shares its research in nutritive value of foods and of the nutritional adequacy of diets and food supplies. It also maintains the Nutrient Data Bank which contains surveys and data on the nutrient values in foods and descriptions of foods. Various consumer materials are available as well as a publications list.

* Nutritionally-Related Chronic Diseases

Beltsville Human Nutrition Research Center
BARC-East, Building 308
Beltsville, MD 20705   (301) 344-2157

This center conducts research on nutrient composition and nutritional qualities of food; performs studies on energy metabolism and nutritional requirements; and develops dietary strategies that can delay the onset of nutritionally-related chronic diseases.

* Nutrition Labels and U.S. RDA

Office of Public Affairs
Food and Drug Administration
5600 Fishers Lane, HFE88
Rockville, MD 20857   (301) 443-3170

A short fact sheet titled *Nutrition Labels and U.S. RDA* explains the evolution of the Recommended Daily Allowances (RDAs) and the intention of nutritional labeling information.

* Nutrition Needs of Mothers and Infants

Children's Nutrition Research Center
at Baylor College of Medicine
1100 Bates St.
Houston, TX 77030   (713) 798-7000

This center focuses on determining the unique nutrient needs of pregnant and lactating women, and of children from conception through early years of development.

* Nutrition: Technical Assistance

Center for Health Promotion and Education
Centers for Disease Control
1600 Clifton Rd., NW
Room SSB249
Atlanta, GA 30333   (404) 329-3492

Through its three divisions--health education, nutrition, and reproductive health-- this center offers technical assistance and expertise in these categories, as well as in health promotion and health education. Primary recipients of technical assistance are official state and local health agencies, schools, and health care delivery settings. The Center maintains a database of health education programs and methods in schools and rural and urban communities, which is part of the Combined Health Information Database (CHID).

* Obesity and Energy Metabolism

Office of Clinical Center Communications
Warren G. Magnuson Clinical Center
NIH, Building 10, Room 5C-305
9000 Rockville Pike
Bethesda, MD 20892   (301) 496-2563

Single copies are available free of a 23-page booklet titled *Obesity and Energy Metabolism* (No. 86-1805) which explains the relationship between too much food and too little exercise. A videotape based on this publication is available and can be purchased or available on a free loan basis.

* Older Adults and Nutrition

Human Nutrition Research Center on
Aging at Tufts University
711 Washington, St.
Boston, MA 02111   (617) 556-3330

This center researches the special nutritional needs of persons as they age, with a view toward enhancing the quality of later life through improved nutrition and health.

* Organic and Natural Foods

Office of Public Affairs
Food and Drug Administration
5600 Fishers Lane, HFE88
Rockville, MD 20857   (301) 443-3170

A short pamphlet titled *The Confusing World of Health Foods* (No. 84-2108) provides general information about foods sold as health foods and about such terms as "organic". *The Consumer's Guide to Food Labels* (No. 85-2083) translates the nutrition information which appears on food labels.

* Pesticide Residues

Office of Pesticide Programs
Environmental Protection Agency
401 M St., SW
Washington DC 20460   (202) 557-7090

EPA administers two Congressionally mandated statutes to control the more than 45,000 pesticide products registered for use in the United States. The EPA monitors the distribution and use of these pesticides, issuing civil or criminal penalties for violations. EPA also sets tolerances or maximum legal limits for pesticide residues on food commodities and feed grains to prevent consumer exposure to unsafe pesticide levels.

* Pick Your Own Fruits and Vegetables

Contact your local USDA Extension Service agent
Many farmers allow consumers to pick produce directly from their fields at substantial savings.

* Recipes and other Nutrition Materials

Consumer Information Center
Department 70
Pueblo, CO 81009

Four new booklets called *Eating Right...The Dietary Guidelines Way*, provide recipes and detailed information on following HNIS nutrition guidelines:

Preparing Foods and Planning Menus Using the Dietary Guidelines. Tips for cooking with less fat, sugar, and sodium, plus a daily guide to food choices. $2.50. Item No. 172-V.
Making Bag Lunches, Snacks, and Desserts Using the Dietary Guidelines. Munchers guide to snacks, tips on reading food labels, and desserts with less fat and sugar. $3.00. Item No. 173-V.
Shopping for Food and Making Meals in Minutes Using the Dietary Guidelines. Quick meal hints, tips on reading food labels, and a shopping guide. $3.00. Item No. 174-V.
Eating Better When Eating Out Using the Dietary Guidelines. Tips for ordering foods "your way", advice on reading menus, and facts and fallacies on fast foods. $1.50. Item No. 175-V.

* Saccharin, Cyclamate and Aspartame

Office of Public Affairs
Food and Drug Administration
5600 Fishers Lane, HFE88
Rockville, MD 20857   (301) 443-3170

The FDA offers information on food additives including free pamphlets such as *Sweetness Minus Calories = Controversy* (No. 85-2205) which gives the legal and scientific histories of these sugar substitutes and other sweeteners.

* Salt and Low-Sodium Diets

Office of Public Affairs
Food and Drug Administration
5600 Fishers Lane, HFE88
Rockville, MD 20857   (301) 443-3170

Free pamphlets about consumption of salt in one's daily diet are available including *A Word About Low-Sodium Diets* (No. 87-2179) which suggests ways consumers can lower sodium intake and lists foods that are naturally low in sodium. A slide set titled "Good Sense About Sodium" which is also available in Spanish, is obtainable through Consumer Affairs Officers in FDA district offices.

* Teenagers and Necessary Nutrition

National Health Information Center
PO Box 1133
Washington, DC 20013   (800) 336-4797 (301) 565-4167 in MD

In its series called "Healthfinders", this clearinghouse makes available for only a $1.00 handling fee a resource pamphlet titled *Adolescent Health Information Materials* which lists various publications and manuals available from the American Dietetic Association, the National Dairy Council, and other private and government sources.

* Vitamins and Recommended Dietary Allowances

Office of Public Affairs
Food and Drug Administration
5600 Fishers Lane, HFE88
Rockville, MD 20857   (301) 443-3170

Single copies are available free of the government's recommended dietary allowances in a pamphlet titled *Some Facts and Myths of Vitamins* (No. 82-2164).

* Vitamins A - K Publications

National Health Information Center
PO Box 1133
Washington, DC 20013   (800) 336-4797 (301) 565-4167 in MD
In its series called "Healthfinder", this clearinghouse lists numerous city and county health departments as well as foundations and public health organizations which offer fact sheets on vitamin A, vitamin B, vitamin C, vitamin D, vitamin E and vitamin K. This four-page "Healthfinder" titled *Vitamins* also lists books and publications pertaining to minerals and vitamin supplements.

* Worksite Nutrition Programs

ODPHP Health Information Center
PO Box 1133
Washington, DC 20013-1133   (800) 336-4797 (301) 565-4167 in MD
A 58-page program for implementing nutrition programs in the workplace and describes what resources employers need to conduct such a health initiative. *Worksite Nutrition: A Decision Maker's Guide* (No. U-0010) can be purchased for $2.00.

Contraception and Pregnancy

Several government-sponsored clearinghouses listed below, for example, the National Center for Maternal and Child Health and the Family Life Information Exchange offer materials published by both federal and state health agencies as well as organizations such as the March of Dimes Birth Defects Foundation. These information centers work in close coordination with many government and private groups and research hubs so they are in a position to refer callers to expert and organizations who can answer questions and concerns.

* Adolescent Pregnancy Programs
Office of Adolescent Pregnancy Programs
Department of Health and Human Services
200 Independence Avenue, SW, Room 736E
Washington, DC 20201   (202) 245-7473
This office promotes adoption as an alternative to early parenting and focuses on teenagers under 18 years of age. Pregnancy prevention strategies and information resources are coordinated by this office.

* Adoption: Decision and Resources
Family Life Information Exchange
P.O. Box 30146
Bethesda, MD 20814   (301) 907-8198
This clearinghouse offers numerous resources on the issue of putting up a child for adoption, including such free publications as *The Adoption Option: A Guidebook for Pregnancy Counselors* (No FP-10000).

* Birth Control and Sterilization Posters
Family Life Information Exchange
P.O. Box 30146
Bethesda, MD 20814   (301) 907-8198
This clearinghouse offers single free copies of several posters including "Spacing Pregnancy Means" (FP-100068) and "Sterilization is Permanent" (FP-100059).

* Birth Control Methods
National Institute of Child Health and Human Development
NIH, Building 31, Room 2A32
9000 Rockville Pike
Bethesda, MD 20892   (301) 496-5133
The National Institute of Child Health and Human Development distributes pamphlets and reports on the various methods of contraception, as well as medical updates on the risks and/or effectiveness of new forms of birth control. The 19-page booklet, *Facts About Oral Contraceptives*, is available free.

* Birth Defects and Toxic Substances
Genetic Toxicology Association
Cleary, Gottlieb, Steen and Hamilton
1725 N St., NW
Washington, DC 20036   (202) 728-2700
The Genetic Toxicology Association promotes the study of mutagenicity (the capacity to induce mutations in living organisms).

* Breastfeeding Information
National Clearinghouse for Maternal and Child Health
38th & R St., NW
Washington, DC 20057   (202) 625-8410
A 22-page booklet is available free, *Breast Feeding* (No. B-30) which encourages lactation and teachers the proper techniques.

* Catalog: Info, Help and Resources for Mothers
National Maternal and Child Health Clearinghouse
38th & R St., NW
Washington, DC 20057   (202) 625-8410
A valuable directory of educational materials, organizations, and resources for expectant and new mothers is available free from this national center. The Third Edition of this 170-page guide is titled *Healthy Mothers Coalition Directory of Educational Materials*.

* Cesarean Childbirth
National Institute of Child Health and Human Development

NIH, Building 31, Room 2A32
9000 Rockville Pike
Bethesda, MD 20892   (301) 496-5133
This institute can provide data and medical information about this health issue. A 13-page booklet, *Facts About Cesarean Childbirth* (No. 431P), discusses cesarean delivery, types of incisions, current thinking about repeat cesarean, and the pros and cons of this method of birth.

* Child Health Info for Prospective and New Parents
National Center for Education in Maternal and Child Health
38th & R St., NW
Washington, DC 20057   (202) 625-8400
The Center responds to information requests from prospective and new parents, consumers, as well as professionals. This clearinghouse provides technical assistance, and develops educational and reference materials. The NCEMCH Resource Center contains professional literature, patient education materials, curricula, audiovisuals, and information about organizations and programs. Major content areas include pregnancy, child and adolescent health, and human genetics.

* Child Safety: CPR, Infant and Child Car Seats
National Health Information Center
P. O. Box 1133
Washington, DC 20013   (800) 336-4797 (301) 565-4167 (in MD)
Child Safety Resource Guide describes currently available publications that offer information for individuals responsible for the care and safety of young people. It is designed for educators looking for materials to support program activities, as well as for the general public. The materials listed focus on injury prevention and give tips and suggestions on protecting children against potential hazards in the home, in cars, on bicycles, and in the water. A short list of coloring and activities books is included, as well as sources of information on cardio-pulmonary resuscitation.

* Cigarettes and the Unborn
Office on Smoking and Health
Technical Information Center
Park Building, Room 1-10
5600 Fishers Lane
Rockville, MD 20857   (301) 443-1690
Now You're Smoking For Two! A Guide to Smoking and Pregnancy (No. 83-50198) is available free.

* Condoms and Effectiveness of other Contraception
Contraception Evaluation Branch
EPN 607, 9000 Rockville Pike
Bethesda, MD 20892   (301) 496-4924
The Contraception Evaluation Branch designs and supports a program of studies to clarify the safety and effectiveness of fertility control. They also provide on-going surveillance of the effectiveness of fertility regulating products and surgical procedures. A major emphasis now is to demonstrate the degree to which barrier contraceptives reduce the risk of sexually transmitted diseases, including AIDS. Staff can refer you to researchers examining a particular birth control method, with most of their research being published in journals.

* Comparing Contraceptives
Office of Consumer Affairs
Food and Drug Administration
Public Inquiries
5600 Fishers Lane (HFE-88)
Rockville, MD 20857   (301) 443-3170
This agency publishes *Comparing Contraceptives* (No. 85-1123), which discusses the possible side effects and effectiveness of nine different types of birth control and also contains a chart.

* Down's Syndrome Information

National Institute of Child Health and Human Development
NIH, Building 31, Room 2A32
9000 Rockville Pike
Bethesda, MD 20892   (301) 496-5133

Single copies of an 18-page booklet, *Facts About Down Syndrome for Women Over 35* (No. 82-536), discusses genetic counseling, and the outlook for a child born with Down's syndrome. This institute can provide more technical and statistical information about this birth defect.

* Drinking When Pregnant

National Clearinghouse for Alcohol and Drug Information
P.O. Box 2345
Rockville, MD 20852   (301) 468-2600

Preventing Fetal Alcohol Effects: A Practical Guide for Ob/Gyn Physicians and Nurses (DHHS No. 81-1163) suggests ways to identify expectant mothers at risk due to alcohol consumption during pregnancy. Fact sheets also available free include "Fetal Alcohol Syndrome" (Order No. MS303 and Order No. MS304).

* Drugs (Legal and Illegal) and Pregnancy

Office of Consumer Affairs
Food and Drug Adminstration
Public Inquiries
5600 Fishers Lane (HFE-88)
Rockville, MD 20857   (301) 443-3170

Single copies are available free of *Drugs and Pregnancy*, (No. 80-3083), which explains how medications, drugs, alcohol and tobacco are shared with the unborn baby. Other related hazards to the fetus are also discussed.

* Eating for Two

Office of Consumer Affairs
Food and Drug Adminstration
Public Inquiries
5600 Fishers Lane (HFE-88)
Rockville, MD 20857   (301) 443-3170

A free booklet, *All About Eating for Two* (No. 84-2183), discusses how pregnancy and breastfeeding affect a woman's nutritional needs.

* Family Planning Promotion

Family Life Information Exchange
P.O. Box 30146
Bethesda, MD 20814   (301) 907-8198

The Family Life Information Exchange has information on family planning, adolescent pregnancy, and adoption. The have brochures and pamphlets, as well as catalogs containing family planning publications. A free newsletter on health education and family planning is also available. Several of their free titles include: *Contraception: Comparing the Options*; *Designing Your Family Planning Education Program* (FP-100003); *Family Planning in Primary Care Settings* (FP-100007).

* Fetal and Newborn Development and Child Health

National Institute of Child Health and Human Development
National Institutes of Health
9000 Rockville Pike
Bethesda, MD 20892   (301) 496-3454

The National Institute of Child Health and Human Development (NICHHD) conducts and supports research on the reproductive, developmental, and behavioral process that determine the health of children, adults, families, and populations. Research for mothers, children, and families is designed to advance knowledge of fetal development, pregnancy, and birth; to identify the prerequisites of optional growth through infancy to adulthood; and to contribute to the prevention and treatment of mental retardation.

* Genetics Research

National Institute of General Medical Sciences
National Institutes of Health
Building 31, Room 4A52
9000 Rockville Pike
Bethesda, MD 20892   (301) 496-7301

NIGMS supports research and research training in the basic biomedical sciences that form the foundation needed to make advances in the understanding of disease. Research focuses on the cellular basis of disease, genetics, pharmacological sciences, physiology and biomedical engineering. For instance, they look at how DNA is replicated or how drugs are metabolized in your body. They have brochures and reports for the general public and professionals on such topics as medicines and genetic diseases.

* Gynecological Health

National Health Information Center
P.O. Box 1133
Washington, DC 20013   (800) 336-4797 (301) 565-4167 in MD

In its series, "Healthfinder", the center publishes *Women's Health* which lists many organizations that provide information on a broad range of topics including gynecological, mitral valve prolapse, osteoporosis. This 6-page reference illustrates the array of organizations which offer expertise and information.

* Healthy Mothers, Healthy Babies

Office of Public Affairs
Health Resources and Services Administration
5600 Fishers Lane, Room 1443
Rockville, MD 20857   (301) 443-2086

The Health Resources and Services Administration offers a free catalog, Current Publications, which lists all the publications films, and videos produced by HRSA's three bureaus: Bureau of Health Care Delivery and Assistance, Bureau of Maternal and Child Health and Resources Development and Bureau of Health Professions.

* Infertility and Population Research

Reproductive Sciences Branch
Center for Population Research
6130 Executive Blvd., Room 603
Bethesda, MD 20892   (301) 496-6515

The Reproductive Sciences Branch supports basic research in reproductive sciences, such as the alleviation of human infertility, curing human reproductive diseases and disorders, development of healthy embryos, and the discovery of safe methods of contraception. Institutional Programs in Reproductive Sciences Research awards grants to leading institutions in the U.S. to help them to establish Program Projects and Research Centers to support research on reproductive sciences. They also support postdoctoral fellowships, institutional training grants, and other awards to facilitate the development and maintenance of reproductive sciences research programs. This Branch also organizes workshops and symposiums in the U.S. and abroad on various topics in the reproductive sciences.

* Infertility and Treatments

Office of Consumer Affairs
Food and Drug Adminstration
Public Inquiries
5600 Fishers Lane (HFE-88)
Rockville, MD 20857   (301) 443-3170

Single copies are available free of the two-page pamphlet, *Infertility and How It's Treated* (No. 83-3136).

* Maternal and Child Health Clearinghouse

National Clearinghouse for Maternal and Child Health
38th & R St., NW
Washington, DC 20057   (202) 625-8410

This clearinghouse is a centralized source of materials and information in the areas of human genetics and maternal and child health. The clearinghouse responds to inquiries, distributes publications, bibliographies, and referral lists, which are compiled on an in-house, online database for related materials.

* Measles and Rubella

National Clearinghouse for Maternal and Child Health
38th & R St., NW
Washington, DC 20057   (202) 625-8410

Birth defects caused by rubella and its prevention through vaccination are discussed in this free 14-page booklet, *Rubella*.

* Nutrition during Pregnancy

National Clearinghouse for Maternal and Child Health
38th & R St., NW
Washington, DC 20057   (202) 625-8410

Food for the Teenager During and After Pregnancy (No. H-75)includes sample menus and other information about diet. *Pregnancy Basics: What You Need to Know and Do to Have a Good Healthy Baby* discusses do's and don'ts and single copies of this 13-page booklet are also available from the Clearinghouse.

* Population Research: Fertility, Contraception

Center for Population Research
Executive Plaza North, Room 604
Bethesda, MD 20892   (301) 496-1101

The Center for Population Research, as part of the National Institute of Child Health and Human Development, is responsible for the extramural effort in population research. It funds research through grants and contracts for studies on fertility, contraception, and population structure and change. The Inter-agency Committee on Population Research, a committee of Federal Agencies, facilitates the exchange of information on population research, which includes producing two free publications: *The Inventory and Analysis of Federal Population Research* which lists all the federally supported population research projects; and *The Inventory of Private Agency Population Research* which lists research projects by private organizations. CPR also advances international cooperation in population research and collaborates with the World Health Organization regarding the development of safe methods of contraception.

* Pregnancy and Childbirth Health Resources

National Health Information Center
P.O. Box 1133
Washington, DC 20013   (800) 336-4797 (301) 565-4167 in MD
In its series, "Healthfinder", the center publishes *Women's Health* which lists many organizations that provide information on a broad range of topics including pregnancy and childbirth. This 6-page reference illustrates the array of organizations which offer expertise and information.

* Pregnancy and Infancy Resources

Pregnancy and Perinatology Branch
National Institute of Child Health and Human Development
Room 643, EPN Building
9000 Rockville Pike
Bethesda, MD 20892   (301) 496-5575
Information on pregnancy, birth, and infant development and disorders is available through the Pregnancy and Perinatology Branch. They have brochures, pamphlets, reports, and information on current research.

* Premature Birth

National Institute of Child Health and Human Development
National Institutes of Health
9000 Rockville Pike
Bethesda, MD 20892   (301) 496-3454
This institute has much information about premature labor and birth including two free booklets: *Little Babies Born Too Soon, Born Too Small* (No. 77-1079) and *Facts About Premature Birth*.

* Prenatal Care: Government's Bestseller

National Clearinghouse for Maternal and Child Health
38th & R St., NW
Washington, DC 20057   (202) 625-8410
This clearinghouse makes available free single copies of *Prenatal Care* (Pub. No. H50), the federal government's popular 98-page "Dr. Spock" which provides basic information to pregnant women on caring for herself and her unborn baby. This booklet (No. 186P) is also available for $2.50 from the Consumer Information Center, Dept. Z, Pueblo, CO 81009. The Spanish version, *Cuidado Prenatal* (Stock No. 017-091-00209-6) is available for $4.50 from the Superintendent of Documents, Government Printing Office, Washington, DC 20402, (202) 783-3238.

* Prenatal Care: Technical Assistance

Center for Health Promotion and Education
Centers for Disease Control
1600 Clifton Rd., NW
Room SSB249
Atlanta, GA 30333   (404) 329-3492
This CDC center offers technical assistance and expertise on reproductive health as well as in health promotion and health education. Primary recipients of technical assistance are official state and local health agencies, schools, and health care delivery settings. The Center maintains a database of health education programs and methods in schools and rural and urban communities, which is part of the Combined Health Information Database (CHID).

* Pregnancy-Related Deaths Investigation

Center for Chronic Disease Prevention and Health Promotion
Centers for Disease Control
1600 Clifton Rd, NE
Bldg 3, Room 117
Atlanta, GA 30333   (404) 639-2838
The National Maternal Mortality Surveillance System is maintained as an avenue for reporting pregnancy-related deaths in the United States. All reported deaths are investigated, and a liaison has been established with local and national organizations of obstetricians and gynecologists to improve obstetric practices.

* Smoking and Pregnancy

National Institute of Child Health and Human Development
NIH, Building 31, Room 2A32
9000 Rockville Pike
Bethesda, MD 20892   (301) 496-5133
This free 7-page booklet, *Facts About Pregnancy and Smoking*, describes the effects of cigarettes on the developing fetus.

* Sonograms and Its Effects on Pregnancy

National Institute of Child Health and Human Development
Office of Research Reporting
Building 31, Room 2A-32
9000 Rockville Pike
Bethesda, MD 20892   (301) 496-5133
This office distributes a 1984 NICHHD conference report entitled, *Diagnostic Ultrasound Imaging in Pregnancy*, which discusses the biophysics and bioeffects of sonograms, clinical applications, epidemiological studies, and the psychological, legal, and ethical dimensions of ultrasound imaging. A brief pamphlet, *The Unknowns of Ultrasound* (No. 83-8201) is also available free.

* Sterilization Operations

Family Life Information Exchange
P.O. Box 30146
Bethesda, MD 20814   (301) 907-8198
Information for Men-Your Sterilization Operation (FP-100014) is available in English and Spanish and includes 3-part consent form used for all federally funded vasectomies. Information for Women-Your Sterilization Operation (No 10015) provides information on tubal ligation and other methods of birth control. It is also available in Spanish.

* Sudden Infant Death Syndrome (SIDS)

National Sudden Infant Death Syndrome Clearinghouse
8201 Greensboro Dr., Suite 600
McLean, VA 22102   (703) 821-8955
This clearinghouse was established to provide information and educational materials on SIDS, apnea, and other related issues. The staff responds to information requests from professionals, families with SIDS-related deaths, and the general public by sending written materials and making referrals. The clearinghouse maintains a library of reference materials and mailing lists of state programs, groups, and individuals concerned with SIDS. Their many publications include bibliographies on SIDS and self-help support groups, a publications catalogue, and a newsletter.

* Teenage Pregnancy Prevention Grants

Adolescent Pregnancy Programs
PHS, Room 736E
200 Independence Ave., SW
Washington, DC 20201   (202) 245-7473
This office awards grants to private and public non-profit organizations to establish and operate voluntary family planning services. The Adolescent Family Life Program supports research projects and innovative family-centered, community-based demonstration projects to provide either care or prevention services for adolescents and their families.

* Toxoplasmosis and Birth Defects

National Institute of Allergy and Infectious Diseases
NIH, Building 31, Room 7A-32
9000 Rockville Pike,
Bethesda, MD 20892   (301) 496-5717
A five-page booklet, *Toxoplasmosis*, (Pub. No. 83-308) discusses the hazards to the fetus of the toxoplasma parasites and suggests precautions to prevent the disease. Single copy available free from the institute.

* Workplace Hazards: Fetal Development and Pregnancy

National Institute for Occupational Safety and Health
4676 Columbia Parkway
Cincinnati, OH 45226   (800) 356-4674
NIOSH is responsible for conducting research to make the nation's workplaces healthier and safer by responding to urgent requests for assistance from employers, employees, and their representatives where imminent hazards are suspected. They conduct inspections, laboratory and epidemiologic research, publish their findings, and make recommendations for improved working conditions to regulatory agencies. NIOSH trains occupational health and safety workers and communicates research results to those concerned.

Stress, Mental Illness, and Family Violence

The National Institute of Mental Health of the National Institutes of Health is a useful starting place for discovering other information resources. Local and state chapters of the National Mental Health Association provide assistance to the mentally ill and their families, and provide help to school systems and local governments. Many county and state governments offer counseling and other services.

* Adolescent Violence and Death

National Technical Information Service
U.S. Department of Commerce
Springfield, VA 22161

Focal Points provides information on violence as a public health problem, particularly in the area of reducing the deaths of those in the 15-24 age group. Stress reduction and other programs that prevent violence are described. This publication (Order No.PB84-158385) is available for $7.00.

* Anger and Aggression

Public Inquiries Branch
National Institute of Mental Health
Parklawn Building
5600 Fishers Lane Room 15C-05
Rockville, MD 20857   (301) 443-4513

This Institute publishes several free pamphlets including *Plain Talk About Dealing with the Angry Child* and *Plain Talk About Adolescence*.

* Biofeedback and Stress Reduction

Public Inquiries Branch
National Institute of Mental Health
Parklawn Building
5600 Fishers Lane Room 15C-05
Rockville, MD 20857   (301) 443-4513

Plain Talk About Biofeedback reviews the medical uses of biofeedback, including its use by psychologists to help tense and anxious clients learn to relax. This pamphlet is available free from the Consumer Information Center, Pueblo, CO 81009. *Plain Talk About Handling Stress* discusses the stages of physical and mental stress, describes the symptoms and offers suggestions for stress reduction. This is available free from the Institute.

* Charla Franca: Como Tratar Al Nino Enojado

Public Inquiries Branch
National Institute of Mental Health
Parklawn Building
5600 Fishers Lane Room 15C-05
Rockville, MD 20857   (301) 443-4513

The Spanish version of *Plain Talk About Dealing With The Angry Child* (Pub No. 81-78 (SP) is available free. The Institute publishes other pamphlets in Spanish.

* Child Abuse Prevention Programs

Clearinghouse on Child Abuse and Neglect
Administration for Children, Youth, and Families
P.O. Box 1182
Washington, DC 20013   (703) 821-2086

The National Center on Child Abuse and Neglect (NCCAN) awards grants to states for a variety of programs dealing with child abuse and neglect; conducts research into the causes, prevention, and treatment of child abuse and neglect; funds demonstration programs to identify the best means of preventing maltreatment and treating troubled families; and funds the development and implementation of training programs. It distributes information through the Clearinghouse on Child Abuse and Neglect Information.

* Child Abuse and Neglect Clearinghouse

Clearinghouse on Child Abuse
and Neglect Information
P.O. Box 1182
Washington, DC 20013   (703) 821-2086

The Clearinghouse on Child Abuse and Neglect Information is a major resource for both professionals and the general public interested in child maltreatment issues. Publications distributed include bibliographies, training materials, and research reviews. The clearinghouse maintains a database (Dialogue File 64)

from which they can retrieve information on specific topics. Contact this office for a free listing of their publications and other resources.

* Child Abuse Resources for Professionals

National Child Abuse and Neglect
Clinical Resource Center
1205 Oneida St.
Denver, CO 80220   (303) 321-3963

This center focuses on clinical issues by providing training and consultation on a fee-for-service basis and through networking of streamlining resources and referrals. Program and case consultation is provided at the Center or by phone (they have a WATS line) for a fee. An annual symposium and a scholars-in-residence program provides professionals and lay persons the opportunity to observe and participate in the Center's activities, which include workshops, seminars, and professional education. The Center's resource library offers audiovisual rentals and a free publications catalog.

* Child Abuse Signs and Symptoms

Clearinghouse on Child Abuse
and Neglect Information
P.O. Box 1182
Washington, DC 20013   (703) 821-2086

Child Abuse and Neglect: An Informed Approach To A Shared Concern is a free pamphlet providing information about detecting child abuse and how to obtain help.

* Child Adoption, Foster Care and Welfare

Children's Bureau
Administration for Children, Youth, and Families
Office of Human Development Services
P.O. Box 1182
Washington, DC 20013   (202) 245-0656

The Children's Bureau funds a range of state-run programs combatting child abuse and neglect, strengthening foster care and adoption services, and supporting other child welfare services.

* Children of Alcoholic Families

National Clearinghouse on Alcohol Information
PO Box 2345
Rockville, MD 20852   (301) 468-2600

A Growing Concern: How to Provide Services for Children of Alcoholic Families discusses issues and strategies for providing help to youngsters from homes with alcoholism. This 52-page booklet (Order No. PH196) is geared more to professionals and caregivers and is free.

* Child Sexual Abuse Info Center

National Resource Center on Child Sexual Abuse
Information Service
106 Lincoln St.
Huntsville, AL 35801   (205) 533-KIDS; (800) KIDS-0006; or

NRCCSA
11141 Georgia Ave.
Wheaton, MD 20902   (301) 949-5000

The NRCCSA is an information, training, and technical assistance center designed for all professionals working in the field of child sexual abuse. They provide an array of services to help professionals better to investigate and manage child sexual
victimization cases. The Information Service handles requests for information, and for a quarterly publication, *Roundtable*, which offers information, updates, and new developments on child abuse. This office also sponsors comprehensive training with national experts and leading professionals.

* Community Mental Health Help

Consumer Information Center
Dept. Z
Pueblo, CO 81009

A Consumer's Guide to Mental Health Services describes the services available from community mental health centers, details different kinds of therapy and mental health professionals, and provides a list of warning signals and tells what to do in a crisis situation. This 21-page booklet is available free.

* Crisis Counseling Grants and Materials

Emergency Services Branch
National Institute of Mental Health
5600 Fishers Lane, Room 11C25
Rockville, MD 20857 (301) 443-4735

The Emergency Services Branch oversees three programs: 1) The Emergency Research Program studies the psychosocial response to mass emergencies; 2) The Crisis Counseling Program administers crisis counseling grants to states in which there has been a Presidentially-declared disaster; 3) The Emergency Preparedness Program plans for alcohol, drug abuse, and mental health disaster-related services nationwide. The program provides technical assistance and public education materials to states and local agencies in times of emergencies, and has three publications designed for non-mental health emergency workers (police, fire, emergency medical personnel) which focus on mental health issues.

* Death and Grieving

National Sudden Infant Death Syndrome Clearinghouse
8201 Greensboro Drive
Suite 600
McLean, VA 22102 (703) 821-8955

The Grief of Children discusses some of the ways that children express grief and that adults can help. Two other short pamphlets available free are *Parents and the Grieving Process* and *Talking to Children About Death.*

* Depression: Diagnosis and Treatments

National Institute of Mental Health
Alcohol, Drug Abuse and Mental Health Administration
5600 Fishers Lane, Room 15C05
Rockville, MD 20857 (301) 443-4515

NIMH conducts research on depression and other mental disorders, distributes information, conducts demonstration programs for the prevention, treatment, and rehabilitation of the mentally ill.

A major media campaign on depression, called Project D/ART (Depression/Awareness, Recognition, Treatment), is being developed by NIMH in collaboration with other organizations to provide information on symptoms, causes, and treatments of various depressive disorders. Many publications and reports are available on various topics for professionals and the general public.

* Depressive Disorders and Antidepressent Drugs

National Institute of Mental Health
5600 Fishers Lane, Room 15C05
Rockville, MD 20857 (301) 443-4515

A free 13-page pamphlet, *Depressive Disorders: Causes and Treatments (No. 83-1081)*, discusses symptoms of depression and the various effective treatments available. *Using Drugs to Life That Dark Veil of Depression (No.84-3140)* discusses various antidepressent drugs and the various side effects of each by generic and trade name. *You Are Not Alone: Facts About Mental Health and Mental Illness* (Pub. No. 85-1178) discusses mood changes, anxiety,and ways to deal with depression. Single copies of each of these booklets are available.

* Elderly Alcohol Abuse

Information Center
National Institute on Aging
2209 Distribution Circle
Silver Spring, MD 20910 (301) 495-3455

Aging and Alcohol Abuse is a one-page information sheet available free from the National Institute on Aging.

* Emotional Problems and Self-Help

National Technical Information Service
US Department of Commerce
Springfield, VA 22161

Self-help Groups As a Vehicle for Helping Individuals Cope with Emotional Problems discusses the potential for helping emotionally troubled individuals. This publication is available for $6.00.

* Family Adjustment and Crisis

Family Information Center
U.S. Department of Agriculture

National Agricultural Library Building,Room 304
Beltsville, MD 20705 (301) 344-3719

This Center has information for the public on family adjustment to change and management of stress, as well as family and individual anxieties concerning midlife crisis and the aging process. Publications for professionals include *Special Reference Briefs* on critical aspects and stages of family life.

* Mental Health Databases

National Institute of Mental Health
Parklawn Building, Room 15C-05
5600 Fishers Lane
Rockville, MD 20857 (301) 443-4515

This Institute maintains databases which index and abstract documents from the worldwide literature pertaining to mental health. In addition to scientific journals, there are references to audiovisuals, dissertations, government documents and reports. Mental Health Abstracts is available on DIALOG and another commerical vendor, BRS, offers the National Institute of Mental Health database.

* Mental Retardation Services

President's Committee on Mental Retardation
330 Independence Ave., SW
Room 4262, North Building
Washington, DC 20201 (202) 245-7634

The President's Committee on Mental Retardation has information on prevention of biomedical and environmental causes of retardation, and family and community support services. Materials are also available on the legal rights of the mentally retarded and employment programs.

* Mental Retardation Research and Clearinghouse

Mental Retardation Research Centers
National Institute of Child Health and Human Development
Executive Plaza North, Room 631
6130 Executive Blvd.
Bethesda, MD 20897 (301) 496-1383

The Mental Retardation Research Centers are designed to further the understanding, treatment, and prevention of mental retardation. They are a combination of organized research and medical service programs, bringing the mentally retarded in contact with medical and behavioral specialists. The Centers offer programs to train medical students and postdoctoral fellows. Contact this office for a list of the Centers and information on current research.

* Phobias and Panic Disorders

National Institute of Mental Health
5600 Fishers Lane, Room 15C05
Rockville, MD 20857 (301) 443-4515

Modern Talking Picture Service,Inc.
Film Scheduling Center
5000 Park Street North
St.Petersburg, FL 33709 (813) 541-5763

A free 40-page pamphlet, *Phobias and Panic* (86-1472), discusses panic disorders, types of phobias, and various kinds of treatments available. The National Audiovisual Center sells and loans free of charge a 58-minute videotape, "Phobias and Panic Disorders."

* Physical Fitness and Mental Health

National Institute of Mental Health
5600 Fishers Lane, Room 15C05
Rockville, MD 20857 (301) 443-4515

Plain Talk About Physical Fitness and Mental Health presents ideas about exercise and its connection to mental stability, particularly for special groups of people. Single copies of this brief brochure (Order No. 84-1364) is available free.

* Runaway Hotline for Parents and Youngsters

(800) 621-4000

The National Runaway Hotline provides information and resources to parents and runaways. It will deliver messages to parents from their children and offer advice to runaways regarding places to go for help. The Hotline operates 24 hours a day, and all information is confidential.

* Runaway and Homeless Youth Shelters

Division of Runaway Youth Programs
Administration for Children, Youth and Families
P.O. Box 1182
Washington, DC 20013 (202) 245-0085

The Division of Runaway Youth Programs provides federal grants to states, communities, and public and private organizations to establish and operate runaway and homeless youth shelters. This year's budget is for $26 million. An annual report is available which lists all the grantees.

* Schizophrenia Research

Schizophrenia Research Branch
Division of Clinical Research
National Institute of Mental Health
Parklawn Building, Room 10C-16
5600 Fishers Lane
Rockville, MD 20857   (301) 443-4707

This research bureau has news of the latest medical research into schizophrenia, however, access to this information is limited to mental health professionals and researchers.

* State Mental Institutions Survey

Surveys and Reports Branch
National Institute of Mental Health
Parklawn Building, Room 18C-07
5600 Fishers Lane
Rockville, MD 20857   (301) 443-4707

This office has data on mental health facilities and generates the annual Census of State Mental Health Hospitals, which provides characteristics of patients.

* Stress and Violent Behavior School Materials

National Health Information Clearinghouse
P.O. Box 1133
Washington, DC 20013-1133   (800) 336-4797 (301) 565-4167 (in MD)

Healthfinders: School Health Materials identifies many posters, audiovisuals, and printed materials on subjects ranging from suicide to divorce geared to grades K-6. Most of the videotapes, comic books and filmstrips are available from non-profit or commercial organizations.

* Stress Information Resources

National Health Information Clearinghouse
P.O. Box 1133
Washington, DC 20012   (800) 336-4797 (301) 565-4167 (in MD)

Healthfinder: Stress Information Resources lists and describes government agencies and private organizations which offer publications and resources related to adolescent and childhood stress, work-related stress, and stress management. This 4-page pamphlet (A0012) is available for $1.00.

* Stress Management Publications

Superintendent of Documents
US Government Printing Office
Washington, DC 20402

Stress Management in Work Settings summarizes scientific evidence and reviews conceptual and practical issues relating to worksite stress management. Order No. 017-033-00428-5 is available for $9.50.
An Evaluation Handbook for Health Education Programs in Stress Management (Order No. PB84-171735) is available for $31 and gives information on how to examine and evaluate stress management programs.

* Wife Beating and Elder Abuse Help Center

Clearinghouse on Family Violence Information
P.O. Box 1182
Washington, DC 20013   (703) 821-2086

This clearinghouse has information on spouse and elder abuse. They have brochures and audiovisual materials available, and an in-house database from which they can retrieve reference materials and organizations involved with family violence.

AIDS, Cancer and Other Diseases

Many of the offices and publications listed here will direct you to numerous non-profit and private organizations which also offer information and expertise. The National Health Information Center, for example, suggests interested individuals contact the American Red Cross for a series of brochures on the "Latest Facts About AIDS" which are produced jointly with the U.S. Public Health Service. Similarly, the National Cancer Institute will refer callers to such national groups as the American Lung Association and the American Heart Association.

* Acne and Skin Disease Prevention and Treatment

National Institute of Arthritis and Musculoskeletal
and Skin Diseases
National Institutes of Health
Building 31, Room 4C05
9000 Rockville Pike
Bethesda, MD 20892   (301) 496-8188
The NIAMS conducts and supports basic and clinical research concerning the causes, prevention, diagnosis, and treatment of a large number of diseases, including acne and skin problems. Reports and brochures for professionals and the general public are available, along with an information specialist who can provide in-depth information on a variety of related topics.

* AIDS (Acquired Immune Deficiency Syndrome) Hotline

AIDS Hotline   (800) 342-2437
For information, pamphlets, and reports about AIDS (Acquired Immune Deficiency Syndrome), call above toll-free number.

* AIDS and Dentistry

Dental Disease Prevention Activity
Center for Prevention Services
Centers for Disease Control
1600 Clifton Road NE
Atlanta, GA 30333   (404) 693-3534
Preventing the Transmission of Hepatitis B, AIDS, and Herpes in Dentistry offers 13 pages of advice on preventive measures for dental health care workers to minimize their risk of the transmission of these diseases to themselves, their families, and patients. Single copies are free.

* AIDS and Sexually Transmitted Diseases Resource Center

(800) 227-8922
The Sexually Transmitted Diseases Hotline provides information and referrals for treatment of sexually transmitted diseases. They can refer callers to clinics, support groups, and other services, and offer brochures and pamphlets. Their hours are 8 am to 8 pm (Pacific Standard Time).

* AIDS Prevention National Clearinghouse:

Posters, Publications, Databases, Videos
National AIDS Information Clearinghouse
PO Box 6003
Rockville, MD 20850   (301) 762-5111 (800) 458-5231 (bulk orders)
A Center for Disease Control service, this clearinghouse has publications, posters, and videos dealing with AIDS which are free of charge. The publications include a fact sheet, guidelines for the prevention of the spread of AIDS in schools and the workplace, and the Surgeon General's report on AIDS. They have two online databases; one dealing with organization, and the other lists unpublished educational materials (no journals).

* AIDS Prevention and Control National Program

Office of Public Affairs
Centers for Disease Control
1600 Clifton Rd.
Atlanta, GA 30333   (404) 693-3534
This government agency, Centers for Disease Control (CDC), is responsible for the prevention and control of AIDS, Acquired Immune Deficiency Syndrome. The CDC provides leadership to the national HIV prevention program by providing technical and financial assistance for HIV prevention activities to state and local health and education agencies and other organizations. They conduct surveillance of HIV infection, associated diseases, and death. The CDC conducts and supports epidemiology and laboratory studies and provides HIV prevention guidelines, recommendations, and training. The CDC performs national public

information activities and evaluates programs. For an HIV operation plan and AIDS packet contact this office.

* AIDS Research Worldwide

National Institute of Allergy
and Infectious Diseases
National Institutes of Health
Building 31, Room 7A32
9000 Rockville Pike
Bethesda, MD 20892   (301) 496-5717
The NIAID conducts and supports research to study the causes of allergic, immunologic, and infectious diseases, and to develop better means of preventing, diagnosing, and treating illness. Some of the studies look at the role of the immune system in chronic diseases, such as arthritis, and at disorders of the immune system, as in asthma. NIAID has become the lead component at NIH for coordinating and conducting AIDS research. Brochures and reports are available on a wide variety of topics.

* AIDS: Surgeon General's Report

AIDS
PO Box 14252
Washington, DC 20044
This detailed 30-page report titled *Surgeon General's Report on Acquired Immune Deficiency Syndrome* discusses the facts about this disease, how it is transmitted, the relative risks of infection, and how to protect yourself against the disease.

* AIDS Videotapes

National Audiovisual Center
8700 Edgeworth Drive
Capitol Heights, MD 20743   (301) 763-1896
A 28-minute video titled "AIDS: Fears and Facts" answers questions most often asked by the general public about this disease.
A short 13-minute videotape, "AIDS and Your Job--What You Should Know" outlines precautions that can be taken to reduce the risk of exposure to the AIDS virus by police, firefighters and other public safety professionals. Another video, "What If The Patient Has AIDS?" describes precautions for health care professionals. Each of these videos cost $55.00.

* Allergic Reactions: Causes and Treatments

Office of Clinical Center Communications
Warren G. Magnuson Clinical Center
NIH, Building 10, Room 5C-305
9000 Rockville Pike
Bethesda, MD 20892   (301) 496-2563
A 25-page pamphlet from the "Medicine for the Layman" series titled *Allergies* (No. 81-1948) discusses the basic mechanism in allergic reactions and the biochemical reactions that occur. This free booklet also addresses the treatment and control of allergies and certain side effects of drugs used in alleviating allergic reactions.

* Allergies: Home, School, and Work

National Audiovisual Center
8700 Edgeworth Drive
Capitol Heights, MD 20743   (301) 763-1896
A slide set, "Coping With Your Allergies At Home, At School, and on the Job", is available for $33.00 which includes 40 color slides, an audiocassette, and script.

* Allergies and Infectious Diseases Research

National Institute of Allergy
and Infectious Diseases
National Institutes of Health

Building 31, Room 7A32
9000 Rockville Pike
Bethesda, MD 20892 (301) 496-5717
The NIAID conducts and supports research to study the causes of allergic, immunologic, and infectious diseases, and to develop better means of preventing, diagnosing, and treating illness. Some of the studies look at the role of the immune system in chronic diseases, such as arthritis, and at disorders of the immune system, as in asthma. NIAID has become the lead component at NIH for coordinating and conducting AIDS research. Brochures and reports are available on a wide variety of topics.

* Allergies Dust and Drugs to Pollen

National Institute of Allergy
and Infectious Diseases
National Institutes of Health
Building 31, Room 7A32
9000 Rockville Pike
Bethesda, MD 20892 (301) 496-5717
A free copy of a 7-page pamphlet, *Allergies: Questions and Answers*, (No. 81-189) answers many general questions about allergies and offers information on their symptoms, prevention, diagnosis, and treatment. This institute offers single copies free of the following publications: *Drug Allergy* (No. 82-703), *Dust Allergy* (No. 83-490); *Insect Allergy* (No. 82-1046); *Mold Allergy* (No. 84-797); *Poison Ivy Allergy* (No. 82-897); *Pollen Allergy* (No. 76-493).

* Alzheimer's and Dementia

Office of Clinical Center Communications
Warren G. Magnuson Clinical Center
NIH, Building 10, Room 5C-305
9000 Rockville Pike
Bethesda, MD 20892 (301) 496-2563
The Brain in "Aging" and Dementia (No. 83-2625) discusses brain anatomy and physiology, the normal process of brain aging, and senility. Vascular dementia and Alzheimer's disease are described as well as research on the causes and treatment.

* Alzheimer's: Long-Term Care

Office of Technology Assessment
600 Pennsylvania Ave., SE
Washington, DC 20510 (202) 228-6688
OTA is assessing existing methods of locating and arranging health and long-term care services for Alzheimer's and dementia patients. The study will identify methods that are successful in some communities and may serve as models for others. Contact Katie Maslow, the project director, for more information.

* Alzheimer's Q & A

National Institute on Aging Information Center
2209 Distribution Circle
Silver Spring, MD 20910 (301) 495-3455
A 12-page free pamphlet, *Q & A: Alzheimer's Disease* (No. 81-1646), addresses fundamental issues related to the causes, symptoms, and treatment of this disease as well as research efforts surrounding it.

* Amyotrophic Lateral Sclerosis

National Institute of Neurological Disorders and Stroke
National Institutes of Health
9000 Rockville Pike
Building 31, Room 8A06
Bethesda, MD 20892 (301) 496-4697
This institute offers information on neurological and communicative disorders including a free 26-page pamphlet titled *Amyotrophic Lateral Sclerosis* (No. 84-916) which discusses the physiology and symptoms of this progressively crippling and fatal disease.

* Apnea and SIDS

National Sudden Infant Death Syndrome Clearinghouse
8201 Greensboro Drive
Suite 600
McLean, VA 22102 (202) 625-8410
This clearinghouse can provide many materials about infantile apnea, sudden infant death syndrome (SIDS), crib death including *Current Research in Sudden Infant Death* and *SIDS Information for the EMT*.

* Arteriosclerosis

National Heart, Lung, and Blood Institute
NIH, Building 31, Room 42-21
9000 Rockville Pike
Bethesda, MD 20892 (301) 496-4236

Cardiovascular diseases including arteriosclerosis are studied by this institute. Free pamphlets are available including *Arteriosclerosis* (No 79-1421) which discusses the development of this disease, risk, factors, and prevention.

* Arthritis and Treatments

Office of Clinical Center Communications
Warren G. Magnuson Clinical Center
NIH, Building 10, Room 5C-305
9000 Rockville Pike
Bethesda, MD 20892 (301) 496-2563
A free 27-page booklet, *Arthritis Today*, (No. 83-1945) explains gout, rheumatoid arthritis, and osteoarthritis, and discusses treatment. A videotape, "Arthritis Today", which covers the same material in the booklet is available on free loan to educators and institutions from the Modern Talking Picture Service, Inc., Film Scheduling Center, 5000 Park Street North, St.Petersburg, FL 33709, (813) 541-5763.

* Arthritis Information Clearinghouse

National Arthritis and Musculoskeletal
and Skin Disease Information Clearinghouse
PO Box 9782
Arlington, VA 22209 (703) 558-4999
This clearinghouse makes available many publications and offers telephone assistance. Many bibliographies are provided: *Directory of Information Sources, 1986* ($4); *Arthritis in Children: An Annotated Bibliography, 1986* ($3); *Arthritis and Employment: A Selected Bibiography, 1984* ($3); *Diet and Arthritis: An Annotated Bibliography, 1986* ($2); *Exercise and Arthritis, 1986* ($4); *Osteoarthritis Patient Education Materials: An Annotated Bibliography* ($3); *Psychosocial Aspects of Rheumatic Diseases: An Annotated Bibliography, 1985* ($3); *Rheumatoid Arthritis Patient Education Materials: An Annotated Bibliography* ($4); and *Sexuality and the Rheumatic Diseases: An Annotated Bibliography* ($3).

* Arthritis, Lyme and other Musculoskeletal Diseases

National Institute of Arthritis and Musculoskeletal
and Skin Diseases
National Institutes of Health
Building 31, Room 4C05
9000 Rockville Pike
Bethesda, MD 20892 (301) 496-8188
The NIAMS conducts and supports basic and clinical research concerning the causes, prevention, diagnosis, and treatment of a large number of diverse diseases, including arthritis, muscle diseases, Lyme disease, and acne. They fund Multipurpose Arthritis Centers which conduct research on various types of arthritis. Reports and brochures for professionals and the general public are available, along with an information specialist who can provide in-depth information on a variety of related topics. Contact this office for a free listing of the Arthritis Centers or for more information.

* Asthma and Other Respiratory Disorders

National Institute of Allergy
and Infectious Diseases
National Institutes of Health
Building 31, Room 7A32
9000 Rockville Pike
Bethesda, MD 20892 (301) 496-5717
A free 11-page report titled *Asthma* (No. 83-525) describes the triggers of asthma attacks and treatment and research on this respiratory disorder. This institute can offer information on sinusitis, tuberculosis and other respiratory problems.

* Blindness and Vision Problems

National Eye Institute
Building 31, Room 6A32
9000 Rockville Pike
Bethesda, MD 20892 (301) 496-5248
NEI conducts, fosters and supports basic and applied research, including clinical trials, related to the cause, natural history, prevention, diagnosis, and treatment of disorders of the eye and visual system. Several brochures and reports are available for the general public and health professionals on a wide variety of related topics as well as more specific concerns such as *Diabetes and Your Eyes*.

* Bone and Orthopedics Research

Musculoskeletal Diseases Program
National Institute of Arthritis and Musculoskeletal
and Skin Diseases
Westwood Building, Room 407
Bethesda, MD 20205 (301) 496-4236
This program focuses on orthopedic research, which includes sports medicine, growth and development of bone and bone cells, as well as head injury. Staff can answer questions regarding current research and treatment issues and

brochures and pamphlets are available through the National Institute of Arthritis and Musculoskeletal and Skin Diseases.

* Bowel Disease and Syndrome

National Digestive Diseases Information Clearinghouse
Box NDDIC
Bethesda, MD 20892 (301) 468-6344
This clearinghouse offers information and publications including *IBD and IBS: Two Very Different Problems* which compares inflammatory bowel disease and irritable bowel syndrome.

* Brain Tumors

National Institute of Neurological Disorders and Stroke
National Institutes of Health
9000 Rockville Pike
Building 31, Room 8A06
Bethesda, MD 20892 (301) 496-4697
Brain Tumors: Hope Through Research (No. 82-504) explains types of tumors, warning symptoms, and treatment including chemotherapy. This is a central information starting place for information on the brain.

* Breast Cancer Prevention and Treatment Clearinghouse

Cancer Information Service
National Cancer Institute
Building 31, Room 10A24, NIH
9000 Rockville Pike
Bethesda, MD 20892 (800) 4-CANCER (800) 492-6600 in MD
Contact CIS for pamphlets, medical updates, organizations, and support groups dealing with breast cancer. *Breast Cancer: We're Making Progress Every Day* (No. 96-2409) summarizes the latest information about breat cancer including surgery, breast reconstruction, and rehabilitation. Single copies of this 12-page pamphlet are available free. *Breast Cancer: What You Should Know* (No. 85-2000) discusses X-ray mammography and other breast cancer screening methods.

* Breast Cancer Videotapes

National Audiovisual Center
8700 Edgeworth Drive
Capitol Heights, MD 20743 (301) 763-1896
Several videotapes can be purchased from the Center including:
"Breast Cancer" and "Breast Cancer: We're Making Progress Everyday" as well as "BSE In Hospitals" which is an instructional program designed to help nurses teach hospitalized women how to perform breast self-examinations.

* Breast Exams and Breast Lumps

Cancer Information Service
National Cancer Institute
Building 31, Room 10A24, NIH
9000 Rockville Pike
Bethesda, MD 20892 (800) 4-CANCER (800) 492-6600 in MD
An illustrated guide for breast self-examination is included in a free 12-page pamphlet titled *Breast Cancer: We're Making Progress* (No. 96-8409). *Questions and Answers About Breast Lumps* (No. 86-2401) describes some of the most common noncancerous breast lumps and what can be done about them.

* Cancer and Afro-Americans

Cancer Information Service
National Cancer Institute
Building 31, Room 10A24, NIH
9000 Rockville Pike
Bethesda, MD 20892 (800) 4-CANCER (800) 492-6600 in MD
What Black Americans Should Know About Cancer (No. 82-1635) is a free 28-page booklet explaining the rates and risks of cancer among Blacks and answers the most often asked questions as well as prevention, detection, treatment, and rehabilitation.

* Cancer-Causing Products

Clearinghouse of Occupational Safety
and Health Information
National Institute of Occupational Safety and Health (NIOSH)
4676 Columbia Pkwy.
Cincinnati, OH 45226 (513) 533-8326 (800) 35-NIOSH
NIOSH distributes a publication that lists the trade name products containing one or more of 16 carcinogens (substances for which evidence indicates a causal relationship between exposure to that substance and cancer). They can also provide you with other reports and information on carcinogens.

* Cancer: Chemotherapy, Radiation, Surgery

Office of Clinical Center Communications
Warren G. Magnuson Clinical Center
NIH, Building 10, Room 5C-305
9000 Rockville Pike
Bethesda, MD 20892 (301) 496-2563
This clinical center which experiments with unproven therapies on cancer patients shares its findings and offers several relevant publications including *Cancer Treatment* (No. 82-1807) and *Radiation Risks and Radiation Therapy* (No. 83-2367).

* Cancer Clearinghouse: AZT to Radon

Office of Cancer Communications
National Cancer Institute
Building 31, Room 10A18
9000 Rockville Pike
Bethesda, MD 20892 (301) 496-5583
The NCI's overall mission is to conduct and support research, training, health information distribution, and other programs with respect to the cause, diagnosis, prevention, and treatment of cancer, and the continuing care of cancer patients and their families. Some of their current research is looking at Azidothymidine (AZT) in relation to AIDS, and the possible link between radon and lung cancer risk. NCI supports an information and education center, an International Cancer Research Databank, as well as national cancer research and demonstration centers.

* Cancer Detection and Diagnostic Imaging

Diagnostic Imaging Research Program
National Cancer Institute
Executive Plaza North, Room 800
Rockville, MD 20892 (301) 496-9531
The Diagnostic Imaging Program supports and administers grants and contracts for extramural research in the field of Diagnostic Imaging. The staff can also answer your questions regarding this medical technology.

* Cancer Information Regional Offices

Cancer Information Service
National Cancer Institute
Building 31, Room 10A18
9000 Rockville Pike
Bethesda, MD 20892 (800) 4-CANCER
The National Cancer Institute has set up offices across the U.S. through which they route the Cancer Information Service calls for those particular areas. These offices offer the same services as the Cancer Question and Answer Hotline (see above). Contact this office for a list of offices and more information.

* Cancer Journal

Superintendent of Documents
Government Printing Office
Washington, DC 20402 (202) 783-3238
The Journal of the National Cancer Institute covers basic and clinical oncology. Published twice monthly, it contains peer-reviewed scientific articles and reports, reviews of technical areas and issues, commentaries and editorials, and a news section. Also included are book reviews and listings, upcoming events, employment opportunities, and grants and fellowships. The cost is $60 per year. For back issues, contact: National Technical Information Service at (800) 336-4700.

* Cancer Literature: Bulletins and Bibliographies

Superintendent of Documents
Government Printing Office
Washington, DC 20402 (202) 783-3238
In addition to *The Journal*, the National Cancer Institute has several other publications. *Cancergrams* are monthly current awareness bulletins in 66 cancer-related subject areas and each issue contains abstracts of recent publications. Cost is between $7.50-$9.00 for a year depending upon subject area. *Oncology Overviews* are specialized bibliographies with abstracts, each referencing up to 500 recent publications. Some of the abstracts include editorial commentary which provides historical background and current research directions. Cost varies between $2.50-$10.00, depending upon topic. *Recent Reviews* are fully indexed and categorized collections of abstracts of 250-400 reviewed articles published during the year. The three volumes cover cancer diagnosis and treatment, carcinogenesis and cancer virology, immunology and biology. Cost varies between $4.00-$22.00 per volume. For back issues, contact: National Technical Information Service, 5285 Port Royal RD, Springfield, VA 22161, (800) 336-4700.

* Cancer Pamphlets and Publications List

Cancer Information Service
National Cancer Institute

Building 31, Room 10A18
9000 Rockville Pike
Bethesda, MD 20892 (800) 4-CANCER
The National Cancer Institute has over one hundred publications available to the general public and health professionals (many are also in Spanish). Topics range from information on smoking to radiation therapy. Contact this office for a list of publications.

* Cancer Prevention Awareness

Office of Cancer Communications
National Cancer Institute
Building 31, Room 10A-18
9000 Rockville Pike
Bethesda, MD 20892 (301) 496-5583
The National Cancer Institute launched the Cancer Prevention Awareness Program which is a national public education effort aimed at reducing the cancer morality rate by 50 percent by the year 2000. The Program provides information through mass media and intermediary organizations to improve public knowledge and attitudes related to cancer and its prevention, and encourages individuals to adopt lifestyles which reduce their risk of developing cancer. NCI is collaborating with Giant Food Inc., a supermarket chain, in a consumer education program entitled "Eat for Health." The study is designed to inform consumers about nutrition, health promotion, and cancer risk reduction, and to test the effectiveness of supermarket nutrition education programs. One of the free pamphlets titled *Everything Doesn't Cause Cancer* (No. 84-2039) answers some common questions about the causes and prevention of cancer as well as methods for testing chemicals and test results. *Good News, Better News, Best News: Cancer Prevention* (No. 84-2671) discusses avoidable cancer risks and gives steps that one can take every day to prevent it.

* Cancer Q&A International Clearinghouse

Service Desk
International Cancer Information Center
National Cancer Institute, NIH
Building 82, Room 103
Bethesda, MD 20892 (301) 496-7403 (800) 4-CANCER
The International Cancer Information Center develops and applies state-of-the-art technology to collect the results of the latest information on cancer research, diagnosis, and treatment. Distributed through online databases, technical journals, and specialized publications (see Cancer Journal and Literature), the information services provide a resource to the most recent cancer information available. Updated monthly, the databases include PDQ, CANCERLIT, and CLINPROT. PDQ's database includes a file that summarizes the most current approaches to cancer treatment, a file of research treatment protocols that are open to patient entry, and a directory of physicians who provide cancer treatment, and health care organizations the have programs of cancer care. CANCERLIT is a comprehensive bibliographic database containing over 650,000 citations and abstracts of published cancer literature. CLINPROT database provides detailed summaries of about 1500 active, experimental cancer therapy protocols from the U.S. and other countries.

* Cancer Research on Causes and Biology

Frederick Cancer Research Facility
P.O. Box B
Frederick, MD 21701 (301) 698-1000
The Frederick Cancer Research Facility, as part of the National Cancer Institute, is the leading center for cancer research. They support research on the causes and biology of cancer, the regulation of given expression, and chemical carcinogenesis. All research information is distributed through NCI.

* Cancer: Spanish Publications

Office of Communications
National Cancer Institute
Building 31, Room 10A18
9000 Rockville Pike
Bethesda, MD 20892 (301) 496-5583
The institute has numerous pamphlets published in Spanish that are available free including: *Los Examenes de Los Senos, Que Debe Saber Sobre Ellos* (No. 82-2138) on breast cancer and *Lo Que Usted Debe Saber Sobre El Cancer* (No. 83-1828) which is a bilingual booklet that answers questions about the causes, prevention, detection and treatment of cancer.

* Cancer: Speakers

Office of Communications
National Cancer Institute
Building 31, Room 10A18
9000 Rockville Pike
Bethesda, MD 20892 (301) 496-5583
This office can give you information on speakers who are available to talk on a variety of topics to the general public, as well as health professionals. The topics

can range from current research to environmental risks. Contact this office for more information on scheduling.

* Cancer Unconventional Treatments

Office of Technology Assessment
600 Pennsylvania Ave., SE
Washington, DC 20510 (202) 228-6590
OTA is working on a study that will summarize available information on the major types of unconventional cancer treatments; describe the legal constraints on their availability; and examine the potential for evaluating these new treatments for safety and effectiveness. Contact Jane Sisk, the project director, for more information.

* Cancer: Videotapes

National Audiovisual Center
8700 Edgeworth Drive
Capitol Heights, MD 20743 (301) 763-1896
Several videos can be purchased including "Cancer and the Environment" which looks at such factors as chemical and industrial pollution, auto emissions, diet, estrogen, and tobacco. "Cancer: What Is It?" provides an overview of cancer and compares the behavior of malignant cells with normal cells. A 27-minute video, "Control and Prevention of Malignant Melanoma: A Program for Melanoma-Prone Families" discusses danger signs, skin self-examination, and prevention techniques of this potentially fatal skin cancer.

* Carcinogens: Annual Report

Public Information Office
National Toxicology Program MD B2-04
PO Box 12233
Research Triangle Park, NC 27709 (919) 541-3991
Single copies of an abridged version of the *Annual Report on Carcinogens* is available. It identifies some 150 substancesand processes and gives summaries of the evidence for their link with cancer in humans and laboratory animals. It also provides information on production, use, population exposed, cities, and federal regulations to safeguard the public.

* Cardiovascular Diseases

National Heart, Lung, and Blood Institute
NIH, Building 31, Room 42-21
9000 Rockville Pike
Bethesda, MD 20892 (301) 496-4236
How Doctors Diagnose Heart Disease (No. 81-753) provides information on screening and treatment of coronary artery disease, including catheterization, electrocardiograms, exercise testing, and cineangiography. Single copies of this pamphlet, which is also published in Spanish, are available free.

* Cerebral Palsy

National Institute of Neurological Disorders and Stroke
National Institutes of Health
9000 Rockville Pike
Building 31, Room 8A06
Bethesda, MD 20892 (301) 496-4697
This center for medical research has information about the latest developments on this disease as well as a free 26-page pamphlet titled *Cerebral Palsy: Hope Through Research* (No. 84-158).

* Chemotherapy and Radiation

Therapy for Head or Neck
National Institute of Dental Research
NIH, Bldg 31, Room 2C-35
9000 Rockville Pike
Bethesda, MD 20892 (301) 496-3583
Patients undergoing radiation therapy for the head or neck, or cancer chemotherapy may benefit from a free 4-page pamphlet, *Radiation, Chemotherapy and Dental Health* (No. 81-2090), which discusses possible dental problems that could occur and also describes important preventive procedures.

* Cholesterol and Coronary Heart Disease

National Cholesterol Education Program
NIH, Building 31, Room 4A-21
9000 Rockville Pike
Bethesda, MD 20892 (301) 230-1340
This clearinghouse of the National Heart, Lung and Blood Institute (NHLBI) works to inform the public about cardiovascular disease. One of many publications available free is *NHLBI Facts About Blood Cholesterol* (No. 86-2696).

* Chronic Disease Prevention

Health and Medicine

Center for Chronic Disease Prevention
and Health Promotion
Centers for Disease Control
1600 Clifton Rd., NE
Bldg 3, Room 117
Atlanta, GA 30333   (404) 693-3534
Begun in 1988, this center was established in the belief that more emphasis was needed on chronic disease prevention if CDC was to accomplish its mission of preventing unnecessary illness, disability, and death. CCDPHP stresses translating research findings into effective community-based programs, strengthening the delivery of preventive health services, and designing programs to meet the needs of minority groups. Units within the center cover smoking and health, nutrition, school health, chronic disease control, reproductive health, diabetes, and surveillance and analysis. The center works with State health departments on breast cancer control projects that promote screening mammography, advanced training for technicians, equipment testing, and peer review. The Preventive Health and Health Services Block Grant helps fund states' efforts to combat chronic diseases and to offer health education. Some interventions are designed to serve the dual purpose of meeting local health needs and providing a model for other programs. The Center has established a newsletter, *Chronic Disease Notes and Reports*, to provide a regular forum for communication.

* Chronic Pain Research and Therapies

National Institute of Neurological Disorders and Stroke
National Institutes of Health
9000 Rockville Pike
Building 31, Room 8A06
Bethesda, MD 20892   (301) 496-4697
One publication offered free to interested individuals is *Chronic Pain: Hope through Research* (No. 82-2406) which summarizes research findings on persistent pain and various therapies including drugs, acupuncture, surgery, electrical stimulation, and also psychological techniques.

* Cirrhosis of the Liver

National Digestive Diseases Information Clearinghouse
Box NDDIC
Bethesda, MD 20892   (301) 468-6344
A free four-page pamphlet titled *Cirrhosis of the Liver* (No. 84-1134) explains preventive measures including alcohol abstinence and other causes, symptoms, diagnosis and treatment.

* Colon Colitis, Diverticulitis, and Cancer

Office of Consumer Affairs
Public Inquiries
Food and Drug Administration
5600 Fishers Lane (HFE-88)
Rockville, MD 20857   (301) 443-3170
The Colon Goes Up, Over, Down, and Out (DHHS Pub. No. 84-1111) discusses how the colon works and is the site of many problems such as colon colitis, diverticulitis, and cancer.

* Cooley's Anemia

National Heart, Lung, and Blood Institute
NIH, Building 31, Room 42-21
9000 Rockville Pike
Bethesda, MD 20892   (301) 496-4236
This Institute offers information on many aspects of cardiovascular disease including a free pamphlet titled *Cooley's Anemia: Prevention Through Understanding* (No. 80-1269) which discusses prevention through testing and genetic counseling.

* Crohn's Disease

National Digestive Diseases Information Clearinghouse
Box NDDIC
Bethesda, MD 20892   (301) 468-6344
Information about ulcerative colitis and Crohn's Disease, clinical symptoms, epidemiological patterns, treatment strategies and experimental therapies are provided by this clearinghouse.

* Dementia Disorders

National Institute of Neurological Disorders and Stroke
National Institutes of Health
9000 Rockville Pike
Building 31, Room 8A06
Bethesda, MD 20892   (301) 496-4697
The Dementias: Hope through Research (No. 81-2252) describes different types of dementias as well as "pseudodementias" and research on the suspected causes of these disorders.

* Depression: Diagnosis and Treatments

National Institute of Mental Health
Alcohol, Drug Abuse and Mental Health Administration
5600 Fishers Lane, Room 15C05
Rockville, MD 20857   (301) 443-4515
NIMH conducts research on depression and other mental disorders, distributes information, conducts demonstration programs for the prevention, treatment, and rehabilitation of the mentally ill. A major media campaign on depression, called Project D/ART (Depression/Awareness, Recognition, Treatment), is being developed by NIMH in collaboration with other organizations to provide information on symptoms, causes, and treatments of various depressive disorders. Many publications and reports are available on various topics for professionals and the general public.

* Diabetes and Cardiovascular Disease

National Heart, Lung, and Blood Institute
NIH, Building 31, Room 42-21
9000 Rockville Pike
Bethesda, MD 20892   (301) 496-4236
Diabetes and Cardiovascular Disease (No. 77-1212) is a free pamphlet that discusses the diabetic's risk of development heart disease and suggests preventive measures.

* Diabetes Control Programs

Division of Diabetes Translation
Office of Chronic Disease
Prevention and Health Promotion
CDC, 1600 Clifton Rd., EO8
Atlanta, GA 30333   (404) 639-1848
This division has cooperative agreements with 30 states to establish Diabetes Control Programs. Through each state's health department, with the Center for Disease Control providing matching funds, these programs are designed for complications specific interventions for diabetics. They examine for eye disease and make appropriate referrals, as well as assist with diabetic pregnancy and lower limb circulation problems. Contact this office for referral to local states of for more information.

* Diabetes Information Center

National Diabetes Information Clearinghouse
Box NDIC
Bethesda, MD 20892   (301) 468-2162
NDIC responds to requests for information about diabetes and its complications and distributes information appropriate to health professionals, people with diabetes and their families, and the general public. They have many publications and bibliographies, as well as *Diabetes Dateline*, a free quarterly current awareness newsletter that features news about diabetes research, upcoming meetings and events, and new publications. NDIC uses the online database CHID (Combined Health Information Database) from which they can reference health information. Some other publications include 300-page *The Diabetes Dictionary* which is available for $1.00 (Spanish version is $2.00); *The Prevention and Treatment of Five Complications of Diabetes, A Guide for Patients with an Introduction to Day-to-Day Management of Diabetes*, and *Self Blood Glucose Monitoring*.

* Diarrhea Prevention and Control

National Digestive Diseases Information Clearinghouse
Box NDDIC
Bethesda, MD 20892   (301) 468-6344
This clearinghouse offers information on this digestive tract disorder including *Diarrhea, Infectious and Other Causes* (No. 86-2749) and a free 12-page pamphlet *Traveler's Diarrhea*.

* Digestive Health and Disease Clearinghouse

National Digestive Diseases Information Clearinghouse
Box NDDIC
Bethesda, MD 20892   (301) 468-6344
NDDIC responds to requests for information about digestive diseases and distributes information to health professionals, people with digestive diseases, and the general public. They have many publications, as well as a news bulletin. NDDIC uses the online database CHID (Combined Health Information Database) from which they can access health information and organizations. Some of their free publication include *Digestive Health and Disease: A Glossary* (No. 86-2750); *Gas in the Digestive Tract* (No. 85-553); *Bleeding in the Digestive Tract* (No. 86-1133); *Facts and Fallacies About Digestive Diseases* (No. 84-2673); *Your Digestive System and How It Works* (No. 86-2681); *Milk Intolerance Due to Lactose Deficiency* (No. 85-2751); and *Heartburn* (No. 86-882).

* Epilepsy and Convulsions

Office of Clinical Center Communications
Warren G. Magnuson Clinical Center

NIH, Building 10, Room 5C-305
9000 Rockville Pike
Bethesda, MD 20892 (301) 496-2563
This clinical center offers a free 24-page report titled *Epilepsy* (No. 82-2369) which discusses types of seizures and medical and surgical therapies.

* Eye Research Experiments Nationwide

National Eye Institute
National Institute of Health
Bldg 31, Room 6A-32
9000 Rockville Pike
Bethesda, MD 20892 (301) 492-5248
Intended for the practitioner, *Clinical Trials Supported by the National Eye Institute* briefly describes 20 ongoing research studies. Included is the current status of the study, the results, any publications that result from the studies, as well as a list of the participating clinical centers.

* Gallstone Disease

National Digestive Diseases Information Clearinghouse
Box NDDIC
Bethesda, MD 20892 (301) 468-6344
Questions about surgery and complications as well as the reasons for the formation of gallstones are addressed in this free 4-page pamphlet titled *Gallstone Disease* (No. 85-2752).

* Head Injury

Musculoskeletal Diseases Program
National Institute of Arthritis and Musculoskeletal
and Skin Diseases
Westwood Building, Room 407
Bethesda, MD 20205 (301) 496-5717
This program focuses on orthopedic research, which includes sports medicine, growth and development of bone and bone cells, as well as head injury. Staff can answer questions regarding current research and treatment issues. Brochures and pamphlets are available through the National Institute of Arthritis and Musculoskeletal and Skin Diseases.

* Head Trauma and Rehab

National Institute of Neurological Disorders and Stroke
National Institutes of Health
9000 Rockville Pike
Building 31, Room 8A06
Bethesda, MD 20892 (301) 496-4697
Head Injury: Hope through Research (No. 84-2478) discusses ways to prevent head injuries and the resulting damage from different types of injuries, as well as rehabilitation techniques.

* Heart Attacks

National Heart, Lung, and Blood Institute
NIH, Building 31, Room 42-21
9000 Rockville Pike
Bethesda, MD 20892 (301) 496-4236
A free 20-page booklet, *Heart Attacks* (No. 86-2700) discusses risk factors, symptoms, and treatment. A videotape based on this publication which offers encouraging evidence that cardiovascular disease death rates have decreased due to changes in diet and lifestyle is available for sale through the National Audiovisual Center, or on free loan to educators and institutions from the Modern Talking Service, Film Scheduling Center, 5000 Park Street North, St Petersburg, FL 33709, (813) 541-5763. *Test Your Healthy Heart I.Q.!* (No. 85-2724) offers over a dozen questions and answers about cardiovascular and pulmonary risk factors.

* Heart Disease: Diagnosis and Treatment

Office of Clinical Center Communications
Warren G. Magnuson Clinical Center
NIH, Building 10, Room 5C-305
9000 Rockville Pike
Bethesda, MD 20892 (301) 496-2563
A free 27-page pamphlet, *The Heart: Diagnosis and Treatment* (No. 81-1809), discusses new findings in clinical cardiology, new techniques to diagnose abnormalities in the pumping function of the heart, and new concepts in treating people who come to the hospital with an acute heart attack.

* Heart Disease Videotapes

National Audiovisual Center
8700 Edgeworth Drive
Capitol Heights, MD 20743 (301) 763-1896
Several videos can be purchased from the Center and some can be rented free from the Modern Talking Picture Service Film Scheduling Center (5000 Park

Street North, St.Petersburg, FL 33709, 813-5431-5763) including "Cholesterol, Diet and Heart Disease", "Heart Attacks", and "Coronary Heart Disease: Roles of Surgery and Balloon Dilatation".

* Herpes Type I and Type II

National Institute of Allergy
and Infectious Diseases
National Institutes of Health
Building 31, Room 7A32
9000 Rockville Pike
Bethesda, MD 20892 (301) 496-5717
This institute offers information and various publications on sexually transmitted diseases including *Genital Herpes* (No. 84-2005) which is also available in Spanish (No. 854-656); and *Sexually Transmitted Diseases* (STDs).

* High Blood Pressure

High Blood Pressure Information Center
4733 Bethesda Ave., Suite 530
Bethesda, MD 20814 (301) 951-3260
The Center is a source of information and educational materials for consumers, providers, and planners of high blood pressure control services. Print and audiovisual materials (for professionals and the public), as well as information on locations and services of community programs and activities are available. The Center can access material through the CHID database. A free newsletter, Info Memo, covers topics of interest concerning blood pressure, cholesterol and smoking and is published as needed. Several free publications available include: *Community Guide to High Blood Pressure* (No. 82-2333); *High Blood Pressure: Things You and Your Family Should Know* (No. 86-2025; also published in Spanish); *High Blood Pressure and What You Can Do About It*; *High Blood Pressure Control Programs at the Worksite* (No. 83-1125).

* Huntington's Disease Research Center

Department of Medical Genetics
Indiana University Medical School
Medical Research Building
975 W. Walnut St.
Indianapolis, IN 46202-5251 (317) 274-2245
The National Institutes of Health and Indiana University Medical Center, Indianapolis, maintain a roster of Huntington's Disease patients and families. Each of the families complete a family history questionnaire, and the statistics are used for research. IUMC also acts as a broker between families and researchers, who can request subjects for a particular project from IUMC's database of patients and families.

* Infectious Diseases

National Institute of Allergy
and Infectious Diseases
National Institutes of Health
Building 31, Room 7A32
9000 Rockville Pike
Bethesda, MD 20892 (301) 496-5717
This institute offers many publications and expertise about diarrhea, bacterial meningitis, the common cold, mononucleosis, herpes, rabies, Rocky Mountain Spotted Fever, schistosomiasis, and other infectious diseases. *Understanding the Immune System* (No. 84-529) is a free 22-page report that discusses antigens, the immune system, disorders (including AIDS), the immunology of transplants, and new diagnostic methods.

* Kidney and Urological Diseases

National Kidney and Urological Diseases
Information Clearinghouse
Box NKUDIC
Bethesda, MD 20892 (301) 468-6345
This clearinghouse responds to inquiries regarding kidney and urological diseases. They can access the CHID (Combined Health Information Database) database to get further information. They have pamphlets, brochures, and reports for the public and professionals, and can refer people to voluntary and professional organizations.

* Kidney Stones

National Institute of Diabetes and Digestive
and Kidney Diseases
NIH, Building 31, Room 9A-04
9000 Rockville Pike
Bethesda, MD 20892 (301) 496-3583
This institute offers several publications free including: *Prevention and Treatment of Kidney Stones* (No. 83-2495) and *Extracorporeal Shock Wave Lithotripsy* (No. 84-859) as well as experts on staff who can answer questions.

Health and Medicine

* Kidney Transplants

National Institute of Diabetes and Digestive
and Kidney Diseases
NIH, Building 31, Room 9A-04
9000 Rockville Pike
Bethesda, MD 20892   (301) 496-3583
This Institute conducts research regarding kidney transplants. The staff can refer you to current researchers, as well as sending you brochures and reports on this procedure.

* Leprosy: Free Treatment

Gillis W. Long Hansen's Disease Center
Carville, LA 70721   (504) 642-4706
The Gillis W. Long Hansen's Disease Center primarily provides Hansen's Disease (leprosy) patients a place to receive a complete evaluation and treatment. Any person with a confirmed diagnosis of leprosy is eligible for admission. The Center conducts an extensive patient care and rehabilitation program, as well as research, training and education activities.

* Mitral Valve Prolapse

National Heart, Lung, and Blood Institute
NIH, Building 31, Room 42-21
9000 Rockville Pike
Bethesda, MD 20892   (301) 496-4236
This institute offers much information to enhance the public's understanding of cardiovascular disease and prevention. One of its free publications is *NHLBI Facts About...Mitral Valve Prolapse.*

* Nerve Regeneration and Brain Transplants

Office of Technology Assessment
600 Pennsylvania Ave., SE
Washington, DC 20510   (202) 228-6677
Recent advances in neuroscience research have enormous potential to improve the lives of millions of Americans. OTA is currently studying the following neuroscience-associated topics: neural transplants and nerve regeneration, including related ethical and legal issues; biological rhythms and shift work; neurotoxicity testing by private and public organizations; and biochemical bases of mental illness. Contact Mark Schaefer, the project director, for more information.

* Parkinson's Disease

National Institute of Neurological Disorders and Stroke
National Institutes of Health
9000 Rockville Pike
Building 31, Room 8A06
Bethesda, MD 20892   (301) 496-4697
Parkinson's Disease: Hope Through Research (No. 83-139) outlines the possible causes and treatments for Parkinson's disease and summarizes both research efforts and therapies.

* Periodontal Gum Disease

Periodontal Disease Centers
National Insstitute of Dental Research
Westwood Building, Room 559
533 Westbard Ave.
Bethesda, MD 20892   (301) 496-7784
This Institute funds the Periodontal Disease Centers which conduct research on the causes, treatment and prevention of periodontal disease. One of the centers focuses on the identification of risk factors. The staff can answer general questions regarding periodontal disease. Several free publications include: *Periodontal (Gum) Disease, Detection and Prevention of Periodontal Disease in Diabetes* (No. 86-1148) *Tooth Decay* (No. 82-1146), *Preventing Tooth Decay: A Guide to Implementing Self-Applied Fluoride Programs in School Settings;* and *Seal Out Dental Decay* (No. 80-1140) which discusses plastic sealants.

* Rare Diseases and Orphan Drugs Clearinghouse

National Information Center for Orphan Drugs and Rare Diseases
450 5th Street NW Room 7103
Washington, DC 20001   (202) 272-3430
This center (NICODARD) responds to inquiries on diseases with a prevalence of 200,000 or fewer cases in the United States. This clearinghouse, sponsored by the Food and Drug Administration, also gathers and disseminates information on medicines not widely researched or available.

* Rheumatic Disease

National Institute of Arthritis and Musculoskeletal Diseases
NIH,Building 31, Room 9A-04
Bethesda, MD 20892   (301) 496-5717

A 43-page reference titled *Rheumatic Diseases and the Older Adult: An Annotated Bibliography, 1986,* contains 86 references with abstracts to the medical literature for physicians, allied health professionals, and others interested in geriatric medicine and rheumatology. It is available for $4.00.

* Sickle Cell Centers

National Sickle Cell Disease Program
7550 Wisconsin Ave., Room 504
Bethesda, MD 20892   (301) 496-6931
This program funds centers to coordinate manpower, research, and facilities by offering a combination of research and demonstration services, screening and education clinics, public and professional education, and counseling and rehabilitation for sickle cell disease.

* Skin Diseases

National Arthritis and Musculoskeletal
and Skin Disease Information Clearinghouse
PO Box 9782
Arlington, VA 22209   (703)558-4999
Living with Epidermolysis Bullosa (No. 84-663), *What You Should Know About Vitiligio* (No. 80-2088) are a sampling of materials available free from this clearinghouse.

* Spina Bifida

National Institute of Neurological Disorders and Stroke
National Institutes of Health
9000 Rockville Pike
Building 31, Room 8A06
Bethesda, MD 20892   (301) 496-4697
Spina Bifida: Hope through Research (No. 86-309) discusses the prevailing views about the causes, diagnosis, and medical care of this congenital spinal cord defect.

* Spinal Cord Injury

National Institute of Neurological Disorders and Stroke
National Institutes of Health
9000 Rockville Pike
Building 31, Room 8A06
Bethesda, MD 20892   (301) 496-4697
This institute offers information about the causes, implications,and outlook for spinal cord injuries and drug therapy, neural prostheses, and rehabilitation.

* Stroke and Brain Disorders Resource Center

National Institute of Neurological Disorders and Stroke
National Institutes of Health
9000 Rockville Pike
Building 31, Room 8A06
Bethesda, MD 20892   (301) 496-4697
NINDS conducts and guides research on the causes, prevention, diagnosis, and treatment of fundamental neurological disorders and stroke and trauma. The Institute gives grants for extramural research, as well as providing fellowships. Other areas of research include cerebral palsy, autism, dyslexia, multiple sclerosis, Parkinson's and Huntington's diseases, and epilepsy. Brochures and pamphlets available free include: *What You Should Know About Stroke and Stroke Prevention* (No. 81-1909) and *Stroke: Hope through Research* (No. 83-2222).

* Tooth Decay Prevention and Treatment

Dental Disease Prevention Activity
Centers for Disease Control
1600 Clifton Rd., NE
Atlanta, GA 30333   (404) 329-1830
The Dental Disease Prevention Activity is a resource for information on prevention activities in the field of dental health. It can provide you with information on fluoridation, periodontal disease, and baby-bottle tooth decay. A list of educational materials is also available including the following free publications: *Fluoridation...Nature's Way To Prevent Tooth Decay* (No. 81-8321) and *Fluoridation is for Everyone* (No. 77-8334).

* Toxic Shock Syndrome

Office of Consumer Affairs
Public Inquiries
Food and Drug Administration
5600 Fishers Lane (HFE-88)
Rockville, MD 20857   (301) 443-3170
A short brochure titled *Toxic Shock Syndrome and Tampons* (No. 85-4169) explains the symptoms and causes of this syndrome.

* Ulcers: Gastric and Duodenal
National Digestive Diseases Information Clearinghouse
Box NDDIC
Bethesda, MD 20892 (301) 468-6344
This clearinghouse can offer information on this disease and makes available
free single copies of such publications as *Peptic Ulcer* (No. 85-3800).

Cigarettes and Chewing Tobacco

* Cholesterol and Smoking Connection

Information Services
Cholesterol/Smoking Information Center
Building 31-A, Room 4A-21
Bethesda, MD 20892   (301) 230-1340
This center maintains a database and materials on blood cholesterol and smoking geared to the public, health professionals and issues pertaining to the workplace.

* Cigarettes: Self Test for Smokers

Office on Smoking and Health
Technical Information Center
5600 Fishers Lane, Room 1-10
Rockville, MD 20857   (301) 443-1690
A Self-Test for Smokers (No. 75-8716) provides a questionnaire to help smokers find out what they know about cigarette smoking. Smoking, Tobacco and Health (No. 87-8397) discusses the health risks and prevalence of smoking as well as tobacco growing, cigarette manufacturing, and marketing. No More Butts, A Guide to Quitting Smoking (No. 83-50199) calls on smokers to recognize their addiction and answers questions about quitting. Each of these publications are available free.

* Clearing the Air

Office of Cancer Communications
National Cancer Institute
Building 31, Room 10A-18
9000 Rockville Pike
Bethesda, MD 20892   (800) 4-CANCER (301) 496-5583
Clearing the Air: A Guide to Quitting Smoking (No.86-1647) suggests various approaches to quit smoking. This 32 page pamphlet is also available in Spanish. Single copies are available free.

* No Smoking in Schools

Office of Cancer Communications
National Cancer Institute
Building 31, Room 10A-18
9000 Rockville Pike
Bethesda, MD 20892   (800) 4-CANCER (301) 496-5583
Smoking Programs for Youth describes school-based programs and curricula, many of which can be adapted by community groups or form the basis for a joint program with local schools. Single copies of this 92-page booklet is available free.

* School Health Education Materials

National Health Information Clearinghouse
P.O. Box 11133   (800) 336-4797
Washington, DC 20012-1133   (301) 565-4167 (in MD and DC)
This clearinghouse publishes Healthfinder: School Health Materials (Grades K-6) which describes numerous audiovisuals, printed materials and posters on alcohol, drug abuse and smoking available from government agencies, private organizations and publishers.

* Smoking Info Specifically for Parents

Office of Smoking and Health
Technical Information Center
Park Building, Room 116
5600 Fishers Lane
Rockville, MD 20857   (301) 443-1690
If Your Kids Think Everybody Smokes, They Don't Know Everybody. A Parent's Guide to Smoking and Teenagers (No. 83-50199) explains why some teenagers become smokers. This four page guide is available free.

* Smoke Reduction On-the-Job

Office of Smoking and Health
Technical Information Center
5600 Fishers Lane, Room 1-10
Rockville, MD 20857   (301) 443-1690
No Smoking: A Decision Maker's Guide to Reducing Smoking at the Workplace discusses the impact of smoking on employees and businesses and describes programs companies have used to restrict or ban smoking at work. This 42-page manual (Order No. W0001) is available, $2 handling fee.

* Smokeless Tobacco and Dangers of Chewing

Dental Disease Prevention Activity
Centers for Disease Control
1600 Clifton Road NE
Atlanta, GA 30333   (404) 693-3534
Smokeless Tobacco Education Resources is an annotated list which includes educational materials on snuff and chewing tobacco available from federal, state and local agencies and from private sources. This 6-page bibliography is available free.

* Smoking and High Blood Pressure

High Blood Pressure Information Center
120/80 National Institutes of Health
Bethesda, MD 20892   (301) 496-1809
A free 24-page reference titled The Physician's Guide: How to Help Your Hypertensive Patients Stop Smoking (NIH No. 84-1271) shows what doctors cando within a busy office practice to persuade hypertensive patients to stop smoking.

* Smoking Cessation and Cancer Prevention

Office of Cancer Communications
National Cancer Institute
Building 31, Room 10A-18
9000 Rockville Pike
Bethesda, MD 20892   (800) 4-CANCER (301) 496-5583
The National Cancer Institute carries out a multi-disciplinary program in smoking and tobacco research and control through the Smoking, Tobacco and Cancer Program. It conducts research in epidemiology and carcinogenesis and carry out interventions to reduce smoking and tobacco use. The program is now supporting large-scale intervention trials in eight areas, some of which are adolescent smoking prevention, mass media approach to smoking prevention, and cessation and smoking among minorities. NCI has begun a multicenter Community Intervention Trial for Smoking Cessation (COMMIT) to test strategies to produce long-term cessation among all cigarette smokers within a community, with particular emphasis on heavy smokers. One of their many publications includes Smoking Programs for Youth (No.81-2156) which describes activities that can be pursued throuugh schools and community groups.

* Smoking Risks and Prevention Clearinghouse

Information Center
National Heart, Lung, and Blood Institute
4733 Westbard Ave., Suite 530
Bethesda, MD 20814   (301) 951-3260
The National Heart, Lung, and Blood Institute sponsors a Smoking Education Information Center which provides services to health professionals and the general public on smoking issues. They provide pamphlets, fact sheets, posters, and other publications, as well as information in response to inquiries. The center can access information on the Combined Health Information Database (CHID). A library and reading room are open to the public, and librarians are available to assist you. The Infomemo contains information on disease prevention, education and control. For a publications list or more information, contact this office.

* Smoking Technical Information Center

Office on Smoking and Health
5600 Fishers Lane, Room 1-10
Rockville, MD 20857   (301) 443-1690
This office offers bibliographic and reference services to researchers through its Technical Information Center (TIC). The TIC publishes and distributes a number of titles in the field of smoking and health, and through its database can provide you with further bibliographic information. TIC's Smoking Studies Section designs and conducts national surveys on smoking behavior, attitude, knowledge, and beliefs regarding tobacco use. Visitors may use the collection between 8:30 am and 5:00 pm EST (call ahead), but reference services are also provided by phone. A free publications listing is also available.

* Smoking: Videotapes and Slides

National Audiovisual Center
8700 Edgeworth Drive
Capitol Heights, MD 20743-3701   (301) 763-1896
Numerous videotapes aimed at all ages groups are available can be purchased or rented including "Pressures to Smoke" and "Resisting Pressures to Smoke". "We Can't Go On Like This" (film and videotape) consists of the following seven

vignettes that are designed to motivate a group to explore why they smoke, recognize the obstacles to quitting, and extinguish the habit: "Crisis"; "Digging Cigarettes"; "The Drag Race"; "Escalation"; "Gambling" "The Ordeal of Arnold Hertz"; "We Can't Go On Like This". "Everyone Can Do Something About Smoking" consists of 127 color slides which explain how organizations can help reduce the smoking problem. Another slide set available is "A Physician Talks About Smoking" which presents the latest information on the health effects so as to better equip health professionals who are asked to speak about the effects of smoking on health.

* Snuff and Chewing Tobacco Risks

Office of Cancer Communications
National Cancer Institute
Building 31, Room 10A-18
9000 Rockville Pike
Bethesda, MD 20892   (800) 4-CANCER (301) 496-5583

In Answer To Your Questions on Smokeless Tobacco discusses the risks of snuff and chewing tobacco. Single copies are free.

* Stop Smoking Posters

Office of Smoking and Health
Technical Information Center
Park Building, Room 116

5600 Fishers Lane
Rockville, MD 20857   (301) 443-1690

Don't Get Hooked!" (15" x 21", color) shows a fish smoking a cigarette caught by a fishing hook. It is also available in Spanish. "This Is A Dumb Bunny" pictures a rabbit smoking a cigarette. "Cigarette Mash" (18" x 23", color) shows multicolored sneakers stamping out cigarettes. These posters are available free.

* Stop Smoking: State and Local Programs

Office on Smoking and Health
Technical Information Center
5600 Fishers Lane, Room 1-10
Rockville, MD 20857   (301) 443-1690

State and Local Programs on Smoking and Health: A Catalog of Local Programs Throughout the Country on Smoking and Health (No.82-50189) is packed with descriptions of cessation clinics, prevention efforts, school programs, community and patient education programs, mass media campaigns, and individual self-help strategies. Single copies of this 151-page catalog are available free.

* Teenage Cigarette Smoking Test

Office of Smoking and Health
5600 Fishers Lane, Room 1-10
Rockville, MD 20857   (301) 443-1690

Teenage Cigarette Smoking Self Test is a quiz designed to help teens understand their feelings about smoking. This free 12-page booklet consists of a leader's guide followed by eight duplicating masters.

Health and Medicine

Aging and America's Elderly

With the dramatic demographic changes occurring, a wider array of government agencies and private organizations are focusing on some aspect of the "graying of America". This section introduces a sampling of resources available which target on the special health needs and problems that go hand-in-hand with the aging process. The House and Senate Aging Committees also should not be overlooked because they study many health issues.

* Accidental Hypothermia
National Institute on Aging Information Center
2209 Distribution Circle
Silver Spring, MD 20910   (301) 495-3455
A free 12-page booklet, *A Winter Hazard for Older People: Accidental Hypothermia* (No. 81-1464), warns elderly persons to protect themselves against a progressive drop in deep body temperature that can be fatal if not detected in time and properly treated.

* Age Pages: Info on Health Concerns
National Institute on Aging Information Center
2209 Distribution Circle
Silver Spring, MD 20910   (301) 495-3455
This NIH Institute publishes dozens of fact sheets, printed on two sides in large type, for the lay audience. This series is termed "Age Pages" and a list for most of the fact sheets titled *Age Page Compilation*, is available free. Some of the "Age Pages" which are free include: *Be Sensible About Salt; Can Life Be Extended?; Considering Surgery?; Health Quackery; Hints for Shopping, Cooking and Enjoying Meals;Osteoporosis: The bone thinner; Prostate Problems: Safety Belt Sense; Senility: Myth or Madness?; Sexuality in Later Life; Stroke;* and *Urinary Incontinence.*

* Aging Magazine
Administration on Aging
Department of Health and Human Services
Room 4643
330 Independence Ave., SW
Washington, DC 20201   (202) 245-0641
Aging Magazine, published quarterly for five dollars per year, focuses on innovative programs and book reviews in the field of aging. This publication is primarily designed for professionals and service providers for the elderly.

* Alzheimer's Q & A
National Institute on Aging Information Center
2209 Distribution Circle
Silver Spring, MD 20910   (301) 495-3455
A 12-page free pamphlet, *Q & A: Alzheimer's Disease* (No. 81-1646), addresses fundamental issues related to the causes, symptoms, and treatment of this disease as well as research efforts surrounding it.

* Brain and Dementia
Office of Clinical Center Communications
Warren G. Magnuson Clinical Center
NIH, Building 10, Room 5C-305
9000 Rockville Pike
Bethesda, MD 20892   (301) 496-2563
The Brain in "Aging" and Dementia (No. 83-2625) discusses brain anatomy and physiology, the normal process of brain aging, and senility. Vascular dementia and Alzheimer's disease are described as well as research on the causes and treatment.

* Brittle Bones
Osteoporosis Booklet
National Institute of Arthritis and Musculoskeletal Diseases
NIH, Building 31, Room 9A-04
Bethesda, MD 20892   (301) 496-5717
Osteoporosis: Cause, Treatment, Prevention (No. 86-2226) discusses this bone-thinning condition. Single copy free with a business-sized self-addressed envelope with $.44 postage.

* Central Clearinghouse
National Institute on Aging
National Institutes of Health
Federal Building, Room 6C12

Bethesda, MD 20892   (301) 496-1752
The National Institute on Aging (NIA) has responsibility for biomedical, social, and behavioral research and training related to the aging process and diseases and other special problems and needs of the aged. NIA continues to work on the Baltimore Longitudinal Study of Aging, which has followed the same 650 men since 1958 to measure the changes with age. NIA encourages and supports research on aging at universities, hospital, medical centers, and other organizations. Funds are made available for these investigations through a variety of grant and contract mechanisms.

* Chinese Publications for the Elderly
National Institute on Aging Information Center
2209 Distribution Circle
Silver Spring, MD 20910   (301) 495-3455
Several fact sheets, printed on two sides in large type, are published in Chinese including: *Arthritis Advice; Cancer Facts for People Over 50; Dealing with Diabetes; Dietary Supplements; Heat, Cold, and Being Old; Minorities and How They Grow Old; Foot Care for Older People; Safe Use of Medicines by Older People;* and *What To Do About the Flu.* Individual copies of these fact sheets are available free.

* Depression: Prevention and Intervention
National Institute of Mental Health
Public Inquiries Branch
Parklawn Building, Room 15C-05
5600 Fishers Lane
Rockville, MD 20857   (301) 443-4513
A free 3-page flier, *Fact Sheet: Depression in the Elderly* (No. 80-0932), pays particular attention to depression as it affects the elderly. It discusses symptoms, physical problems, medications, personal relationships that support and encouragement.

* Elder Abuse and Family Violence
Clearinghouse on Family Violence Information
P.O. Box 1182
Washington, DC 20013   (703) 821-2086
This clearinghouse has information on spouse and elder abuse. They have brochures and audiovisual materials available, and an in-house database from which they can retrieve reference materials and organizations involved with family violence.

* Exercise for Older Americans
National Health Information Center
PO Box 1133
Washington, DC 20013   (800) 336-4797 (301) 565-4167 in MD
In its series called "Healthfinder", this clearinghouse publishes *Exercise for Older Americans* which lists publications and audiovisuals available from government agencies, community organizations, foundations and many other health groups. This resource bulletin includes, for example, the National Parkinson Foundation's free exercise program for Parkinson's patients.

* Geriatrics Career Training and Education Grants
Administration on Aging
Office of Program Development
330 Independence Ave., SW
Washington, DC 20201   (202) 245-0441
The Administration on Aging funds continuing education programs in the field of aging by giving grants to institutions of higher education and professional organizations. For a list of these institutions and organizations, contact this office.

* Gerontology Research: Physical, Mental, Emotional Changes

Gerontology Research Center
Francis Scott Key Medical Center
4940 Eastern Ave.
Baltimore, MD 21224   (301) 550-1707
The bulk of the National Institute on Aging intramural research is conducted at the Gerontology Research Center. In 1958 the Center began the Baltimore Longitudinal Study of Aging which involves 1,000 men and women, who, every two years, spend 2 1/2 days undergoing rigorous testing of their physical, mental, and emotional functions. The Center has laboratories to investigate a broad spectrum of human functions. They, as well as NIA, offer a wide range of pamphlets and reports on aging for professionals and the general public.

* Glaucoma Treatment
Office of Consumer Affairs
Food and Drug Administration (FDA)
5600 Fishers Lane
Rockville, MD 20857   (301) 443-3170
A free 4-page pamphlet, *Keeping An Eye on Glaucoma*, (No.80--3105) discusses the control of glaucoma with drugs and surgery.

* Hearing Aids
Office of Consumer Affairs
Food and Drug Administration (FDA)
5600 Fishers Lane
Rockville, MD 20857   (301) 443-3170
Contact this office for the free FDA publication, *Facts about Hearing and Hearing Aids* and other information about these medical devices. This free 32 page pamphlet (No.79-4016) discusses the causes of and treatment for hearing loss and the selection, use, and care of hearing aids.

* Healthy Older People: Exercise, Nutrition, Medicines
ODPHP Health Information Center
P. O. Box 1133
Washington, DC 20013   (800) 336-4797 (202) 429-9091
Healthy Older People, a public education program on health promotion and aging conducted by the Office of Disease Prevention and Health Promotion (ODPHP), encourages older people to adopt good health habits, concentrating on such areas as exercise, nutrition, injury prevention, smoking, and medicines. A list of broadcast and print materials is available to State and local groups, along with a list of State contacts, who are responsible for coordinating statewide activities. The program includes consumer education, professional education, and technical assistance. A Program Memo maintains information on activities and regional workshops.

* Medicare Claims
Attn: Larry Beasley
Health Care Financing Administration
Room 577, East High Rise Building
6325 Security Boulevard
Baltimore, MD 21207 (Written requests only)
A free 8-page pamphlet, *How To Fill Out A Medicare Claim Form*, provides a step by step explanation of how to fill out this basic form in order to get reimbursed for medical bills.

* Medicare Health Insurance
Local Social Security Office
Several handy pamphlets are available free from local Social Security offices including *A Brief Explanation of Medicare* and *A Guide to Health Insurance for People with Medicare*. Both of these publications discuss what Medicare does and does not cover and discusses Medi-gap and other supplementary private health insurance plans.

* Medicare Videotapes
National Audiovisual Center
8700 Edgeworth Drive
Capitol Heights, MD 20743   (301) 763-1896
Several videotapes are sold by the Audiovisual Center including: "Medicare Magazine"; "Mr. Medicare" and "One Measure of Freedom." "Meet Medicare" is an audiocassette which can also be purchased.

* Older Americans Policies and Programs Review
Federal Council on the Aging
Room 4280 Cohen Building
330 Independence Ave., SW
Washington, DC 202021   (202) 245-2451
The Federal Council on the Aging reviews and evaluates Federal aging policies and programs for the purpose of appraising their value and their impact on the lives of older Americans. They serve as spokesperson on behalf of older Americans by making recommendations about Federal policies and programs.

They inform the public about the problems and needs of the aging by collecting and distributing information, conducting or commissioning studies, and publishing their results and issuing reports. The Council provides public forums for discussing problems by sponsoring conferences, workshops, and other meetings.

* Osteoporosis and Older Women
Office of Consumer Affairs
Food and Drug Administration (FDA)
5600 Fishers Lane
Rockville, MD 20857   (301) 443-3170
Osteoporosis: Calcium and Estrogens (No.85-1117) discusses the causes of this weakening of the bones, especially in older women, and how diet and estrogen treatment can help. Single copies of this 8-page brochure are available free.

* Paget's Bone Disease
National Institute of Arthritis and Musculoskeletal Diseases
NIH, Building 31, Room 9A-04
Bethesda, MD 20892   (301) 496-5717
A free 11-page booklet, *Understanding Paget's Disease* (No 85-2241), describes this disease of the bone, which occurs most frequently between the ages of 50 and 70.

* Positive Approach to Aging
National Institute of Mental Health
Public Inquiries Branch
Parklawn Building, Room 15C-05
5600 Fishers Lane
Rockville, MD 20857   (301) 443-4513
A free four-page pamphlet, *Plain Talk About Aging*, describes the experience of growing old and suggests ways to plan carefully in order to have aging be a positive experience.

* Rheumatic Disease
National Institute of Arthritis and Musculoskeletal Diseases
NIH, Building 31, Room 9A-04
Bethesda, MD 20892   (301) 496-5717
A 43-page reference titled *Rheumatic Diseases and the Older Adult: An Annotated Bibliography, 1986*, contains 86 references with abstracts to the medical literature for physicians, allied health professionals, and others interested in geriatric medicine and rheumatology. It is available for $4.00.

* Safe Use of Medicines
National Clearinghouse for Drug Abuse Information
PO Box 2345
Rockville, MD 20852   (301) 468-2600
A free 26-page guide titled *Elder-Ed: An Education Program for Older Americans: Using Medicines Wisely* (No.78-705) contains information on the do's and don'ts of taking medicines and on generic drugs.

* Sexuality in Later Life
National Institute on Aging Information Center
2209 Distribution Circle
Silver Spring, MD 20910   (301) 495-3455
This double-sided fact sheet titled *Sexuality in Later Life* is one of many "Age Pages" available free from the center.

* Spanish Publications for Elderly
National Institute on Aging Information Center
2209 Distribution Circle
Silver Spring, MD 20910   (301) 495-3455
Several fact sheets, printed on two sides in large type, are published in Spanish including: *Accidents and the Elderly; Crime and the Elderly; Foot Care for Older People;* and *Skin: Getting the Wrinkles Out of Aging*. Individual copies of these fact sheets are available free. A listing of all fact sheets published in various languages titled "Age Pages Compilation" is also available free.

* Wellness and Safety Checklist
ODPHP Health Information Center
P. O. Box 1133
Washington, DC 20013   (800) 336-4797 (202) 429-9091
Healthy Older People Skill Sheets consists of a set of five fact sheets, in large type, giving basic information on nutrition, exercise, smoking,injury prevention, and safe use of medicines. Reproducible slicks (12" x 17"each) also are available. Single sets are available for $2.00. A complimentary set of five "Healthy Older People" posters (10" x 34") which address the same concerns as the skill sheets can also be purchased for $3.00 (minimum order of 5 in any combination).

Health and Medicine

* You and Your Aging Parents

Modern Talking Picture Service
Film Scheduling Center
5000 Park Street North
St. Petersburg, FL 33709 (813) 541-5763

A 58-minute videotape is available on free loan to educators and institutions titled "You and Your Aging Parents". It describes the stresses associated with growing old and addresses the challenge to the "sandwich generation". This video, part of the *Medicine for the Layman* series, is also for sale by the National Audiovisual Center, 8700 Edgeworth Drive, Capitol Heights, MD 20743 (301) 763-1896.

* Vision Impairment

National Eye Institute
NIH, Building 31
Room 6A-32, 9000 Rockville Pike
Bethesda, MD 20892 (301) 496-5248

Age-Related Macular Degeneration (No. 85-2294) explains how the eye works and how the degeneration occurs with the aging process. It tells how patients can check their own eyes and describes laser photocoagulation for treating this disease. Single copies available free.

Handicapped/Disabled Resources

See also Law and Social Justice Chapter

* Associations and Foundations Resource List

National Health Information Center
P.O. Box 1133
Washington, DC 20013-1133   (800) 336-4797 (301) 565-4167 (in MD)
This center provides information and support services offered by national organizations and foundations as well as government services available to individuals with handicaps or disabilities including its free six-page bulletin titled *Healthfinder: Family Care.*

* Braille Books and Computers for Blind

American Printing House for the Blind
1839 Frankfurt Ave.
Louisville, KY 40206   (502) 895-2405
American Printing House for the Blind produces a variety of material for the blind, including books, textbooks, and music in Braille, large type and talking books, flexible records, and cassettes. They also have computer hardware and software and free catalogs both in print and Braille.

* Captioned Movies and Videos for the Hearing Impaired

Modern Talking Pictures
500 Park St., North
St. Petersburg, FL 33709   (813) 541-7571
This company's captioned film/video program provides a free loan service of educational and theatrical films and videos for various groups to assist deaf/hearing impaired persons in educational and recreational pursuits. Comprehensive, free catalogs list over 3,500 films and videocassettes. Language controlled open-captions (subtitles) appear on each film and video.

* Clearinghouse on the Handicapped

Clearinghouse on the Handicapped
Switzer Building, Room 3132
330 C Street SW
Washington, DC 20202   (202) 732-1250
This center, sponsored by the U.S. Department of Health and Human Services, responds to inquiries by referrals to organizations that supply information to and about handicapped individuals. This government clearinghouse also provides material on federal benefits, funding, and legislation for the handicapped.

* Communicative and Deafness Disorders Rehabilitation

Office of Deafness and Communicative Disorders
Rehabilitation Services Administration
330 C St., SW, Room 3033
Washington, DC 20201   (202) 732-1401 (202) 732-1298 TDD
The goal of this branch is to promote improved and expanded rehabilitation services for deaf, hard of hearing, speech impaired, and language disordered individuals. This office, as the liaison to national organizations and agencies concerned with deafness and communicative disorders, provide the following services: 1) they develop policies and standards for state rehabilitation agencies' work with these clients; 2) they review services to these clients by the agencies; and 3) they provide technical assistance to Rehabilitation Services Administration staff.

* Deafness Resource Center and Grants

National Institute on Deafness and
  Other Communicative Disorders
NIH, Building 31, Room 1B62,
9000 Rockville Pike
Bethesda, MD 20892   (301) 496-7243
This--the newest Institute at NIH--funds intramural and extramural research on deafness and communicative disorders. Brochures and reports are available for professionals and the general public, covering a wide range of related topics.

* Development Disabilities and Mental Retardation Research

Office of Research Reporting
National Institute of Child Health and Human Development

NIH, Building 31, Room 2A-32
9000 Rockville Pike
Bethesda, MD 20892   (301) 496-5133
This NIH department can share scientific research and consumer information about various development disabilities, birth defects and related issues.

* Developmental Disabilities Resource Center

National Information System for Health Related Services
Center for Developmental Disabilities
Benson Building, First Floor
Columbia, SC 29208   (800) 922-9234 (800) 922-1107 in SC)
This clearinghouse offers information and makes referrals for parents and professionals concerned with children ages 0-21 with development disabilities or special health care needs. It also can identify federal, state and non-profit agencies in every state in the country.

* Disabilities Information Clearinghouse

Clearinghouse on Disability Information Program
Information and Coordination Staff
U.S Department of Education
Room 3132, Mary Switzer Building
Washington, DC 20202-2524   (202) 732-1723 or (202) 732-1241
This clearinghouse will provide you with a free bibliography of disability publications which are available through other Federal agencies and departments. What follows is a sampling of those publications:

Adult Basic Education Programs for Disabled Adults.
Educating Students with Learning Problems: A Shared Responsibility.
Free Appropriate Public Education for Students with Handicaps: Requirements under Section 504 of the Rehabilitation Act of 1973.
EEO and Affirmative Action for Employment of Handicapped Persons by Federal Contractors.
Employers are Asking about Accommodating Workers with Disabilities. Identifies common barriers in the workplace and provides suggestions for accommodation.
Fact Sheet No. 7, Handicapped Assistance Loans. Explains the qualifications and conditions for loan approval to small business owners with physical handicaps.
Hiring the Mentally Restored Makes Dollars and Sense. Includes the following publications: *Affirmative Action to Employ Mentally Restored People; Eight Questions Employers Ask about Hiring the Mentally Restored; and The Mentally Restored & Work: A Successful Partnership.*
A Summary Guide to Social Security and Supplemental Income with Incentives for the Disabled and Blind. This booklet was designed to assist professionals who need to know the work incentive provisions for working with potential or actual SSI or SSDI beneficiaries.
Facts about Down Syndrome.
Caring about Kids: Helping the Hyperactive Child. Discusses the causes, diagnosis, and treatment of hyperactivity in children.

* Employment Research and Development

Administration Officer
Office of Research and Publications
President's Committee on Employment of the Handicapped
1111 20th Street NW, Room 660
Washington, DC 20036   (202) 653-2087
This advisory committee advocates the elimination of environmental and attitudinal barriers impeding the opportunities of handicapped persons. It offers materials on employment of disabled people, affirmative action, disabled veterans, taxes and disability, youth development. The committee publishes a quarterly information bulletin, *Disabled USA*, and sponsors films, exhibits, a speakers bureau, and public service advertising.

* Free Library Services for Physically Handicapped

National Library Service for the Blind and Physically Handicapped
Library of Congress
Washington, DC 20542   (202) 287-9286
This center works through local and regional libraries to provide free library service to persons unable to read or use standard printed materials because of

visual or physical impairment. A bibliography of Braille and recorded materials on health topics is available as well as *Talking Book Topics*.

* Handicapped Rehabilitation Resources

Superintendent of Documents
Government Printing Office
Washington, DC 20402   (202) 783-3238
Designed for professionals and consumer groups, *The American Rehabilitation*, a quarterly publication from the Rehabilitation Services Administration, covers all aspects of life for handicapped individuals. A subscription is $5 per year.

* Infants with Disabilities Clearinghouse

National Information Clearinghouse for Infants with Disabilities
  and Life-Threatening Conditions
Benson Building, First Floor
Columbia, SC 29208   (800) 922-9234 (800-922-1107 in SC)
This resource center offers help on legal and advocacy issues, financial assistance, community services, parent support and parent education, child protective services, home health services and other assistance to parents and professionals concerned about infants with disabilities.

* Learning Disabilities Clearinghouse

National Information Center for Handicapped Children and Youth
PO Box 1492
Washington, DC 20013   (703) 893-6061   (800) 999-5599
This clearinghouse helps parents of handicapped children, disabled adults, and professionals locate services for the handicapped and information on learning disabilities.

* Parents of Disabled Referral Center

National Information Center for Children and Youth with Handicaps
PO Box 1492
Washington, DC 20013   (703) 893-6061 (800) 999-5599
This clearinghouse helps parents of handicapped children, disabled adults locate services and parent support groups. It also focuses on the needs of rural areas, culturally diverse populations, and severely handicapped people. This center also provides information on vocational/transitional issues, special education, and legal rights and advocacy. It provides fact sheets on specific disabilities including autism, cerebral palsy, hearing impairments, Down's syndrome, epilepsy, learning disabilities, mental retardation, physical disabilities, speech and language impairments, spina bifida, visual impairments.

* Rehabilitation Clearinghouse and Databases

National Rehabilitation Information Center
8455 Colesville Road, Suite 935   (MD only) (301) 588-9284
Silver Spring, MD 20910   (800) 346-2742 (voice and TDD)
This clearinghouse provides information on disability-related research, resources, and products for independent living. It provides fact sheets, resource guides, and technical publications. It produces two bibliographic databases, ABLEDATA and REHABDATA which cover rehabilitation products and technical aids for disabled persons along with generic and brand names, manufacturers, distributors, uses, and costs.

* Rehabilitation Research and Development

Director
National Institute on Disability and Rehabilitation Research
Department of Education
Mary E. Switzer Building, Mail Stop 2305
330 C Street SW
Washington, DC 20202   (202) 732-1134
This institute disseminates information concerning developments in rehabilitation procedures, methods, and devices for people of all ages with physical and mental handicaps, especially those who are severely disabled. Statistical data on disabilities and research funding information are also available.

* Speech and Language Disorders Clearinghouse

National Institute on Deafness and
  Other Communicative Disorders
NIH, Building 31, Room 1B62,
9000 Rockville Pike
Bethesda, MD 20892   (301) 496-7243
This--the newest Institute at NIH--funds intramural and extramural research on communicative disorders. Brochures and reports are available for professionals and the general public, covering a wide range of related topics.

* Telephone Hotlines

The following clearinghouses are equipped to send information, make referrals to organizations as well as state and federal government agencies, and also provide telephone information.

Center for Handicapped Children and Teenagers	(415) 923-3549
Clearinghouse on the Handicapped	(404) 639-3534
Coordinating Council for the Handicapped	(312) 939-3513
Federation of the Handicapped	(212) 206-4250
Information Center for Individuals with Disabilities	(617) 727-5540
Information, Protection and Advocacy Center for Handicapped Individuals	(202) 547-8081
March of Dimes Birth Defects Foundation	(914) 428-7100
National Center for Youth with Disabilities	(800) 333-NCYD
National Information Clearinghouse for Infants with Disabilities and Life-Threatening Conditions	(800) 922-9234
National Institute on Disability and Rehabilitation Research	(202) 732-1134
National Information System for Health Related Services	(800) 922-9234

Medical Devices, RX and Surgery

Contemplating a new treatment for back pain, wondering about donating blood, considering elective surgery? There are many specialists and agencies available to offer their expert opinion to help you make informed decisions with your medical team. A few phone calls can boost your ability to weigh the pros and cons of various medical tests and procedures and learn about the reputation of a hospital or health clinic. Several agencies can provide the latest information on specific medications, their generic equivalents and other therapeutic drugs. Even offices that are established to collect and disseminate data for health professionals on adverse drug reactions and experimental drugs can be accessible to individual consumers.

* Anesthesia and Therapeutic Drug Findings

Pharmacological Sciences Program
National Institute of General Medical Sciences
Building 31, Room 4A52
9000 Rockville Pike
Bethesda, MD 20892　　　　　　　　　(301) 496-7707

This program supports research aimed at providing an improved understanding of biological phenomena and related chemical and molecular processes involved in the actions of therapeutic drugs, anesthetic agents, and their metabolites. This program supports research ranging from synthetic chemistry and basic biological and biochemical studies in molecular pharmacology to comparative studies in cell cultures and laboratory animals, as well as controlled clinical investigations in patients and normal volunteers. Grants are available, including pre- and postdoctoral fellowships. The *Biennial Report* describes the current research awards. The *Annual Report of NIGMS* lists all the various programs and their research highlights.

* Approval of All New Drugs

Center for Drug Evaluation and
　　Research, HFD 100, Room 14B45
5600 Fishers Lane
Rockville, MD 20857　　　　　　　　(301) 443-4330; or

Office of Consumer Affairs
HFD 365, 5600 Fishers Lane
Rockville, MD 20857　　　　　　　　(301) 443-3170

The Center for Drug Evaluation and Research develops policy with regard to the safety, effectiveness, and labeling of all drug products and evaluates new drug applications. It develops and implements standards for the safety and effectiveness of all over-the-counter drugs. It also conducts research and develops scientific standards on the composition, quality, safety, and effectiveness of drugs. A list of guidelines is available to help manufacturers comply with the requirements of the regulations. The staff will respond to requests from information regarding the laws, regulations, policies, and functions of the FDA as it pertains to drugs. Many FDA Consumer Report articles, as well as an FDA Consumer Special Report on drugs, are available to the public.

* Blood Banks and Supply

Information Center
Blood Resource Education Program
4733 Bethesda Ave., Suite 530
Bethesda, MD 20814　　　　　　　　(301) 951-3260

The Blood Resource Education Program, supported by the National Heart, Lung, and Blood Institute, is designed to assure accessibility of an adequate supply of high-quality blood and blood products through studies of resource management, the establishment of a national blood data system, and recommendations concerning the structure and function of the national blood resource system. Contact this office for more information regarding the nation's blood supply.

* Brand Name Drug Directory

Superintendent of Documents
Government Printing Office
Washington, DC 20402　　　　　　　　(202) 783-3238

The *National Drug Code Directory* is divided into four sections which alphabetically lists drugs by product trade name, chemical ingredient, short name, and the National Drug Codes which are specific numbers, assigned to the drugs by the Food and Drug Administration, used for insurance billing purposes. The cost of the directory is $76.

* CAT Scans and Safety of Other Technology

Office of Health Technology Assessment

Department of Health and Human Services
Room 310
5600 Fishers Lane
Rockville, MD 20857　　　　　　　　(301) 443-4990

National Technical Information Service
5285 Port Royal Rd.
Springfield, VA 22161　　　　　　　　(800) 336-4700

This office advises the Secretary of Health and Human Services regarding health care technology issues and makes recommendations with respect to whether specific health care technologies should be reimbursable under federally-financed health programs. The office also considers the safety and effectiveness of the technology. Impending assessments are announced in the Federal Register, and input is sought from appropriate Federal agencies. The final reports are made available to the public through the National Technical Information Service. Reports and abstracts published by the Office of Health Technology Assessment are available individually or in annual volume compilations.

* Construction of Hospitals and Health Facilities

Office of Health Facilities
Health Resources and Services Administration
5600 Fishers Lane, Room 11-03
Rockville, MD 20857　　　　　　　　(301) 443-6560

This office serves as the federal focus for examining capital and financial issues involved in health facilities, and administering insured and guaranteed loan programs for health facilities to determine compliance with assurances made during application for federal construction assistance. Materials are available on a variety of topics, including capital formation in health care facilities and cost containment in hospitals through energy conservation.

* Consumer Information about Medications

The National Health Information Center
P.O. Box 1133
Washington, DC 20013　　(800) 336-4797　(301) 565-4167 in MD

In its series called "Healthfinders", *The Home Medical Library* lists numerous books and references about over-the-counter and prescription drugs including the directory published by the United States Pharmacopoeial Convention titled *USP Drug Information Volume II: Advice for the Patient.*

* Drug Reactions and Pharmaceutical News

Drug Bulletin
Food and Drug Administration
HFI 42, 5600 Fishers Lane
Rockville, MD 20857　　　　　　　　(301) 443-3220

Published on an as-needed basis, the *Drug Bulletin* is free to professionals and the general public interested in learning the latest developments in the drug field, such drug reactions and new medical devices.

* Elderly Chinese and Medications

National Institute on Aging Information Center
2209 Distribution Circle
Silver Spring, MD 20910　　　　　　　(301) 495-3455

Safe Use of Medicines by Older People is a free fact sheet, printed on two sides in large type, and it is published in English and Chinese.

* Electrical Stimulation Medical Devices

Electrophysics Branch
Center for Devices and Radiological Health
12721 Twinbrook Parkway
Rockville, MD 20857　　　　　　　　(301) 443-3840

Health and Medicine

The Electrophysics Branch of conducts research on medical devices involving electrical stimulation to evaluate and examine their safety at the cellular level. They also examine the calibration of microwave ovens. The staff can respond to written requests for information.

* Experimental Drugs for Cancer Treatment

Developmental Therapeutics Program
National Cancer Institute
Executive Plaza North, Room 818
Bethesda, MD 20892   (301) 496-8774

The National Cancer Institute distributes two pharmaceutical publications free of charge: 1) NCI Investigational Drugs (89-2141) is an annual publication which encompasses most of the drugs in clinical trial under NCI auspices. It provides necessary product information to health care providers who utilize investigational drug products. 2) NCI Investigational Drugs-Chemical Information (86-2654) is designed to provide selected relevant chemical and hysical data to investigators involved in various multi-disciplinary studies of drugs which were developed or are being developed by the Developmental Therapeutics Program. The staff is also available to answer your questions related to pharmaceuticals.

* Fraudulent Medical Devices

Office of Consumer Affairs
Food and Drug Administration
Public Inquiries
5600 Fishers Lane
Rockville, MD 20857   (301) 443-3170

The Food and Drug Administration does not have the authority to regulate all medical products but it monitors the marketplace and publishes several pamphlets designed to help consumers spot bogus remedies for arthritis, cancer and medical devices including: The Big Quack Attack: Medical Devices (No. 84-3147); Quackery -- The Billion Dollar "Miracle" Business (No. 85-4200), as well as Back Pain: Ubiquitous, Controversial (No. 84-3147).

* Freedom on Information: Medical Devices

Device Monitoring Branch
Bureau of Medical Devices
8757 Georgia Ave., Room 1222
Silver Spring, MD 20910   (301) 427-8100

The Bureau of Medical Devices reviews medical devices for particular specialties (neurology, cardiovascular, ophthalmic, radiology), and then compiles the reactions and malfunctions into a computer database. Through a Freedom of Information request at the following address, you can receive information regarding a specific medical device. FDA, Freedom of Information, 5600 Fishers Lane, HFI35, Rockville, MD 20857.

* Hospitalization and Treatment at Government's Expense

The Clinical Center
National Institutes of Health
Building 10, Room 2C-146
9000 Rockville Pike
Bethesda, MD 20892   (301) 496-4891

The Clinical Center, as part of the National Institutes of Health, is specially designed to place patient care facilities close to research laboratories to promote the quick transfer of new scientific findings to the treatment of patients. Institutes admit to their units only those patients (upon referral by personal physicians) who have the precise kind or stage of illness under investigation by scientist-clinicians. Contact the Clinic with questions regarding current research.

* Hospital Patients Complaints

Office of Health Facilities
Health Resources and Services Administration
5600 Fishers Lane, Room 11-03
Rockville, MD 20857   (800) 638-0742 (800) 492-0359 (in MD)

The OHF answers questions on the Hill-Burton Free Health Care Program and responds to patient complaints on Hill-Burton facilities via a toll-free hotline. The OHF also maintains an in-house database on Hill-Burton facilities.

* Hospital Procedures and Discharge National Survey

Division of Health Care Statistics
NCHS
3700 East-West Highway, Room 2-63
Hyattsville, MD 20782   (301) 436-8522

This division has three branches which conduct research on long-term, hospital, and ambulatory care.

* Hospitals and Energy Conservation

Design and Energy Branch
Division of Facilities Assistance

and Recovery, Room 11A19
5600 Fishers Lane
Rockville, MD 20857   (301) 443-5410

The Energy and Health Facilities Branch provides information on design and construction criteria and guidelines for health care facilities and provides guidelines on energy conservation of health care facilities. This Branch mostly provides technical assistance to health care facilities with government insured mortgages, though they do have a limited ability to assist those outside this loan portfolio.

* Hospitals Providing Free Care

Office of Health Facilities
Health Resources and Services Administration
5600 Fishers Lane, Room 11-03
Rockville, MD 20857   (800) 638-0742 (800) 492-0359 (in MD)

This hotline is a service of the Bureau of Resources Development, Department of Health and Human Services. It distributes information on applying for Hill-Burton assistance, which provides free or low-cost health care. They can answer questions regarding eligibility guidelines and facilities obligated to provide medical services.

* Inventions and New Medical Treatments

Office of Medical Applications of Research (OMAR)
National Institutes of Health
Building 1, Room 260
Bethesda, MD 20892   (301) 496-1143

OMAR is the focal point within the National Institutes of Health (NIH) for technology assessment and transfer activities. These activities are aimed at facilitating the transfer of results of publicly-funded biomedical research into clinical applications and evaluating these research findings for safety and effectiveness. OMAR co-sponsors Consensus Development Conferences which bring together representatives from various fields to assess the clinical applications of specific medical technologies, and then develop a consensus statement. Past topics include cesarean childbirth and Reye's Syndrome. OMAR also administers the NIH patent program, which promotes the transfer and commercialization of federally funded inventions by the private sector. OMAR disseminates information on new treatment methods and new technology.

* Laser Surgery Information

Consumer Information Center
Pueblo, CO 81009

The FDA's publication entitled The Surgeon's Newest Scalpel is a Laser, is designed for the general public and explains the medical applications of the laser and how it works.

* Laser Surgery Referral Network

National Health Information Center
P.O. Box 1133
Washington, DC 20013   (202) 429-9091   (800) 336-4797 outside Washington, DC

This center can provide you with names of organizations and agencies involved with laser surgery, which can then refer you to experts in the field.

* Lower-Cost Generic Drugs Information

Superintendent of Documents
Government Printing Office
Washington, DC 20402   (202) 783-3238

The publication, Approved Drug Product with Therapeutic Equivalent Evaluation, is designed for public education of prescription drugs and lower-cost substitutes in an effort to help the public and health care agencies control health care costs. The price of the manual is $87.

* Medical Devices: Technical Assistance for Small Businesses

Division of Small Manufacturer's Assistance
Center for Devices and Radiological Health
Food and Drug Administration
5600 Fishers Lane, HF2-220
Rockville, MD 20857   (301) 443-6597

The FDA provides information to small businesses regarding device regulations and what is needed to get approval. The FDA often holds meetings and workshops to offer further assistance. The handbook, A Small Business Guide to FDA, explains how the FDA works and the approval process. This Center provides copies of device regulations and FDA documents, as well as guidelines and aids that simplify manufacturer requirements. The SMA MEMO contains articles and tips on medical device regulations and reports on Center activities.

* Medical Devices Updates

Medical Devices and Radiation Center

Food and Drug Administration
5600 Fishers Lane
Rockville, MD 20857 (301) 443-4690
This center conducts research relating to medical devices, reviews and evaluates medical devices approval application, and develops regulations relating to these devices. They publish two bulletins, the *Medical Devices Bulletin* and the *Radiological Health Bulletin*, both of which cover safety alerts, upcoming research, meetings, and new FDA regulations. These bulletins are designed for the medical industry community. To order the bulletins, write the center or call the editors. Radiological Health Bulletin Editor: (301) 443-5860; Medical Devices Bulletin Editor: (301) 443-5807.

* Medicare's Prescription Drug Benefit

Office of Technology Assessment
600 Pennsylvania Ave., SE
Washington, DC 20510 (202) 228-6590
OTA will study the experience of public and private payers of prescription drugs, including how they set payment rates, promote appropriate use, and control total expenditures. The study will apply this experience to develop methods that the Medicare program might use to pay for multiple- and single-source drugs, and pharmaceutical services. Contact Jane Sisk, the project director, for more information.

* Medicines Affected by Age, Genes, and Diet

National Institute of General Medical Sciences
Building 31, Room 4A52
9000 Rockville Pike
Bethesda, MD 20892 (301) 496-7301
A 62-page booklet titled *Medicines and You* (No.81-2140) describes how your age, your genes, and your diet can affect the way medicines will work in your body. This free report also describes ongoing research on biological reactions to drugs.

* Medicines and the Elderly

National Audiovisual Center
8700 Edgeworth Drive
Capitol Heights, MD 20743 (301) 763-1896
A film or videotape titled "Wise Use of Drugs: A Program for Older Americans" is available for sale and rental. This 30 minute program suggests ways to prevent drug dependence and gives suggestions for productive visits to the doctor to insure the patient is given complete information about prescribed drugs.

* Medicines: Bad Reactions and Complaints

Practitioner Reporting System
Food and Drug Administration
12601 Twinbrook Parkway
Rockville, MD 20852 (800) 638-6725 (301) 881-0256 (in MD)
The Practitioner Reporting System offers a service for health professionals to report problems with drugs or medical devices. A copy of the report goes to the manufacturer, as well as to the Food and Drug Administration.

* Orphan Drugs and Rare Diseases

National Information Center on Orphan Drugs and Rare Diseases
P.O. Box 1133
Washington, DC 20013 (202) 429-9091 (800) 336-4797 outside DC
NICODARD staff, a component of the National Health Information Center, can answer questions on rare diseases and on orphan drugs. The Center is a service of the Office of Disease Prevention and Health Promotion, DHHS, and is sponsored by the Orphan Products Development Board of the Food and Drug Administration. A directory of organizations and educational materials is available from the National Technical Information Service.

* Over-the-Counter Drugs and RX Consumer Info

Office of Public Affairs
Food and Drug Administration
5600 Fishers Lane, HFE88
Rockville, MD 20857 (301) 443-3170
The FDA distributes many brochures and publications which cover a variety of topics, such as drugs, cosmetics, and foods safety and additives. This office will gladly send publications on topics that interest you. The *FDA Consumer*, which contains the latest developments at FDA, can be ordered for $12 per year from the Superintendent of Documents, Government Printing Office, Washington DC 20402, (202) 783-3238.

* Over-the-Counter and RX Drugs Safety

Center for Drug Evaluation and
  Research, HFD 100, Room 14B45
5600 Fishers Lane

Rockville, MD 20857 (301) 443-4330; or

Office of Consumer Affairs
HFD 365, 5600 Fishers Lane
Rockville, MD 20857 (301) 443-3170
The Center for Drug Evaluation and Research develops policy with regard to the safety, effectiveness, and labeling of all drug products and evaluates new drug applications. It develops and implements standards for the safety and effectiveness of all over-the-counter drugs. It also conducts research and develops scientific standards on the composition, quality, safety, and effectiveness of drugs. A list of guidelines is available to help manufacturers comply with the requirements of the regulations. The staff will respond to requests from information regarding the laws, regulations, policies, and functions of the FDA as it pertains to drugs. Many FDA Consumer Report articles, as well as an FDA Consumer Special Report on drugs, are available to the public.

* Pharmaceutical Companies Intelligence

Drug Listing Branch
Food and Drug Administration
5600 Fishers Lane, HFO 334
Rockville, MD 20857 (301) 295-8083
This Food and Drug Administration office compiles many different types of drug-related lists, which can be obtained by writing the Freedom of Information Office listed below. Available lists include drug establishments, private label distributors, prescription drug establishments, over-the-counter and bulk drugs, drug products, and import products. The fee varies, depending upon the list. Freedom of Information, FDA, 5600 Fishers Lane, HFI 35, Rockville, MD 20857, (301) 443-6310.

* Pharmaceutical Exports and Mislabeling

Office of Technology Assessment
600 Pennsylvania Ave., SE
Washington, DC 20510 (202) 228-6590
The U.S. pharmaceutical industry is a major supplier of pharmaceuticals to developing countries, but the industry has been criticized for mislabeling certain drugs sold in those countries. OTA is currently studying whether inappropriate labeling is occurring today to allow health workers in those developing countries to use drugs safely and effectively. Contact Hellen Gelband, the project director, for more information.

* Pharmaceutical Research and Development

Office of Technology Assessment
600 Pennsylvania Ave., SE
Washington, DC 20510 (202) 228-6590
OTA is working on a project to examine trends in the structure, process, and products of pharmaceutical R&D in the U.S., with the goal of developing and implementing a system for estimating and tracking R&D costs over time. The study will also describe the organization of the pharmaceutical R&D enterprise, identifying how costs differ by therapeutic class or biological research area. Contact Judith Wagner, the project director, for more information.

* Pharmacology Experiments and Research

Pharmacological Sciences Program
National Institute of General Medical Sciences
Building 31, Room 4A52
9000 Rockville Pike
Bethesda, MD 20892 (301) 496-7707
This program supports research aimed at providing an improved understanding of biological phenomena and related chemical and molecular processes involved in the actions of therapeutic drugs, anesthetic agents, and their metabolites. This program supports research ranging from synthetic chemistry and basic biological and biochemical studies in molecular pharmacology to comparative studies in cell cultures and laboratory animals, as well as controlled clinical investigations in patients and normal volunteers. Grants are available, including pre- and postdoctoral fellowships. The *Biennial Report* describes the current research awards. The *Annual Report of NIGMS* lists all the various programs and their research highlights.

* Radiation Dose Information

Radiopharmaceutical Internal Dose Information Center
P.O.Box 117
Oak Ridge Associated Universities
Oak Ridge, TN 37821-0117 (615) 576-3450
This center primarily serves researchers at government agencies and nuclear medicine centers as well as private physicians having questions about internal radiation dose calculations, especially those involving radiopharmaceuticals.

* Radiation Safety Alerts

Medical Devices and Radiation
Food and Drug Administration

Health and Medicine

5600 Fishers Lane
Rockville, MD 20857   (301) 443-4690

This center conducts research relating to medical devices, reviews and evaluates medical devices approval application, and develops regulations relating to these devices. They publish two bulletins, the *Medical Devices Bulletin* and the *Radiological Health Bulletin*, both of which cover safety alerts, upcoming research, meetings, and new FDA regulations. These bulletins are designed for the medical industry community. To order the bulletins, write the center or call the editors. Radiological Health Bulletin Editor: (301) 443-5860; Medical Devices Bulletin Editor: (301) 443-5807.

* Second Opinion Surgical Hotline

National Second Surgical Opinion Program
Health Care Financing Administration
330 Independence Ave., SW   (800) 638-6833
Washington, DC 20201   (800) 492-6603 in Maryland only

The National Second Surgical Opinion Program is an information resource for people faced with the possibility of non-emergency or elective surgery. By calling its toll-free number, the staff will help you locate a surgeon or other specialist enrolled in the program who can offer you a second opinion. Pamphlets are available containing questions that patients looking for second opinions should ask.

* Seniors and Safe Use of Medicines

National Clearinghouse for Drug Abuse Information
PO Box 2345
Rockville, MD 20852   (301) 468-2600

A free 26-page guide titled *Elder-Ed: An Education Program for Older Americans: Using Medicines Wisely* (No.78-705) contains information on the do's and don'ts of taking medicines and on generic drugs.

* Silicones and Health

Silicones Health Council (SHC)
1330 Connecticut Ave., NW
Suite 300
Washington, DC 20036   (202) 659-0060

SHC is an organization of organo-silicone manufacturers. The group was formed to coordinate programs dealing with health, environmental and safety issues of interest to the industry and to disseminate scientifically sound information regarding silicones.

* Tranquilizer Warnings

Office of Public Affairs
Food and Drug Administration
5600 Fishers Lane, HFE88
Rockville, MD 20857   (301) 443-3170

A Guide to the Proper Use of Tranquilizers (No. 86-3158) is a free 4-page booklet available on the safe use of this medicines used for treating intense anxiety disorders.

* X-rays and Safety

Office of Consumer Affairs
Food and Drug Administration
Public Inquiries
5600 Fishers Lane
Rockville, MD 20857   (301) 443-3170

Several free pamphlets on radiation are available including: *Primer on Radiation* (No. 79-8099); *Seeking the Safest X-ray Picture* (No. 79-8091); *X-ray Record Card* (No. 80-8024); and *X-rays: Get the Picture on Protection* (No. 80-8088).

Chemicals, Toxics, and Other Health Hazards

* See also Careers and Workplace Chapter
* See also Environment and Nature Chapter

Online databases can be accessed to obtain the latest information on potential health hazards as well as known carcinogens and other dangerous chemicals and substances. In addition, several directories and printouts are available to determine environmental risks to our health in the home, school, and at work.

* Access to Computerized Toxicology Databases

Toxicology Information Program (TIP)
National Library of Medicine
8600 Rockville Pike
Bethesda, MD 20894   (301) 496-6308
TIP was established to provide national access to information on toxicology. The program is charged with setting up computerized databases of information from the literature of toxicology and from the files of both governmental and non-governmental organizations. Among the databases are TOXLINE (Toxicology Information Online) and CHEMLINE, a chemical dictionary file. TIP implemented the TOXNET (Toxicology Data Network) system of toxicologically-oriented data banks, including the HSDB (Hazardous Substances Data Bank), which is useful in chemical emergency response. TIP also supports the Toxicology Information Response Center, which provides reference services to the scientific community.

* Asbestos Clearinghouse

Asbestos Information Association/North America (AIA)
1745 Jefferson Davis Highway
Suite 509
Arlington, VA 22202   (703) 979-1150
This association is the public relations arm of U.S. and Canadian asbestos producers and products manufacturers which provides information on asbestos and health.

* Birth Defects and Cancer: Harmful Chemicals

National Institute of Environmental
 Health Sciences
National Institutes of Health
Public Affairs Office
Research Triangle Park, NC 27709   (919) 541-3345
This NIH institute can share the latest scientific findings on cancer-causing agents.

* Chemicals, Pesticides and Prevention

Center for Environmental Health and Injury Control
Centers for Disease Control
1600 Clifton Road, F29
Atlanta, GA 30333   (404) 488-4102
This center offers free publications on such topics as injury prevention, recreational safety, rodent control, and toxic agent control. You may request a copy of their publications list.

* Dangerous Exposure to Toxins: Experiments

Clinical Biochemistry Branch
Division of Environmental Health Laboratory Sciences
Centers for Disease Control
1600 Clifton Rd.
Atlanta, GA 30333   (404) 488-4132
This research branch of CDC develops, validates and applies laboratory technology which improves the detection, treatment, and prevention of human toxicant exposures and resulting adverse health effects. Contact this office for more information regarding toxicant exposures.

* Environment and Medicine

American Institute of Biological Sciences
730 11th St., NW
Washington, DC 20001   (202) 828-1500
The American Institute of Biological Sciences is a federation of professional societies which promotes all biological sciences, including agriculture, environment and medicine. Publications: *BioScience*.

* Environmental and Occupational Health

Society for Occupational and Environmental Health (SOEH)
P.O. Box 42360
Washington, DC 20015-0360   (202) 762-9319
This society's members include physicians, hygienists, economists, laboratory scientists, academians, and labor and industry representatives.

* Environmental Mutagen Organization

Environmental Mutagen Society (EMS)
Ctr Box X Oak Ridge Natl Lab
Bldg 2001, MS 50
Oak Ridge, TN 37831-6050   (415) 422-5698
The focus of the Environmental Mutagen Society is to encourage the study of mutagens in the human environment particularly as they affect public health. Publications: *Environmental Mutagenesis, EMS Newsletter*.

* Environmental Toxicology

American College of Toxicology
9650 Rockville Pike
Bethesda, MD 20814   (301) 520-0033
The American College of Toxicology is a multidisciplinary society composed of professional having common interests in toxicology. Publications: *Journal of American Toxicology, American College of Toxicology Newsletter*.

* Environmental Toxicology Training and Research

National Institute of Environmental
 Health Sciences
National Institutes of Health
P.O. Box 12233
Research Triangle Park, NC 27709   (919) 541-3345
The National Institute of Environmental Health Sciences supports the National Toxicology Program, as well as research on how living organisms react and adapt to the environment. Some of the research encompasses neuroscience, biophysics, and genetics. They offer training programs for scientists and cooperate with many international organizations.

* Harmful Environment Factors

National Institute of Environmental
 Health Sciences
P.O. Box 12233
Research Triangle Park, NC 27709   (919) 541-3345
The National Institute of Environmental Health Sciences supports nd conducts research focusing on the interaction between humans and potentially toxic agents in their environment. The research concentrates on recognizing, identifying and investigating environmental factors that may be harmful and quantifying those factors. NIEHS research also focuses on developing an understanding of the mechanisms of action of toxic agents on biological systems. Information based on research is transmitted to regulatory agencies, other government agencies, the Congress, industry and the public.

* Latest Findings about Toxics

National Toxicology Program
National Institute of Environmental
 Health Sciences, B2-04
P.O. Box 12233
Research Triangle, NC 27709   (919) 541-3991
The National Toxicology Program's main objectives are to increase the depth of knowledge about the toxicology of chemicals, to evaluate the full range of toxic effects of chemicals, to develop and validate new more effective and efficient assays for toxicity, and to distribute toxicological information resulting from its studies. The *Environmental Health Perspectives* is a scientific journal

Health and Medicine

on the biological effects of environmental agents and the mechanisms through which these agents interact with living systems. The journal can be ordered from Superintendent of Documents, U.S. Government Printing Office, Washington, DC 20402, (202) 783-3238.

* Lead-Based Paint

Reference Supervisor
HUD User
Box 280
Germantown, MD 20874   (800) 245-2691 (301) 251-5154 in DC

This computer-based information service offer personalized literature searches by reference staff on such concerns about housing safety and lead-based paint.

* Local Environmental Health Managers

National Conference of Local Environmental
  Health Administrators (NCLEHA)
Summit County Health Department
1100 Graham Circle
Cuyahoga Falls, OH 44224   (216) 923-4891

The National Conference of Local Environmental Health Administrators promotes efficient and effective local environmental health programs. NCLEHA is affiliated with the National Environmental Health Association.

* On-the-Job Hazards: Registry of 40,000 Chemicals

Toxicological Information Program
Specialized Information Services
National Library of Medicine
8600 Rockville Pike
Bethesda, MD 20894   (301) 496-1131

The Registry of Toxic Effects of Chemical Substances (RTECS) is a database of toxicological information compiled, maintained and updated by the National Institute for Occupational Safety and Health. The RTECS now lists over 40,000 chemicals and the concentrations at which toxicity is known to occur. The printed version is available from Superintendent of Documents, Government Printing Office, Washington, DC 20402, (202) 783-3238. The magnetic computer tape is available from National Technical Information Service, 5285 Port Royal Road, Springfield, VA 22161, (703) 487-4650. The on-line database is available from RTECS, Toxicological Information Program, Specialized Information Services, National Library of Medicine, Bethesda, MD 20894, (301) 496-1131. For additional information, contact: The Editor, RTECS, 4676 Columbia Parkway, Cincinnati, OH 45226, (513) 533-8317.

* Radiation Protection and Measurements

National Council on Radiation Protection and Measurements (NCRP)
7910 Woodmont Ave.
Suite 1016
Bethesda, MD 20814   (301) 657-2652

The National Council on Radiation Protection and Measurements represents the interests of professionals with responsibilities for measuring amounts of and providing protection from nuclear radiation. Publications: *NCRP Report*.

* Risk Analysis

Society for Risk Analysis (SRA)

8000 Westpark Drive
Suite 400
McLean, VA 22101-3101   (703) 790-1745

This society is funded for the purpose of studying and understanding on a scientific basis the risks posed by technological development.

* Risk Reduction of Toxic Chemicals Exposures

National Center for Toxicological Research
Jefferson, AR 72079   (501) 541-4517

This center focuses on the need for increased research to develop better ways of assessing the risk of toxic chemicals to humans, and to help reduce those risks. This center also provides the FDA and other regulatory agencies with the knowledge to make regulatory decisions concerning toxic substances. Research is undertaken by a variety of disciplines, including biochemical and comparative toxicology.

* Toxic and Pesticide Information Hotline

National Pesticide Telecommunications Network   (800) 858-7378

This service of the U.S. Environmental Protection Agency and Texas Tech University is open 24 hours, 7 days a week. It responds to non-emergency questions about the effects of pesticides, toxicology and symptoms, environmental effects, disposal and cleanup, and safe use of pesticides.

* Toxicological Information Program

Specialized Information Services
National Library of Medicine
8600 Rockville Pike
Bethesda, MD 20894   (301) 496-1131

The Registry of Toxic Effects of Chemical Substances (RTECS) is a database of toxicological information compiled, maintained and updated by the National Institute for Occupational Safety and Health. The RTECS now lists over 40,000 chemicals and the concentrations at which toxicity is known to occur. The printed version is available from Superintendent of Documents, Government Printing Office, Washington, DC 20402, (202) 783-3238. The magnetic computer tape is available from National Technical Information Service, 5285 Port Royal Road, Springfield, VA 22161, (703) 487-4650. The on-line database is available from RTECS, Toxicological Information Program, Specialized Information Services, National Library of Medicine, Bethesda, MD 20894, (301) 496-1131. For additional information, contact: The Editor, RTECS, 4676 Columbia Parkway, Cincinnati, OH 45226, (513) 533-8317.

* Workplace Hazards Detection

National Institute for Occupational Safety and Health
4676 Columbia Parkway
Cincinnati, OH 45226   (800) 356-4674

NIOSH is responsible for conducting research to make the nation's workplaces healthier and safer by responding to urgent requests for assistance from employers, employees, and their representatives where imminent hazards are suspected. They conduct inspections, laboratory and epidemiologic research, publish their findings, and make recommendations for improved working conditions to regulatory agencies. NIOSH trains occupational health and safety workers and communicates research results to those concerned.

Medical Research: Clues and Answers

Knowledge about breakthroughs in medical research is not confined to the scientific community. Anyone should look upon organizations and centers engaged in clinical studies and experiments as important information resources to learn about the latest theories which explain the complexities of medicine and health.

* Applications and Answers about NIH Grants

Division of Research Grants
National Institutes of Health
3333 Westbard Ave., Room 449
Bethesda, MD 20892 (301) 496-7441

The Division of Research Grants provides for review of National Institutes of Health grant applications. They collect, store, analyze, and evaluate management and program data needed in the administration of extramural programs. This office disseminated information on the various extramural programs and now have the information on the DRG online system. For guidelines and proposal application, contact this office.

* Artificial Intelligence and Biomedical Applications

Sumex Computer Project
Stanford University Medical Center
233 Medical School Office Building
Stanford, CA 94305 (415) 752-2972

Partially funded by NIH, the Sumex Computer Project is based at Stanford University Medical School to develop and operate a national computing resource for biomedical applications of artificial intelligence in medicine and for basic research in artificial intelligence. Funding from NIH is due to expire in 1991. Contact this office for more detailed information regarding the research program.

* Biomedical Research Projects Underway

Research Resources Information Center
1601 Research Blvd.
Rockville, MD 20850 (301) 984-2870

You may write for the free directory, *Biomedical Research Technology Resources*, which lists all the current biomedical research projects funded through National Institutes of Health and the services available to other researchers (see Biomedical Research Technology Program).

* Biomedical Computing, Engineering and Technologies

Biomedical Research Technology Program
Westwood Building, Room 8A11
National Institutes of Health
5333 Westbard Avenue
Bethesda, MD 20892 (301) 496-5411

NIH's Biomedical Research Technology Program focuses on biomedical computing, biomedical engineering, and technologies for the study of bimolecular and cellular structure and function. Most of the Program's budget is directed to the support of research center grants. Grants are also available for projects of advanced technology related to biomedical research. The research centers are open to outside investigators. Contact this office for a free *Biomedical Research Technology Resources Directory* or grant applications.

* Blacks and Minority Scientists Research Grants

Minority Investigator Research Enhancement Award (MIREA)
Deputy Director, Extramural Activities Program
National Institute of Arthiritis and
  Musculoskeletal and Skin Diseases
Westwood Building, Room 403
Bethesda, MD 20892 (301) 496-7495

Deputy Director, Division of Extramural Activities
National Institute of Diabetes and Digestive
  and Kidney Diseases
Westwood Building, Room 406
Bethesda, MD 20892 (301) 496-7083

The MIREA provides support for faculty members of minority institutions to allow them to collaborate with principal investigators of active research grants funded by the National Institute of Arthritis and Musculoskeletal and Skin Diseases (NIAMS) or the National Institute of Diabetes and Digestive and Kidney Diseases (NIDDK). MIREA is part of an effort to strengthen biomedical research and training in institutions with significant commitments to minorities and thereby to increase the participation of minority scientists in biomedical research.

* Blood and Biological Products Standards

Center for Biologics Evaluation and Research
Food and Drug Administration
Building 29, Room 129
8800 Rockville Pike
Bethesda, MD 20205 (301) 496-3556

The Center for Biologics Evaluation and Research, a regulatory agency for biological products, and conducts research related to the development, manufacture, testing, and use of both new and old biological products. It also conducts research on the preparation, preservation, and safety of blood and blood products. The Center cooperates with other agencies, organizations, universities and, scientists regarding biological products. The information they have is technical in nature.

* Brain Tissue Banks for Neurological and Psychiatric Diseases Research

Dr. Edward D. Bird
Professor of Neuropathology
Mclean Hospital
115 Mill St.
Belmont, MA 02178 (617) 855-3426

Human Specimen Bank
Dr. Wallace W. Tourtellotte
Chief of Neurology Service
V.A.- Wadsworth Medical Center
Building 212, Room 31
Los Angeles, CA 90073 (213) 824-4307

The National Institute of Mental Health and National Institute of Neurological Disorders and Stroke support the Brain Tissue Bank at the Mclean Hospital, Belmont, Massachusetts. Both Institutes also support the Human Specimen Bank at the V.A.- Wadsworth Medical Center, Los Angeles, California. These tissue banking resource collects brain tissues obtained at autopsy, blood serum, and spinal fluid, stores them cryogenically and in formalin, and distributes these materials to research scientists.

* Birth Control: Researching New Contraceptive Methods

Contraception Development Branch
EPN 600, 6130 Executive Blvd.
Rockville, MD 20892 (301) 496-1661

The Contraception Development Branch supports research on the development of new fertility regulating methods with emphasis on improving both effectiveness and acceptability. Some of the research focuses on biological evaluation of new compounds, development of improved vaginal and uterine contraception based on chemical or physical methods, and clinical trials of sex steroids. They collaborate with other national and international organizations, such as The World Health Organization and the Population Council and its International Committee for Contraceptive Research. This Branch also holds workshops on various topics.

* Computer-Assisted Medical Instruction R&D

Lister Hill Center for Biomedical Communications
8600 Rockville Pike
Bethesda, MD 20894 (301) 496-4441

This center is responsible for conducting research and development in computer-assisted instruction, distributed information systems, artificial intelligence and expert systems, and electronic document storage and retrieval. The Center's programs cover six areas: communications engineering, information technology, computer science, audiovisual program development, educational technology, and training and consultation. A publications list is available.

* Genetics and Basic Science Research

National Institute of General Medical Sciences
National Institutes of Health
Building 31, Room 4A52

Health and Medicine

9000 Rockville Pike
Bethesda, MD 20892 (301) 496-7301
NIGMS supports research and research training in the basic biomedical sciences that form the foundation needed to make advances in the understanding of disease. Research focuses on the cellular basis of disease, genetics, pharmacological sciences, physiology and biomedical engineering. For instance, they look at how DNA is replicated or how drugs are metabolized in your body. They have brochures and reports for the general public and professionals on such topics as medicines and genetic diseases.

* Grants from National Institutes of Health
Office of Grants Inquiries
National Institutes of Health
5333 Westbard Ave., Room 449
Bethesda, MD 20892 (301) 496-7441
This offfice can answer your questions regarding policies, applications, procedures, and other information concerning NIH grants.

* Health Sciences International Collaboration
Fogarty International Center for Advanced Studies
in Health Sciences
National Institutes of Health
Building 16, Room 306
Bethesda, MD 20852 (301) 496-2075
This international research center assembles scientists and others in the biomedical, behavioral and related fields for discussion, study, and research relating to the international development of the health science. It also sponsors research programs, conferences, and seminars to further international cooperation and collaboration in the life sciences. FIC oversees the Scholars-in-Residence program and awards fellowships to foreign scientists. Publications are available covering international health care concerns.

* Heart and Lung Transplants
National Heart, Lung, and Blood Institute
National Institutes of Health
Building 31, Room 5A-52
9000 Rockville Pike
Bethesda, MD 10892 (301) 496-4236
This Institute is involved with both intra- and extramural, experimental research regarding transplantation of the heart and lungs. Current research focuses on immune modulation and organ rejection, as well as on long-term preservation of the heart to allow for transplantation. The staff can refer you to current researchers, and can send you brochures and reports on this procedure.

* Laboratory Animals for Medical Research
Division of Research Resources
Science and Health Reports
National Institutes of Health
Westwood Building, Room 857
Bethesda, MD 20892 (301) 496-5545
The Animal Resources Program helps meet the needs of biomedical researchers for high quality, disease-free animals and specialized animal research facilities. The program supports, via grants and contracts, primate research centers and their field stations, primate breeding and supply projects, animal diagnostic laboratories, and a variety of other research projects. The program comprises three subprograms: The Regional Primate Research Centers, Laboratory Animal Sciences, and Biological Models and Materials Resources. Contact this office for more information and a free directory which informs researchers of the resources provided and how to access them.

* Mental Health Grants for Hispanic and Other Minorities
Center for Minority Group Mental Health Programs
National Institute of Mental Health
5600 Fishers Lane, Room 11-95
Rockville, MD 20857 (301) 443-3728
The Minority Group Mental Health Program has two funding components. 1) It funds research and development centers to provide minorities (Hispanic, Asia and Native Americans) an opportunity to conduct research on specific minority concerns. And 2) It funds minority students through the MARC, Minority Fellowship, and Minority Institution Research Development Programs, which are designed to give minorities grants for mental health research.

* Neurophysiology and Computer Systems
Research Services Branch
National Institute of Mental Health
Building 36, Room 2A03
Bethesda, MD 20892 (301) 496-4957
The scientists and engineers of this research branch of NIMH develop experimental design, data processing, and computer programs to help with research in neurophysiology, neurogenetics, and neurochemistry. The researchers can provide consultation in statistical analysis and experimental design, along with information on image processing programs which are available to the public.

* Ongoing NIH Scientific Research Database
Research Documentation Section
Division of Research Grants
National Institutes of Health
5333 Westbard Avenue
Westwood Building, Room 148B
Bethesda, MD 20892 (301) 496-7543
The Computer Retrieval of Information on Scientific Projects (CRISPS) system is designed to provide scientific and associated grant identification information on research currently being done at the National Institute of Health.

* Pharmacology Research
Pharmacology Research Associate Program
National Institute of General Medical Sciences
Westwood Building, Room 919
Bethesda, MD 20892 (301) 496-7301
The PRAP is a small, highly selective intramural activity supported by the National Institute of General Medical Sciences. Each year 11 recently trained scientists are selected for a 2-year period of postdoctoral research in laboratories at NIH and the Alcohol, Drug Abuse, and Mental Health Administration. Associates conduct research under the direction of senior scientists and take course work.

* Research Money: Comprehensive List of Grantees
Health-Related Research and Development
Office of Extramural Research
NIH, Building 1, Room 144
9000 Rockville Pike
Bethesda, MD 20892 (301) 496-5126
This office can answer your questions regarding grants and contracts and direct you to the appropriate office for your research needs. This office also formulates grant award policies and procedures and publishes the *Research Award Index*, a directory of the research awards for each year, available for $92 from the Superintendent of Documents, Government Printing Office, Washington, DC 20402, (202) 783-3238.

Health Costs and Services

Health policy and the health care delivery system are evaluated and reassessed every day. Numerous sources for data and statistics are readily available which can help reveal information on particular medical procedures, hospitals and other aspects of health care.

* Births, Abortions, Deaths Statistics
Division of Vital Statistics
National Center for Health Statistics
3700 East-West Highway, Room 1-44
Hyattsville, MD 20782 (301) 436-8952
This division collects data on births, deaths, abortions, marriages, and divorces, and produces annual data for the U.S., states, countries, and local areas.

* Community Health Services for Homeless, Migrant Farmworkers and Other Populations
Bureau of Health Care Delivery and Assistance
Health Resources and Services Administration
5600 Fishers Lane, Room 7-05
Rockville, MD 20857 (301) 443-2320
The Bureau of Health Care Delivery and Assistance Services focuses nationally on efforts to ensure the availability and delivery of health care services in health manpower shortage areas, to medically underserved populations, and to special services populations, such as migrants or the homeless. The Bureau provides project grants to community-based organizations to meet the health needs of the undeserved or special needs populations.

* Cost of Health Care: Statistics
Office of Public Affairs
Health Care Financing Administration
200 Independence Ave., SW
Room 423-H
Washington, DC 20201 (202) 245-8056; or

Office of Research and Statistics
Social Security Administration
1875 Connecticut Ave., NW
Washington, DC 20009 (202) 965-1234
These offices collect statistics regarding health, health care, and health care financing. They compile and distribute data on a wide variety of topics, such as spending on health care services, the age of recipients of services, and health problems.

* Cost Controls of Medical Technologies
National Center for Health Services Research
5600 Fishers Lane, Room 1825
Rockville, MD 20857 (301) 443-4100
The National Center for Health Services Research conducts and supports research on how health services are made available and how they can be more efficiently and effectively provided. The Office of Health Care Technology Assessment evaluates the effectiveness and application of medical technologies proposed for coverage by public programs. The Intramural Research Program conducts research on such projects as patterns of health cost and use, and the impact of Diagnosis Related Groups (DRG's) on health care. The Extramural Research program sponsors investigator-initiated studies on such issues as health promotion and disease prevention. The NCHSR widely distributes it findings and has a catalog of available publications.

* Cost of Medicaid and Medicare
Health Care Financing Administration
6325 Security Blvd.
Baltimore, MD 21207 (301) 597-3933
This office compiles statistics on Medicaid, health coverage for low-income, and Medicare, health coverage for the elderly. The data are broken down many ways such as populations, expenditures, and utilization. Each year they publish a HCFA statistics booklet which provides significant summary information about health expenditures and HCFA programs.

* Cradle to Grave Health Statistics
National Center for Health Care Statistics
Scientific and Technical Information Branch

3700 East West Highway, Room 1-57
Hyattsville, MD 20782 (301) 436-8500
The National Center for Health Statistics (NCHS) is the Federal Government's principal vital and health statistics agency. It collects, analyzes, and distributes data, conducts research in statistical and survey methodology, and provides technical assistance in the U.S., foreign countries, and for other organizations. They conducted several population-based surveys, such as the National Health Interview Survey and the National Health and Nutrition Examination Survey; and several record-based surveys, such as the National Hospital Discharge Survey and The National Nursing Home Survey. NCHS cooperates with states and other countries to improve the quality and availability of data. A central component of NCHS is to distribute its data, which is done through a series of publications, public use data files, and unpublished tabulations, as well as through journals, conferences, and workshops.

* Doctor Visits National Survey
Division of Health Examination Statistics
National Center for Health Statistics
3700 East-West Hwy., Room 2-58
Hyattsville, MD 20782 (301) 436-7068
This division collects data on health-related matters and administers the National Health and Nutrition Survey, which assesses the health and nutritional status of the general population through direct physical examination.

* Federal Health Policy Evaluations
Information Specialist
DHHS Policy Information Center
Department of Health and Human Services
200 Independence Avenue SW, Room 438-F
Washington, DC 20201 (202) 245-6445
This center identifies, collects, and indexes all program evaluations, studies, and reports of government health programs from such agencies as the General Accounting Office, the Congressional Budget Office, the Office of Technology Assessment. Abstracts of these evaluations are available as well as the annual publication, *Compendium of HHS Evaluation Studies*.

* Health Care Delivery and Health Professions
Office of Public Affairs
Health Resources and Services Administration
5600 Fishers Lane, Room 1443
Rockville, MD 20857 (301) 443-2086
The Health Resources and Services Administration offers a free catalog, *Current Publications*, which lists all the publications films, and videos produced by HRSA's three bureaus: Bureau of Health Care Delivery and Assistance, Bureau of Maternal and Child Health and Resources Development and Bureau of Health Professions.

* Illness and Wellness Status of 50,000 Families
Division of Health Interview Statistics
National Center for Health Statistics
3700 East-West Highway, Room 2-44
Hyattsville, MD 20782 (301) 436-7085
This division administers the National Health Interview Survey, which is the principal source of information on the health, illness, and disability status of non-institutionalized population. The survey focuses on current health topics and is conducted continually in 50,000 households.

* Government Health Programs Report Card
Policy Information Center
U.S. Department of Health and Human Services
200 Independence Ave., SW, Room 438-F
Washington, DC 20201 (202) 245-6445
This center has identified, collected, and indexed the U.S. Department of Health and Human Services' program evaluations and evaluative research reports. Also collected are reports from the DHHS Office of the Assistant Secretary for Planning and Evaluation, the DHHS Inspector General's Office, and the General

Health and Medicine

Accounting Office, the Congressional Budget Office, and the Office of Technology Assessment. A one-page description sheet, including an abstract, is prepared for each study. Copies may be purchased through the National Technical Information Service. Inquiries are answered by telephone, by mail, or by personal assistance. An in-house, online database provides access to the reports by subject and/or sponsoring agency, with custom printouts, including abstracts, available upon request. An annual publication, Compendium of HHS Evaluation Studies, is also available.

* Grants for Health Promotion Projects

ODPHP National Health Information Center
P.O. Box 1133
Washington, DC 20013   (800) 336-4797 (301) 565-4167 (in MD)
The guide, *Locating Funds for Health Promotion Projects*, is designed to assist newcomers on their search for health promotion funding by introducing them to the major tasks involved and information services available. This publication is divided into four major sections. Section I discusses basic principles of fundseeking. Sections II and III discuss where and how to look for health promotion funds, focusing on both private and public sectors. Major foundations and Federal agencies interested in health promotion, as well as local sources are listed. Section IV lists resources--organizations, foundations, publications, and databases--that can be useful to those seeking funds. Also included is an appendix, which includes a glossary, a list of acronyms, a bibliography, and a sample grant application form.

* Marriage and Divorce Statistics

Division of Vital Statistics
National Center for Health Statistics
3700 East-West Highway, Room 1-44
Hyattsville, MD 20782   (301) 436-8952
This division collects data on the number of marriages and divorces as well as statistics of births, abortions, and deaths. It produces annual data for the U.S., states, countries, and local areas.

* Medical Services and Personnel Shortages

National Clearinghouse for Primary Care Information
8201 Greensboro Dr., Suite 600
McLean, VA 22102   (703) 821-8955
This clearinghouse provides information services to support the planning, development, and delivery of ambulatory health care to urban and rural areas where shortages of medical personnel and services exist. Its primary audience is health care providers who work in community health centers. They have a list of publications and can make referrals to other health-related organizations. This clearinghouse also publishes a newsletter, *Primary Care Perspectives*.

* Nurses, Doctors, and Services Availability

Bureau of Health Care Delivery and Assistance
Health Resources and Services Administration
5600 Fishers Lane, Room 7-05
Rockville, MD 20857   (301) 443-2320

The Bureau of Health Care Delivery and Assistance Services focuses nationally on efforts to ensure the availability and delivery of health care services in health manpower shortage areas, to medically underserved populations, and to special services populations. It also administers the National Health Service Corps Program which recruits health care practitioners and places them in areas having shortages of people trained in health-related fields.

* Planned Approach to Community Health (PATCH) Program

Center for Chronic Disease Prevention
and Health Promotion
Centers for Disease Control
1600 Clifton Rd., NE
Bldg 3, Room 117
Atlanta, GA 30333   (404) 639-2838
CCDPHP staff work with State and local health departments and community members to organize local intervention programs. The center provides materials and technical assistance, and the communities invest their time and resources and make the program work. Programs have focused on cholesterol screening and nutrition, smoking cessation, alcohol misuse, and prevention of injuries from falls. The PATCH program also conducts international training conferences.

* Prepaid Medicare Health Care

Deputy Director
Office of Prepaid Health Care
Health Care Financing Administration
Parklawn Building, Room 9-11
330 Independence Avenue SW, Room 436
Washington, DC 20201   (202) 245-0816
This office offers materials on health maintenance organizations (HMOs), specifically the capitation concept under Medicare designed to control health costs. Since this bureau monitors qualified plans, it can serve as an information resource on Medicare prepaid health care plans.

* World Health Policies

Office of International Health
Department of Health and Human Services
5600 Fishers Lane, Room 18-87
Rockville, MD 20857   (301) 443-1774
This office supports the Assistant Secretary for Health in developing policy, and also coordinates activities of the Public Health Service in the field of international health. It works closely with the World Health Organization and other international organizations and oversees PHS participation in over 25 bi-national health agreements. The OIH will respond to questions regarding U.S. participation in international health agreements and programs. A publications list is available.

Drugs and Chemical Dependence
General Sources

* See also Education Chapter
* See also Information from Lawmakers Chapter
* See also Health and Medicine Chapter
* See also Law and Social Justice Chapter

This chapter includes information sources which deal primarily with alcohol and illegal drugs. The first section identifies several different government agencies, private organizations, clearinghouses, and databases which track chemical dependence in the U.S., as well as international trends. Drug-related crime, traffic accidents, and other statistics are also included. The Education and Prevention section offers all sorts of publications and audiovisuals for teachers, counselors, health professionals, parents, and students. Comic books and coloring books for youngsters also are noted, as well as free posters which carry the drug-free message. Many organizations experimenting with different strategies for prevention and detection of drug abuse in school, communities and the workplace are listed. Under Treatment and Rehabilitation you'll find several resources which can provide you with counseling, referrals, and printed materials on the problems of addiction. Al-Anon Family Group Headquarters, for example, with its round-the-clock toll-free number offers help to families dealing with alcoholism. The Psychiatric Institute runs the National Cocaine Hotline and answers questions and provides referrals to drug rehab centers. Both the National Health Information Center and the National Clearinghouse on Alcohol and Drug Information are excellent places to learn about the array of private resources, new organizations, hotlines, and self-help programs for those who need them. Dozens of federal and state government law enforcement agencies, as well as those involved with international drug trafficking enforcement and prosecution, are listed in the last section of this chapter.

* Academic Institutions and Organizational Resources

National Clearinghouse for Alcohol and Drug Information
P.O. Box 2345
Rockville, MD 20852   (301) 468-2600
Single copies of publications are sent free of charge and a publications catalog is available. Examples include:
Directory of Academic Institutions and Organizations: Drug, Alcohol, and Employee Assistance Program Educational Resources -national directory of educational opportunities on subjects relevant to employee assistance, covering academic institutions, national organizations, and state alcohol and drug abuse agencies.

* Afro-American Chemical Dependence

Institute on Black Chemical Abuse
2614 Nicollet Ave.
Minneapolis, MN 55408   (612) 871-7878
This organization offers information, referrals, and materials related to drug abuse among blacks.

* Alcohol and Drug Problems Association

Alcohol and Drug Problems Association of North America
444 N. Capitol St., NW, Suite 706
Washington, DC 20001   (202) 737-4340
This private organization offers information and materials on alcohol and drug abuse.

* Alcohol, Drug Abuse and Mental Health Administration

Alcohol, Drug Abuse and Mental Health Administration
5600 Fishers Lane
Rockville, MD 20857   (301) 443-4797
ADAMHA conducts and supports research on the biological, psychological, behavioral and epidemiological aspects of alcoholism, drug abuse, and mental health and illness; supports the training of scientists to conduct research in the alcoholism, drug abuse and mental heath fields; gathers and analyzes data about the extent of alcohol, drug abuse and mental health problems and the national response to these needs; encourages groups to facilitate and expand programs for the prevention and treatment; and provides information on alcoholism, drug abuse, and mental health to the public and to the scientific community.

* Alcoholism and Health Insurance Coverage

National Institute on Alcohol Abuse and Alcoholism
National Institutes of Health
5600 Fishers Lane, Room 16-95
Rockville, MD 20857   (301) 443-3864

The NIAAA looks at trends relating to treatment of alcoholism and insurance financing issues. It advocates adequate health insurance coverage for alcoholism treatment, and conducts studies on this topic, which are available to the public. The fact sheet, "Health Insurance and Alcoholism" (Order No. MS307) is available free.

* Alcoholism in the Workplace

Association of Labor-Management Administrators
and Consultants on Alcoholism
Suite 1001
4601 N. Fairfax Dr.
Arlington, VA 22209   (703) 522-6272
This organization provides resources for combatting the problems of alcohol abuse in the work environment.

* Alcoholism Magazine for Professionals

Superintendent of Documents
U.S. Government Printing Office
Washington, DC 20402   (202) 783-3238
Alcohol Health and Research World, a magazine published quarterly and available for $8 per year, provides professionals with information regarding current research, prevention, and treatment of alcoholism, and includes comment and opinion section, along with information about upcoming events.

* Alcohol Resources and Bibliographies

National Clearinghouse for Alcohol Information
P.O. Box 2345
Rockville, MD 20852   (301) 468-2600
Single copies of each of these resource bulletins are available free: *Self Help Groups for Professionals and Special Populations* (No. MS330); *FAS (Fetal Alcohol Syndrome) Campaign Coordinators* (No. MS328); *Publishers of Books on Alcohol Topics* (No. MS313); *State and Territorial Alcoholism Program Directors* (No. MS260); *Alcohol-Related Periodicals* (No. MS324); *State and Territorial Occupational Alcoholism Program Consultants* (Order No. MS 324).

* Asian Pacific Americans

National Asian
Pacific American Families Against Drug Abuse
6303 Friendship Ct.
Bethesda, MD 20817   (301) 530-0945
This national organization offers materials and assistance to fight chemical dependence.

Drugs and Chemical Dependence

* Careers in Psychological and Epidemiological Aspects of Chemical Dependence
Chemical Dependence
National Institute on Drug Abuse (NIDA)
5600 Fishers Lane
Rockville, MD 20857   (301) 443-6480
It also supports research training of individuals and institutions who are training individuals in the biological and psychological sciences and epidemiological aspects of drug abuse to enable them to pursue careers in research.

* Child Care Centers at Public Housing Projects
Sherone Ivey
U.S. Department of Housing and Urban Development
  Room 4122
P.O. Box 6424
Rockville, MD 20850   (202) 755-1800
The Public Housing Child Care Demonstration Program helps nonprofit organizations establish child care centers for public housing parents, as well as to determine the change in employability due to the provision of the service

* Children of Alcoholics
National Clearinghouse for Alcohol Information
P.O. Box 2345
Rockville, MD 20852   (301) 468-2600
Children of Alcoholics (Order No. MS 321) and A Growing Concern: How to Provide Services for Children of Alcoholic Families (Order No. PH196) are available free from the clearinghouse.

* Cocaine: Pharmacology and Treatment
National Clearinghouse for Alcohol and Drug Information
P.O. Box 2345
Rockville, MD 20852   (301) 468-2600
These publications are available from the Clearinghouse:
Cocaine: Pharmacology, Effects, and Treatment of Abuse, Research Monograph Series 50, 1984.
Cocaine Addiction: It Costs Too Much, 1985.
The Pharmacology of Cocaine, Research Monograph Series 50, 1984.
Cocaine Use in America: Epidemiologic and Clinical Perspectives, Research Monograph Series 61, 1985.
The Behavioral Pharmacology of Cocaine in Humans, Research Monograph Series 50, 1984.
A Cocaine Bibliography, National Institute on Drug Abuse Research Monograph 8, 1974.

* Community Action Against Addiction
National Clearinghouse on Alcohol and Drug Information
PO Box 2345
Rockville, MD 20892   (301) 468-2600
Communities: What You Can Do About Drug and Alcohol Abuse discusses various strategies for parent groups, schools, and workplaces and details various educational materials available. Single copies of this booklet (No.84-1310) are available free.

* Community Prevention and Education Grants
ACTION
Drug Alliance Office
806 Connecticut Ave., NW
Washington, DC 20525   (202) 634-9757
ACTION supports community-based prevention and education efforts with grants, contracts, conferences, and technical assistance.
Nonprofit organizations and state and local governments are eligible to receive grants from ACTION. An announcement is made in the Federal Register regarding the type of activities that the ACTION grant is available for and organizations are encouraged to apply. ACTION also maintains a mailing list which sends copies of the notices appearing in the Federal Register directly to those on the list. To get the name of your organization on this list, call the number above.

* Community Volunteer Service Programs
ACTION
Drug Alliance Office
806 Connecticut Ave., NW
Washington, DC 20525   (202) 634-9757
ACTION is the principal agency in the Federal Government for administering volunteer service programs. Many of the various components of ACTION, such as Foster Grandparents and VISTA, are involved in community drug abuse education, prevention or treatment programs. The Drug Alliance Office coordinates the agency's drug abuse activities, awards grants that strengthen and expand local volunteer activities combatting illegal drug use among youth and the misuse of prescription and over-the-counter drugs by the elderly, provides

training and technical assistance, and conducts public awareness and education efforts.

* Driving-While-Intoxicated Statistics
National Center for Statistics and Analysis
National Highway Traffic Safety Administration
400 7th Street SW
Washington, DC 20590   (202) 366-9294
The National Center tabulates data on highway traffic accidents and maintains statistics on accidents and fatalities due to alcohol or drug use.

* Drug Abuse and AIDS Helpline
National Institute of Drug Abuse   (800) 662-HELP
NIDA Helpline provides general phone information on drug abuse and on AIDS as it relates to intravenous drug users. This hotline offers referrals to drug rehab centers. Hours: 9 a.m. - 3 a.m. Monday through Friday; 12 p.m. - 3 a.m. on weekends.

* Drug Abuse and AIDS Research
Centers for Disease Control
1600 Clifton Rd., NE
Atlanta, GA 30333   (404) 329-3291
Among the research initiatives underway by CDC are exploring the link between illegal drug use and gang involvement and the co-factors of AIDS, including the possible link to non-intravenous illegal drug use.
training and technical assistance, and conducts public awareness and education efforts.

* Drug Abuse Research
National Institute on Drug Abuse (NIDA)
5600 Fishers Lane
Rockville, MD 20857   (301) 443-6480
NIDA conducts and supports research on the biological, psychological, psychosocial, and epidemiological aspects of drug abuse. It also collaborates with and provides technical assistance to State drug abuse authorities, and encourages State and community efforts in planning, establishing, maintaining, coordinating, and evaluating more effective drug abuse programs.

* Drug Education Council
American Council for Drug Education
Suite 110
204 Monroe St.
Rockville, MD 20850   (301) 294-0600
This clearinghouse offers many publications and other materials on educating youngsters about the dangers of chemical dependence.

* Drug Rehabilitation Services
Office of Human Development Services
U.S. Department of Health and Human Services
200 Independence Ave., SW
Washington, DC 20201   (202) 245-2760
This office provides leadership and direction to human services programs for the elderly, children and youth, families, Native Americans, persons living in rural areas, and handicapped persons. HDS administers rehabilitation services for these groups.

* Drug-Related Highway Accidents Research
National Highway Traffic Safety Administration (NHTSA)
400 Seventh St., SW
Washington, DC 20590   (202) 366-9550
NHTSA is the Federal focal point for the national effort to eliminate driving while intoxicated,, including research on drug-related highway problems.

* Drug Testing to Identify High-Risk Youths
Office of Juvenile Justice and Delinquency Prevention (OJJDP)
Office of Justice Programs
U.S. Department of Justice
633 Indiana Ave., NW
Washington, DC 20531   (202) 724-7782
The OJJDP funds programs such as Urine Testing of Juvenile Detainees to Identify High-Risk Youths, and Drug Testing Guidelines for Juvenile Justice agencies.

* Effective Parenting Skills with High-Risk Youth
Office of Juvenile Justice and Delinquency Prevention (OJJDP)
Office of Justice Programs
U.S. Department of Justice

633 Indiana Ave., NW
Washington, DC 20531 (202) 724-7782
The purpose of Identification and Transfer of Effective Juvenile Justice Projects and Services: Effective Parenting Strategies for Families of High Risk Youth is to reduce delinquency and drug abuse in youth by providing community agencies with information and skills to implement special programs for families of high-risk youth. This project currently is assessing existing family-oriented programs that have demonstrated success in decreasing delinquency, drug use, or associated risk factors.

* Employee Help and Drug Screening
National Clearinghouse for Alcohol and Drug Information
P.O. Box 2345
Rockville, MD 20852 (301) 468-2600
Single copies of publications are sent free of charge and a publications catalog is available. Examples include:
Employee Drug Screening: Detection of Drug Use by Urinalysis - booklet addressing the most asked questions about testing in the workplace.
Urine Testing for Drugs of Abuse - technical and scientific information to assist in the planning and implementation of drug testing programs.

* Hispanic Health Coalition
Coalition of Hispanic Health and Human Services Organizations
1030 15th St., NW, Suite 1053
Washington, DC 20005 (202) 371-2100
COSSMHO offers information, assistance and publications related to drug abuse among the Hispanic community.

* HIV/AIDS Clearinghouse for Federal Employees
Office of Personnel Management (OPM)
1900 E St., NW
Washington, DC 20415 (202) 632-5491
OPM operates an AIDS clearinghouse for education, treatment, and workplace related information, including antidiscrimination.

* House of Representatives Narcotics Committee
U.S. Congress
House Select Committee on Narcotics Abuse and Control
H2-234 House Annex 2
Washington, DC 20515 (202) 226-3040
This special committee investigates drug abuse, conducts hearings in Washington and throughout the country, and publishes numerous studies which are available to the public.

* Inner-City Youth Study
Office of Juvenile Justice and Delinquency Prevention (OJJDP)
Office of Justice Programs
U.S. Department of Justice
633 Indiana Ave., NW
Washington, DC 20531 (202) 724-7782
Patterns of Drug Abuse and Delinquency Among Inner-City Youth is one ongoing study to identify factors that influence involvement in delinquency, drug use and drug sales among a high-risk population.

* Innovative Approaches in Criminal Justice
National Institute of Justice
U.S. Department of Justice
633 Indiana Ave., NW
Washington, DC 20531 (202) 724-7782
National Institute of Justice (NIJ) publishes *A Criminal Justice System Strategy for Treating Cocaine-Heroin Abusing Offenders in Custody, Issues and Practices in Criminal Justice, Arresting the Demand for Drugs; Characteristics of Different Types of Drug Involved Offenders.*

* International Criminal Justice Clearinghouse
National Institute of Justice
U.S. Department of Justice
633 Indiana Ave., NW
Washington, DC 20531 (202) 724-7782
The Institute operates an international information center, the National Criminal Justice Reference Service. Subscribers receive the bimonthly *NIJ Reports*, which includes feature articles on major research developments and abstracts of the latest additions to the NCJRS database, which now numbers more than 100,000 documents.

* Juvenile Justice Clearinghouse
Office of Juvenile Justice and Delinquency Prevention
P.O. Box 6000

Rockville, MD 20850 (800) 638-8736
Publications, research findings, and program evaluations are available as well as specific services including database searches, referrals, conference support, and other juvenile justice products.

* Local Drug Treatment Centers Incentives
Susan Lachter David or Lynn J. Cave
National Institute on Drug Abuse
5600 Fishers Lane, Room 10a-54
Rockville, MD 20857 (301) 443-1124
A NIDA project called Overcoming Barriers to Drug Abuse Treatment in the Community aims to develop a flexible education model for use by communities which have funding and want to establish drug treatment facilities. Local drug treatment personnel will receive NIDA-sponsored training to learn techniques to help make treatment programs more acceptable to the community. This model will be used in communities to educate people about drug treatment with the goal of countering resistance to the establishment of new treatment facilities.

* "McGruff" Crime Prevention Campaign
Bureau of Justice Assistance
U.S. Department of Justice
633 Indiana Ave., NW
Washington, DC 20531 (202) 724-7782
National Crime Prevention (McGruff) Campaign, supported by BJA, develops and disseminates crime prevention materials, provides technical assistance and training, and operates a clearinghouse for information on crime prevention programs, publications, and workshops.

* Mental Health and Chemical Dependence
National Institute of Mental Health (NIMH)
5600 Fishers Lane
Rockville, MD 20857 (301) 443-3877
NIMH supports research on the relationships between mental health and drug or alcohol abuse.

* Minorities and Prevention Grants
Attie Key
Minority Substance Abuse Prevention
U.S. Department of Health and Human Services
Security Lane, Rockwall II
Rockville, MD 20857 (301) 443-0369
This government agencies awards grants for minority substance abuse prevention programs.

* Mothers Against Drunk Driving
Mothers Against Drunk Driving
Central Office
669 Airport Freeway, Suite 310
Hurst, TX 76053 (817) 268-6233
MADD serves as a clearinghouse and advocacy group focusing alcoholism and keeping drunk drivers off the roads. SADD, Students Against Drunk Drivers, is the sister organization of MADD.

* Narcotic Drugs and Psychotropic Substances
International Regulations
Food and Drug Administration
5600 Fishers Lane
Rockville, MD 20857 (301) 443-4480
FDA works with the DEA as a drug regulatory agency. Together, they are responsible for working with the international community (the U.N. and WHO) to ensure appropriate scheduling of narcotic drugs and psychotropic substances.

* National Criminal Survey and Other Statistics
Bureau of Justice Statistics
U.S. Department of Justice
633 Indiana Ave., NW
Washington, DC 20531 (202) 724-7782
The Bureau of Justice Statistics (BJS) maintains statistics about crime, its perpetrators and victims, and the operation of the criminal justice system at the Federal, State and local level. The National Institute of Justice sponsors research on crime and its control and is a central federal resource for information on innovative approaches in criminal justice. BJS publishes *Report to the Nation on Crime and Justice: Second Edition, Profile of State Prison Inmates, 1986, Drug Law Violators, 1980-86: Federal Offenses and Offenders, Drug Use and Crime: State Prison Inmate Survey, 1986, and Survey of Youth in Custody, 1987.*

* National Drug Enforcement Data Clearinghouse
Bureau of Justice Statistics

Drugs and Chemical Dependence

U.S. Department of Justice
633 Indiana Ave., NW
Washington, DC 20531   (202) 724-7782
This clearinghouse gathers existing data on drugs and the justice system, identifies drug enforcement data gaps, and prepares special reports and tabulations of existing drug data.

* Non-Government Drug Abuse Prevention Grants
Ford Foundation
Urban Poverty Programs
320 E. 43rd St.
New York, NY 10017   (212) 573-4634

Robert Wood Johnson Foundation
5530 Wisconsin Avenue
Chevy Chase, MD 20815   (301) 986-9720
These are two large private foundations that award grants for new initiatives in combatting addiction.

* President's Drug Czar
Drug Policy Office
The White House
Washington, DC 20500   (202) 456-6554
The President's White House staff, specifically the Drug Policy Office, focuses on proposed legislation and other efforts in the "War on Drugs."

* Prevention, Intervention and Treatment for Juveniles
Office of Juvenile Justice and Delinquency Prevention (OJJDP)
Office of Justice Programs
U.S. Department of Justice
633 Indiana Ave., NW
Washington, DC 20531   (202) 724-7782
Joint projects between The Research and Program Development Division and the Special Emphasis Division of OJJDP include:
Promising Approaches for the Prevention, Intervention, and Treatment of Illegal Drug and Alcohol Use Among Juveniles is designed to help communities with high rates of adolescent drug and alcohol abuse. The project will identify and review promising juvenile drug programs, develop and test program prototypes and provide training.

* Public Health Services and Resources
Human Resources and Services Administration
5600 Fishers Lane
Rockville, MD 20857   (301) 443-2086
HRSA has leadership responsibility in the Public Health Service for general health services and resource issues relating to access, equity, quality and cost of care. This treatment includes AIDS patients as well as drug or alcohol dependent persons.

* Public Housing Computer Searches and Clearinghouse
Drug Information and Strategy Clearinghouse
U.S. Department of Housing and Urban Development
P.O. Box 6424
Rockville, MD 20850   (800) 245-2691 (301) 251-5154 in DC
An extensive database has been developed. Specialists will conduct computer searches on the topic of interest to you and provide referrals, HUD regulations and legal opinions, resource lists, and a newsletter called *Home Front.*

* Public Housing Modernization Anti-Drug Project
Bill Flood
U.S. Department of Housing and Urban Development
Room 4122
P.O. Box 6424
Rockville, MD 20850   (202) 755-6640
The Comprehensive Improvement Assistance Program provides incentives for comprehensive modernization improvements, some of which may serve to prevent drug activity.

* Public Housing Resident Management Grants
Dorothy Walker
U.S. Department of Housing and Urban Development
Room 4134
P.O. Box 6424
Rockville, MD 20850   (202) 755-6860 (202) 755-3611
This HUD program funds the establishment of resident management groups in public housing.

* Senate Committee

U.S. Senate
Subcommittee on Children
Committee on Labor and Human Resources
Washington, DC 20510   (202) 224-5630
This is one of several subcommittees in the U.S. Senate which focus on some aspect of chemical dependence.

* State Drug Abuse Authorities
List of the drug abuse agencies in each state responsible for drug abuse prevention and treatment services:

Department of Health and Social Services
Office of Alcoholism and Drug Abuse
Pouch H-05-F
Juneau, AK 99811
(907) 586-6201

Department of Mental Health Community Programs
Div. of Mental Illness and Substance Abuse
200 Interstate Park Dr.
P.O. Box 3710
Montgomery, AL 36193
(205) 271-9209

Arkansas Office of Alcohol and Drug Abuse Prevention
1515 W. 7th St., Suite 300
Little Rock, AR 72201
(501) 371-2603

Arizona Department of Health Services
Office of Community Behavioral Health
701 E. Jefferson St., Suite 400A
Phoenix, AZ 85034
(602) 255-1152

Department of Alcohol and Drug Abuse
111 Capitol Mall, Suite 450
Sacramento, CA 95814
(916) 445-0834

Colorado Department of Health
Alcohol and Drug Abuse Division
4210 E. 11th Ave.
Denver, CO 80220
(303) 331-8201

Connecticut Alcohol and Drug Abuse Commission
999 Asylum Ave.
Hartford, CT 06105
(203) 566-4145

Department of Human Services
Office of Health Planning and Development
1875 Connecticut Ave., NW, Suite 836
Washington, DC 20009
(202) 673-7481

Bureau of Alcoholism and Drug Abuse
1901 N. Dupont Hwy.
New Castle, DE 19720
(302) 421-6101

Department of Health and Rehabilitative Services
Alcohol and Drug Abuse Program
1317 Winewood Blvd.
Tallahassee, FL 32301
(904) 488-0900

Georgia Department of Human Resources
Div. of Mental Health and Mental Retardation
Alcohol and Drug Section
878 Peachtree St., NE, Suite 318
Atlanta, GA 30309
(404) 894-6352

Government of Guam
Dept. of Mental Health and Substance Abuse
P.O. Box 8896
Tamuning, GU 96911
(671) 477-9704

Department of Health
Mental Health Div.
Alcohol and Drug Abuse Branch
1250 Punchbowl St.
P.O. Box 3378
Honolulu, HI 96801

(808) 548-4280

Iowa Department of Public Health
Div. of Substance Abuse and Health Promotion
321 E. 12th St.
Lucas State Office Bldg., Fourth Floor
Des Moines, IA 50319
(515) 281-3641

Department of Health and Welfare
Bureau of Substance Abuse and Social Services
450 W. State
Boise, ID 83720
(208) 334-5935

Illinois Department of Alcoholism and Substance Abuse
100 W. Randolph St., Suite 5-600
Chicago, IL 60601
(312) 917-3840

State of Indiana Department of Mental Health
Division of Addiction Services
117 E. Washington St.
Indianapolis, IN 46204
(317) 232-7816

Alcohol and Drug Abuse Services
2700 W. 6th St.
Biddle Bldg.
Topeka, KS 66606
(913) 296-3925

Department for Mental Health/Mental Retardation Services
Div. of Substance Abuse
275 E. Main St.
Health Services Bldg, 1st Floor
Frankfort, KY 40621
(502) 564-2880

Office of Prevention and Recovery from Alcohol and Drug Abuse
2744-B Wooddale Blvd.
P.O. Box 53129
Baton Rouge, LA 70892
(504) 922-0730

Massachusetts Divisions of Substance Abuse Services
150 Tremont St.
Boston, MA 02111
(617) 727-1960

State of Maryland
Addiction Services Administration
201 W. Preston St.
Herbert O'Conor Bldg.
Baltimore, MD 21201
(301) 225-6926

Office of Alcohol and Drug Abuse Prevention
Bureau of Rehabilitation
State House
Station 11
Augusta, ME 04333
(207) 289-2781

Michigan Department of Public Health
Office of Substance Abuse Services
3500 N. Logan St.
P.O. Box 30035
Lansing, MI 48909
(517) 373-8600

Department of Human Services
Chemical Dependency Program Division
444 Lafayette Road
Space Center Bldg., 2nd Floor
St. Paul, MN 55155
(612) 296-3991

Missouri Department of Mental Health
Div. of Alcohol and Drug Abuse
1915 S. Ridge Dr.
P.O. Box 687
Jefferson City, MO 65102
(314) 751-4942

State of Montana Department of Institutions
Alcohol and Drug Abuse Div.
1539 11th Ave.

Helena, MT 59620
(406) 444-2827

Division of Mental Health/Mental Retardation Services
Alcohol and Drug Abuse Section
325 N. Salisbury St.
Albemarle Bldg., Room 1100
Raleigh, NC 27611
(919) 733-4670

North Dakota Department of Human Services
Division of Alcoholism and Drug Abuse
State Capitol/Judicial Wing
Bismarck, ND 58505
(701) 224-2769

Nebraska Department of Public Institutions
Div. of Alcoholism and Drug Abuse
801 W. Van Dorn St.
P.O. Box 94728
Lincoln, NE 68509
(402) 471-2851 or 5583

New Hampshire Office of Alcohol and Drug Abuse Prevention
Hazen Dr.
Health and Welfare Bldg.
Concord, NH 03301
(603) 271-4627

New Jersey Division of Narcotic and Drug Abuse Control
129 E. Hanover St.
CN 362
Trenton, NJ 08625
(609) 292-5760

Behavioral Health Services Division
Substance Abuse Bureau
725 St. Michaels Dr.
P.O. Box 968
Santa Fe, NM 87504
(505) 827-0117

Department of Human Resources
Bureau of Alcohol and Drug Abuse
505 E. King St.
Carson City, NV 89710
(702) 885-4790

New York Division of Substance Abuse Services
Executive Park South
Box 8200
Albany, NY 12203
(518) 457-7629

Bureau of Drug Abuse
30 E. Broad St., Room 295A
Columbus, OH 43215
(614) 466-7893

Oklahoma Department of Mental Health
Alcohol and Drug Programs
4545 N. Lincoln Blvd.
Capitol Station
P.O. Box 53277
Oklahoma City, OK 73152
(405) 521-0044

Office of Alcohol and Drug Abuse Programs
301 Public Service Bldg.
Salem, OR 97310
(503) 378-2163

Pennsylvania Department of Health
Commonwealth and Forster Aves.
P.O. Box 90
Harrisburg, PA 17108
(717) 787-9857

Puerto Rico Department of Addiction Control Services
P.O. Box B-Y
Rio Piedras Station
Rio Piedras, PR 00928
(809) 764-3795

Department of Mental Health/Mental Retardation and Hospitals
Division of Substance Abuse
Substance Abuse Administration Bldg.
Cranston, RI 02920

(401) 464-2091

South Carolina Commission on Alcohol and Drug Abuse
3700 Forest Dr.
Landmark East, Suite 300
Columbia, SC 29204
(803) 734-9520

South Dakota Division of Alcohol and Drug Abuse
523 E. Capitol
Joe Foss Bldg., Room 125
Pierre, SD 57501
(605) 773-3123

Tennessee Department of Mental Health/Mental Retardation
Alcohol and Drug Abuse Services
706 Church St., 4th Floor
Nashville, TN 37219
(615) 741-1921

Department of Health Services
Office of the High Commissioner
HICOM Headquarters
Saipan, Mariana Islands, TT 96950

Texas Commission on Alcohol and Drug Abuse
1705 Guadalupe St.
Austin, TX 78701
(512) 463-5510

Utah State Division of Alcoholism and Drugs
150 W. North Temple
P.O. Box 45500
Salt Lake City, UT 84145
(801) 538-3939

Virginia Department of Mental Health/Mental Retardation
Office of Substance Abuse Services
109 Governor St.
P.O. Box 1797
Richmond, VA 23214
(804) 786-3906

Virgin Islands Division of Mental Health, Alcohol and Drug Dependency
P.O. Box 7309
St. Thomas, VI 00801
(809) 773-1992

Office of Alcohol and Drug Abuse Programs
103 S. Main St.
State Office Bldg.
Waterbury, VT 05676
(802) 241-2170

Washington Department of Social and Health Services
Bureau of Alcoholism and Substance Abuse
Office Bldg. 44W
Olympia, WA 98504
(206) 753-5866

Office of Alcohol and Other Drug Abuse
1 W. Wilson St.
P.O. Box 7851
Madison, WI 53707
(608) 266-3442

Department of Health
Div. of Alcoholism and Drug Abuse
1800 Washington St. E.
Bldg. 3, Room 451
Charleston, WV 25305
(304) 348-2276

Alcohol and Drug Abuse Programs
Hathaway Bldg.
Room 354
Cheyenne, WY 82002
(307) 777-7115 or 7118

* Steroids Abuse

Drug Abuse Prevention Oversight Staff
Office of the Secretary
U.S. Department of Education
400 Maryland Ave., SW, Room 4145
Washington, DC 20202-0100   (202) 732-4599
This office provides materials to schools and communities in developing a comprehensive program to prevent the use of alcohol and other drugs. Revised recently to include statistics and information on alcohol, tobacco, and steroids.*
Toll-free Help Hotlines

* Substance Abuse Databases

National Health Information Clearinghouse
P.O. Box 11133
Washington, DC 20012-1133   (800) 336-4797 (301) 565-4167
The Clearinghouse publishes *Healthfinder: Online Health Information* which identifies databases, many of which contain news about recent medical research and studies on addiction such as DRUGINFO. This online system, available from BRS produced by the College of Pharmacy at the University of Minnesota, covers drug and alcohol use and abuse, including educational, sociological, and psychological aspects and therapies.

* Toll-free Hotlines

Here are some of the primary toll-free numbers.

Alcohol and Drug Referral Hotline	(800) 252-6465
Al-Anon	(800) 344-2666
Child Help - National Child Abuse Hotline	(800) 422-4453
Cocaine Helpline	(800) COCAINE
Forest Service Anonymous Witness Reporting System	(800) 73-CRIME (800)-78-CRIME in CA
Just Say No Foundation	(800) 258-2766 (415) 939-6666 in CA
MADD - Mothers Against Drunk Driving	(800) 438-1240
National AIDS Hotline	(800) 342-2437
National Council of Child Abuse & Family Violence	(800) 222-2000
National Council on Alcoholism Information Line	(800) NCA-CALL
National Hepatitis Hotline	(800) 223-0179
National Institute on Drug Abuse	(800) 662-HELP
National Runaway Switchboard and Suicide Hotline	(800) 621-4000
National Sexually Transmitted Diseases Hotline	(800) 227-8922
No Drugs in the Workplace	(800) 628-DRUG
Parents Anonymous National Office	(800) 421-0353
Parent Resource Institute for Drug Education	(800) 241-7946
PRIDE Drug Information Line	(800) 241-7946
Schools Without Drugs	(800) 624-0100
State High School Associations Target Programs	(800) 366-6667
Suicide and Rape 24-Hour Emergency Services	(800) 333-4444
Tough Love	(800) 333-1069 (215) 348-7090

Education and Prevention

* Academic Institutions and Educational Resources

National Clearinghouse for Alcohol and Drug Information
P.O. Box 2345
Rockville, MD 20852   (301) 468-2600

Single copies of publications are sent free of charge and a publications catalog is available. Examples include the *Directory of Academic Institutions and Organizations: Drug, Alcohol, and Employee Assistance Program Educational Resources*, which includes educational opportunities on subjects relevant to employee assistance, covering academic institutions, national organizations, and State alcohol and drug abuse agencies.

* ACTION Drug Abuse Prevention Nationwide

ACTION
Drug Alliance Office
806 Connecticut Ave., NW
Washington, DC 20525   (202) 634-9757

ACTION sponsors educational prevention programs in the community geared to youth drug abuse prevention. The Regional Offices:

Region I
441 Stuart St., 9th Floor, Boston, MA 02116; (617) 223-4501. Serving: Connecticut, Maine, Massachusetts, New Hampshire, Vermont and Rhode Island

Region II
Jacob J. Javits Federal Bldg., 26 Federal Plaza, Suite 1611, New York, NY 10278; (212) 264-4747. Serving: New Jersey, New York, Puerto Rico and the Virgin Islands

Region III
U.S. Customs House, 2nd & Chestnut Sts., Room 108, Philadelphia, PA 19106; (215) 597-9972. Serving: Kentucky, Maryland, Delaware, Ohio, Pennsylvania, Virginia, West Virginia and Washington, DC.

Region IV
101 Marietta St., NW, Suite 1003, Atlanta, GA 30323; (404) 221-2859. Serving: Alabama, Florida, Georgia, Mississippi, North Carolina, South Carolina and Tennessee.

Region V
10 West Jackson Blvd., 3rd Floor, Chicago, IL 60604; (312) 353-5107. Serving: Illinois, Indiana, Iowa, Michigan, Minnesota and Wisconsin

Region VI
1100 Commerce, Room 6B11, Dallas, TX 75242; (214) 767-9494. Serving: Arkansas, Kansas, Louisiana, Missouri, New Mexico, Oklahoma and Texas

Region VIII
Executive Tower Bldg., Suite 2930, 1405 Curtis St., Denver, CO 80202; (303) 844-2671. Serving: Colorado, Wyoming, Montana, Nebraska, North Dakota, South Dakota and Utah

Region IX
211 Main St., Room 530, San Francisco, CA 94150; (415) 974-0673. Serving: Arizona, California, Hawaii, Nevada, Guam and American Samoa

Region X
1111 Third Ave., Suite 330, Seattle, WA 98101; (206) 442-1558. Serving: Alaska, Idaho, Oregon and Washington

* Adolescent Peer Pressure and Prevention Study

National Clearinghouse for Alcohol and Drug Information
P.O. Box 2345
Rockville, MD 20852   (301) 468-2600

Single copies of publications are sent free of charge and a publications catalog is available. Examples include:

Adolescent Peer Pressure Theory, Correlates, and Program Implications for Drug Abuse Prevention, 1988, 115 pg. book. Looks at constructive ways of channeling peer pressure. Designed to help parents and professionals understand the pressures associated with adolescence, the factors associated with drug use, and other forms of problem behavior. Different peer program approaches, ways in which peer programs can be implemented, and research suggestions are included. *Drug Prevention Curricula: A Guide to Selection and Implementation*, 1988, 76 pg. handbook. Written with the assistance of a distinguished advisory panel, this handbook represents the best current thinking about drug prevention education.

* After-School High Risk Youth

Federal Bureau of Investigation
9th St. and Pennsylvania Ave., NW
Washington, DC 20535   (202) 324-3000

High Risk Youth Program is an FBI effort to establish an after school drug abuse prevention program in conjunction with the Office of Juvenile Justice and Delinquency Prevention (OJJDP), and the Boys and Girls Clubs of America. This program targets high risk youth in the area of drug prevention and education. The program goal is to channel the energies of youth into positive activities which will prepare them to live a drug free life. Activities will be developed which teach or reinforce youth life skills (self esteem, decision making, etc.), drug education, and drug refusal skills. This information will also be incorporated into existing programs, such as vocational training. Information on the High Risk Youth Program can be obtained from your local chapter of Boys and Girls Clubs of America.

* AIDS and IV Drug Users Educational Materials

Office of Substance Abuse Prevention (OSAP)
National Institute on Alcohol Abuse and Alcoholism
5600 Fishers Lane
Rockville, MD 20857   (301) 443-0365

OSAP, in cooperation with the Centers for Disease Control, develops educational materials to reduce the risks of AIDS among IV drug users.

* Alcohol Abuse Prevention and Education

National Clearinghouse for Alcohol Information
P.O. Box 2345
Rockville, MD 20852   (301) 468-2600

The National Clearinghouse for Alcohol and Drug Information (NCADI) is a centralized source for information about the causes and treatment of alcoholism and other drug addiction. They have the latest research results, articles, videos and other print materials. A sampling of free fact sheets available includes: *Alcohol and Safety* (No. MS 311), *Legal Drinking Age Summary 1986* (No. MS308); *Treatment for Alcohol Problems: How to Find Help* (No. MS 299); *Sex-Related Alcohol Effects* (No. MS 247); *Prevention of Alcohol Problems* (No. MS 305) For a $15 annual handling fee, the bimonthly bulletin, *Prevention Pipeline*, can be sent to keep you informed of the latest research, programs, or events. NCADI offers technical support to organizations through use of resource lists, direct mail and materials, as well as outreach to groups.

* Anti-Drug Effort in Workplace

Occupational Safety and Health Administration
200 Constitution Ave., NW
Washington, DC 20210   (202) 523-8017

OSHA aids the anti-drug effort by ensuring safe and healthful working conditions in the Nation's 4.5 million workplaces.

* Audiovisuals Videotapes Center

Drug Abuse Prevention Oversight Staff
Office of the Secretary
U.S. Department of Education
400 Maryland Ave., SW, Room 4145
Washington, DC 20202-0100   (202) 732-4599

During 1987, awards were made to develop and distribute audiovisual materials to elementary and secondary schools for drug abuse education and prevention activities. These materials are close-captioned videotapes with brief teacher guides. Copies of the tapes have been sent to all the Nation's school districts and are also available from the National Clearinghouse for Alcohol and Drug Information (301/468-2600), the National Audio-Visual Center (301/763-1896), and from each of the Regional Centers (Eileen Nicosia, 202/732-2311).

* Boy Scouts

Boys Scouts of America
1325 Walnut Hill Lane
Irving, TX 75038   (214) 580-2000

Boy Scouts of America provides a package of information entitled "Drugs: A Deadly Game."

* Close-Captioned Hearing Impaired Videos

Office of Public Affairs
US Department of Education

Drugs and Chemical Dependence

400 Maryland Ave., SW
Washington, DC 20202   (202) 732-4637
Eight productions, close-captioned for the hearing impaired, have been designed to inform students, attending kindergarten through 12th grade, about the dangers of drug use in an engaging and entertaining manner. Contact this office for further information on borrowing or purchasing these videos.

* College and University Drug-Free Network
Vonnie Veltri
Office of Educational Research and Improvement
U.S. Department of Education
400 Maryland Ave., SW, Room 4145
Washington, DC 20202-0100   (202) 357-6265
The Network of Drug-Free Colleges consists of over 1200 colleges and universities.

* Community Involvement with Workplace Drug Abuse Video
National Audiovisual Center
Customer Service Section
8700 Edgeworth Drive
Capitol Heights, MD 20743-3701   (301) 763-1896

National Clearinghouse for Alcohol and Drug Information
P.O. Box 2345
Rockville, MD 20852   (301) 468-8200
"Finding Solutions" portrays drug abuse in the workplace as a community-wide problem; thus the solutions offered through education and prevention are presented as personal, workplace, and community responsibilities. Specific emphasis is placed on the need to effectively deliver accurate and credible information to the workforce, to promote workplace peer involvement and build community partnerships. It is available for sale and rental.

* Community Prevention and Education Grants
ACTION
Drug Alliance Office
806 Connecticut Ave., NW
Washington, DC 20525   (202) 634-9757
ACTION supports community-based prevention and education efforts with grants, contracts, conferences, and technical assistance.
Nonprofit organizations and state and local governments are eligible to receive grants from ACTION. An announcement is made in the Federal Register regarding the type of activities that the ACTION grant is available for and organizations are encouraged to apply. ACTION also maintains a mailing list which sends copies of the notices appearing in the Federal Register directly to those on the list. To get the name of your organization on this list, call the number above.

* Crime Prevention Resource Center
National Crime Prevention Council
1700 K St., NW, 2nd Floor
Washington, DC 20006   (202) 393-7141
The Council provides a limited number of free documents as well as referrals, statistics, technical assistance and information on crime prevention organizations. It handles the McGruff Crime Prevention Program for the Office of Justice Assistance Programs. and distributes books, videos, kits, and other materials.

* Disruptive Student Behavior Guidance
Office of Drug Education
U.S. Department of Education
400 Maryland Ave., SW
Washington, DC 20202-4101   (800) 624-0100
Information on developing the capability of local schools to prevent and reduce drug and alcohol use and associated disruptive behaviors. Training and technical assistance.

* Don't Drink Posters
National Clearinghouse for Alcohol and Drug Information
P.O. Box 2345
Rockville, MD 20852   (301) 468-2600
Single copies of numerous posters with anti-alcohol messages are available free. Martin Luther King (Order No. AV165, 22" x 15", black and white) carries the message: "Live the Dream...Say No to Alcohol and Drug Abuse. Reverend Jesse Jackson poster (Order No. AV99.1, 22" x 16", black and white) reads: "We can march, run, or crawl to freedom but we cannot stagger to freedom. Help prevent alcohol abuse." Message of this "School" (Order No. AV99.3, 22" x 16", black and white) reads: "Why look school's already hard enough, why would I want to get drunk and make it worse?" An Inner Voice (Order No. AV161, 31" x 19", color) promotes abstinence during pregnancy, with a message targeted to Native Americans but relevant to all audiences.

* Drug Abuse Coloring Books
Office of Public Affairs
Drug Enforcement Administration
U.S. Department of Justice
1405 I Street, NW
Washington, DC 20537
Soozie and Katy is a coloring and activity book for youngsters that describes the appropriate use of legal drugs and the dangers accompanying misuse of medicines.

* Drug Abuse Posters
National Clearinghouse for Alcohol and Drug Information
P.O. Box 2345
Rockville, MD 20852   (301) 468-2600
Posters are available from this Clearinghouse as well as numerous printed materials. "The Head of the Class" and "School Daze" are approximately 22" x 17" and available free.

* Drug Abuse Prevention Manual
National Clearinghouse for Alcohol and Drug Information
P.O. Box 2345
Rockville, MD 20852   (301) 468-2600
Prevention Planning Workbook - Volume 1 and 11 (No. 81-1062 and 81-1061)outline a systematic prevention program planning process. Steps include assessing needs, generating problem statements, identifying goals, setting objectives, identifying activities to meet objectives, identifying resources, and development an evaluation component. Another large manual, *Adolescent Peer Pressure: Theory, Correlates, and Program Implications for Drug Abuse Prevention*, is available free.

* Drug Abuse Resistance Education Project
Federal Bureau of Investigation
9th St. and Pennsylvania Ave., NW
Washington, DC 20535   (202) 324-3000
Drug Abuse Resistance Education (DARE) targets children before they are likely to experiment with drugs, alcohol, and tobacco. This approach attempts to prevent drug use and to reduce drug trafficking by eliminating the demand for drugs. Veteran uniformed law enforcement officers are trained to teach a structured curriculum in school classrooms, an effort that also enhances the image of police officers within the community.

* Drug and Substance Abuse Prevention
National Clearinghouse for Alcohol and Drug Information
P.O. Box 2345
Rockville, MD 20852   (301) 468-2600
The office, created by the Anti-Drug Abuse Act, promotes and distributes prevention materials (posters, kits, resource lists) throughout the country. It develops materials and distributes information from its database on prevention, intervention, and treatment for a wide variety of audiences. OSAP supports community-based prevention programs through grant programs and on-site consultation, as well as the National Clearinghouse for Alcohol and Drug Information.

* Drug Alliance Coalitions and Networks Grants
Drug Alliance Office
ACTION
806 Connecticut Ave., NW
Washington, DC 20525   (202) 634-9757
ACTION awards grants to develop coalitions and partnerships working together to prevent and combat chemical dependence at the community level.

* Drug Education Council
American Council for Drug Education
204 Monroe St., Suite 110
Rockville, MD 20850   (301) 294-0600
ACDE organizes conferences; develops media campaigns; reviews scientific findings; publishes books, a quarterly newsletter, and education kits for physicians, schools and libraries; and produces films. Four-part drug prevention kit sold by ACDE called *Building Drug-Free Schools* provides school staff, parents and community groups with suggestions for developing a workable school drug policy, K-12 curriculum, and community support. The kit consists of three guides ($50) and a film ($275).

* Drug Experts International Speakers Bureau
U.S. Information Agency (USIA)
301 Fourth St., SW
Washington, DC 20547   (202) 485-7700

USIA provides public affairs support through its posts in U.S. embassies in countries where illicit drug production and/or trafficking has been identified as a priority issue. USIA selects key people in the international drug field for professional exchange programs in the U.S.; and schedules seminars, conferences, and other activities for U.S. specialists in drug-related fields before selected audiences in key countries.

* Drug Free America Campaign

National Federation of Parents for Drug-Free Youth
Communication Center
1423 N. Jefferson St.
Springfield, MO 65802   (417) 836-3709

This group has taken a leadership role in the organization of the National Red Ribbon Campaign. The purpose of the campaign is to present a unified and visible commitment toward the creation of a Drug Free America.

* Drug-Free School Recognition Program

James Better
Office of Educational Research and Improvement
U.S. Department of Education
400 Maryland Ave., SW, Room 4145
Washington, DC 20202-0100   (202) 357-6144

Under the Drug-Free School Recognition Program, applications from nominated schools are reviewed by experts in the area of drug and alcohol prevention. The schools or programs selected for recognition are honored at ceremonies in Washington, DC.

* Drug-Free Schools and Communities Coordination

Office of Substance Abuse Prevention (OSAP)
National Institute on Alcohol Abuse and Alcoholism
5600 Fishers Lane
Rockville, MD 20857   (301) 443-0365

OSAP conducts training, technical assistance, data collection, and evaluation activities of programs supported under the Drug Free Schools and Communities Act of 1986. It also supports the development of model, innovative, community-based programs to discourage alcohol and drug abuse among young people.

* Drug-Free Schools Manual

Information Office
U.S. Department of Education
555 New Jersey Avenue, NW   (800) 624-0100
Washington, DC 20208   (202) 659-4854

Schools Without Drugs suggests ways for students, parents, schools and communities can fight drugs and describes working programs. This free 79-page booklet also discusses legal issues faced by educational institutions.

* Drug-Free Workplace Helpline

                                        (800) 843-4971
                              (301) 443-6780 (in MD)

The Workplace Helpline answers questions and provides technical assistance to business, industry, and unions about developing and implementing comprehensive drug-free workplace programs. Corporate executive officers, managers, and union representatives are encouraged to call for assistance. The Helpline provides telephone consultation, resource referrals, networking services, and publications to assist in planning, policy development, and program implementation. They have a four-part videotape series for loan on drugs in the workplace. The hotline operates from 9 am to 8 pm EST (Monday-Friday).

* Drug Information for Community Groups

Drug Alliance Office
ACTION
806 Connecticut Ave., NW
Washington, DC 20525   (202) 634-9757

Some of the publications currently available include: *Meeting the Challenge*, a guide for service clubs; *Take Action Against Drug Abuse: How To Start A Volunteer Anti-Drug Program in Your Community; Just Say No Guide for Older American Volunteers.*

* Drugs At Work Videotapes:

Employee and Employer Versions
National Audiovisual Center
Customer Service Section
8700 Edgeworth Drive
Capitol Heights, MD 20743-3701   (301) 763-1896

National Clearinghouse for Alcohol and Drug Information
P.O. Box 2345
Rockville, MD 20852   (301) 468-8200

"Drugs at Work" is a 23 minute educational documentary which describes costs of drug use for the workplace, the individual, and the public; and examines action being taken by government and private companies. Interviews with drug users who have sought treatment and with experts on drugs in the workplace are included; and government and industry representatives describe federal and corporate programs currently underway. This video is available in both employer and employee versions. It is available for sale and rental.

* Drugs: Fact Sheets

National Clearinghouse for Alcohol and Drug Information
P.O. Box 2345
Rockville, MD 20852   (301) 468-2600

This clearinghouse offers a series of fact sheets giving basic information about the psychological and physiological effects of various drugs. Single copies of these fliers are available: *Hallucinogens and PCP* (ADM83-1306); *Inhalants* (ADM83-1305); *Marijuana* (ADM83-1307); *Opiates* (ADM 83-1308); *Sedatives-Hypnotics* (ADM83-1309); *Stimulants and Cocaine* (ADM 83-1304). Fliers also are available in Spanish.

* Drunk Driving Films and Videotapes

National Audiovisual Center
8700 Edgeworth Drive
Capitol Heights, MD 20743-3701   (301) 763-1896

The National Audiovisual Center sells several videotapes: "Under The Influence" and "Until I Get Caught." "Spirits of America," available for rent and sale, deals with issues, attitudes and standards of American drinking patterns and the historical and cultural aspects associated with them.

* Effective School Programs Newsletter

Drug Abuse Prevention Oversight Staff
Office of the Secretary
U.S. Department of Education
400 Maryland Ave., SW, Room 4145
Washington, DC 20202-0100   (202) 732-4599

Challenge Newsletter: bi-monthly, highlights successful programs, provides the latest research on effective prevention measures, and answers questions about school-based efforts. The newsletter is distributed to superintendents, principals, and parent groups across the country. Contact Charlotte Gillespie, 202/732-3030.

* Elementary School Drug Prevention Videos

National Clearinghouse on Alcohol and Drug Information
P.O. Box 2345
Rockville, MD 20852   (301) 468-2600

The following drug prevention videos are available for loan through one of the above Regional Centers or the National Clearinghouse:

The Drug Avengers. Ten 5-minute animated adventures that urge caution about ingesting unfamiliar substances; encourages students to trust their instincts when they think something is wrong; and show that drugs make things worse, not better.

Fast Forward Future. A magical device allows youngsters to peer into the future and see on a TV screen what will happen if they use drugs and what will happen if they remain drug free.

Straight Up. A fantasy adventure that features information on the effects of drugs, developing refusal skills, building self-esteem, and resisting peer pressure.

* Elementary School Education Resources

National Clearinghouse for Alcohol and Drug Information
P.O. Box 2345
Rockville, MD 20852   (301) 468-2600

The Fact Is...You Can Prevent Alcohol and Other Drug Problems Among Elementary School Children is a 17-page booklet that includes audiovisuals, program descriptions, and professional and organizational resources to assist educators and parents of young children.

* Employee Assistance Programs Videotape

National Audiovisual Center
Customer Service Section
8700 Edgeworth Drive
Capitol Heights, MD 20743-3701   (301) 763-1896

National Clearinghouse for Alcohol and Drug Information
P.O. Box 2345
Rockville, MD 20852   (301) 468-8200

"Getting Help" presents detailed information about the use of Employee Assistance Programs (EAPs) in addressing drug use in the workplace. The film describes the value of EAPs to employees and employers through comments by

Drugs and Chemical Dependence

business, labor, and government leaders, and EAP professionals; presentation of three model programs; and EAP client interviews. It encourages employers to consider EAPs as a tool in combatting drugs at work, and provides employees with reassuring information about the confidentiality and effectiveness of an EAP program. This video is available in both employer and employee versions. It is available for sale and rental.

* Ethnic Minorities and Alcoholism Prevention

National Clearinghouse on Alcohol Information
P.O. Box 2345
Rockville, MD 20852   (301) 468-2600

Numerous fact sheets and other booklets are available free from the clearinghouse: *Alcohol and Black Americans* (No. MS 319); *Alcohol and Hispanics* (No. MS309); *Alcohol and Hispanic Americans* (RP0253); *Alcohol and Native Americans* (No. RP0307); *Self Help Groups for Professionals and Special Populations* (No MS330).

* Ethnic Minorities and Drug Prevention

National Clearinghouse on Drug Abuse Information
P.O. Box 416
Kensington, MD 20785   (301) 443-6500

A Guide to Mobilizing Ethnic Minority Communities for Drug Abuse Prevention provides a case study and a step-by-step approach on how minorities can successfully organize to fight drugs. Single copies are available free.

* Families in Anti-Abuse Action

Families in Action
2296 Henderson Mill Road, Suite 204
Atlanta, GA 30345   (404) 934-6364

This organization operates as an information center with over 200,000 documents pertaining to abuse prevention and publishes *Drug Abuse Update*.

* FBI Substance Abuse Prevention Education

Federal Bureau of Investigation (FBI)
9th St. and Pennsylvania Ave., NW
Washington, DC 20535   (202) 324-3000

Each FBI field office has a Special Agent Drug Demand Reduction Coordinator who provides substance abuse prevention education to youth between the ages of 5 and 18 years. The FBI Coordinator gets involved in existing drug prevention initiatives in schools and may also assist in implementing new programs.

* Federal and Private Sector Employee Programs

National Clearinghouse for Alcohol and Drug Information
P.O. Box 2345
Rockville, MD 20852   (301) 468-2600

Single copies of publications are sent free of charge and a publications catalog is available. Examples include:
Federal Employee Assistance Program - presents goals for the Federal Employee Assistance Program and a suggested model for many private sector employees to use in their workplaces.
Drug Abuse Curriculum for Employee Assistance Professionals - its purpose is to upgrade the knowledge and skills of EAP staff regarding the role of the EAP in identification, referral, and treatment of individuals evidencing problems associated with drug used, and to show them how to use organizational initiatives for prevention, education, and training regarding drug abuse.
Strategic Planning for Workplace Drug Abuse Programs - a guide to help employers plan and organize anti-drug abuse programs for their workplace.

* Federal Employees Drug-Free Workplace Effort

Office of Personnel Management (OPM)
1900 E St., NW
Washington, DC 20415   (202) 632-5491

OPM administers a merit system for Federal employment that includes recruiting, examining, training and promoting people on the basis of their knowledge and skills. The Office's role is to ensure that the Federal Government provides an array of personnel services to applicants and employees. OPM, with the U.S. Department of Health and Human Services, has developed drug-free workplace plans for Federal agencies.

* Handbooks: Schools Without Drugs

Drug Abuse Prevention Oversight Staff
Office of the Secretary
U.S. Department of Education
400 Maryland Ave., SW, Room 4145
Washington, DC 20202-0100   (202) 732-4599

This office provides materials to schools and communities in developing a comprehensive program to prevent the use of alcohol and other drugs. Revised recently to include statistics and information on alcohol, tobacco, and steroids.
Growing Up Drug Free: A Parent's Guide to Prevention, a handbook for parents

to help families take an active role in drug prevention before a problem occurs. Copies are available free of charge. Call 1-800-624-0100 or in the Washington metropolitan area call 732-3627. Books also can be ordered from the National Clearinghouse for Alcohol and Drug Information.

* Hawaiian Natives Education Program Grants

Drug Abuse Prevention Oversight Staff
Office of the Secretary
U.S. Department of Education
400 Maryland Ave., SW, Room 4145
Washington, DC 20202-0100   (202) 732-4599

Organizations, primarily those that serve and represent Hawaiian natives, can receive funds for drug prevention and education activities. Contact Allen King, 202/732-4599.

* High School Drug Prevention Videos

National Clearinghouse on Alcohol and Drug Information
P.O. Box 2345
Rockville, MD 20852   (301) 468-2600

Hard Facts About Alcohol, Marijuana, and Crack. Offers factual information about the dangers of drug use in a series of dramatic vignettes.

Speak Up, Speak Out: Learning to Say No to Drugs. Gives students specific techniques they can use to resist peer pressure and say no to drug use.

Dare to be Different. Uses the friendship of two athletes in their last year of high school to illustrate the importance of goals and values in resisting pressures to use drugs.

Downfall: Sports and Drugs. Shows how drugs affect athletic performance and examines the consequences of drug use, including steroid use, on every aspect of an athlete's life - career, family, friends, sense of accomplishment, and self-esteem.

Private Victories. Illustrates the effects of drug and alcohol use on students and the value of positive peer influences in resisting peer pressure to use drugs.

* High School Student Attitudes and Trends

National Clearinghouse for Alcohol and Drug Information
P.O. Box 2345
Rockville, MD 20852   (301) 468-2600

National Trends in Drug Use and Related Factors Among American High School Students, 1975-1986 (265 pages) discusses trends in drug use and attitudes of high school seniors, based on an annual survey conducted since 1975.

* Indian Elementary and Secondary School Children

Drug Abuse Prevention Oversight Staff
Office of the Secretary
U.S. Department of Education
400 Maryland Ave., SW, Room 4145
Washington, DC 20202-0100   (202) 732-4599

Programs for Indian Youth: Anti-alcohol and drug abuse education and prevention services will be provided to Indian children attending elementary and secondary schools on reservations which are operated by the Bureau of Indian Affairs. Contact Allen King, 202/732-4599.

* Indian Tribes and Tribal Schools Education

Bureau of Indian Affairs (BIA)
U.S. Department of Interior
Washington, DC 20240   (202) 343-4576

The BIA funds drug education and prevention efforts aimed at American Indian youth as well as tribes and tribal schools. The purpose of the program is to heighten awareness of problems of alcohol and drug abuse among American Indians and to make BIA-funded schools drug-free. BIA also administers a program for Indian children on reservations who attend elementary and secondary schools through a memorandum of agreement with the Department of Education.

* Junior High School Drug Prevention Videos

National Clearinghouse on Alcohol and Drug Information
P.O. Box 2345
Rockville, MD 20852   (301) 468-2600.

The following drug prevention videos are available for loan through one of the above Regional Centers or the National Clearinghouse:

Straight at Ya. Tips on peer pressure, saying no and building self-esteem.

Lookin' Good. A two-part series based on actual incidents that convey the dangers of drug use and promote the use of peer support groups.

* Just Say No! Clubs

Just Say No Foundation
1777 N. California Blvd., Room 200   (800) 258-2766
Walnut Creek, CA 94596   (415) 939-6666

These nationwide clubs provide support and positive peer reinforcement to youngsters through workshops, seminars, newsletters, walk-a-thons, and a variety of other activities. Clubs are organized by schools, communities, and parent groups.

* Law Enforcement Officials Speakers Bureau

Executive Office for United States Attorneys
U.S. Department of Justice
Tenth Street and Pennsylvania Avenue NW
Washington, DC 20530   (202) 633-2601

The Department of Justice drug education effort emphasizes the importance of citizen involvement and the participation of local business and industry, law enforcement officials and schools. Public service announcements, lectures, and speeches by US Attorneys on the drug issue and prevention, are common.

* Monthly School Newsletters

Narcotics Education, Inc.
12501 Old Columbia Pike   (301) 680-6740
Silver Spring, MD 20904   (800) 548-8700

This organization provides drug prevention and education materials to the general public. Its catalog of publications is available. Two monthly publications for use in school are titled *The Winner* and *Listen* for use in schools.

* National Prevention Network

National Prevention Network
444 N. Capitol St., NW, Suite 530
Washington, DC 20001   (202) 783-6868

This non-governmental clearinghouse offers materials on chemical dependence abstinence and treatment.

* On-the-Job Drug Testing Videos

National Audiovisual Center
Customer Service Section
8700 Edgeworth Drive
Capitol Heights, MD 20743-3701   (301) 763-1896

National Clearinghouse for Alcohol and Drug Information
P.O. Box 2345
Rockville, MD 20852   (301) 468-8200

"Drug Testing: Handle with Care" describes the options available in designing a drug testing component as part of a comprehensive drug-free workplace program. Procedures addressing the needs of both the employer and the employee, to ensure the accuracy and reliability of test results, for specimen collection and laboratory analysis, and a discussion of the critical role of the Medical Review Officer (MRO) are highlighted. Case studies of public/private, unionized/nonunionized work environments with testing components are presented. This video is available in both employer and employee versions. It is available for sale and rental.

* Parent Group Grants

ACTION
Drug Alliance Office
806 Connecticut Ave., NW
Washington, DC 20525   (202) 634-9757

The Drug Alliance Grants from ACTION are intended to strengthen and expand the efforts of community-based volunteer groups working to prevent drug abuse. These grants support innovative volunteer projects including organization of parent groups.ACTION

* Parent Groups Survey

National Clearinghouse for Alcohol and Drug Information
P.O. Box 2345
Rockville, MD 20852   (301) 468-2600

Parents, Peers and Pot II: Parents in Action, 1983 (160 pages) describes the formation of parent groups in rural, suburban, and urban communities.

* Parents Resource Institute

Parents Resource Institute for Drug Education
50 Hurt Plaza, Suite 210   (800) 241-2746
Atlanta, GA 30303   (404) 577-4500

This information and referral center offers consultant services to parents, parent groups, school personnel and youth. It provides a drug-use survey service, conducts an annual conference, publishes a newsletter, a youth group handbook,

and other publications; and sells and rents books, films, videos, and slide programs.

* Positive Peer Pressure Clubs

Federal Bureau of Investigation (FBI)
U.S. Department of Justice
9th St. and Pennsylvania Ave., NW
Washington, DC 20535   (202) 324-3000

The FBI, DEA, and Department of Education, are jointly assisting selected elementary and middle school officials from five major urban areas establish positive peer pressure clubs, clubs which are drug free and student managed. Students sign a "no use" contract, a requirement for membership in the club, and receive drug education material and a club membership card. Students plan various social events throughout the school year, and members receive discounts from participating merchants in the community.

* Positive Peer Prevention Youth Groups Funding

Drug Alliance Office
806 Connecticut Ave., NW
Washington, DC 20525   (202) 634-9757

Drug Alliance Grants from ACTION have supported positive peer prevention activities for youth; the development of technical assistance materials; organization of youth groups.

* Postsecondary Education and Prevention Grants

Drug Abuse Prevention Oversight Staff
Office of the Secretary
U.S. Department of Education
400 Maryland Ave., SW, Room 4145
Washington, DC 20202-0100   (202) 732-4599

Grants for Institutions of Higher Education (IHEs): This program is divided between two groups. First, the Fund for the Improvement of Postsecondary Education has awarded 297 grants since fiscal year 1987 to institutions of higher education to develop and operate drug education and prevention programs. Second, the Drug-Free Schools and Communities Staff in the Office of Elementary and Secondary Education (OESE) has awarded 138 grants to support preservice or inservice personnel training or demonstration programs in drug and alcohol abuse education and prevention for use in elementary and secondary schools. Discretionary grant program.

* Prevention and Education Resources

National Clearinghouse for the Prevention of Drug and Alcohol Abuse
c/o The Quest
National Center
6655 Sharon Woods Blvd.
Chicago, IL 60611   (312) 787-0977

This non-governmental clearinghouse offers publications and information on chemical dependence.

* Prevention Programs That Work

National Clearinghouse for Alcohol and Drug Information
P.O. Box 2345
Rockville, MD 20852   (301) 468-2600

Prevention Plus: Involving Schools, Parents, and the Community in Alcohol and Drug Education describes in detail the operation of six model prevention programs. Single copies of this 324 page book are available free.

* PTA Involvement in School Prevention Programs

National PTA
700 N. Rush St.
Chicago, IL 60611   (312) 787-0977

The Parents and Teachers Association are active in the drug-free school program and offers materials on education efforts.

* Public Housing Youth Sports Clubs

Barbara Dorf
U.S. Department of Housing and Urban Development
Room 7144
P.O. Box 6424
Rockville, MD 20850   (202) 755-6094

Youth Sports Clubs to Combat Drugs is a program to establish youth sports clubs to stop drug use at public housing sites with severe drug problems.

* Public Service Announcements Available

National Institute on Drug Abuse (NIDA)
5600 Fishers La.
Rockville, MD 20857   (301) 443-1124

Radio, print and television public service announcements are available through NIDA which focus on high school and college students on crack and cocaine and a specially designed message for family members of cocaine users. NIDA also

Drugs and Chemical Dependence

offers two booklets *Cocaine/Crack. The Big Lie,* and *When Cocaine Affects Someone You Love,* designed for family members of cocaine users.

* RADAR: Alcohol and Drug Awareness Centers
National Clearinghouse for Alcohol and Drug Information
P.O. Box 2345
Rockville, MD 20852   (301) 468-2600

NCADI works with and through Regional Alcohol and Drug Awareness Resource (RADAR) Network Centers located in almost every state. NCADI and the RADAR Network have become the national resource system for information on the latest research results, popular press and scholarly journal articles, videos, prevention curricula, print materials, and program descriptions. Most of the materials are provided free.

* Respect for Laws and Legal System Curricula
Office of Juvenile Justice and Delinquency Prevention (OJJDP)
U.S. Department of Justice
633 Indiana Ave., NW
Washington, DC 20531   (202) 724-7782

Law-Related Education (LRE) is a program of instruction designed to provide students with a conceptual as well as a practical understanding of the law and legal processes. Its goal is to equip students with knowledge of both their rights and responsibilities under the law and to foster law-abiding behavior and respect for law enforcement and the justice system. In addition, law student chapters of LRE in 10 states are initiating LRE substance abuse prevention programs in their areas. (TDTAD)

* Satellite Broadcasting on Chemical Dependence
U.S. Information Agency (USIA)
301 Fourth St., SW
Washington, DC 20547   (202) 485-7700

USIA uses satellite broadcasting and the full range of its communications resources, including the Voice of America, a world-wide press service and television production, to carry its message to foreign audiences. It also supports local programs by acquiring and adapting U.S. materials on drug abuse prevention and control for overseas use.

* School and Community Grants
Drug Abuse Prevention Oversight Staff
Office of the Secretary
U.S. Department of Education
400 Maryland Ave., SW, Room 4145
Washington, DC 20202-0100   (202) 732-4599

State and Local Grants Program: This is a formula grant program which allocates funds to States based on school-age enrollment. Funds are to be used for anti-drug abuse efforts in schools and community-based organizations. Contact Allen King, (202) 732-4599.

* School Safety Center
National School Safety Center
16830 Ventura Blvd., Suite 200
Encino, CA 91436   (818) 377-6200

Information and technical assistance on school programs and drugs. Publishes *School Safety.*

* School Health Education Materials
National Health Information Clearinghouse
P.O. Box 11133   (800) 336-4797
Washington, DC 20012-1133   (301) 565-4167 (in MD and DC)

This clearinghouse publishes *Healthfinder: School Health Materials (Grades K-6)* which describes numerous audiovisuals, printed materials and posters on alcohol, drug abuse and smoking available from government agencies, private organizations and publishers.

* Spanish Drug Abuse Information Hotline
For Spanish speaking callers: (800) 66-AYUNDA

The National Drug Abuse Information and Treatment Hotline helps drug users find and use local treatment programs, and acquaints those affected by the drug use of a significant other with much needed support groups and/or services. Referrals are also made to local crisis or information hotlines and support groups. Many pamphlets and brochures on a variety of drug topics are available. The hotline is in service 9 am to 3 am EST (Monday-Friday) and 12 pm to 3 am EST (Saturday-Sunday).

* Substance Abuse Counselors and Health Professionals
Office of Substance Abuse Prevention (OSAP)
National Institute on Alcohol Abuse and Alcoholism
5600 Fishers Lane
Rockville, MD 20857   (301) 443-0365

OSAP supports clinical training programs for substance abuse counselors and other health professionals involved in drug abuse education, prevention, and intervention.

* Teenagers and Alcoholism
National Clearinghouse for Alcohol and Drug Information
P.O. Box 2345
Rockville, MD 20852   (301) 468-2600

This clearinghouse produces many materials geared to youngsters including *Alcohol Problems and Youth,* an annotated reading lists which includes stories, novels and nonfiction for teens. *Is Beer A Four Letter Word?* offers 58 pages of project ideas, materials, and alcohol education concepts to encourage teenagers to initiate alcohol abuse prevention projects. *For Teenages Only: How do You Say 'No' to a Drink?* describes ways to refuse alcoholic beverages without embarrassment. *Buzzy's Rebound* (Order No. PH232) features Fat Albert and the Cosby Kids in a comic book written for pre-adolescents. *Think You don't Have to Drink* (Order No. PH226) provides 8 pages worth of reasons not to consume alcohol. Single copies are available free.

* TARGET: Health Lifestyles for High School Students
National Federation of State High School Associations
P.O. Box 20626
Kansas City, MO 64195   (816) 464-5400

TARGET program designed to cultivate healthy lifestyles among America's youth. The program offers workshops, training seminars, and an information bank on chemical use and prevention. It has a computerized referral service for substance abuse literature and prevention programs.

* Teachers, Counselors and Educational Personnel Training
Drug Abuse Prevention Oversight Staff
Office of the Secretary
U.S. Department of Education
400 Maryland Ave., SW, Room 4145
Washington, DC 20202-0100   (202) 732-4599

Educational Personnel Training Program is a discretionary grant program designed to provide financial assistance to State educational agencies, local educational agencies, and institutions of higher education for programs and activities used to train teachers, administrators, guidance counselors, and other educational personnel on drug and alcohol abuse education and prevention. Contact Allen King, 202/732-4599.

* U.S. Department of Education Regional Centers
Drug Abuse Prevention Oversight Staff
Office of the Secretary
U.S. Department of Education
400 Maryland Ave., SW, Room 4145
Washington, DC 20202-0100   (202) 732-4599

Regional Centers are authorized to: 1) train school teams to assess and combat drug and alcohol abuse problems, 2) assist State educational agencies in coordinating and strengthening alcohol and drug abuse education and prevention programs, 3) assist local educational agencies and institutions of higher education in developing training programs for educational personnel, and 4) evaluate and disseminate information on effective substance abuse, education prevention programs and strategies.

Northeast
12 Overton Ave., Sayville, NY 11782-0403; (516) 589-7022. Serving: Connecticut, Delaware, Maine, Maryland, Massachusetts, New Hampshire, New Jersey, New York, Ohio, Pennsylvania, Rhode Island, and Vermont.

Southeast
The Hurt Bldg., 50 Hurt Plaza, Suite 210, Atlanta, GA 30303; (404) 688-9227. Serving: Alabama, District of Columbia, Florida, Georgia, Kentucky, North Carolina, South Carolina, Tennessee, Virginia, West Virginia, Virgin Islands, and Puerto Rico.

Midwest
2001 N. Claybourn, Suite 302, Chicago, IL 60614; (312) 883-8888. Serving: Indiana, Illinois, Iowa, Michigan, Minnesota, Missouri, Nebraska, North Dakota, South Dakota, and Wisconsin.

Southwest
555 Constitution Ave., Norman, OK 73037; (405) 325-1454, or (800) 234-7972 (outside Oklahoma). Serving: Arizona, Arkansas, Colorado, Kansas, Louisiana, Mississippi, New Mexico, Oklahoma, Texas and Utah.

Western
101 SW Main St., Suite 500, Portland, OR 97204; (503) 275-9479, or (800) 547-6339 (outside Oregon). Serving: Alaska, California, Hawaii, Idaho, Montana, Nevada, Oregon, Washington, Wyoming, American Samoa, Guam, Northern Mariana Islands, and Republic of Palau.

* Women and Alcoholism

National Clearinghouse for Alcohol and Drug Information
P.O. Box 2345
Rockville, MD 20852   (301) 468-2600

Women and Alcohol Problems: Tools for Prevention (Order No. PH220) discusses strategies for prevention and this 27-page free booklet is aimed at the individual and their families, community groups, teachers, and health professionals. *For Women Who Drink* (PH182) offers suggestions on finding treatment. *Preventing Fetal Alcohol Effects: A Practical Guide for Ob/Gyn Physicians and Nurses* (DHHS No. 81-1163) suggests ways to identify expectant mothers at risk due to alcohol consumption during pregnancy.Fact sheets also available free include "Fetal Alcohol Syndrome" (Order No. MS303 and Order No. MS304), "Drinking Patterns and Problems Among Women (Order No. MS 332).

* Workplace Initiatives Research Grants

Grants Management Office
National Institute on Drug Abuse (NIDA)
Room 10-25, 5600 Fishers Lane
Rockville, MD 20857   (301) 443-6480

NIDA supports research on the prevalence, impact, and treatment of drug abuse in the workplace through its research grant programs. Information on the grant application process can be obtained from Information and consultation on specific research topics can be obtained from the Office of Workplace Initiatives, NIDA, Room 10-A-53, 5600 Fishers Lane, Rockville, MD 20857.

* Young Athletes and Drug Prevention

Drug Enforcement Administration (DEA)
U.S. Department of Justice
1405 I St., NW
Washington, DC 20537   (202) 633-1000

Team Up for Drug Prevention With America's Young Athletes is a free booklet for coaches that includes information about alcohol and other drugs, reasons why athletes use drugs, suggested activities for coaches, a prevention program, a survey for athletes and coaches, and sample letters to parents.

Treatment and Rehabilitation

* Alcoholics Anonymous, Alateen, Al-Anon Self-Help

Al-Anon/Alateen
Group Headquarters
P.O. Box 862
Midtown Station
New York, NY 10018   (212) 302-7240

Alcoholics Anonymous
Box 459, Grand Central Station
New York, NY 10163   (212) 473-6200

These two national organizations offer support and help in local communities nationwide.

* Alcoholism in the Workplace

Association of Labor-Management Administrators
 and Consultants on Alcoholism
Suite 109
4601 N. Fairfax Dr.
Arlington, VA 22203   (703) 522-6272

This organization provides resources for combatting the problems of alcohol abuse in the work environment.

* Alaskan Natives Prevention and Treatment Services

Indian Health Service
U.S. Department of Interior
5600 Fishers Lane
Rockville, MD 20857   (301) 443-1087

The Indian Health Service (IHS) coordinates agency resources and services for alcohol and drug abuse prevention, intervention, treatment and aftercare of American Indians as well as Alaska Natives with opportunity for maximum tribal involvement in developing and managing programs to meet their health needs.

* Cocaine and Nar-Anon Self-Help

COCANON Family Groups
P.O. Box 64742-66
Los Angeles, CA 90064   (213) 859-2206

Nar-Anon Family Group Headquarters
World Service Office
P.O. Box 2562
Palos Verdes Peninsula, CA 92704

These two national organizations offer support and help in local communities nationwide.

* Drug and Alcohol Treatment for Disabled

Social Security Administration (SSA)
6401 Security Blvd.
Baltimore, MD 21235   (301) 965-7700

The SSA administers a national program of contributory social insurance. SSA provides extensive services for the disabled, including drug and alcohol treatment.

* Drug Abusers Treatment and Rehab Advocacy

National Institute on Drug Abuse (NIDA)
5600 Fishers Lane
Rockville, MD 20857   (301) 443-6480

NIDA encourages other Federal agencies, national, foreign, State and local organizations, hospitals and volunteer groups to enable them to facilitate and extend programs for the prevention of drug abuse, and for the care, treatment and rehabilitation of drug abusers.

* Drug Rehabilitation Services

Office of Human Development Services
U.S. Department of Health and Human Services
200 Independence Ave., SW
Washington, DC 20201   (202)

This office provides leadership and direction to human services programs for the elderly, children and youth, families, Native Americans, persons living in rural areas, and handicapped persons. HDS administers rehabilitation services for these groups.

* Family-Based Approach and Adolescent Drug Treatment

National Clearinghouse for Alcohol and Drug Information
P.O. Box 2345
Rockville, MD 20852   (301) 468-2600

Single copies of publications are sent free of charge and a publications catalog is available, including *Adolescent Drug Abuse: Analyses of Treatment Research*, which assesses the adolescent drug user and offers theories, techniques, and findings about treatment and prevention. It also discusses family-based approaches.

* Federal Employees with HIV/AIDS

Office of Personnel Management (OPM)
1900 E St., NW
Washington, DC 20415   (202) 632-5491

OPM has also developed guidelines for the Federal government in dealing with employees with HIV/AIDS.

* Gateway Drugs and Treatment

American Psychiatric Press, Inc.
1400 K St., NW, Suite 1101   (800) 368-5777
Washington, DC 20005   (202) 682-6269 (in DC)

Getting Tough on Gateway Drugs is a 330-page book describing the drug problem, the drug-dependence syndrome, the gateway drugs, and some ways that families can prevent and treat drug problems.

* Local Drug Treatment Centers Incentives

Susan Lachter David or Lynn J. Cave
National Institute on Drug Abuse
5600 Fishers Lane, Room 10a-54
Rockville, MD 20857   (301) 443-1124

A NIDA project called Overcoming Barriers to Drug Abuse Treatment in the Community aims to develop a flexible education model for use by communities which have funding and want to establish drug treatment facilities. Local drug treatment personnel will receive NIDA-sponsored training to learn techniques to help make treatment programs more acceptable to the community. This model will be used in communities to educate people about drug treatment with the goal of countering resistance to the establishment of new treatment facilities.

* Local Treatment Program Referrals

National Drug Abuse Hotline   (800) 662-HELP
For Spanish speaking callers: (800) 66-AYUNDA

The National Drug Abuse Information and Treatment Hotline provides drug related information to the general public, helps drug users find and use local treatment programs, and acquaints those affected by the drug use of a significant other with much needed support groups and/or services. Referrals are also made to local crisis or information hotlines and support groups, such as Cocaine Anonymous and Narcotics Anonymous. They provide many pamphlets and brochures on a variety of drug topics. The hotline is in service 9 am to 3 am EST (Monday-Friday) and 12 pm to 3 am EST (Saturday-Sunday).

* Methadone and Anti-Addiction Drugs

Food and Drug Administration
5600 Fishers Lane
Rockville, MD 20857   (301) 295-8029

The FDA's activities are directed toward protecting the health of the Nation against impure and unsafe foods, drugs, and cosmetics, and other potential hazards. The FDA directs educational efforts at the proper use of prescription and over-the-counter drugs. FDA is also responsible for the regulatory restrictions on the dispensing of drugs for treatment, including methadone to treat opiate addiction.

* Native Americans Intervention and Treatment

Bureau of Indian Affairs (BIA)
U.S. Department of Interior
Washington, DC 20240   (202) 343-4576

Through an agreement between BIA and the Indian Health Service, these organizations seek to coordinate agency resources and services for alcohol and drug abuse prevention, intervention, treatment and aftercare of American Indians.

* Spanish Drug Abusers Referral Hotline

For Spanish speaking callers: (800) 66-AYUNDA
The National Drug Abuse Information and Treatment Hotline helps drug users find and use local treatment programs, and acquaints those affected by the drug use of a significant other with much needed support groups and/or services. Referrals are also made to local crisis or information hotlines and support groups. Many pamphlets and brochures on a variety of drug topics are available. The hotline is in service 9 am to 3 am EST (Monday-Friday) and 12 pm to 3 am EST (Saturday-Sunday).

* State Alcohol and Drug Abuse Treatment

National Association of State Alcohol and Drug Abuse Directors
444 N. Capitol St., NW, Suite 520
Washington, DC 20001 (202) 783-6868
This association maintains information on U.S. drug treatment programs and funding.

* Substance Abuse Treatment and Rehab

Health Care Financing Administration (HCFA)
200 Independence Ave., SW
Washington, DC 20201 (202) 245-6113
The financing of the national drug abuse treatment rehabilitation and prevention programs has been a joint effort of Federal and state government and the private sector. Medicare and medicaid will not pay for certain types of treatment for alcohol and/or drug dependency.

* Veterans Alcohol Dependent Treatment Programs

Veteran's Administration
810 Vermont Ave., NW
Washington, DC 20420 (202) 233-2300
The Veteran's Administration offers treatment to veterans for alcohol and drug abuse. The Veteran's Administration currently operates 123 alcohol dependent treatment programs nationwide which provide diagnosis and treatment on both an inpatient and an outpatient basis.

* Veteran's Drug and Alcohol Treatment

Veteran's Administration
810 Vermont Ave., NW
Washington, DC 20420 (202) 233-2300
The Veteran's Administration operates diverse programs to benefit veterans and members of their families. These benefits include education and rehabilitation, including drug or alcohol treatment. Call or write for booklet describing benefits available for veterans and their dependents.

* Veteran's Drug Abusers Halfway Houses and VA Hospitals

Veteran's Administration
810 Vermont Ave., NW
Washington, DC 20420 (202) 233-2300
Additionally, the VA operates 52 specialized drug dependence programs which offer care and treatment for drug abusers in VA hospitals. They also have many contracts with half-way houses in local communities to place veterans with either alcohol or drug dependencies. Information on any of these programs can be obtained by contacting the Veteran's Administration office nearest you.

* Veteran's Hospitals Substance Abuse Research

Veteran's Administration
810 Vermont Ave., NW
Washington, DC 20420 (202) 233-2300
The Veteran's Administration conducts extensive research in the field of substance abuse in the 172 VA hospitals nationwide. They also opened the Clinical Alcoholism Research Center in San Diego in 1985. No grants for research are offered by the Veteran's Administration in the field of alcohol and drug abuse.

* Veteran's Outpatient Treatment

Veteran's Administration
810 Vermont Ave., NW
Washington, DC 20420 (202) 233-2300
After hospitalization for alcohol or drug treatment, veterans may be eligible for outpatient care, or may be authorized to continue treatment or rehabilitation in facilities such as halfway houses or therapeutic communities at VA expense.

* VA Medical Centers Inpatient and Outpatient Care

Veteran's Administration
810 Vermont Ave., NW
Washington, DC 20420 (202) 233-2300
Patients may be admitted to any VA medical center for inpatient care. However, there are specialized VA Alcohol Dependence Treatment Programs and Drug Dependence Treatment Programs for inpatient and/or outpatient care in VA medical centers in the following states:

A denotes Alcoholism Program
D denotes Drug Dependence Program
A & D denote both Alcohol and Drug Dependence Programs

Alabama
700 S. 19th St., Birmingham, AL 35233 (A); (205) 933-8101
Loop Rd., Tuscaloosa, AL 35404 (A); (205) 553-3760

Alaska
235 E. 8th Ave., Anchorage, AK 99501; (907) 271-4555

Arizona
7th St. & Indian School Rd., Phoenix, AZ 85012 (A); (602) 277-5551
500 Hwy. 89 N., Prescott, AZ 86313 (A); (602) 445-4860
S. 6th Ave. at Ajo Way, Tucson, AZ 85723 (A & D); (602) 792-1450

Arkansas
300 E. Roosevelt Rd., Little Rock, AR 72206 (A & D); (501) 661-1202

California
2615 E. Clinton Ave., Fresno, CA 93703 (A); (209) 225-6100
11201 Benton St., Loma Linda, CA 92357 (A); (714) 825-7084
5901 E. 7th St., Long Beach, CA 90822 (A & D); (213) 498-1313
Wilshire & Sawtelle Blvd., West Los Angeles, CA 90073 (A & D); (213) 478-3711
425 S. Hill St., Los Angeles, CA 90013 (A & D); (213) 688-3843
150 Muir Rd., Martinez, CA 94553 (A & D); (415) 228-6800
3801 Miranda Ave., Palo Alto, CA 94304 (A & D); (415) 493-5000
3350 LaJolla Village Dr., San Diego, CA 92161 (A & D); (714) 453-7500
4150 Clement St., San Francisco, CA 94121 (A & D); (415) 221-4810
16111 Plummer St., Sepulveda, CA 91343 (A & D); (213) 891-7711

Colorado
1055 Clermont St., Denver, CO 80220 (A & D); (303) 399-8020
Hwy. 183 off Hwy. 50, Fort Lyon, CO 81038 (A); (303) 456-1260

Connecticut
W. Spring St., West Haven, CT 06516 (A); (203) 932-5711

District of Columbia
50 Irving St., NW, Washington, DC 20422 (A & D); (202) 745-8161/ 8162

Florida
1000 Bay Pines Blvd., N. Bay Pines, FL 33504 (A); (813) 398-6661
Archer Rd., Gainesville, FL 32602 (A); (904) 376-1611
1201 N.W. 16th St., Miami, FL 33125 (A & D); (305) 324-4455

Georgia
1670 Clairmont Rd., Atlanta (Decatur), GA 30033 (A & D); (404) 321-6111
2460 Wrightsboro Rd., Augusta, GA 30910 (A); (404) 724-5116

Illinois
820 S. Damen Ave., Chicago, IL 60680 (A & D); (312) 666-6500
1900 E. Main St., Danville, IL 61832 (A); (217) 442-8000
Roosevelt Rd. & 5th Ave., Hines, IL 60141 (A & D); (312) 343-7200
Buckley Rd., Rt. 137, North Chicago, IL 60064 (A & D); (312) 688-1900

Indiana
1481 W. 10th St., Indianapolis, IN 46202 (A & D); (317) 429-6741
E. 38th St., Marion, IN 46952 (A); (317) 674-3321

Iowa
30th & Euclid, Des Moines, IA 50310 (A); (515) 255-2173

Kansas
4801 Linwood Blvd., Kansas City, MO 64128 (A); (616) 861-4700
4101 S. 4th St. Trafficway, Leavenworth, MO 66048 (A); (913) 682-2000
2200 Gage Blvd., Topeka, KS 66622 (A); (913) 272-3111

Kentucky
Leestown Rd., Lexington, KY 40511 (A); (606) 233-4511

Louisiana
1601 Perdido St., New Orleans, LA 70146 (A & D); (504) 568-0811
510 E. Stoner Ave., Shreveport, LA 71130 (A); (318) 221-8411

Maine
Rt. 17, Togus, ME 04330 (A); (207) 623-8411

Maryland
3900 Loch Raven Blvd., Baltimore 21218 (A & D); (301) 467-9932

Drugs and Chemical Dependence

Massachusetts
200 Springs Rd., Bedford, MA 01730 (A & D); (617) 275-7500
150 S. Huntington Ave., Boston, MA 01230 (A & D); (617) 232-9500
125 Lincoln St., Boston, MA 02111 (D); (617) 223-2020
940 Belmont St., Brockton, MA 02401 (A); (617) 583-4500
Rt. 9, Northampton, MA 01060 (A); (413) 584-4040

Michigan
Southfield & Outer Dr., Allen Park, MI 48101 (A & D); (313) 562-6000
5500 Armstrong Rd., Battle Creek, MI 49015 (A & D); (616) 966-5600

Minnesota
One Veterans Dr., Minneapolis, MN 55417 (A & D); (612) 725-6767
8th St., St. Cloud, MN 56301 (A); (612) 252-1670

Mississippi
Pass Rd., Biloxi, MS 39531 (A); (601) 388-5541
1500 E. Woodrow Wilson Dr., Jackson, MS 39216 (A); (601) 362-4471

Missouri
I 270, St. Louis, MO 63125 (A & D); (314) 487-0400

Nebraska
2201 N. Broad Well, Grand Island, NE 68803 (A & D); (308) 382-3660
600 S. 70th St., Lincoln, NE 68510 (A); (402) 489-3802
4104 Woolworth Ave., Omaha, NE 68105 (A); (402) 346-8800

Nevada
1000 Locust St., Reno, NV 89520 (A & D); (702) 786-7200

New Hampshire
718 Smyth Rd., Manchester, NH 03104 (A); (603) 624-4366

New Jersey
Tremont Ave., East Orange, NJ 07019 (A & D); (201) 676-1000
Knoll Croft Rd., Lyons, NJ 07939 (A); (201) 647-0180

New Mexico
2100 Ridgecrest Dr., SE, Albuquerque, NM 87108 (A); (505) 265-1711

New York
113 Holland Ave., Albany, NY 12208 (A & D); (518) 462-3311
130 W. Kingsbridge Rd., Bronx, NY 10468 (A & D); (212) 584-9000
800 Poly Place, Brooklyn, NY 11209 (A & D); (212) 836-6600
3495 Bailey Ave., Buffalo, NY 14215 (A & D); (716) 834-9200
Fort Hill Ave., Canandaigua, NY 14424 (A); (716) 394-2000
Albany Post Rd., Montrose, NY 10548 (A & D); (914) 737-4400
1st Ave. at E. 24th St., New York, NY 10010 (D); (212) 686-7500

North Carolina
1601 Brenner Ave., Salisbury, NC 28144 (A); (704) 636-2351

Ohio
3200 Vine St., Cincinnati, OH 45220 (A & D); (513) 861-3100
1000 Brecksville Rd., Cleveland, OH 44141 (A & D); (216) 526-3030
1000 Brecksville Rd., Cleveland, OH 44141 (A); (216) 791-3800

Oklahoma
921 N.E. 13th St., Oklahoma City, OK 73104 (A & D); (405) 272--9876
635 W. 11th St., Tulsa, OK 74127 (D); Phone Muskogee: (918) 683-3261

Oregon
Garden Valley Blvd., Roseburg, OR 97470 (A); (503) 672-4411
Hwy. 62, White City, OR 97503 (A); (503) 826-2111

Pennsylvania
Blackhorse Rd., Coatesville, PA 19320 (A & D); (215) 384-7711
University & Woodland Ave., Philadelphia, PA 19104 (A & D); (215) 382-2400
Highland Dr., Pittsburgh, PA 15205 (A); (412) 363-4900
University Dr., Pittsburgh, PA 15240 (D); (412) 683-3000

Puerto Rico
GPO Box 4867, San Juan, PR 00936 (A & D), (809) 758-7575

Rhode Island
Davis Park, Providence, RI 02908 (A & D); (401) 273-7100

South Carolina
109 Bee St., Charleston, SC 29403 (A); (803) 577-5011
1801 Assembly St., Columbia, SC 29201 (A); (803) 776-4000

South Dakota
I 90/Hwy. 34, Fort Meade, SD 57741 (A); (605) 347-2511
5th St., Hot Springs, SD 57747 (A); (605) 745-4101

Tennessee
1030 Jefferson Ave., Memphis, TN 28104 (A & D); (901) 523-8990
Johnson City, Mountain Home, TN 37684 (A); (615) 926-1171
Lebanon Hwy., Murfreesboro, TN 37130 (A); (615) 893-1360

Texas
2400 Gregg St., Big Spring, TX 79720 (A); (915) 263-7361
4500 S. Lancaster Rd., Dallas, TX 75216 (A & D); (214) 376-5451
2003 Holcombe Blvd., Houston, TX 77211 (A & D); (713) 795-4411
7400 Merton Minter Blvd., San Antonio, TX 78284 (A); (512) 696-9660
1901 S. First, Temple, TX 76501 (A); (817) 778-4811
Memorial Dr., Waco, TX 76703 (A); (803) 752-6581

Utah
500 Foothill Blvd., Salt Lake City, UT 84148 (A & D); (801) 582-1565

Vermont
N. Hartland Rd. White River Junction 05001 (A) (802) 295-9363

Virginia
Emancipation Dr., Hampton, VA 23667 (A); (804) 722-9961
1201 Broadrock Rd., Richmond, VA 23249 (D); (804) 230-9011
1970 Roanoke Blvd., Salem, VA 24153 (A); (703) 982-2463

Washington
Gravely Lake Dr. & Veterans Dr., American Lake, Tacoma, WA 89493 (A & D); (206) 582-8440
1660 S. Columbian Way, Seattle, WA 98108 (A & D); (206) 762-1010
3710 S.W. U.S. Veterans Rd., Vancouver, WA 97201 (D); (503) 222-9221

West Virginia
1540 Spring Valley Dr., Martinsburg, WV 25401 (A); (304) 263-0811

Wisconsin
County Trunk E., Tomah, WI 54660 (A); (608) 372-3971
5000 W. National Ave., Milwaukee, WI 53295 (A & D); (414) 384-2000

Wyoming
Fort Rd., Sheridan, WY 82801 (A); (307) 672-3473

Law Enforcement and Prosecution

* Airborne Drug Smugglers Interdiction

Federal Aviation Administration (FAA)
800 Independence Ave., SW
Washington, DC 20591 (202) 267-3484

The FAA assists the anti-drug effort in pinpointing and intercepting airborne drug smugglers by enhanced use of radar, posting aircraft lookouts and tracking the movement of suspect aircraft through air traffic control centers.

* Campaign Against Marijuana Planting

Bureau of Land Management (BLM)
U.S. Department of Interior
Washington, DC 20240 (202) 343-5717

The Campaign Against Marijuana Planting (CAMP) attempts to eliminate the planting of marijuana on public land as well as drug labs that are operated on public land. Information should be called in to either your local office of the Bureau of Land Management, local officials in your area, or the national office listed above.

* Chronic Juvenile Offenders, Victimization of Children

Office of Juvenile Justice and Delinquency Prevention
U.S. Department of Justice
633 Indiana Ave., NW
Washington, DC 20531 (202) 724-7782

The Special Emphasis Division provides technical assistance for Federal, State and local governments, as well as for public and private agencies and individuals in planning, establishing, funding, operating, or evaluating juvenile delinquency prevention programs.

* Counternarcotics Intelligence Center

Central Intelligence Agency (CIA)
Washington, DC 20505 (202) 482-1100

The DCI Counterintelligence Center at CIA headquarters pools intelligence information to help in the search of drug traffickers, in conjunction with FBI, DEA, and other government agencies. The DCI Counternarcotics Center includes representatives from the intelligence community including DEA, FBI, Customs, Coast Guard, NSA and DOD. The Center combines CIA and operations officers who have full access to intelligence on international drug trafficking. Its mission is to use intelligence better to help the policy community address the national security problems caused by narcotics and to help the US government fight international narcotics trafficking.

* Court Security

U.S. Marshals Service
Department of Justice
One Tysons Corner Center
McLean, VA 22102 (703) 285-1100

The Service protects members of the Federal judiciary and court facilities against all forms of terrorism and violent tactics which are routinely encountered. Cases generating broad media and public interest, as well as violent threats to the presiding trial judge, will intensify as law enforcement agencies focus on dangerous drug related investigations.

* Crime Victimization and Compensation

Office for Victims of Crime (OVC)
U.S. Department of Justice
633 Indiana Ave., NW
Washington, DC 20531 (202) 724-7782

This national office provides technical assistance and grants to states to enhance victim compensation and assistance programs.

* Criminal Justice Database and Reference Service

National Criminal Justice Reference Service
P.O. Box 6000
Rockville, MD 20850 (301) 251-5000 (800) 851-3420

The National Criminal Justice Reference System is a computerized database of more than 90,000 criminal-justice-related information sources. Information specialists are available to search the database or to use other research techniques to answer questions.

* Customs Service Air and Marine Interdiction Efforts

U.S. Customs Service (USCS)
1301 Constitution Ave., NW
Washington, DC 20229 (202) 566-8195

The Service is responsible for the processing and regulation of people, carriers, cargo, currency and mail which pass into and out of the United States. Customs has developed innovative inspection, air and marine interdiction programs and works closely with DEA in the development of intelligence and other cooperative drug enforcement efforts.

* Deserts and Public Lands Rangers

Bureau of Land Management (BLM)
U.S. Department of Interior
Washington, DC 20240 (202) 343-5717

The BLM Rangers are involved in arresting drug offenders and investigating illegal drug activity on federal lands. The Field Offices of BLM that are staffed by Rangers are as follows:

Albuquerque
Albuquerque District, P.O. Box 6770, Albuquerque, NM 87197-6770 (505) 766-8281

Barstow
Barstow Resource Area, 831 Barstow Rd., Barstow, CA 92311 (619) 256-3591

Boise
Boise District, 3948 Development Ave., Boise, ID 83705 (208) 334-1582

Blythe
Indio Resource Area, P.O. Box 1591, Blythe, CA 92226 (619) 922-4519

El Centro
El Centro Resource Area, 333 S. Waterman Ave.,El Centro, CA 92243 (619) 352-5842

Folsom
Folsom Resource Area, 63 Natoma St., Folsom, CA 95630 (916) 978-4177

Las Cruces
Las Cruces District, P.O. Box 1420, Las Cruces, MN 88004-1420 (505) 525-1171

Medford
Medford District, 3040 Biddle Rd., Medford, OR 97504 (503) 776-4173

Monticello
San Juan Resource Area, 480 S. First West, Monticello, UT 84535 (801) 587-2201

Needles
Needles Resource Area, 901 Third St., Needles, CA 92363 (619) 326-3896

Palm Desert
Indio Resource Area, P.O. Box 1237, Palm Desert, CA 92261 (619) 346-5101

Ridgecrest
Ridgecrest Resource Area, 1415-A N. Norma St., Ridgecrest, CA 93555 (619) 375-7125

Riverside
California Desert District, 1695 Spruce St., Riverside, CA 92507 (714) 351-6427

Ukiah
Ukiah District, 555 Leslie St., P.O. Box 940 , Ukiah, CA 95482 (707) 462-3873

Yuma
Yuma District, 3150 Winsor Ave., P.O. Box 5680, Yuma, AZ 85364 (602) 726-6300

* Diplomatic Initiatives on Crop Control and Interdiction

Bureau of International Narcotics Matters
U.S. Department of State
2201 C St., NW
Washington, DC 20520 (202) 647-8464

INM has overall responsibility for international drug policy development, program management, and diplomatic initiatives. Its major programs are concerned with bi- and multi-lateral assistance for crop control, interdiction, and

Drugs and Chemical Dependence

related enforcement activities in producer and transit nations. INM also provides narcotics-related development assistance, technical assistance for demand reduction programs, and training for foreign personnel in narcotics enforcement and related procedures to strengthen interdiction and enforcement efforts.

* Drivers Under-the-Influence Detection
National Highway Traffic Safety Administration (NHTSA)
400 Seventh St., SW
Washington, DC 20590   (202) 366-9550
The Drug Recognition Program is a program being conducted by NHTSA and the Bureau of Justice Assistance. It is a means of improving enforcement of drug-impaired driving violations. The program trains police officers as Drug Recognition Experts (DREs), enabling the officers to develop skills in evaluating the drivers condition and securing evidence for conviction. Site selection criteria for this program are outline in a monograph available from the above address.

* Drug Dealer Evictions from Public Housing
U.S. Department of Housing and Urban Development
451 Seventh Ave., SW
Washington, DC 20410   (202) 755-6980
HUD is working with the Attorney General, and the Secretary of HHS as well as local public housing authorities, State and Federal law enforcement officers, and local agencies to achieve drug-free public housing.

* Drug-Free Federal Prisons
Bureau of Prisons
320 First St., NW
Washington, DC 20534   (202) 724-3198
The Bureau of Prisons provides psychological and drug abuse treatment services and places increased emphasis creating drug-free prisons so as to break the link between drug use and crime.

* Drug Labs on Public Lands Investigations
Bureau of Land Management (BLM)
U.S. Department of Interior
Washington, DC 20240   (202) 343-5717
The Campaign Against Marijuana Planting (CAMP) attempts to eliminate the planting of marijuana on public land as well as drug labs that are operated on public land. Information regarding Brochures regarding the Bureau's efforts are available as well as copies of the annual report are available through the Washington, DC office.

* Drug-Related Crime Data
Data Center & Clearinghouse for Drugs & Crime
1600 Research Boulevard
Rockville, MD 20850   (800) 666-3332
Drug enforcement data, information on drug trafficking and illicit drug-related aspects of crime are available from this clearinghouse.

* Drug Seizures and Prosecution
Drug Enforcement Administration (DEA)
U.S. Department of Justice
1405 I St., NW
Washington, DC 20537   (202) 633-1000
DEA investigates and prosecutes suspects connected with illicit drug trafficking. It regulates the legitimate manufacture and distribution of controlled substances. It maintains statistics regarding all Federal illicit drug seizures. It trains narcotics officers in other Federal, State, and local agencies as well as foreign police. DEA operates the El Paso Intelligence Center (EPIC), 24 hour daily national center for operational drug enforcement information. The regional offices are:

Atlanta
Richard B. Russell Federal Building, 75 Spring St. SW, Room 740, Atlanta, GA 30303; (404) 331-4401

Boston
Room G-64 JFK Federal Building, Boston, MA 02203; (617) 565-2800

Chicago
500 Dirksen Federal Building, 219 S. Dearborn St., Chicago, IL 60604

Dallas
1880 Regal Row, Dallas, TX 75235; (214) 767-7151

Denver
721 19th St., Room 316, Denver, CO 80201; (303) 844-3951

Detroit
357 Federal Building, 231 W. Lafayette, Detroit, MI 48226; (313) 226-7290

Houston

333 W. Loop North, Suite 300, Houston, TX 77024; (713) 681-1771

Los Angeles
350 S. Figueroa St., Suite 800, Los Angeles, CA 90071; (213) 894-2650

Miami
8400 NW 53rd St., Miami, FL 33166; (305) 591-4870

Newark
806 Federal Office Building, Newark, NJ 07102; (201) 645-6060

New Orleans
1661 Canal St., Suite 2200, New Orleans, LA 70112; (504) 589-3894

New York
555 W. 57th St., Suite 1900, New York, NY 10019; (212) 399-5151

Philadelphia
10224 William J. Green Federal Building, Philadelphia, PA 19106; (215) 597-9530

Phoenix
One N. First St., Suite 201, Phoenix, AZ 85004; (602) 261-4866

San Diego
402 W. 35th St., National City, CA 92050; (619) 585-4200

San Fransisco
450 Golden Gate Ave., Room 12215, P.O. Box 36035, San Fransisco, CA 94102; (415) 556-6771

Seattle
220 W. Mercer, Suite 301, Seattle, WA 98119; (206) 442-5443

St. Louis
7911 Forsythe Blvd., Suite 500, United Missouri Bank Bldg. St. Louis, MO 63015; (314) 425-3241

Washington, D.C.
400 Sixth St., SW, Room 2558, Washington, DC 20024; (202) 724-7834

* Drugs-in-the Workplace
Federal Bureau of Investigation (FBI)
U.S. Department of Justice
9th St. and Pennsylvania Ave., NW
Washington, DC 20535   (202) 324-3000
Each of the 58 FBI field offices have a Special Agent (SA) Drug Demand Reduction Coordinator to the FBI's drugs-in-the-workplace efforts. The FBI coordinator may assist drug prevention efforts, for example, educational programs; employee assistance programs; supervisory training; and drug testing.

* Drug Smuggling Hotline
Interdiction Committee
U.S. Customs Service
Department of the Treasury
1301 Constitution Ave., NW
Washington, DC 20229   1-(800) BE-ALERT
The Zero Tolerance program helps you notify authorities if you witness drug smuggling activities in your area. By calling the number above, authorities will be contacted, and the network will contact your local federal officials.

* Drug Sniffing Dogs
Canine Training Center
U.S. Customs Service
Department of the Treasury
HCR Box 7
Front Royal, VA 22630   (202) 566-8188
The Customs Canine Enforcement Training Center is about 70 miles west of Washington, D.C., in Front Royal, VA. The dogs and officers are trained by Customs canine enforcement officers with professional experience in the field. The dogs are taught to detect concealed narcotics and dangerous drugs, while the officer is instructed in law enforcement and in detecting the dog's alert signals when contraband is discovered. Dogs are obtained from animal shelters around the country or from individual owners. Canine enforcement teams assigned to seaports and airports alternate between examining aircraft, vessels, baggage, cargo, and mail. Teams stationed at land border crossings devote their time to examining vehicles and merchandise entering the United States.

* Extraditions
U.S. Marshals Service
Department of Justice
One Tysons Corner Center
McLean, VA 22102   (703) 285-1100

408

The Marshals Service acts as the government's arm for reaching out and returning fugitives to the United States to face charges and put an end to their illegal activities.

* FBI Special Agent Drug Demand Reduction

Federal Bureau of Investigation (FBI)
9th St. and Pennsylvania Ave., NW
Washington, DC 20535   (202) 324-3000

The primary responsibility of the FBI is its cooperative efforts with the Drug Enforcement Agency to investigate drug matters and drug trafficking involvement by organized crime. The FBI conducts court authorized electronic surveillance and drug-related financial and public corruption investigations. Each of the 58 FBI field offices have a Special Agent (SA) Drug Demand Reduction Coordinator to carry forward the FBI's Drug Demand Reduction Program and the FBI's drugs-in-the-workplace efforts. These FBI Drug Demand Reduction Coordinators are also listed in the Experts Chapter.

F.B.I. SA Lester L. Amann
U.S. Post Office and Courthouse
5th Floor
445 Broadway
Albany, NY 12201-1219
(315) 422-6951

F.B.I. SA Francis P. Coffey, Jr.
301 Grand Ave., NE
Albuquerque, NM 87102
(505) 247-1555

F.B.I. SA Billy G. Andrews
Suite 6
222 W. 7th Ave.
Anchorage, AK 99513
(907) 276-4441

F.B.I. SA Frank Pickens
77 Forsyth St., SW
Atlanta, GA 30303
(404) 521-3900

F.B.I. SA Joseph Monroe
7142 Ambassador Rd.
Baltimore, MD 21207
(301) 265-8080

F.B.I. SA Lucy Wiggins
Room 1400
2121 Building
Birmingham, AL 35203
(205) 252-7705

F.B.I. SA Paul Cavanaugh
J.F.K. Federal Office Bldg.
Boston, MA 02203
(617) 742-5533

F.B.I. SA Peter F. Trinkwalder
Room 1400
Federal Office Bldg.
111 W. Huron St.
Buffalo, NY 14202
(716) 856-7800

F.B.I. SA Dale Willis
Room 115
U.S. Courthouse and Federal
Office Bldg.
Butte, MT 59702
(406) 782-2304

F.B.I. SA Gerard D. Sullivan
6010 Kenley Lane
Charlotte, NC 28217
(704) 529-1303

F.B.I. SA Terri Beck
Room 905
E.M. Dirksen Federal Office Bldg.
219 S. Dearborn St.
Chicago, IL 60604
(312) 431-1333

F.B.I. SA David L. Lichtenfeld
Room 9023
Federal Office Bldg.
Main St.
Cincinnati, OH 45202
(513) 421-4310

F.B.I. SA John J. Dunn, Jr.
Room 3005
Federal Office Bldg.
1240 E. 9th St.
Cleveland, OH 44199
(216) 522-1400

F.B.I. SA James H. Davis
Suite 1357
Strom Thurmond Federal Bldg.
1835 Assembly St.
Columbia, SC 29201
(803) 254-3011

F.B.I. SA Thomas Westberg
Suite 300
1801 N. Lamar
Dallas, TX 75202
(214) 720-2200

F.B.I. SA Lauryn Samulski
Room 1823
Federal Office Bldg.
Denver, CO 80202
(303) 629-7171

F.B.I. SA Glenda M. Moffatt
P.V. McNamara Federal Office Bldg.
477 Michigan Ave.
Detroit, MI 48226
(313) 965-2323

F.B.I. SA Byron V. MacDonald
Suite C-600
700 E. San Antonio Ave.
El Paso, TX 79901
(915) 533-7451

F.B.I. SA Elden Loeffelholz
Room 4307
Kalanianaole Federal Office Bldg.
300 Ala Moana Blvd.
Honolulu, HI 96850
(808) 521-1411

F.B.I. SA Charles Kearney, Jr.
Suite 200
2500 East T.C. Jester
Houston, TX 77002
(713) 868-2266

F.B.I. SA John Brandt
Room 679
Federal Office Bldg.
575 N. Pennsylvania St.
Indianapolis, IN 46204
(317) 639-3301

F.B.I. SA William E. Booth, Jr.
Suite 1553
Federal Office Bldg.
100 W. Capitol St.
Jackson, MS 39269
(601) 948-5000

F.B.I. SA Polly Butler
4th Floor Oaks V
7820 Arlington Expressway
Jacksonville, FL 32211
(904) 721-1211

F.B.I. SA Dennis J. Glenn
Room 300
U.S. Courthouse
Kansas City, MO 64106
(816) 221-6100

F.B.I. SA A. Wayne Baker
6th Floor
710 Locust St.
Knoxville, TN 37901
(615) 544-0751

F.B.I. SA Thomas L. Anderson
700 E. Charleston Blvd.
Las Vegas, NV 89104
(702) 385-1281

F.B.I. SA Don H. Kidd
Suite 200
2 Financial Centre
10825 Financial Pkwy.
Little Rock, AR 72201
(501) 221-9100

F.B.I. SA Charles D. McCormick
Federal Office Bldg.
11000 Wilshire Blvd.
Los Angeles, CA 90024
(213) 477-6565

F.B.I. SA William S. Cheek, Jr.
Room 500
Federal Office Bldg.
600 Martin Luther King Pl.
Louisville, KY 40202
(502) 583-3941

F.B.I. SA Joseph F. DeBiaggio
Room 841
Clifford Davis Federal Office Bldg.
167 N. Main St.
Memphis, TN 38103
(901) 525-7373

F.B.I. SA Gordon McNeill
16320 NW Second Ave.
N. Miami Beach, FL 33169
(305) 944-9101

F.B.I. SA Dale G. Mueller
Room 700
Federal Office Bldg. and
   U.S. Courthouse
517 E. Wisconsin Ave.
Milwaukee, WI 53202
(414) 276-4684

F.B.I. SA Larry C. Brubaker
392 Federal Office Bldg.
Minneapolis, MN 55401
(612) 339-7861

F.B.I. SA David A. Chaney
One St. Louis Centre
1 St. Louis St.
Mobile, AL 36602
(205) 438-3674

F.B.I. SA Drucilla L. Wells
Gateway 1
Market St.
Newark, NJ 07102
(201) 622-5613

F.B.I. SA Ford W. Cole
Federal Office Bldg.
150 Court St.
New Haven, CT 06510
(203) 777-6311

F.B.I. SA Ronald R. Travis
Suite 2200
1250 Poydras St.
New Orleans, LA 70112
(504) 522-4671

F.B.I. SA Darlene Marley
26 Federal Plaza
New York, NY 10278
(212) 553-2700

F.B.I. SA Joseph G. O'Brien
Room 839
200 Granby St.
Norfolk, VA 23510
(804) 623-3111

F.B.I. SA Dan L. Vogel
Suite 1600
50 Penn Plaza
Oklahoma City, OK 73118
(405) 842-7471

F.B.I. SA Michael F. Mott
Room 7401
Federal Office Bldg. and

U.S. Courthouse
215 N. 17th St.
Omaha, NE 68102
(402) 348-1210

F.B.I. SA Linda E. Lyman
William J. Green, Jr. Federal
Federal Office Bldg.
600 Arch St.
Philadelphia, PA 19106
(215) 629-0800

F.B.I. SA James J. Ryan, Jr.
Suite 400
210 E. Indiaola
Phoenix, AZ 85012
(602) 279-5511

F.B.I. SA Ansel Packer
Room 1300
Federal Office Bldg.
1000 Liberty Ave.
Pittsburgh, PA 15222
(412) 471-2000

F.B.I. SA C. David Robinson
Crown Plaza Bldg.
1500 SW 1st Ave.
Portland, OR 97201
(503) 224-4181

F.B.I. SA John William Davis
200 W. Grace St.
Richmond, VA 23220
(804) 644-2631

F.B.I. SA Thomas P. Griffin
Federal Office Bldg.
2800 Cottage Way
Sacramento, CA 95825
(916) 481-9110

F.B.I. SA Carl A. Schultz
Room 2704
Federal Office Bldg.
1520 Market St.
St. Louis, MO 63103
(314) 241-5357

F.B.I. SA E. Rhead Richards, Jr.
Room 3203
Federal Office Blgd.
125 S. State St.
Salt Lake City, UT 84138
(801) 355-7521

F.B.I. SA Chuck Klafka
Room 433
Old Post Office Bldg.
615 E. Houston
San Antonio, TX 78205
(512) 225-6741

F.B.I. SA Ronald G. Orrantia
Room 6S-31
Federal Office Bldg.
880 Front St.
San Diego, CA 92188
(619) 231-1122

F.B.I. SA Chuck Latting
450 Golden Gate Ave.
San Francisco, CA 94102
(415) 553-7400

F.B.I. SA Annibal Torres-Rivera
Room 526
U.S. Courthouse and Federal
   Office Bldg.
Hato Rey, PR 00918
(809) 754-6000

F.B.I. SA Edward P. Dutko
5401 Paulsen St.
Savannah, GA 31405
(912) 354-9911

F.B.I. SA Patrick Marr Beatie
Room 710

Federal Office Bldg.
915 Second Ave.
Seattle, WA 98174
(206) 622-0460

F.B.I. SA Bobby J. Grooms
535 W. Jefferson St.
Springfield, IL 62702
(217) 522-9675

F.B.I. SA Walter J. Merritt
Room 610
Federal Office Bldg.
500 Zack St.
Tampa, FL 33602
(813) 228-7661

F.B.I. SA Robert Hasychak
Washington Metropolitan Field Office
1900 Half St.
Washington, DC 20535
(202) 324-3000

* Federal Prosecutors

Executive Office for United States Attorneys
U.S. Department of Justice
Tenth Street and Pennsylvania Avenue NW
Washington, DC 20530   (202) 633-2601
The U.S. Attorneys conduct the prosecution in Federal court of drug trafficking and connected illegal activities. They provide coordination of major drug investigations to ensure that the court cases produced will be successfully prosecuted.

* Federal and Local Law Enforcement Prosecutors Coordination

Executive Office for United States Attorneys
U.S. Department of Justice
Tenth Street and Pennsylvania Avenue NW
Washington, DC 20530   (202) 633-2601
Established Law Enforcement Coordinating Committees (LECCs) are composed of the heads of Federal, state and local law enforcement and prosecutorial agencies who collectively assess the crime problems in each district and determine how best to use available resources to attach those problems. Cross-designation of local prosecutors as Federal prosecutors is now a frequent occurrence in cooperative investigations and prosecutions.

* Firearms and Drug Trafficking

Bureau of Alcohol, Tobacco, and Firearms (ATF)
1200 Pennsylvania Ave., NW
Washington, DC 20226   (202) 566-7777
ATF is pursuing drug-related violations of Federal law concerning firearms, destructive devices and explosives. ATF's resources include undercover agents, national response bomb scene investigation teams, an international firearms identification and tracking system, a worldwide explosives incident data bank and tracking capability, auditors, and agents with experience in investigating complex RICO and conspiracy cases.

* Forest Service Anonymous Witness Reporting System

U.S. Forest Service
14th St. & Independence Ave., SW   (800) 73-CRIME
Washington, DC 20250   (800)-78-CRIME (in CA)
"Forest Service National Anonymous Witness Reporting System" is toll free nationwide "hotline" telephone number for the purpose of receiving confidential information related to drug and other criminal law violations occurring in the National Forest System, and providing this information to key contacts in the Forest Service. Rewards of up to $5000 may be given witnesses who report information leading to the seizure of controlled substances and/or for apprehension of suspects.

* Fugitive Apprehension

U.S. Marshals Service
Department of Justice
One Tysons Corner Center
McLean, VA 22102   (703) 285-1100
As the Department of Justice agency with primary investigative responsibility for most Federal fugitives, the Marshals Service devotes considerable resources toward apprehending those fugitives with drug-related charges and backgrounds. The Drug Enforcement Administration has transferred all its fugitive cases to the Service.

* Grants for Public Agencies and Non-Profits

Bureau of Justice Assistance
U.S. Department of Justice
633 Indiana Ave., NW
Washington, DC 20531   (202) 724-7782
The Bureau of Justice Assistance has a Discretionary Grant Program which provides assistance to public agencies and private nonprofit organizations for: 1) demonstration programs that, in view of previous research or experience, are likely to be successful in more than one jurisdiction. 2) Educational and training programs for criminal justice personnel and technical assistance to States and units of local government. 3) Projects that are national or multistate in scope, and that address the 18 authorized purposes of the Anti-Drug Abuse Act of 1986.

* Herbicides for Narcotic Plants International Eradication

Agricultural Research Service (ARS)
Building 3, Beltsville Agricultural Research Center
West Bethesda, MD 20705   (301) 344-2264
ARS works with the State Department's Bureau of International Narcotics Matters and the Drug Enforcement Agency to determine the efficacy as well as the environmental impact of using herbicides in eradicating narcotic plants. The Agricultural Attaches posted in some drug producing countries are involved directly with local narcotic plant eradication programs.

* High-Level Drug Traffickers

Narcotics and Dangerous Drugs Section
Criminal Division
U.S. Department of Justice
Tenth Street and Pennsylvania Avenue NW
Washington, DC 20530   (202) 633-2601
This section investigates and prosecutes high-level drug traffickers and members of criminal organizations involved in the importation, manufacture, shipment or distribution of illicit narcotics and dangerous drugs, with particular emphasis on litigation attacking the financial bases of those criminal organizations.

* Highway Safety and Enforcement Nationwide

National Highway Traffic Safety Administration
400 Seventh St., SW
Washington, DC 20590   (202) 366-9550
The Drug Recognition Program is a program being conducted by NHTSA and the Bureau of Justice Assistance. It is a means of improving enforcement of drug-impaired driving violations. The program trains police officers as Drug Recognition Experts (DREs), enabling the officers to develop skills in evaluating the drivers condition and securing evidence for conviction. The Governors' Highway Safety Representatives and Coordinators may be contacted for those who are interested in exploring the possibilities of implementing this program.

Alabama
Representative: Fred O. Braswell, Director, Dept. of Economic and Community Affairs, 3465 Norman Bridge Rd., P.O. Box 2939, Montgomery, AL 36105-0939; (205) 261-3572
Coordinator: Charles Swindall, Chief, Highway and Traffic Safety, Law Enforcement & Planning Division; (205) 261-5897

Alaska
Representative and Coordinator: T. Michael Lewis, Director, Highway Safety and Planning Agency, Department of Public Safety, P.O. Box N, Juneau, AK 85004; (907) 465-4371

Arizona
Representative and Coordinator: Sarah L. Wuertz, Office of Highway Safety, 3010 N. Second St., Suite 105, Phoenix, AZ 85004; (602) 255-3216

Arkansas
Representative: James T. Clark, Director, Transportation Safety Agency, Justice Bldg., Suite 100, Little Rock, AK 72204
Coordinator: Joyce Patterson, Manager, Traffic Safety Division; (501) 682-2139

California
Representative and Coordinator: Peter O'Rourke, Director, Office of Traffic Safety, Business and Transportation Agency, 700 Franklin Blvd., Suite 330, Sacramento, CA 95823; (916) 445-0527

Colorado
Representative and Coordinator: John Conger, Director, Division of Highway Safety, 4201 E. Arkansas Ave., Denver, CO 80222; (303) 757-9201

Connecticut
Representative and Coordinator: Norman C. Booth, Director of Transportation, Bureau of Highways, 24 Wolcott Hill Road, Wethersfield, CT 06109; (203) 566-4248

Delaware
Representative and Coordinator: Francis A. Ianni, Office of Highway Safety, Suite 363, Thomas Collins Bldg., 540 S. Dupont Hwy., Dover, DE 19901; (302) 736-4475

Drugs and Chemical Dependence

District of Columbia
Representative: John E. Touchstone, Director, Department of Public Works, 2000 14th St., NW, 6th Floor, Washington, DC 20009; (202) 939-8000
Coordinator: Carole Lewis, Highway Safety Program; (202) 939-8018

Florida
Representative: Thomas G. Pelham, Director, Dept. of Community Affairs, 2740 Center View Dr., Tallahassee, FL 32399; (904) 488-6001
Coordinator: Sandra M. Whitmire, Chief, Bureau of Public Safety Management; (904) 488-5454

Georgia
Representative and Coordinator: Minaurd C. McGuire, Governor's Office of Highway Safety, 100 Peachtree St., Suite 2000, Atlanta, GA 30303; (404) 656-6996

Hawaii
Representative: Edward Y. Hirata, Department of Transportation, 869 Punchbowl St., Honoluly, HI 96813; (808) 548-4655
Coordinator: Lawrence Hao, Director, Motor Vehicle Safety Office, 79 S. Nimitiz Hwy., Honoluly, HI 96813; (808) 548-5755

Idaho
Representative: Kermit Kiebert, Idaho Transportation Department, P.O. Box 7129, Boise, ID 83707; (208) 334-3682
Coordinator: Melvin Morgan, Office of Highway Safety; (208) 334-8105

Illinois
Representative: Melvin H. Smith, Division of Traffic Safety, 319 Administration Bldg., 2300 S. Dirksen Pwy., Springfield, IL 62764
Coordinator: Larry Wort, Bureau of Safety Programs; (217) 782-4974

Indiana
Representative: Joy L. Rothrock, State Capitol, Room 210, Indianapolis, IN 46204; (317) 232-4579
Coordinator: Michael J. Smith, Division of Traffic Safety, 801 State Office Bldg., Indianapolis, IN 46204; (317) 232-1299

Iowa
Representative: Gene W. Shepard, Iowa Department of Public Safety, Wallace State Office Bldg., Des Moines, IA 50319; (515) 281-5261
Coordinator: J. Michael Laski, Governor's Traffic Safety Bureau; (515) 281-5224

Kansas
Representative: Horace Edwards, Department of Transportation, State Office Building, Topeka, KS 66612; (913) 296-3461
Coordinator: Dwight Robinson, Transportation Safety Administrator; (913) 296-3756

Kentucky
Representative: W. Michael Troop, State Police Headquarters, 919 Versailles Rd., Frankfort, KY 40601-9980; (502) 695-6300
Coordinator: David H. Salyers, Highway Safety Standards Branch; (502) 695-6356

Louisiana
Representative: Betty Theis, Highway Safety Commission, P.O. Box 66336, Baton Rouge, LA 70896; (504) 925--6991

Maine
Representative and Coordinator: Richard Perkins, Department of Public Safety, 36 Hospital St., Augusta, ME 04330; (207) 289-2581

Maryland
Representative: Richard H. Trainor, Secretary of Transportation, P.O. Box 8755, BWI International Airport, Baltimore, MD 21240-0755
Coordinator: Clyde Pyers, Division of Transportation Safety; (301) 859-7157

Massachusetts
Representative and Coordinator: Tarrance D. Schiavone, Governor's Highway Safety Bureau, 100 Cambridge St., Room 2104, Boston, MA 02202; (617) 727-5074

Michigan
Representative and Coordinator: Karen R. Tarrant, Office of Highway Safety Planning, 300 S. Washington Square, Suite 300, Lansing, MI 48913; (517) 334-7900

Minnesota
Representative: Paul D. Tschida, Department of Public Safety, Transportation Bldg., St. Paul, MN 55155; (612) 296-6642
Coordinator: Thomas A. Boerner, Director of Traffic Safety; (612) 296-3804

Mississippi
Representative and Coordinator: Roy Thigpen, 301 W. Pearl St., Jackson, MI 39203-3085; (601) 949-2225

Missouri

Representative: Nathan Walker, Department of Public Safety, P.O. Box 1406, Jefferson City, Missouri 65102-1406; (314) 751-4161
Coordinator: Richard Echols, Deputy Director; (314) 751-4161

Montana
Representative and Coordinator: Albert E. Goke, Highway Traffic Safety Division, Department of Justice, 303 N. Roberts, Helena, MT 59620; (406) 444-3412

Nebraska
Representative: Margaret Higgins, Department of Motor Vehicles, State House Station 94789, Lincoln, NE 68509; (402) 471-2281
Coordinator: Fred E. Zwonechek, Highway Safety Program Office, State House Station 94612; (402) 471-2515

Nevada
Representative: Wayne Teglia, Department of Motor Vehicles, 555 Wright Way, Carson City, NV 89711-0999; (702) 885-5375
Coordinator: Mary Lynne Allison, Traffic Safety Division; (702) 885-5720

New Hampshire
Representative and Coordinator: John B. McDuffee, Highway Safety Agency, 117 Manchester St., Concord, NH 03301

New Jersey
Representative and Coordinator: William T. Taylor, Office of Highway Traffic Safety, Quakerbridge Plaza, Bldg. 5, CN-048, Trenton, NJ 08625; (609) 588-3750

New Mexico
Representative: Dewey Lonsberry, Highway and Transportation Dept., P.O. Box 1149, Santa Fe, NM 87504-1149; (505) 827-5110
Coordinator: John D. Fenner, Traffic Safety Bureau; (505) 827-0427

New York
Representative: Patricia B. Adduci, Department of Motor Vehicles, Empire State Plaza, Swan St. Bldg., Albany, NY 12228; (508) 474-0841
Coordinator: William G. Rourke, Traffic Safey Committee; (518) 474-5777

North Carolina
Representative and Coordinator: Paul B. Jones, Governor's Highway Safety Program, 215 E. Lane St., Raleigh, NC 27601; (919) 733-3085

North Dakota
Representative: Walter R. Hjelle, Highway Department, 600 E. Boulevard Ave., Bismarck, ND 58505-0178; (701) 224-2581
Coordinator: Joseph Carlson, Driver License & Traffic Safety; (701) 224-2600

Ohio
Representative: William Denihan, Department of Highway Safety, P.O. Box 7167, Columbus, OH 42305; (614) 466-2250
Coordinator: Sandra J. Usher, Office of the Governor's, Highway Safety Representative; (614) 466-2550

Oklahoma
Representative and Coordinator: Jim Rodriguez, Highway Safety Office, 200 NE 21st St., D-1, Oklahoma City, OK 73105; (405) 521-3314

Oregon
Representative and Coordinator: Gil W. Bellamy, Oregon Traffic Safety Commission, State Library Bldg., 4th Floor, Salem, OR 97310; (503) 378-3670

Pennsylvania
Representative: John J. Zogby, Deputy Secretary for Safety Administration, 1200 Transportation & Safety Bldg., Harrisburg, PA 17120; (717) 787-3928
Coordinator: Thomas E. Bryer, Center for Highway Safety, 215 Transportation & Safety Bldg; (717) 787-7350

Puerto Rico
Representative: Engineer Dario Hernandes Torres, Secretary of Transportation and Public Works, Box 41269, Minillas Station, Santurce, PR 00940; (809) 726-6670
Coordinator: Lenidas Ramirex-Pineiro, Traffic Safety Commission, Box 41289, Minillas Station; (809) 726-5290 or (809 726-5150, ext. 3550

Rhode Island
Representative: Matthew J. Gill, Department of Transportation, State Office Bldg., Smith St., Providence, RI 02903; (401) 277-2481
Coordinator: Edward J. Walsh, Gov's Office of Highway Safety, 345 Harris Ave., Providence, RI 02909; (401) 277-3024

South Carolina
Representative and Coordinator: Perry Brown, Office of Highway Safety Programs, 1205 Pendleton St., Room 453, Columbia, SC 29201; (803) 734-0421

South Dakota
Representative: Jeff Stingley, Department of Commerce and Regulation, 910 E. Sioux Ave., Pierre, SD 57501; (605) 773-3661

Coordinator: Mike Kumm, State and Community Programs, Dept. of Commerce and Regulation, 118 W. Capitol Ave., Pierre, SD 57501; (605) 773-3675

Tennessee
Representative: James Evans, Department of Transportation, 505 Deaderick St., Suite 700, Nashville, TN 37219; (615) 741-2848
Coordinator: Larry M. Ellis, Governor's Highway Safety Program; (615) 741-2589

Texas
Representative: Raymond E. Stotzer, Jr., State Dept. of Highways and Public Transportation, 11th and Brazos, Austin, TX 78701; (512) 463-8616
Coordinator: Gary Trietsch, Traffic Safety Section (D-18-TS); (512) 465-6751

Utah
Representative: John T. Neilsen, Department of Public Safety, 4501 S. 2700 West, Salt Lake City, UT 84119; (801) 965-4461
Coordinator: Dick Howard, Highway Safety Division; (801) 965-4410

Vermont
Representative: The Honorable Susan Crampton, Secretary of Transportation, 133 State St., Montpelier, VT 05602; (802) 828-2657
Coordinator: Glen Gershaneck, Exec. Asst. to the Secretary of Transportation, Vermont Highway Safety Program; (802) 828-2657

Virginia
Representative: Donald E. Williams, Department of Motor Vehicles, P.O. Box 27412, Richmond, VA 23269; (804) 257-6602
Coordinator: John T. Hanna, Deputy Commissioner for Transportation Safety; (804) 257-6624

Washington
Representative: Samuel C. McCullum, Traffic Safety Commission, 1000 S. Cherry St., MS/PD-11, Olympia, WA 98504; (206) 753-6197
Coordinator: Julie M. Peterson, Traffic Safety Commission; (206) 753-6197

West Virginia
Representative and Coordinator: James Albert, Criminal Justice & Highway Safety Office, 5790-A MacCorkle Ave., Charleston, WV 25304; (304) 348-8814

Wisconsin
Representative: Ronald R. Fiedler, Department of Transportation, Office of Highway Safety, P.O. Box 7910, 4802 Sheboygan Ave., Madison, WI 53707; (608) 266-1113
Coordinator: Maynard Stoehr; (608) 266-0421

Wyoming
Representative: Richard V. Uthoff, State Highway Safety Engineer, Wyoming Highway Safety Department, P.O. Box 1708, Cheyenne, WY 82002-9019; (307) 777-7296
Coordinator: Donald Pruter, Highway Safety Analysis Engineer

Virgin Islands
Representative and Coordinator: Enrique Richards, Office of Highway Safety, P.O. Box 1847, Fredericsted, St. Croix, Virgin Islands 08804; (809) 772-3025

* Immigration and Naturalization Service (INS)
Immigration and Naturalization Service
425 I St., NW
Washington, DC 20536 (202) 633-4330
The INS is responsible for control of illegal entry of persons along our borders, and assists in apprehending smugglers. The Border Patrol is active in drug abuse education and prevention, conducting demonstrations with "drug sniffing dogs" in classrooms and providing drug education information to students.

* Interagency Law Enforcement Training Center
Federal Law Enforcement Training Center
Glynco, GA 31524 (912) 267-2100
The Center is the interagency training facility serving 63 Federal law enforcement organizations. The major training effort is in the area of basic programs to teach common areas of law enforcement skills to police and investigative personnel. The Center offers selective, highly specialized training programs to State and local officers.

* International Fugitives and International Police
International Criminal Police Organization
U.S. National Central Bureau
Washington, DC 20530 (202) 272-8383
This Bureau serves as the communications link among more than 20,000 state and local law enforcement organizations and as the U.S. liaison to INTERPOL. It investigate large-scale narcotics offenses and apprehends international fugitives often involving arrests and extraditions to the countries where the crimes were committed.

* Justice Department Anti-Drug Coordination
Office of Justice Programs
U.S. Department of Justice
633 Indiana Ave., NW
Washington, DC 20531 (202) 724-7782
This office is responsible for policy coordination and general management responsibilities for five OJP bureaus or offices. The Bureau of Justice Assistance (BJA) offers technical assistance to State and local units of government to control crime and drug abuse and to improve the criminal justice system. The Bureau of Justice Statistics (BJS) maintains statistics about crime, its perpetrators and victims, and the operation of the criminal justice system at the Federal, State and local level. The Office of Juvenile Justice and Delinquency Prevention attempts to prevent drug abuse among youth at high risk. The Office for Victims of Crime oversees the Crime Victims Fund which is money comes from fines of Federal criminals. These funds are made available to each State, the District of Columbia, and six Territories to support expanded and improved State victim assistance and compensation programs. The National Victims Resource Center maintains a data base that describes more than 2,000 victim assistance and family violence programs throughout the country.

* Juvenile Delinquency National Trends
Office of Juvenile Justice and Delinquency Prevention (OJJDP)
Office of Justice Programs
U.S. Department of Justice
633 Indiana Ave., NW
Washington, DC 20531 (202) 724-7782
The Research and Program Development Division sponsors research on national trends in juvenile delinquency and serious juvenile crime, prevention strategies, and the juvenile justice system.

* Juvenile Justice Professionals Training
Office of Juvenile Justice and Delinquency Prevention (OJJDP)
Office of Justice Programs
U.S. Department of Justice
633 Indiana Ave., NW
Washington, DC 20531 (202) 724-7782
The Training, Dissemination, and Technical Assistance Division (TDTAD) is responsible for programs that train personnel who work with juvenile offenders and their families.

* Law Enforcement Explorer Programs
Office of Juvenile Justice and Delinquency Prevention (OJJDP)
Office of Justice Programs
U.S. Department of Justice
633 Indiana Ave., NW
Washington, DC 20531 (202) 724-7782
The Training, Dissemination, and Technical Assistance Division (TDTAD) oversees the Exploring Careers in Law Enforcement and Criminal Justice. About 42,000 youths, both male and female, are involved in Law Enforcement Explorer programs, which recently initiated an anti-substance abuse program.

* Law Enforcement Policy Resource Center
Law Enforcement Policy Resource Center
U.S. Department of Justice
633 Indiana Ave., NW
Washington, DC 20531 (202) 724-7782
The Center develops model policies for law enforcement agencies, as well as program briefs and model legislation regarding issues of interest to law enforcement policy makers.

* Mafia and Organized Crime Investigations
U.S. Marshals Service
Department of Justice
One Tysons Corner Center
McLean, VA 22102 (703) 285-1100
The Marshals Service is a charter member of the Organized Crime Drug Enforcement (OCDE) Task Force with full-time investigators assigned to all 13 task force locations.

* Maritime Drug Smuggling Interdiction
U.S. Coast Guard (USCG)
2100 Second St., SW
Washington, DC 20593 (202) 426-2158
The Coast Guard is the only Federal agency with jurisdiction on the high seas as well as territorial waters and has greatly expanded efforts directed against maritime drug smugglers. USCG ships, boats, planes and helicopters conduct routine drug law enforcement patrols and special operations through the maritime arena. Coast Guard emphasis is on detecting and boarding vessels smuggling illicit drugs while still in transit to the United States. In support of its expansive role in interdiction, the Coast Guard maintains an extensive intelligence organization with heavy emphasis on drug trafficking.

Drugs and Chemical Dependence

* Military Drug Testing Program

Health Affairs
U.S. Department of Defense
Washington, DC 20301-1155   (202) 695-7116

Health Affairs is responsible for drug testing program for the military services. It is also responsible for conducting periodic surveys of illegal drug use among the military.

* Money Laundering Investigations

Internal Revenue Service (IRS)
U.S. Department of Treasury
1111 Constitution Ave., NW
Washington, DC 20224   (202) 488-3100

IRS supports drug law enforcement by pursuing income tax violations and money laundering related to the financial aspects of illegal drug trafficking. IRS agents trace the movement of funds to document the acquisition of forfeitable assets by drug traffickers. Using search warrants, IRS seizes various financial reports, including travel records, money orders, and cashier check receipts, which can reveal the concealment or illegal transfer of financial assets. The information gained through the warrants can lead to assets seizable under statutory forfeiture provisions.

* Narcotics Cultivation in Developing Countries

Agency for International Development (AID)
320 21st St., NW
Washington, DC 20523   (202) 647-1850

AID works with the International Narcotics Matters Bureau at the Department of State in designing and implementing foreign assistance programs related directly and indirectly to drug problems in developing nations. AID assistance is particularly focused on rural development programs in traditional growing regions. The alternative agricultural and other economic pursuits made possible by AID funds are, in many countries, the key to cooperation of eliminating cultivation of illicit narcotics.

* Narcotics Identification Manual

Superintendent of Documents
Government Printing Office
Washington, DC 20402   (202) 783-3238

The manual, *Narcotics Identification Manual*, provides descriptions and color photographs to help you identify narcotics, depressants, stimulants, cannabis, hallucinogens, and crack. Included is a chart listing controlled substances, their uses, and effects. This manual sells for $4.25 (S/N 048-002-00101-0).

* Narcotic Plants Detection and Eradication

National Park Service
U.S. Department of Interior
Washington, DC   (202) 343-7394

The Service is responsible for enforcing the laws on Federal lands which prohibit cultivation of narcotic plants.

* National Forests Marijuana Eradication Program

U.S. Forest Service
14th St. & Independence Ave., SW
Washington, DC 20250   (202) 447-3760

The Forest Service assists Drug Enforcement Agency in the national Domestic Marijuana Eradication and Suppression Program which promotes information sharing and provides training, equipment, investigative and aircraft support to state and local enforcement officers. Some 150 special agents are involved in the Forest Service's Law Enforcement Staff; 650 armed, uniformed, law enforcement officers, who since passage of National Forest Drug Control Act in 1986, have authority under Title 21 arrest drug traffickers and producers.

* National Victims Resource Center

Office for Victims of Crime (OVC)
U.S. Department of Justice
633 Indiana Ave., NW
Washington, DC 20531   (202) 724-7782

A National Victims Resource Center at the National Criminal Justice Reference Service that provides victim-related publications, statistics, research, program referrals, and other information from its computerized data base. The Center collects and maintains information on programs throughout the United States that provide services to victims, on State victim/witness programs that receive funds under VOCA, and on Federal victim/witness programs.

* NOAA Drug Interdiction Efforts

National Oceanic and Atmospheric Administration
U.S. Department of Commerce
Washington, DC 20230   (202) 377-8090

Through the course of their regular activities, NOAA provides detection assistance for drug interdiction efforts.

* On-the-Job Drug Testing Videos

National Audiovisual Center
Customer Service Section
8700 Edgeworth Drive
Capitol Heights, MD 20743-3701   (301) 763-1896

National Clearinghouse for Alcohol and Drug Information
P.O. Box 2345
Rockville, MD 20852   (301) 468-8200

"Drug Testing: Handle with Care" describes the options available in designing a drug testing component as part of a comprehensive drug-free workplace program. Procedures addressing the needs of both the employer and the employee, to ensure the accuracy and reliability of test results, for specimen collection and laboratory analysis, and a discussion of the critical role of the Medical Review Officer (MRO) are highlighted. Case studies of public/private, unionized/nonunionized work environments with testing components are presented. This video is available in both employer and employee versions. It is available for sale and rental.

* Parole and Recidivism Rate

U.S. Parole Commission
5550 Friendship Blvd.
Chevy Chase, MD 20815   (301) 492-5990

The Parole Commission is investigating ways in which they may help break the link between crime and drug use in hopes of both reducing drug use and crime, but also of reducing the recidivism rate.

* Pentagon Drug Policy and Enforcement

U.S. Department of Defense
Office of Drug Policy and Enforcement
Washington, DC 20301-1155   (202) 695-7116

Drug policy and enforcement, including coordination of all DOD activities related to Federal drug abuse eradication; provision of Department resources and support to other agencies for drug law enforcement efforts; military and civilian drug testing policy; advice and assistance to the Secretary of Defense and other officials of the Department on anti-drug abuse aspects of departmental policy, plans and programs.

* Public Lands Special Drug Agents

Bureau of Land Management (BLM)
U.S. Department of Interior
Washington, DC 20240   (202) 343-5717

The Special Agents of BLM are responsible for enforcing Federal laws and regulations relating to the public lands and resources. This includes conducting criminal investigations and the ability to arrest violators. Field Offices staffed by Special Agents include the following:

Alexandria
350 S. Pickett St., Alexandria, VA 22304; (703) 274-0177

Anchorage
701 C St., Anchorage, AK 99513; (907) 376-3264

Billings
222 N. 32nd St., Billings, MT 59103; (406) 657-6201

Boise
3380 Americana Terrace, Boise, ID 83706; (208) 334-1570

Cheyenne
2515 Warren Ave., Cheyenne, WY 82001; (307) 772-2559

Denver
2020 Arapahoe St., Denver, CO 80205; (303) 294-7670

Eugene
1255 Pearl St., Eugene, OR 97440; (503) 687-6661

Folsom
63 Natoma St., Folsom, CA 95630; (916) 985-4474

Jackson
P.O. Box 11248, 300 Woodroe Wilson, Jackson, MS 39213; (601) 960-4405

Las Vegas
4765 Vegas Dr., Las Vegas, NV 89126; (702) 388-6453

Phoenix
3707 N. 7th St., Phoenix, AZ 85011; (602) 241-5554

Portland
825 NE Multnomah St., Portland, OR 97208; (503) 231-6875

Redding
355 Hemsted Dr., Redding, CA 96001; (916) 246-5325

Reno
Federal Office Bldg., 300 Booth St., Reno, NV 89520; (702) 784-5683

Sacramento
Federal Office Building, 2800 Cottage Way, Room E-2841, Sacramento, CA 95825; (916) 978-4759

Salt Lake City
324 S. State St., Salt Lake City, UT 84111-2303; (801) 524-3013

Santa Fe
Federal Office Bldg., South Federal Pl., Santa Fe, NM 87501; (505) 988-6478

* Public Housing Drug Eradication Grants

Howard Mortman
U.S. Department of Housing and Urban Development
Room 4114
P.O. Box 6424
Rockville, MD 20850 (202) 755-9101

HUD's Public Housing Drug Elimination Program - grant program for community-wide drug prevention programs

* Prisoner Detention and Transportation System

U.S. Marshals Service
Department of Justice
One Tysons Corner Center
McLean, VA 22102 (703) 285-1100

All persons arrested and detained by order of the Federal courts for prosecution on violations of Federal laws are placed into the custody of the Marshals Service. The Service's National Prisoner Transportation System is continually required to provide extraordinary security for the movement of major drug dealers to and from scheduled court appearances.

* Prisoners, Paroles, Sentencing Data

Data Center & Clearinghouse for Drugs and Crime
Office of Justice Programs
U.S. Department of Justice
633 Indiana Ave., NW (800) 666-3332
Washington, DC 20531 (202) 724-7782

The Data Center & Clearinghouse for Drugs & Crime was established by Justice Department's Bureau of Justice Statistics and the Bureau of Justice Assistance to provide access to existing data on drug law enforcement and the justice system's treatment of drug offenders and nondrug offenders who are drug users. A sampling of free publications include:

Order Number / Title and Release Date
86223 Prisoners and Alcohol - 1/83
87575 Prisoners and Drugs - 3/83
87068 Report to the Nation - 1st Edition - 83
96501 Examining Recidivism - 85
96132 Pretrial Release and Misconduct - 1/85
97681 Felony Sentencing in 18 Local Jurisdictions - 5/85
99175 Jail Inmates, 1983 - 11/85
100582 Prison Admissions and Releases, 1983 - 86
101043 Sentencing and Time Served - 87
104916 Recidivism of Young Parolees - 5/87
105506 Report to the Nation - 2nd Edition - 88
105743 Sentencing Outcomes in 28 Felony Courts, 1985 - 87
108544 Time Served in Prison and on Parole, 1984 - 12/87
109686 Tracking Offenders, 1984 - 1/88
109926 Profile of State Prison Inmates - 1/88
109929 Pretrial Release and Detention: The Bail Reform Act of 1984 - 2/88
109945 Drunk Driving - 88
110643 Bureau of Justice Statistics Data Report 1987 - 88
111612 Sourcebook of Criminal Justice Statistics, 1987 - 88
111763 Drug Law Violators 1980-1986 - 6/88
111940 Drug Use and Crime - 7/88
113365 Survey of Youth in Custody - 9/88
114746 The Redesigned National Crime Survey: Selected New Data - 1/89
115210 Felony Sentences in State Courts, 1986 - 2/89
115749 Bureau of Justice Statistics Annual Report 1988 - 89
116261 Recidivism of Prisoners Released in 1983 - 3/89
116262 Bureau of Justice Statistics Data Report 1988 - 89
116315 Prisoners in 1988 - 4/89
118311 Federal Criminal Cases, 1980-87 - 7/89
94073 Drug Use and Pretrial Crime in the District of Columbia - 6/84
96668 Probing the Links Between Drugs and Crime - 2/85
98259 Use of Forfeiture Sanctions in Drug Cases - 85
98902 Interpol: Global Help in Fight Against Drugs - 9/85

100737 Drinking and Crime - 86
100741 Heroin - 87
100756 Project DARE: Teaching Kids to Say "No" - 3/86
102632 Employee Drug Testing Policies in Police Departments - 10/86
102668 Drugs and Crime: Controlling Use and Reducing Risk through Testing - 11/86
104555 Drug Trafficking - 87
104556 Drug Testing - 87
104557 Drug Education - 87
104865 Controlling Drug Abuse and Crime: A Research Update - 3/87
106992 Drugs and Crime: Current Federal Research - 8/88
107272 Drug Use Forecasting: New York 1984-1986 - 87
108560 Characteristics of Different Types of Drug Involved Offenders - 88
109957 Attorney General Announces NIJ DUF - 3/88
110423 Drug Use Forecasting Packet - 11/86
113915 A Criminal Justice System Strategy for Treating Cocaine-Heroin Abusing Offenders in Custody - 3/88
114730 Identifying Drug Users and Monitoring Them During Conditional Release - 2/88
115403 Street Level Drug Enforcement - 9/88
117999 In-Prison Programs for Drug-Involved Offenders - 7/89
106663 Intensive Supervision Probation and Parole - 88
113110 Reducing Crime by Reducing Drug Abuse - 6/88
114801 Implementing Project Dare: Drug Abuse Resistance Education - 6/88
116317 Drug Control and System Improvement Discretionary Grant Program - 1/89
116322 TASC: Implementing the Model - 9/88
116323 Treatment Alternatives to Street Crime - 1/88
117432 Drug Recognition Program - 89
117435 Report on Drug Control, 1988 - 89
118317 Estimating the Costs of Drug Testing - Pretrial Testing Program - 6/89
115416 Urinalysis as Part of a Treatment Alternatives to Street Crime Program - 7/88
999092 Data Center & Clearinghouse for Drugs & Crime brochure
999100 Drugs & Crime rolodex card

* Rewards for Information on Drug Traffickers
Tax Evasion

Internal Revenue Service (IRS)
U.S. Department of Treasury
1111 Constitution Ave., NW
Washington, DC 20224 (202) 488-3100

Individuals who have information regarding drug traffickers that is of a financial nature can contact the Internal Revenue Service. If the information leads to a successful trial and unpaid taxes are received by the Internal Revenue Service, the informant is eligible to receive a reward (if the information given to the IRS was not obtainable elsewhere and was instrumental in the conviction). The reward varies and is based upon a percentage of assets retrieved. This is not an anonymous information tip system or reward system, but the IRS maintains that confidentiality is strictly enforced.

* Seized and Forfeited Assets

U.S. Marshals Service
Department of Justice
One Tysons Corner Center
McLean, VA 22102 (703) 285-1100

The Marshal Service is responsible for the centralized management of the National Asset Seizure and Forfeiture Fund which includes uniform management procedures in the care, maintenance and disposal of seized and forfeited assets.

* U.S. Secret Service Involvement

U.S. Secret Service (USSS)
1800 G St., NW
Washington, DC 20223 (202) 535-5708

The USSS is involved in drug law enforcement investigations as a result of their following responsibilities including: any offense against the laws of the U.S. relating to currency, coins, obligations, and securities of the U.S. or of foreign governments; forgery and fraudulent negotiation or redemption of Federal Government checks, bonds, and other obligations or securities of the U.S.; offenders of laws pertaining to electronic funds transfer frauds, credit and debit card frauds, false identification documents or devices, computer access fraud, and U.S. Department of Agriculture food coupons, including authority to participate cares.

* Witness Security Protection

U.S. Marshals Service
Department of Justice
One Tysons Corner Center
McLean, VA 22102 (703) 285-1100

The Federal Government's witness security program entails relocation, identity change and a range of other sophisticated services, including personal protection, in order for witnesses to contribute important testimony in drug court cases.

Law and Social Justice
General Sources

* See also Drug and Chemical Dependence Chapter
* See also Careers and Workplace; Research Grants in Every Field Chapter
* See also Your Community; Money for Communities and Non-Profits Chapter
* See also Health and Medicine Chapter; Stress, Mental Illness and Family Violence Chapter
* See also Government Financial Help for Individuals Chapter
* See also Patents, Trademarks and Copyrights Chapter

The U.S. Department of Justice is the most well-known law enforcement organization of the federal government, particularly with the much-publicized activities of the Antitrust Division, the FBI and the Drug Enforcement Agency. The department is the central collector of local and state crime statistics. Also housed within this large department is the Immigration and Naturalization Service. But there are many other resources including state and federal agencies which provide free legal assistance.

* Adjudication, Arrests and National Statistics

Bureau of Justice Statistics
U.S. Department of Justice
633 Indiana Ave., NW
Washington, DC 20531   (202) 724-7770

The U.S. is one of only a few developed countries that has no national court statistics. There are police statistics compiled annually that show the number of persons arrested in the U.S., and there are national prison statistics compiled annually on the number sent to prison. But there are no nationwide statistics that show what happens between arrest and imprisonment. The BJS National Judicial Reporting Program is a statistical series designed to close this gap in American criminal justice statistics. This program will make it possible to answer numerous questions about felony courts that cannot now be answered, such as:

Nationwide, how many persons were convicted of felonies last year?
How many convicted felons received a jury trial?
What percent of convicted felons were sentenced to prison?
What was the average prison sentence for drug trafficking?

Contact this office to find out more information about the status and availability of new national adjudication statistics.

* Administrative Law and Government Procedures

Administrative Conference of the United States
1220 L St., NW, Suite 500
Washington, DC 20037   (202) 254-7020

This government think tank explores ways to improve federal agencies administer regulations, entitlements, and other programs. The Conference studies adjudication, administrative law, governmental processes, judicial review, regulation, and rulemaking. It publishes *1988 Annual Report* and their newsletter, *Administrative Conference News*, which are available free to the public. Also available is the *Administrative Conference of the United States: A Bibliography 1968-1986*.

* AIDS and the Law

National Institute of Justice
NCJRS, Box 6000
Dept. AID
Rockville, MD 20850   (800) 851-3420 (301) 251-5500 in DC

NIJ has the following publications and others on AIDS and legal issues available. Many of the documents are free of charge, while others are available for a modest fee. When ordering or inquiring about an NIJ publication, refer to its NCJ number.

AIDS and Intravenous Drug Use (AIDS Bulletin). 1988, 6 pp. (NCJ 108620).
AIDS and the Law Enforcement Officer (RIA). 1987, 6 pp. (NCJ 107541).
AIDS in Correctional Facilities: Issues and Options, 3rd Edition. 1988, 286 pp. (NCJ 109943).
The Cause, Transmission, and Incidence of AIDS (AIDS Bulletin). 1987, 4 pp. (NCJ 106678).
Precautionary Measures and Protective Equipment: Developing a Reasonable Response (AIDS Bulletin). 1988, 4 pp. (NCJ 108619).

* Antitrust Violations and Company Investigations

Legal Procedure Unit
Antitrust Division
U.S. Department of Justice
10th St. and Constitution Ave. NW
Room 3233
Washington, DC 20530   (202) 633-2481

A total case history of all antitrust investigations is available to the public. If you wish to know if a particular company is being, or ever has been, investigated for antitrust violations, and what the formal complaints were, you are welcome to thumb through the files. In addition, these files can tell you what types of violations have been investigated and what rulings have been brought down in each case. A complete transcript of pleadings, depositions, and summaries of legal procedures in all cases are available. These files are an invaluable source of legal history and precedents, and a perfect guide to business practices. For a photocopy of any portion of the Antitrust Case files, contact the Legal Procedure Unit at the above address.

* Antitrust Enforcement and the Consumer

Public Affairs
Antitrust Division
U.S. Department of Justice
10th St. & Constitution Ave., NW
Room 3107
Washington, DC 20530   (202) 633-2018

The free publication, *Antitrust Enforcement and the Consumer*, details general information on the how antitrust law helps the consumer, as well as specific descriptions of the Sherman and Clayton Acts, various cases the Justice Department has prosecuted and an explanation of how these violators cheated the consumer. The pamphlet also includes the addresses of all of the regional Antitrust Division offices and all of the Federal Trade Commission's regional offices throughout the country.

* Antitrust and Export Trading

Foreign Commerce Section
Antitrust Division
U.S. Department of Justice
10th St. & Constitution Ave., NW
Room 3264
Washington, DC 20530   (202) 633-2464

The United States' policy on foreign trade is developed and preserved by this office. Their staff and files are an incomparable source of information for anyone interested in United States trade and commerce, or the effect of foreign markets on our economy. Investors and bond salesmen, bankers and businessmen-- anyone who needs up-to-the-minute knowledge, even high-school students reporting on inflation--should start here. Congressmen are constantly in touch with the Foreign Commerce Section before voting on trade bills. Rising politicians who want to stand on their economic platform get their data here; voters should, too. In addition, this Section administers the Export Trading Act and works with the Commerce Department to issue all Export Trading Certificates.

* Antitrust Law and Joint Research Ventures

Superintendent of Documents
U.S. Government Printing Office
Washington, DC 20402   (202) 783-3238

The publication, *Antitrust Guide Concerning Research Joint Ventures*, describes the ways that corporate cooperation on research (joint ventures) can be pursued without violating antitrust laws. The *Guide* is available for $5.50 from the GPO.

* Arson, Burglary, and Other Crime Trends

Uniform Crime Reporting Section
Federal Bureau of Investigation
U.S. Department of Justice
9th & Pennsylvania Ave., NW, GRB
Washington, DC 20535 (202) 324-2614

Crime in the United States, an annual report, taken from over 17,000 law enforcement agencies and 98% of the country, is the ultimate information source on crime. Breaking crime down into 8 basic categories (arson, larceny, burglary, aggravated assault, forgery fraud, drugs, prostitution, gambling) the report gives an exact reading of the criminal trends in our country. It lists the crime rates by state, in rural and urban areas, by gender, race, and age. Police find it an invaluable source for crime analysis and lean on it heavily when projecting the year's budget or discussing allocation of manpower. Public policy makers refer to it when debating new programs or community services. This report is fundamental for making better laws, for helping sociologists chart trends, for journalists writing articles. It can even tell prospective homebuyers how safe their future neighborhood will be. The report includes complete listings of types of weapons used in crimes, motives, victim/offender relationships. Anything you could ever want to know about crime in this country is in this report.

* Arson Control and Clearinghouse

U.S. Fire Administration
16825 South Seton Ave.
Emmitsburg, MD 21727 (301) 447-1122

The Arson Resource Center is available to help answer your questions and locate resources related to arson. It was established several years ago by the U.S. Fire Administration, and has developed an impressive collection of arson-related materials. FEMA personnel and NETC students can borrow materials from the Center, and books and research reports are available to the general public through area libraries (interlibrary loan). Audio-visual and general references are stored in the Center for in-house use. The following publications and source materials on arson are available from the USFA free of charge:

Arson Bibliography (#5-0001)
Arson Lab (#5-0003)
Arson Overview Report ($5-0024)
Arson Victims: Suggestions (#5-0034)
Arson Resource Directory (#5-0087)
Arson Prosecution Issues (#5-0086)
Rural Arson Control (#5-0110)
Establishing an Arson Strike Force (#5-0111)

* Arson Incidents National Database

Arson Information Management Systems (AIMS)
Office of Fire Prevention and Arson Control
U.S. Fire Administration
16825 South Seton Ave.
Emmitsburg, MD 21727 (301) 2247-1200

The Arson Information Management Systems (AIMS) is a computerized database for the recording of data from reported arson cases, and used to facilitate analysis of such data for use by investigators, emergency personnel, law enforcers, and others. For more information on AIMS, contact the office above.

* Arson Prevention Traveling Exhibit

Office of Fire Prevention and Arson Control
Federal Emergency Management Agency
16825 South Seton Ave.
Emmitsburg, MD 21727 (301) 447-1200

Arson Trailers tour the country to provide technical and educational assistance to State, local, and national fire service and community groups. Their public educations demonstrations include fire safety issues, local fire problems, and smoke detector usage and maintenance.

* Art Theft FBI Database

Laboratory Division
Federal Bureau of Investigation
Department of Justice
9th St. & Pennsylvania Ave., NW
Washington, DC 20535 (202) 324-4545

The *National Stolen Art File* is a database which lists all currently missing works of art reported as stolen from either public or private collections in the United States. Contact this office for obtaining information from the file.

* Attorney Training

Attorney General's Advocacy Institute
Executive Office for US Attorneys
U.S. Department of Justice
10th St. & Constitution Ave., NW
Room 1342
Washington, DC 20530 (202) 633-4104

The Advocacy Institute trains Assistant U.S. Attorneys and all U.S. Department of Justice attorneys in trial advocacy. The Institute offers courses on civil, criminal and appellate advocacy, and seminars on such specialized topics as white-collar crime, narcotics, conspiracy, environmental litigation, bankruptcy, land condemnations, public corruption and fraud, civil rights, witness security, and computer fraud.

* Child Abuse Prosecution

National Center for the Prosecution of Child Abuse
1033 N. Fairfax St., Suite 200
Alexandria, VA 22314 (703) 739-0321

The National Center for the Prosecution of Child Abuse provides technical assistance, training, and clearinghouse services to improve the investigation and prosecution of child abuse cases and the procedures for dealing with children who have been victims of physical and sexual abuse. It is designed to help prosecutors dealing with the particular complexities of child abuse cases to safeguard child victims against further trauma during a criminal justice process designed for adults. The Center has produced a manual on the investigation and prosecution of child abuse cases. Contact this Center for more information.

* Child Victimization and the Law

National Institute of Justice
NCJRS, Box 6000
Dept. AID
Rockville, MD 20850 (800) 851-3420 (301) 251-5500 in DC

NIJ has the following publications and others on child victimization and the law. Many of the documents are free of charge, while others are available for a modest fee. When ordering or inquiring about an NIJ publication, refer to its NCJ number.

Guardians Ad Litem in the Criminal Courts. 1988, 64 pp. (NCJ 110006).
Prosecution of Child Sexual Abuse: Innovations in Practice (RIB). 1985, 7 pp. (NCJ 99317).
Prosecuting Child Sexual Abuse: New Approaches (RIA). 1985, 5 pp. (NCJ 102994).
Using Dolls to Interview Child Victims: Legal Concerns and Procedures (RIA). 1988, 6 pp. (NCJ 108470).
When the Victim Is a Child. 1985, 134 pp. (NCJ 97664).

* Cities in Schools: Truancy, Dropouts, Violence

Office of Juvenile Justice
and Delinquency Prevention
U.S. Department of Justice
633 Indiana Ave., NW
Washington, DC 20531 (202) 724-5911

Cities in Schools, a public-private partnership that addresses the problems of dropouts and school violence, is designed to reduce school absenteeism and dropout rates by coordinating services for at-risk youngsters. Five regional offices help serve the 26 operating programs throughout the country and assist other local communities to initiate new Cities in Schools programs.

* Coast Guard Law Books

Law Library
U.S. Coast Guard
U.S. Department of Transportation
2100 2nd St., SW, Room 4407
Washington, DC 20593-0001 (202) 267-2536

This library supports the Coast Guard's enforcement division. Books housed here cover case law, statutory law, and other reference works specific to the Coast Guard's role as enforcer of Federal laws on the high seas and U.S. waters. The library is open to the public.

* Coast Guard Law Enforcement Planning

Planning Branch
Research and Development Staff
Office of Engineering and Development
U.S. Coast Guard
U.S. Department of Transportation
2100 2nd St., SW, Room 6208
Washington, DC 20593-0001 (202) 267-1030

Information can be obtained here about research conducted by the Coast Guard in support of its operations and responsibilities. Areas of study include ice operations, ocean dumping, law enforcement, environmental protection, port safety and security, navigation aids, search and rescue procedures, recreational boating, energy, and advanced marine vehicles. For referral to specific personnel working in these areas, contact the Planning Branch.

* Company Antitrust Compliance or Violation

Antitrust Division

U.S. Department of Justice
10th St. & Constitution Ave., NW
Room 3233
Washington, DC 20530 (202) 633-2481
Under the Business Review procedure, any firm may submit a proposed business activity to the Antitrust Division and receive a statement as to whether the Division would challenge the action as a violation of the federal antitrust laws. In addition, you can obtain copies of all such letters and replies in the *Digest of Business Reviews*, an annual publication of the U.S. Department of Justice. The indexes to the *Digest*, updated yearly, allow easy research of all the letters issued since 1968 according to topic, commodity, or service involved, and name of the requesting party. The *Digest*, annual supplements, and revised indexes are available from the Legal Procedure Unit.

* Conservation Law Enforcement Training

Law Enforcement Division
U.S. Fish and Wildlife Service
4401 N. Fairfax Dr.
Arlington, VA 22203 (703) 358-1949
Through this division, state conservation officers are trained in the area of criminal law as it applies to the enforcement of wildlife protection.

* Consumer Antitrust Complaint

Litigation Section
Antitrust Division
U.S. Department of Justice
10th St. & Constitution Ave. NW
Room 910
Washington, DC 20530 (202) 724-6693
If you wish to register a consumer complaint, call the Litigation Section of the Antitrust Division. The Litigation Section can tell you exactly who to get in touch with to lodge your complaint. They can also tell you if litigation is called for and are responsible for bringing such litigation to bear.

* Corrections and Prisons Clearinghouse

National Institute of Corrections
Bureau of Prisons
U.S. Department of Justice
320 1st St., NW
Washington, DC 20534 (202) 724-3106
This office provides several types of technical assistance to correctional agencies and institutes themselves. They can offer advice on managerial procedures or suggest security improvements. Agencies can seek the NIC's help for any nature of problem they may be having with policy and procedure. If an institution has had a rash of successful escapes, they will send people to investigate the problem and suggest potential solutions. The NIC also trains some state and local managerial or executive officials. Anyone interested in a career in corrections management should also contact them.

* Crime Insurance for Homeowners and Business

Federal Crime Insurance
P.O. Box 6301
Rockville, MD 20850 (800) 638-8780 (301) 251-1660 in DC
The Federal Crime Insurance Program is a federally subsidized program sponsored by the Federal Emergency Management Administration for homeowners and commercial businesses to insure against burglary and robbery. To find out if your state is eligible and for further information, contact the office above. Those living in Maryland outside D.C. should call collect: (301) 251-1660.

* Crime Victims Publications

National Victims Resource Center
Box 6000-AIQ
Rockville, MD 20850 (800) 627-6872 (301) 251-5525 in DC area
The following crime victim-related publications are available free of charge from NVRC:
America's Missing and Exploited Children: Their Safety and Future
Crime Victims: Learning How To Help Them
Crime of Rape
Drunk Driving
Economic Cost of Crime
Elderly Victims
Lifetime Likelihood of Victimization
President's Child Safety Partnership
President's Task Force on Victims of Crime
Preventing Domestic Violence Against Women
Risk of Violent Crimes
Robbery Victims
Sexual Assault: An Overview
Teenage Victims
Violent Crime By Strangers and Non-strangers
Violent Crime Trends

* Criminal Justice Bibliographies

National Criminal Justice Reference Service
National Institute of Justice
U.S. Department of Justice
Box 6000
Rockville, MD 20850 (301) 251-5500
The NCJRS acts as an international clearinghouse and reference center on subjects as diverse as Affirmative Action and Jail-Based Inmate Programs. The NCJRS has a bibliography of hundreds of publications. Contact the NCJRS Distribution Service at the above address, or contact the National Institute of Justice, 633 Indiana Ave., NW, Washington, D.C. 20531; (202) 724-2956.

* Criminal Justice Database

National Crime Information Center
Technical Services Division
Federal Bureau of Investigation
JEH Bldg. NW
Washington, DC 20535 (202) 324-2711
On written request, the National Crime Information Center can provide you with information, on-line, concerning wanted persons, missing persons, stolen property, and computerized criminal histories. Searches and printouts are free.

* Criminal Justice Research

Office of Communication & Research Utilization
National Institute of Justice
U.S. Department of Justice
633 Indiana Ave. NW
Washington, DC 20531 (202) 724-2956 (202) 272-6001
The National Institute of Justice has experts on nearly every field of criminal justice to help you find whatever information you're looking for. If you'd like to set up a Neighborhood Watch in your area, talk to Richard Titus or Lois Mock at (202) 724-7684. Do you want to know about environmental security? The NIJ has a specialist for you. Child abuse, DWI's, incidents of family violence, drug prevention education? They have an expert. The NIJ even has a specialist who can tell you anything you want to know about insanity as a defense in a criminal case.

* Criminal Justice: Schools, TV, Families

National Institute of Justice
NCJRS, Box 6000
Dept. AID
Rockville, MD 20850 (800) 851-3420 (301) 251-5500 in DC
NIJ has these and other videos and publications on crime and the law. Many of the documents are free of charge, while others are available for a modest fee. When ordering or inquiring about an NIJ publication, refer to its NCJ number.
Biology and Crime (Crime File videotape). 1985 (NCJ 97216).
Crime and Mental Disorder (RIB). 1984, 6 pp. (NCJ 94074).
Families and Crime (Crime File videotape). 1986 (NCJ 104208).
The Nature and Patterns of American Homicide. 1985, 73 pp. (NCJ 97964).
Safer Schools--Better Students (videotape). 1985 (NCJ 98687).
TV and Violence (Crime File videotape). 1985 (NCJ 97234).

* DNA Fingerprinting

National Institute of Justice
U.S. Department of Justice
Box 6000
Rockville, MD 20850 (301) 251-5500
NIJ-funded research has produced a new technique for identifying a criminal suspect by analyzing DNA in hair, blood, and other body fluids. The FBI is currently using this technology, which is expected to dramatically increase success in investigating violent crimes such as rape and murder. Another important breakthrough has shown that it is possible to determine blood group types from bone fragments left at the scene of a crime or accident. The research is working on a reliable procedure for grouping ABO antigens in bone. This research will eventually expand into testing for DNA in skeletal remains. Contact NIJ for more information on this new technology.

* Domestic Violence Resource Center

National Victims Resource Center
Box 6000-AIQ
Rockville, MD 20850 (800) 627-6872 (301) 251-5525 in DC
The National Victims Resource Center works as an information clearinghouse for the U.S. Department of Justice's Office of Victims of Crime. Family violence experts can assist callers in finding shelters for beaten women or local support groups. The NVRC also distributes a wide array of free publications. They also administer a library of more than 7,000 victim-related books and articles covering child physical and sexual abuse, victims services, domestic violence, victim-witness programs, and violent crime.

* Drug Abuse Warning Network (DAWN)

Information Systems Unit
Office of Diversion Control
Drug Enforcement Administration
U.S. Department of Justice
1405 Eye St. NW, Room 719
Washington, DC 20537   (202) 633-1316

For those who want to understand and evaluate the scope and magnitude of drug abuse in the United States, this network is an invaluable information source. Whether you are a local public administrator considering programs, a reporter on the heels of a story, or just a concerned parent, the Drug Abuse Warning Network can provide you with needed information. More than 900 hospital emergency rooms and medical examiner facilities supply data to the program. DAWN identifies drugs currently in vogue, determines existing patterns and profiles of abuse/abuser in Standard Metropolitan Statistical Areas, monitors systemwide abuse trends, detects new abuse entities and polydrug combinations, and provides data needed for rational control and scheduling of drugs being abused. It is the full-information source on the drug problem in America.

* Drug Testing and the Law

National Institute of Justice
NCJRS, Box 6000
Dept. AID
Rockville, MD 20850   (800) 851-3420 (301) 251-5500 in DC

NIJ has these and other videos and publications on drug testing and the law. Many of the documents are free of charge, while others are available for a modest fee. When ordering or inquiring about an NIJ publication, refer to its NCJ number.

Drug Surveillance Through Urinalysis (videotape). 1986 (NCJ 100130). V H S, Beta, or 3/4-inch.

Drug Testing (Crime File videotape). 1986 (NCJ 104213). VHS, Beta, or 3//4-inch.

Drug Testing (Crime File study guide). 1986, 4 pp. (NCJ 104556).

Drugs and Crime: Controlling Use and Reducing Risk Through Testing (R I A). 1986, 6 pp. (NCJ 102668).

Police Drug Testing. 1987, 109 pp. (NCJ 105191).

Testing to Detect Drug Abuse (TAP publication). 1986, 2 pp. (NCJ 104282).

* Ethnic Tensions Resolution and Assistance

Community Relations Service (CRS)
U.S. Department of Justice
5550 Friendship Blvd., Suite 300
Chevy Chase, MD 20815   (301) 492-5929

If your community is being torn apart by ethnic disputes or police-citizen conflicts, you may need help from this special service, set up by the Civil Rights Act of 1964. The Community Relations Service exists to resolve such disputes. The agency provides direct conciliation and mediation assistance to communities to facilitate the peaceful, voluntary resolution of racial and ethnic disputes or conflicts, and the peaceful co-existence of police and citizens' groups in the rapidly changing neighborhoods of today's cities. The CRS regularly provides conferences, training workshops, and publications to any and all communities in an attempt to forestall such disputes. However, when tensions do break out, the CRS will initiate whatever steps are necessary to begin making progress toward bringing about a resolution. They normally begin with extensive informal discussions with public or police officials and local community leaders, but if the agency and the parties determine that formal negotiations offer the best hope for a settlement, the agency arranges and mediates the negotiations.

* Explosives and Firearms Tracing Guidebook

Distribution Center
Bureau of Alcohol, Tobacco, and Firearms
U.S. Department of the Treasury
7943 Angus Ct.
Springfield, VA 22153   (703) 455-7801

The free book, *Firearms and Explosives Tracing Guidebook* is designed to assist law enforcement officials in preparing trace requests and determining whether or not firearms or explosives can be traced. Additional materials relating to firearms and explosives identification are included as a reference guide.

* FBI Academy and Careers

Federal Bureau of Investigation
U.S. Department of Justice
J. Edgar Hoover Bldg.
Washington, DC 20535   (202) 324-5352

Federal Bureau of Investigation Academy
Quantico, VA 22135   (703) 640-6131

If you're interested in making a career out of the FBI, here's your chance. Contact the Academy or the FBI directly to obtain information on agent, special agent, or nonagent and managerial positions.

* Federal Law Enforcement Training

Federal Law Enforcement Training Center
U.S. Department of the Treasury
Glynco, GA 31524   (912) 267-2100

Federal Law Enforcement Training Center
Office of Artesia and Marana Operation
U.S. Department of the Treasury
1300 West Richey St.
Artesia, NM 88210   (505) 746-9862

The Centers above are the Federal Government's principal resources for conducting interagency law enforcement training. There are 62 Federal organizations that participate in training at Glynco. Since many individual agencies conduct very specific advanced programs for their own employees, approximately 20 participating organizations have training offices at Glynco, GA, or at the facilities at Marana, AZ and Artesia, NM.

Basic training programs provide training to entry-level Federal uniformed officers in basic law enforcement skills, such as firearms, arrest techniques, principles of law, and driver training. Programs include Immigration and Naturalization Service's Detention Officer Training, U.S. Customs Service Inspector Training, Basic Law Enforcement for Land Management Agencies, Basic Law Enforcement for Indian Police, Border Patrol Training, and Park Police Training, among others. Examples of advanced training for experienced law enforcement officers include Officer Safety and Survival Training, Antiterrorism Management and Contingency Training, National Wildfire Investigation Training, White Collar Crime Training, and Marine Law Enforcement.

* Firearms: State Laws and Published Ordinances

Distribution Center
Bureau of Alcohol, Tobacco, and Firearms
U.S. Department of the Treasury
7943 Angus Ct.
Springfield, VA 22153   (703) 455-7801

The free book, *Firearms: State Laws and Published Ordinances*, outlines the state and local laws and ordinances for firearms of all states, commonwealths, and possessions of the United States. A ready reference table for use with the publication lists key elements of state laws, such as purchaser waiting period, purchaser requirements, license/permit to purchase, license as dealer manufacturer, licensee record-keeping requirements, and local government limits, and where they can be located in the laws and ordinances. State attorneys are also listed if you have state-related questions or problems regarding firearms.

* Forensics Computerized Database

Laboratory Division
Federal Bureau of Investigation
Department of Justice
9th St. & Pennsylvania Ave., NW
Washington, DC 20535   (202) 324-4545

The Forensics Information System is computerized database used to identify all types of forensic evidence. It includes a Rifling Characteristics File which can identify the manufacturer and type of weapon that may have been used to fire a bullet. Other files can be used to identify tire tracks or shoe prints left at the scene of a crime.

* Funding for Criminal Justice Research

Criminal Justice Research Office
U.S. Department of Justice
633 Indiana Ave. NW
Room 900
Washington, DC 20531   (202) 724-7631

Anyone interested in conducting advanced research in any Criminal Justice related fields can apply for funding from this office. Past projects to receive support from this office include studies investigating the impact of the latest technologies on conviction rates.

* Guns and Criminals Videos and Publications

National Institute of Justice
NCJRS, Box 6000
Dept. AID
Rockville, MD 20850   (800) 851-3420 (301) 251-5500 in DC

NIJ has these and other videos and publications on weapons, crime, and the law. Many of the documents are free of charge, while others are available for a modest fee. When ordering or inquiring about an NIJ publication, refer to its NCJ number.

The Armed Criminal in America (RIB). 1986, 5 pp. (NCJ 102827).

The Armed Criminal in America: A Survey of Incarcerated Felons. 1985, p. (NCJ 97099).

Gun Control (Crime File videotape). 1985 (NCJ 97224). VHS, Beta, 3/4-inch.

Gun Control (Crime File study guide). 1985, 4 pp. (NCJ 100740).

Law and Social Justice

* Guns and Firearms Tracing Center
National Tracing Center
Bureau of Alcohol, Tobacco, and Firearms
U.S. Department of the Treasury
3361-F 75th Ave.
Landover, MD 20785 (800) 424-5057
The National Tracing Center provides firearms tracing services to duly authorized law enforcement agencies in the United States and those in many foreign countries. Tracing is the systematic tracking of firearms from manufacturer to purchaser (and/or possessor) for the purpose of aiding law enforcement in identifying suspects involved in criminal violations, establishing stolen status, and proving ownership. 24 Hour Number: (301) 436-8159; Out of Business Records: (800) 424-8201; Special Agent in Charge: (301) 436-8230.

* Habitual Juvenile Offenders
Office of Juvenile Justice
and Delinquency Prevention
U.S. Department of Justice
633 Indiana Ave., NW
Washington, DC 20531 (202) 724-5911
The Serious Habitual Juvenile Offenders Comprehensive Action Program is providing intensive training and technical assistance to 20 communities to help their juvenile justice systems more efficiently identify, adjudicate, supervise, and incarcerate serious habitual juvenile offenders. Contact this office for more information on this program and how its successes might be applied to other communities.

* Heroin Situation Indicators
Office of Intelligence
Drug Enforcement Administration
U.S. Department of Justice
1405 Eye St., NW, Room 1013
Washington, DC 20537 (202) 633-1071
A retail and wholesale heroin price/purity index is available based upon data from the analysis of drug evidence samples submitted to the Drug Enforcement Administration. In addition, reports are available on heroin-related emergency room admissions and deaths from 21 major metropolitan areas scattered throughout the country. These reports are published on a quarterly basis.

* High Seas Law Enforcement
Operational Law Enforcement Division
Office of Law Enforcement and Defense Operations
U.S. Coast Guard
U.S. Department of Transportation
2100 2nd St., SW, Room 3110
Washington, DC 20593-0001 (202) 267-1890
As the primary maritime law enforcement agency for the U.S., the Coast Guard enforces Federal laws, treaties, and international agreements to which the U.S. is a party. The Coast Guard may conduct investigations when violations are suspected, such as smuggling, drug trafficking, or polluting. Empowered to board and inspect vessels routinely as well, the Guard also conducts :"suspicionless" boardings to prevent violations. To report suspicious or questionable activity on boats, or to complain about an improperly conducted boarding, call the Boating Safety Hotline, (800) 368-5647; or (202) 267-0780 in D.C., or contact your local Coast Guard commander. The office listed above can provide you with information about the Coast Guard's law enforcement role and the National Narcotics Border Interdiction System, which coordinates multi-agency and international operations with other countries to suppress narcotics trafficking.

* Hypnosis: Forensic Tool
National Victims Resource Center
Box 6000-AIQ
Rockville, MD 20850 (800) 627-6872 (301) 251-5525 in DC
area
Contact this Center for the free publication, *Forensic Use of Hypnosis*, which details how evidence revealed through hypnosis is used in court cases.

* Identifying Victims of Catastrophic Accidents
FBI Disaster Squad
Identification Division
Federal Bureau of Investigation
U.S. Department of Justice
J. Edgar Hoover Bldg., Room 11255
Washington, DC 20537 (202) 324-5401
The Disaster Squad is expert at identifying victims of catastrophic accidents. Government agencies rely upon them whenever victim identification is a problem. For local law enforcement, private investigators, transportation companies, or even families of the missing, the Disaster Squad can make a thorough analysis through fingerprints, dental records, and other physical evidence, and lay the mystery to rest. Contact this office for more information on the Squads services.

* Inmate Locator Line
Public Information
Bureau of Prisons
U.S. Department of Justice
320 1st St., NW, Room 640
Washington, DC 20536 (202) 724-3198
A special phone service hotline is available for people trying to locate family members or loved ones believed to be incarcerated in local, state, or federal correctional institutions. Call the Inmate Locater Line: (202) 724-3126 between 10 a.m. and 4:30 p.m. EST.

* Inside the FBI
Office of Public Affairs
Federal Bureau of Investigation
U.S. Department of Justice
J. Edgar Hoover Bldg., Room 7116
Washington, DC 20535 (202) 324-5352
If you have a group planning on visiting Washington, D.C., and would like to make the FBI Headquarters a part of that trip, contact the Office of Public Affairs. Guided tours are offered Mondays through Fridays (except holidays) from 9:00 a.m. to 4:00 p.m. No appointments are necessary for groups numbering fifteen or less.

* Jail Overcrowding
National Institute of Justice
NCJRS, Box 6000
Dept. AID
Rockville, MD 20850 (800) 851-3420 (301) 251-5500 in DC
NIJ has videos and publications on prison and jail overcrowding. Many of the documents are free of charge, while others are available for a modest fee. When ordering or inquiring about an NIJ publication, refer to its NCJ number.

* Juvenile Delinquency Risk Factors
Office of Juvenile Justice
and Delinquency Prevention
Research and Program Development Division
U.S. Department of Justice
633 Indiana Ave., NW
Washington, DC 20531 (202) 724-7560
This research division assesses a wide range of risk factors faced by children between the ages of six and 17. Researchers are looking beyond established delinquency correlates--such as age, race, and sex--to investigate more practical factors, such as personality characteristics, drug use, family relationships, school experience, the community environment, peer/gang associations, and juvenile justice sanctions. Contact this division for more information on this research.

* Juvenile Drug Abuse Risk Factors
Office of Juvenile Justice
and Delinquency Prevention
Research and Program Development Division
U.S. Department of Justice
633 Indiana Ave., NW
Washington, DC 20531 (202) 724-7560
This division has researched drug use among juveniles to develop information on high-risk factors for drug use among youth, and on the effectiveness of interventions for preventing or controlling illegal drug use. These studies include recommendations for promising prevention and rehabilitation strategies. Contact this division for more information.

* Law Enforcement Officers: Deaths and Assaults
Uniform Crime Reporting Section
Federal Bureau of Investigation
U.S. Department of Justice
9th & Pennsylvania Ave., NW, GRB
Washington, DC 20535 (202) 324-2614
The publication, *Law Enforcement Officers Killed or Assaulted*, is available from the FBI Crime Reporting Section in three yearly forms: the six-month report, preliminary annual, and annual. Write to the above address for a free copy.

* Law Enforcement Training for State and Local Officers
Federal Law Enforcement Training Center
U.S. Department of the Treasury
Glynco, GA 31524 (912) 267-2345
FLETC's Office of State and Local Law Enforcement conducts over 25 specialized programs both at Glynco and at various sites around the country. Some of these programs include: Child Abuse and Exploitation Investigative Techniques, Managing Juvenile Operations, Schools Are For Effective Police Operations Leading to Improved Children and Youth Services, Cargo Theft Investigations, Fraud and Financial Investigations, Hazardous Waste

Investigations, Prison/Jail Crisis Response Training, Criminal Investigations in an Automated Environment, Fugitive Investigations Training, Advanced Arson for Profit Investigations, and Narcotics Officer Training.

* Lie Detector Tests: Reliability

National Institute of Justice
U.S. Department of Justice
Box 6000
Rockville, MD 20850   (301) 251-5500

To investigate the validity of polygraph examinations in criminal investigations, an NIJ study compared the accuracy of human examiners to that of a computer program in assessing the truth of answers to specific questions. The computer program was found to be just as reliable as that of the human examiners. Contact this Institute for more information on this study and the use of polygraphs in criminal justice.

* Maximum Speed Limit Enforcement

Police Traffic Services Division
Office of Enforcement and Emergency Services
Traffic Safety Programs
National Highway Traffic Safety Administration
U.S. Department of Transportation
400 7th Street, SW, Room 6124
Washington, DC 20590   (202) 366-5440

The National Maximum Speed Limit is 65 miles per hour on certain interstate highways. This office processes annual certifications of maximum speed limit enforcement programs throughout the U.S. and assists states in developing and improving enforcement efforts.

* Missing and Exploited Children Clearinghouse

National Center for Missing and Exploited Children
Publications Department
1835 K St., NW, Suite 600
Washington, DC 20006   (800) 843-5678 (202) 634-9836 in DC

This Center serves as a clearinghouse of information on missing or exploited children; provides technical assistance to citizens and law-enforcement agencies; offers training programs to law-enforcement and social service professionals; distributes photos and descriptions of missing children nationwide; coordinates child protection efforts with the private sector; networks with nonprofit organizations and state clearinghouses; and provides information on effective state legislation to ensure the protection of children. The following publications are available free of charge:
Books:
Child Molesters: A Behavioral Analysis
Child Pornography and Prostitution
Children Traumatized in Sex Rings
Interviewing Child Victims
Investigator's Guide
Parental Kidnapping
Selected State Legislation
Youth at Risk
Brochures:
Child Protection
Child Protection Priorities
For Camp Counselors
Just in Case...You Are Considering Family Separation
Just in Case...You Are Dealing with Grief Following the Loss of a Child
Just in Case...You Are Using the Federal Parent Locator Service
Just in Case...You Need a Babysitter
Just in Case...Your Child Is a Runaway
Just in Case...Your Child Is Missing

* Missing and Exploited Children Hotline

National Center for Missing and Exploited Children
1835 K St., NW, Suite 600
Washington, DC 20006   (800) 843-5678 (202) 634-9836 in DC

This toll-free telephone hotline is open for those who have information missing or exploited children. The TDD hotline for the deaf is 1-800-826-7653.

* Neighborhood Crime Comparison Information

Uniform Crime Reporting Section
Federal Bureau of Investigation
U.S. Department of Justice
9th & Pennsylvania Ave., NW, GRB
Washington, DC 20535   (202) 324-2614

If you'd like to know how safe your prospective new neighborhood is, contact the Uniform Crime Reporting Section. This annual report, *Crime In the United States* contains an exact reading of the crime rates of any city in America (down to the types of crimes committed most frequently in which neighborhoods). Also, local police departments of most major cities have neighborhood crime reports available and will actually rate the safety factor of your new address for you.

* Neighborhood Safety Videos and Publications

National Institute of Justice
NCJRS, Box 6000
Dept. AID
Rockville, MD 20850   (800) 851-3420 (301) 251-5500 in DC

NIJ has these and other publications and videos on crime prevention and the law. Many of the documents are free of charge, while others are available for a modest fee. When ordering or inquiring about an NIJ publication, refer to its NCJ number.
Crime Stoppers: A National Evaluation (RIB). 1986, 5 pp. (NCJ 102292).
The Growing Role of Private Security (RIB). 1984, 5 pp. (NCJ 94703).
Guardian Angels: An Assessment of Citizen Response to Crime: Executive Summary. 1986, 31 pp. (NCJ 1009111).
Improving the Use and Effectiveness of Neighborhood Watch Programs (RIA). 1988, 4 pp. (NCJ 108618).
Neighborhood Safety (Crime file videotape). 1985 (NCJ 97227). VHS, Beta, or 3/4-inch.
Taking a Bite Out of Crime: The Impact of a Mass Media Crime Prevention Campaign. 1984, 78 pp. (NCJ 93350).

* Neighborhood Watch Programs

Office of Crime Prevention
National Institute of Justice
U.S. Department of Justice
633 Indiana Ave. NW
Washington, DC 20531   (202) 724-7684

If you're interested in starting a Neighborhood Watch Program in your town, or want to know how you can make yours better, contact the Neighborhood Watch Specialists at the National Institute of Justice. They will be glad to help you make your neighborhood a safer place.

* New Federal Laws

Office of the Federal Register
National Archives and Records Administration
8th St. & Pennsylvania Ave., NW, Room 8401
Washington, DC 20408   (202) 523-5230

This office receives all the laws enacted by Congress for publication in the *Federal Register* and can provide information regarding these laws. They also publish *United States at Large*, a compilation of laws enacted during a particular year.

* Nuclear Incidents

Emergency Programs Center
U.S. Department of Justice
10th St. & Constitution Ave., NW
Room 6101
Washington, DC 20530   (202) 633-4545

If you would like to know the facts of any case of criminal activity involving nuclear incidents, the files of the Emergency Programs Center is for you. The office of the U.S. Department of Justice coordinates the government's activity in any such case. For instance, if you want the facts on the real-life case of nuclear extortion seen in the movie, *The Falcon and the Snowman*, this is the place to go. Maybe you are interested in writing your own thriller on nuclear espionage; contact the Emergency Programs Center and read accounts of actual incidents to give your writing that tinge of reality. Whatever your interest may be, here's where you'll get the facts.

* Odometer Tampering

Odometer Fraud Staff
Office of Chief Counsel
National Highway Traffic Safety Administration
U.S. Department of Transportation
400 7th Street, SW, Room 5219
Washington, DC 20590   (202) 366-9511

Federal law requires that the seller of a car sign a disclosure statement that the mileage on the odometer is accurate and has not been rolled back. NHTSA enforces the odometer law via inspections and criminal charges. Information on odometer tampering is also available from the Auto Safety Hotline: (800) 424-9393.

* Police-Citizen Conflict Resolution

Community Relations Service (CRS)
U.S. Department of Justice
5550 Friendship Blvd., Suite 300
Chevy Chase, MD 20815   (301) 492-5929

The agency provides direct conciliation and mediation assistance to communities to facilitate the peaceful, voluntary resolution of racial and ethnic disputes or conflicts, and the peaceful co-existence of police and citizens' groups in the rapidly changing neighborhoods of today's cities. They normally begin with extensive informal discussions with public or police officials and local community leaders, but if the agency and the parties determine that formal negotiations offer the best hope for a settlement, the agency arranges and mediates the negotiations.

* Police Use of Deadly Force

Community Relations Service
5550 Friendship Blvd., Room 330
Chevy Chase, MD 20815 (301) 492-5929

There has been a steady increase in cases of community disruption due to minority groups' belief that the police have used deadly force--or a severe degree of non-lethal force-- when it was unwarranted. The booklet, *Police Use of Deadly Force*, provides information that will be useful to citizens and police looking for constructive alternatives to continued hostility and suspicion.

* Prisons and Correctional Institutions Clearinghouse

National Institute of Corrections Information Center
Bureau of Prisons
U.S. Department of Justice
1790 30th St., Suite 130
Boulder, CO 80301 (303) 939-8877

This center is the complete source of information on correctional institutions. They have the data to answer any and all questions. Public policy makers who are considering the economics and potential benefits of a proposed new prison would be wise to get in touch with the NIC, as would construction companies thinking of making a bid on a new site. Politicians, correctional officials, reporters, or even inmates who want to investigate possible reforms should contact this office.

* Prisons: History, Statistics

Public Affairs
Bureau of Prisons
U.S. Department of Justice
320 1st St., NW, Room 640
Washington, DC 20536 (202) 724-3198

The Bureau of Prisons has many publications available to the public. They release an annual *State of the Bureau* report, as well as publications describing new and existing facilities, a history of the development of the federal bureau, and an annual statistical report of the Nation's correctional facilities.

* Protection of the President

Personnel Division
U.S. Secret Service
Department of the Treasury
1800 G St., NW
Washington, DC 20223 (202) 535-5800

Protection is the key mission of the Uniformed Division of the Secret Service. They are responsible for the White House Complex; the Main Treasury Building and Annex and other Presidential offices; the President and immediate family; the official residence of the Vice President and his immediate family; and foreign diplomatic missions as prescribed by statute.

* Racial Disputes Resolution

Community Relations Service (CRS)
U.S. Department of Justice
5550 Friendship Blvd., Suite 300
Chevy Chase, MD 20815 (301) 492-5929

If your community is being torn apart by ethnic disputes or police-citizen conflicts, you may need help from this special service, set up by the Civil Rights Act of 1964. The Community Relations Service exists to resolve such disputes. The agency provides direct conciliation and mediation assistance to communities to facilitate the peaceful, voluntary resolution of racial and ethnic disputes or conflicts, and the peaceful co-existence of police and citizens' groups in the rapidly changing neighborhoods of today's cities. The CRS regularly provides conferences, training workshops, and publications to any and all communities in an attempt to forestall such disputes. However, when tensions do break out, the CRS will initiate whatever steps are necessary to begin making progress toward bringing about a resolution. They normally begin with extensive informal discussions with public or police officials and local community leaders, but if the agency and the parties determine that formal negotiations offer the best hope for a settlement, the agency arranges and mediates the negotiations.

* Recidivism Statistics

Bureau of Justice Statistics
U.S. Department of Justice
633 Indiana Ave., NW
Washington, DC 20531 (202) 724-7770

The National Recidivism Data Base links Bureau of Justice Statistics corrections data with State and FBI criminal history information to derive representative samples of individuals released from State prisons, follow these samples for several years, and produce estimates on the incidence, prevalence, and seriousness of later arrests and dispositions. For information on available statistics on prison recidivism, contact this office.

* RX Drug and Controlled Substances Registration

Registration Section
Office of Compliance and Regulatory Affairs
Drug Enforcement Administration
U.S. Department of Justice
666 11th St., NW, Room 920
Washington, DC 20001 (202) 254-8255

Information is available about registration under the Controlled Substances Act. Every person who manufactures, distributes, or dispenses any controlled substance, or who proposes to engage in the manufacture, distribution, or dispensing of any controlled substance, must register annually with the Registration Branch of the DEA. The names of all registrants are available to the public. A schedule of all controlled substances is also available. In addition, the DEA will investigate any registrant to ensure that they are accountable for the controlled substances handled if presented with requests or evidence which would seem to warrant such investigation.

* Secret Service Special Agents

Personnel Division
U.S. Secret Service
Department of the Treasury
1800 G St., NW
Washington, DC 20223 (202) 535-5800

Special agents for the Secret Service are charged with two missions: protection and investigation. In addition to those protected by the Uniformed Division, the Special Agents guard former Presidents and their spouses, children of former Presidents, visiting heads of foreign states and governments and their spouses, and major Presidential and Vice Presidential candidates. Counterfeiting, forgery, and fraud investigations are also performed by Special Agents. Candidates interested in applying may contact local Secret Service field offices.

* Settlement of Claims Against the Government

Claims Group General Government Division
General Accounting Office
441 G St., NW
Washington, DC 20548 (202) 275-3102

In addition to helping settle claims of one government agency against another, this GAO office also settles claims by and against the United States. Claims may involve individuals, businesses, or foreign, state, and municipal governments. Claims are settled by GAO when the departments and agencies have not been given specific authority to handle their own claims and when they involve 1) doubtful questions of law or fact; 2) appeals of agency actions; 3) certain debts which agencies are unable to collect; and 4) waivers of certain erroneous payments for pay. Contact GAO for more information.

* Special Security Events

Emergency Programs Center
U.S. Department of Justice
10th St. & Constitution Ave., NW
Room 1230
Washington, DC 20530

If you would like to find out about U.S. Department of Justice activities during major outbreaks of civil disorder or domestic terrorism, such as the famous race riots of 1968 or the more recent unrest in Miami, then you may want to check the files of the Emergency Programs Center which coordinates all such activities. This office also has handled such special security events as the Los Angeles and Lake Placid Olympics and the reception of the Cuban refugees into the United States.

* Stolen Pharmaceuticals and Other Drug Theft Office of Intelligence

Drug Enforcement Administration
U.S. Department of Justice
1405 Eye St., NW, Room 1013
Washington, DC 20537 (202) 633-1071

All legal drug handlers registered with the Drug Enforcement Administration are required to report thefts or losses on controlled substances. Stolen supplies from legitimate drug handlers comprise a substantial portion of the illicit drug distribution network. The DEA has a fully updated list of all reports of drug theft. For information contact the Office of Intelligence at the above address or phone number.

* Supreme Court Library

Supreme Court of the United States Library

1 1st St., NE
Washington, DC 20543 (202) 252-3177
A complete working collection of American, English, and Canadian statues, records and briefs dating back to 1832 are contained in this library. Historical and constitutional documents along with the federal tax laws and legislative histories of selected federal acts are also available here. The library is open to the public.

* U.S. Park Police

National Capital Region
National Park Service
U.S. Department of the Interior
1100 Ohio Dr., SW
Washington, DC 20242 (202) 426-6650
The U.S. Park Police have the same authority and powers as the Washington, D.C. metropolitan police. They also act as hosts to park visitors.

* Victimization Statistics

National Victims Resource Center
Box 6000-AIQ
Rockville, MD 20850 (800) 627-6872 (301) 251-5525 in DC
This Center can provide you with nationwide statistics on the victims of crime.

* Violent Criminal Behavior

National Institute of Justice
U.S. Department of Justice
Box 6000
Rockville, MD 20850 (301) 251-5500
NIJ research has examined the relation between early child abuse, neglect, and subsequent violent criminal behavior. Criminal records of substantiated cases of individuals abused as children were compared with criminal records of a matched group of non-abused individuals. The results to date suggest that those who were abused as children did commit more violent offenses as adults than those not abused as children. Contact this office for more information on this topic.

* Whistleblower Hotlines and Government Inspector Generals

Many federal departments and agencies have hotlines, some toll-free numbers, into the office of the Inspector General. The responsibility of the IG is chiefly an in-house auditor looking for fraud, mismanagement, and government waste. These whistleblower hotlines exist to encourage federal employees, state employees, contractors, and citizens to report any allegations.

Department of Agriculture
Office of Inspector General
P.O. Box 23399 (800) 424-9121
Washington, DC 20026 (202) 472-1388

Department of the Army
The Pentagon (800) 572-9000
Washington, DC 20310 (202) 695-1578

Department of Commerce
14th and Constitution Ave., NW
Room 7898-C (800) 424-5197
Washington, DC 20230 (202) 377-2495

Department of Defense
Defense Hotline
The Pentagon (800) 424-9098
Washington, DC 20301-1900 (202) 693-5080

Department of Education
Inspector General Hotline
P.O. Box 23458 (800) 647-8733
Washington, DC 20026 (202) 755-2770

Department of Energy
1000 Independence Ave., SW
Room 5DO39, Forrestal Building
Washington, DC 20585 (202) 586-4073

Department of Health and Human Services
OIG Hotline
P.O. Box 17303 (800) 368-5779
Baltimore, MD 21203-7303 (301) 597-0724

Department of Housing and Urban Development
451 7th St., SW, Room 8254
Washington, DC 20410 (202) 472-4200

Department of the Interior
18th and C Sts., NW, Room 5359 (800) 424-5081

Washington, DC 20240 (202) 343-2424

Department of Justice
Office of Professional Responsibility
10th and Constitution Ave., NW, Room 4304
Washington, DC 20530 (202) 633-3365

Department of Labor
200 Constitution Ave., NW, Room S1303 (800) 424-5409
Washington, DC 20210 (202) 357-0227

Department of State
2201 C St., NW
New State Building, Room 6821
Washington, DC 20520 (202) 647-3320

Department of Transportation
400 7th St., NW, Room 9210 (800) 424-9071
Washington, DC 20590 (202) 366-1461

Department of Treasury
15th and Pennsylvania Ave., NW, Room 2412 (800) 826-0407
Washington, DC 20220 (202) 566-7901

Department of Veterans Affairs
1425 K St., NW
McPherson Building, Room 1100 (800) 368-5899
Washington, DC 20420 (202) 842-5474

Environmental Protection Agency
401 M St., SW
Room 307 NE Mall (800) 424-4000
Washington, DC 20460 (202) 382-4977

Federal Bureau of Investigation
Inspections Division
Washington, DC 20535 (202) 324-2901

General Accounting Office
441 G St., NW (202) 272-5557
Washington, DC 20548 (800) 424-5454

General Services Administration
18th and F Sts., NW, Room 5340 (800) 424-5210
Washington, DC 20405 (202) 566-1780

Merit Systems Protection Board
Office of the Special Counsel
1120 Vermont Ave., NW, Suite 1100 (800) 872-9855
Washington, DC 20005 (202) 653-9125

National Aeronautics and Space Administration
Inspector General
P.O. Box 23089
L'Enfant Station (800) 424-9183
Washington, DC 20026 (202) 755-3402

Office of Personnel Management
1900 E St., NW, Room 6831
Washington, DC 20415 (202) 632-4423

Railroad Retirement Board
Office of Inspector General
Office of Investigation
844 N. Rush St., Room 450 (800) 772-4528
Chicago, IL 60611 (312) 751-4336

Small Business Administration
1441 L St., NW, Room 203
Washington, DC 20416 (202) 653-7557

Tennessee Valley Authority
400 West Summit Hill Drive (800) 323-3835
Knoxville, TN 37902 (615) 632-3550

U.S. Agency for International Development
21st and Virginia Ave.
Room 5644, New State Building
Washington, DC 20523 (202) 235-3528

U.S. Information Agency
Donohoe Building, Room 1100
400 6th St., SW
Washington, DC 20547 (202) 485-8202

* World's Largest Law Library

Law and Social Justice

Law Library
Library of Congress
Washington, DC 20540   (202) 707-5073

As the world's largest and most comprehensive library of foreign, international, and comparative law, the Law Library provides information for all known legal systems including common law, civil law, Roman law, canon law, Chinese law, Jewish and Islamic law, and ancient and medieval law. Specialists with knowledge of more than fifty languages provide reference and research service in all known legal systems. U.S. legislative documents housed here include the *Congressional Record* (and its predecessors), the serial set, a nearly complete set of bills and resolutions, current documents, committee prints, reports, hearings, etc. plus a complete set of U.S. Supreme Court records and briefs and collections of U.S. Court of Appeals records and briefs. The law library has five major divisions:

American-British Law: United States, Australia, Canada, Great Britain, India, New Zealand, Pakistan, certain other countries of the British Commonwealth and their dependent territories, and Eire: (202) 707-5077.

European Law: Nations of Europe and their possessions, except Spain and Portugal: (202) 707-5088.

Hispanic Law: Spain and Portugal, Latin America, Puerto Rico, the Philippines, and Spanish- and Portuguese-language states of Africa: (202) 707-5070.

Far Eastern Law: Nations of East and Southeast Asia including China, Indonesia, Japan, Korea, Thailand, and former British and French possessions in the area: (202) 707-5085.

Near Eastern and African Law: Middle Eastern countries, including the Arab states, Turkey, Iran, and Afghanistan, and all African countries, except Spanish- and Portuguese-language states and possessions: (202) 707-5073.

Courts and Legal Help

* Administration of U.S. Courts

Administrative Office of the United States Courts
811 Vermont Ave., NW
Washington, DC 20544 (202) 633-6097

This Office is responsible for supervision of administrative matters in all courts except the Supreme Court, supervising accounts and practices of the Federal probation offices, certain administrative matters within the Bankruptcy court, and exercises general supervision over administrative matters in offices of the United States magistrates. Information may be obtained from the following offices:

Bankruptcy Division:	(202) 633-6231
Court Administration Division:	(202) 633-6236
Defender Services Division:	(202) 633-6122
Financial Management Division:	(202) 633-6122
General Counsel:	(202) 633-6127
Magistrates Division:	(202) 633-6251
Personnel Division:	(202) 633-6112
Probation Division:	(202) 633-6226
Statistical Analysis and Reports Division:	(202) 633-6094

* Arbitrators and Mediators

Federal Mediation and Conciliation Service (FMCS)
2100 K St., NW
Washington, DC 20427 (202) 653-5300

Through its regional offices and suboffices, FMCS assists federal agencies, private sector employers, and labor organizations in resolving labor-management disputes. When there is no local or state resource available, the parties involved may contact the regional FMCS office to be assigned a qualified mediator or arbitrator, on call 24 hours a day. Upon request, mediators will assist the parties in resolving disputes, and arbitrators will make a final decision. Technical assistance includes training for one or both parties in developing constructive methods of dispute resolution, help in forming committees, and collective bargaining workshops. Contact your local FMCS office for any of these services.

* Bankruptcy Clearinghouse

Administrative Office of the United States Courts
Bankruptcy Division
811 Vermont Ave., NW, Room 1050
Washington, DC 20544 (202) 633-6234

Since the Administrative Office has general supervision for the bankruptcy courts, information on bankruptcy forms, fees, and explanations of the Bankruptcy Act is available.

* Bench Book for District Court Judges

Inter-Judicial Affairs and Information Service Division
Federal Judicial Center
1520 H St., NW
Washington, DC 20005 (202) 633-6365

The *Bench Book for United States District Court Judges* is available to judicial personnel only. This book contains statutes, suggestions, recommendations, and reference materials for judicial proceedings. The book is prepared by the Judicial Center from the guidance of experienced district judges.

* Civil and Criminal District Court Procedures

Superintendent of Documents
Government Printing Office
Washington, DC 20402 (202) 783-3238

Rules of Civil Procedure for the United States District Courts, With Forms. Contains the Rules of Civil Procedure for United States District Courts as promulgated and amended by the Supreme Court to October 1, 1977. $3.75
Rules of Criminal Procedure for the United States District Courts, With Forms. Contains the Rules of Criminal Procedure for the United States District Courts, together with forms as amended to October 1, 1979. $2.25
Federal Rules of Evidence. Sets forth Rules of Evidence for use in proceedings in the courts of the United States and before United States magistrates. $1.50
Federal Rules of Appellate Procedure. Contains the Federal Rules of Appellate Procedure as promulgates and amended by the United States Supreme Court to October 1, 1979, along with the forms adopted by the Court. $1.75

* Constitution and Supreme Court Decisions

Supreme Court of the United States
1 1st St., NE
Washington, DC 20543 (202) 252-3000

The *Constitution of the United States of America: Analysis and Interpretation* includes the text of the Constitution, along with its amendments prefacing annotations of the Supreme Court decisions that are relevant to the way the Constitution is interpreted. The cost is $70.00 and is available from the Superintendent of Documents, Government Printing Office, Washington, D.C. 20402; (202) 783-3238.

* Disabled and Handicapped Persons: Legal Aid

National Association of Protection and Advocacy System
220 Eye Street, NW Suite 150
Washington, DC 20002 (202) 546-8202

Every state and the territories provide legal assistance for the handicapped and developmentally disabled. This national organization also coordinates state agencies for the mentally ill and client assistance program. NAPAS publishes a newsletter titled *Annual Report*. The following is a list of the state protection and advocacy agencies for those with developmental disabilities.

Alabama Disabilities Advocacy Program		(205) 348-4928
Alaska Advocacy Services	(800) 478-1234	(907) 344-1002
American Samoa Client Assistance P&A Program		(684) 633-2418
Arizona Center for Law in the Public Interest		(602) 252-4904
Arkansas Advocacy Services		(501) 371-2171
California Protection and Advocacy Inc.	(800) 952-5746	(916) 488-9950
(818) 546-1631 (415) 839-0811		
Colorado Legal Center		(303) 722-0300
Connecticut Office of P&A	(800) 842-7303	(203) 297-4300
Delaware Disabilities Law Program		(302) 856-0038
District of Columbia Information, Protection, and Advocacy		(202) 547-8081
Florida Advocacy Center for Persons with Disabilities		(904) 488-9070
Georgia Advocacy Office, Inc.	(800) 537-2329	(404) 885-1234
Guam Advocacy Office		(671) 646-9026
Hawaii Protection and Advocacy Agency		(808) 949-2922
Idaho's Coalition of Advocates for the Disabled		(208) 335-5353
Illinois Protection and Advocacy Inc.		(312) 341-0022
Indiana Advocacy Services	(800) 622-4845	(317) 232-1150
Iowa Protection and Advocacy Service, Inc.		(515) 278-2502
Kansas Advocacy and Protection Services	(800) 432-8276	(913) 776-1541
Kentucky Office for Public Advocacy Division	(800) 372-2988	(502) 564-2967
Louisiana Advocacy Center for the Elderly and Disabled		(800) 662-7705
(504) 5522-2337		
Maine Advocacy Services	(800) 452-1948	(207) 377-6202
Maryland Disability Law Center		(301) 333-7600
Massachusetts Disability Law Center		(617) 723-8455
Michigan Protection and Advocacy Service		(517) 487-1755
Minnesota Legal Aid Society of Minneapolis		(612) 332-7301
Mississippi Protection and Advocacy System		(601) 981-8207
Missouri Protection and Advocacy System	(800) 392-8667	(314) 893-3333
Montana Advocacy Program		(406) 444-3889
Nebraska Advocacy Services		(402) 474-3183
Nevada Office of Protection and Advocacy	(800) 992-5715	(702) 789-0233
New Hampshire Disabilities Rights Center		(603) 228-0432
New Jersey Office of Advocacy	(800) 792-8600	(609) 292-9742
New Mexico Protection and Advocacy System	(800) 432-4682	(505) 256-3100
New York Commission on Quality of Care for the Mentally Disabled		
(518) 473-4057		
North Carolina Governor's Advocacy Council for Persons with Disabilities		
(919) 733-9250		
North Dakota Protection & Advocacy Project	(800) 474-2670	(701) 224-2972
Northern Mariana Islands Catholic Social Services		(670) 234-6981
Ohio Legal Rights Service	(800) 282-9181	(614) 466-7284
Oklahoma Protection and Advocacy Agency		(918) 664-5883
Oregon Advocacy Center		(503) 243-2081
Pennsylvania Protection and Advocacy	(800) 692-7443	(800) 238-6222
(717) 236-8110		
Puerto Rico Governor's Office Ombudsman for the Disabled		(809) 766-2333
Rhode Island Protection and Advocacy System		(401) 831-3150
South Carolina Protection and Advocacy System		(800) 922-5225
(803) 782-0639		
South Dakota Advocacy Project, Inc.	(800) 742-8108	(605) 224-8294
Tennessee E.A.C.H. Inc.	(800) 342-1660	(615) 298-1080
Texas Advocacy, Inc.	(800) 252-9108	(512) 454-4816
Utah Legal Center for the Handicapped	(800) 662-9080	(801) 363-1347
Vermont Developmental Disability Law Project		(802) 863-2881
Virginia Department for Rights of the Disabled	(800) 552-3962	(804) 225-2042
Virgin Islands Committee on Advocacy for the Developmentally Disabled		
(809) 772-1200		
Washington Protection and Advocacy System		(206) 324-1521

Law and Social Justice

West Virginia Advocates   (800) 950-5250   (304) 346-0847
Wisconsin Coalition for Advocacy   (608) 267-0214
Wyoming Protection and Advocacy System   (800) 624-7648   (307) 638-7668

* Disaster Victims Legal Services
Federal Emergency Management Agency
P.O. Box 70274
Washington, DC 20024   (202) 646-3484

The *Manual for Disaster Legal Services* has been prepared by FEMA and the Young Lawyers Division (YLD) of the American Bar Association. Its purpose is to orient new and potential volunteers to the FEMA-YLD Program for offering legal services to victims following major disasters. In order to facilitate this orientation, the *Manual* emphasizes schematic diagram, paraphrases statutes and regulations, and simplifies many issues relating to the program.

* Federal Courts Office Procedure
Judicial Center
Inter-Judicial Affairs and Information Services Division
1520 H St., NW
Washington, DC 20005   (202) 633-6365

Office procedures relating to organization and process of the federal courts is defined in a free handbook available only to certain judicial personnel from this office.

* Federal Courts Report
Administrative Office of the United States Courts
811 Vermont Ave., NW
Washington, DC 20544   (202) 633-6097

The business of all the federal courts (except the United States Court of Military Appeals and United States Tax Courts) is included in the *Annual Report of the Director of Administrative Office of the United States Courts*. It is available for $13.00 from the Superintendent of Documents, Government Printing Office, Washington, D.C. 20402; (202) 783-3238.

* Federal Judicial Resource Center
Federal Judicial Center
1520 H St., NW
Washington, DC 20005   (202) 633-6011

The subjects in this service cover civil and criminal procedure, constitutional law and probabilities, and court management. Material on all areas of the federal judicial administration can be obtained by writing the Federal Judicial Center.

* Federal Magistrates
Administrative Office of the United States Courts
Magistrates Division
811 Vermont Ave., NW
Washington, DC 20544   (202) 633-6097

Information and statistics on the offices of the United States magistrates is provided annually to Congress and can be obtained by contacting this Administrative Office of the United States Courts, Magistrates Division.

* Federal Public Defenders
Administrative Office of the United States Courts
811 Vermont Ave., NW
Washington, DC 20544   (202) 633-6097

Under the Criminal Justice Act, the *Federal Public Defenders and Federal Community Defender Organizations by the Districts Courts* is made available to the public. *Annual Reports* are provided by Defender organizations listing their activities.

* Foreigners Visiting Judicial Branch
Federal Judicial Center
Inter-Judicial Affairs and Information Services Division
1520 H St., NW
Washington, DC 20005   (202) 633-6365

Arrangements for official visitors from abroad, along with conducting briefings and assembling materials are conducted in this division.

* Judicial Branch Answer Desk
Federal Judicial Center
Dolly Madison House
1520 H Street, NW
Washington, DC 20005   (202) 633-6011

Call this center to determine how this branch of government can help you or can refer you to the appropriate office, agency, or court.

* Judicial Conference Update
Federal Judicial Center
Center Information Services Office
1520 H St., NW
Washington, DC 20005   (202) 633-6365

The Third Branch is a monthly bulletin that reports to the federal judicial community and other parties on the endeavors of the Judicial Conference. *The Third Branch* also provides a monthly update of changes in federal judicial personnel.

* Judicial Education and Training
Federal Judicial Center
1520 H St., NW
Washington, DC 20005   (202) 633-6011

This Center provides continuing education for federal judicial personnel. It also conducts research, development, and training for the judicial system.

* Judicial Research Reports
Federal Judicial Center
1520 H St., NW
Washington, DC 20005   (202) 633-6365

Research reports, staff papers, manuals, handbooks, and catalogs are publications that are available containing the results of research and analysis done for or by the Center. A publications catalog and other information can be obtained from the Federal Judicial Center.

* Law School Free Legal Clinics
Office of Public Affairs
Legal Services Corporation
400 Virginia Ave. S.W.
Washington, DC 20024   (202) 863-1839

The Law School Clinic Program is an additional source of legal assistance for the poor. A significant achievement of these clinics is their ability to educate students in substantive and procedural law, while providing a service to clients in their local communities.

* Legal Aid and Services Clearinghouse
National Clearinghouse on Legal Services
407 S. Dearborn St.
Chicago, IL 60605   (312) 939-3830

As a grantee of the Legal Services Corporation, this clearinghouse conducts research on computerized databases for LSC funded organizations. They maintain a brief bank and publish two newsletters each month with information on legal briefs. Copies of the briefs are free to LSC organizations, and for a slight fee to the public. Each month they publish Clearinghouse Review, which contains relevant articles and briefs (free to LSC organizations, $75 per year to all others). The clearinghouse also has manuals on public law.

* Legal Services and Problems
Office of Public Affairs
Legal Services Corporation
400 Virginia Ave. S.W.
Washington, DC 20024   (202) 863-1839

If you are in need of legal services, the Office of Public Affairs can direct you to the LSC field office that serves your area. If you feel that you are eligible for services but are denied by the field office, LSC's Public Affairs Office will help you have your complaints investigated.

* Legal Services Corporation Grantees and Contracts
Office of Field Services
Legal Services Corporation
400 Virginia Ave. S.W.
Washington, D.C. 20024   (202) 863-1820

A Fact Book, published yearly by LSC for $25, contains information regarding LSC funding data, program expenditures, and program characteristics, as well as information on national support centers and program services to clients. The Corporation's objective in compiling and issuing this *Fact Book* is to provide a complete and objective profile of legal services programs, which can serve as a reliable reference tool for policy decision-making and further quantitative analysis. A directory of the Legal Services Corporation's contract and grantee agencies is available for $8.

* Legal Services Corporation Opinions
General Counsel's Office
Legal Services Corporation
400 Virginia Ave. S.W.
Washington, D.C. 20024   (202) 863-1820

This office contains the final opinions, briefs, and orders for all cases adjudicated by Legal Services Corporation. All of these documents can be examined during business hours.

* Legal Services Corporation Newsletter

Legal Services Corporation
400 Virginia Ave. S.W.
Washington, DC 20024 (202) 863-1839
Legal Services Board is a quarterly publication which contains information on LSC regulations and activities, as well as articles by Board members. Information is also included on LSC funded organizations.

* Legal Services National Support Centers

Office of Public Affairs
Legal Services Corporation
400 Virginia Ave. S.W.
Washington, DC 20024 (202) 863-1839
The Corporation currently funds sixteen National Support Centers that specialize in various aspects of "poverty law" or in the problems of particular classes of individuals, such as migrants or the elderly. The centers produce publications and provide information relating to their respective areas. In addition they lobby Congress and federal agencies and monitor legislation and regulations of interest to their purported constituencies. The Support Centers, however, provide little or no actual representation of poor clients. Contact this office for more information regarding the individual Support Centers and their areas of interest.

* Mediation Board Publications

Office of Executive Secretary
National Mediation Board
1425 K St., NW, Room 910
Washington, DC 20572 (202) 523-5920
There are three annual subscription mailing lists available from the Board. Costs may be reduced or waived when it is in the public interest to do so.
Subscription List #1, $175: *Annual Reports of the NMB; Certifications and Dismissals; Determination of Craft or Class; Findings Upon Investigation; Emergency Board Reports.*
Subscription List #2, $ 50: *Annual Reports of the NMB; Emergency Board Reports; Determination of Craft or Class.*
Subscription List #3, $ 35: *The Representation Manual and Amendments.*

* Mediation Cases

Legal Services Office
Federal Mediation and Conciliation Service (FMCS)
2100 K St., NW, Room 712
Washington, DC 20427 (202) 653-5305
This office represents FMCS in legal cases. In unusually complex and technical mediation efforts, Legal Services staff participate as part of the mediation team. Contact this office for more information on labor-management conciliation cases.

* Mediation National Board Freedom of Information

National Mediation Board
1425 K St., NW,
Washington, DC 20572 (202) 523-5996
This office handles Freedom of Information Act requests regarding the National Mediation Board.

* Native Americans with Disabilities Legal Aid

Native American DNA-People's Legal Services
P.O. Box 306
Window Rock, AZ 86515 (602) 871-4151
This advocacy group provides legal help to Indians with handicaps and developmental disabilities. * Native

* Probation Practices

Administrative Office of the United States Courts
Probation Division
Washington, DC 20544 (202) 633-6228
The quarterly journal, *Federal Probation*, contains correctional philosophy and practices. The Administrative Office supervises the accounts and practices of the federal probation offices. Contact this office to obtain a copy.

* Public Defenders of U.S. Courts

Administrative Office of the United States Courts
811 Vermont Ave., NW
Washington, DC 20544 (202) 633-6097
Under the Criminal Justice Act, the *Federal Public Defenders and Federal Community Defender Organizations by the Districts Courts* is made available to the public. *Annual Reports* are provided by Defender organizations listing their

activities.

* State Justice Free Newsletter

State Justice Institute News
120 South Fairfax St.
Alexandria, VA 22314 (703) 684-6100
This free quarterly newsletter, *State Justice Institute News*, provides information about SJI grant programs, upcoming conferences, and the grant application process.

* State Justice Grant Categories

State Justice Institute
120 South Fairfax St.
Alexandria, VA 22314 (703) 684-6100
The Institute provides grants, contracts and cooperative agreements to State courts and organizations that can help improve the judicial administration of the State courts. To accomplish this goal, the Institute funds education projects in five categories: 1) Programs of proven merit which support established, exemplary, direct training to State trial and appellate court judges and other court personnel; 2) State initiatives which support state-based training projects developed or endorsed by the State courts for the benefit of judges and other court personnel in a particular state. This would include pre-bench orientation, development of bench books and model plans for career-long education for the judiciary; 3) National and regional training programs which fund projects addressing SJI Special Interest categories, which include seminars on topics that transcend state lines, regional training programs sponsored by national organizations, or specialized training programs for trial court judges; 4) Technical assistance which provides coordination, support services, information distribution, and other activities necessary for the development of effective education programs for judges, such as the development of educational curriculum or distribution of information about continuing judicial education programs; 5) Conferences which fund regional or national conferences that address topics of major concern to state judiciary.

* Supreme Court Document Copies

Library, Supreme Court of the United States
1 1st St., NE
Washington, DC 20543 (202) 252-3177
Supreme Court documents may be copied at the Library, Supreme Court of the United States, or by mail at the cost of $.10 per page by contacting the Photoduplication Service, Library of Congress, Washington, D.C. 20540; (202) 287-5640.

* Supreme Court Information

Supreme Court
Clerk's Office
1 1st St., NE
Washington, DC 20543 (202) 252-3029
The status of pending cases, docket sheet information, and admissions to the Supreme Court bar can be obtained from the Clerk's Office. This office also distributes court opinions.

* Supreme Court Publications

Supreme Court of the United States
Information
Supreme Court Building
1 1st St., NE
Washington, DC 20543 (202) 252-3211
Individual Slip Opinions include all of the Supreme Court's opinions as announced from the bench. They are issued periodically and cost $140.00 a term of Court. *Preliminary Prints* (advance parts) are official United States Reports containing all the opinions with syllabi, indices, tables of cases, and other editorial additions. They are issued periodically and cost $56.00 a term of Court.

* Supreme Court Records

Supreme Court
Clerk's Office
1 1st St., NE
Washington, DC 20543 (202) 252-3029
Supreme Court records are housed in over 20 regional depositories. Contact this office for a list of their locations.

* Tax Court Decisions

United States Tax Court
400 2nd St., NW
Washington, DC 20217 (202) 376-2754
United States Tax Court Reports contain a consolidation of the tax decisions for a month. The yearly subscription cost is $27.50 and is available from the Superintendent of Documents, Government Printing Office, Washington, D.C. 20402; (202) 783-3238.

* Tribal Courts for Native Americans

Office of Tribal Services
Bureau of Indian Affairs
U.S. Department of the Interior
18th and C Sts., NW
Washington, DC 20240   (202) 343-2111

This office serves as a cross between the Health and Human Services, Labor, Justice, and Housing and Urban Development Departments for the Indian population. The needy are paid welfare subsidies and provided job training. This office also operates 19 special federal courts and funds 127 tribal courts, along with administering the police force for Indian reservations, and a rehabilitation program for Indian homes.

Immigration and Naturalization

* "Ask Immigration" Center

Central Office
Immigration and Naturalization Service
425 I Street, NW
Washington, DC 20536   (202) 633-4316

The "Ask Immigration" telephone service system provides pre-recorded information on a wide range of immigration- and citizenship-related topics. This Service is available 24 hours a day, 7 days a week. If you are calling from a location outside the local calling area of the INS office, you will be charged long distance telephone costs. Immigration Information Officers are available to provide personal assistance at the local INS offices listed below during different times of the day. To find out the exact times such assistance is available and the regular business hours for each office, listen carefully to the initial answer message when you call the office in your area and follow the instructions provided. If all you need is an INS form and want it mailed to your address, the initial message will tell you which number on your telephone to press. Leave your name, address, INS form(s) needed, and/or information materials you require. For the Immigration Service to respond promptly to your request, be sure to state your name clearly, spelling it if necessary, and provide your current, complete address. After calling the appropriate state INS office (refer to separate listing of INS state offices), enter one of the number codes below which corresponds to the information about immigration and naturalization that you need.

General Immigration Information:
347 The Immigration & Naturalization Service
370 Where to mail application
161 How to obtain copies of documents (G-639)
271 Visa availability list
142 Appeals & Motions
036 Reporting your change of address (AR-11)
341 The Outreach Program

Immigration Reform and Control Act of 1986 (IRCA):
070 Legalization updates
272 Special agricultural worker program
174 Employer sanctions
372 Systematic alien verification for entitlements program (Project SAVE)
095 Anti-discrimination provisions of the law
090 How to apply for permanent resident status if you resided continuously in the United States since before January 1, 1972 (Updated Registry)

Your Alien Registration Card:
265 Permanent alien registration receipt card
058 Applying for a replacement alien registration receipt card (I-90)
129 If you never received your alien registration receipt card (I-90)

Immigrant Visas and Immigrant Status:
053 Filing petitions to obtain immediate relative status (I-130)
097 Filing petitions to sponsor prospective immigrant employee (I-140)
065 How an alien in the United States may request a change of status to permanent resident status (I-485)
136 When a United States citizen marries a foreign national outside the USA
156 Fiance/fiancee visa (I-129F)
096 How to file joint petitions for spouse to remove conditional basis of their permanent resident status (I-751)
241 Orphan petitions (I-600)
255 Immigration benefits for adoption before 16th birthday (I-130)
172 Application for asylum in the USA (I-589)
354 Permanent residence for beneficiaries of approved asylum applications

Student Visas:
164 Permission to go to school (I-20, I-134)
267 How to maintain your student status
344 Visas for spouse and dependent children of student
131 Student visa extension (I-538)
145 Permission to work (I-538)
252 F-1 Transfer to another school (I-538)
355 M-1 Transfer to another school (I-538)

Nonimmigrant Visas and Nonimmigrant Status:
262 Nonimmigrant or temporary visas
038 Temporary visitor's visa
029 How to request an extension of temporary stay (I-539)
134 Applying for a replacement arrival-departure document I-94 (I-102)
041 Change of status from one nonimmigrant classification to another nonimmigrant classification for purpose of work (I-506)
245 Requirements for classification as nonimmigrant treaty trader E-1

231 Requirements for classification as nonimmigrant treaty investor E-2
364 Requirements for classification as nonimmigrant exchange alien J-1
044 Requirements for classification as nonimmigrant temporary workers H-1, H-2, and H-3, (I-129B)
338 Intracompany transfers L-1 (I-129L, I-129S)
091 Deferred departure status for nationals of the Peoples Republic of China

Undocumented Aliens:
232 How to report aliens illegally in the United States and/or the companies that hire them

Travel Outside the United States:
033 Departure from the USA by permanent residents: reentry permits (I-131)
360 Travel authorization for refugees: Refugee travel documents (I-570)
137 Travel by an alien whose application for permanent resident status is still pending
239 Emergency travel requests
236 Student travel outside the USA

Citizenship and Naturalization:
061 Citizenship and Naturalization requirements (N-400)
153 Residency requirements for naturalization
169 Derivative citizenship for children of U.S. citizens
139 Citizenship for children born outside the United States (N-600)
258 Naturalization based upon military service
159 Replacement of certificate of citizenship or naturalization (N-565)
351 How to file for naturalization on behalf of a child
358 Loss of United States citizenship

* Citizenship Education Videos

Immigration and Naturalization Service
U.S. Department of Justice
425 Eye St., NW, Room 7228
Washington, DC 20536   (202) 633-3320

Schools, community service organizations, churches, or others who wish to run citizenship education programs may borrow any of the several videocassettes available from the INS free of charge. The INS currently has twelve videocassettes available covering topics ranging from a focus on specific articles of the Constitution to the story of the American Flag, from an examination of the electoral process to biographies of George Washington and Abraham Lincoln. All videocassettes will be shipped postage free. A complete list of the available videocassettes and a synopsis of each can also be obtained by writing or calling the INS. In addition, a series of textbooks are available for school districts wishing to include citizenship education in their curriculum. These textbooks come in elementary or secondary reading levels.

* Employers Hotline on Immigrant Employees

Immigration and Naturalization Service
U.S. Department of Justice
425 Eye St., NW, Room 7116
Washington, DC 20536   (800) 777-7700 (202) 633-3228

If you are unsure how the Immigration Reform and Control Act affects you as employer, call this hotline.. This 24-hour, toll-free hotline contains important information, in both English and Spanish, on employee and employer responsibilities and punishments. You can also receive information on legalization requirements and other general information. It will tell you exactly what your responsibilities are both to those workers who are eligible for legalization and those who are not, as well as explain your rights as an employer.

* Farmworkers: English and Spanish Immigration Information

Immigration and Naturalization Service
U.S. Department of Justice
425 Eye St., NW, Room 7116
Washington, DC 20536   (202) 633-3228

If you are unsure how the Immigration Reform and Control Act affects you as a farmworker, call 1-800-777-7700. This 24-hour, toll-free line contains important information, in both English and Spanish, on employee and employer responsibilities and punishments. It can tell you whether or not your employer has treated you fairly and what you can do about it. You can also receive information on alien benefits, legalization requirements, and other general information.

* Immigration and Naturalization State Offices

Each of these state offices operate "Ask Immigration". In addition to these tape recorded messages, staff is available to provide information and send literature in response to telephone requests.

Alaska
Anchorage: (907) 343-7820

Arizona
Phoenix: (602) 261-3122
Tucson: (602) 629-6229

California
Fresno: (209) 487-5091
Los Angeles: (213) 894-2119
Sacramento: (916) 551-2785
San Diego: (619) 557-5570
San Francisco: (415) 705-4411
San Jose: (408) 291-7876

Colorado
Denver: (303) 844-3526

Connecticut
Hartford: (203) 240-3171

District of Columbia
Washington, (Arlington, VA): (703) 235-4055
Washington, (INS Central Office): (202) 633-4316

Florida
Jacksonville: (904) 791-2624
Miami: (305) 536-5741
Tampa: (813) 228-2131

Georgia
Atlanta: (404) 331-5158

Hawaii
Honolulu; (808) 541-1379

Illinois
Chicago: (312) 353-7334

Indiana
Indianapolis: (317) 226-6009

Kentucky
Louisville: (502) 582-6375

Louisiana
New Orleans: (504) 589-6533

Maine
Portland: (207) 780-3352

Maryland
Baltimore: (301) 962-2065

Massachusetts
Boston: (617) 565-3879

Michigan
Detroit: (313) 226-3240

Minnesota
St. Paul: (612) 854-7754

Missouri
Kansas City: (816) 891-0603
St. Louis: (314) 425-4532

Montana
Helena: (406) 449-5288

Nebraska
Omaha: (402) 341-8995

Nevada
Las Vegas: (702) 384-3696

Reno: (702) 784-5427

New Jersey
Newark: (201) 645-4400

New Mexico
Albuquerque: (505) 766-2378

New York
Albany: (518) 472-4621
Buffalo: (716) 849-6760
New York: (212) 206-6500

North Carolina
Charlotte: (704) 523-1704

Ohio
Cincinnati: (513) 684-3781
Cleveland: (216) 522-4770

Oklahoma
Oklahoma City: (405) 231-4121

Oregon
Portland: (503) 221-3006

Pennsylvania
Philadelphia: (215) 597-3961
Pittsburgh: (412) 644-3356

Puerto Rico
San Juan: (809) 766-5280

Tennessee
Memphis: (901) 521-3301

Texas
Dallas: (214) 767-0514
El Paso: (915) 532-0273
Harlingen: (512) 425-7333
Houston: (713) 847-7900
San Antonio: (512) 229-6350

Utah
Salt Lake City: (801) 524-5771

Virginia
Norfolk: (804) 441-3081

Washington
Seattle: (206) 442-5956
Spokane: (509) 353-2129

* Political Asylum

Office of Asylum Affairs
Bureau of Human Rights and Humanitarian Affairs
Department of State
SA-17, Room 520
Washington, DC 20520   (202) 326-6110

This office handles the Department of State's responsibilities regarding political asylum by providing advisory opinions on the cases to the Immigration and Naturalization Service.

* Work Permits for Foreigners

Labor Certification Division
Employment and Training Administration
Department of Labor
200 Constitution Ave., NW, Room N4456
Washington, DC 20210   (202) 535-0163

If an employer wishes to hire foreign workers, he must first obtain a foreign labor certificate, which is a statement from the U.S. Department of Labor stating that there is no U.S. citizen available to fill the job. The Department investigates to make sure that the wages and working conditions of the foreign workers will not seriously affect U.S. workers. An employer applies for a foreign labor certificate through the local state employment service office, which then conducts a job hunt before sending the application form to the area regional office for approval or disapproval.

Discrimination and Civil Rights

* See also Health and Medicine Chapter; Handicapped Resources
* See also Information from Lawmakers Chapter

* Advocates for the Handicapped Clearinghouse

National Information Center for Handicapped Children and Youth
PO Box 1492
Washington, DC 20013   (703) 893-6061 (800) 999-5599
This clearinghouse helps parents of handicapped children, disabled adults, and professionals locate services for the handicapped and information on disabilities.

* Affirmative Action and Hiring the Handicapped

Office of Federal Compliance Programs
Employment Standards Administration
Department of Labor
200 Constitution Ave., NW, Room C3325
Washington, DC 20210   (202) 523-9475
The Rehabilitation Act of 1973 prohibits most employers doing business with the federal government from discriminating in employment against handicapped persons. Employers with contracts in excess of $2,500 must take affirmative action to hire and promote qualified handicapped persons.

* Age Discrimination

U.S. Equal Employment Opportunity Commission
1801 L Street, NW
Washington, DC 20507   (800) 872-3362
Persons 40 years of age or older are protected by the Age Discrimination in Employment Act, which prohibits arbitrary age discrimination in hiring, discharge, pay, promotions, fringe benefits, and other aspects of employment. Retaliation against a person who files a charge of age discrimination, participates in an investigation, or opposes an unlawful practice is also illegal. Contact this office for their free fact sheet and more information on age discrimination.

* Alaskan Natives

Office of Public Affairs
Bureau of Indian Affairs
U.S. Department of the Interior
18th and C Sts., NW
Washington, DC 20240   (202) 343-1711
Some free publications available from the Bureau of Indian Affairs Public Affairs office. Due to the limited supply and small staff, only one copy of each publication may be requested: *Federal Acknowledgment Process, Alaska Natives, American Indian and Alaskan Native Education, Bureau of Indian Affairs Social Services Program, 1980 Census Count of American Indians Employment with BIA, Housing Program for Indians, List of Tribal Entities Recognized and Eligible to Receive Services from the U.S. Bureau of Indian Affairs Federal/Indian Relationship.*

* American Indians Rights

Office of Public Affairs
Bureau of Indian Affairs
U.S. Department of the Interior
18th and C Sts., NW
Washington, DC 20240   (202) 343-1711
The free booklet, *American Indians Today: Answers to Your Questions, 1988,* contains useful information on the Native American Indians and their relationship to the Bureau of Indian Affairs. Programs within the Bureau, including education, health services, and housing are briefly outlined and contain recent statistics. Many questions are answered within the booklet, including the rights of the Indians to own land and have their own governments. A map locates the Indian lands and communities, showing Federal and State Indian Reservations and other Indian groups. An excellent bibliography, prepared by the Smithsonian Institution, is included.

* Asian Americans and Immigrants Discrimination

U.S. Commission on Civil Rights
Clearinghouse Division, Room 700
1121 Vermont Ave., NW
Washington, DC 20425   (202) 376-8105
The Commission is a primary source for civil rights laws and regulations.

Numerous publications are available at no charge from the Commission on Civil Rights and they may also be available at depository libraries including:
Recent Activities Against Citizens and Residents of Asian Descent. Discusses historical discrimination against Asian immigrants and Asian Americans, factors in anti-Asian activity, and specific incidents since 1920 of violence, harassment, and intimidation against persons of Asian descent.

* Business EEOC Assistance Program

Office of Program Operations
U.S. Equal Employment Opportunity Commission
1801 L Street, NW
Washington, DC 20507   (800) 872-3362 (202) 634-7674
The EEOC offers access to equal employment information and provides educational and technical assistance to small and mid-size employers and unions regarding their rights and obligations under federal laws prohibiting discrimination in the workplace. The program stresses such topics as sex and discrimination, sexual harassment, employee selection procedures, recordkeeping requirements, and layoffs. Contact this office for more information on assistance programs.

* Civil Rights Commission Clearinghouse

Robert S. Rankin Civil Rights Library
U.S. Commission on Civil Rights
1121 Vermont Ave., NW, Room 709
Washington, DC 20425   (202) 376-8110
The Civil Rights Memorial Library, located at the Civil Rights Commission's headquarters in Washington, D.C., is a clearinghouse of civil rights information and contains 50,000 reference works, including 400 civil rights and minority issues journals, periodicals, legal journals, 3,500 reels of microfilm, and a comprehensive collection of reports, transcripts, and civil rights texts. It also maintains two online database systems: Ohio College Library Center (OCLC), and Dialog.

* Civil Rights Commission Regional Offices

Eastern Regional Division, 1121 Vermont Ave., NW, Washington, DC 20425; (202) 523-5264

Central Regional Division, Old Federal Office Building, 911 Walnut Street, Room 3103, Kansas City, MO 64106; (816) 374-5253

Western Regional Division, 3660 Wilshire Boulevard, Suite 810, Los Angeles, CA 90010; (213) 894-3437

* Civil Rights Complaints

U.S. Commission on Civil Rights
Complaint Referral
1121 Vermont Ave., NW
Washington, DC 20425   (202) 376-8376
Contact this office or a regional office of the CCR if you have complaints about discrimination and/or the abuse of civil rights.

* Civil Rights Directories and Publications

U.S. Commission on Civil Rights
Clearinghouse Division, Room 700
1121 Vermont Ave., NW
Washington, DC 20425   (202) 376-8105
The following publications are a sampling of those available at no charge from the Commission on Civil Rights. These publications are designed to provide reliable information about civil rights problems and about the laws, procedures, and approaches available for resolving them. A complete *Catalog of Publications* is available free of charge, and those publications that are out of print may be available at depository libraries across the U.S.
Civil Rights Directory. Lists private and public individuals and organizations concerned with civil rights at local, State, Federal, and national levels.
The Economic Progress of Black Men in America. Examines earnings and employment of black men from 1940 to 1980, sources of the earning gap with

Law and Social Justice

white men and effects of civil rights policies.

Police Practices and the Preservation of Civil Rights. A statement expressing concern that violation of civil rights by some police officers is a serious national problem. Includes recommendations for remedy.

* Civil Rights Enforcement

Civil Rights Division
U.S. Department of Justice
10th St. & Constitution Ave., NW
Room 5643
Washington, DC 20530   (202) 633-2151

If you have any questions as to the enforcement of 1964 Civil Rights Act, contact the Civil Rights Division. Information on the history of Civil Rights enforcement, as well as actual case history may be obtained by calling or writing the above address. Note: This office will not have information on the Civil Rights movement or on Dr. Martin Luther King, Jr., except insofar as they pertain to federal investigations or prosecutions.

* Civil Rights Hearings

U.S. Commission on Civil Rights
Clearinghouse Division, Room 700
1121 Vermont Ave., NW
Washington, DC 20425   (202) 376-8376

Transcripts of discussions at conferences, consultations sponsored by the Commission on Civil Rights, and testimony at Commission hearings are available to the public. Commission hearings focus government and public attention on civil rights problems and examine the manner in which Federal authorities discharge their civil rights responsibilities.

* Civil Rights: Proposed Legislation

U.S. Commission on Civil Rights
Office of Staff Director
1121 Vermont Ave., NW
Washington, DC 20425   (202) 523-5571

This office can provide you with current information on civil rights legislation and other relevant issues of civil rights law.

* Civil Rights Updates and Newsletter

U.S. Commission on Civil Rights
1121 Vermont Ave., NW
Washington, DC 20425   (202) 376-8177

Update, a monthly summary of the Civil Rights Commission's projects and activities, is available to the public free of charge. Another free publication, *Perspectives*, is published quarterly to provide varied views and information on civil rights issues.

* Employment Discrimination and Affirmative Action

Equal Opportunity Programs Staff
Justice Management Division
U.S. Department of Justice
10th St. & Constitution Ave., NW
Room 1230
Washington, DC 20530   (202) 633-5049

Do you feel you've been unjustly discriminated against in the workplace? Contact this office and the U.S. Department of Justice will tell you exactly how the annual affirmative action plan affects equal employment opportunity.

* Employment Discrimination: Filing A Complaint

U.S Equal Employment Opportunity Commission
1801 L Street, NW
Washington, DC 20507   (800) 872-3363

If you believe you have been discriminated against by an employer, labor union, or employment agency when applying for a job or on the job because of race, color, sex, religion, national origin, or age, you may file a charge of discrimination with the EEOC. Charges may be filed in person, by mail, or telephone by contacting the nearest EEOC field office or the national office listed above.

* Equal Employment Opportunity Hotline

Equal Employment Opportunity Commission
1801 L Street, NW
Washington, DC 20507   (800) USA-EEOC

This toll-free hotline receives and investigates employment discrimination charges against private employers and state and local governments. The EEOC Attorney-of-the-Day can offer telephone guidance to callers with their questions about alleged discrimination.

* Equal Employment Opportunity Offices Nationwide

Albuquerque Area Office, 505 Marquette, NW, Suite 1105, Albuquerque, NM 87102; (505) 766-2061

Atlanta District Office, 75 Piedmont Avenue, NE, Suite 1100, Atlanta, GA 30335; (404) 331-6093

Baltimore District Office, 109 Market Place, Suite 4000, Baltimore, MD 21202; (301) 962-3932

Birmingham District Office, 2121 Eighth Avenue, North, Suite 824, Birmingham, AL 35203; (205) 731-0082

Boston Area Office, JFK Federal Building, Room 409-B, Boston, MA 02203; (617) 565-3200

Buffalo Local Office, 28 Church Street, Room 301, Buffalo, NY 14202; (716) 846-4441

Charlotte District Office, 5500 Central Avenue, Charlotte, NC 28212; (704) 567-7100

Chicago District Office, 536 South Clark Street, Room 930-A Chicago, IL 60605; (312) 353-2713

Cincinnati Area Office, 550 Main Street, Room 7015, Cincinnati, OH 45202; (513) 684-2851

Cleveland District Office, 1375 Euclid Avenue, Room 600, Cleveland, OH 44115; (216) 522-2001

Dallas District Office, 8303 Elmbrook Drive, Dallas, TX 75247; (214) 767-7015

Denver District Office, 1845 Sherman Street, 2nd Floor, Denver, CO 80203; (303) 866-1300

Detroit District Office, 477 Michigan Avenue, Room 1540, Detroit, MI 48226; (313) 226-7636

El Paso Area Office, 700 East San Antonio Street, Room B-406 El Paso, TX 79901; (915) 534-6550

Fresno Local Office, 1313 P Street, Suite 103, Fresno, CA 93721; (209) 487-5793

Greensboro Local Office, 324 West Market Street, Room B-27, P.O. Box 3363, Greensboro, NC 27401; (919) 333-5174

Greenville Local Office, 300 East Washington Street, Suite B-41 Greenville, SC 29601; (803) 233-1791

Honolulu Local Office, 677 Ala Moana Blvd., Suite 404, Honolulu, HI 96850; (808) 541-3120

Houston District Office, 405 Maine Street, 6th Floor, Houston, TX 77002; (713) 653-3320

Indianapolis District Office, 46 East Ohio Street, Room 456, Indianapolis, IN 46204; (317) 226-7212

Jackson Area Office, 100 West Capitol Street, Suite 721, Jackson, MS 39269; (601) 965-4537

Kansas City Area Office, 911 Walnut, 10th Floor , Kansas City, MO 64106; (816) 426-5773

Little Rock Area Office, 320 West Capitol Avenue, Suite 621, Little Rock, AR 72201; (501) 378-5060

Los Angeles District Office, 3660 Wilshire Boulevard, 5th Floor, Los Angeles, CA 90010; (213) 251-7278

Louisville Area Office, 601 West Broadway, Room 613, Louisville, KY 40202; (502) 582-6082

Memphis District Office, 1407 Union Avenue, Suite 502, Memphis, TN 38104; (901) 521-2617

Miami District Office, Federal Building, One Northeast First Street, 6th Floor, Miami, FL 33132; (305) 536-4491

Milwaukee District Office, 310 West Wisconsin Avenue, Suite 800, Milwaukee, WI 53203; (414) 291-1111

Minneapolis Local Office, 220 Second Street South, Room 108, Minneapolis MN 55401-2141; (612) 370-3330

Nashville Area Office, 404 James Robertson Parkway, Suite 1100

Nashville, TN 37219; (615) 736-5820

Newark Area Office, 60 Park Place, Room 301, Newark, NJ 07102; (201) 645-6383

New Orleans District Office, 701 Loyola Avenue, Suite 600, New Orleans, LA 70113; (504) 589-2329

New York District Office, 90 Church Street, Room 1501, New York, NY 10007; (212) 263-7161

Norfolk Area Office, 200 Granby Mall, Room 412, Norfolk, VA 23510; (804) 441-3470

Oakland Local Office; 1333 Broadway, Room 430, Oakland, CA 94612; (415) 273-7588

Oklahoma Area Office, 200 NW 5th Street, Room 703, Oklahoma City, OK 73102; (405) 231-4911

Philadelphia District Office, 1421 Cherry Street, 10th Floor, Philadelphia, PA 19102; (215) 597-7784

Phoenix District Office, 4520 N. Central Avenue, Suite 300, Phoenix, AZ 85012-1848; (602) 261-3882

Pittsburgh Area Office, 127 West Hargett Street, Suite 500, Raleigh, NC 27601; (919) 856-4064

Richmond Area Office, 400 North 8th Street, Room 7026, Richmond, VA 23240; (804) 771-2692

San Antonio District Office, 5410 Fredericksburg Road, Suite 200, San Antonio, TX 78229; (512) 229-4810

San Diego Local Office, 880 Front Street, Room 4S-21, San Diego, CA 92188; (619) 293-6288

San Francisco District Office, 901 Market Street, Suite 500, San Francisco, CA 94103; (415) 995-5049

San Jose Local Office, 280 South First Street, Room 4150, San Jose, CA 95113; (408) 291-7352

Savannah Local Office, 10 Whitaker Street, Suite B, Savannah, GA 31401; (912) 944-4234

Seattle District Office, 1321 Second Avenue, 7th Floor, Seattle, WA 98101; (206) 422-0968

St. Louis District Office, 625 N. Euclid Street, 5th Floor, St. Louis, MO 63108; (314) 425-6585

Tampa Area Office, 700 Twiggs Street, Room 302, Tampa, FL 33602; (813) 228-2310

Washington Field Office, 1717 H Street, NW, Suite 400, Washington, DC 20006; (202) 653-6197

* Equal Opportunity and Non-Discrimination
Information Handling and Support Facilities
General Accounting Office
P.O. Box 6015
Gaithersburg, MD 20877   (202) 275-6241
A Compilation of Federal Laws and Executive Orders for Nondiscrimination and Equal Opportunity Programs (#HRD-78-138) is a free 72-page book that can help companies avoid employment discrimination problems. It cites 87 laws and orders relating to equal rights in employment practices, as well as in the provision of services. Each citation briefly describes the law or order, identifies what type of discrimination it prohibits and to whom it applies, and which agencies enforce it.

* Equal Work Equal Pay
U.S. Equal Employment Opportunity Commission
1801 L Street, NW
Washington, DC 20507   (800) 872-3362 (202) 634-6831
Women and men who perform substantially equal work in the same establishment are covered by the Equal Pay Act, which prohibits employers from discriminating in pay because of sex and from reducing the wages of either sex to comply with the law. A violation may exist where a different wage is paid to a predecessor or successor employee of the opposite sex. Retaliation against a person who files a charge of equal pay discrimination, participates in an investigation, or opposes an unlawful employment practice also is illegal. Contact this office for a free fact sheet or to file a complaint.

* Fair Housing Local and State Agencies
U.S. Commission on Civil Rights
Clearinghouse Division, Room 700
1121 Vermont Ave., NW
Washington, DC 20425   (202) 376-8105
The Commission is a primary source for civil rights laws and regulations. Numerous publications are available at no charge from the Commission on Civil Rights and they may also be available at depository libraries including: *Directory of State and Local Fair Housing Agencies.* For 91 State and local governmental agencies, describes classes protected under the pertinent fair housing law and unlawful discriminatory housing practices.

* Housing Discrimination
Housing and Civil Enforcement Section
Civil Rights Division
U.S. Department of Justice
10th St. & Constitution Ave., NW
Room 7525
Washington, DC 20530   (202) 633-4715
If you feel you've been denied housing due to racial, sexual, or religious discrimination, contact the Housing and Civil Enforcement Section of the U.S. Department of Justice. Their advisers can tell you if and what action is warranted in your case, and they can also refer you to local agencies for the help you need. This office is also responsible for bringing civil actions in federal courts whenever there is reasonable cause to believe that a person or group is denying housing unjustly due to discrimination.

* Minorities and Women: Last Hired, First Fired
U.S. Commission on Civil Rights
Clearinghouse Division, Room 700
1121 Vermont Ave., NW
Washington, DC 20425   (202) 376-8105
The Commission is a primary source for civil rights laws and regulations. Numerous publications are available at no charge from the Commission on Civil Rights and they may also be available at depository libraries including: *Last Hired, First Fired: Layoffs and Civil Rights.* Examines the effects of seniority as applied to layoffs of minority and female workers.

* Minority Hiring Statistics
U.S. Equal Employment Opportunity Commission
Survey Division, 9th Floor
1801 L Street, NW
Washington, DC 20507   (202) 363-4948
EEOC compiles minority employment statistics for the following groups: private employment; unions; state and local governments; elementary and secondary education; health services; clericals; service-oriented industries; and skilled and craft industries. The database is searchable by occupation, industry, and region--state, county, or city. Searches and printouts are available free of charge.

* Native Americans with Disabilities Legal Aid
Native American DNA-People's Legal Services
P.O. Box 306
Window Rock, AZ 86515   (602) 871-4151
This advocacy group provides legal help to Indians with handicaps and developmental disabilities. * Native

* Native Americans Rights
Office of Public Affairs
Bureau of Indian Affairs
U.S. Department of the Interior
18th and C Sts., NW
Washington, DC 20240   (202) 343-1711
The free booklet, *American Indians Today: Answers to Your Questions, 1988,* contains useful information on the Native American Indians and their relationship to the Bureau of Indian Affairs. Programs within the Bureau, including education, health services, and housing are briefly outlined and contain recent statistics. Many questions are answered within the booklet, including the rights of the Indians to own land and have their own governments. A map locates the Indian lands and communities, showing Federal and State Indian Reservations and other Indian groups. An excellent bibliography, prepared by the Smithsonian Institution, is included.

* Pregnancy Discrimination
U.S. Equal Employment Opportunity Commission
1801 L Street, NW
Washington, DC 20507   (800) 872-3363 (202) 634-6831
Discrimination on the basis of pregnancy, childbirth, or related medical conditions constitutes unlawful sex discrimination. Women affect by pregnancy or related conditions must be treated in the same manner as other applicants or employees with similar abilities or limitations. Contact EEOC for more

information on hiring, pregnancy and maternity leave, child care, health insurance, fringe benefits, and filing charges of discrimination.

* Religious Discrimination

U.S. Commission on Civil Rights
Clearinghouse Division, Room 700
1121 Vermont Ave., NW
Washington, DC 20425   (202) 376-8105

The Commission is a primary source for civil rights laws and regulations. Numerous publications are available at no charge from the Commission on Civil Rights and they may also be available at depository libraries including:
Religion in the Constitution: A Delicate Balance. Addresses the issues of religious discrimination.

* School Desegregation and Textbooks

U.S. Commission on Civil Rights
Clearinghouse Division, Room 700
1121 Vermont Ave., NW
Washington, DC 20425   (202) 376-8105

The Commission is a primary source for civil rights laws and regulations. Numerous publications are available at no charge from the Commission on Civil Rights and they may also be available at depository libraries including:
Fair Textbooks: A Resource Guide. Lists materials aimed at reducing biases in textbooks, organizations, publishers, and their guidelines.
New Evidence on School Desegregation. This report analyzes data from 125 school districts for 1967 to 1985 to see the extent of racial imbalance in schools.

* Sex Discrimination and Filing Complaints

U.S. Commission on Civil Rights
Clearinghouse Division, Room 700
1121 Vermont Ave., NW
Washington, DC 20425   (202) 376-8105

The Commission is a primary source for civil rights laws and regulations. Numerous publications are available at no charge from the Commission on Civil Rights and they may also be available at depository libraries including:
Guide to Federal Laws and Regulations Prohibiting Sex Discrimination. Summarizes Federal laws, policies, and regulations banning sex discrimination and tells how to file complaints.

* Voting Rights

U.S. Commission on Civil Rights
Clearinghouse Division, Room 700
1121 Vermont Ave., NW
Washington, DC 20425   (202) 376-8105

The Commission is a primary source for civil rights laws and regulations. Numerous publications are available at no charge from the Commission on Civil Rights and they may also be available at depository libraries including:
Citizen's Guide to Understanding the Voting Rights Act. Explains the provisions of the 1965 Voting Rights Act, and how individuals may make complaints and comments.
The Voting Rights Act: Unfulfilled Goals. An evaluation of the status of minority voting rights in jurisdictions covered by the original provision of the 1965 act.

Who Owes Money to Whom

Any public or private company, organization, and for that matter, any individual, who borrows money and offers an asset as collateral, must file with the state at the Office of Uniform Commercial Code (UCC). A filing is made for each loan and each of the documents is available to the public. To obtain these documents is a two-step process. The first step is to request a search to see if there are any filings for a certain company. The fee for such a search usually is under $10.00. Then you will want to request copies of each of these documents. The cost for each document averages only a few dollars. This Office of Uniform Commercial Code is part of the state government and usually is located near or in the same office as the Office of Corporations which falls under the Secretary of State.

The initial search of records will provide:
   o the number of listings under one name;
   o the file number for each of the listings;
   o the date and time of filing; and
   o the name and address of the debtor.

Each UCC filing will disclose:
   o a description of the asset placed as collateral; and
   o the name and address of the secured party.

This disclosure not only provides insight into the financial security of an individual or organization, but it can also give a picture of their assets. Remember, this information is available on any public or private company or individual. The next time your brother-in-law asks you for money for a new business venture, it probably is worth the investment of a few dollars for a UCC search to see whether your relative owes money to others.

Most states will ask if you would like certified or non-certified information. Certification means that they will stand by the accuracy of the information if it is used in a court or other legal proceeding. For most cases business researchers will not need the extra procedure of certification.

Farm Loan Filings

A new law, the Food and Security Act of 1986, involves filings on crop and livestock loans. Not all states have adopted this law. However, those which have must set up an automated central filing system under the Office of Uniform Commercial Code. Many states have not adopted the law because of the expense involved in setting up the system. Under this system the office must be able to provide information on filings in 24 hours. The purpose of the system is to notify those who purchase crops from growers if the farmer has already offered that crop as collateral.

UCC Request Forms

Some states provide you with current information about recent filings over the telephone, but others will only accept your request if it is stated on a standard UCC Form. And still others will respond if you send your request in writing but will give you a discount if your query is on an official UCC Form. Most all states use UCC Form 11 for requesting information. Copies of UCC Forms for all 50 states can be obtained by calling Forms, Inc. (1-800-854-1080). The cost for any amount under 100 is sixty cents a form.

Online Access

With online capabilities one can usually search by such categories as: personal or commercial debtor, type of amendments, name of secured part, name of assigned party, and type of collateral. The following states offer online access to their files: California, Colorado, Florida, Mississippi, Montana, South Dakota, Texas, Utah, and Washington.

California, New Jersey, and New York are in the process of installing laser optical image computer systems.

Exceptions

Louisiana is the only state that has not adopted the Uniform Commercial Code. Some parishes (counties) require filings. In Georgia these filings are maintained by the Clerk of the Superior Court.

Uniform Commercial Code Offices

Alabama
Uniform Commercial Code Division, Secretary of State, Room 536, State Office Building, Montgomery, AL 36130; (305) 261-5231. Searches: Requests must be submitted in writing. The charge is $5.00 for name searches submitted on Alabama Form UCC-11, $7.00 for searches submitted by letter and $1 for each additional listing. Copies of Documents: Available for $1 per page. (Only farm filings are computerized at this time.) Farm Filings: Call (205) 261-5971. List of new farm filings published every month.

Alaska
Uniform Commercial Code Division, Department of Commerce, 3601 C Street, Suite 1132, Anchorage, AK 99503; (907) 762-2104. Searches: Requests must be submitted in writing on an Alaska Form UCC-11. The charge is $5.00 per listing. Copies of Documents: Available for $15.00 for all documents in a file (This charge includes search fee.). Farm Filings: Maintained by the County Circuit Court.

Arizona
Uniform Commercial Code Department, Secretary of State, 1700 W. Washington, Phoenix, AZ 85007; (602) 253-8221. Searches: Requests must be submitted in writing. The charge is $6.00 per name plus 50 cents per listing for copying fee. Copies of Documents: Available for 50 cents a page. Farm Filings: Maintained by the County Circuit Court.

Arkansas
Uniform Commercial Code, Secretary of State, Room 25, Little Rock, AR 72201; (501) 682-5078. Searches: Requests must be submitted in writing on a Arkansas Form UCC-11. The charge is $5.00 per debtor name. Copies of Documents: Available for $5.00 for the first three pages. Each additional page is $1.00. Farm Filings: Contact Central Farm Filings (501) 682-3458 for information. Requests for searches must be submitted on an EFS-1 form. The charge is $10.00 for 1 to 5 names and $20.00 for 6 to 10 names.

California
Uniform Commercial Code Division, Secretary of State, P.O. Box 1738, Sacramento, CA 95808; (916) 445-8061. Searches: Request must be submitted in writing. Charge is $11.00 per name. For $30.00 a one name search will be conducted and all documents copied. Copies of Documents: Available for $1.00 for the first page and 50 cents for every additional page. Farm Filings: If you

do not find them at the state level, remember some are filed with the county government (there is no standard procedure in California).

Colorado

Uniform Commercial Code Division, Secretary of State, 1560 Broadway, Suite 200, Denver, CO 30202; (303) 894-2243. Searches: A telephone information searches of two debtor's names (last four filings of each) is available at no cost. These searches are not certified. The charge for written requests is $7.00 for a search of the first year of filings for one debtor name. For each year after there is an additional $2.00 charge. A computer printout will be sent to verify the search. Copies of Documents: Available for $1.25 per page. Farm Filings: Maintained at the County Court Recorder. Online Access: Call Patti Webb at (303) 894-2227 or (303) 894-2228 for information on orientation classes for new accounts. They offer several subscription packages: 3 months for $300, 1 year for $1000 with 15 minute access time each call, 1 year for $5000 with private telephone number, and 1 year for $10,000 with direct computer hookup, which allows user to connect as many as 8 computer terminals to the system.

Connecticut

Uniform Commercial Code Division, Secretary of State, 30 Trinity Street, Hartford, CT 06106; (203) 566-4021. Searches: Request must be submitted in writing. The charge is $6.00 for request submitted on a Connecticut Form UCC-11. The charge for requests submitted by letter is $11.00. Requests received by Federal Express or Express Mail are given priority. Copies of Documents: The charge for the first three pages is $3.00, each additional page is $3.00. Farm Filings: They are not available at this time, but as computerization of this office progresses they will be. Maintained now by the County Recorder.

Delaware

Uniform Commercial Code Section, P.O. Box 793, John G. Townsend Building, Dover, DE 19903; (302) 736-4279 (Choose 8 for UCC recorded message, choose 0 for a UCC service representative). Searches: Requests must be submitted in writing. $10 per search. Copies of Documents: Available for $2 per page. Farm Filings: Maintained by this office.

District of Columbia

Recorder of Deeds, 515 D Street N.W., Washington, D.C. 20001; (202) 727-5374. Searches: Requests must be submitted in writing. The charge is $15.00 for each secured party. Copies of Documents: Available for $1.00 per page, plus $1.00 for certification.

Florida

Uniform Commercial Code Division, Department of State, P.O. Box 5588, Tallahassee, FL 32314; (904) 487-6845. Searches: Call 904-487-6063. The staff will search three names at no cost. For printed verification a written request must be submitted. The charge is $7.50 per name and DBA's (Doing Business As) $15.00. Copies of Documents: Available for $1.00 per page. Farm Filings: Filings are maintained by the County Circuit Court. Online Access: UCC Division, 409 E. Gaines Street, Tallahassee, FL 32399; (904) 487-6001. Write or call and they will send you an information booklet that describes the service they have available through CompuServe. The cost for online service is $25.00 per hour.

Georgia

The State of Georgia does not maintain Uniform Commercial Code Filings. Contact the Clerk of Superior Court at the County level for these filings.

Hawaii

Uniform Commercial Code, Bureau of Conveyance, P.O. Box 2867, Honolulu, HI 96803; (808) 548-3108. Searches: Requests must be submitted in writing on a Hawaii Form UCC-3 or any states UCC-11. The charge is $1.00 per debtor name, plus an additional 50 cents per listing. Copies of Documents: Available for 50 cents per page. Farm Filings: Maintained by this office.

Idaho

Uniform Commercial Code Division, Secretary of State, State House, Boise, ID 83720; (208) 334-3191. Searches: Information may be requested by phone or in writing. The charge is $7.00 for phone requests and $6.00 for written requests. An additional $1.00 is charged if the request is not submitted on an Idaho UCC-4 Form. Copies of Documents: The charge for copying all documents involved in a search is $6.00. Farm Filings: A 24-hour Expedite Service is available for these filings. The charge is $17.00.

Illinois

Uniform Commercial Code Division, Secretary of State, Centennial Building, Room 30, 2nd & Edwards Street, Springfield, IL 62756; (217) 782-7518. Searches: All requests must be in writing. The charge for requests on non-standard forms is $10.00. Requests submitted on a Illinois Form UCC-11.7 is $5.00. Copies of Documents: The charge is 50 cents per page. Farm Filings: If you do not find them at the state level remember some are filed with the county government. (There is no standard procedure in Illinois.) Payment for searches and copies may be charged to VISA or Master Charge. Microfilm: Copies of all documents filed within the month are available on a subscription basis for $2.50 a month. Daily Computer Printout Listing: Available for $2.50 a

month. Online Access: For information write the above office. A brochure explaining the system will be sent to you.

Indiana

Uniform Commercial Code Division, Secretary of State, State House, Room 105, Indianapolis, IN 46204; (317) 232-6393. Searches: All searches must be requested in writing. An Indiana Form UCC-11 is preferred. The charge is $1.00 per debtor's name and 50 cents for each filing. All requests for searches received by Federal Express or Express Mail are given a priority. Copies of Documents: The charge is 50 cents per page and $1.00 for certification. Farm Filings: If you do not find them at the state level remember some are filed with the county government. (There is no standard procedure in Indiana.)

Iowa

Uniform Commercial Code Division, Secretary of State, Hoover Building, Des Moines, IA 50319; (515) 281-3326. Searches: Information may be requested by phone or in writing. The cost of a phone search is $5.00, plus $1.00 for a printout. The charge for a non-standard request is $6.00 and $5.00 for a request submitted on an Iowa Form UCC-11. Copies of Documents: The fee is $1 for each copy requested. Farm Filings: Maintained by this office.

Kansas

Uniform Commercial Code Division, Secretary of State, State House, Topeka, KS 66612; (913) 296-3650. Searches: Phone requests are accepted from those holding an account with the UCC. The charge for phone requests is $15.00 per name for verbal information and $5.00 for an order. The charge for written requests is $5.00. If staffing permits, all requests are filled within 24 hours. Copies of Documents: The charge is a $1.00 a page. There is no additional charge for certification. Farm Filings: This office has handled farm filings since 1984. Filings prior to that year are maintained by the County Register of Deeds.

Kentucky

Uniform Commercial Code Division, Office of Secretary of State, State Capitol Building, Frankfort, KY 40601; (501) 564-2848 Ext. 16. Searches: All searches of UCC filings are conducted by outside agencies. The UCC Division will provide a list of these agencies. Farm Filings: Filings are maintained by the County Circuit Court.

Louisiana

The state of Louisiana has not adopted the Uniform Commercial Code. Filings may be maintained at the Parish (county) level.

Maine

Uniform Commercial Code Division, Secretary of State, State House Station 101, Augusta, ME 04333; (207) 289-4177. Searches: All requests must be submitted in writing. The charge is $5.00. Copies of Documents: The charge is $1.00 for each document. Farm Filings: Maintained by this office.

Maryland

Uniform Commercial Code Division, State Department of Assessments and Taxation, 301 West Preston Street, Baltimore, MD 21201; (301) 225-1340. Searches: The State of Maryland does not conduct searches. If you write the above address, they will provide a list of title companies that do provide that service. Farm Filings: Maintained by this office.

Massachusetts

Uniform Commercial Code Division, Secretary of State, Room 17101, 1 Ashburton Place, Boston, MA 02108; (617) 727-2860. Searches: Requests must be submitted in writing on a Form UCC-11 (any states form is acceptable). The charge is $5.00 for an information computer printout and $10.00 for computer printout with face page. (These charges are due to change with the present legislature.) Requests sent by Federal Express or Express Mail are given priority. Copies of Documents: The charge is $2.00 per page and $3.00 for certification. Farm Filings: Maintained by this office. Online Access: Plans are to offer this capability by mid-1989.

Michigan

Uniform Commercial Code Section, P.O. Box 30197, Lansing, MI 48909-7697; (517) 322-1495. Searches: Telephone requests are handled on an expedite basis. The charge is $25.00. You must have an account number with the UCC Section to obtain this service. The charge for requests submitted on non-standard forms is $6.00. Requests submitted on a Michigan Form UCC-11 is $3.00. Requests sent by Federal Express or Express Mail are given priority. Copies of Documents: The charge is $1.00 per page and $1.00 for certification. Farm Filings: Filings are maintained by the County Recorder of Deeds.

Minnesota

Uniform Commercial Code Division, Secretary of State, 180 State Office Building, St. Paul, MN 55155; (612) 296-2434. Searches: Requests must be submitted in writing. The charge for a request submitted on a Minnesota Form UCC-11 is $7.00. The charge for a request submitted on a non-standard form is $12.00. These charges include information on 5 listings and/or 5 copies. The charge for additional listings is 50 cents a listing. Copies of Documents: Available for 50 cents a page. The charge for certified copies is $1.00. Farm

Filings: Available from the County Recorder of Deeds unless the debtor is a non-resident or a corporation and then they are filed with the UCC Division.

Mississippi

Uniform Commercial Code Division, Secretary of State, P.O. Box 136, Jackson, MS 39205; (601) 359-1350. Searches: Phone information is available at no cost. Information available by phone is: approximate number of filings, secured party, file numbers, and date and time of filing. The charge for written requests submitted on Mississippi Form UCC-11 is $5.00. The charge for written requests submitted on non-standard forms is $10.00. Copies of Documents: Available for $2.00 a pages. Farm Filings: Farm Filings are maintained by the above office. Online Access: Contact Deborah Boler (601) 359-1350. The cost is approximately $50 a month.

Missouri

Uniform Commercial Code Division, Secretary of State, P.O. Box 1159, Jefferson City, MO 65102; (314) 751-2360. Searches: Information searches will be given over the phone. These searches are not certified and are free of charge. (This service is not available on Mondays or the day after a holiday.) The charge for written requests is $4.00 Copies of Documents: Available for $4.00 per listing. Farm Filings: Maintained by the County Recorder.

Montana

Uniform Commercial Code Bureau, Secretary of State, Capitol Station, Helena, MT 59620; (406) 444-5368. Searches: Requests for searches will be accepted by phone. The charge is $5.00, the same as for a written request. All searches are conducted the day of the request. Copies of Documents: Available for 50 cents a page. The charge for certification is $2.00. Farm Filings: Maintained in this office. Online Access: Contact Linda Watson (406) 444-5368. She will send you an information brochure. The charge for a search is $2.00. Computer must be IBM compatible.

Nebraska

Uniform Commercial Code Division, P.O. Box 95104, 301 Centennial Mall S., Lincoln, NE 68509; (402) 471-4080. Searches: The charge for requests by phone is $1.00 per debtor's names. No verification is sent. The charge for written requests is $3.00. A computer printout containing a list of the filings is sent to the requester. Copies of Documents: Available for 50 cents per page. The charge for certification is $4.00. Farm Filings: Maintained by the county government, but the above office will submit a request for a search for you. The county will bill you directly for its service. Magnetic Tape: Considering offering magnetic tape copies of UCC filings with 30 day updates.

Nevada

Uniform Commercial Code Division, Secretary of State, Capitol Complex, Carson City, NV 89710; (702) 885-5298. Searches: Only written requests for information will be accepted. The charge is $6.00 for a request submitted on a Nevada Form UCC-3. The charge for requests submitted on a non-standard form is $6.30. For an additional $10.00 your request will be expedited. This fee must be paid with a separate check. Copies of Documents: Available for $1.00 per page and an additional $6.00 for certified copies. Farm Filings: Maintained at the office of the County Recorder.

New Hampshire

Uniform Commercial Code Division, Secretary of State, State House, Room 204, 107 N. Main Street, Concord, NH 03301; (603) 271-3276 or 271-3277. Searches: Requests must be submitted in writing. The charge for a request submitted on a New Hampshire Form UCC-11 is $3.00. The charge for a request submitted on a non-standard form is $4.00. Copies of Documents: Available for 50 cents per file. Farm Filings: Maintained by this office.

New Jersey

Uniform Commercial Code Division, State Department, State Capitol Building, CN300, Trenton, NJ 08625; (609) 530-6426. Searches: Requests must be submitted in writing on a New Jersey Form UCC-1 or a security agreement signed by the debtor. The charge is $25.00. Expedite Service is available for $5. The requester pays the express mail expense. Copies of Documents: Available for $1.00 per page. Farm Filings: Maintained by the county and the state. At the county level you will want to check with the County Recorder.

New Mexico

Uniform Commercial Code Division, Bureau of Operations, Secretary of State, Executive Legislative Building, Room 400, Santa Fe, NM 87503; (505) 827-3600. Searches: The State of New Mexico does not do searches, but they will provide you with a list of abstract companies that are authorized to do so. Farm Filings: This office located at the same address with conduct a search for $15.00. Their phone number is (505) 827-3610. They will follow-up the verbal report with a written statement. Online Access: Available soon.

New York

Uniform Commercial Code Division, Secretary of State, P.O. Box 7021, Albany, NY 12231; (518) 474-4763. Searches: Requests must be submitted in writing. For requests submitted on a New York Form UCC-11 the charge is $7.00. For requests submitted on non-standard forms the charge is $12.00. Copies of Documents: Available for 50 cents per page. Farm Filings: Maintained by both the state and the County Recorder.

North Carolina

Uniform Commercial Code Division, Secretary of State, 300 N. Salisbury Street, Raleigh, NC 27611; (919) 733-4205. Searches: Requests must be submitted in writing, preferably on a North Carolina Form UCC-11. The charge is $8.00. All requests are handled within 24 hours of receipt. Copies of Documents: Available for $1.00 per page. Farm Filings: Maintained by this office and the County Recorder.

North Dakota

Uniform Commercial Code Division, Secretary of State, State Capitol, Bismark, ND 58505; (701) 224-2900. Searches: Requests must be submitted in writing preferably on a North Dakota UCC-11. The charge is $5.00. Copies of Documents: Available for $5.00 for the first three pages and $1.00 a page for additional pages. Farm Filings: The Central Notice staff will take requests for searches over the phone for crop and livestock filings. The charge is $2.00. Written requests are the same as stated above. Farm equipment and real estate filings are optional and may be maintained by the state or the County Recorder of Deeds.

Ohio

Uniform Commercial Code Division, Secretary of State, 30 E. Broad Street, 14th Floor, Columbus, OH 43266-0418; (614) 466-9316. Searches: Phone requests for information are not certified and are free of charge. Written requests should be submitted on an Ohio Form UCC-11. The charge is $9.00. It takes 6 months for these searches to be conducted. Expedite service is available for $19.00. These requests are processed in 5 working days. Copies of Documents: Available for $1.00 per page. Farm Filings: Maintained by the County Recorder.

Oklahoma

Uniform Commercial Code Office, Oklahoma County Clerk, 320 Robert S. Kerr, Room 105, Oklahoma City, OK 73102; (405) 278-1521. Searches: Requests must be submitted in writing. The charge is $5.00. Copies of Documents: Available for $1.00 per page. The charge for certified copies is $1.00. Farm Filings: Maintained by this office.

Oregon

Uniform Commercial Code Division, Secretary of State, Room 41, State Capitol, Salem, OR 97310; (503) 378-4146. Searches: Requests must be submitted in writing, preferably on a Oregon Form UCC-25R. The charge is $3.75 per debtor's name. Copies of Documents: Available for $1.50 per page. Farm Filings: Maintained by this office. The charge for a search is $15.00 per name. Monthly reports by agricultural product code are available on microfilm or paper copy.

Pennsylvania

Uniform Commercial Code Division, Corporation Bureau, State Department, 308 N. Office Building, Harrisburg, PA 17120; (717) 787-8712. Searches: Requests for searches must be submitted in writing on a Pennsylvania Form UCC-11. The charge is $5.00. Copies of Documents: Available for $1.00 per page. Farm Filings: Maintained by this office.

Rhode Island

Uniform Commercial Code Division, Secretary of State, 270 Westminster Mall, Providence, RI 02903; (401) 277-2521. Searches: Requests must be submitted in writing. The charge is $5.00. Copies of Documents: Available for 50 cents per copy. Farm Filings: Maintained by the City Recorder of Deeds.

South Carolina

Uniform Commercial Code Division, Secretary of State, P.O. Box 11350, Columbia, SC 29211; (803) 734-2175. Searches: Requests must be submitted in writing, preferably on a South Carolina Form UCC-4. The charge is $5.00 per debtor name. Priority is given to requests received by Express Mail or Federal Express. Copies of Documents: Available for $1.00 per page. Farm Filings: Maintained by County Recorder.

South Dakota

Central Filing System, Secretary of State, 500 E. Capitol, Pierre, SD 57501; (605) 773-4422. Searches: Telephone requests for searches are accepted from those with prepaid deposit accounts. Written requests are accepted on any UCC standard request form. The charge is $4.00. Copies of Documents: Available for 50 cents per page. Farm Filings: Maintained by this office. Online access at no charge is available. Online Access: Available by subscription. Average charge is 50 to 60 cents a search. The system can be used by those with IBM compatible computers and Hayes compatible modems.

Tennessee

Uniform Commercial Code Section, Secretary of State, J.K. Polk Building, Suite 1800, Nashville, TN 37219; (615) 741-3276. Searches: Requests must be submitted in writing, preferably on a Tennessee Form UCC-11. The charge is $5.00. Copies of Documents: Available for $1.00 per copy. Farm Filings: Maintained by this office and County Recorder. It is necessary to check with both offices.

Information on People, Companies, and Mailing Lists

Texas

Uniform Commercial Code, Secretary of State, P.O. Box 13193, Capitol Station, Austin, TX 78711; (512) 462-1155. Searches: The charge for a search requested by phone is $25.00. The charge for written requests submitted on Texas Form UCC-11 is $10.00. The charge for written requests submitted on a non-standard form is $25.00. Copies of Documents: Available for $1.50 per page with a $5.00 minimum charge. The charge for certification is an additional $5.00. Farm Filings: Maintained by the above office. Online Access: It is projected to be available by the Fall of 1988. For further information contact: Jacob Young (512) 463-5609.

Utah

Uniform Commercial Code Division, Business Regulation Department, 160 East Third Street, Salt Lake City, UT 84110; (801) 530-6020. Searches: The charge is $10 per debtor name. Copies of Documents: Available for 30 cents per page, minimum of $1.00. Farm Filings: Central Filings maintained these files. Phone requests are accepted. The charge is $5.00. Online Access: Available on a subscription basis. The charge is $25.00 per month. Contact Peter VanAlstine (801) 530-6027 for further information. Computer must be IBM compatible.

Vermont

Uniform Commercial Code, Secretary of State, Pavillion Office Building, Montpelier, VT 05602; (802) 328-2388. Searches: Requests for searches must be submitted in writing on a Vermont Form UCC-11. The charge is $5 per debtor name, plus 50 cents for an information sheet containing debtor's name, secured party, file number, and date and time filed. Copies of Documents: Available for $2.00 per page. Farm Filings: Central Filings Section maintains these files. Contact the above address. The charges for searches is the same, but they do accept phone requests for searches.

Virginia

Uniform Commercial Code Division, State Corporation Commission, P.O. Box 1197, Richmond, VA 23209; (804) 786-3689. Searches: Requests for searches must be submitted in writing. The charge is $6.00 per debtor name. Copies of Documents: Available for $1.00 per page. There is an additional charge of $6.00 for certification. Farm Filings: Maintained by this office and the County Recorder.

Washington

Uniform Commercial Code Division, Department of Licensing, P.O. Box 9660, 405 Black Lake Place, Olympia, WA 98502; (206) 753-2523. Searches: Requests must be submitted in writing. The charge is $4.00 for all the listings of one debtor. Copies of Documents: Available for $8.00. This includes search fee, plus copies of all documents for one debtor. Farm Filings: Maintained in this office. Microfilm: Copies of each days filings are available for $5.00 per day. Online Access: Contact Shirley Wheelock for information on how to set up a prepaid account. Subscription availability is limited at this time.

West Virginia

Uniform Commercial Code Division, Secretary of State, West Wing, Room 131, State Capitol Building, Charleston, WV 25305; (304) 345-4000. Searches: Phone requests for information are accepted. The charge is $5.00. Written requests are preferred. The charge is $2.00. Copies of Documents: Available for $1.00 for the first page, additional pages are 75 cents. The charge for certification is $5.00. Farm Filings: Maintained by the County Recorder.

Wisconsin

Uniform Commercial Code Division, Secretary of State, Madison, WI 53707; (608) 266-3087. Searches: Phone requests for information are accepted. The charge is $5.00 per filing. The charge for written requests is $5.00 per debtor name. Copies of Documents: Available for $1.00 per document. Certification is an additional 50 cents. Farm Filings: Maintained by the County Register of Deeds.

Wyoming

Uniform Commercial Code, Secretary of State, State Capitol Building, Cheyenne, WY 82002; (307) 777-6924. Searches: Phone requests for information are accepted for 2 debtor names. The charge is $5.00 per debtor name. The charge for written requests is the same. Copies of Documents: Available for 50 cents per page. Farm Filings: Maintained by this office and the County Recorder.

Professional People and Local Businesses

Buried within each state government are several and sometimes dozens of offices where individuals as well as business establishments must register in order to perform certain types of services and commercial activities. State laws require accountants, architects, concert promoters, employment agencies, podiatrists and numerous other professionals to register. The data derived from these regulatory boards provide unique opportunities for researchers and marketing executives to obtain demographic data, mailing lists and even competitive information.

Mailing Lists

Mailing lists offer the biggest potential from these offices. The unusual as well as the mundane are available in a variety of formats. Not only are many of these lists not accessible commercially, if they are, you can get them from the states cheaper and usually without restrictions. In other words, you can purchase a state list once, and use it over and over again. Commercial list brokers will never let you do this. Here is a sampling of mailing lists:

o 1 cent per name for all dentists in Kentucky;
o free directory of real estate agents in Arizona;
o $40 for a list of all nurses in Colorado;
o a mailing list of all contractors in Arkansas for $10;
o 2 cents per name for all swimming pool dealers in Florida;
o a listing of librarians in Georgia;
o 4 cents a name for all the psychologists in California;
o $100 for a computer tape of all accountants in Florida;
o $1.45 per 1,000 names for all medical practices in Illinois; or
o free list of all attorneys in Maine.

Most every state provides mailing labels in the form of cheshire or pressure sensitive labels. In many cases, the charge is nominal.

Common Lists and Specialized Rosters

Every state maintains a variety of standard rosters. Some states keep as few of 20 lists and others have over 100. Names of licensed professionals and business establishments available from most every state include:

o medical professionals
o accountants
o real estate agents and brokers
o veterinarians
o barbers
o insurance agents
o architects
o nursing homes
o cosmetologists
o hearing aid dealers
o social workers
o lawyers

After reviewing the rundown of all 50 states and District of Columbia licensing boards, you will be amazed at the variety of lists that are within easy reach. In most cases you can obtain printouts for such licensed services as:

o burglar alarm contractors in Maine
o tow truck operations in Minnesota
o hat cleaners in Ohio
o ski areas in Michigan
o day care centers in New York
o security guards in New Hampshire
o outfitters in Colorado

Computer Tapes and Diskettes: Selections and Sorting Options

Many states can provide the information on magnetic tape and some are beginning to offer data on IBM PC compatible diskettes. Most every state will allow you to select names by zip code or county whether the licensee is active or inactive. Some states will allow you to select certain demographic characteristics, such as years of formal education.

Markets and Demographics

With a little creativity and resourcefulness, the information at licensing boards can provide pertinent clues in formulating a market profile. For example, you can determine:

o which counties have the highest concentration
    of psychologists;
o what is the average number of years of schooling for real
    estate agents in certain zip codes;
o for the past 10 years which zip codes have experienced the
    fastest growth for accountants;
o the number of out-of-state licensed paralegals;
o which counties have the most podiatrists or veterinarians per
    capita; or,
o how many insurance agents are there in a given county.

Some states have the capability of performing historical analysis, while others will supply you with the raw data.

Competitive Intelligence

Depending upon the type of business you are investigating, pertinent competitive information may be ferreted from state licensing boards. For example, if you are a dentist, mobile home dealer, nursing home administrator or real estate broker, you could plot how many competitors you are up against in a given zip code or county. Or, you may be able to determine how many opticians work for an eye care chain, or tax consultants for a given tax preparer.

Organization of Licensing Boards

Approximately half of the states have a central office which is responsible for all licensed professions. For such states it is a relatively easy process to obtain information because it is all generated from a single source. However, the other states make this task difficult. Typically, each separate independent

Information on People, Companies, and Mailing Lists

board maintains information for one profession. The only connection these agencies have to the state government is that their board members are appointed by the governor.

States With Restrictions

Six states have laws that place certain stipulations on the use of their lists of licensed professionals. In these cases the data may not be used for commercial purposes. Iowa, Montana, New York, North Dakota, Rhode Island and Washington have such restrictions. The District of Columbia, Hawaii and Kansas do not release addresses but will provide names.

State Licensing Boards

Alabama

Contact: State Occupational Information Coordinating Commission (SOICC), Bell Building, 207 Montgomery St. #400, Montgomery, AL 36130 (205) 261-2990. This office offers the publication, *Licensed Occupation*, which contains addresses for all state licensing boards. Licensing Boards/Professions: Accountants, Aircraft Personnel, Architects, Attorney-at-Law, Auctioneers, Audiologists, Speech Pathologists, Bar Pilots, Water Transportation Personnel, Boxer and Wrestler Trainers, Classroom Teachers, Coal Mine Foremen/Mine Electricians, Cosmetologists, Counselors, Dentists, Dental Hygienists, Chiropractors, Doctors of Medicine, Physician's Assistants, Surgeon's Assistants, School Bus Drivers, Embalmer/Funeral Directors, Engineer-in-Training and Professional Engineers, Land Surveyors, Firefighters, Foresters, General Contractors, Hearing Aid Specialists, Heating and Air Conditioning Contractors, Insurance Agents, Interior Designers, Landscape Architects, Landscape Horticulturist/Planters, Pest Control Operators and Fumigators, Tree Surgeons, Law Enforcement Personnel, Nurses, Nursing Home Administrators, Optometrists, Pharmacists, Physical Therapists, Physical Therapist Assistants, Plumbers, Podiatrists, Polygraph Examiners, Psychologists, Real Estate Brokers, Security Salespersons, Social Workers, Veterinarians. Types of Lists Available: Format of information available varies from board to board. Rosters are free of charge from some boards. Computer Printouts: Available on a cost recovery basis from some boards. Mailing Labels: Available on a cost recovery basis from some Boards. Requester must supply labels. Magnetic Tape: Some board make available tapes on a cost recovery basis plus $15 for the tape. Data can be sorted by Zip Code, county and city. For further information regarding data processing capabilities contact: Rick Courson or Deryl Flowers (205) 261-3100.

Alaska

Contact: Division of Occupational Licensing, Department of Commerce and Economic Development, State of Alaska, PO Box D, Juneau, AK 99811-0800 (907 465-2534. The above office serves as the central licensing agency for the state. Licensing Boards/Professions: State Athletic Commission, Architects, Engineers, Land Surveyors, Audiologists, Barbers and Hairdressers, Chiropractors, Collection Agencies, Construction Contractors, Concert Promoters, Dental Professionals, Dispensing Opticians, Electrical Administrators, Geologists, Guides, Hearing Aid Dealers, Marine Pilots, Physicians, Morticians, Naturopaths, Nursing, Nursing Home Administrators, Optometrists, Pharmacists, Physical Therapists, Psychologists, Public Accountants, Veterinarians. Types of Lists Available: Directories are available for each profession for $5 to $20 each (Names and addresses included). Magnetic Tape: Requester must supply tape plus $40 per hour computer time.

Arizona

Contact: Arizona Department of Revenue, 1700 West Washington, Phoenix, AZ 85007 (602) 542-4576. This office publishes *A Guide To State Licensing Requirements*, which contains addresses for all state licensing boards. Licensing Boards/Professions: Pharmacists, Physical Therapists, Podiatrists, Psychologists, Chiropractors, Dentists, Teachers, Homeopathic Specialists, Veterinarians, Medical Examiners, Radiologic Technicians, Naturopathic Physicians, Nurses, Opticians, Optometrists, Osteopaths, Barbers, Cosmetologists, Department of Racing, Real Estate Brokers, Contractors, Technical Registrators, Insurance Agents, Physician Assistants, Liquor Licensees, Nursing Care Administrators. Types of Lists Available: (Since format of information varies from board to board, examples of two boards are given.) Board of Nursing Directory is available at no cost. It contains names and addresses. Medical Examiners Directory is available for $10 and lists names and addresses.

Arkansas

Contact: Administrative Office, Secretary of State, State Capitol Building, Little Rock, AR 72201 (501) 682-2345. This office can direct you to the proper licensing authority. The Arkansas Industrial Development Commission (One State Capitol Mall, Little Rock, AR 72201, (501) 371-1121, publishes *Taking Care of Business in Arkansas: A Directory of Guidelines and Resources*, which contains the addresses for the following licensing agencies. Licensing Boards/Professions: Architects, Abstracters, Accountants, Barber Examiners,

Burial Association, Funeral Directors, Contractors, Cosmetologists, Dental Examiners, Electricians, Speech Pathologists, Audiologists, Nurses, Pharmacists, Real Estate Brokers, Savings & Loan Institutions, Veterinary Engineers, Land Surveyors, Athletic Trainers, Chiropractors, Collection Agencies, Counselors, Embalmers, Foresters, Landscape Architects, Manufactured Home Builders, Physicians, Opticians, Optometrists, Podiatrists, Psychologists, Sanitarians, Social Workers, Soil Classifiers, Therapy Technologists. Types of Lists Available: Since the format of information varies from board to board, examples include the Board of Nursing Roster which contains three rosters for $20 each (RNs, LPNs, and LPTNs). Computer Printout: List of all contractors is available for $10 with selections by Zip Code and type of contractor. Requester is charged $10 plus computer time for this service. Floppy Disk: Master file available if staffing permits. Requester must provide disk plus pay computer time charges.

California

Contact: State of California, Department of Consumer Affairs, 1020 N. St., Sacramento, CA 95814 (916) 445-1254 (N. CA), (415) 620-4360 (San Francisco Bay area), (213) 557-0967 (So. CA). This office can provide you with the publication, *California License Handbook* ($10.75) which contains addresses for all state licensing boards. Licensing Boards/Professions: Professional Engineers, Cosmetologists, Fabric Care Technicians, Physical Therapists, Medical Quality Assurance, Physician's Assistants, Chiropractors, Acupuncture Specialists, Accountants, Psychologists, Registered Nurses, Pharmacists, Architects, Funeral Directors, Embalmers, Landscape Architects, Veterinarians, Animal Health Technicians, Home Furnishings Decorators, Collection and Investigative Agents, Dentists, Dental Auxiliaries, Barbers, Behavioral Scientists, Optometrists, Shorthand Reporters, Structural Pest Control Operators, Athletic Trainers, Vocational Nurses, Psychiatric Technicians, Osteopaths, Electronic Repair Dealers, Personnel Services, Geologists and Geophysicists, Dispensing Opticians/Contact Lens Examiners, Respiratory Care Specialists, Nursing Home Admistrators, Podiatrists, Hearing Aid Dispensers, Speech Pathologists, Audiologists, Tax Preparers. Computer Printout: Lists of licensees of each profession available for four cents per name, with a minimum charge of $50 per agency. Mailing Labels: Cheshire and Avery Labels available. Same charge as printout. Magnetic Tape: The basic rate is three cents per name, with a minimum charge of $50 per agency. There is a $30 charge per tape with selection choices available by Zip Code and county order. For special data processing orders: Data Processing Special Jobs Unit, Department of Consumer Affairs, 1020 N. Street, Room 577, Sacramento, CA 95814 (916) 323-7018.

Colorado

Contact: Department of Regulatory Agencies, State Services Building, Room 110, 1525 Sherman Street, Denver, CO 80203 (303) 866-4456. The above office serves as the state central licensing agency. Licensing Board/Professions: Accountants, Architects, Banking, Barbers, Cosmetologists, Chiropractors, Dentists, Electricians, Engineers, Hearing Aid Dealers, Insurance Agents, Land Surveyors, Mobile Home Dealers, Nurses, Nursing Home Administrators, Optometrists, Outfitters, Pharmacists & Pharmacies, Physical Therapists, Physicians, Plumbers, Psychologists, Race Tracks & Events, Realtors, Savings & Loans, Securities, Ski Lifts Operators, Social Workers, Veterinarians. Computer Printouts: Complete master file costs $3500.00. Individual lists of professionals available for 50 cents a page. Magnetic Tape: Complete master file also costs $3500.00. Mailing Labels: Requester must provide labels and cost is $1 for 36 names. Contact for Independent Boards: Department of Regulatory Agencies, State Services Building, Room 110, 1525 Sherman Street, Denver, CO 80203 (360) 866-4456. This office can provide you with the publication *Doing Business In Colorado* ($3) which contains addresses for the Department of Health (Emergency Medical Technicians, Radiographers, Speech Pathologists), Department of Institutions (Alcohol & Drug Counselors, Psychiatric Technicians).

Connecticut

Contact: Occupational Licensing Division, Department of Consumer Products, 165 Capitol Avenue, Hartford, CT 06106 (203) 566-3290. This office serves as the licensing division for the following occupations. Licensed Occupations: Electricians, Plumbers, Heating and Cooling Specialists, Well Drillers, Elevator Installers, Home Improvement Contractors, Arborists, TV and Radio Repair Specialists. Computer Printouts: Available on a cost recovery basis. Mailing Labels: Pressure sensitive and cheshire labels available on a cost recovery basis. Data can be sorted in alphabetical or Zip Code order. Licensed Health Professions: Contact Phillip Mollison, Department of Health Services, 150 Washington St., Hartford, CT 06106 (203) 566-2038 (this office serves as a central licensing agency for the following health professions): Physicians, Dentists, Optometrists, Osteopaths, Naturopaths, Homeopaths, Chiropractors, Psychologists, Registered Nurses, Licensed Practical Nurses, Dental Hygienists, Registered Physical Therapists, Hypertrichologists, Audiologists, Speech Pathologists, Podiatrists, Hairdressers, Barbers, Embalmers, Funeral Directors, Sewer Cleaners, Sewer Installers, Sewer Install/Clean, Registered Sanitarians, Nursing Home Administrators, Hearing Aid Dealers, Opticians, Veterinarians, Occupational Therapists, Medical Group Shops. Computer Printouts: Costs are $65 minimum charge first 5,000 names, $5 per 1,000 thereafter. Mailing Labels: Pressure sensitive cost $65 minimum charge first 1,000 names, $10 per 1,000 thereafter. Cheshire labels cost $65 minimum charge first 5,000 names, $5 per 1,000 thereafter. Magnetic Tape: The cost is $65 per profession plus $25 for the tape. $3500 for all professions, plus $25 for the tape. Selection choices include sorting by Zip Code and city. Other Licensed Professions: Contact Professional Licensing Division, 165 Capitol Avenue, Hartford, CT 06106 (203) 566-1814: Architects, Landscape Architects, Engineers, Engineers-in-Training, Land

Surveyors, Pharmacists, Patent Medicine Distributors, Mobile Manufactured Home Parks. Computer Printouts: Also available on a cost recovery basis. Mailing Labels: Cheshire and pressure sensitive label available on a cost recovery basis. Data can be sorted in alphabetical or Zip Code order. For further information regarding computer printouts and mailing label order contact Jerry Riley, (203) 566-2538.

Delaware

Contact: Division of Professional Regulation, PO Box 1401, O'Neil Building, Dover, Delaware 19903 (302) 736-4522. This office serves as the administrative agency for the following state licensing boards and commissions. Licensed Professionals: Architects, Accountants, Landscape Architects, Cosmetologists, Barbers, Podiatrists, Chiropractors, Dentists, Electricians, Adult Entertainment, Physicians, Nurses, Real Estate Brokers, Harness Racing, Land Surveyors, Private Employment Agencies, Gaming Control, Athletic (Wrestling and Boxing), Deadly Weapons Dealers, Nursing Home Administrators, Funeral Directors, Social Workers, Speech Pathologists, Hearing Aid Dealers, Audiologists, Psychologists, Veterinarians, Optometrists, Occupational Therapists, Pharmacists, River Boat Pilots, Thoroughbred Racing. Computer Printouts: All lists are available for $25 except for the nursing roster which costs $40.00. Magnetic Tape: All professions cost $25 each, except nursing roster which costs $40.00. Mailing Labels: Self-adhesive labels cost same price as printouts. Lists can be sorted alphabetically or by Zip code.

District of Columbia

Contact: Department of Consumer and Regulatory Affairs, 614 H Street NW, Washington, DC 20001 (202) 727-7170. The above office serves as the state central licensing agency. Licensing Board/Professions: Accountants, Architects, Barbers, Cosmetologists, Dentists, Dietitian, Electricians, Funeral Directors, Physicians, Nurses, Nursing Home Administrators, Occupational Therapists, Optometrists, Pharmacists, Physical Therapists, Plumbers, Podiatrists, Engineers, Psychologists, Real Estate Agents, Refrigeration and Air Conditioning Specialists, Social Workers, Steam and Other Operating Engineers, Veterinarians. Types of Lists Available: Rosters of all professionals available but include name only because addresses and phone numbers are confidential.

Florida

Contact: Florida Department of Professional Regulation, Attn: Ms. Chiquita Spikes, 130 N. Monroe St., Tallahassee, FL 32301 (904) 488-8860. This office serves as the central administrative agency for the state licensing boards. Licensing Boards/Professions: Accountants, Architects, Barbers, Chiropractors, Construction Industry, Cosmetologists, Dentists, Dispensing Opticians, Electrical Contractors, Professional Engineers and Land Surveyors, Landscape Architects, Funeral Directors and Embalmers, Medical Examiners, Hearing Aid Dispensers, Naturopathics, Nursing Home Administrators, Nurses, Optometrists, Osteopaths, Pharmacists, Pilot Commissioners, Podiatrists, Psychologists, Real Estate Brokers, Veterinarians, Acupuncture Technicians, Radiological Health Technicians, Laboratory Services, Entomology Specialists, Emergency Medical Personnel, Licensure and Certification (Swimming Pools), Banking and Finance. Computer Printout: List is available for $5.08 per 1000 names, plus $55 set up fee for the computer time. Mailing Labels: Pressure Sensitive Labels cost $20 per 1000 names, plus a $55 set up fee for computer time. Cheshire Labels - Print cost is same as for computer printout. Magnetic Tape: Cost is $100 per file. There is a charge of $100 set-up fee plus a $13.65 per reel cost. Selection choices can be run by county or Zip Code order.

Georgia

Contact: Examining Board Division, Secretary of State, 166 Pryor Street, SW, Atlanta, GA 30303 (404) 656-1776. This office can refer you to the appropriate state examining board and provide you with the publication, *Joint Secretary Rules For Licensing*, which contains addresses for all the boards. Licensing Boards/Professions: Accountants, Architects, Athletic Trainers, Auctioneers, Barbers, Chiropractors, Construction Industry, Cosmetologists, Professional Counselors, Social Workers, Marriage and Family Therapists, Dietitians, Dentists, Engineers, Land Surveyors, Foresters, Funeral Directors/Embalmers, Geologists, Hearing Aid Dealers and Dispensers, Landscape Architects, Librarians, Physicians, Nurses, Nursing Home Administrators, Occupational Therapists, Dispensing Opticians, Optometrists, Pharmacists, Physical Therapists, Podiatrists, Polygraph Testers, Practical Nurses, Private Detectives and Security Agencies, Psychologists, Recreation Specialists, Sanitarians, Speech Pathologists, Audiologists, Used Car Dealers, Used Motor Vehicle Dismantlers, Rebuilders, and Salvage Dealers, Veterinarians, Water and Wastewater Treatment Plant Operators and Laboratory Analysts. Computer Printouts: Available for each profession for 3 cents a name. Mailing Labels: Cheshire labels available for 3 cents a name. Individual licensing boards must be contacted for selection choices.

Hawaii

Contact: Office of the Director, Department of Commerce and Consumer Affairs, PO Box 541, Honolulu, HI 96809 (808) 548-4100. The above office serves as the central administrative agency for the state licensing boards. Licensing Boards/Professions: Accountants, Acupuncture Specialists, Barbers, Boxers, Chiropractors, Contractors, Cosmetologists, Dental Examiners, Detectives and Guards, Electricians and Plumbers, Elevator Mechanics, Engineers, Architects, Land Surveyors, Landscape Architects, Hearing Aid Dealers and Fitters, Massage Specialists, Physicians, Motor Vehicle Industry, Motor Vehicle Repair Technicians, Naturopaths, Nurses, Nursing Home Administrators,

Dispensing Opticians, Optometrists, Osteopaths, Pest Control Operators, Pharmacists, Physical Therapists, Psychologists, Real Estate Brokers, Speech Pathologists, Audiologists, Veterinarians, Embalmers/Funeral Directors, Collection Agencies, Commercial Employment Agencies, Mortgage and Collection Servicing Agents, Mortgage Brokers and Solicitors, Port Pilots, Subdivision, Time Sharing, Travel Agents. Computer Printouts: List of names of licensees are available for 25 cents a page. These lists do not contain addresses because of privacy act considerations.

Idaho

Contact: State of Idaho, Department of Self-Governing Agencies, Bureau of Occupational Licenses, 2404 Bank Drive #312, Boise, ID 83705-2598 (208) 334-3233. This office can direct you to one or all of the following state licensing boards. Licensing Boards/Professions: Accountants, Athletic Directors, Bartenders, Engineers, Land Surveyors, Dairy Products, Dentistry, Geologists, Physicians, Architects, Barbers, Chiropractors, Cosmetologists, Counselors, Dentists, Environmental Health Specialists, Hearing Aid Dealers and Fitters, Landscape Architects, Morticians, Nursing Home Administrators, Optometrists, Podiatrists, Psychologists, Social Workers, Outfitters and Guides, Pharmacists, Public Works Contractors, Real Estate Brokers. Types of Lists Available: Format of information available varies from board to board. Computer Printout: Lists available for all professions on a cost recovery basis. Mailing Labels: Some boards have Cheshire labels available; charges are determined on a cost recovery basis. Magnetic Tape: Some boards can provide data on tape; charges are determined on a cost recovery basis and requester must provide tape. Some boards can sort data by Zip Code, county, and educational fields.

Illinois

Contact: State of Illinois, Department of Registration and Education, 320 West Washington, Third Floor, Springfield, IL 62786 (217) 785-0920. This office serves as the central state licensing agency for the following professions. Licensed Professions: Athletic Trainers, Architects, Barbers, Cosmetologists, Chiropractors, Collection Agencies, Controlled Substance Specialists, Dentists and Dental Auxiliaries, Polygraph Testers, Detectives, Embalmers, Funeral Directors, Land Sales, Land Surveyors, Physicians, Nurses, Nursing Home Administrators, Occupational Therapists, Optometrists, Pharmacists, Physical Therapists, Podiatric Physicians, Boxing and Wrestling, Engineers, Psychologists, Service Corporations, Accountants, Real Estate Brokers and Salespersons, Roofing Contractors, Shorthand Reporters, Social Workers, Structural Engineers, Veterinarians. Computer Printouts: Available for all professions. Basic computer cost is $38.22 plus $1.45 per 1,000 names. Mailing Labels: Available for all professions at same cost. Magnetic Tape: Available for all professions at same cost. Requester must supply tape. Microfiche: Available for all professions at same cost as printout. (Alphabetical sequence only) Data can be sorted by Zip code and county.

Indiana

Contact: Indiana Professional Licensing Agency, 1021 State Office Building, Indianapolis, IN 46204 (317) 232-3997. This office can direct you to one or all of the following state licensing boards. Licensing Boards/Professions: Accountants, Architects, Auctioneers, Barbers, Beauticians, Boxers, Engineers and Land Surveyors, Funeral Directors, Plumbers, Real Estate Agents, TV-Radio and Watch Repair Technicians. Computer Printouts: Format of information varies from board to board, however, most boards can provide a computer printout or a roster of licensed professionals for free or on a cost recovery basis. Mailing Labels: Boards with computerized records can provide mailing labels on a cost recovery basis. Licensed Health Professionals: Contact Indiana Health Professional Bureau, 1 America Square #1020, Indianapolis, IN 82067 (317 232-2960 for the following medical specialties: Chiropractors, Dentists, Health Facility Administrators, Medical Licensing, Nurses, Optometrists, Pharmacists, Sanitarians, Speech Pathologists, Audiologists, Psychologists, Veterinarians, Hearing Aid Dealers, Podiatrists, Physical Therapists. Computer Printouts: Available for all professions. Costs associated with the production of a list are .273 cents per computer second (50-70 seconds is normal), $3 per list job set-up charge, 10 cents per page and actual postage costs plus 10% handling costs. Mailing Labels: Available for all professions; costs are the same as for printouts except for per page charge. Labels are 1 cents per label printed. Selection choices are available sorted by license number, Zip Code, county, current or expired status, and residence or outside of Indiana. Policy on Release of Names: Explanation of why the list is required must accompany request. Commercial requests, and requests for charitable solicitation will be denied.

Iowa

Contact: Director of Professional Licensure, Iowa State Board of Health, Lucas State Office Building, Des Moines, IA 50319 (515) 281-4401. This office serves as a central licensing agency for the following health professionals. It can also provide referral service to the independent boards listed below. Licensed Professionals: Dietitians, Funeral Directors and Embalmers, Hearing Aid Dealers, Nursing Home Administrators, Optometrists, Opthalmology Dispensers, Podiatrists, Psychologists, Physical and Occupational Therapists, Occupational Therapist Assistants, Social Workers, Speech Pathologists and Audiologists, Respiratory Care Therapists, Barbers, Cosmetologists, Chiropractors, Nurses, Physicians, Dentists, Pharmacists, Veterinarians. Computer Printouts: Each list costs $12 set-up fee, 10 cents per thousand for sort, plus $7.50 per thousand names. Mailing Labels: Each list costs $7.50 per thousand, 15 cents per thousand for sort, plus $3 for shipping and handling for pressure sensitive labels. Magnetic Tape: Each list costs $12 set-up fee, 10 cents per thousand for sort, plus $16 for tape. Selection choices for printouts, mailing labels, and tapes can be sorted alphabetically by county ($30 additional) or by Zip Code. Other Licensed Professionals: Contact Professional Licensing Regulation Division, Department of Commerce, 1918 SE Hulsizer, Ankeny, IA 50021. This office can direct you to one or all of the following state licensing boards: Accountants, Engineers and Land Surveyors, Landscape Architects, Architects, Real Estate Agents. Types of Lists Available: The format of information varies from board to board. Computer Printouts: Available from some boards on a cost recovery basis. Mailing Labels: Pressure Sensitive and cheshire labels available from some boards on a cost recovery basis. Data can be sorted by Zip Code, county and city.

Kansas

Contact: Publication Division, Secretary of State, State Capitol, 2nd Floor, Topeka, KS 66612 (913 296-3489. This office can provide you with the publication, *Kansas Directory*, which gives addresses for all state licensing boards. Licensing Boards: Abstracters, Accountants, Adult Care Home Administrators, Apprenticeship Council (Operating Engineers, Plumbers and Pipefitters, Carpenters, Electrical Workers), Attorneys, Banking, Barbers, Cosmetologists, Court Reporters, Dentists and Dental Auxiliaries, Educators, Emergency Medical Services, Fire Protection Personnel Standards and Education, Healing Arts Specialists, Hearing Aid Dispensers, Insurance Agents, Land Surveyors, Embalmers/Funeral Directors, Nurses, Optometrists, Pharmacists, Physical Therapists, Podiatrists, Professional Practices, Proprietary Schools, Real Estate Agents, Technical Professions (Engineers, Architects, Landscape Architects, Veterinarians. Types of Lists Available: Kansas has an "Open Records Act" which prohibits the release of licensees' names and addresses.

Kentucky

Contact: Division of Occupations and Professions, Secretary of State, PO Box 456, Frankfort, KY 40602 (502) 564-3296. This office can direct you to one or all of the following state licensing boards. Licensing Boards/Professions: Hearing Aid Dealers, Nurses, Proprietary Education (Private Schools), Psychologists, Social Workers, Speech and Audiologists. Computer Printouts: Available for each profession for 10 cents a page. Mailing Labels: Pressure sensitive labels are available for each profession for 10 cents a page (8 labels to a page). Other Licensed Professionals: Contact Kentucky Occupational Information Coordinating Committee, 275 East Main Street - 2 Center, Frankfort, KY 40621 (502) 564-4258. This office will serve as a referral agency to the following boards and can provide you with the publication, *Occupations - Careers Requiring A License or Certificate 1986-1987*, which identifies the licensing boards which cover the following professionals: Accountants, Agriculture Specialists, Architects, Auctioneers, Bar Examiners, Barbers, Chiropractors, Dentists, Teacher Education, Vocational Rehabilitation Specialists, Financial Institutions, Hairdressers, Cosmetologists, Emergency Medical Technicians Services, Radiation and Product Safety Specialists, Housing/Buildings/Construction, Insurance Agents, Medical Licensure Supervisors, Mines and Minerals, Natural Resources and Environmental Protection Specialists, Nursing Home Administrators, Ophthalmic Dispensers, Optometric Examiners, Pharmacists, Physical Therapists, Podiatrists, Polygraph Examiners, Professional Engineers and Land Surveyors, Real Estate Agents, Veterinarians. Computer Printouts: Most boards can provide lists on a cost recovery basis. Mailing Labels: Most boards can provide labels on a cost recovery basis.

Louisiana

Contact: Office of Commerce and Industry, Department of Commerce, Baton Rouge, LA 70801 (504) 342-5388. This office can provide you with the publication, *Reference Guide of Permits and Licenses Louisiana*, which identifies all the state licensing agencies. Licensing Boards/Professions: Acupuncture Assistants, Adoption Agencies, Adult Day Care Administrators, Agricultural Consultants, Alcoholic Beverages Solicitors, Ambulatory Surgical Centers, Animal Food Manufacturers, Quarantined Cattle Feedlot, Arborists, Archaeological Investigators, Architects, Auctioneers, Banking, Barbers, Beauticians, Bedding and Furniture Upholsterers, Beer Distributors, Blind Business Enterprise Operators, Blood Alcohol Analysts, Embalmers/Funeral Directors, Accountants, Shorthand Reporters, Chiropractors, Pesticide Applicators, Driving School Instructors, Sewage/Construction Contractors, Cotton Buyers, Credit Unions, Waste-Salvage Oil Operators, Custom Meat Processing Plants, Cut Flower Dealers, Dairy Product Retailers, Day Care Centers, Fuels Dealers, Dentists, Detention Centers, Drug Manufacturers, Egg Marketers, Electroloysis Technicians, Embalmers, Emergency Medical Technicians, Emergency Shelter Care Centers, Employment Service Agencies, Equine Infection Anemia, Explosives, Family Support Counselors, Feed Manufacturers, Fertilizer Manufacturers, Fireworks, Fire Protection Sprinkler Systems, Food Manufacturing, Foster Care, Grain Dealers, Handicapped Group Homes, Hazardous Waste, Health Care Facilities, Hearing Aid Dealer, Hemodialysis Clinic, Home Health Centers, Horse Racing, Horticulturists, Hospitals, Housing, Independent Laboratories, Sewage System Installers, Insurance, Landscape Architects, Nurses, Lime Manufacturers, Liquefied Gas Distributors, Liquor, Livestock Dealers, Maternity Homes, Mental and Substance Abuse Clinics, Midwives, Nursing Home Administrators, Nursery Stock Dealers, Occupational Therapists, Optometrists, Pesticide Dealers, Pharmacists, Physical Therapists, Physicians, Physician Assistants, Plant Breeders, Plumbers, Podiatrists, Solid Waste Processors, Seafood Distributors, Psychologists, Radiation Therapists, Radio and Television Repair Technicians, Radiologic Technologists, Real Estate Brokers, Rehabilitation Centers, Sanitarians, Social Workers, Speech Pathologists and Audiologists, Veterinarians, Voice Stress Analysts. Types of Lists Available: Most of the state licensing agencies do not

have computer generated reports but directories are available for most professions.

Maine

Contact: Department of Professional and Financial Regulation, State House Station 35, Augusta, ME 04333 (207) 289-2217. This office can direct you to one or all of the following state licensing boards. The publication, *Maine Directory of Occupational Licensing*, can be obtained from the Division of Economic Analysis and Registration Division, Department of Labor, State House Station Nr. 54, Augusta, ME 04333 (207) 289-2271. This publication lists all the state licensing boards. Licensing Boards/Professions: Veterinarians, Itinerant Vendors, Bureau of Banking, Consumer Credit Protection Services, Insurance Agents, Athletic Trainers, Real Estate Agents, Geologists and Soil Scientists, Solar Energy Auditors, Hearing Aid Dealers and Fitters, Accountants, Arborists, Barbers, Commercial Drivers Education Instructors, Speech Pathologists and Audiologists, Auctioneers, Electricians, Funeral Directors, Foresters, Dietitians, Nursing Home Administrators, Oil and Solid Fuel Installers, Substance Abuse Counselors, Manufactured Housing (mobile home parks), River Pilots, Physical Therapists, Plumbers, Psychologists, Social Workers, Radiological Technicians, Occupational Therapists, Respiratory Care Therapists, Nurses, Dentists, Chiropractors, Osteopaths, Podiatrist, Physicians, Engineers, Attorneys. Types of Lists Available: Rosters are available free for the health professionals as well as attorneys. Computer Printout: Available for most of the professions on a cost recovery basis. Telephone numbers are included. Mailing Labels: Pressure sensitive labels are available for most of the professions for 4 cents a name.

Maryland

Contact: Division of Maryland Occupational and Professional Licensing, 501 St. Paul Place, 9th Floor, Baltimore, MD 21202 (301) 333-6209. This office serves as a central licensing agent for the following professionals. Licensed Professionals: Architects, Master Electricians, Engineers, Foresters, Hearing Aid Dealers, Landscape Architects, Pilots, Plumbers, Land Surveyors, Public Accountants, Second Hand Dealers, Precious Metal and Gem Dealers, Pawnbrokers, Real Estate Agents and Brokers, Home Improvement Contractors, Barbers and Cosmetologists, Racing. Referral to the licensing agency for Collection Agencies, Mortgage Brokers and Insurance Agents can be provided by the office listed above. Computer Printout: Lists of all professions are available and cost is determined by the number of names on the list and computer time. Mailing Labels: Cheshire labels are available for all professions. Cost is determined by the number of names plus computer time. Magnetic Tape: Available for all professions; cost is determined by amount of computer time used and the cost of the tape. Selection choices for computer printouts, mailing labels and tapes can be sorted in Zip Code or county order. All requests must be submitted in writing addressed to the attention of Joseph Roggenkamp at the office noted above. Other Licensed Professions: Office of Boards and Commissions, Department of Health and Mental Hygiene, 201 W. Preston Street, Baltimore, MD 21202 (301 225-5837. This office can direct you to the appropriate board which licenses health and other professionals: Audiologists, Chiropractors, Dentists, Dietitians, Electrologists, Medical Examiners, Morticians, Nurses, Nursing Home Administrators, Optometrists, Occupational Therapists, Pharmacists, Physical Therapists, Podiatrists, Professional Counselors, Psychologists, Environmental Sanitarians, Speech Pathologists, Social Workers, Well Drillers, Water Work and Waste System Operators. Computer Printouts: Lists are available of all professions on a cost recovery basis. Mailing Labels: Cheshire labels are available for all of the professions on a cost recovery basis. Magnetic Tape: Tapes are available for all of the professions on a cost recovery basis. Selection choices for printouts, mailing labels, and tapes can be sorted by Zip Code and county.

Massachusetts

Contact: Tom Forsyth, Computer Service, Division of Registration, Room 1510, 100 Cambridge Street, Boston, MA 02202 (617) 727-2076. The above office can direct you to one or all of the following state licensing boards. It can also provide you with information on the types of lists available. Licensing Boards/Professions: Electrologists, Gas Fitters, Hair Dressers, Health Officers, Landscape Architects, Licensed Practical Nurses, Nursing Home Administrators, Optometrists, Physician's Assistants, Podiatrists, Pharmacists, Plumbers, Psychologists, Real Estate Brokers, Registered Nurses, Sanitarians, Speech Language Pathologists, Audiologists, Social Workers, TV-Repair Technicians, Physical Therapists, Occupational Therapists, Athletic Trainers, Architects, Barbers, Barber Shops, Certified Public Accountants, Chiropractors, Dental Hygienists, Dentists, Dispensing Opticians, Pharmacies, Electricians, Embalmers, Engineers, Veterinarians. Computer Printouts: Lists of all professionals are available. The cost is 50 cents a page or 1 cent per name (minimum of $20). Mailing Labels: Pressure sensitive labels are available at a charge of $20 for the list 1,000 names and $30 for each additional 1,000 names. Magnetic Tape: Available for all professions; fee is the same as for mailing labels. Data can be sorted alphabetically or by Zip Code.

Michigan

Contact: Michigan Department of License and Regulation, PO Box 30018, Lansing, MI 48909 (517) 373-1870. This office serves as a central licensing agency for the following professions. Licensing Board/Professions: Accountants, Architects, Barbers, Athletic Control (Wrestlers and Boxers), Builders, Carnival Amusement Rides, Cosmetologists. Contact the department noted above for details about directories, computer printouts, mailing labels and tapes.

Minnesota

Contact: Small Business Assistance Office, Minnesota Department of Energy and Economic Development, 900 American Center Building, 150 East Kellogg Boulevard, St. Paul, MN 55101 (612) 296-3871. This office can publishes the *Minnesota Directory*, which contains the addresses of all the state licensing boards. Licensing Boards/Professions: Abstracters, Accountants, Adjusters, Alarm and Communications Contractors, Architects, Assessors, Attorneys, Auctioneers, Bailbondsmen, Barbers, Beauticians, Boiler Operators, Boxing Related Occupations, Brokers, Building Officials, Burglar Installers, Chiropractors, Clergy, Cosmetologists, Dentists, Dental Assistants, Dental Hygienists, Private Detectives, Electricians, Energy Auditors, Engineers, Financial Counselors/Financial Planners, Funeral Directors/Embalmers/Morticians, Hearing Aid Dispensers, Racing, Insurance Agents, Investment Advisors, Landscape Architects, Land Surveyors, Midwives, Notary Public, Nursing Home Administrators, Optometrists, Osteopathic Physicians, Pawnbrokers, Peace Officers, Pharmacists, Physical Therapists, Physicians, Surgeons, Physician's Assistants, High Pressure Pipefitters, Plumbers, Podiatrists, Practical Nurses, Precious Metal Dealers, Process Servers, Psychologists, Real Estate Brokers, Registered Nurses, Rehabilitation Consultants, Sanitarians, Securities Brokers, Tax Preparers, Teachers, Tow Truck Operators, Transient Merchants, Veterinarians, Water Conditioning Contractors and Installers, Water and Waste Treatment Operators, Water Well Contractors/Explorers/Engineers. Types of Lists Available: Some boards have free rosters available. Computer Printouts: All boards have printouts available on a cost recovery basis. Mailing Labels: Labels are available on a cost recovery basis; for further information contact Debbie Fobboda, Data Processing Center, (612) 297-2552.

Mississippi

Contact: Secretary of State, PO Box 136, Jackson, MS 39205 (601) 359-3123. The publication, *Official And Statistical Register*, which is available from the above office, gives addresses of all state licensing boards. Licensing Boards/Professions: Agricultural Aviation Pilots, Architects, Landscape Architects, Athletic Trainers, Funeral Directors, Chiropractors, Dentists, Physicians, Nurses, Nursing Home Administrators, Optometrists, Pharmacists, Physical Therapists, Psychologists, Veterinarians, Bar Admissions, Barbers, Cosmetologists, Engineers and Land Surveyors, Foresters, Polygraph Examiners, Public Accountants, Public Contractors, Real Estate Agents. Types of Lists Available: Rosters are available from most boards on a cost recovery basis.

Missouri

Contact: Division of Professional Registration, Department of Economic Development, PO Box 1335, Jefferson City, MO 65102 (314) 751-2334. This office can direct you to one or all of the following state licensing boards. Licensing Boards/Professions: Accountants, Architects/Engineers/Land Surveyors, Athletic Trainers, Barbers, Chiropractors, Cosmetologists, Professional Counselors, Dentists, Embalmers/Funeral Directors, Healing Arts Specialists, Employment Agencies, Hearing Aid Dealers/Fitters, Nurses, Optometrists, Podiatrists, Pharmacists, Real Estate Agents, Veterinarians, Insurance Agents, Nursing Home Administrators, Lawyers (Supreme Court), Dental Hygienists, Physicians, Physical Therapists, Speech Pathologists and Audiologists, Psychologists. Types of Lists Available: Format of information varies from board to board. For data on health professionals, contact Mary Neutzler, Department of Health, PO Box 570, Jefferson City, MO 65102 (314) 751-6279. Computer Printouts: Available at a cost of 50 cents a page. Mailing Labels: Pressure sensitive labels are available for $45 for the first 1,000, $60 for the second 1,000, and $30 for each 1,000 thereafter. Magnetic Tape: Available at a base cost of $100, plus $25 for the first 1,000, $20 for each 1,000 thereafter (user must supply tape). Selection choices for printouts, labels, and tape are available sorted by Zip Code, county or out-of- state. Other licensing boards offer printouts and mailing labels on a cost recovery basis. Data may be sorted by Zip Code or county.

Montana

Contact: Professional and Occupational Licensing, Business Regulation, Department of Commerce, 1424 Ninth Avenue, Helena, MT 59620-0407 (406) 444-3737. The above office can refer you to one or all of the following licensing boards. Licensing Boards/Professions: Accountants, Acupuncture, Architects, Athletic Trainers, Banks, Barbers, Beer Distributors, Chiropractors, Cosmetologists, Dental Hygienists, Dentists, Denturists, Electricians, Electrologists, Employment Agencies, Engineers and Land Surveyors, Fire Protection Equipment, Hearing Aid Dispensers, Horse Racing, Insurance, Landscape Architects, Lawyers, Librarians, Medical Doctors, Morticians, Nurses, Nursing Home Administrators, Occupational Therapists, Operating Engineers (Boiler) Optometrists, Osteopathic Physicians, Pawnbrokers, Pharmacy, Physical Therapists, Plumbers, Podiatrists, Polygraph Examiners, Private Investigators, Private Schools, Psychologists, Contractors, Radiologic Technologists, Real Estate Brokers and Salesmen, Sanitarians, Securities Brokers and Salesmen, Social Workers and Counselors, Speech Pathologists and Audiologists, Taxidermists, Tourist Campground and Trailer Courts, Veterinarians, Water Well Drillers. Computer Printouts: List of each profession is available but user sign a disclaimer stating the names will not be used for commercial purposes.

Nebraska

Contact: Bureau of Examining Boards, Nebraska Department of Health, PO Box 95007, Lincoln, NE 68509 (402) 471-2115. This office can direct you to the appropriate state health licensing agency. Licensing Boards/Health Professions: Athletic Trainers, Advanced Emergency Medical Technicians, Audiologist/Speech Pathologists, Cosmetologists, Chiropractors, Dentists/Dental Hygienists, Embalmers/Funeral Directors, Hearing Aid Instrument Dealers and Fitters, Pharmacists, Podiatrists, Optometrists, Physical Therapists, Nurses, Nursing Home Administrators, Massage Specialists, Occupational Therapists, Professional Counselors, Psychologists, Respiratory Care Specialists, Social Workers, Sanitarians, Veterinarians. Computer Printouts: Printouts are available on a cost recovery basis. Mailing Labels: Pressure sensitive labels available on a cost recovery basis. For further information call Health Data Processing (402) 471-2337. Other Licensing Boards/Professions: Contact state operator at (402) 471-2311 to be connected with the board which licenses the following professions: Accountants, Engineers/Architects, Barbers, Abstracters, Appraisers, Land Surveyors, Landscape Architects, Manufactured Housing.

Nevada

Contact: State of Nevada Executive Chamber, Capitol Complex, Carson City, NV 89710 (702) 486-4500. This office can direct you to the appropriate licensing boards for specific professionals. Licensing Boards/Professions: Accountants, Architects, Athletic Trainers, Audiologists and Speech Pathologists, Barbers, Chiropractors, Contractors, Cosmetologists, Dentists, Engineers and Land Surveyors, Funeral Directors and Embalmers, Hearing Aid Specialists, Homeopaths, Landscape Architects, Liquefied Petroleum Gas Distributors, Marriage and Family Counselors, Physicians, Naturopathic Healing Arts Specialists, Nurses, Dispensing Opticians, Optometrists, Oriental Medicine, Osteopaths, Pharmacists, Physical Therapists, Podiatrists, Private Investigators, Psychologists, Racing, Shorthand Reporters, Taxicab Drivers, Veterinarians. Computer Printouts: Available from most boards for a nominal fee. Data can be sorted by Zip Code and out-of-state.

New Hampshire

Contact: SOICC of New Hampshire, 643 Old Sun Cook Road, Concord, NH 03301 (603) 228-9500. This office can provide you with the publication, *Licensed Certified and Registered Occupations in New Hampshire*, which contains addresses for all state licensing boards. Licensing Boards/Professions: Accountants, Public Health Service (Emergency Medical Technicians), Engineers/Architects/Land Surveyors, Supreme Court (Attorneys), Auctioneers, Insurance (Bailbondsmen), Barbers, Cosmetologists, Chiropractors, Court Reporters, Dentists, Drivers Education Instructors, Electricians, Funeral Directors/Embalmers, Engineers, Physicians, Pari-mutuel (Racing), Private Security Guards, Lobbyists, Nurses, Nursing Home Administrators, Occupational Therapists, Optometrists, Psychologists, Pesticide Control Operators, Pharmacists, Plumbers, Podiatrists, Real Estate Agents, Teacher Agents, Veterinarians, Water Supply and Pollution Control Operators. Types of Lists Available: Format of information varies from board to board. Rosters are available from many boards free of charge, nominal fee charged by some boards.

New Jersey

Contact: Frank Klein, Centralized Licensing, Division of Consumer Affairs, Richard Hughes Justice Complex, CN152, Trenton, NJ 08625 (609) 292-4670. This office can direct you to one or all of the following state licensing boards. Licensing Boards/Professions: Accountants, Architects, Barbers, Beauticians, Dentists, Electrical Contractors, Marriage Counselors, Plumbers, Morticians, Nurses, Opthalmic Dispensing Technicians, Optometrists, Pharmacists, Physical Therapists, Professional Engineers and Landscape Surveyors, Professional Planners, Psychological Examiners, Shorthand Reporters, Veterinarians, Public Movers and Warehousemen, Acupuncture Specialists, Landscape Architects, Athletic Trainers, Hearing Aid Dispensers, Chiropractors, Opthomologists. Computer Printouts: Printouts are available on a cost recovery basis. Mailing Labels: Cheshire mailing labels available on a cost recovery basis. Use of lists must be beneficial to state or licensee.

New Mexico

Contact: Regulation and Licensing Department, PO Drawer 1388, Santa Fe, NM 87504-1388 (505) 827-6318. This office serves as the state central licensing agency and publishes *Licensing Information for Professional and Occupational Boards and Commissions*, which contains addresses for all the licensing boards. Licensing Boards/Professions: Accountants, Architects, Athletic Promoters, Barbers, Chiropractors, Cosmetologists, Dentists, Engineers and Land Surveyors, Landscape Architects, Physicians, Nurses, Nursing Home Administrators, Occupational Therapists, Optometrists, Osteopaths, Pharmacists, Physical Therapists, Podiatrists, Polygraphers, Private Investigators, Psychologists, Realtors, Thanatopractice, Veterinarians. Computer Printout: Available for 10 cents a name. Mailing Labels: Cheshire labels available for 15 cents a name. Selection choice for printouts and mailing labels are available in alphabetical order.

New York

Contact: New York State Education Department, Division of Professional Licensing, Cultural Education Center, Empire State Plaza, Albany, NY 12230 (518) 474-3917, (800) 342-3729. This office serves as the state central licensing agency for the following professions. Licensed Professionals: Acupuncture Specialists, Architects, Audiologists, Certified Shorthand Reporters, Chiropractors, Dentists, Landscape Architects, Land Surveyors, Massage Therapists, Physicians, Osteopaths, Nurses, Occupational Therapists, Opthalmic Dispensers, Optometrists, Pharmacists, Physical Therapists, Podiatrists, Professional Engineers, Psychologists, Public Accountants, Social Workers, Speech Pathologists, Veterinarians. Computer Printouts: Available for 25 cents per page. All requests must be presented as Freedom of Information Act

Information on People, Companies, and Mailing Lists

requests and user must give reason for use. State law prohibits lists to be used for commercial or fund raising purposes.

North Carolina

Contact: North Carolina Center for Public Policy Research, PO Box 430, Raleigh, NC 27602 (919) 832-2839. This office publishes *Boards, Commissions, And Councils* for $15.00. This pamphlet contains addresses for the following state licensing agencies. Licensing Boards/Professions: Alarm Systems, Architects, Auctioneers, Barbers, Boiler Operators, Accountants, Chiropractors, Cosmetologists, Registered Counselors, Dental, Electrical Contractors, Foresters, General Contractors, Hearing Aid Dealers and Fitters, Landscape Architects, Landscape Contractors, Law Examiner, Manufactured Housing, Marital and Family Therapists, Physicians, Navigators and Pilots, Morticians, Nurses, Nursing Home Administrators, Opticians, Optometrists, Osteopaths, Pesticide Operators, Pharmacists, Physical Therapists, Plumbers and Heating Specialists, Podiatrists, Practicing Psychologists, Private Protective Services, Professional Engineers and Land Surveyors, Public Librarians, Real Estate, Refrigeration Techicians, Sanitarians, Social Workers, Speech and Language Pathologists, Structural Pest Control Operators, Veterinarians, Waste Water Treatment Operators, Water Treatment Facility Operators. Computer Printouts: Available from some boards for $20 per 1,000 names. Mailing Labels: Pressure sensitive labels available for $20 per thousand. Selection choices for printouts and mailing labels can be sorted by Zip Code and county.

North Dakota

Contact: North Dakota Legislative Council Library, 2nd Floor, State Capitol, Bismarck, ND 58505 (701) 224-2916. This office can publishes *State Of North Dakota Boards And Commissions*, which gives addresses for all state licensing boards. Licensing Boards/Professions: Abstracters, Accountants, Aeronautics, Architects, Athletic Trainers, Audiologists and Speech Pathologists, Barbers, Chiropractors, Cosmetologists, Dentists, Dietetians, Electricians, Embalmers, Emergency Medical Services, Professional Engineers and Land Surveyors, Hearing Aid Dealers and Fitters, Massage Therapists, Physicians, Nurses, Nursing Home Administrators, Occupational Therapists, Optometrists, Pharmacists, Physical Therapists, Plumbers, Podiatrists, Private Investigators, Private Police Security, Psychologists, Real Estate Agents, Respiratory Care Specialists, Social Workers, Professional Soil Classifiers, Veterinarians, Water Well Contractors. Types of Lists Available: Directories available free from some boards. Computer Printouts: Available from most boards on a cost recovery basis. Mailing Labels: Pressure sensitive labels available from most boards on a cost recovery basis. Selection choice for printout and labels only available in alphabetical order. Requester must disclose reason for use.

Ohio

Contact: State of Ohio, Department of Administrative Services, Division of Computer Services, 30 East Broad Street, 40th Floor, Columbus, OH 43266-0409 (614) 466-8029. This office can provide detailed information on computerized information. Licensed Professionals: Wholesale Distributors of Dangerous Drugs, Terminal Distributor of Dangerous Drugs, Pharmacists, Certified Public Accountants, Public Accountants, Pharmacists Interns, Registered Barbers, Barber Shops, Beauty Shops, Schools, Managing Cosmetologists, Cosmetologists, Manicurists, Instructors, Architects, Landscape Architects, Practical Nurses, Registered Nurses, Surveyors, Engineer and Surveyors, Dentists, Dental Hygienists, Doctors of Osteopathy, Doctors of Medicine, Doctors of Surgical Podiatry, Chiropractors, Midwives, Embalmers, Funeral Directors, Embalmer and Funeral Directors, Hat Cleaners, Dry Clearners, Hotel-Motels, Public Employment Agencies, Auctioneers, Private Investigators, Auction Business, Auction Firms. Computer Printouts: Available for 7.5 cents per name, minimum of $75.00. Mailing Labels: Cheshire labels are available for 7.5 cents per name and Pressure Sensitive labels are available for 8.2 cents per name. Magnetic Tape: Available for 7.5 cents per name for the first 10,000 names, 5 cents per name for 10,000 to 50,000 names. Requester must supply tape or the charge is $20 per tape. Selection choices are available sorted by Zip Code and county.

Oklahoma

Contact: Allan Wright, Governor's Office, State Capitol, Oklahoma City, OK 73105 (405) 521-2342 or State Information Operator (405) 521-1601. The above office can direct you to all state licensing agencies. Licensing Board/Professions: Accountants, Real Estate Agents, Physicians, Foresters, Horse Racing, Medicolegals, Nursing Homes, Nurses, Optometrists, Osteopaths, Physicians, Pharmacists, Polygraph Examiners, Private Prison Industry, Psychologists, Shorthand Reporters, Social Workers, Speech Pathologists, Veterinarians, Landscape Architects, Architects, Bar Association, Chiropractors, Cosmetologists, Dentists, Embalmers and Funeral Directors. Computer Printouts: Available from many of the boards for a nominal fee (ie, accountants $20). Mailing List: Available from many of the boards on cost recovery basis (ie, accountants $115). Other Licensed Professionals: Contact Occupational Licensing, OK State Health Department, PO Box 53551, Oklahoma City, OK 73152 (405) 271-5217. The above office can direct you to the following state licensing agencies: Barbers, Hearing Aid Dealers, Electricians, Water and Waste Treatment Plant Operators, Alarm Companies. Computer Printouts: Available for 9 cents a name. Mailing Labels: Cheshire mailing labels are available on a cost recovery basis. Selection choices can be sorted by Zip Code and county.

Oregon

Contact: Department of Economic Development, Smnall Business Advocates, 595 Cottage St. NE, Salem, OR 97310 (800) 547-7842 or (800) 233-3306 (Oregon).

The above office can direct you to one or all of the following state licensing boards or send out the *Fact Book*, a pamphlet which contains names and addresses of all licensing boards. Licensing Boards/Professions: Accountants, Architects, Barbers and Hairdressers, Builders (Builders, Contractors), Building Codes Division (Licensing of Building Trades), Consolidated Boards (Collection Agencies, Debt Consolidators, Geologists, Landscape Architects, Landscape Contractors, and TV/Radio Service Dealers, Engineering Examiners, Financial Institutions, Fire Marshal, Insurance Agents, Maritime Pilots, Real Estate Agents, Tax Practitioners. Computer Printouts: Available from some boards (ie, Accountancy $75). Mailing Labels: Pressure Sensitive labels available from some boards (ie, Accountancy $75). Magnetic Tape: Available from some boards on a cost recovery basis (ie, Accountancy $75). Data can be sorted by Zip Code.

Pennsylvania

Contact: Bureau of Professional and Occupational Affairs, Secretary of State, 618 Transportation and Safety Building, Harrisburg, PA 17105-2644 (717) 787-8505. The above office can direct you to one or all of the following state business related licensing boards. Licensing Boards/Professions: Accountants, Architect, Auctioneer, Barber, Cosmetology, Funeral Directors, Landscape Architects, Professional Engineers, Real Estate, Vehicles. Licenses Health Professions: Contact Bureau of Professional and Occupational Affairs, Secretary of State, 618 Transportation and Safety Building, Harrisburg, PA 17120 (717) 783-1400. This office can direct you to one or all of the following state health related licensing boards: Dentists, Physicians, Nurses, Nursing Home Administrators, Occupational Therapists, Optometrists, Osteopaths, Pharmacists, Physical Therapists, Podiatrists, Psychologists, Speech-Language and Hearing Specialists, Veterinarians, Navigators. Computer Printouts: Available on bond paper bound into a book. Cost includes $71 set-up fee plus, .005 per name for entire state or entire file, .03 per name for selected counties within PA. Magnetic Tape: Available for $96 set-up fee (tape provided by Bureau), .005 per name for entire state or entire file, .03 per name for selected counties within the state. Data can be sorted by Zip Code, county and license number. For further information contact Mary Sibrava (717) 787-8503.

Rhode Island

Contact: Rhode Island Occupational Information Coordinating Commission, 22 Hayes Street, Room 133, Providence, RI 02908 (401) 272-0830. The above office publishes the *Rhode Island Handbook of Licenses - Certified and Regulated Information* which costs $8.50. Licensing Boards/Professions: Nurses Aides, Health Facilities, Psychologists, Respiratory Therapists, Sanitarians, Speech Pathologists, Veterinarians, Physical Therapists, Plumbers, Podiatrists, Prosthetists, LPNs, RNs, Nursing Home Administrators, Occupational Therapists, Opticians, Optometrists, Osteopaths, Physician Assistants, Embalmers/Funeral Directors, Hairdressers, Cosmetologists, Manicurists, Massage Therapists, Physicians, Midwives, Acupuncturists, Athletic Trainers, Audiologists, Barbers, Barber Shops, Chiropractors, Dentist, Dental Hygienist, Electrologist, Architects, Coastal Resource Management, Engineers and Land Surveyors. Types of Lists Available: Rosters available free from some boards. Computer Printouts: Available from some boards on a cost recovery basis (ie, Registered Nurses $140; Architects $21). State stipulates that lists may not be used for commercial purposes.

South Carolina

Contact: South Carolina State Library, 1500 Senate Street, Columbia, SC 29211 (803) 734-8666. They will direct you to the proper licensing board. Licensing Boards/Professions: Accountants, Architects, Auctioneers, Barbers, Morticians, Chiropractors, Contractors, Cosmetologists, Dentists, Engineers, Environmental Systems (Well Diggers), Foresters, Funeral Services, Landscape Architects, Physicians, Nurses, Nursing Home Administrators, Occupational Therapists, Opticians, Optometrists, Pharmacists, Physical Therapists, Professional Counselors, Marriage and Family Therapists, Psychologists, Real Estate Agents, Sanitarians, Home Builder, Social Workers, Speech Pathologist/Audiologists, Veterinarians, Athletic Trainers (Boxing and Wrestling), Geologists. Computer Printouts: Available on a cost recovery basis (Nursing 5 cents a name). Mailing Labels: Cheshire and pressure sensitive labels available on a cost recovery basis (Nursing 3 - 7 cents a label). Data can be sorted by Zip Code.

South Dakota

Contact: Department of Commerce and Regulation, 910 E. Sioux, Pierre, SD 57501 (605) 773-3178. South Dakota Medical and Osteopath Examiners, 1323 A. Minnesota Avenue, Sioux Falls, SD 57104 (605) 336-1965. The above office can direct you to one or all of the following state licensing boards. Licensing Boards/Professions: Physicians, Osteopaths, Physician's Assistants, Physical Therapists, Medical Corporations, Emergency Technicians, Abstracters, Accountants, Barbers, Chiropractors, Cosmetologists, Electricians, Engineers/Architects, Funeral Directors, Hearing Aid Dispensers, Medical/Osteopaths, Nurses, Nursing Home Administrators, Optometrists, Pharmacists, Plumbers, Podiatrists, Psychologists, Real Estate Agents, Social Workers, Veterinarians. Computer Printout: Complete list of all above listed professionals available for $15. Mailing Labels: Available for all doctors for $60. Hard copy directories are available for $25 each.

Tennessee

Contact: Division of Regulatory Boards, Department of Commerce and Insurance, 500 James Robertson Parkway, Nashville, TN 37219-5322 (615) 741-3449. This office can direct you to one or all of the following state licensing boards. Licensing Boards/Professions: Accountants, Architects and Engineers,

Auctioneers, Barbers, Collection Services, Contractors, Cosmetologists, Funeral Directors and Embalmers, Land Surveyors, Motor Vehicle Salesmen and Dealers, Personnel Recruiters, Pharmacists, Polygraph Examiners, Real Estate. Types of Lists Available: Format of information varies from board to board. Rosters: Available from most boards at a nominal fee. Other Licensed Health Professionals: Division of Health Related Professions, Department of Health and Environment, 287 Plus Park Blvd Complex, Nashville, TN 37217 (615) 367-6220. Professions include: Dentists, Dental Hygienists, Podiatrists, Physicians, Physician's Assistants, Osteopaths, Optometrists, Veterinarians, Nursing Home Administrators, Dispensing Opticians, Chiropractors, Social Workers, Hearing Aid Dispensers, Registered Professional Environmentalists, Marital and Family Counselors, Speech Pathology/Audiologists, Occupational and Physical Therapists, X- Ray Technicians, Registered Nurses, Licensed Practical Nurses. Types of Lists Available: Rosters are available from most boards at a nominal fee.

Texas

Contact: Texas Department of Commerce, Office of Business Permit Assistance, PO Box 12728, Capitol Station, Austin, TX 78711 (512) 320-0110, (800) 888-0511. This office can provide you with the publication, *A Brief Guide To Business Regulations And Services In Texas*. Licensing Boards/Professions: Accountants, Architects, State Bar of Texas, Barbers, Cosmetologists, Morticians, Educators, Public Safety, Chiropractors, Psychologists, Dentists, Real Estate Agents, Engineers, Veterinarians, Insurance Agents, Land Surveyors, Landscape Architects, Fitting and Dispensing of Hearing Aids, Private Investigators and Private Security Agencies, Polygraph, Vocational Nurses, Nursing, Nursing Home Administrators, Physicians, Optometrists, Structural Pest Control Operators, Pharmacists, Physical Therapists, Plumbers, Podiatrists, Professional Counselors, Dietitians, Speech-Language Pathology and Audiology. Computer Printouts: Printouts available from most boards on a cost recovery basis. Mailing Labels: Cheshire and pressure sensitive labels available from many boards on a cost recovery basis. Data can be sorted by Zip Code, city, county and out-of-state.

Utah

Contact: Division of Occupational and Professional Licensing, Department of Business Regulation, Heber M. Wells Building, 160 East 300 South/PO Box 45802, Salt Lake City, UT 84145-0801 (801) 530-6628. Licensing Boards/Professions: Accountants, Architects, Barbers, Cosmetologists, Electrologists, Chiropractors, Podiatrists, Dentists, Dental Hygienists, Embalmers, Funeral Directors, Pre-Need Sellers, Engineers, Land Surveyors, Physicians, Surgeons, Naturopaths, Registered Nurses, Licensed Practical Nurses, Nurse Midwives, Nurse Anesthetists, Nurse Specialists, Prescriptive Practice Specialist, IV Therapists, Optometrists, Osteopaths, Pharmacists, Pharmacies, Manufacturing Pharmacies, Shorthand Reporters, Veterinarians, Health Facility Administrators, Sanitarians, Morticians, Physical Therapists, Psychologists, Clinical Social Workers, Conduct Research on Controlled Substance, Marriage and Family Therapists, Master Therapeutic Recreational Specialists, Speech Pathologists, Audiologists, Occupational Therapists, Hearing Aid Specialists, Massage Therapists, Massage Establishments, Acupuncture Practitioners, Physician Assistants, Dieticians, Contractors. Computer Printouts: Available for all professions at a cost of $25 each. Mailing Labels: Cheshire labels available for all professions at a cost of $75.00.

Vermont

Contact: Division of Licensing and Registration, Secretary of State, Pavillion Office Building, Montpelier, VT 05602 (802) 828-2363. The above office can direct you to one or all of the following state licensing boards. Licensing Boards/Professions: Accountants, Architects, Barbers, Boxing Control, Chiropractors, Cosmetologists, Dentists, Engineers, Funeral Directors/Embalmers, Land Surveyors, Medical Board (Physicians, Podiatrists, Real Estate Brokers, Veterinarians, Physical Therapists, Social Workers, Physician Assistants, Motor Vehicle Racing, Nurses, Nursing Home Administrators, Opticians, Optometrists, Osteopaths, Pharmacies, Pharmacist, Psychologists, Private Detectives, Security Guards, Radiological Technicans. Computer Printouts: Available for all professions for 1 cent a name. Mailing Labels: Pressure sensitive labels available for 1 cent a name. Data can be sorted by ZIP Code and active or inactive status.

Virginia

Contact: Virginia Department of Commerce, 3600 W. Broad Street, Richmond, VA 23230 (804) 367-8500. The above office serves as a central licensing agency. It can also provide you with the publication, *Business and Occupational Regulation in Virginia*. Licensed Professions: Accountants, Architects, Auctioneers, Audiologists, Barbers, Boxers, Contractors, Commercial Driver Training Schools, Employment Agencies, Professional Engineers, Geologists, Hairdressers, Harbor Pilots, Hearing Aid Dealers and Fitters, Landscape Architects, Nursing Home Administrators, Librarians, Opticians, Polygraph Examiners, Private Security Services, Real Estate Brokers, Speech Pathologists, Land Surveyors, Water and Wastewater Works Operators, Wrestlers. Computer Printouts: Available for all professions on a cost recovery basis. Mailing Labels: Cheshire and Pressure Sensitive labels available for all professions on a cost recovery basis. Licensed Health Professions: Contact Receptionist, Health Professionals (804) 662-0000. The office listed above can provide you with phone numbers for the following licensing boards: Dentists, Funeral Directors/Embalmers, Physicians, Medical/Legal Assistants, Nurses, Optometrists, Pharmacists, Psychologists, Professional Counselors, Social Workers, Veterinarians. Types of Lists Available: Contact the data processing

Office for complete information (804) 662-9936.

Washington

Contact: Department of Licensing, Licensing Division, Attn: Jo Waidely, PO Box 9649, Olympia, WA 98504 (206) 586-4561. The above office serves as a central licensing agency. Licensed Professions: Acupuncturists, Auctioneers, Architects, Barbers, Camp Club Registration/Salespersons, Chiropractors, Cosmetology Schools/Instructors, Cosmetologists, Manicurists, Collection Agencies, Debt Adjusters/Agencies, Dentists, Dental Hygienists, Drugless Therapeutic-Naturopaths, Employment Agencies/Managers, Professional Engineers, Engineers-in-Training, Land Surveyors, Engineering Corporations/Partnerships, Escrow Officers/Agents, Firearms Dealers, Embalmers, Apprentice Embalmers, Funeral Directors, Funeral Establishments, Hearing Aid Dispensers/Trainees, Land Development Registration, Landscape Architects, Massage Operators, Midwives, Notary Publics, Nursing Home Administrators, Occularists, Occupational Therapists, Dispensing Opticians, Optometrists, Osterpaths, Osteopathic Physician/Surgeon, Osteopathic Physician Assistants, Physicians, Surgeons, Physician's Assistants, Limited Physician, Podiatrists, Practical Nurses, Psychologists, Physical Therapists, Real Estate (Brokers, Salespersons, Corporations, Partnerships, Branch Offices), Land Development Representatives, Registered Nurses, Timeshare Registration & Salespersons, Veterinarians, Animal Technicians. Computer Printouts: Available for all professions on a cost recovery basis. Mailing Labels: Pressure sensitive labels available for all professions on a cost recovery basis. Magnetic Tape: Available on a cost recovery basis. The State prohibits use of lists for any commercial activity.

West Virginia

Contact: Administrative Law Division, Secretary of State, State Capitol, Charleston, WV 25305 (304) 345-4000. The above office can direct you to one or all of the following state licensing boards. Licensing Boards/Professions: Accountants, Architects, Barbers, Beauticians, Chiropractors, Dentists, and Dental Hygienists, Embalmers and Funeral Directors, Engineers, Foresters, Hearing-Aid Dealers, Landscape Architects, Land Surveyors, Law Examiners, Physicians, Practical Nurses, Registered Nurses, Nursing Home Administrators, Occupational Therapists, Optometrists, Osteopaths, Pharmacists, Physical Therapists, Psychologists, Radiologic Technicians, Real Estate Agents, Sanitarians, State Water Resources, Veterinarians. Computer Printouts: Available from all boards at a cost of 10 cents per page, plus $1.00.

Wisconsin

Contact: Department of Regulation and Licensing, Office of Document Processing, PO Box 8935, Madison, WI 53708 (608) 266-2112. The above office can direct you to one or all of the following state licensing agencies. Licensed Professions: Accountants, Animal Technicians, Architects, Architects, Engineers, Barbers, Bingo Organizations, Morticians, Chiropractors, Cosmetologists, Distributors of Dangerous Drugs, Dental Hygienists, Dentists, Interior Designers, Private Detectives, Drug Manufacturers, Electrologists, Professional Engineers, Funeral Directors, Hearing Aid Dealers/Fitters, Land Surveyors, Manicurists, Physicians, Surgeons, Nurse Midwives, Registered Nurses, Licensed Practical Nurses, Nursing Home Administrators, Optometrists, Pharmacists, Physical Therapists, Physician's Assistants, Podiatrists, Psychologists, Raffle Organizations, Real Estate Brokers, Beauty Salons, Electrolysis Salons, Veterinarians. Computer Printouts: Available for all professions at a cost of $15 for the first 1,000 names, $3.50 for each additional 1,000 names. Magnetic Tape: Available for all professions at a cost of $15 for the first 1,000 names, $3.50 for each additional 1,000 names. Tape charge is $15. Data may be sorted by Zip Code or in state only.

Wyoming

Contact: Governor's Office, State Capitol, Cheyenne, WY 82002 (307) 777-7434. This office can direct you to one or all of the following state licensing boards. Licensing Boards/Professions: Funeral Directors/Embalmers, Health Service Administrators, Buyers and Purchasing Agents, Shorthand Reporters, Medical Record Technicians, Accountants and Auditors, Claims Adjusters, Appraisers, Engineers, Architects, Surveyors, Interior Designers and Decorators, Medical Laboratory Workers, Dental Laboratory Technicians, Opticians, Radiological Technicians, Respiratory Technicians, Quality Control Inspectors, Security Salespeople, Insurance Agents, Real Estate Agents, Physicians, Physician's Assistants, Chiropractors, Pharmacists, Occupational Therapists, Activity Therapists, Physical Therapists, Speech Pathologist and Audiologist, Veterinarian, Optomistrist, Dietitians, Dentists, Dental Hygienists, Registered Nurses, Licensed Practical Nurses, Emergency Medical Technicians, Nurse's Aides, Medical Assistants, Counselors, Lawyers, Legal Assistants, Cosmetologists and Barbers. Types of Lists Available: Format of information varies from board to board. Rosters are available to non-profit organizations for free and at a nominal fee for commercial organizations. Computer Printouts: Available on a cost recovery basis from many boards. Mailing Labels: Available on a cost recovery basis from many boards.

Driver's Licenses and Motor Vehicles

Mailing lists galore and plentiful market research data derived from state motor vehicle departments offer the potential for increasing your bottom line. Did you ever want to know how many 40-year old males in Boston wear contact lenses, or perhaps obtain the names and addresses of all Arizonians who own Cadillacs? Well, it is within the realm of possibilities.

Believe it or not, those long lines that drive us crazy when registering a car or renewing a driver's license have a bright side. Each person in line turns over to the state a wealth of information about him or herself. This data -- name, address, age, physical characteristics, and buying patterns--are the stuff of which customer lists, market studies, and demographic analyses are made. While states charge you for this information, it will cost a fraction of what you would spend if you hired some sharp marketing consultant to unearth the data.

Take the example of my friend, Ron, a mechanic for expensive foreign cars in Wilmington, Delaware. One day Ron got tired of watching his boss laugh all the way to the bank and decided he wanted to open a shop of his own. Through the state he was able to obtain printouts of all owners of Audis, BMWs, and Mercedes in his area. Armed with this information, Ron ultimately was able to obtain a small business loan, open a shop, and now is making more than I'd care to admit.

Many states maintain files not only on autos, but also on boats and recreational vehicles. This data can be of further help in targeting potential customers. It doesn't take business brilliance to deduce that a person living in Palm Beach, who owns several high-ticket imported cars and has a 37-foot Hatteras yacht, is a potential customer for a home security company.

Many states will sort through their driver's license database by age and sex for an additional charge and provide a listing, for example, of all females between the ages of 18 and 45 years living in a particular district. If you are launching a magazine aimed at working women, this is priceless marketing intelligence. The same holds true for older persons who have special senior citizen identifiers and for young males who are eligible for the Selective Service.

These data are used in countless ways by researchers for compiling statistics on health issues, and of course, used by the government for manufacturer recalls or warranty programs, and emission studies. Insurance companies, financial institutions, and other businesses thrive on this cross-sectioning of the body public.

Information derived from a state's automobile owner registration master file is usually available in two formats -- magnetic tape or computer printouts. Most states prefer sending you a tape for larger files, while printouts are allowed for shorter sorts. In addition, some states offer mailing labels for an additional charge.

The most likely sorting options include: an entire state file; all vehicles within a county; vehicle type (2-door, 4-door, 4-wheel drive) by state or county; and vehicle make or year by state or county.

Driver's license information can usually be extracted to provide: name and license number (only); name, license number, and address; and a variety of other factors regarding age or sex. All states charge for this information, usually per 1,000 entries plus a set-up fee, but the potential for increasing your profits by using this valuable data will far outweigh the costs.

There are a few states which do not allow access to this data. These are Connecticut, South Dakota, Rhode Island, New Jersey, Indiana, Hawaii, Georgia, and Arkansas. Utah, North Carolina, and Montana are the three states which will not divulge drivers license information but will turn over vehicle registration files. And three states, Pennsylvania, New Mexico and Kansas, will only give you the information under very specific circumstances. That leaves 38 states which are wide open.

Motor Vehicle Offices

Alabama

Drivers: Alabama Department of Public Safety, Drivers License Division, P.O. Box 1471, Montgomery, AL 36192; (205) 261-4400. Services: Individual records can be retrieved for $4.00 per record.

Owners: Alabama Department of Revenue, Vehicle Registration, 212 Folsom Administration Building, 64 N. Union St., Montgomery, AL 36130; (205) 271-3250. Services: A magnetic tape or printout is available. Data can be sorted by owner's name, address, make, model and year for 3.4 million vehicles. Cost is $22 per thousand and computer time cost.

Alaska

Drivers: Division of Motor Vehicles, 5700 E. Tudor, Anchorage, AK 99507; (907) 269-5572. Services: Nothing available. A bill is currently in the legislature to make files confidential.

Owners: Same as above.

Arizona

Drivers: Arizona Motor Vehicles Division, 1801 W. Jefferson St., Phoenix, AZ 85007; (602) 255-7567. Database: Arizona Drivers - provides name and address of 1,160,000 female drivers and 1,368,000 male drivers. Arizona Revised Statute 23-210J allows for distribution of this information on machine-readable tape only. Services: Data can be sorted by reportable categories. Cost is $1,800.

Owners: Arizona Motor Vehicles Division, 1801 W. Jefferson St., Room 230M, Phoenix, AZ 85007; (602) 255-7567. Database: Arizona Drivers - contains owner's name and address plus make, model, year, tag and license numbers for 1,655,833 cars and 875,000 other vehicles. Services: A mailing list is available for $3,300, or a computer tape can be purchased and data sorted by make, model or year. Tape cost is $.10 per name with $600 minimum order.

Arkansas

Drivers: Arkansas Office of Motor Vehicle Registration, P.O. Box 1272, Little Rock, AR 72203; (501) 682-7060. Services: license information is protected under the Privacy Act. A release must be signed by a driver before that data can be released.

Owners: Arkansas Office of Motor Vehicle Registration, P.O. Box 1272, Little Rock, AR 72203; (501) 682-4702. Database: Arkansas Automobile Owners - contains owner's name and address plus make, model, year and license number for over 15 million automobiles and approximately 300,000 million other vehicles including motorcycles and boats. Services: No data tapes released. Records are open for public inspection at the office only.

California

Drivers: Department of Motor Vehicles, P.O. Box 942869, Sacramento, CA 94269; (916) 732-7723. Services: Individual records can be requested, must identify the name and address of the driver.

Owners: Department of Motor Vehicles, P.O. Box 942869, Sacramento, CA 94269; (916) 732-7463. Database: California Automobile Owners - contains owner's name and address as well as make, model, year, tag and license numbers of 13 million automobiles and 650,000 motorcycles. Services: This file must be purchased in its entirety (i.e., information of all motorcycles cost $22,750 and registration records for automobiles costs approximately $400,000).

Colorado

Drivers: Colorado Motor Vehicle Division, Traffic Records, 140 W. 6th Ave., #100, Denver, CO 80204; (303) 620-4111. Database: Colorado Drivers - contains name, address, license number of 2.5 million drivers. It is available in three files: minor, provisional, and adult permits. Services: One time single run only of name, address and license number only. The cost of $25 per 1,000 names with a $1,000 minimum.

Owners: Colorado Motor Vehicle Division, Traffic Records, 140 W. 6th Ave., #100, Denver, CO 80204; (303) 620-4111. Database: Colorado Owners - contains name and address. Services: One time single run only of name, address and license number only. The cost of $25 per 1,000 names with a $1,000 minimum.

Connecticut

Drivers and Owners: Connecticut State Department of Motor Vehicles, 60 State Street, Wethersfield, CT 06109; (203) 566-3830. Data are confidential.

Delaware

Drivers: Delaware Motor Vehicles Division, P.O. Box 698, Dover, DE 19903; (302) 736-4421. Database: Delaware Drivers - provides name, address, height, weight and other drivers license information except hair color of 490,000 drivers. Services: Some ready made programs available. Any additional programming requires additional charges.

Owners: Delaware Motor Vehicle Division, P.O. Box 698, Dover DE 19903; (302) 736-4421. Database: Delaware Drivers - provides owner's name and address along with make, model, year, title number, expiration date of 500,000 registration cars, motorcycles or trucks. Services: A data tape can be purchased with sorting of reportable variables for $325 plus $.01 per name.

District of Columbia

Drivers: District of Columbia, Department of Public Works Information Office, 301 C. St. N.W., Room 1025, Washington, D.C. 20001; (202) 727-6761. Database: District of Columbia Drivers - contains name, address, suspensions, sex, social security number, height, type of permit, license number, expiration dates, restrictions, of 800,000 drivers. Services: Computer tapes and printouts available. Data can be sorted by categories but not recommended. Cost is $1,700.

Owners: District of Columbia, Department of Public Works Information Office, 301 C. St. N. W., Room 1025, Washington, D.C. 20001; (202) 727-5604. Database: District of Columbia Owners - contains owner's name, address, make, model, year, tag number, and registration number of 263,290 vehicles. Services: computer tape available, data can be sorted by category. Cost is $900.

Florida

Drivers: Florida Highway Safety and Motor Vehicles Department, Neil Kirkman Building, Tallahassee, FL 32301; (904) 488-6710. Database: Florida Drivers - contains name, address, and birth date of over 9 million drivers. Services: No sorting is available. A computer tape or printout can be obtained for $.02 per name (tape); $.03 per name (printout).

Owners: Florida Highway Safety and Motor Vehicles Department, Neil Kirkman Building, Tallahassee, FL 32301; (904) 488-6710. Database: Florida Automobile Owners - provides owner's name and address plus make, model, year, tag number and class code for 7 million cars and 5 million other vehicles. Services: no sorting is available, data available on a computer tape or printout. Cost is $.02 per name (tape); $.03 per name (printout).

Georgia

Drivers and Owners: Motor Vehicle Department, Trinty Washington Bldg, Atlanta, GA 30334; (404) 656-4100. No data released.

Hawaii

Drivers and Owners: Division of Motor Vehicles and Licenses, 1455 S. Beretainia St., Honolulu, HI 96814; (808) 942-3745. No data released.

Idaho

Drivers: Idaho Department of Transportation, P.O. Box 7129, Boise, ID 83707; (208) 334-8742. Database: Idaho Drivers - provides name, sex, birthdate, weight, address, zip code, license type, expiration date, restrictions, issue data and county, and county of residence of 944,001 drivers. Services: Data may be selected by sex, age or range of ages, and county of residence. The cost is $30 per 1,000 names with a $200 minimum charge.

Owners: Idaho Department of Transportation, P.O. Box 7129, Boise, ID 83707; (208) 334-8742. Database: Idaho Owners - provides owner's name, address, make, model, year, issue and expiration date. Services: Data can be selected by registration type, and/or county of issuance. Computer tape and printout available. Cost is $200 minimum charge and $30 per 1,000 names.

Illinois

Drivers: Illinois Secretary of State, Drivers Services Division, 2701 S. Dirksen Parkway, Springfield, IL 62723; (217) 782-1978. Database: Illinois Drivers - contains name, address, sex, date of birth, license issue and expiration date of 8 million drivers. Services: Data can be sorted by various categories and provided on a computer tape for $200 plus $20 per 1000 names, or on a printout for $.50 per page (15,000 names or less).

Owners: Illinois Secretary of State, Centennial Building, Room 414, Springfield, IL 62756; (217) 782-0029. Database: Illinois Automobile Owners - provides owner's name and address, make, model and year of over 6 million passenger cars and over 2 million other vehicles. Services: Complete records are available. Data can be sorted by various categories. Computer tapes available for $200 plus $20 per 1000; computer printouts for $.50 per pate (15,000 names or less).

Indiana

Drivers and Owners: Data not released. Indiana Bureau of Motor Vehicles, 100 N. Senate Ave. Indianapolis, IN 46204.

Iowa

Drivers: Iowa Department of Transportation, Drivers Services, Lucas State Office Building, Des Moines, IA 50319; (515) 281-6315. Database: Iowa Drivers - provides name, address, date of birth, height, weight, restrictions, issue and expiration dates, license number, and restrictions of 2.5 million drivers. Services: Data are listed in order by license number. Data cannot be sorted. Computer tapes available $370 (Tapes must be provided by requester).

Owners: Iowa Department of Transportation, Office of Vehicle Registration, Lucas State Office Building, Des Moines, IA 50319; (515) 281-4875. Database: Iowa Automobile Owners - provides complete description of vehicle for 4.2 million cars and other vehicles. Services: Data tapes available for $.39 per thousand names plus $14.00 for each tape, computer time charge for sorts and a $20.00 set up fee.

Kansas

Drivers and Owners: Data tapes not released for commercial purposes. Kansas Department of Revenue, 200 Docking State Office Building, Topeka, KS 66612; (913) 296-7074.

Kentucky

Drivers: Kentucky Transportation Cabinet, Division of Driver Licensing, State Office Building, Frankfort, KY 40622; (502) 564-4864. Database: Kentucky Drivers - provides name, address, and date of birth of over 2.4 million drivers. Services: Data can be sorted by various categories. Computer tapes or printouts are available for $.01 per name plus $510 for programming and computer costs. Mailing labels are available for $2.45 per thousand plus above charges.

Owners: Kentucky Transportation Cabinet, Division of Motor Vehicle Licensing, State Office Building, Room 205, Frankfort, KY 40622. Database: Kentucky Automobile Owners - provides owner's name and address along with make, model and year for over 2 million vehicles. Services: Data can be sorted by various categories. Computer tapes and printouts available for $.02 per name plus programming costs. Mailing labels can be purchased for $3.50 per thousand plus programming costs.

Louisiana

Drivers: Louisiana Department of Public Safety and Corrections, P.O. Box 66614, Baton Rouge, LA 70896; (504) 925-6239. Database: Louisiana Drivers - provides name, address, height, weight, sex, date of birth of 2.7 million drivers. Services: Computer tape and printout available. Data can be sorted by variables. Cost is $.02 per name plus $500.

Owners: Louisiana Department of Public Safety and Corrections, P.O. Box 66612, Baton Rouge, LA 70896; (504) 825-67239. Database: Louisiana Owners - provides owner's name, address, make, model and year, date of acquisition, color, new or used for 4.5 million vehicles. Services: Computer tape and printout available for $.02 per record and $500.

Maine

Drivers: Maine Motor Vehicle Division, Secretary of State, 26 Child St., Augusta, ME 04333; (207) 289-5553. Database: Maine Drivers - provides name, address, birth date, and sex of 800,000 drivers. Services: Data available on computer tape, printout for $.25 per name. Mailing labels are available for an extra charge.

Owners: Maine Motor Vehicles Division, Secretary of State, 26 Child St., Augusta, ME 04333; (207) 289-5553. Database: Maine Automobile Owners - contains owner's name and address, birth date as well as make, model, year, identification number for 700,000 registered vehicles. Services: Data can be sorted by variables and can be purchased on computer tape, printout or mailing labels for $.03 per name.

Maryland

Drivers: Maryland Motor Vehicle Administration, 6601 Ritchie Highway, Room 200, Glen Burnie, MD 21062; (301) 768-7665. Database: Maryland Drivers -

Information on People, Companies, and Mailing Lists

contains name, address, birth date, height, weight, and identification number of over 2 million drivers. Services: data can be sorted by variables and available on computer tape for $350 plus a $25 application fee and processing costs.

Owners: Maryland Motor Vehicle Administration, 6601 Ritchie Highway, Room 200, Glen Burnie, MD 21062; (301) 768-7665. Database: Maryland Automobile Owners - provides owner's name and address along with make, model and year for nearly 3,000,000 passenger cars and 3 million other vehicles. Some insurance information is included.

Massachusetts
Drivers: Massachusetts Registry of Motor Vehicles, 100 Nashua Street, Boston, MA 02114; (617) 727-3716. Database: Massachusetts Automobile Drivers - provides name, address, social security number/license number, date of birth, and height of 4 million drivers. Services: Data can be sorted by all variables except sex. The cost is $200 for the first 1,000 names and $30 per 1,000 records thereafter. Data is available on computer tape or printout (for less than 30,000 names).

Owners: Massachusetts Registry of Motor Vehicles, 100 Nashua Street, Boston, MA 02114; (617) 727-3716. Database: Massachusetts Automobile Owners - contains owner's name and address along with make, model and year of 5 million vehicles. Services - Sorting of data is available, for instance, by particular insurance company the owner carries. The cost is $200 for the first 1,000 names and $30 per 1,000 records thereafter. Data is available on computer tape or printout (for less than 30,000 names).

Michigan
Drivers: Michigan Department of State, Data Processing Division, Lansing, MI 48918; (517) 322-1583. Database: Michigan Drivers - provides names, address, birth date, and sex of 6 million drivers. Services: Data may be selected by sex, birth date, county, city, and zip code at a cost of $64 per 1,000 names versus $16 per 1,000 names unsorted. There is a $400 minimum charge. Data can be purchased on computer tape or printout.

Owners: Michigan Department of State, Data Processing Division, Lansing, MI 48918; (517) 322-1583. Database: Michigan Automobile Owners - provides owner's name and address with year, make and model of 5.5 million passenger cars and 4.5 million other vehicles. Services: The cost for sorting is $64 per 1,000 names versus $16 per 1,000 unsorted names. There is a $5,000 minimum charge. Data can be purchased on computer tape or printout.

Minnesota
Drivers: Minnesota Department of Public Safety, Driver/Vehicle Services Division, Transportation Building, St. Paul, MN 55155; (612) 297-2442. Database: Minnesota Drivers - provides name, address, and sex of 3 million drivers. Services: Data cannot be sorted, there is an extra fee if more information is required. Data is available on computer tape for $25,000 plus a $5,000 security deposit which is refunded after one year.

Owners: Minnesota Department of Public Safety, Driver/Vehicle Services Division, Transportation Building, St. Paul, MN 35155; (612) 296-2832. Database: Minnesota Automobile Owners - contains owner's name and address along with make, model, and year for 3 million cars and 1.1 million other vehicles. Services: Certain data can be sorted. Data are available on computer tape or printout. There is a $500 minimum plus $8 per 1,000 names.

Mississippi
Drivers: Mississippi Department of Public Safety/Data Processing, P.O. Box 958, Jackson, MS 39205; (601) 987-1212. Database: Mississippi Drivers - contains name, address, birth date, race and sex of over 1,794,000 drivers. Services: Data cannot be sorted. The entire file must be purchased for $250 plus $15 per reel.

Owners: Mississippi State Tax Commission Network, P.O. Box 960, Room 220, Jackson, MS 39205; (601) 359-117. Database: Mississippi Automobile Owners - provides a complete file, including owner's name and address, make, model, year of 1.6 million registered vehicles. Services: Data can be sorted and made available on computer tape or printout. Fees range from $1,000 - $2,000. Mailing labels available for an extra charge.

Missouri
Drivers: Missouri Department of Revenue, Information Services Bureau, P.O. Box 41, Jefferson City, MO 65105; (314) 751-5486. Database: Missouri Drivers - contains name, address, sex, birth date, height, weight, eye color, restrictions, license number, class, and county of 3 million drivers. Services: Data available on computer tape or printouts for $1,000, plus $35 per hour plus $20 per 1,000. Mailing labels available for an extra charge $2 per 1,000.

Owners: Missouri Department of Revenue, Information Services Bureau, P.O. Box 41, Jefferson City, MO 65105; (314) 751-5486. Database: Missouri Owners - provides name and address of registered owners plus make, model, year, number of cylinders, type of fuel, license expiration date, and year for over 3 million cars and 2 million other vehicles. Services: Data available on computer tape or printout. Cost: $100 plus $35 per hour and $20 per 1,000. Mailing labels available for an extra fee of $2.00 per 1,000.

Montana
Drivers: Data not made available.

Owners: Montana Motor Vehicle Division, 925 Main St., Deer Lodge, MT 59722; (406) 846-1423. Database: Montana Automobile Owners - provides owner's name and address along with year, make, model, body, color, serial number, second owner for over one million registered vehicles. Services--Data available on computer tape and printout. The cost is $200 for the first 10,000 names and $2.00 per 1,000 names thereafter.

Nebraska
Drivers: Nebraska Department of Motor Vehicles, P.O. Box 94789, Lincoln, NE 68509; (402) 471-3909. To receive information you must provide the correct date of birth, or license number for each record requested. The cost is $1.75 per record.

Owners: Nebraska Department of Motor Vehicles, P.O. Box 94789, Lincoln, NE 68509. Database: Nebraska Automobile Owners - provides listing by make, model, and year which includes owner's name and address for 856,000 passenger cars and 650,000 other vehicle owners. Services: Data can be provided on computer tape and printout for $12 per 1,000 or $300 minimum.

Nevada
Drivers: Nevada Department of Motor Vehicles, 555 Wright Way, Carson City, NV 89711; (702) 885-5380, or (702) 885-5375. Database: Nevada Drivers - provides name, address, date of birth, height, weight, for more than one million drivers. Services: Data can be sorted by county, zip code, date of birth and made of car. Data available on computer tape or printout (up to 1,000,000 names). Mailing labels available for an extra fee. Cost is $2,500 for the entire file or $15 per 1,000 for a partial listing.

Owners: Contains owner's name, address along with make, model and year for one million registered vehicles. Data may also be selected by county, ZIP Code and make of car. Cost: Computer tape is available for $2,500 or portions prorated $15 per thousand. A printout is available up to 1,000,000 records. Also available on mailing labels.

New Hampshire
Drivers: New Hampshire Department of Safety, Data Processing, 10 Hazen Drive, Concord, NH 03305; (603) 271-2314. Database: New Hampshire Drivers - consists of name, address, physical characteristics, social security number, issue and expiration date and restriction of 720,000 drivers. Services: Data can be sorted by sex or age. Data provided on computer tape or printout. Prices vary, depending on data requested and size of the file. The entire file is available on microfiche for $50.00

Owners: New Hampshire Department of Safety, Data Processing, 10 Hazen Drive, Concord, NH 03305; (603) 271-2314. Database: New Hampshire Owners - contains owner's name and address along with make, model and year for 815,628 passenger cars and 517,606 other vehicles. Services: Data can be sorted by zip code, model or make. Data available on computer tape or printout (extra charge). Fees vary depending on request. Entire file available on microfiche for $50.00.

New Jersey
Drivers and Owners: Data not available for purchase. Must write in for individual records. New Jersey Division of Motor Vehicles, 25 S. Montgomery St., Trenton, NJ 08660; (609) 292-6500.

New Mexico
Drivers and Owners: Data cannot be sold for commercial purposes. New Mexico Taxation and Revenue Department, Motor Vehicle Division, P.O. Box 1028, Santa Fe, NM 87504; (505) 827-2294.

New York
Drivers and Owners: Data tapes not available for purchase. Must write in for individual records at $2.50 per record. State Department of Motor Vehicles, Empire State Plaza, Room 433, Albany, NY 12228; (518) 449-3419.

North Carolina
Drivers: No records released.

Owners: North Carolina State, Information Processing Service, 3700 Old Wake Forest Road, Raleigh, NC 27609; (919) 733-555. Database: North Carolina Automobile Owners - provides owner's name and address, second owner's name, make, model, year, plate classification, license number and weight of vehicle of 5.5 million registered vehicles. Services: Data can be sorted by model, year, make, county, zip code and other variables. The cost is $250 for the first 12,500 records and $20 per 1,000 records thereafter.

North Dakota
Drivers: North Dakota Drivers License and Traffic Safety Division, 600 E. Blvd. Ave., Bismark, ND 58505; (701) 224-2601. Database: North Dakota Drivers - provides name, address, date of birth, and license number of 450,000 drivers. Services: Special sort/extraction is available. The cost is $9 per 1,000 names with a $250 minimum. Mailing labels available for an extra fee.

Owners: North Dakota Motor Vehicles Department, Capitol Grounds, Bismark, ND 58505; (701) 224-2725. Database: North Dakota Automobile Owners - contains owner's name and address along with make, model and year of 419,000 passenger cars and 370,000 other vehicles. Services: Data can be sorted by variables and provided on computer printout tape for $50 plus $20 per 1,000 names. Mailing labels available for an extra fee.

Ohio

Drivers: Ohio Bureau of Motor Vehicles, Data Services, P.O. Box 16520, Columbus, OH 43216; (614) 752-7695. Database: Ohio Drivers - includes name, address, sex, date of birth, height, weight, hair color, eye color, zip code, some restrictions, for over 8 million registered drivers. Services: Data can be sorted by variables. Data available on computer tape for $.075 per record. Mailing labels are $.08 each.

Owners: Ohio Bureau of Motor Vehicles, Data Services, P.O. Box 16520, Columbus, OH 43216; (614) 752-7695. Database: Ohio Automobile Owners - provides owner's name and address along with make, model, year, license number, and expiration date for over 6 million registered vehicles. Services: Data can be sorted by variables. Available on computer tape or printout at $.075 per record. Mailing labels provided for $.08 each.

Oklahoma

Drivers and Owners: Data tapes not sold. Individual records available for $1.00 each. Oklahoma Tax Commission, Motor Vehicle Division, 2501 N. Lincoln Blvd., Oklahoma City, OK 73194; (405) 521- 3217.

Oregon

Drivers: Oregon Department of Transportation, Motor Vehicles Division, 1905 Lana Ave. N.E., Salem, OR 97314; (503) 378-6995. Database: Oregon Drivers - contains name, address, sex, age, and year of birth for over 2 million drivers. Services: Data can be sorted and provided on computer tape for $165 or printout for $190 plus $28 for box of paper.

Owners: Oregon Department of Transportation, Motor Vehicles Division, 1905 Lana Ave. N.E., Salem, OR 97314; (503) 378-6995. Database: Oregon Automobile Owners - contains owner's name and address along with make, model, and year for over two million registered vehicles. Services: Data can be sorted by variables, data available on computer tape ($165), or printout ($190 plus $28 for box of paper).

Pennsylvania

Drivers and Owners: Data only available with a special request. Not available for commercial purposes. Bureau of Drivers Licenses Information, Box 2691, Harrisburg, PA 17105; (717) 787-2158.

Rhode Island

Drivers and Owners: Data not available to the public. Department of Motor Vehicles, State Office Building, Providence, RI 02903; (401) 277-2970.

South Carolina

Drivers: South Carolina Highway Department, P.O. Box 1498, Columbia, SC 29216; (803) 737-1209. Database: South Carolina Drivers - provides name, address, birth date, license number, and restrictions of 1.8 million drivers. Services: Data may be sorted by last name, zip code, tag number as well as automobiles and/or motorcycles for 100,000 records. Computer tapes or printouts are available for $1,200.

Owners: South Carolina Highway Department, P.O. Box 1498, Columbia, SC 29216; (803) 737-1084. Database: South Carolina Automobile Owners - contains name and address of 700,000 registered vehicle owners along with make, year and serial number. Services: Data may be sorted by last name, zip code, tag number as well as automobile and/or motorcycles. Requests must be in by the 10th of the month and printouts are run the last week of the month. Charges vary from $500 to $1,200. Printouts available up to 100,000 names.

South Dakota

Drivers and Owners: Data not released. Division of Motor Vehicles, 118 W. Capitol St., Pierre, SD 57501; (605) 773-4129.

Tennessee

Drivers: Department of Safety Information System, 150 Foster Ave., Nashville, TN 37210; (615) 251-5322. Database: Tennessee Drivers - contains name, address, date of birth, sex and physical characteristics of approximately 3 million drivers. Services: Data can be sorted by category. Computer tapes, printouts and mailing labels are available for a minimum $500 plus $.10 per record.

Owners: Department of Revenue, Management Systems Division, Andrew Jackson Building, Room 402, 500 Deaderick St., Nashville, TN 37242; (615) 741-2411. Database: Tennessee Automobile Owners - contains owner's name, address, model, make, year, tag number of approximately 4 million vehicles. Services: Computer tapes, printouts, and mailing labels available for $300 minimum, plus $100 set up fee plus $20.05 per 1,000 names.

Texas

Drivers: Texas Department of Public Safety, Attn. L.I. and V.I., P.O. Box 4087, Austin, TX 78773; (512) 465-2186. Database: Texas Drivers - provides name, address, date of birth, license number, for over 12 million drivers. Services: Data can be sorted by category. Data provided on computer tape for $27,000 for the entire file, or $2.25 per 1,000.

Owners: State Department of Highway and Public Transportation, Division of Motor Vehicles, 40th and Jackson, Austin, TX 78779; (512) 465-7531. Database: Texas Automobile Owners - contains owner's name and address along with make, model, and year, previous owner, lien holder for 14 million vehicles. Services: Sorting is not available. Data available on computer tape for $4,000 plus $.30 per 1,000.

Utah

Drivers: Data not released.

Owners: Utah State Tax Commission, Data Processing, 160 E. 300 South St., Salt Lake City, UT 84134. Database: Utah Automobile Owners - provides owner's name and address along with make, model and year for 1.9 million vehicles. Services: Data can be sorted and made available on computer tape for $300 to $400.

Vermont

Drivers: Vermont Department of Motor Vehicles, 120 State Street, Montpelier, VT 05603; (802) 828-2020. Database: Vermont Drivers - contains name, address, physical characteristics, license number and date of birth of 397,093 drivers. Services: Full identification must be provided in order to obtain information. Cost is $2.50 for each record.

Owners: Vermont Department of Motor Vehicles, 120 State Street, Montpelier, VT 05603; (802) 828-2020. Database: Vermont Automobile Owners - provides owner's name and address along with make, model, and year for 310,000 passenger cars and 300,000 other vehicles. Services: Must provide vehicle identification to obtain information. Cost is $2.50 for each record.

Virginia

Drivers: Data not released.

Owners: Dealer & Records Division, P.O. Box 7412, Richmond, VA 23269;; (804) 367-0455. If you provide the license number they will provide the information. Initial fee of $3,000 plus $5.00 per record.

Washington

Drivers: Department of Licensing, Highways/Licensing Building, Olympia, WA 98504; (206) 753-7397. Database: Washington Drivers - provides driver's name, date of birth, and address of registered drivers. Services: Sorting is available. A written request is required and an agreement must be signed. Each program is custom made. The charge is $3,680 plus tax.

Owners: Department of Licensing, Highways/Licenses Building, Olympia, WA 98504; (206) 753-7379. Database: Washington Automobile Owners - contains owner's name, address, make, model, year and class of vehicle. Services: It can be sorted alphabetically by owner's name, address, make, model, year and class of vehicle. It can be sorted alphabetically by owner's name or state or county. A written request is required and an agreement must be signed. Each program is custom made. The charge is $3,680 plus tax.

West Virginia

Drivers: West Virginia Department of Motor Vehicles, 1800 Washington St., East Charleston, WV 25305; (304) 348-2723. Database: West Virginia Drivers - provides name, address, height, weight, race, sex, and date of birth of 1.4 million drivers. Services: Data can be sorted and provided on computer tape or printout. Cost is $1,350.

Owners: West Virginia Department of Motor Vehicles, 1800 Washington St. East Charleston, WV 25305; (304) 348-2723. Database: West Virginia Automobile Owners - contains owner's name and address along with make, model, and year of 1,200,000 passenger cars and 246,000 other vehicles. Services: Data can be sorted and provided on computer tape or printout for $1,350.

Wisconsin

Drivers: Wisconsin Department of Transportation, 4802 Sheboygan Ave., Madison, WI 53711; (608) 266-2237. Database: Wisconsin Drivers - provides an alphabetical list of name, address, date of birth, sex and drivers record for 3.8 million drivers. Services: Data available on computer tape or printout for $2,600.

Owners: Wisconsin Department of Transportation, 4802 Sheboygan Ave., Madison, WI 53711; (608) 266-2237. Database: Wisconsin Owners- provides owner's name and address plus make, model and year of 2.3 million passenger cars and 1.7 million other vehicles. Services: Data cannot be sorted. Entire file must be purchased on computer tape for $2,600.

Wyoming

Drivers: Wyoming Department of Revenue and Taxation, 122 West 25th Street, Cheyenne, WY 82002; (307) 777-5259. Database: Wyoming Driver - provides name, address, date of birth, Social Security Number, status, expiration, and issuance date for 500,000 drivers. Services: Cost for magnetic tape: $1 per record with a $100 minimum. All requests must be approved by the Commission.

Owners: Wyoming Department of Revenue and Taxation, 122 West 25th Street, Cheyenne, WY 82002; (307) 777-6511. Individual record searches with a written request. Cost $2 per search.

Other Info Sources On People

Here are trail guides for genealogy research as well as all the major federal government sources for locating individuals. Also refer to the other sections in this chapter, specifically Who Owes Money to Whom and Driver's Licenses and Motor Vehicles which identify other sources for gathering information on the family clan or next door neighbors.

* Army Active Personnel Locator
U.S. Department of the Army
Worldwide Locator, EREC
Ft. Benjamin Harrison, IN 46249-5301 (800) 444-3333 (317) 542-4211
To locate a missing relative in the active army, contact this service. There is a small fee for the search.

* Army Discharged Personnel Locator Service
National Personnel Records Center
9700 Page Blvd.
St. Louis, MO 63132-5200 (314) 263-7201
To locate a relative or friend who is has been discharged from the Army, or who is deceased, contact the above office. The locator service's records go back to 1912; you may be able to find out what your great, great grandfather did in the Army. There is a small fee for the search.

* Army Personnel Locator
U.S. Army Worldwide Locator
ELREC
Fort Benjamin Harrirson, IN 46249 (317) 542-4211 (recording)
To locate a long lost relative who is still on active duty in the Army, contact this office by letter. There is a small fee for their services. The telephone recording will give you information on the procedure and the data they need from you to initiate their search.

* Army Reserve and Retiree Locator
Army Reserve Personnel Center
U.S. Department of the Army
9700 Page Blvd.
St. Louis, MO 63132-5200 (314) 263-7828
To locate a missing relative in the Army reserve (who is not assigned to a unit), or to locate a living Army retiree, contact this office. There is a small fee for the search.

* Biographical Directory of the U.S. Congress 1774-1989
Superintendent of Documents
Government Printing Office
Washington, DC 20402 (202) 783-3238
The Biographical Directory of the U.S. Congress 1774-1989, contains authoritative biographies of the more than 11,000 men and women who have served in the U.S. Congress from 1789 to 1989, and in the Continental Congress between 1774 and 1789. Many features include a listing of all chairmen of standing committees, all major formal leadership positions, bibliographic citations, and major revisions of political party affiliations reflecting the latest scholarship. You'll also find complete rosters of State congressional delegations for the First through 100th Congresses. This bicentennial edition is the most comprehensive *Biographical Directory of the United States Congress* ever issued. The latest edition published at the beginning of the 101st Congress is available through the Government Printing Office for $82.

* Congressional Directory
Superintendent of Documents
Government Printing Office
Washington, DC 20402 (202) 783-3238
The *Congressional Directory* has been the official handbook for the Congress since 1821 and is also widely used by Federal agency officials and the general public. Its contents include lists of addresses, rooms, and phone numbers of Members, biographical sketches of Members, Capitol officers and officials, committees, departments, and information on diplomatic offices and statistics. It also includes lists of members of the press admitted to the House and Senate galleries. The *1989-1990 Official Congressional Directory of the 101st Congress* is available for $15 in paperback, $20 in hardback, and $25 for a hardback copy with a thumb index.

* Family and Military Genealogy
Military Reference Branch
National Archives and Records Administration
8th St. & Pennsylvania Ave., NW
Washington, DC 20408 (202) 523-4804
The National Archives holds military service records and veterans' benefits records (pensions and bounty-land application files) for service performed from the Revolution (1775) through the early 20th century. The Archives does not have Confederate pension records, which were authorized by some southern states. To order photocopies of military service records, you must use National Archives Trust Fund Form 80 and submit a separate form for each file requested. You can obtain copies of this form and additional information about military service records from the Reference Services Branch at (202) 523-3218. Your order must contain the following information: soldier's full name; period/war in which he/she served; state from which he/she served; branch of service; and whether the service was with the Union or Confederate forces.

* Federal Campaign Finance Law Complaints
Federal Election Commission
999 E Street, NW
Washington, DC 20463 (202) 376-5140
If you believe a violation of the Federal campaign finance law has taken place, you may file a complaint with the Federal Election Commission. Send the Commission a letter explaining why you believe the law may have been violated, describe the specific facts and circumstances, and name the individuals or organizations responsible. The letter must be sworn to, signed, and notarized. Complaints of alleged violations receive case numbers and are called MURs, Matters Under Review.

* Federal Elections Clearinghouse
Federal Election Commission
999 E Street, NW
Washington, DC 20463 (202) 376-5670
The Election Clearinghouse assists election officials and the general public by responding to inquiries concerning the electoral process, publishing research, and conducting workshops on all matters related to Federal election administration.

* Federal Elections Library
Federal Election Commission Library
999 E Street, NW
Room 801
Washington, DC 20463 (202) 376-5312
The FEC Library's collection includes basic legal research tools and materials dealing with political campaign finance, corporate and labor political activity, and campaign finance reform. The Library staff prepares indexes to Advisory Opinions and Matters Under Review (MURs), as well as a "Campaign Finance and Federal Election Law Bibliography," which are available for purchase from the FEC's Public Records Office.

* Federal Employees' Personnel Records
National Personnel Records Center
National Archives and Records Administration
111 Winnebago Street
St. Louis, MO 63118 (314) 425-5722
Federal employees' personnel records are transferred and stored in the National Personnel Records Center. The Center can answer questions regarding the information available, and can provide copies of documents. Contact the Center for more information.

* Financial Disclosure Database on Federal
Candidates
Federal Election Commission
Data Systems Development Division

Information on People, Companies, and Mailing Lists

999 E Street, NW
Washington, DC 20463 (202) 376-3140
The FEC maintains a computer database of information from all reports filed by political committees, individuals, and other entities since 1972. The data is sorted into indexes which permit a detailed analysis of campaign finance activity and, additionally, provide a tool for monitoring contribution limitations. The data can be searched by specific candidate or contributor. By contacting this office, individuals can have searches done on twenty names or less free of charge. For searches of more than 20 names, cost varies depending on computer time needed.

* Genealogy Reference
Main Reading Room
Library of Congress
Washington, DC 20540 (202) 707-5521
Located on the first floor of the Thomas Jefferson Building, the main reading room contains material on American history, economics, fiction, language and literature, political science, government documents, and sociology. A reference collection for these materials is also housed there. These reading rooms are not equipped to answer reference questions over the telephone, but will provide information on their collections, hours of operation, and the like.
Local History and Genealogy/(202) 707-5537

* Genealogy Research
Reference Services Branch
8th St. & Pennsylvania Ave., NW
Room 205
Washington, DC 20408 (202) 523-3218
Using Records in the National Archives for Genealogical Research is a free, 25-page brochure which explains a little about genealogical research in general, and then outlines the genealogical records in the National Archives. It includes the necessary information in order to research your request.
Guide to Genealogical Research in the National Archives is available for $25 and contains information about individuals whose names appear in census records, military service and pension files, ship passenger and arrival lists, land records, and many other types of records. This Guide shows how to tap this rich resource, explaining what types of records are preserved in the National Archives and what specific information about individuals is included in each type of record. For more information on genealogical research, contact the Reference Services Branch.

* Genealogical Workshops
Education Branch
National Archives and Records Administration
8th St. & Pennsylvania Ave., NW, Room 505
Washington, DC 20408 (202) 523-4867
Genealogical workshops are offered quite frequently by the Education Branch of the National Archives. The topics covered include census records, passenger lists, naturalization records, military service records, as well as many other genealogical topics. Each workshop lasts three hours and costs $10. Call or write for a complete workshop schedule.

* Historical Documentary Editions 1988
National Historical Publications and Records Commission
National Archives and Records Administration
8th St. & Pennsylvania Ave., NW, Room 300
Washington, DC 20408 (202) 523-3092
This free catalog lists and describes all the documentary editions supported by the Commission with funds or by formal endorsement. These editions represent a major, long-term effort to make the nation's important documents widely available for study and research. Each title includes a brief description, as well as ordering information.

* Inmate Locator Line
Public Information
Bureau of Prisons
U.S. Department of Justice
320 1st St., NW, Room 640
Washington, DC 20536 (202) 724-3198
A special phone service hotline is available for people trying to locate family members or loved ones believed to be incarcerated in local, state, or federal correctional institutions. Call the Inmate Locator Line: (202) 724-3126 between 10 a.m. and 4:30 p.m. EST.

* Military and Civilian Employment Records
National Personnel Center
9700 Page Blvd.
St. Louis, MO 63232 (314) 263-7201

This Center holds both military and civilian Federal personnel records dating from 1900 to the present. The Center prefers written requests for reference assistance.

* Military Pension Genealogy Searches
General Reference Branch
National Archives and Records Administration
Washington, DC 20408 (202) 523-3059
This office holds military service and pension records of people who served prior to 1900. The office accepts written requests only. Ask for *Form NATF 80*.

* Military Records 19th Century On
Suitland Reference Branch
National Archives and Records Administration
Washington, DC 20409 (202) 763-7410
This office holds historical material, including Land Office records, military personnel records dating prior to 1900, State Department personnel overseas post records since 1935, the Japanese war relocation records, records of the U.S. military government of Germany and Japan, as well as records of all military actions dating from the Revolutionary War through 1963. The office provides reference assistance in locating historical material, and will answer reference questions both in writing and by phone.

* Military Reference
Office of the National Archives
National Archives and Records Administration
8th St. & Pennsylvania Ave., NW, Room 13W
Washington, DC 20408 (202) 523-3340
The Military Reference Branch maintains records of military personnel separated from the U.S. Air Force, Army, Coast Guard, Marine Corps, Navy, Confederate States, volunteers, as well as veterans records. The publication, *Military Service Records in the National Archives of the United States*, provides a detailed list of the holdings and pertinent details about the records.

* Military Service Genealogy Searches
General Reference Branch
National Archives and Records Administration
Washington, DC 20408 (202) 523-3059
This office holds military service and pension records of people who served prior to 1900. The office accepts written requests only. Ask for *Form NATF 80*.

* National Driver Register
National Driver Register (NTS-24)
Traffic Safety Programs
National Highway Traffic Safety Administration
U.S. Department of Transportation
400 7th Street, SW, Room 5119
Washington, DC 20590 (202) 366-4800
The *National Driver Register* is a central, computerized index of state records on drivers whose operator licenses have been revoked, denied, or suspended for more than 6 months. Data includes name, birthdate, height, weight, eye color, date and reason for action, and date of reinstatement. Applications for driver licenses are routinely checked against the register, and states exchange information via an electronic system.

* Personal Census Records Service
Personal Census Service Branch
Bureau of the Census
Pittsburgh, KS 66762 (316) 231-7100

The Census History Staff
Data User Services Division
Bureau of the Census
U.S. Department of Commerce
Washington, DC 20233 (301) 763-7936
The Bureau of the Census employs a staff to search the Federal censuses of population from 1900 on, stored at Pittsburgh, Kansas, and provide, for a fee, official transcripts of personal data from these records to individuals who lack other birth or citizenship documents. Government agencies and employers often accept these transcripts as evidence of age and place of birth for obtaining employment, social security benefits, old age assistance, passports, naturalization papers, or delayed birth certificates, and for other purposes. The personal information recorded in these censuses may be furnished only upon the written request of the named individual or his or her legal representative. Application forms, with detailed information, can be obtained by contacting either office above.

* Photographs of Every Member of Congress
The Superintendent of Documents

452

Government Printing Office
Washington, DC 20402 (202) 275-3030

The *Congressional Pictorial Directory* contains photographs of the President, Vice President, members of the Senate and House, Officers of the Senate and House, Officials of the Capitol, and a list of the Senate delegations and an alphabetical list of senators and representatives. The paperback edition is $4.24, and the hardback copy is $14.00.

* Presidential Political Appointments: The "Plum" Book

Senate Government Affairs Committee
Dirksen Office Building, Room S-340
Washington, DC 20510 (202) 224-3791

Superintendent of Documents
Government Printing Office
Washington, DC 20402 (202) 275-3030

U.S. Policy and Supporting Positions, more commonly known as the *Plum Book*, lists some 3,000 political appointment jobs and describes the type of appointment, tenure, grade, and salary. It is available for sale at the Superintendent of Documents for $14 per copy.

* Prisoners of War and Reclassification

U.S. Department of Defense
Force Management and Personnel
The Pentagon, Room 3E767
Washington, DC 20301-4000 (202) 695-7402

For information on conscientious objectors and POW's, including reclassification and discharge data, contact the above office.

* Prisoner-of-War Records

Military Services Branch
National Archives and Records Administration
8th St. & Pennsylvania Ave., NW, Room 13W
Washington, DC 20408 (202) 523-3340

This Branch has information regarding Prisoner-of-War records through the Civil War, and can also direct you to the proper office for information regarding prisoners-of-war through the Vietnam War.

* Salaries and Expenses of Congressmen, Congresswomen, and Their Employees

House Document Room
H-226 Capitol Bldg.
Washington, DC 20515 (202) 225-3456

The *Report of the Clerk of the House* includes the salaries of House members' staffs, committee staffs, and House officers and employees. This quarterly report includes a listing of House expenditures.

* Salaries and Expenses of U.S. Senators and Their Staff

Senate Document Room
B-04 Senate Hart Office Building
Washington, DC 20510 (202) 224-7860

The biannual *Report of the Secretary of the Senate* lists Senate expenditures and details the salaries of senators' staff, members, committee staff members, and officers and employees of the Senate.

* Selective Service Registration Status

Registration Information Office
P.O. Box 4638
North Suburban, IL 60197-4638 (800) 621-5388

If you have any questions regarding an individual's status and the requirement to register, call or write this office.

* Ship Passenger Arrival Lists

Reference Services Branch
National Archives and Records Administration
8th St. & Pennsylvania Ave., NW
Washington, DC 20408 (202) 523-3218

The National Archives compiles ship passenger arrival records dating from 1820 for most east and gulf coast ports, a few lists dating from 1800 for Philadelphia, and from the 1890's for San Francisco and Seattle. Archives staff can conduct searches if you know the full name of the passenger, the port of entry, and the approximate date of arrival.

* State Access to Financial Disclosure Database

Federal Election Commission
Public Records Office
999 E Street, NW
Washington, DC 20463 (202) 376-3140

Under the State Access Program, individuals and organizations in 15 states now have immediate online access to several standard FEC computer indexes which provide descriptive information on all registered political committees, the total receipts and disbursements of committees, and a listing of all PAC contributions to federal candidates. Participating states with operational terminals within their State Election Offices include: Arizona, Colorado, Connecticut, Georgia, Illinois, Iowa, Massachusetts, Michigan, New Jersey, New Mexico, Ohio, Tennessee, Vermont, Washington, and Wisconsin.

* State Election Finance Records

Federal Election Commission
Public Records Office
999 E Street, NW
Washington, DC 20463 (202) 376-3155, (800) 424-9530

Researchers can obtain campaign finance reports from the records office in each state. Contact this FEC office to order a list of the names, addresses, and phone numbers of national and state disclosure offices.

* Vietnam Casualty Computer Printout

Center for Electronic Records
National Archives and Records Administration
Washington, DC 20408 (202) 523-3267

This office holds all Federal records on computer disk, which include all recent DOD records and the casualty lists from the Vietnam War. Copies may be purchased.

Information on People, Companies, and Mailing Lists

Information On Any Company

When many researchers are doing investigations on companies they often rely only on two major information sources:

> Public Companies = US Securities and Exchange
> Commission Filings

> Privately Held Companies = Dun & Bradstreet
> Reports

Although many people still depend heavily on the Securities and Exchange Commission (SEC) and Dun & Bradstreet (D & B), these two resources have severe limitations. The Securities and Exchange Commission has information on approximately only 10,000 public companies in the United States. However, according to the IRS and the US Bureau of the Census (both agencies count differently), there are between 5,000,000 and 12,000,000 companies in the country. So you can see that the SEC represents only a small fraction of the universe. Also, if you are interested in a division or a subsidiary of a public corporation and that division does not represent a substantial portion of the company's business, there will be no information on their activities on file at the SEC. This means that for thousands of corporate divisions and subsidiaries it is necessary to look beyond the SEC.

D & B Won't Jail You For Not Telling The Truth But The Government Will

The problems with Dun & Bradstreet reports are more significant than the shortcomings of company filings at the SEC. The main drawback is that D & B reports have been established primarily for credit purposes and are supposed to indicate the company's ability to pay its bills. Therefore, you will find information from current creditors about whether a business is late in its payments, which may or may not be a useful barometer to evaluate the company.

If there is additional financial information in these reports, you should also be aware of who in the company provides D & B with information and their motives. The information contained in these reports does not carry the legal weight of the company information registered with the Securities and Exchange Commission. If a company lies about any of the information it turns over to the SEC, a corporate officer could wind up in jail. Dun & Bradstreet, however, collects its information by telephoning a company and asking it to provide certain information voluntarily. The company is under no obligation to comply and, equally important, is under no obligation to D & B to be honest. Unlike the government, Dun & Bradstreet cannot prosecute.

If a competitor or someone were interested in acquiring Information USA, Inc., for example, probably the first step would be to obtain any financial data about this privately held company. In this hypothetical case, Information USA, Inc. might be interested in such a sale or perhaps want to impress the competition. Consequently, the information supplied to Dun & Bradstreet most likely would be the sanitized version which I would want outsiders to see. My only dilemma would be in remembering what half truths we told D & B last year so

that our track record would appear consistent. However, Information USA, Inc. would not and does not play such games with its financial information filed with the Maryland Secretary of State.

This is why resourceful researchers are starting to appreciate the value of the thousands of non-traditional information sources such as public documents and industry experts.

Where To Start: SEC

The first question to resolve is whether the company you are gathering intelligence about is a public corporation. If it is, you should get your hands on copies of the company's SEC filings. The fastest way to make this determination is to call either of the two major private SEC document retrieval companies. Both firms have toll-free numbers and offer this service free of charge.

Bechtel Information Services
SEC/Express
9430 Key West Avenue
Rockville, MD 20850
(800) 231-3282
(301) 738-1400

Disclosure Inc.
5161 River Road Building 60
Bethesda, MD 20816
(800) 638-8241
(301) 951-1300

If the company in question files with the Securities and Exchange Commission, the least you should do is to obtain a copy of the Annual Report, known as 10-K. This disclosure form will give you the most current description of the company's activities along with their annual financial statement.

Financial Statements In Addition To The Annual Report

In addition to the 10-K you may also want to see the company's most current financial statements by obtaining copies of all 10-Q's filed since their last 10-K. 10-Q's are basically quarterly financial statements which will bring you up-to-date since the last annual report.

The two other documents which may be of immediate interest are the 8-K's and the Annual Report to Stockholders. An 8-K will disclose any major developments that have occurred since the last annual report, such as information about a takeover or major lawsuit. The Annual Report to Stockholders, the glossy quasi-public relations tool that is sent to all those who own stock in the company, can provide another component in assembling a company's profile. The most interesting item in this report, which is not included in the 10-K Annual Report, is the message from the President. This message often provides insights about the company's future plans.

Obtaining Copies of SEC Documents

The fastest way to get SEC documents is through one of the many document retrieval companies which provide this service. In addition to the two major firms mentioned above, other companies that specialize in quickly obtaining corporate SEC filings include:

1) Cunningham & Hamlette
   3815-B W Street SE
   Washington, DC 20020
   (202) 789-2151

2) Warren O. Flood Filing Service
   1209 Tuckerman Street NW
   Washington, DC 20011
   (202) 289-0239

3) FACS Info Service, Inc.
   157 Fisher Avenue
   Eastchester, NY 10709
   (212) 379-2330 (NYC)
   FAX (914) 779-7038

4) Federal Document Retrieval, Inc.
   810 Fist Street, N.E., Suite 600
   Washington, DC 20002
   (202) 789-2233

5) Meredith Hurt & Associates
   11526 Maple Ridge Road
   Reston, VA 22090
   (202) 628-9628

6) Research Information Services
   501 Capitol Court, NE
   Capitol, Suite 200
   Washington, DC 20002
   (202) 737-7111

7) Charles E. Simon & Company
   1333 H Street NW, Suite 500
   Washington, DC 20005
   (202) 289-5300

8) Washington Service Bureau
   655 15th Street NW, Room 275
   Washington, DC 20005
   (202) 833-9200

9) Washington Document Service
   450 5th Street NW, Suite 1110
   Washington, DC 20001
   (202) 628-5200

10) Vickers Stock Research Corp.
    450 5th Street NW, Room 910
    Washington, DC 20001
    (202) 626-4951

You can also go to one of the four major SEC Document Rooms to see any public filing. These reference rooms are located in Washington, DC, New York City, Chicago, and Los Angeles.

If the company headquarters or main office is located in the area served either by the Atlanta, Boston, Denver, Fort Worth, or Seattle regional offices, the 10-K and other documents can be examined at the appropriate SEC office. For the exact location of any of the regional offices mentioned contact:

Office of Public Affairs
US Securities and Exchange Commission
450 5th Street NW, Room 1012
Washington, DC 20549
(202) 272-2573

One way to obtain free copies of these reports is to call the company directly and tell them you are a potential investor. Many public corporations are set up to respond to this sort of inquiry.

Before you order any of these SEC filings, it is wise to ask for the total number of pages contained in each of the documents you want to obtain. Most of these document retrieval firms charge by the page and, no doubt, you don't want to be surprised if a company's amendment to its 10-K happens to run 500 pages in length.

Once you have the SEC documents you can then explore the additional sources described below.

Clues At The State Level About Privately Held Companies Plus Divisions And Subsidiaries Of Public Corporations

The following sources are designed primarily to help you gather information on privately held companies or those divisions and subsidiaries of public corporations which are not contained in documents filed with the US Securities and Exchange Commission. However, the sources described here will enhance your work in collecting data on all types of companies. If the company in question is not publicly owned, the next step is to turn your attention to the appropriate state government offices. All companies doing business in any state leave a trail of documentation there. The number of documents and the amount of detail vary widely depending upon the state regulations and the type of company.

One of the main reasons you should begin your search with the state government is that it may take longer to retrieve the information from the state offices than from other checkpoints which are described in this Section.

Puzzling Together Bits of Information

Remember that only the US Securities and Exchange Commission documents fulfill the purpose of providing you with information on your competitor or acquisition candidate. All other government documents are generated to comply with some law or policy, such as pollution control, consumer protection, or tax collection. Because of this, government bureaucrats who collect and analyze these documents have no idea just how valuable the information can be to you. Do not expect that the data contained in other government documents will be presented in a way that automatically will suit your particular needs. Furthermore, no single document will provide all the information about a corporate entity that you are after.

The strategy is to get any information whatever because each piece might contribute to your overall information mosiac. Although a full profit and loss statement will be out of reach, the office of uniform commercial code can tell you to whom the company owes money and a description of the corporation's assets. The state office of corporations may not give you the total sales figure, but if the company is headquartered out of state, it may tell you the corporation's total sales in that state and what percentage this is of its total. With a little bit of

Information on People, Companies, and Mailing Lists

algebra you can estimate the total sales.

If it were as easy as making one phone call and getting complete financial information on any company, everyone would be doing it. Your competitive advantage lies in getting information that other people don't know about or are too lazy to get.

In the event you intend to dig around at the state level, the following three offices are a must. They offer the biggest potential for the least amount of effort:

1) Office of Corporations

Every corporation, whether it is headquartered or has an office in a state, must file some information with a state agency. The corporations division or office of corporations usually is part of the office of the Secretary of State. When a company incorporates or sets up an office in the state, it must file incorporation papers, or something similar, which provides--at a minimum--the nature of the business, the names and addresses of officers and agents, and the amount of capital stock in the company. In addition to this registration, every company must file some kind of annual report. These annual reports may or may not contain financial data. Some states require sales figures, and others ask just for asset figures.

2) Office of Uniform Commercial Code

Any organization, and for that matter, any individual, which borrows money and offers an asset as collateral, must file within the state at the office of uniform commercial code. A filing is made for each loan and each of the documents is available to the public. To obtain these documents is a two step process. First, one must request a search to see if there are any filings for a certain company. The fee for a search is usually under $10.00. Such a search will identify the number of documents filed against the company. You then will have to request copies of each of these documents. The cost for each document averages only a few dollars. This office of uniform commercial code usually is located in or near to the same office of corporations.

3) State Securities Office

The US Securities and Exchange Commission in Washington, DC regulates only those corporations which sell stock in their company across state lines. There is another universe of corporations which sells stock in their companies only within state lines. For such stock offerings, complete financial information is filed with the state securities regulator. These documents are similar to a those filed at the US Securities and Exchange Commission. But remember that the documents vary from one state to the next and, equally important, the requirement of filing an annual report differs from state to state. Usually a telephone call to the office in charge can tell you whether a particular company has ever offered stock intrastate. If so, you are then in a position of getting copies of these filings. Usually the Secretary of State's office can refer you to the state's securities regulator.

Finding The Right State Office

Because of the multitude of differences between the 50 state governments, expect to make half a dozen calls before you locate the right office. Several starting places are described below with the simplest ones listed first.

1) State Government Operator

The AT&T information operator can give you the telephone number for the state government operator, and then in turn you can ask for the phone number of the specific government office.

2) State Department of Commerce

Now that every state is aggressively trying to get companies to expand or relocate to their state, these departments can serve as excellent starting points because they are familiar with other government offices which regulate business. Many times these departments have established a "one-stop office" with a separate staff on call to help business find whatever information it needs.

3) State Capitol Library

By asking the state government operator to connect you to the state capitol library, a reference librarian can identify the state agency which can best respond to your queries.

4) Directories

If you intend to dig around various state government offices on more than just an infrequent basis, you might consider purchasing a state government directory. Usually the state office of Administrative Services is the place that will sell you a directory, or you might want to contact the state bookstore. If you want to purchase a directory that covers all 50 states, consider:

State Executive Directory ($125)
Carroll Publishing Company
1058 Thomas Jefferson Street NW
Washington, DC 20007
(202) 333-8620

Tracking The Trail of Company Information In Other State Offices

The three offices described earlier are only the starting places for information on companies. There are dozens of other state agencies that are brimming with valuable bits of data about individual corporations; however, these sources require a bit more care because they can be used only under certain circumstances or require extra resourcefulness.

1) Utility and Cable TV Regulators

Utility companies are heavily regulated by state agencies, and as a result there is a lot of financial and operational information that is accessible. Most people know that gas and electric companies fall into this category, but you may not be aware that this also applies to water companies, bus companies, rail systems, telephone companies, telecommunication companies, and cable TV operators.

2) Other State Regulators

State government is very similar to the federal government in that its function is to regulate many of the activities of the business community. In those states where state laws and enforcement are very effective, Uncle Sam relies on those states to enforce the federal laws. For example, the US Food and Drug Administration will use the records from the state of New Jersey for information on pharmaceutical manufacturers instead of sending out its own team of federal data collectors. The US Environmental Protection Administration will use state records in those states that have strict environmental statutes rather than using its own resources.

3) Financial Institutions

Banks, savings and loans, credit unions and other financial institutions all file information with the state bank regulator. Many of these organizations are also regulated by federal agencies so what you get from the state office often will be a copy of the form filed with the federal government.

4) Environment Regulators
Most every state has an office which regulates pollutants in the air, water and ground. Such departments are similar to the US Environmental Protection Agency in Washington, DC and monitor whether any new or old business is polluting the environment. If the company you are investigating has plans to build a new plant in the state, get ready to collect some valuable information. Before construction can begin, the company must file information with the state environmental protection agency. These documents will detail the size of the plant, what kind of equipment it will use, and how much this equipment will be used. With such information, other manufacturers in the same business can tell exactly what the capacity and estimated volume of the plant will be. Sometimes there will be three separate offices with authority over air, water or solid waste. Each will collect basically the same information, and they can be used, one against each other, to ensure that you get all the information you need.

5) Department of Commerce/Economic Development
As mentioned earlier, each state is now actively trying to attract and develop business development within the state. The state's office of economic development or department of commerce is normally charged with this responsibility. To attract business to the state, this agency has to know all about existing business throughout the state, which all translates into who is doing what, how successful they are, and how large the company is. At a minimum, the economic development office can probably provide you with information on the number of employees for a given company. They will also be aware what other government offices in the state keep records about the industry or company which interests you. The experts at this state agency are similar to the 100 industry analysts at the US Department of Commerce and can serve as excellent resources for collecting government information on an industry.

6) State Government Contractors
Although many states are not accustomed to sharing information with researchers, you should be able to obtain details about any purchase the state makes. If the company in question sells to the state, you should get copies of their contracts. Just like the federal government which makes all this procurement information available, the state which spends public funds guarantees that the public has a right to know how the money is being spent. You may have to enforce your rights under the state law which is equivalent to the federal Freedom of Information Act.

7) Minority and Small Business
Many states maintain special offices which track minority firms and other small companies. These offices can be helpful not only in identifying these businesses but may also be able to tell you the size or products of a given business. The small business office and possibly a separate minority business division normally fall under the state department of commerce.

8) Attorney General
The state Attorney General's office is the primary consumer advocate for the state against fraudulent practices by businesses operating within the state. So, if the company you are investigating is selling consumer services or products, it would be worth the effort to check with this office. In some states the attorney generals have begun to concentrate on certain areas. For example, the office in Denver specializes in gathering information on companies selling energy saving devices, and the one in New York investigates companies with computerized databases which provide scholarship information.

9) Food and Drug Companies
Any company which produces, manufactures or imports either food or drug products is likely to come under the jurisdiction of the state food and drug agency. This office makes routine inspection of facilities and the reports are generally accessible; however, a Freedom of Information Act request is sometimes necessary.

Country and Local Sources

County and local sources can prove to be the biggest bucket of worms as far as information sources go. Unlike state government where there are 50 varieties to choose from, there are over 5,000 different jurisdictions at the local level. Here are some basic checkpoints that can enhance your information gathering efforts.

Local Newspapers: Business Editors

The local newspaper can provide the best leads for anything you are investigating at the local level. It is perhaps the best source mentioned in this book. A well-placed telephone call to the business editor or the managing editor, if there is not a business section, can prove to be most useful. In smaller towns, and even in suburbs of larger cities where there are suburban newspapers, a local business generates a good deal of news. A local reporter often knows the company like no one else in the country. The company executives usually are more open with the local media because they like to show off about how big they are, how much the company is growing, etc. A reporter is also likely to know company employees who can corroborate or refute the executive's remarks.

Ask the local newspaper if you can get copies of all articles written about the company in question. After you review them, call the reporter to see what additional information may be stored in his or her head.

Other Checkpoints

It is worth fishing for information in a number of other places, including agencies and private organizations.

1) Chamber of Commerce
Talking to someone on the research staff or the librarian can help you identify sources within the community about a company. A friendly conversation with Chamber executives can also provide insight into a company's financial position and strategies.

2) Local Development Authority
Many local communities, counties, and regional areas have established development authorities to attract business and industry to their area. They operate pretty much the same as the state department of economic development described above, and as a result collect a lot of data about the businesses in their area.

3) Local Courts
Civil and criminal court actions can provide excellent source material for company investigations. Perdue chicken company, a private corporation in Maryland, revealed its annual sales figures while fighting Virginia sales tax in the courts. A recent search revealed four financial-related suits filed against a large privately held political campaign fundraising firm in McLean,

Virginia. If you are not in close proximity to the court, it may be worthwhile to hire a local freelance reporter or researcher. In most jurisdictions there are chronological indexes of both civil and criminal cases which are kept by the clerk of the court. These indexes record all charges or complaints made, the names of the defendants and plaintiffs in the event of civil cases, the date of the filing, the case number, and the disposition if one has been reached. Armed with the case number you can request to see the case files from the clerk.

Federal Regulators

The federal offices identified in the preceding section on market studies also are excellent sources for information on companies. Industry specialists within the federal government are likely to have information on companies or can refer you to other sources which may have just the information you need.

The 26 government agencies listed here are those that are involved with regulating industries and/or the companies within those industries. The information held at each federal office varies from agency to agency; however, most of the offices maintain financial or other information that most researchers would consider sensitive.

Airlines, Air Freight Carriers, and Air Taxis
Office of Community and Consumer Affairs
US Department of Transportation
400 7th Street SW, Room 10405
Washington, DC 20590
(202) 366-2220

Airports
Air Traffic Service Division
National Flight Data Center, Room 634
Federal Aviation Administration, ATO-250
800 Independence Avenue SW
Washington, DC 20591
(202) 267-9311

Bank Holding Companies and State Members of the Federal Reserve System
Freedom of Information Act Office
Board of Governors of the Federal Reserve System
20th Street & Constitution Avenue NW, Room B1122
Washington, DC 20551
(202) 452-3684

Banks, National
Communications Division
Comptroller of the Currency
490 L'Enfant Plaza East SW
Washington, DC 20219
(202) 447-1800

Barge and Vessel Operators
Financial Analysis, Tariffs
Federal Maritime Commission
1100 L Street NW
Washington, DC 20573
(202) 523-5876

Cable Television System Operators
Cable TV Bureau
Federal Communications Commission
1919 M Street NW
Room 242
Washington, DC 20554
(202) 632-7480

Colleges, Universities, Vocational Schools, and Public Schools
Office of Educational Research & Improvement
U.S. Department of Education
555 New Jersey NW, Room 300

Washington, DC 20208-5641
(202) 357-6651

Commodity Trading Advisors
Commodity Pool Operators and Futures Commission Merchants
Commodity Futures Trading Commission
2033 K Street, NW
Washington, DC 20581
(202) 254-8630

Consumer Products
Corrective Actions Division
US Consumer Product Safety Commission
5401 Westbard Avenue
Bethesda, MD 20816
(301) 492-6608

Electric and Gas Utilities and Gas Pipeline Companies
Federal Energy Regulatory Commission
US Department of Energy
825 North Capitol Street NE, Room 9204
Washington, DC 20426
202) 357-8370

Exporting Companies
Office of Export Trading Companies Affairs
US Department of Commerce
14th & Constitution Avenue, Room 1223
Washington, DC 20230
(202) 377-5131

Federal Land Bank and Production Credit Associations
Farm Credit Administration
1501 Farm Credit Drive
McLean, VA 22102-5090
(703) 883-4000

Foreign Corporations
World Traders Data Report
US Department of Commerce
Washington, DC 20230
(202) 377-3181

Government Contractors
Federal Procurement Data Center
4040 North Fairfax Drive, Room 900
Arlington, VA 22203
(703) 235-1634

Hospitals and Nursing Homes
National Center for Health Statistics
3700 East-West Highway
Hyattsville, MD 20782
(301) 436-8500

Land Developers
Office of Interstate Land Registration
US Department of Housing and Urban Development
451 7th Street SW, Room 6262
Washington, DC 20410
(202) 755-7077

Mining Companies
Mine Safety and Health
US Department of Labor
4015 Wilson Boulevard
Arlington, VA 22203
(703) 235-1452

Non-Profit Institutions
US Internal Revenue Service
Freedom of Information Reading Room
1111 Constitution Avenue NW, Room 1563
P.O. Box 388, Ben Franklin Bldg.
Washington, DC 20044
(202) 566-3770

Nuclear Power Plants
Nuclear Regulatory Commission
1717 H Street NW
Washington, DC 20555
(301) 492-7715

Pension Plans

Division of Inquiries and Technical Assistance
Office of Pension and Welfare Benefits Programs
US Department of Labor
200 Constitution Avenue NW, N5658
Washington, DC 20210
(202) 523-8776

Pharmaceutical, Cosmetic and Food Companies

Associate Commissioner for Regulatory Affairs
US Food and Drug Administration
5600 Fishers Lane
Rockville, MD 20857
(301) 443-1594

Pesticide and Chemical Manufacturers

US Environmental Protection Agency
Office of Pesticides and Toxic Substances
401 M Street SW
Washington, DC 20460
(202) 382-2902

Radio and Television Stations

Mass Media Bureau
Federal Communications Commission
1919 M Street NW, Room 222
Washington, DC 20554
(202) 632-6485

Railroads, Trucking Companies, Bus Lines, Freight Forwarders, Water Carriers, Oil Pipelines, Transportation Brokers, Express Agencies

US Interstate Commerce Commission
12th & Constitution Avenue NW, Room 4126
Washington, DC 20423
(202) 275-7231

Savings and Loan Associations

Federal Home Loan Bank Board
1700 G Street NW
Washington, DC 20552
(202) 377-6000

Telephone Companies, Overseas Telegraph Companies, Microwave Companies, Public Land and Mobile Service

Common Carrier Bureau
Federal Communications Commission
1919 M Street NW, Room 500
Washington, DC 20554
(202) 632-6910

Suppliers And Other Industry Sources

If all of the above sources fail to provide information you need on a given company, your last resort is to go directly into the industry and try to extract the information by talking with insiders.

The two reference sources along with your telephone---an essential and perhaps the best research tool---that will help you track down industry specialists include:

1) **Trade Associations** are identified in *Encyclopedia of Associations* - (Gale Research Co., Book Tower, 835 Penobsot Building, Detroit, MI 48277, (313) 961-2242, (800) 223-GALE);

2) **100 Industry Analysts** at the US Department of Commerce. Government Industry Analysts who cover industries such as athletic goods, dairy products or truck trailers.

Your first step is to begin casting around for someone in the industry who knows about the company in question. When hunting for an expert, it is essential that you remain determined and optimistic about eventually finding one or several individuals who will be "information jackpots."

People who know their industry will be able to give you the details you need about any company (i.e., its size, sales, profitability, market strategies). These sources probably will not be able to give you the precise figure that is on the balance sheet or profit and loss statement, but they will offer a very educated guess which is likely to be within 10 to 20% of the exact figure. And usually this estimate is good enough for anyone to work with.

The real trick is finding the right people---the ones who know. Talk to them and get them to share their knowledge with you.

Where Else To Look For Industry Experts

Industry experts are not concentrated in Washington, DC but are located all over the world, so you need to exercise some common sense to figure out where to find them. Here are some general guidelines.

1)Industry Observers
These are specialists on staff at trade associations, think tanks, and at the US Department of Commerce and other government agencies. Anyone who concentrates on an industry has familiarity with the companies that comprise that industry.

2)Trade Magazines
You will find that there is at least one magazine which reports on every industry. The editors and reporters of these trade publications also are well acquainted with individual companies.

3)Suppliers
Most industries have major suppliers which must know about the industry they service and the companies within that industry. For example, the tire manufacturers anticipate every move among automakers well before any other outsiders. Suppliers also have to know the volume of every manufacturer to whom they sell or intend to sell to because of the obvious repercussions on the supplier's business. Every company is like this, even Information USA, Inc. We are basically a publisher, and if you talk to our printers, you would get a pretty good picture of exactly what we are doing.

Company Case Studies and Databases

1) Company Case Studies For As Little As $2.00 Each

Case studies of major and minor companies as well as subsidiaries of public companies can provide valuable competitive intelligence. Thousands of such cases are identified in a $7.50 publication titled *Directory of Harvard Business School Cases and Related Course Materials 1986-87*. A supplement to the directory, covering the period between April 1987 and January 1988 is available for $5.00.

HBS Publications Division
Operations Department
Boston, MA 02163
(617) 495-6117

2) Government and Commercial Databases

ABI/Inform, Disclosure, and Management Contents are just a few of the online databases which provide quick access to information about all types of companies. Additional leads for gathering intelligence about companies can be derived from diverse databases maintained by the US government, many of which are identified in the *Federal Database Finder* (Information USA, Inc.).

Complete Financials On Franchising Companies

Franchising companies, whether public or privately held, must file detailed financial information in 14 different states. These state statutes create excellent opportunities for gathering competitive and marketing data as outlined below.

Inside Information

If the company of interest is a franchise organization, a great deal of financial information for their average franchisee is available in addition to their corporate profit and loss statements and balance sheets. A typical table of contents for a filing includes:

o biographical information on persons affiliated with the franchisor
o litigation
o bankruptcy
o franchisees' initial franchise fee or other initial payment
o other recurring or isolated fees and payments
o the franchisee's initial investment
o obligations of the franchisee to purchase or lease from designated sources
o obligations of the franchisee to purchase or lease in accordance with specifications or from approved suppliers
o financing arrangements
o obligations of the franchisor: other supervision, assistance or services
o territorial rights
o trademarks, service marks, trade names, logotypes and commercial symbols
o patents and copyrights
o obligation of the franchisee to participate in the actual operation of the franchise business
o restrictions on goods and services offered by the franchisee
o term, renewal, termination, repurchase, modification, assignment and related information
o agreements with public figures
o actual, average, projected or forecasted franchisee sales, profits and earnings
o information regarding franchises of the franchisor
o financial statements
o contracts
o standard operating statements
o list of operational franchisees
o estimate of additional franchised stores
o company-owned stores
o estimate of additional company-owned stores
o copies of contracts and agreements

Market Information and Franchising Trends

The franchise information packet often includes information on the results of their market studies which establish the need for their product or service. These can provide valuable market information as well as forecasts for potential markets. Is the ice cream boom over? A quick check into Ben and Jerry's forecast for future stores will give you a clue of what the experts think.

Franchise companies are often the first to jump current trends and fads in the US, for example, ice cream shops and diet centers. You can get an instant snapshot of such a trend by reviewing the marketing section of a franchise agreement.

Career Opportunities

If you ever wondered how much it would cost to open up your own bookstore, restaurant, video store, or most any other kind of venture, you can get all the facts and figures you need without paying a high-priced consultant or tipping your hand to your current employer. Just take a look at a franchise agreement from someone in a similar line of business. You can even discover the expected salary level.

New Business for Suppliers

If you are looking to sell napkins, Orange Julius or computer services to Snelling & Snelling, their franchise statements will disclose what kind of agreements they currently have with similar suppliers.

State Checkpoints for Franchising Intelligence

To obtain franchise agreements from the 14 states that require such disclosure, simply call one or more of the offices listed below and ask if a specific company has filed. Copies of the documentation are normally sent in the mail with a copying charge of $0.05 to $0.10 a page.

California
Department of Corporations, 1115 11th Street, Sacramento, 95814, (916) 445-7205

Hawaii
Department of Commerce, Business Registration Department, 1010 Richards Street, Honolulu, 96813, (808) 548-5317

Illinois
Franchise Division, Office of Attorney General, 500 South Second Street, Springfield, 62706, (217) 782-1279

Indiana
Franchise Division, Secretary of State, One North Capitol Street, Suite 560, Indianapolis, 46204, (317) 232-6681

Maryland
Assistant Attorney General, Maryland Division of Securities, Munsey Building, 7 North Calvert Street, 18th Flr, Baltimore, 21202, (301) 576-6360

Minnesota
Minnesota Department of Commerce, 500 Metro Square Building, St. Paul, 55101, (612) 296-2594

New York
Bureau of Investor and Protection Securities, New York State Department of 120 Broadway, New York, 10272, (212) 341-2446

North Dakota
Franchise Examiner, Office of Securities Commissioner, Capitol Building, Ninth Floor, Bismarck, 58505, (701) 224-2910

Oregon
Corporation Division, Commerce Building, Salem, 97310, (503) 378-4387

Rhode Island
Securities Section, Banking Division, 233 Richmond Street, Providence, 02903-4231, (401) 277-2405

South Dakota
Franchise Administrator, Division of Securities, State Capitol, Pierre, 57501,

(605) 773-4013

Virginia
Franchise Section, Division of Securities and Retail Franchising, 1229 Bank Street, Richmond, 23219, (804) 786-7751

Washington
Department of Licensing, Securities Division, Business and Professions

Administration, 111 W. Wilson Street, P.O. Box 1768, Olympic, 98504, (206) 753-6928

Wisconsin
Franchise Investment Division, Wisconsin Securities Commission, PO Box 1768, Madison, 53701, (608) 266-3414

Companies In Your State

State documents on 9,000,000 public and private companies have hit the computer age. Nine states already offer online access to their files and 15 states intend to follow suit within the next year. Computerized records are such a major issue with state officials who administer corporate division offices that they have placed online access on their annual convention agenda. Furthermore, 27 states will make their complete file available on magnetic tape, and, I should say, at bargain prices. And if you are not computerized, all but a few states offer free telephone research services. Here are a dozen ways to ferret out current information on companies:

* a list of companies by SIC code within a given
      state or county
* names and addresses of a company's officers
      and directors
* a list of all new companies incorporated in
      a given week or month
* the location of any company with a single
      phone call
* a mailing list of 300,000 companies for $100
* the availability of a given company name
* a complete list of non-profit organizations
* list of companies by city, zip, date of
      incorporation, or size of capital stock
* a mailing list of limited partnerships
* a listing of companies on which a given
      individual is an officer or board member
* a listing of trademarks for a given state
* what companies in a given state are subsidiaries
      of a given company

Financial Data and Other Documents on File

Although there are variations, most all states maintain the following documents for every company doing business in their state: Certificate of Good Standing; Articles of Incorporation; Reinstated Articles of Incorporation; Articles of Amendment; Articles of Merger; Articles of Correction; Articles of Dissolution; Certificate of Incorporation; Certificate of Authority; and, Annual Report (which contains list of officers and directors).

All states require corporations to file the original Articles of Incorporation, a yearly annual report and amendments to the Articles of Incorporation. Clerks can provide you with certifications of good standing stating that the corporation has complied with the regulation to file a yearly annual report. A certificate of good standing does not assure financial stability, but is only a statement that the corporation has abided by the law. You may obtain a statement of name availability if you are searching for a name for your new corporation. Most states require prepayment for copies of documents. You can mail them a blank check stipulating the amount not to exceed a certain amount. You may want to call the phone information number for details before sending in your written request.

Only a few states require financial information in their annual reports. However, every state requires companies to list the value of the capital stock in their Articles of Incorporation.

Some states, such as Massachusetts used to require financial data in the past, so it may be useful to request annual reports of previous years.

Data on Six Different Types of Companies

The types of companies required to file documents with the state include: Domestic Companies (those incorporated within the state), Foreign Companies (those incorporated in another state, but doing business in the state), Partnerships, Limited Partnerships, Non-Profit Organizations, Business Names (incorporated and non-incorporated firms). It should be emphasized here that all public and private companies as well as subsidiaries of public corporations are required to reveal this information.

Company Information Available in Numerous Formats

Each state provides information about corporations in some or all of the following formats:

1) Telephone, Mail and Walk-In Services:
Telephone information lines have been established in all but one state to respond to inquiries regarding the status of a specific corporation. North Dakota stands alone as the only state that does not give any information over the phone. It accepts only written requests and charges a nominal fee for documents. New Jersey is the only state that charges for its phone service. The NJ Expedite Service allows you to receive information over the phone and charge the cost of the service to your credit card. Another option for New Jersey company information is to have it sent via Western Union's electronic mail service.

Telephone operators can verify corporate names, identify the resident agent and his address, the date of incorporation, the type of corporation (foreign, domestic, etc.), and the amount of capital stock. Often these operators can either take your request for documents on file pertaining to a corporation or they can refer you to the appropriate number. Names of officers and directors are never given over the phone. This information is usually contained in a company's annual report, copies of which can be requested by phone or letter.

These state telephone lines tend to be quite busy. It is not unusual for the larger offices of a corporation to answer over 1200 inquiries a day. Persistence and patience are essential on your part. Requests for copies of documents usually require prepayment. You can mail them a blank check stipulating the amount not to exceed a certain amount. You may want to call the phone information number for details before sending in your written request.

Walk-in service, with access to all documents, is an option in every state. However, if you do not want to do the research yourself, most every state can suggest private firms which will obtain the pertinent data for you.

2) Mailing Labels:

The following six states will print mailing labels of companies on file: Arizona, Idaho, Maine, New Mexico, Mississippi, and Nebraska. However, over half the states will sell you a computer tape of their files, from which mailing labels can be generated easily by a good mailhouse or service bureau.

3) Computer Tape Files:
Currently 27 states will provide you with magnetic tapes of their corporate files. The cost is very reasonable, and in many cases the state will require the user to supply blank tapes.

4) Custom Services:
Many of the states provide custom services with outputs ranging from computer printouts and magnetic tape files to statistical tables. Such services are a valuable way to obtain specific listings of corporations such all non-profit corporations or all companies within a given SIC code. Most states that offer this option compute cost by figuring time, programming time, and printing expense.

5) New Companies:
Most all of the states offer some type of periodic listing of newly formed companies. As a rule, these can be purchased on a daily, weekly, or monthly subscription basis.

6) Microfiche and Microfilm:
Eleven of the states will also sell you copies of their documents on microfiche or microfilm at a nominal fee.

7) Online Access:
As mentioned earlier, nine states now provide online access to their files, and 15 other states are in the active planning stages. The states currently with online systems include:

o Alaska - available through Motznik Computer Service
o Arizona - their only customer for this service is Dun and Bradstreet
o Florida - available through CompuServe
o Georgia - available through Information America
o Illinois - available through Mead Data Central
o Missouri - available through Mead Data Central
o New Mexico - available through New Mexico Technet
o Oklahoma - their only customer for this service is Dun and Bradstreet
o Texas - available through Information America

State Corporation Divisions

Alabama
Division of Corporation, Secretary of State, 524 State Office Building, Montgomery, AL 36130, (205) 261-5324; Selected Publications: *Guide to Incorporation*. Phone Information: (205) 261-5324. Files can be searched by title only. Copies of Documents on File: Available for $1.50 per page plus $1.50 for certified copies. Mailing Labels: No. Magnetic Tape: No. Microfiche: No. New Corporate Listings: No. Custom Searches: No. Online Access: No. Number of Active Corporations on File: Figures not available.

Alaska
Office of Banking, Securities and Corporation, Division of Economic Enterprise, Department of Commerce and Economic Development, PO Box D, Juneau, AK 99811, (907) 465-2570. Selected Publications: *Establishing Business in Alaska* ($3). Phone Information: (907) 465-2530. Copies of Documents on File: Complete corporate record (Articles of Incorporation, annual report, amendments, etc.). Certified copies cost $5, list of Officers and Directors cost $1, Certificate of Status cost 60 cents. Mailing Labels: No. Magnetic Tape: Copy of complete master file, excluding Officers and Directors is priced at $100.00. Requester must supply blank tape. Microfiche: No. New Corporate Listings: Bimonthly listing of new corporations costs $120/year. (Address written request to the attention of Kris Kuaana). Custom Searches: No. Online Access: Available on subscription basis for $50/month plus $50/hour access time from Motznik Computer Service Inc., 3701 Mountain View Drive, Anchorage, AK 99508, (907) 276-6254. Custom Searches and Mailing Labels: Available by type of corporation, SIC code, and zip code, 3 cents a name plus $40 selection

charge. Number of Active Corporations on File: 19,000.

Arizona
Department of Corporations Secretary of State, 1200 W Washington, Phoenix, AZ 85007, (602) 542-3026. Selected Publications: *How to File Articles for Non-Profits and Profits*. Phone Information: (602) 255-4285. Copies of Documents on File: Cost 50 cents per page, $5 for certified copies. Mailing Labels: No. Magnetic Tape: Master File $400. Requester must supply blank tape. Microfiche: All corporations statewide $70.00. New Corporate Listing: Monthly Listing of New Domestic Companies ($150). Custom Searches: Categories include city name, type of corporation, and zip code. Contact: Data Center at (602) 255-1734. Other: Hard copy printouts of active and inactive corporations $400.00. Online Access: No. Number of Corporations on File: 96,000.

Arkansas
Corporations, Secretary of State, State Capitol, Little Rock, AR 72201, (501) 682-5151. Selected Publications: *Corporate Guide*. Phone Information: (501) 682-5151. Copies of Documents on File: Call (501) 371-3622 for copies at 50 cents a page plus $1 for certified copies. Mailing Labels: Master list 2 cents a name. Magnetic Tape: Master file 2 cents a name. Microfiche: No. New Corporate Listing: Statistics only. Custom Searches: Categories include foreign, domestic, profit, and non-profit corporations. Cost: 2 cents a name, 50 cents a page. Online Access: Only Dunn and Bradstreet at this time. Contact Philip Hoots at (501) 371-5818. Number of Corporations on File: 60,000.

California
Corporations, Supervisor of Records, Secretary of State, 1230 J Street Sacramento, CA 95814, (916) 324-1485. Selected Publications: Listing available. Phone Information: Corporate Status call (916) 445-2900; Name Availability at (916) 322-2387, Forms and Samples at (916) 445-0620. Copies of Documents on File: Cost is 30 cents a page, plus $2 for certified copies (written requests only). Mailing Labels: No. Magnetic Tape: Yes. Categories: Active $2,450; Active Stock $2,055; Active Non-Stock $430; Active Non-Stock by Classification $185 per page. Microfiche: No. Custom Searches: Computer generated listing of Active $2,170, Active Stock $1,810, Active Non-Stock $360, Active Non-Stock by Classification $150 per list. Contact: Patricia Gastelum, Management Services Division, Information Systems Section, 1230 J Street, Suite 242, Sacramento, CA 95814, (916) 445-0948. All orders must be submitted in writing. Online Access: No. Number of Corporations on File: 1,050,000.

Colorado
Corporate Division, Secretary of State, 1560 Broadway, Suite 200, Denver, CO 80202, (303) 866-2361. Selected Publications: None. Phone Information: (303) 866-2360. Copies of Documents on File: Cost is 50 cents a page. Mailing Labels: No. Magnetic Tape: Available on cost recovery basis. Categories: Foreign and Domestic. Microfiche: Available at $1.00 a sheet (includes Summary of Master Computer File, total of 60 sheets). New Corporate Listings: Weekly List of New Corporations is priced at $125 (written request only). Custom Searches: Yes. Categories: Foreign and Domestic available on a cost recovery basis. Online Access: Available on January 1, 1988. Contact Karen Jackson, (303) 866-5238. Number of Corporations on File: 175,000.

Connecticut
Corporate UCC Division, 30 Trinity Street, Hartford, CT 06106, (203) 566-2448. Selected Publications: None. Phone Information: (203) 566-8570. Copies of Documents on File: Fees start at $4.00. Written requests only. Mailing Labels: No. Magnetic Tape: Copy of master file $100.00. Requester must provide tapes. Microfiche: No. New Corporate Listing: No. Custom Searches: No. Online Access: Not at this time. Number of Corporations on File: 325,000.

Delaware
Division of Corporations, Secretary of State, Dover, DE 19903, (302) 736-3073. Selected Publications: *Incorporating in Delaware*. Phone Information: (302) 736-3073. Copies of Documents on File: Available at $1 a page plus $10 for certification. Mailing Labels: No. Magnetic Tape: No. Microfiche: No. New Corporate Listings: Monthly New Corporation Listing ($10 a month). Custom Searches: Yes. Categories include foreign and domestic which are available on cost recovery basis. Online Access: Not available. Number of Active Corporations on File: 178,000.

District of Columbia
Corporations Division, Consumer and Regulatory Affairs, 614 H Street, N.W., Room 407, Washington, DC 20001, (202) 727-7278. Selected Publications: *Guideline and Instruction Sheet for Profit, Non-Profit, Foreign, or Domestic*. Phone Information: (202) 727-7283. Copies of Documents on File: Available for $5 each (all copies certified). Mailing Labels: No. Magnetic Tape: No. Microfiche: No. New Corporate Listings No. Custom Searches: No. Online Access: Possibly available in 1988. Number of Corporations on File: 60,000.

Florida
Division of Corporations, Secretary of State, PO Box 6327, Tallahassee, FL 32314, (904) 487-6000. Selected Publications: *Copy of the Law Chapter 607* (corporate law). Phone Information: (904) 488-9000. Copy of Documents on File: Available at 50 cents a page. Microfiche: Yes. Categories: Officers and Directors, Registered Agents $65; Domestic Corporations $75; Foreign,

Information on People, Companies, and Mailing Lists

Non-Profit, Limited Partnerships, Trademarks $50 (addresses are included). Magnetic Tape: No. New Corporate Listings: No. Custom Searches: No. Online Access: Available on CompuServe (614-457-8600). Address written request to Attn: Public Access, Division of Corporations. Ask for a CompuServe Intro-Pak. Charge for connect time is $25 per hour. Number of Corporations on File: 678,000.

Georgia

Division of Business Services and Regulation, Secretary of State, Suite 306, West Tower #2, Martin Luther King Drive, S.E., Atlanta, GA 30334, (404) 656-2185. Selected Publications: None. Phone Information: (404) 656-2185. Copies of Documents on File: Available at $10 and all copies certified. Mailing Labels: No. Magnetic Tape: Master file available on cost recovery basis. Microfiche: No. New Corporate Listings: Quarterly Listing of New Corporations on magnetic tape (cost determined at time of request). Custom Searches: No. Online Access: Available by subscription through Information America. Contact Jim Prim at (404) 892-1800. Number of Active Corporations on File: 750,000 to 1,000,000.

Hawaii

Business Registration Division, Department of Commerce and Consumer Affairs, PO Box 40, Honolulu, HI 96810, (808) 548-6111. Selected Publications: None. Phone Information: (808) 548-6111. Copies of Documents on File: Available at 25 cents a page, plus 10 cents a page for certified copies. Mailing Labels: No. Magnetic Tape: No. Microfiche: No. New Corporate Listing: Daily printout available but only for walk-ins. Custom Searches: No. Online Access: No. Number of Active Corporations on File: 34,000.

Idaho

Corporate Division, Secretary of State, Room 203, Statehouse, Boise, ID 83720, (208) 334-2300. Selected Publications: *Idaho Corporation Law*. Phone Information: (208) 334-2300. Copies of Documents on File: Available at 25 cents per page, $2 for certified copies. Mailing Labels: Profit Corporations only at $100. Magnetic Tape: Copy of master file available on cost recovery basis. Microfiche: Call (208) 334-2300 for Non-Profit Corporations ($75), Profit and Non-Profits ($75). Custom Searches: Available at same price and categories as microfiche. New Corporate Listing: No. Online Access: No. Number of Corporations on File: 28,000.

Illinois

Corporations Division, Centennial Building, Room 328, Springfield, IL 62756, (217) 782-6961. Selected Publications: *Guide for Organizing (Domestic, Non-profit, or Foreign)*. Phone Information: (217) 782-7880. Copies of Documents on File: Available at 50 cents a page plus $5 for certified copies. Minimum order is $5. Mailing Labels: No. Magnetic Tape: Yes. Categories: Domestic and Foreign cost $1,355; Not-for-Profit cost $300.00. Microfiche: Yes. Categories: Same as for magnetic tape. Cost determined at time of request. New Corporate Listings: Daily List costs $318 per year; Monthly List priced at $175 per year. Custom Searches: No. Other: Certified List of Domestic and Foreign Corporations (Address of Resident Agent included) costs $75 for two volumes. Online Access: Available from Mead Data Central (LEXIS), 9393 Springboro Pike, PO Box 933, Dayton, OH 45401, (800) 227-9597. Number of Active Corporations on File: 227,000.

Indiana

Office of Corporation, Secretary of State, Room 155, State House, Indianapolis, IN 46204, (317) 232-6582. Selected Publications: None. Phone Information: ***(317) 232-658). Copies of Documents on File: Available at 30 cents a page. Mailing Labels: No. Magnetic Tape: No. Microfiche: No. New Corporate Listings: Daily Listing is published biweekly for $20 a month. Custom Searches: No. Online Access: No. This office hopes to be online and have greater search capabilities by 1988. Number of Active Corporations on File: 180,000.

Iowa

Corporate Division, Secretary of State, Hoover State Office Building, Des Moines, IA 50319, (515) 281-5204. Selected Publications: None. Phone Information: (515) 281-5204. Copies of Documents on File: Available at $1 a page; certified copies cost $5. Mailing Labels: No. Magnetic Tape: Master file costs $35 and requester must supply tape. Microfiche: No. New Corporate Listings: No. Custom Searches: Searches by Chapters of Incorporation (profit, non-profit, etc.). Cost determined at time of request. Online Access: No. Number of Active Corporations on File: 130,000.

Kansas

Corporate Division, Secretary of State, Capitol Building, Second Floor, Topeka, KS 66612, (913) 296-4564. Selected Publications: *Instruction Sheets*. Phone Information: (913) 296-4564. Copies of Documents on File: Available at 50 cents a page plus $7.50 for certified copies (written requests only). Mailing Labels: No. Magnetic Tape: No. Microfiche: No. New Corporate Listings: No. Custom Searches: Available in near future. Online Access: No. Number of Active Corporations on File: 66,000. The office has just computerized and expects to have more capabilities in the future.

Kentucky

Corporate Division, Secretary of State, Room 152, Capitol Building, Frankfort, KY 40601, (502) 564-2848. Selected Publications: *Rules & Laws Manual* ($8).

Phone Information: (502) 654-7330. Copies of Documents on File: Available on cost recovery basis. Mailing Label: No. Magnetic Tape: No. Microfiche: No. New Corporate Listings: Available for $50 a month. Custom Searches: No. Online Access: No. Number of Active Corporations on File: 85,000.

Louisiana

Corporate Division, Secretary of State, 7051 Florida Boulevard, Baton Rouge, LA 70806, (504) 925-4704. Selected Publications: *Corporate Law Book* ($4.75). Phone Information: (504) 925-4704. Copies of Documents on File: Available starting at $10. Mailing Label: No. Magnetic Tape: Available in the future. Microfiche: No. New Corporate Listing: Weekly Newsletter costs 57 cents per week. (Requester must supply large pre-addressed envelope). Custom Searches: No. Online Access: Available in the future. For the latest update contact Mrs. Cumbo at (504) 925-4716. Number of Active Corporations on File: N/A.

Maine

Information and Report Section, Bureau of Corporations, Secretary of State, State House Station 101, Augusta, ME 04333, (207) 289-4195. Selected Publications: *Corporate Law G* (requester must supply stamped self-addressed envelope); *Guide to Completing Forms of Incorporation* (Blue Guide). Phone Information: (207) 289-4195. Copies of Documents on File: Available for $1 a page, plus $1 for certified copies. Mailing Labels: No. Magnetic tape: Copy of master file available on cost recovery basis. Microfiche: No. New Corporate Listings: Monthly Corporations Listing costs $8. Custom Searches: Available on a cost recovery basis. Categories: Call (207) 289-4190 for searches on location, type of corporation, dates of incorporation, dissolutions. Online Access: Will be available in the near future. Number of Active Corporations on File: 35,000.

Maryland

Corporate Charter Division, Department of Assessments and Taxation, 301 W. Preston Street, Baltimore, Maryland 21201, (301) 225-1330. Selected Publications: *Guide to Corporations*. Phone Information: (301) 225-1330. Copies of Documents on File: Available for $1 a page, plus $6 for certified copies. Mailing Labels: No. Magnetic Tape: Not yet available. Microfiche: No. New Corporate Listings: Monthly Corporate Computer Printout costs $25 a month. Custom Searches: Not at this time. Online Access: Near future. Number of Active Corporations on File: 120,000. This office is in the process of automating their system and hope to have further capabilities in the future.

Massachusetts

Corporate Division, Secretary of State, 1 Ashburton Place, Boston, MA 02108, (617) 727-2850. Selected Publications: *Organizing a Business Corporation, Organizing a Non-Profit Corporation, When You Need Information About Corporations in Massachusetts, Choose a Name for Your Business, Compendium of Corporate Law* ($12). Phone Information: (617) 727-2850. Copies of Documents on File: Available for 80 cents a page, $10 for certified copies. Mailing Labels: No. Magnetic Tape: Cost is $150 for copy of master file and requester must supply four tapes. Microfiche: No. New Corporate Listings: Quarterly Filings cost $40 a quarter. Custom Searches: Not at this time. Other: Printout of all corporations on file in 11 volumes costs $35. Online Access: Available in the future. Number of Corporations on File: 290,000.

Michigan

Corporation Division, Corporation and Securities Bureau, Michigan Department of Commerce, PO Box 30054, 6546 Mercantile, Lansing, MI, 48909, (517) 334-6302. Selected Publications: *Checklist of Responsibility, Guide to Starting a Business in Michigan*. Phone Information: (517) 334-6304. Copies of Documents on File: Available at 75 cents per page, $5 for certified copies. (Request a price list.) Mailing Labels: No. Magnetic Tape: No. Microfiche: Available for 75 cents per fiche; reel of microfilm cost $10 (Annual Report). New Corporate Listings: Monthly Listing costs $12 per month. Custom Searches: No. Online Access: Available in the future. Number of Corporations on File: 222,618.

Minnesota

Corporate Division, Secretary of State, 180 State Office building, St. Paul, MN 55155, (612) 296-2803. Selected Publications: *Guide to Chapter 302A*. Phone Information: (612) 296-2803. Copies of Documents on File: Available for $1 per document, $5 for certified copies. Mailing Labels: Yes. Categories: Domestic, Limited Partnerships, Non-profits, Foreign, Foreign Limited, Foreign Non-profits, Trademarks, Business Trusts. Cost determined at time of request. Magnetic Tape: No. Microfiche: Available documents on file (Articles of Incorporation, annual reports, amendments) cost 21 cents sheet plus filing or retrieval fees. New Corporate Listings: Daily Log costs approximately $15. Custom Searches: Available on a cost recovery basis. Contact Mary Beth Steinwall at (612) 296-3266. Categories same as for mailing labels. Online Access: Available in the future. Number of Corporations on File: 156,000.

Mississippi

Office of Corporations, Secretary of State, PO Box 136, 401 Mississippi Street, Jackson, MS 39205, (601) 359-1350. Selected Publications: *Laws Relating to Business Corporations, Professional Corporations, Business Development Corporations, Small Business Investment Companies, Non-Profit and Non Share Corporations, Savings and Loan Associations*. Phone Information: (601) 359-1350. Copies of Documents on File: Available at $1 a page plus $5 for certified copies. Mailing Labels: Available beginning July 1, 1987. Magnetic Tape: Yes, beginning July 1, 1987. Microfiche: No. New Corporate Listings: Monthly Listing costs $25, Weekly Listing is priced at $8 (prepayment required). Custom Searches: Available from July 1, 1987. Online Access: Yes, beginning July 1, 1987. Number of Active Corporations on File: 65,000. This office is converting to automated system with advanced search capabilities.

Missouri

Corporate Division, Secretary of State, 301 High Street, PO Box 77, Jefferson City, MO 65102, (314) 751-4194. Selected Publications: *Corporation Handbook.* Phone Information: (314) 751-4153. Copies of Documents on File: Available at 50 cents per page plus $5.00 for certified copies. Mailing Labels: No. Magnetic Tape: Cost is between $50 and $100 for copy of master file, plus $20 for tape. Microfiche: No. New Corporate Listings: No. Custom Searches: No. Online Access: Available through Mead Data Central (LEXIS), 9393 Springboro Pike, PO Box 933, Dayton, OH 45401, (513) 865-6800. Number of Active Corporations on File: 110,000.

Montana

Corporate Department, Secretary of State, Capitol Station, Helena, MT 59620, (406) 444-3665. Selected Publications: None. Phone Information: (406) 444-3665. Copies of Documents on File: Available on a cost recovery basis. Mailing Labels: No. Magnetic Tape: No. Microfiche: No. New Corporate Listings: No. Custom Searches: No but can search by name of corporation and name of director only. Online Access: No. Number of Corporations on File: 300,000.

Nebraska

Corporate Division, Secretary of State, State Capitol, Lincoln, NE 68509, (402) 471-4079. Selected Publications: None. Phone Information: (402) 471-4079. Copies of Documents on File: Available for $1 per page, $10 for certified copies. Mailing Labels: Available on a cost recovery basis. Contact Mr. Englert at (402) 471-2554. Magnetic Tape: Available on a cost recovery basis. Also contact Mr. Englert. Microfiche: No. New Corporate Listings: Available upon request. Custom Searches: No. Online Access: No. Number of Active Corporations on File: 80,000.

Nevada

Office of Corporations, Secretary of State, Capitol Complex, Carson City, NV 89710, (702) 885-5203. Selected Publications: *Book of Statutes.* Phone Information: Corporate Status call (702) 885-5105; General Info call (702) 885-5203. Copies of Documents on File: Available for $1 per page, $5 for certified copies. Written request only, prepayment required (send a blank check stating limit). Mailing Labels: No. Magnetic Tape: Copy of master file available, cost determined at time of request. Microfiche: No. New Corporate Listings: Monthly Listing of New Corporations costs $20 a month. Custom Searches: Yes. Searches may be done by location of resident agent. Cost determined at time of request. Other: A three volume listing of corporations on file is published twice a year which includes names of active and inactive corporations but not addresses. Online Access: No. Number of Active Corporations on File: 47,000.

New Hampshire

Corporate Division, Secretary of State, State House, Room 204, Concord, NH 03301, (603) 271-3244. Selected Publications: *How to Start a Business, New Hampshire Corporate Law.* Phone Information: (603) 271-3246. Copies of Documents on File: Available for $1 per page, plus $1 for certified copies. Mailing Labels: No. Magnetic Tape: No. Microfiche: Master File of Corporations, 66 sheets, 30 cents a sheet (updated monthly). New Corporate Listings: Monthly Subscriber List costs $11 plus postage. Custom Searches: No. Other: Booklet lists all non-profit corporations will be offered for sale on July 1, 1987. Online Access: No. Number of Active Corporations on File: 22,000.

New Jersey

Commercial Recording Division, Secretary of State, 125 W. State Street, Trenton, NJ 08625, (609) 530-6400. Selected Publications: *Corporate Filing Packet.* Phone Information: General Information call (609) 530-6405; Forms call (609) 292-0013); Expedite Service call (609) 984-7107. There is a charge for standard information, $2 look-up fee for each request plus $5 expedite fee. User may use VISA or Master Charge for payment. Answers available by phone, mail or Western Union Electronic Mail. Copies of Documents on File: Available for $1 per page plus $15 for certified copies. Mailing Labels: No. Magnetic Tape: Depends on justification. Microfiche: No. New Corporate Listings: Monthly List of Corporations costs $100 per month. Custom Searches: Numerous search capabilities are available. Each request is reviewed on individual basis. Requester is billed for computer time. Online Access: Available in the future. Number of Active Corporations on File: 500,000.

New Mexico

Corporation Division, PO Drawer 1269, Santa Fe, NM 87504, (505) 827-4502. Selected Publications: None. Phone Information: (505) 827-4504. Copies of Documents on File: Available on a cost recovery basis. Mailing Labels: No. Magnetic Tape: No. Microfiche: No. New Corporate Listings: No. Custom Searches: No. Online Access: Available through New Mexico Technet, 4100 Osuna N.E., Albuquerque, NM 87109, (505) 345-6555. Custom Searches: Yes. Categories: Corporate Name, Domestic or Foreign, Profit or Non-profit, Date

of Incorporation, Active or Inactive, Identification Number, Amount of Capital Stock, Principal Office Address, Officers and Directors Names (includes addresses, Social Security numbers and titles), Name of Incorporators, Registered Agent and Office, Good Standing Status, Parent/Subsidiary Information. Number of Active Corporations on File: 50,000.

New York

Bureau of Corporations, Secretary of State, 162 Washington Avenue, Albany, NY 12231, (518) 474-6200. Selected Publications: *Corporate Handbook* (lists services only), *Extract of Laws for Incorporating.* Phone Information: (518) 474-6200. Copies of Documents on File: Available for 50 cents per page, $2 for certified copies (soon to be changed). Mailing Labels: No. Magnetic Tape: No. Microfiche: No. New Corporate Listing: Available daily, monthly, and biannually, called Report of Corporations, by subscription only. Online Access: Available in the near future. Number of Corporations on File: 1,000,000.

North Carolina

Division of Corporation, Secretary of State, 300 N. Salisbury Street, Raleigh, NC 27611, (919) 733-4201. Selected Publications: *Guidelines for Forming a Business, Corporation Laws* ($8.18 plus postage and handling). Phone Information: (919) 733-4201. Copies of Documents on File: Available for $1 per page, $2 for certified copies. Mailing Labels: No. Magnetic Tape: Available on cost recovery basis. Categories: All active corporations, foreign, domestic, non-profit, and profit. Microfiche: No. New Corporate Listings: Available for $20 a month. Custom Searches: Yes. Categories: Type of Corporation, Professional Corporations, Insurance Corporations, Banks, and Savings and Loans. Online Access: Available in 1988. Number of Active Corporations on File: 150,000.

North Dakota

Corporation Division, Secretary of State, Capitol Building, Bismarck, ND 58505, (701) 224-2905. Selected Publications: *North Dakota Business Corporation Act Statute* $3. Phone Information: No. Copies of Documents on File: Search of records cost $2, four pages for $1, $10 for certified copies. (Written requests). Mailing Labels: No. Magnetic Tape: No. Microfiche: No. New Corporate Listings: Monthly Corporation List costs $10. Custom Searches: No. Online Access: No. Number of Active Corporations on File: 24,000. This office is not computerized.

Ohio

Corporation Division, Secretary of State, 30 East Broad Street, 14th Floor, Columbus, OH 43266-0418, (614) 466-3910. Selected Publications: *Corporate Checklist.* Phone Information: Corporate Status call (614) 466-3910; Name Availability call (614) 466-0590. Copies of Documents on File: Contact (614) 466-1776. Available for $1 per page, $5 for certified copies. Mailing Labels: No. Magnetic Tape: No. Microfiche: No. New Corporate Listing: Call (614) 466-8464. Weekly County-Wide Listing costs 25 cents a page, Weekly Statewide Listing costs 10 cents a page ($25-$30 a month). Custom Searches: Yes. Categories: location (county), Foreign, Domestic, Profit, Non-Profit. $125. Online Access: No. Number of Active Corporations on File: 350,000.

Oklahoma

Corporations, Secretary of State, 101 State Capitol Building, Oklahoma City, OK 73105, (405) 521-3048. Selected Publications: None. Phone Information: (405) 521-3048. Copies of Documents on File: Available for $1 per page, $5 for certified copies. Mailing Labels: No. Magnetic Tape: Complete master file costs $2,400. Microfiche: No. New Corporate Listings: Monthly Charter List costs $150 a month, plus Amendments $250 a month. Custom Searches: Yes. Categories: Total of 18 (Profit, Non-profit, Foreign, Domestic, etc.) Online Access: Presently only Dunn and Bradstreet has access. Possibly will be available to others within a year. Number of Active Corporations on File: 172,000.

Oregon

Corporation Division, Department of Commerce, 158 12th Street N.E., Salem, OR 97310, (503) 378-4166. Selected Publications: *Starting a Business in Oregon, Types of Filings.* Phone Information: (503) 378-4166. Copies of Documents on File: Available for $3 a copy, $3 to $9 for certified copies. Mailing Labels: No. Magnetic Tape: Complete masterfile costs $190. Contact William Gifford at (503) 373-7920. Requester must provide tape or charge will be an additional $20 a tape. Microfiche: No. New Corporate Listings: Statistical Report of New Corporations. Custom Searches: Yes. Numerous categories with a minimum charge of $150. Address inquiries to Attn: Laura Cooper. Online Access: Yes. Contact Laura Cooper (503-373-7920). Charges include $100 for hookup, $70 monthly fee, plus telephone charges and computer time. Number of Corporations on File: 80,000.

Pennsylvania

Corporation Bureau, Department of State, 308 N. Office Building, Harrisburg, PA 17120, (717) 787-1997. Selected Publications: *Corporate Guide* (currently under revision). Phone Information: (717) 787-1057. Copies of Documents on File: Available for $1 per page, $5 search fee, $7.50 for certified copies. Mailing Labels: No. Magnetic Tape: Copy of master file available for $400 per tape, Requester must supply three blank tapes. Microfiche: No. New Corporate Listings: County or area listing available for 25 cents per name. Custom Searches: Yes. Categories: Non-Profit, Domestic, Foreign, county location,

Information on People, Companies, and Mailing Lists

Limited Partnerships, Fictitious name, Trademarks, Foreign Non-profits, Cooperatives, Professional Corporations (25 cents per name). Online Access: Available in the near future. Number of Corporations on File: 540,000.

Rhode Island

Corporations Division, Secretary of State, 270 Westminster Mall, Providence, RI 02903, (401) 277-3040. Selected Publications: None. Phone Information: (401) 277-3040. Copies of Documents on File: Available for 15 cents per page, $2 for certified copies. Mailing Labels: No. Magnetic Tape: No. Microfiche: No. New Corporate Listings: No. Custom Searches: No. Online Access: No. Number of Active Corporations on File: 50,000.

South Carolina

Division of Corporations, Secretary of State, PO Box 11350, Columbia, SC 29211, (803) 734-2150. Selected Publications: None. Phone Information: (803) 734-2158. Copies of Documents on File: Available for $1 per page, $2 for certified copies. Mailing Labels: No. Magnetic Tape: No. Microfiche: No. New Corporate Listing: Special request only; contact Christine Sox at (803) 734-2161. Custom Searches: No. Online Access: No. Number of Active Corporations on File: 60,000.

South Dakota

Corporate Division, Secretary of State, 500 East Capitol, Pierre, SD 57501, (605) 773-4845. Selected Publications: None. Phone Information: (605) 773-4845. Copies of Documents on File: Available for 50 cents per page, $5 for certified copies. Mailing Labels: No. Magnetic Tape: No. Microfiche: No. New Corporate Listings: No. Custom Searches: No. Online Access: No. Number of Active Corporations on File: 20,000.

Tennessee

Office of Secretary of State, Services Division, Suite 500, James K. Polk Building, Nashville, TN 37219-5040, (615) 741-2286. Select Publications: *Handbook*. Phone Information: (615) 741-2286. Copies of Documents on File: Available for 25 cents per page, $2 for certified copies (call 615-741-6488). Mailing Labels No. Magnetic Tape: Yes. Categories: All Corporations, Foreign, Domestic, Profit, Non-Profit, Banks, Credit Unions, Cooperative Associations. Cost determined at time of request. (615-741-0584). Microfiche: No. New Corporate Listings: Monthly New Corporation Listing on a cost recovery basis (call 615-741-1111). Custom Searches: Yes. Categories: Same as for magnetic tape at a cost of 25 cents a page (3 corporations on a page). Contact (615) 741-0584. Online Access: This option is under consideration. Number of Active Corporations on File: 100,000.

Texas

Corporation Section, Statute Filing Division, Secretary of State, PO Box 13697, Austin, TX 78711, (512) 463-5586. Selected Publications: *Filing Guide to Corporations*. (Written requests only.) Phone Information: (512) 463-5555. Copies of Documents on File: Available for 55 cents for first page, 15 cents for each additional page, $1 a page for certified copies. Mailing Labels: No. Magnetic Tape: No. Microfiche: Names of officers and directors available. Cost determined at time of request. New Corporate Listings: Weekly Charter Update costs $27.50 per week. Custom Searches: No. Online Access: Available through Information America (404-892-1800). Contact Linda Gordon at (713) 751-7900. Number of Active Corporations on File: 400,000.

Utah

Corporations and UCC, Division of Business Regulations, P.O. Box 45801, 160 East 300 S, Second Floor, Salt Lake City, UT 84145-0801, (801) 530-6012. Selected Publications: *Going into Business* (only available for walk-ins). Phone Information: (801) 530-4849. Copies of Documents on File: Available for 30 cents a page, $10 for certified copies. Mailing Labels: No. Magnetic Tape: Yes. Categories: Profit, Non-Profit, Foreign, Domestic. Cost includes computer time and programming fee. Microfiche: No. New Corporate Listing: Weekly New Corporation List 30 cents a page, New Doing Business As (DBA) List 30 cents a page. Custom Searches: Yes. Categories: Same as for Magnetic tape. Cost includes printing charge of 30 cents a page plus computer time and programming fee. Online Access Possibly in the future. Number of Active Corporations on File: 60,000.

Vermont

Corporate Division, Secretary of State, Pavillion Office Building, Montpelier, VT 05602-2710, (802) 828-2386. Selected Publications: *Doing Business in Vermont*. Phone Information: (802) 828-2386. Copies of Documents on File: Available for 10 cents per page, $5 for certified copies. Mailing Labels: No. Magnetic Tape: No. Microfiche: Yes. New Corporate Listings: Yes. Monthly New Corporations and Trade names $5 a month. Doing Business As (DBA) $20. Out-of-State Corporations $100. Custom Searches: Yes. Categories: Foreign, Domestic, Non-profits, by date of registration. Cost is 1 cent a name. Online Access: No. Number of Active Corporations on File: 17,000.

Virginia

Clerk of Commission, State Corporation Commission, Secretary of State, Richmond, VA 23209, (804) 786-7141. Selected Publications: Explanatory handouts. Phone Information: (804) 786-3733. Copies of Documents on File: Available for $1 per page, $3 for certified copies. Mailing Labels: No. Magnetic Tape: Possibly in the future. Microfiche: No. New Corporate Listings: No. Custom Searches: Yes. Categories: Foreign, Domestic, Non- profit, Professional corporation, Non-Stock, Public Service, Cooperatives. Available on cost recovery basis. Online Access: Not at this time. Number of Active Corporations on File: 128,000.

Washington

Corporate Division, Secretary of State, 505 East Union (PM-21), Olympia, WA 98504, (206) 753-7120. Selected Publications: *Corporation Date Book* (contains forms and outlines procedures and laws) $14. Phone Information: (206) 753-7115. Copies of Documents on File: Call (206) 586-2061 to leave recorded message for document orders. Fees are $1 a document. Mailing Labels: No. Magnetic Tape: No. Microfiche: Cost is $10 a month per set. New Corporate Listings: No except for statistical sheet. Custom Searches: No. Online Access: No. Number of Active Corporations on File: 105,000.

West Virginia

Corporate Division, Secretary of State, Room 139 West, State Capitol, Charleston, WV 25305, (304) 342-8000. Selected Publications: None. Phone Information: (304) 342-8000. Copies of Documents on File: Available for 50 cents per page, $10 for certified copies. Mailing Labels: No. Magnetic Tape: No. Microfiche: No. New Corporate Listing: Monthly Report costs $5. Custom Searches: No. Online Access: No. Number of Active Corporations on File: 38,000.

Wisconsin

Corporate Division, Secretary of State, PO Box 7846, Madison, WI 53707, (608) 266-3590. Selected Publications: *Booklet of Statutes Governing Incorporation* ($2.50). Phone Information: (608) 266-3590. Copies of Documents on File: Available for 40 cents per page, $2 for certified copies. Mailing Labels: No. Magnetic Tape: No. Microfiche: Yes. Monthly New Corporations costs $11 a month. New Corporate Listing: Yes (see microfiche entry). Custom Searches: No. Online Access: No. Number of Active Corporations on File: Not available.

Wyoming

Corporate Division, Secretary of State, State of Wyoming, Capitol Building, Cheyenne, WY 82002, (307) 777-7311. Selected Publications: *Wyoming Business Corporation Act* ($3). Phone Information: (307) 777-7311. Copies of Documents on File: Available for 50 cents for first 10 pages then 15 cents a page, $3 for certified copies. Mailing Labels: No. Magnetic Tape: Yes. Categories: Trademarks, New Domestic, New Foreign all available on a cost recovery basis. Information cannot be used for solicitation. Submit written request with letter of purpose. Microfiche: No. New Corporate Listings: Yes. (See magnetic tape entry). Custom Searches: Yes. Categories: Trademarks 25 cents per name and address, New Domestic $120 or $80 if in-state request, New Foreign $120 or $80 if instate request. Information cannot be used for solicitation. Submit written request with letter of purpose. Online Access: No. Number of Active Corporations on File: 24,300.

State Company Directories

Market Info, Mailing Lists, Databases Available From State Company Directories

Would you like to know what kind of computing systems and software 24,000 manufacturing firms in California use? Or where you could find out what materials 7,000 manufacturers in North Carolina need for their manufacturing processes? Or which of 2,700 manufacturers in Nevada have contracts with the federal government? You can get quick answers to these questions and more in the state directories of manufacturing companies.

These directories contain valuable information concerning what products are bought, sold, and distributed in each state. At the very least, each directory lists the companies' names, addresses, phone numbers, products, and SIC codes, and is cross-referenced by company name, location, and SIC code/product. So, if you want to find out which companies in Tennessee manufacture a certain type of electronic component and where they are located, all you have to do is look it up in the product index. If you want to find out what manufacturing firms are operating in a certain town or county, the geographic index will tell you. These directories can be invaluable for targeting new market areas, monitoring industry trends, developing more effective mailing lists, and much more.

The majority of these directories are put out by the individual state's Chamber of Commerce or Department of Economic Development, while private publishing firms compile and distribute the rest. The price and sophistication of these directories vary widely from state to state. While some, like Montana's, may offer only the basic information mentioned above, others, like the Illinois directory, will also include key personnel, CEO, parent company, employment figures, import/export market, computer system used, and more. Prices range from no charge for North Dakota's directory, all the way to $250 for Alabama's five volume set. Most of the prices listed below include shipping and handling, and state sales tax where applicable.

Many of these directories are also available in database formats and differ widely in cost. While there are some real bargains, such as Rhode Island's directory of 2,600 firms on diskette for $20, some, like Colorado's of 4,700 firms, will cost you $1,000. Before ordering any of these databases, make sure that the software is compatible with your own system. Mailing labels for many of the directories are also available, and many states allow you to chose the companies you want for your mailing list on a cost per label basis.

List of State Company Directories

Alabama
Alabama Development Office, Research Division, State Capitol, 135 S. Union Street, Montgomery, AL 36130; (205) 263-0048. $250/5 volumes. Listing of 5,000 companies includes name, address, phone, CEO, year established, employee figures, product lines, parent company, import/export, and SIC code. Cross-referenced by company name, location, product, parent company, international trade, and SIC code. Available on diskette or tape database format for $42 +3 cents per entry + cost of software.

Alaska
Alaska Center for International Business, University of Alaska, 4201 Tudor Center Drive, Suite 120, Anchorage, AK 99508; (907) 561-2322. $13.90. *The*

Alaska Trade Directory, a listing of 150 Alaska companies and industries that import or export, includes name, address, phone, CEO, key personnel, market area, product/service, and SIC code. Cross-referenced by company name and product/SIC code.

Arizona
Phoenix Chamber of Commerce, 34 West Monroe, Suite 900, Phoenix, AZ 85003; (602) 254-5521. $64.72. Listing of 3,200 companies includes name, address, phone, CEO, employee figures, market area, products, and SIC code. Cross-referenced by company name, location, market area, and products/SIC code.

Arkansas
Arkansas Industrial Development Foundation, P.O. Box 1784, Little Rock, AR 72203; (501) 682-1121. $31.60. Listing of 2,500 companies includes name, address, phone, contact person, parent company, products, and SIC code. Cross-referenced by company name, location, and product/SIC code.

California
Database Publishing Company, 523 Superior Avenue, Newport Beach, CA 92663; (800) 888-8434. $151. Listing of 24,000 companies includes name, address, phone, CEO, key personnel, sales volume, year established, parent company, products, computer brand used, import/export, employee figures, and SIC code. Cross-referenced by company name, location, products, and SIC code. Available on diskette for $975.

Colorado
Business Research Division, University of Colorado, Campus Box 420, Boulder, CO 80309; (303) 492-8227. $60. Listing of 4,700 companies includes name, address, phone, employee figures, market area, CEO, products, and SIC code. Cross-referenced by company name, location, and SIC code. Available in database format for $1,000. Mailing labels: $200/set.

Connecticut
Connecticut Labor Department, Employment Security Division, attn: Business Management, 200 Folly Brook Boulevard, Weathersfield, CT 06109; (203) 566-2120. $22. The 1984 directory of 4,000 companies includes name, address, products, and SIC code. Cross-referenced by company name, location, products, and SIC codes. A quarterly updated listing available for $7/year.

McRAE's Industrial Directories, 817 Broadway, 3rd Floor, New York, NY 10003; (800) 622-7237. $129.50. Listing of 8,200 CT and RI manufacturing firms includes name, address, phone, parent company, key personnel, employee figures, size, products, and SIC code. Cross- referenced by company name, location, and SIC code.

Delaware
Delaware State Chamber of Commerce, One Commerce Center, Suite 200, Wilmington, DE 19801; (302) 655-7221. $45 for state Chamber members; $55 for non-members. The directory of commerce and industry, listing over 6,000 companies, includes name, address, phone, CEO, employee figures, products/services, and SIC code. Cross-referenced by company name, location, and SIC code. Mailing labels: 10 cents/company.

Florida
Florida Chamber of Commerce, P.O. Box 11309, Tallahassee, FL 32302; (904) 222-2831. $65. Listing of over 10,000 companies includes name, address, phone, CEO, employee figures, products, import/export, and SIC code. Cross-referenced by company name, location, and SIC code. Available in database format, diskette or tape, for 12 cents/company or about $1,200. Mailing labels: 5 cents/company or $556 for entire directory.

Georgia
Georgia Department of Industry and Trade, Directory Section, P.O. Box 1776, Atlanta, GA 30301; (404) 656-3619. $40. Listing of 5,410 companies includes name, address, phone, market area, parent company, key personnel, employee figures, year established, products, and SIC code. Cross-referenced by company name, location and SIC code.

Information On People, Companies, and Mailing Lists

Hawaii

Chamber of Commerce of Hawaii, 735 Bishop Street, Honolulu, HI 96813; (808) 522-8800. $22. The 1984 edition of over 150 companies includes name, address, phone, contact person, product, and SIC code. Cross-referenced by company name, location, and SIC code. A 1989 edition is in the planning stages.

Idaho

Center for Business Development & Research, University of ID Moscow, ID 83842; (208) 885-6611. Available by the fall of 1989, the new directory of over 1,500 manufacturers will include name address, phone, CEO, product/service, import/export, employee figures, and SIC code. Cross-referenced by company name, location, and SIC code. Will also be available on diskette. Prices not yet fixed.

Illinois

Harris Publishing Company, 2057-2 Aurora Road, Twinsburg, OH 44087; (800) 321-9136. $103.50. Listing of over 20,000 companies includes name, address, phone, CEO, employee figures, computer brand used, year established, sales volume, product, and SIC code. Cross-referenced by company name, location, product, and SIC code. Diskette format, containing 9,000 companies with 20 or more employees, available for $295.

Indiana

Harris Publishing Company, 2057-2 Aurora Road, Twinsburg OH 44087; (800) 321-9136. $79.50. Listing of over 8,000 companies includes name, address, phone, CEO, employee figures, year established, annual sales, computer brand used, products, and SIC code. Cross-referenced by company name, location, product, and SIC code. Diskette format, containing 6,000 companies with 10 or more employees, available for $245.

Iowa

Iowa Department of Economic Development, Research Section, 200 East Grand Avenue, Des Moines, IA 50309; (515) 281-3925. $40. Listing of over 3,500 companies includes name, address, phone, CEO, purchasing agent, parent company, employee figures, product, and SIC code. Cross-referenced by company name, location, product, and SIC code.

Kansas

Kansas Department of Commerce, 400 West 8th Street, Suite 500, Topeka, KS 66603; (913) 296-3481. $35. Listing of 3,800 companies includes name, address, phone, contact person, parent company, employee figures, product, and SIC code. Cross-referenced by company name, location, product, and SIC code.

Kentucky

Department of Economic Development, Maps & Publications, 133 Holmes Street, Frankfort, KY 40601; (502) 564-4715. $30. Listing of 3,600 companies includes name, address, phone, CEO, year established, employee figures, products, and SIC code. Cross-referenced by company name, location, and SIC code.

Louisiana

Department of Commerce & Industry, P.O. Box 94185, Baton Rouge, LA 70804-9185; (504) 342-5361. $48. Listing of 3,000 companies includes name, address, phone, CEO, purchasing agent, marketing area, import/export, products, and SIC code. Cross-referenced by company name, location, and SIC code. Database format available sometime in 1989.

Maine

Maine Manufacturing Directory, Tower Publishing Company, 34 Diamond Street, P.O. Box 7220, Portland, ME 04112; (800) 431-2665 in-state; (207) 774-9813 out-of-state. $27.50. Listing of 2,200 companies includes name, address, phone, three contact persons, employee figures, gross sales, product, and SIC code. Cross-referenced by company name, location, and SIC code. Mailing labels: $55 for first 1,000, then 5 cents each.

Maryland

Office of Maryland Magazine, Redwood Tower, 9th Floor, 217 East Redwood Street, Baltimore, MD 21202; (301) 333-6600. $35. Listing of 2,500 companies includes name, address, phone, employee figures, year established, annual sales, products, key personnel, and SIC code. Divided into sections by company name, location, industry, import/export, products, and SIC code. Mailing labels: $125/set.

Massachusetts

George D. Hall Publishing Company, 50 Congress Street, Boston, MA 02109; (617) 523-3745. $59.60 in-state; $56.95 out-of-state. Listing of 6,600 companies includes name, address, phone, CEO, sales volume, employee figures, products, and SIC code. Cross-referenced by company name, location, and product. Database format on diskette for any 3,000 companies available for $400.

Michigan

Harris Publishing Company, 2057-2 Aurora Road, Twinsburg, OH 44087; (800) 321-9136. $103.50. Listing of 14,000 companies includes name, address, phone, CEO, employee figures, computer brands used, year established, products, and SIC code. Cross-referenced by company name, location, product, and SIC code. Diskette format, containing 7,000 companies with 20 or more employees, available for $295.

Michigan

National Information Systems, 11300 Rupp Drive, Burnsville, MN 55337; (612) 894-9494. $83.49. Listing of 9,000 companies includes name, address, phone, contact person, employee figures, sales volume, year established, products, and SIC code. Cross-referenced by company name, location, and product/SIC code.

Mississippi

Mississippi Research & Development Center, 3825 Ridgewood Road, Jackson, MS 39211; (601) 982-6606. $50. Listing of 2,600 companies includes name, address, phone, CEO, key personnel, employee figures, parent company, products, international trade, and SIC code. Cross- referenced by company name, location, product, and SIC code. Available on diskette for $400, and $100 for yearly update.

Missouri

Harris Publishing Company, 2057-2 Aurora Road, Twinsburg, OH 44087; (800) 321-9136. $78.50. Listing of 8,000 companies includes name, address, phone, CEO, employee figures, computer brand used, year established, product, and SIC code. Cross-referenced by company name, location, product, and SIC code. Diskette format, containing 4,800 companies with 10 or more employees, available for $245.

Montana

Department of Commerce, Business Assistance Division, 1424 9th Avenue, Helena, MT 59620; (406) 444-3923. $20. Listing of 2,500 companies includes name, address, phone, owner, size classification, products, and SIC code. Cross-referenced by company name, location, product, and SIC code.

Nebraska

Nebraska Department of Economic Development, P.O. Box 94666, Lincoln, NE 68509; (402) 471-3784. $30. Listing of 1,800 companies includes name, address, phone, CEO, parent company, employee figures, import/export, products, and SIC code. Cross-referenced by company name, location, and product/SIC code. Available on IBM compatible diskette for $150.

Nevada

Gold Hill Publishing Company, P.O. Drawer F, Virginia City, NV 89440; (702) 847-0222. $48 out-of-state; $50.70 in-state. Listing of 2,700 companies includes name, address, phone, parent company, CEO, key personnel, fax #, square footage occupied, sales volume, products, import/export, federal contracts, year established, years in NV, products, and SIC code. Cross-referenced by company name, location, and product/SIC code. Available on diskette for $125.

New Hampshire

Department of Research & Economic Development, Industrial Development Office, 105 Loudon Road, P.O. Box 856, Concord NH 03301; (603) 271-2591. $29.75. Listing of 4,800 companies includes name, address, phone, CEO, ranking officers, year established, sales volume, import/export, products, and SIC code. Cross-referenced by company name, location, and product/SIC code. Available on IBM compatible diskette for $250/set of 4 + $4.74 postage & handling.

New Jersey

Commerce Register, Inc., 190 Godwin Avenue, Midland, NJ 07432; (800) 221-2172. $82.50. Listing of 11,000 companies includes name, address, phone, key personnel, sales volume, products, employee figures, square footage and acreage occupied, year established, SIC code, and bank, accountants, and law firms used. Cross-referenced by company name, location, and product/SIC code. Available on diskette for $153 minimum charge, depending on number of listings ordered.

New Mexico

Economic Development & Tourism Department, Joseph M. Montoya Building, 1100 St. Francis Drive, Santa Fe, NM 87503; (505) 827-0274. $20. Listing of 1,800 companies includes name, address, phone, CEO, employee figures, products/services, and SIC code. Cross-referenced by company name, location, and product/SIC code.

New York

MacRAE's Industrial Directories, 817 Broadway, 3rd Floor, New York, NY 10003; (800) 622-7237. $129.50. Listing of 14,000 companies includes name, address, phone, key personnel, size classification, products, location, and SIC code.

North Carolina

North Carolina Department of Commerce, Department DM, P.O. Box 25249, Raleigh, NC 27611; (919) 733-5146. $52.50. Due out 4/89, the new edition of 7,000 companies includes name, address, phone, CEO, year established, employee figures, parent company, import/export, product, and purchasing and product SIC codes. Cross-referenced by company name, location, parent company, product, products purchased, and import/export capabilities. Available on IBM magnetic tape database format for $1,000.

North Dakota

North Dakota Economic Development Commission, Liberty Memorial Building, State Capitol Grounds, Bismarck, ND 58505; (701) 224-2810. No charge. Listing of over 600 companies includes name, address, phone, contact person, employee figures, products, and SIC code. Cross-referenced by company name, location, and product/SIC code.

Ohio

Harris Publishing Company, 2057-2 Aurora Road, Twinsburg, OH 44087; (800) 321-9136. $113.50. Listing of 18,000 companies includes name, address, phone, CEO, employee figures, year established, annual sales, computer brand used, products, and SIC code. Cross-referenced by company name, location, product, and SIC code. Diskette format, containing 8,700 companies with 20 or more employees, available for $298.

Oklahoma

Oklahoma Department of Commerce, 6601 Broadway Extension, Building #5, Marketing Division, Oklahoma City, OK 73116; (405) 843-9770, ext. 207. $40. Listing of 4,500 companies includes name, address, phone, owner's name, employee figures, product, and SIC code. Cross-referenced by company name, location, product, and SIC code.

Oregon

Oregon Economic Development Department, 595 Cottage Street NE, Salem, OR 97310; (503) 373-1200. $60. Listing of 7,500 companies includes name, address, phone, employee figures, parent company, CEO, import/export, products, and SIC code. Cross-referenced by company name, product, and SIC code. Available in database formats and mailing labels at variable cost.

Pennsylvania

Harris Publishing Company, 2057-2 Aurora Road, Twinsburg, OH 44087; (800) 321-9136. $113.50. Listing of 18,000 companies includes name, address, phone, CEO, employee figures, computer brand used, year established, products, and SIC code. Cross-referenced by company name, location, product, and SIC code. IBM compatible diskette format, containing 8,800 companies with 20 or more employees, available for $299.50.

Rhode Island

Department of Economic Development, Research Division, 7 Jackson Walkway, Providence, RI 02903; (401) 277-2601. No charge for RI residents; $15 for non-residents. Listing of 2,600 companies includes name, address, phone, CEO, employee figures, parent company, products, and SIC code. Cross-referenced by company name, location, and SIC code. Available on MacIntosh compatible diskette for $20.

South Carolina

State Development Board, P.O. Box 927, Columbia, SC 29209; (803) 737-0400. Attn: directory sales. $35. Listing of 3,200 companies includes name, address, phone, CEO, purchasing agent, employee figures, product line, parent company, and SIC code. Cross-referenced by company name, location, product, and SIC code. Available on IBM compatible diskette for $1,000.

South Dakota

Governor's Office of State Development, Capitol Lake Plaza, Pierre, SD 57501; (605) 773-5032. $20. Listing of 700 companies includes name, address, phone, trade name, employee figures, CEO, purchasing agent, sales manager, products, and SIC code. Cross-referenced by company name, location, and SIC code. Mailing labels: $20/set.

Tennessee

M. Lee Smith Publishers & Printers, P.O. Box 2678, Arcade Station, Nashville, TN 37219; (615) 242-7395. $67.80 in-state; $64 out-of-state. Due out 3/89, listing of 5,300 companies includes name, address, phone, parent company, key personnel, employee figures, marketing area, computer brand used, products, and SIC code. Available in database format, magnetic tape or diskette: $100 conversion fee, then $250 per 1,000 chosen. Mailing labels: $175 per 1,000.

Texas

University of Texas, Bureau of Business Research, P.O. Box 7459, Austin, TX 78713; (512) 471-1616. $110. Two volume directory of 15,500 companies includes name, address, phone, key personnel, year established, sales volume, employee figures, market area, import/export, products, and SIC code. Volume 1 lists companies by name; volume 2 by product/SIC code. Available on diskette for $400 per 2,000 companies.

Utah

Utah Economic Development Division, 6150 State Office Building, Salt Lake City, UT 84114; (801) 538-3036. $22. Listing of 2,600 companies includes name, address, phone, employee figures, products, and SIC code. Cross-referenced by company name and SIC code. Available in dBase 3 database format, high or low density diskettes, for $22.

Vermont

Agency of Development & Community Affairs, Pavillion Office Building, Montpelier, VT 05602; (802) 828-3221. $10. Listing of 1,300 companies includes name, address, phone, CEO, parent company products trade names, products exported, employee figures, retail/mailorder/or wholesale distribution, and SIC code. Cross-referenced by company name, location, and product/SIC code. Soon available as on-line database.

Virginia

Virginia Chamber of Commerce, 9 South 5th Street, Richmond, VA 23219; (804) 644-1607. $69.93 in-state; $67 out-of-state. Listing of 4,000 companies includes name, address, phone, CEO, employee figures parent company, products, and SIC code. Cross-referenced by product, SIC code, county, and city. Available in ASCII and ABCDIC magnetic tape database formats for $225. Mailing labels vary in price.

Washington

Database Publishing Company, 523 Superior Avenue, Newport Beach, CA 92663; (800) 888-8434. $80. Listing of 3,800 companies includes name, address, phone, CEO, key personnel, sales volume, year established, parent company, products, computer brand used, employee figures, import/export, product, and SIC code. Cross-referenced by company name, location, products, and SIC code. Diskette format variable in price.

West Virginia

Governor's Office of Community & Industrial Development, Room R-150, State Capitol, Charleston, WV 25305; (304) 348-0350. $40. Listing of 1,200 companies includes name, address, phone, CEO, employee figures, computer brand used, year established, products, and SIC code. Cross-referenced by company name, location, product, and SIC code.

Wisconsin

WMC Service Corporation, P.O. Box 352, 501 East Washington Street, Madison, WI 35701; (608) 258-3400. $94.50 in-state; $90 out-of-state. Listing of 9,000 companies includes name, address, phone, CEO, year established, computer brand used, employee figures, parent company, fax #, import/export, out-of-state affiliates, products, and SIC code. Cross-referenced by company name, location, product, and SIC code. Available on IBM compatible diskette for $495, which also includes a copy of the Wisconsin Service Companies Directory.

Wyoming

Economic Development & Stabilization Board, 3rd Floor, 122 West 25th Street, Cheyenne, WY 82002; (307) 777-7284. No charge. Listing of 250 companies includes name, address, phone, CEO, market area, employee figures, product, and SIC code. Cross-referenced by company name, location, and SIC code.

State Securities and Stockbrokers

State Securities Offices Offer Company Information, Mailing List of Brokers and More

The offices of state security regulators offer financial data on thousands of companies which are not required to file with the U.S. Securities and Exchange Commission as well as the names, addresses, financial data, and consumer information on thousands of stockbrokers and broker-dealers.

State regulation of the sale of securities in the United States began in 1911 when the Kansas legislature passed the first securities law. North Carolina enacted a law the same year; Arizona and Louisiana did so in 1912. By 1919, 32 states had followed suit. Now, all states and the federal government have laws regulating the sale of corporate securities, bonds, investment contracts and stocks.

The reason for these laws is simple enough: they protect the public, unfamiliar with the intricacies of investing, against deceitful promoters and their often worthless stocks. This is the same type of function that the US Securities and Exchange Commission performs in Washington, DC. The United States covers companies trading stocks across state boundaries, and the states cover companies trading stocks within their state. The laws--called Blue Sky laws--prevent speculative schemes "which have no more basis than so many feet of blue sky," according to the Commerce Clearing House Blue Sky Law Reports.

The Blue Sky Law is usually administered by each state's Securities Commission or Securities Division. Securities to be sold within a state must register with this office. If the issuer is a corporation, for example, it must submit the following information:

o articles of incorporation
o purpose of proposed business
o names and addresses of officers and directors
o qualifications and business history of applicant - detailed financial data

Each state, however, has numerous exemptions. Securities issued by national banks, savings and loan associations, non-profit organizations, public utilities, and railroads are usually exempt from the Blue Sky laws, as are securities listed on the stock exchange, those issued by companies registered with the U.S. Securities and Exchange Commission, and those issued by foreign governments with which the U.S. has diplomatic relations.

Securities offices also require broker--dealer firms, the agents (or sales representatives), and investments advisers wanting to work in the state to file applications.

Agents wanting to work in one or more states now apply for registration by filing with National Association of Securities Dealers' Central Registration Depository (CRD). To keep the CRD current, agents must submit all pertinent employment and application changes. All state securities offices are hooked up to the CRD through computer terminals and use them to monitor agents registered or applying to register in their jurisdictions as well as any complaints filed against individuals.

In 1989, most states will also use the system for registration of broker-dealer firms. Information kept in the repository will include registration applications, amendments to applications, complaints on file, and so forth. The purpose is to reduce the amount of paperwork for the states and to promote more uniformity. As of mid December, 1988, only eight states had not yet signed up to participate: Arizona, Arkansas, Florida, Michigan, Nebraska, New Hampshire, New Jersey and North Dakota. Most are expected to switch in 1989.

The system is not set to accept broker-dealers' audited financial statements or annual reports so applicants will have to continue to file in the states requiring them. The broker-dealer phase of the CRD is scheduled to be ready in February 1989. Several states are now trying to determine what, if any, information they will require broker-dealers to file with their securities divisions. Most of those states that have made a decision said they will continue to require annual financial reports to be filed with their offices.

Below are the names, addresses and telephone numbers for the state securities offices. Most of these offices will routinely provide information over the phone on whether specific companies, agents, or broker-dealers are registered in their states. Requests for more detailed information may have to be submitted in writing.

Securities Offices

Alabama
Securities Commission, 144 Commerce St., Second Floor, Montgomery, AL 36130; (205) 261-2984.

Alaska
Division of Banking, Securities and Corporations, Department of Commerce and Economic Development, Ninth Floor, State Office Building, 333 Willoughby, PO Box D, Juneau, AK 99811; (907) 465-2521.

Arizona
Securities Division, Arizona Corporation Commission, 120 West Washington, St., Phoenix, AZ 85007; (602) 542-4242.

Arkansas
Securities Department, Heritage West Building, Third Floor, 201 West Markham, Little Rock, AR 72201; (501) 371-1011.

California
Securities Regulation Division, Department of Corporations, 600 South Commonwealth Ave., Suite 1600, Los Angeles, CA 90005; (213) 736-2741.

Colorado
Division of Securities, Department of Regulatory Agencies, 1560 Broadway, Suite 1450, Denver, CO 80202; (303) 894-2320.

Connecticut
Securities and Business Investments Division, Department of Banking, Securities and Business, 44 Capitol Ave., Hartford, CT 06106; (203) 566-4560.

Delaware
Division of Securities, Department of Justice, 820 North French St., Wilmington, DE 19801; (302) 571-2515.

District of Columbia
Division of Securities, DC Public Service Commission, 450 5th St., NW, Suite

820, Washington, D.C. 20001; (202) 626-5105.

Florida
Division of Securities and Investor Protection, Department of Banking and Finance, Office of Comptroller, The Capitol, Tallahassee, FL 32399; (904) 488-9805.

Georgia
Business Services and Regulations, Office of Secretary of State, Suite 315 West Tower, Two Martin Luther King Dr., Atlanta, GA 30334; (404) 656-2894.

Hawaii
Business registration Division, Department of Commerce and Consumer Affairs, 1010 Richards St., PO Box 40, Honolulu, HI 96810; (808) 548-5319.

Idaho
Securities Bureau, Department of Finance, 700 West State St., Boise, ID 83720; (208) 334-3684.

Illinois
Securities Department, Office of Secretary of State, 90 South Spring St., Springfield, IL 62704; (217) 782-2256.

Indiana
Securities Division, Office of Secretary of State, One North Capitol, Suite 560, Indianapolis, IN 46204; (317) 232-6681.

Iowa
Securities Bureau, Office of Commissioner of Insurance, Lucas State Office Building, Des Moines, IA 50319; (515) 281-4441.

Kansas
Office of Securities Commissioner, Landon State Office Building, 900 SW Jackson St., Suite 552, Topeka, KS 66612; (913) 296-3307.

Kentucky
Division of Securities, Department of Financial Institutions, 911 Leawood Dr., Frankfort, KY 40601; (502) 564-2180.

Louisiana
Securities Commission, 315 Louisiana State Office Building, 325 Loyola Ave., New Orleans, LA 70112; (504) 568-5515.

Maine
Securities Division, Bureau of Banking, Department of Professional and Financial Regulation, State House Station 121, Augusta, ME 04333; (207) 582-8760.

Maryland
Division of Securities, Office of Attorney General, The Munsey Building, 18th Floor, Calvert and Fayett Streets, Baltimore, MD 21202; (301) 576-6360.

Massachusetts
Securities Division, Department of Secretary of State, 1719 John W. McCormack Building, One Ashburton Place, Boston, MA 02108; (617) 727-3548.

Michigan
Corporation and Securities Bureau, Department of Commerce, 6546 Merchantile Way, Lansing, MI 48909; (517) 334-6200.

Minnesota
Registration and Licensing Division, Department of COmmerce, 50 Metro Square Building, 7th & Robert Sts., St. Paul, MN 55101; (612) 296-4026.

Mississippi
Securities Division, Office of Secretary of State, 41 Mississippi St., Jackson, MS 39205; (601) 359-1350.

Missouri
Office of Secretary of State, 301 West High St., Jefferson City, MO 66102; (314) 751-4136.

Montana
Securities Department, State Auditor's Office, 126 North Sanders, Room 270, Helena, MT 59601; (406) 444-2040.

Nebraska
Bureau of Securities, Department of Banking and Finance, 301 Centennial Mall S., Lincoln, NE 68509; (402) 471-3445.

Nevada
Securities Division, Office of Secretary of State, 2501 East Sahara Ave., #201, Las Vegas, NV 89158; (702) 486-4400.

New Hampshire
Office of Securities Regulation, 157 Manchester St., Concord, NH 03301; (603) 271-1463.

New Jersey
Bureau of Securities, Division of Consumer Affairs, Department of Law and Public Safety, Two Gateway Center, 8th Floor, Newark, NJ 07102; (201) 648-2040.

New Mexico
Securities Division, REgulation and Licensing Department, Bataan Memorial Building, Room 165, Santa Fe, NM 87503; (505) 827-7705.

New York
Bureau of Investor Protection and Securities, Department of Law, 12 Broadway, 23rd Fl., New York, NY 10271; (212) 341-2722.

North Carolina
Securities Division, Department of State, 300 N Salisbury St., #404, Raleigh, NC 27611; (919) 733-3924.

North Dakota
Office of Securities Commissioner, 9th Fl. State Capitol, Bismark, ND 58505; (701) 224-2910.

Ohio
Division of Securities, Department of Commerce, 77 South High St, 22nd Fl., Columbus, OH 43266; (614) 644-7381.

Oklahoma
Department of Securities, 2401 North Lincoln Blvd., 4th Fl., Oklahoma City, OK 73152; (405) 521-2451.

Oregon
Division of Finance and Corporate Securities, Department of Insurance and Finance, 21 Labor Industries Bldg., Salem, OR 97310; (503) 378-4385.

Pennsylvania
Securities Commission, Division of Licensing and Compliance, 1010 North Seventh St., Second Floor, Harrisburg, PA 17102; (717) 787-8061.

Rhode Island
Securities Division, Department of Business Regulation, 233 Richmond St., #232, Providence, RI 02903; (401) 277-3048.

South Carolina
Securities Division, Department of State, 1205 Pendelton St., #501, Columbia, SC 29201; (803) 734-1087.

South Dakota
Division of Securities, Department of Commerce and Regulation, 910 East Sioux, Pierre, SD 57501; (605) 773-4823.

Tennessee
Division of Securities, Department of Commerce and Insurance, 1808 West End Bldg., Nashville, TN 37219; (615) 741-3187.

Texas
State Securities Board, 1800 San Jacinto St., Austin, TX 78711; (512) 474-2233.

Utah
Securities Division, Department of Business Regulation, P.O. Box 45802, Salt Lake City, UT 84145; (801) 530-6600.

Vermont
Securities Division, Department of Banking & Insurance, 38 State St., 2nd Fl., Montpelier, VT 05602; (802) 828-3420.

Virginia
Division of Securities and Retail Franchising, State Corporation Commission, PO Box 1197, Richmond, VA 23209; (804) 786-7751.

Washington
Securities Division, Department of Licensing, PO Box 648, Olympia, WA 98504; (206) 753-6928.

West Virginia
Securities Division, State Auditor's Office, Room W-118, State Capitol, Charleston, WV 25305; (304) 348-2257.

Wisconsin

Office of Commissioner of Securities, 111 West Wilson St., Madison, WI 53701; (608) 266-3431.

Wyoming

Securities Division, Office of the Secretary of State, State Capitol Building, Cheyenne, WY 82002; (307) 777-7370.

Hospitals and Nursing Homes

All states maintain records on health care facilities and nursing homes. Licensing offices maintain the most current information on a wide range of such facilities. In smaller states, one division is usually charged with the responsibility for licensing and certifying health care facilities. Larger states usually divide licensing duties among several bureaus.

In addition to hospitals and nursing homes, states license and certify home health agencies, ambulatory surgical centers, birthing centers, college infirmaries, alcohol and drug rehabilitation centers, renal dialysis centers, abortion clinics, HMO's, independent clinical laboratories, and cerebral palsy treatment homes. Separate rosters are often available for those which have become voluntarily certified: home health care agencies, hospice, independent physical therapists, mobile X-ray providers, and rural health clinics.

Such offices will usually answer questions concerning health care facilities and alternative care programs for the elderly. Many also offer directories listing registered facilities and related information to help the public in choosing a facility. These offices also investigate complaints and take action against facilities found to be in violation of health, nutrition, and safety standards.

Among the other documents available for public inspection are those associated with the initial filing for state certification, reapplication if there has been any change in ownership, and written notification if there have been changes in the number of beds available or services offered other than those for which the initial license was issued.

Information is easily available of the name and address of each facility, the administrator, phone number, number of beds, In some states, the number of beds is further broken down into those for acute care, bassinets, and Medicare or Medicaid beds.

Information available from state health care licensing offices is helpful not only for persons seeking the best health care in their state, but also for sales representatives, real estate developers, pharmaceutical companies, linen, uniform and food service companies, cable television firms, and anyone else with a product or service in the health care, rehabilitation, or nursing home areas.

Certificate Of Need

To ensure that each person has access to adequate health care and nursing home facilities and to ensure that such facilities do not place profit above care, many have what is called a Certificate of Need (CON) program. Such programs require each health care facility in a state to file a CON to defend the need for such a facility in that area.

CON were required under the 1976 National Health Planning Act. Originally, under CON, the federal government reviewed all state Medicare payment requests, but has since discontinued the requirement. States are unregulated and each is charged with determining Medicare eligibility.

In a regulatory capacity, CON programs are used to review the number of medical care facilities, providers, or services within a state and to determine which areas have too few or too many facilities or services available to the public. CON tends to protect the little guy. For example, CON checks the number of nursing home beds to make sure that there are not too many that smaller nursing homes cannot compete and are driven into bankruptcy.

Without a CON Program, any hospital or nursing home could be built, and there would be a tendency to overbuild, resulting in underutilization. Also, if there are too many hospital beds, services, or health facilities, potential investors would look elsewhere to invest their capital.

CON not only regulates the number of beds and health facilities, but also high ticket medical equipment such as magnetic imaging equipment and special surgical lasers. These items are very expensive, and states usually buy as few as possible and transport them to facilities rather than locating them in just one permanent place. CON programs review facilities and equipment based upon a threshold value.

How CON Works

Before a health care facility or nursing home can open, it must furnish the state with a letter of intent, an application form listing its cost, potential customers, and other specifics about the facility (hospital, nursing home, rehabilitation center, etc.). Most states publish this information in a monthly newsletter and costs for this information varies. The letters are published to allow public input into the decisionmaking process and because many of these decisions involve the financial backing of state tax dollars.

Who Uses CON

Because of the large amounts of money involved in the health care industry, the information provided in CON letters of intent is valuable to a great number of businesses and professionals, including: insurance companies, architects, engineers, lawyers, medical newsletters, equipment suppliers, support services, accountants, health consultants, construction companies, and news reporters.

Consultants may use CON information to determine which states have strict regulations for health facilities or to see how successful applications are filled out. A company looking to build a long-term care facility might search for an area where the CON rules are less stringent. Insurers and lawyers use the data to target both facilities and patients, while engineers and architects are able to get the jump on the competition by regularly monitoring CON requests.

What follows is a listing of those offices within the states that provide health care licensing and Certificate of Need (CON) information.

Information on People, Companies, and Mailing Lists

Health Services

Arizona

Department of Health Services, Birch Hall, 411 N. 24th St., Phoenix, AZ 85008; (602) 220-6407. Licenses: home health agencies, non- federal hospitals, supervisory care homes, nursing care institutions, ambulatory surgical centers, outpatient treatment clinics, free standing facilities, rural health clinics, portable x-ray units, rehabilitation clinics, infirmaries, special hospitals, end stage renal disease and transplant centers. Provides free listings including name, address, phone number, administrator, type of ownership of each facility. Application forms are public information.

Certificate of Need: None.

California

Department of Health Services, Licensing and Certification, 714 P. St., Room 823, Sacramento, CA 95814; (916) 445-2070. Licenses: hospitals, skilled nursing facilities, intermediate care facilities, primary care clinics, home health agencies, mental health facilities and rehabilitative hospitals. There are 21 district offices. 11 located in Los Angeles. Each district office keeps files which can be inspected by the public. A health facilities directory is available for $7.60.

Certificate of Need: Obsolete January 1, 1988.

Georgia

Department of Human Resources, Standards and Licensure Section, 878 Peachtree St. N.E., Suite 803, Atlanta, GA 30309; (404) 894-7505. Licenses: hospitals, nursing homes, intermediate care homes, home health agencies, residential treatment centers, ambulatory surgical centers, end stage renal disease centers. For each type of facility a listing detailing the name, address, phone number, number of beds and name of the administrator is available. The listings vary in price ranging from $3.00 - $5.00. Application forms are public information.
Certificate of Need: Georgia State Health Planning Agency, 4 Executive Park Dr. N.E., Suite 2100, Atlanta, GA 30329; (404) 894-4899. Publication: *"Projects on Hand"* a monthly subscription with information on proposed projects. It includes the facility name, location, brief description of the project, proposed cost and deadline for decision.

Hawaii

Department of Health, Hospital and Medical Facilities Branch, P.O. Box 3378, Honolulu, HI 96801; (808) 548-5935. Licenses: hospitals, skilled nursing and intermediate care facilities. A free directory for each type of facility is available.

Certificate of Need: State Health Planning Office, 335 Merchant St., Room 214, Honolulu, HI 96803; (808) 548-4050. Publication: a free monthly newsletter is issued listing applications received and the status of each project.

Idaho

Bureau of Facility Standards, Licensing and Certification, Department of Health and Welfare, 450 W. State St., Boise, ID 83720; (208) 334-6627. Licenses: hospitals, skilled nursing homes, end stage renal disease facilities, comprehensive outpatient rehabilitation facilities, ambulatory surgical centers, physical therapists, rural health clinics, hospice agencies, home health agencies, shelter homes, intermediate care for the mentally retarded. Free listings are available for each type of facility containing name, address, administrator, number of beds, types of services. Application forms are public information. Annual reports also available with a written request.

Certificate of Need: None.

Iowa

Department of Inspection Appeals, Division of Health Facilities, Lucas Office Building, Des Moines, IA 50319; (215) 281-4244. Licenses: all health care facilities including long term care, residential and intermediate care, skilled nursing facilities. A directory listing all health care facilities by county is available. It is free and provides the name, address, phone number, administrator, number of beds, state license number of each facility. Also available: results from surveys, complaint investigation reports. Application forms released with a written request.

Certificate of Need: Certificate of Need Program, State Health Department, Lucas State Office Building, Des Moines, IA 50319; (515) 281-4344. Specific questions on a project will be answered on the phone. No publications issued at this time.

Kansas

Department of Health and Environment, Landon State Office Building, 900 S. W. Jackson, Suite 1001, Topeka, KS 66620; (913) 296-1270. Licenses: hospitals, home health agencies, rehabilitation centers, ambulatory surgical centers, psychiatric hospitals, recuperation centers. Two directories available, *Hospitals* ($4.00) and *Nursing Homes* ($2.00) each containing the name, address, phone number, license expiration date and administrator of each facility. Application forms available with written request.

Certificate of Need: None.

Kentucky

Division of Licensing and Regulation, 275 E. Main St., CHR Building, 4th Floor, East, Frankfort, KY 40621; (502) 564-2800. Licenses: hospitals, nursing homes, personal care homes, family care centers, day care centers, child placing centers, mental health centers, ambulances, ambulatory care centers, nonmedical alcohol and mental health facilities. Directories available for different levels of care, each includes the name, address, phone number, administrator, number of beds, description of service, type of ownership for each facility. Charge is $.10 per page. For specific information from an application form, a request must be made to the Director.

Certificate of Need: Commission for Health Economics Control, 275 E. Main St., Frankfort, KY 40621; (502) 564-6620. Publication: free newsletter contains any letters of intent, relevant dates, listing of applications going on public notices; actions taken at the previous meetings, listing of all applications currently in process.

Louisiana

Division of Licensing and Certification, P.O. Box 3767, Baton Route, LA 70821; (504) 342-5774. Licenses: hospitals, home health care agencies, day care centers, nursing homes, adult day care, substance abuse centers, ambulatory surgical centers, laboratories, adoption facilities and respite care facilities. Individual information packets for each area are available. Prices range from $2.00 - $5.00. Due to budget cuts not all packets are kept current, information can be given over the telephone. All information from application forms is confidential.

Certificate of Need: None.

Maine

Division of Licensing and Certification, State House Station 11, Augusta, ME 04333; (207) 289-2606. Licenses: hospitals, ambulatory surgical centers, rehabilitation facilities, end state renal disease facilities, home health facilities, hospices, independent laboratories, physical therapists, portable x-ray services, rural health clinics. A directory is issued each year ($5.00) with the name, address, phone number, administrator and number of beds given for each facility.

Certificate of Need: Division of Project Review, John D. Dickens, Director, Office of Health Planning and Development, Department of Human Services, State House Station 11, 151 Capitol St., Augusta, ME 04333; (207) 289-2716. Publication: free monthly 17 page report containing information on all projects under consideration. Includes a brief description of the project, capital expenditures and a listing of decisions rendered.

Michigan

Michigan Department of Health, Division of Licensing and Certification, 3500 N. Logan St., Lansing, MI 48909; (517) 335-8505. Licenses: nursing homes, hospitals, homes for the aged, mental health facilities. Free directory available containing the name, address, phone number and number of beds for each facility. Application forms are public information.

Certificate of Need: Division of Health Facility Construction, Department of Public Health, 3500 N. Logan St., Lansing, MI 48909; (517) 335-8504. Publication: free monthly newsletter, reports on which projects have been approved and the total dollar amount.

Minnesota

Department of Health, Health Resources Division, 717 S.E. Delaware St., P.O. Box 9441, Minneapolis, MN 55440; (612) 623-5000. Licenses: hospitals, nursing homes, board care, ambulatory surgical centers, skilled nursing homes, independent laboratories, portable x-ray facilities, outpatient physical therapy, home health agencies. A directory ($15.00) is published containing the name, address, phone number, administrator and kind of ownership of each facility. Application files are open for public inspection - for copies a written request is required and there is a charge.

Certificate of Need: None.

Mississippi

State Department of Health, Division of Health Facility Licensure and Certification, P.O. Box 1700, Jackson, MS 39215; (601) 960-7769. Licenses: hospitals, skilled nursing care facilities, personal care homes, ambulatory surgical facilities, home health agencies, independent laboratories, rehabilitation agencies, rural health clinics, physical therapists, end stage renal disease facilities. Free directory available providing the name, address, license number, number of beds and governing authority of each facility. All license application information is confidential.

Certificate of Need: Division of Planning and Resource Development, State Department of Health, P.O. Box 1700, Jackson, MS 39215; (601) 960-7884. Publication: free newsletter reports various kinds of information on projects that have been approved or disapproved.

Missouri

Bureau of Hospital Licensure and Certification, Department of Health, P.O. Box 570, Jefferson, MO 65102; (314) 751-6302. Licenses: hospitals, ambulatory surgical centers, certified comprehensive outpatient rehabilitation facilities, certified independent laboratories, certified outpatient rehabilitation facilities, certified portable x-ray providers, certified renal dialysis facilities, regional centers for the developmentally disabled, trauma centers. A directory of hospitals and related health services is available. It lists the facility name, address, administrator and type of service. Information from an application form must be requested in writing.

Certificate of Need: State Health Planning and Development Agency, 1738 E. Elm St., Jefferson City, MO 65101; (314) 751-6403. Publication: a free quarterly report is published with information on current letters of intent, project name, description, estimated cost, date submitted and approval date.

Nebraska
Department of Health, Division of Standards, P.O. Box 95007, State Office Building, Lincoln, NE 68509; (402) 471-2946. Licenses: hospitals, nursing homes, boarding homes, clinics, end stage renal disease facilities. A free roster is distributed providing the name and address of each facility, the administrator, number and types of beds is also given. All application forms are available to the public.

Certificate of Need: Section of Hospitals and Medical Facilities, Nebraska Department of Health, P.O. Box 95007, Lincoln, NE 68509; (402) 471-2105 or Keith N. Larsen, Director, Nebraska HealthNetwork, 301 Centennial Mall South, Lincoln, NE 68509; (402) 471-3495. Nebraska HealthNetwork is a division of the Nebraska State Department of Health. It provides weekly updates of the Certificate of Need Status Reports. Reports can be sent on a weekly, bimonthly or monthly basis. Charges vary $30.00 - $130.00 depending on type of service.

Nevada
Bureau of Regulatory Health Services, 505 E. King St., Room 202, Carson City, NV 89710; (702) 885-4475. Licenses: hospitals, skilled nursing homes, intermediate care facilities, group homes, adult day care. Listing of facilities available containing the name, address, administrator and number of beds for each facility. Cost $4.00. Application forms are public information.

Certificate of Need: Division of Health Resources and Cost Review, 505 King St., # 603, Carson City, NV 89710; (702) 885-4176. Publication: letters of intent and applications can be inspected by the public. If copies are needed, there is a copying charge.

New Jersey
Department of Health, Licensing Certification and Standards, CN 367, Trenton, NJ 08625; (609) 588-7725. Licenses: hospitals, nursing homes, boarding homes, home health agencies, portable x-ray facilities, special hospitals, ambulatory surgical centers, family planning clinics, abortion clinics, HMOs, and psychiatric hospitals. A hospital directory is available ($2.00) all other for $1.00.

Certificate of Need: Department of Health, CN 360, Trenton, NJ 08625; (609) 292-9382. Publication: none. Files are available to the public for inspection. No regular mailings provided.

New Mexico
Licensing Health Related Facilities, P.O. Box 968, Santa Fe, NM 87504; (505) 827-0020. Licenses: all health facilities: hospitals, nursing homes, x ray labs, home health agencies, ambulatory surgical centers, psychiatric hospitals, intermediate care facilities, transplant centers, rural health clinics, rehabilitation centers, maternity homes, day care centers, boarding homes. A free roster is distributed including the name, address, name of directory, ownership information and capacity of each facility.

Certificate of Need: None.

New York
New York State Department of Health, Bureau of Health Care Services, Corning Tower Building, Room 1970, Rockefeller Empire State Plaza, Albany, NY 12237; (518) 474-2006. Licenses: home health agencies, long term home health care programs. No directories or listings available. Applications are public information.

Bureau of Hospital Services, Corning Tower Building, Room 2038, Rockefeller Empire State Plaza, Albany, NY 12237; (518) 473-7557. Licenses: hospitals. A hospital directory is available ($3.00) from: Health Education Service, Health Research Inc., P.O. Box 7126, Albany, NY 12224 (518) 439-7286.

Certificate of Need: Bureau of Project Management, N.Y. State Department of Health, Room 1717, Tower Building, Empire State Plaza, Albany, NY 12237. Information on a particular project can be obtained from the Freedom of Information Office at the address above. Letters of intent are not published.

North Carolina
Health Care Facilities Branch, 701 Barbour Dr., Raleigh, NC 27603; (919) 733-6225. Licenses: hospitals, nursing homes, ambulatory surgical facilities, home health agencies, hospices, abortion clinics, cardiac rehabilitation facilities. Separate directories are available: *Hospitals* ($1.50); *Nursing Homes* ($1.50); *Home Health Agencies and Hospices* ($1.50); *Ambulatory Surgical Facilities* (free);

Abortion Clinics (free), *Cardiac Rehabilitation Facilities* (free). Each directory includes the name, address, phone number, administrator, number of beds, license number for each facility. All information from application forms is made public.

Certificate of Need: Certificate of Need, Department of Human Resources, Division of Facilities Services, 701 Barbour Dr., Raleigh, NC 27603. Publication: a monthly report is published that describes projects that have been approved or denied. Annual reports from hospitals and nursing homes can be obtained from this office.

Ohio
Bureau of Medical Information, 246 N. High St., P.O. Box 118, Columbus, OH 43266; (614) 466-7857. Licenses: hospitals, home health agencies, nursing homes, hospices. A free directory, *Nursing Homes, Rest Homes, Homes for the Aged, and Other Certified Facilities in Ohio,* is available. It contains the address, phone number, skilled or rest home classification, number of beds, and type of ownership for each facility. Information from application forms is made public.

Certificate of Need: Office of Resource Development, OH Department of Health, P.O. Box 118, Columbus, OH 43266; (614) 466-3325. Publication: a free monthly report lists notices of intent, applications received and decisions rendered.

Oklahoma
State Department of Health, Institutional Services, 1000 N.E. 10th St., P.O. Box 53551, Oklahoma City, OK 73152; (405) 271-6868. Licenses: hospitals, alcohol treatment centers, ambulatory surgical centers, end stage renal disease facilities, home health facilities, hospices, laboratories, outpatient physical therapists, x-ray providers, nursing homes and ambulances. A *Hospital and Related Facilities Directory* ($6.00) provides the name, address and administrator for each facility. Information from application forms is made public once approved.

Certificate of Need: Oklahoma Health Planning Commission, P.O. Box 53551, Oklahoma City, OK 74152; (405) 271-5161. Publication: a free monthly notice provides information on the applications received and the actions taken by the Commission.

Oregon
Health Care Services, P.O. Box 231, Portland, OR 97207; (503) 229-5686. Licenses: hospitals, community based health facilities, nursing homes. A listing of nursing homes ($5.00) is available providing the name, address, phone number, administrator and number of beds for each facility.

Certificate of Need: Office of Health Policy, 3886 Beverly St. N.E., Suite 19, Salem, OR 97305; (503) 378-4684, (800) 255-7007. Publication: a free monthly newsletter updates the status of applications and the results of reviews.

Pennsylvania
Department of Health, Division of Hospitals, Room 532, Health and Welfare Building, Harrisburg, PA 17120; (717) 783-1288. Licenses: hospitals, ambulatory surgical facilities. Information from application forms is made public. A free directory is available from: Health Data Center, P.O. Box 90, Harrisburg, PA 17108 (717) 783-2548. Some data is available on magnetic tape. Division of Long Term Care, Room 526, Harrisburg, PA 17120 (717) 787-1816. Licenses: nursing homes. A free directory provides general information including name, address, ownership, type of facility of each facility. Information from application forms is made public.

Certificate of Need: Pennsylvania Department of Health, Bureau of Planning, Division of Need Review, Room 1023, Health and Welfare Building, Harrisburg, PA 17120; (717) 787-5601. Publication: a monthly report lists letters of intent, the name, address, CON# and a brief description of each project. Cost $25.00/year.

Rhode Island
Department of Health, 75 Davis St., Room 306, Providence, RI 02809; (401) 277-2566. Licenses: nursing homes, hospitals, laboratories, group homes (mental retardation), sheltered homes, home health agencies, organized ambulatory care, free standing ambulatory care, HMOs. A free listing is available with the name, address, administrator, level of care and license number of each facility.

Certificate of Need: Medical Care Standards, 75 Davis St., Providence, RI 02908. Publication: various reports published containing information on on-going reviews, and applications submitted. Also publishes a listing of hospitals with their short and long range plans.

South Carolina
Division of Health Licensing, Department of Health and Environmental Control (DHEC), 2600 Bull St., Columbia, SC 29201; (803) 734-4680. Licenses: all health care facilities. A free directory is available. All information from application forms is made public.

Certificate of Need: Certificate of Need Division, Bureau of Health Facilities, Department of Health and Environmental Control, 2600 Bull St., Columbia, SC

29201; (803) 734-4690. Publication: a monthly bulletin containing a listing and the status of CON applications under review. Cost $120.00/year.

South Dakota

Licensure and Certification Program, Division of Public Health, 523 E. Capitol, Pierre, SD 57501; (605) 773-3364. Licenses: hospitals, ambulatory surgical centers, chemical dependent treatment centers, maternity homes, nursing homes, supervised personal care. A free directory includes the name, address, administrator and number of beds for each facility. Information from application forms is confidential.

Certificate of Need: Licensure and Certification Program, CON Division, Department of Health, FOSS Building, 523 E. Capitol, Pierre, SD 57501; (605) 773-3364. A bill is currently in the legislature to eliminate CON.

Tennessee

Board for Licensing Health Care Facilities, 283 Plus Park Blvd., Nashville, TN 37217; (615) 367-6303. Licenses: hospitals, nursing homes, home health agencies, residential homes for the aged, institutional homes for the aged, ambulatory surgical treatment centers, home health agencies. Three directories available for grouped areas. Each is free and contains the name, address, phone number, license fee, number of beds, date of license and license number for each facility. All information from application forms is public.

Certificate of Need: Tennessee Health Facilities Commission, Realtors Building, 306 Gay St., Nashville, TN 37219; (615) 741-2364. Publication: a monthly report is published with information on CON applications, decisions and upcoming projects. Cost is $35.00/year.

Texas

Department of Health, Hospital and Professional Licensure Division, 1100 W. 49th St., Austin, TX 78756; (512) 458-7531. Licenses: hospitals. A directory, updated monthly, provides the name, address, administrator, license bed, facility type, number of beds, expiration of each facility. Cost is $16.23. Information from application forms is available with a written request. There is a copying charge per page.

Quality Standards Division, 1100 W. 49th St., Austin, TX 78756; (512) 458-7611. Licenses: nursing homes, custodial care homes, adult day care facilities, maternity homes, facilities for the mentally retarded. A free directory of long term care facilities is provided. Information from application forms is made public.

Certificate of Need: None.

Utah

Bureau of Health Facilities Licensure, Utah Department of Health, P.O. Box 16660, Salt Lake City, UT 84116; (801) 538-6152. Licenses: hospitals, nursing homes, residential care facilities, end stage renal disease facilities, home health agencies, abortion clinics, surgical centers, birthing centers, mental disease facilities. A free directory includes a listing of: residential care facilities, hospitals, home health agencies, end stage renal disease and nursing care facilities. Each includes the name, address, phone number and number of beds for each facility.

Certificate of Need: None.

Virginia

Department of Health, Division of Licensure and Certification, 1013 Madison Building, 109 Grover St., Richmond, VA 23219; (804) 786-2081. Licenses: hospitals, facilities for mental health, nursing homes, intermediate care facilities for mentally retarded, psychiatric hospitals, outpatient surgical hospitals, hospices, renal dialysis units, home health agencies, comprehensive outpatient rehabilitation facilities, laboratories, portable x-ray units, physical therapists. A free directory is distributed: Health Care Facilities Licensed or Certified by the Virginia Department of Health. Information from application forms is made public.

Certificate of Need: Director, Division of Resources Development, Virginia Department of Health, 109 Governor St., Richmond, VA 23219; (804) 786-7463. Information on projects that have been approved can be obtained with a written request. Information released includes the name, a brief description and the capital expenditure of a particular project.

Washington

Office of Licensing and Certification, 1112 S. Quince St., Olympia, WA 98504; (206) 753-4064. Licenses: boarding homes, child care facilities, home health agencies, hospices, alcohol treatment centers, birthing centers, eye banks, hospitals, psychiatric hospitals, residential treatment centers. Free directories are available for some types of facilities. Information included in the directory includes: license number, owner, type, number of beds, address and phone number. For information from an application form, the request must be made in writing.

Certificate of Need: Department of Social and Health Services, Certificate of Need Program, MS OB-43E, Olympia, WA 98504; (206) 753-5854. Publication: on an irregular basis, a list of approved projects is released.

West Virginia

Health Facilities Licensure and Certification, P & G Building, 1800 Washington St., East, Charleston, WV 25305; (304) 348-0050. Licenses: hospitals, nursing homes, personal care homes, mental health facilities, birthing centers, medical model adult day care centers, non-profit corporate guardianship (for behavioral problems). Three directories are available ($3.00 each): nursing homes, hospitals, personal care homes. Each includes the name, address, administrator and telephone number of each facility. For specific information from an application form, a written request is required.

Certificate of Need: Health Care Cost Review Authority, Certificate of Need, 100 Dee Dr., Charleston, WV 25311; (304) 343-3701. Publication: A free weekly newsletter is published. It includes letters of intent, application decisions, list of projects determined to be not reviewable and hearing notices.

Wisconsin

Department of Health and Social Services, Bureau of Quality Compliance, 1 West Wilson St., Room 150, Madison, WI 53701; (608) 266-2055. Licenses: hospitals, nursing homes and home health agencies. Each has its own directory ($5.00), with information on the type of ownership, name, address, administrator, county and number of beds of each facility. All information from application forms is made public.

Certificate of Need: Bureau of Planning and Development, 1 West Wilson St., Madison, WI 53701; (608) 266-0433. Publication: a free monthly newsletter lists notices of intent and describes current projects for nursing homes only.

Wyoming

Department of Health and Social Services, Division of Health and Medical Services, Cheyenne, WY 82002; (307) 777-7121. Licenses: hospitals, nursing homes, boarding homes, diagnostic centers, outpatient rehabilitation facilities, birthing centers. An annual directory (free) is published. It lists medical facilities, addresses number of beds, ownership information and percent occupancy of each facility.

Certificate of Need: None.

Food and Drug Companies

If you are seeking information on sanitation or safety conditions at a particular restaurant, fast food franchise, or meatpacking facility and don't want to wade through masses of information maintained by the federal government, you can always start at the state level. All state departments of health have a division that oversees the inspection and certification of food processing, storing, and serving facilities in the state.

This information might be valuable if you were interested in buying into a facility or if you have a new product that you want to market in a specific area, say sanitation shields for salad bars. Conversely, having state records can add weight to your argument if you want to close an offensive facility down, say a slaughterhouse or noisy neighborhood bar.

Among the types of facilities most state offices regulate are:

o food processing plants
o food storage facilities
o non-alcoholic bottling plants
o public accommodations (AL)
o vending machines (CT)
o school lunch programs (NH)
o bed and breakfast facilities (NH)
o wineries (OR)

License and inspection forms are a matter of public record in most states and may be obtained by submitting a Freedom of Information Act (FOI) request. The license form will include the address of the facility, the owner's name, and the number of people employed at the facility. Inspection forms provide information on:

o structure of facility
o construction of equipment
o condition of equipment
o sanitation procedures
o how products are handled
o type of labeling
o type of packaging
o safety violations

Forty states will provide computer printouts. Missouri, Louisiana, Nebraska, New Mexico, Oklahoma, and Washington are in the process of computerizing their inspection and licensing data. Unfortunately, none of the states will provide mailing labels.

State offices responsible for regulating the manufacture, distribution, and sale of drugs can provide computer listings of the facilities that they license and inspect.

The types of facilities most often regulated are:

o pharmacies
o drug manufacturers
o drug wholesalers
o medical device manufacturers
o research institutions using controlled
   substances or hazardous materials

Food And Drug Offices

Alabama
Department of Public Health, Division of Environmental Health, 434 Monroe St., Room 317, Montgomery, AL 63130; (205) 261-5003. This agency acts as a consultative agency. Most inspections done at the county level. Overseas the inspections of food plants and warehouses. Lists are maintained at the county level. Inspection forms can be requested through the department's legal office.

Alabama State Board of Pharmacy, 1 Perimeter Park South, Suite 425 South, Birmingham, AL 35243; (205) 967-0130. Application and inspection records are confidential. A computer listing of pharmacies is available under certain circumstances. Printout: $25.00, mailing labels $55.00.

Alaska
Department of Environmental Conservation, Division of Environmental Health, P.O. Box O, Juneau, AK 99801; (907) 465-2609. Licenses and inspects restaurants, food processors, storage facilities, public accommodations, bottling companies. Some information stored on the computer, some lists may be available.

Department of Commerce and Economic Development, Division of Occupational Licensing, P.O. Box D-LIC, Juneau, AK 99811. Licenses and inspects pharmacies, drug manufacturers and wholesalers. Lists $5.00.

Arizona
State Department of Health Services, Sanitation Section, 3008 N. 3rd St., Suite 207, Phoenix, AZ 85012; (602) 255-1203. Most inspections and permits issued on the county level. This office inspects institutions contracted by FDA and include: wholesale food manufacturers. The county is responsible for retail food and food processors. A mailing list is available for those places it inspects (around 100).

State Board of Pharmacy, 5060 N. 19th Ave. Suite 101, Phoenix, AZ 85015; (602) 255-5125. Licenses and inspects: pharmacies, drug wholesalers and manufacturers. Inspection reports are available to the public. Information can be retrieved and a computer printout provided. A mailing list is available and can be sorted in any form needed.

Arkansas
Department of Health, Division of Sanitarian Services, 4815 West Markham, Little Rock, AR 72205; (501) 661-2171. Provides management to county agencies for inspection of retail food operations. The state is responsible for inspecting canning plants, bottling plants and manufactured milk plants. It has a contract with FDA to inspect their inventories. With a Freedom of Information request, a listing of any type of plant can be obtained. Inspection reports can also be obtained through a Freedom of Information request.

Board of Pharmacy, P.O. Box 55356, Little Rock, AR 72205; (501) 661-2833. Inspects and licenses retail pharmacies, drug manufacturers, wholesalers and medical device manufacturers. Computer listings available with a written request. Application forms are public information.

California
State Department of Health Section, Food and Drug Branch, Room 400, 714 P. St., Sacramento, CA 95814; (916) 445-2263. Licenses and inspects: food, drug and medical device manufacturers, processors and packagers. Information from application forms is generally available unless the firm is under current investigation for possible violations of the law that could result in civil or criminal investigation. Computer listings, including a listing of warehouses, will become available once the computer system is in operation.

State Board of Pharmacy, 1020 N. St., Sacramento, CA 95814; (916) 323-7018. Licenses and inspects pharmacies and drug wholesalers. A mailing list of the entire file is available. The list can be sorted by county. Minimum order $50.00.

Colorado
Colorado Department of Health, Division of Consumer Protection, 4210 E. 11th Ave., Denver, CO 80220; (303) 331-8250. There is no licensing program on the state level. This office inspects: food processors, manufacturers and warehouses. Data is not on computer, no mailing lists available at this time.

Board of Pharmacy, 1525 Sherman St., Room 128, Denver, CO 80203; (303) 866-2526. Licenses and inspects pharmacies. A mailing list of pharmacies is available for $20.00. Mailing labels are produced in alphabetical order only ($20.00, you supply the labels).

Information on People, Companies, and Mailing Lists

Connecticut

State Department of Consumer Protection, Food Division, State Office Building, 165 Capitol Ave., Hartford, CT 06106; (203) 566-3388. Licenses non-alcoholic beverage manufacturers, bakeries, frozen dessert manufacturers and vending machines. Inspects all food warehouses whether licensed or not plus those listed above. Information from application forms is public. Listings available of licensed establishments.

State Department of Consumer Protection, Division of Drug Control, State Office Building, 165 Capitol Ave., Hartford, CT 06106; (203) 566-2294. Licenses and inspects drug manufacturers and wholesalers. Mailing lists not provided, routine inspection reports can be obtained.

Professional Licensing Division, Commission of Pharmacy, State Office Building, Room G1A, Hartford, CT 06106; (203) 566-4832. Provides computer lists or labels for pharmacists and pharmacies. Requests must be made in writing and approved by the Board. Lists can be sorted into: alphabetical, numerical or zip code order. Costs: labels $100.00, printouts $50.00.

Delaware

State Department of Public Health, Office of Food Protection, 802 Silver Lake Blvd. Robbins Building, Dover, DE 19901; (302) 736-4731. Issues permits to food processors and some manufacturers. Most inspections are done at the county level. A listing is maintained only for milk processors and farm haulers.

State Department of Health and Social Services, Office of Pharmaceutical Control, 802 Silver Lake Building, Robbins Building, Dover, DE 19901; (302) 736-4708. Licenses pharmacies, manufacturers and distributors. Listings sold under certain circumstances.

District of Columbia

Department of Consumer Regulatory Affairs, Business Regulations Administration, Food Protection Branch, 614 H Street, NW, Washington, D.C. 20001; (202) 727-7250. Inspects and licenses all manufacturers of food products. No computer listings available. Company files with names and addresses are open to the public.

Board of Pharmacy, Department of Consumer and Regulatory Affairs, Pharmaceutical and Medical Control Division, 614 H Street, NW, Washington, D.C. 20001; (202) 727-7223. Licenses all pharmacies in District of Columbia. A computer listing available with a written request.

Florida

State Department of Agriculture and Consumer Services, Bureau of Food Grade and Standards, 3125 Conner Building M-A, Tallahassee, FL 32399; (904) 488-3951. Licenses food processors, distributors, and retail stores. Can provide computer lists of each and can sort buy 16 categories. Information from application forms is public.

State Department of Health and Rehabilitative Services, Pharmacy Program Office, 1317 Winewood Blvd. Tallahassee, FL 32399; (904) 487-1257. Licenses and inspects drug wholesalers, repackers, manufacturers, cosmetic manufacturers, device manufacturers, complimentary drug distributors. With a written request, a list of each type is provided free. License application forms may be available to the public, decisions are made on a case by case basis.

Georgia

Department of Agriculture, Consumer Protection Field Forces Division, 19 Martin Luther King Drive, Atlanta, GA 30334; (404) 656-3627. Licenses and inspects food processors, producers, distributors and warehouses. Mailing lists available $30.00 per list. Sorting into various categories is available.

Board of Pharmacy, 166 Pryor St. S.W., Atlanta, GA 30303; (404) 656-3912. Licenses and inspects pharmacies, drug manufacturers, wholesalers. A mailing list is available in alphabetical order for $.02 per name. License application information is public.

Idaho

State Department of Health and Welfare, Food Quality Control Section, State House, Boise, ID 83720; (208) 334-5938. Consults with local health departments and monitors their performance. Inspections are done at the local level. The State Food Program Coordinator can answer general questions about an establishment or will find out specific information upon request.

Board of Pharmacy, 500 S. 10th St., Boise, ID 83720; (208) 334-2356. Licenses and inspects drug manufacturers, wholesalers, distributors, repackers and non-pharmacy outlets. Mailing lists available: pharmacies $10.00 (mailing labels $25.00) all others the same price. Lists can be sorted into zip code order or by type of facility.

Illinois

Department of Public Health, Division of Food, Drugs and Devices, 525 W. Jefferson St., Springfield, IL 62761; (217) 785-2439. There is no licensing program in Illinois. This office inspects: bottling plants, candy and cookie manufacturers, bakeries, warehouses, processors. Computer listings are available by type for $.10 per page. Inspection forms including a description summary are available for $.10 per page. This office also inspects drug manufacturers and medical device manufacturers. No directory is available, but a computer listing may be released upon written request.

State Board of Pharmacy, 100 W. Randolph, Chicago, IL 60601; (312) 917-4573. Licenses and inspects pharmacies, drug manufacturers, wholesalers and distributors of controlled substances. Mailing lists not available.

Hawaii

State Department of Health, Kinau Hale Building, 1250 Punchbowl St., P.O. Box 3378, Honolulu, HI 96801; (808) 548-3280. Food Products Section: inspects for misbranded and adulterated products and medical devices. Mailing lists not available. Sanitation Branch: licenses and inspects food processors, warehouses, manufacturers and bottling plants. No mailing lists. Inspection reports available upon request.

State Board of Pharmacy, 1010 Richards St., P.O. Box 3469, Honolulu, HI 96801; (808) 548-3086. Inspects and licenses pharmacies. A roster is available for $9.00.

Indiana

State Board of Health, Division of Retail and Manufactured Foods, 1330 West Michigan St., P.O. Box 1964, Indianapolis, IN 46206; (317) 633-0618. Licenses and inspects food processors, bottling plants, warehouses, manufacturers. Mailing lists are not disseminated for commercial purposes.

Bureau of Consumer Protection, 1010 Richards St., P.O. Box 3469, Honolulu, HI 96801; (317) 633-8553. Licenses and inspects drug manufacturers, processors, relabelers, packagers and wholesalers once a year. For specific information concerning a particular company, write a letter with your specific question to the Office of Legal Affairs at the same address.

State Board of Pharmacy, 1 American Square, Suite 1020, P.O. Box 82067, Indianapolis, IN 46282; (317) 232-2960. Licenses and inspects pharmacies only. Free mailing lists available.

Iowa

State Department of Inspections and Appeals, Food Products Control, Lucas Building, Des Moines, IA 50319; (515) 281-6538. Licenses and inspects all food related business. Computer listings are available for $12.00 per listing. Limited sorting of files available.

Board of Pharmacy, 1209 East Court, Des Moines, IA 50319; (515) 281-5944. Licenses and inspects pharmacies, drug manufacturers and distributors. Mailing lists are available. Requests must be made in writing. Minimum order $20.00, sorting available by several categories. Mailing labels also available.

Kansas

State Department of Health and Environment, Division of Health, Food Service, Drug and Lodging Section, 109 S.W. 9th St., Suite 604, Topeka, KS 66612; (913) 296-1500. Licenses all food services, inspects food and drug manufacturers, bakeries, bottling plants and warehouses. Requests for mailing lists must be made in writing.

Board of Pharmacy, Landon State Office Building, 900 Jackson St., Room 513, Topeka, KS 66612; (913) 296-4056. Licenses and inspects pharmacies, distributors, retail dealers, analytical laboratories for controlled substances and research institutions using controlled substances. Before a mailing list is released, the Board must give its approval. Application forms are in most cases open to the public for review.

Kentucky

Cabinet for Human Resources, Division of Food and Sanitation, 275 East Main St., Frankfort, KY 40621; (502) 564-3722. Licenses and inspects food service establishments, retail food markets, vending machines, bottling companies, frozen food lockers, shellfish repackers, food salvage dealers. Mailing lists are available with no sorting possible.

Board of Pharmacy, 1228 U.S. 27 South, Frankfort, KY 40601; (502) 564-3833. Licenses and inspects drug manufacturers, wholesalers, pharmacies. Computer listings or labels available in zip code order, county or alphabetical order. Must be prepaid $35.00. All records public information.

Louisiana

State Department of Health and Human Resources, Food and Drug Control Unit, P.O. Box 3776, Baton Rouge, LA 70821; (504) 568-5402. Licenses and inspects warehouses, manufacturers, distributors and repackers. Computer listings available soon.

Board of Pharmacy, 5615 Corporate Blvd. Suite 8E, Baton Rouge, LA 70808; (504) 949-7545. Licenses and inspects pharmacies and manufacturers. All information included on application forms is public. Listings not available.

Maine

State Department of Agriculture, Division of Regulations, State House Station 28, Augusta, ME 04333; (207) 289-3841. Licenses and inspects: food processors, bakeries, bottling plants, warehouses, mobile vendors and retail stores. Computer listings available $1.00 per sheet. Sorting can be done by type only.

Board of Pharmacy, 1 Northwood Road, Lewiston, ME 04240; (207) 783-9769. Licenses and inspects pharmacies and drug manufacturers. Mailing lists available $25.00.

Maryland

Department of Health and Mental Hygiene, Division of Food Control, 201 W. Preston St., Baltimore, MD 21201; (301) 333-3163. Acts as a consultant to counties for their inspection programs, provides back-up support and guidance. Inspects and licenses warehouses, food processors, and distributors. Computer listings available but not for commercial purposes.

Department of Health and Mental Hygiene, Drug Control Division, 201 W. Preston St., Baltimore, MD 20201; (301) 333-3000. Inspects pharmacies and some drug manufacturers. Works with the Board of Pharmacy. Application information is open to the public for review.

Board of Pharmacy, 201 W. Preston St., Baltimore, MD 21201; (301) 225-5910. Licenses pharmacies and drug manufacturers. Mailing lists or labels available $40.00.

Massachusetts

Department of Public Health, Division of Food and Drugs, 305 South St., Jamaica Plain, MA 02130; (617) 522-3700 est. 395. Licenses and inspects food processors, warehouses, bottled water plants, bakeries, distributors. Computer listings can be generated with a Freedom of Information request. There is a per page charge.

State Board of Pharmacy, State Office Building, Government Center, 100 Cambridge St., Boston, MA 02202; (617) 727-7390. Licenses pharmacies and wholesalers. License applications information is public. A mailing list, labels or magnetic tape can be purchased, sorted by zip code or alphabetical order. A written request is required. The typical cost is $100.00. Contact Tom Forsythe (617) 727-3056.

Michigan

Department of Agriculture, Food Division, P.O., Box 30017, Lansing, MI 48909; (517) 373-1060. Licenses and inspects food processors, canners, distributors, warehouses and grocery stores. Computer listings are available, the charge is based on size of run. The file can be sorted by county, region, zip code or alphabetical order.

Board of Pharmacy, P.O. Box 30018, Lansing, MI 48909; (517) 373-0620. Licenses and inspects pharmacies, drug manufacturers, wholesalers, and distributors. Computer lists can be generated for $.20 per page with a $20.00 minimum.

Minnesota

Department of Agriculture, Food Inspection Department, 90 W. Plato Blvd., St. Paul, MN 55107; (612) 296-1592. Licenses and inspects food manufacturers, processors, wholesalers, warehouses, retail stores. For information concerning the availability of mailing lists contact the Minnesota Trade Office at (612) 297-4222.

Board of Pharmacy, 2700 University Ave., West #107, St. Paul, MN 55114; (612) 642-0541. Licenses and inspects drug manufacturers, wholesalers, pharmacies. Mailing lists and labels available through the State Documents Office at (612) 297-3000. Information from application forms is public.

Mississippi

State Department of Health, Division of Sanitation, P.O. Box 1700, Jackson, MS 39215; (601) 960-7689. Licenses and inspects bottling plants, warehouses and wastewater installers. Permits are issued to food service establishments, recreational vehicle parks, and milk plants. Computer lists are available for a fee, contact the Office of Public Records, (601) 960-7667.

State Board of Pharmacy, Suite 1165, C & F Plaza, 2310 Hwy. 80 West, Jackson, MS 39204; (601) 354-6750. Licenses and inspects drug manufacturers, wholesalers and pharmacies. Listing and mailing labels available ($100.00/listing; $150.00/labels). Information contained on license applications is public.

Missouri

State Department of Health, Bureau of Community Sanitation, 1730 Elm St., Jefferson City, MO 65102; (314) 751-6095. Licenses frozen dessert manufacturers and distributors, non-alcoholic bottlers, manufacturers and distributors, hotels and motels. Inspects retail food establishments, food plants and warehouses. Currently entering information into a computer system. Lists will become available fall, 1988.

State Board of Pharmacy, 3523 North Ten Mile Dr., Jefferson City, MO 65102; (314) 751-2334. There is no licensing or inspection regulations for drug wholesalers or distributors. The Board licenses and inspects pharmacies only. Mailing lists are $15.00; labels $20.00 for the first 1000 entries, $5.00 each thousand after. Listings can be sorted by type or by zip code.

Montana

State Department of Health and Environmental Sciences, Food and Consumer Safety Bureau, W. F. Cogswell Building, Capitol Station, Helena, MT 59620; (406) 444-2408 Licenses and inspects food warehouses, manufacturers, packagers and processors. Mailing lists available on a limited basis.

State Board of Pharmacy, 510 1st Ave. N., Suite 100, Great Falls, MT 59401; (406) 761-5131. Licenses and inspects drug wholesalers and manufacturers. Lists not available by Montana law. Records can be inspected onsite.

Nebraska

Licenses and inspects food manufacturers, processors, retail stores and warehouses. Files are open to the public but the only way to obtain a listing is to visit the office and copy the information.

Bureau of Examining Boards, State Department of Health, 301 Centennial Mall South, P.O. Box 95007, Lincoln, NE 68509; (402) 471-2115. Licenses pharmacies only. Wholesalers and distributors are not licensed. Listings can be sorted into hospital or community pharmacies for a fee.

Nevada

State Department of Human Resources, Bureau of Regulatory Health Services, 505 East King St., Carson City, NV 89710. Licenses all food establishments, processors and manufacturers. A computer section is presently being set up. No listings available at this time. All application information is available to the public. This department also licenses and inspects drug manufacturers. There are so few that a hand written list can be obtained. All financial information is confidential.

State Board of Pharmacy, 1201 Terminal Way, Suite 212, Reno, NV 89502; (702) 322-0691. Licenses and inspects drug wholesalers, manufacturers and pharmacies. Computer listings available, prices vary. Information from application forms is confidential.

New Hampshire

State Department of Health and Welfare, Environmental Sanitation Program, Health and Welfare Building, 6 Hazen Drive, Concord, NH 03301; (603) 271-4589. New Hampshire does not inspect food processors or warehouses. It licenses restaurants, grocery stores and school lunch programs. Files are open to the public on a case by case basis. Lists are available free upon written request.

State Board of Pharmacy, Health and Welfare Building, 6 Hazen Drive, Concord, NH 03301; (603) 271-2350. Licenses and inspects pharmacies, wholesalers, distributors and manufacturers of controlled drugs. Computer lists available $50.00; application forms are public information.

New Jersey

State Health Department, Consumer Health Services, Food and Milk Program, CN-364, Trenton, NJ 08625; (609) 984-1367. Licenses and inspects all food and cosmetic wholesalers, processors and distributors. Computer listings available $40.00 to $50.00 depending on request.

Division of Narcotic Abuse and Drug Control, CN-364, Trenton, NJ 08625; (609) 984-1308. Licenses and inspects drug manufacturers and packagers. Listings available for $16.00.

Board of Pharmacy. 1100 Raymond Blvd., Newark, NJ 07102; (201) 648-2433. Licenses and inspects pharmacies. Mailing list and labels available. Information from application forms is public.

New Mexico

State Department of Health and Environment, Environmental Improvement Division, P.O. Box 968, Santa Fe, NM 87504; (505) 827-2850. Licenses dairy farms and restaurants only. Inspects food processors, warehouses and bottling plants. Currently working on a computer system to include a master list of all companies.

New York

State Department of Agriculture and Markets, Division of Food Inspection Services, Capital Plaza, One Winners Circle, Albany, NY 12235; (518) 457-5368. Licenses and inspects food processors, refrigerated warehouses, salvagers, and distributors. No lists can be released. Certain information from the application or inspection form can be disclosed.

Board of Pharmacy, Cultural Education Center, Room 3035, Albany, NY 12230; (518) 474-3848. Licenses and inspects pharmacies, manufacturers, distributors, wholesalers and repackagers. Computer listing available for $120.00 with a written request and letter of intent. Information from the application form available only to government agencies or for a legal matter.

North Carolina

State Department of Agriculture, Food and Drug Protection Division, 1 Edenton St., P.O. Box 27647, Raleigh, NC 27611; (919) 733-7366. Under a contract with FDA, this office licenses and inspects wholesale food manufacturers, warehouses,

Information on People, Companies, and Mailing Lists

bottling plants and bakeries. Computer listings are available. They can be sorted by type of company, county, town or by inspector. Inspection reports available with a written Freedom of Information request.

Board of Pharmacy, P.O. Box H, Carrboro, NC 27510; (919) 942-4454. Licenses and inspects pharmacies. Computer lists available upon written request.

North Dakota
Department of Health and Consolidated Laboratories, Division of Food Inspection, 1220 Missouri Ave., Bismarck, ND 58501. Licenses and inspects retail food establishments, bed and breakfast facilities, vending operations. Under contract with FDA to inspect warehouses and processors. Computer listings can be requested and are charged a processing fee. Contact: Deb Larson (701) 224-2382.

State Board of Pharmacy, P.O. Box 1354, Bismarck, ND 58502; (701) 258-1535. Licenses and inspects all pharmacies and wholesale manufacturers. Mailing lists available for $10.00 each. Information from application forms is public.

Ohio
Department of Agriculture, Division of Foods, Dairies and Drugs, 8995 E. Main St., Reynoldsburg, OH 43068; (614) 466-1450. Licenses and inspects food processors, warehouses, grocery stores, bottling plants and bakeries. Computer listings can be generated, sorted by county or commodity. The cost per page is $.22.

State Board of Pharmacy, 65 South Front St., Room 504, Columbus, OH 43266; (614) 466-4143. Licenses and inspects pharmacies, drug wholesalers, distributors, industrial first aid rooms. Mailing lists available, sorted by county or type of license. Mailing labels available for an extra charge.

Oklahoma
State Department of Health, Food Protection Service, P.O. Box 53551, Oklahoma City, OK 73152; (405) 271-5243. Licenses and inspects food processors, bottling plants, warehouses, salvage warehouses, dairy plants, farms, distributors and packagers. Computer listings sorted by type and class available. Cost varies.

State Board of Pharmacy, 4545 N. Lincoln, Suite 112, Oklahoma City, OK 73105; (405) 521-3815. Licenses and inspects pharmacies, wholesalers, manufacturers and packagers. Information just being input into a computer system. All files are public information.

Oregon
Department of Agriculture, Food and Dairy Division, 635 Capitol St., N.E., Salem, OR 97310; (503) 378-3790. Licenses and inspects food processors, retail stores, bakeries, warehouses, bottling plants and wineries. Computer listings available, can be sorted by size and type. Cost is $55.00 plus $.01 per name.

Board of Pharmacy, 1400 S.W. 5th Ave., P.O. Box 231, Portland, OR 97207; (503) 229-5849. Licenses and inspects drug manufacturers, pharmacies, wholesalers, retail outlets with over the counter drugs. Pharmacy list available $75.00/ labels $80.00.

Pennsylvania
State Department of Agriculture, Bureau of Food and Chemistry, 2301 N. Cameron St., Harrisburg, PA 17120; (717) 787-4315. Licenses and inspects bakeries, bottling plants and warehouses. Mailing lists not available, some information can be provided over the telephone.

State Department of Health, Division of Drugs, Devices and Cosmetics, Health and Welfare Building, 7th and Forster Sts., P.O. Box 90, Harrisburg, PA 17120; (717) 787-2307. Licenses and inspects drug, cosmetic and device manufacturers. Computer listings can be generated with various sorts. The cost varies on length of run.

Board of Pharmacy, P.O. Box 2649, Harrisburg, PA 17105. Licenses and inspects pharmacies. Computer listings available-the entire file costs $71.00 plus $.005 per name. For a county sort the cost is $71.00 plus $.03 per name.

Rhode Island
State Department of Health, Division of Food Protection and Sanitation, 75 Davis St., Providence, RI 02908; (401) 277-2750. Licenses and inspects food processors, wholesalers and food service establishments, vending machines and warehouses. Computer listings are available for a fee.

State Department of Health, Division of Drug Control, 75 Davis St., Providence, RI 02908. Licenses and inspects drug manufacturers, wholesalers, retailers, pharmacies, some devices and cosmetics. No lists produced.

South Carolina
Department of Health and Environmental Control, Division of Dairy Foods and Bottling Plants, J. Marion Sims Building, 2600 Bull St., Columbia, SC 29201; (803) 734-4970. Inspects soft drink bottling plants and dairy farms. Computer listings and mailing labels available. $10.00 per listing plus a $3.50 set up charge for sorting the file.

Department of Agriculture, Laboratory Division, 1101 William St., P.O. Box 11280, Columbia, SC 29201; (803) 737-2070. Inspects non-meat manufacturers and warehouses. Listings can be provided, but data is not computerized so that sorting the file is not possible.

State Board of Pharmaceutical Examiners, 1026 Sumter St., P.O. Box 11927, Columbia, SC 29211; (803) 734-1010. Currently licenses pharmacies, will soon include manufacturers and wholesalers. Files are open to the public. Computer lists and labels available. $.03 per address and $5.00 computer charge. Listing can be sorted by type (community, independent), county or zip code. Contact: Joelle Snyder, (803) 734-3826.

South Dakota
Department of Commerce and Regulation, Division of Commercial Inspection, 118 W. Capitol St., Pierre, SD 57501. There is no licensing program, listings not available. This office inspects wholesalers, warehouses and bottling plants.

Department of Agriculture, Division of Regulatory Services, Anderson Building, 445 East Capitol, Pierre, SD 57501; (605) 773-3724. Inspects milk plants, pesticide producers, fertilizer producers and nurseries.

State Board of Pharmacy, P.O. Box 518, Pierre, SD 57501; (605) 224-2338. Licenses pharmacies only. Listings available $20.00. Files open to the public.

Tennessee
State Department of Agriculture, Division of Quality and Standards, Ellington Agricultural Center, Melrose Station, P.O. Box 40627, Nashville, TN 37204. The Food and Drug Administration maintains all information and inspection files on warehouses, processors, bottling plants, bakeries, grain elevators, and produce warehouses. The state office will refer you to the appropriate federal office.

Board of Pharmacy, 1808 West End Building, Nashville, TN 37219; (615) 741-2718. Licenses and inspects drug wholesalers, distributors, manufacturers, and pharmacies. Prices for computer listings vary. Average cost $20.00. Can be sorted into zip code, county or alphabetical order.

Texas
Department of Health, Division of Food and Drugs, 1100 W. 49th St., Austin, TX 78756; (512) 458-7248. Licenses and inspects food manufacturers, bottling plants, bakeries, and retail food markets. Computer listings can be generated for a reasonable fee. Can be sorted by county or zip code order. Inspection form information must be requested under the Freedom of Information Act.

Also licenses and inspects drug manufacturers, packagers and distributors. Listings are available.

State Board of Pharmacy, 8505 Cross Park Drive, Suite 110, Austin, TX 78754; (512) 832-0661. Licenses and inspects pharmacies. Computer lists and labels available. Sorting is possible, the price depends on need.

Utah
Department of Agriculture, Bureau of Consumer Services, Division of Food, 350 N. Redwood Road, Salt Lake City, UT 84116; (801) 533-4124. Licenses and inspects manufacturers, processors, retail stores and warehouses. Computer listings can be generated for $5.00 and sorted into broad categories.

Board of Pharmacy, Heber Wells Building, 160 East 300 South, Salt Lake City, UT 84111; (801) 530-6628. Licenses and inspects pharmacies, wholesalers, manufacturers. Printed lists are available for $25.00; labels $75.00.

Vermont
Department of Health and Human Services, Environmental Health Division, 60 Main St., Burlington, VT 05401; (802) 863-7220. Licenses and inspects bakeries, restaurants, delis, mobil food units, food and lodging establishments. Inspects on a complaint basis only: bottling plants, warehouses and food processors. Computer lists can be generated, there is a minimum charge of $5.00 with an additional cost of $.04 per page.

State Department of Agriculture, Dairy Division, 116 State Street, Montpelier, VT 05602; (802) 828-2433. Licenses and inspects dairy farms, milk plants, dairy processors, warehouses (dairy) retail stores and the plant industry (feed, seed, and fertilizer). Computer lists can be generated upon request.

State Board of Pharmacy, c/o Secretary of State, Pavillion Office Building, Montpelier, VT 05602; (802) 828-2372. Licenses and inspects pharmacies and wholesalers. Listings available at $5.00 each plus $.03 per name. Labels the same cost. Lists can be sorted into alphabetical order, license number or zip code order.

Virginia
State Department of Agriculture, Bureau of Food Inspection, 1100 Bank St., P.O. Box 1163, Richmond, VA 23209; (804) 786-3520. Licenses and inspects food processors, warehouses, storage plants. Information available on a firm's history and inspection information. Computer listings can be generated for a processing fee.

State Board of Pharmacy, 1601 Rolling Hills Dr., Richmond, VA 23229; (804) 662-9911. Licenses and inspects pharmacies, drug manufacturers, wholesalers and any company handling controlled substances. For a listing, the request must be made in writing. Lists can be sorted into zip code, alphabetical or license number order. Labels can also be ordered. All licensure information is confidential.

Washington

State Department of Agriculture, Dairy and Food Division, 406 General Administration Building, Olympia, WA 98504; (206) 753-5042. Company files are not up to date. Data is in the process of being entered into a new computer system. Lists of food processors and warehouses could become available in 1 to 2 years.

Board of Pharmacy, 319 East 7th Ave. FF-21, Washington Education Association Building, Olympia, WA 98504; (206) 753-6834. Licenses and inspects pharmacies, drug wholesalers, manufacturers and animal shelters. For a computer list or mailing labels send a written request. Sorting the file is possible. The cost is $25.00 - $30.00.

West Virginia

State Health Department, Environmental Health Services, State Office Building #3, 1800 Washington St. East., Charleston, WV 25305; (304) 348-2981. Licenses and inspects food processors, bakeries, canneries, candy manufacturers and bottling plants. Computer listings can be generated.
State Board of Pharmacy, 150 Rockdale Road, Follansbee, WV 26037; (304) 527-1270. Licenses and inspects pharmacies, drug distributors and manufacturers. Computer printouts or labels available. Can sort into alphabetical or zip code order. Cost varies.

Wisconsin

Department of Agriculture, Trade and Consumer Protection, Food Division, 801 West Badger Road, P.O. Box 8911, Madison, WI 53708; (608) 266-7240. Licenses and inspects food processors, warehouses, bottling plants, dairy farms and bakeries. Computer lists are available for some types of establishments. There is a processing fee. Sorting is available to a limited extent.

State Department of Regulation and Licensing, P.O. Box 8935, Madison, WI 53708; (608) 266-2112. Licenses and inspects pharmacies, manufacturers, and distributors. Computer listings and labels available from the Renewal Document Office (608) 266-0627. Cost $15.00 for the first 1000 names, $3.50 each additional 1000.

Wyoming

Department of Agriculture, Food and Drug Section, 2219 Carey Ave. Cheyenne, WY 82001; (307) 777-6587. Licenses and inspects food processors, warehouses and distributors. Computer lists are not generated. There is a list of firms who voluntarily agree to have their names released. Most firms in Wyoming are small.

State Board of Pharmacy, 1720 South Poplar St., Casper, WY 82601; (307) 234-0294. Inspects pharmacies, wholesalers and distributors (of controlled substances only). Listings are not available. Files are open to the public.

Utility Companies

A consulting firm in New Jersey was interested in working out a deal between an electrical company that needed extra power to meet increasing consumer demands, and some private companies that had the ability to generate and sell their extra power. By determining the power needs and financial resources of the utility company, the consulting firm could then match them up with the appropriate power sources in private industry, and along the way save the public utility company millions of dollars by not having to build expensive new power plants of their own. But how did this consulting firm discover the operational and financial background of the electric company to draw up their proposals? The State Utility Regulatory Commission was their source.

If a company provides a service that its state considers a public utility, it must, at the very least, provide detailed financial statements and annual reports to the state's Utility Regulatory Commission. The URC's role is to ensure that utility companies follow the state operating guidelines and make their annual findings available to the public.

The one thing you can count on about utility regulation commissions across the U.S. is that they are all different. The utilities they regulate, the information they gather, and the way they are set up all vary from state to state. For example, where Tennessee regulates the standard utilities--transportation, water and sewer, electricity, gas, and telephone--South Dakota regulates all of these along with warehouses and elevators. And while West Virginia will provide you only with a utility's balance sheets and annual reports, Vermont will give you all that plus a company's tariff information, informal complaints, and special contracts, along with the state regulatory commission's proceedings reports.

Many state utility regulatory commissions have different divisions for each type of utility. Telecommunications, for example, generally includes the following divisions: local and long distance telephone, radio common carriers, resellers, cable televison, and coin operated pay telephones. Fixed utilities often include gas, electricity,, water, sewer, and refuse. Many states, like Utah and Pennsylvania, also have transportation divisions that regulate trucking, railroads, taxicabs, buses, and so forth. Some states regulate utilities not regulated in other states, such as cotton gins in Oklahoma, and elevators in South Dakota.

Information in the Public Utility Commission (PUC) files is meant for and mostly used by consumers--whether individual or commercial--for the purposes of estimating and comparing costs, but the financial information kept on file at commissions contains a wealth of information invaluable to the entrepreneur. In many states, utilities file reports on sales volume, details on revenues raised and customer base, balance sheets, and service reliability and responsiveness, all of which is important for targeting your competition, and developing market studies, mailing lists, and much more. And most state commissions have much of this information on file in hard copy, but some have begun transferring it into computer formats and will do customized searches based on your specific needs.

Utility Commissions

Alabama

Wallace Tidmore, Secretary of the Commission, Public Service Commission, Box 991, Montgomery, AL 36101; (205) 261-5209. Utilities Regulated: Local and long distance telephone, radio common carriers and resellers; some gas, electric and water (investor owned); transportation (rail, buses, taxis, trucks); gas pipeline (for safety only). Examples of Information on File: annual reports and other financial information. Format of Files and Costs: Hard copy, but efforts to automate are underway. No charge for simple requests; charge on a cost recovery basis for extensive searches. Listing of Regulated Companies: Yes. No charge. Publications Available: *Annual Report* and *First Monday* which lists PSC news. No charge.

Alaska

Ray Wipperman, Public Utilities Commission, 420 L Street, Suite 100, Anchorage, AK 99501; (907) 276-6222. Utilities Regulated: telephone, radio common carriers, some cable television, electricity, gas, water, sewer, steam, garbage, and refuse. Examples of Information on File: Fully regulated companies file tariff and financial information. Format of Files and Costs for Information: Hard copy. Cost for duplicating $0.25 per page. Listing of Regulated Companies: Yes. $5 per copy. Other Publications Available: *Notices*, published twice weekly lists public notices on tariff filings, etc. $40 per year. *Order List*, published weekly, lists all orders issued, $25 per year.

Arizona

Nancy Dempsey, Docket Control Center, Arizona Corporation Commission, 1200 W. Washington Street, Phoenix, AZ 85007; (602) 542-4251. Utilities Regulated: Water, sewer, irrigation, gas, electricity, and telephone. Examples of Information on File: Annual reports; applications called Certificates of Convenience and Necessity, which cover changes in rates; geographic area; and tariffs. Format of Files and Costs for Information: From 1986 to present, files are hard copy; before 1985 copies are on microfilm. Costs are $0.50 per page for staff to copy, and $0.10 if requestor comes in to the office to make copies. Listing of Regulated Companies: Yes. No charge. Other Publications Available: *Water News*, lists types of cases relating to water. No charge. *Hearing Notices*, lists dates and times and specific information about hearings. No charge. *Hearing Calendar*, lists weekly dates and times of hearings. No charge.

Arkansas

Jan Sanders, Secretary, Public Service Commission, P.O. Box C400, Little Rock, AR 72203; (501) 682-2051. Utilities Regulated: Electricity, telephone, gas, and water. Examples of Information on File: Annual Reports; complaints, rate and tariff information. Format of Files and Costs for Information: Hard copy and older records are on microfilm. Costs are $0.10 per page for duplicating for over 10 pages and $0.10 per fiche (60 pages). Listing of Regulated Companies: Yes. $0.10 per page (approximately 13 pages). Other Publications Available: *Daily Log*, weekly agenda of the Commission, *Pending Rate Report*, prepared weekly, this lists upcoming rate hearings. Both available for $0.10 per page.

California

Office of the Director, Public Utilities Commission, Consumer Affairs Branch, 505 Van Ness Ave., Room 4300, San Francisco, CA 94102; (415) 557-0647. Utilities Regulated: Local and long distance telephone, telegraph, mobile telephone, cellular telephone facilities and resellers, gas, electricity, water, steam, gas pipeline, sewer, and intra-state transportation. Examples of Information on File: Annual Reports, applications, case files (orders, pleadings, correspondence, exhibits, transcripts). Format of Files and Costs of Information; Hard copy. $0.20 per page. Listing of Regulated Companies: Yes. Lists by type of company, and prices vary for each list from $1 to $10. For information contact the Documents Section (415) 557-1812. Other Publications Available: *Agendas for Meetings*, $75 per year; *Daily Calendar* $125 per year; *Bi-Weekly Calendar*, $50 per year; *Transportation Calendar*, $75 per year; and the *Annual Report*, no charge.

Colorado

Information Center, Public Utilities Commission, Department of Regulatory Agencies, 1580 Logan St., Office Level 2, Denver, CO 80203; (303) 894-2000. Utilities Regulated: water and electricity (investor owned), gas (distribution companies only and inspection of new pipeline), telephone (all local and long distance only in Colorado), transportation (taxis and hauling for hire). Examples of Information on File: Annual reports, current operating tariffs, changes in rates or tariffs, etc. Format for Files and Costs for Information: Files are microfilmed daily. Charge is $0.20 per printed page. Customized computer searches also available on cost recovery basis. Directory of Regulated Companies: Yes. $0.20 per printed page. Other Publications Available: *Weekly Agenda* which details the Commission's agenda, is available at $0.20 per page through the Executive Secretary, at the above address.

Connecticut
Barney Spector, Director, Consumer Services Division, Public Utility Control, 1 Central Park Plaza, New Britain, CT 06051; (203) 827-1553. Utilities Regulated: Electricity, gas, water, local and cellular telephone, and cable television. Examples of Information on File: Annual reports, complaints, all financial information, etc. Format of Files and Costs for Information: Hard copy files available for $0.25 per page. Listing of Regulated Companies: Yes. $0.25 per page. Other Publications Available: None.

Delaware
Jim Hazel, Public Information Officer, Public Service Commission, 1560 South Dupont Highway, P.O. Box 457, Dover, DE 19903; (302) 736-4247. Utilities Regulated: Electricity, telephone, water, cable television, new car franchises. Examples of Information on File: Quarterly financial report, new service or elimination of existing service, rate changes, issuance of stock. Format of Files and Costs for Information: Hard copy files 1987-89. Prior files on microfiche. Copies are available for $0.25 each. Listing of Regulated Companies: Yes. no charge. Other Publications Available: *Annual Report*. No charge.

District of Columbia
Office of the Secretary, Service Commission, 450 5th Street, N.W., Suite 800, Washington, D.C. 20001; (202) 626-5120. Utilities Regulated: Electricity, gas, local telephone. Examples of Information on File: Annual Reports, other periodic accounting information, new tariffs or amendments. Format of Files and Costs for Information: Hard copy files plus some computerized records. $0.15 per copy. Listing of Regulated Companies: Yes. No charge. Other Publications Available: *Annual Report*, *Quarterly Newsletter* available from consumer services.

Florida
Steve Tribble, Director of Records and Reporting, Public Service Commission, 101 E. Gaines Street, Tallahassee, FL 32399-0850; (904) 488-7238. Utilities Regulated: Local and long distance telephone, coin-operated telephones, resellers and interexchange carriers, water, sewer, and investor owned gas and electric companies. Limited jurisdiction over rural and municipally owned gas and electric companies. Examples of Information on File: Monthly general operating reports, earnings and rate changes. and complaints. Format of Files and Costs for Information: Hard copy files. $1 per page. Directory of Regulated Companies: Yes. $1 per page. Other Publications Available: *Summary of Orders*, and *Report of New Dockets* are both published weekly for $20.80 annually each.

Georgia
Executive Director's Office, Public Service Commission, 244 Washington St., Atlanta, GA 30334; (404) 656-4501. Utilities Regulated: local telephone, electric, gas, radio common carriers, transportation. Examples of Information on File: Annual reports, changes in names, changes in management. Format of Files and Costs for Information: Hard copy, $0.25 per page. Listing of Regulated Companies: Yes. Listings of all companies by type. $0.25 per page. Other Publications Available: *Annual Report*. No charge.

Hawaii
Norman Lee, Chief Engineer, Public Utilities Commission, 465 S. King St., Kekuanaoa Building, Room 103, Honolulu, HI 96813; (808) 548-3990. Utilities Regulated: Local and cellular telephone, radio common carriers, electricity, gas, water, sewer, trucking, and intra-state transportation. Examples of Information on File: Monthly financial reports, and annual reports. Format of Files and Costs for Information: Currently hard copy but computerization of files underway. $0.25 per page plus postage. Listing of Regulated Companies: Yes. But the commission will not duplicate and mail lists. Other Publications Available: *Annual Report*. $3.85.

Idaho
Commission Secretary, Public Utilities Commission, State House, Boise, Idaho 83720; (208) 334-3143. Utilities Regulated: Telephone, gas, electricity, water, and trucking. Examples of Information on File: applications for rate increases, financial statements. Format of Files and Costs for Information: Hard copy, $0.15 per page. Listing of Regulated Companies: Yes. No charge. Other Publications Available: *Annual Report*. No charge. *Summary List of Cases*. Published monthly, free of charge.

Illinois
Chief Clerk's Office, Public Utilities Commission, 527 E. Capitol Avenue, Springfield, IL 62794; (217) 782-2024. Utilities Regulated: Local and long distance telephone, radio common carriers, customer-owned pay telephones, gas, electricity, water and sewer, gas pipeline, railroad, bus, towing and tractor-trailer haulers. Examples of Information on File: Annual reports and other general information. Format of Files and Costs for Information: Hard copy. Files over two years old on microfilm. $0.25 per page. Directory of Regulated Companies: Yes. $0.35 per page. Other Publications Available; *Agenda*, published bi-weekly, lists the commission's agenda. No charge. *Annual Report*, is in three parts--utilities, appendix to utilities, and transportation--and sells for $10 each.

Indiana
Public Information Office, Utility Regulatory Commission, State Office Building, Room 913, Indianapolis, IN 46204; (317) 232-2713. Utilities Regulated: Local telephone, WATS resellers, telephone cooperatives, interexchange carriers, radio common carriers, gas, gas transportation companies, electricity, steam, water, and sewer. Examples of Information on File: Rates and charges, tariffs, financial reports, and all changes. Format of Files and Costs for Information: Hard copy. $0.20 per page and $2 to mail. Listing of Regulated Companies: Yes. No charge. Other Publications Available: The commission's *Annual Report* and other general information.

Iowa
Iowa State Utilities Board, Department of Commerce, Utilities Division, Lucas State Office Building, Des Moines, IA 50319; (515) 281-5979. Utilities Regulated: Local and long distance telephone, telegraph, investor-owned gas and electricity. Examples of Information on File: Annual Reports and all financial information. Format of Files and Costs for Information: Hard copy. $0.50 for first three pages and $0.15 thereafter. Listing of Regulated Companies: Yes. $0.50 per page. Other Publications Available: *Annual Report* that includes filings and description of proceedings.

Kansas
Director of Public Affairs, Corporation Commission, Utilities Division, Docking State Office Building, 4th Floor, Topeka, KS 66612-1571; (913) 296-3391. Utilities Regulated: local and long distance telephone, electricity, gas and water. Examples of Information on File: Annual reports and all records of proceedings. Format of Files and Costs for Information: Hard copy and older records on microfilm. 1-10 pages, $0.10 per copy and costs decrease as number of pages increases. Also actual charges for postage. Listing of Regulated Companies: Yes. But must certify that the list will not be used for solicitation.

Kentucky
Public Service Commission, 730 Schenkel Lane, Box 615, Frankfort, KY 40602; (502) 564-3940. Utilities Regulated: Local and long distance telephone, WATS resellers, radio common carriers, cellular telephone, electricity, gas, water, and sewer. Examples of Information on File: Annual reports, tariffs, and applications for changes. Format of Files and Costs for Information: Hard copy plus older files are on microfilm. $0.10 a page for hard copy and $0.50 for microfilm. Postage extra. Listing of Regulated Companies: Yes. $10.00. Other Publications Available: Bimonthly PSC update listing all cases filed, hearings, and decisions for an annual fee of $65.

Louisiana
Secretary of the Commission, Public Service Commission, One American Place, Suite 1630, Baton Rouge, LA 70825; (504) 342-4416. Utilities Regulated: Local, long distance, and cellular telephone, long distance facility-based carriers, and pay telephones; electricity, gas and water. Examples of Information on File: Tariff information on all regulated companies. Format of Files and Costs for Information: Hard copy. $0.25 per page. $1 per page for transcriptions of hearings. Listing of Regulated Companies: Yes. No charge.

Maine
Mary Broad, Public Utilities Commission, 242 State Street, Station 18, Augusta, ME 04333-0018; (207) 289-3831. Utilities Regulated: Local exchange telephone, radio common carriers, resellers, cellular telephone; electricity, gas, and water. Examples of Information on File: Annual reports, financial statements, transfer of stock or rate changes. Format of Files and Costs for Information: Hard copy. Computerization is underway. $0.20 per page. Listing of Regulated Companies: Yes. No charge. Other Publications Available: *Monthly Docket*, $10 semiannually, *Weekly Agenda*, $12 semiannually, and copies of all orders and decisions, $73 semiannually.

Maryland
Director of Consumer Assistance and Public Affairs, Public Service Commission, The American Building, 231 Baltimore St., Baltimore, MD 21202; (301) 333-6028. Utilities Regulated: Gas, electricity, water, sewer, and resellers of long distance telephone service. Examples of Information on File: Financial information, annual reports, and tariff information. Format of Files and Costs for Information: Hard copy. Computerization underway. $0.20 per page and actual charges for postage. Listing of Regulated Companies: Yes. No charge.

Massachusetts
Secretary of the Department of Public Utilities, Department of Public Utilities, Leverett Saltonstall Building, Government Center, 100 Cambridge St., Boston, MA 02202; (617) 727-3500. Utilities Regulated: Trucks, buses, and railroad; gas, water and voluntary holding companies for electricity. Examples of Information on File: Annual reports and financial statements. Format of Files and Costs for Information: Hard copy. $0.20 per page. Listing of Regulated Companies: Yes, within the department's annual report. No charge.

Michigan
Executive Secretary, Public Service Commission of the Department of Commerce, P.O. Box 30221, Lansing, MI 48909; (517) 334-6445. Utilities Regulated: Local and long distance telephone, electricity, independent meter testers, gas and water. Examples of Information on File: Tariffs, annual reports,

Information on People, Companies, and Mailing Lists

audit information, and filings to the commission. Format of Files and Costs for Information: Hard copy and older records are on microfilm. Actual costs for copying plus $0.02 per page and actual postage costs. Listing of Regulated Companies: Yes. Same costs as for other records. Other Publications Available: Yes. Individuals may subscribe to listings of orders, agendas, and minutes; fees vary.

Minnesota

Department of Public Service, Public Utilities Commission, 780 American Center Building, 150 E. Kellogg Blvd., St. Paul, MN 55101; (612) 296-7124. Utilities Regulated: Local and inter-LATA telephone, pay telephone, electricity, and gas. Examples of Information on File: Annual financial reports, tariffs, and case files. Format of Files and Costs for Information: Hard copy. $0.25 per page for copies. Listing of Regulated Companies: Yes. $0.25 per page. Other Publications Available: Yes. The Commission's *Biennial Report* and the summary of hearings. No charge.

Mississippi

Brian Ray, Public Service Commission, P.O. Box 1174, Jackson, MS 39215-1174; (601) 961-5400. Utilities Regulated: Land-line telephone, radio common carriers, personal paging systems, WATS resellers, interstate telephone, electricity, gas, water, and sewer. Examples of Information on File: Annual reports, tariffs, financial information, and proceedings before the commission. Format of Files and Costs for Information: Hard copy now but a case-tracking system is being implemented so within the year everything will be computerized. $0.50 per page. Listing of Regulated Companies: Yes. $0.50 per page. Other Publications Available: *Monthly Docket*, discusses monthly business before the commission. No charge.

Missouri

Secretary of the Commission, Public Service Commission, P.O. Box 360, Jefferson City, MO 65102; (314) 751-7494. Utilities Regulated: Local telephone, inter-exchange facility-based carriers, inter-exchange resellers, pay telephones, electricity, gas, water, and sewer. Examples of Information on File: Applications, financial information, complaints, annual reports, etc. Format of Files and Costs for Information: Hard copy and some records are computerized. Can perform some custom searches; charges vary. Copying costs are $0.30 per page or $1 for certified copies plus $0.10 per page. Listing of Regulated Companies: Yes. No charge. Other Publications Available: *Tariff Filing Docket*, lists tariff matters. Published weekly. $24 per year. *Weekly Docket* lists hearings coming up the next week. No charge.

Montana

Dennis Crawford, Public Service Commission, 2701 Prospect Ave., Helena, MT 59620-2601; (406) 444-6199. Utilities Regulated: Local and long distance telephone, electricity, water and sewer, gas, and intra-state oil pipeline. Examples of Information on File: annual reports, special reports, rules, regulations, and tariffs. Format of Files and Costs for Information: Hard copy. Older orders are on microfilm. $0.30 per page if staff does research, and $0.15 if requestor does research. Listing of Regulated Companies: No. Other Publications Available: Commission's *Annual Report*. Actual costs.

Nebraska

Public Service Commission, 300 the Atrium, 1200 N St., P.O. Box 94927, Lincoln, NE 68509; (402) 471-3101. Utilities Regulated: Local and long-distance telephone and motor carriers. Examples of Information on File: Annual reports, financial information, tariffs, proceedings of hearings. Format of Files and Costs for Information: Hard copy. $0.25 for copying, no mailing charges. Listing of Regulated Companies: Yes. No charge. Other Publications Available: *Service Rate Questionnaire* gives information about customers. No charge.

Nevada

Public Affairs Specialist, Public Service Commission, Capitol Complex, 727 Fairview Drive, Carson City, NV 89710; (702) 885-4180. Utilities Regulated: Electricity, gas, telephone, water and sewer, various motor carriers, and railroad. Examples of Information on File: Annual reports, insurance and operating certificates, rates and tariffs. Format of Files and Costs for Information: Hard copy and microfilm for older copies. $0.25 a page. Listing of Regulated Companies: Yes, alphabetical and by utility. No charge. Other Publications Available: No.

New Hampshire

Executive Director, Public Utilities Commission, 8 Old Suncook Rd., Concord, NH 03301; (603) 271-2431. Utilities Regulated: Gas, electricity, telephone, sewer, water, steam. Examples of Information on File: Service reliability, financial information, records of responsiveness and responsiblity. Format of Files and Costs for Information: Hard copy. $0.50 per page. Listing of Regulated Companies: Yes. $0.50 per page. Other Publications Available: *Biennial Report for the Legislature*.

New Jersey

Board of Public Utilities, 2 Gateway Center, Newark, NJ 07102; (201) 648-2026. Utilities Regulated: Electricity, gas, water, sewer, solid waste. Examples of Information on File: Tariff information, annual reports on revenue, expenses, and capitalization. Format of Files and Costs for Information: Hard copy for

regulations. Copies are $1 per page. Annual reports are computerized. listing of Regulated Companies: Yes. $1 per page. Other Publications Available: *Case File Report*, published weekly. $120 per year. *Agenda*, published monthly. Price varies according to number of pages.

New Mexico

Records Office, Public Service Commission, P.O. Box 2205, Santa Fe, NM 87504-2205; (505) 827-6940. Utilities Regulated: Gas, electricity, water, and sewer. Examples of Information on File: tariffs, annual reports, hearing proceedings. Format of Files and Costs for Information: Hard copy and microfilm. $0.15 per page on paper, $0.25 per copy of film. Film to film copies are available. Listing of Regulated Companies: Yes. $0.15 per page. Other Publications Available: None.

New York

Central Files, Public Service Commission, 3 Empire State Plaza, Albany, NY 12223; (518) 474-7080. Utilities Regulated: Water, gas, electricity, telephone. Examples of Information on File: Annual reports, financial statements, performance material. Format of Files and Costs for Information: Hard copy. Older records on microfilm. Copy of complete fiche set $1.50. Listing of Regulated Companies: Yes. No charge. Other Publications Available: *Financial Statistics of Major Utilities*, $6 reproduction costs.

North Carolina

Clerk's Office, Utilities Commission, Box 29510, Raleigh, NC 27626-0520; (919) 733-7680. Utilities Regulated: Electricity, telephone, gas, water, and sewer, transportation, and radio common carriers. Examples of Information on File: Annual reports, applications, rates, and comments from orders issues. Format of Files and Costs for Information: Hard copy. $0.20 per page. Transcription of testimony is $1 per page. Listing of Regulated Companies: Yes. $0.20 per page. Other Publications Available: *North Carolina Public Utilities Law Book--Rules and Regulations*, $20, *Orders and Decisions*, published annually. Actual cost.

North Dakota

Secretary of the Commission, Public Service Commission, 12th Floor, State Capitol, Bismark, ND 58505; (701) 224-2400. Utilities Regulated: Electricity, gas, telephone, and transportation. Examples of Information on File: Annual reports, financial information, and rate case information. Format of Files and Costs for Information: Hard copy. Older records on microfilm. $0.25 per page if research is involved and $0.10 per page for duplicating. Other Publications Available: No.

Ohio

Fiscal Office, Public Utilities Commission, 180 E. Broad St., Columbus, OH 43266-0573; (614) 466-3016. Utilities Regulated: Bridges, heating and cooling, inter-urban railroad, water transportation, pipelines, sewage, electricity, natural gas, railroad, water works, and telephone. Examples of Information on File: Annual reports. Format of Files and Costs for Information: Two years of hard copy, and prior years on microfilm. $0.15 per page for paper copies and $0.35 per page for film. Listing of Regulated Companies: Yes. $0.15 per page. Other Publications Available: Yes. *Annual Report*. No charge.

Oklahoma

Office Manager, Oklahoma Corporation Commission, Public Utilities Division, Room 500, Jim Thorpe Office Building, Oklahoma City, OK 73105; (405) 521-3908. Utilities Regulated: Electricity, gas, telephone, water, and cotton gins. Examples of Information on File: All information connected with case hearing or filing, annual reports, audit reports, and applications. Format of Files and Costs for Information: Hard copy, but computerization is underway. $0.25 per page or $7.50 per document. Listing of Regulated Companies: Yes. $0.50 per page. Other Publications Available: *Annual Report*. No charge.

Oregon

Public Information Office, Public Utilities Commission, Labor and Industries Building, Salem, OR 97310; (503) 378-5849. Utilities Regulated: Trucking, electricity, gas, water, and telephone. Examples of Information on File: Financial and operational information. Format of Files and Costs for Information: Hard copy, microfilm, and magnetic tape. $0.25 for first 10 pages and $0.10 per page thereafter. Listing of Regulated Companies: Yes. No charge. Other Publications Available: General information pamphlets.

Pennsylvania

Public Utilities Commission, P.O. Box 3265, Harrisburg, PA (717) 783-1740. Utilities Regulated: Gas, electricity, water, sewer, communications, and intra-state transportation. Examples of Information on File: Annual reports, updated tariff information, and other periodic reports on a variety of matters. Format of Files and Costs for Information: Hard copy and records are currently being computerized. Cost is 75 cents per page. Customized searches are available. Listing of Regulated Companies: Available for 75 cents per page. Other Publications Available: None.

Rhode Island

Commission Clerk's Office, Public Utilities Commission, 100 Orange St., Providence, RI 02903; (401) 277-3500. Utilities Regulated: Gas, electricity, telephone, water, sewer, cable television, and trucking. Examples of Information on File; Annual reports, materials from rate hearings, and complaints. Format of Files and Costs for Information: Hard copy. Microfilming is underway. $0.25 per page. Listing of Regulated Companies: Yes. No charge. Other Publications Available: No.

South Carolina

Executive Director, Public Service Commission, 111 Doctor's Circle, P.O. Drawer 11649, Columbia, SC 29211; (803) 737-5135. Utilities Regulated: Gas, electricity, telecommunications, water and wastewater, and transportation. Examples of Information on File: Quarterly financial reports, rate-of-return, sales, and cost information. Format of Files and Costs for Information: Hard copy. $0.25 per copy. Listing of Regulated Companies: Yes, within the commission's annual report. $2.

South Dakota

Geoff Simon, Public Utilities Commission, 500 E. Capital Avenue, Pierre, SD 57501; (605) 773-3201. Utilities Regulated: Telephone, electricity, gas, transportation, warehouses, and elevators. Examples of Information on File: tariffs, monthly reports on financial matters and rate filings. Format of Files and Costs for Information: Hard copy available for 15 cents per page. Listing of Regulated Companies: Available at no charge. Other Publications Available: *Annual Report*. No charge. Agendas of Commission meetings are available, but there is no distribution system in place.

Tennessee

Public Utilities Commission, 460 James Robertson Pky., Nashville, TN 37219; (615) 741-2125. Utilities Regulated: Transportation, water/sewer, electricity, gas, telephone. Examples of Information on File: annual reports, rate and tariff information, ad valorum tax reports, other financial records. Format of Files and Costs for Information: Hard copy available for 25 cents per page for copies. Transcripts are $1.50 per page. Customized searches available for an additional charge for computer time. Listing of Regulated Companies: Yes. No charge. Other Publications Available : *Annual Report*, no charge. *Agenda* of cases. Send a self-addressed stamped envelope.

Texas

Public Utility Commission, 78000 Shoal Creek Blvd., Suite 400 North, Austin, TX 78757; (512) 458-0100. Utilities Regulated: Electricity, local telephone, and AT&T long distance telphone. Examples of Information on File: Annual reports, financial information, tarrif information, and transcripts of commission hearings. Format of Files and Costs for Information: Hard copy and older records on microfilm. Cost is 85 cents for the first page and 15 cents for each additional page for each file. Listing of Regulated Companies: Yes, $5 each. Other Publications Available: News releases, new filings, and agendas available for $30 per year. *PUC Bulletin* contains examiners report and orders issued by the Commission available for $50 per year. *Substantive Rules* is a loose-leaf edition of all rules issued by the Commission are available for $25 per year.

Utah

Floy Wilcox, Public Service Commission, 160 East 300 South, Salt Lake City, UT 84111; (801) 530-6716. Utilities Regulated: Electricity, gas, water, transportation, telephone. Examples of Information on File: Annual Reports, complaints, petitions, requests for agency action. Format of Files and Costs for Information: Hard copy and microfilm for older records are available for 50 cents per page. Listing of Regulated Companies: Yes, at no charge. Other Publications Available: *Telecommunications Orders, Gas and Electric Orders, Transportation Orders* are available for $200 per year each.

Vermont

Public Service Board, 120 State St., Montpelier, VT 05602; (802) 828-2358. Utilities Regulated: Gase, electricity, telephone, water, cable television. Examples of Information on File: Proceedings, tariff information, annual reports, informal complaints, special contracts. Format of Files and Costs for Information: Hard copy and microfilm are available for 10 cents per page. Listing of Regulated Companies: Available at no charge. Other Publications Available: *Board Decisions*, 10 cents per page. This publication will soon go online and there will be a subscription charge.

Virginia

Division of Energy Regulation, State Corporation Commission, P. O. Box 1197, Richmond, VA 23209. Utilities Regulated: Electricity, gas, water, sewer, telephone. Examples of Information on File: Financial and operational information, transmission applications. Format of Files and Costs for Information: Hard copy and older records are on microfilm available for $1 per page. Other Publications Available: *Annual Report*. No charge.

Washington

Public Utilities Commission, Chandler Plaza Building, 1300 S. Evergreen Park Dr., SW, Olympia, WA 98504; (206) 753-6423. Utilities Regulated: Electricity, telephone, telecommunications, water, gas, transportation. Examples of Information on File: Balance sheets and annual reports. Format of Files and Costs for Information: Hard copy is available for 12 cents per page. All files will be computerized in the near future. Listing of Regulated Companies: Available for 12 cents per page. Other Publications Available: *Transportation Docket*, published monthly, no charge. *Utilities Docket*, published weekly, no charge.

West Virginia

Public Service Commission, P.O. Box 812, Charleston, WV 25323; (304) 340-0300. Utilities Regulated: Telephone, gas water, sewer, railroad, electricity, gas pipelines, and motor carriers. Examples of Information on File: Annual reports, financial statements. Format of Files and Costs for Information: Hard copy and microfilm available for 20 cents per pages.

Wisconsin

Public Service Commisssion, P.O. Box 7854, Madison, WI 53707; (608) 267-7915. Utilities Regulated: Gas, electricity, telephone, water, sewer. Examples of Information on File: Annual reports, tariffs, and rules. Format of Files and Costs for Information: Hard copy available at 15 cents per page. Listing of Regulated Companies: Available for 15 cents per page. Other Publications Available: *Annual Report*, meetings schedules and minutes. No charge.

Wyoming

Steve Oxley, Public Service Commission, Herschler Building, 122 W. 25th St., Cheyenne, WY 82002; (307) 777-7427. Utilities Regulated: Electricity, gas, pipelines, telephone, telegraph, radio common carriers, water, railroad, motor carriers. Examples of Information on File: Rates, conditions of service, contracts, financial conditions. Format of Files and Costs for Information: Hard copy available for 25 cents per page. Listing of Regulated Companies: Yes at $2 per copy. Other Publications Available: *Utility Rate Book*, rates of fixed utilities. $20 per year.

Information on People, Companies, and Mailing Lists

Weights and Measures

Looking for a mailing list of all delicatessens in the state? This office is likely to have it for you. The same is true for any other organization which uses a scale for commercial purposes, including gas stations, pharmacies, and dairies.

Every time you buy a half pound of corned beef or gas up the car, you rely on the accuracy of the scale behind the counter or meter on the pump. These and thousands of other measuring devices are used with confidence every day by businesses and consumers, most never questioning the accuracy of the information. Who then is charged with making sure a pound is a pound and an inch an inch?

All commercial measuring devices are regularly inspected by agents of your state office of weights and measures. In addition, such offices are the official keepers of state standards of mass, length, and volume traceable to those maintained by the National Institute of Standards and Technology (formerly the National Bureau of Standards).

These offices are staffed by professionals who can answer questions as simple a child's homework assignment or as complicated as determining the best method of sale for a particular commodity. Many types of businesses rely on the expertise of these offices: defense industries, scale companies, and store-front businesses such as fabric shops, railroads, feed stores, and so on.

In general, most agents of a state office of weights and measures conduct on-site inspections of equipment at commercial businesses and manufacturing plants, ensuring that measuring devices are being used correctly and are being maintained so as to ensure their accuracy. Investigators also inspect scales used to weigh trucks and other vehicles used for transporting goods from factory or farm to market. Among the measuring devices inspected on a regular basis are: gasoline and air pumps, gas storage tanks, dairies, truck scales, pharmacy scales, and those used by commercial businesses.

The offices also field and investigate numerous complaints, most questioning the accuracy of fuel pumps. State agents also enforce standards of the Fair Packaging and Labeling Act. This law, passed by Congress in 1966, standardized the packaging and labeling of products so that they are packaged in containers of approximate similar size and labeled so as not to mislead.

Virtually every commercial transaction involves the use of weights and measures, so the state files are extensive. Given the number of transactions, even a slight measurement error can add up to thousands of dollars. Most state offices will provide business addresses and the type and capacity of measuring devices owned by companies on their files.

The following is a listing of state offices of weights and measures.

Weights and Measures Offices

Alabama
Don E. Stagg, Director, Weights and Measures Division, Alabama Department of Agriculture, P.O. Box 3336, Montgomery, AL 36193; (205) 261-2614.

Alaska
Department of Labor, Weights and Measures Division, Office Park, Juneau, AK 99801; (907) 465-4870.

Arizona
Ray Helmick, Chief, Arizona Weights and Measures Division, 1951 W. North Lane, Phoenix, AZ 85021; (602) 255-5211. ***

Arkansas
San F. Hindsman, Director, Bureau of Standards, Division of Weights and Measures, 4608 West 61st Street, Little Rock, AR 72209; (501) 371-1759.

California
Darrell A. Guensler, Acting Assistant Director, Division of Measurement Standards, California Department of Food and Agriculture, 8500 Fruitridge Rd., Sacramento, CA 95826; (916) 366-5119.

Colorado
Mr. Davis Wallace, Chief, Measurement Standard Securities, Department of Agriculture, 3125 Wyandot, Denver, CO 80211; (303) 866-2845.

Connecticut
Allan M. Nelson, Chief, Weights and Measures Division, Department of Consumer Protection, State Office Building, Room G17, 1665 Capitol Ave., Hartford, CT 06106; (203) 566-5230.

Delaware
Eugene Keeley, Supervisor, Office of Weights and Measures, 2320 South Dupont Hwy., Dover, DE 19901; (302) 736-4811.

District of Columbia
Earl E. Maxwell, Chief, Department of Consumer and Regulatory Affairs, Weights, Measures and Markets Division, 1110 U. St., N.E., Washington, D.C. 20020; (202) 767-7923.

Florida
Mr. Wayne Ball, Chief, Bureau of Weights and Measures, Department of Agriculture and Consumer Services, 3125 Conner Blvd. Lab Complex, Tallahassee, FL 32301; (904) 488-9140.

Georgia
Martin Coile, Director, Weights and Measures Laboratory, Atlanta Farmers Market, Forest Park, GA 30050; (404) 363-7611.

Hawaii
George E. Mattimore, Administrator, Measurement Standards, Department of Agriculture, 725 Ilalo St., Honolulu, HI 96822; (808) 548-7152.

Idaho
Lyman D. Holloway, Chief, Bureau of Weights and Measures, Department of Agriculture, 2216 Kellogg Lane, Boise, ID 83712; (208) 334-2345.

Illinois
Sidney A. Colbrook, Weights and Measures Program Manager, Bureau of Product Inspection and Standards, Department of Agriculture, 801 Sangamon Ave., Springfield, IL 62706; (217) 785-8312.

Indiana
Robert W. Walker, Director of Weights and Measures, State Board of Health, 1330 West Michigan St., Indianapolis, IN 46206; (317) 633-0350; (317) 633-0350.

Iowa
James O'Conner, Supervisor, Weights and Measures Division, Department of Agriculture and Land Stewardship, Henry A. Wallace Building, Des Moines, IA 50319; (515) 281-6716.

Kansas
Deverne Phillips, State Sealer, Division of Inspections, Kansas State Board of Agriculture, 2016 West 37th St., Topeka, KS 66611; (907) 465-4870.

Kentucky
Charles L. Prebble, Director, Division of Weights and Measures, Department of Agriculture, 106 West Second St., Frankfort, KY 40601 ; (502) 564-4870.

Louisiana

Ronald Harold, Director, Louisiana Weights and Measures, Department of Agriculture, P.O. Box 44456, Capitol Station, Baton Rouge, LA 70804; (504) 925-3780.

Maine

Clayton F. Davis, Director, Agriculture Inspections Division, Division of Regulation, Station 28, Augusta, ME 04333; (207) 289-3841.

Maryland

Richard L. Thompson, Chief, Weights and Measures Section, Department of Agriculture, 50 Harry S. Truman Parkway, Annapolis, MD 21401; (301) 841-5790.

Massachusetts

Virgil Glenn, Supervising Inspector, Massachusetts Division of Standards, One Ashburton Place, Boston, MA 02108; (617) 727-3480.

Michigan

Edward Heffron, Chief, Food Division, Department of Agriculture, Ottawa Tower North, Box 30017, Lansing, MI 48909; (517) 373-1060.

Minnesota

Edward Skluzacek, Director, Division of Weights and Measures, State of Minnesota, Department of Public Service, 2277 Highway 36, St. Paul, MN 55113; (612) 341-7200.

Mississippi

William P. Elkridge, Director, Weights and Measures Division, Mississippi Department of Agriculture and Commerce, 1603 Walter Sillers Building, P.O. Box 1609, Jackson, MS 39205; (601) 359-3670.

Missouri

Lester Barrows, Director, Weights and Measures Division, Department of Agriculture, P.O. Box 630, Jefferson City, MO 65102; (314) 751-4278.

Montana

Steven H. Meloy, Bureau Chief, Bureau of Weights and Measures, Department of Commerce, 1424 9th Ave., Helena, MT 59620; (406) 444- 3164.

Nebraska

Steven A. Malone, Director, Division of Weights and Measures, Department of Agriculture, State Office Building, 301 Centennial Mall South, Lincoln, NE 68509; (402) 741-2341.

Nevada

Knute D. Pennington, Chief Deputy State Sealer, Bureau of Weights and Measures, Department of Agriculture 1266 S. Stewart St., Reno, NV 89712; (702) 789-0166.

New Hampshire

Roy Howard, Director, Bureau of Weights and Measures, Department of Agriculture, Caller Box 2042, Concord, NH 03302; (603) 271-3700.

New Jersey

Thomas W. Kelly, State Superintendent, State Office of Weights and Measures, 187 West Hanover St., Trenton, NJ 08625; (609) 292-4615.

New Mexico

Fred A. Gerk, Chief, Standards and Consumer Services, Department of Agriculture, Department 3170, P.O. Box 30005, Las Cruces, NM 88003; (505) 646-1616.

New York

John J. Bartfai, Director, Bureau of Weights and Measures, Department of Agriculture, Building 7-A, 1220 Washington Ave., Albany, NY 12235; (518) 457-3452.

North Carolina

David N. Smith, Director, Consumer Standards Division, Department of Agriculture, P.O. Box 27647, Raleigh, NC 27611; (919) 733-3313.

North Dakota

Bruce Niebergall, Director, North Dakota Public Service Commission, Department of Weights and Measures, State Capitol, Bismark, ND 58505; (701) 224-2400.

Ohio

Bruce Litzenberg, Chief, Division of Weights and Measures, Ohio Department of Agriculture, 8995 East Main St., Reynoldsburg, OH 43068; (614) 866-6361.

Oklahoma

Ray Elliot, Director, Marketing Industry Division, Oklahoma Department of Agriculture, 2800 North Lincoln Blvd., Oklahoma City, OK 73105; (405) 521-3864.

Oregon

Kendrick J. Simila, Administrator, Measures Standard Division, Department of Agriculture, 635 Capitol St., N.E., Salem, OR 97310; (503) 378-3792.

Pennsylvania

John Yahner, Director, Bureau of Standard Weights and Measures, Department of Agriculture, 2301 North Cameron St., Harrisburg, PA 17110; (717) 787-6772.

Rhode Island

Lynda Agresti Maurer, Sealer of Weights and Measures, Department of Labor, Division of Professional Regulations, 220 Elmwood Ave., Providence, RI 02907; (401) 457-1863.

South Carolina

Charles T. Smith, Director, Consumer Services Division, Department of Agriculture, P.O. Box 11280, Columbia, SC 29211; (803) 734-2210.

South Dakota

James Melgaard, Director, Division of Consumer Inspection, 118 West Capitol, Pierre, SD 57501; (605) 773-3697.

Tennessee

Jimmy Hopper, Director, Weights and Measures, Department of Agriculture, Box 40627, Melrose Station, Nashville, TN 37204; (615) 360-0160.

Texas

Charles E. Forester, Supervisor of Weights and Measures, Department of Agriculture, Box 12847, Stephen F. Austin Building, Austin, TX 78711; (512) 463-7610.

Utah

Edison J. Stephens, Deputy Commissioner, State Department of Agriculture, 350 North Redwood Road, Salt Lake City, UT 84116; (801) 533-4109.

Vermont

Trafford F. Brink, Director, Division of Weights and Measures and Retail Inspection, Department of Agriculture, 116 State Street, Montpelier, VT 05602; (802) 828-2436.

Virginia

James F. Lyles, Bureau Chief, Weights and Measures Section, Department of Agriculture and Consumer Services, P.O. Box 1163, Room 403, Richmond, VA 23209; (804) 786-2476.

Washington

Steuart Delaney, Acting Chief, Section of Weights and Measures, Department of Agriculture, 2747 29th Ave. S.W., Tumwatter, WA 98502; (206) 753-5042.

West Virginia

James T. Rardin, Acting Director, Division of Weights and Measures, Department of Labor, 1800 Washington St., East, Motor Vehicles Building, Charleston, WA 25305; (304) 348-7890.

Wisconsin

Robert W. Probst, Director, Bureau of Weights and Measures, Wisconsin Department of Agriculture, Trade and Consumer Protection, 801 W. Bayder Rd., Madison, WI 53708; (608) 266-2227.

Wyoming

William H. Hovey, Manager, Consumer/Compliance Division, Department of Agriculture, 2219 Carey Ave., Cheyenne, WY 82002; (307) 777-6591.

Insurance Companies and Salesmen

An insurance company wants to compare their rates to those of their competitors. A software company with a new time saving product needs the names of all the 1,500 insurance companies in Minnesota for a mailing list. Someone shopping for auto insurance wants to see sample policies from five different insurance companies in her area before she makes a final decision. A prospective insurance buyer wants to know how many complaints have been lodged against a certain company before he signs on the dotted line. All of this information and more can be found at the State Insurance Offices.

Although the kinds of information available at each of these offices varies from state to state, all except Colorado and Hawaii have listings of the insurance companies in their state, and only 9 states--Arkansas, Georgia, Hawaii, Louisiana, Maryland, Montana, New York, Texas, and Washington--do not compile comprehensive listings of the in-state insurance agents. About thirty states will provide you with these listings in the form of a computer printout and/or mailing labels. California, Indiana, and Kansas also offer these listings on computer tape or diskettes.

Most state offices also handle consumer complaints and make their findings available to the public. Illinois, for example, not only compiles a "Complaint Rating List" that will tell you the number of complaints filed against a company, they also calculate "Complaint Ratios," which show the number of complaints versus the amount of insurance a company writes. If a company writes 100 policies and has 20 complaints, chances are you shouldn't buy a policy from them. But these "Complaint Ratios" can also be used by insurance companies to find out which of their competitors' policies produce the highest number of complaints. This is invaluable information for a company that plans to sell a new type of policy and wants a market study.

When an company wants to sell certain commercial or personal lines of insurance, they must file the policy forms and endorsements at the state office. Individuals can request copies of these policies before they make a purchase to compare rates from one company to another. Some states, in fact, publish "Premium Comparison Manuals" for personal auto and homeowners policies. For the rate charts listed in these manuals, each insurance company must take the same policy situation, such as a three bedroom house or a twenty-seven year old driver, and prepare a rate estimate for an insurance policy.

Some state offices also require insurance companies to file their "Rate Manuals" which show their brokers how to estimate their company's insurance premiums. These are valuable sources of information for both the consumer and competitor. And if you are interested in looking into a company's history--when it was first licensed, owners and former owners-- many state offices can furnish you with that information, too.

Insurance Divisions

Alabama

Insurance Department, 135 S. Union St., Montgomery, AL 36130/(205) 264-3550. Insurance Companies Documents on File: Available for $1 a page plus mailing costs from Blue Print Services, P.O. Box 1383, Montgomery, AL 36109/(205) 263-4865. Listing of Insurance Companies: "Annual Report" (List of all licensed insurance companies) is available at no charge. Number of Licensed Insurance Companies: 1,300. Licensed Agents Listing of Agents: Published yearly and available at no cost. Listing does not contain addresses. Number of Licensed Agents: Not available.

Alaska

Insurance Division Commerce and Economic Development Department, PO Box D, Juneau, AK 99811/(907) 465-2515. Insurance Companies Documents on File: Cost recovery basis Listing of Insurance Companies: Available for $25. Number of Licensed Insurance Companies: 1,050. Licensed Agents List of Agents: Available for $25. Number of Agents: 2,800.

Arizona

Insurance Department, 801 E. Jefferson, Phoenix, AZ 85034/(602) 255-4783. Insurance Companies Documents on File: Available for 50 cents per page. Requests must be submitted in writing. Listing of Insurance Companies: Contained in Annual Report, which is published yearly. Cost is $10. Prepayment required. (602) 255-5995 Number of Licensed Insurance Companies: over 2,000. Licensed Agents List of Agents: A computer printout is available by line of insurance. Cost is 3 cents a name. Average cost is $400. (602) 255-5605. Number of Agents: over 30,000.

Arkansas

Insurance Department, 400 University Tower Bldg, Little Rock, AR 72204/(501) 371-1813. Insurance Companies Documents on File: Available for $1 a page. Listing of Insurance Companies: 1,400. Licensed Agents List of Agents: Not Available. (501) 371-1421. Number of Agents: 24,000.

California

Insurance Department, Business, Transportation and Housing Agency, 600 S. Common Wealth Ave, L.A., CA 90005/(213) 736-2552. Insurance Companies Documents on File: Annual/Quarterly Statements are available to public at a cost of 50 cents per page plus sales tax up to four pages, then an outside copy service must be brought in. There is a one dollar fee per document certification. Listing of Insurance Companies: Lists are available, either in printout format (Cheshire labels) or magnetic tape format. Cost for list of all admitted companies is $30. Other lists, including breakdowns of different classes of insurance carriers or license types are also available at prices ranging from approximately $350 to $800. Interested parties should contact the Department's Electronic Data Processing Bureau, at (916) 445-3642 to request an order form. Number of Licensed Insurance Companies: 1,344. Licensed Agents List of Agents: Available by calling (916) 322-3555. Number of Agents: Not available.

Colorado

Insurance Division, 112 E. 14th St., Denver, CO 80203/(303) 866-3201. Insurance Companies Documents on File: Available to the public for 25 cents per page, but a visit to the office is necessary. Listing of Insurance Companies: A current listing is not available. The only listing available is dated 1982. Number of Licensed Companies: 1,500 Licensed Agents List of Agents: Available by calling (303) 866-3205.Lists are sorted by line of insurance and the cost is $100 a list. Number of Agents: Not available.

Connecticut

Insurance Department, 165 Capitol Ave, Hartford, CN 06106/(203) 566- 3017. Insurance Companies Documents on File: A visit to the office is necessary to copy documents. Listing of Insurance Companies: List is printed twice a year and is available for $10.75. All requests must be submitted in writing and be prepaid. Number of Licensed Companies: 939. Licensed Agents List of Agents: Lists are available by calling (203) 566-8357. Lists are sorted by authority, company, and locality. Cost of each list is $100. Number of Agents: Not available.

Delaware

Insurance Department, 841 Silver Lake Blvd, Dover, DE 19901/(302) 736-4251. Insurance Department, 841 Silver Lake Blvd, Dover, DE 19901/ (302) 736-4251.Insurance Companies Documents on File: Documents are available by contacting Budget Print (302) 674-1146. Cost is $1.50 per page. Listing of Insurance Companies: Cheshire or pressure sensitive labels are available for $75.00. Computer printouts are available on a cost recovery basis. Number of Insurance Companies: 1,500. Licensed Agents List of Agents: Available by contacting 302- 736-4251. Number of Agents: 80,000.

District of Columbia

Insurance Administration, Consumer and Regulatory Affairs Dept., 614 H St NW, DC 20001/(202) 727-7419. Insurance Companies Documents on File: Documents may be reviewed and copied in the office. Listing of Insurance

Companies: A free listing is available. Number of Insurance Companies: Not available. Licensed Agents List of Agents: No listing available. Number of Licensed Agents: Not available.

Florida
Insurance and Treasurer Department, Chief Executive Office, 1716 Larson Building, Tallahassee, FL 32300/(904) 488-5262. Insurance Companies Documents on File: Copies are available for 50 cents per page and $5 for certified copies. Listing of Insurance Companies: Complimentary copy of Year List of All Insurance Companies Licensed to Do Business in State of Florida available upon written request. Annual Report also contains listing. Number of Insurance Companies; 1,800. Licensed Agents List of Agents: List is sorted by type of insurance. They categorize 67 types of insurance. Computer printouts are available on a cost recovery basis, as are magnetic tape formats and gummed labels. Number of Agents: 169,458.

Georgia
Insurance Commissioner, 200 Predmont Ave, Atlanta, GA 30334/(404) 656-2074. Insurance Companies Documents on File: Annual Statements are available. Listing of Insurance Companies: Computer printouts are available for $30. Number of Insurance Companies: 1,438. Licensed Agents List of Agents: No list available (404) 656-2100. Number of Agents: 48,000.

Hawaii
Commerce and Consumer Affairs Department, Insurance Division, Box 3614, 1010 Richards St, Honolulu, HI 96811/(808) 548-4564. Insurance Companies Documents on File: Available for 25 cents per page. List of Insurance Companies: No listing available. Number of Insurance Companies: 760. Licensed Agents List of Agents: No listing available. Number of Agents: 730 general agents.

Idaho
Insurance Department, 500 S. 10th, Boise, ID 83720/(208) 334-2250. Insurance Companies Documents on File: Available for 50 cents per page. Listing of Insurance Companies: Company Listing available for $7.50. This order must be prepaid. Number of Insurance Companies: 1,500. Licensed Agents (208) 334-2250 List of Agents: Computer printout available for $100. Pressure Sensitive labels available for $100. List and labels can be sorted by line of insurance or ZIP code. Number of Agents: 10,500.

Illinois
Insurance Department, 320 W. Washington St., 4th Floor, Springfield, IL 62767/(217) 782-4515. Insurance Companies Documents on File: Available for $1.00 a page. Listing of Insurance Companies: Annual Statement available quarterly. Computer Information 217-782-3045: Printout available for $100. Magnetic tape or diskette available for $100. Requester must supply tape or diskette. Pressure sensitive labels can be run on a cost recovery basis if requester supplies labels. Cheshire labels also available on a cost recovery basis. All computer runs are in ZIP code order. Number of Insurance Companies: 1,719. Licensed Agents List of Agents: (217) 782-3045 Computer printouts available for $100. Magnetic tape or diskette available for $600. Requester must supply tape or diskette. Cheshire labels available for $1,000. All computer runs are in ZIP code order. Number of Agents: 69,000.

Indiana
Insurance Department, 509 State Office Bldg., Indianapolis, IN 46204/(317) 232-2405. Phone Information: (317) 232-2392. Documents on File: Available for 25 cents per page. Listing of Insurance Companies: Monthly computer run available for $25.00. This listing contains name of company, address, phone number, and type of insurance. Computer generated labels and listings on magnetic tape or diskette will be available in the near future. Number of Insurance Companies: 1,678. Licensed Agents List of Agents: Computer listing will be available in near future. Microfiche, which is processed monthly, available for $300. Number of Agents: 86,000.

Iowa
Commerce Department, Insurance Division, Lucas State Office Building, Des Moines, IA 50319/ (515) 281-4033. Insurance Companies Documents on File: Documents can be reviewed in the office and may be copied for a minimal charge. Listing of Insurance Companies: Available for $3.00. Number of Insurance Companies: 1,487. Licensed Agents (515) 281-4037 List of Agents: Computer printout available on a cost recovery basis. Pressure sensitive labels available on a cost recovery basis. Customized listing or labels may be sorted by type of insurance, ZIP Code, county, or company. Number of Agents: 52,580.

Kansas
Kansas Insurance Department, 420 S. West 9th St, Topeka, KS 66612/(913) 296-3071. Insurance Companies Documents on File: Documents can be copied on a cost recovery basis. Listing of Insurance Companies: Kansas Insurance Company Directory available free of charge. Listing available on magnetic tape if requester supplies the tape. (Kansas forbids use of public information for solicitation purposes.) Number of Insurance Companies: 1,200. Licensed Agents List of Agents: Customized lists of agents by company, line of business or location are available on a cost recovery basis. Number of Agents: 27,000.

Kentucky
Department of Insurance, PO Box 517, Frankfort, KY 40602/(502) 564-3630. Insurance Companies Documents on File: (502) 564-6081 Call and then submit written request and prepayment. Documents will be copies for $1 a page. Average cost is $50 or $60. Listing of Insurance Companies: Directory available for $40. Pressure sensitive labels available for $40. Number of Insurance Companies: 1,300. Licensed Agents (502) 564-6002 List of Agents: Computer printouts are available in many formats but due to computer limitations no listing of all agents is available. The following listings are available for $5 each: ZIP Code, Company Name, and Lines of Insurance. Number of Agents: 43,000.

Louisiana
Insurance Department, PO Box 94214, Baton Rouge, LA 70804-9214/(504) 342-5900. Insurance Companies Documents on File: A written request must be submitted for all documents. All documents are available for $1 per page. Listing of Insurance Companies: Report of the Commissioners of Insurance is available at no charge. It contains name, address and telephone number of all insurance companies. Number of Insurance Companies: 1,690. Licensed Agents List of Agents: No list of agents is available. Names may be obtained by visiting the office. Number of Agents: 70,000.

Maine
Insurance Bureau Business, Occupational and Professional Regulation Department, State House Station 35, Augusta, ME 04333/(207) 289-3101. Insurance Companies Documents on File: Documents will be copied as staffing permits on a cost recovery basis. Listing of Insurance Companies: (207) 289-2217 Written request required. Computer printout available on a cost recovery basis. Printouts can be sorted by ZIP code, alphabetical, county, or type of insurance. Pressure sensitive labels available for 4 cents a name. Number of Insurance Companies: 700. Licensed Agents List of Agents: (207) 289-2217 Computer printout available on a cost recovery basis. Pressure sensitive labels available for 4 cents a name. Number of Agents: 8,000.

Maryland
Insurance Division, Licensing and Regulation Department, 501 St. Paul PL. Baltimore, MD 21202/(301) 333-6300. Insurance Companies Documents on File: Available for $1 per page. Listing of Insurance Companies: Annual Directory available for $1.50. Number of Insurance Companies: 1,600. LICENSED AGENTS (301) 333-4039 List of Agents: No listing available. Number of Agents: 65,000-70,000.

Massachusetts
Insurance Division, Consumer Affairs and Business Regulations Executive Office, 100 Cambridge St 18th Fl, Boston, MA 02202/(617) 727-5503. Insurance Companies Documents on File: Copies of documents may be obtained on a cost recovery basis. Listing of Insurance Companies: Computer printout available for 40 cents a page. Number of Insurance Companies: 900. Licensed Agents (617) 727-3536 List of Agents: Available 1989. Number of Agents: 45,000.

Michigan
Insurance Bureau, Licensing and Regulations Department, PO Box 30220, Lansing, MI 48909/(517) 373-9273. Insurance Companies Documents on File: Office will copy up to 14 pages free, over 15 pages documents are copies on a cost recovery basis. Listing of Insurance Companies: Computer printouts available for 20 cents per page. Number of Insurance Companies: 110. Licensed Agents List of Agents: Computer printout available for 20 cents per page. Average cost is $90. Number of Agents: 65,000.

Minnesota
Insurance Division, Minnesota Department of Commerce, 500 Metro Square Building, St. Paul, MN 55101/(612) 296-4026. Insurance Companies Documents on File: Copies available for 50 cents per page. Listing of Insurance Companies: State Document Division, 117 University Avenue, St. Paul, MN 55155/(612) 297-3000. Photocopied listing available for $17.70 plus tax and handling cost. Mailing list office, Debbie Sabota (612) 297-2552. Number of Insurance Companies: 1,500. Licensed Agents List of Agents: Contact Mailing List Office listed above. Number of Agents: 38,000-40,000.

Mississippi
Insurance Department, PO Box 79, Jackson, MS 29205/(601) 359-3576. Insurance Company Documents on File: Copies of documents available on a cost recovery basis if staffing permits. Listing of Insurance Companies: Computer printout available for $300. Pressure sensitive labels available for $360. Cheshire labels available for $300. Number of Insurance Companies: 1,673. Licensed Agents List of Agents: Available from the Mississippi Association of Life Underwriters, P.O.Box13649, Jacksonville, MS 39236/(601) 981-1522. Labels, printouts or tapes available for $600. Number of Agents: 20,000.

Missouri
Insurance Division; Regulatory Agencies, PO Box 690, Jefferson City, MO 65102/(314) 751-2562. Insurance Companies Documents on File: A Book of documents available for $5. Listing of Insurance Companies: Computer printout and pressure sensitive labels available on a cost recovery basis. Number of

Information on People, Companies, and Mailing Lists

Insurance Companies: 1,200. Licensed Agents List of Agents: Computer printout and pressure sensitive labels available on a cost recovery basis. Number of Agents: 64,000.

Montana

Insurance Commissioner, PO Box 4009, Helena, MT 59604-4009/(406) 444-2040. Insurance Companies Documents on File: Documents can be copies for 50 cents per pages as staffing permits. Listing of Insurance Companies: Computer printout available for $6.25 plus postage. Number of Insurance Companies: 1,300. Licensed Agents List of Agents: No listing available. Names may be viewed by visiting the office. Number of Agents: 8,310.

Nebraska

Insurance Department, PO Box 94699, Lincoln, NE 68509/(402) 471-2201. Insurance Companies Documents on File: Available for 50 cents per page. Listing of Insurance Companies: Computer printouts, pressure sensitive labels, or magnetic tape can be obtained for $50. Computerized information can be sorted by ZIP code, alphabetical, or by line of insurance. Summary of Insurance Business is available annually for $10. It lists amount of premiums each company collects and the volume of business. Licensed Agents List of Agents: Computer printouts, pressure sensitive labels or magnetic tape are available for $100. Computerized information can be sorted by ZIP code, alphabetical, or by line of insurance. Number of Agents: 13,000.

Nevada

Insurance Division, Commerce Department, Capitol Complex, Carson City, NV 89710/(702) 885-4270. Insurance Companies Documents on File: Available for 50 cents per page. Listing of Insurance Companies: Computer printouts, cheshire and pressure sensitive labels and diskettes available on a cost recovery basis. Computerized information can be sorted by ZIP code, alphabetical, or city. Number of Insurance Companies: 1,380. Licensed Agents List of Agents: Same as for insurance companies. Number of Agents: 17,000.

New Hampshire

Insurance Department, 169 Manchester St., Concord, NH 03301/(603) 271-2261. Insurance Companies Documents on File: Documents may be viewed by visiting the above office. List of Insurance Companies: A printout titled Licensed Companies is available on a cost recovery basis. Number of Insurance Companies: 780. Licensed Agents List of Agents: Computer printout available for $100. Number of Agents: 3,500.

New Jersey

Insurance Department, 201 E. State St, CN 325, Trenton, NJ 08625/(609) 292-5371. Insurance Company Documents on File: Available for $1.50 a page. Listing of Insurance Company: Commissioners Annual Report contains a listing of insurance companies. Number of Insurance Companies: 1,065 Licensed Agents List of Agents: (609) 987-2046 List is available on a cost recovery basis. Number of Agents: Not available.

New Mexico

Insurance Division, Corporation Commission, PO Drawer 1269, Santa Fe, NM 87504-1269/(505) 827-4542. Insurance Companies Documents on File: Documents will be copied on a cost recovery basis. Listing of Insurance Companies: Directory of Insurance Companies available free of charge. Number of Insurance Companies: 1,500. Licensed Agents List of Agents: Computer printout available for $400. Pressure sensitive labels available for $200. Number of Agents: 12,000.

New York

Insurance Department, Empire State Plaza, Building 1, Albany, NY 12257/(518) 474-6615. Insurance Companies Documents on File: Available for 50 cents per page. Listing of Insurance Companies: (518) 474-4557 Directory of Licensed Insurance Companies available for $1.00. Number of Insurance Companies: 1,000. Licensed Agents List of Agents: Lists are not available for commercial purposes. Number of Agents: 120,000.

North Carolina

Insurance Department, Box 26387, 430 N. Salisbury St., Raleigh, NC 27611/(919) 733-7343. Insurance Companies Documents on File: Available for 50 cents per page. Average cost is $40-$50. Listing of Insurance Companies: Computer printout is available for $5.00. Number of Insurance Companies: 1,100. Licensed Agents (919) 733-7487 List of Agents: Available for $135.00 for the first 5,000 names, for every additional 1,000 the cost is $5.00. Lists may be sorted by company, line of insurance, resident or nonresident, and ZIP. Number of Agents: 26,267.

North Dakota

Insurance Department, Capitol Building, 5th Floor, Bismark, ND 58505/(701) 224-2440. Insurance Companies Documents on File: Available for 20 cents per page. Listing of Insurance Companies: Computer printout is available for $16.80. Pressure sensitive labels are available for $100.00. Number of Insurance Companies: 1,300. Licensed Agents List of Agents: Pressure sensitive labels and computer printout are available for $20 plus 2 cents a name. List may be sorted by resident or nonresident and line of insurance. Number of Agents: 10,000.

Ohio

Insurance Department, 2100 Stella Court, Columbus, OH 43266-0566/(614) 481-5735. Insurance Companies : Documents on File: Available for 50 cents per page. Listing of Insurance Companies: Authorized list of Insurance Companies is available free of charge. This list contains names only. Computer printouts, pressure sensitive labels and magnetic tape are available on a cost recovery basis. Lists can be sorted by types of insurance, foreign or domestic, ZIP Code, and city. All requests must be submitted in writing. Licensed Agents List of Agents: Computer printout and pressure sensitive labels are available on a cost recovery basis. Number of Agents: 54,000.

Oklahoma

Insurance Department, 408 Will Rogers Building, Oklahoma City, OK 73105/(405) 521-2828. Insurance Companies Documents on File: Contact Gary Woodard (405) 521-3966. Listing of Insurance Companies: (405) 521-4164 Annual Report and Directory is available for $10. Computer printouts and pressure sensitive labels available on a cost recovery basis. Magnetic tape available for $25 plus 1 cent per record. Lists may be sorted by line of insurance or ZIP code. Licensed Agents List of Agents: Computer printouts and pressure sensitive labels available on a cost recovery basis. Number of Agents: 30,000.

Oregon

Insurance Division, Commerce Department, 158 12th Street NE, Salem, OR 97310/(503) 378-4271. Insurance Companies Documents on File: Available for 50 cents per page. Listing of Insurance Companies: Directory available for $2.50. Number of Insurance Companies: 1,432. Licensed Agents List of Agents: Computer printout is available for $25.00. Pressure sensitive labels are available for $50.00. Number of Agents: 19,000.

Pennsylvania

Insurance Department, 1311 Strawberry Square, Harrisburg, PA 17105/(917) 787-2735. Insurance Companeis Documents on File: Available for 25 cents per page. Listing of Insurance Companies: Listing is available for $20.00. Number of Insurance Companies: 1,400. Licensed Agents List of Agents: (717) 787-3840 Complete listing available for 2,500. List is available by line of insurance or alphabetically. Number of Agents: 150,000.

Rhode Island

Insurance Division, Business Regulations Department, 100 North Main Street, Providence, RI 02903/(401) 277-2223. Insurance Companies Documents on File: Available for 20 cents per page. Average cost is $32. Listing of Insurance Companies: Annual Report is available for $15. It contains names and addresses of all insurance companies. Number of Insurance Companies: 900. Licensed Agents : List of Agents: Available on a cost recovery basis. Number of Agents: 25,000.

South Carolina

Insurance Department, P.O. Box 100, Columbia, SC 29202-3105/(803) 737-6160. Insurance Companies Documents on File: Available by written request for $25.00. Listing of Insurance Companies: Master list of all licensed companies is available for $5. Pressure sensitive labels are available on a cost recovery label. Number of Insurance Companies: 1,260. Licensed Agents (803) 737-6095 List of Agents: Listing available for 3 cents per name. Pressure sensitive labels are available for 6 cents per label. Number of Agents: 40,000.

South Carolina

Insurance Division, Commerce and Regulations Department, 500 East Capitol, Pierre, SD 57501/(605) 773-3563. Insurance Companies Documents on File: Available for 75 cents per page. Listing of Insurance Companies: Computer printout and pressure sensitive labels are available for $25. Number of Insurance Companies: 1,200. Licensed Agents List of Agents: Computer printouts are available for $200. Pressure sensitive labels are available for $250. Number of Agents: 11,000.

Tennessee

Commerce and Insurance Department, 1808 West End Building, Nashville, TN 37219/(615) 741-1692. Insurance Companies Documents on File: All documents may be viewed in the office. Listing of Insurance Companies: Quarterly listing of companies available for free. The listing contains addresses, type of insurance, and ZIP code. Number of Insurance Companies: 1,439. Licensed Agents List of Agents: List may be copied in the office. Number of Agents: 65,000.

Texas

Insurance Board, 1110 San Jacinto, Austin, TX 78701-1998/(512) 463-6425. Insurance Companies Documents on File: Available for 50 cents per page. Listing of Insurance Companies: Company Book contains address, phone number, assets, and liabilities. It is available for $10.73. Licensed Agents List of Agents: Not available. Number of Agents: 100,000.

Utah

Insurance Department, P.O. Box 45803, Salt Lake City, UT 84145/(801) 530-6403 Insurance Companies Documents on File: Available for 25 cents per page. Listing of Insurance Companies: Computer printouts are available for $1.00 a sheet. Average cost is $50. Pressure sensitive labels are available for $10 per page. Average cost is $140. Number of Insurance Companies: 1,450. Licensed Agents List of Agents: Pressure sensitive labels are available for $350. Number of Agents: 16,500.

Vermont

Department of Banking and Insurance, 120 State Street, Montpelier, VT 05602/(802) 828-3301. Insurance Companies Documents on File: Documents may be viewed in the office. Listing of Insurance Companies: Available free of charge. Number of Insurance Companies: 1,000. Licensed Agents List of Agents: Computer printouts, mailing labels and magnetic tape available on a cost recovery basis. Number of Agents: 7,200.

Virginia

Insurance Bureau, State Corporation Commission, 1220 Bank Street, P.O. Box 1197, Richmond, VA 23219/(804) 786-3741. Insurance Companies Documents on File: Available for $1 per page. Listing of Insurance Companies: Available free of charge. Number of Insurance Companies: 1,300. Licensed Agents List of Agents: Available by company. Each list is $5. Number of Agents: Not available.

Washington

Insurance Commissioner, Insurance Building, MSAQ-21, Olympia, WA 98504/(206) 753-2418. Insurance Companies Documents on File: Documents available for $20. Listing of Insurance Companies: Available on a cost recovery basis. Number of Insurance Companies: 1,300. Licensed Agents List of Agents: No list available. The state law forbids the use of names for commercial purposes. Number of Agents: 25,000.

West Virginia

Insurance Department, 2100 Washington St East, Charleston, WV 25305/(304) 348-2100. Insurance Companies Documents on File: Available for 50 cents per page. Listing of Insurance Companies: Commissioners Annual Report contains names and addresses. It is available for $10.00. Number of Insurance Companies: 1,000. Licensed Agents (304) 348-3386 List of Agents: Written request required. Computer printout available for $60.00. Pressure sensitive labels available for $60.00. Number of Agents: 20,000.

Wisconsin

Insurance Commission, P.O. Box 7573, Madison, WI 53707-7873/(608) 267-9456. Insurance Companies Documents on File: Available for 20 cents per page. Listing of Insurance Companies: Computer printout available for $50.00. Listing can be searched by ZIP code, county, line of insurance, company, and resident or nonresident. Licensed Agents (608) 266-8699 List of Agents: Available for $50.00. It can be searched by ZIP code, county, line of insurance, company and resident or nonresident. Number of Agents: 50,000.

Wyoming

Insurance Department, 122 West 25th Street, Cheyenne, WY 82002- 0440/(307) 777-7401. Insurance Companies Documents on File: Available for $1.00 per page plus postage. Average cost $100. Listing of Insurance Companies: Computer printouts available for $50.00. Number of Insurance Companies: 970. Licensed Agents (307) 777-7319 List of Agents: Computer printout is available for $50.00. Number of Agents: 3,100.

Information on People, Companies, and Mailing Lists

Federal Mailing Lists

Listed below are a number of mailing lists available from the federal government. This does not represent all available mailing lists but only the more popular ones. Remember that anywhere the government collects names and addresses, that information theoretically is available to the public. Keep this in mind as you review the other chapters in this book.

At the end of each description below is a vendor code. The complete name and address for vender codes are at the end of the mailing list descriptions.

Abstract Newsletter Subscribers
Contains 14,000 subscribers to the National Technical Information service newsletter service which covers the most recent research findings in 26 areas of industrial, technological, and sociological interest. Format: Off-line; Price: $100/per thousand names; Vendor: NTIS.

Agexporter (formerly Foreign Agriculture)
A monthly magazine targeted at business firms selling United States farm products overseas. Provides timely information on overseas trade opportunities, including reports on marketing activities and how-to's of agricultural exporting. List ID: FA-2E; 460 paid subscribers; Vendor: GPO.

Airman's Information Manual
Subscription provides the fundamentals required in order to fly in the United States National Airspace System. It also contains items of interest to pilots concerning health and medical facts, factors affecting flight safety, a pilot/controller glossary of terms used in the Air Traffic Control System, and information on safety, accident and hazard reporting. List ID: BFAP-2D; 9,134 paid subscribers; Vendor: GPO.

Alcohol Health and Research World
Presents current research findings; prevention, treatment, and training program descriptions; and observations with opinions from those working at the base level to provide services to persons affected by alcohol-related problems. List ID: AHRW-2Q; 5,932 paid subscribers; Vendor: GPO.

Area Wage Survey
These bulletins report on earnings in 70 major metropolitan areas for occupations common to a wide variety of establishments, including office clerical, professional and technical, maintenance, custodial, and material movement occupations. List ID: AWS-2B; 327 paid subscribers; Vendor: GPO.

Business America, The Magazine of International Trade
A biweekly publication designed to help American exporters penetrate overseas markets by providing them with timely information on opportunities for trade and methods of doing business in foreign countries. List ID: CRTD-2E; 4,632 paid subscribers; Vendor: GPO.

Branch Office Deposits
The Office of Thrift Supervision contains street addresses for home offices and branch offices of 3,196 FSLIC insured institutions. Zip codes are not included. Format: Tape; Price: $150; Vendor: FHLBB.

Business Conditions Digest
Prepared in the Statistical Indicators Division of the Bureau of Economic Analysis, the Digest presents almost 500 economic indicators in a form convenient for analysis with different approaches to the study of current business conditions and prospects (e.g., the national income model, the leading indicators, and anticipations and intentions), as well as for analysts who use combinations of these approaches. List ID: BCD-2G; 4,123 paid subscribers; Vendor: GPO.

Cancergrams
Current awareness bulletins in numerous cancer-related subject areas; Vendor : GPO.

Catalog of Federal Domestic Assistance
A Government-wide summary of financial and nonfinancial Federal programs, projects, services, and activities that provide assistance or benefits to the American public administered by departments and establishments of the Federal Government. Describes the type of assistance available and the eligibility requirements for the particular assistance being sought, with guidance on how to apply. Also intended to improve coordination and communication between the Federal Government and State and local governments. List ID: COF89-1X; 4,456 paid subscribers; Vendor: GPO.

Census and You (formerly Data User News)
A monthly newsletter for users of Census Bureau statistics, which gives up-to-date information on Bureau programs, products and services and the latest news about demographic and economic data. List ID: DUN-2G; 2,941 paid subscribers; Vendor: GPO.

Census and You Mailing List (formerly Data User News)
Listing of the 394 free subscribers to the "Data User News", which contains news highlights of current products available from the U.S. Bureau of the Census. Format: Tape; Price: $10; Vendor: CENSUS.

Children Today
Reports on Federal, State, and local services for children, child development, health and welfare laws, and other news pertinent to child welfare in the United States. List ID: CT-2S; 5,201 paid subscribers; Vendor: GPO.

Commerce Business Daily: Synopsis of United States Government Proposed Procurement, Sales, and Contract Awards
The Synopsis is of particular value to firms interested in bidding on U.S. Government purchases, surplus property offered for sale, or in seeking subcontract opportunities from prime contractors. It lists current information received daily from military and civilian procurement offices. List ID: COBD-2P; 42,106 paid subscribers; Vendor: GPO.

Commercial Info Management (CIMS)
CIMS is a decentralized database of the U.S. Dept. of Commerce that matches subscribing U.S. firms with foreign companies and governments interested in purchasing U.S. goods and services. Information connecting buyers and sellers is transmitted via telecommunications between U.S. posts in foreign counties and District Offices in the U.S. District Offices maintain data on the size, products and export capabilities of companies in their area. Format: Off-line; Price: $500 for entire list; Vendor: COMMERCE.

Committee on Scientific & Technical Information
List of individuals who have requested copies of the index by 22 major categories of National Technical Information Service reports that were developed and endorsed by the Committee on Scientific and Technical Information. Format: Off-line; Price: $100/per thousand; Vendor: NTIS.

Congressional Record
A verbatim report on Congressional debates and other proceedings. List ID: CR-3A; 1,698 paid subscribers. List ID: CRM-3A (Microfiche); 70 paid subscribers; Vendor: GPO.

Consumer Directory - Catalog
CERN-II is a directory of more than 2,000 organizations involved in consumer education or protection. Groups listed range from government agencies to university programs at the national, state, or local level. Retrieval information

includes: address, phone number, contact person, type of organization (25 categories), staff size, funding, subject areas covered, etc. Format: Off-line; Price : Free; Vendor: GSA-CIC.

Cumulative List of Organizations

Lists contributions of organizations which are deductible under Section 170(c) of the Internal Revenue Code of 1954. List ID: CL-1L; 5,075 paid subscribers; Vendor: GPO.

Current Housing Reports

H-111. Housing Vacancies. Quarterly reports and an annual issue which give percent distributions of rental vacancies and homeowner vacancies, by facilities, number of rooms, monthly rent asked and sales price asked, etc., compared with same quarter of previous year.
H-121. Housing characteristics. Occasional reports of data for the country as a whole and for regions on selected characteristics of housing. List ID: CHR-2Q; 211 paid subscribers; Vendor: GPO.

Current Wage Development

Presents wage and benefit changes that result from collective bargaining settlements and unilateral management decisions. Also includes statistical summaries and special reports on wage trends. List ID: CWD-2M; 650 paid subscribers; Vendor :GPO.

Customs Bulletin and Decisions

Contains regulations, rulings, decisions, and notices concerning Customs and related matters of the United States Court of Appeals for the Federal Circuit and the United States Court of International Trade. List ID: CB-2E; 1,041 paid subscribers; Vendor: GPO.

Customs Regulations of the United States

Contains regulations made and published for the purpose of carrying out customs laws administered by the United States Customs Service. List ID: CRUS-1F; 3,710 paid subscribers; Vendor: GPO.

DOD FAR Supplement

This Department of Defense supplement to the Federal Acquisition Regulation contains guidelines on the provisions, clauses, and cost principles authorized for DOD contracts, as well as the procedures and actions necessary for awarding and administering the contracts. List ID: DFARS-1A; 4,806 paid subscribers; Vendor: GPO.

Domestic Mail Manual

Designed to assist Postal Service customers in obtaining maximum benefits from domestic postal services. It includes applicable regulations and information about rates and postage, classes of mail, special services, wrapping and mailing requirements, and collection and delivery services. List ID: DOM-2S; 8,631 paid subscribers; Vendor: GPO.

Economic Indicators

Gives pertinent economic information on prices, wages, production, business activity, purchasing power, credit, money and Federal finance. List ID: ECIN-2G; 4,766 paid subscribers; Vendor: GPO.

Education Statistics Mailing List

Contains over 5,000 individuals who have requested material from the National Center for Education Statistics. Format: Tape; Price: See Vendor; Vendor: NCES.

EIA Publication New Releases (DOE-EIA-0204)

Contains 14 categories of users of U.S. Energy Department's Energy Information Administration publications with approximately 13,000 names. Format: Off-line; Price: Cost Recovery; Vendor: EIA.

Employment and Earnings

Current data on employment, hours, and earnings for the United States as a whole, for States, and for more than 200 local areas. List ID: EMEA-2M; 3,485 paid subscribers; Vendor: GPO.

Export Administration Regulations

Subscription service consists of a compilation of official regulations and policies governing the export licensing of commodities and technical data. List ID: EAR88-1A; 8,385 paid subscribers; Vendor: GPO.

FAA Aviation News

Designed to help airmen become safer pilots, this publication gives updates and major Federal Aviation Administration rule changes and proposed Changes, as well as refresher information on flight rules, maintenance airworthiness, avionics, accident analysis, and other related topics. Covers all types of aircraft, including helicopters, balloons, gliders, antique, sport and experimental. List ID: FAN-2D; 15,032 paid subscribers; Vendor: GPO.

FDA Consumer

Covers information written especially for consumers about Food and Drug Administration regulatory and scientific decisions, and about the safe use of products regulated by FDA. List ID: FDAP-2G; 23,942 paid subscribers; Vendor: GPO.

Federal Acquisition Regulations

The Federal Acquisition Regulation (FAR) is the primary regulation used by Federal Executive Branch agencies purchasing supplies and services. List ID: FEACR-1A; 13,757 paid subscribers; Vendor: GPO.

The Federal Labor-Management and Employee Relations Consultant

Presents current information in the field of labor-management and employee relations. List ID: FLMC-2G; 365 paid subscribers; Vendor: GPO.

Federal Procurement Data Center

This database contains two million records pertaining to federal procurement actions from 1979 to present. Information is on contracts totaling $25,000 or more and also includes the purchasing or contracting office, date of award, principal place of performance and dollars obligated. Format: Tape, hard copy, gummed labels, microfiche; Price: variable; Vendor: FPDC.

Federal Register

Provides a uniform system for making available to the public regulations and legal notices issued by Federal agencies. These include Presidential proclamations and Executive orders and Federal agency documents having general applicability and legal effect, documents required to be published by Act of Congress and other Federal agency documents of public interest.
List ID: FR-3A; 17,085 paid subscribers; Vendor: GPO.
List ID: MFFR-3A Microfiche; 1,129 paid subscribers.

Federal Trainer

Contains news and features pertaining to programs for training Federal employees. List ID: FEDT-2Q; 164 paid subscribers; Vendor: GPO.

Fishery Bulletin

Publishes original research papers, and occasionally, reviews of topical interest, in the broad discipline of fishery science. Research fields of particular interest are ecology, oceanography, and limnology; mariculture; ocean pollution; physiology, behavior and taxonomy of marine organisms, particularly fishes; technology; gear development; and economics. List ID: FB-2D; 214 paid subscribers; Vendor: GPO.

Foreign Economic Trends and Their Implications for the United States

Includes key economic indicators, a brief summary of the state of the economy of the subject country, the current situation and economic trends, industrial report, agricultural report, foreign trade situation, living costs, monetary situation, and conclusions and implications for the United States. List ID: ECTR-2B; 845 paid subscribers; Vendor: GPO.

Foreign Traders Index (FTI)

A directory of manufacturers, service organizations, agent representatives, retailers, wholesalers, distributors and cooperatives in 130 countries outside the U.S. Data are maintained by the International Trade Administration at the U.S. Department of Commerce. It provides the nature of business, name of officers, size, employees and establishment date. FTI is restricted to U.S. use. It is current for 5 years and is updated quarterly. Format: Tape, hard copy, gummed labels; Price: Varies, 25 cents/per name; Vendor: ITA.

Foreign Trade Reports FT990

Highlights of United States export and import trade. List ID: FT990-2M; 380 paid subscribers; Vendor: GPO.

Information on People, Companies, and Mailing Lists

FSS Agency Rehabilitation
The General Services Administration sells this mailing list which totals some 1,000 addresses. Format: Tape; Price: $50/per reel; Vendor: GSA-MLIC.

FSS Excess Property
The General Services Administration sells this mailing list which totals some 2,000 addresses. Format: Tape; Price: $50/per reel; Vendor: GSA-MLIC.

FSS Publications
The General Services Administration sells this mailing list which totals 47,000 addresses. Format: Tape; Price: $50/per reel; Vendor: GSA-MLIC.

FSS Procurement Bidders
The General Services Administration sells this mailing list which totals some 47,000 addresses. Format: Tape; Price: $50/per reel; Vendor: GSA-MLIC.

FSS Property Rehabilitation
The General Services Administration sells this mailing list which totals some 1,000 addresses. Format: Tape; Price: $50/per reel; Vendor: GSA-MLIC.

FSS Surplus Personal Property Zone (Regions 4 & 5)
Some 24,000 addresses comprise this General Services Administration mailing list. Surplus property auctioned by the federal government consists of hand and machine tools, office machines and supplies, furniture, hardware, motor vehicles, confiscated boats, airplanes and construction equipment. Format: Tape; Price: $50/per reel; Vendor: GSA-MLIC.

FSS Surplus Personal Property Zone (Regions 6 & 7)
Some 9,000 addresses comprise this General Services Administration mailing list. Surplus property auctioned by the federal government consists of hand and machine tools, office machines and supplies, furniture, hardware, motor vehicles, confiscated boats, airplanes and construction equipment. Format: Tape; Price: $50/per reel; Vendor: GSA-MLIC.

FSS Surplus Personal Property Zone (Regions 8 - 10)
Some 38,000 addresses comprise this General Services Administration mailing list. Surplus property auctioned by the federal government consists of hand and machine tools, office machines and supplies, furniture, hardware, motor vehicles, confiscated boats, airplanes and construction equipment. Format: Tape; Price: $50/per reel; Vendor: GSA-MLIC.

FSS Surplus Personal Property Defaulted Bidders
Some 4,000 addresses comprise this General Services Administration mailing list. Surplus property auctioned by the federal government consists of hand and machine tools, office machines and supplies, furniture, hardware, motor vehicles, confiscated boats, airplanes and construction equipment. Format: Tape; Price: $50/per reel; Vendor: GSA-MLIC.

FSS Surplus Personal Property Zone (Regions 1, 2, 3)
Some 19,000 addresses comprise this General Services Administration mailing list. Surplus property auctioned by the federal government consists of hand and machine tools, office machines and supplies, furniture, hardware, motor vehicles, confiscated boats, airplanes and construction equipment. Format: Tape; Price: $50/per reel; Vendor: GSA-MLIC.

Futures All Firm Directory
The National Future Association directory contains an alphabetical listing of the four categories of futures traders: Commodity Trading Advisors, Commodity Pool Operators, Futures Commission Merchants, and Introducing Brokers. Addresses and phone numbers are included. Format: Off-line; Price: $10-$25; Vendor: NFA.

Government Unit Name and Address File
Contains names, addresses, and geographic codes of local governments in the census for the years ending in 2 and 7. Format: Tape; Price: $140/per reel; Vendor: CENSUS 2.

GPO Sales Publications Reference File
A guide to current publications offered for sale by the Superintendent of Documents arranged by GPO stock numbers; Superintendent of Documents classification numbers; and alphabetically by subjects, titles, agency series and report numbers, key words and phrases, and personal authors. List ID: PRF-2N; 441 paid subscribers; Vendor : GPO.

GSA Rocky Mountain Bulletin
The General Services Administration sells this mailing list which totals some 3,000 addresses. Format: Tape; Price: $50/per reel; Vendor: GSA-MLIC.

GSA Training (Classes)
The General Services Administration sells this mailing list which totals some 26,000 names and addresses. Format: Tape; Price: $50/per reel; Vendor: GSA-MLIC.

Harmonized Tariff Schedules of the U.S. Annotated
For use in classifying imported merchandise for rate of duty and statistical purposes. List ID: TSA88-1A; 9,673 paid subscribers; Vendor: GPO.

Humanities
Published by the National Endowment for the Humanities, this publication describes the NEH program, projects, and issues in the humanities. Gives recent grants, deadlines, and useful information for applicants seeking funds. List ID: NR-2N; 3,671 paid subscribers; Vendor: GPO.

ICC Interstate Carrier Listing
Provides names, addresses, phone number, and motor carrier number of 51,000 active motor carriers. Types of carriers included in file are: railroads, trucking co., bus lines, freight forwarders, water carriers, property brokers, rate bureaus, and private carriers. Format: Tape $45, Hard copy $100; Price: Cost recovery; Vendor: ICC.

ICD-9-CM International Classification of Diseases, 9th Revision, Clinical Modification, 3rd Edition:
Volumes 1 and 2; 47,684 paid subscribers; List ID: ICDP-1C.
Volume 3, Procedures Tabular List and Alphabetic Index; 108 paid subscribers; List ID: ICDH-1C.

Internal Revenue Bulletin
Announces official Internal Revenue Service rulings, Treasury Decisions, Executive Orders, legislation, and court decisions pertaining to internal revenue matters. List ID: IRB-2E; 5,027 paid subscribers; Vendor: GPO.

International Flight Information Manual
Primarily designed as a preflight and planning guide for use by United States non-scheduled operators, business and private aviators contemplating flights outside of the United States. List ID: IFM89-1F; 1,016 paid subscribers; Vendor: GPO.

International Mail Manual
List ID: IMM-2S; 4,603 paid subscribers; Vendor: GPO.

Journal of the National Cancer Institute
An up-to-the-minute, reliable and comprehensive source of critical news and information on the latest developments in cancer research and treatment, including: prevention, clinical trials, immunology, molecular and tumor cell biology, biochemistry, carcinogenesis, epidemiology, biological response modifiers, cancer control, drug development, pharmacology, and many other fields. List ID: JNCI-2E; 2,232 paid subscribers; Vendor: GPO.

Lists of Parties Excluded from Federal Procurement or Nonprocurement Programs
List ID: CLDSC-2M; 959 paid subscribers; Vendor: GPO.

Management
Focuses attention on important developments in the Office of Personnel Management. List ID: CSJ-2Q; 1,793 paid subscribers; Vendor: GPO.

Manual on Uniform Traffic Control Devices for Streets and Highways
This manual provides detailed uniform standards for all signs, markings and devices placed on, over, or adjacent to a street or highway. Included are general specifications of sizes, shapes and colors, as well as sections on guide signs,

pavement markings, traffic control signals, and islands. List ID: N-523-2A; 6,415 paid subscribers; Vendor: GPO.

Marine Fisheries Review

A review of developments and news of the fishery industries prepared in the National Marine Fisheries Service, United States Department of Commerce. List ID: MFR-2M; 177 paid subscribers; Vendor: GPO.

Master Cross Reference List

Part I, Logistics Reference No. to NSN; 379 paid subscribers; List ID: MCR01-2Q

Part II, NIIN to Logistics Reference No.; 463 paid subscribers; List ID: MCR02-2Q

Part III, FSCM and Logistics Reference to NSN; 212 paid subscribers; List ID: MCR03-2Q; Vendor: GPO

Monthly Catalog of United States Government Publications

Lists the publications printed and processed during each month. It includes the publications sold by the Superintendent of Documents, those for official use, and those sent to Depository Libraries. List ID: MC89-1F; 1,242 paid subscribers; Vendor: GPO.

Monthly Energy Review

Illustrates current and historical statistics on United States production, storage, imports and consumption of petroleum, natural gas, and coal. List ID: MER-2B; 1,273 paid subscribers; Vendor: GPO.

Monthly Labor Review

Includes articles on labor force, wages, prices, productivity, economic growth, and occupational injuries and illnesses. Regular features include a review of developments in industrial relations, book reviews, and current labor statistics. List ID: MLR-2D; 6,976 paid subscribers; Vendor: GPO.

National Library of Medicine Audiovisuals Catalog

List ID: MAC89-1S; 251 paid subscribers; Vendor: GPO.

Nuclear Safety

Through this periodical the Energy Department provides concise and authoritative evaluation of scientific and technological developments relating to nuclear safety as they emerge from atomic research and development programs. List ID: NS-2N; 535 paid subscribers; Vendor: GPO.

Occupational Outlook Quarterly

A periodical to help young people, employment planners, and guidance counselors keep abreast of current occupational and employment developments. List ID: OOQ-2R; 22,730 paid subscribers; Vendor: GPO.

OSHA Standards and Regulations

Volume I, General Industry Standards and Interpretations; 5,056 paid subscribers; List ID: OSH01-1A

Volume II, Maritime Standards; 1,380 paid subscribers; List ID: OSH02-1A;

Volume III, Construction Industry Standards and Interpretations; 4,579 paid subscribers; List ID: OSH03-1A

Volume IV, Other Regulations and Procedures; 1,631 paid subscribers; List ID: OSH04-1A

Volume V, Field Operations Manual; 1,029 paid subscribers; List ID: OSH05-1A

Volume VI, Industrial Hygiene Technical Manual; 1,102 paid subscribers; List ID: OSH06-1A; Vendor: GPO

Official Gazette of the United States Patent and Trademark Office: Patents

Contains the patents, Patent Office notices, and designs issued each week. List ID: OG-2D; 2,313 paid subscribers; Vendor: GPO.

Official Gazette of the United States Patent and Trademark Office: Trademarks

Contains Trademarks, Trademark Notices, Marks Published for Opposition, Trademark Registrations Issued, and Index of Registrants. List ID: OGT-2D; 1,565 paid subscribers; Vendor: GPO.

Official Summary of Security Transactions and Holdings

Made up of securities holdings figures showing owners, relationships to issues, amounts of securities bought or sold by each owner, their individual holdings at the end of the reported month, and types of securities. List ID: OSST-2G; 916 paid subscribers; Vendor: GPO.

Postal Bulletin

Contains current orders, instructions and information relating to the United States Postal Service, and Commemorative Stamp Posters. List ID: POB-2E; 3,062 paid subscribers; Vendor: GPO.

Resources in Education

List ID: RIE-2M; 933 paid subscribers; Vendor: GPO.

Schedule B: Statistical Classification of Domestic and Foreign Commodities Exported from the United States

Contains approximately 40,007 digit commodity classifications, based on the organization framework of the Tariff Schedules of the United States, Annotated, to be used by shippers in reporting export shipments from the United States and for use in compiling official statistics on exports of merchandise from the United States. List ID: SCHB-1A; 28,436 paid subscribers; Vendor: GPO.

Schizophrenia Bulletin

Facilitates the dissemination and exchange of information about schizophrenia and provides abstracts of the recent literature on the subject. List ID: SB-2Q; 2,160 paid subscribers; Vendor: GPO.

SEC Monthly Statistical Review

Includes statistical summaries of new securities, securities sales, common stock prices, stock transactions, and other phases of securities exchange. List ID: STBU-2M; 375 paid subscribers; Vendor: GPO.

Survey of Current Business

Gives information on trends in industry, the business situation, outlook, and other points pertinent to the business world. List ID: SCUB-2D; 7.031 paid subscribers; Vendor: GPO.

Vendor List

The following is an alphabetical listing of government agencies according to their vendor symbols noted above.

CENSUS

Customer Service, Census Bureau
Data Services Division
Washington, DC 20233
(202) 763-4100

COMMERCE

Department of Commerce
World Traders Data Reports Section
14th St. & Constitution Ave., NW
Washington, DC 20230
(202) 377-3181

EIA

Energy Information Administration
Freedom of Information Office
Department of Energy
1000 Independence Ave., SW, 1G051
Washington, DC 20462
(202) 586-5955

FPDC

Federal Procurement Data Center
4040 N. Fairfax Drive, # 900
Arlington, VA 22203
(703) 235-1326

GSA-CIC

Information on People, Companies, and Mailing Lists

Consumer Information Center
General Services Administration
Room G142/18th and F St., NW
Washington, DC 20405
(202) 566-1794

GSA-MLIC
GSA/BSC
819 Taylor St., Room 11A05
Ft. Worth, TX 76102
(817) 334-3284

GPO
Superintendent of Documents
U.S. Government Printing Office
Washington, DC 20401
Prices and Selections:
Cheshire labels: $85.00 per 1,000
 minimum list user charge of $300 per order
Pressure sensitive labels: $5.30 per 1,000
Key coding (up to 5 digits): $2.00 per 1,000
No geographic selections available. No foreign lists available.
Shipping charges: $10.00 to $15.00.

ICC
Interstate Commerce Commission
Section of System Development
12th & Constitution, NW, #1349
Washington, DC 20423
(202) 275-7682

IRS
Internal Revenue Service Headquarters
Department of the Treasury
1111 Constitution Ave., NW
Washington, DC 20224
(202) 488-3100

ITA
International Trade Administration or
District Office
U.S. Department of Commerce
Washington, DC 20230
(202) 377-8246

MINING
Mining Information Division
Mine Safety & Health Administration
P.O. Box 2537
Denver, CO 80225
(303) 236-2729

NCES
National Center for Education Statistics/
Data Systems Branch
555 New Jersey Ave., NW, #300
Washington, DC 20208
(202) 357-6651

NFA
National Future Association
200 West Madison
Chicago, IL 60606
(312) 781-1300

NTIS
National Technical Information Service
5285 Port Royal Road
Springfield, VA 22161
(703) 487-4812

OTS
Office of Thrift Supervision
1700 G St., NW
Washington, DC 20552
(202) 416-2751

Federal Auctions and Surplus Property

Looking for a bargain? Year round, the federal government offers hundreds of millions of dollars worth of property and goods--from animals to real estate--at remarkable prices. The Customs Service sells seized property--jewelry, camera, rugs--anything brought in from another country. The IRS auctions off everything imaginable--boats, cars, businesses. The U.S. Postal Service sells unclaimed merchandise, including lots of books.

There is one story to inspire: a New Yorker bought surplus parachutes from the Pentagon and became a supplier selling clothesline cord. If you are looking for a business, try the Small Business Administration, which sells equipment and businesses it has acquired through foreclosure. Want a good deal on a house? U.S. Department of Housing and Urban Development offers repossessed homes--sometimes for practically nothing--on government foreclosures.

Very few people know about these unique bargains because the federal government doesn't advertise them. Described below are 30 of Uncle Sam's Red Tag Specials. Contact the appropriate offices for more information. And remember, if you don't find what you want, stay at it. This is ongoing and new merchandise and property are coming in all the time.

* Burros and Horses: Bureau of Land Management
Office of Public Affairs
Bureau of Land Management
U.S. Department of the Interior
Room 5600, 18th & C Sts., N.W.
Washington, DC 20240 (202) 343-4724
Or contact your local Bureau of Land Management office. The "Adopt-a-Horse" program is aimed at keeping wild herds at in the West at manageable levels, and allows individuals around the country to purchase a wild horse for $125 or a burro for $75. Representatives of the BLM travel around the country, so that you don't have to travel to Wyoming to participate. The only qualifications for adoption are that you have appropriate facilities to house the animal, that you are of legal age in your state, and that you have no record of offenses against animals. The horses and burros may not be used for any exploitative purposes such as rodeos or races, nor may they be re-sold. Upon adoption, you sign an agreement to that effect, and no title of ownership is given until one year after an adoption. Animals are usually from two to six years in age, and must be trained. The offices listed above have brochures on the "Adopt-a-Horse" program with more details.

* Christmas Trees, Seedling, Wooden Poles and Posts: Bureau of Land Management
U.S. Department of the Interior
Bureau of Land Management
Forestry Division
18th & C Sts., N.W.
Washington, DC 20240 (202) 653-8864
Contact your local Bureau of Land Management (BLM), U.S. Department of Interior. In the 11 Western states, the Bureau of Land Management has a program for obtaining low-cost Christmas trees from Federal lands. By contacting your local BLM office, you may obtain a permit for a nominal fee (usually between $3 -$5) to cut a tree for your own use. You will be given a map with directions as to which are permissible areas for tree-cutting. Non-profit organizations may also qualify.

In addition, under the Minor Forest Products program, you may collect or cut specified small trees for use as poles or posts; or, you may obtain cactus or plant seedlings from areas of natural growth where there are abundant supplies-- again at a very low cost. These items are free for non-profit organizations. Permits for commercial usage may also be available.

Alaska
222 W. 7th Ave. #13, Anchorage, AK 99513-7599 (907) 271-5555.

Arizona
3007 N 7th St., P.O. Box 16563, Phoenix, AZ 85011 (602) 241-5504.

California
2800 Cottage Way, E-2841, Sacramento, CA 95825 (916) 978-4746.

Colorado
2850 Youngfield St., Lakewood, CO 80215 (303) 236-1700.

Eastern States
350 S. Pickett St., Alexandria, VA 22304 (703) 461-1369.

Idaho
3380 Americana Terrace, Boise, ID 83706 (208) 334-1771.

BIFC: Boise Interagency Fire Center, 3905 Vista Ave., Boise, ID 83705 (208) 389-2457.

Montana
222 N. 32nd St., P.O. Box 36800, Billings, MT 59107 (406) 255-2913.

Nevada
850 Harvard Way, P.O. Box 12000, Reno, NV 89520 (702) 328-6386.

New Mexico
120 Post Office and Federal Bldg., P.O. Box 1449, Santa Fe, NM 87504-1449 (505) 988-6316.

Oregon
825 N.E. Multnomah St., P.O. Box 2965, Portland, OR 97208 (503) 231-6274.

Phoenix
PTC: Phoenix Training Center, 5050 N. 19th Ave., Suite 300, Phoenix, AZ 85015 (602) 241-2651.

Utah
324 South State St., CFS Financial Center Bldg., Suite 301, Salt Lake City, UT 84111-2303 (801) 539-4021.

Wyoming
2515 Warren Ave., P.O. Box 1828, Cheyenne, WY 82003 (307) 772-2111.

* FHA Money May Be Waiting For You
DHUD-Shares
541 7th Street, SW
Washington, DC 20410 (202) 755-5616
If you or someone in your family has successfully payed off a mortgage on a house, there may be money waiting for you at the Department of Housing and Urban Development. HUD oversees the Federal Housing Administration (FHA) which insures mortgages that your bank lends to house buyers. Each year FHA

predicts how many people will default on their loans, and based on that prediction, they calibrate how much mortgage insurance home buyers will pay during that year. If it turns out that there are fewer loan defaults than FHA predicted, those borrowers that have continued to pay their mortgages have what are called "Mutual Mortgage Dividend" checks coming to them upon completion of the loan agreement.

Another way you may qualify for an FHA insurance refund is to have taken out, say, a 30 year mortgage and payed the entire FHA insurance premium up front instead of in installments over the entire period of the loan. If you have completed the loan agreement in less than 30 years, you may have money coming back to you since you didn't use the insurance for the entire 30 years you've already paid for. In most cases, though, you have to carry a loan for at least 7 years to qualify for a dividend, and the longer you have a loan, the more likely it is that you will qualify for a dividend check.

In these cases where you prepay all of your mortgage insurance premium up front, your bank should let you know that you may eventually be eligible for a mutual mortgage refund upon fulfillment of the loan agreement. Also, after you have paid off your loan, your bank should notify HUD, who in turn should notify you if you have any refund coming, usually within six months. However, if HUD cannot locate you, they will add your name to a list of other individuals who cannot be located but have HUD money coming to them.

Through the Freedom of Information Act many individuals have gotten their hands on copies of this list from HUD and gone around the country tracking down the people and charging them fees to recover this HUD money. Depending on the size of the original loan, your dividend refund could be several thousand dollars, and since some of these "bounty hunters" may ask for up to 50% of the refund just for making a phone call that you could make yourself, you could be losing out on a substantial sum of money by letting them do it.

If you feel you may have money coming to you, or if a member of your family who took out a mortgage is now deceased and you are an heir, try to locate the original loan contract number, and then make a few calls.

* Firewood: U.S. Forest Service

U.S. Forest Service
Department of Agriculture
12th & Independence Aves. S.W.
Box 96090
Washington, D.C. 20090-6090

Contact your nearest National Forest Office. In any National Forest, you may pick up downed or dead wood for firewood, after requesting a permit from the Forest of your choice. You may phone to request the permit, and must have it in your possession while collecting the wood. The Forest Service allows you to gather six cords worth of wood--equal to 12 pick-up truck loads. Wood may not be collected for commercial purposes.

Northern Region

Federal Building, 200 East Broadway St., P. O. Box 7669, Missoula, MT 59807 (406) 329-3511. Includes Idaho and Montana.

Intermountain Region

Federal Building, 324 25th St., Ogden, UT 84401 (801) 625-5354. Includes Idaho, Nevada, Utah, and Wyoming.

Southern Region

1720 Peachtree Rd. N.W., Atlanta, GA 30367 (404) 347-4191. Includes Alabama, Arkansas, Florida, Georgia, Kentucky, Louisiana, Mississippi, North Carolina, Puerto Rico and the Virgin Islands, South Carolina, Tennessee, Texas, Virginia.

Rocky Mountain Region

11177 West Eighth Ave., P.O. Box 25127, Lakewood, CO 80225 (303) 236-9431. Includes Colorado, Nebraska, South Dakota, Wyoming.

Pacific Southwest Region

630 Sansome St., San Francisco, CA 94111 (415) 556-0122. For California.

Pacific Northwest Region

319 SW Pine St., P.O. Box 3623, Portland, OR 97208 (503) 221-2877. Includes Oregon and Washington.

Southwestern Region

Federal Building, 517 Gold Ave. S.W., Albuquerque, NM 87102 (505) 842-3292.

Eastern Region

310 West Wisconsin Ave., room 500, Milwaukee, WI 53203 (414) 291-3693. Includes Illinois, Indiana, Ohio, Michigan, Minnesota, Missouri, New Hampshire,

Maine, Pennsylvania, Vermont, West Virginia, Wisconsin.

Alaskan Region

Federal Office Building, 709 West Ninth St., P.O. Box 21628, Juneau, AK 99802 (907) 586-8863.

* Homes: Department of Agriculture (USDA)

USDA, FmHA
Single Family Housing Division
14th & Independence Aves., S.W.
Washington, DC 20250   (202) 382-1474

Contact your local Farmers Home Administration Office. There are 1900 around the country. The Farmers Home Administration, part of the Department of Agriculture, makes low-interest loans available to qualified applicants to purchase homes or farms in rural areas (among other things). They are also charged with disposing of properties that are foreclosed. First, the Farm Home Administration makes any necessary repairs to the properties, then offers them for sale to people who have the same qualifications as those applying for FmHA loans. (Based on income, credit worthiness and other criteria). Eligible applicants also qualify to purchase the properties at special low FmHA interest rates (as low as 1%). If no eligible applicants purchase a property, it is then put up for sale to the general public at competitive prices. If the property is not sold within 10 days, it is reduced by 10%. Sales to the general public may be through FmHA offices or through private real estate brokers. FmHA "eligible applicants" must reside on the property purchased; but other buyers may use it for investment or rental purposes. A separate program applies for farms.

* Homes: Department of Housing and Urban Development

U.S. Department of Housing and Urban Development
451 7th St. S.W.
Washington, DC 20410-4000;

Consult your local newspapers for HUD listings; or, your regional HUD office, listed below; or, the real estate broker of your choice.

HUD's Property Disposition facilities are located within ten regional offices and various field offices around the country. Contact the nearest office for details (see listing below). Frequently, HUD will advertise upcoming auctions of foreclosed properties in a local newspaper. The properties may be apartments, condominiums, or various kinds of single- family homes. The condition of these properties varies widely, including some that are little more than shells; and that, of course, affects the price. Some may be located in less than desirable neighborhoods; but others may end up being bargains, either as investments or personal residences. Bids are placed through private real estate brokers, who then submit them to HUD. The highest bidder wins. Five per cent of the sale offer is required as earnest money and must accompany the bid. Bidders must furnish their own financing. HUD stresses that properties sell "as is," so it is up to a potential buyer to determine the value and condition, although the listings will state major problems.

Newspaper ads list houses that will be available for the next ten days, as well as others that did not sell in previous auctions. Listings include addresses, number of bedrooms and bathrooms, and suggested prices. Remember that HUD contracts are binding and non-negotiable: once your bid has won, there's no turning back.

HUD Region I (Boston)

Thomas P. O'Neill Federal Building, 10 Causeway St., Boston, MA 02222-1092. 617-565-5234. Field offices are located in: Bangor, ME; Burlington, VT; Hartford, CT; Manchester, NH; and Providence, RI. Ask for Property Distribution Division in these offices.

Region II (New York)

HUD New York Regional Office, 26 Federal Plaza, New York, NY 10278-0068. 212-264-8068. Field offices located in: Albany, NY; Buffalo, NY; Camden, NJ; Hato Rey, PR; and Newark, NJ.

Region III (Philadelphia)

HUD Philadelphia Regional Office, Liberty Square Building, 105 South Seventh St., Philadelphia, PA 19106-3392, 215-597-2560. Field offices located in: Baltimore, MD; Charleston, WV; Pittsburgh, PA; Richmond, VA; Washington, D.C.; and Wilmington, DE.

Region IV (Atlanta)

HUD Atlanta Regional Office, Richard B. Russell Building, 75 Spring St., S.W., Atlanta, GA 30303-3388, 404-331-5136. Field offices located in: Birmingham, AL; Columbia, SC; Coral Gables, FL; Greensboro, NC; Jackson, MS; Jacksonville, FL; Knoxville, TN; Louisville, KY; Memphis, TN; Nashville, TN; Orlando, FL; and Tampa, FL.

Region V (Chicago)

HUD Chicago Regional Office, 300 South Wacker Dr., Chicago, IL 60606-6765, (312) 353-5680. Also 547 West Jackson Boulevard, Chicago, IL 60606-5760, (312) 353-6236. Field offices are located in: Cincinnati, OH; Cleveland, OH; Columbus, OH; Detroit, MI; Flint, MI; Grand Rapids, MI; Indianapolis, IN; Milwaukee, WI; Minneapolis/St. Paul, MN; and Springfield, IL.

Region VI (Fort Worth)

HUD Fort Worth Regional Office, 1600 Throckmorton, P.O. Box 2905 Fort Worth, TX 76113-2905, (817) 885-5401. Field Offices are located in: Albuquerque, NM; Dallas, TX; Houston, TX; Little Rock, AR; Lubbock, TX; New Orleans, LA; Oklahoma City, OK; San Antonio, TX; Shreveport, LA; and Tulsa, OK.

Region VII (Kansas City)

HUD Kansas City Regional Office, Professional Building, 1103 Grand Ave., Kansas City, MO. Field offices are located in: Des Moines, IA; Omaha, NE; St. Louis, MO; Topeka, KS.

Region VIII (Denver)

HUD Denver Regional Office, Executive Tower Building, 1405 Curtis St., Denver, CO 80202-2349, (303) 844-4513. Field offices are located in: Casper, WY; Fargo, ND; Helena, MT; Salt Lake City, UH; and Sioux Falls, SD.

Region IX (San Francisco)

One North First St., Suite 400, Phoenix, AZ 85004-2360, (602) 261-4156. Field offices are located in: Fresno, CA; Honolulu, HI; Las Vegas, NV; Los Angeles, CA; Phoenix, AZ; Reno, NV; Sacramento, CA; San Diego, CA; Santa Ana, CA; and Tucson, AZ.

HUD San Francisco Regional Office, Phillip Burton Federal Building and U.S. Courthouse, 450 Golden Gate Avenue, P.O. Box 36003, San Francisco, CA 94102-3448, (415) 556-4752. Indian Programs only.

Region X (Seattle)

HUD Seattle Regional Office, Arcade Plaza Building, 1321 Second Ave., Seattle, WA 98101-2054, (206) 442-5414. Field offices are located in: Anchorage, AK; Boise, ID; Portland, OR; and Spokane, WA.

* Homes: H.U.D. Urban Homesteading Program

U.S. Department of Housing and Urban Development
Urban Homesteading Division
Office of Community Planning and Development
451 7th St., S.W, Washington, DC 20410-7000   (202) 755-5324
Contact: Regional HUD offices (listed above); or, your city or county Housing and Community Development Office. This program is available through certain qualified localities in a state which acquires HUD, VA, or other foreclosed homes for the purpose of renovating them and improving neighborhoods. The homes are virtually given away to people who must, in turn, finance the renovation and live in the home. Low-interest, government-financed loans are available to do the rehabilitation. This can be a great bargain, but the program is limited in scope to 157 local communities around the country and only a few homes may be available each year. Also, there are income limits for people participating in the program.

Here's how the program works (details may vary in different communities): First, you must contact your regional HUD office (listed above) or the Housing and Community Development division of your city or county to find out if any communities in your area participate in the Homesteading program. If they do, and you qualify, you fill out an application and, if three or more persons qualify for the same property, your name may then be placed in a lottery or a similar system providing an equitable selection system be used.) If your name is drawn as a winner, you then pay $10 for the home. However, you must have a stable income and employment, and possess sufficient cash for settlement costs, as well as possess a good credit rating. "Open Houses" are held for perspective applicants to view and to determine the extent of renovation or repairs needed. Low-interest financing is accomplished through the local government, which uses Federal funding to support it. You may choose from a list of contractors provided by your local government, and all work is completed before you move in. You may also perform the work yourself. Your remodeling costs basically become your mortgage on the home and you must live there for five years, bringing the house up to code within three years. Applicants must be 18 years of age, U.S. citizens, or registered aliens with permanent resident status, and not have been a homeowner within the previous three years.

* Homes: Veterans Administration

U.S. Veterans Administration
810 Vermont Ave., N.W.
Washington, DC 20420   (202) 233-4000
Contact local Veterans Administration Office, or real estate broker. Watch newspaper ads in local papers for listings of foreclosed properties. The National Veterans Administration office in Washington, DC is not directly involved in handling the sales; for any inquiries you will be referred to a real estate broker or local VA office.

The Veterans Administration sells foreclosed properties through private real estate brokers. Properties are frequently advertised in local newspapers, giving information such as address, number of bedrooms and bathrooms, particular defects in the property, and price. Almost any real estate agent can show you the property. Local VA offices are the best source of information on the procedures involved in purchasing these properties. In some cases, they will also directly send you lists of properties currently available in your area. Others will not, referring you to a broker. In either case, you must go through an agent to purchase the house, since the process is very much like a regular real estate transaction . Except, remember, once you have put a bid on a house and won, there is no negotiating or turning back. Houses come "as is" with no guarantees, so it is important to inspect them carefully. Some are located in less than desirable neighborhoods, but there are bargains to be had as well. (Prices may drop on homes that are not sold in a certain period of time. VA financing is possible, but you get a 10% discount for paying cash).

* Houses and Other Property From Failed Savings and Loan Companies

Resolution Trust Corporation
Washington, DC 20429   (202) 789-6316 (800) 431-0600
As a result of the hundreds of failed US Savings and Loan institutions the US Government has on had over 30,000 real property assets is it attempting to auction off at the best available price. The inventory contains approximately 12,000 single family homes 2,500 commercial properties and 800 parcels of undeveloped land.

* Miscellaneous Property: U.S. Customs Service

Northrop Worldwide Aircraft Services
U.S. Customs Support Division
P.O. Box 2065
Lawton, OK 73502-2065   (405) 357-9194.
Northrop Worldwide Aircraft Services, under contract with the U.S.Customs Service, auctions forfeited and confiscated general merchandise, including vehicles, on a nationwide basis. Items include everything from vessels--both pleasure and commercial--to aircraft, machinery, clothes (in both commercial and individual quantities), real estate, jewelry, household goods, precious stones, food products, liquor, furniture, and high technology equipment. Public auctions and sealed and open bid methods are all used.

For $50 dollars per year you can subscribe to a mailing list of items to be auctioned nationwide; or you may subscribe to a list limited to one region of the country for $25. You will then receive fliers with descriptions of items available in upcoming auctions. Regions are divided as follows: General, Northeast sales; Southeast Sales; Northwest sales; and Southwest sales. Send your name, address, telephone number, and a money order to the above address. Allow six to eight weeks for the first flier to arrive. The fliers will then arrive three weeks prior to the viewing period and will tell you when and where the items are available for inspection and details of auction procedures. Catalogs are also available with additional details. For sealed bids, a deposit equal to 20% of the total bid must be submitted along with the bid.

U.S. Customs auctions are held every nine weeks in the following cities: Los Angeles, CA; Del Rio, TX; Laredo, TX; Nogales, AZ; Brownsville, TX; Miami, FL; Edinburg, TX; Chicago, IL; Houston, TX.

U.S. Customs auctions are held every six weeks in the following cities: Jersey City, NJ; El Paso, TX; San Diego, CA; Yuma, AZ.

* Miscellaneous Property: U.S. Department of Defense

The Defense Reutilization Marketing Service
P.O. Box 1370
Battle Creek, MI 49016-1370   (616) 961-7331
Imagine what kinds of items are used , then discarded, by a government department as big as the Defense Department: literally everything from recyclable scrap materials and weapons accessories, to airplanes, ships, trains, and motor vehicles; to wood and metalworking machinery, agricultural equipment, construction equipment, communications equipment and medical, dental and veterinary supplies. Not to forget photographic equipment, chemical products, office machines, food preparation and serving equipment, musical instruments, textiles, furs, tents, flags, and live animals. No activated items with military applications are included. Neither are real estate or confiscated items such as sports cars or luxury goods.

Goods sold are either surplus or not usable by other government agencies. First priority is given to designated groups which qualify for donations. The rest is then put up for public sale. By contacting the Defense Reutilization Marketing Service at the above address or telephone, you can receive a booklet called *How to Buy Surplus Personal Property* which explains what DOD has for sale and how to bid for it. The Defense Department also lists notices of Sealed Bid property

Government Auctions and Surplus Property

sales in the Commerce Business Daily, available from the Superintendent of Documents, Government Printing Office, Washington, DC 20402-9325; (202) 783-3238.

Sales are conducted by regional Defense Reutilization and Marketing Region (DRMR) sales offices which coordinate sales in their geographical area. Listed below are addresses and telephone numbers of the regional offices, which can direct you further as to exactly where items are physically sold. Local sales are by auction, spot bid, or on a retail basis. Auctions are held where there are relatively small quantities of a variety of items. Spot bids are made through forms submitted in the course of a sale--usually when the property is something with a high demand or interest. The retail sales offer small quantities at fixed, market-level prices.

Large quantities of goods are usually sold by sealed bid, which you submit by mail, along with a deposit, on a form you obtain in a catalog which describes the items. (You receive the catalogs once you are on the mailing list.) Recyclable materials are usually sold by this method. You can be put on a mailing list to receive advance notice of DOD sales in your region, but if you don't make any bids after two notifications it will probably be removed unless you make an additional request to remain on the list. You can also be placed on a National Bidders List for sales throughout the country. By contacting the DOD Bidders Control Office, P.O. Box 1370, Battle Creek, MI 49016-1370, (616) 961-7331 or 961-7332. People under age 18 and members of the U.S. Armed Forces, including civilian employees, are not eligible to participate in these sales.

Following are the Defense Reutilization and Marketing sales offices:

DRMR - Columbus, P.O. Box 500, Blacklick, OH 43004-0500, (614) 238-2114. This region includes: MN, WI, MI, IA, NE, KS, MO, IL, IN, OH, WV, VA, DE, NJ, PA, , MD, CT, NY, RI, MA, ME, VT, NH, and District of Columbia

DRMR - Memphis, 2163 Airways Blvd., Memphis, TN 38114-0716, (901) 775-6417. This region includes: TX, OK, AR, LA, MS, AL, TN, KY, GA, FL, SC, NC.

DRMR - Ogden, P.O. Box 53, Defense Depot Ogden, Ogden, UT 84407-5001, (801) 399-7257. This region includes: ND, SD, MT, WY, ID, UT, CO, AZ, NM, WA, OR, NV, CA.

You can also take advantage of DOD sales if you live outside the United States. The DOD booklet, *How to Buy Surplus Personal Property*, lists addresses for various regions around the world.

* Miscellaneous Property: U.S. Postal Service

U.S. Postal Service
475 L'Enfant Plaza, S.W.
Washington, DC 20260-3100   (202) 268-2000

Contact the Dead Letter Branches listed below for undeliverable goods; or your local Postmaster for Vehicle Maintenance Facilities and surplus property auctions.

The Postal Service holds auctions of unclaimed merchandise which includes a wide range of property--from electronic and household items--to clothes, jewelry, linens, toys, all types of equipment, and lots of books. Sales are handled through five dead letter branches throughout the country listed below. However, the highest-value items such as art works, are sold through private auctioneers. Contact your local Postmaster to ask about their auctions of surplus property and used vehicles. The used vehicle sales can be good bargains, since the vehicles are somewhat fixed up, painted, and occasionally in good condition. Some jeeps, for instance, may sell for between $1200 and $1500. The sales are conducted by 225 Vehicle Maintenance Facilities around the country.

The dead letter items are usually sold in lots of similar goods, with the volume or quantity varying widely. Prices depend on what the goods are and the number of people bidding at a particular auction. You can get on a mailing list to receive advance notice of auctions, including information on when items may be viewed ahead of time. There may be a minimum bid required, such as $20; and often cash is the only acceptable payment. Bidders are responsible for removing the items purchased.

A flier for a recent Postal Service auction of unclaimed and damaged merchandise in St. Paul, Minnesota advises that only those already on an established check register may pay by check; otherwise, cash is required. It also advised that potential bidders to bring their own containers-- boxes, crates, and bags--for packing. The Postal Service in San Francisco, California, recently announced that books, jewelry, sound recordings, speakers, and cabinets, as well as miscellaneous merchandise would be available.

Eastern Region

U. S. Postal Service Claims and Inquiry, Room 531 A, 2970 Market St., Philadelphia, PA 19104, (215) 895-8140. Includes Pennsylvania, Southern New Jersey, Maryland, Delaware, Ohio, Kentucky, part of Indiana, Virginia, West Virginia, North Carolina, and South Carolina.

Central Region

U.S. Postal Service Dead Letter Office, 443 Fillmore, St. Paul, MN 55107, (612) 293-3089. Includes Minnesota, Michigan, Wisconsin, North Dakota, South Dakota, Wyoming, Colorado, Nebraska, Iowa, Indiana, and Illinois.

Northeast Region

U.S. Postal Service Dead Parcel Office, 380 W. 33rd St. New York, NY 10001, (212) 330-2931. Includes: New York, Massachusetts, Puerto Rico, Connecticut, New Hampshire, New Jersey, and Rhode Island.

Southern Region

U.S. Postal Service Undeliverable Mail Branch, P.O. Box 44161, Atlanta, GA 30336-9506, (404) 344-1625. Auction location is 730 Great Southwest Parkway, Atlanta, GA. Includes: Georgia, Florida, Louisiana, Tennessee, Arkansas, Mississippi, Oklahoma, Texas, and parts of South Carolina.

Western Region

U.S. Postal Service Claims and Inquiries, 1300 Evans Ave., Room 293, San Francisco, CA 94188-9664, (415) 550-5400. Auctions are held at 228 Harrison St., San Francisco, CA. Includes: Alaska, Oregon, Idaho, California, Washington, Nevada, Utah, Arizona, New Mexico, part of Texas, and Hawaii.

* Miscellaneous Property: General Services Administration Property

U.S. General Services Administration
18th and F. Sts., N.W.
Washington, DC 20405   (202) 557-7785

Contact your local GSA office listed below. The GSA disposes of surplus property for most of the government agencies, and has items ranging from vehicles and scrap metals, to office furniture, office and industrial equipment, data processing equipment, boats, medical equipment, waste paper and computers; as well as aircraft, railroad equipment, agricultural equipment, textiles, food waste, photographic equipment, jewelry, watches, and clothing.

You can have your name placed on a mailing list to receive advance notices of auctions at no cost. Sales are conducted as regular auctions, spot auctions (where bids are submitted on-the-spot in writing) and by sealed bid (written on a form and mailed in). For auctions and spot bids, you will have two days prior to the sale to view and inspect property, and one week prior for sealed bids. For sealed bid items you receive a catalog, once your are on the mailing list, describing the merchandise. Announcements come out as property is accumulated, with March to October being the busiest period. The highest bidder wins in all cases.

Prices may range from way below wholesale for some items to close-to-market prices for others, especially automobiles and boats. Cars tend to be common American-made brands, such as Tempos, Citations, and Reliances. Prices for 4-6 year-old cars may range from around $1500 to $3000 depending on the condition. Payment may be by cash, cashier's checks, money orders, traveler's checks, government, or credit union checks; but any personal or business checks must be accompanied by an Informal Bank Letter guaranteeing payment. Full payment must be made by the following day, and bidders are responsible for removal of all property. To bid in GSA auctions, you must register at the site and obtain a bidder number. Once you are on the bidders mailing list, you must bid at least once while receiving five mailings or your name will be removed from the list. Then you must contact the appropriate office again to continue receiving mailings.

Some recent listings for a GSA sale in Bismarck, North Dakota included the following items: miscellaneous kitchen equipment, meat slicers, coffee makers, cameras, film, binoculars, screens, paper, postage meter, nuts and bolts, typewriters, lettering set, mailboxes, lamps, and a streetlight

For information about GSA auctions in your area, contact one of the regional offices listed below:

National Capitol Region

(Washington DC and vicinity)
6808 Loisdale Rd., Building A, Springfield, VA 22150, (703) 535-7084, or (703) 557-7796, for a recording.

Region I (Boston)

GSA, Surplus Sales Branch, 10 Causeway St., 9th Floor, Boston, MA, (617) 565-7316.

Region II (New York)

GSA Surplus Sales Branch, 26 Federal Plaza, Room 20-2016, New York, NY, 10278, (212) 264-4824, or (212) 264-4823, for a recording.

Region III (Philadelphia)

GSA Surplus Sales Branch, 9th and Market Sts., Philadelphia, Pennsylvania 19107, (215) 597-5671 or (215) 597-SALE for a recording.

Region IV (Atlanta)

GSA Surplus Sales Branch, 75 Spring St. SW Atlanta, Georgia 30303 (404) 331-0972.

Region V (Chicago)

230 S. Dearborn St., Chicago, Illinois 60604 (312) 353-6061 or (312) 353-0246 for a recorded announcement.

Region VI (Kansas)

GSA Surplus Sales Branch, 6F BPS 4400, College Blvd. Suite 175, Overland Park, Kansas 66211.

Region VII (Ft. Worth)

GSA Surplus Sales Branch, 819 Taylor St., Ft. Worth, Texas 76102 (817) 334-2351.

Region VIII (Denver)

GSA Surplus Sales Branch, Denver Federal Center Building 41, Denver, Colorado 80225 (303) 236-7705.

Region IX (San Francisco)

GSA Surplus Sales Branch, 525 Market St., 32nd Floor, San Francisco, California 94105 (415) 974-9189.

Region X (Washington)

GSA Surplus Sales Branch GSA Center, Auburn, Washington 98002 (206) 931-7562.

* Miscellaneous Property: Internal Revenue Service (IRS)

Call the IRS National Information Hotline (800) 424-1040
The hotline can tell you which local office to call. The property sold by the IRS is seized from delinquent taxpayers rather than being used or surplus government property. Many kinds of merchandise are put up for auction, including real estate, vehicles, and office and industrial equipment. Sales are by both sealed bids and public auction. Regarding property sales, the IRS warns that land may still be redeemed by the original owner up to 180 days AFTER you, the bidder, purchase it at an auction; and therefore no deed is issued until this time period has elapsed. Buildings on land being sold by the IRS are NOT open for inspection by a potential buyer unless permission is granted by the taxpayer/owner.

Payment may be by cash, certified check, cashier's check, or money order. In some cases, full payment is required the day of the sale. Otherwise, a 20% downpayment (or $200, whichever is greater) is needed to hold the property, with the balance due at a specified time from the date of the sale, not to exceed one month.

* Miscellaneous Property: U.S. Marshals Service

U.S. Marshals Service
Seized Assets Division
Department of Justice
Constitution Ave. & 10th St., N.W.
Washington, DC 20530
Contact your local Sunday newspaper for auction notices in the legal section, or the nearest U.S. Marshals Office under U.S. Department of Justice. Usually the Marshals Office is located in the Federal Building of a city.

In 1989, the Drug Enforcement Agency expects to collect $1 billion worth of property from convicted drug dealers. This figure will be up from what has already been a sixfold increase in property seizures in the past two years. The U.S. Marshals Service , which holds crime-related property accumulated in Federal drug-related and other confiscations, auctions much of this off to the public through 94 offices around the country. Items sold include everything from entire working businesses, to cars, houses, jewelry, rare coin and stamp collections, apartment complexes, and restaurants. Recently, an old Virginia estate which had belonged to George Washington's chaplain was sold by the U.S. Marshals Service for $5.4 million! A Lamborghini automobile went for $91,850 in Texas. The government is not giving these properties away by any means, but bargains are possible as well as opportunities to purchase some exotic goodies. Confiscated viable businesses are managed by the Service until the time of the auction in order to keep up or increase the businesses' value.

Auctions are not scheduled regularly, but occur when items accumulate. Auctions may be conducted by private auctioneers or the Marshals Service itself. No mailing list is kept to notify you individually, and there is no national listing of

items, since new properties are seized daily and adjudication of drug-related cases may take years. Payment at these auctions is by cash, certified check, or special arrangements when large amounts of money are involved. One note, the Marshals Service checks out people paying for large items with cash to make sure the government is not re-selling things to drug dealers. The Marshals Service also auctions off property seized by the Drug Enforcement Agency.

* Natural Resources Sales Assistance

Small Business Administration
1441 L Street, NW
Washington, DC 20416 (202) 653-6533
The federal government sells surplus real and personal property and natural resources, such as timber. SBA works with government agencies which are selling the property and resources to assure that small businesses have an opportunity to buy a fair share of them. Contact your nearest SBA office for more information or the SBA Answer Desk (800) 368-5855.

* Real Estate: General Services Administration Property Sales

General Services Administration (800) GSA-1313
Call this toll-free number for national listing of properties, and then contact local GSA office for the area you are interested in.

* Real Estate: Small Business Administration (SBA)

U.S. Small Business Administration
Portfolio Management Division
1441 L St., N.W.
Washington, DC 20416 (202) 653-6900
Contact your local SBA office located in 10 Regional Offices around the country with dozens of District Offices. The SBA auctions off properties of people who have defaulted on home loan payments in SBA-sponsored programs. Listings of auctions are printed in local newspapers, usually in the Sunday edition in the classified section. Merchandise is identified as SBA property and sold by private auctioneers. Items sold range from office furniture and equipment to buildings or entire bakeries, drycleaners, or other businesses. There may be parts or whole businesses available. The auctioneer may have an entire auction of SBA items, or a mixture of things from various sources. You may request to bid by sealed bid if you desire; and a deposit is required. Payment is by cash or certified check. If you are interested in certain categories of merchandise, you may have your name placed on a mailing list for auctions of that particular item. SBA Regional Offices follow:

Dallas: 8625 King George Dr., Dallas, TX 75235-3391 (214) 767-7643.

Kansas City: 911 Walnut St., 13th Floor, Kansas City, MO 64106 (816) 462-2989.

Denver: 999 18th St.,Ste. 701, Denver, CO 80202 (303) 294-7001.

San Francisco: 450 Golden Gate Ave,San Francisco, CA (415) 556-7487.

Seattle: 2615 4th Ave.,Room 440, Seattle, WA 98121 (206) 442-5676.

Boston: 60 Batterymarch St., 10th Floor, Boston, MA 02110 (617) 451-2030.

New York: 26 Federal Plaza, Room 31-08, New York, NY 10278.

King of Prussia: 475 Allendale Rd., Suite 201, King of Prussia, PA 19406 (215) 962-3750.

Atlanta: 1375 Peachtree St. N.E., 5th Floor, Atlanta, GA 30367-8102 (404) 347-2797.

Chicago: 230 Dearborn St., Room 510, Chicago,IL 60604-1593 (312) 353-0359.

* Ships: Maritime Administration

U.S. Department of Transportation
Office of Ship Operations
Maritime Administration
400 7th St., S.W.
Washington, DC 20590 (202) 366-5111
When the government decides that a merchant ship is no longer needed or useable, it may put that ship up for sale by auction, through a sealed bid procedure. It is sold to the highest bidder usually for its scrap value.

* Timber Sales for Small Business

Small Business Administraiton
1441 L St NW
Washington, DC 20416 (202) 653-6533
The U.S. Government regularly sells timber from the federal forests managed by

the U.S. Forest Service, Department of Agriculture, and the Bureau of Land

Government Auctions and Surplus Property

Management, Department of Interior. On occasion, timber also is sold from federally-owned forests which are under the supervision of the Department of Defense, the Department of Energy, and the Tennessee Valley Authority, and the Department of the Interior. The SBA and these agencies work together to ensure full opportunity for concerns to bid on federal timber sales. SBA and the sales agencies jointly set aside timber sales for bidding by small concerns when it appears that, under open sales, small business would not obtain a fair share at reasonable prices. Contact your SBA office for further information.

Donations To Non-Profit Organizations

* Art Exhibits
Smithsonian Institution
1100 Jefferson Dr., S.W., Room 316
Washington, DC 20560 (202)357-3168

The Smithsonian can bring art to you, whether you live in a major metropolitan area or a rural one. The Traveling Exhibition Service may sponsor over 100 different exhibits at any given time in museums and other locations around the country. The exhibitions range from popular culture, to fine arts, photography, historical exhibits, or topics of interest to children. The collections are from other museums and institutions, sometimes including the Smithsonian, and are most frequently sent to other museums, libraries, historic homes, or even schools and community centers. The bigger exhibits that require special security arrangements go only to museums equipped to handle them.

* Books
Library of Congress
Exchange and Gift Division
1st & Independence Sts., S.E.
Madison Building, Room 303
Washington DC 20540 (202)707-9511

Government agencies, educational institutions, and other non-profit organizations may qualify to obtain free books from the U.S. Library of Congress. Someone from the organization must choose which books are desired, and supply the Library with pre-addressed franking labels. Congressional offices will help educational institutions such as universities and schools obtain these labels. Non-profit organizations may submit bids to purchase books. There is no limit on the number of books a group may order.

* Federal Property To Homeless Organizations
U.S. Department of Health and Human Services
Public Health Service
Division of Health Facilities Planning
Parklawn Building, Room 17A10
5600 Fishers Lane
Rockville, MD 20857 (301)443-2265

If you are part of a non-profit organization ministering to the homeless, the government is currently (as of summer of 1989) taking applications for eligible groups to receive excess or unused federal buildings or land for homeless people. The program is administered by a combination of the Department of Department of Housing and Urban Development, which screens applications, the General Services Administration, which makes the properties available, and the Department of Health and Human Services, which reviews applications. Every Monday, the *Federal Register* (available from libraries or by subscription) lists which federal properties are available and where. Post Offices may also have listings on their bulletin boards. An organization has 90 days after that listing to apply for property. Eligibility is on a first come first serve basis, after certain other criteria is filled. That criteria is outlined in The Federal Register. If you think that your organization qualifies, you may contact the above number to request an application packet. The homeless program is putting on the back burner a previous program offering surplus federal land to organizations involved with certain health programs.

* Food and Surplus Commodities
USDA Food Distribution Program
Food and Nutrition Service
3101 Park Center Dr.
Alexandria, VA 22302 (703) 756-3660

Non-profit groups with tax-exempt status may apply for surplus commodities held by the Agriculture Department, such as grain (usually flour), oils, and sometimes milk and cheese. The large quantities of surplus cheese and milk that existed a couple of years ago are largely depleted. The items available depend somewhat on which foods are currently in surplus. Contact your state distribution agency, frequently the state Department of Agriculture, Department of Education, or Administrative Services, or the above address.

* Foreign Gifts
General Services Administration
Property Management Division
Crystal Mall Building #4,
Washington, DC 20406 (202)257-1234

Non-Presidential gifts from foreign countries to U.S. government agencies or their representatives may be displayed by the recipient in his government office, then purchased by him at an officially assessed value. If the gift is not purchased, it may end up in a State Surplus Property office, where the general public can get a chance to buy it. Watches and jewelry are commonly available, along with books, sculptures, and various artifacts. But the souvenir from Anwar Sadat to Jimmy Carter during the Middle East peace talks goes to the U.S. Archives and possibly later to the Jimmy Carter Library.

Items desired by non-profit organizations should be requested through your local Surplus Property Office, which can then contact the GSA about a donation. You can find a list of foreign gifts given to government agencies published yearly in the *Federal Register*.

* Miscellaneous Property
General Services Administration
Office of Property Management
Room 701 Crystal Mall Building, #4
Washington, DC 20406 (202) 557-1234

Or contact your local State Office of Surplus Property. The General Services Administration will donate items it handles to qualifying non-profit organizations which request it. Your State Office of Surplus Property, also called Office of Purchasing, Property Control, or General Services, makes the determination whether your group qualifies, then contacts the GSA to obtain it. There may be a fee for handling and service. Groups eligible can include public agencies, and non-profit educational, public health, elderly, or homeless organizations.

* Tools for Schools
Defense Industrial Plant Equipment Center
DIPEC-OID
Memphis, TN 38114-5051 (901)775-6593

This program of the Defense Logistics Agency loans used industrial equipment no longer needed by the military or military contractors to qualifying non-profit educational institutions. The equipment must be over $5000 in value and includes such things as saws, milling equipment, drilling equipment, and grinding equipment. Loans are for five year periods, but may be renewed indefinitely.

The receiving institution must pay for the cost of transportation, packaging and handling, plus any necessary repairs. Some equipment comes "as is" and may be inoperable; other items sometimes show up almost unused. The equipment generally dates from between 1950 to 1970, but in some cases it can be of superior quality than its modern equivalent. The Defense Industrial Plant Equipment Center advises looking first hand at equipment before ordering it.

* Travel Aboard An Icebreaker
Ice Operations Division
U.S. Coast Guard Headquarters
Washington, DC 20593
Attn: Lt. Wayne Roberts

The Coast Guard evaluates scientific projects to determine if they qualify for a selected scientist to ride along with one of the two Coast Guard Icebreakers that travel to the Arctic and Antarctica. Selections for the Antarctic trip are actually made by the National Science Foundation (1800 G St. N.W., Washington, DC (202) 357-9859). Most travelers are sponsored by government or educational organizations, but the Coast Guard is interested in any appropriate, professional project and will consider other applications as well. They can also be flexible on their itinerary to accommodate projects. Travelers must pay for use of the ship and helicopter time, although sometimes scientists on short missions may not have to reimburse these costs. Contact the address above for applications.

State Government Auctions

The following is a descriptive listing of state government offices which offer acutions or donations of surplus property.

State List of Auctions

Alabama

Alabama Surplus Property, P.O. Box 210487, Montgomery, Alabama 36121, (205)277-5866. Alabama auctions off a variety of items about three times per year, including office equipment, heavy machinery (such as milling machines and drill presses), and vehicles, including cars, trucks, boats, and tractors. Trailers, medical equipment, tires, dossiers, and lathes are also sold. The state advertises upcoming auctions in local newspapers, but you can also be put on a mailing list. Payment can be by cash, cashier's check, or personal check with a bank letter of credit. Items are available for viewing two days prior to the auction. No bids by mail.

Alaska

Office of Surplus Property, 2400 Viking Dr., Anchorage, Alaska 99501, (907)465-2172, general information; (907)279-0596, mailing list information. Alaska's Division of General Services and Supply sells surplus office equipment, including furniture and typewriters, every Tuesday from 8:30 am to 12:pm, and from 1:30 pm to 4:00 pm in a garage sale fashion with prices marked for each item. For items costing over $100, cash or cashiers checks are required. Vehicles, at various locations throughout the state, are sold during sealed bid auctions twice a year, in the spring and fall. Payment is by cashiers check after you have been notified of your winning bid.

Arizona

Office of Surplus Property, 1537 W. Jackson St., Phoenix, Arizona 85007, (602)542-5701. About four times per year, Arizona auctions off everything from vehicles to miscellaneous office equipment and computers. Items are sold by lots rather than individually; and prices, especially cars, can be below blue book price, depending upon opening bids. Vehicles range from empty frames to Jaguars. A mailing list is maintained. Individual cities and county governments in Arizona also hold their own surplus auctions.

Arkansas

State Marketing and Redistribution Office, 6620 Young Rd., Little Rock, AR 72201, (501)565-8645. Arkansas conducts both bid and retail, fixed price sales of surplus items. On Wednesdays, between 7:30 am and 3:00 pm, buyers may view and purchase items, which include office machines, tables, and tires, valued at under $300. Larger, more valuable items, including vehicles, medical equipment, mobile homes, and machine shop and automotive supplies, are auctioned off. You must bid three times to keep your name on the mailing list. The state also conducts sealed bids by mail. No personal checks are accepted for sealed bids. All items are sold "as is," with no guarantees implied or stated.

California

State of California, Office of Fleet Administration, 1416 10th St. Sacramento, CA 95814, (916)445-7527. California sells surplus office equipment or other supplies only to schools and other non-profit or educational institutions. However, once a month the General Services Department of the state holds auctions at Sacramento or Los Angeles State Garages of surplus automobiles. Vehicles may include sedans, cargo and passenger vans, pick-ups (mostly American-made). Viewing is available prior to the auction. You can receive 2 weeks advance notice by getting on the mailing list. Payment is by cash, cashiers check, or certified check. Personal checks are also accepted, but items may not be picked up until the check has cleared. No out-of-state checks. Prices vary greatly, and some vehicles have required minimum bids.

California Highway Patrol, Used Vehicle Sales Office, 2812 Meadowview Rd., Sacramento, CA 95814, (916)421-0285. CHP auctions off vehicles such as Crown Victorias, Chevy Capris, Dodge Diplomats, 4x4's, Mustangs, and many more. Most have air conditioning, power steering, and power brakes. Minimum bids are stated on a recorded telephone message. The auction is by sealed bids which are opened at 3:00 pm daily; winners may be present or notified by telephone. Payment is by cashiers check, certified check, or, money order only--no personal checks or cash accepted. Inspection is available between 8:00 am and 4:00 pm.

Colorado

Department of Correctional Industries, 100 East 66th Ave. Denver, CO 80221, (303)428-5297. Several times a year, Colorado auctions off its surplus property, excepts for motor vehicles, which are not sold to the public. Auctions are pre-announced in newspaper ads, and a mailing list is also maintained. The auctions are not held on a regular basis; rather, only when items accumulate. If you are on the mailing list, you will receive a couple of weeks advanced notice. Non-profit organizations have first choice of state surplus items, which can include typewriters, desks, computers, file cabinets, hospital beds, and much more.

Connecticut

60 State St. Rear, Old Wethersfield, CT 06109, (203)566-7018, or (203)566-7190. The state holds tag sales on a daily basis between noon and 3:45pm. Items vary from day to day. Vehicles are auctioned separately 8 or 9 times per year, with newspaper ads giving advance notice. These auctions are usually on the second Saturday of the month. Vehicles commonly available include Ford LTD's, Plymonth Horizons, and Chevrolet Chevettes, and may be viewed one hour prior to the auction. Buyers may also purchase a brochure with vehicle descriptions for $3.

Delaware

Division of Purchasing, P.O. Box 299, Delaware City, DE 19706, (302)834-4550. About three to five times each year Delaware publicly auctions off vehicles, office furniture, and other surplus or used property. Vehicles include school buses, paddle boats, vans, pick-up trucks, and sedans. Prices depend on the condition of the item and how many people are bidding for it. Vehicles may be inspected and started up prior to the auction, but may not be driven. You may get on a mailing list to be advised of upcoming auctions.

District of Columbia

The District of Columbia Property Division, (202)767-7989. DC holds vehicle auctions once a month at 8:00 am at Blue Plains. Vehicles include cars, trucks, buses, ambulances, and boats. Inspection and viewing is available one hour prior to the auction. Prices and conditions of vehicles vary greatly. No mailing list is kept.

District of Columbia Office of Property Control, (202)767-7586. Three times per year, this office auctions off items which include clothing, typewriters, cabinets, tools, refrigerators, and more at the DC Police Training Academy facility. No mailing list is kept, but advance notices are placed in The Washington Post. Viewing of items is allowed the day of the sales. Cash only is accepted.

Florida

Department of General Services, 813 A Lake Bradford Rd. Tallassee, Florida. 32304, (904)488-5272. DGS holds daily public retail-type sales of various items, excluding vehicles, between 9:00 am and 4:00 pm. Items left over from the sales are then put up for auction. Auctions are held every other Friday at 9:00 am. Items include office supplies, computers, medical equipment, mowers, calculators, typewriters, couches, desks, chairs, tables, air conditioners, black boards, and filing cabinets. Items are offered both individually and by lot, and payment can be by cash or personal check (Florida residents only). The merchandise may be viewed the day before the auction. No mailing list is kept, but ads are placed in local newspapers the Sunday before the auctions are held.

Department of General Services, 813 B Lake Bradford Rd., Tallahassee, FL 32304, (904)488-4452. General Service's Division of Motor Pool auctions off vehicles by sealed bid once a year. Newspaper ads run one month before the auction, containing descriptive information and viewing schedules. Vehicles are of various types, including both confiscated and used state vehicles.

Department of Motor Vehicles and Watercraft, 1-800-843-8781, in Florida; and (904)772-0110, out-of-state. MVW also sells surplus items, including motorcars and boats. Automobile auctions take place anywhere from 8 to 10 times per year, with dates set 4 to 6 weeks in advance at various auction locations throughout the state. Industrial equipment is also included, along with various kinds of used and confiscated vans, trucks, cars, and Blazers. Boats are auctioned twice a year and include pleasure and fishing boats. Items may be viewed two days prior to the auction, and by contacting MVW you can be put on their mailing list.

Georgia

State of Georgia, Department of Administrative Services, Purchasing Division, Surplus Property Services 1050 Murphy Ave, S.W. Atlanta, Georgia 30310, (404)756-4800. Georgia auctions vehicles, including sedans, wagons, trucks, vans, buses, and cement mixers; also shop equipment, generators, typewriters, copiers, computers, tape recorders, and other office equipment; as well as audio-visual equipment, cameras, electronic equipment, and air conditioners. They keep a mailing list and also advertise the auctions in local newspapers. Merchandise may be inspected two days before an auction, which are held on the third Wednesday of a month--but not necessarily every month. Vehicles may be started up, but not driven. Sealed bids are also used, and deposits are required with these. For auctions, items are payable with cash or check with sufficient I.D. if the amount is under $501.00. For personal or business checks in amounts over $501.00, property will be held until the check clears. A recent Georgia auction offered 40 sedans between 3 and 15 years old, 30 pick-up trucks from 5 to 22 years old, vans dating from 1965 to 1989, tires, tractors, farm equipment, shop equipment, office equipment, and 3 lots of televisions.

Hawaii

Hawaii does not conduct surplus sales at the state level.

Idaho

Bureau of Supplies, 801 Reserve St., Boise, ID 83712, (208)334-2468. Every year the Bureau of Supplies auctions off surplus items,including cars, equipment, televisions, chairs, office equipment, desks, and typewriters. Items are sold individually. Local checks are accepted as payment with two IDs. The Bureau maintains a mailing list and also advertises auctions in local newspapers.

Illinois

Office of Property Control, 3550 Great Northern Ave., Springfield, IL 62707, (217)793-1813. Two or three times per year this office auctions off vehicles and property. Property includes office equipment, desks, chairs, typewriters, restaurant equipment, calculators, cameras, refrigerators, and filing cabinets. The office maintains a mailing list and also advertises the auctions in advance in local newspapers. Prices vary widely, but below- market prices are available. Illinois auctions off vehicles by sealed bid only.

Indiana

State Surplus Property Section, 545 W. McCarty St., Indianapolis, IN 46225-1239, (317)232-0134: warehouse; (317)232-1365: office. Indiana holds auctions as items accumulate, mostly through sealed bids, which are opened monthly and sold to the highest bidder. You can get on the mailing list for items in your area of interest, then physically inspect the merchandise and obtain a bid package. You will be asked to fill out a form specifying what category of items you are interested in bidding on. This procedure is for surplus property, such as office equipment, computers, farming equipment, real estate, scrap metal, computer equipment, and hospital equipment. Vehicles are sold on the first Thursday of each month at 11;00am by public auction. Payment is by cash, certified check, cashiers check, or money order. No personal checks or letters of credit are accepted. Items purchased must be removed from premises by 8:00 pm the day of the auction. A recent auction in Indianapolis included such surplus items as radio base stations, laboratory equipment, computer hardware, gas masks, and stop watches; and also confiscated items, including stoves, refrigerators, antique furniture and dishes, radios, televisions, bicycles, jewelry, microwaves, cellular phones, and VCR's.

Iowa

Department of Natural Resources, Wallace State Office Bldg., Des Moines, IA 50319, (515)281-5145. The Department of Natural Resources holds an auction every year to dispose of items such as boats, fishing rods, tackle boxes, guns, and other fishing and hunting equipment, as well as office equipment. Payment is by cash or check with appropriate identification. There is no mailing list, but auctions are advertised in local newspapers.

Vehicle Dispatchers Garage, 301 E. 7th, Des Moines, IA, 50319, (515)281-5121. The Department of Transportation holds auctions three to four times per year at 9:00 am on Saturdays. They mostly sell patrol cars, pickups, trucks, and sometimes newer confiscated vehicles. Most have at least 68,000 miles of travel on them, and prices vary widely. A deposit of $200 is required on the day of the sale, with full payment due by the following Thursday. Payment may be made by cash or check with an accompanying letter of credit. Viewing is possible Friday all day and Saturday morning prior to the sale.

Kansas

Kansas State Surplus Property, P.O. Box 19226, Topeka, KS 66619-0226, (913)296-2334. The State Surplus Property office sells sedans, snow plows, and everything they have, from staples to bulldozers. Other merchandise may include confiscated cars from drug raids, office typewriters, and even a buffalo. Property is first offered to other state agencies at set prices, and whatever is left over is

opened to public sale at the same prices. Prices tend to be competitive, for example, $5000 cars selling for $2400. Items not sold by auction are sold by sealed bids, with a catalog available containing descriptions of items and where they are located. To obtain copies of catalogs describing sealed bid items, send several self addressed 6 x 9 inch envelopes with $1 each to the above address.

Kentucky

Kentucky Office of Surplus Property, 501 Home St., Frankford, KY 40601, (502)564-4836. Kentucky holds public auctions on Saturdays every two or three months (there were 9 in 1988). Items may include vehicles, desks, chairs, calculators, typewriters, file cabinets, tape recorders, electronic equipment, couches, beds, and lawnmowers, to name a few. Merchandise may be viewed the day before an auction. The office maintains a mailing list and also advertises upcoming auctions in local newspapers. Some items are auctioned by sealed bids. Property is payable by cash, check, or money order.

Louisiana

Division of Administration, Louisiana Property Assistance Agency, 1059 Brickyard Lane, Baton Rouge, LA 70804, (504)342-6849. Public auctions are held on the second Saturday of every month at 9:00 am at 1502 North 17th St. Items may be viewed the week before. Property sold ranges from medical and office equipment, to boats, shop equipment, typewriters, file cabinets, pinball machines, bicycles, televisions, adding machines, and chairs, and vehicles such as Chevy Impalas, Dodge Chargers, Ford Escorts, and pickup trucks. All items are sold "as is" and "where is." Payment is required in full the day of the auctions, but no personal or company checks are accepted. In addition, all merchandise must be removed within five days after the sale. Auctions are conducted by Brown's Auction Company, P.O. Box 1508 Eunice, LA 70535, (318)546-70535.

Maine

Office of Surplus Property, Station 95, Augusta, ME 04333, (207)289-5750. Five or six times per year, Maine publicly auctions off vehicles on the grounds of the Augusta Mental Health Institute. You must register to be able to bid, and then you will automatically be notified of upcoming auctions. Vehicles may include police cruisers, pick-up trucks, Buick Regals, snowmobiles, lawn mowers, and heavy equipment, such as large trucks, graders, and backhoes. Inspection is allowed between 8:00 am and 10:00 am the day of the auctions, which are always held on Saturdays. Vehicles may be started up but not driven. Personal checks, money orders, certified checks, and cash are all accepted. Office equipment and other non-vehicles items are sold by tag sale once per month, and prices are negotiable. Exact date, place, and time of auctions are announced in local newspapers, but there is no mailing list. Payment is due for both vehicles and other items the day of the auction or sale.

Maryland

Maryland does not sell surplus property directly to the public. Office furniture and the like are sold or donated to non-profit organizations or state agencies, and vehicles are sold to dealers only. Call: (301)799-0440.

Massachusetts

Massachusetts State Purchasing Agency, One Ashburton Place, Boston, MA, 02108, (617)727-2920. About six times per year, Massachusetts holds public auctions of surplus property. The State Purchasing Agency places ads in The Boston Globe on the Sunday prior to each of the auctions, which are normally held on Saturdays. Vehicles sold include sedans, wagons, vans, and pick-ups with an average age of four years. Conditions range from good to junk. Viewing is available the day before the auction from 9:00 am to 4:00 pm. No start-ups allowed. The state does not auction other surplus property.

Michigan

State of Michigan, Department of Management and Budget, State Surplus Property, 3353 N. Logan, Lansing, MI 48913, (517)335-8444. The state auctions off all kinds of office furniture , household goods, machinery, livestock, and vehicles, such as sedans, buses, trucks, and boats. Auctions are held at different locations for different categories of property. The State Surplus Property Office sends out yearly calendars with auction dates and information. Double check dates because additions or changes may occur. Payment may be made by cash or check and should include the 4% state sales tax. No refunds are made. Inspections of merchandise are available either the day before or the morning of an auction.

Minnesota

Minnesota Surplus Operations Office, 5420 Highway 8, New Brighton, MN 55112, (612)296-5177; toll-free Hotline: 800-296-1056, in-state only. Minnesota holds about 17 auctions per year at different locations around the state. They sell vehicles such as old patrol cars, passenger cars, trucks, vans, suburbans, and trucks, as well as tractors, boats, snowmobiles and outboard motors. The state also auctions off furniture, office equipment, kitchen equipment, tools, and confiscated items such as vehicles, computers, jewelry, car stereos and radios, and other personal effects. Many of these items are sold far under market price. You may be put on a mailing list to receive a calendar for the schedule of upcoming auctions for the year. Inspections of property are held at 9:300 am, an hour and a half before the auction begins; and payment is by personal check, cash, or money order.

Mississippi

Bureau of Surplus Property, P.O. Box 5778, Whitfield Rd., Jackson, MS 39208, (601)939-2050. Once a year, Mississippi auctions off such items as machinery, textiles, ammunition boxes, and unrepairable vehicles. Merchandise may be viewed the day before, and is payable by cash, check with proper I.D., possibly including a bank letter of credit, or certified check.

Department of Public Safety, P.O. Box 958, Jackson, MS 39205, (601)987-1453. Once or twice a year, the State Department of Public Safety auctions off working vehicles when they accumulate. They have mostly Ford and Chevy patrol cars, and only occasionally vans and other types of vehicles. Most have at least 100,000 miles on them. Recent average prices have ranged from $1200 to $1500. Payment must be in cash or cashiers check--no personal checks. The balance is due the day of the auction. You may have your name put on a mailing list to receive notices of auctions.

Missouri

State Of Missouri, Surplus Property Office, 117 N. Riverside Dr. Jefferson City, MO 65102, (314)751-3415. Twice a year, Missouri holds regular public auctions twice per year, as well as holding sealed bid auctions of merchandise located at various places in the state. Items include office equipment and vehicles. You can be put on a mailing list to receive notices of upcoming auctions, plus they are advertised in local newspapers. For regular auctions, inspection is available the day of the auction; and sealed bid items may be viewed two or three days before the deadline. Items may be sold by lot or individually. Payment may be made by cash or personal check.

Montana

Property and Supply Bureau, 930 Lyndale Ave., Helena, MT 59620, (406)444-4514. Montana holds a vehicle auction once a year, of about 300 state vehicles. These auctions are advertised in local newspapers prior to the auction. In addition, the state offers other property for sale each month - on the second Friday of the month. The sales include items such as office supplies, computers, chairs, tables, and vehicles including trucks, vans, sedans, highway patrol cars, and more. Payment can be by cash, business check, or bank check.

Nebraska

Nebraska Office of Administrative Services, Material Division, Surplus Property, P.O. Box 94901, Lincoln, NE 68509, (402)479-4890. Three or four times a year, Nebraska auctions off office furniture, computers, couches, and more. Separate auctions are held for vehicles and heavy equipment-- also about three or four times per year. Auctions are advertised in newspapers and on radio, and a mailing list is also kept. Sealed bid auctions are held for property such as scrap iron, wrecked vehicles, guard posts, and tires. Items are available for viewing two days prior to the auctions, which are held on Saturdays at 5001 S. 14th St. Payment can be made by cash or check.

Nevada

Nevada State Purchasing Division, Kinkead Bldg., Room 400 Capitol Complex, Carson City, NV 89710, (702)885-4070. About once a year, Nevada holds a sale on the second Saturday in August of such items as calculators, desks, cabinets, tables, chairs, scrap metal, weapons, waste oil and laboratory equipment. The sale is on a first come, first serve basis, with minimum prices marked on the property. Occasionally, prices of unsold items are reduced up to 50%. Vehicles, including motorcycles, as well as slot machines, are sold by auction separately and are available for inspection the day before. Vehicles are also auctioned by sealed bid, and you can be put on a mailing list to receive notice of auctions of 19 categories of merchandise, including heavy equipment, boats, and planes. Once you have requested to place your name on the mailing list, if you do not subsequently bid on two consecutive occasions, it will be removed. Payment is by cash or local check with proper I.D. No out of state checks accepted. For vehicles, you can put down a 5% deposit with two weeks to complete payment.

New Hampshire

Office of Surplus Property 78 Regional Dr., Building 3, Concord, NH 03331, (603)271-2126. New Hampshire holds two auctions per year of vehicles and other equipment, such as office furniture and machines, and refrigerators. Vehicles, which include Omnis, cruisers, pickups, and vans, may be viewed the day before the auction, while other merchandise can be viewed on the same day just before the auction. A mailing list is maintained, and ads are also placed in local newspapers prior to the auctions. Acceptable payment includes cash and certified funds.

New Jersey

New Jersey Purchase and Property Distribution Center, 1620 Stuyvestant Ave. Trenton, NJ 08628, (609)530-3300. New Jersey auctions off used state vehicles such as Chevy Chevettes, Dodge vans, various types of compacts, and occasionally buses and heavy equipment. Frequency of auctions depends on availability; however, in the Spring of '89, auctions were being held every other week. Vehicles may be inspected and started up the day before the auction from 9:00 am to 12:00 pm, and from 1:00 pm to 3:00 pm. Payment is by cash, money order, or certified check. No personal checks. A 10% deposit is required to hold a vehicle, and then the successful bidder has five days to complete payment and remove the vehicle. To be advised of auctions, put your name on the mailing list by calling or writing the address and phone number above. A recent vehicle auction in New Jersey offered a variety of Dodge and Chevy vehicles , ages ranging from three to thirteen years, with mileages from 50,000 to 130,000. Other surplus items are not put up for public auction; rather they are offered to other state agencies.

New Mexico

New Mexico Highway and Transportation Department, SB-2, P. O. Box 1149, Santa Fe, NM, 87504-1149, (505)827-5580. About once a year, on Saturday at the end of September, New Mexico auctions off vehicles, including sedans, loaders, backhoes, snow removal equipment, pick-ups, vans, four-wheel drives, and tractors. They have some office equipment as well. You may place your name on a mailing list to receive the exact date of the auction and descriptions of merchandise up for bidding. Items may be inspected the day before the auction. Payment is by cash, checks with proper I.D., money orders, or cashier's checks. No credit cards.

New York

State of New York Office of General Service, Bureau of Surplus Property, Building # 18, State Office Building Campus, Albany, NY 12226, (518)457-6335. The Office of General Services holds auctions continuously in locations around the state. Surplus and used office equipment, scrap material, agricultural items (even unborn cows). Medical, photographic, institutional and maintenance equipment are sold through sealed bids, usually in lots of varying size. To participate in a sealed bid, you place your name on a mailing list for items in seven different categories, then make your bid by mail. The highest bidder wins and is notified by mail. Mailings give as much information as possible about the items being auctioned; but state officials stress that merchandise is sold "as is" and advise viewing property in person before making a bid. A ten percent deposit is required with each sealed bid. Vehicles are sold by public auction and may include cars, trucks, buses, tractors, bulldozers, mowers, compressors, plows, sanders, and other highway maintenance and construction equipment. Large items are sold individually, and smaller equipment, such as chain saws, is more likely to be sold in lots. These auctions take place about 55 times per year. Payment may be made by certified check or cash. A ten percent deposit will hold a vehicle until the end of the day.

North Carolina

State Surplus Property, P.O. Box 33900, Raleigh, NC 27636-3900, (919)733-3889. North Carolina auctions off surplus merchandise located across the state, including vehicles and office equipment, by sealed bid. Office equipment includes furniture, typewriters, desks, and chairs; and vehicles include Reliances, Crown Victorias, Mustangs, and vans. For a fee of $15 you can be placed on a mailing list to receive weekly advisories of what is for auction, with a description of the item and its condition. Otherwise, if you visit the warehouse in person, you can pick up free samples of bid listings and look at lists of prices that items sold for in previous auctions. The warehouse is located on Highway 54 - Old Chapel Hill Road. Payment is by money order or certified check, and you have 10 days to pay for your merchandise and 30 days to pick it up. Items may be inspected two weeks before an auction from Monday to Friday between 8:00 am and 5:00 pm.

On Tuesdays, the warehouse is closed between 1:00 pm and 3:00 pm when the bids are opened and the public is then invited to attend.

North Dakota

Surplus Property Office, P.O. Box 7293, Bismarck, ND 58502, (701)224-2273. Once a year the Office of Surplus Property auctions surplus office furniture and equipment, as well as vehicles and scrap materials. Merchandise may be viewed the morning of the auction. Cash, cashiers checks, or money orders are acceptable forms of payment. Personal or business checks are accepted only with a bank letter of credit.

Ohio

Office of State and Federal Surplus Property, 226 N. Fifth St., Columbus, OH 43215, (614)466-5052. Ohio holds public auctions and sealed bid sales on a wide range of office machines and equipment, furniture, and vehicles. The sealed bid sales are held at various locations around the state for inoperable vehicles. These may be inspected any time after you receive your bid invitation in the mail. Other vehicle auctions are held three times a year, with inspections available the day before. Vehicles may include sedans, trucks, vans, 4x4s, boats, mowers, tractors, and chain saws. At the time of the auction, a 25% downpayment is required, with the balance due by the following Monday (auctions are held on Saturdays). For the sealed bid auctions, payment must be by money order or certified check.

Oklahoma

Central Purchasing, State Capitol, Oklahoma City, OK 73105, (405)521-3046, general information only for public auctions; (405)521-3835, for information on sealed bids; (405)521-2126, to get your name on a mailing list. Oklahoma auctions off vehicles as they accumulate. The state advertises upcoming auctions in local newspapers. Vehicles often have from 80,000 to 100,00 miles on them and vary in condition. Celebrities and Dodge Aires are commonly sold, but an occasional gem will slip in, like the fully-loaded candy apple red Corvette, with only 5,000 miles on it that showed up one day. Agencies most likely to have auctions are : Department of Human Services (vehicles and other items); Wildlife Department (vehicles); Department of Public Safety (vehicles); and the Department of Transportation (vehicles). The state advises that you contact each agency separately for details. Sealed bid auctions of all kinds of merchandise are also held. You may request your name to be placed on a mailing list, but if you do not bid three times, it will be removed. Otherwise, visit the office to view a catalog of listings.

Oregon

Department of Surplus Property, 1655 Salem Industrial Dr. N.E. Salem, OR 97310, (503)378-3131 (Salem area). About three times a year, Oregon auctions off both vehicles and other equipment, such as office furniture. Merchandise may include snow plows, horse trailers, computer equipment, or shop equipment. Although some are "junk," other items are in excellent condition, and bargains may be found. To be placed on the mailing list, send a stamped, self-addressed envelope to the address listed above. Ads are also placed in local newspapers in the areas where the auction will be held, giving the date and location of the auction. The procedure is to register and obtain a bidder number, which you hold up when you are making a bid. At the same time as you register, you must show some form of identification, and then you may pay for merchandise with a 10% down payment; the balance due within three working days. Personal checks are accepted, but no title of ownership is sent until the check clears the bank. The vehicle and general merchandise auctions are usually held on the same day, one in the morning, one in the afternoon.

Pennsylvania

General Services Department, Bureau of Vehicle Management 2221 Forster St. Harrisburg, PA 17105, (717)783-3132. Once a month, the DGS auctions off all kinds of vehicles, especially Aires, Chevettes, Cavaliers, Omnis, Cherokees, and Ford LTDs. Many have mileages under 100,000, and ages commonly range from 1979 to 1986. An inspection period begins two weeks before an auction on Monday through Friday from 8:00 am to 5:00 pm at the storage facility located at 22nd & Forster Sts. in Harrisburg. If you request an application, you may have your name put on a mailing list for advance advisories of auctions for a period of one year. A $100 deposit is required (cash or annual surety bonds only) if you win a bid, with full payment due within five working days by cashier's check, certified check, or postal money order. No personal or company checks accepted.

Bureau of Supplies and Surplus, Department of General Services, 2221 Forster St. Harrisburg, PA 17105, (717)787-4083. The Bureau of Supplies and Surplus of the General Services Department sells such items as office furniture and machines, including typewriters, desks, chairs, sectional furniture, filing cabinets, copy machines, dictaphones, and calculators. This merchandise is first offered to other state agencies, then put up for public sale after five days. There is no mailing list for notification of upcoming auctions, but ads are placed in the local newspapers in the area where an auction will be held. However, you can be put on a mailing list for some specific items such as heavy equipment. Property is sold at set prices. You may call to find out what items are currently for sale, or visit the warehouse between 8:00 am and 3:45 pm Monday through Friday.

Rhode Island

Department of Administration, Division of Purchase, 301 Promenade St., Providence, RI 02908, (401)277-2375. Rhode Island's Division of Purchase auctions off its surplus vehicles and office equipment, as well as other items. Items vary widely from auction to auction, and you should write to the address below to request an application to bid. Most bids are by the sealed bid system, where you send in your bid by mail. Categories of merchandise include: police and military supplies; automobile and transportation; aircraft and airfield; food and food products; builders supplies; medical equipment; electronics and data processing items; furniture and furnishings; office machines; and office supplies. Auctions for homes are held separately.

South Carolina

Division of General Services, 1441 Boston Ave., West Columbia, SC 29169, (803)739-5490. South Carolina sells items ranging from vehicles, to office and heavy equipment. Property is collected in monthly cycles and offered first to state agencies before being put up for sale to the public. No mailing list is kept, but you can visit the warehouse on 1441 Boston Ave. in West Columbia, which is open between 8:00 am and 4:30 pm Monday through Friday. Prices are tagged; there is no auction. Every other month, the General Services Division holds public auctions of items by lot for State, Federal,and Wildlife Department property. A mailing list is kept for advance advisories and property descriptions. There is a $10 fee to receive the mailings. Items can be inspected, and you are advised to make notes of the numbers of property you are interested in, then to check back to inquire if it is still available, since state agencies have first choice.

South Carolina Public Transportation Department, P.O. Box 191, Columbia SC 29202, (803)737-6635, for general information; (803)737-1488, for mailing list. About every five weeks, the South Carolina Department of Public Transportation holds auctions of its used and surplus vehicles, which include everything from patrol cars, trucks, and passenger cars, to highway equipment. To have your name put on a mailing list of upcoming auctions, call the number above. Payment is by cash, check or money order. Banking information will be requested for personal checks. Vehicles may be viewed on the Monday and Tuesday before the auctions, which are always held on a Wednesdays at 10 am.

South Dakota

Bureau of Administration, State Property Management, 701 East Sioux Ave., Pierre, SD 57501, (605)773-4935. Twice a year, in the spring and fall, the Department of Transportation holds public auctions for office equipment and vehicles,including Chevy Citations and pick-ups. Vehicles have over 100,000 miles on them and sell for well under market price. You may visually inspect the vehicles prior to the auction, but you may not enter them. However, during the auction, the vehicles are started and demonstrated. Auctions are located wherever the most property has accumulated in the state. Terms are cash only on the day of sale.

Tennessee

Department of General Services Property Utilization, 6500 Centennial Blvd., Nashville, TN 37209, (615)741-1711. Tennessee auctions off surplus vehicles, office equipment, and machinery of various kinds--milling machines, lathes, welders, and metal working equipment. The vehicles are of all types, including dump trucks, pick-ups, sedans, and station wagons. Auctions are held twelve times a year in Jackson, Dandridge, Nashville, and Chattanooga. No mailing list is kept, but the auctions are advertised in local newspapers. Items are available for inspection the day before the auction. Payment can be in cash, cashier's checks, or certified check.

Texas

Texas State Purchasing and General Services Commission, 1711 San Jacinto, P.O. Box 13047, Capitol Station, Austin, TX 78711-3047, (512)463-3445. Every two months, Texas auctions off vehicles, office furniture and machines, and highway equipment. You must apply to be put on the mailing list, which will give you a brief description of items available at the next auction. You may call the agency selling the property to arrange to inspect it; however, merchandise is available for inspection two hours before the auction, held at the Austin City Coliseum. Items are mostly used state property, although some is confiscated as well. You must register to bid beforehand. Payment on a winning bid is due at the end of the auction. Cash, cashiers check, certified check, money order, bank draft with Letter of Credit, or personal or company check with Letter of Credit are acceptable forms of payment. Items sold on site must be removed the day of the sale. Texas also holds sealed bid auctions, where you make a bid by mail. First, you indicate what category of property you are interested in, and they will send you bid forms and descriptions of items in that category. Sealed bid participants are notified by letter if winning bids and the exact amount due. Deposits for non-winners are returned. Also, each of the Texas state agencies hold local sales, for which each has its own mailing list.

Utah

Utah State Surplus Office, 522 South 700 West, Salt Lake City, UT 84104, (801)533-5883. Four or five times a year, Utah auctions of vehicles off and office furniture, as well as heavy equipment, whenever property accumulates. Most items are sold by public auction, although sealed bid auctions are sometimes held as well. Most of the public auctions are held in Salt Lake City at the address above, although some are occasionally held in other parts of the state. You may request your name be put on a mailing list to receive advance notice of auctions. Property may be viewed prior to an auction. Acceptable forms of payment are cash, cashier's check, and personal checks up to $100 with two forms of I.D. Payments must be in full on the day of the auction.

Vermont

Vermont Central Surplus Property Agency, RD #2, Box 520, Montpelier, VT 05602, (802)828-3394. Vermont sells low-priced surplus office furniture and machines on retail basis between 8:00 am and 4:00 pm daily at the Central Garage on Barre Montpelier Rd. Items include desks, chairs, file cabinets, and book shelves. Twice a year, vehicles, which may include police cruisers, dump trucks, and pick-ups, are sold by public auction, on a Saturday in May and September. A mailing list is kept to advise you in advance of upcoming auctions. Local newspapers also advertise them. Vehicles may be inspected the Friday

Government Auctions and Surplus Property

before an auction. Payment is up to the auctioneer, who is a private contractor. Usually, checks must be bank-certified, and a deposit is required to hold any vehicle not paid for in full the day of the auction. The balance is due by the following Tuesday by 3:00 pm.

Virginia

State Surplus Property, P.O. Box 1199, Richmond, VA 23209, (804)786-3876. Virginia auctions off everything but jewelry and land, including vehicles, office equipment and furniture, computers, tractors, bulldozers, dump trucks, pick-ups, and vans. Scrap metal, tires, and batteries are sold separately. Sales are by both public auction and sealed bid. There are sealed bid offerings every week, and as many as two auctions per week. Auction sites are at various locations around the state. You may place your name on a mailing list for both public auctions and sealed bid auctions; the sealed bid method is used when there are fewer than 100 items available. Inspections are allowed the day before the auction and again for a couple of hours on the day of the auction. For sealed bid items, you may call for more details on the items offered for sale.

Washington

Office of Commodity Redistribution, 2805 C St. S.W., Building 5, Door 49, Auburn, WA 98001, (206)931-3931. Washington holds auctions of used state vehicles, conducts "silent bids" (auctions where the bids are written rather than spoken), and also sells surplus materials by sealed bid (bids are placed through the mail) via catalogs. The vehicles are auctioned about every three months and include all kinds of used state conveyances, from patrol cars, to trucks and passenger cars, most having over 100,000 miles. There are few new luxury or confiscated type vehicles. The "silent bids" are held once a month, and include large quantities of office furniture sold by the pallet, with the exception of typewriters, which are sold individually. You may visit the warehouse to inspect the items beforehand. Payment may be made by cashiers check, money order, or cash, but no personal checks. For the sealed bids, you may request a catalog of merchandise, which includes everything from vehicles, to scrap material, office equipment, computers, clothes, cleaning fluids, tools, and pumps. For any of these sales, you may request to be put on the mailing list at the address above.

West Virginia

West Virginia State Agency Surplus Property, 2700 Charles Ave., Dunbar, WV 25064, (304)348-3456. Each month, West Virginia auctions off such items as chairs, desks, telephones, computers, typewriters, office equipment and furniture, and other miscellaneous property, as well as vehicles. The vehicles range from police cruisers to Cavaliers, Mustangs, some Crown Victorias, and an occasional Mercedes, in varying conditions. Inspection is available the week before the auction from 8:30 am to 6:00 pm. Payment may be by personal check, business check, or certified check, but no cash. Payment is due in full the same day. For sealed bids, payment is due within one week after a bid has won. Deposits, usually 20% of a bid, are returned to unsuccessful bidders, or in the case of winning bids, applied to the purchase price.

Wisconsin

Department of Transportation, Hill Farm Building, 4802 Sheboygan Ave. Madison, WI 53707, (608)266-3965. The Department of Transportation continuously sells a variety of merchandise from its warehouse in Madison. These items vary greatly from week to week, but may include work tables, desks, files, calculators and other office equipment and furniture, as well as vehicles. Call ahead before visiting the facility to view the property, which is sold at set prices.

Wisconsin Department of Administration, P.O. Box 7880, Madison, WI 53708, (608)266-8024. The Department of Administration holds vehicle auctions every month--usually with around 100 vehicles, including passenger vehicles, vans, trucks, and station wagons, all of different makes and models. The vehicles are usually at least four years old, or have at least 70,000 miles on them. You may have your name placed on a mailing list for advance notice of auctions; however, the auctions are also advertised in local newspapers. Payment is by cash, personal check, cashiers check, or money order. No credit cards. The full amount is due the day of the auction.

Wyoming

State Motor Pool, 723 West 19th, Cheyenne, WY 82002, (307)777-7247. Although it donates most of its surplus property to other state agencies, Wyoming does auction off its surplus vehicles, which may include pick-ups, vans, sedans, and jeeps. Most, though, have high mileage--from 50 to 60 thousand, up to 100,000 miles, but not always. You can have your name placed on a mailing list to receive advance notices of auctions, which are held when items accumulate. The state also advertises in local newspapers. Inspection of the vehicles is available between 3:00 pm and 6:00 pm the Friday before the auction, which is usually held on Saturdays. Payment depends on the auctioneer who is a private contractor. Usually, cash or check with proper I.D. are acceptable. Some cars go for well below market value, but others may be bidded up in price, depending on the mood of the crowd.

Unclaimed Money

In the United States today, experts believe that about five billion dollars in unclaimed money is collecting dust in state Abandoned Property offices. Some of the monetary items that end up in a state's possessions after being declared abandoned by the holding institution include:

* forgotten bank accounts
* uncashed stock dividends
* insurance payments
* safe deposit boxes
* utility deposits
* travelers checks
* money orders

People move away, lose track of investments, or die, and the accounts or funds, after a set amount of time--frequently five years--are reported to the state Treasurer's Escheats, Comptroller's, or Revenue office. The state then tries to track down the owners and return the money.

If you think financial property may be held by your state, the first step is to contact the appropriate office (a state by state list follows) to find out whether your name is listed. Or, in the case of the estate of a deceased person, the listing would be under his/her name. You will then fill out a claim form which you must return together with the required identification or proof of ownership. Requirements for proving ownership may vary according to the amount of the claim and the complications involved, but frequently states will ask for such things as copies of driver's licenses, social security numbers, and bank account numbers and passbooks. Most require that the information be notarized. A few states have limitations on how long they keep abandoned property before turning it over to state coffers, but most keep it indefinitely. Some also pay interest on the money if the property was originally interest-bearing.

Honest Finders vs. Vultures

The states currently owe money from abandoned property to an estimated one in ten people in the country, according to attorney David Epstein. But many states do not have the resources to investigate every case, and do little more than advertise names of owners in local newspapers. The resulting gap is sometimes filled by professional "finders" or "heir searchers" who find the owners themselves and charge a fee or commission in exchange for returning it. They can obtain lists, legally in most cases but sometimes surreptitiously, of the names of the owners from the state offices, then conduct their own search. Because of cases where these finders have charged excessive fees to people for returning their own money, and because of the strain their demands have put on some already over-burdened state offices, the finders have a shady reputation in some quarters. One state office, for example, refers to them as "bounty hunters," and another calls them "vultures." Many state offices feel that the finders infringe on the owner's right to have their money returned with no charge involved, which is the goal of the state.

But Paula Smith, Director of the Texas Abandoned Property Office and head of the informal National Association of Abandoned Property Administrators, says that since the states never find 100% of the owners, there is a place for honest finders. For example, if a state is unable to locate the owner of a sizable property that he didn't even know about, and a finder does the job, then a service has been performed. Many states, such as Texas, limit the amount of commission a finder may charge; and others have confidentiality laws that prevent them from aiding finders in any way.

One of the biggest obstacles states face, according to Ms. Smith, is obtaining the cooperation of the banks, insurance companies, and other institutions in reporting properties to them. Despite laws that govern how a holding institution should deal with dormant accounts, they are often low priority items in a business, she explains; and a state must sometimes work hard to convince them that it is best qualified to return the money.

With $5,000,000,000 (that's billion) in property sitting around out there, clearly many people have an interest in what happens to it. Finders, keepers, states and businesses all have something at stake, and the losers will be those who fail to take advantage of the services that the states offer.

State Listing of Unclaimed Property Offices

Alabama

Department of Revenue and Unclaimed Property, 1021 Madison Ave. P.O. Box 1911, Montgomery, AL 36131; (205) 261-2500. Alabama sends notices to the last known addresses of people whose unclaimed property has reverted to the Department of Revenue. The state also advertises in local newspapers four times a year - in a total of 63 different publications. In Alabama only owners, heirs or those possessing power of attorney will receive the property once it has been rightfully claimed. It usually takes about three weeks for the claimant to receive his money once the claim has been approved. The state has no statute of limitations on how long it can hold unclaimed property.

Alaska

Alaska Department of Revenue, Income and Excise Audit Division, Unclaimed Property Section, P.O. Box S.A. Juneau, AK 99811-0400 ; (907) 465-4653. Alaska publishes names of unclaimed property owners in the three major newspapers, sends the information to state

legislators, and contacts local news services in order to try to find the owners. They have a three person office, and the person in charge of refunds also makes efforts to investigate the whereabouts of owners. Alaska is currently holding an estimated 20,000 items of unclaimed property.

Arizona

Arizona Department of Revenue, Unclaimed Property, 1600 West Monroe, Phoenix, AZ 85007; (602) 542-3908. Twice a year the state runs advertisements in local newspapers with the names of people who have unclaimed property. Claimants need three pieces of I.D. to identify themselves as the rightful owners. In the case of an estate or property of a deceased person, a copy of the will is also required. Currently over 60,000 people have abandoned property in Arizona.

Arkansas

Auditor of the State, Unclaimed Property Division, 230 State Capitol, Little Rock, AR 72201; (501) 682-6030. Arkansas publishes the names of owners yearly in local newspapers, and also sends letters to the last known address of each person. In 1988 the state held "The Great Arkansas Treasure Hunt " which featured TV spots in an effort to locate owners. There are currently 7 thousand unclaimed accounts or other properties in Arkansas, dating from 1979. Arkansas is one of the few states where the unclaimed property reverts to general revenue after three years in the Unclaimed Property Office. The state will deal only with the actual owner of the property and not with other parties, including those endowed with power of attorney. Finders are restricted to a ten per-cent commission of the total retrieved. Refunds are usually sent out within about two weeks of approval.

California

...laimed Property Office, P.O. Box 942850, Sacramento, CA 94250-5873; ...6) 323-2827, Toll free (800) 992-4647 (CA only). In California the law requires the state to advertise unclaimed properties. However, according to Tom Holland, who heads the Unclaimed Property Office, they no longer have a special locator unit, due to budget cuts. The office uses radio and television advertisements, as well as newspaper advisories to locate owners. A person inquiring about abandoned property in California can get an instant answer by phone from the Office's computer. However, they still need to fill out a claim form and show proof of identity once they have determined that the property they are looking for is in the hands of the state. Mr. Holland says that soon State Banks will provide public access to the state data base in order to broaden the availability of information about unclaimed property. There are four hundred finders in California trying to get a piece of the considerable action in a state with over a million unclaimed properties worth four million dollars. They can come to the state's office and look up information on microfiche, but are limited to a ten per cent commission. In addition, the state will only make checks out amounting to 10 per-cent for a finder, while sending the remaining 90 per-cent directly to the owner.

Colorado

Colorado State Treasurer, Division of Unclaimed Property, 1560 Broadway, Suite 630, Denver, CO 80202; (303) 894-2449. Colorado has a statute of limitations of 20 years before unclaimed property be claimed by the state. Once a year, the state places the names of owners whose accounts they received the previous year in local newspapers. Colorado will deal only with owners. Finders may obtain a list of property owners for a $10 fee, but no research is available to them. The Unclaimed Property Office will only send checks directly to owners. Returns usually go out within two to four weeks of approval. Colorado, like other states, also stipulates that no owner is obligated to pay a finder a commission until the funds have been held by the state for 24 months or longer. The state currently holds 30,000 names on file of unclaimed property owners.

Connecticut

Treasury Department, 55 Elm St., Hartford, CT 06106; (203) 566-5516. Connecticut lists names of owners in local newspapers and also has a new in-house locator. The state has about ten million dollars that is currently unclaimed - approximately 30,000 owners. Returns are made out to owners only, or to someone with power of attorney.

Delaware

Delaware State Escheator, P.O. Box 8931, Wilmington, DE 19899; (302) 571-3349. Delaware requires different kinds of proof of ownership, depending on the kind or amount of the claim. After approval, a return is usually mailed out in about six to eight weeks. The state publishes names of owners in local newspapers, or notifies county authorities in unusual cases. Delaware will send returns in joint names of finder and owner.

District of Columbia

Department of Finance and Revenue, Unclaimed Property Division, 300 Indiana Ave. N.W., Room 5008, Washington, D.C. 20001; (202) 727-0063. The District of Columbia requires the usual proof of ownership, plus social security numbers to identify owners. They get out the returns in about four to six weeks. D.C. places advertisements in newspapers, produces some radio and TV spots, as well as sending out letters to owners and placing lists of owners in public libraries. They do not have a locating unit. D.C. currently holds $20 million in unclaimed property since 1981, and finders are limited to 10% commission. Finders must wait until the District government has held an account for seven months before they can contract to recover it.

Florida

Office of Comptroller, Division of Finance, Abandoned Property Section, Tallahassee, FL 32399-0350; (904) 487-0510. Florida deals with owners and other parties, but finders must be licensed private investigators. Returns are made out only to owners or investigators. They currently have between three and four hundred thousand dollars worth of unclaimed property.

Georgia

Georgia Department of Revenue, Unclaimed Property Office, 270 Washington St. Room 405, Atlanta, GA 30334 (no phone). Georgia is in the process of upgrading its office and soon hopes to speed up its return time on claims. Claimants may write, telephone, or come in and view lists in order to determine if they have property in the office. The next step is to fill out a claim form and return it with the necessary documentation and proof of identity. Checks are then sent out within a month. As part of its upgrading, the Georgia office also has more resources to locate owners, through records searches and outreach programs at state public events and placing lists in state Tax Commissioners' offices. They also place advertisements in 159 county newspapers. Georgia holds property in perpetuity and does not pay interest. The office is currently holding about 65,000 names on file - a total of $35 million dating from 1973. However, they are also holding some safe deposit box items that date back to the 1800's. There are currently no restrictions on finders.

Hawaii

Director of Finance, State of Hawaii, Unclaimed Property Section, Honolulu, HI 96810; (808) 5489-7578. Hawaii lists property owners names in local papers and attempts to locate people by phone. The state currently has between 160 and 170 thousand names of people who have not claimed their property. The amounts range from a few cents to hundreds of thousands of dollars. Hawaii does deal with finders, in providing lists of owners names, etc, but the state will send out checks only to owners. People inquiring about unclaimed property may do so by phone, but a written request is required if there is more than one account.

Idaho

Ms. Mary Weirick, State Tax Commission, 700 West State St., P.O. Box 36, Boise, ID 83722; (208) 334-7623. Idaho publishes a list of names twice a year in local newspapers, and runs continuous lists in some publications. In addition, some local radio stations announce 20 names per week in cooperation with the state. Also, they now have a full-time locator in the office to find potential owners. The state deals with finders and will sell them a list of properties worth $200 and above, but it requires that any property be held for two years by the state before a commission may be charged. After that, checks may be mailed to finders.

Illinois

Department of Financial Institutions, 421 East Capitol Ave., Springfield, IL 62706; (217) 782-8463. Illinois requests that inquiries to the office be in writing to facilitate their research. After approval, returns usually take about three months. The state advertises the names of owners in the newspapers of the county of each owner's last known address. They currently have over one million names. Finders are required to send the contract with the owners to the state office for approval; and they are limited to 50% of the first $1000 and 10% of everything above that. Checks are sent only to owners.

Indiana

Abandoned Property Section, 219 State House, Indianapolis, IN 46204-2794; (317) 232-6348. Indiana has a statute of limitations of 25 years before unclaimed property reverts to the Common School Fund. After approval, returns take about six to eight weeks. The state runs newspaper advertisements as well as television spots in an effort to find owners. Finders must submit the contract with the owners for approval by the state, and checks are sent directly to the owners. Also, finders are limited to 10% commission for amounts over $1000 and to 1/3rd under $1000.

Iowa

Great Iowa Treasure Hunt, Treasurer's Office, Hoover Building, State Capitol Complex, Des Moines, IA 50319; (515) 281-5540. Iowa publishes owners' names in local newspapers twice a year, and has representatives at the State and County Fairs to disseminate information. They use radio and TV advertisements for larger claims - $100 and over. Iowa currently has close to 74 thousand unclaimed properties. The office takes anywhere from 60 to 120 days to make the returns once the claim is approved.

Kansas

State Treasurer's Office, 900 Southwest Jackson, Suite 201, Topeka, KS 66612-1235; (913) 296-3171, or Toll-free 1-800-432-0386 (KS only). Kansas will take phone or written inquiries about lost properties. They pay owners directly. Currently there are over 200,000 unclaimed properties in the state. The Treasurer's office makes attempts by mail and through public gatherings to find owners.

Kentucky

Revenue Cabinet, Station 62, Frankfort, KY 40620; (502) 564-4722. Kentucky successfully processes 250 claims per year. They place advertisements in local newspapers, produce press releases, and run radio and television announcements in attempts to locate owners. In addition, they try to find people by mail. Kentucky requests all inquiries to be in writing (although they have even discovered people attempting fraud by using fake letterhead); and finders need a power of attorney or other legal document. Returns are sent to owners only. The office says they hope to see new legislation soon to control finders' fees.

Louisiana

Unclaimed Property Section, P.O. Box 91010, Baton Rouge, LA 00821; (504) 925-7537.

Maine

Treasurer's Department, Abandoned Property Division, House Station 39, Augusta, ME 04333; (207) 289-2771. Maine accepts either phone or written inquiries, and will have a return in about a week from approval, although stock returns take longer. Since 1979, there has been no statute of limitation on the length of time the office will hold funds. Finders cannot collect commissions on properties held less than two years and after that they are limited to 15%. Maine uses advertising and personal letters to try to locate owners, and they are in the process of being able to actively investigate their unclaimed properties.

Maryland

Comptroller of the Treasury, Unclaimed Property Section, 301 West Preston St., Baltimore, MD 21201; (301) 225-1700. Maryland has no statute of limitations governing the length of time property is held. The office has been in existence since 1966 and deals with both finders and owners.

Massachusetts

Commonwealth of Massachusetts, Treasury Department, Unclaimed Property Division, 50 Franklin St., 2nd Floor, Boston, MA 02110. Massachusetts, whose office has been in existence since 1955, pays interest to owners on interest-earning property. They publish names in local newspapers every year to try to locate owners. Once ownership has been established, the office pays returns in about four to six weeks. The state does not give returns to finders.

Michigan

Michigan Department of the Treasury, Escheats Division, Lansing, MI 48922; (517) 334-6550. Michigan has a statute of limitations of seven years after abandonment for amounts under $50. The office is not computerized so they have no current figures for how much property is being held, but they do get the returns out within several weeks. They have no capacity for investigation. For finders, they need a private detective's license, and the office makes out checks depending on what kind of settlement has been made.

Minnesota

Minnesota Department of Commerce, Office of Unclaimed Property, 500 Metro Square, St. Paul, MN 55101-2118; (612) 296-2568, Toll free 1-800-652-9747 within the state but outside Minneapolis/St.Paul area. Minnesota has about 150,000 properties currently unclaimed. Inquiries may be made by phone or in writing, and specific documentation will be required. Four to six weeks are needed to process returns. Searchers can collect for owners if proper documents are presented, but there is a 10 % limit on commissions unless there is a prior agreement between the owner and the searcher.

Mississippi

Mississippi Treasurer's Office, Unclaimed Property Division, P.O. Box 138, Jackson, MS 39205; (601) 359-3600. Mississippi pays interest on accounts - 5% on interest-bearing accounts and 1% on everything else. They currently hold $5.4 million in unclaimed funds. The state sets a limit of 33 1/3 % commission for finders, but expects new legislation to restrict that amount further. The state is required by law to publish the names of owners each year and letters are mailed to their last known addresses. It usually takes about six weeks for returns to be processed, if all the information has been properly supplied by the claimant.

Missouri

Department of Economic Development, Unclaimed Property, Box 1272, Jefferson City, MO 65102; (314) 751-0840. Missouri pays interest on interest-bearing accounts; and finders can collect their percentages with no limitations. The office tries to locate owners through publications, mailings and some searches, but they do not have investigative capability.

Montana

State Of Montana Department of Revenue, Abandoned Property Section, Mitchell Bldg. Helena, MT 59620; (406) 444-2425. Montana's one-person office cannot conduct extensive investigations to find property owners, but they do advertise items over $100 in the county of the person's last known address. There are currently between 70 and 100 thousand accounts unclaimed. Returns are made to finders with legal contracts or power of attorney.

Nebraska

Nebraska State Treasurer's Office, Property Capitol Building, Lincoln, NE 68509; (402) 471-2455. Nebraska publishes the names of property owners in local newspapers, sends out letters, and conducts research in an effort to locate the rightful owners. The office will deal with owners only and issues checks to them alone.

Nevada

State of Nevada, Unclaimed Property Division, State Mail Room, Las Vegas, NV 89158; (702) 486-4140, or Toll free 1-800-521-0019 (NV only). Nevada currently has between 50 and 60 thousand unclaimed properties, the vast majority of which are under $500. They prefer inquiries to be made in writing and will make returns in about three weeks. The state allows finders to make claims after the state has tried for two years to locate the rightful owner. The finders are then limited to ten per-cent commission, and the checks are sent separately to the finder and the owner. Nevada advertises in local papers as part of its efforts to locate the owners.

New Hampshire

New Hampshire State Treasurer's Office, Abandoned Property Division, State House Annex Room 121, Concord, NH 03301; (603) 271-2619. After advertising an abandoned property for two years, New Hampshire can go to court and have the account escheated to the county involved, with 15% going to a general State Treasurer's fund. After the two year period, the owner needs a special bill in the state legislature to retrieve his money. The State advertises once again in the newspaper prior to escheatment, and they research large accounts. New Hampshire does not recognize finders; any agreement between a finder and owner is unenforceable for 24 months after a property is turned over to the state, and then the escheatment process takes over.

New Jersey

New Jersey Supervisor of Escheats, 1 West State Street, 3rd Floor CN 214,

Trenton, NJ 08625; (609) 292-2121. New Jersey will not supply lists of owners' names to finders. They pay no interest and are a custodial state. Their efforts to find owners consist mostly of running newspaper advertisements.

New Mexico

New Mexico Taxation and Revenue Department, P.O. Box 630, Santa Fe, NM 87509-0630; (505) 827-0767. New Mexico holds properties for 25 years; after that they escheat to the General Fund for Schools. Objects such as those found in safe deposit boxes can be auctioned when they are turned over to the state, but a New Mexico spokesperson says that so far that has never happened. The state currently holds between 180-200,000 names, dating back to 1959 and totaling about $8 million. They advertise owners' names statewide and send letters to the last known addresses. Finders are subject to a gross receipts tax, but there is no limit on the commission they may charge.

New York

Administrator, Office of Unclaimed Funds, Alfred E. Smith Bldg. 9th Floor, Albany, NY 12236; (518) 473-0824, Toll free 1-800- 221-9311 (NY only). From New York's hotline or regular phone number, owners can find out immediately if their property has been turned over to the state. Then they will need to fill out the appropriate forms with proof of identification, which will vary for different kinds of property. Interest is paid for the first five years at the U.S. Treasury rate. There are currently seven million names of unclaimed property owners in the state, with funds amounting to two billion dollars. New York is very active in its efforts to find owners. Besides sending out letters (about three thousand per week), they have a mobile outreach program, where office personnel travel to various locations with all the computerized information, and visit senior citizens centers, malls, fairs, etc. They say this has been very successful in locating owners, whereas pilot projects to try to match names with the Department of Motor Vehicles and the Taxation and Finance Department have been less successful. The state is "not thrilled" with finders and feels that owners should be able to reclaim their property free of charge. Finders fees are limited to 15% and the office encourages people to deal directly with them.

North Carolina

Administrator, Escheat and Abandoned Property Section, Department of State Treasurer, 325 N. Salisbury St., Raleigh, NC 27611; (919) 733-6876. In North Carolina, the Abandoned Property Section can return funds in less than two weeks in uncomplicated situations. By law, they must send lists of owners names to clerks of the State Supreme Court in each county and to local newspapers. They also use computer matches with the Department of Motor Vehicles, and they have a locator unit as well. Currently, North Carolina holds over 5 million dollars in abandoned monies. Finders must be licensed private investigators and must state their fees in a contract with the owner. Commissions are limited to 25%.

North Dakota

North Dakota Unclaimed Property Division, 6th Floor, State Capitol, Bismark, ND 58505; (701) 224-2805. North Dakota publicizes abandoned properties in local newspapers, radio, television, through mailings to last known addresses, and booths at the State Fair. They accept inquiries by phone or mail, and then require claim forms to be filled out with appropriate documents attached. Once approved, returns usually take about two weeks. The state sends checks only to owners and has a two-year waiting period before finders can contract on a property. Finders' fees are limited to 25% of the total amount. Interest earned by abandoned properties goes to a common school fund.

Ohio

Chief, Division of Unclaimed Funds, Department of Commerce, 2 Nationwide Plaza, 4th Floor, Columbus, OH 43215; (614) 644-6226. In Ohio, the published lists of owners' names includes a coupon that they can fill out to expedite their claim. Returns could take from eight weeks to three months, depending on the complications involved. Ohio also has an outreach program where the office sends representatives to state and county fairs, shopping malls and other public events. This includes visiting sites of the Governor's "Capital for the Day" program where he picks a town to spend the day in to conduct business. The state currently has 2.8 million names on file, with funds amounting to 77 million dollars. It pays interest of 6% on amounts over $25. Ohio is unusual in that the Unclaimed Funds Division operates on the money it is holding, at no cost to the government. The state's Department of Development also uses unclaimed funds to guarantee loans that stimulate economic development. In addition, the original holding institutions in Ohio are only required to turn 10% of the unclaimed funds over to the state, and they use the money to invest at market value. The claimant still receives the full amount owed to him. The Ohio office must hold funds for two years before finders can make contracts on them, and their fees are restricted to 10%. Checks are paid to owners only unless another party has the power of attorney.

Oklahoma

Oklahoma Tax Commission, Unclaimed Property Section, 2501 Lincoln Blvd., Oklahoma City, OK 73194-0010; (405) 521-4275. Oklahoma is a custodial state and keeps unclaimed properties in perpetuity. The state currently holds $25 million worth of these monies. They publicize names in local newspapers twice a year and intend to have a locator service in the near future. If a finder has a power of attorney, he can submit a claim and there is currently no limit on the amount of commission he can charge.

Government Auctions and Surplus Property

Oregon

Oregon Division of State Lands, 1600 State Street, Salem, OR 97310; (503) 378-3805. Oregon will hold unclaimed property for 25 years, and then it becomes part of the School Fund. Interest earned also goes to the Fund. The state sends letters to the last known addresses of owners and advertises in local newspapers. They also publish an information packet for consumers explaining the procedures involved for claiming abandoned property. The state sends checks jointly to finders and owners and there are currently no restrictions on the amount of commission finders may charge.

Pennsylvania

Supervisor, Abandoned and Unclaimed Property Section, Pennsylvania Department of Revenue, 2850 Turnpike Industrial Park, Middletown, PA 17057; (717) 986-4641, or Toll free 1-800-222-2046 (PA only). Procedures and proof required to reclaim property depend on the type and size of the property, and whether the claimant is the owner, heir or estate. Since 1983, the state has collected $100 million from 400,000 accounts. Pennsylvania checks its list of names against state tax records to help locate people and sends out notices for amounts over $100. The state also lists the names of owners in local newspapers, and passes lists on to General Assembly members. In addition, they have an outreach program that travels to public functions around the state looking for owners, and they have found one in five people on their list in this manner. In Pennsylvania there are no restrictions on finders.

Rhode Island

State Of Rhode Island, Unclaimed Property Division, P.O. Box 1435, Providence, RI 02901; (401) 277-6505. Rhode Island takes about three to four weeks to return lost funds once the claim is made. Callers to the state office may find out immediately from the computerized listing if they actually have money there, and then must follow up with the proper identification. The state pays simple interest - 5% on interest-bearing accounts and 1% on non interest- bearing accounts. They send out letters to the last known addresses of owners, place advertisements in all the state newspapers, and run television and radio spots advertising names of owners. They also have an outreach program, where representatives of the Unclaimed Property Office travel to public functions around the state to try to locate people. The state says this program has been very effective. In March of 1988 Rhode Island advertised six thousand names of property owners and was able to locate half of them. Searchers are on their own here - they receive no help from the state, nor are there restrictions on the fees they may charge.

South Carolina

Abandoned Property Office, South Carolina Tax Commission, P.O. Box 125, Columbia, SC 29214; (803) 737-4771. In South Carolina, a claimant looking for lost property can go to the holding institution - that is, the original business where the account or money was located - within the first sixty days after his funds have been declared abandoned. Then, he must look for them in the state office. Twice a year the office runs advertisements in county newspapers, with names of people known to have lived in each county. They also travel to the State Fair and shopping malls around the state in search of owners, as well as mail letters to the last known addresses. South Carolina currently holds $18 million in abandoned property, representing 250,000 accounts. In 1989, lists of owners' names were made available to the public for the first time, but the office will not duplicate or mail copies. Finders fees have also been limited to 15% for the first time, and the state now mandates it must hold a property for two years before a finder can contract to recover it.

South Dakota

Ms. Ruby Douglas, Abandoned Property, State Treasurer's Office, 500 East Capitol, Pierre, SD 57501; (605) 773-3378. Inquiries may be by phone or in writing to the office, which can do an immediate computer search to determine if a claimant's property is being held there. Then, the claimant must submit whatever proof is required and complete the necessary paperwork. A simple claim may be returned within one week. South Dakota has a successful outreach program that travels to state and county fairs with a specially-made list of names that is posted so the public may easily read it. In the past two years, they have tripled their refunds as a result of the program. In addition, the office lists names in local newspapers. Finders are limited to 25% commission and the office pays returns directly to owners only. No lists of names are made available for heir-finding purposes, although anyone who wants to see the names may come to the office by appointment only.

Tennessee

State of Tennessee, Unclaimed Property Division, Andrew Jackson State Office Bldg. 11th floor, Nashville, TN 37219; (615) 741-6499. In Tennessee the Unclaimed Property Division pays only to estates in the case of money belonging to a deceased person. In all cases, they require suitable proof identification such as proof of address, social security number, etc. Returns take approximately three weeks. Interest is paid only if the original holder paid it as well. Tennessee advertises names of owners in local newspapers, sends letters to last known addresses, matches its list with other state agencies, and searches current telephone directories in an effort to locate them. Further efforts may be made in cases of large accounts. Since 1979, $26 million worth of abandoned property has been reported to the state office, of which $8 million has been returned. The office currently holds $18 million worth of property. Finders must make appointments with the office to view lists of names, and they are frequently booked months in advance. Any contract made between a finder and owner must be approved by the state; and contracts are only valid after the state has held the property for one year. Finders are restricted to 10% commission.

Texas

Unclaimed Money Fund, P.O. Box 12608, State Treasurer's Office, Austin, TX 78711; (512) 463-4630, or Toll free 1-800-321-CASH (TX only). Texas claimants follow procedures similar to those in most states - that is, filling out claim forms, providing notarized documentation of ownership, and submitting driver's license or social security numbers. Returns take about 90 days to process. The state has a locator service to find owners, and also advertises names in local newspapers. The Treasurer's office has received two million accounts over the past 25 years, representing over $ 206 million. Finders are limited to 10% commission; and the Treasurer's office advises people who have been contacted by a finder to check with them first before paying someone a fee to return their money. Money never claimed in Texas goes to a Foundation School Fund, or to the State general revenue. However, claimants can retrieve their funds at any time.

Utah

Utah Unclaimed Property Division, 219 State Capitol, Salt Lake City, UT 84114; (801) 538-1043. Utah pays interest on accounts that were interest-bearing when they came from the bank, such as certificates of deposit; but other items such as savings accounts are closed out by the bank. The state advertises in the paper names they received in the past six months and publicizes on radio and television. They also run a booth at the State Fair and maintain a locator in the office. The state has over 150,000 unclaimed properties at the present time, of which 8000 are over $25. Searchers or finders can apply with a valid power of attorney and checks are issued either to owners or those with power of attorney. No agreement between owners and fee-finders is enforceable until the state has held the property for two years.

Vermont

State Treasurer's Office, Abandoned Property Division, 133 State St., Montpelier, VT 05602; (802) 828-2301. Vermont sends out letters to owners of property worth $25 or more. If the amount is over $50, the state runs advertisements in local newspapers for two consecutive weeks. They have no other investigative capability due to the very small size of the office. Vermont has collected about two million dollars worth of unclaimed property since 1965, and currently holds between 16 and 18 thousand properties. Finders can only contract with owners after the state has held a property for twelve months.

Virginia

Department of the Treasury, Division of Unclaimed Property, P.O. Box 3 R, Richmond, VA 23207; (804) 225-2393, or Toll free 1-800-468-1088 (VA only). Virginia requires a claimant to submit proof of whatever information the state received from the holder. For example, someone claiming money in a savings account would have to produce a passbook or other proof of ownership of that account. In most cases, returns are made within two to three weeks. The state pays interest if the original holder was also paying it. There is a 5 % limit. In Virginia, unclaimed property information is classified as confidential, so the state cannot release information to finders. Private agreements between finders and owners are limited to a 10% commission for the finder. In addition, the property must be held for 36 months before such a contract is recognized. Approximately 400-500 thousand names are currently on file with the abandoned property office, and the state is holding some $92 million.

Washington

State of Washington Department of Revenue, Unclaimed Property Office, P.O. Box 448, Olympia, WA 98507; (206) 586-2736. Washington has an automated system that enables the office to respond immediately to inquiries about unclaimed property. Their list dates back to 1955. The office attends county and state fairs to locate owners, and hopes to branch out soon to malls and other public locations as well. The staff searches telephone books and recently found the owner of $149,000 by looking in the telephone directory. She had not even known the money was owed to her. They also place advertisements in local newspapers every six months and send out notices. They say that efforts to advertise through the broadcast media have not been very successful. Washington pays interest if an account was previously interest-bearing; and continues to pay the same rate. The state currently holds about $60 million in unclaimed property, from about 500,000 owners. Last year, it paid out over one million dollars in returns, out of the eight to ten million it received. Washington is one of the most restrictive states for finders, limiting them to 5% commission and subjecting them to the confidentiality law which limits what information the office can reveal about abandoned property owners. As a result, they say they have few problems with heir-finding.

West Virginia

Treasurer of the State, Unclaimed Property Division, State Capital, Charleston, WV 25305; (304) 343-4000. West Virginia has a two-person office for unclaimed property, so the efforts they can make to locate owners are minimal, and returns may take some time. By law, however, the state must advertise the names in local newspapers. There are no regulations on finders, but the office does not supply lists of names. Finders can view the names by visiting the office, but no information except names and addresses is released unless an owner has authorized it.

Wisconsin

Office of the State Treasurer, Unclaimed Property Division, P.O. Box 2114, Madison, WI 53701-2114; (608) 267-7977. The Wisconsin office prefers written inquiries about lost properties, including as accurate a description as possible. Once a claim is approved by the Unclaimed Property Division and the Attorney General's office, returns are made within six to eight weeks. The state pays interest if the account was interest-bearing in the first place. For properties over $50, Wisconsin runs newspaper advertisements listing the names of owners. The office is able to perform only limited research. They search current telephone directories, and try to check social security numbers with the Department of Revenue. Finders are limited to 20% commission as of May 1988. They may purchase a list of names and view the records in the office, but checks are made out only in the names of the owners.

Wyoming

Abandoned Property Division, Wyoming State Treasury Office, State Capital Building, Cheyenne, WY 82002; (307) 777-7408. Wyoming's Abandoned Property Office currently deals mainly with lost insurance claims. However, new legislation is expected soon to bring the state in line with the uniform abandoned property law. But currently, other holders are not required to report abandoned funds to the state. The claim procedures for recovering the insurance money is similar to what other states require - that is, proof of policy number, address, etc. Returns are usually made in one week. Currently Wyoming holds 5000 names on its unclaimed list. Wyoming has a five year statute of limitations, after which funds that are still unclaimed revert to a Common School Fund and are no longer claimable. Finders can come into the office to view the list of names and there are no restrictions on the amount of commission they may charge. However, finders have no access to property until the account has been held by the state for two years.

Small Business and Entrepreneuring
Federal Starting Places

* See also Business and Industry Chapter
* See also Selling to the Government Chapter
* See also Information on People, Companies, and Mailing Lists Chapter
* See also Economics, Demographics, and Statistics Chapter
* See also International Trade Chapter
* See also Patents, Trademarks and Copyrights Chapter

Here you will discover that the U.S. Small Business Administration is not the only federal agency that provides financial and managerial assistance to small businesses and entrepreneurs. For example, trade remedy relief is the responsibility of the U.S. International Trade Commission and the National Science Foundation offers small firms R&D opportunities. After you become more familiar with the Answer Desk, incubator programs, FTC rules, certified lenders, and other federal help, you may want to move on to the next section, State Starting Places and Money. You'll probably find a lot of help close by in the state capitol and in other major metropolitan areas besides Washington, D.C. State governments are increasingly responsive to small business and offer many services.

* Advocacy and Small Business
Office of Advocacy
U.S. Small Business Administration
1441 L St., NW, Room 1012
Washington, DC 20416   (202) 653-6533
As the watchdog for small business within the federal government, this office carries out the following: researching the effect of federal laws, programs, regulation, and taxation on small business and making recommendations to federal agencies for appropriate adjustments to meet the needs of small business; conducting economic studies and statistical research into matters affecting small business and evaluating future opportunities, problems, and needs of small business; and serving as a conduit through which small business can make suggestions and comment on policy. Available for sale from the U.S. Government Printing Office, The State of Small Business: A Report of the President, contains the most current information on small business performance in the economy. Also issued from this office is the Small Business Advocate, a monthly newsletter that reports on small business issues and actions of the Office of Advocacy. It is available through Advocacy's Office of Information by calling (202) 634-7600. For more information contact the office above.

* Answer Desk
Office of Advocacy
U.S. Small Business Administration
1725 Eye St., NW, Room 414   (800) 368-5855
Washington, DC 20416   (202) 653-7561
The Small Business Answer Desk helps callers with questions on how to start and manage a business, where to get financing, and other information needed to operate and expand a business. This toll-free hotline is provided by SBA's Office of Advocacy and operates from 8:30 a.m. to 5:00 p.m. EST, Monday through Friday.

* Broadcast Entrepreneurs: Purchasing and Technical Assistance
Consumer Assistance and Small Business Division
Office of Public Affairs
Federal Communications Commission
1919 M St., NW, Room 254
Washington, DC 20554   (202) 632-7000
The CASB Division will provide you with personal assistance in locating information concerning FCC rules, policies, procedures, and guidance concerning participation in FCC rulemaking proceedings. In addition, this office provides specialized to assistance to those interested in becoming involved in the small business telecommunications industry. They will walk you through the purchasing procedures, identify resources for financial and technical assistance, and perform license status checks for applicants. The Public Affairs office also coordinates broadcast ownership workshops, which cover these topic and more, every year across the country. Contact CASB for more information.

* Business Assistance--Directory of Federal and State
National Technical Information Service
Department of Commerce
5285 Port Royal Rd.

Springfield, VA 22161   (703) 487-4650
The Directory of Federal and State Business Assistance describes more than 180 Federal and 500 state programs. Each entry gives a summary of the service offered, a telephone number and address, and eligibility requirements if any. These programs are designed to help new and growing companies compete more effectively in domestic and international markets. Uses of this directory can include how to get funding for a company's research and development; where to get mail lists of potential overseas business buyers; who provides venture money; and what Federal and state contacts offer free management consulting. The Directory is available for $29.00. Contact the Sales Desk to place an order or request the free information brochure, PR-801.

* Business Assistance Newsletter
Public Affairs
Minority Business Development Agency
114th and Constitution Ave. NW
Room 6707
Washington, DC 20230   (202) 377-1936
Minority Business Today is a free monthly publication which highlights interesting articles, educational opportunities, loan information, and grant awards, as well as procurement and publications information, relating to minority businesses. Also included is information on international trade and Minority Business Development Centers.

* Business Loans from the SBA
Contact your local SBA office or the Small Business Answer Desk Listed in this Section.
SBA offers two basic types of business loans: guaranteed loans which are made by private lenders, usually banks, and guaranteed up to 90 percent by SBA; and SBA direct loans which are available only to applicants unable to secure an SBA guaranteed loan. Business Loans from the SBA is a brochure available from your SBA office which gives information on these two types of loans, how to apply for a loan, terms of loans, collateral, eligibility requirements, and general size standards.

* Capital Formation for Small Businesses
The Office of Small Business Policy
Division of Corporation Finance
U.S. Securities and Exchange Commission
450 5th St., NW
Washington, DC 20549   (202) 272-2644
The Securities and Exchange Commission's main responsibility under the securities laws is to protect investors and to make sure the capital markets operate fairly and orderly. However, the Commission is careful not to let its regulations impair capital formation by small businesses. Therefore, the SEC has taken a number of steps to help small businesses raise capital and to ease the burden of undue regulations under the federal securities laws. The Commission is continually examining other ways to meet these goals. For more information, contact this office.

* Coal Operator Assistance

Small Coal Operator Assistance
Land Resources
Natural Resources Management
Resource and Development
Tennessee Valley Authority
Norris, TN 37828   (615) 632-1753

To ensure more competition and reasonable prices, TVA reserves a portion of its coal purchases for small producers. In addition, the TVA provides mining and reclamation technical assistance to small coal producers. The program is also involved in non-coal mineral abandoned mine reclamation. The percentage of contracts awarded to coal suppliers is evaluated based on the capability of the company to comply with TVA's mine reclamation programs.

* Contract Loans

Contact your local SBA office or the Small Business Answer Desk   listed in this section.

The Contract Loan Program (COL) is a short term line of credit, without a revolving feature. It is available under SBA's guaranty loan program solely to finance the estimated cost of labor and material needed to perform on a specific contract. Detailed information can be obtained from the SBA office in your area.

* Definition of a Small Business

Contact your local SBA office or the Small Business Answer Desk   listed in this section.

SBA generally defines a small business as one which is independently owned and operated and is not dominant in its field. Most small, independent businesses or individuals starting a business are eligible for SBA assistance. To be eligible for SBA loans and other assistance, a business must meet a size standard set by the SBA. Specific size standard information is available through any SBA office around the country.

* Development Company Loans

Contact your local SBA office or the Small Business Answer Desk listed in th is section.

Development Company Loans are made to development organizations approved by SBA for the purpose of fostering economic growth in rural and urban areas. Growth is measured primarily by job creation and retention. Loan proceeds are used by development companies to assist small business concerns with plant acquisition, construction, conversion, or expansion, including the acquisition of machinery and equipment. Contact the nearest SBA office for more information on these loans.

* Disaster Assistance

Contact your local SBA office or the Small Business Answer Desk listed in th is section.

Natural disasters, such as hurricanes, floods, tornados, and earthquakes, often cause hardship to business and individuals. When the U.S. President or SBA Administrator declares a specific area to be a disaster area, two types of loans are offered by SBA: Physical Disaster Loans and Economic Injury Disaster Loans. To obtain the pamphlets *Disaster Loans for Homes and Personal Property, Economic Injury Disaster Loans for Small Businesses*, and *Physical Disaster Business Loans*, or for more information, contact your local SBA office.

* Economic Database

Office of Economic Research
Office of Advocacy
U.S. Small Business Administration
1725 Eye St., NW, Room 414
Washington, DC 20416   (202) 634-7550

The *Small Business Data Base* (SBDB) is an integrated effort for developing and organizing data on the role of small business in the U.S. Economy. It is designed to meet the needs of the research community for analyzing cause and effect relationships of small business problems and progress. *The Small Business Data Base: A User's Guide* provides an overview of Data Base files and applications, as well as methods of accessing the *Small Business Data Base*. It is designed to acquaint the first-time user with the diversity of possible uses with the SBDB. To obtain this guide or for more information, contact the office above.

* Environmental Protection Agency Small Business Ombudsman

Small Business Ombudsman
Environmental Protection Agency
401 M Street SW
Washington, DC 20460   (202) 382-3090

The Small Business Ombudsman in the EPA Office of the Administrator provides various services to help small business comply with EPA regulations. The Ombudsman serves as information services and advocate for small business

interests in the regulatory development process. It helps these small businesses with their individual problems.

* EPA-Help Hotline for Small Business

Environmental Protection Agency
401 M Street SW
Washington, DC 20460   (800)368-5888 (202) 557-1938

The Small Business Hotline is an EPA-based hotline that gives advice and information to small businesses on complying with EPA regulations. It deals with problems encountered by small-quantity generators of hazardous waste and other small businesses with environmental concerns.

* Expanding SBA Services to Business

Office of Private Sector Initiative
U.S. Small Business Administration
1441 L Street, NW, Room 317
Washington, DC 20416   (202) 653-7880

The Private Sector Initiatives Program is a cooperative, outreach program designed to increase the effectiveness of SBA programs, particularly in providing management training and publications to the small business community. It combines the resources of trade associations, corporations, foundations, and professional societies with those of SBA in responding to the changing needs of small business. The main focus of this program is enlarging the capability of SBA to provide valuable services to small businesses through cooperative, jointly-sponsored activities with the private sector, particularly at reduced cost. Some of the ways the private sector helps SBA in delivering these services is by co-sponsoring management training programs (courses, conferences, clinics, seminars, and workshops), providing speakers, panelists, and moderators for training programs, and offering one-on-one counseling to small business persons. For additional information on this program, contact your SBA office or the office above.

* Facts About Small Businesses

Office of Business Development
U.S. Small Business Administration
1441 L St., NW, Room 317
Washington, DC 20416   (202) 653-6881

Contact this office above to obtain any the following fact sheets:

Seasonal Line of Credit Program (#4)
Contract Loan Program (#6)
Handicapped Assistance Loans (#7)
Small Business Institute Program (#11)
SCORE/ACE (#16)
Loans to Small General Contractors (#17)
Management and Technical Assistance 7(j) Program (#20)
Surety Bond Guarantee Program (#21)
Secondary Market Program - Fact Sheet for Lenders (#24)
Section 504 - Certified Development Company Program (#25)
Small Business Solar Energy and Conservation Loan Program (#29)
Interest Rate Policy (#30)
Section 8(a) Program (#36)
Facts About Certified and Preferred Lender Programs (#38)
Facts about SBA (#39)
Facts about Small Business (#40)
International Trade Assistance (#42)
Small Business Development Centers (#43)
Facts About Black-Owned Small Businesses (#44)
Facts About Women-Owned Small Businesses (#45)
Facts About Hispanic-Owned Small Businesses (#47)
Facts About Firms Owned by Asians, American Indians, and Other Minorities (#48)
Private Sector Initiatives Program (#49)
Guaranteed Loans to Employee Trusts (#50)
SBA Export-Revolving Line of Credit (#51)
Small Business Innovation Research (SBIR) Program (#52)
Loans for Vietnam-Era and Disabled Veterans (#53)

* Small Business Administration Field Offices

SBA field offices are comprised of regional offices (RO), district offices (DO), branch offices (BO), post-of-duty offices (POD), and disaster area offices (DAO). The regional offices are located in 10 major cities around the country and each directs a number of district offices within the region. Regional offices do not make individual loans or offer specific assistance to individuals or companies. District offices are the real contact point for small businesses needing information or assistance. Each district office is staffed by a team of experts in the lending, procurement, and management assistance areas who have the responsibility to consider loan applications, to offer individual management assistance, and to coordinate other small business services. Branch offices and post-of-duty offices have a smaller staff than district offices and are not quite as full-serviced. Disaster area offices are located in four cities around the country

Small Business and Entrepreneuring

and each provides disaster assistance for their individual regions to small business owners.

Region 1

Augusta
40 Western Ave., Room 512, Augusta, ME 04330; (207) 622-8378

Boston
60 Batterymarch St., 10th Floor, Boston, MA 02110; (617) 451-2030

Boston
10 Causeway St., Room 265, Boston, MA 02114; (617) 565-5590

Concord
55 Pleasant St., Room 210, Concord, NH 03301-1257; (603) 225-1400

Hartford
330 Main St., 2nd Floor, Hartford, CT 06106; (203) 240-4700

Montpelier
87 State St., Room 205, Montpelier, VT 05602; (802) 828-4474

Providence
380 Westminster Mall, 5th Floor, Providence, RI 02903; (401) 528-4586

Springfield
1550 Main St., Room 212, Springfield, MA 01103; (413) 785-0268

Region 2

Albany
445 Broadway, Room 261, Albany, NY 12207; (518) 472-6300

Buffalo
111 W. Huron St., Room 1311, Buffalo, NY 14202; (716) 846-4301

Camden
2600 Mt. Ephrain Ave., Camden, NJ 08104; (609) 757-5183

Elmira
333 E. Water St., 4th Floor, Elmira, NY 14901; (607) 734-8130

Hato Rey
Carlos Chardon Ave., Room 691, Hato Rey, PR 00918; (809) 753-4002

Melville
35 Pinelawn Rd., Room 102E, Melville, NY 11747; (516) 454-0750

New York
26 Federal Plaza, Room 31-08, New York, NY 10278; (212) 264-7772

New York
26 Federal Plaza, Room 3100, New York, NY 10278; (212) 264-4355

Newark
60 Park Place, 4th Floor, Newark, NJ 07102; (201) 645-2434

Rochester
100 State St., Room 601, Rochester, NY 14614; (716) 263-6700

St. Croix
4C & 4D Este Sion Frm, Room 7, St. Croix, VI 00820; (809) 778-5380

St. Thomas
Veterans Drive, Room 283, St. Thomas, VI 00801; (809) 774-8530

Syracuse
100 S. Clinton St., Room 1071, Syracuse, NY 13260; (315) 423-5383

Region 3

Baltimore
10 N. Calvert St., 3rd Floor, Baltimore, MD 21202; (301) 962-4392

Charleston
550 Eagan St., Suite 309, Charleston, WV 25301; (304) 347-5220

Clarksburg
168 W. Main St., 5th Floor, Clarksburg, WV 26301; (304) 623-5631

Harrisburg
100 Chestnut St., Suite 309, Harrisburg, PA 17101; (717) 782-3840

King of Prussia

475 Allendale Rd., Suite 201, King Prussia, PA 19406; (215) 962-3846

King Prussia
475 Allendale Rd., Suite 201, King Prussia, PA 19406; (215) 962-3750

Pittsburgh
960 Penn Ave., 5th Floor, Pittsburgh, PA 15222; (412) 644-2780

Richmond
400 N. 8th St., Room 3015, Richmond, VA 23240; (804) 771-2617

Washington
1111 18th St., 6th Floor, Washington, DC 20036; (202) 634-4950

Wilkes-Barre
20 N. Pennsylvania Ave., Room 2327, Wilkes-Barre, PA 18701; (717) 826-6497

Wilmington
844 King St., Room 5207, Wilmington, DE 19801; (302) 573-6294

Region 4

Atlanta
1375 Peachtree St., NE, 5th Floor, Atlanta, GA 30367-8102; (404) 347-2797

Atlanta
1720 Peachtree Rd., NW, 6th Floor, Atlanta, GA 30309; (404) 347-2441

Birmingham
2121 8th Ave., N., Suite 200, Birmingham, AL 35203-2398; (205) 731-1344

Charlotte
222 S. Church St., Room 300, Charlotte, NC 28202; (704) 371-6563

Columbia
1835 Assembly St., Room 358, Columbia, SC 29202; (803) 765-5376

Coral Gables
1320 S. Dixie Hwy, Suite 501, Coral Gables, FL 33146; (305) 536-5521

Gulfport
One Hancock Plaza, Suite 1001, Gulfport, MS 39501-7758; (601) 863-4449

Jackson
100 W. Capitol St., Suite 322, Jackson, MS 39269-0396; (601) 965-4378

Jacksonville
400 W. Bay St., Room 261, Jacksonville, FL 32202; (904) 791-3782

Louisville
600 Federal Place, Room 188, Louisville, KY 40202; (502) 582-5976

Nashville
404 James Robertson Pkwy, Suite 1012, Nashville, TN 37219; (615) 736-5881

Statesboro
52 N. Main St., Room 225, Statesboro, GA 30458, (912) 489-8719

Tampa
700 Twiggs St., Room 607, Tampa, FL 33602; (813) 228-2594

W. Palm Beach
5601 Corporate Way S., Suite 402, W. Palm Beach, FL 33407; (305) 689-3922

Region 5

Chicago
230 S. Dearborn St., Room 510, Chicago, IL 60604-1593; (312) 353-0359

Chicago
219 S. Dearborn St., Room 437, Chicago, IL 60604-1779; (312) 353-4528

Cincinnati
550 Main St., Room 5028, Cincinnati, OH 45202; (513) 684-2814

Cleveland
1240 E. 9th St., Room 317, Cleveland, OH 44199; (216) 522-4180

Columbus
85 Marconi Blvd., Room 512, Columbus, OH 43215; (614) 469-6860

Detroit
477 Michigan Ave., Room 515, Detroit, MI 48226; (313) 226-6075

Eau Claire
500 S. Barstow Commo, Room 37, Eau Claire, WI 54701; (715) 834-9012

Indianapolis
575 N. Pennsylvania St., Room 578, Indianapolis, IN 46204-1584; (317) 269-7272

Madison
212 E. Washington Ave., Room 213, Madison, WI 53703; (608) 264-5261

Marquette
300 S. Front St., Marquette, MI 49885; (906) 225-1108

Minneapolis
100 N. 6th St., Suite 610, Minneapolis, MN 55403-1563; (612) 370-2324

Milwaukee
310 W. Wisconsin Ave., Suite 400, Milwaukee, WI 53203; (414) 291-3941

Springfield
511 W. Capitol St., Suite 302, Springfield, IL 62704; (217) 492-4416

Region 6

Albuquerque
5000 Marble Ave., NE, Room 320, Albuquerque, NM 87100; (505) 262-6171

Austin
300 E. 8th St., Room 520, Austin, TX 78701; (512) 482-5288

Corpus Christi
400 Mann St., Suite 403, Corpus Christi, TX 78401; (512) 888-3331

Dallas
8625 King George Dr., Bldg. C, Dallas, TX 75235-3391; (214) 767-7643

Dallas
1100 Commerce St., Room 3C-36, Dallas, TX 75242; (214) 767-0605

El Paso
100737 Gateway W., Suite 320, El Paso, TX 79902; (915) 541-7586

Ft. Worth
819 Taylor St., Room 10A27, Ft. Worth, TX 76102; (817) 334-3613

Harlingen
222 E. Van Buren St., Room 500, Harlingen, TX 78550; (512) 427-8533

Houston
2525 Murworth, Suite 112, Houston, TX 77054; (713) 660-4401

Little Rock
320 W. Capitol Ave., Room 601, Little Rock, AR 72201; (501) 378-5871

Lubbock
1611 Tenth St., Suite 200, Lubbock, TX 79401; (806) 743-7462

Marshall
505 E. Travis, Room 103, Marshall, TX 75670; (214) 935-5257

New Orleans
1661 Canal St., Suite 2000, New Orleans, LA 70112; (504) 589-6685

Oklahoma City
200 NW 5th St., Suite 670, Oklahoma City, OK 73102; (405) 231-4301

San Antonio
7400 Blanco Rd., Suite 100, San Antonio, TX 78216; (512) 229-4535

Shreveport
500 Fannin St., Room 8A-08, Shreveport, LA 71101; (318) 226-5196

Region 7

Cedar Rapids
373 Collins Rd. NE, Room 100, Cedar Rapids, IA 52402-3118; (319) 399-2571

Des Moines
210 Walnut St., Room 749, Des Moines, IA 50309; (515) 284-4422

Kansas City
1103 Grand Ave., 6th Floor, Kansas City, MO 64106; (816) 374-3419

Kansas City
911 Walnut St., 13th Floor, Kansas City, MO 64106; (816) 426-2989

Omaha
11145 Mill Valley Rd., Omaha, NB 68154; (402) 221-4691

Springfield
620 S. Glenstone St., Suite 110, Springfield, MO 65802-3200; (417) 864-7670

St. Louis
815 Olive St., Room 242, St. Louis, MO 63101; (314) 425-6600

Wichita
220 E. Waterman St., 1st Floor, Wichita, KS 67202; (316) 269-6571

Region 8

Casper
100 East B St., Room 4001, Casper, WY 82602-2839; (307) 261-5761

Denver
999 18th St., Suite 701, Denver, CO 80202; (303) 294-7001

Denver
721 19th St., Room 407, Denver, CO 80202-2599; (303) 844-2607

Fargo
657 Second Ave. N, Room 218, Fargo, ND 58108-3086; (701) 239-5131

Helena
301 S. Park, Room 528, Helena, MT 59626; (406) 447-5381

Salt Lake City
125 S. State St., Room 2237, Salt Lake City, UT 84138-1195; (801) 524-5800

Sioux Falls
101 S. Main Ave., Suite 101, Sioux Falls, SD 57102-0527; (605) 336-2980

Region 9

Agana
Pacific Daily News Bldg., Room 508, Agana, GM 96910; (671) 472-7277

Fresno
2202 Monterey St., Suite 108, Fresno, CA 93721; (209) 487-5189

Honolulu
300 Ala Moana, Room 2213, Honolulu, HI 96850; (808) 541-2990

Las Vegas
301 E. Steward St., Room 301, Las Vegas, NV 89125; (702) 388-6611

Los Angeles
350 S. Figueroa St., 6th Floor, Los Angeles, CA 90071; (213) 894-2956

Phoenix
2005 N. Central Ave., 5th Floor, Phoenix, AZ 85004; (602) 261-3732

Reno
50 S. Virginia St., Room 238, Reno, NV 89505; (702) 784-5268

Sacramento
660 J St., Room 215, Sacramento, CA 95814; (916) 551-1445

San Diego
880 Front St., Room 4-S-29, San Diego, CA 92188; (619) 557-5440

San Francisco
211 Main St., 4th Floor, San Francisco, CA 94105-1988; (415) 974-0642

San Francisco
450 Golden Gate Ave., San Francisco, CA 94102; (415) 556-7487

Santa Ana
901 W. Civic Ctr Dr., Room 160, Santa Ana, CA 92703; (714) 836-2494

Tucson
300 W. Congress St., Box FB-33, Tucson, AZ 85701; (602) 629-6715

Region 10

Anchorage
8th & C Sts., Room 1068, Anchorage, AK 99501; (901) 271-4022

Boise
1020 Main St., Suite 290, Boise, ID 83701; (208) 334-1696

Portland
1220 SW Third Ave., Room 676, Portland, OR 97204-2882; (503) 221-2682

Seattle

Small Business and Entrepreneuring

2615 4th Ave., Room 440, Seattle, WA 98121; (206) 442-5676

Seattle
915 Second Ave., Room 1791, Seattle, WA 98174-1088; (206) 442-5534

Spokane
W. 920 Riverside Ave., Room 651, Spokane, WA 99210; (509) 456-3783

Region 11

Atlanta
120 Ralph McGill St., 14th Floor, Atlanta, GA 30308; (404) 347-3771

Fairlawn
15-01 Broadway, 1st Floor, Fairlawn, NJ 07410; (201) 794-8195

Grand Prairie
2306 Oak Lane, Suite 110, Grand Prairie, TX 75051; (214) 767-7571

Sacramento
1825 Bell St., Suite 208, Sacramento, CA 95825; (916) 978-4578

* Films on Small Business

National Audiovisual Center
National Archives and Records Administration
Customer Services, Section PY
8700 Edgeworth Drive
Capitol Heights, MD 20743-3701   (301) 763-1896

A number of films on small business topics are available for sale and sometimes for rental purposes. *The 1986 Media Resource Catalog* contains a list of the titles. To obtain the free catalog, contact this office.

* Financial Management and Your Business

Superintendent of Documents
U.S. Government Printing Office
Washington, DC 20402   (202) 783-3238

Financial Management: How to Make a Go of Your Business contains information required to familiarize the small business owner/manager with the basic concepts of financial management. Tips on financial planning, cash-flow management, forecasting and obtaining capital, and other topics are covered. It is available for $2.50.

* Food and Drug Small Business Assistance

Small Business Coordinator
Food and Drug Administration
5600 Fishers Lane
Room 1372, HFC 50
Rockville, MD 20857   (301) 443-1583

The FDA has established the Division of Small Manufactures Assistance to help small companies learn about and comply with FDA regulations. This office can explain FDA procedures and provide assistance in dealing with the FDA. For a free copy of A Small Business Guide to FDA or more information contact this office.

* Franchise and Business Opportunities Rules

Federal Trade Commission
Marketing Practices
6th & Pennsylvania Ave., NW
Washington, DC 20580   (202) 326-3128

Under the FTC's Franchise and Business Opportunities Rule, sellers of franchises and business opportunities are required to give prospective buyers a disclosure document containing specific information about the franchise and any earning claims. For more information on this regulation, contact this office or your regional FTC.

* Incubators

Office of Private Sector Initiatives
U.S. Small Business Administration
1441 L St., NW, Room 317
Washington, DC 20416   (202) 653-7880

A small business incubator is a flexible method of encouraging the development of new businesses and fostering local economic development. Incubators are facilities in which a number of new and growing businesses operate under one roof with affordable rents, sharing services and equipment, and having equal access to a wide range of professional, technical, and financial programs. For more information, contact your nearest SBA office or the office listed above.

* Indian Business Development

Office of Trust and Economic Development
Bureau of Indian Affairs
U.S. Department of the Interior
18th and C Sts., NW
Washington, DC 20240   (202) 343-5831

Indian tribes and small businesses may receive technical assistance and financial backing through this office. The Bureau spends more than $10 million annually to develop Indian business enterprises.

* International Visitors Program

International Visitors Liaison
U.S. Small Business Administration
1441 L Street, NW, Room 100
Washington, DC 20416   (202) 653-6393

The growing influx of foreign visitors to SBA reflects the growing world-wide interest in small business and the appreciation of small business contributions to national economies. SBA personnel are pleased to meet with government officials, embassy personnel, private sector individuals, educators, students, and other interested parties. Program policies, administration, and operational aspects can be shared through consultation, observation, and briefing sessions. If you are interested in attending a half-day, full-day, or two-day session, contact this office.

* Lenders Programs

Office of Financial Institutions
U.S. Small Business Administration
1441 L St., NW, Room 804
Washington, DC 20416   (202) 653-2585

Under the Certified Lenders Program, the lenders, acting under SBA supervision, handle much of the necessary paperwork and review client financial status - thereby speeding up loan processing and freeing SBA personnel for other assistance to small businesses. Under SBA's Preferred Lenders Program, the lenders handle all loan paperwork, processing, and servicing. For more detailed information, contact the SBA office in your area or the office above.

* Lending and Bonding for Minority Business

Minority Business Resource Center (MRBC)
Small and Disadvantaged Business Utilization (SDBU)
Director of Civil Rights
Office of the Secretary of Transportation
U.S. Department of Transportation
400 7th Street, SW, Room 9410
Washington, D.C. 20590   (202) 366-2852

This office offers short-term lending and bonding assistance to small businesses in the transportation industry. The Short-term Lending Program offers loans at prime interest rates, while the Bonding Assistance Program enables small firms to obtain bonding in support of transportation-related contracts. Entrepreneurs can contact MBRC for information and certification details.

* Management and Technical Assistance

Office of Minority Small Business
and Capital Ownership
U.S. Small Business Administration
1441 L St., NW, Room 602
Washington, DC 20416   (202) 653-6407

The SBA initiates, organizes, and maintains a management counseling service for small firms in the 8(a) program. Under this authority, SBA places grants, agreements, and contracts with qualified individuals, profit-making firms, state and local governments, educational institutions, and some non-profit organizations to furnish management and technical aid to SBA clients and other eligible small firms. Some of the services performed are accounting, marketing, engineering, and bookkeeping. Eligible recipients of development assistance are generally firms in SBA's 8(a) contracting program, socially or economically disadvantaged individuals, or small firms located in areas of high concentration of unemployed and low-income individuals. If you are interested in providing technical or management assistance to eligible small firms, contact the office above. If you are interested in receiving technical or management assistance, contact the SBA field office in your area.

* Medical Devices: Technical Assistance for Small Businesses

Division of Small Manufacturer's Assistance
Center for Devices and Radiological Health
Food and Drug Administration
5600 Fishers Lane, HF2-220
Rockville, MD 20857   (301) 443-6597

The FDA provides information to small businesses regarding device regulations and what is needed to get approval. The FDA often holds meetings and workshops to offer further assistance. The handbook, *A Small Business Guide to FDA*, explains how the FDA works and the approval process. This Center provides copies of device regulations and FDA documents, as well as guidelines and aids that simplify manufacturer requirements. The *SMA MEMO* contains articles and tips on medical device regulations and reports on Center activities.

* Minority Business Development Centers

Public Affairs
Minority Business Development Agency
Department of Commerce
14th St. and Constitution Ave. NW
Room 6707
Washington, DC 20230   (202) 377-1936

MBDA funds a nationwide network of 100 Minority Business Development Centers--in large minority population areas--to help minority-owned firms needing assistance in counseling, accounting, administration, business planning, inventory control, negotiations, referrals, networking, construction, and marketing. The MBDC offers entrepreneurs managerial and technical assistance for bonding, bidding, estimating, financing, procurement, international trade, franchising, acquisitions, mergers, joint ventures, and leverage buyouts. The MBDC provides vital business information from corporations, trade associations, export management companies, and federal, state, and local government agencies. The MBDC also identifies minority-owned firms for contract opportunities with state and local government agencies, and private institutions. Business referral services are provided free of charge. The MBDCs, however, generally charge nominal fees for specific management and technical assistance services.

* Minority Business Development- State and Local Offices

Minority Business Development Agency
Department of Commerce
14th St. and Constitution Ave., NW
Washington, DC 20230   (202) 377-2414

The following is list of state and local offices which are concerned with minority business development. You may contact these offices for more information about the services and assistance they can provide.

* Minority Business Program Development

Office of Program Development
Minority Business Development Agency
Department of Commerce
14th St. and Constitution Ave., NW
Room 5096
Washington, DC 20230   (202) 377-5770

The office is responsible for designing and developing all MBDA programs, and identifying private and public sector resources in connection with the delivery of direct and indirect assistance to develop the minority business community. The Private Sector Division develops programs to encourage the creation and growth of business opportunities within the private sector by providing funding to business and trade associations, foundations, corporations, financial and education institutions, and other private sector organizations. The Public Sector Division is responsible for program development, oversight, and implementation of Federal, state, and local programs that impact on minority business enterprise.

* Minority Business Purchasing

National Minority Supplier Development Council
1412 Broadway, 11th Floor
New York, NY 10018   (212) 944-2430

The National Minority Supplier Development Council works with 47 Councils throughout the U.S. to promote the use of minority-owned firms. They assist firms in developing and marketing their capabilities, and acts as a liaison between minority companies and companies which wish to purchase their products or services. Contact the Council for more information.

* Minority Business Regional Assistance

Public Affairs
Minority Business Development Agency
Department of Commerce
14th St. and Constitution Ave. NW
Room 6707
Washington, DC 20230   (202) 377-1936

The Minority Business Development Agency conducts most of its activities through its six Regional Offices and four District Offices:

Atlanta
1371 Peachtree St., NE, Suite 505, Atlanta, GA 30309; (404) 347-4091

Chicago
55 East Monroe St., Suite 1440, Chicago, IL 60603; (312) 353-0182

Dallas
1100 Commerce St., Room 7B23, Dallas, TX 75242; (214) 767-8001

New York
26 Federal Plaza, Room 37-20, New York, NY 10278; (212) 264-3262

San Francisco
221 Main St., Room 1280, San Francisco, CA 94105; (415) 974-9597

Washington
14th and Constitution Ave. NW, Room 6723, Washington, D.C. 20230; (202) 377-8275

District Offices:

Boston
Room 418, 10 Causeway St., Boston, MA 02222; (617) 565-6850

Los Angeles
Suite 201, 977 N. Broadway, Los Angeles, CA 90057; (213) 894-7157

Miami
Room 928, 51 SW., 1st Ave., Miami, FL 33130; (305) 536-5054

Philadelphia
Room 10128, 600 Arch St., Philadelphia, PA 19106; (215) 629-9841

* Minority Business Week

Minority Enterprise Development Week
Minority Business Development Agency
Department of Commerce
14th St. and Constitution Ave., NW
Room 5073
Washington, DC 20230   (202) 377-5196

Minority Enterprise Development Week--MED Week--is an annual celebration to honor the contributions of minority entrepreneurs and those individuals and organizations who actively support minority business development. It is celebrated the first full week in October, and includes workshops, seminars, an Awards Gala, as well as a Marketplace where public and private sector buyers meet with minority vendors.

* Minority Research

Research Division
Minority Business Development Agency
Department of Commerce
14th St. and Constitution Ave., NW
Room 5701
Washington, DC 20230   (202) 377-4671

This Division conducts research on minority businesses and issues related to them. A complete listing of research studies is available for free by contacting this office.

* Minority Small Business

Contact your local SBA office or the Small Business Answer Desk listed in this section.

Members of minority groups who own or are interested in owning small businesses are eligible for all SBA programs. In addition, SBA offers special programs to assist members of minority groups who want to start small businesses or expand existing ones. Contact your SBA office for additional information.

* Money, Management, and Marketing

Office of Business Development
U.S. Small Business Administration
1441 L St., NW, Room 317
Washington, DC 20416   (202) 653-6881

Focus on the Facts is a series of information sheets issued by SBA which includes those listed below. To obtain copies, contact the office above.

How to Raise Money for a Small Business (#1)
How to Start a Small Business (#2)
Planning...The Most Important Ingredient (#3)
Knowing Your Market (#4)
Information...The Key to Success (#5)
How to Price Your Products and Services (#6)
Opportunities in Exporting (#7)
How to Start a Home-Based Business (#8)

* Patent Licensing Opportunities

National Patent Program
Room 401, Building 005
BARC-West
Beltsville, MD 20705   (301) 344-2518

Small Business and Entrepreneuring

Government patents resulting from agricultural research discoveries are available for licensing to U.S. companies and citizens. Licenses are offered on a non-exclusive, exclusive, and co-exclusive basis. Non-exclusive licenses are generally granted when no large investment to market a product is expected. Exclusive and co-exclusive licenses are granted when substantial investment is required. Fees for licenses are negotiable. An annual catalog listing all patents available for license plus technical abstracts is available. The necessary regulations and forms are included.

* Publications on Small Business

U.S. Small Business Administration
P.O. Box 15434
Fort Worth, TX 67119

SBA has a collection of over 100 business booklets which are sold for a nominal fee (most are under $2.00). These publications address the most important business topics and answer the questions most asked by prospective and existing business owners. The topics include financial management and analysis, general management and planning, crime prevention, marketing, personnel management, and new products, ideas, and inventions. Some of the booklets are listed below. A free *Directory of Business Development Publications* and order forms can be received by contacting your local SBA office or by calling the Small Business Answer Desk at 1-800-368-5855. To order any of the publications below send your request to the Fort Worth, Texas address in this listing.

Financial Management and Analysis
ABC's of Borrowing: $1.00
Profit Costing and Pricing For Manufacturing: $1.00
Basic Budgets for Profit Planning: $0.50
Understanding Cash Flow: $1.00
A Venture Capital Primer for Small Business: $0.50
Accounting Services for Small Service Firms: $0.50
Analyze Your Records to Reduce Costs: $0.50
Budgeting in a Small Business Firm: $0.50
Sound Cash Management and Borrowing: $0.50
Recordkeeping in a Small Business: $0.50
Break Even Analysis: A Decision Making Tool: $1.00
A Pricing Checklist for Small Retailers: $0.50
Pricing Your Products and Services Profitably: $1.00

General Management and Planning
Effective Business Communications: $0.50
Locating or Relocating Your Business: $1.00
Problems in Managing a Family-Owned Business: $0.50
Business Plan for Small Manufacturers: $1.00
Business Plan for Small Construction Firms: $1.00
Planning and Goal Setting for Small Business: $0.50
Fixing Production Mistakes: $0.50
Should You Lease or Buy Equipment: $0.50
Business Plan for Retailers: $1.00
Choosing a Retail Location: $1.00
Business Plan for Small Service Firms: $0.50
Going into Business: $0.50
How to Get Started With a Small Business Computer: $1.00
The Business Plan For Home - based Business: $1.00
How to Buy or Sell a Business: $1.00
Purchasing for Owners of Small Plants: $0.50
Buying for Retail Stores: $1.00
Small Business Decision Making: $1.00
Business Continuation Planning: $1.00
Developing a Strategic Business Plan: $1.00
Inventory Management: $0.50
Techniques for Problem Solving: $1.00
Techniques for Productivity Improvement: $1.00
Selecting the Legal Structure for your Business: $0.50
Evaluating Franchise Opportunities: $0.50
Starting a Retail Travel Agency: $1.00
Small Business Risk Management Guide: $1.00

Crime Prevention
Reducing Shoplifting Losses: $0.50
Curtailing Crime--Inside and Out: $1.00
A Small Business Guide to Computer Security: $1.00

Marketing
Creative Selling: The Competitive Edge: $0.50
Marketing for Small Business: An Overview: $1.00
Is the Independent Sales Agent For You: $0.50
Marketing Checklist for Small Retailers: $1.00
Research Your Market: $1.00
Selling by Mail Order: $1.00
Market Overseas With U.S. Government Help: $1.00
Advertising: $1.00

Personnel Management
Checklist for Developing a Training Program: $0.50
Employees: How to Find and Pay Them: $1.00

Managing Employee Benefits: $1.00

New Products/Ideas/Inventions
Can You Make Money With Your Idea or Invention: $0.50
Introduction to Patents: $0.50

* Research and Development

Office of Small Business Research and Development
National Science Foundation
Room 1250
1800 G St., NW
Washington, DC 20550   (202) 357-7464

This office offers information and guidance on NSF programs and research opportunities for small firms involved in research and technology.

* Research and Development Funding for

Small Business
National Technical Information Service
Department of Commerce
5285 Port Royal Rd.
Springfield, VA 22161   (703) 487-4650

The *Small Business Guide to Federal Research and Development Funding Opportunities* provides you with direct contacts to U.S. Government offices that contract out research and development work. It is written for smaller businesses with strong scientific and technical competence that want to do research and development work with the government. Highlighted is the Small Business Innovation Research (SBIR) Program. This program requires agencies to set aside a portion of the R&D awards for small businesses. This guide gives you steps to obtaining Federal R&D funding, an overview of Federal laboratory research efforts, criteria companies must meet, and certain laws and regulations that affect small business participation. Contact the Sales Desk to place your order or request the free information brochure, *PR-801*.

* Research Studies in Small Business

Office of Economic Research
Office of Advocacy
U.S. Small Business Administration
1725 I St., NW, Room 414
Washington, DC   (202) 634-7550

The Office of Advocacy conducts and coordinates applied research in a variety of areas important to small business to promote policies that strengthen the performance of American small business. *The Catalog of Completed Research Studies* is a listing of SBA contracted research studies completed between 1978 and 1986, with over 200 studies covering a broad scope of small business topics and issues, including studies on finance and credit, capital formation, taxes and regulation, government competition and procurement, job creation, innovation, and women and minority business ownership. Contact the office above to obtain this catalog.

* Seasonal Line of Credit

Contact your local SBA office or the Small Business Answer Desk listed in this section.

The Seasonal Line of Credit program is a short-term loan available under SBA's guaranty program to finance an increase in the trading assets (receivables and inventory) of eligible small businesses arising from a seasonal upswing in business. For additional information on this program, contact the nearest SBA office in your area.

* SEC Policy

The Office of Small Business Policy
Division of Corporation Finance
U.S. Securities and Exchange Commission
450 5th St., NW
Washington, DC 20549   (202) 272-2644

This office directs the SEC's small business rulemaking goals, reviews and comments on the impact the SEC rule proposals have on small issuers, and serves as a liaison with Congressional committees, government agencies, and other groups concerned with small business. Information on security laws that pertain to small business offerings may be obtained from this office.

* Section 8(a) Program

Contact your local SBA office or the Small Business Answers Desk listed in this section.

Through the 8(a) Program, small companies owned by socially and economically disadvantaged persons can obtain federal government contracts and other assistance in developing their business. Under the 8(a) Program, SBA acts as the prime contractor and enters into all types of federal government contracts (including, but not limited to, supply, services, construction, research and development) with other government departments and agencies, and negotiates subcontracts for small companies in the 8(a) Program. Contact your SBA office for more information.

* Service Corps of Retired Executives Association (SCORE)

Service Corps of Retired Executives Association
1825 Connecticut Ave., NW, Suite 503
Washington, DC 20009   (202) 653-6279

SCORE is an independent, voluntary, non-profit association funded almost exclusively by the SBA. It is made up to over 13,000 men and women from all walks of business management, most of whom are retired, who volunteer their services to small businesses seeking managerial assistance. SCORE volunteers work in each district office and their services are free. They provide small-business community assistance in the form of one-on-one and team counseling and nominal-fee workshops. The Active Corps of Executives (ACE) is closely coordinated with SCORE. ACE volunteers are not yet retired and volunteer their services in counseling and training to supplement those offered by the retired SCORE counselors. For more information on the SCORE and ACE, contact the office above, or the SBA office in your area.

* Small Business and the SEC

Publications Section
Printing Branch, Stop C-11
U.S. Securities and Exchange Commission
Washington, DC 20549   (202) 272-7040

The free booklet, *Q&A: Small Business and the SEC*, discusses capital formation and the federal securities laws and is designed to help you understand some of the basis, necessary requirements that apply when you wish to raise capital by selling securities. It answers such questions as:

What are the federal securities laws?
Is any special help available for a small business that wants to sell its securities?
Should my company "go public"?
How does my small business "go public"?
If my company becomes "public," what are its disclosure obligations?
Are there legal ways to sell securities without registering with   the SEC?
Are there state law requirements in addition to those under the   federal securities laws? and
Where can I go for more information?

* Small Business Development Centers (SBDCs)

Contact you local SBA office or the Small Business Answer Desk listed in this section.

Small Business Development Centers are located in 46 states, the District of Columbia, Puerto Rico, and the Virgin Islands. These centers provide quality assistance, counseling, and training to prospective and existing business owners. They also provide managerial and technical help, research studies, and other types of specialized assistance.

* Small Business Innovation Research (SBIR) Program

Office of Innovation, Research and Technology
U.S. Small Business Administration
1441 L St., NW, Room 500
Washington, DC 20416   (202) 653-7875

The Small Business Innovation Research (SBIR) Program came into existence with the enactment of the Small Business Innovation Development Act of 1982. Under SBIR, agencies of the federal government with the largest research and development budgets are mandated to set aside a legislated percentage each year for the competitive award of SBIR funding agreements to qualified high technology small business concerns. SBA was designated as the federal agency having unilateral authority and responsibility for coordinating and monitoring the government-wide activities of the SBIR program and reporting on its results annually to Congress. In line with this responsibility, SBA publishes the *SBIR Pre-Solicitation Announcement* quarterly. The *PA* contains pertinent information on the program and specific data on upcoming SBIR solicitations. To obtain the *SBIR Pre-Solicitation Announcement*, call (202) 653-6458, and for further information, contact the office above.

* Small Business Institutes (SBIs)

Contact your local SBA Office or the Small Business Answer Desk listed in th is section.

SBIs are organized through the SBA on almost 500 college campuses and universities around the nation. The institutes are staffed by senior business administration students and their faculty advisors and offer free guidance and assistance to troubled small firms. Contact your local SBA district office to obtain the name and telephone number of the SBI nearest you.

* Small Business Investment Companies (SBICs)

Finance and Investment Division
U.S. Small Business Administration

1441 L St., NW, Room 808
Washington, DC 20416   (202) 653-2806

SBA licenses, regulates, and provides financial assistance to privately owned and operated Small Business Investment Companies. Their major function is to make "venture" or "risk" investments by supplying equity capital and extending unsecured loans and loans not fully collateralized to small enterprises which meet their investment criteria. SBA also licenses a specialized type of SBIC solely to help small businesses owned and managed by socially or economically disadvantaged persons. This type of SBIC is a Section 301(d) SBIC, formerly referred to as a MESBIC (Minority Enterprise SBIC). For more information or to obtain the free brochure, *Small Business Investment Companies: The SBIC Program*, contact the office above.

* Solar Energy and Conservation Loans

Contact your local SBA office or the Small Business Answer Desk listed in th is section.

Financial assistance is provided to small business concerns engaged in the engineering, manufacturing, distributing, marketing, installing, or servicing of energy measures designed to conserve the Nation's energy resources. Detailed information can be obtained from the SBA office in your area.

* Starting and Managing a Business From Your Home

Superintendent of Documents
U.S. Government Printing Office
Washington, DC 20402   (202) 783-3238

The publication, *Starting and Managing a Business From Your Home*, provides descriptions of products and services to help you start your home-based business. It includes a questionnaire to help you decide if you are the typical entrepreneur, and also gives helpful information on managing your business, including tips on structure, recordkeeping, taxes, and insurance. It is available for $2.00 from GPO

* Surety Bonds

Contact your local SBA office or the Small Business Answer Desk listed in this section.

Through its Surety Bond Guarantee Program, the SBA helps to make the bonding process accessible to small and emerging contractors, including minorities who find bonding unavailable to them. The SBA is authorized to guarantee to a qualified surety up to 90 percent of losses incurred under bid, payment, or performance bonds issued to contractors on contracts valued up to $1.25 million. These contracts may be for construction, supplies, manufacturing, or services provided by either a prime or subcontractor for government or non-government work. This program is administered through SBA's 10 regional offices and participating surety companies and agents throughout the nation.

* Trade Remedy Assistance for Small Businesses

The Trade Remedy Assistance Office
U.S. International Trade Commission
500 E St., SW
Washington, DC 20436   (202) 252-2200

Small businesses are often adversely affected by U.S. trade laws, which may allow foreign products to flood the U.S. market and unfairly compete with U.S. businesses which sell similar products. The ITC, however, provides technical assistance under U.S. trade remedy laws to eligible small businesses which have experienced such effects. To qualify, businesses must have neither adequate resources nor the financial ability to obtain qualified outside assistance. ITC staff is available to meet with eligible small businesses to discuss the petition process and to help organize and assemble relevant background material. The office has assisted eligible small businesses at the preinstitution stage in analyzing their trade-related problems and deciding which statutes may offer relief. Technical assistance may include the review of initial drafts submitted by the eligible small business and advice on additions, deletions, and possible alternative presentations, leading to the final preparation of the petition for filing with the ITC. Such assistance also includes discussion of relevant ITC precedents and publications.

* Transportation Small Business Assistance

Public Assistance Office
Interstate Commerce Commission
12th St. and Constitution Ave., NW
Washington, DC 20423   (202) 275-7597

The Commission maintains a Public Assistance Office to help the small business owner or transportation firm in such matters as how to file protests on rates, how to file new operating authority or extensions, or how to get adequate service where there is none.

* Veterans Assistance

Contact your local SBA office or the Small Business Answer Desk listed in this section.

The SBA makes special efforts to help veterans get into business or expand existing veteran-owned small firms. Acting on its own or with the help of

Small Business and Entrepreneuring

veterans organizations, the SBA sponsors special business training workshops for veterans. The SBA also sponsors special computer-based training and long-term entrepreneurial programs for veterans. Each SBA office has a veterans affairs specialist to help give veterans special consideration with loans, training, and/or procurement. The *Veterans Handbook*, which outlines the Agency's special consideration programs for veterans, is also available from SBA district and regional offices.

* Vietnam-Era and Disabled Veterans Loans

Contact your local SBA office or the Small Business Answer Desk listed in this section.

Under a special appropriation, funds are available for direct loans to disabled and Vietnam-era veterans. These loans can be made only when financing is not available from other sources on reasonable terms. These loans may be made to establish a small firm or assist in the operation or expansion of an existing business. The administrative ceiling on these loans is $150,000. While all qualified veterans receive special consideration in connection with applications for SBA assistance, most loans are made by financial institutions and many are guaranteed by SBA. Whenever a guaranteed loan or other reasonable credit is available, the SBA cannot make a direct loan.

* Women's Business Ownership

Office of Women's Business Ownership
U.S. Small Business Administration
1441 L St., NW, Room 414
Washington, DC 20416   (202) 653-8000

This office was formed to implement a national policy to support women entrepreneurs. Its primary functions include developing and coordinating a national program to increase the number and success of women-owned businesses while making maximum use of existing government and private sector resources; researching and evaluating the special programmatic needs of current or potential women business owners, and develop and test ways of meeting them; working with federal, state, and local governments to ensure that they consider women's business ownership in their program areas.

State Starting Places and Money

Who Can Use State Money?

All states require that funds be used solely by state residents. But that shouldn't limit you to exploring possibilities only in the state in which you currently reside. If you reside in Maine, but Massachusetts agrees to give you $100,000 to start your own business, it would be worth your while to consider moving to Massachusetts. Shop around for the best deal.

Types of Money And Help Available

Each state has different kinds and amounts of money and assistance programs available, but these sources of financial and counseling help are constantly being changed. What may not be available this year may very well be available next. Therefore, in the course of your exploration, you might want to check in with the people who operate the business "hot-lines" to discover if anything new has been added to the states' offerings.

Described below are the major kinds of programs which are offered by most of the states.

Information

Hotlines or One-Stop Shops
Hotlines or One-Stop Shops are available in many states through a toll-free number that hooks you up with someone who will either tell you what you need to know or refer you to someone who can. These hotlines are invaluable -- offering information on everything from business permit regulations to obscure financing programs. Most states also offer some kind of booklet that tells you to how to start-up a business in that state. Ask for it. It will probably be free.

Small Business Advocates
Small Business Advocates operate in all fifty states and are part of a national organization (the National Association of State Small Business Advocates) devoted to helping small business people function efficiently with their state governments. They are a good source for help in cutting through bureaucratic red tape.

Funding Programs

Free Money
Free Money can come in the form of grants, it and works the same as free money from the federal government. You do not have to pay it back.

Loans
Loans from state governments work in the same way as those from the federal government -- they are given directly to entrepreneurs. Loans are usually at interest rates below the rates charged at commercial institutions and are also set aside for those companies which have trouble getting a loan elsewhere. This makes them an ideal source for riskier kinds of ventures.

Loan Guarantees
Loan Guarantees are similar to those offered by the federal government. For this program the state government will go to the bank with you and co- sign your loan. This, too, is ideal for high risk ventures which normally would not get a loan.

Interest Subsidies On Loans
Interest Subsidies On Loans is a unique concept not used by the federal government. In this case the state will subsidize the interest rate you are charged by a bank. For example, if the bank gives you a loan for $50,000 at 10% per year interest, your interest payments would be $5,000 per year. With an interest subsidy you might have to pay only $2,500 since the state would pay the other half. This is like getting the loan at 5 percent instead of 10 percent.

Industrial Revenue Bonds or General Obligation Bonds
Industrial Revenue Bonds or General Obligation Bonds are a type of financing that can be used to purchase only fixed assets, like a factory or equipment. In the case of Industrial Revenue Bonds the state will raise money from the general public to buy your equipment. Because the state acts as the middleman, the people who lend you the money do not have to pay federal taxes on the interest they charge you. As a result, you get the money cheaper because they get a tax break. If the state issues General Obligation Bonds to buy your equipment, the arrangement will be similar to that for an Industrial Revenue Bond except that the state promises to repay the loan if you cannot.

Matching Grants
Matching Grants supplement and abet federal grant programs. These kinds of grants could make an under-capitalized project go forward. Awards usually hinge on the usefulness of the project to its surrounding locality.

Loans To Agricultural Businesses
Loans to Agricultural Businesses are offered in states with large rural, farming populations. They are available solely to farmers and/or agribusiness entrepreneurs.

Loans To Exporters
Loans to Exporters are available in some states as a kind of gap financing to cover the expenses involved in fulfilling a contract.

Energy Conservation Loans
Energy Conservation Loans are made to small businesses to finance the installation of energy-saving equipment or devices.

Special Regional Loans
Special Regional Loans are ear-marked for specific areas in a state that may have been hard hit economically or suffer from under-development. If you live in one of these regions, you may be eligible for special funds.

High Tech Loans
High Tech Loans help fledgling companies develop or introduce new products into the marketplace.

Loans To Inventors

Small Business and Entrepreneuring

Loans to Inventors help the entrepreneur develop or market new products.

Local Government Loans
Local Government Loans are used for start-up and expansions of businesses within the designated locality.

Childcare Facilities Loans
Childcare Facilities Loans help businesses establish on-site day care facilities.

Loans To Women And/Or Minorities
Loans to Women and/or Minorities are available in almost every state from funds specifically reserved for economically disadvantaged groups.

Many federally funded programs are administered by state governments. Among them are the following programs:

SBA 7(A) Guaranteed and Direct Loan Program
The SBA 7(A) Guaranteed and Direct Loan Program can guarantee up to 90% of a loan made through a private lender (up to $500,000), or make direct loans of up to $150,000.

SBA 504
The SBA 504 establishes Certified Development Companies whose debentures are guaranteed by the SBA. Equity participation of the borrower must be at least 10%, private financing 60% and CDC participation at a maximum of 40%, up to $500,000.

SBIR Grants
SBIR Grants award between $20,000 to $50,000 to entrepreneurs to support six months of research on a technical innovation. They are then eligible for up to $500,000 to develop the innovation.

Small Business Investment Companies
Small Business Investment Companies (SBIC) license, regulate and provide financial assistance in the form of equity financing, long-term loans, and management services.

Community Development Block Grants
Community Development Block Grants are available to cities and counties for the commercial rehabilitation of existing buildings or structures used for business, commercial, or industrial purposes. Grants of up to $500,000 can be made. Every $15,000 of grant funds invested must create at least one full-time job, and at least 51% of the jobs created must be for low-and moderate-income families.

Urban Development Action Grants
Urban Development Action Grants, funded by the Department of Housing and Urban Development, are awarded to communities which then loan the proceeds at flexible rates to eligible businesses. Projects whose total costs are less than $100,000 are not eligible. UDAG funds should leverage at least three to four times their amount in private sector investment.

Farmers Home Administration (FmHA) Emergency Disaster Loans
Farmers Home Administration (FmHA) Emergency Disaster Loans are available in counties where natural disaster has substantially affected farming, ranching or aquaculture production.

FmHA Farm Loan Guarantees
FmHA Farm Loan Guarantees are made to family farmers and ranchers to enable them to obtain funds from private lenders.

Funds must be used for farm ownership, improvements, and operating purposes.

FmHA Farm Operating Loans
FmHA Farm Operating Loans to meet operating expenses, finance recreational and nonagricultural enterprises, to add to family income, and to pay for mandated safety and pollution control changes are available at variable interest rates. Limits are $200,000 for an insured farm operating loan and $400,000 for a guaranteed loan.

FmHA Farm Ownership Loans
FmHA Farm Ownership Loans can be used for a wide range of farm improvement projects. Limits are $200,000 for an insured loan and $300,000 for a guaranteed loan.

FmHA Soil And Water Loans
FmHA Soil and Water Loans must be used by individual farmers and ranchers to develop, conserve, and properly use their land and water resources and to help abate pollution. Interest rates are variable; each loan must be secured by real estate.

FmHA Youth Project Loans
Youth Project Loans enable young people to borrow for income-producing projects sponsored by a school or 4H club.

Assistance Programs

Management Training
Management Training is offered by many states in subjects ranging from bookkeeping to energy conservation.

Business Consulting
Business Consulting is offered on almost any subject. Small Business Development Centers are the best source for this kind of assistance.

Market Studies
Market Studies to help you sell your goods or services within or outside the state are offered by many states. They all also have State Data Centers which not only collect demographic and other information about markets within the state, but also have access to federal data which can pinpoint national markets. Many states also provide the services of graduate business students at local universities to do the legwork and analysis for you.

Business Site Selection
Business Site Selection is done by specialists in every state who will identify the best place to locate a business.

Licensing, Regulation, and Permits
Licensing, Regulation, and Permits information is available from most states through "one-stop shop" centers by calling a toll-free number. There you'll get help in finding your way through the confusion of registering a new business.

Employee Training Programs
Employee Training Programs offer on-site training and continuing education opportunities.

Research And Development
Research and Development assistance for entrepreneurs is a form of assistance that is rapidly increasing as more and more states try to attract high technology-related companies. Many states are even setting up clearing houses so that small

businesses can have one place to turn to find expertise throughout a statewide university system.

Procurement Programs
Procurement Programs have been established in some states to help you sell products to state, federal, and local governments.

Export Assistance
Export Assistance is offered to identify overseas markets. Some states even have overseas offices to drum up business prospects for you.

Assistance In Finding Funding
Assistance in Finding Funding is offered in every state, particularly through regional Small Business Development Centers. They will not only identify funding sources in the state and federal governments but will also lead you through the complicated application process.

Special Help For Minorities And Women
Special Help for Minorities and Women is available in almost every state to help boost the participation of women and minorities in small business ventures. They offer special funding programs and, often, one-on- one counseling to assure a start-up success.

Venture Capital Networking
Venture Capital Networking is achieved through computer databases that hook up entrepreneurs and venture capitalists. This service is usually free of charge. In fact, the demand for small business investment opportunities is so great that some states require the investor to pay to be listed.

Inventors Associations
Inventors Associations have been established to encourage and assist inventors in developing and patenting their products.

Annual Governors' Conferences
Annual Governors' Conferences give small business people the chance to air their problems with representatives from state agencies and the legislature.

Small Business Development Centers
Small Business Development Centers, funded jointly by the federal and state governments, are usually associated with the state university system. SBDC's are a god-send to small business people. They will not only help you figure out if your business project is feasible, but also help you draw up a sensible business plan, apply for funding, and check in with you frequently once your business is up and running to make sure it stays that way.

Tourism
Tourism programs are prominent in states whose revenues are heavily dependent on the tourist trade. They are specifically aimed at businesses in the tourist industries.

Small Business Institutes
Small Business Institutes at local colleges use senior level business students as consultants to help develop business plans or plan expansions.

Technology Assistance Centers
Technology Assistance Centers help high tech companies and entrepreneurs establish new businesses and plan business expansions.

On-Site Energy Audits
On-Site Energy Audits are offered free of charge by many states to help control energy costs and improve energy efficiency for small businesses. Some states also conduct workshops to encourage energy conservation measures.

Minority Business Development Centers
Minority Business Development Centers offer a wide range of ser-vices from initial counseling on how to start a business to more complex issues of planning and growth.

State Starting Places

Alabama

General Information

Alabama Development Office, State Capitol, 135 South Union Street, Montgomery, AL 36130, (205) 263-0048. Answers general inquiries about Alabama's programs. "Small Business is Big Business in Alabama" is a free packet with information on assistance programs, sources of financing, a licensing handbook, and tips on preparing business and financial plans.

Small Business Advocate, c/o Alabama Development Office, State Capitol, 135 South Union Street, Montgomery, AL 36130, (205) 263-0048. Assistance in cutting bureaucratic red tape. Information and expertise in dealing with state, federal and local agencies.

Small Business Development Centers

The following offices offer free and fee-based services to new and expanding businesses:

Auburn: Auburn University, Small Business Development Center, 226 Thach Hall, Auburn, AL 36849, (205) 826-4220.

Birmingham: The University of Alabama at Birmingham, Small Business Development Center, 901 South 15th Street, UC Building #4, Room 143, Birmingham, AL 35294, (205) 934-6760.

Florence: The University of North Alabama, Small Business Development Center, School of Business, Florance, AL 35632, (205) 760-4234.

Huntsville: Northeast Alabama Regional SBDC, Alabama A&M University and the, University of Alabama in Huntsville, 225 Church Street, N.W., Huntsville, AL , 35804, (205)535-2061.

Huntsville: Alabama High Technology Assistance Center, The University of Alabama in Huntsville 336 Morton Hall, Huntsville, AL 35899, (205) 895-6409.

Jacksonville: Jacksonville State University, Small Business Development Center, College of Commerce and Business Administration, Jacksonville, AL 36265, (205) 231-5271.

Livingston: Livingston University, Small Business Development Center, Station 35 Livingston, AL 35470, (205) 652-9661, ext. 439.

Mobile: The University of South Alabama, Small Business Development Center College of Business/Management Studies, Mobile, AL 36688, (205) 460-6004.

Montgomery: Alabama State University, Small Business Development Center, 915 South Jackson Street, Montgomery, AL 36195, (205) 269-1102.

Troy: Troy State University, Small Business Development Center, Sorrell College of Business, Troy, AL 36082, (205) 566-7665.

Tuscaloosa: Alabama International Trade Center, The University of Alabama, P.O. Box 1996, Tuscaloosa, AL 35487, (205) 348-7621.

Tuscaloosa: The University of Alabama, Small Business Development Center P.O. Box J, Tuscaloosa, AL 35487, (205) 348-7011.

Tuskegee: Tuskegee University, Small Business Development Center, School of Business, Tuskegee, AL 36088, (205) 727-6307.

Alaska

General Information

Division of Business Development, Alaska Department of Commerce and Economic Development, P.O. Box D, Juneau, AK 99811, (907)465-2018, or 3601 C Street, Suite 722, Anchorage, AK 99503, (907) 563-2165. Answers general inquiries. A free booklet, "Establishing a Business in Alaska," provides information on assistance programs, licensing requirements, taxation, labor laws, financial assistance programs, and state sources of information.

Small Business Advocate, Division of Business Development, Department of Commerce and Economic Development, P.O. Box D, Juneau, AK 99811, (907) 465-2018. Assistance in cutting bureaucratic red tape. Information and expertise in dealing with state, federal, and local agencies.

Small Business Development Centers

The following offices offer free and fee-based services to new and expanding businesses:

Anchorage: Small Business Development Center, Statewide Administrative Office, 430 West 7th Avenue, Suite 115, Anchorage, AK 99501, (907) 274-7232, or 800 478-7232 outside Anchorage.

Anchorage: Anchorage SBDC Office, University of Alaska Anchorage, 430 West 7th Avenue, Suite 115, Anchorage, AK 99501, (907) 274-7232.

Fairbanks: Fairbanks SBDC Office, University of Alaska, Downtown Center, 510 2nd Avenue, Suite 316, Fairbanks, AK 99701, (907) 456-1701; or 800-478-1701 outside Fairbanks.

Juneau: Juneau SBDC Office, University of Alaska Southeastern, 1108 F Street, Juneau, AK 99801, (907) 463-3789; 800-478-3789 outside Juneau.

Ketchikan: Ketchikan SBDC Site, Ketchikan College, 7th and Madison, Ketchikan, AK 99901.
Kodiak: Kodiak SBDC Site, Kodiak College, P.O. Box 946, Kodiak, AK 99615, (907) 486-3099.

Kotzebue: Kotzebue SBDC Site, Chukchi College, P.O. Box 297, Kotzebue, AK 99752.

Nome: Nome SBDC Site, Northwest College, Pouch 400, Nome, AK 99762, Bethel SBDC Site, Kuskokwim College, P.O. Box 368, Bethel, AK 99559, (907) 453-4509.

Sitka: Sitka SBDC Site, Islands College, 1101 Sawmill Creek Boulevard, Sitka, AK 99835.

Soldotna: Kenai SBDC Site, Kenai Peninsula College, P.O. Box 848, Soldotna, AK 99669, (907) 262-5801.

Valdez: Valdez SBDC Site, Prince William Sound Community College/Valdez Chamber of Commerce P.O. Box 2418, Valdez, AK 99686, (907) 835-5109.

Arizona

General Information

Arizona Office of Economic Development, Department of Commerce, State Capitol, 1700 West Washington, Phoenix, AZ 85007, (602) 255-5374.

State Small Business Advocate, Arizona Department of Commerce, Fourth Floor, Capital Towers, 1700 West Washington, Phoenix, AZ 85007, (602) 255-5371. Assistance in cutting bureaucratic red tape. Information and expertise in dealing with state, federal, and local agencies.

Small Business Development Centers

The following offices offer free and fee-based services to new and expanding businesses:

Arizona: Gateway Community College SBDC, 3901 East Van Buren, Aloha #150, Phoenix, AZ 85008, (602) 392-5220.

Lake Havasu: Mojave SBDC, 1977 West Acoma Boulevard, Lake Havasu City, AZ 86403, (602) 873-2683.

Phoenix: Rio Salado SBDC, 7611 West Thomas, (Westridge Mall), Phoenix, AZ 85075, (602) 849-1077.

Sierra Vista: Cochise College SBDC, 901 N. Colombo, Room 411, Sierra Vista, AZ 85635, (602) 459-9778.

Stafford: Eastern Arizona College SBDC, 1111 Thatcher Boulevard, Stafford, AZ 85446, (602) 428-7603.

Arkansas

General Information

Small Business Clearinghouse, Arkansas Industrial Development Commission,

One Capitol Mall, Little Rock, AR 72201, (501) 682-7500. "Small Business Information Clearinghouse Summaries" is a spiral-bound notebook that summarizes the states' programs agency by agency.

Small Business Advocate, Coordinator, Small Business Programs, Arkansas Industrial Development Commission, One State Capitol Mall, Room 4C300, Little Rock, AR 72201, (501) 371-5273. Assistance in cutting bureaucratic red tape. Information and expertise in dealing with state, federal, and local agencies.

Small Business Development Centers

The following offices offer free and fee-based services to new and expanding businesses:

Arkadelphia: Small Business Development Center, Henderson State University, P.O. Box 7624, Arkadelphia, AR 71923, (501) 246-5511, ext. 327.

Beebe: Small Business Development Center, Arkansas State University - Beebe, P.O. Drawer H, Beebe, AR 72012, (501) 882-6452, ext. 26.

Conway: Small Business Development Center, University of Central Arkansas, College of Business Administration, Conway, AR 72032, (501) 450-3190.

Fayetteville: Small Business Development Center, University of Arkansas at Fayetteville, College of Business, BA 117, Fayetteville, AR 72701, (501) 575-5148.

Jonesboro: Small Business Development Center, Arkansas State University, Drawer 2650, Jonesboro, AR 72467, (501) 972-3517.

Little Rock: Small Business Development Center, Central Office, University of Arkansas at Little Rock, 100 South Main, Suite 401, Little Rock, AR 72201, (501) 371-5381.

Searcy: Small Business Development Center, Harding University, Department of Business and Economics, Searcy, AR 72143, (501) 268-6161, ext. 497.

California

General Information

Office of Small Business, California Department of Commerce, 1121 L Street, Suite 501, Sacramento, CA 95814, (916) 445-6545. Offers workshops, seminars, individual counseling, and publications.

Office of Local Development, California Department of Commerce, 1121 L Street, Suite 600, Sacramento, CA 95814, (916) 322-1398. Provides case studies, handbooks, slide presentations, on-site training workshops, and seminars on a wide range of topics, including: downtown revitalization, industrial development, streamlining the local permit process, and financing.

Office of Business Development, California Department of Commerce, 1121 L Street, Suite 600, Sacramento, CA 95814, (916) 322-5665. Identifies available locations for business development in California and provides site-specific information on regional economic trends, labor supply, wage rates, real estate prices, infrastructure needs, transportation costs, regulations, taxes, tax-exempt bond financing, and government-sponsored job training.

California Commission for Economic Development, Office of the Lieutenant Governor, State Capitol, Room 1028, Sacramento, CA 95814, (916) 445-8994. Publishes "Doing Business in California: A Guide for Establishing Business." Cost: $3.00.

Small Business Advocate, 1120 North Street, Sacramento, CA 95814, (916) 322-6108. Provides assistance in cutting bureaucratic red tape and information and expertise in dealing with state, federal, and local agencies.

Small Business Development Centers

The following offices offer free and fee-based services to new and expanding businesses:

Oakland: East Bay Small Business Development Center, 2201 Broadway, Suite 814, Oakland, CA 94612, (415) 893-4114.

Los Angeles: Los Angeles Small Business Development Center, 550 S. Vermont, 3rd Floor, Los Angeles, CA 90020, (213) 387-3010.

San Diego: San Diego Small Business Development Center, 110 West C Street #1600, San Diego, CA 92101, (619) 232-0124.

Chico: Tri-County Small Business Assistance Center, 1001 Willow Street, Chico, CA 95927, (916) 893-8732.

Aptos: Central Coast Small Business Assistance Center, 6500 Soquel Drive, Aptos, CA 95003, (408) 479-6136.

Crescent: North Coast Small Business Resource Center, 250 Leavitt Mall, Crescent City, CA 95531, (707) 464-2168.

Colorado

General Information

Colorado Office of Small Business, Office of Economic Development, 1625 Broadway, Suite 1710, Denver, CO 80202, (303) 892-3840, Hotline 1-800-323-7798 in Colorado. Offers information, assistance and referrals for Colorado's small business owners and operators. The Small Business Hotline provides access to the Colorado Business Clearinghouse, a computerized database that contains information on over 2,000 business resources.

Colorado Office of Business Development, Office of Economic Development, 1625 Broadway, Suite 1710, Denver, CO 80202, (303) 892-3840. Provides information and assistance to local economic development organizations, assists in retaining and expanding existing businesses, and responds to out-of-state inquiries concerning expanding or relocating in Colorado.

State Small Business Advocate, Office of Economic Development, Suite 1710, 1625 Broadway, Denver, CO 80202, (303) 892-3840. Provides assistance in cutting bureaucratic red tape and information and expertise in dealing with state, federal, and local agencies.

Small Business Development Centers

Alamosa: Small Business Development Center, Adams State College, Alamosa, CO 81002, (719)589-7199.

Aurora: Small Business Resource Center, Community College of Aurora, 791 Chambers Road, #302, Aurora, Co 80011, (303) 360-4745.

Colorado Springs: Small Business Development Center, Pikes Peak Community College - CO Springs Chamber, 100 Chasestone Ctr., Box B, Colorado Springs, CO 80901, (719) 635-1551.

Delta: Small Business Development Center, Delta Montrose Vocational School, 1765 U.S. Highway 50, Delta, CO 81416, (303) 874-7671.

Denver: Small Business Development Center (Central Office), 600 Grant Street, Suite 505, Denver, CO 80203, (303) 894-2422.

Denver: Small Business Development Center, Community College of Denver, 600 Grant Street, Suite #505, Denver, CO 80203, (303) 894-2425.

Denver: Small Business Development Center, Denver Chamber of Commerce, 1600 Sherman-Annex, Denver, CO 80203, (303) 534-2525.

Fort Morgan: Small Business Resource Center, Morgan Community College, 300 Main Street, Fort Morgan, CO 80701, (303) 867-3351.

Glenwood: Small Business Resource Center, Colorado Mountain College, P.O. Box 10001 PB, Glenwood Springs, CO 81602, 1-800-621-1647.

Lakewood: Small Business Development Center, Red Rocks Community College, 13300 W. 6th Ave., Dept. 22, Lakewood, CO 80401, (303) 989-7290 .

Lamar: Small Business Resource Center, Lamar Community College, 2400 S. Main, Lamar, CO 81052, (719) 366-2248.

Littleton: Small Business Development Center, Arapahoe Community College, 5900 S. Santa Fe Drive, Littleton, CO 80120, (303) 797-5985.

Pueblo: Small Business Development Center, Pueblo Community College, 900 W. Orman Ave., Pueblo, CO 81004, (719) 549-3224.

Trinidad: Small Business Resource Center, 600 Prospect Street, Davis Building, Trinidad, CO 81082 (719) 846-5645.

Westminister: Small Business Development Center, Front Range Community College, 3645 W. 112 Ave., Westminister, CO 80030, (303) 466-8811, Ext. 345.

Connecticut

General Information

Office of Small Business Services, Department of Economic Development, 210 Washington Street, Hartford, CT 06106, (203) 566-4051. Offers a One Stop Licensing Center for call-in or drop-in service. Publishes "Establishing a Business in Connecticut," a free booklet for ready reference to state licensing laws.

Small Business Advocate, Department of Economic Development, 210 Washington Street, Hartford, CT 06106, (203) 566-4051. Provides assistance in cutting bureaucratic red tape, and information and expertise in dealing with state, federal, and local agencies.

Small Business Development Centers

The following offices offer free and fee-based services to new and expanding businesses:

Storrs: Connecticut Small Business Development Centers, State Headquarters, University of Connecticut, 368 Fairfield Road, U-41, Room 422, Storrs, CT 06268, (203) 486-4135.

Bridgeport: Small Business Development Center, Bridgeport Regional Business Council, 180 Fairfield Avenue, Bridgeport, CT 06601, (203) 335-3800.

Bridgeport: Small Business Development Center, University of Bridgeport, 141 Linden Avenue, Bridgeport, CT 06601, (203) 576-4249.

Danielson: Small Business Development Center, Quinebaug Valley Community College, P.O. Box 59, Maple Street, Danielson, CT 06239, (203) 774-1130, ext. 309.

West Hartford: Small Business Development Center, University of Connecticut, West Hartford Campus, 1800 Asylum Avenue, West Hartford, CT 06117, (203) 241-4986.

New Haven: Small Business Development Center, Greater New Haven Chamber of Commerce, 195 Church Street, New Haven, CT 06506, (203) 787-6735.

Groton: Small Business Development Center, University of Connecticut, Administration Building, RM 308, Avery Point, Groton, CT 06340, (203) 449-1188.

Stamford: Small Business Development Center, SACIA, Landmark Square, Stamford, CT 06901, (203) 359-3220.

Waterbury: Small Business Development Center, University of Connecticut, Kirschbaum Library, Room 108, 32 Hillside Avenue, Waterbury, CT 06701, (203) 757-1231.

Delaware

General Information

Delaware Development Office, 99 Kings Highway, P.O. Box 1401, Dover, DE 19903, (302) 736-4271. Offers referrals to appropriate state agencies and other organizations. Free tabloid, "Small Business Start-Up Guide," is available.

Small Business Advocate, Delaware Development Office, 99 Kings Highway, P.O. Box 1401, Dover, DE 19903, (302) 736-4271. Provides assistance in cutting bureaucratic red tape, and information and expertise in dealing with state, federal, and local agencies.

Small Business Development Centers

The following offices offer free and fee-based services to new and expanding businesses:

Dover: Delaware Small Business Development Center, Kent County Administration Building, 414 Federal Street, Dover, DE 19901, 1-800-222-2279 in Kent and Sussex counties only.

Newark: Delaware Small Business Development Center, Suite 005 Purnell Hall, University of Delaware, Newark, DE 19716, (302) 451-2747.

District of Columbia

General Information

Office of Business and Economic Development, District Building, 1111 E Street, N.W., Washington, D.C. 20004, (202) 727-6600. Offers a wide range of technical and financial assistance programs.

Small Business Development Centers

The following offices offer free and fee-based services to new and expanding businesses:

Washington: Howard University (Central Office), Small Business Development Center, 6th & Fairmont Street, N.W., Suite 128, Washington, D.C. 20059, (202) 636-5150.

Washington: George Washington University, Small Business Development Center, 720 20th Street, N.W., Suite SL 101, Washington, D.C. 20052, (202) 994-7463.

College Park: University of Maryland, Small Business Development Center,

Small Business and Entrepreneuring

College of Business and Management, College Park, MD 20814, (301) 454-5072.

Bethesda: Montgomery College, Small Business Development Center, 7815 Woodmont Avenue, Bethesda, MD 20814, (301) 656-7482.

Fairfax: George Mason University, Small Business Development Center, 4400 University Drive, Fairfax, VA 22030, (703) 323-2568.

Florida

General Information

Bureau of Business Assistance, Department of Commerce, Division of Economic Development, G-26 Collins Building, Tallahassee, FL 32399, (904) 488-9357, 1-800 342-0771 in Florida. The Business Services Section operates a toll-free information and referral service for current and potential small business owners. They also sponsor workshops and business forums and an annual Small Business Development Workshop that brings together local, state, and federal agency representatives.

Small Business Advocate, Florida Department of Commerce, G-27 Collins Building, Tallahassee, FL 32399, (904) 487-4698. Assistance in cutting bureaucratic red tape. Information and expertise in dealing with state, federal, and local agencies.

Small Business Development Centers

The following offices offer free and fee-based services to new and expanding businesses:

Boca Raton: Small Business Development Center, Florida Atlantic University, School of Public Administration, College of Business and Public Administration, Boca Raton, FL 33431, (305) 338-2239.

Cocoa: Small Business Development Center, 1519 Clearlake Road, Cocoa, FL 32922, (305) 631- 3368.

Deland: Small Business Development Regional Center, Stetson University, School of Business Administration, P.O. Box 8417, Deland, FL 32720, (904) 734-1066.

Fort Lauderdale: Fort Lauderdale Small Business Development Center, 220 Southwest 2nd Avenue, Fort Lauderdale, FL 33301, (305) 355-5211.

Fort Myers: Small Business Development Center, West Thomas Howard Hall, Rooms 203 & 204, Ft. Myers, FL 33907, (813) 489-4140.

Fort Pierce: Small Business Development Center, Indian River Community College, 3209 Virginia Avenue, Fort Pierce, FL 33482, (305) 468-4700, ext. 4756.

Ft. Walton: Small Business Development Center, 414 Mary Esther Cutoff, Ft. Walton Beach, FL 32548, (904) 244-1036.

Gainesville: Small Business Development Center, 1031 Northwest 6th Street, Suite B1, Gainesville, FL 32601, (904) 337-5621.

Jacksonville: Small Business Development Center, University of North Florida, College of Business, 4567 St. John's Bluff Road, South, Building 11, Room 2197, Jacksonville, FL 32216, (904) 646-2476.

Key West: Small Business Development Center, Florida Keys Community College, #1 Keylime Square, Key West, FL 33040, (305) 294-8481.

Miami: Small Business Development Center, Florida International University, Division of Continuing Education, Trailer MO1, Tamiami Campus, Miama, FL 33199, (305) 554-2272.

Miami: Small Business Development Center, Bay Vista Campus (North Miami Campus), Academic Building #1, Room 350, Miami, FL 33181, (305) 940-5790.

Orlando: Small Business Development Center, University of Central Florida, 12424 Research Parkway, Suite 400-B, Orlando, FL 32726, (305) 658-6859.

Ocala: Small Business Development Center, P.O. Box 1388, Ocala, FL 33620, (904) 854-2333, ext. 557.

Palm Beach Gardens: Small Business Development Center, Palm Beach Community College, North Campus, 3160 PGA Boulevard, Palm Beach Gardens, FL 33410, (305) 627-4278.

Panama City: Small Business Development Center, Florida State University, 4917 North Bay Drive, Panama City, FL 32405, (904) 872-4655.

Pembroke Pines: Small Business Development Center, Broward Community College, 7200 Hollywood Boulevard, Pembroke Pines, FL 33024, (305) 987-0100.

Pensacola: State Coordinator, Florida Small Business Development Centers,

University of West Florida, Building 38, Pensacola, FL 32514, (904) 474-3016.

Pensacola: Small Business Development Center, University of West Florida, College of Business, Building 8, Pensacola, FL 32514, (904) 474-2908.

St. Petersburg: Small Business Development Center, University of South Florida, St. Petersburg Campus, 830 First Street South, Room 113, St. Petersburg, FL 33701, (813) 893- 9529.

Sarasota: Small Business Development Center, 5700 Tamiami Trail, Sarasota, FL 33580, (813) 355-7671.

Tallahassee: Small Business Development Center, Florida Agricultural and Mechanical University, P.O. Box 708, Commons Building, Room 7, Tallahassee, FL 32307, (904) 599-3407.
Tallahassee: Small Business Development Center, Florida State University, 1605 East Plaza Drive, Suite 1, Tallahassee, FL 32308, (904) 644-6524.

Tampa: Small Business Development Center, University of South Florida, Room 3331, Tampa, FL 33620, (813) 974-4274.

Georgia

General Information

Georgia Department of Community Affairs, 1200 Equitable Building, 100 Peachtree Street, N.W., Atlanta, GA 30303, (404) 656-6200. Provides information on financing programs and other services offered by the state government.

Business Council of Georgia, 1280 South CNN Center, Atlanta, GA 30303, (404) 223-2264. The Business Council is a clearinghouse for information and makes referrals to the Georgia Department of Labor, the Georgia Department of Industry and Trade, and other agencies. The council often acts as a liaison between businesses and local chambers of commerce.

Georgia Small Business Association, 1280 South CNN Center, Atlanta, GA 30335, (404) 223-2285. GSBA is a statewide membership organization that promotes the interests of small businesses. It keeps members informed of pending legislation, changes in law/regulations, provides management assistance and advice, provides information, makes referrals, and provides a variety of other services for small businesses.

Small Business Advocate, Department of Administrative Services, West Tower, Room 1302, 200 Piedmont Avenue, Southeast, Atlanta, GA 30334, (404) 656-6315.

Small Business Development Centers

The following offices offer free and fee-based services to new and expanding businesses:

Albany: Southwest Georgia SBDC, 501 N. Slappey Boulevard, Albany, GA 31702, (912) 439-7232.

Athens: Small Business Development Centers (State Office), Chicopee Complex, University of Georgia, Athens, GA 30602, (404) 542-5760.

Athens: North Georgia Regional Center SBDC, Chicopee Complex, 1180 East Braod Street, Athens, GA 30602, (404) 542-7436.

Atlanta: Atlanta SBDC, Georgia State University, 1 Park Place South, Suite 1055, Atlanta, GA 30303, (404) 658-3550.

Brunswick: Coastal Area SBDC, Brunswick Junior College, Altama at Fourth, Brunswick, GA 31523, (912) 264-7343.

Central Savannah River SBDC: Augusta College, 1061 Catherine Street, Augusta, GA 30910, (404) 737-1790.

Columbus: West Georgia SBDC, 18 Ninth Street, Heritage Tower, Suite 105, Columbus, GA 31901, (404) 571-7433.

Dublin: Central Georgia Branch Office SBDC, 1009 Bellevue Avenue, Dublin, GA 31021, (912) 272-5546.

Gainsville: Gainesville Junior College Subcenter SBDC, Gainesville, GA 30503, (404) 535- 6318.

Lawrenceville: Gwinnett Area Subcenter SBDC, 1230 Atkinson Road, Lawrenceville, GA 30245, (404) 963-4902.

Macon: Central Georgia SBDC, P.O. Box 169, Macon, GA 32198, (912) 741-8023.

Marietta: Kennesaw College SBDC, P.O. Box 444, Marietta, GA 30061, (404) 429-2800.

Milledgeville: Central Georgia Branch Office SBDC, 130 South Jefferson Street, Milledgeville, GA 31061, (912) 453-9311.

Morrow: South Metro Atlanta SBDC, Clayton State College, P.O. Box 285, Morrow, GA 30260, (404) 961-3414.

Rome: Northwest Georgia SBDC, Floyd Junior College, P.O. Box 1864, Rome, GA 30163, (404) 295-6324.

Savannah: Coastal Georgia Savannah Center SBDC, P.O. Box 8343, Savannah, GA 31412, (912) 264-2533.

Statesboro: Southeast Georgia SBDC, Georgia Southern College, Landrum Center Box 8156, Statesboro, GA 30460, (912) 681-5194.

Valdosta: South Georgia SBDC, Valdosta State College Pound Hall, (North Campus), Valdosta, GA 31698, (912) 333-5966.

Hawaii

General Information

Small Business Information Service, Department of Business and Economic Development, P.O. Box 2359, Honolulu, HI 96804, (808) 548-7645. Assists both new and existing businesses with information on government permit and license requirements, government procurement, sources of alternative financing, marketing, preparing a business plan, and available entrepreneurship training programs.

Small Business Advocate, Department of Business Economic Development, 250 South King Street, Honolulu, HI 96813, (803) 548-4347.

Idaho

General Information

Idaho Department of Commerce, Division of Economic Development, 700 West State Street, Boise, ID 83720, (208) 334-2470.

Small Business Advocate, Department of Commerce, State House, Boise, ID 83720, (208) 334-2470.

Small Business Development Centers

The following offices offer free and fee-based services to new and expanding businesses:

Boise: Idaho Small Business Development Center (State Office), Boise State University, College of Business, 1910 University Drive, Boise, ID 83725, (208) 385-1640; 1-800-225-3815 in Idaho.

Boise: Idaho Small Business Development Center, Ida-Ore Planning and Development Association, 7270 Potomac Drive, Boise, ID 83704, (208) 323-1154.

Hayden: Idaho Small Business Development Center, Panhandle Area Council, 11100 Airport Drive, Hayden, ID 83835, (208) 772-0587.

Lewiston: Idaho Small Business Development Center, Lewis Clark State College, 8th Avenue and 6th Street, Lewiston, ID 83501, (208) 799-2465.

Mountain Home: Idaho Small Business Development Center, Elmore County Business Resource Center, 190 S. 4th East, Mountain Home, ID 83647, (208) 587-2142.

Pocatello: Idaho Small Business Development Center, Idaho State University, 427 N. Main, Suite A, Pocatello, ID 83204, (208) 232-4921.

Twin Falls: Idaho Small Business Development Center, CSI/Region IV, P.O. Box 1844, Twin Falls, ID 833303, (208) 734-6586.

Illinois

General Information

Small Business Assistance Bureau, Illinois Department of Commerce and Community Affairs, State of Illinois Center, 100 West Randolph Street, Suite 3-400, Chicago, IL 60601, (312) 917-7179; Hotline 1-800-252-2923 in Illinois. The Small Business Hotline is a "one-stop shop" for small business information. It offers quick, personalized answers to business owners' questions. Also available, "How to Start a Small Business in Illinois," a comprehensive start- up guide.

Small Business Advocate, Small Business Assistance Bureau, Illinois Department

of Commerce and Community Affairs, Suite 3-400, 100 West Randolph, Chicago, IL 60601, (312) 917-2829. Assistance in cutting bureaucratic red tape. Information and expertise in dealing with state, federal, and local agencies.

Small Business Development Centers

The following offices offer free and fee-based services to new and expanding businesses. There are so many SBDC's in Illinois that only center names, towns, and telephone numbers are given:

Aledo: Aleco Chamber of Commerce, Aledo, IL, (309) 582-5373.

Aurora: Waubonsee Community College, Aurora, IL, (312) 892-3334, Ext. 141.

Bloomington: Illinois State University, McLean County Chamber of Commerce, Bloomington, IL, (309) 829-6632.

Canton: Spoon River College, Canton, IL, (309) 647-4647, Ext. 320.

Carbondale: Southern Illinois University, Carbondale, IL, (618) 536-2424.

Cartersville: John A. Logan Community College, Cartersville, IL, (618) 985-6384.

Centralia: Kaskaskia College, Centralia, IL, (618) 532-2049.

Champaign: Parkland College, Champaign, IL, (217) 351-2200, Ext. 556.

Chicago: Back of the Yards Neighborhood Council, Chicago, IL, (312) 523-4419.

Chicago: CANDO, Chicago, IL, (312) 845-9645.

Chicago: Chicago Labor Institute, Chicago, IL, (312) 853-3477.

Chicago: Chicago State University, Chicago, IL, (312) 995-3944.

Chicago: Greater North Pulaski Economic DevelopmentCommission, Chicago, IL, (312) 384- 2262.

Chicago: Greater Southwest Development Corporation, Chicago, IL, (312) 436-4448.

Chicago: Greater Westside Development Corporation, Chicago, IL, (312) 436-4448.

Chicago: Hyde Park-Kenwood Development Corporation, Chicago, IL, (312) 667-3932.

Chicago: Cosmopolitan Chamber of Commerce, Chicago, IL, (312) 786-0212.

Chicago: SAMCOR Development Corporation, Chicago, IL, (312) 261-1888.

Chicago: Daley College, Chicago, IL, (312) 838-4876.

Chicago: Neighborhood Institute, Chicago, IL, (312) 933-0200.

Chicago: Truman College, Chicago, IL, (312) 989-6112.

Chicago: University Village Association, Chicago, IL, (312) 243-4045.

Chicago: University of Illinois/Chicago, Chicago, IL, (312) 996-2608.

Chicago: Olive-Harvey Community College, Chicago, IL, (312) 660-4839.

Chicago: North River Commission/Lawrence Avenue Development Corporation, Chicago, IL (312) 478-0202.

Chicago: Southeast Chicago Development Commission, Chicago, IL, (312) 731-8755.

Chicago: Little Village Chamber of Commerce, Chicago, IL, (312) 521-5387.

Danville: Danville Area Community College Economic Development Corporation, Danville, IL, (217) 442-7232.

Decatur: Richland Community College, Decatur, IL, (217) 875-7215.

DeKalb: Northern Illinois University, DeKalb, IL, (815) 753-1403.

Dixon: Sauk Valley Community College, Dixon, IL, (815) 288-5511, Ext. 320.

East St. Louis: Illinois State Office Building (State Office), East St. Louis, IL, (618) 875-9300, Ext. 395.

Edwardsville: Southern Illinois University, Edwardsville, IL, (618) 692-2929.

Elgin: Elgin Community College, Elgin, IL, (312) 888-6906.

Geneseo: Geneseo Chamber of Commerce, Geneseo, IL, (309) 944-4740.

Glen Ellyn; College of DuPage, Glen Ellyn, IL, (312) 858-2800.

Godfrey: Lewis & Clark Community College, Godfrey, IL, (618) 466-3411, Ext. 434.

Grayslake: College of Lake County, Grayslake, IL, (312) 223-3633.

Ina: Rend Lake Community College, Ina, IL, (618) 437-5353.

Joliet: Joliet Junior College, Joliet, IL, (815) 727-6544, Ext. 1319.

Kankakee: Kankakee Community College, Kankakee, IL, (815) 933-0374.

Kewanee: Business Resource Assistance Center, Kewanee, IL, (309) 852-5671.

Macomb: Macomb Area Chamber of Commerce, Macomb, IL, (309) 837-4855.

Macomb: Western Illinois University, Macomb, IL, (309) 298-1128.

Moline: Black Hawk Community College, Quad Cities Chamber of Commerce, Moline, IL, (309) 762-3661.

Monmouth: Maple City Business and Technology Center, Monmouth, IL, (309) 734-4664.

Oglesby: Illinois Valley Community College, Oglesby, IL, (815) 223-1740.

Olney: Illinois Eastern Community Colleges, Olney, IL, (618) 395-3011.

Peoria: Bradley University, Peoria, IL, (309) 677-2309.

Oak Park: Mid-Metro Economic Development Group, Oak Park, IL, (312) 524-8770.

Quincy: John Wood Community College, Quincy, IL, (217) 228-5510.

Rockford: Rock Valley College, Rockford, IL, (815) 968-4087.

Springfield: Lincoln Land Community College, Capital Area SBDC, Springfield, IL, (217) 492-4772.

Ullin: Shawnee College, Ullin, IL, (618) 634-9618.

University Park: Governor's State University, University Park, IL, (312) 534-3713.

Worth: Moraine Valley Community College, Worth, IL, (312) 371-2210, Ext. 310.

Indiana

General Information

Small Business Advocate, Office of Business Regulatory Ombudsman, Indiana Department of Commerce, Suite 700, One North Capitol, Indianapolis, IN 46204-2243, (317) 232-5295.

Small Business Development Centers

The following offices offer free and fee-based services to new and expanding businesses:

Bloomington: Bloomington SBDC, 1821 West Third, Bloomington, IN 47401, (812) 339-8937.

Columbus: Columbus SBDC, 4920 North Warren Drive, Columbus, IN 47203, (812) 379-4041.

Columbus: Columbus SBDC, 4920 North Warren Drive, Columbus, IN 47203, (812) 379-4041.

Evansville: Evansville SBDC, 100 N.W. Second Street, Suite 202, Evansville, IN 47708, (812) 425-7232.

Fort Wayne: Fort Wayne SBDC, 1830 Wayne Trace, Fort Wayne, IN 46803, (219) 426-0040.

Indianapolis: SBDC Lead Center, One North Capitol, Suite 200, Indianapolis, IN 46204-2248, (317) 634-1690.

Indianapolis: Indianapolis SBDC, 1317 West Michriver, Indianapolis, IN 46202, (317) 274- 8200.

Kokomo: Kokomo-Howard County SBDC, P.O. Box 731, Kokomo, IN 46901, (317) 457-5301.

LaPorte: Northwest Indiana SBDC, 611 1/2 Michigan Avenue, Suite 2A, LaPorte, IN 46350, (219) 326-7232.

Madison: Madison Area SBDC, 301 East Main Street, Madison, IN 47250, (812) 265-2956.

Merrillville: Northwest Indiana SBDC, 3700 East Lincoln Highway., Merrillville, IN 46410, (219) 942-3496.

Muncie: East Central SBDC, 401 South High Street, Muncie, IN 47305, (317) 284-8144.

New Albany: Southern Indiana SBDC, 1702 East Spring Street, P.O. Box 653, New Albany, IN 47150, (812) 945-0054.

Richmond: Richmond-Wayne County Area SBDC, 600 Promenade, Richmond, IN 47374, (317) 962- 2887.

South Bend: South Bend SBDC, 300 North Michigan, South Bend, IN 46601, (219) 282-4350.

Terre Haute: Terre Haute Area SBDC, Indiana State University, Terre Haute, IN 47809, (812) 237-3232.

West Lafayette: West Lafayette SBDC, 1291 E Cumberland Avenue, P.O. Box 2378, West Lafayette, IN 47906, (317) 497-1108.

Iowa

General Information

Iowa Department of Economic Development, 200 East Grand Avenue, Des Moines, IA 50309, (515) 281-3251; CALL ONE: 1-800-532-1216 in Iowa only.

Small Business Advocate, Small Business Division, Iowa Department of Economic Development, 200 East Grand Avenue, Des Moines, IA 50309, (515) 281-8324.

Small Business Development Centers

The following offices offer free and fee-based services to new and expanding businesses:

Ames: SBDC Administrative Office, 137 Lynn Avenue, Ames, IA 50010, (515) 292-6351.

Ames: Iowa State University SBDC, Iowa State University, 137 Lynn Avenue, Ames, IA 50010, (515) 292-6355.

Audobon: Audobon Branch Office, 405 Washington Street, Audobon, IA 50025, (712) 563-3165.

Cedar Falls: University of Northern Iowa SBDC, University of Northern Iowa, 127 Seerley Hall, Cedar Falls, IA 50614, (319) 273-2696.

Council Bluffs: Iowa Western SBDC, Western Community College, 2700 College Road, Box 4C, Council Bluffs, IA 51502, (712) 325-3260.

Creston: Southwestern SBDC, Southwestern Community College, Highway 34 and South Cherry, 500 East Taylor, Creston, IA 50801, (515) 782-4161.

Davenport: Eastern Iowa SBDC, Eastern Iowa Community College, 304 West Second Street, Davenport, IA 52801, (319) 322-4499.

Des Moines: Drake University SBDC, Drake University, 210 Aliber Hall, Des Moines, IA 50311, (515) 271-2655.

Dubuque: Northeast Iowa SBDC, Dubuque Area Chamber of Commerce, 770 Town Clock Plaza, Dubuque, IA 52001, (319) 588-3350.

Iowa City: University of Iowa SBDC, University of Iowa, Oakdale Campus, 106 Technology Innovation Center, Iowa City, IA 52242, (319) 335-4057.

Mason City: North Iowa Area SBDC, North Iowa Area Community College, 500 College Drive, Mason City, IA 50401, (515) 421-4342.

Ottumwa: Indian Hills SBDC, Indian Hills Community College, Grandview and Elm, Ottumwa, IA 52501, (515) 683-5127.

Sious City: Western Iowa Tech SBDC, Western Iowa Tech Community College, 5001 E. Gordon Drive, Box 265, Sioux City, IA 51102, (712) 276-0380.

Spencer: Iowa Lakes SBDC, Iowa Lakes Community College, Gateway North Shopping Center, Highway 71 North, Spencer, IA 51301, (712) 262-4213.

West Burlington: Burlington Branch Office, Southeastern Community College, Drawer F, West Burlington, IA 52665, (319) 752-2731, Ext. 103.

Kansas

General Information

Kansas Department of Commerce, Capitol Tower Office Building, 400 West 8th Street, Suite 500, Topeka, KS 66603-3957, (913) 296-3483. Offers a "One-Stop Clearinghouse" for obtaining permits and applications necessary for establishing and operating a business.

Small Business Advocate, Director, Existing Business, Department of Commerce, 400 Southwest Eighth, Suite 500, Topeka, KS 66603-3957, (913) 296-3481.

Small Business Development Centers

The following offices offer free and fee-based services to new and expanding businesses:

Wichita: SBDC (State Coordinating Office), The Wichita State University, 021 Cointon Hall, Box 148, Wichita, KS 67208, (316) 689-3193.

Emporia: SBDC, Emporia State University, 1200 Commercial, 207 Cremer Hall, Emporia, KS 66801, (316) 343-1200, Ext. 308.

Hays: SBDC, Fort Hays State University, 1401 S. Main Street, Hays, KS 67601, (913) 628- 5340.

Overland Park: SBDC, Johnson County Community College, 12345 College at Quivira, OCB 257, Overland Park, KS 66210, (913) 469-3878.

Manhattan: SBDC, Kansas State University, 204 Calvin Hall, Manhattan, KS 66506, (913) 532- 5529.

Pittsburg: SBDC, Pittsburg State University, The Institute for Economic Development, Shirk Hall, Pittsburg, KS 66762, (316) 231-8267 or 231-7000, Ext. 4920.

Lawrence: SBDC, University of Kansas, 342 E. Summerfield Hall, Lawrence, KS 66045, (913) 864-7557.

Topeka: SBDC, Washburn University, 110 Henderson Learning Center, Topeka, KS 66621, (913) 295-6305.

Wichita: SBDC, Wichita State University, River Park Place, 727 N. Waco, Suite 580, Wichita, KS 67203, (316) 263-2929.

Kentucky

General Information

Kentucky Business Information Clearinghouse, Kentucky Commerce Cabinet, Department of Economic Development, Capital Plaza Tower, Frankfort, KY 40601, (502) 564-4252; 1-800-626-2250 in Kentucky only. This office handles requests for business licensing and permit information, referrals to other state, federal and local government agencies, and problems with government red tape.

Small Business Advocate, Small Business Division, Department of Economic Development, Business Information Clearninghouse, 22nd Floor, Capital Plaza Tower, Frankfort, KY 40601, (502) 564- 4252.

Small Business Development Centers

The following offices offer free and fee-based services to new and expanding businesses:

Ashland: Ashland SBDC, Boyd-Greenup County Chamber of Commerce Bldg., P.O. Box 830, 207 15th Street, Ashland, KY 41105-0830, (606) 329-8011.

Bowling: Bowling Green SBDC, Western Kentucky University, 245 Grise Hall, Bowling Green, KY 42101, (502) 745-2901.

Cumberland: Southeast SBDC, Southeast Community College, Rm. 113 Chrisman Hall, Cumberland, KY 40823, (606) 589-4514.

Cumberland: Southeast SBDC, Southeast Community College, Rm. 113 Chrisman Hall, Cumberland, KY 40823, (606) 589-4514.

Elizabethtown: SBDC, 238 West Dixie Highway, Elizabethtown, KY 42701, (502) 765-6737.

Highland Heights: North Kentucky SBDC, Northern Kentucky University, BEP Center 463, Highland Heights, KY 41076, (606) 572-6524.

Hopkinsville: Hopkinsville SBDC, Pennyrile Area Development District, 300 Hammond Drive, Hopkinsville, KY 42240, (502) 886-8666.

Lexington: Central Kentucky SBDC, University of Kentucky, Rm. 11 Porter

Building, Lexington, KY 40506-0205, (606) 257-7666.

Louisville: Bellarmine College SBDC, Bellarmine College, School of Business, Newburg Road, Louisville, KY 40205, (502) 452-8282.

Louisville: University of Louisville SBDC (Technology Specialized Center), University of Louisville, Center for Entrepreneurship and Technology, School of Business -- Belknap Campus, Louisville, KY 40292, (502) 588-7854.

Morehead: Morehead SBDC, Morehead State University, Butler Hall, Morehead, KY 40351, (606) 783-2895.

Murray: West Kentucky SBDC, Murray State University, College of Business and Public Affairs, Murray, KY 42071, (502) 762-2856.

Owensboro: Owensboro SBDC, 3860 U.S. Hwy. 60 West, Owensboro, KY 42301, (502) 926-8085.

Pikeville: Pikeville SBDC, 222 Hatcher Court, Pikeville, KY 41501, (606) 432-5848.

Somerset: South Central SBDC, Eastern Kentucky University, 216 Popular Avenue, Somerset, KY 42501, (606) 678-5520.

Louisiana

General Information

Louisiana Department of Economic Development, P.O. Box 94185, Baton Rouge, LA 70804-9185, (504) 342-5359.

Small Business Advocate, Community Development Division, Louisiana Department of Commerce & Industry, Box 94185, Baton Rouge, LA 70804-9184.

Small Business Development Centers

The following offices offer free and fee-based services to new and expanding businesses:

Baton Rouge: Capital (Southern University), Small Business Development Center, 9613 Interline Avenue, Baton Rouge, LA 70809, (504) 922-0998.

Hammond: Southeastern Louisiana University, Small Business Development Center, College of Business Administration, SLU Station, Box 522, Hammond, LA 70402, (504) 549-3831.

Lafayette: University of Southwestern Louisiana, Small Business Development Center, College of Business Administration, Box 4372, Lafayette, LA 70504, (318) 231-5751.

Lake Charles: McNeese State University, Small Business Development Center, College of Business Administration, Lake Charles, LA 70609, (318) 475-5529.

Monroe: Louisiana Small Business Development Center (State Director), Northeast Louisiana University, Monroe, LA 71209-6435, (318) 342-2464.

Monroe: Northeast Louisiana University, Small Business Development Center, College of Business Administration, Monroe, LA 71209, (318) 342-2129.

Natchitoches: Northwestern State University, Small Business Development Center, College of Business Administration, Natchitoches, LA 71497, (318) 357-5611.

New Orleans: International Trade Center, 368 Business Administration, University of New Orleans, Lakefront Campus, New Orleans, LA 70148, (504) 286-7197.

New Orleans: Loyola University, Small Business Development Center, College of Business Administration, Box 134, New Orleans, LA 70118, (504) 865-3474.

New Orleans: Southern University, Small Business Development Center, College of Business Administration, New Orleans, LA 70126, (504) 282-4401, Ext. 308.

New Orleans: University of New Orleans, Small Business Development Center, College of Business Administration, Lakefront Campus, New Orleans, LA 70148, (504) 286-6978.

Ruston: Louisiana Tech University, Small Business Development Center, Box 10318, Tech Station, Ruston, LA 71272-0046, (318) 257-3537.

Shreveport: LSU-Shreveport, Small Business Development Center, College of Business Administration, 1 University Place, Shreveport, LA 71115, (308) 797-5144.

Thibodaux: Nicholls State University, Small Business Development Center, College of Business Administration, P.O. Box 2015, Thibodaux, LA 70310, (504) 448-4242.

Small Business and Entrepreneuring

Maine

General Information

Business Answers, Department of Economic and Community Development, Station #59, Augusta, ME 04333; 1-800-872-3838 in Maine only. Serves as a central clearinghouse of information regarding business assistance programs and services available to state businesses.

Small Business Advocate, Maine Department of Economic & Community Development, Station 59, 193 State Street, Augusta, ME 04333, (207) 289-2658; 1-800-541-5872 outside Maine.

Small Business Development Centers

The following offer free and fee-based services to new and expanding businesses:

Auburn: SBDC, Androscoggin Valley Council of Governments, 70 Court Street, Auburn, ME 04210, (207) 783-9186.

Bangor: SBDC, Eastern Maine Development Corporation, 10 Franklin Street, Bangor, ME 04401, (207) 942-6389.

Caribo: SBDC, Northern Maine Regional Planning Commission, P.O. Box 779, Caribou, ME 04736, (207) 498-8736.

Machias: SBDC, University of Maine at Machias, Math and Science Building, Machias, ME 04654, (207) 255-3313.

Portland: BDC (Administrative Office), University of Southern Maine, Center for Research and Advanced Study, 246 Deering Avenue, Portland, ME 04102,(207) 780-4420.

Winslow: SBDC, Northern Kennebec Regional Planning Commission, 7 Benton Avenue, Winslow, ME 04902, (207) 873-0711.

Wiscasset: SBDC, Coastal Enterprises, Inc., P.O. Box 268, Wiscasset, ME 04578, (207) 882- 7552.

Maryland

General Information

Maryland Business Assistance Center, 217 East Redwood Street, Baltimore, MD 21202, (301) 333- 6975; Hotline; 1-800-OK-GREEN in Maryland only. A direct link to state services including public financing, facility location, state-funded employee training, government procurement assistance, help with licensing and permit processing, and information on starting a business.

Small Business Advocate, Department of Economic and Employment Development, 45 Calvert Street, Annapolis, MD 21401, (301) 974-3514. Assistance in cutting bureaucratic red tape. Information and expertise in dealing with state, federal, and local agencies.

Small Business Development Centers

The following offices offer free and fee-based services to new and expanding businesses:

Baltimore: Small Business Development Centers (Administrative Office), Department of Economic and Employment Development, 217 East Redwood Street, Baltimore, MD 21202, (301) 333-6996.

Baltimore: Central Maryland Regional SBDC, 123 West 24th Street, Baltimore, MD 28218, (301) 889-5772.

Elkton: Eastern Maryland Regional SBDC, 107 Railroad Avenue, Elkton, MD 21921, (301) 392- 3366; 1-800-321-6413 in Maryland only.

Hagerstown: Western Maryland Regional SBDC, Potomac Edison Co., Downsville Pike, Hagerstown, MD 21740, (301) 790-6179.

Waldorf: Southern Maryland Regional SBDC, 235 Smallwood Village Center, Waldorf, MD 20601, (301) 932-4155.

Massachusetts

General Information

Massachusetts Office of Business Development, 100 Cambridge Street, Boston, MA 02202, (617) 727-3221; SPIRIT: 1-800-632-8181 in Massachusetts only. Operates the "SPIRIT" Business Line, a toll-free, direct hot-line service to answer business-related questions.

Small Business Development Centers

The following offices offer free and fee-based services to new and expanding businesses:

Amherst: SBDC (State Office), 205 School of Management, University of Massachusetts, Amherst, MA 01003; (413) 549-4903, Ext. 303.

Boston: SBDC, Minority Business Training and Resource Center, 625 Huntington Avenue, Boston, MA 02115; (617) 734-0094.

Chestnut Hill: SBDC Metro Boston Regional Office, Boston College, 96 College Road -- Rahner House, Chestnut Hill, MA 02167; (617) 552-4091.

Fall River: SBDC Southeastern Regional Office, 200 Pocasset Street, P.O. Box 2785, Fall River, MA 02722; (617) 673-9783.

Lowell: SBDC Northeastern Regional Office, University of Lowell, 450 Aiken Street, Lowell, MA 01854; (617) 458-7261.

Springfield: SBDC Western Massachusetts Regional Office, 101 State Street, Suite #323, Springfield, MA 01103; (413) 737-6712.

Worcester: SBDC Central Massachusetts Regional Office, Graduate School of Management, Clark University, 950 Main Street, Worcester, MA 01610; (617) 793-7615.

Michigan

General Information

Michigan Business Ombudsman, P.O. Box 30107, Lansing, MI 48909; (517) 373-6241. 1-800-232-2727 in Michigan. Acts as a mediator in resolving regulatory disputes between business and the various state departments and also provides consultation and referral services. The ombudsman also serves as a "one-stop" center for business permits.

Small Business Advocate, Michigan Department of Commerce, P.O. Box 30225, Lansing, MI 48909; (517) 335-4720. Assistance in cutting bureaucratic red tape. Information and expertise in dealing with state, federal and local agencies.

Small Business Development Centers

The following offices offer free and fee based services to new and expanding businesses.

Ann Arbor: Ann Arbor Innovation Center SBDC, 912 North Maine Street, Ann Arbor, MI 48104; (313) 662-0550

Battle Creek: Kellogg Community College SBDC, 450 North Avenue, Battle Creek, MI 49016; (616) 965-3931, Ext. 223

Bay City: Bay Area Chamber of Commerce SBDC, 901 Saginaw, Bay City, MI 48708; (517) 893- 4567

Big Rapids: West Central Community Growth Alliance SBDC, 110 Elm Street, Big Rapids, MI 49307; (616) 796-7031

Detroit: Detroit Economic Growth Corporation SBDC, First National Building, Suite 600, Detroit, MI 48226; (313) 963-2940

Detroit: SBDC State Administrative Office, Wayne State University, 2727 Second Avenue, Detroit, MI 48201; (313) 577-4848

Escanaba: Central Upper Peninsula SBDC, 2415 14th Avenue, South, Escanaba, MI 49829; (906) 786-9234

Flint: Flint Area SBDC, 708 Root Street, Flint, MI 48503; (313) 232-7101

Grand Rapids: Grand Rapids SBDC, 66 North Division, Grand Rapids, MI 49503; (616) 242-6613

Harrison: Region 7B Community Growth Alliance SBDC, 402 N. First Street, Harrison, MI 48625; (517) 539-2173

Houghton: Michigan Technological University SBDC, Houghton, MI 49931; (906) 482-7206

Kalamazoo: Kalamazoo SBDC, 130 N. Kalamazoo Mall, Kalamazoo, MI 49007; (616) 343-1150

Marlette: Thumb Area SBDC, 3270 Wilson Street, Marlette, MI 48453; (517) 635-3561

Midland: Midland County Growth Council SBDC, 300 Rodd Street, Midland, MI 48640; (517) 839-9901

Monroe: Monroe SBDC, 1555 S. Raisinville Road, Monroe, MI 48161; (313) 242-7300

Mt. Clemens: Macomb County Business Assistance Center, 115 South Groesbeck, Mt. Clemens, MI 48043; (313) 469-5118

Mt. Pleasant: Middle Michigan SBDC, 111 S. University Street, Mt. Pleasant, MI 48858; (517) 772-2858

Muskegon: Muskegon/Oceana SBDC, 349 W. Webster Avenue, Room 104, Muskegon, MI 49440; (616) 726-4848

Onaway: Northeast Michigan Consortium SBDC, P.O. Box 711, Onaway, MI 49765; (517) 733-8548

Pontiac: Oakland County Economic Development Group, Executive Office Building, 1200 North Telegraph, Pontiac, MI 48053; (313) 858-0732

Scottville: Manistee-Mason SBDC, West Shore Community College, 3000 N. Stiles Road, Scottville, MI 49454-0277 (616) 845-6211 or 723-8356

Southgate: Downriver SBDC, 15100 Northline Road, Southgate, MI 48193; (313) 281-0700

Traverse City: Traverse Bay Area SBDC, 202 East Grandview Parkway, P.O. Box 387, Traverse City, MI 49685; (616) 947-5075

Minnesota

General Information

Minnesota Small Business Assistance Office, 900 American Center Building, 150 East Kellogg Boulevard, St. Paul, MN 55101; (612) 296-3871; Hotline: 1-800-652-9747. Small business and business licensing assistance. Provides accurate, timely and comprehensive information and assistance to businesses in all areas of start-up, operation, and expansion. Referrals to other state agencies.

Small Business Advocate, Minnesota Small Business Assistance Office, 900 American Center, 150 Kellogg Boulevard, St. Paul, MN 55101; (612) 296-3871.

Small Business Development Centers

The following offices offer free and fee-based services to new and expanding businesses:

Bemidji: Bemidji State University SBDC, 14th and Birchmont Drive, Bemidji, MN 56601-2699; (218) 755-2750.

Brainerd: Brainerd TI SBDC, 300 Quince Street, Brainerd, MN 56401; (218) 828-5302, 1-800- 247-2574 in Minnesota.

Chaska: College of St. Thomas Enterprise Center (State Office), 1107 Hazeltine Boulevard, Chaska, MN 55318; (612) 448-8810.

Duluth: University of Minnesota-Duluth SBDC, 150 School of Business and Economics, Duluth, MN 55812; (218) 726-8761.

Mankato: Mankato State University SBDC, P.O. Box 14, Mankato, MN 56001; (507) 389-1648.

Marshall: Southwest State University SBDC, Marshall, MN 562588; (507) 537-7440.

Moorhead Moorhead State University SBDC, 1104 Seventh Avenue South, Moorhead, MN 56560; (218) 236-2289.

St. Cloud: St. Cloud State University SBDC, First Avenue South and Seventh Street, St. Cloud, MN 56301; (612) 255-4842.

St. Paul: College of St. Thomas SBDC, 23 Empire Drive, St. Paul, MN 55103; (612) 223-8663.

St. Paul: University of Minnesota Extension Service, Small Business Development Center, Dept. of Agriculture and Applied Economics, 248 Classroom Office Building, 1994 Bedford Avenue, St. Paul, MN 55108; (612) 625-1715.

Winona: Winona State University SBDC, Somsen Hall, Eighth and Jackson, Winona, MN 55987; (507) 457-5088.

Small Business Development Centers

The following offices offer free and fee-based services to new and expanding businesses:

Columbus: SBDC, Mississippi University for Women, Box W-239, Columbus, MS 39701; (601) 329-4750.

Greenwood: Northwest Regional SBDC, P.O. Box 3244, 305 W. Market Street, Greenwood, MS 38930; (601) 846-4230.

Hattiesburg: Southeast Regional SBDC, Pearl River Community College, Forest County Vocational Technical Center, P.O. Box 16235, Hattiesburg, MS 39402-6235; (601) 544-0010.

Jackson: SBDC Department of Economic Development, 1300 Walter Sillers Building, P.O. Box 849, Jackson, MS 39205; (601) 359-3421.

Jackson: SBDC/Foreign Trade Institute, Millsaps College, P.O. Box 15395, Jackson, MS 39210; (601) 354-5201, Ext. 407.

Jackson: Mississippi Small Business Development Center, Administrative Office, 3825 Ridgewood Road, Jackson, MS 39211; (601) 982-6395.

Long Beach: SBDC, University of Southern Mississippi, USM-Gulf Park, Long Beach, MS 39560; (601) 865-4578.

Meridian: East Central Regional SBDC, P.O. Box 4398, 5500 Highway 19N, Meridian, MS 39304
(483-8241, Ext. 616.

Mississippi State: SBDC Mississippi State University, P.O. Drawer 5288, 240 McCool Hall, College of Business & Industry, Mississippi State, MS 39762; (601) 325-3817.

Tupelo: Northeast Regional SBDC, P.O. Box 203, 1018 N. Gloster Street, Tupelo, MS 38802; (601) 844-5413.

University: Small Business Development Center, The Univeristy of Mississippi, University, MS 38677; (601) 234-2120.

Missouri

General Information

Missouri Business Assistance Center, Department of Economic Development, P.O. Box 118, Jefferson City, MO 65102, First-Stop Shop: 1-800-523-1434. The First-Stop Shop number for Missouri residents serves to link business owners and state government and provides information on state rules, regulations, licenses, and permits. The Business Assistance Center provides information and technical assistance to start-up and existing businesses on available state and federal programs.

Federal Information Center, Federal Building, 1520 Market Street, Kansas City, MO 64106, 1-800- 892-5808 in Missouri; or Federal Information Center, Federal Building, 1520 Market Street, St. Louis, MO 63103, 1-800-392-7711 in Missouri. Both locations offer information regarding Missouri programs for business people.

Small Business Advocate, Department of Economic Development, P.O. Box 118, Jefferson City, MO 65102; (314) 751-4982. Assistance in cutting bureaucratic red tape. Information and expertise in dealing with state, federal, and local agencies.

Small Business Development Centers

The following offices offer free and fee-based services to new and expanding businesses:

Cape Girardeau SBDC, 222 N. Pacific, Cape Girardeau, MO 63701; (314) 651-2963.

Columbia: School of Business, University of Missouri, 1700 University Place, Columbia, MO 65211; (314) 882-7096.

Columbia: SBDC & Missouri Cooperative Extension Service, 821 Clark Hall, University of Missouri, Columbia, MO 65211; (314) 882-4321.

Flat River: SBDC, Mineral Area College, Flat River, MO 63601; (314) 686-4104.

Jefferson City: SBIR and High Tech Program, 301 W. High, Room 770, P.O. Box 118, Jefferson City, MO 65102; (314) 751-3906.

Joplin: SBDC, Missouri Southern State College, 107 Matthews Hall, 3950 Newman Road, Joplin, MO 64801; (417) 625-9319.

Kansas City: SBDC, Rockhurst College, 5225 Troost Avenue, Kansas City, MO 64110; (816) 926-4572.

Small Business and Entrepreneuring

Kirksville: SBDC, Northeast Missouri State University, 205 E. Patterson, Kirksville, MO 63501; (816) 785-4307.

Poplar Bluff: SBDC & Business School, Three Rivers Community College, Poplar Bluff, MO 63901; (314) 686-4104.

Maryville: SBDC, Northwest Missouri State University, 515 N. Main Street, Maryville, MO 64468; (816) 562-1701.

Rolla: Center for Technology Development, 306 Harris Hall, University of Missouri-Rolla, Rolla, MO 65401; (314) 341-4004.

Rolla: SBDC, Engineering Management Building, University of Missouri-Rolla, Rolla, MO 65401; (314) 341-4561.

Springfield: SBDC & Center for Business Research, 901 S. National, P.O. Box 88, Southwest Missouri State University, Springfield, MO 65804; (417) 836-5658.

Warrensburg: Center for Technology & Small Business Development, Central Missouri State University, Warrensburg, MO 64093; (816) 429-4402.

Warrensburg: Center for Technology & Business, #80 Grinstead Hall, Central Missouri State University, Warrensburg, MO 65804; (816) 429-4402.

Montana

General Information

Business Assistance Division, Department of Commerce, 1424 Ninth Avenue, Helena, MT 59620; (406) 444-3923. "A Guide to Montana's Economic Development Assistance Program," which lists state and federal agencies and other sources of business assistance is available at no charge.

Division of Small Business Advocacy and Business Licensing, Department of Commerce, 1424 Ninth Avenue, Helena, MT 59620, 1-800-221-8015 (in-state only). Offers a toll-free number for licensing and permit questions. Also acts as an advocate for small businesses.
Small Business Advocate, Business Assistance Division, Department of Commerce, 1424 Ninth Avenue, Helena, MT 59620; (406) 444-4380. Assistance in cutting bureaucratic red tape. Information and expertise in dealing with state, federal, and local agencies.

Small Business Development Centers

The following offices offer free and fee-based services to new and expanding businesses:

Helena: Small Business Development Center, Business Assistance Division, Department of Commerce, 1424 Ninth Avenue, Helena, MT 59620; (406) 444-4780.

Glendive: Small Business Development Sub-center, c/o Dawson Community College, P.O. Box 421, Glendive, MT 59330; (406) 365-2377.

Nebraska

General Information

Department of Economic Development, Research Division, P.O. Box 94666, 301 Centennial Mall South, Lincoln, NE 69509; (402) 471-3782; 800-426-6505 in state. One-Stop Business Assistance Program: Provides information on technical assistance, regulations licenses, and taxes as well as marketing, patents, and business counseling.

Department of Economic Development, Small Business Division, P.O. Box 94666, 301 Centennial Mall South, Lincoln, NE 69509; (402) 471-3111. Offers technical assistance to small businesses and acts as a clearinghouse for information on other state services. Activities include acting as a link between business and government contracts, promoting exports of Nebraska products to foreign markets, maintaining a job training liaison to coordinate labor training with industrial location and expansion, maintaining business finance consultants in outreach offices, and providing information on federal programs such as Community Development Block Grants, SBA loans, and FmHA Business and Industry loans.

Small Business Advocate, Small Business Division, P.O. Box 94666, 301 Centennial Mall South, Lincoln, NE 68509, 402-471-3742. Assistance in cutting bureaucratic red tape. Information and expertise in dealing with state, federal, and local agencies.

Small Business Development Centers

The following offices offer free and fee-based services to new and expanding businesses:

Chadron: Chadron SBDC, Administration Building, Chadron State College, Chadron, NE 69337; (308) 432-6282.

Lincoln Lincoln SBDC, 1237 R Street, Suite 203, Lincoln, NE (402) 472-3358; 1-800-742-8800 in Nebraska.

North Platte: North Platte SBDC, 416 N. Jeffers, Room 26, Mid Plains Community College, North Platte NE 69101; (308) 534-5115.

Omaha: University of Nebraska at Omaha (State Office), 1313 Farnam-on-The-Mall, Suite 132, Omaha, NE 68182-0164; (404) 554-2521 (8381).

Peru: Peru SBDC, Industrial Arts Building, Room 27, Peru State College, Peru, NE 68421; (402) 872-3815.

Scottsbluff: Scottsbluff SBDC, 1721 Broadway, Room 408, Nebraska Public Power Building, Scottsbluff, NE 69361; (308) 635-7513.

Wayne: Wayne SBDC, Connell Hall, Wayne State College, Wayne, NE 68787; (402) 375-2004.

West Campus Kearney: Kearney SBDC, Business Department Office Building, Kearney State College, West Campus Kearney, NE 68849; (308) 234-8344.

Nevada

General Information

State of Nevada Commission on Economic Development, Capitol Complex, Carson City, NV 89710; (702) 885-4325; 1-800-336-1600 in Nevada. Publishes a pamphlet, "Backing Business in Nevada," which lists state resources for business retention and expansion. Acts as a clearinghouse for information and technical assistance. Operates several business assistance programs and performs advertising and public relations activities on behalf of Nevada business.

Small Business Advocate, Nevada Office of Community Services, Capitol Complex, Suite 116, 1100 East William, Carson City, NV 89710; (702) 885-4602.

Small Business Development Centers

The following offices offer free and fee-based services to new and expanding businesses:

Elko: Elko Small Business Development Center, Northern Nevada Community College, 901 Elm St., Elko, NV 89801; (702) 738-8493.

Las Vegas: Las Vegas Small Business Development Center, College of Business and Economics, University of Nevada -- Las Vegas, 4505 Maryland Pkwy., Las Vegas, NV 89154; (702) 739- 3362.

Reno: Reno Small Business Development Center, College of Business Admin., Rm. 411, University of Nevada, Reno, NV 89577; (702) 784-1717.

New Hampshire

General Information

Small Business Advocate, Department of Resources and Economic Development, Division of Economics, Prescott Park, 105 Loudon Rd., Concord, NH 03301.

Small Business Development Centers

The following offices offer free and fee-based services to new and expanding businesses:

Durham: Seacoast SBDC Sub-center, Kingman Farm, University of New Hampshire, Durham, NH 03824; (603) 743-3995.

Franconia: North Country SBDC Sub-Center, P.O. Box 189, Franconia, NH 03580; (603) 862- 8742.

Keene: Keene SBDC Sub-Center, Blake House, Keene State College, Keene, NH 03431; (603) 352-1909, ext. 238.

Manchester: Small Business Development Center (State Office), University Center, Room 311, 400 Commercial St., Manchester, NH 03101; (603) 743-3995; 1-800-322-0390 in New Hampshire only.

Manchester: Merrimack Valley SBDC Sub-Center, 400 Commercial St., Room 311, Manchester, NH 03101 ; (603) 625-4522.

Plymouth: Plymouth SBDC Sub-Center, Hyde Hall, Plymouth State College, Plymouth, NH 03264; (603) 536-5000, ext. 2526.

New Jersey

General Information

Office of Small Business Assistance, Capital Place One, 200 S. Warren Street, CN 835, Trenton, NJ 08625; (609) 984-4442. Advice on expansion and business start-ups, and marketing and procurement assistance are some of the services available to small businesses. The office also offers seminars throughout the state as part of its outreach program.

Small Business Advocate, Office of Business Advocacy, Capital Place One, 200 S. Warren Street, CN 823, Trenton, NJ 08625; (609) 292-0700. Assistance in cutting bureaucratic red tape. Information and expertise in dealing with state, federal, and local agencies.

Small Business Development Centers

The following offices offer free and fee-based services to new and expanding businesses:

Atlantic: Atlantic County Community College SBDC, 1535 Bacharach Blvd., Atlantic City, NJ 08401; (609) 343-4810.

Camden: Rutgers SBDC, Camden Campus, Victor Building, Room 200 C, Point and Pearl Sts., Camden, NJ 08102; (609) 757-6221.

Newark: New Jersey Small Business Development Center, Rutgers Graduate School of Management, 180 University Ave., Newark, NJ 07102; (201) 648-5950.

Newark: Rutgers SBDC, Newark Campus, 180 University Ave., Newark, NJ 07882; (201) 648- 5950.

New Brunswick: Drop In Center, Middlesex County Regional Chamber of Commerce, 10 Livingston Ave., New Brunswick, NJ 08901; (201) 545-3300.

Trenton: Mercer County Community College SBDC, P.O. Box B, Trenton, NJ 08690; (609) 586- 4800, ext. 469.

Union: Brookdale Community College SBDC, Newman Springs Rd., Lincroft, NJ 07738; (201) 842-1900. Ext. 551; Kean College SBDC, Morris Ave. and Conant, Union, NJ 07083; (201) 527-2413.

Washington: Skylands SBDC, Warren County Community College Commission, Route 57 West, RD #1 Box 55A, Washington, NJ 07882; (201) 689-7613.

New Mexico

General Information

Business Development Section, Department of Economic Development and Tourism, Joseph Montoya Building, 1100 St. Francis Drive, P.O. Box 20003, Sante Fe, NM 87503; (505) 827-0300.

Small Business Advocate, Department of Economic Development and Tourism, Joseph Montoya Building, P.O. Box 20003, 1100 St. Francis Drive, Santa Fe, NM 87503; (505)-827-0300. Assistance in cutting bureaucratic red tape. Information and expertise in dealing with state, federal, and local agencies.
As of printing time, New Mexico does not have any Small Business Development Centers. However, many community Colleges have business assistance centers that entrepreneurs can contact for help.

New York

General Information

Businesss Opportunity Center, New York State Department of Economic Development, Business Opportunity Center, Albany, NY 12245, 1-800-STATE NY. A special service that offers fast, up- to-date information on the State's business development programs and can help in making contact with appropriate agencies.

Small Business Advocate, Director of Advocacy, New York State Department of Economic Development, 1515 Broadway, 51st floor, New York, NY 10036; (212) 309-0466.

Small Business Development Centers

The following offices offer free and fee-based services to new and expanding businesses:

Albany: State University of New York SBDC (State Office), State University Plaza, Albany, NY 12246, 1-800-732-SBDC.

Albany: SUNY at Albany SBDC, Draper Hall, 107, 135 Western Ave., Albany, NY 12222; (518) 442-5577.

Binghamton: SUNY at Binghamton SBDC, Vestal Parkway East, Binghamton, NY 13901; (607) 777- 4024.

Brooklyn: Long Island University School of Business SBDC, Humanities Building, 7th Floor, 1 University Plaza, Brooklyn, NY 11201; (718) 852-1197.

Buffalo: State University College at Buffalo SBDC, HB 228, 1300 Elmwood Ave., Buffalo, NY 14222; (716) 878-4030.

Farmingdale: State University Agricultural and Technical College SBDC, Laffin Administration Building, Room 007, Farmingdale, NY 11735; (516) 420-7930, or 420-2765.

Jamestown: Jamestown Community College SBDC, P.O. Box 20, Jamestown, NY 14702-0020; (716) 665-5220.

New York: Pace University SBDC, Pace Plaza, New York, NY 10038; (212) 488-1901.

Plattsburgh: State University College at Plattsburgh SBDC, c/o T.A.C., Plattsburgh, NY 12901; (518) 564-2214.

Sanborn: Niagara County Community College SBDC, c/o T.A.C., 3111 Saunders Settlement Rd., Sanborn, NY 14132; (716) 693-1910.

Stone Ridge: Ulster County Community College SBDC, Stone Ridge, NY 12484; (914) 687-0768.

Syracuse: Greater Syracuse Incubator Center, 1201 East Fayette St., Syracuse, NY 13210; (315) 475-0083.

Utica: State University College of Technology at Utica/Rome SBDC, P.O. Box 3050, Utica, NY 13504-3050; (315) 792-7432.

Watertown: Jefferson Community College SBDC, Watertown, NY 13601; (315) 782-9262.

North Carolina

General Information

North Carolina Department of Commerce, Small Business Development Division, 430 N. Salisbury St., Raleigh, NC 27603; (919) 733-4151. Coordinates state small business assistance programs and financing. Includes pooled industrial revenue bonds, a certified SBA Development Company, and a long-term, fixed-rate financing program. Also provides information and referral services to small firms and prospective entrepreneurs and acts as advocate for the state's small business community.

Small Business Advocate, Small Business Development Division, North Carolina Department of Commerce, Dobbs Building Room 2019, 430 North Salisbury St., Raleigh, NC 27611; (919) 733-7980. Assistance in cutting bureaucratic red tape. Information and expertise in dealing with state, federal, and local agencies.

Small Business Development Centers

Boone: SBTDC, Northwestern Regional Center, Appalachian State University, Boone, NC; (704) 262-2095.

Charlotte: SBTDC, Southern Piedmont Regional Center, University of North Carolina-- Charlotte, Charlotte, NC; (704) 597-9851.

Cullowhee: SBTDC, Western Regional Center, Western Carolina University, Cullowhee, NC; (704) 227-7494.

Elizabeth: SBTDC Northeastern Regional Center, Elizabeth City State University, Elizabeth City, NC; (919) 335-3247.

Fayetteville: SBTDC, Cape Fear Regional Center, Fayetteville State University, Pembroke State University, Methodist University, Campbell University, Fayetteville, NC; (919) 486- 1727.

Greenville: SBTDC, Eastern Regional Center, East Carolina University, Greenville, NC; (919) 757-6157.

Greensboro: University of North Carolina - Greensboro, North Carolina A & T State, Greensboro, NC; (919) 334-7005.

Raleigh: SBTDC Headquaters Office, University of North Carolina, 4509 Creedmoor Rd., Suite 201, Raleigh, NC 27612; (919) 733-4643; 1-800-2580-UNC in North Carolina.

Raleigh: SBTDC, Research Triangle Park Regional Center, University of North Carolina-Chapel Hill, Raleigh, NC; (919) 733-4643.
Wilmington: SBTDC, Southeastern Regional Center, University of North

Small Business and Entrepreneuring

Carolina - Wilmington, Wilmington, NC; (919) 395-3744.

Winston-Salem: SBTDC, Northern Piedmont Regional Center, Winston-Salem State University, Winston-Salem, NC.

North Dakota

General Information

Center for Innovation and Business Development, Box 8103, University Station, Grand Forks, ND 58202; (701) 777-3132. The "Do It Yourself" Entrepreneur Kit is a step-by-step guide, with optional software, to writing your own business and marketing plan. It is targeted to new manufacturing ventures producing new products or technology, but the guide can also be relevant to many entrepreneurs, academics, and business professionals.

Small Business Advocate, North Dakota Development Commission, Liberty Memorial Building, Bismarck, ND 58501; (701) 224-2810. Assistance in cutting bureaucratic red tape. Information and expertise in dealing with state, federal, and local agencies.

Small Business Development Centers

The following offices offer free and fee-based services to new and expanding businesses:

Bismark: State SBDC Office, Economic Development Commission, Business Development Assistance Division, Liberty Memorial Building, Bismarck, ND 58505; (701) 224-2810.

Dickinson: Dickinson Regional Center SBDC, 314 3rd Ave. West, Drawer L, Dickinson, ND 58602; (701) 227-2096.

Fargo: Fargo Regional Center SBDC, North Dakota State University, Box 5437, Fargo, ND 58105; (701) 237-7374.

Grand Rapids: Grand Forks Regional Center SBDC, Minnkota Power, 1822 Mill Road, Grand Forks, ND 58201; (701) 795-4227.

Jamestown: Jamestown Regional Center SBDC, 121 First Avenue West, P.O. Box 1530, Jamestown, ND 58402; (701) 252-4830.

Minot: Minot Regional Center SBDC, 1020 20th Avenue Southwest, P.O. Box 940, Minot, ND 58702; (701) 852-8861.

Ohio

General Information

Ohio Department of Development, P.O. Box 1001, Columbus, OH 43266-0101; (614) 644-8748; 1-800- 248-4040, in Ohio. The Ohio One-Stop Business Permit Center provides new entrepreneurs with licensing and permit information and directs them to the proper department for specific aid.

Small Business Advocate, Small And Developing Business Division, Ohio Department of Development, 30 East Broad St., 23rd Floor, P.O. Box 100, Columbus, OH 43266-0101; (614) 466-2718. Assistance in cutting bureaucratic red tape. Information and expertise in dealing with state, federal, and local agencies.

Small Business Development Centers

The following offices offer free and fee-based services to new and expanding businesses:

Columbus: Ohio Small Business Development Center (state office), Ohio Department of   Development, P.O. Box 1010, Columbus, OH 43266-0101; (614) 466-5111; 1-800-282-1085, in Ohio.

Oklahoma

General Information

Teamwork Oklahoma, 6601 Broadway Extension, Oklahoma City, OK 73116; (405) 843-9770; 1-800-522- OKLA, in Oklahoma. Acquaints businesspersons or potential businessperson with the many financial and consulting services available in Oklahoma.

Small Business Advocate, Oklahoma Department of Commerce, Five Broadway, Executive Park, 6001 Broadway Ext. Oklahoma City, OK 73116-8214. Assistance in cutting bureaucratic red tape. Information and expertise in dealing with state, federal, and local agencies.

Small Business Development Centers

The following offices offer free and fee-based services to new and expanding businesses:

Ada: East Central State University, Small Business Development Center, 1036 East Tenth, Ada, OK 74820; (405) 436-3190.

Alva: Northwestern Oklahoma State University, Small Business Development Center, Alva, OK 73717; (405) 327-5883.

Durant: State Office, Southeastern Oklahoma State University, Small Business Development Center, 517 University, Durant, OK 74701; (405) 924-0277.

Edmond: Central State University, Small Business Development Center, 100 North University Blvd., Edmond, OK 73034; (405) 341-2980, ext. 2836.

Emid: Enid Subcenter, Small Business Development Center, 1216 W. Willow, Suite A, Enid, OK 73707; (405) 237-4810.

Lawton: Lawton Subcenter, Small Business Development Center, Federal Bldg., Room 311, 431 E Ave., Lawton, OK 73501; (405) 248-4946.

Midwest: Rose State College, Small Business Development Subcenter, Procurement Specialty   Center, Tom Steed Bldg., Room 218, 6420 S.E. 15th., Midwest City, OK 73110; (405) 733-7348.

Muskogee: Muskogee Subcenter, Small Business Development Center, 4th and West Broadway, Muskogee, OK 74401; (918) 647-4019.

Poteau: Poteau Satellite Center, Small Business Development Center, Carl Albert Junior College, 1507 South McKenna, Poteau, OK 74953; (918) 647-4019.

Tahlequah: Northeastern State University, Small Business Development Center, Tahlequah, OK 74464; (918) 458-0802.

Tulsa: University of Tulsa, Small Business Development Subcenter, Enterprise Development Center, 600 South College Ave., Tulsa, OK 74104; (918) 592-2700.

Weatheerfor: Southwestern Oklahoma State University, Small Business Development Center, 100 Campus Dr., Weatheerfor, OK 73096; (405) 774-1040.

Oregon

General Information

Department of Economic Development, Business Development Division, 595 Cottage St. N.E., Salem, OR 97310; (503) 373-1225. Provides information to business investors on land, buildings, financing,and other relevant issues. Provides consulting services for manufacturing and processing companies with problems. Supports local economic development organizations in expansion efforts. Manages the Oregon Enterprize Zone program which offers property tax relief incentives in 30 specified regions, and a computer-based inventory of available industrial sites and buildings in the state. The Division maintains regional offices in six locations around the state.

Office of Small Business Advocate, Department of Economic Development, 595 Cottage St. N.E., Salem, OR 97310; (503) 373-1200. Assistance in cutting bureaucratic red tape. Information and expertise in dealing with state, federal, and local agencies.

Small Business Development Centers

The following offices offer free and fee-based services to new and expanding businesses:

Albany: Small Business Development Center, Linn-Benton Community College, 6500 S.W. Pacific Blvd., Albany, OR 97321; (503) 967-6112.

Ashland: Small Business Development Center, Southern Oregon State College/Ashland, Regional Services Institute, Ashland, OR 97520; (503) 482-5838.

Beaverton: Small Business Development Center, Portland Community College, Center for Entrepreneurial Ventures, 15245 N.W. Greenbrier Pkwy., Beaverton, OR 97006; (503) 645- 8183.

Bend: Small Business Development Center, Central Oregon Community College, 2600 N.W. College Way, Bend, OR 97701; (503) 385-5524.

Coos Bay: Small Business Development Center, Southwestern Oregon Community College, 1988 Newmark St., Coos Bay, OR 97420; (503) 888-2525, ext. 259.

Depoe: Small Business Development Center, Oregon Coast Community College, Service Dist., P.O. Box 29, Mall 101, Suite A, Depoe Bay, OR 97341-0029; (503) 765-2627.

Eugene: Small Business Development Center Network, 1059 Willamette St., Eugene, OR 97401; (503) 726-2250.

Eugene: Small Business Development Center, Lane Community College, 1059 Willamette St., Eugene, OR 97401; (503) 726-2255.

Grants Pass: Small Business Development Center, Rogue Community College, 206 N.E. 7th, Grants Pass, OR 97526; (503) 474-0762.

Gresham: Small Business Development Center, Mt. Hood Community College, 26000 S.E. Stark St., Gresham, OR 97030; (503) 667-7658.

Klamath: Small Business Development Center, Oregon Institute of Technology, 3201 Campus Dr., Klamath Falls, OR 97601; (503) 883-7556 or 883-7562.

La Grande: Small Business Development Center, Eastern Oregon State College, Regional Services Institute, La Grande, OR 97850; (503) 963-1391.

Medford: Small Business Development Center, Southern Oregon State College/Medford, 229 N. Bartlett, Medford, OR 97501; (503) 772-3478.

Ontario: Small Business Development Center, Treasure Valley Community College, 173 S.W. 1st St., Ontario, OR 97914; (503) 889-2617.

Oregon: Small Business Development Center, Clackamas Community College, 108 8th St., Oregon City, OR 97045; (503) 656-4447.

Pendleton: Small Business Development Center, Blue Mountain Community College, 37 S. Dorian, Pendleton, OR 97801; (503) 276-6233.

Portland: Small Business Development Center, Portland State University, Small Business International Trade Program, P.O. Box 751, 615 S.W. Harrison, Portland, OR 97207; (503) 464-3257.

Portland: Small Business Development Center, Portland Community College, 221 N.W. 2nd Ave., 3rd Floor, Portland, OR 97209; (503) 273-2828.

Rosenburg: Small Business Development Center, Umpqua Community College, 744 S.E. Rose, Roseburg, OR 97470; (503) 672-2535.

Salem: Small Business Development Center, Chemedeta Community College, 365 Ferry St. S.E., Salem, OR 97301; (503) 399-5181.

Seaside: Small Business Development Center, Clatsop Community College, 1240 S. Holladay, Seaside, OR 97138; (503) 738-3347.

The Dalles: Small Business Development Center, Treaty Oak Community College, Service District, 212 Washington, The Dalles, OR 97058; (503) 296-1173.

Tillamook: Small Business Development Center, Tillamook Bay Community College, Service District, 401B Main St., Tillamook, OR 97141; (503) 842-2551.

Pennsylvania

General Information

Business Resource Network, Room 404, Forum Building, Harrisburg, PA 17120; (717) 783-5700. Acts as a clearinghouse to assist small business in finding resources and services available in the state.

Small Business Advocate, Office Of Enterprise Development, Business Resource Network, 404 Forum Building, Harrisburg, PA 17120; (717) 783-5700. Assistance in cutting bureaucratic red tape. Information and expertise in dealing with state, federal, and local agencies.

Small Business Development Centers

The following offices offer free and fee-based services to new and expanding businesses:

Bethlehem: Small Business Development Center, Lehigh University, 301 Broadway, Bethlehem, PA 18015; (215) 758-3980.

Clarion Small Business Development Center, Clarion University of Pennsylvania, Dana Still Building, Clarion, PA 16214; (814) 226-2060.

Erie: Small Business Development Center, Gannon University, Carlisle Building, 3rd Floor, Erie, PA 16541; (814) 871-7714.

Latrobe: Small Business Development Center, St. Vincent College, Alfred Hall, 4th Floor, Latrobe, PA 15650; (412) 537-4572.

Lewisburg: Small Business Development Center, Bucknell University, 310 Dana Engineering Building, Lewisburg, PA 17837; (717) 524-1249.

Loretto Small Business Development Center, St. Francis College, Raymond Hall, Loretto, PA 15940; (814) 472-3200.

Middletown: Small Business Development Center, Pennsylvania State University at Harrisburg, The Capital College, Crags Building, Route 230, Middletown, PA 17057; (717) 948-6069.

Philadelphia: State Director's Office, Pennsylvania Small Business Development Centers, 423 Vance Hall, University of Pennsylvania, Philadelphia, PA 19104-6374; (215) 898-1219.

Philadephia: Small Business Development Center, LaSalle University, 20th and Olney Ave., Philadelphia, PA 19141; (215) 951-1416 or 951-1735.
Philadelphia: Small Business Development Center, Temple University, Room 481, Ritter Hall, Annex 004-00, Philadelphia, PA 19122; (215) 787-7280.

Philadephia: Small Business Development Center, University of Pennsylvania, The Wharton School, 409 Vance Hall, Philadelphia, PA 19104-6357; (215) 898-4861.

Pittsburgh: Small Business Development Center, Duquesne University, Rockwell Hall, Room 10, Concourse, 600 Forbes Aves., Pittsburgh, PA 15282; (412) 434-6233.

Pittsburgh: Small Business Development Center, University of Pittsburgh, Room 343, Mervis, Pittsburgh, PA 15260; (412) 648-1544.

Scranton: Small Business Development Center, University of Scranton, 415 N. Washington Ave., Scranton, PA 18503; (717) 961-7588.

Wilkes-Barre: Small Business Development Center, Wilkes College, Hollenback Hall, 192 S. Franklin St., Wilkes-Barre, PA 18766; (717) 824-4651, ext. 4340.

Rhode Island

General Information

Rhode Island Department of Economic Development, 7 Jackson Walkway, Providence, RI 02903; (401) 277-2601. Maintains three separate divisions: Financial Services, 2) The Business Action Center, and 3) Small Business Development Division.

Small Business Advocate, Advisory Commission, Good Neighbor Alliance Corp., 1664 Cranston St., Cranston, RI 02920. Assistance in cutting bureaucratic red tape. Information and expertise in dealing with state, federal, and local agencies.

Small Business Development Centers

The following offices offer free and fee-based services to new and expanding businesses:

Kingston: Small Business Development Center State Headquarters, University of Rhode Island, 346 Ballentine Hall, Kingston, RI 02882-0806; (401) 792-2451.

Providence: Small Business Development Center, Downtown Providence Office, 270 Weybosset St., Providence, RI 02903; (401) 831-1330.

Smithfield: Small Business Development Center, Bryant College, Smithfield, RI 02917; (401) 232-6111.

Providence: Opportunities Industrialization Center Office, One Hilton St., Providence, RI 02905; (401) 272-4400.

Woonsocket: Small Business Development Center, Woonsocket Office, Greater Woonsocket Chamber Of Commerce, One Marquette Plaza, 9th Floor, Woonsocket, RI 02895; (401) 762-1730.

Newport: Small Business Development Center, Newport Office, Admiral's Gate Tech Center, 221 Third St., Newport, RI 02840; (401) 849-6900.

South Carolina

General Information

Enterprise Development Department, South Carolina State Development Board, P.O. Box 927, Columbia, SC 29202; (803) 737-0400. Stimulates the formation and growth of new businesses. Step-by-step information on starting a new business in South Carolina is provided in the "Business Formation and Expansion Manual," a free publication. Provides a network of services for development of business plans, offers assistance to small businesses on individual problems, and establishes a regional network for women-owned businesses. Technical assessments are available as well as educational and training programs and financial and marketing assistance.

Small Business Advocate, Industry-Business and Community Services, South Carolina Development Board, P.O. Box 927, Columbia, SC 29202; (803) 734-1400. Assistance in cutting bureaucratic red tape. Information and expertise in dealing with state, federal, and local agencies.

Small Business and Entrepreneuring

Small Business Development Centers

The following office offers free and fee-based services to new and expanding businesses:

Columbia: Small Business Development Center, College of Business Administration, University of South Carolina, Columbia, SC 29208; (803) 777-5118.

South Dakota

General Information

Small Business Advocate, Governor's Office of Economic Development, 711 Wells Ave., Pierre, SD 57501; (605) 773-5032. Assistance in cutting bureaucratic red tape. Information and expertise in dealing with state, federal, and local agencies.

Small Business Development Centers

The following offices offer free and fee-based services to new and expanding businesses:

Vermillion: State Headquarters, South Dakota Small Business Development Center, USD School of Business, 414 East Clark St., Vermillion, SD 57069; (605) 677-5272.

Sioux Falls: Small Business Development Center, Chamber of Commerce Office, 231 S. Phillips, Room 365, Sioux Falls, SD 57102; (605) 339-3366.

Aberdeen: Small Business Development Center, Chamber of Commerce Office, 516 South Main, P.O. Box 1179, Aberdeen, SD 57401; (605) 225-2860.

Watertown: Small Business Development Center, First District Association of Local Governments, 124 First Ave. N.W., P.O. Box 1207, Watertown, SD 57201; (605) 394-5725.

Rapid City: Small Business Development Center, Executive Suites, 2100 S. 7th St., Suite 227, P.O. Box 5628, Rapid City, SD 57701; (605) 394-5725.

Tennessee

General Information

Office of Small Business, Department of Economic and Community Development, 320 Sixth Ave. North, Nashville, TN 37219; (615) 741-1888. Serves as an advocate for the small business community. Acts as a clearinghouse on programs and projects in both the public and private sectors that assist small business.

Small Business Advocate, Department of Economic and Community Development, 7th Floor, 320 Sixth Ave. Nort, Nashville, TN 37219; (615) 741-2626. Assistance in cutting bureaucratic red tape. Information and expertise in dealing with state, federal, and local agencies.

Small Business Development Centers

The following offices offer free and fee-based services to new and expanding businesses:

Chattanooga: Small Business Development Center, Chattanooga State Technical Community College, 100 Cherokee Blvd., Chattanooga, TN 37405; (615) 752-4308.

Cookville: Small Business Development Center, Tennessee Technological University, College of Business, Cookeville, TN 38505; (615) 372-3648.

Dyersburg: Small Business Development Center, Dyersburg State Community College, Office of Extension Services, P.O. Box 648, Dyersburg, TN 38024; (901) 286-3267.

Jackson: Small Business Development Center, Jackson State Community College, 2046 North Parkway Street, Jackson, TN 38301; (901) 424-5389.

Johnson City: Small Business Development Center, East Tennessee State University, P.O. Box 23, 440 A, College of Business, Johnson City, TN 37614; (615) 929-6984.

Knoxville: Small Business Development Center, State Technical Institute at Knoxville, P.O. Box 22990, Business/Community Services, Knoxville, TN 37933; (615) 971-5210.

Martin: Small Business Development Center, University of Tennessee at Martin, School of Business Administration, Martin, TN 38238; (901) 587-7236.

Memphis: Small Business Development Center, Office of the State Director, Memphis State University, Memphis, TN 38152; (901) 678-2500.

Memphis: Small Business Development Center, Memphis State University, 320 South Dudley, Memphis, TN 38104; (901) 527-1041.

Morristown: Small Business Development Center, Walters State Community College, Business/Industrial Services, Morristown, TN 37813-1999; (615) 581-2121.

Murfreesboro: Small Business Development Center, Middle Tennessee State University, School of Business, Murfreesboro, TN 37132; (615) 898-2745.

Nashville: Small Business Development Center, Tennessee State University, School of Business, Nashville, TN 37203; (615) 251-1178.

Texas

General Information

Texas Department of Commerce, Small Business Division, P.O. Box 12728, Austin, TX 78711; (512) 472-5059. Provides business counseling for both new and established firms. Helps firms locate capital, state procurement opportunities, and resources for management and technical assistance. An Office of Business Permit Assistance serves as a clearinghouse for permit-related information throughout the state and refers applicants to appropriate agencies for permit and regulatory needs.

Small Business Advocate, Texas Department of Commerce, Small Business Division, P.O. Box 12728, Austin, TX 78711; (512) 472-5059. Assistance in cutting bureaucratic red tape. Information and expertise in dealing with state, federal, and local agencies.

Utah

General Information

Small Business Advocate, Utah Small Business Development Center, University of Utah, Suite 418, 660 South 200 East, Salt Lake City, UT 84111. Assistance in cutting bureaucratic red tape. Information and expertise in dealing with state, federal, and local agencies.

Vermont

General Information

Vermont Economic Development Department, 109 State Street, Montpelier, VT 05602; (802) 828- 3221; 1-800-622-4553, in-state.

Small Business Advocate, Vermont Agency of Development and Community Affairs, Montpelier, VT 05602; (802) 828-3211. Assistance in cutting bureaucratic red tape. Information and expertise in dealing with state, federal, and local agencies.

Small Business Development Centers

Burlington: State Small Business Development Office, Morrill Hall, University of Vermont, Burlington, VT 05405-0106; (802) 656-4479.

Morrisville: Small Business Development Center, UVM Extension Service, RFD 1, Box 2280, Morrisville, VT 05661; (802) 773-3349.

Rutland: Small Business Development Center, UVM Extension Service, Box 489, Rutland, VT 05701; (802) 773-3349.

St. Johnsbury: Small Business Development Center, UVM Extension Service, HCR 31, Box 436, St. Johnsbury, VT 05819; (802) 748-5512.

West Brattleboro: Small Business Development Center, UVM Extension Service; (SBDC Resource Center), Box 2430, 411 Western Ave., West Brattleboro, VT 05301; (802) 257-7967.

Winooski: Small Business Development Center, UVM Extension Service, 4A Laurette Drive, Winooski, VT 05404; (802) 655-9540.

Woodstock: Small Business Development Center, UVM Extension Service, Town Hall, 31 The Green, Woodstock, VT 05091; (802) 457-2664.

Virginia

General Information

Department of Economic Development, Office of Small Business and Financial

Services, 1000 Washington Building, Richmond, VA 23219; (804) 786-3791. Helps new or expanding business by answering questions about licensing, taxes, regulations, assistance programs, etc. The office can also locate sources of information in other state agencies, and it also can identify sources of help for business planning, management, exporting, and financing.

Virginia Employment Commission Economic Information Services Division, 703 East Main St., P.O. Box 1358, Richmond, VA 23211; (804) 786-3047. Publishes the "Virginia Business Resource Directory," a comprehensive source of information on every aspect of doing business in the state, from business planning, management and personnel issues to sources of finance, marketing assistance, and regulations and licences.

Small Business Advocate, Office of Small Business and Financial Services, Virginia Department of Economic Development, 1000 Washington Building, Richmond, VA 23219; (804) 786-3791. Assistance in cutting bureaucratic red tape. Information and expertise in dealing with state, federal, and local agencies.

Small Business Development Centers

The following offices offer free and fee-based services to new and expanding businesses:

Fairfax: Small Business Development Center, George Mason University, Entrepreneurship Center. 4400 University Dr., Fairfax, VA 22030; (703) 323-2568.

Washington

Business Assistance Division, Department of Trade and Economic Development, 101 General Administration Building, AX-13, Olympia, WA 98504; (206) 586-3021

Small Business Development Centers

Bellingham: Small Business Development Center, College of Business and Economics, Western Washington University, 417 Parks Hall, Bellingham, WA 98225; (206) 676-3899.

Everett: Small Business Development Center, 917 134th St. S.W., Everett, WA 98204; (206) 745-0430.

Moses Lake: Small Business Development Center, Big Bend Community College, 28th and Chanute, Moses Lake, WA 98837-3299; (509) 762-5351.

Olympia: Small Business Development Center, 1000 Plum, P.O. Box 1427, Olympia, WA 98507; (206) 573-5616.

Pasco: Small Business Development Center, Columbia Basin College, 2600 North 20th, Pasco, WA 99320; (509) 735-6222.

Pullman: State Headquarters, Small Business Development Center, 441 Todd Hall, Pullman, WA 99164-4740; (509) 335-1576.

Pullman: Small Business Development Center, Washington State University, 441 Todd Hall, Pullman, WA 99164-4740; (509) 335-7869.

Seattle: Small Business Development Center, 180 Nickerson, Suite 310, Seattle, WA 98109; (206) 464-5450.

Seattle: Small Business Development Center, Rainier Business Assistance Center, 2620 Rainier Avenue South, Seattle, WA 98144; (206) 721-2026.

Spokane: Small Business Development Center, Freeway Plaza Building, #150, Spokane, WA 99204; (509) 456-2781.

Tacoma: Small Business Development Center, 735 St. Helens Avenue, Tacoma, WA 98402; (206) 272-7232.

Vancouver: Small Business Development Center, Columbia River EDC, 404 East 15th St., Vancouver, WA 98663; (206) 693-2555.

Wenatchee: Small Business Development Center, Wenatchee Valley College, 25 North Wenatchee, Wenatchee, WA 98801; (509) 662-0414.

Yakima: Small Business Development Center, 303 East D St. #2, Yakima, WA 98901; (509) 575- 2284.

West Virginia

General Information

Small Business Development Center, State Capitol Complex, Charleston, WV 24305; (304) 348- 2960. Acts as a one-stop resource center for information and

assistance in filing state and federal forms and coordinates assistance programs with other agencies.

Small Business Advocate, Director, Small Business Development Center, Capitol Complex, Charleston, WV 24305; (304) 348-2960. Assistance in cutting bureaucratic red tape. Information and expertise in dealing with state, federal, and local agencies.

Small Business Development Centers

The following offices offer free and fee-based services to new and expanding businesses:

Eau Clair: Small Business Development Center, University of Wisconsin--Eau Claire, 113 Schneider Hall, Eau Claire, WI 54701; (715) 836-5636.

Green Bay: Small Business Development Center, University of Wisconsin--Green Bay, Library Learning Center, Green Bay, WI 54301; (414) 465-2662.

Kenosha: Small Business Development Center, University of Wisconsin--Parkside, 234 Tallent Hall, Kenosha, WI 53141; (414) 553-2047.

Lacrosse: Small Business Development Center, University of Wisconsin--LaCrosse, School of Business, Administration, Lacrosse, WI 54601; (608) 785-8782.

Madison: Small Business Development Center, University of Wisconsin--Madison, 905 University Ave., Madison, WI 53715; (608) 263-2221.

Madison: State Headquarters, Small Business Development Center, University of Wisconsin Extension, 432 North Lake Street, Madison, WI 53706; (608) 263-7812.

Milwaukee: Small Business Development Center, University of Wisconsin--Milwaukee, 929 N. Sixth St., Milwaukee, WI 53203; (414) 227-3240.

Oshkosh: Small Business Development Center, University of Wisconsin--Oshkosh, 157 Clow Faculty Bldg., Oshkosh, WI 54901; (414) 424-1435.

Stevens Point: Small Business Development Center, University of Wisconsin--Stevens Point, Old Main Building, Stevens Point, WI 54481; (715) 346-2004.

Wyoming

General Information

Small Business Advocate, Economic Development and Stabilization Board, Herschler Building, Cheyenne, WY 82002; (307) 777-7287. Assistance in cutting bureaucratic red tape. Information and expertise in dealing with state, federal, and local agencies.

Small Business Development Centers

The following offices offer free and fee-based services to new and expanding businesses:

Casper: State Director, Wyoming Small Business Development Center, State Network Office, 130 North Ash, Suite A, Casper, WY 82601; (307) 235-4825.

Casper: Small Business Development Center/CC, 130 North Ash, Suite A, Casper, WY 82601; (307) 325-4827.

Cheyenne: Small Business Development Center/LCCC, 1400 E. College Drive, Cheyenne, WY 82007; (307) 778-5222.

Laramie: Small Business Development Center/UW, Box 3275, University Station, Laramie, WY 82071; (307) 766-2363.

Gillette: Small Business Development Center, SC-Gillette, 720 W. 8th, Gillette, WY 82716; (307) 686-0297.

Powell: Small Business Development Center/NWCC, 146 S. Bent, Suite 103, Powell, WY 82435; (307) 734-3746.

Rock Springs: Small Business Development Center/WWCC, 544 Broadway, Rock Springs, WY 82901; (307) 362-8107.

Douglas: Small Business Development Center, WEC-Douglas, P.O. Box 1028, Douglas, WY 82330; (307) 358-4090.

Lander: Small Business Development Center/CWC, 360 Main, Lander, WY 82520; (307) 332-3394.

Federal Money for Business

* See also Careers and Workplace; Research Grants in Every Field Chapter

The following is a description of the grants, loans and direct payments which are available to small businesses, inventors, researchers, and other interested parties from the federal government. The information is taken from the *Catalog of Federal Domestic Assistance* which is published by the U.S. Government Printing Office in Washington, D.C. The number next to the title description is the reference number listed in the *Catalog*. Contact the office listed below the title for more information about any of these money programs.

* Commodity Loans and Purchases (Price Supports) 10.051

Cotton, Grain and Rice Price Support Division
Agriculture Stabilization and Conservation Service
U.S. Department of Agriculture
P.O. Box 2415
Washington, DC 20013   (202) 447-7641
To improve and stabilize farm income, to assist in bringing about balance between supply and demand of the commodities, and to assist farmers in the orderly marketing of their crops. Types of assistance: direct payments, loans. Estimate of annual funds available: $ 995,610,000.

* Cotton Production Stabilization 10.052 (Cotton Direct Payments)

Commodity Analysis Division
Agricultural Stabilization and Conservation Service
P.O. Box 2415
U.S. Department of Agriculture
Washington, DC 20013   (202) 447-6734
To assure adequate production for domestic and foreign demand for fiber, to protect income for farmers, to hold down Federal costs, to enhance the competitiveness of U.S. cotton for domestic mill use and export, and to conserve our natural resources. Types of assistance: direct payments. Estimate of annual funds available: $ 1,469,526,000.

* Dairy Indemnity Program 10.053

Emergency Operations and Livestock Program Division Agricultural Stabilization and Conservation Service
Department of Agriculture
P.O. Box 2415
Washington, DC 20013
To protect dairy farmers and manufacturers of dairy products who through no fault of their own, are directed to remove their milk, milk cows or dairy products from commercial markets because of contamination from pesticides which have been approved for use by the Federal government. Types of assistance: direct payments. Estimate of annual funds available: $ 545,000.

* Emergency Conservation Program (ECP) 10.054

Agricultural Stabilization and Conservation Service
Department of Agriculture
P.O. Box 2415
Washington, DC 20013   (202) 447-6221
To enable farmers to perform emergency conservation measures to control wind erosion on farmlands, or to rehabilitate farmlands damaged by wind erosion, floods, hurricanes, or other natural disasters. Types of assistance: direct payments. Estimate of annual funds available: $ 13,021,000.

* Feed Grain Production Stabilization 10.055 (Feed Grain Direct Payments)

Commodity Analysis Division
Agricultural Stabilization and Conservation Service
Department of Agriculture
P.O. Box 2415
Washington, DC 20013   (202) 447-4417
To assure adequate production for domestic and foreign demand, to protect income for farmers, to hold down Federal costs, to enhance the competitiveness of United States exports. Types of assistance: direct payments. Estimate of annual funds available: $ 5,016,696,000.

* Wheat Production Stabilization 10.058 (Wheat Direct Payments)

Commodity Analysis Division
Agricultural Stabilization and Conservation Service
Department of Agriculture
P.O. Box 2415
Washington, DC 20013   (202) 447-4146
To assure adequate production for domestic and foreign demand, to protect income for farmers, to hold down Federal costs, to enhance the competitiveness of U.S. exports, to compact inflation, and to conserve our natural resources. Types of assistance: direct payment. Estimate of annual funds available: $ 641,480,000.

* National Wool Act Payments 10.059 (Wool and Mohair Incentive Payments)

Commodity Analysis Division
Agricultural Stabilization and Conservation Service
Department of Agriculture
P.O. Box 2415
Washington, DC 20013   (202) 475-4645
To encourage increased domestic production of wool at prices fair to both producers and consumers in a way that has the least adverse effect on domestic and foreign trade and to encourage producers to improve the quality and marketing of their wool and mohair. Types of assistance: direct payment. Estimate of annual funds available: $ 83,800,000.

* Water Bank Program 10.062

Agricultural Stabilization and Conservation Service
Department of Agriculture
P.O. 2415
Washington, DC 20013   (202) 447-6221
To conserve surface waters; preserve and improve the Nation's Wetlands; increase migratory waterfowl habitat in nesting, breeding and feeding areas in the U.S.; and secure environmental benefits for the Nation. Types of assistance: direct payment. Estimate of annual funds available: $ 10,409,000.

* Agricultural Conservation Program (ACP) 10.063

Agricultural Stabilization and Conservation Service
Department of Agriculture
P.O. Box 2415
Washington, DC 20013   (202) 447-6221
Control of erosion and sedimentation, encourage voluntary compliance with federal and state requirements to solve point and nonpoint source pollution, improve water quality, encourage energy conservation measures, and assure a continued supply of necessary food and fiber for a strong and healthy people and economy. Types of assistance: direct payment. Estimate of annual funds available: $ 228,479,000.

* Forestry Incentives Program (FIP) 10.064

Agricultural Stabilization and Conservation Service
Department of Agriculture
P.O. Box 2415
Washington, DC 20013   (202) 447-6221
To bring private non-industrial forest land under intensified management; to increase timber production; to assure adequate supplies of timber; and to enhance other forest resources through a combination of public and private investments on the most productive sites on eligible individual or consolidated ownerships of efficient size and operation. Types of assistance: direct payment. Estimate of annual funds available: $ 14,203,000.

* Rice Production Stabilization 10.065 (Rice Direct Payments)

Commodity Analysis Division
Agricultural Stabilization and Conservation Service
Department of Agriculture
P.O. Box 2415
Washington, DC 20013 (202) 447-5954

To assure adequate production for domestic and foreign demand to protect income for farmers, to hold down federal costs, to enhance the competitiveness of U.S. exports, and to conserve our natural resources. Types of assistance: direct payment. Estimate of annual funds available: $ 733,550,000.

* Emergency Livestock Assistance 10.066

Emergency Operations and Livestock Programs Division
Agricultural Stabilization and Conservation Service
Department of Agriculture
P.O. Box 2415
Washington, DC 20013 (202) 447-5621

To provide emergency feed assistance to eligible livestock owners, in a state, county, or area approved by the Executive Vice President, CCC, where because of disease, insect infestation, flood, drought, fire, hurricane, earthquake, storm, hot weather, or other natural disaster, a livestock emergency exists. Types of assistance: direct payment. Estimate of annual funds available: $ 820,000,000.

* Grain Reserve Program 10.067 (Farmer-Held and Owned Grain Reserve)

Cotton, Grain and Rice Price Support Division
Agricultural Stabilization and Conservation Service
Department of Agriculture
P.O. Box 2415
Washington, DC 20013 (202) 382-9886

To insulate sufficient quantities of grain from the market to increase price to farmers. Types of assistance: direct payment. Estimate of annual funds available: $ 498,229,000.

* Rural Clean Water Program (RWCP) 10.068

Conservation and Environmental Protection Division
Agricultural Stabilization and Conservation Service
Department of Agriculture
P.O. Box 2415
Washington, DC 20013 (202) 447-6221

To achieve improved water quality in the most cost-effective manner possible in keeping with the provisions of adequate supplies of food, fiber, and a quality environment. Types of assistance: direct payment. Estimate of annual funds available: $ 316,000.

* Conservation Reserve Program (CRP) 10.069

Conservation and Environmental Protection Division
Agricultural Stabilization and Conservation Service
Department of Agriculture
P.O. Box 2415
Washington, DC 20013 (202) 447-6221

To protect the Nation's long-term capability to produce food and fiber; to reduce soil erosion; to reduce sedimentation; to improve water quality; to create a better habitat for fish and wildlife. Types of assistance: direct payment. Estimate of annual funds available: $ 736,316,000.

* Colorado River Salinity Control (CRSC) 10.070

Conservation and Environmental Protection Division
Agricultural Stabilization and Conservation Service
Department of Agriculture
P.O. Box 2415
Washington, DC 20013 (202) 447-6221

To provide financial and technical assistance to: identify salt source areas; develop project plans to carry out conservation practices to reduce salt loads; install conservation practices to reduce salinity levels, and carry out research education and demonstration activities. Types of assistance: direct payment. Estimate of annual funds available: $ 3,034,000.

* Emergency Loans 10.404

Administrator, Farmers Home Administration
Department of Agriculture
Washington, DC 20013 (202) 382-1632

To assist family farmers, ranchers and aquaculture operators with loans to cover losses resulting from major and/or natural disasters. Types of assistance: loan guarantee. Estimate of annual funds available: $ 600,000,000.

* Farm Operating Loans 10.406

Director, Farmer Programs Loan Making Division
Farmers Home Administration
Department of Agriculture
Washington, DC 20250 (202) 382-1632

To enable operators of not larger than family farms through the extension of credit and supervisory assistance, to make efficient use of their land, labor, and other resources. Types of assistance: loan guarantee. Estimate of annual funds available: $ 3,498,109,000.

* Farm Ownership Loans 10.407

Administrator, Farmers Home Administration
Department of Agriculture
Washington, DC 20250 (202) 382-1632

To assist eligible farmers, ranchers, and aquaculture operators, including farming cooperatives, corporations, partnerships, and joint operations through the extension of credit to become owner-operators of not larger than family farms. Types of assistance: loan guarantee. Estimate of annual funds available: $ 819,000,000.

* Rural Rental Housing Loans 10.415

Administrator, Farmers Home Administration
Department of Agriculture
Washington, DC 20250 (202) 382-1604

To provide economically designed and constructed rental and cooperative housing and related facilities suited for independent living for rural residents. Types of assistance: loan guarantee. Estimate of annual funds available: $ 554,900,000.

* Soil and Water Loans (SW Loans) 10.416

Administrator, Farmers Home Administration
Department of Agriculture
Washington, DC 20250 (202) 382-1632

To facilitate improvement, protection, and proper use of farmland by providing adequate financing and supervisory assistance for soil conservation; water resource development; conservation and use. Types of assistance: loan guarantee. Estimate of annual funds available: $ 11,000,000.

* Indian Tribes and Tribal Corporation Loans 10.421

Director, Community Facilities Division
Farmers Home Administration
Department of Agriculture
Washington, DC 20250 (202) 382-1490

To enable tribes and tribal corporations to mortgage lands as security for loans from the Farmers Home Administration to buy additional land within the reservation. Types of assistance: loan guarantee. Estimate of annual funds available: $ 2,000,000.

* Business and Industrial Loans 10.422

Administrator, Farmers Home Administration
Department of Agriculture
Washington, DC 20250 (202) 447-7967

To assist public, private, or cooperative organizations (profit or nonprofit), Indian tribes or individuals in rural areas to obtain quality loans for the purpose of improving, developing or financing business, industry, and employment and improving the economic and environment climate in rural communities including pollution abatement and control. Types of assistance: loan guarantee. Estimate of annual funds available: $ 95,700,000.

* Industrial Development Grants (IDG) 10.424

Director, Community Facilities Loan Division
Farmers Home Administration
Department of Agriculture
Washington, DC 20250 (202) 382-1490

To facilitate the development of business, industry, and related employment for improving the economy in rural communities. Types of assistance: grants. Estimate of annual funds available: $ 6,500,000.

* Rural Rental Assistance Payments (Rental Assistance) 10.427

Administrator, Farmers Home Administration
Department of Agriculture
Washington, DC 20250 (202) 382-1604

To reduce the rents paid by low-income families occupying eligible Rural Rental Housing (RRH) Rural Cooperative Housing (RCH), and Farm Labor Housing (LH) projects financed by the Farmers Home Administration through its

Sections 515, 514, and 516 loans and grants. Types of assistance: direct payment. Estimate of annual funds available: $ 275,310,000.

* Interest Rate Reduction Program 10.437

County Supervisor, Farmers Home Administrator (in the county where the farming is located); or write FMHA, USDA
Washington, DC 20250

To aid not larger than family sized farms in obtaining credit when they are temporarily unable to project a positive cash flow without a reduction in the interest rate. Types of assistance: loan guarantee. Estimate of annual funds available: $ 17,000,000.

* Farm Credit System Farm Land Acquisition Program (FCS Demonstration Project) 10.438

Lender or FmHA County Supervisor in county where farming operation is located; or write for location to:
FMHA, USDA
Washington, DC 20250

To help farm credit banks certified eligible by the Farm Credit Assistance Board to sell inventory properties. This program will reduce the interest rate for qualified applicants to purchase eligible farm credit system inventory farm property. The loan limit is $300,000. Interest rates can be reduced four or five percent. Types of assistance: loan guarantee. Estimate of annual funds available: $ 5,000,000.

* Intermediary Relending Program 10.439

Farmers Home Administration
Room 6321
South Agriculture Building
Washington, DC 20250   (202) 475-4100

To finance business facilities and community development. Types of assistance: loans. Estimate of annual funds available: $ 14,000,000.

* Crop Insurance 10.450

Manager, Federal Crop Insurance Corporation
Department of Agriculture
Washington, DC 20250   (202) 447-6795

To improve economic stability of agriculture through a sound system of crop insurance by providing multi-peril insurance for individual producers of commercially grown commodities against unavoidable causes of loss such as adverse weather conditions, fire insects or other natural disasters. Types of assistance: insurance. Estimate of annual funds available: $ 1,670,500,333.

* Foreign Agricultural Market Development and Promotion 10.600

Assistant Administrator
Commodity and Marketing Programs
Foreign Agricultural Service
Department of Agriculture
Washington, DC 20250   (202) 447-4761

To create, expand, and maintain markets abroad for U.S. agricultural commodities. Types of assistance: direct payment. Estimate of annual funds available: $ 33,039,240.

* Targeted Export Assistance (TEA) 10.601

Assistant Administrator
Commodity and Marketing Programs
Foreign Agricultural Service
Department of Agriculture
Washington, DC 20250   (202) 447-4761

To counter or offset the adverse effect on the export of a U.S. agricultural commodity or the product thereof a subsidy,import quota, or other unfair foreign trade practice. Types of assistance: direct payment. Estimate of annual funds available: $ 200,000,000.

* Rural Electrification Loans and Loan Guarantees (REA) 10.850

Administrator, Rural Electrification Administration
Department of Agriculture
Washington, DC 20250   (202) 382-9540

To assure that people in eligible rural areas have access to electric services comparable in reliability and quality to the rest of the nation. Types of assistance: loan guarantee. Estimate of annual funds available: $ 622,050,000.

* Rural Telephone Loans and Loan Guarantees (REA) 10.851

Administrator, Rural Electrification Administration
Department of Agriculture
Washington, DC 20250   (202) 382-9540

To assure that people in eligible rural areas have access to telephone service comparable in reliability and quality to the rest of the nation. Types of assistance: loan guarantee. Estimate of annual funds available: $ 239,250,000.

* Rural Telephone Bank Loans (Rural Telephone Bank) 10.852

Governor, Rural Telephone Bank
Department of Agriculture
Washington, DC 20250   (202) 382-9540

To provide supplemental financing to extend and improve telephone service in rural areas. Types of assistance: loan. Estimate of annual funds available: $ 177,045,000.

* Rural Economic Development Loans and Grants 10.854

Administrator, Rural Electrification Administration
Department of Agriculture
Washington, DC 20250   (202) 382-9540

To promote rural economic development and job creation projects, including funding for project feasibility studies, start-up costs, incubator projects, and other reasonable expenses for the purpose of fostering rural development. Types of assistance: loans, grants. Estimate of annual funds available: $ 1,092,000.

* Great Plains Conservation 10.900

Deputy Chief for Programs
Soil Conservation Service
Department of Agriculture
P.O. Box 2890
Washington, DC 20013   (202) 447-4527

To conserve and develop the Great Plains soil and water resources by providing technical and financial assistance to farmers, ranchers, and others in planning and implementing conservation practices. Types of assistance: direct payment. Estimate of annual funds available: $ 12,286,000.

* Trade Adjustment Assistance 11.109

Daniel F. Harrington
U.S. Department of Commerce
Office of Trade Adjustment Assistance
International Trade Administration
14th & Constitution Ave.
Washington, DC   (202) 377-3373

To provide trade adjustment assistance to firms and industries adversely affected by increased imports. Types of assistance: grants. Estimate of annual funds available: $ 4,199,000.

* Fishermen's Contingency Fund (Title IV) 11.408

Chief, Financial Services Division
National Marine Fisheries Service
1335 East West Hwy
Silver Spring, MD 20910   (301) 427-2396

To compensate U.S. commercial fishermen for damage/loss of fishing gear and 50 percent of resulting economic loss due to oil and gas related activities in any area of the Outer Continental Shelf. Types of assistance: direct payments. Estimate of annual funds available: $ 726,000.

* Fishing Vessel and Gear Damage Compensation Fund (Section 10) 11.409

Chief, Financial Services Division
Attn: National Marine Fisheries Service
Department of Commerce
1335 East West Hwy
Silver Spring, MD 20910   (301) 427-2396

To compensate U.S. fishermen for the loss, damage, or destruction of their vessels by foreign fishing vessels and their gear by any vessel. Types of assistance: direct payment. Estimate of annual funds available: $ 947,000.

* Fishing Vessel Obligation Guarantees 11.415

Chief, Financial Services Division
National Marine Fisheries Service
Department of Commerce
1335 East West Hwy
Silver Spring, MD 20910   (301) 427-2390

To provide government guarantees of private loans to finance or upgrade U.S. fishing vessels or shoreside facilities. Types of assistance: loan guarantee. Estimate of annual funds available: $ 130,000,000.

* Minority Business Development Centers (MBDC) 11.800
Assistant Director, Office of Program Development
Rm 5096, Minority Business Agency
Department of Commerce
14th & Constitution Ave, NW
Washington, DC 20230   (202) 377-5770
To provide business development services for a minimal fee to minority firms and individuals interested in entering, expanding or improving their efforts in the marketplace. Types of assistance: grants. Estimate of annual funds available: $ 23,167,000.

* American Indian Program (AIP) 11.801
Assistant Director, Office of Program Development
Room 5096, Minority Business Development Agency
Commerce, 14th 7 Constitution Ave.
Washington, DC 20230   (202) 377-5770
To provide business development service to American Indians and individuals interested in entering, expanding or improving their efforts in the marketplace. Types of assistance: Grants. Estimate of annual funds available: $ 1,485,000.

* Minority Business and Industry Association - Minority Chambers of Commerce (MB and IA/C of C) 11.802
Asst. Director, Office of Program Development
Rm 5096, Minority Business Development Agency
Commerce, 14th & Constitution Ave, N.W.
Washington, DC 20230   (202) 377-5770
To provide financial assistance for Minority Business and Industry Association/Minority Chambers of Commerce (MB and IA/C of C) which act as advocates for their members and the minority community. Types of assistance: grants. Estimate of annual funds available: $ 1,420,000.

* Procurement Technical Assistance for Business Firms (Procurement Technical Assistance (PTA) 12.002
Defense Logistics Agency
Cameron Station, Office of Small and
Disadvantaged Business Utilization (DLA-U)
Room 4C112
Alexandria, VA 22304-6100   (202) 274-6471
To assist eligible entities in the payment of the costs of establishing and carrying out new Procurement Technical Assistance Programs and maintaining existing Procurement Technical Assistance Programs. Types of assistance: grants. Estimate of annual funds available: $ 6,789,868.

* Special Loans for National Health Service Corps Members to Enter Private Practice (National Health Service Corps Private Practice Loans) 13.973
Dr. Audrey F. Manley, Director
National Health Service Corps
Health Resources and Services Administration
Parklawn Bldg. Rm 7A-39
5600 Fishers Lane
Rockville, MD   (301) 443-2900
To assist members of the National Health Service Corps (NHSC) in establishing their own private practice in a health manpower shortage area. Types of assistance: direct loan. Estimate of annual funds available: $ 247,000.

* Interest Reduction Payments-Rental and Cooperative Housing for Lower Income Families (236) 14.103
Director, Office of Multifamily Housing Management
Department of Housing and Urban Development
Washington, DC 20410   (202) 426-3968
To provide good quality rental and cooperative housing for persons of low- and moderate-income by providing interest reduction payments in order to lower their housing costs. Types of assistance: direct payments. Estimate of annual funds available: $ 625,651,000.

* Mortgage Insurance-Construction or Substantial Rehabilitation of Condominium Projects (234(d) Condominiums) 14.112
Insurance Division, Office of Insured Multifamily Housing Development, HUD
Washington, DC 20410   (202) 755-6223
To enable sponsors to develop condominium projects in which individual units will be sold to home buyers. Types of assistance: loan guarantee. Estimate of annual funds available: $ 0.

* Mortgage Insurance - Homes (203(b)) 14.117
Director, Insured Family Development Division
Office of Single Family Housing, HUD
Washington, DC 20410   (202) 755-6700
To help families undertake home ownership. Types of assistance: loan guarantee. Estimate of annual funds available: $ .3672E+11.

* Mortgage Insurance-Land Development (title X) 14.125
Director, Single Family Development Division
Office of Insured Single Family Housing, HUD
Washington, DC 20410   (202) 755-6700
To assist the development of subdivisions on a sound economical basis. Types of assistance: loan guarantee. Estimate of annual funds available: $ 73080930.

* Mortgage Insurance-Cooperative Projects (213 Cooperatives) 14.126
Insurance Division, Office of Insured
Multifamily Housing Development, HUD
Washington, DC 20410   (202) 755-6223
To make it possible for nonprofit cooperative ownership housing corporations or trusts to develop or sponsor the development of housing projects to be operated as cooperatives. Types of assistance: loan guarantee. Estimate of annual funds available: $ 0.

* Mortgage Insurance-Manufactured Home Parks (207(m) Manufactured Home Parks) 14.127
Insurance Division, Office of Insured Multifamily
Housing Development
Department of Housing and Urban Development
Washington, DC 20410   (202) 755-6223
To make possible the financing of construction or rehabilitation of manufactured home parks. Types of assistance: loan guarantee. Estimate of annual funds available: $ 0.

* Mortgage Insurance-Hospitals (242 Hospitals) 14.128
Insurance Division, Office of Insured Multifamily
Housing Development, HUD
Washington, DC 20410   (202) 755-6223
To make possible the financing of hospitals. Types of assistance: loan guarantee. Estimate of annual funds available: $ 217,858,000.

* Mortgage Insurance-Nursing Homes, Intermediate Care Facilities and Board and Care Homes (232 Nursing Homes) 14.129
Insurance Division, Office of Insured Multifamily
Housing Development, HUD
Washington, DC 20412   (202) 755-6223
Types of assistance: loan guarantee. Estimate of annual funds available: $ 233,419,000.

* Mortgage Insurance-Purchase of Sales-Type Cooperative Housing Units (213 Sales) 14.132
Director, Single Family Development Division
Office of Insured Family Housing, HUD
Washington, DC 20410   (202) 755-6700
To make available, good quality, new housing for purchase by individual members of a housing cooperative. Types of assistance: loan guarantee. Estimate of annual funds available: $ 0.

* Mortgage Insurance-Purchase of Units in Condominiums (234(c)) 14.133
Director, Single Family Development Division
Office of Insured Single Family Housing, HUD
Washington, DC 20410   (202) 755-6700
To enable families to purchase units in condominium projects. Types of assistance: loan guarantee. Estimate of annual funds available: $ 2,716,191,000.

Small Business and Entrepreneuring

* Mortgage Insurance-Rental Housing (207)   14.134
Insurance Division, Office of Insured Multifamily
Housing Development, HUD
Washington, DC 20410   (202) 755-6223
To provide good quality rental housing for middle income families. Types of assistance: loan guarantee. Estimate of annual funds available: $ 9,337,000.

* Mortgage Insurance-Rental Housing for Moderate Income Families and Elderly, Market Interest Rate (221(d)(3) and (4) Multifamily - Market Rate Housing) 14.135
Insurance Division, Office of Insured Multifamily
Housing Development, HUD
Washington, DC 20410   (202) 755-6223
To provide good quality rental or cooperative housing for moderate income families and the elderly. Types of assistance: loan guarantee. Estimate of annual funds available: $ 233,419,000.

* Mortgage Insurance-Rental Housing for the Elderly (231) 14.138
Insurance Division, Office of Insured
 Multifamily Housing Development, HUD
Washington, DC 20410   (202) 755-6223
To provide good quality rental housing for the elderly. Types of assistance: loan guarantee. Estimate of annual funds available: $ 15,561,000.

* Mortgage Insurance-Rental Housing in Urban Renewal Areas (220 Multifamily) 14.139
Insurance Division, Office of Insured
 Multifamily Housing Development, HUD
Washington, DC 20410   (202) 755-6223
To provide good quality rental housing in urban renewal areas, code enforcement areas, and other areas designated for overall revitalization. Types of assistance: loan guarantee. Estimate of annual funds available: $ 24,898,000.

* Property Improvement Loan Insurance for Improving All Existing Structures and Building of New Nonresidential Structures (Title I) 14.142
Director, Title I Insurance Division, HUD
Washington, DC 20410   (202) 755-6880
To facilitate the financing of improvements to homes and other existing structures and the building of new nonresidential structures. Types of assistance: loan guarantee. Estimate of annual funds available: $ 1,138,000,000.

* Supplemental Loan Insurance - Multifamily Rental Housing 14.151
Insurance Division, Office of Insured Multifamily
 Housing Development, HUD
Washington, DC 20411   (202) 755-6223
To finance repairs, additions and improvements to multifamily projects, group practice facilities, hospitals, or nursing homes already insured by HUD or held by HUD. Types of assistance: loan guarantee. Estimate of annual funds available: $ 31,123,000.

* Mortgage Insurance for the Purchase or Refinancing of Existing Multifamily Housing Projects (Section 223(f) Insured Under Section 207) 14.155
Office of Insured Multifamily Housing Development
Insurance Division, HUD
Washington, DC 20410   (202) 755-6223
To provide mortgage insurance to lenders for the purchase or refinancing of existing multifamily housing projects, whether conventionally financed or subject to federally insured mortgages. Types of assistance: loan guarantee. Estimate of annual funds available: $ 11,719,000.

*** Housing for the Elderly or Handicapped (202) 14.157
Assisted Elderly and Handicapped Housing Division**
Office of Elderly and Assisted Housing, HUD
Washington, DC 20410   (202) 426-8730
To provide for rental or cooperative housing and related facilities (such as central dining) for the elderly or handicapped. Types of assistance: loan. Estimate of annual funds available: $ 480,106,000.

* Operating Assistance for Troubled Multifamily Housing Projects (Flexible Subsidy Fund) (Troubled Projects) 14.164
Chief, Program Support Branch
Management Operations Division, Office of
Multifamily Housing Management, HUD
Washington, DC 20420   (202) 755-5654
To provide assistance to restore or maintain the physical and financial soundness of certain projects assisted or approved for assistance under the National Housing Act or under the Housing and Urban Development Act of 1965. Types of assistance: grants, direct payments. Estimate of annual funds available: $ 38,150,000.

* Mortgage Insurance-Two Year Operating Loss Loans, Section 223(d) (Two Year Operating Loss Loans) 14.167
Office of Insured Multifamily Housing Development
Insurance Division Housing, HUD
Washington, DC 20410   (202) 755-6223
To insure a separate loan covering operating losses incurred during the first two years following the date of completion of a multifamily project with a HUD insured first mortgage. Types of assistance: loan guarantee. Estimate of annual funds available: $ 49,796,000.

* Multifamily Coinsurance (Section 223(f); Section 221(d); Section 232) 14.173
Office of Insured Multifamily Housing Development
Coinsurance Division, HUD
Washington, DC 20410   (202) 426-7113
Under the coinsurance programs, HUD authorizes approved lenders to coinsure mortgage loans. In exchange for the authority to perform the required underwriting, servicing, management and property disposition functions, approved lenders assume responsibility for a portion of any insurance loss on the coinsured mortgage. Types of assistance: loan guarantee. Estimate of annual funds available: $ 855,870,000.

* Housing Development Grants 14.174
Director, Development Grants Division
Rm. 6110 Office of Elderly and Assisted Housing, HUD
451 7th St. SW
Washington, DC 20410   (202) 755-6142
To support the construction or substantial rehabilitation of rental housing in areas experiencing severe shortages of decent rental housing opportunities for families and individuals without other reasonable and affordable housing alternatives in the private market. Types of assistance: grants. Estimate of annual funds available: $ 20,000,000.

* Supporting Housing Demonstration Program (Transitional Housing; Permanent Housing for Handicapped Homeless Persons) 14.178
Morris Bourne, Director, Transitional Housing Staff
Office of Housing, HUD
451 7th St. SW,
Washington, DC 20410   (202) 755-9075
To develop innovative approaches for providing housing and supporting services to facilitate the transition to independent living for homeless persons who are capable of making the transition with in 24 months, and to provide permanent housing for handicapped persons. Types of assistance: grants, direct payments. Estimate of annual funds available: $ 80,000,000.

* Protection of Ships from Foreign Seizure (Fishermen's Protection Act) 19.201
Ronald J. Bettauer, Asst. Legal Adviser for
 International Claims and Investment Disputes
Office of the Legal Adviser
Department of State
Washington, DC 20520   (202) 632-7810
To reimburse U.S. fishermen whose vessels are seized by a foreign country on the basis of: claims to jurisdictions not recognized by the U.S.; claims to jurisdictions recognized by the U.S. but exercised in a manner inconsistent with international law as recognized by the U.S.; any general claim to exclusive fisher management with conditions and restrictions. Types of assistance: insurance. Estimate of annual funds available: $ 1,453,966.

* Fishermen's Guaranty Fund (Section 7) 19.204
Office of Fisheries Affairs
Bureau of Oceans and International Environmental
 and Scientific Affairs, Rm. 5806

Department of State
Washington, DC 20520 (202) 647-2009
To provide for reimbursement of losses incurred as a result of the seizure of a U.S. commercial fishing vessel by a foreign country on the basis of rights or claims in territorial waters or on the high seas which are not recognized by the United States. Types of assistance: insurance. Estimate of annual funds available: $ 2,266,400.

* Construction-Differential Subsidies (CDS) 20.800
Associate Administrator for Maritime Aids
Maritime Administration, DOT
400 7th St. SW
Washington, DC 20590 (202) 366-0364
To promote the development and maintenance of the U.S. Merchant Marine by granting financial aid to equalize cost of construction of a new ship in a U.S. shipyard with the cost of constructing the same ship in a foreign shipyard. Types of assistance: direct payment. Estimate of annual funds available: $ 464,000.

* Federal Ship Financing Guarantees (Title XI) 20.802
Associate Administrator for Maritime Aids
Maritime Administration, DOT
Washington, DC 20590 (202) 366-0364
To promote construction and reconstruction of ships in the foreign trade and domestic commerce of the U.S. by providing government guarantees of obligations so as to make commercial credit more available. Types of assistance: loan guarantee. Estimate of annual funds available: $ 26,500,000.

* Maritime War Risk Insurance (Title XII, MMA, 1936) 20.803
Edmond J. Fitzgerald, Director
Office of Trade Analysis and Insurance
Maritime Administration, DOT
Washington, DC 20590 (202) 366-2400
To provide war risk insurance whenever it appears to the Secretary of Transportation that adequate insurance for water-borne commerce cannot be obtained on reasonable terms and conditions from licensed insurance companies in the U.S. Types of assistance: insurance. Estimate of annual funds available: $ 265,000.

* Operating-Differential Subsidies (ODS) 20.804
Associate Administrator for Maritime Aids
Maritime Administration, DOT
400 7th St. SW
Washington, DC 20590 (202) 366-0364
To promote development and maintenance of the U.S. Merchant Marine by granting financial aid to equalize cost of operating a U.S. flag ship with cost of operating a competitive foreign flag ship. Types of assistance: direct payment. Estimate of annual funds available: $ 218,100,000.

* Capital Construction Fund (CCF) 20.808
Associate Administrator for Maritime Aids
Maritime Administration, DOT
Washington, DC 20590 (202) 366-0364
To provide for replacement vessels, additional vessels or reconstructed vessels, built and documented under the laws of the US for operation in the US foreign, Great Lakes or noncontiguous domestic trades. Types of assistance: direct payment. Estimate of annual funds available: $ 251,000.

* Supplementary Training 20.810
Bruce J.Carlton, Director
Office of Maritime Labor and Training
Maritime Administration, DOT
Washington, DC 20590 (202) 366-5755
To train seafarers in shipboard firefighting, diesel propulsion and other such essential subjects related to safety and operations where this training is not or cannot be provided by the industry directly. Types of assistance: other. Estimate of annual funds available: $ 542,000.

* Construction Reserve Fund 20.812
Associate Administrator for Maritime Aids
Maritime Administration, DOT
Washington, DC 20590 (202) 366-0364
To promote the construction, reconstruction, reconditioning or acquisition of merchant vessels which are necessary for national defense and to the development of U.S. commerce. Types of assistance: direct payment. Estimate of annual funds available: $ 62,000.

* Payments for Essential Air Services 20.901
Director, Office of Aviation Analysis, P-50
DOT, 400 7th St., SE
Washington, DC 20590 (202) 366-1030
To provide air transportation to eligible communities by subsidizing air service. Types of assistance: direct payment. Estimate of annual funds available: $ 25,140,000.

* Arts and Artifacts Indemnity 45.201
Alice M. Wheliham, Indemnity Administrator
Museum Program, National Endowment for the Arts
Washington, DC 20506 (202) 682-5442
To provide for indemnification against loss or damage for eligible art works, artifacts and objects. Types of assistance: Insurance. Estimate of annual funds available: $ 0.

* Scientific, Technological and International Affairs (STIA) 47.053
Asst. Director, Directorate for Scientific, Technological and International Affairs
National Science Foundation
1800 G St., NW
Washington, DC 20550 (202) 357-7631
To provide opportunities for small high-technology business firms to participate in NSF-supported research. Types of assistance: grants. Estimate of annual funds available: $ 35,291,000.

* Loans for Small Business (Business Loans 7(a)(11)) 59.003
Director, Office of Business Loans, SBA
1441 L St., NW
Washington, DC 20416 (202) 653-6470
To provide loans to small business owned by low-income persons or located in areas of high unemployment. Types of assistance: loans, loan guarantee. Estimate of annual funds available: $ 57,000,000.

* Management and Technical Assistance for Socially and Economically Disadvantaged Businesses (7(j) Development Assistance Program) 59.007
Associate Administrator for Minority Small Business
1441 L St., NW, Room 602
Washington, DC 20416 (202) 653-6475
To provide management and technical assistance through qualified individuals, public or private organizations to existing or potential businesses which are economically and socially disadvantaged or which are located in areas of high concentration of unemployment. Types of assistance: grants. Estimate of annual funds available: $ 8,080,000.

* Physical Disaster Loans (7(b) Loans(DL)) 59.008
Disaster Assistance Division, SBA
1441 L St., NW
Washington, DC 20416 (202) 653-6879
To provide loans to the victims of designated physical-type disasters for uninsured loans. Types of assistance: loans, loan guarantee. Estimate of annual funds available: $ 280,000,000.

* Small Business Investment Companies (SBIC; MESBIC) 59.011
Director, Office of Investment, SBA
1441 L St., NW
Washington, DC 20416 (202) 653-6584
To provide funds to small business investment companies that make equity and venture capital investments in small business and provide advisory services and counseling to small business. Types of assistance: loans, loan guarantee. Estimate of annual funds available: $ 154,000,000.

* Small Business Loans (Regular Business Loans - 7(a) Loans) 59.012
Director, Office of Business Loans, SBA
1441 L Street, NW
Washington, DC 20416 (202) 653-6470
To provide guaranteed loans to small business which are unable to obtain financing in the private credit marketplace, but can demonstrate an ability to

repay loans granted. Types of assistance: loan guarantee. Estimate of annual funds available: $ 2,621,000,000.

* State and Local Development Company Loans (501 and 502 Loans) 59.013

Office of Economic Development, SBA
1441 L St. NW, Room 720
Washington, DC 20416 (202) 653-6416

To make federal loans to state and local development companies to provide long-term financing to small business concerns located in their areas. Types of assistance: loan guarantee. Estimate of annual funds available: $ 35,000,000.

* Bond Guarantees for Surety Companies (Surety Bond Guarantee) 59.016

James Parker, Jr., Director
Office of Surety Guarantees, SBA
4040 North Fairfax Dr.
Arlington, VA 22203 (703) 235-2900

To guarantee surety bonds issued by commercial surety companies for small contractors unable to obtain a bond without a guarantee. Types of assistance: insurance. Estimate of annual funds available: $ 1,250,000,000.

* Handicapped Assistance Loans (HAL-1 and HAL-2) 59.021

Director, Office of Business Loans, SBA
1441 L. St. NW
Washington, DC 20416 (202) 653-6470

To provide loans and loan guaranties for nonprofit sheltered workshops and other similar organizations that produce goods and services. Types of assistance: loans, loan guarantee. Estimate of annual funds available: $ 17,000,000.

* Small Business Energy Loans 59.030

Office of Business Loans, SBA
1441 L St. NW
Washington, DC 20416 (202) 653-6470

To provide loans to small business concerns to finance plant construction, expansion, conversion or startup. Types of assistance: loan guarantee. Estimate of annual funds available: $ 5,000,000.

* Veterans Loan Program (Veterans Loans) 59.038

Director, Office of Business Loans, SBA
1441 L St., NW
Washington, DC 20416 (202) 653-6470

To provide loans to small businesses owned by Vietnam-era and disabled veterans. Types of assistance: loans. Estimate of annual funds available: $ 17,000,000.

* Certified Development Company Loans (504 Loans) 59.041

Office of Economic Development, SBA
Room 720, 1441 L St., NW
Washington, DC 20416 (202) 653-6416

To assist small business concerns by providing long-term financing for fixed assets through the sale of debentures to private investors. Types of assistance: loan guarantee. Estimate of annual funds available: $ 330,000,000.

* Foreign Investment Guaranties 70.002

Robert L. Jordan, Information Officer
Overseas Private Investment Corporation
Washington, DC 20527 (202) 457-7093

To guarantee loans and other investment made by eligible US investors in friendly developing countries and areas. Types of assistance: loan guarantee. Estimate of annual funds available: $ 175,000,000.

* Foreign Investment Insurance (Political Risk Insurance) 70.003

Robert L. Jordan, Information Officer
Overseas Private Investment Corporation
Washington, DC 20527 (202) 457-7093

To insure investments of eligible U.S. investors in developing friendly countries and areas, against the risks of inconvertibility, expropriation, war, revolution and insurrection, certain types of civil strife, and business interruption. Types of assistance: insurance. Estimate of annual funds available: $ 2,470,000,000.

* Direct Investment Loans (Dollar Loans) 70.005

Robert Jordan, Information Officer
Overseas Private Investment Corporation
Washington, DC 20527 (202) 457-7093

To make loans for projects in developing countries sponsored by or significantly involving U.S. small business or cooperatives. Types of assistance: loans. Estimate of annual funds available: $ 23,000,000.

* Energy-Related Inventions 81.036

George Lewitt, Director
Office of Energy Related Inventions
National Institute of Standards and Technology
Gaithersburg, MD 20899 (301) 975-5500

To encourage innovation in developing non-nuclear energy technology by providing assistance to individual and small business companies in the development of promising energy-related inventions. Types of assistance: grants, other. Estimate of annual funds available: $ 4,850,000.

* Energy Extension Service 81.050

Ronald W. Bowes, Chief
Energy Management and Extension Branch, DOE
(CE-221), Forrestal Bldg.
1000 Independence Ave, SW
Washington, DC 20585 (202) 586-8288

To encourage individuals and small establishments to reduce energy consumption and convert to alternative energy sources. Types of assistance: grants. Estimate of annual funds available: $ 3,844,000.

* Office of Minority Economic Impact Loans (OMEI Direct Loans for DOE Bid or Proposal Preparation) 81.063

Kenneth Workman
Office of Minority Economic Impact
MI-3.2, DOE, Forrestal Bldg., Room 5B-110
Washington, DC 20585 (202) 586-1594

To provide direct loans to minority business enterprises (MBE) to assist them in financing bid or proposal preparation costs they would incur in pursuing DOE work. Types of assistance: loans. Estimate of annual funds available: $ 850,000.

Franchising

One of the safer ways to launch a new business is by purchasing a franchise. Franchises have a significantly lower failure rate than other new enterprises because most franchise arrangements include the business experience and expertise normally lacking in new business owners. The following organizations and publications will help you find the right franchise for you.

Organizations

Federal Trade Commission
Bureau of Consumer Protection
Division of Enforcement
Pennsylvania Avenue at 6th Street, NW
Washington, DC 20580   (202) 326-2970, Craig Tregillus
The Federal Trade Commission enforces federal laws pertaining to business franchising. The Bureau of Consumer Protection publishes several free papers and guides designed to aid franchisers and franchisees in complying with federal regulations, including an explanation of the FTC disclosure rule. These free publications include:

Franchise and Business Opportunities. A four-page guide about what to consider before buying a franchise.

The Franchise Rule: Questions and Answers. A one-page summary of the disclosure rule and penalties for infractions by the franchiser.

Franchise Rule Summary. A seven-page, detailed technical explanation of the federal disclosure rule, which requires franchisers to furnish a document (with information on twenty topics) to the potential franchisee before a sale. This includes an explanation and description of the Uniform Franchise Offering Circular (UFOC) required in fourteen states.

International Franchise Association
1350 New York Avenue, NW
Washington, DC 20005   (202) 628-8000, Buzzy Gordan
Founded in 1960, the International Franchise Association (IFA) has more than 600 franchiser members, including thirty-five overseas. IFA members are accepted into the organization only after meeting stringent requirements regarding number of franchises, length of time in business, and financial stability. The IFA offers about twenty-five educational conferences and seminars yearly, including an annual convention and a legal symposium. There is a program on financing and venture capital designed to bring together franchisers and franchisees. Each year the association also sponsors several trade shows, open to the public, so that franchisers may attract potential franchisees. There is a library, but as yet no database, for members. Mr. Buzzy Gordon, Public Relations Officer, will answer inquiries from the public and make referrals for speakers, courses, and resources on franchising. The IFA also publishes:

Investigate Before Investing. A thirty-two-page booklet offering tips on evaluating a franchise. $3.00

Answers to the 21 Most Commonly Asked Questions About Franchising. Informative pamphlet for newcomers to the field. $1.00

How to be a Franchisor. Step-by-step details on how to launch a franchise, including details on legal and operational

procedures. Cost is $5.95

Is Franchising For You?. A self-evaluation guide for potential franchisers. $3.95

FTC Franchising Rule: The IFA Compliance Kit. A kit in a three-ring binder, with updates on all advisory opinions issued by FTC, this publication provides an overview of disclosure requirements, together with checklists and comparisons. $80.00

U.F.O.C. Guidelines. Instructions for completing the Uniform Franchise Offering Circular, this was prepared by the Midwest Securities Commissioners Association for use by franchisors in meeting state and federal disclosure requirements. $10.00

Directory of Membership. Listings of all International Franchise Association members. $3.95

U.S. Department of Commerce
International Trade Administration
14th Street and Constitution Avenue, NW
Washington, DC 20230   (202) 377-0342
This office provides comprehensive information of interest to franchisers and franchisees. It has published the following guidebooks, which may be ordered from the U.S. Government Printing Office, Superintendent of Documents, Washington, D.C. 20402:

Franchise Opportunities Handbook. A bible of franchising information, this 390-page directory includes detailed listings of 1,265 companies, facts about the franchising industry, guidance for investing in a franchise, resource listings of helpful agencies and organizations, and a bibliography. Cost is $15.00; it is available from U.S. Government Printing Office, Superintendent of Documents, Washington, D.C. 20402; (202) 783-3238.

Franchising in the Economy--1986-88. A detailed ninety-three page survey, with numerous charts and statistics on the international growth of franchising. Includes information on types of franchise companies, minority enterprises, and sales figures for retail and service firms. $5.25

Franchise Experts

Brian Bond
Business Development Office
U.S. Small Business Administration
1441 L Street, NW
Washington, DC 20005   (202) 653-6881
Coordinator of a coalition between the International Franchising Association (IFA) and the Small Business Administration (SBA), Mr. Bond is available to answer questions and provide assistance to regional offices of the SBA. He is currently developing training materials and seminars, as well as a database system for regional/district offices, such as the one now in use in the Chicago area.

Andrew Kostecka
Commodity Industry Specialist
Office of Service Industries
International Trade Administration

Small Business and Entrepreneuring

U.S. Department of Commerce
14th Street and Constitution Avenue, NW
Washington, DC 20230   (202) 377-0342
The federal government's leading expert on franchising, Mr. Kostecka is the compiler of the annual *Franchise Opportunities Handbook*. He can guide potential franchisers to reputable consulting firms and can provide assistance and referrals to resources for franchisees. He is a frequent speaker at franchise seminars, trade and business association conferences, and educational seminars throughout the world.

Complete Financials On Franchising Companies

Franchising companies, whether public or privately held, must file detailed financial information in 14 different states. These state statutes create excellent opportunities for gathering competitive and marketing data as outlined below.

Competitive Information

If the company of interest is a franchise organization, a great deal of financial information for their average franchisee is available in addition to their corporate profit and loss statements and balance sheets. A typical table of contents for a filing includes:

* biographical information on persons affiliated
    with the franchisor
* litigation
* bankruptcy
* franchisees' initial franchise fee or other initial payment
* other recurring or isolated fees and payments
* the franchisee's initial investment
* obligations of the franchisee to purchase or lease from
    designated sources
* obligations of the franchisee to purchase or lease in
    accordance with specifications or from approved suppliers
* financing arrangements
* obligations of the franchisor: other supervision, assistance
    or services
* territorial rights
* trademarks, service marks, trade names, logotypes and
    commercial symbols
* patents and copyrights
* obligation of the franchisee to participate in the actual
    operation of the franchise business
* restrictions on goods and services offered by the franchisee
* term, renewal, termination, repurchase, modification,
    assignment and related information
* agreements with public figures
* actual, average, projected or forecasted franchisee sales,
    profits and earnings
* information regarding franchises of the franchisor
* financial statements
* contracts
* standard operating statements
* list of operational franchisees
* estimate of additional franchised stores
* company-owned stores
* estimate of additional company-owned stores
* copies of contracts and agreements

Market Information and Future Trends

The franchise information packet often includes information on the results of their market studies which establish the need for their product or service. These can provide valuable market information as well as forecasts for potential markets. Is the ice cream boom over? A quick check into Ben and Jerry's forecast for future stores will give you a clue of what the experts think.

Franchise companies are often the first to jump current trends and fads in the U.S., for example, ice cream shops and diet centers. You can get an instant snapshot of such a trend by reviewing the marketing section of a franchise agreement.

Career Opportunities

If you ever wondered how much it would cost to open up your own bookstore, restaurant, video store, or most any other kind of venture, you can get all the facts and figures you need without paying a high-priced consultant or tipping your hand to your current employer. Just take a look at a franchise agreement from someone in a similar line of business. You can even discover the expected salary level.

New Business for Suppliers

If you are looking to sell napkins, Orange Julius or computer services to Snelling & Snelling, their franchise statements will disclose what kind of agreements they currently have with similar suppliers.

State Checkpoints for Franchising Intelligence

To obtain franchise agreements from the 14 states that require such disclosure, simply call one or more of the offices listed below and ask if a specific company has filed. Copies of the documentation are normally sent in the mail with a copying charge of $0.05 to $0.10 a page.

California
Department of Corporations
1115 11th Street
Sacramento, CA 95814   (916) 445-7205

Hawaii
Department of Commerce
Business Registration Department
1010 Richards Street
Honolulu, HI 96813   (808) 548-5317

Illinois
Franchise Division
Office of Attorney General
500 South Second Street
Springfield, IL 62706   (217) 782-1279

Indiana
Franchise Division
Secretary of State
One North Capitol Street, Suite 560
Indianapolis, IN 46204   (317) 232-6681

Maryland
Assistant Attorney General
Maryland Division of Securities
Munsey Building
7 North Calvert Street, 18th Flr
Baltimore, MD 21202   (301) 576-6360

Minnesota
Minnesota Department of Commerce
500 Metro Square Building
St. Paul, MN 55101   (612) 296-2594

New York

Bureau of Investor and Protection Securities
New York State Department of
120 Broadway
New York, NY 10272   (212) 341-2446

North Dakota
Franchise Examiner
Office of Securities Commissioner
Capitol Building, Ninth Floor
Bismarck, ND 58505   (701) 224-2910

Oregon
Corporation Division
Commerce Building
Salem, OR 97310   (503) 378-4387

Rhode Island
Securities Section, Banking Division
233 Richmond Street
Providence, RI 02903-4231   (401) 277-2405

South Dakota
Franchise Administrator, Division of Securities

State Capitol
Pierre, SD 57501   (605) 773-4013

Virginia
Franchise Section
Division of Securities and Retail Franchising
1229 Bank Street
Richmond, VA 23219   (804) 786-7751

Washington
Department of Licensing
Securities Division
Business and Professions Administration
111 W. Wilson Street
P.O. Box 1768
Olympic, WA 98504   (206) 753-6928

Wisconsin
Franchise Investment Division
Wisconsin Securities Commission
PO Box 1768
Madison, WI 53701   (608) 266-3414

Business and Industry
General Sources

* See also Experts Chapter
* See also Science and Technology Chapter
* See also Small Business and Entrepreneuring Chapter
* See also International Trade Chapter
* See also Law and Social Justice Chapter
* See also Energy Chapter

This chapter covers big business and major industries in the U.S., such as telecommunications, mining, transportation, railroads, and shipping. Because businesses in these industries are regulated by the federal government, a significant amount of revealing information about them is often available to the public, including financial reports, safety records, business volumes, and violations of industry regulations. But you'll also find other important sources on consumer relations, hiring incentives, child care, and even help in converting your business to the metric system.

* Alcohol Production Regulations
Wine and Beer Branch
Office of Compliance Operations
Bureau of Alcohol, Tobacco, and Firearms
U.S. Department of the Treasury
1200 Pennsylvania Ave., NW
Washington, DC 20226   (202) 566-7626

Distilled Spirit and Tobacco Branch
Office of Compliance Operations
Bureau of Alcohol, Tobacco, and Firearms
U.S. Department of the Treasury
1200 Pennsylvania Ave., NW
Washington, DC 20226   (202) 566-7531

These offices regulate basic permit requirements under the Federal Alcohol Administration, as well as the use, bulk sales, bottling, labeling, and advertising of wine, beer, and distilled spirits. Regulations for the sale and production of distilled spirits are also outlined in the booklet, *Laws and Regulations under the Federal Alcohol Administration Act*, available from the Bureau's Distribution Center at 7943 Angus Ct., Springfield, VA 22153.

* Alcohol, Tobacco, and Firearms Regulation Research
National Laboratory Center
Bureau of Alcohol, Tobacco, and Firearms
U.S. Department of the Treasury
1401 Research Blvd.
Rockville, MD 20850   (301) 294-0410

Laboratory services for the Bureau are conducted at the National Laboratory Center in Rockville, MD, and at regional locations in Atlanta, GA, and San Francisco, CA, in the areas of compliance and law enforcement. All alcohol-containing products sold in the United States and imported to this country are analyzed at these laboratories, and tobacco products are examined for tax classification. Specialists also investigate firearms, explosives, and arson evidence at the forensic labs. Crime lab scientists are also trained at this facility.

* Alcohol, Tobacco, and Firearms Regulations Update
Wine and Beer Branch
Bureau of Alcohol, Tobacco, and Firearms
U.S. Department of the Treasury
1200 Pennsylvania Ave.,
Washington, DC 20226   (202) 566-7626

In April and October, this office publishes the *Unified Agenda* in the *Federal Register*. The *Agenda* outlines regulations that have been issued, are being proposed, or are being reviewed within a six month period by the entire Bureau to give the public ample notice of all regulatory activities. Contact this office for additional information.

* Alcohol, Tobacco, and Firearms Statistics
Public Affairs Branch
Office of Congressional and Media Affairs
Bureau of Alcohol, Tobacco, and Firearms
U.S. Department of the Treasury
1200 Pennsylvania Ave., NW
Washington, DC 20226   (202) 566-7135

The free booklet, *Ready Reference Statistics*, outlines the Bureau's statistical activities. Alcohol statistics include moonshine seizures; beer, wine, and distilled spirits production; the number of licensees and permittees; and federal excise tax rates. The U.S. viticulture areas (areas where wine may be produced) are also listed. The tobacco section outlines production and tax rates. Also included is the number of domestic, imported, and exported manufacturers of firearms by type, as well as a listing of the number of registered weapons by state and type.

* Alcohol Trade Laws
Trade Affairs Branch
Office of Industry Compliance
Bureau of Alcohol, Tobacco, and Firearms
U.S. Department of the Treasury
1200 Pennsylvania Ave., NW, Room 6209
Washington, DC 20226   (202) 789-3081

The Trade Affairs Branch informs industry of the provisions of the Federal Alcohol Administration Act, as well as issues of product compliance, permits applications, and Bureau opinions relating to the Act.

* Bureau of Alcohol, Tobacco, and Firearms Publications
Distribution Center
Bureau of Alcohol, Tobacco, and Firearms
U.S. Department of the Treasury
7943 Angus Ct.
Springfield, VA 22153   (703) 455-7801

The following is a sampling of free publications from the ATF Distribution Center:

Index of Materials Required by the Freedom of Information Act
Public Use Forms
Information to Claimants
Distilled Spirits for Fuel Use
Payment of Tax by Electronic Fund Transfer
Importation of Distilled Spirits, Wines, and Beer
Beverage Distilled Spirits Plants and Breweries Authorized to Operate
Bonded Wineries and Bonded Wine Cellars Authorized to Operate
Information for Specially Denatured Spirits Applicants
Information for Tax-Free Alcohol Applicants
Distribution and Use of Denatured Alcohol/Rum and formulas for Denatured Alcohol/Rum
Liquor Laws and Regulations for Retail Dealers
Instructions - Application for FAA Act Basic Permits: Wholesalers and Importers
Firearms Curios and Relics List
Federal Firearms Licensee Information
Importation of Arms, Ammunition, and Implements of War
Bomb Threats and Physical Security Planning

* Business Assistance Service
Office of Business Liaison
Department of Commerce
14th St. and Constitution Ave., NW
Room 5898C
Washington DC 20230   (202) 377-3176

The Business Assistance Service provides information and guidance on programs throughout the Federal Government. The Service can answer such questions as:

How can I sell my products or services to the Federal Government?
Where do I find overseas buyers?
Where can I get Federal business loans?

The Business Assistance staff maintains a network of interagency contacts so that they can quickly provide you with current information on a wide range of subjects. People with specific questions about government programs can also find the answers by contacting the Business Assistance staff.

* Business Briefings and Speakers

Office of Business Liaison
Department of Commerce
14th St. and Constitution Ave., NW
Room 5898C
Washington DC 20230 (202) 377-3176

This office has an Outreach Program which organizes a series of briefings for the business community. These briefings serve a dual purpose of promoting the Department's activities to business and allowing Commerce officials to be familiar with business perspectives. The briefings are free and are held in Washington, D.C. Speaking requests from business organizations are also routinely handled through this office. Sending Commerce officials across the country, promoting Departmental programs, and listening to concerns of business allows OBL to extend its outreach.

* Business Community Representation

Chamber of Commerce of the United States
1615 H St., NW
Washington, DC 20062 (202) 659-6000

The Chamber of Commerce is generally regarded as the spokesgroup for United States business. It is the world's largest business federation composed of more than 180,000 companies plus several thousand other organizations such as local and state chambers of commerce and trade and professional associations. It has an environmental department. Publications: *Nation's Business, The Business Advocate.*

* Business Reference Service

Library
Department of Commerce
14th St. & Constitution Ave., NW
Washington DC 20230 (202) 377-5511

The Department of Commerce's Library is open to the public, 1:00 p.m. to 4 p.m., Monday through Friday. Their collection is business oriented, and the staff is available to direct you to appropriate resources.

* Business Services Directory

Office of Business Liaison
Department of Commerce
14th St. and Constitution Ave., NW
Room 5898C
Washington DC 20230 (202) 377-3176

The *Business Services Directory* gives you a brief description of all the programs of the Department of Commerce, including phone numbers, and is used by the business community to find sources of information within the Department. Those in business can see the activities of the various programs and how they relate to their particular business. This free directory is available from the office listed above.

* Commerce Libraries

Library
Department of Commerce
14th St. & Constitution Ave., NW
Washington, DC 20230 (202) 377-5511

Many libraries within the Department of Commerce are open to the public and have collections specific to the concerns of the various Bureaus. You can contact the libraries directly regarding hours of operations, and questions on various topics:

NOAA
Library and Information Services, National Oceanic and Atmospheric Administration, 6009 Executive Blvd., Rockville, MD 20852; (301) 443-8330

NIST
Research Information Center, National Institute of Standards and Technology, Administration Bldg. 101, Room E106, Gaithersburg, MD 20899; (301) 975-3052

Patent and Trademark Office
Scientific Library, Patent and Trademark Office, 2021 Jefferson Davis Hwy., Arlington, VA 22202; (703) 557-2955

Census Bureau

Library, Bureau of the Census, Federal Office Bldg. No. 3, Room 2455, Washington D.C. 20233; (202) 763-5042

* Commercial and Industrial Conservation

Distributer and Marketing Services
Power, 1101 Market St.
4S136X Missionary Ridge Pl.
Chattanooga, TN 37402 (615) 751-5103

The TVA offers businesses, industries, and other nonresidential power users free, in-depth energy conservation audits upon request, with loans available for those businesses and industries which carry out measures recommended in the audits. The program assists with water heating, space heating, and air conditioning as end uses. Contact this office for more information on energy audits and conservation.

* Consumer Affairs

Office of Consumer Affairs
Department of Commerce
14th St. and Constitution Ave., NW
Room 5718
Washington DC 20230 (202) 377-5001

The office provides advice and technical assistance to businesses on problems and issues of concern to consumers. Through cooperative projects among businesses, consumers, and local and state governments, this office works to improve companies' customer relations and the quality of goods and services. OCA also helps businesses deal with customer concerns about advertising, warranties, complaint-handling, credit, and products safety, as well as helping them establish ways to involve consumers in the development of product safety and performance standards. OCA also mediates between consumers and businesses on complaints and inquiries, helping businesses to reach equitable resolutions to such complaints.

* Consumer Information and Complaint Centers

The Interstate Commerce Commission has three regional offices which serve a variety of functions, one of which is to answer inquiries and assist the public with concerns regarding interstate bus, trucking, and railroad companies. The most frequent calls involve moving companies.

Eastern
Interstate Commerce Commission, 3535 market St., Room 16400, Philadelphia, PA 19104; (215) 596-4040. States served: AL, CT, DE, D.C., FL, GA, KY, MA, MD, ME, MS, OH, PA, NC, NH, NJ, NY, RI, SC, TN, VA, VT, WV.

Central
Interstate Commerce Commission, Everett McKinley Dirken Building, 219 South Dearborn St., Room 1304, Chicago, IL 60604; (312) 353-6204. States served: AR, IA, IL, IN, KS, LA, MI, MO, MN, NE, ND, OK, SD, TX, WI.

Western
Interstate Commerce Commission, 211 Maine St., Suite 500, San Francisco, CA 94105; (415) 974-7125. States served: AK, AZ, CA, CO, ID, MT, NV, NM, OR, UT, WA, WY.

* Consumer Rule Guides For Businesses

Federal Trade Commission
Public Reference Branch, Room 130
6th & Pennsylvania Ave., NW
Washington, DC 20580 (202) 326-2222

The FTC publishes the following guides for businesses to help them comply with the most current consumer trade rules and regulations, on everything from offering layaways to the Federal warranty law.

Business Guide to the Federal Trade Commission's Mail Order Rule
Businessperson's Guide to Federal Warranty Law
Direct Marketer's Guide to Labeling Requirements Under the Textile and Wool Acts
Complying with the Credit Practices Rule
Guides for the Jewelry Industry
Handling Customer Complaint: In-House and Third-Party Strategies
How to Write Readable Credit Forms
Offering Layaways
Payments and Services
Rules and Regulations Under the Hobby Protection Act
Textile and Wool Acts
Writing a Care Label: How to Comply with the Amended Care Labeling Rule
Writing Readable Warranties

* Gifts-in-Kind Program

Office of Private Sector Development
Peace Corps
1990 K St., NW
Washington, DC 20526 (202) 254-6360

Business and Industry

The Peace Corps allows corporations to donate materials if a need for them materials exists. Contact this office for more information on the donation process.

* Explosives: Laws and Regulations
Distribution Center
Bureau of Alcohol, Tobacco, and Firearms
U.S. Department of the Treasury
7943 Angus Ct.
Springfield, VA 22153   (703) 455-7801
ATF laws and regulations for firearms are described in the free book, *ATF: Explosives Law and Regulations*. Commerce in explosives is highlighted, describing licenses and permits, business conduct, records and reports, storage, exemptions, and unlawful acts. The impact of the regulations on the fireworks industry is also discussed.

* Hiring Incentives for Employers of Veterans
Assistant Secretary for Veterans
Employment and Training
Department of Labor
200 Constitution Ave., NW, Room S1313
Washington, DC 20210   (202) 523-9116
As a hiring incentive, the Veterans Administration will pay an employer half of a Veteran's entry wages up to $10,000 for up to nine months or fifteen months for a veteran with a disability rating of 30% or more. A veteran must have served during the Korean Conflict or the Vietnam Era, and have been unemployed for 10 to 15 weeks. Employers must certify that they intend to hire the veteran upon completion of training. Adequate training facilities must be available; wages and benefits must be no less than those normally paid; and training cannot be for a position for which the Veteran already qualifies. Veterans and employers alike must apply for certification with any local job service office or VA Regional Office.

* Infrastructure Technologies
Office of Technology Assessment
600 Pennsylvania Ave., SE
Washington, DC 20510   (202) 228-6939
Public works infrastructure, which includes roads, bridges, sewers, etc., provides essential services--moving people and goods, supplying water, and disposing of waste. And there is little disagreement about the urgency of repair, maintenance, or new construction of these vital systems. OTA is currently studying how technological, institutional, and financial alternatives could be combined to meet the challenges posed by infrastructure needs that might be required in the Federal role. Contact Edith Page, the project director, for more information.

* Interstate Commerce Commission
Interstate Commerce Commission
12th St. & Constitution Ave., NW
Washington, DC 20423   (202) 275-7252
The Interstate Commerce Commission was created as an independent regulatory agency by act of February 4, 1887 to regulate commerce. ICC's responsibilities include regulation of carriers engaged in transportation in interstate commerce and in foreign commerce to the extent that it takes place within the U.S. Surface transportation under the Commission's jurisdiction includes railroads, trucking companies, bus lines, freight forwarders, water carriers, transportation brokers, and a coal slurry pipeline. The regulatory laws vary depending on the type of transportation; however, they generally involve certification of carriers seeking to provide transportation for the public, rates, adequacy of service, purchases, and mergers. The Commission assures that the carriers it regulates will provide the public with rates and services that are fair and reasonable.

* ICC Library
Interstate Commerce Commission
12th St. and Constitution Ave., NW, Room 3392
Washington, DC 20423   (202) 275-7328
The Interstate Commerce Commission's library is open to the public, and its collection focuses on transportation and transportation law. You must sign in with the building guard before going up to the library.

* Metric Conversion Assistance
Office of Metric Programs
Department of Commerce
14th St. and Constitution Ave., NW
Room 4841
Washington DC 20230   (202) 377-0944
This office coordinates Federal metric transition to promote consistency in agency plans, policies, and practices. It identifies and helps remove barriers that inhibit or block metric transition in federal, state, or local rules, standards and codes, or regulations. It also provides technical and general information about the metric system and its use to businesses, educators, the news media, and the

general public. There are several free brochures and pamphlets available from the Office explaining the metric system and metric conversions.

* National Association of Manufacturers
National Association of Manufacturers (NAM)
1776 F St., NW
Washington, DC 20006   (202) 637-3000
The National Association of Manufacturers is a voice for industry at the national level. Members are manufacturing companies from throughout the United States. Publications: *Enterprise, PAC Manager*.

* Donations to the Peace Corps
Peace Corps
1990 K St., NW
Washington, DC 20526   (202) 254-6360
The Peace Corps offers corporations donate materials if a need for them materials exists. Contact this office for more information on the donation process.

* On-Site Child Care
Women's Bureau
Department of Labor
200 Constitution Ave., NW, Room S3309
Washington, DC 20210   (202) 523-6652
The free publication, *Employers and Child Care: Benefiting Work and Family*, is designed for employers and employees concerned with developing programs and policies to assist in quality and cost-efficient child care programs while parents are at work. Created to help in a vast array of situations, it provides guidance to those who wish to improve employee productivity and business' ability to recruit and retain the best workers. It is designed for people who are concerned about fulfilling two essential and often conflicting responsibilities--working and caring for their families.

* Pulp and Paper Industry
Technical Association of the Pulp and Paper Industry (TAPPI)
Box 105112, Technology Park
Atlanta, GA 30348   (404) 446-1400
The Technical Association of the Pulp and Paper Industry consists of individual professionals working in pulp, paper, packaging, converting and nonwovens industries. Publications: *TAPPI Journal*.

* Science and Technical Business References
Science and Technology Division
Reference Section
Library of Congress
Washington, DC 20540   (202 707-5580
Informal series of reference guides are issued free from the Science and Technology Division under the general title, *LC Science Tracer Bullet*. These guides are designed to help readers locate published material on subjects about which they have only general knowledge. New titles in the series are announced in the weekly Library of Congress *Information Bulletin* that is distributed to many libraries including:

80-3   Automotive Electronics
80-6   Lasers and Their Applications
80-19 Industrial Robots
81-9   Cable Television (Cable TV)
82-5   Jet Engines and Jet Aircraft
84-7   Biotechnology
87-9   Microcomputers
87-12 Optical Disc Technology

* Space Management Research
Office of Real Property Development
Public Buildings Service
General Services Administration
18th and F Sts., NW, Room 2313
Washington, DC 20405   (202) 566-0059
Information on space management research studies which emphasize efficiency and cost productiveness can be obtained by contacting this office.

* Statistics Reports
Publications
Office of the Secretary
Interstate Commerce Commission
12th St. and Constitution Ave., NW
Washington, DC 20423   (202) 275-7833
This office compiles and publishes statistics on the various modes of transportation.

Annual

Transport Statistics in the United States. Detailed data on traffic, operations, equipment, finances, and employment for carriers subject to the Interstate Commerce Act.

A-300 Wage Statistics of Class I Freight Railroads in the United States-Calendar Year. Number of employees, service hours, and compensation by occupational group: Executive, Officials, and Staff Assistants; Professional and Administrative; Maintenance-of-Way and Structures; Maintenance of Equipment and Stores, etc.

Quarterly

Large Class I Motor Carriers of Property Selected Earnings Data. Operating revenues, net carrier operating income, net income, revenue tons hauled, operating ratio and rate of return.

Class I Freight Railroads Selected Earnings Data. Railway operating revenues, net railway operating income, income before extraordinary items, net income, revenue ton-miles of freight, and rate of return.

Large Class I Motor Carriers of Passengers Selected Earnings Data. Operating revenues, net carrier operating income, net income, revenue passengers carried, operating ratio, and rate of return.

Large Class I Household Goods Carriers Selected Earnings Data. Operating revenues, net carrier operating income, net income, revenue tons hauled, operating ratio and rate of return.

Monthly

M-350 Preliminary Report of Railroad Employment, Class I Line-Haul Railroads. Number of employees at middle of month, group totals.

* Tax Credits for Employers of Targeted Groups

Employment and Training Administration
Department of Labor
200 Constitution Ave., NW, Room S2322
Washington, DC   20210   (202) 523-6871

The Targeted Jobs Tax Credit Program offers employers a credit against their tax liability for hiring individuals from nine target groups that have traditionally had difficulty obtaining and holding jobs. Groups include disadvantaged youths, the handicapped, disadvantaged veterans, ex-offenders, and recipients of state and federal assistance. An employer must request certification for the individual prior to starting work. The credit applies only to employees hired into a business or trade. For more information contact your local Employment Service offices or your local Internal Revenue Service office.

Airlines

* Air Carrier Market Data and Statistics

Public Reference Room
Research and Special Programs Administration
U.S. Department of Transportation
400 7th Street, SW, Room 4201
Washington, D.C. 20590   (202) 366-4888

Start with this office for market data, financial information, and traffic statistics on air carrier passenger and cargo operations. Information is compiled by DOT from schedules that air carriers file, and some data is stored in a computerized database. For the publication, *Air Carrier Traffic Statistics*, contact the Transportation Systems Center in Cambridge. (See that entry.)

* Air Traffic Plans and Requirements

Air Traffic Plans and Requirements
Federal Aviation Administration
Department of Transportation
800 Independence Ave., SW, Room 400 East
Washington, DC 20591   (202) 267-3136

The air traffic control system tracks flights automatically and tags each one with a small block of information written electronically on the radar scope used by air traffic controllers. The data block includes aircraft identity, altitude and ground speed, and transponder code. Contact this office for more information.

* Air Traffic System Errors

Quality Assurance Division
Air Traffic Services
Federal Aviation Administration
Department of Transportation
800 Independence Ave., SW, Room 416
Washington, DC 20591   (202) 267-9205

All system errors are logged on a central file chronologically by region. The file consists of reports identifying anything wrong in the air traffic service terminal. Contact this FAA office for more information on system errors.

* Aircraft Accident Data: U.S. Air Carrier Operations

National Technical Information Services
5285 Port Royal Road
Springfield, VA 22161

The *Annual Review of Aircraft Accident Data: U.S. Air Carrier Operations* contains statistical tabulations of data compiled from reports of accidents involving revenue operations of U.S. air carriers in a particular calendar year. The report is divided into sections according to the Part of the Code of Federal Regulations under which the aircraft were flown when the accidents occurred (14 CFR Part 121 or 14 CFR Part 135). The Part 135 section is further divided into scheduled and non-scheduled operations. Information provided within each section includes a list of accidents, tabulations of injuries, types of accidents, accident causes and related factors, and accident rates. Comparisons are made of data for the given year to averages of accident data for several prior years. The publication is available for a fee from the office above. Call (703) 487-4650 for single copies and microfiche; or (703) 487-4630 for an annual subscription.

* Aircraft Accident Investigations

Biomedical and Behavioral Science Division
Office of Aviation Medicine
Federal Aviation Administration
Department of Transportation
800 Independence Ave., SW, Room 400 East
Washington, DC 20591   (202) 267-3136

This office analyses medical data associated with victims of aviation accidents.

* Aircraft Accident Prevention

Accident Prevention Staff
General Aviation Division
Flight Standards Service
Federal Aviation Administration
Department of Transportation
800 Independence Ave., SW, Room 2322
Washington, DC 20591   (202) 366-6321

The staff provides national guidance and policy on accident prevention in general aviation. For information on available publications, tapes, slides, seminars, and speakers, contact the office at the above address.

* Aircraft Accident Reports

Accident/Incident Analysis Branch
Air Traffic Service
Federal Aviation Administration
Department of Transportation
800 Independence Ave., SW, Room 417D
Washington, DC 20591   (202) 267-9612

Accidents and incidents involving aircraft are documented in a central file maintained by this FAA branch. Contact this office for more information on the information in these files.

* Aircraft Accidents

Safety Analysis Division
Office of Aviation Safety
Federal Aviation Administration
Department of Transportation
800 Independence Ave., SW
Washington, DC 20591   (202) 267-9149

The division can provide you with information on general aviation accidents and near mid-air collisions.

* Aircraft Accident Statistics

Safety Data Branch
Flight Standards
National Field Office
Federal Aviation Administration
Department of Transportation
P.O. Box 25082, AVN-121B
Oklahoma City, OK 73125   (405) 680-6420

The FAA maintains statistics on the following: general aviation accident information; incidents (little damage or minor injury) of both air carrier and general aviation; service difficulty reports; and enforcement data and violations. Contact this office for more information.

* Aircraft Flight Data and Voice Recorders Investigations

Engineering Services Division
Bureau of Technology
National Transportation Safety Board
800 Independence Avenue, SW, Room 826
Washington, DC 20594   (202) 382-6686

For information on aircraft flight data and voice recorders examined by the NTSB, contact the office above.

* Aircraft Maintenance Data

Maintenance Analysis Center Section
AVN-140
Federal Aviation Administration
Department of Transportation
Aeronautical Center
P.O. Box 25082
Oklahoma City, OK 73125   (405) 680-6495

Information and statistics are available regarding aircraft include maintenance surveillance, mechanical interruptions, and inflight mechanical problems.

* Aircraft Noise

Noise Abatement Division
Office of Environment and Energy
Federal Aviation Administration
Department of Transportation
800 Independence Ave., SW, Room 432
Washington, DC 20591   (202) 267-3553

This FAA division conducts research on reducing noise levels of new aircraft, and retrofitting older aircraft to reduce noise levels.

* Aircraft Standards and Statistics Data Base

Management Standards and Statistics Division
Federal Aviation Administration
AMS-400
Department of Transportation
800 Independence Ave., SW

Washington, DC 20591 (202) 267-8063
The FAA maintains several computerized data files on a variety of aviation-related subjects such as: aviation safety, air traffic, aviation schools, commercial and government ownership and operation of aircraft, aircraft repair stations, FAA facilities, and procurement. While the FAA does not conduct searches of these files for anyone outside the agency, they will copy any file you designate onto a blank tape that you provide for $38.

* Airline Antitrust Violations
Aviation Analysis
Federal Aviation Administration
Department of Transportation
800 Independence Ave., SW, Room 10223
Washington, DC 20591 (202) 267-4382
The office investigates airline mergers and interlocks, unfair methods of competition among carriers, and also determines antitrust immunity. Contact this FAA office for more information on airline antitrust issues.

* Airline Data
Office of Aviation Information Management
Research and Special Programs Administration
U.S. Department of Transportation
400 7th Street, SW, Room 4125
Washington, DC 20590 (202) 366-9059
The Aviation Information Management (AIM) program collects information on the financial operations of air carriers. Government, industry, and the general public may access this information. Database functions are housed at the Transportation Systems Center (see entry) but this office can serve as liaison for access to air carrier reports and data requiring DOT approval for release.

* Airline Passenger Safety
Community and Consumer Liaison Division
Office of Public Affairs
Federal Aviation Administration
Department of Transportation
800 Independence Ave., SW
Washington, DC 20591 (202) 267-3481
Airline passengers who have inquiries or complaints regarding airplane safety should contact this office.

* Airlines General Inquiries
Office of Public Affairs
Federal Aviation Administration
Department of Transportation
800 Independence Ave., SW
Washington, DC 20591 (202) 267-3481
Questions and information requests about the aviation industry can be directed to this FAA office.

* Airline Transportation Data Files
Center for Electronic Records
National Archives and Records Administration
8th St. & Pennsylvania Ave., NW, Room 20E
Washington, DC 20408 (202) 523-3267
This center has information regarding airline transportation from the U.S. Department of Transportation and the Civil Aeronautics Board. Contact the Center for a detailed listing of the data available.

* Airmen and Aircraft Registry
Airmen and Aircraft Registry
Federal Aviation Administration
Department of Transportation
Mike Monroney Aeronautical Center
P.O. Box 25082
Oklahoma, OK 73125 (405) 680-4331
The FAA keeps permanent records on all U.S. civil aircraft and airmen (students, private, commercial and airline transport). The Registry also issues and monitors certificates to air carrier personnel involved in international civil aviation. Contact this office for information on these records, along with the registration records of all civil aircraft.

* Airport Security
Airport Security Program
Civil Aviation Security Service
Federal Aviation Administration
Department of Transportation
800 Independence Ave., SW, Room 319
Washington, DC 20591 (202) 267-9863

The FAA ensures the presence of law enforcement in U.S. airports, and approves the security programs of all airports under FAR 107. It also certifies walk-through detection devices.

* Airport Standards
Design and Operational Criteria Division
Office of Airport Standards
Federal Aviation Administration
Department of Transportation
800 Independence Ave., SW, Room 614
Washington, DC 20591 (202) 267-3446
This office can provide you with information on standards required for constructing and operating airports. Such standards include size, length, separation between runways, snow and ice control, and crash and fire rescue equipment. Contact this office for more information.

* Air Travelers' Rights and Complaints
Consumer Affairs Division
Intergovernmental and Consumer Affairs
Governmental Affairs
Office of the Secretary of Transportation
U.S. Department of Transportation
400 7th Street, SW
Washington, D.C. 20590 (202) 366-2220
If your problem cannot be resolved directly with the airline, contact this office for information on air travelers' rights and for assistance in resolving problems with airlines and charter flights. Complaints about delayed or canceled flights, reservations, lost baggage, smoking, refunds, and overbooking can also be handled here.

* Annual Review of Aircraft Accidents
National Technical Information Services
5285 Port Royal Road
Springfield, VA 22161 (703) 557-4650
The *Annual Review of Aircraft Accident Data: U.S. General Aviation* contains statistical tabulations of data compiled from reports of accidents involving U.S. general aviation aircraft in a particular calendar year. The report is divided into sections according to the type of aircraft and also according to the purpose for which aircraft was being used at the time of an accident. Within each section, tabulations provide data describing the types, causes, and circumstances of accidents. Accident rates (total and fatal) are provided, as are comparisons of the data of the given year to averages of accident data for several prior years. This publication is available from the office above. Call (703) 487-4650 for single copies and microfiche; or (703) 487-4630 for an annual subscription.

* Aviation Equipment Specifications
Engineering and Specifications Division
Office of Airport Standards
Federal Aviation Administration
Department of Transportation
800 Independence Ave., SW, Room 614
Washington, DC 20591 (202) 267-3826
This office can supply you with information on specifications for the manufacturing and installation of such aviation equipment as visual aides associated with aircraft landing and taxiing, runway lights, approach lights, beacons, and so forth.

* Aviation Forecasts
Aviation Forecasts Branch
Office of Aviation Policy
Federal Aviation Administration
Department of Transportation
800 Independence Ave., SW, Room 935F
Washington, DC 20591 (202) 267-3103
The following publications are available through this office (free of charge, depending on availability; otherwise you will be referred to the Government Printing Office, where they can be purchased):

Federal Aviation Administration Aviation Forecast. This microfiche provides 12-year projections on all aspects of aviation, including total aircraft, total airborne, statute miles of U.S. air carriers, hours flown in general aviation, and fuel consumed.

Terminal Area Forecasts. This microfiche provides 10-year projections on 400 specific airports including in-plane passengers, and operations of air carriers.

* Aviation History
Agency Historian
Office of Public Affairs
Federal Aviation Administration

Business and Industry

Department of Transportation
800 Independence Ave., SW, Room 907A
Washington, DC 20591 (202) 267-3478
The FAA Historian can provide you with information on almost any aspect of the history of American aviation.

* Aviation Medicine
Biomedical and Behavioral Science Division
Office of Aviation Administration
Federal Aviation Administration
Department of Transportation
800 Independence Ave., SW, Room 325
Washington, DC 20591 (202) 267-3535
The FAA conducts aeromedical research on in the following areas:
-Psychology: evaluates spatial disorientation and visual perception in the aviation environment;
-Physiology: performance and health of aircrew and air traffic controllers under diverse environmental conditions;
-Toxicology: toxic hazards such as pesticides used in aerial application, products of combustion and ionizing radiation from air shipment of radioactive cargo in the high-altitude environment;
-Protection and survival: studies of techniques for lessening or preventing crash injuries, developing concepts and evaluating survival equipment used under adverse physical conditions, establishing human physical limitations of civil aviation operations, and evaluating emergency procedures for downed aircraft.

* Aviation News
FAA General Aviation News
General Aviation and Commercial Division
Flight Standards Service, AFS-800
Federal Aviation Administration
Department of Transportation
800 Independence Ave., SW, Room 325
Washington, DC 20591 (202) 267-8212
The bimonthly publication, *Aviation News*, is a safety magazine for general aviation pilots (for more information about content, contact the above office). It is available for $13 per year from the Government Printing Office, Superintendent of Documents, Washington, DC 20402; (202) 783-3238.

* Aviation Policy
Information Systems Branch
Policy Analysis Division, APO-130
Office of Aviation Policy and Plans
Federal Aviation Administration
Department of Transportation
800 Independence Ave., SW, Room 937C
Washington, DC 20591 (202) 267-3374
Reports and other data are generated by approximately 18 databases to aid in aviation policy decisions on such matters as the activities of airlines, seat belt configurations, and the number of airports in the United States.

* Aviation Procedures Periodicals
Superintendent of Documents
U.S. Government Printing Office
Washington DC 20402 (202) 783-3238
The following two periodicals from GPO contain the current internal directives of the Federal Aviation Administration:

Flight Services Handbook. Describes the procedures and terms used by personnel providing assistance and communications services ($46/subscription, #950-032-00000-6).

Data Communications Handbook. Describes teletypewriter operating procedures, applicable international teletypewriter procedures, and continuous U.S. Service weather schedules ($34/subscription, #950-004-00000-2).

* Aviation Publications
U.S Department of Transportation
M-443.2
Washington, DC 20590
Write to the above address to order free copies of the annual *Guide to Federal Aviation Administration Publications* (FAA-APA-PG-11). For approval of more that 10 copies, write to: Federal Aviation Administration, Department of Transportation, 800 Independence Ave., SW, APA-230, Washington, DC 20591. Many of the publications listed are free.

* Aviation Statistics--General
Information Analysis Branch
Management Standards and Statistics Division
Office of Management Systems

Federal Aviation Administration
Department of Transportation
800 Independence Ave., SW, Room 607
Washington, DC 20591 (202) 267-8063
Historical and current aviation statistics are available on such subjects as: air traffic activities, number of aircraft, flying hours, pilots, and passengers. For a listing of available publications, contact the above office.

* Bird Strikes
Airport Safety Data Group
Office of Airport Standards
Federal Aviation Administration
Department of Transportation
800 Independence Ave., SW, Room 615
Washington, DC 20591 (202) 267-8792
Birds being accidentally sucked into jet engines is a serious aviation hazard. Contact this office for information on where bird strikes occur.

* Commuter and Air Taxi Services
Commuter and Air Taxi Branch
Transportation Division
Office of Flight Operations
Federal Aviation Administration
Department of Transportation
800 Independence Ave., SW, Room 303
Washington, DC 20591 (202) 267-8086
Contact this office for information regarding policy, regulations, and directives for commuter and air taxi aircraft. A list is available of air taxi operators and commercial operators of small aircraft.

* Consumer Complaints
Community and Consumer Liaison Division
Office of Public Affairs
Federal Aviation Administration
Department of Transportation
800 Independence Ave., SW
Washington, DC 20591 (202) 267-3481
Complaints involving such aviation issues as safety, noise, pesticide spraying, or broken seat belts can be directed to this office.

* Consumer Rights on Airlines
Government Printing Office
Superintendent of Documents
Washington DC 20402 (202) 783-3238
Fly Rights is an easy-to-read booklet that explains the rights and responsibilities of air travellers. It is available at nominal cost from the GPO.

* Educational Resources in Aviation
Aviation Education Officer
Federal Aviation Administration
Department of Transportation
800 Independence Ave., SW
Washington, DC 20591 (202) 267-3469
The FAA's Aviation Education Program offers volunteer assistance to the nation's schools through the following programs: career guidance; tours of airports, control towers, and other facilities; classroom lectures and demonstrations; aviation safety information; aviation education resource materials; computerized clearinghouse of aviation and space information; aviation science instruction programs for home/school computers; "Partnerships-in-Education" activities; and teachers' workshops. Write to the above office for more information.

* Essential Air Passenger Service
Aviation Analysis
Federal Aviation Administration
Department of Transportation
800 Independence Ave., SW, Room 5100
Washington, DC 20591 (202) 267-5903
This office guarantees that certain cities will be served by airlines. It also represents community views. Contact this office for more information on airport service.

* Essential Air Service
Office of Aviation Analysis
Policy and International Affairs
Office of the Secretary of Transportation
U.S. Department of Transportation
400 7th Street, SW
Room 6401

Washington, D.C. 20590 (202) 366-5903
The Departments's Essential Air Service Program ensures that certain cities will be served by air transportation. The program establishes subsidy levels, selects carriers, processes applications to change service levels, and reviews fitness of carriers. Contact the office listed for information about this program.

* Federal Aviation Administration Academy
Federal Aviation Administration
Department of Transportation
P.O. Box 25082, AAC-900
Oklahoma, OK 73125 (405) 680-6900
The Academy is the principal source of technical information on U.S. civil aviation. It conducts training for FAA personnel through resident or correspondence courses and occasional on-site training. Air traffic training is available for specialists who man the FAA airport traffic control towers, air route traffic control center, and flight service stations. Electronic training is also available for engineers and technicians who install and maintain navigation and traffic control communications facilities. Initial and recurrent training is also conducted for air carrier and general operations inspectors. The Academy provides air navigation facilities and flight procedures analysis to flight inspection personnel.

* Films and Videos on Aviation
Public Inquiry Center
Federal Aviation Administration
Department of Transportation, APA-230
Washington, DC 20591 (202) 267-3481
The FAA has a free catalog of films and videos which are aimed primarily at the aviation community. They describe the kinds of programs and measures that can be taken collectively to increase the safety, capacity, and efficiency of the U.S. national airspace system--in areas ranging from air traffic control to aeromedical research, meteorology, and safety. Most of the titles listed in the catalog are available in both 16mm film and 1/2" VHS videocassette. There is no charge for borrowing these FAA titles, and no admission may be charged to any audiences viewing the programs. These titles may also be purchased. For a copy of the *FAA Film/Video Catalog*, contact this office.

* Financial Analysis of Airline Industry
Aviation Analysis
Federal Aviation Administration
Department of Transportation
800 Independence Ave., SW, Room 5100
Washington, DC 20591 (202) 267-5903
Financial studies and evaluations of the air transportation industry are available on such subjects as profit margin trends, aircraft cost and performance, domestic jet trends, fuel trends, carrier lenders, passenger yield, used aircraft sales, aircraft seating trends, and airline employment.

* Flight Procedures
Flight Procedures Branch
Federal Aviation Administration
Department of Transportation
P.O. Box 25082
AVN-220900
Oklahoma, OK 73125 (405) 680-3382
The branch develops and maintains instrument flight procedures.

* General Inquiries
Office of Public Affairs
Federal Aviation Administration
Department of Transportation
800 Independence Ave., SW
Washington, DC 20591 (202) 267-3481
The stating place for any information on airlines, airports and aircraft.

* Human Factors: Aviation Research
Civil Aeromedical Institute
Federal Aviation Administration
Department of Transportation
Mike Monroney Aeronautical Center
P.O. Box 25082
Oklahoma, OK 73125 (405) 680-4806
CAMI conducts research to identify human factor causes of aircraft accidents, prevent future accidents, and make accidents that do occur more survivable. Contact this Institute for more information on this research.

* International Air Transportation
Office of International Aviation
Policy and International Affairs

Office of the Secretary of Transportation
U.S. Department of Transportation
400 7th Street, SW, Room 6402
Washington, D.C. 20590 (202) 366-2423
This office studies and develops U.S. policy with regard to international aviation. It ensures cooperation between U.S. and foreign-flag airlines and negotiates air service agreements with other countries.

* International Aviation
Bureau of Economic and Business Affairs
Department of State
2201 C St., NW, Room 5531
Washington, DC 20520 (202) 647-7973
In handling all international aviation negotiations and agreements, this office works on expanding aviation markets overseas, aviation security, and other issues relating to international aviation, such as assisting airlines in operating overseas and monitors agreements thereof. Information is available on these topics.

* Medical Certification of Airmen
Civil Aeromedical Institute
Federal Aviation Administration
Department of Transportation
Mike Monroney Aeronautical Center
P.O. Box 25082
Oklahoma, OK 73125 (405) 680-4806
CAMI operates a program for the medical certification of airmen, and educates pilots and physicians in matters related to aviation safety. It is also responsible for developing and producing brochures, slides, and training films for distribution to aviation groups and organizations. Contact CAMI for more information on certification or these education programs.

* National Airport System Plan
Office of Airport Planning and Programming
National Planning Division
Federal Aviation Administration
Department of Transportation
800 Independence Ave., SW, Room 617
Washington, DC 20591 (202) 267-3451
Contact this office for statistical information on the National Airport System.

* National Flight Data
National Flight Data Center
Airspace--Rules and Aeronautical Information Division
Air Traffic Service
Federal Aviation Administration
Department of Transportation
800 Independence Ave., SW, Room 634
Washington, DC 20591 (202) 267-9311
This Center can provide you with information on all civilian airports (and those military airports with joint usage), navigation aids, and procedures for the national airspace system. The Center also maintains a database which contains such items as the latitude and longitude of airports, airport runways, records of obstruction to air navigation, flight planning information, bearing and distance information, and records of hazards to air navigation.

* Pilot's Aeromedical Standards
Medical Specialties Division
Office of Aviation Medicine
Federal Aviation Administration
Department of Transportation
800 Independence Ave., SW, Room 324
Washington, DC 20591 (202) 267-3802
Contact this FAA division for information on policy, regulations, and standards for medical certificates required for a pilot's license.

* Pilot Schools
U.S. Government Printing Office
Superintendent of Documents
Washington DC 20402 (202) 783-3238
The *List of Certified Pilot Schools* provides you with an up-to-date directory of pilot training schools in the U.S. It is available for $1.75 from the GPO (#050-007-00763-9).

* Radio Frequency Systems Compatibility
Spectrum Engineering Division
Systems Research and Development Service
Federal Aviation Administration
Department of Transportation
800 Independence Ave., SW, Room 500

Business and Industry

Washington, DC 20591   (202) 267-9710

The FAA ensures that radio systems have frequencies on which to operate that are compatible with other frequencies. Work is also done in conjunction with international organizations on plans for future radio systems.

* Relocation Assistance Near Airports

Community and Environmental Needs Division
Office of Airport Planning and Programming
Federal Aviation Administration
Department of Transportation
800 Independence Ave., SW, Room 616
Washington, DC 20591   (202) 267-3263

The division assists airport owners involved with airport development projects provide uniform and equitable treatment of persons displaced from their homes and businesses due to federal or federally-assisted programs. Assistance is also available on environmental impact and noise.

* Security

Civil Aviation Security Service (ACS 400)
Federal Aviation Administration
Department of Transportation
800 Independence Ave., SW, Room 320
Washington, DC 20591   (202) 267-9075

The office is a source of information and expertise on the following airport security issues: domestic and foreign aircraft hijacking; bomb threats at airports and on airplanes; compliance and enforcement of regulations; prevention of attempts; explosives and explosive devices found at airports and on airplanes; international crimes involving civil aviation; information on numbers of people screened, numbers of weapons found, and weapon detection devices.

* Small Business Procurement

Small Business Specialist Procurement Division

AAC-70A
Federal Aviation Administration
Department of Transportation
Mike Monroney Aeronautical Center
P.O. Box 25082
Oklahoma, OK 73125   (405) 680-4391

The office provides FAA contracting and procurement support for spare parts, modifications and service contracts for the fleet of aircraft, and their air navigation and communication gear operated by the FAA.

* Standards and Statistics Data Base

Management Standards and Statistics Division
Federal Aviation Administration
AMS-400
Department of Transportation
800 Independence Ave., SW
Washington, DC 20591   (202) 267-8063

The FAA maintains several computerized data files on a variety of aviation-related subjects such as: aviation safety, air traffic, aviation schools, commercial and government ownership and operation of aircraft, aircraft repair stations, FAA facilities, and procurement. While the FAA does not conduct searches of these files for anyone outside the agency, they will copy any file you designate onto a blank tape that you provide for $38.

* Tariffs and Routes

Aviation Analysis
Federal Aviation Administration
Department of Transportation
800 Independence Ave., SW, Room 10223
Washington, DC 20591   (202) 267-4382

Contact this office for information regarding carriers' passenger and cargo operations.

Communications

* Amateur Radio Operators
National Technical Information Service
5285 Port Royal Road
Springfield, VA 22161 (703) 487-4600
A database of all the Federal Communications Commission's licensed amateur radio operators is available through NTIS. This magnetic tape file contains records on over 450,000 operators, including names, addresses, ages, station locations, and other licensing information. This Amateur Radio Service Master File (PB 83-220-889), available for $625 (6,250 BPI) or for $825 (BPI), is updated weekly.

* Amateur Radio Services
Consumer Assistance Branch
Federal Communications Commission
Gettysburg, PA 17326 (717) 337-1212
The FCC's Amateur Radio Services is comprised of three parts--amateur Service, amateur-satellite service, and Radio Amateur Civil Emergency Radio (RACES). During times of national crises, licensed amateur stations can assist local governments in coordinating emergency efforts. Those interested in becoming a licensed ARS operator must take a qualifying exam. Over 450,000 licensed individuals in the U.S. are ARS members.

* Applications & Publications
Services & Supply Branch
Federal Communications Commission
1919 M Street, NW, Room B-10
Washington, DC 20554 (202) 632-7272
This office will provide you with any FCC licensing application forms, construction permits, and instructional publications on how to conform with FCC guidelines.

* Auxiliary Services Branch
Federal Communications Commission
2025 M Street, NW, Room 7310
Washington, DC 20554 (202) 632-6485
Documents on File: FM Booster Stations, International, Intercity Relays, Remote Pickups, Translator Relays, Studio Transmitter Link, and so on. Hours of Operation: Monday through Friday, 1:00 p.m. to 5:00 p.m.

* Broadcast Ownership Reference Room
Federal Communications Commission
1919 M Street, NW, Room 234
Washington, DC 20554 (202) 632-6993
Documents on File: Commercial and Non-Commercial Ownership Reports for Station a.m., FM, and TV, Contract Files, and Network Affiliation Agreements. Hours of Operation: Monday through Friday, 9:00 a.m. to 4:30 p.m.

* Broadcast Regulations
Mass Media Bureau
Federal Communications Commission
1919 M Street, NW, Room 314
Washington, DC 20554 (202) 632-6460
The Mass Media Bureau has three major responsibilities: 1) regulating a.m., FM, and television broadcast stations and related facilities; 2) administering and enforcing cable TV rules; and 3) licensing private microwave radio facilities used by cable systems.
The Bureau also processes applications for licenses or other filings, analyzes complaints, and conducts investigations.

* Broadcast Violations
Field Operations Bureau
Federal Communications Commission
1919 M Street, NW, Room 734
Washington, DC 20554 (202) 632-6980
FOB is the FCC's primary point of contact with the public. Field office personnel nationwide interact with consumers, radio communications users, and the telecommunications industry through enforcement and public service activities. The Field Operations Bureau detects violations of radio regulations, monitors transmissions, inspects stations, investigates complaints of radio interference, and issues violations notices. It also examines and licenses radio operators; processes applications for painting, lighting, and placing antenna towers; and furnishes direction-finding aids for ships and aircraft in distress. The bureau maintains over 30 field offices across the country.

* Business Radio Services
Licensing Division
Federal Communications Commission
Route 116
Gettysburg, PA 17326 (717) 337-1212
The FCC authorizes and licenses all Business Radio Services used in commercial activity. Over 640,000 businesses in the U.S., from mail couriers to exterminators to plumbers, use radio services as part of their operations and must be licensed by the FCC. Updated daily, these files are available on database and can be accessed through SAFE, or at an access terminal by visiting the FCC office in person.

* Cable Television
Federal Communications Commission
File Room Number 2
1919 M Street, NW, Room 248
Washington, DC 20554 (202) 632-6993
Documents on File: FCC Form 325 Schedule 2, Physical System Data, Reference to files that are filed by county, state, and/or operator legal name. Hours of Operation: Monday through Friday, 9:00 a.m. to 4:30 p.m.

* Cable Television
Federal Communications Commission
File Room Number 1
1919 M Street, NW, Room 244
Washington, DC 20554 (202) 632-6993
Documents on File: Correspondence Files, FCC Form 325 Schedule 1, Community Unit Data, 76.12 Registration (letter), 76.400 Ownership Change (Letters), Cable Antenna Relay Services (CARS), Cable Show Cause Orders, (CSC) Files, Cable Special Relief (CSR), and Cross-Ownership Files. Hours of Operation: Monday through Friday, 9:00 a.m. to 4:30 p.m.

* Cellular Reference Room
Federal Communications Commission
1919 M Street, NW, Room 209
Washington, DC 20554 (202) 632-6400
Documents on File: Pending Cellular Applications, Petitions. Hours of Operation: Tuesday, Thursday, and Friday, 1:00 p.m. to 4:00 p.m.

* Common Carrier Bureau Reference and File Rooms
Federal Communications Commission
Accounting and Audits Division
Public Reference Room
2000 L Street, NW, Room 812
Washington, DC 20554 (202) 634-1861
Documents on File: Accounts and Subaccounts, Continuing Property Records, Disposition Units, Pension Filings, Official Correspondence, Computer II Public Files, Depreciation Rates, Filings, Docket 86-111 Implementation Filings, Contracts between Carriers, and Affiliations Waiver Requests dealing with Accounting and Reporting. Hours of Operation: Monday through Friday, 9:00 a.m. to 4:00 p.m.

* Common Carrier Regulations
Common Carrier Bureau
Federal Communications Commission
1919 M Street, NW, Room 500
Washington, DC 20554 (202) 632-6910
This office regulates wire and radio communications common carriers--paging, digital electronic message service, point-to-point microwave, multipoint distribution service, rural radio, cellular radio, offshore radio, international fixed radio, international fixed public radio, telephone, telegraph, and satellite companies. It also processes applications for licenses or other filings, analyzes related complaints, and conducts investigations into common carrier-related problems.

* Communications and Information Policy
Public Information
National Telecommunications and

Information Administration
Department of Commerce
14th St. and Constitution Ave., NW
Room 4898
Washington, DC 20230 (202) 377-1551

The National Telecommunications and Information Administration's policy recommendations affect the nation's economic and technological advancement in the telecommunications industry. This includes common carrier, telephone, broadcast, and satellite communications systems. It is involved with regulatory changes that have led to increased competition in common carrier operations and the growing overlap between telecommunications and computers. In the information field, NTIA focuses attention on issues of privacy and security and the impact of U.S. and international privacy legislation on the flow of electronic data across national boundaries. Contact this office for more information.

* Communications Networks and New Technologies

Office of Technology Assessment
600 Pennsylvania Ave., SE
Washington, DC 20510 (202) 228-6774

Recent advances in information storage and transmission technologies, occurring in a new deregulated and intensely competitive economic climate, are rapidly changing the Nation's communication networks. OTA is studying the role of the Federal government in this area, along with how to coordinate them, resolve potential conflicts between them, and examine new communication systems abroad and their potential relationships to the U.S. systems. Contact Linda Garcia, the project director, for more information.

* Consumer Complaints: Television, Broadcast Radio

Complaints & Investigations Branch
Federal Communications Commission
2025 M Street, NW, Room 8210
Washington, DC 20554 (202) 632-7048

This office handles consumer complaints involving commercial, non-commercial and cable TV, and broadcast radio. These complaints generally involve transmission interference problems, complaints about indecent language, and commercial sponsorship regulations. Complaints about billing, programming, and scheduling are handled by the local governments and stations themselves.

* Database Search Service

Spectrum Analysis and Frequency
Engineering (SAFE)
11166 Main Street, Suite 100
Fairfax, VA 22030 (703) 359-8470

The FCC has contracted SAFE to provide the public with a search and retrieval service for all information contained in the FCC database files. For example, they could give you the names of all the businesses within a 70 mile radius of Washington, DC, that use mobile radios in their operations, or even equal opportunity employment statistics for TV stations in Dallas, Texas. They provide on-line access to the databases for $54 per hour, and or they will do customized searches for $55 per hour plus the cost of materials. Data is available on computer tape, floppy disks, paper, and mailing labels. For a complete description of the FCC's databases and costs of searches, contact SAFE.

* Domestic Facilities Division

Federal Communications Commission
Public Reference Room
2025 M Street, NW, Room 6220
Washington, DC 20554 (202) 634-1860

Documents on File: Point to Point Microwave, Digital Electronic Message Services, Multi-Point Distribution Services, Space Stations, Section 214, and Equipment Registration. Hours of Operation: Monday through Thursday, 8:30 a.m. to 12:30 PM, 1:30 PM to 3:00 PM.

* Electric Borrowers Operations Database

Public Information Office
Rural Electrification Administration
U.S. Department of Agriculture
Washington, DC 20250 (202) 382-1255

The Rural Electrification Administration (REA) Database contains financial and statistical information about the operations of approximately 2,160 REA electric and telephone borrowers individually and as a group. The following information can be retrieved about each borrower: outstanding loans, REA debit service repayments, balance sheet items, revenue and expense items, operating statements, and sales statistics. REA maintains a variety of files containing information, ranging from loan statistics to accounting data. Searches and printouts are available free of charge. Tapes can be purchased for a cost-recovery fee, and hard copy reports are also available.

* Electronic Equipment Authorization

Equipment Authorization Branch
Federal Communications Commission

7435 Oakland Mills Road
Columbia, MD 21046 (301) 725-1585

All electronic equipment must be approved by the FCC before it is marketed in or imported into the U.S. The FCC's equipment authorization program also includes procedures for approving telephone equipment connected to public telephone network and for advance approval of over-the-air subscription (pay) TV systems before their authorization for use. The FCC also maintains and constantly updates a database of the equipment it authorizes. For more information on equipment application guidelines and regulations, contact EAB.

* Enforcement

Common Carrier Bureau
Federal Communications Commission
2025 M Street, NW, Room 6202
Washington, DC 20554 (202) 632-7553

This office handles consumer complaints involving communications services provided by interstate common carriers, which include voice, record, data, video and facsimile transmissions via wire, microwave, satellite, radio marine cable, optical fiber, and other facilities. The majority of complaints generally concern a carrier's rates or practices or the accuracy of a service charge or billing practice. Contact this office for more information on lodging a complaint.

* Enforcement Reference Room

Federal Communications Commission
2025 M Street, NW, Room 8210
Washington, DC 20554 (202) 632-6968

Documents on File: Station Complaint Files, Congressional Correspondence, Files, and Network Correspondence Files. Hours of Operation: Monday through Friday, 9:00 a.m. to 5:00 p.m.

* Equal Employment Opportunity

Federal Communications Commission
2025 M Street, NW, Room 7218
Washington, DC 20554 (202) 632-6968

Documents on File: FCC Form 395 Reports (Broadcast Stations and Cable Employment Units), Submissions that Cable Companies File in the Certification Process, Labor Force Statistics, Correspondence to and from Broadcast Stations and Cable Employment Units, and Cable Certification Process Results. Hours of Operations: Monday through Friday, 8:00 a.m. to 4:30 PM.

* Emergency Broadcast System

Federal Communications Commission
1919 M Street, NW, Room 840
Washington, DC 20554 (202) 632-3906

The Emergency Broadcast System (EBS) was originally developed to be used by the President in times of national crisis or war. EBS may now also be used by state and local officials in all 50 states, the District of Columbia, Puerto Rico, the Virgin Islands, American Samoa, and Guam to disseminate warning and instructions to the public in situations threatening life and property. Nationally, the EBS, which can be activated only by the White House, is designed to enable the President to speak to the nation within 10 minutes of his request. Contact this office for more information.

* Experimental Radio Service

Frequency Liaison Branch
Federal Communications Commission
1919 M Street, NW, Room 7326
Washington, DC 20554 (202) 653-8141

The FCC's Experimental Radio Service permits the public to experiment with new uses of radio frequencies. Individuals or manufacturers wishing to conduct research involving radiowave propagation equipment must be licensed by the FCC. For more information on the application procedures or on the database maintained on all experimental radio licenses granted, contact this office.

* Fairness/Political Programming Branch

Federal Communications Commission
2025 M Street, NW, Room 8202
Washington, DC 20554 (202) 632-6968

Documents on File: Correspondence and Rulings on Fairness/Political Programming Complaints. Hours of Operation: Monday through Friday, 8:00 a.m. to 5:30 p.m.

* FCC Information Bulletins and Fact Sheets

Federal Communications Commission
Consumer Assistance and Small Business Division
Office of Public Affairs
1919 M Street, NW
Washington, DC 20554 (202) 632-7000

If you are looking for general information about communications issues or background material about the FCC, you may want to obtain copies of the following bulletins from this office. Single copies only are supplied free of charge.

Bulletins:
How to Apply for a Broadcast Station
Mass Media Services
The FCC in Brief
Radio Stations and Other Lists
Private Radio Services
Evolution of Wire and Radio Communications
Station Identification and Call Signs
Frequency Allocation
Memo to All Young People Interested in Radio
Cable Television
Field Operation Bureau

Fact Sheets:
Low Power Television (LPTV)
Multipoint Distribution Service (MDS)
Instructional Television Fixed Service (ITFS)
Direct Broadcast Service (DBS)
Cellular Radio
Satellite Program Scrambling
Indecency/Obscenity
Exparte'
Dial-a-Porn
FCC Fee Information
Specialized Mobile Radio Service (SMRS)

* FCC Mass Media Bureau Reference and File Sources

Federal Communications Commission
Mass Media
Pubic Reference Room
1919 M Street, NW, Room 239
Washington, DC 20554   (202) 632-6485
Documents on File: Station License Files, New Applications, Assignments and Transfers, Engineering Files, Construction Permits, LPTV, and ITFS. Hours of Operation: Monday through Friday, 10:00 a.m. to 4:30 p.m.

* FCC News Releases Recording

Federal Communications Commission
News Media Division
Office of Public Affairs
1919 M Street, NW
Washington, DC 20554   (202) 632-0002
The Office of Public Affairs' recorded message will provide you with information on the latest news releases concerning the FCC and the telecommunications industry.

* FCC Open Meetings

Federal Communications Commission
1919 M Street, NW, Room 856
Washington, DC 20554   (202) 632-7000
The general public is welcome to attend and observe all Commission meetings, except when the Commission finds that the public interest requires otherwise. This office can provide you with the free brochure, *A Guide To Open Meetings*, which outlines how FCC meetings work and where to obtain information on their findings.

* FCC Record of Actions

U.S. Government Printing Office
Superintendent of Documents
Washington, DC 20402   (202) 783-3238
The *FCC Record* provides a comprehensive, timely, and cost-effective source of FCC actions, including all texts released to the public daily through the FCC Office of Public Affairs. It contains a table of contents, a popular name case table, table of docket numbers, DA and FCC numbers, a list of cases by locale, and an alphabetical subject index. In addition, the *FCC Record* contains some public notices, speeches, and staff papers, and is available every two weeks through the GPO at an annual subscription rate.

* FCC Research and Copy Service

Federal Communications Commission
1919 M Street, Room 246
Washington, DC 20037   (202) 857-3815
Any documents on file at the FCC's library or reference rooms listed below can be researched and copied for you for a fee by ITS, Inc. ITS charges $22 per hour for research, and $.08 per page for photocopying. Documents located in the Private Radio Licensing Division must be ordered from ITS, Inc., 1270 Fairfield Road, Gettysburg, PA 17325; (717) 337-1433.

* FCC Rules and Regulations

U.S. Government Printing Office
Superintendent of Documents
Washington, DC 20402   (202) 783-3238
The volumes of *FCC Rules and Regulations* must be purchased from the GPO, rather directly from the FCC. In addition to the FCC Rules, the GPO has available for purchase the following publications and documents often requested by customers:

Communications Act of 1934 (including amendments)
Volumes of FCC Reports and Decisions
FCC Annual Reports
Federal Register
Code of Federal Regulations

* FCC Rules On-line

Federal Communications Commission
1919 M Street, NW, Room 230
Washington, DC 20554   (202) 632-4128
By visiting the FCC in person can you have the most up-to-date information on the complete FCC rules and regulations through the Automated FCC Rules Reference System. This system provides the only on-line computer access to FCC rules and regulations, and can be accessed free of charge at designated computer terminals at the FCC.

* FCC Telephone Directory

Federal Communications Commission
1919 M Street, NW
Washington, DC 20554   (202) 857-3800
Issued on a quarterly basis, the FCC's telephone directory is available for $2.50 by mail or $1.00 if you pick it up in person. This directory can be a very useful research tool not only because it includes FCC telephone and room numbers of staff members, but also because it contains functional listings which identify key telephone numbers by subject areas.

* Federal Communications Commission Reference Room

Dockets Reference Room
1919 M Street, NW, Room 239
Washington, DC 20554   (202) 632-7569
The Dockets Reference Room maintains files on all rulemaking proceedings, docket files, transcripts of hearing proceedings, decisions, briefs, depositions, interrogatories, and ex parte comments. If you cannot visit the docket room in person, the FCC's copying service, ITS, Inc., will reproduce any documents you wish and send them to you for a fee.

* Federal Telecommunications Resource

Interdepartment Radio Advisory Committee (IRAC)
National Telecommunications and Information Administration
14th St. and Constitution Ave., NW
Room 1605
Washington, DC 20230   (202) 377-0319
Radio frequency spectrum management is the concern of NTIA's Office of Spectrum Management (OSM). By statute, NTIA manages the Federal government's use of the radio spectrum, while the Federal Communications Commission is responsible for non-Federal usage. OSM processes nearly 100,000 frequency assignment actions every year. It chairs and provides administrative and analytic support to the Interdepartment Radio Advisory Committee (IRAC). The IRAC is the central advisory body to NTIA regarding Federal Government radio spectrum management and use.

* Foreign Press and Radio Translations

Foreign Broadcast Information Service
National Technical Information Service
Department of Commerce
5282 Port Royal Rd.
Springfield, VA 22161   (703) 487-4630
The subscription, *Foreign Press and Radio Translations*, provides a daily (paper copy) or weekly (microfiche copy) publication featuring news accounts, commentaries, and government statements from foreign broadcasts, press agency transmissions, newspapers, and periodicals published in the previous 48 to 72 hours. The selections available are the following:

People's Republic of China
Eastern Europe
Soviet Union
East Asia
Near East and South Asia
Latin America
Western Europe

Business and Industry

Sub Saharan Africa

The paper copy is available for $360 annually, and the microfiche copy for $150. Contact the Subscription Department to place an order or request a free information brochure *PR-376*.

* Formal Complaints and Investigations

Federal Communications Commission
2025 M Street, NW, Room 6206
Washington, DC 20554 (202) 632-4890
Documents on File: Formal Complaints and Related Pleadings, Interlocking Directorate Reports and Applications, Pole Attachment Complaints and Related Pleadings, Pole Attachment State Certifications, Enforcement Proceedings which include: mergers, acquisitions, and transfers of control files. Hours of Operation: Monday through Friday, 9:00 a.m. to 5:00 p.m.

* Industry Analysis

Federal Communications Commission
Public Reference Room
1919 M Street, NW, Room 537
Washington, DC 20554 (202) 632-0745
Documents on File: Reports required by FCC Rules and Regulations, Administrative Reports, Annual Reports to Stockholders, FCC Form 492, Rate of Return Report, Statistics of Communications Common Carriers, Quarterly Operating Data of Telephone and Telegraph Carriers, Switched Access Reports, Equal Access Implementation Reports, NECA - Pool Results, Local Exchange Rates, Monthly Bypass Request Report - AT&T, Lifeline Link-Up Reports, IAD Reports, General Reference Material from Sources. Hours of Operation: Monday through Friday, 9:00 a.m. to 1:00 p.m., 2:00 p.m. to 5:00

* Informal Complaints and Public Inquiries Branch

Federal Communications Commission
2025 M Street, NW, Room 6202
Washington, DC 20554 (202) 632-4890
Documents on File: Informal Written Telephone Related Complaints and Public Information. Hours of Operation: Monday through Friday, 8:00 a.m. to 5:00 p.m.

* International Broadcasting Service

Federal Communications Commission
2025 M Street, NW, Room 8120-A
Washington, DC 20554 (202) 254-3394
The IBS sets aside a portion of the radio spectrum for stations wishing to broadcast to foreign countries. Currently, IBS regulates 18 such stations, most of which are religious-oriented. Additionally, IBS negotiates telecommunications agreements with foreign countries. Contact this office for more information.

* International Communications

Bureau of International Communications
and Information Policy
Department of State
2201 C St., NW, Room 6317
Washington, DC 20520 (202) 647-8345
As the principal advisor to the Secretary of State on international telecommunications policy issues affecting U.S. foreign policy and national security, this bureau coordinates with other U.S. Government agencies and the private sector in formulating and implementing international policies relating to communications and information technologies. CIP provides guidance and instructions to U.S. representatives to such international organizations as the International Telecommunications Satellite Organization, the International Maritime Satellite Organization, The Information, Computers, and Communications Policy Committee of the Organization for Economic Cooperation and Development, and the International Telecommunication Union. Through bilateral negotiations and multilateral programs, CIP promotes the principles of free enterprise and the free flow of communication.

* International Communications Regulation

Federal Communications Commission
International Facilities Division
1919 M Street, NW, Room 533
Washington, DC 20554 (202) 632-7834
Documents on File: International Microwave Point-to-Point Files, International Fixed Radiotelephone Files, International Fixed Radiotelegraph Files, International Space Station Files, Recognized Private Operating Agency Files, Uniform Settlement Policy Files, Submarine Cable Landing License Files, International Earth Station Files, Transborder Earth Station Files, Section 214, INTELSAT, and Comsat Documents, Rulemakings, Rulings, Assignments of Licenses, Transfer of Control, and Temporary Authorities. Hours of Operation: Monday through Friday, 8:00 a.m. to 1:00 p.m., 2:00 p.m. to 5:00 p.m.

* International Telecommunications

Office of International Affairs
National Telecommunications and
Information Administration
14th St., NW, Room 4090
Washington, DC 20230 (202) 377-1304
This office is responsible for developing International Communications policy. OIA works to minimize unnecessary Federal and foreign government interference in the efficient functioning of international telecommunications markets. It also seeks to identify and, where feasible, lessen foreign obstacles to U.S. trade in telecommunications and information services and products. To do this, OIA assesses the communications policies of other nations and cooperates with the State Department in preparing U.S. positions before various international forums, such as the International Telecommunication Union and the Organization for Economic Cooperation and Development. Also, OIA reviews a wide rage of issues pertinent to regulatory and legislative proceedings. Contact this office for more information on international communications.

* Legislative Affairs

Office of Legislative Affairs
Federal Communications Commission
1919 M Street, NW, Room 808
Washington, DC 20554 (202) 632-6405
If you have questions concerning congressional testimony, current bills, or other legislative matters related to the FCC, this office has two attorneys on staff who specialize in mass media and common carrier law to answer your questions.

* Marine Radio Services

Aviation & Marine Branch
Federal Communications Commission
2025 M Street, NW, Room 5114
Washington, DC 20554 (202) 632-7175
The FCC regulates the Marine Radio Services for the safety and operational communications of non-federal maritime activities, including U.S. vessels that traverse international waters and land stations in the Maritime Mobile Radio Service. This office also regulates the Aviation Radio Services for nongovernment use of radio for aeronautical radionavigation, search and rescue, and other safety operations.

* Master Frequency File Database

Frequency Liaison Office
Federal Communications Commission
2025 M Street, NW, Room 7320
Washington, DC 20554 (202) 653-8141
The Master Frequency File contains information on the identification, location, and technical characteristics of almost 900,000 radio and television broadcast stations, satellite stations, land mobile and microwave stations, and all other types of radio frequency transmitters. Information on each facility includes name of owner, mailing address, height of transmitting towers, power, frequency, number of mobile units, and much more. This file is available for sale from NTIS on microfiche or magnetic tape, or specialized searches can be arranged through Spectrum Analysis and Frequency Engineering (SAFE), 11166 Main Street, Suite 100, Fairfax, VA 22030; (703) 359-8470.

* Mobile Services Division

Federal Communications Commission
Public Reference Room
1919 M Street, NW, Room 628
Washington, DC 20554 (202) 632-6400
Documents on File: Station Files, Maps, Diagrams, Petitions, Co-Channel Searches and Background Material Pending Files, and Cellular Granted Station Files. Hours of Operation: Monday through Thursday, 8:00 a.m. to 12:00 p.m.

* National Telecommunications

and Information Administration
National Telecommunications and Information Administration
Department of Commerce
14th St. and Constitution Ave., NW
Room 4898
Washington, DC 20230 (202) 377-1551
This Administration's broad goals include formulating policies to support the development and growth of telecommunications, information and related industries, furthering the efficient development and use of telecommunications and information services, providing policy and management for Federal use of the electromagnetic spectrum, and providing telecommunications facilities grants to public service users. NTIA employs 287 people and has an annual budget of $35,104,000.

* Policy and Program Planning

Federal Communications Commission

1919 M Street, NW, Room 544
Washington, DC 20554   (202) 632-9342
Documents on File: Petitions in Non-Docketed Proceedings, Comments and
Replies in Non-Docketed Proceedings, Applications for Review, Petitions for
Declaratory Rulings/Comments and Replies, Petitions for Waiver/Comments
and Replies, CEI Plans/Comments and Replies. Hours of Operation: Monday
through Friday, 9:00 a.m. to 5:30 p.m.

* Political Programming Rules

Political Programming
Federal Communications Commission
2025 M Street, NW, Room 8202
Washington, DC 20554   (202) 632-7586
This office can answer questions concerning political programming rules and
regulations. For example, if a station lets a legally qualified candidate for public
office use, its broadcast facilities must give "equal opportunities" to other
candidates for the same office. This office can also tell you about programming
costs for political candidates, who are all entitled to "lowest unit charges" for use
of broadcast or cable TV facilities during the 45 days preceding a primary and
the 60 days preceding a general election.
Contact this office for more information.

* Private Radio Reference Room

Federal Communications Commission
1270 Fairfield Road
Gettysburg, PA 17325   (717) 337-1311
Documents on File: Land Mobile and GMRS Applications, Microwave
Applications, AViation Ground Applications, Marine Coast Applications, all
Dismissals, Copies of Special Temporary Authorities (STA) or Transfers of
Control. Hours of Operation: Monday through Friday, 8:00 a.m. to 4:30 p.m.

* Private Radio Licensing

Licensing Division
Federal Communications Commission
Gettysburg, PA 17326   (717) 337-1212
For information on the status of any pending applications for FCC private radio
licenses, contact this office.

* Private Radio Regulations

Private Radio Bureau
Federal Communications Commission
2025 M Street, NW, Room 5002
Washington, DC 20554   (202) 632-6940
This office regulates radio stations serving the communications needs of
businesses, individuals, nonprofit organizations, and state and local governments,
including the following uses: private land mobile, private operational fixed
microwave, aviation, marine, personal, amateur, and disaster. It also processes
applications for licenses or other filings, analyzes complaints, and conducts
investigations.

* Public Access Link (PAL)

Equipment Authorization Branch
Federal Communications Commission
7435 Oakland Mill Road
Columbia, MD 21046   (301) 725-1585
The Public Access Link (PAL) provides computerized information on the status
of pending applications and technical information on granted authorizations.
The system remains on-line continuously, providing a twenty-hour service to the
public. You can also access the FCC "Bulletin Board" of recent Commission
actions which might impact on the equipment authorization program, a list of
testing laboratories which have filed required information with the FCC, and
grantee and manufacturer codes assigned for equipment identification. For
direct, on-line hook-up with your modem, call (301) 725-1072.

* Public Service Workshops and Seminars

Federal Communications Commission
1919 M Street, NW, Room 725
Washington, DC 20554   (202) 634-1940
The FCC conducts free seminars and workshops across the country to help the
public identify and resolve telecommunications-related interference problems.
For example, the FCC will train TV service technicians, telephone companies
and manufacturers, and power company technicians how to eliminate
interference in consumer-related products and services. Also, the FCC will
conduct seminars by special request from any group which needs help addressing
interference-related problems. Examples of special requests include Cable
television companies, Taxi Cab Associations, and hospital paging users. For
more information on having a seminar address your group, contact the FCC.

* Public Service Reference

Federal Communications Commission
1919 M Street, NW, Room 728
Washington, DC 20554   (202) 632-7240
Documents on File: Commercial Radio Operator Application Files and Bulletins
Concerning Radio Operator Matters.

* Purchasing and Technical Assistance for
   Broadcast Entrepreneurs

Consumer Assistance and Small Business Division
Office of Public Affairs
Federal Communications Commission
1919 M St., NW, Room 254
Washington, DC 20554   (202) 632-7000
The CASB Division will provide you with personal assistance in locating
information concerning FCC rules, policies, procedures, and guidance concerning
participation in FCC rulemaking proceedings. In addition, this office provides
specialized to assistance to those interested in becoming involved in the small
business telecommunications industry. They will walk you through the
purchasing procedures, identify resources for financial and technical assistance,
and perform license status checks for applicants. The Public Affairs office also
coordinates broadcast ownership workshops, which cover these topic and more,
every year across the country. Contact CASB for more information.

* Radio-Frequency (RF) Radiation

Office of Engineering and Technology
Federal Communications Commission
2025 M Street, NW, Room 7130
Washington, DC 20554   (202) 632-7060
Every transmitting device emits Radio Frequency (RF) radiation, and levels
which exceed FCC standards can be a serious health risk. If you have questions
about RF radiation in your community or workplace, contact the FCC for a free
consumer information package on RF radiation, along with technical surveys and
investigations of certain transmitters across the country.

* Rulemaking Changes at the FCC

The Secretary
Federal Communications Commission
1919 M Street, NW, Room 222
Washington, DC 20554   (202) 632-6410
The FCC is interested in any experiences, judgments, or insights you might have
that would shed light on issues and questions raised in an inquiry or rulemaking.
To obtain guidelines on how to submit your ideas on any FCC rulemaking
changes, contact this office.

* Tariff Legal Documents

Federal Communications Commission
1919 M Street, NW, Room 518
Washington, DC 20554   (202) 632-6387
Documents on File: Notices of Proposed Rulemakings, Petitions against Tariffs
(including comments and replies), Petitions for Reconsideration (including
comments and replies), Access Tariffs, Petitions dealing with Access Tariff,
Applications for Review (comments and replies).

* Tariff Review Public Reference Room

Federal Communications Commission
1919 M Street, NW, Room 513
Washington, DC 20554   (202) 632-6387
Documents on File: Multipoint Distribution Service (MDS), American
Telephone and Telegraph Company, Access Service Tariffs by Bell Operating
Companies, National Exchange Carrier Association, and Independent Telephone
Companies, Western Union Telegraph Company, International Record Carriers,
and other Overseas Carriers, Specialized Common Carriers, Satellite Carriers,
Microwave Carriers, Maritime Carriers, Facilities for CATV and Wide Spectrum
Service, and Mobile Radiotelephone Service. Hours of Operation: Monday
through Friday, 1:30 p.m. to 4:30 p.m.

* Tax Breaks For Broadcasting Entrepreneurs

Consumer Assistance and Small Business Division
Office of Public Affairs
Federal Communications Commission
1919 M Street, NW, Room 254
Washington, DC 20554   (202) 632-7260
If an owner of a broadcast or cable facility sells that station to a minority-owned
purchaser, the FCC can permit the seller to defer the payment of capital gains
tax, generally for 2 to 3 years. The FCC defines minority-ownership as consisting
in excess of 50 per cent of controlling interest. Also, shareholders in a minority-
controlled broadcast or cable entity are eligible for tax certificates upon the sale
of their shares, provided that their interest was acquired to assist in the financing
of the acquisition of the facility. The FCC may also issue tax certificates in
transfers to limited partnerships where the general partner is a minority

individual and owns more than 20 per cent interest in the broadcast or cable facility. For more information, contact CASB.

* Telecommunications Expertise for Public Service Groups

Public Telecommunications Facilities Program
National Telecommunications
  and Information Administration
Department of Commerce
14th St. and Constitution Ave., NW
Room 4625
Washington, DC 20230   (202) 377-5802

By identifying public service telecommunications needs, NTIA assists schools, hospitals, libraries, policy, fire departments, and government agencies in using advanced telecommunications systems and technology to achieve their goals.

* Telecommunications Publications

Publications Information
National Telecommunications
  and Information Administration
Department of Commerce
14th St. and Constitution Ave., NW
Room 4625
Washington, DC 20230   (202) 377-5802

A catalog is available which lists all the reports available from NTIA. Most are technical research studies, but several deal with communications policies and standards. In 1988, NTIA issued *TELECOM 2000*, the first comprehensive review and analysis of U.S. telecommunications policy in 20 years, as well as a number of reports regarding new computer-related communications and information services, expansion of broad-band and cable television systems, and customer options, high-definition television, and other topics.

* Telecommunications Research

Institute for Telecommunications Sciences
National Telecommunications
  and Information Administration
Department of Commerce
325 Broadway
Boulder, CO 80303   (303) 497-3572

As the chief research and engineering arm of NTIA, the Institute for

Telecommunication Sciences supports Administration Telecommunication objectives such as enhanced domestic competition, improved foreign trade opportunities for U.S. telecommunication firms, and more efficient and effective use of the radio frequency spectrum. ITS also serves as a principal Federal resource for assistance in solving problems of other Federal agencies, state and local governments, private corporations and associations, and international organizations. ITS conducts research in spectrum use analysis, telecommunication standards development, telecommunication systems performance, telecommunication systems planning and applied research. The *Annual Technical Progress Report* describes in more detail the research conducted, as well as listing the publications available.

* Telephone Utility Systems

Assistant Administrator--Telephone
Rural Electrification Administration
U.S. Department of Agriculture
Room 4056 South Building
Washington, DC 20250   (202) 382-9554

The USDA lends money to approximately 1,000 rural telephone companies and maintains a staff knowledgeable in both operations and equipment.
Consumer Complaints: Telephones, Faxes

* Transcripts of FCC Hearings

Capital Hill Reporting, Inc.
1825 K Street, NW, Suite 1122
Washington, DC 20006   (202) 466-9500

Transcripts of hearings, FCC Official Court Reporting Service, and Transcripts of Court hearings may be obtained by contacting this office.

* Video/Audio Tape Recordings of FCC Open Meetings

The Prism Corporation
4400 Jennifer Street, NW, Suite 200
Washington, DC 20015   (202) 686-8250

Video and audio tape recordings of Commission open meetings, official sessions, and FCC tutorials, are available to the public only from a this private contractor on a fee basis. Customers may buy blank tapes from this office or provide their own. Customers should be prepared to provide date of meetings, and, when appropriate, agenda number, unless they want this office to perform a search for a fee.

Shipping and Fishing

* Aids to Navigation

Office of Navigation Safety and Waterways Services
U.S. Coast Guard
U.S. Department of Transportation
2100 2nd St., SW, Room 1116
Washington, DC 20593-0001 (202) 267-1965

The Coast Guard maintains aids to navigation such as lighthouses and lights, buoys, beacons, fog signals, and long-range radionavigation aids like LORAN-C and OMEGA. The aids are established to assist navigators in plotting safe courses on waters under U.S. jurisdiction and in certain international areas. The seven volumes of *Light Lists*, which detail the navigation aids in seven geographic areas, are available at varying cost from the Superintendent of Documents, Government Printing Office, Washington, D.C. 20402; (202) 783-3238. The *LORAN-C User Handbook*, which explains the radionavigation system and how to use it, is also available from GPO for $4.75.

* Boating Correspondence Course

U.S. Government Bookstore
World Savings Building
720 N. Main St.
Pueblo, CO 81003 (719) 544-3142

Designed for boaters who can't attend a boating class, *The Skipper's Course* covers basic navigation, legal requirements, anchoring, weather, emergency procedures, boat handling, and safety. A certificate of completion is awarded. Stock No: 050012002258. Price: $6.50.

* Bridges Over Navigable Waters

Bridge Administration Division
Office of Navigation Safety and Waterways Services
U.S. Coast Guard
U.S. Department of Transportation
2100 2nd St., SW, Room 1408
Washington, DC 20593-0001 (202) 267-0368

Bridges and causeways spanning navigable waterways in the U.S. are subject to Coast Guard safety regulations concerning their construction, operation, and maintenance. This office oversees bridge engineering and issues permits. For further details, contact the division listed above.

* Certificates of Documentation for Vessels

Vessel Documentation Branch
Merchant Vessel Inspection and Documentation Division
Office of Marine Safety, Security, and Environmental Protection
U.S. Coast Guard
U.S. Department of Transportation
2100 2nd St., SW, Room 1312
Washington, DC 20593-0001 (202) 267-1492

Most commercial vessels of 5 or more net tons used on U.S. waters must be documented. Commercial vessels engaged in foreign trade and recreational boats of that size, may be documented at the option of the owner. Also, undocumented vessels equipped with propulsion machinery are required to be numbered by their individual states. Lending institutions regard a documented vessel to be a more secure form of collateral, thus making bank financing easier to obtain. Considered a form of international registration, the *Certificate of Documentation* may also make customs entry and clearance easier in foreign ports. The initial documentation fee is about $100. *Certificates of Documentation* are issued by the Coast Guard at documentation offices around the U.S. The office listed above can provide you with the address of the one nearest you.

* Coast Guard Courses and Textbooks

Coast Guard Auxiliary National Board, Inc.
9949 Watson Industrial Park
St. Louis, MO 63126

The following are textbooks used in Coast Guard Auxiliary public education courses. They can be ordered by writing to the above address, or you can get each textbook by taking the course of the same title through the Coast Guard. To find out where courses are offered near you, call the Courseline at (800) 336-BOAT; or (800) 245-BOAT in VA.

Boating Skills and Seamanship. Boating laws and regulations, boat handling, and navigation ($8.00).
Sailing and Seamanship. Same basic text as above, geared to sailboats ($8.00).
Advanced Coastal Piloting. How to read charts, plot courses, predict tides, and use navigation aids ($8.00).

* Coast Guard Regulations

Marine Safety Council
U.S. Coast Guard
U.S. Department of Transportation
2100 2nd St., SW, Room 3600
Washington, DC 20593-0001 (202) 267-1477

Rules and regulations proposed by the Coast Guard are taken under consideration and studied by this Council. Hearings are held at Coast Guard headquarters in D.C. and at other locations around the country. Announcements appear Monday through Friday in the *Federal Register*. For further information, contact the Council.

* Coast Guard Rescue Service

SAR Database Manager
Search and Rescue Division
Office of Navigation Safety and Waterways Services
U.S. Coast Guard
U.S. Department of Transportation
2100 2nd St., SW, Room 1422
Washington, DC 20593-0001 (202) 267-1579

The Search and Rescue (SAR) program maintains a comprehensive system of resources to save lives and prevent personal injury and property damage on the navigable waters of the U.S. This system includes rescue vessels, aircraft, and communication facilities. A cooperative international distress response system is also maintained for incidents on the high seas. For more information about the Guard's SAR program, contact the branch listed above.

* Coast Guard Reserve

Office of Readiness and Reserve
U.S. Coast Guard
U.S. Department of Transportation
2100 2nd St., SW, Room 5101 (202) 267-2350

In time of war or national emergency, the Coast Guard Reserve provides trained individuals and units for active duty. The Reserve also assists the Guard in peacetime missions during domestic emergencies and peak operations. The *Coast Guard Reservist Magazine*, available free from the office listed above, provides bimonthly news and human interest stories about Coast Guard Reservists and their activities.

* Coastal Zone Management

Office of Ocean and Coastal Resource Management
National Ocean Service
National Oceanic and Atmospheric Administration
Department of Commerce
1825 Connecticut Ave., NW
Room 706
Washington, DC 20235 (202) 673-5111

To balance the needs for preserving and developing the resources in the U.S. coastal zone, the National Ocean Service, through its Office of Ocean and Coastal Resource Management, provides the coordination and expertise at the Federal level needed for effective management of these coastal resources. NOS has begun to expand the technical assistance provided to States and territories, emphasizing special area management planning, coastal hazards mitigation, cost-effective coastal management, and the simplification of permit processes for coastal activities.

* Commercial Fisheries Clearinghouse

Public Affairs
National Marine Fisheries Service
National Oceanic and Atmospheric Administration
Department of Commerce
1335 East-West Hwy.
Silver Spring, MD 20910 (202) 427-2370

The National Marine Fisheries Service manages the country's stocks of saltwater fish and shellfish for both commercial and recreational interests. NMFS administers and enforces the Magnuson Fishery Conservation and Management Act to assure that fishing stays within sound biological limits, and that U.S. commercial and recreational fishermen have the opportunity to harvest all the available fish within these limits. Several hundred Fisheries Service scientists conduct research relating to these management responsibilities in science and research centers in 15 states and the District of Columbia. Many of these laboratories have evolved a major field of interest, and have special knowledge of the fish in their geographical area that leads to predictions of abundance,

Business and Industry

economic forecasts, and direct assistance to sport fishermen and commercial fishing businesses. Each of the science and research centers of the National Marine Fisheries Service has their own area of expertise and knowledge of the fish in their area. Contact them directly regarding questions or publications requests.

* Commercial Vessel Inspections
Merchant Vessel Inspection and Documentation Division
Office of Marine Safety, Security, and Environmental Protection
U.S. Coast Guard
U.S. Department of Transportation
2100 2nd St., SW, Room 1400
Washington, DC 20593-0001   (202) 267-2978

The Coast Guard administers and enforces safety standards for the design, construction, equipment, and maintenance of commercial vessels and offshore structures on the Outer Continental Shelf. Foreign vessels subject to U.S. jurisdiction must also meet the required standards. Boardings are conducted to detect and prevent violations. Safety regulations cover such ship characteristics as hull structure, watertight integrity, fire safety, and navigation instrumentation. Records, mostly computerized, are kept on these inspections at district Coast Guard offices. For general information or referral to a records inspection facility near you, contact the division listed.

* Crew Certification
Licensing and Evaluation Branch
Merchant Vessel Personnel Division
Office of Marine Safety, Security, and Environmental Protection
U.S. Coast Guard
U.S. Department of Transportation
2100 2nd St., SW, Room 1210
Washington, DC 20593-0001   (202) 267-0218

To ensure that vessels are safely and sufficiently crewed with properly trained personnel, the Coast Guard develops safe manning standards for commercial vessels and administers a system for evaluation and licensing. Crew requirements on a vessel depend on factors such as route, tonnage, horsepower, and type of trade. The rules and regulations for licensing are included in the *Code of Federal Regulations*, Title 46, parts 10-14. Licensing and exams are given in applicable professional fields at regional examination centers around the country. Contact your local Coast Guard office or the branch listed above for referral to the center nearest you.

* Fish Exports
Office of Trade and Industry Services
National Marine Fisheries Service
National Oceanic and Atmospheric Administration
Department of Commerce
1335 East-West Hwy., Room 6212
Silver Spring, MD 20910   (301) 427-2379

This office assists seafood exporters by providing trade leads, conducting sales missions, doing market studies, and organizing "how to export" seminars. It helps industry by improving their access to markets in other countries. The Service provides inspection services for fishery commodities for export and issues official U.S. Government certificates attesting to the findings.

* Fisheries Technical Reports
Scientific Publications Office
National Marine Fisheries Service
National Oceanic and Atmospheric Administration
Department of Commerce
7600 Sand Point Way N.E.
Seattle, WA 98115   (206) 526-6107

This office prepares the following scientific and technical publications having to do with fisheries:

Fishery Bulletin. Publishes original research reports and technical notes on investigations in fishery science, engineering, and economics. Quarterly, $16 per year.
Marine Fisheries Review. Publishes review articles, original research reports, significant progress reports, technical notes, and new articles on fisheries science, engineering, and economics, commercial and recreational fisheries, marine mammal studies, and foreign fisheries developments. Quarterly, $7 per year.
NOAA Technical Reports. Publishes scientific investigations that document long-term continuing programs of NMFS, technical papers of general interest intended to aid conservation and management, as well as many other topic areas. Indexes are available. Issued irregularly, price varies.

* Fishery Products Grading and Inspection
Utilization Research and Services
National Marine Fisheries Service
National Oceanic and Atmospheric Administration
Department of Commerce

1335 East-West Hwy., Room 6142
Silver Spring, MD 20910   (301) 427-2355

The National Marine Fisheries Service conducts a voluntary seafood inspection program on a fee-for-service bases. A wide range of inspection services are available to any interested party, including harvesters, processors, food-service distributors, and importers and exporters. These services include vessel and plant sanitation inspection, product evaluation (in-plant and warehouse lot), product specification review, label review, laboratory analyses (microbiological tests, chemical contaminant/indices of decomposition, species identification), training, and education and information. This office has a great deal of information concerning inspections, grading of products, and regulations. They also publish a document listing fishery products that have been produced in fish establishments approved by the National Marine Fisheries Service.

* Fisheries Research
Office of Research and Environmental Information
National Marine Fisheries Service
National Oceanic and Atmospheric Administration
Department of Commerce
1335 East-West Hwy., Room 6310
Silver Spring, MD 20910   (301) 427-2367

Contact this office for information regarding fisheries research. Topics covered include acid rain and pollution, aquaculture information, diseases of fish, ecology and fish recruitment, fishing methods, and resource abundance.

* Fishery Statistics
Office of Research and Environmental Information
National Marine Fisheries Service
National Oceanic and Atmospheric Administration
Department of Commerce
1335 East-West Hwy., Room 8313
Silver Spring, MD 20910   (301) 427-2328

The Fisheries Statistics Division publishes statistical bulletins on marine recreational fishing and commercial fishing, and on the manufacture and commerce of fishery products. Annual publications available from this Office include the following:

Marine Recreational Fishery Statistics
Frozen Fishery Products
Processed Fishery Products
Imports and Exports of Fishery Products
Fish Meal and Oil

An annual publication titled, Fisheries of the United States, is prepared by the Fisheries Statistics Division, and includes information on U.S. commercial fishery landings, U.S. exclusive economic zone catches, world fisheries, imports and exports, U.S. supply, and per capita fish consumption. This publication is available through Superintendent of Documents, Government Printing Office, Washington, D.C. 20402; (202) 783-3832.

* Fisheries Trade and Industry Services
Office of Trade and Industry Services
National Marine Fisheries Service
National Oceanic and Atmospheric Administration
Department of Commerce
1335 East-West Hwy.
Silver Spring, MD 20910   (301) 427-2351

This office conducts activities designed to improve the competitiveness of the U.S. fishing industry in domestic and world markets and to enhance the safety and quality of U.S. seafood products. Programs include identification of industry trade issues and problems, financial assistance in the form of loan guarantees, insurance programs, a capital construction fund, and research and development grants, administration of fishery marketing councils, administration of inspection and grading programs, and research and development of product safety, quality and use.

* Fishing Multi-Lateral Agreements
Bureau of Oceans and International Environmental
and Scientific Affairs
Department of State
2201 C St., NW, Room 5806
Washington, DC 20520   (202) 647-2335

This office negotiates fishing agreements with countries who want to fish within the U.S. economic zone, along with agreements with countries within whose zone the U.S. would like to fish. They are also responsible for multi-lateral agreements dealing with fishing on the high seas, with particular attention to conservation issues. Information is available on these agreements and on fishery concerns in general.

* Fishing Vessels International Claims
Assistant Legal Advisor for International Claims
Office of the Legal Advisor

Department of State
2201 C St., NW
Washington, DC 20520   (202) 832-7810

The Fishermen's Protective Act provides for reimbursement for financial loss to owners of vessels registered in the United States for fines paid to secure the release of vessels seized for operation in waters not recognized as territorial waters by the United States. No registration or payment of premiums is required prior to the seizure in order to qualify for reimbursement.

* Foreign Fish Catches

Office of International Affairs
National Marine Fisheries Service
National Oceanic and Atmospheric Administration
Department of Commerce
1335 East-West Hwy. , Room 7624
Silver Spring, MD 20910   (301) 427-2272

For information regarding foreign fishing catches (allocations) or foreign fisheries in general contact the Office of International Affairs.

* High Seas Law Enforcement

Operational Law Enforcement Division
Office of Law Enforcement and Defense Operations
U.S. Coast Guard
U.S. Department of Transportation
2100 2nd St., SW, Room 3110
Washington, DC 20593-0001   (202) 267-1890

As the primary maritime law enforcement agency for the U.S., the Coast Guard enforces Federal laws, treaties, and international agreements to which the U.S. is a party. The Coast Guard may conduct investigations when violations are suspected, such as smuggling, drug trafficking, or polluting. Empowered to board and inspect vessels routinely as well, the Guard also conducts :"suspicionless" boardings to prevent violations. To report suspicious or questionable activity on boats, or to complain about an improperly conducted boarding, call the Boating Safety Hotline, (800) 368-5647; or (202) 267-0780 in D.C., or contact your local Coast Guard commander. The office listed above can provide you with information about the Coast Guard's law enforcement role and the National Narcotics Border Indiction System, which coordinates multi-agency and international operations with other countries to suppress narcotics trafficking.

* International Marine Environmental Efforts

Environmental Coordination Branch
Marine Environmental Response Division
Office of Marine, Safety, Security, and Environmental Protection
U.S. Coast Guard
U.S. Department of Transportation
2100 2nd St., SW, Room 1202
Washington, DC 20593-0001   (202) 267-0421

Information is available here on the Coast Guard's role in international marine environmental efforts, such as representation in the U.N. International Maritime Consultative Organization. For further information on cooperative environmental efforts, contact the branch listed.

* Marine Advisory Service

National Sea-Grant College Program
National Oceanic and Atmospheric Administration
Department of Commerce
1335 East-West Hwy.
Silver Spring, MD 20910   (202) 377-8090

Operated through the Sea-Grant Colleges, the marine advisory service consists of agents and specialists who are experts in areas such as seafood technology, marine economics, coastal engineering, commercial fishing, recreation, and communications. These specialists provide a link between the people who live and work in coastal areas and researchers in the universities. They sponsor workshops, conferences, and seminars on marine issues for the public and representatives of industry and government agencies. They talk to high school science classes, as well as publish bulletins, fact sheets, newsletters, technical papers, and audio-visual materials concerning marine affairs. The following is a list of Sea-Grant Colleges, and people you can contact for more information.

* Maritime Affairs

Office of Maritime and Land Transport
Department of State
2021 C St., NW, Room 5826
Washington, DC 20520   (202) 647-5840

This office is involved with all matters concerning maritime affairs, including unions, shipping regulations, the exporting and importing of cargo, and rights of passage. They also take part in the negotiations and agreements on these issues and monitor them to make sure the agreements are followed.

* Marine Environmental Information

Pollution Response Branch
Marine Environmental Response Division
Office of Marine Safety, Security,
and Environmental Protection
U.S. Coast Guard
U.S. Department of Transportation
2100 2nd St., SW, Room 2104
Washington, DC 20593-0001   (202) 267-0518, (202) 267-2611

This office responds to requests for marine environmental protection information from Congress and other federal agencies, state agencies, schools, industries, and the general public. Data is available on laws relating to the protection of the marine environment, incidents involving releases of oil or other hazardous substances, and federally funded spill response operations.

* Marine Mammals Protection Enforcement

Office of Protected Resources
National Marine Fisheries Service
National Oceanic and Atmospheric Administration
Department of Commerce
1335 East-West Hwy.
Silver Spring, MD 20910   (301) 427-2322

The Marine Mammal Protection Act commits the United States to long-term management and research programs to conserve and protect these animals. Marine mammals may be taken for scientific research, public display, and incidentally to commercial fishing. The National Marine Fisheries Service grants or denies requests for exemptions, issues permits, carries out research and management programs, enforces the Act, participates in international programs, and issues rules and regulations to carry out its mission to conserve and protect marine mammals. An annual report is available for the Office of Protected Resources, which gives detailed information regarding the activities of the Office. This office can also provide you with copies of the Act, and two publications: *First Aid For Stranded Marine Mammals*, and *Proceedings of the Workshop to Review and Evaluate Whale Watching Programs and Management Needs*.

* Marine Pollutants

Office of Oceanography and Marine Assessments
National Ocean Service
National Oceanic and Atmospheric Administration
Department of Commerce
6001 Executive Blvd.
Rockville, MD 20852   (301) 443-8487

This office surveys and monitors the oceans, U.S. coastal waters and the Great Lakes to produce data and information products that are critically important for offshore oil and gas exploration, dredging operations, coastal and offshore construction, seafloor mining, waste disposal management, and for protecting the marine environment from the adverse effects of ocean and coastal pollution.

* Mariners Weather Log

National Oceanographic Data Center
National Oceanic and Atmospheric Administration
Universal Building Room 412
Washington, DC 20235   (202) 673-5549

The Mariners Weather Log is a unique source of information on marine weather and climate and their effects on operations at sea. Published quarterly by the National Oceanographic Data Center, the *Mariners Weather Log* provides comprehensive coverage of major storms of the North Atlantic and North Pacific, reports and annual summaries on tropical cyclones, information on the National Weather Service's Marine Observation Program, selected shipboard gale and wave observations, and general articles about weather and climate, hazards and safety precautions, and related marine lore. An annual subscription is available for $6 from the Superintendent of Documents, Government Printing Office, Washington, D.C. 20402; (202)783-3238.

* Marine Technology

Library
Coast Guard Research and Development Center
U.S. Coast Guard
U.S. Department of Transportation
Avery Point
Groton, CT 06340-6096   (203) 441-2648

Marine research is conducted here in areas such as ice technology, navigation instrumentation technology, ocean dumping surveillance, pollution, search and rescue techniques, and marine fire and safety technology. This library is a good starting point for obtaining specific information about what research is done by the Center and for referrals to appropriate experts.

* Marine Technology Society

2000 Florida Avenue, NW
Suite 500
Washington, DC 20009   (202) 462-7557

This non-profit organization is dedicated to providing information about marine science and engineering. It is divided into 14 geographical sections in the U.S.

Business and Industry

and Canada, and each section holds monthly meetings, at which brief technical presentations are given. The Society has 31 professional committees that sponsor technical conferences, workshops, and short courses that are open to members and nonmembers. The staff can provide you with technical information and referrals. The Society publishes the *Journal of the Marine Technology Society*, a quarterly publication that presents technical activities of the Society, papers, conferences summaries, book reviews, and so on. It is available free of charge to members and for $5 for nonmembers.

* Maritime Trade Statistics

Trade Analysis Division (MAR-570)
Office of Trade and Analysis and Insurance
Maritime Administration
U.S. Department of Transportation
400 7th Street, SW
Washington, DC 20590   (202) 366-2282

Records on federally subsidized shipping companies are maintained by this Division. Information includes vessel name, port dates, and crew costs. The public can visit the document inspection room or write for information.

* Nautical Charts

Chart Distribution Branch
National Ocean Service
National Oceanic and Atmospheric Administration
Department of Commerce
Riverdale, MD 20737   (301) 436-6990

The National Ocean Service produces approximately 1,000 nautical charts for navigation in U.S. estuarine waters and navigable inland waterways, the Great Lakes, and the 2 1/2 million square miles of coastal waters of the United States and its possessions. NOAA *Chart and Map Catalogs* describe nautical charts which are listed in a series of four catalogs, one for each region of the U.S. ocean and coastal waters. NOAA bathymetric maps and special purpose charts are listed in a single catalog. A sixth catalog is a guide to NOAA nautical products and services. The catalogs contain a brief description of each nautical chart, bathymetric map, special purpose chart, and chart-related publication produced by the NOS. They also include the price of the chart of publication, other information needed to select and order nautical charting products, and a list of NOAA chart sales facilities and authorized commercial chart sales agents. Contact this office for your free catalogs.

* Oceanographic Data and Publications

National Oceanic and Atmospheric Administration
Department of Commerce
1825 Connecticut Ave., NW
Washington, DC 20235   (202) 673-5549

The National Oceanographic Data Center has a free publications list which includes technical reports and bulletins, as well has a variety of data reports pertaining to oceanographic research.

* Oceanographic Information

National Oceanographic Data Center
National Environmental Satellite, Data
and Information Service
National Oceanic and Atmospheric Administration
Department of Commerce
1825 Connecticut Ave., NW
Washington, DC 20235   (202) 673-5549

The National Oceanographic Data Center provides global coverage of oceanographic data and services. NODC's databases cover physical and chemical properties of the world's oceans, seas, and estuaries, plus information on selected continental shelf and coastal waters. Researchers using NODC data range from industrial scientists through local, state, and national government investigators, to university or academic personnel. Information is available in various forms: publications computer plots, computer printouts, magnetic tapes and floppy disks. Simple questions usually can be answered without charge by telephone or mail, but more complicated ones requiring research or computer processing usually carry a fee.

* Oceanographic Corps Jobs

Commission Personnel Division
NOAA Corps
National Oceanic and Atmospheric Administration
Department of Commerce
11400 Rockville Pike
Rockville, MD 20852   (301) 443-8616

The NOAA Corps is the uniformed service of the Department of Commerce responsible for operating and managing NOAA's fleet of hydrographic, oceanographic, and fisheries-research ships and for supporting NOAA scientific programs. Engineering, computer science, mathematics, and science baccalaureate or higher degree graduates are sought for positions in the Corps.

* Ocean Pollution Information Network

Ocean Pollution Data and
Information Network/ CCRO
National Oceanographic Data Center
National Oceanic and Atmospheric Administration
1825 Connecticut Ave., NW
Washington, DC 20235   (202) 673-5539

The Ocean Pollution Data and Information Network facilitates user access to ocean pollution data and information generated by 11 participating Federal departments and agencies. OPDIN provides a wide range of products and services to researchers, managers, and others who need data and information about ocean pollution. OPDIN is managed by the Central Coordination and Referral Office (CCRO). The CCRO maintains a directory of Federal ocean pollution data and information systems and services, lists of ocean pollution scientists and managers and their fields of expertise, and annually-updated catalogs of Federal marine pollution research, development, and monitoring projects. The CCRO also provides information and advice about ocean pollution data management and processing, as well as copies of catalogs, directories, technical reports, data inventories, and data products.

* Oil and Chemical Spills Hotline

National Response Center (NRC)
Marine Environmental Response Division
Office of Marine Safety, Security, and Environmental Protection
U.S. Coast Guard
U.S. Department of Transportation
2100 2nd St., SW, Room 2611   (800) 424-8802
Washington, DC 20593   (202) 267-2188

The NRC receives reports of oil and hazardous substance spills, investigates incidents, initiates civil penalty actions, monitors cleanups, and coordinates federally funded spill response operations. NRC's National Strike Force assists federal coordinators on the scene in responding to pollution accidents. For further details, or to report information, contact the Center toll-free.

* Panama Canal Dredging

Engineering and Construction Bureau
Dredging Division
c/o Panama Canal Commission
APO Miami, FL 34011-5000   (507) 52-4500

The Dredging Division is responsible for maintenance and construction dredging; slide removal; inspection and maintenance of the Atlantic breakwater; operation and maintenance of navigational aids; the detection, containment, recovery, and disposal of oil pollution in Canal operating areas; and the removal and control of aquatic weeds through the use of chemical and biological means. For more information on the dredging operations, contact this office.

* Panama Canal Economic and Market Research

Economic Research and Market Development Division
The Office of Executive Planning
c/o Panama Canal Commission
APO Miami 34011-5000   (507) 52-7961

As an agency of the U.S. Government, the Panama Canal Commission has a legal obligation to operate on a break-even basis, recovering all costs of operating, maintaining, and improving the Canal through tolls revenue. The agency tries to have a high standard of service at the lowest possible cost. As a reflection of this, toll rates have gone up only four times since the Canal opened in 1914. Operating costs are very carefully controlled so that it provides an economic advantage to world trade on many routes. Even if other world trade routes may be shorter in distance, the Canal remains competitive because of its reliable, cost-effective service. For more information on operating costs, contact this office.

* Panama Canal Traffic Data

Economic Research and Market Development Division
The Office of Executive Planning
c/o Panama Canal Commission
APO Miami 34011-5000   (507) 52-7961

The Panama Canal is a vital link in the world transportation chain. A large share of world trade passes through the Canal over any of the world's major trade routes. In 1988, 156.5 million long tons of cargo moved through the Canal aboard 12,318 oceangoing vessels. More than 690,962 vessels have crossed the waterway, carrying more than 4 billion long tons of the world's goods from one ocean to the other. For more information or compilations of Canal traffic data, contact this office.

* Panama Canal Vessel Emergency Response Management

Marine Director
Marine Bureau
c/o Panama Canal Commission
APO Miami, FL 34011-5000   (507) 52-4500

For information on marine operations including inspections, piloting, locks, traffic management, canal services, marine safety, canal operations and maritime training, contact this Bureau. The Commission's marine risk management team is devoted to the prevention of and response to accidents involving vessels carrying hazardous cargoes. The team consists of an experienced fireman, a licensed marine engineer, a safety generalist, an experienced chemist, and lead by an experienced active duty U.S. Coast Guard officer. This team is also responsible for updating the Commission's Vessel Emergency Response Plan and in conducting vessel emergency training exercises.

* Port Regulations

Port Safety and Security Division
Office of Marine Safety, Security, and Environmental Protection
U.S. Coast Guard
U.S. Department of Transportation
2100 2nd St., SW, Room 1104
Washington, DC 20593-0001   (202) 267-0489

Coast Guard Captains of the Port enforce rules and regulations concerning the safety and security of ports and the anchorage and movement of vessels. This includes supervising cargo transfers and storage; conducting harbor patrols and facility inspections; establishing security zones; and surveying to prevent water pollution. The Division also administers a licensing and registration program for deepwater ports transferring oil from tankers to shore via pipelines. For information on regulations and operations, contact the division listed.

* Protection of Ships From Seizure

Assistant Legal Advisor for International Claims
Office of the Legal Advisor
Department of State
2201 C St., NW
Washington, DC 20520   (202) 832-7810

The Fishermen's Protective Act provides for reimbursement for financial loss to owners of vessels registered in the United States for fines paid to secure the release of vessels seized for operation in waters not recognized as territorial waters by the United States. No registration or payment of premiums is required prior to the seizure in order to qualify for reimbursement.

* Saint Lawrence Seaway Statistics

Office of Trade and Traffic Development
Saint Lawrence Seaway Development Corporation
400 7th Street, SW, Room 5424
Washington, DC 20590   (202) 366-0091

This office keeps statistics on traffic in the Great Lakes/Seaway system. Data is recorded on the number of vessels and their size, type, cargo, and nationality. Cargo vessel statistics are published in the *Annual Traffic Report in the Saint Lawrence Seaway*.

* Saint Lawrence Seaway Publications

Public Affairs Office
Saint Lawrence Seaway Development Corporation
U.S. Department of Transportation
180 Andrews Street
Massena, NY 13662-1763   (315) 764-3232

Free publications about the Seaway are available by contacting this office. Some of the titles available include the following:

Annual Traffic Report in the Saint Lawrence Seaway. Cargo vessel statistics for traffic between Montreal and Lake Erie.
Pleasure Craft Guide: The Seaway. Information on boating in the St. Lawrence River.
The Saint Lawrence Seaway. General and historical information in French and English, including port data, schedules, and tourist information.
The Saint Lawrence Seaway Annual Report.
Seaway Regulations. Includes regulations and toll schedule, operating manual, and chart booklet.

* Sea-Grant Colleges

Office of Oceanic Research Programs
National Oceanic and Atmospheric Administration
Department of Commerce
1335 East-West Hwy.
Silver Spring, MD 20910   (202) 377-8090

The National Sea Grant College Program is a national network of over 300 colleges, universities, research institutions, and consortia working in partnership with industry and the federal government to support Great Lakes and marine research, education, and extension services. This program provides support for institutions engaged in comprehensive marine research, education, and advisory service programs, supports individual projects in marine research and development, and sponsors education of ocean scientists and engineers, marine technicians, and other specialists at selected colleges and universities.

* Sea Grant Depository

National Sea Grant Depository
Pell Library Building
University of Rhode Island
Bay Campus
Narragansett, RI 02882   (401) 792-6114

The National Sea Grant Depository is a clearinghouse for all Sea Grant publications. The scope of the collection includes a wide variety of marine topics, such as oceanography, marine education, aquaculture, fisheries, coastal zone management, recreation, and law. The collection includes journal reprints, technical and advisory reports, books, manuals, directories, annual reports, conference proceedings, and newsletters. The Depository provides reference and online search services, and welcomes telephone, mail and inter-library loan requests. The Depository will loan documents, but does not distribute the publications (they refer you to the authors). A quarterly publication, *Sea Grant Abstracts*, includes abstracts of all the new publications received by the Depository. Contact the Depository for more information.

* Ship Construction

Office of Ship Construction (MAR-720)
Maritime Administration
U.S. Department of Transportation
400 7th Street, SW, Room 6422
Washington, DC 20590   (202) 366-1880

Contact this office for information on the cost of and market for shipbuilding. The difference between the cost of constructing ships here and abroad are also examined.

* Small Passenger Vessel Safety

Marine Inspection Office
Your Local Coast Guard Office

Most small passenger vessels (less than 100 tons and carrying more than 6 people) are required to adhere to certain Coast Guard safety regulations. These include having a safety orientation procedure for passengers (announcement or placard), posting of emergency instructions, a life preserver for every person on board, and a Coast Guard safety certification. Marine Inspection Offices around the country issue the certificates. To find an Inspection Office near you, or to report a violation or complaint, call the Boating Safety Hotline (800) 368-5647; or (202) 267-0780 in D.C.

* Sockeye Odyssey and Other Films

National Oceanic and Atmospheric Administration
Department of Commerce
14th St. and Pennsylvania Ave., NW
Room 6013
Washington, DC 20230   (202) 377-8090

A brochure is available which lists motion picture films produced by the National Oceanic and Atmospheric Administration. Most NOAA productions are available in both motion picture and video formats. Unless noted, these films are not available directly from NOAA. To borrow prints without charge, except for return postage, write to: Modern Talking Pictures, 6000 Park Street North, St., Petersburg, FL 33709. These films are heavily booked, so you must send your request as early as possible. The following is a list of their titles:

Sockeye Odyssey
The Awesome Power
The Great American Fish Story
The Great American Fish Story- The West
The Great American Fish Story- The Northeast
The Great American Fish Story- The South
The Great American Fish Story- The Lakes and Rivers
Down to the Monitor
Estuary
*FAMOUS- Boundary of Creation**
*Give Me The Tides**
Global Weather Experiment
*Longlines: An Undersea Investigation**
NOAA Corps- The Seventh Service
Trashing The Oceans

*Available directly from NOAA. Contact the office listed above for a free catalog.

* Updates for Mariners

District Commander
Your local Coast Guard Office

The free *Local Notice to Mariners* is issued weekly by each Coast Guard District. Intended for small craft owners, it advises you of changes in the status of aids to navigation (buoys, radiobeacons, etc.); chart updates; drawbridge operations; and safety warnings for particular areas. This *Local Notice* often includes temporary changes not included in the Defense Mapping Agency's *Notice to Mariners*. To order a subscription for the *Local Notice*, send a written request to the District

Business and Industry

Commander of your local Coast Guard office. For referral to the correct address, call the Boating Safety Hotine (800) 368-5647; or (202) 267-0780 in D.C.

* U.S. Merchant Marine Academy

U.S. Merchant Marine Academy
Maritime Administration
U.S. Department of Transportation-Kings Point
Long Island, NY 11024   (516) 773-5000

Future merchant marine officers are trained here in navigation instrumentation, ship maneuvering, ship management, and communications. The Academy also administers a Federal assistance program for maritime academies in California, Maine, Massachusetts, Michigan, New York, and Texas.

* War Risk Insurance for Ships

Marine Insurance Division
Office of Trade and Analysis and Insurance
Maritime Administration
U.S. Department of Transportation

400 7th Street, SW, Room 8121
Washington, DC 20590   (202) 366-4161

The War Risk Insurance Program insures operators and seamen against losses from hostile action if commercial insurance is not available to them. The program covers loss of life and materials due to war or nuclear detonation.

* Waterways Traffic Regulation

Commander G-NSP
Vessel Traffic Services Branch
Office of Navigation Safety and Waterways Services
U.S. Coast Guard
U.S. Department of Transportation
2100 2nd St., SW, Room 1410
Washington, DC 20593-0001   (202) 267-0407

To ensure the safe and orderly passage of vessels, cargo, and people, Vessel Traffic Services in major ports oversee the movement of vessels and install necessary safety equipment. Traffic is monitored closely during hazardous conditions and bad weather. To locate the Vessel Traffic Service nearest you, contact the branch listed above or your local Coast Guard office.

Mining

* Abandoned Mine Land Reclamation
Office of Surface Mining Reclamation and Enforcement
U.S. Department of the Interior
1951 Constitution Ave., NW
Washington, DC 20240   (202) 343-5365
The surface mining law requires that operators pay a reclamation fee for each ton of coal produced. These fees are deposited with the U.S. Treasury in a fund called the Abandoned Mine Reclamation Fund and are used to reclaim sites that were mined and left unreclaimed before the surface mining law was enacted in 1977. Fifty percent of the fees collected in a state that has approved reclamation and regulatory programs is returned to that state for use in its reclamation program. The other fifty percent is the Federal share. This portion is used by the Office of Surface Mining Reclamation and Enforcement to address public health and safety emergencies caused by past mining practices, and to fund high-priority reclamation projects in non-program states. To obtain your state contact for the abandoned mine land reclamation program, contact the office above.

* Bureau of Mines Field Facilities
Bureau of Mines
U.S. Department of the Interior
2401 E St., NW
Washington, DC 20241   (202) 634-1004

Alabama
Tuscaloosa Research Center, University of Alabama Campus, P.O. Box L, Tuscaloosa, AL 35486; (205) 759-9440

Alaska
Alaska Field Operations Center, 201 E. 9th Ave., Suite 101, Anchorage, AK 99501; (907) 271-2454

Colorado
Intermountain Field Operations Center, P.O. Box 25086, Building 20, Denver Federal Center, Denver, CO 80225; (303) 236-0421
Minerals Availability Field Office, Building 20, Denver Federal Center, Denver, CO 80225; (303) 236-5200
Denver Research Center, P.O. Box 25086, Building 20, Denver Federal Center, Denver, CO 80225; (303) 236-0697

Minnesota
Twin Cities Research Center, 5629 Minnehaha Ave. S., Minneapolis, MN 55417; (612) 725-4610

Missouri
Rolla Research Center, P.O. Box 280, 1300 Bishop Ave., Rolla, MO 65401; (314) 364-3169

Nevada
Reno Research Center, 1605 Evans Ave., Reno, NV 89512; (702) 784-5261

Oregon
Research Center, 1450 Queen Ave., SW, Albany, OR 97321; (503) 967-5893

Pennsylvania
Pittsburgh Research Center, Cochrans Mill Rd, P.O. Box 18070, Pittsburgh, PA 15236; (412) 892-6601

Texas
Helium Field Operations, 1100 South Fillmore, Amarillo, TX 79101; (806) 376-2602

Utah
Salt Lake City Research Center, 729 Arapeen Dr., Salt Lake City, UT 84108; (801) 524-6100

Washington
Spokane Research Center, E 315 Montgomery Ave., Spokane, WA 99207; (509) 484-1610
Western Field Operations Center, E. 360 Third Ave., Spokane, WA 99202; (509) 456-7905

* Minerals Management Service Field Offices

Atlantic Region
381 Elden St., Suite 1109, Herndon, VA 22070-4817; (703) 787-1113

Alaska Region
949 E. 36th Ave., Suite 604, Anchorage, AK 99508-4302; (907) 261-4070

Gulf of Mexico Region
1201 Elmwood Park Blvd., New Orleans, LA 70123-2394; (504) 736-2595

Pacific Region
1340 W. 6th St., Los Angeles, CA 90017; (213) 894-3389

Rocky Mountains
Royalty Management Program Accounting Center and Central Service Center, 6th Ave. and Kipling St., Bldg. 85, Lakewood, CO 80225; (303) 231-3162

* Bureau of Mines State Activities Directory
Chief, Office of State Activities
Bureau of Mines
U.S. Department of the Interior
2401 E St., NW
Washington, DC 20241   (202) 634-1107
The following offices are sources of information on state mineral activity:

Alaska
Regional Office of State Activities, Bureau of Mines, U.S. Department of the Interior, P.O. Box 550, Juneau, AK 99802-0550; (907) 364-2111

Denver
Regional Office of State Activities, Bureau of Mines, U.S. Department of the Interior, Denver Federal Center, Bldg. #20, P.O. Box 25086, Denver, CO 80225-0086; (303) 236-0435

Pittsburgh
Regional Office of State Activities, Bureau of Mines, U.S. Department of the Interior, Cochrans Mill Rd., P.O. Box 18070, Pittsburgh, PA 15236-0070; (412) 892-4423/(412) 892-4422

Reno
Regional Office of State Activities, Bureau of Mines, U.S. Department of the Interior, Reno Research Center, 1605 Evans Ave., Reno, NV 89512-2295; (702) 784-5215

Spokane
Regional Office of State Activities, Bureau of Mines, U.S. Department of the Interior, E. 360 Third Ave., Spokane, WA 99202-1413; (509) 353-2720

Tuscaloosa
Regional Office of State Activities, Bureau of Mines, U.S. Department of the Interior, University of Alabama Campus, P.O. Box L, University, AL 35486-9777; (205) 759-9465; (205) 759-9466

Tucson
Regional Office of State Activities, Bureau of Mines, U.S. Department of the Interior, 210 E. 7th St., Tucson, AZ 85705-8454; (602) 629-5111

Twin Cities
Regional Office of State Activities, Bureau of Mines, U.S. Department of the Interior, 5629 Minnehaha Ave., S., Minneapolis, MN 55417-3099; (612) 725-4534; (612) 725-4535

* Bureau of Mines Publications
Superintendent of Documents
Government Printing Office
Washington, DC 20420   (202) 783-3238
Publications of the Bureau of Mines in an annotated bibliography of new publications by the Bureau of Mines. Included in this monthly flyer are listings of free publications, open file reports, and outside publications available concerning the mineral industry. The annual subscription price is $11.00, and the single copy price is $1.00 (S/N 724-004-00000-8).

* Bureau of Reclamation Regional Offices
Bureau of Mines
U.S. Department of Interior
1951 Constitution Avenue, NW
Washington, DC 20240   (202) 343-4953
Here are the regional offices which enforce strip mining and reclamation laws:

Business and Industry

Lower Colorado Region: Box 427, Nevada Hwy. and Park St., Boulder City, NV 89005; (702) 293-8420

Mid-Pacific Region
2800 Cottage Way, Sacramento, CA 95825; (916) 978-4919

Pacific Northwest Region
Box 043, 550 W. Fort St., Boise, ID 83724; (208) 334-1938

Upper Colorado Region
Box 11568, 125 S. State St., Salt Lake City, UT 84147; (801) 524-5403

Great Plains Region
Box 36900, 316 N. 26th St., Billings, MT 59107; (406) 657-6218

* Census of Minerals Industries Bibliography
Superintendent of Documents
Government Printing Office
Washington, DC 20402 (202) 783-3238
The Census of Mineral Industries, 1987, Geographic Series is featured in this bibliography, as well as the Industry Series subscription service.

* Claims on Federal Lands
Energy and Mineral Resources
Bureau of Land Management
U.S. Department of the Interior
18th and C Sts., NW
Washington, DC 20240 (202) 343-4201
The brochure, *Staking a Mining Claim on Federal Lands*, describes the procedure you would follow to stake a mining claim on public lands. Claims are granted to individuals for particular pieces of land, valuable for specific mineral deposits. Questions concerning the definition of a mining claim and the technicalities of recording and maintaining mining claims are also covered.

* Coal Ash Producers
American Coal Ash Association
1000 16th St., NW
Suite 507
Washington, DC 20036 (202) 659-2303
This association is comprised by companies which are producers of fly ash from the combustion of coal and are interested in promoting its use.

* Coal Mining and Environmental Protection
Office of Public Affairs
Office of Surface Mining Reclamation and Enforcement
1951 Constitution Avenue, NW
Washington, DC 20240 (202) 343-4953
This office works to protect people and the environment from the side-effects of coal mining, while continuing to regulate coal mining. Lands that were affected by past coal mining operations must be repaired if left unreclaimed or abandoned. Technical assistance is provided to states so that they can perform their responsibilities under the surface mining law. State personnel are trained in the technical aspects of surface mining, such as soil compaction, revegetation, and groundwater hydrology, so that they can better enforce regulations.

* Deep Seabed Mining
Ocean Minerals and Energy Division
National Ocean Service
National Oceanic and Atmospheric Administration
Department of Commerce
1825 Connecticut Ave., NW
Washington, DC 20235 (202) 673-5121
Extensive information is available on deep seabed mining, which includes the annual report to Congress and an updated environmental assessment of NOAA deep seabed mining licensees' exploration plans. This office can provide you with information regarding the research conducted concerning the environmental impact of the mining, as well as information on the regulations and licenses.

* Energy and Mineral Resources
Office of Energy and Marine Geology
U.S. Geological Survey
National Center, MS 915
Reston, VA 22092 (703) 648-6470
Investigations of the nature, extent, and origin of the Nation's coal, oil and gas, oil shale, uranium, and geothermal resources are basic to this office's research efforts. Acquired data are placed in computerized databases, such as the National Coal Resources Data System.
Environmental Mining Research

* Environmental Technology Division
Bureau of Mines
U.S. Department of the Interior
2401 E St., NW
Washington, DC 20241 (202) 634-1263
Researchers at the Bureau of Mines are working on low-cost ways to deal with the problem of acid drainage at abandoned mines. They are developing computer programs to predict potential drainage at new mines. The Bureau's environmental research also addresses the problem of solid waste disposal and soil and water contaminated by metals. Technologies are developed that will reduce or remove the threats that these wastes pose.

* Films on the Mining Industry
Office of Technology Transfer
Bureau of Mines
U.S. Department of the Interior
2401 E St., NW, MS 6201
Washington, DC 20241 (202) 634-1224
This office publishes a listing of films and videos on topics related to the mineral industry. Topics include safer coal mining equipment, mine shaft smoke and fire protection system, and a retractable diamond bit system for core drilling, among others. All of the films and videos may be purchased or can be borrowed free of charge.

* Gold Prospecting
Publications Department
Bureau of Mines
U.S. Department of the Interior
18th and C Sts., NW, Room 2647
Washington, DC 20240 (202) 343-5520
The publications department of the Bureau of Mines distributes the free booklet, *How To Mine and Prospect for Gold.*

* Indian Lands and Minerals
Office of Trust and Economic Development
Bureau of Indian Affairs
U.S. Department of the Interior
18th and C Sts., NW
Washington, DC 20240 (202) 343-5831
This office manages some 53 million acres of land held in trust by the United States for Indians. Tribes are helped in protecting their lands and in developing their forest, water, mineral, and energy resources.

* International Mineral Data
Superintendent of Documents
Government Printing Office
Washington, DC 20402 (202) 783-3238
The *Minerals Yearbook, 1985: Volume 111 (Area Reports: International)* contains the latest available mineral data from more than 150 foreign countries and discusses the importance of minerals to the economies of these nations. It reviews the international minerals industry in general and its relationship to the world economy. 1987 (S/N 024-004-02179-9, $36.00).

* Materials Research: Wear and Corrosion
Research Division
Bureau of Mines
U.S. Department of the Interior
2401 E St., NW
Washington, DC 20241 (202) 634-1210
Advanced materials research is being conducted to eliminate wear and corrosion within the minerals industry through the use of ceramics, high-performance plastics, high-tech metals and alloys, and composites. Bureau scientists are also developing new coatings to protect equipment from the heat, corrosive chemicals, and abrasive materials found in mills, smelters, refineries, and furnaces.

* Metals and Mining Producers
American Mining Congress (AMC)
1920 N St., NW
Suite 300
Washington, DC 20036 (202) 861-2800
The American Mining Congress is an industry association of producers of metals, coal industrial and agricultural minerals; manufacturers of mining and mineral processing machinery, equipment and supplies; and mining engineering firms. Publications: *American Mining Congress Journal.*

* Mine Map Repositories
Office of Public Affairs
Surface Mining Reclamation and Enforcement
U.S. Department of the Interior

1951 Constitution Ave., NW
Washington, DC 20240 (202) 343-4953

The Mine Map Repositories were established in 1970 and are responsible for collecting and archiving mine maps both east and west of the Mississippi River and in Alaska. The brochure, *Mine Map Repositories*, provides information and statistics on the mine map repository facilities of the Office of Surface Mining Reclamation and Enforcement. The five repositories are listed with their addresses and phone numbers. They are located in Pittsburgh, PA, Wilkes-Barre, PA, Denver, CO, Spokane, WA, and Juneau, AK.

* Mineral Resource Films

Audiovisual Library
Office of Public Affairs
Bureau of Mines
U.S. Department of the Interior
2401 E St., NW
Washington, DC 20241 (202) 343-5512

This office's brochure, *Mineral Resource Films*, lists information on borrowing and scheduling films and videocassettes, along with National distribution centers. Films available cover such topics as copper, cast iron, silver, mine fire control, the minerals challenge, wealth out of waste, tungsten, lead, boron, gold, and platinum.

* Mine Companies and Property Ownership Maps

Division of Program Information and Analysis
Surface Mining Reclamation and Enforcement
U.S. Department of the Interior
1951 Constitution Ave., NW
Washington, DC 20240 (202) 343-5907

Valuable information is available from the mine maps available through the mine map repositories of the Office of Surface Mining Reclamation and Enforcement. Mine and company names, water sources, property ownership of adjoining companies and towns, latitudes and longitudes, coal outcrop seam designations, openings and emergency exits of mines, and gas and power lines are some of the topics covered. This information can be useful to local developers, engineering firms, and energy interests, as well as private citizens.

* Mine Map Repositories

Office of Public Affairs
Surface Mining Reclamation and Enforcement
U.S. Department of the Interior
1951 Constitution Ave., NW
Washington, DC 20240 (202) 343-4953

The Mine Map Repositories were established in 1970 and are responsible for collecting and archiving mine maps both east and west of the Mississippi River and in Alaska. The brochure, *Mine Map Repositories*, provides information and statistics on the mine map repository facilities of the Office of Surface Mining Reclamation and Enforcement. The five repositories are listed with their addresses and phone numbers. They are located in Pittsburgh, PA, Wilkes-Barre, PA, Denver, CO, Spokane, WA, and Juneau, AK.

* Mine Maps

Division of Program Information and Analysis
Surface Mining Reclamation and Enforcement
U.S. Department of the Interior
1951 Constitution Ave., NW
Washington, DC 20240 (202) 343-5907

Valuable information is available from the mine maps available through the mine map repositories of the Office of Surface Mining Reclamation and Enforcement. Mine and company names, water sources, property ownership of adjoining companies and towns, latitudes and longitudes, coal outcrop seam designations, openings and emergency exits of mines, and gas and power lines are some of the topics covered. This information can be useful to local developers, engineering firms, and energy interests, as well as private citizens.

* Mineral Commodity Summaries 1989

Minerals Information Office
Bureau of Mines/U.S. Geological Survey
U.S. Department of the Interior
18th and C Sts., MS 2647-MIB
Room 2647
Washington, DC 20240 (202) 343-5520

Mineral Commodity Summaries 1989 lists the statistics available for 82 commodities, including domestic production and uses; salient statistics - United States; recycling; import sources; tariff; depletion allowance; government stockpile; events and trends; world mine production, reserves and reserve base; world resources; and substitutes. The expert's name and phone number of each report is also listed.

* Mineral Commodity Information

Minerals Information Office
Bureau of Mines/U.S. Geological Survey
U.S. Department of the Interior
18th and C Sts., MS 2647-MIB
Room 2647
Washington, DC 20240 (202) 343-5520

The Minerals Information Office is staffed by mineral experts who distribute a wide variety of mineral-related information and publications to meet and support the needs of the public, as well as government agencies and the scientific and industrial sectors. The staff provides information on the most current as well as past published reports pertaining to minerals, mining, processing, and research, as well as updated listings of current reports.

* Mineral Deposits Database

Minerals Information Office
Bureau of Mines/U.S. Geological Survey
U.S. Department of the Interior
18th and C Sts., MS 2647-MIB
Room 2647
Washington, DC 20240 (202) 343-5520

The *Personal Computer Advanced Deposit Information Tracking System Mineral Deposit Data Base* contains information on 3,000 domestic and foreign (market economy countries) mining operations, including operation data (name, company, locations, etc.) and operation status (operation type, processing and milling methods, capacity, etc.). The database covers 34 critical and strategic commodities, representing those deposits most significant in terms of value and tonnage.

* Mineral Deposits Distribution

Mineral Resources
Geologic Inquiries
U.S. Geological Survey
907 National Center
Reston, VA 22092 (703) 648-4383

The U.S.Geological Survey assesses the distribution of the mineral resources of the United States, especially strategic and critical commodities, and studies the processes that control the occurrence of mineral deposits. New techniques and methods useful in the search for these resources are continually being developed.

* Mineral Commodity Information

Minerals Information Office
Bureau of Mines/U.S. Geological Survey
U.S. Department of the Interior
18th and C Sts., MS 2647-MIB
Room 2647
Washington, DC 20240 (202) 343-5520

The Minerals Information Office is staffed by mineral experts who distribute a wide variety of mineral-related information and publications to meet and support the needs of the public, as well as government agencies and the scientific and industrial sectors. The staff provides information on the most current as well as past published reports pertaining to minerals, mining, processing, and research, as well as updated listings of current reports.

* Mineral Commodity Summaries 1989

Minerals Information Office
Bureau of Mines/U.S. Geological Survey
U.S. Department of the Interior
18th and C Sts., MS 2647-MIB
Room 2647
Washington, DC 20240 (202) 343-5520

Mineral Commodity Summaries 1989 lists the statistics available for 82 commodities, including domestic production and uses; salient statistics - United States; recycling; import sources; tariff; depletion allowance; government stockpile; events and trends; world mine production, reserves and reserve base; world resources; and substitutes. The expert's name and phone number of each report is also listed.

* Mineral Policy Analysis

Policy Analysis
Information and Analysis Division
Bureau of Mines
U.S. Department of the Interior
2401 E St., NW
Washington, DC 20241 (202) 634-1292

Bureau economists prepare special studies that analyze issues involving minerals in the United States. An ongoing assessment of the Nation's "mineral position" is conducted. Specialists examine factors that affect the competitiveness of the U.S. mineral industry and its contribution to the Nation's economy. Environmental regulations are also evaluated as to their impact on U.S. mineral production.

Business and Industry

* Mineral Processing Research

Minerals and Materials Science
Bureau of Mines
U.S. Department of the Interior
2401 E St., NW
Washington, DC 20241   (292) 634-1233

This office looks for ways to improve mineral processing operations by cutting costs and recovering more minerals contained in ores. A variety of processing methods are studied, including crushing, grinding, flotation, smelting, solvent extraction, and leaching. Their research also includes long-range efforts to apply high technology to mineral processing.

* Mineral Production and Consumption

Information and Analysis Division
Bureau of Mines
U.S. Department of the Interior
2401 E St., NW
Washington, DC 20241   (202) 634-7131

The Bureau of Mines collects information about minerals from U.S. mining companies and mineral processing plants. Mineral production and consumption is monitored throughout the world through contacts with foreign governments, U.S. embassies, international publications, and visits to mines overseas. The Bureau employs 11 state mineral specialists through cooperative data collection agreements with the states. Three regional field offices and nine research centers also gather information. The data is then made available to the public via reports, books, and computer disks.

* Mineral Resource Films

Audiovisual Library
Office of Public Affairs
Bureau of Mines
U.S. Department of the Interior
2401 E St., NW
Washington, DC 20241   (202) 343-5512

This office's brochure, *Mineral Resource Films*, lists information on borrowing and scheduling films and videocassettes, along with National distribution centers. Films available cover such topics as copper, cast iron, silver, mine fire control, the minerals challenge, wealth out of waste, tungsten, lead, boron, gold, and platinum.

* Mineral Resources

Mineral Resources
Geologic Inquiries
U.S. Geological Survey
907 National Center
Reston, VA 22092   (703) 648-4383

The U.S.Geological Survey assesses the distribution of the mineral resources of the United States, especially strategic and critical commodities, and studies the processes that control the occurrence of mineral deposits. New techniques and methods useful in the search for these resources are continually being developed.

* Minerals and Mining Bibliography

Superintendent of Documents
Government Printing Office
Washington, DC 20402   (202) 783-3238

Bureau of Mines publications and mineral industry publications are featured. Books describing the coal mining industry, gold availability, and the wilderness mineral potential are included. Free.

* Minerals: Data, Industries, and Technology

Publication Distribution
Bureau of Mines
U.S. Department of the Interior
Cochrans Mills Rd.
P.O. Box 18070
Pittsburgh, PA 15236   (412) 892-4338

The Bureau of Mines publishes several reports of investigations and information circulars that are free of charge to those interested in mineral research. *Mineral Industry Surveys* are published monthly, quarterly, and annually, presenting data on various minerals and metals. Reprints from *Minerals Yearbook 1987* are available and report on the mineral industry in the United States and abroad. *Minerals Facts and Problems* covers the technology used in the extraction and processing of minerals.

* Minerals of Critical and Strategic Importance

Research Division
Bureau of Mines
U.S. Department of the Interior

2401 E St., NW
Washington, DC 20241   (202) 634-1210

An emphasis within the Bureau of Mines' Research Division is reducing the Nation's dependence on imports for certain minerals that have key defense and industrial applications. The Bureau is developing ways to recover strategic and critical minerals from mineral processing wastes and to recycle these minerals. Key minerals of this type include cobalt, chromium, manganese, and platinum.

* Minerals Management Service Field Offices

Bureau of Mines
U.S. Department of Interior
1951 Constitution Avenue, NW
Washington, DC 20240   (202) 343-4953

U.S. Department of Interior has the following regional offices:

Atlantic Region
381 Elden St., Suite 1109, Herndon, VA 22070-4817; (703) 787-1113

Alaska Region
949 E. 36th Ave., Suite 604, Anchorage, AK 99508-4302; (907) 261-4070

Gulf of Mexico Region
1201 Elmwood Park Blvd., New Orleans, LA 70123-2394; (504) 736-2595

Pacific Region
1340 W. 6th St., Los Angeles, CA 90017; (213) 894-3389

Rocky Mountains
Royalty Management Program Accounting Center and Central Service Center, 6th Ave. and Kipling St., Bldg. 85, Lakewood, CO 80225; (303) 231-3162

* Minerals Research

Research Division
Bureau of Mines
U.S. Department of the Interior
2410 E St., NW
Washington, DC 20241-0001   (202) 634-1210

Research is being conducted here to find cheaper, more efficient ways of mining and processing minerals. Robotics and advanced automation is also being researched for use in mining operations. Immediate problems in the industry are also studied, such as improvement of equipment and procedures.

* Minerals Yearbooks Bibliography

Superintendent of Documents
Government Printing Office
Washington, DC 20402   (202) 783-3238

Yearbooks on metals and minerals are listed, as well as reports on the domestic and international industry. Free.

* Mine Safety

Health, Safety, and Mining Technology
Bureau of Mines
U.S. Department of the Interior
2401 E St., NW
Washington, DC 20241   (292) 634-1251

The Bureau is studying ways to improve mine safety and to eliminate the health risks of mining. One of the areas of emphasis is finding ways to reduce a miner's exposure to respirable dust, which causes black lung and other respiratory diseases. Studies in safety precautions help companies build more stable mines with better roof support systems and more efficiently detect flammable gases and ignition sources. Research on automation and robotics to do the more hazardous jobs is also being done.

* Mines Library

Bureau of Mines
U.S. Department of the Interior
2401 E St., NW, Room 127
Washington, DC 20241   (202) 634-1116

The Bureau of Mines' Library contains a wealth of technical information involving the mineral industry. Reference librarians are available to answer questions by phone or mail. Topics include state and county mineral data, mineral supply and demand analysis, congressional reports pertaining to minerals, oil and gas reports, and market studies. Free mineral publications published by the Bureau of Mines are also available. The hours of the library are 7:45 a.m. to 4:15 p.m., Monday through Friday.

* Mines Technology Transfer

Office of Technology Transfer
Bureau of Mines
U.S. Department of the Interior

2401 E St., NW, MS 6201
Washington, DC 20241   (202) 634-1224
The Technology Transfer Group distributes information on mining industry issues in many ways. *Technology Transfer* is a newsletter announcing the latest technology and research in mining. Free conferences are also held around the country on a variety of topics, such as advanced materials research and new technology for minerals. To be placed on the mailing list, contact the office above.

* Mining and Prospecting On Public Land
Minerals and Geology Mgmt.
U.S. Department of Agriculture
Forest Service, Box 96090
Washington, DC 20090-6090   (703) 235-8010
Since passage of the Mining Law of 1872, qualified prospectors have been allowed to search for mineral deposits on public domain lands.

* Offshore Geologic Resources
Geologic Inquiries
U.S. Geological Survey
907 National Center
Reston, VA 22092   (703) 648-4383
Using remotely sensed data, including sidescan sonar and other geophysical surveys, and direct sampling, the USGS studies the geology and assesses the potential mineral and energy resources of the continental margins and the Exclusive Economic Zone of the United States (200 miles from the coastline) and its territories. Also identified are geologic features that must be considered in the selection of sites for offshore drilling platforms and pipelines.

* Offshore Minerals Leasing
Offshore Minerals Management
Mineral Management Service
U.S. Department of the Interior
18th and C Sts., NW
Washington, DC 20240   (202) 343-3530
The Mineral Management Service leases the rights to explore and develop oil and gas on Federal lands of the continental shelf. The "shelf" is made up of the submerged offshore areas lying seaward of the territorial sea to a depth of 200 meters (656 feet) and beyond that area to that depth which allows for mineral exploration. The brochure, *Leasing Energy Resources on the Outer Continental Shelf*, explains the leasing procedure and gives a history of the program.

* Offshore Minerals Management
Mineral Management Service
U.S. Department of the Interior
18th and C Sts., NW
Washington, DC 20240   (202) 343-3530
The Mineral Management Service leases the rights to explore and develop oil and gas on Federal lands of the continental shelf. The "shelf" is made up of the submerged offshore areas lying seaward of the territorial sea to a depth of 200 meters (656 feet) and beyond that area to that depth which allows for mineral exploration. The brochure, *Leasing Energy Resources on the Outer Continental Shelf*, explains the leasing procedure and gives a history of the program.

* Strip Mining and Reclamation
Office of Public Affairs
Office of Surface Mining Reclamation and Enforcement
U.S. Department of Interior
1951 Constitution Avenue, NW
Washington, DC 20240   (202) 343-4953
This office works to protect people and the environment from the side-effects of coal mining, while continuing to regulate coal mining. Lands that were affected by past coal mining operations must be repaired if left unreclaimed or abandoned. Technical assistance is provided to states so that they can perform their responsibilities under the surface mining law. State personnel are trained in the technical aspects of surface mining, such as soil compaction, revegetation, and groundwater hydrology, so that they can better enforce regulations.

* Strip Mining Enforcement Offices
Office of Surface Mining Reclamation and Enforcement
U.S. Department of Interior
1951 Constitution Avenue, NW
Washington, DC 20240   (202) 343-4953

Albuquerque
625 Silver Ave., SW, Suite 310, Albuquerque, NM 87102; (505) 766-1486

Appalachia
350 Elaine Dr., Suite 2300, Lexington, KY 40504; (606) 233-2792

Ashland
Federal Bldg., Room 120, 1430 Greenup Ave., Ashland, KY 41101; (606) 325-4735

Beckley
101 Harper Park Dr., Beckley, WV 25801; (304) 255-5265

Birmingham
280 W. Valley, Room 302, Homewood, AL 35209; (205) 731-0890

Big Stone Gap
P.O. Box 626, Big Stone Gap, VA 24219; (703) 523-4303

Casper
Federal Bldg., 100 East B St., Room 2128, Casper, WY 82601-1918; (307) 261-5776

Columbus
2242 S. Hamilton Rd., Columbus, OH 43232; (614) 866-0578

Chattanooga
900 Georgia Ave., Room 30, Chattanooga, TN 37402; (615) 752-5175

Charleston
603 Morris St., Charleston, WV 25301; (304) 347-7158

Denver
Bldg. 20, Room B2015, P.O. Box 25065, Denver CO 80225; (303) 236-0331

Eastern
Ten Parkway Center, Pittsburgh, PA 15220; (412) 937-2828

Harrisburg
Harrisburg Transportation Ctr., Third Fl., Suite 3C, 4th and Market Sts., Harrisburg, PA 17101; (717) 782-4036

Hazard
516 Village Lane, Hazard, KY 41701; (606) 439-5843

Indianapolis
Minton-Capehart Federal Bldg., 575 N. Penn St., Room 301, Indianapolis, IN 46204; (371) 226-6700

Johnstown
Penn Traffic Bldg., Room 20, 319 Washington St., Johnstown, PA 15901; (814) 533-4223

Kansas City
1103 Grand Ave., Room 502, Kansas City, MO 64106; (816) 374-6405

Knoxville
530 Gay St., Suite 500, Knoxville, TN 37902; (615) 673-4504

Lexington
340 Legion Dr., Suite 28, Lexington, KY 40504; (606) 233-7327

London
P.O. Box 1048, London, KY 40741; (606) 878-6440

Lebanon
Two Acre Task Force: P.O. Box 487, Lebanon, VA 24266; (703) 889-4032

Madisonville
Segebarth Bldg., Box F, 2100 N. Main St., Madisonville, KY 42431; (502) 825-4500

Morgantown
P.O. Box 886, Morgantown, WVA 26507; (304) 291-4004

Norris
P.O. Box 295, Norris, TN 37828; (615) 632-1699

Olympia
Columbia Commons, 3773 C Martini Way East, Suite 104, Olympia, WA 98506; (206) 753-9538

Pikesville
Division of Audit Management, First National Bank, Room 608B, 334 Main St., Pikesville, KY 41505; (606) 432-4123

Prestonburgh
P.O. Box 306, 2664 West Mountain Parkway, West Prestonburg, KY 41618; (606) 866-1291

Business and Industry

Springfield
600 East Monroe St., Room 20, Springfield IL 62701; (217) 492-4495

Tulsa
5100 East Skelley Dr., Suite 550, Tulsa, OK 74135; (918) 581-6430

Wilkes-Barre
20 N. Penn. Ave., Suite 3323, Wilkes-Barre, PA 18701; (717) 826-6726

Western
1020 15th St., 2nd Fl., Brooks Towers, Denver, CO 80202; (303) 564-4380

General Transportation

* Accident Briefs (Non-major Accident Reports)

Public Inquiries Section
National Transportation Safety Board
800 Independence Avenue, SW, Room 805F
Washington, DC 20594 (202) 382-6735

Reports of accidents in brief or summary format are issued for all aviation accidents and for all non-major railroad, highway, pipeline, and marine accidents investigated by or for the NTSB, for which probable cause is determined. The accident reports are issued in a publication containing up to 200 individual reports, which identify the facts, conditions, circumstances, and probable cause for each accident. The publication may include other statistical data such as tabulations by type of accident, phase of operation, casual factors, and injuries. For information on ordering these publications, which are available for a fee, contact the office above.

* Accident Investigations

Bureau of Accident Investigation
National Transportation Safety Board
800 Independence Avenue, SW
Washington, DC 20594 (202) 382-6800

Bureau of Field Operations
National Transportation Safety Board
800 Independence Avenue, SW
Washington, DC 20594 (202) 382-6820

The Bureaus of Accident Investigation and Field Operations investigate or cause to be investigated all aviation and selected surface transportation accidents and incidents; develop proposed probable cause(s) of accidents; formulate recommendations to minimize their recurrence; and prepare detailed reports for use by other government agencies, the Congress, the transportation industry, and the traveling public. The Bureau of Accident Investigation manages the investigations of major transportation accidents--those accidents for which multidisciplinary teams (go-teams) are sent to the accident site. The Bureau of Field Operations manages the investigations of the smaller-scale accidents that are usually investigated by one person from the Safety Board. For more information, contact the appropriate office listed above.

* Accident Reports (Major)

Public Inquiries Section
National Transportation Safety Board
800 Independence Avenue, SW, Room 805F
Washington, DC 20594 (202) 382-6735

Detailed narrative reports which contain the facts, conditions, circumstances, analysis, conclusions, and probable cause of major aviation, railroad, highway, pipeline, and marine accident investigations are issued for all accidents which resulted in a major investigation. Major accident reports are issued irregularly and are available for a fee from the National Technical Information Service (NTIS). For information on ordering, contact the office above.

* Alaska Pipeline

Alaska Natural Gas Pipeline Project
Office of Pipeline Safety
Research and Special Programs Administration
U.S. Department of Transportation
400 7th Street, SW
Washington, DC 20590 (202) 366-4556

Contact this office for information about the plans, programs, policies, and regulation concerning the Alaska pipeline.

* Alternative Fuels Initiative

Office of Engineering
Urban Mass Transit Administration
400 7th St., SW, Room 6431
Washington, DC 20590 (202) 366-0090

Since 1988, UMTA's Office of Engineering has been involved in the effort to replace today's conventional fuels with cleaner-burning alternative fuels, such as methanol, ethanol, and compressed natural gas. For more information, contact the office at the above address.

* Appealing Transportation Licensing Decisions

Office of Administrative Law Judges
National Transportation Safety Board
800 Independence Avenue, SW, Room 822
Washington, DC 20594 (202) 382-6760

This office provides the initial forum for the review of appeals from the suspension, amendment, modification, revocation, or denial of any operation certificate or license issued by the Secretary of Transportation under the Federal Aviation Act of 1958. The primary purpose of this function is to assure fair and impartial review when appeals are taken from safety enforcement certificate actions by the Administrator of the Federal Aviation Administration against airmen or certificate holders or from denials of pilot applications for airman medical certificates. For more information on the process involved, contact the office above.

* Automobile Fuel Economy

Motor Vehicle Requirements Division
Office of Market Incentives
Rulemaking
National Highway Traffic Safety Administration
U.S. Department of Transportation
400 7th Street, SW, Room 5320
Washington, DC 20590 (202) 366-0486

NHTSA issues fuel economy standards and collects information on the technological and economic capabilities of automobile manufacturers to maximize fuel efficiency. Contact this office for information and referrals.

* Auto Safety Hotline

Office of Defects Investigation (NEF-10)
National Highway Traffic Safety Administration
U.S. Department of Transportation
400 7th Street, SW, Room 5326 (800) 424-9393
Washington, DC 20590 (202) 366-0123

This toll-free hotline is accessible in all 50 states, Puerto Rico, and the Virgin Islands. Consumers may call to report automobile safety problems or to request information on recalls, defects, investigations, child safety seats, tires, drunk driving, crash test results, seat belts, air bags, odometer tampering, and other related topics. Staff will also make referrals to state and other agencies. Also ask about the New Car Assessment Program (NCAP), which provides comparable data on the frontal crashworthiness of selected new vehicles.

* Aviation Accident Data on Computer Tape

Accident Data Branch
National Transportation Safety Board
800 Independence Avenue, SW, Room 834
Washington, DC 20594 (202) 382-6672

Computerized tapes containing public data on aircraft accidents are available. Contact the office above for information on ordering the tapes.

* Certificate and License Appeals

Office of Administrative Law Judges
National Transportation Safety Board
800 Independence Avenue, SW, Room 822
Washington, DC 20594 (202) 382-6760

The Safety Board serves as the "court of appeals" for any airman or mariner whenever certificate action is taken by the Federal Aviation Administrator or the U.S. Coast Guard Commandant. The Board's administrative law judges hear, consider, and issue initial decisions on appeals from FAA certificate actions taken under Section 602(b), 609 and 501(c) of the Federal Aviation Act of 1958, as amended. Judges' decisions may be appealed to the five-member Board by the airman or FAA. The Board's review of the appeal encompasses the transcripts of the proceeding, the judge's decision, and appeal briefs submitted by the parties. For more information, contact the office above.

* Consumer Liaison

Office of Public Interest Groups
Intergovernmental and Consumer Affairs
Governmental Affairs
Office of the Secretary of Transportation
U.S. Department of Transportation
400 7th Street, SW
Washington, DC 20590 (202) 366-1524

This office acts as a liaison between Congress, state and local governments, business and industry, and public interest groups to ensure that their needs are considered when Department policy decisions are made. Public and private

Business and Industry

organizations can contact this office to communicate needs and comment on DOT programs and regulations.

* Consumer Transportation Issues

Office of Public Interest Groups
Intergovernmental and Consumer Affairs
Governmental Affairs
Office of the Secretary of Transportation
U.S. Department of Transportation
400 7th Street, SW
Washington, D.C. 20590   (202) 366-1524

This office acts as a liaison between Congress, state and local governments, business and industry, and public interest groups to ensure that their needs are considered when Department policy decisions are made. Public and private organizations can contact this office to communicate needs and comment on DOT programs and regulations.

* Economic Analysis of Transportation Policy

Office of Economics (P-30)
Policy and International Affairs
Office of the Secretary of Transportation
U.S. Department of Transportation
400 7th Street, SW, Room 10305
Washington, D.C. 20590   (202) 366-4416

Staff in this office analyze transportation policy issues to assess their economic and institutional implications. Studies focus on energy and environmental concerns, safety, the handicapped, user charges, and Federal assistance. Contact this office to determine what reports are available and how to obtain them.

* Economic Studies of Transit Industry

Industry, Economics and Finance Division
Office of Economics
Policy and International Affairs
Office of the Secretary of Transportation
U.S. Department of Transportation
400 7th Street, SW, Room 10223
Washington, D.C. 20590   (202) 366-5412

Financial and economic studies of the transportation industry are prepared by this office. Air transportation is emphasized, but other modes are also evaluated. Report topics include mergers, regional marketing studies, gross receipts at airports, and intelligent vehicle highway systems. Contact this office to determine if a study has been prepared on your subject.

* Employment in Transportation

Central Employment Office
Office of Personnel
U.S. Department of Transportation
400 7th St., SW, Room 9113
Washington, DC 20590   (202) 366-9394

Employment inquiries for positions in Washington, D.C., should be submitted to this office. Regional and district offices handle employment in their areas. Civil Service positions include air traffic controller; electronics maintenance technicians; civil, aeronautical, automotive, electronic, and highway engineers; and administrative, management, and clerical positions.

* Freedom of Information

Freedom of Information Act Division
Office of the General Counsel
Office of the Secretary of Transportation
U.S. Department of Transportation
400 7th Street, SW, Room 5432
Washington, D.C. 20590   (202) 366-4542

Inspection of some DOT documents which have proprietary information may require formal Freedom of Information Act (FOIA) requests. Each administration within DOT has a FOIA office. The central office listed here can supply you with addressees and contacts for submittal of FOIA requests.

* Handicapped Assistance and Mass Transit

Office of Research, Training,
and Rural Transportation
Urban Mass Transit Administration
400 7th St., SW, Room 6102
Washington, DC 20590   (202) 366-4995

UMTA is involved in a Congressionally-mandated project with the National Easter Seals Committee to study accessibility problems faced by the handicapped who use mass transit. The office runs a series of demonstrations on improved arrangements to help the handicapped.

* Hazardous Material Transportation Accidents

Information Systems Division (DHM-63)
Office of Hazardous Materials Transportation
Research and Special Programs Administration
U.S. Department of Transportation
400 7th Street, SW, Room 8112
Washington, DC 20590   (202) 366-4555

This division collects and analyzes accident data from transporters of hazardous materials by highway, rail, air, and water and from container manufacturers. Information stored in the database includes the hazardous material involved, transporter name and mode, packaging used, cause of accident, and results. Contact the above office for searches. There may be a charge.

* Lending and Bonding for Small Business

Minority Business Resource Center (MRBC)
Small and Disadvantaged Business Utilization (SDBU)
Director of Civil Rights
Office of the Secretary of Transportation
U.S. Department of Transportation
400 7th Street, SW, Room 9410
Washington, D.C. 20590   (202) 366-2852

This office offers short-term lending and bonding assistance to small businesses in the transportation industry. The Short-term Lending Program offers loans at prime interest rates, while the Bonding Assistance Program enables small firms to obtain bonding in support of transportation-related contracts. Entrepreneurs can contact MBRC for information and certification details.

* Mass Transit Program Evaluation

Program Evaluation Division
Urban Mass Transit Administration
Department of Transportation
400 7th St., SW, Room 9306
Washington, DC 20590   (202) 366-1727

This office can provide you with information on its recent and on-going evaluations of projects and programs implemented by UMTA. For information on earlier evaluations, refer to UMTRIS (see separate listing).

* NTSB Annual Report to Congress

Public Inquiries Section
National Transportation Safety Board
800 Independence Avenue, SW, Room 805F
Washington, DC 20594   (202) 382-6735

NTSB's *Annual Report* to the U.S. Congress details the major activities of the NTSB aviation, railroad, highway, pipeline, and marine safety during the previous calendar year. The biennial additions also include an appraisal, evaluation, and review, and recommendations for legislative and administrative action and change, with respect to transportation safety. It is available free from the office above.

* NTSB Directives

Public Inquiries Section
National Transportation Safety Board
800 Independence Avenue, SW, Room 805F
Washington, DC 20594   (202) 382-6735

NTSB Directives is a manual of orders and notices, which identify NTSB organization, policies, and procedures. The directives are updated as NTSB organization, policies, and procedures change. They are available for a fee from the office above.

* NTSB General Information

Public Inquiries Section
National Transportation Safety Board
800 Independence Avenue, SW, Room 805F
Washington, DC 20594   (202) 382-6735

The pamphlet, *The National Transportation Safety Board*, provides you with general information on the mission and responsibilities of the NTSB and how it accomplishes these responsibilities. It is available free from the office above.

* NTSB Regional Offices

Office of Government and Public Affairs
National Transportation Safety Board
800 Independence Avenue, SW
Washington, DC 20594   (202) 382-6600

To obtain the addresses and telephone numbers of NTSB's ten regional offices located around the country, contact the office above.

* Pipeline Safety

Office of Pipeline Safety (OPS)
Research and Special Programs Administration

U.S. Department of Transportation
400 7th Street, SW
Washington, DC 20590 (202) 366-4572

OPS establishes and enforces safety standards for the transportation of gas and other hazardous materials by pipeline. A computerized reporting system is maintained to collect and analyze accident and incident data from pipeline operators. Accident reports include the operator's name, the hazardous material involved, description of the accident, and results. For database searches, contact the office listed. There may be a charge.

* Private Sector Initiatives in Mass Transit

Office of Private Sector Initiatives
Office of Budget and Policy
Urban Mass Transit Administration
Department of Transportation
400 7th St., SW, Room 9300
Washington, DC 20590 (202) 366-1666

This office encourages private sector involvement in mass transit throughout the United States. Specifically, they work through the following four areas:

Competitive Contracting: Local transit authorities are encouraged to open the provisioning of services up to private sector competition.

Entrepreneurial Services: Groups in the private sector are encouraged to start self-sustaining transit services (such as taxi and bus) in cooperation with local transit authorities.

Joint Development: Federal assistance is available to help plan public/private sector joint ventures at transit facilities.

Demand Management Program: Federal funds are available to encourage local employers and merchants to develop techniques to help manage transportation and mobility problems in their areas.

* Public Docket

Public Inquiries Section
National Transportation Safety Board
800 Independence Avenue, SW, Room 805F
Washington, DC 20594 (202) 382-6735

The Safety Board's Public Inquiries Section maintains a public docket at the Board's headquarters in Washington, D.C. The docket contains the records of all Board investigations, all safety recommendations, and all safety enforcement proceedings. These records are available to the public and may be reviewed or duplicated for public

* Public Hearings on Accidents

Public Inquiries Section
National Transportation Safety Board
800 Independence Avenue, SW, Room 805F
Washington, DC 20594 (202) 382-6735

Following an accident, the Board may decide to hold a public hearing to collect added information and to air in a public forum the issues involved in an accident. Contact the office above for more information on obtaining accident reports from the hearings.

* Public Private Transportation Network

(800) 522-7786

This technical support and information system draws on the expertise of private sector operators and other experts in the transportation field. In addition to these speakers, the Network also arranges seminars.

* Regulations of the NTSB

Public Inquiries Section
National Transportation Safety Board
800 Independence Avenue, SW, Room 805F
Washington, DC 20594 (202) 382-6735

Regulations of the NTSB are published in the *Federal Register* and codified in the *Code of Federal Regulations*, Chapter VIII, Title 49 - Transportation. These regulations are issued irregularly as procedures change. They are available free from the office above. Contact the office above for information on ordering the regulations.

* Research Abstracts

Manager, UMTRIS
Transportation Research Board
National Research Council
2101 Constitution Ave., NW
Washington, DC 20418 (202) 334-2995

Twice annually UMTRIS publishes the *Urban Transportation Abstracts* which provide all the new references added to the it transportation research database during the preceding six months. Each issue is divided into five sections:

Abstracts of Reports and Journal Articles, Summaries of New and Ongoing Research, Source Index, Author/Investigator Index, and Retrieval Term Index. Summer and winter issues can be purchased individually, or through an annual subscription fee of $55.

* Research Bibliography Services

Manager, UMTRIS
Transportation Research Board
National Research Council
2101 Constitution Ave., NW
Washington, DC 20418 (202) 334-2995

Urban Mass Transit Research Information System provides computerized, online responses to transit inquiries. A computer-generated bibliography, including abstract of articles, reports, and summaries of new and ongoing research, can be created for almost any subject related to mass transportation. UMTRIS is now providing a new, low-cost extension to its online capability. Because transportation professionals are often interested in the same current problems, UMTRIS has made available, at a nominal fee, copies of the database literature searches that have been recently completed and may be of interest to other professionals.

* Safety Institute

Transportation Safety Institute (DMA-60)
Research and Special Programs Administration
U.S. Department of Transportation
6500 South MacArthur Blvd.
Oklahoma City, OK 73125 (405) 680-3153

The Institute supports the Department's efforts to reduce transportation accidents. It develops and conducts training programs for Federal, state, and local governments; industry; and foreign personnel. Courses are offered in aviation, highway, marine, pipeline, and railroad safety; materials analysis; transportation security; and other subjects.

* Safety Monitoring of the Trucking Industry

Motor Carrier Information and Analysis (HIA-10)
Office of Motor Carriers
Federal Highway Administration
U.S. Department of Transportation
400 7th St., SW, Room 3104
Washington, DC 20590 (202) 366-4023

FHWA motor carrier programs address licensing interstate and intrastate commercial truck and bus drivers and enforce uniform safety regulations for commercial motor vehicles and their cargo. Driver and vehicle tests and inspections are designed to determine safety performance on the road, and follow-up reviews are conducted when problem areas are identified. The Cargo Security Program regulates the movement of dangerous cargoes on the Nation's highways. This includes hazardous wastes, explosives, flammables, and other volatile materials. Permits are issued to regulate packaging, labeling and transporting of these materials. The transport of migrant workers is also regulated.

Carrier data by state can be obtained from the office listed above. Some information in printout form is available on a cost basis, with price varying according to the information requested. Driver and vehicle tests and inspections are conducted in the field by Motor Carrier Safety and Field Operations, Office of Motor Carriers, FHWA, USDOT, 400 7th St., SW, Room 3408, Washington, D.C. 20590; (202) 366-2952.

* Safety Publications

Public Inquiries Section
National Transportation Safety Board
800 Independence Avenue, SW, Room 805F
Washington, DC 20594 (202) 382-6735

The Safety Board makes public all of its actions and decisions in the form of accident reports, special studies, statistical reviews, safety recommendation and press releases. Details on available publications can be obtained by writing to the office above.
use.

* Safety Recommendations

Public Inquiries Section
National Transportation Safety Board
800 Independence Avenue, SW, Room 805F
Washington, DC 20594 (202) 382-6735

Safety Recommendations are issued by the NTSB as a result of the investigation of transportation accidents and other safety problems. Recommendations usually identify a specific problem uncovered during an investigation of an accident or other safety problems and specify how to correct the situation. Such recommendations are directed to the organization best able to act on the problem, whether it is private or public. These recommendations are issued when a problem is identified, and are distributed individually and in a monthly publication. Contact the office above for information on ordering the recommendations.

* Speeches of the NTSB Members of the Board

Public Inquiries Section
National Transportation Safety Board
800 Independence Avenue, SW, Room 805F
Washington, DC 20594 (202) 382-6735

The Members of the Board are frequently asked to speak before Congressional Committees and state, local, and private organizations. Their prepared statements enunciate NTSB's positions on transportation issues. The topics of these statements vary depending on the organization before which they are speaking. Speech texts are issued irregularly. They are available free from the office above. When ordering, specify the date of the speaking engagement and the committee or organization before which the speech was made.

* Spill Maps

Public Inquiries Section
National Transportation Safety Board
800 Independence Avenue, SW, Room 805F
Washington, DC 20594 (202) 382-6735

Spill maps are developed on selected transportation accidents involving hazardous materials. The maps identify how the hazardous materials spread based on environment in the subject accident. Spill maps are issued irregularly. They are available free from the office above until limited supplies are exhausted. For information on ordering the maps, contact the office above.

* State Motor Vehicle Inspections

Records and Motor Vehicle Services Division (NTS-43)
National Highway Traffic Safety Administration
U.S. Department of Transportation
400 7th Street, SW
Washington, DC 20590 (202) 366-2676

NHTSA's Motor Vehicle Inspection Program is aimed at providing car owners with preventative information on what repairs are needed to achieve greater safety, lower pollution, and better mileage. The annual *Study of the State Motor Vehicle Inspection Program* is available from this office.

* Technical Transportation Information

Technology Sharing Program (DRT-1)
Office of Research and Technology
Research and Special Programs Administration
U.S. Department of Transportation
400 7th Street, SW
Washington, D.C. 20590-0001 (202) 366-4208

The RSPA develops and coordinates a comprehensive transportation information service. Contact this office for referrals and details on DOT programs, projects, contacts, available technical information on transportation-related topics. Technological areas include energy, security, emergency preparedness, and safety.

* Technology Exchange Programs

International Cooperative Division and Secretariat (P-25)
Office of International Transportation and Trade
Office of the Secretary of Transportation
U.S. Department of Transportation
400 7th Street, SW
Washington, D.C. 20590 (202) 366-4368

DOT participates in a number of cooperative programs with other countries to exchange mutually beneficial transportation research data and state-of-the-art technical information. Areas of exchange include highway technology; ports and inland waterways; railway technology; and search and rescue operations. China and the Soviet Union are among the countries participating. Contact this office for information about these programs.

* Transit Environments

Environment Division
Policy and International Affairs
Office of the Secretary of Transportation
U.S. Department of Transportation
400 7th Street, SW, Room 9217
Washington, D.C. 20590 (202) 366-4366

This is the DOT contact point for environmental issues. Staff can provide you with information and referrals on such subjects as highway beautification, transportation architecture, bicycle paths, historic preservation activities, and environmental impact statements.

* Transportation Library

Library (M-493)
Office of the Secretary of Transportation
U.S. Department of Transportation
400 7th Street, SW, Room 2200
Washington, D.C. 20590 (202) 366-0746

An extensive collection of literature on all aspects of transportation is housed here. Reading rooms are also available in regional offices around the country. Contact the specific administration of interest. Law Library: (202) 366-0749.

* Transportation of Hazardous Materials

Office of Hazardous Materials Transportation
Research and Special Programs Administration
U.S. Department of Transportation
400 7th Street, SW
Washington, DC 20590-0001 (202) 366-2301

This office can provide you with information on the transportation of hazardous materials by highway, rail air, and water. Data is collected directly from industry and also via compliance inspections by field staff. The quarterly *Hazardous Material Newsletter* is available free from the office above.

* Transportation Systems Center

Technical Information Center-Library
Transportation Systems Center (TSC)
Research and Special Programs Administration
U.S. Department of Transportation
Kendall Square, 55 Broadway
Cambridge, MA 02142 (617) 494-2306

TSC is the DOT's multimodal research and analysis center to address national transportation and logistics issues. With contractual participation by industry and academia, it conducts technical, socio-economic, and human-factor studies on which the Department's transportation policy decisions are based. Areas of research include safety, security, transportation infrastructure, system modernization, and information technology relevant to transportation system operations. Research covers highways, rail, air, and water. The Center maintains statistics and a transportation information database. There is no central point for distribution of reports, publications, data tapes, and other information available from the Center, so contact the Library above for referral to the appropriate source within the Center for the information you need.

* University Research on Transportation

Office of University Research (P-34)
Policy and International Affairs
Office of the Secretary of Transportation
U.S. Department of Transportation
400 7th Street, SW
Washington, D.C. 20590 (202) 366-0190

Grants are made to institutions of higher learning to establish and administer transportation research centers. Issues for study are determined by the Department. This office can provide you with a list of universities that receive federal money for this purpose.

* Urban Mass Transit Administration

Department of Transportation
400 7th St., SW
Washington, DC 20590 (202) 366-4040

UMTA assists in the development of improved mass transportation facilities, equipment, techniques, and methods; encourages the planning and establishment of area-wide urban mass transportation systems; and provides assistance to state and local governments in financing such systems.

* Urban Mass Transportation Research

Manager, UMTRIS
Transportation Research Board
National Research Council
2101 Constitution Ave., NW
Washington, DC 20418 (202) 334-2995

The Urban Mass Transportation Research Information Service is a computerized database on worldwide transportation research. Administered by the Transportation Research Board (TRB), it covers all phases of conventional, new, and automated public transportation. UMTRIS features database storage/retrieval of abstracts of technical papers, journal articles, research reports, computer program descriptions, and statistical sources, as well as state-of-the-art bibliographies. Descriptions of ongoing research, especially that sponsored by UMTA, are also included. UMTRIS offers the public nearly 20,000 information references to ongoing and completed research activities, and adds 2,000 new references annually to the database. In addition to serving as the central source of technical information to the public and private sectors, UMTRIS also serves as an institutional memory for UMTA projects and project reports. The database can be searched online by any computer with a modem through DIALOG Information Services File 63. UMTRIS is supported by a National Network of Transportation Libraries (18), and they serve both as repositories that house and make UMTA documents available to the general public, as well as document delivery centers that provide UMTRIS users with full text copies of citations retrieved from the database.

* Vehicle Manufacturer Safety Compliance

Vehicle Manufacturer Safety Compliance (NEF-30)
Enforcement
National Highway Traffic Safety Administration
U.S. Department of Transportation
400 7th Street, SW
Washington, DC 20590   (202) 366-2832

To ensure that foreign and domestic vehicle and equipment manufacturers comply with federal motor vehicle safety standards, this office performs compliance testing, inspections, and investigations involving about 150 performance requirements and nearly 3000 equipment items.

* Vehicle Research and Testing

Vehicle Research and Test Center
Research and Development
National Highway Traffic Safety Administration
U.S. Department of Transportation
P.O. BOX 37
East Liberty, OH 43319   (513) 466-4521

NHTSA evaluates the effectiveness of Federal Motor Vehicle Safety Standards. This engineering facility performs tests to obtain basic data used to establish standards for safety and fuel efficiency of motor vehicles.

Highways, Waterways and Railways

* AMTRAK: National Railroad Passenger Corporation

AMTRAK
60 Massachusetts Ave., NE
Washington, D.C. 20002　　　　　　　　(202) 383-3000
AMTRAK was created in 1970 to provide a balanced national transportation system by developing, operating, and improving U.S. intercity rail passenger service.

* AMTRAK Financial and Operating Statistics

AMTRAK
Office of Public Affairs
60 Massachusetts Ave., NE
Washington, D.C. 20002　　　　　　　　(202) 906-3860
No rail passenger system in the world makes a profit; therefore, AMTRAK does require government assistance in the form of an annual appropriation. However, AMTRAK has made significant progress in reducing its dependence on federal support while at the same time improving the quality of service. The Annual Report provides operating statistics and financial statements, which cover operations, cashflows, and changes in capitalization.

* AMTRAK Passenger Services

AMTRAK
60 Massachusetts Ave., NE
Washington, D.C. 20002　　　　　　　　(202) 906-2733
The Passenger Services Department handles all of the onboard service aspects of AMTRAK, including all of its employees across the country.

* AMTRAK Customer Relations

AMTRAK
60 Massachusetts Ave., NE
Washington, D.C. 20002　　　　　　　　(202) 906-2121
You may call or write the Customer Relations Office concerning any comments or problems with AMTRAK service. Please include your ticket receipt and dates of travel to help with the resolution of your problem.

* AMTRAK Tickets or Travel Information

AMTRAK
60 Massachusetts Ave., NE
Washington, D.C. 20002　　　　　　　　(800) USA-RAIL
For information regarding tickets or travel on AMTRAK, call 1-800-USA-RAIL. AMTRAK also publishes a travel planner which provides travel tips and services, as well as a listing AMTRAK's vacation packages.

* Annual Report of Interstate Transportation Companies

Bureau of Accounts' Public Reference Room
Interstate Commerce Commission
12th St. and Constitution Ave., NW, Room 3378
Washington, DC 20403　　　　　　　　(202) 275-7356
Annual reports of companies regulated by the ICC contain revealing information concerning those companies, including annual income, balance sheets, expenses, types of equipment owned, and much more. These documents may be examined by the public in the Reference Room from 8:30 a.m. to 5:00 p.m. weekdays,and photocopies of these reports, at a cost of $.60 per page, with a $3.00 minimum charge per order, may be obtained by writing the Office of the Secretary, Room 2215, ICC, Washington, DC, 20423.

* Applications of Motor Carriers

Motor and Rail Docket File
Office of the Secretary
Interstate Commerce Commission
12th St. & Constitution Ave., NW
Room 1221
Washington, DC 20423　　　　　　　　(202) 275-7285
As required by the Motor Carrier Act, all motor carriers must be willing to give a copy of its application package to anyone willing to pay the $10.00 fee. These packages include information on the type of authority requested from the ICC, the type of business run by the applicant, a history of the applicant's business, and more. Contact this office for more information on examining these applications.

* Assistance to Foreign Highways

International Highway Programs (HPI-10)
Associate Administrator for Policy
Federal Highway Administration
U.S. Department of Transportation
400 7th St., SW
Washington, DC 20590　　　　　　　　(202) 366-0111
FHWA administers programs which provide assistance and advice to foreign governments engaged in highway engineering and administration. Projects have included technical assistance in fabricating bridge segments, value engineering skills, development of transportation systems, materials testing, quality control, and skid testing. Through the International Visitors Program, highway specialists from over 40 countries receive training. Countries that have participated include China, Indonesia, Haiti, Kuwait, Dubai, and Saudi Arabia. Two publications available from this office are *World of Technology for Sharing* and *Highway Community on the Occasion of the 18th World Road Congress*.

* Automotive Trade Statistics

Machinery and Transportation Equipment Branch
Machinery and Equipment Division
Office of Industries
U.S. International Trade Commission
500 E St., SW, Room 500
Washington, DC 20436　　　　　　　　(202) 252-1380
The compilation and publication of the following two series of data began in response to congressional and general public interest. Series A relates to all motor vehicles--passenger automobiles, trucks, buses, and so forth--and is published annually each Spring. Series B relates to new passenger automobiles only and is published annually each Fall.
　　Automotive Trade Statistics, 1964-1984: Factory Sales, Imports, Exports, Apparent Consumption, and Trade Balances with Canada and All Other Countries for all motor vehicles.
　　Automotive Trade Statistics, 1964-1984: Factory Sales, Imports, Exports, Apparent Consumption, and Trade Balances with Canada and All Other Countries for passenger automobiles only.

* Bridges Over Navigable Waters

Bridge Administration Division
Office of Navigation Safety and Waterways Services
U.S. Coast Guard
U.S. Department of Transportation
2100 2nd St., SW, Room 1408
Washington, DC 20593-0001　　　　　　(202) 267-0368
Bridges and causeways spanning navigable waterways in the U.S. are subject to Coast Guard safety regulations concerning their construction, operation, and maintenance. This office oversees bridge engineering and issues permits. For further details, contact the division listed above.

* Cargo Insurance

Office of the Secretary
Interstate Commerce Commission
12th St. and Constitution Ave., NW, Room 2215
Washington, DC 20423　　　　　　　　(202) 275-7428
All motor common carriers of property and freight forwarders are required to maintain cargo insurance for the protection of the shipping public. Under this protection, the insurance company is directly liable to a shipper or consignee for any cargo claim for which the motor carrier or freight forwarder may be legally liable. No limitations in the policy itself, such as deductibles, may be used as a defense by the insurance companies against claims filed under this Commission's prescribed cargo endorsements. Railroads are not required to maintain cargo insurance. The name of the insurance company may be obtained by writing the Office of the Secretary.

* Commission Reports and Orders Certification

Public Records Room
Interstate Commerce Commission
1176 G St., NW, Room 1312
Washington, DC 20423　　　　　　　　(202) 275-1295
All Commission Reports and Orders are available to the public at a slight cost ($.60 per page) and can be received by contacting the Public Records Room.

* Computerized Data Base of Railroads
Office of Transportation Analysis
Interstate Commerce Commission
12th St. and Constitution Ave., NW, Room 3219
Washington, DC 20423   (202) 275-7684
The Office of Transportation Analysis maintains a computerized data base of railroad contract summaries, which include shipper names on agricultural commodities.

* Crashworthiness
Office of Crashworthiness Research (NRD-10)
Research and Development
National Highway Traffic Safety Administration
U.S. Department of Transportation
400 7th Street, SW
Washington, DC 20590   (202) 366-4862
Research is conducted on vehicle crashworthiness and crash avoidance. To determine how drivers and passengers fare in head-on collisions, information is collected on seat belts, air bags, child safety restraints, motorcycle helmets, fuel systems, rearview mirrors, tires, door locks, seats, bumpers, and school busses. The annual publication, *Federal Motor Vehicle Safety Standards and Regulations*, is available for $82.00 from the Government Printing Office. Superintendent of Documents, Washington, DC 20402; (202) 783-3238. New Car Assessment Program information on selected models is available from the Auto Safety Hotline: (800) 424-9393.

* Diesel Fuel Recording
Interstate Commerce Commission
12th St. and Constitution Ave., NW
Washington, DC 20423   (202) 275-6787
This recording states the average diesel fuel price each week after a survey is taken of fuel stations across the country.

* Driver and Pedestrian Research
Office of Driver and Pedestrian Research (NRD-40)
Research and Development
National Highway Traffic Safety Administration
U.S. Department of Transportation
400 7th Street, SW
Washington, DC 20590   (202) 366-9591
This office studies factors affecting the safety of drivers and pedestrians. Research areas include determining the causes of unsafe driving and developing countermeasures; the effectiveness of vehicle occupant safety restraints; the effect of alcohol and drugs; the safety concerns of bicycles, motorcycles, and mopeds; driver license standards; and young drivers. This office can refer you to staff researching the topic of your interest.

* Funded Traffic Safety Projects
Evaluation Staff (NTS-02.1)
Traffic Safety Programs
National Highway Traffic Safety Administration
U.S. Department of Transportation
400 7th Street, SW
Washington, DC 20590   (202) 366-2759
Once known as the National Project Reporting System, funded project information collected by this office from each state is stored in a database. Projects are funded in areas such as occupant safety and alcohol. Findings are assembled annually in a published report providing an overview of the projects, their status, and how funding is apportioned, such as amounts to each project and within each project, amount to education, to enforcement, and to other areas. Contact the Evaluation Staff for details.

* Hazardous Material Transportation Accidents
Information Systems Division (DHM-63)
Office of Hazardous Materials Transportation
Research and Special Programs Administration
U.S. Department of Transportation
400 7th Street, SW, Room 8112
Washington, DC 20590   (202) 366-4555
This division collects and analyzes accident data from transporters of hazardous materials by highway, rail, air, and water and from container manufacturers. Information stored in the database includes the hazardous material involved, transporter name and mode, packaging used, cause of accident, and results. Contact the above office for searches. There may be a charge.

* Highway Beautification
Environment Division
Policy and International Affairs
Office of the Secretary of Transportation
U.S. Department of Transportation

400 7th Street, SW, Room 9217
Washington, DC 20590   (202) 366-4366
This is the DOT contact point for environmental issues. Staff can provide you with information and referrals on such subjects as highway beautification, transportation architecture, bicycle paths, historic preservation activities, and environmental impact statements.

* Highway Construction Accident Prevention
Office of Highway Safety (HHS-21)
Associate Administrator for Safety and Operations
Federal Highway Administration
U.S. Department of Transportation
400 7th St., SW
Washington, DC 20590   (202) 366-1153
Highway construction safety programs are funded to remove, relocate, or shield roadside obstacles; to identify and correct hazards at railroad crossings; and to improve signing, pavement markings, and signalization. For information and referral, contact the Office of Highway Safety. The following publications are also available:

Highway Safety Improvement Programs, Annual Report
Status Report of Federal Funds Used for Highway Safety Programs.

Several other reports prepared by this office are available from National Technical Information Service, 5285 Port Royal Road, Springfield, VA 22161; (703) 487-4650. A sampling of titles follows:

Inexpensive Accident Countermeasures at Narrow Bridges
Legibility and Driver Response to Selected Lane and Road Closure Barricades
Re-Evaluation of Traffic Control at Non-Signalized Intersections
Rollover Potential of Vehicles on Embankments, Sideslopes, and Other Roadside Features; Railroad-Highway Grade Crossing Signal Visibility Improvement Program, Final Report
Constant Warning Time Devices for Railroad-Highway Crossings: Technical Summary
Studies of the Road Marking Code

* Highway Contractors and Subcontractors
Office of Civil Rights
Federal Highway Administration
U.S. Department of Transportation
400 7th St., SW
Washington, DC 20590   (202) 366-0693
This office monitors compliance with civil rights laws by requiring contractors and subcontractors of Federal highway projects to submit employment data. Equal opportunity issues are also addressed in the Disadvantaged Business Enterprise Program, which awards contracts and subcontract commitments to small and minority businesses, and in FHWA's Historically Black Colleges and Universities Programs. Data from contractor filings and a list of contractors and subcontractors, by state or county, are available from this office. You can also obtain a copy of *FHWA's Historically Black Colleges and Universities Programs*, a publication with details about those programs.

* Highway Environment
Environmental Policy Division (HEV-1)
Office of Right-of-Way and Environment
Federal Highway Administration
U.S. Department of Transportation
400 7th St., SW
Washington, DC 20590   (202) 366-2045
FHWA assesses environmental impact so that highways are located, constructed, and designed in cooperation with environmental concerns. Water and air quality, noise abatement, vegetation management, corrosion control, and preserving wildlife are some of the factors considered. For more information on FHWA efforts in these areas, contact the office listed above.

* Highway Publications
Office of Public Affairs (HPA-1)
Federal Highway Administration
U.S. Department of Transportation
400 7th St., SW
Washington, DC 20590   (202) 366-0660
The *FHWA Publications Index*, free from Public Affairs, is a useful guide to current reports, manuals, and summaries generated by programs of the Federal Highway Administration. The *Index* provides contact addresses and telephone numbers for obtaining the publications from offices within FHWA or from NTIS and GPO. The titles listed below are available directly from Public Affairs:

Motor Carrier Activities of the FHWA
U.S. Highways
Commercial Motor Vehicle Safety Act of 1986
FHWA News
The Single License Requirement for Truck and Bus Drivers

Business and Industry

* Highways Research Center
Technical Information Center-Library
Transportation Systems Center (TSC)
Research and Special Programs Administration
U.S. Department of Transportation
Kendall Square, 55 Broadway
Cambridge, MA 02142   (617) 494-2306

TSC is the DOT's multimodal research and analysis center to address national transportation and logistics issues. With contractual participation by industry and academia, it conducts technical, socio-economic, and human-factor studies on which the Department's transportation policy decisions are based. Areas of research include safety, security, transportation infrastructure, system modernization, and information technology relevant to transportation system operations. Research covers highways, rail, air, and water. The Center maintains statistics and a transportation information database. There is no central point for distribution of reports, publications, data tapes, and other information available from the Center, so contact the Library above for referral to the appropriate source within the Center for the information you need.

* Highway Statistics
Office of Highway Information Management (HPM-1)
Associate Administrator for Policy
Federal Highway Administration
U.S. Department of Transportation
400 7th St., SW, Room 3306
Washington, DC 20590   (202) 366-0180

This office is the centralized source for highway statistics compiled by FHWA. The *Highway Statistics Summary*, updated every ten years, summarizes historical information on the Nation's highway system, its users, and Federal, State, and local highway funding. You can also obtain statistics and information on personal, regional, and national travel trends; fuel usage and taxes; road user and motor vehicle taxes; toll bridges, roads, tunnels, and ferries in the U.S.; traffic volume; driver licenses; and yearly statistical summaries. Contact this office to be added to the mailing list for a free subscription to *Monthly Motor Fuels Reported by State*, which indicates trends in gasoline sales.

* Highway Traffic Safety Records
Technical Reference Division (NAD-52)
Office of Administrative Operations
National Highway Traffic Safety Administration
U.S. Department of Transportation
400 7th Street, SW
Washington, DC 20590   (202) 366-2768

NHTSA reports and records are available for public inspection at this location, and database searches can be requested for a fee. Holdings include vehicle research and test reports; investigation reports on accidents and defects; recall information; compliance reports; consumer complaints; consumer advisories; filmed records of research and tests; NHTSA *Technical Reports*; engineering specifications; and certification information. Both light and heavy highway vehicles are covered. Call ahead to ensure that the records you need will be on hand.

* Interstate Commerce Commission
Interstate Commerce Commission
12th St. & Constitution Ave., NW
Washington, DC 20423   (202) 275-7252

The Interstate Commerce Commission was created as an independent regulatory agency by act of February 4, 1887 to regulate commerce. ICC's responsibilities include regulation of carriers engaged in transportation in interstate commerce and in foreign commerce to the extent that it takes place within the U.S. Surface transportation under the Commission's jurisdiction includes railroads, trucking companies, bus lines, freight forwarders, water carriers, transportation brokers, and a coal slurry pipeline. The regulatory laws vary depending on the type of transportation; however, they generally involve certification of carriers seeking to provide transportation for the public, rates, adequacy of service, purchases, and mergers. The Commission assures that the carriers it regulates will provide the public with rates and services that are fair and reasonable.

* Interstate Commerce Commission Register
Superintendent of Documents
Government Printing Office
Washington, DC 20402   (202) 783-3238

The *ICC Register* is a daily summary of motor carrier applications and of decisions and notices issued by the ICC. Subscription information is available from GPO.

* Interstate Commerce Publications
Office of Government and Public Affairs
Interstate Commerce Commission
12th St. and Constitution Ave., NW, Room 4111
Washington, DC 20423   (202) 275-7252

A complete list of publications, including explanatory material on the operation and activities of the ICC and on special consumer-related fields, such as household goods movements and small shipments, is available. This list may be obtained by calling or writing this office.

* Interstate Commerce Speakers
Office of Government and Public Affairs
Interstate Commerce Commission
12th St. and Constitution Ave., NW, Room 4111
Washington, DC 20423   (202) 275-7252

Speakers are available to discuss subjects relating to the Commission's organization, operations, procedures, and regulations.

* Legal Assistance
Office of the Secretary
Interstate Commerce Commission
12th St. and Constitution Ave., NW, Room 2215
Washington, DC 20423   (202) 275-7428

To assist claimants in disputes, the Commission requires all motor carriers to designate an agent for service of legal process in each state into or through which they operate. The name of this process agent may be obtained by writing to the Office of the Secretary.

* Maximum Speed Limit
Police Traffic Services Division
Office of Enforcement and Emergency Services
Traffic Safety Programs
National Highway Traffic Safety Administration
U.S. Department of Transportation
400 7th Street, SW, Room 6124
Washington, DC 20590   (202) 366-5440

The National Maximum Speed Limit is 65 miles per hour on certain interstate highways. This office processes annual certifications of maximum speed limit enforcement programs throughout the U.S. and assists states in developing and improving enforcement efforts.

* Motor and Rail Dockets
Office of the Secretary
Motor and Rail Docket File Room
Interstate Commerce Commission
12th St. and Constitution Ave., NW, Room 1221
Washington, DC 20423   (202) 275-7285

All the Commission's decisions and other legal documents are available for public inspection in the Office of the Secretary.

* National Driver Register
National Driver Register (NTS-24)
Traffic Safety Programs
National Highway Traffic Safety Administration
U.S. Department of Transportation
400 7th Street, SW, Room 5119
Washington, DC 20590   (202) 366-4800

The *National Driver Register* is a central, computerized index of state records on drivers whose operator licenses have been revoked, denied, or suspended for more than 6 months. Data includes name, birthdate, height, weight, eye color, date and reason for action, and date of reinstatement. Applications for driver licenses are routinely checked against the register, and states exchange information via an electronic system.

* Northeast Corridor Rail Project
Public Affairs
Federal Railway Administration
Department of Transportation
400 7th St., SW, Room 3413
Washington, DC 20590   (202) 366-0366

Now in its final stages, the project is a major track upgrading on AMTRAK's main line from Washington, DC to Boston. The goal of the upgrading is to produce the best high-speed passenger railroad in the United States. This office can be contacted for information regarding current progress.

* Occupants Displaced by Highway Construction
Office of Right-of-Way (HRW-22)
Office of Right-of-Way and Environment
Federal Highway Administration
U.S. Department of Transportation
400 7th St., SW, Room 3219
Washington, DC 20590   (202) 366-0342

This office administers FHWA's lead role in implementing the Uniform Relocation Assistance and Real Property Acquisition Policies Act. When Federally funded highway construction projects involve displacing residents from acquired property, this Act sets policies for purchase of the land and relocating the people on it. The publication, *Your Rights and Benefits as Displaced Under the Federal Relocation Assistance Program*, is available from this office.

* Pedestrian Safety
Geometric and Roadside Design Branch
Engineering Division
Office of Engineering Program Development
Federal Highway Administration
U.S. Department of Transportation
400 7th St., SW, Room 3128
Washington, DC 20590 (202) 366-1315

Highway design and roadside facilities are studied by this office to determine their impact on pedestrians and bicyclists. The publication, *Pedestrian and Bicycle Facilities*, provides you with information about the roadside designs and structures used in safety-related applications.

* Public Tariff File
Tariff Examining Branch
Bureau of Traffic
Interstate Commerce Commission
12th St. and Constitution Ave., NW, Room 4360
Washington, DC 20423 (202) 275-7462

The Bureau of Traffic monitors tariff publication, filing, and interpretation, and suspends any unreasonable or unlawful tariffs before they become effective. The tariffs are available for public inspection by contacting the Tariff Examining Branch.

* Rail and Service Abandonments
Office of Transportation Analysis
Interstate Commerce Commission
12th St. and Constitution Ave., NW, Room 3100
Washington, DC 20423 (202) 275-6854

No line of railroad may be abandoned and no rail service discontinued unless the Commission has a certificate of public convenience and necessity authorizing the abandonment or discontinuance. The Notice of Intent must be filed with the Commission at least 15 days, but not more than 30 days, prior to the filing of the abandonment application. The public may become a party to this proceeding by filing a protest, which the Commission will then investigate. For more information, contact the Office of Transportation Analysis.

* Railroad Accidents
System Support Division
Safety, RRS 22
Federal Railway Administration
Department of Transportation
400 7th St., NW
Washington, DC 20590 (202) 366-2760

The division maintains data accessible to the public regarding railroad accidents on a computer database, as well as in the following free publications:

Accident-Incident Bulletin (annual)
Railroad Highway Crossing Accident-Incident and Inventory Bulletin
Summary of Accidents Investigated by the Federal Railway Administration (1987)
Railroad Employee Fatalities Investigated by the Federal Railway Administration (quarterly)
Railroad Accident Investigation Reports (National Transportation Safety Board)

* Railroad Freight and Operations
Office of Information and Systems
Office of Policy
Federal Railroad Administration
Department of Transportation
400 7th Street, SW, RRP-20
Washington, DC 20590 (202) 366-0366

This office studies the use of freight cars, accounting and financial systems of railroads, coal rates, grain transportation, and mergers. Available for purchase is the yearly series *Carload Waybill Statistics (Report TD1)*, a compilation of rail freight statistics calculated annually showing traffic flows by commodity across broad geographic areas (including from Canada). You can order this report through the National Technical Information Service, or contact the above office for more information. *Freight Commodity Statistics* is available for purchase from the Association of American Railroads, and contact the above office for more information. The public use computer tape of the *Carload Waybill Sample* is available for purchase from ALK Associates, Inc., 1000 Herrontown Rd., Princeton, NJ 08540. Attn: Database Mgr.

* Railroad Information

Public Affairs
Federal Railway Administration
Department of Transportation
400 7th St., SW, Room 3413
Washington, DC 20590 (202) 366-0366

Contact the Public Affairs for additional information on FRA programs, publications, and activities.

* Railroad Research and Development
Office of Research and Development
Federal Railway Administration
Department of Transportation
400 7th St., SW, Room 8305
Washington, DC 20590 (202) 366-9601

Call this office for information on the latest trends in railway technology and thinking. Topics include developments to improve track and track bed structures; work to reduce the effects of accidents involving tank cars carrying hazardous materials; efforts to gain a better understanding of equipment failures; development of less expensive and more effective grade crossing techniques; and research into human factors in train operation.

* Railroad Safety
Office of Safety
Federal Railway Administration
Department of Transportation
400 7th St., SW, Room 8314
Washington, DC 20590 (202) 366-0521

This office inspects tracks, equipment, signals, and general railroad operations. It investigates accidents and complaints, and makes routine investigations. The office has jurisdiction over such areas as locomotives, signals, safety appliances, power brakes, hours of service, transportation of explosives; and human factors in rail operations. The free publication, *Safety Report*, lists federal government actions to improve railroad safety. It includes statistical compilations of accidents; incident reports, federal safety regulations, orders and standards issues by the Federal Railroad Administration; evaluation of the degree of their observance; summary of outstanding problems; analysis and evaluation of research and related activities; a list of completed or pending judicial actions for the enforcement of any safety rules, regulations, orders, or standards issued; and recommendations for additional legislation. The publication is available by contacting Public Affairs, Federal Railway Administration, Department of Transportation, 400 7th St., SW, Room 3413, Washington, D.C. 20590; (202) 366-0366.

* Rail Transit Safety
Office of Safety
Urban Mass Transit Administration
400 7th St., SW, Room 6432
Washington, DC 20590 (202) 366-2896

UMTA's rapid- and light-rail transit safety system is made up of the following aspects: 1) Safety Information--Reporting and Analysis System--developing a new rapid rail transit accident/incident reporting system; 2) System Safety--disseminating pertinent information to individuals working in the field of mass transit; 3) Drug and Alcohol Abuse information; and 4) Information on State Transit Programs.

* Rates and Charges
Bureau of Traffic
Rates and Informal Cases Section
Interstate Commerce Commission
12th St. and Constitution Ave., NW, Room 4310
Washington, DC 20423 (202) 275-7358

A tariff is a schedule of rates and charges, and each carrier must file a copy with the ICC. If you have a complaint with a company regarding the charges, contact the Bureau of Traffic for assistance. They may be able to help resolve the matter quickly.

* Road Signs
Traffic Control Development Applications Division (HTO-21)
Traffic Control Systems
Traffic Operations Division
Office of Safety and Operations
Federal Highway Administration
U.S. Department of Transportation
400 7th St., SW
Washington, DC 20590 (202) 366-2184

Efforts by this division improve the effectiveness and uniformity of such traffic control devices as road signs, signal lamps, and highway markings throughout the country. Standards are developed for designing signs and using other traffic control devices. The meanings of road signs and markings are described in *Road Symbol Signs*, which can be obtained by contacting the office listed above. Two other publications on the subject, listed below, are available from the

Business and Industry

Superintendent of Documents, U.S. Government Printing Office, Washington, D.C. 20402; (202) 783-3238:

Manual on Uniform Traffic Control Devices, ($22.00)
Standard Highway Signs Book, ($30.00)

* Special Permission Authority

Special Permission Board
Bureau of Traffic
Interstate Commerce Commission
12th St. and Constitution Ave., NW, Room 4338
Washington, DC 20423 (202) 275-7395

Companies must give the ICC one day's notice for new or reduced rates and five to seven working days for increased rates or fares. You must contact the Special Permission Board to shorten the time period.

* Traffic Accident Data

Performance Evaluation Branch
Office of Highway Safety
Federal Highway Administration
U.S. Department of Transportation
400 7th St., SW
Washington, DC 20590 (202) 366-2159

Statistics are kept here on fatal and injury accident rates for the Nation's highways. An extensive list of publications related to accidents and highway safety is also maintained. Call or write this office to request the data you need.

* Tariff Instructional Manual

Tariff Section
Bureau of Traffic
Interstate Commerce Commission
12th St. and Constitution Ave., NW, Room 4363A
Washington, DC 20423 (202) 275-7462

The Tariff Instructional Manual is intended as a guide for carriers wishing to publish their own tariffs. It includes only the essentials and will require some adjustment to meet individual needs. This outlines the rules and regulations and offers several examples. They also include information on frequent problems and define some of the terms used in the tariff application.

* Transportation of Hazardous Materials

Office of Hazardous Materials Transportation
Research and Special Programs Administration
U.S. Department of Transportation
400 7th Street, SW
Washington, DC 20590-0001 (202) 366-2301

This office can provide you with information on the transportation of hazardous materials by highway, rail air, and water. Data is collected directly from industry and also via compliance inspections by field staff. The quarterly *Hazardous Material Newsletter* is available free from the office above.

* Transportation Safety Institute

Transportation Safety Institute (DMA-60)
Research and Special Programs Administration
U.S. Department of Transportation
6500 South MacArthur Blvd.
Oklahoma City, OK 73125 (405) 680-3153

The Institute supports the Department's efforts to reduce transportation accidents. It develops and conducts training programs for Federal, state, and local governments; industry; and foreign personnel. Courses are offered in aviation, highway, marine, pipeline, and railroad safety; materials analysis; transportation security; and other subjects.

* Transport Statistics in the United States

Publications
Interstate Commerce Commission
12th St. and Constitution Ave., NW
Washington, DC 20423 (202) 275-7833

This is an annual report which contains statistics of railroads and motor carriers. It includes a complete breakdown of finances, expenses and equipment, as well as service statistics. The tables are compiled from reports filed with the Commission by railroads and motor carriers.

* Waterways Traffic Regulation

Commander G-NSP
Vessel Traffic Services Branch
Office of Navigation Safety and Waterways Services
U.S. Coast Guard
U.S. Department of Transportation
2100 2nd St., SW, Room 1410
Washington, DC 20593-0001 (202) 267-0407

To ensure the safe and orderly passage of vessels, cargo, and people, Vessel Traffic Services in major ports oversee the movement of vessels and install necessary safety equipment. Traffic is monitored closely during hazardous conditions and bad weather. To locate the Vessel Traffic Service nearest you, contact the branch listed above or your local Coast Guard office.

Selling To The Government

See also Small Business and Entrepreneuring Chapter

Federal and state governments buy practically every product from broom handles to tires. They hire the services of more consultants and writers than a multinational corporation. Most agencies and departments have special offices with sole responsibility for procurement. And, because both state and federal governments are eager to help small businesses, launching your business with a government contract is one way to get it off the ground without investing a lot of capital. And, remember the public--meaning you--has the right to see government contracts and discover, for instance, how many toilet seats the Pentagon purchased last year.

* Airline, Hotel, Train Services

Superintendent of Documents
U.S. Government Printing Office (GPO)
Washington, DC 20402　　　　　　　　(202) 783-3238
The GSA contracts with the airline industry and hotel/motel establishments to provide reduced rates for federal employees traveling on official business. The *Federal Travel Directory* contains the schedules, fares, and telephone reservation numbers of those airlines, as well as guidelines for using AMTRAK, and lists American lodging accommodations by state and city; foreign, by country and city. Information should be verified when making specific reservations. The *Directory* incorporates the *Federal Hotel-Motel Discount Directory*, previously a subscription and a single sales publication. Monthly; subscription price $57.00/year, single copy $9.50, (722-006-00000-3).

* Architect-Engineer Services

Office of Design and Construction (PQS)
General Services Administration
18th and F Sts.
Washington, DC 20405　　　　　　　　(202) 566-1888
GSA awards contracts for design services to the most highly qualified architect/engineer firms. *Architect/Engineer Services* is a booklet which gives information on this topic, including who is eligible for GSA professional services contracts, how to find out about potential GSA projects, what types of contracts are available, and where and how to apply. To obtain this booklet, contact the office above.

* Army Weapons Systems and Prime Contractors

U.S. Government Printing Office
Superintendent of Documents
Washington, DC 20402-6518　　　　　　(202) 783-3238
The Department of the Army publishes the *Army Weapons Systems Handbook*, which contains photographs and descriptions of the major weapons systems in the Army, their program status, and a list of the prime contractors involved. It also gives information on the Soviet counterparts. A copy can be ordered through the Government Printing Office for a moderate charge.

* Art and Historic Preservation

Art and Historic Preservation Division
General Services Administration
18th and F Sts., NW, Room 1300
Washington, DC 20405　　　　　　　　(202) 566-1256
This division oversees three programs which include the Art-in-Architecture Program, the Fine Arts Program, and the Historic Preservation Program. Under the Art-in-Architecture Program, GSA regional offices commission mural and sculptures for newly constructed public buildings. Artists are selected in cooperation with the National Endowment for the Arts (NEA). NEA-appointed panels, consisting of local civic and art-oriented representatives and the project architect, recommend artists to GSA. The Fine Arts Program is responsible for the conservation and maintenance of art which pre-dates the Art-in-Architecture Program. The Historic Preservation Program ensures that historic structures are rehabilitated and preserved for continued federal use and public enjoyment. A list of these buildings is available, along with information on many historic structures.

* Ballistic Missiles Procurement

U.S. Department of the Army
Strategic Defense Command
Public Affairs Office
P.O. Box 1500
Huntsville, AL 35807-3801　　　　　　(205) 895-3887

This Command conducts advanced research and development in the fields of radar, interceptors, optics, and other technical aspects of ballistic missile defense. It publishes fact sheets on the various research programs of the Command, and booklets entitled *Doing Business with the U.S. Army Strategic Defense Command* and *U.S. Army--First in Space and Strategic Defense*. Write or call to request a copy.

* Bid Protest for Government Contracts

Information Handling and Support Facilities
General Accounting Office
P.O. Box 6015
Gaithersburg, MD 20877　　　　　　　(202) 275-6241
The GAO resolves disputes between agencies and bidders for government contracts, including grantee award actions. The free publication, *Bid Protests at GAO: A Descriptive Guide*, contains information on GAO's procedures for determining legal questions arising from the awarding of government contracts. Contact this office for more information on bid protests on government contracts.

* Certificate of Competency

Contact your local SBA office or
Small Business Answer Desk
U.S. Small Business Administration
1725 Eye St., NW Room 414
Washington, DC 20416　　　(202) 653-7561 or (800) 368-5855
If a small firm is the low bidder on a federal contract, but the contracting officer questions the firm's ability to perform the contract, the contracting agency must refer the firm to SBA for a *Certificate of Competency* (COC). When a firm applies for a COC, SBA makes an on-site study of the firm's facilities, management, performance record, and production capacity in relationship to the contract in question. If SBA determines that the firm is capable of performing the contract within the required time period, the SBA issues a COC attesting to that fact. The contracting officer must then award the contract to the small firm. This authority is a valuable tool for small businesses judged capable of meeting the contract requirements. Contact your SBA office for more information.

* Commerce Business Daily

Superintendent of Documents
Government Printing Office
Washington DC 20402　　　　　　　　(202) 783-3238
Commerce Business Daily is a daily list of government procurement invitations, contract awards, subcontracting leads, sales of surplus property, and foreign business opportunities, as well as certain foreign government procurements. The annual subscription cost is $261 for first-class mail, or $208 for second-class. *CBD* is available on-line from a sizable list of contractors who are named in the lower left-hand corner of the front page of each *CBD* edition. Call (202) 377-0632 for additional information.

* Competitive Bidding

Office of Public Affairs
Legal Services Corporation
400 Virginia Ave. S.W.
Washington, D.C. 20024　　　　　　　202-863-1839
Legal Services Corporation is developing and implementing a system for the competitive award of all grants and contracts for the provision of services. They will be educating prospective providers of legal services and their communities about the availability of federal funds. LSC will also be developing mediation, arbitration, and other dispute resolution programs.

Selling To The Government

* Construction Contracts

Office of Procurement - PP
Public Buildings Service
General Services Administration
18th and F Sts., NW
Washington, DC 20405 (202) 566-0907

Contracts for construction or repairs and alterations are awarded to the lowest responsive and responsible bidder on the basis on competitive sealed bids. Competitive negotiations may be used when warranted. Notice of contracts are placed in local newspapers, various trade journals, technical publications serving the construction industry, and the *Commerce Business Daily*. Notices are also sent to those who are on the bidder's mailing list. Each of GSA's PBS regional offices maintains mailings lists of interested prospective bidders. Firms may apply by contacting the nearest Business Service Center.

* Contract Appeals

Board of Contract Appeals (G)
General Services Administration
18th and F Sts., NW
Washington, DC 20405 (202) 566-0720

The GSA Board of Contract Appeals works to resolve disputes arising out of contracts with GSA, the U.S. Departments of Treasury, Education, and Justice, and other independent government agencies. The Board also hears and decides bid protests arising out of government-wide automated data processing (ADP) procurements. A contractor may elect to use either the GSA Board or the General Accounting Office for resolution of an ADP bid protest. Contractors may elect to have their appeals processed under the Board's accelerated procedures if the claim is $50,000 or less, or under the small claims procedure if the claim is $10,000 or less. Contractors may also request that a hearing be held at a location convenient to them. With the exception of small claims decisions, contractors can appeal adverse Board decisions to the U.S. Court of Appeals for the Federal Circuit. For more information, contact the office above.

* Contracting with the Defense Logistics Agency

Public Affairs (DLA-B)
Defense Logistics Agency
Cameron Station
Alexandria, VA 22304-6100 (202) 274-6135

This office has information on all Defense Logistics Agency business and activities, and a pamphlet on it mission, *The ABC's of DLA*. It also offers a *DLA Index to Publications*, a *DLA Index to Forms*, and the brochure, *An Identification of Commodities Purchased by the Defense Logistics Agency*. Write or call to request free copies.

* Contracting Research and Development with

the Defense Department
Defense Technical Information Center
DTIC, Attn: FDRB
Cameron Station
Alexandria, VA 22304-6145 (202) 274-7633

DTIC is the clearinghouse for the U.S. Department of Defense's collection of scientific and technological research and development information. The booklet entitled *Registration and Certification for Scientific and Technical Services* will explain who is eligible to use the Center's services and how to register as a user. The manual also contains a list of contractors, their offices and phone numbers, and information on the potential contractor program. The *Handbook for Users* and the *Green and White* brochure (DTIC-BC-1) explain the two major databases available to contractors and potential contractors: one for completed research and technological reports and one for ongoing research and development information. Write or call for more information and free copies of the brochures.

* Contracts and Small Business Activities

Procurement and Supply Department
The U.S. Postal Service
475 L'Enfant Plaza, SW, Room 4541
Washington, DC 20260 (202) 268-4040

Contact this office for information on contracts and small business activities through the U.S. Postal Service.

* Daily Procurement News

Superintendent of Documents
U.S. Government Printing Office
Washington, DC 20402 (202) 783-3238

Each weekday, the *Commerce Business Daily* gives a complete listing of products and services wanted by the U.S. government--products and services that your business may be selling. Each listing includes the following: the product or service, along with a short description; name and address of the agency; deadline for proposals or bids; phone number to request specifications; and the solicitation number of the product or service needed. Many business concerns, including small businesses, incorporate *CBD* review into their government

marketing activities. To obtain a $208.00/year subscription, contact the office above. Two-year and 6-month subscriptions are also available.

* Debarred Government Contractors

Superintendent of Documents
Government Printing Office
Washington, DC 20401
(202) 783-3238

The *Debarred List* is a quarterly publication listing those people or businesses currently debarred from doing business with the government for violation of various public contract acts.

* Defense Contractor Fraud Hotline

The Pentagon
Washington, DC 20301 (202) 693-5080, (800) 424-4098

Call this number to report fraud or corruption by anyone working for a Department of Defense contractor. The Hotline people are eager to supply your office with posters, brochures, and wallet size cards displaying their number.

* Doing Business with the Department of Veterans Affairs

Office of Acquisition and Materiel Management (93D)
Department of Veterans Affairs
810 Vermont Ave., NW
Washington, DC 20420 (202) 233-7611

The brochure, *Doing Business with the Department of Veterans Affairs*, is available free from this office. It includes information on doing business with an individual Medical Center, the Marketing Center, and the VA Central Office. Information on small business programs and the DVA contracting activities is also provided, along with a solicitation mailing list application. Contact the office above to obtain a copy.

* Doing Business With the Federal Government

Office of Publications
General Services Administration
18th and F Sts., NW
Washington, DC 20405 (202) 566-1235

The publication, *Doing Business With the Federal Government*, explains procurement policies, procedures, and programs. It also lists procurement offices by agency, and their 12 GSA Business Service Centers. It is available from your local Business Service Center, or the address listed above. Additional copies can be ordered from the Superintendent of Documents. U.S. Government Printing Office, Washington, D.C. 20402.

* Doing Business with the Military

Director, Office of Small and
Disadvantaged Business Utilization
Undersecretary of Defense for Acquisition
The Pentagon, Room 2A340
Washington, DC 20301 (202) 694-1151

This office has an information package on how to sell to the Department of Defense. It contains a booklet of rules and regulations in selling to the military, a booklet listing all the procurement offices worldwide, and a subcontracting directory. Write or call to request a copy.

* Education Grants and Contracts Service

Office of Management
U.S. Department of Education
400 Maryland Ave.
Washington, DC 20202 (202) 732-2804

This office publishes the pamphlet, GCMS: Grants and Contracts Management System, which gives you over-all information about the on-line information system which monitors the educational grant and procurement contract awards of the U.S. Department of Education. It also contains a telephone list of contacts within the system to call for information and inquiries on the status of your application. For information concerning GCMS, contact the Director, Management Support Division, Grants and Contracts Service, (202) 732-2773.

* Federal Contracts Database

Federal Procurement Data Center
4040 N. Fairfax Dr., Suite 900
Arlington, VA 22203 (703) 235-1326

This Center distributes consolidated information about federal purchases, including research and development. FPDC can tell you how much the federal government spent last quarter on products and services, which agencies made those purchases, and who the contractors were. FPDC summarizes this information through two types of reports: the FPDC standard report and the FPDC special report. The standard report is a free, quarterly compilation containing statistical procurement information in "snapshot" form for over 60 federal agencies, as well as several charts, graphs, and tables which compare procurement activities by state, major product and service codes, method of procurement, and contractors. The report further includes quarterly and year-to-year breakdowns of amounts and percentages spent on small, women-owned, and minority businesses. Special reports are prepared upon request for a fee, based on computer and labor costs. They are tailored to the specific procurement information needs of the user and analyze 25 data elements, or categories, which can be cross-tabulated in numerous ways. A special report can help you analyze government procurement and data trends, identify competitors, and locate federal markets for individual products or services. Contact the office listed above for further information.

* Federal Equipment Data Center

Federal Equipment Data Center
4040 N. Fairfax Dr., Suite 900
Arlington, VA 22203 (703) 235-2870
GSA's Federal Equipment Data Center maintains a current inventory of owned and leased general purpose data processing equipment as reported by over 60 federal agencies. In addition to maintaining a master ADP database, the FEDC produces reports to satisfy the need for geographical and market analyses. These data allow federal managers to review equipment profiles semiannually in the report, *Automatic Data Processing Equipment in the U.S. Government*, which includes charts and graphs profiling the Federal inventory by manufacturer, federal agency, systems and components. Special reports to meet specific data requirements can be produced on request. Further information about the FEDC reports and/or capabilities can be obtained from the office above.

* Federal Supply Schedules

Schedule Information Center
General Services Administration
FFNI - FSS, Room 634
Washington, DC 20406 (703) 557-8177
When economical to do so, Federal agencies can purchase an item directly from a contractor under the Federal Supply Schedule Program. This program provides federal agencies with sources for products and services such as furniture, electric lamps, appliances, photographic and duplicating equipment and supplies, athletic equipment, laboratory equipment and supplies, and audio and video recording equipment and supplies. Schedules are indefinite-quantity contracts usually established for a term of one to three years, and payment is made directly to the contractor by the ordering agency. Solicitations for bids under the Federal Supply Schedule program are advertised in the *Commerce Business Daily*. For more information, contact this office.

* Federal Systems Integration and Management Center

Federal Systems Integration
and Management Center
General Services Administration
5203 Leesburg Pike, Suite 400
Falls Church, VA 22041-3467 (703) 756-4300
This Center provides technical and acquisition assistance to federal agencies in the application of information systems and technology. FEDSIM acquires, manages, and uses computer and data communications systems needed to support federal information systems. For further information, contact the above office.

* Federal Vendor Payment System

Office of the Assistant Commissioner Field Operations
Financial Management Service
U.S. Department of the Treasury
401 14th St., SW
Washington, DC 20227 (202) 287-0311
"Vendor Express" enables Federal agencies to make electronic payments through the Automated Clearinghouse system to firms providing goods and services to the Federal Government. Clear information is provided to identify the payments. Within two years, FMS expects to make a significant number of all such Federal vendor payments via electronics.

* Fraud Hotline at Uncle Sam's Chief Housekeeper

Office of Inspector General
General Services Administration
18th and F Sts., NW
Washington, DC 20405 (202) 566-0450
Toll-Free Hotline Number: (800) 424-5210 Local Hotline Number: (202) 566-1780. This 24-hour hotline number is designed to assist those who wish to report alleged fraud, waste, abuse, and mismanagement. For more information contact the Office of Inspector General at the General Services Administration, the federal government's chief housekeeper.

* Fraud Hotline at Government's Chief Auditor

Fraud Prevention Group
General Accounting Office
600 E St., NW, Suite 1000
Washington, DC 20548
(202) 272-5557/8 (DC area); or 800-424-5454
The GAO runs a hotline to encourage reports of potential problems in government programs involving waste, fraud, abuse, and illegal actions. The Fraud Prevention Group tries to identify root causes and recurring patterns of illegal activities in order to see how they can best be detected and prevented. The group also probes agency information or accounting systems and programs for weaknesses that invite or allow fraud.

* General Services Administration Publications

Office of Publications
General Services Administration
18th and F Sts., NW
Washington, DC 20405 (202) 566-1235
GSA's *Annual Report* is available free from this office. The report includes general information about GSA, along with a financial statement. Also available free from this office is *What is GSA?*, a booklet which gives information on the various Services within GSA. For information on obtaining these and other publications contact the office listed above.

* Government Contracts for Small Business

Office of Small and Disadvantaged
Business Utilization
Department of Labor
200 Constitution Ave., NW, Room S1004
Washington, DC 20210 (202) 523-9148
This office was created to ensure that small and disadvantaged businesses are provided maximum opportunities to participate in government contracting activities for supplies and services. To this end, it conducts outreach programs and seminars for these business, and acts as a liaison with the Small Business Administration.

* Highway Contractors and Subcontractors

Office of Civil Rights
Federal Highway Administration
U.S. Department of Transportation
400 7th St., SW
Washington, DC 20590 (202) 366-0693
This office monitors compliance with civil rights laws by requiring contractors and subcontractors of Federal highway projects to submit employment data. Equal opportunity issues are also addressed in the Disadvantaged Business Enterprise Program, which awards contracts and subcontract commitments to small and minority businesses, and in FHWA's Historically Black Colleges and Universities Programs. Data from contractor filings and a list of contractors and subcontractors, by state or county, are available from this office. You can also obtain a copy of *FHWA's Historically Black Colleges and Universities Programs*, a publication with details about those programs.

* How the Government Acquires Land

Office of Publications
General Services Administration
18th and F Sts., NW
Washington, DC 20405 (202) 566-1235
The brochure, *How the Government Acquires Land*, answers questions most frequently asked by owners of real property selected by GSA for public building construction projects. It explains the agency's policy for determining public needs, selecting sites, arriving at a fair price to pay owners, and acquiring the property needed for public use. If your land is required by the federal government for constructing a public building, you will be paid a fair price for your property and compensated for any inconveniences^@government purchases,%^@^Ct of government property, travel by federal employees, defense materials, pubic buildings and space, supply and procurement, public utilities, transportation, utilization and disposal of property, and other programs and activities of GSA. New FPMR or amendments are published in the *Federal Register* and are accumulated in the *Code of Federal Regulations in Title 41, Chapter 101*. Both documents are available from GPO.

* Repairing and Rehabilitating Federal Personal Property

See above Local Help for Selling to the Government
The GSA attempts as much as possible to repair and rehabilitate personal property, such as furniture or office machines, for further federal use. FSS awards contracts for services which include electrostatic spray painting of metal furniture, refinishing of wood furniture, typewriter repair, tire retreading, and general auto repair. Federal agencies may contract for their own repair and maintenance services only if an FSS contract is not available. The majority of contracts are awarded to small and minority businesses, workshops for the blind and severely handicapped, and Federal Prison Industries, Inc. For further

Selling To The Government

information, contact one of the GSA Business Service Centers.

* Selling to the Army: Small Business

U.S. Army Materiel Command
Small and Disadvantaged Business
Utilization Office
5001 Eisenhower Ave.
Alexandria, VA 22333 (202) 274-8185

A series of brochures is available for small and women-owned businesses on how to sell their products and services to the Army. *How to Do Business with AMC* lists the commodity commands and each Small Business Office at each command. *Selling to the Military, Small Business Specialists,* and *Small Business Subcontracting* all cover information on the application process through the Department of Defense. Also available are brochures explaining finance regulations for small businesses and how to prepare offers. Write or call for free copies.

* Selling to Navy Exchanges

Navy Resale and Services Support Office
Ft. Wadsworth
Staten Island, NY 10305-5097 (718) 390-3503

This office supplies the brochure, *The Navy Resale System*, which explains how to sell to the Navy military exchanges. Call or write for a free copy.

* Selling to the General Services Administration

Office of Publications
General Services Administration
18th and F Sts., NW
Washington, DC 20405 (202) 566-1235

To get the most for its money in its multi-billion-dollar-a-year operations, GSA actively seeks new bidders and increased competition for its supply and service contracts. The brochure, *Contracting Opportunities With GSA*, outlines what those contracts buy and how and where to begin the bidding process to become a GSA supplier. Contact your Business Service Center to obtain this brochure.

* Selling to the Government Newsletter

Office of Client Relations
General Services Administration
18th and F Sts., NW, Room 6011
Washington, DC 20405 (202) 523-1200

This office provides customer services to its clients. For more information or to obtain a copy of its bi-monthly newsletter, the Alert Bulletin, contact the office above.

* Selling to the Marine Corps

Commandant of the Marine Corps
Morale Welfare Recreation Support Center
Quantico, VA 22134 (703) 640-3800

This office supplies fact sheets list Marine Corps installations worldwide and explaining how to sell to the military exchanges on those installations.

* Selling to NASA

National Aeronautics and Space Administration
Office of Small and Disadvantaged
Business Utilization, Code K
Washington, DC 20546 (202) 453-2088

Selling To NASA outlines for you the procurement process, marketing your capabilities, special assistance programs for small and disadvantaged businesses, NASA field installations, and a listing of NASA small/minority business personnel. For a free copy, contact this office.

* Selling to National Park Concessions

Concessions Division
National Park Service
U.S. Department of the Interior
1100 L St., NW
Washington, DC 20005 (202) 343-1550

For information on providing goods and services on a contractual basis with the National Park Service, contact the office above.

* Selling to the Government Printer

Superintendent of Documents
Government Printing Office
Washington, DC 20402 (202) 275-3030

Joint Committee on Printing

The Capitol, Room S-151
Washington, DC 20510 (202) 224-5241

Issued by the Joint Committee on Printing for the use of government departments and agencies in the procurement of paper stock for printing, these standards consist of three parts. They are also of value and interest to paper manufacturers, printing establishments, and others concerned with paper standards and specifications. *Part 1* contains detailed standard specifications; *Part 2* gives the standards to be used in testing; and *Part 3* consists of the definitive color standards for all mimeograph, duplicator, writing, manifold, bond ledger, and index papers (color standards for other classes of paper will be prepared and issued as such standards are developed). Subscription service includes supplementary material for an indeterminate period and is available for $22.00 from the Superintendent of Documents.

* Selling to the Tennessee Valley Authority

Purchasing
Tennessee Valley Authority
6th and Chestnut St.
Chattanooga, TN 37402 (615) 751-5610

The TVA buys both products and services from private businesses. The services they procure include the transfer, disposal and shipping of equipment, materials, supplies, and fuels, along with management services. TVA purchases are principally for construction and operation of electric power plants and transmission systems, the construction of dams and locks, and the development and experimental production of fertilizers. Other items required include electrical generating equipment, such as turbogenerators, steam-generating units, nuclear plant equipment, hydraulic turbines and generators, transformers, boilers, piping systems, and switchgear. Raw materials bought include coal, coke, and nuclear fuel. Also bought are electrical and electronic supplies, equipment and spare parts, communications equipment, structural and milled steel, phosphate rock and chemicals, and items for medical laboratory, and photographic purposes.

* Selling to the U.S. Arms Control Agency

U.S. Arms Control and Disarmament Agency
Attn: A/CON
320 21st St., NW
Washington, DC 20451 (202) 235-2388

Those seeking to do business with the U.S. Arms Control and Disarmament Agency or to obtain information on research contracts should contact the Contracting Office.

* Selling to the U.S. Army: Commodity Commands

U.S. Army Materiel Command
Public Affairs
5001 Eisenhower Ave.
Alexandria, VA 22333 (202) 274-8010

The U.S. Army Materiel Command encompasses seven commodity commands which contract for both products and research and development. The Materiel Command buys everything the soldier uses, both personally and in his job. The commodity commands include the Armament, Munitions and Chemical Commmand; the Aviation Systems Command; the Communications-Electronics Command; the Laboratory Command (which contracts for research); the Missile Command; the Tank-Automotive Command; and the Troop Support Command (includes portable sanitary equipment, food, and uniforms). Call or write for a free brochure explaining what the Material Command encompasses.

* Selling to the U. S. Department of Education

Grants and Contracts Service
Office of Management
U.S. Department of Education
400 Maryland Ave.
Washington, DC 20202 (202) 732-2804

This office serves as the primary link between the U.S. Department of Education and those in the private sector who wish to obtain grants for education and contracts for business firms and non-profit organizations. A brochure entitled "Doing Business with the Department of Education" outlines the procedure necessary to secure a grant or contract. Over 50 percent of the contracts are awarded to small businesses, small disadvantaged businesses, labor surplus area businesses, small and small disadvantaged subcontractors, and women-owned businesses. Some of the areas under contract include feasibility studies, travel agency services, data collection, public relations, arts/graphics, print/binding, and computer (ADP) entry and transmission services, to name just a few.

* Selling to the U.S. Department of Housing and Urban Development

Office of Procurement and Contracts
Room 5260
Department of Housing and Urban Development
Washington, DC 20410 (202) 755-5294

This office is responsible for purchasing all supplies, equipment, and services to fulfill Headquarters' logistical, administrative, and program requirements. Some of the areas where contracts are awarded include ADP software development and systems maintenance, HUD building operation and maintenance, technical assistance to HUD program recipients, housing research, and special studies.

Office of Small and Disadvantaged Business Utilization, Room 10226, Department of Housing and Urban Development, Washington, DC 20410, (202) 755-1428
This office provides direct HUD contracting and subcontracting opportunities to businesses and organizations, which include small businesses, firms in labor surplus areas, women-owned businesses, and historically black colleges and universities. For more information on HUD's procurement program, contact this office and ask for their free brochure, "Doing Business with HUD."

* Selling to the U.S. Department of Labor

Office of Small and Disadvantaged
Business Utilization
Department of Labor
200 Constitution Ave., NW, Room S1004
Washington, DC 20210   (202) 523-9148
What the U.S. Department of Labor Buys is intended to acquaint prospective contractors with the Department's mission and programs, and to assist them in understanding the its acquisition process, identifying business opportunities and contact points, and determining the appropriate sources form which detailed information and guidance may be obtained.

* Selling to the U.S. Department of State

Superintendent of Documents
Government Printing Office
Washington, DC 20402   (202) 783-3238
A Guide To Doing Business With The Department of State, is designed to familiarize small, minority, and female-owned businesses with the Department's procurement program, lists user-office contacts under the various categories of products and services; all Federal Offices of Small and Disadvantaged Business Utilization; available subcontracting opportunities; and contacts for trade and investment-related issues.

* Selling to the U.S. International Trade Commission

Contracting and Procurement Division
U.S. International Trade Commission
500 E St., SW
Washington, DC 20436   (202) 252-1730
This ITC division can provide you with information on contract and procurement opportunities.

* Selling to the U.S. Securities and Exchange Commission

The Office of Administrative Services
U.S. Securities and Exchange Commission
450 5th St., NW
Washington, DC 20549   (202) 272-7000
For information about contracts contact this office.

* Selling to VA Canteen Service

Veterans Canteen Service
Merchandise Support Division (133B1)
Department of Veterans Affairs
810 Vermont Ave., NW
Washington, DC 20420   (202) 376-8140/8142

The Veterans Canteen Service (VCS) provides food and other service activities at VA medical centers for the comfort and well-being of the patients. The brochure, *Selling to the Veterans Canteens,* provides information on VCS' buying procedures. For more information contact the office above.

* Small and Disadvantaged Business

Small and Disadvantaged Business
Utilization
U.S. Department of Agriculture
Room 124 W. Administration Bldg.
Washington, DC 20250   (202) 447-7177
Through this office, the USDA provides assistance to small, disadvantaged, and women-owned businesses wishing to do business with the USDA. This office expands procurement for and provides technical and financial assistance to labor surplus area concerns and small, minority, and women-owned businesses for increasing use of these businesses as subcontractors. Write or call for the free booklet, "Selling to the USDA," which covers all aspects of the USDA's procurement process.

* Small and Disadvantaged Businesses

Office of Small and Disadvantaged Business Utilization
National Science Foundation
1800 G St., NW, Room 1250
Washington, DC 20550   (202) 357-7875
This office provides information and guidance to small, minority, and women-owned companies seeking procurement opportunities with NSF or its major contractors.

* Small and Disadvantaged Business Utilization

Office of Small and Disadvantaged Business Utilization
General Services Administration
18th and F Sts., NW
Washington, DC 20405   (202) 566-1021
Each federal agency with procurement authority is required by law to maintain this office to promote participation of these firms in government procurement. Consult your Business Service Center or the office listed above for further information.

* Small and Disadvantaged Business Utilization

Office of Small and Disadvantaged Business Utilization
General Services Administration
18th and F Sts., NW
Washington, DC 20405   (202) 566-1021
Each federal agency with procurement authority is required by law to maintain this office to promote participation of these firms in government procurement.

* Small Business Pentagon Procurement Assistance

Small Business Office
Defense Fuel Supply Center
5010 Duke St.
Cameron Station, Building 8
Alexandria, VA 22314-6160   (202) 274-7428
This Small Business Office will refer potential contractors to the major buying centers within the Defense Logistics Agency for the commodity or service they wish to market. They have two standard brochures, *Selling to the Military* and *Guide to Preparation.* Write or call for free copies.

* Small Business Procurement

Office of Procurement
U.S. Department of the Treasury
1500 Pennsylvania Ave., NW
Room 1458
Washington, DC 20220   (202) 566-9616
The free booklet, *Selling to the Department of the Treasury,* discusses the opportunities available to businesses in the contracting of supplies, materials, equipment, and services to the Department. Procurement offices are listed for each of the Bureau, including regional offices. *What Treasury Buys* is also a valuable publication listing all of the items purchased by each of the Bureaus. *Small Business Contracting Directory* lists all of the current subcontractors and the item provided.

* Small Business Subcontracting Directory

Superintendent of Documents
U.S. Government Printing Office
Washington, DC 20402   (202) 783-3238
Designed to aid small businesses interested in subcontracting opportunities within the Department of Defense, the *Small Business Subcontracting Directory* is an indispensable guide arranged alphabetically by State and includes the name and address of each current DOD prime contractor as well as the product or service being provided to DOD. It also includes the name and telephone number for each Small Business Liaison Officer who knows what the subcontracted products and services are, what the prime contracting firm has purchased in the past, what it is presently purchasing, and what it may be planning to purchase in the future. It is available for $7.00 through GPO.

* Software Development and Information Technology Center

Office of Software Development
and Information Technology
General Services Administration
5203 Leesburg Pike, Suite 1100
Falls Church, VA 22041-3467   (703) 756-6151
This office solves problems for other Federal agencies on a reimburseable basis by offering techniques, publications, and experienced staff to assist in the areas of software management, IRM planning, and office automation systems. Contract opportunities are available to firms with expertise in specialties such as software conversion, software engineering, information resources planning, and office automation. For general information, contact the Center at the address

listed above; for more specific information call the appropriate office listed below: Federal Software Management Support Center: (703) 756-4500; Federal IRM Planning Support Center: (703) 756-4000; Federal Office Automation Support Center: (703) 756-6900.

* Subcontract Assistance

Contact your local SBA office or
Small Business Answer Desk
U.S. Small Business Administration
1725 Eye St., NW Room 414
Washington, DC 20416   (202) 653-7561 or (800) 368-5855

SBA develops subcontracting opportunities for small business by maintaining close contact with large business prime contractors and referring qualified small firms to them. The SBA has developed agreements and close working relationships with hundreds of prime contractors who cooperate by offering small firms opportunities to compete for their subcontracts. In addition, to complete SBA's compliance responsibilities, commercial market representatives monitor prime contractors in order to assess their compliance with laws governing subcontracting opportunities for small businesses.

* Subcontracting Opportunities for Small Business

Office of Small and Disadvantaged
Business Utilization, Code K
National Aeronautics and Space Administration
Washington, DC 20546   (202) 453-2088

Subcontracting with NASA prime contractors is an important source of revenue for many companies, both small and large. For example, of the $5.6 billion awarded to NASA prime contractors in FY 83, $1.9 billion was channeled on to subcontractors, with over $600 million going to small businesses. Special contract clauses are included in most NASA prime contracts which require the prime contractor to maximize small business subcontracting opportunities. Most of the major contractors have small business representatives assigned to assist small companies in understanding and responding to the prime contractor, and many also produce special publications which can be helpful to those interested in subcontracting. The above office can provide you with more information on the subcontracting process, along with a free directory of NASA's 120 top prime contractors, which lists each contractor's name, address, contact person, phone and fax numbers, and product or service.

* Subcontracting Opportunities for Small Business

Office of Small and Disadvantaged
Business Utilization, Code K
National Aeronautics and Space Administration
Washington, DC 20546   (202) 453-2088

Subcontracting with NASA prime contractors is an important source of revenue for many companies, both small and large. For example, of the $5.6 billion awarded to NASA prime contractors in FY 83, $1.9 billion was channeled on to subcontractors, with over $600 million going to small businesses. Special contract clauses are included in most NASA prime contracts which require the prime contractor to maximize small business subcontracting opportunities. Most of the major contractors have small business representatives assigned to assist small companies in understanding and responding to the prime contractor, and many also produce special publications which can be helpful to those interested in subcontracting. The above office can provide you with more information on the subcontracting process, along with a free directory of NASA's 120 top prime contractors, which lists each contractor's name, address, contact person, phone and fax numbers, and product or service.

* Specifications and Standards of the Federal Government

Specifications Section
General Services Administration
7th and D Sts., SW, Room 6654
Washington, DC 20407   (202) 472-2205

The booklet, *Guide to Specifications and Standards of the Federal Government*, gives you information on the types, use, and purposes on specifications and standards. It is available free through the office listed above.

* Submitting Unsolicited Proposals

General Manager, Procurement policies
and Programs Division
U.S. Postal Service Headquarters
475 L'Enfant Plaza SW
Washington, DC 20260-6201   (202) 252-1730

The Postal Service is always willing to look at new ideas that will help improve mail service. Breakthroughs can come from creative individuals working in business or alone, with insight to see a problem as no one else has. The Postal Service has set up criteria to identify and review the more promising proposals. An unsolicited proposal--an offer that is not in response to a formal solicitation--must be submitted in writing and must include specific information if you want the Postal Service to consider it.

* U.S. Government and Purchasing Sales Directory

Superintendent of Documents
U.S. Government Printing Office
Washington, DC 20402   (202) 783-3238

Published by the SBA, the *U.S. Government and Purchasing Sales Directory* is a major resource for a small business that wants to sell to the federal government or buy property being sold by the government. The small business owner will find in the *Directory* an alphabetical listing of the products and services bought by the military departments, and a separate listing or the civilian agencies. Both sections are keyed to the purchasing offices that buy such products and services. The *Directory* also includes an explanation of the ways in which the SBA can help a business obtain government prime contracts and subcontracts, data on government sales of surplus property, and comprehensive descriptions of the scope of the increasingly important government market for research and development.

* U. S. Postal Service Procurement Manual

Communications Department
U.S. Postal Service
475 L'Enfant Plaza, SW
Washington, DC 20260   (202) 268-2143

This manual establishes uniform policies and procedures relating to procuring facilities, equipment, supplies and services under the authority of Chapter 4, Title 39, United States Code. The subscription costs $103.00 domestic, and $128.75 foreign from: Superintendent of Documents, Government Printing Office, Washington, D.C. 20402-0001; (202) 783-3238.

* Vendor Sales to Military Exchanges Headquarters

Army and Air Force Exchange Service
Attn: PA-I
P.O. Box 660202
Dallas, TX 75266   (214) 780-2763

This office supplies the brochure, *Facts for Vendors*, which explains how to sell to the Army and Air Force military exchanges. Call or write for free copies.

International Trade
Selling Overseas

* See also Economics, Demographics and Statistics Chapter
* See also Vacations and Business Travel Chapter
* See also Small Business and Entrepeneuring Chapter
* See also Agriculture and Farming Chapter

The federal and state governments are the best sources of help and information for businesses, both large and small, looking to sell their goods and products overseas. You can get free or low-cost assistance with financing, marketing, accounting, licensing assistance, overseas representation, and even exporting insurance. And, if you want to take advantage of the new opportunities developing in Eastern Europe, the U.S. Department of Commerce now has a special office to help you--the Eastern European Business Information Center.

* Administrative Law Judges
Office of Administrative Law Judges
U.S. International Trade Commission
500 E St., SW, Room 213
Washington, DC 20436 (202) 252-1691
This office holds evidence hearings on cases involving such products as baldness remedies, genetically engineering hormones, computer chips, and plastic screw anchors. For more information contact this office.

* Agent/Distributor Service
U.S. and Foreign Commercial Service
International Trade Administration
U.S. Department of Commerce, Room H2106
Washington, DC 20230 (202) 377-5777
ITA's Agent/Distributor Service gives you an opportunity to show your product literature to potential agents and distributors abroad. This personalized search for qualified foreign representatives will identify up to six prospects who have examined your product literature and expressed interest in representing your product. Contact this office for more information.

* Antiboycott Compliance
Office of Antiboycott Compliance
Bureau of Export Administration
Department of Commerce
14th St. and Constitution Ave., NW
Room 6098
Washington, DC 20230 (202) 377-2381
This office develops and implements policies and measures for opposing foreign boycotts against countries friendly to the United States. The law specifically prohibits U.S. companies from complying with unsanctioned foreign boycotts against countries friendly to the U.S. OAC conducts investigations of alleged violations, prepares cases for settlement, and provides support in the event of criminal prosecution or civil litigation of cases. The office also provides advice to the business community on the statutory requirements and implementing regulations. The booklet, U.S. Antiboycott Laws Regulation Of Participation In Foreign Boycotts, provides some general information concerning antiboycott compliance, and is available at no charge.

* Antitrust Protection
Office of Export Trading Company Affairs
International Trade Administration
U.S. Department of Commerce
Washington, DC 20230 (202) 377-5131
The Commerce Department, which implements the ETC Act, can grant immunity from federal and state criminal and civil prosecution for export activities. The ETC Act also provides significant disincentives against private actions. To examine the ETC Act program, contact this ITA office.

* Arab Boycott
Antiboycott Compliance Staff
International Trade Administration
U.S. Department of Commerce
14th & Constitution, NW, Room 6098
Washington, DC 20230 (202) 377-2004

For assistance and information on how to comply with the Arab Boycott laws, contact this office.

* Basic Guide to Exporting
Government Printing Office
Superintendent of Documents
Washington, DC 20402 (202) 783-3238
The Basic Guide to Exporting provides you with a detailed, step-by-step guide through the exporting process. It fills you in on everything you need to know about developing an export strategy, finding economical market research, pricing for profits, shipping overseas, export documentation, traveling abroad, answering overseas inquiries, making an overseas sales contact, using an export management company, antitrust, copyrights, trade secrets, technology licensing, getting paid for overseas sales, joint ventures, patents, licensing exports, financing overseas sales, foreign sales corporations, government assistance to exporters, and a wealth of other useful information. It is available for $8.50 (s/n 003-009-00487-0) from GPO.

* Bonded Merchandise Carriers
Public Information Office
U.S. Customs Service
Department of the Treasury
P.O. Box 7407
Washington, DC 20044 (202) 566-8195
A brochure, Notice to Carriers of Bonded Merchandise, outlines the precautions you must take in the shipment of bonded goods into the United States. Bonded merchandise is delivered directly to the Customs officer in charge at the port of destination.

* Bridge Data Tables
Office of Tariff Affairs and Trade Agreements
U.S. International Trade Commission
500 E St., SW, Room 404
Washington, DC 20436 (202) 252-1592
The office publishes concordances and trade tables which provide U.S. import and export trade data for the past five years under the harmonized Commodity Description and Coding System. The Commission expects the international trade community to make extensive use of the so-called "bridge data tables" as the United States moves to the Harmonized System.

* Broadcast Services
Office of Public Affairs Personnel
U.S. Department of Commerce
14th St & Constitution, NW
Washington, DC 20230
The Department of Commerce has the following broadcast services:
Hard News and Economic Report (202) 393-4100
Weekly Features (202) 393-4102
Commerce News Announcements (202) 393-1847

* Cargo Importation Guidelines
Division of Cargo Enforcement
Office of Inspection and Control
U.S. Customs Service
Department of the Treasury
1301 Constitution Ave., NW, Room 4141

Washington, DC 20229   (202) 566-5354
This office establishes guidelines and policies for the importation of all cargo, both from air and sea vessels. Staff can answer your questions regarding specific import requirements.

* Caribbean Basin Business Promotion

U.S. and Foreign Commercial Service
International Trade Administration
U.S. Department of Commerce
14th St. & Constitution, NW, Room HCHB1066
Washington, DC 20230   (202) 377-5777
The US&FCS carries out the Caribbean Basin Initiative (CBI) by assisting U.S. firms in identifying business opportunities in Central America and the West Indies. It also established a CBI Business Promotion Council to apply private sector expertise to problems in the Caribbean Basin. Contact this office for more information.

* Caribbean Basin Employment and Trade

Bureau of International Economic Affairs
Department of Labor
200 Constitution Ave., NW, Room S5355
Washington, DC 20210   (202) 523-7597
The annual report, *Trade and Employment Effects of the Caribbean Basin Economic Recovery Act*, describes the provisions included in the CBERA, along with the benefits they provide to beneficiary countries. It also analyzes changes in U.S. trade with CBERA countries, and looks at trends in U.S. employment in those industries which have undergone the most significant changes in trade flows. Contact this office for more information on the report.

* Caribbean Basin Trade Policy

Trade Reports Division
Office of Economics
U.S. International Trade Commission
500 E St., SW, Room 602
Washington, DC 20436   (202) 252-1216
Staff monitors the impact of the Caribbean Basin Economic Recovery Act on U.S. industries and consumers and studies several other issues, including the effects of the act on investment in Caribbean countries. ITC economists have traveled to four Caribbean countries to obtain firsthand information on how the act affected their production and exports. For more information on this trade act contact the above office.

* Catalog & Video/Catalog Exhibitions

U.S. and Foreign Commercial Service
International Trade Administration
U.S. Department of Commerce, Room H2106
Washington, DC 20230   (202) 377-5777
You can send your product literature or promotional video on tour abroad to U.S. embassies or consulates, where your materials will be displayed to interested potential buyers and representatives. In this way, as an exporter you gain market exposure for products or services without the cost of traveling overseas. Contact this office for more information.

* Commerce Business Daily

Superintendent of Documents
Government Printing Office
Washington, DC 20402   (202) 783-3238

Office of Publications
International Trade Administration
Department of Commerce
14th & Constitution, NW
Washington, DC 20230   (202) 377-0632
Commerce Business Daily (CBD) is a daily list of government procurement invitations, contract awards, subcontracting leads, sales of surplus property, and foreign business opportunities, as well as certain foreign government procurements. The annual subscription cost is $261.00 for first-class mail and $208.00 second-class. A six-month trial subscription costs $130.00 for first-class and $104.00 for second-class. *CBD* is available on-line from a sizable list of contractors named in the lower left-hand corner of the front page of each edition. Contact ITA for additional information, or GPO to order a subscription.

* Commercial Information Management System

U.S. and Foreign Commercial Service
International Trade Administration
U.S. Department of Commerce
14th St & Constitution, NW, Room H2106
Washington, DC 20230   (202) 377-5777

The Commercial Information Management System (CIMS) electronically links all the economic and marketing information of the different offices worldwide, speeding delivery of vital business data. Through CIMS and a variety of other resources, US&FCS can develop individually tailored information packages on foreign business and economic climate; import regulations; tariff and non-tariff barriers; domestic and foreign competition; individual competitors and competitive factors; distribution practices; how products are promoted in the market; policies and product standards; end-users; and more. It is also possible to identify foreign agents, distributors, importers, manufacturers, retailers, government purchasing officials, and end-users interested in a product or service. US&FCS will provide names, contacts, telex and telephone numbers, cable addresses, product or service specialties, year established, number of employees, and relative size--all tailored to individual specifications. For more information on CIMS contact, this office.

* Commodity and Chemical Product Reports

Office of the Secretary
U.S. International Trade Commission
500 E St., SW
Washington, DC 20436   (202) 252-1000
The Commission publishes results of investigations concerning various commodities and subjects, along with a series of reports on chemicals. For information on specific reports and how to obtain them, contact this office.

* Comparison Shopping Service

U.S. and Foreign Commercial Service
International Trade Administration
U.S. Department of Commerce, Room H2106
Washington, DC 20230   (202) 377-5777
Check out your overseas competition through this personalized product shopping service available in selected markets abroad. US&FCS in-country staff will conduct on-the-spot surveys to determine key marketing facts about your product and its competition, including sales potential, comparable products, distribution channels, going price, competitive factors, and qualified purchasers. For more information on the comparison shopping service, contact this ITA office.

* Competitive Assessments of U.S. Industries

Office of Public Affairs
U.S. Department of Commerce
International Trade Administration
14th & Constitution, NW, Room H3414
Washington, DC 20230   (202) 377-3808
Competitive Assessments of U.S. Industries are studies of the competitiveness of selected U.S. industries as compared with their foreign counterparts. These assessments were prepared by International Trade Administration industry analysts with the assistance in particular cases of other U.S. Government agencies, industry associations, and various private sector groups and individuals. Assessments of more than 45 industries or industry sectors have been published as of June 1989. For an up-to-date listing of each study, contact this office.

* Construction Industry Statistics

Superintendent of Documents
Government Printing Office
Washington, DC 20402   (202) 783-3238
The bimonthly publication, *Construction Review*, carries virtually all of the U.S. Government's statistics pertaining to the construction industry. An annual subscription is $21.00, and $26.25 foreign. A single copy is $3.50, and $4.38 foreign. Contact GPO to order.

* Congressional Information Requests On Unfair Trade Practices

Office of the Secretary
U.S. International Trade Commission
500 E St., SW, Room 112
Washington, DC 20436   (202) 252-1000
The Commission is required to make available to the President and to the Committee on Ways and Means of the House of Representatives and to the Committee on Finance of the Senate, whenever requested, all information at its command and is directed to make such investigations and reports.

* Counseling Services

Washington, D.C. Branch Office
International Trade Administration
U.S. Department of Commerce
14th St & Constitution NW, Room HCHB1066
Washington, DC 20230   (202) 377-3181
Individualized export counseling services of a trade specialist are available to you free of charge. Most business clients work with one trade specialist in their local office throughout their exporting experience. This close working relationship enables your trade specialist to develop an in-depth understanding of your export

needs. Trade specialists can develop marketing packages for your company, individually tailored to your specific products or services and oriented to your marketing goals. The Washington, D.C., Branch Office counsels visitors to the capital and schedules appointments with Department officials.

* Country Desk Officers

International Economic Policy Unit
International Trade Administration
U.S. Department of Commerce
14th St & Constitution, NW
Washington, DC 20230   (202) 377-3022

Country desk officers are an excellent source of information on trade potential in specific countries. Every country in the world has a country desk officer assigned to it. These specialists can look at the needs of an individual U.S. firm wishing to sell in a particular country in the full context of that country's overall economy, trade policies, and political situation, and also in light of U.S. policies toward that country. Desk officers keep up-to-date on the economic and commercial conditions in their assigned countries. Each collects information on the country's regulations, tariffs, business practices, economic and political developments, trade data and trends, market size, and growth. In this way, each keeps tabs on the country's potential as a market for U.S. products, services, and investments. They also seek to remove obstacles to U.S. commercial activities in their assigned countries, and work with the ITA district offices in counseling businesses and arranging seminars on trade and investment opportunities in their assigned countries. The Country Desk is organized as follows:

Headquarters: (202) 377-3022
GATT Division: (202) 377-3681
International Organizations: (202) 377-3227
U.S. Trade by Region--
Africa: (202) 377-2175
Canada: (202) 377-3101
Caribbean Basin & Mexico: (202) 377-5327
Eastern Europe: (202) 377-2645
European Community: (202) 377-5276
Israel Information Center: (202) 377-4652
Japan: (202) 377-4527
Near East: (202) 377-4441
Pacific Basin: (202) 377-4008
PRC. Hong Kong: (202) 377-3583
South America: (202) 377-2436
South Asia: (202) 377-2954
USSR: (202) 377-4655
Western Europe: (202) 377-5341

* Customs Audit Activities

Office of Regulatory Audit
U.S. Customs Service
Department of the Treasury
1301 Constitution Ave., NW, Room 2311
Washington, DC 20229   (202) 566-2812

Components that are sent from the U.S. to be assembled in a foreign country and then returned to the U.S. for sale are audited by this office. All claims of importers and exporters are also investigated. The manual, *807 Guide: Import Requirements on Articles Assembled Abroad from U.S. Components*, will also clarify the provisions. This publication may be obtained from the Public Information Office, U.S. Customs Service, P.O Box 7407, Washington, D.C. 20044.

* Customs Bonded Warehouses

Entry Rulings Branch
Office of Regulations and Rulings
U.S. Customs Service
Department of the Treasury
1301 Constitution Ave., NW, Room 2215
Washington, DC 20229   (202) 566-5856

Payment of duty is not required on goods stored, manipulated, or manufactured in a Customs bonded warehouse. The importer and warehouse proprietor incur liability under a bond. Contact the Customs office nearest you for more specific information. Provisions are also outlined in the brochure, *U.S. Customs Bonded Warehouse*, available from the Public Information Office, U.S. Customs Service, P.O. Box 7407, Washington, DC 20044.

* Customs Bulletin and Decisions

Superintendent of Documents
Government Printing Office
Washington, DC 20402   (202) 783-3238

Customs Bulletin and Decisions is a subscription service which contains regulations, rulings, decisions, and notices concerning Customs and related matters of the United States Court of Appeals for the Federal Circuit and the United States Court of International Trade. The price is $114.00 per year. (S/N 748-002-00000-6)

* Customs: Current Issues

Information Services Division
U.S. Customs Service
Department of the Treasury
1301 Constitution Ave., NW
Washington, DC 20229   (202) 566-3962

Customs Today is the official magazine of the U.S. Customs Service employees. Issues feature efforts of the Customs Service in the areas of drug enforcement, import and export analysis, and the automated systems used in these areas.

* Customs District Rulings Program

Area Director of Customs
U.S. Customs Service
Department of the Treasury
New York Seaport
6 World Trade Center
New York, NY 10048   (212) 466-5817

The importing public may submit a request for a binding classification ruling for a prospective shipment under the *Harmonized Tariff Schedule*. Ruling requests must be in writing and must contain a statement of all relevant facts relating to the transaction. District Officers in other parts of the country will also assist you.

* Customs Laboratories

Office of Laboratories and Scientific Services
U.S. Customs Service
Department of the Treasury
1301 Constitution Ave., NW, Room 7113
Washington, DC 20229   (202) 566-5853

The U.S. Customs Laboratories system includes the headquarters facility and seven field laboratories in New York, Savannah, New Orleans, Los Angeles, San Francisco, Chicago, and San Juan. It also operates a nearly full service laboratory in an 18-wheel trailer truck. Analysis is often needed to determine the country of origin of anything from pistachio nuts to steel. State-of-the-art technology is used. On a typical day, a Customs chemist may analyze a steel plate for allowing elements, determine whether a cheese was made from goat's or cow's milk, test an electric motor to determine its horsepower, or examine a suitcase for heroin residue as evidence of smuggling. Approximately 80,000 samples are studied annually.

* Customs Regulations of the United States

Superintendent of Documents
Government Printing Office
Washington, DC 20402   (202) 783-3238

A basic manual and supplementary material are part of the subscription service, *Customs Regulations of the United States*, which contains regulations made and published to carry out customs laws administered by the U.S. Customs Service. The yearly subscription price is $40.00. (S/N 948-006-00000-6)

* Customs Regulations Retrieval System

Office of Regulations and Rulings
U.S. Customs Service
Department of the Treasury
1301 Constitution Ave, NW, Room 2321
Washington, DC 20229   (202) 566-5095

The *Legal Precedent Retrieval System* is a research tool designed to assist users in identifying and recovering rulings and decisions of the office above and the National Import Specialist, New York Seaport Area. It consists of two parts: the *Keyword Directory* and the *Keyword Worksheet*. The *Directory* is a comprehensive index to classification, value, drawback, bonds, entry, carrier, marking, penalty, and other rulings. The *Keyword Worksheet* serves as a means of verifying if a particular keyword you are interested in exists within the system before you begin a comprehensive study of your subject matter. The *Decisions/Rulings Microfiche* is also available as a companion system to the LPRS.

* Defense-Critical Industrial Imports

Assistant Secretary for Industrial
Resources Administration
Bureau of Export Administratoin
Department of Commerce
14th St. and Constitution Ave., NW
Room 3878
Washington, DC 20230   (202) 377-4506

This office is responsible for policies and programs related to the defense industrial base. Its activities in this area include reviewing the impact of imports on defense-critical industries to ensure that defense contractors receive priority in obtaining raw materials and components in short supply.

* District Export Councils

U.S. and Foreign Commercial Service
International Trade Administration

International Trade

U.S. Department of Commerce
14th St. & Constitution, NW, Room HCHB1066
Washington, DC 20230   (202) 377-5777
The local district offices expand their own services through District Export Councils (DECs), composed of nearly 1,700 volunteer businesspersons across the nation. These DECs give U.S. companies opportunities to meet with seasoned exporters, who sponsor counseling sessions, seminars, trade missions, and other trade events. The district offices also cooperate with state governments in their export programs. Contact this office for more information.

* Drawback: Commodity Tax Remittance

Entry Rulings Branch
Office of Regulations and Rulings
U.S. Customs Service
Department of the Treasury
1301 Constitution Ave., NW
Washington, DC   (202) 566-5856
"Drawback" is a situation in which a duty or tax, lawfully collected, is refunded or remitted, wholly or partially, because of a particular use made of the commodity on which the duty or tax was collected. The rationale for drawback has always been to encourage American commerce or manufacturing. It permits the American manufacturer to compete in foreign markets without the handicap of including in his costs, and consequently in his sales price, the duty paid on imported merchandise. For a more complete discussion of drawback, obtain the flyer *Drawback: A Duty Refund on Certain Exports* from the Public Information Office, U.S. Customs Service, P.O. Box 7407, Washington, D.C. 20044.

* Duty Assessment and Tariff Classification

Office of Trade Operations
U.S. Customs Service
Department of the Treasury
1301 Constitution Ave., NW, Room 1334
Washington, DC 20229   (202) 566-5307
This office determines the value of merchandise imported into the United states and sets the rate of duty to be paid. Duty or tariff classification can also be obtained in writing to the district where the merchandise will be reported or where the importer will be doing business. For further information in this area, obtain the flyer, *Tariff Classification of Prospective Imports*, from the Public Information Office, U.S. Customs Service, P.O. Box 7407, Washington, D.C. 20044.

* Duty Removal on Imports from Developing Countries

Office of the Secretary
U.S. International Trade Commission
500 E St., SW, Room 112
Washington, DC 20436   (202) 252-1000
The ITC advises the U.S. President of the probable economic effect of preferential removal of the duty on imports from designated developing countries on the U.S. domestic industry and consumers. Contact this office for information on current and past studies, along with economic trade issues with developing countries.

* Eastern Europe Business Information Center

Eastern Europe Business Information Center
U.S. Department of Commerce
14th and Constitution Ave, NW Room 6043
Washington, DC 20230   (202) 377-2645
This office serves as a clearinghouse for information on opportunities in Eastern Europe, and on U.S. Government programs supporting private enterprise, trade and investment in Eastern Europe. It is also a referral point for voluntary assistance programs. It will encourage development of economically sound proposals for the Polish-American and Hungarian-American Enterprise Funds.

* East-West Trade Policy

Bureau of Economic and Business Affairs
Department of State
2001 C St., NW, Room 3819
Washington, DC 20520   (202) 647-2875
This office, as one of two offices in International Trade Controls, has broad responsibilities for the conduct of U.S. economic policy, including between the U.S. and the USSR. It is primarily responsible, however, for the negotiation of strategic trade agreements with newly industrialized nations, along with being charged with the administration of worldwide foreign policy export controls. Information is available on importing or exporting products, as well as on doing business with foreign countries.

* East-West Trade Report

Trade Reports Division
Office of Economics

U.S. International Trade Commission
500 E St., SW, Room 602
Washington, DC 20436   (202) 252-1216
The ITC monitors imports into the United States from 16 nonmarket-economy countries and makes a report at least once each calendar quarter on the effect of such imports on the production of like or directly competitive articles in the United States and on employment within the industry. Contact this office for more information on these reports.

* Economic Analyses of U.S. Trade Policy

Office of Economics
U.S. International Trade Commission
500 E St., SW, Room 602
Washington, DC 20436   (202) 252-1216
Economic analyses helps the ITC perform its two main functions: investigating the effects of imports on competing U.S. industries and providing expert advice to Congress and the President on international economic issues. Contact this office for more information.

* Electronics Importers/Brokers Seminars

Public Service Division
Federal Communications Commission
1919 M Street, NW, Room 725
Washington, DC 20554   (202) 634-1940
The FCC conducts free training seminars for electronics importers and brokers to show them how to comply with FCC rules and regulations for electronic equipment coming into the country. To find out more about arranging a seminar for your company, contact the FCC.

* European Technology and U.S. Trade

Office of Technology Assessment
600 Pennsylvania Ave., SE
Washington, DC 20510   (202) 228-6354
The OTA is currently studying how the European Commission's Single Market Act and the technology projects of Europe affect U.S. manufacturers and trade, particularly in high-technology sectors like microelectronics, computers, and telecommunications equipment. The study is comparing how technology development in chosen industrial sectors has worked in both Europe and East Asia, and assessing the conditions under which governmental participation and collaboration between firms, universities, and government has succeeded or failed. Contact Julie Gorte, the project director, for more information.

* Export Administration Publications

Export Seminar Staff
Office of Export Licensing
Bureau of Export Administraiton
Department of Commerce
14th St. and Constitution Ave., NW
Room 1608
Washington, DC 20230   (202) 377-8731
The following free information publications are available through the Export Seminar Staff:
Exports by Mail
Export Licensing Infformation and Assistance
Distribution License:
-How to Conduct a Systems Review
-How to Prepare for an OEL Systems Review
-Pre-License Consultation
The Export License: How to Fill Out the Application--A step-by-step guide using Form BXA-622P
U.S. Antiboycott Laws Regulation of Participation in Foreign Boycotts
Inter-Agency and Inter-Governmental Review Procedure

The following publications are available for sale from: Superintendent of Documents, Government Printing Office, Washington, D.C. 20402; (202) 783-3238:

Export Administration Annual Report, FY 1988 ($7.00)
1989 Annual Foreign Policy Report to the Congress ($4.25)
U.S. Export Administration Regulations ($87.00)

* Export Administration Regulations

Superintendent of Documents
Government Printing Office
Washington, DC 20402   (202) 783-3238
The Export Administration Regulations is a comprehensive guide to the rules controlling exports of U.S. products and answers questions on export licensing requirements. At no additional cost, subscribers receive supplementary *Export Adminstration Bulletins* which explain recent policy changes and provide replacement pages to keep your set of regulations up-to-date. The *Regulations* are available for $87.00.

* Export Advice Hotline

(800) 343-4300

For information and advice on exporting your products or services, call this hotline and ask for Operator 940. This operator will take your name and address, and a U.S. Department of Commerce trade specialist will contact you.

* Export Control for Strategic and Dual Use Technology

Office of International Trade Control
Bureau of Economic and Business Affairs
Department of State
2201 C St., NW, Room 3529
Washington, DC 20520 (202) 647-1625

This office provides foreign policy guidance pertaining to U.S. export controls for national security and foreign policy purposes and for non-stategic trade with Eastern Europe, Soviet Union, the Peoples Republic of China, and other non-marker economy countries. It represents the Department of State in advising the Department of Commerce on U.S. foreign policy aspects of U.S. strategic export control under the Export Administration Act.

* Export Enforcement

Office of Export Enforcement
Bureau of Export Administration
Department of Commerce
14th St., and Constitution Ave., NW
Room 4616
Washington, DC 20230 (202) 377-8252

This office investigates suspected export control violations and conducts criminal and administrative investigations in the United States. The Office conducts pre-license and post-shipment checks overseas and provides regional export enforcement support to U.S. Embassies. OEE also coordinates with the U.S. Customs Service on investigative activities and seizure of goods.

* Exporter Assistance

Exporter Assistance Staff
Office of Export Licensing
Bureau of Export Administration
Department of Commerce
14th St. and Constitution Ave., NW
Room 1099D
Washington, DC 20230 (202) 377-4811

This office's experts can help solve or answer most of your questions about how to apply for an export license. By telephone or mail these experts can help you prepare license applications and guide you through export regulations. Business, industry, and government will always get fast and courteous assistance to help them comply with U.S. Export Control Laws. *The Export License*, a step-by-step guide to filling out the export liceense application, is available free-of-charge.

* Exporter Seminars

Export Seminar Staff
Bureau of Export Administration
Department of Commerce
14th St. and Constitution Ave., NW
Room 1608
Washington, DC 20230 (202) 377-8731

One way that the Bureau of Export Administration distributes information necessary to businesses on the export regulations is in the form of Exporter Seminars. These seminars are held in cities all across the country, one each month, as well as an annual update conference in Washington, D.C. Seminar instructors are experienced export licensng, policy, and enforcement officials. In addition to conducting the training sessions, they meet privately with individual attendees to answer questions and discuss specific export licensing problems. A three-day conprehensive seminar teaches the exporter how to use and interpret the *Export Administration Regulations*, fill out export license applications, and use the Commodity Control List. The program also updates exporters on export legislation and regulation and provides detailed coverage of distribution licensing and internal control programs, GTE and GLR licensing, termporary exports, parts and components requirements, technical data transfers, and more. Also conducted are overseas seminars on export licensing for importers and reexporters of U.S. commodities. Contact this office for a schedule of seminars and further information.

* Export Information System (XIS)

Contact your local SBA office or
Small Business Answer Desk
U.S. Small Business Administration
1725 Eye St, NW Room 414
Washington, DC 20416 (202) 653-7561 or (800) 368-5855

The SBA's Export Information System provides an initial screening of world markets to determine the export potential of a commodity or manufactured product, and contains data on exports and imports supplied by members of the United Nations. SBA offices use the XIS to assist small firms in finding markets for their product overseas, in evaluating trends in those markets, and in assessing the types of competition in specific country markets. Contact your SBA office for more information.

* Export Legal Advice Network (ELAN)

Contact your local SBA office or
Small Business Answer Desk
U.S. Small Business Administration
1725 Eye St, NW Room 414
Washington, DC 20416 (202) 653-7561 or (800) 368-5855

The Export Legal Assistance Network (ELAN) is a cooperative program between SBA and the Federal Bar Association. ELAN provides free, one-time legal consultations to new-to-export small companies. The FBA maintains rosters of attorneys in 40 cities who are knowledgeable in export-related legal matters and available to assist small firms. For more information on ELAN, contact the SBA office in your area.

* Export License Application and Information Network*

Office of Export Licensing
Bureau of Export Administration
Department of Commerce
14th St. and Constitution Ave., NW
Room 1099D
Washington, DC 20230 (202) 377-4811

Export License Application and Information Network (ELAIN) offers U.S. exporters a fast and convenient way to submit license applications to Commerce. This time-saving service accepts export license applications electronically for all Western country destinations. On receipt, the Commerce Department will review, process, and issue the license electronically for all commodities except supercomputers.

* Export License Tracking

Office of Export Licensing
Bureau of Export Administration
Department of Commerce
14th St. and Constitution Ave., NW
Washington, DC 20230 (202) 377-2753

The System for Tracking Export License Applications (STELA) answers the question most frequently asked by business: "What is the status of my license application?" Call STELA for a brief recorded message with up-to-the-minute status report on your case. STELA's automated voice response system can be accessed using a push-button phone. STELA can also give exporters authority to ship their goods for those applications approved without conditions. For information on how to use STELA, or if you want to know your case number, call the number listed above.

* Export Licensing

Office of Export Licensing
Bureau of Export Administration
Department of Commerce
14th St. and Constitution Ave., NW
Room 1093
Washington, DC 20230 (202) 377-8536

This office processes all export license applications and issues all export licenses for commodities and technical data controlled for national security, foreign policy, and short supply reasons. The office also administers the international import certificate and delivery verification system. OEL provides assistance to the business community, directs the Bureau's Export Seminar Program, and works with foreign licensing officer counterparts to harmonize licensing procedures.

* Export Licensing Newsletter

Office of Export Licensing
Bureau of Export Administration
Department of Commerce
14th St. and Constitution Ave., NW
Room 1608
Washington, DC 20230 (202) 377-8731

Office of Export Licensing Insider is a free quarterly newletter published by the Office of Export Licensing, which contains information about OEL, licensing procedures, publications, and seminars, as well as a Q&A section concerning a specific export licensing area.

* EXPORT NOW

Public Affairs Office
International Trade Administration
U.S. Department of Commerce
14th St. & Constitution, NW

Washington, DC 20230   (202) 377-3808

With the dollar substantially declining against the currencies of U.S. major trading partners, the government's efforts to open world markets to U.S. goods has paid off. As American products improve in quality and became more price-competitive abroad, exports become increasingly important in the U.S. economy. Recognizing that this economic climate was ideal for improving the position of U.S. companies in the world markets, then-president, Ronald Reagan, launched the EXPORT NOW program. This major public and private sector cooperative campaign encourages U.S. business firms to take advantage of a window of opportunity that has opened for them to reach fresh markets, increase profits, expand product lines, and create new jobs for Americans. EXPORT NOW especially focuses attention on the export opportunities and resources awaiting small and medium-size companies. Contact this ITA office for more information on participation in EXPORT NOW.

* Export Revolving Line of Credit Loan (ERLC)

Contact your local SBA office or
Small Business Answer Desk
U.S. Small Business Administration
1725 Eye St, NW Room 414
Washington, DC 20416   (202) 653-7561 or (800) 368-5855

To assist small businesses in exporting their products and services abroad, SBA has established the Export Revolving Line of Credit Loan Program (ERLC). Any number of withdrawals and repayments can be made as long as the dollar limit of the line is not exceeded and the disbursements are made within the stated maturity period. For more information on eligibility, use of proceeds, amount of loan, maturity, interest rates, fees, collateral, special program requirements, and how to apply, contact your SBA office.

* Export Seminars and Workshops

U.S. and Foreign Commercial Service
International Trade Administration
U.S. Department of Commerce, Room H2106
Washington, DC 20230   (202) 377-5777

Trade specialists can keep you posted on upcoming export workshops, conferences, and seminars in your area, as well as on domestic and overseas trade events that offer good potential for promoting your products or services. Contact this office for more information on export seminars and workshops.

* Export Trade Resource Directory

Superintendent of Documents
U.S. Government Printing Office
Washington, DC 20402   (202) 783-3238

Partners in Export Trade is a directory for export trade contacts published by the U.S. Department of Commerce containing a listing of over 4500 firms, including many ETCs and EMCs, manufacturers, producers, and service organizations. It is available from GPO for $11.00 (s/n 003-009-00512-4).

* Export Trading Companies

Office of Export Trading Company Affairs
International Trade Administration
U.S. Department of Commerce
14th St & Constitution NW
Washington, DC 20230   (202) 377-5131

If you are a firm looking to expand sales by exporting, you can hire an Export Trading Company (ETC), or Export Management Company (EMC) to market and sell your products for you, and save you time and money. The ITA sponsors these companies through conferences, workshops, and presentations. Some of the expertise and other advantages offered by ETCs and EMCs include the following:

Services Offered: Many ETCs and EMCs provide a multitude of services, including market research; appointing overseas distributors or commission representatives; exhibiting a client's products at international trade shows; and handling financing, shipping, and documentation. All the U.S. manufacturer has to do is fill the order. Most ETCs and EMCs are small firms which provide personal, one-on-one service.

Market Knowledge: Their ability to identify and understand the diversities inherent with different markets is almost infinite. Regional traders cover many markets and geographical areas and help ETCs and EMCs adjust their services according to particular environments.

Product Specialization: Most successful ETCs and EMCs specialize in one or more product areas. Both their product expertise and, more importantly, their knowledge of distribution structures in foreign markets focus on the specific interest of their clients.

Efficiencies of Scale: ETCs and EMCs have specialized personnel with international backgrounds, who use resources that are generally available only to the export departments of larger firms. However, small firms are not the only ones that benefit from efficiencies of scale--anyone can profit whenever an ETC or EMC can efficiently export a product at a lower cost than the manufacturer.

Some benefits of using an ETC/EMC include language expertise, experience in financial and banking relations, and familiarity with regulations of importing countries.

Shipping Efficiency: ETCs and EMCs can consolidate the products of several suppliers in one shipment, frequently negotiating better freight rates than most individual manufacturers can obtain for themselves.

There are more than 1,500 ETCs and EMCs in the United States. Potential exporters should develop a list of those ETCs and EMCs which specialize in exporting the types of products proposed to be sold overseas. For assistance in locating and selecting the proper ETC/EMC, contact your nearest ITA district office, or contact the office above.

* Export Trading Company Act of 1982

Office of Export Trading Company Affairs
International Trade Administration
U.S. Department of Commerce
Washington, DC 20230   (202) 377-5131

The Export Trading Company Act of 1982 is an information packet containing fact sheets on some of the ways Title III of the ETC Act can help U.S. firms gain a competitive edge on foreign markets. Topics include shippers' associations, trade associations and the ETC Act, technology licensing and the ETC Act, and the Webb-Pomerene Act and the ETC Act. For a copy, contact this office.

* Export Trading Company (ETC) Guidebook

Superintendent of Documents
U.S. Government Printing Office
Washington, DC 20402   (202) 783-3238

The *Export Trading Company (ETC) Guidebook* is intended to assist those considering starting or expanding exporting through the various forms of an ETC as encouraged by the ETC Act. This *Guidebook* will also facilitate your review of the ETC Act and export trading options and serve as a planning tool for your business by showing you what it takes to export profitably and how to start doing it. It is available for $8.00 (s/n 003-009-00523-0) from GPO.

* Export Training Programs

Contact your local SBA office or
Small Business Answer Desk
U.S. Small Business Administration
1725 Eye St, NW Room 414
Washington, DC 20416   (202) 653-7561 or (800) 368-5855

Export training programs are cosponsored by SBA district offices with the U.S. Department of Commerce and others interested in international trade. Emphasis is placed on the practical application of successful exporting procedures to small business. Contact your SBA office for more information.

* Feasibility Studies: Exports and Foreign Trade

United States Trade and Development Program
320 21st St., NW
Washington, DC 20523   (703) 875-4357

The United States Trade and Development Program (TDP) conducts feasibility studies on foreign development programs, enabling a client foreign government to determine whether a development project is technically and economically feasible. The study also identifies products and services likely to be needed for the project, and serves as a guide for American firms possibly able to meet these needs. Contact the office for further information on feasibility studies and other informational programs. Contact the office for a copy of their latest *Congressional Presentation*.

* Fees for US&FCS Services

U.S. and Foreign Commercial Service
International Trade Administration
U.S. Department of Commerce
14th St. & Constitution, NW, Room H2106
Washington, DC 20230   (202) 377-5777

Custom services, such as Comparison Shopping, *Commercial News USA*, CIMS, and participation in trade events and other activities, carry participation fees, which are kept as low as possible so that smaller businesses can participate. Counseling services are free of charge. Contact this office for more information on fees.

* Foreign Availability Assessments

Office of Foreign Availability
Bureau of Export Administration
Department of Commerce
14th St. and Constitution Ave., NW
Room SB-701
Washington, DC 20230   (202) 377-8074

This office conducts foreign availability assessments to determine if a foreign item is comparable to a good or technology that is controlled for national security purposes, and to determine if it is available in fact from non-U.S. sources. Foreign availability of a controlled item exists when a foreign item of comparable quality is available in fact to proscribed countries in sufficient quantities so that continued control of U.S. exports of the item would be ineffective in achieving its purposes. Foreign availability studies are performed to assess new and on-going foreign policy controls, to evaluate proposed national security controls, to support licensing decisions, and assess foreign availability claims from any source for decontrol. Exporters can submit requests to have an item decontrolled.

* Foreign Buyer Program

U.S. and Foreign Commercial Service
International Trade Administration
U.S. Department of Commerce, Room H2106
Washington, DC 20230   (202) 377-5777

An excellent method for exporters to contact prime business is through the US&FCS Foreign Buyer Program. If you have no time to travel overseas, you can participate in a ITA-supported trade show here in the U.S. which is the next best way to meet qualified foreign customers. The US&FCS promotes these shows worldwide to attract foreign buyer delegations, manages an International Business Center, and counsels participating U.S. firms. Contact this ITA office for more information on the Foreign Buyer Program.

* Foreign Competition

The Office of Investigations
U.S. International Trade Commission
500 E St., SW, Room 615
Washington, DC 20436   (202) 252-1161

The ITC investigates issues relating to U.S. and foreign customs laws; the volume of importation in comparison with domestic production and consumption; the conditions, causes, and effects relating to competition of foreign industries with those of the United States; and all other factors affecting competition between U.S. and imported articles.

* Foreign Economic Impact on U.S. Employment

Office of International Economic Affairs
Bureau of International Labor Affairs
200 Constitution Ave., NW, Room S5325
Washington, DC 20210   (202) 523-7610

The Labor Department's foreign economic research program evaluates the effects of foreign economic developments on the earnings and employment of U.S. workers. This includes quantitative analysis of the impact of policies on international trade, investment, and technology transfer. Often undertaken in response to congressionally-mandated studies or to requests from other executive branch agencies, research is conducted by staff economists and supplemented by outside research contractors. A complete list of the research is available by contacting this office.

* Foreign Economic Trends

Superintendent of Documents
Government Printing Office
Washington, DC 20402   (202) 783-3238

Foreign Economic Trends presents business and economic developments and the latest economic indicators for almost 100 countries. They are prepared on an annual or semiannual basis by the U.S. Foreign Service. More than 100 reports are issued each year. An annual subscription is $55.00 from the Superintendent of Documents or single copies are available for $1.00 from the Department of Commerce, Publications Distribution, H1617M, Washington, DC 20230; (202) 377-5494.

* Foreign Export Policy

Office of Technology and Policy Analysis (OTPA)
Bureau of Export Administration
Department of Commerce
14th St. and Constitution Ave., NW
Washington, DC 20230   (202) 377-4188

This office develops and implements overall policies for the licensing of exports. It provides policy guidance and technical expertise for a wide range of technologies and country specific issues. OTPA is responsible for technical support in the reviews of both the U.S. and the International Control Lists, and integration of the Military Critical Technologies List.

* Foreign Loan Statistics

Office of Data Management
Office of the Assistant Secretary
for International Affairs
U.S. Department of the Treasury
1500 Pennsylvania Ave., NW
Washington, DC 20220   (202) 566-2969

Publications are available on foreign loans made by the U.S. Government. The reports are entitled Active Foreign Credits of the U.S. Government, Contingent Foreign Liabilities of the U.S. Government, and Amounts Due and Unpaid 90 Days or More on Foreign Credits of the U.S. Government. These are available for ready reference in the Library of Congress.

* Foreign Market Research

U.S. and Foreign Commercial Service
International Trade Administration
U.S. Department of Commerce, Room H2106
Washington, DC 20230   (202) 377-5777

If you want to know how your industry's products are selling around the world, which markets are growing the fastest, which ones are changing, or which ones want to buy more of your products, the U.S. and Foreign Commercial Service (US&FCS) has the answers for a large number of U.S. industries. US&FCS can provide highly specific analysis of your target markets, tailored to your industry and potential customers. Experienced research analysts continually collect and analyze business and economic data overseas. They search for specific export opportunities and identify market trends affecting trade, investment, and other issues of concern to U.S. businesses interested in trading abroad. The US&FCS develops extensive research on a wide variety of overseas markets. Concise, customized reports can be provided for an industry or country, in print or on diskettes. This wealth of international marketing data is available to you through your nearest US&FCS office. For more information on foreign market research, contact this office.

* Foreign Money Markets

Foreign Exchange and Gold Operations
U.S. Department of the Treasury
1500 Pennsylvania Ave., NW, Room 5037
Washington, DC 20220   (202) 566-2773

This office monitors the foreign money markets for the Department of the Treasury. Contact them for more information.

* Foreign Trade and Investment Policy

Deputy Assistant Secretary for Trade and Investment Policy
Office of the Assistant Secretary
of the Treasury for International Affairs
U.S. Department of the Treasury
1500 Pennsylvania Ave., NW
Washington, DC 20220   (202) 566-2748

This office formulates trade and investment policies. Responsibilities in this area also include international trade, international investment, East-West Policy, trade finance, and commodity policy.

* Foreign Trade Zones

Public Information Office
U.S. Customs Service
Department of the Treasury
P.O. Box 7407
Washington, DC 20044   (202) 566-8195

Foreign or "free" trade zones are secured areas legally outside a nation's customs territory. Their purpose is to attract and promote international trade and commerce. The free pamphlet, Foreign Trade Zones, describes the advantages of using them, how they are established, how the Customs Service is involved, what may be placed in them, what may be done in them, how is merchandise entered from a zone for U.S. consumption, and other information sources.

* Free-Trade Agreements

The Trade Reports Division
Office of Economics
U.S. International Trade Commission
500 E St., SW, Room 602
Washington, DC 20436   (202) 252-2126

The ITC conducts some very complex, sophisticated studies regarding trade. One of these investigations, for example, examines the pros and cons of initiating negotiations with Japan to explore the possibility of the United States-Japan free-trade agreement. The ITC is also conducting a similar study involving possible free-trade agreements with Taiwan, the Republic of Korea, the Association of Southeast Asian Nations, and the entire Pacific Rim. For more information concerning these studies and other free-trade issues, contact this office.

* Global Competitiveness of Selected Industries

Office of the Secretary
U.S. International Trade Commission
500 E St. SW
Washington, DC 20436   (202) 252-1000

To assess the global competitiveness of selected industries, the ITC has conducted studies which cover textiles, steel, automotive parts, optical fibers, and

International Trade

oilseeds. Contact this office for more information concerning these studies and other issues of competition.

* Great Stores of the World

Trade Development Unit
International Trade Administration
U.S. Department of Commerce
14th St & Constitution NW
Washington, DC 20230   (202) 377-1461

A special marketing program for consumer goods, "Great Stores of the World," brings U.S. sellers into direct, one-on-one contact with buyers from major department and specialty store chains overseas. Travel and appointments are arranged by the specialists to save time for the seller and to make sure he meets the right customers. Contact this office for more information on this program.

* Harmonized Tariff Schedule

Public Information Office
U.S. Customs Service
Department of the Treasury
P.O. Box 7407
Washington, DC 20044   (202) 566-8195

The leaflet, *Harmonized Tariff Schedule of the United States*, describes this system which classifies tariffs of international goods. This schedule, used by importers, exporters, Customs statisticians, and others, places all goods of a single commodity under one code. It saves time and money for those involved in international trade because goods do not have to be recoded and redescribed as they move from country to country and from system to system. To receive additional information on HTS, there is a monthly subscription service that will supply you with a handbook and monthly updates. *Commodity Classification - Harmonized System Handbook* is $79 per year from the Government Printing Office, Washington, D.C. 20402. Your local Customs office can also be a source for additional information.

* Harmonized Tariff Schedule of the United States

Office of Tariff Affairs and Trade Agreements
U.S. International Trade Commission
500 E St., SW, Room, 404
Washington, DC 20436   (202) 252-1592

The ITC annually issues the Harmonized Tariff Schedule of the United States, which contains the U.S. tariff schedules and related matters and considers questions concerning the arrangement of such schedules and the classification of articles. The schedule and its periodic supplements which update its provisions contain about 8,700 legal classifications and cover each article that may be imported into the United States.

* Historical Trade Information

The Office of the Secretary
U.S. International Trade Commission
500 E St., SW
Washington, DC 20436   (202) 252-1000

The office has been a depository for historical information on the Commission since 1916. Contact this office for information on its holdings.

* Importation Under Bond

Public Information Office
U.S. Customs Service
Department of the Treasury
P.O. Box 7407
Washington, DC 20044   (202) 566-8195

Temporary importation under bond (TIB) is a procedure whereby, under certain conditions, merchandise may be entered into the Customs territory temporarily free of duty by posting a bond. In the bond, the importer agrees to export or destroy the merchandise within a specified time or pay liquidated damages, generally equal to twice the normal duty. The booklet, *Temporary Importation Under Bond*, explains the bond exportation requirements and the classes of goods involved.

* Imported Articles Subsidized or Sold at Less Than Fair Value

The Office of Investigations
U.S. International Trade Commission
500 E St., SW, Room 615
Washington, DC 20436   (202) 252-1161

The ITC conducts investigations to determine whether there is reasonable indication of material injury to, threat of material injury to, or the establishment of, an industry in the U.S. by reason of imports of foreign merchandise allegedly being subsidized or sold at less than fair value. For information on current and past investigations, contact this office.

* Imported Merchandise Database

Office of Automated Commercial Systems Operations
U.S. Customs Service
Department of the Treasury
1301 Constitution Ave., NW
Washington, DC 20229   (202) 566-9838

ACS, the comprehensive importation tracking system of the U.S. Customs Service, is used by inspectors, import specialists, cashiers, entry control and enforcement personnel, customs brokers, importers, carriers, port authorities, service centers, and other government agencies. *Automated Broker Interface* (ABI) within the system allows the user to interface directly with the Custom's computer and transmit entry and entry summary data on imported merchandise. The system is voluntary and is available to both large and small businesses. Brokers who are not automated may submit data through a service bureau. The brochure, *ACS Overview*, outlines the program.

* Importing Guidelines

Superintendent of Documents
Government Printing Office
Washington, DC 20402   (202) 783-3238

The publication, *Importing into the United States*, provides useful information for both United States importers and foreign exporters. Sections within the book include entry of goods, invoices, assessment of duty, classification and value, marking, special requirements, fraud, and foreign trade zones. The price is $4.25. (S/N 048-002-00103-6)

* Importing of Articles from Developing Countries

Public Information Office
U.S. Customs Service
Department of the Treasury
P.O. Box 7407
Washington, DC 20044   (202) 566-8195

Generalized System of Preferences (GSP) is a system used by many developed countries to help developing nations improve their financial or economic condition through export trade. It provides for the duty-free importation of a wide range of products from certain countries which would otherwise be subject to customs duty. The free pamphlet, *GSP and the Traveler*, lists popular tourist items eligible for duty-free treatment under GSP and the beneficiary countries.

* Importing Pleasure Boats

Carrier Rulings Branch
Office of Regulations and Rulings
U.S. Customs Service
Department of the Treasury
1301 Constitution Ave., NW, Room 2137
Washington, DC 20229   (202) 566-5706

When a pleasure boat or yacht arrives in the United States, the first landing must be at a Customs port or designated place where Customs service is available. The pamphlet, *Pleasure Boats*, explains the Customs formalities involving pleasure boats to help you plan your importation and reporting requirements, overtime charges, and provides other information relating strictly to pleasure boats. You can get a copy of *Pleasure Boats* from the Public Information Office, U.S. Customs Service, P.O. Box 7407, Washington, D.C. 20044.

* Import Quotas

Quota Section
Office of Trade Operations
U.S. Customs Service
Department of the Treasury
1301 Constitution Ave., NW, Room 2379
Washington, DC 20229   (202) 566-8592

Import quotas and the commodities subject to them are regulated by this office. An import quota is defined as a quantity control on imported merchandise for a certain period of time. There are two types of import quotas: absolute and tariff-rate. Absolute quotas limit the quantity of goods that may enter the commerce of the U.S. in a specific period. Tariff-rate quotas permit a specified quantity of imported merchandise to be entered at a reduced rate of Customs duty during the quota period. For further information, contact the Public Information Office, U.S. Customs Service, P.O. Box 7407, Washington, D.C. 20044, and request a copy of the free flyer, *Import Quotas*.

* Import Relief Case Documents

Docket Room
Office of the Secretary
U.S. International Trade Commission
500 E St., SW
Washington, DC 20436   (202) 252-1802

Publications in this collection date back to January 1961 and relate to the Commission's investigation of cases in which U.S. industries sought "import relief." Industries investigated include nonrubber footwear, zippers, mushrooms, stainless steel, wrapper tobacco, nuts, bolts and screws. Case documentation is available.

* Import Requirements
Public Information Office
U.S. Customs Service
Department of the Treasury
P.O. Box 7407
Washington, DC 20044 (202) 566-8195

The free booklet, *Import Requirements*, provides a general explanation of import requirements. This publication is valuable to those interested in going into an importing business or for a person who may be importing something for personal use only and not for resale. The arrival and entry of goods, customs examination of goods, protesting of the decision, mail shipments, restricted merchandise, and a review of the Foreign Assets Control Regulations are outlined.

* Industry Adjustment to Import Competition
The Office of Investigations
U.S. International Trade Commission
500 E St., SW, Room 615
Washington, DC 20436 (202) 252-1161

On behalf of an industry, a firm, a group of workers, or other representatives of an industry, the ITC will conduct investigations to determine whether an article is being imported in such increased quantities as to be a substantial cause or threat of serious injury to the domestic industry producing an article like or directly competitive with the imported article. Contact this office for more information on import competition.

* International Capital Banking Statistics
Office of Data Management
Office of the Assistant Secretary for International Affairs
U.S. Department of the Treasury
1500 Pennsylvania Ave., NW, Room 5127
Washington, DC 20220 (202) 566-5473

Treasury International Capital Forms are filed for the purpose of gathering timely information on international capital movements. Banks, other depository institutions, International Banking Facilities, bank holding companies, brokers, and dealers in the United States must file reports. The organizations describe liabilities to, or claims on, foreigners, whether they are individuals or institutions. The Federal Reserve Bank of New York acts as the agent and receives the filed reports. The address is International Reports Division, International Reports and Support Dept., 4th Fl., Federal Reserve Bank of New York, 33 Liberty St., New York, NY 10045.

* International Capital Nonbanking Statistics
Office of Data Management
Office of the Assistant Secretary for International Affairs
U.S. Department of the Treasury
1500 Pennsylvania Ave., NW, Room 5127
Washington, DC 20220 (202) 566-5473

International Capital Nonbanking Forms provide information on the liability and claim positions of the United States with respect to foreign countries. This aids in determining the financial position of the United States and the movement of capital between the United States and foreign countries. Unlike the International Capital Banking Forms, these forms are filed by exporters, importers, industrial commercial concerns, nonbanking financial institutions, and foreign sales corporations. The Federal Reserve Bank of New York acts as the agent for the collection of these forms. The address is: International Reports Division, Federal Reserve Bank of New York, 33 Liberty St., New York, NY 10045.

* International Commodities
Office of Commodity Policy
Office of the Assistant Secretary for International Affairs
U.S. Department of the Treasury
1500 Pennsylvania Ave., NW, Room 5423
Washington, DC 20220 (202) 566-2561

This office monitors international commodity developments of such products as wheat and meat imports, tropical timber, iron ore, copper, cocoa, coffee, and sugar. They also stay abreast of activity involving the International Rubber Agreement, the United Nations Conference on Trade and Development Commodities Issues, oceans policy, the world oil market, and international energy policy.

* International Competitiveness
Office of Industries
U.S. International Trade Commission
500 E St., SW
Washington, DC 20436 (202) 252-1296

This office studies the international competitiveness of U.S. producers in such areas as textile mill products, oilseeds, steel sheet and strip, auto parts, optical fibers, certain vegetables, and steel. For more information on these studies contact this office.

* International Construction
International Construction Unit
International Trade Administration
U.S. Department of Commerce
14th St & Constitution NW
Washington, DC 20230 (202) 377-1461

For major projects abroad, the International Construction unit assists U.S. planning, engineering, and construction firms with bids and contracts. It works with the U.S. Export-Import Bank and the multilateral development banks and is a clearinghouse for information on major projects worldwide.

* International Economic Review
Trade Reports Division
Office of Economics
U.S. International Trade Commission
500 E St., SW, Room 602
Washington, DC 20436 (202) 252-1216

The "International Economic Review," a monthly review of trade and policy developments, provides information on significant economic and policy developments abroad that may affect U.S. commerce. The review is distributed to Members of Congress and the public on request.

* International Economic Policies
International Economic Policy
International Trade Commission
U.S. Department of Commerce
14th & Constitution, NW
Washington, DC 20230 (202) 377-3022

The International Economic Policy (IEP) sector, seeking to increase U.S. trade and investment, identifies foreign barriers to commerce and takes part in negotiations to remove them. It also searches for U.S. commercial opportunities overseas and counsels U.S. businesses. Some recent activities of IEP include the following:

prepared U.S. positions for the U.S.-Soviet Joint Commercial Commission meeting in Moscow and supported the Secretary of Commerce's participation in its discussions; participated in negotiations that led to the U.S.-Canada Free Trade Area Agreement;

conducted seminars throughout the U.S. to introduce the American business community to the U.S.-Israel Free Trade Area Agreement;

and negotiated renewal of an agreement with China on industrial cooperation in electronics and telecommunications.

* International Mail Imports
Public Information Office
U.S. Customs Service
Department of the Treasury
P.O. Box 7407
Washington, DC 20044 (202) 566-8195

Mail subject to Customs examination from overseas is the topic of discussion in the free brochure, *International Mail Imports*. All possible questions on this mail are answered, including claims, amount of duty, exemptions of duty, packages mailed while traveling abroad, returned merchandise, and damaged and replaced articles.

* International Monetary Affairs
Deputy Assistant Secretary for International Monetary Affairs
Office of the Assistant Secretary
of the Treasury for International Affairs
U.S. Department of the Treasury
1500 Pennsylvania Ave., NW, Room 3222
Washington, DC 20220 (202) 566-5232

All aspects of the international money markets are monitored by this office. This includes the gold market, international bank lending, foreign exchange market developments, and the International Monetary Fund.

* International Negotiations
Office of Multilateral Affairs
International Economic Policy
International Trade Commission
U.S. Department of Commerce
14th & Constitution, NW
Washington, DC 20230 (202) 377-3022

This office takes part in negotiations involving a number of countries, such as the 96-nation Uruguay Round of trade negotiations. It assists in matters related to the United Nations Conference on Trade and Development (UNCTAD) and the

International Trade

Organization for Economic Cooperation and Development. The office also coordinates Commerce Department positions on unfair-trade-practice cases.

* International Price Indexes: Export and Import

Office of Prices and Living Conditions
Bureau of Labor Statistics
Department of Labor
600 E St., NW, Room 3302
Washington, DC 20212 (202) 272-5025

This office measures change in the prices of commodities exported from and imported into the United States. Quarterly price indexes are available for all exported and imported items and major subgroups, such as food, beverages and tobacco, crude materials except fuels, animal and vegetable oils, fats and waxes, chemicals, manufactured goods, machinery and transport equipment, and miscellaneous manufactured articles.

* International Trade Assistance and Publications

Office of International Trade
U.S. Small Business Administration
1441 L St., NW, Room 501A
Washington, DC 20416 (202) 653-7794

This office provides information and assistance to small business owners completely new to exporting and those already exporting but planning to expand their markets. OIT works closely with SBA field offices in providing a range of outreach and educational programs. Contact this office for more information or to obtain a free copy of their publication, *The Exporter's Guide to Federal Resources for Small Business*. Another publication issued from this office, *Market Overseas with U.S. Government Help*, is available for $1.00 by writing to SBA, P.O. Box 15434, Fort Worth, TX 76119.

* International Trade Commission Annual Report

Office of the Secretary
U.S. International Trade Commission
500 E St., SW
Washington, DC 20436 (202) 252-1000

An annual report to the Congress of various Commission activities is available to the public. Included in the report is a message from the Acting Chairman, a summary of completed investigations, a discussion of various studies, each organizational unit's annual activities, and management and finance information.

* International Trade Commission Official Records

The Office of the Secretary
U.S. International Trade Commission
500 E St., SW
Washington, DC 20436 (202) 252-1000

This office compiles and maintains the ITC's official records, such as petitions, briefs, and other legal documents. It also issues the Commission's notices, reports, and orders, and schedules and participates in all ITC meetings and hearings.

* International Trade Loans

Contact your local SBA office or
Small Business Answer Desk
U.S. Small Business Administration
1725 Eye St, NW Room 414
Washington, DC 20416 (202) 653-7561 or (800) 368-5855

The International Trade Loan program has been established to help more small businesses both compete more effectively with import competition, as well as significantly expand existing export markets. For more information on these loans, including the amount of loan, percentage of guaranty, eligibility, collateral, and maturity, contact the SBA office in your area.

* International Trade Publications

Office of the Secretary
U.S. International Trade Commission
500 E St., SW
Washington, DC 20436 (202) 252-1806

"Publications and Investigations of the United States Tariff Commission and United States International Trade Commission" is an index of all publications issued by both agencies since their inception. The booklet, "Selected Publications of the United States International Trade Commission," contains selected documents through 1988 and dating back to 1917. Publications may be ordered 24 hours a day, 7 days a week by calling (202) 252-1809. Requests for publications which are out of print should be taken up in writing or in person with the Secretary's Office above.

* International Trade Statutes

The Trade Remedy Assistance Office
U.S. International Trade Commission

500 E St., SW
Washington, DC 20436 (202) 252-2200

This office can provide you with information on the trade statues that the ITC administers. When appropriate, this office makes referrals to other offices within the ITC and to other agencies responsible for administering particular trade laws. It also receives inquiries from Congress, Government agencies, law firms, trade associations, the press, and academia.

* International Trade Studies

Office of the Secretary
U.S. International Trade Commission
500 E St., SW, Room 112
Washington, DC 20436 (202) 252-1000

Following requests from the U.S. President, the House Ways and Means Committee, the Senate Finance Committee, either branch of the Congress, or on its own motion, the ITC conducts studies, investigations, and research projects on a broad range of topics relating to international trade. Public reports of these studies, investigations, and research projects are issued in most cases. The Commission also keeps informed of the operation and effect of provisions relating to duties or other import restrictions of the United States contained in various trade agreements. Occasionally, the Commission is required by statute to perform specific trade-related studies.

* Market Disruption From Communist Countries

The Office of Investigations
U.S. International Trade Commission
500 E St., SW, Room 615
Washington, DC 20436 (202) 252-1161

The Commission conducts investigations to determine whether increased imports of an article produced by a Communist country are causing market disruption in the United States. If there is a positive determination of disruption, the President may take action which would apply only to imports of the article from the Communist country.

* Market Share Reports

U.S. Department of Commerce
National Technical Information Service
5285 Port Royal Road
Springfield, VA 22161 (703) 487-4650

Market Share Reports provide exporters and market analysts with data on import of manufactured products into foreign countries' markets and the shares supplied by the United States and eight leading suppliers. While the data dated from 1983, it is nevertheless the latest available. There are eighty-eight reports in the *Country Series*, and 1,500 *Commodity Series Reports*. *Country Reports* are $11.00 each, and *Commodity Reports* are $10.00 each. For a free publications catalog, contact the above office.

* Marking of Country of Origin on U.S. Imports

Entry Rulings Branch
Office of Regulations and Rulings
U.S. Customs Service
Department of the Treasury
1301 Constitution Ave., NW, Room 2137
Washington, DC 20229 (202) 566-5856

The brochure, *Marking of Country of Origin on U.S. Imports*, acquaints manufacturers and exporters in other nations with the country of origin marking requirements for goods imported into the United States. It describes forms of marking, marking of combined articles, marking of containers, special markings on certain articles, and items that do not require marking. To receive this brochure, contact Public Information, U.S. Customs Service, P.O. Box 7407, Washington, DC 20044.

* Matchmakers/Trade Missions

U.S. and Foreign Commercial Service
International Trade Administration
U.S. Department of Commerce, Room H2106
Washington, DC 20230 (202) 377-5777

Trade events can be a profitable part of your marketing plan. You can invest as much money and effort as you choose, depending on your strategy. Trade events can be as simple as sending your product catalogs overseas or as intense as participating in a major international exhibition. You can meet potential customers in person, or send your catalog "on tour" via the Matchmakers and Trade Missions programs. Take the guesswork out of international business travel by joining a Foreign Commercial Service "Matchmaker" delegation or trade mission to target markets selected for their high potential for your particular industry. US&FCS will accompany you overseas, arrange a full schedule of individual appointments with qualified foreign agents, distributors, or customers, and provide complete logistical and promotional support. You'll meet senior industry leaders and government officials who can make on-the-spot decisions. US&FCS also sponsors state- and industry-organized trade missions. Contact this office for more information on the "Matchmakers" and the Trade Missions programs.

* Matchmaker Trade Missions

Office of International Trade
U.S. Small Business Administration
1441 L St., NW, Room 501A
Washington, DC 20416   (202) 653-7794
Cosponsored by SBA and the U.S. Department of Commerce, this program arranges direct contact for American firms with potential partners in new international markets. Contact the office above or your SBA office for more information.

* Monetary Instruments: Imported or Exported

Smuggling Investigations Division
U.S. Customs Service
Department of the Treasury
1301 Constitution Ave., NW
Washington, DC 20229   (202) 566-8005
Guidelines of the Customs Service give no limitation on the amount of monetary instruments which may be brought into or taken out of the United States. However, if you plan to transport or are involved in the transport of more than $10,000, you must file a report (Customs Form 4790) with the Customs Service. Monetary instruments include U.S. or foreign coin, currency, travelers checks, money orders, and negotiable instruments or investment securities in bearer form.

* Multilateral Bank Foreign Assistance Projects

Major Projects Reference Room
International Trade Administration
U.S. Department of Commerce
14th St & Constitution NW
Washington, DC 20230   (202) 377-4876
The Major Projects Reference Room keeps detailed project documents on multilateral bank and U.S. Government foreign assistance projects. It is open to the public by appointment.

* Nuclear Export and Import Control

Nuclear Energy and Energy Technology Affairs
Bureau of Oceans and International Environmental
and Scientific Affairs
Department of State
2201 C St., NW, Room 7820
Washington, DC 20520   (202) 647-4101
This office works closely with the Nuclear Regulatory Commission with regard to the licensing requests for nuclear imports and exports. They also study the development and transfer of nuclear technology in foreign countries. This office monitors the Nuclear Non-Proliferation Treaty, making sure that the countries which signed the treaty are following its regulations. They also oversee the export and import of items which are not nuclear, but which could be used for nuclear purposes, such as super computers. The export of these items must follow the guidelines set in the Nuclear Non-Proliferation Treaty.

* Office of the United States Trade Representative

Winder Building
600 17th St., NW
Washington, DC 20506   (202) 395-3515
This office develops and coordinates U.S. international trade, commodity, and direct investment policy, and leads or directs negotiations with other countries on such matters. There are two offices, one in Washington, D.C., and the other in Geneva, Switzerland. The U.S. Trade Representative is a Cabinet-level official with the rank of ambassador who acts as the principal trade adviser, negotiator, and spokesperson for the President on trade and related investment matters.

* Operation of the Trade Agreements Program

Office of the Secretary
U.S. International Trade Commission
500 E St., SW
Washington, DC 20436   (202) 252-1000
The annual report, Operation of the Trade Agreements Program, highlights major developments in U.S. trade policy in 1987, including the realignment of exchange rates among the major industrialized countries, the bilateral free-trade arrangement with Canada, and the start of Harmonized Commodity Description and Coding System. The report also includes data on U.S. trade under the Generalized System of Preferences program and the Caribbean Basin Initiative, a comprehensive review of developments within the GATT and other multilateral forums, and actions taken under U.S. trade law. The report covers details of trade relations with seven major trading partners. To obtain a copy of this report and others, contact this office.

* Overseas Business Reports

Superintendent of Documents
Government Printing Office
Washington, DC 20402   (202) 783-3238
Overseas Business Reports include current and detailed marketing information, trade outlooks, statistics, regulations, and marketing profiles for most countries. The annual subscription from GPO is $14.00, and $17.50 for foreign mail orders. Single copies are available from the Department of Commerce, Publications Distribution, H1617M, Washington, D.C. 20230; (202) 377-5494.

* Overseas Contracts Bidding

Office of Trade Development
International Trade Administration
U.S. Department of Commerce
14th & Constitution, NW
Washington, DC 20230   (202) 377-1461
U.S. firms in need of assistance bidding on large project contracts abroad should contact this office.

* Overseas Marketing Magazine

U.S. and Foreign Commercial Service
International Trade Administration
U.S. Department of Commerce, Room H2106
Washington, DC 20230   (202) 377-5777
Commercial News USA is distributed overseas to the foreign customers and business partners you may want to reach. It has helped thousands of U.S. companies begin or expand their sales in international markets. For $250, you can showcase your product or service in this export promotion catalog-magazine which is distributed to more than 100,000 pre-screened foreign agents, distributors, government purchasing officials, and end-users worldwide. Responses from interested readers will come directly to you--address coded for easy identification. Exporters may submit a black-and-white photo and a brief description of their product or service. For more information about *Commercial News USA*, contact your nearest U.S. Department of Commerce District Office, or call (800) 343-4300, and ask for Operator 940, or contact the office above.

* Overseas Trade Specialists

U.S. and Foreign Commercial Service
International Trade Administration
U.S. Department of Commerce
14th St. & Constitution, NW, Room H2106
Washington, DC 20230   (202) 377-5777
Because US&FCS commercial officers understand firsthand the problems that U.S. companies encounter in their efforts to trade abroad, they are in a strong position to provide a range of services to help companies sell overseas. Trade specialists do on-the-spot market research overseas, including customized individual studies; search for sales leads and qualified agents and distributors for your product; make appointments with key buyers and government officials; and counsel firms frustrated by trade barriers. They speak the host-country language, understand local customs, traditions, and trade regulations, and can be a particularly valuable resource when you're visiting overseas markets in person. Contact this office to discuss your marketing needs with an overseas trade specialist.

* Research Methods

Investigation Support Division
Office of Economics
U.S. International Trade Commission
500 E St., SW, Room 602
Washington, DC 20436   (202) 252-1216
ITC staff use economic models to determine the effects of certain tariffs and quotas on imports. In addition to providing estimates of supply and characteristics of demand in all final investigations, these ITC economists provide estimates to outside parties to investigations prior to Commission hearings so that these parties are able to review and comment on the estimates. In final investigations, staff economists also include estimates of the effect of dumping on the price and volume of sales of domestic products. Estimates are based on methodology developed in this office. Contact this office for more information on tariffs and import quotas.

* Restraining Foreign Exports

Import Administration
International Trade Administration
U.S. Department of Commerce
14th & Constitution, NW
Washington, DC 20230   (202) 377-1780
ITA's Import Administration administers programs under which foreign governments agree to restrain exports of certain products to the United States. Through consultations with foreign governments, and monitoring, the Import

International Trade

Administration makes sure trade agreements are followed. Contact this office for more information.

* Service Sector Markets Overseas

Services Unit
International Trade Administration
U.S. Department of Commerce
14th St & Constitution NW
Washington, DC 20230 (202) 377-1461

Because the U.S. is very competitive in the services sector, the Services Unit plays an important role in trade promotion efforts. This office provides information on the operation of services sectors in other countries and on specific trade opportunities. Contact this office for more information.

* Services for Exporters

U.S. and Foreign Commercial Service
International Trade Administration
U.S. Department of Commerce
14th & Constitution NW, Room H2106
Washington, DC 20230 (202) 377-5777

U.S. companies are strategically positioned to profit from exporting their products and services to many nations, but selling goods and services in foreign markets doesn't have to be complicated and confusing. Firsthand knowledge of overseas markets and the exporting process can greatly increase your company's chances for exporting success. However, finding the information and advice you need to enter--and succeed--in world markets can be a major problem. So, the U.S. and Foreign Commercial Service has trade professionals around the world dedicated to your export success. Experts are available to help you export your goods or services in virtually all major world markets, and offer highly effective services to help you every step of the way. For more information on services for exporters, contact this office.

* Smuggling Investigations

Smuggling Investigations Division
U.S. Customs Service
Department of the Treasury
1301 Constitution Ave., NW
Washington, DC 20229 (202) 566-8005

Special agents within the U.S. Customs Service are assigned to duty stations all over the world to detect international smuggling. They have recovered art and archeological objects and have made arrests for cargo theft, and for narcotics and arms smuggling.

* Starting Points for Overseas Trading

U.S. and Foreign Commercial Service
International Trade Administration
U.S. Department of Commerce
14th St. & Constitution, NW, Room HCHB1066
Washington, DC 20230 (202) 377-3181

The first stop a U.S. company should make to take advantage of government export programs is the nearest Commerce Department (ITA) district office. Through the district office, a company has access to all assistance available in the Commerce Department, including practical information about overseas market opportunities, developed by commercial officers abroad and by industry and country desk officers in Washington, D.C. The district offices can also direct companies toward other government and private sector export services. Each office is headed by a director and supported by trade specialists and other staff. These professionals help company decision makers gain a basic understanding of profitable opportunities in exporting and assist them in evaluating the company's market potential overseas. To find out how the Foreign Commercial Service's programs can benefit your company, call your nearest U.S. Department of Commerce District Office listed as follows:

Alabama/Birmingham (205) 731-1331
Alaska/Anchorage (907) 271-5041
Arizona/Phoenix (602) 261-3285
Arkansas/Little Rock (501) 378-5794
California/Los Angeles (213) 209-7104
    Santa Ana (714) 836-2461
    San Diego (619) 557-5395
    San Francisco (415) 556-5860
Colorado/Denver (303) 844-3246
Connecticut/Hartford (203) 240-3530
Delaware/Served by Philadelphia (215) 962-4980
District of Columbia (202) 377-3181
Florida/Miami (305) 536-5267
    Clearwater (813) 461-0011
    Jacksonville (904) 791-2796
    Orlando (407) 648-1608
    Tallahassee (904) 488-6469
Georgia/Atlanta (404) 347-7000
    Savannah (912) 944-4204
Hawaii/Honolulu (808) 541-1782

Idaho/Boise (208) 334-3857
Illinois/Chicago (312) 353-4450
    Palatine (312) 397-3000
    Rockford (815) 987-8123
Indiana/Indianapolis (317) 269-6214
Iowa/Des Moines (515) 284-4222
Kansas/Wichita (316) 269-6160
Kentucky/Louisville (502) 582-5066
Louisiana/New Orleans (504) 589-6546
Maine/Augusta (207) 622-8249
Maryland/Baltimore (301) 962-3560
Massachusetts/Boston (617) 565-8563
Michigan/Detroit (313) 226-3650
    Grand Rapids (616) 456-2411
Minnesota/Minneapolis (612) 348-1638
Mississippi/Jackson (601) 965-4388
Missouri/St. Louis (314) 425-3302-4
    Kansas City (816) 426-3141
Montana/Served by Denver (303) 844-3246
Nebraska/Omaha (402) 221-3664
Nevada/Reno (702) 784-5203
New Hampshire/Served by Boston (617) 565-8563
New Jersey/Trenton (609) 989-2100
New Mexico/Santa Fe (505) 827-0264
    Albuquerque (505) 766-2386
New York/New York (212) 264-0634
    Buffalo (716) 846-4191
    Rochester (716) 263-6480
North Carolina/Greensboro (919) 333-5345
North Dakota/Served by Omaha (402) 221-3664
Ohio/Cincinnati (513) 684-2944
    Cleveland (216) 522-4750
Oklahoma/Oklahoma City (405) 231-5302
    Tulsa (918) 581-7650
Oregon/Portland (503) 221-3001
Pennsylvania/Philadelphia (215) 962-4980
    Pittsburgh (412) 644-2850
Puerto Rico/San Juan (809) 766-5555
Rhode Island/Providence (401) 528-5104
South Carolina/Columbia (803) 765-5345
    Charleston (803) 724-4361
South Dakota/Served by Omaha (402) 221-3664
Tennessee/Nashville (615) 736-5161
    Memphis (901) 521-4137
Texas/Dallas (214) 767-0542
    Austin (512) 482-5939
    Houston (713) 229-2578
Utah/Salt Lake City (801) 524-5116
Vermont/Served by Boston (617) 565-8563
Virginia/Richmond (804) 771-2246
Washington/Seattle (206) 442-5616
    Spokane (509) 353-2922
West Virginia/Charleston (304) 347-5123
Wisconsin/Milwaukee (414) 291-3473
Wyoming/Served by Denver (303) 844-3246

Business Libraries:
Most district offices maintain extensive business libraries containing the Commerce Department's latest reports. See the listing of district offices above.

* Tariff Summaries

Office of Tariff Affairs and Trade Agreements
U.S. International Trade Commission
500 E St., SW, Room 404
Washington, DC 20436 (202) 252-1592

From time to time, the ITC prepares and publishes a series of summaries of trade and tariff information. These summaries contain descriptions (in terms of the Tariff Schedules of the United States) of the thousands of products imported into the United States, methods of production, and the extent and relative importance of U.S. consumption, production, and trade, together with certain basic factors affecting the competitive position and economic health of domestic industries.

* Technical Advisory Committees

Technical Support Staff
Office of Technology and policy Analysis
Bureau of Export Administration
Department of Commerce
14th St. and Constitution Ave., NW
Room 4086
Washington, DC 20230 (202) 377-2583

Technical Advisory Committees (TAC) provide advice and assistance with questions involving technical matters, worldwide availability, and actual utilization of production technology, licensing procedures which affect the level of export controls applicable to any goods or technology, and exports subject to multilateral controls in which the U.S. participates. You can get more information on the TACs from this office.

* Technology, Innovation, and U.S. Trade

Office of Technology Assessment
600 Pennsylvania Ave., SE
Washington, DC 20510 (202) 228-6354

The international diffusion of technology has resulted in increased competition from a growing number of countries, in a widening array of products, and cut into the market share of U.S. manufacturers. OTA is currently examining how changes in the competitiveness of U.S. manufacturing industries affect the ability of the U.S. economy to create new jobs in various sectors. The study will also assess how technology, coupled with strategic responses by U.S. firms, could reverse the erosion of U.S. market shares. Contact Julie Gorte, the project director, for more information.

* Textile Import Affairs

Textiles Division
Office of International Trade
Bureau of Economic and Business Affairs
Department of State
2201 C St., NW, Room 2835
Washington, DC 20520 (202) 647-1998

This office represents the State Department in interagency programs that monitor and implement the U.S. Import Control Program. The United States currently has 38 bilateral agreements dealing with textiles, including yarn, garments, and such home furnishings as rugs and drapes.

* Textile Quota Reports

Office of Textiles and Apparel
International Trade Administration
U.S. Department of Commerce
14th & Constitution, NW, Room H3100
Washington, DC 20230 (202) 377-3080

Textile Quota Reports provide textile and apparel data in units of quantity and value for cotton, wool, man-made fiber, and vegetable fibers, except cotton and silk blend manufactures. Eleven separate reports are available monthly in microfiche only. One month costs $20.00, or $240.00 annually. To order, contact this office.

* Trade and Competitiveness Laws

Office of Congressional Liaison
U.S. International Trade Commission
500 E St., SW, Room 718
Washington, DC 20436 (202) 252-1151

The Omnibus Trade and Competitiveness Act is the most comprehensive revision of U.S. trade law since the inception of the General Agreement on Tariffs and Trade (GATT). The Act amends several of the statutes administered by the Commission and, in addition, requires the ITC to conduct several industry competitiveness investigations.

* Trade and Tariff Summaries

Office of the Secretary
U.S. International Trade Commission
500 E St., SW
Washington, DC 20436 (202) 252-1000

The annual report, Summaries of Trade and Tariff Information, covers the operation of the ITC's trade agreements program. The report contains information on U.S. participation in multilateral trade negotiations and agreements, as well as related material on foreign economic and trade developments and the administration of U.S. trade laws. Contact this office for specific information regarding these agreements.

* Trade and Technical Literature

U.S. and Foreign Commercial Service
International Trade Administration
U.S. Department of Commerce, Room H2106
Washington, DC 20230 (202) 377-5777

For the latest information on trade practices and new technology--including handbooks, periodicals, and buyer's guides--check the *Trade and Technical Literature* section in each issue of *Commercial News USA*.

* Trade Development Industry Officers

Trade Development Unit
International Trade Administration
U.S. Department of Commerce
14th St & Constitution NW
Washington, DC 20230 (202) 377-1461

ITA's Trade Development unit promotes the trade interests of industry sectors and offers information on markets and trade practices worldwide. The industry

specialists promote exports of their industries through marketing seminars, foreign buyer groups, executive trade missions, business counseling, and information on market opportunities. They work directly with their industries, trade associations, and state development agencies to plan international marketing programs and develop policy negotiations aimed at attacking trade barriers and opening up markets. The industries are grouped as follows:

AEROSPACE
This office assists the U.S. aerospace industry in maintaining and expanding its contribution to U.S. trade. This office operates the Aerospace Product Information Centers, which are designed to provide market exposure for small companies at international trade shows. It also sponsors conferences and organized trade shows.
Aerospace: (202) 377-8228

AUTOMOTIVE and CONSUMER GOODS
These offices analyze trends within the automotive industry and more than 125 consumer goods industries. It analyzes trade and regulatory policy issues affecting these industries and promotes their international competitiveness.
Automotive: (202) 377-0823
Consumer Goods: (202) 377-0337

BASIC INDUSTRIES
The following offices assist industries that account for more than $1 trillion in domestic shipments, including non-ferrous and ferrous metals, chemicals and allied products, lumber, wood and paper products, domestic construction, petroleum, coal and other energy products, biotechnology, and advanced composite materials.
Chemicals and Allied Products: (202) 377-0128
Forest Products and Domestic Construction: (202) 377-0384
Energy: (202) 377-1466
General Industrial Machinery: (202) 377-5445
Metals, Minerals, and Commodities: (202) 377-0575
Special Industrial Machinery: (202) 377-0302
Instrumentation: (202) 377-5466

CAPITAL GOODS AND INTERNATIONAL CONSTRUCTION
This office works to strengthen the competitive position of U.S. capital goods and international construction industries.
International Construction: (202) 377-5225

SCIENCE AND ELECTRONICS
This unit supports high technology industries, emphasizing competitive analyses and export trade opportunities. It is also preparing an in-depth analysis of the competitiveness of the U.S. semiconductor and electronics industries.
Computer and Business Equipment: (202) 377-0572
Microelectronics & Instrumentation: (202) 377-2587
Telecommunications: (202) 377-4466

SERVICES
This unit works to improve the international competitive position of U.S. service industries through policy analysis and promotion.
Services Industries: (202) 377-3575
Medical Services: (202) 377-0550

TEXTILES AND APPAREL
This unit chairs and staffs the interagency Committee for the Implementation of Textile Agreements (CITA) which exercises U.S. rights under multilateral and bilateral textile agreements. The Office monitors imports of textiles and apparel to ensure compliance with bilateral agreements and to prevent domestic market disruption. CITA also considers recommendations for consultation calls with foreign governments and helps negotiate and implement bilateral agreements.
Textiles: (202) 377-5078

TRADE ADJUSTMENT ASSISTANCE
This unit helps trade-injured firms and industries become more competitive with foreign firms.
Exporting Trade Companies: (202) 377-5131

TRADE INFORMATION AND ANALYSIS
As ITA's primary macro-economic analysis arm, this unit conducts long- and short-term research and analyses on these issues: trade legislation, bilateral and multilateral trade negotiations, U.S. direct investment overseas, foreign direct investment in the U.S., LDC debt problems and currency fluctuations, and international finance issues. Major publications include *U.S. Industrial Outlook*, and *U.S. Trade Performance and Outlook*.
Trade Information Analysis: (202) 377-1316

Export Statistics and Trade Data (Foreign): (202) 377-4211
Export Statistics and Trade Data (Domestic): (202) 377-4211

* Trade Development Seminars

Trade Development Unit
International Trade Administration
U.S. Department of Commerce
14th St & Constitution NW

Washington, DC 20230   (202) 377-1461

Trade development seminars have focused on Far East aerospace markets, biotechnology in Europe and Japan, worldwide construction and engineering, and selling auto parts to the Japanese and to Korea. Executive missions have gone to Asia, Europe, and South America for auto parts, telecommunications, supercomputers, and aerospace. Buyer groups for computers, textile products, and apparel have received special handling. Contact this office for more information about trade development seminars.

* Trade Information and Analysis

Trade Information and Analysis Office
Trade Development Office
International Trade Administration
U.S. Department of Commerce
14th St & Constitution NW
Washington, DC 20230   (202) 377-2456

U.S. businesses that need assistance in their market planning should contact this ITA office. They distribute and analyze international trade and investment data for U.S. businesses to use in export promotions and trade policy. The office also produces economic and econometric analyses, industry statistics, and trade, finance, and investment data and studies--especially for multiple groups of industries. U.S. and foreign country trade data can be accessed through ITA's district offices.

* Trade Information Contacts

Office of the United States Trade Representative
600 17th St., NW
Washington, DC 20506   (202) 395-3230

The best initial contact point for inquiries of the Office of the United States Trade Representative is the Public Affairs Office. They can answer questions, supply information or direct researchers to appropriate other offices.

* Trade Injury Assistance

Trade Adjustment Division
Trade Development Office
International Trade Administration
U.S. Department of Commerce
14th St & Constitution NW
Washington, DC 20230   (202) 377-1461

The Trade Adjustment division provides technical assistance to firms and industries that have been injured by imports. Contact this office for information on available assistance.

* Trademarks, Trade Names, and Copyrights

Office of Regulations and Rulings
U.S. Customs Service
Department of the Treasury
1301 Constitution Ave., NW, Room 2104
Washington, DC 20229   (202) 566-5765

This office records trademarks, tradenames, and copyrights with the U.S. Customs Service for the purpose of prohibiting the importation of certain articles. It also sets forth the procedures for the disposition of articles bearing prohibited marks or names, and copyrighted or piratical articles, including release to the importer in certain cases.

* Trademark Information for Travelers

Public Information Division
U.S. Customs Service
Department of the Treasury
P.O. Box 7407
Washington, DC 20044   (202) 566-8195

Company trademarks of restricted and unrestricted merchandise for importation into the U.S. are listed in the following categories in this pamphlet: clothing, perfumes, lenses and other optical goods, watches and clocks, jewelry and precious metalware, tape recorders and musical instruments, and shoes. Some companies restrict the quantity of merchandise or have not given consent for the importation.

* Trade Leads, Analysis, International Markets

Public Affairs Office
International Trade Administration
U.S. Department of Commerce
14th St. & Constitution, NW
Washington, DC 20230   (202) 377-3808

Published every two weeks by the International Trade Administration, the trade magazine, *Business America*, offers exporting advice and how-to information, including worldwide trade leads, country-to-country marketing guidance, incisive economic analyses, advance notice of planned exhibitions of U.S. products worldwide, and success stories of selected American business firms in the field of exporting. A special issue of *Business America* provides a roadmap to guide

prospective exporters toward people in the government who can help them obtain export know-how and information about overseas markets. For a copy, contact the office above; and for a annual subscription ($40), contact the Government Printing Office, Superintendent of Documents, Washington, D.C. 20402; (202) 783-3238.

* Trade Negotiations Advice

Office of Tariff Affairs and Trade Agreements
U.S. International Trade Commission
500 E St., SW, Room 404
Washington, DC 20436   (202) 252-1592

The ITC advises the U.S. President on the probable economic effect on domestic industry and consumers of modification of duties and other barriers to trade that may be considered for inclusion in any proposed trade agreement with foreign countries.

* Trade Opportunities in Overseas Markets

U.S. and Foreign Commercial Service
International Trade Administration
U.S. Department of Commerce, Room H2106
Washington, DC 20230   (202) 377-5777

The US&FCS has a program to find the best outlets for your products in overseas markets. To locate ready and willing international customers interested in your type of product or service, contact a trade specialist through this office who can provide you with details on specifications, quantities, end-use, delivery, and bid deadlines. These leads are available electronically or in printed form through a variety of public and private sources. Contact this office for more information.

* Trade-Related Employment Issues

Bureau of International Labor Affairs
Department of Labor
200 Constitution Ave., NW, Room S2235
Washington, DC 20210   (202) 523-6043

The Bureau of International Labor Affairs represents the Department of Labor in the development of international economic and trade policies that affect the welfare of U.S. workers. This role includes conducting research on trade-related employment issues, coordinating advice received from Labor Advisory Committees on Trade authorized by the Trade Agreements Act of 1979, and acting as a liaison between other federal departments, agencies, and organized labor. The Bureau is also a member of various interagency committees charged with trade policy functions, and continues to participate in the formulation of U.S. immigration policy.

* Trade Remedy Assistance

The Trade Remedy Assistance Office
U.S. International Trade Commission
500 E St., SW
Washington, DC 20436   (202) 252-2200

If a U.S. business has experienced adverse effects from U.S. trade laws, such as loss of sales due to increased sales of foreign products in the U.S., they may be able to get assistance to remedy the situation. This office can provide you with general information on the remedies and benefits available to businesses under U.S. trade laws. For more information on eligibility and the types of assistance available, contact this office.

* Trade Shows

U.S. and Foreign Commercial Service
International Trade Administration
U.S. Department of Commerce, Room H2106
Washington, DC 20230   (202) 377-5777

Meet potential customers face-to-face, sell your products and services, and assess the competition at trade shows around the world. At US&FCS-certified international trade fairs, you'll receive special services to enhance your market promotion efforts. US&FCS-organized exhibitions offer you the facility to identify potential agents and distributors in addition to a targeted marketing campaign for your products. Contact this office for more information.

* Trade Statistics

Statistical Services Division
Office of Data Systems
U.S. International Trade Commission
500 E St., SW, Room 615-P
Washington, DC 20436   (202) 252-1171

The ITC responds daily to inquiries for trade data and assists in evaluating data reliability. Four statistical bulletins summarizing import and export information for use in the trade community are available. Compiling statistical data allows the ITC to compare export, import, and domestic production statistics. In conjunction with other agencies, the Commission is working to develop concepts for an international commodity code for reporting transactions in international trade and to report them to the Congress.

* Trade Statistics

U.S. and Foreign Commercial Service
International Trade Administration
U.S. Department of Commerce, Room H2106
Washington, DC 20230 (202) 377-5777

Your trade specialist can provide you with up-to-date marketing data on thousands of individual products and markets in more than 200 countries. This statistical information is gathered from both U.S. and U.N. sources, using sophisticated and flexible software programs that allow the data to be extracted by dollar value, quantity, unit value, market share percentage, and varying time frames. For more information on trade statistics, contact this office.

* Tropical Products

Office of Food Policy and Programs
Bureau of Economic and Business Affairs
Department of State
2201 C St NW, Room 3640
Washington, DC 20520 (202) 647-3090

This office works closely with GATT and commodity organizations regarding tropical products, and monitors several international agreements. Although not in agreement with other countries regarding what constitutes a tropical product, this office handles cocoa, cotton, coffee, bananas, sugar, tea, jute, and other hard fibers. This office can provide information regarding these products and agreements.

* Unfair Import Investigations

Office of Unfair Import Investigations
U.S. International Trade Commission
500 E St., SW, Room 401
Washington, DC 20436 (202) 252-1561

As a representative of the public interest, this office ensures that complete records of import investigations are developed, and that the relevant issues are briefed for the administrative law judges and the Commission. Investigative attorneys from this office actively participate with private parties throughout investigations. The investigative staff represents the public interest rather than the private interests of a complainant or respondent. Businesses seek protection through this office from alleged infringement of intellectual property rights in a host of different industries.

* Unfair Trade Practices

The Office of Investigations
U.S. International Trade Commission
500 E St., SW, Room 615
Washington, DC 20436 (202) 252-1161

The ITC investigates unfair import trade practices, which include unlawful, unfair methods of competition and unfair acts in the importation or sale of products in the U.S. The threat or effect of these practices is often to destroy or injure a domestic industry, prevent the establishment of such an industry, or restrain or monopolize trade and commerce in the United States. Most complaints involve allegations of patent, copyright, or trademark infringement, while other investigations include alleged violation of the antitrust laws, misappropriation of trade secrets, passing off, and false advertising. If the Commission determines that a violation of the statute has occurred, the ITC excludes the articles involved from entry into the U.S., or it may issue cease-and-desist orders directing the company engaged in such violation to cease and desist from engaging in such unfair methods or acts.

* Unfair Trade Practices

Import Administration
International Trade Administration
U.S. Department of Commerce
14th & Constitution, NW
Washington, DC 20230 (202) 377-1780

The Import Administration sector provides a process for American manufacturers and workers to ask the government to determine whether they are the victims of unfair trade practices and to help them solve the problem. These unfair practices usually involve foreign subsidies and dumping (selling in the U.S. at less than fair value), which harm the competitive ability of efficient U.S. producers that do not have the benefit of government subsidies or a protected home market. Contact this office for more information.

* U.S. Industrial Outlook

Office of Trade Development
International Trade Administration
U.S. Department of Commerce
14th & Constitution, NW
Washington, DC 20230 (202) 377-1461

Each year, Trade Development publishes the *U.S. Industrial Outlook*, which contains analyses and forecasts of domestic and international trends for more than 300 U.S. manufacturing and service industries.

* U.S. Export Administration Regulations

Superintendent of Documents
Government Printing Office
Washington, DC 20402 (202) 783-3238

U.S. Export Administration Regulations is a loose-leaf compilation of regulations that exporters must familiarize themselves with in order to conduct their export business. Annual subscribers receive supplementary *Export Administration Bulletins* which explain recent policy changes and provide replacement pages to keep the set of regulations up-to-date. An annual subscription is $87.00, and foreign mail is $108.75. Single copies of bulletins are $8.00. Contact GPO for ordering information.

* U.S. Multilateral Trade Negotiations

Office of Industries
U.S. International Trade Commission
500 E St., SW
Washington, DC 20436 (202) 252-1296

This office conducts research in support of U.S. multilateral trade negotiations, such as the Uruguay Round. A current project will evaluate the probable effects of liberalizing tariff and nontariff measures.

* U.S. Trade Centers

U.S. and Foreign Commercial Service
International Trade Administration
U.S. Department of Commerce, Room H2106
Washington, DC 20230 (202) 377-5777

US&FCS Trade Centers in Tokyo, Seoul, Mexico City, and London are available for your company's special promotions for a small fee. These Trade Centers also organize specialized exhibitions on themes targeting special opportunities in the local marketplace. Contact this office for additional information on the trade centers.

* Vehicle Importation

Public Information Division
U.S. Customs Service
Department of the Treasury
P.O. Box 7407
Washington, DC 20044 (202) 566-8195

The pamphlet, *Importing a Car*, outlines the provisions for dutiable entry or free entry of automobiles, trucks, and motorcycles. Prior arrangements, documentation, safety and emissions standards, and federal tax guidelines are also discussed.

* Vessel Owners and Masters: Customs Rules

Public Information Office
U.S. Customs Service
Department of the Treasury
P.O. Box 7407
Washington, DC 20044 (202) 566-8195

Masters or vessel owners may incur penalties for violations of United States Customs laws, including violations committed by members of their crews. The brochure, *Notice to Masters of Vessels*, notifies the masters of proper precautions in the areas of arrival and entry, and merchandise in order to avoid penalties for violations.

* World Traders Data Reports

U.S. and Foreign Commercial Service
International Trade Administration
U.S. Department of Commerce, Room H2106
Washington, DC 20230 (202) 377-5777

For your export endeavors to be successful, your trading partners abroad must be reliable and qualified. To assess the reliability of potential customers or representatives, the US&FCS can provide you with *World Traders Data Reports*. Your trade specialist can prepare up-to-date, made-to-order background checks of your potential trading partners. Your *World Traders Data Report* will include background information on the foreign firms you select, their standing in the local business community, credit worthiness, and overall reliability and suitability as trade contacts. Contact this office for additional information on these reports.

Overseas Financing, Investing, and Insurance

Conducting business and investing overseas doesn't have to be a complete gamble. To help promote overseas development, the federal government has created plenty of assistance programs to insure your investments, check the credit status of your business partners, finance your projects, and even advise you about the political climate of any country. Whether you are looking for export loans, foreign labor trends, or travel advisories for your next trip, you'll find what you need below.

* Agribusiness and Foreign Development

Office of Business Development
Overseas Private Investment Corporation
1615 M St., NW
Washington, DC 20527   (202) 457-7010

The Overseas Private Investment Corporation is working closely with the Department of Agriculture, the Agribusiness Council, United States cooperative organizations, and others to facilitate the transfer of agribusiness development know-how to raise the efficiency of food systems in the emerging nations. OPIC provides pre-investment assistance, project financing, and insurance. Contact this OPIC office for more information.

* Agriculture Exports

Export-Import Bank of the United States
811 Vermont Ave., NW
Washington, DC 20571   (202) 566-8860

In cooperation with the U.S. Department of Agriculture, Eximbank assists the export of American agricultural commodities, agricultural equipment, seeds and chemicals, and storage and processing facilities. Contact this office for more information.

* Applying for Financing

Vice President for Finance
Overseas Private Investment Corporation
1615 M St., NW
Washington, DC 20527   (202) 457-7178, (800) 424-6742

The sponsor of a potential project interested in obtaining financing should provide OPIC with a copy of the business plan for the proposed project. The plan should include:
-A general description of the project
-Identity, background, and the audited financial statements of the project's proposed principal owners and management
-Planned sources of supply, anticipated output and markets, distribution channels, competition, and the basis for projecting market share
-Summary of project costs and sources of procurement of capital goods and services
-Proposed financing plan, including the amount of the proposed OPIC participation, and financial projections
-Brief statement of the contribution the business is expected to make to local economic and social development

OPIC's staff is pleased to work with investors to structure a financing package to satisfy the diverse requirements and goals of all parties. Contact this office for more information on applying for financing.

* Contractors & Exporters Insurance

Applications Office
Overseas Private Investment Corporation
1615 M St., NW
Washington, DC 20527   (202) 457-7059

OPIC insures against wrongful callings of bid, performance or advance payment guaranties, and other guaranties, usually issued in the form of bank standby letters of credit. OPIC also provides suppliers of goods and services with political risk protection against loss of or damage to physical assets, as well as protection against unresolved contractual disputes with the foreign buyer. Insurance offered under this program can protect a wide range of U.S. companies in such service industries as engineering, drilling, hotel and hospital management, construction, computer, and telecommunications services. Exporters of such goods as heavy machinery, turbines, computers, medical equipment, irrigation equipment, meters, storage tanks, and vehicles are also eligible for coverage. The types of goods and services listed above are examples of the many contracting and exporting activities covered by OPIC insurance under this program. Other types of goods and services not listed here are eligible as well. Contact this office for more information.

* Credit Checks

Computer Applications/Office Automation
Export-Import Bank of the United States
811 Vermont Avenue, NW
Washington, DC 20571   (202) 566-4690

Contact this office to obtain information on Eximbank's credit files on thousands of foreign firms which have had experience with Eximbank. The information provided is helpful to companies new to foreign markets.

* Development Contribution

Vice President for Finance
Overseas Private Investment Corporation
1615 M St., NW
Washington, DC 20527   (202) 457-7178, (800) 424-6742

When considering a proposed project, OPIC must look at how it will contribute to the economic and social development of the host country. They will examine such factors as:
-Increased availability of goods and services of better quality or at lower cost
-Development of skills through training
-Transfer of technological and managerial skills
-Foreign exchange earnings or savings
-Host country tax revenues
-Increases in stimulation of other local enterprises

OPIC will also consider the environmental effects of ventures to which it supports. Contact this office for more information on the required developmental contributions.

* Economic Developments in Exporting

Office of Policy and Planning
Export-Import Bank of the United States
811 Vermont Ave., NW
Washington, DC 20571   (202) 566-8861

This office monitors economic developments that may affect the Bank's operations. It also conducts the policy planning and research work of the Bank, and reviews and evaluates the Bank's programs and policies. For more information, contact the office above.

* Eligibility Criteria for Investments

Applications Officer
Overseas Private Investment Corporation
1615 M St., NW
Washington, DC 20527   (202) 457-7059

Investment can be insured if it is used to enlarge or modernize an existing plant and equipment, or for additional working capital in an expanded business. Coverage for investment to own an existing enterprise is available if the investor plans to help fund expansion of the enterprise. There is no fixed form which an investment must take to be eligible for coverage. For more information on eligible investment, contact this OPIC office.

* Eligibility Criteria for Investors

Applications Officer
Overseas Private Investment Corporation
1615 M St., NW
Washington, DC 20527   (202) 457-7059

There is no requirement that the project in which the insured investment is made be a project owned or controlled by U.S. investors. However, insurance can be issued only to "eligible investors." OPIC can therefore insure an investment by an eligible investor in a project controlled by foreign interests, but it is only the investment which is insured, not the entire project. Eligible investors are defined as:
- Citizens of the United States
- Corporations, partnerships, or other associations created under the laws of the United States, or any state or territory of the United States, which are substantially beneficially owned by U.S. citizens

- A foreign business at least 95% owned by investors eligible under the above

Contact this office for more information on eligibility of investors.

* Energy Industry: Overseas Investment

Office of Corporate Communications
Overseas Private Investment Corporation
1615 M St., NW
Washington, DC 20527   (202) 457-7059

OPIC provides insurance for most types of investments in energy exploration and development. For more information, OPIC's *Energy Industry* brochure is available from this office.

* Enterprises Eligible for Finance Program

Vice President for Finance
Overseas Private Investment Corporation
1615 M St., NW
Washington, DC 20527   (202) 457-7178(800) 424-6742

Financing is provided for a wide range of enterprises under terms and conditions that are flexible enough to permit sound development projects to be achieved. Eligible enterprises include manufacturing, agricultural production, fishing, forestry, mining, energy development, storage, processing, and certain service industries providing the host country with exceptional developmental benefits. Certain industries involving significant capital investment, such as commercial hotels, tourist facilities, leasing companies and equipment maintenance and distributorship facilities, are also financed. Projects in the poorer developing countries and those involving smaller U.S. firms or cooperatives as sponsors are of particular interest. Contact OPIC for more information.

* Equity and Equity Participating Investments

Vice President for Finance
Overseas Private Investment Corporation
1615 M St., NW
Washington, DC 20527   (202) 457-7178, (800) 424-6742

As well as providing debt capital, OPIC provides permanent capital through capital stock investments and the purchase of a project's debentures convertible to stock. In these cases owners share their equity in a project with OPIC. This permits them to reduce their exposure to risk and, by improving the project's capital base, often makes it possible to obtain substantially more debt capital for the project as well. OPIC is very selective in its equity investment program as making investments such as these usually involves greater risk than being a secured creditor of a project. Contact this office for more information on equity and equity participating investments.

* Eximbank Annual Report

Office of Public Affairs and Publications
Export-Import Bank of the United States
811 Vermont Ave., NW, Room 1203
Washington, DC 20571   (202) 566-8990

The *Annual Report of the Export-Import Bank of the United States* can be obtained from the office above. Some of the information provided includes financial statements and a management report.

* Eximbank Electronic Bulletin Board

811 Vermont Avenue, NW
Washington, DC 20571   (202) 566-4699

Call this number above to access Eximbank's Bulletin Board System for electronic communications.

* Eximbank Project Analysis

Engineering Division
Export-Import Bank of the United States
811 Vermont Ave., NW
Washington, DC 20571   (202) 566-8802

The Engineering Division evaluates the technical feasibility of proposed projects and monitors projects in progress. Contact this office for further information.

* Eximbank Publications and Public Affairs

Office of Public Affairs and Publications
Export-Import Bank of the United States
811 Vermont Ave., NW, Room 1203
Washington, DC 20571   (202) 566-8990

This office is responsible for the Bank's press information and press relations, and for distributing its publications. For more information, contact the office above.

* Expropriation Insurance

Applications Officer

Overseas Private Investment Corporation
1615 M St., NW
Washington, DC 20527   (202) 457-7059

According to OPIC insurance contracts, expropriatory action that can be insured includes nationalization of an enterprise, the taking of property, and various situations which might be described as "creeping expropriation." Any action that is taken by the government in the country where the project is taking place is considered expropriatory if it has a specified impact on either the properties or the operations of the foreign project, or on the rights or financial interests of the insured investor. Expropriatory action must continue for at least one year, six months for contracts covering oil and gas projects, and three months or less in contracts covering institutional loans. Important limitations in the definition of expropriatory action include exceptions for proper regulatory or revenue actions taken by host governments and actions provoked or instigated by the investor or foreign enterprise. Insurance against risks that apply only to a specific project may be available upon request and will be rated individually. OPIC's compensation is according to the book value of the investment or loan as of the date of expropriation. OPIC makes sure the coverage does not allow an equity investor to keep its ownership interest and to be compensated for expropriatory actions. Contact this office for more information on expropriation coverage.

* Export Briefing Programs

Export-Import Bank of the U.S.
811 Vermont Avenue, NW
Washington, DC 20571   (202) 566-4490

Eximbank offers briefing programs to the small business community. The programs include group briefings and individual discussions held both within the Bank and around the country about how the Eximbank can help small businesses succeed in exporting their goods and services. For scheduling information, contact this office.

* Export Finance and Insurance

Office of Public Affairs and Publications
Export-Import Bank of the United States
811 Vermont Ave., NW, Room 1203
Washington, DC 20571   (202) 566-8990

The *Program Selection Guide* summarizes the major features of Eximbank's export finance and insurance programs. It was designed so that you can easily determine the program most appropriate for specific export transactions. The exact terms are controlled solely by the policy, commitment, or guarantee issued to the exporter or financial institution. You can get a free copy of this booklet from the office above.

* Export-Import Banking Hotline

Business Advisory Service
Export-Import Bank of the U.S.
811 Vermont Avenue, NW
Washington, DC 20571   (800) 424-5201

To encourage small businesses to sell overseas, the Export-Import Bank maintains this special office to provide information on the availability and use of export credit insurance, guarantees, direct and intermediary loans extended to finance the sale of U.S. good and services abroad. Call this toll-free number for more information.

* Export-Import Insurance Claims

Claims and Recoveries Division
Export-Import Bank of the United States
811 Vermont Ave., NW
Washington, DC 20571   (202) 566-8822

This office processes claims filed under the Bank's guarantee and insurance programs and is responsible for collections and recoveries. Contact the office for more information.

* Export-Import Library

Export-Import Bank of the United States
811 Vermont Ave., NW, Room 1373
Washington, DC 20571   (202) 566-8320

The Library contains information on economics, finance, exports credits, business, and statistics. Contact the office above for more information.

* Exporting Services

Export-Import Bank of the United States
811 Vermont Avenue, NW
Washington, DC 20571   (202) 566-4490

Each of Eximbank's export support programs is available to cover exports of services, and two are specially designed for services exports. The Engineering Multiplier Program provides medium-term financing for initial services contracts, such as feasibility studies and preconstruction design engineering services, for projects that could produce significant follow-on orders for U.S. exports. The special FCIA Services Industry Policy provides repayment protection for service companies that receive regular progress payments from their foreign customers on terms of up to 180 days. Eximbank also extends its loan and guarantee support to assist U.S. exports for Operations and Maintenance contracts to bring foreign projects up to their performance potential.

* Export Insurance

Insurance Division
Export-Import Bank of the United States
811 Vermont Ave., Room 919
Washington, DC 20571   (202) 566-4490

The Insurance Division is responsible for the Bank's export credit insurance programs that are administered by the Foreign Credit Insurance Association (FCIA). Contact this office for more information.

* Export Seminars

Export-Import Bank of the United States
Office of Pubic Affairs
811 Vermont Avenue, NW
Washington, DC 20571   (202) 566-4490

Eximbank offers the following briefing and instructional seminars on various topics relating to import/export financing. Space is limited for these seminars, so make your reservations as early as possible. Each seminar is held in Washington, D.C., and is free of charge.

One-Day Briefing Program: Designed to give exporters and others an introduction to the programs of the Export-Import Bank and the Foreign Credit Insurance Association, and how they may be used to enhance export sales efforts.

Two-Day Briefing Program: Offered free of charge for bankers and others, these seminars are useful for those who have some knowledge of the Eximbank and FCIA, but need to be brought up to date on recent program changes.

Four-Day Training Seminar: Designed to give bankers, exporters, and others a working knowledge of the programs of Eximbank and FCIA. Time is also devoted to programs of other U.S. government and international agencies that support exports. Opportunities are given to meet with members of Eximbank's staff.

For an schedule of upcoming seminars, contact the above office.

* Finance Program

Vice President for Finance
Overseas Private Investment Corporation
1615 M St., NW
Washington, DC 20527   (202) 457-7178, (800) 424-6742

OPIC achieves its finance program through direct loan, loan guaranty, and equity techniques that provide medium- to long-term funding and permanent capital to ventures involving significant equity and management participation by U.S. businesses. OPIC's loans and loan guaranties normally are provided in the form of "project financing," which is based primarily on the economic, technical, marketing, and financial soundness inherent in the project. OPIC can provide a significant portion of medium- and long-term funds for financing in countries where conventional financial institutions often are reluctant or unable to lend on such a basis. Because its programs support private sector investments in financially viable projects, OPIC does not offer concessional terms usually associated with government-to-government lending, nor does it offer financing of export sales unrelated to long-term investment in overseas business. Questions concerning financing for specific projects or preliminary applications should be addressed to the above OPIC office.

* Financing Techniques for Foreign Investment

Vice President for Finance
Overseas Private Investment Corporation
1615 M St., NW
Washington, DC 20527   (202) 457-7178, (800) 424-6742

OPIC's financing programs include the following:

Direct Loans. This program provides financing for smaller projects from OPIC's own funds. These loans generally range in amount from $500,000 to $6 million. This source of funding may be used only for financing projects sponsored by or significantly involving U.S. small businesses or cooperatives.

Guaranteed Loans. This program is for major corporations not eligible for direct loans, and small businesses and cooperatives investing in large projects. Typical OPIC loan guaranties range from $2 million to $25 million, but can be as large as $50 million.

Contact this office for more information on OPIC's financing techniques.

* Foreign Credit Insurance Regional Offices

FCIA, 40 Rector Street, 11th Floor, New York, NY 10006; (212) 277-7020. Areas served: New England, New York, New Jersey, Pennsylvania, Delaware, District of Columbia, Maryland, and Virginia.

FCIA, 20 North Clark Street, Suite 910, Chicago, IL 60602; (312) 641-1915. Areas served: Ohio, Indiana, Michigan, Illinois, Wisconsin, Minnesota, North Dakota, South Dakota, Iowa, Missouri, Nebraska, Kansas, Kentucky, and West Virginia.

FCIA, Wells Fargo Center, Suite 2580, 333 South Grand Ave., Los Angeles, CA 90071; (213) 687-3890. Areas served: Alaska, Washington, Oregon, California, Hawaii, Nevada, Arizona, Montana, Wyoming, Colorado, and Utah.

FCIA, Texas Commerce Tower, 600 Travis, Suite 2860, Houston, TX 77002; (713) 227-0987. Areas served: Louisiana, Oklahoma, Arkansas, New Mexico, North Carolina, South Carolina, Texas, Mississippi, and Tennessee.

FCIA, World Trade Center, 80 Southwest 8th St., Miami, FL 33130; (305) 372-8540. Area served: Florida, Alabama, Georgia, Puerto Rico, and Virgin Islands.

* Foreign Geographic Loan Areas

Export-Import Bank of the United States
811 Vermont Ave., NW, Room 1203
Washington, DC 20571   (202) 566-8990

The four foreign geographic area divisions administer the Bank's medium and long-term lending and guarantee activities. Loan officers process requests for assistance, perform financial analysis, and maintain contact with other participant countries in the OECD export credit arrangement. Contact the appropriate office above for further information:

Africa and Middle East: (202) 566-8011
Asia: (202) 566-8885
Europe and Canada: (202) 566-8813
Latin America: (202) 566-8943

* Foreign Investment Opportunities Update

Public Affairs
Overseas Private Investment Corporation
1615 M St., NW
Washington, DC 20527   (202) 457-7093

TOPICS is a free newsletter that contains information about specific investment opportunities and trends in various countries. To get on the mailing list, contact the above OPIC office.

* Export-Import Bank of the United States

811 Vermont Ave., NW, Room 1203
Washington, DC 20571   (202) 566-8990

Export-Import Bank of the United States is an independent, corporate agency of the U.S. Government, chartered by Congress. The principal legislation governing its operations is the Export-Import Bank Act of 1945, as amended through October 15, 1989, and the Government Corporation Control act. Eximbank's agent, the Foreign Credit Insurance Association (FCIA) offers several types of credit insurance policies to cover the risks of non-payment on export credit transactions, such as sales of products and services, leasing of equipment, and consignments in foreign countries.

* How Can the Export-Import Bank Help You

Office of Public Affairs and Publications
Export-Import Bank of the United States
811 Vermont Ave., NW, Room 1203
Washington, DC 20571   (202) 566-8990

Contact the office above to see how Eximbank can assist you.

* Importing-Exporting Legislation

Office of Congressional and External Affairs
Export-Import Bank of the United States
811 Vermont Ave., NW, Room 929
Washington, DC 20571   (202) 566-8806

This office is Eximbanks's liaison with other U.S. government agencies, interagency bodies, and the U.S. Congress. It is also responsible for Eximbank's legislative affairs. Contact the office above for more information.

* Inconvertibility Insurance

Applications Officer
Overseas Private Investment Corporation
1615 M St., NW
Washington, DC 20527   (202) 457-7059

OPIC's inconvertibility coverage assures that earnings, capital, principal and interest, and other payments, can continue to be transferred into U.S. dollars under the same exchange regulations and practices that were in effect at the time the insurance was issued. If a blockage occurs, the insured can exchange local currency for dollars. Blockage can be either "active" (e.g. new, more restrictive regulations by exchange control authorities that denies access to foreign exchange) or "passive" (e.g. authorities fail to act on an application for foreign exchange within the specified time period). OPIC makes dollar payments when it receives local currency. The coverage does not protect against devaluation of a country's currency. Contact this office for more information on inconvertibility coverage.

* Insurance Policies for First-Time Exporters

Export-Import Bank of the United States
811 Vermont Ave., NW
Washington, DC 20571   (202) 566-4490, (800) 424-5201

Through FCIA, Eximbank offers a short-term insurance policy geared to meet the particular credit requirements of smaller, less experienced exporters. Under the policy, the Export-Import Bank assumes 95% of the commercial and 100% of the political risk involved in extending credit to the exporter's overseas customers. This policy frees the smaller exporter from "first loss" commercial risk deductible provisions that are usually found in regular insurance policies. The special coverage is available to companies which are just beginning to export or have an average annual export credit sales volume of less than $750,000 for the past two years.

* Investor Information Service (IIS)

Investor Information Service
Overseas Private Investment Corporation
1615 M St, NW
Washington, DC 20527   (202) 457-7010

For American businesses considering overseas ventures, obtaining basic information about foreign countries and their business environments is an important first step. Unfortunately, this is often a difficult process, and frequently takes a lot of time, given all the different sources of information and the resulting research required. To assist U.S. firms in gathering such information, as well as assisting the flow of information about developing countries to potential U.S. investors, OPIC created the Investor Information Service (IIS). IIS is a publications clearinghouse that provides interested companies and individuals with easy "one-stop-shopping" for basic business, economic, and political information commonly sought when considering investment overseas. The materials, which are gathered into "kit" form, are obtained from various U.S. Government agencies, foreign governments, and international organizations. These source materials cover the economies, trade laws, business regulations and attitudes, political conditions, and investment incentives of specific developing countries and areas. The information kits packaged by IIS are categorized by individual countries as well as major geographic regions. At present, IIS kits are available for more than 100 developing countries and 16 regions. Each information kit generally contains the following country-specific publications:

Background Notes. Describe a country's land, people, history, government, political conditions, economy and foreign relations.

Foreign Economic Trends and Their Implications for the United States. Discusses the economic and financial conditions of a country, and explains how they could affect U.S. overseas business.

Overseas Business Reports. Contain information on a country's trade patterns, industry trends, distribution and sales channels, natural resources, infrastructure, and trade regulations.

Post Report. Contains practical information on living and travelling in a country.

Investment Climate Statement. Summarizes those laws, policies, and changes in a country's economic climate that may affect existing or new U.S. direct investment.

Foreign Labor Trends. Discusses employment trends, union activities, and relations between labor, government, and industry.

Travel Advisories. Provides information on travel conditions, restrictions, and document requirements.

Maps. Show transportation networks, economic activities, and land utilization.

Foreign Publications. Outline legal codes and discuss business regulations, investment incentives, and other related topics.

This country-specific data is supplemented by a package of information describing the organization, programs and publications of various U.S. Government agencies and international organizations concerned with international trade and investment. Descriptions of the following organizations are generally included in the package:

Agency for International Development (AID)
Export-Import Bank of the United States (Ex-Im)
Foreign Credit Insurance Association (FCIA)
Inter-American Development Bank (IDB)
International Finance Corporation (IFC)
Overseas Private Investment Corporation (OPIC)
U.S. Department of Commerce

U.S. Trade and Development Program (TDP)

IIS works continually to identify and collect new publications to add to its information kits. Documents are selected on the basis of their content, cost, and utility to potential investors. The Service's publications inventory, which contains more than 1,300 items in all, is updated regularly to ensure that kit materials are current. IIS provides investors with a general overview of countries, and helps them know how to get more information from various internationally-oriented organizations. It is not, however, a research and analysis service. Telephone orders by credit card can be made by calling (202) 457 7010, or (800) 424-6742. For an IIS brochure and order form, contact this OPIC office listed above.

* Investment Eligibility Criteria for Countries

Applications Officer
Overseas Private Investment Corporation
1615 M St., NW
Washington, DC 20527   (202) 457-7059

OPIC programs are available to cover U.S. private investments in over 100 countries which have been determined to be "less developed friendly countries and areas," and with which the U.S. has agreements to operate OPIC programs. Insurance investments in developing countries with high per-capita incomes is restricted to projects sponsored by U.S. small businesses or co-operatives, projects involving minerals or energy, construction projects, and other projects judged by OPIC's Board of Directors to merit insurance, such as those offering important development or trade benefits. OPIC can only insure investment in countries with which there is an intergovernmental agreement. Contact this office for more information.

* Investment Missions Program

Public Affairs
Overseas Private Investment Corporation
1615 M St., NW
Washington, DC 20527   (202) 457-7011

OPIC leads five investment missions each year to encourage and makes easier private American investment in developing countries. Mission participants meet with high level government officials and attend briefing sessions with the U.S. Ambassador, Embassy staff and local business leaders. Most importantly, individual business appointments with potential joint-venture partners and other local executives with expertise in a company's specific field of interest are prearranged by OPIC. For more information on upcoming missions activities, contact this office.

* Levels and Cost of Coverage

Applications Officer
Overseas Private Investment Corporation
1615 M St., NW
Washington, DC 20527   (202) 457-7059

OPIC insurance contracts generally require the insurance premium to be paid annually in advance. Premiums are computed for each type of coverage based on the maximum insured amount and a current insured amount which may be elected by the investor on a yearly basis. Contact this office for information on the base rates for different industries, including manufacturing/services projects, institutional loans, natural resource projects, oil and gas projects, and contractor & exporters coverages.

* Medium- and Long-Term Export Loans and Guarantees

Office of Public Affairs and Publications
Export-Import Bank of the United States
811 Vermont Ave., NW, Room 1203
Washington, DC 20571   (202) 566-8990

The brochure, *Medium- and Long-Term Export Loans and Guarantees* provides information on the types of commitments, eligible markets, eligible exports, master agreements, and repayment terms under Eximbank's programs. Contact this office for your free copy.

* Mutually Beneficial Investments

Applications Officer
Overseas Private Investment Corporation
1615 M St., NW
Washington, DC 20527   (202) 457-7059

When investors apply for insurance, they are asked to supply data on how the project will affect the host countries' development, including information on job creation, skill development, balance of payments effects, taxes and host government revenues, and contributions to basic human needs. In addition to its broad mandate to support only investment "sensitive and responsive" to development needs, OPIC has a legislative mandate to foster private initiatives and competition and to discourage monopolistic practices. OPIC examines any laws or agreements conferring monopoly rights, special tax or tariff protection, and any other factors which restrict competition. The effect of a proposed investment on U.S. employment and the U.S. balance of payments is closely examined by OPIC. For more information on applying for investment insurance, contact the above office.

* New Venture Insurance Program

Applications Officer
Overseas Private Investment Corporation
1615 M St., NW
Washington, DC 20527   (202) 457-7059

All of OPIC's insurance and guaranty obligations are backed by the full faith and credit of the United States of America, as well as OPIC's own substantial financial reserves. Insurance is available for new ventures or to expand existing enterprises. OPIC insures investments in qualified projects in less developed friendly countries or areas against loss due to specific political risks. OPIC's statute authorizes it to insure against the following risks:

-Inability to convert into dollars local currency received by the   investor as profits or earnings or return of the original   investment.
-Loss of investment due to expropriation, nationalization, or   confiscation by action of a foreign government.
-Loss of income and loss of assets due to political violence, i.e.,   war, revolution, insurrection, or civil strife.

Contact this office for more information about OPIC's insurance program.

* Oil, Mineral, Gas Investment Insurance

Insurance Department
Overseas Private Investment Corporation
1615 M St., NW
Washington, DC 20527   (202) 457-7200

OPIC offers highly flexible and innovative coverage for investment in mineral exploration and development (including processing where it is an integral part of a development project); for oil and gas exploration, development and production; for construction and other contracting projects; for cross-border lease transactions and for institutional loans. For more information on these programs, contact the office above.

* Overseas Investment Information Hotline

Pre-Investment Services
Overseas Private Investment Corporation
1615 M St., NW
Washington, DC 20527   (202) 457-7010, Toll-free (800) 424-6742

OPIC promotes economic growth in developing countries by encouraging U.S. private investment in those nations through two principal programs: (1 insurance of investment against certain political risks and (2 financing U.S.-sponsored enterprises through direct loans and/or loan guaranties. OPIC also offers several pre-investment services. For further information on OPIC programs and services, and for dates of future investment seminars and missions, contact this office.

* Overseas Investment Publications

Office of Corporate Communications
Overseas Private Investment Corporation
1615 M St., NW
Washington, DC 20527   (202) 457-7059

OPIC publications include the following:

Annual Report
Programs for Contractors & Exporters
Insurance Handbook
Investor Information Service
Finance Handbook
Small Business Guide
Country List
Claims History
Guidelines for Broker/Agent Participation

For additional information on OPIC, free copies of these publications are available on request from the above office.

* Overseas Private Investment Corp. Country & Area List

Information Officer
The Overseas Private Investment Corporation
1615 M St., NW
Washington, DC 20527   (202) 457-7200

In general, OPIC's insurance and finance programs are operable in the following countries and areas. Coverages may be limited in higher income areas, indicated by an asterisk. The countries and areas are as follows:

Anguilla, Antigua/Barbuda, Argentina, Aruba*, The Bahamas*, Bahrain*, Bangladesh, Barbados*, Belize, Benin, Bolivia, Botswana, Brazil, Burkina Faso, Burundi, Cameroon, Cape Verde, Central African Republic, Chad, China, China (Taiwan), Colombia, Congo, Cook Islands, Costa Rica, Cote d'Ivoire, Cyprus, Djibouti, Dominica, Dominican Republic, Ecuador, Egypt, El Salvador, Equatorial Guinea, Fiji, French Guiana, Gabon, Gambia, Ghana, Greece,

Grenada, Guatemala, Guinea, Guinea-Bissau, Guyana, Haiti, Honduras, India, Indonesia, Ireland, Israel*, Jamaica, Jordan, Kenya, Korea, Lebanon, Lesotho, Liberia, Madagascar, Malawi, Malaysia, Mali, Malta*, Mauritania, Mauritius, Morocco, Mozambique, Nepal, Netherlands Antilles*, Niger, Nigeria, Northern Ireland, Oman*, Pakistan, Papua New Guinea, Philippines, Portugal, Qatar*, Rwanda, St. Kitts-Nevis, St. Lucia, St. Vincent/Grenadines, Sao Tome and Principe, Saudi Arabia*, Senegal, Sierra Leone, Singapore*, Somalia, Sri Lanka, Sudan Swaziland, Syria, Tanzania, Thailand, Togo, Tonga, Trinidad & Tobago*, Tunisia, Turkey, Uganda, Uruguay, Western Samoa, Yemen Arab Republic, Yugoslavia, Zaire, and Zambia.

Investors interested in up-to-date information on OPIC services available in specific countries and areas, as well as information regarding program availability in countries not listed should contact OPIC directly.

* Political Violence Insurance

Applications Officer
Overseas Private Investment Corporation
1615 M St., NW
Washington, DC 20527   (202) 457-7059

Losses resulting from violent acts taken to achieve a political objective, such as declared or undeclared war, hostile action by national or international forces, civil war, revolution, insurrection, or civil strife (Coverage for civil strife is optional) are compensated. Losses resulting from an effort to hinder, combat, or defend against such violent acts are covered as well. However, acts to achieve labor or student objectives are not covered. Two different types of coverage for loss due to political violence are available. An investor may request either or both:

Business Income Coverage (BIC). BIC covers income losses when the insured's assets are damaged by political violence. The policy can be modified to include coverage for locations outside the insured's facility. The insured are compensated according to their expected net income plus their continuing, normal operating costs. OPIC will also pay for expenses that reduce business income loss, such as renting a temporary facility. Compensation is paid until the business is back on its feet and productive, or for one year, whichever comes first.

Assets. The property used for the project can be insured against loss due to political violence. The basic measure of compensation is the original cost of the property, unless it would cost less to repair or replace it, or if damaged equipment can still be used, the reduction in the fair market value of the asset. A replacement cost coverage is also available, which provides compensation up to twice the lost equipment's original cost, provided the equipment is actually replaced in the host country.

Contact this office for more information on these types of coverage for loss due to political violence.

* Registering for Contractors & Exporters Programs

Finance Department
Overseas Private Investment Corporation
1615 M St., NW
Washington, DC 20527   (202) 457-7179

To register for OPIC programs for contractors and exporters write a brief letter to OPIC requesting registration and identifying:

-Your company, its address, and ownership
-The project, the host country, the purchasing entity or owner,   and, if known, the parties providing the financing for the   project
-The date for submission of bids and/or commencement of work and   the expected duration of the project
-The approximate dollar value of the project to be bid or   negotiated, and the types and amounts of coverage you are   requesting
-If relevant, the U.S. licensed insurance broker associated with   this registration whom you wish to designate as the "broker of record". You may also designate a "standing broker of record"   so that, until the designation is canceled, the broker may   receive commissions on all eligible OPIC Contractors and Exporters Program transactions.

Contact the above office for additional information.

* Registering Your Investment

Office of Corporate Communications
Overseas Private Investment Corporation
1615 M St., NW
Washington, DC 20527   (202) 457-7059

OPIC's policy is to insure new investment only. To be eligible for this OPIC insurance, an investor must fill out a *Request for Registration for Political Risk Investment Insurance* (OPIC Form No. 50) to be used in filing for registration of your proposed investment. To avoid jeopardizing your eligibility for OPIC insurance for your investment, be sure to register your investment before it is made or irrevocably committed. A request for a *Registration Letter* must contain the following information:

-The identity of the investor
-Citizenship eligibility of the investor
-Country or territory in which the investment is to be made
-Brief description of the project
-Statement that the investment has neither been made nor irrevocably committed
-Type of investment contemplated, the kind of insurance coverages desired, and an estimate of the amounts under each coverage

There is no registration fee. For more information, or to receive an application for insurance, contact this OPIC office.

* Relationships with Other Financing Institutions

Vice President for Finance
Overseas Private Investment Corporation
1615 M St., NW
Washington, DC 20527   (202) 457-7178, (800) 424-6742

OPIC's finance program is designed to complement and supplement the lending and investing facilities of commercial banks; local, regional, and international development banks and investment funds; and such entities as the Export-Import Bank of the United States and the Agency for International Development. To encourage such joint participation, OPIC will advise and assist U.S. sponsors in securing debt and equity financings from these institutions.

* Small Business Assistance Hotline

Export-Import Bank of the United States
811 Vermont Ave., NW
Washington, DC 20571   (800) 424-5201

Small business exporters can call this hotline for assistance from the Eximbank, or for information on their special programs for small businesses.

* Small Business Exporting Resources

Superintendent of Documents
U.S. Government Printing Office
Washington, DC 20401   (202) 783-3238

The *Exporter's Guide to Federal Resources for Small Businesses*, is available through the GPO for a nominal fee.

* Small Business Services

Finance Department
Overseas Private Investment Corporation
1615 M St., NW
Washington, DC 20527   (202) 457-7178, (800) 424-OPIC

OPIC is directed in its legislation to show preference to smaller investors. Recognizing that such investors may lack experience in overseas investment, OPIC officers are prepared to render special assistance to small businesses. Also, OPIC will accept business from these smaller investors through qualified insurance brokers to whom OPIC will pay a limited brokerage commission. For program information, call toll-free (outside of the Washington, DC, area).

* Small Contractors' Guaranty Program

Finance Department
Overseas Private Investment Corporation
1615 M St., NW
Washington, DC 20527   (202) 457-7179

OPIC offers a finance program to assist small business contractors who have difficulty getting a financial institution to issue standby letters of credit or other instruments used as performance and advance payment guaranties for projects overseas. U.S. investors and financial institutions interested in the Small Contractors' Guaranty Program should address their inquiries (including questions regarding eligibility criteria, rates and application procedures) to the above office.

* The Opportunity Bank

Opportunity Bank
Overseas Private Investment Corporation
1615 M St., NW
Washington, DC 20527   (202) 457-7010, (800) 424-6742

A major stumbling block in the developing world's attempt to attract U.S. investment capital arises from the limited flow of information between potential U.S. equity investors and likely sponsors of investment projects in the developing countries. To help remedy this problem, OPIC has created the Opportunity Bank, a pre-investment services to U.S. investors. It is a computerized data system which matches the interests of U.S. companies with the needs and requirements of projects in the developing world. For further information, or to register your firm, contact the above office. FAX: (202) 331-4234.

* U.S. Borrowers Loans and Guarantees

United States Division
Export-Import Bank of the United States
811 Vermont Ave., NW, Room 901
Washington, DC 20571   (202) 566-8819

This division is responsible for loans and guarantees to U.S. borrowers, specifically the Working Capital Guarantee Program and transactions approved under Section 1912 of the Bank's 1978 legislation. Section 1912 allows Eximbank to help an American company compete for a domestic sale against a foreign firm backed by unfairly subsidized financing from a foreign export credit agency. For more information contact the office above.

* Working Capital Guarantees

United States Division
Export-Import Bank of the United States
811 Vermont Ave., NW
Washington, DC 20571   (202) 566-8819

The Working Guarantee Program seeks to expand U.S. exports by encouraging lenders to make working capital loans to U.S. businesses for various export-related productions and marketing activities. For more information on program description, eligible exporters, eligible lenders, and so forth, contact the office above.

Economics, Demographics and Statistics
General Sources

* See also Information on People, Companies, and Mailing Lists Chapter
* See also Current Events and Homework Chapter
* See also Expert Chapter

During a recent hearing on Capitol Hill, a congressman questioned a Bureau of the Census official why so much money needs to be spent collecting census data when all the information is contained in the popular paperback, *Information Please Almanac*. Of course, all this information comes from the Census Bureau which conducts surveys and the decennial census. This attitude is typical of those who have no idea that the U.S. Government is the largest producer of data in the world, and that anyone else selling it is probably getting it from Uncle Sam. The major publication which identifies many of the statistical sources from the federal government is the *Statistical Abstract of the U.S.* Be sure you look through the Experts Chapter where thousands of data experts are listed by name and telephone number.

* 1990 Census Block-Numbered Maps
Customer Services Branch
Data User Services Division
Bureau of the Census
Washington, DC 20233   (301) 763-4100
The 1990 census block-numbered map series includes county-wide maps prepared on the smallest possible number of map sheets at the maximum practical scale. The 1990 map series will depict each county (or county equivalent) on one or more map sheets--depending on the areal size and shape of the county, the number of blocks in the county, and the density of the block pattern--that will allow displaying all block numbers and feature identifiers, as well as show the county boundary and the MCDs/CCDs, places, and census tracts/BNAs in the county. Each county will consist of one or more parent sheets at a single scale, plus insets of densely settled geographic areas as required. As a result, the maps for counties could be at different scales. Insets will be single sheets at a larger scale. In densely developed areas where an inset will not fit on one sheet, multiple-sheet insets will be used. An index showing the map sheet and inset coverage will be included. The standard sheet size planned for all maps is 36" x 42" with a maximum 32" x 32" map display area. Data users must purchase these maps from the Census Bureau; they will not be printed and sold through the Government Printing Office (GPO) as in 1980. The maps will be produced by map plotting equipment on paper by Census Bureau staff.

* 1990 Census Introduction
Customer Services Branch
Data User Services Division
Bureau of the Census
Washington, DC 20233   (301) 763-4100
The brochure, *Your Introduction to the 1990 Census*, describes why there will be a 1990 census, what is involved, what will be asked of individuals, how the questionnaires are processed, and what the 1990 census will tell us. Contact this office to receive a free copy of the brochure.

* 1990 Tabulation and Publication Report
Customer Services Branch
Data User Services Division
Bureau of the Census
Washington, DC 20233   (301) 763-4100
The *1990 Census of Population and Housing Tabulation and Publication Program* report describes the 1990 census tabulation and publication program for the 50 States and the District of Columbia. While it is impossible to anticipate all user needs in a changing environment, the Census Bureau designed the 1990 census tabulation and publication program to meet a variety of data needs for different segments of the data user community. Highlights in the report include information on questionnaire content, sample design and disclosure avoidance, dissemination media, map products, data products, custom data products, how to obtain 1990 census data products, and a dictionary of geographic terms. For further information about the report, or to order a free copy, contact the Customer Services Branch. If you want more information about the tabulation and publication program, contact the Data Products Branch, Decennial Planning Division, Census Bureau, Washington, D.C. 20233; (301) 763-4908.

* 1986 Population Estimates
and 1985 Per Capita Income Estimates
Customer Services (Diskettes)
Data User Services Division
Bureau of the Census
Washington, DC 20233   (301) 763-4100
Available computer diskettes cover the 1986 population estimates for sub-county governmental units. The data include total population (April 1, 1980); per capita income (sample data, 1979); population estimates (July 1, 1986); and per capita income estimates for 1985 for about 39,000 governmental units. Diskettes are available by groups of bordering States. To request a data diskette, contact Customer Services and they will mail ordering information to you for the diskette files of interest to you.

* X-11.2 and X-11.2Q Seasonal Adjustments
Customer Services (Diskettes)
Data User Services Division
Bureau of the Census
Washington, DC 20233   (301) 763-4100
Two improved versions of the Census-developed X-11 and 11.Q seasonal adjustment software programs are now available which adjust series that range from 3 to 30 years. They are based on the ratio-to-moving average method which provides a moving average and includes trend-cycle curves, ratios of trend-cycle estimates, and estimates of seasonal factors from those ratios. The X-11.2 program adjusts monthly series with a variety of options for adjusting special characteristics. It provides substantial practical flexibility with respect to the kinds of series that can be adjusted. Included in the package are trading and holiday routines, diagnostic plots for output, and a table of the final combined adjustment. The adjusted data can be output to a pre-specified file. The X-11.2Q program adjusts quarterly series and follows the same basic procedures as the X-11.2 program. The trading day and holiday routines are not included, and some options differ somewhat. To request a data diskette, contact Customer Services and they will mail ordering information to you for the diskette files of interest to you.

* Agriculture, Economic, and Government Areas
Data User Services Division
Customer Services
Bureau of the Census
U.S. Department of Commerce
Washington, DC 20233   (301) 763-4100
The following agriculture, economic, and government areas statistical publications are free from this office.

Guide to the 1982 Census of Agriculture and Related Statistics
A Review of the 1982 Census of Agriculture
Guide to the 1982 Economic Censuses and Related Statistics (also available as a separate 20-minute video tape on a loan basis)
An Overview of the 1982 Economic Censuses is free from the Bureau of the Census
Guide to Service Industry Statistics and Related Data

* American Housing Survey 1985 on CD-ROM
Customer Services
Data User Services Division
Bureau of the Census
Washington, DC 20233   (301) 763-4100

The *American Housing Survey* (AHS) is the largest regular national sample survey that describes people and their homes in the United States. It is sponsored by the Department of Housing and Urban Development (HUD) and conducted by the U.S. Census Bureau which uses interviews to gather information on approximately 42,000 individual housing units and the households that occupy them. The 1985 Core file is in both ASCII SDF (flat) file and SAS formats (PC SAS Version 6.03). The files are microdata files containing the results of each individual interview in the national survey. The technical documentation that comes with the disc is very detailed. It sells for $125; the technical documentation alone is $40. For a brochure containing additional ordering information, contact Customer Services.

* Approved Recurring Reports Bulletin

Office of Information Management
and Statistics (70Y-723B)
Department of Veterans Affairs
810 Vermont Ave., NW
Washington, DC 20420   (202) 233-6837

The *Approved Recurring Reports Bulletin* includes a list of reports which have been cleared by the Reporting Policy & Review Service for data collection or have been discontinued since the last printed issue. Contact the office above to obtain a copy.

* Automated Geographic Support System

Chief, Geography Division
Bureau of the Census
Washington, DC 20233

This interagency project was created to produce geographic products for the 1990 census. The geographic component of the new generation of computer-based approaches for taking the 1990 census is called the TIGER System (Topologically Integrated Geographic Encoding & Referencing System). The TIGER File will provide geographic products and services for the 1990 decennial census from a totally automated single source. This means that all mapping and geoprocessing will be in complete agreement. In conjunction with the U.S. Geological Survey, the Geography Division developed a computer-readable map file for the whole United States, providing the most complete and accurate set of maps ever prepared for the U.S.--and the first from a computer file. The TIGER System will be used to produce publication quality maps on high precision computer-driven map production devices to accompany the data files for the census bureau's 1990 decennial publication programs. For detailed information on the TIGER System, ask for the *Tiger Tales Presentation* from your regional Census office or the office listed above.

* Automated Management Information System

Reporting Systems Division
Office of Information Management and Statistics
Department of Veterans Affairs
810 Vermont Ave., NW
Washington, DC 20420   (202) 233-6825

The Automated Management Information System (AMIS) is an agency-wide system designed to meet the Department of Veterans Affairs' statistical reporting needs. Contact the office above for further information.

* Bureau of the Census

Bureau of the Census
U.S. Department of Commerce
Washington, DC 20233   (301) 763-4040

The Bureau of the Census takes a census of the U.S. population every 10 years, and they keep the information collected from individual persons, households, or establishments strictly confidential and use it only for statistical purposes. The agency collects, tabulates, and publishes a wide variety of statistical data about the people and the economy of the U.S. These data are utilized by the Congress, the executive branch, and by the public generally in the development and evaluation of economic and social programs. Its principal functions include: 1) decennial censuses of population and housing, 2) quinquennial censuses of agriculture, State and local governments, manufacturers, mineral industries, distributive trades, construction industries, and transportation, 3) current surveys that provide information on many of the subjects covered in the censuses at monthly, quarterly, annual, or other intervals, 4) compilation of current statistics on U.S. foreign trade, including data on imports, exports, and shipping, 5) special censuses at the request and expense of States and local government units, 6) publication of estimates and projections of the population, 7) current data on population and housing characteristics; and 8) current reports on manufacturing, retail and wholesale trade, services, construction, imports and exports, State and local government finances and employment, and other subjects.

April 1, 1990, marks 200 years of census taking in America. A national census has been taken every ten years in the United States since 1790. Mandated by the U.S. Constitution, the decennial census is the basis for determining how many seats each state will fill in the House of Representatives. The census provides important social and economic information about our people and our nation. Many federal, state, and local government programs, private corporations, and community agencies use census data. Each census portrays America, and over

the years the census has revealed a great deal about how our country has changed as we have grown from a young agrarian nation of about 4 million people clustered along the Eastern seaboard to a complex post-industrial society of nearly 250 million spread across the continent and beyond.

Techniques for taking the census have steadily improved over the past two centuries. The 1990 Census will rely heavily on computerization in field operations, processing, geography, data tabulations, and products. The 1990 Census is likely to be the most accurate census in U.S. history. Issues such as census undercount and the homeless population will be particularly important in the coming census.

* Business Economics- Publications and Databases

Public Information
Bureau of Economic Analysis
U.S. Department of Commerce
1401 K St., NW, Room 713
Washington DC 20230   (202) 523-0777

A User's Guide to BEA Information contains program descriptions and entries for specific products and services, including publications, computer tapes, diskettes, and other information services. The first, general section of the *Guide* describes the products and services that cut across the range of BEA's work. The following sections describe the products and services related to BEA's four program areas: National economics, regional economics, international economics, and other tools for measuring, analyzing, and forecasting. Some highlights include the following:

Survey of Current Business. A monthly journal containing estimates and analyses of U.S. economic activity. Includes the *Business Situation*, a review of current economic developments and articles pertaining to the national, regional, and international economic accounts and related topics ($18 per year).

Business Conditions Digest. A monthly publication containing tables and charts for more than 300 series, including business cycle indicators and other series that help evaluate economic conditions. Features the composite indexes of leading, coincident, and lagging indicators ($44 per year).

Handbook of Cyclical Indicators. Series descriptions and data for 1947-1982 for all series that appear in *Business Conditions Digest*. Includes an explanation of how the composite indexes are constructed ($21.95).

Business Statistics: 1986-. Monthly or quarterly data for 1983-1986 and annual data for 1961-1986 for series that appear in *Survey of Current Business* (16.00).

Evaluation of the GNP Estimates. An evaluation of the GNP estimates, covering the reliability of estimates, sources of error and types of statistical improvement, status of source data, documentation of methodology, release schedules, and security before release ($5.00).

Gross State Product, Annual Estimates, 1963-1986-. These estimates are the counterpart of gross domestic product and provide the most comprehensive measure of State production now available. The estimates are for the 50 States, nine BEA regions, and the United States, and for 61 industries ($100 computer tape, $40 diskettes).

* Business and Industry Data Centers

Data User Services Division
Customer Services
Bureau of the Census
U.S. Department of Commerce
Washington, DC 20233   (301) 763-4100

The Census Bureau initiated a pilot project to stimulate the use of economic data by establishing 15 Business and Industry Data Centers, economic counterparts to the network of State Data Centers. Contact this office for a free listing of these centers.

* Consultation Over the Telephone

Data User Services Division
Customer Services
Bureau of the Census
U.S. Department of Commerce
Washington, DC 20233

Subject-matter specialists from all areas of the Census Bureau may be consulted by telephone. For detailed statistical information route calls as follows:

Government, Commerce, and Industry
Agriculture Data: (301) 763-1113
Business Data (Retail, Wholesale, Services): (301) 763-7564
Construction Statistics: (301) 763-7163
Foreign Trade Data: (301) 763-5140
State Exports: (301) 763-5708
Government Data: (301) 763-7366
Industry Data: (301) 763-7800
Manufacturers Data: (301) 763-7666

Economics, Demographics and Statistics

Population, Housing, and Income
Housing Data: (301) 763-2881
International Statistics: (301) 763-2870
Neighborhood Statistics: (301) 763-2358
Population Data: (301) 763-5002
Special Demographic Studies: (301) 763-7720

Government, Commerce, and Civic
Relations: (301) 763-2436/(TTY 763-5020)

* CD-ROM Products to Come
Customer Services
Data User Services Division
Bureau of the Census
Washington, DC 20233 (301) 763-4100

The Census Bureau will continue to produce its popular large data files in CD-ROM format. Future CD-ROM products include:

1986 County Business Patterns
1988 County and City Data Book
1987 Census of Agriculture
1990 Tiger/Line Extract Files
1990 Census of Population and Housing

* CD-ROM Test Disc 2
Customer Services
Data User Services Division
Bureau of the Census
Washington, DC 20233 (301) 763-4100

The CD-ROM Test Disc 2 was produced in February 1988 and is the model for future CD-ROM discs containing summary data. It contains two statistical data files: *Census of Agriculture, 1982: Final County Data*, and *Census of Retail Trade, 1982: ZIP Code File*. Both files are in dBase III format. Producing CD-ROMs in this format lets users access the files with many other commercial software packages. The documentation that comes with the disc contains an abstract, a glossary, a State-county code list, a questionnaire facsimile, technical information relating to the file, and a layout of the file. The cost is $125. Contact this office for a brochure containing additional ordering information.

* Census Bureau Library
Library
Bureau of the Census
U.S. Department of Commerce
Washington, DC 20233 (301) 763-5042

The Census Bureau Library collection contains general statistical information, population areas statistics, demographics, migration, foreign country censuses, and the complete collection of census publications. It is open to the public, and photocopying equipment is available.

* Census Bureau's Online Data System
Data Access and Use Staff
Data User Services Division
Bureau of the Census
Washington, DC 20233 (301) 763-2074

CENDATA is the Census Bureau's on-line service, available commercially for access from remote terminals or microcomputers, that carries selected current data, press releases, and publication lists from Bureau programs. If you need the most recent population estimates for states, counties, incorporated places, and selected towns and townships use CENDATA. CompuServe and DIALOG, information service companies, are offering CENDATA to their customers. Contact this office for more information about CENDATA content and on-line services, or call CompuServe: (800) 848-8199; or DIALOG Information Services: (800) 334-2564.

* Census Data Diskettes
Customer Services (Diskettes)
Data User Services Division
Bureau of the Census
Washington, DC 20233 (301) 763-4100

The data diskettes are available from the Bureau of the Census. These files are generated on an IBM Personal Computer and can be used with compatible microcomputers using the PC DOS 1.1 or higher operating systems. Contact this office for a complete listing of those available.

* Census Data On CD-ROM
Customer Services
Data User Services Division
Bureau of the Census
Washington, DC 20233 (301) 763-4100

The Census Bureau now makes several of its large databases available in microcomputer format. To use Compact Disc - Read Only Memory (CD-ROM) you will need a personal computer, a CD-ROM reader, and the appropriate CD-ROM software for your system. The discs are standard 4 3/4" size and are compatible with all CD-ROM readers. If you are interested in learning more about the software and hardware requirements of CD-ROM technology, request an Information Packet from this office. To demonstrate CD-ROM products, Census Bureau analysts have written various software programs for public access. The software is available to users from the following two sources:

-An electronic bulletin board accessed by modem on (301) 763-1568.
-You can obtain CD-ROM software from the University of Tennessee. This clearinghouse has information on software packages available for use with the Census Bureau's CD-ROMs and also maintains a list of private software vendors who sell software developed to access the CD-ROMs. For information from the clearinghouse, contact: Department of Marketing, Logistics, and Transportation, 316 Stokley Management Center, University of Tennessee, Attn: Center for Electronic Data Analysis, Knoxville, TN 37996; (615) 974-5311.

* Census Depository Libraries
Data User Services Division
Customer Services
Bureau of the Census
U.S. Department of Commerce
Washington, DC 20233 (301) 763-4100

There are nearly 1,500 Government and Census depository libraries; these include large public and university libraries that will have census reports in their reference collections. The holdings in the Census Bureau's library are complete. To contact the library call (301) 763-5042. A listing entitled *Government and Census Depository Libraries Holding Census Bureau Reports* is free from the Census Bureau.

* Census/Equal Employment Opportunity Special File
Customer Services Branch
Data User Services Division
Bureau of the Census
Washington, DC 20233 (301) 763-4100

This special computer tape file will provide sample census data to support affirmative action planning for equal employment opportunity. The file will contain tabulations showing detailed occupations and educational attainment data by age. These data will also be cross tabulated by sex, Hispanic origin, and race. Data will be provided for all counties, MSAs, and places of 50,000 or more inhabitants. For more information on this special computer tape files, contact this office.

* Census Newsletter
Superintendent of Documents
U.S. Government Printing Office
Washington, DC 20402 (202) 378-3238

Census and You brings you the latest news about Census Bureau products and programs. This monthly newsletter cuts through the complexities of Government statistical programs and tells you where to find the statistics you need on the latest trends in various areas, what products fit your needs, how to get in touch with the experts, where to turn locally for information, and what programs the Census Bureau is planning now and how to be sure your views are heard. It is available from the Government Printing Office for $12.00. To FAX orders or inquiries, dial (202) 275-0019.

* Census of Agriculture Diskettes
Customer Services (Diskettes)
Data User Services Division
Bureau of the Census
Washington, DC 20233 (301) 763-4100

These diskettes include data from the *1987 Census of Agriculture Advance Reports* for each State and each county with ten or more farms. County and State data items include: farms by size, land use, value of agricultural products sold, selected expense items, operator characteristics, major livestock and poultry inventories and sales, and selected crops by State. The *1987 Census of Agriculture Preliminary Reports* for each State is available for all States.

* Census Products and Services
Data User Services Division
Customer Services
Bureau of the Census
U.S. Department of Commerce
Washington, DC 20233 (301) 763-4100

The *Census Catalog & Guide 1989* is a one-stop guide that tells you where to look for every Census Bureau data product and service. In it you'll find information on every report, microfiche, computer tape, floppy disk, and map issued, 1980-1988; explanations of the censuses and surveys of business, manufacturing, and population--plus all the others; and lists of over 5,000 sources of assistance--Census Bureau specialists, other Federal statistical offices, State and local agencies, and private companies. There also is a nationwide list of Government and Census depository libraries. The book sells for $21.00. To FAX orders or inquiries, dial (202) 275-0019. International customers should add 25% to the cost.

* Census Regional Offices

The regional offices of the Census Bureau play a vital role in the work of the Census Bureau. They offer educational, inquiry, and reference services to Federal, State, and local government agencies; minority organizations; businesses; libraries; educational institutions; community service organizations; the media; and the general public. Information services specialists in the offices assist data users across the country by furnishing information about Census Bureau reports and tape files, and making presentations at workshops and conferences. The Census Awareness and Products Program (CAPP) staff in all 12 offices can help:

Atlanta
1365 Peachtree St., NE, Room 638; Atlanta, GA 30309; (404) 347-2274

Boston
Federal Office Building, Room 553, 10 Causeway St., Boston, MA 02116; (617) 565-7078

Charlotte
222 S. Church Street, Suite 505, Charlotte, NC 28202-3220; (704) 521-4400

Chicago
175 W. Jackson Boulevard, Room 557, Chicago, IL 60604-2689; (312) 409-4619

Dallas
1100 Commerce Street, Room 3C54, Dallas, TX 75242; (214) 767-7105

Denver
7655 W. Mississippi Ave., P.O. Box 26750, Denver, CO 80226; (303) 979-7750

Detroit
Federal Building and U.S. Courthouse, Room 565, 231 Lafayette St., Detroit, MI 48226; (313) 354-4654

Kansas City
One Gateway Center, Fourth and State Streets, Kansas City, KS 66101; (816) 891-7562

Los Angeles
11777 San Vicente Boulevard, Room 810, Los Angeles, CA 90049; (818) 904-6513

New York
Federal Office Building, Room 37-130, 26 Federal Plaza, New York, NY 10278; (212) 264-4730

Philadelphia
105 South 7th Street, 1st Floor, Philadelphia, PA 19106-3395; (215) 597-8313

Seattle
101 Stewart St., Suite 500, Seattle, WA 98101-1098; (206) 728-5314

* Census Reports
Data User Services Division
Customer Services
Bureau of the Census
U.S. Department of Commerce
Washington, DC 20233   (301) 763-4100

The Bureau publishes a number of guides, catalogs, indexes, Factfinders, and other user aids. Most of these materials are available for reference as well as purchase; some are free. Printed reports for the individual economic censuses usually consist of separate series for industries, geographic areas, subjects, and special reports. Some of the series are designated as preliminary and will appear several months before corresponding final reports. Preliminary reports have limited detail, however, and their figures are subject to change in the final reports. Copies of printed reports can also be obtained on microfiche.

* Census Schedules Available to the Public
National Archives and Records Service
Reference Services Branch
7th and Pennsylvania Avenue, NW
Washington, DC 20408   (202) 523-3220

The U.S. population census records contain a wealth of information about people. They are useful in learning about one's ancestors and about local social and economic conditions at various times in history. Microfilm copies of the original population schedules, form 1790 through 1910 are open to the public at the National Archives and its regional center and at many libraries in various parts of the United States. Most now have facilities for making paper copies from the microfilm.

* Census Statistical Areas Committees

Census statistical areas committees consist of local data users with an interest in the census statistical areas programs. These committees exist in all metropolitan statistical areas and some other counties. The committee memberships represent the data users within the community by including planners, representatives from the business community, government agencies, the media, minority organizations, and neighborhood associations. The local census statistical areas committees play an important part in defining geographic statistical areas. The committees recommend or approve the boundaries for statistical reporting units. Each local committee selects a census statistical areas key person as a liaison between the Bureau of the Census and the committee for these programs. For the key person in your area, contact the Census Bureau regional office nearest you.

* Census Telephone Contacts
Data User Services Division
Customer Services
Bureau of the Census
U.S. Department of Commerce
Washington, DC 20233   (301) 763-4100

Telephone Contacts for Data Users is free from the Census Bureau.

* Census Tract/Block Numbering Area Outline Maps
Customer Services Branch
Data User Services Division
Bureau of the Census
Washington, DC 20233   (301) 763-4100

These maps will show census tract/block numbering area boundaries and numbers and the features and feature names underlying these boundaries (for example, the boundaries and names of counties, county subdivisions, and places). The scale of the maps will be determined such that the number of map sheets for each area will be minimal, but will vary by area. For densely settled areas, where the census tract/block numbering area numbers and boundary features cannot be shown, the Census Bureau will issue insets at a larger scale. These maps will be available in both electrostatic plotter version and a printed version. Data users who do not wish to wait for the printed maps can purchase these maps from the Census Bureau for a fee. Data users who want printed maps can purchase the printed maps from the Superintendent of Documents, beginning in 1992. Until then, contact the office above for more information.

* Census University Curriculum Support
User Training Branch
Data User Services Division
Bureau of the Census
U.S. Department of Commerce
Washington, DC 20233   (301) 763-4100

The Bureau has a Census Curriculum Support Project, designed to help university instructors teach about census concepts, methodologies, and products. The Bureau prepares such items as instructors' guides, application exercises, bibliographies, and visual aides. For further information, contact this division.

* Clearinghouse for Census Data Services
Customer Services Branch
Data User Services Division
Bureau of the Census
Washington, DC 20233   (301) 763-4100

The National Clearinghouse for Census Data Services is a referral service for users needing special assistance in obtaining and using statistical data and related products prepared by the Census Bureau. Organizations registered with the Clearinghouse offer assistance ranging from informational services, such as seminars or workshops, to technical services such as providing tape copies or performing geocoding. A list is available.

* Consumer Expenditure and Family Budgets
Consumer Expenditure Surveys Division
Office of Prices and Living Conditions
Bureau of Labor Statistics
U.S. Department of Labor
600 E St., NW, Room 4216
Washington, DC 20212   (202) 272-5156

The *Consumer Expenditure Studies*, a continuing annual survey of consumer expenditures and income, is the basic source of data for the revision of items and weights in the market basket of consumer purchases to be priced for the Consumer Price Index. Selected data is classified by income class, family size, and other demographic and economic characteristics of consumer units. Coverage includes the urban population of the U.S. through 1983, and the total population in 1984 and after.

Economics, Demographics and Statistics

* Consumer Price Index and Labor Data on Computer Diskette

BLS Office of Publications
U.S. Department of Labor
441 G St., NW, Room 2831A
Washington, DC 20212 (202) 523-7827

Computer diskettes offer an easy-to-use way to manipulate data for economists, other social scientists, researchers, managers, and policymakers with an interest in measuring employment, prices, productivity, injuries and illnesses, and wages. BLS diskette users need an IBM-compatible microcomputer and Lotus 1-2-3 Version 1A or Version 2. Each diskette contains the named data series and a brief technical description that highlights regular revisions, if any, and typical uses for statistics. A flyer is available which describes the diskettes available and their cost.

* Consumer Price Index Within 24 hours

National Technical Information Service
U.S. Department of Commerce
5285 Port Royal Road
Springfield, VA 22151 (703) 487-4630

A Consumer Price Index data summary is available by mailgram within 24 hours of the CPI release. It provides unadjusted and seasonally adjusted U.S. City Average data for All Urban Consumers and for Urban Wage Earners and Clerical Workers. The cost of this service is $145.00 per year.

* Consumer Prices

Office of Prices and Living Conditions
Bureau of Labor Statistics
U.S. Department of Labor
600 E St., NW, Room 3216
Washington, DC 20212 (202) 272-5160

The Labor Department measures consumer price changes for a predetermined market basket of consumer goods and services for two population groups: all urban consumers, and urban wage earners and clerical workers. The fixed market basket includes 382 entry level items representing all goods and services purchased for everyday living by all urban residents. Monthly and bimonthly indexes are available for various geographic regions.

* Consumer Purchasing Power Index

Superintendent of Documents
Government Printing Office
Washington, DC 20402 (202) 783-3238

Each monthly issue of the *Consumer Price Index Detailed Report* provides a comprehensive summary of price movements for the month, plus statistical tables, charts, and technical notes. The report covers two indexes, the Consumer Price Index for All Urban Consumers, and the Consumer Price Index for Wage Earners and Clerical Workers. The indexes reflect data for the U.S. city average and selected areas. An annual subscription is available for $21.00.

* Cost-Of-Living Studies

Office of Prices and Living Conditions
Bureau of Labor Statistics
U.S. Department of Labor
600 E St., NW, Room 4013
Washington, DC 20212 (202) 272-5096

Available information includes in-depth research reports on various aspects of price measurement, such as adjustment for quality change and cost-of-living indexes. Data is also available on price indexes for different demographic groups and for the service industry, as well as improved estimation techniques for price indexes.

* Cost-Reimbursable Surveys from Census

Special Census Staff
Demographic Surveys Division
Bureau of the Census
U.S. Department of Commerce
Washington, DC 20233 (301) 763-7854

Upon request the Census Bureau conducts cost-reimbursable surveys and special studies for Federal agencies on such topics as employment, health, housing, crime, and consumer expenditures. It also performs similar work for educational institutions, qualified private organizations, and takes special censuses requested by local governments needing up-to-date census figures. Contact this division for more information.

* County and City Data Book

Superintendent of Documents
Government Printing Office
Washington, DC 20402-9325 (202) 783-3238

The *County and City Data Book* is your one-stop, official source for county and city data. You can profile or compare thousands of cities and counties. It gives you quick access to comprehensive data including maps for each state highlighting metropolitan counties and cities with 25,000 or more inhabitants. It answers these questions:

What percentage of your county's population is made up of persons 65 years old and over?
Which county in your state experienced the largest increase in business establishments?
How many building permits authorized new housing in your city?

The subjects covered include agriculture, bank deposits, business, climate, crime, electric bills, employment, government finances, health care, housing, personal income, population, poverty, vital statistics, and many more. The book sells for $36.00. To FAX orders or inquiries, call (202) 275-0019. International customers should add 25% to the cost.

* County and City Data Books: 1983 & 1988

Customer Services (Diskettes)
Data User Services Division
Bureau of the Census
Washington, DC 20233 (301) 763-4100

The 1988 and 1983 files provide a compendia of data from the *1980 Census of Population and Housing*, the *1982 and 1977 Economic Censuses*, the *1982 and 1978 Census of Agriculture*, and other data from a variety of Federal government, private agency, and national association sources. Some data items included are vital statistics, government employment, climate, and social security. A free sampler diskette for the *1988 County & City Data Book* is available on request. Note that free sampler diskettes previewing the 1988 edition are available from Customer Services.

* County Business Patterns on Diskette

Customer Services (Diskettes)
Data User Services Division
Bureau of the Census
Washington, DC 20233 (301) 763-4100

Data on diskette are available annually for every U.S. county--1983 to 1986--and show number of establishments, employment, and payroll, for industries in the Standard Industrial Classification (SIC) levels: two-digit State and county level, 2-, 3-, and 4-digit at U.S. level. Software is not provided.

* County Household Estimates on Diskette

Customer Services (Diskettes)
Data User Services Division
Bureau of the Census
Washington, DC 20233 (301) 763-4100

This series presents estimates of households for counties. The 1985 estimates include average population for households, population totals, revised county population estimates for States. A section on methodology is also available. To request a data diskette, contact Customer Services and they will mail ordering information to you for the diskette files of interest to you.

* County Subdivision Maps

Customer Services Branch
Data User Services Division
Bureau of the Census
Washington, DC 20233 (301) 763-4100

These maps will show the names and boundaries of all counties (or county equivalent) and subdivisions in each State, as well as all places for which the Census Bureau tabulates data for the 1990 census. They also will depict American Indian reservations, including off-reservation trust lands, tribal jurisdiction statistical areas in Oklahoma, tribal designated statistical areas, Alaska Native Regional Corporations, and Alaska Native village statistical areas. All boundaries will be as of January 1, 1990. These maps will be available first in electrostatic plotter version and later in a printed form. The electrostatic plotter paper sheet size will be about 36" x 42" and the scale will be 1:500,000. These maps will be produced on a State basis and sold by the Census Bureau upon user request. Later, these maps will be printed and bound in the State reports for various series. In the reports, these maps will be partitioned into multiple, page-size sheets and the scale will vary between States. The printed reports can be purchased through the Superintendent of Documents, Government Printing Office, Washington, DC 20402-9325; (202) 783-3238.

* County-to-County Migration

Customer Services Branch
Data User Services Division
Bureau of the Census
Washington, DC 20233 (301) 763-4100

Computer files will be issued by State, providing summary records for all intrastate county-to-county migration streams and significant interstate county-to-county migration streams. Each record will include codes for the geographic

618

area of origin, codes for the geographic area of destination, and selected characteristics of the persons who made up the migration stream. For more information on these special computer tape files, contact this Census office.

* Current Economic Data

Data User Services Division
Customer Services
Bureau of the Census
U.S. Department of Commerce
Washington, DC 20233   (301) 763-4100

The Census Bureau's integrated program of current surveys produced data supporting key indicators of monthly economic performance and quarterly GNP calculations covering most goods producing sectors. The Bureau has taken steps to improve and expand its economic products and services in a number of areas. The Bureau improved current merchandise trade data by reinstituting seasonal adjustments of monthly imports and exports, generating new tabulations of state-of-shipment for exports, providing monthly graphic information on trade performance, and publishing data for imports (c.i.f. basis) and imports (customs basis) simultaneously. Contact this office for more information the economic data products from Census.

* Current Employment Analyses

Office of Employment and Unemployment Statistics
Bureau of Labor Statistics
U.S. Department of Labor
441 G St., NW, Room 2486
Washington, DC 20212   (202) 523-1944

Labor force statistics from the *Current Population Survey* provide a comprehensive body of information on the employment and unemployment experience of the nation's population, classified by age, sex, race, and a variety of other characteristics. The data is published in a variety of sources, including the monthly news release, *The Employment Situation*, and the monthly periodical, *Employment and Earnings*. Data uses include economic indicators, measure of potential labor supply, and evaluation of wage rates and earnings trends for specific demographic groups.

* Current Wage Developments

Superintendent of Documents
Government Printing Office
Washington, DC 20402   (202) 783-3238

Each monthly issue of *Current Wage Developments* includes selected wage and benefit changes, work stoppages, major agreements that expire during the next month, calendar of features, and statistics on compensation changes. The cost is $15.00 per year. For more information on this data, contact Office of Compensation and Working Conditions, Bureau of Labor Statistics, U.S. Department of Labor, 441 G St., NW, Room 2021, Washington, DC, 20212; (202) 523-1382.

* Economic Bulletin Board

Office of Business Analysis
U.S. Department of Commerce
14th St. and Constitution Ave., NW
Room 4887
Washington DC 20230   (202) 377-1986

The Economic Bulletin Board is a one-stop source for current economic information. It has the latest releases from the Bureau of Economic Analysis, the Bureau of the Census, the Bureau of Labor Statistics and other Federal agencies. The Bulletin Board includes summaries of economic news from the Department of Commerce, economic indicators, GNP, Consumer Price Index, and special economic studies and reports, as well as listings of new publications and databases. The Bulletin Board is available 24 hours a day. Contact the office listed above for more information regarding the Bulletin Board and subscription fees.

* Economic Data

Center for Electronic Records
National Archives and Records Administration
8th St. & Pennsylvania Ave., NW, Room 20E
Washington, DC 20408   (202) 523-3267

The Center has a vast amount of economic data from various government agencies, such as the Bureau of Economic Analysis, Agencies for Economic Opportunity and Legal Services, Economic Stabilization Programs, Economics, Statistics, and Cooperative Service, and the Bureau of the Census. Contact this office for a complete listing of information available from each agency.

* Economic Growth and Industry Employment Projections

Office of Economic Growth and Employment Projections
Bureau of Labor Statistics
U.S. Department of Labor

601 D St., NW, Room 4000
Washington, DC 20212   (202) 272-5381

Projections of U.S. economic growth and industry employment provides a framework for studying the factors affecting long-range economic growth. Data available include projections of total gross national product (GNP), demand and income composition of GNP, and aggregate components of demand specified by 160 industry groups under alternative assumptions for basic economic variables and government economic policies. Reference period for projections is for approximately 10 years ahead.

* Economic Indicators

Public Information
Bureau of Economic Analysis
U.S. Department of Commerce
1401 K St, NW, Room 713
Washington DC 20230   (202) 523-0777

The Bureau of Economic Analysis can provide you with basic information on such key issues as economic growth, inflation, regional development, and the Nation's role in the world economy. BEA's current national, regional, and international estimates usually appear first in news releases. The information is available to the general public in three forms: on recorded telephone messages, online through the Economic Bulletin Board, and in *BEA Reports*. The recorded messages are available 24 hours a day for several days following release. The usual time of release (eastern standard time) and the telephone numbers to call are as follows:

Leading Indicators: The message is updated weekly, usually on Monday, to include recently available component data. Release time: 8:30 a.m. Call (202) 898-2450.

Gross National Product. Release time: 8:30 a.m. Call (202) 898-2451.

Personal Income and Outlays. Release time: 10:00 a.m. Call (202) 898-2452.

Merchandise Trade, Balance of Payments Basis or U.S. International Transactions. Release time: 10:00 a.m. Call (202) 898-2453.

News releases are available on the Economic Bulletin Board shortly after their release. Selected estimates and articles are also available. The Bulletin Board is available by subscription from the National Technical Information Service, 5285 Port Royal Rd., Springfield, VA 22161; (703) 487-4630. The *BEA Reports* present information contained in BEA news releases and are mailed the day after estimates are released. An annual subscription can be ordered from the Bureau. Contact the Public Information Office listed above for more information and a list of release dates for BEA estimates.

* Economic Monitoring

The Office of Economic Analysis
U.S. Securities and Exchange Commission
450 5th St., NW
Washington, DC 20549   (202) 272-7104

The SEC's Office of Economic Analysis deals with the economic and practical issues that affect the Commission's regulatory activities. To accomplish this, it builds and maintains different computer databases, designs programs to access data, and develops and tests research methods. The staff looks at how market regulations affect issuers, broker-dealers, investors, and the economy in general. The office also closely watches the national market structure and regulation changes that affect the ability of small businesses to raise capital. Significant developments in the marketplace are analyzed, as are new trends in the securities market and new types of securities. Results of the studies are occasionally published with the Commission's approval. For more information on current and past studies, contact this office.

* Economic Policy Development

U.S. Department of Commerce
14th St. and Constitution Ave., NW
Room 4850
Washington DC 20230   (202) 377-2235

Economic Affairs analyzes economic developments, develops economic policy options and oversees the collection and distribution of a major share of Federal government economic and business developments; promotes efforts to improve productivity; and analyzes supply and demand for strategic materials.

* Economic Reports

What follows is a list of the Federal Reserve Banks across the U.S., along with their free consumer publications available:

Board of Governors of the Federal Reserve System
Publications Services, MS-138
20th St. & Constitution Ave., NW
Washington, DC 20551   (202) 452-3244

Economics, Demographics and Statistics

Consumer Handbook on Adjustable Rate Mortgages. Explains adjustable rate mortgages and some of the risks and advantages.
Consumer Handbook to Credit Protection Laws. Tells how consumer credit laws can help in shopping for and applying for credit and in keeping a good credit record.
Consumer's Guide to Mortgage Closings. Explains the mortgage closing process.
Consumer's Guide to Mortgage Lock-Ins. Describes various aspects of mortgage lock-ins.
Consumer's Guide to Mortgage Refinancing. Discusses the process and some of the risks and advantages to mortgage refinancing.
Federal Reserve Glossary. Defines many of the terms used in monetary policy and in bank supervision.
Guide to Business Credit and the Equal Credit Opportunity Act. Advises consumers of their rights under the Act when applying for a business loans and helps consumers prepare effective loan presentations.
Guide to Federal Reserve Regulations. Explains the goals and scope of Federal Reserve regulations.
How to File a Consumer Credit Complaint. Tells how to file a complaint against a bank.
If You Use a Credit Card. Explains federal law safeguards against lost cards, what to do about unsatisfactory goods purchased with credit cards, and how to compute and compare credit card charges.

Federal Reserve Bank of Atlanta
Public Information Department
104 Marietta St. NW
Atlanta, GA 30303-2713 (404) 521-8788
Economic Review. A bimonthly publication presenting new research and articles on the economy of the Southeast.

Federal Reserve Bank of Boston
Bank and Public Services Department
600 Atlantic Ave.
Boston, MA 02106 (617) 973-3459
Checkpoints. Explains how to write, deposit, and cash checks; also available in Spanish and Portuguese.
Consumer Education Catalog. Lists consumer education materials published by the System.
New England Economic Indicators. Quarterly report of statistical data for the nation and New England states.
New England Economic Review. Publishes articles of broad economic interest six times a year.

Federal Reserve Bank of Chicago
Public Information Center
230 S. LaSalle St.
Chicago, IL 60690 (312) 322-5111
Economic Perspectives. Bimonthly publication on banking, business, and agriculture.
Seventh District Economic Data. Provides statistical data on population, business, agriculture, foreign trade, and finance for the five states of the 7th Federal Reserve District.

Federal Reserve Bank of Cleveland
Public Information Department
P.O. Box 6387
Cleveland, OH 44101 (216) 579-2047
Economic Review. Quarterly publication featuring monetary, economic, and banking topics of district and national interest.
Economic Trends (Chartbook). Charts latest economic statistics and briefly discusses the current economy.

Federal Reserve Bank of Dallas
Public Affairs Department
Station K
Dallas, TX 75222 (214) 651-6289 or 6266
Agricultural Highlights. Discusses regional agricultural developments.
District Highlights. Quarterly analysis of district economic and financial developments.
Economic Review. Bimonthly publication of articles on economic and financial topics.
Energy Highlights. Summarizes developments in the energy industry; four times a year.

Federal Reserve Bank of Kansas City
Public Affairs Department
925 Grand Ave.
Kansas City, MO 64198 (816) 881-2402
Economic Review. Discusses a variety of economic and financial topics; 10 issues per year.

Federal Reserve Bank of Minneapolis
Public Affairs
250 Marquette Ave.
Minneapolis, MN 55480 (612) 340-2446
Agricultural Credit Conditions. Quarterly survey of district farm economy.
Consumer Credit Protection: Do You Know Your Rights? Easy-to-understand summary of consumers' credit protection rights.

District Economic Conditions. Analyzes nonfarm economic activity of the district and each state; quarterly.
Quarterly Review. Includes feature articles on the district economy.
Your Credit Rights. Contains learning activities on establishing and using credit; intended for consumer groups and teachers.

Federal Reserve Bank of New York
Public Information Department
33 Liberty Street
New York, NY 10045 (212) 720-6134
Consumer Credit Regulators (Fedpoints 17). Reviews the responsibilities of the 12 federal organizations charged with administering consumer regulations.
Quarterly Review. Reports on business activities and the money and bond markets.

Federal Reserve Bank of Philadelphia
Public Information Department
P.O. Box 66
Philadelphia, PA 19105 (215) 574-6115
Business Outlook Survey. Reports on manufacturing in the district and provides forecasts for the next six months; monthly.
Business Review. Bimonthly articles for readers with a general interest in economics.
Buying Treasury Securities. Provides basic information on investing in Treasury bills, notes, and bonds.
Electronic Banking for Today's Consumer. Explains electronic services such as ATMs, direct deposit, bill-paying services, and point-of-sale terminals, as well as consumer protections of Regulation E.
Fair Debt Collection Practices Act. Summarizes the main provisions of the Act.
Give Yourself Credit. Guides consumers through various credit protection laws.
How the New Equal Credit Opportunity Act Affects You. Outlines the Act's main provisions for consumers.
Plastic Fraud: Getting a Handle on Debit and Credit Cards. Discusses consumer awareness concerning credit and debit card fraud and the regulations protecting consumers.
Quarterly Regional Economic Report. Analyzes the economy of the district.
Your Credit Rating. Describes the importance of credit histories and consumers' rights when using credit, including ways to correct records.

Federal Reserve Bank of Richmond
Public Services Department
P.O. Box 27622
Richmond, VA 23261 (804) 697-8000
Black Banks. Profiles operating revenue and distribution by profit/loss size of black banks.
Community Affairs Officers at Federal Reserve Banks. Outlines the Community Affairs Officer's role, duties, and responsibilities, particularly those related to the Community Reinvestment Act.
Cross Sections. Quarterly reviews of business and economic developments.

Federal Reserve Bank of St. Louis
Public Information Office
P.O. Box 442
St. Louis, MO 63166 (314) 444-8421
Agriculture: an Eighth District Perspective. Quarterly summary of national and district agricultural developments.
Annual U.S. Economic Data. Provides selected economic statistics.
Business: An Eighth District Perspective. Summarizes national and district business developments.
Review. Examines national and international economic developments; analyzes various sectors of the district; ten issues per year.

Federal Reserve Bank of San Francisco
Public Information Department
P.O. Box 7702
San Francisco, CA 94120 (415) 974-2163
Give Yourself Credit. Guides the consumer through various credit protection laws.
Review. Discusses selected economic, banking, and financial topics; quarterly.

* Economic Census in the U.S.
Data User Services Division
Customer Services
Bureau of the Census
U.S. Department of Commerce
Washington, DC 20233 (301) 763-4100
Taken every 5 years, the economic censuses include the manufacturing, service, construction, and mineral industries; retail and wholesale trade; transportation; agriculture; and governments. For more information on the censuses of the U.S. economy, contact this office.

* Economic Studies
The Office of Economic Analysis
U.S. Securities and Exchange Commission
450 5th St., NW
Washington, DC 20549 (202) 272-7104

The following are just a few of the many economic studies that are available from the SEC. Contact this office to obtain one of the following or a complete listing of all the reports available:

Spillover Effects of Shelf Registration
Transcript of Proceedings in the Matter of: Economic Forum on Tender Offers
Institutional Ownership, Tender Offers, and Long-Term Investments
The Economics of Any-or-All, Partial, and Two-Tier Tender Offers
Shark Repellents and Stock Prices: The Effects of Anti-takeover Amendments Since 1980
Eurodollar Bonds: Alternative Financing for United States Companies
Do Bad Bidders Become Good Targets?

* Economists: Regional, National, International

Public Information
Bureau of Economic Analysis
U.S. Department of Commerce
1401 K St., NW
Washington DC 20230   (202) 523-0777

The Bureau can provide you with an extensive list of telephone numbers of economists who can be contacted for information pertaining to their area of expertise. The list includes a wide rage of economic issues within national, regional, and international economics.

* Education-Related Surveys

Data User Services Division
Customer Services
Bureau of the Census
U.S. Department of Commerce
Washington, DC 20233   (301) 763-4100

In the educational field, a set of surveys provide information about principals and teachers, teacher supply and demand, staffing patterns, working conditions in the schools, policies of schools and school districts, and other data. Contact this office for more information on educational surveys.

* Elderly Statistics

Data User Services Division
Customer Services
Bureau of the Census
U.S. Department of Commerce
Washington, DC 20233   (301) 763-4100

The Census Bureau, playing a major role in collecting, publishing, and distributing statistics on the older population, is cosponsor of the new Federal Interagency Forum on Aging-Related Statistics, as are the National Institute on Aging and the National Center for Health Statistics. Contact this office for more information on available statistics.

* Employment and Unemployment: Monthly Data and Estimates

Office of Employment and Unemployment Statistics
Bureau of Labor Statistics
441 G St., NW, Room 2919
Washington, DC 20212   (202) 523-1694

This office collects, analyzes, and publishes detailed industry data on employment, wages, hours, and earnings of workers on payrolls of non-agricultural business establishments. It also publishes monthly estimates of state and local area unemployment for use by federal agencies in allocating funds as required by various federal laws. In addition, the office provides current data on occupational employment for most industries for economic analysis and for vocational guidance and education planning.

* Exhibits and Conventions at Census

User Training
Bureau of the Census
U.S. Department of Commerce
Washington, DC 20233   (301) 763-2370

For information on exhibits and conventions, contact this office.

* Factfinder for the Nation

Customer Services Branch
Data User Services Division
Bureau of the Census
Washington, DC 20233   (301) 763-4100

The *U.S. Bureau of the Census Factfinder for the Nation* describes, in a series of reports, the range of Census Bureau materials available on a given subject and suggests some of their uses. *Factfinders* are published on an irregular basis as topical brochures that may be used individually, in groupings of related topics, or as a complete series:

No. 1. *Statistics on Race and Ethnicity*. 4 pp. 1981. Out of print. 1 microfiche.

No. 2. *Availability of Census Records About Individuals*. 4 pp. 1983. .25.
No. 3. *Agricultural Statistics*. 4 pp. 1983. Out of print. 1 microfiche.
No. 4. *History and Organization*. 12 pp. 1988 .40.
No. 5. *Reference Sources*. 12 pp. 1988. .30.
No. 6. *Housing Statistics*. 4 pp. 1981 .25.
No. 7. *Population Statistics*. 4 pp. 1981. .25.
No. 8. *Census Geography--Concepts and Products*. 8 pp. 1985. .30.
No. 9. *Construction Statistics*. 4 pp. 1983. .25.
No. 10. *Retail Trade Statistics*. 4 pp. 1983. .25.
No. 11. *Wholesale Trade Statistics*. 4 pp.. 1983. .25.
No. 12. *Statistics on Service Industries*. 4 pp. 1983. .25.
No. 13. *Transportation Statistics*. 4 pp. 1983. .25.
No. 14. *Foreign Trade Statistics*. 4 pp. 1978. Out of print. 1 microfiche.
No. 15. *Statistics on Manufacturers*. 4 pp. 1983. .25.
No. 16. *Statistics on Mineral Industries*. 4 pp. 1983. .25.
No. 17. *Statistics on Governments*. 4 pp. 1983. .25.
No. 18. *Census Bureau Programs and Products*. 16 pp. 1985. .40.
No. 19. *Enterprise Statistics*. 4 pp. 1983. .25.
No. 20. *Energy and Conservation Statistics*. 4 pp. 1980. Out of print. 1 microfiche.
No. 21. *International Programs*. 4 pp. 1981. .25.
No. 22. *Data for Small Communities*. 12 pp. 1986. .40.

These *Factfinders* are available from Customer Services. A 25% discount is available on orders of 100 copies or more sent to a single address.

* Federal Budget: Economic Impact

Publications Office
Congressional Budget Office
House Office Building Annex #2
Second and D Streets, SW
Washington, DC 20402   (202) 226-2809

All information published by CBO is available to the public in print form only. Most analysis results in publications, but there are also working papers and memoranda available. Among the major on-going publications at CBO are the following:

Economic Forecasts. This biannual forecast of the American economy focuses on such issues as unemployment, interest and inflation rates, the gross national product, and the overall short- and long-term outlook for the entire economy.

Baseline Budget Projections. These biannual baseline projections start with the most recently completed budgetary decisions made by Congress and show the effect on the budget if no new policy decisions were made during the next five years. These baselines act as a benchmark when considering spending and taxing policies.

Bill Cost Estimates. CBO prepares cost estimates for nearly every public bill reported by Congressional committees and shows how these legislative proposals would affect spending or revenues over the next five years.

Analysis of the President's Budget. CBO publishes an analysis of the President's annual budget that examines the scope and impact of the Administration's revenue and spending proposals.

Scorekeeping. CBO provides Congress with up-to-date tabulations of Congressional action on revenue and spending bills in order to measure the status of Congressional actions against targets or limits set in the budget.

Annual Report on Budget Options. This annual report includes a discussion of national budget priorities. It examines alternative ways to reduce the deficit and provides specific spending and revenue options for Congress to consider.

The Sequestration Report. This biannual advisory report provides CBO's economic assumptions of real economic growth, estimates budget base levels according to current spending and taxing law and the effects on deficit targets, and calculates the amount of money to be sequestered to eliminate any excess.

* Federal Economic Policy

Office of the Assistant Secretary
of the Treasury for Economic Policy
U.S. Department of the Treasury
1500 Pennsylvania Ave., Nw
Washington, DC 20220   (202) 566-2551

Under the Secretary of the Treasury, this office recommends economic policy and formulates policies that have general significance for the nation's economy.

* Finding and Using the Data

Census Office of Public Affairs
U.S. Department of Commerce
Federal Office Building No. 3, Rm. 2705
Washington, DC 20233   (301) 763-4040

Census Bureau products are available in a variety of places. Libraries across the country have printed reports, and an increasing number have microfiche. Current publications are kept for reference and order at the 12 Bureau of the

Economics, Demographics and Statistics

Census regional offices and the 47 U.S. Department of Commerce district offices. Summary-tape, public-use microdata, and geographic reference files, and flexible diskettes, as well as those microfiche (including recent out-of-print reports), maps, and publications not sold by the GPO can be ordered from the Census Bureau. Help is also available through the Bureau's national headquarters. Copies of products and materials generally can be purchased from the Census office above or from the Superintendent of Documents, U.S. Government Printing Office, Washington, DC 20402; (202) 378-3238.

* Fiscal and Federal Budget Alternatives

Publications Office
Congressional Budget Office
House Office Building Annex #2
Second and D Streets, SW
Washington, DC 20515   (202) 226-2809

CBO has published thousands of papers since its inception in 1974, and all are available to the general public. These reports are written to provide Congress with budget-related information and with analyses of alternative fiscal, budgetary, and programmatic policies. A listing of all CBO publications is available from the CBO Publications Office. All publications are available from that office, and many are available from GPO. CBO studies fall into categories including U.S. economy and fiscal policy; federal budget; commerce, industry, and trade; social programs; national security; and government operations. Superintendent of Documents, U.S. Government Printing Office, Washington, D.C. 20402; (202) 275-3030.

* Financial Statistics

Division of Research and Statistics
Federal Reserve System, Room B3048
20th St. & Constitution Ave., NW
Washington, DC 20551   (202) 452-3301

Economic and financial information is available on such topics as government finances, business conditions, wages, prices, and productivity. A variety of reports and studies are published regularly. Contact this office or any Federal Reserve Bank for more information on available financial statistics.
Federal Reserve System Resource Materials

* Foreign Investment Statistics

International Investment Division
Bureau of Economic Analysis
Department of Commerce
1401 K St., NW, Room 1008
Washington DC 20230   (202) 523-0659

BEA's international economics program encompasses international transactions accounts (balance of payments) and the direct investment estimates. The international transactions accounts, which measure U.S. transactions with foreign countries, include merchandise trade, trade in services, the current-account balance, and capital transactions. The direct investment estimates cover estimates of U.S. direct investment abroad and foreign direct investment in the United States, income and other flows associated with these investments, and other aspects of the operations of multinational enterprises. Contact this office for further information on direct investment and international services.

* Foreign Money Markets

Foreign Exchange and Gold Operations
U.S. Department of the Treasury
1500 Pennsylvania Ave., NW, Room 5037
Washington, DC 20220   (202) 566-2773

This office monitors the foreign money markets for the Department of the Treasury. Contact them for more information.

* Foreign Portfolio Investment

Office of Foreign Portfolio Investment Survey
Office of the Assistant Secretary
of the Treasury for International Affairs
U.S. Department of the Treasury
1500 Pennsylvania, Ave., NW
Washington, DC 20220   (202) 566-5297

Once every five years, this office conducts a survey of foreign portfolio investment within the United States. The next survey will be conducted in 1990.

* General Accounting Office

General Accounting Office
441 G St., NW
Washington, DC 20548   (202) 275-2812

GAO assists the Congress, its committees, and its members in carrying out their legislative and oversight responsibilities; carries out legal, accounting, auditing, and claims settlement functions of federal government programs and operations; and makes recommendations designed to provide for more efficient and effective government operations.

* General Accounting Office Annual Report

Information Handling and Support Facilities
General Accounting Office
P.O. Box 6015
Gaithersburg, MD 20877   (202) 275-6241

The GAO's *Annual Report to Congress* highlights its efforts for the present fiscal year. It contains budget information, a list of recommendations to Congress, and a catalog of Audit Reports issued during the fiscal year. As with most GAO publications, the annual report is available free of charge for the first five copies ordered (thereafter, $2 per copy).

* General Accounting Office Reports

Information Handling and Support Facilities
General Accounting Office
P.O. Box 6015
Gaithersburg, MD 20877   (202) 275-6241

Each month the Comptroller General sends a list of GAO reports and testimony issued or released during the previous month to Congress, its committees, and its members. Up to 5 copies of each GAO report are provided free of charge, and $2 is charged for each additional copy.

* Geography of the Census

Data User Services Division
Customer Services
Bureau of the Census
U.S. Department of Commerce
Washington, DC 20233   (301) 763-4100

The Bureau collects and publishes data for two kinds of geographical areas:

Governmental
-the United States, Puerto Rico, and outlying areas under U.S. sovereignty or jurisdiction
-States, counties, and county equivalents
-incorporated places (e.g., cities, villages) and minor civil divisions (MC's) of counties (such as townships)
-congressional districts and election precincts
-American Indian reservations and Alaska Native villages

Statistical
-four census regions (Northeast, South, Midwest, and West) and nine census divisions, all of which are groupings of States
-Metropolitan areas
-census country divisions in States where minor civil division boundaries are not satisfactory for statistical purposes
-census designated places
-urbanized areas
-census tracts and block numbering areas averaging about 4,000 people
-census blocks--generally equivalent to city blocks
-enumeration districts--census administrative areas, averaging around 700 inhabitants, where block statistics are not available
-block groups--counterparts to enumeration districts, averaging 900 population, in areas with census blocks
-Neighborhoods--subareas locally defined by participants in the Bureau's Neighborhood Statistics Program
-ZIP Codes--Postal Service administrative areas independent of either governmental or other statistical areas.

In the census of retail trade, the Bureau publishes data for central business districts (CAD's) and major retail centers outside CAD's; in the census of governments, for school districts and other special districts; and in foreign trade and international research, for countries and world areas. Generally, survey data are published only for the larger areas, such as the U.S., its regions, and some States, while census data are made available for smaller areas as well. Contact this office for more information on Census geography.

* Government Auditing Standards

Superintendent of Documents
Government Printing Office
Washington, DC 20548   (202) 275-9359

Revised and updated in 1988, the *Yellow Book--Government Auditing Standards* (#02000000243-3) carries standards for audits of government organizations, programs, activities and functions; and of government money received by contractors, non-profit organizations, and other non-government organizations. The standards are to be followed by auditors and audit organizations where regulated by law, regulation agreement, or policy. The statements pertain to the auditors' professional quality, quality of audit effort, and the character of professional and meaningful audit reports. $3.50.

* Government Income and Expenses: Monthly

Superintendent of Documents
Government Printing Office

Washington, DC 20402 (202) 783-3238
For monthly information on the U.S. Government's monthly income and
expenses, subscribe to the publication, *Monthly Treasury Statement of Receipts
and Outlays of the United States Government*. The annual price is $22.00 (S/N
748-009-00000-1).

* Government Transactions

Government Division
Bureau of Economic Analysis
U.S. Department of Commerce
1401 K St., NW
Washington DC 20230 (202) 523-0715

BEA's national economics program encompasses the government transactions on
a national income and product accounting basis, which include estimates of
government receipts, expenditures, and surplus of deficit. The estimates are
prepared separately for Federal and for State and local governments. Contact
the office listed above for further information.

* Guide to the 1987 Economic Censuses and Related Statistics

Customer Services Branch
Data User Services Division
Bureau of the Census
Washington, DC 20233 (301) 763-4100

The *Guide to the 1987 Economic Censuses and Related Statistics* describes the
scope, coverage, classification system, data items, and publications for each of the
economic censuses and the related surveys that provide monthly and annual data.
It also reviews other Census Bureau data series that provide information of value
to economic statistics users. Single copies are free from this office.

* Detailed Census Information

For detailed information about the contents of specific censuses, programs, or
publications, contact the following offices:

General Trade
Retail Trade: (301) 763-7038
Wholesale Trade: (301) 763-5281
Service Industries: (301) 763-7039
Transportation: (301) 763-4634
Establishment Data: (301) 763-5281
Truck, commodity surveys: (301) 763-4364

Manufacturers
Durable Goods: (301) 763-7304
Nondurable Goods: (301) 763-2510
Mineral Industries: (301) 763-5938
Construction Industries: (301) 763-5435

Minority- and Women-Owned
Businesses: (301) 763-5517
Enterprise Statistics: (301) 763-5470
Puerto Rico and other U.S. possessions: (301) 763-5656

* Homeless Statistics

1990 Census Promotion Office
U.S. Bureau of the Census
U.S. Department of Commerce
Washington, DC 20233 (301) 763-1990

The number of homeless, vagrants, and transients has increased in the last ten
years since the 1980 Census. The Census Bureau has two operations designed
to count the homeless. A "shelter and street night" count will take place that
counts people in hotels and motels identified beforehand as shelters for the
homeless, or that cost $12 or less per night. It also includes "emergency" shelters
and open locations in the streets, parks, and other areas not intended for
habitation. The Census Bureau plans to encourage those who work with the
homeless, and the homeless themselves, to apply to do the enumeration.

* Hours and Earnings Monthly Survey

Office of Employment and
Unemployment Statistics
Bureau of Labor Statistics
U.S. Department of Labor
441 G St., NW, Room 2919
Washington, DC 20212 (202) 523-1694

A monthly survey provides hours and earnings data collected from payroll
records of business establishments. The data available includes gross hours and
earnings of production or nonsupervisory workers in 454 industries, and overtime
hours in 323 manufacturing industries. The data are published in a variety of
sources, and are used as economic indicators, wage negotiations, and economic
research and planning.

* Income and Program Participation Survey

Data User Services Division
Customer Services
Bureau of the Census
U.S. Department of Commerce
Washington, DC 20233 (301) 763-4100

New information on important aspects of household economic activity has
continued to emerge from the *Survey of Income and Program Participation*
(SIPP), including more detailed observations on income flows and frequency of
participation in government assistance programs. Special reports issued from
SIPP were *Who's Helping Out--Support Networks Among American Families*, and
Pensions: Worker Coverage and Retirement Income. For information on these
special reports, or questions about the *Survey of Income and Program
Participation*, contact this office.

* Industry and Employment Projections

Office of Economic Growth and
Employment Projections
Bureau of Labor Statistics
U.S. Department of Labor
601 D St., NW, Room 4414
Washington, DC 20212 (202) 272-5278

State and area employment data classified by industry division, and gross weekly
hours and earnings for production and related workers in manufacturing is
available, as is other data, including demographic employment/unemployment,
monthly labor force and unemployment, occupational employment, and area
wage surveys.

* Industry-Occupation Employment Matrix

Office of Economic Growth and Employment Projections
Bureau of Labor Statistics
U.S. Department of Labor
601 D St., NW, Room 4000
Washington, DC 20212 (202) 272-5283

The National Industry-Occupation Employment Matrix provides detailed
information on the distribution of occupational employment by industry.
Coverage is for over 650 detailed occupations--wage and salary, self-employed,
and unpaid family workers, and wage and salary workers only for over 300
detailed industries.

* Information Management and Statistics

Office of Information Management and Statistics (70Y) Department of
Veterans Affairs
810 Vermont Ave., NW
Washington, DC 20420 (202) 233-2423

This office is the information management and statistical research branch of the
VA. It provides statistical data and analyses to VA management of budgeting,
program management, and policy formulation, and coordinates the Agency's
internal, interagency, and public use reporting needs. OIM&S is also responsible
for VA-wide information resources management policy, paperwork management,
records management, forms and correspondence management policy, and mail
and travel policy. Contact the office above for more information. Contact this
office for information on obtaining the following publications:

Summary of Medical Programs. Presents facility specific program data.
Trend Data. An annual publication which presents up to 25 years of data related
to VA activities.

* Industry Productivity Measurements

Industry Productivity and Technology Studies
Office of Productivity and Technology
U.S. Department of Labor
200 Constitution Ave., NW
Washington, DC 20210(202) 523-*****

The Industry Productivity Measurement Program develops annual indexes of
productivity for individual industries. Available data include annual indexes of
output per employee hour, output per employee, output, employment, and
employee hours, as well as annual indexes of industry multifactor productivity
(labor and capital combined). Data are published in a variety of sources,
including the annual bulletin, *Productivity Measures for Selected Industries*.

* Industry Wage Statistics

Office of Compensation and Working Conditions
Bureau of Labor Statistics
U.S. Department of Labor
441 G St., NW, Room 2026
Washington, DC 20212 (202) 523-1160

Data available from industry surveys include averages and distributions of
straight-time earnings for representative occupations--nationwide, regions,

Economics, Demographics and Statistics

selected areas--by size of establishment and other characteristics, depending on industry and how they were studied. Published in summaries and in *Industry Wage Surveys*, the data are useful for wage and salary administration, union contract negotiation, arbitration, and government policy considerations.

* Information Services Specialists

Data User Services Division
Customer Services
Bureau of the Census
U.S. Department of Commerce
Washington, DC 20233   (301) 763-4100

Customer Services staff and subject specialists at Bureau headquarters, as well as information services specialists in its regional offices, are equipped to answer questions about census and survey data and provide personalized attention to your needs. To receive a telephone contact list, contact the office above.

* Interindustry Economics

Interindustry Economics Division
Bureau of Economic Analysis
U.S. Department of Commerce
1401 K St., NW, Room 608
Washington DC 20230   (202) 523-0792

Input-output accounts for the United States show how industries interact--providing input to, and taking output from, each other--to produce the GNP. *Benchmark tables, based largely on the economic census, are prepared every 5 years. Annual tables are prepared using basically the same procedures as used for the benchmark tables, but with less comprehensive and less reliable source data. For more information contact the office listed above.

* Internal Auditing

Information Handling and Support Facilities
General Accounting Office
P.O. Box 6015
Gaithersburg, MD 20877   (202) 275-6241

The free book, *Accounting Principles and Standards for Federal Agencies* (#123095), provides guidance for internal auditing in federal agencies.

* International Comparisons of Productivity, Labor Costs, Economic Indicators, and Unemployment

International Training Division
Office of Productivity and Technology
Bureau of Labor Statistics
U.S. Department of Labor
200 Constitution Ave., NW, Room S1310
Washington, DC 20210   (202) 523-9231

This office develops comparisons of productivity and labor costs to assess U.S. economic performance relative to other countries. Data available include indexes of output per employee hour, hourly compensation, and unit labor costs in manufacturing. The coverage includes 11 industrial countries plus regional groupings. Also available are data concerning labor force, employment, and unemployment for foreign countries, by selected characteristics, approximating U.S. concepts. This office also makes comparisons of prices, compensation costs, and other major economic indicators in industrial countries.

* International Energy Economic Research

Office of Regional and Resources Policy
Office of the Assistant Secretary
of the Treasury for International Affairs
U.S. Department of the Treasury
1500 Pennsylvania Ave., NW
Washington, DC 20220   (202) 566-5071

This office under the Secretary of the Treasury studies international energy resources and technology and their impact on the United States' economy.

* International Finance

Division of International Finance
Federal Reserve System
MS-16, Room 1242
20th St. & Constitution Ave., NW
Washington, DC 20551   (202) 452-3614

For information relating to foreign financial markets, international banking, U.S./international transactions, international development, world payments, and economic activity, contact this office.

* International Price Indexes: Export and Import

Office of Prices and Living Conditions
Bureau of Labor Statistics
U.S. Department of Labor

600 E St., NW, Room 3302
Washington, DC 20212   (202) 272-5025

This office measures change in the prices of commodities exported from and imported into the United States. Quarterly price indexes are available for all exported and imported items and major subgroups, such as food, beverages and tobacco, crude materials except fuels, animal and vegetable oils, fats and waxes, chemicals, manufactured goods, machinery and transport equipment, and miscellaneous manufactured articles.

* International Statistics

Data User Services Division
Customer Services
Bureau of the Census
U.S. Department of Commerce
Washington, DC 20233   (301) 763-4100

The Bureau published demographic statistics for the world's 206 countries in cooperation with the Agency for International Development and also developed international data bases on AIDS, youth, and aging for developing countries. Also, the Census Bureau is assisting 25 countries in planning, conducting, or analyzing population censuses.

* International Visitors Program

International Visitors Program
Bureau of the Census
U.S. Department of Commerce
Washington, DC 20233   (301) 763-2839

The International Visitors Program provides an opportunity for consultation with experts at the Census Bureau. Consultation sessions can last for a day to a week. Workstudy tours are also available, generally lasting two to six weeks. Statistical consultations are offered on surveys, data processing, and technical and analytical aspects of census and survey taking.

* Labor Statistics Availability

Division of Information Services
Bureau of Labor Statistics
U.S. Department of Labor
441 G St., NW, Room 2831A
Washington, DC 20212   (202) 523-1221

The Bureau of Labor Statistics can provide you with a tentative release schedule for BLS major economic indicators. The schedule lists the information available (i.e., employment situation, consumer price index, productivity and costs, etc.), as well as the date and time of the information release. The *BLS Update* also contains the release dates for the quarter.

* Local Area Employment and Unemployment

Office of Employment and Unemployment Statistics
Bureau of Labor Statistics
U.S. Department of Labor
441 G St., NW, Room 2083
Washington, DC 20212   (202) 523-1038

This office provides laborforce, employment, and unemployment data estimated by state employment security agencies. These data are used primarily to allocate federal funds to local jurisdiction. The coverage includes annual average data with demographic detail for 50 states, the District of Columbia, 30 large metropolitan areas, and 11 of their central cities, and monthly data to include 50 states, 330 areas, 3,100 counties, and 500 cities of 50,000 or more. The data are published in a variety of sources, including the annual bulletin, *Geographic Profile of Employment and Unemployment*, and the monthly periodical, *Employment and Earnings*.

* Longitudinal Employment Surveys

Office of Economic Research
Bureau of Labor Statistics
U.S. Department of Labor
441 G St., NW, Room 2026
Washington, DC 20212   (202) 523-1347

Every couple of years, this office updates *The National Longitudinal Surveys*, which study employment profiles of certain age groups . The groups include: young women who were 14-24 in 1968; mature women who were 30-44 in 1967; and youth who were 14-21 in 1979. Information available includes labor market activities, characteristics of jobs, earnings, unemployment, social and demographic characteristics, education, and training.

* Mapping Algorithms

Customer Services Branch
Data User Services Division
Bureau of the Census
Washington, DC 20233   (301) 763-4100

The Census Bureau is making the FORTRAN source code routines available that it used to produce TIGER maps on its Unisys 1100 Series mainframe computers, so that experienced FORTRAN systems analysts can learn how Census mapping algorithms work. However, the routines will not run on any computer system without extensive additional programming, and the Bureau will not support the routines, nor answer questions about them. If you would still like to obtain these algorithms to assist you in your own programming efforts, you can order them on computer tape together with documentation on the TIGER data structure for $600 from the office above.

* Map Products from Census

Customer Services Branch
Data User Services Division
Bureau of the Census
Washington, DC 20233   (301) 763-4100

Superintendent of Documents
Government Printing Office
Washington, DC 20402-9325   (202) 783-3238

Each of the following map types will be available for purchase separately. Listed are descriptions of the map products offered through the 1990 census program. This listing includes only those maps that will be sold separately; it does not include maps that will be prepared and included in the printed reports.

* Market News Reports

Information Staff
Agricultural Marketing Service
U.S. Department of Agriculture
Room 3510, South Building
P.O. Box 96456
Washington, DC 20090-6456   (202) 447-8998

Skilled market reporters gather and document marketing information that is distributed quickly throughout the U.S. via telephone recorders, newspapers, radio, television, and in printed reports. The reports are available for seven commodities: dairy, tobacco, cotton, fruits and vegetables, livestock, grain, and poultry, and they contain information on supply and demand and shipping point reports that cover prices paid by types of sale. Much of the information is gathered and distributed by local field offices via satellite.

* Monetary Affairs

Bureau of Economic and Business Affairs
Department of State
2201 C St., NW, Room 4830
Washington, DC 20520   (202) 647-5935

This office evaluates foreign policy aspects of the functioning of the International Monetary System and examines international banking and taxation issues. A member of the Joint IMF-IBID, this office also conducts multilateral negotiations of rescheduling of foreign debts to the United States.

* National Income and Wealth Economics

National Income and Wealth Division
Bureau of Economic Analysis
U.S. Department of Commerce
1401 K St., NW, Room 800
Washington DC 20230   (202) 523-0669

The national income and product accounts show the value and composition of the Nation's output and the distribution of incomes generated in its production. The accounts include estimates of gross national product (GNP), GNP price measures, the goods and services that make up GNP in current and constant dollars, national income, personal income, and corporate profits. Contact the office listed above for more information.

* New Census Materials

Data User Services Division
Customer Services
Bureau of the Census
U.S. Department of Commerce
Washington, DC 20233   (301) 763-4100

The Monthly Product Announcement is a free listing of every new report, computer tape, microfiche, and so forth, from the Census Bureau complete with price and ordering information, as it is issued. It is available from Customer Services office above.

* Online Economic Indicators

BLS Electronic News Releases Service
Bureau of Labor Statistics
U.S. Department of Labor
441 G St., NW, Room 2822
Washington, DC 20212   (202) 523-1913

Economic indicators from the Bureau of Labor Statistics are available electronically at the time of their release. There is no charge for the data. Users pay only for the actual computer time used. More than 100 releases a year are available online, including monthly releases on consumer and producer prices, earnings, employment and unemployment, as well as quarterly releases on productivity, employment costs, collective bargaining, and import and export price indexes.

* Policy and Procedures Manual

Information Handling and Support Facilities
General Accounting Office
P.O. Box 6015
Gaithersburg, MD 20877   (202) 275-6241

The GAO publishes the Policy and Procedures Manual for Guidance of Federal Agencies, the official medium through which the Comptroller announces principles, standards, and related requirements for accounting to be observed by the federal departments and agencies. Formation report forms designed by these agencies for the collection of information from the public are required to be cleared by GAO before they may be issued. The review and clearance functions are to ensure that information is obtained with minimum burden on those businesses required to provide the information, to eliminate duplicate data collection efforts, and to ensure that collected information is tabulated so as to maximize its usefulness.

* Population and Housing 1980

Superintendent of Documents
U.S. Government Printing Office
Washington, DC 20402   (202) 378-3238.

The 1980 Census of Population and Housing: Users' Guide (PHC80-R1) includes a text and several supplements, a glossary, and table-finding guides. It is available from the GPO.

* Population and Housing Statistics

Data User Services Division
Customer Services
Bureau of the Census
U.S. Department of Commerce
Washington, DC 20233   (301) 763-4100

The following population and housing publications are available free from Census: Neighborhood Statistics From the 1980 Census; and Subject Index to Current Population Reports, series P-23, No. 109.

* Population Bulletin

The Population Reference Bureau, Inc.
Circulation Department
777 14th St., NW
Washington, DC 20005   (202) 639-8040

Population Bulletin Vol. 44, No. 1, April 1989 discusses the Census Bureau's plans for taking the 1990 Census, looks back on 200 years of census taking in America, and details such key aspects of the 1990 Census as the questionnaire, census geography, and data dissemination plans. It also examines certain important issues in the coming census. The Population Bulletin is published four times a year and is distributed to members of the Population Reference Bureau. To order a copy of the Bulletin, or to join PRB, contact the office listed above.

* Population Estimates Software

Customer Services (Diskettes)
Data User Services Division
Bureau of the Census
Washington, DC 20233   (301) 763-4100

This software package contains a series of programs, internal documentation, and a practice set of county-level data for the State of New Jersey. It permits users to compute population estimates using their own data according to several Census Bureau approved methods. To request a data diskette, contact Customer Services and they will mail ordering information to you for the diskette files of interest to you.

* Population Survey

Data User Services Division
Customer Services
Bureau of the Census
U.S. Department of Commerce
Washington, DC 20233   (301) 763-4100

The Current Population Survey continues to generate the Nation's official measures of employment, unemployment, income, and poverty. Plans are in the works to redesign the survey early in the 1990s. The Bureau continues working with agencies sponsoring other recurring surveys on such topics as consumer expenditures, housing, crime, job training, and health, including the development of data on Acquired Immune Deficiency Syndrome (AIDS). For more information about the current population survey, contact this Census office.

* Prices and Living Conditions

Office of Prices and Living Conditions

Economics, Demographics and Statistics

Bureau of Labor Statistics
U.S. Department of Labor
600 E St., NW, Room 3205
Washington, DC 20212   (202) 272-5036
This office develops a wide variety of information on prices in retail and primary markets and conducts research to improve the measurement of price change. The program also includes Consumer Price Indexes, Producer Price Indexes, and export and import price indexes for U.S. foreign trade. The Bureau can also provide you with information on its studies of consumer expenditures, income assets, and liabilities of all U.S. families.

* Private Sector Productivity

Productivity Research Division
Office of Productivity and Technology
Bureau of Labor Statistics
U.S. Department of Labor
200 Constitution Ave., NW, Room S4315
Washington, DC 20210   (202) 523-6010
This office develops measures for the business, non-farm business, and manufacturing sectors of the economy, as well as for nonfinancial corporations. Available information includes quarterly and annual levels, indexes, and percent changes for output per hour for all persons and related measures, such as unit labor cost, real and current dollar compensation per hour, and unit labor payments. Monthly employment and employee hour data are available.

* Producer Prices and Price Indexes

Office of Prices and Living Conditions
U.S. Department of Labor
600 E St., NW, Room 5210
Washington, DC 20212   (202) 272-5113
This office provides measures of changes in prices received by producers at the level of the first commercial transaction for many commodities and a few services. Price indexes are available for virtually all industries in the mining and manufacturing sectors. *Producer Price Indexes* is a monthly periodical, which includes a comprehensive report on price movements for the month, plus regular tables and technical notes. A subscription is available for $29.00 per year from: Superintendent of Documents, Government Printing Office, Washington, DC 20402; (202) 783-3238.

* Productivity and Technology Statistics

Office of Productivity and
Technology Studies
Bureau of Labor Statistics
U.S. Department of Labor
200 Constitution Ave., NW, Room S4320
Washington, DC 20210   (202) 523-9244
This office is responsible for three major research programs. The productivity program compiles and analyzes productivity and related statistics on the U.S. business economy and its major sectors, and on individual industries and government. The technological studies program investigates trends in technology and their impact on employment and productivity. And the international labor statistics program compiles and analyzes data on productivity and related factors in foreign countries for comparison with the U.S. experience. The free directory, *BLS Publications on Productivity and Technology*, lists all the publications of each program.

* Productivity and Technology Trends

Office of Productivity and Technology
Bureau of Labor Statistics
U.S. Department of Labor
200 Constitution Ave., NW, Room S4325
Washington, DC 20210   (202) 523-9394
To better understand the factors under lying productivity change, this office measures productivity trends in the economy, major sectors, industrial industries, and government. The staff also investigates and can provide you with information on the nature and effect of technological change within industries and across industry lines.

* Program Evaluation

Program Evaluation & Methodology Division
General Accounting Office
Room 5868
441 G St. NW
Washington, DC 20548   (202) 275-1854
This office evaluates the effectiveness of virtually any government program. These evaluations focus on both improving government, and introducing innovations in the evaluation of such programs. The Division encourages and maintains contacts with evaluation professionals in other federal agencies, universities, professional societies, and state and local governments, and fosters improved communication within the evaluation community. It makes available a series of papers introducing such topics as how to design program evaluations, and how to conduct survey questionnaires.

* Prototype TIGER/Line File Diskette

Customer Services (Diskettes)
Data User Services Division
Bureau of the Census
Washington, DC 20233   (301) 763-4100
The file on this 1.2 megabyte high-density diskette represents a prototype of the TIGER/Line files released for the entire U.S. in 1989. The diskette presents an extract of the 1988 Dress Rehearsal Census TIGER database for Boone County, Missouri. It contains political boundaries (as of January 1, 1987), 1988 Dress Rehearsal statistical area boundaries, feature names and classification codes, alternate feature names, latitude/longitude coordinates (shape records), and address ranges with associated ZIP Codes for streets within the Columbia, Missouri area. To request a data diskette, contact Customer Services and they will mail ordering information to you for the diskette files of interest to you.

* Public Debt of the United States: Monthly

Superintendent of Documents
Government Printing Office
Washington, DC 20402   (202) 783-3238
For a monthly description of the public debt of the United States Government, subscribe to *Monthly Statement of the Public Debt of the United States*. The price is $19.00 (S/N 748-008-00000-4).

* Public-Use Microdata Sample for the Older Population

Customer Services Branch
Data User Services Division
Bureau of the Census
Washington, DC 20233   (301) 763-4100
The Census Bureau is considering producing this product to meet the increasing demand for data on the older population. This file could be used to generate sufficient data, especially for the oldest age groups, to construct detailed cross tabulations by age, sex, race, and other characteristics. Contact this office for more information.

* Regional Economic Forecast

Regional Economic Analysis Division
Bureau of Economic Analysis
U.S. Department of Commerce
1401 K St., NW, Room 308
Washington DC 20230   (202) 523-0946
BEA's regional economics program provides estimates, analyses, and projections by region, State, metropolitan statistical area, and county. Data available includes personal income, wage and salary income and employment, and proprietors' income and employment. Estimates of total and per capita personal income are used by the Federal government in formulas to distribute funds to States and local areas, by State and local governments for revenue projections, and by businesses in marketing and plant location studies. BEA also maintains econometric models to forecast annual changes in economic activity and to analyze the impacts of projects and programs. In conjunction with the projections work, BEA has developed estimates of gross state product. Contact this office for more information.

* Report Guidelines for GAO

Superintendent of Documents
General Accounting Office
DHIS, P.O. 6015
Gaithersburg, MD 20877   (202) 275-6241
The *Checklist for Report Writers and Reviewers* (#091096) standardizes the report format and shows how it should be organized. It breaks a GAO report down to its components--cover, transmittal letter, digest--and poses questions to use in judging how well each was written. The booklet includes reminders of GAO reporting policies, principles taught in Producing Organized Writing and Effective Reviewing (POWER), recurring reporting problems, and technical reporting requirements. Another publication, *From Auditing to Editing* (#095119), is a guide for teaching report writing. Each book is free for the first five copies, and $2 for each additional one.

* Resources, Community, and Economic Development

Resources, Community, and Economic Development Division
General Accounting Office
441 G St. NW, Room 4919
Washington, DC 20548   (202) 275-3567
As with most sections of GAO, this section does most of its work in the form of reports requested specifically by the Congress. However, the division does share its reports, testimony and studies with interested groups outside the government. This division coordinates GAO's work in the areas of food, domestic housing and community development, environmental protection, land use planning arrangement and control, transportation systems and policies, and water and water-related programs. The division also provides GAO audit coverage at the

Departments of Agriculture, Commerce, Energy, Housing and Urban Development, Interior, and Transportation; the Army Corps of Engineers (civil function); the Environmental Protection Agency; the Small Business Administration; the Interstate Commerce, Federal Maritime and Federal Communications Commissions; the National Railroad Passenger Corporation (Amtrak); the Washington Metropolitan Area Transit Authority; the U.S. Railway Association; the Civil Aeronautics Board; the Federal Emergency Management Agency; and a variety of boards, commissions, and quasi-governmental entities.

* Revenue from Public Lands

Management Services
Bureau of Land Management
U.S. Department of the Interior
18th and C Sts., NW
Washington, DC 20240   (202) 343-4864

This office collects and disburses revenues and receipts generated from public lands. The Bureau of Land Management is a primary generator of revenues in the Federal government, with more than $800 million collected annually from a variety of sources, including timber sales, sale of public lands, grazing leases, right-of-way leases, permits, and mineral receipts.

* Seminars at the Census Bureau

User Training Branch
Data User Services Division
Bureau of the Census
U.S. Department of Commerce
Washington, DC 20233   (301) 763-1510

Seminars are available for librarians, government personnel, and for the general public to help you identify the types of statistical data available from Census and other Federal agencies as well as how to use these data. Seminars last from one-half day to four days, and there is a nominal fee. Current courses include:

Statistical Resources for Librarians and Information Specialists: An Introduction
An Introduction to CD-ROM
Understanding and Using the TIGER System
CENDATA: The Census Bureau's Online Information Service

From time to time the Bureau also trains people in preparing population projections and estimates, and on special topics. Contact the office above for information on fees and scheduling.

* Special Computer Tape Files

Customer Services Branch
Data User Services Division
Bureau of the Census
Washington, DC 20233   (301) 763-4100

The Census Bureau will produce and release several special computer tape files in 1993 to meet unique data needs. Others may be produced based on user demand and availability of resources. Contact this office for a list of these upcoming files.

* Special Services of the Census

The Director
Bureau of the Census
Washington, DC 20233

The Bureau of the Census can provide you with special services on a cost-reimbursable basis, such as designing and carrying out sample surveys (including collecting data by mail or field enumeration), providing population estimates and projections, making special tabulations of data collected in censuses and surveys, and giving other technical assistance. The Bureau of the Census may act as consultant to or agent for groups on special statistical problems. Inquiries concerning special services should be addressed to the office above.

* Special Tabulations Program

William Downs
Housing and Household Economic Statistics Division
Bureau of the Census
U.S. Department of Commerce
Washington, DC 20233   (301) 763-8553

This division handles specialized needs of the data user that are not met through the 1990 standard data products or the User-Defined Areas Program. Such needs include specialized cross tabulations, product formats, or geographic areas which require splitting blocks. The computer process for this program generally involves retabulating data from the confidential internal record files. The Census Bureau prepares these special tabulations on a user-fee basis. The Census Bureau will provide free estimates of the cost and time required to produce a special tabulation. To obtain these estimates, the user must provide specific information on the proposed data content as well as the geographic areas. Contact this office for more information on available special services.

* State and Metropolitan Area Data Book

Superintendent of Documents
Government Printing Office
Washington, DC 20402-9325   (202) 783-3238

The *State and Metropolitan Area Data Book* contains statistics for states, metropolitan statistical areas, 738 component counties, and 510 central cities. You can use this edition to find the areas that are growing the fastest, with the highest median family income, or the most college graduates, to determine where your metro area ranks in amount of Federal contracts, retail sales, or service receipts, or to track past employment trends by industry between areas or patterns within an area. The book also contains explanatory notes, and source citations for finding additional information. The book sells for $28.00. To FAX orders or inquiries, call (202) 275-0019. International customers should add 25% to the cost.

* State and Metropolitan Area Data Book 1988 on Diskettes

Customer Services (Diskettes)
Data User Services Division
Bureau of the Census
Washington, DC 20233   (301) 763-4100

These diskettes present selected data from the book. There are over 1,800 variables for states, about 300 for metropolitan areas and component counties, and over 80 for central cities. A wide variety of subject areas are included. Sources include the Bureau of the Census and several other national agencies both public and private. Note that free sampler diskettes previewing this product are available from Customer Services. To request a data diskette, contact Customer Services and they will mail ordering information to you for the diskette files of interest to you.

* State Data Centers

Data User Services Division
Customer Services
Bureau of the Census
U.S. Department of Commerce
Washington, DC 20233   (301) 763-4100

The Census Bureau began the State Data Center program to make statistical information more readily available to the public. There are State Data Centers (in almost all States, the District of Columbia, the Virgin Islands, and Puerto Rico) and private and public organizations registered with the Bureau's National Clearinghouse for Census Data Services located throughout the country. The Bureau furnishes data products, training in data access and use, technical assistance, and consultation to States. For more information on the State Data Center Program, call (301) 763-1580. Listings of the centers are available upon request from the Census division listed above.

* Statistical Abstract of the United States

Superintendent of Documents
Government Printing Office
Washington, DC 20402-9325   (202) 783-3238

The official *Statistical Abstract of the United States* is the one reference book to have in your home, office, school, or library. It is an extensive collection of statistics on social, economic and political subjects from over 200 sources. It includes source notes for each table and a guide to statistical publications for more information, a list of telephone contacts for key Federal statistical agencies, a special section on State rankings, a comprehensive index, many graphs and tables depicting analytical percents and rankings, and the latest available official data--quoted and used by experts in every field. The 1989 paper edition is $26.00, and the 1989 cloth edition is $32.00. To FAX orders or inquiries, call (202) 275-0019. International customers should add 25% to the cost.

* Statistical Briefs

Data User Services Division
Customer Services
Bureau of the Census
U.S. Department of Commerce
Washington, DC 20233   (301) 763-4100

The Bureau produces the *Statistical Brief Series*--short, nontechnical presentations on such policy-related topics as child care, pension coverage, computer usage, consumer markets in China, and housing in selected metropolitan areas. Briefs are distributed to audiences ranging from Congress and government officials to the general public. Contact this office for more information.

* Statistical Methodology

Data User Services Division
Customer Services
Bureau of the Census
U.S. Department of Commerce
Washington, DC 20233   (301) 763-4100

Economics, Demographics and Statistics

Internationally recognized researchers recently worked with Census Bureau specialists on a variety of statistical challenges. Studies included economic development in ghettos, undercount adjustment, value of fringe benefits, effect of income fluctuations on poverty rates, improving state-to-state migration estimates, and recalibration of earlier occupation and industrial classification to make them more compatible with 1980 census data. Contact this office for more information on these statistical studies.

* Statistics Services
    Data User Services Division
    Customer Services
    Bureau of the Census
    U.S. Department of Commerce
    Washington, DC 20233   (301) 763-4100
Population, housing, business, agriculture, government finances, foreign trade--the Bureau of the Census gathers data on these and many other subjects. Do you need statistics like the following?

Which areas have the fastest growing populations?
What is the average value of houses in my neighborhood?
How do shoe sales in my area compare with sales in other parts of the country?
How many acres of wheat did farmers grow in my county?
How much money did my county government spend on road maintenance last year, and how did that compare with the neighboring counties?
How well do imports and exports balance in U.S. trade with the Mideast?

For more information on these and other statistics, contact this service division.

* Supplementary Reports
    Customer Services Branch
    Data User Services Division
    Bureau of the Census
    Washington, DC 20233   (301) 763-4100
Supplementary reports present special compilations of census data dealing with specific population and housing subjects as well as for sub-groups of the population. The types of reports vary from census to census. Some examples of supplementary reports being considered for 1990 are *Advance Estimates of Social, Economic, and Housing Characteristics*; *Social, Economic, and Housing Characteristics for Redefined Metropolitan Statistical Areas*; graphic chartbooks; thematic maps portraying 1990 census data; and an atlas of census maps that will contain the printed publication maps. Contact this office for more information.

* Teaching Materials From Census
    Data User Services Division
    Customer Services
    Bureau of the Census
    U.S. Department of Commerce
    Washington, DC 20233   (301) 763-4100
CCSP Update keeps college instructors informed about new resources, teaching materials, and projects for students. It is available for no cost from the Census Bureau.

* Thematic Statistical Maps
    Customer Services Branch
    Data User Services Division
    Bureau of the Census
    Washington, DC 20233   (301) 763-4100
The maps, which the Census Bureau issues as part of the GE-50 map series, usually depict a wide variety of statistical topics. In the past, the Census Bureau issued these maps as a single sheet wall map. Similar maps also appeared in selected printed report series as page-size maps. For more information on statistical maps, contact this office.

* TIGER Data Base
    Cafe, Geography Division
    Bureau of the Census
    Washington, DC 20233
The TIGER database contains digital data for all 1990 census map features (such as roads, railroads, and rivers) and the associated collection geography (such as census tracts and blocks), political areas (such as cities and townships), feature names and classification codes, alternate feature names, 1980 and 1990 census geographic area codes, Federal Information Processing Standard codes, and within metropolitan areas, address ranges and ZIP Codes for streets. Contact this office for more information on the TIGER database.

* TIGER/Line Comments
    State and Regional Programs Staff
    Data User Services Division
    Bureau of the Census
    Washington, DC 20233

The Bureau of the Census would like to find out how you are using TIGER/Line data, especially your specific applications. Please send your comments to this address.

* TIGER/Line Files
    Customer Services Branch
    Data User Services Division
    Bureau of the Census
    Washington, DC 20233   (301) 763-1580
The TIGER database is not available to the public; however, TIGER/Line Files are. The TIGER/Line File is an extract of selected geographic and cartographic information from the TIGER database. The normal geographic coverage for a TIGER/Line File is a county. Each file contains appropriate census geographic area codes, latitude/longitude coordinates, the name and type of the feature, the relevant census feature class code identifying the feature segment by category and, for portions of metropolitan and highly populated areas, the address ranges and associated ZIP Codes for each side of a street segment. The files can be combined to cover the whole nation. The TIGER/Line Files are available to data users as follows:

1) The prototype version of the TIGER/Line file for each county in the U.S. has been released. These files contain digital data for all census map features as well as the 1990 census collection geography, such as census tracts and blocks, and 1980 census political boundaries.

2) The current version of the TIGER/Line file is known as the precensus version. These files contain updates to the political boundaries to January 1, 1988, and provide some address range enhancements resulting from the Census Bureau's address list development work in urban areas. In addition, the Bureau has added permanent record numbers, as well as Federal Information Processing Standards Codes for minor civil divisions/census county divisions and places, and American Indian Reservations and have made some minor modifications to the record format. The version replaces the prototype version.

3) In 1991, the Bureau will release the census version of the TIGER/Line file which will include updates to the political boundary information to January 1, 1990, contain corrections (i.e. additions or deletions) to map features made during the census, identify voting districts where appropriate, and modify the geographic area codes to reflect the areas for which 1990 data will be tabulated.

The public can use a TIGER/Line file to combine the geographic and cartographic data of a TIGER/Line file with other statistical information--such as population, housing, income, or any other type of data--using either mainframe or personal computers and appropriate software for various applications. Some examples of its uses are mapping/thematic mapping, geocoding of spatially-referenced data for marketing research, routing, address matching, redistricting, and applications into geographic information systems.

All precensus TIGER/Line files are available on 9 track, 1600 bi or 6250 bi computer tape, ASCII or EBCDIC, labeled. The precensus TIGER/Line files are available on computer tape. The price of the computer tapes is $200 for the first county ordered in each state, plus $25 for each additional county in that state. The data set for the entire United States is $87,450, with Puerto Rico and Other Outlying Areas it is $90,150. Documentation for the files can also be obtained separately for $5. The precensus TIGER/Line files are also available on CD-ROM (Compact Disc - Read Only Memory) that can record 650 megabytes of data. The discs are standard size and are compatible with all CD-ROM readers in your personal computers. The price of the CD-ROMs is $250 each. To order the TIGER/Line files write to the Customer Services Branch, or to charge your order to your VISA or Master Card, or to establish a deposit account, call the number listed above. Tapes can also be ordered by sending a prepaid order, payable to Commerce-Census, to the above address.

* TIGER System Reference Materials Unpublished
    Data Developments
    Data User Services Division
    Bureau of the Census
    Washington, DC 20233   (301) 763-4100
A series of unpublished papers, as referenced in the TIGER/LINE technical documentation, are available for sale at the single-package price of $5. For a listing of the titles included in the package, and to receive an ordering form contact this office.

* Trade Product Classification
    Data User Services Division
    Customer Services
    Bureau of the Census
    U.S. Department of Commerce
    Washington, DC 20233   (301) 763-4100
The Census Bureau has prepared for implementation of the complex new Harmonized System of trade product classification. Meetings were held to inform exporters of the changes, and domestic product classifications were produced to support better analyses of production and trade flows. Researchers

are studying the statutory request for constant-dollar information on U.S. merchandise trade. Contact this office for more information.

* Treasury Bulletin

Superintendent of Documents
Government Printing Office
Washington, DC 20402   (202) 783-3238

Treasury Bulletin is a quarterly synopsis of Treasury activities, covering financial operations, budget receipts and expenditures, debt operations, cash income and outgo, internal revenue collections, capital movements, yields of long-term bonds, ownership of Federal securities, and other Treasury activities. The annual subscription price is $20.00 (S/N 748-007-00000-8).

* Types of Data Files

Customer Services Branch
Data User Services Division
Bureau of the Census
Washington, DC 20233   (301) 763-4100

The Bureau of the Census gathers data on many subjects, but only a fraction of this information is published. To help meet needs not met by these regular publication sources, the Census Bureau maintains an extensive holding of data in computerized form. Almost 1,500 separate data files are available, the majority of which are products of the Bureau's regular data collection and tabulation programs. The types of files include:

Summary Data. Resemble information in published reports; however, data files are often more detailed and cover more geographic areas.

Public-Use Microdata Samples. Include records for unidentifiable individual observations--persons, households, and housing units in a form that protects the confidentiality of the responses, but allows users to design their own tabulations. The Census Bureau does limit the sample size and geographic identification on microdata files.

Geographic Reference Files. List geographic codes associated with specific areas; present computerized representations of maps; and relate various geographic concepts to Census Bureau geography.

Special Tabulations. Statistical information specially prepared by the Census Bureau at the request and expense of the user. These data are furnished on computer tape, printouts, or microfiche, and cannot be sold by the Census Bureau as a standard product for approximately 6 months after completion.

For a brief description of selected tape files and a list of files issued within the past five years showing the number of tape reels, price of technical documentation and references to the Data Development containing a more detailed file description, contact the office listed above.

* User-Defined Areas

Adrienne Quasney
Decennial Planning Division
Bureau of the Census
U.S. Department of Commerce
Washington, DC 20233   (301) 763-4282

This program gives the Census Bureau a generalized capability to produce data based on locally specified geographic areas not available in census tabulations and publications. Through this program, participants will be provided population and housing data for their specified area on a user-fee basis. The primary objective of the program is to process requests for data for specialized geography efficiently to ensure timely delivery of the program products for reasonable user fees. If you are interested in obtaining further information about the User-Defined Areas Program, contact the office above.

* Voting District Outline Maps

Customer Services Branch
Data User Services Division
Bureau of the Census
Washington, DC 20233   (301) 763-4100

The maps in this series will show voting district numbers and boundaries as well as the underlying features such as roads, railroads, and rivers. They also will show the boundaries and names of counties, county subdivisions, and places. The mapping unit will be a county with a variable scale. The maps will not be printed. They will be produced only for counties in those States that participated

in Phase 2 of the Voting District Program. These maps will be produced using map plotting equipment on paper by Census Bureau staff. Contact this office for more information on obtaining these maps.

* Wage and Price Indexes on Computer Tape

Bureau of Labor Statistics
U.S. Department of Labor
441 G St., NW, Room 1077
Washington, DC 20212   (202) 523-7827

BLS major data series are available on magnetic tape. The standard format is 9-track, 6250 BPI. In addition to the data files listed, BLS makes some microdata tapes and also prepares customized data files on a cost-for-service basis. Available data files include consumer expenditures, consumer price index, export-import price indexes, and labor force, as well as many others. A brochure is available which describes the tapes, ordering information, and the cost of each tape.

* Wage Surveys: Area, Industry and White Collar Earnings

Office of Compensation and Working Conditions
Bureau of Labor Statistics
U.S. Department of Labor
441 G St. NW, Room 2021
Washington, DC 20210   (202) 523-1763

This office conducts three different types of wage surveys. The area and industry surveys provide annual data on averages and distributions of earnings for selected occupations in major industry groups in metropolitan areas. The white-collar salary survey is the annual *Professional, Administrative, Technical, and Clerical Survey* which is used in the Federal pay-setting process and provides data on salaries in white-collar occupations from a national sample of establishments.

* Women Worker Data

Office of Publications
Bureau of Labor Statistics
U.S. Department of Labor
441 G St., NW, Room 2421
Washington, DC 20212   (202) 523-1221

This office publishes a wide array of information about women in the labor force. This information is presented to the public through a variety of publications, including news releases, periodicals, bulletins, reports, tapes, and diskettes. The pamphlet, *Where to Find BLS Statistics on Women*, identifies the particular publications in which specific data services may be found, along with information on how to obtain BLS publications. The data includes information labor force status, employment, and unemployment, earnings and hours of work, education, occupational injuries and illness, and unpublished data.

* Workshops on Census Data

Data User Services Division
Customer Services
Bureau of the Census
U.S. Department of Commerce
Washington, DC 20233   (301) 763-4100

The Bureau conducts workshops for data users. For more information, contact Data User Training Program at (301) 763-1510, or contact the office above.

* World Population Data Base

International Demographic Data Center
Scuderi Building, Room 614
U.S. Census Bureau
Washington, DC 20233   (301) 763-4086

The World Population database contains population data for the overall world, its regions (i.e. Latin America, Asia, etc.) and 200 individual countries. Population statistics include total population, estimated projections, growth rate, migratory rate, and crude (number per 1,000) birth and death rates. Data is collected from a survey conducted every two years. The latest statistics were added in 1989, and the time span covered is 1950 through 2050 (projections). Contact this office for free searches and print-outs or to purchase tapes.

State Crime Statistics

* See also Law and Social Justice Chapter

You wouldn't put your kid in a day care center near an outdoor drug market or buy a fast-food franchise in an area where the crime rate is ten times the national average, but how can you stay away from areas if the crime statistics aren't common knowledge? Among the largest databases maintained by states are those pertaining to crime and to law enforcement. These statistics provide a fairly accurate profile of how an area is affected by crime and how the police and the criminal justice system react.

The data are valuable for students and researchers, political aspirants, real estate companies, urban planners, journalists, private rehabilitation facilities, burglar alarm and security services firms, and, in particular, any business seeking a fairly safe place from which to operate.

Before drawing conclusions from state crime data, a number of factors should be considered, including:

o Strength of local police departments
o Economic profile
o Density and size of the area and surrounding communities
o Cultural factors such as education, recreation, ethnic makeup and religion
o Attitudes of residents toward police, crime
o Policies and characteristics of other components in the law enforcement system
o Organization and cooperation of adjoining and overlapping police departments
o Membership and attitudes toward special police organizations
o Climate
o Standards of appointments to local police force
o Crime reporting practices
o Age makeup

Crime statistics are available from all but three states. Only Louisiana, North Dakota, and Tennessee do not provide statistics on crime. For those states, the U.S. Department of Justice can provide you with some data. Call 800-732-3277 for Justice Statistics and 800-638-8736 for Juvenile Statistics.

Examples of the type of data available from your state office include:

o number of juveniles arrested in your state for possession of illegal drugs
o number of shoplifting convictions in your county
o incidents of white-collar crime in major metropolitan areas
o number of armed robberies that have occurred in the last three years

Most states have publications that report crime data. Thirty-four states publish Annual Reports. Connecticut publishes a *Quarterly Report*. Arkansas, Colorado, and Connecticut publish reports in addition to their *Annual Report*. The following states publish reports containing information on crime: California,

District of Columbia, Kansas, Maryland, Missouri, Montana, North Carolina, Ohio, South Carolina, South Dakota, Vermont Most reports are in the form of statistical tables with an introduction explaining how to use the information and a summary. Tables are presented on such categories as crime, arrests, process, personnel, expenditures, and correctional actions. Other categories may include adult felony arrest offenses, adult misdemeanor offenses, adult probation, juvenile probation. They are published on a yearly basis and most are available at no cost.

Each state's annual crime and delinquency report summarizes data pertaining to its own criminal justice system. Information is available on a state-wide or county-wide basis. In addition, some states will retrieve data not available in published sources if requested in writing. Usually there is a fee for such services.

Computer printouts are available from 36 states. California, Colorado, Idaho, and Illinois require a fee for this service. To obtain a printout in District of Columbia you must submit a Freedom of Information At Request. Oregon has only standard output reports available, whereas the other states will do some individualized searching for data The following states will produce data only upon special request: Connecticut, Tennessee, Kentucky, Maryland, Montana, New Hampshire, and North Carolina.

Data are available on magnetic tape from North Carolina and Wisconsin.

Though West Virginia's files are not computerized, they will search manually for data. Rhode Island and Washington are in the process of computerizing their files and hope to be able to provide printouts in 1989.

List of State Crime Statistics Offices

Alabama
Uniform Crime Reporting Program, 858 S. Court St., Montgomery, AL 36130; (205) 832-4930. Publications and Services: Crime in Alabama Annual Report; computer printouts of selected data provided if readily available for no charge.

Alaska
Department of Public Safety, Information Systems, Uniform Crime Reporting Section, 5700 E. Tudor St., Anchorage, AK 99507; (907) 269-5659. Publication and Services: Crime in Alaska Annual Report; most data is on the computer, but printouts not provided at this time.

Arizona
Department of Public Safety, Uniform Crime Reporting Section, P.O. Box 6638, Phoenix, AZ 85005; (602) 223-2222. Publication and Services: Arizona Uniform Crime Annual Report, computer printouts of selected data provided at no charge.

Arkansas
Crime Information Center, Uniform Crime Reporting Section, 1 Capitol Mall, Room 4D 200, Little Rock, AR 72201; (501) 682-2222. Publications and Services; A Public Opinion Report from the Arkansas Crime Poll, Crime in Arkansas Annual Report; computer printouts of selected data provided at no charge.

California

Department of Justice, Bureau of Criminal Statistics and Special Services, P.O. Box 903427, Sacramento, CA 94203; (916) 739-5598. Publications and Services: Crime and Delinquency in California, Criminal Justice Profile; computer printouts of selected data provided for a fee in some cases.

Colorado

Department of Public Safety, Division of Criminal Justice, 700 Kipling St., Suite 300, Denver, CO 80215; (303) 239-4442. Publications and Services: Public Opinion Survey, Risk Assessment Study, Judicial Survey Study, Community Corrections Annual Report; computer printouts of selected data provided, there may be a fee.

Connecticut

Department of Public Safety, Department of State Police, Uniform Crime Reporting Program, Crimes Analysis Division, 294 Colony St., Meriden, CT 06450; (203) 238-6575. Publications and Services: Annual Uniform Crime Report, Crime in Connecticut, Quarterly Report. Computer printouts of selected data not normally available, but would consider a special request.

Delaware

Delaware State Police, State Bureau of Identification, P.O. Box 430, Dover, DE 19903; (302) 736-5878. Publications and Services: Crime in Delaware Annual Report; monthly computer printouts available of various statistics on the state and county level. Contact: Statistical Analysis Center, 60 La Plaza, Dover, DE 19901; (302) 736-4626.

District of Columbia

Metropolitan Police Department, Crime Research and Analysis Section (CRAS), Room 3125, 300 Indiana Ave., NW, Washington, D.C. 20001; (202) 727-4100. Publications and Services: Statistical Report of Crime Index Offenses and Arrests (published monthly and annually). Computer printouts of selected data provided with a freedom of information request.

Florida

Department of Law Enforcement, Uniform Crime Reporting Section, P.O. Box 1489, Tallahassee, FL 32302; (904) 488-5221. Publication and Services: Crime in Florida Annual Report, computer printouts of selected data available at no charge.

Georgia

Georgia Bureau of Investigation, Georgia Crime Information Center, P.O. Box 370748, Decatur, GA 30037; (404) 244-2607. Publication and Services: Georgia Criminal Justice Data Annual Report, computer printouts of selected data provided at no charge.

Hawaii

Criminal Justice Data Center, 465 S. King St., Room 101, Honolulu, HI 96813; (808) 548-2090. Publication and Services: Crime in Hawaii Annual Report; computer printouts of selected data may be available, depends on request.

Idaho

Criminal Identification Bureau, 6062 Corporal Lane, Boise, ID 83704; (208) 334-2537. Publication and Services: Uniform Crime Reporting Program Annual Report; computer printouts of selected data provided for a fee.

Illinois

Department of State Police, Division of Forensic Services and Identification, Bureau of Identification, 726 South College, Springfield, IL 62704; (312) 793-8550. Publication and Services: Crime in Illinois Annual Report, computer printouts of selected data provide for a fee.

Indiana

Indiana State Police, Data Section, 100 N. Senate, Room 111, Indianapolis, IN 46204; (317) 232-8289. Publication and Services: No annual report, computer printouts of selected data provided with a special request.

Iowa

Department of Public Safety, Research and Development Bureau, Wallace State Office Building, Des Moines, IA 50317; (515) 281-5042. Publication and Services: Iowa Uniform Crime Annual Report; several computer printouts prepared and distributed upon request. No individual research available.

Kansas

Statistical Analysis Center, Kansas Bureau of Investigation, 1620 Tyler, Topeka, KS 66612; (913) 232-6000. Publication and Services: Crime in Kansas Annual Report, no computer searching available to the public.

Kentucky

State Police, Records Section. 1250 Louisville Road, Frankfort, KY 40601; (502) 227-8717. Publications and Services: Crime in Kentucky; computer printouts of selected data available in special circumstances, depending upon request.

Louisiana

State Police, Office of Public Affairs, Box 66614, Baton Rouge, LA 70896; (504) 925-6202. Publications and Services: No publications or services available from this office. Statistics must come from the FBI in Washington, D.C.

Maine

Uniform Crime Reporting, 36 Hospital St., Station # 42, Augusta, ME 04333; (207) 289-2025. Publications and Services: Crime in Maine Annual Report; computer printouts of selected data is limited.

Maryland

Maryland State Police, CR-CR, Uniform Crime Reporting, 1200 Reistertown Road, Pikesville, MD 21208; (301) 653-4212. Publications and Services: Crime in Maryland, Battered Spouse Annual Report; Racial, Religious and Ethnic Crimes; computer printouts not generally available, with a written request data can be extracted.

Massachusetts

Commissioner of Public Safety, 1010 Commonwealth Ave., Boston, MA 02215; (617) 566-4500. Publications and Services: Crime in Massachusetts Annual Report, no computer services available.

Michigan

Department of State Police, 7150 Harris Drive, Lansing, MI 48913; (517) 373-6510. Publications and Services: Crime in Michigan Annual Report; computer services not available to the public.

Minnesota

Criminal Justice Information System, Bureau of Criminal Apprehension, 1246 University Ave., St. Paul, MN 55104; (612) 296-6953. Publications and Services: Annual Report; computer printouts of selected data provided at no charge.

Mississippi

City of Jackson Police Department, Box 17, Crime Analysis Unit, Jackson, MS 39205; (601) 987-1212. Publication and Services: State of Mississippi is not a central agency for collecting crime statistics. Major source of statistical information is the City of Jackson Police Department which publishes an Annual Report. No computer services provided.

Missouri

State Highway Patrol, Criminal Records Division, P.O. Box 568, Jefferson City, MO 65102; (314) 751-3313. Publications and Services: Missouri Crime Index Report, data is not computerized, no printouts available.

Montana

Montana Board of Crime Control, 303 N. Roberts, Helena, MN 59620; (406) 444-3604. Publications and Services: Crimes of Montana ($4.00); computer printouts of selected data provided upon written request.

Nebraska

Commission on Law Enforcement and Criminal Justice, 301 Centennial Mall South, P.O. Box 94946, Lincoln, NE 68509; (402) 471-2194. Publications and Services: Crime In Nebraska Annual Report; computer printouts of selected provided at no charge.

Nevada

No central agency within the state; each county has a sheriffs department (17 in all) that keeps records; main county department to list: Nevada Highway Patrol, 555 Wrightway, Carson City, NV 89701; (702) 885-5300.

New Hampshire

Department of Safety, Uniform Crime Reports, Hazen Drive, Concord, NH 03301; (603) 271-2509. Publications and Services: Crime In New Hampshire Annual Report, computer printouts of selected data provided upon written request.

New Jersey

Division of State Police, Uniform Crime Reporting Unit, Box 7068, West Trenton, NJ 08628; (609) 882-2000. Publications and Services: Crime In New Jersey Annual Report, computer printouts of selected data provided at no charge.

New Mexico

Department of Corrections, Data Processing, 1422 Paseo de Peralta, Santa Fe, NM 87503; (505) 827-8606. Publications and Services: Annual Report; computer printouts of selected data provided at no charge.

New York

Division of Criminal Justice Services, Executive Park Tower, Stuyvesant Plaza, Albany, NY 12203; (518) 457-8393. Publications and Services: Crime and Justice Annual Report, no computer services available.

North Carolina

Division of Criminal Information, 407 Blount St., Raleigh, NC 27601; (919) 733-3171. Publications and Services: Crime in North Carolina ($15.00); computer printouts of selected data provided upon special request. Magnetic tapes available for a fee.

North Dakota

State Crime Bureau, P.O. Box 1054, Bismark, ND 58502; (701) 221-6180. Publications and Services: No annual report; no computer services provided.

Ohio

Governor's Office of Criminal Justice Services, Capitol Square, 65 East State Street, Suite 312, Columbus, OH 43215; (614) 466-5126. Publications and Services: Crime and Arrest Data by County (computer printout); computer printout of selected data within limitations.

Oklahoma

Oklahoma State Bureau of Investigation, Northeast 36th At Eastern, P.O. Box 11497, Oklahoma City, OK 73136; (405) 427-5421. Publications and Services: Crime in Oklahoma Annual Report, computer printouts of selected data provided at no charge.

Oregon

State Executive, Law Enforcement Data System, 155 Collage St. N.E., Salem, OR 97310; (503) 378-3057. Publications and Services: Report of Criminal Offenses and Arrests Annual Report, no computer services available, but standard output reports can be obtained.

Pennsylvania

Pennsylvania State Police, Commission on Crime and Delinquency, 1800 Elmerton Ave., Harrisburg, PA 17120; (717) 787-5152. Publications and Services: Crime In Pennsylvania Annual Report; computer printouts of annual data is provided at no charge.

Rhode Island

Governor's Justice Commission, 222 Quaker Lane, West Warwick, RI 02893; (401) 277-2620. Publications and Services: Serious Crime in Rhode Island Annual Report ($5.00), data not computerized until 1989, no services available.

South Carolina

South Carolina Law Enforcement Division, Uniform Crime Reporting, P.O. Box 21398, Columbia, SC 29221. Publications and Services: Crime in South Carolina ($3.00), computer printouts of selected data provided at no charge.

South Dakota

Division of Criminal Investigation, 500 E. Capitol St., Pierre, SD 57501; (605) 773-3331. Publications and Services: Crime in South Dakota, computer printouts of certain data available. Not all data computerized at this point.

Tennessee

Crime Information Center, P.O. Box 100940, Nashville, TN 37210; (615) 741-0430. Publications and Services: no crime reports issued, information not maintained on a computer.

Texas

Department of Public Safety, Statistical Services, Uniform Crime Reporting, Crime Records, Box 4143, Austin, TX 78765; (512) 465-2000. Publications and Services: Crime In Texas Annual Report, computer printouts of selected data provided at no charge.

Utah

Department of Public Safety, Commission on Criminal and Juvenile Justice, 4501 South 2700 West, Salt Lake City, UT 84119; (801) 538- 1031. Publications and Services: Crime in Utah Annual report, computer services not available.

Vermont

Vermont Criminal Information Center, P.O. Box 189, Waterbury, VT 05676; (802) 244-8763. Publications and Services: Vermont Crime Report, computer printouts of partial data can be provided at no charged. Only partial databases are searchable.

Virginia

Department of State Police, P.O. Box 27472, Richmond, VA 23261; (804) 674-2000. Publications and Services: Crime in Virginia Annual Report, computer printouts of selected data provided at no charge.

Washington

Washington Association of Sheriffs and Police Chiefs, Box 826, Olympia, WA 98507; (206) 459-6386. Crime in Washington State Annual Report; special requests for sorted data is not normally accepted at this time. New computer in 1989 should be able to handle individual requests.

West Virginia

Department of Public Safety, Uniform Crime Reporting Division, 725 Jefferson Road, Charleston, WV 25309; (304) 746-2192. Publications and Services: Crime in West Virginia Annual Report, no computer services available, but data can be retrieved manually and staff will fill requests as needed.

Wisconsin

Wisconsin Statistical Analysis Center, 30 West Mifflin St., Madison, WI 53702; (608) 266-3323--Publication and Services: Crimes and Arrests Annual Report; computer printouts of selected data provided at no charge. Data also available on magnetic tape.

Wyoming

Criminal Justice Information Section, 316 W. 22nd St., Cheyenne, WY 82002; (307) 777-7523--Publications and Services: Uniform Crime Annual Report; computer printouts of selected data provided at no charge.

State Labor Offices

* See also Careers and Workplace Chapter

Labor market information departments are an overlooked resource within state governments. These little-known offices can provide current, customized data such as:

- which cities have the highest concentration of restaurants or credit agencies;
- how many Hispanic males were living in Bridgeport, Connecticut in 1987;
- which zip codes have the fastest growing population of working women in managerial positions;
- the name, address and size of each new business or business expansion in a given state;
- which US counties offer the highest entry level salaries for market research analysts.

Two reasons for tapping state government labor offices for market and demographic data are that in most cases the information is free and less than one year old.

Source of Data

The primary function of each state labor information office is to collect data in conjunction with the federal government in order to produce employment, unemployment, occupational and wage information. The most interesting data sources, are state unemployment contribution forms filled out by every employer in the state. This form is filed quarterly revealing total wages and number of employees for companies by SIC code in each city and county.

In addition, each state also compiles data showing future manpower needs within the state. By studying labor trends, economic conditions and school enrollments, these agencies project the future supply and demand for up to 1,000 different occupations. Many offices also supplement their information with data from the US Bureau of Census as well as other state data collection agencies to provide additional studies and forecasts.

More Current Than Federal Data

If you are a user of the Census Bureau's *County Business Patterns,* you are aware that the latest information available is for 1984, and 1985 data will be out around July 1987. But, are you aware that right now you can obtain basically the same information from most states that was collected in the second quarter of 1986? This information is 18 months more current than Census data. If you are looking for personal income figures by state, county or city, the latest available data from the federal government dates back to 1984. Moreover, the majority of personal income is made up of wage data which is available from most states for June 1986.

Also remember that all data, such as state unemployment information, are passed on to the federal government for publication, but are available from state governments several weeks before being released from Washington.

State Data More Detailed, Cheaper and Accessible Than Federal Data

Unemployment rate data are released by the US Bureau of Labor Statistics for approximately 150 major cities. However, the state of Connecticut alone can provide unemployment data for 169 cities. If you are looking for salary by type of occupation, the Bureau of the Census covers about 400 occupations in their 1980 data. But state governments will cover up to one thousand occupations based on 1985 or even 1986 data.

Reagan Administration policies combined with the public's increased reliance on traditional federal data sources have caused many of major federal statistical agencies to increase prices and to decrease services. In contrast, using state labor information centers is like walking into virgin data territory. Most everything is still free from these offices, and state employees are eager to do a lot of free research for those who call. In a conversation I had with the labor information office in Ohio, the director recounted how a local bank requested demographic data for a few dozen zip codes in a three state area. Not only did the state office assemble this information but also gave it to the bank on diskettes...all for free.

Multiple Uses of Labor Market Data

State labor data provide an endless array of uses, but here are some of the primary applications.

1) Marketing:
The marketing information available from the states is overwhelming. The data cover both the consumer and industrial markets. It can be used for determining your current market size as well as identifying new or emerging marketing opportunities. For example, you can find:

- monthly employment and average wages by SIC code, by county,
- annual employment for up to 1,000 occupations, by county, by SIC code,
- which counties have the highest concentration of hairdressers making over $20,000 per year,
- how many bartenders are working in a given city,
- how many hotels with fewer than 100 employees operate in a given city,
- what are the fastest growing jobs or industries in any county or city,
- one year projections (1987) of demographic data for each city and county, or
- five to ten year projections of industries and occupations by city and county.

Many labor market information centers also offer special market studies to cover specific industries which may be important within the state. You can get free studies covering the hospital industry, ski industry, finance industry and many high tech related industries.

2) Company Information:

These offices can tell you how many companies in a given SIC code are located in any county or city. States also can provide the median salary and average starting salary for up to one thousand different jobs, and can even tell you how many people are employed in all these companies by type of job. Many states keep information on any company which is a newcomer to the state or undertaking major business expansion. And, most every state can give you the number of employees for any manufacturer in the state.

3) Business Location:

Whether you are establishing a new plant, a real estate business or fast food franchise, these offices can help you locate the best location with regards to labor availability, customer availability and competition. The state labor experts can furnish specifics on how many college graduates, typists or computer programmers with 3 years of experience are looking for work in any given area; or how many are unemployed and looking for work, or how many are working for other companies in the area and their salaries. You can discover what wages are being paid by your competitors in the area for these jobs. Some states volunteer to provide information on union activity in any area. Some states can give you an indication of the work ethic of potential employees. Work ethic can be quantified by showing the number of days off taken by specific employees in certain industries. And if your customers are going to be consumers or businesses in the area, these labor market specialists can share estimates on your potential clientele.

4) Employee Development:

If you are worried about the availability of skilled employees for the future growth of your business, these offices can forecast for you the exact number of people who will be available from school training programs and other employers. This can help you determine if your business will have to move to another location or begin an in-house training program to ensure a plentiful supply of trained labor.

5) Labor Negotiations:

You can find out what the average entry wage for a typist is in your area or what the average fringe benefit package looks like for businesses in your industry. What is the maximum amount of days off allowed for sick leave in your industry? How many companies in your industry offer paid dental care? Answers to these and other employee benefit questions can be useful leverage in negotiating employee benefit packages.

6) Affirmative Action, EEOC and Government Contracts:

Organizations which have to comply with EEOC and affirmative action criteria can get all the data necessary from these offices. Labor force data for any area can pinpoint how many women, Hispanics, etc., are in the labor force for various occupations. Such data can be compared with a company's current employee demographics. This information can be useful when seeking government contracts. Also, remember that many government contracts are set aside for those companies in high unemployment areas. This data, too, can be obtained from these offices to see if you qualify.

7) Economic Analysis:

If you are interested in any local area economic forecasting or economic monitoring, this is a ideal place to start. All of these offices have monthly and quarterly newsletters which plot economic health down to the city and county level. If your business is dependent on the economic conditions of a specific region, state, city or county, this approach is an easy way to keep your finger on the pulse of what is happening.

8) Careers and Job Search:

An important function of each of these offices is to provide career and job counseling information. If you are looking for a job, each office has access to a state database which identifies available job openings throughout the state. They project which jobs will be in demand in the next 10 to 20 years. And more importantly, the future supply is projected for these positions so that you can more easily spot important opportunities. Moreover, you can obtain the starting salaries and median wages for approximately a thousand occupations in hundreds of industries. Many states give out free books designed for job seekers, as well as information on how to participate in training programs and vocational education opportunities.

9) Computer Formats and Special Services:

You must remember that no two states operate in the same manner or generate identical data. Although many offer the same reports, some may break down the data into 2-digit SIC codes and others into 4-digit SIC codes. What you must never forget is that although one state may NOT provide the data in the format you need, this does not rule out the possibility when dealing with other states. A few states now have their data online and more are beginning to offer diskettes and computer tapes. But if a state labor office says it does not provide computer readable formats, you may be able to convince them to let you be the first. These offices all seem to be very flexible and not heavily encumbered in bureaucracy.

Be sure to investigate any special services which may be offered by the state. Some offer free sources on how to interpret and use labor data and others provide customized affirmative action reports.

State Labor Offices

Alabama

Department of Industrial Relations, Research & Statistics Division, 649 Monroe St., Montgomery, AL 36130, (205) 261-5461; Selected Publications: *Affirmative Action Data, Career Exploration Guide, Monthly Labor Market, Metro Area Occupational Trends to 1995, Occupational Supply/Demand Components, Alabama's High Technology Industries, Annual Average Labor Force, Area Trends in Employment and Unemployment, Youth in Alabama*; Computer Readable Formats: No; Custom Research: Limited amount available free.

Alaska

Department of Labor, Research and Analysis, P.O. Box 25501, Juneau, AK 99802, (907) 465-4500; Selected Publications: *Economic Trends, Fish Harvesting Employment, Planning Information, Population Projections, Occupational Information, Directory of Apprenticeships, Statistical Quarterly, Wage Rates*; Computer Readable Formats: No; Custom Research: Limited amount available free.

Arizona

Department of Economic Security, Research Administration, 1300 W. Washington St., Phoenix, AZ 85007, (602) 255-3871; Selected Publications: *Affirmative Action Planning Information, Annual Planning Information, Applying for Government Jobs, Arizona Economic Outlook, Arizona Labor Market Newsletter, Arizona Licensed Occupation Requirements, Arizona Occupational Employment Forecasts, Arizona Occupational Profiles, Career Decision Making, Careers Today-Electronics, Choosing a Vocational School, Employer Wage Survey, Employment Interview Guide, Finding a Job in the Wants Ads, Helpful Hints for Job Seekers, Job Search Tips for Women, Map of Major Employers, The Resume, Small Employer Wage Survey, Supply/Demand-Occupational Projections and Training Data, Summer Jobs For Students*; Computer Readable Formats: No; Custom Research: Most everything is free.

Arkansas

Employment Security Division, Research and Analysis Section, P.O. Box 2981, Little Rock, AR 72203, (501) 371-1541; Selected Publications: *Annual Planning Information, Annual Report of the Employment Security Division, Arkansas Labor Force Statistics, Covered Employment and Earnings, Affirmative Action Programs, Statistical Review, Current Employment Developments, Monthly Employment Trends, Monthly County Labor Market Information, AR Wage Survey, Construction Wage Rates in Arkansas, Directory of Licensed Occupations, Job Hunters Guide to AR, Occupational Trends, Staffing Patterns*; Computer Readable Formats: No;

Custom Research: Limited amount available free.

California

Employment Development Department, Employment Data & Research, 7000 Franklin St., #1100, Sacramento, CA 95828, (916) 427-4656; Selected Publications: *Annual Planning Information, Labor Market Quarterly, Labor Market Information for Affirmative Action Programs, Apprentice Information Guide, California Occupational Guides, Guide to Job Exploration, Health Careers Handbook, How to Use Labor Market Information for Career Decision Making, Occupational Outlook Handbook, Projections of Employment By Industry and Occupation*; Computer Readable Formats: Yes; Custom Research: Most everything is free.

Colorado

Department of Labor and Employment, Labor Market Information Section, 1330 Fox St., Denver, CO 80204, (303) 866-6326; Selected Publications: *Affirmative Action Packets, Annual Planning Information Report, Monthly Colorado Labor Force Review, Employment and Wages Quarterly, Occupational Employment Outlook 1985-1990, Job Bank Wage Listing, Occupational Employment in Selected Industries, Quarterly Occupational Supply/Demand Outlook*; Computer Readable Formats: No; Custom Research: Free on a limited basis.

Connecticut

Department of Labor, Office of Research and Information, 200 Folly Brook Blvd, Wethersfield, CT 06109, (203) 566-3472; Selected Publications: *Manpower Development and Planning Report, Annual Planning Information, The Occupational Outlook, New Manufacturing Firms, Occupations in Demand, Labor Market Review, Job Scope, Occupational Projections and Training Data*; Computer Readable Formats; No: Custom Research: Free.

Delaware

Labor Department, Occupational and Labor Market Information Office, University Office Plaza, Newark, DE 19714, (302) 368-6962; Selected Publications: *Annual Labor Force Report, Annual Labor Force Unemployment Statistics, Annual Number of Employers and Employers and Total Wages, Delaware Labor Supply and Demand: Occupational and Industrial Projections, Delaware Labor Market Trends Decade of the 80's, Delaware Labor Market 1985 in Brief, Delaware and Wilmington Labor Market Trends Quarterly*; Computer Readable Formats: Soon; Custom Research: Limited amount available free.

District of Columbia

Employment Services Department, Labor Market Information, Room 201, 500 C St., NW, Washington, DC 20001, (202) 639-1175; Selected Publications: *Annual Planning Information, Comparison of Tax Rates in Washington Metro Area, DC Directory of Volunteer Opportunities for Youth, Directory of 200 Major Employers, Occupational Employment in Selected Industries, Annual Population Estimates By Census Tract, Jobs and Occupations in 1990*; Computer Readable Formats: No; Custom Research: Charge for large projects, all others free.

Florida

Department of Labor and Employment Security, Division of Labor, Employment and Training, Bureau of Research and Information, 2574 Seagate Drive, Tallahassee, FL 32301, (904) 488-1048; Selected Publications: *Affirmative Action Statistical Packets, Florida Employment Statistics, Florida Industry and Occupational Employment 1995, Florida Occupational Employment in Hospitals, Labor Force Summary, Labor Market Trends, Occupational Employment in Federal Government, Occupations Employment in the Finance, Insurance and Real Estate Industry, Occupational Employment in the Services Industry, Occupational Wage Surveys*; Computer Readable Formats: No; Custom Research: Limited amount available free.

Georgia

Department of Labor, Labor Information Systems, 254 Washington St., SW, Atlanta, GA 30334, (404) 656-3177; Selected Publications: *Area Labor Profiles, Civilian Labor Force Estimates, GA Directory of Labor Market Information, GA Employment and Earnings, GA Employment and Wages, GA Labor Market Trends, GA Occupational Employment, Civilian Labor Force Estimates, Data on Labor Availability, Data on Occupational Supply and Demand, Earnings by Industry and Area, Labor Force Characteristics, Data on Employment Service Applicants and Openings*; Computer Readable Formats: No; Custom Research: Charge for Large projects, all others free.

Hawaii

Labor Market and Employment Services Branch, Labor & Industrial Relations Dept., 830 Punchbowl St., Honolulu, HI 96813, (808) 548-6999; Selected Publications: *Study of Displaced Sugar Workers, Demand Occupations, Employment Outlook for Industries and Occupations, Job Hunters's Guide, Labor Force Data, Affirmative Action Programs, Licensed Occupations, Occupational Employment Statistics, Occupational Illness and Injuries*; Computer Readable Formats: No; Custom Research: Free.

Idaho

Department of Employment, Research and Analysis Bureau, 317 Main St., Bosie, ID 83735, (208) 334-2755; Selected Publications: *Affirmative Action Statistics, Annual Planning Information Report, Area Employment Newsletter, Census Profiles of Idaho Cities and Counties, Employment and Wages by Industry in Idaho,*

County Economic Profiles, Idaho Economic Forecast, Idaho Opportunities, Local Area Personal Income; Computer Readable Formats: No; Custom Research: Most everything is free.

Illinois

Employment Security Bureau, Research and Analysis, 910 South Michigan, 14th Fl., Chicago, IL 60605, (312) 793-2316; Selected Publications: *Labor Market Review, Labor Market Trends, Affirmative Action Information, Occupational Employment Statistics, Occupational Projections, Wage Survey, Where Workers Work in Chicago, Commuting Patterns in Illinois, Illinois Employment*; Computer Readable Formats: Yes; Custom Research: Limited amount available free.

Indiana

Employment Security Division, Labor Market Information, 10 N. Senate Ave., Indianapolis, IN 46204, (317) 232-7701; Selected Publications: *Monthly Labor Market Letter, Monthly Establishment Summary, Monthly County Employment Patterns, Non-MSA Establishment Employment, Labor Force Statistics, Covered Employment and Payrolls, Affirmative Action Information Handbooks, Regional Economic Profiles, Occupational Employment Projections 1990, Occupational Wage Surveys, Occupations In Demand, Hours and Earnings of Production Workers*; Computer Readable Formats: No; Custom Research: Limited amount available free.

Iowa

Department of Employment Services, Labor Market Information Unit, 1000 E. Grand Ave., Des Moines, IA 50319, (515) 281-8182; Selected Publications: *Labor Force Employment and Unemployment Information, Labor Market Information for Service Delivery Areas, Wage Surveys, Labor Market Information for Affirmative Action Programs, Occupational Employment Statistics, Industry/Occupational Projections, Iowa Labor Supply/Demand Analysis, Career Guides, Hours and Earning for Production Workers, Employment and Wage Data by Industry, Job Insurance Benefits*; Computer Readable Formats: Yes; Custom Research: Free.

Kansas

Department of Human Resources, Division of Employment & Training, Research & Analysis Section, 401 Topeka Ave., Topeka, KS 66603, (913) 296-5058; Selected Publications: *Occupational Staffing Patterns, Financing Job Insurance, Characteristics of Exhaustees, Kansas Business Births and Deaths, Kansas Job Guides, Annual Planning Information, Kansas Wage Survey, Average Wage by Industry, Affirmative Action Packet, Annual Report to Vocational Education, Labor Market Review, Report on Employment-Hours and Earnings, Labor Force Estimates, Kansas Job Insurance Claims, Employment by Area and Industry, Characteristics of Unemployment by County, Wage Surveys*; Computer Readable Formats: No; Custom Research: Charge for large projects, all others free.

Kentucky

Department of Employment Services, Research & Statistics, CHR Bldg 2W, Frankfort, KY 40621, (502) 564-7976; Selected Publications: *Non-Agricultural Wage and Salary Employment, Kentucky Labor Market Newsletter, Estimate of Production Workers and Average Hours and Earnings, Labor Force Estimates, Occupational Outlook, Career Outlook and Opportunities, Occupational Profiles, Labor Area Summary, Labor Area Profile, Annual Planning Information, Affirmative Action, Labor Supply Estimates, Monthly Report of Workers Laid Off as a Result of Imports, Characteristics of Unemployed, Average Covered Monthly Workers in Manufacturing by Industry Division and County, Total Wages by Industrial Division and County, Average Weekly Wages by Industrial Division and County*; Computer Readable Formats: No; Custom Research: Limited amount available free.

Louisiana

Department of Employment Security, Research and Statistics Unit, P.O. 44094, Baton Rouge, LA 70804, (504) 342-3141; Selected Publications: *Annual Employment and Wages, Monthly Labor Market Information, Manpower for Affirmative Action, Annual Planning Report, Occupational Employment Statistics, Average Weekly Wage, LA Occupational Injuries and Illnesses*; Computer Readable Formats: Limited; Custom Research: Limited amount available free.

Maine

Bureau of Employment Security, Division of Economic Analysis, 20 Union St., Augusta, ME 04330, (207) 289-2271; Selected Publications: *Labor Market Digest Monthly, Employment Situation, The Month in Brief, Employment Situation Summary, Maine Hospital Wage Survey, Maine Occupational Staffing Patterns in Hospitals-Government-Manufacturing-Nonmanufacturing-Trade, Careers In Maine Woods*; Computer Readable Formats: Yes; Custom Research: Charge for larger projects, all others free.

Maryland

Department of Human Resources, Research and Analysis, Employment and Training, 1100 N. Eutaw St., Baltimore, MD 21201, (301) 383-5007; .PA Selected Publications: *Affirmative Action Data, Career Decision Making, Civilian Labor Force Employment and Unemployment by Place of Residence, Claims Processed for Unemployment Insurance Benefits, Computer-Health-Food Service-High Technology Careers in Maryland, Current Employment Statistics, Labor Market Dimensions, Employment and Payrolls Covered by the Unemployment Insurance Law of Maryland, Employment and Unemployment Watch, Maryland Local Area*

Economics, Demographics and Statistics

Labor Market Analysis, Maryland Occupational Staffing Patterns, Maryland Rural Manpower Report, Occupational Wage Information, Wage Information Directory, Your Job Search-Four Steps to Success; Special Services: Recorded messages providing information on topics ranging from How To Get A Job to the latest employment statistics. Computer Readable Formats: No. Customer Research: Limited amount available free.

Massachusetts

Division of Employment Security, Job Market Research, Charles F. Hurley Building, Boston, MA 02114, (617) 727-6531; Selected Publications: *Planning Data: Massachusetts and Associated SMA's, Employment and Wages, Massachusetts Employment Review, Massachusetts Profiles, Occupational Profiles of Manufacturing Industries, Structure of Massachusetts Job Market, High Technology in Massachusetts, Employment in the Mini-Computer Industry, Health Services Industry Employment, Biomedical-Biotechnical Employment, Business Support Services Employment, Scientific Instruments Industries, Tourism in Berkshire County, Your First Job, Job Search Resources, New England Economic Indicators;* Computer Readable Formats: No; Custom Research; Free.

Michigan

Employment Security Commission, Bureau of Research and Statistics, 7310 Woodward Ave., Detroit, MI 48202, (313) 876-5439; Selected Publications: *Affirmative Action Information Report, Annual Planning Information, Claims Counter, Covered Employment Statistics, Monthly Labor Market Review, Motor Vehicles and Related Industries, Occupations in Education, Michigan Manufacturing Industries, Occupational Wage Information, Quarterly Job Openings Report;* Computer Readable Formats: Limited; Custom Research: Limited amount available free.

Minnesota

Department of Jobs and Training, Research Office, 390 North Robert St., St. Paul MN 55101, (612) 296-8716; Selected Publications: *Monthly Review of Labor and Economic Conditions, Minnesota Employment Outlook to 1990, Important MN Occupations by Industry, MN Hospitals and Nursing Homes Salary Survey, MN Wage Data By Industry and Size of Firm, Employment and Wage Data By County;* Computer Readable Format: Soon; Custom Research: Charge for large projects, all others free.

Mississippi

Employment Security Commission, Labor Market Information Department, 1520 West Capitol St., Jackson, MS 39215, (601) 961-7424; Selected .PA Publications: *Annual Labor Force Averages, Annual Report, Employment and Job Openings 1995, Farm Income and Expenditures, Affirmative Action Programs, Monthly Labor Market Data, Labor Market Trends, Mississippi's Business Population, Mississippi Fringe Benefit Survey, Mississippi High Technology in Prospective, Occupational Employment and Job Openings by Unit of Analysis, Personal Income by Major Sources, Quarterly Labor Market Summary, Transfer Payments by Major Sources;* Computer Readable Formats: Yes; Customer Research: Limited amount available free.

Missouri

Division of Employment Security, Research & Analysis, P.O. Box 59, Jefferson City, MO 65104, (314) 751-3602; Selected Publications: *Monthly Labor Area Trends, Labor Market Information for Affirmative Action Programs, Wages Paid in Selected Occupations, Employment Outlook to 1990;* Computer Readable Formats: Soon; Custom Research: Free.

Montana

Department of Labor and Industry, Research & Analysis Bureau, P.O. Box 1728, Helena, MT 59624, (406) 444-2430; Selected Publications: *Quarterly Employment and Labor Force, Monthly Statistics in Brief, Annual Planning Information, Women in the 80's, Employment Wages and Contributions, Montana Supply and Demand Report, Wage Survey, Montana Apprenticeable Occupations, Industry/Occupation Projections, A Plant Closure Study;* Computer Readable Formats: No; Custom Research: Limited Amount available free.

Nebraska

Department of Labor, Labor Market Information, 550 South 16th St., Lincoln, NE 68505, (402) 475-8451; Selected Publications: *Quarterly Employment and Wages, Monthly Labor Area Summary, Women in Numbers, Occupational Employment Statistics by Industry, Monthly Labor Force, Affirmative Action, Employment and Earnings Report, Survey of Average Hourly Wage Rates, Occupational Newsletter, Nebraska Job Prospects;* Computer Readable Formats: No; Custom Research: Limited amount available for free.

Nevada

Employment Security Department, Employment Security Research Section, 500 E Third St., Carson City, NV 89713, (702) 885-4550; Selected Publications: *Quarterly Economic Update, Nevada Wage Survey, Nevada Affirmative Action, Occupational Projections, Licensed Occupations, Occupational Training Directory, High Profile Occupations, Job Finding Techniques;* Computer Readable Formats: Limited; Custom Research: Limited amount available free.

New Jersey

Labor Department, Labor Market Information Office, John Fitch Plaza CN110, Trenton, NJ 08625, (609) 292-7376; Selected Publications: *Regional Labor Market Reviews, Regional Labor Market Newsletters, .PA Compendium of New Jersey Wage Surveys, Employment and Economy Newsletter, Employment Trends, Economic Indicators Monthly;* Computer Readable Formats: No; Custom Research: Limited amount available free.

New Hampshire

Employment Security Department, Economic Analysis and Reports, 32 South Main St., Concord, NH 03301, (603) 224-3311; Selected Publications: *Annual Planning Information, Annual Planning Information SMA's, Annual Planning Information for Hillsboro County, Community Patterns NH, Economic Conditions, Employment and Wages by County, Employment and Wages SMA's, Employment and Wages by Planning Region, Fact Book: Cities and Towns, Firms By Size, Local Area Unemployment Statistics, NH Affirmative Action Data, NH Labor Supply and Demand, NH Occupational Outlook 1995, Wages Offered for Job Openings;* Computer Readable Formats: Soon; Custom Research: Free.

New Mexico

Department of Employment Security, Economic Research and Analysis, P.O. Box 1928, Albuquerque, NM 87103, (505) 841-8645; Selected Publications: *Monthly Labor Market Review, Labor Force Employment and Unemployment, Nonagricultural Wage and Salary Employment, Facts and Figures about New Mexico, Hours and Earnings Estimates, Albuquerque Small Employer Wage Survey, Occupational Manpower Needs to 1990, Jobs to 1990, Area Job Market Flyers, How To Look For A Job, Women Workers in New Mexico, Large Employers in New Mexico by County;* Computer Readable Formats: Limited; Customer Research: Limited amount available for free.

New York

Department of Labor, Division of Research & Statistics, State Office Bg. Campus #12, Albany, NY 12240, (518) 457-3800; Selected Publications: *Affirmative Action Data, Agricultural Employment Bulletin, Annual Labor Area Report, Calendar of Collective Bargaining, Labor Force by Occupation and Selected Demographic Groups, Commutation Patterns for Counties and SMA's, Consumer Price Index for Selected Areas and Population Groups, County Profiles: Socio-Economic Characteristics, Current Population Survey Data, Directory of Employee Organizations in New York State, Earnings and Hours in Selected Industries, Employment Trends, High Technology Industries in New York State, Hiring Specifications, Characteristics of Individuals on Unemployment by Zip Code, Occupational Brief, Occupational Projections, Occupations in High Technology Industries, Planning Information for Vocational Education, Statistics on Work Stoppages;* Computer Readable Formats: Soon; Custom Research: Charge for large projects, all others free.

North Carolina

Employment Security Commission, Labor Market Information Division, P.O. Box 25903, Raleigh, NC 27611, (919) 733-2936; Selected Publications: *Monthly Claimsletter, Announced New and Expanding Manufacturing Firms, NC Preliminary Civilian Labor Force Estimates, .PAL State and Local Labor Summaries, Labor Market Newsletter, Active Job Applicants by County, NC Insured Employment and Wage Payments Quarterly, Registered Applicants and Job Openings, Employment Projections for SMSA's and Planning Regions, Follow-Up Survey of NC High School Graduates by County, Manpower Information for Affirmative Action Programs, North Carolina Employment Projects, NC Labor Force Estimates by County, Area, and State, Wage Rates in Selected Occupations, Fringe Benefit Practices in Manufacturing Industries;* Computer Readable Formats: No; Custom Research: Limited amount available free.

North Dakota

Job Service, Research and Statistics, P.O. Box 1537, Bismarck, ND 58502, (701) 224-3048; Selected Publications: *Monthly Labor Market Advisor, Occupations Wage Surveys and Benefits for Major Cities, Occupational Projections to 1990, Employment Surveys by Major City, Annual Planning Report;* Computer Readable Formats: No; Custom Research: Charge for large amounts, all others free.

Ohio

Bureau of Employment Services, Labor Market Information Division, 145 South Front St., Columbus, OH 43216, (614) 466-8806; Selected Publications: *Monthly Labor Market Review, County Labor Force Reports, Labor Force Estimates, Metropolitan Profile, Occupational Projections 1995, Ohio Occupational Almanac, Summary of Unemployment Compensation Activities, Trends in Rate in Covered Unemployment, Composition of Unemployment Benefits and Recipients, Composition of Job Seekers, Composition of Job Placements, Summary of Ohio Worker Training Program Activities;* Computer Readable Formats: Yes; Custom Research: Charge for large projects, all others free.

Oklahoma

Oklahoma Employment Security Commission, Economic Analysis, 2401 N. Lincoln Blvd., Oklahoma City, OK 73105, (405) 557-7104; Selected Publications: *Manpower Information for Affirmative Action, Annual Report to the Governor, Oklahoma Population Reports, Handbook of Employment Statistics, County Employment and Wage Data, Labor Market Reviews Newsletter, Occupational Wage Surveys, OK Monthly Economic Newsletter;* Computer Readable Formats: Yes; Custom Research: Charge for large projects, all other free.

Oregon

Employment Division, Research and Statistics, 875 Union NE, Salem, OR 97311,

(503) 378-8656; Selected Publications: *Affirmative Action Programs, Agricultural Employment, Average Weekly Earnings-Hours, Business and Employment Outlook, Monthly Local Labor Trends, Occupational Program Planning System Oregon Industrial Outlook, Oregon Wage Information*; Computer Readable Formats: No; Custom Research: Charge for large projects, all others free.

Pennsylvania

Department of Labor & Industry, Research & Statistics Division, 7th & Foster Sts., Harrisburg, PA 17121, (717) 787-2114; Selected Publications: *Civilian Work Force Data by Labor Market Area of Residence, Annual Average Labor Force Data, Civilian Labor Force Series by Labor Market Area, PA Labor Market Areas Ranked on Basis of Rate of Unemployment, PA Unemployment Fact Sheet, Directory of Occupational Wage Information, Occupational Trends and Outlook for Total Civilian Employment, Industry Trends and Outlook 1995, Women in the Labor Force, Youth in the Labor Force, Occupations Employment in Hospital Finance-Insurance-Real Estate-Mining-Construction-Service Industries, Annual Planning Information, Affirmative Action Report, Labor Market Job Guides, Directory of Licensed Occupational Information Systems, Labor Demand-Supply Relationships, Career Guide, Labor Market Letters, PA Employment and Earnings, Vocational Preparation Job Characteristics and Outlook, PA's Microcomputer Occupational Information System, Hours and Earnings, Current Trends in Employment and Wages in PA Industries*; Computer Readable Formats: Yes; Custom Research: Charge for large projects, all others free.

Rhode Island

Department of Employment Security, Research and Statistics, 24 Mason St., Providence, RI 02903, (401) 277-3700; Selected Publications: *RI Employment Newsletter, Quarterly Labor Supply and Demand Report, Employment and Wages by City and Industry, Annual Planning Information, Manpower Information for Affirmative Action Programs, Employment In RI Hospitals, Job Openings by 9 Digit DOT Codes, Characteristics of Active Job Applicants*; Computer Readable Format: No; Custom Research: Free.

South Carolina

Employment Security Commission, Labor Market Information Division, P.O. Box 995, Columbia, SC 29202, (803) 737-2660; Selected Publications: *SC Job Search Assistance Guide, Labor Market Review, Employment Trends, Occupational Projections 1990, Labor Force in Industry, Employment and Wages in SC*; Computer Readable Formats: Limited; Custom Research: Charge for large projects, all others free.

South Dakota

Department of Labor, Labor Market Information Center, 700 Illinois North, Pierre, SD 57501, (605) 622-2314; Selected Publications: *Labor Bulletin, Occupational Wage Information, Occupational Outlook Handbook, Employment and Earnings, Affirmative Action Package, Statewide Job Listings*; Computer Readable Formats: Yes; Custom Research: Limited amount available free.

Tennessee

Department of Employment Security, Research and Statistics Division, 519 Cordell Hull Bldg., Nashville, TN 37219, (615) 741-3639; Selected Publications: *Monthly Available Labor, Monthly Labor Force Summary, Annual Planning Information, Affirmative Action Programs, Commuting Patterns, Occupational Information System, Tennessee Employment Projections 1990, Tennessee Youth Report, Veterans in Tennessee, Women in the Labor Force, Tennessee High School Graduates*; Computer Readable Formats: Limited; Custom Research: Limited amount available free.

Texas

Texas Employment Commission, Economic Research & Analysis Dept., TEC Building, Austin, TX 78778, (512) 463-2616; Selected Publications: *Civilian Work Force Estimates, Current Population Survey, Nonagricultural Wage and Salary Employment Estimates, Average Hours and Earnings Data, Employment and Wages by Industry and County, Affirmative Action Packets, Characteristics of the Unemployed, Agricultural Employment Estimates, Special Reports on Women, Youth and Veterans, Regional Reports, Labor Demand Projects by 1990, Occupational Employment Statistics*; Computer Readable Formats: Limited; Custom Research: Charge for large projects, all others free.

Utah

Utah Department of Employment Security, Labor Market Information Services, P.O. Box 11249, Salt Lake City, UT 84147, (801) 533-2293; Selected Publications: *Helpful Hints for Job Seekers, Licensed Occupations in Utah, Monthly Utah Labor Market Report, Utah's Service Economy, Utah Directory of Business and Industry, Women in Utah Labor Force*; Computer Readable Formats: On a limited basis. Custom Research: Free.

Vermont

Department of Employment and Training, Labor Market Information, P.O. Box 488, Montpelier, VT 05602, (802) 229-0311; Selected Publications: *Woman's Guide to Apprenticeship, National Apprenticeship Program, Occupations in Demand, Directory of Manufacturers, Labor Market Area Bulletins, Occupational Staffing Patterns, Profile of Active Applicants, Vermont Labor Force, Wage and Fringe Benefit Survey*; Computer Readable Formats: No; Custom Research: Free.

Virginia

Virginia Employment Commission, Economic Information Services Division, P.O. Box 1358, Richmond, VA 23211, (804) 786-8222; Selected Publications: *Labor Force by Sex and Minority Status, Commuting Patterns, Data on Public Schools, Economic Assumptions for the US and VA, Economically Disadvantaged Data, Employment and Training Indicators, Employment and Wages in Establishments, Employment and Wages in VA, Monthly Employment Hours and Earnings, Monthly Labor Force Estimates, Monthly Labor Market Trends, Licensed Occupations in VA, List of Employers By Size, Occupations in Virginia, Size Codes:Number of Employers by Size Groups, Social Indicators for Planning and Evaluations, Survey of Manufacturing, State and County Veteran Population, 1990 State Industry and Occupational Projections, Trends in Employment-Hours and Earnings, Quarterly Virginia Economic Indicators, Virginia Business Resource Directory, VA Job Service Data.*

Washington

Employment Security Group, Labor Market and Economic Analysis Branch, 212 Maple Park LMEA, Olympia, WA 98504, (206) 438-4804; Selected Publications: *Affirmative Action Information, Annual Demographic Information, Area Wage Survey, Employment and Payrolls in Washington, Occupational Profiles and Projections, Labor Market Monthly*; Computer Readable Formats: Some; Custom Research: Large projects are charged on a contract basis.

West Virginia

Employment Security Department, Labor and Economic Research, 120 California Ave., Charleston, WV 25305, (304) 348-2660; Selected Publications: *Annual Planning Information for 4 Metropolitan Areas, West Virginia Women in the Labor Force, Labor Market Trends, Current Conditions of the WV Natural Gas Industry, Occupational Employment in the Finance, Insurance and Real Estate Industries, WV Economic Summary, Licensed Occupations in West Virginia*; Computer Readable Formats: No. Custom Research: Limited amount available free.

Wisconsin

Department of Industry, Labor and Human Relations, Bureau of Labor Market Information, P.O. Box 7944, Madison, WI 53707, (608) 266-2439; Selected Publications: *Wisconsin Statistics-A Directory of Sources, Monthly Employment Newsletter, Monthly Wisconsin Economic Indicators, Wisconsin Industry Projections to 1990, County Commuting Patterns, Program Planning Information for Wisconsin, Wage Survey of 410 Occupations for SMA's*; Computer Readable Formats: Some; Custom Research: Charge for large projects, all others free.

Wyoming

Employment Employment Security Commission, Research & Analysis, P.O. Box 2760, Casper, WY 82602, (307) 235-3642; Selected Publications: *Occupational Employment Statistics: Manufacturing and Hospitals, Occupational Employment Statistics, Annual Planning Report, Wyoming's Annual Planning Report, Wyoming's Covered Employment and Wage Data, Labor Force Trends, Applicants and Job Openings in Wyoming, Affirmative Action Package*; Computer Readable Format: No; Custom Research: Limited amount available.

State Health Statistics

* See also Health and Medicine Chapter

Vital And Infectious Disease Statistics

The last few years have witnessed explosive growth in products and services aimed at the health-conscious baby-boomers and their aging parents. In order to market products and services, many business use state health statistics and records. State health data are used to great success by insurance companies, individual medical providers and doctor groups, private health care clinics and rehabilitative service centers, diet and natural food producers, pharmaceutical and cosmetic companies, and even publishers.

A state's health care registration system is often the best place to start researching specific health data for an entire state's population. In addition each, state makes available its annual health report in a number of formats.

Some insurance companies use this information to steer away from areas where cancer rates are too high or to zero-in on areas where rates are lower than the national norm. Along this same line, a new doctor might search for an area where there is a greater demand for his or her specific medical expertise.

Exercise equipment manufacturers can use the data to target upscale, "yuppie" markets for their sales campaigns -- or identify clusters of older hospitals with on-site physical therapy facilities that might need new equipment. Other examples include:

- how many people have cancer, diabetes, or high blood pressure by zip code
- hospitals with CAT scans and other sophisticated medical equipment
- vaccination records to find which homes have babies, preschoolers, grade schoolers, etc.
- names, addresses and neighborhoods with the most senior citizens
- names and addresses of ambulatory care facilities and state-funded birth control/venereal disease counseling clinics
- neighborhoods not immediately serviced by existing drug stores

Data are collected and used to assess the current status of health and health care in a state and to help state officials better anticipate future health care needs and resources. In addition, the information provides baseline data for medical research, charts population shifts, and identifies specific groups, communities, neighborhoods, etc. for special state and federal health programs.

Annual reports, available from state vital statistics departments, contain information on births, deaths, marriages and divorces, with narrative and graphic highlights of emerging demographic and health issue trends.

Annual reports from a state's office of epidemiology contain specific data on the incidence of notifiable communicable diseases and related information reported by area physicians, hospitals and health clinics.

Computer printouts of selected data provide the most current health and health care information in detail, much of which does not make it into a state's annual reports. Data can be sorted and printed to assist individuals and businesses with statistical research projects. Most states are staffed with experts to help with individual research requests.

All states but Alaska, Iowa, Maine, Nebraska, and South Dakota provide computer printouts of selected data. The following states provide information on magnetic tape of diskette for a fee: Arizona, California, Connecticut, Georgia, Illinois, Indiana, Maryland, New York, Texas, Utah, Washington, and Wyoming.

Offices For Vital And Infectious Disease Statistics

Alabama
Department of Health, Bureau of Vital Statistics, 434 Monroe St., Room 204, Montgomery, AL 36130, (205) 261-5033.--Publications: *Annual Report*; Services: computer printout of selected data.

Division of Disease Control, Epidemiology Division, Department of Health, 434 Monroe St., Montgomery, AL 36130, (205) 261-2650.-- Publications: *Annual Report*; Services: computer printout of selected data.

Alaska
State Department of Health, Division of Public Health, P.O. Box H-06, Juneau, AK 99881, (907) 465-3090.--Publications: *Annual Report*.

State Department of Health, Office of Epidemiology, P.O. Box 240249, Anchorage, AK 99524, (907) 561-4406.--Publications: *Annual Report*.

Arizona
Department of Health Services, Office of Planning, 1740 West Adams St., Phoenix, AZ 8500, (602) 255-1216.--Publications: *Abortion Surveillance Report, Accidental Deaths in Arizona, Health Status and Vital Statistics*; Services: will provide aggregate data on computer printout or tape.

Department of Health Services, Office of Infectious Diseases, Epidemiology, 3008 N. 3rd St., Phoenix, AZ 85012, (602) 230-5927.-- Publications: *Communicable Diseases in Arizona*; Services: computer printout of selected data.

Arkansas
Department of Health, Office of Vital Statistics, State Health Building, 4815 W. Markham, Little Rock, AR 72205, (501) 661-2371.-- Publications: *Annual Report*; Services: computer printouts available for certain items for a processing fee.

Department of Health, Epidemiology Program, Division of Health Maintenance, 4815 W. Markham, Little Rock, AR 72205, (501) 661-2264.-- Publications: *Annual Report*; Services: computer printout of selected data.

California
Department of Health Services, Division of Health Statistics, 714 P. St., Sacramento, CA 95814, (916) 445-1010.-- Publications: *Vital Statistics of California* ($20.00), *General Fertility Rates and Age-Specific Live Births by Age of Mother* ($3.50), *Age-Specific Death Rates and Mortality Indexes for California Counties* (free), *Five Leading Causes of Death by Sex and Age* ($2.50), *Suicides in California* (3.50), *Multiples Causes of Death* ($2.50), *California's Nonlicensed Marriages -- A First Look at Their Characteristics* ($3.50), *Birth, Fetal Death, and Death Certificate Data Quality Study* ($3.50), *Health Practices Among California Adults* (3.50), *California Occupational*

Mortality ($20.00); Services: computer printouts, magnetic tapes and diskettes for a fee.

Department of Health Services, Epidemiological Studies and Surveillance Section, 2151 Berkeley Way, Berkeley, CA, 94704, (415) 540-2518.-- Publications: weekly and monthly reports issued; Services: none at this time.

Colorado

Department of Health, 4210 East 11th Ave., Denver, CO 80220, (303) 331-4875.-- Publications: *Colorado Vital Statistics*; Services: computer printout of extracted data. Minimum charge $25.00.

Department of Health, Division of Disease Control & Environmental Epidemiology, 4210 East 11th Ave., Denver, CO 80220, (303) 331-8330.--Publications: *Colorado Disease Bulletin, Annual Report*; Services: computer printout of selected data.

Connecticut

Department of Health Services, Division of Health Surveillance and Planning, 150 Washington St., Hartford, CT 06106, (203) 566-1115.--Publications: *Annual Report*; Services: computer printouts and machine readable forms for a fee.

Department of Health Services, Epidemiology Program, 150 Washington St., Hartford, CT 06106, (203) 566-5058.--Publications: various statistical reports; Services: computer printouts from 1987 data and 1988 as it becomes available.

Delaware

Department of Health and Social Services, Office of Vital Statistics, P.O. Box 637, Dover, DE 19903, (302) 736-4721.--Publications: *Annual Report* to become available with 1988 data; Services: computer printout of selected data through the Center for Health Statistics.

Bureau of Disease Prevention, Division of Public Health, P.O. 637, Dover, DE 19903, (302) 736-5617.--Publications: *Monthly Surveillance Report*; Services: computer printout of data can be generated.

District of Columbia

Department of Human Services, Research and Statistics Division, 425 I St. N. W., Washington, DC 20001, (202) 727-0707.--Publications: *Annual Report*; Services: computer printout of selected data tables.

Preventive Health Services Administration, 1875 Connecticut Ave. N.W., Washington, DC 20009, (202) 673-6756.--Publications: quarterly reports issued by individual offices; Services: computer printouts of selected data.

Florida

Department of Health and Rehabilitative Services, Vital Statistics Services, 1217 Pearl St., Jacksonville, FL 32231, (904) 359-6963.--Publications: *Florida Vital Statistics, Vital News and Quarterly Vital Statistics Report, Florida Accidental Death Statistics, Florida Trends in Chronic Disease Mortality*; Services: data recently computerized, printouts available in the future.

Department of Health and Rehabilitative Services, 1317 Winewood Blvd. Tallahassee, FL 32399, (904) 488-2905. -Publications: *Quarterly Report, Florida Morbidity Statistics*. Services: computer printouts of selected data. Magnetic tapes with special request.

Georgia

Department of Human Resources, Division on Public Health, Administrative Services, Vital Statistics, 878 Peachtree St., N.E., Atlanta, GA 30309, (404) 894-6482, (404) 894-6482.--Publications: *Annual Report*; Services: computer printouts of selected data $25.00 minimum, magnetic tapes $50.00 minimum.

Department of Human Resources, Division of Public Health, Epidemiology Department, 878 Peachtree St. N.E., Atlanta, GA 30309, (404) 894-6531.--Publications: *Communicable Disease Morbidity Annual Report, Annual Report*, Services: computer printouts on certain selected statistics.

Hawaii

Department of Health, Research and Statistics, Kinau Hale Building, 1250 Punchbowl St., Honolulu, HI 96801, (808) 548-6454.-- Publications: *Annual Report*; Services: computer printouts of selected data.

Department of Health, Epidemiology Branch, Kinau Hale Building, 1250 Punchbowl St., Honolulu, HI 96801, (808) 548-5986.--Publications: *Annual Report*; Services: data recently computerized, printouts of certain data available.

Idaho

Department of Health and Welfare, Bureau of Vital Statistics, Statehouse, Boise, ID 83720, (208) 334-5976.--Publications: *Annual Report*; Services: computer printouts of selected data.

Department of Health and Welfare, Bureau of Preventive Medicine, Statehouse, Boise, ID 83720, (208) 334-5930.--Publications: *Biweekly Disease Surveillance Report, Annual Report*; Services: new software being piloted, computer printouts will be available.

Illinois

Department of Public Health, Department of Vital Records, Division of Data Processing, 525 W. Jefferson, Springfield, IL 62761, (217) 782-2049.--Publications: *Annual Report*; Services: computer printouts of selected data, magnetic tapes of birth/death data for a fee.

Department of Public Health, Division of Infectious Diseases, 525 W. Jefferson, Springfield, IL 62761, (217) 785-7165 --Publications: no published reports; Services: computer printouts available.

Indiana

State Board of Health, Division of Public Health Statistics, 1330 West Michigan St., P.O. Box 1964, Indianapolis, IN 46206, (317) 633-0276.--Publications: *Vital Statistics Summary, Indiana Abortion Report, Indiana Health Profile, Indiana County Population Estimates, Indiana Population Changes*; Services: computer printouts and tapes available for a fee.

State Board of Health, Disease Intervention, 1330 West Michigan St., P.O. Box 1964, Indianapolis, IN 46206, (317) 633-8414.--Publications: *Annual Report*; Services: computer printouts if data exists.

Iowa

Department of Public Health, Statistic Services, Lucas State Office Building, Des Moines, IA 50319, (515) 281-4945.--Publications: *Annual Report*; Services: only yearly data tables. No computer printouts.

Department of Public Health, Epidemiology Section, Lucas State Office Building, Des Moines, IA 50319, (515) 281-5424.--Publications: *Annual Report*; Services: data computerized as of 1987. Computer printouts for last year's data only.

Kansas

Department of Health and Environment, Office of Communication Services, Forbes Field, Topeka, KS 66620, (919) 296-1414.--Publications: *Annual Report*; Services: computer printouts of selected data.

Department of Health and Environment, Bureau of Epidemiology, Suite 605, Mills Building, 109 S.W. 9th St., Topeka, KS 66612, (919) 296-5586 --Publications: *Annual Report*; Services: data in the process of being computerized, printouts not available at this time.

Kentucky

Cabinet for Human Resources, Health Data Branch, 275 East Main St., Frankfort, KY 40621, (502) 564-2757.--Publications: monthly report, year-end summary table; Services: computer printouts of selected data.

Cabinet for Human Resources, Division of Epidemiology, 275 East Main St., Frankfort, KY 40621, (502) 564-3418.--Publications: monthly and year end summary reports; Services: computer printouts of selected data.

Louisiana

Department of Health and Human Resources, Public Health Statistics, P.O. Box 60630, New Orleans, LA 70821, (504) 568-5458.--Publications: *Annual Report*; Services; computer printouts if data is complete (not all data computerized).

Department of Health and Human Resources, Office of Epidemiology, P.O. Box 60630, New Orleans, LA 70821, (504) 568-5005.--Publications: *Annual Report*; Services: computer printout of 87 data only.

Maine

Bureau of Health, Vital Statistics, 222 State St., Augusta, ME 04333, (207) 289-3184.--Publications: *Annual Report* ($7.00); Services: no computer printouts available.

Economics, Demographics and Statistics

Bureau of Health, Division of Disease Control, 157 Capitol St., Augusta, ME 04333, (207) 289-3591.--Publications: weekly report; Services: new computer system being installed, printouts not available at this time.

Maryland
Department of Health and Mental Hygiene, Center for Health Statistics, 201 West Preston St., Baltimore, MD 21201, (301) 225-5974.--Publications: *Vital Statistics Preliminary Report*; Services: computer printouts of selected data, magnetic tape requests must be cleared through the Chief, Vital Statistics.

Department of Health and Mental Hygiene, Communicable Diseases Surveillance, 201 West Preston St., Baltimore, MD 21201, (301) 225-6712.--Publications: *Annual Report*; Services: computer printouts depends on the type of information requested.

Massachusetts
Department of Public Health, Division of Health Statistics and Research, 153 Tremont, 5th Floor, Boston, MA 02111, (617) 727-0752.--Publications: *Annual Report*; Services: computer printouts of selected data.

Department of Public Health, Epidemiology Program, 305 South St., Boston, MA 02130, (617) 522-3700.--Publications: *Annual Report*; Services: computer printouts of selected data.

Michigan
Department of Public Health, Office of State Registrar, Center for Health Statistics, Statistical Services Section, P.O. Box 30035, Lansing, MI 48909, (517) 335-8656.--Publications: *Health Statistics Pocket Guide, Abortions in Michigan, Cancer Incidence and Mortality, Michigan Perinatal Effectiveness Index, Infant and Maternal Health Statistics, Michigan Health Statistics* ($11.00); Services: computer printouts with a written request for a fee.

Department of Public Health, Division of Disease Surveillance, P.O. Box 30036, Lansing, MI 48909, (517) 335-8163.--Publications: weekly report; Services: no computer reports at this time.

Minnesota
State Health Department, Center for Health Statistics, 717 Delaware St., S.E. Minneapolis, MN 55414, (612) 623-5353.--Publications: *Annual Report*; Services: computer printouts of selected data.

State Health Department, Acute Epidemiology Department, 717 Delaware St., S.E. Minneapolis, MN 55414, (612) 623-5414.--Publications: various statistical reports on all reportable diseases; Services: computer printouts of summary data.

Mississippi
Department of Health, Vital Records Division, Statistical Services, P.O. Box 1700, 2423 N. State St., Jackson, MS 39205, (601) 960-7635.--Publications: *Annual Report*; Services: computer printouts of specific information require a written request.

Department of Health, Office of Epidemiology, P.O. Box 1700, Jackson, MS 39205, (601) 960-7725.--Publications: annual case tabulations; Services: computer printouts for reasonable requests only.

Missouri
Department of Health, Vital Records Department, P.O. Box 570, Jefferson City, MO 65101, (314) 751-6381.--Publications: *Annual Report*; Services: computer printouts of selected data.

Department of Health, Bureau of Communicable Disease Control, 1730 E. Elm St., Jefferson City, MO 65102, (314) 751-6128.--Publications: data recently computerized, computer printouts if data exists.

Montana
Department of Health, Bureau of Records and Vital Statistics, Helena, MT 59620, (406) 444-4228.--Publications: *Annual Report*; Services: computer printouts of selected data.

Department of Health and Environmental Sciences, Communicable Disease Section of Preventive Health Services Bureau, Cogswell Building, Helena, MT 59620, (406) 444-4740.--Publications: *Annual Report*; Services: computer printouts of current and previous years only.

Nebraska
Department of Health, Vital Statistics Department, P.O. Box 95007, Lincoln, NE 68509, (402) 471-2871.--Publications: *Annual Report*;

Services: data not computerized, the Health Data and Statistical Research Department will help with statistical information on the phone.

Department of Health, Division of Disease Control, P.O. Box 95007, Lincoln, NE 68509, (402) 471-2937.--Publications: *Nebraska Morbidity Report*; Services: data not computerized, only monthly data available.

Nevada
Department of Human Resources, Division of Health, Section of Vital Statistics, 505 East King St., Carson City, NV 89710, (702) 885-4480.--Publications: *Vital Statistics Report*; Services: computer printouts on selected data.

Department of Human Resources, Office of Communicable Diseases, 505 East King St., Carson City, NV 89710, (702) 885-4800.--Publications: *Annual Report*; Services: data currently being entered into their computer. No printouts until 1989.

New Hampshire
Department of Health and Welfare, Bureau of Vital Records, Health and Human Services Building, 6 Hazen Drive, Concord, NH 03301, (603) 271-4651.--Publications: *Annual Report*; Services: computer printouts with a special request for a fee.

Department of Health and Welfare, Bureau of Communicable Disease Control, Health and Human Services Building, 6 Hazen Dr., Concord, NH 03301, (603) 271-4477.--Publications: monthly bulletin; Services: computer printouts for selected data.

New Jersey
Department of Health, Vital Statistics Department, CN 360, Trenton, NJ 08625, (609) 984-5506.--Publications: *Annual Report*; Services: computer printouts for a fee.

Department of Health, Division of Epidemiology and Disease Control, University Office Plaza, CN 369, Trenton, NJ 08625, (609) 588-7500.--Publications: No annual report, files open to the public for research purposes; Services: Only 1987 data computerized as of July 1988.

New Mexico
Department of Health and Environment, Public Health Division, Health Statistics Division, Vital Statistics Program P.O. Box 968, Santa Fe, NM 87504, (505) 827-2539.--Publications: *Annual Report*; Services: computer printouts of selected data.

Department of Health and Environment, Office of Epidemiology P. O. Box 968, Santa Fe, NM 87504, (505) 827-0006.--Publications: weekly report, working on an annual report for 1987 data; Services: computer printout by disease, county, or month.

New York
Department of Health, Vital Statistics Office, Tower Building, Empire State Plaza, Albany, NY 12237, (518) 474-3055.--Publications: *Annual Report*; Services: computer printouts and magnetic tapes available with a written request.

Department of Health, Bureau of Communicable Disease Control, Empire State Plaza, Albany, NY 12237, (518) 474-3187.--Publications: *Annual Report*; Services: depending on the purpose of the request, computer searches can be done.

North Carolina
Department of Human Resources, Division of Health Services, 225 N. McDowell St., Raleigh, NC 27611, (919) 733-3421.-- Publications: *Annual Report*; Services: computer printouts beginning with 1987 data only.

North Dakota
Department of Health, Administrative Services Section, Second Floor, Judicial Wing, State Capitol, Bismarck, ND 58505, (701) 224-2360.--Publications: *Annual Report*; Services: computer searches and printouts.

Department of Health, Division of Disease Control, State Capitol, Bismarck, ND 58505, (701) 224-2378.--Publication: *Annual Report*; Services: computer searches and printouts.

Ohio
Department of Health, Statistical Analysis Unit, 8th Floor, 650 S. Front St., Columbus, OH 43266, (614) 466-7545.--Publications: *Annual Report*; Services: computer searches and printouts.

Oklahoma

Department of Health, Division of Data Management, 1000 N.E. 10th St., P.O. Box 53551, Oklahoma City, OK 73152, (405) 271-4542.--Publications: *Annual Report*; Services: computer searches and printouts for a fee.

Department of Health, Office of Communicable Diseases, 1000 N.E. 10th St., P.O. Box 53551, Oklahoma City, OK 73152, (405) 271-4060.--Publications: *Annual Summary and Monthly Bulletin*; Services: computer searches and printouts.

Oregon

State Health Department, Center for Health Statistics, P.O. Box 116, Portland, OR 97207, (503) 229-5895.--Publications: *Oregon Vital Statistics, Induced Termination of Pregnancy, Oregon Deaths Due to Drugs and Alcohol, Teen Pregnancy, Maternal and Infant Death: Characteristics of Oregon's Indochinese Refugees, Oregon Health Trends* (quarterly newsletter).

State Health Department, Division of Epidemiology, P.O. Box 116, Portland, OR 97202, (503) 229-5792.--Publications: *Health Status Monitoring*; Services: computer searches and printouts of selected data.

Pennsylvania

Department of Health, Health Statistics and Research, State Health Data Center, P.O. Box 90, Harrisburg, PA 17120, (717) 787-6436.--Publications: *Annual Report*; Services: computer searches and printout requests must be made in writing. Costs are $150.00 for one year, $75.00 for each additional year.

Department of Health, Division of Epidemiology, Health and Welfare Building, 7th and Forster Sts., P.O. Box 90, Harrisburg, PA 17120, (717) 787-3350.--Publications: *Annual Report*; Services: computer searches and printouts.

Rhode Island

Department of Health, Vital Records, Room 101, 75 Davis St., Providence, RI 02908, (401) 277-2812.--Publications: *Annual Report*; Services: computer printouts there is a special request. Not all data available on computer, fee depends on the computer time required.

Department of Health, Office of Disease Control, 75 Davis St., Providence, RI 02908, (401) 277-2362.--Publications: *Disease Bulletin* published monthly and year to date totals; Services: computer searches and printouts available for year years 1987 and partial 1988.

South Carolina

Department of Health and Environmental Control, Office of Vital Records and Public Health Statistics, 2600 Bull St., Columbia, SC 29201, (803) 734-4810.--Publications: *Annual Report*; Services: computer searches, printouts. Fee depends on the size of the run.

Department of Health and Environmental Control, Communicable Disease Control Section, 2600 Bull St., Columbia, SC 29201, (803) 734-5010.--Publications: no annual report, various minor disease reports issued, Services: computer searches, printouts of data from 1985 to current month.

South Dakota

State Health Department, Center for Health Policy and Statistics, Joe Foss Bldg., Pierre, SD 57501, (605) 773-3361.--Publications: *Annual Report*; Services: not all data on computer, cannot provide printouts.

State Health Department, Communicable Disease Program, Center for Health Policy and Statistics, Joe Foss Bldg., Pierre, SD 57501, (605) 773-3361.--Publications: *Annual Report*; Services: not all data on computer, cannot provide printouts at this time.

Tennessee

Department of Health and Environment, Center for Health Statistics, Information and Referral Unit, C2 242, Cordell Hull Building, Nashville, TN 37219, (615) 741-1954.--Publications: *Annual Report*; Services: computer searches and printouts at no charge.

Department of Health and Environment, Center for Health Statistics, Communicable Diseases, Information and Referral Unit, C2 242, Cordell Hull Building, Nashville, TN 37219, (615) 741-1954.--Publications: *Annual Report*, Services: computer searches and printouts at no charge.

Texas

Department of Health, Bureau of Vital Statistics, Statistical Services Division, 1100 West 49th St., Austin, TX 78756, (512)458-7111.--Publications: *Texas Vital Statistics*; Services: computer searches, printouts available, there is a programming charge. Magnetic tapes sold under circumstances. A committee meets regularly to review tape requests.

Department of Health, Bureau of Epidemiology, 1100 West 49th St., Austin, TX 78756, (512) 458-7455.--Publications: *Reported Morbidity and Mortality in Texas*; Services: computer searches and printouts with a written request.

Utah

Department of Health, Bureau of Policy Planning and Analysis, Health Information Center, 288 North 1460 West, Salt Lake City, UT 84116, (801) 538-6111.--Publications: *Annual Summary Report*; Services: computer searches, printouts and magnetic tapes.

Department of Health, Bureau of Epidemiology, P.O. Box 16660, Salt Lake City, UT 84116, (801) 538-6191.--Publications: monthly report, annual summary; Services: not all data on computer, printouts not available.

Vermont

Department of Health and Human Services, Vital Records Statistics, 60 Main St., Burlington, VT 05401.--Publications: *Annual Report*; Services: computer searches and printouts.

Department of Health and Human Services, Division of Epidemiology, 60 Main St., Burlington, VT 05401.--Publications: *Annual Report*; Services: computer searches and printouts.

Virginia

Department of Health, Center for Health Statistics, P.O. Box 1000, Richmond, VA 23208, (804) 786-6228.--Publications: *Annual Report*; Services: limited amount of data on computer, computer printouts if data exists.

Department of Health, Office of Epidemiology, James Madison Building, 109 Governor St., Richmond, VA 23219, (804) 786-6261.--Publications: monthly report with year to date totals; Services: computer searches, printouts available.

Washington

Department of Social and Health Services, Division of Vital Statistics, Office Building #2, Olympia, WA 98504, (206) 586-6029.--Publications: *Vital Statistics and Induced Terminations of Pregnancy*; Services: Computer searches for selected data, magnetic tapes for $125.00 per year.

West Virginia

State Health Department, State Office Building, 1800 Washington St. Charleston, WV 25305, (304) 348-9100.--Publications: *Annual Report*; Services: computer printout of selected data.

State Health Department, Epidemiology and Health Promotion, Surveillance and Disease Control, State Office Building, 1800 Washington St. East, Charleston, WV 25305, (304) 348-5358.--Publications: no annual report; Services: data recently computerized, computer printouts for 1987 to present.

Wisconsin

Department of Health and Social Services, Vital Statistics Department, 1 West Wilson St., Madison, WI 53701, (608) 266-1939.--Publications: *Annual Report*; Services: computer printouts for selected data with a special written request.

Department of Health and Social Services, Division of Health, Community Health and Prevention, 1 West Wilson St., Madison, WI 53701, (608) 267-9003.--Publications: *Annual Report*; Services: computer printouts requests must be made in writing.

Wyoming

Department of Health and Social Services, Division of Health and Medical Services, Vital Records Services, Cheyenne, WY 82002, (307) 777-7591.--Publications: *Vital Statistics*; Services: computer searches, printouts and magnetic tapes. Costs: $25.00 for a simple request, $300-$350 for each magnetic tape.

Department of Health and Social Services, Division of Health and Medical Services, Preventive Medicine, Hathaway Building, Cheyenne, WY 82002.--Publications: *Epidemiologic Bulletin* (monthly). Services: computer searches and printouts.

Highway Accident Statistics

* See also Your Community Chapter
* See also Business and Industry Chapter

A car runs a red light and slams into your brand new Jeep Cherokee, doing $1,500 worth of damage. You shout, they shout, a police officer comes and files an accident report. Guess what? You've just become part of your state's traffic accident database. Not just your name, mind you, but every little detail about the accident will be entered into a computer file and stored for posterity -- or until someone asks the state for the information.

A state accident database is a file made up of reports completed by all law enforcement agencies which investigate accidents. While it might seem that this data should be confidential, it is freely available to engineers, lobbyists, courts, safety organizations, and such citizen-action groups as Mothers Against Drunk Drivers (MADD).

In most instances, the computerized system can be searched and printouts provided by a number of variables.

* The Human Element: driver sex, age, equipment used by age, sex, charged driver violations, pedestrian age.

* Environmental Elements: accident type vs. highway conditions, traffic control vs. accident site, accident type vs. weather, and accident type vs. light conditions.

* Accident Characteristics: county, month of year, time of day, rural/urban road system, hit and run severity, holiday accidents, fatal accidents, alcohol involved, property damage, fires/type of car, accidents caused by animals in the highway.

Our research indicates that state highway accident database searches can be tailored to individual requests within reason. In some states, state employees will perform computer searches and provide printouts--all free of charge. Other states charge up to $150 per hour or require a Freedom of Information Act request.

The only states not providing data searches and printouts are: Alaska, Hawaii, Mississippi, Oklahoma, South Dakota, and Wisconsin.

A statewide accident summary and a breakdown of accident problems by specific areas can be obtained by contacting that state offices listed below.

Highway Department Offices

Alabama
Alabama Highway Department, Accident Identification and Surveillance Section, Traffic Engineering, 1409 Coliseum Blvd., Montgomery, AL 36130; (205) 261-6128. Publications and Services: *Alabama Traffic Accident Facts*; accident database can be searched, sorted and a printout produced. The cost is $50.00 per run.

Alaska
Department of Transportation, Demand Public Facilities, P.O. Box Z-2500, Juneau, AK 99811; (907) 465-2777. Publication: *Annual Report* (free). There are no computer services available due to limited staff.

Arizona
Arizona Department of Transportation, Traffic Records Unit, 1739 W. Jackson Ave., Phoenix, AZ 85007; (602) 255-7724. Publications and Services: *Arizona Traffic Accident Summary*; accident database can be searched, sorted and a printout provided at no charge.

Arkansas
Arkansas Transportation Safety Agency, Traffic Safety Division, Justice Bldg. Suite 100, Little Rock, AR 72201; (501) 682-5993. Publications and Services: *Statewide Accidents*; accident database can be searched, sorted and a printout provided at no charge.

California
Caltrans, Tasas Unit, 1120 N. St., P.O. Box 1499, Room 4123, Sacramento, CA 95807; (916) 445-2543. Publications and Services: *Accident Data on California Highways* ($2.50); accident database can be searched, sorted and a printout provided on a cost recovery basis.

Colorado
Department of Highways, Traffic Staff, 4201 E. Arkansas Ave., Denver, CO 80222; (303) 757-2385. Publications and Services: *Accidents and Rates on State Highways* ($5.00); accident database can be searched, sorted and a printout provided for a substantial charge for businesses, free to government agencies.

Connecticut
Department of Transportation, Planning Inventory and Data, Bureau of Planning, 24 Wolcott Hill Road, P.O. Drawer A, Wethersfield, CT 06109; (203) 665-0072. Publications and Services: *Connecticut Univariate Distribution Report*; accident database can be searched, sorted and a printout provided at no cost with a written request.

Delaware
Department of Public Safety, Delaware State Traffic Section, P.O. 438, Dover, DE 19903; (302) 736-5933. Publications and Services: *Annual Report*; accident database can be searched, sorted and a printout provided at no cost.

District of Columbia
Traffic Analysis, Traffic Enforcement Bureau, 501 New York Ave., NW, Washington, D.C. 20001; (202) 727-6533. Publications and Services: *Annual Report*; computer printouts of sorted and selected data available.

Florida
Department of Highway Safety and Motor Vehicles, Office of Management and Planning, Neil Kirkman Bldg., Tallahassee, FL 32301; (904) 488-3666. Publications and Services: *Florida Traffic Accident Facts*; accident database can be searched, sorted and a printout provided at no cost.

Georgia
Department of Public Safety, Accident Reporting, P.O. Box 1456, Atlanta, GA 30371; (404) 624-7660. Publications and Services: *Annual Report*; accident database can be searched, sorted and a printout provided at no cost.

Hawaii
Department of Transportation, Traffic Branch, 869 Punchbowl St., Honolulu, HI 96813; (808) 548-3215. Publications and Services: *Major Traffic Accidents in Hawaii*; accident database cannot be searched at this time, but printouts will become available in the future.

Idaho
Office of Highway Safety, Idaho Transportation Department, P.O. Box 7129, Boise, ID 83707; (208) 334-3533. Publications and Services: *Idaho Traffic Accident Analysis*; accident database can be searched, sorted and a printout provided at no cost.

Illinois
Department of Transportation, Division on Traffic Safety, 2300 S. Dirksen Parkway, Springfield, IL 62764; (217) 782-2575. Publications and Services: *Accident Facts*; accident database can be searched, sorted and a printout provided at no cost.

Indiana

State Police Data Section, State Office Building, 100 N. Senate Avenue, Indianapolis, IN 46204; (317) 232-1293. Publications and Services: *Summary of Motor Vehicle Traffic Accidents*; accident database can be searched, sorted and a printout provided on a cost recovery basis. A written request is required.

Iowa

Iowa Department of Transportation, Driver Safety and Improvement, Lucas State Office Building, Des Moines, IA 50319; (515) 281-5012. Publications and Services: *Accident Facts*; accident database can be searched, sorted and a printout provided for a cost recovery fee.

Kansas

Department of Transportation, Office of Traffic Safety, Docking Building, Topeka, KS 66612; (913) 296-3756. Publications and Services: *Yearly Summary*; accident database can be searched, sorted and a printout provided at no cost.

Kentucky

State Police, Records Section, 1250 Louisville Road, Frankfort, KY 40601; (502) 227-8717. Publications and Services: *Accident Facts Book*; accident database can be searched, sorted for the last five years and a printout provided at no charge.

Louisiana

Department of Public Safety and Corrections, Highway Safety Commission, 265 S. Foster Dr., P.O. Box 66336, Baton Rouge, LA 70896; (504) 925-6991. Publications and Services: *Louisiana Traffic Accident Information*; accident database can be searched, sorted and a printout provided with a written special request at no charge.

Maine

Department of Public Safety, Information Systems, 36 Hospital St., Augusta, ME 04333; (207) 289-3396. Publications and Services: *Maine Breakdown of Accident and Injury Codes*; accident database can be searched, sorted and a printout provided at no cost.

Maryland

State Highway Administration, Bureau of Accident Studies, 350 S. Hammonds Ferry Rd., Glen Burnie, MD 21061; (301) 859-7513. Publications and Services: no annual reports issued, staff will supply data tailored to individual needs within reasonable requests. There is normally no charge, but depends on the amount of data requested.

Massachusetts

Registry of Motor Vehicles, 100 Nashua St., Boston, MA 02114; (617) 727-3716. Publications and Services: last annual report published in 1981. Accident database can be searched, sorted and a printout provided in most cases. There is a fee for the data retrieval service.

Michigan

Michigan State Police, Traffic Services, Analysis Section 7150 Harris Drive, Lansing, MI 48913; (519) 322-1969. Publications and Services: *Traffic Accident Facts Book*; for computer printouts of selected data, a Freedom of Information request is required.

Minnesota

Department of Public Safety, Office of Traffic Safety, Room 207, Transportation Bldg., St. Paul, MN 55155; (612) 296-6953. Publications and Services: *Crash Facts*; accident database can be searched, sorted and a printout provided at no cost.

Mississippi

Department of Public Safety, Statistical Bureau, P.O. Box 958, Jackson, MS 39205; (601) 987-1262. Publications and Services: *Traffic Accident and Enforcement Activities*; no computer printouts available at this time.

Missouri

State Highway Patrol, Traffic Division, P.O. Box 568, Jefferson City, MO 65102; (314) 751-3313. Publications and Services: *Missouri Traffic Crashes*; accident database can be searched, sorted and a printout provided with a special request.

Montana

Montana Highway Patrol, Records Bureau, 303 N. Roberts, Helena, MT 59620; (406) 444-3278. Publications and Services: *Annual Report*; accident database can be searched, sorted and a printout provided at no cost.

Nebraska

Department of Roads, Highway Safety Division, Accident Records Highway Safety, P.O. Box 94669, Lincoln, NE 68509; (402) 479-4645. Publications and Services: *Traffic Accident Facts*; accident database can be searched, sorted and a printout provided depending on need at no cost.

Nevada

Department of Transportation, Safety Engineering, 1263 S. Stewart St., Carson City, NV 98712; (702) 885-3469. Publications and Services: *Nevada Traffic Accidents*; accident database can be searched, sorted and a printout provided for a cost recovery charge.

New Hampshire

Department of Safety, Data Processing, 10 Hazen Drive, Concord, NH 03305; (603) 271-2131. Publications and Services: *Annual Accident Statistics*; accident database can be searched, sorted and a printout provided for a fee. Magnetic tapes can be purchased with instruction on how to convert data onto a diskette.

New Jersey

Department of Law and Public Safety, Division of Highway Traffic Safety, Quackerbridge Plaza. Building 5, 3rd floor, CN 048, Trenton, NJ 08625; (609) 588-3750. Publications and Services: no annual report issued; accident database can be searched, sorted and a printout provided at no cost.

New Mexico

Highway and Transportation Department, Traffic Safety Bureau, P.O. Box 5824, Montoya Building, Santa Fe, NM 87502; (505) 827-3226. Publications and Services: *New Mexico Traffic and Crash Data*; accident database can be searched, sorted and a printout provided at no cost.

New York

State Department of Motor Vehicles, Statistical Services, Empire State Plaza, Albany, NY 12228; (518) 474-0679. Publications and Services: *Summary of Motor Vehicle Accidents*; accident database can be searched, sorted and a printout provided for $25.00 per calendar year.

North Carolina

Division of Motor Vehicles, Collision Reports, 1100 New Bern Ave., Raleigh, NC 27697; (919) 733-7250. Publications and Services: *Traffic Accident Facts*; accident database can be searched, sorted and a printout provided for a fee from: Highway Safety Research Center, CB #3430, UNC Campus, Chapel Hill, NC 27599 (919) 962-2202.

North Dakota

State Highway Department, Drivers License and Traffic Safety Division, Accident Records Section, 600 East Boulevard Ave., Bismarck, ND 58505; (701) 224-4352. Publications and Services: *Accident Facts*; accident database can be searched, sorted and a printout provided at no cost.

Ohio

Department of Highway Safety, Public Information Office, 240 Parsons Ave. Columbus, OH 43215; (614) 466-2550. Publications and Services: *Accident Facts*; accident database can be searched, sorted and a printout provided at no cost.

Oklahoma

Department of Public Safety, Services and Records Division, P.O. Box 11415, Oklahoma City, OK 73136; (405) 424-4011. Publications and Services: *Summary of Motor Vehicles Traffic Collisions*; *Oklahoma Traffic Accident Fact Book* ($3.00 each); no computer printouts available, for specific information call and request data over the phone.

Oregon

Traffic Data Unit, 2001 Front St., Salem, OR 97310; (503) 378-6537. Publications and Services: *Traffic Accident Rate on the State Highway System*; accident database can be searched, sorted and a printout provided for a fee.

Pennsylvania

Department of Transportation, Center for Highway Safety, Room 215, Transportation and Safety Building, Harrisburg, PA 17120; (717) 787-3393. Publications and Services: *Traffic Accident Facts and Statistics*; accident database can be searched, sorted and a printout provided at no cost.

Rhode Island

Department of Transportation, Planning Section, State Office Building, Smith Street, Providence, RI 02903; (401) 277-2694. Publications and Services: *Annual Report*; accident database can be searched, sorted and a printout provided with a special request.

South Carolina

Department of Highways, Safety Office, P.O. Box 191, Columbia, SC 29202; (803) 737-1162. Publications and Services: *South Carolina Traffic Accidents*; accident database can be searched, sorted and a printout provided at no cost.

South Dakota

Department of Transportation, Accident Records, 118 W. Capitol, Pierre, SD 57501; (605) 773-3868. Publications and Services: *Facts Book*; no computer services or printouts available.

Tennessee

Department of Safety, 1150 Foster Ave., Nashville, TN 37210; (615) 251-5220. Publications and Services: *Accident Facts Book, Annual Report*; accident database can be searched, sorted and a printout provided on a cost recovery basis.

Texas

Department of Public Safety, Statistical Services, Box 4087, Austin, TX 78773; (512) 465-2000. Publications and Services: *Motor Vehicle Traffic Accidents, A Look at DWI... Accidents, Victims, Arrests*; accident database can be searched, sorted and a printout provided for a cost recovery fee.

Utah

Department of Transportation, Division of Traffic Safety, 4501 South, 2700 West, Salt Lake City, UT 84119; (801) 965-4284. Publications and Services: *Utah Annual Safety Report*; accident database can be searched, sorted for data after 1980 and printouts provided at no cost.

Vermont

Agency for Transportation, Planning Research Division, 133 State St., Montpelier, VT 05602. Publications and Services: *Vermont Accident Facts*; accident database can be searched, sorted and printouts provided at no cost.

Virginia

Department of Transportation, Traffic Engineering, 1401 E. Broad St., Richmond, VA 23219; (206) 786-2969. Publications and Services: *Accident Summary Book*; accident database can be searched, sorted and printout provided upon special request. There may be a charge.

Washington

Department of Transportation, Public Transportation Plan, Safety Data Planning, Olympia, WA 98504; (206) 753-6005. Publications and Services: *Washington State Department of Transportation Highway Traffic Report*; accident database can be searched, sorted and a printout provided. There may be a fee.

West Virginia

Department of Highways, Traffic Engineering Division, 1900 Washington St. East, Charleston, WV 25305; (304) 348-3063. Publications and Services: *West Virginia Accident Data*; accident database can be searched, sorted and a printout provided for a fee.

Wisconsin

Department of Transportation, Bureau of Driver Licenses, P.O. Box 7917, Madison, WI 53707; (608) 266-2237. Publications and Services: *Accident Facts*; computer printouts not normally available.

Wyoming

Highway Safety Branch, Wyoming Highway Department, P.O. Box 1708, 5300 Bishop Boulevard, Cheyenne, WY 82002; (307) 777-7296. Publications and Services: *Wyoming Comprehensive Report on Traffic Accidents*; accident database

State Data Centers

Approximately 1,300 organizations nationwide receive data from the U.S. Bureau of the Census and in turn disseminate the information to the public free of charge or on a cost recovery basis. These organizations are called state data centers and serve as ideal information sources for both local and national markets. The centers listed in this report are the major offices for each state. If you are looking for national markets, start with a center in your state. If you are searching for local market data, contact the center located in the relevant area.

Demographics and Target Market Identification

State data center offices are most frequently used for obtaining information on target markets. For instance, the Army and Navy used such services to identify which areas are populated with large numbers of teenagers in order to open recruiting offices and focus their advertising campaign. Avon door-to-door sales reps used state data center generated demographic maps to identify homes with highest potential. L. L. Bean relied on a center to determine large Hispanic populations for a special promotion of outdoor recreational products. These offices could provide current data including:

- The age distribution within a given county
- Moving patterns for particular geographical areas
- The number of wells and mobile homes in 85 counties
- How many gravel pits in the state of Montana
- Counties with the highest rate of illegitimate children
- Analysis of why certain stores in an auto parts chain are doing better than others
- Demographic profile of a person in need of child care
- The top 25 markets by zip code
- The number of male secretaries in a dozen contiguous counties.

Forecasting Future Markets

The biggest opportunities often lie in knowing the future of a market. Many of the state data centers have developed specific software for analyzing Census and other data to project growth of specific markets. Here is a sampling of what some centers can do:

- Population projections for every three years to the year 2020 (done by California center)
- State population changes by the year 2000
- What year the white population will not be in the majority
- The number of teenagers by the next century
- Series of economic indicators for plotting future economic health in state (Oklahoma center provides such data).

Site Location

Another major area of interest is in providing information to companies considering relocating into a state. Because most states are aggressively trying to attract business, numerous customized services receive a high priority. Local centers can provide information such as the number of fast food restaurants in the area and the best location for another one. And some states, like Arkansas, have special site evaluation software which can manipulate Census data to show the demographic characteristics for market radiuses which are 2, 5 or 10 miles from a given site. Oklahoma and other states have free data sheets covering every community in their state which are loaded with specifics for choosing a location. Their reports contain data on:

- Distance from major cities
- Population: past and future
- Climate
- Municipal services
- Utilities
- Labor market analysis
- List of major manufacturers
- List of major employers
- Transportation
- Commercial services
- Major freight lines and truck terminals
- Educational facilities
- Financial institutions
- Tax structure
- Housing and churches
- Medical facilities
- Retail business in city
- Industrial financial assistance
- Water analysis report
- Recreational facilities
- Wholesale business in city
- Items deserving special consideration

Professional and Personal Relocation

The same services that are intended to help businesses relocate also can be useful to individuals and professionals. For example, if you are looking for a place to start an orthodontics practice, a local data center could determine which counties and cities have the most affluent families with young people--a prime market for braces. Also, if you get an offer for a new job in another city, obtaining a data sheet on the local community like the one described above provides insight into the types of housing, schools, churches, and recreational facilities available.

Business Proposals Plus Loan and Grant Applications

If you are looking for money for either a grant, a loan or even venture money, data centers can provide the information needed for proposal writing. Grantors must have such information as what percent of people live below poverty line, and banks want to know current business patterns for a new enterprise when seeking a loan. These sorts of data can be obtained easily from these centers.

Economics, Demographics and Statistics

Level of Detail

Because the data centers use information from other sources in addition to the Bureau of Census, the level of detail will vary according to subject area as well as the state and office contacted. Much of the Census data can be provided at the state, county, city, census tract and block group level (which is normally even smaller than a zip code). Data according to zip code are also available for many categories of information. All states also have the public use micro data sample, which do not contain aggregate data but actual questionnaire information filled out by respondents. They can be manipulated into any kind of special detail required.

Custom Work, Workshops and Other Services

A lot of work performed by the data centers is customized in nature. The organizations collect data from other federal and state sources to enhance their Census information. Many have arrangements with other state data centers to send any computer file needed to do special analysis. This is how local centers can provide national information or inter-market comparisons. Some centers will even perform custom census projects for clients, which means raw data collection for market research.

Free and low cost workshops about services and information opportunities are sponsored in some areas for potential users. These workshops are important at the local level because in the past they were readily available from the Bureau of Census, but recent budget cuts have reduced their frequency and increased their price. Because of the centers' familiarity of census data, these offices are excellent starting places for most any information search.

Formats

Data centers offer some of the most sophisticated formats you are likely to find from public organizations. They all provide computer tapes, off-the-shelf reports, custom reports from computer analysis, and quick answers over the telephone. Most are also set up to provide custom analysis and/or raw data on computer diskettes, and some -- like Ohio -- have developed a PC database from which they can generate standard reports and down load onto diskettes. Colorado and other states are beginning to make data accessible on-line.

Prices

Although the U.S. government provides most of the data to these centers, the feds do not interfere with fee schedules. Most offices try to give out information free, but some charge on a cost recovery basis. Some states do not charge for the first so many pages of a report but charge a nominal fee for additional pages. Some say they have a minimum fee of $20 for customized computer runs. It is interesting that these centers sell you computerized data cheaper than the U.S. Bureau of the Census in Washington. In contrast to the Bureau's fee of $140, Illinois and Georgia only charge $50 for a data tape file, and in Florida the cost is $15 for a file.

In the dozens of interviews we conducted with these centers about the complicated market research reports they have provided to clients, the highest figure we found they ever charged was $2,000.00. That amount of money would buy virtually nothing from most marketing consultants.

State Data Centers

Below is a roster of data centers in all 50 states as well as the District of Columbia, Puerto Rico and Virgin Islands. Some of these Census Bureau information providers are based in state departments and agencies, universities, business colleges, and libraries. Each center listed below includes the name and phone number of the data expert.

Alabama
Center for Business and Economic Research, University of Alabama, P.O. Box AK, Tuscaloosa, AL 34587, Ms. Annette Walters (205) 348-6191

Alabama Department of Economic and Community Affairs, Office of State Planning, P.O. Box 2329, 3465 Norman Bridge Road, Montgomery, AL 36105-0939, Mr. Gilford Gilder (205) 284-8775

Alabama Public Library Service, 6030 Monicello Drive, Montgomery, AL 36130, Ms. Hilda Dent (205) 277-7330

Alaska
Alaska State Data Center, Research and Analysis, Department of Labor, P.O. Box 25504, Juneau, AK 99802-5504, Mr. Greg Williams (907) 465-4500

Office of Management and Budget, Division of Strategic Planning, Pouch AD, Juneau, AK 99811, Mr. Gregg Ericson (907) 465-3573

Department of Education, Division of Libraries and Museums, Alaska State Library, Pouch G, Juneau, AK 99811-0571, Mr. Lou Coatney (907) 465-2942

Department of Community & Regional Affairs, Division of Municipal & Regional Assistance, P.O. Box BH, Juneau, AK 99811, Mr. Doug Griffin (907) 465-4750

Institute for Social & Economic Research, University of Alaska, 707 "A" Street, Suite 206, Anchorage, AK 99501, Mr. Jack Kruse (907) 278-4621

Arizona
Arizona Department of Economic Security, 1300 West Washington, P.O. Box 6123-045Z, Phoenix, AZ 85005, Ms. Betty Jeffries (602) 255-5984

Center for Business Research, College of Business Administration, Arizona State University, Tempe, AZ, 85287, Mr. Tom Rex (602) 965-3961

College of Business Administration, Northern Arizona University, Box 15066, Flagstaff, AZ 86011, Dr. Joseph Walka (602) 523-3657

Federal Documents Section, Department of Library, Archives, and Public Records, Capitol, Third Floor, 1700 West Washington, Phoenix, AZ 85007, Ms. Holly Penix (602) 621-4121

Arkansas
Center for Information Services, University of Arkansas-Little Rock, 2801 South University, Little Rock, AR 72204, Ms. Sarah Breshears (501) 371-1973

Arkansas State Library, 1 Capitol Mall, Little Rock, AR 72201, Ms. Mary Honeycutt (501) 371-2150

Research & Analysis Section, Arkansas Employment Security Division, P.O. Box 2981, Little Rock, AR 72201, Mr. Herman Sanders (501) 371-1543

California
State Census Data Center, Department of Finance, 1025 P Street, Room 83, Sacramento, CA 95814, Ms. Linda Gage, Director (916) 322-4651

Sacramento Area COG, 106 K Street, Suite 200, Sacramento, CA 95814, Mr. Bob Faseler (916) 441-5930

Association of Bay Area Governments, Metro Center, 8th and Oak Streets, P.O. Box 2050, Oakland, CA 94604, Ms. Patricia Perry (415) 464-7937

Regional Research Institute of Southern California, 600 S. Commonwealth Street, Los Angeles, CA 90005, Mr. Tim Douglas (213) 385-1000

San Diego Association of Governments, Security Pacific Plaza, 1200 3rd Avenue, Suite 524, San Diego, CA 92101, Ms. Karen Lamphere (619) 236-5353

State Data Center Program, University of California-Berkeley, 2538 Channing Way, Berkeley, CA 94702, Ms. Ilona Einowski/Ann Gerkin (415) 642-6571

Colorado

Division of Local Government, Colorado Department of Local Affairs, 1313 Sherman Street, Room 520, Denver, CO 80203, Mr. Reid Reynolds / Ms. Rebecca Picasso (303) 866-2156

Business Research Division, Graduate School of Business Administration, University of Colorado- Boulder, Boulder, CO 80309 , Mr. Gerald Allen (303) 492-8227

Natural Resources & Economics, Department of Agriculture, Colorado State University, Fort Collins, CO 80523, Ms. Sue Anderson (303) 491-5706

Documents Department, The Libraries, Colorado State University, Fort Collins, CO 80523, Ms. Karen Fachan (303) 491-5911

Connecticut

Comprehensive Planning Division, Connecticut Office of Policy and Management, 80 Washington Street, Hartford, CT 06106, Mr. Theron Schnure (203) 566-8285

Government Documents, Connecticut State Library, 231 Capital Avenue, Hartford, CT 06106, Mr. Albert Palko (203) 566-4971

Processing Center, Institute for Social Inquiry, University of Connecticut, U-164, Storrs, CT 06268, Ms. Marilyn Potter (203) 486- 4440

Delaware

Delaware Development Office, 99 Kings Highway, P.O. Box 1401, Dover, DE 19903, Ms. Judy McKinney (302) 736-4271

College of Urban Affairs and Public Policy, University of Delaware, IEC Building, Room 131, Wyoming Road, Newark, DE 19716, Mr. Ed Ratledge (302) 451-8405

District of Columbia

District of Columbia, Data Services Division, Mayor's Office of Planning, Room 313, Presidential Bldg., 415 12th Street, N.W., Washington, DC 20004, Mr. Albert Mindlin (202) 727-6533

Metropolitan Washington Council of Governments, 1875 I Street, N.W., Suite 200, Washington, DC 20006, Mr. John McClain/Ms. Jenean Johanningmeier (202) 223-6800

Florida

Florida State Data Center, Executive Office of the Governor, Office of Planning & Budgeting, 304 Carlton Building, Tallahasse, FL 32301 , Mr. Steve Kimble (904) 487-2814

Center for the Study of Population, Institute for Social Research, 654 Bellemy Building, Florida State University, Tallahassee, FL 32306, Dr. Ike Eberstein (904) 644-1762

State Library of Florida, R.A. Gray Building, Tallahassee, FL 32399, Ms. Evelyn Turkinton (904) 487-2651

Georgia

Division of Demographic & Statistical Services, Georgia Office of Planning and Budget, 270 Washington Street, S. W., Room 608, Atlanta, GA 30334, Mr. Tom Wagner/Ms. Robin Kirkpatrick (404) 656-0911

Documents Librarian, Georgia State University, University Plaza, Atlanta, GA 30303, Ms. Gayle Christian, (404) 658-2185
Robert W. Woodruff Library for Advanced Studies, Emory University, Atlanta, GA 30322, (404) 727- 6880

Main Library, University of Georgia, Athens, GA 30602, Ms. Susan C. Field (404) 542-0664

Georgia Department of Community Affairs, Office of Research & Information, 40 Marietta St., N.W., 8th Floor, Atlanta, GA 30303, Mr. Paul Lycett (404) 656-5526

Documents Librarian, State Data Center Program, Albany State College, 504 College Drive, Albany, GA 31705, Ms. Juanita Miller (912) 681-5117

State Data Center Program, Mercer University Law Library, Mercer University, Macon, GA 31207, Mr. Steve Thorpe (912) 744-2667

Data Services, University of Georgia Libraries, 6th Floor, Athens, GA 30602, Ms. Hortense Bates (404) 542-0727

Price Gilbert Memorial Library, Georgia Institute of Technology, Atlanta, GA 30332, Mr. Richard Leacy (404) 894-4519

Hawaii

Hawaii State Data Center, State Dept. of Planning & Economic Development, Kamamalau Building, Room 602A, 250 S. King Street, Honolulu, HI 96813, Mailing Address: P.O. Box 2359, Honolulu, HI 96804, Mr. Robert Schmitt, State Statistician/Mr. Bob Stanfield (808) 548-3082

Electronic Data Processing Division, State Department of Budget and Finance, Kalanimoku Building, 1151 Punchbowl Street, Honolulu, HI 96813, Mr. George Matsuo (808) 548-2618

Idaho

Idaho Department of Commerce, State Capital Bldg., Rm. 108, Boise, ID 83720, Dr. David Porter, Administrator (208) 334-2470/Mr. Alan Porter (208) 334-4714

Institutional Research, Room 319, Business Building, Boise State University, Boise, ID 83725, Mr. Don Canning (208) 385-1613

The Idaho State Library, 325 West State Street, Boise, ID 83702, Mr. Charles Bolles, State Librarian,(208) 334-2150

Idaho Population Project, Campus Box 8450, Idaho State University, Pocatello, ID 83209, Dr. Paul Zelus (208) 236-2351.

Illinois

Division of Planning and Financial Analysis, Illinois Bureau of the Budget, William Stratton Building, Rm. 605, Springfield, IL 62706, Ms. Ann Geraci (217) 782-3500.

Community Research Services, Department of Sociology, Anthropology & Social Work, Illinois State University, 205 N. University Street, Normal, IL 61761, Dr. Roy Treadway (309) 438-5946.

Center for Governmental Studies, Northern Illinois University, Social Science Research Bldg., DeKalb, IL 60115, Ms. Ruth Anne Tobias, (815) 753-1901, x221

Regional Research and Development Service, Southern Illinois University at Edwardsville, Box 1456, Edwardsville, IL 62026, Mr. Charles Kofron (618) 692-3500

Chicago Area Geographic Information Study, Room 2102, Building BSB, P.O. Box 4348, University of Ilinois at Chicago, Chicago, IL 60680, Mr. Jim Bash, (312) 996-5274

Indiana

Indiana State Library, Indiana Data Center, 140 North Senate Avenue, Indianapolis, IN 46204, Mr. Ray Ewick, Director/ Ms. Sandi Thompson, (317) 232-3733

Indiana Business Research Center, Indiana University, 10th and Fee Lane, Bloomington, IN 47405, Dr. Morton Marcus, (812) 335-5507

Indiana Business Research Center, P.O. Box 647, 801 West Michigan, B.S. 4005, Indianapolis, IN 46223, Ms. Carol Rogers, (317) 274-2205

Division of Economic Analysis, Indiana Department of Commerce, 1 North Capital, Suite 700, Indianapolis, IN 46204, Mr. Charles Sim, Director (317) 232-8959

Iowa

Research Section, Iowa Department of Economic Development, 200 E. Grand Avenue, Des Moines, IA 50309, Mr. Doug Getter, (515) 281-3825

State Library of Iowa, Historical Building, East 12th and Grand, Des Moines, IA 50319, Ms. Linda Maurer (515) 281-4102

Center for Social and Behavioral Research, University of Northern Iowa, Cedar Falls, IA 50614, Dr. Robert Kramer, (319) 273-2105

Census Services, Iowa State University, 320 East Hall, Ames, IA 50011, Dr. Willis Goudy (515) 294- 8337

Laboratory for Political Research, University of Iowa, 345 Shaeffer Hall, Iowa City, IA 52242, Mr. Jim Grifhorst, (319) 353-3103

Census Data Center, Department of Public Instruction, Grimes State

Economics, Demographics and Statistics

Office Building, Des Moines, IA 50319, Mr. Steve Boal (515) 281-4730

Small Business Development Center, College of Business, 210 Aliber Hall, Drake University, Des Moines, IA 50311, Ms. Carolyn Ramsay (515) 271-2655

Ballou Library, Buena Vista College, Strom Lake, IA 50588, Dr. Barbara Palling, (712) 794- 2127.

Kansas
State Library, Room 343-N, State Capitol Building, Topeka, KS 66612, Mr. Marc Galbraith (913) 296- 3296

Division of the Budget, Room 152-E, State Capitol Building, Topeka, KS 66612, Mr.Dana Ferrell (913) 296-2436

Institute for Public Policy and Business Research, 607 Blake Hall, The University of Kansas, Lawrence,KS 66045-2960, Mr. Robert Glass (913) 864-3123

Center for Urban Studies, Box 61, Wichita State University, Wichita, KS 67208, Mr. Mark Glaser (316) 689-3737

Population Research Laboratory, Department of Sociology, Kansas State University, Manhattan, KS 66506, Mr. Donald Adamchak (913) 532-6865

Kentucky
Urban Studies Center, College of Urban & Public Affairs, University of Louisville, Louisville, KY 40292, Ms. Shirley Demos (502) 588-6626

Office of Policy & Management, State of Kentucky, Capitol Annex, Frankfort, KY 40601, Mr. William Hintze (502) 564-7300

State Library Division, Department for Libraries & Archives, 300 Coffeetree Road, P.O.Box 537, Frankfort, KY 40601, Ms. Brenda Fuller (502) 875-7000

Louisiana
Louisiana State Planning Office, Department of Administration, P.O. Box 94095, Baton Rouge, LA 70804, Ms. Karen Paterson (504) 342-7410

Division of Business and Economic Research, University of New Orleans, Lake Front, New Orleans, LA 70122, Mr. Vincent Maruggi (504) 286-6248

Division of Business Research, Louisiana Tech University, PO Box 10318, Ruston, LA 71272, Dr. Edward O'Boyle (318)257-3701

Reference Department, Louisiana State Library, PO Box 131, Baton Rouge, LA 70821, Mrs. Blanche Cretini (504) 342-4918

Experimental Statistics Department, 173 Agriculture Administration Building, Louisiana State University, Baton Rouge, LA 70803, Mr. George Tracy (504) 388-8303

Maine
Division of Economic Analysis and Research, Maine Department of Labor, 20 Union Street, Augusta, ME 04330, Mr. Raynold Fongemie, Director, Ms. Jean Martin (207) 289-2271

Maine State Library, State House Station 64, Augusta, ME 04333, Mr. Gary Nichols (207) 289- 3561

Maryland
Maryland Department of State Planning, 301 West Preston Street, Baltimore, MD 21201,Mr. Arthur Benjamin (301) 225-4450

Computer Science Center, University of Maryland, College Park, MD 20742, Mr. John McNary (301) 454- 6030

Government Reference Service, Pratt Library, 400 Cathedral Street, Baltimore, MD 21201, Ms. Susan Arrington (301) 396-5328

Massachusetts
Massachusetts Institute for Social and Economic Research, 117 Draper Hall, University of Massachusetts, Amherst, MA 01003, Dr. Patricia Madson (413) 545-0176

Massachusetts Institute for Social and Economic Research, Box 219, The State House, Boston, MA 02133, Mr. William Murray (617) 727-3237

Michigan
Michigan Information Center, Department of Managment & Budget, Office of Revenue and Tax Analysis, PO Box 30026, Lansing, MI 48909, Dr. Laurence Rosen (517) 373-2697

MIMIC/Center for Urban Affairs, Wayne State University, 5229 Cass Avenue, Detroit, MI 48202, Dr. Mark Neithercut (313) 577-2180

The Library of Michigan, Government Documents Service, PO Box 30007, Lansing, MI 48909, Ms. F. Anne Diamond (517) 373-1593

Minnesota
State Demographic Unit, Minnesota State Planning Agency, Room 101, Capitol Square Bldg., 550 Cedar Street, St. Paul, MN 55101, Mr. Thomas Giograms (612) 296-4886.

Minnesota Analysis and Planning System, University of Minnesota-St. Paul, 475 Coffey Hall, 1420 Eckles Avenue, St. Paul, MN 55108, Mr. Randy Cantrell (612) 624-7767

Interagency Resource & Information Center, Department of Education, 501 Capitol Square Building, St. Paul, MN 55101, Ms. Patricia Tupper (612) 296-0595

Mississippi
Center for Population Studies, The University of Mississippi, Bondurant Bldg., Rm 3W, University, MS 38677, Dr. Max Williams, Director (601) 232-7288

Governor's Office of Federal-State Programs, Department of Community Development, 301 West Pearl Street, Jackson, MS 39203-3096, Mr. Glen Duckworth (601) 949-2219

Missouri
Planning Section, Missouri Coordinating Board for Higher Education, 101 Adams Street, Jefferson City,MO 65101, Ms. Sara Oqawa (314) 751-2361

Office of Administration, 124 Capitol Building, PO Box 809, Jefferson City, MO 65102, Mr. Ryan Burson (314) 751-2345

Montana
Census and Economic Information Center, Montana Department of Commerce, 1424 9th Avenue, Capitol Station, Helena, MT 59620-0401, Ms. Patricia Roberts (406) 444-2896

Montana State Library, 1515 East 6th Avenue, Capitol Station, Helena, MT 59620, Mr. Harold Chambers (406) 444-3004

Bureau of Business and Economic Research, University of Montana, Missoula, MT 59812, Ms. Maxine Johnson (406) 243-5113

Survey Research Center, Wilson Hall, Rm. 1-108, Montana State University, Bozeman, MT 59717, Ms. Lee Faulkner, (406) 994-4481

Nebraska
Bureau of Business Research, 200 CBA, The University of Nebraska-Lincoln, Lincoln, NE 68588, Dr. Donald Pursell/Mr. Jerry Deichert (402) 472-2334

Policy Research Office, PO Box 94601, State Capitol, Rm. 1321, Lincoln, NE 68509-4601, Mr. Andrew Cunningham (402) 471-2414

Nebraska Library Commission, 1420 P Street, Lincoln, NE 68508, Mr. John L. Kipischke (402) 471-2045

The Central Data Processing Division, Department of Administration Services, 1306 State Capitol, Lincoln, NE 68509, Mr. Skip Miller (402) 471-2065

Nevada
Nevada State LIbrary, Capitol Complex, 401 North Carson, Carson City, NV 89710, Ms. Joan Kerschner/Mr. Donald Thompson (702) 885-5160

Department of Data Processing, Capitol Complex, Blasdell Building, Rm. 304, Carson City, NV 89710, Mr. Bob Rigsby (702) 885-4091

New Hampshire
Office of State Planning, 2-1/2 Beacon Street, Concord, NH 03301, Mr. Jim McLaughlin (603) 271-2155

New Hampshire State Library, Park Street, Concord, NH 03301, Ms. Shirley Gray Adamovich (603) 271- 2392

Office of Biometrics, University of New Hampshire, James Hall, 2nd

Floor Durham, NH 03824, Mr. Owen Durgin (603) 862-1700

New Jersey
New Jersey Department of Labor, Division of Planning & Research, CN 388-John Fitch Plaza, Trenton, NJ 08625-0388, Ms. Connie O. Hughes (609) 984-2593

New Jersey State Library, 185 West State Street, CN 520, Trenton, NJ 08625-0520, Ms. Judith S. Rowe (609) 452-6052

Princeton-Rutgers Census Data Project, Princeton University Computer Center, 87 Prospect Avenue, Princeton, NJ 08544, Ms. Judith S. Rowe (609) 452-6052

Princeton-Rutgers Census Data Project, Center for Computer & Information Services, Rutgers University, CCIS-Hill Center, Busch Campus, PO Box 879, Piscataway, NJ 08854, Ms. Gertrude Lewis, (201) 932-2483

New Mexico
Economic Development and Tourism Department, 1100 St. Francis Drive, Santa Fe, NM 87503, Ms. Carol Selleck (505) 827-0276

New Mexico State Library, PO Box 1629, Santa Fe, NM 87503, Ms. Norman McCallan (505) 827- 2033

Information Services Division, General Service Department, 715 Alta Vista, Santa Fe, NM 87503, Ms. Bonnie Drake (505) 827-8524

Bureau of Business and Economic Research, University of New Mexico, Albuquerque, NM 87131, Ms. Lynn Wombold (505) 277-2216

Center for Business Research & Services, Box 3CQ, New Mexico State University, Las Cruces, NM 88003, Dr. Kathleen Brook, (505) 646-4905

New York
Division of Economic Research & Statistics, New York Department of Commerce, 1 Commerce Plaza, Room 905, 99 Washington Avenue, Albany, NY 12245, Mr. Peter Ansell, Asst. Deputy Commissioner/Mr. Michael Batutis, Chief Demographer (518) 474-6005

Cornell Institute for Social and Economic Research (CISER), Cornell University, 323 Uris Hall, Ithaca, NY 14853-7601, Ms. Ann Gray (607) 255-1358

Nelson A. Rockefeller Institute of Government, 411 State Street, Albany, NY 12203, (518) 255-1358

Law and Social Sciences Unit, New York State Library, Cultural Education Center, Empire State Plaza, Albany, NY 12230, Ms. Elaine Scheerer (518) 474-5128/Ms. Mary Redmond (518) 474-3940

North Carolina
North Carolina Office of State Budget and Management, 116 West Jones Street, Raleigh, NC 27611, Ms. Francine Ewing, Director of State Data Center (919) 733-7061

State Library, North Carolina Department of Cultural Resouces, 109 East Jones Street Raleigh, NC 27611, Ms. Delores Porter (919) 966-3343

Institute for Research in Social Science, University of North Carolina, Manning Hall 026A, Chapel Hill, NC 27514, Ms. Diana McDuffie/Mr. Jack Beggs (919) 966-3346

Land Resources Information Service, Division of Land Resources, PO Box 27687, Raleigh, NC 27611, Ms. Karen Siderelis (919) 733-2090

North Dakota
Department of Agricultural Economics, North Dakota State University, Morrill Hall, Room 224, PO Box 5636, Fargo, ND 58105, Mr. Gary Goreham/ Dr. Richard Rathge (701)237-8621

Office of Intergovernment Assistance, State Capitol, 14th Floor, Bismarck, ND 58505, Mr. Jim Boyd (701) 224-2094

Department of Geography, University of North Dakota, Grand Forks, ND 58202, Dr. Floyd Hickok (701) 777-4593

North Dakota State Library, Liberty Memorial Building, Capitol Grounds, Bismarck, ND 58505, Ms. Margaret Stefanak (701) 224-2290

Ohio
Ohio Data Users Center, Ohio Department of Development, State Office Tower Building, 26th Floor, 30 E. Broad Street, Columbus, OH

43266-0101, Mr. Barry Bennett (614) 466-2115

Oklahoma
Oklahoma State Data Center, Oklahoma Department of Commerce, #5 Broadway Executive Park, 6601 Broadway Extension, Oklahoma City, OK 73116-8214, Ms. Karen Selland (405) 843-9770

Oklahoma Department of Libraries, 200 N.E. 18th Street, Oklahoma City, OK 73105, Mr. Steve Beleu (405) 521-2502

Oregon
Intergovernmental Relations Division, Executive Department, 155 Cottage Street, N.E., Salem, OR 97310, Ms. Lana Holman (503) 378-3732

Oregon State Library, State Library Building, Salem, OR 97310, Mr. Graig Smith (503) 378- 4502

Bureau of Governmental Research & Service, University of Oregon, Hendricks Hall, Room 340, PO Box 3177, Eugene, OR 97403, Ms. Karen Seidel (503) 686-5232

Center for Population Research and Census, Portland State University, PO Box 751, Portland, OR 97207, Mr. Ed Shafer (503) 229-3922

Oregon State Housing Division, Department of Commerce, 110 Labor & Industries Bldg., Salem, OR 97310, Mr. Mike Murphy (503) 378-5953

Pennsylvania
Institute of State and Regional Affairs, Pennsylvania State University at Harrisburg, Middletown, PA 17057, Mr. Bob Surridge (717) 948-6336

Pennsylvania State Library, Forum Building, Harrisburg, PA 17120, Mr. John Gerswindt (717) 787-2327

Governor's Office of Budget and Administration, Bereau of Management Services, 903 Health & Welfare Building, Harrisburg, PA 17120, Mr. Ray Kasper (717) 787-1764

Puerto Rico
Puerto Rico Planning Board, Minillas Government Center, North Bldg., Avenida De Diego, PO Box 41119, San Juan, PR 00940, Mr. Nolan Lopez (809) 728-4430, x2664 or 3876

General Library, University of Puerto Rico, Road #2, Mayaguez, PR 00708, Prfa. Grace Quinones Seda (809) 834-4040

Biblioteca Carnegie, Avda. Ponce de Leon, Parada 2, San Juan, PR 00901, Sra. Carmen Martinez (809) 724-1046

Rhode Island
Rhode Island Statewide Planning Program, 265 Melrose Street, Room 203, Providence, RI 02907, Mr. Chet Symanski (401) 277-2656

Rhode Island Department of State Library Services, 95 Davis Street, Providence, RI 02908, Mr. Frank Iacona (401) 277-2726

Social Science Data Center, Brown University, PO Box 1916, Providence, RI 02912, Ms. Lauralee Thompson (401) 863-2550

Office of Municipal Affairs, Rhode Island Department of Administration, 275 Westminister Mall, Providence, RI 02903, Mr. Paul Egan (401) 277-2886

Office of Evaluation, Rhode Island Department of Health, 75 Davis Street Room 409, Providence, RI 02908, Mr. Jay Buechner (401) 277-2550

South Carolina
Division of Research and Statistical Services, South Carolina Budget and Control Board, Rembert Dennis Bldg. Room 337, Columbia, SC 29201, Mr. Bobby Bowers/Mr. Mike Macfariane (803) 734-3782

South Carolina State Library, PO Box 11469, Columbia, SC 29211, Ms. Mary Toll (803) 734- 8666

South Dakota
Business Research Bureau, School of Business, University of South Dakota, 414 East Clark, Vermillion, SD 57069, Ms. DeVee Dykstra (605) 677-5287

Documents Department, South Dakota State Library, Department of Education and Cultural Affairs, 800 N. Illinois Ave., Pierre, SD 57501, Ms. Margaret Betzpaletz (605) 773-3131

Economics, Demographics and Statistics

Labor Market Information Center, South Dakota Department of Labor, 607 North 4th Street Box 1730, Aberdeen, SD 57402-4730, Ms. Mary Susan Vickers (605) 622-2314

Vital Records Program, South Dakota Department of Health, Foss Building, Pierre, SD 57501, Ms. Jan Smith (605) 773-3355

Rural Sociology Department, South Dakota State University, Scobey Hall Room 226, Brookings, SD 57007, Dr. Jim Satteriee (605) 688-3693

Tennessee
Tennessee State Planning Office, John Sevier State Office Bldg., 500 Charlotte Ave. Suite 307, Nashville, TN 37219, Mr. Charles Brown (615) 741-1676

Center for Business and Economic Research, College of Business Administration, University of Tennessee, Room 100, Glocker Hall, Knoxville, TN 37996-4170, Ms. Betty Vickers (615) 974-5441

TEXAS
State Data Center, Texas Advisory Commission on Intergovernmental Relations, Sam Houston Building, 201 E 14th Street, Austin, TX 78711. Mailing address: PO Box 13206 (ACIR), Capitol Station, Austin, TX 78711, Ms. Susan Szaniszlo (512) 463-1812

Department of Rural Sociology, Texas A & M University System, Special Services Building, College Station, TX 77843, Dr. Steve Murdock (409) 845-5115 or 5332

Texas Natural Rsources Information System, (TNRIS), PO Box 13087, Austin, TX 78711, Mr. Sam McCullock (512) 463-8346

Texas State Library and Archive Commission, PO Box 12927, Capitol Station, Austin, TX 78711, Ms. Bonnie Grobar (512) 463-5455

Utah
Office of Planning & Budget, State Capitol, Rm. 116, Salt Lake City, UT 84114, Mr. Brad Barber, Director/Ms. Natalie Gochnour (801) 533-6082

Bureau of Economic and Business Research, 401 Garff Building, University of Utah, Salt Lake City, UT 84112, Ms. Ronda Brinkerhoff (801) 581-6333

Population Research Laboratory, Utah State University, UMC 07, Logan, UT 84322, Mr. Yun Kim (801) 750-1231

Department of Employment Security, 174 Social Hall Avenue, PO Box 11249, Salt Lake City, UT 84147, Mr. Ken Jensen (801) 533-2372

Vermont
Office of Policy Research and Coordination, Pavilion Office Building, 109 State Street, Montpelier, VT 05602, Mr. Bernard Johnson / David Healy (802) 828-3326

Center for Rural Studies, University of Vermont, 25 Hills Building, Burlington, VT 05405-0090, Mr. Tom Arnold (802) 656-3021

Vermont Department of Libraries, 111 State Street, Montpelier, VT 05603, Ms. Patricia Klinck, Sate of Librarian (802) 828-3265

Vermont Agency of Dvelopment and Community Affairs, Pavilion Office Building, 109 State Street, Montpelier, VT 05602, Mr. Jed Guertin (802) 828-3211

Virginia
Department of Planning & Budget, 445 Ninth Street Office Bldg., PO Box 1422, Richmond, VA 23211, Mr. Larry Robinson (804) 786-8624

Tayloe Murphy Institute, University of Virginia, Dynamics Bldg., 4th Floor, 2015 Ivy Road, Charlottesville, VA 22903, Dr. Michael Spar (804) 971-2661

Virginia State Library, 12th and Capitol Streets, Richmond, VA 23219, Mr. Jim Martinelli (804) 786- 2175

Virgin Islands
Department of Commerce of the Virgin Islands, P.O. Box 6400, St. Thomas, VI 00802, Ms. Charlotte Amalie, Mr. James Pobicki (809) 774-8784

Washington
Estimation & Forecasting Unit, Office of Financial Management, Insurance Bldg., AQ-44, Olympia, WA 98504-0202, Mr. Lawrence Weisser (206) 586-2808

Documents Section, Washington State Library, AJ-11, Olympia, WA 98504, Ms. Ann Bregent (206) 753- 4027

Puget Sound Council of Govts., 215 1st Avenue South, Seattle, WA 98104, Ms. Cam McIntosh (206) 464- 7532

Social Research Center, Department of Rural Sociology, Rm. 133, Wilson Hall, Washington State Univeristy, Pullman, WA 99164, Dr. Annabel Cook (509) 335-1511

Department of Sociology, Demographic Research Laboratory, Western Washington University, Belligham, WA 98225, Mr. Lucky Tedrow,Director (206) 676-3617

Technical Information Services, University Library, Eastern Washington University, Cheney, WA 99004, Mr. Jay Rae (509) 359-7894

Department of Sociology, Central Washington University, Ellensburg, WA 98926, Mr. John R. Dugan (509) 963-3131

West Virginia
Community Development Division, Governor's Office of Community and Industrial Development, Capitol Complex, Building 6, Room 553, Charleston, WV 25305, Ms. Mary C. Hariess (304) 348-4010

Reference Library, West Virginia State Library Commission, Science and Cultural Center, Capitol Complex, Charleston, WV 25305, Ms. Karen Goff (304) 348-2045

Office of Health Services Research, Department of Community Health, West Virginia University, 900 Chestnut Ridge Road, Morgantown, WV 26505, Ms. Valerie Frey-McClung (304) 293-2601

Wisconsin
Demographic Services Center, Department of Administration, 101 S. Webster St., 6th Floor, PO Box 7868, Madison, WI 53707-7868, Ms. Nadene Roenspies, Mr. Robert Naylor (608) 266- 1927

Department of Rural Sociology, University of Wisconsin, 1450 Linden Drive, Rm. 316, Madison, WI 53706, Ms. Doris Slesinger/Mr. Tom Godfrey (608) 262-1515

Wyoming
Institute for Policy Research, University of Wyoming, PO Box 3925, Laramie, WY 82071, Mr. Fred G. Doll (307) 766-5141

Department of Administration and Fiscal Control, Emerson Building, Cheyenne, WY 82002, Mr. Phil Kiner, Director, Research & Statistics (307) 777-7504

State Statistical Abstracts

For years researchers have been aware of the importance of keeping around the latest edition of the *Statistical Abstract of the United States* (available for $25 from Superintendent of Documents, US GPO, Washington, DC 20402, (202) 783-3238). Now if you are interested in local or regional opportunities, trends or markets, most every state government offers their own *State Statistical Abstract* or something comparable. Most of the states produce their abstract on a annual basis. There are only 8 states which do not publish abstracts: Arkansas, Delaware, Kansas, Massachusetts, New Hampshire, Texas, Virginia, Wisconsin.

Tables and graphs are used to illustrate the performance of the economy. Where comparisons can be made, state, regional, and national data can be compared. Market analysts, businesses and researchers will find the following kinds of information in a statistical abstract:

o how many of Fortune magazine's top 500 companies
  have manufacturing plants in the state;
o the number of jobs directly or indirectly related to
  exports;
o largest sources of personal income;
o number of people employed in
  agricultural/non-agricultural jobs;
o how a state ranks in population and land size;
o number of acres of forest land;
o number of airports, number privately owned;
o number of registered aircraft;
o changes in population-age distribution;
o percentage of 17 and 18 year olds graduating from
  high school;
o number of state universities, vocational schools;
o motor vehicle registrations;
o crime rates; and
o traffic fatalities.

Similar to the *Statistical Abstract of the US* in providing important data in charts and tables, these state abstracts offer important leads to more detailed sources of information. Although the specific charts and tables many not offer the exact detail of data you require on a particular topic, they will identify the offices which generate this type of information. By contacting the specific office you are likely to get the precise data you require. They can't publish everything they have in a single statistical abstract, but they can dig it out of their files for you.

Statistical Abstract Offices

Alabama
University of Alabama, Center for Business and Economic Research, P.O. Box Ak, Tuscaloosa, AL   35487, (205) 263-0048--Publication: *Economic Abstract of Alabama* ($40.00).

Alaska
Alaska Department of Labor, Research and Analysis, P.O. Box 25501, Juneau, AK   99802, (907) 465-4500--Publication: *Statistical Quarterly* (free).

Arizona
Arizona Department of Economic Security Research Administration, P.O. Box 6123, Phoenix, AZ   85005, (602) 255-3616--Publication:

Labor Market Information-Annual Planning Information (free).

California
Department of Finance, 1025 P. St., Room 83, Sacramento, CA   95814, (916) 322-2263--Publication: *California Statistical Abstract* (free).

Colorado
University of Colorado, Business Research Division, Graduate School of Business Administration, Campus Box 420, Boulder, CO   80309, (303) 866-3386-Publication: *Statistical Abstract of Colorado* ($45.00).

Connecticut
Office of Policy and Management, Budget and Financial Management Division, 80 Washington St., Hartford, CT   06106, (203) 566-8342--Publication: *Economic Report of the Governor* (free).

District of Columbia
Mayor's Office, Office of Policy, Office of Statistics, District Building, 1350 Pennsylvania Ave. N.W., Washington, DC   20005, (202) 727-6319--Publication: *Indices* ($5.00).

Florida
University Presses of Florida, 15 N.W. 15th St., Gainesville, FL 32603, (904) 392-1351--Publication: *Florida Statistical Abstract* ($19.95).

Georgia
Georgia Office of Planning and Budget, 270 Washington St., Room 608, Atlanta, GA   30334, (404) 656-3820--Publications: *Georgia Descriptions and Data - A Statistical Abstract* ($7.50).

Hawaii
State of Hawaii, Business and Economic Development, P.O. Box 2359, Honolulu, HI   96804, (808) 548-3060--Publication: *State of Hawaii Statistical Abstract* ($15.00).

Idaho
Secretary of State, Room 203, State House, Boise, ID   83720, (208) 334-3900-- Publication: *Idaho Blue Book* ($5.00).

Illinois
University of Illinois, Bureau of Economic and Business Research, 1206 S. 6th St., 428 Commerce West, Champaign, IL   61820, (217) 333-2330--Publication: *Statistical Abstract* ($27.00).

Indiana
Indiana Department of Commerce, Division of Economic Analysis, One North Capitol, Suite 700, Indianapolis, IN   46204, (317) 232-3953--Publication: *The Indiana Economy: A Primer* (free).

Iowa
Iowa Development Commission, 200 Grand Ave., Des Moines, IA   50309, (515) 281-3555-- Publication: *Statistical Profile of Iowa* (free).

Kentucky
Cabinet for Economic Development, 133 Holmes St., Frankfort, KY 40601, (502) 564-4715--Publication: *Kentucky Economic Statistics* (free).

Maine
Business Development Office, State House Station #59, Augusta, ME 04333, (207) 289-3195--Publication: *Maine Statistical Summary* (free).

Maryland
Department of Economic and Employment Development, P.O. Box 447, Bladensburg, MD   20710, (301) 333-6953--Publication: *Statistical Abstract* ($22.00).

Michigan
Wayne State University, Bureau of Business Research, School of Business Administration, Detroit, MI   48202, (313) 577-4505--Publication: *Michigan Statistical Abstract* ($22.50).

Minnesota

State Planning Administration, 300 Centennial Building, 658 Cedar St., St. Paul, MN 55155, (612) 296-8282--Publication: *Pocket Data Book* (free).

Mississippi

Mississippi State University, Division of Business Research, College of Business and Industry, Drawer 5288, Mississippi State, MS 39762, (601) 325-3221--Publications: *Mississippi Statistical Abstract* ($29.50).

Missouri

University of Missouri, B & PA Research Center, 10 Professional Building, Columbia, MO 65211, (314) 882-4805--Publications: *Statistical Abstract* ($20.00).

Montana

Department of Commerce, Census and Economic Information Center, 1424 9th Ave. Helena, MT 59620, (406) 444-4393--Publication: *Montana Statistical Abstract* (free).

Nebraska

Department of Economic Development, Research Division, P.O. Box 94666, Lincoln, NE 68509, (402) 471-3111--Publication: *Nebraska Statistical Handbook* ($6.00).

Nevada

Nevada Planning and Intergovernmental Affairs, 1100 E. Williams, Room 120, Capitol Complex, Carson City, NV 89710, (702) 885-5977--Publication: *Statistical Abstract* ($15.00).

New Jersey

Office of Economic Policy, New Jersey Department of Commerce, 20 W. State St., Trenton, NJ, (609) 292-1890--Publication: *New Jersey Profile* (free).

New Mexico

State Budget Division, Room 432, State Capitol Building, Santa Fe, NM 87503, (505) 827-3640--Publication: *Status of the State* (free).

New York

Rockefeller Institute of Government, 411 State St., Albany, NY 12203, (518) 472-1300-- Publication: *New York Statistical Yearbook* ($20.00).

North Carolina

Office of the State Budget, 116 W. Jones St., Raleigh, NC 27603, (919) 733-7061--Publications: *North Carolina State Statistical Abstract* ($4.00).

North Dakota

The Bureau of Business and Economic Research, College of Business and Public Administration, Box 8255, University of North Dakota, Grand Forks, ND 58202, (701) 777-3365--Publications: *North Dakota Statistical Abstract* (price not determined).

Ohio

Ohio Data Users, P.O. Box 1001, Columbus, OH 43266, (614) 466-2115--Publication: *County Profiles* ($50.00).

Oklahoma

University of Oklahoma, CEMR (Center for Economic and Management Research), College of Business Administration, 307 W. Brooks St., Norman, OK 73019, (405) 624-5108--Publications: *Statistical Abstract* ($20.00).

Oregon

Economic Development Department, 595 Cottage St. N.E., Salem, OR 97310, (503) 373-1280--Publication: *Oregon Statistical Profile* ($3.00).

Pennsylvania

State Data Center, State University at Harrisburg, Capitol College, Middletown, PA 17057, (717) 948-6336--Publication: *Statistical Abstract* ($15.00).

Rhode Island

Department of Economic Development, 7 Jackson Walkway, Providence, RI 02903, (401) 277-2601--Publication: *Rhode Island Basic Economic Statistics* (free).

South Carolina

Division of Research and Statistical Services, 1000 Assembly St., Rembert C. Dennis Building, Suite 425, Columbia, SC 29201, (803) 734-3793--Publication: *South Carolina Statistical Abstract* ($17.00).

South Dakota

Businesses Research Bureau, School of Business, The University of South Dakota, 414 East Clark St., Vermillion, SD 57069, (605) 677-5287--Publications: *South Dakota Economic and Business Abstract* ($5.00); *The Demography and Socio-Economic Characteristics of South Dakota and Its Economic Regions* ($3.00).

Tennessee

University of Tennessee, Center for Business and Economic Research, S. 100 Glocker Hall, College of Business Administration, Knoxville, TN 37996, (615) 974-5441--Publication: *Tennessee State Statistical Abstract* ($30.00).

Texas

Department of Commerce, Research and Planning Division, State Data Center, P.O. Box 12728, Austin, TX 78711, (512) 463-1166--Publication: (in the process of assembling data for a statistical abstract).

Utah

University of Utah, bureau of Economic and Business Research, P.O. Box 8066, Salt Lake City, UT 84108, (801) 538-1027--Publication: *Annual Economic Report* (free).

Vermont

Agency of Development and Community Affairs, Montpelier, VT 05602, (802) 828-3211--Publication: *Vermont Selected Statistics* (free).

Washington

Department of Revenue, Office of the Forecast Council, Evergreen Plaza, Room 300, Olympia, WA 98504, (206) 753-2061--Publication: *Economic and Revenue Forecast for Washington State* ($10.00).

West Virginia

Chamber of Commerce, Research and Strategic Planning, P.O. Box 2789, Charleston, WV 25330, (304) 342-1115--Publication: *West Virginia Economic Statistical Profile* ($50.00).

Wyoming

Wyoming State Government, Research and Statistics Division, 302 Emerson Blvd. Cheyenne, WY 82002, (307) 777-7504--Publication: *The Wyoming Data Handbook* (Free).

State Forecasting Centers

State planning offices can provide vast quantities of local market information, demographic data, and company intelligence -- more than you would believe possible. Every state has a bureau equivalent to a planning office to assist the Governor in charting future economic change. Of course, the quantity of information varies from one state to the next as does the sophistication in methods of gathering and analyzing data. However, most information is generated to support decision making for policies and legislative initiatives which will affect the current and future status of the state economy. These blueprints for the future usually include plans for attracting new businesses and industries as well as improving the quality of housing, education and transportation.

It should be noted that there is a wide disparity in the research and strategic focus of these state planning offices. The position of this function within the state bureaucratic structure often provides clues about the scope of its mission. In most states this forecasting operation is housed in the Department of Economic Development or in a separate policy office under the Governor's office. However, in our survey of all fifty states we discovered this crucial function in unexpected places. In South Carolina, for example, there is a special Commission on the Future within the Lieutenant Governor's office and in Texas a comparable office falls under the jurisdiction of the state comptroller.

The types of information available from these offices are outlined below.

Business Expansion and Economic Outlook

If you currently do business in a state or intend to establish a business there, it would be wise to learn about the Governor's long-term strategy. Keep in mind that no one is more concerned about the state's future than this elected official. If your company sells to farmers, inquire at the planning office about the Governor's agricultural policies. If your firm relies on high tech complementary businesses, see whether there is a plan to attract high tech companies. Or if you are interested in consumer markets, be aware of demographic projections conducted by the planning agency for the state as well as for specific regions and counties. Many states appear to be charting future population patterns on a regular basis as is evident with the sampling of publications noted here.

Indiana: *Some Aspects of Demographic Change in Indiana from 1980 to 2000*
California: *California's Economic Future -- Building New Foundations for a Competitive Society*
Michigan: *Population Projections for Michigan to the Year 2010*
Utah: *Utah 2000*
Nebraska: *Nebraska Industry -- A Survey of Concerns, Needs and Future Plans*
New Jersey: *Annual Economic Forecast*

Demographics and Market Studies

Most of these offices are aware of the current demographic situation within their state. They also continually monitor the major industries in the state as well as emerging industries. Their data usually are derived from a combination of federal, state and locally generated information. Sometimes these offices are part of the state data center program run by the U.S. Bureau of the Census. Demographic studies as well as state statistical abstracts are readily available.

Arizona: *Community Profiles*
Montana: *County Profiles*
Washington DC: *Housing Monographs by Ward*
Nevada: *Community Profiles -- Demographic Facts*
New Hampshire: *Changes in Households and Households Size for Towns and Cities*
Iowa: *A Statistical Profile of Iowa*
Maryland: *State Statistical Abstract*

These state planning offices often produce in-depth market studies on diverse topics:

Arizona: *Aerospace in Arizona -- An Assessment of Market Opportunities*
Delaware: *Food Processors, Banking,* and *Automotive Just-In-Time Suppliers*
Maryland: *Impact of Professional Sports on the Maryland Economy*
Michigan: *Machine Tool Industry Update*
Missouri: *Home Health Care and the Homemaker*
Nebraska: *Profit Opportunities in Nebraska for Manufacturers of Pet Food*
New York: *Statistical Profile of the Printing and Publishing Industry*
Florida: *Monthly Tourist Surveys*
Virginia: *High Technology Communications in Virginia*

Company Information and Industry Directories

Many of these offices are responsible for maintaining information on the companies which are located within their state. It is not unusual for the state to collect the following data on every manufacturer and corporation:

- Name of company;
- Address and telephone number;
- Names of principal officers;
- Types of products or services produced;
- Number of employees; and
- Sales estimate.

You stand to learn more about a company, especially its financial picture, if the business in question received some type of economic assistance from the state. After all, once a company takes taxpayer money, the public has a right to know. There is a growing number of companies that fall into this category. Recently we received a list of over 100 firms which obtained financial assistance from Pennsylvania just during the past year.

Other handy resources available from many state planning offices are company directories, many of them concentrate on one industry sector.

Economics, Demographics and Statistics

Kansas: *Directory of Kansas Warehouse and Distribution Centers*
Michigan: *Michigan Private 100*
Montana: *Consumer Products Buyer's Directory*
Oregon: *Directory of Oregon Electronic Products*

Databases and Special Services

Because these planning agencies share their forecasts and statistical data with other offices within the state government, often the data are readily available to the public, usually for free or on a cost recovery basis. Already many have established customized databases, some of which permit direct online access. Examples include:

* Idaho's database linking entrepreneurs with investors;
* Colorado's community profiles database covering 63 counties and 260 municipalities;
* Florida's nine public access databases; and
* Nevada's computerized databank on land availability, labor resources and economic statistics.

Difficulties Tracking Down Forecasting Data

Since numerous offices within a state are engaged in forecasting expect to run into some obstacles. Don't be discouraged if, when you contact one office for specific market data, you are told there is "no way" they would keep such information. The odds are that some other state bureaucrat has the information, so always patiently ask for other offices you could call. For example, practically every state publishes a directory of manufacturers, but it may not be produced by the planning office but by some other agency across town. This holds true when hunting for statistical information, markets studies, and databases.

State Planning Offices

The address and telephone numbers are included for the primary planning offices in each state as well as the District of Columbia. The publications listed with the office do not represent the entire universe of hardcopy data available. These titles are included only when the office is capable of providing us with a current listing. There are states which have publications but do not have any sort of catalog. For those states you must request data under specific topic headings.

Alabama
Alabama Department of Economic and Community Affairs, 3465 Norman Bridge Road, P.O. Box 2939, Montgomery, AL 36105, (205) 284-8910---Publications: *Annual Report*.

Alaska
State Planning Office, Division of Policy, Commerce & Economic Development, Office of Management and Budget, P.O. AD, Juneau, AK 99811, (907) 465-3568.

Arizona
Arizona Department of Commerce, State Capitol, 1700 West Washington, Phoenix, AZ 85007, 602-255-5371---Publications: *Annual Report, Arizona Annual Economic Profile, Arizona Department of Commerce Services Directory, Aerospace in Arizona-An Assessment of Market Opportunities, Arizona Developments Quarterly Newsletter, Directory of High Technology Companies, Guide to Establishing a Business in Arizona, High Technology in Arizona-A Market Analysis of Suppliers, Maquiladora Opportunities in Arizona, Arizona Chamber Directory, Arizona Agribusiness Profiles, Arizona Community Profiles* ($18), *Arizona Indian Profiles, Arizona Industrial Profiles* ($8), *Arizona Regional Profiles, Arizona Mail Street Newsletter, Common Questions About Planning Newsletter, Planning and Zoning Handbook* ($20), *Rural Economic Development Resource Directory* ($5), *Financial Resources for Business Development, Request for Proposal Handbook, Twenty Questions About Bldg, Arizona's Changing Economy* ($5), *Bi-Weekly Report of Federal and State*

Proposals Under Review, Clearinghouse Manual, Federal Assistance Award Data System Report, Local Government Funding Paper, Arizona Energy Data Report, Community Energy Profile Handbook, Arizona Energy Quarterly Newsletter, So-Easy Energy Saving Packet, Energy Checklist, Ease the Squeeze Driving Hints, Apartment Energy Conservation Guide, Home Energy Conservation Guide, Mobile Home Energy Conservation Guide, Energy Fact Sheets, Arizona Exporters Directory, Arizona Export Statistics, Arizona World Trade Review Quarterly Newsletter, Directory of International Services.

Arkansas
Office of Industrial Development, State of Arkansas, #1 Capitol Mall, Little Rock, AR 72201, (501) 682-1121---Publications: *Breaking Down Old Walls-Laying a New Foundation, Annual Report.*

California
Commission on Economic Development, State of California, State Capitol, Room 1028, Sacramento, CA 95814, (916) 445-1025---Publications: *Annual Report, Doing Business in California-A Guide for Establishing a Business* ($2), *Child Care-The Bottom Line* ($.50), *An International Trade Policy for California* ($2), *Poisoning Prosperity-The Impact of Toxics in California's Economy* ($5), *Assessment of Reduced Revenue on California Local Law Enforcement* ($2), *California-Inventing the Future Through Investment and Innovation, California's Economic Future-Building New Foundations for a Competitive Society.*

Colorado
State of Colorado, Division of Commerce and Development, Department of Local Affairs, 1313 Sherman St., Room 523, Denver, CO 80203, (303) 866-2205---Publications: *Directory of Services, State Newsletter.* Other Services: Community Profiles Database, covering 63 counties and 260 municipalities.

Connecticut
Connecticut Department of Economic Development, 210 Washington St., Hartford, CT 06106, (203) 566-4094--Publications: *Annual Report.*

Delaware
Delaware Development Office, State of Delaware, Executive Department, 99 Kings Highway, P.O. Box 1401, Dover, DE 19903, (302) 736-4271---Publications: *Three-Year Capital Budget Plan, Delaware Data Book, Comparison of Estimated State and Local Family Tax Burdens, Small Business Start-Up Guide,* and *Procurement Guide, Industries Under Study: Banking, Automotive "Just-In-Time" Suppliers, Food Processors, Polymer Producers, Business Services and Air Transportation Services.* Other Services: Business Research Section maintains an extensive library of data resources and responds to requests for economic, demographic and travel information. Selective online access available to a computerized real estate file. A computerized hotel reservation system is also available.

District of Columbia
Office of Planning, Deputy Mayor for Economic Development, Government of the District of Columbia, Washington, DC 20004, (202) 727-6492---Publications: *Census Tract Map* ($2), *Citizen's Guide to Zoning, Comprehensive Plan and Land Use Map, Development Process in the District of Columbia* ($50), *District of Columbia Zoning Map* ($3), *Market Assessment for Downtown Washington, Housing Monograph by Ward, Population Monograph by Ward, Land Use Monograph by Ward, 1982 Housing Unit Estimates Washington, DC, Planning for the Future/The Ward Planning Process, Proposal to Establish Development Zones East of the Anacostia River, Population Estimates Washington, DC, Connecticut Avenue Corridor Study, Anacostia Metro Station Action Plan, Benning Road Action Plan, Fort Totten Metro Station Action Plan, Fourteenth Street and Potomac Avenue Metro State Area Action Plan, Howard Gateway Action Plan, New York Avenue Industrial Corridor Action Plan, Rhode Island Avenue Metro Station Action Plan, Taylor and Upshur Street Action Plan, Street Address Directory* ($4), *The State of the Wards Report.*

Florida
Bureau of Economic Analysis, Florida Department of Commerce, Division of Economic Development, Tallahassee, FL 32301, (904) 487-2971---Publications: *Monthly Tourist Surveys, County Comparisons, Florida and the Other Forty-Nine, Agency Functional Plan, Information Resources Technology Plan, Economic Intelligence Monthly, A Guide to Florida Environmental Permitting, Agency Functional Plan, Annual Summary of Florida's International Trade.* Special Services: Nine public access databases, and customized research requests.

Georgia
Office of Planning and Budget, 270 Washington Street, S.W., Atlanta, GA 30334, (404) 656-3820---Publications: *Governor's Policy Statement, Memos from Growth Issues Resources Council.*

Hawaii
Planning and Economic Development, Kamamalu Building, 250 S. King St., Honolulu, HI 96814, (808)-548-4347.

Idaho

Department of Commerce, Room 108, State Capitol, Boise, ID 83720, (208) 334-3417---Publications: *Economic Development Agenda.*

Illinois

Illinois Department of Commerce and Community Affairs, 620 East Adams Street, Springfield, IL 62701, (217) 782-3233 --Publications: *Blueprint for the Future, Annual Statistics Report.*

Indiana

Indiana Economic Development Council, One North Capitol, Suite 425, Indianapolis, IN 46204, (317) 631-0871---Publications: *Annual Economic Report, The Futures of Indiana-Trends Affecting Economic Change 1986-2000, Indiana's Infrastructure Strategy-An Outline for Action, A Preliminary Review of Alternative Utility Regulatory Approaches, 1986 Indiana Economic Development Congress, Defining Vocational Education, Some Aspects of Demographic Change in Indiana-1980 to 2000 Youth Entering the Workforce, Vocational Education: Who Are The Students, Do Vocational and Academic Programs Compete for a Student's Time?, Indiana Vocational Education at Selected Schools, Vocational Education in Indiana, Vocational Education and Economic Development in Indiana, A Future of Learning and Work, The Investment Effects of Indiana's Preliminary Tax Abatement Programs, An Evaluation of Property Tax Abatement in Indiana, Looking Back-The Update of Indiana's Strategic Economic Development Plan.*

Iowa

Iowa Department of Economic Development, 200 East Grand Avenue. Des Moines, IA 50309, (515) 281-3251---Publications: *Statistical Profile of Iowa, Economic Developments.*

Kansas

Department of Economic Development Research, 400 W 8th St. 5th Floor, Topeka, KS 66603, (913) 296-3564---Publications; *Annual Report, Directory of Kansas Manufacturers and Products ($35), Directory of Kansas Warehouse and Distribution Centers, Directory of Kansas Job Shops, Fortune 500 Facilities in Kansas, Kansas Manufacturing Firms in Exports, Kansas Association Directory, Firms Headquartered In Kansas, Kansas New and Expanding Manufacturers, Kansas Economic Development Statutes, Commercial Guide to Industrial Development.*

Kentucky

Center for Business & Economic Development, 302 Matthews Building, College of Business and Economics, University of Kentucky, Lexington, KY 40506, (606) 257-7664---Publications: *Annual Economic Report.*

Louisiana

State Planning Office, Division of Administration, P.O. Box 94095, Baton Rouge, LA 70804, (504) 342-7410.

Maine

Economic and Community Development Office, State House Station 59, Augusta, ME 04333, (207) 289-2656.

Maryland

Division of Research, Department of Economic and Community Development, 45 Calvert St., Annapolis, MD 21401, (301) 974-3629---Publications: *The Impact of Professional Sports on the Maryland Economy, An Econometric Analysis of Variations in Workers' Compensation Rates, The Fiscal Impact of Professional Sports, The Economic Impact of the Preakness on the Maryland Economy, Workers' Compensation Insurance, Competitive Rating in Workers' Compensation Insurance, The Economic Impact of the University of Maryland's Football Program, Report of the Special Advisory Committee on Professional Sports and the Economy, Maryland Statistical Abstract, Workers' Compensation in Maryland, Technical Notes on 27 Issues in Workers' Compensation, Workers' Compensation in Maryland, Workers' Compensation Summary of Major Studies, Prompt Payment of Temporary Total Disability Benefits, Maryland Workers' Compensation Claims Experience, Workers' Compensation Medical Claims and Benefits Written Opinions, A Comparative Analysis of Accident Patterns by Industry and by State, Report of the Governor's Commission to Study the Workers' Compensation System, Addendum to the Report of the Governor's Commission to Study the Workers' Compensation System, A Preliminary Feasibility Study of Ferry Service on the Chesapeake Bay, A Guide to the Calculation of Workers' Tax Payments, The Impact of the Commercial Fishing Industry on the Maryland Economy, Telecommunications Taxation, Selected Economic Indications-Monthly.*

Massachusetts

Governor's Office of Economic Development, State House 109, Boston, MA 02133, (617) 727-1130---Publications: *Creating the Future: Opportunity, Innovation and Growth in the Massachusetts Economy.*

Michigan

Business Research Office, Department of Commerce, State of Michigan, P.O. Box 30225, Lansing, MI 48909, (517) 373-7401:

Publications: *Business Guide to Understanding Michigan Sales and Use Tax, Comparison with Illinois, Comparison with Indiana, Comparison with Kentucky, Comparison with Ohio, Comparison with Tennessee, Comparison with Wisconsin, County Business Climate Overview and Highlights for each of 83 Counties, Food Processing Overview, Michigan as a Place to do Business-A Review of Recent Studies, Michigan's Labor Force Characteristics, Michigan's Market Potential, Michigan Property Tax System-Overview of the, Ontario-Brief Look at Augusta, Ontario vs. Michigan-A Comparison, Review of Michigan Taxes, Crain's Detroit Business List of Top Privately Held Companies, Crain's Detroit Business List of Top Publicly Held Companies, Fortune 500 Companies Headquartered in Michigan, Michigan Private 100, The Michigan 100, Employment Size Study, Industrial Construction Trends by County, Industrial Real Estate Market Survey, Michigan Economic Update, Michigan Economy-Overview, New Business Incorporations, New Capital Expenditures in Michigan, Population Projections for Michigan to the Year 2010, Questions & Answers About Small Business, REMI Employment Multipliers, US Dept. of Commerce, Bureau of Economic Analysis Projections, Metal Fabricating Industry Study, Michigan Chemical Industry-An Overview, Michigan Machine Tool Industry Update, Michigan Machinery Industry Overview, Michigan Service Industry Overview, Michigan-State of the Future, Plastics Industry, Basic Business Sources-SMU Business Library, Business Reference Sources-Library of Michigan, Business Taxes in Michigan, The Case for Michigan, Commercial Redevelopment Act, Community Growth Alliances, Export Assistance, Food Processing Opportunities in Michigan, Forest Products Opportunities in Michigan, Governor's Commission on Jobs and Economic Development Adopts Labor Training, Labor Training, Leader in Automated Systems Manufacturing, Michigan-The Leader in Metalworking, Michigan's Expanding Plastics Industry, Michigan's Improving Business Future, Michigan Main Street-Downtown Revitalization Assistance, Property Tax Incentives, Small Business Centers, State Financial Assistance.*

Minnesota

State Planning Agency, Administration, 300 Centennial Bldg., 658 Cedar St., St. Paul, MN 55155, (612) 296-3985---Publications: *Minnesota State Hospital Facilities and Alternative Use, Minnesota State Hospital Use and Cost, A Profile of Minnesota State Hospital Employees, The Economic Impact of Minnesota State Hospitals, Public Opinions About State Hospitals, Residents/Patients in Minnesota State Hospitals, Opinions and Recommendations for the Minnesota State Hospital System, Minnesota State Hospitals-Executive Summary, Mental Health Commission Report, Studies of the Academies for the Deaf and the Blind, Disabilities and Technology, Real Homes Real Education Real Job: A New Way of Thinking.*

Mississippi

Mississippi Research and Development Center, 3825 Ridgewood Rd., Jackson, MS, 39211, (601) 982-6489---Publications: *Bibliography of Publications, Budget Facts: Facts on Financing Mississippi State Government, Catalog of Audiovisual Materials Available on Loan, Checklist for New Manufacturers in Mississippi, A Comparison of the 1980 Census Count in Mississippi with the Mississippi Research and Development Center's 1980 County Population Projections, Directory of Master Parent Companies of Mississippi Manufacturers, Electrical Peak Demand Control System, Factors Affecting the Location of Technology Intensive Industries, Facts and Figures, Handbook of Selected Data for Mississippi, Highlights of Mississippi's Changing Economy, How to Develop a Business Plan, Industrial Incentives, Major Government Regulations Affecting Small Retail Business in Mississippi, Mississippi County Data Bank, Mississippi Industrial Services Communicator, Mississippi Manufacturers Directory ($35), Mississippi Manufacturing Atlas, Mississippi's Public Junior College Vocational-Technical Courses of Interest to Industry, R & D Economic Brief, R & D Annual Report, Services for Mississippi Businesses.*

Missouri

Missouri Office of Administration, Division of Budget and Planning, P.O. Box 809, Jefferson City, MO 65102, (314) 751-2345---Publications: *Missouri Demographic and Economic Profile, An Analysis of the Missouri Agribusiness Sector, Missouri's Statewide Economic Development Planning Program, A Directory of Missouri Data Sources, An Economic Analysis of Energy Supply and Demand in Missouri, Export Trade of the State of Missouri, Home Health Care and The Homemaker, Housing Program Utilization in Missouri, Missouri Housing Situation, Missouri Transportation System: Condition, Capacity and Impediments to Efficiency, Transportation Trends, Potential Industrial Opportunities for Missouri's Resource Base, A User's Guide to Missouri Maps.*

Montana

Business Assistance Division, Department of Commerce, State of Montana, 1424 9th Ave., Helena, MT 59620, (406) 444-3923 ---Publications: *County Profiles, Montana Statistical Abstract, Montana Manufacturers and Products Directory, Business and Industrial Location Guide, Consumer Products Buyers' Directory.*

Nebraska

Nebraska Department of Economic Development, P.O. Box 94666-State Office Bldg., 301 Centennial Mall South, Lincoln, NE 98509, (402) 471-3111 (800-426-6505)---Publications: *The Ethanol Distilling Industry-An Industrial Opportunity in Nebraska, Pharmaceuticals and Related Industries: Opportunities in Nebraska, Threshold Estimates and Other Tools for Retail Analysis, Frozen Potato and Onion Processing Opportunities in Nebraska,*

Economics, Demographics and Statistics

Investment of Nebraska Public Pension Funds, Nebraska as a World Class Center for Communications Industry, Equity Capital for Nebraska Small Business, Nebraska Visitors Survey, Nebraska Industry: A Survey of Their Concerns, Needs & Future Plans, Characteristics of Nebraska Immigrants and Outmigrants, 1984 Nebraska Air Service Study, The Nebraska Economic Indicators Survey, Hazardous Waste in Nebraska, Profit Opportunities in Nebraska for Manufacturers of Pet Food, Opportunities for Nebraska Businesses in India, Nebraska Profit Opportunities for Manufacturers of Scientific, Measuring and Controlling Instruments, Vegetable Production, Processing and Marketing in Nebraska, Service as a Leading Sector in Economic Development, Nebraska's Economic Performance, Building Prosperity: Nebraska Economic Development Strategy, Nebraska Statistical Handbook ($6.00), Nebraska Facts and Figures, Nebraska Directory of Manufacturers and their Products ($20.00), Nebraska Community Profiles.

Nevada

Commission on Economic Development, State of Nevada, Capitol Complex, Carson City, NV, (702) 885-4325---Publications: *State Plan for Economic Diversification and Development, Nevada Industrial Directory, Community Profiles-Demographic Facts, Quarterly Newsletter, State Economic Development Brochure, The Nevada Development Handbook.* Other: Development of a statewide database to provide access to information about land availability, labor sources and economic statistics.

New Hampshire

Office of State Planning, State of New Hampshire, Executive Department, 2 1/2 Beacon St., Concord, NH 03301, (603) 271-2155---Publications: *Current Year Population for New Hampshire Communities, Selected Economic Characteristics for New Hampshire Municipalities, Current Estimates and Trends in New Hampshire's Housing Supply Update-Annual, New Hampshire Population Projections for Counties and Municipalities, Current Estimates and Trends in New Hampshire's Housing Supply-1970-1981, New Hampshire Population Trends, Changes in Households and Household Size for Towns and Cities in New Hampshire, Taxable Valuation Per Person in New Hampshire Communities.*

New Jersey

Office of Economic Analysis, State of New Jersey, 1 West State St. Trenton, NJ 08625, (609) 292-1890---Publications: *Economic Report of the Governor-Annual, Economic Forecast-Annual.*

New Mexico

Economic Development Department, 1100 St. Francis Drive, Santa Fe, NM 87503, (505) 827-0302---Publications: *Annual Report, New Mexico USA (Economic Development), The New Mexico Rio Grande Research Corridor, New Mexico Magazine, The New Mexico Manufacturing Directory, The New Mexico Fact Book, Community Surveys, Brochure on International Trade, Brochure on Writing a Business Plan, Financial Resources in New Mexico.*

New York

Bureau of Business Research, NYS Department of Economic Development, Room 910, One Commerce Plaza, Albany, NY 12245, (518) 474-8670---Publications: *The Alpine Ski Industry in New York State, The Apparel Industry in New York State-A Statistical Profile, Business Trends in New York State-Monthly, Economic Trends in Selected Metropolitan Areas of New York State, Financial Services Industries in New York State, Industrial Development Bond report, New York State Business Fact Book Supplement-Annual, New York State Tax Structure-State Taxes-Local Taxes outside NYC, Local Taxes New York City, Personal Income in Areas and Counties of New York State-Annual, Profile of People, Jobs and Housing for New York State-New York City-Each County, A Statistical Profile of the Printing and Publishing Industry in New York State, A Statistical Report on High Technology Industries in New York State, Summaries of Selected Business and Business Climate Surveys, Summary of Business Statistics-Quarterly and Annual, Tax Incentives and Financing for Industrial Location, Tax Incentives-New York State, Tax Incentives-New York City.*

North Carolina

Office of Policy and Planning, NC Department of Administration, 116 Jones St., Raleigh, NC 27611, (919) 733-4131.

North Dakota

North Dakota Scanning Network, State of North Dakota, Office of the Governor, Bismark, ND 58505, (701) 224-2810--Publications: *Prairie Scans,* a newsletter identifying important issues and problems the state may face in the future. North Dakota Economic Development Commission, Liberty Memorial Building, Bismark, ND 58505, (701) 224-2810---Publications: *Annual Planning Report, North Dakota Economic Indicators, New Wealth Creating in North Dakota, North Dakota Growth Indicators, North Dakota Taxes, Available Buildings in North Dakota, North Dakota Economic Development Commission Work Plan, Financial and North Dakota, Resources and North Dakota, Manufacturers and North Dakota, Network Newsletter.*

Ohio

State of Ohio, Department of Development, P.O. Box 1001, Columbus,

OH 43216, (614) 466-2609---Publications: *Annual Report.*

Oklahoma

Oklahoma Futures Commission, Department of Commerce, 6601 Broadway Extension, Oklahoma City, OK 73116, (405) 843-9770---Publications: *Five Year Plan.*

Oregon

Oregon Economic Development Department, 595 Cottage Street, NE, Salem, OR 97310, (503) 373-1200---Publications: *Starting a Business in Oregon, A Summary of Oregon Taxes, Financial Incentives for Business Expansion:Building the Long-Term Financing Gap for Small Business, Directory of Manufacturing Plants, Oregon County Economic Indicators ($3), Oregon Economic Development Revenue Bonds, Directory of Oregon Manufacturers ($60), Oregon Industrial and Commercial Announced Investments, Oregon Economic Trends Project ($50), Oregon International Trade Directory ($30), Exporter's Handbook ($25), Helping Export Firms, Personalized Export Panel, Asia Representatives Office, Directory of Oregon Electronic Products, Directory of Oregon Industrial Equipment and Supplies, Directory of Forest Products Equipment and Services.*

Pennsylvania

Pennsylvania Department of Commerce, 446 Forum Bldg., Harrisburg, PA 17120, (717) 783-1132---Publications: *Annual Report.*

Rhode Island

Rhode Island Statewide Planning Program, 265 Melrose St., Providence, RI 02907, (401) 277-2601---Publications: *State Guide Plan and Strategic Plan, The Housing Report of the Governor's Human Services Advisory Council, Interim Ground Transportation Plan-Year 2010, Access Update-Telecommunications Device for the Deaf in State Government, Forensic Services Security Issues, Quonset State Airport Master Plan, Jerusalem Master Plan, Hazard Mitigation Plan, Ocean State Outdoors-Recreation and Conservation Strategies for Rhode Island, Highway Jurisdiction in Rhode Island, Methods for Calculating Vehicle Miles of Travel in Rhode Island, Transportation and Land Use, Rhode Island Coastal Resources Management Program, Water Resources Issues in Land Use Policy, Reevaluation of Statewide Travel Demand Model, Federally Assisted Rental Housing, Quonset State Airport Master Plan, Unified Work Program for Transportation Planning, Work Program 1987-1988, Policy Statement-Proposals for New or Restructured Public Transit Facilities or Service, Port of Galilee-A Case Study of Port Redevelopment, The Feasibility of Closing Ladd Center, Unified Work Program for Transportation Planning, Siting High-Level Nuclear Waste Repositories, Ocean State Outdoors-Recreation and Conservation Strategies for Rhode Island.*

South Carolina

Commission on the Future of South Carolina, Office of Lieutenant Governor, Post Office Box 142, Columbia, SC 29202, (803) 734-2080.

South Dakota

Governor's Office of Economic Development, Capitol Lake Plaza, Pierre, SD 57501, (605) 773-5032 ---Publications: *Economic Development Programs, Directory of Manufacturers and Processors ($20),*

Tennessee

Department of Economic and Community Development, 320 Sixth Ave., North, Nashville, TN 37219, (615) 741-1888 ---Publications: *Economic Growth in Tennessee, Tennessee Economic Statistics, Tennessee Population.*

Texas

Comptroller of Public Accounts, LBJ State Office Building, Austin, TX 78774, (512) 463-1778---Publications: *Annual Financial Report, 1988-1989 Biennial Revenue Estimate, Taxes and Texas: A National Survey on Alternatives and Comparisons, Texas Fees-Putting a Price on State Services, Quarterly Survey of Business Expectations in Texas, Sales and Franchise Tax Exemptions, Time of Change-Time of Choice, State Government's Use of Outside Services, Decontrolling Natural Gas-The Impact on Texas Prices and Tax Revenue, The High Finance of Higher Education, The Petroleum Industry and the Texas Sales Tax, The Geography of State Spending, Productivity Ideas and Cost Cutting Alternative to Control of State Budget Growth, Hazardous Waste in Texas, The Geography of Texas Taxes.*

Utah

Data Resources Section, Office of State Planning and Budget, State of Utah, 116 Capitol Bldg, Salt Lake City, UT 84114, (801) 533-6082---Publications: *1987 Baseline Projections, Economic Report to the Governor, State of Utah Revenue Forecast (quarterly), Utah Data Guide (quarterly), Budget in Brief (annual), Capital Budget (annual), Historic and Projected Long Tern Revenues and Expenditures, Historic Analysis of Preliminary Taxes, The Impact of the Gramm-Rudman-Hollings Deficit Reduction Act, The Import of the Tourism- Travel and Recreation Industry in Utah, The Importance of the Agricultural Industry in Utah, Retail Sales and Service Analysis, Flooding and Landslides in Utah-An Economic Impact Analysis, The Economic and Demographic Impacts of the Intermountain Power Project, Final Socio-economics Technical Report-Utah Basin Synfuels Development, Utah-2000,*

Energy-2000, Socioeconomic Impacts of the Boulder to Bullfrog Road Improvement, The Economic Issues Surrounding the Vitro Remedial Action Alternatives, Utah Facts, Utah Directory of Business and Industry, Utah Export Directory, Utah Economic Development Plan, Utah Economic and Business Review, Construction Report (quarterly), *Statistical Abstract of Utah.*

Vermont

Office of Policy Research and Coordination, Pavillion Office Building, 109 State St., Montpelier, VT 05602, (802) 828-3326---Services and Responsibilities: Monitor Trends and Anticipate the Impact of Evolving Technologies such as Telecommunications, Provide Staff for the Governor's Council of Economic Advisors, Data on Vermont's Economy.

Virginia

Governor's Office, Department of Economic Development, 1000 Washington Building, Richmond, VA 23219, (804) 786-3791---Publications: *Virginia Facts and Figures 1987, Economic Developments-A Statistical Summary, Quarterly Economic Development Report, High Technology Communications in Virginia, Corporate Headquarters in Virginia, Metalworking Industries-Advantages of a Virginia Location, High Technology-Biomedical and Related Industries-Advantages of a Virginia Location, Printing Industry-Cost Savings in Virginia, Virginia Small Business Financing Authority, High Technology Applied Here, Virginia-Local Taxes on Manufacturers, Virginia-Export Management/Trading Companies, International Business Services Directory, Mountains of Hardwood-Virginia's Southern Mountain Region, Virginia-A Guide to Establishing a Business, Are You Ready? A Guide to Community Preparedness for Industrial Development in Virginia, Manufacturing in Virginia, Allegheny County-Clifton Forge-Covington-Virginia-A New Thrust for Industry, The Virginia Economy, Foreign Investment in Virginia.*

Washington

Washington State, Department of Trade and Economic Development, 101 General Administration Bldg., Olympia, WA 98504, (206) 753-5630---Publications: *The Washington State Input-Output Study for 1982, Foreign Exports and the Washington Economy, The Aquaculture Industry in Washington State-An Economic Overview, Washington State Department of Trade and Economic Development-The First Two Years.*

West Virginia

Research and Strategic Planning, Department of Industrial and Community Development, 1900 Washington St., East Bldg. 6, Room 504, Charleston, WV 25305, (304) 348-3810.

Wisconsin

Bureau of Research, Department of Development, 123 West Washington Ave., P.O. Box 7970, Madison, WI 53707, (608) 267-9214---Publications: *Profiles in Success-Wisconsin Business Developments, New Industries and Plant Expansions Reported in Wisconsin, Models of State Entrepreneurial Development Programs, Youth Unemployment in Wisconsin, Entrepreneurial Culture in Wisconsin, Out-of-State Certified Minority Businesses, Industrial Revenue Bond Financing in Wisconsin, Analysis of State Investment Board Investments to Enhance the Wisconsin Economy, Biennial Report on Tax Incremental Financing, Industrial Revenue Bond Financing, Economic Development Lending Activities of the Wisconsin Housing Development Authority, Wisconsin Long-range Economic Forecast 1985-1995, An Economic Analysis of Wisconsin Regions, Advertising Conversion Results 1983 and 1986, Ozone Air Quality Management and Economic Development in Southeastern Wisconsin, The Relationship of State and Local Government Spending and Taxing to Economic Performance-An Econometric Analysis of the States from 1972 to 1984, Labor Management Cooperation in Wisconsin, The Wisconsin Tourism Industry-Analysis of Market Share and Trends, The Economic Development Potential of the Service Sector Industries in Wisconsin, A Statistical Profile of Minority Population, Employment and Business Ownership in Wisconsin, Development Preparedness Task Force, Task Force Tourism Funding, The Flow of Federal Funds to Wisconsin, Exchange Rate and Interest Rates Effects on Wisconsin Employment, Management Assistance and Business Growth in Wisconsin, A Comparative Study of US and Wisconsin Productivity-Analysis of Manufacturing Industries 1963-1982, Employment Potential of Wisconsin Industry Groups-An Analysis and Industry Classification, Local Economic Development in Wisconsin.*

Wyoming

Economic Development and Stabilization Board, Herschler Building, 3rd Floor, Cheyenne, WY 82002, (307) 777-7284---Publications: *Wyoming, Directory of Manufacturing and Mining, Public Financing for Wyoming Business, Mineral Yearbook.*

Foreign Policy

* See also Economics, Demographics and Statistics Chapter
* See also Experts Chapter
* See also Current Events Reports and Homework Chapter
* See also Drug and Chemical Dependence; Law Enforcement Chapter
* See also International Trade Chapter
* See also Law and Social Justice; Immigration Chapter
* See also Vacations and Business Travel Chapter

The U.S. Department of State, the Agency for International Development (AID), and nearly half a dozen other government agencies study the changing political, social, and economic situations in every region of the world. All this intelligence is spun off into all sorts of studies and reports as well as such informative and readable material as *Background Notes* and *GIST*. If you are considering travel abroad, information about a country's history and culture is readily available. Anyone doing research on a particular region of the world can benefit from using the historical resources available as well as the country desk officers who track daily developments abroad. International treaties, peace and conflict resolution, international organizations such as the World Bank, also erase boundaries for obtaining information about our increasingly inter-dependent world. International agreements from Law of the Sea to the Nuclear Test Ban Treaty are spelled out in materials that the average person can understand. You'll also find plenty of public information on weapons systems and other aspects of the U.S. military.

* Advisory Commission on Public Diplomacy

United States Advisory Commission on Public Diplomacy
United States Information Agency
301 Fourth St., SW, Room 600
Washington, DC 20547   (202) 485-2457
The seven Presidentially-appointed Commissioners oversee the operations of USIA and make a yearly report of findings and recommendations to the President, Congress, the Secretary of State, the Director of USIA, and the American people. The free report, which describes all the USIA functions, is available from this office.

* African Countries and US Foreign Policy

Public Affairs
Department of State
2201 C St., NW, Room 3509
Washington, DC 20520   (202) 647-7371
This Bureau develops implementation of U.S. policy in 46 Sub-Sahara African countries. The Office advises the Secretary of State on foreign policy issues, especially those focusing on democracy, economics, and human rights. Information is available on each of the countries, including *Background Notes*, foreign economic trend reports, and GIST summaries.

* Agency for International Development Library

Development Information Center
Room 105 SA-18
U.S. Agency for International Development
Washington, DC 20523-1801   (703) 875-4818
The library collections include: reference collection of current and retrospective runs of the major AID program documents and financial reports, such as *Congressional Presentations, Country Development Strategy Statements, Action Plans, Policy Papers, Current Technical Service Contracts and Grants*, and *U.S. Overseas Loans and Grants*, also the current *AID Handbook*; microfiche collection; historical off-site collection; Women in Development collection; current book collection of commercial publication, directories, yearbooks, and reports from other bilateral and international development agencies, private voluntary organizations, and research institutions which deal with current development issues. Access is through an online catalog. Although the library contains some information on development in general, most materials relate to AID-supported research and projects. The library holdings focus on those countries in which AID has or has had project or program activities, and on those subjects related to the Agency's work. If you are flexible about the countries and topics you are willing to investigate, you will have a much better chance of finding relevant information. A list of countries with AID missions is available in AID's *Project History List*, by Country Name in a black binder located on the right as you enter the library.

* Agriculture Assistance

Office of Agriculture
Bureau for Science and Technology, Room 409, SA-18
U.S. Agency for International Development
Washington, DC 20523-1809   (703) 875-4300
This office provides technical leadership in the broad range of activities related to international agriculture development.
The focus of the AID's agriculture, rural development, and nutrition program is to increase the incomes of the poor and to expand the availability and consumption of food while maintaining and enhancing a country's natural resource base. For more information or to obtain a copy of *A Program Guide to the Office of Agriculture, Bureau for Science and Technology*, contact the office above.

* A.I.D. Information

Development Information Center
Room 105 SA-18
U.S. Agency for International Development
Washington, DC 20523-1801   (703) 878-4818
Information about the structure and administration of the AID is available from the series of *AID Handbooks* from the above reference section of the library. General information about AID's plans in a particular country can be found in the *Country Development Strategy Statements* (CDSS's) in the serials room. Also in the serials room are *Congressional Presentations* (CPs) and *Annual Budget Submissions* (ABSs), which contain financial information on AID projects. Information on all phases on AID projects is available in project documents (PD's). Call (703) 875-INFO for general directions concerning AID.

* A.I.D. Magazine and Newsletter

Office of Publications
Agency for International Development
320 21st St., NW
Washington, DC 20523   (202) 647-4330
The Agency for International Development publishes a free quarterly newsletter, *AID Highlights*, which describes a different AID program in each issue. This publication is designed for those in the general public interested in Agency activities. *Frontlines* is a monthly newspaper, available to Agency staff and retirees that also highlights the current activities of the AID.

* A.I.D. Reference Services

Development Information Center
Room 105 SA-18
U.S. Agency for International Development
Washington, DC 20523-1801   (703) 875-4818
The library's holding of AID documents catalogued since 1974 are available on microfiche and can be read on microfiche readers in the library. Hard copies or microfiche copies of documents can be ordered from AID's Document and Information Handling Facility in Bethesda, MD. The library's historical (pre-1974) documents are stored off-site, but may be retrieved upon request at the reference desk (be sure to have a full citation and complete call number). For more information, contact the office above.

* A.I.D. Speakers Bureau

Office of Public Liaison
Bureau for External Affairs
Agency for International Development
320 21st St., NW
Washington, DC 20623 (202) 647-4213

Speakers within the AID organization are available to address meetings and conferences. A wide variety of topics can be discussed, including women's issues, health, economic policy, agriculture, world hunger, and disaster relief. A letter must be sent to the office above outlining the format of the meeting, the number of people attending, the location of the meeting, and the subject of the presentation. A minimum of two weeks is needed to secure a speaker.

* Alien Registration Information

Central Office
Immigration and Naturalization Service
425 I Street, NW
Washington, DC 20536 (202) 633-4316

Publications and tape recorded messages about immigration are available from this central office. However, field offices operate in most states and these local phone numbers appear in the Law and Social Justice Chapter and, of course, are easy to obtain from the directory assistance operators. When calling the tape recorded telephone number, (202) 633-4316, enter one of the number codes below which corresponds to the information about immigration and naturalization that you need:

265 Permanent alien registration receipt card
058 Applying for a replacement alien registration receipt card (I-90)
129 If you never received your alien registration receipt card (I-90)

* American and Foreign Teachers Exchange Program

Office of Academic Programs
United States Information Agency
301 Fourth St., SW, Room 353
Washington, DC 20547 (202) 485-2555

The Advising, Teaching, and Specialized Programs Division serves overseas education advising centers, foreign exchange students in the U.S., and administers the International Student Exchange Program for one-to-one exchange of university students. Its Teacher Exchange Branch arranges one and two way exchanges of U.S. and foreign teachers, and summer seminars for U.S. teachers to study abroad. Free brochures and applications are available.

* American Books Overseas Distribution

Book Programs Division
Office of Cultural Centers and Resources
Bureau of Educational and Cultural Affairs
United States Information Agency
301 Fourth St., SW, Room 320
Washington, DC 20547 (202) 485-2896

USIA helps in the translation, publication, and promotion of American books overseas. The Promotion Branch organizes traveling book exhibits and supports an American presence at international book fairs. The Field Operations Branch supports the translation and publication of a broad range of titles, mostly in the social sciences and humanities.

* American Business and A.I.D. Coordination

Office of Private Sector Coordination
Agency for International Development
320 21st St., NW
Washington, DC 20523 (202) 647-9100

This office assists, coordinates, and advises on the involvement of the U.S. business community with AID to achieve Agency objectives. Cooperative projects between AID and the U.S. business community within AID's guidelines are encouraged. Contact this ofice for more information.

* American Experts Overseas Lecture Tour

Office of Program Coordination and Development
United States Information Agency
301 Fourth St., SW, Room 550
Washington, DC 20547 (202) 485-2764

AmParts are experts in a field--usually economics, international affairs, literature, the arts, U.S. political and social processes, sports, science, or technology--sent abroad by USIA to meet with groups or individual professional counterparts. Recruited on the basis of requests of USIA staff in other countries, AmParts often engage in informal lecture/discussions with small groups, grant media interviews, or speak before larger audiences. Those interested in the American Participant program are invited to submit a brief letter indicating times of availability, along with a curriculum vitae and at least two lecture topics with brief talking points. A free brochure on the program is available from this office.

* American Foreign Policy Information Clearinghouse

Office of Public Communications
Bureau of Public Affairs
Department of State
2201 C St., NW, Room 5819
Washington, DC 20520 (202) 647-6575

This bureau issues various publications covering U.S. foreign relations, some of which are free. You can be placed on the mailing list and will receive publications in your area of interest as soon as they are off the presses. Call or write for a complete catalog of publications. Some free publications include:

GIST series. Two page summaries of U.S. policy on specific issues affecting the foreign relations of the U.S.
Current Policy series. Texts of U.S. foreign policy speeches by the President, Vice President, Secretary of State, and senior Department of State officials.
Special Report series. Reviews of analyses of major issues currently affecting the foreign relations of the U.S.
Selected Documents series. Compilations of official documents on subject related to the foreign policy of the U.S.
Historical Issues series. Basic histories of the major events and diplomatic negotiations underlying current issues.

* American Publications Translated and Distributed Worldwide

Superintendent of Documents
Government Printing Office
Washington, DC 20402 (202) 783-3238

The United States Information Agency publishes many teaching materials, including books, maps, complete teaching modules, and 14 magazines in 20 languages. By law most USIA publications may be distributed only in foreign countries. However, by congressional action, two magazines are available in the United States. *English Teaching Forum,* a quarterly for English teachers worldwide, is published by USIA's English Language Programs Division. *Problems of Communism* is a bi-monthly forum for American and foreign scholars discussing communist and socialist affairs. It is published in English and Spanish. Both these magazines are available through the GPO.

* American Schools and Hospitals Abroad

Bureau for Food and Peace
and Voluntary Assistance
U.S. Agency for International Development
Washington, DC 20523 (703) 875-4535

Each year this Bureau gives grants on a competitive basis to private, non-profit schools, hospitals, and libraries known for their excellence in demonstrating U.S. ideas and practices of education and medicine to citizens of other countries. Grant recipients must by U.S.-based, tax-exempt, private citizens' organizations which have founded and/or sponsor overseas institutions on a continuing basis. Eligible schools must be for secondary or higher level educations, while hospitals must conduct medical education and research. Grants are made to the U.S. sponsors for the exclusive benefit of the overseas institutions and customarily carry matching or cost-sharing provisions. Contact the office above for more information.

* American Studies for Foreigners

Division of Study of the U.S.
United States Information Agency
301 Fourth St., SW, Rom 256
Washington, DC 20547 (202) 485-2557

The Division for the Study of the U.S. promotes foreign education through conferences, seminars, exchange programs for foreign educators, grants, and development of school resource materials. The Academic Specialist Branch provides grants for American teachers to instruct their peers at foreign educational institutions. Contact this office for more information.

* Aquaculture and Fishing in Third World

Fisheries Specialist
Office of Programming and Training Support
Peace Corps
1990 K St., NW
Washington, DC 20526 (202) 254-3402

In helping people help themselves, fishery specialists provide information and techniques to farmers and fishermen on stocking, managing, feeding, and harvesting fish.

* Arctic and Antarctic International Policy

Office of Polar Affairs
Bureau of Oceans and International Environmental
and Scientific Affairs
Department of State
2201 C St., NW, Room 5801

Washington, DC 20520   (202) 647-3262

This office is concerned with all issues concerning the Arctic and Antarctic, including the environment and marine life, such as whales and seals. They are also closely involved with the many science stations located on the Antarctic.

* Assistance to Foreign Highways

International Highway Programs (HPI-10)
Associate Administrator for Policy
Federal Highway Administration
U.S. Department of Transportation
400 7th St., SW
Washington, DC 20590   (202) 366-0111

FHWA administers programs which provide assistance and advice to foreign governments engaged in highway engineering and administration. Projects have included technical assistance in fabricating bridge segments, value engineering skills, development of transportation systems, materials testing, quality control, and skid testing. Through the International Visitors Program, highway specialists from over 40 countries receive training. Countries that have participated include China, Indonesia, Haiti, Kuwait, Dubai, and Saudi Arabia. Two publications available from this office are *World of Technology for Sharing* and *Highway Community on the Occasion of the 18th World Road Congress*.

* Bilateral and Multilateral International Aid Donors

Donor Coordination
Bureau for Program and Policy Coordination
Agency for International Development
320 21st St., NW, Room 3645
Washington, DC 20523   (202) 647-8342

This Bureau coordinates AID policies and programs with other bilateral assistance donors, United Nations development organizations, and multilateral development banks. In close collaboration with State, Treasury, and other interested government agencies, the Bureau reviews programs, budgets, and staffing of the international development organizations. Recommendations are made on the U.S. Government's position regarding these matters, and guidance is provided to U.S. representatives to these organizations.

* Binational Libraries and Cultural Centers Worldwide

Library Programs Division
Bureau of Educational and Cultural Affairs
United States Information Agency
301 Fourth St., SW, Room 314
Washington, DC 20547   (202) 485-2915

USIA maintains or supports 156 libraries and reading rooms in 95 countries, as well as library programs at 111 binational centers in 24 countries. Collections focus on fostering foreign understanding of U.S. people, history, and culture. A bi-weekly bibliography, listing 80-100 titles on international relations and developments in the U.S., is one of many library services provided for the overseas posts, including reference and research assistance.

* Black Medical Schools and International Development

Office of Research and University Relations
Bureau for Science and Technology, Room 309, SA-18
U.S. Agency for International Development
Washington, DC 20523   (703) 875-4005

AID has initiated a program to increase participation by historically black medical schools in AID-supported international activities. The program links each of four participating medical schools with a major U.S. School of Public Health that already has extensive overseas experience. Through a set of Joint Memoranda of Understanding (JMOU), program support grants have been awarded to the eight participating institutions to increase their capacity to provide technical assistance to AID field missions in implementing health, population, and nutrition policies and strategies. Contact this office for more information.

* Business Development Teaching Overseas

Peace Corps
1990 K St., NW
Washington, DC 20526   (202) 254-4940

Volunteers teach new ways of conducting business and trade by introducing basic accounting skills, administration, and marketing to farmers, fisherman, and village women.

* Caribbean and Latin America Field Project Histories

Inter-American Foundation
1515 Wilson Blvd.
Rosslyn, VA 22209   (703) 841-3855

IAF is compiling 267 project file-based histories and 13 field- based project histories which outline the background, results, and lessons learned of each of IAF's funded projects in Latin America and the Caribbean. These histories are valuable research tools for those interested in development efforts in these regions.

* Caribbean Basin Employment and Trade

Office of International Economic Affairs
Bureau of International Economic Affairs
Department of Labor
200 Constitution Ave., NW, Room S5355
Washington, DC 20210   (202) 523-7597

The annual report, *Trade and Employment Effects of the Caribbean Basin Economic Recovery Act*, describes the provisions included in the CBERA, along with the benefits they provide to beneficiary countries. It also analyzes changes in U.S. trade with CBERA countries, and looks at trends in U.S. employment in those industries which have undergone the most significant changes in trade flows. Contact this office for more information on the report.

* Center for the Study of Foreign Affairs

Foreign Service Institute
1400 Key Blvd., Room 304
Arlington, VA 22209   (703) 875-5183

The Center for the Study of Foreign Affairs aims to enrich traditional Foreign Service training by keeping government officials in many agencies abreast of emerging foreign policy concepts. Its program of conferences, research, and publications combines new perspectives developed by private scholarship with the practical experience of foreign affairs personnel. The Center publishes full-length studies of various foreign policy issues in its Study of Foreign Affairs series, many of which are based on conferences and workshops held at the Center.

* Central Intelligence Agency Information

Public Affairs
Central Intelligence Agency   (703) 351-2053
Washington, DC 20505   (703) 482-7676

The Public Affairs office can provide declassified information and respond to inquiries.

* Central Intelligence Agency Reports Published Before 1980

Photoduplication Service
Library of Congress
Washington, DC 20540   (202) 707-5650

The Library of Congress distributes CIA reports that have been released to the public. These reports detail foreign government structures, trade news, economic conditions, and industrial development. Orders must be prepaid or charged to a standing account at the Library of Congress. For $13 the Photoduplication Service can also provide you with a list of CIA reports available. Reports can be purchased on microfilm for $24 per reel.

* Childhood Communicable Disease Control

Health Programmer
Office of Programming and Training Coordination
Peace Corps
1990 K St., NW
Washington, DC 20526   (202) 254-8400

The Peace Corps has developed child survival programs that train parents as well as children with curricula designed to teach better nursing skills, with an emphasis on vaccination.

* Child Survival in the Third World

User Services
A.I.D. Document & Information Handling Facility
7222 - 47th Street
Chevy Chase, MD 20815   (301) 951-7191

The child health publications listed below can be viewed in the Library on microfiche, and paper copies may be obtained from the address above. Note that document identification call numbers follow the identification number. Their telefax number is (301) 951-9624.

The A.I.D. Diarrheal Disease Control Strategy (Oral Rehydration Therapy and Related Interventions). Washington, D.C.; U.S. Agency for International Development, 1986. (616.3427.A288) (PN-AAX-052).
Birth Spacing and Child Survival. Maine, Deborah and Regina McNamara. Sponsored by the U.S. Agency for International Development, Bureau for Science and Technology, Office of Population, New York: Columbia University, Center for Population and Family Health, 1985. (613.94.M225) (PN-AAV-575).
Child Survival: A Third Report to Congress. Washington, D.C.: U.S. Agency for International Development, 1987. (613.0432.C536 1987) (PN-AAZ-401).
Child Survival: Risks and the Road to Health. Galway, Katrina, Brent Wolff and Richard Sturgis. Sponsored by the U.S. Agency for International Development, Bureau for Science and Technology, Office of Population. Columbia, MD:

Westinghouse Company, Institute for Resource Development, Inc. 1987. (362.19892.G183) (PN-AAX-157).

Child Survival Strategy, 1987-1990: Bureau for Africa, U.S. Agency for International Development. Washington, D.C.: U.S. Agency for International Development, Bureau for Africa, Office of Technical Resources, 1987. (613.0432.C536) (PD-AAU-969).

Health and Family Planning in Community-Based Distribution Programs. Mawer, Maria, Sandra Huffman, Deborah Cebula and Richard Osbor, eds. Sponsored by the U.S. Agency for International Development, Bureau for Science and Technology, Office of Population, Boulder, CO: Westview Press, 1985. (362.1.W356) (PN-AAT-004).

Immunizations. Primary Health Care Issues Series. Sabin, Edward and wayne Stinson. Washington, D.C: American Public Health Association, 1981. (614.47.I33) (PN-AAJ-782).

Notes From the Field: A.I.D.-Supported Oral Rehydration Therapy Activities. Sanghvi, Tina and Patricia E. Scully. Proceedings from the International Conference on Oral Rehydration Therapy, 2nd, Washington, D.C., December 10-13, 1985. Washington, D.C.: Creative Associates, Inc. for the U.S. Agency for International Development, 1985. (616.3427.S225) (PN-AAU-137).

* Child Survival Action Program
Office of Health
Bureau for Science and Technology, Room 709, SA-18
U.S. Agency for International Development
Washington, DC 20523 (703) 875-4600

Each year, fourteen to fifteen million children in developing countries die of disease and malnutrition before they reach the age of five. In February 1985, A.I.D. demonstrated its commitment to helping these children by establishing the Child Survival Action Program (CSAP) to deliver simple, inexpensive, and proven technologies to save the lives of these children and to improve their prospects for a healthy future. A.I.D.'s child survival strategy includes four basis interventions: oral rehydration therapy (ORT), immunization, birth spacing, and better infant and child nutrition. For information on CSAP, contact the office above.

* CIA Catalog of Maps and Publications
Public Affairs
Central Intelligence Agency
Washington, DC 20505 (703) 351-2053

The CIA declassifies many of its maps which are available from the National Technical Information Service, 5285 Port Royal Road, Springfield, VA 22161 (703) 487-4650. The catalog, titled *CIA Maps and Publications Released to the Public*, is available free from the CIA. Some of the titles include *The Impact of Gorbachev's Policies on Soviet Economic Statistics* (NTIS SOV 88-10049); *Chiefs of State and Cabinet Members of Foreign Governments* (NTIS LDA-CS 88-001); and *The World Factbook* (NTIS PB 88-928009)

* Citizenship and Naturalization
Central Office
Immigration and Naturalization Service
425 I Street, NW
Washington, DC 20536 (202) 633-4316

Publications and tape recorded messages about immigration are available from this central office. However, field offices operate in most states and these local phone numbers appear in the Law and Social Justice Chapter and, of course, are easy to obtain from the directory assistance operators. When calling the tape recorded telephone number, (202) 633-4316, enter one of the number codes below which corresponds to the information about immigration and naturalization that you need:

061 Citizenship and Naturalization requirements (N-400)
153 Residency requirements for naturalization
169 Derivative citizenship for children of U.S. citizens
139 Citizenship for children born outside the United States (N-600)
258 Naturalization based upon military service
159 Replacement of certificate of citizenship or naturalization (N-565)
351 How to file for naturalization on behalf of a child
358 Loss of United States citizenship

* Commercial Library Program Publications List
Foreign Affairs Information Management Center
2201 C St., NW, Room 3239
Department of State
Washington, DC 20520 (202) 647-1062

This list provides a wide-ranging selection of publications useful to commercial reference facilities. It contains annotated bibliographies of directories, buyers' guides, yearbooks, atlases, etc., in general and in special product areas. State manufacturing and industrial directories are included, as are telex directories.

* Conflict Resolution
United States Institute of Peace
1550 M St. N.W.

Washington, DC 20005 (202) 457-2700

The Jeanette Rankin library program supports the expansion of the Institute's and the nation's information resources on issues in the fields of peace and international conflict management. The Institute also conducts the annual National Peace Essay Contests for high school students, and has many television and other media projects on such subjects as the history of U.S.--USSR summitry and issues and ideas in peacemaking. Publications of the Institute include the biennial report; the bimonthly Journal which provides information on the Institute's programs and achievements and increases public knowledge of important projects and points of view; and *In Brief*, a new series highlighting results from Institute projects, as well as books and papers.

* Cooperatives and Credit Unions
Office of Private and Voluntary Cooperation
Bureau for Food for Peace
& Voluntary Assistance, Room 310, SA-8
U.S. Agency for International Development
Washington, DC 20523 (703) 875-4647

U.S. cooperatives provide business services and outreach in cooperative development to underdeveloped countries for their U.S. membership. These organizations support the participation of rural and urban poor people in their countries' development. These organizations are not charitable or fund-raising groups and rely almost exclusively on AID funding for their international programs.

* Country and Territory Info Pamphlets
Superintendent of Documents
Government Printing Office
Washington, DC 20402 (202) 783-3238

Background Notes, a series of short, factual pamphlets about various countries and territories of the world, plus selected international organizations, contain up-to-date information on each country's people, culture, geography, history, government, political conditions, economy, defense, and foreign relations with other countries, including the United States. A reading list provides additional sources of information about the country, and travel notes, maps, and occasional photographs are often included. A complete set can be purchased from the Government Printing Office for $32.00.

* Country "Desks"
Country Desk Officers
Department of State
2201 C St., NW
Washington, DC 20520 (202) 647-4000

The State Department's Country Desk Officers are responsible for following all activities in their assigned countries, from the political, economic, and social perspectives. These officers are in contact with the embassies; deliver and receive documents from the embassies; and write reports on the current activities in the country. The officers can provide the most current information available about their country. Call the number above and ask for the country you wish to find information about. Also see the Expert Chapter for a complete roster giving the name and phone number of the country specialists.

* Country Intelligence and Research Coordination
Department of State
Bureau of Intelligence and Research
2201 C St., NW, Room 8732
Washington, DC 20520 (202) 647-2404

This bureau coordinates programs of intelligence, research, and analysis for the State Department and for other Federal agencies, and produces intelligence studies and current intelligence analyses essential to foreign policy determination and execution. The Office of Research maintains a liaison with cultural and educational institutions on a wide range of matters relating to Government contractual and private foreign affairs research.

* Cultural and Educational International Exchange
Office of Public Liaison
United States Information Agency
301 Fourth St., SW, Room 602
Washington, DC 20547 (202) 485-2355

The USIA distributes the free *Directory of Resources for Cultural and Educational Exchanges and U.S. Information*, a treasure trove of information on cultural and educational exchange programs in the U.S. The directory provides contacts and background information of government agencies and non-profit and private organizations which sponsor exchange programs.

* Development Aid Policy and Budget
Bureau for Program and Policy Coordination
Agency for International Development
320 21st St., NW
Washington, DC 20523 (202) 647-9110

International Relations and Defense

AID's program and budget is formulated and revised as needed by the Bureau for Program and Policy Coordination. This Bureau presents the Agency's program to Congress, and reviews country program strategies and project proposals. The Bureau develops economic assistance policies, provides guidance on long-range program planning, economic analysis, sector assistance strategies, and project analysis and design.

* Development Information System

Center for Development Information and Evaluation
Bureau for Program and Policy Coordination
U.S. Agency for International Development
Washington, D.C. 20523-1801   (703) 875-4818

This Center operates and maintains the A.I.D. Development Information System (DIS), which provides online access to development assistance experience from almost 9,000 A.I.D.-funded projects and over 50,00 A.I.D.-generated technical, evaluation, and research reports. The *A.I.D. Technical Reports* is a monthly acquisitions list which presents citations recently added to the DIS of technical reports from Agency sponsored projects and activities. The *A.I.D. Project Descriptions* is a quaterly acquisitions list which presents abstracts of grant agreements, project design documents, and project identification documents recently added to the DIS. Citations are organized by sector and within sector by title. Contact the office above for further information.

* Diplomatic Archives in Foreign Countries

Office of the Historian
Bureau of Public Affairs
S A-1, Room 3100
Department of State
Washington, DC 20520   (202) 663-1122

The publication, *Public Availability of Diplomatic Archives in Foreign Countries*, lists each country and its archival rules, requirements, and documents made available. A list of important published works on archival sources is also available.

* Drug War

Bureau of International Narcotics Matters
Department of State
2201 C St., NW, Room 7331
Washington, DC 20520   (202) 647-6642

To coordinate the worldwide effort to halt the production and flow of illegal drugs to the United States, this bureau works closely with foreign governments and international organizations. Under bilateral agreements and international treaties, it provides technical and material assistance to foreign governments for such programs as eradication of narcotics crops, destruction of illicit laboratories, and training of antinarcotics interdiction personnel.

* East Asia and Pacific Region Clearinghouse

Bureau of East Asia and Pacific Affairs
Department of State
Public Affairs, Room 5310
2201 C St., NW
Washington, DC 20520   (202) 647-2538

This Bureau is responsible for U.S. relations with the countries in East Asia and the Pacific, which include Australia, New Zealand, China, Indonesia, Malaysia, Brunei, Singapore, Japan, North and South Korea, Philippines, the Pacific Islands, Taiwan, Thailand, Burma, Vietnam, Laos, and Cambodia. This office advises the Secretary on foreign policy issues, especially those focusing on democracy, economics, and human rights. Information is available such as Background Notes, GIST, and speeches and agreements relating to these countries.

* Economic and Social Conditions Worldwide

Center for Development Information and Evaluation
Agency for International Development
PPC/CDIE, SA-18
Washington, DC 20523-1801   (703) 875-4818

The Economic and Social Data System (ESDS) contains statistical information gathered from government agencies and organizations from around the world. Countries worldwide are characterized according to the Country's economy, financial situation, demographics, poverty indicators, labor force, social factors, and the levels of education, nutrition, health, and food. This database is for use by AID employees and contractors only.

* Economic Development in the Third World

Office of Rural and Institutional Development
Bureau for Science and Technology, Room 608, SA-18
U.S. Agency for International Development
Washington, DC 20523   (703) 875-4710

This office's goal is to create broadly based and sustainable economic growth and the active economic participation of the poor in underdeveloped countries. The

staff of economists, anthropologists, and social and management scientists work on policy and institutional change and technology transfer in three key areas: employment and enterprise development; decentralization and public management; and natural resources and regional economic systems analysis and management. Contact this office for more information.

* Economic Development Projects Involving Women

Women in Development
Office of Training and Program Support
Peace Corps
1990 K St., NW
Washington, DC 20526   (202) 254-8890

This office ensures that Peace Corps programs are designed to fully integrate women into the economic development process of their countries and communities. This office provides programming, training, and evaluation to the field workers. *The Exchange*, a quarterly newsletter, is published and distributed to 6,000 volunteers and staff in the field, with a focus on projects involving women.

* Economic Policy

Bureau of International Organization Affairs
Department of State
2201 C St., NW, Room 5328
Washington, DC 20520   (202) 647-2506

This office, as coordinator of U.S. economic policy within the United Nations, is responsible for the analysis and handling of international economic issues as they arise in international organizations, especially those in force in the U.N. system.

* Economic Support Fund

Office of Planning and Budgeting
Bureau for Program and Policy Coordination
Agency for International Development
320 21st St., NW, Room 3756
Washington, DC 20523   (202) 647-9110

The Economic Support Fund supports U.S. economic, political, and security interests and advances U.S. foreign policy objectives. The resources that ESF provides curb the spread of economic and political disruption and help friends and allies to deal with threats on their security and independence. ESF is flexible economic assistance provided on a grant or loan basis. It may be used to sustain economic activity to address basic development needs, or to improve the basic framework of the existing system.

* Education Development in Developing Countries

Office of Education
Bureau for Science and Technology, Room 609
U.S. Agency for International Development
Washington, DC 20523   (703) 875-4700

This office helps developing countries more efficiently allocate and use of their education resources, especially at the primary school level. To improve the quality of education, the office also develops appropriate and effective teaching technologies. And by developing educational communications and social marketing systems, researchers help improve AID's health and agriculture extension services. Contact the office above for further information.

* Energy Development in Developing Countries

Office of Energy
Bureau for Science and Technology
U.S. Agency for International Development
Washington, DC 20523   (703) 875-4203

With the AID's Missions and Regional Bureaus, this office helps assisted countries develop appropriate energy services. The *Program Plan*, available from the office above, explains the programs of this office in pursuit of that goal and how the Office is organized to implement those programs.

* Energy Publications

User Services
AID Document & Information Handling Facility
7222-47th Street
Chevy Chase, MD 20815   (301) 951-7191 ext. 9624

The following reports of the Office of Energy, Bureau for Science and Technology, can be obtained from the office above (the Document no. follows the Office of Energy Report no.):

New Direction for A.I.D., Renewable Energy Activities. February 1988 (88-01; PN-ABB-532).
Assessment of Integrated Coal Gasification Combined Cycle Technology for India. May 1988 (88-06; PN-AAZ-893).
The A.I.D. Experience with Independent Power Generation. August 1988 (88-14; PN-ABB-535).

Options to Increase Private Participation in Electric Power Development in A.I.D.-Assisted Countries. December 1987 (88-15; PN-ABB-536).

* European and Canadian Affairs

Department of State
2201 C St., NW, Room 5229
Washington, DC 20520   (202) 647-6925

This office studies and guides government to government foreign relations with the Soviet Union, Canada, and Eastern and Western Europe. Their work involves economic affairs, OECD, and NATO. This office can provide information with regard to the above.

* Farmer-to-Farmer Program

Agriculture Sector Specialist
Office of Training and Program Support
Peace Corps
1990 K St., NW
Washington, DC 20526   (202) 254-3402

Working in collaboration with the Agency for International Development (AID) and Volunteers in Overseas Cooperative Assistance (VOCA), the Peace Corps has added this program to its Agriculture Sector. This office provides specific short-term (30 to 120 days) technical assistance to countries whose requests are approved in such areas as dairy production, vegetable production, and vegetable handling.

* Fishing Multi-Lateral Agreements

Bureau of Oceans and International Environmental
and Scientific Affairs
Department of State
2201 C St., NW, Room 5806
Washington, DC 20520   (202) 647-2335

This office negotiates fishing agreements with countries who want to fish within the U.S. economic zone, along with agreements with countries within whose zone the U.S. would like to fish. They are also responsible for multi-lateral agreements dealing with fishing on the high seas, with particular attention to conservation issues. Information is available on these agreements and on fishery concerns in general.

* Fishing Vessels International Claims

Assistant Legal Advisor for International Claims
Office of the Legal Advisor
Department of State
2201 C St., NW
Washington, DC 20520   (202) 832-7810

The Fishermen's Protective Act provides for reimbursement for financial loss to owners of vessels registered in the United States for fines paid to secure the release of vessels seized for operation in waters not recognized as territorial waters by the United States. No registration or payment of premiums is required prior to the seizure in order to qualify for reimbursement.

* Food For Peace Program

Bureau for Food for Peace and Voluntary Assistance
Room 260, SA-8
U.S. Agency for International Development
Washington, DC 20523   (703) 875-4801

To obtain information on the Food for Peace Program, contact the office above to receive a copy of the *Food for Peace 1987 Annual Report.*

* Foreign Attitudes of USA

Office of Research
United States Information Agency
301 Fourth St., SW, Room 352
Washington, DC 20547   (202) 485-2965

Assessing foreign attitudes is one of USIA's prime responsibilities. A daily summary of worldwide media reaction to events of concern to the United States is used throughout the official diplomatic community. The research staff also amasses information for use by the White House, the Department of State, government agencies and USIA staff in assessing issues. Interested persons can obtain USIA research reports from depository libraries throughout the country. A list of these libraries is available.

* Foreign Aid Development Reports

Center for Development Information and Evaluation (CDIE)
Bureau for Program and Policy Coordination
U.S. Agency for International Development
Washington, DC 20523   (703) 875-4818

This Center's evaluation publications series includes a broad range of subjects of interest to those working in international development. The series comprises project impact evaluations, program evaluations, special studies, program design

and evaluation methodology reports, and discussion papers. The *CDIE Evaluation Publications List* is arranged by general subject category and by type of report within each category or subcategory. Each document has an identification number and is available in hard copy or on microfiche. A partial list of the documents follows below.

A.I.D. Assistance to Local Government: Experience and Issues. November 1983, No. 17 (PN-AAL-026).

Agricultural Policy Analysis and Planning: A Summary of Two Recent Analyses of A.I.D.-Supported Projects Worldwide. August 1988, No. 55 (PN-AAX-205).

Agricultural Research in Northeastern Thailand. May 1982, No. 34 (PN-AAJ-615).

An Evaluation of the African Emergency Food Assistance Program in Chad. 1984-1985, June 1987, No. 48 (PN-AAL-091).

Development Assistance and Health Programs: Issues of Sustainability. October 1987, No. 23 (PN-AAL-097).

Private Sector: Ideas and Opportunities -- A review of Basic Concepts and Selected Experience. June 1982, No. 14 (PN-AAJ-618).

Private Volunteer Organizations and the Promotion of Small-Scale Enterprise. July 1985, No. 27 (PN-AAL-055).

The Impact of Irrigation on Development: Issues for Comprehensive Evaluation Study. October 1980, No. 9 (PN-AAJ-208).

Reaching the Rural Poor: Indigenous Health Practitioners Are There Already. March 1979, No. 1 (PN-AAG-685).

Rural Development: Lessons From Experience -- Highlights of the Seminar Proceedings. January 1989, No. 25 (PN-AAX-214).

Strengthening the Agriculture Research Capacity of the Less Developed Countries: Lessons From A.I.D. Experience. September 1983, No. 10 (PN-AAL-020).

Study of Family Planning Program Effectiveness. April 1979, No. 5 (PN-AAG-672).

Universities for Development: Report of the Joint Indo-U.S. Impact Evaluation of the Indian Agricultural Universities. September 1988, No. 68 (PN-AAX-206).

Women in Development: A.I.D.'s Experience, 1973-1985. Vol. I, Synthesis Paper, March 1987, No. 18 (PN-AAL-087).

For more information or to obtain the CDIE Evaluation Publications List, contact the office above.

* Foreign Aid Effectiveness and Assessment

National Security and International Affairs Division
General Accounting Office
441 G St. NW, Room 5055
Washington, DC 20548   (202) 275-5518

This office serves as GAO's lead division for the international affairs issues. This division provides GAO audit coverage for the Department of State, the Agency for International Development, the International Development Cooperation Agency, the Central Intelligence Agency, the Export-Import Bank of the United States, the U.S. Information Agency, and the Panama Canal Commission, as well as for the international activities of numerous other federal entities. International Division personnel staff GAO's overseas offices.

* Foreign Aid Projects Database

Development Information Center
Room 105 SA-18
U.S. Agency for International Development
Washington, DC 20523-1801   (703) 875-INFO

The Development Information System (DIS) contains information on A.I.D. projects, programs, policies, and research, as well as associated project, research, and technical documents. Anyone can search DIS databases through the easy-to-use MenuDOS system on the library's public computer terminal. Records can be located by subject, author, title, project number, date, project status, or bibliographic type (e.g. project paper, evaluation, research report). All of these fields can be combined during one search. The MenuDIS quick reference guide to the right of the terminal can help you with your search. For more information on A.I.D.'s three main databases, "Document," "Project," and "Library Catalog," contact the office above.

* Foreign Disaster Assistance

Office of U.S. Foreign Disaster Assistance
Agency for International Development
320 21st St., NW, Room 1262A
Washington, DC 20523   (202) 647-8924

International Relations and Defense

The office administers AID's overseas disaster assistance program. The office involves other U.S. Government agencies, voluntary and international organizations, and the U.S. private sector to meet the demands of disaster relief, rehabilitation, preparedness, early warning, and mitigation in countries stricken or threatened by natural or man-made disasters, including earthquakes, floods, cyclones, volcanoes, accidents, and civil strife. OFDA provides technical assistance and training for the development of government disaster assistance programs, technology transfer for improved prediction and warning systems, and material and personnel resources for emergency relief and rehabilitation.

* Foreign Economic Aid Projects

Document Information and Handling Facility
Agency for International Development
7222 47th St., Suite 102
Chevy Chase, MD 20815 (301) 951-7191

Reports containing information on AID's projects may be obtained from the above facility for a minimal fee. One may also wish to subscribe to *Research and Development Abstracts* for a listing of available material for $10 per year.

* Foreign Economic Impact on U.S. Employment

Office of International Economic Affairs
Bureau of International Labor Affairs
200 Constitution Ave., NW, Room S5325
Washington, DC 20210 (202) 523-7610

The Labor Department's foreign economic research program evaluates the effects of foreign economic developments on the earnings and employment of U.S. workers. This includes quantitative analysis of the impact of policies on international trade, investment, and technology transfer. Often undertaken in response to congressionally-mandated studies or to requests from other executive branch agencies, research is conducted by staff economists and supplemented by outside research contractors. A complete list of the research is available by contacting this office.

* Foreign Language Training

Defense Language Institute
Foreign Language Center
Non-Resident Division
Presidio of Monterey, CA 93944 (408) 647-5000

The Defense Language Institute is one of the world's largest language training centers. The holdings of its library--over 100,000 books in 50 languages--are available through a national inter-library loan program. The non-resident division offers foreign language courses for sale. A catalog of the languages available may be obtained for $5.25. Write or call for brochures on the Institute and information regarding inter-library loans.

* Foreign Policy Briefings and Speakers

Office of Public Programs
Bureau of Public Affairs
2201 C St NW, Room 5831
Department of State
Washington, DC 20520 (202) 647-1710

Foreign policy briefings are arranged on request for interested groups to the extent that resources permit. These briefings can be on a variety of topics, such as foreign economic environment or human rights.

* Foreign Policy Public Forums

Office of Public Programs
Bureau of Public Affairs
Department of State
2201 C St., NW, Room 5831
Washington, DC 20520 (202) 647-2234

The State Department encourages public dialogue on foreign policy topics through nationwide public appearances by Department officials. The following is a list of public programs available:

Conferences - National foreign policy conferences are scheduled throughout the year for leaders from business, labor, government, and other organizations. Regional foreign policy conferences are held several times a year in major cities. These day-long meetings involve senior department officials, a variety of local co-sponsoring organizations, and flexible formats to encourage the free exchange of information and opinions.

Seminars - Foreign policy seminars attract 30 to 40 specialists from the private sector together with Department officials for informal discussions. The Bureau offers 1 or 2 day seminars for business executives and media representatives, emphasizing international economic and other foreign policy issues.

Liaison with Nongovernmental Organizations - NGO liaison is initiated and maintained with national organizations interested in foreign policy issues. Briefings on these issues are organized for NGO leaders and staffers and other special interest groups.

* Foreign Press Centers

Washington Foreign Press Center
529 Fourteenth St., NW, Suite 898
Washington, DC 20045 (202) 724-1640

New York Foreign Press Center
110 E. 59th St.
New York, NY 10022 (212) 826-4722

Los Angeles Foreign Media Liaison Office
11000 Wilshire Blvd.
Los Angeles, CA 90024 (213) 209-7693

Press offices in Washington, DC, New York, and Los Angeles assist foreign journalists, resident and visiting, in acquiring press credentials and gaining access to newsmakers.

* Foreign Service Career Counseling

Personnel Office
Special Services Branch
United States Information Agency
301 Fourth St., SW, Room 525
Washington, DC 20547 (202) 485-2628

Information on career opportunities in the Foreign Service is available from this office.

* Foreign Studies of America and English

Division for the Study of the U.S.
Office of Academic Programs
Bureau of Educational and Cultural Affairs
United States Information Agency
301 Fourth St., SW, Room 256
Washington, DC 20547 (202) 485-2562

USIA supports academic programs for the study of America, as well as the study of the English language. It acts as liaison between American and foreign universities, academic associations, and scholars, and supports 200 cultural centers and binational centers in 100 countries for the study of the English language. It publishes teaching materials in many languages and numerous publications, including "English Teaching Forum," a professional quarterly for English teachers worldwide. It also sponsors many seminars, institutes, study tours, exchange programs and curriculum support geared to the study of America in foreign countries.

* Forest Management and Education Worldwide

Natural Resources Sector
Office of Training and Programming Support
Peace Corps
1990 K St., NW
Washington, DC 20526 (202) 254-8400

Working in 38 countries, forestry specialists design and execute forest management plans designed to help combat the overcutting, droughts, and deserts that are beginning to threaten many tropical forests around the world. They also help establish nurseries, curricula in environmental education, and skills in tropical fruit cultivation.

* Forestry, Environment, and Natural Resources

Office of Forestry, Environment and Natural Resources
Bureau for Science and Technology, Room 509 SA-18
U.S. Agency for International Development
Washington, DC 20523-1812 (703) 875-4106

To maximize the amount of development that is sustainable, the Agency is working toward networking of worldwide development planning. This office's strategy includes providing technical assistance to government and non-government agencies working toward the development of national environmental policy and programs which will contribute to sustainable economic development; and to provide assistance in research and the transfer of appropriate technologies. For more information or to obtain the *User's Guide to the Office of Forestry, Environment and Natural Resources*, contact the office above.

* Fulbright Foreign Policy Scholarships

Office of Academic Programs
The Bureau of Educational and Cultural Affairs
United States Information Agency
301 Fourth St., SW, Room 234
Washington, DC 20547 (202) 485-7360

This office develops and runs all academic programs of USIA, including the best-known educational exchange, the Fulbright Scholarship program. About 5,000 Fulbright grants are awarded each year to American students, teachers, and scholars to work abroad and to foreign citizens to teach, study, and conduct research in the U.S. In addition to the Fulbright program, the Academic Exchange Programs Division of this office administers grants to private agencies conducting complementary programs to the Fulbright academic exchanges, and has responsibilities for foreign research centers, Fulbright commissions, and seminars for foreign Fulbright students. Contact this office for more information and application forms for the Fulbright program.

* Geographic Boundaries and Disputes

Office of the Geographer
Bureau of Intelligence and Research
Department of State
2201 C St., NW, Room 8742
Washington, DC 20520   (202) 647-2022
This office distributes several publications which contain a variety of geographical information. Some of them include:

Geographic Notes. Contains brief analyses of current issues relevant to United States foreign policy. These analyses provide a geographical perspective on such foreign policy-related topics such as boundary, sovereignty, and territorial disputes.
International Boundary Studies. This is a series of specific boundary papers.

* Geographic Bureaus

Agency for International Development
320 21st St., NW
Washington, Dc 20523
These Bureaus are the principal AID line offices with responsibility for the planning, formulation, and management of United States economic development and/or supporting assistance programs in their respective areas overseas. An annual budget of proposed Bureau activities is submitted for approval, and a program and budget is presented to Congress through the Bureau of Program and Policy Coordination. The Bureaus also represent the agency before the press and public as required.

Bureau for Africa: (202) 647-9232
Bureau for Latin America and the Caribbean: (202) 647-8246
Bureau for Asia and Near East: (202) 647-9119

* Grants for International Research Development

Office of Research and University Relations
Bureau of Science and Technology
Agency for International Development
Washington, DC 20523   (703) 875-4094
AID links the land grant universities with the historically black colleges and universities both in the United States and abroad in an effort of cooperation. Research grants, usually in the amount of $100,000, are given in the areas of health, agriculture, rural development and nutrition to historically black colleges and universities in 30 countries. The presidentially appointed Board for International Food and Agricultural Development formulates policy and projects to foster the working relationship of agricultural universities in AID programs. Research projects are listed in the *Commerce Business Daily* for which colleges and universities can compete. Unsolicited research proposals by individuals are also considered, but only a limited number are accepted. For information on the guidelines for these proposals, contact the above office.

* Grassroots Assistance to Africa

African Development Foundation
1625 Massachusetts Ave., NW, Suite 600
Washington, DC 20036   (202) 673-3916
This is a non-profit, government corporation formed to support self-help development activities in economically depressed communities in Africa and to promote friendship between Africa and the U.S. The Foundation makes grants, loans, and loan guarantees to Africans engaged in peaceful development efforts. Call the number listed to request a free African Development information packet and for further information about the Foundation.

* Health Development

Office of Health
Bureau for Science and Technology
Room 709, SA-18
U.S. Agency for International Development
Washington, DC 20523   (703) 875-4600
This office serves as AID's principal source of technical expertise and assistance on international health issues and projects. Contact this office for more information, or to obtain a copy of the *Directory of the Office of Health, Bureau for Science and Technology.*

* High Seas Law Enforcement

Operational Law Enforcement Division
Office of Law Enforcement and Defense Operations
U.S. Coast Guard

U.S. Department of Transportation
2100 2nd St., SW, Room 3110
Washington, DC 20593-0001   (202) 267-1890
As the primary maritime law enforcement agency for the U.S., the Coast Guard enforces Federal laws, treaties, and international agreements to which the U.S. is a party. The Coast Guard may conduct investigations when violations are suspected, such as smuggling, drug trafficking, or polluting. Empowered to board and inspect vessels routinely as well, the Guard also conducts :"suspicionless" boardings to prevent violations. To report suspicious or questionable activity on boats, or to complain about an improperly conducted boarding, call the Boating Safety Hotline, (800) 368-5647; or (202) 267-0780 in D.C., or contact your local Coast Guard commander. The office listed above can provide you with information about the Coast Guard's law enforcement role and the National Narcotics Border Indiction System, which coordinates multi-agency and international operations with other countries to suppress narcotics trafficking.

* Historian of the State Department

Bureau of Public Affairs
Columbia Plaza Office Building
2401 E St., NW, Room 3100
Department of State
Washington, DC 20520   (202) 663-1122
The office of the Historian has twin missions: to compile and publish the official diplomatic record of the United States in the series *Foreign Relations of the United States*; and to prepare policy-related historical research studies for the key officers of the Department of State. *Foreign Relations of the United States* is a multi-volume series in which the Historian's staff seeks, arranges, and edits principal papers which comprise the record of American foreign policy. Although principally based on State Department records, the series also is derived from White House files, the archives of other agencies, and, where relevant, papers and recollections of former officials. Resources and the pace at which the documents are declassified determine the rate at which the series is published. The office also publishes the American Foreign Policy series which contains texts of official messages, addresses, statements, reports, and communications which best convey the objectives of U.S. foreign policy.

* Historically Black Colleges and International Development Research

Office of Research and University Relations
Bureau for Science and Technology, Room 309, SA-18
U.S. Agency for International Development
Washington, DC 20523   (703) 875-4005
AID's Historically Black Colleges and Universities (HBCUs) Research Program seeks to take advantage of the strong interest of HBCUs in development assistance activities. Through this program, AID hopes to involve researchers from HBCUs in the problems of developing countries. Inclusion in the research program is determined through an AID formal review process. Contact this office for more information.

* Housing in Developing Countries

Office of Housing and Urban Programs
Bureau for Private Enterprise
Agency for International Development
320 21st St., NW
Washington, DC 20623   (202) 647-8298
This program facilitates private financing for shelter for lower income families in developing countries by guaranteeing repayment to U.S. lenders for projects requested by these countries. Innovative programs are financed, such as upgrading the provisions of sewerage, potable water, electricity, and home improvements. Basic urbanized lots are financed for the construction of family dwellings, and low-cost, expandable core housing units are made available.

* Human Rights Violations Worldwide Department of State

Bureau of Human Rights and Humanitarian Affairs
2201 C St., NW, Room 7802
Washington, DC 20520   (202) 647-1383
Country Reports on Human Rights in 1989 covers the human rights practices of all nations that receive U.S. foreign assistance, those nations that do not receive it but are members of the United Nations, and those few nations that are not members of the U.N. Each country's section begins with a brief description of the country, including information on political parties and security forces. It then is broken down into several area. The first deals with respect for human rights and includes information on political killings, disappearances, torture, and denial of public trial. Other sections include information on respect for civil liberties, such as freedom of speech, press and religion, respect for political rights and worker rights, as well as information on discrimination. This annual report can be purchased from the Government Printing Office, Superintendent of Documents, Washington, D.C. 20402; (202) 783-3238.

* Immigrant Visas and Immigrant Status

International Relations and Defense

Central Office
Immigration and Naturalization Service
425 I Street, NW
Washington, DC 20536   (202) 633-4316
Publications and tape recorded messages about immigration are available from this central office. However, field offices operate in most states and these local phone numbers appear in the Law and Social Justice Chapter and, of course, are easy to obtain from the directory assistance operators. When calling the tape recorded telephone number, (202) 633-4316, enter one of the number codes below which corresponds to the information about immigration and naturalization that you need:

053 Filing petitions to obtain immediate relative status (I-130)
097 Filing petitions to sponsor prospective immigrant employee (I-140)
065 How an alien in the United States may request a change of status to permanent resident status (I-485)
136 When a United States citizen marries a foreign national outside the USA
156 Fiance/fiancee visa (I-129F)
096 How to file joint petitions for spouse to remove conditional basis of their permanent resident status (I-751)
241 Orphan petitions (I-600)
255 Immigration benefits for adoption before 16th birthday (I-130)
172 Application for asylum in the USA (I-589)
354 Permanent residence for beneficiaries of approved asylum applications

* Impact of Human Rights Activities on Foreign Policy

Department of State
Bureau of Human Rights and Humanitarian Affairs
2201 C St., NW, Room 7802
Washington, DC 20520   (202) 647-1383
This bureau ensures that consideration of human rights is a regular part of U.S. foreign policy decision-making, as expressed through direct contacts between the U.S. and individual countries, quiet diplomacy, and continuous public activity. In the 1970's, Congress passed a series of laws linking human rights conditions in specific countries to actions by the U.S. government, such as most-favored-nation tariff status, U.S. government credits guaranties, and economic and military assistance. Congress has mandated that this bureau submit an annual report reviewing human rights practices country by country.

* Industry Productivity Trends

Industry Productivity Studies Division
Office of Productivity and Technology
Department of Labor
200 Constitution Ave., NW, Room S4320
Washington, DC 20210   (202) 523-9219
This office looks at a variety of technological trends. One study analyzes major impending changes in products, materials, and production methods in selected industries; their present and future applications; and their effect on output, productivity, employment, skill levels, training, and occupational requirements. Another study analyzes technological changes that have major effects on more than one industry. Coverage includes selected innovations such as computers and numerical control of machine tools, with an emphasis on innovations that will be important in the next five to 10 years.

* Intelligence: The Acme of Skill

Public Affairs
Central Intelligence Agency
Washington, DC 20505   (703) 351-2053
Two free CIA brochures are available to the public include *Intelligence: The Acme of Skill*, and *The Factbook on Intelligence*.

* Inter-American Affairs

Public Affairs
Bureau of Inter-American Affairs
Department of State
2201 C St., NW, Room 5911
Washington, DC 20520   (202) 647-4727
This bureau prepared foreign policy documents relating to U.S. relations with all countries of the Western Hemisphere except Canada. The documents focus on issues revolving around democracy, human rights, economic policy, narcotics, and promotion of U.S. security commercial interests. A wide variety of information, including *Background Notes* and GIST, concerning these countries is available.

* Inter-American Foundation Publications

Inter-American Foundation
Publications Office
1515 Wilson Blvd.
Rosslyn, VA 22209   (703) 841-3876
The following is a sampling of the free titles published in English, Spanish, and Portuguese.

The Inter-American Foundation and the Small- and Micro-Enterprise Sector

What to Think About Cooperatives: A Guide From Bolivia
In Support of Women: Ten Years of Funding by the Inter-American Foundation
A Review of the Inter-American Foundation's Support for Health Activities
Bottom-up Development in Haiti
The Inter-American Foundation in the Making
In Partnership with People: An Alternative Development Strategy
Grassroots Development
Inter-American Foundation Annual Report.
Direct to the Poor: An Anthology of articles from Grassroots Development.

* Inter-American Grassroots Development Video Series

West Glen Communications, Inc.
1430 West Broadway
New York, NY 10018
The following videos, which are part of the Inter-American Foundation's "Grassroots Development Video Series," are available for sale or on loan. Each video is $22.95 from West Glen Communications at the above address, or on loan from Modern Talking Picture Service, 500 Park Street North, St. Petersburg, FL 33709.

A Cooperative Without Borders: The First Step (21 minutes). Depicts the struggle of a group of Mexican migrant workers and their hope for the future to improve economic conditions as an alternative to migration (1987). Teacher's guide available.

The Women's Construction Collection (13 minutes). The story of 25 unemployed women selected from the poorer neighborhoods of Kingston, Jamaica, and trained in construction trades (1986).

Alpacas: An Andean Gamble (28 minutes). The peasant community of Aquia, Peru, bets on its future by repopulating its communal highlands with alpacas. Teachers' guide available.

* International Aid Public Information

Office of Public Inquiry
Bureau for External Affairs
Agency for International Development
320 21st St., NW
Washington, DC 20523   (202) 647-1850
For further information on the programs and projects within the Agency, contact the office above.

* International Aid Report to Congress

Office of Public Inquiry
Bureau for External Affairs
Agency for International development
320 21st St., NW
Washington, DC 20523   (202) 647-1850
Congressional Presentation is a seven volume document that describes the AID program of each developing country. Statistical information is included for present and prior years. Copies are available in limited supply from the above office and are also available for use at the Center for Development Information and Evaluation, 1601 N. Kent St., Room 105, Arlington, VA; (703) 875-4818.

* International Air Transportation

Office of International Aviation
Policy and International Affairs
Office of the Secretary of Transportation
U.S. Department of Transportation
400 7th Street, SW, Room 6402
Washington, DC 20590   (202) 366-2423
This office studies and develops U.S. policy with regard to international aviation. It ensures cooperation between U.S. and foreign-flag airlines and negotiates air service agreements with other countries.

* International Conferences Coordination

Bureau of International Organization Affairs
Department of State
2201 C St., NW, Room 1517
Washington, DC 20520   (202) 647-6875
This office organizes over 700 intergovernmental conferences each year. They accredit all participating delegations and decide who represents the U.S. and what information is allowed to be shared.

* International Development Resource Materials

Development Information Center
Room 105 SA-18
U.S. Agency for International Development
Washington, DC 20535-1801   (703) 875-4818

The AID Library also has a collection of non-AID materials. You can identify materials acquired after April 1984 using the on-line catalog in the Development Information System, and earlier acquisitions will be found in the card catalog.

* International Law Library
Law Library
Library of Congress
Washington, DC 20540   (202) 707-5073

As the world's largest and most comprehensive library of foreign, international, and comparative law, the Law Library provides information for all known legal systems including common law, civil law, Roman law, canon law, Chinese law, Jewish and Islamic law, and ancient and medieval law. Specialists with knowledge of more than fifty languages provide reference and research service in all known legal systems. U.S. legislative documents housed here include the *Congressional Record* (and its predecessors), the serial set, a nearly complete set of bills and resolutions, current documents, committee prints, reports, hearings, etc. plus a complete set of U.S. Supreme Court records and briefs and collections of U.S. Court of Appeals records and briefs. The law library has five major divisions:

American-British Law

United States, Australia, Canada, Great Britain, India, New Zealand, Pakistan, certain other countries of the British Commonwealth and their dependent territories, and Eire: (202) 707-5077.

European Law

Nations of Europe and their possessions, except Spain and Portugal: (202) 707-5088.

Hispanic Law

Spain and Portugal, Latin America, Puerto Rico, the Philippines, and Spanish- and Portuguese-language states of Africa: (202) 707-5070.

Far Eastern Law

Nations of East and Southeast Asia including China, Indonesia, Japan, Korea, Thailand, and former British and French possessions in the area: (202) 707-5085.

Near Eastern and African Law

Middle Eastern countries, including the Arab states, Turkey, Iran, and Afghanistan, and all African countries, except Spanish- and Portuguese-language states and possessions: (202) 707-5073.

* International Visitors Program
Bureau of Educational and Cultural Affairs
United States Information Agency
301 Fourth St., SW, Room 255
Washington, DC 20547   (202) 485-7217

Some 2,600 foreign leaders from many fields are invited each year by USIA to meet with their counterparts in the United States, either joining group projects or an individually tailored program to learn about our society. In addition to these visits, partially or wholly funded by USIA, another 2,500 Voluntary Visitors participate in similar programs, traveling at their own or their governments' expense.

* International Youth Exchange
The Bureau of Educational and Cultural Affairs
United States Information Agency
301 Fourth St., SW, Room 357
Washington, DC 20547   (202) 485-7299

This office administers grants to non-profit organizations for international educational and cultural exchanges for youths 15 to 25 years of age. Organizations wishing to become sponsors, or individuals wishing to be put in contact with sponsoring organizations, can receive free information from this office.

* Junior Foreign Service Officer Trainee Program
Personnel Office
Special Services Branch
United States Information Agency
301 Fourth St., SW, Room 525
Washington, DC 20547   (202) 485-2628

Each December the Foreign Service Officer Examination is held at many locations in this country and overseas to screen candidates for the Junior Officer Trainee Program. Date, locations, and other information is available from this office.

* Latin American/Caribbean Foreign Assistance
Inter-American Foundation
Program Office
1515 Wilson Blvd.
Rosslyn, VA 22209   (703) 841-3855

The Inter-American Foundation database monitors projects that receive IAF funding, and can be search by the following areas: type of project, urban/rural area, type of beneficiary, whether it generates income, and more. Contact this office for more information on the database or searching the files.

* Law of the Sea Treaty
Office of Oceans Law and Policy
Bureau of Oceans and International Environmental
   and Scientific Affairs
Department of State
2201 C St., NW, Room 5805A
Washington, DC 20520   (202) 647-9098

In working out policy regarding use of the world's oceans, this office monitors countries to see if they conform to the Law of the Sea Treaty, and negotiate U.S. policy regarding the Treaty. This is a large treaty with over 300 articles, dealing with such issues as uses of the outer continental shelf, pollution, fishing, use of Straits and territorial zones. The United States, however, has not signed the treaty due to concerns about the seabed mining article.

* Limited Resource Farming Projects
Agriculture Sector Specialist
Office of Training and Program Support
Peace Corps
1990 K St., NW
Washington, DC 20526   (202) 254-3402

The Peace Corps' agricultural specialists provide personnel and services to 46 countries, and have recently become especially proficient in bee-keeping projects. They help teach and establish crop production techniques, basic production research, small animal husbandry, and are currently developing a project for iguana production in Honduras. This project, though, is only in the early planning stages and would not be implemented until the 1990s; it is being designed as a food resource and forest preservation program. They also work closely with volunteers in the U.S. and abroad to share culturally related information regarding such topics such as limited resource farming practices here and abroad.

* Marine Environmental Efforts
Environmental Coordination Branch
Marine Environmental Response Division
Office of Marine, Safety, Security, and Environmental Protection
U.S. Coast Guard
U.S. Department of Transportation
2100 2nd St., SW, Room 1202
Washington, DC 20593-0001   (202) 267-0421

Information is available here on the Coast Guard's role in national marine environmental efforts, such as representation in the U.N. International Maritime Consultative Organization. For further information on cooperative environmental efforts, contact the branch listed.

* Marine Science and International Policy
Office of Marine Science and Polar Affairs
2201 C St., NW, Room 5801
Department of State
Washington, DC 20520   (202) 647-3262

This office handles international marine environment concerns, from the protection of whales to cleaning up oil spills, by negotiating bilateral and multilateral agreements.

* Maritime Trade Statistics
Trade Analysis Division (MAR-570)
Office of Trade and Analysis and Insurance
Maritime Administration
U.S. Department of Transportation
400 7th Street, SW
Washington, DC 20590   (202) 366-2282

Records on federally subsidized shipping companies are maintained by this Division. Information includes vessel name, port dates, and crew costs. The public can visit the document inspection room or write for information.

* Narcotics Cultivation Worldwide
Bureau for Program and Policy Coordination
Agency for International Development
320 21st Street NW
Washington, DC 20523   (202) 647-1850

AID in conjunction with other international agencies collects data about narcotics growing areas of the world and attempts channel economic development for narcotics producing areas into alternative crops and rural development. AID missions are involved in research for developing and testing alternative crops. Other agencies are responsible for the monitoring of enforcement and eradication of illegal narcotics cultivation.

* Natural Resources and the Environment

User Services
A.I.D. Document & Information Handling Facility
7222-47th Street
Chevy Chase, MD 20815   (301) 951-7191/-9624

The following documents may be viewed in the Library on microfiche. Hard copies may be obtained from the address above. Note document identification numbers are included. Also, AID publishes a collection of *Country Environmental Profiles* which may assist persons doing research on the environmental issues of a specific country. A listing of these *Country Environmental Profiles* is available at the reference desk of the Library.

Arid and Semiarid Rangelands: Guidelines for Development. Handbook/Manual/Guide, 1987. PN-AAY-730.

Ecological Development in the Humid Topics: Guidelines for Planners. AID Supported Study by the Winrock International Institute of Agricultural Development, 1987. PN-ABB-421.

Economics and Biological Diversity: Developing and Using Economic Incentives to Conserve Biological Resources. AID Supported Study, Nov. 1988. PN-ABA-988 (Not available on microfiche).

Environment and Natural Resources. A.I.D. Policy Paper. Apr. 1988. PN-AAV-464.

Forest for the Trees: Government Policies and the Misuse of Forest Resources. AID Supported Study, May 1988. PN-ABB-973 (Not available on microfiche).

Progress in Conserving Tropical Forests and Biological Diversity in Developing Countries: The 1987 Annual Report to Congress on the Implementation of Sections 118 and 119 of the Foreign Assistance Act, as amended. AID Program Document, 27 June 1988. PN-AAY-764.

Thailand Natural Resources Profile: Is the Resource Base for Thailand's Development Sustainable? AID Environmental Assessment, Jan. 1987. PD-AAY-099.

* Near Eastern and South Asian Countries Update

Bureau of Near Eastern and South Asian Affairs
Department of State
2201 C St., NW, Room 4515
Washington, DC 20520   (202) 647-5151

This office develops United States foreign policy for the countries within their jurisdiction, and advises the Secretary on these countries. They follow political, social, and economic developments and prepare policy papers. *Background Notes* and GIST summaries are available on the various countries, as well as foreign policy papers and speeches.

* Newspapers and Periodicals Worldwide

Library of Congress
Washington, DC 20540   (202) 707-5650

Hundreds of different newspapers and periodicals from all fifty states and countries around the world are available on microfilm for $24 for domestic and $27 for foreign publications. Subscriptions are available or single issues can be ordered. Orders must be prepaid or charged to a standing account at the Library of Congress.

* Nonimmigrant Visas and Nonimmigrant Status

Central Office
Immigration and Naturalization Service
425 I Street, NW
Washington, DC 20536   (202) 633-4316

Publications and tape recorded messages about immigration are available from this central office. However, field offices operate in most states and these local phone numbers appear in the Law and Social Justice Chapter and, of course, are easy to obtain from the directory assistance operators. When calling the tape recorded telephone number, (202) 633-4316, enter one of the number codes below which corresponds to the information about immigration and naturalization that you need:

262 Nonimmigrant or temporary visas
038 Temporary visitor's visa
029 How to request an extension of temporary stay (I-539)
134 Applying for a replacement arrival-departure document I-94 (I-102)
041 Change of status from one nonimmigrant classification to another nonimmigrant classification for purpose of work (I-506)
245 Requirements for classification as nonimmigrant treaty trader E-1
231 Requirements for classification as nonimmigrant treaty investor E-2
364 Requirements for classification as nonimmigrant exchange alien J-1
044 Requirements for classification as nonimmigrant temporary workers H-1, H-2, and H-3, (I-129B)

338 Intracompany transfers L-1 (I-129L, I-129S)
091 Deferred departure status for national of the Peoples Republic of China

* Non-Violent Conflict Resolution Grants

United States Institute of Peace
1550 M St. N.W.
Washington, D.C. 20005   (202) 457-1700

The Grants Program provides financial support to nonprofit organizations, official public institutions, and individuals to fund projects on various themes and topics of interest. Past projects have included the role of third-party negotiators in the resolution of regional conflicts, religious and ethical questions in war and peace, and the use of non-violent sanctions in confronting political violence. Call or write for more information regarding grant application procedures.

* Nutrition and Health Education in Developing Countries

Health Programmer
Office of Training and Programming Support
Peace Corps
1990 K St., NW
Washington, DC 20526   (202) 254-8400

Volunteers work to teach modern health-care techniques through programs on vaccination and hygiene and nursing. They design health curricula as well as teaching basic elements of nutrition.

* Nutrition and Food Science

Office of Nutrition
Bureau for Science and Technology, Suite 411, SA-18
U.S. Agency for International Development
Washington, D.C. 20523-1808   (703) 875-4003

This office's resources are invested at the "cutting edge" of nutrition science, food science, and technology and in creating mechanisms for adapting food and nutrition content to specific conditions and needs of host countries. As a result of these efforts, the Office has created programs in three major categories: child survival, household food security, and nutribusiness. The *1989 Interim Directory: Sustained Enhanced Nutritional Status for Everyone* (SENSE) will help you better understand this Bureau's nutrition programs. For more information on the Office of Nutrition, or to obtain a copy of the *Directory*, contact the office above.

* Opportunities for Women in Developing Countries

International Women's Program
Bureau of International Organization Affairs
Department of State
2201 C St., NW, Room 4334A
Washington, DC 20520   (202) 647-1155

Working through the United Nations Commission, this office strives to improve the lives of women in developing countries. Toward this end, this office develops and introduces resolutions to the U.N., and focuses on such issues as increasing literacy, equality in the law, and the availability of credit information.

* Organization of American States (OAS)

Documents Officer
Permanent Mission of the U.S.A. to the
   Organization of American States
Department of State
2201 C St., NW, Room 6489
Washington, DC 20520   (202) 647-8650

The Documents Officer can provide you with all reference documents and other general information concerning the Organization of American States.

* Organization of the U.S. State Department

Bureau of Public Affairs
Department of State
2201 C St., NW, Room 5819
Washington, DC 20520   (202) 647-6575

Department of State Today is a free publication which outlines the general organization of the State Department, including descriptions of the various Bureaus and their responsibilities. A list of public services is available, along with a section of charts, maps, and tables.

* Panama Canal Crisis Hotline

Office of the Ombudsman
Panama Canal Commission
APO Miami 43011-5000   (507) 52-3412

The Office of the Ombudsman handles administrative problems, inefficiencies, and policy conflicts existing within the Panama Canal Commission and other US Government agencies on the Isthmus of Panama resulting from the Treaty. The office does its best to improve employee morale and their quality of life. Due to the recent political unrest in Panama, a "hotline" was established to help employees, dependents, area residents and others previously employed with U.S. Federal agencies on the Isthmus, work through their concerns and hardships. For more information, contact this office.

* Panama Canal Dredging Division

Engineering and Construction Bureau
Dredging Division
c/o Panama Canal Commission
APO Miami, FL 34011-5000   (507) 52-4500

The Dredging Division is responsible for maintenance and construction dredging; slide removal; inspection and maintenance of the Atlantic breakwater; operation and maintenance of navigational aids; the detection, containment, recovery, and disposal of oil pollution in Canal operating areas; and the removal and control of aquatic weeds through the use of chemical and biological means. For more information on the dredging operations, contact this office.

* Panama Canal Economic and Market Research

Economic Research and Market Development Division
The Office of Executive Planning
c/o Panama Canal Commission
APO Miami 34011-5000   (507) 52-7961

As an agency of the U.S. Government, the Panama Canal Commission has a legal obligation to operate on a break-even basis, recovering all costs of operating, maintaining, and improving the Canal through tolls revenue. The agency tries to have a high standard of service at the lowest possible cost. As a reflection of this, toll rates have gone up only four times since the Canal opened in 1914. Operating costs are very carefully controlled so that it provides an economic advantage to world trade on many routes. Even if other world trade routes may be shorter in distance, the Canal remains competitive because of its reliable, cost-effective service. For more information on operating costs, contact this office.

* Panama Canal Environmental Safeguards

Sanitation Branch
General Services Bureau
Panama Canal Commission
APO Miami 34011-5000

The Sanitation Branch carries out measures to control disease carrying organisms and environmental sanitation measures essential to maintaining a high standard of public health which can be enjoyed by Panama Canal Commission employees and their families. There is an effort to control insect vector and vermin by nonchemical methods. For more information, contact the above office.

* Panama Canal Logistical Support

Office of Logistical Support
General Services Bureau
Panama Canal Commission
4400 Dauphine St.
New Orleans, LA 70146-6800   (504) 948-5299

The Logistical Support Division provides centralized procurement, inventory management, warehousing, distribution, contract administration, and supply and property disposal support to Canal operations. For more information, contact this office.

* Panama Canal Publications and Audiovisuals

The Office of Public Affairs
c/o Panama Canal Commission
APO Miami 34011-5000   (507) 52-3165

The Office of Public Affairs has available various publications including the *Panama Canal 75th Anniversary Commemorative Album* and *The Panama Canal Spillway* as well as press releases, brochures, and other matters of related interest are distributed to the work force and the public at large. A broad range of photographic and audio-visual support services were created as well. A limited number of projection prints are available for loan to individuals and groups interested in the canal and its operation. All films are 16mm color and sound. Individuals may obtain video tapes of all subjects by submitting a blank tape in the desired format and the payment of a transfer charge. Some examples of the available films for general audiences are as follows:

The Task That Never Ends. 1984. Depicts the on going job of maintaining and improving the channel of the Panama Canal, widening, deepening and straightening the water route.

The Vital Link. 1986. Depicts the role of the Panama Canal in world commerce with a layman's introduction to the people and methods of Canal operations. Details of lockages, traffic control, and communications at the crossroads of the world.

1986 Landslide. 1987. Shows the resumption of the Cucaracha Slide in October, 1986. Measures taken to maintain Canal traffic while the obstruction was removed and remedial actions taken.

Some examples of the available films of special interest to engineers and mechanical craftsmen include the following:

Locks Overhaul - Strut Arms. 1981. A detailed description of strut arm removal prior to gate or bullwheel removal and replacement.

Locks Overhaul - Bullwheels. 1982. A detailed description of bullwheel removal and replacement.

There are also films of special interest to canal operating personnel. Films are available in both Spanish and English. For a complete listing of films produced by the Panama Canal Commission, contact the above office.

* Panama Canal Traffic Data

Economic Research and Market Development Division
The Office of Executive Planning
c/o Panama Canal Commission
APO Miami 34011-5000   (507) 52-7961

The Panama Canal is a vital link in the world transportation chain. A large share of world trade passes through the Canal over any of the world's major trade routes. In 1988, 156.5 million long tons of cargo moved through the Canal aboard 12,318 oceangoing vessels. More than 690,962 vessels have crossed the waterway, carrying more than 4 billion long tons of the world's goods from one ocean to the other. For more information or compilations of Canal traffic data, contact this office.

* Panama Canal Treaty Implementation

Office of the Secretary
Panama Canal Commission
2000 L St., NW, Room 550
Washington, DC 20036-4996   (202) 634-6441

On September 7, 1977, the United States and the Republic of Panama signed the Panama Canal Treaty of 1977. The Treaty provided for the establishment of the Panama Canal Commission on October 1, 1979, to assume certain operational responsibilities for the Canal until December 31, 1999. When the Treaty terminates on December 31, 1999, the Republic of Panama shall assume total responsibility for the management, operation, and maintenance of the Panama Canal, which shall be turned over in operating condition and free of liens and debts, except as the two parties may otherwise agree. Of the permanent current work force, 84 percent are Panamanians. For more information, contact this office.

* Panama Canal Vessel Emergency Response Management

Marine Director
Marine Bureau
c/o Panama Canal Commission
APO Miami, FL 34011-5000   (507) 52-4500

For information on marine operations including inspections, piloting, locks, traffic management, canal services, marine safety, canal operations and maritime training, contact this Bureau. The Commission's marine risk management team is devoted to the prevention of and response to accidents involving vessels carrying hazardous cargoes. The team consists of an experienced fireman, a licensed marine engineer, a safety generalist, an experienced chemist, and lead by an experienced active duty U.S. Coast Guard officer. This team is also responsible for updating the Commission's Vessel Emergency Response Plan and in conducting vessel emergency training exercises.

* Peace and International Conflict Resolution Clearinghouse

Education and Public Information Program
United States Institute of Peace
1550 M St. N.W.
Washington, D.C. 20005   (202) 457-2700

The Jeanette Rankin library program supports the expansion of the Institute's and the nation's information resources on issues in the fields of peace and international conflict management. The Institute also conducts the annual *National Peace Essay Contests* for high school students, and has many television and other media projects on such subjects as the history of U.S.--USSR summitry and issues and ideas in peacemaking. Publications of the Institute include the biennial report; the bimonthly *Journal* which provides information on the Institute's programs and achievements and increases public knowledge of important projects and points of view; and *In Brief*, a new series highlighting results from Institute projects, as well as books and papers.

* Peace Corps Environment Education Curricula

Natural Resources Sector
Office of Training and Program Support
Peace Corps
1990 K St., NW
Washington, DC 20526   (202) 254-8400

International Relations and Defense

In charge of the forestry sector, natural resources encompasses wildlife management, national parks management, soil conservation, and environmental education curricula.

* Peace Corps Reference Manuals

Information Collection and Exchange (ICE)
Office of Training and Program Support
Peace Corps
1990 K St., NW
Washington, DC 20526   (202) 254-7386

The Peace Corps publishes a number of handbooks and materials written by their experienced Peace Corps volunteers which are designed to assist new volunteers abroad:

Community Health Education in Developing Countries
Cooperatives
Disaster Procedures
Freshwater Fish Pond Culture and Management
A Glossary of Agricultural Terms
Health and Sanitation Lessons--Africa
Pesticide Safety
The Photonovel--A Tool for Development
Programming and Training for Small Farm Grain Storage
Self-Help Construction of One-Story Buildings
Water Purification, Distribution, and Sewage Disposal

* Political Asylum

Office of Asylum Affairs
Bureau of Human Rights and Humanitarian Affairs
Department of State
SA-17, Room 520
Washington, DC 20520   (202) 326-6110

This office handles the Department of State's responsibilities regarding political asylum by providing advisory opinions on the cases to the Immigration and Naturalization Service.

* Population Planning

Office of Population
Bureau for Science and Technology, Room 811, SA-18
U.S. Agency for International Development
Washington, DC 20523-1819   (703) 875-4402

Here population projects are designed to strengthen USAID assistance to country family planning programs worldwide. The projects fall into two broad categories: those which support current family planning service delivery, and research to enhance future efforts in the population field. Contact the office above for more information.

* Private Voluntary Organizations

Office of Private and Voluntary Cooperation
Bureau for Food for Peace & Voluntary Assistance
Room 260, SA-8
U.S Agency for International Development
Washington, DC 20523   (703) 875-4801

AID has long recognized the important contribution made by private voluntary organizations (PVOs) to development efforts in the Third World. According to AID, PVOs are tax-exempt non-profit organizations which receive some portion of their annual revenue from the private sector (demonstrating their private nature) and receive voluntary contributions of money, staff time, or in-kind support from the general public (a demonstration of their voluntary nature). For information on AID available to PVOs, grants reserved for registered PVOs, and for general information, contact the office above. Also ask for a copy of *The AID-PVO Partnership: Sharing Goals and Resources in the Work of Development*.

* Problems of Communism and Socialism

Superintendent of Documents
Government Printing Office
Washington, DC 20402   (202) 783-3238

The United States Information Agency publishes many teaching materials, including books, maps, complete teaching modules, and 14 magazines in 20 languages. By law most USIA publications may be distributed only in foreign countries. However, by congressional action, two magazines are available in the United States. *English Teaching Forum*, a quarterly for English teachers worldwide, is published by USIA's English Language Programs Division. *Problems of Communism* is a bi-monthly forum for American and foreign scholars discussing communist and socialist affairs. It is published in English and Spanish. Both these magazines are available through the GPO.

* Radio Free Europe/Radio Liberty

Board for International Broadcasting

1201 Connecticut Avenue, NW, Suite 400
Washington, DC 20036   (202) 254-8050

The Board for International Broadcasting's annual reports, available free of charge to the public, cover Radio Free Europe's and Radio Liberty's research, audience, technical facilities, future plans, and more. RFE's Research and Analysis Department is the largest center in the West for research on Eastern Europe. RAD's analytical staff produce papers in English on a broad range of subjects, including the internal situations in the countries to which RFE broadcasts. Also available are situation and background reports, along with special publications covering timely topics in those countries. RL publications covering activities in the Soviet Union are also available, including research reports and bulletins, and press surveys and monitoring reports. Contact this office for more information on how to order these research publications.

* Radio Free Europe/Radio Liberty Library

Reference Library
1775 Broadway
New York, NY 10019   (202) 397-5354

This library contains over 17,000 volumes, 3,000 reels of microfilm, 355 subscriptions to periodicals and newspapers in English, Russian, and other languages, and RFE/RL Archival Material.

* Refugees, Permanent Residents, Students, and Aliens Travel

Central Office
Immigration and Naturalization Service
425 I Street, NW
Washington, DC 20536   (202) 633-4316

Publications and tape recorded messages about immigration are available from this central office. However, field offices operate in most states and these local phone numbers appear in the Law and Social Justice Chapter and, of course, are easy to obtain from the directory assistance operators. When calling the tape recorded telephone number, (202) 633-4316, enter one of the number codes below which corresponds to the information about immigration and naturalization that you need:

033 Departure from the USA by permanent residents: reentry permits (I-131)
360 Travel authorization for refugees: Refugee travel documents (I-570)
137 Travel by an alien whose application for permanent resident status is still pending
239 Emergency travel requests
236 Student travel outside the USA

* Refugee Resettlement and Asylum

Bureau of Refugee Programs
Department of State
2201 C St., NW, Room 5824
Washington, DC 20520   (202) 647-3964

At the center of a cooperative effort between the State Department, other Government agencies, private voluntary organizations, and international agencies, this bureau provides assistance to refugees in countries of first asylum, and to implement the admission policies to the United States for refugee resettlement. Some of the programs for which this bureau is responsible include relief and repatriation of refugees, and the selection, processing, and training of refugees to be admitted to the United States.

* Resolution of Human Rights Violations

Bureau of International Organization Affairs
Department of State
2201 C St., NW, Room 4334A
Washington, DC 20520   (202) 647-2708

This office focuses on human rights issues within the United Nations, with the hope of improving the state of human rights in foreign countries. They also oversee U.N. human rights organizations and write U.S. government replies to accusations of U.S. human rights violations.

* Sahel Development Program

Sahel Desk
Bureau for Africa, Room 3491
Agency for International Development
Washington, DC 20523   (202) 647-5991

AID participates in a long-term program for the development of the Sahelian region of West Africa. The objectives of the Sahel Development Program are to promote regional food self-reliance and self-sustaining economic growth. The program is coordinated, planned, and designed by the Club du Sahel, comprised of nine Sahel states: Mali, Chad, Niger, Burkina Fasco, Senegal, Mauritania, Cape Verde, the Gambia, and Guinea-Bissau; the United States; and over 20 participating governments and international organizations.

* Science and Technology Development

Bureau for Science and Technology, Room 4942
U.S. Agency for International Development
Washington, DC 20523-0057 (202) 647-1827

Multi-disciplinary science expertise from this office work closely with regional and field staffs, offering needed technical assistance, and serve as a link to U.S. and international development specialists. A major responsibility is to identify and support research having interregional or worldwide implications and research on the "cutting edge" of technology generation, such as biotechnology and the use of genetic engineering techniques. Contact this office for more information or to obtain its brochure, *Science and Technology in the Agency for International Development.*

* Science Capacity-Building in Third World

Office of the Science Advisor
Agency for International Development
Washington, DC 20523 (703) 875-4444

This office coordinates the more innovative and collaborative approaches to the problems and processes of development research, technology transfer, and related capacity-building programs and activities in the development of Third World countries. Scientific and technological needs and opportunities in developing countries are identified, and resources are found to meet those needs from the United States and foreign public and private sources. Effective communication is ensured between the United States scientific and technological capacities and the development programs in which the United States participates.

* Seabed Mining, Outer Continental Shelf and Other Ocean Policies

Office of Oceans Law and Policy
Bureau of Oceans and International Environmental
and Scientific Affairs
Department of State
2201 C St., NW, Room 5805A
Washington, DC 20520 (202) 647-5123

This series of studies deals with a variety of topics concerning the seas, such as sea boundaries, straight baselines, and national maritime claims. Call or write for copies of specific studies and more information.

* Small Business Contracts with A.I.D.

Office of Small and Disadvantaged Business Utilization
Agency for International Development
Washington, DC 20523-1414 (703) 875-1551

Information and other handout materials are provided for AID procurement for small and disadvantaged businesses. A weekly bulletin is published that lists the current need of the agency. For a packet of information on the requirements for securing business with AID, write to the office above.

* State Department Speakers

Office of Public Programs
Bureau of Public Affairs
Department of State
2201 C St NW, Room 5831
Washington, DC 20520 (202) 647-2234

Speaking engagements are arranged with organizations throughout the country. To make the best use of the speakers' time, the bureau normally tries to schedule other events during trips, such as media interviews, informal discussion with community leaders, and visits to academic institutions.

* State of World Peace Survey

United States Institute of Peace
1550 M St. N.W.
Washington, D.C. 20005 (202) 457-1700

The Institute has decided to undertake a task of presenting critical information on the state of peace worldwide to the American public and to the international community. A number of valuable studies are available in areas such as human rights and global ecology. The Institute's report will be a periodically updated survey seeking to identify trends, causes, and consequences of armed international conflict on a region-by-region basis. In addition, efforts will be made to standardize methods of statistical reporting on the state of world peace.

* Student Visa Information

Central Office
Immigration and Naturalization Service
425 I Street, NW
Washington, DC 20536 (202) 633-4316

Publications and tape recorded messages about immigration are available from this central office. However, field offices operate in most states and these local phone numbers appear in the Law and Social Justice Chapter and, of course, are easy to obtain from the directory assistance operators. When calling the tape recorded telephone number, (202) 633-4316, enter one of the number codes

below which corresponds to the information about immigration and naturalization that you need:

164 Permission to go to school (I-20, I-134)
267 How to maintain your student status
344 Visas for spouse and dependent children of student
131 Student visa extension (I-538)
145 Permission to work (I-538)
252 F-1 Transfer to another school (I-538)
355 M-1 Transfer to another school (I-538)

* Teaching in the Third World

Education Sector
Office of Programming and Training Support
Peace Corps
1990 K St., NW
Washington, DC 20526 (202) 254-8400

Volunteers are trained to teach people of other cultures by experienced educators. Programs are planned here to fit the basic needs of the countries being served.

* Technology Assessment Reports

Office of Technology Assessment
Publications Order
U.S. Congress
Washington, DC 20510-8025 (202) 224-8996

These OTA publications are available through the office above, the Government Printing Office, and the National Technical Information Service. To find out correct ordering information and prices, along with brief summaries of the following studies, contact the OTA office above and request their current publications catalog.

Africa Tomorrow: Issues in Technology, Agriculture, and U.S. Foreign Aid (TM-F-31)
Continuing the Commitment: Agricultural Development in the Sahel (F-308)
Enhancing the Quality of U.S. Grain for International Trade (F-399)
Grain Quality in International Trade: A Comparison of Major U.S. Competitors (F-402)
A Review of U.S. Competitiveness in Agriculture Trade (TM-TET-29)
Sustaining Tropical Forest Resources: Reforestation of Defraded Lands (BP-F-18)
Sustaining Tropical Forest Resources: U.S. and International Institutions (BP-F-19)

* Technology Transfer in the Third World

Office of the Science Advisor
U.S. Agency for International Development
Room 320, SA-18
Washington, DC 20523-1818 (703) 875-4444

This office responds to the interest of Congress in supporting innovative, collaborative approaches in Third World development research and technology transfer. A small, highly competitive research grant program funds the more experimental and less widely known technologies that might later be incorporated into AID's mainstream programs. This grant program is designed to encourage the involvement of scientists in the developing countries. The office also helps support a National Academy of Sciences program to establish research networks among institutions in the developing countries that can identify underexploited resources of potential economic value. Contact the office above for more information.

* Trade Agreements

Developed Countries Trade Division
Bureau of Economic and Business Affairs
Department of State
2201 C St., NW, Room 3822
Washington, DC 20520 (202) 647-1162

In handling the U.S. relationship with developed countries regarding bilateral and multilateral trade agreements, this offices examine all aspects of trade, such as restrictions on exports, customs, and licensing requirements. Information is available on these agreements and other issues concerning trade with these developed countries.

* Trade-Related Employment Issues

Department of Labor
200 Constitution Ave., NW, Room S2235
Washington, DC 20210 (202) 523-6043

The Bureau of International Labor Affairs represents the Department of Labor in the development of international economic and trade policies that affect the welfare of U.S. workers. This role includes conducting research on trade-related employment issues, coordinating advice received from Labor Advisory Committees on Trade authorized by the Trade Agreements Act of 1979, and acting as a liaison between other federal departments, agencies, and organized labor. The Bureau is also a member of various interagency committees charged with trade policy functions, and continues to participate in the formulation of U.S. immigration policy.

* Training Engineers Overseas

Office of Programming and Training Support
Peace Corps
1990 K St., NW
Washington, DC 20526   (202) 254-8400

Civil, mechanical, mining, environmental, and metallurgical engineers help train people to develop water, sanitation, and transportation systems, as well as building bridges and roads.

* Transportation Technology Exchange

International Cooperative Division and Secretariat (P-25)
Office of International Transportation and Trade
Office of the Secretary of Transportation
U.S. Department of Transportation
400 7th Street, SW
Washington, D.C. 20590   (202) 366-4368

DOT participates in a number of cooperative programs with other countries to exchange mutually beneficial transportation research data and state-of-the-art technical information. Areas of exchange include highway technology; ports and inland waterways; railway technology; and search and rescue operations. China and the Soviet Union are among the countries participating. Contact this office for information about these programs.

* Travel Advisories and Alerts for Unstable Countries

Overseas Citizens Services
Department of State
2201 C St., NW, Room 4800
Washington, DC 20520   (202) 647-5225

This office can provide you with visa requirements for U.S. citizens wishing to travel to foreign countries. They stress that this information is subject to change and that the definitive information regarding visas can come only from the foreign embassies. This taped message lists all the countries, their current visa requirements, travel advisories for the countries, as well as the embassies' phone numbers.

* Treaties and International Agreements

Office of Legal Advisor
Department of State
2201 C St., NW, Room 5420
Washington, DC 20520   (202) 647-2044

Information on treaties and international agreements to which the U.S. is a party is prepared by the Office of Legal Advisor. The following publications can be purchased from the Superintendent of Documents, Government Printing Office, Washington, DC 20402; (202) 783-3238:

United States Treaties and Other International Agreements. This multivolume series presents the texts of all treaties and other international agreements of the U.S. entered into force since January 1, 1950. It contains the official, legal texts of agreements in their original languages, with English translations when necessary.

Treaties and Other International Agreements of the United States of America, 1776 - 1949. This contains the texts of bilateral, multilateral, and other international agreements entered into by the United States.

Treaties in Force. Lists the treaties and other international agreements in effect for the United States on record in the Department of State at the beginning of each year ($16.00).

Treaties and Other International Acts Series (TIAS). TIAS provides in pamphlet form the texts of treaties and international agreements to which the U.S. is a party. Purchase is by subscription or single copy ($89.00 per year).

* United Nations Documents and Reference

Bureau of International Organization Affairs
Department of State
2201 C St., NW, Room 3428
Washington, DC 20520   (202) 647-6878

This office performs general reference on United Nations matters for the State Department. There is limited availability for U.N. documents.

* United Nations Educational Scientific and Cultural Organizations (UNESCO) UNESCO Affairs

Bureau of International Organization Affairs
Department of State
2201 C St., NW, Room 5331
Washington, DC 20520   (202) 647-6878

Although the United States withdrew from UNESCO in 1984, it still maintains a foreign service officer observes UNESCO and reports their activities to the State Department. This office can provide you with general information regarding UNESCO.

* United Nations Special Agencies

Office of Technical Specialized Agencies
Bureau of International Organization Affairs
Department of State
2201 C St., NW, Room 5331
Washington, DC 20520   (202) 647-2330

In overseeing U.S. relationships with United Nations technical and specialized organizations, this office is responsible for planning, coordinating, and implementing U.S. policy toward these organizations and other programs within the United Nations. They work closely with other offices, governmental agencies, and organizations.

* University Expertise in International Development

Office of Research and University Relations
Bureau for Science and Technology, Room 309, SA-18
U.S. Agency for International Development
Washington, DC 20523   (703) 875-4005

U.S. universities are the primary centers which generate knowledge and the development of skills essential to the U.S. role in development assistance. The overseas missions of AID in particular need to be able to draw upon the scientific community in order to apply the most current technical expertise and judgment to mission plans and programs. In response to this need, AID has established a Joint Career Corps (JCC) to encourage certain exchanges of work assignments between university faculty and Agency staff. Candidates proposed by their universities must be tenured faculty, at least at the Associate Professor level, with established scientific reputations, leadership qualities, and the ability to provide both technical and policy related advice to missions and high-level host country officials. Contact this office for more information.

* Urban Development in Third World

Office of Housing and Urban Programs
Bureau for Private Enterprise
Agency for International Development
320 21st St., NW
Washington, DC 20523   (202) 647-8298

This office supports a program of research and technical assistance in urban development. New tools are developed and applied to the analysis of urban issues and urban investment strategies to strengthen their effectiveness.

* U.S. Exports to Developing Countries

Commercial, Legislative and Business Affairs
Bureau of Economic and Business Affairs
Department of State
2201 C St., NW, Room 6822
Washington, DC 20520   (202) 647-1942

This office acts as a clearinghouse within the State Department for general questions concerning international business exporting and U.S. Government programs to support U.S. business and exports. It also works with the U.S. Department of Commerce to support U.S. commercial assistants working in 140 U.S. embassies overseas.

* U.S. Foreign Policy News Summary

Bureau of Public Affairs
2201 C St., NW, Room 5815A
Department of State
Washington, DC 20520   (202) 647-6575

Update From State is a new bimonthly publication dedicated to informing the public about the policies, operations, and diplomatic efforts of the Department of State and the Foreign Service. It includes material on the full range of international affairs, interviews, and articles by key foreign policymakers, and a list

* U.S. Foreign Policy Press Materials

Press and Publications Service
Bureau of Programs
United States Information Agency
301 Fourth St., SW, Room 406
Washington, DC 20547   (202) 485-2257

USIA prints materials to project an accurate image of the United States and its foreign policy abroad, and to combat disinformation and the communist threat. The Wireless File, a radioteletype network which now can also be accessed computer-to-computer, sends five regional transmissions of policy statements and interpretation each weekday. Each contains 20,000 to 30,000 words in English, but also includes Spanish, French, and Arabic portions, and is sent to U.S.

personnel abroad for background information and to distribute to foreign opinion leaders and news media. The Express File transmits material from the Wireless directly into the news rooms of foreign media. This division also distributes articles, photographs, the Dateline America news-feature service, and a monthly Soviet propaganda alert. USIA also prints 14 magazines and commercial bulletins in 20 languages, mostly at foreign locations. Generally, they contain reprints from American periodicals for distribution abroad. Publications printed in Washington, D.C., are *America Illustrated*, a monthly printed in Russian; *Topic*, published six times a year for sub-Saharan Africa, in English and French; *Dialogue*, a quarterly devoted to American culture and ideas, printed in English, French, and Spanish, as well as other translations put out by field posts; *Economic Impact*, an English and Spanish quarterly; *English Teaching Forum*, a quarterly for English teachers around the world; and *Problems of Communism*. The latter two are available in the United States through the Government Printing Office. Other magazines printed overseas are *al-Majal*, an Arabic monthly; *Span*, an English monthly published in India; and *Trends*, a Japanese bi-monthly. USIA also distributes pamphlets and leaflets in more than 100 countries.

* U.S. Information Agency Library

United States Information Agency
301 Fourth St., SW, Room 135
Washington, DC 20547   (202) 485-8947
The Washington library of USIA houses a varied collection, including a Russian language section. Access is restricted: permission to use the library can be obtained through the Office of Congressional and Public Liaison, address above, Room 602, (202) 485-2355.

* U.S. Representation at International Organizations

Bureau of International Organization Affairs
Department of State
2201 C St., NW, Room 6334
Washington, DC 20520   (202) 647-6575
This bureau explains United States' foreign policy positions to other nations and does the day-in and day-out work of representing the U.S. and presenting U.S. policies at the United Nations. They work with many international organizations, such as the International Labor Organization, and take part in over 700 international conferences each year.

* U.S. Role in United Nations

United States Mission to the United Nations
799 United Nations Plaza
New York, NY 10017   (212) 415-4404
This office can provide information regarding the activities and positions of U.S. representatives as well as the delegations of other countries at the United Nations.

* U.S.-Soviet Exchange Initiative

President's U.S.-Soviet Exchange Initiative
United States Information Agency
301 Fourth St., SW, Room 751
Washington, DC 20547   (202) 485-1548
This office is implementing the General Exchanges Agreement signed by the U.S. and the Soviet Union in 1985 to resume academic, cultural, and performing artists exchanges, officially suspended since 1979. It is also charged with facilitating a new, extensive initiative to foster direct contact between their citizens, endorsed by the leaders of both countries. Guidance is provided to private-sector groups interested in establishing exchanges in the areas of performing arts, exhibitions, education, health, sports, television, film, youth, citizen and professional counterparts.

* Visa Information for Aliens

Visa Services
Department of State
Bureau of Consular Affairs
Columbia Plaza Office Building
2401 E St., NW, Room 1353
Washington, DC 20520   (202) 647-0510
This office provides visa information for citizens of foreign countries who wish to come to the United States for a temporary stay, such as for studies, tourism, or medical treatment. To obtain a visa you must contact the nearest American embassy or consulate. This office can direct you to the closest place, as well as inform you of documents necessary for the application process.

* Voice of America International Broadcasting

Office of External Affairs
Voice of America
United States Information Agency
330 Independence Ave., SW, Room 1547
Washington, DC 20547   (202) 485-6231

On the air since 1942, VOA has built an audience of more than 127 million adults, listening to some 1200 hours of broadcasting a week in 43 languages. With 34 studios at headquarters in Washington, DC, three more in New York, one in Los Angeles, and one in Miami, VOA beams programs worldwide through a satellite network. VOA maintains news bureaus in 26 cities, and uses part-time correspondents in many countries to supplement its own staff. Radio Marti broadcasts seven days a week to Cuba, and a test of TV Marti has been funded. Information on the VOA and its program schedules is available. Forty-five-minute tours of VOA facilities are given weekdays, except holidays. Call for reservations.

* Voice of America Facilities

Office of Engineering and Technical Operations
Voice of America
United States Information Agency
330 Independence Ave., SW, Room 3348
Washington, DC 20547   (202) 485-8048
The Voice of America has a Master Control and Network Control Center in Washington, DC, facilities in New York City, Chicago, Los Angeles, and Miami, 107 transmitters worldwide, and 15 satellite circuits to use in reaching audiences all over the globe. A Satellite Interconnect System (SIS) is in the beginning phases of operation and will eventually improve reception of VOA broadcasts in many remote areas. The public can receive free of charge information on the technical operations of VOA, including a descriptive leaflet on SIS, a table of VOA relay stations, showing the locations, transmitters, power range, and area reached, and a frequency schedule.

* Voluntary Relief Organizations Reports

Bureau for Food for Peace and Voluntary Assistance
Room 260, SA-8
U.S. Agency for International Development
Washington, DC 20523   (703) 875-4801
Voluntary Foreign Aid Programs: Report of American Voluntary Agencies Engaged in Overseas Relief and Development Registered with the Agency for International Development describes the general nature of the work being carried out by the Private and Voluntary Organizations (PVOs) which are registered with AID. Included is such information as a PVO's geographic focus and sectorial concentration, as well as summaries of support, revenue, and expenditures. Contact the office above to obtain a copy.

* War Risk Insurance for Ships

Marine Insurance Division
Office of Trade and Analysis and Insurance
Maritime Administration
U.S. Department of Transportation
400 7th Street, SW, Room 8121
Washington, DC 20590   (202) 366-4161
The War Risk Insurance Program insures operators and seamen against losses from hostile action if commercial insurance is not available to them. The program covers loss of life and materials due to war or nuclear detonation.

* Water and Sanitation Assistance and Training

Office of Training and Program Support
Peace Corps
1990 K St., NW
Washington, DC 20526   (202) 254-8890
This office works at encouraging and implementing better methods of sanitation and water purification.

* Who's Who in the Diplomatic Community

Bureau of Public Affairs
Department of State
2201 C St., NW, Room 5815A
Washington, DC 20520   (202) 647-9859
The Bureau of Public Affairs publishes a sales catalog, which lists their publications, as well as ordering information. The following publications are also available from the Superintendent of Documents Government Printing Office, Washington, D.C. 20402; (202) 783-3238.

Department of State Bulletin ($4.50 a month/ $25 per year). This official monthly record of U.S. foreign policy provides the public, Congress, and government agencies with information on developments in U.S. foreign relations and on the work of the State Department. The Bulletin includes major addresses and news conferences of the President and the Secretary, statements before congressional committees, special features and articles on international affairs, selected press releases, and a list of treaties and other agreements to which the United States is or may become a party.

Diplomatic List ($14). Prepared quarterly, the Diplomatic List includes the names of the members of the diplomatic staffs of all missions and their spouses, as well as the addresses and phone numbers of the foreign missions.

Employees of Diplomatic Missions ($13). This quarterly publication lists all the members of the technical, administrative, and service staffs of more than 130 foreign missions. It gives the employee's name, function, and home address.

Key Officers of Foreign Service Posts ($10). Produced three times a year, this publication lists all key officers at Foreign Service posts whom business representatives would most likely need to contact. Addresses and phone numbers are included.

State Department Organizational Directory ($6.50). It includes detailed organizational listings of State, AID, ACDA, and the U.S. Information Agency, with titles, names, and phone numbers. There is a directory of services listing available services within the Department of State.

Update From State (free). A new bimonthly publication dedicated to informing the public about the policies, operations, and diplomatic efforts of the Department of State and the Foreign Service.

* Women in Development Program

Development Information Center
Room 105 SA-18
Agency for International Development
Washington, DC 20523-1801   (703) 875-4818

Contact this Center for information on AID's Women in Development subject collection of papers and documents assembled and organized by the AID Women in Development Office. Access is through a handlist. Call (703) 875-INFO for general AID information.

* Women Empowerment in Third World

Bureau for Program and Policy Coordination
Agency for International Development
320 21st St., NW, Room 3725A
Washington, DC 20523   (202) 647-3992

Women in developing countries play a significant role in economic production, family support, and the overall development process of the national economies. Bilateral aid is therefore administered to give particular attention to the programs, projects, and activities that tend to integrate women and improve their status in these countries. Materials on experiences within this program are available through the Center for Development Information and Evaluation, 1601 N. Kent St., Room 105, Arlington, VA (703) 875-4818.

* Work Permits for Foreigners

Labor Certification Division
Employment Service
Employment and Training Administration
Department of Labor
200 Constitution Ave., NW, Room N4456
Washington, DC 20210   (202) 535-0163

If an employer wishes to hire foreign workers, he must first obtain a foreign labor certificate, which is a statement from the U.S. Department of Labor stating that there is no U.S. citizen available to fill the job. The Department investigates to make sure that the wages and working conditions of the foreign workers will not seriously affect the wages and working conditions of U.S. workers. An employer applies for a foreign labor certificate through the local state employment service office, which then conducts a job hunt before sending the application form to the area regional office for approval or disapproval.

* WORLDNET Radio and Television Satellite Network

Public Liaison
Television and Film Service
United States Information Agency
601 D St., NW
Washington, DC 20547   (202) 376-1127

The first live global satellite television network, WORLDNET now reaches every continent, transmitting five days a week. Designed to link overseas posts and embassies with Washington and to provide news and feature programming for foreign broadcast media, WORLDNET allows the U.S. to explain our foreign policy with new immediacy and to act quickly in response to global events. "Dialogues" are an innovative way to demonstrate American press freedom by linking American newsmakers electronically with foreign journalists in unrehearsed, live "telepress conferences." The network utilizes Intelsat and regional satellites. Nearly 200 U.S. embassies, consulates, and cultural centers around the world are equipped with antennae to receive WORLDNET programming and distribute it to local broadcasters. A free brochure on WORLDNET is available. On August 22, 1988, RIAS-TV joined RIAS (Radio in the American Sector), a 40- year-old U.S.-German cooperative effort. With a Washington bureau and access to WORLDNET programming, as well as American network footage, and the ability to originate programs, RIAS-TV is reaching large audiences in both East and West Germany, and by cable, West Berlin.

Arms Control and World Peace

Ongoing negotiations between the superpowers to reduce the arsenals of the United States and the Soviet Union are coordinated in this country by the U.S. Arms Control and Disarmament Agency (ACDA). This federal agency also takes the lead in other efforts to reduce the risk of war, for example, in verification of other countries' compliance of the Nuclear Non-Proliferation Treaty and other international agreements. Information about these developments as well as technical materials are identified here. Weapons sales to foreign governments as well as technology transfer, and treaties must win the approval of the U.S. Senate so the Armed Services Committee and other congressional panels serve as additional information sources which often provide a different approach to the objectives of the president and the ACDA.

* Current and Future Negotiations
Bureau of Strategic Programs
Arms Control and Disarmament Agency
320 21st St., NW
Washington, DC 20451 (202) 647-6566
This office coordinates with other agencies on research and policy studies to support the development of a comprehensive and effective arms control program. The Bureau also conducts external research on the technical and political implications of current and proposed negotiating options. This research supports implementation of existing agreements, ongoing negotiations, and planning for future negotiations.

* Defense Systems Impact on Arms Control
Defense Programs & Analysis
Bureau of Nuclear and Weapons Control
Arms Control and Disarmament Agency
320 21st St., NW
Washington, DC 20451 (202) 647-3466
Arms Control Impact Statement, an annual report to Congress, contains details on certain weapons systems and analyses on the impact that such systems have on arms control agreements, treaties, and negotiations. Those weapon systems include nuclear weapon-related programs, defense programs which exceed specified cost ceilings, and other technology and weapons systems which the Executive Branch certifies as having significant effects on arms control. Impact statements are intended to be of value to the executive branch, to the Congress, and to the general public in evaluating the arms control implications of the development of major U.S. nuclear and non-nuclear weapons systems. Impact statements are intended to enhance the likelihood that arms control considerations become and remain integral to the decision making process on major U.S. defense programs, and that ACDA be instrumental in the process. Contact this office to obtain a copy of this annual publication.

* Diplomatic Coordination
Office of Public Affairs
Arms Control and Disarmament Agency
320 21st St., NW, Room 5843
Washington, DC 20451 (202) 647-8677
As part of an interagency public diplomacy group, this office prepares, coordinates, and publishes materials to support the Administration's conduct of public diplomacy activities. ACDA also provides guidance on arms control matters to press spokesmen of other Federal agencies, assists in preparation of information for use abroad, conducts special programs and conferences for nongovernmental organizations and the news media, and conducts briefings for media representatives, visiting students, and scholars.

* Disarmament Activities and Documents
Superintendent of Documents
Government Printing Office
Washington, DC 20402 (202) 783-3238
Each volume of ACDA's historical series, *Documents on Disarmament*, contains complete details on significant arms control and disarmament activities by printing the textual materials of treaties, agreements, laws, reports, statements, resolutions, communiques, proposals, declarations, and speeches of both U.S. and foreign origin.

* Economic Analysis of Arms Control Programs
Defense Programs and Analysis Division
Bureau of Nuclear and Weapons Control
Arms Control and Disarmament Agency
320 21st St. NW
Washington, DC 20451 (202) 647-3466

This division is responsible for the Agency's economic analysis of defense and arms control programs, and the analysis of weapons technology. Contact them for more information on these issues.

* Economic Impact of Arms Reduction Treaties
Office of Public Affairs
U.S. Arms Control and Disarmament Agency
320 21st St., NW, Room 5843
Washington, DC 20451 (202) 647-8677
Research relevant indirectly to negotiation support and directly to assessing the economic impact of treaties and agreements is an important part of ACDA's activities. They analyze the economics of defense strategies, and are currently building data banks on worldwide defense and economic information. One of the objectives of arms control is the reduction of global military expenditures, and research in support of this objective includes analyses of the economic impact of the INF Treaty, defense spending and national budgets, and military procurement. ACDA economists review Soviet and Eastern European countries' national accounts, and prepare an annual submission on U.S. defense spending for the U.N. military expenditures reporting program. For questions regarding economics research, contact this office.

* Europe
Theater Affairs Division
Bureau of Strategic Programs
Arms Control and Disarmament Agency
320 21st St. NW
Washington, DC 20451 (202) 647-6566
The task of arms control in Europe is to reduce the danger of war. Contact this bureau for more information on the various ACDA to bring about this goal.

* Foreign Military Sales
Defense Security Assistance Agency
The Pentagon, Room 4D720
Washington, DC 20301-2800 (202) 697-8108
This office administers the Foreign Military Sales (FMS) Program, which deals with U.S. government sales of defense articles and services to foreign governments. A free booklet containing information on the Program and the U.S. Defense Security Assistance Agency is available upon request.

* Foreign Weapon Sales Statistics
Comptroller/DMD
Defense Security Assistance Agency
The Pentagon, Room 4B659
Washington, DC 20301-2800 (202) 697-2440
This office publishes a free annual publication, *Foreign Military Sales, Foreign Military Construction Sales, and Military Assistance Facts*, which contains information and detailed statistics on all grant programs, sales, and Federal financing of security assistance to foreign countries. Write or call for a copy.

* INF Treaty Q & A
Office of Public Affairs
Arms Control and Disarmament Agency
320 21st St., NW, Room 5843
Washington, DC 20451 (202) 523-2801
Understanding the INF Treaty reviews the post-World War II history leading up to the treaty, its negotiation, ratification, and implementation. This 36-page booklet provides the historical context to NATO's 1979 two-track decision, a history of the negotiations themselves, the ratification process that took place in both countries, an overview of the inspection and elimination procedures that are now being implemented, and an addendum that addresses may questions

frequently asked about the INF Treaty.

* Legal Advice on Arms Control Treaties

The Office of the General Counsel
Arms Control and Disarmament Agency
320 21st St., NW
Washington, DC 20451   (202) 647-3582

This office is responsible for all matters of domestic and international law relevant to ACDA's work. It provides advice and assistance in drafting and negotiating arms control treaties and agreements, and on questions regarding their approval by Congress, and their implementation, interpretation, ratification, and revision. Attorneys from the office also serve as legal advisers on U.S. arms control negotiating delegations. The office also handles the legal aspects of Agency policies and operations in the areas of personnel, ethics, security, patents, contracts, procurement, and fiscal and administrative matters.

* Military Equipment Export Licenses

Office of Munitions Control
Bureau of Politico-Military Affairs
Department of State, SA-6
Washington, DC 20520   (703) 875-6650

Being responsible for the licensing and regulation of commercial exports of military equipment and services, this office develops policy guidance on munitions exports, and registers all U.S. exports of arms, ammunition, and implements of war.

* Multilateral Arms Control Negotiations

Bureau of Multilateral Affairs
Arms Control and Disarmament Agency
320 21st St. NW
Washington, DC 20451   (202) 647-5999

This office develops arms control policy, strategy, and tactics for ongoing multilateral arms control negotiations, and provides organizational support, delegation staffing, and Washington backstopping for multilateral negotiations, such as multilateral and bilateral chemical weapons negotiations and the First Committee of the United Nations General Assembly. Contact this bureau for more information relevant to multilateral affairs.

* Newsletter

Office of Public Affairs
Arms Control and Disarmament Agency
320 21st St., NW, Room 5832
Washington, DC 20451   (202) 523-2801

Arms Control Update, an eight-page, serially-published ACDA newsletter, reviews recent developments in arms control and contains excerpts from administration statements on U.S. arms control policy. Recent issues contain broad overviews of U.S. arms control activities and information about other, more in-depth, publications. Contact this office to receive a free subscription.

* Non-Proliferation Evaluation

International Nuclear Affairs Division
Bureau of Nuclear and Weapons Control
Arms Control and Disarmament Agency
320 21st St. NW
Washington, DC 20451   (202) 647-3466

This division provides advice, assessments, and policy recommendations on the international relations aspects of nonproliferation. It also assesses each proposed agreement for peaceful cooperation and provides ACDA views on U.S. nuclear export control issues.

* Non-Proliferation Treaty Compliance

Office of Non-Proliferation and Export Policy
Bureau of Oceans and International Environmental
  and Scientific Affairs
Department of State
2201 C St., NW, Room 7828
Washington, DC 20520   (202) 647-4812

Concerned with non-proliferation policy, this office makes sure that materials having nuclear weapons potential are not exported without careful consideration of the Nuclear Non-Proliferation Treaty.

* Nuclear Risk Reduction Center

Nuclear Risk Reduction Center
Bureau of Politico-Military Affairs
Department of State
2201 C St., NW, Room 7532
Washington, DC 20520   (202) 647-0025

The United States Nuclear Risk Reduction Center and its Soviet counterpart have been established to reduce the risk of conflict that might result from accident, misinterpretation, or miscalculation.

* Nuclear Technologies

Nuclear Safeguards and Technology Division
Bureau of Nuclear and Weapons Control
Arms Control and Disarmament Agency
320 21st St. NW
Washington, DC 20451   (202) 647-3466

This division provides advice and policy recommendations on safeguard systems, nuclear fuel cycles, and the technology aspects of nonproliferation. It also assesses the safeguards and nonproliferation implications of emerging technologies. Contact this division for more information.

* Peace and International Conflict Grants

Jennings Randolph Program for International Peace
United States Institute of Peace
1550 M St. N.W.
Washington, D.C. 20005   (202) 457-1700

This Program provides fellowships to scholars and leaders in peace to undertake research and other appropriate forms of communication on issues of international peace and the management of international conflict. The Fellowship Program has three levels: Jennings Randolph Distinguished Fellows are individuals whose careers show extraordinary accomplishment concerning questions of international peace; United States Institute of Peace Fellows are individuals also of accomplishment, but of somewhat less eminence; and United States Institute of Peace Scholars are individuals working on doctoral dissertations in the field.

* Policy Coordination

Bureau of Strategic Programs
Arms Control and Disarmament Agency
320 21st St. NW
Washington, DC 20451   (202) 647-6566

This office is responsible for U.S.-Soviet nuclear arms control. In coordination with other U.S. agencies, it develops U.S. nuclear arms control policies for Presidential approval, supports negotiations on nuclear arms control, and provides analytical support for these efforts. Its responsibilities also include consultation and coordination with allied and other foreign governments on U.S./Soviet arms control negotiations. This bureau maintains the official record of all relevant documents, speeches, significant comments, and general material related to bilateral arms control and negotiations.

* Politico-Military Considerations

Bureau of Politico-Military Affairs
Department of State
2201 C St., NW, Room 7320
Washington, DC 20520   (202) 647-1256

The bureau advises the Secretary of State on the military aspects of various foreign policy matters, such as arms control negotiations, regional security arrangements, security assistance, arms sales programs, and technology transfers. It has primary responsibility for coordinating U.S. arms sales, military assistance, and Economic Support Fund programs to other nations. With a role in ongoing arms control negotiations, the bureau prepare talks with he Soviets on reduction of strategic nuclear weapons, defense and space issues, and nuclear testing. It also is involved in multilateral negotiations to ban chemical weapons and reduce conventional forces in Europe.

* Press Releases

Office of Public Affairs
Arms Control and Disarmament Agency
320 21st St., NW, Room 5843
Washington, DC 20451   (202) 523-2801

This office publishes and distributes a daily compilation of press clippings; dispatches a daily cable containing selected press releases on arms control to U.S. Diplomatic posts overseas; and supplies numerous updates of arms control topics in its *Issues Brief* series. Contact this office for more information on these news releases.

* Proposals in U.S. Congress

Office of Congressional Affairs
Arms Control and Defense Agency
320 21st St. NW
Washington, DC 20451   (202) 523-3796

This office responds to congressional interest in arms control and negotiations by arranging briefings and consultations between ACDA officials and Members of Congress and staff; arranging arms control seminars for Congressional staff with ACDA officials and officials from other agencies; working with Congressional committee staffs in arranging hearings at which ACDA officials appear as witnesses; and distributing informational material on arms control issues to Members of Congress and their staffs. In response to requests from

Senators and staff, this office provides information and coordinated briefings, seminars, and speakers.

* Proposed Arms and Technology Transfers

Arms Transfer Division
Bureau of Nuclear and Weapons Control
Arms Control and Disarmament Agency
320 21st St. NW
Washington, DC 20451   (202) 647-3466

This office assesses the arms control implications of proposed arms transfers and technology transfers, and represents the Agency in the preparation of the Administration's annual security assistance programs. This office also participates in the implementation of the Missile Technology Control Regime. Contact this office for more information concerning arms transfer.

* Proposed Weapons Sales Analysis

Office of Security Assistance and Sales
Bureau of Politico-Military Affairs
Department of State
2201 C St., NW, Room 7418
Washington, DC 20520   (202) 647-7774

OASA sets policy regarding transfer or sales of arms to foreign countries with respect to geographic regions and the technology allowed in the regions. They also deal with the transfer of arms regarding their purpose for use, as well as third country transfers, where a country who bought arms from the U.S. wants to sell these arms to another country. This office handles munitions control which concerns the licensing of items with military applications. Working closely with the Department of Defense on many of these areas, OSAS also helps in formulating the budget for military needs.

* Public Information on Arms Control Policies

Office of Public Affairs
Arms Control and Disarmament Agency
320 21st St., NW, Room 5843
Washington, DC 20451   (202) 523-2801

This office distributes and coordinates public information on arms control and disarmament. The staff works to ensure accurate and complete media coverage of U.S. arms control policies, and makes the public aware of arms control activities through speaking engagements and publications. This office also responds to information requests, and provides Agency leaders with advice on public perceptions of U.S. arms control policies.

* Safeguards and Arms Control Research

Office of Public Affairs
U.S. Arms Control and Disarmament Agency
320 21st St., NW, Room 5843
Washington, DC 20451   (202) 647-8677

ACDA's sponsored external research covers a wide range of arms control issues, such as verification, nuclear safeguards, nuclear test ban monitoring, and crisis stability issues. Specific examples of projects include Retrieval of Public Statements on Verification, and a Computer Model for Simulating Conventional Warfare. Conferences and seminars on related issues are also arranged. Contact this office for more information on these projects and other on-going external research.

* Soviet Compliance with Arms Control Agreements

Office of Public Affairs
Arms Control and Disarmament Agency
320 21st St., NW, Room 5843
Washington, DC 20451   (202) 523-2801

The President's annual *Report on Soviet Noncompliance* to Congress presents in detail an evaluation of Soviet actions with respect to arms control obligations. Annually, ACDA also prepares for the President to submit to the Congress the report, *Adherence to and Compliance with Agreements*. This report contains details of the process by which the U.S. Government ensures U.S. compliance with its arms control obligations, detailed responses to Soviet charges of U.S. noncompliance, and an evaluation of other nations' compliance with international arms control agreements.

* Speakers on Arms Control

Office of Public Affairs
Arms Control and Disarmament Agency
320 21st St., NW, Room 5843
Washington, DC 20451   (202) 647-8677

Officers of the U.S. Arms Control and Disarmament Agency will address audiences in all parts of the country if speaking engagements can be worked into their schedules.

* Status of Current Arms Control Activities

Office of Public Affairs
Arms Control and Disarmament Agency
320 21st St., NW, Room 5843
Washington, DC 20451   (202) 523-2801

Each year the President is required to send to the Congress an annual report on the activities of ACDA and the nation's arms control agenda. The report includes a complete review of arms control and disarmament goals, research, and activities, as well as appraisals of the status and prospects of arms control negotiations and of arms control measures in effect. Contact this office of more information on this report.

* Treaty Verification Operations

Operations Analysis Division
Bureau of Verification & Intelligence
Arms Control and Disarmament Agency
320 21st St., NW
Washington, DC 20451   (202) 647-8091

The ACDA VAX computer helps evaluate and improve treaty verification procedures, assess treaty compliance, and verify provisions of proposed treaties, along with other facets of negotiation support. One of the VAX programs, for example, keeps track of all arms control-related external research conducted throughout the U.S. Government. All agencies are informed of on-going research to ensure that no duplication of work occurs. Contact this office for more information on computer aided research and arms control.

* Verification of Soviet Compliance

Bureau of Verification and Intelligence
Arms Control and Disarmament Agency
320 21st St. NW
Washington, DC 20451   (202) 647-8091

This bureau provides a focal point within ACDA and the U.S. Government for formulating U.S. arms control verification policy and for assessing Soviet compliance with arms control agreements.

* Weapons Reduction Research and Arms Control Options

Office of Public Affairs
U.S. Arms Control and Disarmament Agency
320 21st St., NW, Room 5843
Washington, DC 20451   (202) 647-8677

Research, both short-run and long-run, on all aspects of arms control and disarmament is one of the Arms Control and Disarmament Agency's principal functions. While most research projects support the immediate requirements of ongoing negotiations, others have been directed toward the goal of a world free from war and the dangers of armaments. Over the years, ACDA has accumulated a wealth of information on every conceivable aspect of arms control and disarmament. ACDA also coordinates research and studies by or for other government agencies, and analyzes selected defense programs for their arms control implications. Contact this office for information on specific research topics.

* World Peace Assessment

United States Institute of Peace
1550 M St. N.W.
Washington, DC 20005   (202) 457-1700

The Institute has decided to undertake a task of presenting critical information on the state of peace worldwide to the American public and to the international community. A number of valuable studies are available in areas such as human rights and global ecology. The Institute's report will be a periodically updated survey seeking to identify trends, causes, and consequences of armed international conflict on a region-by-region basis. In addition, efforts will be made to standardize methods of statistical reporting on the state of world peace.

* Worldwide Military Expenditures and Arms Transfers

Superintendent of Documents
Government Printing Office
Washington, DC 20402   (202) 783-3238

This annual publication provides a compilation of annual military and other relevant statistics for each of 145 countries over a decade, as well as essays on pertinent topics and special analyses. Military data include military spending, numbers of armed forces, and arms exports and imports in value and quantity terms. Comparative economic data include gross national product, central government expenditures, population, and total exports and imports. This publication also provides worldwide military and other relevant statistics for the period 1979-1986, as well as arms transfer data through 1987.

Military and National Security

* See also Information from Lawmakers Chapter
* See also Selling to the Government Chapter
* See also Science and Technology Chapter

The military-industrial complex is vast and many of the research and development centers and laboratories identified below are useful information sources. Defense procurement and contracts are included here as well as in the Selling to the Government chapter. Military installations, personnel, spending, and other dimensions to the armed forces are contained in this chapter. There are 108 House and Senate committees and subcommittees that not only oversee the Pentagon but also have the last word on the defense budget. Policy concerning weapons sales and technology transfer to foreign governments are also addressed in the preceding section on arms control and disarmament.

* Aeromedical Research
Strughold Aeromedical Library
U.S. Department of the Air Force
School of Aerospace Medicine
Brooks Air Force Base, TX 78235   (512) 536-3725
This library will provide inter-library loans, and can help you identify reports and refer you to the appropriate source.

* Aeronautical Systems Clearinghouse
Aeronautical Systems Division
Office of Public Affairs
Department of the Air Force
Wright-Patterson Air Force Base, OH 45433   (513) 255-3334
This office develops and acquires aeronautical systems, their components, and related aerospace equipment, including aircraft engines, airborne communications systems, special reconnaissance projects, and interpretation facilities. Fact sheets are available for each of the 200 programs administered by the agency. Write or call the above office for a free brochure describing the Division's mission.

* Aeronautics Research: Air Force
U.S. Department of the Air Force
Arnold Engineering Development Center
Air Force Systems Command
Arnold Air Force Base, TN 37389 (615) 454-5586
This center has test laboratories in which atmospheric conditions, orbital, space flight, and ballistic conditions can be simulated. A brochure on the base, its programs, and mission, along with fact sheets on technical subjects, including wind tunnels, aeropropulsion systems, and rocket test facilities can be obtained by writing or calling the above office.

* Aerospace Research Library
Information Management Division
National Air and Space Museum, Room 3100
Smithsonian Institute
Washington, DC 20560   (202) 357-3133
The Museum has a research library devoted to books and journals on aviation history, space exploration history, and science and technology in the fields of astronomy, astrophysics, engineering, geology, and space medicine.

* Aerospace Structures
Aerospace Structures Information
and Analysis Center
U.S. Department of the Air Force
WRDC/FIBR
Wright-Patterson AFB, OH 45433   (513) 255-6688
This Center is a central point for the collection and distribution of aerospace structures information. It maintains a library of reports done by various government agencies, and can refer you to other libraries and sources. Requests for specific information are served for researchers or contractors with a "need to know" status. Write or call for How to Get It: A Guide to Defense-related Information Sources and a free brochure describing the Center, its services, and user eligibility.

* Aircraft Armament Research
Munitions Systems Division
U.S. Air Force Systems Command
Elgin Air Force Base, FL 32542   (904) 882-3931
This Command conducts research, development, testing, and evaluation of guns and other aircraft weapons, explosives, chemical-biological weapons, and missile systems. The office will respond to requests for information on specific technical topics.

* Aircraft Test Flights
Air Force Flight Test Center
Public Affairs Office
Edwards Air Force Base, CA 93523-5000   (805) 277-3510
This office can supply you with fact sheets on all aircraft tested on its facilities, the history of the Test Center, significant historical events, and biographies of famous people associated with the base.

* Air Force Aeronautical Systems
U.S. Department of the Air Force
Aeronautical Systems Division
Public Affairs Office
Wright-Patterson Air Force Base, OH 45433-6503   (513) 255-2725
The Public Affairs Office's brochure, What's Happening at ASD, lists the major programs in all the Aeronautical Systems Division offices, the contractors involved, and the program status. Also available is a brochure describing the five laboratories which make up the Wright Research and Development Center: aeropropulsion and power, flight dynamics, materials, avionics, and electronic technology.

* Air Force Aviation History
U.S. Department of the Air Force
Air Force Central Visual Information Library
Norton Air Force Base, CA 92409-5996   (714) 382-2493
This library will loan copies from their collection, which includes visual productions of documentaries, training materials, the history of aviation, and W.W.II and Korean War produced by the Air Force.

* Air Force Casualty Reporting
U.S. Department of the Air Force
Casualty Matters
Headquarters, AFMPA/DPMC
Randolph Air Force Base, TX 78150-6001   (512) 652-3305
To obtain information on Air Force personnel who are injured, deceased, missing in action, or taken prisoner, call the above number 24-hours a day, 7 days a week.

* Air Force Directives, R & D, Goals
U.S. Department of the Air Force
Air Force Information for Industry Office
5001 Eisenhower Ave.
Alexandria, VA 22333   (202) 247-9305
The Air Force Information for Industry Office offers information, assistance, and resources to aid potential contractors in doing business with the Air Force. You may write or call their office. The following are among the free publications

available:

Air Force Logistics Needs, Mission Element Need Statements (MENS), Program Element Descriptive Summaries, Program Management Directive, R & D Planning Summaries, Technical Objective Documents, Technology Needs Documents, and *Selling to the United States Air Force.*

* Air Force Historical Records

Air Force Historical Research Center
HQUSAFHRC/HD
Maxwell Air Force BASE, AL 36112   (205) 293-6678

This is the principal repository for Air Force historical records. It holds the most extensive collection of documentary source material on the history of U.S. military action. The Center is open to researchers and scholars, and provides research services.

* Air Force Historical Research Library

Secretary of the U.S. Air Force
Public Resource Library
The Pentagon, Room 5C945
Washington, DC 20330-1000   (202) 697-4100

The Resource Library is able to answer a broad range of Air Force related questions and has printed material available such as biographies of prominent Air Force generals, fact sheets on Air Force related topics (such as aircraft, weapons systems, missions), and "Speech Inserts" from key speeches by Air Force leadership.

* Air Force Housekeeping Programs

U.S. Air Force Engineering Service Center
Public Affairs Office
Tyndall Air Force Base, FL 32403-6001   (904) 283-6476

This Center conducts research and forms Air Force policy for the managing of food services, laundry services, and billeting on Air Force bases worldwide. They can provide fact sheets on their programs and engineering activities.

* Air Force Military History

Office of Air Force History
HQUSAF/CHOR, Building 5681
Bolling Air Force Base, DC 20332   (202) 767-0412

This office has a small library and archives on Air Force military history going back to the Civil War era, and is available to researchers and scholars. It has holdings on microfilm of the Air Force Historical Research Center in Alabama. It offers a brochure on Air Force research programs with opportunities for research fellowships, and a publications list.

* Air Force Patents

The Judge Advocate General
Patents Division, AF/JACP
1900 Half St., SW
Washington, DC 20324-1000   (202) 475-1386

This office grants licenses for commercial use of government-owned patents. For information on the patents available, contact the above office.

* Air Force Procurement

U.S. Air Force
Air Force Information for Industry Office (AFIFIO)
5001 Eisenhower Ave.
Alexandria, VA 22333   (202) 274-9305

This office maintains a research and development, technical reading room open to DOD contractors, and will provide research and development planning and requirement documents to qualified users. The office can also give information on the Air Force Potential Contractors Program, which was instituted to facilitate technology transfer between the military and industry. Write or call for the free brochure explaining eligibility requirements and how to access the reading room, as well as how to enroll in the Potential Contractors Program and gain access to the Defense Technology Information Center.

* Air Force Research Grants

Office of Scientific Research
U.S. Air Force
Bolling Air Force Base
Washington, DC 20332   (202) 767-4943

This office accepts proposals for scientific research and requests for grants. Write or call for copies of the *Research Interest* pamphlet, the *Proposer's Guide*, the *Grant Brochure* (which lists the types of grants available), and technical brochures on Air Force research programs.

* Air Force Special Missions

Headquarters
U.S. Air Force Reserve
Public Affairs Office
Robins Air Force Base, GA 31098   (212) 9266721

Write for photographic reproductions of Air Force aircraft, including the one and only C130 spray mission airplane used for drug enforcement and control. The office also has fact sheets available containing little known but interesting data on other special missions of the Air Force Reserve, including the Central American support flights.

* Airport Security: Hijacking, Bomb Threats

Civil Aviation Security Service (ACS 400)
Federal Aviation Administration
Department of Transportation
800 Independence Ave., SW, Room 320
Washington, DC 20591   (202) 267-9075

The FAA ensures the presence of law enforcement in U.S. airports, and approves the security programs of all airports under FAR 107. It also certifies walk-through detection devices. The office is a source of information and expertise on the following airport security issues: domestic and foreign aircraft hijacking; bomb threats at airports and on airplanes; compliance and enforcement of regulations; prevention of attempts; explosives and explosive devices found at airports and on airplanes; international crimes involving civil aviation; information on numbers of people screened, numbers of weapons found, and weapon detection devices.

* Air Warfare and Missile Systems Research

U.S. Navy
Naval Weapons Support Center
Public Affairs Office
Crane, IN 47522   (812) 854-2511

This Center conducts research and development, testing, and evaluation on air warfare and missile systems. Write or call for their free brochure containing vital statistics on the Center, its mission, and personnel, and which lists major contractors in the local area. Copies of technical reports may be ordered from the Center, a list of reports is also available.

* American Military History 15th Century On

Army Military History Institute
Carlisle Barracks, PA 17013-5008   (717) 245-3611

The Institute collects original source material on American military history dating as far back as the 15th Century, and holds over one million catalogued items. The Institute provides research and reference assistance to researchers on site and by written and telephone request.

* Ammunition, Combat, Weapons Testing

U.S. Army
Public Affairs Office (AMSTE-PA)
Aberdeen Proving Ground, MD 21005   (301) 278-3840

This facility conducts research, development, and testing of weapons, systems, ammunition, and combat and support vehicles. Their pamphlet entitled *This is TECOM* explains the Command, its mission, organization, structure, history, and methods of testing. The booklet *Facts and Figures* provides statistics on property values, energy consumption, number of employees, and population figures. Both are free upon request.

* Army Active Personnel Locator

U.S. Department of the Army
Worldwide Locator, EREC
Ft. Benjamin Harrison, IN 46249-5301   (317) 542-4211

To locate a missing relative in the active army, contact the above office; the toll free number is 1-800-444-3333. There is a small fee for the search.

* Army Aircraft Worldwide

U.S. Department of the Army
Aviation Systems Command
Federal Center
4300 Goodfellow Blvd.
St. Louis, MO 63120-1798   (314) 263-1164

This Command maintains all Army aircraft. It publishes a booklet entitled AVSCOM - Worldwide, containing facts and figures on troops, world locations, resources, and assets of the Command. To obtain a free copy, write or call the above office.

* Army and Air Force Base Exchanges Procurement

Army and Air Force Exchange Service
P.O. Box 222305
Dallas, TX 75222   (214) 780-2011

This office handles procurement of resale merchandise for Army and Air Force base exchanges in the continental United States. Write or call for free fact sheets on the Service and a *Vendor's Fact Book* explaining how to sell to the exchanges.

* Army and Navy Historic Photographs
Still Picture Branch
National Archives and Records Administration
Washington, DC 20408 (202) 523-3236
This office holds photographs from all Federal agencies, including the historical Matthew Brady Civil War collection, and Army and Navy photographs from Word War II. Copies may be obtained at cost.

* Army Budget and Forces
Community Relations Division
U.S. Army Public Affairs
The Pentagon, Room 2E631
Washington, DC 20310 (202) 679-2707
The Posture of the Army and the *Department of the Army Budget Estimates Fiscal Year 1989* is published annually and contains information on the status and direction of Army forces and the budget overview. Write or call to obtain a copy of the statement.

* Army Computer Procurement
Public Affairs Office
U.S. Army Information Systems Selection
  and Acquisition Agency
2461 Eisenhower Ave.
Alexandria, VA 22331 (202) 325-9762
This office is responsible for the procurement of all Army computer systems. Write for its fact sheet which describes the agency's mission, philosophy, and procurement process.

* Army Corps of Engineers Historical References
U.S. Army Corps of Engineers
Attn: Office of History
Humphreys Engineering Center
Ft. Belvoir, VA 22060-5577 (202) 355-3554
This office will respond to reference inquiries regarding the history of the Army Corps of Engineers. Permission is granted to serious researchers for the use of its archival library, which maintains historical documents dating from the beginning of the Corps. Recent information is available on the Corps' involvement in the 1989 Alaskan oil spill, the California earthquake, and Hurricane Hugo. The office publishes numerous books and reports and a free list of publications is available on request. The Center extends an open invitation for visitors to drop in.

* Army Discharged Personnel Locator Service
National Personnel Records Center
9700 Page Blvd.
St. Louis, MO 63132-5200 (314) 263-7201
To locate a relative or friend who is has been discharged from the Army, or who is deceased, contact the above office. The locator service's records go back to 1912; you may be able to find out what your great, great grandfather did in the Army.
There is a small fee for the search.

* Army Engineers' Environmental Publications
U.S. Army Corps of Engineers
Public Affairs
20 Massachusetts Ave., NW
Washington, DC 20314 (202) 272-0011
The Corps offers free brochures on a wide variety of subjects, including archaeology, camping, environment, erosion control, flood control, flood plain management, history, safety, waste-water treatment and water supply. For a publications list, call or write the above office.

* Army Exploration Maps
Cartographic and Architectural Branch
National Archives and Records Administration
Washington, DC 20408 (202) 756-6700
This office provides reference service on maps and architectural drawings in its holdings, which include survey maps, early Army exploration maps of the Old West dating from 1860. Call or write for assistance.

* Army Historical Publications
U.S. Army Center for Military History
20 Massachusetts Ave., NW
Washington, DC 20314-2000 (202) 272-0295
The Army Center for Military History publishes books, monographs and series

on Army military related history. A small sampling of the selections include *The Military and the Media*, *The Final Years*, a series on the Korean War, the Vietnam era, and a series on World War II. Write or call to order their 50-page brochure listing over 200 publications.

* Army Historical Research
U.S. Army Center of Military History
Historical Resources Branch
20 Massachusetts Ave., NW
Washington, DC 20314-0200 (202) 274-8290
The Army Center of Military History maintains a library and archives which may be used by serious researchers. For information about use of the library and its holdings, write or call the above office.

* Army Medical Library
Stimson Library
U.S. Department of the Army
Academy of Health Science
Building 2840, Room 106
Ft. Sam Houston, TX 78234-6100 (512) 221-5932
This library will provide inter-library loans, answer information requests, or give referrals to serious researchers. The collection is particularly good on physical therapy, health care administration, and materials on Army medical history.

* Army Medical Research
U.S. Department of the Army
Army Medical Research and Development Command
Attn: SGRD-PA
Fort Detrick
Frederick, MD 21701 (301) 663-2732
This Command conducts research and development in medical sciences, supplies, and equipment. Write or call for free copies of the brochure describing the Command, a quarterly newsletter, and the *Broad Agency Announcement* describing the research areas for which they solicit and instructions for submitting proposals.

* Army Patents
Patents, Copyrights and Trademarks Division
U.S. Army Legal Services Agency
5611 Columbia Pike, Room 332A
Falls Church, VA 22041-5013 (202) 756-2617
This office grants licenses for commercial use of government-owned patents. For information on the patents available and the cooperative research and development agreements with Army regional laboratories, contact the above office.

* Army Personnel Locator
U.S. Army Worldwide Locator
ELREC
Fort Benjamin Harrison, IN 46249 (317) 542-4211
To locate a long lost relative who is still on active duty in the Army, contact this office by letter. There is a small fee for their services. The telephone recording will give you information on the procedure and the data they need from you to initiate their search.

* Army Procurement
U.S. Army
Technical Industrial Liaison Office (TILO)
5001 Eisenhower Ave.
Alexandria, VA 22333 (202) 274-8948
This office maintains a research and development, technical reading room open to DOD contractors, and will provide research and development planning and requirement documents to qualified users. The office can also give information on the Army Potential Contractors Program, which was instituted to facilitate technology transfer between the military and industry. Write or call for the free brochure explaining eligibility requirements and how to access the reading room, as well as how to enroll in the Potential Contractors Program and gain access to the Defense Technology Information Center.

* Army Recruitment Audiovisuals
Army Recruiting Support Command
Cameron Station, Building 6
Alexandria, VA 22304 (202) 274-6666
Civic groups may request the Army's recruiting films for community fairs and youth events. The Army has a traveling slide projection show with short subject presentations on American history, the Federal government, development of the English language, Army basic training, and the Army nursing program. Write to the above address for information on the exhibit's availability.

* Army Research Grants

U.S. Army Research Office
P.O. Box 12211
Research Triangle Park, NC 27709   (919) 549-0641

This office considers requests for support of basic scientific research from educational institutions and nonprofit organizations. Write or call for a free pamphlet entitled *Broad Agency Announcement*, which describes the type of research being solicited by the Army and how to apply for a grant.

* Army Research Labs, Speakers on Technology

U.S. Department of the Army
Laboratory Command Headquarters
AMSLC-PA
2800 Powder Mill Rd.
Adelphi, MD 20783-1145   (301) 394-3590

This Command oversees the work of the seven major U.S. Army research laboratories. A brochure on the laboratories' missions and programs is available, and the Command can provide public speakers for civic groups in the field of technology development. Write or call for information.

* Army Reserve and Retiree Locator

Army Reserve Personnel Center
U.S. Department of the Army
9700 Page Blvd.
St. Louis, MO 63132-5200   (314) 263-7828

To locate a missing relative in the Army reserve (who is not assigned to a unit), or to locate a living Army retiree, contact this office. There is a small fee for the search.

* Army Speakers Bureau

Community Relations Division
U.S. Army Public Affairs
The Pentagon, Room 2E631
Washington, DC 20310   (202) 697-2707

The Army supplies speakers on a wide range of subjects to civic groups across the country, including chaplains, doctors, and nutritionists. They have experts in their Wildlife and Environment Conservation Program and Drug and Alcohol Abuse Program who will speak to you about how to start and run your own community programs. Contact your nearest Army installation, or the above office, for a referral.

* Army Technology Transfer and Commercialization

U.S. Department of the Army
Army Research Office
P.O. Box 12211
Triangle Park, NC 27709-2211   (919) 549-0641

The Army Research Office sponsors programs to further technology development and technology transfer in the United States. Its Technology Transfer Program allows private industry to enter into patent agreements with the Army, making possible the commercialization of Army technological findings. Write or call for free brochures and information describing these programs.

* Army Weapons Systems and Prime Contractors

U.S. Government Printing Office
Superintendent of Documents
Washington, DC 20402-6518   (202) 783-3238

The Department of the Army publishes the *Army Weapons Systems Handbook*, which contains photographs and descriptions of the major weapons systems in the Army, their program status, and a list of the prime contractors involved. It also gives information on the Soviet counterparts. A copy can be ordered through the Government Printing Office for a moderate charge.

* Astronomy: Naval Observatory

Naval Observatory
34th and Massachusetts Ave.
Washington, DC 20392-5100   (202) 653-1541

Monday night tours are conducted at the Observatory; call for reservations. A tour brochure and fact sheets on topics such as telescopes, planetariums, and astronomy may be obtained by writing or calling the above office.

* Atomic Era Veterans Hotline

Defense Nuclear Agency
Public Affairs Office
6801 Telegraph Rd.
Alexandria, VA 22310-3398   800-462-3683

This toll free number is for "atomic" era veterans and their families to call for information on whether he or she was exposed to dangerous radiation in the course of their military duty. Call or write for more information.

* Atmospheric Nuclear Test Era

Defense Nuclear Agency
Public Affairs Office
6801 Telegraph Rd.
Alexandria, VA 22310-3398   (202) 325-7095

The Agency maintains a public reading room holding information and historical documents pertaining to the atmospheric nuclear testing era. Appointments are required. This specific reading room is administered by the Nuclear Test Personnel Review Program of the Department of Defense.

* Aviation History

Information Management Division
National Air and Space Museum, Room 3100
Smithsonian Institute
Washington, DC 20560   (202) 357-3133

The Museum archives have photographs, manuscripts, and personal papers related to major figures in aviation history from the turn of the century to the present. Holdings include NASA "moon shots," and the official collection of Air Force photographs dating back from 1955 to the earliest days of aviation, including both World Wars and the Korean War. Write for their information brochure.

* Aviation Services

U.S. Army Aviation Systems Command
4300 Goodfellow Blvd.
Attn: AMSAV-Z
St. Louis, MO 63120-1798   (314) 263-1164

This Command is responsible for depot activities and services, serving all four branches of the military. The Command has a Speakers Bureau which responds to requests from civic organizations, of any age group, to speak on scientific and technological topics, as well as the varied personal hobbies of its members. Write or call for free brochures describing the Command's mission, programs, and functions.

* Ballistic Missiles Procurement

U.S. Department of the Army
Strategic Defense Command
Public Affairs Office
P.O. Box 1500
Huntsville, AL 35807-3801   (205) 895-3887

This Command conducts advanced research and development in the fields of radar, interceptors, optics, and other technical aspects of ballistic missile defense. It publishes fact sheets on the various research programs of the Command, and booklets entitled *Doing Business with the U.S. Army Strategic Defense Command* and *U.S. Army--First in Space and Strategic Defense*.

* Ballistic Research and Engineering

Ballistic Research Laboratories
314 Ryan Building
Aberdeen Proving Ground, MD 21005-5066   (301) 278-6954

This is an advanced technology laboratory conducting basic and applied research in mathematics, physics, chemistry, biophysics, and engineering related to defense ballistics. A brochure describing the laboratory and its programs will be available in the spring of 1990. Write or call for more information.

* Base Closures and Economic Impact

Office of Economic Adjustment
U.S. Department of Defense
The Pentagon, Room 4C767
Washington, DC 20301-4000

The Office of Economic Adjustment assists local communities, areas or states affected by U.S. Department of Defense actions, such as base closures, establishment of new installations, and cutbacks or expansion of activities. It publishes a number of free publications on these issues, including *Communities in Transition*, *Economic Recovery*, and *Twenty-five Years of Civilian Re-use*. Write or call for more information.

* Bases Overseas

Foreign Military Rights Affairs
International Security Affairs
Department of Defense
The Pentagon, Room 4D830
Washington, DC 20301   (202) 695-6386

This office can supply you with information on the status of negotiations for U.S. bases in foreign countries. Write or call for assistance.

* Biological Defense Research

International Relations and Defense

U.S. Department of the Army
Dugway Proving Ground
Public Affairs Office
Dugway, UT 84022 (801) 831-2102
This facility conducts biological defense research and field and lab tests to evaluate chemical and radiological weapons and defense systems. Its technical library can be made accessible to approved researchers; requests for technical reports are handled on a case by case basis. Write or call for a brochure describing the installation.

* Biological Research in Medical Defense
U.S. Army Medical Research Institute
for Infectious Diseases
Public Affairs Office
Fort Detrick, MD 21701 (301) 663-2285
This Institute conducts research on biological agents of military significance and development of vaccines, anti-toxins, toxoids and drugs for medical defense. Write or call for a free brochure on the Institute; copies of technical reports are also available.

* Burial of Veterans
Superintendent
Arlington National Cemetery
Arlington, VA 22211 (202) 695-3191
Many veterans are eligible to be buried at Arlington. Write or call this office for information on eligibility requirements and procedures.

* Casualty Reporting: Army
Casualty Services Division
U.S. Department of the Army
Hoffman Building, Room 920
Alexandria, VA 22331 (202) 325-7990
The Casualty Services Division is responsible for the Army's casualty reporting and notification system worldwide, and provides a survivor and next-of-kin assistance program. The office is available for calls 24 hours a day, seven days a week. A free brochure is available explaining their procedures.

* Ceramics and Metals Research
U.S. Department of the Army
Army Materials and Mechanics Research Center
Watertown, MA 02172 (617) 923-5278
This Center specializes in research regarding metals and ceramics. It maintains a library open to approved researchers, and copies of technical reports are available upon request. Write or call for free brochures describing the Center, its mission, and programs.

* Chemical and Biological Weapons
U.S. Department of the Army
Public Affairs Office STEDP-PA
Dugway Proving Ground, UT 84022-5000
This facility conducts biological defense research, and field and lab tests to evaluate chemical and radiological weapons and defense systems. A post guide, economic impact statement, and fact sheets on the history of the post, its mission, and the ranger training program are available. Write or call for free copies.

* Chemical Defense, Bald Eagles and Peregrine Falcons
U.S. Department of the Army
Chemical Research Development
and Engineering Center
Aberdeen Proving Ground, MD 21010-5423 (301) 671-4345
While the Center's primary mission is concerned with research on chemical defensive material, the Center has become very involved in wildlife conservation programs because of its location on the Chesapeake Bay. The Center is especially experienced in a Bald Eagle program and a Peregrine Falcon program. Fact sheets on these and other wildlife issues may be obtained by writing or calling the above office.

* Chemical Defense Technologies
U.S. Army Medical Research Institute
of Chemical Defense
Attn: SGRD-UV-R
Aberdeen Proving Ground, MD 21010-5425 (301) 671-3653
This Institute conducts research, development, testing, and evaluation of medical/chemical defense technologies. Write or call for a free brochure describing the work of the Institute and a list of technical reports.

* Chemical Propulsion Resource Center
The Johns Hopkins University

Applied Physics Laboratory
Chemical Propulsion Information Agency (CPIA)
Johns Hopkins Rd.
Laurel, MD 20707 (301) 992-7307
CPIA provides products, specialized reference service, database searches, and copies of technical reports on all areas of chemical propulsion. Write or call for a free pamphlet explaining their services and how to become a subscriber. Note, however, that this service is primarily for DOD contractors.

* Civil Air Patrol
HQ Civil Air Patrol
U.S. Department of the Air Force
Office of Public Affairs
Maxwell AFB, AL 3611-5572 (205) 293-5463
The Civil Air Patrol has three main missions: 1) emergency services; 2) aerospace education; and 3) a cadet program for high school students. Write or call for a leaflet explaining the programs and benefits of membership.

* Civil Engineering and Construction Research
Naval Civil Engineering Laboratory
Naval Construction Battalion Center
U.S. Department of the Navy
Port Hueneme, CA 93043 (805) 982-4493
This Center is the principal research, development, test, and evaluation center for shore and sea-floor facilities and for support of Navy and Marine Corps construction forces. The Public Affairs Office of the Center has a brochure on the Laboratory's mission, programs, and personnel entitled *Tech Activities*. There are also two procurement offices located at the Center. Write or call the above office for further information.

* Coast Guard Reserve
Office of Readiness and Reserve
U.S. Coast Guard
U.S. Department of Transportation
2100 2nd St., SW, Room 5101 (202) 267-2350
In time of war or national emergency, the Coast Guard Reserve provides trained individuals and units for active duty. The Reserve also assists the Guard in peacetime missions during domestic emergencies and peak operations. The *Coast Guard Reservist Magazine*, available free from the office listed above, provides bimonthly news and human interest stories about Coast Guard Reservists and their activities.

* Cold Environments Research
U.S. Army Corps of Engineers
Army Cold
Regions Research and Engineering Laboratory
72 Lyme Rd.
Hanover, NH 03755-1290 (603) 646-4100
This Laboratory conducts research on living, working, traveling, and building in cold environments. A Speakers Bureau will provide experts to speak before civic groups. Write or call for brochures explaining the mission and programs, and how to do business with the Laboratory.

* Communications and Electronic Government Contracts
U.S. Army Communications-Electronics Command
Ft. Monmouth, NJ 07703 (201) 532-1088
This Command is concerned with research, development and acquisition of communications tactical data, command and control systems, and the components and materials of electronic communications. Its Technical/Industrial Liaison and Special Projects Office will supply information and literature on Advance Planning Briefings for Industry and how to do business with CECOM.

* Conscientious Objectors and Reclassification
U.S. Department of Defense
Force Management and Personnel
The Pentagon, Room 3E767
Washington, DC 20301-4000 (202) 695-7402
For information on conscientious objectors and POW's, including reclassification and discharge data, contact the above office.

* Contracting with the Defense Logistic Agency
Public Affairs (DLA-B)
Defense Logistics Agency
Cameron Station
Alexandria, VA 22304-6100 (202) 274-6135
This office has information on all Defense Logistics Agency business and activities, and a pamphlet on it mission, *The ABC's of DLA*. It also offers a *DLA*

Index to Publications, a *DLA Index to Forms*, and the brochure, *An Identification of Commodities Purchased by the Defense Logistics Agency.*

* Contracting Research and Development with the Defense Department
Defense Technical Information Center
DTIC, Attn: FDRB
Cameron Station
Alexandria, VA 22304-6145   (202) 274-7633

DTIC is the clearinghouse for the U.S. Department of Defense's collection of scientific and technological research and development information. The booklet entitled *Registration and Certification for Scientific and Technical Services* will explain who is eligible to use the Center's services and how to register as a user. The manual also contains a list of contractors, their offices and phone numbers, and information on the potential contractor program. The *Handbook for Users* and the *Green and White* brochure (DTIC-BC-1) explain the two major databases available to contractors and potential contractors: one for completed research and technological reports and one for ongoing research and development information.

* Construction Productivity Partnership
U.S. Army Corps of Engineers
Public Affairs Office
20 Massachusetts Ave., NW
Washington, DC 20314-1000   (202) 272-0010

The Army Corps of Engineers sponsors the Construction Productivity Advancement Research Program (CPAR), in which the Corps joins in partnership with city government, public utilities, or private industry to fund research which will benefit the U.S. construction industry as a whole. Write or call for their booklet describing the program and participation guidelines.

* Contractors and Government Procurement
Defense Logistics Agency
Defense Contract Administration Service (DCAS)
Cameron Station
Alexandria, VA 22304-6100   (202) 274-6135

The nine regional offices of this Service provide post-award contract administration. Booklets are available which explain the services of the agency and the procedure for obtaining a government contract, and the staff will answer questions on current contractors and contracts. Contact your regional office or the above office to locate the office nearest you.

* Correcting Errors in Air Force Records
Air Force Board for the
  Correction of Military Records
U. S. Department of the Air Force
The Pentagon
Washington, DC 20330   (202) 692-4726

This Board handles appeals for correction of Air Force military records containing errors or unjust information. Write or call for the appropriate application forms.

* Correcting Errors in Army Records
Army Board for Correction of
  Military Records
U.S. Department of the Army
The Pentagon
Washington, DC 20310-1803   (202) 697-9515

This Board handles appeals for correction of Army military records containing errors or unjust information. Write or call for the appropriate application forms.

* Correcting Errors in Navy Records
Board for the Correction
  of Naval Records
U.S. Department of the Navy
Arlington Navy Annex, Room 2432
Washington, DC 20370   (202) 694-1765

This Board handles appeals for correction of Navy military records containing errors or unjust information. Write or call for the appropriate application forms.

* Cost Comparison of Soviet and U.S. Defense Activities
Public Affairs
Central Intelligence Agency
Washington, DC 20505   (703) 351-2053

The CIA declassifies many of its publications including *A Dollar Cost Comparison of Soviet and U.S. Defense Activities, 1968-1978* which is available from the Library of Congress Photoduplication Service, Washington, DC 20540 (202) 707-5650. More recent studies such as *1988 USSR Defense Industries*

(SOV88-10043) are sold through the National Technical Information Service, 5285 Port Royal Road, Springfield, VA 22161 (703) 487-4650; or the Government Printing Office, Washington, DC 20402 (202)783-3238. A publications catalog titled *CIA Maps and Publications Released to the Public* is available free.

* Critical and Strategic Mineral Commodities
Minerals Information Office
Bureau of Mines/U.S. Geological Survey
U.S. Department of the Interior
18th and C Sts., MS 2647-MIB
Room 2647
Washington, DC 20240   (202) 343-5520

The *Personal Computer Advanced Deposit Information Tracking System Mineral Deposit Data Base* contains information on 3,000 domestic and foreign (market economy countries) mining operations, including operation data (name, company, locations, etc.) and operation status (operation type, processing and milling methods, capacity, etc.). The database covers 34 critical and strategic commodities, representing those deposits most significant in terms of value and tonnage.

* Defense Budget and Military Spending Reports
National Technical Information Service
Springfield, VA 22161   (703) 487-4650

The Service has both paper copy and microfiche copy of Department of Defense budget reports, including *Program Acquisition Costs by Weapons System*; *Construction Programs*; *Research, Development, Test and Evaluation Program*; and *Procurement Programs*. For price and ordering information, write or call the above office.

* Defense Contractor Fraud Hotline
The Pentagon   (202) 693-5080
Washington, DC 20301   (800) 424-4098

Call this number to report fraud or corruption by anyone working for a Department of Defense contractor. The Hotline people are eager to supply your office with posters, brochures, and wallet size cards displaying their number.

* Defense Data Worldwide Network
Ada Information Clearinghouse
c/o IIT Research Institute
4600 Forbes Blvd.
Lanham, MD 20706   (703) 685-1477

This organization supplies comprehensive services and information to Ada database users worldwide. It offers a free quarterly newsletter, a calendar of events, a list of resources for reusing the Ada code, information on how to access the *Defense Data Network*, a list of Ada compilers, a list of Ada serial publications, a list of classes and seminars, a free monthly handout on new products and tools for Ada, a catalog of college courses, and two bulletin boards with comprehensive Ada information. Call or write for an information packet explaining their services and resources.

* Defense Department General Information
Directorate for Public Communication
U.S. Department of Defense
The Pentagon, Room 2E777
Washington, DC 20301-1400   (202) 697-5737

This office answers general questions concerning the work of the Department of Defense, including defense spending and defense policy. Upon request, the office can supply copies of major speeches delivered by officials in the Office of the Secretary of Defense, reports issued by the Office, and fact sheets on defense issues. Write or call for more information.

* Defense Department Manpower Statistics
Washington Headquarter Services
Directorate for Information Operations
  and Reports
1215 Jefferson Davis Hwy., Suite 1204
Arlington, VA 22202-4302   (202) 746-0786

A free catalog is available which lists this office's publications covering DOD manpower statistics, including financial management data, logistic data, health care statistics, and prime contract award data. Write or call to order a copy.

* Defense Department Organization and Functions
Directorate for Organizational
  and Management Planning
Department of Defense
The Pentagon, Room 3A326
Washington, DC 20301-1100   (202) 6978-9330

This office publishes the *Defense Organizational and Functions Guidebook*, which outlines the functions of the major components of the U.S. Department of

Defense. It contains a functional statement citing the pertinent charter and detailed information on the authority and responsibilities of each organization, including an organizational chart. To request a free copy, write or call the above office.

* Defense Energy Consumption
Defense Energy Policy Directorate
Office of the Assistant Secretary of Defense
DEF/P&L/L(EP
The Pentagon, Room 1D760
Washington, DC 20301-3000　　　　　　(202) 697-2500
This office can provide you with wholesale petroleum data and facility energy consumption data. Inquiries will be answered on a cost recovery basis.

* Defense Maps and Charts Toll-free Number
Defense Mapping Agency
Combat Support Center
Attn: Customer Assistance Office　　　　(800) 826-0342
Washington, DC 20315-0010　　　　　　(301) 227-2495
The Defense Mapping Agency makes available at cost a broad range of maps and charts. There are four categories available: aeronautical, topographic, hydrographic, and digital (lists those products available on magnetic tape). Each map costs $2.75 each.

* Defense Monthly Magazine
American Forces Information Service
1735 N. Lynn St.
Arlington, VA 22209　　　　　　　　　(202) 274-4847
The Information Service publishes *Defense 90*, a bi-monthly magazine devoted to defense issues and policy. You can order it through the U.S. Government Printing Office, Superintendent of Documents, Washington, DC 20402; (202) 783-3238.

* Defense Technical Information and Referral Center
Defense Technical Information Center
Cameron Station
Alexandria, VA 22304-6145　　　　　　(202) 274-3848
DTIC maintains a *Referral Data Bank Directory* of major resource and holding centers in the Department of Defense. Write or call the above office for more information.

* Dictionary of Military Terms
U.S. Government Printing Office
Superintendent of Documents
Washington, DC 20402-6518　　　　　　(202) 783-3238
The Joint Staff has published a comprehensive *Dictionary of Military and Associated Terms*, available for approximately $15.00. Contact the Government Printing Office for current price and ordering information.

* Doing Business with the Military
Director, Office of Small and
　　Disadvantaged Business Utilization
Undersecretary of Defense for Acquisition
The Pentagon, Room 2A340
Washington, DC 20301　　　　　　　　(202) 694-1151
This office has an information package on how to sell to the Department of Defense. It contains a booklet of rules and regulations in selling to the military, a booklet listing all the procurement offices worldwide, and a subcontracting directory.

* Electromagnetic Technology
Directorate for Public Communication
U.S. Department of Defense
The Pentagon, Room 2E777
Washington, DC 20301-1400　　　　　　(202) 697-5737
This office can provide you with general information about electromagnetic technology, including annual reports, newsletters and fact sheets, and will make referrals for you if you need more detailed information.

* Excavation and Dredging Regulation
Regulatory Branch
U.S. Army Corps of Engineers
20 Massachusetts Ave., NW, Room 6235
Washington, DC 20314　　　　　　　　(202) 272-0199
You must obtain a Corps permit if you plan to locate a structure, excavate, or discharge dredged or fill material in waters of the United States, including wetlands, or if you plan to transport dredged material for the purpose of

dumping it into ocean waters. Contact the appropriate District Engineer office for current information and to apply for a permit. You may contact the above office for addresses and telephone numbers of the District offices.

* Federal Helium Stockpile
Helium Operations
Bureau of Mines
U.S. Department of the Interior
2401 E St, NW
Washington, DC 20241　　　　　　　　(202) 634-4734
The Bureau of Mines' Federal Helium Program provides helium for the current and foreseeable needs of essential government activities and assists individual enterprises with the production and distribution of helium. Approximately 300 million cubic feet of helium is withdrawn annually from the Bureau's Cliffside Helium Storage Reservoir near Amarillo, Texas. After purification, this helium is distributed to federal agencies, the private helium industry, and to university and college research facilities.

* Federal Technological Resources Directory
National Technical Information Service
Springfield, VA 22161　　　　　　　　(703) 487-4650
The *Directory of Federal Technological Resources* listing all federal resources for services, expertise, and facilities of interest to engineers, scientists, and technology-oriented businesses may be ordered from this service for a moderate charge.

* Film Footage
U.S. Department of Defense
Motion Media Records Center
Building 248
Norton Air Force Base, CA 92409-0218　(714) 382-2307
This Center holds Army, Navy, and Marine Corps stock footage from 1964 to the present. Contact the National Archives for footage from prior years. They will assist researchers, educators, or commercial enterprises in locating specific scenes for a moderate fee. Call or write for their free brochure describing the holdings and how to access the Center.

* Flight Testing and Aerial Support Systems
Air Force Flight Test Center
Air Force Systems Command
U.S. Department of the Air Force
Edwards Air Force Base, CA 93523　　　(805) 277-3510
This Test Center conducts advanced development programs in flight testing and evaluation of new aircraft, rocket propulsion systems, aerial support systems (parachutes, delivery and recovery systems), and the training of research pilots. Its technical library may be made available for approved researchers. Fact sheets on the history, mission, aircraft, and space shuttle, as well as photographs of the base and aircraft are available at no charge upon request.

* Foreign Language Training
Defense Language Institute
Foreign Language Center
Non-Resident Division
Presidio of Monterey, CA 93944　　　　(408) 647-5000
The Defense Language Institute is one of the world's largest language training centers. The holdings of its library--over 100,000 books in 50 languages--are available through a national inter-library loan program. The non-resident division offers foreign language courses for sale. A catalog of the languages available may be obtained for $5.25. Write or call for brochures on the Institute and information regarding inter-library loans.

* Foreign Military Sales
Defense Security Assistance Agency
The Pentagon, Room 4D720
Washington, DC 20301-2800　　　　　　(202) 697-8108
This office administers the Foreign Military Sales (FMS) Program, which deals with U.S. government sales of defense articles and services to foreign governments. A free booklet containing information on the Program and the U.S. Defense Security Assistance Agency is available upon request.

* Foreign Weapon Sales Statistics
Comptroller/DMD
Defense Security Assistance Agency
The Pentagon, Room 4B659
Washington, DC 20301-2800　　　　　　(202) 697-2440
This office publishes a free annual publication, *Foreign Military Sales, Foreign Military Construction Sales, and Military Assistance Facts*, which contains information and detailed statistics on all grant programs, sales, and Federal financing of security assistance to foreign countries. Write or call for a copy.

* Freedom of Information Access

Defense Intelligence Agency
Attn: RTS-1B
Washington, DC 20340-3299   (202) 373-8361

For access to information held by the Defense Intelligence Agency and subject to the provisions of the Freedom of Information Act, contact this office. A brochure, *Brief History of DIA*, which gives information on the various functions and the mission of the agency is available upon request.

* Fuel Suppliers and Consumption in the Military

Public Affairs Office
Defense Fuel Supply Center
Defense Logistics Agency
Cameron Station
Alexandria, VA 22304-6160   (202) 274-6450

This office will supply information on almost anything you will want to know concerning fuel supply in the military. The staff will explain how to contract for the Strategic Petroleum Reserve, and how to request information under the Freedom of Information Act, such as statistics on fuel consumption patterns in the military and copies of current contracts with major suppliers.
You may request a free copy of their *Fact Book*, which tells how much was spent on fuel throughout the Department of Defense, the sources of supply, and how the fuel was allocated. It includes line graphs and pie charts, with a national geographic distribution breakdown.

* Genealogy Searches Military Service

General Reference Branch
National Archives and Records Administration
Washington, DC 20408   (202) 523-3059

This office holds military service and pension records of people who served prior to 1900. The office accepts written requests only. Ask for *Form NATF 80*.

* Geotechnical Research

U.S. Army Corps of Engineers
Waterways Experiment Station
Attn: PSTIAC
3909 Halls Ferry Rd.
Vicksburg, MS 39180   (601) 634-2504

A component of the Geotechnical Lab, the Pavements and Soil Trafficability Information Analysis Center (PSTIAC) provides products and specialized reference services to the public. The staff can be tasked to provide evaluative engineering and/or analytical service on pavements, trafficability, vehicle mobility, and terrain, primarily relevant to military needs. Database searches are performed on a cost recovery basis, and requests are approved on a case by case basis. The Station's library participates in the national inter-library loan system, and copies of technical reports are distributed on a first come, first served basis. (Reports are thereafter available from DTIC.) The Public Affairs Office can provide a summary of publications, fact sheets on the Center's programs, brochures on subject areas, and a comprehensive book entitled *Summary of Capabilities* describing the Center's work. Time on the Center's super computer is available for sale to academic researchers.

* Government Films, Videos, and Slides

National Audio-Visual Center
8700 Edgeworth Dr.
Capital Heights, MD 20743   (301) 763-1891

This is the sole source from which to purchase all U.S. government produced films, video tapes and slide sets. Write or call their office for a list of the specialty catalogs available; the catalogs are free, the products are for sale.

* Guided Missiles and Rocket Launching

Naval Ordnance Missile Test Facility
White Sands Missile Range, NM 88002   (505) 678-2101

This facility is used for the testing and evaluation of guided missiles, and endo- and exo-atmospheric research in rocket launching. Write or call for a free brochure detailing the type of research conducted on the facility and its range capabilities.

* High Seas Law Enforcement

Operational Law Enforcement Division
Office of Law Enforcement and Defense Operations
U.S. Coast Guard
U.S. Department of Transportation
2100 2nd St., SW, Room 3110
Washington, DC 20593-0001   (202) 267-1890

As the primary maritime law enforcement agency for the U.S., the Coast Guard enforces Federal laws, treaties, and international agreements to which the U.S. is a party. The Coast Guard may conduct investigations when violations are suspected, such as smuggling, drug trafficking, or polluting. Empowered to board and inspect vessels routinely as well, the Guard also conducts :"suspicionless" boardings to prevent violations. To report suspicious or questionable activity on boats, or to complain about an improperly conducted boarding, call the Boating Safety Hotline, (800) 368-5647; or (202) 267-0780 in D.C., or contact your local Coast Guard commander. The office listed above can provide you with information about the Coast Guard's law enforcement role and the National Narcotics Border Indiction System, which coordinates multi-agency and international operations with other countries to suppress narcotics trafficking.

* History Museums in U.S. and Germany

U.S. Army Center of Military History
Attn: DAMH-HSM
20 Massachusetts Ave., NW
Washington, DC 20314-0200   (202) 272-0310

The Army Center of Military History administers 73 public museums throughout the U.S. and West Germany. Write or call the above office for a list of museum locations and collections.

* Installations Public Works Construction

U.S. Department of the Army
Public Affairs Office
Construction Engineering Research Laboratory
P.O. Box 4005
Champaign, IL 61824-4005   (217) 373-7216

This office has copies of technical reports on research related to the construction, operation, maintenance, and repair of public works facilities at military installations. For a free brochure detailing your nearest Construction Engineering Research Laboratory and where to obtain reports, contact this office.

* Joint Chiefs of Staff

Historical Division
Joint Chiefs of Staff
U.S. Department of Defense
The Pentagon, Room 1A
Washington, DC 20318-0400   (202) 697-3088

This office publishes a number of military history series and volumes, including *Joint Chiefs of Staff and National Policy (1945-1954)* and *The Chairmen of the Joint Chiefs of Staff*, discussing the evolution of the office and profiles of its chiefs. Write or call the above office for prices and availability of the publications.

* Land and Aeronautical Target Survivability

Survivability/Vulnerability Information Analysis Center
WRDC/FIVS/SURVIAC
Wright-Patterson AFB, OH 45433   (513) 255-4840

SURVIAC maintains and operates a database of non-nuclear survivability/vulnerability data, information, methodologies, models, and analyses relating to U.S. and foreign land and aeronautical targets. The Center is a source for products, specialized reference services, database searches, and technical reports offered on a cost recovery basis. Contact SURVIAC to order services or obtain general information.

* Largest Defense Contractors

Directorate for Information Operations and Reports
Washington Headquarters Services
1215 Jefferson Davis Hwy., Suite 1204
Arlington, VA 22202   (202) 746-0786

This office publishes such reports as *100 Companies Receiving the Largest Dollar Volume of Prime Contract Awards* and the *Atlas/Data Abstract for the United States and Selected Areas*, which contains a map showing all the military installations and a compendium of Department of Defense statistics for each state. Write or call for their free catalog list all their publications available through the Government Printing Office.

* Lawrence Livermore Computer Facility

Visitors Center
Lawrence Livermore National Laboratory
Greenville Road
Livermore, CA 94550   (415) 422-9797

The National Laboratory conducts public tours of its computing center. You must, however, be 18 years of age or older. For information, contact the Visitors Center.

* Lawrence Livermore National Laboratory

Laboratory Communications and
    Public Information
Lawrence Livermore National Laboratory

7000 East Ave. (Mail Stop L-404)
Livermore, CA 94550 (415) 422-4599

The Laboratory maintains a library accessible to researchers able to demonstrate a "need to know." The collection includes reports, texts, and journals on biomedicine, physics, energy, and military weapons design. Their *Rainbow* brochure outlines the programs, functions, and mission of the laboratory, and *Science and Engineering on the Grand Scale* gives an overview of each laboratory department. Free booklets on a broad range of subjects are available, including physics, the national magnetic fusion energy computing center, biomedical cancer research, solar energy research, and history of the National Laboratory and its role in weapons research.

* Logistics Research

U.S. Army
Ordnance Center and School Library
(AMATSL-SE-LI)
Aberdeen Proving Ground, MD 21004 (301) 278-5615

The Center's school has several technical libraries devoted to military logistics, supply and maintenance, which are open to approved researchers. For information on their holdings and accessibility, contact the above office.

* Marine Corps Historical Research and Internships

U.S. Marine Corps Historical Center
Building 58, Navy Yard
9th and M Sts., SE
Washington, DC 20374-0580 (202) 433-3840

The Historical Center encompasses a museum, library, archives, reference section, a world historical section, and publishing department. The library is open to serious researchers. The Center sponsors an internship program whereby students may earn college credit for performing research work at the Center. Write or call for brochures describing both the museum and the library; a free publications catalog is also available.

* Marine Corps Information Clearinghouse

Commandant for the Marine Corps
Headquarters, U.S. Marine Corps
Washington, DC 20380-0001 (202) 694-2680

This office publishes material describing Marine Corps programs, personnel, and budget. Publication indexes and checklists are also available for a small fee. Write for information.

* Medical History Research

National Museum of Health and Medicine
Building 54, South Wing
Walter Reed Army Medical Center
Washington, DC 20606-6000 (202) 576-2348

The museum maintains an archives and a behind-the-scenes collection available for serious researchers. Write or call for brochures and information on the collection and for information on the tax-exempt, non-profit foundation headed by Surgeon General Dr. Koop for a new national health museum.

* Medical Scholarships through the Air Force

U.S. Department of the Air Force
Headquarters, USAF-RT/RS (512) 652-4334
Randolph Air Force Base, TX 78155 (800) 531-5980

The Air Force offers Health Professions Scholarships in return for military service obligation. Contact the above office or call toll-free number for further information.

* Microcomputers and Semiconductors

Reliability Analysis Center (RAC)
U.S. Department of the Air Force
U.S. Department of Defense
P.O. Box 4700
Rome, NY 13440-8200 (315) 337-0900

Evaluation engineering, analytical services, products, and specialized reference services are provided by RAC in the areas of microcircuits, semiconductors, nonelectric devices, and electronic modules. Reliability and maintainability data on planned and operational systems and equipment is stored in a database. A user's catalog, searches, and technical reports can be obtained on a cost recover basis.

* Military Academies

Training and Education
Manpower, Installation and Logistics
U.S. Department of Defense
The Pentagon, Room 3B930
Washington, DC 20301 (202) 695-2618

To meet a portion of the long-range requirement for career military officers the U.S. Military Academy, U.S. Naval Academy, and the U.S. Air Force Academy were established. These schools offer curricula specifically designed to train students as professional officers. For more information on these academies, contact them at the following addresses:

U.S. Military Academy, West Point, NY 10996; (914) 267-4041
U.S. Naval Academy, Annapolis, MD 21402; (301) 267-4361
U.S. Air Force Academy, USAFA, CO 80840; (719) 472-4040

* Military and Civilian Employment Records

National Personnel Center
9700 Page Blvd.
St. Louis, MO 63232 (314) 263-7201

This Center holds both military and civilian Federal personnel records dating from 1900 to the present. The Center prefers written requests for reference assistance.

* Military Archives

U.S. Department of Defense
Still Media Records Center
Code SSRC-PSa
Building 168 Naval Imaging Command
Anacostia Naval Station
Washington, DC 20374 (202) 433-2166

This photographic archives/library maintains photographs and a ready access slide file for all four branches of the military. Its holdings date from 1954 to the present, and include pictures of ships, tanks, missiles, rockets, the Grenada invasion, military exercises in Honduras, and the largest official collection of Vietnam photography available. Research assistants are available to help patrons, and the Center will do research for a small fee.

* Military Records 19th Century On

Suitland Reference Branch
National Archives and Records Administration
Washington, DC 20409 (202) 763-7410

This office holds historical material, including Land Office records, military personnel records dating prior to 1900, State Department personnel overseas post records since 1935, the Japanese war relocation records, records of the U.S. military government of Germany and Japan, as well as records of all military actions dating from the Revolutionary War through 1963. The office provides reference assistance in locating historical material, and will accept reference questions both in writing and by phone.

* Military Traffic Management

Military Traffic Management Command
U.S. Department of Defense
5611 Columbia Pike
Falls Church, VA 22041 (202) 756-1242

This Command manages all DOD freight and passenger movement in the United States, and all Army transport activities worldwide; however, the Command's expertise and responsibilities are considerably more complex and far-ranging. Upon request, this office will supply you with a 25-page brochure entitled *Ensuring Combat Power Gets to Its Place of Business*, an information brief on specific traffic management topics and projects, a copy of their *Traffic Management Progress Report* (published quarterly), and a pamphlet on how to do business with the Command. All are free of charge.

* Minerals of Critical and Strategic Importance

Research Division
Bureau of Mines
U.S. Department of the Interior
2401 E St., NW
Washington, DC 20241 (202) 634-1210

An emphasis within the Bureau of Mines' Research Division is reducing the Nation's dependence on imports for certain minerals that have key defense and industrial applications. The Bureau is developing ways to recover strategic and critical minerals from mineral processing wastes and to recycle these minerals. Key minerals of this type include cobalt, chromium, manganese, and platinum.

* Mine Sweeping and Other Naval Coastal Activities

Naval Coastal Systems Center
U.S. Department of the Navy
Panama City, FL 32407 (904) 234-4011

The Center is involved in research and development in support of naval missions and operations in the coastal (Continental Shelf) regions, including mine sweeping, diving and salvage, and amphibious operations. Experts may be obtained from their Speakers Bureau to talk on naval research and development issues, and their office will make every effort to answer specific questions from serious researchers. Write or call for a brochure describing their work and programs, and for information on their Tour Program for civic groups.

* Missile and Space Launchers

1st Strategic Aerospace Division
Office of Public Affairs
Vandenberg Air Force Base, CA 93437   (805) 866-3595

This center conducts developmental and operational testing of missile and space launchers. It is the only launch facility in the U.S. for ICBM's, and the only facility to have launched into polar orbit. The public is invited to its annual open house, held usually in the spring. Fact sheets on the base, its mission, programs, and history can be obtained by writing or calling the above office.

* Missile and Weapons Testing

Office of Public Affairs
Pacific Missile Test Center
Code 113
Point Mugu, CA 93042   (805) 989-8094

This Center tests and evaluates Naval weapons systems and devices and provides logistics and training support. Included are guided missiles, rockets, free-fall weapons, fire control and radar systems, drones and target drones, electronic devices, countermeasures equipment, test planning, simulations, and data collection. Reports are available only through Freedom of Information Act requests. For further details, contact Public Affairs.

* Missile Research

U.S. Army Missile Command
Redstone Arsenal, AL 35898   (205) 678-2101

This Command conducts research and development on rockets, guided missiles, air defense weapons systems, meteorology, missile launching, and associated equipment. Write or call for a free brochure on the Command and its history, and a pamphlet on how to do business with the Command. Copies of technical reports are also available upon request.

* Missile Testing Center

U.S. Department of the Army
Public Affairs Office
Building 122
White Sands Missile Range, NM 88002-5047   (505) 678-1134

This research and missile testing center invites the public to an open house twice a year, which includes a visit to the "Trinity Site" where the first atomic detonation took place. The center publishes a brochure and fact sheets on its history, mission, and wide range of programs. The test range also functions as a wildlife preserve. Write or call for their free publications and information on open house days.

* Museum of Health and Medicine

National Museum of Health and Medicine
Building 54, South Wing
Walter Reed Army Medical Center
Washington, DC 20606-6000   (202) 576-2348

The museum is open to the public every day of the week, and features exhibits illustrating health and disease in their social and historical contexts. You may see organ specimens dating from the Civil War, the bullet that killed President Lincoln, a famous collection of microscopes dating from their invention, and currently an "interactive" exhibit on AIDS and another on "Headache Art"-- migraine sufferers' depiction on paper on what a migraine headache is like. Write or call for a free brochure on the museum and its hours.

* National Guard Bands

National Guard Bureau
Attn: NGB-PAC
4501 Ford Ave.
Alexandria, VA 22301-1457   (202) 756-1923

Local National Guard units provide bands, color guards, and flight demonstrations for community events upon request of civic groups. The Guard also sponsors annual open houses and conducts tours of the local bases. A Speakers Bureau will provide experts to speak on defense and local issues, and the Guard sponsors orientation trips for civic leaders. Call or write for more information on the Guard's varied community assistance programs, including the loan of equipment to civic groups.

* National Guard Statistical Information

National Guard Bureau
NSB-PA, Room 23261
The Pentagon
Washington, DC 20310-2500   (202) 695-0421

The Guard publishes a brochure entitled *National Guard Updates* which discusses the Federal and State mission, force structure, overseas deployments, and personnel statistics, and an *Annual Review* of its work and accomplishments. Write or call for a free copy.

* National Guard Posters and History

National Guard Bureau
Attn: PAH
The Pentagon
Washington, DC 20310-2500   (202) 695-0421

Posters and lithographs of historical events involving the Guard, which date from 1636 to the present, are available free of charge. This office will provide advice and help in obtaining information on specific Guard Units.

* Naval Air Procurement

Naval Air Engineering Center
U.S. Department of the Navy
Lakehurst, NJ 08733-5000   (201) 323-2011

This Center conducts research, development, testing, and evaluation of aircraft launching and landing equipment and airborne weapons systems. Write or call the Center for copies of a mission statement, historical background sheet, and information on contracting.

* Naval Avionics Development Center

U.S. Department of the Navy
Naval Air Development Center
Code 094, Small Business Office
Warminster, PA 18974   (215) 441-2456

This laboratory researches, develops, tests, and evaluates naval avionic systems. Write or call for their free pamphlet, *Doing Business with the Naval Air Development Center*.

* Naval Avionics Procurement

Naval Avionics Center
Public Affairs Office
6000 E. 21st St.
Indianapolis, IN 46219   (317) 353-7600

This Center conducts research and development on avionics and related equipment. Call or write for free brochures describing the Center, its programs, statistics on its employees, and a booklet on *How to Do Business with NAC*.

* Naval Construction Battalion Center

U.S. Department of the Navy
Naval Construction Battalion Center
Port Hueneme, CA 93043   (805) 982-4493

This is the training center for the Navy's Construction Battalion (the "Seabees"). The Center has a base guide, a profile sheet giving statistical information on the base, and a brochure on the history of the Center, which was founded during W.W. II. They will accept written or phone requests for information.

* Naval Guided Weapons Systems

U.S. Department of the Navy
Public Affairs Office
Naval Ship Weapon Systems Engineering Station
Port Hueneme, CA 93043   (805) 982-7972

This Station conducts research and development, testing, and evaluation on ships'guided weapons systems. To obtain information about the station, its programs, and activities, write or call for the booklets, *NSWSES, Your Navy in Ventura County*, and a copy of their 25th anniversary magazine containing articles about the various departments.

* Naval Historical Research

Naval Historical Center
Washington Navy Yard
Washington, DC 20374   (202) 433-2210

The Navy Historical Center's research library and operational archives is open to private researchers. Its holdings include a still photographic collection of over 225,000 views and an art collection of over 8,000 pieces. Write or call for their free catalog of books in print, which includes an 8-volume series *Dictionary of American Naval Fighting Ships* and a 9-volume series *Naval Documents of the American Revolution*.

* Naval Observatory Library

34th and Massachusetts Ave.
Washington, DC 20392-5100   (202) 653-1541

The Naval Observatory's research library is open to the public by appointment. Its holdings include many rare books on astronomy as well as the current literature. A list of publications is available at no charge, which includes the *Astronomical Almanac*, the *Nautical Almanac*, the *Air Almanac*, the *Almanac for Computers*, *Astronomical Phenomena*, various periodicals, and reference materials.

International Relations and Defense

* Naval Patents
Deputy Counsel
Office of the Chief of Naval Research
(Intellectual Property)
800 N. Quincy St.
Arlington, VA 22217-5000   (202) 696-4000

This office grants licenses for commercial use of government-owned patents. For information on the patents available for licensing, contact the above office.

* Naval Reservists
Naval Reserve Recruiting Office
Naval Reserve Center
U.S. Department of the Navy
U.S. Department of Defense
2600 Powder Mill Road   (301) 394-2510
Adelphi, MD 20783-1198   (301) 394-2510

Naval Reservists are prepared for mobilization with equipment and training programs that parallel those of the regular Navy, including participation in fleet exercises. The Recruiting Office can provide information and brochures about the Reserve.

* Navy Band
U.S. Navy Band
Public Affairs Office
Washington Navy Yard
Washington, DC 20374-1052   (202) 433-2394

The U.S. Navy Concert Band and its specialty units--including the Commander's Trio, Windjammers, Tuba-Euphonium Quartet, Sea Chanters, Country Current, and the Commodores--are available to perform at community events nationwide. Units of the band perform a wide range of musical styles, from jazz, folk, and blue grass to classical chamber and cocktail music. Write or call for information on how to request the Band.

* Navy Budget and Forces Summary
Comptroller of the Navy, NCB32
Crystal City Mall, No. 2, Room 606
Statistical and Report Branch
Washington, DC 20350-1100   (202) 697-7819

This office publishes a *Budget and Forces Summary* covering the overall Navy budget for current and prior years, and a projection for the coming year. It contains a complete breakdown of the appropriations. Write or call for a free copy.

* Navy Exchanges Procurement
Navy Resale and Services Support Office
Naval Station New York
Staten Island, NY 10305-5097   (718) 390-3700

This office handles procurement of resale merchandise for Navy exchanges and commissary stores. Write or call for the free "Guide for Doing Business with the Navy Resale System."

* Navy Information Clearinghouse
U.S. Navy
Office of Information
The Pentagon
Washington, DC 20350-1200   (202) 695-6915

This office answers a broad range of general questions pertaining to Navy affairs. It can also supply a copy of the *Navy Fact File* containing general information on ships, aircraft and weapons systems, ship programs, and other statistics.

* Navy Medical Research
Naval Medical Research and Development Command
Attn: Code 40C
Bethesda, MD 20814   (202) 295-1453

This Command conducts research, development, testing, and evaluation in diving medicine, submarine medicine, aviation medicine, fleet health care, infectious diseases, and dental health. A list of their technical reports is available upon request.

* Navy Procurement
Navy Acquisition, Research and
  Development Information Center (NARDIC)
5001 Eisenhower Ave.
Alexandria, VA 22333   (202) 274-9315

This Center maintains a research and development, technical reading room open to DOD contractors, and will provide research and development planning and requirement documents to qualified users. The Center can also give information on the Navy Potential Contractors Program, which was instituted to facilitate technology transfer between the military and industry. Write or call for the free brochure explaining eligibility requirements and how to access the reading room, as well as how to enroll in the Potential Contractors Program and gain access to the Defense Technology Information Center.

* Navy Ship Historic Plans
Cartographic and Architectural Branch
National Archives and Records Administration
Washington, DC 20408   (202) 756-6700

This office compiles the plans of all U.S. Navy ship since the Navy was founded. Call or write for assistance.

* Night Vision Research
Office of Public Affairs
Night Vision and Electro-Optics
  Laboratories (NVEOL)
Fort Belvoir, VA 22060-5677   (703) 664-5066

NVEOL conducts research and development into electro-optical low-energy lasers, all-weather systems, infrared, radiation, visionics, and image intensification. The laboratories provide the Army with equipment to enable it to carry out nocturnal operations efficiently. This office can offer information and referral on laboratory programs.

* Nuclear Armaments Research
U.S. Army Armament Research
and Development Command
Dover, NJ 07901-5001   (201) 724-4021

This Command conducts research, development, life-cycle engineering, and initial acquisition of various nuclear and non-nuclear weapons and ammunition. The Command accepts requests for information on specific technical topics on a case-by-case basis. Write or call for their information pamphlet and brochures on the research center and current programs.

* Patents Owned by Uncle Sam
National Technical Information Service
U.S. Department of Commerce
5285 Port Royal Rd.
Springfield, VA 22161   (703) 487-4650

This Service has a list of government patents available for licensing, as well as copies of all patents issued by the U.S. Patent Office. Call or write for ordering information.

* Pension Genealogy Searches
General Reference Branch
National Archives and Records Administration
Washington, DC 20408   (202) 523-3059

This office holds military service and pension records of people who served prior to 1900. The office accepts written requests only. Ask for *Form NATF 80*.

* Pentagon Budget Statistics
Office of Assistant Secretary of Defense
Public Affairs
The Pentagon, Room 2E777
Washington, DC 20301-1400   (202) 697-5737

This office can furnish you with copies of the book *Construction Programs (C-1)*, *DOD Budget for Fiscal Year 1989*, the *Annual Report to Congress*, and the *Defense '89 Almanac*, which gives statistics on manpower, organization charts, force charts, DOD budget, and international relations data. Write or call for free copies.

* Pentagon Products and Services
National Technical Information Service
Springfield, VA 22161   (703) 487-4650

This agency collects and publishes the results all government-sponsored research carried out by corporations, universities, and government agencies. The *Products and Services Catalog* gives an overview of the agency's services, and describes by subject the reports, subscription newsletters, database and microfiche services available. The catalog is free; publications and services may be purchased at cost. Write or telephone the above office for more information.

* Photographic Archives
Still Picture Branch (NNSP)
National Archives Records Administration
Eighth and Pennsylvania Ave., NW, Room 18N
Washington, DC 20408   (202) 523-3236

The archives holds the official photographic collection for the Army, Navy, and Marine Corps dating 1955 back to the founding of the country. Patrons can order photographic reproductions and posters for a small fee. Write or call for a price sheet, a "Select List" of period topics--including The Civil War, World War II, the Old West, the American Revolution, and American Cities--and a catalog entitled *War and Conflict*.

* Photographic Archives of U.S. Military

U.S. Department of Defense
Still Media Records Center
Anacostia Naval Station, Building 168
Washington, DC 20374-1681   (202) 433-2168

This Center holds over one million negatives from all four military services, dating from the mid-1950s to present. Its archives are open to the public (appointments are preferred), and copies of negatives may be purchased. The Center maintains a research file by subject, and the staff will do research on a fee basis.

* Plastics and Adhesives Research

Plastics Technical Evaluation Center
U.S. Army Armament Research, Development
  and Engineering Center (ARDEC)
Building 355-N
Picatinny Arsenal, NJ 07806-5000   (201) 724-4021

Technical information related to plastics, adhesives, and organic matrix composites is generated, evaluated, stored, and distributed at this Center, with an emphasis on performance and properties. Computerized databases are maintained on the compatibility of polymers with propellants and explosives and on materials deterioration. The Center provides services on a fee basis, including consulting, state-of-the-art studies, handbooks, analysis, evaluation, and bibliographic and literature searches. To arrange for services or to get information, contact PLASTEC at the number listed above.

* Plastics: Adhesives and Sealants Expert

Arthur Landrock
PLASTEC
U.S. Army/ARDEC
Building 355-N
Picatinny Arsenal, NJ 07806-5000   (201) 724-4021

Mr. Landrock, a materials engineer at PLASTEC, is an expert frequently consulted nationwide in the fields of adhesives and sealants. He has authored two books, including *Adhesives Technology Handbook* from Noyse Publications.

* Potential Military Contracts

Directorate for Public Communications
Office of Assistant Secretary of Defense
  for Public Affairs
The Pentagon, Room 2E777
Washington, DC 20301   (202) 697-6462

This Public Affairs office will answer your general questions regarding the Defense Advanced Research Projects Agency (DARPA), which supports high-risk, high-payoff programs for research and technology development. Brochures available include the *Defense Advanced Research Projects Agency* updated annually, *Information, Science and Technology Office Research Programs* which lists current research programs, and the report, *Strategic Computing: Fourth Annual Report November 1988*. All are free upon request, as well as press releases on major events sponsored by DARPA. Write or call also for their *User's Guide for Potential Contractors*.

* President's National Security Council

National Security Council
Old Executive Office Building
17th St. and Pennsylvania Ave., NW
Washington, DC 20506   (202) 395-4974

The NSC is responsible to assess and appraise the objectives, commitments, and risks of the United States in relation to our actual and potential military, economic, and political power, in the interest of national security, and to consider policies on matters of common interest to the department and agencies of the Government, and to make such recommendations and reports to the President as it deems appropriate or as the President may require. Council members are the President, the Vice President, the Secretary of State, and the Secretary of Defense, as prescribed by statute. The Chairman, Joint Chiefs of Staff, and the Director of Central Intelligence are statutory advisors. The Council's staff is headed by the Executive Secretary and provides day-to-day support for the President and his Assistant for National Security Affairs.

* Prisoners of War and Reclassification

U.S. Department of Defense
Force Management and Personnel
The Pentagon, Room 3E767
Washington, DC 20301-4000   (202) 695-7402

For information on conscientious objectors and POW's, including reclassification and discharge data, contact the above office.

* Radiobiology Research

Armed Forces Radiobiology Research Institute
Defense Nuclear Agency
National Naval Medical Center, Building 42
Bethesda, MD 20814   (202) 295-1210

The Institute conducts tours of the facility, and makes its library available to approved researchers. Its *Annual Report* summarizes the current work being performed in radiobiological research, and a brochure explains the Institute and its various programs. Both are free upon request.

* Relocation Assistance

Realty Services Division
Corps of Engineers Real Estate
U.S. Army Corps of Engineers
Attn: CERE-R
Washington, DC 20314-1000   (202) 272-0517

This office administers the Uniform Relocation Assistance Act for the Department of the Army. The Act provides benefits to landowners, tenants, businesses, and farmers who must move or must move property as a result of government acquisition of real property for Federal projects. Benefits include reimbursement for moving, costs, replacement housing, and direct losses. For further information, contact the Realty Services Division.

* Research and Development for Small Business

U.S. Army Laboratory Command
2800 Powder Mill Road
Attn: AMSLC-SP
Adelphi, MD 20783   (202) 394-1076

The Command has a collection of hand-outs relating to Army research and development programs. These free pamphlets intended for small businesses include the *Laboratory Command Small Business Guide, Unsolicited Proposal Guide*, and *Technical/Industrial Liaison Guide*.

* Research and Development Standards or Military Contractors

Tri-Service Industry Information Center
5001 Eisenhower Ave.
Alexandria, VA 22333   (202) 274-8948

This office provides information on research and development, planning, and requirements information to suppliers of military equipment for the Army, Navy, and Air Force. To enter the research center, you must have a DOD contract and a personal security clearance. Write or call to obtain brochures on how to use the center and for its publications, including *Air Force Logistics Needs, Mission Element Need Statements (MENS), Program Element Descriptive Summaries, Program Management Directive, R&D Planning Summaries, Technical Objective Documents Technology Needs Documents*, and *Selling to the United States Air Force*.

* Retirement Home

Public Relations
U.S. Soldiers' and Airmen's Home
3700 North Capitol St., NW
Washington, DC 20317   (202) 722-3386

The Home was established for retired or discharged enlisted and warrant officer personnel, men and woman, who have served 20 years or more in the Army or Air Force; or who have a service-connected disability preventing them from earning a living; or who have served during periods of war and have a nonservice connected disability preventing their earning a livelihood. For general information and brochures, contact the office listed above. For admissions, call (202) 722-3336. For information about the U.S. Soldiers' and Airmen's Home National Cemetery, contact the following address: 21 Harewood Road, NW, Washington, DC 20011; (202) 695-3190.

* ROTC: Reserve Officers Training Corps

Training and Education
Manpower, Installation and Logistics
U.S. Department of Defense
The Pentagon, Room 3B930
Washington, DC 20301   (202) 695-2618

The Reserve Officers Training Corps (ROTC) program is conducted at over 500 U.S. colleges and universities and is the single largest source of officers for the Armed Forces, both career and non-career. For further details about ROTC, contact the office listed above.

* Science and Engineering Army Apprenticeships

U.S. Department of the Army
Chemical Research Development
  and Engineering Center

Aberdeen Proving Ground, MD 21010-5423   (301) 671-4345

This Center sponsors a science and engineering apprenticeship program for high school students, summer "associateships" for high school faculty, and a faculty research and engineering program for university level scientists. The Center further welcomes requests from high schools for assistance with "Science Fairs" not only locally, but at the national and regional level.

* Science Fairs and Research Grants

U.S. Department of the Army
Army Research Office
P.O. Box 12211
Triangle Park, NC 27709-2211   (919) 549-0641

This office administers the nation-wide Science Fair program, which sponsors science competition at the high school level, and the Defense Research Initiative, which is a competitive grant program for government funding of university research. Write or call for free brochures and information describing these programs.

* Selective Service Fact Sheets:
Deferments, Exemptions, Etc.

Public Affairs
Selective Service System
1023 31st St., NW
Washington, DC 20435   (202) 724-0790

The Selective Service System provides free to the public fact sheets which contain information on certain aspects of the Selective Service System.

Aliens and Dual Nationals
Federal Student Aid, Job Training Benefits and Federal Employment
Postponements, Deferments, Exemptions
Selective Service and the Immigration Reform and Control Act of 1986

* Selective Service Regulations

Public Affairs
Selective Service System
1023 31st St., NW
Washington, DC 20435   (202) 724-0790

The documents listed below are usually available in the government documents section of major libraries:
Military Selective Service Act of June 24, 1948. This is the law under which the Selective Service System operates.
Code of Federal Regulations. Selective Service Regulations are contained within.

* Selective Service Registration:
Induction, Claims, and Appeals

Public Affairs
Selective Service System
1023 31st St., NW
Washington, DC 20435   (202) 724-0790

The booklet, *Information for Registrants*, furnishes information about Selective Service responsibilities, and registrant rights and obligations. It also explains the induction, claims, and appeals process. To obtain a copy, contact this office.

* Selective Service Registration Status

Registration Information Office
P.O. Box 4638
North Suburban, IL 60197-4638   (800) 621-5388

If you have any questions regarding an individual's status and the requirement to register, call or write this office.

* Selective Services Semiannual Update

Public Affairs
Selective Service System
1023 31st St., NW
Washington, DC 20435   (202) 724-0790

Every six months, the Selective Service System publishes a summary of its program. Copies of the report can be obtained from this office.

* Selling to the Army: Commodity Commands

U.S. Army Materiel Command
Public Affairs
5001 Eisenhower Ave.
Alexandria, VA 22333   (202) 274-8010

The U.S. Army Materiel Command encompasses seven commodity commands which contract for both products and research and development. The Materiel Command buys everything the soldier uses, both personally and in his job. The commodity commands include the Armament, Munitions and Chemical Command; the Aviation Systems Command; the Communications-Electronics Command; the Laboratory Command (which contracts for research); the Missile

Command; the Tank-Automotive Command; and the Troop Support Command (includes portable sanitary equipment, food, and uniforms). Call or write for a free brochure explaining what the Material Command encompasses.

* Selling to the Army: Small Business

U.S. Army Materiel Command
Small and Disadvantaged Business
Utilization Office
5001 Eisenhower Ave.
Alexandria, VA 22333   (202) 274-8185

A series of brochures is available for small and women-owned businesses on how to sell their products and services to the Army. *How to Do Business with AMC* lists the commodity commands and each Small Business Office at each command. *Selling to the Military*, *Small Business Specialists*, and *Small Business Subcontracting* all cover information on the application process through the Department of Defense. Also available are other free brochures explaining finance regulations for small businesses and how to prepare offers.

* Selling to the Marine Corps

Commandant of the Marine Corps
Morale Welfare Recreation Support Center
Quantico, VA 22134   (703) 640-3800

This office supplies fact sheets list Marine Corps installations worldwide and explaining how to sell to the military exchanges on those installations.

* Selling to Navy Exchanges

Navy Resale and Services Support Office
Ft. Wadsworth
Staten Island, NY 10305-5097   (718) 390-3503

This office supplies the brochure, *The Navy Resale System*, which explains how to sell to the Navy military exchanges. Call or write for a free copy.

* Service Classification:
Aliens, Conscientious Objectors, Ministers

Selective Service System
1023 31st. St., NW
Washington, DC 20435   (202) 724-0820

Classification is the process of determining who is available for military service and who is deferred or exempted from such service. Classification categories include conscientious objectors, ministers, veterans, and alien and dual nationals. For more information, contact this office.

* Small Business Pentagon Procurement Assistance

Small Business Office
Defense Fuel Supply Center
5010 Duke St.
Cameron Station, Building 8
Alexandria, VA 22314-6160   (202) 274-7428

This Small Business Office will refer potential contractors to the major buying centers within the Defense Logistics Agency for the commodity or service they wish to market. They have two standard brochures, *Selling to the Military* and *Guide to Preparation*. Write or call for free copies.

* Small Business and Disadvantaged Procurement

Small Business Office
U.S. Department of Defense
The Pentagon
Washington, DC 20301   (202) 697-9383

This office will supply information and guidance to small and disadvantaged businesses. Free copies are available of a list of the 700 DOD procurement offices and a book listing the major prime DOD contractors and the products and services they provide. Write or call their office to get on the solicitors' mailing list.

* Software Development and Technology

Data and Analysis Center for Software (DACS)
P.O. Box 120
Utica, NY 13503   (303) 336-0937

DACS provides products and specialized reference services on software development and maintenance programs. Subsets of its database can be obtained on hard copy or magnetic tape. Database searches and copies of technical reports are furnished on a cost recovery basis. Write or call for a free products and services brochure containing ordering and price information.

* Solid State Laser Research

Documents Office
Naval Research Laboratory (NRL)
Code 2628

4555 Overlook Ave., SW
Washington, DC 20375-5000 (202) 767-2949
The Laboratory conducts research on low- and medium-power solid state lasers and infrared detectors. Technical reports can be obtained on the research from National Technical Information Service, 5285 Port Royal Road, Springfield, VA 22161; (703) 487-4650. A few are available from NRL directly. Contact the Documents Office for details.

* Space and Missile Product Engineering
Office of Public Affairs
Western Space and Missile Center
U.S. Department of the Air Force
U.S. Department of Defense
Vandenberg AFB, CA 93437-6021 (805) 866-3016
Research, development, and product engineering in support of U.S. space and missile programs are conducted at this Center. Work focuses on radar, telemetry, electro-optics, communications range and mission control, weather timing, aircraft impact location, and data handling. Contact the Office of Public Affairs for information and referral.

* Space and Missile Test Range Research
ESMC/CC
Patrick Air Force Base, FL 32925 (407) 494-5933
This center conducts research and development activities in test range instrumentation and provides support for the Defense Department's missile and space programs. This involves radar, trajectory computers, tracking and target analysis, communications, timing and firing systems, telemetry, and data storage. For more information, contact research and development staff at the address listed above.

* Space Technology Research
U.S. Air Force Space Technology Center
Kirtland Air Force Base, NM 87117-6008 (505) 846-1911
This Center oversees the work of the three major Air Force research laboratories: the Weapons Laboratory at Kirtland; the Astronautics Laboratory at Edwards Air Force Base, California; and the Geophysics Laboratory at Hanscom Air Force Base, Massachusetts. Free fact sheets on all three labs and their programs are available from this Center, including fact sheets on the SDI program, the relay mirror experiment, the Alpha chemical laser experiment, "Brilliant Pebbles" research, optics research, microwaves, plasma physics, and nuclear weapons effects research. The Center offers a Speakers Bureau of experts and intern programs for outside researchers.

* Speakers Bureau: Chemical Weapons
U.S. Department of the Army
Chemical Research Development
and Engineering Center
Aberdeen Proving Ground, MD 21010-5423 (301) 671-4345
While the Center's mission is to conduct research on chemical defense materials, it also provides a variety of programs involving the Center in the civic and scientific communities. Through its Speakers Bureau the Center will provide experts on scientific and technological topics. Write or call for a brochure explaining the laboratory, the Center's programs, and statistics on the post. Interested persons from the business and scientific community may call or write to be added to their mailing list for Advance Planning Briefings to Industry and notices of conferences and seminars.

* Specifications and Standards
Naval Publications and Forms Center
U.S. Department of Defense
5801 Tabor Ave.
Philadelphia, PA 19120-5099 (215) 697-2179
This Center is the DOD's distribution point for unclassified specifications and standards used to determine requirements for military procurement. Military personnel can obtain the *Index of Specifications and Standards* from this Center. The general public can obtain it from the Government Printing Office, Superintendent of Documents, Washington, D.C. 20402; (202) 783-3238. Contact the Center for the Following types of information:

Military specifications and standards
Federal specifications and standards
Qualified product lists
Military handbooks
Air Force-Navy aeronautical specifications and standards
Air Force specifications
Air Force specifications bulletins
Air Force-Navy aeronautical bulletins

* Star Wars and Other Defense Research Information
Office of Assistant Secretary of Defense

Public Affairs
Directorate for Defense Information
Pentagon 2E765
Washington, DC 20301-1400 (202) 695-3886
This office can supply you with fact sheets, press releases, and reports on defense programs such as Star Wars, the DOD Laser and Space Program, and the Defense Advanced Research Projects Agency (DARPA) activities, and related Congressional activity. Staff can also direct you in making FOIA requests for Defense contract information.

* Surplus Property from Defense Department
Defense Reutilization and Marketing Service
Public Affairs Office
P.O. Box 1370
Battle Creek, MI 49016-1370 (616) 961-7331
This office manages and disposes of surplus property from all Department of Defense agencies. Many items are for sale by public auction. Write or call for free pamphlets on how to buy DOD surplus property and applications for the national bidders mailing list. For local sales, contact the nearest DRMS office or the above office for a referral.

* Tactical Weapons: Database Searches for Contractors
GACIAC/IIT Research Institute
10 W. 35th St.
Chicago, IL 60616 (312) 567-4345
This organization offers user guides, a bi-monthly bulletin, and complex database searches on tactical weapons guidance and control, information, and analysis. Write or call for further information; requesters must be registered DOD contractors.

* Technical Assistance to Foreign Countries
U.S. Army Corps of Engineers
Attn: CEMP-MG
20 Massachusetts Ave., NW
Washington, DC 20314-1000 (202) 272-0641
Through its Foreign Military Sales Program, the Army Corps of Engineers can provide a full range of services to foreign governments, including construction management, research and development, procurement, training, and engineering design. For information, contact the above office.

* Technical Exchange Between Government and Industry
Government Industry Data Exchange Program
GIDEP Operations Center
Corona, CA 91720-5000 (714) 736-4677
GIDEP is a data exchange program between government and industry. Members have access to five databases, grouped by subject: Failure Experience; Engineering; Reliability, Maintainability, and Quality; Metrology; and Value Engineering. In addition, GIDEP has a newsletter and an *Urgent Data Request System*. For a free information package on program services, membership, and application forms, write or call the above office.

* Technical Expertise at Federal Labs
Defense Technical Information Center
Cameron Station, DTIC-BC
Alexandria, VA 22304-6145 (202) 274-6434
The Defense Technical Information Center maintains a Domestic Technology Referral Data Base, supplying a broad referral to federal laboratories and their areas of expertise. The service is available to all legitimate requesters; the requester need not be a "registered user." Call or write for information.

* Technology Research Army Libraries
U.S. Army Materiel Command
Information Systems Command
Public Affairs Office
Timberlake, AZ (602) 538-8609
Each Army Materiel Command installation has a technological library. It is usually possible to gain access to the library if you obtain prior approval. Contact your local AMC for information, or the above office for a referral to your closest installation.

* Technology Transfer and Systems Engineering
Director of Publications, DRI-P
Defense Systems Management College
Ft. Belvoir, VA 22060-5426 (703) 664-5082
This College publishes 28 books and a bi-monthly magazine entitled *Program Manager* (subscription, $7.50 per year). Titles include *Systems Engineering Management Guide* (a Government Printing Office all-time best-seller), *Cost Estimating*, *Subcontract Management Guide*, *Skill in Communications*, and *Program Office Guide to Technology Transfer*. All apply to acquisition and

program management. Write for a free publications list explaining where to purchase them, stock numbers, and prices. The editor will also supply a sample copy of the *Program Manager* upon written request.

* Technology Transfer Competitiveness
Administrator
Federal Laboratory Consortium
P.O. Box 545
Sequim, WA 98382　　　　(206) 683-1005

The mission of the Consortium is to facilitate technology transfer among government, business, and academic entities in order to foster American economic and technological competitiveness. It sponsors conferences and seminars and publishes a free monthly newsletter (currently no charge). For very specific questions from bona fide researchers who find themselves at an impasse, the Consortium will conduct a database search to refer the inquirer to an appropriate lab. Write or call for a free general information packet explaining the organization, how to access its services, facilities available for testing, and examples of technology transfers.

* Test Flight History
Air Force Flight Test Center
Air Force Systems Command
U.S. Department of the Air Force
Edwards Air Force Base, CA 93523　　　(805) 277-3510

The History Office on Edwards Air Force Base has an archival library of history documents about the base. Videotapes of historical events are also available for viewing on site. Call or write the above office for information on its holdings.

* Time: Naval Observatory's Atomic Clock
Atomic Clock
National Observatory
24th and Massachusetts Ave.
Washington, DC 20392-5100　　　(202) 653-1541

The Observatory's Master Clock is the source for all standard time in the United States. For the correct time, call the number above, or dial 1-900-410-TIME if you are outside of the D.C. area.

* Training Methods Speakers Bureau
U.S. Army Research Institute for
　Behavioral and Social Sciences
5001 Eisenhower Ave.
Alexandria, VA 22333　　　(202) 274-8683

The Institute conducts research for the military on educational and training methods and organizational effectiveness. Requests may be made to its Speakers Bureau for experts in the field. Copies of its published reports may be obtained through the Defense Technology Information Center.

* Training Military Doctors
Uniformed Services University of Health Sciences
U.S. Department of Defense
4301 Jones Bridge Road, Room A1045
Bethesda, MD 20814　　　(202) 295-3049

Physicians for the military services and for the Public Health Service are educated at this institution. In addition to a school of medicine and graduate and continuing education programs, the university incorporates the Military Medical Education Institute which provides combat training for health care professionals in the military service. You can obtain information and brochures from the above address.

* Underwater Defense Systems Research
Office of Public Affairs
Naval Underwater Systems Center
U.S. Department of the Navy
U.S. Department of Defense
Newport Laboratory
Newport, RI 02840　　　(401) 841-2182

Underwater warfare systems and components, undersea surveillance systems, navigation systems, and related technologies are developed, tested, and analyzed at the Center. The Office of Public Affairs sometimes has publications on hand or can refer you to appropriate information sources within the Center.

* U.S. Military Installations Atlas
Directorate for Information Operations and Reports
Washington Headquarters Services
1215 Jefferson Davis Hwy., Suite 1204
Arlington, VA 22202　　　(202) 746-0786

The *Atlas/Data Abstract for the United States and Selected Areas* contains a map showing all the military installations and a compendium of Department of Defense statistics for each state. Write or call for their free catalog list all their publications available through the Government Printing Office.

* Vendor Sales to Military Exchanges
Headquarters
Army and Air Force Exchange Service
Attn: PA-I
P.O. Box 660202
Dallas, TX 75266　　　(214) 780-2763

This office supplies the brochure, *Facts for Vendors*, which explains how to sell to the Army and Air Force military exchanges. Call or write for free copies.

* Vietnam Casualty Computer Printout
Center for Electronic Records
National Archives and Records Administration
Washington, DC 20408　　　(202) 523-3267

This office holds all Federal records on computer disk, which include all recent DOD records and the casualty lists from the Vietnam War. Copies may be purchased.

* Voluntary Draft and Selective Service Compliance
Selective Service System
1023 31st St., NW
Washington, DC 20435　　　(202) 724-0820

Applicants for Title IV federal student aid, Job Training Partnership Ace benefits, and those young men seeking employment with the federal government who are required to register must be in compliance with the registration requirement in order to be eligible for those programs. For more information, contact this office.

* Waterways and Wetlands R & D
Research and Development Division
U.S. Army Corps of Engineers
CERD-ZA
Washington, DC 20314-1000　　　(202) 272-0254

Contact this office for information and referral on Corps of Engineers research and development into reservoir water quality; coastal ecology; aquatic plant control; environmental impact of development projects; designing dams, locks, and other hydraulic structures for earthquakes; river ice and winter navigation; battlefield environment; Army installations; and combat engineering.

* Weapons Lab Super Computer Center
U.S. Air Force Super Computer Center
Kirtland Air Force Base, NM 87117-6008　　(505) 646-5354

The Super Computer Center is administered by the Weapons Laboratory. Academic researchers sponsored by the Department of Defense may have access to the Cray 1 and Cray 2 super computer services and a bi-monthly newsletter. Write or call for their brochure on how to subscribe for time on the computer, eligibility for use, and prices.

* Weapons Museum
U.S. Army Ordnance Museum
Aberdeen Proving Ground
Aberdeen, MD 23005　　　(301) 278-3602

This museum holds the free world's largest collection of military weapons and paraphernalia, including captured W.W. II German V-2 rockets, the one and only atomic cannon, and handguns with curved barrels to shoot around corners. It's open to the public Tuesday through Sunday, and admission is free. You can also write for their pamphlet, *Welcome to the U.S. Army Ordnance Museum.*

Science and Technology
General Sources

* See also Experts Chapter
* See also Current Events and Homework Chapter
* See also Economics, Demographics, and Statistics Chapter
* See also Patents, Trademarks and Copyrights Chapter

Part of the reason we are suffering from an information explosion can be attributed to technology. About 90 percent of all scientific knowledge has been generated since 1950. And, according to the U.S. Department of Commerce, this knowledge is expected to double again in the next ten to fifteen years. Technology, once again, has recaptured the interest and investment of both American business and the public. In 1982, *Time* magazine selected the computer as its "Man of the Year," and in 1984 Ronald Reagan signed into law a congressional resolution designating September 30 through October 6 as National High Tech Week. This section will introduce you to the major sources of information about technology throughout the government, including those located at the National Technical Information Service (NTIS) and the Science and Technology Reading Room at the Library of Congress. Through these sources you'll find sources of information on everything from Alzheimer's disease and genetic fingerprinting to supercomputers and commercial biotechnology.

* 3 Million Science and Technical Books

Science and Technology Division
Library of Congress
Washington, DC 20540 (202) 707-5639
The Science and Technology collection contains more than 3 million scientific and technical books and pamphlets and 3 million technical reports, including those issued by the Department of Energy, NASA, the Department of Defense, and other government agencies. The collections, which are particularly strong in aeronautical materials, contain first editions of Copernicus and Newton and the personal papers of the Wright Brothers and Alexander Graham Bell. Computer terminals provide principal access to the collections. Special scientific finding aids, such as abstracting and indexing journals, are part of the division's reference collection. This Division also prepares an informal series of reference guides called *Tracer Bullets*, which are available free upon request. More extensive bibliographies are published from time to time.

* Adolescent Health

Office of Technology Assessment
600 Pennsylvania Ave., SE
Washington, DC 20510 (202) 228-6590
OTA is working on a project to assess the health status of adolescents 10 to 18 years old and identify factors that put adolescents at risk for health problems, including racial and ethnic backgrounds, socioeconomic status, gender, and developmental stage. Particular attention will be paid to the availability, effectiveness, and accessibility of health services for adolescents. Contact Denise Dougherty, the project director, for more information.

* Agrichemical Contaminations of Groundwater

Office of Technology Assessment
600 Pennsylvania Ave., SE
Washington, DC 20510 (202) 228-6516
To assess agricultural technology that may reduce groundwater contamination, OTA is reviewing data and literature on extent, types, and sources of agrichemical contamination, and on hydrogeological, crop type, and cropping system relationships.
The study will also assess likely impacts of these new technologies, especially on the environment farm economics, rural communities, and the structure of agriculture. Contact Alison Hess, the project director, for more information.

* Alzheimers and Other Dementias

Office of Technology Assessment
600 Pennsylvania Ave., SE
Washington, DC 20510 (202) 228-6688
OTA is assessing existing methods of locating and arranging health and long-term care services for alzheimers and dementia patients. The study will identify methods that are successful in some communities and may serve as models for others. Contact Katie Maslow, the project director, for more information.

* American Association for the Advancement of Science

1333 H Street NW
Washington, D.C. 20005 (202) 326-6400
The largest scientific organization in the country with membership exceeding 136,000, this association was formed to promote increased public understanding of science and technology. Its activities are divided regionally and by field of interest, and it also sponsors international events such as its annual meeting which brings together scientists from all over the world. The Association can provide information about major scientific and technological issues, and staff will help you locate both specialists and printed materials. It publishes *Science* magazine as well books about topics of immediate scientific interest, as well as directories and other materials of interest to its members.

* Association for Computing Machinery

11 West 42nd Street
New York, NY 10036 (212) 869-7440
This large educational and scientific society is concerned with all aspects of computer science and its applications. The Association's 32 Special Interest Groups (SIGs) and numerous local chapters throughout the US provide members with a variety of forums and continuing education programs. The SIGs focus on subjects ranging from Automata and Computability Theory (ACT) to Software Engineering (SIGSOFT). Each group holds an annual conference, the proceedings of which are published by the Association, and publishes 11 journals covering different aspects of R&D and application in the computer field. A free publications catalog is available.

* Association of Science-Technology Centers (ASTC)

1413 K Street NW, 10th Floor
Washington, D.C. 20005 (202) 371-1171
This association of science museums promotes public understanding of science and technology. It publishes a quarterly calendar of museum exhibits. ASTC sponsors conferences which are open to the public. It sells surveys about computers, along with a bimonthly newsletter.

* Biotechnology and a Global Economy

Office of Technology Assessment
600 Pennsylvania Ave., SE
Washington, DC 20510 (202) 228-6692
OTA is currently working on a study to identify current U.S. capabilities in various applications of biotechnology and compare these capabilities with efforts underway internationally. They will also address trade, export, and international intellectual property issues relevant to the safe and timely commercialization of products derived from biotechnology. Cooperative ventures between U.S. and Japanese and Western European firms will also be assessed, along with international agreements and technology transfer mechanisms. Contact Kevin O'Connor, the project director, for more information.

* Commercial Low-Level Radioactive Waste

Office of Technology Assessment
600 Pennsylvania Ave., SE
Washington, DC 20510   (202) 228-6852
OTA is working on a project to analyze the Federal effort and State progress in
implementing the Low-Level Radioactive Waste Policy Amendments Act, which
identifies Federal activities needed to help States meet milestones for developing
disposal facilities. Contact Gretchen Hund McCabe, the project director, for
more information.

* Communications Networks and New Technologies

Office of Technology Assessment
600 Pennsylvania Ave., SE
Washington, DC 20510   (202) 228-6774
Recent advances in information storage and transmission technologies, occurring
in a new deregulated and intensely competitive economic climate, are rapidly
changing the Nation's communication networks. OTA is studying the role of the
Federal government in this area, along with how to coordinate them, resolve
potential conflicts between them, and examine new communication systems
abroad and their potential relationships to the U.S. systems. Contact Linda
Garcia, the project director, for more information.

* Computerized Data File Directory

Directory of Computerized Datafiles
National Technical Information Service
Department of Commerce
5285 Port Royal Rd.
Springfield, VA 22161   (703) 487-4650
The annual, *Computerized Data File Directory* contains more than 1,300 source
files for unique Federal numeric and text data. This publication offers its readers
a single, convenient reference to important datafiles prepared by a variety of
Federal agencies. The cost is $55.00. Call the Sales Desk to place an order or
ask for a free information brochure *PR-629*.

* Computer Software Directory

Directory of Computer Software
National Technical Information Service
Department of Commerce
5285 Port Royal Rd.
Springfield, VA 22161   (703) 487-4650
This directory contains detailed descriptions of software applications and tools.
Information has been compiled in cooperation with hundreds of U.S.
Government agencies. More than 1,700 programs are arranged under 21 subject
headings. Full indexes by subject, hardware, language, and sponsoring agency
are included. Agencies providing programs include the National Library of
Medicine, Environmental Protection Agency, Department of Defense, the
Department of Energy, plus many others. The cost is $55.00. Contact the Sales
Desk of place an order or ask for a free information brochure *PR-261*.

* Congressional Fellowships

Personnel Office
Office of Technology Assessment
Congress of the United States
Washington, DC 20510
OTA awards up to six fellowships each year, providing an opportunity for
individuals of demonstrated outstanding ability to gain a better understanding of
science and technology issues facing Congress, along with the ways in which
Congress establishes national policy related to these issues. Applications must
be received by January 31. Stipends range from $28,000 to $55,000, depending
upon background and experience. For further information, write this office.

* Current Technology Assessment Activities

Publishing Office
Office of Technology Assessment
600 Pennsylvania Ave.
SE, Washington, DC 20510   (202) 224-8996
Free upon request, this booklet provides Members of Congress with brief
summaries of OTA's current work projects and their anticipated completion
dates.

* Digital Spatial Data and Mapping Software

U.S. Geological Survey
Reston-ESIC
507 National Center
Reston, VA 22092   (703) 648-6045
The U.S. Geological Survey's Earth Science Information Center (ESIC) now
offers inventories of digital spatial data sets and cartographic applications
software in two bound listings. These inventories provide up-to-date
bibliographic descriptions of data sets and software available from federal, state,
and local government agencies and the private sector.

Sources for Digital Spatial Data. Describes more than 500 data sets containing
spatially referenced base or thematic categories of data. The data sets are
indexed by geographic area of coverage and cross-indexed by type of data.

Sources for Software for Computer Mapping and Related Disciplines. Describes
more than 700 subroutines, programs, and systems that can be used in geographic
information systems, map and chart plotting and construction, image processing
and analysis, surveying, photogrammetry, data modeling and analysis, coordinate
conversion, and other applications. Each publication is $22.

* Defense Nuclear Waste and

Contamination Cleanup
Office of Technology Assessment
600 Pennsylvania Ave., SE
Washington, DC 20510   (202) 228-6862
Today there is a large backlog of high-level, transuranic, low-level, hazardous,
and mixed nuclear waste at the 15 facilities in the Department of Energy's
nuclear weapons complex. OTA is currently studying how best to clean up this
nuclear waste problem using technologies for waste management and
minimizations. Contact Peter Johnson, the project director, for more
information.

* Digital Spatial Data Applications Cooperation

U.S. Geological Survey
Reston-ESIC
507 National Center
Reston, VA 22092   (703) 648-6899
If your organization is involved in digital spatial data applications, the Earth
Science Information Center invites you to contribute information about your
holdings. Your data and software may be valuable to other users.

* Drug Labeling in Developing and

Newly-Industrialized Countries
Office of Technology Assessment
600 Pennsylvania Ave., SE
Washington, DC 20510   (202) 228-6590
The U.S. pharmaceutical industry is a major supplier of pharmaceuticals to
developing countries, but the industry has been criticized for mislabeling certain
drugs sold in those countries. OTA is currently studying whether inappropriate
labeling is occurring today to allow health workers in those developing countries
to use drugs safely and effectively. Contact Hellen Gelband, the project director,
for more information.

* Education Technologies

Office of Technology Assessment
600 Pennsylvania Ave., SE
Washington, DC 20510   (202) 228-6936
New curriculum requirements, shortages of qualified teachers in some subjects,
sparse student enrollment in some regions, and rising costs for educational
services contribute to an increasing need for effective methods for providing
instruction. OTA is currently studying these problems and the various
technological options, their costs, effectiveness, and tradeoffs, in the K-12 school
setting. Contact Linda Roberts, the project director, for more information.

* Emerging Agricultural Technology

Office of Technology Assessment
600 Pennsylvania Ave., SE
Washington, DC 20510   (202) 228-6521
OTA is studying the emerging agricultural technologies for the 1990s and the
structure of the research system that gives rise to these technologies, which
include biotechnology, information technology, and low input technology for the
food and agricultural sector. Contact Mike Phillips, the project director, for
more information.

* Energy Systems Vulnerability

Office of Technology Assessment
600 Pennsylvania Ave., SE
Washington, DC 20510   (202) 228-6427
A study is underway at OTA to assess the vulnerability of certain energy
producing and delivery systems--electricity, natural gas, and refined oil products--
to disruption by either terrorist actions or massive natural disasters. Contact
Alan Crane, the project director, for more information.

* Environmental Research Technology Transfer

Center for Environmental Research Information
Environmental Protection Agency
401 M St., SW
Washington DC 20460   (513) 569-7562

The Office of Research and Development of the EPA has centralized most of its information distribution and technology transfer activities in the Center for Environmental Research Information listed above. CERI also serves as a central point of distribution for ORD research results and reports.

* European Technology and U.S. Trade

Office of Technology Assessment
600 Pennsylvania Ave., SE
Washington, DC 20510   (202) 228-6354

The OTA is currently studying how the European Commission's Single Market Act and the technology projects of Europe affect U.S. manufacturers and trade, particularly in high-technology sectors like microelectronics, computers, and telecommunications equipment. The study is comparing how technology development in chosen industrial sectors has worked in both Europe and East Asia, and assessing the conditions under which governmental participation and collaboration between firms, universities, and government has succeeded or failed. Contact Julie Gorte, the project director, for more information.

* Federal Laboratory Consortium (FLC)

U.S. Department of Agriculture
Extension Service
14th & Independence Ave., S.W.
Room 3865, South Building
Washington, D.C. 20250-0900   (202) 447-7185

FLC is a national network of 300 individuals from federal laboratories and centers across the country. Members are responsible for assessing the technologies developed at their facility and then passing that knowledge onto industry, government, and the general public. Through the FLC the public can gain access to all unclassified research conducted by the federal government. The FLC director can refer you to an FLC member in your specialty or geographical area. Its *Federal Laboratory Directory 1985* provides data on 388 federal laboratories with ten or more full-time professionals engaged in R&D. Information is provided about staff size,
mission, and major scientific or testing equipment. The Directory can be obtained for free from the NTIS, 5285 Port Royal Rd., Springfield, VA 22161, (703) 487-4600.

* Forensic Uses of DNA Tests

Office of Technology Assessment
600 Pennsylvania Ave., SE
Washington, DC 20510   (202) 228-6690

OTA is working on a project to gather technical information on the reliability of the various genetic techniques, assess costs and procedural uses raised by the rapid adoption of forensic genetic testing, and outline issues that will emerge as the genetic tests are more widely used. Contact Robyn Nishimi, the project director, for more information.

* Genetic Testing in the Workplace

Office of Technology Assessment
600 Pennsylvania Ave., SE
Washington, DC 20510   (202) 228-6690

OTA is now studying the state-of-the-art technologies used by employers for genetic screening and monitoring, which includes a survey of the 500 largest U.S. industries, to largest utilities, and 11 major unions to determine the current nature and extent of employer testing. Also being examined is the impact of genetic testing; relevant ethical issues; and legal issues, including employment discrimination. Contact Robyn Nishimi, the project director, for more information.

* Health Services Research

Health Services Research (152)
Department of Veterans Affairs
810 Vermont Ave., NW
Washington, DC 20420   (202) 233-2666

The goal of this research is to improve the effectiveness and efficiency of the Department of Veterans Affairs health care delivery system. Health services researchers develop and distribute information designed to help clinicians, investigators, and administrators select medical interventions and administrative actions that are most appropriate to the Agency's mission: the provision of quality medical care services to the veteran patient.

* High-Temperature Superconductivity

Office of Technology Assessment
600 Pennsylvania Ave., SE
Washington, DC 20510   (202) 228-6270

The availability of high-temperature superconducting materials offers potential for practical use of superconductors in computers, transportation, and electric power systems, as well as many new applications not possible with the traditional low-temperature materials. OTA is currently working on a project to evaluate the U.S. research and development agenda for these materials, the technical and

economic barriers facing potential applications, and the processing/manufacturing requirements for delivering products using these materials. Contact Greg Eyring, the project director, for more information.

* Ice Navigational Technology

Planning Branch
Research and Development Staff
Office of Engineering and Development
U.S. Coast Guard
U.S. Department of Transportation
2100 2nd St., SW, Room 6208
Washington, DC 20593-0001   (202) 267-1030

Information can be obtained here about research conducted by the Coast Guard in support of its operations and responsibilities. Areas of study include ice operations, ocean dumping, law enforcement, environmental protection, port safety and security, navigation aids, search and rescue procedures, recreational boating, energy, and advanced marine vehicles. For referral to specific personnel working in these areas, contact the Planning Branch.

* Information Technology and Research

Office of Technology Assessment
600 Pennsylvania Ave., SE
Washington, DC 20510   (202) 228-6766

Advanced information technology is having a major impact on the conduct of science and engineering research in nearly all disciplines--supercomputers, high resolution color displays, artificial intelligence software, and more. OTA is assessing the impact of advanced information technology on research, with particular emphasis on Federal programs to provide access to supercomputers and the Federal role in developing a national scientific network. Contact Fred Weingarten, the project director, for more information.

* Infrastructure Technologies

Office of Technology Assessment
600 Pennsylvania Ave., SE
Washington, DC 20510   (202) 228-6939

Public works infrastructure, which includes roads, bridges, sewers, etc., provides essential services--moving people and goods, supplying water, and disposing of waste. And there is little disagreement about the urgency of repair, maintenance, or new construction of these vital systems. OTA is currently studying how technological, institutional, and financial alternatives could be combined to meet the challenges posed by infrastructure needs that might be required in the Federal role. Contact Edith Page, the project director, for more information.

* Institute of Electrical and Electronics Engineers

IEEE Headquarters
345 East 47th Street
New York, NY 10017   (212) 705-7867

This large engineering society focuses on advancing the theory and practice of electrical engineering, electronics, computer engineering and computer science. IEEE consists of 30 technical societies corresponding to essentially every recognized discipline or interest area. There are, for example, societies for biomedical engineering, control systems, communications, and power engineering. The largest is the IEEE Computer Society. Staff at IEEE can respond to questions and refer you to members in regional chapters around the US. One of the organization's main functions is publishing technical literature, and presently it is credited with publishing 15% of the world's technical papers in the electrical and electronic fields. Each Society publishes one or more technical periodicals, usually called *Transactions* or *Journals*, which cover such fields as aerospace and electronic systems, electron devices, lightwave technology, microwave theory and techniques, and quantum electronics. The primary periodical is *IEEE Spectrum* which contains state-of-the-art news, reviews, and application articles of interest to many engineers and scientists. Call (212) 705-7890 for information on technical activities; and (201) 981-1393 for publications from the Piscataway, NJ, Service Center.

* Japanese Technical Resources

Directory of Japanese Technical Resources
National Technical Information Service
Department of Commerce
5285 Port Royal Rd.
Springfield, VA 22161   (703) 487-4650

The directory, *Japanese Technical Resources*, allows government, industry, and the academic community to find U.S. sources of Japanese high-technology information. It is divided into four parts: 1) an alphabetical list of commercial organizations that collect, abstract, translate, or distribute Japanese technical information; 2) a list of government agencies with programs and services involving Japanese technical information; 3) a list of libraries that have extensive holdings of Japanese technical information; and 4) a list of Japanese technical reports translated by the U.S. Government and available to the public. It is available for $36.00.

Science and Technology

* Materials Research: Wear and Corrosion
Research Division
Bureau of Mines
U.S. Department of the Interior
2401 E St., NW
Washington, DC 20241 (202) 634-1210
Advanced materials research is being conducted to eliminate wear and corrosion within the minerals industry through the use of ceramics, high-performance plastics, high-tech metals and alloys, and composites. Bureau scientists are also developing new coatings to protect equipment from the heat, corrosive chemicals, and abrasive materials found in mills, smelters, refineries, and furnaces.

* Medical Research
Medical Research Service
Veterans Health Services and Research Administration Department of Veterans Affairs
810 Vermont Ave., NW
Washington, DC 20420 (202) 233-5041
VA efforts in this area fall into two broad categories: research on medical, dental, and psychiatric problems that are specific to the veteran population (spinal cord injury, Agent Orange, etc); and research on general health problems that are particularly prevalent among veterans (e.g., alcoholism, aging, and schizophrenia). Most of the investigators are VA clinicians and the close links between research and patient care functions give the research program a clinical orientation that is directly related to its goal of providing quality medical care to the veteran patient. For more information, contact the office above.

* Medical Waste
Office of Technology Assessment
600 Pennsylvania Ave., SE
Washington, DC 20510 (202) 228-6854
OTA is currently studying medical waste handling and disposal as comparisons of incineration and alternative management technologies and their associated risks, along with waste reduction and recycling options for medical waste management. Contact Kathryn Wagner, the project director, for more information.

* Medicare's Prescription Drug Benefit
Office of Technology Assessment
600 Pennsylvania Ave., SE
Washington, DC 20510 (202) 228-6590
OTA will study the experience of public and private payers of prescription drugs, including how they set payment rates, promote appropriate use, and control total expenditures. The study will apply this experience to develop methods that the Medicare program might use to pay for multiple- and single-source drugs, and pharmaceutical services. Contact Jane Sisk, the project director, for more information.

* Mines Technology Transfer
Office of Technology Transfer
Bureau of Mines
U.S. Department of the Interior
2401 E St., NW, MS 6201
Washington, DC 20241 (202) 634-1224
The Technology Transfer Group distributes information on mining industry issues in many ways. *Technology Transfer* is a newsletter announcing the latest technology and research in mining. Free conferences are also held around the country on a variety of topics, such as advanced materials research and new technology for minerals. To be placed on the mailing list, contact the office above.

* National Referral Center
Library of Congress
Washington, D.C. 20540 (202) 707-567
NRC maintains an online data bank of more than 12,000 qualified organizations or individuals willing to provide information to the general public on topics in science, technology, and the social sciences. The Center can refer you to appropriate associations, government agencies, literature and databases. Staff will perform computer searches and send you a printout free of charge. A typical citation contains the name of the resource person or group, mailing address, telephone number, areas of interest, special collections, databases, publications and special services.

* Neuroscience Advances
Office of Technology Assessment
600 Pennsylvania Ave., SE
Washington, DC 20510 (202) 228-6677
Recent advances in neuroscience research have enormous potential to improve the lives of millions of Americans. OTA is currently studying the following neuroscience-associated topics: neural transplants and nerve regeneration,

including related ethical and legal issues; biological rhythms and shift work; neurotoxicity testing by private and public organizations; and biochemical bases of mental illness. Contact Mark Schaefer, the project director, for more information.

* New Energy Technologies and Developing Countries
Office of Technology Assessment
600 Pennsylvania Ave., SE
Washington, DC 20510 (202) 228-6267
OTA is currently working on a study to examine how technology can contribute to the goal of sound and productive energy development in the world's poorer countries, and the role of U.S. policy and the relevant international organizations in encouraging the rapid adoption of improved technologies. Contact Joy Dunkerley, the project director, at OTA for more information.

* NTIS Data Base Searches
Selected Research in Microfiche (SRIM)
National Technical Information Service
5285 Port Royal Rd.
Springfield, VA 22161 (703) 487-4929
Selected Research in Microfiche (SRIM) automatically provides selected technical reports as they are issued. Using SRIM, customers design (or select) their own subscription parameters, choosing from more than 350 subject topics. They then receive all reports that fall within their selections. Customers pay only $1.25 for each report they receive. Call SRIM Product Manager to start your subscription or request the free information brochure, *PR-271*.

* NTIS Index
National Technical Information service
Department of Commerce
5285 Port Royal Rd.
Springfield, VA 22161 (703) 487-4650
NTIS Title Index is a microfiche list that provides an economical means of locating reports for sale from NTIS. It cites titles, order numbers, and prices of reports input into NTIS for a two-year period. A key-word-out-of-context title listing index is provided along with a personal author index and an order/report number index. The price for a two-year subscription is $400. Call the Sales Desk to place an order or request the free information brochure, *PR-567*.

* NTIS Products
National Technical Information Service
Department of Commerce
5285 Port Royal Rd.
Springfield, VA 22161 (703) 487-4630
The NTIS information products and services presented in this section give you ready access to the results of both U.S. and foreign government-sponsored research. The U.S. Government alone invests billions of dollars in research and development and engineering programs. Much of the resulting knowledge and technology is available through NTIS. And in the case of applied technology, this information can be of great value because it is not proprietary and may be used freely. The following newsletters are available through NTIS:

Weekly Abstracts Newsletters. These weekly bulletins present summaries of the most recent U.S. and foreign government research and development and engineering results. Prices range from $95- $125 depending upon subject area. For more information, request the free brochure, *PR-797*.

Computers, Control & Information Theory Abstract Newsletter. This bulletin provides early notice of new software and datafiles as they are received by the Federal Computer Products Center. It also includes abstracts of Government research in computers and information theory. A subscription is available for $125 per year. For more information, request the free brochure, *PR-797*.

Tech Notes. This is a monthly service providing access to the Federal laboratory activities and resources. An NTIS Tech Notes subscription provides selected *Fact Sheets* on the latest U.S. government-developed technologies and know-how. This low-cost service provides concise, illustrated one page announcements describing new processes, instruments, materials, equipment, software, services, and techniques. Each month more than 100 fact sheets are arranged under twelve subject headings. A subscription is available for $157 per year. For more information request the free brochure, *PR-365*.

Government Reports Announcements and Index Journal. This journal is issued twice monthly for those who want to see all of the research and development and engineering results announced annually by NTIS. Its comprehensive coverage provides 2,500 results within each issue. Entries are arranged under 38 major subject headings and then further sorted within more than 350 subheadings. A subscription is available for $420 per year. For more information, request the free information brochure, *PR-195*.

* NTIS Product Services Catalog

National Technical Information Service
Department of Commerce
5285 Port Royal Rd.
Springfield, VA 22161   (703) 487-4650
NTIS Product Services Catalog describes the bulletins, journals, catalogs, and
directories produced by NTIS and available for sale. It also includes descriptions
of more than eighty subscription items produced by other government agencies
and made available from NTIS. Call for your free copy.

* Office of Technology Assessment
Publications and Reports

Office of Technology Assessment
Publications Order
U.S. Congress
Washington, DC 20510-8025   (202) 224-8996
These OTA publications are available through the office above, the Government
Printing Office, and the National Technical Information Service. To find out
correct ordering information and prices, contact the OTA office above and
request their current publications catalog. Free executive summaries of each of
these reports are available from this office.

Agriculture and Forestry

Acid Rain and Transported Air Pollutants: Implications for Public Policy (0-204)
Africa Tomorrow: Issues in Technology, Agriculture, and U.S. Foreign Aid (TM-F-31)
Agricultural Postharvest Technology and Marketing Economics Research (TM-F-21)
Assessing Biological Diversity in the United States: Data Considerations (BP-F-39)
An Assessment of the U.S. Food and Agricultural Research System (F-155)
Commercial Biotechnology: An International Analysis (BA-218)
Continuing the Commitment: Agricultural Development in the Sahel (F-308)
Drugs in Livestock Feed (F-91)
Emerging Food Marketing Technologies (F-79)
Energy From Biological Processes (E-124)
Enhancing Agriculture in Africa: A Role for Development Assistance (F-356)
Enhancing the Quality of U.S. Grain for International Trade (F-399)
Environmental Contaminants in Food (F-103)
Food Information Systems (F-35)
Grain Quality in International Trade: A Comparison of Major U.S. Competitors (F-402)
Grassroots Conservation of Biological Diversity in the United States (BP-F-38)
Grassroots Development: The African Development Foundation (F-378)
Impacts of Applied Genetics: Micro-Organisms, Plants, and Animals (HR-132)
Impacts of Technology on U.S. Cropland and Rangeland Productivity (F-166)
Innovative Biological Technologies for Lesser Developed Countries (BP-F-29)
Integrated Renewable Resource Management for U.S. Insular Area (F-325)
Nutrition Research Alternatives (F-74)
Open Shelf-Life Dating of Food (F-94)
Organizing and Financing Basic Research To Increase Food Production (F-49)
Perspectives on Federal Retail Food Grading (F-47)
Pest Management Strategies in Crop Protection (F-98)
Pesticide Residues in Food (F-398)
Plants: The Potential for Extracting Protein, Medicines, and Other Useful Chemicals (BP-F-23)
A Review of U.S. Competitiveness in Agriculture Trade (TM-TET-29)
Sustaining Tropical Forest Resources: Reforestation of Defraded Lands (BP-F-18)
Sustaining Tropical Forest Resources: U.S. and International Institutions (BP-F-19)
Technologies To Benefit Agriculture and Wildlife (BP-F-34)
Technologies To Maintain Biological Diversity (F-330)
Technologies To Sustain Tropical Forest Resources (F-214)
Technology and the American Economic Transition (TET-283)
Technology, Public Policy, and the Changing Structure of American Agriculture (F-285)
Technology, Public Policy, and the Changing Structure of American Agriculture: A Special Report for the 1985 Farm Bill (F-272)
Technology, Renewable Resources, and American Crafts (BP-F-27)
Water-Related Technologies for Sustainable Agriculture in U.S. Arid/Semiarid Lands (F-212)
Water-Related Technologies for Sustainable Agriculture in U.S. Arid/Semiarid Lands: Selected Foreign Experience (BP-F-20)
Wetlands: Their Use and Regulation (0-206)
Wood Use: U.S. Competitiveness and Technology (ITE-210)

Biological Applications

Alternatives to Animal Use In Research, Testing, and Education (BA-273)
Artificial Insemination: Practice in the United States (BP-BA-48)
Assessment of Technologies for Determining Cancer Risk From the Environment (H-138)
Commercial Development of Tests for Human Genetic Disorders (Staff Paper)
Commercial Biotechnology: An International Analysis (BA-218)
Federal Policies and the Medical Devices Industry (H-229)
Federal Regulation and Animal Patents (Staff Paper)
Hearing Impairment and Elderly People (BP-BA-30)
Humane Gene Therapy (BP-BA-24)
Impacts of Applied Genetics: Micro-Organisms, Plants, and Animals (HR-132)

Impacts of Neuroscience (BP-BA-24)
Infertility: Medical and Social Choices (BA-358)
Innovative Biological Technologies for Lesser Developed Countries (BP-F-29)
Institutional Protocols for Decisions About Life-Sustaining Treatments (BA-389)
Life-Sustaining Technologies and the Elderly (BA-306)
Loosing a million minds: Confronting the Tragedy of Alzheimer's Disease and Other Dementias (BA-323)
Mapping Our Genes: Genome Projects - How Big, How Fast? (BA-373)
Methods for Locating and Arranging Health and Long-Term Care for Persons With Dementia (BA-403)
New Developments in Biotechnology: Field-Testing Engineered Organisms: Genetic and Ecological Issues (BA-350)
New Developments in Biotechnology: Ownership of Human Tissue and Cells (BA-337)
New Developments in Biotechnology: Patenting Life (BA-370)
New Developments in Biotechnology: Public Perceptions in Biotechnology (BP-BA-45)
New Developments in Biotechnology: U.S. Investment in Biotechnology (BA-360)
Preventing Illness and Injury in the Workplace (H-256)
Reproductive Health Hazards in the Workplace (BA-266)
The Role of Genetic Testing in the Prevention of Occupational Disease (BA-194)
Status of Biomedical Research and Related Technology for Tropical Diseases (H-258)
Technologies for Detecting Heritable Mutations in Human Beings (H-298)
Technologies for Managing Urinary Incontinence (HCS-33)
Technology and Aging in America (BA-264)
Transgenic Animals (Staff Paper)
World Population and Fertility Planning Technologies: The Next 20 Years (HR-157)

Defense

Advanced Space Transportation
Alternative Cargo Policies (BP-O-36)
Anti-Satellite Weapons, Countermeasures, and Arms Control (ISC-281)
Arms Control in Space (BP-ISC-28)
An Assessment of Alternative Economic Stockpiling Policies (M-36)
Ballistic Missile Defense Technology (ISC-254)
Big Dumb Boosters: A Low Cost Transportation Option (Background Paper)
The Border War On Drugs (0-336)
Commercial Newsgathering From Space (TM-ISC-40)
Defending Secrets, Sharing Data: New Locks and Keys for Electronic Information (CIT-310)
The Defense Technology Base: Introduction and Overview (ISC-374)
Directed Energy Missile Defense in Space (BP-ISC-26)
The Effects of Nuclear War (NS-89)
Energy Technology Transfer to China (TM-ISC-30)
International Cooperation and Competition in Civilian Space Activities (ISC-239)
Launch Options for the Future: A Buyer's Guide (ISC-383)
Monitoring and Preventing Accidental Radiation Release at the Nevada Test Site
MX Missile Basing (ISC-140)
New Structural Materials Technologies: Opportunities for the Use of Advanced Ceramics and Composites (TM-E-32)
New Technologies for NATO: Implementing Follow-On Forces Attack (ISC-309)
Nuclear Proliferation and Safeguards (E-48)
Piloted Space Transportation Technologies
Reducing Launch Operations Costs: New Technologies and Practices (TM-ISC-28)
Remote Sensing and the Private Sector: Issues for Discussion (TM-ISC-20)
Review of the FAA 1982 National Airspace System Plan (STI-176)
Scientific Validity of Polygraph Testing: A Research Review and Evaluation (TM-H-15)
SDI: Technology, Survivability, and Software (ISC-353)
Seismic Verification of Nuclear Testing Treaties (ISC-361)
Space Stations and the Law: Selected Legal Issues (BP-ISC-41)
Strategic Materials: Technologies To Reduce U.S. Import Vulnerability (ITE-248)
Taggants in Explosives (ISC-116)
Technologies for NATO's Follow-On Forces Attack Concept (ISC-312)
Technology and East West Trade (ISC-101)
Technology and East West Trade: An Update (ISC-209)
Technology Transfer to China (ISC-340)
Technology Transfer to the Middle East (ISC-173)
UNISPACE '82: A Context for International Cooperation and Competition (TM-ISC-26)
U.S.-Soviet Cooperation in Space (TM-STI-27)

Education and Training

Alternatives to Animal Use in Research, Testing, and Education (BA-273)
Automation and the Workplace: Selected Labor, Education, and Training Issues (TM-CIT-25)
Automation of America's Offices (CIT-287)
Computer Technology in Medical Education and Assessment (BP-H-1)
Computerized Manufacturing Automation: Employment, Education, and the Workplace (CIT-235)
Demographic Trends and the Scientific and Engineering Work Force (TM-SET-35)
Displaced Homemakers: Programs and Policy (ITE-292)
Educating Scientist and Engineers: Grade School to Grad School (SET-377)
Elementary and Secondary Education for Science and Engineering (TM-SET-41)

Science and Technology

Higher Education for Science and Engineering (BP-SET-62)
Informational Technology and Its Impact on American Engineers (CIT-187)
Life-Sustaining Technologies and the Elderly (BA-306)
Plant Closing: Advance Notice and Rapid Response (ITE-321)
Potential Office Hazards and Controls (Contractor Report)
Power On! New Tools for Teaching and Learning (SET-379)
Preventing Illness and Injury in the Workplace (H-256)
Reproductive Health Hazards in the Workplace (BA-266)
Research Funding As An Investment: Can We Measure the Returns? (TM-SET-36)
Role of Technology in the Education, Training, and Retraining of Adult Workers (Contractor Document)
Technology and Handicapped People (H-179)
Technology and Structural Unemployment: Reemploying Displaced Adults (ITE-250)
Trade Adjustment Assistance: New Ideas for an Old Problem (ITE-346)
Transportation of Hazardous Materials (SET-304)
Transportation of Hazardous Materials: State and local Activities (SET-301)

Energy and Mineral Resources

Advanced Material by Design: New Structural Materials Technologies (E-351)
Analysis of Laws Governing Access Across Federal Lands: Options for Access in Alaska (M-82)
Application of Solar Technology to Today's Energy Needs (E-66)
An Assessment of Alternative Economic Stockpiling Policies (M-36)
An Assessment of Development and Production Potential of Federal Coal Leases (M-150)
An Assessment of Information System Capabilities Required to Support U.S. Materials Policy Decision (M-40)
An Assessment of Oil Shale Technologies (M-118)
Benefits of Increased Use of Continuous Casting by the U.S. Steel Industry (TM-ISC-2)
Changing Energy Structure of U.S. Industry
Coal Exports and Port Development (TM-0-8)
Coastal Effects of Offshore Energy Systems (0-37)
Commercialization High-Temperature Superconductivity (ITE-388)
Conservation and Solar Energy Programs of the Department of Energy: A Critique (E-120)
Copper: Technology and Competitiveness (E-367)
The Direct Use of Coal: Prospects and Problems of Production and Combustion (E-86)
Electric Power-Wheeling and Dealing: Technological Considerations for Increasing Competition (E-409)
Energy and Efficiency of Building in Cities (E-168)
Energy From Biological Processes (E-124)
Energy Technology Transfer to China (TM-ICS-30)
Engineering Implications to Chronic Materials Scarcity (M-44)
Enhanced Oil Recovery Potential in the United States (E-59)
Environmental Protection in the Federal Coal Leasing Program (E-237)
The Future of Liquefied Natural Gas Imports (E-110)
Gas Potential From Devonian Shales of the Appalachian Basin (E-57)
Gasohol (TM-E-1)
A History and Analysis of the Federal Prototype Oil Shale Leasing Program (M-119)
Increased Automobile Fuel Efficiency and Synthetic Fuels: Alternatives for Reducing Oil Imports (E-185)
Industrial and Commercial Cogeneration (E-192)
Industrial Energy Use (E-198)
Management of Fuel and Nonfuel Minerals in Federal Lands (M-88)
Marine Applications for Fuel Cell Technology (TM-0-37)
Marine Minerals: Exploring Our New Ocean Frontier (O-342)
Materials and Energy From Municipal Waste (M-93)
New Electric Power Technologies: Problems and Prospects for the 1990's (E-246)
New Structural Materials: Opportunities for the Use of Advanced Ceramics and Composites (TM-E-32)
Nuclear Power in an Age of Uncertainty (E-216)
Nuclear Powerplant Standardization: Light Water Reactors (E-134)
Nuclear Proliferation and Safeguards (E-48)
Ocean Thermal Energy Conversion (O-62)
Oil and Gas Technologies for the Arctic and Deepwater (O-270)
Oil Production in the Arctic National Wildlife Refuge: The Technology and the Alaskan Oil Context (E-394)
Oil Transportation by Tankers: An Analysis of Marine Pollution and Safety Measures (O-9)
Patterns and Trends in Federal Coal Lease Ownership, 1950-80 (TM-M-7)
Potential Effects of Section 3 of the Federal Coal Leasing Amendments Act of 1976 (E-300)
Power Frequency and Electromagnetic Fields: Exposure, Effects, Research and Regulation (BP-E-53)
Recent Developments in Ocean Thermal Energy (TM-O-3)
Residential Energy Conservation (E-92)
Solar Power Satellite Systems (E-144)
Starpower: The U.S. and the International Quest for Fusion Energy (E-338)
Strategic Materials: Technologies to Reduce U.S. Import Vulnerability (ITE-248)
Technical Options for Conservation of Metals (M-97)
Technologies for Improving Minerals Royalty Management
Technologies for Prehistoric and Historic Preservation (E-319)
Technologies for Underwater Archaeology and Maritime Preservation (BP-E-37)

Technology for Soviet Energy Availability (ISC-153)
A Technology Assessment of Coal Slurry Pipelines (E-60)
Technology Transfer to the Middle East (ISC-173)
Transportation of Liquefied Natural Gas (TM-E-12)
U.S. Natural Gas Availability: Conventional Gas Supply Through the Year 2000 (TM-E-12)
U.S. Natural Gas Availability: Gas Supply Through the Year 2000 (E-245)
U.S. Oil Production: The Effect of Low Oil Prices (E-348)
U.S. Vulnerability to an Oil Import Curtailment: The Oil Replacement Capability (E-243)
Western Surface Mine Permitting and Reclamation (E-279)
World Petroleum Availability: 1980-2000 (TM-E-5)

Environment and Pollution

Acid Rain and Transported Air Pollutants: Implications for Public Policy (O-204)
Are We Cleaning Up? 10 Superfund Case Studies (ITE-362)
Assessing Contractor Use In Superfund (BP-ITE-51)
Assessment of Technologies for Determining Cancer Risks From the Environment (H-138)
The Direct Use of Coal: Prospects and Problems of Production and Combustion (E-86)
Environmental Containments in Food (F-103)
Environmental Protection in the Federal Coal Leasing Program (E-237)
An Evaluation of Options for Managing Greater-Than-Class-C Low-Level Radioactive Waste (BP-0-40)
From Pollution to Prevention: A Progress Report on Waste Reduction (ITE-347)
Habitability of the Love Canal Area: An Analysis of the Technical Basis for the Decision on the Habitability of the Emergency Declaration Area (TM-M-13)
Impacts of Applied Genetics: Micro-Organisms, Plants, and Animals (HR-132)
Issues in Medical Waste Management (BP-O-49)
Managing the Nation's Commercial High-Level Radioactive Waste (O-171)
Marine Applications for Fuel Cell Technology (TM-O-37)
Monitoring and Preventing Accidental Radiation Release at the Nevada Test Site
Municipal Solid Waste Management
New Clean Air Act Issues (O-412)
Nonnuclear Industrial Waste: Classifying for Hazards Management (TM-M-9)
Ocean Incineration: Its Role in Managing Hazardous Waste (O-313)
Oil and Gas Technologies for the Arctic and Deepwater (O-270)
Oil Transportation by Tankers: An Analysis of Marine Pollution and Safety Measures (O-9)
Passive Smoking in the Workplace: Selected Issues (Staff Paper)
Protecting the Nation's Groundwater From Contamination (O-233)
Serious Reduction of Hazardous Waste (ITE-317)
Superfund Strategy (ITE-252)
Technologies and Management Strategies for Hazardous Waste Control (M-196)
Technologies for Prehistoric and Historic Preservation (E-319)
Technologies for the Preservation of Prehistoric and Historic Landscapes (BP-E-44)
Technologies for Reducing Dioxin in the Manufacture of Pulp and Paper
Technologies for Underwater Archaeology and Maritime Preservation (BP-E-37)
Technology and Oceanography: An Assessment of Federal Technologies for Oceanographic Research and Monitoring (O-141)
Trade Adjustment Assistance: New Ideas for an Old Program (ITE-346)
Transportation of Hazardous Materials (SET-304)
Transportation of Hazardous Materials: State and Local Activities (SET-301)
Urban Ozone and the Clean Air Act: Problems and Proposals for Change (Staff paper)
Wastes in Marine Environments (O-334)
Wetlands: Their Use and Regulation (O-206)

Health

Abstracts of Case Studies in the Health Technology Case Study Series (P-225)
Acid Rain and Transported Air Pollutants: Implications for Public Policy (O-204)
AIDS and Health Insurance: An OTA Survey (Staff Paper)
Artificial Insemination: Practice in the United States (BP-BA-48)
Assessing the Efficacy and Safety of Medical Technologies (H-75)
Assessment of Four Common X-Ray Procedures (BP-H-14)
Assessment of Technologies for Determining Cancer Risks From the Environment (H-138)
Assistive Devices for Severe Speech Impairments (HCS-26)
Biology, Medicine, and Bill of Rights (CIT-371)
Blood Policy and Technology (H-260)
Boston Elbow (HCS-29)
Cancer Testing Technology and Saccharin (H-55)
Costs and Effectiveness of Screening for Cervical Cancer in the Elderly (Contractor Paper)
Children's Mental Health: Problems and Services (BP-H-33)
Costs and Effectiveness of Screening for Cholesterol in the Elderly (Contractor Paper)
Colorectal Cancer Screening in the Elderly (Staff Paper)
Commercial Biotechnology: An International Analysis (BA-218)
Compensation for Vaccine-Related Injuries (TM-H-6)
Computer Technology in Medical Education and Assessment (BP-H-1)
Contact Lenses (HCS-31)
Cost-Effectiveness Analysis of Influenza Vaccine (H-152)
The Cost-Effectiveness of Digital Subtraction Angiography in the Diagnosis of Cerebrovascular Disease (HCS-34)

Industry

Science and Technology

Policy Implications of the Computed Tomography (CT) Scanner: An Update (BP-H-8)
Power Frequency and Electromagnetic Fields: Exposure, Effects, Research, and Regulation (BP-E-53)
Preventing Illness and Injury in the Workplace (H-256)
R&D in the Maritime Industry (BP-O-35)
Reproductive Health Hazards in the Workplace (BA-266)
Role of Technology in the Education, Training, and Retraining of Adult Workers (Contractor Document)
Safe Skies for Tomorrow: Aviation Safety in a Competitive Environment (SET-381)
Safer Skies With TCAS: Traffic Alert and Collision Avoidance System (SET-431)
Scientific Use of Supercomputers (BP-CIT-31)
Services in the U.S. Balance of Payments 1982-84: Documentation of OTA Estimates (Working Paper)
Strategies for Medical Technology Assessment (H-181)
Technology and Steel Industry Competitiveness (M-122)
Technology and Structural Unemployment: Reemploying Displaced Adults (ITE-250)
Technology and the American Economic Transition (TET-283)
Technology and the Future of the U.S. Construction Industry
Technology, Innovation, and Regional Economic Development (STI-238)
Technology, Innovation, and U.S. Trade
Technology, Trade, and the U.S. Residential Construction Industry (TET-315)
Transgenic Animals (Staff Paper)
Transportation of Hazardous Materials: State and Local Activities (SET-301)
U.S. Industrial Competitiveness: A Comparison of Steel, Electronics, and Automobiles (ISC-135)
The U.S. Textile and Apparel Industry: A Revolution in Progress (TET-332)
Wood Use: U.S. Competitiveness and Technology (ITE-210)

Information Technology and Services

An Assessment of Alternatives for a National Computerized Criminal History System (CIT-161)
An Assessment of Information System Capabilities Required To Support U.S. Materials Policy Decision (M-40)
Automation and the Workplace: Selected Labor, Education, and Training Issues (TM-CIT-25)
Automation of America's Offices (CIT-287)
Biology, Medicine, and the Bill of Rights (CIT-371)
Book Preservation Technologies (O-375)
Costs and Effectiveness of Screening for Cervical Cancer in the Elderly (Contractor Paper)
Children's Mental Health: Problems and Services (BP-H-33)
Costs and Effectiveness of Screening for Cholesterol in the Elderly (Contractor Paper)
Colorectal Cancer Screening in the Elderly (Staff Paper)
Communications Systems for an Information Age (CIT-407)
Computer-Based National Information Systems: Technology and Public Policy Issues (CIT-146)
Computerized Manufacturing Automation: Employment, Education, and the Workplace (CIT-235)
Copyright and Home Copying
Costs of AIDS and Other HIV Infections: Review of the Estimates (Staff Paper)
Criminal Justice, New Technologies, and the Constitution (CIT-366)
Defending Secrets, Sharing Data: New Locks and Keys for Electronic Information (CIT-310)
Democratic Governance Through Information and Communications Technologies (BP-CIT-59)
Do Insects Transmit AIDS? (Staff Paper)
Educating Scientists and Engineers: Grade School to Grad School (SET-377)
Effects of Information Technology on Financial Services Systems (CIT-202)
Efficacy and Cost Effectiveness of Psychotherapy (BP-H-6)
Electronic Delivery of Public Assistance Benefits: Technology Options and Policy Issues (BP-CIT-47)
The Electronic Supervisor: New Technology, New Tensions (CIT-333)
Elementary and Secondary Education for Science and Engineering (TM-SET-41)
Energy Technology Transfer to China (TM-ISC-30)
Federal Government Information Technology: Electronic Record Systems and Individual Privacy (CIT-296)
Federal Government Information Technology: Electronic Surveillance and Civil Liberties (CIT-293)
Federal Government Information Technology: Management, Security, and Congressional Oversight (CIT-297)
Federal Government Information Technology: The Social Security Administration and Information Technology (CIT-311)
Federal Response to AIDS
Higher Education for Science and Engineering (BP-SET-52)
Impact of Randomized Clinical Trials on Health Policy and Medical Practice (BP-H-22)
Implications of Electronic Mail and Message Systems for the U.S. Postal Service (CIT-183)
The Information Context of Premanufacture Notices (BP-H-17)
Information Technology R&D: Critical Trends and Issues (CIT-268)
Informational Technology and Its Impact on American Education (CIT-187)
Informing the Nation: Federal Information Dissemination in an Electronic Age (CIT-396)
Intellectual Property Rights in an Age of Electronics and Information (CIT-302)
International Cooperation and Competition in Civilian Space Activities (ISC-239)

Medical Testing and Health Insurance (H-384)
MEDLARS and Health Information Policy (TM-H-11)
Patent-Term Extension and the Pharmaceutical Industry (CIT-143)
Payment for Physician Services: Strategies for Medicare (H-294)
Plant Closing: Advance Notice and Rapid Response (ITE-321)
Policy Implications of Medical Information Systems (H-56)
Power On! New Tools for Teaching and Learning (SET-379)
A Preliminary Assessments of the National Crime Information Center and the Computerized Criminal History System (I-80)
The Quality of Medical Care: Information for Consumers (H-386)
Radiofrequency Use and Management: Impacts From the World Administrative Radio Conference of 1979 (CIT-163)
Review of Postal Automation Strategy: A Technical and Decision Analysis (TM-CIT-22)
Role of Technology in the Education, Training, and Retraining of Adult Workers (Contractor Document)
Science, Technology, and the Constitution (BP-CIT-43)
Science, Technology, and the First Amendment (CIT-369)
Scientific Validity of Polygraph Testing: A Research Review and Evaluation (TM-H-15)
Screening for Open-Angle Glaucoma in the Elderly (Staff Paper)
Selected Electronic Funds Transfer Issues: Privacy, Security and Equity (BP-CIT-12)
Strategies for Medical Technology Assessment (H-181)
Technology and Structural Unemployment: Reemploying Displaced Adults (ITE-250)
The Use of Preventative Services by the Elderly (staff Paper)

International Trade, Competition, and Cooperation

Arms Control in Space (BP-ISC-28)
Civilian Space Policy and Applications (STI-177)
Civilian Space Stations and U.S. Future in Space (STI-241)
Commercial Biotechnology: An International Analysis (BA-218)
Copper: Technology and Competitiveness (E-367)
Energy Technology Transfer to China (TM-ISC-30)
Enhancing Agriculture in Africa: A Role for Development Assistance (F-356)
Enhancing the Quality of U.S. Grain for International Trade (F-399)
Grain Quality in International Trade: A Comparison of Major U.S. Competitors (F-402)
International Competition in Services: Banking, Building, Software, Know-How (ITE-328)
International Competitiveness in Electronics (ISC-200)
International Cooperation and Competition in Civilian Space Activities (ISC-239)
Paying the Bill: Manufacturing and America's Trade Deficit (ITE-390)
A Review of U.S. Competitiveness in Agricultural Trade (TM-TET-29)
Salyut: Soviet Steps Toward Permanent Human Presence in Space (TM-STI-14)
Services in the U.S. Balance of Payments 1982-84: Documentation of OTA Estimates (Working Paper)
Starpower: The U.S. and the International Quest for Fusion Energy (E-338)
Technology and East-West Trade (ISC-101)
Technology and East-West Trade: An Update (ISC-209)
Technology and Soviet Energy Availability (ISC-153)
Technology and Structural Unemployment: Reemploying Displaced Adults (ITE-250)
Technology, Innovation, and U.S. Trade
Technology, Trade, and the U.S. Residential Construction Industry (TET-315)
Technology Transfer to China (ISC-340)
Technology Transfer to the Middle East (ISC-173)
Trade in Services: Exports and Foreign Revenues (ITE-316)
UNISPACE '82: A Context for International Cooperation and Competition (TM-ISC-26)
U.S. - Soviet Cooperation in Space (TM-STI-27)

Oceans and Water Resources

Alternative Cargo Policies (BP-O-36)
An Assessment of Maritime Trade and Technology (O-220)
The Border War on Drugs (TM-O-8)
Coal Exports and Port Development (TM-O-8)
Costal Effects of Offshore Energy Systems (O-37)
Establishing a 200-Mile Fisheries Zone (O-46)
An Evaluation of Options for Managing Greater-Than-Class-C Low-Level Radioactive Waste (BP-O-40)
Extending Cabotage Policy to All Commercial Maritime Activities in the EEZ
Integrated Renewable Resource Management for U.S. Insular Areas (F-325)
Issues in Medical Waste Management (BP-O-49)
Marine Applications for Fuel Cell Technology (TM-O-37)
Marine Minerals: Exploring Our New Ocean Frontier (O-342)
Municipal Solid Waste Management
Ocean Incineration: Its Role in Managing Hazardous Waste (O-313)
Ocean Margin Drilling (TM-O-4)
Ocean Thermal Energy Conversion (O-62)
Oil and Gas Technologies in the Arctic and Deepwater (O-270)
Oil Transportation by Tankers: An Analysis of Marine Pollution and Safety Measures (O-9)
Protecting the Nation's Groundwater From Contamination (O-233)
R&D in the Maritime Industry (BP-O-35)
Recent Developments in Ocean Thermal Energy (TM-O-3)
Technologies for Underwater Archaeology and Maritime Preservation (BP-E-37)

Technology and Oceanography: An Assessment of Federal Technologies for Oceanographic Research and Monitoring (O-141)
Transportation of Liquefied Natural Gas (O-53)
Use of Models for Water Resources Management, Planning, and Policy (O-159)
Using Desalination Technologies for Water Treatment (BP-O-46)
Wastes in Marine Environments (O-334)
Wetlands: Their Use and Regulation (O-206)

Science and Technology, Research and Development

Advanced Materials by Design: New Structural Materials Technologies (E-351)
Alternatives to Animal Use in Research, Testing, and Education (BA-273)
Anti-Satellite Weapons, Countermeasures, and Arms Control (ISC-281)
Assessment of Technologies for Determining Cancer Risks From the Environment (H-138)
An Assessment of the United States Food and Agriculture Research System (F-155)
Ballistic Missile Defense Technology (ISC-254)
Biology, Medicine, and the Bill of Rights (CIT-371)
Blood Policy and Technology (H-260)
Book Preservation Technologies (O-375)
Cancer Testing Technology and Saccharin (H-55)
Civilian Space Policy and Applications (STI-177)
Civilian Space Stations and U.S. Future in Space (STI-241)
Commercial Biotechnology: An International Analysis (BA-218)
Commercial Development of Tests for Human Genetic Disorders (Staff Paper)
Commercializing High-Temperature Superconductivity (ITE-388)
Criminal Justice, New Technologies, and the Constitution (CIT-366)
Demographic Trends and the Scientific and Engineering Work Force (TM-SET-35)
Education Scientists and Engineers: Grade School to Grad School (SET-377)
Elementary and Secondary Education for Science and Engineering (TM-SET-41)
Energy Technology Transfer to China (TM-ISC-30)
Federal Regulations and Animal Patents (Staff Paper)
Global Models, World Futures, and Public Policy (R-165)
Human Gene Therapy (BP-BA-32)
Identifying and Regulating Carcinogens (BP-H-42)
Impacts of Applied Genetics: Micro-Organisms, Plants, and Animals (HR-132)
Impacts of Neuroscience (BP-BA-24)
Information Technology R&D: Critical Trends and Issues (CIT-268)
Microelectronics R&D (BP-CIT-40)
New Developments in Biotechnology: Field Testing Engineered Organisms: Genetic and Ecological Issues (BA-350)
New Developments in Biotechnology: Ownership of Human Tissues and Cells (BA-337)
New Developments in Biotechnology: Patenting Life (BA-370)
New Developments in Biotechnology: Public Perceptions of Biotechnology (BP-BA-45)
New Developments in Biotechnology: U.S. Investment in Biotechnology (BA-360)
New Structural Material Technologies: Opportunities for the Use of Advanced Ceramics and Composites (TM-E-32)
Patent-Term Extension and the Pharmaceutical Industry (CIT-143)
Power On! New Tools for Teaching and Learning (SET-379)
R&D in the Maritime Industry (BP-O-35)
The Regulatory Environment for Science (TM-SET-34)
Research Funding As An Investment: Can We Measure the Returns? (TM-SET-36)
The Role of Genetic Testing in the Prevention of Occupational Disease (BA-194)
Salyut: Soviet Steps Toward Permanent Human Presence in Space (TM-STI-14)
Science, Technology, and the Constitution (BP-CIT-43)
Science, Technology, and the First Amendment (CIT-369)
Scientific Use of Supercomputers (BP-CIT-31)
Scientific Validity of Polygraph Testing: A Research Review and Evaluation (TM-H-15)
SDI: Technology, Survivability, and Software (ISC-353)
Seismic Verification of Nuclear Test Ban Treaties (ISC-361)
Space Science Research in the United States (TM-STI-19)
Status of Biomedical Research and Related Technology for Tropical Diseases (H-258)
Technologies for Detecting Heritable Mutations in Human Beings (H-298)
Technology Transfer at the National Institutes of Health (TM-H-10)
Technology Transfer to China (ISC-340)
Transgenic Animals (Staff Paper)

Space

Advanced Space Transportation Technologies
Anti-Satellite Weapons, Countermeasures, and Arms Control (ISC-281)
Arms Control in Space (BP-STI-28)
Ballistic Missile Defense Technology (ISC-254)
Big Dumb Boosters: A Low Cost Transportation Option (Background Paper)
Civilian Space Policy and Applications (STI-177)
Civilian Space Stations and U.S. Future in Space (STI-241)
Commercial Newsgathering From Space (TM-ISC-40)
Directed Energy Missile Defense in Space (BP-ISC-26)
International Cooperation and Competition in Civilian Space Activities (ISC-239)
Launch Options for the Future: A Buyer's Guide (ISC-383)
Piloted Space Transportation Technologies
Reducing Launch Operations Costs: New Technologies and Practices (TM-ISC-28)
Remote Sensing in the Private Sector: Issues for Discussion (TM-ISC-20)

Salyut: Soviet Steps Toward Permanent Human Presence in Space (TM-STI-14)
SDI: Technology, Survivability, and Software (ISC-353)
Seismic Verification of Nuclear Test Ban Treaties (ISC-361)
Solar Power Satellite Systems (E-144)
Space Science Research in the United States (TM-STI-19)
Space Stations and the Law: Selected Legal Issues (BP-ISC-41)
UNISPACE '82: A Context for International Cooperation and Competition (TM-ISC-26)
U.S. - Soviet Cooperation in Space (TM-STI-27)

Transportation

Advanced Space Transportation Technologies
Airport and Air Traffic Control Systems (STI-175)
Airport System Development (STI-231)
Automated Guideway Transit: An Assessment of Personal Rapid Transit and Other New Systems (T-8)
Big Dumb Boosters: A Low Cost Transportation Option (Background Paper)
The Border War On Drugs (O-336)
Changes in the Future Use and Characteristics of the Automobile Transportation System (T-83)
Civilian Space Policy and Applications (STI-177)
The Direct Use of Coal: Prospects and Problems of Production and Combustion (E-86)
Energy From Biological Processes (E-124)
An Evaluation of Railroad Safety (T-61)
Gasohol (TM-E-1)
Gearing Up for Safety: Motor Carrier Safety in a Competitive Environment (SET-382)
Safer Skies With TCAS: Traffic Alert and Collision Avoidance System (SET-431)
Impact of Advanced Air Transport Technology: Pt.1-Advanced High-Speed Aircraft (T-112)
Impact of Advanced Air Transport Technology: Pt.2-Air Cargo (BP-T-10)
Impact of Advanced Air Transport Technology: Pt.3-Air Services to Small Communities (T-170)
Impact of Advanced Air Transport Technology: Pt.4-Financing and Program Alternatives for Advanced High-Speed Aircraft (BP-T-14)
Impact of Advanced Group Rapid Transit Technology (T-106)
Increased Automobile Fuel Efficiency and Synthetic Fuels: Alternatives for Reducing Oil Imports (E-185)
Launch Options for the Future: A Buyer's Guide (ISC-383)
Managing the Nation;s Commercial High-Level Radioactive Waste (O-171)
Mandatory Passive Restraints in Automobiles: Issues and Evidence (BP-H-15)
Oil Transportation by Tankers: An Analysis of Marine Pollution and Safety Measures (O-9)
Piloted Space Transportation Technologies
Reducing Launch Operations Costs: New Technologies and Practices (TM-ISC-28)
Review of the FAA 1982 National Airspace System Plan (STI-176)
Safe Skies for Tomorrow: Aviation Safety in a Competitive Environment (SET-381)
Strategic Materials: Technologies to Reduce U.S. Import Vulnerability (ITE-248)
A Technological Assessment of Coal Slurry Pipelines (E-60)
Transportation of Hazardous Materials (SET-304)
Transportation of Hazardous Materials: State and Local Activities (SET-301)
U.S. Passenger Rail Technologies (STI-222)
Wastes in Marine Environments (O-334)

* Pharmaceutical Research and Development

Office of Technology Assessment
600 Pennsylvania Ave., SE
Washington, DC 20510   (202) 228- 6590

OTA is working on a project to examine trends in the structure, process, and products of pharmaceutical R&D in the U.S., with the goal of developing and implementing a system for estimating and tracking R&D costs over time. The study will also describe the organization of the pharmaceutical R&D enterprise, identifying how costs differ by therapeutic class or biological research area. Contact Judith Wagner, the project director, for more information.

* Science Information Tracer Bullets

Science and Technology Division
Reference Section
Library of Congress
Washington, DC 20540   (202) 707-5580

Informal series of reference guides are issued free from the Science and Technology Division under the general title, *LC Science Tracer Bullet*. These guides are designed to help readers locate published material on subjects about which they have only general knowledge. New titles in the series are announced in the weekly Library of Congress *Information Bulletin* that is distributed to many libraries. The following is a list of *Tracer Bullets* currently available:

TB No.Title

80-1 Green Revolution
80-3 Automotive Electronics
80-4 Aging
80-5 Low-Level Ionizing Radiation:

Science and Technology

* Ozone Depletion and Greenhouse Effect

Office of Technology Assessment
600 Pennsylvania Ave., SE
Washington, DC 20510   (202) 228-6845

OTA is currently studying the major contributors to climate change, ozone depletion, and the greenhouse effect for both the developed and developing world. OTA will identify areas where gains in efficiency, product substitution, conservation, or other options can slow climate change. Contact Rosine Bierbaum, the project director, for more information.

* Patent, Trademark, and Copyright Monitoring

National Patent Council

Crystal Plaza One, 2001 Jefferson Davis Highway, Suite 301, Arlington, VA 22202; (703) 521-1669. The Council provides general information about patents, trademarks, and copyrights, answering just about any question you may have, or will make referrals to other sources of information.

Intellectual Property Owners, Inc.

1255 23rd St., NW, #850, Washington, DC 20037; (202) 466-2396. IPO is a non-profit trade association representing people who own patents, trademarks, and copyrights. It gathers and disseminates information on legislative and regulatory matters, and monitors international events and intellectual property developments. It publishes the *IPO News* which keeps members up- to-date on developments in the field.

Patent Office Society

Commissioner of Patents and Trademarks, 2021 Jefferson Davis Highway, Crystal City, VA 22202; (703) 557-6103, or (703) 557-5698. This professional society for patent examiners promotes the patent system to the general public. It publishes the *Journal of the Patent Office Society* and the *Official Gazette*. The *Official Gazette* is printed every Tuesday for those trying to secure patents. It can be purchased from the Government Printing Office.

Commissioner of Patents and Trademarks

Public Service Center, Office of Patents & Trademarks, 2021 Jefferson Davis Highway, Crystal City, VA 20231; (703) 557-5168. The Center publishes a newsletter that includes a listing of publications and brochures put out by the Patent and Trademark Office. The staff tries to answer all questions such as finding the right office or locating publications. Patent specifications and drawings, as well as trademarks, are $1.50 each. You must have the patent or trademark number.

Search Room--Patents

2021 Jefferson Davis Highway, Crystal City, VA 22202; (703) 557-2276, (703) 557-7800 for general information; (703) 557-2955 for the Scientific Library. This service will search for any patent, and give the vendor's name, the issue date, and the title. You can also go in and search all patents in any field. The Scientific Library contains all US and foreign patents and is open to the public.

Search Room--Trademarks

2021 Jefferson Davis Highway, Crystal City, VA 22202; (703) 557-3281. To search a trademark, you must either go to this office or call the Trademark Library at (703) 557-3281, which is open to the public.

Trademark Information Office

2021 Jefferson Davis Highway, Crystal City, VA 22202; (703) 557-7800. This office will answer questions on different aspects of trademarks, and make available a booklet describing trademarks and what the Patents and Trademarks Office does.

Copyright Office

Reference & Bibliographic Section, Library of Congress, Washington, DC 20559; (202) 479-0700. This office will research the copyright you need and send you the information by mail. Requests must be in writing and you must specify exactly what it is you need to know.

United States Trademark Association

6 East 45th Street, New York, NY 10017; (212) 986-5880. The USTA keeps abreast of all aspects of the trademark field. Forums, educational meetings and an annual meeting are held. It maintains a comprehensive library that offers access to source material on all aspects of trademarks. Publications include *The*

Trademark Reporter, The Executive Newsletter, and over 50 bulletins which are published each year, reporting on general news, publications, and events related to trademark law, advertising, marketing, and design.

American Intellectual Property Law Association

2001 Jefferson Davis Highway, Suite 203, Arlington, VA 22202; (703) 521-1680. AIPLA tries to promote better understanding of the patent, trademark, and copyright systems. Its law library is open to the public which makes available a wide range of material on patents. Publications include *AIPLA Bulletin* ($40/year), *AIPLA Quarterly Journal* ($45/year), and *An Overview of Intellectual Property* ($.25/pamphlet).

* Rural Development and Information Age Technology

Office of Technology Assessment
600 Pennsylvania Ave., SE
Washington, DC 20510   (202) 228-6774

OTA is currently studying how rural America is affected by the information age. The study will help Congress formulate plans for revitalizing the rural economy in a way that takes advantage of technological developments. Contact Linda Garcia, the project director, for more information.

* Rural Health Care

Office of Technology Assessment
600 Pennsylvania Ave., SE
Washington, DC 20510   (202) 228-6590

OTA is currently reviewing and evaluating past and current rural health care efforts; examining how medical technologies have been and might be diffused into rural areas; and identifying policies that might improve the quality, affordability, and accessibility of rural health care. Contact Elaine Power, the project director, for more information.

* Science, Technology, and Social Science Data Base

General Reading Rooms
Library of Congress
Washington, DC 20540   (202) 707-5522

The *Science, Technology, and Social Science Database* is a computerized directory of more than 14,000 organizations or individuals who will provide information to the general public on topics primarily in science, technology, and the social sciences. Citations generally contain the name of the organization or person, mailing address, telephone number, areas of interest, special collections, publications, and special services.

* Securities Markets and Information Technology

Office of Technology Assessment
600 Pennsylvania Ave., SE
Washington, DC 20510   (202) 228-6772

Fundamental changes are taking place in the securities and related financial markets that will affect the structure and operations of the exchanges, the links between markets, the nature of the products traded, and the strategies by which they are traded. OTA is currently studying the role that information technologies--computers and telecommunications--play in these accelerating changes. Contact Vary Coates, the project director, for more information.

* Technical Bibliographies

Published Searches
National Technical Information Service
Department of Commerce
5285 Port Royal Rd.
Springfield, VA 22161   (703) 487-4650

Published Searches contains bibliographies available on more than 3,000 topics from NTIS and 23 international information sources. These specialized bibliographies are created not only from material announced by NTIS, but also from published scientific journal articles gathered from 23 other international information sources. Each bibliography is chosen for its current interest to a particular audience. Most titles are updated annually. For a copy of the NTIS Published Search Master Catalog listing more the 3,000 titles, contact NTIS and ask for *PR-186.*

* Technical Memoranda

Publishing Office
Office of Technology Assessment
600 Pennsylvania Ave., SE
Washington, DC 20510   (202) 224-8996

Issued at the request of Members of Congress, OTA *Technical Memoranda* are issued on specific subjects analyzed in recent OTA reports or in projects currently in process at OTA.

* Technology Assessment Background Papers

Publishing Office
Office of Technology Assessment
600 Pennsylvania Ave., SE
Washington, DC 20510   (202) 224-8996

Useful to a variety of different parties, the information in the *Background Papers* supports formal OTA assessments or is an outcome of internal exploratory planning and evaluation. The papers are free of charge, and can be requested through this office.

* Technology Assessment with Patents

Office of Documentation Information
Patent and Trademark Office
Department of Commerce
1921 Jefferson Davis Hwy., Room 304
Arlington, VA 22202   (703) 557-5652

The Technology Assessment and Forecast (TAF) Program's mission is to stimulate the use and enhance the usability of the more than 27 million documents which make the categorized U.S. patent file. The PTO has assembled the TAF database which covers all U.S. patents. The PTO extracts meaningful information about the U.S. patent file from the TAF database, analyzes the information, and makes it available in a variety of formats. Users of TAF information include patent attorneys, researchers, PTO employees and other government agencies. Patent information from the TAF database is distributed to users through publications, such as *Patent Profiles* and *Technology Assessment and Forecast Reports*, as well as through custom patent reports and statistical reports. Contact this office for more information on the TAF database, and ordering information for TAF publications.

* Technology Catalogs

National Technical Information Service
Department of Commerce
5285 Port Royal Rd.
Springfield, VA 22161   (703) 487-4650

Each of the *Federal Technology Catalogs: Guides to New and Practical Technologies* contains more than 1,000 summaries of selected processes, instruments, materials, equipment, software, services, and techniques. In conjunction with Federal agencies and their laboratories, key practical and applied results are screened for interest to U.S. engineers, research and development managers, and business planners. Most entries give a telephone contact for further detailed information or for specific technical discussion. Each catalog is subdivided into 23 subject headings making it easy to scan for exact references. Each entry includes full bibliographic information, full summaries, and how to obtain additional information. Catalogs are available for each year going back to 1981, and range in price from $27 to $36.00. Contact the Sales Desk to place an order or request the free information brochure, *PR-801.*

* Technology Commercialization

Office of Commercial Affairs
Technology Administration
Department of Commerce
14th St. and Constitution Ave., NW
Room 4203
Washington DC 20230   (202) 377-4743

This office works with industry to develop a consensus regarding technology opportunities and foreign competitive challenges. OCA facilitates cooperative joint ventures with U.S. industry in areas of research and technology development, and aims to improve the ability of U.S. industry to access federally-funded technology. This office also provides specific assistance in targeting and coordinating information activities in areas such as Japanese science and technology and metric conversion. Key activities include facilitating the adoption of flexible computer-integrated manufacturing by small- and medium-sized businesses by encouraging the establishment of private sector-funded joint centers and by working with other federal agencies and industry to remove barriers and create incentives. Contact this office for more information.

* Technology Exchange Programs

International Cooperative Division and Secretariat (P-25)
Office of International Transportation and Trade
Office of the Secretary of Transportation
U.S. Department of Transportation
400 7th Street, SW
Washington, DC 20590   (202) 366-4368

DOT participates in a number of cooperative programs with other countries to exchange mutually beneficial transportation research data and state-of-the-art technical information. Areas of exchange include highway technology; ports and inland waterways; railway technology; and search and rescue operations. China and the Soviet Union are among the countries participating. Contact this office for information about these programs.

Science and Technology

* Technology, Innovation, and U.S. Trade

Office of Technology Assessment
600 Pennsylvania Ave., SE
Washington, DC 20510 (202) 228-6354

The international diffusion of technology has resulted in increased competition from a growing number of countries, in a widening array of products, and cut into the market share of U.S. manufacturers. OTA is currently examining how changes in the competitiveness of U.S. manufacturing industries affect the ability of the U.S. economy to create new jobs in various sectors. The study will also assess how technology, coupled with strategic responses by U.S. firms, could reverse the erosion of U.S. market shares. Contact Julie Gorte, the project director, for more information.

* Technology Policy

Office of Technology Policy
Technology Administration
Department of Commerce
14th St. and Constitution Ave., NW
Room 4818
Washington DC 20230 (202) 377-1581

This office analyzes and advocates the removal of technical and non-technical barriers to the commercialization of technology, including such macroeconomic policies as antitrust, trade, product liability, tax. regulatory, and intellectual property laws. The OTP staff also evaluate civilian technology trends and commercial potential in the U.S., and assesses options for greater cooperation among industry, government, and academia. This office assists state, local, and regional organizations in their support of technology-oriented companies and institutions through a clearinghouse with information on the initiatives and experiences of these organizations to date. Contact this office for more information on technology policy.

* Technology, Productivity, and Innovation

Technology Administration
Department of Commerce
14th St. and Constitution Ave., NW
Room 4824
Washington DC 20230 (202) 377-1984

This administration identifies opportunities or barriers affecting U.S. commercial innovation, quality, productivity, and manufacturing, and advocates Federal policies and programs to eliminate governmentwide statutory, regulatory, or other barriers to the rapid commercialization of U.S. science and technology. The Technology Administration represents U.S. commercial interests in international science and technology agreements and forums, and promotes joint efforts involving business, industry, educational institutions, and state and local organizations to encourage technology commercialization.

* Technological Risks and Opportunities for Future U.S. Energy Supply and Demand

Office of Technology Assessment
600 Pennsylvania Ave., SE
Washington, DC 20510 (202) 228-6275

The OTA is currently studying the current views of the U.S. future energy outlook to identify key technical uncertainties and risks that affect the validity of these views, and to evaluate energy policy options for dealing with these uncertainties and risks. Contact Steven Plotkin, the project director, for more information.

* Technology Resources Directory

National Technical Information Service
Department of Commerce
5285 Port Royal Rd.
Springfield, VA 22161 (703) 487-4650

The *Directory of Federal Laboratory and Technology Resources* guides readers to hundreds of Federal agencies, laboratories, and engineering centers willing to share their expertise, equipment--and sometimes even their facilities--to aid in U.S. research efforts. The current edition contains detailed summaries of more than 1,000 unique resources, including descriptions of some 90 technical information centers. The name, address, and telephone number of a personal contact is listed for each entry, along with a detailed descriptive summary. The directory is available for $36.00. Contact the Sales Desk to place an order or to request the free information brochures, *PR-746* and *PR-801*.

* Technology to Counter Terrorism

Office of Technology Assessment
600 Pennsylvania Ave., SE
Washington, DC 20510 (202) 228-6429

OTA is examining what current R&D--such as explosives detection technology-- is applicable to countering terrorism. The study will identify promising lines of work for further utilization and assess the effectiveness of translating successful technology into actual protection of U.S. citizens, officials, and property. Contact Anthony Fainberg, the project director, for more information.

* Technology Transfer Competitiveness

Technology Transfer Competitiveness
Administrator
Federal Laboratory Consortium
P.O. Box 545
Sequim, WA 98382 (206) 683-1005

The mission of the Consortium is to facilitate technology transfer among government, business, and academic entities in order to foster American economic and technological competitiveness. It sponsors conferences and seminars and publishes a free monthly newsletter (currently no charge). For very specific questions from bona fide researchers who find themselves at an impasse, the Consortium will conduct a database search to refer the inquirer to an appropriate lab. Write or call for a free general information packet explaining the organization, how to access its services, facilities available for testing, and examples of technology transfers.

* Training in the Workplace and

U.S. Competitiveness
Office of Technology Assessment
600 Pennsylvania Ave., SE
Washington, DC 20510 (202) 228-6352

Currently, OTA is exploring the connections between new workplace technologies, employee training, and competitiveness. The study will examine such topics as national investment in training; demographic changes in the work force; employee training in countries that are major industrial competitors of the U.S.; and policy questions concerning existing Federal programs. Contact Wendell Fletcher, the project director, for more information.

* Unconventional Cancer Treatments

Office of Technology Assessment
600 Pennsylvania Ave., SE
Washington, DC 20510 (202) 228-6590

OTA is working on a study that will summarize available information on the major types of unconventional cancer treatments; describe the legal constraints on their availability; and examine the potential for evaluating these new treatments for safety and effectiveness. Contact Jane Sisk, the project director, for more information.Part of the reason we are suffering from an information explosion can be attributed to technology. About 90 percent of all scientific knowledge has been generated since 1950. And, according to the US Department of Commerce, this knowledge is expected to double again in the next ten to fifteen years. Technology, once again, has recaptured the interest and investment of both American business and the public. In 1982 Time magazine selected the computer as its "Man of the Year," and in 1984 President Reagan signed into law a congressional resolution designating September 30 through October 6 as National High Tech Week.

Aerospace Technology

* Advanced Fighter Technology

Ames Research Center
P.O. Box 273
Edwards, CA 93523   (805) 258-8381

Researched is being conducted on the Advanced Fighter Technology Integration (AFTI) F-111 program. The AFTI F-111 features a smooth surface variable camber Mission Adaptive Wing (MAW) which the pilot can adjust depending on flight conditions.

* Aerospace Commercial Assistance

Boeing/Peat Marwick
Commercial Space Group
600 Maryland Avenue, SW
Suite 455
Washington, DC 20024   (202) 479-4240

In 1986, NASA contracted with the Boeing Company and Peat Marwick to provide professional support to companies interested in exploring the potential benefits of space by providing the following services at no charge: current space activity briefings; concept formulation; technical planning and feasibility studies; experiment design assistance; market research; economic feasibility and business planning; financial alternatives and tax analysis; and links with other expertise in academia, industry, or NASA. If you are interested in pursuing a specific project or need assistance in space-related commercial areas, contact this office.

* Aerospace Commercialization Agreements

National Aeronautical and Space Administration
Office of Commercial Programs
Code C/PAO
Washington, DC 20546   (202) 453-1123

NASA uses a number of innovative and functional agreements which provide private industry with assistance, services, and facilities to help reduce the risks associated with their commercial space ventures. This family of agreements include:

Joint Endeavor Agreements: Involving no exchange of funds between NASA and the private company, JEAs are designed to encourage early space ventures and demonstrate the use of space technology to meet marketplace needs. Private industry funds the experiments and NASA provides transportation and other services.

Space Systems Development Agreements: SSDAs provide industry with a deferred payment schedule for Shuttle launch services. This allows the entrepreneur to have a more favorable cash flow during a time when capital investment costs are typically the greatest.

Technical Exchange Agreements: TEAs are designed for companies interested in applying microgravity or other technologies to their commercial operations, but who are not yet ready to commit to a specific space flight experiment or venture. Under the agreement, NASA and a company agree to exchange technical information and cooperate in the conduct and analysis of ground-based research programs. The company funds its own participation, while at the same time gaining direct access to and results from NASA facilities and research.

* Aerospace Commercialization Publications

Office of Commercial Programs
National Aeronautics and Space Administration
Code C/PAO
Washington, DC 20546   (202) 453-1123

The following publications on the commercial applications of space are available from this office:

Spinoff: An illustrated summary of NASA's major aeronautical and space programs, their goals and directions, their contributions to American scientific and technological growth, and their potential for practical benefits in new products and processes.
Aerospace Spinoffs: Twenty-Five Years of Technology Transfer.
Commercial Use of Space: A New Economic Strength for America.
NASA Commercial Programs: A Progress Report 1988.

* Aerospace Commercial Users Catalog

Commercial Development Division (Code CC)
Office of Commercial Programs
National Aeronautics and Space Administration
Washington, DC 20546   (202) 453-1123

This catalog, *Accessing Space: A Catalog of Process Equipment, and Resources for Commercial Users*, provides a broad range of information for the commercial developer of space seeking to understand and experience the areas of microgravity research and remote sensing. This publication provides an inventory along with information about the equipment and facilities that are being used and developed for commercial space applications.

* Aerospace Technology Briefs

Office of Commercial Programs
National Aeronautical and Space Administration
Code C/PAO
Washington, DC 20546   (202) 453-1123

Each issue of NASA's *Tech Briefs* contains concise descriptions of newly developed products and processes arising from NASA research and development efforts, and identifies and highlights information on new aerospace technologies which appear to have potential non-aerospace uses. Once you've identified a specific technology you are interested in, you can request a *Technology Support Package*, which provides more detailed information. Contact this office to be put on the *Tech Briefs* mailing list.

* Ames Research Center

National Aeronautics and Space Administration
Moffett, CA 94035   (415) 965-5091

Located in the heart of "Silicon Valley" at the southern end of San Francisco Bay, Ames specializes in scientific research, exploration, and applications aimed toward creating new technology for the Nation. The center's major program responsibilities are concentrated in computer science and applications, computational and experimental aerodynamics, flight simulation, flight research, hypersonic aircraft, rotorcraft and powered-lift technology, aeronautical and space human factors, life sciences, space sciences, solar system exploration, airborne science and applications, and infrared astronomy. The center also supports military programs, the Space Shuttle, and various civil aviation projects. The center's laboratories are equipped to study solar and geophysical phenomena, life evolution and life environmental factors, and to detect life on other planets.

* Astronaut Candidates

Astronaut Selection Office
Mail Code AHX
Johnson Space Center
Houston, TX 77058

NASA accepts applications on a continuous basis and selects astronaut candidates as needed. Civilians and military personnel are considered for the one-year training program. Current regulations require that preference be given to U.S. citizens when they are available. Contact this office for more information on pilot astronaut or mission specialist opportunities.

* Automated Space Flight

Office of Space Science and Applications
National Aeronautics and Space Administration
400 Maryland Avenue, SW
Washington, DC 20546

The NASA automated space flight program is directed toward scientific investigations of the solar system using ground-based, airborne, and space techniques, including rockets, Earth satellites, and deep space probes. This office oversees research and development activities leading to programs that demonstrate the application of space systems, space environment, and space-related or derived technology for the benefit of the world. These activities involve such disciplines as weather and climate, pollution monitoring, Earth resources survey, and Earth and ocean physics.

* Big Bang Theory

Goddard Space Flight Center
Greenbelt, MD 20771   (301) 286-6255

The Cosmic Background Explorer (COBE), a spacecraft built at Goddard, will be deployed to test the "Big Bang" theory about the origins of our universe, and gain answers to such questions as What started the formation of galaxies? And what caused galaxies to be arranged in giant clusters? Contact Goddard for more information concerning the project.

Science and Technology

* Black Holes, Quasars, and Exploding Galaxies
Goddard Space Flight Center
Greenbelt, MD 20771 (301) 286-6255
The Gamma Ray Observatory (GRO) will try to study the processes that propel the energy-emitting objects of deep space: exploding galaxies, black holes, and quasars. One of the instruments used in this study is the Energetic Gamma-Ray Experiment Telescope. Contact Goddard for more information.

* Balloon Projects at NASA
Goddard Space Flight Center
Wallops Flight Facility
Wallops Island, VA 23337 (804) 824-1579
Wallops manages and coordinates NASA's Scientific Balloon Projects using thin film, helium-filled balloons to provide approximately 45 scientific missions each year. When fully inflated, the balloons can expand to nearly 600 feet in diameter with a volume of more than 50 million cubic feet. Contact Wallops for more information.

* Business in Space
Office of Commercial Programs
National Aeronautics and Space Administration
400 Maryland Avenue, SW, Code C
Washington, DC 202546 (202) 453-1030
This office provides the focus within NASA for an agency-wide program to expand U.S. private sector investment and involvement in civil space activities. The office is responsible for programs actively supporting new, high technology commercial space ventures, the commercial application of existing aeronautics and space technology, and expanding commercial access to available NASA capabilities and services.

* Centers for the Commercial Development of Space
Office of Commercial Programs
Commercial Development Division
National Aeronautics and Space Administration
Washington, DC 20546 (202) 453-1123
NASA's 16 Centers for the Commercial Development of Space are non-profit consortia of industry, universities, and government which conduct space-based, high-technology research and development in specific areas ranging from materials processing to remote sensing. These CCDS serve as incubators for future commercial space ventures, enabling their industrial affiliates to explore the economic value of space in a program where financial and technical risks are shared. For more information on becoming an industrial affiliate, contact one of the following centers:

Center for Advanced Materials
Battelle Columbus Laboratories, 505 King Avenue, Columbus, OH 43201-2693; (614) 424-7240.

Center for Macromolecular Crystallography
University of Alabama-Birmingham, THT-Box 79, University Station, Birmingham, AL 35294; (205) 934-5329.

Consortium for Materials Development in Space
University of Alabama-Huntsville, Research Institute Building, Huntsville, AL 35899; (205) 895-6620.

Center for Advanced Space Propulsion
University of Tennessee Space Institute, P.O. Box 1385, Tullahoma, TN 37388-8897; (615) 454-9294.

Center for Space Processing of Engineering Materials
Vanderbilt University, Box 6309-Station B, Nashville, TN 37235; (615) 322-7047.

Center for Development of Commercial Crystal Growth in Space
Center for Advanced Materials Processing
Clarkson University, Potsdam, NY 13676; (315) 268-2336.

Space Vacuum Epitaxy Center
University of Houston, Science and Research Building I, 4800 Calhoun, Houston, TX 77204; (713) 749-3701.

Center for Mapping
Ohio State University, 1958 Neil Avenue, Columbus, OH 43210-1247; (614) 292-6642.

Center for Space Automation and Robotics
University of Wisconsin-Madison, 1357 University Avenue, Madison, WI 53706; (608) 262-5524.

Space Power Institute
Auburn University, 231 Leach Center, Auburn, AL 36849-5320; (205) 826-5894

Center for Materials for Space Structures

Case Western Reserve University, School of Engineering, 10900 Euclid Avenue, Cleveland, OH 44106; (216) 368-4222.

Center for Bioserve Research
University of Colorado-Boulder, School of Aerospace Engineering, Campus Box 429, Boulder, CO 80309; (303) 492-7613.

Center for Autonomous & Man-Controlled Robotic & Sensing Systems (CAMRSS)
Environmental Research Institute of Michigan, P.O. Box 8618, Ann Arbor, MI 48107-8618; (313) 994-1200.

Center for Cell Research
Pennsylvania State University, 465 N. Frear Laboratory, University Park, PA 16802; (814) 865-2408.

Center for Space Power
Space Research Center, Zachry Building, Room 218, Texas A&M University, College Station, TX 77843; (409) 845-7441.

ITD Space Remote Sensing Center
Bldg. 1103, Suite 118, Stennis Space Center, MS 39529; (601) 688-2509.

* Industrial Applications Centers

Indianapolis
Aerospace Research Applications Center, 611 N. Capitol Avenue, Indianapolis, IN 46204; (317) 262-5003.

Durant
Central Industrial Applications Center, P.O. Box 1335, Durant, OK 74702; (405) 924-5094.

Pittsburgh
NASA Industrial Applications Center, 823 William Pitt Union, Pittsburgh, PA 15260; (412) 648-7000.

Los Angeles
NASA Industrial Applications Center, Research Annex, Room 200, University of Southern California, 3716 South Hope Street, Los Angeles, CA 90007; (213) 743-8988.

Tolland
NERAC, Inc., New England Research Applications Center, One Technology Drive, Tolland, CT 06084; (203) 872-1749.

Raleigh
North Carolina Science and Technology Research Center, P.O. Box 12235, Research Triangle Park, NC 27709; (919) 549-0671.

Alachua
Technology Applications Center, One Progress Boulevard, Box 24, Alachua, FL 32615; (904) 462-3913.

Lexington
NASA/UK Technology Applications Program, 109 Kinkead Hall, University of Kentucky, Lexington, KY 40506; (606) 257-6322.

Baton Rouge
NASA/SU Industrial Applications Center, P.O. Box 9221, Department of Computer Science, Southern University, Baton Rouge, LA 70813; (504) 771-2060.

* Challenger Center for Space Science Education
1101 King St.
Suite 190
Alexandria, VA 22314 (703) 683-9740
The Challenger Center, founded as a living memorial to the *Challenger* crew, plans to construct a series of simulated space environment centers linked to museums, science centers, and school districts throughout the world through a comprehensive, international endowment program. The first center, the Challenger Center Space-Life Station, will be build in the Washington, D.C., area, and will serve as headquarters for the network. An educator membership is available that includes a journal, newsletter, updates, and conference information.

* Commercial Flight Program
Office of Commercial Programs
National Aeronautics and Space Administration
Code C/PAO
Washington, DC 20546 (202) 453-1123
Under this program, businesses can gain access to NASA space capabilities and use the unique environment of space to conduct investigations that may lead to new, high-value products and technological advances. Certain portions of the

Space Shuttle, Spacelab, and the Space Station Freedom payloads, for example, are being set aside for commercial uses.

* Commercial Payloads Video

Office of Commercial Programs
Commercial Development Division
National Aeronautics and Space Administration
Washington, DC 20546 (202) 453-1123

NASA's Commercial Development Division is producing a videotape which shows how commercial payloads on spacecraft are developed, managed, and processed. The film is designed to provide viewers with a perspective on the basic flow of payload processing from concept, through ground processing, to post-mission analysis. It will be available through NASA's Headquarters, Centers for the Commercial Development of Space, and Field Centers.

* Commercial Programs Advisory Committee

National Aeronautics and Space Administration
Office of Commercial Programs
Washington, DC 20546 (202) 453-1123

As a subcommittee of the NASA Advisory Council, the CPAC assists NASA by reviewing policies and programs, and recommending strategies to implement the national space policy goals to promote greater investment and participation by the U.S. private sector in America's civil space program. The Committee holds meetings that are open to the public. A free brochure, *Charting the Course: U.S. Space Enterprise and Space Industrial Competitiveness*, which includes highlights of the Committee's findings, is available.

* Commercial Programs Newsletter

Office of Commercial Programs
National Aeronautics and Space Administration
Code C/PAO
Washington, DC 20546 (202) 453-1123

The free bimonthly publication, *Office of Commercial Programs Newsletter*, covers the latest news related to the NASA's commercial programs, including new publications, projects, committee meetings, grants, congressional actions, and technology transfer. For more information on obtaining copies, contact this office.

* Computer Software Management and Information Center

University of Georgia
382 E. Board Street
Athens, GA 30602 (404) 542-3265

NASA and other government agencies develop many types of computer programs that frequently can be adapted--with little or no modification--to secondary uses, often remote from their original purpose. In the interests of national productivity, COSMIC offers adaptable programs to business and industry at a fraction of their original cost. COSMIC publishes, in four different formats, a catalog of the some 1,400 programs available for purchase: on microfiche ($10); printed copies ($25); on IBM PC-compatible diskettes ($30); and on computer magnetic tape ($50).

* Deep Space Network

Jet Propulsion Laboratory
4800 Oak Grove Drive
Pasadena, CA 91109 (818) 354-7006

JPL operates the worldwide deep space tracking and data acquisition network (DSN). As part of its DSN facilities, JPL oversees the use of the world's largest satellite receiving dishes located near Death Valley, California, measuring over 90 meters in diameter each.

* Dryden Flight Research Facility

Ames Research Center
Hugh L. Dryden Flight Research Facility
P.O. Box 273
Edwards, CA 93523 (805) 258-8381

Located at in the Mojave Desert about 80 miles north of Los Angeles, California, Ames-Dryden has developed a unique and highly specialized capability for conducting flight research programs. The facility was actively involved in the Approach and Landing Tests of the Space Shuttle Orbiter Enterprise and continues to support Shuttle landings from space. Currently, Ames-Dryden is conducting research on the X-29 program in a variety of advanced aero technologies, including forward swept wings, aeroelastic tailoring, and thin supercritical wings.

* Earth Observing System (EOS)

Goddard Space Flight Center
Greenbelt, MD 20771 (301) 286-8955

Eos, the Earth Observing System, is a planned NASA program for observing the Earth from space using unmanned platforms in conjunction with the Space Station. Its goal is to understand the Earth as an integrated system. The platform will be equipped with remote sensing instruments, and launched into polar orbit so that all parts of the globe can be viewed. Contact Goddard for more information.

* Goddard Space Flight Center

Greenbelt, MD 20771 (301) 286-6255

Located 10 miles northeast of Washington, D.C., Goddard's research is centered in six space and Earth Science laboratories and in the management, development, and operation of several near-Earth space systems: The Hubble Space Telescope will become an important astronomical telescope in space when deployed by the Space Shuttle to study the stars, planets, and interstellar space. The Upper Atmosphere Research Satellite will be launched to look back at Earth's atmosphere to help understand its composition and dynamics. As part of the Space Station program, Goddard will develop the detailed design, construction, and test and evaluation of the automated free-flying polar platform and provisions for instruments and payloads to be attached externally to the Space Station.

* Hubble Space Telescope

Goddard Space Flight Center
Greenbelt, MD 20771 (301) 286-6255

When deployed by the Space Shuttle, the Hubble Space Telescope will become an important astronomical telescope in space. Its movements will be controlled from Goddard's Space Telescope Operations Control Center, as the observatory's five scientific instruments study the stars, planets, and interstellar space. The Space Telescope Science Institute in Baltimore, Maryland, will analyze much of the data generated from the Hubble Space Telescope.

* Jet Propulsion Laboratory

4800 Oak Grove Drive
Pasadena, CA 91109 (818) 354-7006

Located 20 miles northeast of Los Angeles, California, JPL is engaged in activities associated with deep space automated scientific missions--engineering subsystem and instrument development, and data reduction and analysis required in deep space flight. Current NASA flight projects under JPL include Voyager, Galileo, Magellan, and the Mars Observer. JPL also designs and tests flight systems, including complete spacecraft, and provides technical direction to contractor organizations. JPL also operates the worldwide deep space tracking and data acquisition network (DSN) and maintains a substantial technology program to support present and future NASA flight projects.

* Langley Research Center

Hampton, VA 23665-5225 (804) 864-6123

Located about 100 miles south of Washington, D.C., Langley's primary mission is the research and development of advanced concepts and technology for future aircraft and spacecraft systems, with particular emphasis on environmental effects, performance, range, safety, and economy. Examples of this research are projects involving flight simulation, composite structural materials, and automatic flight control systems. Work is continuing in the development of technology for avionic systems for reliable operations in terminal areas of the future. Efforts continue to improve supersonic flight capabilities for both transport and military aircraft. The center also works with the general aviation industry to help solve problems concerning aircraft design and load requirements and to improve flight operations. Langley's newest major project is developing technology for the National Aero-Space Plane.

* Manned Space Flight Research

Lyndon B. Johnson Space Center
Houston, TX 77058 (713) 483-3671

Located 20 miles southeast of downtown Houston, Texas, the Johnson Center is NASA's primary center for design, development, and testing of spacecraft and related systems for manned flight; selection and training of astronauts; planning and conducting manned missions; and extensive participation in the medical, engineering, and scientific experiments carried aboard space flights. Johnson has program management responsibility for the Space Shuttle program and the Space Station, along with the interfaces between the two. The Johnson Center also directs the operations of the White Sands Test Facility in Las Cruces, New Mexico, which supports the Space Shuttle propulsion system, power system, and materials testing.

* Marshall Space Flight Center

Huntsville, AL 35812 (216) 433-6043

Located in Huntsville, Alabama, the Marshall Center, along with being NASA's launch vehicle development center, manages projects involving scientific investigation and application of space technology to the solution of problems on Earth. The Center provides the Shuttle orbiter's engines, the external tank that carries liquid hydrogen and liquid oxygen for those engines, and the solid rocket

Science and Technology

boosters that assist in lifting the Shuttle orbiter from the launch pad. Marshall's Orbital Maneuvering Vehicle will be carried into orbit also by the Shuttle to perform a number of activities, including moving satellites from one orbit to another. Marshall will also design the living and working, laboratory, and life support modules for the Space Station, along with an environmental control system.

* Michoud Assembly Facility
P.O. Box 29300
New Orleans, LA 70189   (504) 257-2601
Located about 15 miles east of downtown New Orleans, Louisiana, Michoud's primary mission is the systems engineering, engineering design, manufacture, fabrication, and assembly for the Space Shuttle external tank.

* NASA Activities Newsletter
Superintendent of Documents
Government Printing Office
Washington, DC 20402   (202) 783-3238
NASA Activities covers current agency highlights, including new programs and projects, personnel activities, field center news, relevant legislation, community activities, and more. It is available by subscription from GPO for $8.00 per year.

* NASA Formal Series Reports
National Technical Information Service
Springfield, VA 22161   (703) 487-4630
Through NTIS you can obtain full copies of scientific and technical reports produced by NASA. Original copies of these reports are sent to you as they are printed, even before they are announced to the general public by NASA. You can order reports under one of the ten following categories: Aeronautics, Astronautics, Chemistry and Materials, Engineering, Geosciences, Life Sciences, Mathematical and Computer Sciences, Physics, Social Sciences, and Space Sciences. Price per copy is $15.

* NASA Headquarters
400 Maryland Avenue, SW
Washington, DC 20546   (202) 453-1000
NASA Headquarters manages the space flight centers, research centers, and other installations that make up the National Aeronautics and Space Administration. The staff at Headquarters determine the programs and projects; establish management policies, procedures, and performance criteria; evaluate progress; review and analyzes all phases of the aerospace program.

* NASA Monetary Awards for Inventions
Staff Director
Inventions and Contributions Board
National Aeronautics and Space Administration
Washington, DC 20546   (202) 453-2890
NASA makes monetary awards to individuals or organizations for scientific or technical contributions which have been used and have proven to be of verifiable value to NASA. Many qualified contributions have been produced during the performance of contracts for NASA. Contact this office for information concerning the criteria for eligibility and the procedure for submitting an application for an award.

* NASA Patent Bibliography
National Technical Information Service
5285 Port Royal Road
Springfield, VA 22101   (703) 487-4600
The *NASA Patent Abstracts Bibliography*, a semiannual updated compendium of over 4,000 NASA patented inventions, is published as a service to companies, firms, and individuals seeking new licensable products for the commercial market. For convenience, each issue has a separately bound *Abstract Section* ($13.75 per issue) and *Index Section* ($29 per copy). The *Abstract Section* covers only the indicated 6 month period, while the *Index Section* is cumulative, covering all NASA-owned inventions announced since May 1969.

* NASA Procurement Report
National Aeronautics and Space Administration
Office of Procurement
Code HM
Washington, DC 20546   (202) 453-2130
The *NASA Semiannual Procurement Report* presents summary data on all NASA procurement actions and detailed information on contracts, grants, agreements, and other procurements over $25,000 awarded by NASA during a six month period. Contact this office for your free copy.

* NASA STAR Journal
National Technical Information Service

Springfield, VA 22161   (703) 487-4630
The *NASA STAR Journal* is a microfiche copy of NASA's biweekly *STAR* journal, which indexes and abstracts all of NASA's research and development results, as well as other research and engineering related to aerodynamics and space. The price is $70 per year for 24 issues.

* National Space Technology Laboratories
NSTL, MS 39529
Located near Bay St. Louis, Mississippi, NSTL's main mission is the support of Space Shuttle main engine and main orbiter propulsion system testing. NSTL is also a center of excellence in the area of remote sensing and is involved in Earth sciences programs of national and international significance, which are conducted at its Earth Resources Laboratory. NSTL also conducts data systems and commercial utilization studies in support of the Space Station.

* Oceans and Space
Goddard Space Flight Center
Greenbelt, MD 20771   (301) 286-8955
NASA's Laboratory for Oceans at Goddard works to expand the applications of space technology in oceanographic research by demonstrating new research uses of satellite data and by initiating new flight instrument concepts for satellite flight missions.

* Ozone and Chlorofluorocarbons
Goddard Space Flight Center
Greenbelt, MD 20771   (301) 286-8955
Using such tools as Goddard's Total Ozone Mapping Spectrometer (TOMS) aboard the Nimbus-7 Spacecraft, NASA conducts research missions over Antarctica and Arctic regions to measure ozone, aerosol profiles, and other constituents of the atmosphere. Recent studies look at the relationship between fluorocarbons and ozone holes in the atmosphere. Contact Goddard for more information.

* Propulsion Systems Research
Lewis Research Center
21000 Brookpart Road
Cleveland, OH 44135   (216) 433-2942
Located about 20 miles southwest of Cleveland, Ohio, Lewis is NASA's leading center for research, technology, and development in aircraft propulsion, space propulsion, space power, and satellite communication. Lewis has the responsibility for developing the largest space power system ever designed to provide the electrical power necessary to accommodate the life support systems and research experiments to be conducted aboard the Space Station. In addition, Lewis will support the Station in other major areas, such as auxiliary propulsion systems and communications. Other facilities here include a zero-gravity drop tower, wind tunnels, space environment tanks, chemical rocket thrust stands, and chambers for testing jet engine efficiency and noise.

* Robot Space Retrieving Equipment
Goddard Space Flight Center
Greenbelt, MD 20771   (301) 286-8955
NASA is developing an autonomous free flying robot for retrieving equipment or a spacewalking astronaut drifting in separated flight near the Space Station. Recent test flights have been flown from the Space Shuttle's cargo bay. Contact Goddard for more information.

* Spacecraft and Launch Vehicles
Office of Space Operations
National Aeronautics and Space Administration
400 Maryland Avenue, SW, Code T
Washington, DC 20546   (202) 453-2019
This office tracks activities involving aeronautical research aircraft, space launch vehicles, and spacecraft. It also acquires and distributes technical and scientific data from these spacecraft. Contact this office for more information on this subject.

* Space Exploration
Office of Exploration
National Aeronautics and Space Administration
400 Maryland Avenue, SW, Code Z
Washington, DC 20546   (202) 453-8928
The office develops long range plans for exploration and expansion of human presence beyond Earth into the solar system, along with a roadmap which provides opportunities and options leading to the commitment to national space exploration initiatives by 1992.

* Space Launches
John F. Kennedy Space Center

Kennedy Space Center, FL 32899   (407) 867-2201

Located on the east coast of Florida, 150 miles south of Jacksonville, the Kennedy Space Center serves as the primary center within NASA for the test, checkout, and launch of space vehicles, which presently includes the launch of manned and unmanned vehicles at Kennedy, Cape Canaveral, and Vandenberg Air Force base in California. The Center is also responsible for the assembly, checkout, and launch of Space Shuttle vehicles and their payloads, landing operations, and the turn-around of Space shuttle orbiters between missions.

* Space Research and Technology

Office of Aeronautics and Space Technology (OAST)
National Aeronautics and Space Administration
400 Maryland Avenue, SW, Code R
Washington, DC 20546   (202) 453-2693

This office plans, directs, executes, evaluates, documents, and distributes the results of NASA research and technology development programs. These programs are conducted primarily to demonstrate the feasibility of a concept, structure, or component system which may have general application to the nation's aeronautical and space objectives. For information on specific research programs, contact this NASA office.

* Space Shuttle and Spacelab

Office of Space Flight
National Aeronautics and Space Administration
400 Maryland Avenue, SW, Code M
Washington, DC 20546   (202) 453-1132

To permit humans to explore space and perform missions which will lead to increased knowledge and the quality of life on Earth, this office directs the development of space transportation and the required supporting systems for humans to perform missions in space. One of the major program now underway is the Space Shuttle, and this office is responsible for scheduling Space Shuttle flights, including the Spacelab. This office also develops financial plans and pricing structures for these flights; provides services to users; manages expendable launch services and upper stages; and manages of NASA's advanced program activities.

* Space Station

Office of Space Station
National Aeronautics and Space Administration
400 Maryland Avenue, SW, Code S
Washington, DC 20546   (202) 453-2015

This office manages and directs all aspects of NASA's Space Station program whose goal is to develop a permanently manned Space Station by the mid 1990s; to encourage other nations to participate in the Space Station program; and to promote private sector investment in space through enhanced space-based operational capabilities.

* Space-Type Freeze-Dehydrated Foods

GEWA Visitor Center Gift Shop
Goddard Space Flight Center
Greenbelt, MD 20771   (301) 286-6476

The Gift Shop at Goddard sells samples of foods that astronauts eat during space flights. The food, however, is for sale only in the Gift Shop--no mail orders. Other companies that can provide you with information on space-type, freeze dried foods include the following: Spaceland Enterprises, Inc., 1970 Carroll Ave., San Francisco, CA 94124; and Sky-Lab Foods, Inc., 177 Lake Street, White Plains, NY 10604.

* Satellite-Aided Search and Rescue

Goddard Space Flight Center
Greenbelt, MD 20771   (301) 286-6256

In a cooperative project sponsored by the U.S., Canada, France, and the Soviet Union, NASA is working on a satellite system, SARSAT, that greatly reduces the time required to rescue air, sea, and other distress victims and to find victims which otherwise might not be found. Contact Goddard for more information.

* Satellite Repair In Space

Goddard Space Flight Center
Greenbelt, MD 20771   (301) 286-8955

The Satellite Servicing Project is working on ways to expand the operational life of satellites to be launched in the future. Not only does this project repair satellites, it also allow for planned routine maintenance calls in space which will maximize the longevity of the satellites and save money. Contact Goddard for more information.

* Space Telescope Science Institute

Johns Hopkins Homewood Campus
Baltimore, MD 21218   (301) 338-4757

Located in Baltimore, Maryland, STSI plans and conducts science operations for the Edwin P. Hubble Space Telescope, a cooperative venture between NASA and the European Space Agency (ESA). Scheduled for launch aboard the Space shuttle, the telescope spacecraft will orbit the Earth at approximately 350 miles sending data and receiving commands through NASA's Tracking and Data Relay Satellite System.

* Super-Maneuverable Jet Fighter

Ames Research Center
Hugh L. Dryden Flight Research Facility
P.O. Box 273
Edwards, CA 93523   (805) 258-8381

Ames-Dryden is testing a specially instrumented F-18 fighter jet to investigate high alpha or high angle of attack flight which may result in airplanes capable of "supermaneuvers." Contact Ames for more information.

* Technology Transfer Statistics

Office of Commercial Programs
National Aeronautical and Space Administration
Washington, DC 20546   (202) 453-1123

NASA is currently studying the economic impact of their technology transfer programs in both the aerospace industry and the nation at large. When completed, the study will be available through this office. For more information on the study, contact this office.

* Technology Utilization Officers

Technology Utilization Division
NASA Scientific and Technical Information
Facility
P.O. Box 8757
Baltimore, MD 21240

Within the NASA technology transfer network, Technology Utilization Officers (TUOs) are placed at each of NASA's field centers. They work with industry, providing information on new technologies developed at the center and matching and cross-correlating NASA technologies with industrial needs. They also provide a link to NASA's engineers and scientists, who can help clients locate, adapt, and implement NASA technology. The following is a list of the NASA field centers and their technology utilization officers.

Ames Research Center, Mail Code 223-3, Moffett Field, CA 94035/Larry Milov/(415) 694-6471.

Goddard Space Flight Center, Mail Code 702, Greenbelt, MD 20771/Donald Friedman/(301) 286-6242.

Lyndon B. Johnson Space Center, Mail Code EA4, NASA Road One, Houston, TX 77058/Dean Glenn/(713) 483-3809

Langley Research Center, Mail Stop 139A, Hampton, VA 23665/John Samos/(804) 865-3281.

Marshall Space Flight Center, Code AT01, MSFC, AL 35812/Ismail Akbay/(205) 544-2223.

Lewis Research Center, Mail Stop 7-3, 21000 Brookpark Road, Cleveland, OH 44135/Daniel Soltis/(216) 433-5567.

Jet Propulsion Laboratory, Mail Stop 156-211, 4800 Oak Grove Drive, Pasadena, CA 91109/Norman Chalfin/(818) 354-2240.

National Space Technology Laboratories, Code GA-00, NSTL Station, MS 39529/Robert Barlow/(601) 688-1929.

John F. Kennedy Space Center, Mail Stop PT-TPO-A, Kennedy Space Center, FL 32899/Thomas Hammond/(305) 867-3017.

NASA Resident Office-JPL, Mail Stop 180-801, 4800 Oak Grove Drive, Pasadena, CA 91109/Gordon Chapman/(818) 354-4849.

* Tethered Satellite System

Marshall Space Flight Center
Huntsville, AL 35812   (216) 433-6043

Marshall manages the Tethered Satellite System, expected to be in orbit by 1990, which will be carried by the Space Shuttle into space and suspended from the orbiter's cargo bay on a tether to study electrodynamic phenomena and the Earth's upper atmosphere for magnetospheric, atmospheric, and gravitational data.

* Tracking and Data Relay Satellite System

Goddard Space Flight Center
Greenbelt, MD 20771   (301) 286-6255

Voice and data transmissions between Earth and orbital regions are multiplying rapidly, and to accommodate this communications growth NASA is building a new Earth-to-orbit and orbit-to-Earth communications link called the Tracking and Data Relay Satellite System. When completed, TDRSS, along with two other communications satellites, will comprise NASA's Space Network, and will be one of the biggest advances in space communications technology to date. For more information, contact Goddard.

* Transonic Wind Tunnels

Science and Technology

Langley Research Center
Hampton, VA 23665-5225   (804) 864-6123
Included in Langley's research labs are a variety of wind tunnels covering the entire Mach-number speed range. The National Transonic Facility is a new cryogenic wind tunnel providing a unique opportunity for conducting high Reynolds number research at subsonic and transonic speeds.

* Upper Atmosphere Research Satellite (UARS)
Goddard Space Flight Center
Greenbelt, MD 20771   (301) 286-8955
To investigate current upper atmospheric changes, UARS will provide for the first time the global data required in probing the chemistry, dynamics, and radiative inputs of the stratosphere and mesosphere. Contact Goddard for more information.

* Wallops Flight Facility
Goddard Space Flight Center
Wallops Island, VA 23337   (804) 824-1579
A part of Goddard Space Flight Center, Wallops manages and implements NASA's sounding rocket projects which use suborbital rocket vehicles to accommodate approximately 50 scientific missions each year. Approximately 100-150 rocket launches are conducted each year from the Wallops Island site. In cooperative and commercial projects, Wallops provides support which includes launching, tracking, aircraft flights, and data reduction, to various segments of the Department of Defense and commercial and educational ventures. Wallops also conducts Earth and ocean physics, ocean biological and atmospheric science field experiments; satellite correlative measurements; and developmental projects for new remote sensor systems.

* X-Ray Astrophysics
Goddard Space Flight Center
Greenbelt, MD 20771   (301) 286-8955
When completed, NASA's X-ray Astrophysics Facility (AXAF) will permit astronomers to extend their observations of the cosmos beyond the normal visible band to the X-ray region of the spectrum, providing valuable new information on phenomena spanning our Milky Way galaxy and stretching to the farthest reaches of the known universe. Contact Goddard for more information.

Geology and Earth Science

* Drilling Core Library

Core Library
U.S. Geological Survey
MS 975, Building 810
Box 25046, Federal Center
Denver, CO 80225   (303) 236-1931

The USGS Core Library collects, stores, and makes available to the public valuable core material from boreholes drilled for oil and gas. The cores are collected from a variety of public and private sources, most of them being from the Rocky Mountain and the Great Plains regions. The cores are processed into core slabs, a more usable and easily archived form. You can examine the processed cores at the facility.

* Earth Science Bibliography

Superintendent of Documents
Government Printing Office
Washington, DC 20402   (202) 783-3238

Earthquake and volcano publications are listed in this bibliography. *Earthquakes and Volcanoes*, a bimonthly subscription service is featured at an annual cost of $6.50. The *Preliminary Determination of Epicenters* subscription service is listed at a yearly cost of $14.00. Space and satellite publications are also included. Free.

* Earth Science Information Centers

Reston-ESIC
U.S. Geological Survey
507 National Center
Reston, VA 22092   (703) 648-6045

The Earth Science Information Office operates a nationwide information and sales service for the results of earth science research, maps, and related products and publications. A network of Earth Science Information Centers provides information about geologic, hydrologic, topographic, and land-use maps; books and reports; aerial, satellite, and radar images and related products; earth science and map data in digital form and related applications software; and geodetic data. ESIC offices can take orders for such customized products as aerial photographs and orthophotoquads, digital cartographic data, and geographic names gazetteers. These centers also function as over-the-counter dealers for USGS books and maps.

Anchorage
ESIC, U.S. Geological Survey, 4230 University Dr., Room 101, Anchorage, AK 99508-4664; (907) 561-5555

Anchorage
ESIC, U.S. Geological Survey, U.S. Courthouse, Room 113, 222 W. 7th Ave., #53, Anchorage, AK 99513-7546; (907) 271-4307

Denver
ESIC, U.S. Geological Survey, 169 Federal Building, 1961 Stout St., Denver, CO 80294; (303) 844-4169

Lakewood
ESIC, U.S. Geological Survey, Box 25046, Federal Center, MS 504, Denver, CO, 80225-0046; (303) 236-5829

Los Angeles
ESIC, U.S. Geological Survey, Federal Building, Room 7638, 300 N. Los Angeles St., Los Angeles, CA 90012; (213) 894-2850

Menlo Park
ESIC, U.S. Geological Survey, Building 3, MS 532, 345 Middlefield Rd., Menlo Park, CA 94025; (415) 329-4309

Reston
ESIC, U.S. Geological Survey, 507 National Center, Reston, VA 22092; (703) 648-6045

Rolla
ESIC, U.S. Geological Survey, 1400 Independence Rd., MS 231, Rolla, MO 65401; (314) 341-0851

Salt Lake City
ESIC, U.S. Geological Survey, 8105 Federal Building, 125 S. State St., Salt Lake City, UT 84138; (801) 524-5652

San Francisco

ESIC,U.S. Geological Survey, 504 Custom House, 555 Battery St., San Francisco, CA 94111; (415) 556-5627

Spokane
ESIC, U.S. Geological Survey, 678 U.S. Courthouse, W. 920 Riverside Ave., Spokane, WA 99201; (509) 353-2524

Stennis Space Center
ESIC, U.S. Geological Survey, Bldg. 3101, Stennis Space Center, MS 39529; (601) 688-3544

Washington, D.C.
ESIC, U.S. Geological Survey, Department of the Interior Building, 18th & C Sts., NW, Room 2650, Washington, DC 20240; (202) 343-8073

* Earth Science Teaching Materials

Geologic Inquiries Group
U.S. Geological Survey
907 National Center
Reston, VA 22092   (703) 648-4383

Packets of geological teaching aids for different grade levels and geographic location are available from the Geologic Inquiries Group and from the Earth Science Information Centers listed elsewhere in this book. These packets include lists of reference materials, various maps and map indexes, and a selection of general interest publications. Requests for teachers packets should be sent on school letterhead, indicating the grade level and subject of interest.

* Environmental Geology

Geologic Division
U.S. Geological Survey
National Center, MS 911
Reston, VA 22092   (703) 648-6600

The U.S. Geological Survey conducts geologic mapping and gathers other basic information about the Nation's geologic framework and the processes that have shaped it. Scientists also determine the age and distribution of different types of rocks, climatic changes and their effect on land and water resources, and variations in the Earth's gravity and magnetic field.

* Geodetic Information

National Geodetic Data Center
National Ocean Service
National Oceanic and Atmospheric Administration
Department of Commerce
11400 Rockville Pike
Rockville, MD 20852   (301) 443-8631

The National Geodetic Data Center collects, maintains, publishes, and distributes a complete range of information pertaining to the National Geodetic Reference System, including data on vertical and horizontal geodetic survey stations, geodetic control diagrams for the conterminous United States, Alaska, and Hawaii, gravity values for over 1 million points, calibration base line data, astronomic and Doppler satellite data, computer programs for geodetic applications, and geodetic publications and historical records. NGDC has catalogs available describing a variety of maps, slide sets, and educational tools which are appropriate for both technical and non-technical audiences. Data is broken down into ten categories: solid earth geophysics, earthquake seismology, geomagnetic survey data, marine geological data, marine geophysical data, solar-terrestrial data, solar activity data, geomagnetic variations data, ionospheric data and glaciology. Databases, bulletins, and reports are available within each category. A *Directory of Data Services* lists researchers who can be contacted for technical information about data and products.

* Geologic Names Committee

U.S. Geological Survey
National Center, MS 902
Reston, VA 22092   (703) 648-4311

The Geologic Names Committee defines and recommends policy and rules governing stratigraphic nomenclature and classification for the USGS. *Stratigraphic Notes* is published to announce changes in official geologic names usage. Lexicons are compiled that show domestic geologic names usage, and a file is maintained of geologic names reserved future use.

* Geologic Inquiries

Science and Technology

U.S. Geological Survey
National Center, MS 907
Reston, VA 22092   (301) 648-4383
To obtain technical information on such geologic topics as earthquakes and volcanoes, energy and mineral resources, the geology of specific areas, and geologic maps, contact this office.

* Geologic Science

Office of Scientific Publications
Geologic Division
U.S. Geological Survey
National Center, MS 904
Reston, VA 22092   (703) 648-6077
This office reviews all scientific publications in the geologic field for scientific accuracy. Both internal and outside publications are analyzed. All must comply with the Geological Survey's standards.

* Geophysical and Solar-Terrestrial Information

National Geophysical Data Center
National Oceanic and Atmospheric Administration
Department of Commerce
325 Broadway
Boulder, CO 80303   (303) 497-6215
The National Geophysical Data Center combines in a single center all data activities in the fields of solid earth geophysics, marine geology and geophysics, and solar-terrestrial physics. NGDC produces numerous publications which catalog and document data. In addition, NGDC has available a variety of maps, slide sets, and educational tools which are appropriate for both technical and non-technical audiences.

* International Geology

Geologic Division
U.S. Geological Survey
National Center, MS 917
Reston, VA 22092   (703) 648-6047
Through scientific cooperation and exchange programs, this office coordinates geologic activities and research with other countries, including developing nations.

* Landslide Information

Landslide Information Center
U.S. Geological Survey
Box 25046, MS 966, Federal Center
Denver, CO 80225   (303) 236-1599
This center responds to inquiries on landslide research and maintains files of landslide documents, newspaper clippings, and photographs that may be examined or photocopied at the Center.

* Earthquakes and Other U.S. Geological Survey Publications

U.S. Geological Survey
Book and Report Sales
Box 25425
Denver, CO 80225   (303) 236-7476
This is a listing of some of the general interest publications available through the U.S. Geological Survey. They are free unless otherwise indicated.

The Antarctic and its Geology
Earthquakes
Eruptions of Hawaiian Volcanoes: Past, Present and Future ($4.00)
Eruptions of Mount St. Helens: Past, Present, and Future ($2.75)
Geologic History of Cape Cod, Massachusetts
Geology of Caves
The Great Ice Age
The Interior of the Earth

Landforms of the United States
Marine Geology: Research Beneath the Sea
Our Changing Continent
Permafrost
Safety and Survival in an Earthquake
The San Andreas Fault
Volcanoes
Geysers
Natural Steam for Power
Elevations and Distances in the United States
Geologic Maps: Portraits of the Earth
Steps to the Moon
Tree Rings: Timekeepers of the Past

* U.S. Geological Survey Regional Information Offices

Anchorage
Public Inquiries Office, U.S. Geological Survey, Room 101, 4230 University Dr., Anchorage, AK 99508-4664; (907) 271-4320

Anchorage
Public Inquiries Office, U.S. Geological Survey, Federal Building, Room E-146, Box 53, 701 C St., Anchorage, AK 99513; (907) 271-4307

Denver
Public Inquiries Office, U.S. Geological Survey, Federal Building, Room 169, 1961 Stout St., Denver, CO 80294; (303) 844-4169

Los Angeles
Public Inquiries Office, U.S. Geological Survey, Federal Building, Room 7638, 300 N. Los Angeles St., Los Angeles, CA 90012: (213) 894-2850

Menlo Park
Public Inquiries Office, U.S. Geological Survey, Building 3 (Stop 533), Room 3128, 345 Middlefield Rd., Menlo Park, CA 94025; (415) 329-4390

Reston
Public Inquiries Office, U.S. Geological Survey, 503 National Center, Room IC402, 12201 Sunrise Valley Dr., Reston, VA 22092; (703) 648-6892

Salt Lake City
Public Inquiries Office, U.S. Geological Survey, Federal Building, Room 8105, 125 South State St., Salt Lake City, UT 84138; (801) 524-5652

San Francisco
Public Inquiries Office, U.S. Geological Survey, Customhouse, Room 504, 555 Battery St., San Francisco, CA 94111; (415) 556-5627

Spokane
Public Inquiries Office, U.S. Geological Survey, U.S. Courthouse, Room 678, West 920 Riverside Ave., Spokane, WA 99201; (509) 456-2524

Washington, D.C.
Public Inquiries Office, U.S. Geological Survey, Main Interior Building, 2600 Corridor, 18th and C Sts., NW, Washington, DC 20240; (202) 343-8073

* Volcanoes and Earthquakes

Science and Technology Division
Reference Section
Library of Congress
Washington, DC 20540   (202 707-5580
Informal series of reference guides are issued free from the Science and Technology Division under the general title, *LC Science Tracer Bullet*. These guides are designed to help readers locate published material on subjects about which they have only general knowledge. New titles in the series are announced in the weekly Library of Congress *Information Bulletin* that is distributed to many libraries. Two relevant *Tracer Bullets* currently available are: TB *81-14 Volcanoes*, and TB *89-8 Earthquakes & Earthquake Engineering*.

National Institute of Standards and Technology

A good idea often isn't good enough anymore. As U.S. firms have discovered in international markets, innovation by itself does not ensure commercial success. Unless a new technology is quickly translated into an efficiently manufactured, high-quality product, a faster-acting competitor is likely to capitalize on the advance and reap most of the market returns. The National Institute of Standards and Technology (NIST), formerly the National Bureau of Standards, as a world-class center for science and engineering research, is uniquely positioned to help U.S. firms strengthen their competitive performance.

NIST has been a valuable behind-the-scenes partner of industry and academia, providing the standards and measurement techniques that foster technological advance, domestic and international commerce, and, ultimately, economic progress. NIST is also responsible for speeding innovation and accelerating the adoption of new technologies and new ideas by U.S. companies. That's why about half of the organization's scientists and engineers focus their work on the fastest-moving and, perhaps, most commercially attractive areas of science: advanced materials, electronics, superconductivity, automation, computing, biotechnology, and thin-layer technology.

The National Institute of Standards and Technology provides advisory and consulting services to assist government and industry in the development of standards. As the national reference for physical measurement, NIST produces measurement standards data necessary to create, make, and sell U.S. products and services at home and abroad. Staff work with industry and consumers at every level. Generally, a staffer can lead you to major companies, research centers, experts, and literature. Listed below are the NIST laboratories and centers which can provide you with scientific and technological services as well as measurement, instrumentation and standards information.

* Advanced Measurement Techniques

Office of Physical Measurement Services
National Measurement Laboratory
National Institute of Standards and Technology
B362 Physics Bldg.
Gaithersburg, MD 20899 (301) 975-2005

The National Measurement Laboratory develops advanced measurement techniques for complex physical and chemical systems for use in areas such as chemical manufacturing, waste disposal, biotechnology, and environmental studies. Contact this office for more information.

* Alloys: New and Improved

Metallurgy Division
Institute for Materials Science and Engineering
National Institute of Standards and Technology
B261 Materials Bldg
Gaithersburg, MD 20899 (301) 975-5963

The Institute for Materials Science and Engineering explores and quantifies processing technologies to produce new and improved alloys. For more information, contact this division.

* Applications Portability Profile

Systems and Software Technology Division
National Computer Systems Laboratory
National Institute of Standards and Technology
B266, Bldg. 225
Gaithersburg, MD 20899 (301) 975-3290

The ability to move or port an application from one operating system environment to another is important for cost effective computing. The National Computer Systems Laboratory is working with users and industry to define and implement the Applications Portability Profile (APP), a group of standard elements, including database management, data interchange, network services, user interfaces, and programming services. Workshops for vendors and users are sponsored to explore common requirements for software portability, and to reach agreements on common ways to implement the standards that are being developed. Contact this office for more information on portability and workshops.

* Applied Mathematics

Center for Applied Mathematics
National Engineering Laboratory
National Institute of Standards and Technology
Gaithersburg, MD 20899 (301) 975-2732

The Center for Applied Mathematics conducts research and supports NIST activities and other Federal agencies in selected fields of the mathematical and computer sciences. The Center also develops such mathematical tools as scientific software, statistical models and computational methods, mathematical handbooks, and manuals. Contact this office for more information.

* Atomic Mapping

Center for Analytical Chemistry
National Measurement Laboratory
National Institute of Standards and Technology
A309 Chemistry Bldg.
Gaithersburg, MD 20899 (301) 975-3143

The National Measurement Laboratory has developed a tool for "atomic mapping" of the magnetic characteristics of material surfaces. A boon to the $40 billion magnetic recording industry, the instrument will be produced commercially by a U.S. firm. Contact this Center for more information on atomic mapping.

* Automated Manufacturing Data Handling

Automated Manufacturing Research Facility
Center for Manufacturing Engineering
National Institute of Standards and Technology
Building 220, Room B433
Gaithersburg, MD 20899 (301) 975-3400

In a very real sense, the cornerstone of the "factory of the future" will be information. The hardware of the facility--robots, machine tools and sensors-- is very visible, but the ability to generate, store, retrieve, and transfer information accurately and on time will be just as important as any hardware. Special features of this unseen part of the Automated Manufacturing Research Facility include the use of distributed databases and a data communications system. Contact this facility for more information on the on-going data handling projects.

* Automated Manufacturing Data Preparation

Automated Manufacturing Research Facility
Center for Manufacturing Engineering
National Institute of Standards and Technology
Building 220, Room B433
Gaithersburg, MD 20899 (301) 975-3400

At the Automated Manufacturing Research Facility, research is underway to determine exactly what sorts of data are required by a factory's manufacturing and inspection systems, and how these data can be generated automatically by the various data preparation systems in use in the facility. Contact this facility for more information on this research.

* Building Environment

Building Environment Division
Center for Building Technology
National Engineering Laboratory

National Institute of Standards and Technology
Gaithersburg, MD 20899   (301) 975-5851

The Building Environment Division develops fundamental data, measurement techniques, test methods, and models for the design, construction, and operation of the building envelope and building mechanical and electrical systems. The division also develops software performance criteria, interface standards, and test methods needed to make effective use of modern computer-aided design hardware and software and database management systems within the disaggregated construction industry. Sample outputs for the division include testing and rating procedures and computer models for the performance of heating and air conditioning systems, predictive models for estimating peak heating/cooling requirements and annual building energy use, and indoor air quality, criteria for improving thermal performance of insulating materials, and criteria for measuring and improving the lighting in buildings. The division also has computer aids to assist in formulating building standards and expert systems. Contact this office for more information.

* Building Materials Research

Building Materials Division
Center for Building Technology
National Engineering Laboratory
National Institute of Standards and Technology
Gaithersburg, MD 20899   (301) 975-6706

The Building Materials Division conducts laboratory, field and analytical research and develops methods for evaluating the performance and durability of building materials and components. The division also develops chemical, physical, microstructural, and mechanical characterization procedures and mathematical methods for describing microstructures for building materials. Also, the division conducts voluntary laboratory inspection and proficiency sample programs to aid maintenance of quality in execution of standard tests on materials used in building and highway construction. Contact this office for guidelines for selecting building materials, or for more information on the on-going research in building materials.

* Building Technology

Center for Building Technology
National Engineering Laboratory
National Institute of Standards and Technology
Gaithersburg, MD 20899   (301) 975-5900

The Center for Building Technology is the national building research laboratory. It works cooperatively with other organizations, private and public, to improve building practices. It conducts laboratory, field, and analytical research. It develops technologies to predict, measure, and test the performance of building materials, components, systems, and practices. This knowledge is required for responsible and cost effective decisions in the building process and cannot be obtained through proprietary research and development. The Center provides technologies needed by the building community to achieve the benefits of advanced computation and automation. It does not distribute building standards or regulations, but its technologies are widely used in the building industry and adopted by governmental and private organizations which have standards and codes responsibilities. Contact this Center for more information.

* Building Technology Presentations and Symposia

Center for Building Technology
National Engineering Laboratory
National Institute of Standards and Technology
B250 Building Research Building
Gaithersburg, MD 20899   (301) 975-5900

Staff at the Center for Building Technology make a number of presentations at professional societies and at technical meetings of building community organizations. Also, the center presents a monthly series of Building Technology Symposia, in cooperation with other organizations concerned with building research and practice. Contact this Center for further information.

* Calibration Services

Center for Manufacturing Engineering
National Engineering Laboratory
National Institute of Standards and Technology
Building 220, Room B322
Gaithersburg, MD 20899   (301) 975-3400

The Center for Manufacturing Engineering maintains the national standards for the length, force, and a number of subsidiary standards. It offers primary calibration services for these standards. Under unique circumstances, the Center accepts especially complex or sensitive measurement assignments of national significance. Contact this Center for more information.

* Center for Analytical Chemistry Services

Center for Analytical Chemistry
National Institute of Standards and Technology
A309 Chemistry Bldg.
Gaithersburg, MD   (301) 975-3145

The availability of Center for Analytical Chemistry analytical expertise to other institutions is an important service function. In addition to service analyses, the Center is frequently called upon to consult or advise, to provide various metrological calibrations of a chemical nature on a wide variety of industrial and research materials, and to provide analytical services of a unique nature such as compositional mapping, depth profiling, or ultra-trace analysis. These services are available to private industry when the uniqueness of the Center capability has been demonstrated, and similar services are not available in the private sector. Contact this office for more information.

* Center for Analytical Chemistry Technical Activities

Center for Analytical Chemistry
National Institute of Standards and Technology
A309 Chemistry Bldg.
Gaithersburg, MD 20899   (301) 975-3145

Center for Analytical Chemistry Technical Activities annual report summarizes the technical activities in the Inorganic Analytical Research Division, the Organic Analytical Research Division, and the Gas and Particulate Science Division. In addition, it describes certain special activities in the Center, including quality assurance and voluntary standardization coordination. Contact this office for a free copy.

* Center for Manufacturing Engineering

Center for Manufacturing Engineering
National Engineering Laboratory
National Institute of Standards and Technology
Gaithersburg, MD 20899   (301) 975-3400

The Center for Manufacturing Engineering provides competence and develops technical data, findings, and standards in manufacturing engineering, mechanical metrology, automation, robotics, control technology, and precision mechanical engineering to support the discrete parts manufacturing industries. Contact this office for more information on the research and developments at the Center.

* Ceramic and Metal Powder Production

Office of Nondestructive Evaluation
Institute for Materials Science and Engineering
National Institute of Standards and Technology
B344 Materials Bldg.
Gaithersburg, MD 20899   (301) 975-5727

The *Nondestructive Evaluation Technical Activities 1989* annual report reviews the technical activities and developments at NIST, including ceramic and metal powder production and consolidation, formability of metals, composites processing and interfaces, and standards and methods. Also included are listings of the various seminars and invited talks which were presented in 1989. A listing of the Office's publications are also available. For a free copy contact:

* Ceramics Program

Ceramics Division
Institute for Materials Science and Engineering
National Institute of Standards and Technology
A256 Materials Bldg
Gaithersburg, MD 20899   (301) 975-6119

The Institute for Materials Science and Engineering conducts a high-tech ceramics program geared to help U.S. industry stay competitive in the worldwide race to expand production and application of these materials. Direct your inquiries to the above office.

* Chemical Engineering Center

Center for Chemical Engineering
National Engineering Laboratory
National Institute of Standards and Technology
Gaithersburg, MD 20899   (303) 497-5108

The Center for Chemical Engineering performs research in process metrology, thermophysical properties of fluids and solids, and unit operations and processes; provides measurement practices and standards, fundamental engineering data, calibration and measurement services, and engineering science for the chemical and related industries, academe, and Government.

* Chemical Process Research

Chemical Process Metrology Division
Center for Chemical Engineering
National Engineering Laboratory
National Institute of Standards and Technology
Gaithersburg, MD 20899   (301) 975-2601

Research is on-going in the Chemical Process Metrology Division to develop measurement standards and provide measurement services for flow (volume and mass rates), liquid density, liquid volume, and humidity. Experimental and theoretical research is conducted to characterize fluid behavior.

* Chemical Reference Laboratory

Center for Analytical Chemistry
National Measurement Laboratory
National Institute of Standards and Technology
A309 Chemistry Bldg.
Gaithersburg, MD 20899 (301) 975-3143
The National Measurement Laboratory serves as the nation's reference laboratory for the more than 250 million chemical composition measurements made each day in the United States for industrial process control, environmental protection, toxic substances control, and health services. Working with a U.S. firm, the National Measurement Laboratory designed a new instrument for more efficient and more accurate separation and analysis of chemical elements in a sample. Contact this Lab for more information.

* Chemical Research

Center for Analytical Chemistry
National Institute of Standards and Technology
A309 Chemistry Bldg.
Gaithersburg, MD (301) 975-3145
Current programs at the Center for Analytical Chemistry include the following: Clinical Standards, Environmental Standards, Metal Standards, Gas Standards, Biomaterial Standards, Acid Rain, Environmental Analysis, Particle Analysis, Specimen Banking, and Nutrient Analysis. Research interests include atom reservoirs, bioanalytical sensors, bioanalytical techniques, compositional mapping, electrochemical techniques, high resolution chromatography, laboratory automation, laser enhanced ionization in flames, and multicomponent analysis. Contact this Center for more information about research interests or the center's current programs.

* Commercialization of Advanced Technology

Director,
National Institute of Standards and Technology
Manufacturing Technology Centers Program
Bldg. 220, Room B111
Gaithersburg, MD 20899 (301) 975-3414
Through the Advanced Technology Program, NIST is directed to speed the commercialization of new technology and the development of new, generic manufacturing techniques. NIST may support or participate in research consortia to develop and test new equipment or production processes, provided that they are "generic" to a particular industry or group of industries. The program will be aimed at small- to mid-sized, high technology firms or consortia. The idea is to "leverage" the relatively small financial resources of NIST by using the Institute's support to encourage private investment in each project. For more information, contact this office.

* Computer and Telecommunications Standards Assistance

Information Systems Engineering Division
National Computer Systems Laboratory
National Institute of Standards and Technology
A266 Technology Bldg.
Gaithersburg, MD 20899 (301) 975-3262
The National Computer Systems Laboratory helps computer manufacturers, communications companies, and domestic and international standards-writing groups to produce and test standards for off-the-shelf compatibility of computer and related telecommunications systems. Contact this NIST division for more information.

* Computer Assistance for Organizations

National Computer Systems Laboratory
National Institute of Standards and Technology
B154 Technology Bldg.
Gaithersburg, MD 20899 (301) 975-2822
The National Computer Systems Laboratory works on techniques and tools to help organizations make effective use of computers and information technology, reduce training costs, and improve productivity. Contact this Lab for more information.

* Computer Information Technology

National Computer Systems Laboratory
National Institute of Standards and Technology
B154 Technology Bldg.
Gaithersburg, MD 20899 (301) 975-2822
Computers are indispensable tools of the Information Age. Current uses, however, tap neither the full potential of rapidly improving hardware and software, nor the growing opportunities arising from new telecommunications technology that can simultaneously transmit data, image, and voice signals. The National Computer Systems Laboratory is helping to ensure that the manufacturers and users of information technology will reap the anticipated benefits--better products, the growth of markets, and production applications of information technology. Beyond providing technical assistance, NCSL serves

government and industry by developing standards, test methods, and computer security measures. It consists of the following divisions:

Information Systems Engineering Division, A266 Technology Bldg.; (301) 975-3262
Systems and Software Technology Division, B266 Technology Bldg.; (301) 975-3290
Computer Security Division, A216 Technology Bldg.; (301) 975-2934
Systems and Network Architecture Division, B217 Technology Bldg.; (301) 975-3643
Advanced Systems Division, A224 Technology Bldg.; (301) 975-2900

* Computer Security Consulting

Computer Security Division
National Computer Systems Laboratory
National Institute of Standards and Technology
A216, Bldg. 225
Gaithersburg, MD 20899 (301) 975-2929
The National Computer Systems Laboratory (NCSL) provides federal agencies with advice and assistance in computer security planning, training, and related activities. With the National Security Agency, NCSL reviews and comments on agency security plans for sensitive, unclassified systems. Regular workshops, meetings, and a national computer security conference comprise the ongoing program to facilitate the interchange of ideas, needs, guidance, and standards.

* Computer Systems Consulting

National Computer Systems Laboratory
National Institute of Standards and Technology
B154 Technology Bldg.
Gaithersburg, MD 20899 (301) 975-2822
The National Computer Systems Laboratory (NCSL) consults with federal agencies to solve technical problems. Carried out on a cost-reimbursable basis, projects are selected for their broad applicability to federal agency information processing and their contributions to NCSL programs. The professional staff is uniquely qualified to address technical problems in computer security, software engineering, advanced computer systems, database management and graphics systems, and distributed processing. For specific information on how NCSL's products, services, and expertise can help your organization, contact this laboratory.

* Cooperative Data Programs

Reference Center
Standard Reference Data
National Institute of Standards and Technology
A323 Physics Building
Gaithersburg, MD 20899 (301) 975-2208
The need for high quality data far exceeds the resources of the Standard Reference Data Program. as a result, NIST participates in numerous cooperative data projects which have been set up to meet the needs. In a typical project, the NIST technical centers work together with an outside group, such as a technical society, industry group, or government agency to develop databases. Contact this Center for more information.

* Cooperative Research With NIST Experts

Cooperative Research Program
National Institute of Standards and Technology
A363 Physics Bldg.
Gaithersburg, MD 20899 (301) 975-4505
Researchers from industry and universities regularly work in NIST laboratories with Institute experts on projects of mutual interest. For example, engineers, machinists, and computer specialists from private companies, other government agencies, and universities have joined NIST researchers to develop the quality control techniques and the computer software interface standards needed for the automated factory of the future. For information on conducting cooperative research at the Institute write or call David Edgerly, or call the individual division listed previously that applies to your interests directly.

* Data Evaluation Centers

An important part of the National Standard Reference Data System is the data evaluation centers active in major areas of physics, chemistry, and materials science. These centers represent a long-term commitment to assessing and improving the quality of data in each area. Each of the centers maintains a close working relationship with other government agencies, private-sector organizations, and international groups active in its area. The centers welcome inquiries and opportunities for cooperative projects. The data centers are, unless otherwise indicated, located at the National Institute of Standards and Technology, Gaithersburg, MD 20899.

Chemistry
Aqueous Electrolyte Data Center, A164 Chemistry Building
Chemical Kinetics Information Center, A147 Chemistry Building

Science and Technology

Chemical Thermodynamics Data Center, A158 Chemistry Building
Fluids Mixtures Data Center, Mail Code 774.00, National Institute of Standards and Technology, Boulder, CO 80303
Ion Kinetics and Energetics Data Center, A147 Chemistry Building
Molten Salts Data Center, Rensselaer Polytechnic Institute, Department of Chemistry, Troy, NY 12181
Radiation Chemistry Data Center, University of Notre Dame, Radiation Laboratory, Notre Dame, IN 46556
Thermodynamics Research Center, Texas A&M University, College Station, TX 77843-3111

Materials Science

Alloy Phase Diagram Data Center, B150 Materials Building
Center for Information and Numerical Analysis and Synthesis, Purdue University, 2595 Yeager Road, West Lafayette, IN 47906
Corrosion Data Center, B259 Materials Building
Crystal Data Center, A207 Materials Building
Phase Diagrams for Ceramists Data Center, A229 Materials Building
Tribology Information Center, A247 Materials Building

Physics

Atomic Collision Cross Section Data Center, Joint Institute for Laboratory Astrophysics, University of Colorado, Boulder, CO 80309
Atomic Energy Levels Data Center, A167 Physics Building
Atomic Transition Probabilities Data Center, A267 Physics Building
Fundamental Constants Data Center, B258 Metrology Building
Molecular Spectra Data Center, B268 Physics Building
Photon and Charged-Particle Data Center, C311 Radiation Physics Building

* Earthquake Safety

Center for Building Technology
National Engineering Laboratory
National Institute of Standards and Technology
B250 Building Research Bldg.
Gaithersburg, MD 20899   (301) 975-5900

The National Engineering Laboratory uses a specially designed computerized facility to test how full-scale bridge and building components would perform in earthquakes. Contact this Center for more information.

* Electromagnetic Technology

Electromagnetic Technology Division
Center for Electronics & Electrical Engineering
National Engineering Laboratory
National Institute of Standards and Technology
Gaithersburg, MD 20899   (303) 497-5341

The Electromagnetic Technology Division provides national reference standards and measurement services required to determine the characteristics of optical guided-wave systems and lasers. Contact this office for more information.

* Electronic Publishing

Systems and Software Technology Division
National Computer Systems Laboratory
National Institute of Standards and Technology
B266, Bldg. 225
Gaithersburg, MD 20899   (301) 975-3290

The National Computer Systems Laboratories' Electronic Publishing Laboratory assists federal agencies in the selection and use of publishing systems by demonstrating the capabilities and limitations of different publishing technologies. Laboratory demonstrations focus on electronic publishing and the role of standards in electronic document processing and interchange. To visit the laboratory, contact the office above.

* Electronics & Electrical Engineering

Center for Electronics & Electrical Engineering
National Engineering Laboratory
National Institute of Standards and Technology
Gaithersburg, MD 20899   (301) 975-2220

This Center conducts research and development in the field of electronic and electrical materials, devices, instruments, and systems. The Center develops engineering data, measurement methods, theory, physical standards, and associated technology, and provides technical services, national reference standards, and engineering measurement traceability for the benefit of government, industry, and the scientific community. Contact this office for more information.

* Emerging Technologies in Manufacturing Engineering

Center for Manufacturing Engineering
National Engineering Laboratory
National Institute of Standards and Technology
B119 Technology Bldg.
Gaithersburg, MD 20899(301) 975-2300

Emerging Technologies in Manufacturing Engineering is an internal report produced by the managers and staff of the Center for Manufacturing Engineering for planning purposes only. It represents their current best thinking about emerging technologies in manufacturing engineering, the impact these technologies will have on their programs, and the directions their programs will go if sufficient resources are available. The emerging technologies discussed are those that they believe will require increased support and leadership from CME in coming years. Contact this office for a free copy.

* Energy Efficient Chemical Separation

Chemical Engineering Science Division
Center for Chemical Engineering
National Engineering Laboratory
National Institute of Standards and Technology
Gaithersburg, MD 20899   (303) 497-6944

The Chemical Engineering Science Division creates mass transfer models and heat transfer codes for new, energy efficient separation concepts.

* Energy-Related Inventions Program

Office of Energy-Related Inventions
National Engineering Laboratory
National Institute of Standards and Technology
Gaithersburg, MD 20899   (301) 975-5500

The National Institute of Standards and Technology evaluates all promising nonnuclear energy-related inventions, particularly those submitted by independent inventors and small companies for the purpose of obtaining direct grants for their development from the Department of Energy. The Energy-Related Inventions Program provides an opportunity for inventors to obtain Federal assistance in developing and commercializing their inventions. For a leaflet answering questions about qualifying, the evaluation process, types of assistance, patent policy, and other frequently asked questions about the program; and to request an Evaluation Request Form, contact the office above.

* European Community Approach to Standards Development

Office of Standards Code and Information
A629 Administration Bldg.
Gaithersburg, MD 20899   (301) 975-4029

The Commission of the European Communities (EC) is acting swiftly to turn the 12-member countries into a single integrated market of 320 million people by the end of 1992. EC legislation dealing with standardization is likely to have a profound effect on U.S. exports. *A Summary of the New European Community Approach to Standards Development* contains a list of EC and U.S. government contacts for information on various aspects of EC activities related to standardization. For a copy, send a self-addressed mailing label to Patrick Cooke at the address above.

* Fire Center Research Grants

Center for Fire Research
National Institute of Standards and Technology
Building 224, Room A247
Gaithersburg, MD 20899   (301) 975-6850

The Center for Fire Research (CFR) awards, mostly to universities, about 25 research grants annually that are integrated with the in-house program by CFR technical monitors who have related project responsibilities. Contact this Center for more information on the research grants. FIREDOC is the automated database of the Fire Research Information Services bibliographic collection. The collection contains national and international fire research reports, books, journal articles and conference proceedings. FIREDOC contains the references and, if possible, abstract and keywords. The full text of the document is not included in the database. FIREDOC is available 23 hours per day, Monday through Friday. It is not available between 8:30 a.m. and 9:30 a.m. eastern time. On Saturdays and Sundays it is available 24 hours per day. For detailed instructions on how to access the database and how to perform bibliographic searches, you can get the *FIREDOC User's Manual* for $11.95 from National Technical Information Service, 5285 Port Royal Rd., Springfield, VA 22161; (703) 487-4650. For additional information, call Nora Jason at the NIST office above.

* Fire Measurement and Research Developments

Fire Measurement and Research Division
Center for Fire Research
National Engineering Laboratory
National Institute of Standards and Technology
Gaithersburg, MD 20899   (301) 975-6866

Contact this division for information on studies which identify and measure potentially harmful combustion products and their effects on living organisms, and studies to develop less flammable furnishings.

* Fire Research and Consulting

Center for Fire Research

National Institute of Standards and Technology
Building 224, Room A247
Gaithersburg, MD 20899   (301) 975-6850

The Center for Fire Research (CFR) provides technical support to voluntary standards and codes groups, the engineering and design community, the building industry, fire services, and fire protection organizations. It also provides scientifically-based recommendations to other government agencies on fire-related issues. CFR also conducts fire research for private industry when CFR facilities or expertise are unique and when the requested research complements the on-going CFR program. Contact this Center for more information.

* Fire Research Center

Center for Fire Research
National Engineering Laboratory
National Institute of Standards and Technology
Gaithersburg, MD 20899   (301) 975-6850

This Center performs and supports research to provide the scientific and technical basis for reducing fire losses and the cost of fire protection. The Center's technical promotes the development and widespread use of scientifically-based fire protection engineering practices, promote the continued advance in knowledge of the physics and chemistry behind actual fires, and maintain the technical capability for timely response to current fire problems. The Center maintains a definitive fire research information center for its use and as a resource for the fire community. The Center also manages a grants program for basic and applied fire research to complement in-house research. For more information, contact this Center.

* Fire Research Computer Bulletin Board

The Center for Fire Research
National Institute of Standards and Technology
Building 224, Room A247
Gaithersburg, MD 20899   (301) 975-6850

The Center for Fire Research Computer Bulletin Board is a public access computer bulletin board featuring computer programs developed by the Center for Fire Research. The bulletin Board also contains information on FIREDOC and Center for Fire Research activities. You will find fire simulation programs developed at the Center, information on upcoming activities at the Center, including conferences, workshops and seminars, a listing of recent reports from the Center, and more. Contact this Center for more information on accessing the bulletin board.

* Fire Research Publications, 1987

National Technical Information Service
Springfield, VA 22161

Interested in the combustion toxicity of various plastics? cigarette fire-safety? sprinklers? smoke control? soot formation? The NIST Center for Fire Research issued publications and articles on these topics and many others, all of which are compiled in the bibliography, *Fire Research Publications, 1987*. NIST conducts research on how fires start and spread and how they can be detected and suppressed. This research leads to realistic material test methods, cost-effective fire safety design concepts, and new methods of fire control and extinguishment. Copies are $14.95 prepaid through the office above.

* Fire Safety

Center for Fire Research
National Engineering Laboratory
National Institute of Standards and Technology
A247 Polymer Bldg.
Gaithersburg, MD 20899   (301) 975-6850

The National Engineering Laboratory develops computer-based models and engineering tools that predict fire and its effects for use by the fire protection and building communities in designing safer buildings. Contact this Center for more information.

* Fire Safety in Transportation Vehicles

Fire Measurement and Research Division
Center for Fire Research
National Engineering Laboratory
National Institute of Standards and Technology
Gaithersburg, MD 20899   (301) 975-6866

This division makes recommendations for upgrading fire safety of mass transportation vehicles such as subway cars and trains.

* Fire Science and Engineering

Fire Science and Engineering Division
Center for Fire Research
National Engineering Laboratory
National Institute of Standards and Technology
Gaithersburg, MD 20899   (301) 975-6869

This Division develops new methods for determining fire hazard and risk and extends them into engineering practice. The division provides information and analytical methods for advancing the science of fire protection, develops comprehensive and user-friendly computer models of fire and its effects within complex structures, performs experiments and analysis on the growth and spread of fire on materials and within structures, and develops measurement techniques and analyses to study the dynamics of water in putting out fires. Sample outputs include a fire hazard assessment method that addresses smoke transport and the behavior and effects on people, a handbook of smoke control, an improved room fire growth computer model, and a salt water analog technique for determining the motion of smoke in complex structures. Contact this division for more information on fire science and engineering developments.

* Fracture and Deformation Research

Materials Reliability Division
Institute for Materials Science and Engineering
National Institute of Standards and Technology
Division 430
Boulder, CO 80303   (303) 497-3268

Understanding how and why structural materials fail--the aim of the Materials Reliability Division--can yield enormous benefits. When used in the design and fabrication of structure, detailed, quantitative knowledge of the mechanics of fracture and deformation can improve safety and reliability, increase productivity, and even avert disaster, such as bridge collapses and railroad derailments that stem from stresses and flows in materials. The division's staff studies nonlinear fracture mechanics, arc physics, acoustoelasticity, the mechanics of composite materials, and the relationship between the structure, properties, and mechanical behavior of materials. Materials are examined over a wide range of temperatures. The division conducts studies for other government agencies and provides technical services to industry and public and private research institutions. For more information, contact this NIST division.

* GATT Standards Code Activities of the National Bureau of Standards 1987

Office of Standards Code and Information
A629 Administration Bldg.
Gaithersburg, MD 20899   (301) 975-4029

GATT Standards Code Activities of the National Bureau of Standards 1987 is an annual report that describes NIST's role over the past year as the official U.S. GATT (General Agreement on Tariffs and Trade) inquiry point for information on standards and certification activities that might significantly affect U.S. trade. The NIST effort included coordinating comments on proposed foreign regulations, translating of foreign texts, and operating the GATT "hotline" (301/975-4041, not toll free) that provides the latest information on foreign notifications from the GATT Secretariat in Geneva, Switzerland. The 1987, highlights were participation in the GATT Standards Code meeting on information exchange and the ISONET (International Organization for Standardization Information Network) workshop on international trade; publication of an introduction to standardization, certification, and laboratory accreditation; and background research for the Canadian Free Trade Agreement. Contact the office above to obtain a copy.

* Guest Researcher Opportunities in Building Technology

Center for Building Technology
National Engineering Laboratory
National Institute of Standards and Technology
Building 226, Room B226
Gaithersburg, MD 20899   (301) 975-5900

The Center for Building Technology performs cooperative research with other organizations, private and public. There are many opportunities for engineers, scientists, and students from private and public organizations to participate in CBT research:

-Research Associates (from industry and academia),
-Guest Researchers (from U.S. and international organizations),
-Postdoctoral Research Associates (selected by National Academies),
-Engineers and Scientists from State and local governments,
-Visiting Scholars from universities, and
-Cooperative and Summer Students

Contact this office for more information on guest researcher opportunities.

* HAZARD I

National Fire Protection Association
One Stop Data Shop
Batterymarch Park
Quincy, MA 02269

National Technical Information Service
Springfield, VA 22161

Center for Firesafety Studies

Science and Technology

Worcester Polytechnic Institute
Worcester, MA 01609

Center for Fire Research
Room A-247, Building 224
Gaithersburg, MD 20899

HAZARD I is a method for predicting the hazards to the occupants of a building from a fire therein. Within prescribed limits, *HAZARD I* allows you to predict the outcome of a fire in a building populated by a representative set of occupants in terms of which persons successfully escape and which are killed, including the time, location, and likely cause of death for each. Specific applications vary, but some include material/product performance evaluation, fire reconstruction and litigation, evaluation of code changes or variances, fire department pre-planning, and extrapolation of fire test data to additional physical configurations. *HAZARD I* consists of a three volume report and a set of computer disks and costs $225 per copy from the National Fire Protection Association or the National Technical Information Service. Training programs are planned for a variety of target groups at the Center for Firesafety Studies. For more information, contact the Center for Fire Research.

* Hydrocarbon Engineering Properties

Office of Standard Reference Data
National Institute of Standards and Technology
A323 Physics Building
Gaithersburg, MD 20899   (301) 975-2208

A new database for calculating viscosity, density, and other important engineering property data of hydrocarbons--natural gas, petroleum, and organic materials, including mixtures of fluids--has been developed by NIST. The "DDMIX" database was developed as part of a research project sponsored by an industry consortium of petroleum, chemical, and gas processing firms. Available on a floppy disk for personal computers, it provides rapid access to important information on the storage and transportation of fluids, and for the design of new chemical processes. Among other things, the program allows users to calculate quickly various thermodynamic and transport properties of fluid mixtures. To order the *DDMIX--Mixture Property Program (1988), NIST Standards Reference Database 14*, a floppy disk for personal computers for $400, contact the office above.

* Industrial Quality Control

Office of Standard Reference Materials
National Measurement Laboratory
National Institute of Standards and Technology
B311 Chemistry Bldg.
Gaithersburg, MD 20899   (301) 975-2012

The National Measurement Laboratory contributes to improved industrial quality control by developing Standard Reference Materials and calibrating equipment and devices. Contact this office for more information.

* Information Resource Dictionary System

Information Systems Engineering Division
National Computer Systems Laboratory
National Institute of Standards and Technology
A226 Bldg. 225
Gaithersburg, MD 20899   (301) 975-3262

The Information Systems Engineering Laboratory research initiative resulted in the Information Resource Dictionary System (IRDS) standard and an IRDS prototype, a software system that records, stores, and processes information about an organization's data and data processing resources. The IRDS enables federal government users to improve productivity by identifying information resources that can be shared within an organization and between organizations. Contact this office for more information on IRDS and its uses.

* Information Systems Engineering Assistance

Information Systems Engineering Division
National Computer Systems Laboratory
National Institute of Standards and Technology
A226, Bldg. 225
Gaithersburg, MD 20899   (301) 975-3262

The Information Systems Engineering Division supports standards development and provides technical assistance to government and industry in data administration; data management; computer graphics; geographic information systems; standards validation; and programming language technologies. Contact this division for more information on available assistance.

* Information Technology Research

Information Systems Engineering Division
National Computer Systems Laboratory
National Institute of Standards and Technology
A266 Technology Bldg.
Gaithersburg, MD 20899   (301) 975-3262

The National Computer Systems Laboratory conducts research on parallel processing performance, speech recognition, and other rapidly evolving applications of information technology to provide a basis for standards development.

* Information Technology Standards

Information Systems Engineering Division
National Computer Systems Laboratory
National Institute of Standards and Technology
A266 Technology Bldg.
Gaithersburg, MD 20899   (301) 975-3262

The National Computer Systems Laboratory helps the information technology industry and users develop cost-effective national and international standards for open systems that erase incompatibility barriers and allow exchange of information between the systems of different manufacturers. Contact this division for more information.

* Integrated Services Digital Networks

Advanced Systems Division
National Computer Systems Laboratory
National Institute of Standards and Technology
A224, Bldg. 225
Gaithersburg, MD 20899   (301) 975-2904

The National Computer Systems Laboratory investigates standards and develops conformance test methods for Integrated Services Digital Networks (ISDN), a new telecommunications technology that makes it possible to send and receive voice, data, and image signals simultaneously over digital telephone networks. NCSL established the North American ISDN User's Forum to create a strong user voice in the implementation of ISDN. Contact this office for more information.

* Law Enforcement Standards Laboratory

Law Enforcement Standards Laboratory
National Engineering Laboratory
National Institute of Standards and Technology
Gaithersburg, MD 20899   (301) 975-2757

The Law Enforcement Standards Laboratory conducts research and provides technical services to the U.S. Department of Justice and State and local governments in support of law enforcement agencies. The division develops standards for police bullet-resistant equipment, handguns, shotguns, communications equipment, physical security equipment, tear gas devices, speed measuring devices, and evidential breath testers. The division also provides guides for selecting and applying commercial intrusion systems, facsimile equipment, and protective equipment. Technical reports on various related subjects such as handgun ammunition, blood/breath alcohol analysis, and arson investigation, are available. Contact this laboratory for more information.

* Low-Alloy Steel Calibration Standards

Office of Standard Reference Materials
National Institute of Standards and Technology
B311 Chemistry Bldg.
Gaithersburg, MD 20899   (301) 975-6776

NIST has developed a new graded series of seven low-alloy steel standards for calibrating optical emission and x-ray fluorescence spectrometers. Great care has been used in preparing these materials to obtain a high level of homogeneity to meet the demands of new, highly precise instruments used in the quality control of alloy materials. *Standard Reference Materials* (SRM's) 1761-1767, prepared in consultation with ASTM and industry, are available for $135 each in the form of disks approximately 34 mm in diameter and 19 mm thick. To obtain information on the certified values of each disk, or to order the new graded series of calibration standards, contact the office above.

* Malcolm Baldrige National Quality Awards

National Institute of Standards and Technology
Inquiries Unit
E128 Administration Bldg.
Gaithersburg, MD 20899

A goal of the National Institute of Standards and Technology is to aid firms in building a competitive advantage. NIST manages the annual Malcolm Baldrige National Quality Awards to work towards this goal. Winning firms achieve continuous improvement in their manufacturing processes and final products. They, like formidable foreign competitors, have succeeded in meshing efficiency, flexibility, quality, and innovation in a single operation. Contact this office for more information on the awards.

* Manufacturing Engineering Publications

Center for Manufacturing Engineering
National Engineering Laboratory
National Institute of Standards and Technology
B119 Technology Bldg.
Gaithersburg, MD 20899(301) 975-2300

The current edition of the *Publications of the Center for Manufacturing Engineering* covers the period January, 1978 through December, 1988. This listing reflects the diversity of scientific and technical problems which have been attacked over the past ten years in fulfillment of the Center's mission. Publications, indexed by subject area, cover research done by the Center in the areas of high precision dimensional measurement and precision engineering; robotics and intelligent machines; manufacturing data description, data administration, and information processing; and sensors for manufacturing processes. Contact this Center for a free copy.

* Manufacturing Engineering Research

Center for Manufacturing Engineering
National Engineering Laboratory
National Institute of Standards and Technology
Building 220, Room B322
Gaithersburg, MD 20899   (301) 975-3400

NIST is recognized as the Nation's finest general purpose scientific and engineering laboratory. The mission of the Center for Manufacturing Engineering is to bring the resources of this laboratory to bear on the standards and measurements problems associated with America's discrete parts manufacturing. In fulfillment of its mission, the Center conducts active programs of research in the areas of high precision dimensional measurement; sensing and measurement of force, sound, vibration, and surface finish characteristics; and application of advanced control and sensing techniques to automated machines, manufacturing systems, and robot manipulators. Contact this Center for more information on current research.

* Manufacturing Technology Centers Program

Director,
National Institute of Standards and Technology
Manufacturing Technology Centers Program
Bldg. 220, Room B111
Gaithersburg, MD 20899   (301) 975-3414

To bring automated manufacturing technology to small- and mid-sized manufacturing firms, NIST has begun a manufacturing technology centers program. The program is designed to establish regional centers that will help these companies improve their technical capabilities and competitiveness. Their central activity is working hands-on with small and mid-size firms to 1) determine their particular technology needs; 2) develop a technology up-grade plan; 3) assist with business and financial planning to make the up-grade possible; and 4) help in the implementation of the new technology. The program will help to move new technology into the marketplace and will accelerate adoption of well-established "off-the-shelf" technologies to improve competitiveness of U.S.-based firms. The Centers invite inquiries from small and mid-sized manufacturers who want to find out more about their services. For more information about the program, or for phone numbers contact the above office.

* Materials Science

Materials Science and Engineering Laboratory
National Institute of Standards and Technology
B309 Materials Bldg
Gaithersburg, MD 20899   (301) 975-5658

Without new and better materials, technological progress would come to a halt. Increasingly, advances in fields ranging from electronics to construction depend on the mastery of an almost infinitesimally small domain, the arrangements of atoms and molecules that determine material properties. MSEL's research staff investigate all classes of advanced materials: ceramics, polymers, composites, and metallic alloys. The results are data, measurement tools, and services for understanding, improving, predicting, and controlling the processing and performance of materials. From autos to aerospace, improved materials are changing our lives. Car bodies and airplane parts are being made from polymer composites. Unconventional processing or synthesizing techniques are giving metal, ceramic, and polymer alloys increased strength or unusual properties. The laboratory consists of the following divisions:

Office of Nondestructive Evaluation, B344 Materials Bldg; (301) 975-5727
Ceramics Division, A256 Materials Bldg.; (301) 975-6119
Fracture and Deformation Division, 430.0 NIST, Boulder, CO 80303; (303) 497-3251
Polymers Division, A305 Polymer Bldg.; (301) 975-6762
Metallurgy Division, B261 Materials Bldg.; (301) 975-5963
Reactor Radiation Division, A106 Reactor Bldg.; (301) 975-6210

* Materials Science and Engineering Laboratory Annual Report

Director
Materials Science and Engineering Laboratory
National Institute of Standards and Technology
B309 Materials Bldg.
Gaithersburg, MD 20899   (301) 975-5658

The *Materials Science and Engineering Laboratory Annual Report* describes in detail the technical activities of each of the Laboratory's major units and is available on request from the Lab above.

* Mathematical Analysis

Mathematical Analysis Division
Center for Applied Mathematics
National Engineering Laboratory
National Institute of Standards and Technology
Gaithersburg, MD 20899   (301) 975-2702

The Mathematical Analysis Division provides consulting services in applied economics. The Division also performs research and collaborates in the application of mathematical analysis, mathematical modeling, and requisite computer-based methods to science and engineering. Contact this division for more information on the services offered, or the research conducted.

* Mathematical Software

Scientific Computing Division
Center for Applied Mathematics
National Engineering Laboratory
National Institute of Standards and Technology
Gaithersburg, MD 20899   (301) 975-3816

The Center for Applied Mathematics puts out the *Guide to Available Mathematical Software*. Contact this office to obtain a copy.

* Measurement Technology

National Measurement Laboratory
National Institute of Standards and Technology
A309 Chemistry Bldg.
Gaithersburg, MD 20899   (301) 975-3143

The National Measurement Laboratory's researchers subscribe to the maxim: If a process cannot be measured or a product characterized, then it is not completely understood. Their work takes them to the frontiers of the physical and chemical sciences, the birthplace of many new technologies. And it takes them to the manufacturing floor, where their technical understanding is translated into sensors, analytical methods, and other tools required for efficient production of high-technology materials and products. NML also coordinates the U.S. measurement system with those of other nations, facilitating international trade. It consists of the following centers:

Center for Basic Standards, B160 Physics Bldg.; (301) 975-4203
Center for Radiation Research, C229 Radiation Physics Bldg.; (301) 975-6090
Center for Chemical Physics, A363 Physics Bldg.; (301) 975-4500
Center for Analytical Chemistry, A309 Chemistry Bldg.; (301) 975-3143
Office of Standard Reference Data, A323 Physics Bldg.; (301) 975-2200
Office of Standard Reference Materials, B311 Chemistry Bldg.; (301) 975-2012
Office of Physical Measurement Services, B362 Physics Bldg.; (301) 975-2005

* Metals Quality and Cost

Metallurgy Division
Institute for Materials Science and Engineering
National Institute of Standards and Technology
B261 Materials Bldg
Gaithersburg, MD 20899   (301) 975-5963

The Institute for Materials Science and Engineering works with the U.S. metals industry and other federal laboratories to develop and exploit technologies that will improve the quality and reduce the cost of domestic steel, aluminum, and other metals. For more information, contact this division.

* National Computer Systems Laboratory Newsletter

National Computer Systems Laboratory
National Institute of Standards and Technology
B154 Technology Bldg.
Gaithersburg, MD 20899   (301) 975-2832

Published every six weeks, the *National Computer Systems Laboratory Newsletter* includes information on conferences, Federal Information Processing Standards, and NCSL special publications. Contact this office for more information on the *NCSL Newsletter*.

* National Engineering Laboratory

National Engineering Laboratory
National Institute of Standards and Technology
B119 Technology Bldg.
Gaithersburg, MD 20899   (301) 975-2300

Scores of studies have emphasized the importance of manufacturing to the competitive position of U.S. industry. The National Engineering Laboratory researchers are making accelerated efforts to provide the measurements and technology U.S. firms need to compete in burgeoning markets for ever faster semiconductors and optical communications equipment. On NEL's agenda are safety, public health, and the environment, as reflected in studies of fire prevention, evaluations of alternatives to ozone-depleting chlorofluorocarbons, and research supporting development of effective building regulations. It consists of the following centers:

Science and Technology

Center for Computing and Applied Mathematics, A438 Administration Bldg.; (301) 975-2728
Center for Electronics and Electrical Engineering, B358 Metrology Bldg.; (301) 975-2220
Center for Manufacturing Engineering, B322 Metrology Bldg.; (301) 975-3400
Center for Building Technology, B250 Building Research Bldg.; (301) 975-5900
Center for Fire Research, A247 Polymer Bldg.; (301) 975-6850
Center for Chemical Engineering, 770.0, NIST, Boulder, CO 80303; (303) 497-5108

* National Innovation Workshops
Office of Energy-Related Inventions
National Engineering Laboratory
National Institute of Standards and Technology
Gaithersburg, MD 20899   (301) 975-3694
The Office of Energy-Related Inventions conducts a series of National Innovation Workshops for inventors and small businesses. Contact this office for more information.

* National Measurement Standards
Center for Basic Standards
National Measurement Laboratory
National Institute of Standards and Technology
B160 Physics Bldg.
Gaithersburg, MD 20899   (301) 975-4203
The National Measurement Laboratory maintains and improves national standards for mass, length, time, temperature, and electric current. Inquiries should be directed to this Center.

* National Technical Information Service
National Technical Information Service
Springfield, VA 22161   (703) 487-4650
The National Institute of Standards and Technology publications are sold by the National Technical Information Service. They can supply microfiche, or paper copy from microfiche, at any time. *Federal Information Processing Standards*, *NIST Interagency Reports* (a special series of interim or final reports on work performed by NIST for outside sponsors), and *Grant/Contract Reports* are available only from NTIS. Place orders on (800) 336-4700. For more information call the office above.

* Neutron-Scattering Experiments
Reactor Radiation Division
Institute for Materials Science and Engineering
National Institute of Standards and Technology
Bldg. 235 Room A106
Gaithersburg, MD 20899   (301) 975-6226
Neutron-scattering methods of research permit studies of bulk samples, often yielding information on submicroscopic materials behavior and structure that is unsurpassed in detail and accuracy. Division scientists are engaged in a broad research program aimed at understanding and measuring the structure and properties of virtually all classes of materials used by industry, including high-temperature superconductors, advanced ceramics, catalysts, artificially structured materials, hydrogen in metals, and others that hold promise for high-technology applications. They are also furthering the uses of neutron diffraction and radiography for nondestructive evaluation. Other activities include efforts to develop new instrumentation and to strengthen the theoretical foundation of neutron-scattering research. Contact the office above for information on free services, including descriptive literature, telephone or on-site descriptions of the facilities, and discussion of problems.

* NIST List of Publications by Subject Category
National Institute of Standards and Technology
U.S. Department of Commerce
Publications and Program Inquiries
E128 Administration Bldg.
Gaithersburg, MD 20899   (301) 975-3058
A complimentary abridged journal of research, the *NIST List of Publications by Subject Category* compiles the NIST publications that are available, along with ordering information. It also contains a listing of depository libraries and a listing of Department of Commerce District Offices, two other sources of NIST publications.

* NIST Nonperiodical Technical Publications
Superintendent of Documents
Government Printing Office
Washington, DC 20402   (202) 783-3283
The National Institute of Standards and Technology nonperiodical publications include:

Monographs. Major contributions to the technical literature on various subjects related to the Institute's scientific and technical activities.

Handbooks. Recommended codes of engineering and industrial practice (including safety codes) developed in cooperation with interested industries, professional organizations, and regulatory bodies.

Special Publications. Includes proceedings of conferences sponsored by NIST, NIST annual reports, and other special publications appropriate to this grouping such as wall charts, pocket cards, and bibliographies.

Applied Mathematics Series. Mathematical tables, manuals, and studies of special interest to physicists, engineers, chemists, biologists, mathematicians, computer programmers, and others engaged in scientific and technical work.

National Standard Reference Data Series. Provides quantitative data on the physical and chemical properties of materials, compiled from the world's literature and critically evaluated.

Building Science Series. Disseminates technical information developed at the Institute on building materials, components, systems, and whole structures. The series presents research results, test methods, and performance criteria related to the structural and environmental functions and the durability and safety characteristics of building elements and systems.

Technical Notes. Studies or reports which are complete in themselves but restrictive in their treatment of a subject. Analogous to monographs but not so comprehensive in scope or definitive in treatment of the subject area. Often serve as a vehicle for final reports of work performed at NIST under the sponsorship of other government agencies.

Voluntary Product Standards. Developed under procedures published by the Department of Commerce, these standards establish nationally recognized requirements for products, and provide all concerned interests with a basis for common understanding of the characteristics of the products. NIST administers this program as a supplement to the activities of the private sector standardizing organizations.

Consumer Information Series. Practical information, based on NIST research and experience, covering areas of interest to the consumer. Easily understandable language and illustrations provide useful background knowledge for shopping in today's technological marketplace.

Order the above NIST publications from the Government Printing Office above.

* NIST Research Reports
Public Information Division
National Institute of Standards and Technology
A903 Administration Bldg.
Gaithersburg, MD 20899   (301) 975-2762
NIST Research Reports is a special publication which includes a research update, a listing of new NIST publications, and a conference calendar. It also includes specific NIST research reports of general public interest. Contact this office to obtain a copy.

* Nondestructive Evaluation Research
Office of Nondestructive Evaluation
Institute for Materials Science and Engineering
National Institute of Standards and Technology
B344, Materials Bldg.
Gaithersburg, MD 20899   (301) 975-5727
Nondestructive evaluation (NDE) is concerned with inspecting structures and products such as nuclear reactors, aircraft, and pipelines--an essential component of safety programs. Researchers are also concerned with monitoring important properties and characteristics of materials while they are being processed. In this capacity, NDE provides the information necessary for guiding or controlling production processes, assuring uniform high-quality products, and reducing waste. Contact the office above for more information.

* Non-Energy Invention Assistance
Office of Non-Energy Inventions
National Engineering Laboratory
National Institute of Standards and Technology
Gaithersburg, MD 20899   (301) 975-5500
The National Institute of Standards and Technology is developing a new program to reach out to individuals. Any inventor will be able to submit an invention to NIST for evaluation, so long as it is non-nuclear. Drawing on a national network of science and engineering consultants, NIST--for *free*--will evaluate the technical feasibility and marketability of the invention: Will it work? Will anyone buy it? Recommendations for support will go elsewhere for marketing assistance or development grants. This program is not yet operational as it is awaiting congressional approval, but if you wish to submit a non-energy invention to the

program, you may put your name on a waiting list. For more information, contact the office above.

* Open Systems Interconnection Technology

Systems and Network Architecture Division
National Computer Systems Laboratory
National Institute of Standards and Technology
B217, Bldg. 225
Gaithersburg, MD 20899   (301) 975-3618

The National Computer Systems Laboratory supports private industry and government through testing and standards implementation activities. For example, the Laboratory established OSINET, a cooperative government/industry research network which tests commercial Open Systems Interconnection (OSI) technology products to see how well they operate together. Contact this division for more information about the program to advance the standards necessary for effective integrated network management.

* Optical Disk Media

Advanced Systems Division
National Computer Systems Laboratory
National Institute of Standards and Technology
A224, Bldg. 225
Gaithersburg, MD 20899   (301) 975-2904

The National Computer Systems Laboratory is developing a testing methodology that predicts life expectancy of optical disk media. This research will assist government managers in planning how long information may safely be stored on these media. Contact this office for more information.

* Origins of Historical Artifacts

Materials Science and Engineering Laboratory
National Institute of Science and Technology
B309 Materials Bldg.
Gaithersburg, MD 20899   (301) 975-5658

In a remote Asian village, an archaeologist unearths a bronze art object. Though the object appears similar to many discovered in other excavations, a basic question must be answered before it can be catalogued or displayed in a museum: Where did it originate? More specifically, where did the raw materials come from that make up the object? One of the most useful techniques of tracing an ancient artifact or verifying the authenticity of a piece is lead isotope ratio analysis. Scientists at the National Institute of Standards and Technology are using the technique in collaboration with museum researchers who seek to pinpoint just where precious art pieces come from. For more information, contact this laboratory.

* Phase Diagram Databases

Institute for Materials Science and Engineering
National Institute of Standards and Technology
B309 Materials Bldg
Gaithersburg, MD 20899   (301) 975-5658

The Institute for Materials Science and Engineering works with professional societies to develop phase diagram databases that will help improve processing control and use of metals, ceramics, and polymers. For more information, contact this Institute.

* Photoduplicated Copies of NBS Publications

Photoduplication Service
Library of Congress
Washington, DC 20540   (202) 287-5640

Photoduplicated copies of many old National Bureau of Standards publications can be purchased from this Library of Congress service.

* Polymer Composites

National Institute of Standards and Technology
A209 Polymer Building
Gaithersburg, MD 20899   (301) 975-6837

Researchers in industry, universities, and government are invited to participate in an NIST research program that addresses the most critical barriers in high-performance polymer composite processing which producers must overcome to meet increasing international competition. The U.S. market for high technology plastic products is expected to grow. The United States now has the technological lead in the use of high performance polymer composites in defense and aerospace applications. In high-volume mass markets, however, U.S. industries face intense competition. For more information, contact Donald L. Hunston at the above office.

* Polymer Science

Polymers Division
Institute for Materials Science and Engineering
National Institute of Standards and Technology

A305 Polymer Bldg
Gaithersburg, MD 20899   (301) 975-6762

The uses of polymers and polymer-based composites are virtually unlimited, and the materials are even displacing metals in many structural and high-performance applications, including automobiles and commercial and military aircraft. Advances in polymer science have paced important technological developments. The Polymers Division supports U.S. industries that produce, process, or use synthetic polymers. Its basic research programs are devoted to strengthening the scientific foundation that sustains continued advances in this important class of materials. These programs are designed according to the perceived needs of industry. The division is developing novel sensors for monitoring viscosity, flow, molecular orientation, and mixing. For more information on polymers research, contact this NIST division.

* Protecting Computerized Information

Computer Security Division
National Computer Systems Laboratory
National Institute of Standards and Technology
A216 Technology Bldg.
Gaithersburg, MD 20899   (301) 975-2934

The National Computer Systems Laboratory develops standards and guidelines for protecting computerized information from threats of all kinds--operator error, power losses, natural disasters, and unauthorized users. Contact this division for more information.

* Quality Assurance

Center for Building Technology
National Engineering Laboratory
National Institute of Standards and Technology
Building 226, Room B226
Gaithersburg, MD 20899   (301) 975-5900

The Center for Building Technology provides a quality assurance program for over 1000 public and private construction materials testing laboratories nationwide that is relied upon by owners, designers, builders, and State and local governments responsible for buildings and transportation facilities. Contact this Center for more information on the Quality Assurance Program.

* Radiation Measurements

Center for Radiation Research
National Measurement Laboratory
National Institute of Standards and Technology
C229 Radiation Physics Bldg.
Gaithersburg, MD 20899   (301) 975-6090

The National Measurement Laboratory designs dosimeters used to assure accurate measurement of radiation for diagnostic and therapeutic uses, personnel monitoring, and the production of materials. Contact this Center for more information on radiation measurement.

* Radiation Research

Center for Radiation Research
National Institute of Science and Technology
C229 Radiation Physics Bldg
Gaithersburg, MD 20899   (301) 975-6090

The Center for Radiation Research develops and maintains the scientific competencies and experimental facilities necessary to provide the Nation with a central basis for uniform physical measurements, measurement methodology, and measurement services in the areas of near infra-red radiation, optical radiation, ultraviolet radiation, and ionizing radiation; provides government, industry, and the academic community with essential calibrations for field radiation measurements needed in such applied areas as nuclear power, lighting, solar radiation processing, advanced laser development, and radiation protection for public safety; and carries out research in order to develop improved radiation standards, new radiation measurement technology, and improved understanding of atomic, molecular, and ionizing radiation processes, and to elucidate the interaction of radiation and particles with inanimate and biological materials. Contact this Center for a copy of the annual report summarizing the activities that were carried out in 1989, and listing publications, talks, and professional interactions.

* Research and Testing Facilities

National Institute of Standards and Technology
Department of Commerce
E128 Administration Bldg.
Gaithersburg, MD 20899   (301) 975-3058

The NTIS has some of the premier research and testing facilities in the United States, several of which are unequaled anywhere in the world. To aid firms in building a competitive advantage, NIST makes available for cooperative and proprietary work its varied research and testing facilities at its headquarters in Gaithersburg, Maryland, and its site in Boulder, Colorado. To contact a facility, see the previous listing of centers and laboratories. The following is a listing of some of the special facilities that are available to conduct research at various centers and laboratories:

Science and Technology

Center for Analytical Chemistry

Research Reactor
NIST has a 20-megawatt research reactor used in materials research, molecular structure determination, and neutron activation analysis. This analysis is applicable to a wide variety of biomedical problems such as nutrition, the role of trace elements in human development, bioaccumulation, the role of trace elements in disease processes, investigations of metal-containing drugs, and utilization of cold neutrons.

Microprobe Facilities
The Center's microanalysis facilities are among the most advanced and complete in the world. Instruments include an analytical electron microscope, ion microprobe, secondary ion mass spectrometer, time of flight secondary ion mass spectrometer, laser microprobe mass analyzer, and a Raman microprobe. The latter two instruments provide molecular information from micro-regions and offer great potential in biomedical applications.

Trace Element Facilities
The Center for Analytical Chemistry has a wide variety of instruments used for the determination of trace element concentrations in virtually any matrix. These instruments include the following: atomic absorption spectrometer, spark atomic emission spectrometer, inductively coupled plasma spectrometer, dc plasma spectrometer, laser enhanced ionization spectrometer, spark source mass spectrometer, thermal ionization mass spectrometer, electrochemical analyzers, neutron activation analysis

Trace Organic Analysis
The Center performs basic and applied research in many areas of organic analysis. They have a variety of research instruments for this research.

Specimen Bank Research Facility
This facility contains separate clean areas for organic and inorganic sample preparation, biohazard hoods, cryogenic homogenization apparatus, and low temperature storage facilities. The specimen bank project is part of a multi-agency program in environmental monitoring and health research.

Ultrapure Reagents Facility
Modern trace analysis requires the use of high-purity reagents to minimize contamination problems commonly associated with measurements at parts-per-million and lower levels. A new reagents facility has been completed for the preparation of key trace analytical reagents.

Center for Manufacturing Engineering

Automated Manufacturing Research Facility
This facility is the major national laboratory for research in automated manufacturing. The facility provides a "test-bed" where researchers from NIST, industrial firms, universities, and other government agencies can work together on projects of mutual interest. Their research concentrates on the standards and measurement techniques required for successful automated manufacturing. The supporting technology for future computer integrated manufacturing systems are developed.

Center for Applied Mathematics

Consolidated Scientific Computing System
This major computation facility provides services through telecommunications links.

Evans and Sutherland PS-300 Dynamical Graphics System
This facility provides local display at video rates and includes 3-D perspective and orthographics projections, zoom, rotation and scaling on three axes, and variable-depth contrast. Transformed data may be transmitted back to the host computer after graphical treatment is completed. The system offers a "window" capability for difficult mathematical operations, such as the problem of visualizing a large data set at some intermediate stage of a large scale computation.

Perkin-Elmer 3230 Minicomputer
This facility is best suited to moderate-size scientific software development and limited production computing. A major feature of the 3230 is its wide I/O bandwidth which supports large local memory graphics terminals.

Raster Technologies ONE/380 Graphics System
This facility provides high resolution color raster images of three-dimensional objects or 24-bit color imaging data. The objects may be point clouds, wire frames, or solid objects with hidden surface removal, and lighting models for solid rendering. Local object manipulations include perspective or orthographic projections, translation, rotation, and scaling in three axes. All local operational parameters can be recovered by the host computer. High level graphics software available for major host computers at NIST supports this terminal. Applications

include CAD/CAM rendering, four-dimensional data using color as the fourth dimension, and interaction with mathematical models through surface rendering.

Center for Electronics & Electrical Engineering

Data Converter Testing Facility
This facility offers regular calibration service for static parameters of high-accuracy A/D and D/A converters, particularly for linearity and differential linearity measurements. The facility also includes testing of data converters under certain dynamic conditions, e.g., settling time measurements and noise measurements.

High Voltage Measurement Facility
This facility provides tests at high voltages requiring accurate measurements and sensitive diagnostics. The equipment includes high-speed photographic equipment for electrical breakdown diagnostics, Kerr effect electro-optical equipment for space charge diagnostics, equipment for partial discharge measurements, and equipment for dielectric loss measurements. Additionally, precision dividers provide for high voltage measurements under steady-state and transient conditions.

Semiconductor Processing Facility
This facility occupies about 4,000 sq. ft. of space, half of it clean room space, and has the capability of state-of-the-art semiconductor processing for research applications. It produces specialized test specimens, experimental samples, customized device prototypes, and carefully prepared materials under extremely well-controlled and flexible conditions.

Antenna Scanning Facility
The planar, near-field antenna scanning range in Boulder, Colorado, represents the state-of-the-art in measurement accuracy for such facilities, utilizing a highly accurate verified technique. It can be used to characterize antennas of various types indoors, at lower cost, at high accuracies, and with more resultant information than that yielded by conventional outdoor antenna range techniques. It can also be used for measurements not possible inn other types of facilities. Using theory, new measurement techniques, and computer software, a laser interferometer controlled probe precisely scans the antenna under test to determine near-field antenna parameters which are then converted to the desired far-field characteristics.

Center for Manufacturing Engineering

Automated Manufacturing Research Facility
This facility is a research laboratory for study of the measurement and standards problems of the "factory of the future." An extensive network of computers makes up the real-time control, distributed data administration, and manufacturing engineering elements of the facility. Research is currently supported on sensors, real-time control, deterministic metrology, production management and scheduling, data administration, communications, and preparation of manufacturing data.

Acoustical Anechoic Chamber
This facility provides a free-field environment for research and calibrations on measurement of the directivity of sound sources and the directional response of microphones and sensor arrays.

Center for Building Technology

Large Scale Structural Test Facility
This facility, with a 45 foot reaction wall and its 12-million pound capacity universal testing machine, is capable of testing large-scale structural components 60-feet in length. Specimens can also be subjected to lateral loading up to 1 million pounds. It is the largest facility of its kind in the free world.

Tri-Directional Structural Testing Facility
This facility is a unique computer-controlled apparatus capable of applying forces or displacements in three directions simultaneously to large-scale structural components and systems. This facility currently supports NIST's research role in developing seismic design and construction standards for reducing the hazards of earthquakes.

Environmental Chambers
These facilities support development of thermal performance modeling techniques required for predicting human comfort, energy efficiency, and fire safety in buildings. The chambers can automatically control temperatures with automatic humidity control.

Calibrated Hot-Box Facility
This facility provides precise measurements of heat, air, and moisture transfer through full-scale building wall and roof sections including door and window openings. The facility can simulate worldwide climatic conditions through the use of temperature, humidity, and air control. The measurements provide the basis for standard measurement methods used in private laboratories.

Five Story Plumbing Research Facility
This facility, with its high-speed preprogrammed computerized data acquisition systems, is used to study the performance of and develop measurement methods for plumbing fixtures, water supply, and waste drainage systems. The technology developed is used in building codes and standards.

Reverberation Chamber
This facility is used to develop sound pressure coefficients and to calibrate test equipment in other laboratories. The chamber supports research to define the acoustical parameters for building materials and spaces and to develop models and test methods for evaluating acoustical performance.

Construction Materials Reference Laboratories
In conjunction with other laboratories, this facility serves over 1,000 public and private laboratories nationwide by providing proficiency samples, inspections, and field test methods for cost effective quality assurance in materials.

Outdoor Energy Conservation Test Site
This facility includes a passive solar test house containing over 400 sensors and transducers for measuring the thermal performance of such solar features as clerestory windows, mass storage wall, and direct-gain cell. Six single-room test houses provide data on heat exchange. Other facilities study solar heat pumps and domestic hot water systems.

Image Analysis Laboratory
This facility has two special-purpose image analysis computers and cameras for obtaining images and converting them into digital form. The facility is used extensively in studies of materials degradation involving images from the scanning electron microscope or photographs of surfaces of full-scale structures.

Center for Fire Research

Fire Test Building
This facility is designed for large scale fire experiments. Smoke abatement equipment permits large fires to be conducted safely without pollution of the environment. Some of the experimental capabilities are single room fire experiments; room-corridor fire experiments; rate of heat release (small to large scale including material samples, single items of furniture, full size rooms); fire endurance furnace with unique high rate of temperature increase capability; room-corridor smoke travel experiments; and two-story smoke travel experiments.

NIST Annex
This facility serves as a field station for experiments not readily accommodated in the main laboratories. Some of the experimental capabilities include multiroom single story structure for smoke movement studies; two story, four bay, steel frame structure for studies of steel framing movement and deflection and floor/ceiling performance with significant fire exposures; compartment fire facility for studying vent flows; sprinkler facility for droplet distribution studies; small scale gas-well simulation blow-out experiment; small scale aircraft cabin fire experiment.

Center for Fire Research Laboratory Facilities
The Center for Fire Research Laboratories' facilities include Lateral Ignition and Flame Spread Test for wall materials; vertical flame heat transfer rig; salt water smoke movement analog facilities; Fire Simulation Laboratory with dedicated mini-computer and high resolution graphics capability; apparatus for combustion product toxicity studies; Fire Research Information Service--a library of over 30,000 fire research documents; droplet imaging system for size and velocity distribution measurements in sprays.

National Measurement Laboratory

Free-Electron Laser User Facility
This laboratory is constructing a national free-electron laser user facility for research in physics, chemistry, biophysics, materials science, and medical sciences.

Materials Science and Engineering Laboratory
The specialized facilities include an array of metals and ceramics laboratories for controlled materials synthesis and process; a 12-million-pound test rig for evaluating large-scale mechanical material properties; experimental stations for studying arc-welding processes; specialized small-angle and texture x-ray diffractometers particularly suited for polymer characterization; and a 20-megawatt reactor for neutron scattering experiments.

Cold Neutron Research Facility
This facility is the nation's first for "cold Neutron" studies, filling a serious void in the nation's materials science and engineering research. The facility provides beams of deeply penetrating low-energy neutrons, essential for important experiments that are impractical or even impossible with conventional neutron sources. The facility is available to all U.S. users for the study of materials research, molecular structure determination, and neutron activation analysis.

Center for Chemical Engineering

Gas Flow Measurement Facility/Boulder
This facility measures the flow rate of gas on a mass basis. Gas flows through the meter to be tested and then is condensed by passing the gas through a cryogenic system and into a weigh tank. The time integrated mass flow rate passing through the test meter is the same as the mass accumulated in the weigh tank. This facility provides high accuracy and the only mass-based continuous gas flow measurement in the world.

Water Flow Facilities
These facilities employ weighing and timing techniques as the means to make primary determination of the quantity of water flowing through the device or system under test.

Advanced Systems Division

CD-ROM Technology Evaluation Laboratory
The Compact Disk-Read Only Memory technology evaluation laboratory provides a site where Federal users can evaluate CD-ROM hardware and retrieval systems. More than 25 CD-ROM disks and 6 CD-ROM players have been installed; the National Computer Systems Laboratory solicited disk and equipment donations for the laboratory from the private sector. Other available CD-ROM databases include library catalogs, journal indexes, zip code directories, dictionaries, and product catalogs. CD-ROM drives and interfaces include systems manufactured by Phillips, Toshiba, Hitachi, and Sony.

* Research Associate Program
> Office of Research and Technology Applications
> National Institute of Standards and Technology
> Room A537, Administration Bldg.
> Gaithersburg, MD 20899   (301) 975-3087

The National Institute of Standards and Technology's Research Associate Program is an effective means for the transfer of technology, and in particular, measurement technology. The Program offers the opportunity to work under the supervision of and consult with NIST professionals of recognized stature in their fields, makes available the extensive laboratory and related facilities at NIST, and is an effective means of communicating industrial views and needs directly to NIST. Contact this office for more detailed information.

* Research of the National Institute of Standards and Technology
> Superintendent of Documents
> Government Printing Office
> Washington, DC 20402-9371   (202) 783-3238

For $13.00 a year, you can't afford not to know what's going on at the Nation's Measurement Science Laboratory. The *Journal of Research of the National Institute of Standards and Technology* brings you up-to-date scientific articles and information on NIST research and development in physics, chemistry, engineering, mathematics, and computer sciences. Papers cover a broad range of subjects, with major emphasis on measurement methodology and the basic technology underlying standardization. Also included from time to time are survey articles on topics closely related to the Institute's technical and scientific programs, cooperative research opportunities and grants, conference reports, and more. The journal is issued six times a year. Contact GPO to subscribe.

* Robotics Demonstrations
> Center for Manufacturing Engineering
> National Engineering Laboratory
> National Institute of Standards and Technology
> Gaithersburg, MD 20899   (301) 975-3414

Demonstrations of robot-tended machining workstations, and inspection machines, as well as demonstrations of optical measurement of surface finish are presented for the public. To schedule a tour, contact this Center.

* Robot Systems Division
> The Robot Systems Division
> Center for Manufacturing Engineering
> National Engineering Laboratory
> National Institute of Standards and Technology
> Gaithersburg, MD 20899   (301) 975-3418

The Robot Systems Division develops and maintains competence in robotics, real-time sensory interactive control technology, robot programming languages and standards, and interface standards for computer-integrated manufacturing systems and advanced robotic systems. The division conducts research into new techniques of sensing and control, sensory data processing, and uses databases, communications, world models, robot programming languages and techniques, interactive graphics for programming and intelligent, real-time control for industrial military, space, and construction applications. Work is on-going to develop experimental hardware and software, and measures of system performance for a wide variety of robot applications. Research in robot safety,

Science and Technology

robot assembly of parts, tools, and fixtures, and applications of intelligent control to military and industrial systems is performed. Contact this division for more information.

* Scientific Computer Users Newletter

Computer Planning and Analysis
Center for Applied Mathematics
National Engineering Laboratory
National Institute of Standards and Technology
Gaithersburg, MD 20899 (301) 975-3801

The Office of Computer Planning and Analysis puts out a bi-monthly newsletter for scientific computer users. Contact this office for more information on subscriptions.

* Scientific Computing Services

Scientific Computing Division
Center for Applied Mathematics
National Engineering Laboratory
National Institute of Standards and Technology
Gaithersburg, MD 20899 (301) 975-3816

The Scientific Computing Division provides consulting services; performs research, and collaborates in the application of computer science and technology to computation problems in physical science and engineering at NIST.

* Semiconductor Industry

Center for Manufacturing Engineering
National Engineering Laboratory
National Institute of Standards and Technology
B322 Metrology Bldg.
Gaithersburg, MD 20899 (301) 975-3400

The National Engineering Laboratory (NEL) helps the semiconductor industry improve the quality, cost, and reliability of U.S. manufactured semiconductor devices through new measurement methods and calibration services. NEL is developing, with a major electronics firm, a computerized "expert" system to help process engineers pinpoint probable causes of errors in semiconductor manufacturing.

* Small Business Specialist

Small Business Specialist
National Institute of Standards and Technology
U.S. Department of Commerce
Gaithersburg, MD 20899 (301) 975-6343

NIST's small business specialist is the contact for small businesses who wish to use the services of the National Institute of Standards and Technology.

* Small-Scale Advanced Manufacturing

Center for Manufacturing Engineering
National Engineering Laboratory
National Institute of Standards and Technology
B119 Technology Bldg.
Gaithersburg, MD 20899(301) 975-2300

Small job shops--operations with fewer than 50 employees--make up about 85 percent of U.S. metal fabrication facilities and account for about 75 percent of all U.S. metal fabrication. They are running substantially behind their overseas competitors in the use of modern technology. The National Institute of Standards and Technology is working to answer questions such as What modern technologies are commercially available, affordable, and useful to the small job shop? and What return on investment might be expected? To help answer these questions, NIST is using its own job shop to conduct an experiment in the practical implementation of computer-integrated manufacturing. Contact this Center for more information.

* Speech Recognition Research

National Computer Systems Laboratory
National Institute of Standards and Technology
B154 Technology Bldg.
Gaithersburg, MD 20899 (301) 975-2822

Computers that understand spoken language and can carry on conversations with humans are a science fiction staple. But in reality, comprehending and responding to spoken language is a difficult process for most computers. Interactions between people and machines still are limited mostly to communicating through mechanical means such as a keyboard. NIST researchers are developing improved algorithms and software for phonetically-based recognition of speech and ways to measure the performance of automatic speech recognizers. Basic research as well as measurement methods are needed to advance the technology. For more information on speech recognition research, contact this laboratory.

* Standards Certification Activities in the United States

Office of Standards Code and Information
A629 Administration Bldg.
Gaithersburg, MD 20899 (301) 975-4029

Certification programs, considered a vital link between product standards and actual products, have significant impact on the marketplace. *The ABC's of Certification Activities in the United States* describes the different types of programs or schemes used to produce written assurance that a product or service conforms to a standard or specification. A sequel to *The ABC's of Standards-Related Activities in the United States* (1987), the new report provides a further introduction to certification for those not familiar with this important standards-related activity. Included are descriptions of product quality; self certification; third-party certification; federal, state, international, and regional programs; choice of standards; certification methodology; and certification marks. The report also addresses some of the potential problems with certification programs. To obtain a copy send a self-addressed mailing label to Maureen A. Breitenberg at the above address.

* Standards for Federal Government Certification Programs

Superintendent of Documents
Government Printing Office
Washington, DC 20402-9371 (202) 783-3238

Federal Government Certification Programs is a guide for manufacturers, distributors, state and local government officials, importers, consumers, and others concerned with standards and procedures used in federal certification programs. It contains information on manufactured products, agricultural commodities, medical services--devices and drugs, defense procurement items, transportation, and the voluntary inspection and uniform grading of such food items as dairy products, meats, and produce. Each entry describes the scope and nature of the program, lists the testing and inspection practices, standards used, methods of identification and enforcement, reciprocal recognition or acceptance of certification, and a contact point in the federal agency. The updated directory is a joint effort by NIST and the U.S. Department of Agriculture. The directory costs $12 prepaid through GPO.

* Standard Reference Data

Reference Center
Standard Reference Data
National Institute of Standards and Technology
A323 Physics Building
Gaithersburg, MD 20899 (301) 975-2208

The Standard Reference Data Program aims to provide reliable, well-documented data to scientists and engineers for use in technical decision making, research and development. Experts in the physical, chemical, and materials sciences critically evaluate data that result from experimental measurements, calculations, and theory. The evaluations are carried out through a network of data centers, projects, and cooperative programs that comprise the National Standard Reference Data System. Experienced researchers in each area assess the accuracy of the data reported in the literature, prepare compilations, and recommend best values. The outputs are widely distributed as publications and computer-readable databases. Some of the databases are also accessible via on-line data systems. For a free complete catalog of publications and databases, contact the office above.

* Standard Reference Data Grants

Reference Center
Standard Reference Data
National Institute of Standards and Technology
A323 Physics Building
Gaithersburg, MD 20899 (301) 975-2208

Each year, the Standard Reference Data Program, in cooperation with other government funding agencies, administers a grant program aimed at involving experts in universities, industry, and government in data evaluation projects. This competitive program focuses on high priority short-term projects within the overall chemistry, physics, and materials scope of the program. Contact this office for more information and application procedures.

* Standard Reference Materials Catalog

Office of Standard Reference Materials
National Institute of Science and Technology
B311 Chemistry Bldg
Gaithersburg, MD 20899 (301) 975-6776

Nearly 1,000 Standard Reference Materials available from NIST are listed in the *NBS Standard Reference Materials Catalog 1988-89*. The materials, certified for specific *chemical and physical properties, include cements, ores, metals, glass, plastics, food, and environmental and clinical items. The expanded list of nutrition and health standards includes materials to calibrate instruments to detect marijuana in a human urine sample and to improve the precision of tests for elevated levels of the enzyme aspartate aminotransferase (AST) to detect heart attacks. Two new micro-length standards also are listed. The first commercial space-made product, 10-Micrometer Polystyrene Spheres, is available on a glass slide to calibrate microscopes. The second commercial space-made product, 30 Micrometer Polystyrene Spheres, is a new measurement standard for powder manufacturers. Also available is a series of seven individual low-alloy steels widely used in industry. Contact the office above to obtain the catalog.

* Standard Technical Data

Office of Standard Reference Data
National Measurement Laboratory
National Institute of Standards and Technology
A323 Physics Bldg.
Gaithersburg, MD 20899 (301) 975-2200

The National Measurement Laboratory provides reliable technical data required by industry, government, and academia to increase the effectiveness of U.S. science and technology. For information on this data, contact this office.

* State Technology Programs Clearinghouse

Director,
National Institute of Standards and Technology
Manufacturing Technology Centers Program
Bldg. 220, Room B111
Gaithersburg, MD 20899 (301) 975-3414

This clearinghouse gathers and analyzes information on the many State and local technology development programs across the nation. The idea is to develop a central base of information on what programs are available, what has been tried, and what the results have been. The clearinghouse will be a resource for state and local governments when deciding on new technology policies. The information will be shared through workshops and other mechanisms. For more information, contact this office.

* Statistical Engineering Services

Statistical Engineering Division
Center for Applied Mathematics
National Engineering Laboratory
National Institute of Standards and Technology
Gaithersburg, MD 20899 (301) 975-2840

The Statistical Engineering Division provides consulting services in the application of mathematical statistics to physical science experiments and engineering tests. The division conducts studies of computational methods and prepares reports, manuals, handbooks, and tools for statistical computing. The outputs include the Handbook for Development and Implementation of Measurement Assurance Programs, and DATAPLOT computer software for data analysis and model building. Contact this division for more information.

* Structures Research

Structures Division
Center for Building Technology
National Engineering Laboratory
National Institute of Standards and Technology
Gaithersburg, MD 20899 (301) 975-6048

The Structures Division conducts laboratory, field, and analytical research in structural and earthquake engineering, investigates structural failures, characterizes normal and extreme loads on buildings occurring during construction and in service, develops design criteria for reduction of damage caused by natural hazards, and develops advanced computation methods for evaluating static and dynamic response of structures. Work is on-going to enhance building safety. Sample outputs include technical data and design criteria for loads on buildings and technical data for building performance in earthquakes. Contact this division for more information.

* Technology Extension Programs

Director,
National Institute of Standards and Technology
Manufacturing Technology Centers Program
Bldg. 220, Room B111
Gaithersburg, MD 20899 (301) 975-3414

The NIST is making efforts to forge new ties to the many State and local technology extension services that have been created throughout the country. NIST can establish cooperative agreements with state or local programs to develop programs that transfer federally developed technology to business within their area. State and local extension services typically emphasize business advice rather than dealing with sophisticated technology. Ties with NIST will help to coordinate the state and local extension services with federal technology transfer programs. Through workshops, seminars, and other mechanisms, NIST plans to help technology extension agents make the best use of federal resources.

* Technology Services

Technology Services
National Institute of Standards and Technology
A363 Physics Bldg.
Gaithersburg, MD 20899 (301) 975-4500

For many U.S. businesses, the tools for building a competitive advantage already exist--in other firms, in university or federal laboratories, or even in off-the-shelf technology available from suppliers. The National Institute of Technology and Standard's industrial technology services, a still evolving array of outreach programs, aim to get the productivity-enhancing equipment and methods to the companies that need them. Technology Services provides technical support, and in some cases financial assistance, to U.S. industry, especially small and medium-sized businesses, to facilitate the commercialization of products based on new scientific discoveries. Among the services are

-Providing technical support and financial assistance to regional centers for transferring manufacturing technology to small and medium-sized firms.

-Developing Standard Reference Materials and Standard Reference Data and calibrating equipment and devices to aid in improving industrial quality control.

-Promoting technology innovation by technically evaluating innovations, inventions, and new technologies.

-Providing technical assistance to private, local, national, and international standards-writing organizations to ensure equity in the marketplace.

Contact the office above for more information on the available services.

* The Journal of Research of the National Bureau of Standards

Superintendent of Documents
Government Printing Office
Washington, DC 20402-9371 (202) 783-3238

The proceedings of a 1987 symposium, *Accuracy in Trace Analysis--Accomplishments, Goals, Challenges*, have been reprinted in this special edition of the journal. The 4-day event at NIST covered such topics as the history of trace analysis, robotics in the chemistry lab, measuring vitamins in foods, and the use of microwaves to dissolve samples. The proceedings consist of nearly 140 technical reports. This special edition is $3.00 prepaid through GPO.

* Thermochemical Tables Available Online

Office of Standard Reference Data
National Institute of Standards and Technology
A323 Physics Bldg.
Gaithersburg, MD 20899 (301) 975-2208

The third edition of the (Joint-Army-Navy-Air Force) *JANAF Thermochemical Tables*, published by NIST, has been computerized to provide scientists and engineers with rapid access to information on the performance of materials at high temperatures. The database is available to subscribers on STN International (Scientific and Technical Network), an on-line private sector retrieval service offered worldwide. The numerical data can be used to make quick performance calculations for chemical reactors such as rocket engines, air pollution control equipment, internal combustion engines, coal gasifiers, and furnaces. The database is designed to list in one table all of the values for a given property of a chemical compound when the values for that compound appear in more than one tabulation. Information can be obtained by chemical name, the formula, or by the *Chemical Abstracts Registry Number*. For information on the new JANAF file through STN, contact the office above.

* Thermophysical Computer Programs

Thermophysics Division
Center for Chemical Engineering
National Engineering Laboratory
National Institute of Standards and Technology
Gaithersburg, MD 20899 (303) 497-3257

The Thermophysics Division creates computer programs for the calculation of thermodynamic and transport properties of industrial chemicals and fuels (for improved commercial exchange of fluids and process design).

* Tours of the Facilities

Tours
National Institute of Standards and Technology
Gaithersburg, MD 20899 (301) 975-3585

Free tours of the various facilities at NIST are given on Thursdays at 9:30 a.m. They generally last for two hours, and the public is welcome, but should schedule reservations in advance through Jan Hauber at the office above.

Patents, Trademarks and Copyrights

* See also Science and Technology Chapter
* See also International Relations and Defense Chapter

If you are looking for patent information the Patent and Trademark Office listed below is the place to go. If you want to do patent research outside of the Washington, DC area the Patent Office can suggest local libraries which carry their information. You should also be aware that for $6.00 the Patent Office can provide you with a disclosure statement which can protect your idea for 2 years. It is not a patent, but for many it is a good inexpensive way to get started until you find out whether your idea is saleable. Copyright information is available from the Library of Congress which is described here.

* Business Patents and Protection

Office of Business Practices
Bureau of Economics and Business Affairs
Department of State
2201 C St., NW, Room 3531A
Washington, DC 20520   (202) 647-1486

This office deals with intellectual property rights, including computer chip and copyright protection. They conduct bilateral and multilateral negotiations and have an ongoing relationship with intellectual property rights conventions. This office also deals with international relations pertaining to international trade laws.

* Copyright Examining Practices

Copyright Office
Certifications and Documents
Library of Congress
Washington, DC 20559   (202) 707-6800

The *Compendium II of Copyright Office Practices* is intended as a general guide for those with special interest in copyright examining practices which concern the registration of applications for copyright under the 1976 Copyright Act. It is available for $51 from the Superintendent of Documents, Government Printing Office, Washington, D.C. 20402; (202) 783-3238.

* Copyright Research Service

Copyright Office
Reference and Bibliographic Section
Library of Congress
Washington, DC 20559   (202) 707-6850

For a fee of $10 per hour or part thereof, the Copyright Office will research the copyright you need and send you the information by mail. Requests must be in writing, and you must specify exact details you require.

* Copyright Royalty Tribunal

Copyright Royalty Tribunal
1111 20th St. NW
Washington, DC 20036   (202) 653-5175

This agency makes adjustments for copyright royalty rates for records, jukeboxes, and some cable television transmissions.

* Copyright Royalty Tribunal Meetings

Copyright Royalty Tribunal
1111 20th St. NW
Washington, DC 20036   (202) 653-5175

Notices of agency meetings are announced 30 days in advance, and hearing notices are published in the *Federal Register*. The trade press then publicizes the proceedings.

* Copyrights

Copyright Office
Library of Congress
Washington, DC 20559   (202) 707-6540

The Library of Congress Copyright Office grants exclusive rights to reproduce or prepare derivative works on the copyrighted work in copies or on phonorecords and to distribute them to the public by sale, rental, lease, or loan. Copyrightable works include books, periodicals, and other literary works; musical compositions, song lyrics, dramas, and dramatico-musical compositions; pantomimes and choreographic works; pictorial, graphic, and sculptural works; motion pictures and other audiovisual works; and sound recordings. The Library

provides information on copyright registration procedures and copyright card catalogs covering more than 16 million works that have been registered since 1870.

* Creative and Analytical Thinking Skills

Commissioner of Patents and Trademarks
Patent and Trademark Office
Department of Commerce
2121 Crystal Dr., Room 1101C
Arlington, VA 22202   (703) 557-1610

Project XL is a PTO outreach program designed to encourage the development of analytical and creative thinking and problem-solving skills among America's youth. The principal focus of this effort is on the promotion of educational programs that teach critical and creative thinking. They present national and regional conferences, and established an Education Roundtable, an open forum and nation discussion network. This office distributes an information guide called *The Inventive Thinking Project*, designed to channel students in grades K-12 into the inventive thinking process through the creation of their own unique inventions or innovations. They are also in the process of developing an educator's resource guide and a special curriculum. Contact this office for more information about Project XL and the assistance and products they have available.

* Intellectual Property Rights

Office of Business Practices
Bureau of Economics and Business Affairs
Department of State
2201 C St., NW, Room 3531A
Washington, DC 20520   (202) 647-1486

This office deals with intellectual property rights, including computer chip and copyright protection. They conduct bilateral and multilateral negotiations and have an ongoing relationship with intellectual property rights conventions. This office also deals with international relations pertaining to international trade laws.

* Invention, Evidence of Conception

Commissioner of Patents and Trademarks
Patent and Trademark Office
Department of Commerce
2121 Crystal Dr.
Arlington, VA 22202   (703) 557-3225

A Disclosure Document is evidence of the dates of conception of inventions. A paper disclosing an invention and signed by the inventor may be forwarded to the Patent and Trademark Office. It will be retained for two years, and then destroyed unless it is referred to in a separate letter in a related patent application filed within two years. The Disclosure Document is not a patent application, and the date of its receipt in the Patent and Trademark Office will not become the effective filing date of any patent application subsequently filed. These documents will be kept in confidence by the Patent and Trademark Office. In addition to the $6 fee, the Disclosure Document must be accompanied by a stamped, self-addressed envelope and a separate paper in duplicate, signed by the inventor, stating that he/she is the inventor and requesting that the material be received for processing under the Disclosure Document Program.

* Inventions for Licensing

Government Inventions for Licensing
Abstract Newsletter
National Technical Information Service
5285 Port Royal Rd.
Springfield, VA 22161   (703) 487-4630

The newsletter, *Inventions for Licensing*, provides weekly coverage of inventions from all Federal agencies. Each issue provides full summaries of inventions U.S. companies can review to discover business opportunities. More than 1,200 inventions are announced annually. A study of the inventions granted in the past year shows that 54% of inventions licensed go to smaller businesses; some inventions require only small amounts of development before they are ready to market; large and small firms have added new product lines using these inventions; and new companies have been started using this Government technology. A subscription is available for $225 per year. Contact the Subscription Department to place an order or to request a free brochure *PR-801*.

* Inventors Conference and Exposition
Office of Public Affairs
Patent and Trademark Office
Department of Commerce
2011 Crystal Dr., Room 208B
Arlington, VA 22202 (703) 557-3341
An annual conference is sponsored by the Patent and Trademark Office, and includes speakers, exhibits, and seminars. The conference is usually held in May, and is advertised in a wide variety of journals. Contact the Office of Public Affairs for more information.

* Literary Works Copyright Entries Catalogs
Superintendent of Documents
Government Printing Office
Washington, DC 20402 (202) 783-3238
The following copyright catalogs, which list materials registered only during the period covered by each issue, are available on microfiche only and are sold as individual subscriptions:
Part 1: Nondramatic Literary Works (quarterly) $11.00 per year.
Part 2: Serials and Periodicals (semi-annually) $5.00 per year.

* Patent Academy
Patent and Trademark Office
Department of Commerce
One Crystal Park, Room 502
Arlington, VA 22202 (703) 557-2086
The Patent Academy provide training to patent examiners on all aspects of the patent application process. Although designed for Patent and Trademark Office employees, the Academy is also open to the public. A complete schedule of the topics covered in the four phase program and the fees associated with each phase is available from the Academy.

* Patent and Trademark Copies
Patent and Trademark Office
Department of Commerce
Washington, DC 20231 (703) 557-7800
Printed copies of any patent, identified by its patent number, may be purchased from the Patent and Trademark Office at a cost of $1.50 each, postage free, except plant patents in color, which are $6.00 each. Send your check or money order with the patent number to the address listed above.

* Patent and Trademark Office
Department of Commerce
20211 Jefferson Davis Highway
Arlington, VA 22202 (703) 557-3341
The Patent and Trademark Office provides patent and trademark protection to inventors and businesses for their inventions and corporate and product identifications. Through the preservation, classification, and distribution of patent information, PTO encourages innovation and the scientific and technical advancement of American industry. It examines applications and grants patents on inventions, and maintains search files of U.S. and foreign patents for public use, and supplies copies of patents and official records to the public. It performs similar functions for trademarks.

* Patent and Trademark Publications
Superintendent of Documents
Government Printing Office
Washington, DC 20402 (202) 783-3238
The following is a list of Patent and Trademark publications available through the Government Printing Office:

Annual Indexes. An index of the patents issued each year is published in two volumes, one an alphabetical index of patentees and the other an index by subject matter of inventions. An annual index of trademarks contains an alphabetical index of trademark registrants, registration numbers, dates published, classification of goods for which registered, and decisions published during the calendar year. Prices vary from year to year.

General Information Concerning Patents. Contains a vast amount of general information concerning the application for and granting of patents expressed in non-technical language for the layman ($2.00).

Manual of Classification. A loose-leaf volume listing the numbers and descriptive titles of the more than 390 classes and 115,00 subclasses used in the subject classification ($49.00).

Manual of Patent Examining Procedure. A loose-leaf manual which serves primarily as a detailed reference work on patent examining practice and procedure for the Patent Examining Corps ($70.00).

Patent Attorneys and Agents Registered to Practice Before the U.S. Patent and Trademark Office. An alphabetically and geographically arranged listing of patent attorneys and agents registered ($17.00).

Patent Official Gazette. The official journal of the Patent and Trademark Office relating to patents. Issued each Tuesday, simultaneously with the weekly issuance of patents, it contains a selected figure of the drawings and an abstract of each patent granted, indexes of patents, lists of patents available for license or sale, and general information such as orders, notices, changes in rules, and changes in classification ($270.00).

37 Code of Federal Regulations ($13.00).

Story of the Patent and Trademark Office ($3.50).

Trademark Official Gazette. The official journal of the Patent and Trademark Office relating to trademarks. Published every Tuesday, it contains an illustration of each trademark published for opposition, a list of trademarks registered, classified list of registered trademarks, and Patent Office notices ($302.00).

Trademark Manual of Examining Procedures ($14.00).

* Patent Applications
Superintendent of Documents
Government Printing Office
Washington, DC 20402 (202) 783-3238
The publication, *General Information Concerning Patents*, gives you an overview of the Patent and Trademark Office, as well as the patent application procedures. Included are application forms, and information regarding the filing fees, petitions, and foreign patents. It is available through the Government Printing Office.

* Patent Applications for Other Countries
Office of Public Affairs
Patent and Trademark Office
Department of Commerce
2011 Crystal Dr., Room 208B
Arlington, VA 22202 (703) 557-3341
The Patent Cooperation Treaty is presently adhered to by 39 countries, including the United States, and facilitates the filing of applications for patents on the same invention in member countries by providing, among other things, for centralized filing procedures and a standardized application format. The Paris Convention for the Protection of Industrial Property provides that each country guarantee to the citizens of the other countries the same rights in patent and trademark matters that it gives to its own citizens. The treaty provides for the right of priority in the case of patents, trademarks, and industrial designs. Currently 93 countries, including the United States, adhere to the treaty.

* Patent Attorneys, List of
Superintendent of Documents
Government Printing Office
Washington, DC 20402 (202) 783-3238
An alphabetically and geographically arranged listing of patent attorneys and agents registered to practice before the U.S. Patent and Trademark Office is available through GPO for $17.00.

* Patent Bibliographies
National Technical Information Service
Department of Commerce
5285 Port Royal Road
Springfield, VA 22161 (703) 487-4640
The Patent and Trademark Office produces and leases many machine-readable patent databases that are processed and offered to the public through commercial systems. The primary patent database, the Patent Full Text Database, has several subfiles. These are not to be construed as "legal" patent searches. Contact the Sales Desk for more information or the free brochure, *PR-186*.

* Patent Catalogs to Government-Owned Inventions
Catalogs of Government Inventions for Licensing
National Technical Information Service

Patents, Trademarks and Copyrights

Department of Commerce
5285 Port Royal Rd.
Springfield, VA 22161 (703) 487-4650
The annual *Patent Catalog To Government-Owned Inventions* offers unique patent licensing opportunities. The catalogs are subdivided into 43 subject headings, making it easy to scan for exact references. Each entry includes a detailed summary inventor information, and information on obtaining backup material. Catalogs for each year going back to 1981 are available with prices ranging from $33-$45.00. Contact the Sales Desk to place an order or to request the free information brochure, *PR-801*.

* Patent Depository Libraries

Office of Patent Depository Library Programs
Patent and Trademark Office
Department of Commerce
1921 Jefferson Davis Hwy, Room 306
Arlington, VA 22202 (703) 557-9686
The following libraries, designated as Patent Depository Libraries, receive current issues of U.S. Patents and maintain collections of earlier-issued patents. The scope of these collections varies from library to library, ranging from patents of only recent years to all or most of the patents issued since 1790. These patent collections, which are organized in patent number sequence, are available for use by the public free of charge. In addition, each of the PDLs offer supplemental reference publications of the U.S. Patent Classification System, including the *Manual of Classification, Index to the U.S. Patent Classification, Classification Definitions*, and provides technical staff assistance in their use to aid the public. CASSIS (Classification and Search Support Information System), which provides direct, on-line access to Patent and Trademark Office data is available at all PDLs.

* Patent Drawings

Cartographic and Architectural Branch
National Archives and Records Administration
8th St. & Pennsylvania Ave., NW
Washington, DC 20408 (202) 756-6700
This collection consists of patent drawings from the period between 1835-1871. An index is available to help you search through the collection. All the drawings are on microfilm and are available for $22. Copies can be made of the drawings at a cost of $1.60 a running foot. The drawings are available for viewing 8:00 a.m. to 4:20 p.m., Monday through Friday, at the Branch Office, 841 South Pickett St., Alexandria, Virginia.

* Patent Licensing Opportunities

National Patent Program
Room 401, Building 005
BARC-West
Beltsville, MD 20705 (301) 344-2518
Government patents resulting from agricultural research discoveries are available for licensing to U.S. companies and citizens. Licenses are offered on a non-exclusive, exclusive, and co-exclusive basis. Non-exclusive licenses are generally granted when no large investment to market a product is expected. Exclusive and co-exclusive licenses are granted when substantial investment is required. Fees for licenses are negotiable. An annual catalog listing all patents available for license plus technical abstracts is available. The necessary regulations and forms are included.

* Patent Search

Patent Office Search Room
Patent and Trademark Office
Department of Commerce
2021 Jefferson Davis Hwy.
Arlington, VA 22202 (703) 557-2276
The Patent and Trademark Office has a classification system in which patents are divided into classes and subclasses of subjects, covering all items from the simple to the complex. This system permits any individual to locate and examine all existing patents in any field of technology. The Patent Search Room is open to the public Monday-Friday 8a.m.-8p.m. Computer terminals are available for your search, as well as staff to assist you in using the facilities. You can make copies of patents at a cost of 15 cents per page.

* Patents on Seeds

Plant Variety Protection Office
Commodities Scientific Support Division
AMS, NAL, Room 500
Beltsville, MD 20705 (301) 344-2518

Unique seeds, with few exceptions, that are sexually reproduced can be protected by patents. The protection, which extends for 18 years, provides owners with exclusive rights to sell, reproduce, export, and produce the seed.

* Royalty Payments

Copyright Royalty Tribunal
1111 20th St. NW
Room 450
Washington, DC 20036 (202) 653-5175
In addition to records, jukeboxes, and some cable television transmissions, the Tribunal also sets terms and rates of royalty payments for the use of nondramatic works and pictorial, graphic, and sculptural works by public broadcasting stations. In addition, the Tribunal makes distribution of royalty fees for cable television and jukeboxes. Contact this office for more information on royalty payments.

* Satellite Home Viewer Act of 1988

Copyright Royalty Tribunal
1111 20th St. NW
Washington, DC 20036 (202) 653-5175
Under the Satellite Home Viewer Act of 1988, the Tribunal distributes royalty fees to copyright owners.

* Technology Assessment with Patents

Office of Documentation Information
Patent and Trademark Office
Department of Commerce
1921 Jefferson Davis Hwy., Room 304
Arlington, VA 22202 (703) 557-5652
The Technology Assessment and Forecast (TAF) Program's mission is to stimulate the use and enhance the usability of the more than 27 million documents which make the categorized U.S. patent file. The PTO has assembled the TAF database which covers all U.S. patents. The PTO extracts meaningful information about the U.S. patent file from the TAF database, analyzes the information, and makes it available in a variety of formats. Users of TAF information include patent attorneys, researchers, PTO employees and other government agencies. Patent information from the TAF database is distributed to users through publications, such as *Patent Profiles* and *Technology Assessment and Forecast Reports*, as well as through custom patent reports and statistical reports. Contact this office for more information on the TAF database, and ordering information for TAF publications.

* Trademark Search

Trademark Search Library
Patent and Trademark Office
Department of Commerce
2011 Jefferson Davis Hwy., Room 2C08
Arlington, VA 22202 (703) 557-3281
A record of all active trademark registrations and pending applications is maintained by the PTO to help determine whether a previously registered mark exists which could prevent the registration of an applicant's mark. The Trademark Search Library is open to the public free of charge Monday through Friday, 8:00 a.m. to 5:30 p.m. The PTO cannot advise prospective applicants of the availability of a particular mark prior to the filing of an application. The applicant may hire a private search company or law firm to perform a search if a search is desired before filing an application and the applicant is unable to visit the search library. The PTO cannot recommend any such companies, but the applicant may wish to consult listings for "Trademark Search Services" in the telephone directories or contact local bar associations for a list of attorneys specializing in trademark law.

* Tribunal Hearing Transcripts

Copyright Royalty Tribunal
1111 20th St. NW
Washington, DC 20036 (202) 653-5175
All transcripts of Tribunal hearings and meetings are available to the public upon request.

Agriculture and Farming
Management and Productivity

* See also Experts Chapter
* See also International Trade
* See also Information from Lawmakers Chapter
* See also Environment and Nature Chapter
* See also Careers and Workplace; Research Grants in Every Field Chapter

Most farmers, ranchers, and growers are aware of only a fraction of the resources available from the federal government but consumers, chefs, gardeners, and ordinary folks know even less about the help and information readily accessible from the U.S. Department of Agriculture (USDA). A local telephone call to your USDA extension service will bring instantaneous advice on how to get rid of a wasp's nest or termites. Extension services in local communities offer classes on a wide range of other topics such as career opportunities to hydroponic farming. The National Agricultural Library is another mammoth information center with its numerous databases and publications. Youngsters between the ages of 10 to 20 years are eligible for start-up USDA loans to launch businesses ranging from lawn-moving services to roadside produce stands. Incentives for agriculture cooperatives and new alternative approaches to farming also can be exploited. The government along with many land grant colleges and universities can share the latest research findings about soil and water conservation, farmland preservation, crop yields, or genetic engineering. In addition to farming, aquaculture, forestry information, there are answers to questions concerning the quality of meat, poultry, dairy, produce and other food that reaches the supermarket.

Family farmers, agricultural cooperatives, medium size growers, to corporate agribusiness all can benefit from the technical expertise, resources, loan and loan guarantee programs, and other incentives offered by numerous government offices. Efforts to modernize farming in developing countries, notably by the Peace Corps, are included in the International Relations and Defense Chapter.

* AGRICOLA Database

National Agricultural Library
Reference Branch, Room 111
10301 Baltimore Blvd.
Beltsville, MD 20782 (301) 344-4479
The bibliographic database consists of records for literature citation of journal articles, monographs, theses, patents, software, audiovisual materials, and technical reports relating to all aspects of agriculture. It also includes materials not in the NAL collection. Access to AGRICOLA is available on-site, on a cost-recovery basis and online through DIALOG and BRS, and on CD-ROM from several vendors. For more information contact NAL at the above address.

* Agricultural Diseases Database

Emergency Programs Information Center Data Bank
Veterinary Services, APHIS
U.S. Department of Agriculture
6505 Belcrest Rd.
Hyattsville, MD 20782 (301) 436-8687
The Emergency Program Information Center (EPIC) maintains a computerized database with bibliographic information for all literature stored on microfilm by the center. The EPIC Data Bank consists of worldwide literature covering diseases of livestock and poultry exotic to the U.S. Complete services, including bibliographic printouts and copies of cited articles, are primarily for personnel working in Federal and cooperating State animal disease-control and eradication programs. Users outside APHIS are generally only provided citations; however, requests are handled on an individual basis. The center has prepared standard bibliographies on 17 different topics, which are available to the general public. The PIC Brucellosis file is included in the AGRICOLA system.

* Agriculture and Food Marketing Revolution

Yearbook Editor, Publications
U.S. Department of Agriculture
Room 535-A
Washington, DC 20250 (202) 447-9173
Each year, the USDA publishes a yearbook which explores one theme in depth. The 1988 yearbook, Marketing U.S. Agriculture, written by experts from farms, industry, universities, and government, describes the revolution in the food marketing system caused by new technology, social changes, and increased competition for world markets.

* Agricultural Chemicals

National Agricultural Chemicals Association (NACA)

1155 15th St., NW
Madison Building
Suite 900
Washington, DC 20005 (202) 296-1585
The National Agricultural Chemicals Association consists of companies producing chemical controls for fungi, rodents, pests and weeds.

* Agricultural Environmental Engineering

American Society of Agricultural Engineers (ASAE)
2950 Niles Rd.
St. Joseph, MI 49085 (616) 429-0300
The American Society of Agricultural Engineers is the national association for engineers working on problems of importance to agricultural interests including irrigation and other large scale projects with environmental significance. Publications: Agricultural Engineering, ASAE Standards, Transactions of the ASAE.

* Agricultural Pests and Insects

Public Awareness, LPAS
APHIS
U.S.Department of Agriculture
Federal Building, Room 700
6505 Belcrest Road
Hyattsville, MD 20782 (301) 436-7799
The following is a sampling of fact sheets intended for consumers, farmers, scientists, journalists, and others. All publications are free; however, if ordering multiple quantities, an explanation is requested. Mediterranean Fruit Fly (August 1985). For farmers and the generalpublic, it describes the appearance and life cycle of the fly, and explains how eradication is accomplished by survey, regulatory actions, and control.
International Programs in APHIS (January 1983). For the general public, it describes protective measures taken worldwide to prevent spread of agricultural pests and diseases through imports and exports. Lists APHIS overseas offices and their activities.

* Agricultural Productivity

Eastern Regional Research Center
600 E. Mermaid Lane
Philadelphia, PA 19118 (215) 233-6400
Through basic, applied, and developmental research, scientists at nine research centers at ERRC are involved with projects to improve productivity of animals and crop plants and reduce losses; develop new and improved products and

processing technology; upgrade nutritional value; open new and expand existing domestic and foreign markets; reduce marketing costs; eliminate health-related problems; and minimize energy consumption.

* Alternative Agricultural Opportunities

Executive Officer
Local Extension Service
U.S. Department of Agriculture
Room 340A Administration Building
Washington, DC 20250 (202) 447-4111

The USDA operates an extension program in 3,165 counties located in all of the 50 states and the U.S. territories. Federal, state, and local governments share in financing and conducting cooperative extension educational programs to help farmers, processors, handlers, farm families, communities, and consumers apply the results of food and agricultural research including Alternative Agricultural Opportunities, which helps farmers use a distinctive approach to alternative crop and livestock enterprises to integrate marketing, management, and production factors into a total business plan.

* Alternative Farming Systems

U.S. Department of Agriculture
10301 Baltimore Blvd.
Beltsville, MD 20705 (301) 344-3704

This center covers organized farming or gardening that includes low-input, sustainable, or regenerative agriculture. Conservation tillage and other cultivation practices, such as intercropping, crop rotation, and use of green manures, are also covered.

* American Agriculture News Service

News Features (202) 488-8358

This recorded message gives you daily news announcements on a variety of agriculture-related topics.

* Animal and Manmade Fibers and Textiles

Fibers and Textiles
U.S. Department of Agriculture
10301 Baltimore Blvd.
Beltsville, MD 20705 (301) 344-3719

This center covers natural and manmade fibers, textiles and apparel, fashion design and merchandizing, and home furnishings. Library users may also access the Fiber Files for both soft fiber crops and for animal fibers.

* Animal Welfare

Animal Welfare
U.S. Department of Agriculture
10301 Baltimore Blvd.
Beltsville, MD 20705 (301) 344-3704

This center handles matters of animal care and handling, as well as housing and caging, training guides and manuals for animal care personnel, ethical issues involving animals, legislation, and regulation, and testing alternatives for drug toxicology studies.

* Aquaculture and Fish Farming

Aquaculture
U.S. Department of Agriculture
10301 Baltimore Blvd.
Beltsville, MD 20705 (301) 344-3704

This center covers culture of aquatic plants and animals in freshwater, brackish water, and marine environments. Examples include catfish farming, oyster culture, freshwater prawn culture, and trout farming. Staff can also answer questions about animal parasitology. Patrons can use AquaRef, a system containing aquaculture information on computer.

* Bees and Beekeeping

Honeybee Breeding Genetics
and Physiology Research Lab
U.S. Department of Agriculture
ARS, 1157 Ben Hur Rd.
Baton Rouge, LA 70820 (504) 766-6064

Scientists are currently at work trying to protect the beekeeping industry and the public from the advent of the Africanized bees that are due to arrive in mid 1990. Research projects include use of a toxic substance that will attract bees and kill them, a repellent that will keep these aggressive bees from stinging, and ways of protecting commercial queen bee farms from invasion of Africanized bees.

* Biotechnology and Genetic Engineering

Biotechnology
U.S. Department of Agriculture

10301 Baltimore Blvd.
Beltsville, MD 20705 (301) 344-3704

Subject areas covered by this center include genetic engineering, plant and animal tissue culture, single cell protein, immobilized enzymes, legislation and regulations, transgenic animals, and detoxification using microbes.

* Business Start-Up Loans for 10-20 Year Olds

Production Loan Division
U.S. Department of Agriculture
Farmers Home Administration
Washington, DC 20250 (202) 382-1632

The USDA lends up to $5,000 to youths from 10 to 20 years of age. The loans can be used to support both farm and non-farm ventures, such as small cropfarming, livestock farming, roadside stands, and custom work. They are normally made in conjunction with youth groups and require parental consent.

* Chemical and Fertilizer Hotline

Chemical Referral Center (800) CMA-8200
(202) 887-1315 (DC and collect calls from AK)

This toll-free service provides non-emergency referrals to companies that manufacture chemicals and to state and federal agencies for health and safety information and information regarding chemical regulations. It operates 9 a.m. to 6 p.m. eastern time.

* Commodities Market News

Information Staff
Agricultural Marketing Service
U.S. Department of Agriculture
Room 3510, South Building
P.O. Box 96456
Washington, DC 20090-6456 (202) 447-8998

Skilled market reporters gather and document marketing information that is distributed quickly throughout the U.S. via telephone recorders, newspapers, radio, television, and in printed reports. The reports are available for seven commodities: dairy, tobacco, cotton, fruits and vegetables, livestock, grain, and poultry, and they contain information on supply and demand and shipping point reports that cover prices paid by types of sale. Much of the information is gathered and distributed by local field offices via satellite.

* Communicable Diseases Affecting Cattle and Poultry

Animal and Plant Health Inspection Service
U.S. Department of Agriculture
Room 320-E
Washington, DC 20250 (202) 447-5193

A staff of specialists studies communicable diseases and pests affecting livestock and poultry.

* Compost and Improved Soil

Soil Microbial Systems
U.S. Department of Agriculture
Building 318, Room 108 BARC-E
Beltsville, MD 20705 (301) 344-3163

This office provides technical assistance on the production and use of compost, soil, and microbes.

* Crop and Soil Agronomy

American Society of Agronomy (ASA)
677 South Segoe Rd.
Madison, WI 53711 (608) 273-8080

The American Society of Agronomy promotes the acquisition and diffusion of knowledge concerning the nature and interrelationship of plants, soils and the environment. Publications: *Agronomy Journal, Crops and Soils, Journal of Environmental Quality, Journal of Agronomic Education, Agronomy News*.

* Crop Insurance Coverage

Manager
Federal Crop Insurance Corporation
U.S. Department of Agriculture
Washington, DC 20250 (202) 447-4603
OR: Your local crop insurance agent

The USDA runs a crop insurance program to improve the economic stability of agriculture through a sound system of crop insurance that provides multiple-peril insurance for individual farmers to ensure a basic income against droughts, freezes, insects, and other natural causes of disastrous crop losses. Any owner or operator of farmland who has an insurable interest in a crop in a county where insurance is offered on that crop is eligible unless the land is not classified for insurance purposes.

* Educational Programs: Farmers and their Families

Executive Officer
U.S. Department of Agriculture
Room 340A Administration Building
Washington, DC 20250   (202) 447-4111

The USDA operates an extension program in 3,165 counties located in all of the 50 states and the U.S. territories. Federal, state, and local governments share in financing and conducting cooperative extension educational programs to help farmers, processors, handlers, farm families, communities, and consumers apply the results of food and agricultural research. The Extension Service has targeted 9 national initiatives to provide a new focus for educational efforts.

Alternative Agricultural Opportunities: Helps farmers use a distinctive approach to alternative crop and livestock enterprises to integrate marketing, management, and production factors into a total business plan.

Building Human Capital: Helps people develop marketable job skills, make informed career decisions, and expand available opportunities.

Competitiveness and Profitability of American Agriculture:
To enhance farmers' competitiveness and profitability, Extension helps farmers improve production, finance, and management skills; develop new technology; adjust profitability to global market changes; and strengthen business and support systems.

Conservation and Management of Natural Resources: Helps people benefit from natural ecosystems without destroying them, sustain a productive natural resource base, market natural resource goods and services, and formulate and implement sound public policies.

Family and Economic Well-Being: Helps families manage finances and make sound financial decisions; confront and deal with such problems as alcohol and drug abuse, teenage pregnancy, and unemployment; and develop strategies for retirement.

Improving Nutrition, Diet, and Health: Extension offers up-to-date information about the relationship of dietary practices to lifestyle factors; the safety, quality, and composition of foods; and consumers' needs and perceptions about the food industry.

Revitalizing Rural America: In cooperation with local governments, Extension programs emphasize how to increase competitiveness and efficiency of rural programs, explore methods to diversify local economies and attract new business, adjust to impact of change, develop ways to finance and deliver services, and train leaders to make sound policy decisions for rural communities.

Water Quality: Work with consumers, producers and local government to learn more about the importance of high-quality ground water and the conservation of water resources. Emphasis is also put on the effects of agricultural chemicals and contaminants on water quality.

Youth at Risk: Extension is helping expand youth outreach resources to meet the needs of youth, develop programs for the most susceptible youth populations, provide leadership and job skills, and increase training of professionals and volunteers to work in communities to prevent and treat problems.

* Emerging Agricultural Technology

Office of Technology Assessment
600 Pennsylvania Ave., SE
Washington, DC 20510   (202) 228-6521

OTA is studying the emerging agricultural technologies for the 1990s and the structure of the research system that gives rise to these technologies, which include biotechnology, information technology, and low input technology for the food and agricultural sector. Contact Mike Phillips, the project director, for more information.

* Erosion Control

Information Division
U.S. Department of Agriculture
ASCS, P.O. Box 205
Kansas City, MO 64141   (202) 447-5237

The Agricultural State Conservation Service (ASCS) directs a number of conservation programs to preserve and improve American farmland:
Conservation Reserve Program (CRP): Targets the most fragile farmland by encouraging farmers to stop growing crops on land designated by conservationists as "highly erodible" and plant grass or trees on it instead. The farmer receives rent on the land for a term of ten years. Cost-share programs are also available for permanent planting of grass and trees in these areas.

* Farm Credit Administration Freedom of Information Act Requests

Freedom of Information Act Officer
Farm Credit Administration
1510 Farm Credit Drive
McLean, VA 22102   (202) 883-4056

Contact the office above for Freedom of Information Act requests.

* Farm Credit Administration Library

Library
Farm Credit Administration
1501 Farm Credit Drive
McLean, VA 22102   (202) 883-4296

For information on obtaining reference material through inter-library loan, contact the office above.

* Farm Money and Credit Reports

Office of Congressional and Public Affairs
Farm Credit Administration
1501 Farm Credit Drive
McLean, VA 22102   (703) 883-4056

Information on obtaining publications and documents can be obtained from the office above. Some of the documents it has which are available include news releases issued since January 1, 1972, biographies of Farm Credit Administration officials, and speeches by FCA officials. Other publications include:

FCA Handbook - Statutes & Regulations (fee charged)
FCA Examination Manual (Set fee Charged)
FCA Bulletin (Published 10 days after each meeting of the FCA Board)
FCA Report (Published on an as-needed basis)
FCA Orders
FCA Money and Credit Market Report
FCA Organization Chart
FCA Board Policies
FCA Annual Report

* Farming Cooperatives

Agricultural Cooperative Service
U.S. Department of Agriculture
Washington, DC 20250   (202) 653-6976

The USDA will assist any group interested in starting or developing agricultural cooperatives, and will also work with them to solve organizational, operational, or management problems. They will also help a cooperative expand export markets.

* Farming Profitability and Competitiveness

Executive Officer
Local Extension Service
U.S. Department of Agriculture
Room 340A Administration Building
Washington, DC 20250   (202) 447-4111

The USDA operates an extension program in 3,165 counties located in all of the 50 states and the U.S. territories. Federal, state, and local governments share in financing and conducting cooperative extension educational programs to help farmers, processors, handlers, farm families, communities, and consumers apply the results of food and agricultural research including Competitiveness and Profitability of American Agriculture: To enhance farmers' competitiveness and profitability, Extension helps farmers improve production, finance, and management skills; develop new technology; adjust profitability to global market changes; and strengthen business and support systems.

* Farmer-Owned Lending Institutions

Office of Congressional and Public Affairs
Farm Credit Administration
1501 Farm Credit Drive
McLean, VA 22102   (703) 883-4056

The Farm Credit System is a network of farmer-owned lending institutions and specialized service organizations. More than 70 years ago Congress created the System to provide American agriculture with a dependable source of credit at competitive rates. Today the System provides about one-third of the total credit used by America's farmers, ranchers, and their cooperatives. The *Farm Credit System 1989 Information Guide*, which provides information on the Farm Credit System, including a list of the System's banks, is available free from the office above.

* Farmland Conservation Efforts

Information Division
U.S. Department of Agriculture
ASCS, P.O. Box 205
Kansas City, MO 64141   (202) 447-5237

The Agricultural State Conservation Service (ASCS) directs a number of conservation programs to preserve and improve American farmland: Conservation Reserve Program (CRP): Targets the most fragile farmland by encouraging farmers to stop growing crops on land designated by conservationists as "highly erodible" and plant grass or trees on it instead. The farmer receives rent on the land for a term of ten years. Cost-share programs are also available for permanent planting of grass and trees in these areas. Agricultural Conservation Program (ACP): This program is designed to solve soil, water, and related resource problems through costsharing. ACP assistance is available to install soil-saving practices, including terraces, grass, sod waterways,other measures to control erosion. It also helps reduce sediment, chemicals, and livestock waste that contaminate streams and lakes.

* Farmland Natural Disaster Relief
Office of Government and Public Affairs
U.S. Department of Agriculture
Washington, DC 20250   (202) 447-3298

This free publication provides an overview of USDA's disaster assistance programs. It describes types of assistance available and where to apply for assistance. Local extension agents in each county can approve disaster applications for the following: conservation structures (when located on eligible lands); rehabilitation of farm lands destroyed by disaster; crop payment subsidies for disruption caused by disaster to regular crop schedules; sale of animal feed at below market price in emergency situations; animal grazing on reserve or conservation lands in emergency situations; donation of animal feed to Indian reservations when needed; and donation of grain to migratory wildfowl domains. The federal government will also remove debris from a major disaster from publicly- or privately-owned lands or waters.

* Farm Management and Improvements
The National Fertilizer Research Center
Tennessee Valley Authority
Muscle Shoals Reservation
Muscle Shoals, AL 35660   (205) 386-2598

The TVA is involved in a broad range of agricultural services. Thousands of demonstration farms have been created to test agricultural improvements. Current research focuses on farm management and record-keeping, planning and specialization, new crops, weed and pest control, and marketing, as well as continued improvements in fertilizer use and production practices. Current agricultural programs include developing alternative fuels from hardwood trees and farm crops, along with recycling nutrients found in farm and municipal waste.

* Farm Products Cash Value
Northern Regional Research Center
U.S. Department of Agriculture
ARS, 1815 N. University St.
Peoria, IL 61604   (309) 685-4011

The research goal of this center is to increase the cash value of farm products in domestic and foreign markets through improved quality and safety of food and feed, enhanced use of plant materials as renewable resources, and increased efficiency of crop production.

* Fertilizer and Chemical Development
The National Fertilizer Development Center
Tennessee Valley Authority
Muscle Shoals Reservation
P.O. Box 1010
Muscle Shoals, AL 35660   (205) 386-2593

The National Fertilizer Development Center plans and manages research and development programs for new and improved fertilizers and processes for their manufacture; for testing and demonstrating methods of chemical and organic fertilizer use as an aid to soil and water conservation and to the improved use of agricultural and related resources; and for operating and maintaining facilities to serve as a national laboratory for research and development in chemistry and chemical engineering related to fertilizers essential to national defense. The center conducts research to develop improved technology for converting cellulousic materials, including trees, to ethanol and other chemicals. Currently, there is an emphasis to demonstrate ways to minimize pollution problems during the handling and use of fertilizers in order to protect the environment.

* Financial Assistance For Rural
   Residents and Communities
Farmers Home Administration (FmHA)
U.S. Department of Agriculture
Washington, DC 20250   (202) 447-4323

FmHA provides financial assistance to rural people and communities that cannot obtain commercial credit at affordable terms. Applicants must be unable to obtain credit from usual commercial sources. Examples of the types of loans available are Emergency Loans, Youth Project Loans, Housing Repair Loans and Grants, and Business and Industry Loan Guarantees.

* Forest Insect and Disease Management
Contact: your State Forester or the state office

of the U.S. Forest Service, usually located in the state capitol.

To reduce loss and damage to forests and lands by forest insects and diseases, the USDA provides technical and financial assistance in prevention, detection, evaluation, and suppression of forest insect and disease outbreaks on state and private lands.

* Great Plains Conservation Work
Soil Conservation Service
U.S. Department of Agriculture
Washington, DC 20250   (202) 382-1868

Land users living in the Great Plains states can seek assistance from the Soil Conservation Service (SCS), which offers technical assistance and cost-sharing funds to farmers, ranchers, and other land users in the Great Plains. Cost-share rates can range up to 80 percent for urgently needed conservation work. Contact SCS or your local Soil Conservation Office.

* Gypsy Moth Control
Printing and Distribution Management Branch, APHIS
U.S. Department of Agriculture
Federal Building, Room G-100
6505 Belcrest Rd.
Hyattsville, MD 20782   (301) 436-7176

The following publication is available free of charge from APHIS: *Don't Move the Gypsy Moth* (July 1985). This tells how to make sure outdoor household articles don't spread gypsy moths.

* Horticulture Clearinghouse
U.S. Department of Agriculture
10301 Baltimore Blvd.
Beltsville, MD 20705   (301) 344-3704

This center covers technical horticultural or botanical question, economic botany, wild plants of possible use, herbs, bonsai, and floriculture.

* Hydroponic Farming
Environmental Research Laboratory
2601 East Airport Dr.
Tucson, AZ 85706   (602) 741-1990

This lab can provide you with information and expertise on hydroponics, the process of growing crops without soil.

* Insects Identification and Control
Contact your local USDA
Extension Service agent

Technical assistance is available to help you identify and eliminate any problems you may have caused by insects and bugs. You are encouraged to catch one of the insects which are causing the problem and send it in for analysis. Contact your local Extension Service for more information.

* Livestock and Veterinary Services
Livestock and Poultry Sciences
Room 217, Bldg. 200
Beltsville Agricultural Research Center
Beltsville, MD 20705   (301) 344-3431

Specialists study many topics, including domestic animal diseases, beef production, dairy production, foreign animal diseases, poultry production and diseases, production of sheep and fur-bearing animals, swine production, and livestock facilities.

* Livestock Rangeland
Rangeland Resources
Bureau of Land Management
U.S. Department of the Interior
1725 I St., NW
Washington, DC 20006   (202) 653-9193

The Bureau of Land Management has administration of 170 million acres of public lands where livestock graze. About 18,800 ranchers and farmers graze livestock on BLM-managed lands. A majority of these permittees have small (less than 100 head) or medium (100 to 500 head) livestock operations.

* Multiple Uses of Crops
Critical Agricultural Materials
U.S. Department of Agriculture
10301 Baltimore Blvd.
Beltsville, MD 20705   (301) 344-3454

This center covers new crops or new uses for old crops, including forest products and especially crops from which "natural rubber" can be produced.

* National Agriculture Clearinghouse

National Agricultural Library
U.S. Department of Agriculture
10301 Baltimore Blvd.
Beltsville, MD 20705   (301) 344-3755

The National Agricultural Library (NAL) has established 12 specialized information centers to provide enhanced services to its current clientele, as well as to develop new service relationships with the public and private sectors. Aside from agricultural researchers, centers also serve educators, consumers, and the private sector. Each center has a coordinator responsible for planning the center's activities, including reference services, collection development, developing information products, coordinating outreach activities, and establishing distribution networks.

* National Agriculture Library Services

National Agricultural Library (NAL)
10301 Baltimore Blvd.
Beltsville, MD 20705   (301) 344-3755

NAL provides comprehensive information services for the food and agricultural sciences through a variety of sources, which include bibliographies, personal reference services, loans, photocopies, and online data files. Services are provided to agricultural colleges, research institutions, government agencies, agricultural associations, industry, individual scientists, and the general public. NAL cooperates with the Library of Congress and the National Library of Medicine to provide access to publications worldwide in the agricultural, chemical, and biological sciences. NAL houses one of the largest collections in the free world on agricultural subjects--1.6 million volumes--including biology, chemistry, nutrition, forestry, soil sciences, and much more.

* Patent Licensing Opportunities

National Patent Program
Room 401, Building 005
BARC-West
Beltsville, MD 20705   (301) 344-2518

Government patents resulting from agricultural research discoveries are available for licensing to U.S. companies and citizens. Licenses are offered on a non-exclusive, exclusive, and co-exclusive basis. Non-exclusive licenses are generally granted when no large investment to market a product is expected. Exclusive and co-exclusive licenses are granted when substantial investment is required. Fees for licenses are negotiable. An annual catalog listing all patents available for license plus technical abstracts is available. The necessary regulations and forms are included.

* Patents on Seeds

Plant Variety Protection Office
Commodities Scientific Support Division
AMS, NAL, Room 500
Beltsville, MD 20705   (301) 344-2518

Unique seeds, with few exceptions, that are sexually reproduced can be protected by patents, The protection, which extends for 18 years, provides owners with exclusive rights to sell, reproduce, export, and produce the seed.

* Pesticide and Quarantine Programs

Animal and Plant Health Inspection Service
Plant Protection and Quarantine
6505 Belcrest Rd.
Hyattsville, MD 20782   (301) 436-7799

The USDA helps states and growers control or eradicate pests and diseases that cause plant loss. APHIS cooperates with state agencies to establish quarantines, pesticide spray programs, or release of sterile insects to reduce pest populations.

* Pesticides Database

Pesticides Information Retrieval System
Environmental Protection Agency
401 M St., SW
Washington DC 20460   (202) 554-1404

This computer database provides public access to current information on over 36,000 pesticide products. The system development has been jointly funded by USDA and EPA and is managed by Purdue University.

* Pesticide Information Hotline

National Pesticide Telecommunications Network   (800) 858-7378

This service of the U.S. Environmental Protection Agency and Texas Tech University is open 24 hours, 7 days a week. It responds to non-emergency questions about the effects of pesticides, toxicology and symptoms, environmental effects, disposal and cleanup, and safe use of pesticides.

* Pesticide Products Inventory

Office of Pesticide Programs
Environmental Protection Agency
401 M St., SW
Washington DC 20460   (202) 557-7090

EPA administers two Congressionally mandated statutes to control the more than 45,000 pesticide products registered for use in the United States. The EPA monitors the distribution and use of these pesticides, issuing civil or criminal penalties for violations. EPA also sets tolerances or maximum legal limits for pesticide residues on food commodities and feed grains to prevent consumer exposure to unsafe pesticide levels.

* Pesticides Rules and Regulations

Environmental Protection Agency
401 M Street SW
Washington, DC 20460   (703) 557-4434

The Pesticides Docket provides public access to documentation for each Registration Standard under development when the Agency begins review of data for the Registration Standard or upon publication of a notice setting out the list and sequence of Registration Standards. The docket contains documentation of pre-special and special reviews of pesticides, memoranda, all comments, correspondence, documents, proposals, or other materials concerning a pending pesticide regulatory decision provided to the Agency by a person or party outside of government (other than confidential business information).

* Plant and Entomological Services

Information Staff
Beltsville Agricultural Research Service
U.S. Department of Agriculture
Room 307, Bldg. 307, BARC West
Beltsville, MD 20705   (301)344-2264

Specialists study and can provide you with information on biological control of pests, corn and sorghum production, crop mechanization and pest control equipment, crop pollination, bees and honey, insect control, forage crop production, range management, plant genetics and breeding, pesticide use and impacts, plant pathology, weed control, small grains production, sugar crop production, and plant physiology.

* Plant Breeders Protection

Plant Variety Protection Office
U.S. Department of Agriculture
National Agricultural Library Building
AMS, Room 500
10301 Baltimore Blvd.
Beltsville, MD 20705   (301) 344-2518

Federal legislation protects the ownership rights of breeders of plants that reproduce through seeds. The Agricultural Marketing Service will certify whether or not a new variety is entitled to patent protection.

* Post-Harvest Processing

Southern Regional Research Center
U.S. Department of Agriculture
1100 Robert E. Lee Blvd.
ARS, Box 19687
New Orleans, LA 70197   (504) 589-7022

Research at this center relates primarily to post-harvest processing, product enhancement, and the safety and use of agricultural commodities produced in the southern U.S.

* Production, Coops, and Marketing Groups

Your local Extension Agent or
Office for the Assistant Secretary
Science and Education Department
U.S. Department of Agriculture
Washington, DC 20250   (202) 447-5923

The USDA will provide educational and technical assistance to any agricultural production or marketing association, group, or cooperative. They provide the latest USDA land grant university research findings, discuss new technology, and share the results of feasibility studies, market analysis reports, and the development of new products and markets.

* Quarterly Report to Congress

Current Information Branch,
Agricultural Research Service
U.S. Department of Agriculture
Building 005
Beltsville, MD 20705   (301) 344-3547

The free *Quarterly Report To Congress* summarizes research findings of projects conducted by USDA. Reports cover livestock, poultry, crops, insect pest control, soil and water resources, human nutrition, post-harvest technology, and commercial uses for commodities.

Agriculture and Farming

* Safe Pesticide Enforcement

Association of American Pesticide Control Officials (AAPCO)
2004 Le Suer Rd.
Richmond, VA 23229 (804) 288-8181
The Association of American Pesticide Control Officials is comprised of state, municipal and federal officials throughout North America interested in a uniform approach to the enforcement of laws controlling the proper and safe use of pesticide chemicals.

* Seed Quality and Inspection Labs

Federal Seed Lab
U.S. Department of Agriculture
Beltsville, MD 20705 (301) 344-2089
The federal government can test seeds to determine their quality and whether they are free from contamination. They will also prosecute any agent that transfers contaminated or mislabeled seed from state to state. Seeds are examined by or at a state agent's request, and there may be some fee involved.

* Soil and Farmland Protection Programs

Soil Conservation Service (SCS)
U.S. Department of Agriculture
P.O. Box 2890
Washington, DC 20013 (202) 447-4543
Soil surveys are used not only for conservation purposes but also to identify suitable lands for a wide variety of uses, from maintaining crops to urban uses. Information about soil helps prevent major construction mistakes and misuse of land that can be productively put to use. Soil maps identify flood-prone areas and sources of water pollutants.

* Soil Conservation Technical Expertise

Soil Conservation Service (SCS)
U.S. Department of Agriculture
P.O. Box 2890
Washington, DC 20013 (202) 447-4543
Technical expertise is available in such areas as irrigation, drainage, landscape architecture, construction, sanitary and water quality, and hydrology.

* Soil, Water, and Air Sciences

ARS Information Staff
U.S. Department of Agriculture
Room 307-A, Building 005
Beltsville, MD 20705 (301) 344-2264
Specialists study such topics as environmental quality, erosion and sedimentation, soil fertility and plant nutrition, organic wastes, pesticide degradation, water use efficiency and tillage practices, and weed control. Contact the ARS staff for answers to questions on these and other conservation-related topics.

* State-based Farming Research

Cooperative State Research Service
Aerospace Bldg.
901 D. St., SW
Washington, DC 20251 (202) 447-2929
More than half of the publicly funded agricultural research in the U.S. is conducted at State Agricultural Experiment Stations (SAES), located on land-grant universities in each state and territory in the U.S. The SAES serve as an early warning system for problems and opportunities. Such advancements as iodized salt, fluoride toothpaste, and mineral and vitamin additives for food came from these laboratories. Scientists are involved with experiments to reduce food costs for the consumer, reforest our landscape with genetically improved trees free from insects and diseases, produce leaner meat, control pests, prevent acid rain, and fight insect pests. Since the SAES are located at the land-grant universities, the Cooperative Extension Service readily transfers research to the classroom and to citizens.

* Technology Assessment Reports

Office of Technology Assessment
Publications Order
U.S. Congress
Washington, DC 20510-8025 (202) 224-8996
These OTA publications are available through the office above, the Government Printing Office, and the National Technical Information Service. To find out correct ordering information and prices, along with brief summaries of the following studies, contact the OTA office above and request their current publications catalog.

Agriculture and Forestry
Africa Tomorrow: Issues in Technology, Agriculture, and U.S. Foreign Aid (TM-F-31)

Agricultural Postharvest Technology and Marketing Economics Research (TM-F-21)
Assessing Biological Diversity in the United States: Data Considerations (BP-F-39)
An Assessment of the U.S. Food and Agricultural Research System (F-155)
Commercial Biotechnology: An International Analysis (BA-218)
Continuing the Commitment: Agricultural Development in the Sahel (F-308)
Drugs in Livestock Feed (F-91)
Emerging Food Marketing Technologies (F-79)
Energy From Biological Processes (E-124)
Enhancing Agriculture in Africa: A Role for Development Assistance (F-356)
Enhancing the Quality of U.S. Grain for International Trade (F-399)
Grain Quality in International Trade: A Comparison of Major U.S. Competitors (F-402)
Grassroots Conservation of Biological Diversity in the United States (BP-F-38)
Grassroots Development: The African Development Foundation (F-378)
Impacts of Applied Genetics: Micro-Organisms, Plants, and Animals (HR-132)
Impacts of Technology on U.S. Cropland and Rangeland Productivity (F-166)
Innovative Biological Technologies for Lesser Developed Countries (BP-F-29)
Pest Management Strategies in Crop Protection (F-98)
Pesticide Residues in Food (F-398)
Plants: The Potential for Extracting Protein, Medicines, and Other Useful Chemicals (BP-F-23)
A Review of U.S. Competitiveness in Agriculture Trade (TM-TET-29)
Sustaining Tropical Forest Resources: Reforestation of Defraded Lands (BP-F-18)
Sustaining Tropical Forest Resources: U.S. and International Institutions (BP-F-19)
Technologies To Benefit Agriculture and Wildlife (BP-F-34)
Technologies To Maintain Biological Diversity (F-330)
Technologies To Sustain Tropical Forest Resources (F-214)
Technology and the American Economic Transition (TET-283)
Technology, Public Policy, and the Changing Structure of American Agriculture (F-285)
Technology, Public Policy, and the Changing Structure of American Agriculture: A Special Report for the 1985 Farm Bill (F-272)
Technology, Renewable Resources, and American Crafts (BP-F-27)
Water-Related Technologies for Sustainable Agriculture in U.S. Arid/Semiarid Lands (F-212)
Water-Related Technologies for Sustainable Agriculture in U.S. Arid/Semiarid Lands: Selected Foreign Experience (BP-F-20)
Wetlands: Their Use and Regulation (0-206)
Wood Use: U.S. Competitiveness and Technology (ITE-210)

* Tobacco Inspection

Tobacco Division
U.S. Department of Agriculture
AMS, P.O. Box 96456
Washington, DC 20090-6456 (202) 447-2567
Tobacco sold at auction in designated U.S. markets, along with imported tobacco (except cigar and oriental varieties), are inspected.

* Transportation Services for Agricultural Products

Office of Transportation
U.S. Department of Agriculture
P.O. Box 96575
Washington, DC 20090-6575 (202) 653-6060
This office recognizes that transportation facilities are an integral part of the agribusiness system. Farmers, shippers, farm organizations and local or state agencies who wish to bring about changes in freight service or rates for food products can seek assistance through this office.

* TVA Fertilizer R & D

National Fertilizer Development Center
Resource Development
Tennessee Valley Authority
Muscle Shoals Reservation
Muscle Shoals, AL 35660 (205) 386-2593
At its National Fertilizer Development Center, TVA operates the world's leading facility for developing new fertilizer technology. Major objectives of this program have been to reduce energy requirements for fertilizer production and increase the efficiency of fertilizer use. Also, emphasis is on an environmental initiative aimed at avoiding an adverse environmental impact from fertilizer production, distribution, and use. Various activities with agricultural colleges and fertilizer industries take place, including model plant compliance demonstrations and educational audiovisuals.

* U.S. Agriculture Department Resources

Information Office
U.S. Department of Agriculture
Office of Public Affairs, Room 402-A
Washington, DC 20250 (202) 447-4614
The information staff can help you get the facts you need. USDA also publishes a variety of publications. Some of the general, more helpful ones are:

Fact Book of Agriculture. Published annually, this monograph details the mission of the many USDA agencies, and provides a plethora of information about agriculture in the U.S.
How to Get Information from USDA: Lists sources of information in the USDA agencies.
Your United States Department of Agriculture: Provides some history of the USDA and describes how this huge agency serves farms, local communities, as well as the world agricultural communities.
Report of the Secretary of Agriculture: Published annually, this report gives a summary of progress and initiatives for thepolicy making agencies in USDA-- great source of "what's new" at the USDA.

* Water Quality and Natural Resources Education

Executive Officer
Local Extension Service
U.S. Department of Agriculture
Room 340A Administration Building
Washington, DC 20250   (202) 447-4111

The USDA operates an extension program in 3,165 counties located in all of the 50 states and the U.S. territories. Federal, state, and local governments share in financing and conducting cooperative extension educational programs to help farmers, processors, handlers, farm families, communities, and consumers apply the results of food and agricultural research, including Conservation and Management of Natural Resources, which helps people benefit from natural ecosystems without destroying them, sustain a productive natural resource base, market natural resource goods and services, and formulate and implement sound

public policies. Water Quality: Work with consumers, producers and local government to learn more about the importance of high-quality ground water and the conservation of water resources. Emphasis is also put on the effects of agricultural chemicals and contaminants on water quality.

* Water Quality and Preservation

U.S. Department of Agriculture
Deputy for Programs, SCS
Box 2890
Washington, DC 20013   (202) 447-4527

The USDA manages a variety of water resource programs to aid landowners and agricultural operators use existing water resources wisely. These programs also promote reclamation and preservation of water sources that have been contaminated or allowed to fall into disrepair. USDA will provide technical and financial assistance for approved projects that meet its criteria.

* Wood Pests

Your local Forest Service or
Extension Office, or
Forest Insect and Disease Research
U.S. Department of Agriculture
FS, Room 609 RP-E
Arlington, VA 22209   (703) 235-8065

The USDA provides technical assistance for insect and diseases to wood, whether it is in use, stored, wood products, or urban trees. All insect and disease suppression projects must meet specific criteria for federal participation.

Food Quality and Distribution

* See also Health and Medicine; Food Facts, Nutrition and Diets Chapter
* See also Consumer Chapter

* Beef and Meat Grading and Certification

Meat Grading and Certification Branch
U.S. Department of Agriculture
AIMS, Room 2638-S
Washington, DC 20250   (202) 382-1246

All meat is federally inspected on a mandatory basis. All other product grading is voluntary. Grading of meat, poultry, eggs, and dairy products and fresh and processed fruits and vegetables is provided on request for a fee. For further information, contact the appropriate office.

* Cotton, Dairy, Produce, Meat Regulations

Agricultural Marketing Service
U.S. Department of Agriculture
Information Staff, AMS
P.O. Box 96456
Washington, DC 20090-6456   (202) 447-6766

This office regulates the following segments of the agricultural industry: cotton, dairy products, fruits and vegetables, some livestock, poultry, grains, seeds, and also tobacco.

* Crop Yields and Food Research

Beltsville Agricultural Research Center (BARC)
Room 227, Building 003, BARC-W
U.S. Department of Agriculture
Beltsville, MD 20705   (301) 344-3078

BARC is among the largest and most diversified agricultural complexes in the world. About 900 scientists and technicians who specialize in a wide variety of research projects, have a long list of accomplishments to their credit. Animal researchers study livestock diseases, animal nutritional needs, and animal genetics and physiology. Plant specialists seek greater crop yields by breeding plants that use light and nutrients more efficiently. Broad research topics include animals, insects, plants, soil, air water, human nutrition, and family resources.

* Dairy Products Grading and Inspection

Dairy Grading Branch
Dairy Division, Room 2750
U.S. Department of Agriculture
Washington, DC 20250   (202) 475-5530

All eggs (liquid or frozen) are federally inspected on a mandatory basis. All other product grading is voluntary. Grading of meat, poultry, eggs, and dairy products and fresh and processed fruits and vegetables is provided on request for a fee. For further information, contact the appropriate office.

* Emergency Relief and Excess Food

Commodity Operations Division
U.S. Department of Agriculture
ASCS, Room 5755 South Building
Washington, DC 20250   (202) 477-5074

The Commodity Credit Corporation buys, stores, and distributes such commodities as dry milk, wheat, rice, and corn, which are acquired through price support programs. The commodities are sent overseas as donations, distributed to domestic food programs, or given to relief agencies in times of emergencies.

* Food and Nutrition Information Center

Food and Nutrition Service
U.S. Department of Agriculture
10301 Baltimore Blvd.
Beltsville, MD 20705   (301) 344-3719

This center acquires books, journal articles, and audiovisual materials pertaining to human nutrition, food service management, and food science. Items in the FNIC collection are listed in AGRICOLA, NAL's computerized bibliographic database, which can be accessed through Dialog (800-3-DIALOG) or BRS (800-345-4BRS). FNIC also has a unique demonstration center for food and nutrition microcomputer software. The extensive collection of dietary analysis, nutrition education, and food service programs is available for on-site review by appointment only.

* Food Distribution Process Studies

Commodities Scientific Support Division
AMS, Box 96456
U.S. Department of Agriculture
Washington, DC 20090-6456   (202) 447-2704

Studies are available on a wide variety of markets covering all aspects of the distribution process: wholesaling, packaging, transportation, and more. For a listing of studies available, contact the above office.

* Food Inspection and Official Standards

Food Safety and Inspection Service
U.S. Department of Agriculture
Information Division, Room 327-E
Washington, DC 20250   (202) 447-9113

This office inspects all meats, poultry, and egg products shipped interstate and abroad, and ensures that labels on these products are truthful. They also develop official grade standards for meat, poultry, eggs, dairy products, and fresh and processed fruits and vegetables.

* Food Irradiation Safety

Food Irradiation
U.S. Department of Agriculture
10301 Baltimore Blvd.
Beltsville, MD 20705   (301) 344-3719

This center covers the use of ionizing radiation to process foods. Print and audio-visual aids are available in food science, nutrition, safety and wholesomeness, labeling, economics, and other subjects.

* Food Poisoning or Improper Packaging

Food Safety and Inspection Service
U.S. Department of Agriculture
Washington, DC 20250   (800) 535-4555

This service takes calls from consumers on cases of meat or poultry food poisoning or complaints about meat or poultry spoilage due to improper packaging or processing. They can also provide you with health-oriented information on safe handling and storage of meats and poultry.

* Food Safety and Supply

Western Regional Research Center
U.S. Department of Agriculture
ARS, 800 Buchanan St.
Albany, CA 94710   (415) 486-3421

Research here is generally focused on food problems. Scientists try to increase agricultural productivity through preventing loss and ensuring safety of the food supply and improving market quality of agricultural products. They also have a program to find new means to convert agricultural materials to value-added food and nonfood products.

* Free Food For Non-Profit Institutions

Food Distribution Program
Food and Nutrition Service
3101 Park Center Dr., Room 502
Alexandria, VA 22302   (703) 756-3680

Charitable and rehabilitation institutions are usually eligible to receive surplus commodities stored by USDA. The commodities available are dairy products, grain oil, and peanuts.

* Grading and Inspecting Poultry

Poultry Grading Branch
AMS Poultry Division
U.S. Department of Agriculture
Room 3938, South Building
Washington, DC 20250   (202) 447-3272

All poultry are federally inspected on a mandatory basis. Tobacco sold at auction in designated U.S. markets, along with imported tobacco (except cigar and oriental varieties), are also inspected. All other product grading is voluntary. Grading of meat, poultry, eggs, and dairy products and fresh and processed fruits and vegetables is provided on request for a fee. For further information, contact the appropriate office.

* Grading Food Products

Agricultural Marketing Service
U.S. Department of Agriculture
Washington, DC 20250   (202) 447-8998

USDA provides producers, packers, processors, shippers, wholesalers, and consumers with official certification of the quality of food and farm products to aid in establishing a market value for the product. For most commodities a fee is charged to cover the cost of the service, and the service may be conducted during packing or processing or at supply depots. The official grading or inspection certificate is accepted as prima facie evidence in court.

* Grain Inspection

Federal Grain Inspection Service
Administrator, FGIS
U.S. Department of Agriculture
Room 1094 South Building
Washington, DC 20250   (202) 382-0219

This office establishes federal standards for grain and performs inspections to ensure compliance. They also regulate the weighing of all grain for export.

* Livestock Health and Safety

Packers and Stockyards Administration
Room 3039 South Building
Washington, DC 20250   (202) 382-9528

This office regulates trade practices of businesses involved in marketing livestock, meat, and poultry.

* Meat and Poultry Hotline

Food Safety and Inspection Service
U.S. Department of Agriculture
Washington, DC 20250   (800) 535-4555

This service takes calls from consumers on cases of meat or poultry food poisoning or complaints about meat or poultry spoilage due to improper packaging or processing. They can also provide you with health-oriented information on safe handling and storage of meats and poultry.

* Nutritional Labeling

Meat and Poultry Standards and
Labeling Division, FSIS
U.S. Department of Agriculture
300 C St., SW, Room 311
Washington, DC 20250   (202) 447-6043

The USDA is responsible for labeling requirements for meat and poultry only, and this is done on a voluntary basis.

* Packers and Stockyards Program

Packers and Stockyards Administration
U.S. Department of Agriculture
Washington, DC 20250   (202) 447-7051

The USDA's packers and stockyards specialists work with private producers and trade organizations to investigate complaints and file any complaint on violations of fair and open competition in the marketing of livestock.

* Perishable Agricultural Commodities

PACA Branch
Agricultural Marketing Service
U.S. Department of Agriculture
Washington, DC 20250   (202) 447-2890

The USDA's Agricultural Marketing Service (AMS) prohibits unfair trading practices among buyers and sellers of perishable items. The AMS will provide advice on your rights and responsibilities and try to bring disputing parties together for informal settlements.

* Pick Your Own Fruits and Vegetables

Contact your local USDA Extension
Service agent

Many farmers allow consumers to pick produce directly from their fields at substantial savings.

* Processed Fruits and Vegetables Inspection

Processed Products Branch
Food and Vegetable Division, AMS
U.S. Department of Agriculture
Box 96456

Washington, DC 20090-6456   (202) 447-4693

Grading of meat, poultry, eggs, and dairy products and fresh and processed fruits and vegetables is provided on request for a fee. For further information, contact this office.

* Protection From Animal Pests and Diseases

Animal and Plant Health Inspection Service
Veterinary Services,
U.S. Department of Agriculture
Washington, DC 20250   (202) 436-5533

For control or eradication of livestock/poultry pest or disease, a state government or industry can receive cooperation from the federal government to establish quarantines, vaccination procedures, and destruction of diseased or exposed animals.

* Quality Control Regulations

Marketing Order Administration Branch
U.S. Department of Agriculture
AMS/FV, P.O. Box 96465
Washington, DC 20090-6456   (202) 447-2491

This office administers programs that give growers the authority to work together to develop dependable markets for their products. Methods used include establishing minimum quality standards to keep inferior products from depressing markets for an entire crop, research and promotion projects to improve production, and volume controls to stabilize the short-term rate of commodity shipments.

* Seed Quality and Inspection Labs

Federal Seed Lab
U.S. Department of Agriculture
Beltsville, MD 20705   (301) 344-2089

The federal government can test seeds to determine their quality and whether they are free from contamination. They will also prosecute any agent that transfers contaminated or mislabeled seed from state to state. Seeds are examined by or at a state agent's request, and there may be some fee involved.

* Technology Assessment Reports

Office of Technology Assessment
Publications Order
U.S. Congress
Washington, DC 20510-8025   (202) 224-8996

These OTA publications are available through the office above, the Government Printing Office, and the National Technical Information Service. To find out correct ordering information and prices, along with brief summaries of the following studies, contact the OTA office above and request their current publications catalog.

Food Information Systems (F-35)
Nutrition Research Alternatives (F-74)
Open Shelf-Life Dating of Food (F-94)
Organizing and Financing Basic Research To Increase Food Production (F-49)
Perspectives on Federal Retail Food Grading (F-47)
Pesticide Residues in Food (F-398)

* Transportation Food Containers

Office of Transportation
Director, International Division
U.S. Department of Agriculture
P.O. Box 96575
Washington, DC 20090-6575   (202) 653-6275

This office regulates the standards for manufacture of container equipment used to move agricultural products between the U.S. and foreign countries.

* Volume Food Buyers

Agricultural Marketing Service
U.S. Department of Agriculture
Washington, DC 20250   Poultry Division: (202) 447-7693

USDA specialists work with volume food buyers in developing specifications for food commodities using specifications, grades, and standards that have been developed by USDA for this purpose. Graders examine food and certify the food buyers' purchases prior to delivery. Any processor, wholesaler, retailer, hospital, restaurant, governmental agency, educational institution, airline, or other public or private group buying food in large quantities may ask USDA for their inspection services by contacting this office.

* Wholesale Food Distribution

Marketing Facilities Branch
U.S. Department of Agriculture
AMS, Room 2649-S, Box 96456

Washington, DC 20090-6456   (202) 447-8317

This office performs general research aimed at getting food on the table more cheaply by working with wholesale food distribution facilities and farmers markets to reduce the price spread between what the farmer gets for his products and what the consumer pays.

* Wholesalers and Volume Food Buyers

Special Inspection Services
Agricultural Marketing Service
U.S. Department of Agriculture
Washington, DC 20250   Dairy Products: (202) 447-3245

USDA specialists work with volume food buyers in developing specifications for food commodities using specifications, grades, and standards that have been developed by USDA for this purpose. Graders examine food and certify the food buyers' purchases prior to delivery. Any processor, wholesaler, retailer, hospital, restaurant, governmental agency, educational institution, airline, or other public or private group buying food in large quantities may ask USDA for their inspection services by contacting this office.

Fruits and Vegetables Fresh: (202) 447-5870   Processed: (202) 447-4693
Meat: (202) 382-1116
Poultry Division: (202) 447-7693

* World Food Donations

Agency for International Development
Food for Peace
State Annex #2
Washington, DC 20523   (202) 875-4901

By working with groups like CARE and the World Food Program, the Food For Peace program helps needy people abroad by sending food and other agricultural commodities.

Trade and Marketing

* See also the International Trade Chapter
* See also the Experts Chapter

* Agricultural Analyses and Forecasts

Economic Research Service and
National Agricultural Statistical Service
U.S. Department of Agriculture
Box 1608   (800) 999-6779
Rockville, MD 20850   (202) 447-7017

Several publications are available which provide information about the world trade situation. *Situation and Outlook Reports* provide analyses and forecasts of all major agricultural commodities and such related topics as finance, farm inputs, land values, and world regional developments (each year and are available in one-year ($10), two-year $19 or three-year $27 subscriptions); *Agricultural Statistics Reports* estimate production, stocks, inventories, disposition, utilization, and prices of about 40 agricultural commodities and other items such as labor and farm numbers; *The Journal of Agricultural Economics Research* his journal covers technical research in agricultural economics, including econonometric models and statistics focusing on methods employed and results of USDA economic research ($7/year; two years: $13, and three years:$18).

* Agricultural/Food Trade Policy

Bureau of Economic and Business Affairs
Department of State
2201 C St., NW, Room 3427
Washington, DC 20520   (202) 647-3090

This office handles agricultural trade issues and agreements, including the General Agreement on Tariffs and Trade (GATT) negotiations. Besides monitoring such food commodities as coffee, cocoa and jute, this office also is responsible for foreign policy aspects of food aid and shipment, and acts as liaison with the Department of Agriculture.

* Agricultural Import Quotas

Foreign Agricultural Service
Information Services
U.S. Department of Agriculture
Room 5074 South Building
Washington DC 20250   (202) 447-3448

This office regulates the imports of beef, dairy products, and other commodities by administering quotas imposed by the President.

* Agricultural Industry Investigations

Office of Investigations
U.S. International Trade Commission
500 E St., SW, Room 615
Washington, DC 20436   (202) 252-1161

This office coordinates the ITC's investigations involving antidumping, reviews, escape-clause and market disruptions, and determinations of whether imports of agricultural products are interfering with programs of the U.S. Department of Agriculture. For more information regarding these investigations, contact this office.

* Agricultural Trade and Marketing

Agricultural Trade and Marketing
U.S. Department of Agriculture
10301 Baltimore Blvd.
Beltsville, MD 20705   (301) 344-3704

This center covers agricultural trade and marketing, trade policies, barriers, trade agreements and negotiations, agricultural domestic policy and international trade, and many other trade-related matters. Staff can also answer questions relating to the economics of urbanization and urban policies in developing countries.

* Agriculture Exports Clearinghouse

Information Division
Foreign Agricultural Service
U.S. Department of Agriculture
5074 South Building
Washington, DC 20250   (202) 447-3448

For supply and demand information of agricultural products in other countries, contact the above office.

* Animal and Pet Import and Export Restrictions

Import--Export Staff Veterinary Services
APHIS/U.S. Department of Agriculture
6505 Belcrest Rd.
Hyattsville, MD 20782   (301) 436-8590

The USDA will provide certification to exporters or importers of animals and animal products, or pet birds to prevent the introduction of agricultural pests and diseases from foreign countries into the U.S. and to aid exporters meeting foreign importers standards.

* Electronic Export Data Available

Special Programs Division
U.S. Department of Agriculture
Office of Information
Room 536-A
Washington, DC 20250   (202) 447-5505

Daily, weekly, and monthly reports showing foreign trade opportunities, exports to major markets, highlights of trade and production, import/export prices, and policy developments are available electronically through USDA's Electronic Dissemination of Information (EDI) systems.

* Expert Export Assistance

FAS Coordinator
U.S. Department of Agriculture
Room 4951 South Building
Washington, DC 20050   (202) 447-7103

The USDA's Foreign Agricultural Service offers private companies and cooperatives assistance in marketing their products overseas. The Agricultural Information and Marketing Service (AIMS), for example, provides foreign trade opportunities and contacts to U.S. food and agricultural businesses by collecting and publicizing information on foreign buyers and advertising U.S. export availability. The export marketing services offered include Trade Leads, Buyer Alert, Foreign Buyer Lists, and U.S. Supplier Lists. This material is available in print or through various computer information suppliers, for a charge, depending on the information you request.

* Export Publications and Manuals

FAS Information Services
Room 5922
U.S. Department of Agriculture
Washington, DC 20250   (202) 447-7937

The Foreign Agricultural Service issues various reports and publications each year based on information from agricultural attaches and counselors stationed around the world.

AgExporter. This monthly magazine features articles which analyze conditions affecting trade and highlighting market development and export promotion. $11 U.S., $14 foreign.

World Agricultural Production Report. Monthly report of USDA production estimates for grain, cotton, and oilseeds in major countries and selected regions of the world. Free.

Agricultural Trade Offices: One-Stop Service Overseas. Directory of U.S. agricultural trade offices and what they do to assistexporters of U.S. food and agricultural products. Free.

U.S. Farmer's Export Arm. Describes the services of the FAS. Free.

Partners in Trade Promotion. Directory and description of the FAS market development cooperator program. Free.

Agriculture's Emissaries Overseas. Directory and description of agricultural counselor/attache offices overseas. Free.

Food and Agricultural Export Directory. Listing of export services and key contacts in the export business. Free.

U. S. Export Sales. Weekly report that summarizes sales and exports of selected U.S. agricultural commodities by country bases on reports from private exporters. Free. For more information call (202) 477-3273.

Free brochures also are available on such topics as FAS agricultural trade offices and attaches abroad, export financing, Public Law 480, technical requirements for export products, and the FAS market development program.

* Farm Export Information Round-the-Clock

Agriculture and Farming

Information Division
U.S. Department of Agriculture
Room 5074, FAS
Washington, DC 20250   (202) 447-3448

News reports announcing agreements and allocations for farm exports are available by facsimile. Also, 24-hour information is available on export credit guarantee activities and on Export Enhancement Program (EEP) news. The Weekly Roundup of World Production and Trade offers current news items and trade statistics on various commodities, along with a summary of recent developments in world production and trade.

* Export Opportunities For Small and Minority Businesses

Minority and Small Business Program
U.S. Department of Agriculture
FAS, Room 4951-S
Washington, DC 20250-1000   (202) 382-9498

This program provides small and minority companies with a broad range of support services and assistance in selling their products overseas.

* Farm Imports and Exports

ERS/NASS
U.S. Department of Agriculture
Box 1608
Rockville, MD 20850   (800) 999-6779 (202) 447-7017

Foreign Agricultural Trade of the United States updates the quantity and value of U.S. farm exports and imports, plus price trends. Subscriptions for one year cost $20, two years $39, and three years $57.00.

* Import Interference With Agricultural Programs

The Office of Investigations
U.S. International Trade Commission
500 E St., SW, Room 615
Washington, DC 20436   (202) 252-1161

At the direction of the U.S. President, the ITC conducts investigations to determine whether any articles are being or are about to be imported into the U.S. under such conditions and in such quantities as to have a negative effect on the U.S. Department of Agriculture's programs for agricultural commodities or products. If investigation find that import interference exists, the U.S. President may decide to restrict the imports in question by imposing either import fees or quotas.

* International Trade Shows

High Value Products Division, FAS
U.S. Department of Agriculture
Room 4951-S
Washington, DC 20250-1000   (202) 447-7103

The USDA offers a cost-effective service for U.S. firms to explore foreign markets. FAS organizes national pavilions in major international food shows throughout the world. Participation includes individual booths, lounge, advance public relations work, product shipment, and customs clearance for the show. Copies of the current trade show calendar are available.

* Market Prospects Overseas

Information Division
FAS, U.S. Department of Agriculture
Room 5922-S
Washington, DC 20250-1000   (202) 447-7937

A series of background publications describing market prospects for U.S. food and farm products in many countries is available from this office.

* Plant Import and Export Restrictions

Plant Protection Quarantine Unit
Room 632, APHIS
U.S. Department of Agriculture
6505 Belcrest Rd.
Hyattsville MD 20782   (301) 436-8447

The USDA will provide certification to exporters or importers of plants and plant products as well as animals and animal products, or pet birds to prevent the introduction of agricultural pests and diseases from foreign countries into the U.S. and to aid exporters meeting foreign importers standards.

* World Agricultural Databases

Economic Research Service Databases
U.S. Department of Agriculture
ERS/NASS
P.O. Box 1608
Rockville, MD 20850   (800) 999-6779

The Economic Research Service has developed more than 60 databases dealing in a wide variety of U.S. and world agricultural economics topics. Data products are shipped on DOS-compatible discs or on unlabeled, 9-track 6250 b.p.i. magnetic tapes as appropriate. A complete listing of ERS electronic products and ordering information is available by contacting the above center.

* World Agricultural Trade Database

Chief, Trade and Marketing Branch
Foreign Agricultural Service
U.S. Department of Agriculture
Washington, DC 20250   (202) 382-1294

The Foreign Agricultural Service (FAS) maintains a database of selected foreign agricultural trade information for the U.S. and 100 nations that conduct agricultural trade. The database contains information from a variety of sources, including United Nations trade tapes from the Food and Agriculture Organization and data from the Bureau of the Census. Examples of retrievable information include long-term U.S. exports by destination; foreign country import and export data; foreign production, supply, and distribution of agricultural products; and other export marketing information. Searches and print-outs are provided on a cost-recovery basis. Staff prefers request by phone so that they can discuss your needs and thereby supply you with appropriate information.

* World Competition

Yearbook Editor, Publications
U.S. Department of Agriculture
Room 535-A
Washington, DC 20250   (202) 447-9173

Each year, the USDA publishes a yearbook which explores one theme in depth. The 1988 yearbook, *Marketing U.S. Agriculture*, written by experts from farms, industry, universities, and government, describes the revolution in the food marketing system caused by new technology, social changes, and increased competition for world markets.

State Agriculture Information

In most states, agriculture is the leading industry. Farming has become highly specialized, and modern farmers and agribusinesses must stay abreast of a wide range of current data: crop prices, price and production projections, field statistics, test results, and more. The U.S. Department of Agriculture publishes the greatest number of reports and surveys in such areas, routinely publishing data on crop conditions, long- and short-term weather forecasts, research developments, and current and projected market conditions for specific crops at home and abroad. Decisions involving billions of dollars are made each year based on this information.

USDA reports are most often used to track crop and livestock production and prices and to maximize production by ensuring that the best equipment and storage techniques are used for each crop. But the federal government does not hold a monopoly on agricultural information. States also collect and disseminate a great deal of farm data, and obtaining information from a state agency is generally less time-consuming and expensive than going through the USDA offices in Washington, D.C.

Market News and Surveys

Individual states contribute to the Market News Service. Major wire services, newspapers, and radio stations use this service to track developments in agriculture. The service is used by virtually all persons involved in the sale or purchase of grain, livestock, poultry, or poultry products, as well as by insurance and investment companies and government agencies.

State agencies often make available employment and income surveys -- publications providing information of farms and the families who operate them, the quality of services provided, income generated from all sources, and analysis of this data. Special state agricultural directories are also a good source of information, providing the name, address, and telephone number of every agricultural producer in a state by commodity. They also include data on production levels, acreage, and farm dollar values for each commodity.

Information on Agribusiness and Growers

In terms of collecting information on agricultural companies, most states maintain a computerized licensing and product registration system and will provide mailing lists for a minimum fee. Included in the databases are names and addresses of agricultural processors, distributors, and manufacturers, as well as all registered products. States maintain records on the number of products and licenses held by each company, and inspection reports for retailers, wholesalers, and packagers are usually available for a fee. In addition, some states require that you file a Freedom of Information Act request to obtain this information.

Marketing or Agricultural Development Programs

State agriculture offices may offer their biggest help in promoting products grown within a state. Each state has a marketing and development program to protect, conserve, and develop state agriculture and natural resources. The objectives of such programs are to develop new and existing markets (including foreign) for state agricultural products and to ensure that state farms and ranches are using the best production techniques available. These offices also:

* improve agricultural profitability by encouraging the development of value-added products and new, high-value crops.

* encourage and support research issues impacting upon agricultural growth within the state.

* serve as clearinghouses for trade leads and provide various support services for state farmers and agribusinesses, including grading, inspection, promotion, and market intelligence.

* assist the agricultural producer, processor, shipper and exporter to expand trade volume and to broaden marketing areas, to reduce distribution and transportation costs, and to gain freer access to foreign markets.

To obtain overseas contracts, companies have their name and product(s) registered in the state export directory (free). Foreign investors and importers look to state directories for new ideas and areas in which to expand their business interests.

State departments of agriculture also rent booths at agricultural trade shows both at home and overseas. For example, if you have a small seafood company or are in the pasta and noodle business, renting a booth through the state at the Japan Food Show will go a long way to promote your product and may net you a tax-free trip to the Orient as well.

States also help promote your product overseas and may prove valuable in helping your small businesses expand through foreign franchises. Another example: a popular soft yogurt company was able to franchise in several overseas markets with the help of the Maryland State Agricultural Department.

Statistical Reporting Service (SRS)

The purpose of SRS is to collect and disseminate current statistics on the nation's agriculture. SRS maintains a network of 44 field offices which service all 50 states through cooperative agreements with state departments of agriculture or state universities. These State Statistical Offices (SSOs) regularly survey thousands of farmers, ranchers, and agribusinesses that voluntarily provide data on a confidential basis.

Statisticians consolidate these reports with field observations, objective yield measurements, and other data to produce state farm and ranch estimates. These data are then forwarded to SRS headquarters in Washington, D.C., where they are combined and released as a national profile. In addition, SRS issues about 300 national and 9,000 state farm reports each year. The reports provide broad coverage of agriculture,

Agriculture and Farming

including 120 crops and 45 livestock items.

State Agricultural Offices

The following is a list of state agricultural departments and the products and services they can provide:

Alabama

Agricultural Statistics Service, M.L. Dantzler, Box 1071, Montgomery, AL 36192; (205) 832-7263. Publications: *Alabama Farm Facts* (issued twice monthly): *Agricultural Prices*; *Crop Production or Forecasts, Intended & Actual Plantings, and Grain Stocks*; *Fruits, Nuts and Vegetables*; *Livestock Numbers, Production, Slaughter and Milk*; *Poultry and Eggs*; *Broiler Report* (issued each Wednesday); *Crop Weather* (issued each Monday, March-December); *County Data: Cattle, Hogs, Poultry, Corn, Cotton, Hay, Oats, Peanuts, Sorghum Grain, Soybeans, Wheat*; *Alabama Agricultural Statistics, Fact Sheet on Alabama Agriculture, Alabama Agriculture Perspective.*

Department of Agriculture and Industries, P. O. Box 3336, Montgomery, AL 36193; (205) 261-5872. Publications: *Fruit and Vegetable Direct Marketing Directory, Alabama Farmers' Bulletin, Ag Talk, The Alabama Food and Agricultural Export Directory.*

Alaska

State Statistical Service, D.A. Brown, Box 799, Palmer, AK 99645; (907) 745-4272. Publications: *Alaska Agricultural Statistics*; *Alaska Farm Reporter* (monthly); *Crop Weather* (weekly).

Department of Natural Resources, Division of Agriculture, P.O. Box 949, Palmer, AK 99645. Publication: *Alaska Agricultural Statistics.*

Arizona

Agricultural Statistics Service, B. L. Bloyd, 201 East Indianola, Suite 250, Phoenix, AZ 85012; (602) 241-2573. Publications: *Arizona Agricultural Statistics, Crop Release, Livestock Release, Crop and Weather Report.*

Arizona Commission of Agriculture and Horticulture, 1688 West Adams, Phoenix, AZ 85007; (602) 255-4373. Annual Report.

Arkansas

Agricultural Statistics Service, D. H. Von Steen, Box 1417, Little Rock, AR 72203; (501) 378-5145. Publications: *Arkansas Farm Report* (issued twice a month); *Weather and Crop Bulletin*; *Weekly Broiler* (weekly); *County Estimates*; *Agricultural Statistics for Arkansas.*

Cooperative Extension Service, University of Arkansas, P.O. Box 391, Little Rock, AR 72203; (501) 373-2500. Publication: Annual Report of Accomplishments.

California

Agricultural Statistics Service, H. J. Tippett, Box 1258, Sacramento, CA 95806; (916) 551-1533. Publications: *California Agriculture*; *Exports of California Agricultural Products*; *California Agricultural Export Directory*; *Summary of County Agricultural Commissioners' Reports*; *Field Crop Statistics*; *Prices Received by California Producers for Farm Commodities*; *Fruit and Nut Acreage, Fruit and Nut Statistics, Grape Acreage Bulletin*; *Grapes, Raisins, and Wine*; *Walnuts, Raisins, and Prunes, Vegetable Crops*; *Livestock Statistics*; *Eggs, Chickens, and Turkeys*; *Dairy Industry Statistics, Complete set of County Agricultural Commissioner Report Data, Commodity by County.*

State of California, Food and Agriculture, 1220 N. St., Sacramento, CA 94271; (916) 445-8614. Programs: Agricultural Export Program (AEP): first of its kind by a state, AEP provides assistance, service,and support in developing sales in foreign markets. It is a five year matching funds partnership in which the costs of foreign maarket development are equally shared between the California Department of Food and Agriculture and program cooperators. The program is open to all private companies, marketing boards,and commissions or associations who are producers, processors, or marketers of California agricultural products. The AEP program is developing its own "California specific" trade lead network which will electronically provide information on buyer leads, best market prospects, trade barriers, and export assistance.

Colorado

Agricultural Statistics Service, C. A. Hudson, Box 17066, Denver, CO 80217; (303) 964-0250. The Colorado Legislature has eliminated funding for agricultural statistics. Requests should be made to the Department of Agriculture, Public Information Officer, Jim Miller (303) 866-2811.

Colorado Department of Agriculture, 1525 Sherman St., Denver, CO 80203; (303) 866-2811. Programs: 1) Homestead Protection: makes agricultural credit available to farmers allowing farmers to redeem a portion of their homestead through a purchase of the property. 2) The Department administers the Colorado Agricultural Development Authority which makes low interest loans to producers. 3) Project ARC (Agricultural Resources in Colorado): rebate funds are offered to assist farmers with the identification and promotion of innovative agricultural practices. Publications: *Update/Outlook* (bi-monthly); *AgImpact* (quarterly).

Connecticut

For Connecticut agricultural statistics, contact the Marketing Division at the Connecticut Department of Agriculture below. Connecticut Department of Agriculture, State Office Building, Room 273, 165 Capitol Ave., Hartford, CT 06106; (203) 566-4667. Program: Joint Venture Program: $50,000 in matching funds is available to agricultural commodity groups and organizations for promotion of "Connecticut Grown" products. Publications: *Connecticut Grown, Annual Report, Farm Fresh Directory, Connecticut Sugarhouses, Connecticut Wineries, Pick Your Own: Orchards, Vegetables, Christmas Trees, Berries*; *Connecticut Farmers Markets, Export Directory, Hay List, Fair List, Connecticut Agricultural Directory, Connecticut Agricultural Statistics,* and the *Apple Fact Sheet.*

Delaware

The Agricultural Statistics Service is combined with the State of Maryland office. For specific data requests, refer to the Maryland Agricultural Statistics Office.

Delaware Department of Agriculture, 2320 S. Dupont Highway, Dover, DE 19901. Publication: *Delaware Agricultural Statistics.*

Florida

Agricultural Statistics Services, R. L. Freie, 1222 Woodward St., Orlando, FL 32803; (305) 648-6013. Publication: *Florida Agricultural Statistics.*

Commissioner of Agriculture, Mayo Building, Tallahassee, FL 32399-0800. Publications: *Annual Report*; *Agricultural Groups Directory*; *Dollars and $ense*; *Statistical Livestock Roundup.*

Georgia

Agricultural Statistics Service, L. E. Snipes, Stephens Federal Building, Suite 320, Athens, GA 30613; (404) 546-2236. Publications: *Georgia Farm Report* includes the following reports: Crop production, Grain stocks, Vegetable production, Fruit production, Prices received and paid by farmers, Hog inventory, Pig crop, Egg production, Hatchery data, Milk production, Livestock slaughter, Cash receipts, Farm Labor; *Weather and Crops*; *Weekly Hatchery*; *Georgia Agricultural Facts, Georgia Poultry Facts.*

Department of Agriculture, Capitol Square, Atlanta, GA 30334; (404) 656-3645, (800) 282-5852. Publications: *Farmers and Consumers Market Bulletin.*

Hawaii

Agricultural Statistics Service, A. R. Davis, State Department of Agriculture Building, 1428 S. King St., Honolulu, HI 96822; (808) 548-7155. Publication: *Hawaii Agricultural Statistics.*

Department of Agriculture, P.O. Box 22159, Honolulu, HI 96822; (808) 548-7109. Programs: 1) Agricultural Loan Program: credit is available to qualified farmers, partnerships, corporations,and agricultural cooperatives to promote agricultural development in Hawaii. 2) New Farmer Program: provides financial assistance through initial start-up loans to new farmers. 3) Orchard Development Program: allows tax relief to qualified orchardists during the developmental period of certain fruit and nut crops. 4) Aquaculture Loan Program: provides loans for the development of aquaculture enterprises. Independent. 5) Sugar Grower Loan Program: provides supplementary direct loans to independent sugar growers to cover deficits during current period of insufficient national protection against foreign sugar imports. 6) Agricultural and New Farmer Loan Program: loans to encourage the development of agricultural enterprises in the State. Publications: *Annual Report, Hawaii Agricultural and Food Products Export Directory.*

Idaho

Agricultural Statistics Service, R. C. Max, Box 1699, Boise, ID 83701; (208) 334-1507. Publication: *Annual Report, Agriculture in Idaho.*

Idaho Department of Agriculture, Marketing and Development, P.O. Box 790, Boise, ID 83701; (208) 334-2718. Program: Rural Rehabilitation Loans: this lending program helps stabilize rural

Idaho by providing funds to small family farmers and to youths who want to continue in agricultural pursuits. Publication: *Department of Agriculture Annual Report*.

Illinois

Agricultural Statistics Service, F. S. Barrett, Box 19283, Springfield, IL 62794; (217) 492-4295. Publications: *Illinois Farm Report*, Illinois Weather and Crop Reports: Fruit, Vegetables, Meat Animals, Poultry, Milk, Prices, and the *Farm Employment Report*.

Department of Agriculture, Division of Administrative Services, State Fairgrounds, P.O. Box 4906, Springfield, IL 62708; (217) 782-2172. Programs: Illinois Grain Insurance Corporation (IGIC): provides full protection to Illinois farmers who store their grain in country elevators; "T by 2000". This program is a nationwide model aimed at controlling soil erosion of fragile lands by the turn of the century. Publication: *Illinois Agricultural Statistics Annual Summary*.

Indiana

Agricultural Statistics Service, R. W. Gann, Agricultural Administration Building, Purdue University, West Lafayette, IN 47907; (317) 494-8371. Publication: *Indiana Agricultural Statistics*.

Indiana Department of Commerce, Office of the Commissioner of Agriculture, One North Capitol, Suite 700, Indianapolis, IN 46204; (317) 232-8770. Programs: 1) Hoosier Homestead and Hoosier Business Award Programs: farms and businesses that have been a working factor in the same family for at least 100 years receive an award. 2) Treasurer's Farm Program (TFP) provides low interest loans to farmers facing cash flow difficulties. Publications: *Guide to Direct Sources of Indiana Agricultural Products, Directory to Cottage Industries, Agricultural Export Directory, Hay and Straw Directory*.

Iowa

Agricultural Statistics Service, D. M. Skow, 210 Walnut St., Des Moines, IA 50309; (515) 284-4340. Publications: *Preparing Crop and Livestock Estimates, Annual Statistical Report*.

Secretary of Agriculture, Wallace Building, Des Moines, IA 50319; (515) 281-5681. Programs: Agricultural Diversification Program: assists farms with an alternative crop and livestock program. Agricultural Development Authority: assists beginning farmers in acquiring agricultural land, property, and agricultural improvements by offering loans at low interest rates.

Kansas

Agricultural Statistics Service, M.E. Johnson, Room 290, 444 S.E. Quincy St., Topeka, KS 66683; (913) 295-2600. *Annual Statistical Report*.

State Board of Agriculture, 109 S.W. 9th St., Topeka, KS 66612; (913) 296-3536.

Kentucky

Agricultural Statistics Service, D. D. Williamson, Box 1120, Louisville, KY 40601; (502) 582-5293. Publications: *AGRI-NEWS, Crop Reports, Livestock Reports, Dairy Reports, Poultry Reports, Price Reports, Miscellaneous Reports, Crop Weather, County Estimates*.

Department of Agriculture, 7th Floor, Capital Plaza Tower, Frankfort, KY 40601; (502) 564-4896, (800) 372-7602 (consumer line). Program: FARMLOT (800-327-6568): free marketing service to persons across the state who are interested in buying and/or selling farm commodities as well as receiving regional up-to-date farm market prices. Publication: *Kentucky Agricultural Statistics*.

Louisiana

Agricultural Statistics Service, B. A. Nelson, Box 5524, Alexandria, LA 71307. Publication: *Statistical Report*.

Department of Agriculture and Forestry, P.O. Box 94302, Baton Rouge, LA 70804; (504) 342-7011. Program: Farm Youth Loan Program: provides loan and loan guarantees to youths who are involved in an organized school program in agriculture. Publication: *Market Bulletin*.

Maine

For specific statistical information on Maine's agricultural products contact the Commissioner's Office of the Department of Agriculture, Food and Rural Resources (207) 289-3871.

Department of Agriculture, Food and Rural Resources, Commissioner's Office, State House Station 28, Augusta, ME 04333; (207) 289-3871. Publications: *Suggested Guidelines in Managing Maine's Most Common Infectious and Parasitic Disease of Livestock, Peat Task Force Report, How to Organize Agricultural Marketing Cooperatives, Annual Report on the Main Agricultural Fairs, Report of Energy Use in Agriculture Task Force, Farm Financing in Maine, Saving Energy in Rural Maine or Who is Doing What on the Farm, Maine Small Farm Statistics, Useable Waste Products for the Farm*.

Maryland

Agricultural Statistics Service, M. B. West, 50 Harry S. Truman Parkway, Suite 202, Annapolis, MD 21401; (301) 841-5740. Publications: *Maryland Agricultural Statistics*.

Maryland Department of Agriculture, 50 Harry S. Truman Parkway, Annapolis, MD 21401; (301) 841-5700. Publication: *The Maryland Department of Agriculture Yesterday, Today and Tomorrow; Agricultural Maryland*.

Massachusetts

For specific agricultural statistics, contact the Department of Food and Agriculture listed below.

Massachusetts Department of Food and Agriculture, 100 Cambridge, Boston, MA 02202; (617) 727-3018. Programs: Municipal Farmland Identification Program: information on available farmland will be mapped and on record. It provides the communities and farmers with an inventory on the possible crop production of an area and assists in planning decisions. Agricultural Preservation Restriction Program: protects diminishing farmland resources through the purchase of Agricultural Preservation Restrictions, commonly known as development rights.

The Department is currently initiating its own, complimentary data-collection program which will be transformed into a reliable computerized data base. Publications: *Massachusetts Agriculture Annual Report. The Fresh Connection* - a newsletter designed to help local growers find new markets, and to help improve communications between local producers and restaurant chefs.

Michigan

Agricultural Statistics Service, D. J. Fedewa, Box 20008, Lansing, MI 48901; (517) 377-1831. Publication: *Michigan Agricultural Statistics*.

Department of Agriculture, P.O. Box 30017, Lansing, MI 48909; (517) 373-1104. Program: Agricultural Assistance Network: provides assistance to Michigan farmers and related agribusinesses facing financial hardship as a result of economic crisis. A toll free hotline (1-800-346-FARM) is available to anyone with problems related to loans, human service needs, legal referrals, and financial farm management. Publications: *Accomplishments Report, MDA This Week, The Economics of Food and Agriculture in Michigan*.

Minnesota

Agricultural Statistics Service, C. G. Rock, Box 7068, St. Paul, MN 55107; (612) 296-2230. Publications: *Agri-View, Minnesota Weekly Crop-Weather Report, Potato Stocks, Monthly Turkey Report, Minnesota Agricultural Statistics Book*.

Department of Agriculture, 90 West Plato Blvd. Saint Paul, MN 55107; (612) 297-1551. Publication: *Minnesota Agriculture*.

Mississippi

Agricultural Statistics Service, G. R. Knight, Box 980, Jackson, MS 39205; (601) 965-4575. Publication: *Mississippi Agricultural Statistics*.

Mississippi Department of Agriculture and Commerce, P.O. Box 1609, Jackson, MS 39215; (601) 354-6734. Publication: *Annual Report*.

Missouri

Agricultural Statistics Service, D. M. Bay, P.O. Box L, Columbia, MO 65205; (314) 875-5233. Publications: *Missouri Agricultural Finance Survey, Annual Crop Summary, Farm Facts, Agricultural Statistics, County Agri-facts* for each county.

Missouri Department of Agriculture, P.O. Box 630, Jefferson City, MO 65102; (314) 751-4645. Publication: *Missouri Farm Facts*.

Montana

Agricultural Statistics Service, L. H. Pratt, Box 4369, Helena, MT 59604; (406) 449-5303. Publication: *Agricultural Statistics Bulletin*.

Department of Agriculture, Agriculture/Livestock Building, Capitol Station, Helena, MT 59620; (406) 444-3144. Programs: Agricultural Assistance Program: provides confidential one-on-one assistance to financially distressed farmers and ranchers (800) 722-FARM; Agricultural Development: makes grants and low interest rate loans available to rural youth organizations and other qualified farmers and ranchers. Publications: *Legal Aspects of Difficult Choices, Farm & Ranch Debt, Junior Agricultural Loan Program, Rural Assistance Loan Program*,

Agriculture and Farming

Agricultural Loan Linked Deposit Program, Agricultural Assistance Program, and *Farm/Ranch Hotline.*

Nebraska

Agricultural Statistics Service, J. L. Aschwege, Box 81069, Lincoln, NE 68501; (402) 471-5541. Publication: *Nebraska Agricultural Statistics.*

Department of Agriculture, Nebraska Agricultural Development, P.O. Box 94947, Lincoln, NE 68509; (402) 471-4876, (800) 422-6692. Publication: *Nebraska Agriculture.*

Nevada

Agricultural Statistics Service, C. R. Lies, Box 8880, Reno, NV 89507; (702) 784-5584. Publication: *Annual Statistical Summary.*

Nevada State Department of Agriculture, Box 11100, Reno, NV 89510; (702) 789-0180. Publication: *Nevada and Its Agriculture.*

New England

Maine, New Hampshire, Vermont, Connecticut, Rhode Island, Massachusetts, 22 Bridge St., P.O. Box 1444, Concord, NH 03301; (603) 224-9639. Publications: *Ag Review Monthly, Crop Acreage and Production,* and *Crop Weather.*

New Hampshire

New Hampshire Department of Agriculture, Caller Box 2042, Concord, NH 03302; (603) 271-3688. No reports published.

New Jersey

Agricultural Statistics Service, J. R. Gibson, CN-330 New Warren St., Trenton, NJ 08625; (609) 292-6385. Publications: *Farm Facts, Weekly Weather Crop, Annual Vegetable Summary, Fertilizer Report.*

Department of Agriculture, Health and Agriculture Building, CN-330, Trenton, NJ 08625; (609) 292-8896. Programs: administers nine commodity councils dedicated to research, education and agricultural promotion. Agricultural Development Program: through a variety of tours and educational activities, this program informs the non-farming public about New Jersey's agriculture. Publication: *New Jersey Agriculture.*

New Mexico

Agricultural Statistics Service, D. G. Gerhardt, Box 1809, Las Cruces, NM 88004; (505) 523-8168. Publications: *New Mexico Agri-Info, Weekly Crop Weather, Crop Acreages and Production, Livestock Inventory and Production, Chile Summary, Grape Summary, New Mexico Agricultural Statistics.*

New Mexico Department of Agriculture, NMSU Campus, Box 3189, Las Cruces, NM 88003; (505) 646-2804. Programs: Rangeland Protection Program: implements brush control programs on lands within the state. ADC Program: assists agricultural producers with the control of prairie dogs and kangaroo rats on rangeland, planted pastures, and field crops. Publications: *Biennial Report, New Mexico Agricultural Export Directory.*

New York

Agricultural Statistics Service, G. W. Suter, 1 Winners Circle, Albany, NY 12235; (518) 457-5570. Publication: *New York Agricultural Statistics.*

New York Department of Agriculture and Markets, 1 Winners Circle, Albany, NY 12235; (518) 457-4492. Program: Institutional Procurement Assistance Program (1-800-NY-CROPS) assists state institutional facilities in purchasing foods grown, produced,and processed in the state. The program utilizes a computerized database of farmers, institutional buyers, and food wholesalers to provide buyers and sellers with detailed information on sources and marketing opportunities for New York State fresh fruits and vegetables. Publications: *New York Agriculture 2000, Frontiers for Agriculture: An Action Agenda for New York State, Annual Report,* and *New York Wine Guide.*

North Carolina

Agricultural Statistics Service, Box 27767, Raleigh, NC 27611; (919) 856-4394. Publication: *Agriculture in North Carolina.*

North Carolina Department of Agriculture, Raleigh, NC 27611; (919) 733-4216. Program: Public Affairs Department features reports on agricultural business violations; Market NewsLine: a new electronic version of market news that transmits instant reports on farm market prices, supply and demand information,and weather. Publication: *Agricultural Review.*

North Dakota

Agricultural Statistics Service, R. F. Carver, Box 3166, Fargo, ND 58102; (701) 237-5771. Agricultural Statistics.

Department of Agriculture, State Capitol, Bismarck, ND 58505; (701) 224-2231. Programs: Northern Crops Institute: established to foster cooperation of farm commodity and agri-business organizations. Centennial Farm Award Program: awards given to families who have retained ownership of their farm for 100 years or more. Publication: *North Dakota Biennial Report.*

Ohio

Agricultural Statistics Service, H. L. Carter, 200 N. High St., Columbus, OH 43215; (614) 469-5590. Publication: *Ohio Agricultural Statistics.*

Ohio Department of Agriculture, 65 South Front St., Columbus, OH 43215; (614) 466-2732. Programs: Ohio Farm Financial Management Program: offers seminars on Farm Financial Management In Time of Stress; a $500,000 grant is being used to help farmers with new financing techniques using a computer generated program. International Trade Program: designed to foster international trade relationships between foreign buyers and Ohio agribusiness firms via a trade-leads match-making service. The focus of this program is toward small businesses.

Oklahoma

Agricultural Statistics Section, R. P. Bellinghausen, 2800 N. Lincoln Blvd. Oklahoma City, OK 73105; (405) 525-9226. Publication: *Oklahoma Agricultural Statistics.*

State Department of Agriculture, 2800 North Lincoln Blvd., Oklahoma City, OK 73105; (405) 521-3861. Publication: *The Oklahoma Department of Agriculture and You.*

Oregon

Agricultural Statistics Service, P.M. Williamson, 1220 S.W. 3rd Avenue, Portland, OR 97204; (503) 221-2131. Publication: *Oregon Agriculture and Fisheries Statistics.*

Department of Agricultural and Resource Economics, Oregon State University, Corvallis, OR 97331; (503) 754-2942. Publications: *Farming and Ranching in Oregon, Oregon County and State Agricultural Estimates, Commodity Data Sheets* for: grains, hay, field crops, tree fruits and nuts, small fruits and berries, vegetables and truck crops, specialty products, livestock and poultry.

Pennsylvania

Agricultural Statistics Service, W. C. Evans, 2301 N. Cameron St., Harrisburg, PA 17110; (717) 787-3904. Publications: *Crop and Livestock Annual Summary, Keystone Digest, Special Dairy Report, Broilers, Annual Manufactured Dairy, Machinery Custom Rates, Mushroom Report, Weekly Crop and Weather Round-Up.*

Department of Agriculture, 2301 North Cameron St., Harrisburg, PA 17110; (717) 787-4694. Publication: *Annual Report.*

Rhode Island

For specific agricultural statistics in Rhode Island contact the office listed below.

Rhode Island Department of Environmental Management, Division of Agriculture and Marketing, Roger Williams Building, 22 Hayes St., Providence, RI 02908; (401) 277-2781. Programs: Purchase of Development Rights: designed to retain agricultural land by purchasing right to develop the land for purposes other than agriculture. Farm, Forest and Open Space: encourages the maintenance of Rhode Island's productive agriculture and forestland. The use value assessment is based on the current use of land rather than the potential development value. Publications: *Weekly Wholesale and Retail Market Reports, Seasonal Crop and Apple Market Reports,* Pick-Your-Own brochures and information, Farmers Market brochures and information, Crop Brochures featuring Nutritional, Storage, Buying and Cooking information on Rhode Island grown crops. *Rhode Island Agricultural Statistics, Export Directory.*

South Carolina

Agricultural Statistics Service, H. J. Power, Box 1911, Columbia, SC 29202; (803) 765-5333. Publication: *Market Bulletin.*

Department of Agriculture, P.O. Box 11280, Columbia, SC 29211; (803) 734-2210. Publications: *Annual Report,* individual reports: Tobacco, Soybean, Cattle, Beef, Pork, Peach, Watermelon, Egg, Peanut and Tomato, *Commodity Promotions and Consumer Information, Poultry Grading, Fruit and Vegetables, Ag Study Tours, Small Farms, Fruit and Vegetable Market News, International Trade, Livestock Market News, Consumer Services.*

South Dakota

Agricultural Statistics Service, J.C. Ranek, Box V, Sioux Falls, SD 57117; (605) 765-5333. Publications: *Crop and Livestock Reporter, Crop-Weather Summary, South Dakota Agriculture, South Dakota's Rank in Agriculture.*

Department of Agriculture, Anderson Building, 445 E. Capitol, Pierre, SD 57501; (605) 773-5032. Program: Adult Farm and Ranch Business Management Program: assists farmers and ranchers in developing a farm accounting system. Publication: *Statewide Annual Report, South Dakota Agriculture, Horizons.*

Tennessee

Agricultural Statistics Service, C. R. Brantner, Box 41505, Nashville, TN 37204; (615) 736-5136. Publications: *Tennessee Weather and Crops, Tennessee Farm Facts, Agricultural Statistics.*

Department of Agriculture, Ellington Agricultural Center, P.O. Box 40627, Nashville, TN 37204; (615) 360-0160. Program: Overseas Market Program: new-to-export companies receive counseling via state-sponsored educational seminars and individual meetings with marketing personnel. Advise is also available on international financing. Publications: *Producer to Consumer Directory, Tennessee Hay Directory,* and *Tennessee Agriculture: A Century Farms Perspective.*

Texas

Agricultural Statistics Service, D. S. Findley, Box 70, Austin, TX 78767; (512) 482-5581. Publications: *Texas Agricultural Facts, Texas Historic Livestock Statistics, Texas Historic Crops Statistics, Texas County Statistics, Texas Custom Rates Statistics, Texas Citrus Tree Inventory Survey, Weekly Crop-Weather, Monthly Citrus, Monthly Onions, Quarterly Vegetable Acreage, Monthly Cattle on Feed, Weekly Broilers.*

Department of Agriculture, P.O. Box 12847, Austin, TX 78711; (512) 463-7624. Program: International Marketing Program: this network ties into the USDA's computerized trade lead system that spans the world to gather buyer inquiries on a daily basis. Publications: *Texas Agriculture Facts, Gazette, Taste of Texas.*

Utah

Agricultural Statistics Service, D. J. Gneiting, Box 25007, Salt Lake City, UT 84125; (801) 524-5003. Publications: *Utah Agriculture, Weekly Crop-Weather.*

Department of Agriculture, 350 North Redwood Road, Salt Lake City, UT 84116; (801) 533-5421. Programs: Computerized Branding: Utah is the first state to have a computerized brand renewal system which processed 24,000 brands in one year. Agricultural Resource Development Loan (ARDL): low interest loans to establish conservation practices. Resource Inventory and Monitoring Systems (RIMS): loans to implement soil and water conservation. Publications: *Market News, Biennial Report.*

Vermont

Vermont Department of Agriculture, State Office Building, 116 State St., Montpelier, VT 05602; (802) 828-2419. Contact: Office of Information for various free directories and brochures including: *Hay Directory* and *Specialty Foods Directory.*

Agricultural Statistics: Vermont is included in the New England State Statistical Office. Contact: New England State Statistical Office, P.O. Box 1444, Concord, NH 03301; (603) 224-9639.

Virginia

Agricultural Statistics Service, C. A. Dunkerley, Box 1659, Richmond, VA 23213; (804) 786-3500. Publications: *Crops and Livestock, Poultry, Milk and Dairy, Prices and Income, Virginia Agricultural Statistics, Tobacco Sales.*

Department of Agriculture and Commerce, Post Office Box 1163, Richmond, VA 23213; (804) 786-2373. Program: Rural Virginia Development Foundation: researches and evaluates potential venture investment opportunities, established a computerized information exchange system statewide - tel-o-auction, to promote livestock sales. Publications: *Bulletin, Year in Review.*

Washington

Agricultural Statistics Service, D. A. Hasslen, Box 609, Olympia, WA 98507; (206) 586-8919. Publication: *Washington Statistical Bulletin.*

Department of Agriculture, 406 General Administration Building AX-41, Olympia, WA 98504; (206) 586-6108. Publications: *Washington State Food and Agricultural Suppliers Directory, Biennial Report, Washington Agricultural Exports Statistical Bulletin.*

West Virginia

Agricultural Statistics Service, J. J. Brueggen, 4720 Brenda Lane, Charleston, WV 25312; (304) 348-2217. Publications: *West Virginia Mountain State Reporter, West Virginia Crop Weather Bulletin, West Virginia Agricultural Statistics.*

Department of Agriculture, State Capitol, Charleston, WV 25303; (304) 348-3708. Publication: *The Market Bulletin.*

Wisconsin

Agricultural Statistics Service, C. D. Spencer, Box 9160, Madison, WI 53715; (608) 264-5317. Publication: *Washington Agricultural Statistics.*

Department of Agriculture, 801 W. Badger Rd., P.O. Box 8911, Madison, WI 53708; (608) 266-2939. Publications: *Direct Marketing Guide, Take Home Guide.*

Wyoming

Agricultural Statistics Service, S. J. Hundley, Box 1148, Cheyenne, WY 82003; (307) 772-2181. Publications: *Biweekly Ag Statistics, Winter Wheat Variety, Winter Wheat County Estimates, Barley County Estimates, Hay County Estimates, Sheep and Lamb Loss, Crop Weather Report, Wyoming Agricultural Statistics.*

Department of Agriculture, 2219 Carey Avenue, Cheyenne, WY 82002; (307) 777-6792. Publications: *Your Agriculture Business Plan, Annual Statistical Report, Agricultural Trade Directory, Wyoming Agricultural Production: A History, Working With Agricultural Lenders: Understanding the Loan Approval Process, Agricultural Loan Volume and Market Shares by Lender, Wyoming Farm and Ranch Finance Survey, Credit for Wyoming Agricultural and Commercial Sectors, Wyoming Farm and Ranch Land Market, Costs of Producing Crops, Prices Received by Wyoming Farmers and Ranchers.*

Energy
General Sources

* See also Experts Chapter
* See also Current Events and Homework Chapter
* See also Careers and Workplace; Research Grants in Every Field Chapter
* See also Economics, Demographics and Statistics Chapter
* See also Environment and Nature Chapter
* See also Housing and Real Estate Chapter
* See also Weather and Maps Chapter
* See also Science and Technology Chapter
* See also Housing and Real Estate Chapter

Finding new and more efficient sources and uses of energy is one of the most pressing issues facing the world today. Here you'll find information leads on everything from international energy agreements to how you can better insulate your home to lower your heating bills. Not only can you find out about the newest energy-related legislation or the newest developments in geothermal power, but you'll also find sources on such volatile issues as nuclear reactor safety and offshore oil exploration. Whether you're a business that needs an energy audit or a student doing a report on solar energy, these up-to-date resources will provide you with the answers.

* Alcohol Fuel Plant Permits
Distribution Center
Bureau of Alcohol, Tobacco, and Firearms
U.S. Department of the Treasury
7943 Angus Ct.
Springfield, VA 22153   (703) 455-7801
The free booklet, *Alcohol Fuel Plants*, outlines the general provisions of the alcohol fuel plant permit system. Questions and answers are included to clarify certain points in reference to alcohol fuel plant application and operations. If you need further information, contact the Bureau's Regional Office located in your state.

* Alcohol Fuel Production Loans
Office of Alcohol Fuels
Conservation and Renewable Energy
U.S. Department of Energy
1000 Independence Ave., SW, Room 5F-086
Washington, DC 20585   (202) 586-9791
Contact this office for information on the Energy Security Act's loan guarantee program (Title II Renewable Energy), designed in part to encourage the private sector to construct alcohol fuel production facilities. The office also monitors the remaining cooperative agreements and feasibility studies under this program.

* Appliance Labeling
Building Equipment Division
Conservation and Renewable Energy
U.S. Department of Energy
1000 Independence Ave., SW, Room 5H-048
Washington, DC 20585   (202) 586-9123
Energy guide labels, required by law to be on the back of all major appliances, provide information as to energy efficiency and cost of operation of the particular equipment. Contact this office for information on the Appliance Standards Program.

* Appliance Testing and Evaluation
Building Equipment Division
Building and Community Systems
Conservation and Renewable Energy
U.S. Department of Energy
1000 Independence Ave., SW, Room 5H-048
Washington, DC 20585   (202) 586-9123
DOE's Building Equipment Division develops or modifies test procedures for measuring energy saving design procedures in major household appliances. The office also develops minimum energy efficiency standards for these appliances. Contact the office for further information.

* Appropriate Technology Assistance Service
U.S. Department of Energy

P.O. Box 2525
Butte, MT 59702-2525   (800) 428-2525
                                                      (800) 428-1718 (MT)
National Appropriate Technology Assistance Service (NATAS) provides tailored information and technical and commercialization assistance by toll-free telephone or mail.

* Architecture and Engineering
Buildings Systems Division
Buildings and Community Systems
Conservation and Renewable Energy
U.S. Department of Energy
1000 Independence Ave., SW, Room 5E-098
Washington, DC 20585   (202) 586-9449
The Buildings Systems Division distributes information and runs outreach programs on energy efficient buildings. The work of this Division focuses on how systems, subsystems, and components of buildings function independently and how they interact. This Division also develops and promotes research on construction and operation methods and standards for application to new or existing structure. Contact this office for more detailed program information and information on available publications. Also contact the National Energy Information Center and the National Technical Information Service for more information.

* Atmospheric Fluid Dynamics
Pacific Northwest Laboratory
Richland Operations Office, DOE
P.O. Box 999
Richland, WA 99352   (509) 375-3870
This office collects and manages research on atmospheric fluid dynamics as they apply to design, performance, and operation of wind turbines. Recent work includes wind turbine wake research, microscale turbulence analyses for dynamic stress load studies, flow characterization, and micrositing in complex terrain. This laboratory has performed wind energy resource assessments for the U.S. and has also developed an international wind energy resource assessment. Contact this office for more detailed information on its projects.

* Audit and Accounting Files
Division of Public Affairs
Federal Energy Regulatory Commission
825 North Capitol Street, NE
Washington, DC 20426   (202) 357-8055
Contact this office for information on examining the accounting files and FERC audits of gas, electric, and oil companies.

* Automobile Fuel Economy
Motor Vehicle Requirements Division
Office of Market Incentives
Rulemaking
National Highway Traffic Safety Administration

U.S. Department of Transportation
400 7th Street, SW, Room 5320
Washington, DC 20590   (202) 366-0486
NHTSA issues fuel economy standards and collects information on the technological and economic capabilities of automobile manufacturers to maximize fuel efficiency. Contact this office for information and referrals.

* Biofuels
Biofuels and Municipal Waste Technology Division
Conservation and Renewable Energy
U.S. Department of Energy
1000 Independence Ave., SW, Room 5H-072
Washington, DC 20585   (202) 586-4679
DOE researchers provide the technology base for the production of cost-competitive liquid and gaseous fuels from biomass resources. During the early stages of biofuels development, DOE provides leadership and sponsors long-term, high-risk research and development (R&D). As technology is developed, industry's level of cooperation and cost sharing increases. Finally, when the technology is sufficiently advanced and the economics are sufficiently defined, industry assumes responsibility for commercialization of the developed technology. Contact this office for the program summary and other program information.

* Biomass Feedstock Fuels
Biofuels and Municipal Waste Technology Division
U.S. Department of Energy
1000 Independence Ave., SW, Room 5H-095
Washington, DC 20585   (202) 586-4679
This office directs long-term research and development into increasing supplies of biomass feedstocks. Researchers also develop conversion technologies for producing heat, gas, and liquid fuels from a variety of biomass and municipal waste feedstocks. They also investigate aquatic, herbal, and wood crops with potential for increased biomass yields, as well as related systems. Regional programs focus on technology transfer and matching local feedstocks to conversion technologies.

* Bulletins: Ocean Thermal to Wind Power
Science and Technology Division
Reference Section
Library of Congress
Washington, DC 20540   (202) 707-5580
Informal series of reference guides are issued free from the Science and Technology Division under the general title, *LC Science Tracer Bullet*. These guides are designed to help readers locate published material on subjects about which they have only general knowledge. New titles in the series are announced in the weekly Library of Congress *Information Bulletin* that is distributed to many libraries. The following is a list of *Tracer Bullets* currently available:

80-7 Solar Energy
80-8 Electric & Hybrid Vehicles
80-12 Ocean Thermal Energy
80-16 Synthetic Fuels
81-5 Wind Power
81-13 Wood As Fuel
83-9 Geothermal Energy

* Computer Control of Power Systems
Computer Systems Section
Power System Control Center
Tennessee Valley Authority
2N 10A Power Control Center
Chattanooga, TN 37401   (615) 751-8678
The Computer Systems Section develops and maintains the software systems that control such functions as economic dispatch, automatic generation control, and logging. Telemetered information from TVA's plants, substations, and from interconnection points with utilities is analyzed and processed to help the load coordinators determine the most economical and reliable method to run the power system. Personnel also are responsible for program development and maintenance of the software for the five area dispatch control centers and a microwave alarm logger.

* Conservation Technology Transfer
Energy Management and Extension Branch, CE-221
Office of State and Local Assistance Programs
U.S. Department of Energy
1000 Independence Ave., SW
Washington, DC 20585   (202) 586-8288
The Energy Extension Service helps market and transfer energy conservation technology and information to businesses. Contact this office to find more out about the information and technology available.

* Consumer Countries
Consumer Country Affairs
Bureau of Economics and Business Affairs
Department of State
2201 C St., NW, Room 3336
Washington, DC 20520   (202) 647-4017
This office deals with energy-consuming countries--countries that use more energy than they produce. The primary portfolio is dealing with the International Energy Agency in Paris, which was begun in response to the oil crisis. This office, which coordinates policy regarding energy and energy crises, is broken down into the various energy sources (oil, natural gas, coal, nuclear, solar, wind and electricity) with each looking at the stock and emergency preparedness. They also each follow a handful of countries and track international organizations. With the Department of Energy and Commerce, they try to sell energy when they can.

* Consumers and Energy Issues
Congressional, Intergovernmental and Public Affairs
U.S. Department of Energy
1000 Independence Ave., SW, Room 8G-026
Washington, DC 20585   (202) 586-5573
This office analyzes how Department of Energy policies affect the public energy consumer. It is a source of referral for specific program information to other offices in the Department of Energy.

* Consumption Statistics
Energy End-Use Division
Energy Markets and End Use
Energy Information Administration
U.S. Department of Energy
1000 Independence Ave., SW, Room 1F-093
Washington, DC 20585   (202) 586-1112
This office compiles statistics on energy consumption in U.S. residential, commercial, industrial, and transportation sectors by sector and by fuel type. Contact this office for more information and available publications.

* Deep Seabed Mining
Ocean Minerals and Energy Division
National Ocean Service
National Oceanic and Atmospheric Administration
Department of Commerce
1825 Connecticut Ave., NW
Washington, DC 20235   (202) 673-5121
Extensive information is available on deep seabed mining, which includes the annual report to Congress and an updated environmental assessment of NOAA deep seabed mining licensees' exploration plans. This office can provide you with information regarding the research conducted concerning the environmental impact of the mining, as well as information on the regulations and licenses.

* Defense Energy Emergencies
Energy Emergency Operations
International Affairs and Energy Emergencies
U.S. Department of Energy
1000 Independence Ave., SW, Room 8F0973
Washington, Dc 20585   (202) 586-1311
This office conducts programs to ensure that the U.S. can meet its defense energy needs and that government and industry can continue their essential functions in a catastrophic emergency. It works to reduce U.S. vulnerability to such emergencies and to help improve energy emergency decision making. Contact this office for more detailed information.

* Department of Energy Annual Report
Office of Public Affairs
U.S. Department of Energy
1000 Independence Ave., SW, Room 8G-096
Washington, DC 20585   (202) 586-8325
The Division of Budget and Administration prepares the U.S. Department of Energy's annual budget and *Annual Report*. For copies of these and other Department of Energy Publications, please contact the office of Public Affairs, a good starting point for any quest for information from the Department of Energy.

* Diesel Fuel Recording
Interstate Commerce Commission
12th St. and Constitution Ave., NW
Washington, DC 20423   (202) 275-6787
This recording states the average diesel fuel price each week after a survey is taken of fuel stations across the country.

* DOE Budget

Office of the Controller
Office of Management and Administration
U.S. Department of Energy
1000 Independence Ave., SW, Room 4A-139
Washington, DC 20585 (202) 586-4171

The free publication, *Budget Highlights*, summarizes, in statistics and narrative description, the current budget and programs of the Department of Energy.

* DOE Energy Research

Office of Energy Research
U.S. Department of Energy
1000 Independence Ave., SW, Room J-304
Washington, DC 20585 (301) 586-5430

The Office of Energy Research gives advice on Department of Energy research programs, university-based education and training activities, as well as grants and other forms of energy assistance. Contact this office for available program information, including the publication, *Programs of the Office of Energy Research*, which provides a summary of office research and education programs.

* DOE Public Reading Rooms

U.S. Department of Energy
Public Reading Room
1000 Independence Ave., SW, Room 1E-90
Washington, DC 20585 (800) 638-8081

A variety of program documents are available at DOE Public Reading Rooms and Information Offices listed below. Nuclear Regulatory Commission materials are available at the listed NRC Local Public Document rooms. For further information about the Local Public Document Room Program, call the above office.

Albuquerque
Operations Office, National Atomic Museum, P.O. Box 5400, Kirtland Air Force Base, E, Albuquerque, NM 87115; (505) 844-8443

Boston
Support Office, U.S. Department of Energy, 10 Causeway Street, Room 1197, Boston, MA 02222-1035; (617) 565-7700

Chicago
Operations Office, Building 201, 9800 South Cass Ave., Argonne, IL 60439; (312) 972-2010

Idaho
Operations Office, Public Reading Room, 1776 Science Drive, Idaho Falls, ID 83402, (208) 526-1144

Nevada
Operations Office, Public Reading Room, U.S. Department of Energy, P.O. Box 98518, Las Vegas, NV 89193-8518; (702) 295-1563

Oak Ridge
Operations Office, Federal Building, Oak Ridge, TN 37830; (615) 576-1046

Richland
Operations Office, Federal Building, Room 157, Richland, WA 99352; (509) 376-8583

San Francisco
Operations Office, Wells Fargo Bank Building, 1333 Broadway, Oakland, CA 94612; (415) 273-4428

Savannah River
Operations Office, DOE Public Documents Reading Room, Gregg-Graniteville Library, Second Floor, University of South Carolina-Aiken, 171 University Parkway, Aiken, SC 29801; (803) 648-6851 x320

* Donation of Energy-Related Laboratory Equipment

University and Industry Programs
Office of Field Operations Management
U.S. Department of Energy
1000 Independence Ave., SW
Washington, DC 20585 (202) 586-1634

Used energy equipment is donated to nonprofit educational institutions of higher learning for use in appropriate programs. Contact the office for further information and details.

* Economics and Statistics

Economics and Statistics Division
Office of Energy Markets and End Use
Energy Information Administration
U.S. Department of Energy
1000 Independence Ave., SW, Room 1F-077
Washington, DC 20585

This office compiles economic and financial energy statistics, including domestic and international trends.

* Electric Power Data

Electric Power Division
Coal, Nuclear, Electric and Alternate Fuels
Energy Information Administration
U.S. Department of energy
1000 Independence Ave., SW, Room 2G-053
Washington, DC 20585 (202) 586-9863

This office collects analytical data on electric power supply, including capacity, generation, distribution, fuel use, finances, and rates. It also prepares projections of capacity, generation, fuel use, costs, rates, financial requirements, and distribution of electric power. The effects of policy and regulatory actions on the electric utilities' rates, costs, capacity, generation, distribution, finance, and consumption of input fuels are also studied. Contact this office for more information.

* Electric Power Supply and Rates

Transmission and Consumer Service
Distributer and Marketing Services
MR5S
Chattanooga, TN 37402-2801 (615) 751-6886

TVA has a goal to operate a more competitive power system by not increasing its power rates for its consumers for three years. Rate stability in 1988 avoided a 6 percent rate increase and resulted in $300 million in savings for consumers. For information on electric power supply and rates, or to receive brochures with coal and electricity statistics, including breakdowns of monthly residential and industrial electric bills, and the use of TVA revenue dollars, contact this office.

* Electric Utility Systems

Administrator
Rural Electrification Administration
U.S. Department of Agriculture
Room 4051 (202) 382-9542

USDA lends money to about 1,000 rural electric companies and maintains a staff that is knowledgeable on both operations and equipment.

* Emergencies

Energy Emergency Plans and Integration
International Affairs and Energy Emergencies
U.S. Department of Energy
1000 Independence Ave., SW, Room GH-060
Washington, DC 20585 (202) 586-4000

This office develops energy emergency plans and responses to energy emergencies, and manages international cooperation in response to energy emergencies. Contact this office for more detailed information.

* Emergency Policy

Energy Policy and Evaluation
International Affairs and Energy Emergencies
U.S. Department of Energy
1000 Independence Ave., SW, Room GE-362
Washington, DC 20585 (202) 586-2442

This office defines, analyzes, and coordinates energy emergency policy issues, focusing on resolving problems that may hinder effective U.S. responses to energy emergencies. This office also assesses the impact of proposed responses on all levels of government, private industry, and individuals. Contact the office for further information.

* Energy and Mineral Resources

Office of Energy and Marine Geology
U.S. Geological Survey
National Center, MS 915
Reston, VA 22092 (703) 648-6470

Investigations of the nature, extent, and origin of the Nation's coal, oil and gas, oil shale, uranium, and geothermal resources are basic to this office's research efforts. Acquired data are placed in computerized databases, such as the National Coal Resources Data System.

* Energy Extension Services

Energy Management and Extension Branch, CE-221
Office of State and Local Assistance Programs
U.S. Department of Energy
1000 Independence Ave., SW
Washington, DC 20585 (202) 586-8288

The Energy Extension Service (EES) provides small-scale energy users, such as individuals, small businesses, and local governments, with personalized information and on-site technical assistance for practical energy conservation, including the uses of renewable energy resources. All states, as well as U.S. territories and the District of Columbia, offer this conservation assistance.

* Energy Information Administration
U.S. Department of Energy
1000 Independence Ave., SW, Room E1-231
Washington, DC 20585   (202) 586-1094
The Energy Information Administration's *Annual Report* provides a good summary of the Administrations' structure and key informational contacts within the offices.

* Energy Information Directory
National Energy Information Center
Energy Information Administration
U.S. Department of Energy
1000 Independence Ave., SW, Room E1-231
Washington, DC 20585   (202) 586-8800
The National Energy Information Center is the central distribution point for most U.S. Department of Energy publications, including the free *Energy Information Administration Publications Directory: A Users Guide*. The *Directory* includes current program information sources; an index of DOE, State, and Federal Agency contacts; a directory of DOE technical information with descriptions of computerized databases and other resources; Congressional Committees and Subcommittees that have jurisdiction over various components of the Civilian Radioactive Waste Management Program; and DOE Public Reading Rooms and Information Offices, and NRC local public document rooms; and listings of selected publications. Also ask for the latest edition of the *Energy Information Directory*, a comprehensive guide to energy information in the Federal government. The NEIC should be an early contact in any energy research project.

* Energy Information Center, National
National Energy Information Center
U.S. Department of Energy
1000 Independence Ave., SW, Room E1-231
Washington, DC 20585   (202) 586-8800
A suggested early contact for any energy research project, this is the central clearinghouse for energy information and assistance. The Center is a detailed and comprehensive source of information about energy data and information.

* Energy-Saving Equipment in Buildings
Building Equipment Division
Conservation and Renewable Energy
U.S. Department of Energy
1000 Independence Ave., SW, Room 5H-048
Washington, DC 20585   (202) 586-9123
This Division supplies the private sector with the technological base on which to develop and test high efficiency energy equipment used in operating residential and commercial buildings. This office is also responsible for administration of the Appliance Standards Program. Contact this office for more information.

* Energy Science Research
Accelerator and Fusion Research Division
Lawrence Berkeley Laboratory
1 Cyclotron Road
Mail stop 50A/5104
Berkeley, CA 94720   (414) 486-5771
The Lawrence Berkeley Laboratory undertakes a wide ranging research program in Energy Sciences, which includes geology, chemistry, materials sciences, physics and engineering. LBL pursues basic research and seeks ways of practical application of the basic results. The work of this division of the Laboratory is designed to reflect Energy Department priorities in finding ways to explore and recover energy resources, as well as protecting people and the environment from possible hazards. Contact the above office for further information.

* Environmental Impact Statements
Office of National Environmental Policy Act
     Project Assistance
Environment, Safety, and Health
U.S. Department of Energy
1000 Independence Ave., SW, Room 3E-080
Washington, DC 20585   (202) 586-4610
NEPA documents prepared for DOE activities are reviewed and approved through this office to determine whether DOE programs require Environmental Impact Statements. This office also reviews energy-related Environmental Impact Statements from other agencies. Contact this office for more detailed information.

* Environmental Issues and Energy Development
Office of Environmental Analysis
Assistant Secretary for Environment, Safety and Health
U.S. Department of Energy
1000 Independence Ave., SW, Room 4G-036
Washington, DC 20585   (202) 586-2061
This office analyzes proposed environmental policies, laws, and regulations to determine their effects on energy development and use. The office also assesses the potential impact on the environment of energy technologies being developed by the Department of Energy, along with the potential impact of national energy strategies at both the national and regional level. Contact the office for more detailed information.

* Environmental Protection, International
Bureau of Oceans and International Environmental and
     Scientific Affairs
Department of State
2201 C St., NW, Room 4325
Washington, DC 20520   (202) 647-9266
This office looks at international environmental issues and concerns, such as pollution, acid rain, global climate changes, the ozone, and toxic waste. They monitor bilateral and multilateral agreements, and work with other agencies in trying to develop ways to handle these environmental concerns.

* Federal Energy Management
Federal Energy Management Program
Office of Conservation and Renewable Energy
U.S. Department of Energy
1000 Independence Ave., SW
Washington, DC 20585   (202) 586-1145
This office coordinates the Federal government's energy management efforts. The *FEMP Update*, published quarterly by the FEMP, provides information that will assist Federal managers in their energy management responsibilities. Contact this office above for further information, or to obtain a copy of FEMP's *Annual Operating Plan for Fiscal Year 1989*.

* Federal Energy Policy
Commerce Clearing House, Inc.
4025 West Peterson Ave.
Chicago, IL 60646   (312) 940-4600
The *Federal Energy Guidelines* is a set of loose-leaf publications dealing primarily with DOE programs, certain other Federal energy activities, and general data regarding energy policy are produced from an automated data base. Nongovernment offices can obtain a subscription by contacting the office above.

* Federal Energy Regulatory Commission
Federal Energy Regulatory Commission
Division of Public Affairs
825 North Capitol Street, NE, Room 2214
Washington, DC 20426   (202) 357-8055
This office can supply you with information on the work of the Federal Energy Regulatory Commission, FERC. This office can also assist you in obtaining copies of FERC official documents.

* Federal Energy Regulatory Commission Publications
Reference and Information Services Branch
Federal Energy Regulatory Commission
825 North Capitol Street, NE, Room 1000
Washington, DC 20426   (202) 357-8118
The *Federal Energy Regulatory Commission Publications Directory* provides descriptions, sources, stock numbers, and prices, when applicable, of the latest editions of publications and staff reports issued by the Federal Energy Regulatory Commission or the former Federal Power Commission. Contact the office above to obtain a free copy.

* Films on Energy Issues
Audiovisual Branch
Office of Public Affairs
U.S. Department of Energy
1000 Independence Ave., SW, Room 8-096
Washington, DC 20585   (202) 586-8325
This office can provide you with information on availability of Department of Energy motion pictures and multimedia presentations.

* Financial Statistics and Projections
Economics and Statistics Division
Energy Markets and End Use
Energy Information Administration
U.S. Department of Energy

1000 Independence Ave., SW, Room 1F-077
Washington, DC 20585   (202) 586-1441
This office compiles economic and financial energy statistics and projections, and periodic assessments of the U.S. energy situation are made. Additionally, it evaluates and interprets current trends and events in the U.S. and international energy situations. For available information and publications, contact this office.

* Fuel Economy and State Motor Vehicle Inspections

Records and Motor Vehicle Services Division (NTS-43)
National Highway Traffic Safety Administration
U.S. Department of Transportation
400 7th Street, SW
Washington, DC 20590   (202) 366-2676
NHTSA's Motor Vehicle Inspection Program is aimed at providing car owners with preventative information on what repairs are needed to achieve greater safety, lower pollution, and better mileage. The annual *Study of the State Motor Vehicle Inspection Program* is available from this office.

* Fuel Efficiency and Vehicle Research and Testing

Vehicle Research and Test Center
Research and Development
National Highway Traffic Safety Administration
U.S. Department of Transportation
P.O. BOX 37
East Liberty, OH 43319   (513) 666-4511
NHTSA evaluates the effectiveness of Federal Motor Vehicle Safety Standards. This engineering facility performs tests to obtain basic data used to establish standards for safety and fuel efficiency of motor vehicles.

* Genetic Research

Life Sciences Program
Lawrence Berkeley Laboratory
One Cyclotron Rd.
Mail Stop 50A/5104
Berkeley, CA 94720   (414) 486-5771
The Life Sciences Program at the Lawrence Berkeley Laboratory undertakes research into genes and related aspects of genetic structure. It also researches radiobiology, nuclear medicine, biotechnology, and cellular and molecular damage caused by energy-related environmental hazards. Contact this office for more detailed information on its programs.

* Geothermal Energy

Geothermal Technology Division
Conservation and Renewable Energy
U.S. Department of Energy
1000 Independence Ave., SW, Room 5H-065
Washington, DC 20585   (202) 586-5340
Geothermal energy technology improvements are needed before the more difficult resources--moderate-temperature hydrothermal fluids, geopressured brines, hot dry rock, and magma--can compete economically with conventional power generation technologies. Until these technologies become available for industry use, this resource cannot meet its full potential in the Nation's energy supply mix. This division supports geothermal technology development and transfer through government/industry cooperation. Research that promises future economic expansion of geothermal development and use is given priority. Contact this office for more information and the program summary.

* Grand Coulee and Other Dams

Commissioner's Office
Bureau of Reclamation
U.S. Department of the Interior
18th and C Sts., NW
Washington, DC 20240   (202) 343-4157
Across the West, the Bureau of Reclamation annually supplies over 210,000 billion gallons of water to more than 23 million people for municipal, industrial, and agricultural use. The best known Reclamation projects are the Grand Coulee Dam on the Columbia River and the Hoover Dam on the Colorado River. Project water is delivered to almost 10 million acres of farmland to produce crops valued at $7.5 billion annually. The Bureau's non-polluting hydroelectric powerplants supply electricity to 17 million persons. Reclamation reservoirs also provide millions of visitors with facilities for fishing, swimming, picnicking, and sightseeing.

* Heat Pump Program

Residential Energy Services Program
Tennessee Valley Authority
3N 45B Signal Place
1101 Market St.
Chattanooga, TN 37402-2801   (615) 751-5261
TVA and participating local power distributors offer a heat pump program to encourage the installation of energy-efficient heat pumps in existing residential dwellings. The plan includes an on-site inspection to ensure the heat pump is correctly installed. In addition, distributors may offer such incentives as cash payments, electric bill credits, or low-interest loans. Loans may be used for approved weatherization improvements, such as attic and floor insulation and storm windows, installed along with a heat pump. No down payment is required, and customers may take up to 10 years to repay the loans.

* Home Energy Audits

Residential and Commercial Conservation Branch, CE-222
Office of State and Local Assistance Programs
U.S. Department of Energy
1000 Independence Ave, SW
Washington, DC 20585   (202) 586-1733
Through the Residential Conservation Service, eligible gas and electric customers can request that their large utility companies give them home energy audits and related services to help them use energy more efficiently. Owners and renters of single-family residences and multifamily residences in buildings with up to four units are being targeted for this service. Given a free energy audit of their premises and cost information on recommended energy-saving measures, residents would take energy-saving actions. Contact this office for more information.

* Household Energy Consumption and Expenditures, 1987

Office of Energy Markets and End Use
Energy End Use Division
Energy Information Administration
U.S. Department of Energy
1000 Independence Ave., SW, Room 1F-093
Washington, DC 20585   (202) 586-1122
Household Energy Consumption and Expenditures, 1987 is the second report based on 1987 RECS data. The 1987 RECS, the seventh in a series of national surveys of households and their energy suppliers, provides baseline information on how households in the United States use energy. A randomly selected set of housing units that includes single-family detached homes, townhouses, apartment buildings, condominiums, and mobile homes were selected for the survey. Data from the RECS and a companion survey, the Residential Transportation Energy Consumption Survey, are available to the public in published reports such as this one and on public use tapes.

* Housing Energy Characteristics 1987

Office of Energy Markets and End Use
Energy End Use Division
Energy Information Administration
U.S. Department of Energy
1000 Independence Ave., SW, Room 1F-093
Washington, DC 20585   (202) 586-1122
Housing Characteristics 1987 is the first of a series of reports based on data from the 1987 RECS, the seventh in the series of national surveys of households and their energy suppliers. These surveys provide baseline information on how households in the United States use energy. Contact this office for more information.

* Hydroelectric Power

Resource Management
Bureau of Reclamation
U.S. Department of the Interior
P.O. Box 25007
Denver CO 80225   (303) 236-3289
The Bureau of Reclamation is currently operating 49 powerplants at different sites throughout the West. For further information on the impact of hydroelectric power and the Bureau's efforts, contact this office.

* Hydroelectric Power Films

U.S. Army Corps of Engineers
Directorate of Information Management
Visual Information Branch
20 Massachusetts Ave., NW
Washington, DC 20314   (202) 272-0017
This office maintains a still photographic library and offers a free film loan and video distribution program. The Corps has educational and public relations films on their recreational facilities, navigation, flood control, hydro-electric power, and environmental systems. Write for information on the how to participate in the program.

* Industrial Energy Bibliography

Office of Scientific and Technical Information
Department of Energy
P.O. Box 62
Oak Ridge, TN 37831   (615) 576-1196
The *Technical Reports Bibliography* is the first annotated publication containing information on all scientific and technical reports sponsored by the DOE

Industrial Energy Conservation Program during the years 1974-1987. Contact this office for information on ordering.

* Industrial Energy Conservation
National Technical Information Service
5285 Port Royal Road
Springfield, VA 22161 (703) 557-4660
The monthly publication, *Industrial Energy Conservation*, announces the current worldwide information on all aspects of energy conservation in industry, including alternative energy sources; improved materials, equipment, and processes; waste heat recovery; and industrial waste management. This publication contains the abstracts of DOE reports, journal articles, conference papers, patents, theses, and monographs added to the Energy Data Base (EDB) during the past month. Also included is information obtained through acquisition programs or interagency agreements and through the International Energy Agency's Energy Technology Data Exchange or government-to-government agreements. The digests in *IEC* and other citations to information on energy conservation in industry technologies back to 1974 are available for on-line searching and retrieval on EDB. Current information, added daily to EDB, is available to DOE and its contractors through the DOE Integrated Technical Information System. Customized profiles can be developed to provide current information to meet each user's needs. The entire Energy Data Base is available on commercial on-line retrieval systems. (Order #PB89-93390011).

* Industrial Energy Technologies
Office of Industrial Programs
Deputy Assistant Secretary for Conservation
U.S. Department of Energy
1000 Independence Ave., SW, Room 5F-043
Washington, DC 20585 (202) 586-9487
Here researchers develop new energy technologies for improved energy efficiency in the industrial process and greater fuel flexibility. This office can supply you with several basic reports describing what programs are being undertaken. Reports on the results of their studies are available from the National Technical Information Service.

* Industrial Programs: Research in Progress
National Technical Information Service
U.S. Department of Commerce
5285 Port Royal Rd.
Springfield, VA 22161 (703) 557-4660
The report, *Office of Industrial Programs: Research in Progress* contains summaries for currently active projects supported by the Office of Industrial Programs. The report was prepared from the DOE Research-in-Progress database maintained by the Office of Scientific and Technical Information. Write to the office above to obtain a copy of this report.

* Institutional Energy Conservation Grants
Institutional Conservation Programs Branch, CE-231
Office of State and Local Assistance Programs
U.S. Department of Energy
1000 Independence Ave., SW
Washington, DC 20585 (202) 586-8034
Public and private nonprofit schools and hospitals can get matching, cost-shared grants to make detailed energy analyses and energy-saving capital improvements. The government will contribute 50 percent of the cost of these conservation projects, and in certain hardship cases, they may provide more. Contact this office for more information.

* Integrated Technical Information System
U.S. Department of Energy
Office of Scientific and Technical Information
P.O. Box 62
Oak Ridge, TN 37831 (615) 576-1222
The Integrated Technical Information System (ITIS), developed by the DOE, provides access to DOE databases in the Energy Data Information System; information merging for customized information products; and electronic mail, a communications link among OSTI, DIE, and contractor offices. Library specialists, information managers, and researchers can work from remote terminals to search various databases on ITIS. Contact the office above for more information.

* International Annual Energy Outlook
National Energy Information Center
Energy Information Center
U.S. Department of Energy
1000 Independence Ave., SW, Room E1-231
Washington, DC 20585 (202) 586-1181

The *Annual Energy Outlook* is a survey of the U.S. and world energy situation. It includes projections of production and prices in the U.S. and overseas. Contact NEIC for information on obtaining a copy of the report.

* International Energy Affairs
International Research and Development Policy
International Affairs and Energy Emergencies
U.S. Department of Energy
1000 Independence Ave., SW, Room 7A-029
Washington, DC 20585 (202) 586-6777
This office coordinates and assists the development of energy research and development cooperation involving the United States and other nations. Contact the office for more detailed information.

* International Energy Data
International and Contingency Information Division
Energy Markets and End Use
Energy Information Administration
U.S. Department of Energy
1000 Independence Ave., SW, Room 1H-087
Washington, DC 20585 (202) 586-1130
This Branch compiles international energy information, including current international energy market assessments, international energy projections, contingency planning studies, prices, distribution, and other quick response or special purpose analyses. In addition, the Branch reports U.S. energy data to international organizations. Contact office for information on its research reports and publications.

* International Energy Analysis
Office of Energy Markets and End Use
Energy Information Administration
U.S. Department of Energy
1000 Independence Ave., SW, Room 1H-087
Washington, DC 20585 (202) 586-1130
This office forecasts international energy supply and demand under various assumptions of international institutional arrangements and other international factors. Contact this office for more detailed program information.

* Lawrence Berkeley Laboratory
Lawrence Berkeley Laboratory
One Cyclotron Rd.
Berkeley, CA 94720 (414) 486-5771
Lawrence Berkeley Laboratory is a multi-program national laboratory run by the University of California under contract to the U.S. Department of Energy. It undertakes a wide range of unclassified research activities, including Accelerator and Fusion Research, Applied Science, Life Science, Earth Science, Energy Sciences, Engineering, General Sciences, Information and Computing Sciences, Materials and Chemical Sciences, Nuclear Science and Physics. The Laboratory describes its function as being four-fold: research, education, developing and operating national experimental facilities, and fostering productive relations between LBL research programs and private industry. Contact the Public Affairs office for copies of their annual report and catalog of programs.

* Legislation
Division of Public Affairs
Federal Energy Regulatory Commission
825 North Capitol Street, NE
Washington, DC 20426 (202) 357-8055
You can get information on energy-related legislative matters under consideration by Congress, after release by the Committee or Member of Congress involved. For more information current or past legislation, contact this office.

* Legislation on Energy Issues
Congressional and Intergovernmental Affairs
U.S. Department of Energy
1000 Independence Ave., SW, Room 8E-070
Washington, DC 20585 (202) 586-5466
Daily actions by Congress on energy legislation, are tracked through this office, and the staff can provide you with current status of the legislation. The office prepares briefing books and issues papers for Department of Energy witnesses, and compiles membership lists of Congressional committees concerned with DOE programs. The office also prepares and distributes reports of all daily energy related Congressional activity. Contact this office for more information on current energy legislation.

* Libraries, Energy
The Energy Library
U.S. Department of Energy

1000 Independence Ave., SW, Room GA-138
Washington, DC 20585   (202) 586-9534
This library compiles material on administrative and regulatory matters, non-nuclear research and development and alternative energy sources. The following are the major libraries of the Department of Energy:

Federal Energy Regulatory Commission Library, 825 N. Capitol Street, NW, Room 8502, Washington, D.C. 20426; (202) 307-5479. Focuses on regulatory matters.

Germantown Branch, U.S. Department of Energy, Germantown Branch, Room 6034, Washington, D.C. 20585; (301) 353-4301. This library focuses on material on nuclear energy and fossil fuels, energy research, and environmental protection, safety and emergency preparedness.

* Liquid Biomass Fuels in Vehicles

Office of Alcohol Fuels
U.S. Department of Energy
1000 Independence Ave., SW, Room 5G-086
Washington, DC 20585   (202) 586-9791
Contact this office for information on the use of liquid biomass fuels in vehicles. The office handles market analysis, market testing, research and development, and commercialization programs involving these fuels. It consolidates information about federal alcohol fuel efforts and education activities designed to increase public awareness and use of alcohol fuels. For further information on available publications, contact this office.

* Load Management

Marketing Services
3N45B Signal Pl.
Tennessee Valley Authority
1101 Market St.
Chattanooga, TN 37402-2801   (615) 751-5247
The TVA, in cooperation with power distributors, is trying out a number of ways to flatten out the peaks in consumer power demand, which requires the use of more expensive generating facilities. One of these load management demonstrations involves remote controlled "cycling" of hot water heaters and space-conditioning units in homes. About 120,000 remote switches have been installed for power distributors to investigate larger capacity storage small element water heaters.

* Load Research

Load Research Efforts
Tennessee Valley Authority
Power, 1100 Market St.
2N-48A Signal Place
Chattanooga, TN 37402-2801   (651) 751-6741
Researchers are currently sampling TVA power customers to determine when and how much electricity they consume. Homes and businesses are monitored to determine hourly load information, which will be gathered for studies of cost of service, rate design, and planning and marketing. Contact this office for more information on power usage statistics in the TVA regions.

* Marketing Federally Generated Power

Power Marketing Coordination
Office of the Assistant Secretary
Conservation and Renewable Energy
U.S. Department of Energy
1000 Independence Ave., SW, Room 8G-061
Washington, DC 20585   (202) 586-5581
Contact the above office for information on the marketing of power generated at Federal facilities. The Judicial Administrations are listed below:

Alaska Power Administration, Robert J. Cross, Administrator, P.O. Box 020050, Juneau, AK 99802-0050; (907) 586-7405
Bonneville Power Administration, James Jura, Administrator, P.O. Box 3621, Portland, OR 97208; (503) 230-5101
Washington, D.C. Office, Lee Johnson, Assistant Administrator, FORSTL, Room 8G033; (202) 586-5640
Southeastern Power Administration, Harry C. Geisinger, Administrator, Samuel Elbert Building, Elberton, GA 30635; (404) 283-9911
Southwestern Power Administration, Ronald H. Wilkerson, Administrator, P.O. Box 1619, Tulsa, OK 74101; (918) 581-7474
Western Area Power Administration, William Clagett, Administrator, P.O. Box 3402, 1627 Cole Boulevard, Golden, CO 80401; (303) 231-1513

* Markets and End Use

Office of Energy Markets and End Use
Energy End Use Division
Energy Information Administration
U.S. Department of Energy
1000 Independence Ave., SW, Room 1F-093

Washington, DC 20585   (202) 586-1122
Here research produces models for short-and medium-term energy demand in end use sectors: residential, industrial, commercial, and transportation. The research includes regional and demographic breakdowns, analyses of market penetration, the impact of conservation, and new technologies. The office can provide you with reports detailing its programs, as well as some subject reports.

* Maximum Speed Limit

Police Traffic Services Division
Office of Enforcement and Emergency Services
Traffic Safety Programs
National Highway Traffic Safety Administration
U.S. Department of Transportation
400 7th Street, SW, Room 6124
Washington, DC 20590   (202) 366-5440
The National Maximum Speed Limit is 65 miles per hour on certain interstate highways. This office processes annual certifications of maximum speed limit enforcement programs throughout the U.S. and assists states in developing and improving enforcement efforts.

* Mineral Geology

Office of Energy and Marine Geology
U.S. Geological Survey
National Center, MS 915
Reston, VA 22092   (703) 648-6470
Investigations of the nature, extent, and origin of the Nation's coal, oil and gas, oil shale, uranium, and geothermal resources are basic to this office's research efforts. Acquired data are placed in computerized databases, such as the National Coal Resources Data System.

* Minorities and Energy Programs

National Minority Energy Information Clearinghouse
U.S. Department of Energy
1000 Independence Ave., SW, Room 5R-110
Washington, DC 20585   (202) 586-5876
This Clearinghouse is a centralized repository for information about energy programs and the economic impact of those programs on minorities, minority businesses, and minority educational institutions. The following services are available from the Clearinghouse: research, referrals, information transfer, selective distribution of information, and searches of minority energy information retrieval systems as well as commercial and other Federal databases.

* National Energy Information Center

Energy Information Administration
U.S. Department of Energy
1000 Independence Ave., SW, Room 1F-048
Washington, DC 20585   (202) 586-8800
The National Energy Information Center can provide you with statistical and analytical data, information, and referral assistance on virtually an energy-related issue. The Center operates the EIA microfilm control center, providing access to data collection surveys and historical documents available to the public.

* National Energy Information Center

U.S. Department of Energy
Forestall Bldg., EI-22
1000 Independence Ave., SW, Room 1F048
Washington, DC 20585   (202) 252-8800
National Energy Information Center (NEIC) Energy Information Administration's data and projections on energy productions, consumption, prices, and supplies, are available by mail or telephone.

* National Energy Software Center

U.S. Department of Energy
National Energy Software Center
Argonne National Laboratory
9700 South Cass Ave.
Argonne, IL 60439   (312) 972-7250
The National Energy Software Center, NESC, is DOE's software information and distribution center. It is operated by Argonne National Laboratory for DOE's Office of Scientific and Technical Information, OSTI, which is responsible for establishing policy and providing oversight for DOE's software sharing activities. Software exchange and information center activities for the U.S. Nuclear Regulatory Commission are carried with support from the NRC's Office of Resource Management. NESC provides a central computer software information and resource facility in support of DOE and NRC research and development programs. It also serves as a focal point for intra-agency sharing of software and for the transfer and exchange of computer technology to other U.S. and foreign agencies, as well as to the U.S. private sector. Contact the office above for more information.

* New Energy Technologies and Developing Countries

Office of Technology Assessment
600 Pennsylvania Ave., SE
Washington, DC 20510 (202) 228-6267

OTA is currently working on a study to examine how technology can contribute to the goal of sound and productive energy development in the world's poorer countries, and the role of U.S. policy and the relevant international organizations in encouraging the rapid adoption of improved technologies. Contact Joy Dunkerley, the project director, at OTA for more information.

* News Releases

National Energy Information Center, EI-231
Energy Information Administration
Room 1F-048, Forestall Building
Washington, DC 20585 (202) 586-8800

EIA New Releases is published six times per year and contains information on issues of special interest, periodicals, machine- readable files, and how to order EIA publications.

* Ocean Energy

Wind and Oceans Technologies Division
Conservation and Renewable Energy
U.S. Department of Energy
1000 Independence Ave., SW
Washington, DC 20585 (202) 586-5630

Here researchers develop technologies to harness ocean energy in a cost-effective and environmentally safe manner. Researchers look to develop ocean energy technology to the point where businesses accurately assess whether applications of the technology are viable energy conversion alternatives, or supplements, to systems currently in use. Contact this office for more program information.

* Petroleum Overcharge Refunds

Office of Hearings and Appeals
U.S. Department of Energy
1000 Independence Ave., SW, Room 6G-087
Washington, DC 20585 (202) 586-2094

Cash refunds are available to any people, business firms, and governments that purchased refined petroleum products in the U.S. between August 1973 and January 1981. This office distributes millions of dollars in oil overcharges collected through the DOE enforcement program between those years. This office can give you further details.

* Petroleum Price Regulation

Economic Regulatory Administration
Press Office
U.S. Department of Energy
1000 Independence Ave., SW, Room 8G-087
Washington, DC 20585 (202) 586-5810

This office serves as the first public contact point for information on petroleum enforcement actions for crude oil price and allocation regulations prior to January 28, 1981. ERA also regulates natural gas imports and exports; administers programs for the conversion of oil- and gas-fired utilities to alternate fuels; and licenses both exports of electricity from the United State and transmission lines crossing U.S. borders. Contact this office for more information.

* Photovoltaic Materials and Devices

Solar Energy Technologies
Deputy Assistant Secretary for Renewable Energy
Conservation and Renewable Energy
U.S. Department of Energy
1000 Independence Ave., SW, Room 5F-081
Washington, DC 20585 (202) 586-6223

This office conducts research and development leading toward potentially low-cost, advanced photovoltaic materials and devices which are environmentally sound. Contact this office for more program information.

* Photovoltaics

Photovoltaics Technology Division
Conservation and Renewable Energy
U.S. Department of Energy
1000 Independence Ave., SW, Room 5F-081
Washington, DC 20585 (202) 586-1720

Researchers are currently developing photovoltaic technology--which converts sunlight directly into electricity--for the large-scale generation of economically competitive electric power in the U.S. Eventually photovoltaic energy products will significantly contribute to the mix of renewable energy sources on which the U.S. will depend. Contact this office for its program summary.

* Power Control Centers

Power Control Center
Tennessee Valley Authority
2N 10A Power Control Center
Chattanooga, TN 37401 (615) 751-8678

TVA's five area dispatch control centers (ADCCs) monitor the 15,000 miles of transmission lines across which power is carried to the distributors of TVA power and large industries in the Valley. The dispatchers at the ADCCs and the load coordinators at the Power System Control Center work together to coordinate the maintenance of the transmission network to ensure the safety of the men working on the lines, and to make sure there are no transmission lines scheduled to be out of service that would cause an interruption in power service.

* Power Information Center

Interagency Advanced Power Group (IAPG)
c/o CSR, Inc.
1400 Eye Street, NW, Suite 600
Washington, DC 20005 (202) 842-7600

The Interagency Advanced Power Group (IAPG) promotes the exchange of information in advanced power fields by 1) maintaining a database of projects sponsored by its member agencies (Army, Navy, Air Force, NASA, and DOE); and 2) arranging semiannual meetings in the following areas of interest: chemical, electrical, magnetohydrodynamics, mechanical, nuclear, solar, and systems R&D. Members of industry and academia who are frequently invited to serve as presenters or participants at these meetings can receive IAPG publications by subscribing to NTIS. Membership and associated benefits are free to employees of the IAPG member agencies.

* Power System Control

Power System Control Center
Tennessee Valley Authority
2N 10A
Chattanooga, TN 37401

TVA provides a reliable supply of power at the lowest possible cost to the consumers. This center manages the resources needed to meet the daily load of the TVA power system, the largest in the U.S. Through control of generation, interchange transactions with other utilities, and load management, the staff at the Center ensures that the residents and industrial customers have ample power on hand to meet their needs.

* Press Services

Press Secretary to the Secretary, DOE
U.S. Department of Energy
Office of Communications
FORSTL, CP-60, Room 8G087
Washington, DC 20585 (202) 586-8325

DOE's Press Service produces news releases and answers inquiries from the media of a general nature in all program areas, including nuclear energy and national defense programs within DOE. The office also arranges press conferences and media interviews for the Secretary of Energy and other DOE officials.

* Producing Countries

Office of Energy Producer - Country Affairs
Bureau of Economics and Business Affairs
Department of State
2201 C St., NW, Room 3329
Washington, DC 20520 (202) 647-3985

This office handles all foreign affairs concerning energy producing countries. Subjects studies include OPEC, natural gas, uranium, as well as the importing and exporting of oil and gas.

* Publications

Public Affairs
Division of Public Affairs
U.S. Department of Energy
1000 Independence Ave., SW, Room 8G048
Washington, DC 20585 (202) 586-6827

This office writes and publishes the DOE's newspaper, *DOE This Month* and produces written material describing DOE programs and policies in a variety of formats, including speech texts, talking points, letters to editors, magazine/journal articles, and fact sheets. Contact this office for more information on the publications available from DOE.

* Publications--Free

Publications Branch
Technical Information Center
Department of Energy

P.O. Box 62
Oak Ridge, TN 37831   (615) 576-1301
Contact TIC office for a complete listing of their free publications.

* Regulation

Federal Energy Regulatory Commission
Office of External Affairs
825 North Capitol Street, NE
Washington, DC 20426   (202) 357-8055
The free *Annual Report of the Federal Energy Regulatory Commission* details last year's energy regulatory activities of the FERC, as well as giving a summary of the structure and functions of each office within FERC.

* Regulation Hotline

Office of Congressional Affairs
Energy Regulatory Commission
U.S. Department of Energy
1000 Independence Ave., SW
Washington, DC 20585   (202) 357-8055
Call this office for information on energy regulation matters.

* Regulatory Files

Division of Public Affairs
Federal Energy Regulatory Commission
825 North Capitol Street, NE
Washington, DC 20426   (202) 357-8055
Records and files of the Federal Energy Regulatory Commission are available for public inspection or copying at FERC's North Capitol Street office. Contact the office of Public Affairs for more detailed information on consulting records. The following is a summary of the available information:

-All filings submitted to the Commission which comprise formal records. This includes applications, petitions and other pleadings requesting FERC action; responses, protests, motions, contracts, briefs, rate schedules, tariffs and related filings; and FERC staff correspondence relating to any proceedings.
-Transcripts of hearings, hearing exhibits, proposed testimony and exhibits filed with the Commission but not yet offered or received in evidence.
-Administrative law judges' actions, orders, and correspondence in connection with FERC proceedings.
-Commission orders, notices, opinions, decisions, letter orders, and approved Commission minutes.
-Agendas and lists of actions taken at Commission meetings, which are open to the public.
-Environmental impact statements prepared by FERC staff pursuant to the National Environmental Policy Act of 1969.
-Agendas, minutes, and draft papers relating to the National Power Survey, Natural Gas Policy Council and other FERC advisory committee meetings, all open to the public.
-Filings and recordings in court proceedings to which the Commission is a party and FERC correspondence with the courts.
-News releases and announcements issued by FERC.
-Subject index of Commission actions.

* Regulatory Information

Division of Public Affairs
Federal Energy Regulatory Commission
825 North Capitol Street, NE, Room 2214
Washington, DC 20426   (202) 357-8055
Contact this office for general or specific information on any of the regulatory activities of the Federal Energy Regulatory Commission.

* Renewable Energy Information Hotline

P.O. Box 8900
Silver Spring, MD 20907   (800) 523-2929
Conservation and Renewable Energy Inquiry and Referral Service (CAREIRS) answers for the general public by toll-free telephone or mail. Call (800) 462-4983 in Pennsylvania, or (800) 233-3071 in Alaska & Hawaii.

* Renewable Energy Publications

Solar Energy Research Institute
Technical Inquiry Service
1617 Cole Boulevard
Golden, CO 80401-3393
You can get any of the following series of documents on the renewable energy programs sponsored by the Department of Energy at no charge by writing the office above.

Solar Building Program Summaries
Wind Energy
Energy Storage and Distribution

Solar Thermal Energy
Biofuels
Geothermal Energy
Photovoltaic Energy
Ocean Energy

* Renewable Energy Publications

Conservation and Renewable Energy Inquiry
and Referral Service (CAREIRS)
Renewable Energy Information
Box 8900
Silver Spring, MD 20907   (800) 523-2929
The following are some of the free energy information publications available through the above CAREIRS service. Bulk copies are not available. The service asks that each request be limited to 8 publications.

Fact Sheets
FS 105 *Alternative Heat Sources for Heat Pumps*
FS 109 *Planning for a Homeowner Installation*
FS 110 *Converting a Home to Solar Heat*
FS 113 *Solar Energy Systems Consumer Tips*
FS 115 *Solar Heat Storage*
FS 118 *Solar Energy and You (for middle grades)*
FS 120 *Earth-Sheltered Houses*
FS 124 *Sunspaces and Solar Greenhouses*
FS 135 *Wind Energy Systems*
FS 141 *Energy Efficient Lighting*
FS 142 *Insulation*
FS 150 *Municipal Resource Recovery*
FS 176 *Solar Energy and Your Home: Questions and Answers*
FS 178 *Low-Cost Passive and Hybrid Solar Retrofits*
FS 183 *Facts About Ethanol*
FS 185 *Residential Indoor Air Pollution*
FS 190 *Movable Insulation*
FS 203 *Caulking and Weatherstripping*
FS 207 *Buying an Energy Efficient House*
FS 208 *Moisture Control in Your Home*
FS 214 *Biofuels as a Source of Energy*
FS 216 *Improving the Energy Efficiency of Windows*
FS 217 *Small-Scale Hydropower Systems*
FS 218 *Learning About Energy Conservation (for elementary grades)*
FS 220 *Landscaping for Energy-Efficient Homes*

Books and Brochures
SD 107 *Tips for Energy Savers*
SD 109 *Regional Guidelines for Building Passive and Energy Conserving Homes*
SD 115 *Protecting Solar Access for Residential Development*
SD 133 *Site Planning for Solar Access*

Bibliographies
DC 150 *Renewable Energy Reading List for Young Adults*
DC 169 *Passive Solar Construction - Design and Performance*
DC 175 *Wind Energy*
DC 189 *Photovoltaics Stand Alone Applications Reading List*

* Renewable Energy Technologies

Conservation and Renewable Energy Inquiry
and Referral Service (CAREIRS)
P.O. Box 8900   (800) 523-2929
Silver Spring, MD 20907   (800) 233-3071 (AK and HI)
CAREIRS provides information on the full spectrum of renewable energy technologies and energy conservation, including active/passive solar, solar thermal, photovoltaics, wind, biomass, alcohol fuels, hydroelectric, geothermal, and ocean thermal energy. In addition, the Service maintains contact with a nationwide network of public and private organizations that specialize in highly technical or regionally specific information. Telephone service is available 9 a.m. to 5 p.m. Eastern Standard Time.

* Renewable Energy Technologies

Deputy Assistant Secretary for Renewable Energy
Conservation and Renewable Energy
U.S. Department of Energy
1000 Independence Ave., SW, Room 5H-095
Washington, DC 20585   (202) 586-8084
This office conducts research and development of biomass energy technology, energy from municipal waste, and geothermal/small hydropower energy technology. They emphasize the development of renewable technology with potential to increase significantly the Nation's supply of fuel, heat, and electricity. Contact the office for program information.

* Research and Technology Development

Program Integration Analysis Division
Office of Energy Research

U.S. Department of Energy
1000 Independence Ave., SW, Room F-327
Washington, DC 20585 (301) 353-3122
The Office of Energy Research undertakes advanced and fundamental research to support the Energy Department's long-term energy technology development. *Programs of the Office of Energy Research* describes the Office's research activities in sufficient detail to enable researchers to understand current Energy Department research programs. A copy is available free through the office.

* Research Facilities

Office of Energy Research
Office of Field Operations Management
U.S. Department of Energy
1000 Independence Ave., SW, Room 7B-040
Washington, DC 20585 (202) 586-5447
The *Capsule Review of DOE Research and Development and Field Facilities* surveys DOE research facilities, with brief descriptions of the work of the various offices.

* Residential Energy Conservation Database

Office of Energy Markets and End Use
Energy End Use Division
Energy Information Administration
U.S. Department of Energy
1000 Independence Ave., SW, Room 1F-093
Washington, DC 20585 (202) 586-1122
The database, *Technical Documentation, 1984 Residential Energy Consumption Survey and 1985 Residential Transportation Energy Consumption Survey*, contains data concerning energy consumption in the U.S. residential sector. The *RECS* data file contains basic data concerning housing unit characteristics, including weather and weighing variables. The file contains 5,611 sample households from the contiguous U.S. representing 85.8 million weighted households. The 1985 *RTECS* data provide information on how energy is used in households for personal transportation based on the number and type of vehicles per household and, for each vehicle, annual miles traveled, gallons of fuel consumed, type of fuel used, price paid for fuel, and vehicle miles-per-gallon. Contact this office for more information on these databases.

* Short-Term and Long-Term Energy Statistics

Energy Analysis and Forecasting Division
Energy Markets and End Use
Energy Information Administration
U.S. Department of Energy
1000 Independence Ave., SW, Room 1H-055
Washington, DC 20585 (202) 586-6160
This division compiles statistics on both short-term (up to 18 months) and the long-term (primarily within the next 15 years) energy supply and demand. Contact this office for more information.

* Solar Building Technology

Solar Building Technology Program
Conservation and Renewable Energy
U.S. Department of Energy
1000 Independence Ave., SW
Washington, DC 20585 (202) 586-6436
Research from this office provides the solar and buildings industries with the technology needed to develop reliable solar systems that can contribute significantly to a building's space heating, hot water, cooling, and lighting requirements at competitive costs. Major research activities are aimed at improving the overall effectiveness of solar water and space heating systems, increasing solar cooling system performance, increasing daylighting system contributions, and increasing overall building energy contributions from individual solar heating, cooling, and daylighting technologies through systems integration. These activities are planned and executed in close cooperation with the solar and building industries to ensure that the results can readily be adopted by the private sector. Contact this office for further information.

* Solar Energy and Wind Information

National Climatic Data Center
National Oceanic and Atmospheric Administration
Department of Commerce
Federal Building
Asheville, NC 28801 (704) 259-0682
The National Climatic Data Center has a great deal of information regarding solar energy and wind data. Information includes solar radiation averages, measurements, and sunshine averages, as well as wind statistics. Reference manuals and indexes are also available. Prices vary depending upon the information requested. The Center can provide you with more detailed information regarding the data available.

* Solar Energy Research

Solar Energy Research Institute
1617 Cole Boulevard
Golden, CO 80401 (303) 231-7303
SERI is the lead organization for advanced solar research and development in the U.S. Its Technical Inquiry Service responds to questions related to SERI's research and the solar research conducted in other laboratories and universities from the scientific, industrial, and business communities. Central inquiry and referral services are provided to the general public through the Conservation and Renewable Energy Inquiry and Referral Service, (CAREIRS). The Document Distribution Service, (303) 231-1243, responds to requests for single copies, prior to NTIS announcements, of selected SERI-produced technical reports and publications in hard copy format for a fee. Contact the above office for more information.

* Solar Technical Information Service

Solar Energy Research Institute
1617 Cole Boulevard
Golden, CO 80401 (303) 231-7303
Solar Energy Research Institute Technical Inquiry Service (SERI/TIS) solar technical information requested by scientific and industrial professional by telephone or mail.

* Solar Thermal Technology

Solar Thermal Technology Division
Conservation and Renewable Energy
U.S. Department of Energy
1000 Independence Ave., SW, Room 5H-021
Washington, DC 20585 (202) 586-8103
Here researchers are looking to improve the overall performance of solar thermal systems and provide cost-effective energy options that are strategically secure and environmentally sound. Major research activities include energy collection technology, energy conversion technology, and systems and applications technology for both CR and DR systems. This research is being conducted through research laboratories in close coordination with the solar thermal industry, utility companies, and universities. This research program is also pursuing the development of critical components and subsystems for improved energy collection and conversion devices.

This development follows two basic paths: 1) For CR systems, critical components include stretched membrane heliostats, direct absorption receivers (DARs), and transport subsystems for molten salt heat transfer fluids. These components offer the potential for a significant reduction in system costs; and 2) For DR systems, critical components include stretched membrane dishes, reflux receivers, and Stirling engines. These components will significantly increase system reliability and efficiency, which will reduce costs.

The major thrust of the program is to provide electric power; however, there is an increasing interest in the use of concentrated solar energy for such applications as detoxifying hazardous wastes and developing high-value transportable fuels. These potential uses of highly concentrated solar energy still require additional experiments to prove concept feasibility. The research's goal of economically competitive energy production from solar thermal systems is being cooperatively addressed by both industry and government. Contact this office or the Solar Energy Research Institute for more information and a copy of the program summary.

* Spent Fuel Options

Nuclear Power
Tennessee Valley Authority
1101 Market St.
Chattanooga, TN 37401 (615) 751-8689
The TVA, in a cooperative effort with various utilities, is studying alternative facilities needed to store spent fuel and radioactive waste from TVA nuclear plants. Contact this office for more information on radioactive waste storage.

* State Energy Conservation

Energy Management and Extension Branch, CE-221
Office of State and Local Assistance Programs
U.S. Department of Energy
1000 Independence Ave., SW
Washington, DC 20585 (202) 586-8288
To reduce the growth rate of energy demand, States voluntarily participate in a cooperative effort with the U.S. Department of Energy (DOE), which provides technical and cost-shared financial assistance, while the states develop and implement comprehensive plans for achieving specific energy goals. At present, all states, as well as the District of Columbia and U.S. territories, participate in this conservation program.

* Statistics

National Energy Information Center
Energy Information Administration
U.S. Department of Energy

1000 Independence Ave., SW, Room E1-231
Washington, DC 20585   (202) 252-8800
This Center can provide you with National energy statistics and general data services. Contact them for more information on the types available.

* Systems Vulnerability
Office of Technology Assessment
600 Pennsylvania Ave., SE
Washington, DC 20510   (202) 228-6427
A study is underway at OTA to assess the vulnerability of certain energy producing and delivery systems--electricity, natural gas, and refined oil products-- to disruption by either terrorist actions or massive natural disasters. Contact Alan Crane, the project director, for more information.

* Technical Information
Office of Scientific and Technical Information
U.S. Department of Energy
P.O. Box 62
Oak Ridge, TN 37831   (615) 576-1192
Both DOE-originated information and worldwide literature regarding advances in subjects of interest to DOE researchers are collected, processed, and distributed through this office. The major databases in this system are available within the United States through commercial on-line systems and to those outside the United States through formal governmental exchange agreements.

* Technical Energy Information
Office of Scientific and Technical Information
U.S. Department of Energy
P.O. Box 62
Oak Ridge, TN 37831   (615) 576-1541
Office of Scientific and Technical Information, Technical Information Center (OSTI/TIC) access to bibliographic databases for the government, contractors, libraries, and research institutions, and supplies reports to the National Technical Information Service for sale to the public, contacted by mail or telephone.

* Technical Information Center
U.S. Department of Energy
P. O. Box 62
Oak Ridge, TN 37831   (615) 576-6837
The Technical Information Center distributes energy information resulting from DOE-funded research and development, as well as relevant technical literature produced worldwide for use by the DOE community. The Center also maintains the DOE Energy Data Base (EDB) with over 1.8 million citations to technical energy literature, and the central DOE Research-in-Progress (RIP) database. It also publishes abstract journals and bibliographies and provides on-line retrieval through DOE-RECON. Contact this office for more information on the Center's information services.

* Technological Risks and Opportunities for
Future U.S. Energy Supply and Demand
Office of Technology Assessment
600 Pennsylvania Ave., SE
Washington, DC 20510   (202) 228-6275
The OTA is currently studying the current views of the U.S. future energy outlook to identify key technical uncertainties and risks that affect the validity of these views, and to evaluate energy policy options for dealing with these uncertainties and risks. Contact Steven Plotkin, the project director, for more information.

* Technology Hotline
National Appropriate Technology
  Assistance Service (NATAS)
U.S. Department of Energy
P.O. Box 2525
Butte, MT 59702-2525   (800) 428-2525
                                        (800) 428-1718 (MT)
Both businesses and consumers can call this toll-free hotline for information on implementing energy-saving technologies. NATAS provides more detailed technical assistance than other programs and helps entrepreneurs develop appropriate technology.

* Tennessee Valley Authority
Power Control Center
Tennessee Valley Authority
2N 10 A Power Center
Chattanooga, TN 37401   (615) 751-8678
The TVA serves an area in the southeast U.S. consisting of 91,000 square miles and over seven million residents in parts of seven states. TVA has a total generating capacity in excess of 32,000 megawatts, made up of 11 operating coal-fired power plants, two licensed nuclear plants, 29 hydro plants, four combustion

turbine installations, and the Raccoon Mountain Pumped-Storage Plant. The TVA works toward achieving competitive power rates, a reliable transmission system, research on clean-coal technology, industrial development in the region, improved quality and costs, and excellent fossil and hydro facilities performance.

* TVA Energy Publications
Distributer Marketing Services
Governmental and Public Affairs
Tennessee Valley Authority
1101 Market St., SP3N
Chattanooga, TN 37402-2801   (615) 751-5160
TVA provides publications on energy for research studies and the general public. They contain general information on the TVA and also specific information on such subjects as dams and steam plants, nuclear power, energy alternatives, and energy conservation, including buying guides for appliances. Though solar energy projects are no longer being carried out at TVA, you can still obtain information on past research.

* Unleaded Gas and Fuels Hotline
Environmental Protection Agency
Region I
JFK Federal Bldg.   (800) 821-1237
Boston, MA 02203   (800) 631-2700 (MA)
The Unleaded Fuel Tank Hotline is an enforcement-related line that takes calls about tampering with vehicles, pumps, and other problems related to unleaded fuels. It provides this service for Region I states: Connecticut, Massachusetts, New Hampshire, Rhode Island, Vermont.

* Water Heater Program
Residential Energy Services Program
Tennessee Valley Authority
1101 Market St.
3N 45B Signal Place
Chattanooga, TN 37402-2801   (615) 751-5261
The TVA's water heater program is designed to encourage homeowners in the region to install electric water heaters in new and existing homes. The program, available through local power distributors, offers participation incentives, which include cash payments, credits on electric bills, or financing. Water heater distributors may also offer free or reduced-cost water heaters, or make special offers for maintenance or installation. Loans may be used for a heat pump and related items such as electronic air cleaners, programmable thermostats, and extended warranties. No down payment, and the loan may be repaid over a period of up to 10 years.

* Weatherization Assistance
Weatherization Assistance Programs Branch, CE-232
U.S. Department of Energy
1000 Independence Ave., SW
Washington, DC 20585   (202) 586-2204
To reduce high fuel costs for heating and air conditioning, low-income families, the elderly, and the handicapped can receive assistance to weatherize their homes and apartments. Those in need can have caulking and weatherstripping, storm windows, attic insulation, and heating system improvements installed at little or no charge. Contact this office or your state energy office for more detailed information on this assistance.

* Wind Energy Test Center
Solar Energy Research Institute (SERI)
1617 Cole Boulevard
Golden, CO 80401   (303) 231-7111
SERI's Wind Energy Test Center is the focal point for wind technology research activities in the U.S. The objective is to establish a technology base in a support industry in confirming the viability of wind energy as an alternative energy source. Basic research in wind turbine dynamics is conducted to understand the random nature of the wind, characterize its complex interaction with the wind turbine, and determine the effects of this interactions on performance, structural loads reliability and lifetime. Research is also scheduled to establish the feasibility of such technological advances as high performance airfoils, variable speed generators, and controls. Cooperative research and test programs with the wind industry will also take place over the next 5 years. SERI can provide you with information on its current activities and publications.

* State and Territorial Energy Offices

Alabama
Science, Technology, and Energy Division, P.O. Box 2939, Montgomery, AL 36105-0939

Alaska
Department of Community and Regional Affairs, 949 East 36th Ave., Suite 400, Anchorage, AK 99508

American Samoa
Territorial Energy Office, Office of the Governor, Pago Pago, American Samoa 96799

Arizona
Dept. of Commerce, 1700 West Washington, 5th Floor, Phoenix, AZ 85007

Arkansas
Energy Office, One State Capitol Mall, Little Rock, AR 72201

California
Energy Commission, 1516 Ninth Street, Sacramento, CA 95814

Colorado
Office of Energy Conservation, 112 East 14th Ave., Denver, CO 80203

Connecticut
Office of Policy and Management, Energy Division, 80 Washington St., Hartford, CT 06106

Delaware
Energy Office, P.O. Box 1401, Dover, DE 19901

District of Columbia
Energy Office, 613 G Street, NW, 5th Floor, Washington, DC 20001

Florida
Governor's Energy Office, 214 South Bronough St., Tallahassee, FL 32399-0001

Georgia
Office of Energy Resources, 270 Washington, SW, Room 615, Atlanta, GA 30334

Guam
Energy Office, P.O. Box 2950, Agana, Guam 96910

Hawaii
State Energy Division, Dept. of Planning and Economic Development, 335 Merchant Street, Room 109, Honolulu, HI 96813

Idaho
Dept. of Water Resources, Division of Energy Resources, 1301 North Orchard, Boise, ID 83720

Illinois
Dept. of Energy and Natural Resource, 325 West Adams, Room 300, Springfield, IL 62706

Indiana
Dept. of Commerce, Division of Energy Policy, One North Capitol, Suite 700, Indianapolis, IN 46204-2243

Iowa
Dept. of Natural Resources, Energy and Geological Division, Wallace State Office Building, Des Moines, IA 50319

Kansas
Research and Energy Analysis Division, Kansas Corporation Commission, State Office Building, 4th Floor, Topeka, KS 66612

Kentucky
Energy Cabinet, P.O. Box 11888, Lexington, KY 40578-1916

Louisiana
Dept. of Natural Resources, P.O. Box 44124, Baton Rouge, LA 70804

Maine
Office of Energy Resources, State House Station No. 53, Augusta, ME 04333

Maryland
Energy Office, 301 West Preston Street, Suite 903, Baltimore, MD 21201

Massachusetts
Executive Office of Energy Resources, 100 Cambridge Street, Room 1500, Boston, MA 02202

Michigan
Public Service Commission, P.O. Box 30228, Lansing, MI 48909

Minnesota
Dept. of Energy and Economic Development, 900 American Center Building, 150 East Kellogg Boulevard, St. Paul, MN 55101

Mississippi
Dept. of Energy and Transportation, 510 George Street, Suite 300, Jackson, MS 39202

Missouri
Dept. of Natural Resources and Conservation, Division of Energy, P.O. Box 176, Jefferson City, MO 65102

Montana
Dept. of Natural Resources and Conservation, Energy Division, 1520 East Sixth St., Helena, MT 59620

Nebraska
Energy Office, P.O. Box 95085, State Capitol Building, 9th Floor, Lincoln, NE 68509

Nevada
State Office of Community Services, Capitol Complex, Carson City, NV 89710

New Hampshire
Governor's Energy Office, 2 1/2 Beacon St., Concord, NH 03301

New Jersey
Division of Energy Planning and Conservation, 101 Commerce St., Newark, NJ 07102

New Mexico
Dept. of Minerals and Natural Resources, 525 Camino de los Marquez Santa Fe, NM 87503

New York
State Energy Office, Two Rockefeller Plaza, Albany, NY 12223

North Carolina
Dept. of Commerce, Energy Division, P.O. Box 25249, Raleigh, NC 27611

North Dakota
Office of Intergovernmental Assistance, State Capitol Building, Bismarck, ND 58505

Ohio
Office of Energy Conservation, Ohio Dept. of Development, 77 South High Street, 24th Floor, Columbus, OH 43266-0413

Oklahoma
Dept. of Commerce, Division of Community Affairs and Development, 6601 Broadway Extension, Oklahoma City, OK 73116

Oregon
Dept. of Energy, 625 Marion Street, NE, Salem, OR 97310-0831

Pennsylvania
Energy Office, P.O. Box 8010, Harrisburg, PA 17102

Rhode Island
Office of Energy Assistance, 275 Westminister Mall, Providence, RI 02903

South Carolina
Governor's Division of Energy, Agriculture, and Natural Resources, 1205 Pendleton Street, 3rd Floor, Columbia, SC 29211

South Dakota
Energy Office, 217 1/2 West Missouri, Pierre, SD 57501

Tennessee
Energy Division, Department of Economic and Community Development, 320 Sixth Ave., North, 6th Floor, Nashville, TN 37219-5308

Texas
Energy Management Center, Governor's Office of Budget and Planning, P.O. Box 12428, Capitol Station, Austin, TX 78711

Utah
Energy Office, 355 West North Temple, Three Triad Center, Suite 450, Salt Lake City, UT 84180-1204

Vermont
Department of Public Services, State Office Building, Montpelier, VT 05602

Virginia
Department of Mines, Minerals, and Energy, 2201 West Broad Street, Richmond, VA 23220

Washington
State Energy Office, 809 Legion Way SE, Olympia, WA 98504

West Virginia
Governor's Office of Community and Industrial Development, 1204 Kanawha Blvd. East, 2nd Floor, Charleston, WV 25301

Energy

Wisconsin
Division of Energy and Intergovernmental Relations, 101 South Webster Street, Madison, WI 53707

Wyoming
Economic Development and Stabilization Board, Herschler Building,, East Wing, 3rd Floor, Cheyenne, WY 82002

Mariana Islands
Office of Energy and Environment, P.O. Box 340, Saipan, Mariana Islands 96950

Puerto Rico
Office of Energy, P.O. Box 41089, Minillas Station, Santurce, Puerto Rico 00940

Virgin Islands
Energy Office, Room 233, Building 3, Lagoon Complex, Fredericksted, St. Croix, U.S. Virgin Islands 0084

Fossil Fuels: Oil, Coal, and Natural Gas

* Alaska Natural Gas Pipeline

Alaska Natural Gas Pipeline Project
Office of Pipeline Safety
Research and Special Programs Administration
U.S. Department of Transportation
400 7th Street, SW
Washington, DC 20590   (202) 366-4556
Contact this office for information about the plans, programs, policies, and
regulation concerning the Alaska pipeline.

* Atmospheric Fluidized Bed Combustion

Fluidized Bed Combustion Projects
Tennessee Valley Authority
Power, P.O. Box 1010
CEB-2W201A
Muscle Shoals, AL 35660   (615) 751-7438
This office can provide you with up-to-date information on atmospheric fluidized
bed combustion, a new technology which burns pulverized coal at a lower
temperature than conventional pulverized coal technology in a bed of limestone
particles, resulting in lower nitrogen oxide emissions. The by-product is more
easily disposed of, and therefore, it is more environmentally desirable. A 160
megawatt atmospheric fluidized bed demonstration plant was recently completed
in Paducha, Kentucky, at the Shaunyee Plant.

* Clean Coal Technology

Clean Coal Technology
Demonstration Project
U.S. Department of Energy
1000 Independence Ave., NW, FE-22
Washington, DC 20585   (202) 586-7165
Through DOE's Clean Coal Technology (CCT) Demonstration Program, the
most promising of the advanced coal-based technologies are being moved into
the marketplace through demonstration. The demonstration effort is at a large
enough scale to generate all data needed by the public sector to judge the
commercial potential of the processes being developed. These technologies will
reduce or eliminate the economic and environmental impediments that limit the
full use of coal, and will work toward resolving the conflict between the
increasing use of coal and the growing concern about the environmental impact
of such use. Contact the above office for further information, including a copy
of their report *Clean Power From Clean Coal*.

* Coal Combustion and Control Systems

Fossil Energy
U.S. Department of Energy
1000 Independence Ave., SW, Room C2156
Washington, DC 20585   (301) 353-4348
This office oversees research in atmospheric and pressurized fluidized bed
combustion, coal-water mixtures, coal preparation and advanced combustion
techniques. The office also develops advanced environmental control technology,
including management of solid wastes produced by advanced fossil energy
technologies. Contact the office for further program information.

* Coal Energy Research

Research and Development
Power and Business Operations
Missionary Ridge Place, 3N41A
1101 Market St.
Chattanooga, TN 37402-2801   (615) 751-7438
This office can provide you with information on TVA's two most promising
technologies for better use of coal: fluidized bed combustion, and advanced
sulfur dioxide control technology to capture sulfur in conventional coal-fired
boilers.

* Coal Liquefaction

Pittsburgh Energy Technology Center
P.O. Box 10940
Pittsburgh, PA 15236   (412) 892-6128
This laboratory conducts research and development in coal liquefaction,
alternative fuels, coal slurries, advanced combustion, magnetohydrodynamics,
coal preparation, flue gas cleanup, and university coal research. Contact this
office for available information on its research.

* Coal Supply and Demand

Coal Division
Coal, Nuclear, Electric and Alternate Fuels
Energy Information Administration
U.S. Department of Energy
1000 Independence Ave., SW, Room 2G-053
Washington, DC 20585   (202) 586-9880
This office monitors all supply and demand aspects of coal, including production,
prices, and distribution. It identifies and analyses coal reserves; examines new
technologies for deriving energy from coal; and, studies existing and proposed
legislation and regulations affecting coal supply and demand. Contact this office
for more program information.

* Coal Use Technology Database

Pittsburgh Energy Technology Center
P.O. Box 10940
Pittsburgh, PA 15236   (412) 892-6144
Contact this office for information on its database on emerging coal use
technologies.

* Defense Energy Consumption

Defense Energy Policy Directorate
Office of the Assistant Secretary of Defense
DEF/P&L/L(EP
The Pentagon, Room 1D760
Washington, DC 20301-3000   (202) 697-2500
This office can provide you with wholesale petroleum data and facility energy
consumption data. Inquiries will be answered on a cost recovery basis.

* Defense Energy Consumption

Defense Energy Policy Directorate
Office of the Assistant Secretary of Defense
DEF/P&L/L(EP
The Pentagon, Room 1D760
Washington, DC 20301-3000   (202) 697-2500
This office can provide you with wholesale petroleum data and facility energy
consumption data. Inquiries will be answered on a cost recovery basis.

* Energy and Mineral Resources

Office of Energy and Marine Geology
U.S. Geological Survey
National Center, MS 915
Reston, VA 22092   (703) 648-6470
Investigations of the nature, extent, and origin of the Nation's coal, oil and gas,
oil shale, uranium, and geothermal resources are basic to this office's research
efforts. Acquired data are placed in computerized databases, such as the
National Coal Resources Data System.

* Export Assistance for Coal
and Coal Technologies Industry

National Technical Information Service
U.S. Department of Commerce
Springfield, VA 22161
The *Guide to federal Export Assistance Activities Applicable to the U.S. Coal and
Coal Technologies Industry* provides coal and coal technology firms with a single
reference source for identifying U.S. government agencies, programs, and
contacts that might aid in exporting. The *Guide* contains an in-depth discussion
of the eight major agencies offering export assistance and identifies pertinent
activities performed by other federal agencies that might assist coal and coal
technologies exporters. Write to the office above to obtain a copy.

* Fossil Energy Developments

Communications Staff
Fossil Energy, FE-5
U.S. Department of Energy
Washington, DC 20585   (202) 586-6503
Fossil Energy Review provides an update of key events in the Department of
Energy's Fossil Energy program. It is published as part of the Office of Fossil
Energy's technology transfer efforts conducted in response to the
Stevenson-Wydler Technology Innovation Act of 1980 and the Technology

Transfer act of 1986. Contact this office or the Government Printing Office for subscription availability.

* Fossil Energy Research

Western Research Institute (WRI),
P.O. Box 3395, University Station
Laramie, WY 82071   (307) 721-2211
This fossil energy research center specializes in environmental assessment, extraction process development, and fuels upgrading. Research efforts focus on conversion of oil shale, tar sands, coal, and waste products to useful hydrocarbon products and environmentally acceptable wastes. Contact this Institute for more information on fossil energy.

* Fossil Fuel Research Solicitations

National Institute for Petroleum
and Energy Research (NIPER)
P.O. Box 2128
Bartlesville, OK 74005   (918) 337-4375
NIPER solicit fossil fuel technology research not only from government agencies, but from the private sector as well. Contact this office for more information.

* Fossil Fuel Technology

National Institute for Petroleum
and Energy Research (NIPER)
P.O. Box 2128
Bartlesville, OK 74005   (918) 337-4375
This office conducts research and development covering all phases of liquid fossil fuel technology. This program includes research on petroleum extraction using enhanced oil recovery methods and improved drilling technology; the extraction of natural gas from Western tight sands; processing and thermodynamic properties of conventional oils, as well as liquid products made from coal, oil shale, and tar sands; recycling of waste lubricating oil; and improving automotive engine emissions. Databases on crude oil analyses, alternative fuels, enhanced oil recovery are maintained, and the public has free access to them. Contact this office for more information on fossil fuel technology and accessing information on the Institute's databases.

* Fuel Suppliers and Consumption in the Military

Public Affairs Office
Defense Fuel Supply Center
Defense Logistics Agency
Cameron Station
Alexandria, VA 22304-6160   (202) 274-6450
This office will supply information on almost anything you will want to know concerning fuel supply in the military. The staff will explain how to contract for the Strategic Petroleum Reserve, and how to request information under the Freedom of Information Act, such as statistics on fuel consumption patterns in the military and copies of current contracts with major suppliers. You may request a free copy of their *Fact Book*, which tells how much was spent on fuel throughout the Department of Defense, the sources of supply, and how the fuel was allocated. It includes line graphs and pie charts, with a national geographic distribution breakdown.

* Naval Petroleum Reserves

Office of Naval Petroleum and Oil Shale Reserves
Fossil Energy
U.S. Department of Energy
1000 Independence Ave., SW, Room 3H-076
Washington, DC 20585   (202) 586-4685
This office oversees the operations of the Naval Petroleum and Oil Shale Reserves, including the protection, conservation, maintenance, and production of Reserves. A Naval petroleum reserve program has existed since before the Second World War. Contact the above office for information or references to further information on the program.

* Offshore Geologic Resources

Geologic Inquiries
U.S. Geological Survey
907 National Center
Reston, VA 22092   (703) 648-4383
Using remotely sensed data, including sidescan sonar and other geophysical surveys, and direct sampling, the USGS studies the geology and assesses the potential mineral and energy resources of the continental margins and the Exclusive Economic Zone of the United States (200 miles from the coastline) and its territories. Also identified are geologic features that must be considered in the selection of sites for offshore drilling platforms and pipelines.

* Offshore Oil and Gas Leasing

Offshore Minerals Management

Mineral Management Service
U.S. Department of the Interior
18th and C Sts., NW
Washington, DC 20240   (202) 343-3530
The Mineral Management Service leases the rights to explore and develop oil and gas on Federal lands of the continental shelf. The "shelf" is made up of the submerged offshore areas lying seaward of the territorial sea to a depth of 200 meters (656 feet) and beyond that area to that depth which allows for mineral exploration. The brochure, *Leasing Energy Resources on the Outer Continental Shelf*, explains the leasing procedure and gives a history of the program.

* Offshore Oil Lease Revenues

Land Resources Division
National Park Service
U.S. Department of the Interior
1100 L St., NW
Washington, DC 20005   (202) 523-5252
The National Park System is able to purchase land for its use with the revenues received from off-shore oil leases. Revenues from these leases also are credited to the Land and Water Conservation Fund and the Historic Preservation Fund for efforts in these areas.

* Oil and Gas Leasing
on the Outer Continental Shelf

Offshore Minerals Management
Mineral Management Service
U.S. Department of the Interior
18th and C Sts., NW
Washington, DC 20240   (202) 343-3530
The Mineral Management Service leases the rights to explore and develop oil and gas on Federal lands of the continental shelf. The "shelf" is made up of the submerged offshore areas lying seaward of the territorial sea to a depth of 200 meters (656 feet) and beyond that area to that depth which allows for mineral exploration. The brochure, *Leasing Energy Resources on the Outer Continental Shelf*, explains the leasing procedure and gives a history of the program.

* Oil and Gas Leasing on Public Lands

Energy and Mineral Resources Division
Bureau of Land Management
U.S. Department of the Interior
18th and C Sts., NW
Washington, DC 20240   (202) 343-4201
Public lands are available for oil and gas leasing only after they have been evaluated through the Bureau of Land Management. In areas where development of oil and gas resources would conflict with the protection or management of other resources or public land uses, mitigating measures are identified and may appear on leases as either stipulations to uses or as restrictions on surface occupancy. Two types of leases are issued: competitive and noncompetitive.

* Oil and Gas Royalties

Royalty Management
Mineral Management Service
U.S. Department of the Interior
Kipling at Sixth Ave., Bldg. 85
Lakewood, CO 8025   (303) 231-3058
The Royalty Management Program collects and accounts for bonuses, rentals, and royalties due on the Outer Continental Shelf, federal offshore, and Indian mineral leases. It then distributes the money to States, Indians, or other Federal agencies. Owners of federal and Indian leases are required, by regulation and lease terms, to pay an annual lease rental fee and/or monthly royalties or profit share on the value of minerals removed or sold from a lease.

* Oil and Natural Gas:
Production, Marketing, Legislation

Office of Economic Analysis
Policy, Planning and Analysis
U.S. Department of Energy
1000 Independence Ave., SW, Room 7H-063
Washington, DC 20585   (202) 586-5667
This office prepares analyses and advises the Secretary of Energy on government policies affecting the discovery, production, refining, marketing, and consumption of oil and natural gas. This promotes free market policies and regulatory reform, thereby increasing the economic efficiency of oil and natural gas markets, increasing domestic consumer welfare, and reducing the Nation's vulnerability to energy supply disruptions. To accomplish this objective, the staff currently prepares analyses of natural gas legislation, restrictions on Alaskan oil exports, acquisition/drawdown policies for the Strategic Petroleum Reserve, domestic refinery policy, tax reform policy, and the Crude Oil Windfall Profits Tax. Contact this office for information on the availability of these and other reports and program information.

* Oil, Gas, and Shale Technology

Oil, Gas, and Shale
Fossil Energy
U.S. Department of Energy
1000 Independence Ave., SW, Room D122
Washington, DC 20585 (301) 353-2877

This office is responsible for Federal technology programs for recovery of natural gas from hydrocarbon reserves, Eastern gas shales, and Western tight gas sands; for the recovery of methane from coal; and for recovery of other unconventional gas resources. The office is also responsible for the advancement of the science and engineering database for gas extraction technologies. Contact this office for program information.

* Oil Potential in the U.S.
Oil, Gas, Shale and Special Technologies

Office of Fossil Energy
U.S. Department of Energy
1000 Independence Ave., SW
Washington, DC 20585 (301) 353-2877

The document, *Federal Oil Research: A Strategy for Maximizing the Producibility of Known U.S. Oil*, summarizes the current American oil situation. It traces Federal programs designed to maximize U.S. oil potential, and describes the program's present status. Contact the above office for further information.

* Oil Recyclers

National Oil Recyclers Association (NORA)
1891 Preston White Drive
P.O. Box 2459
Reston, VA 22091 (703) 620-4700

The National Oil Recyclers Association is comprised of primary producers of recycled used oil fuel. Its purpose is to represent the interests of used oil recyclers to the Environmental Protection Agency to ensure regulations on used oil are carried out and to encourage recycling.

* Oil Shale Conversion

Oil, Gas, and Shale Technology
Fossil Energy
U.S. Department of Energy
1000 Independence Ave., SW, Room D122
Washington, DC 20585 (301) 353-3514

This office is involved with oil shale conversion to liquid fuels, including the development of a sound technology base for surface and in-situ processes and the investigation of improved environmental mitigation strategies and systems. Call or write the above office for more information.

* Outer Continental Shelf Oil and Gas

Operations Management
Offshore Minerals Management
Mineral Management Service
U.S. Department of the Interior
18th and C Sts., NW
Washington, DC 20240 (202) 343-3530

Management of the oil and gas operations following leasing agreements with the Mineral Management Service is outlined in the publication, *Managing Oil and Gas Operations on the Outer Continental Shelf*. This booklet describes activities through the drilling and production process to lease relinquishment.

* Petroleum Industry Interest Group

American Petroleum Institute (API)
1220 L St., NW
Washington, DC 20005 (202) 682-8000

The American Petroleum Institute is the petroleum industry trade association representing major oil companies, independent oil producers and fuel distributors, and service-station owners. It publishes extensive statistics about the industry. Publications: *Petroleum Today, Washington Report*.

* Petroleum Information Systems

Petroleum Marketing Division
Oil and Gas
Energy Information Administration
U.S. Department of Energy
1000 Independence Ave., SW, Room 2G-051
Washington, DC 20585 (202) 586-5986

This office compiles information on crude oil and refined petroleum product prices and the industry market. The office can provide you with regular statistical reports on heating oil, gasoline, and other refined product prices and on sales of fuel oil and kerosene. Contact this office for available information and publications.

* Petroleum Overcharge Refunds

Office of Hearings and Appeals
U.S. Department of Energy
1000 Independence Ave., SW, Room 6G-087
Washington, DC 20585 (202) 586-2094

Cash refunds are available to any people, business firms, and governments that purchased refined petroleum products in the U.S. between August 1973 and January 1981. This office distributes millions of dollars in oil overcharges collected through the DOE enforcement program between those years. This office can give you further details.

* Petroleum Research

Bartlesville Project Office
U.S. Department of Energy
P.O. Box 1398
Bartlesville, OK 74001 (918) 336-2400

This Center is involved with research and engineering in petroleum and natural gas, including the improvement and demonstration of technologies in exploration, producing, refining, and use. A database on crude oil production and marketed fuel properties is also maintained. Research into automobile fuels is also undertaken. Contact this office for information on the database.

* Petroleum Statistics

Petroleum Supply Division
Oil and Gas
Energy Information Administration
U.S. Department of Energy
1000 Independence Ave., SW, Room 2G-020
Washington, DC 20585 (202) 586-5844

This office compiles statistics and projections for crude oil and refined petroleum products, including their availability, production, imports, processing, transportation, stocks, and distribution. For available information and publications, contact this office.

* Pipeline Safety

Office of Pipeline Safety (OPS)
Research and Special Programs Administration
U.S. Department of Transportation
400 7th St., SW
Washington, DC 20590 (202) 366-4572

OPS establishes and enforces safety standards for the transportation of gas and other hazardous materials by pipeline. A computerized reporting system is maintained to collect and analyze accident and incident data from pipeline operators. Accident reports include the operator's name, the hazardous material involved, description of the accident, and results. For database searches, contact the office listed. There may be a charge.

* Public Lands Oil and Gas Leasing

Energy and Mineral Resources Division
Bureau of Land Management
U.S. Department of the Interior
18th and C Sts., NW
Washington, DC 20240 (202) 343-4201

Public lands are available for oil and gas leasing only after they have been evaluated through the Bureau of Land Management. In areas where development of oil and gas resources would conflict with the protection or management of other resources or public land uses, mitigating measures are identified and may appear on leases as either stipulations to uses or as restrictions on surface occupancy. Two types of leases are issued: competitive and noncompetitive.

* Small Coal Operator Assistance

Small Coal Operator Assistance
Land Resources
Natural Resources Management
Resource and Development
Tennessee Valley Authority
Norris, TN 37828 (615) 632-1753

To ensure more competition and reasonable prices, TVA reserves a portion of its coal purchases for small producers. In addition, the TVA provides mining and reclamation technical assistance to small coal producers. The program is also involved in non-coal mineral abandoned mine reclamation. The percentage of contracts awarded to coal suppliers is evaluated based on the capability of the company to comply with TVA's mine reclamation programs.

* Strategic Petroleum Reserve

New Orleans Project Management Office
Oak Ridge Operations Office
Department of Energy

900 Commerce Rd. East
New Orleans, LA 71023   (504) 734-4201

Petroleum Reserves
Fossil Energy
U.S. Department of Energy
1000 Independence Ave., SW, Room 3G-072
Washington, DC 20585   (202) 586-4415

The Strategic Petroleum Reserve was established to provide a stock of petroleum products to serve as at least a partial cushion in case of another cut off of oil products from overseas. Reports on the reserve and its progress are available from the above offices. The New Orleans office can answer specific questions on project implementation, site locations, construction, technical problems, and related matters, and the Washington office can provide you with information on the project's overall direction.

* Strategic Petroleum Reserve: Quarterly Report

Office of Petroleum Reserves
Assistant Secretary for Fossil Energy
U.S. Department of Energy
1000 Independence Ave., SW, Room 3G-024
Washington, DC 20585   (202) 586-4410

Strategic Petroleum Reserve: Quarterly Report details the current status of the Strategic Petroleum Reserve project, designed to have a stock on hand of petroleum in case of future supply disruptions. Contact the office of the National Energy Information Center for information on availability.

* Underground Storage Tank Regulations

Environmental Protection Agency
401 M Street SW
Washington, DC 20460   (202) 475-9720

The Underground Storage Tank (UST) Docket provides public access to regulatory information supporting the Agency's regulatory action on USTs. As of April 1, 1987, there are seven dockets: (1) UST Notification Form; (2) Technical Standards for USTs Containing Petroleum; (3) Financial Responsibility Requirements for USTs Containing Petroleum; (4) State Program Approval; (5) Report to Congress on Exempt Tanks; (6) Consolidated Rules of Practice Governing the Administrative Assessment of Civil Penalties and Revocation or Suspension of Permits; and (7) Financial Responsibility Requirements for USTs Containing Hazardous Substances.

* World Petroleum Prices

Energy Plastics Branch
Energy and Chemicals Division
U.S. International Trade Commission
500 E St., SW, Room 513
Washington, DC 20436   (202) 252-1342

This office can provide you with the study, *Possible Effects of Changing World Crude Petroleum Prices.*

Nuclear Energy and Waste

* Abnormal Occurrences at Nuclear Facilities
Superintendent of Documents
Government Printing Office
Washington, DC 20402   (202) 783-3238
The NRC prepares a quarterly *Report to Congress on Abnormal Occurrences* which also serves to communicate significant event information to licensees, other government agencies, and the public. This publication reports abnormal occurrences, which are unscheduled incidents or events which the NRL determined significant from the standpoint of public health and safety, involving facilities and activities regulated by the NRL and those regulated by the agreement states. For more information on the content of the reports, contact the Office of Analysis and Evaluation of Operational Data, Nuclear Regulatory Commission, Washington, DC 20555; (301) 492-9809. Contact GPO for ordering information.

* Accidents and Incidents
Division of Operational Events Assessment
Office of Nuclear Reactor Regulation
Nuclear Regulatory Commission
Room 11 E1
Washington, DC 20055   (301) 492-1163
This division implements programs and procedures to systematically assess and screen daily reactor events; to provide daily reports; to recommend immediate corrective plant-specific and generic actions; and to coordinate the follow-up to events by assigning and tracking follow-up actions. This Division maintains and administers "on-call officer" roster to assure notification of management for events requiring prompt actions. They also respond to emergencies, and serve as the Incident Assessment Team contact.

* Antitrust Review of Nuclear Industry
Office of the General Counsel
Nuclear Regulatory Commission
Room 3H1
Washington, DC 20555   (301) 492-1532
During the licensing process, the NRC and the Attorney General conduct antitrust reviews of license applications, and an antitrust hearing may be required. Contact this office for more information on past or current antitrust reviews.

* Atomic Safety and Licensing Appeal Panel
Nuclear Regulatory Commission
4530 East-West Highway
Room 534A
Bethesda, MD 20814   (301) 492-7662
Three-member appeal boards are selected from this panel to review individual licensing board decisions. These include proceedings for the licensing of nuclear power plants and other nuclear facilities. The Appeal Board decision is subject only to judicial review in a Federal court of appeals.

* Atomic Safety and Licensing Board Panel
Nuclear Regulatory Commission
4530 East-West Highway
Room 422
Bethesda, MD 20814   (301) 492-7814
Three-member licensing boards are drawn from this panel. They are made up of lawyers and others with expertise in various technical and environmental fields to conduct public hearings on applications to build and operate nuclear power plants and other matters related to the possession and use of nuclear facilities and materials.

* Atomic Vapor Laser Isotope Separation
Advanced Technology Projects
  and Technology Transfer
Uranium Enrichment
Nuclear Energy
U.S. Department of Energy
1000 Independence Ave., SW, Room A171
Washington, DC 20585   (301) 353-4781
This office researches and develops techniques to process atomic vapor laser isotope separation (AVLIS). More detailed information is available from the above office.

* Audiovisuals, Nuclear Waste
Information Services Division
Office of Civilian Radioactive Waste Management
U.S. Department of Energy
1000 Independence Ave., SW
Washington, DC 20585   (202) 586-5722
The *OCRWM Audiovisual Directory* lists abstracts of videotapes, audiocassettes, slides and films on the subject of waste management. These products are available for loan to Federal, State, and local governments; Indian Tribes; the media; professionals; and the general public. The directory contains both current and historical footage and features citation listings numerically and alphabetically by titles. The directory also indexes products by subject keywords. In addition to a printed directory, the information is available online through the *OCRWM Product Record System*.

* Citizen's Guide to U.S. Nuclear Regulatory Commission
Public Affairs
Nuclear Regulatory Commission
Washington, DC 20402   (301) 492-0240
The *Citizen's Guide to U.S. Nuclear Regulatory Commission Information* is designed to acquaint the public with the availability of information pertaining to the licensing and regulation of nuclear energy, and of all commercial high-level and low-level radioactive waste and uranium recovery activities in the United States.

* Construction Permits for Nuclear Facilities
Office of Nuclear Reactor Regulation
Nuclear Regulatory Commission
Room 1201
Washington, DC 20555   (301) 492-1270
Obtaining an NRC construction permit is the first objective of a utility or other company seeking to operate a nuclear power reactor or other nuclear facility under NRC licensing authority. The process begins with the filing and acceptance of an application, generally comprising many volumes of data, covering both safety and environmental considerations, in accord with NRC requirements and guidance. Contact this office for more information concerning the construction permit process.

* Criminal Incidents
Emergency Programs Center
U.S. Department of Justice
10th St. & Constitution Ave., NW
Room 6101
Washington, DC 20530   (202) 633-4545
If you would like to know the facts of any case of criminal activity involving nuclear incidents, the files of the Emergency Programs Center is for you. This office of the U.S. Department of Justice coordinates the government's activity in any such case. For instance, if you want the facts on the real-life case of nuclear extortion seen in the movie, *The Falcon and the Snowman*, this is the place to go. Maybe you are interested in writing your own thriller on nuclear espionage; contact the Emergency Programs Center and read accounts of actual incidents to give your writing that tinge of reality. Whatever your interest may be, here's where you'll get the facts.

* Daily Nuclear Documents
Public Document Room
Nuclear Regulatory Commission
2120 L. Street, NW
Washington, DC 20037   (202) 634-3273
The *PDR Daily Accession List* describes agency documents that are made publicly available each weekday. There is ordinarily at least a two-to-three-week delay in the public availability of new documents. The PDR collection includes all publicly available forms of communication generated by NRC or sent to NRC by the companies and institutions it regulates. The Accession Lists are organized by NRC topics, and all documents appropriate to a topic and their file location are listed in one place. A free publication, *How to Use The Public Document Room's Daily Accession List*, is available from the office above, and explains the *Daily Accession List*, the PDR request policy, as well as the classification scheme.

* Decommissioning Nuclear Facilities
Remedial Action Program Information Center
Oak Ridge National Laboratory (ORNL)

P.O. Box 2008, Building 2001
Oak Ridge, TN 37831-6050   (615) 576-0568
The *Nuclear Facility Decommissioning and Site Remedial Action* database serves as a comprehensive source of technical information relevant to the DOE Remedial Action Program, under which nuclear facilities are decommissioned and cleaned up. Computerized literature searches of RAPIC databases are available upon request at no charge.

* Energy Software Center

National Energy Software Center
Nuclear Regulatory Commission
Argonne National Laboratory
9700 South Cass Avenue
Argonne, IL 60439   (708) 972-2000
The National Energy Software Center is the Nuclear Regulatory Commission's software information and distribution center. The Center acquires, processes, packages, maintains, and distributes computer programs and data compilations developed under the sponsorship of NRC and other government agencies. Bulletins describing recent software acquisitions are issued bimonthly, and abstracts containing information on all software in the NESC collection are published annually. Package costs vary, and a current price list is available from NESC.

* Environmental Review of Proposed Nuclear Facilities

Office of Nuclear Reactor Regulation
Nuclear Regulatory Commission
Room 12d1
Washington, DC 20555   (301) 492-1270
An environmental review begins with an analysis of the consequences to the environment of the construction and operation of the proposed nuclear facility at the proposed site. Upon completion of the analysis, a draft Environmental Statement is published and distributed to all interested parties. Comments are then taken into account in the preparation of a final Environmental Statement. During this same period, the NRC is conducting analysis and preparing a report on the site suitability aspects of the proposed licensing action. Contact this office more information on the review process and reports.

* Exhibits, Nuclear Waste

U.S. Department of Energy
Office of Civilian Radioactive Waste Management
ERAP/ISD (RW-43) (Exhibits)
Washington, DC 20585
OCRWM has one full-size (9' X 20') exhibit and several tabletop (3' X 8') exhibits which describe the radioactive waste management program. These exhibits are used at public meetings and events around the country.

* Export and Import Controls

Nuclear Energy and Energy Technology Affairs
Bureau of Oceans and International Environmental
  and Scientific Affairs
Department of State
2201 C St., NW, Room 7820
Washington, DC 20520   (202) 647-4101
This office works closely with the Nuclear Regulatory Commission with regard to the licensing requests for nuclear imports and exports. They also study the development and transfer of nuclear technology in foreign countries. This office monitors the Nuclear Non-Proliferation Treaty, making sure that the countries which signed the treaty are following its regulations. They also oversee the export and import of items which are not nuclear, but which could be used for nuclear purposes, such as super computers. The export of these items must follow the guidelines set in the Nuclear Non-Proliferation Treaty.

* Export-Import Licensing

International Programs
Nuclear Regulatory Commission
Room 3H1
Washington, DC 20555   (202) 492-0347
This NRC office formulates and recommends policies concerning nuclear exports and imports, international safeguards, international physical security, nonproliferation matters, and international cooperation and assistance in nuclear safety and radiation protection. NRC is responsible for licensing the import or export of nuclear-related materials and equipment. This export authority extends to production and utilization facilities, to special nuclear and source material, to byproduct materials, and to certain nuclear-related components and other material.

* Freedom of Information Act Requests

Office of Administration
Nuclear Regulatory Commission
7920 Norfolk Ave., Room 378C

Bethesda, MD 20814   (301) 492-8133
All Freedom of Information Act Requests should be addressed to the Office listed above.

* Fuel Cycle Plants and Material Safety

Industrial and Medical Nuclear Safety Division
Office of Nuclear Material Safety and Safeguards
Nuclear Regulatory Commission
Room 6H1
Washington, DC 20555   (301) 492-3426
This office analyzes health physics, radiation and nuclear safety, quality, licensing, and follow-up review of all fuel cycle plants. Contact this office for more information on its studies.

* Fusion Energy and Basic Science Research

General Sciences
Lawrence Berkeley Laboratory
One Cyclotron Rd.
Mail Stop 50A/5104
Berkeley, CA 94720   (414) 486-5771
The General Sciences section of the Lawrence Berkeley Laboratory researches the basic nature of matter to provide basic understanding of the elements of the universe, making progress possible in many fields of science. Of particular interest in the work of this division is investigation of the potential development of nuclear fusion energy sources. Contact this office for more information.

* Fusion Technology

Office of Fusion Energy
Energy Research
U.S. Department of Energy
1000 Independence Ave., SW, Room T204
Washington, DC 20585   (301) 353-3347
The office works to develop sound physical and engineering technological foundations needed for the design, construction, and operation of complex nuclear fusion experiments and facilities. Contact the office for more detailed program information.

* Gas Centrifuge and Isotope Separation Research

Uranium Enrichment Advanced Technology Project
U.S. Department of Energy
1000 Independence Ave., SW, Room A-171
Washington, DC 20585   (301) 353-4781
This project conducts research and development of gas centrifuge technology and advanced isotope separation techniques. It publishes an annual report which covers statistical information pertaining to uranium research and development. Contact the office for further information.

* High-Level Nuclear Waste

High-Level Waste Management Division
Office of Nuclear Material Safety and Safeguards
Nuclear Regulatory Commission
Room 4H1
Washington, DC 20555   (301) 492-3404
This Division develops and manages the Agency's program for the licensing, inspection, and regulation of the Department of Energy's high-level waste repository program. They also provide the lead for all Agency activities under the Nuclear Waste Policy Act.

* Inspection of Nuclear Reactors

Nuclear Reactor Regulation
Nuclear Regulatory Commission
Room 12D1
Washington, DC 20402   (301) 492-1274
A basic element in NRC reactor regulation is the inspection of licensed reactor facilities to determine the state of reactor safety, to confirm that the operations are in compliance with the provisions of the license, and to ascertain whether other conditions exist which have safety implications serious enough to warrant corrective action. The NRC conducts a program to deal with unsafe or potentially unsafe events or conditions which occur at individual plant sites or other facilities involving licensed operation ("reactive" inspections).

* Interim Waste Storage

Superintendent of Documents
U.S. Government Printing Office
Washington, DC 20402   (202) 783-3238
The Monitored Retrievable Storage Review Commission's report, *Nuclear Waste: Is There A Need For Federal Interim Storage?*, reflects the Commission's extensive technical work and public policy deliberations. It is available for sale from the office above.

* International Reactor Development

Office of Technology Support Program
U.S. Department of Energy
1000 Independence Ave., SW, Room H407
Washington, DC 20585   (301) 353-3609

Under the Civilian Reactor Technology Support Program, this office coordinates and cooperates with other Federal agencies in developing and executing international programs for power reactor development. Contact this office for more information.

* Justifying Nuclear Energy

Office of Program Support
Nuclear Energy
U.S. Department of Energy
1000 Independence Ave., SW, Room 5A-157
Washington, DC 20585   (301) 353-5462

This office is responsible for justifying and defending DOE's Nuclear Energy programs before internal agency, Office of Management and Budget (OMB), and Congressional reviews. More detailed information is available from the above office.

* Licensee Event Reports

Superintendent of Documents
Government Printing Office
Washington, DC 20402   (202) 783-3238

Licensee Event Report Compilation is a monthly publication which contains summaries of reported operational information submitted to the NRC by nuclear powerplant licensees in accordance with Federal regulations. The summaries are arranged alphabetically by facility name and chronologically by event data for each facility, with components, system, and keyword indexes following the summaries. The complete documents are available for review at the Public Document Room, Nuclear Regulatory Commission, 2120 L Street, NW, Washington, DC 20037; (202) 634-3273.

* Licensing Nuclear-Related Operations

Office of Nuclear Reactor Regulation
Nuclear Regulatory Commission
Room 12 D1
Washington, DC 20402   (301) 492-1270

The Nuclear Regulatory Commission grants licenses for nuclear power operations and other possession and use of nuclear materials, including the transportation and disposal of nuclear materials and wastes. Contact this office for more information on the licensing process.

* Limited Work Authorization

Office of Nuclear Reactor Regulation
Nuclear Regulatory Commission
Room 12 D1
Washington, DC 20555   (301) 492-1270

The NRC may decide to grant a Limited Work Authorization to an applicant in advance of a final decision on the construction permit, in order to allow certain work to begin at the site. Such a step could save seven months' construction time.

* Liquid Metal Fast Breeder Reactor

Office of Technology Support Program
U.S. Department of Energy
1000 Independence Ave., SW, Room H407
Washington, DC 20585   (301) 353-3609

This office is the principal point of contact for information on the National Liquid Metal Fast Breeder Reactor (LMFBR). Program details are available from the above office.

* Low-Level Nuclear Waste

Division of Low-Level Waste Management and Decommissioning
Office of Nuclear Material Safety and Safeguards
Nuclear Regulatory Commission
Room 5E1
Washington, DC 20555   (301) 492-3340

This division directs the NCR's program for the licensing, inspection, and regulation to assure safety and quality associated with the management, treatment, and commercial disposal of low-level nuclear waste.

* Marketing Support for Nuclear Programs

Office of Marketing Technology Deployment
and Strategic Planning
Uranium Enrichment

Nuclear Energy
U.S. Department of Energy
1000 Independence Ave., SW, Room A170
Washington, DC 20585   (301) 353-4610

This office is oversees marketing activities which support uranium enrichment programs. It is also responsible for the preliminary design and construction planning for a potential Atomic Vapor Laser Isotope Separation (AVLIS) production plant. More detailed information is available from the above office.

* Material Review and Licensing

Medical, Academic, and Commercial Use Safety Branch
Division of Industrial and Medical Nuclear Safety
Office of Nuclear Material Safety and Safeguards
Nuclear Regulatory Commission
Room 6 H24
Washington, DC 20555   (301) 492-3418

This Branch conducts health physics, radiation safety, and other appropriate analyses, licensing, and follow-up review of byproduct, medical, academic, industrial, and other source and special nuclear materials, including the preparation of environmental assessments and impact statements, determination of quality evaluations of sealed sources and devices, and licensing of exempt distribution of consumer products.

* NRC Docket Breakdown

Public Document Room
Nuclear Regulatory Commission
2120 L Street, NW
Washington, DC 20555   (202) 634-3273

Each organization engaged in a nuclear activity licensed and regulated by NRC is assigned a docket (case) number. Documents exchanged between NRC and the license applicant or licensee are filed together under that number. The docket files are open to the public in the Public Documents Room.

* Nuclear Regulatory Commission

Office of Governmental and Public Affairs
Nuclear Regulatory Commission
Washington, DC 20555   (301) 492-0240

This office serves as a public inquiry point for information on the following:

-Licensing (including decommissioning) of commercial nuclear power plants and other nuclear facilities and the possession and use of nuclear materials for medical, industrial, educational, and research purposes.
-Inspections and investigations designed to assure that licensed activities are conducted in compliance with the agency's regulations and other requirements and enforcement of compliance.
-Search in the areas of safety, safeguards, and environmental assessment and the establishment of regulations, standards, and guidelines governing the use of nuclear facilities and materials.
-Safeguarding nuclear facilities and materials from diversion or sabotage.
-Implementation of agency responsibilities under the Nuclear Waste Policy Act of 1982 (high-level radioactive wastes), the Low-Level Radioactive Waste Policy Act of 1980, and the Uranium Mill Tailings Radiation Control Act of 1978.
-Packaging of radioactive materials for transport.

* Open and Closed Meetings of the NRC

Office of the Secretary
Nuclear Regulatory Commission
Washington, DC 20555   (301) 492-1969

The public is welcome to observe all Commission meetings, unless a meeting is closed because it involves one or more of the "exempted" subjects described in NRC Regulations. "Exempted" subjects usually involve classified information, investigations, enforcement actions, internal rules and practices, or personnel matters. Advance notices of Commission meetings are published in the *Federal Register*, posted in the Public Document Room, and mailed to those on a regular list. Contact the Office of the Secretary to be added to the list. Current information on scheduled Commission meetings may be obtained by calling the recorded message number: (301) 492-0292. Transcripts are made of Commission meetings. These are available in the Public Document Room for inspection or duplication.

* Operating Statistics on Nuclear Plants

Licensed Operating Reactors
Superintendent of Documents
Government Printing Office
Washington, DC 20402   (202) 783-3238

Also referred to as the "Gray Book," *Monthly Operating Units Status Reports* provides data on the operation of nuclear units as timely and accurately as possible. It contains three sections: highlights and statistics for commercial operating units, detailed information on each unit, and an appendix for miscellaneous information such as spent fuel storage capabilities.

* Operations Analysis

Nuclear Operations Analysis Center
Nuclear Regulatory Commission
P .O. Box Y
Oak Ridge National Laboratory
Oak Ridge, TN 37831　　　　　　　(615) 574-0393

The Nuclear Operations Analysis Center performs analysis tasks, as well as information-gathering activities, for the Nuclear Regulatory Commission. It conducts a number of tasks related to the analysis of nuclear power experience, including an annual operation summary for U.S. power reactors, generic case studies, plant operating assessments, and risk assessments. NOAC also publishes staff studies and bibliographies, disseminates monthly nuclear power plant operating event reports, and cooperates in the preparation of Nuclear Safety.

* Peaceful Uses of Nuclear Technology

Office of Nuclear Technology and Safeguards
Bureau of Oceans and International Environmental
 and Scientific Affairs
Department of State
2201 C St., NW, Room 7828
Washington, DC 20520　　　　　　　(202) 647-3310

Concerned with peaceful uses of nuclear power, such as nuclear energy, this office negotiates cooperative agreements with other countries for the safe functioning of nuclear reactors, and also becomes involved where nuclear reactor accidents occur.

* Power Plant Emissions

Radioactive Emissions Standards
Office of Radiation Programs
Environmental Protection Agency
401 M St., SW, Room NE108
Washington DC 20460　　　　　　　(202) 475-9600

The EPA, with a number of other federal agencies, protects the public from unnecessary exposure to ionizing radiation. EPA's major responsibilities are to set radioactive emissions standards and exposure limits, assess new technology, and monitor radiation in the environment in four areas: radiation from nuclear accidents, radon emissions, land disposal of radioactive waste, and radiation in groundwater and drinking water. The EPA fulfills these responsibilities by setting emissions standards for nuclear power plants, and for radionuclides in drinking water and in the air. EPA also prescribes work practices to reduce emissions of radon from underground uranium mines, develops radioactive waste disposal standards, and issues guidance to limit occupational exposure.

* Public Participation in Nuclear Licensing

Atomic Safety and Licensing Board Panel
Nuclear Regulatory Commission
Room 422
4350 East-West Highway
Bethesda, MD 20814　　　　　　　(301) 492-7814

As part of the licensing process, a mandatory public hearing is carried out by a three-member Atomic Safety and Licensing Board, which then makes an initial decision as to whether a construction permit should be granted. A notice of a public hearing is published in the Federal Register and in local newspapers, giving 30 days for members of the public to petition to intervene in the proceeding.

* Radiation in Vicinity of Reactors

NRC TLD Direct Radiation Monitoring Network
Government Printing Office
Superintendent of Documents
Washington, DC 20402　　　　　　　(202) 783-3238

This quarterly publication provides the status and results of the NRC thermoluminescent dosimeter (TLD) direct radiation monitoring. It presents the radiation levels measured in the vicinity of NRC licensed facility sites throughout the country.

* Radioactive Waste Management

U.S. Department of Energy
Office of Civilian Radioactive Waste Management
Office of External Relations and Policy
Information Services Division
1000 Independence Ave., SW, Mail Stop RW-43
Washington, DC 20585　　　　　　　(202) 586-5722

Radioactive Waste Management is a monthly publication that provides digests of current information available on the topics of spent fuel transport and storage, radioactive effluents from nuclear facilities, techniques of processing radioactive waste, remedial actions and environmental aspects of radioactive waste management. Those wishing to receive this publication should call (703) 487-4630 and request document number PB88-902900.

* Radioactive Waste Management Bulletin

U.S. Department of Energy
Office of Civilian Radioactive Waste Management
Office of External Relations and Policy
Information Services Division
1000 Independence Ave., SW, Mail Stop RW-43
Washington, DC 20585　　　　　　　(202) 586-5722

The *OCRWM Bulletin*, a monthly publication, provides information about OCRWM program activities, milestones, events, publications, and documents to assist interested individuals in keeping abreast of the radioactive waste management program. In addition, the text of the *Bulletin* is available on *INFOLINK*.

* Reactor Construction Surveillance

Division Of License Performance and Quality Evaluation
Office of Nuclear Reactor Regulation
Nuclear Regulatory Commission
Room 10H1
Washington, DC 20555　　　　　　　(301) 492-1004

This Division develops and implements a program for assuring quality and reliability of reactor license facilities design, fabrication, construction, testing, and operation.

* Reactor Inventory in the U.S.

Office of Scientific and Technical Information
Nuclear Energy
U.S. Department of Energy
1000 Independence Ave., SW, Room 5A-157
Washington, DC 20585　　　　　　　(202) 586-6684

Nuclear Reactors Built, Being Built or Planned is a survey of American nuclear reactors in operation, under construction or planned. Contact this office for a copy.

* Reactor Safeguards Advisory Committee

Advisory Committee on Reactor Safeguards
Nuclear Regulatory Commission
Room 440
Washington, DC 20555　　　　　　　(301) 492-4516

This statutory body of 15 scientists and engineers reviews and makes recommendations to the Commission on all applications to build or operate nuclear power reactors and on related nuclear safety matters. The ACRS provides advice to the Commission on potential hazards of proposed safety standards. The ACRS reviews requests for pre-application site and standard plant approvals, for each application for a construction permit or an operating license for power reactors, and for applications for licenses to construct or operate test reactors.

* Reactor Safety Research

Division of Systems Research
Office of Nuclear Regulatory Research
Nuclear Regulatory Commission
Room 369
Washington, DC 20555　　　　　　　(301) 492-3500

This Division plans, develops, and directs comprehensive safety research programs for predicting nuclear reactor and plant systems behavior under normal, accident, and severe accident conditions. Responsibilities include evaluating challenges to containments, development of accident source terms, performance and review of probable risk assessments, and accident sequence analysis. Contact this office for more information on the research.

* Reactors and National Security

Office of New Production Reactors
U.S. Department of Energy
1000 Independence Ave., SW, Room 7A-175
Washington, DC 20585　　　　　　　(202) 586-5733

To meet national security requirements, this office acquires and constructs new production reactors, along with developing a strategy to consider their safety, quality, environmental, and performance. Contact this office for further information.

* Reactor Training Center

NRC Technical Training Center
Nuclear Regulatory Commission
Osborne Office Center
Chattanooga, TN 37411　　　　　　　(615) 855-6500

The NRC Technical Training Center was established to develop and implement policy and programs for technical training of NCR staff. The TTC provides technical training in broad areas of reactor technology and specialized technical training.

* Regulation Dockets

Superintendent of Documents
Government Printing Office
Washington, DC 20402   (202) 783-3238
Title List of Documents Made Publicly Available contains descriptions of the information received and generated by the Nuclear Regulatory Commission. The information includes docketed material associated with civilian nuclear power plants and material received and generated by the Commission pertinent to its role as a regulatory agency. "Docketed" refers to the system by which the Commission maintains its regulatory records. A monthly subscription price is available for $108.00 per year.

* Regulation Hotline

     (800) 368-223
     (202) 479-0487 (in D.C.)
DOE's toll-free hotline announces upcoming technical meetings of DOE and the Nuclear Regulatory Commission (NRC). The public is invited to attend these meetings, and may call the 800 telephone number to determine the date, time and location of the meetings. A telephone recording service has also been established to announce upcoming meetings related to the waste management program of the NRC. The number is (800) 368-5642, ext. 20436. Washington, D.C., area residents should call 492-0436.

* Regulation Public Documents

Nuclear Regulatory Commission
2120 L. Street, NW
Washington, DC 20037   (202) 634-3273
The Public Document Room maintains over 1.5 million agency documents in hard copy and microfiche. The majority of these documents relate to the licensing and inspection of nuclear facilities and to the use, transport and disposal of nuclear materials. There is generally about a two week processing delay before documents are available in the PDR. The PDR files are open for public use, and reference librarians assist on-site patrons in their use. The reference staff also respond to telephone and letter requests. The PDR on-line catalog contains citations to public documents received after October 1978, and the computer searches are free of charge. In addition, the Commission has approximately 100 local Public Document Rooms around the country. Call the office above for information on the locations.

* Regulatory and Technical Reports

Government Printing Office
Superintendent of Documents
Washington, DC 20402   (202) 783-3238
Regulatory and Technical Reports is a quarterly compilation, cumulated annually with the fourth quarter, of regulatory and technical reports and conference proceedings issued by the NRC staff and contractors. Contact GPO for ordering information.

* Regulatory Bulletins

Division of Information Support Services
Nuclear Regulatory Commission
Washington, DC 20555   (202) 275-2060
Generic Letters, Bulletins, and *Information Notices* are written NRC notifications sent to groups of licensees that identify specific problems, developments, or other matters of interest of which licensees should be aware or for which the NRC is calling for or recommending specific steps be taken by the licensees. These technical documents are placed in the Public Document Room, and can be automatically sent to interested groups or organizations who are on the mailing list.

* Regulatory Enforcement

Office of Enforcement, 7H1
Nuclear Regulatory Commission
Washington, DC 20402   (301) 492-0741
This office develops policies and programs for enforcement of NRC requirements. It manages major enforcement actions and assesses the effectiveness and uniformity of enforcement actions taken by the regional offices. Enforcement powers include notices of violation, fines, and orders for license modification, suspension, or revocation.

* Regulatory Guides

Superintendent of Documents
Government Printing Office
Washington, DC 20402   (202) 783-3238
Nuclear Regulatory Commission regulatory guides describe methods acceptable to the NRC staff of implementing specific parts of the Commission's regulations and, in some cases, describe techniques used by the staff in evaluating specific problems or postulated accidents. Guides also may advise applicants regarding information the NRC staff needs in reviewing applications for permits and licenses. Comments on the guides are encouraged. The following guides are currently issued. *Division 1: Power Reactor Guides; Division 2: Research and Test Reactor Guides; Division 3: Fuels and Materials Facilities Guides; Division 4: Environmental and Siting Guides; Division 5: Materials and Plant Protection Guides; Division 6: Product Guides; Division 7: Transportation Guides; Division 8: Occupational Health Guides; Division 9: Antitrust and Financial Review Guides; Division 10: General Guides.*

* Regulatory Library

Nuclear Regulatory Commission
7920 Norfolk Avenue
Room 190
Bethesda, MD 20814   (301) 492-8501
The Nuclear Regulatory Commission's library is open to the public, and its focus is on nuclear energy. Reference staff are available to assist you.

* Regulatory Publications

Superintendent of Documents
Government Printing Office
Washington, DC 20402   (202) 783-3238
Nuclear Regulatory Commission Issuances is a monthly publication containing opinions, decisions, denials, memorandum, and orders of the Commission, the Atomic Safety and Licensing Appeal Board, the Atomic Safety and Licensing Board, and the Administrative Law Judge. A subscription is available for $102.00 per year ($5.50 per copy). Semiannual and Quarterly indexes are also available.

* Regulatory Research

Office of Nuclear Regulatory Research
Nuclear Regulatory Commission
Room 254
Washington, DC 20555   (301) 492-3700
The Nuclear Regulatory Commission is mandated by law to conduct an extensive conformatory research program in the areas of safety, safeguards, and environmental assessment. In addition, the agency establishes regulations, standards, and guidelines governing the various licensed uses of nuclear facilities and materials.

* Repository for Nuclear Waste

Yucca Mountain Information Office
P.O. Box 69
Beatty, NV 89003   (702) 553-2130
The Nuclear Waste Policy Amendments Act of 1987 named Yucca Mountain, Nevada as the only candidate site to be characterized for a repository. Contact this DOE office for further information.

* Safeguards

Division of Safeguards and Transportation
Office of Nuclear Safety and Safeguards
Nuclear Regulatory Commission
Room 4E
Washington, DC 20555   (301) 492-3365
This Division develops overall agency safeguards policy and conducts safeguards licensing, inspection, and regulatory functions applicable to nuclear materials, nonreactor facilities, transportation of nuclear materials, and nonreactor inspection activities.

* Safeguards Inspection

Division of Reactor Inspection and Safeguards
Office of Nuclear Reactor Regulation
Nuclear Regulatory Commission
Room 9EI
Washington, DC 20555   (301) 492-0903
This Division performs special reactor inspection, vendor inspections, reactor safeguards licensing, and regulatory effectiveness reviews, and quality assurance reviews for reactors. This Division also performs inspections in response to allegations and reports of defective and substandard components and equipment in nuclear service or being offered for nuclear service.

* Safety Review for Nuclear Plants

Office of Nuclear Reactor Regulations
Nuclear Regulatory Commission
Room 8EI
Washington, DC 20555   (301) 492-0884
An applicant for a nuclear plant construction permit lays out the proposed nuclear plant design in *Preliminary Safety Analysis Report* (PSAR). The NRC staff examines the applicant's PSAR to determine whether the plant design is safe and consistent with NRC rules and regulations; whether valid methods of calculation were employed and accurately performed; and whether the applicant

has conducted its analysis and evaluation in sufficient depth and breadth to support staff approval as to assured adequate levels of safety.

* Speakers, Nuclear Waste

Yucca Mountain Project Office
U.S. Department of Energy
P.O. Box 98518
Las Vegas, NV 89193-8518   (702) 794-7920

Members of the OCRWM program staff are available to speak to various groups interested in the radioactive waste management program. Qualified speakers can discuss the OCRWM program in general or address specific topics of special interest to a particular organization. To request a speaker from the Speakers' Bureau in the Nevada Project Office, contact the office above.

* Spent Fuel Options

Nuclear Power
Tennessee Valley Authority
1101 Market St.
Chattanooga, TN 37401   (615) 751-8689

The TVA, in a cooperative effort with various utilites, is studying alternative facilites needed to store spent fuel and radioactive waste from TVA nuclear plants. Contact this office for more information on radioactive waste storage.

* Standards for Nuclear Safety

Division of Engineering
Office of Nuclear Regulatory Research
Nuclear Regulatory Commission
Room 254
Washington, DC 20555   (301) 492-3800

This Division plans, develops, and directs comprehensive research programs and standards development for nuclear safety in the design, qualification, construction, inspection, testing, operation, and decommissioning of nuclear power plants. This office maintains liaison and provides technical input to other Federal agencies, the American National Standards Institute, professional societies, and international organizations.

* State Nuclear Programs

State, Local and Indian Tribe Programs
Office of Governmental and Public Affairs
Nuclear Regulatory Commission
Room 3D21
Washington, DC 20555   (301) 492-0321

This office plans and directs NRC's program of cooperation and liaison with States, local governments, interstate and Indian Tribe organizations. They also develop and direct administrative and contractual programs for coordinating and integrating Federal and State regulatory activities.

* Supply and Demand: Nuclear and Alternative Fuel

Nuclear and Alternate Fuels Division
Coal, Nuclear, Electric and Alternate Fuels
Energy Information Administration
U.S. Department of Energy
1000 Independence Ave., SW, Room BG-057
Washington, DC 20585   (202) 586-2009

The office prepares, analyzes, and projects the availability, production, cost, processing, transportation, and distribution of nuclear and alternate energy sources, including solar, wind, and wood. Contact this office for more information and publications.

* Three Mile Island

Three Mile Island Program
Nuclear Energy
U.S. Department of Energy
1000 Independence Ave., SW, Room E461
Washington, DC 20585   (301) 353-3456

This office manages DOE's Three Mile Island Research and Development Programs. Contact the office for further information.

* TVA Nuclear Power Plants

Nuclear Power
Tennessee Valley Authority
1101 Market St.
Chattanooga, TN 37402-2801   (615) 751-8689

TVA has two licensed nuclear plants with a total of five reactors in operation. Two additional plants, with a total of four reactors, are under construction. The division's responsibilities include demonstrating safe and reliable performance, making sure that operating plants to meet or exceed industry standards of excellence, increasing productivity and reliability of nuclear units to meet or

exceed the industry average, and maintaining a competitive human resources program.

* Uranium Mine Clean Up

Uranium Mill Tailings Remedial Action Project Office
Albuquerque Operations Office
Department of Energy
P.O. Box 5400
Albuquerque, NM 87115   (505) 353-2585

This office performs clean-up activities at 24 inactive uranium mill tailings sites and associated vicinity properties in 11 States and the Navajo Indian Reservation. After clean-up is completed, the sites will be owned by DOE and licensed by the Nuclear Regulatory Commission. You can get further information on Department of Energy nuclear waste management programs from the above office.

* Uranium Mining and the Environment

Grand Junction Projects Office (GJPO)
Idaho Operations Office
U.S. Department of Energy
P.O. Box 2567
Grand Junction, CO 81502   (303) 242-8621

This office assesses the environmental effects of uranium mining and milling operations, and manages uranium leases on lands under DOE control. This office also provides geoscientific support in characterizing sites under consideration as repositories under DOE's Civilian Radioactive Waste Management Program. It also participates in international technical exchanges under several programs administered by the Organization for Economic Cooperation and Development's Nuclear Energy Agency and the International Atomic Energy Agency. Contact this office for further information on DOE nuclear waste management programs.

* Waste Advisory Committee

Advisory Committee on Nuclear Waste
Nuclear Regulatory Commission
Room 2G1
Washington, DC 20555   (301) 492-0240

The Advisory Committee on Nuclear Waste is an independent committee established by the Commission to provide it with advice and recommendations concerning all aspects of nuclear waste management for which the NRC has responsibility. Its primary focus is on waste disposal, but its work also includes other aspects of waste management, such as the handling, processing, transportation, storage, and safeguarding of nuclear wastes, including spent fuel, nuclear wastes mixed with other hazardous substances, and uranium mill tailings.

* Waste Background Information

U.S. Department of Energy
Office of Civilian Radioactive Waste Management
Office of External Relations and Policy
Information Services Division
Mail Stop RW-43
1000 Independence Ave., SW
Washington, DC 20585   (202) 586-5722

The *OCRWM Backgrounders* provide current background information on program facts, issues and initiatives. *Backgrounders* are published periodically by the Office of External Relations and Policy and are distributed to individuals and organizations on the *OCRWM Bulletin* mailing list and by individual requests.

* Waste Clean Up

Office of Remedial Action and Waste Technology
Nuclear Energy
1000 Independence Ave., SW, Room E435
Washington, DC 20585   (301) 353-5006

This office provides plans, develops, and executes DOE programs for civilian nuclear waste treatment and low-level waste management. It also works to clean up and decommission both contaminated DOE and legislatively-authorized non-Government facilities and sites. Beneficial uses of nuclear waste byproducts are also studied. Further information on Department of Energy nuclear waste management programs can be obtained from the above office.

* Waste Management

Information Services Division
Office of Civilian Radioactive Waste Management
U.S. Department of Energy
1000 Independence Ave., SW, Room 5A-051
Washington, DC 20585   (202) 586-2835

The *Publications Catalog, Office of Civilian Radioactive Waste Management,* is a detailed summary of office reports and studies on nuclear waste management. This catalog provides citations of selected technical and public information on nuclear waste management. The free brochure, *Managing the Nation's Nuclear Waste*, is also available from this office.

* Waste Management Factsheets

U.S. Department of Energy
Office of Civilian Radioactive Waste Management
Office of External Relations and Policy
Information Services Division
Mail Stop RW-43
1000 Independence Ave., SW
Washington, DC 20585   (202) 586-5722

OCRWM has published factsheets that describe the overall OCRWM program, the repository program, the monitored retrievable storage (MRS) system and the transportation program.

* Waste Management Publications

U.S. Department of Energy
Office of Civilian Radioactive Waste Management
Office of External Relations and Policy
Information Services Division
Mail Stop RW-43
1000 Independence Ave., SW
Washington, DC 20585   (202) 586-5722

The OCRWM publications catalog contains abstracts of printed documents on the topic of high-level radioactive waste management that are of interest to Federal, State and local government officials and staff; affected Indian Tribes; advisory groups; special interest groups; the media; information science professionals; and students and the general public. The catalog features citation listings alphabetically by titles, an index by keywords and an index by corporate authors. In addition to a printed catalog, the information is available online through the *OCRWM Product Record System*.

Climate and Forecasts

See also Science and Technology; Geology and Earth Science Chapter
See also Current Events and Homework Chapter

The National Weather Service is a well-known federal institution but the general public probably is unaware of the Landslide Information Center and other government offices which track and analyze climate changes. General information and technical materials on other "Acts of God" such as volcano eruptions and earthquakes are identified in the Science and Technology Chapter. Many agencies are using the most sophisticated methods for cartography from the National Archives to the National Air and Space Administration. By and large the primary distributor of all sorts of maps is the U.S. Geological Survey.

* Acid Rain, Aerosols, and Climate Impact
Environmental Research Laboratory
National Oceanic and Atmospheric Administration
Department of Commerce
8060 13th St.
Silver Spring, MD 20910   (301) 427-7684
The Air Resources Laboratory performs weather research to understand and predict human influences on the environment, especially those involving atmospheric transport and dispersion of pollutants such as acid rain and ozone to distances up to thousands of kilometers. The ARL also monitors and interprets trends in natural and man-made substances, such as CO425, halocarbons, aerosols, and ozone which can potentially modify the climate. In addition, ARL studies solar radiation for its role in climate change. An annual report is available, which describes in more detail the current research being undertaken at ARL.

* Aeronomy Research
Earth's Atmosphere Research
Environmental Research Laboratories
National Oceanic and Atmospheric Administration
Department of Commerce
325 Broadway
Boulder, CO 80303   (303) 497-6286
The Aeronomy Laboratory studies the physical and chemical processes of the Earth's atmosphere to advance our capability for monitoring, predicting, and controlling these processes. Recent emphasis is on the greenhouse effect, stratospheric and tropospheric ozone.

* Air Quality and Atmospheric Research
Environmental Sciences Group
Environmental Research Laboratories
National Oceanic and Atmospheric Administration
Department of Commerce
325 Broadway
Boulder, CO 80303   (303) 497-6286
The Environmental Sciences Group includes the Climate Research Program (studies of short- and long-term climate change), the Weather Research Program (research to improve short-range weather predictions and warning, especially regarding storm systems and flash floods), the Weather Modification Program (evaluations of data from various states' weather modification programs), and the Program for Regional Observing and Forecasting Services (transfer of technology such as interactive computer workstations to operational agencies like the National Weather Service). Contact the Public Affairs Office for more information about the programs.

* Atmospheric Sciences Central Library
Central Library
National Oceanic and Atmospheric Administration
Department of Commerce
6009 Executive Blvd.
Rockville, MD 20852   (301) 443-8330
The library maintains a collection of books, journals, technical reports, microfiche, and compact discs to support research in the atmospheric sciences, oceanography, geophysics, and related disciplines. The library uses a wide array of products and services to meet its clientele's needs. Computers provide for information retrieval and bibliographic control of materials. Online services include access to hundreds of databases, which are available through systems such as Dialog, BRS, NEXIS, and LEXIS. The library's facilities and collection are available for the general public to use on-site during normal business hours.

* Beaches and Resort Weather Forecasts
Cape Cod, MA	(617) 771-0500
Key West, FL	(305) 296-2011
Miami, FL	(305) 661-5065
Myrtle Beach, SC	(803) 744-3207
Nags Head, NC	(919) 995-5610
Ocean City, MD	(301) 289-3223
Orlando, FL	(305) 851-7510
Rehoboth, DE	(302) 856-7633
St Augustine/Daytona, FL	(904) 252-5575
St Petersburg/Tampa, FL	(813) 645-2506
Virginia Beach, VA	(804) 853-3013

* Climatic Information
National Climatic Data Center
National Environmental Satellite, Data and Information Service
Department of Commerce
Federal Building
Asheville, NC 28801   (704) 259-0682
The National Climatic Data Center compiles and distributes global historical climate information. It is the collection center for all United States weather records and the world's largest climate data center. Many millions of weather facts are stored in NCDC's computer banks, available for quick response. Nearly one-third of the inquiries received are from attorneys seeking to establish circumstances surrounding legal events. Simple questions can be answered on the phone; however, those requests which need detailed digging may carry a research charge. Much data is available free or by fee in printed form.

* Cumulative Climatic Data Summaries
National Climatic Data Center
National Environmental Satellite, Data & Information Service
National Oceanic and Atmospheric Administration
Department of Commerce
Federal Building
Asheville, NC 28801   (704) 259-0682
Local Climatological Data is a monthly and annual publication for each of approximately 290 National Weather Service stations. Each issue includes daily and monthly temperatures, dew point temperatures, heating and cooling degree days, weather, precipitation, snowfall, pressure, wind, sunshine, and sky cover. Three-hourly weather observations and hourly precipitation data are also presented for most stations. *Climatological Data* is a monthly and annual publication issued for each state containing much the same information. Contact this office for current prices.

* Cyclones and Other Oceanographic Forecasts
National Oceanographic Data Center
National Oceanic and Atmospheric Administration
Universal Building Room 412
Washington, DC 20235   (202) 673-5549
The Mariners Weather Log is a unique source of information on marine weather and climate and their effects on operations at sea. Published quarterly by the National Oceanographic Data Center, the *Mariners Weather Log* provides comprehensive coverage of major storms of the North Atlantic and North Pacific, reports and annual summaries on tropical cyclones, information on the National Weather Service's Marine Observation Program, selected shipboard gale and wave observations, and general articles about weather and climate, hazards and safety precautions, and related marine lore. An annual subscription is available for $6 from the Superintendent of Documents, Government Printing Office, Washington, D.C. 20402; (202)783-3238.

* Environmental Satellite Systems

National Environmental Satellite,
Data And Information Service
National Oceanic and Atmospheric Administration
Department of Commerce
Federal Office Bldg. 4
Washington, DC 20233   (202) 763-4690

The National Environmental Satellite, Data and Information Service manages the nation's civil earth observing satellite systems for meteorology and oceanography. NESDIS operates low-altitude polar-orbiting satellites and high-altitude geostationary satellites which together monitor weather and surface conditions over the entire globe each day, providing advance warning of hurricanes, flash floods, and other severe weather conditions. Its satellites play an increasingly important role in monitoring global climate changes and such related phenomena as changes in ozone distribution over the Earth, plus changes in the marine environment. Contact this office for more information regarding satellite and data topics.

* Environmental Research Publications

Environmental Research Laboratories
National Oceanic and Atmospheric Administration
Department of Commerce
325 Broadway
Boulder, CO 80303   (303) 497-6286

As the research arm of NOAA, the Environmental Research Laboratories support the present responsibilities and the development of future services of NOAA. Programs include investigation of ocean processes and their interactions with the atmosphere; studies of the ocean environment as it is affected by waste disposal and development of energy and food resources; atmosphere and ocean research on weather and climate change; and much, much more. *Environmental Research Laboratories Publication Abstracts* lists all scientific and technical papers and reports available in a given year, as well as ordering information. The *Abstracts* are arranged alphabetically by Laboratory, and an author index is included.

* Floods: Audiovisuals

Public Affairs
National Weather Service
Department of Commerce
8060 13th. St., Room 1326
Silver Spring, MD 29010   (301) 427-8090

The National Weather Service has films, videotapes, slide programs, and informational pamphlets dealing with floods. Contact the Public Affairs Office for more information.

* Greenhouse Effect, Ozone and Related Research

Environmental Research Laboratories
National Oceanic and Atmospheric Administration
Department of Commerce
325 Broadway
Boulder, CO 80303   (303) 497-6286

The Environmental Research Laboratories conducts an integrated program of fundamental research, related technology development, and services to improve understanding and prediction of the geophysical environment comprising the oceans and inland waters, the lower and upper atmosphere, the space environment, and the Earth. Activities at its laboratories address such major areas as stratospheric and tropospheric ozone, the greenhouse effect and atmospheric chemistry, acid rain sources, transport and deposition, ocean role in climate, meteorological phenomena, solar disturbances, and computer modeling of oceanic conditions. Contact this office for more information about the Laboratories.

* Hurricanes and Tropical Weather Research

Environmental Research Laboratories
Atlantic Oceanographic and Meteorological Laboratory
National Oceanic and Atmospheric Administration
Department of Commerce
34301 Rickenbacher Causeway
Miami, FL 33149   (305) 361-4300

The Atlantic Oceanographic and Meteorological Laboratory performs tropical weather research to improve the description, understanding, and prediction of hurricanes, and to explore methods for modifying them. AOML's oceanographic studies focus on exchanges of energy and matter through the air-sea interface, and hydrothermal processes of mineralization at seafloor spreading centers. An annual report is available which describes the research conducted at AOML, including a listing of the technical reports published by AOML researchers.

* Mariners Weather Log

National Oceanographic Data Center
National Oceanic and Atmospheric Administration
Universal Building Room 412
Washington, DC 20235   (202) 673-5549

The Mariners Weather Log is a unique source of information on marine weather and climate and their effects on operations at sea. Published quarterly by the National Oceanographic Data Center, the *Mariners Weather Log* provides comprehensive coverage of major storms of the North Atlantic and North Pacific, reports and annual summaries on tropical cyclones, information on the National Weather Service's Marine Observation Program, selected shipboard gale and wave observations, and general articles about weather and climate, hazards and safety precautions, and related marine lore. An annual subscription is available for $6 from the Superintendent of Documents, Government Printing Office, Washington, D.C. 20402; (202)783-3238.

* Meteorological National Center

National Meteorological Center
National Weather Service
National Oceanic and Atmospheric Administration
Department of Commerce
5400 Auth Rd., Room 101
Camp Springs, MD 20033   (301) 763-8016

At the National Meteorological Center (NMC) in Maryland, more than 100,000 weather observations are incorporated daily into models of the atmosphere to produce weather forecasts from 48 hours to as far as 10 days ahead. Monthly and seasonal predictions of temperature and precipitation over North America also are produced. NMC guidance goes to National Weather Service facilities in every part of the nation where it helps meteorologists and hydrologists prepare local warnings and forecasts.

* Meteorologists Society

American Meteorological Society (AMS)
45 Beacon St.
Boston, MA 02108   (617) 227-2425

The American Meteorological Society certifies consulting meteorologists and grants a Seal of Approval to television and radio meteorologists. Publications: *Journal of Climate and Applied Meteorology, Journal of Atmospheric Sciences, Journal of Physical Oceanography, Meteorological and Geoastrophysical.*

* Meteorology and Climate Analysis

ASRL-Meteorology
Environmental Protection Agency
Research Triangle Park, NC 27711

This library's major field of interest is the meteorological aspects of air pollution, including model development and application, climatic analysis, and geophysical studies. The library holds a collection of climatic data material consisting of approximately 4,000 climatic data material reports on microfiche, over 400 rolls of film of synoptic data, surface and vorticity charts, and a large body of topographic maps.

* National Environmental Data Clearinghouse

NEDRES Office
National Oceanic And Atmospheric Administration
Department of Commerce
1825 Connecticut Ave., NW, Room 412
Washington, DC 20235   (202) 673-5548

The National Environmental Data Referral Service (NEDRES) is designed to provide convenient, economical, and efficient access to widely scattered environmental data. NEDRES is a publicly available service which identifies the existence, location, characteristics, and availablilty conditions of environmental data sets. NEDRES database contains only descriptions, not the actual data. It is a national network of federal, state, and private organizations cooperating to improve access to environmental data. Major subject categories include climatology and meteorology, oceanography, geophysics and geology, geography, hydrology and limnnology, terrestrial resources, toxic and regulated substances, and satellite remotely sensed data. NEDRES also produces the following printed catalogs with references to available environmental data on selected topics and regions:

Finding the Environmental Data You Need (free)
NEDRES Memorandum of Agreement (free)
NEDRES Database User Agreement (free)
NEDRES Data Base User Guide (7.50)
Guideline for the Description of Environmental Data Files for the Nedres Database (10.00)
North American Climatic Data Catalog: Part 1 (10.00)
North American Climatic Data Catalog: Part 2 (10.00)
Satellite Remote Sensing of the Marine Environment: Literature and Data Sources (10.00)
Coastal and Estuarine Waters of California, Oregon, and Washington (10.00)
Chesapeake Bay and Adjacent Wetlands
Chesapeake Bay Environmental Data Directory (free to federal and state agencies)
Environmental Data Review (free)

Weather and Maps

For more information on the NEDRES database and the user charges, contact the office listed above.

* Oceanographic Data and Publications

National Oceanic and Atmospheric Administration
Department of Commerce
1825 Connecticut Ave., NW
Washington, DC 20235   (202) 673-5549

The National Oceanographic Data Center has a free publications list which includes technical reports and bulletins, as well has a variety of data reports pertaining to oceanographic research.

* Oceanographic Information

National Oceanographic Data Center
National Environmental Satellite, Data
   and Information Service
National Oceanic and Atmospheric Administration
Department of Commerce
1825 Connecticut Ave., NW
Washington, DC 20235   (202) 673-5549

The National Oceanographic Data Center provides global coverage of oceanographic data and services. NODC's databases cover physical and chemical properties of the world's oceans, seas, and estuaries, plus information on selected continental shelf and coastal waters. Researchers using NODC data range from industrial scientists through local, state, and national government investigators, to university or academic personnel. Information is available in various forms: publications computer plots, computer printouts, magnetic tapes and floppy disks. Simple questions usually can be answered without charge by telephone or mail, but more complicated ones requiring research or computer processing usually carry a fee.

* Permafrost, Ice Age and Other Publications

Book and Report Sales
Box 25425
Denver, CO 80225   (303) 236-7476

This is a listing of some of the general interest publications available through the U.S. Geological Survey. They are free unless otherwise indicated.

The Great Ice Age
The Interior of the Earth
Landforms of the United States
Marine Geology: Research Beneath the Sea
Our Changing Continent
Permafrost
Geysers
Glaciers: A Water Resource

* Satellites and Other Instruments for

Atmosphere, Geodesy, Navigational Study
Office of Legislative Affairs
National Oceanic and Atmospheric Administration
Department of Commerce
14th St. and Constitution Ave., NW
Room 6228   (800) 648-6209
Washington, DC 20230   (202) 842-7460 (DC area)

The National Oceanic and Atmospheric Administration (NOAA) has a free *Product Information Catalog* (PIC) which lists over 600 products related to the atmosphere, oceans, navigation, fisheries, mammals, geodesy, satellites, and other environmental concerns. These products span the range from simple pamphlets to technical reports. Each listing includes price and ordering information. NOAA has designed a system, the NOAA Information Service (NIS) to provide high-speed, automated retrieval of the PIC via an electronic database management system. A NOAA Information Specialist will answer inquiries about NOAA products and services and make in-house referrals to technical representatives. Call (206) 526-9403 in Washington State.

* Satellite Data

National Climate Center
National Environmental Satellite, Data,
and Information Service
National Oceanic and Atmospheric Administration
Department of Commerce
World Weather Building, Room 100
Washington, DC 20233   (301) 763-8111

The Satellite Data Services Division (SDSD) of the National Climatic Data Center manages a database of environmental satellite data and information and provides products from this database to requesters. A unique source of data and information, the environmental database contains film imagery and digital data collected by a number of environmental satellites from 1960 to the present. It includes data from NOAA's operational environmental satellites and selected data from NASA and the Department of Defense. While much of the data is nominally meteorological, its oceanographic applications have been very extensive, and the data and information has been of interest to agronomists, hydrologists, and geologists. Contact the office listed above for more information on the data and services available.

* Space Environment Research

Space Environment Laboratory
Environmental Research Laboratories
National Oceanic and Atmospheric Administration
Department of Commerce
325 Broadway
Boulder, CO 80303   (303) 497-3313

The Space Environment Laboratory provides real-time space environment monitoring and forecasting services, develops techniques for improving forecasts of solar disturbances and their effect on the near-Earth space environment, and conducts research in solar-terrestrial physics. An annual report is available which goes into more detail about the Laboratory, the research conducted, and lists the technical reports published.

* Severe Storms Forecast Center

National Severe Storms Forecast Center
National Weather Service
National Oceanic and Atmospheric Administration
Department of Commerce
601 E. 12th St.
Kansas City, MO 64106   (816) 426-5922

The National Severe Storms Forecast Center is the office responsible for forecasting tornadoes and severe thunderstorms throughout the contiguous United States. In addition to this, NSSFC prepares aviation forecasts and advisories to aircraft in-flight, weather analyses based on interpretation of satellite data, and national weather summaries. The national weather summaries are issued twice daily and are distributed nationally for use by radio, television, newspapers, and other media interests. They are written in narrative form and contain information on significant weather that has occurred in the Nation. An extensive list of technical reports is available from NSSFC, most of which deal with tornado and severe thunderstorm forecasting.

* Solar Energy and Wind Information

National Climatic Data Center
National Oceanic and Atmospheric Administration
Department of Commerce
Federal Building
Asheville, NC 28801   (704) 259-0682

The National Climatic Data Center has a great deal of information regarding solar energy and wind data. Information includes solar radiation averages, measurements, and sunshine averages, as well as wind statistics. Reference manuals and indexes are also available. Prices vary depending upon the information requested. The Center can provide you with more detailed information regarding the data available.

* Storms and Natural Disaster Detection

National Ocean Service
National Oceanic and Atmospheric Administration
Department of Commerce
6001 Executive Blvd.
Rockville, MD 20852   (301) 443-8487

The Office of Oceanography and Marine Assessments surveys and monitors the oceans, U.S. coastal waters, estuarine waterways, and the Great Lakes to produce data and information products that describe the physical properties of these waters for a wide range of engineering and navigational applications. This office also conducts studies to assess the environmental impact of human activities in U.S. coastal waters. Many of these marine data and information products are essential for protecting life and property from storms and other destructive natural forces. Other marine products, such as predictions of the times and heights of tides and descriptions of tidal currents, are vital for safe navigation.

* Undersea Research

National Undersea Research Program
National Oceanic and Atmospheric Administration
Department of Commerce
6010 Executive Blvd.
Rockville, MD 20852   (301) 443-8391

The National Undersea Research Program develops programs and provides support to scientists and engineers for the study of biological, chemical, geological, and physical processes in the world's oceans and lakes. NURP assist researchers in conducting what are considered by NOAA and the marine community to be crucial research programs. In order to execute these programs, NURP provides investigators with a suite of the modern undersea facilities including submersibles, habitats, air and mixed gas SCUBA, and remotely operated vehicles. A major part of the research program is carried out by a network of National Undersea Research Centers. Contact this office for more information on the research conducted or the research centers.

* Weather Data Archive and Analyses

Selective Guide to Climatic Data Sources
National Climatic Data Center
National Oceanic and Atmospheric Administration
Department of Commerce
Federal Building
Asheville, NC 28801   (704) 259-0682

The *Selective Guide to Climatic Data Sources* is designed to assist potential users of climatological information by acquainting them with the various forms in which these data are archived and the products or publications that are prepared from these data. Each listing contains the file name, format, contents, and an abstract. The Data Center also has the ability to prepare other statistical tabulations, climatological analyses, and special studies other than those listed in the *Guide*. Further information on the cost for preparing such specialized products, or the cost for items listed in the *Guide*, may be obtained from the Data Center. A meteorologist is available to assist you in locating appropriate data or answering your questions.

* Weather Films and Publications

National Weather Service
National Oceanic and Atmospheric Administration
Department of Commerce
8060 13th St., Room 1326
Silver Spring, MD 20910   (301) 427-8090

A list of films, videotapes, and slides, as well as brochures is available from the National Weather Service. These publications deal with tornados, thunderstorms, floods, and hurricanes. Contact this office for your free list.

* Weather Forecasts

National Weather Service
National Oceanic and Atmospheric Administration
Department of Commerce
8060 13th St., Room 1326
Silver Spring, MD 20910   (301) 427-8090

A listing is available of the weather information phone numbers for major cities throughout the U.S., as well as several resort towns. Recordings are available at most National Weather Service offices. For a listing of these phone numbers, see the city's telephone directory under "United States Government, Department of Commerce, National Weather Service" or "Weather." Large capacity weather information recordings are operated by telephone companies at some locations with forecasts supplied by the National Weather Service. For these listings, turn back to the first page of this chapter.

* Weather Maps

Public Affairs
National Oceanic and Atmospheric Administration
Department of Commerce
14th St. and Constitution Ave., NW
Room 6013
Washington, DC 20230   (202) 377-8090

This office has free copies of the weekly series of daily weather maps. The maps include the highest and lowest temperatures chart, and the precipitation areas and amounts chart. Annual subscriptions are available for $60 per year. Contact the Public Affairs Office for more information.

* Weather Forecasts for U.S. Cities

Albany, NY	(518) 476-1122
Albuquerque, NM	(505) 243-1371
Atlanta, GA	(404) 936-1111
Birmingham, AL	(205) 942-8430
Bismarck, ND	(701) 223-3700
Boise, ID	(208) 342-8303

Boston, MA	(617) 567-4670
Buffalo, NY	(716) 634-1615
Caribou, ME	(207) 496-8931
Charleston, WV	(304) 344-9811
Cheyenne, WY	(307) 635-9901
Chicago, IL	(312) 298-1413
Cincinnati, OH	(513) 241-1010
Cleveland, OH	(216) 931-1212
Columbia, SC	(803) 796-8710
Denver, CO	(303) 639-1212
Des Moines, IA	(515) 288-1047
Detroit, MI	(313) 941-7192
Elko, NV	(702) 738-3018
El Paso, TX	(915) 778-9343
Eugene, OR	(503) 484-1200
Fort Worth, TX	(817) 336-4416
Great Falls, MT	(406) 453-5469
Indianapolis, IN	(317) 222-2362
International Falls, MN	(218) 283-4615
Jackson, MS	(601) 936-2121
Jacksonville, FL	(904) 757-3311
Little Rock, AR	(501) 834-0316
Los Angeles, CA	(213) 554-1212
Louisville, KY	(502) 363-9655
Lubbock, TX	(806) 762-0141
Memphis, TN	(901) 757-6400
Miami, FL	(305) 661-5065
Milwaukee, WI	(414) 744-8000
Minneapolis, MN	(612) 452-2323
New Orleans, LA	(504) 465-9212
New York City, NY	(212) 315-2705
Oklahoma City, OK	(405) 360-8106
Omaha, NE	(402) 571-8111
Philadelphia, PA	(215) 627-5578
Phoenix, AZ	(602) 957-8700
Pittsburgh, PA	(412) 644-2881
Portland, ME	(207) 775-7781
Portland, OR	(503) 236-7575
Raleigh, NC	(919) 860-1234
Redding, CA	(916) 221-5613
Reno, NV	(702) 793-1300
Salt Lake City, UT	(801) 575-7669
San Antonio, TX	(512) 828-3384
San Francisco, CA	(415) 936-1212
Savannah, GA	(912) 964-1700
Seattle, WA	(206) 526-6087
Sheridan, WY	(307) 672-2345
Shreveport, LA	(318) 635-7575
Sioux Falls, SD	(314) 928-1198
St. Louis, MO	(314) 928-1198
Topeka, KS	(913) 234-2592
Washington, DC	(202) 936-1212
Wichita, KS	(316) 942-3102

* World Climate Data

National Climatic Data Center
National Oceanic And Atmospheric Administration
Department of Commerce
Federal Building
Asheville, NC 28801   (704) 259-0682

The National Climatic Data Center has a wide variety of world climate data sources, some of which include *Climates of the World, World Weather Records, Monthly Climatic Data for the World, Defense Department Foreign Data*, and *Foreign Data Publications Collection*. They also have several guides and catalogs on world weather. Contact the Center for more information on these and other publications and their current price list.

Maps and Geography

* Aeronautical Charts

Chart Distribution Branch
National Ocean Service
National Oceanic and Atmospheric Administration
U.S. Department of Commerce
Riverdale, MD 20737   (301) 436-6990

The National Ocean Service Distribution Branch provides NOAA aeronautical charts and chart-related publication for the U.S. Air Space System. NOAA aeronautical charts depict navigation data and flight regulation information critically important for flight planning, flight navigation, landings and take-offs, and air traffic control. The *Catalog of Aeronautical Charts and Related Publications* contains a brief description of each aeronautical chart and chart-related publication produced by the NOS, as well as aeronautical charts produced by the U.S. Defense Mapping Agency for civilian use. It also includes the price of the chart or publication, other information needed to select and order aeronautical chart products, and a list of NOAA chart sales facilities and authorized commercial chart sales agents.

* Airborne-Geophysical Information

Branch of Geophysics
U.S. Geological Survey
MS 964, Box 25046
Denver Federal Center
Denver, CO 80225   (303) 236-1343

State index maps and information about available aeromagnetic and aerodiometric maps and profiles can be obtained from this office.

* Antarctic Maps

Distribution Branch
U.S. Geological Survey
Building 810
Denver Federal Center, Box 25286
Denver, CO 80225   (800) USA-MAPS

Antarctic maps are available that show contour intervals of 200 meters and bathymetric information for coastal areas. The 1:250,000 -scale topographic maps are the primary map source for the planning, logistic support, and multidisciplinary investigations of the U.S. Antarctic Research Program. In the 1:500,000 series, the satellite imagery was recorded by NASA's Landsat, including the coastal areas of Wilkes Land and Enderby Land.

* Atlas of Military Installations in U.S.

Directorate for Information Operations and Reports
Washington Headquarters Services
1215 Jefferson Davis Hwy., Suite 1204
Arlington, VA 22202   (202) 746-0786

The *Atlas/Data Abstract for the United States and Selected Areas* contains a map showing all the military installations and a compendium of Department of Defense statistics for each state. Write or call for their free catalog list all their publications available through the Government Printing Office.

* Automatic Mapping Program

National Technical Information Service
U.S. Department of Commerce
5285 Port Royal Road
Springfield, VA 22151   (703) 487-4650

The Cartographic Automatic Mapping Program performs many cartographic functions and can be used in conjunction with the World Data Bank II noted below. CAM software, microfiche, and documents are available from NTIS.

* Cadastral Survey Publications

Branch of Cadastral Survey Development, SC 678
Bureau of Land Management Service Center
U.S Department of the Interior
Denver Federal Center, Bldg. 50
P.O. Box 25047
Denver, CO 80225-0047

The following publications on surveying are available from this office:

Surveying Our Public Lands. Informative account of survey history, the growth of the public domain, the rectangular survey system, and the role of the federal cadastral surveyor (Free, #P-25).

Surveys and Surveyors of the Public Domain. To be used as an aid in training cadastral surveyors in the application of surveying principles, survey laws and their formation, and a study of the people who performed the surveys ($8.00, #P-140).

Preparation of Special Instructions. A required quasi-legal document authorizing a cadastral survey or resurvey. This book contains important guidelines for the proper and adequate preparation of this and other related documents ($1.85, #P-171).

Durability of Bearing Trees. Prepared as a guide for cadastral surveyors and others involved in the search for old bearing trees as well as identifying and evaluating various species of trees for marking new bearing trees ($1.40).

Manual of Surveying Instructions, 1973. Describes in detail all aspects of how cadastral surveys are made in conformance to statutory law and its judicial interpretation ($16.00, Superintendent of Documents, Government Printing Office, S/N 024-011-00052-6).

Selected Computations of Astronomical Computations. Discusses the following topics: Motion of the Earth, Solar Time, Sidereal Time, 24-Hour Clock, Time Signals, Azimuth Determination, Polaris, Selected Examples for Azimuth Determination - Sun, Polaris Observation for Azimuth, Equatorial Star Identification Equatorial Star/Hour Angle Observation (Free, #T/N 318).

* Cartographic Archives

Cartographic and Architectural Branch
Special Archives Division
National Archives and Records Administration
8th St. & Pennsylvania Ave., NW
Washington, DC 20408   (703) 756-6700

The Cartographic and Architectural Branch has over 11 million maps, charts, aerial photographs, architectural drawings, patents, and ship plans, which constitute one of the world's largest accumulations of such documents. The Branch holds architectural and engineering drawings created by civilian and military agencies. All the holdings can be examined in the research room at 841 South Pickett St., Alexandria, VA, from 8:00 a.m. to 4:30 p.m., Monday through Friday. Reproductions can be furnished for a fee.

* Cartographic Research and Experimental Maps

Geographic and Cartographic Research
National Mapping Division
U.S. Geological Survey
National Center, MS 521
Reston, VA 22092   (703) 648-4505

The U.S. Geological Survey acquires, stores, and uses geographic data in studies that combine geographic analyses with new cartographic concepts and techniques. New types of cartographic data and experimental maps result and are used to solve environmental problems and to aid in resource management.

* Central Cartographer: Defense Mapping Agency

Defense Mapping Agency
Combat Support Center
Attn: Customer Assistance Office
Washington, DC 20315-0010 (301) 227-2495; or toll free: (800) 826-0342

The Defense Mapping Agency makes available at cost a broad range of maps and charts. There are four categories available: aeronautical, topographic, hydrographic, and digital (lists those products available on magnetic tape). Each map costs $2.75 each. Write or call to order copies.

* China Map

Public Affairs Office
Central Intelligence Agency
Washington, DC 20505   (703) 351-2053

The Central Intelligence Agency Cartographic Automated Mapping Program and World Data Bank have generated a one-page multi-colored map which incorporates the new Pinyin (phonetic alphabet) spelling of names that became effective in 1979. The gazetteer on the reverse side of the map includes both the Pinyin and Wade-Giles rendition of geographic names. This Pinyin Edition (S/N 041-015-00106-0) can be purchased from the Government Printing Office, Washington, DC 20402; (202) 783-3238.

* CIA Catalog of Declassified Maps
Public Affairs
Central Intelligence Agency
Washington, DC 20505 (703) 351-2053
The CIA declassifies many of its maps which are available from the National Technical Information Service, 5285 Port Royal Road, Springfield, VA 22161 (703) 487-4650. The catalog, titled *CIA Maps and Publications Released to the Public*, is available free from the CIA.

* CIA World and Country Maps
Public Affairs
Central Intelligence Agency
Washington, DC 20505 (703) 351-2053
Hundreds of maps generated by the Central Intelligence Agency are sold through NTIS. There are country maps as well as maps of continents are available. smaller geographical areas and city maps such as Moscow and Vicinity; Middle East Area Oilfields and Facilities; Israeli Settlement in the Gaza Strip; South Africa: Industrial Activity and Production; Africa Ethnolinguistic Groups.

* Comet Haley Atlas
Superintendent of Documents
Government Printing Office
Washington, DC 20402 (202) 783-3238
Census statistics publications are listed in this bibliography. One may send for the Railroad Maps of North America, featuring 5,000 maps and surveys. Weather and political atlases are listed, as well as an atlas to the Comet Haley. Free.

* Digital Cartography
Earth Science Information Center
U.S. Geological Survey
507 National Center
Reston, VA 22092 (703) 648-6045
U.S. Geodata is the effort of the U.S. Geological Survey to expand its mapping program with digital cartography, involving the collection, storage, processing, analysis, and display of map data with the aid of computers. This includes a collection of planimetric, elevation, and geographic names information. This data may be combined with other data for cartographic applications. Users are able to plot their own maps with appropriate software. Calculations can be performed related to spatial analysis.

* Digital Spatial Data and Mapping Software
U.S. Geological Survey
Reston-ESIC
507 National Center
Reston, VA 22092 (703) 648-6045
The U.S. Geological Survey's Earth Science Information Center (ESIC) now offers inventories of digital spatial data sets and cartographic applications software in two bound listings. These inventories provide up-to-date bibliographic descriptions of data sets and software available from federal, state, and local government agencies and the private sector.

Sources for Digital Spatial Data. Describes more than 500 data sets containing spatially referenced base or thematic categories of data. The data sets are indexed by geographic area of coverage and cross-indexed by type of data.

Sources for Software for Computer Mapping and Related Disciplines. Describes more than 700 subroutines, programs, and systems that can be used in geographic information systems, map and chart plotting and construction, image processing and analysis, surveying, photogrammetry, data modeling and analysis, coordinate conversion, and other applications. Each publication is $22.

* Digital Spatial Data Applications Cooperation
U.S. Geological Survey
Reston-ESIC
507 National Center
Reston, VA 22092 (703) 648-6899
If your organization is involved in digital spatial data applications, the Earth Science Information Center invites you to contribute information about your holdings. Your data and software may be valuable to other users.

* Earth Observation System
Customer User Services
Earth Resources Observation System Data Center (EROS)
U.S. Geological Survey
Sioux Falls, SD 57198 (605) 594-6511
Aerial photographs are available from this center for most geographical regions of the country. Prices range from $6 to $65, depending on whether they are black and white or color photographs. Contact this office for ordering information.

* Earth-Science Films
Visual Information Services Group
U.S. Geological Survey
790 National Center
Reston, VA 22092 (703) 648-4376
The Visual Information Services Group provides earth-science movies on a free-loan, short-term (2 or 3 day) basis to educational institutions and professional and scientific societies.

* Geographic Boundaries and International Disputes
Office of the Geographer
Bureau of Intelligence and Research
Department of State
2201 C St., NW, Room 8742
Washington, DC 20520 (202) 647-2022
This office distributes several publications which contain a variety of geographical information. Some of them include:

Geographic Notes. Contains brief analyses of current issues relevant to United States foreign policy. These analyses provide a geographical perspective on such foreign policy-related topics such as boundary, sovereignty, and territorial disputes.
International Boundary Studies. This is a series of specific boundary papers.

* Geographic Data and Research
Geographic and Cartographic Research
National Mapping Division
U.S. Geological Survey
National Center, MS 521
Reston, VA 22092 (703) 648-4505
The U.S. Geological Survey acquires, stores, and uses geographic data in studies that combine geographic analyses with new cartographic concepts and techniques. New types of cartographic data and experimental maps result and are used to solve environmental problems and to aid in resource management.

* Geographic Names Information
Branch of Geographic Names
U.S. Geological Survey
National Center, MS 523
Reston, VA 22092 (703) 648-4547
The USGS Branch of Geographic Names maintains a national research, coordinating, and information center to which all problems and inquiries concerning domestic geographic names can be directed. This office compiles name information, manages a names data repository, maintains information files, and publishes materials on domestic geographic names. The USGS, in cooperation with the Board on Geographic Names, maintains the *National Geographic Names Data Base* and compiles *The National Gazetteer of the United States of America* on a state-by-state basis.

* Geological Cartography Exhibits
Exhibits Committee
U.S. Geological Survey
790 National Center
Reston, VA 22092 (703) 648-4357
Exhibits illustrating recent work in cartography, geography, geology, water resources, and other aspects of the USGS research are available to scientific associations for professional meetings and conferences. Contact this office for availability and scheduling information.

* Geological Survey Field Records Collection
Field Records
U.S. Geological Survey
MS 914, Building 20
Box 25046, Federal Center
Denver, CO 80225 (303) 236-1005
The Field Records collection consists of the original materials produced by the USGS during its field investigations. Holdings include 15,600 notebooks, 2,000 folders, 2,400 map groups, and 60,000 aerial photographs. Upon gaining approval, you may examine these records at the Denver Library or make arrangements for the materials to be sent to a more convenient USGS library.

* Geologic Maps Hotline
Distribution Branch
U.S. Geological Survey
Building 810
Denver Federal Center, Box 25286
Denver, CO 80225 (800) USA-MAPS

Weather and Maps

Geologic maps are made by USGS as part of a continuing program of examining geological structure, mineral resources, and products. These maps range in scale from 1:20,000 to 1:2,5000,000, depending on the type of information shown.

Geologic Quadrangle Maps. Show the bedrock, surficial, or engineering geology of selected quadrangles in the United States.
Black-and-White or Multicolor Miscellaneous Field Studies Maps. Are preliminary reports on geologic aspects of mineral and environmental studies. *Mineral Investigations Resource Maps.* Feature mineral distribution of metallic and nonmetallic minerals.
Geophysical Investigations Maps. Show the results of surveys to measure geomagnetism, gravity, and radioactivity in selected areas of the country.
State Geologic Maps. Show rock types and named geologic units exposed at the surface, geologic faults, anticlines, and synclines.
Antarctic Geologic Maps. Define rock type and named units of exposed and inferred rocks in ice-free areas.
Oil, Gas, and Coal Investigations Maps.

* Geologic Names Committee
U.S. Geological Survey
National Center, MS 902
Reston, VA 22092   (703) 648-4311
The Geologic Names Committee defines and recommends policy and rules governing stratigraphic nomenclature and classification for the USGS. *Stratigraphic Notes* is published to announce changes in official geologic names usage. Lexicons are compiled that show domestic geologic names usage, and a file is maintained of geologic names reserved future use.

* Ground Water, Floods and Other Hydrologic Investigative Maps
Distribution Branch
U.S. Geological Survey
Building 810
Denver Federal Center, Box 25286
Denver, CO 80225   (800) USA-MAPS
Hydrologic investigations atlases are either black and white or multicolor maps showing a wide range of water-resources information, such as depth to ground water, floods, irrigated acreage, producing aquifers, availability of water on Indian lands, surface-water discharge to the oceans, chemical or mineral content of water, surface impoundments, and water temperature.

* Land Use and Land Cover Maps
Distribution Branch
U.S. Geological Survey
Building 810
Denver Federal Center, Box 25286
Denver, CO 80225   (800) USA-MAPS
Land use maps and land cover maps are available for most of the United States. Land use maps refer to human uses of the land (housing and industry) and land cover maps describe the vegetation, water, natural surface, and construction on the land surface. The scale used ranges from 1:100,000 for a few maps in the Western states to 1:250,000 for most other maps.

* Library of Congress Geography and Map Resources
Geography and Map Division
Library of Congress
Washington, DC 20540   (202) 707-6277
The Library's cartographic collections, which include 4 million maps, nearly 51,000 atlases, 500 globes, and some 8,000 reference books, are the largest and most comprehensive in the world. The collections include atlases published over the last five centuries covering individual continents, countries, states, counties, and cities as well as the world. Official topographic, geologic, soil, mineral, and resource maps and nautical and aeronautical charts are also available for most countries. There are also complete LANDSAT microimage data sets of images produced by several satellites revolving around the Earth. Subscription information on the microfiche data sets is available from EOSAT, 4300 Forbes Blvd., Lanham, MD 20706; (800) 344-9933.

* Mapping Research Reference Collection
National Mapping Division Research Reference Collection
U.S. Geological Survey
521 National Center
Reston, VA 22092   (703) 648-4562
The National Mapping Division Office of Research maintains a collection of over 3,000 technical reference works in the fields of cartography and geography. The collection also includes the National Mapping Division Historical Archives, containing over 150,000 sheets. Functioning primarily to support research of the National Mapping Division, it is also open for use by other USGS personnel and the public. Items may be borrowed by the public through inter-library loans at local libraries.

* Maps and Atlases: United States and Foreign
Superintendent of Documents
Government Printing Office
Washington, DC 20402   (202) 783-3238
Census statistics publications are listed in this bibliography. One may send for the Railroad Maps of North America, featuring 5,000 maps and surveys. Weather and political atlases are listed, as well as an atlas to the Comet Haley. Free.

* Maps of Moon and Planets
Distribution Branch
U.S. Geological Survey
Building 810
Denver Federal Center, Box 25286
Denver, CO 80225   (800) USA-MAPS
The USGS established an astrogeology program on behalf of NASA to support lunar and planetary exploration. Many maps of the Moon, Mars, Venus, and Mercury are available.

* Maps: Technical Information
Geologic Inquiries
U.S. Geological Survey
National Center, MS 907
Reston, VA 22092   (301) 648-4383
To obtain technical information on such geologic topics as earthquakes and volcanoes, energy and mineral resources, the geology of specific areas, and geologic maps, contact this office.

* Meteorological Topographic Maps
ASRL-Meteorology
Environmental Protection Agency
Research Triangle Park, NC 27711
This library's major field of interest is the meteorological aspects of air pollution, including model development and application, climatic analysis, and geophysical studies. The library holds a collection of climatic data material consisting of approximately 4,000 climatic data material reports on microfiche, over 400 rolls of film of synoptic data, surface and vorticity charts, and a large body of topographic maps.

* Mine Companies and Property Ownership Maps
Division of Program Information and Analysis
Surface Mining Reclamation and Enforcement
U.S. Department of the Interior
1951 Constitution Ave., NW
Washington, DC 20240   (202) 343-5907
Valuable information is available from the mine maps available through the mine map repositories of the Office of Surface Mining Reclamation and Enforcement. Mine and company names, water sources, property ownership of adjoining companies and towns, latitudes and longitudes, coal outcrop seam designations, openings and emergency exits of mines, and gas and power lines are some of the topics covered. This information can be useful to local developers, engineering firms, and energy interests, as well as private citizens.

* Mine Map Repositories
Office of Public Affairs
Surface Mining Reclamation and Enforcement
U.S. Department of the Interior
1951 Constitution Ave., NW
Washington, DC 20240   (202) 343-4953
The Mine Map Repositories were established in 1970 and are responsible for collecting and archiving mine maps both east and west of the Mississippi River and in Alaska. The brochure, *Mine Map Repositories*, provides information and statistics on the mine map repository facilities of the Office of Surface Mining Reclamation and Enforcement. The five repositories are listed with their addresses and phone numbers. They are located in Pittsburgh, PA, Wilkes-Barre, PA, Denver, CO, Spokane, WA, and Juneau, AK.

* National Atlas Updates
Distribution Branch
U.S. Geological Survey
Building 810
Denver Federal Center, Box 25286
Denver, CO 80225   (800) USA-MAPS
The *National Atlas of the United States* (1970) contains 765 maps and charts on 335 pages. Out of print and no longer for sale, it can still be found in most libraries. However, separate sheets of selected reference maps and thematic maps from the *Atlas* are available from the USGS. Some of the sheets have been updated. Some updated thematic maps include potential natural vegetation (1985), monthly average temperature (1986) monthly minimum temperature

(1986), monthly maximum temperature (1986), networks of ecological research (1983), and territorial growth (1986).

* National Gazetteer of the United States of America

Books and Open File Reports
U.S. Geological Survey
Box 25425, Federal Center
Denver, CO 80225 (303) 236-7476

The National Gazetteer of the United States of America is a geographic dictionary of place and feature names, published on a state-by-state basis. It includes a glossary of terms and abbreviations, a map of counties in a state, and an alphabetical listing of USGS topographic quadrangle maps of the state, in addition to the information contained in the *National Geographic Names Data Base*. Also listed are names of features from other historical sources. Variant names are listed and cross-referenced to their official names. A variant name is any other known name or spelling applied to a feature other than the official name.

* National Mapping Activities

National Mapping Division
U.S. Geological Survey
National Center, MS 516
Reston, VA 22092 (703) 648-5748

The National Mapping Program of the U.S. Geological Survey compiles, updates, and prints topographic maps as well as thematic maps that combine topographic data with other spatial data, such as geology, hydrology, rainfall, land use, and population. Four regional Mapping Centers, located in Reston, VA, Rolla, MO, Denver, CO, and Menlo Park, CA, are responsible for map production and for coordinating joint mapping activities with other Federal and State agencies. Maps are sold through the Earth Science Information Centers and through private dealers.

* National Mapping System

Distribution Branch
U.S. Geological Survey
Building 810
Denver Federal Center, Box 25286
Denver, CO 80225 (800) USA-MAPS

The USGS National Mapping System is a rich source of numerous types of maps. The brochure, *Catalog of Maps*, describes in detail the different maps available. Contact either the above office for a price list or one of the Earth-Science Information Centers for more information on the maps available.

* National Park Maps

Technical Information Center
National Park Service
Denver Service Center
12795 W. Alameda Parkway
P.O. Box 25287
Denver, CO 80225-0287 (303) 969-2130

The Technical Information Center has been designated by the National Park Service as the central repository for all National Park Service-generated planning, design, and construction maps, drawings, and reports as well as related cultural, environmental, and other technical documents. Bibliographic data on aerial photography is also maintained. The Center reproduces and delivers copies of the available materials for the Service, other agencies, and the public, both here and abroad. Today, the system has a holding of 100,000 data records, which represent about 500,000 microfilm aperture cards of maps, plans, and drawings; 1,000 records of resource and site aerial photography; and 25,000 planning, design, environmental, cultural resource, and natural resource documents.

* Nautical Charts

Chart Distribution Branch
National Ocean Service
National Oceanic and Atmospheric Administration
U.S. Department of Commerce
Riverdale, MD 20737 (301) 436-6990

The National Ocean Service produces approximately 1,000 nautical charts for navigation in U.S. estuarine waters and navigable inland waterways, the Great Lakes, and the 2 1/2 million square miles of coastal waters of the United States and its possessions. NOAA *Chart and Map Catalogs* describe nautical charts which are listed in a series of four catalogs, one for each region of the U.S. ocean and coastal waters. NOAA bathymetric maps and special purpose charts are listed in a single catalog. A sixth catalog is a guide to NOAA nautical products and services. The catalogs contain a brief description of each nautical chart, bathymetric map, special purpose chart, and chart-related publication produced by the NOS. They also include the price of the chart of publication, other information needed to select and order nautical charting products, and a list of NOAA chart sales facilities and authorized commercial chart sales agents. Contact this office for your free catalogs.

* Photoimage Maps

Distribution Branch
U.S. Geological Survey
Building 810
Denver Federal Center, Box 25286
Denver, CO 80225 (800) USA-MAPS

Photoimage maps are published in three types: orthophotomaps, orthoquads, and border maps of US./Mexico and U.S/Canada. Satellite (Landsat) image maps are multi-color photograph-like maps made from data collected by Earth resources satellites. They are available for selected areas in about half of the states, along with such areas as Antarctica, the Bahamas, and Iceland.

* Portraits of the Earth

U.S. Geological Survey
Book and Report Sales
Box 25425
Denver, CO 80225 (303) 236-7476

Geologic Maps: Portraits of the Earth is one of many maps available from the U.S. Geological Survey.

* Railroad Maps of North America

Superintendent of Documents
Government Printing Office
Washington, DC 20402 (202) 783-3238

Census statistics publications are listed in this bibliography. One may send for the Railroad Maps of North America, featuring 5,000 maps and surveys. Weather and political atlases are listed, as well as an atlas to the Comet Haley. Free.

* Scholarly Sources on Cartography

Smithsonian Institution Press
Dept. 900
Blue Ridge Summit, PA 17214 (717) 794-2148

Produced by the Woodrow Wilson International Center for Scholars, the *Guides to Scholarly Sources* are designed to be descriptive, evaluative surveys of source materials. The Guide titled *Cartography and Remote Sensing* is divided into two parts. Part I examines area collections - libraries; archives and manuscript depositories; art, film, music, and map collections; and data banks. Part II focuses on pertinent activities of Washington-based organizations, public and private. Given for each are its related functions, materials and products.

* Space Photographs

Customer Services
Earth Resources Observation System Data Center (EROS)
U.S. Geological Survey
Sioux Falls, SD 57198 (605) 594-6511

The EROS Data Center maintains photographs from many of the space missions, including those of the space shuttle, Apollo, and Gemini. Contact the center directly for information concerning specific topics.

* State Topographic Maps

Earth Science Information Center
U.S. Geological Survey
507 National Center
Reston, VA 22092 (703) 648-6045

Two types of directories are now available listing topographic maps for each state. *An Index to Topographic and Other Map Coverage* and its companion, *Catalog of Topographic and Other Published Maps*, contain information on the types of state maps that are available. The *Index* shows you how to locate your general area of interest and then the specific location and name of the area for which you want a map in each state. The *Catalog* lists cities and geographic areas for which maps are available.

* Topographic and Topographic-Bathymetric Maps

Distribution Branch
U.S. Geological Survey
Building 810
Denver Federal Center, Box 25286
Denver, CO 80225 (800) USA-MAPS

Topographic maps of the USGS use brown contours to show the shape and elevation of the terrain. The maps show and name prominent natural and man-made features. The best known USGS maps are those of the 7.5-minute, 1:24,000-scale quadrangle series. Fifteen-minute maps are also available, particularly for the Hawaiian Islands, but some detail is omitted or generalized. Other topographic maps include the U.S. 1:100,000 scale series, county map series, U.S. 1:250,000-scale series, state map series, National Park series, and shaded-relief maps.

On the topographic-bathymetric maps, contour lines show elevations of the land areas above sea level, and isobaths (depth contours) show the form of the land below the water. Some bathymetric maps also show magnetic and gravity data.

Weather and Maps

The combined map serves the needs of oceanographers, marine geologists, land use planners, physical scientists, conservationists, and others having an interest in management of the coastal zone, the wetlands, and the offshore environment.

* U.S. Geological Survey Photographs

Photographic Library, MS 914
U.S. Geological Survey
Box 25046, Federal Center
Denver, CO 80225   (303) 236-1010

The Photographic Library of the U.S. Geological Survey contains a special collection of approximately 250,000 photographs. The Library may be used by the public as well as by personnel of other government agencies. Persons who wish to obtain prints, copy negatives, and duplicate transparencies from the collection are encouraged to visit the library. If this is not possible, the staff will prepare lists of specific photographs in response to requests. Many photographs are selected by searching U.S. Geological Survey publications and are identified by title and number of the publication as well as the number of the page and plate of the figure found. To obtain information on purchasing prints, negatives, or transparencies, contact the library directly.

* U.S. Geological Survey: New Publications

Branch of Data Systems
U.S. Geological Survey
National Center, MS 582
Reston, VA 22092   (703) 648-6045

New Publications of the U.S. Geological Survey is a free monthly catalog of new publications released by the U.S. Geological Survey. To be placed on the mailing list, contact the office above.

* Weather Maps

Public Affairs
National Oceanic and Atmospheric Administration
U.S. Department of Commerce
14th St. and Constitution Ave., NW
Room 6013
Washington, DC 20230   (202) 377-8090

This office has free copies of the weekly series of daily weather maps. The maps include the highest and lowest temperatures chart, and the precipitation areas and amounts chart. Annual subscriptions are available for $60 per year. Contact the Public Affairs Office for more information.

* World Data Bank II

National Technical Information Service
U.S. Department of Commerce
5285 Port Royal Road
Springfield, VA 22151   (703) 487-4650

The CIA produced a cartographic data base which represents natural and man-made features of the world in a digital format. Approximately six million points are contained on five separate geographic area files. All four volumes (PB 87-184-768) on magnetic tape can be purchased from NTIS.

Environment and Nature
General Sources

* See also Careers and Workplace; Research Grants in Every Field Chapter
* See also Current Events and Homework Chapter
* See also Energy Chapter
* See also Health and Medicine Chapter
* See also Vacations and Business Travel Chapter

Ozone depletion, dioxins, chemical dumps, medical waste, and the disappearance of tropical rain forests are just a few of the environmental issues making news headlines daily. These and other topics, including the tug-of-war between conservation and development, are covered in this chapter. Besides the hundreds of Environmental Protection Agency sources, you'll also find several interest and lobby groups which are useful sources on practically any environmental issue, from details about proposed Clean Air Act amendments to municipal garbage incinerators and indoor air quality. Bird watchers and naturalists will find a complete state-by-state listing of the National Wildlife Refuges here, but should also browse through the Vacations and Business Travel Chapter for information on National Parks and other points of interest.

* Acoustical and Noise Control
National Association of Noise Control Officials (NANCO)
53 Cubberley Rd.
Trenton, NJ 08618   (609) 984-4161
The National Association of Noise Control Officials consists of employees of the federal and state governments, consultants, scientists and students concerned with acoustical control in the environment. Publications: *Vibrations*.

* Agricultural Environmental Engineering
American Society of Agricultural Engineers (ASAE)
2950 Niles Rd.
St. Joseph, MI 49085   (616) 429-0300
The American Society of Agricultural Engineers is the national association for engineers working on problems of importance to agricultural interests including irrigation and other large scale projects with environmental significance. Publications: *Agricultural Engineering, ASAE Standards, Transactions of the ASAE*.

* Aircraft Noise
Noise Abatement Division
Office of Environment and Energy
Federal Aviation Administration
U.S. Department of Transportation
800 Independence Ave., SW, Room 432
Washington, DC 20591   (202) 267-3553
This FAA division conducts research on reducing noise levels of new aircraft, and retrofitting older aircraft to reduce noise levels.

* Arctic and Antarctic Science Stations
Office of Polar Affairs
Bureau of Oceans and International Environmental
    and Scientific Affairs
Department of State
2201 C St., NW, Room 5801
Washington, DC 20520   (202) 647-3262
This office is concerned with all issues concerning the Arctic and Antarctic, including the environment and marine life, such as whales and seals. They are also closely involved with the many science stations located on the Antarctic.

* Army Corps of Engineers Publications
U.S. Army Corps of Engineers
Public Affairs
20 Massachusetts Ave., NW
Washington, DC 20314   (202) 272-0011
The Corps offers free brochures on a wide variety of subjects, including archaeology, camping, environment, erosion control, flood control, flood plain management, history, safety, waste-water treatment and water supply. For a publications list, call or write the above office.

* Artificial Light and Bio-Environmental Research
International Bio-Environmental Foundation
15300 Ventura
Suite 405
Sherman Oaks, CA 91436   (818) 907-5483
The International Bio-Environmental Foundation consists of scientists studying the biological effects of atmospheric ions, electromagnetic fields, noise and artificial light.

* Asbestos Ombudsman Clearinghouse
Environmental Protection Agency
401 M St., SW   (800) 368-5888
Washington DC 20460   (703) 557-1938 (in VA)
The assigned mission of the Asbestos Ombudsman Clearinghouse is to provide to the public sector, including individual citizens and community services, information on handling and abatement of asbestos in schools, the workplace, and the home. In addition, interpretation of the asbestos-in-school requirements, and publications are provided to explain recent legislation. More specifically, the EPA Asbestos Ombudsman receives complaints and requests for information and provides assistance with regard to them.

* Asbestos Quality Assurance Lab and Hotline
Asbestos Technical Information Service   (800) 334-8571/Ext. 6741
The Asbestos Technical Information Service is part of the Quality Assurance Program in Bulk Asbestos Analysis Sampling at Research Triangle Park. It is a service for laboratories in need of technical information on asbestos. The service will also direct private citizens who have general questions concerning asbestos to the proper channels.

* Asbestos Regulations
Toxic Substances Control Act Information
Environmental Protection Agency
401 M St., SW
Washington DC 20460   (202) 554-1404
This service can provide you with technical information on asbestos, as well information on regulations and publications.

* Attorneys General Environmental Enforcement
National Association of Attorneys General
444 North Capitol St., NW
Suite 403
Washington, DC 20001   (202) 628-0435
The National Association of Attorneys General provides a forum for the exchange of information and experience among chief legal officers of the fifty states and five other jurisdictions; fosters interstate cooperation on legal and law enforcement issues; and conducts policy research and analysis of issues pertaining to the states and territories.

Environment and Nature

* Automated Laboratory Library
Central Regional Laboratory (CRL) Library
839 Bestgate Rd.
Annapolis, MD 21401 (301) 388-2090
This library was established in support of the Regional Laboratory which started in Annapolis in 1964. The subjects in the collection focus on biology, chemistry, ecology, engineering, hazardous waste hydrology, and oceanography. To serve the highly diversified expertise of the laboratory scientists and engineers, material is provided in aquatic biology, analytical chemistry, automated laboratory techniques, industrial wastewater monitoring, toxic and hazardous substances, and mathematical modelling. A special collections covers the Chesapeake Bay.

* Basic Sciences Clearinghouse
Library Services Office
Research Triangle Park, NC 27711 (919) 541-2777
The Research Triangle Park (RTP) library's collection concentrates on chemical toxicity, all aspects of air pollution as well as the basic sciences, with some coverage of business and economics. Databases maintained here include BRS, CAS On-line, DIALOG, Hazardline, Hazardous Waste Database, and NLM.

* Business Community and Environmental Concerns
Chamber of Commerce of the United States
1615 H St., NW
Washington, DC 20062 (202) 659-6000
The Chamber of Commerce is generally regarded as the spokesgroup for United States business. It is the world's largest business federation composed of more than 180,000 companies plus several thousand other organizations such as local and state chambers of commerce and trade and professional associations. It has an environmental department. Publications: *Nation's Business, The Business Advocate.*

* Clearinghouse
Office of Information Resources Management
Environmental Protection Agency
401 M St., SW, PM-218B
Washington DC 20460 (202) 382-5224
The EPA's *Information Resources Directory* (IRD) includes both descriptive subject and programmatic listings of EPA databases and models, hotlines and clearinghouses, dockets and libraries, documents, and individual contacts. Where appropriate, it also lists selected environmental information resources outside of the Agency. The first page of each section gives a synopsis of the type of information found in the section, describes how the information is arranged, provides a sample entry, and lists sources. This a free publication from the office above.

* Coastal Zone Management
Office of Ocean and Coastal Resource Management
National Ocean Service
National Oceanic and Atmospheric Administration
Department of Commerce
1825 Connecticut Ave., NW, Room 706
Washington, DC 20235 (202) 673-5111
To balance the needs for preserving and developing the resources in the U.S. coastal zone, the National Ocean Service, through its Office of Ocean and Coastal Resource Management, provides the coordination and expertise at the Federal level needed for effective management of these coastal resources. NOS has begun to expand the technical assistance provided to States and territories, emphasizing special area management planning, coastal hazards mitigation, cost-effective coastal management, and the simplification of permit processes for coastal activities.

* Coast Guard Environmental Protection
Planning Branch
Research and Development Staff
Office of Engineering and Development
U.S. Coast Guard
U.S. Department of Transportation
2100 2nd St., SW, Room 6208
Washington, DC 20593-0001 (202) 267-1030
Information can be obtained here about research conducted by the Coast Guard in support of its operations and responsibilities. Areas of study include ice operations, ocean dumping, law enforcement, environmental protection, port safety and security, navigation aids, search and rescue procedures, recreational boating, energy, and advanced marine vehicles. For referral to specific personnel working in these areas, contact the Planning Branch.

* Community-College Environmental Curricula Grants
National Workforce Development Staff
Office of Research and Development
Environmental Protection Agency
401 M St., SW, Room NE312
Washington DC 20460 (202) 382-2573
The National Workforce Development Staff awards money to community colleges to support the development of environment-related curriculum, allowing these colleges to then train State employees. The office also awards fellowships to State employees to continue their education concerning the environment. The fellowship applications are given out through the individual States. Contact this office for more information.

* Conservation and Environmental Trends
Conservation Foundation, The
255 23rd St., NW
Washington, DC 20037 (202) 293-4800
The Conservation Foundation is a research and public education organization promoting wise use of the earth's resources. It conducts research and educational programs in land use, air pollution control, toxic substances, water resources, environmental dispute resolution, and reports periodically on environmental conditions and trends. Publications: *Conservation Foundation Letter.*

* Conservation Districts
National Association of Conservation Districts
1025 Vermont Ave., NW
Suite 730
Washington, DC 20005 (202) 346-5995
The National Association of Conservation Districts has a membership consisting of local subdivisions of governments which work to conserve and develop land, water, forests, wildlife, and related natural resources.

* Consumer Publications
Public Information Center
Environmental Protection Agency
401 M St., SW, PM-211 B
Washington DC 20460 (202) 475-7751
The EPA's Public Information Center maintains a wide selection of publications on major environmental topics. The materials distributed by the Center are nontechnical and have been prepared as sources of general environmental information for the public. Technical documents are available through the EPA Library, the National Technical Information Service, or the publishing office within EPA. The *Public Information Center Publications List* is updated monthly and is free.

* County Governments Environmental Activities
National Association of Counties (NACo)
440 1st St., NW
8th Floor
Washington, DC 20001 (202) 393-6226
NACO serves as a forum for improving the nation's county governments and to communicate the county viewpoint to national officials. NACo acts as a liaison with other levels of government, serves as a national advocate for counties, and achieves a public understanding of the role of counties in the intergovernmental system.

* Dial-A-Regulation
Environmental Protection Agency
401 M St., SW, Room W1035
Washington DC 20460 (202) 523-5022
A recorded message of *Federal Register* highlights gives a summary of documents appearing in the next day's issue, including new regulations.

* Drinking Water Programs
Office of Drinking Water
Environmental Protection Agency
401 M St., SW, Room E1011
Washington, DC 20460 (202) 382-5543
This EPA office develops national programs, technical policies, and regulations for water pollution control and water supply. It also administers part of the Safe Drinking Water Act.

* Ecological Modeling
International Society for Ecological Modeling
North American Chapter
School of Natural Resources
Ohio State University
Columbus, OH 43210 (614) 292-2265
This society consists of individuals interested in constructing mathematical models of air, water, and environmental pollution problems.

* Ecology Research

National Ecology Center
U.S. Fish and Wildlife Service
2627 Redwing Rd.
Fort Collins, CO 80526-2899   (303) 226-9100
The center conducts research, develops new tools, and transfers information so that scientists can better understand and manage fish and wildlife resources, habitats, and ecosystems. All endangered marine mammal research is performed here. Workshops are held in refuge management and habitat model development for those within the Interior Department and scientists in Federal and State agencies and foreign countries. Studies are reported in the Center's *Biological Report* series and through extension education brochures.

* Ecological Society

Ecological Society of America (ESA)
730 11th St., NW
Suite 400
Washington, DC 20001   (202) 628-1500
The Ecological Society of America is a professional society of individuals interested in the study of living things in relation to their environments. ESA is a member society of the American Institute of Biological Sciences. Publications: *Bulletin of the Ecological Society of America, Ecology, Ecological Monographs*.

* Economic Impact of Environmental Laws

National Environmental Development Association (NEDA)
605 14th St., NW
Washington, DC 20005   (202) 638-1230
The National Environmental Development Association consists of companies and others concerned with the impact of environmental legislation on business and industrial profits. Publications: *Balance*.

* Educational Materials and Programs

Environmental/Energy Education
Land Resources Division
Resource Development
Tennessee Valley Authority
Norris, TN 37828   (615) 632-1640
Much of TVA's environmental education effort is accomplished through university-based environmental education centers. The TVA has worked with several universities and colleges across the Valley and seven states to develop environmental education teaching aids and programs for schools, along with workshops for teachers. At the national level, the TVA has been involved in coordinating programs with the Environmental Protection Agency. In addition, TVA offers teacher workshops and interpretive programs for groups at Land Between the Lakes, an experimental area for schools and the public to study total resource management. Contact this office of more information on the TVA's environmental education programs.

* Education Materials from the EPA

Public Information Center
Environmental Protection Agency
401 M St., SW, PM-211 B
Washington DC 20460   (202) 475-7751
Environmental Education Materials For Teachers and Young People is a free annotated list of educational materials on environmental issues. Entries include diverse materials ranging from workbooks and lesson plans to newsletters, films, and computer software intended for young people. Educational materials available from sources other than EPA are listed alphabeticaly following the name of their sponsoring organization or group. A separate listing of selected EPA publications and other material available from EPA's Public Information Center is included in this pamphlet, as well as a short descriptive list of environmental education resource facilities. Contact this office to order your free copy.

* Educator Associations

American Society for Environmental Education
Box 800
Wheeler Professional Park
Hanover, NH 03755   (603) 448-6697

North American Association for Environmental Education
Box 400
Troy, OH 45373   (513) 698-6493
These two organizations assist and support the work of individuals and groups engaged in environmental education, research, and service.

* Educators

Association for Environmental Engineering Professors
Dept. of Civil Engr.
University of Texas, EJC 8.6

Austin, TX 78712   (512) 471-5602
This association is comprised of individuals working or teaching in the fields of health, the environment, air and water resources, and related areas.

* Endangered Resource Defense Council

National Resources Defense Council
122 E. 42nd St.
New York, NY 10168   (212) 949-0049
This organization is dedicated to protecting endangered natural resources and improving the quality of human environment. Areas of concentration are air and water pollution, nuclear safety, land use, urban environment, toxic substances control, resource management, wilderness and wildlife protection, and coastal zone management. Publications: *The Amicus Journal*.

* Enforcement and Investigations

National Enforcement Investigations Center Library (NEIC)
Building 53, Box 25277
Denver Federal Center
Denver, CO 80225   (303) 236-5122
This library's collection comprises case files, technical reports, data compilations, and background information used to develop the basis for field studies and enforcement actions; research and development reports on municipal, industrial, and agricultural pollution abatement practices; enforcement conference documents and environmental law materials; technical reference materials covering chemistry, pesticides, toxic substances, air technology, and hazardous wastes. Databases maintained here inlclude BRS, CDS, CIS, Consent Decree System, DIALOG, FINDS, Ground Water On-line, HWDMS, ISI, LEXIS/NEXIS, NLM, PCS, SFFAS, STORET, VV-Text, and Westlaw.

* Enforcement of Environmental Laws

Civil Enforcement
Enforcement and Compliance Monitoring
Environmental Protection Agency
401 M St., SW, Room W1035
Washington DC 20460   (202) 382-4137
When regulated entities fail to comply voluntarily with EPA requirements, the EPA, in partnership with State agencies, can take a number of enforcement actions. These alternatives include compliance promotion; administrative money penalties; negotiated compliance schedules; and ultimately, judicial enforcement involving criminal proceedings in federal court. Contact this office for more information regarding enforcement of environmental laws.

* Engineers

American Academy of Environmental Engineers
132 Holiday Court
Suite 206
Annapolis, MD 21401   (301) 266-3311
The American Academy of Environmental Engineers is a professional organization comprised of sanitary and environmental engineers. Publications: *AAEE Roster, The Diplomate*.

* Environmental Defense Fund

Environmental Defense Fund Inc. (EDF)
444 Park Ave., South
New York, NY 10016   (212) 686-4191
This organization of lawyers, scientists and economists is dedicated to protecting environmental quality and public health. EDF pursues responsible reform of public policy in resource conservation, toxic chemicals, water resources, air quality, land use and wildlife, working through research and public education, and judicial, administrative, and legislative action. Publications: *EDF letter*.

* Environmental Educators

American Society for Environmental Education
Box 800
Wheeler Professional Park
Hanover, NH 03755   (603) 448-6697
ASEE is a professional organization for environmental educators at all educational levels from primary school to graduate university studies.

* Environmental Impact Statements

Special Programs and Analysis Division
Office of Federal Activities
Environmental Protection Agency
401 M St., SW, Room 2119
Washington DC 20460   (202) 382-5075
This office reviews and completes a compliance check on *Environmental Impact Statements* (EISs) to ensure that they meet the criteria required of an EIS. They comment on the impact statement and then publish it in the *Federal Register*. These *Statements* are documents required of Federal agencies by the National

Environment and Nature

Environmental Policy Act for major projects or legislative proposals significantly affecting the environment. A tool for decision making, they describe the positive and negative effects of the undertaking and lists alternative actions. This office can also refer you to a Federal agency responsible for an *Environmental Impact Statement* on a specific topic.

* Environmental Engineering and Technology

Office of Environmental Engineering and Technology
Office of Research and Development
Environmental Protection agency
401 M St., SW, Room W635E
Washington, DC 20460   (202) 382-2600

Research in environmental engineering and technology studies pollution from industrial and municipal sources, and analyzes alternative control technologies. Examples of research includes exploring innovative techniques for removing and disposing of pollutants, and developing cost-effective methods of providing safe drinking water.

* EPA Bibliography

National Technical Information Service
5825 Port Royal Rd.
Springfield, VA 22161   (703) 487-4650

EPA Publications Bibliography, Quarterly Abstract Bulletin is a quarterly update listing and indexing EPA technical reports and journal articles added to the NTIS collection during the preceding quarter. The fourth issue of each year contains bibliographic citations with abstracts for the preceding quarter and cumulative indexes for the calendar year. Single copies are $25, and a yearly subscription is $90.

* EPA Freedom of Information Requests

Freedom of Information Officer
Environmental Protection Agency
401 M St., SW, Room W227
Washington DC 20460   (202) 382-4048

All Freedom of Information requests should be addressed to the Officer listed above.

* EPA Libraries

EPA Headquarters Library
401 M St., SW
Room 2904 WSM
Washington, DC 20460

The EPA Headquarters Library provides information services covering a wide range of environmental and related subjects of interest to EPA staff and the general public. Major areas include air and radiation, chemistry, hazardous waste, management, noise abatement, pesticides, resource recovery, solid waste, toxicology, wastewater treatment, water quality, and water supply. Databases maintained here include CAS On-line, CIS, DIALOG, Ground Water On-line, Hazardous Waste Database, ISI, LEXIS/NEXIS, NLM, and Newsnet. The library's special collection covers hazardous waste.

There are 28 EPA network libraries located in Headquarters, and all regional offices and laboratories to support the EPA offices. The libraries and other information services contain a combined collection of over 128,900 books, 5,088 journals subscriptions, 357,146 hard copy reports, 3,166,500 documents on microfilm and microfiche, 9,000 journal article reprints, and 2,000 maps. A free publication, *Guide to EPA Libraries And Information Services*, lists each of the libraries, as well as their location, collection emphasis, loan policy, and the services they offer. What follows is a list of the EPA's regional libraries:

Region 1 Library

JFK Federal Bldg., Boston, MA 02203; (617) 565-3300. The EPA Region I Library's collection still reflects some older New England river basin reports, but has been extensively developed in the areas of air pollution & control, pesticides & toxic substances, groundwater, solid & hazardous waste, health effects, water pollution & control. Databases maintained here include BRS, CAS On-line, CIS, DIALOG, Ground Water On-line, Hazardous Waste Database, and LEXIS/NEXIS. Special collections include the Hazardous Waste collection, Envirofiche since 1980, New England materials: Connecticut, Maine, Massachusetts, New Hampshire, Rhode Island, and Vermont.

Region 2 Library

26 Federal Plaza, New York, NY 10278; (212) 264-2881. This library embraces all aspects of EPA's environmental mission. Databases maintained here include DIALOG, Hazardous Waste Database, and ISI. Its general collection covers human resources management.

Region 2 Field Office Library

Edison, NJ 08837
This library includes materials on all EPA programs: air, solid waste, hazardous waste, toxic substances, pesticides, water, and radiation.

Region 3 Library

841 Chestnut St., Philadelphia, PA 19107; (215) 597-0580. This Center (IRC) provides information support for a wide range of environmental programs and activities conducted by the Regional office. It also serves as an information resource for the general public. Subject areas include air pollution, pesticides, employee development, radiation, environmental law, toxic substances, hazardous waste, toxicology, management, water pollution, and wetlands. Databases maintained here include CIS, DIALOG, Ground Water On-line, Hazardline, Hazardous Waste Database, and LEXIS/NEXIS. There are also special collections on wetland ecology and hazardous waste and law. In addition, a special effort is made to acquire published information on environmental conditions and trends within the five states and the District of Columbia which comprise Region 3.

Region 4 Library

345 Courtland St., NE, Atlanta, GA 30365-2401; (404) 347-4216. The Region 4 Library provides a full range of library and information services, covering subjects from air and water pollution to toxics and hazardous waste with a variety of technical reports, reference books, journals, and online computer services. Databases maintained here include CAS On-line, CIS, DIALOG, Dun & Bradstreet, Hazardous Waste Database, ISI, LEXIS/NEXIS, NLM, NPIRS, and OHS.

Region 5 Library

230 South Dearborn St., Room 1670, Chicago, IL 60604; (312) 353-2022. The subject areas of this library's collection cover air pollution, air quality, groundwater, hazardous waste, noise, pesticides, recycling and resource recovery, solid waste management, toxic substances, water pollution, water quality, and water supply (drinking water). The emphasis is on the Great Lakes and the six states in the Region: Illinois, Indiana, Michigan, Minnesota, Ohio, and Wisconsin. Databases maintained here include BRS, CIS, DIALOG, Ground Water On-line, Hazardous Waste Database, ISI, LEXIS/NEXIS, NLM, and ORBIT.

Region 6 Library

1445 Ross Ave., Allied Bank Tower, Dallas, TX 75202-2733; (214) 655-6444. The EPA Region 6 Library includes materials on all EPA programs: air pollution, radiation, hazardous waste, solid waste, noise, toxic substances, pesticides, and water pollution.

Region 7 Library

726 Minnestoa Ave., Kansas City, KS 66101; (913) 236-2828. The Region 7 Library provides information on a wide range of environmental subjects of interest to the Regional staff and the general public. Subject areas include agricultural pollution, air pollution, environmental law, hazardous waste, pesticides, radiation, solid waste management, water pollution, water quality, and water supply. Databases maintained here include CIS, Hazardous Waste Database, LEXIS/NEXIS, NLM, and Watstore.

Region 8 Library

999 18th St., Suite 1300, Denver, CO 80202-22413; (303) 293-1444. The Region 8 Library includes materials on all EPA programs: air, water, hazardous and solid waste, pesticides, toxic substances, noise and radiation, particularly as they relate to the states within the Region. In addition, because the Rocky Mountain area is rich in energy resources, the library collects material relating to energy resource development and its relationship to the environment. And finally, to support other Agency programs, the collection incorporates publications relating to economics, planning, transportation, management and employee development. Databases maintained here include CARL, CIS, DIALOG, Ground Water On-line, and Hazardous Waste Database.

Region 9 Library

215 Fremont St., 6th Floor, San Francisco, CA 94105. The Region 9 Library's major subject areas include air pollution and control, pesticides, environmental health and safety, radiation, hazardous waste, research and development, law, solid waste. Databases maintained include CIS, DIALOG, Hazardline, and Hazardous Waste Database. Special collections here include Environmental Impact Statements, hazardous waste, and speeches given by EPA Senior Staff.

Region 10 Library

1200 Sixth Ave., Seattle, WA 98101; (206) 442-1289. The Region 10 Library's holdings include monographs, serials, a basic environmental law collection, EPA reports (both hard copy and microfiche), and local and state government reports. The collection was originally heavily oriented toward water pollution, but has since been developed to encompass all other areas of environmental quality. Databases maintained here include CIS, DIALOG, Ground Water On-line, Hazardous Waste Database, LEXIS/NEXIS, and NLM. Special collections include Environmental Impact Statements and hazardous waste.

* EPA Newsletter

Superintendent of Documents
Government Printing Office
Washington DC 20402   (202) 783-3238

Published six times a year, the *EPA Journal* presents articles concerning the environment, State and local actions, and EPA activities. A subscription is available for $8.00 per year. For more information concerning the EPA Journal contact: Editor, *EPA Journal*, 401 M St, SW, A-107, Washington D.C. 20460: (202) 382-4393.

* Equipment Manufacturers

Environmental Industry Council (EIC)
1825 K St., NW
Suite 210
Washington, DC 20006　　　　　　　　　　(202) 331-7706
The Environmental Industry Council consists of corporations which manufacture environmental protection equipment and materials.

* Exposure to Toxic Substances

Exposure Evaluation Division
Office of Toxic Substances
Environmental Protection Agency
401 M St., SW, Room E315B
Washington, DC 20460　　　　　　　　　　(202) 382-4241
This EPA division studies human and environmental exposure to chemical substances in support of OTS risk assessment activities. EED provides standards, guidance, and rule deveopment. It reviews available information relevant to chemical exposure to humans and develops guidelines for epidemiological data.

* Greenhouse Effect

Office of Technology Assessment
600 Pennsylvania Ave., SE
Washington, DC 20510　　　　　　　　　　(202) 228-6845
OTA is currently studying the major contributors to climate change, ozone depletion, and the greenhouse effect for both the developed and developing world. OTA will identify areas where gains in efficiency, product substitution, conservation, or other options can slow climate change. Contact Rosine Bierbaum, the project director, for more information.

* Guide to the Environmental Protection Agency

Public Information Center
Environmental Protection Agency
401 M St., SW, PM-211B
Washington, DC 20460　　　　　　　　　　(202) 475-7551
Your Guide to the United States Environmental Protection Agency describes how the EPA is addressing the major environmental problems that confront the U.S. It looks at the organization, and the laws for which the EPA is responsible, as well as providing a listing of regional offices and research facilities. Contact this office for your free copy.

* Gulf Breeze Environmental Center

Environmental Research Laboratory (ERL) Library
Sabine Island
Gulf Breeze, FL 32561　　　　　　　　　　(904) 932-5311
The Gulf Breeze Environmental Research Laboratory (GBERL) library provides information services to GBERL employees and the general public. The library's subject areas include aquatic toxicology, microbiology, genetic engineering, pathobiology, marine ecology, and pesticide science. Databases maintained here include DIALOG and Ground Water On-line.

* Health Effects of Chemicals

Health and Environmental ReviewDivision
Office of Toxic Substances
Environmental Protection Agency
401 M St., SW, Room E617
Washington, DC 20460　　　　　　　　　　(202) 382-4241
The Health and Environmental Review Division studies the hazards posed by new chemicals to human health and the environment, and for integrating these studies with exposure information from other EPA divisions.

* Health Risks and the Environment

Office of Health Research
Research and Development
Environmental Protection Agency
401 M St., SW, Room 3100
Washington DC 20460　　　　　　　　　　(202) 382-5900
This office conducts health assessment research which provides an integrated, scientific basis for evaluating environmental risks and effects stemming from exposure to various substances, and provides data needed to estimate human mortality and illness caused by pollutants.

* Hotlines: EPA State and Local Site-Specific

Region II　　　　　　　　　　　　　　(800) 732-1223

This is a local hotline that provides site-specific regulatory information on Resource Conservation and Recovery Act only in the Region II areas of New York, New Jersey, Puerto Rico, and the Virgin Islands.

Region III　　　　　　　　　　　　　　(800) 438-2474
The EPA Region III Hotline provides general information on Agency programs to the public and makes referrals as needed. It provides this information for all Region III states: Washington, D.C., Delaware, Maryland, Pennsylvania, Virginia, and West Virginia.

Region IV　　　　　　　　　　　　　　(800) 241-1754
The EPA Region IV Hotline provides general information on Agency programs to the public and makes referrals as needed. It provides this information for all Region IV states: Alabama, Florida, Georgia, Kentucky, Mississippi, North Carolina, South Carolina, and Tennessee.

Region V　　　　　　　(800) 621-8431 (800) 572-2515 (IL)
The EPA Region V Hotline provides general information on Agency programs to the public and makes referrals as needed. It provides this information for all Region V states: Indiana, Michigan, Illinois, Minnesota, Ohio, and Wisconsin.

Region VII
The Region VII Hotline provides general information on Agency programs to the public and makes referrals a needed. It provides this information for all Region VII states: Iowa, Kansas, Missouri, and Nebraska. Kansas: (800) 221-7749; Nebraska, Iowa, and Missouri: (800) 223-0425.

Region VII　　　　　　　　　　　　　　(800) 223-0424
The Resource Conservation and Recovery Act Hotline in Region VII provides information on implementation of RCRA in Iowa.

Region VIII　　　　　　　　　　　　　　(800) 525-3022
The Region VIII Hotline provides general information on Agency programs to the public and makes referrals as needed. It provides this information for all Region VIII states: Colorado, Montana, North Dakota, South Dakota, Utah, and Wyoming.

Region IX　　　　　　　　　　　　　　(800) 231-3075
This is a local hotline that provides site-specific regulatory information on Resource Conservation and Recovery Act only in the Region IX areas of Arizona, California, Hawaii, Nevada, Guam, and Samoa.

* Impact of Technology

Institute of Environmental Sciences (IES)
940 East Northwest Highway
Mt. Prospect, IL 60056　　　　　　　　　　(312) 255-1561
The Institute of Environmental Sciences consists of individuals concerned with the affect on men, materials, and equipment of the use of advanced technology. Publications: *Journal of Environmental Sciences*.

* Indian Affairs Field Offices

Bureau of Indian Affairs
U.S. Department of the Interior
Code 130, Room 4627N
Washington, DC 20240　　　　　　　　　　(202) 343-1710
For information on American Indian lands, address your correspondence to: Area Director, Bureau of Indian Affairs, followed by the address listed below.

Alaska
P.O. Box 3-8000, Juneau, AK 99802; (907) 586-7177. Serving: Alaska

Arizona
P.O. Box M, Window Rock, AZ 86515; (602) 871-5151, ext. 5106. Serving: Navajo Reservations only, Arizona, Utah, and New Mexico
P.O.Box 10, Phoenix, AZ 85001; (602) 241-2305. Serving: Arizona, Nevada, Utah, and Idaho

California
Federal Office Building, 2800 Cottage Way, Sacramento, CA 95825; (916) 484-4682. Serving: California

Minnesota
Chamber of Commerce Building, 15 South Fifth St., 10th Floor, Minneapolis, MN 55402; (612) 349-3631. Serving: Minnesota, Iowa, Michigan and Wisconsin

Montana
316 North 26th St., Billings, MT 59101; (406) 657-6315. Serving: Montana and Wyoming

New Mexico
P.O. Box 26567, Albuquerque, NM 87125-6567; (505) 766-3170. Serving: Colorado and New Mexico

North Dakota
115 4th Ave., SE, Aberdeen, SD 57401; (605) 226-7261. Serving: Nebraska, North Dakota, and South Dakota

Environment and Nature

Oklahoma

WCD-Office Complex, P.O. Box 368, Anadarko, OK 73005; (405) 247-6673. Serving: Kansas and West Oklahoma
Old Federal Building, 5th & Okmulgee St., Muskogee, Oklahoma 74401; (918) 687-2296. Serving: East Oklahoma

Oregon

Federal Building, 1002 N.E. Holladay St., Portland, OR 97232-4182; (503) 231-6702. Serving: Oregon, Washington, and Idaho

Virginia

1000 N. Glebe Road, Arlington, VA 22201; (703) 235-3006. Serving: New York, Maine, Louisiana, Florida, North Carolina, Mississippi, Connecticut, and Rhode Island

* Innovative/Alternative Environmental Clearinghouse

Innovative/Alternative Projects   (304) 293-4191
This Clearinghouse provides information on innovative and alternative projects to enable communities and grant applicants to identify and contact other sources with experience in technologies.

* Inspector General's Whistle Blower Hotline

Environmental Protection Agency
401 M St., SW
Washington DC 20460   (800) 424-4000
The Inspector General's Whistle Blower Hotline receives reports of EPA-related waste, fraud, abuse, or mismanagement from public and from EPA and other government employees. All calls are kept confidential. The Hotline operates Monday through Friday, 10:00 a.m. to 3:00 p.m.(EST).

* Insular Islands Assistance

Territorial and International Affairs
U.S. Department of the Interior
18th and C Sts., NW
Washington, DC 20240   (202) 343-4822
Technical assistance in the areas of social, political, and economic development is given to the Insular Islands by this office. The office is no longer involved in the government of the islands.

* Interior Department Freedom of Information

Freedom of Information Appeals Officer
Department of the Interior
18th and C Sts., NW, Room 2248
Washington, DC 20240   (202) 343-5339
Each bureau under the Department of the Interior has a separate office that handles concerns under the Freedom of Information Act. If you wish to obtain the officer's name within a particular bureau or wish to file with the central office, contact the officer above.

* International Environmental Conservation

Office of Ecology, Health and Conservation
Bureau of Oceans and International
  Environmental and Scientific Affairs
Department of State
2201 C St., NW, Room 4325
Washington, DC 20520   (202) 647-2418
This office handles matters in two basic areas: 1) the conservation of nature and natural resources, such as wildlife, plant issues, and tropical deforestation; 2) international health issues, particularly AIDS. This office also works with other agencies in developing an international approach for the United States in dealing with these problems. Recently, they have been looking at debt leverage in third world countries to set aside land for new parks or to protect habitats.

* International Environment Policy

Bureau of Oceans and International Environmental
  and Scientific Affairs
Department of State
2201 C St., NW, Room 7831
Washington, DC 20520   (202) 647-1561
International political and economic relationships are increasingly affected by science and technology and by environmental issues. This bureau deals with U.S. foreign policy such specialized fields as nuclear physics, marine science, biotechnology, global climate, acid rain, and wildlife conservation. The bureau also manages bilateral science and technology agreements with ten countries and guides the development and implementation of several hundred other science and technology arrangements.

* International Marine Environmental Efforts

Environmental Coordination Branch

Marine Environmental Response Division
Office of Marine, Safety, Security, and Environmental Protection
U.S. Coast Guard
U.S. Department of Transportation
2100 2nd St., SW, Room 1202
Washington, DC 20593-0001   (202) 267-0421
Information is available here on the Coast Guard's role in international marine environmental efforts, such as representation in the U.N. International Maritime Consultative Organization. For further information on cooperative environmental efforts, contact the branch listed.

* International Marine Science and Policy

Office of Marine Science and Polar Affairs
2201 C St., NW, Room 5801
Department of State
Washington, DC 20520   (202) 647-3262
This office handles international marine environment concerns, from the protection of whales to cleaning up oil spills, by negotiating bilateral and multilateral agreements.

* Land Use Engineering

Division of Engineering
Bureau of Land Management
U.S. Department of the Interior
1725 I St., NW
Washington, DC 20006   (202) 653-8811
For technical information concerning environmental engineering of roads, buildings, and recreational structures, contact the above office.

* Law Library

EPA Law Library
401 M St., SW
Room 2902
Washington, DC 20460   (202) 382-5919
The EPA Law Library provides information services to the Agency's legal and enforcement personnel, and to the ten Regional Counsels. The collection contains approximately 9,000 volumes of legal and law-related material concentrating on Federal law, with special emphasis on administrative and environmental law. Included are statutes, codes, regulations, case reports, digests, citators, and legal reference sources, as well as looseleaf services, newspapers, and 70 current law reviews and periodicals.

* Leak Detection Technologies

Leak Detection Technology Association
1801 K St., NW
Suite 800
Washington, DC 20006   (202) 835-2355
This association is composed of businesses involved in environmental protection and safe-guarding human health through the development and use of leak detection technology.

* Legislation

Environmental Legislative Library
832 West Tower, 401 M St., SW
Washington, DC 20460   (202) 382-5425
The Legislative Library primarily supports the Office of Legislative Analysis, but also provides information for other EPA staff on request. The collection consists primarily of federal environmental legislation and related federal information. The library is mainly geared to the current Congress, but there are many older documents in the collection. The library responds to reference requests from EPA staff; supplies copies of Congressional documents when possible; tracks status of current environmental legislation; and compiles current status of pending environmental legislation organized by subject area. Databases maintained include Legi-Slate and the Congressional Quarterly Data Base (CQ)

* Local Government Environmental Activities

International City Managers Association (ICMA)
1120 6th St., NW, Suite 300
Washington, DC 20005   (202) 626-4600
The purposes of ICMA are to enhance the quality of local government and to nurture and assist professional local government administrators in the U.S. and other countries.

* Medicine and Clinical Ecology

American Academy of Environmental Medicine (AAEM)
Box 16106
Denver, CO 80216   (303) 622-9755

The American Academy of Environmental Medicine is comprised of people studying the effects of the environment on human health. Publications: Archives of Clinical Ecology.

* Minnesota-Based Environmental Lab
Environmental Research Laboratory Library
6201 Congdon Boulevard
Duluth, MN 55804
This library's major fields of interest are analytical chemistry, fisheries biology, and water pollution. Its general collections cover analytical chemistry and fisheries biology.

* Minority and Disadvantaged Small Business Hotline
Office of Small and Disadvantaged Business Utilization
Environmental Protection Agency
401 M St., SW   (800) 368-5888
Washington DC 20460   (202) 557-7015 (DC area)
The Small Business Hotline is an EPA-based hotline that gives advice and information to small businesses on complying with EPA regulations. It deals with problems encountered by small-quantity generators of hazardous waste and other small businesses with environmental concerns.

* Monitoring Pollution
Office of Modeling, Monitoring Systems
  and Quality Asssurance
Research and Development
Environmental Protection Agency
401 M St., SW, Room 3702
Washington DC 20460   (202) 3822-5767
This office provides data on monitoring systems and quality assurance research which develops standardized methods to measure and monitor pollutants.

* Monitoring Systems Lab
Environmental Monitoring Systems
Laboratory Library
944 E. Harmon Ave.
Las Vegas, NV 89109   (702) 798-2648
The Environmental Monitoring Systems Laboratory develops, evaluates, and applis methods and strategies for monitoring the environment. Major program areas include advanced analytical methods, advanced monitoring methods, exposure assessment, monitoring network design, quality assurance, radiation monitoring, and special projects. The library's general collections cover nuclear science and quality assurance. The special collection covers hazardous waste.

* Municipal and Business Practices Environmental Impact
INFORM
381 Park Ave. South
New York, NY 10016   (212) 689-4040
INFORM is a not-for-profit organization that conducts field level research of business and municipal practices affecting the environment. It is the aim of INFORM to identify institutional sources of environmental problems and then to determine positive steps toward reducing or eliminating those problems.

* Mutagens
Environmental Mutagen Society (EMS)
Ctr Box X Oak Ridge Natl Lab
Bldg 2001, MS 50
Oak Ridge, TN 37831-6050   (415) 422-5698
The focus of the Environmental Mutagen Society is to encourage the study of mutagens in the human environment particularly as they affect public health. Publications: *Environmental Mutagenesis, EMS Newsletter*.

* National Environmental Data Network
National Environmental Data Referral Service
NEDRES Office
National Oceanic And Atmospheric Administration
Department of Commerce
1825 Connecticut Ave., NW, Room 412
Washington, DC 20235   (202) 673-5548
The National Environmental Data Referral Service (NEDRES) is designed to provide convenient, economical, and efficient access to widely scattered environmental data. NEDRES is a publicly available service which identifies the existence, location, characteristics, and availablility conditions of environmental data sets. NEDRES database contains only descriptions, not the actual data. It is a national network of federal, state, and private organizations cooperating to improve access to environmental data. Major subject categories include climatology and meteorology, oceanography, geophysics and geology, geography, hydrology and limnnology, terrestrial resources, toxic and regulated substances,

and satellite remotely sensed data. For more information on the NEDRES database and the user charges, contact the office listed above. NEDRES also produces the following printed catalogs with references to available environmental data on selected topics and regions:

Finding the Environmental Data You Need (free)
NEDRES Memorandum of Agreement (free)
NEDRES Database User Agreement (free)
NEDRES Data Base User Guide (7.50)
Guideline for the Description of Environmental Data Files for the Nedres Database (10.00)
North American Climatic Data Catalog: Part 1 (10.00)
North American Climatic Data Catalog: Part 2 (10.00)
Satellite Remote Sensing of the Marine Environment: Literature and Data Sources (10.00)
Coastal and Estuarine Waters of California, Oregon, and Washington (10.00)
Chesapeake Bay and Adjacent Wetlands
Chesapeake Bay Environmental Data Directory (free to federal and state agencies)
Environmental Data Review (free)

* Natural Landmarks Registry
National Registry of Natural Landmarks
National Registry Branch
National Park Service
U.S. Department of the Interior
1100 L St., NW
Washington, DC 20005   (202) 343-9536
The Park Service conducts natural region studies to identify areas that are of potential national significance. These areas are then studied in the field by scientists. Natural areas considered of national significance are cited by the Secretary of the Interior as eligible for recognition as Registered Natural Landmarks. The owner may apply for a certificate and bronze plaque designating the site.

* Natural Resources Library
Natural Resources Library
U.S. Department of the Interior
18th and C Sts., NW
Washington, DC 20240   (202) 343-5815
Information is provided to the general public on such topics as Native American Indians, mining and minerals issues, land reclamation and management, fish and wildlife, water resources, parks and outdoor recreation, and the preservation of scenic and historic sites. The library is open from 7:45 a.m. to 5:00 p.m., Monday through Friday. Computer searches can also be performed by their reference librarians.

* Noise Control Engineering
Institute of Noise Control Engineering (INCE)
Box 3206, Arlington Branch
Poughkeepsie, NY 12603   (914) 462-4006
The Institute of Noise Control Engineering is a professional organization concerned with the advancement of noise control technology with particular emphasis on engineering solutions to environmental noise problems. Publications: *Noise Control Engineering, Journal of Noise/News*.

* Occupational Health and the Environment
Society for Occupational and Environmental Health (SOEH)
P.O. Box 42360
Washington, DC 20015-0360   (202) 762-9319
This society's members include physicians, hygienists, economists, laboratory scientists, academians, and labor and industry representatives.

* Oregon-Based Environmental Lab
Environmental Research Laboratory Library
200 SW 35th St.
Corvallis, OR 97333   (503) 757-4731
The Corvallis Environmental Research Laboratory (CERL) Library was established in 1966with an emphasis on marine, estuarine, and fresh water quality, air and terrestrial research. At present the laboratory has three branches: Toxics and Pesticides, Hazardous Materials, and Water, and the Air. Research concerns acid precipitation and its effects on the ecosystem, wildlife toxicology, genetic engineering, wetlands, and hazardous waste. Databases maintained here include CIS, DIALOG, and NLM. General collections of the library include acid rain, air pollution-ecology, biology, estuarine research, genetic engineering, wetlands, wildlife toxicology. The library's special collection covers acid rain.

* Outer Continental Shelf Management
Offshore Minerals Management
Mineral Management Service
U.S. Department of the Interior

18th and C Sts., NW
Washington, DC 20240 (202) 343-3530
Management of the oil and gas operations following leasing agreements with the Mineral Management Service is outlined in the publication, *Managing Oil and Gas Operations on the Outer Continental Shelf*. This booklet describes activities through the drilling and production process to lease relinquishment.

* Park Service Technical Information

Technical Information Center
National Park Service
Denver Service Center
12795 W. Alameda Parkway
P.O. Box 25287
Denver, CO 80225-0287 (303) 969-2130
The Technical Information Center has been designated by the National Park Service as the central repository for all National Park Service-generated planning, design, and construction maps, drawings, and reports as well as related cultural, environmental, and other technical documents. Bibliographic data on aerial photography is also maintained. The Center reproduces and delivers copies of the available materials for the Service, other agencies, and the public, both here and abroad. Today, the system has a holding of 100,000 data records, which represent about 500,000 microfilm aperture cards of maps, plans, and drawings; 1,000 records of resource and site aerial photography; and 25,000 planning, design, environmental, cultural resource, and natural resource documents.

* Pipeline Safety

Office of Pipeline Safety (OPS)
Research and Special Programs Administration
U.S. Department of Transportation
400 7th Street, SW
Washington, DC 20590 (202) 366-4572
OPS establishes and enforces safety standards for the transportation of gas and other hazardous materials by pipeline. A computerized reporting system is maintained to collect and analyze accident and incident data from pipeline operators. Accident reports include the operator's name, the hazardous material involved, description of the accident, and results. For database searches, contact the office listed. There may be a charge.

* President's Council on Environmental Quality

Council on Environmental Quality
722 Jackson Place, NW
Washington, DC 20503 (202) 395-5750
This office was established by the National Environmental Policy Act of 1969 to formulate and recommend national policies to promote the improvement of the quality of the environment. There are three members on the Council appointed by the President by and with the consent of the Senate. The Council's major responsibilities are to provide opinion and policy advice to the President on environmental matters, to act with White House advisors and other agencies to develop international environmental policy, to interact as a liaison with representatives of foreign governments and international organizations about global environmental issues, to assist in coordinating federal environmental programs that involve more than one agency, to act in the review process for proposed legislation on environmental quality, and to prepare the annual *Environmental Quality Report* on environmental activities of all levels of government and of private entities.

* Professionals on Environmental Issues

National Association of Environmental Professionals
Box 9400
Washington, DC 20016 (202) 229-7171
The National Association of Environmental Professionals consists of people involved in environmental planning, assessment, management, review, and research. it awards the CEP (Certified Environmental Professional) designation. Publications: *The Environmental Professional*.

* Public Access to EPA Actions

Environmental Protection Agency
401 M St., SW
Washington DC 20460 (202) 382-5926
The Public Information Reference Unit provides public access to regulatory information supporting the EPA's actions administered under the Clean Air Act and the Clean Water Act. Records are submitted to this office by the programs within EPA or the regions for public inspection and photocopying. This office also has information supporting other EPA regulations issued under the following statutes: Resource Conservation & Recovery Act, Safe Drinking Water Act, Noise Control Act, and the Marine Protection, Research and Sanctuaries Act.

* Public Policy

Association of Environmental Scientists and Administrators

2718 Southwest Kelly
Suite C-190
Portland, OR 97204 (503) 295-4885
AESA was created to represent the goals and interests of environmental professionals and to foster discussion of environmental public policy issues.

* Quality Assurance

Office of Modeling, Monitoring Systems
and Quality Asssurance
Research and Development
Environmental Protection Agency
401 M St., SW, Room 3702
Washington DC 20460 (202) 382-5767
This office provides data on monitoring systems and quality assurance research which develops standardized methods to measure and monitor pollutants.

* Radiation Protection and Measurements

National Council on Radiation Protection and Measurements
7910 Woodmont Ave.
Suite 1016
Bethesda, MD 20814 (301) 657-2652
The National Council on Radiation Protection and Measurements represents the interests of professionals with responsibilities for measuring amounts of and providing protection from nuclear radiation. Publications: *NCRP Report*.

* Radon and Radiation Control

Office of Radiation Programs
Environmental Protection Agency
401 M St., SW, Room NE108
Washington DC 20460 (202) 475-9600
The EPA, with a number of other federal agencies, protects the public from unnecessary exposure to ionizing radiation. EPA's major responsibilities are to set radioactive emissions standards and exposure limits, assess new technology, and monitor radiation in the environment in four areas: radiation from nuclear accidents, radon emissions, land disposal of radioactive waste, and radiation in groundwater and drinking water. The EPA fulfills these responsibilities by setting emissions standards for nuclear power plants, and for radionuclides in drinking water and in the air. EPA also prescribes work practices to reduce emissions of radon from underground uranium mines, develops radioactive waste disposal standards, and issues guidance to limit occupational exposure.

* Radon: Citizen's Guide

Public Information Center
Environmental Protection Agency
401 M St., SW, PM-211 B
Washington DC 20460 (202) 475-7751
A Citizen's Guide to Radon helps readers understand the radon problem and decide if they need to take action to reduce radon levels in their homes. It explains what radon is, how it is detected, and what the results mean. Contact this office for your free copy.

* Radon Indoors

Radon Division
Office of Radiation Programs
Environmental Protection Agency
401 M St., SW, Room NE200
Washington DC 20460 (202) 475-9622
The EPA's indoor radon program assists States in identifying areas with high indoor radon levels, researches, demonstrates, and evaluates techniques to reduce radon levels, and establishes standard methods for measuring radon levels. Contact this office for more information on radon standards.

* Reclamation Bibliography

Superintendent of Documents
Government Printing Office
Washington, DC 20402 (202) 783-3238
Publications on priorities within the Bureau are listed, including the safety of dams and a water measurement manual used in irrigation and municipal water facilities.

* Regional Environmental Councils

National Association of Regional Councils (NARC)
1700 K St., NW, Suite 1306
Washington, DC 20006 (202) 457-0710
The NARC consists of regional councils of local governments, governmental agencies, libraries and organizations which are interested in regionalism as an approach to meeting problems that cross local governmental boundaries such as economic development, transportation and environmental management.

* Regulations

Environmental Protection Agency
401 M St., SW
Washington DC 20460   (202) 783-3238

Single copies of *Federal Registers* with environmental regulations can be obtained from this office.

* Regulatory Information References

Environmental Protection Agency
401 M St., SW
Washington DC 20460   (202) 382-5926

PIRU provides public access to regulatory information supporting the Agency's actions administered under (1) the Clean Air Act (primarily the State Implementation Plans), and (2) the Clean Water Act (primarily the Effluent Limitation Guidelines). Records are submitted to PIRU (indexed) by the programs within EPA or the Regions for public inspection and photocopying. PIRU also has information supporting other EPA regulations issued under the following statutes: Resource Conservation & Recovery Act (RCRA), Safe Drinking Water Act, Noise Control Act, and The Marine Protection, Research and Sanctuaries Act.

* Research Center

Andrew W. Briedenbach Environmental
Research Center Library
26 W. St. Clair St.
Cincinnati, OH 45268   (513) 569-7703

The major subjects in this library's collection are bacteriology, biology, biotechnology, chemistry, engineering, hazardous wastes, hydrobiology, microbiology, solid waste management, toxicology, water pollution, and water quality. Databases maintained here include BRS, CAS On-line, CIS, DIALOG, Dun & Bradstreet, Hazardous Waste Database, LEXIS/NEXIS, NLM, Toxline, and Toxnet. General collections include bacteriology, biology, biotechnology, microbiology, physics, solid waste management. This library's special collections cover the environment, Canada, legal issues, hazardous waste, and solid waste.

* Research Labs

Environmental Research Laboratories
National Oceanic and Atmospheric Administration
Department of Commerce
325 Broadway
Boulder, CO 80303   (303) 497-6286

The Environmental Research Laboratories conducts an integrated program of fundamental research, related technology development, and services to improve understanding and prediction of the geophysical environment comprising the oceans and inland waters, the lower and upper atmosphere, the space environment, and the Earth. Activities at its laboratories address such major areas as stratospheric and tropospheric ozone, the greenhouse effect and atmospheric chemistry, acid rain sources, transport and deposition, ocean role in climate, meteorological phenomena, solar disturbances, and computer modeling of oceanic conditions. . *Environmental Research Laboratories Programs and Plans* is a free publication which contains highlights of Laboratory accomplishments and abbreviated summaries of immediate objectives. More comprehensive and detailed descriptions of activities, results, and plans may be found in the laboratories' annual reports.

* Research and Technology Transfer

Center for Environmental Research Information
Environmental Protection Agency
401 M St., SW
Washington DC 20460   (513) 569-7562

The Office of Research and Development has centralized most of its information distribution and technology transfer activities in the Center for Environmental Research Information listed above. CERI also serves as a central point of distribution for ORD research results and reports.

* Resident Environmental Education

Environmental/Energy Education
Land Between The Lakes
Resource and Development
Tennessee Valley Authority
Golden Pond, KY 42231   (502) 924-1606

The Youth Station and Brandon Spring at Land Between The Lakes operates the residential education program to promote better environmental understanding, aesthetic appreciation, and man's place in nature. These dorm-style activity areas are open year-round and accommodate kindergarten through college-level groups. Groups are welcome to carry out their own programs, or the staff can help in developing them. Activities include canoeing, pond studies, and nature walks. With Murray (Kentucky) State University Center for Environmental Education, the staff provides additional workshops for area teachers and in-service students.

* Resource Conservation & Recovery Act Docket

Environmental Protection Agency
401 M Street SW
Washington, DC 20460   (202) 475-9327

This Docket provides public access to regulatory information supporting the Agency's actions under RCRA. Records support Federal Register notices, Delisting Petitions, and other Office of Solid Waste (OSW) publications. RCRA Docket publishes a semiannual catalog of frequently requested documents. The RCRA Docket staff performs two primary functions: maintaining the docket and responding to information requests. The activities which are required for each function include maintaining the RCRA Docket, tracking regulations, organizing and storing information, and distributing and ordering documents.

* Resource Conservation and Recovery Hotline

CERCLA/RCRA Hotline
Environmental Protection Agency
401 M St., SW   (800) 424-9346
Washington DC 20460   (202) 382-3000

This hotline answers questions concerning the Resource Conservation and Recovery Act, Superfund, and hazardous waste regulations. Requests for certain documents from the *Federal Register* and public laws are also handled in addition to referral to appropriate contacts. See also RCRA/CERCLA Hotline and Superfund Hotline.

* Right to Know Information Center (PIC)

Environmental Protection Agency
401 M St., SW
Washington DC 20460   (202) 382-2080

The Public Information Center answers inquiries from the public about EPA, its programs, and activities and offers a variety of general, non-technical information materials.

* Risk Analysis Society

Society for Risk Analysis (SRA)
8000 Westpark Drive
Suite 400
McLean, VA 22101-3101   (703) 790-1745

This society is funded for the purpose of studying and understanding on a scientific basis the risks posed by technological development.

* Risk Assessment Improvements

International Life Sciences Institute - Risk Science Institute (RSI)
1126 16th St., NW
Washington, DC 20036   (202) 659-3306

The primary goal of the Risk Science Institute (RSI) is to improve risk assessment by strengthening the scientific principles on which assessments are based. RSI has adopted the following objectives to achieve this goal: 1) To develop and distribute new scientific knowledge; and 2) To involve the best scientific talent wherever it is found.

* Risk Comparison and Setting Environmental Priorities

Office of Policy, Planning and Evaluation
Environmental Protection Agency
401 M St., SW, Room M3002
Washington, DC 20460   (202) 382-2747

Comparing Risks and Setting Environmental Priorities documents the result of the first year of three Comparative Risk Projects sponsored on a demonstration basis. The projects use risk information in an integrated approach to identify and to assess environmental issues, to set priorities among these issues, and to develop appropriate strategies to manage these problems. Contact this office for your free copy.

* Safe Drinking Water Hotline

Environmental Protection Agency
401 M St., SW
Washington DC 20460   (800) 426-4791

The Safe Drinking Water Hotline responds to questions concerning the Safe Drinking Water Act, Water Standards, Regulations, and the Underground Injection Program. It will also provide selected publications relevant to these issues. It operates Monday through Friday, 8:30 a.m. to 4:30 p.m. (EST).

* Sea-Grant Colleges

Office of Oceanic Research Programs
National Oceanic and Atmospheric Administration
Department of Commerce
1335 East-West Hwy.
Silver Spring, MD 20910   (202) 377-8090

The National Sea Grant College Program is a national network of over 300 colleges, universities, research institutions, and consortia working in partnership with industry and the federal government to support Great Lakes and marine research, education, and extension services. This program provides support for institutions engaged in comprehensive marine research, education, and advisory service programs, supports individual projects in marine research and development, and sponsors education of ocean scientists and engineers, marine technicians, and other specialists at selected colleges and universities.

* Small Business EPA-Help Hotline

Environmental Protection Agency
401 M Street SW   (800) 368-5888
Washington, DC 20460   (202) 557-1938

The Small Business Hotline is an EPA-based hotline that gives advice and information to small businesses on complying with EPA regulations. It deals with problems encountered by small-quantity generators of hazardous waste and other small businesses with environmental concerns.

* Small Business EPA Ombudsman

Small Business Ombudsman
Environmental Protection Agency
401 M Street SW
Washington, DC 20460   (202) 382-3090

The Small Business Ombudsman in the EPA Office of the Administrator provides various services to help small business comply with EPA regulations. The Ombudsman serves as information services and advocate for small business interests in the regulatory development process. It helps these small businesses with their individual problems.

* Space Environment and Solar-Terrestrial Physics

Space Environment Laboratory
Environmental Research Laboratories
National Oceanic and Atmospheric Administration
U.S. Department of Commerce
325 Broadway
Boulder, CO 80303   (303) 497-3313

The Space Environment Laboratory provides real-time space environment monitoring and forecasting services, develops techniques for improving forecasts of solar disturbances and their effect on the near-Earth space environment, and conducts research in solar-terrestrial physics. An annual report is available which goes into more detail about the Laboratory, the research conducted, and lists the technical reports published.

* Technology Assessment Reports

Office of Technology Assessment
Publications Order
U.S. Congress
Washington, DC 20510-8025   (202) 224-8996

These OTA publications are available through the office above, the Government Printing Office, and the National Technical Information Service. To find out correct ordering information and prices, along with brief summaries of the following studies, contact the OTA office above and request their current publications catalog.

Agriculture and Foresty
Acid Rain and Transported Air Pollutants: Implications for Public Policy (O-204)
Africa Tomorrow: Issues in Technology, Agriculture, and U.S. Foreign Aid (TM-F-31)
Environmental Contaminants in Food (F-103)
Integrated Renewable Resource Management for U.S. Insular Area (F-325)
Technologies To Maintain Biological Diversity (F-330)
Technologies To Sustain Tropical Forest Resources (F-214)
Technology and the American Economic Transition (TET-283)
Water-Related Technologies for Sustainable Agriculture in U.S. Arid/Semiarid Lands (F-212)
Water-Related Technologies for Sustainable Agriculture in U.S. Arid/Semiarid Lands: Selected Foreign Experience (BP-F-20)
Wetlands: Their Use and Regulation (O-206)

* Tennessee Valley Authority Environmental Policy

Environmental Quality Staff
Tennessee Valley Authority
Summer Place Building
Knoxville, TN 37902-6604   (615) 632-6578

Environmental protection and enhancement are a natural part of all TVA programs that affect the water, air, and land. This office provides centralized environmental guidance and direction to the entire agency, and is TVA's point of contact with Federal and State environmental regulators. To ensure meaningful citizen involvement in TVA's environmental activities and decisions, this office conducts periodic meetings with members of the environmental community to discuss matters of mutual nterest. The public is also kept informed through advertised public meetings and the news media.

* Terminology amd Acronyms

Public Information Center
Environmental Protection Agency
401 M St., SW, PM-211 B
Washington DC 20460   (202) 475-7751

The free *Glossary of Environmental Terms and Acronym List* is designed to provide you with an explanation of the more commonly used environmental terms appearing th EPA publications, news releases, and other Agency documents. The terms and definitions in this publication were selected to give the user a general sense of what a term or phrase means in relatively non-technical language. Contact this office for your free copy.

* Territorial and International Affairs

Territorial and International Affairs
U.S. Department of the Interior
18th and C Sts., NW
Washington, DC 20240   (202) 343-4822

International affairs within the Department of the Interior are handled by this office. If more than one Bureau is involved in an international effort, this office acts as the coordinator and liaison between the Department and the foreign constituent.

* Training Clearinghouse

Environmental Protection Agency
401 M St., SW
Washington DC 20460   (202) 475-6678

The national clearinghouse for all Agency training activities, from environmental science to enforcement to personal and professional development. The Institute focuses on in-house training, but serves as the Agency's training "broker" with other Federal agencies, State, and local governments, associations, and environmental organizations. Contact this Institute for more information on specific training programs.

* Transit Environments

Environment Division
Policy and International Affairs
Office of the Secretary of Transportation
U.S. Department of Transportation
400 7th Street, SW, Room 9217
Washington, DC 20590   (202) 366-4366

This is the DOT contact point for environmental issues. Staff can provide you with information and referrals on such subjects as highway beautification, transportation architecture, bicycle paths, historic preservation activities, and environmental impact statements.

* TVA Natural Resources Protection

Resource Development
Tennessee Valley Authority
400 W. Summit Hill Dr.
Knoxville, TN 37921   (615) 632-6367

The TVA's work with natural resources involves the whole range of environmental concerns. Today, with 20 million acres of forests in the Valley, TVA is working to adapt computer-age management to this valuable resource. TVA lakes and their 11,000 miles of shoreline provide an extensive resource for waterfowl protection, game management, and fisheries research. Industrial development and increased population intensify the necessity of protecting the natural environment. Research and testing continue to seek better ways to protect air and water; to dispose of and make use of wastes; to plan for the wise use and management of land; and to protect and preserve water tables and mineral resources, along with free-flowing streams, plants, and animal life.

* Undersea Research

National Undersea Research Program
National Oceanic and Atmospheric Administration
Department of Commerce
6010 Executive Blvd.
Rockville, MD 20852   (301) 443-8391

The National Undersea Research Program develops programs and provides support to scientists and engineers for the study of biological, chemical, geological, and physical processes in the world's oceans and lakes. NURP assist researchers in conducting what are considered by NOAA and the marine community to be crucial research programs. In order to execute these programs, NURP provides investigators with a suite of the modern undersea facilities including submersibles, habitats, air and mixed gas SCUBA, and remotely operated vehicles. A major part of the research program is carried out by a network of National Undersea Research Centers. Contact this office for more information on the research conducted or the research centers.

* Water Quality Criteria

Criteria and Standars Division
Office of Water Regulations and Standards
Environmental Protection Agency
401 M St., SW, Room E829
Washington, DC 20460   (202) 475-7301

The Clean Water Act requires each state to set water quality standards for every dignifician body of surface water within its borders. To set these standards, states specify the uses of each body of water (such as drinking water, recreation, commercial fishing), and restrict pollution to levels that permit those uses. The EPA assists the states in setting these standards and monitors them to make sure they meet the minimum required.

* Woodsy Owl and Children's Materials

U.S. Department of Agriculture
Forest Service, P.O. Box 96090
Washington, DC 20090-6090   (202) 475-3785

To increase children's awareness of our delicate environment, the Forest Service's Woodsy Owl campaign has a variety of free materials available, including coloring sheets, detective sheets, song sheets, patches, *Woodsy Owl on Camping* (brochure), and stickers.

Environment and Nature

Water and Air Quality

* Acid Rain and Aquatic Species Chart
Superintendent of Documents
Government Printing Office
Washington, DC 20402   (202) 783-3238
The wall chart, *Acid Rain: The Effect on Aquatic Species*, illustrates the survival of selected aquatic species in an acidic environment. Information is given on acid rain, its causes, and the effect on aquatic life. Measures 17 by 22 inches (S/N 024-010-00675-7, $3.25).

* Acid Rain Program
Atmospheric Deposition Analysis
Water Resources Division
U.S. Geological Survey
National Center, MS 416
Reston, VA 22092   (703) 648-6875
The Geological Survey, in cooperation with other Federal agencies and many State agencies, is participating in a coordinated nationwide program to monitor the chemical composition of precipitation and selected streams and lakes that are now or may be affected by acid rain. Selected watersheds are also being studied to gain a better understanding of the hydrologic and geochemical processes that determine whether or not acid rain will ultimately affect the quality of water coming from the watershed.

* Aerosol and Indoor Environment
American Association for Aerosol Research
Indoor Environment Program
1 Cyclotron Rd.
Berkeley, CA 94720   (919) 541-6736
This group promotes the research of small particles suspended in gases.

* Air Pollution and State Motor Vehicle Inspections
Records and Motor Vehicle Services Division (NTS-43)
National Highway Traffic Safety Administration
U.S. Department of Transportation
400 7th Street, SW
Washington, DC 20590   (202) 366-2676
NHTSA's Motor Vehicle Inspection Program is aimed at providing car owners with preventative information on what repairs are needed to achieve greater safety, lower pollution, and better mileage. The annual *Study of the State Motor Vehicle Inspection Program* is available from this office.

* Air Pollution Control Policy
State and Territorial Air Pollution Program Administrators
444 North Capitol St., NW
Suite 306
Washington, DC 20001   (202) 624-7864
STAPPA consists of state and local officials concerned with air pollution abatement and remedial response.

* Air Pollutants, Asbestos and Consumer Safety Hotline
Consumer Product Safety Commission Hotline
5401 Westbard Avenue
Bethesda, MD 20207   (800) 638-2772
The CPSC hotline provides information on consumer safety and guidelines on exposure to formaldehyde, asbestos, and air pollutants. They offer copies of studies and other related documents.

* Air Pollution Control Association
Air Pollution Control Association (APCA)
Box 2861
Pittsburgh, PA 15230   (412) 621-1090
The Air Pollution Control Association collects and distributes information about air pollution and its control. It publishes *APCA Journal*.

* Air Pollution Emissions Hotline
Control Technology Center Hotline   (919) 541-0800
The Control Technology Center Hotline is the component of EPA's Air Toxics Strategy. The Hotline provides information to State and local pollution control agencies on sources of emissions of air toxics. It operates Monday through Friday, 8:00 a.m. to 4:30 p.m. (EST).

* Air Quality and Climate Change
Atmospheric Sciences Department
Tennessee Valley Authority
Resource Development
Chemical Engineering Bldg.
Muscle Shoals, AL 35660   (205) 386-2556
The TVA is working on a large scale air pollution control program. A current report, *How Clean Is Our Air?*, evaluates the levels of traditional air pollutants, as well as discussing emerging air quality issues, which include regional oxident pollution, acidic deposition, indoor air quality, toxic air pollutants, and climate change. A full-scale report will focus on various specific regional programs that address these issues. One example, the Middle Tennessee Ozone Study, is investigating the levels and sources of ozone in the greater Nashville metropolitan area as a cooperative effort between the TVA and the Tennessee Division of Air Pollution Control. Contact this office for more information on the study and the regional air quality control programs.

* Air Quality Planning and Standards
Office of Air Quality Planning and Standards
Environmental Protection Agency
Research Triangle Park, NC 27711   (919) 541-5618
This office develops national standards for air quality, emission standards for new stationary and mobile sources, and emission standards for hazardous pollutants. Contact this office for information on specific standards.

* Air Quality Standards Library
Office of Air Quality Planning
and Standards (OAQPS) Library
826 Mutual Plaza, MD-16
Research Triangle Park, NC 27711   (919) 541-5618
This library focuses on air pollution and control technology, including material on costs, chemical technology, minerals, and statistics. The reference collection emphasizes chemistry and engineering.

* Air Resources Laboratory
Environmental Research Laboratory
National Oceanic and Atmospheric Administration
Department of Commerce
8060 13th St.
Silver Spring, MD 20910   (301) 427-7684
The Air Resources Laboratory performs weather research to understand and predict human influences on the environment, especially those involving atmospheric transport and dispersion of pollutants such as acid rain and ozone to distances up to thousands of kilometers. The ARL also monitors and interprets trends in natural and man-made substances, such as CO425, halocarbons, aerosols, and ozone which can potentially modify the climate. In addition, ARL studies solar radiation for its role in climate change. An annual report is available, which describes in more detail the current research being undertaken at ARL.

* Air Risk Hotline
Pollutant Assessment Branch, MD-13
Environmental Protection Agency
Research Triangle Park, NC 27711   (919) 541-0888
The primary purpose of the Air Risc Hotline is to provide an initial quick response based upon available health and exposure data and the expertise of EPA and its contractors.

* Air Toxics Information Clearinghouse
National Air Toxics Information Clearinghouse
MD-13
Environmental Protection Agency
Research Triangle Park, NC 27711   (919) 541-0850
The National Air Toxics Information Clearinghouse (NATICH) assists states in developing air toxics programs and setting emission levels.

* Aquatic Plants
Aquatic Biology Department
Resource Development
River Basin Operations
Water Resources

Tennessee Valley Authority
311 Broad St.
Chattanooga, TN 37402-2801   (615) 751-7324

TVA's two major weapons for controlling the spread of pesky aquatic plants, such as Eurasian watermilfoil, spiny-leaf naiad, and hydrilla in its reservoirs, is the winter and summer draw downs and the selective spraying of herbicides. Reservoir levels may be lowered several feet in the late summer to dry out and kill the roots of these plants embedded in shallow areas of the reservoirs; while at other times, lake levels may be held higher than normal to prevent sunshine from penetrating to the bottom and thus prevent germination and growth of new colonies. Selective use of approved herbicides in high priority use areas, such as swimming beaches, developed shoreline, and marinas, is another effective control method. Several experimental control strategies also are being tested on TVA lakes. One of the most promising is a cooperative effort between TVA and the U.S. Army Corps of Engineers. TVA proposes to conduct large scale demonstrations on Guntersville reservoir on the use of Grass Carp, hydrilla fly, a fungus to control watermilfoil, and other methods being currently tested on a smaller scale by the Corps Waterways Experiment Station.

* Aquatic Toxicology and Water Quality Research

Environmental Research Laboratory Library
College Station Rd.
Athens, GA 30613   (404) 546-3302

The Athens Environmental Research Laboratory (ERL) Library provides information services covering a wide range of environmental and management subjects. Subject areas include aquatic toxicology, microbiology, biology, pesticides, chemistry, water pollution, engineering, and water quality. Databases maintained here include CIS, DIALOG, and Ground Water On-line.

* Atmospheric Research and Air Quality

Environmental Sciences Group
Environmental Research Laboratories
National Oceanic and Atmospheric Administration
Department of Commerce
325 Broadway
Boulder, CO 80303   (303) 497-6286

The Environmental Sciences Group includes the Climate Research Program (studies of short- and long-term climate change), the Weather Research Program (research to improve short-range weather predictions and warning, especially regarding storm systems and flash floods), the Weather Modification Program (evaluations of data from various states' weather modification programs), and the Program for Regional Observing and Forecasting Services (transfer of technology such as interactive computer workstations to operational agencies like the National Weather Service). Contact the Public Affairs Office for more information about the programs.

* Auto Emission Controls Manufacturers

Manufacturers of Emission Controls Association (MECA)
1707 L St., NW
Suite 520
Washington, DC 20036   (202) 296-4797

The Manufacturers of Emission Controls Association represents the common interests of companies manufacturing emission control equipment throughout the United States. Publications: *Environmental Industry Council*.

* Auto Exhaust Systems Manufacturers

Automotive Exhaust Systems Manufacturers Council
300 Sylvan Ave.
Box 1638
Englewood Cliffs, NJ 07632   (201) 569-8500

This council was formed by a group of companies making exhaust system parts to expand the market for their products and monitor noise and emission control legislation.

* Bibliography: Water Pollution and Resources

Superintendent of Documents
Government Printing Office
Washington, DC 20402   (202) 783-3238

Water conservation and management books are featured. The *National Water Summary* books on hydrologic events and the subscription service, *Soil and Water Conservation News*, are among the selections. Free.

* Boulder Canyon and Other Water Projects

Office of Public Affairs
Bureau of Reclamation
U.S. Department of the Interior
P.O. Box 25007
Denver Federal Center
Denver, CO 80225   (303) 236-7000

Contact the office above for their recent publications listing. Topics available include the following: annual reports and project data from the Bureau, Boulder Canyon Project reports, design standards, engineering manuals, research reports, technical records, and design and construction records, and other reports on subjects such as canals, dams, economic planning, environment, geology and rock mechanics, hydrology, and safety.

* Chesapeake Bay Regional Library

Central Regional Laboratory (CRL) Library
839 Bestgate Rd.
Annapolis, MD 21401   (301) 266-9180

This library was established in support of the Regional Laboratory which started in Annapolis in 1964. The subjects in the collection focus on biology, chemistry, ecology, engineering, hazardous waste hydrology, and oceanography. To serve the highly diversified expertise of the laboratory scientists and engineers, material is provided in aquatic biology, analytical chemistry, automated laboratory techniques, industrial wastewater monitoring, toxic and hazardous substances, and mathematical modelling. A special collections covers the Chesapeake Bay.

* Clean Air Act

Air Docket
Environmental Protection Agency
401 M St., SW, Room M 1500
Washington DC 20460   (202) 382-7548

The Air Docket provides public access to regulatory information which supports the Agency's actions administered under the Clean Air Act. The docket consists of files containing a series of file folders for each category of documents. Most of the records are on microfilm. Contact this office for more information.

* Clean Air Regulations Docket

Central Docket
Environmental Protection Agency
401 M Street SW
Washington, DC 20460   (202) 382-7548

The Central Docket provides public access to regulatory information which supports the Agency's actions administered under the Clean Air Act. The docket consists of files containing a series of file folders for each category of documents. Most of the records are on microfilm.

* Clean Lakes Clearinghouse

Environmental Protection Agency
401 M St., SW, WH-553
Washington DC 20460   (202) 382-7111

The main purpose of the Clean Lakes Clearinghouse is to collect, organize, and distribute information on lake restoration, protection, and management to researchers, EPA personnel, lake managers, and State and local governments. The clearinghouse has a bibliographic database from which they can search specific topic areas. Contact this office for more information.

* Coal Ash Producers

American Coal Ash Association
1000 16th St., NW
Suite 507
Washington, DC 20036   (202) 659-2303

This association is comprised by companies which are producers of fly ash from the combustion of coal and are interested in promoting its use.

* Dams and Steam Plants

Governmental and Public Affairs
Community Relations
Tennessee Valley Authority
400 W. Summit Hill Dr.
Knoxville, TN 37902   (615) 632-2101

Washington Representative
Tennessee Valley Authority
412 1st St, Room 300
Washington, DC 20444   (202) 479-4412

The TVA has constructed a system of dams and reservoirs to promote navigation on the Tennessee River and its tributaries, and to control destructive flood waters in the Tennessee and Mississippi drainage basins, and to also produce electric power. Citizens are welcome to tour and visit the dams and steam plants.

* Dam Safety

Engineering and Research
Bureau of Reclamation
U.S. Department of the Interior
P.O. Box 25007
Denver, CO 80225   (303) 236-6988

Environment and Nature

Safety of dams will continue to be a Bureau of Reclamation priority. The Department revises safety ratings annually, based on the latest technical information available for each dam operated by the Bureau.

* Deep Seabed Mining

Ocean Minerals and Energy Division
National Ocean Service
National Oceanic and Atmospheric Administration
Department of Commerce
1825 Connecticut Ave., NW
Washington, DC 20235   (202) 673-5121

Extensive information is available on deep seabed mining, which includes the annual report to Congress and an updated environmental assessment of NOAA deep seabed mining licensees' exploration plans. This office can provide you with information regarding the research conducted concerning the environmental impact of the mining, as well as information on the regulations and licenses.

* Drinking Water Rules and Regulations

Environmental Protection Agency
401 M Street SW
Washington, DC 20460   (202) 475-9598

The Drinking Water Docket currently contains information on the following regulatory phases: (1) Volatile Organic Chemical (VOC) (Phase I); (2) Fluoride (Phase IIA); (3) Synthetic Organic Chemicals (SOC) (Phase II); (4) Surface Water Treatment Rule (SWTR); and (5) Radionuclides (Phase III). Others will be developed as new Maximum Contaminant Level Goals (MCLG) and Maximum Contaminant Levels (MCL) are proposed. These materials include appropriate *Federal Register* notices, letters, public hearing transcripts, National Drinking Water Advisory Council materials, public comments, technical support documents, and other materials.

* Effluent Guidelines

Office of Water Regulations and Standards
Environmental Protection Agency
401 M St., SW
Washington DC 20460   (202) 382-7120

The Clean Water Act was designed to control the discharge of pollution into U.S. waters. Any industry that pumps waste water into U.S. waters must have a permit. The EPA develops effluent guidelines which set pollution limits for specific industries.

* Emissions Hotline

Control Technology Center Hotline   (919) 541-0800

The Control Technology Center Hotline is the component of EPA's Air Toxics Strategy. The Hotline provides information to State and local pollution control agencies on sources of emissions of air toxics. It operates Monday through Friday, 8:00 a.m. to 4:30 p.m. (EST).

* English and Spanish Publications

Book and Report Sales
Box 25425
Denver, CO 80225   (303) 236-7476

This is a listing of some of the general interest publications available through the U.S. Geological Survey. They are free unless otherwise indicated.

Glaciers: A Water Resource
Ground Water
Ground Water and the Rural Homeowner
Rain: A Water Resource (Also available in Spanish)
River Basins of the United States
Save Water....Save Money
Water in the Urban Environment: Erosion and Sediment
The Water of the World
Water Use in the United States
What Is Water? (Also available in Spanish)
Why Is the Ocean Salty? (Also available in Spanish)

* Groundwater and Contaminants

Robert S. Kerr Environmental Research
Laboratory Library
P.O. Box 1198
Ada, OK 74820   (405) 332-8800

The Robert S. Kerr Environmental Research Laboratory (RSKERL) is the Agency's center of expertise for investigation of the soil and subsurface environment. Important areas of research at RSKERL include the study of the chemical and microbial contamination of groundwater and the mathematical and computer modeling of both the movement of groundwater and the influence of various contaminants in this area of the environment. Sources of pollution, as well as migration and degradation of pollutants, are all topics of concern at RSKERL. Databases maintained here include Ground Water On-line.

* Groundwater Management

Resource Management
Bureau of Reclamation
U.S. Department of the Interior
P.O. Box 25007
Denver CO 80225   (303) 236-3289

A priority of the Bureau of Reclamation is groundwater management. The Bureau continues to work with state, regional, and local entities in support of the theory that the responsibility for groundwater management, allocation, and protection rests with the states. Several programs are focused on coordinating the use of surface water and groundwater, desalinization and improvement of water quality, control of high water tables through drainage, and technical assistance to other governmental agencies.

* Groundwater Quality and Conservation

Groundwater Management Districts Association
1125 Maize Rd.
Colby, KS 67701   (913) 462-3915

The Groundwater Management Districts Association consists of districts, consulting organizations and individuals concerned with the management and conservation of water resources. It provides information transfer between members.

* Halogenated Solvents

Halogenated Solvent Industry Alliance (HSIA)
1225 19th St., NW
Suite 300
Washington, DC 20036   (202) 223-5890

The Halogenated Solvent Industry Alliance consists of producers, users, distributors and equipment manufacturers in the halogenated solvent industry. It was established to develop constructive programs on legislative and regulatory problems involving halogenated solvents.

* Hydroelectric Power

Resource Management
Bureau of Reclamation
U.S. Department of the Interior
P.O. Box 25007
Denver CO 80225   (303) 236-3289

The Bureau of Reclamation is currently operating 49 powerplants at different sites throughout the West. For further information on the impact of hydroelectric power and the Bureau's efforts, contact this office.

* Hydrographic Research

Commission Personnel Division
NOAA Corps
National Oceanic and Atmospheric Administration
Department of Commerce
11400 Rockville Pike
Rockville, MD 20852   (301) 443-8616

The NOAA Corps is the uniformed service of the Department of Commerce responsible for operating and managing NOAA's fleet of hydrographic, oceanographic, and fisheries-research ships and for supporting NOAA scientific programs. Engineering, computer science, mathematics, and science baccalaureate or higher degree graduates are sought for positions in the Corps.

* Hydrologists Institute

American Institute of Hydrology (AIH)
3416 University Ave., SE
Suite 200
Minneapolis, MN 55414   (612) 379-0901

The American Institute of Hydrology registers and certifies hydrologists and hydrogeologists.

* Industrial Gas Cleaning

Industrial Gas Cleaning Institute
1707 L St., NW
Suite 570
Washington, DC 20036   (202) 296-4797

The Industrial Gas Cleaning Institute is a member of the Environmental Industry Council. Members are manufacturers of industrial air pollution control equipment for stationary sources.

* Industrial Waste Waters

Water Pollution Control Federation (WPCF)
601 Wythe St.
Alexandria, VA 22314-1994   (703) 684-2400

The Water Pollution Control Federation consists of regional associations of individuals concerned with the disposal of domestic and industrial waste waters. Publications: *Operations Forum, Highlights*.

* Lake Protection and Restoration

Clean Lakes Program
Office of Water Regulations and Standards
Environmental Protection Agency
401 M St., SW
Washington DC 20460   (202) 382-7105
The EPA's Clean Lakes Program provides technical and financial assistance to States for programs dealing with lake restoration and protection.

* Lead and Your Drinking Water

Public Information Center
Environmental Protection Agency
401 M St., SW, PM-211 B
Washington DC 20460   (202) 475-7751
The free brochure, *Lead and Your Drinking Water*, explains the dangers of lead in your drinking water, how it gets there, and steps you can take to remove the lead.

* Local Air Pollution Control

Association of Local Air Pollution Control Officials
444 North Capitol St., NW
Washington, DC 20001   (202) 624-7864
The Association of Local Air Pollution Control Officials represents the common interests of air pollution officials throughout the United States.

* Local Air Pollution Control Hotline

Best Available Control Technology
Lowest Achievable Emission Rate Clearinghouse
Environmental Protection Agency
Research Triangle Park, NC 27711   (919) 541-5432
This Clearinghouse was established to enable State and local air pollution control agencies to exchange information on BACT/LAER determinations for new or modified sources, and to facilitate more consistent emission levels.

* Marine, Coastal, Estuarine Water Quality

Environmental Research Laboratory Library
South Ferry Rd.
Narragansett, RI 02882   (401) 782-3025
The Environmental Research Laboratory Narragansett (ERLN), with its field station in Newport, Oregon, is the EPA's center for marine, coastal, and estuarine water quality research. General collections cover aquatic toxicology, biological oceanography, biomedical science, coastal research, fisheries biology, marine biology, marine ecology, marine organisms. The special collections cover: O Estuarine and marine disposal and discharge of complex wastes, dredged materials, and other wastes; O Water use designation and quality criteria for estuarine and marine water and sediment; O Environmental assessment of ocean discharge.

* Marine Environment and Ocean Dumping

Office of Marine and Estuarine Protection
Environmental Protection Agency
401 M St., SW
Washington DC 20460   (202) 382-7166
This office carries out the duties covered under the Marine Protection, Research and Sanctuaries Act, which is designed to protect the marine environment from the harmful effects of ocean dumping. The Act establishes a permit program to ensure that ocean dumping does not cause degradation of the marine environment. Contact this office for more information on ocean dumping regulation.

* Marine Pollutants

Office of Oceanography and Marine Assessments
National Ocean Service
National Oceanic and Atmospheric Administration
Department of Commerce
6001 Executive Blvd.
Rockville, MD 20852   (301) 443-8487
This office surveys and monitors the oceans, U.S. coastal waters and the Great Lakes to produce data and information products that are critically important for offshore oil and gas exploration, dredging operations, coastal and offshore construction, seafloor mining, waste disposal management, and for protecting the marine environment from the adverse effects of ocean and coastal pollution.

* Motor Vehicle Emissions

Motor Vehicle Emissions Laboratory Library
2565 Plymouth Rd.
Ann Arbor, MI 48105   (313) 668-4311
This library provides information services concentrated on automotive engineering to EPA staff and the general public. Subject areas include air pollution from mobile sources, alternative alcohol fuels, and motor vehicle retrofit devices.

* Municipal, Recreation, Industrial Water Supply

U.S. Department of Agriculture
Deputy for Programs, SCS
Box 2890
Washington, DC 20013   (202) 447-4527
The USDA manages a variety of water resource programs to aid landowners and agricultural operators use existing water resources wisely. These programs also promote reclamation and preservation of water sources that have been contaminated or allowed to fall into disrepair and to monitor recreation, municipal, and industrial water supply.

* National Ocean Service

National Oceanic and Atmospheric Administration
Department of Commerce
6001 Executive Blvd.
Rockville, MD 20852   (301) 443-8487
The Office of Oceanography and Marine Assessments surveys and monitors the oceans, U.S. coastal waters, estuarine waterways, and the Great Lakes to produce data and information products that describe the physical properties of these waters for a wide range of engineering and navigational applications. This office also conducts studies to assess the environmental impact of human activities in U.S. coastal waters. Many of these marine data and information products are essential for protecting life and property from storms and other destructive natural forces. Other marine products, such as predictions of the times and heights of tides and descriptions of tidal currents, are vital for safe navigation.

* National Water Conditions Monthly Update

Hydrologic Information Unit
Water Resources Division
U.S. Geological Survey
419 National Center
Reston, VA 22092   (703) 648-6817
National Water Conditions is a monthly summary of hydrologic conditions in the United States and southern Canada. Subscriptions are free upon application.

* Ocean and Coastal Pollution

Office of Oceanography and Marine Assessments
National Ocean Service
National Oceanic and Atmospheric Administration
Department of Commerce
6001 Executive Blvd.
Rockville, MD 20852   (301) 443-8487
This office surveys and monitors the oceans, U.S. coastal waters and the Great Lakes to produce data and information products that are critically important for offshore oil and gas exploration, dredging operations, coastal and offshore construction, seafloor mining, waste disposal management, and for protecting the marine environment from the adverse effects of ocean and coastal pollution.

* Ocean Dumping Surveillance and Marine Technology

Library
Coast Guard Research and Development Center
U.S. Coast Guard
U.S. Department of Transportation
Avery Point
Groton, CT 06340-6096   (203) 441-2648
Marine research is conducted here in areas such as ice technology, navigation instrumentation technology, ocean dumping surveillance, pollution, search and rescue techniques, and marine fire and safety technology. This library is a good starting point for obtaining specific information about what research is done by the Center and for referrals to appropriate experts.

* Oceanic Long-Range Planning

American Oceanic Organization (AOO)
Box 513
Edgewater, MD 21037   (301) 261-9491
The American Oceanic Organization serves to encourage long-range government planning in such areas of oceanology as pollution control and resources development. Members are drawn from government agencies, universities, Congress and industry.

Environment and Nature

* Oceanographic Corps Jobs
Commission Personnel Division
NOAA Corps
National Oceanic and Atmospheric Administration
Department of Commerce
11400 Rockville Pike
Rockville, MD 20852   (301) 443-8616
The NOAA Corps is the uniformed service of the Department of Commerce responsible for operating and managing NOAA's fleet of hydrographic, oceanographic, and fisheries-research ships and for supporting NOAA scientific programs. Engineering, computer science, mathematics, and science baccalaureate or higher degree graduates are sought for positions in the Corps.

* Ocean Pollution Information Network
Ocean Pollution Data and
  Information Network/ CCRO
National Oceanographic Data Center
National Oceanic and Atmospheric Administration
1825 Connecticut Ave., NW
Washington, DC 20235   (202) 673-5539
The Ocean Pollution Data and Information Network facilitates user access to ocean pollution data and information generated by 11 participating Federal departments and agencies. OPDIN provides a wide range of products and services to researchers, managers, and others who need data and information about ocean pollution. OPDIN is managed by the Central Coordination and Referral Office (CCRO). The CCRO maintains a directory of Federal ocean pollution data and information systems and services, lists of ocean pollution scientists and managers and their fields of expertise, and annually-updated catalogs of Federal marine pollution research, development, and monitoring projects. The CCRO also provides information and advice about ocean pollution data management and processing, as well as copies of catalogs, directories, technical reports, data inventories, and data products.

* Oil and Chemical Spills Hotline
National Response Center (NRC)
Marine Environmental Response Division
Office of Marine Safety, Security, and Environmental Protection
U.S. Coast Guard
U.S. Department of Transportation
2100 2nd St., SW, Room 2611   (800) 424-8802
Washington, DC 20593   (202) 267-2188
The NRC receives reports of oil and hazardous substance spills, investigates incidents, initiates civil penalty actions, monitors cleanups, and coordinates federally funded spill response operations. NRC's National Strike Force assists federal coordinators on the scene in responding to pollution accidents. For further details, or to report information, contact the Center toll-free.

* Paper Industry Air and Stream Pollution
National Council of the Paper Industry for Air
  and Stream Improvements
260 Madison Ave.
New York, NY 10016   (212) 532-9000
The National Council of the Paper Industry for Air and Stream Improvements is a technical organization devoted to finding solutions to environmental protection problems in the manufacture of pulp, paper and wood products in industrial forestry.

* Pollution Control Equipment Manufacturers
Process Equipment Manufacturers Association (PEMA)
7297 Lee Highway
Suite N
Falls Church, VA 22042   (703) 533-0286
PEMA consists of companies engaged in the manufacturing of and supply of equipment for food, chemical, pulp and paper, water and water processing, air pollution control, etc.

* Pollution Control Financing
Council of Pollution Control Financing Agencies
1225 Eye St., NW
Suite 300
Washington, DC 20005   (202) 682-3996
This council is for state and local government agencies and other organizations which are interested in financing and economic incentives for pollution control facilities, both public and private.

* Pollution Liability Insurance
Pollution Liability Insurance Association (PLIA)
1333 Butterfield Rd.
Suite 100
Downers Grove, IL 60515   (312) 969-5300

PLIA is a reciprocal pool reinsuring pollution liability policies written by member insurance companies.

* Pollution Response Operations
Pollution Response Branch
Marine Environmental Response Division
Office of Marine Safety, Security,
  and Environmental Protection
U.S. Coast Guard
U.S. Department of Transportation
2100 2nd St., SW, Room 2104   (202) 267-0518
Washington, DC 20593-0001   (202) 267-2611
This office responds to requests for marine environmental protection information from Congress and other federal agencies, state agencies, schools, industries, and the general public. Data is available on laws relating to the protection of the marine environment, incidents involving releases of oil or other hazardous substances, and federally funded spill response operations.

* Project Skywater: Cloud Seeding
Cloud Seeding - Project Skywater
Water Augmentation Group, Code D-3720
Research and Laboratory Services Division
Bureau of Reclamation
U.S. Department of the Interior
P.O. Box 25007
Denver, CO 80225-0007   (303) 236-4346
Project Skywater is a weather modification project which attempts to change natural phenomena such as clouds, rain, snow, hail, lightning, thunderstorms, tornadoes, fog, and hurricanes so they are more beneficial or less destructive. Under Project Skywater, various domestic cloud seeding programs have been undertaken, including the Sierra Nevada Cooperative Program, the Colorado River Augmentation Demonstration Program, the Southwest Cooperative Demonstration Program, the Tennessee Valley Authority Cooperative Program, the Arizona Snowpack Augmentation Program, and the Colorado River Enhanced Snowpack Test. Foreign assistance programs are also underway with the Canary Islands (Spain), Morocco, and Thailand.

* Regional Hydrologists
Water Resources Division
U.S. Geological Survey
409 National Center
Reston, VA 22092   (703) 648-5215
The U.S. Geological Survey has the following hydrologist field offices:

Northeastern Region
Regional Hydrologist, U.S. Geological Survey, 433 National Center, Reston, VA 22092; (703) 648-5817. Serving: CT, DE, IL, IN, ME, MD, MA, MI, MN, NH, NJ, NY, OH, PA, RI, VT, VA, DC, WV, WI

Southeastern Region
Regional Hydrologist, U.S. Geological Survey, Richard B. Russell Federal Bldg., 75 Spring St., SW, Room 772, Atlanta, GA 30303; (404) 331-5174. Serving: AL, AR, FL, GA, KY, LA, MS, NC, PR, SC, TN, Virgin Islands

Central Region
Regional Hydrologist, U.S. Geological Survey, Mail Stop 406, Box 25046, Denver Federal Center, Lakewood, CO 80225; (303) 236-5920. Serving: CO, IA, KS, MO, MT, NE, NM, ND, OK, SD, TX, UT, WY

Western Region
Regional Hydrologist, U.S. Geological Survey, 345 Middlefield Rd., Mail Stop 470, Menlo Park, CA 94025. Serving: AK, AR, CA, Guam, HI, ID, NV, OR, WA

* Rural Non-Source Water Pollution
U.S. Department of Agriculture
Deputy for Programs, SCS
Box 2890
Washington, DC 20013   (202) 447-4527
The USDA manages a variety of water resource programs to aid landowners and agricultural operators use existing water resources wisely. The Rural Clean Water Program to reduce non-source water pollution is one of its programs.

* Safe Drinking Water Hotline
Environmental Protection Agency
401 M Street SW
Washington, DC 20460   (800) 426-4791
The Safe Drinking Water Hotline responds to questions concerning the Safe Drinking Water Act, Water Standards, Regulations, and the Underground Injection Program. It will also provide selected publications relevant to these issues. It operates Monday through Friday, 8:30 a.m. to 4:30 p.m. (EST).

* Sea-Grant Colleges

Office of Oceanic Research Programs
National Oceanic and Atmospheric Administration
Department of Commerce
1335 East-West Hwy.
Silver Spring, MD 20910   (202) 377-8090

The National Sea Grant College Program is a national network of over 300 colleges, universities, research institutions, and consortia working in partnership with industry and the federal government to support Great Lakes and marine research, education, and extension services. This program provides support for institutions engaged in comprehensive marine research, education, and advisory service programs, supports individual projects in marine research and development, and sponsors education of ocean scientists and engineers, marine technicians, and other specialists at selected colleges and universities.

* Spray Equipment Manufacturers

National Spray Equipment Manufacturers Association
550 Randall Rd.
Elyria, OH 44035   (216) 988-9411

The NSEMA serves as a technical forum for safety and environmental matters pertaining to the spray finishing industry.

* State Drinking Water Programs

State Programs Division
Office of Drinking Water
Environmental Protection Agency
401 M St., SW, Room E1101
Washington DC 20460   (202) 382-5526

This office oversees the drinking water regulations that are part of the Clean Water Act at the regional and State level. They make sure a State's standards meet at least the minimum requirements of the law, and they are also responsible for their enforcement.

* Unleaded Gas and Fuels Hotline

Environmental Protection Agency
Region I
JFK Federal Bldg.   (800) 821-1237
Boston, MA 02203   (800) 631-2700 (MA)

The Unleaded Fuel Tank Hotline is an enforcement-related line that takes calls about tampering with vehicles, pumps, and other problems related to unleaded fuels. It provides this service for Region I states: Connecticut, Massachusetts, New Hampshire, Rhode Island, Vermont.

* Volatile Emissions Control Clearinghouse

Volatile Organic Compounds/Reasonably
Achievable Control Technology (VOC) Clearinghouse
Environmental Protection Agency
Research Triangle Park, NC 27711   (919) 541-5625

This Clearinghouse is intended to control VOC emissions by facilitating the exchange of technical data and experience to control emissions.

* Wastewater Treatment Clearinghouse

Small Flows Clearinghouse
613 N. Spruce St.
Morgantown, WV 26505   (800) 624-8301

The National Small Flows Clearinghouse provides information on wastewater treatment technologies for small communities. This clearinghouse was mandated by the Clean Water Act Amendments of 1977.

* Water Conservation

U.S. Department of Agriculture
Deputy for Programs, SCS
Box 2890
Washington, DC 20013   (202) 447-4527

The USDA manages a variety of water resource programs to aid landowners and agricultural operators use existing water resources including Resource Conservation and Development which encourages state and local governments and non-profit organizations to develop programs to accelerate water conservation and development.

* Water Contamination by Metals

Environmental Technology Division
Bureau of Mines
U.S. Department of the Interior
2401 E St., NW
Washington, DC 20241   (202) 634-1263

Researchers at the Bureau of Mines are working on low-cost ways to deal with the problem of acid drainage at abandoned mines. They are developing computer programs to predict potential drainage at new mines. The Bureau's environmental research also addresses the problem of solid waste disposal and soil and water contaminated by metals. Technologies are developed that will reduce or remove the threats that these wastes pose.

* Water Data Exchange (NAWDEX)

National Water Data Exchange
Water Resources Division
U.S. Geological Survey
National Center, MS 421
Reston, VA 22092   (703) 648-5677

The National Water Data Exchange is a confederation of Federal and non-Federal water-oriented organizations working together to improve access to available water data. Information on sites for which water data is available, the types of data available, and the organizations that store the data is available from NAWDEX.

* Water Online and Other Databases

Environmental Research Laboratory Library
College Station Rd.
Athens, GA 30613   (404) 546-3302

The Athens Environmental Research Laboratory (ERL) Library provides information services covering a wide range of environmental and management subjects. Subject areas include aquatic toxicology, microbiology, biology, pesticides, chemistry, water pollution, engineering, and water quality. Databases maintained here include CIS, DIALOG, and Ground Water On-line.

* Water Pollution and Hydrobiology Clearinghouse

Andrew W. Briedenbach Environmental
Research Center Library
26 W. St. Clair St.
Cincinnati, OH 45268   (513) 569-7703

The major subjects in this library's collection are bacteriology, biology, biotechnology, chemistry, engineering, hazardous wastes, hydrobiology, microbiology, solid waste management, toxicology, water pollution, and water quality. Databases maintained here include BRS, CAS On-line, CIS, DIALOG, Dun & Bradstreet, Hazardous Waste Database, LEXIS/NEXIS, NLM, Toxline, and Toxnet. General collections include bacteriology, biology, biotechnology, microbiology, physics, solid waste management. This library's special collections cover the environment, Canada, legal issues, hazardous waste, and solid waste.

* Water Pollution Control

Association of State and Interstate Water Pollution Control Administrators (ASIWPCA)
444 North Capitol St., NW
Suite 330
Washington, DC 20001   (202) 624-7782

This association is comprised of chief water pollution control administrators from the states, District of Columbia, U.S. possessions and interstate agencies. It establishes objectives, policies and standards for state water pollution control.

* Water Quality Assessment

Office of Water Quality
Water Resources Division
U.S. Geological Survey
National Center, MS 412
Reston, VA 22092   (703) 648-6884

The National Water Quality Assessment Program is designed to address a wide range of water-quality issues that include chemical contamination, acidification, eutrophication, salinity, sedimentation, and sanitary quality. The program strives to provide nationally consistent descriptions of current water-quality conditions and to define long-term trends in water quality.

* Water Quality Federal Association

Federal Water Quality Association (FWQA)
c/o WH 547, U.S. EPA
401 M St., SW
Washington, DC 20460   (202) 833-8383

The Federal Water Quality Association is affiliated with the Water Pollution Control Federation. Members consist of federal employees, consultants, and industry and association representatives concerned with sewage and industrial water treatment and disposal.

* Water Quality Networks

Office of Water Quality
Water Resources Division
U.S. Geological Survey
National Center, MS 412
Reston, VA 22092   (703) 648-6884

Environment and Nature

The National Water-Quality Networks Program describes and appraises the Nation's water resources. The largest of these networks is the National Stream Quality Accounting Network (NASQAN), which consists of more than 400 sampling sites used to measure a comprehensive list of physical and chemical characteristics on a quarterly or bimonthly schedule to fulfill information needs of national and regional water resources planners and managers. Other networks within the program include the Radiochemical Surveillance Network, the Tritium Network, and the Hydrologic Bench-Mark Network. This last network monitors the natural streamflow and water quality of small river basins that are known to be relatively little affected by man's activities.

* Water Research Grants

Chief Hydrologist
Water Resources Division
U.S. Geological Survey
National Center, MS 409
Reston, VA 22092 (703) 648-5215

The Water Research Grants Program is a national program of grants to support technology development and research in major water resource problem areas. State Water Resources Research and Technology Institutes, qualified educational institutions, private foundations, private firms, individuals, and agencies of local or state governments are eligible to receive grants on a dollar-for-dollar matching basis for research concerning any aspect of a water-resource related problem deemed to be in the national interest.

* Water Resources Activities

Hydrologic Information Unit
Water Resources Division
U.S. Geological Survey
419 National Center
Reston, VA 22092 (703) 648-6817

The current hydrology program in each state is outlined in a series of pamphlets entitled *Water-Resources Activities of the Geological Survey in (State)*. Pamphlets are available through the regional hydrologists offices listed elsewhere in this book.

* Water Resources: National Survey

National Water Summary Branch
Water Resources Division
U.S. Geological Survey
National Center, MS 407
Reston, VA 22092 (703) 648-6851

The National Water Summary Program brings together information about the availability, quantity, quality, and use of water resources and organizes it in ways to show the Nation's water resources condition to national, state, and local officials and to the general public. *National Water Summary Reports* are published annually.

* Water Resources Association

American Water Resources Association (AWRA)
5410 Grosvenor Lane
Suite 220
Bethesda, MD 20814 (301) 493-8600

The American Water Resources Association is a multidisciplinary, non-profit, scientific and education association dedicated to research, planning, management, development and education in water resources. AWRA is a member society of the Renewable Natural Resources Foundation. Publications: *Hydata News, Water Resources Bulletin*.

* Water Resources Congress

Water Resources Congress (WRC)
3800 North Fairfax Drive
Suite 7
Arlington, VA 22203 (703) 525-4881

The Water Resources Congress is a federation of associations, government agencies and private firms concerned with land and water use, conservation, and control. Publications: *Washington Report*.

* Water Resources Information

Hydrologic Information Unit
Water Resources Division
U.S. Geological Survey
National Center, MS 419
Reston, VA 22092 (703) 648-6817

Contact this office for requests for general information on water resources of an area or the Nation and on activities of the Water Resources Division.

* Water Resources Library

Departmental Library

Bureau of Reclamation
U.S. Department of the Interior
P.O. Box 25007, D7923I
Denver Federal Center
Denver, CO 80225-0007 (303) 236-6963

This library within the Bureau of Reclamation holds a wealth of information on the Bureau's water conservation activities. Library materials may be used only at the library or may be checked out through the inter-library loan system at your local library. Key topics include hydrology engineering, groundwater management, dam safety, soil mechanics, and business related issues.

* Water Problems Nationwide

Interstate Conference on Water Problems (ICWP)
2300 M St., NW
Suite 800
Washington, DC 20037 (202) 466-7287

The Interstate Conference on Water Problems consists of state and regional agencies, non-profit organizations and universities concerned with conservation, development and administration of water and land-related resources. Publications: *ICWP Policy Statement & Bylaws, Washington Report*.

* Water Purifiers and Other Equipment

Water Quality Association
4151 Naperville Rd.
Lisle, IL 60532 (312) 369-1600

The WQA is a not-for-profit association representing firms and individuals engaged in the design, manufacture, production, distribution and sale of equipment, products, supplies and services for providing quality water for specific uses in residential, commercial, industrial and institutional establishments.

* Watershed Protection

U.S. Department of Agriculture
Deputy for Programs, SCS
Box 2890
Washington, DC 20013 (202) 447-4527

The USDA manages a variety of water resource programs to aid landowners and agricultural operators use existing water resources wisely including Watershed Protection Projects which provides flood management prevention; watershed protection; agricultural water management.

* Water Supply and Waste Water Treatment

National Environmental Training Association (NETA)
8687 Via de Ventura
Suite 214
Scottsdale, AZ 85258 (602) 951-1440

The National Environmental Training Association consists of trainers of personnel in the field of air and noise pollution and hazardous waste control, water supply and waste water treatment. Publications: *NETA Newsletter*.

* Water Supply, Flood Plain Management

U.S. Army Corps of Engineers
Public Affairs
20 Massachusetts Ave., NW
Washington, DC 20314 (202) 272-0011

The Corps offers free brochures on a wide variety of subjects, including archaeology, camping, environment, erosion control, flood control, flood plain management, history, safety, waste-water treatment and water supply. For a publications list, call or write the above office.

* Water Supply Situation

Resource Management
Bureau of Reclamation
U.S. Department of the Interior
P.O. Box 25007
Denver Federal Center
Denver, CO 80225 (303) 236-3289

The Bureau assists water users and development agencies in reviewing state and federal water laws in an ongoing effort to conserve the Nation's water supply.

* Western Reservoirs and Water Projects Photographs

Visual Communication Services
Bureau of Reclamation
U.S. Department of the Interior
P.O. Box 25007
Denver Federal Center
Denver, CO 80225 (303) 236-6973

Photographs depicting Bureau of Reclamation activities may be borrowed from this office. Videocassettes, slide shows, black and white photos, and color slides are available, showing water and power activities, such as recreation, irrigation, agriculture, research, and reservoirs, within the Western region.

* Western Water Quality and Supply
Engineering and Research
Bureau of Reclamation
U.S. Department of the Interior
P.O. Box 25007
Denver, CO 80225   (303) 236-6988

The Bureau of Reclamation provides programs and leadership to improve water quality, to eliminate environmental pollution and protect Western water supplies from other threats of pollution. Other related programs include fish and wildlife enhancement, reduction of salinity and other pollutants in streams and reservoirs, agricultural drainage control, and protection against contamination of underground and surface water sources.

* Wetlands Protection
Office of Wetlands Protection
Environmental Protection Agency
401 M St., SW
Washington DC 20460   (202) 475-7791

This office implements EPA statutory responsibilities in the Clean Water Act as they relate to the filling of wetlands and other aquatic resources. Designed to raise the importance of wetlands, this office works with other governmental bodies to encourage wetlands protection.

* Wild and Scenic Rivers
Land and Renewable Resources
Bureau of Land Management
U.S. Department of the Interior
18th and C Sts., NW
Washington, DC 20240   (202) 343-4896

The Bureau of Land Management manages about 2,200 miles of the Wild and Scenic River System, primarily in the western United States. These areas are located in the directory, *Recreation Guide to BLM Public Lands*, available from the Office of Public Affairs, Bureau of Land Management, U.S. Department of the Interior, Washington, D.C. 20240.

* Undersea Research
National Undersea Research Program
National Oceanic and Atmospheric Administration
Department of Commerce
6010 Executive Blvd.
Rockville, MD 20852   (301) 443-8391

The National Undersea Research Program develops programs and provides support to scientists and engineers for the study of biological, chemical, geological, and physical processes in the world's oceans and lakes. NURP assist researchers in conducting what are considered by NOAA and the marine community to be crucial research programs. In order to execute these programs, NURP provides investigators with a suite of the modern undersea facilities including submersibles, habitats, air and mixed gas SCUBA, and remotely operated vehicles. A major part of the research program is carried out by a network of National Undersea Research Centers. Contact this office for more information on the research conducted or the research centers.

Forests and Land Conservation

See also Business and Industry Chapter
See also Vacations and Business Travel Chapter

* Abandoned Mine Land Reclamation

Office of Surface Mining Reclamation and Enforcement
U.S. Department of the Interior
1951 Constitution Ave., NW
Washington, DC 20240 (202) 343-5365
The surface mining law requires that operators pay a reclamation fee for each ton of coal produced. These fees are deposited with the U.S. Treasury in a fund called the Abandoned Mine Reclamation Fund and are used to reclaim sites that were mined and left unreclaimed before the surface mining law was enacted in 1977. Fifty percent of the fees collected in a state that has approved reclamation and regulatory programs is returned to that state for use in its reclamation program. The other fifty percent is the Federal share. This portion is used by the Office of Surface Mining Reclamation and Enforcement to address public health and safety emergencies caused by past mining practices, and to fund high-priority reclamation projects in non-program states. To obtain your state contact for the abandoned mine land reclamation program, contact the office above.

* Agents and Rangers for Public Lands

Office of Public Information
Bureau of Land Management
U.S. Department of the Interior
18th and C Sts., NW
Washington, DC 20240-0001 (202) 343-5717
As a caretaker of more than 300 million acres, the BLM manages and protects these lands and the resources associated with them. BLM has highly trained Special Agents and uniformed rangers to enforce applicable Federal laws on public lands. Special agents are responsible for conducting criminal investigations and making arrests. Rangers primarily patrol the public lands where they prevent law violations and assist stranded visitors. Contact the office above for the pamphlet *Protecting Public Land Resources* for a listing of Field Offices to contact for employment.

* Bureau of Land Management State Offices

Bureau of Land Management
U.S. Department of the Interior
Washington, DC 20240 (202) 343-5717
Specific information about opportunities to enjoy the benefits of the public lands and resources can best be obtained from the state office responsible for the areas of interest:

Alaska
Bureau of Land Management, 701 C St., P.O.Box 13, Anchorage, AK 99513; (907) 271-5555

Arizona
Bureau of Land Management, 3707 N 7th St., Phoenix, AZ 85014; (602) 241-5504

California
Bureau of Land Management, Federal Building, Room E-2841, 2800 Cottage Way, Sacramento, CA 95825; (916) 484-4724

Colorado
Bureau of Land Management, 2850 Youngfield St., Lakewood, CO 80215; (303) 236-1700. Also serves Kansas

Eastern States
Bureau of Land Management, 350 South Pickett St., Alexandria, VA 22304; (703) 274-0190. Serves states bordering and east of the Mississippi River),

Idaho
Bureau of Land Management, 3380 Americana Terr., Boise, ID 83706; (208) 331-1771

Montana
Bureau of Land Management, 222 N 32nd Street, P.O. Box 36800, Billings, MT 59107; (406) 657-6561. Also serves North Dakota and South Dakota

Nevada
Bureau of Land Management, 300 Booth St., P.O. Box 12000, Reno, NV 89520; (702) 784-5311

New Mexico
Bureau of Land Management, South Federal Pl., P.O. Box 1449, Santa Fe, NM 87501; (505) 988-6316. Also serves Oklahoma and Texas.

Oregon
Bureau of Land Management, 825 NE Multnomah St., P.O. Box 2965, Portland, OR 97208; (503) 231-6274. Also serves Washington.

Utah
Bureau of Land Management, 324 South State Street, Suite 301, Salt Lake City, UT 84111-3146; (801) 524-5311

Wyoming
Bureau of Land Management, 2515 Warren Ave., P.O. Box 1828, Cheyenne, WY 82001; (307) 772-2111. Also serves Nebraska.

* Bureau of Reclamation Regional Offices

Bureau of Mines
U.S. Department of Interior
1951 Constitution Avenue, NW
Washington, DC 20240 (202) 343-4953
Here are the regional offices which enforce strip mining and reclamation laws:

Lower Colorado Region
Box 427, Nevada Hwy. and Park St., Boulder City, NV 89005; (702) 293-8420

Mid-Pacific Region
2800 Cottage Way, Sacramento, CA 95825; (916) 978-4919

Pacific Northwest Region
Box 043, 550 W. Fort St., Boise, ID 83724; (208) 334-1938

Upper Colorado Region
Box 11568, 125 S. State St., Salt Lake City, UT 84147; (801) 524-5403

Great Plains Region
Box 36900, 316 N. 26th St., Billings, MT 59107; (406) 657-6218

* Cadastral Survey

Branch of Cadastral Survey Development
Bureau of Land Management
U.S. Department of the Interior
1725 I St., NW
Washington, DC 20240 (202) 653-8798
The Office of Cadastral Surveys is responsible for the creation, restoration, marking, and defining of the boundaries of public lands. Under the cadastral system, the public domain is plotted into a grid of squares, each approximately 6 miles to the side, called "townships." In recent years, modern technology has replaced the traditional "chain" measuring tape with electronic instruments. Microwave, light wave, laser beam, photogrammetry, and gyroscopic orientations are among the scientific mediums integrated in the cadastral surveyor's array of working tools.

* Christmas Trees - Free

Division of Forestry
Bureau of Land Management
U.S. Department of the Interior
Washington, DC 20240 (202) 653-8864
The BLM officials issue permits to cut Christmas trees for a nominal fee on Bureau of Land Management-administered lands in the 11 Western states and Alaska. Free-use permits are available from the Bureau to non-profit organizations for timber and trees to be used exclusively by that organization. This excludes the resale of any free timber or trees by those organizations.

* Cooperative Forest Fire Control

Fire Protection Staff
U.S. Department of Agriculture
Forest Service, P.O. Box 96090
Washington, DC 20090-6090 (202) 235-8039

State and Federal governments cooperate to protect non-federal timberland, potential timberland, certain non-forested watershed lands, and other rural lands from serious fire damage. For information, contact a regional forester or area Forest Service director or the above office.

* Cooperative Forest Insect and Disease Management

Contact: your State Forester or the state office
of the U.S. Forest Service, usually located
in the state capitol.

To reduce loss and damage to forests and lands by forest insects and diseases, the USDA provides technical and financial assistance in prevention, detection, evaluation, and suppression of forest insect and disease outbreaks on state and private lands.

* Erosion Control

Information Division
U.S. Department of Agriculture
ASCS, P.O. Box 205
Kansas City, MO 64141 (202) 447-5237

The Agricultural State Conservation Service (ASCS) directs a number of conservation programs to preserve and improve American farmland:
Conservation Reserve Program (CRP): Targets the most fragile farmland by encouraging farmers to stop growing crops on land designated by conservationists as "highly erodible" and plant grass or trees on it instead. The farmer receives rent on the land for a term of ten years. Cost-share programs are also available for permanent planting of grass and trees in these areas.

* Federal Lands Energy Leasing

Offshore Minerals Management
Mineral Management Service
U.S. Department of the Interior
18th and C Sts., NW
Washington, DC 20240 (202) 343-3530

The Mineral Management Service leases the rights to explore and develop oil and gas on Federal lands of the continental shelf. The "shelf" is made up of the submerged offshore areas lying seaward of the territorial sea to a depth of 200 meters (656 feet) and beyond that area to that depth which allows for mineral exploration. The brochure, *Leasing Energy Resources on the Outer Continental Shelf*, explains the leasing procedure and gives a history of the program.

* Fire and Land Management

Fire and Aviation Management
Bureau of Land Management
U.S. Department of the Interior
1725 I St., NW
Washington, DC 20006 (202) 653-8800

BLM's fire management program is divided into two areas: wildfire suppression and prescribed fire. Wildfire suppression includes all aspects of preparing for, detecting, and fighting wildland fire, and for rehabilitation of severely burned areas. Fire is also used under prescribed conditions to help achieve land management objectives. An average of 700 prescribed (intentionally set and controlled) fires are conducted each year by BLM to make room for new forage for livestock and wildlife. They are also used to prepare a site for seeding or the planting of seedlings.

* Fire Safety Bibliography

Superintendent of Documents
Government Printing Office
Washington, DC 20402 (202) 783-3238

Fire safety publications are listed, including improving the fire safety of cigarettes and the effect of cigarettes on the ignition of furnishings. Free.

* Forest Fire Reports

Aviation and Fire Management
U.S. Department of Agriculture
Current Forest Fire Situation
Washington, DC 20013 (703) 235-8666

This office can provide you with information on forest fires anywhere in the U.S.

* Forest Management and Education Worldwide

Natural Resources Sector
Office of Training and Programming Support
Peace Corps
1990 K St., NW
Washington, DC 20526 (202) 254-8400

Working in 38 countries, forestry specialists design and execute forest management plans designed to help combat the overcutting, droughts, and deserts that are beginning to threaten many tropical forests around the world.

They also help establish nurseries, curricula in environmental education, and skills in tropical fruit cultivation.

* Forest Products Utilization

Cooperative Forestry
Forest Service
U.S. Department of Agriculture
Room 125-A CW P.O. Box 2417
Washington, DC 20013 (202) 235-2212

Technical assistance is available to wood processors and harvesters of wood products in cooperation with private consultants and state agencies.

* Forest Ranger Recruitment

Forest Service
U.S. Department of Agriculture
Recruitment
P.O. Box 2417
Washington, DC 20013 (703) 235-2730

Contact this office for information on a career as a forest ranger.

* Forest Research and Technical Expertise

Deputy for Research
Forest Service
U.S. Department of Agriculture
Box 90690
Washington, DC 20090-6090 (202) 447-6665

Basic research is conducted by a large staff on such topics as forest insects and diseases, forest fire and atmosphere sciences, forest resource economics, biodiversity, global climate change, watershed and aquatic habitat, range and wildlife ecology, wood chemistry and fiber products, and structural and forest system engineering.

* Forests and Land Management

Forestry Division
Bureau of Land Management
U.S. Department of the Interior
1725 I St., NW
Washington, DC 20006 (202) 653-8864

The Bureau of Land Management administers 90 million acres of forested lands, most of which are in Alaska. In the lower 48 states, some 26 million acres are managed, including 21 million acres of woodlands and 5 million acres of commercial forest lands.

* Forests Near TVA Reservoirs

River Basin Operations
Land Resources
Natural Resources Management
Forest Resource Development
Tennessee Valley Authority
Norris, TN 37828 (615) 632-1631

The Forest Resource Development staff maintains forests around TVA's reservoirs to prevent development and thereby protect the water from siltation. The forests are kept in good health to allow for hunting--within the bounds of state regulations--and recreational parks. The Service also creates jobs and encourages economic development by assisting industry in utilizing forest resources. The staff also works with state agencies in reforestation efforts and fire control programs.

* Gold Prospecting

Publications Department
Bureau of Mines
U.S. Department of the Interior
18th and C Sts., NW, Room 2647
Washington, DC 20240 (202) 343-5520

The publications department of the Bureau of Mines distributes the free booklet, *How To Mine and Prospect for Gold.*

* Great Plains Conservation Work

Soil Conservation Service
U.S. Department of Agriculture
Washington, DC 20250 (202) 382-1868

Land users living in the Great Plains states can seek assistance from the Soil Conservation Service (SCS), which offers technical assistance and cost-sharing funds to farmers, ranchers, and other land users in the Great Plains. Cost-share rates can range up to 80 percent for urgently needed conservation work. Contact SCS or your local Soil Conservation Office.

Environment and Nature

* Indian Land Trust
Office of Trust and Economic Development
Bureau of Indian Affairs
U.S. Department of the Interior
18th and C Sts., NW
Washington, DC 20240   (202) 343-5831
This office manages some 53 million acres of land held in trust by the United States for Indians. Tribes are helped in protecting their lands and in developing their forest, water, mineral, and energy resources.

* Land Management Library
Bureau of Land Management Library, SC 324A
U.S. Department of the Interior
Denver Federal Center
P.O. Box 25007
Denver, CO 80225   (303) 236-6649
A vast collection of information on issues concerning land management is available to the public through this library. The reference staff and an automated card catalog system aid researchers in exploring the following topics: cadastral engineering; forest resources management; land reserve studies; legislation and public land laws; range management; watershed management; mineral, oil, and gas leasing; oil shale; and conservation and use of public lands.

* Land Use and Land Cover Maps
Distribution Branch
U.S. Geological Survey
Building 810
Denver Federal Center, Box 25286
Denver, CO 80225   (800) USA-MAPS
Land use maps and land cover maps are available for most of the United States. Land use maps refer to human uses of the land (housing and industry) and land cover maps describe the vegetation, water, natural surface, and construction on the land surface. The scale used ranges from 1:100,000 for a few maps in the Western states to 1:250,000 for most other maps.

* Livestock Rangeland
Rangeland Resources
Bureau of Land Management
U.S. Department of the Interior
1725 I St., NW
Washington, DC 20006   (202) 653-9193
The Bureau of Land Management has administration of 170 million acres of public lands where livestock graze. About 18,800 ranchers and farmers graze livestock on BLM-managed lands. A majority of these permittees have small (less than 100 head) or medium (100 to 500 head) livestock operations.

* Minerals Management Service Field Offices
Bureau of Mines
U.S. Department of Interior
1951 Constitution Avenue, NW
Washington, DC 20240   (202) 343-4953
U.S. Department of Interior has the following regional offices:

Atlantic Region
381 Elden St., Suite 1109, Herndon, VA 22070-4817; (703) 787-1113

Alaska
949 E. 36th Ave., Suite 604, Anchorage, AK 99508-4302; (907) 261-4070

Gulf of Mexico
1201 Elmwood Park Blvd., New Orleans, LA 70123-2394; (504) 736-2595

Pacific Region
1340 W. 6th St., Los Angeles, CA 90017; (213) 894-3389

Central Region
6th Ave. and Kipling St., Bldg. 85, Lakewood, CO 80225; (303) 231-3162

* Mining Claims on Federal Lands
Energy and Mineral Resources
Bureau of Land Management
U.S. Department of the Interior
18th and C Sts., NW
Washington, DC 20240   (202) 343-4201
The brochure, *Staking a Mining Claim on Federal Lands*, describes the procedure you would follow to stake a mining claim on public lands. Claims are granted to individuals for particular pieces of land, valuable for specific mineral deposits. Questions concerning the definition of a mining claim and the technicalities of recording and maintaining mining claims are also covered.

* National Firefighting Coordination
Fire and Aviation Management
Bureau of Land Management
U.S. Department of the Interior
1725 I St., NW
Washington, DC 20006   (202) 653-8800
The goal of the Boise Interagency Fire Center is to provide the nationwide coordination of fire support activities among Federal and state firefighting agencies. The Fire Center is also called upon to help during many types of natural disasters when local, state, and regional resources are exhausted.

* National Park Off-shore Oil Leases Revenues
Land Resources Division
National Park Service
U.S. Department of the Interior
1100 L St., NW
Washington, DC 20005   (202) 523-5252
The National Park System is able to purchase land for its use with the revenues received from off-shore oil leases. Revenues from these leases also are credited to the Land and Water Conservation Fund and the Historic Preservation Fund for efforts in these areas.

* National Park Service Regional Offices
National Park Service
U.S. Department of the Interior
1100 L St., NW
Washington, DC 20005   (202) 523-5252
Here are the contact points for the field offices of the National Park Service.

Alaska
2525 Gambell St., Room 107, Anchorage, AK 99503; (907) 261-2690

Mid-Atlantic
Second and Chestnut Sts., Philadelphia, PA 19106; (215) 597-2284. Serving: PA, VA, WV, DE, MD

Midwest
1709 Jackson St., Omaha, NE 68102; (402) 221-3431. Serving: NE, MO, KS, IA, IL, IN, WI, MI, MN, OH

National Capital
1100 Ohio Dr., SW, Washington, DC 20242; (202) 485-9813

North-Atlantic
15 State St., Boston, MA 02109-3572; (617) 565-8841. Serving: NY, NJ, CT, RI, MA, NH, VT, ME

Pacific Northwest
83 South King St., Suite 212, Seattle, WA 98104; (206) 442-5565. Serving: WA, OR, ID

Rocky Mountains
12795 W. Alameda Pkwy, P.O. Box 25287, Denver, CO 80225; (303) 969-2875. Serving: MT, ND, SD, WY, UT, CO

Southeast
75 Spring St., Atlanta, GA 30303; (404) 331-5185. Serving: MS, TN, AL, GA, FL, SC, NC, KY, Virgin Is., PR

Southwest
P.O. Box 728, Santa FE, NM 87504-0728; (505) 988-6388. Serving: NM, TX, LA, OK, AR

Western
450 Golden Gate Ave., P.O. Box 36063, San Francisco, CA 94102; (415) 556-4196. Serving: CA, AZ, NV, HI, Guam, Northern Marianas Is., Am Samoa, Micronesia, Marshall Is., Palau.

* Native American Indians Land Rights
Office of Public Affairs
Bureau of Indian Affairs
U.S. Department of the Interior
18th and C Sts., NW
Washington, DC 20240   (202) 343-1711
The free booklet, *American Indians Today: Answers to Your Questions, 1988*, contains useful information on the Native American Indians and their relationship to the Bureau of Indian Affairs. Programs within the Bureau, including education, health services, and housing are briefly outlined and contain recent statistics. Many questions are answered within the booklet, including the rights of the Indians to own land and have their own governments. A map locates the Indian lands and communities, showing Federal and State Indian Reservations and other Indian groups. An excellent bibliography, prepared by the Smithsonian Institution, is included.

* Public Lands National Parks

Division of Interpretation
National Park Service
U.S. Department of the Interior
1100 L St., NW, Room 2101
Washington, DC 20240   (202) 523-5270

The National Park Service assists its facilities in planning and carrying out their exhibits and visitor programs. Their future plans include more involvement in environmental education programs to be offered at the Park Service sites.

* Public Lands Oil and Gas Leasing

Energy and Mineral Resources Division
Bureau of Land Management
U.S. Department of the Interior
18th and C Sts., NW
Washington, DC 20240   (202) 343-4201

Public lands are available for oil and gas leasing only after they have been evaluated through the Bureau of Land Management. In areas where development of oil and gas resources would conflict with the protection or management of other resources or public land uses, mitigating measures are identified and may appear on leases as either stipulations to uses or as restrictions on surface occupancy. Two types of leases are issued: competitive and noncompetitive.

* Public Lands Photos

Forestry, Range, Realty
Office of Public Affairs
Bureau of Land Management
U.S. Department of the Interior
18th and C Sts., NW
Washington, DC 20240   (202) 343-5717

Thousands of black and white photographs and color slides are available, including forestry, realty, minerals, and range subjects.

* Public Lands Recreation

Office of Public Affairs
Bureau of Land Management
U.S. Department of the Interior
18th and C Sts., NW
Washington, DC 20240   (202) 343-5717

In recognition of the importance of outdoor recreation to Americans, *Recreation 2000 Executive Summary* sets forth the commitment of the Bureau of Land Management to the management of outdoor recreation resources in the public lands. The plan highlights the areas in which the Bureau intends to concentrate future efforts, such as visitor information, resource protection, land ownerships, partnerships, volunteers, tourism programs, facilities, and permits, fees, and concessions.

* Public Land Renewable Resources Management

Land and Renewable Resources
Bureau of Land Management
U.S. Department of the Interior
18th and C Sts., NW
Washington, DC 20240   (202) 343-4896

The Bureau of Land Management issues leases, rights-of-way, and use permits for a wide variety of public lands including parks; power transmission and distribution lines; petroleum products collection and transmission systems.

* Public Lands Revenue: Grazing, Timber Sales, Mining

Management Services
Bureau of Land Management
U.S. Department of the Interior
18th and C Sts., NW
Washington, DC 20240   (202) 343-4864

This office collects and disburses revenues and receipts generated from public lands. The Bureau of Land Management is a primary generator of revenues in the Federal government, with more than $800 million collected annually from a variety of sources, including timber sales, sale of public lands, grazing leases, right-of-way leases, permits, and mineral receipts.

* Public Land Statistics

Office of Public Information
Bureau of Land Management
U.S. Department of the Interior
18th and C Sts., NW
Washington, DC 20240-0001   (202) 343-5717

The publication, *Public Land Statistics*, contains valuable information regarding the land administered by the Bureau of Land Management. Tables include the following topics: land disposition and use, range management, resource conservation and development, forest management, wildlife habitat management,

wild horse and burro management, cultural resource management, outdoor recreation, areas of critical environmental concern, energy and mineral resources, public land surveys, fire protection, and finance.

* Smokey Bear and Fire Prevention

Smokey Bear Headquarters
U.S. Forest Service
1621 N. Kent St.
Room 1001 RPE
Rosslyn, VA 22209   703-235-8666

To make children aware of the campaign to fight forest fires, the Forest Service makes a variety of materials available to children, including posters, signs, patches, bookmarks, bumper stickers, and comic books.

* Soil and Farmland Protection Programs

Soil Conservation Service (SCS)
U.S. Department of Agriculture
P.O. Box 2890
Washington, DC 20013   (202) 447-4543

Soil surveys are used not only for conservation purposes but also to identify suitable lands for a wide variety of uses, from maintaining crops to urban uses. Information about soil helps prevent major construction mistakes and misuse of land that can be productively put to use. Soil maps identify flood-prone areas and sources of water pollutants.

* Soil and Land Conservation

Soil Conservation Society of America (SCSA)
7515 Northeast Ankeny Rd.
Ankeny, IA 50021   (515) 289-2331

The Soil Conservation Society of America promotes better land use and management and publishes the *Journal of Soil and Water Conservation*.

* Soil Conservation Technical Expertise

Soil Conservation Service (SCS)
U.S. Department of Agriculture
P.O. Box 2890
Washington, DC 20013   (202) 447-4543

Technical expertise is available in such areas as irrigation, drainage, landscape architecture, construction, sanitary and water quality, and hydrology.

* State Soil-Saving Conservation

Information Division
U.S. Department of Agriculture
ASCS, P.O. Box 205
Kansas City, MO 64141   (202) 447-5237

The Agricultural State Conservation Service (ASCS) directs a number of conservation programs to preserve and improve American farmland:
Agricultural Conservation Program (ACP): This program is designed to solve soil, water, and related resource problems through costsharing. ACP assistance is available to install soil-saving practices, including terraces, grass, sod waterways, and other measures to control erosion. It also helps reduce sediment, chemicals, and livestock waste that contaminate streams and lakes.

* Soil, Water, and Air Sciences

ARS Information Staff
U.S. Department of Agriculture
Room 307-A, Building 005
Beltsville, MD 20705   (301) 344-2264

Specialists study such topics as environmental quality, erosion and sedimentation, soil fertility and plant nutrition, organic wastes, pesticide degradation, water use efficiency and tillage practices, and weed control. Contact the ARS staff for answers to questions on these and other conservation-related topics.

* Strip Mining and Reclamation

Office of Public Affairs
Office of Surface Mining Reclamation and Enforcement
U.S. Department of Interior
1951 Constitution Avenue, NW
Washington, DC 20240   (202) 343-4953

This office works to protect people and the environment from the side-effects of coal mining, while continuing to regulate coal mining. Lands that were affected by past coal mining operations must be repaired if left unreclaimed or abandoned. Technical assistance is provided to states so that they can perform their responsibilities under the surface mining law. State personnel are trained in the technical aspects of surface mining, such as soil compaction, revegetation, and groundwater hydrology, so that they can better enforce regulations.

Environment and Nature

* Strip Mining Enforcement Offices Nationwide

Office of Surface Mining Reclamation and Enforcement
U.S. Department of Interior
1951 Constitution Avenue, NW
Washington, DC 20240   (202) 343-4953
The following are field offices of DOI's Surface Mining and Reclamation Office:

Albuquerque
625 Silver Ave., SW, Suite 310, Albuquerque, NM 87102; (505) 766-1486

Appalachia
350 Elaine Dr., Suite 2300, Lexington, KY 40504; (606) 233-2792

Ashland
Federal Bldg., Room 120, 1430 Greenup Ave., Ashland, KY 41101; (606) 325-4735

Beckley
101 Harper Park Dr., Beckley, WV 25801; (304) 255-5265

Birmingham
280 W. Valley, Room 302, Homewood, AL 35209; (205) 731-0890

Big Stone Gap
P.O. Box 626, Big Stone Gap, VA 24219; (703) 523-4303

Casper
Federal Bldg., 100 East B St., Room 2128, Casper, WY 82601-1918; (307) 261-5776

Columbus
2242 S. Hamilton Rd., Columbus, OH 43232; (614) 866-0578

Chattanooga
900 Georgia Ave., Room 30, Chattanooga, TN 37402; (615) 752-5175

Charleston
603 Morris St., Charleston, WV 25301; (304) 347-7158

Denver
Bldg. 20, Room B2015, P.O. Box 25065, Denver CO 80225; (303) 236-0331

Eastern
Ten Parkway Center, Pittsburgh, PA 15220; (412) 937-2828

Harrisburg
Harrisburg Transportation Ctr., Third Fl., Suite 3C, 4th and Market Sts., Harrisburg, PA 17101; (717) 782-4036

Hazard
516 Village Lane, Hazard, KY 41701; (606) 439-5843

Indianapolis
Minton-Capehart Federal Bldg., 575 N. Penn St., Room 301, Indianapolis, IN 46204; (371) 226-6700

Johnstown
Penn Traffic Bldg., Room 20, 319 Washington St., Johnston, PA 15901; (814) 533-4223

Kansas City
1103 Grand Ave., Room 502, Kansas City, MO 64106; (816) 374-6405

Knoxville
530 Gay St., Suite 500, Knoxville, TN 37902; (615) 673-4504

Lexington
340 Legion Dr., Suite 28, Lexington, KY 40504; (606) 233-7327

London
P.O. Box 1048, London, KY 40741; (606) 878-6440

Lebanon
Two Acre Task Force: P.O. Box 487, Lebanon, VA 24266; (703) 889-4032

Madisonville
Segebarth Bldg., Box F, 2100 N. Main St., Madisonville, KY 42431; (502) 825-4500

Morgantown
P.O. Box 886, Morgantown, WVA 26507; (304) 291-4004

Norris
P.O. Box 295, Norris, TN 37828; (615) 632-1699

Olympia
Columbia Commons, 3773 C Martini Way East, Suite 104, Olympia, WA 98506; (206) 753-9538

Pikesville
Division of Audit Management, First National Bank, Room 608B, 334 Main St., Pikesville, KY 41505; (606) 432-4123

Prestonburgh
P.O. Box 306, 2664 West Mountain Parkway, West Prestonburg, KY 41618; (606) 866-1291

Springfield
600 East Monroe St., Room 20, Springfield IL 62701; (217) 492-4495

Tulsa
5100 East Skelley Dr., Suite 550, Tulsa, OK 74135; (918) 581-6430

Wilkes-Barre
20 N. Penn. Ave., Suite 3323, Wilkes-Barre, PA 18701; (717) 826-6726

Western Region
1020 15th St., 2nd Fl., Brooks Towers, Denver, CO 80202; (303) 564-4380

* Timber and Woodland Analysis

River Basin Operations
Natural Resources Management
Land Resources
Forestry Resource Development
Tennessee Valley Authority
Norris, TN 37828   (615) 632-1631
This Land Resources group has developed a number of user-friendly, reliable, PC software programs, which allow the public, the timber industry, and consultants to analyze timber supply, inventory, and finances by providing growth and yield information. Inventory processing helps foresters to determine maximum financial returns by calculating, for example, the optimal time to schedule harvesting. To stay abreast of all new technologies, this resource group also conducts safety seminars, field days, and hardware demonstrations, and to stay abreast of all new technology.

* Tree Growing and Lumber Bibliography

Superintendent of Documents
Government Printing Office
Washington, DC 20402   (202) 783-3238
Tree publications are listed, including those of interest to tree growers and the lumber industry. Also featured is a guide to Christmas Tree diseases and books listing the tropical timbers of the world. Free.

* Urban Land Use Management

Urban Land Institute
1090 Vermont Ave., NW
Suite 300
Washington, DC 20005   (202) 289-8500

The Urban Land Institute consists of developers, architects, and public officials organized to provide accurate, unbiased information useful to land planners and developers. The organization publishes *Land Use Digest, Project Reference File, Urban Land.*

* Wetlands and Land Conservation

Information Division
U.S. Department of Agriculture
ASCS, P.O. Box 205
Kansas City, MO 64141   (202) 447-5237
The Agricultural State Conservation Service (ASCS) directs a number of conservation programs: plant trees, improve timberstands, prevent loss of wetlands for migratory waterfowl, and control water pollution.

* Wildland Fire Database

FIREBASE Operations
U.S. Department of Agriculture Forest Service
Boise Interagency Fire Center
3905 Vista Ave.
Boise, ID 83705   (208) 389-2604
FIREBASE is a collection of bibliographic citations and abstracts of wildland fire-related information. The database is international in scope and topic include wildland fire detection; prevention and suppression; fire management analysis; planning and training; and fire statistics, indexes, and hazards.

* Youth Conservation Corps Regional Offices

Washington Office
Youth Program Officer
National Park Service

U.S. Department of the Interior
Room 4415, P.O. Box 37127
1100 L St., NW
Washington, DC 20013-7127 (202) 343-5514
Youngsters interested to gain experience in environmental protection can contact the nearest field office of the National Park Service listed below to inquire about summer job opportunities:

Alaska
2525 Gambell St., Room 107, Anchorage, AK 99503; (907) 261-2690

Mid-Atlantic
Second and Chestnut Sts., Philadelphia, PA 19106; (215) 597-2284. Serving: PA, VA, WV, DE, MD

Midwest
1709 Jackson St., Omaha, NE 68102; (402) 221-3431. Serving: NE, MO, KS, IA, IL, IN, WI, MI, MN, OH

National Capital
1100 Ohio Dr., SW, Washington, DC 20242; (202) 485-9813

North-Atlantic
15 State St., Boston, MA 02109-3572; (617) 565-8841. Serving: NY, NJ, CT, RI, MA, NH, VT, ME

Pacific Northwest
83 South King St., Suite 212, Seattle, WA 98104; (206) 442-5565. Serving: WA, OR, ID

Rocky Mountains
12795 W. Alameda Pkwy, P.O. Box 25287, Denver, CO 80225; (303) 969-2875. Serving: MT, ND, SD, WY, UT, CO

Southeast
75 Spring St., Atlanta, GA 30303; (404) 331-5185. Serving: MS, TN, AL, GA, FL, SC, NC, KY, Virgin Is., PR

Southwest
P.O. Box 728, Santa FE, NM 87504-0728; (505) 988-6388. Serving: NM, TX, LA, OK, AR

Western
450 Golden Gate Ave., P.O. Box 36063, San Francisco, CA 94102; (415) 556-4196. Serving: CA, AZ, NV, HI, Guam, Northern Marianas Is., Am Samoa, Micronesia, Marshall Is., Palau.

Fish and Wildlife

* See also Vacations and Business Travel Chapter

* Acid Rain and Aquatic Species Chart
Superintendent of Documents
Government Printing Office
Washington, DC 20402   (202) 783-3238

The wall chart, *Acid Rain: The Effect on Aquatic Species,* illustrates the survival of selected aquatic species in an acidic environment. Information is given on acid rain, its causes, and the effect on aquatic life. Measures 17 by 22 inches (S/N 024-010-00675-7, $3.25).

* Alaska Fish and Wildlife Research
Alaska Fish and Wildlife Research Center
U.S. Fish and Wildlife Service
1011 E. Tudor Rd.
Anchorage, AK 99503   (907) 786-3512

The Alaska Fish and Wildlife Research Center in Anchorage, in association with its field stations in Kodiak and Fairbanks, is responsible for planning and conducting research on fish, wildlife, and their habitats in Alaska. Areas of research include: the status and trends of marine mammal populations; the distribution, abundance, and population trends of coastal and marine birds; waterfowl population dynamics; productivity and stock of anadromous fish; advanced technology and its use in studying arctic and subarctic fish and wildlife; and identifying and resolving conflicts between wildlife and the utilization of Alaska's natural resources.

* Arctic and Antarctic Science Stations
Office of Polar Affairs
Bureau of Oceans and International Environmental
  and Scientific Affairs
Department of State
2201 C St., NW, Room 5801
Washington, DC 20520   (202) 647-3262

This office is concerned with all issues concerning the Arctic and Antarctic, including the environment and marine life, such as whales and seals. They are also closely involved with the many science stations located on the Antarctic.

* Bald Eagles and Peregrine Falcons
U.S. Department of the Army
Chemical Research Development
  and Engineering Center
Aberdeen Proving Ground, MD 21010-5423   (301) 671-4345

While the Center's primary mission is concerned with research on chemical defensive material, the Center has become very involved in wildlife conservation programs because of its location on the Chesapeake Bay. The Center is especially experienced in a Bald Eagle program and a Peregrine Falcon program. Fact sheets on these and other wildlife issues may be obtained by writing or calling the above office.

* Banded Waterfowl Recovery
Office of Migratory Bird Research
Pawtuxent Wildlife Research Center
U.S. Fish and Wildlife Service
Laurel, MD 20708   (301) 498-0300

If you happen to capture, find, or shoot a banded bird is obtained, you should remove the band, flatten and tape it securely to a piece of heavy paper or cardboard, and mail it to the address above. Include the following information: 1) Names and address of person sending the band: 2) All numbers and letters on the band (in case the band is lost from the envelope); 3) Date the band was obtained; 4) Place where band was found (mileage and direction from the nearest town, including County and State); 5) How the band was obtained (on a bird shot, found dead, etc.). Mark the envelope *Hand Cancel.*

* Birds Bibliography
Superintendent of Documents
Government Printing Office
Washington, DC 20402   (202) 783-3238

This listing includes booklets on the Atlantic Barrier Islands and their plant and animals life, the Chesapeake Bay's bird population, and field guide to fifty birds to observe in your own town. The Duck Stamp Collection subscription service is also outlined. Free.

* Bird Strikes
Airport Safety Data Group
Office of Airport Standards
Federal Aviation Administration
Department of Transportation
800 Independence Ave., SW, Room 615
Washington, DC 20591   (202) 267-8792

Birds being accidentally sucked into jet engines is a serious aviation hazard. Contact this office for information on where bird strikes occur.

* Birds, Buffalo, and Other Publications
U.S. Fish and Wildlife Service
4401 N. Fairfax Dr.
Arlington, VA 22203   (703) 358-1711

For a free listing of general interest publications from the Fish and Wildlife Service, contact the office above. General interest publications are available free of charge, but when ordering more than five publications, the need must be justified. Titles include the following:

American Bald Eagle
America's Sea Turtles
Attracting and Feeding Birds
Chesapeake Bay
Conservation Notes on American Buffalo
Ducks at a Distance
Duck Stamp Story
Endangered Species
Facts about Federal Wildlife Laws
Lead Poisoning in Waterfowl
People and Wildlife-Public Involvement in Fish and Wildlife Administration
Waterfowl Regulations

Also available is a *Wildlife Biologue Series* of various species of wildlife, including endangered species. The series includes a one page life history of the species. They are free of charge when ordering under five copies. Contact the above office for a listing.

* Buffalo and Cattle Refuges
Division of Refuges
U.S. Fish and Wildlife Service
4401 N. Fairfax Dr.
Arlington, VA 22203   (703) 358-1744

Buffalo and Texas longhorn cattle, as well as deer and elk, can be enjoyed at wildlife refuges maintained by the U.S. Department of the Interior. Wichita Mountains in Oklahoma and Fort Niobrara in Nebraska preserve these animals in their natural habitat. The government periodically auctions these animals to the public at these locations. For more information, contact the refuge managers directly: Fort Niobrara National Wildlife Refuge, Hidden Timber Route, HC 14, Box 67, Valentine, NE 69201; (402) 376-3789. Witchita Mountains Wildlife Refuge, Rt. 1, Box 448, Indiahoma, OK 73552; (405) 429-3222. You can see Buffalo also at the National Bison Range in Moiese, Montana. For more information on this refuge, contact National Bison Range, Moiese, MT 59824; (406) 644-2211.

* Captive Breeding of Endangered Species
Patuxent Wildlife Research Center
U.S. Fish and Wildlife Service
Laurel, MD 20708   (301) 498-0300

The Endangered Species Branch at Patuxent conducts research on several endangered species in their native habitats throughout the United States and its territories. Current studies focus on such species as the Puerto Rican parrot, California condor, Hawaiian forest birds, Kirtland's warbler, and eastern timber wolf. Along with studying the endangered species, the scientists breed them in captivity for release to bolster wild populations. Key endangered species, as well as closely related surrogate species, are maintained for captive propagation research. The physiological, behavioral, and veterinary characteristics of these species are evaluated to gain a better understanding of possible biological problems as well as to assist with management of the species in the wild.

* Coastal Zone Conservation and Naturalists
American Littoral Society (ALS)

Sandy Hook
Highlands, NJ 07732 (201) 291-0055
The American Littoral Society promotes the study and conservation of the coastal zone habitat. Publications: *Coastal Reported, Underwater Naturalist.*

* Conservation Law Enforcement Training
Law Enforcement Division
U.S. Fish and Wildlife Service
4401 N. Fairfax Dr.
Arlington, VA 22203 (703) 358-1949
Through this division, state conservation officers are trained in the area of criminal law as it applies to the enforcement of wildlife protection.

* Duck and Geese Population
North American Waterfowl Management Plan
U.S. Fish and Wildlife Service
Federal Bldg., Fort Snelling
Twin Cities, MN 55111 (612) 290-3131
The United States and Canada have joined forces to reverse the decline in certain populations of ducks and geese. This plan has inspired cooperation between Federal, Provincial, and State governments, as well as private conservation agencies in the two countries. Joint ventures, formed among public and private corporations, are developing economic incentives to change land use practices, striking agreements with private landowners, and improving water management.

* Duck Stamps
Federal Duck Stamp Office
U.S. Fish and Wildlife Service
4401 N. Fairfax Drive
Arlington, VA 22203 (703) 358-2020
The Federal Duck Stamp program has become one of the most successful conservation programs ever initiated. To date, over 350 million duck stamp dollars have gone to preserve over 4 million acres of wetland refuges for North American waterfowl. A sheet of duck stamps from 1987-1988, Redheads, can be purchased for $10.00, as well as the 1988-1989 Snow Goose stamps. The 1989-1990 Lesser Scaup stamps are available for $12.50. To order your Duck Stamps, contact U.S. Postal Service, Philatelics Sales Division, Washington, D.C. 20265-9997.
Subscriptions to the Duck Stamp Collection are available at $12 each from the Superintendent of Documents. The collection includes a data sheet on each duck stamp issued since the first one in 1934. Each sheet includes a photograph of the stamp and original art, short biography of the artist, names of the designers and engravers, inscription, first date of sale, and number of stamps sold. The subscription service provides the entire collection to date plus one update per year for an indeterminate period of time.

* Duck Stamp Design Competition
Federal Duck Stamp Office
U.S. Fish and Wildlife Service
4401 N. Fairfax Drive
Arlington, VA 22203 (703) 358-2020
Each year, a Duck Stamp Design Competition is held, with the winning design chosen by a panel of waterfowl and art experts. Any artist can enter the contest by submitting a 7 X 10 inch waterfowl design and paying an entry fee. The winner receives a pane of stamps bearing his or her design. Winning artists also sell prints of their prize entries which are eagerly sought by collectors.

* Duck Stamp Collection Subscription
Federal Duck Stamp Office
U.S. Fish and Wildlife Service
4401 N. Fairfax Drive
Arlington, VA 22203 (703) 358-2020
The Federal Duck Stamp program has become one of the most successful conservation programs ever initiated. To date, over 350 million duck stamp dollars have gone to preserve over 4 million acres of wetland refuges for North American waterfowl. A sheet of duck stamps from 1987-1988, Redheads, can be purchased for $10.00, as well as the 1988-1989 Snow Goose stamps. The 1989-1990 Lesser Scaup stamps are available for $12.50. To order your Duck Stamps, contact U.S. Postal Service, Philatelics Sales Division, Washington, D.C. 20265-9997. Subscriptions to the Duck Stamp Collection are available at $12 each from the Superintendent of Documents. The collection includes a data sheet on each duck stamp issued since the first one in 1934. Each sheet includes a photograph of the stamp and original art, short biography of the artist, names of the designers and engravers, inscription, first date of sale, and number of stamps sold. The subscription service provides the entire collection to date plus one update per year for an indeterminate period of time.

* Ecosystems and Wildlife Habitat Models
National Ecology Center

U.S. Fish and Wildlife Service
2627 Redwing Rd.
Fort Collins, CO 80526-2899 (303) 226-9100
The center conducts research, develops new tools, and transfers information so that scientists can better understand and manage fish and wildlife resources, habitats, and ecosystems. All endangered marine mammal research is performed here. Workshops are held in refuge management and habitat model development for those within the Interior Department and scientists in Federal and State agencies and foreign countries. Studies are reported in the Center's *Biological Report* series and through extension education brochures.

* Ecological Society
Ecological Society of America (ESA)
730 11th St., NW
Suite 400
Washington, DC 20001 (202) 628-1500
The Ecological Society of America is a professional society of individuals interested in the study of living things in relation to their environments. ESA is a member society of the American Institute of Biological Sciences. Publications: *Bulletin of the Ecological Society of America, Ecology, Ecological Monographs.*

* Endangered Wildlife and Plants
Office of Endangered Species
U.S. Fish and Wildlife Service
4401 N. Fairfax Dr.
Arlington, VA 22203 (703) 358-2161
The Fish and Wildlife Service follows a formal procedure in determining which species should be placed on the *U.S. List of Endangered and Threatened Wildlife and Plants*. The proposed ruling is published in the *Federal Register*, and after a suitable period for public comment and possible revision, it is published as a final rule. To obtain a listing of the endangered and threatened wildlife and plants and other information on this topic, contact the office above.

* Environmental Defense Fund
Environmental Defense Fund Inc. (EDF)
444 Park Ave., South
New York, NY 10016 (212) 686-4191
This organization of lawyers, scientists and economists is dedicated to protecting environmental quality and public health. EDF pursues responsible reform of public policy in resource conservation, toxic chemicals, water resources, air quality, land use and wildlife, working through research and public education, and judicial, administrative, and legislative action. Publications: *EDF letter.*

* Exotic and Warm Water Fish Husbandry
National Fisheries Research Center
U.S. Fish and Wildlife Service
7920 NW 71 St.
Gainesville, FL 32606 (904) 378-8181
Exotic and warm water fish of the southeastern United States and the Gulf Coast are studied at the National Fisheries Research Center in Gainesville, Florida, and at its field station in Marion, Alabama. Research of fish husbandry of southeastern fishes is also conducted. Aquatic weed control as it relates to the survival of these fishes is also a priority.

* Fish and Marine Life Bibliography
Superintendent of Documents
Government Printing Office
Washington, DC 20402 (202) 783-3238
Fisheries and fish research publications are featured in this bibliography, along with marine fish posters of the California, Great Lakes, and Gulf and South Atlantic waters.
Free.

* Fish and Wildlife Technical Publications
Office of Information Transfer
U.S. Fish and Wildlife Service
1025 Pennock Pl., Suite 212
Fort Collins, CO 80524 (303) 493-8401
Many technical publications are produced by the U.S. Fish and Wildlife Service. Copies of publications are available to selected individuals or organizations concerned with environmental issues.

Resource Publication
Fish and Wildlife Leaflet
Investigations in Fish Control
Fish Disease Leaflet
North American Fauna
Fish and Wildlife Research
Fish and Wildlife Technical Report
Biological Report

Environment and Nature

Fisheries Review and *Wildlife Review* are also available on a subscription basis from the Superintendent of Documents, Government Printing Office. *Fisheries Review* is $16.00/year and *Wildlife Review* is $22.00/year.

* Fish and Wildlife Year 2000
Office of Public Affairs
Bureau of Land Management
U.S. Department of the Interior
18th and C Sts., NW
Washington, DC 20240 (202) 343-5717

The full-color brochure, *Fish and Wildlife 2000: A Plan for the Future*, describes the future management plan of the public lands and their resources. These resources include recreation, range, forest, minerals, watershed, fish and wildlife, wilderness and natural, scenic, scientific, educational, and cultural values. A strategic plan is outlined, including the management of wildlife habitats, fisheries habitats, threatened and endangered species, and human resources.

* Fish and Wildlife Cooperative Research
Cooperative Fish and Wildlife
Research Units Center
U.S. Fish and Wildlife Service
4401 N. Fairfax Dr.
Arlington, VA 22203 (703) 358-1709

Cooperative fish and wildlife research field stations are located at various universities throughout the country. Research finds answers to a broad spectrum of fish and wildlife management questions, from habitat requirements of individual species to the effects of development projects on populations of fish and wildlife. Graduate education is provided to resource managers at the M.S. and Ph.D. levels and in-service training and continuing education is given to employees of conservation agencies. Technical assistance is made available to fish and wildlife resource managers and to the public. For a complete listing of field stations, contact the office above.

* Fish and Wildlife Photographs
Audio Visuals
U.S. Fish and Wildlife Service
18th and C Sts., NW
Washington, DC 20240 (202) 343-5611

The Audio Visual Department of the U.S. Fish and Wildlife Service has an extensive collection of both black and white pictures and color slides of fish and wildlife. There is no charge for their lending service, which extends 30 or 90 days. If the photographs or slides are used in publications, the photographer and the U.S. Fish and Wildlife Service must be given credit.

* Fish Disease and Chemical Cures
National Fisheries Research Center
U.S. Fish and Wildlife Service
P.O. Box 818
LaCrosse, WI 54602-0818 (608) 783-6451

The National Fisheries Research Center at LaCrosse, Wisconsin, has been designated by the Fish and Wildlife Service to negotiate registration for fishery chemicals with regulatory agencies. Pesticides are registered with the U.S. Environmental Protection Agency, and therapeutants for controlling fish diseases are registered with the U.S. Food and Drug Administration. Once a fishery chemical is registered by the Federal government, states will generally allow the use of that chemical for fish culture and management.

* Fisheries Contaminant Research
National Fisheries Contaminant Research Center
U.S. Fish and Wildlife Service
Rt. 2, 4200 New Haven Rd.
Columbia, MO 65201 (314) 875-5399

All fisheries contaminant research under the U.S. Fish and Wildlife Service, except for the Great Lakes area, is conducted at the National Fisheries Contaminant Research Center and its eight field stations. The Center is actively studying the effects of pesticides and other contaminants on aquatic ecosystems. Research equipment is designed to study the long-term effects of contaminants on growth, life stages, and biochemistry of fishes and other aquatic forms under realistic pollution conditions. The Center has capabilities to conduct special studies of national concern with striped bass, Atlantic and Pacific salmon, grayling, and Arctic char. Scientists and special groups are welcome at the Center, and special arrangements can be made for visiting scientists to conduct cooperative research with laboratory investigators.

* Fish Hatcheries Scientific Advice
Office of Information Transfer
U.S. Fish and Wildlife Service
1025 Pennock Pl., Suite 212
Fort Collins, CO 80524 (303) 493-8401

This office distributes technical information to scientists, refuge managers, and fish hatchery managers within and outside of the U.S. Fish and Wildlife Service. At office meetings scientists present research findings and provide technical advice to others. In turn, they have a rare opportunity to meet the users of their findings face to face. Information is also transferred through synthesis documents, which bring together information from a variety of sources on a particular topic of interest. Each package is then distributed to a specific audience, such as refuge managers or fish hatchery managers. Contact the office above to be placed on the mailing list for periodic announcements of new publications.

* Fish Health Research
National Fisheries Center
U.S. Fish and Wildlife Service
Box 700
Kearneysville, WV 25430 (304) 725-8461 x5333

The National Fisheries Center and its five field stations are world-renowned as a focal point for fish health research and fisheries development. Studies include nutrition, genetics, diseases, management technology, and technical services. The facility contains a training academy of fish husbandry.

* Fish Information and Exhibits
National Fisheries Center
U.S. Fish and Wildlife Service
Box 700
Kearneysville, WV 25430 (304) 725-7061

The National Fisheries Center in Leetown, West Virginia, continually initiates programs of interest to the general public. Visitors can enjoy a large exhibit area with numerous displays showing the importance of fish, water, and the environment to mankind. There is an information counter with brochures and other materials and a separate aquarium building and outside display pools with various species of live fish. Also at the facility is an environmental education section with a meeting/classroom and crafts workshop. The facility is free to the public.

* Grain Surpluses for Wildlife
Commodities Operations
U.S. Department of Agriculture
ASCS, Room 2415
Washington, DC 20013 (202) 447-6500

Upon request of the U.S. Department of the Interior, bulk grain is available in emergency situations to feed wildlife and birds as long as grain surpluses exist.

* Great Lakes Fish Spawning and Survival
National Fisheries Research Center
U.S. Fish and Wildlife Service
1451 Green Rd.
Ann Arbor, MI 48105 (313) 994-3331

The primary objective of the National Fisheries Research Center in Ann Arbor and its eight biological stations and research vessels is to develop the knowledge and technical basis for assessing, protecting, enhancing, and rehabilitating the valuable resources and habitats of the Great Lakes. Laboratory experiments provide information on how natural and man-induced changes in the lakes may affect important fish populations. Particular emphasis is placed upon the spawning requirements, survival of early life stages, and forage requirements of important species such as lake trout.

* Marine Environmental Pollution Response
Pollution Response Branch
Marine Environmental Response Division
Office of Marine Safety, Security,
and Environmental Protection
U.S. Coast Guard
U.S. Department of Transportation
2100 2nd St., SW, Room 2104 (202) 267-0518
Washington, DC 20593-0001 (202) 267-2611

This office responds to requests for marine environmental protection information from Congress and other federal agencies, state agencies, schools, industries, and the general public. Data is available on laws relating to the protection of the marine environment, incidents involving releases of oil or other hazardous substances, and federally funded spill response operations.

* Marine Life Posters
Superintendent of Documents
Government Printing Office
Washington, DC 20402 (202) 783-3238

The following is a list of Marine Life Posters available from the National Marine Fisheries Service through the Government Printing Office. The posters are printed on washable non-glare plasticized paper, and cost $5.50 each.

Marine Fishes of the California Current and Adjacent Waters
Marine Fishes of the Gulf and South Atlantic
Fishes of the Great Lakes
Mollusks and Crustaceans of the Coastal U.S.

* Marine Mammals Rescue and Protection

Office of Protected Resources
National Marine Fisheries Service
National Oceanic and Atmospheric Administration
Department of Commerce
1335 East-West Hwy.
Silver Spring, MD 20910   (301) 427-2322

The Marine Mammal Protection Act commits the United States to long-term management and research programs to conserve and protect these animals. Marine mammals may be taken for scientific research, public display, and incidentally to commercial fishing. The National Marine Fisheries Service grants or denies requests for exemptions, issues permits, carries out research and management programs, enforces the Act, participates in international programs, and issues rules and regulations to carry out its mission to conserve and protect marine mammals. An annual report is available for the Office of Protected Resources, which gives detailed information regarding the activities of the Office. This office can also provide you with copies of the Act, and two publications: *First Aid For Stranded Marine Mammals*, and *Proceedings of the Workshop to Review and Evaluate Whale Watching Programs and Management Needs.*

* Marine Technology Society

Marine Technology Society
2000 Florida Avenue, NW
Suite 500
Washington, DC 20009   (202) 462-7557

This non-profit organization is dedicated to providing information about marine science and engineering. It is divided into 14 geographical sections in the U.S. and Canada, and each section holds monthly meetings, at which brief technical presentations are given. The Society has 31 professional committees that sponsor technical conferences, workshops, and short courses that are open to members and nonmembers. The staff can provide you with technical information and referrals. The Society publishes the *Journal of the Marine Technology Society*, a quarterly publication that presents technical activities of the Society, papers, conferences summaries, book reviews, and so on. It is available free of charge to members and for $5 for nonmembers.

* Migratory Bird Research

Migratory Birds Research Branch
Patuxent Wildlife Research Center
U.S. Fish and Wildlife Service
Laurel, MD 20708   (301) 498-0300

Research at Patuxent on migratory game birds includes methods of assessing the status of various species, discovering reasons for declines in particular bird populations, and investigating relationships between bird populations and environmental variables to determine ecologically sound resource management techniques. Non-game migratory bird research at Patuxent studies particular habitat requirements for breeding, migration, and wintering.

* National Fisheries Library

U.S. Fish and Wildlife Service
P.O. Box 818
LaCrosse, WI 54602-0818   (608) 783-6451

The Center's library has the world's most complete collection of publications on fishery chemicals, their use, and their effects on the environment. Computer hook-ups provide access to over 200 databases.

* National Wildlife Refuges Visitor's Guide

Office of Public Affairs
U.S. Fish and Wildlife Service
18th and C Sts., NW
Washington, DC 20240   (202) 343-5634

National Wildlife Refuges: A Visitor's Guide is a listing of all of the National Wildlife Refuges that provide visitor opportunities; not all of the refuges in the system are included. A map locating each of these refuges is featured, along with public facilities, including visitor's centers, foot trails, auto tours, bicycling, boating, environmental study areas, hunting, fishing, camping, picnicking, swimming, and food and lodging. For a state-by-state listing of these refuges, see the listing below under "Wildlife Refuges National System."

* Naturalists Society

American Society of Naturalists (ASN)
Division of Biological Sciences
University of Kansas
Lawrence, KS 66045   (913) 864-3763

The American Society of Naturalists is a professional association of biological scientists with particular interests in the environmental sciences. Publications: *The American Naturalist*.

* Nature Study Society

American Nature Study Society (ANSS)
5881 Cold Brook Rd.
Homer, NY 13077   (607) 749-3655

The American Nature Study Society is concerned with the study of nature and with conservation education. Publications: *Nature Study*.

* National Wildlife Federation

National Wildlife Federation (NWF)
1412 16th St., NW
Washington, DC 20036   (202) 797-6800

This conservation education organization is dedicated to creating and encouraging an awareness for wise and proper management of soil, air, water, forests, minerals, plant life, and wildlife by extensive education programs, newsletters, and litigation of environmental disputes.

* Nuisance Fish Control

National Fisheries Research Center
U.S. Fish and Wildlife Service
P.O. Box 818
LaCrosse, WI 54602-0818   (608) 783-6451

The National Fisheries Research Center at La Crosse, along with its field station at Hammond Bay, Michigan, have played an important role in the development and registration of toxicants that are useful for controlling populations of the dreaded sea lamprey, a predator of Great Lakes fishes. Intensive research and control efforts have greatly reduced the sea lamprey population through the use of larval lampricides. The Center is also responsible for all research under the U.S. Fish and Wildlife Service to control nuisance fish.

* Ocean and Coastal Pollution

Office of Oceanography and Marine Assessments
National Ocean Service
National Oceanic and Atmospheric Administration
Department of Commerce
6001 Executive Blvd.
Rockville, MD 20852   (301) 443-8487

This office surveys and monitors the oceans, U.S. coastal waters and the Great Lakes to produce data and information products that are critically important for offshore oil and gas exploration, dredging operations, coastal and offshore construction, seafloor mining, waste disposal management, and for protecting the marine environment from the adverse effects of ocean and coastal pollution.

* Ocean and Marine Technology

Marine Technology Society (MTS)
1825 K St., NW
Suite 203
Washington, DC 20006   (202) 775-5966

The Marine Technology Society is an ocean-oriented, multidisciplinary, international professional society which was formed to encourage the development of the technology, education, operational expertise and public awareness needed to advance study int he marine science and technology field.

* Parrots, Gray Whale and 2,700 Videos and Films

National Audiovisual Center
8700 Edgeworth Dr.
Capitol Heights, MD 20743-3701   (800) 638-1300

The National Audiovisual Center contains more than 2,700 titles of videocassettes, films and slide/sound programs. Among them are some wonderful presentations produced by the National Park Service and the U.S. Fish and Wildlife Service. Materials may be rented or purchased. Contact the AV Center for specific information.
Some titles include:

Everglades: Seeking a Balance
Gulf Island Beaches, Bays, Sands, and Bayous
California Gray Whale
Environmental Awareness
Giant Sequoia
One Man's Alaska
Sanctuary: The Great Smoky Mountains
Crater Lake
Yellowstone
Washington, DC: Fancy Free
Glacier Bay
Bighorn Canyon Experience
Cape Cod

Environment and Nature

What is a Mountain?
Living Waters of the Big Cypress
National Parks: Our Treasured Lands
Mt. McKinley
America's Wetlands
Parrots of Luquillo
Where the Fish Will Be
Patuxent Wildlife Research Center
Minnesota Valley National Wildlife Refuge

* Patuxent Wildlife Center Film

National Audiovisual Center
8700 Edgeworth Dr.
Capitol Heights, MD 20743-3701   (800) 638-1300

This film informs the viewers about the wildlife research activities at the Patuxent Wildlife Research Center in Laurel, Maryland. It describes the wildlife research on endangered species, environmental contaminants, migratory waterfowl, and urban wildlife carried on at the center and at field stations around the world. This 20 minute film is available on 16mm film, and on Beta and VHS videocassettes. The film can be rented for $40.00 or purchased for $210.00. The videocassettes can be purchased for $95.00 each.

* Restoring America's Wildlife

Superintendent of Documents
Government Printing Office
Washington, DC 20402   (202) 783-3238

Illustrated with photographs and paintings by nationally known artists, *Restoring America's Wildlife 1937-1987* describes the impact of modern wildlife management on nearly a score of popular species and describes the many economic and recreational opportunities created by the Pittman-Robertson Federal Aid in Wildlife Restoration Act. 1986 (S/N 024-010-00671-4, $20.00).

* Salmon and Other Pacific Fish

National Fisheries Research Center
U.S. Fish and Wildlife Service
Building 204, Naval Station Puget Sound
Seattle, WA 98115-5007   (206) 526-6654

Fishery research problems of the Pacific Coast, except for those of Alaska, are solved at the National Fisheries Research Center in Seattle, Washington, and at its field stations in Cook, Washington, Nordland, Washington, and Reno, Nevada. Projects involving the study of Pacific salmon, trout, and steelhead provide valuable information to the economy of the Pacific Northwest and to the recreational fishing of this area. The Center has two main research groups: fish health and environment, and fish ecology. Willard Field Station near Cook, Washington, studies fish living in the Columbia River Basin and the effects of many hydropower projects in the area. The Marrowstone Field Station in Nordland, Washington, is the U.S. Fish and Wildlife Service's only marine laboratory where salmon and steelhead are studied as they leave their native streams and enter the oceans. The third field station in Reno, Nevada, works with threatened and endangered species native to the area.

* Saltwater Fish and Shellfish Stocks

Public Affairs
National Marine Fisheries Service
National Oceanic and Atmospheric Administration
Department of Commerce
1335 East-West Hwy.
Silver Spring, MD 20910   (202) 427-2370

The National Marine Fisheries Service manages the country's stocks of saltwater fish and shellfish for both commercial and recreational interests. NMFS administers and enforces the Magnuson Fishery Conservation and Management Act to assure that fishing stays within sound biological limits, and that U.S. commercial and recreational fishermen have the opportunity to harvest all the available fish within these limits. Several hundred Fisheries Service scientists conduct research relating to these management responsibilities in science and research centers in 15 states and the District of Columbia. Many of these laboratories have evolved a major field of interest, and have special knowledge of the fish in their geographical area that leads to predictions of abundance, economic forecasts, and direct assistance to sport fishermen and commercial fishing businesses.

* Sierra Club

Sierra Club
730 Polk St.
San Francisco, CA 94109   (415) 981-8634

The aim of the Sierra Club is to explore, enjoy and protect the wild places of the earth, to promote responsible use of the earth's ecosystems and resources, and to restore the quality of the natural and human environment by using lawful means. Publications: *Sierra, National News Report, Energy Report.*

* U.S. Fish and Wildlife Regional Offices

U.S. Fish and Wildlife Service
4401 N. Fairfax Dr.
Arlington, VA 22203   (703) 343-5333

Here are the field offices of the Interior Department's Fish and Wildlife Service.

Region 1
Lloyd 500 Building, Suite 1692, 500 NE Multnomah St., Portland, OR 97232; (503) 231-6118

Region 2
Box 1306, Albuquerque, NM 87103; (505) 766-2321

Region 3
Federal Building, Fort Snelling, Twin Cities, MN 55111; (612) 725-3563

Region 4
Richard B. Russell Federal Building, 75 Spring St., SW, Atlanta, GA 30303; (404) 331-3588

Region 5
One Gateway Center, Suite 700, Newton Corner, MA 02158; (617) 965-5200

Region 6
Box 25486, Denver Federal Center, Denver, CO 80225; (303) 236-7920

Region 7
1101 E. Tudor Rd., Anchorage, AK 99503; (907) 786-3542

Region 8
Matomic Building, Mail Stop 527, Washington, DC 20240; (202) 653-8791

* Vertebrate Research

Biological Survey/National Ecology Center
U.S. Fish and Wildlife Service
U.S. Department of the Interior
Museum of Natural History Building
10th and Constitution Ave., NW
Washington, DC 20560   (202) 357-1930

This laboratory performs systematic and ecological studies of vertebrates and their communities, particularly in their relationship to land use practices. Studies also include work with endangered species. Qualified researchers may inquire about possible study through the laboratory.

* Volunteers: Fish and Wildlife Service

U.S. Fish and Wildlife Service
4401 N. Fairfax Dr.
Arlington, VA 22203   (703) 343-5333

Would you like to spend some time banding birds at a national wildlife refuge, feeding fish at a national fish hatchery, or doing research in a laboratory? Then consider volunteering with the U.S. Fish and Wildlife Service. There are no age requirements; however, anyone under 18 must have written parental approval. Young people under 16 years of age are encouraged to volunteer as part of a supervised group, such as a Boy Scout troop, Girl Scout troop, or 4H Club. Contact one of the U.S. Fish and Wildlife regional offices for possible volunteer programs in your area.

* Waterfowl and Migratory Birds

Northern Prairie Wildlife Research Center
U.S. Fish and Wildlife Service
P.O. Box 2096
Jamestown, ND 58402   (701) 252-5363

This research center gathers information to improve the management of migratory birds, particularly waterfowl west of the Mississippi River. Results of their studies are applied to National Wildlife Refuges and other Federal, State, and private lands. Field and experimental studies are conducted from the headquarters near Jamestown, North Dakota, and through field stations at Woodworth, North Dakota; Davis, California; and La Crosse, Wisconsin. Studies are also conducted on the ecology of the prairie pothole and upper Mississippi River areas.

* Waterfowl Hunting Regulations

Office of Migratory Bird Management
U.S. Fish and Wildlife Service
4401 N. Fairfax Dr.
Arlington, VA 22203   (703) 358-1714

Aerial surveys of waterfowl breeding populations and habitats, post-hunting surveys, and the banding program provide useful biological data for developing annual waterfowl hunting regulations. Before the rules are set, the current waterfowl picture is presented to the public through news releases, publication of proposed regulations in the *Federal Register*, and a series of late July and early

August public meetings where survey data and Fall flight forecasts are reviewed. The decisions of each state are then published in the *Federal Register*.

* Wetlands and Wintering Waterfowl

National Wetlands Research Center
U.S. Fish and Wildlife Service
1010 Gause Blvd.
Slidell, LA 70458 (504) 646-7564
This center focuses on research and development studies of issues related to the protection, restoration, and management of wetlands, with an emphasis on wintering waterfowl. The Center gathers data on plant and animal ecology in both managed and natural wetland systems. Most current information is published in the *Biological Report* series. Field stations are located in Baton Rouge, LA, Corpus Christi, TX, and Vicksburg, MS.

* Wetlands Protection

Office of Wetlands Protection
Environmental Protection Agency
401 M St., SW
Washington DC 20460 (202) 475-7791
This office implements EPA statutory responsibilities in the Clean Water Act as they relate to the filling of wetlands and other aquatic resources. Designed to raise the importance of wetlands, this office works with other governmental bodies to encourage wetlands protection.

* Whale Watching

Office of Protected Resources
National Marine Fisheries Service
National Oceanic and Atmospheric Administration
Department of Commerce
1335 East-West Hwy.
Silver Spring, MD 20910 (301) 427-2322
The Marine Mammal Protection Act commits the United States to long-term management and research programs to conserve and protect these animals. The National Marine Fisheries Service grants or denies requests for exemptions, issues permits, carries out research and management programs, enforces the Act, participates in international programs, and issues rules and regulations to carry out its mission to conserve and protect marine mammals. An annual report is available for the Office of Protected Resources, which gives detailed information regarding the activities of the Office. This office can also provide you with copies of the Act, and two publications: *First Aid For Stranded Marine Mammals*, and *Proceedings of the Workshop to Review and Evaluate Whale Watching Programs and Management Needs*.

* Wild Burros and Horses for Adoption

Office of Public Information
Bureau of Land Management
U.S. Department of the Interior
18th and C Sts., NW
Washington, DC 20240-0001 (202) 343-5717
Wild burros and horses that roam on public lands are put up for adoption after a short time to decrease their numbers. If you are interested in adopting one of these animals, you should contact a local BLM adoption center, and there is a fee of $125 per horse and $75 per burro. You must also transport the animals home and provide for their future upkeep. The booklet, *So You'd Like to Adopt A Wild Horse Or Burro?*, answers many of the questions you might have when handling this responsibility. Contact the office above for the adoption centers near you.

* Wildlife Contaminant Research

Environmental Contaminants Research Branch
Patuxent Wildlife Research Center
U.S. Fish and Wildlife Service
Laurel, MD 20708 (301) 498-0300
Research on environmental contaminants is one of the major efforts at the Patuxent Wildlife Research Center. Field research is conducted at contaminated sites and demonstrates the relation between the presence of contaminants in the environment or tissues of a wildlife species and the degree of risk to the species. Controlled laboratory studies measure effects of mixtures of chemical contaminants on growth, survival, reproduction, metabolism, behavior, and well-being.

* Wildlife Disease Control

National Wildlife Health Research Center
U.S. Fish and Wildlife Service
6006 Schroeder Rd.
Madison, WI 53711 (608) 271-4640
This center offers services and conducts activities to prevent and control wildlife diseases. Workshops and seminars are sponsored at the Center and other locations throughout the country. The information produced through research

findings and field observations is issued in the form of original articles in scientific journals, *Service Research Information Bulletins*, brochures, and special communications projects. A video presentation on lead poisoning in migratory birds was recently produced that is now widely used by the conservation community.

* Wildlife Habitats on Public Lands

Wildlife and Fisheries Division
Bureau of Land Management
U.S. Department of the Interior
1725 I St., NW
Washington, DC 20006 (202) 653-9202
Wildlife habitats for more than 3,000 species are managed on public lands by the Bureau of Land Management. Included in this count are 140 threatened or endangered plant and animal species. The Bureau also protects and manages the key riparian areas along 85,000 miles of streams. BLM manages habitats for one out of every five big game animals in the United States, including caribou, brown and grizzly bears, desert bighorn sheep, moose, mule deer, and antelope.

* Wildlife Import Restrictions

Publications Unit
U.S. Fish and Wildlife Service
4401 N Fairfax Dr.
Arlington, VA 22203 (703) 358-1711
Before travelling overseas, learn what items cannot be imported. Write for a copy of *Facts About Federal Wildlife Laws* and a list of protected species at the above address.

* Wildlife Refuge National System

Refuges and Wildlife
U.S. Fish and Wildlife Service
18th and C Sts., NW
Washington, DC 20240 (202) 343-5333
The National Wildlife Refuge System is a network of United States lands and waters managed specifically for the enhancement of wildlife. Refuges are vitally important for they provide food, water, shelter, and space for approximately 60 endangered species and hundreds of species of birds, mammals, reptiles, amphibians, fish, and plants. Over 440 refuges, encompassing over 90 million acres in 49 states and five trust territories, now comprise the system. An estimated 30 million people visit these lands annually:

Alabama
Bon Secour, P.O. Box 1650, Gulf Shores, AL 36542; (205) 968-8623. Choctaw, Box 808, 2704 Westside College Ave., Jackson, AL 36545; (205) 246-3583. Eufaula, Rte. 2, Box 97-B, Eufaula, AL 36027; (205) 687-4065. Wheeler (Blowing Wind Cave, Fern Cave, Watercress Darter), Rte. 4, Box 250, Decatur, AL 35603; (205) 353-7243.

Alaska
Alaska Maritime (Alaska Peninsula Unit, Bering Sea Unit, Chukchi Sea Unit, Gulf of Alaska Unit), 202 West Pioneer Ave., Homer, AK 99603; (907) 235-6546. Aleutian Islands Unit, Box 5251, Naval Air Station Adak, FBO Seattle, WA 98791; (907) 592-2406. Alaska Peninsula (Becharof), P.O. Box 277, King Salmon, AK 99613; (907) 246-3339. Arctic, Box 20, 101-12th Ave., Fairbanks, AK 99701; (907) 456-0250. Innoko, Box 69, McGrath, AK 99627; (907) 524-3251. Izembek, Box 127, Cold Bay, AK 99571; (907) 532-2445. Kanuti, Box 11, 101-12th Ave., Fairbanks, AK 99701; (907) 456-0329. Kenai, 2139 Ski Hill Road, Soldotna, AK 99669-2139; (907) 262-7021. Kodiak, 1390 Buskin River Rd., Kodiak, AK 99615; (907) 487-2600. Koyukuk, P.O. Box 287, Galena, AK 99741; (907) 656-1231. Nowitna, P.O. Box 287, Galena, AK 99741; (907) 656-1231. Selawik, P.O. Box 270, Kotzebue, AK 99572; (907) 442-3799. Tetlin, P.O. Box 155, Tok, AK 99780; (907) 883-5312. Togiak, P.O. Box 270, Dillingham, AK 99576; (907) 842-1063. Yukon Delta, P.O. Box 346, Bethel, AK 99559; (907) 543-3151. Yukon Flats, Box 14, 101-12th Ave., Fairbanks, AK 99701; (907) 456-0440.

Arizona
Buenos Aires, P.O. Box 109, Sasabe, AZ 85633; (602) 823-4251. Cabeza Prieta, 1611 N. Second Ave., Ajo, AZ 85321; (602) 387-6483. Cibola, P.O. Box AP, Blythe, CA 92226; (602) 857-3253. Havasu, P.O. Box 3009, Needles, CA 92363; (619) 326-3853. Imperial, P.O. Box 72217, Martinez Lake, AZ 85365; (602) 783-3371. Kofa, P.O. Box 6290, 356 W. 1st, Yuma, AZ 85366-6290; (602) 783-7861. San Bernardino, Rural Rte. 1. Box 228R, Douglas, AZ 85607; (602) 364-2104.

Arkansas
Felsenthal (Overflow), P.O. Box 1157, Crossett, AR 71635; (501) 364-3167. Holla Bend (Logan Caves), Box 1043, 115 S. Denver St., Russellville, AR 72801; (501) 968-2800. N.E. Arkansas Refuges, P.O. Box 279, Turrell, AR 72384; (501) 343-2595. Big Lake, P.O. Box 67, Manila, AR 72442; (501) 564-2429. Cache River, P.O. Box 279, Turrell, AR 72384; (501) 343-2595. Wapanocca, P.O. Box 279, Turrell, AR 72384; (501) 343-2595. White River, Box 308, 321 W. 7th St., De Witt, AR 72042; (501) 946-1468.

California

Cibola, P.O. Box AP, Blythe, CA 92226; (602) 857-3253. Havasu, P.O. Box 3009, Needles, CA 92363; (619) 326-3853. Imperial, P.O. Box 72217, Martinez Lake, AZ 85365; (602) 783-3371. Kern (Bitter Creek, Blue Ridge, Hopper Mountain, Pixley, Seal Beach), P.O. Box 670, Delano, CA 93216-0219; (805) 725-2767, (805) 725-5284. Klamath Basin Refuges (Bear Valley (OR), Clear Lake, Klamath Forest (OR), Lower Klamath (OR & CA), Tule Lake, Upper Klamath (OR)), Rte. 1, Box 74, Tule Lake, CA 96134; (916) 667-2231. Modoc, P.O. Box 1610, Alturas, CA 96101; (916) 233-3572. Sacramento (Butte Sink WMA, Delevan, Willow Creek-Lurline WMA), Rte. 1, Box 311, Willows, CA 95988; (916) 934-2801. Salton Sea, P.O. Box 120, Calipatria, CA 92233; (619) 348-5278, (619) 348-5310. Tijuana Slough (Coachella Valley, Sweetwater Marsh), P.O. Box 335, Imperial Beach, CA 92032; (619) 575-1290. San Francisco Bay (Antioch Dunes, Castle Rock, Ellicott Slough, Farallon, Humboldt Bay, Salinas Lagoon, San Pablo Bay), P.O. Box 524, Newark, CA 94560; (415) 792-0222. San Luis (East Grasslands WMA, Grasslands WMA, Kesterson, Merced, San Joaquin River), P.O. Box 2176, Los Banos, CA 93635; (209) 826-3508.

Colorado
Alamosa/Monte Vista, P.O. Box 1148, Alamosa, CO 81101; (303) 589-4021. Arapaho (Bamforth (WY), Hutton Lake (WY), Pathfinder (WY)), P.O. Box 457, Walden, CO 80480; (303) 723-8202. Browns Park, 1318 Hwy. 318, Maybell, CO 81640; (303) 365-3613.

Connecticut
Salt Meadow, P.O. Box 307, Charlestown, RI 02813; (401) 364-9124. Stewart B. McKinney, U.S. Federal Bldg., Room 210, 915 Lafayette Blvd., Bridgeport, CT 06604; (203) 579-5617.

Delaware
Bombay Hook, Rte. 1, Box 147, Smyrna, DE 19977; (302) 653-9345. Prime Hook, Rte. 3, Box 195, Milton, DE 19968; (302) 684-8419.

Florida
Arthur R. Marshall Loxahatchee (Hobe Sound), Rte. 1, Box 78, Boynton Beach, FL 33437; (407) 732-3684. Chassahowitzka (Crystal River, Egmont Key, Passage Key, Pinellas), 7798 S. Suncoast Blvd., Homosassa, FL 32646; (904) 382-2201. Florida Panther (Ten Thousand Lakes), 2629 S. Horseshoe Dr., Naples, FL 33942; (813) 643-2636. J.N. "Ding" Darling (Caloosahatchee, Island Bay, Matlacha Pass, Pine Island), One Wildlife Dr., Sanibel, FL 33957; (813) 472-1100. Lake Woodruff, P.O. Box 488, DeLeon Springs, FL 32028; (904) 985-4673. Lower Suwannee (Cedar Keys), P.O. Box 1193 C, Chiefland, FL 32626; (904) 493-0238. Merritt Island (Pelican Island, St. Johns), P.O. Box 6504, Titusville, FL 32780; (305) 867-0667. National Key Deer (Crocodile Lake, Great White Heron, Key West), P.O. Box 510, Big Pine Key, FL 33043; (305) 872-2239. St. Marks, P.O. Box 68, St. Marks, FL 32355; (904) 925-6121. St. Vincent, P.O. Box 447, Apalachicola, FL 32320; (904) 653-8808.

Georgia
Eufaula, Rte. 2, Box 97-B, Eufaula, AL 36027; (205) 687-4065. Okefenokee (Banks Lake), Rte. 2, Box 338, Folkston, GA 31537; (912) 496-7366. Piedmont, Rte. 1, Box 670, Round Oak, GA 31038; (912) 986-5441. Savannah Coastal Refuges (Blackbeard Island, Harris Neck, Pinckney Island (SC), Savannah, Tybee, Wassaw, Wolf Island), P.O. Box 8487, Savannah, GA 31412; (912) 944-4415.

Hawaii
Hawaiian and Pacific Islands Complex, P.O. Box 50167, 300 Ala Moana Blvd., Honolulu, HI 96850; (808) 541-1201. Hakalau Forest, 154 Waianuenue Ave., Federal Bldg., Room 219, Hilo, HI 96720; (808) 969-9909. Kilauea Point, P.O. Box 87, Kilauea, Kauai, HI 96754; (808) 828-1413. Remote Island Refuges (Baker Island, Hawaiian Islands, Howland Island, Jarvis Island, Johnston Atoll, Rose Atoll), P.O. Box 50167, 300 Ala Moana Blvd., Honolulu, HI 96850; (808) 541-1201. Wetlands Refuges (Hanalei, Huleia, James C. Campbell, Kakahaia, Pearl Harbor), P.O. Box 50167, 300 Ala Moana Blvd., Honolulu, HI 96850; (808) 541-1201.

Idaho
Deer Flat, P.O. Box 448, Nampa, ID 83653; (208) 467-9278. Kootenai, HCR 60, Box 283, Bonners Ferry, ID 83805; (208) 267-3888. Southeast Idaho Refuge Complex (Oxford Slough WPA), 1246 Yellowstone Ave., A-4, Pocatello, ID 83201-4372; (208) 237-6615. Bear Lake, 370 Webster, Box 9, Montpelier, ID 83254; (208) 847-1757. Camas, 2150 E. 2350 N., Hamer, ID 83245; (208) 662-5423. Grays Lake, 74 Grays Lake Rd., Wayan, ID 83285; (208) 574-2755. Minidoka, Rte. 4, P.O. Box 290, Rupert, ID 83350; (208) 436-3589.

Illinois
Chautauqua (Meredosia), Rte. 2, Havana, IL 62644; (309) 535-2290. Crab Orchard, P.O. Box J, Carterville, IL 62918; (618) 997-3344. Mark Twain, 311 North 5th St., Suite 100, Great River Plaza, Quincy, IL 62301; (217) 224-8580. Annada District, P.O. Box 88, Annada, MO 63330; (314) 847-2333. Brussels District, P.O. Box 142, Brussels, IL 62013; (618) 883-2524. Wapello District, Rte. 1, Wapello, IA 52653; (319) 523-6982. Upper Mississippi River National Wildlife and Fish Refuge, 51 East 4th St., Winona, MN 55987; (507) 452-4232. Savanna District, Post Office Bldg., Savanna, IL 61074; (815) 273-2732.

Indiana
Muscatatuck, Rte. 7, Box 189A, Seymour, IN 47274; (812) 522-4352.

Iowa
DeSoto, Rte. 1, Box 114, Missouri Valley, IA 51555; (712) 642-4121. Union Slough, Rte. 1, Box 52, Titonka, IA 50480; (515) 928-2523. Upper Mississippi River National Wildlife and Fish Refuge, 51 East 4th St., Winona, MN 55987; (507) 452-4232. McGregor District, P.O. Box 460, McGregor, IA 52157; (319) 873-3423.

Kansas
Flint Hills, P.O. Box 128, Hartford, KS 66854; (316) 392-5553. Kirwin, Rte. 1, Box 103, Kirwin, KS 67644; (913) 543-6673. Quivira, Rte. 3, Box 48A, Stafford, KS 67578; (316) 486-2393.

Louisiana
Bogue Chitto (Breton, Delta), 1010 Gause Blvd., Bldg. 936, Slidwell, LA 70458; (504) 646-7555. Cameron Prairie, Rte. 1, Box 643, Bell City, LA 70630; (318) 598-2216. Catahoula, P.O. Drawer Z, Rhinehart, LA 71363-0201; (318) 992-5261. D'Arbonne (Upper Ouachita), P.O. Box 3065, Monroe, LA 71201; (318) 325-1735. Lacassine (Shells Keys), Rte. 1, Box 186, Lake Arthur, LA 70549; (318) 774-5923. Lake Ophelia, P.O. Box 256, Marksville, LA 71351; (318) 253-4131. Sabine, Hwy. 27, 3000 Main St., Hackberry, LA 70645; (318) 762-3816. Tensas River, Rte. 2, Box 295, Tallulah, LA 71282; (318) 574-2664.

Maine
Moosehorn (Cross Island, Carlton Pond WPA, Franklin Island, Seal Island, Sunkhaze Meadows), P.O. Box 1077, Calais, ME 04619; (207) 454-3521. Petit Manan, P.O. Box 279, Milbridge, ME 04658; (207) 546-2124. Pond Island, Northern Blvd., Plum Island, Newburyport, MA 01950; (508) 465-5753. Rachel Carson, Rte. 2, Box 751, Wells, ME 04090; (207) 646-9226.

Maryland
Blackwater (Martin, Susquehanna), Rte. 1, Box 121, Cambridge, MD 21613; (301) 228-2692. Chincoteague, Box 62, Chincoteague, VA 23336; (804) 336-6122. Eastern Neck, Rte. 2, Box 225, Rock Hall, MD 21661; (301) 639-7056. Patuxent, Rte. 197, Laurel, MD 20708; (301) 498-0300.

Massachusetts
Great Meadows (John Hay (NH), Massasoit, Monomoy, Nantucket, Oxbow, Wapack (NH)), Weir Hill Rd., Sudbury, MA 01776; (508) 443-4661. Parker River (Pond Island (ME), Thacher Island), Northern Blvd., Plum Island, Newburyport, MA 01950; (508) 465-5753. Rachel Carson, Rte. 2, Box 751, Wells, ME 04090; (207) 646-9226.

Michigan
Seney (Harbor Island, Huron), Seney, MI 49883; (906) 586-9851. Shiawassee (Michigan Islands, Wyandotte), 6975 Mower Rd., Rte. 1, Saginaw, MI 48601; (517) 777-5930.

Minnesota
Agassiz, Middle River, MN 56737; (218) 449-4115. Big Stone, 25 NW 2nd St., Ortonville, MN 56278; (612) 839-3700. Minnestoa Valley, 4101 E. 80th St., Bloomington, MN 55420; (612) 854-5900. Minnesota Wetlands Complex, Rte. 1, Box 76, Fergus Falls, MN 56537; (218) 739-2291. Morris WMD, Rte. 1, Box 208, Mill Dam Rd., Morris, MN 56267; (612) 589-1001. Detroit Lakes WMD, Rte. 3, Box 47D, Detroit Lakes, MN 56501; (218) 847-4431. Fergus Falls WMD, Rte. 1, Box 76, Fergus Falls, MN 56537; (218) 739-2291. Litchfield WMD, 305 North Sibley, Litchfield, MN 55355; (612) 693-2849. Rice Lake (Mille Lacs, Sandstone), Rte. 2, Box 67, McGregor, MN 55760; (218) 768-2402. Sherburne, Rte. 2, Zimmerman, MN 55398; (612) 389-3323. Tamarac, Rural Rte., Rochert, MN 56578; (218) 847-2641. Upper Mississippi River Complex, P.O. Bldg., Box 2484, La Crosse, WI 54602; (608) 784-5540. Upper Mississippi River National Wildlife and Fish Refuge (IA, IL, MN, WI), 51 East 4th St., Winona, MN 55987; (507) 452-4232. Winona District, 51 East 4th St., Winona, MN 55987; (507) 452-4232.

Mississippi
Mississippi Sandhill Crane, 7200 Coane Ln., Gautier, MS 39553; (601) 497-6322. Noxubee, Rte. 1, Box 142, Brooksville, MS 39739; (601) 323-5548. Yazoo (Hillside, Mathews Brake, Morgan Brake, Panther Swamp), Rte. 1, Box 286, Hillandale, MS 38748; (601) 839-2638.

Missouri
Mingo, Rte. 1, Box 103, Puxico, MO 63960; (314) 222-3589. Squaw Creek, P.O. Box 101, Mound City, MO 64470; (816) 442-3187. Swan Lake, P.O. Box 68, Sumner, MO 64681; (816) 856-3323.

Montana
Benton Lake, P.O. Box 450, Black Eagle, MT 59414; (406) 727-7400. Bowdoin (Black Coulee, Creedman Coulee, Hewitt Lake, Lake Thibadeau), P.O. Box J, Malta, MT 59538; (406) 654-2863. Charles M. Russell (Hailstone, Halfbreed Lake, Lake Mason, Nichols Coulee, UL Bend, War Horse), P.O. Box 110, Lewistown, MT 59457; (406) 538-8706. Fort Peck Wildlife Station, P.O. Box 166, Fort Peck, MT 59223; (406) 526-3464. Jordan Wildlife Station, P.O. Box 63, Jordan, MT 59337; (406) 557-6145. Sand Creek Wildlife Station, P.O. Box 89, Roy, MT 59471; (406) 464-5181. Lee Metcalf, P.O. Box 257, Stevensville, MT 59870; (406) 777-5552. Medicine Lake (Lamesteer), HC 51, Box 2, Medicine Lake, MT 59247; (406) 789-2305. National Bison Range (Nine-Pipe, Pablo), Moiese, MT 59824; (406) 644-2211. Northwest Montana WMD (Swan River),

780 Creston Hatchery Rd., Kalispell, MT 59901; (406) 755-7870, (406) 755-9311. Red Rock Lakes, Monida Star Rte., Box 15, Lima, MT 59739; (406) 276-3347.

Nebraska
Crescent Lake (North Platte), HC 68, Box 21, Ellsworth, NE 69340; (308) 762-4893. DeSoto, Rte. 1, Box 114, Missouri Valley, IA 51555; (712) 642-4121. Fort Niobrara/Valentine, Hidden Timber Route, HC 14, Box 67, Valentine, NE 69201; (402) 376-3789. Valentine, Hidden Timber Route, HC 14, Box 67, Valentine, NE 69201; (402) 376-3789. Rainwater Basin WMD, P.O. Box 1686, Kearney, NE 68847; (308) 236-5015.

Nevada
Desert National Wildlife Range (Amargosa Pupfish Station), 1500 North Decatur Blvd., Las Vegas, NV 89108; (702) 646-3401. Ash Meadows, P.O. Box 2660, Pahrump, NV 89041; (702) 372-5435. Pahranagat, Box 510, Alamo, NV 89001; (702) 725-3417. Ruby Lake, Ruby Valley, NV 89833; (702) 779-2237. Sheldon, P.O. Box 111, Room 308, U.S. Post Office Bldg., Lakeview, OR 97630; (503) 947-3315. Stillwater (Anaho Island, Fallon), P.O. Box 1236, Fallon, NV 89406-1236; (702) 423-5128.

New Hampshire
John Hay, Weir Hill Rd., Sudbury, MA 01776; (508) 443-4661. Wapack, Weir Hill Rd., Sudbury, MA 01776; (508) 443-4661.

New Jersey
Edwin B. Forsythe (Brigantine Division), Great Creek Rd., Box 72, Oceanville, NJ 08231; (609) 652-1665. Barnegat Division, 70 Collinstown Rd., Barnegat, NJ 08005; (609) 698-1387. Great Swamp, Pleasant Plains Rd., RD 1, Box 152, Basking Ridge, NJ 07920; (201) 647-1222. Killcohook, Suite 104, Scott Plaza 2, Philadelphia, PA 19113; (215) 521-0662. Supawna Meadows, RD 3, Box 540, Salem, NJ 08079; (609) 935-1487.

New Mexico
Bitter Lake, P.O. Box 7, Roswell, NM 88201; (505) 622-6755. Bosque del Apache, P.O. Box 1246, Socorro, NM 87801; (505) 835-1828. San Andres, P.O. Box 756, Las Cruces, NM 88001; (505) 382-5047. Sevilleta, General Delivery, San Acacia, NM 87831; (505) 864-4021. Grulla, P.O. Box 228, Umbarger, TX 79091; (806) 499-3382. Las Vegas, Rte. 1, Box 399, Las Vegas, NM 87701; (505) 425-3581. Maxwell, P.O. Box 276, Maxwell, NM 87728; (505) 375-2331.

New York
Iroquois, P.O. Box 517, Casey Rd., Alabama, NY 14003; (716) 948-9154. Montezuma, 3395 Rte. 5/20 East, Seneca Falls, NY 13148; (315) 568-5987. Wertheim (Amagansett, Conscience Point, Elizabeth A. Morton, Lido Beach, Oyster Bay, Seatuck, Target Rock), P.O. Box 21, Shirley, NY 11967; (516) 286-0485.

North Carolina
Alligator River (Currituck), P.O. Box 1969, Manteo, NC 27954; (919) 473-1131. Pea Island, (919) 987-2394. Great Dismal Swamp, 3100 Desert Rd., P.O. Box 349, Suffolk, VA 23434; (804) 986-3705. Mackay Island, P.O. Box 31, Knotts Island, NC 27950; (919) 429-3100. Mattamuskeet (Cedar Island, Pungo, Swanquarter), Rte. 1, Box N-2, Swanquarter, NC 27885; (919) 926-4021.

North Dakota
Arrowwood (Chase Lake, Slade), Rural Rte. 1, Pingree, ND 58476; (701) 285-3341. Long Lake, Rural Rte. 1, Box 23, Moffit, ND 58560; (701) 387-4397. Valley City WMD, Rural Rte. 1, Valley City, ND 58072; (701) 845-3466. Audubon, Rural Rte. 1, Coleharbor, ND 58531; (701) 442-5474. Lake Ilo, Dunn Center, ND 58626; (701) 548-4407. Des Lacs (Lake Zahl), P.O. Box 578, Kenmare, ND 58746; (701) 385-4046. Crosby WMD, P.O. Box 148, Crosby, ND 58730; (701) 965-6488. Lostwood, Rural Rte. 2, Box 98, Kenmare, ND 58746; (701) 848-2722. Devils Lake WMD (Lake Alice, Sullys Hill National Game Preserve), P.O. Box 908, Devils Lake, ND 58301; (701) 662-8611. J. Clark Salyer, Box 66, Upham, ND 58789; (701) 768-2548. Kulm WMD, P.O. Box E, Kulm, ND 58456; (701) 647-2866. Tewaukon, Rural Rte. 1, Cayuga, ND 58013; (701) 724-3598. Upper Souris, Rural Rte. 1, Foxholm, ND 58738; (701) 468-5467.

Ohio
Ottawa (Cedar Point, West Sister Island), 14000 W. State Rte. 2, Oak Harbor, OH 43449; (419) 898-0014.

Oklahoma
Little River (Little Sandy), P.O. Box 340, Broken Bow, OK 74728; (405) 584-6211. Salt Plains, Rte. 1, Box 76, Jet, OK 73749; (405) 626-4794. Sequoyah (Oklahoma Bat Caves), Rte. 1, Box 18A, Vian, OK 74962; (918) 773-5251. Tishomingo, Rte. 1, Box 151, Tishomingo, OK 73460; (405) 371-2402. Washita (Optima), Rte. 1, Box 68, Butler, OK 73625; (405) 664-2205. Wichita Mountains Wildlife Refuge, Rte. 1, Box 448, Indiahoma, OK 73552; (405) 429-3221.

Oregon
Klamath Forest and Upper Klamath, Rte. 1, Box 74, Tule Lake, CA 96134; (916) 667-2231. Lewis and Clark, HC 01, Box 910, Ilwaco, WA 98624-9707; (206) 484-3482. Malheur, HC 72, Box 245, Princeton, OR 97721; (503) 493-2612. Sheldon/Hart Mountain Complex, P.O. Box 111, Room 308, U.S. Post Office Bldg., Lakeview, OR 97630; (503) 947-3315. Sheldon, P.O. Box 111, Room 308, U.S. Post Office Bldg., Lakeview, OR 97630; (503) 947-3315. Hart Mountain,

P.O. Box 111, Room 308, U.S. Post Office Bldg., Lakeview, OR 97630; (503) 947-3315. Umatilla (Cold Springs, McKay Creek), P.O. Box 239, Umatilla, OR 97882; (503) 922-3232. McNary, P.O. Box 308, Burbank, WA 99323; (509) 547-4942. Toppenish, Rte. 1, Box 1300, Toppenish, WA 98948; (509) 865-2405. Western Oregon Refuge Complex, 26208 Finley Refuge Rd., Corvallis, OR 97333; (503) 757-7236. Ankeny, 2301 Wintel Rd., Jefferson, OR 97352; (503) 327-2444. Baskett Slough, 10995 Hwy. 22, Dallas, OR 97338; (503) 623-2749. William L. Finley (Bandon Marsh, Cape Meares, Oregon Islands, Three Arch Rocks), 26208 Finley Refuge Rd., Corvallis, OR 97333; (503) 757-7236.

Pennsylvania
Erie, RD 1, Wood Duck Ln., Guys Mills, PA 16327; (814) 789-3585. Tinicum National Environmental Center (Killcohook (NJ)), Suite 104, Scott Plaza 2, Philadelphia, PA 19113; (215) 521-0662. Supawna Meadows (NJ), RD 3, Box 540, Salem, NJ 08079; (609) 935-1487.

Puerto Rico
Caribbean Islands (Buck Island (Virgin Islands), Cabo Rojo, Culebra, Desecheo, Green Cay (Virgin Islands), Sandy Point (Virgin Islands)), Box 510, Carr. 301, KM 5.1, Boqueron, PR 00622; (809) 851-7258.

Rhode Island
Ninigret (Block Island, Pettaquamscutt Cove, Sachuest Point, Salt Meadow (CT), Trustom Pond), P.O. Box 307, Charlestown, RI 02813; (401) 364-9124. Stewart B. McKinney, U.S. Federal Bldg., Room 210, 915 Lafayette Blvd., Bridgeport, CT 06604; (203) 579-5617.

South Carolina
Cape Romain, 390 Bulls Island Rd., Awendaw, SC 29429; (803) 928-3368. Carolina Sandhills, Rte. 2, Box 330, McBee, SC 29101; (803) 335-8401. Pee Dee, P.O. Box 780, Wadesboro, NC 28170; (704) 694-4424. Pinckney Island, P.O. Box 8487, Savannah, GA 31412; (912) 944-4415. Santee, Rte. 2, Box 66, Summerton, SC 29148; (803) 478-2217.

South Dakota
Lacreek, HWC 3, Box 14, Martin, SD 57551; (605) 685-6508. Lake Andes (Karl E. Mundt), Rural Rte. 1, Box 77, Lake Andes, SD 57356; (605) 487-7603. Madison WMD, P.O. Box 48, Madison, SD 57042; (605) 256-2974. Sand Lake (Pocasse), Rural Rte. 1, Box 25, Columbia, SD 57433; (605) 885-6320. Waubay, Rural Rte. 1, Box 79, Waubay, SD 57273; (605) 947-4521.

Tennessee
Cross Creeks, Rte. 1, Box 556, Dover, TN 37058; (615) 232-7477. Hatchie (Chickasaw, Lower Hatchie), P.O. Box 187, Brownsville, TN 38012; (901) 772-0501. Reelfoot (Lake Isom), Rte. 2, Hwy. 157, Union City, TN 38261; (901) 538-2481. Tennessee, P.O. Box 849, Paris, TN 38242; (901) 642-2091.

Texas
Anahuac (Moody), P.O. Box 278, Anahuac, TX 77514; (409) 267-3337. McFaddin/Texas Point, P.O. Box 609, Sabine Pass, TX 77655; (409) 971-2909. Aransas (Matagorda), P.O. Box 100, Austwell, TX 77950; (512) 286-3559. Attwater Prairie Chicken, P.O. Box 518, Eagle Lake, TX 77434; (409) 234-5940. Brazoria (Big Boggy), P.O. Box 1088, Angleton, TX 77516-1088; (409) 849-6062. San Bernard, P.O. Box 1088, Angleton, TX 77516-1088; (409) 849-6062. Buffalo Lake (Grulla (NM)), P.O. Box 228, Umbarger, TX 79091; (806) 499-3382. Muleshoe, P.O. Box 549, Muleshoe, TX 79347; (806) 946-3341. Hagerman, Rte. 3, Box 123, Sherman, TX 75090-9564; (214) 786-2826. Laguna Atascosa, P.O. Box 450, Rio Hondo, TX 78583; (512) 748-3607. Lower Rio Grande Valley/Santa Ana Complex, 320 N. Main, Room A-103, McAllen, TX 78501; (512) 630-4636.

Utah
Fish Springs, P.O. Box 568, Dugway, UT 84022; (801) 522-5353. Ouray (Bear River Migratory Bird Refuge), 1680 W. Hwy. 40, Room 1220, Vernal, UT 84078; (801) 789-0351.

Vermont
Missisquoi, P.O. Box 163, Swanton, VT 05488; (802) 868-4781.

Virginia
Back Bay (Plum Tree Island), 4005 Sandpiper Rd., P.O. Box 6286, Virginia Beach, VA 23456; (804) 721-2412. Chincoteague (Wallops Island), Box 62, Chincoteague, VA 23336; (804) 336-6122. Eastern Shore of Virginia (Cedar Island, Fisherman Island), RFD 1, Box 122B, Cape Charles, VA 23310; (804) 331-2760. Great Dismal Swamp (Nansemond), 3100 Desert Rd., P.O. Box 349, Suffolk, VA 23434; (804) 986-3705. Mason Neck (Featherstone, Marumsco), 14416 Jefferson Davis Hwy., Suite 20A, Woodbridge, VA 22191; (703) 690-1297. Presquile, P.O. Box 620, Hopewell, VA 23860; (804) 458-7541.

Washington
Columbia (Saddle Mountain), 735 E. Main St., P.O. Drawer F, Othello, WA 99344; (509) 488-2668. McNary, P.O. Box 308, Burbank, WA 99323; (509) 547-4942. Nisqually (San Juan Islands), 100 Brown Farm Rd., Olympia, WA 98506; (206) 753-9467. Coastal Refuges Office (Dungeness, Protection Island, Washington Islands), P.O. Box 698, Sequim, WA 98382; (206) 457-8792. Ridgefield (Pierce Ranch, Steigerwald Lake), 301 N. Third St., P.O. Box 457, Ridgefield, WA 98642; (206) 887-4106. Toppenish, Rte. 1, Box 1300, Toppenish, WA 98948; (509) 865-2405. Turnbull, S. 26010 Smith Rd., Cheney, WA 99004;

(509) 235-4723. Umatilla, P.O. Box 239, Umatilla, OR 97882; (503) 922-3232.
Willapa (Lewis and Clark (OR)), HC 01, Box 910, Ilwaco, WA 98624-9707;
(206) 484-3482. Julia Butler Hansen (Formerly Columbian White-tailed Deer),
P.O. Box 566, Cathlamet, WA 98612; (206) 795-3915. Conboy Lake, P.O. Box
5, Glenwood, WA 98619; (509) 364-3410.

Wisconsin

Horicon (Fox River, Gravel Island, Green Bay), W. 4279 Headquarters Rd.,
Mayville, WI 53050; (414) 387-2658; Necedah, Star Rte. West, Box 386, Necedah,
WI 54646; (608) 565-2551. Upper Mississippi River Complex, P.O. Bldg., Box
2484, La Crosse, WI 54602; (608) 784-5540. Trempealeau, Rte. 1, Trempealeau,
WI 54661; (608) 539-2311. Upper Mississippi River National Wildlife and Fish
Refuge, 51 East 4th St., Winona, MN 55987; (507) 452-4232. La Crosse District,
P.O. Bldg., Box 415, La Crosse, WI 54601-0415; (608) 784-3910.

Wyoming

Bamforth, P.O. Box 457, Walden, CO 80480; (303) 723-8202.   Hutton Lake,
P.O. Box 457, Walden, CO 80480; (303) 723-8202.   National Elk Refuge, P.O.
Box C, Jackson, WY 83001; (307) 733-9212. Pathfinder, P.O. Box 457, Walden,
CO 80480; (303) 723-8202. Seedskadee, P.O. Box 67, Green River, WY 82935;
(307) 875-2187.

* Wildlife Refuge Regional Offices

Region 1

Lloyd 500 Bldg., Suite 1692, 500 NE Multnomah St., Portland, OR 97232; (503)
231-6118, (503) 231-6214.

Region 2

P.O. Box 1306, Albuquerque, NM 87103; (505) 766-2321, (505) 766-1829.

Region 3

Federal Bldg., Fort Snelling, Twin Cities, MN 55111; (612) 725-3563, (612) 725-
3507.

Region 4

Richard B. Russell Federal Bldg., 75 Spring St., SW, Atlanta, GA 30303; (404)
331-3588, (404) 331-0833.

Region 5

One Gateway Center, Suite 700, Newton Corner, MA 02158; (617) 965-5100,
(617) 965-9222.

Region 6

Box 25486, Denver Federal Center, Denver, CO 80225; (303) 236-7920, (303)
236-8145. Region 7, 1011 E. Tudor Rd., Anchorage, AK 99503; (907) 786-3542,
(907) 786-3538.

* Wildlife Society

Wildlife Society
5410 Grosvenor Lane
Bethesda, MD 20814   (301) 897-9770

The Wildlife Society is devoted to the protection of United States wildlife
resources. The Society is a member of the Renewable Resources Foundation.
It publishes *Journal of Wildlife Management, The Wildlifer, Wildlife Society
Bulletin.*

* World Wildlife Fund

World Wildlife Fund (WWF)
1250 24th St., NW
Washington, DC 20037   (202) 293-4800

The World Wildlife Fund is the leading private organization in the U.S. working
internationally to protect endangered wildlife and wildlands. World Wildlife
Fund emphasizes field activities and practical, rigorously planned, scientifically
based conservation projects. It protects endangered wildlife and tropical forest
habitats through a mix of grants and the direct programmatic activities of its staff.

* Youth Conservation Corps

United States Youth Conservation Corps
U.S. Fish and Wildlife Service
National Park Service
Washington, DC 20240   (202) 343-5951

The Youth Conservation Corps is a summer employment program for young
men and women, ages 15 through 18, who work, learn, and earn wages
accomplishing needed conservation work on public lands. The program is also
administered by the Forest Service of the U.S. Department of Agriculture.
Projects include constructing trails, building campground facilities, planting trees,
collecting litter, clearing streams, improving wildlife habitats, and office work.
Limited positions are available.

Hazardous and Solid Waste

* See also Health and Medicine; Chemicals,Toxics, and Other Health Hazards Chapter

* 45,000 Pesticide Products Inventory
Office of Pesticide Programs
Environmental Protection Agency
401 M St., SW
Washington DC 20460   (202) 557-7090
EPA administers two Congressionally mandated statutes to control the more than 45,000 pesticide products registered for use in the United States. The EPA monitors the distribution and use of these pesticides, issuing civil or criminal penalties for violations. EPA also sets tolerances or maximum legal limits for pesticide residues on food commodities and feed grains to prevent consumer exposure to unsafe pesticide levels.

* Abandoned Mines Acid Drainage Disposal
Environmental Technology Division
Bureau of Mines
U.S. Department of the Interior
2401 E St., NW
Washington, DC 20241   (202) 634-1263
Researchers at the Bureau of Mines are working on low-cost ways to deal with the problem of acid drainage at abandoned mines. They are developing computer programs to predict potential drainage at new mines. The Bureau's environmental research also addresses the problem of solid waste disposal and soil and water contaminated by metals. Technologies are developed that will reduce or remove the threats that these wastes pose.

* Agricultural Chemicals Association
National Agricultural Chemicals Association (NACA)
1155 15th St., NW
Madison Building
Suite 900
Washington, DC 20005   (202) 296-1585
The National Agricultural Chemicals Association consists of companies producing chemical controls for fungi, rodents, pests and weeds.

* Animal Poison Control Hotline
National Animal Poison Control Center   (217) 333-3611
The National Animal Poison Control Center, at The University of Illinois, provides 24-hour consultation in diagnosis and treatment of suspected or actual animal poisonings or chemical contaminations. Its emergency response team will rapidly investigate such incidents in North America, and perform laboratory analysis of feeds, animal specimens, and environmental materials for toxicants and chemical contaminants.

* Chemical and Solid Waste Transportation
Chemical Waste Transportation Council (CWTC)
1730 Rhode Island Ave., NW
Suite 1000
Washington, DC 20036   (202) 659-4613
The Chemical Waste Transportation Council represents the interests of companies engaged in the business of hauling chemical wastes. The Council is affiliated with the National Solid Wastes Management Association.

* Chemical and Toxic Assessments
Chemical Assessment Desk
Office of Toxic Substances
Environmental Protection Agency
401 M St., SW
Washington DC 20460   (202) 382-3442
The Chemical Assessment Desk provides technical consultation from the Office of Toxic Substances and promotes communication within EPA on chemical assessment information.

* Chemical Ecology
International Society of Chemical Ecology
101 T.H. Morgan Building
University of Kentucky
Lexington, KY 40506   (606) 257-2652

The International Society of Chemical Ecology was formed to promote understanding the origin, function and significance of natural chemicals interacting among organisms. Publications: *Journal of Chemical Ecology.*

* Chemical Engineers
American Institute of Chemical Engineers (AICHE)
345 East 47th St.
New York, NY 10017   (212) 705-7538
The American Institute of Chemical Engineers is a national society for chemical engineers. The Institute is a member society of the American Association of Engineering Societies. Publications: *AICHE Journal, Chemical Engineering, Progress, Chemical Engineering Faculties, Directory of Chemical Engineering Consultants, International Chemical.*

* Chemical Hazards Management Bibliography
Superintendent of Documents
Government Printing Office
Washington, DC 20402   (202) 783-3238
Hazardous and toxic waste management are topics within this bibliography. A pocket guide to chemical hazards and a septic
systems and ground-water protection guide are featured. Free.

* Chemical Health and Safety Hotline
Chemical Referral Center(800) CMA-8200 (202) 887-1315 (in DC)
This toll-free service provides non-emergency referrals to companies that manufacture chemicals and to state and federal agencies for health and safety information and information regarding chemical regulations. It operates 9 a.m. to 6 p.m. eastern time. Residents in Arkansas can call (202) 887-1315 collect.

* Chemical Risk Management
Chemical Control Division
Office of Toxic Substances
Environmental Protection Agency
401 M St., SW, Room E513
Washington DC 20460   (202) 382-3749
This office performs the risk management functions for the Office of Toxic Substances. They manage the new chemical and biotechnology programs.

* Chemicals and Environmental Science
American Chemical Society (ACS)
1155 16th St., NW
Washington, DC 20036   (202) 872-4600
The American Chemical Society is a national professional association of chemists that supports the development of all branches of chemistry. Publications: *Environmental Science & Technology.*

* Chemicals' Impact on Eagles and Falcons
U.S. Department of the Army
Chemical Research Development
and Engineering Center
Aberdeen Proving Ground, MD 21010-5423   (301) 671-4345
While the Center's primary mission is concerned with research on chemical defensive material, the Center has become very involved in wildlife conservation programs because of its location on the Chesapeake Bay. The Center is especially experienced in a Bald Eagle program and a Peregrine Falcon program. Fact sheets on these and other wildlife issues may be obtained by writing or calling the above office.

* Chemists Institute
American Institute of Chemists
7315 Wisconsin Ave.
Bethesda, MD 20814   (301) 652-2447
The American Institute of Chemists is a professional association of chemists in academe, industry and government. Publications: *Chemist.*

* Chemical Transportation Emergency Hotline

Environment and Nature

Chemtrec Hotline
Chemical Transportation Emergency Center
American Chemical Manufacturers Association   (800) 424-9300
The Chemtrec Hotline is a 24-hour Chemical Transportation Emergency Center operated as a public service by the Chemical Manufacturers Association. The Hotline identifies unknown chemicals, provides advice on proper initial response methods and procedures for specific chemicals and situations, and offers assistance in establishing contact with shippers, carriers, manufacturers, special product response teams.

* Commercial Low-Level Radioactive Waste

Office of Technology Assessment
600 Pennsylvania Ave., SE
Washington, DC 20510   (202) 228-6852
OTA is working on a project to analyze the Federal effort and State progress in implementing the Low-Level Radioactive Waste Policy Amendments Act, which identifies Federal activities needed to help States meet milestones for developing disposal facilities. Contact Gretchen Hund McCabe, the project director, for more information.

* Defense Nuclear Waste and Contamination Cleanup

Office of Technology Assessment
600 Pennsylvania Ave., SE
Washington, DC 20510   (202) 228-6862
Today there is a large backlog of high-level, transuranic, low-level, hazardous, and mixed nuclear waste at the 15 facilities in the Department of Energy's nuclear weapons complex. OTA is currently studying how best to clean up this nuclear waste problem using technologies for waste management and minimizations. Contact Peter Johnson, the project director, for more information.

* Dioxin Hotlines

The following hotlines provide callers with information on dioxin and related concerns for contaminated areas in New York, New Jersey, and Missouri:

New Jersey: (800) 346-5009
New York: (800) 722-1223
Missouri: (800) 892-5009

* Dyestuffing Manufacturing and Environmental Hazards

United States Operating Committee on ETAD
1330 Connecticut Ave., NW
Suite 300
Washington, DC 20036   (202) 659-0600
The United States Operating Committee on ETAD is the operating arm of the Ecological and Toxicological Association of the Dyestuffs Manufacturing Industry concerned with environmental and health hazards in the manufacture, processing, shipping, use and disposal of members' products.

* Emergency Plans for Acutely Toxic Chemicals

Emergency Planning & Community Right to Know   (800) 535-0202
                                                     (202) 479-2449
This EPA hotline provides communities with help in preparing for accidental releases of toxic chemicals. Communities can call to obtain interim guidelines regarding *Acutely Toxic Chemicals*. These guidelines cover Organizing a Community, Developing a Chemical Contingency Plan, and gathering site-specific information. The hotline also provides a list of more than 400 acutely toxic chemicals.

* Environmental Mutagen Organization

Environmental Mutagen Society (EMS)
Ctr Box X Oak Ridge Natl Lab
Bldg 2001, MS 50
Oak Ridge, TN 37831-6050   (415) 422-5698
The focus of the Environmental Mutagen Society is to encourage the study of mutagens in the human environment particularly as they affect public health. Publications: *Environmental Mutagenesis, EMS Newsletter*.

* Fishery Chemicals Research

National Fisheries Research Center
U.S. Fish and Wildlife Service
P.O. Box 818
LaCrosse, WI 54602-0818   (608) 783-6451
The National Fisheries Research Center at LaCrosse, Wisconsin, has been designated by the Fish and Wildlife Service to negotiate registration for fishery chemicals with regulatory agencies. Pesticides are registered with the U.S. Environmental Protection Agency, and therapeutants for controlling fish diseases are registered with the U.S. Food and Drug Administration. Once a fishery chemical is registered by the Federal government, states will generally allow the use of that chemical for fish culture and management.

* Formaldehyde Association

Formaldehyde Institute
1330 Connecticut Ave., NW
Washington, DC 20036   (202) 659-0060
This Institute consists of users and producers of formaldehyde concerned with health and environmental problems associated with it.

* Garbage Management and Engineering

American Society of Sanitary Engineers (ASSE)
Box 40326
Bay Village, OH 44140   (216) 835-3040
The American Society of Sanitary Engineers is a national association of engineers working on sanitary projects such as liquid waste collection, processing and disposal. Publications: *ASSE Yearbook, Newsletter*.

* Geologic Hazards and Hazardous Waste

Geologic Inquiries
U.S. Geological Survey
911 National Center
Reston, VA 22092   (703) 648-4380
This division evaluates environmental hazards which are associated with earthquakes, volcanoes, floods, droughts, toxic materials, landslides, subsidence, and other ground failures. Methods of hazards prediction are developed through the study of the Earth's internal structure. Engineering problems are identified and solved, including problems in the selection of sites for power stations, highways, bridges, dams, and hazardous waste disposal.

* Hazardous and Solid Waste State Management

Association of State and Territorial Solid Waste
   Management Officials
444 North Capitol St., NW
Suite 345
Washington, DC 20001   (202) 624-5828
The Association of State and Territorial Solid Waste Management Officials consists of directors and support staff of state and territorial solid and hazardous waste programs.

* Hazardous Materials Technical Hotline

Hazardous Materials Technical Center   (800) 638-8958
                                             (301) 468-8858
This center provides various services related to hazardous materials, including a clearinghouse technical inquiry line, a newsletter for the Department of Defense about hazardous materials, maintenance of a collection of publications on hazardous management, and abstracting and publishing of literature related to hazardous materials. The services provided are free only to the Department of Defense; others must pay a fee to use them.

* Hazardous Material Transportation Accidents

Information Systems Division (DHM-63)
Office of Hazardous Materials Transportation
Research and Special Programs Administration
U.S. Department of Transportation
400 7th Street, SW, Room 8112
Washington, DC 20590   (202) 366-4555
This division collects and analyzes accident data from transporters of hazardous materials by highway, rail, air, and water and from container manufacturers. Information stored in the database includes the hazardous material involved, transporter name and mode, packaging used, cause of accident, and results. Contact the above office for searches. There may be a charge.

* Hazardous Materials Transportation Hotline

U.S. Department of Transportation Department Hotline
400 7th Street, SW, Room 8112
Washington, DC 20590   (202) 366-4488
This Department of Transportation Hotline provides informational assistance pertaining to federal regulations for transportation of hazardous materials. This includes those regulations contained in CFR-49.

* Hazardous Waste Bibliography

and Technology Transfer
Office of Solid Waste and Emergency Response
Environmental Protection Agency
401 M St., Sw
Washington DC 20460   (202) 382-6940

Hazardous and Solid Waste

This bibliography, prepared by the Technology Transfer Task Force, lists and abstracts the most important technical materials that should be readily available to all Federal and State hazardous waste staffs and their contractors. It assigns each document a level of importance as primary reference documents for Federal and State headquarters, regional, and field staffs. Contact this office to obtain a copy.

* Hazardous Waste Cleanup Services

Hazardous Waste Services Association (HWSA)
1333 New Hampshire Ave.
Suite 1100
Washington, DC 20036 (202) 833-1294

The Hazardous Waste Services Association consists of companies involved in the generation, treatment, transportation, disposal and storage of industrial wastes and equipment and services suppliers. Publications: *Wasteline*.

* Hazardous Waste Hotline

RCRA/Superfund Hotline
Environmental Protection Agency
401 M St., SW
Washington DC 20460 (800) 424-9346
(202) 382-3000

Under the Resource Recovery and Conservation Act, the EPA is responsible for identifying general and specific categories of hazardous wastes, developing standards, and enforcing compliance with those standards. Hazardous wastes regulated under RCRA include toxic substances, caustics, pesticides, and other flammable, corrosive, or explosive materials. EPA establishes criteria for classifying land disposal facilities according to their environmental acceptability and publishes a national inventory of unacceptable facilities. Contact this hotline for more information on hazardous wastes and the regulations associated with them.

* Hazardous Waste Ombudsman Hotline

Hazardous Waste Ombudsman Program
Environmental Protection Agency
401 M St., SW
Washington DC 20460 (202) 475-9361

EPA has established this office to handle complaints from the public and regulated community, and to assist them in resolving problems concerning any program or requirement under the hazardous waste law. The Hazardous Waste Ombudsman Program assists citizens and the regulated community who have had problems voicing a complaint or getting a problem resolved about hazardous waste issues. It serves as a last resort to the RCRA/CERCLA Hotline.

* Hazardous Waste Risk Assessment

Resources for the Future - Center for Risk Management
1616 P St., NW
Washington, DC 20036 (202) 328-5000

The Center for Risk Management undertakes a comprehensive program of fundamental research, policy analysis, education, and outreach related to the management of environmental risks in modern society. It deals with problems associated with air and water pollutants, pesticides, toxic substances, hazardous wastes, and climate modification.

* Hazardous Waste Treatment Council

Hazardous Waste Treatment Council (HWTC)
1919 Pennsylvania Ave., NW
Suite 300
Washington, DC 20006 (202) 296-0778

The Hazardous Waste Treatment Council is a trade association of waste disposal firms employing high technology treatment techniques rather than land disposal.

* Industrial Chemical Manufacturers

Industrial Chemical Research Association (ICRA)
1811 Monroe
Dearborn, MI 48124 (313) 563-0360

The Industrial Chemical Research Association consists of manufacturers, marketers, researchers, formulators and suppliers of industrial chemicals. It promotes research, safe practices and increased selling efficiency in the industrial chemicals industry.

* Industrial Chemical Producers

Acrylonitrile Group
c/o Hadley and McKenna
1815 H St., NW, Suite 1000
Washington, DC 20006-3604 (202) 296-6300

The Acrylonitrile Group represents all of the producers of the industrial chemical acrylonitrile used to make plastics and fibers.

* Maine Cleanup Hotline

McKin Site Hotline, Maine, Region I (207) 657-2087

The McKin Site Hotline provides information on Cleanup Efforts at Superfund Site in Grey, ME.

* Medical Waste and Recycling

Office of Technology Assessment
600 Pennsylvania Ave., SE
Washington, DC 20510 (202) 228-6854

OTA is currently studying medical waste handling and disposal as comparisons of incineration and alternative management technologies and their associated risks, along with waste reduction and recycling options for medical waste management. Contact Kathryn Wagner, the project director, for more information.

* Methyl Chloride Industry

Methyl Chloride Industry Alliance (MCIA)
2315 M St., NW
Washington, DC 20037 (202) 659-0900

The Methyl Chloride Industry Alliance serves the industry relative to government regulation of methyl chloride and other matters under the Toxic Substances Control Act (TSCA).

* Metropolitan Sewerage Agencies

Association of Metropolitan Sewerage Agencies (AMSA)
1015 18th St., NW
Suite 1002
Washington, DC 20036 (202) 659-9161

The Association of Metropolitan Sewerage Agencies consists of sewerage agencies in areas with more than 250,000 people. It serves to exchange technical data and deals with the federal government on environmental and regulatory matters. Publications: *AMSA Monthly Report, Law Digest*.

* National Response Center Hotline

Coast Guard Hotline (800) 424-8802
(202) 426-2675

This Department of Transportation National Response Center can be used to report spills of oil and other hazardous materials where required. It can also be used to report incidents in transportation where hazardous materials are responsible for death, serious injury, property damage in excess of $50,000 or continuing danger to life and property.

* New Pesticide Registration

Registration Division
Office of Pesticide Programs
Pesticides and Toxic Substances
Environmental Protection Agency
401 M St., SW
Washington DC 20460 (202) 557-7410

EPA registers new pesticides to ensure that when properly used they will not present "unreasonable" risks to human health or the environment (based on an assessment of economic, social, and environmental costs and benefits). Contact this office for more information.

* Northeast Industrial Waste Clearinghouse

Northeast Industrial Waste Exchange (800) 237-2481
(315) 422-6572

The Northeast Industrial Waste Exchange provides information on waste exchange in the Northeast but with access to other areas. This exchange joins those who generate waste with those who desire waste. *(For Region 1,3, NJ, OH, MI).

* Nuclear Waste Hydrology

Nuclear Waste Program
Water Resources Division
U.S. Geological Survey
National Center, MS 410
Reston, VA 22092 (703) 648-5719

Hydrologic and geologic research and field studies are conducted to develop better understanding of radionuclide transport in ground-water systems. The program also supports Interior's role in the national high-level nuclear waste repository program, providing information on the management of low-level nuclear waste.

* Nuclear Waste Management

American Nuclear Energy Council
410 1st St., SE
Washington, DC 20003 (202) 484-2670

Environment and Nature

This council's members consist of companies engaged in some aspect of the nuclear fuel cycle, from mining to engineering and fabrication to waste disposal. The council represents the industry point of view to Congress and federal agencies.

* Ocean Dumping

Office of Marine and Estuarine Protection
Environmental Protection Agency
401 M St., SW
Washington DC 20460   (202) 382-7166

This office carries out the duties covered under the Marine Protection, Research and Sanctuaries Act, which is designed to protect the marine environment from the harmful effects of ocean dumping. The Act establishes a permit program to ensure that ocean dumping does not cause degradation of the marine environment. Contact this office for more information on ocean dumping regulation.

* Oil and Chemical Spills Hotline

National Response Center (NRC)
Marine Environmental Response Division
Office of Marine Safety, Security, and Environmental Protection
U.S. Coast Guard
U.S. Department of Transportation
2100 2nd St., SW, Room 2611   (800) 424-8802
Washington, DC 20593   (202) 267-2188

The NRC receives reports of oil and hazardous substance spills, investigates incidents, initiates civil penalty actions, monitors cleanups, and coordinates federally funded spill response operations. NRC's National Strike Force assists federal coordinators on the scene in responding to pollution accidents. For further details, or to report information, contact the Center toll-free.

* Oil Spills and Hazardous Waste Response Hotline

Coast Guard Hotline
U.S. Coast Guard
U.S. Department of Transportation
2100 2nd St., SW, Room 2611   (800) 424-8802
Washington, DC 20593   (202) 426-2675

This Department of Transportation National Response Center can be used to report spills of oil and other hazardous materials where required. It can also be used to report incidents in transportation where hazardous materials are responsible for death, serious injury, property damage in excess of $50,000 or continuing danger to life and property.

* PCBs and Asbestos Hotline

Toxic Substances Control Act Hotline
Environmental Protection Agency
401 M St., SW
Washington DC 20460   (202) 554-1404

The Toxic Assistance Office at EPA will answer questions and offer general and technical assistance on the Toxic Substances Control Act. Staff will help to obtain guidance on TSCA regulations, including guidance on PCBs and asbestos issues. Publications are also available through the hotline.

* Pesticides and Toxic Substances Library

Office of Toxic Substances Library
401 M St., SW
Washington, DC 20460   (202) 382-3944

Part of the Office of Pesticides and Toxic Substances, the OTS Library houses collections relevant to toxic substances. The library also maintains some pesticides publications. Hours of operation are Monday through Friday, 8:00 a.m. to 4:30 p.m. Databases maintained here include DIALOG, NLM, STN, and CIS.

* Pesticide Information Hotline

National Pesticide Telecommunications Network   (800) 858-7378
(806) 743-3091 (TX)

This service of the U.S. Environmental Protection Agency and Texas Tech University is open 24 hours, 7 days a week. It responds to non-emergency questions about the effects of pesticides, toxicology and symptoms, environmental effects, disposal and cleanup, and safe use of pesticides.

* Pesticides Database

Pesticides Information Retrieval System
Environmental Protection Agency
401 M St., SW
Washington DC 20460   (202) 554-1404

This computer database provides public access to current information on over 36,000 pesticide products. The system development has been jointly funded by USDA and EPA and is managed by Purdue University.

* Pesticide Producers Association

Pesticide Producers Association (PPA)
1200 17th St., NW
Washington, DC 20036   (202) 857-9800

The Pesticide Producers Association represents the interests of pesticide formulators and manufacturers.

* Pesticides Rules and Regulations

Environmental Protection Agency
401 M Street SW
Washington, DC 20460   (703) 557-4434

The Pesticides Docket provides public access to documentation for each Registration Standard under development when the Agency begins review of data for the Registration Standard or upon publication of a notice setting out the list and sequence of Registration Standards. The docket contains documentation of pre-special and special reviews of pesticides, memoranda, all comments, correspondence, documents, proposals, or other materials concerning a pending pesticide regulatory decision provided to the Agency by a person or party outside of government (other than confidential business information).

* Pipeline Safety

Office of Pipeline Safety (OPS)
Research and Special Programs Administration
U.S. Department of Transportation
400 7th Street, SW
Washington, DC 20590   (202) 366-4572

OPS establishes and enforces safety standards for the transportation of gas and other hazardous materials by pipeline. A computerized reporting system is maintained to collect and analyze accident and incident data from pipeline operators. Accident reports include the operator's name, the hazardous material involved, description of the accident, and results. For database searches, contact the office listed. There may be a charge.

* Poison Control Center Hotline

National Poison Control Center   (202) 625-3333

The National Poison Control Center Hotline is operated by Georgetown University Hospital in Washington, D.C. It provides information on accidental ingestion of chemicals, poisons, or drugs.

* Radioactive and Radon Exposure

Office of Radiation Programs
Environmental Protection Agency
401 M St., SW, Room NE108
Washington DC 20460   (202) 475-9600

The EPA, with a number of other federal agencies, protects the public from unnecessary exposure to ionizing radiation. EPA's major responsibilities are to set radioactive emissions standards and exposure limits, assess new technology, and monitor radiation in the environment in four areas: radiation from nuclear accidents, radon emissions, land disposal of radioactive waste, and radiation in groundwater and drinking water. The EPA fulfills these responsibilities by setting emissions standards for nuclear power plants, and for radionuclides in drinking water and in the air. EPA also prescribes work practices to reduce emissions of radon from underground uranium mines, develops radioactive waste disposal standards, and issues guidance to limit occupational exposure.

* Railroad Hazardous Spills Hotline

Bureau of Explosives Hotline
Association of American Railroads
19th and M Streets, NW
Washington, DC 20036   (202) 639-2222

The Bureau of Explosives Hotline is run by the Association of American Railroads and is a 24-hour emergency number which can be sued for assistance for hazardous materials incidents involving railroads and often contacted through CHEMTREC.

* Recycling Information

Public Information Center
Environmental Protection Agency
401 M St., SW, PM-211 B
Washington DC 20460   (202) 4475-7751

Recycling Works! is a free booklet that provides information about successful recycling programs initiated by state and local agencies. It also describes private recycling efforts and joint recycling ventures of government and businesses.

* Resource Conservation & Recovery Act (RCRA)

Environmental Protection Agency
401 M St., SW

Washington, DC 20460 (202) 475-9327

The Resource Conservation & Recovery Act (RCRA) Docket provides public access to regulatory information supporting the EPA's actions under RCRA. Records support *Federal Register* notices, *Delisting Petitions*, and other Office of Solid Waste publications. RCRA Docket publishes a semiannual catalog of frequently requested documents titled, *A Catalog of Hazardous and Solid Waste Publications.* Contact this office for more information on these and other RCRA documents.

* Resource Recovery Emergency Response Hotline

RCRA On-Scene Coordinators Hotline (214) 767-2666

The Resource Conservation and Recovery Act On-Scene Coordinators Hotline in Region VI responds 24 hours a day to questions and to reports of chemical spills and other emergencies for all Region VI states: Arkansas, Louisiana, New Mexico, Oklahoma, and Texas.

* Safe Pesticide Enforcement

Association of American Pesticide Control Officials (AAPCO)
2004 Le Suer Rd.
Richmond, VA 23229 (804) 288-8181

The Association of American Pesticide Control Officials is comprised of state, municipal and federal officials throughout North America interested in a uniform approach to the enforcement of laws controlling the proper and safe use of pesticide chemicals.

* Sanitary Engineers

Conference of State Sanitary Engineers (CSSE)
150 East Main St.
Westminster, MD 21157 (301) 876-8440

CSSE coordinates the public health engineering activities of the official state and territorial health organizations. Members are officials of state and territorial agencies concerned with the environment. It publishes *CSSE News.* waste programs.

* Solid Waste Management Clearinghouse

Andrew W. Briedenbach Environmental
Research Center Library
26 W. St. Clair St.
Cincinnati, OH 45268 (513) 569-7703

The major subjects in this library's collection are bacteriology, biology, biotechnology, chemistry, engineering, hazardous wastes, hydrobiology, microbiology, solid waste management, toxicology, water pollution, and water quality. Databases maintained here include BRS, CAS On-line, CIS, DIALOG, Dun & Bradstreet, Hazardous Waste Database, LEXIS/NEXIS, NLM, Toxline, and Toxnet. General collections include bacteriology, biology, biotechnology, microbiology, physics, solid waste management. This library's special collections cover the environment, Canada, legal issues, hazardous waste, and solid waste.

* Solid Waste Transportation Council

Chemical Waste Transportation Council (CWTC)
1730 Rhode Island Ave., NW
Suite 1000
Washington, DC 20036 (202) 659-4613

The Chemical Waste Transportation Council represents the interests of companies engaged in the business of hauling chemical wastes. The Council is affiliated with the National Solid Wastes Management Association.

* State Solid Waste Management

Association of State and Territorial Solid Waste
Management Officials
444 North Capitol St., NW
Suite 345
Washington, DC 20001 (202) 624-5828

The Association of State and Territorial Solid Waste Management Officials consists of directors and support staff of state and territorial solid and hazardous

* Superfund and Resource Conservation Hotline

CERCLA/RCRA Hotline (800) 424-9346
(202) 382-3000

This hotline answers questions concerning the Resource Conservation and Recovery Act, Superfund, and hazardous waste regulations. Requests for certain documents from the *Federal Register* and public laws are also handled in addition to referral to appropriate contacts. See also RCRA/CERCLA Hotline and Superfund Hotline.

* Superfund Cleanup Alternatives

Alternative Treatment Technology Information Center
Environmental Protection Agency

401 M St., SW (800) 424-9346
Washington DC 20460 (202) 382-5747 (DC area)

The Alternative Treatment Technology Information Center is an information center designed to serve the needs of EPA staff as well as other individuals and groups involved with Superfund cleanup activities and alternative technology development and use. Contact this Center for more information on its information and services.

* Superfund Compensation and Liability Regulations

Environmental Protection Agency
401 M Street SW
Washington, DC 20460 (202) 382-3046

The Superfund Docket provides public access to information supporting all regulatory decisions issued under the Comprehensive Environmental Response, Compensation, Liability Act of 1980 (CERCLA) as amended. This includes records of proceeding under the Emergency Planning and Community Right to Know Act of 1986, Title III of the Superfund Amendments and Reauthorization Act (SARA) of 1986. The Docket also includes CERCLA guidance documents and information supporting rulemaking under authority of Section 3012 of the Resource Conservation & Recovery Act.

* Superfund Hotline

Environmental Protection Agency
401 M St., SW (800) 424-9346
Washington DC 20460 (202) 382-3000 (DC area)

This hotline answers questions concerning the Resource Conservation and Recovery Act, Superfund, and hazardous waste regulations. Requests for certain documents from the *Federal Register* and public laws are also handled in addition to referral to appropriate contacts. The hotline operates 8:30 a.m. to 7:30 p.m. (EST).

* Toxicology Databases and Clearinghouse

Andrew W. Briedenbach Environmental
Research Center Library
26 W. St. Clair St.
Cincinnati, OH 45268 (513) 569-7703

The major subjects in this library's collection are bacteriology, biology, biotechnology, chemistry, engineering, hazardous wastes, hydrobiology, microbiology, solid waste management, toxicology, water pollution, and water quality. Databases maintained here include BRS, CAS On-line, CIS, DIALOG, Dun & Bradstreet, Hazardous Waste Database, LEXIS/NEXIS, NLM, Toxline, and Toxnet. General collections include bacteriology, biology, biotechnology, microbiology, physics, solid waste management. This library's special collections cover the environment, Canada, legal issues, hazardous waste, and solid waste.

* Toxic Sites Voluntary Cleanup

Clean Sites Inc. (CSI)
1199 N. Fairfax St.
Alexandria, VA 22314 (703) 683-8522

Clean Sites Inc. (CSI) is an independent, non-profit corporation established in 1984 by a coalition of environmental, industry and government groups. Its objective is to accelerate the voluntary cleanup of hazardous waste sites that threaten public health and the environment throughout the United States.

* Toxic Substances Control Act Hotline

Environmental Protection Agency
401 M Street SW
Washington, DC 20460 (202) 554-1404

The Toxic Assistance Office at EPA will answer questions and offer general and technical assistance on the Toxic Substances Control Act. Staff will help you obtain guidance on TSCA regulations including guidance on PCBs and asbestos issues.

* Toxic Substances Non-Confidential Information

Office of Toxic Substances
Non-Confidential Information Center
401 M St., SW (EPA7565)
Northeast Mall, Room B002
Washington, DC 20460 (202) 382-3944

This office's library covers chemical literature in areas of biotechnology, health, chemical industry and process technology, international chemical control, ecology, and pesticides.

* Toxic Substances Rules and Regulations

Office of Toxic Substances
Environmental Protection Agency
401 M Street SW
Washington, DC 20460 (202) 382-3587

Environment and Nature

The Office of Toxic Substances (OTS) Public Information Office houses the official copies of all OTS administrative records supporting regulatory decisions promulgated under the Toxic Substances Control Act (TSCA). The Public Information Office also maintains original materials submitted by industry in compliance with TSCA regulations. The contents of the dockets vary according to the proposed regulation and the particular Section of the Act which is being promulgated. However, generally all dockets contain the following types of supporting documentation: *Federal Register* notices; various health, environmental, and exposure assessment documents; published references; communications; and test data.

* Transportation of Hazardous Materials

Office of Hazardous Materials Transportation
Research and Special Programs Administration
U.S. Department of Transportation
400 7th Street, SW
Washington, DC 20590-0001   (202) 366-2301

This office can provide you with information on the transportation of hazardous materials by highway, rail air, and water. Data is collected directly from industry and also via compliance inspections by field staff. The quarterly *Hazardous Material Newsletter* is available free from the office above.

* Underground Storage Tanks

Office of Underground Storage Tanks
Solid Waste and Emergency Response
Environmental Protection Agency
401 M St., SW, Room 2107
Washington DC 20460   (202) 382-4756

Storage tanks for volatile liquids have been buried underground to reduce the risk of fire and explosion, but leaking tanks are a major source of groundwater contamination and a great risk to human health and the environment. The EPA has issued regulations addressing leak detection, corrective action requirements, standards for new tanks, and other tank management practices. This Office can provide you with details concerning leaking tanks, as well as information regarding the cleanup required.

* Underground Storage Tank Docket

Environmental Protection Agency
401 M Street SW
Washington, DC 20460   (202) 475-9720

The Underground Storage Tank (UST) Docket provides public access to regulatory information supporting the Agency's regulatory action on USTs. As of April 1, 1987, there are seven dockets: (1) UST Notification Form; (2) Technical Standards for USTs Containing Petroleum; (3) Financial Responsibility Requirements for USTs Containing Petroleum; (4) State Program Approval; (5) Report to Congress on Exempt Tanks; (6) Consolidated Rules of Practice Governing the Administrative Assessment of Civil Penalties and Revocation or Suspension of Permits; and (7) Financial Responsibility Requirements for USTs Containing Hazardous Substances.

* Waste Management and Sanitation

National Society of Professional Sanitarians
Dept. of Health
Box 570
Jefferson City, MO 65102   (314) 751-6095

This organization is composed of professionals involved in all aspects of environmental and public health.

* Waste Reduction and Minimization Hotline

Waste Minimization Hotline, Region III
Environmental Protection Agency
841 Chestnut St.
Philadelphia, PA 19107   (800) 826-5320
                                (800) 334-2467 (PA)

The Waste Minimization Hotline provides technical assistance and education on waste minimization. It provides this information for all Region III states: Washington, D.C., Delaware, Maryland, Pennsylvania, Virginia, and West Virginia.

Government Records and Privacy

**A Citizen's Guide on Using the Freedom of Information Act and
the Privacy Act of 1974 to Request Government Records**

Introduction

*A popular Government without popular information or the means
of acquiring it, is but a Prologue to a Farce or a Tragedy or
perhaps both. Knowledge will forever govern ignorance, and a
people who mean to be their Governors, must arm themselves
with the power knowledge gives.* -- James Madison

The Freedom of Information Act (FOIA) established a
presumption that records in the possession of agencies and
departments of the Executive Branch of the United States
government are accessible to the people. This was not always
the approach to federal information disclosure policy. Before
enactment of the Freedom of Information Act in 1966, the
burden was on the individual to establish a right to examine
these government records. There were no statutory guidelines
or procedures to help a person seeking information. There
were judicial remedies for those denied access.

With the passage of the FOIA, the burden of proof shifted
from the individual to the government. Those seeking
information are no longer required to show a need for
information. Instead, the "need to know" standard has been
replaced by a "right to know" doctrine. The government now
has to justify the need for secrecy.

The FOIA sets standards for determining which records must
be made available for public inspection and which records can
be withheld from disclosure. The law also provides
administrative and judicial remedies for those denied access to
records. Above all, the statute requires federal agencies to
provide the fullest possible disclosure of information to the
public.

The Privacy Act of 1974 is a companion to the FOIA. The
Privacy Act regulates federal government agency record keeping
and disclosure practices. The Act allows most individuals to
seek access to federal agency records about themselves. The
Act requires that personal information in agency files be
accurate, complete, relevant, and timely. The Act allows the
subject of a record to challenge the accuracy of the information.
The Act requires that agencies obtain information directly from
the subject of the record and that information gathered for one
purpose not be used for another purpose. As with the FOIA,
the Privacy Act provides civil remedies for individuals whose
rights have been violated.

Another important feature of the Privacy Act is the
requirement that each federal agency publish a description of
each system of records maintained by the agency that contains
personal information. This prevents agencies from keeping
secret records.

The Privacy Act also restricts the disclosure of personally
identifiable information by federal agencies. Together with the
FOIA, the Privacy Act permits disclosure of most personal files
to the individual who is the subject of the files. The two laws
restrict disclosure of personal information to others when
disclosure would violate privacy interests.

While both the FOIA and the Privacy Act encourage the
disclosure of agency records, both laws also recognize the
legitimate need to restrict disclosure of some information. For
example, agencies may withhold information classified in the
interest of national defense or foreign policy, trade secrets, and
criminal investigatory files. Other specifically defined categories
of confidential information may also be withheld.

The essential feature of both laws is that they make federal
agencies accountable for information disclosure policies and
practices. While neither law grants an absolute right to
examine government documents, both laws provide a right to
request records and to receive a response to the request. If a
requested record cannot be released, the requester is entitled
to a reason for the denial. The requester has a right to appeal
the denial and, if necessary, to challenge it in court.

These procedural rights granted by the FOIA and the Privacy
Act make the laws valuable and workable. The disclosure of
government information cannot be controlled by arbitrary or
unreviewable actions.

Which Act To Use

The access provisions of the FOIA and the Privacy Act overlap
in part. The two laws have different procedures and different
exemptions. As a result, sometimes information exempt under
one law will be disclosable under the other.

In order to take maximum advantage of the laws, an individual
seeking information about himself or herself should normally
cite both laws. Requests by an individual for information that
does not relate solely to himself or herself should be made
under the FOIA.

Congress intended that the two laws be considered together in
the processing of requests for information. Many government
agencies will automatically handle requests from individuals in
a way that will maximize the amount of information that is
disclosable. However, a requester should still make a request
in a manner that is most advantageous and that fully protects
all available legal rights. A requester who has any doubts about
which law to use should always cite both the FOIA and the
Privacy Act when seeking documents from the federal
government.

The Scope of the Freedom of Information Act

The federal Freedom of Information Act applies to documents
held by agencies in the executive branch of the federal
Government. The executive branch includes cabinet
departments, military departments, government corporations,

Freedom of Information Act (FOIA)

government controlled corporations, independent regulatory agencies, and other establishments of the executive branch.

The FOIA does not apply to elected officials of the federal government, including the President, Vice President, Senators, and Congressmen, or the federal judiciary. The FOIA also does not apply to private companies; persons who received federal contracts or grants; tax-exempt organizations; or state or local governments.

All States and some localities have passed laws like the FOIA that allow people to request access to records. In addition, there are other federal and state laws that may permit access to documents held by organizations not covered by the FOIA.

What Records Can Be Requested Under FOIA?

The FOIA requires agencies to publish or make available some types of information. This includes: (1) Description of agency organization and office addresses; (2) statements of the general course and method of agency operation; (3) rules of procedure and descriptions of forms; (4) substantive rules of general applicability and general policy statements; (5) final opinions made in the adjudication of cases; and (6) administrative staff manuals that affect the public. This information must either be published or made available for inspection and copying without the formality of an FOIA request.

All other "agency records" may be requested under the FOIA. However, the FOIA does not define "agency record." Material that is in the possession, custody, or control of an agency is usually considered to be an agency record under the FOIA. Personal notes of agency employees may not be agency records. A record that is not an "agency record" will not be available under the FOIA.

The form in which a record is maintained by an agency does not affect its availability. A request may seek a printed or typed document, tape recording, map, computer printout, computer tape, or a similar item.

Of course, not all records that can be requested must be disclosed. Information that is exempt from disclosure is described below in the section entitled "Reasons Access May Be Denied Under the FOIA."

The FOIA carefully provides that a requester may ask for records rather than information. This means that an agency is only required to look for an existing record or document in response to an FOIA request. An agency is not obliged to create a new record to comply with a request. An agency is not required to collect information it does not have. Nor must an agency do research or analyze data for a requester.

Requesters may ask for existing records. Requests may have to be carefully written in order to obtain the information that is desired. Sometimes, agencies will help a requester identify the specific document that contains the information being sought. Other times, a requester may need to be creative when writing an FOIA request in order to identify an existing document or set of documents containing the desired information.

There is a second general limitation on FOIA request. The law requires that each request must reasonably describe the records being sought. This means that a request must be specific enough to permit a professional employee of the agency who is familiar with the subject matter to locate the record in a reasonable period of time.

Because different agencies organize and index records in different ways, one agency may consider a request to be reasonably descriptive while another agency may reject a similar request as too vague. For example, the Federal Bureau of Investigation has a centrex index for its primary record system. As a result, the FBI is able to search for records about a specific person. However, agencies that do not maintain a central name index may be unable to conduct the same type of search. These agencies may reject a similar request because the request does not describe records that can be identified.

Requesters should make their requests as specific as possible. If a particular document is required, it should be identified as precisely as possible, preferably by date and title. However, a request does not have to be that specific. A requester who cannot identify a specific record should clearly explain his or her needs. A requester should make sure, however, that the request is broad enough to cover the information that is needed.

For example, assume that a requester wants to obtain a list of toxic sites near his home. A request to the Environmental Protection Agency for all records on toxic waste would cover many more records than are needed. The fees for such a request might be very high, and it is possible that the request might be rejected as too vague.

A request for all toxic waste sites within three miles of a particular address is very specific. But is unlikely that EPA would have an existing record containing data organized in that fashion. As a result, the request might be denied because there is no existing record containing the information.

The requester might do better to ask for a list of toxic waste sites in his city, county, or state. It is more likely that existing records might contain this information. The requester might also want to tell the agency in the request letter exactly what information is desired. The additional explanation will help the agency to find a record that meets the request.

Many people include their telephone number in their requests. Sometimes questions about the scope of a request can be resolved quickly when the agency employee and the requester talk. This is an efficient way to resolve questions that arise during the processing of FOIA requests.

It is to everyone's advantage if requests are as precise and as narrow as possible. The requester benefits because the request can be processed faster and cheaper. The agency benefits because it can do a better job of responding to the request. The agency will also be able to use its scarce resources to respond to more requests. The FOIA works best when both the requester and the agency act cooperatively.

Making an FOIA Request

The first step in making a request under the FOIA is to identify the agency that has the records. An FOIA request must be addressed to a specific agency. There is no central government records office that services FOIA requests.

Often, a requester knows beforehand which agency has the desired records. If not, a requester can consult a government directory such as the *United States Government Manual*. This manual has a complete list of all the federal agencies, a description of agency functions, and the address of each agency. A requester who is uncertain about which agency has the records that are needed can make FOIA requests at more than one agency.

All agencies normally require that FOIA requests be in writing. Letters requesting records under the FOIA can be short and simple. No one needs a lawyer to make an FOIA request. Appendix 1 of this Guide contains a sample request letter.

The request letter should be addressed to an agency's FOIA officer or to the head of the agency. The envelope containing the written request should be marked "Freedom of Information Act Request" in the bottom left- hand corner.

There are three basic elements to an FOIA request letter. First, the letter should state that the request is being made under the Freedom of Information Act. Second, the request should identify the records that are being sought as specifically as possible. Third, the name and address of the requester must be included.

In addition, under the 1986 amendments to the FOIA, the fees chargeable vary with the status or purpose of the requester. As result, requesters may have to provide additional information to permit the agency to determine the appropriate fees. Different fees can be charged to commercial users, representatives of the news media, educational and noncommercial scientific institutions, and individuals. The next section explains the new fee structure in more detail.

There are several optional items that are often included in an FOIA request. The first is the telephone number of the requester. This permits an agency employee processing a request to talk to the requester if necessary.

A second optional item is a limitation on the fees that the requester is willing to pay. It is common for requesters to ask to be contacted if the charges will exceed a fixed amount. This allows a requester to modify or withdraw a request if the cost is too high.

A third optional item sometimes included in an FOIA request is a request for waiver or reduction of fees. The 1986 amendments waived or reduced the rules for fee waivers. Fees must be waived or reduced if disclosure of the information is in the public interest because it is likely to contribute significantly to public understanding of the operations or activities of the government and is not primarily in the commercial interest of the request. Decisions about granting fee waives are separate from and different from decisions about the amount of fees that can be charged to requesters.

Requesters should keep a copy of their request letter and related correspondence until the request has been fully resolved.

Fees and Fee Waivers

FOIA requesters may have to pay fees covering some or all of the costs of processing their request. As amended in 1986, the law establishes three types of charges that may be imposed on requesters. The 1986 law makes the process of determining the applicable fees more complicated. However, the new rules reduce or eliminate entirely the cost for small, noncommercial requests.

First, fees can be imposed to recover the costs of copying documents. All agencies have a fixed price for making copies using copying machines. Requesters are usually charged the actual cost of copying computer tapes, photographs, or other nonstandard documents.

Second, fees can also be imposed to recover the costs of searching for documents. This includes the time spent looking for material responsive to a request. Requesters can minimize search charges by making clear, narrow requests for identifiable documents whenever possible.

Third, fees can be charged to recover review costs. Review is the process of examining documents to determine whether any portion is exempt from disclosure. Before the effective date of the 1986 amendments, no review charges were imposed on any requester. Effective April 25, 1987, review charges may be imposed on commercial requesters only. Review charges only include costs incurred during the initial examination of a document. An agency may not charge for any costs incurred in resolving issues of law or policy that may arise while processing a request.

Different fees apply to different categories of requesters. There are three basic groups of FOIA requesters. The first includes representatives of the news media, and educational or noncommercial scientific institutions whose purpose is scholarly or scientific research. Requesters in this category who are not seeking records for commercial use can only be billed for reasonable standard document duplication charges. A request for information from a representative of the news media is not considered to be for commercial use if the request is in support of a news gathering or dissemination function.

The second group includes FOIA requesters seeking records for commercial use. Commercial use is not defined in the law, but generally includes profit making activities. Commercial users pay reasonable standard charges for document duplication, search, and review.

The third group of FOIA requesters includes everyone not included in either of the first two groups. People seeking information for their own use, public interest groups, and non-profit organizations are examples of requesters who fall into the third group. Charges for these requests are limited to reasonable standard charges for document duplication and search. No review charges may be imposed. The 1986 amendments did not change the fees charged to these requesters.

Small requests are free to requesters in the first and third groups.

This includes all requesters except commercial users. There is no charge for the first two hours of search time and the first 100 pages of documents. Noncommercial requesters who limit their requests to a small number of easily found records will not pay any fees at all.

In addition, the law also prevents agencies from charging fees if the cost of collecting the fee would exceed the amount collected. This limitation applies to all requests, including those seeking documents for commercial use. Thus, if the allowable charges for any FOIA request are small, no fees are imposed.

Each agency sets charges for duplication, search, and review based on its own costs. The amount of these charges is included in the agency FOIA regulations. Each agency also sets its own threshold for minimum charges.

The 1986 FOIA amendments changed the law on fee waivers. The new rules require that fees must be waived or reduced if disclosure of the information is in the public interest because

Freedom of Information Act (FOIA)

it is likely to contribute significantly to public understanding of the operations or activities of the government and is not primarily in the commercial interest of the requester.

The new rules for fees and fee waivers have created some confusion. Determinations about fees are separate and apart from determinations about eligibility for fee waivers. For example, a news reporter may only be charged duplication fees and may ask that the duplication fees be waived. There is no need for a reporter to ask for a waiver of search and review costs because search and review costs are not charged to reporters.

Only after a requester has been categorized to determine applicable fees does the issue of a fee waiver arise. A requester who seeks a fee waiver should include a separate request in the original request letter. The requester should describe how disclosure will contribute to the public understanding of the operations or activities of the government. The sample request letter in the appendix includes optional language asking for a fee waiver.

Any requester may ask for a fee waiver. Some will find it easier to qualify than others. A news reporter who is charged only duplication costs may still ask that the charges be waived because of the public benefits that will result from disclosure. Representatives of the news media and public interest groups are very likely to qualify for a waiver of fees. Commercial users will find it more difficult to qualify.

The eligibility of other requesters will vary. A key element in qualifying for a fee waiver is the relationship of the information to public understanding of the operations or activities of government. Another important factor is the ability of the requester to convey that information to other interested members of the public. A requester is not eligible for a fee waiver solely because of indigence.

Requirements for Agency Responses

Each agency is required to determine within ten days (excluding Saturdays, Sundays, and legal holidays) after the receipt of a request whether to comply with the request. The actual disclosure of documents is required to follow promptly thereafter. If a request for records is denied in whole or in part, the agency must tell the requester the reasons for the denial. The agency must also tell the requester that there is a right to appeal any adverse determination to the head of the agency.

The FOIA permits agencies to extend the time limits up to ten days in unusual circumstances. These circumstances include the need to collect records from remote locations, review large numbers of records, and consult with other agencies. Agencies are supposed to notify the requester whenever an extension is invoked.

The statutory time limits for responses are not always met. Agencies sometimes receive an unexpectedly large number of FOIA requests at one time and are unable to meet the deadlines. Some agencies assign inadequate resources to FOIA offices. The Congress does not condone the failure of any agency to meet the law's limits. However, as a practical matter, there is little that a requester can do about it. The courts have been reluctant to provide relief solely because the FOIA's time limits have not been met.

The best advice to requesters is to be patient. The law allows a requester to consider a request to be denied if it has not been decided within the time limits. This permits the requester to file an administrative appeal. However, this is not always the best course of action. The filing of an administrative or judicial appeal does not normally result in any faster processing of the request.

Agencies generally process requests in the order in which they were received. Some agencies will expedite the processing of urgent requests. Anyone with a pressing need for records should consult with the agency FOIA officer about how to ask for expedited treatment of requests.

Reasons Access May Be Denied Under the FOIA

An agency may refuse to disclose an agency record that falls within any of the FOIA's nine statutory exemptions. The exemptions protect against the disclosure of information that would harm national defense or foreign policy, privacy of individuals, proprietary interests of business, functioning of government, and other important interests.

A record that does not qualify as an "agency record" may be denied because only agency records are available under the FOIA. Personal notes of agency employees may be denied on this basis.

An agency may withhold exempt information, but it is not always required to do so. For example, an agency may disclose an exempt internal memorandum because no harm would result from its disclosure. However, an agency is not likely to agree to disclose an exempt document that is classified or that contains a trade secret.

When a record contains some information that qualifies as exempt, the entire record is not necessarily exempt. Instead, the FOIA specifically provides that any reasonably segregable portions of a record must be provided to a requester after the deletion of the portions that are exempt. This is a very important requirement because it prevents an agency from withholding an entire document simply because one line or one page is exempt.

Exemption 1: Classified Documents

The first FOIA exemption permits the withholding of properly classified documents. Information may be classified to protect it in the interest of national defense or foreign policy. Information that has been classified as "Confidential," "Secret," or "Top Secret" under the procedures of the Executive Order on Security Classification can qualify under the first exemption.

The rules for classification are established by the President and not the FOIA or other law. The FOIA provides that, if a document has been properly classified under the President's rules, the document can be withheld from disclosure.

Classified documents may be requested under the FOIA. An agency can review the document to determine if it still requires protection. In addition, the Executive Order on Security Classification establishes a special procedure for requesting the declassification of documents. If a requested document is declassified, it can be released in response to an FOIA request. However, a document that was formerly classified may still be exempt under other FOIA exemptions.

Exemption 2: Internal Personnel Rules and Practices

The second FOIA exemption covers matters that are related solely to an agency's internal personnel rules and practices. As interpreted by the courts, there are two separate classes of documents that are generally held to fall within exemption two.

First, information relating to personnel rules or internal agency practices is exempt if it is a trivial administrative matter of no genuine public interest. A rule governing lunch hours for agency employees is an example.

Second, internal administrative manuals can be exempt if disclosure would risk circumvention of law or agency regulations. In order to fall into this category, the material will normally have to regulate internal agency conduct rather than public behavior.

Exemption 3: Information Exempt Under Other Laws

The third exemption incorporates into the FOIA other laws that restrict the availability of information. To qualify under exemption three, a statute must require that matters be withheld from the public in such a manner as to leave no discretion to the agency. Alternatively, the statute must establish particular criteria for withholding or refer to particular types of matters to be withheld.

One example of a qualifying statute is the provision of the Tax Code prohibiting the public disclosure of tax returns and tax law designating identifiable census data as confidential. Whether a particular statute qualifies under Exemption 3 can be a difficult legal determination.

Exemption 4: Confidential Business Information

The fourth exemption protects from public disclosure two types of information: trade secrets and confidential business information. A trade secret is a commercially valuable plan, formula, process, or device. This is a narrow category of information. An example of a trade secret is the recipe for a commercial food product.

The second type of protected data is commercial or financial information obtained from a person and privileged or confidential. The courts have held that data qualifies for withholding if disclosure by the government would be likely to harm the competitive position of the person who submitted the information. Detail information on a company's marketing plans, profits, or costs can qualify as confidential business information. Information may also be withheld if disclosure would be likely to impair the government's ability to obtain similar information in the future.

Only information obtained from a person other than a government agency qualifies under the fourth exemption. A person is an individual, a partnership, or a corporation. Information that an agency created on its own cannot normally be withheld under exemption four.

Although there is no formal requirement under the FOIA, many agencies will notify a submitter of business information that disclosure of the information is being considered. The submitted can file suit to block disclosure under the FOIA. Such lawsuits are generally referred to as "reverse" FOIA lawsuits because the FOIA is being used in an attempt to prevent rather than to require disclosure of information. A reverse FOIA lawsuit may be filed when a submitter of documents and the government disagree whether the information is confidential.

Exemption 5: Internal Government Communications

The FOIA's fifth exemption applies to internal government documents. One example is a letter from one government department to another about a joint decision that has not yet been made. Another example is a memorandum from an agency employee to his supervisor describing options for conducting the agency's business.

The purpose of the exemption is to safeguard the deliberative policymaking processes of government. The exemption encourages frank discussions of policy matters between agency officials by allowing supporting documents to be withheld from public disclosure. The exemption also protects against premature disclosure of policies before final adoption.

While the policy behind the fifth exemption is well-accepted, the application of the exemption is complicated. The fifth exemption may be the most difficult FOIA exemption to understand and apply. For example, the exemption protects the policymaking process, but it does not protect purely factual information related to the policy process. Factual information must be disclosed unless it is inextricably intertwined with protected information about an agency decision.

Protection for the decision making process is appropriate only for the period while decisions are being made. Thus, the fifth exemption has been held to distinguish between documents that are predecisional and therefore may be protected, and those which are post-decisional and therefore not subject to protection. Once a policy is adopted, the public has a greater interests in knowing the basis for the decision.

The exemption also incorporates some of the privileges that apply in litigation involving the government. For example, papers prepared by the government's lawyers are exempt in the same way that papers prepared by private lawyers for clients are not available through discovery in civil litigation.

Exemption 6: Personal Privacy

The sixth exemption covers personnel, medical, and similar files the disclosure of which would constitute a clearly unwarranted invasion of personal privacy. This exemption protects the privacy interests of individuals by allowing an agency to withhold from disclosure intimate personal data kept in government files. Only individuals have privacy interests. Corporations and other legal persons have no privacy rights under the sixth exemption.

The exemption requires agencies to strike a balance between an individual's privacy interests and the public's right to know. However, since only a clearly unwarranted invasion of privacy is a basis for withholding, there is a perceptible tilt in favor of disclosure in the exemption. Nevertheless, the sixth exemption makes it hard to obtain information about another individual without the consent of the individual.

The Privacy Act of 1974 also regulates the disclosure of personal information about individuals. The FOIA and the Privacy Act overlap in part, but there is no inconsistency. Individuals seeking records about themselves should cite both laws when making a request. This ensures that the maximum amount of disclosable information will be released. Records that can be denied to an individual under the Privacy Act are not necessarily exempt under the FOIA.

Exemption 7: Law Enforcement

The seventh exemption allows agencies to withhold law enforcement records in order to protect the law enforcement process from interference. The exemption was amended slightly in 1986, but it still retains six specific subexemptions.

Exemption (7)(A) allows the withholding of law enforcement records that could reasonably be expected to interfere with enforcement proceedings. This exemption protects active law enforcement investigations from interference through premature disclosure.

Exemption (7)(B) allows the withholding of information that would deprive a person of a right to a fair trial or an impartial adjudication. This exemption is rarely used.

Exemption (7)(C) recognizes that individuals have a privacy interest in information maintained in law enforcement files. If the disclosure of information could reasonably be expected to constitute an unwarranted invasion of personal privacy, the information is exempt from disclosure. The standards for privacy protection in Exemption 6 and Exemption (7)(C) differ slightly. Exemption (7)(C) refers only to unwarranted invasions of personal privacy rather than to clearly unwarranted invasions.

Exemption (7)(D) protects the identity of confidential sources. Information that could reasonably be expected to reveal the identity of a confidential source is exempt. A confidential source can include a state, local, or foreign agency or authority, or a private institution that furnished information on a confidential basis. In addition, the exemption protects information furnished by a confidential source if the data was compiled by a criminal law enforcement authority during a criminal investigation or by an agency conducting a lawful national security intelligence investigation.

Exemption (7)(E) protects from disclosure information that would reveal techniques and procedures for law enforcement investigations or prosecutions or that would disclose guidelines for law enforcement investigations or prosecutions if disclosure of the information could reasonably be expected to risk circumvention of the law.

Exemption (7)(F) protects law enforcement information that could reasonably be expected to endanger the life or physical safety of any individual.

Exemption 8: Financial Institutions

The eighth exemption protects information that is contained in or related to examination, operating, or condition reports prepared by or for a bank supervisory agency such as the Federal Deposit Insurance Corporation, or the Federal Reserve, or similar agencies,.

9. Exemption 9: Geological Information

The ninth FOIA exemption covers geological and geophysical information, data, and maps about wells. This exemption is rarely used.

FOIA Exclusions

The 1986 amendments to the FOIA gave limited authority to agencies to respond to a request without confirming the existence of the requested records. Ordinarily, any proper request must receive an answer stating whether there is any responsive information, even if the requested information is exempt from disclosure.

In some narrow circumstances, acknowledgement of the existence of a record can produce consequences similar to those resulting from disclosure of the record itself. In order to avoid this type of problem, the 1986 amendments established three "record exclusions." However, these exclusions do not broaden the ability of agencies to withhold documents.

The exclusions allow agencies to treat certain exempt records as if the records were not subject to the FOIA. Agencies are not required to confirm the existence of three specific categories of records. If those records are requested, agencies may state that there are no disclosable records responsive to the request. However, these exclusions give agencies no authority to withhold additional categories of information from the public.

The first exclusion is triggered when a request seeks information that is exempt because disclosure could reasonably be expected to interfere with a current law enforcement investigation. There are specific prerequisites for the application of this exclusion. First, the investigation in question must involve a possible violation of criminal law. Second, there must be a reason to believe that the subject of the investigation is not already aware that the investigation is underway. Third, disclosure of the existence of the records -- as distinguished from contents of the records -- could reasonably be expected to interfere with enforcement proceedings.

When all three of these conditions are present, an agency may respond to an FOIA request for investigatory records as if the records are not subject to the requirements of the FOIA. In other words, the agency's response does not have to reveal that it is conducting an investigation.

The second exclusion applies to informant records maintained by a criminal law enforcement agency under the informant's name or personal identifier. The agency is not required to confirm the existence of these records unless the informant's status has been officially confirmed. This exclusion helps agencies to protect the identity of confidential informants. Information that might identify informants has always been exempt under the FOIA.

The third exclusion applies only to records maintained by the Federal Bureau of Investigation which pertain to foreign intelligence, counterintelligence, or international terrorism. When the existence of those type of records is classified, the FBI may treat the records as not subject to the requirements of FOIA.

This exclusion does not apply to all classified records on the specific subjects. It only applies when the records are classified and when the existence the records is also classified. Since the underlying records must be classified before the exclusion is relevant, agencies have no new substantive withholding authority.

In enacting these exclusions, congressional sponsors stated that it was their intent that agencies must inform FOIA requesters that these exclusions are available for agency use. Requesters who believe that records were improperly withheld because of the exclusions can seek judicial review.

Administrative Appeal Procedures

Whenever an FOIA request is denied, the agency must inform

the requester of the reasons for the denial and the requester's right to appeal the denial to the head of the agency. A requester may appeal the denial of a request for a document or for fee waiver. A requester may contest the type or amount of fees that were charged. A requester may appeal any other adverse determination including a rejection of a request for failure to describe adequately the documents being requested. A requester can also appeal because the agency failed to conduct an adequate search for the documents that were requested.

A person whose request was granted in part an denied in part may appeal the partial denial. If an agency has agreed to disclose some but not all of the requested documents, the filing of an appeal does not affect the release of the documents that are disclosable. There is no risk to the requester in filing an appeal.

The appeal to the head of an agency is a simple administrative appeal. A lawyer can be helpful, but no one needs a lawyer to file an appeal. Anyone who can write a letter can file an appeal. Appeals to the head of the agency often result in the disclosure of some records that have been withheld. A requester who is not convinced that the agency's initial decision is correct should appeal. There is no charge for filing an appeal.

An appeal is filed by sending a letter to the head of the agency. The letter must identify the FOIA request that is being appealed. The envelope containing the letter of appeal should be marked in the lower left hand corner with the words "Freedom of Information Act Appeal."

Many agencies assign a number to all FOIA requests that are received. The number should be included in the appeal letter, along with the name and address of the requester. It is a common practice to include a copy of the agency's initial decision letter as part of the appeal, but this it not required. It can also be helpful for the requester to include a telephone number in the appeal letter.

An appeal will normally include the requester's arguments supporting disclosure of the documents. A requester may include any facts or any arguments supporting the case for reversing the initial decision. However, an appeal letter does not have to contain any arguments at all. It is sufficient to state that the agency's initial decision is being appealed. Appendix 1 includes a sample appeal letter.

The FOIA does not set a time limit for filing an administrative appeal of an FOIA denial. However, it is good practice to file an appeal promptly. Some agency regulations establish a time limit for filing an administrative appeal. A requester whose appeal is rejected by an agency because it is too late may refile the original FOIA request and start the process again.

A requester who delays filing an appeal runs the risk that the documents could be destroyed. However, as long as an agency is considering a request or an appeal, the agency must preserve the documents.

An agency is required to make a decision on an appeal within twenty days (excluding Saturdays, Sundays, and federal holidays). It is possible for an agency to extend the time limits by an additional ten days. Once the time period has elapsed, a requester may consider a that the appeal has been denied and may proceed with a judicial appeal. However, unless there is an urgent need for records, this is not always the best course of action. The courts are not sympathetic to appeals based solely on an agency's failure to comply with the FOIA's time limits.

Filing a Judicial Appeal

When an administrative appeal is denied, a requester has the right to appeal the denial in court. An FOIA appeal can be filed in the United States District Court in the district where the requester lives. The requester can also file suit in the district where the documents are located or in the District of Columbia. When a requester goes to court, the burden of justifying the withholding of documents is on the government. This is a distinct advantage for the requester.

Requesters are sometimes successful when they go to court, but the results vary considerably. Some requesters who file judicial appeals find that an agency will disclose some documents previously withheld rather than fight about disclosure in court. This does not always happen, and there is no guarantee that the filing of a judicial appeal will result in any additional disclosure.

Most requesters require the assistance of an attorney to file a judicial appeal. A person who files a lawsuit and substantially prevails may be awarded reasonable attorney fees and litigation costs reasonably incurred. Some requesters may be able to handle their own appeal without an attorney. Since this is not a litigation guide, details of the judicial appeal process have been not included. Anyone considering filing an appeal can begin by reviewing the provisions of the FOIA on judicial review.

The Privacy Act of 1974

The Privacy Act of 1974 provides safeguards against an invasion of privacy through the misuse of records by federal agencies. In general, the Act allows citizens to learn how records are collected, maintained, used, and disseminated by the federal government. The Act also permits individuals to gain access to most personal information maintained by federal agencies and to seek amendment of any incorrect or incomplete information.

The Privacy Act applies to personal information maintained by agencies in the executive branch of the federal government. The executive branch includes cabinet departments, military departments, government corporations, government controlled corporations, independent regulatory agencies, and other establishments in the executive branch. Agencies subject to the Freedom of Information Act (FOIA) are also subject to the Privacy Act. The Privacy Act does not generally apply to records maintained by state and local governments or private companies or organizations.

The Privacy Act grants rights only to United States citizens and to aliens lawfully admitted for permanent residence. As a result, foreign nationals cannot use the Act's provisions. However, foreigners may use the FOIA to request records about themselves.

The only records subject to the Privacy Act are records about individuals that are maintained in a system of records. The idea of a "system of records" is unique to the Privacy Act and requires explanation.

The Act defines a "record" to include most personal information maintained by an agency about an individual. A record contains information about education, financial transactions, medical history, criminal history, or employment history. A system of records is a group of records from which information is actually retrieved by name, social security number, or other identifying symbol assigned to an individual.

Some personal information is not kept in a system of records. This information is not subject to the provisions of the Privacy Act, although access may be requested under the FOIA. Most personal information in government files is subject to the Privacy Act.

The Privacy Act also establishes general records management requirements for federal agencies. In summary, there are five basic requirements that are more relevant to individuals.

First, agencies must establish procedures allowing individuals to see and copy records about themselves. An individual may also seek to amend any information that is not accurate, relevant, timely, or complete. The rights to inspect and to correct records are the most important provisions of the Privacy Act. This Guide explains in more detail how an individual can exercise these rights.

Second, agencies must publish notices describing all systems of records. The notices include a complete description of personal-data record keeping policies, practices, and systems. This requirement prevents the maintenance of secret record systems.

Third, agencies must make reasonable efforts to maintain accurate, relevant, timely, and complete records about individuals. Agencies are prohibited from maintaining information about how individuals exercise rights guaranteed by the First Amendment to the U.S. Constitution unless maintenance of the information is specifically authorized by statute or relates to authorized law enforcement activity.

Fourth, the Act establishes rules governing the use and disclosure of personal information. The Act specifies that information collected for one purpose may not be used for another purpose without notice to or the consent of the subject of the record. The Act also requires that agencies keep a record of some disclosures of personal information.

Fifth, the Act provides legal remedies that permit individuals to seek enforcement of rights under the Act. In addition, there are criminal penalties that apply to federal employees who fail to comply with the Act's provisions.

Locating Records

There is no central index of federal government records. An individual who wants to inspect records about himself or herself must first identify which agency has the records. Often, this will not be difficult. For example, an individual who was employed by the federal government knows that the employing agency or the Office of Personnel Management maintains personnel files.

Similarly, an individual who receives veterans' benefits will normally find the related records at the Veterans Administration or at the Defense Department. Tax records are maintained by the Internal Revenue Service, social security records by the Social Security Administration, passport records by the State Department, etc.

For those who are uncertain about which agency has the records that are needed, there are several sources of

information. First, an individual can ask an agency that might maintain the records. If that agency does not have the records, it may be able to identify the proper agency.

Second, a government directory such as the *United States Government Manual* contains a complete list of all federal agencies, a description of agency functions, and the address of the agency and its field offices. An agency responsible for operating a program normally maintains the records related to that program.

Third, a Federal Information Center can help to identify government agencies, their functions, and their records. These Centers, which are operated by the General Services Administration, serve as clearinghouses for information about the federal government. There are several dozen Federal Information Centers throughout the country.

Fourth, the Office of Federal Register publishes an annual compilation of system of records notices for all agencies. These notices contain a complete description of each record system maintained by each agency. The compilation -- which is published in five large volumes -- is the most complete reference for information about federal agency personal information practices. The information that appears in the compilation is also published occasionally in the *Federal Register*.

The compilation -- formally called Privacy Act Issuance -- maybe difficult to find. Copies will be available in some federal depository libraries and possibly in other libraries as well. Although the compilation is the best single source of detailed information about personal records maintained by the federal agencies, it is not necessary to consult the compilation before making a Privacy Act request.

A requester is not required to identify the specific system of records that contains the information being sought. It is sufficient to identify the agency that has the records. Using information provided by the requester, the agency will determine which system of records has the files that have been requested.

Those who request records under the Privacy Act can help the agency by identifying the type of records being sought. Large agencies maintain dozens or even hundreds of different record systems. A request is processed faster if the requester tells the agency that he or she was employed by the agency, was the recipient of benefits under an agency program, or had other specific contacts with the agency.

Making a Privacy Act Request for Access

The fastest way to make a Privacy Act request is to identify the specific system of records. The request can be addressed to the system manager. Few people do this. Instead, most people address their requests to the head of the agency that has the records or the agency's Privacy Act Officer. The envelope containing the written request should be marked "Privacy Act Request" in the bottom left-hand corner.

There are three basic elements to a request for records under the Privacy Act. First, the letter should state that the request is being made under the Privacy Act. Second, the letter should include the name, address, and signature of the requester. Third, the request should describe as specifically as possible the records that are wanted. Appendix 1 includes a sample Privacy Act request letter. It is a common practice for an individual seeking records about himself or herself to make the request both under the Privacy Act of 1974 and the Freedom of Information Act. See the discussion in the front of this Guide about which act to use.

A requester can describe the records by identifying a specific system of records by describing his or her contacts with an agency, or by simply asking for all records about himself or herself. The broader and less specific a request is, the longer it may take for an agency to respond.

It is a good practice for a requester to describe the type of records that he or she expects to find. For example, an individual seeking a copy of his service record in the Army should state he was in the Army and include the approximate dates of service. This will help the Defense Department narrow its search to record systems that are likely to contain the information being sought. An individual seeking records from the Federal Bureau of Investigation may ask that files in specific field offices be searched in addition to the FBI's central office files. The FBI dose not routinely search field office records without a specific request.

Agencies generally require requesters to provide some proof of identity before records will be disclosed. Agencies may have different requirements. Some agencies will accept a signature; others may require a notarized signature. If an individual goes to the agency to inspect records, standard personal identification may be acceptable. More stringent requirements may apply if the records being sought are especially sensitive.

Agencies will inform requesters of a special identification requirements. Requesters who need records quickly should first consult regulations or talk to the agency's Privacy Act Officer to find out how to provide adequate identification.

An individual who visits an agency office to inspect a Privacy Act record may wish to bring along a friend or relative to review the record. When a requester brings another person, the agency may ask the requester to sign a written statement authorizing discussion of the record in the presence of that person.

It is a crime to knowingly and willfully request or obtain records under the Privacy Act under false pretenses. A request for access under the Privacy Act can be made only by the subject of the record. An individual cannot make a request under the Privacy Act for a record about another person. The only exception is for a parent or legal guardian who can request records for a minor or a person who has been declared incompetent.

Fees

Under the Privacy Act, fees can be charged only for the cost of conveying records. No fees may be charged for the time it takes to search for the records or the time it takes to review the records to determine if any exemptions apply. This is a major difference from the FOIA. Under the FOIA, fees can sometimes be charged to recover search costs and review costs. The different fee structure in the two laws is one reason many requesters seeking records about themselves cite both laws. This minimizes allowable fees.

Many agencies will not charge fees for making copies of files under the Privacy Act, especially when the files are small. If paying the copying charges is a problem, the requester should explain in the request letter. An agency can waive fees under the Privacy Act.

Requirements for Agency Responses

Unlike FOIA, there is no fixed time when an agency must respond to a request for access to records under the Privacy Act. It is good practice for an agency to acknowledge receipt of a Privacy Act request within ten days and to provide the requested records within thirty days.

At many agencies, FOIA and Privacy Act requests are processed by the same personnel. When then is a backlog of requests, it takes longer to receive a response. As a practical matter, there is little that a requester can do when an agency response is delayed. Requesters can be patient.

Agencies generally process requests in the order in which they were received. Some agencies will expedite the processing of urgent requests. Anyone with a pressing need for records should consult the agency Privacy Act Officer about how to ask for expedited treatment of requests.

Reasons Access May Be Denied Under the Privacy Act

Not all records about an individual must be disclosed under the Privacy Act. Some records may be withheld to protect important government interests such as national security or law enforcement.

The Privacy Act exemptions are different from the exemptions of the FOIA. Under the FOIA, any record may be withheld from disclosure if it contains exempt information when a request is received. The decision to apply an FOIA exemption is made only after a request has been made. In contrast, Privacy Act exemptions apply not only to records but to systems of records. Before an agency can apply a Privacy Act exemption, the agency must first issue a regulation stating that there may be exempt records in that system of records. Thus, there is a procedural prerequisite for the application of the Privacy Act exemptions.

Without reviewing agency regulations, it is hard to tell whether particular Privacy Act records are exempt from disclosure. However, it is a safe assumption that any system of records that qualifies for an exemption has been exempted by the agency.

Since most record systems are not exempt, the exemptions are not relevant to most requests. Also, agencies do not automatically rely upon the privacy Act exemptions unless there is a specific reason to do so. Thus, some records that are exempt may be disclosed upon request.

Because Privacy Act exemptions are complex and used infrequently, most requesters need not worry about them. The exemptions are discussed here for those interested in the law's details and for reference when an agency withholds records. Anyone interested in more information about the Privacy Act's exemptions can begin by reading the relevant sections of the Act. The complete text of the Act is reprinted in the Appendix to this Guide.

The Privacy Act's exemptions differ from those of the FOIA in another important way. The FOIA is mostly a disclosure law. Information exempt under the FOIA is exempt from disclosure only. That is not true under the Privacy Act. It imposes many separate requirements on personal records. No system of records is exempt from all Privacy Act requirements.

Freedom of Information Act (FOIA)

For example, no system of records is ever exempt from the requirement that a description of the system be published. No system of records can be exempted from the limitations on disclosure of the records outside the agency. No system is exempt from the requirement to maintain an accounting for disclosures. No system is exempt from the restriction against the maintenance of unauthorized information on the exercise of First Amendment rights. All systems are subject to the requirement that reasonable efforts be taken to assure that records disclosed outside the agency be accurate, complete, timely, and relevant. Agencies must maintain proper administrative controls and security for all systems. Finally, The Privacy Act's criminal penalties remain fully applicable to each system of records.

1. General Exemptions

There are two general exemptions under the Privacy Act. The first applies to all records maintained by the Central Intelligence Agency. The second general exemption applies to selected records maintained by an agency or component whose principal function is any activity pertaining to criminal law enforcement. Records of these criminal law enforcement agencies can be exempt under the Privacy Act if the records consists of (A) information compiled to identify individual criminal offenders and which consist only of identifying that and notations of arrests, the nature and disposition of criminal charges, sentencing, confinement, release, and parole or probation status: (B) criminal investigatory records associated with an identifiable individual; or (C) reports identifiable to a particular individual compiled at any stage from arrest through release from supervision.

Systems of records subject to these general exemptions may be exempted from many of the Privacy Act's requirements. Exemption from the Act's access and correction provisions is the most important. Individuals have no right under the Privacy Act to ask for a copy of records that are generally exempt or to seek correction of erroneous records.

In practice, these exemptions are not as expansive as they sound. Most agencies that have exempt records will accept and process Privacy Act requests. The records will be reviewed on a case-by-case basis. Agencies will often disclose any information that does not require protection. Agencies also tend to follow a similar policy for requests for correction.

Individuals interested in obtaining records from the Central Intelligence Agency or from law enforcement agencies should not be discouraged from making requests for access. Even if the Privacy Act access exemption is applied, portions of the records may still be disclosable under the FOIA. This is a primary reason individuals should cite both the Privacy Act and the FOIA when requesting records.

The general exemption from access does not prevent requesters from filing a lawsuit under the Privacy Act when access is denied. The right to sue under the FOIA is not changed because of a Privacy Act exemption.

2. Specific Exemptions

There are seven specific Privacy Act exemptions that can be applied to many systems of records. Records subject to these exemptions are not exempt from as many of the Act's requirements as are the are the records subject to the general exemptions. However, records exempt under the specific exemptions are exempt from the Privacy Act's access and correction provisions. Nevertheless, since the access and correction exemptions are not always applied when available, those seeking records should not be discouraged from making a request. Also, the FOIA can be used to seek access to records exempt under the Privacy Act.

The first specific exemption covers record systems containing information that is properly classified. Classified information is also exempt from disclosure under the FOIA. Information that has been classified in the interest of national defense or foreign policy will normally be unavailable under either the FOIA or the Privacy Act.

The second specific exemption applies to systems of records containing investigatory material compiled for law enforcement purposes other than material covered by the general law enforcement exemption. The specific law enforcement exemption is limited when -- as a result of the maintenance of the records -- an individual is denied any right, privilege, or benefit to which he or she would be entitled by federal law or for which he or she would otherwise be entitled. In such a case, disclosure is required except where disclosure would reveal the identity of a confidential source who furnished information to the government under an express promise that the identity of the source would be held in confidence. If the information was collected from a confidential source before the effective date of the Privacy Act (September 27, 1975), an implied promise of confidentiality is sufficient to permit withholding of the identity of the source.

The third specific exemption applies to systems of records maintained in connection with providing protective services to the President of the United States or other individuals who receive protection from the Secret Service.

The fourth specific exemption applies to systems of records required by statute to be maintained and used solely as statistical records.

The fifth specific exemption covers investigatory material compiled solely to determine suitability, eligibility, or qualifications for federal civilian employment, military service, federal contracts, or access to classified information. However, this exemption applies only to the extent that disclosure of information would reveal the identity of a confidential source who provided the information under a promise of confidentiality.

The sixth specific exemption applies to systems of records that contain testing or examination of material used solely to determine individual qualifications for appointment or promotion in federal service, but only when disclosure would compromise the objectivity or fairness of the testing or examination process. Effectively, this exemption permits withholding of questions used in employment tests.

The seven specific exemption covers evaluation material used to determine potential for promotion in the armed services. The material is only exempt to the extent that disclosure would reveal the identity of a confidential source who provided the information under a promise of confidentiality.

3. Medical Records

Medical records maintained by federal agencies -- for example, records at Veterans Administration hospitals -- are not formally exempt from the Privacy Act's access provisions. However, the Privacy Act authorizes a special procedure for medical records that operates, at least in part, like an exemption.

Agencies may deny individuals direct access to medical records, including psychological records, if the agency deems it necessary. An agency normally reviews medical records requested by an individual. If the agency determines that direct disclosure is unwise, it can arrange for disclosure to a physician selected by the individual or possibly to another person chosen by the individual.

4. Litigation Records

The Privacy Act's access provisions include a general limitation on access to litigation records. The Act does not require an agency to disclose to an individual any information compiled in reasonable anticipation of a civil action or proceeding. This limitation operates like an exemption, although there is no requirement that the exemption be applied to a system of records before it can be used.

Administrative Appeal Procedures for Denial of Access

Unlike the FOIA, the Privacy Act does not provide for an administrative appeal of the denial of access. However, many agencies have established procedures that will allow Privacy Act requesters to appeal a denial of access without going to court. An administrative appeal is often allowed under the Privacy Act, even though it is not required, because many individuals cite both the FOIA and Privacy At when making a request. The FOIA provides specifically for an administrative appeal, and agencies are required to consider an appeal under the FOIA.

When a privacy Act request for access is denied, agencies usually inform the requester of any appeal rights that are available. If no information on appeal rights is included in the denial letter, the requester should ask the Privacy Act Officer. Unless an agency has established an alternative procedure, it is possible that an appeal filed directly with the head of the agency will be considered by the agency.

When a request for access is denied under the Privacy Act, the agency explains the reason for the denial. The explanation must name the system of records and explain which exemption is applicable to the system. An appeal may be made on the basis that the record is not exempt, that the system of records has not been properly exempted, or that the record is exempt but no harm to an important interest will result if the record is disclosed.

There are three basic elements to a Privacy Act appeal letter. First, the letter should state that the appeal is being made under the Privacy Act of 1974. If the FOIA was cited when the request for access was made, the letter should state that the appeal is also being made under the FOIA. This is important because the FOIA grants requesters statutory appeal rights.

Second, a Privacy Act appeal letter should identify the denial that is being appealed and the records that were withheld. The appeal letter should also explain why the denial of access is improper or unnecessary.

Third, the appeal should include the requester's name and address. It is good practice for a requester to also include a telephone number when making an appeal. Appendix 1 includes a sample letter of appeal.

Amending Records Under the Privacy Act

The Privacy Act grants an important right in addition to the ability to inspect records. The Act permits an individual to request a correction of a record that is not accurate, relevant, timely, or complete. This remedy allows an individual to correct errors and to prevent those errors from being disseminated by the agency or used unfairly against the individual.

The right to seek a correction extends only to records subject to the Privacy Act. Also, an individual can only correct errors contained in a record that pertains to himself or herself. Records disclosed under the FOIA cannot be amended through the Privacy Act unless the records are also subject to the Privacy Act. Records about unrelated events or about other people cannot be amended unless the records are in a Privacy Act file maintained under the name of the individual who is seeking to make the correction.

A request to amend a record should be in writing. Agency regulations explain the procedures in greater detail, but the process is not complicated. A letter requesting an amendment of a record will normally be addressed to the Privacy Act Officer of the agency or to the agency official responsible for the maintenance of the record system containing the erroneous information. The enveloped containing the request should be marked "Privacy Act Amendment Request" on the lower left corner.

There are five basic elements to a request for amending a Privacy Act record.

First, the letter should state that it is a request to amend a record under the Privacy Act of 1974.

Second, the request should identify the specific record and the specific information in the record for which an amendment is being sought.

Third, the request should state why the information is not accurate, relevant, timely, or complete. Supporting evidence may be included with the request.

Fourth, the request should state what new or additional information, if any, should be included in place of the erroneous information. Evidence of the validity of the new or additional information should be included. If the information in the file is wrong and needs to be removed rather than supplemented or corrected, the request should make this clear.

Fifth, the request should include the name and address of the requester. It is a good idea for the requester to include a telephone number. Appendix 1 includes a sample letter requesting amendment of a Privacy act record.

Appeals and requirements for Agency Responses

An agency that receives a request for amendment under the Privacy Act must acknowledge receipt of the request within ten days (not including Saturdays, Sundays, and legal holidays). The agency must promptly rule on the request.

The agency may make the amendment requested. If so, the agency must notify any person or agency to which the record had previously been disclosed of the correction.

If the agency refuses to make the change requested, the agency

Freedom of Information Act (FOIA)

must inform the requester of: (1) the agency's refusal to amend the record; (2) the reason for refusing to amend the request; and (3) the procedures for requesting a review of the denial. The agency must provide the name and business address of the official responsible for conducting the review.

An agency must decide an appeal of a denial of a request for amendment within thirty days (excluding Saturdays, Sundays, and legal holidays), unless the time period is extended by the agency for good cause. If the appeal is granted, the record will be corrected.

If the appeal is denied, the agency must inform the requester of the right to judicial review. In addition, a requester whose appeal has been denied also has the right to place in the agency file a concise statement of disagreement with the information that was the subject of the request for amendment.

When a statement of disagreement has been filed and an agency is disclosing the disputed information, the agency must mark the information and provide copies of the statement of disagreement. The agency may also include a concise statement of its reasons for not making the requested amendments. The agency must also give a copy of the statement of disagreement to any person or agency to whom the record had previously been disclosed.

Finding a Judicial Appeal

The Privacy Act provides a civil remedy whenever an agency denies access to a record or refuses to amend a record. An individual may sue an agency if the agency fails to maintain records with accuracy, relevance, timeliness, and completeness as is necessary to assure fairness in any agency determination and the agency makes a determination that is adverse to the individual. An individual may also sue an agency if the agency fails to comply with any other Privacy Act provision in a manner that has an adverse effect on the individual.

The Privacy Act protects a wide range of rights about personal records maintained by federal agencies. The most important are the right to inspect records and the right to seek correction of records. Other rights have also been mentioned here, and still others can be found in the text of the Act. Most of these rights can become the subject of litigation.

An individual may file a lawsuit against an agency in the federal district court in which the individual lives, in which the records are situated, or in the District of Columbia. A lawsuit must be filed within two years from which the basis for the lawsuit arose.

Most individuals require the assistance of an attorney to file a judicial appeal. An individual who files a lawsuit and substantially prevails may be awarded reasonable attorney fees and litigation costs reasonably incurred. Some requesters may be able to handle their own appeal without an attorney. Since this is not a litigation guide, details about the judicial appeal process have not been included. Anyone considering filing an appeal can begin by reviewing the provisions of the Privacy Act on civil remedies.

Appendices

Appendix 1: Sample Request and Appeal Letter

A.   Freedom of Information Act Request Letter

Agency Head [or Freedom of Information Act Officer]
Name of Agency
Address of Agency
City, State, Zip Code
Re: Freedom of Information Act Request.

Dear   :
         This is a request under the Freedom of Information Act.
         I request that a copy of the following documents [or documents containing the following information] be provided to me: [identify the documents or information as specifically as possible].
         In order to help determine my status to assess fees, you should know that I am (insert a suitable description of the requester and the purpose of the request).

[Sample requester descriptions:
         a representative of the news media affiliated with the newspaper (magazine, television station, etc.) and this request is made as part of new gathering and not for a commercial use.
         affiliated with an educational or noncommercial scientific institution and this request is made for a scholarly or scientific purpose.
         an individual seeking information for personal use and not for a commercial use.
         affiliated with a private corporation and am seeking information for use in the company business.]
         [Optional] I am willing to pay fees for this request up to a maximum of $. If you estimate that the fees will exceed this limit, please inform me first.
         [Optional] I request a waiver of all fees of this request. Disclosure of the requested information to me is in the public interest because it is likely to contribute significantly to public understanding of the operations or activities of the government and is not primarily in my commercial interest. [Include a specific explanation.]
         Thank you for your consideration of this request.
              Sincerely,
                        Name
                        Address
                        City, State, Zip Code
                        Telephone number [Optional]

B.   Freedom of Information Act Appeal Letter

Agency Head or Appeal Officer
Name of Agency
Address of Agency
City, State, Zip Code
Re: Freedom of Information Act Appeal

Dear   :
         This is an appeal under the Freedom of Information Act.
         On (date), I requested documents under the Freedom of Information Act. My request was assigned the following identification number:On (date), I received a response ;to my request in a letter signed by (name of official). I appeal the denial of my request.
         [Optional] The documents that were withheld must be disclosed under the FOIA because * * *.
         [Optional] I appeal the decision to deny my request for a waiver of fees. I believe that I am entitled to a waiver of fees. Disclosure of the documents I requested is in the public interest because the information is likely to contribute significantly to public understanding of the operations or activities of government and is not primarily in my commercial interests. (Provide details)
         [Optional] I appeal the decision to require me to pay review costs for this request. I am not seeking the documents for a commercial use. (Provide details)
         [Optional] I appeal the decision to require me to pay search charges for this request. I am a reporter seeking information as part of news gathering and not for commercial use.
         Thank you for your consideration of this appeal.
              Sincerely,
                        Name
                        Address
                        City, State, Zip Code
                        Telephone number [Optional]

C.   Privacy Act Request for Access Letter

Privacy at Officer [or System of Records Manager]
Name of Agency
City, State, Zip Code
Re: Privacy Act Request for Access.

Dear   :
         This is a request under the Privacy Act of 1974.
         I request a copy of any records [or specifically named records] about me maintained at your agency.
         [Optional] To help you to locate my records, I have had the following contacts with your agency: [mention job applications, periods of employment, loans or agency programs applied for, etc.).
         [Optional] Please consider that this request is also made under the Freedom of Information Act. Please provide any additional information that may be available under the FOIA.
         [Optional] I am wiling to pay fees for this request up to a maximum of $. If you estimate that the fees will exceed this limit, please inform me first.
         [Optional] Enclosed is [a notarized signature or other identifying document] that will verify my identity.
         Thank you for your consideration of this request.
              Sincerely,
                        Name
                        Address

City, State, Zip Code
Telephone number [Optional]

D. Privacy Act Denial of Access Letter

Agency Head or Appeal Officer
Name of Agency
City, State, Zip Code
Re: Appeal of Denial of Privacy Act Access Request.

Dear   :

This is an appeal under the Privacy Act of the denial of my request for access to records.

On (date), I requested access to records under the Privacy Act of 1974. My request was assigned the following identification number: .

On (date), I received a response to my request in a letter signed by (name of official). I appeal the denial of my request.

[Optional] The records that were withheld should be disclosed to me because * * *.

[Optional] Please consider that this appeal is also made under the Freedom of Information Act. Please provide any additional information that may be available under the FOIA.

Thank you for your consideration of this appeal.

Sincerely,
Name
Address
City, State, Zip Code
Telephone number [Optional]

E. Privacy Act Request to Amend Records

Privacy Act Officer [or System of Records Manager]
Name of Agency
City, State, Zip Code
Re: Privacy Act Request to Amend Records

Dear   :

This is a request under the Privacy Act to amend records about myself maintained by your agency.

I believe that the following information is not correct: [Describe the incorrect information as specifically as possible].

The information is not (accurate) (relevant) (timely) (complete) because * * *.

[Optional] Enclosed are copies of documents that show that the information is incorrect.

I request that the information be [deleted] [changed to read:]

Thank you for your consideration of this request.

Sincerely,
Name
Address
City, State, Zip Code
Telephone number [Optional]

F. Privacy Act Appeal of Refusal to Amend Records

Agency Head or Appeal Officer
Name of Agency
City, State, Zip Code
Re: Privacy Act Request to Amend Records

Dear   :

This is an appeal made under the Privacy Act of the refusal of your agency to amend records as I requested.

On (date), I was informed by (name of official) that my request was rejected. I appeal the rejection of my request.

The rejection of my request for amendment was wrong because * * *.

[Optional] I enclose additional evidence that shows that the records are incorrect and that the amendment I requested is appropriate.

Thank you for your consideration of this appeal.

Sincerely,
Name
Address
City, State, Zip Code
Telephone number [Optional]

Freedom of Information Act (FOIA)

Federal FOIA Offices

The Office of Information and Privacy (OIP) is the principal contact point within the executive branch for advice and policy guidance on matters pertaining to the administration of the Freedom on Information Act (FOIA). Through OIP's FOIA Counselor Service, experienced FOIA attorneys are available to respond to FOIA-related inquiries at Department of Justice, Office of Information and Privacy, 10th & Constitution Ave., NW, Room 7238, Washington, DC 20530, (202) 633-3642.

The following list contains the principal FOIA legal and administrative contacts at all federal agencies dealing regularly with FOIA matters. In some instances (e.g., the Department of Defense), all major agency components are listed individually under the agency. In other instances (e.g., the Food and Drug Administration), major agency components are listed separately. In still other instances (e.g., the Department of Labor), no components are listed, as it is the agency's preference that all FOIA contacts be made through its main FOIA office.

All telephone numbers are FTS numbers unless a local area code is shown. Where both the legal and the administrative contacts (marked "L" and "A," respectively) are at the same address, the common address follows the name of the administrative contact. OIP should be notified whenever there is a change in a legal or administrative contact or any change in title, telephone number, or address.

ACTION
Steward A. Davis (202-634-9333) (L)
Deputy General Counsel
Ulysses G. Parnell (202-634-9242) (A)
Management Analysis Division
806 Connecticut Ave., NW
Washington, DC 20525

Administrative Conference of the United States
Gary J. Edles (202-254-7020) (L)
General Counsel
2120 L St., NW, Suite 500
Washington, DC 20037

Agriculture Department
Kenneth E. Cohne (202-447-8164) (L)
Assistant General Counsel
Room 2321, South Bldg.
Washington, DC 20250-1400

Milton E. Sloane (202-447-8164) (A)
FOIA/PA Coordinator
Room 536A, Administration Bldg.
Washington, DC 20250

American Battle Monuments Commission
Col. William E. Ryan (202-272-0536) (A)
Director of Operations and Finance
20 Massachusetts Ave., NW, Room 5127
Washington, DC 20314-0300

Appalachian Regional Commission
Joseph E. Napolitano (202-673-7822) (A)
Special Assistant to the Co-Chairman
1666 Connecticut Ave., NW
Washington, DC 20235

Arms Control and Disarmament Agency
Frederick Smith, Jr. (202-647-3442) (A)
Information/Privacy Officer
320 21st St., NW, Room 5731
Washington, DC 20451

Board for International Broadcasting
John A. Lindburg (202-254-8040) (L)
General Counsel
1201 Connecticut Ave., NW
Washington, DC 20036

Central Intelligence Agency
W. George Jameson (703-874-3112) (L)
Associate General Counsel
Office of General Counsel
John H. Wright (703-351-2770) (A)

Information and Privacy Coordinator
Office of Information Services
Washington, DC 20505

Commerce Department
Eric Moll (202-377-5391) (L)
Chief, General Law Division
J. Randall Blumenschein (202-377-3271) (A)
Chief, Mgt. Support Division
Washington, DC 20230

Commission on Civil Rights
William H. Gillers (202-376-8514) (L)
Solicitor
1121 Vermont Ave., NW, Room 606
Washington, DC 20425

Commodity Futures Trading Commission
Glynn L. Mays (202-254-9880) (L)
Senior Assistant General Counsel
Edward W. Colbert (202-254-3382) (A)
Assistant Sec'y to the Commission
2033 K St., NW
Washington, DC 20581

Consumer Product Safety Commission
Alan C. Shakin (202-492-6980) (L)
Assistant General Counsel
Todd A. Stevenson (202-492-5785) (A)
FOI Officer
5401 Westbard Ave.
Washington, DC 20207

Council on Environmental Quality
Edward Yates (202-395-5754) (A)
Staff Attorney
Office of the General Counsel
722 Jackson Pl, NW
Washington, DC 20503

Customs Service
Kathryn C. Peterson (202-566-8681) (L)
Chief, Disclosure Law Branch
Gerald Crowley (202-566-8681) (A)
Paralegal Specialist
1301 Constitution Ave., NW
Washington, DC 20229

Defense Department
Maurice E. White (202-695-6804) (L)
Senior Attorney
OGC/LC, Room 3E988
Charlie Y. Talbott (202-697-1180) (A)
Chief, FOI Division

OASD (PA), Room 2C757
The Pentagon
Washington, DC 20301

Air Force
Susan P. Hotchkiss (202-475-7637) (L)
HQ USAF/JACL
Washington, DC 20324-1000

Richard C. Harding (202-694-4075) (L)
HQ USAF/JACM, Room eE409
John C. Wren (202-695-6552) (L)
Office of General Counsel, Room 4c941
Barbara Carmichael (202-695-4992) (A)
SAF/AADADF, Room 4A1088C
The Pentagon
Washington, DC 20330

Army
B.A. Wilkinson (202-697-8029) (L)
Office of General Counsel, Room 2E725
The Pentagon
Washington, DC 20310-0104

Janet W. Charvat (202-694-4316) (L)
Administrative Law Division
The Pentagon, Room 2E433
Washington, DC 20310-2200

Edith M. Miley (202-325-6163) (A)
FOIA/PA Division
USAISC-P (ASQNS-OP-F)
Room 1146, Hoffman 1
Alexandria, VA 22331-0301

Marine Corps
Darrell L. Moore (202-694-2510) (L)
Judge Advocate Division
HQMC (JAR), Room 1102
B.L. Thompson (202-694-4008) (A)
Management Information Systems Div.
HQMC (Code MI-10), Rm. 4327, Navy Annex
Washington, DC 20380

Navy
Jane Virga (202-325-9860) (L)
Office of the Judge Advocate General
200 Stovall St.
Alexandria, VA 22332

Roger T. McNamara (202-692-7172) (L)
Office of General Counsel, Room 480
Crystal Plaza 5
Washington, DC 20360-5110

Gwen R. Aitken (202-697-1459) (A)
CNO (OP-09B30)
The Pentagon, Room 5E521
Washington, DC 20350-2000

Defense Intelligence Agency
Robert S. Gonzales (202-697-3945) (L)
Assistant General Counsel
The Pentagon, Room 2E238
Robert C. Hardzog (202-373-8361) (A)
Chief, FOIA/PA Staff, RTS-1B
Washington, DC 20340

Defense Logistics Agency
Dave Henshall (202-274-6234) (A)
Administrative Management Branch
DLA-XAM, Cameron Station
Alexandria, VA 22304-6100

Education Department
Robert Wexler (202-732-2690) (L)
Office of the General Counsel, Rm. 4122
Alexia J. Roberts (202-732-4568) (A)
Office of Public Affairs, Rm. 2089
FOB 6, 400 Maryland Ave., SW
Washington, DC 20202

Energy Department
Ralph D. Goldenberg (202-586-8665) (L)
Assistant General Counsel
John H. Carter (202-586-5955) (A)
1000 Independence Ave., SW

Washington, DC 20585

Environmental Protection Agency
Marlyne Lipfert (202-382-5460) (L)
Office of General Counsel (LE-132G)
Jeralene G. Green (202-382-4048) (A)
FOIA Officer (A-101)
401 M St., SW
Washington, DC 20460

Equal Employment Opportunity Commission
Nicholas M. Inzeo (202-634-6592) (L)
Assistant Legal Counsel
2401 E St., NW, Room 214
Washington, DC 20507

Executive Office of the President, Office of Administration
Arnold Intrater (202-456-2273) (L)
General Counsel
472 Old Executive Office Bldg.
Washington, DC 20500

Nell W. Doering (202-395-3367) (A)
Chief, Records & Pubs. Mgt. Branch
2200 New Executive Office Bldg.
Washington, DC 20503

Export-Import Bank
Stephen G. Glazer (202-566-8864) (L)
Associate General Counsel
811 Vermont Ave., NW, Rm. 957
Washington, DC 20571

Farm Credit Administration
James M. Morris (202-883-4020) (L)
Office of General Counsel
Ronald H. Erickson (883-4113) (A)
FOI Officer
Office of Cong. and Public Affairs
1501 Farm Credit Dr.
McLean, VA 22102-5090

Federal Communications Commission
Lawrence S. Schaffner (202-632-6990) (L)
Assistant General Counsel
1919 M St., NW, Room 622
Washington, DC 20554

Federal Deposit Insurance Corporation
Thomas A. Schulz (202-898-7267) (L)
Assistant General Counsel
M. Jane Williamson (202-898-3712) (A)
Assistant Executive Secretary
550 17th St., NW
Washington, DC 20429

Federal Election Commission
Vincent J. Convery, Jr. (202-376-5690) (L)
Office of General Counsel
Fred S. Eiland (202-376-3155) (A)
FOI Officer
999 E St., NW
Washington, DC 20463

Federal Emergency Management Agency
Lorri L. Jean (202-646-4093) (L)
Associate General Counsel, Rm. 840
Linda M. Keener (202-646-3840) (A)
FOI/PA Specialist, Rm. 840
500 C St., SW
Washington, DC 20472

Federal Energy Regulatory Commission
Kathleen McDonough (202-357-8002) (L)
Office of General Counsel, Rm. 4400
Victoria R. Calvert (202-357-8088) (A)
Director, Public Affairs, Rm. 9200
825 N. Capitol St., NE
Washington, DC 20426

Federal Home Loan Bank Board
William L. Van Lenten (202-906-6773) (L)
Assistant General Counsel
1700 G St., NW

Washington, DC 20552

Federal Home Loan Mortgage Corporation
Keith H. Earley (202-759-8414) (L)
Assistant General Counsel
P.O. Box 4115
Reston, VA 22090

Federal Labor Relations Authority
William E. Persina (202-382-0781) (L)
Acting Solicitor, Rm. 222
David L. Feder (202-382-0834) (A)
Assistant General Counsel, Suite 326
500 C St., SW
Washington, DC 20424

Federal Maritime Commission
Joseph C. Polking (202-523-5725) (A)
Secretary
1100 L St., NW, Room 11101
Washington, DC 20573

Federal Mediation & Conciliation Service
Ted M. Chaskelson (202-653-5305) (L)
General Counsel
2100 K St., NW
Washington, DC 20427

Federal Mine Safety & Health Review Commission
Richard Baker (202-653-5625) (L)
Executive Director
1730 K St., NW, Room 614
Washington, DC 20006

Federal Reserve Board
Elaine M. Boutilier (202-452-2418) (L)
Legal Division
20th & C Sts., NW, Room B1051B
Washington, DC 20551

Federal Trade Commission
Marc Wineman (202-326-2451) (L)
Assistant to General Counsel
Yvette Lewis-Byrd (202-326-2402) (A)
Sixth St. & Pennsylvania Ave., NW
Washington, DC 20580

Food and Drug Administration
Gerald H. Deighton (202-443-1812) (A)
5600 Fishers Lane, (HFI-30)
Rockville, MD 20857

Foreign Claims Settlement Commission
Judith H. Lock (202-653-6155) (A)
Administrative Officer
1111 20th St., NW, Room 400
Washington, DC 20579

General Accounting Office
Nola Casieri (202-275-1970) (A)
441 G St., NW, Room 6800
Washington, DC 20548

General Services Administration
Helen C. Maus (202-566-1460) (L)
Attorney-Advisor
Barbara M. Williams (202-566-1643) (A)
18th & F Sts., NW
Washington, DC 20405

Health & Human Services Department
Mary M. McNamara (202-475-0153) (L)
Office of the General Counsel
Rm. 5362, Cohen Bldg.
330 Independence Ave., SW
Russell M. Roberts (202-472-7453) (A)
Director, FOIA/Privacy Division
Rm. 645F, HHH Bldg.
200 Independence Ave., SW
Washington, DC 20201

Housing & Urban Development Department
Charles M. Farbstein (202-755-7137) (L)
Assistant General Counsel, Rm. 10254
Doris Warner (755-6980) (A)

Office of Public Affairs, Rm. 10132
451 7th St., SW
Washington, DC 20410

United States Information Agency
Lorie J. Nierenberg (202-485-8827) (L)
Assistant General Counsel
Lola L. Secora (202-485-7499) (A)
FOIA/PA Officer
301 4th St., SW
Washington, DC 20547

Inter-American Foundation
Charles M. Berk (202-841-3812) (L)
General Counsel
Melvin Asterken (202-841-3869) (A)
FOI Officer
1515 Wilson Blvd.
Rosslyn, VA 22209

Interior Department
John D. Trezise (202-343-5216) (L)
Assistant Solicitor
18 & E Sts., NW
Washington, DC 20240

Internal Revenue Service
Peter V. Filpi (202-566-4109) (L)
Assistant Chief Counsel
John Fuhrman (202-566-3359) (A)
Chief, FOIA/PA Branch
1111 Constitution Ave., NW
Washington, DC 20224

International Development Cooperation Agency
Jan Miller (202-647-8218) (L)
Assistant General Counsel for Employee
      & Public Affairs, Rm. 6892
James L. Harper (202-647-1850) (A)
Office of Public Inquiries, Rm. 5756
320 21st St., NW
Washington, DC 20523

International Trade Commission
W.W. Gearhart (202-252-1091) (L)
Assistant General Counsel
Kenneth R. Mason (202-252-1000) (A)
Secretary to the Commission
500 E St., SW
Washington, DC 20436

Interstate Commerce Commission
Robert S. Burk (202-275-7312) (L)
General Counsel, Rm. 5211
S. Arnold Smith (202-275-7076) (A)
FOIA/PA Officer, Rm. 3132
12th & Constitution Ave., NW
Washington, DC 20423

Justice Department
Richard L. Huff (202-633-FOIA) (L)
Daniel J. Metcalfe
Co-Directors, Rm. 7238
Office of Information & Privacy
Washington, DC 20530

Rhonda S. Gaines (202-633-1938) (A)
FOIA/PA Section, Rm. B-327
Justice Management Division
Washington, DC 20530

Antitrust Division
Leo D. Neshkes (202-633-2692) (A)
FOIA/PA Officer, Rm. 3232
Washington, DC 20530

Bureau of Prisons
Renee Barley (202-724-3062) (A)
FOIA/PA Officer, Rm. 767 HOLC
Washington, DC 20534

Civil Division
Elizabeth A. Pugh (202-633-3178) (L)
Federal Programs Branch, Rm. 3646
Leonard Schaitman (202-633-3441) (L)
Appellate Staff, Rm. 3614

James M. Kovakas (202-633-2319) (A)
FOIA/PA Office, Rm. 3343
Washington, DC 20530

Civil Rights Division
Nelson D. Hermilla (202-633-4209) (A)
Chief, FOI/PA Branch, Rm. 7266
Washington, DC 20530

Criminal Division
L. Jeffrey Ross (202-786-4637) (A)
Chief, FOI/PA Unit, Rm. 3126 BOND
Washington, DC 20005

Drug Enforcement Administration
John H. Langer (202-633-1396) (A)
Chief, FOI Section, Rm. 200 EYE
Washington, DC 20537

Executive Office for U.S. Attorneys
Margaret A. Smith (202-272-9826) (A)
Attorney-in-Charge, Rm. 6410 PAT
Washington, DC 20530

Federal Bureau of Investigation
Emil P. Moschella (202-324-5520) (A)
Chief, FOI/PA Section, Rm. 6296 JEH
Washington, DC 20535

Immigration & Naturalization Service
Russell A. Powell (202-633-1554) (A)
FOIA/PA Section, Rm. 5056 CAB
Washington, DC 20536

Land & Natural Resources Division
Anne H. Shields (202-633-2586) (A)
Section Chief, Rm. 2133
Washington, DC 20530

Marshals Service
Florastine P. Graham (202-307-9054) (A)
FOI/PA Officer
600 Army Navy Drive
Arlington, VA 22202-4210

Parole Commission
Janice G. McLeod (202-492-5959) (A)
5550 Friendship Blvd., Rm. 420
Chevy Chase, MD 20815

Tax Division
J. Brian Ferrel (202-724-6423) (L)
Assistant Chief, CTS, Central Region
Rm. 6124 JCB
Pamela Jones (202-724-7419) (A)
FOIA Unit, Rm. 6823 JCB
Washington, DC 20530

Labor Department
Miriam McD. Miller (202-523-8188) (L)
Office of the Solicitor, Rm. N-2428
200 Constitution Ave., NW
Washington, DC 20210

Legal Services Corporation
Joanne Gretch (202-863-1823) (L)
FOIA Officer
400 Virginia Ave., SW
Washington, DC 20024-2751

Library of Congress
Dorothy M. Schrader (202-707-8380) (L)
General Counsel
William C. Froelich (202-707-8380) (A)
Copyright Office, Dept. 17
1st St. & Independence Ave., SE
Washington, DC 20540

Merit Systems Protection Board
Michael K. Martin (202-653-8261) (L)
Office of the General Counsel
Michael H. Hoxie (202-653-7200) (A)
Director, Information Services Div.
1120 Vermont Ave., NW
Washington, DC 20419

National Aeronautics & Space Administration
George E. Reese (202-453-2465) (L)
Associate General Counsel (Code GG)
Patricia M. Riep (202-453-2939) (A)
FOIA Officer (Code LN)
400 Maryland Ave., SW
Washington, DC 20546

National Credit Union Administration
Hattie M. Ulan (202-682-9630) (L)
Office of the General Counsel
1776 G St., NW
Washington, DC 20456

National Endowment for the Arts
Arthur A. Warren (202-682-5418) (L)
Deputy General Counsel
1100 Pennsylvania Ave., NW
Washington, DC 20506

National Endowment for the Humanities
Rex O. Arney (202-786-0322) (L)
General Counsel
1100 Pennsylvania Ave., NW
Washington, DC 20506

National Labor Relations Board
John W. Hornbeck (202-254-9350) (L)
Office of the General Counsel, Rm. 1107
John J. Toner (202-254-9430) (A)
Associate Executive Secretary, Rm. 701
1717 Pennsylvania Ave., NW
Washington, DC 20570

National Mediation Board
Ronald M. Etters (202-523-5944) (L)
General Counsel
1425 K St., NW, Suite 910
Washington, DC 20572

National Railroad Passenger Corporation (AMTRAK)
William F. Erkelenz (202-383-3975) (L)
General Solicitor
Medaris W. Oliveri (202-383-2728) (A)
FOIA Officer
400 N. Capitol St., NW
Washington, DC 20001

National Science Foundation
Lewis E. Grotke (202-357-9435) (L)
Assistant General Counsel, Rm. 501
Maryellen Schoolmaster (202-357-9494) (A)
FOIA Officer, Rm. 527
1800 G St., NW
Washington, DC 20550

National Security Agency
Vito T. Potenza (301-688-6054) (L)
Assistant General Counsel/Litigation
James V. Pasquarelli (301-688-6527) (A)
Chief, Information Policy Division
Ft. George C. Meade, MD 20755-6000

National Security Council
Nicholas Rostow (202-456-6538) (L)
Legal Adviser
368 Old Executive Office Bldg.
Nancy V. Menan (202-395-3103) (A)
Senior Director of FOI
375 Old Executive Office Bldg.
Washington, DC 20506

National Transportation Safety Board
Ronald S. Battocchi (202-382-6546) (L)
Office of General Counsel, Rm. 818
B. Michael Levins (202-382-6700) (A)
Bureau of Administration, Rm. 802
800 Independence Ave., SW
Washington, DC 20594

Nuclear Regulatory Commission
Mary Katharine Hembree (202-492-1559) (L)
Attorney, Office of General Counsel
Linda L. Robinson (202-492-8133) (A)
Chief, FOI/LPDR

Washington, DC 20555

Occupational Safety & Health Review Commission
Earl R. Ohman, Jr. (202-634-4015) (L)
General Counsel
Linda A. Whitsett (202-634-7943) (A)
1825 K St., NW
Washington, DC 20006

Office of Federal Inspector for Alaskan Natural Gas Pipeline
Nancy M. Ellett (202-586-4669) (A)
Administrative Officer, Code FA-1
1000 Independence Ave., SW
Washington, DC 20585

Office of Management & Budget
Mac Reed (202-395-5600) (L)*
Assistant General Counsel
464 Old Executive Office Bldg.
Darrell A. Johnson (202-395-7250) (A)
Assistant Director for Administration
9026 New Executive Office Bldg.
Washington, DC 20503

* For policy guidance on the Privacy Act
and on FOIA fee matters, contact OMB's
Robert N. Veeder, at 202-395-4814

Office of Personnel Management
Kathleen O. Martin (202-632-4632) (L)
Office of the General Counsel
Charles R. Chesek (202-632-2860) (A)
1900 E St., NW
Washington, DC 20415

Office of Science & Technology Policy
Barbara J. Diering (202-395-7347) (A)
Special Assistant
5013 New Executive Office Bldg.
Washington, DC 20506

Office of U.S. Trade Representative
Dorothy S. Balaben (202-395-3432) (A)
FOIA Officer
600 17th St., NW
Washington, DC 20506

Office of the Vice President
Diane G. Weinstein (202-456-2326) (L)
Counselor to the Vice President
271 Old Executive Office Bldg.
Washington, DC 20501

Overseas Private Investment Corporation
Herbert A. Glaser (202-457-7015) (L)
Office of the General Counsel
1615 M St., NW
Washington, DC 20527

Panama Canal Commission
John L. Haines, Jr. (011-507-527511) (L)
General Counsel
(Balboa, Panama)
APO Miami, FL 34011-5000

Barbara A. Fuller (202-634-6441) (A)
Assistant to the Secretary for
    Commission Affairs
2000 L St., NW, Suite 550
Washington, DC 20036-4996

Peace Corps
Robert L. Martin (202-254-3114) (L)
Associate General Counsel
John M. von Reyn (202-254-6020) (A)
1990 K St., NW
Washington, DC 20526

Pension Benefit Guaranty Corporation
Philip R. Hertz (202-778-8821) (L)
Office of the General Counsel, Rm. 7218
E. William Fitzgerald (202-778-8840) (A)
Disclosure Officer, Rm. 7106
2020 K St., NW

Washington, DC 20006

Pennsylvania Avenue Development Corporation
Staff (202-724-9091)
1331 Pennsylvania Ave., NW
Suite 1220 North
Washington, DC 20004

Postal Service
Charles D. Hawley (202-268-2971) (L)
Assistant General Counsel
Philip J.G. Skelly (202-268-2924) (A)
Records Officer
475 L'Enfant Plaza West, SW
Washington, DC 20260

Railroad Retirement Board
Karl T. Blank (312-386-4941) (L)
Bureau of Law
LeRoy F. Blommaert (312-386-4548) (A)
FOIA Officer
844 Rush St.
Chicago, IL 60611

Securities & Exchange Commission
Richard M. Humes (202-272-2454) (L)
Assistant General Counsel
Hannah R. Hall (202-272-7422) (A)
FOIA Officer
450 5th St., NW
Washington, DC 20549

Selective Service System
Henry N. Williams (202-724-1167) (L)
General Counsel
1023 31st St., NW
Washington, DC 20435

Small Business Administration
Mona K. Mitnick (202-653-6762) (L)
Office of General Counsel
Beverly K. Linden (202-653-6460) (A)
Chief, Office of FOI/PA
1441 L St., NW
Washington, DC 20416

Social Security Administration
David Harty (625-3133) (L)
Office of General Counsel
Rm. 614, Altmeyer Bldg.
Timothy D. Robertson (202-625-2736) (A)
FOIA Officer, Rm. 4100 Annex
6401 Security Blvd.
Baltimore, MD 21235

State Department
Mary Catherine Malin (202-647-3022) (L)
Attorney-Adviser, Rm. 4427A
Frank M. Machak (202-647-7740) (A)
FOIA Coordinator, Rm. 1239
2201 C St., NW
Washington, DC 20520

Tennessee Valley Authority
Maureen H. Dunn (615-632-4131) (L)
Assistant General Counsel
James A. Carmichael (615-632-8018) (A)
Manager, Office of Public Affairs
400 West Summit Hill Dr.
Knoxville, TN 37902

Transportation Department
Robert I. Ross (202-366-9154) (L)
Office of General Counsel (C-10)
Rebecca H. Lima (202-366-4542) (A)
Chief, FOIA Division (A-32)
400 7th St., SW
Washington, DC 20590

Treasury Department
Raymond J. McKenna (202-566-2327) (L)
Office of General Counsel, Rm. 1414
Karne B. Cameron (202-566-2789) (A)
Disclosure Officer, Rm. 1054
1500 Pennsylvania Ave., NW

Washington, DC 20220

Veterans Affairs Department
Thomas Gessell (202-233-3584) (L)
Office of General Counsel (024K)
Lynn H. Covington (202-233-3616) (A)

Director, PMRS (73)
810 Vermont Ave., NW
Washington, DC 20420

The White House
C. Boyden Gray (202-456-2632) (L)
Counsel to the President
1600 Pennsylvania Ave., NW
Washington, DC 20500

Freedom of Information Act (FOIA)

State FOIA Offices

How To Use State Open Records Laws - Freedom of Information

Just as the Freedom of Information Act, enacted by Congress in 1966, gave individuals the right to request and receive information held by the federal government, all states have laws giving the public access to their government records. Many of these laws, often called the Open Record laws, are modeled after the federal act.

The state statutes have some similarities. What is covered under the act, for example, invariably includes all books, maps, photographs and other documents made or received by any government agency in transaction with public business. And just as the federal act has exemptions to the rules, so do the state laws. While most of them exempt personnel, medical and other personal files, as well as criminal intelligence information and "trade secrets," there are less common ones. For example, in South Dakota, commercial fertilizer reports are exempt. In Florida, information provided to an agency for the purpose of ride-sharing arrangements is exempt, and in New Hampshire, meat inspection records are closed.

Companies can get a wide range of information from the state's Open Records laws. Here are a few examples of how these laws have been successfully used at the state level:

Bookstore Gets School Reading List
In Maryland, a bookstore used the state Open Records Law to obtain the required reading list for various courses at the state university in order to stock those books for the coming school year.

Plumber Opens Up Contractng Info
A plumbing company in New York that was the unsuccessful bidder for a project was granted access through the Open Records Law to the successful bid proposal as well as the agency's findings.

Environmental Group Obtains Damaging Drinking Water Study
In New York, an environmental group was able to get reports, analyses, and records concerning soil borings regarding a drinking water treatment plant prepared by a consulting firm for the City of Niagara Falls.

Hospital Gets Billing Practices of Competitors
In Illinois, a hospital in the same markets as another hospital was able to get info on its competitive billing practices concerning ambulance service.

Advertiser Gets State's Mailing List
Through the Open Records Law in Mississippi, a company wishing to expand its advertising list was able to get a list of all the state residents who had a driver's license.

The way laws are administered varies. Some states have time limits for agencies to respond to requests -- usually between three and 10 working days; others do not. Some states have administrative review processes available to individuals who have been denied their request. In other states a person's only recourse is to go court. Some laws state whether or not the motive of the requester is relevant in allowing access to records; some provide sanctions for violations of the statutes, others do not.

In addition, several states publish pamphlets explaining their law and how to file a request for records. New York, for example, has a Committee on Open Government composed of members from the government and the public. It furnishes advice to agencies, the public and the news media and annually reports its recommendations and observations to the governor and the legislature. Unlike the federal act, which has been amended only a few times, state acts are often changed on a frequent basis.

Information on a state's FOIA can usually be obtained from the office of attorney general. Listed below are their addresses, telephone numbers, and some information about the laws and their exemptions. The common exemptions -- personal records, criminal investigation files, library and academic files -- are not listed for each state. Some of the exemptions that are listed are exempted by other state laws.

States may charge fees to cover the cost of searches and/or the cost of copying records.

State Freedom of Information Offices

Alabama
Office of Attorney General, Alabama State House, 11 S. Union St., Montgomery, AL 36130/205-261-7300. Exemptions include income tax returns, records of child care facilities, certain conservation and natural resource information.

Alaska
Office of Attorney General, Department of Law, P.O. Box K - State Capitol, Juneau, AK 99811/907-465-3600. Exemptions because of other state laws include: geological and other information submitted for persons applying to lease or buy land, reports, logs and surveys held by the Department of Natural Resources relating to oil wells for which a permit to drill was issued by the department, information contained in audit reports or tax returns. There is no time limit for responding to requests.

Arizona
Office of Attorney General, 1275 W. Washington, Phoenix, AZ 85997/602-542-4266. Exemptions include consumer fraud reports, racketeering investigations, minutes of executive sessions of public bodies.

Arkansas
Office of Attorney General, 210 E. Markham St., Heritage West Building, Little Rock, AR 72201/501-371-2007. Exemptions include state income tax records, grand jury minutes. Records specifically declared open include motor vehicle citations and blood alcohol tests, payroll records of covered bodies and juvenile court records. Records must be made available within three working days at the time of the request.

California
Office of Attorney General, Department of Justice, P.O. Box 944255, Sacramento, CA 94244-2550/916-322-3360. Exemptions include requests for bilingual election materials, records of regulation of financial institutions, records of utility systems development or market or crop reports, real estate appraisals, statements of finances required by licensing agency. Agencies have 10 working days to comply with request. If denied access, an individual may request a review with the Information Practices Coordinator.

Colorado

Office of Attorney General, 1525 Sherman St. - Third floor, Denver, CO 80203/303-866-3611. Access may be denied for information pertaining to licensing, specific details of state research projects, real estate appraisals by the state before any purchase. Records must be turned over within three working days after a request is made.

Connecticut

Freedom of Information Commission, 97 Elm St. - Rear, Hartford, CT 06106/203-566-5682. Exemptions include real estate appraisals, collective bargaining, anti-trust investigations, states sales and use tax. Any person denied the records requested may appeal to the Freedom of Information Commission.

Delaware

Office of Attorney General, 820 N. French St. - Eighth floor, Wilmington, DE., 19801/(302)571-2500. Exemptions include labor negotiations, anonymous contributors to charity, records of permits for concealed weapons.

District of Columbia

Office of Corporate Counsel, District Building, 1350 Pennsylvania Ave., N.W., Washington, D.C. 20004/202-727-6248. Exemptions include information related to civil anti-trust investigations, fire loss information furnished by insurer to fire marshal. Records declared open include names, salaries, title and dates of employment of all employees or officers of the mayor and an agency.

Florida

Office of Attorney General, The Capitol, Tallahassee, FL 32399-1050/904-487-1963. Exemptions include home addresses, phone numbers and photos of law enforcement personnel. Records held legally open include autopsy reports, inspection records of nursing homes compiled by the Department of Health, appraisal reports of land acquisitions made by a city, vote sheets, final orders and other documents of the Public Service Commission.

Georgia

Office of Attorney General, Department of Law, 132 State Judicial Building, Atlanta, GA, 404-656-3300. Exemptions include tax returns, medical peer review group records. Records declared to be confidential by court decision or attorney general's opinions include: salary information of county employees contained only in personnel files and not included as part of another public record.

Hawaii

Department of Attorney General, Hawaii State Capitol, Room 405, Honolulu, HI 96813/808-548-4740. Exemptions through other state laws include applications for licenses to manufacture or sell motor vehicles, fire investigation records of county fire chiefs may be withheld. There is no time limit for responding to requests.

Idaho

Office of Attorney General, Boise, ID 83722/208-334-2400. Exemptions include papers filed with the judicial council or masters appointed by the supreme court concerning removal, discipline or retirement of judges or justices.

Illinois

Office of Attorney General, State of Illinois, Springfield, IL 62706/217-782-1090. Exemptions include taxpayer information, research data, proposals and bids for contracts, grants and agreements, architects' and engineers' plans.

Indiana

Office of Attorney General, 219 State House, Indianapolis, IN 46204/317-232-6201. Exemptions include information concerning research conducted under the auspices of institutions of higher learning. Information that may be withheld includes negotiations in progress with industrial, research, or commercial prospects.

Iowa

Office of Attorney General, Department of Justice, Hoover Building, Des Moines, IA, 50319/515-281-5164. Exemptions include: appraisal information for possible public land purchase, Iowa Development Commission information on industrial prospects in negotiations, and financial statements submitted to the state Commerce Commission. Records that have been legally open include the Book of Accounts required to be kept by county auditors, and jury lists.

Kansas

Office of Attorney General, Kansas Judicial Center - Second floor, Topeka, KS 66612-1597/913-296-2215. Exemptions include appraisals of property, software programs, well samples, logs and surveys, census and research records, and records of utility customers.

Kentucky

Office of Attorney General, Capitol Building, Frankfort, KY 40601/502-564-7600. Exemptions include details of possible real estate acquisitions, prospective locations of unannounced business. Records legally open include coroner's reports, tax records in the custody of the property valuation administrator, records of disciplinary actions of the state board of medical licensure. A public body must respond in three working days to a request.

Louisiana

Office of Attorney General, Department of Justice, 234 Loyola Building --Seventh floor, New Orleans, LA 70112-2096/504-568-5575. Exemptions include tax return information, financial institution records, confidential mineral reports, records in control of supervisor of public funds. Records held open under the law includes: budget requests of a city parish, records of associations of public officials. An agency has three days to respond to a request.

Maine

Office of Attorney General, State House Station - Six, Augusta, ME 04333/207-289-3661. Exemptions include materials prepared exclusively for labor negotiations, information on hazardous waste. Records legally opened include private appraisal reports obtained by the Bureau of Parks and Recreation in connection with proposed land acquisitions. A public official has 10 days to respond to a request.

Maryland

Office of Attorney General, Munsey Building, Calvert and Fayette Streets, Baltimore, MD 21202-1909/301-576-6300. Records that may be withheld include details of state research projects, real estate appraisals made for state. Records that must be withheld include confidential financial, geological, data, professional licensing records of individuals. Response to a request must not exceed 30 days.

Massachusetts

Office of Attorney General, One Ashburton Place, Boston, MA 02108/617-727-2200. Exemptions include real estate appraisals, name and address of any person contained in an application to carry firearms.

Michigan

Department of Attorney General, 525 W. Ottawa St., Lansing, MI 48913/517-373-1110. Exemptions include public bids, real estate appraisals, archaeological site information, records of any campaign committee. A public body has five working days to respond to a request.

Minnesota

Office of Attorney General, 102 Capitol Building, St. Paul, MN 55155/612-296-6196. Exemptions include property complaint data, real estate appraisals, social recreation data, energy and financial data, public safety data.

Mississippi

Office of Attorney General, P.O. Box 220, Jackson, MS 39205/601-359- 3680. Exemptions include individual tax records, certain appraisal records, archaeological records, commercial and financial records.

Missouri

Office of Attorney General, Supreme Court Building, Jefferson City, MO 65102/314-751-3321. Exemptions include records of state militia, records of national guard, records of labor negotiations.

Montana

Office of Attorney General, Justice Building, 215 N. Sanders, Helena, MT 59620/406-444-2026. Exemptions include unfair trade practices investigations, artificial insemination information, certain vehicle accident reports, reports of financial institutions to the Department of Commerce, and tax records. There is no time limit for responding to a request.

Nebraska

Office of Attorney General, 2115 State Capitol Building, Lincoln, NE 68509/ 402-471-2682. Exemptions include appraisal and negotiation records concerning purchase or sale of property, sales and use tax records, income tax records.

Nevada

Office of Attorney General, Heroes Memorial Building, Carson City, NV 89710/702-647-4170. Exemptions include certain vital statistics, certain divorce records, certain prison commission records.

New Hampshire

Office of Attorney General, State Capitol Annex, 25 Capitol St., Concord, NH 03301-6397/603-271-3658. Exemptions include certain bank records, Cancer Commission records, certain records of Human Rights Commission, records of malpractice claims, certain tax information. Records legally open include city real estate records, salary information of school boards.

New Jersey

Office of Attorney General, Richard Highes Complex Center, CN-080, Trenton, NJ 08625/609-292-4919. Exemptions include cancer incidence reports, certain records of casino Control Commission, Health Department Research Studies, audits of life insurance companies.

New Mexico

Office of Attorney General, P.O. Box 1508, Santa Fe, NM 87504/505-827-6000. Exemptions include certain historical or educational materials, certain vital statistics.

Freedom of Information Act (FOIA)

New York

Department of State, Committee On Open Government, 162 Washington Ave., Albany NY 12231/518-474-2518. Exemptions include records that if disclosed would impair contract awards and collective bargaining. An agency must respond to a request within five business days of receipt of request.

North Carolina

Department of Justice, P.O. Box 629, Raleigh, NC 27602-0629/919-733-3377. Exemptions include certain bank records, commercial feed information, communicable disease records, national guard records, tax records.

North Dakota

Office of Attorney General, State Capitol, Bismark, ND 58505/701-224-210. Exemptions include air pollution records, health department studies, medical review records, legislative investigation records, veterans' records. Records legally open include medical coroner's records, school district records, State Highway Department records, Water Conservation Commission records, state engineer records, records of charitable records on file with the secretary of state.

Ohio

Office of Attorney General, State Office Tower, 30 E. Broad St., Columbus, OH 43266-0410/614-466-4320. Exemptions include victim impact statements, tax information, statistics concerning veterans' exposure to caustic agents. Records legally open include city jail logs, employee address and payroll records of township trustees, complaints filed with the Division of Real Estate.

Oklahoma

Office of Attorney General, State of Oklahoma, Room 112 State Capitol, Oklahoma City, OK 73105/405-521-3921. Exemptions include income tax returns filed with the Oklahoma Tax Commission, certain bank records, income tax records, motor vehicle accident reports.

Oregon

Department of Justice, Justice Building, Salem, OR 97310/503-378-4400. Exemptions include records received or compiled by the superintendent of banks, mortality studies, motor vehicle accident reports, bank examinations, corporate tax information, personal property tax returns.

Pennsylvania

Office of Attorney General, Strawberry Square, 16th floor, Harrisburg, PA 17120/717-787-3391. Exemptions include records of the state ethics commission, records of the Judicial Inquiry and Review Board, records of the PA Crime Commission. Records legally open include salaries and employment addresses of Commonwealth employees.

Rhode Island

Department of Attorney General, 72 Pine St., Providence, RI 02903/401-274-4400. Exemptions include charitable contributions requesting anonymity, collective bargaining, all tax returns, real estate appraisals and engineering feasibility estimates.

South Carolina

Office of Attorney General, Rembert C. Dennis Building, P.O. Box 11549, Columbus, SC 29211/803-734-3970. Exemptions include income tax returns, certain records of the Board of Financial Institutions, Board of Denistry records, contagious disease records, certain information given to the Securities Commission, State Development Board records. Each public body has 15 days to respond to a written request.

South Dakota

Office of Attorney General, 500 E. Capitol, State Capitol Building, Pierre, SD 57501/605-773-3215. Exemptions include commercial fertilizer reports, taxpayer information, hospital inspection information, savings and loan association records.

Tennessee

Office of Attorney General, 450 James Robertson Parkway, Nashville, TN 37219-5025/615-741-6474. Exemptions include appraisal of real and personal property, bank examinations, records of the Medical Review Committee, tax records.

Texas

Office of Attorney General, Supreme Court Building, Austin, TX 78711-2548/512-463-2100. Exemptions include real and personal property appraisals and purchase price, agency reports concerning the supervision of financial institutions, geological information concerning wells, personal property tax records, sales use tax records.

Utah

Office of Attorney General, 236 State Capitol, Salt Lake City, UT 84114/801-533-5261. Exemptions include income tax returns, certain Insurance Commission records, certain Liquor Control Commission records, motor vehicle accident reports, sales tax returns, savings and loan association records.

Vermont

Office of Attorney General, 109 State Street, Montpelier, VT 05602/802-828-3171. Exemptions include tax return records, real estate appraisals, contract negotiation records. A right to appeal a request denial to the agency head exists.

Virginia

Office of Attorney General, 101 N. 8th St., Richmond, VA 23219/804-786-2071.

Washington

Public Disclosure Commission, 403 Evergreen Plaza, Mail Stop F-42, Olympia, WA 98505-3342/206-753-1111. Exemptions include taxpayer information, real estate appraisals, research data, information identifying archaeological sites, bank exams, salary and fringe information survey.

West Virginia

Office of Attorney General, Charleston, WV 25305/303-348-2021. Exemptions include motor vehicle accident reports, labor dispute records, tax returns, bar disciplinary records.

Wisconsin

Department of Justice, 123 W. Washington Ave., P.O. Box 7857, Madison, WI 53707-7857/608-266-3076. Exemptions include air pollution control records, savings bank exams, public utility accident reports.

Wyoming

Office of Attorney General, 123 Capitol Building, Cheyenne, WY 82002/307-777-7841. Exemptions may include details of research projects, real estate appraisals. Other statutory exemptions include motor vehicle accident reports, hospital inspection records, use tax records.

Tracking Federal Legislation

The U.S. Congress is accustomed to answering questions and sharing information with the public. Here is how you can quickly learn about any bill or resolution pending before the House of Representatives or Senate:

Free Legislation Database

This Bill Status Office can tell you within seconds the latest action on any federal legislation. Every bill and resolution for the current session as well as all House and Senate legislation dating back to 1975 are contained in LEGIS, a computerized database. When you call, it is best to give a key word or phrase (i.e., product liability, hazardous waste) which will help the congressional aides search LEGIS. This office can provide such detailed information as:

Have any bills been introduced covering a given topic?
Who is the sponsor of the bill?
How many cosponsors are there?
When was it introduced?
Which committees have the bills been referred to?
Have any hearings been held?
Has there been any floor action?
Has a similar bill been introduced in the other chamber?
Has there been any action on the other side of the Hill?
Have the House and Senate agreed to a compromise bill?
Has the bill been sent to the White House?
Has the President signed or vetoed the bill?
What is the PL (public law) number?

Telephone assistance is free, and printouts from LEGIS are available for $.20 per page but must be picked up at the Bill Status Office. However, by making arrangements with your Representative's or Senator's office, you can avoid this nominal charge and also have the printout mailed to your home or office. Contact: LEGIS, Office of Legislative Information, House Office Building Annex 2, 3rd & D Streets, SW, Room 696, Washington, D.C. 20515; (202)-225-1772.

Bill Sponsor's Legislative Assistant

The aide to the Senator or Representative who is the sponsor of a particular bill is the best person to contact next. The Bill Status Office can tell you the sponsor, and the Capitol Hill Switchboard at (202) 224-3121 can transfer you to the appropriate office; then ask to speak to the person in charge of the particular bill. Usually, this congressional aide will offer to send you a copy of the bill, a press announcement, and other background information. Don't loose this opportunity to get your first of many predictions about the likelihood of the bill becoming law.

Committee Staff

Committees and subcommittees are the real work centers of the Congress. After you touch base with the Bill Status Office (LEGIS), it is wise to double-check that information with the House or Senate committees which have jurisdiction over the legislation you are tracking. The Capitol Hill Switchboard at (202) 224-3121 can connect you with any committee. Once you reach the committee staffer who handles the bill in question, you are now in a position of obtaining the following information:

Are hearings expected to be held?
Has the subcommittee or committee chair promised a vote on the measure?
What is the timetable for committee "markup" and consideration of amendments?
What is the Administration's position on the legislation?
Has the committee filed its report on the bill?
Is there any action on a similar proposal on the other side of the Hill?

You can get free copies of House bills, resolutions, and House committee reports by sending a self-addressed mailing label to the House Document Room, U.S. Capitol, Room H-226, Washington, D.C. 20515; (202) 225-3456. Similarly, you can direct your requests for Senate documents to the Senate Document Room, Senate Hart Bldg., Rm B-04, Washington, D.C. 20510; (202) 224-7860. Public laws, often called slip laws, can be obtained from either the House or Senate Document Rooms, but call the Bill Status Office to get the public law number. You can get printed copies of hearings by contacting the committee which conducted the inquiry, but expect several months lag time before it becomes available.

If the legislation you are concerned about is scheduled for action on the floor of the House or Senate, you can monitor its activity by the hour by listening to the following recorded messages:

House of Representatives Cloakroom
Democrat   (202) 225-7400
Republican (202) 225-7430

Senate Cloakroom
Democrat   (202) 224-8601
Republican (202) 224-8541

Play Constituent

Your Representative's or Senator's office also can help with your questions about specific bills, particularly when you have difficulty getting through to committee or subcommittee staffers. Remember that Members of Congress are eager to serve their constituents, especially for simple requests such as sending you copies of bills or new public laws. The Capitol Hill Switchboard Operator at (202) 224-3121 can connect you with the Washington office of your Representative and Senators.

Additional Tools for Monitoring Federal Legislation

There are sophisticated variations of the free LEGIS database described above. One reason for the growth of commercial databases is that direct online access to LEGIS is limited to Members of Congress and their staff. The following databanks cover every bill or resolution pending before the current session:

* Bill Text Tracking System

This database contains the current full text of all pending federal legislation. Unlike the three databases noted below, this online system provides the latest language of the legislation (i.e., reflecting committee or floor amendments) but does not give information about the status of the bill. Contact: Washington On-Line, Inc., 507 8th Street SE, Washington, D.C. 20003; (202) 543-9101.

* Electronic Legislative Search System

This online system tracks all current federal legislation (as well as all 50 states) and also provides introductory bill summaries and legislative histories. Contact: Commerce Clearinghouse, 4025 W. Peterson Avenue, Chicago, IL 60646, (312) 583-8500.

* Legi-Slate

This computerized system provides information based primarily on the *Congressional Record*, the official edited transcript of the House and Senate floor proceedings. This database also contains committee schedules, all recorded votes and analyses voting patterns. Contact: Legi-Slate, Washington Post Co., 111 Massachusetts Ave., NW, Suite 520, Washington, D.C. 20001; (202) 898-2300.

* Washington Alert Service

This database covers all bills introduced in the U.S. Congress and includes information on committee schedules, release of committee reports and other documents, all recorded votes as well as full text of the publication, *CQ Weekly Report*. Contact: Congressional Quarterly, 1414 22nd Street NW, Washington, D.C. 20037; (202)887-8500.

There are plenty of specialized trade publications designed to help lobbyists stay apprised of developments on the Hill. Online access is available to some of these newsletters, for instance, the Bureau of National Affairs' *Daily Tax Advance* and *Daily Congressional and Presidential Calendar* (BNA OnLine, 1227 25th St., NW, Rm. 3-268, Washington, D.C. 20037; Contact Wendy Casey, (800) 862-4636 or (202) 452-4132). Another example is Budgetrack, a database produced by the editors of *Aviation Week and Space Technology*, which monitors the budget for the U.S. Defense Department and NASA from presidential submission to final congressional action (Budgetrack is available online from Data Resources, Inc., 1750 K St., NW, Washington D.C. 20006).

The American Enterprise Institute, the Brookings Institution, and other Washington-based think tanks generate position papers on specific legislative initiatives and often will share their information with the public. Other useful outside sources which can shed light on activities on the Hill are both small, specialized trade associations and large ones, for example, the National Paint and Coating Association and the U.S. Chamber of Commerce. How successful you are at getting these organizations to help you depends in large measure on how good you are on the telephone.

Congressional Experts

An estimated 4,000 legislative assistants and committee aides fall into the category of "professional staff." Because these congressional aides often draft bills and amendments and play a critical role in the negotiations with special interest groups, they are valuable sources of information, but some are much more open and candid than others. When dealing with these experts, remember they are at the beck and call of an elected official. It doesn't hurt to appeal to their egos and offer to call them when they aren't quite so busy.

Investigations and Special Reports

There are approximately 50 congressional committees and subcommittees which do not have legislative authority but serve as watchdogs with responsibility for reviewing existing laws. Some examples include the Senate Permanent Subcommittee on Investigations, House Select Committee on Aging, the Joint Economic Committee, and the House Science and Technology Subcommittee on Investigations and Oversight. These congressional panels conduct full-scale hearings on a wide range of subjects. A complete listing of these committees appears in the U.S. Congress Committees section. Some hearings conducted by the House Energy and Commerce Subcommittee on Oversight and Investigations during 100th Congress include the following examples:

"Biotechnology: Vaccine Development"
"EPA's Asbestos Regulations"
"Sulfites"
"Ground Water Monitoring"
"Unfair Foreign Trade Practices"
"SEC and Corporate Audits"
"SEC: Oversight of the Edgar System"

Several reports issued in 1985 by this House Subcommittee on Oversight and Investigations include:

The Computer Revolution and the US Labor Force
*Drug Diversion: Prescription Drug Diversion and the
    American Consumer
Industrial Import Shock: Policy Challenges of the 80s*

Many of these committees will put you on their mailing lists to receive notices of upcoming hearings as well as their *Committee Calendar*, which lists all of the hearings held during the previous year.

Congressional Caucuses

Approximately 100 non-legislative caucuses formed by Members of Congress serve as in-house think tanks. Some of these coalitions, such as the Congressional Clearinghouse on the Future provide information to the public. The House Steel Caucus, the Senate Coal Caucus, the Congressional Port Caucus, and others work to get their particular legislative initiatives through the Congress. The staff directors of these organizations can be good sources because these congressional aides have access to all government studies and also have close contact with industry and special interests that the caucus is going to bat for.

Many of these "informal groups" dissolve after work on its legislative priorities is completed, so you should expect that these organizations come and go. A list of these organizations appear next in U.S. Congress Committees section. Note that the Capitol Hill Switchboard at (202) 224-3121 or your Member of Congress can help you find out if a particular special interest caucus exists. A list of the current caucuses appears in the U.S. Congress Committee section.

Federal Agencies Legislative Affairs Offices

Every federal department and agency has an office which makes the Administration's case for the President's proposed budget or legislation. These offices within the executive branch usually are termed the "Offices of Legislative Affairs," which concentrate on particular bills, in contrast to an agency's own Office of Congressional Relations, which tends to respond to requests made by lawmakers or their staff. The office of legislative affairs also makes available written testimony by agency officials who appeared as witnesses at congressional hearings.

Arms of Congress

In addition to the 47 House and Senate committees, the following four organizations produce volumes of information and reports to aid lawmakers. These studies and recommendations by these arms of Congress are available to the public.

* **Congressional Budget Office**
  House Office Building Annex 2
  2nd and D Streets SW
  Washington, DC 20515   (202) 226-2800
Scorekeeping reports, special studies and other economic assessments are all available free to the public.

* **Congressional Research Service**
  Library of Congress
See also the Current Events and Homework Chapter for a comprehensive listing of all CRS studies which cover practically every current event topic. You must arrange to get copies of any CRS publications must be arranged through your Member of Congress.)

* **General Accounting Office**
  Information Office Room 7721
  441 G Street NW
  Washington, DC 20548   (202) 275-2812
Reports and audit information about every government program.

* **Office of Technology Assessment**
  U.S. Congress
  Information Center
  Washington, DC 20510   (202) 228-6150
Studies and executive summaries are available on a whole range of subjects.

U.S. Congress Committees

There is virtually *no* subject that is ignored by some office of the legislative branch of the federal government. Why? The voters back home raise all sorts of concerns with their elected officials. Every special interest group lobbies for this or that. And, each year the President proposes a federal budget which effects every taxpayer. Since Congress controls the government's purse strings, lawmakers ultimately decide the fate of practically every issue facing the country.

Every subject, from aquaculture to zinc, is monitored by some congressional employee. And many committees have authority over all these subjects. Over 100 House and Senate committees and subcommittees oversee the defense; the Department of Housing and Urban Development is subject to the jurisdiction of over 84 committees; and 54 House panels and 21 Senate panels have responsibility for some aspect of the "War on Drugs." Using the seven phone call rule, you will find someone who can be a useful information source. It may be an aide who works directly for a Senator or Congressman, a subcommittee staffer who serves either the Democratic or Republican Members of that subcommittee, an employee at one of the special interest congressional organizations such as the Senate Wine Caucus, or a specialist at the Congressional Research Service or one of the other think tanks of the legislative branch.

The staff at the committees, subcommittees, special interest caucuses, and other congressional organizations listed here can all share their expertise over the phone, refer you to other specialists, and send publications to you free of charge. Congress tends to be particularly responsive to information requests because most every legislator wants your vote.

Telephone Connection with Lawmakers and Staff

Although there is no central office for the U.S. Congress, the central switchboard operators at (202) 224-3121 can connect you with every Washington office of every Senator, every member of the House of Representatives, every committee, and most of the in-house congressional caucuses. To contact members of the Senate staff call or write the Senate Locator, U.S. Capitol, Washington, D.C. 20510; (202) 224-3207, or the House Locator, U.S. Capitol, Washington, D.C. 20515; (202) 225-6514. You needn't bother with room numbers and office buildings when writing to various offices. Simply address correspondence to any Senator or Senate office, followed by U.S. Capitol, Washington, D.C. 20510; and for any Member of the House or House committee, write the U.S. Capitol, Washington, D.C. 20515.

Senate Legislative Committees

The work of drafting and considering legislation is done largely by 16 "standing" or permanent committees. They evaluate proposed federal laws authored by individual Senators, the executive branch, and outside organizations and experts. Each bill and resolution are usually referred to the appropriate committee or committees, which may report a bill out in its original form, favorably or unfavorably, recommend amendments, or allow the proposed legislation to die in committee without action. Committees are divided into subcommittees which conduct hearings, consider and amend legislation, and may either approve or reject the bills. On behalf of the Senate, these committees, with rare exception, determine what reaches the floor. In the process they modify--sometimes extensively--proposals referred to them.

In addition, committees serve as congressional watchdogs of the executive branch. Each committee's jurisdiction determines its oversight of the organization and operations of the executive branch agencies--for knowing how efficiently and effectively the agencies perform their duties, and for knowing whether and how they are carrying out the intent of the laws enacted by Congress. Under the Senate's "advise and consent" responsibility, these committees decide whether or not to confirm the President's nominees to the executive and judicial branches.

These legislative committees produce reams of studies, committee reports, published hearings, and the committee staff are specialists in the areas which fall within the committee's jurisdiction. Both the majority committee staff, currently the Democrats who control the Senate, and the minority staff, the Republican committee staff, operate independently of one another and both can provide different viewpoints on issues, predictions about the fate of particular bills, and suggest people to contact both in the executive branch and organizations lobbying for or against pending legislation.

* Senate Committee on Agriculture, Nutrition and Forestry

Suite SR-328 Russell Senate Office Building
Washington, DC 20510   (202) 224-2035
Topics covered: agriculture; forestry and forest reserves; farm credit; school nutrition; and food stamp programs.

Subcommittees:
Agricultural Credit
Agricultural Production and Stabilization of Prices
Agricultural Research, and General Legislation
Conservation and Forestry
Domestic and Foreign Marketing and Product Promotion
Nutrition and Investigations
Rural Development and Rural Electrification

* Senate Committee on Appropriations
Suite S-128 Capitol

Washington, DC 20510   (202) 224-7282
Topics covered: appropriations of revenues for executive agencies and Federal programs.

Subcommittees:
Agriculture and Related Agencies/(202) 224-7240
Commerce, Justice, State, and Judiciary/(202) 224-7277
Defense/(202) 224-7255
District of Columbia/(202) 224-2731
Energy and Water Development/(202) 224-7260
Foreign Operations/(202) 224-7284
HUD-Independent Agencies/(202) 224-7231
Interior and Related Agencies/(202) 224-7214
Labor, Health and Human Services, Education, and Related Agencies/(202) 224-7288
Legislative Branch/(202) 224-7338
Military Construction/(202) 224-7276
Transportation and Related Agencies/(202) 224-0330
Treasury, Postal Service, and General Government/(202) 224-6280

* Senate Committee on the Armed Services
Suite SR-228 Russell Senate Office Building
Washington, DC 20510   (202) 224-3871
Topics covered: military and defense matters.

Subcommittees:
Strategic Forces and Nuclear Deterrence
Conventional Forces and Alliance Defense
Projection Forces and Regional Defense
Defense Industry and Technology
Readiness, Sustainability, and Support
Manpower and Personnel

* Senate Committee on Banking, Housing, and Urban Affairs
Suite SD-534 Dirksen Senate Office Building
Washington, DC 20510   (202) 224-7391
Topics covered: banks and other financial institutions; public and private housing; Federal monetary policy; urban development; mass transit; and certain foreign trade matters.

Subcommittees:
Housing and Urban Affairs/(202) 224-6348
International Finance and Monetary Policy
Securities
Consumer and Regulatory Affairs
[The rest of the subcommittees can be reached at (202) 224-7391.]

* Senate Committee on the Budget
SD-621 Dirksen Senate Office Building
Washington, DC 20510   (202) 224-0642
Topics covered: coordination of appropriations and revenues in Federal budget. This committee has no subcommittees.

* Senate Committee on Commerce, Science, and Transportation
Suite SD-508 Dirksen Senate Office Building
Washington, DC 20510   (202) 224-5115
Topics covered: regulation of interstate transportation, including railroads, buses, trucks, ships, pipelines, and civil aviation; Coast Guard; Merchant Marine; science and technology research policy; communications; non-military aeronautical and space sciences; coastal zone management; and oceans policy.

Subcommittees:
Aviation
Communications
Consumer
Foreign Commerce and Tourism
Merchant Marine
Science, Technology, and Space
Surface Transportation
National Ocean Policy Study

* Senate Committee on Energy and Natural Resources
Suite SD-364 Dirksen Senate Office Building
Washington, DC 20510   (202) 224-4971
Topics covered: regulation, conservation, and research and development of all forms of energy; mining; national parks; wilderness areas and historical sites; and territorial possessions of the U.S.

Subcommittees:
Energy Regulation and Conservation
Energy Research and Development
Mineral Resources Development and Production
Public Lands, National Parks and Forests
Water and Power

* Senate Committee on Environment and Public Works
Suite SD-458 Dirksen Senate Office Building
Washington, DC 20510   (202) 224-6176
Topics covered: environmental protection; water resources and flood control; public works and buildings; highways; and noise pollution.

Subcommittees:
Environmental Protection
Nuclear Regulation
Superfund, Ocean and Water Protection
Toxic Substances, Environmental Oversight, Research and Development
Water Resources, Transportation and Infrastructure

* Senate Committee on Finance
Suite SD-205 Dirksen Senate Office Building
Washington, DC 20510   (202) 224-4515
Topics covered: taxes; tariffs; import quotas; old-age and survivors insurance; Medicare; unemployment insurance; general revenue sharing.

Subcommittees:
Energy and Agricultural Taxation
Health for Families and the Uninsured
International Debt
International Trade
Medicare and Long Term Care
Private Retirement Plans and Oversight of the Internal Revenue Service
Social Security and Family Policy
Taxation and Debt Management

* Senate Committee on Foreign Relations
Suite SD-419 Dirksen Senate Office Building
Washington, DC 20510   (202) 224-4651
Topics covered: foreign policy; treaties; diplomatic affairs; United Nations.

Subcommittees:
African Affairs
East Asian and Pacific Affairs
European Affairs
International Economic Policy, Trade, Oceans and Environment
Near Eastern and South Asian Affairs
Terrorism, Narcotics, and International Communications
Western Hemisphere and Peace Corps Affairs

* Senate Committee on Governmental Affairs
Suite SD-340 Dirksen Senate Office Building
Washington, DC 20510   (202) 224-4751
Topics covered: budget and accounting matters; organization and reorganization of executive branch; intergovernmental relations; municipal affairs of the District of Columbia; civil service; postal service; and the census.

Subcommittees:
Federal Services, Post Office, and Civil Service/(202) 224-2254
General Services, Federalism, and the District of Columbia/(202) 224-4718
Government Information and Regulation/(202) 224-9000
Oversight of Government Management/(202) 224-3682
Permanent Subcommittee on Investigations/(202) 224-3721

* Senate Committee on the Judiciary
Suite SD-224 Dirksen Senate Office Building
Washington, DC 20510   (202) 224-5225
Topics covered: Federal courts and judges; civil rights and civil liberties; constitutional amendments; interstate compacts; legislative apportionment; antitrust and monopoly; and immigration and naturalization.

Subcommittees:
Antitrust, Monopolies and Business Rights/(202) 224-5701
Constitution/(202) 224-5573
Courts and Administrative Practice/(202) 224-4022
Immigration and Refugee Affairs/(202) 224-7878
Patents, Copyrights, and Trademarks/(202) 224-8178
Technology and the Law/(202) 224-3406

* Senate Committee on Labor and Human Resources
Suite SD-428 Dirksen Senate Office Building

Information from Lawmakers

Washington, DC 20510   (202) 224-5375
Topics covered: education, labor, health, and public welfare.

Subcommittees:
Aging
Children, Family, Drugs and Alcoholism
Education, Arts, and Humanities
Employment and Productivity
Handicapped
Labor

* Senate Committee on Rules and Administration
Suite SR-305 Russell Senate Office Building
Washington, DC 20510   (202) 224-6352
Topics covered: rules of the Senate; Senate employees; management of the Senate; Federal elections; Presidential succession; the Smithsonian Institution; the Library of Congress. The Committee has no subcommittees.

* Senate Committee on Small Business
Suite SR-428A Russell Senate Office Building
Washington, DC 20510   (202) 224-5175, FAX: 224-5619
Topics covered: measures relating to small businesses generally, and to the Small Business Administration.

Subcommittees:
Competition and Antitrust Enforcement
Export Expansion
Government Contracting and Paperwork Reduction
Innovation, Technology, and Productivity
Rural Economy and Family Farming
Urban and Minority-Owned Business Development

* Senate Committee on Veterans' Affairs
Suite SR-414 Russell Senate Office Building
Washington, DC 20510   (202) 224-9126
Topics covered: veterans' affairs, including pensions, medical care, life insurance, education, and rehabilitation. This Committee has no subcommittees.

Senate Think Tanks and Committees

Congressional studies and policy options are byproducts of these Senate committees. Usually established for a limited period of time, these committees ordinarily deal with more specific issues and problems than do the legislative committees. The political party organizations are permanent committees, but others are usually established for a specific period of time or until the project for which they have been created has been completed. Most select committees may investigate, study, and make recommendations, but they have no authority to make legislation. The Select and Special Committees of the Senate are as follows:

Special Committee on Aging
Room SD G-41 Dirksen Senate Office Building; Washington, DC 20510; (202) 224-5364.

Select Committee on Ethics
Room SH-220 Hart Senate Office Building; Washington, DC 20510; (202) 224-2981.

Select Committee on Indian Affairs
Room SH-838 Hart Senate Office Building; Washington, DC 20510; (202) 224-2251; FAX: 224-2309.

Select Committee on Intelligence
Room SH-211 Hart Senate Office Building; Washington, DC 20510; (202) 224-1700.

Senate Impeachment Trial Committee
SH-902D Hart Senate Office, Building; Washington, DC 20510; (202) 224-5471.

Democratic Policy Committee
Rooms S-118 and S-318 The Capitol; Washington, DC 20510; (202) 224-5551 and (202) 224-2939.

Democratic Senatorial Campaign Committee
430 South Capitol St., SE; Washington, DC 20003; (202) 224-2447; FAX: 485-3120.

National Republican Senatorial Committee
425 Second St., NE; Washington, DC 20001; (202) 675-6000; FAX:675-6058.

Conference of the Minority
Room SH-405 Hart Senate Office Building; Washington, DC 20510; (202) 224-2764.

Republican Policy Committee
Room SR-347 Russell Senate Office Building; Washington, DC 20510; (202) 224-2946.

House of Representatives Legislative Committees

The work of drafting and considering legislation is done largely by 22 committees. The jurisdictions of the House committees are similar to the 16 Senate committees; however, the House subcommittees usually play a much more important role than their Senate counterparts. The committees and subcommittees, with rare exception, determine what legislation will be considered by the entire House. In the process they modify--sometimes extensively--proposals referred to them. The committees, like the Senate committees, serve as congressional watchdogs of the executive branch. They oversee the organization and operations of the executive branch agencies--for knowing how efficiently and effectively the agencies perform their duties, and for knowing whether and how they are carrying out the intent of the laws enacted by Congress. These legislative committees are tremendous generators of information on all the issues over which they have jurisdiction, and both the committee and subcommittee staff are accessible and useful contacts.

* House Committee on Agriculture
1301 Longworth House Office Building
Washington, DC 20515   (202) 225-2171
Topics covered: agriculture and forestry measures, including farm credit, crop insurance, soil conservation, rural electrification, domestic marketing, and nutrition.

Subcommittees:
Conservation, Credit, and Rural Development
Cotton, Rice, and Sugar
Department Operations, Research, and Foreign Agriculture
Domestic Marketing, Consumer Relations, and Nutrition
Forests, Family Farms, and Energy
Livestock, Dairy, and Poultry
Tobacco and Peanuts
Wheat, Soybeans, and Feed Grains

* House Committee on Appropriations
H-218 Capitol Building
Washington, DC 20515   (202) 225-2771
Topics covered: appropriation of revenue for executive agencies and Federal programs and activities.

Subcommittees:
Commerce, Justice, State, The Judiciary, and Related Agencies/(202) 225-3351
Defense/(202) 225-2847
District of Columbia/(202) 225-5338
Energy and Water Development/(202) 225-3421
Foreign Operations, Export Financing, and Related Programs/(202) 225-2041
Interior and Related Agencies/(202) 225-3081
Labor, Health and Human Services, Education, and Related Agencies/(202) 225-3508
Legislative/(202) 225-5338
Military Construction/(202) 225-3047
Rural Development, Agriculture, and Related Agencies/(202) 225-2068
Transportation/(202) 225-2141
Treasury, Postal Service, and General Government/(202) 225-5834
VA, HUD, and Independent Agencies/(202) 225-3241

* House Committee on Armed Services
2120 Rayburn House Office Building
Washington, DC 20515   (202) 225-4151

Topics covered: defense matters, including procurement practices, weapons systems, manpower, military intelligence, naval petroleum reserves, and military applications of nuclear energy.

Subcommittees:
Investigations
Military Installations and Facilities
Military Personnel and Compensation
Procurement and Military Nuclear Systems
Readiness
Research and Development
Seapower and Strategic and Critical Materials

* House Committee on Banking, Finance, and Urban Affairs
2129 Rayburn House Office Building
Washington, DC 20515 (202) 225-4247
Topics covered: banking and currency legislation; international financial organizations; public and private housing.

Subcommittees:
Consumer Affairs and Coinage
Domestic Monetary Policy
Economic Stabilization
Financial Institutions Supervision, Regulation, and Insurance
General Oversight and Investigations
Housing and Community Development
International Development, Finance, Trade, and Monetary Policy
Policy Research and Insurance

* House Committee on the Budget
214 House Office Building Annex I
Washington, DC 20515 (202) 226-7200
Topics covered: coordination of spending and revenues in Federal budget.

Subcommittees:
Budget Process, Reconciliation, and Enforcement
Community Development and Natural Resources
Defense, Foreign Policy and Space
Urgent Fiscal Issues
Human Resources
Economic Policy, Projections, and Revenues

* House Committee on the District of Columbia
1310 Longworth House Office Building
Washington, DC 20515 (202) 225-4457
Topics covered: Municipal affairs and administration of the District of Columbia.

Subcommittees:
Fiscal Affairs and Health
Government Operations and Metropolitan Affairs
Judiciary and Education

* House Committee on Education and Labor
2181 Rayburn House Office Building
Washington, DC 20515 (202) 225-4527
Topics covered: education and labor legislation, including vocational rehabilitation, minimum wage legislation, and school lunch programs.

Subcommittees:
Elementary, Secondary, and Vocational Education
Employment Opportunities
Health and Safety
Human Resources
Labor-Management Relations
Labor Standards
Postsecondary Education
Select Education

* House Energy and Commerce Committee
2125 Rayburn House Office Building
Washington, DC 20515 (202) 225-2927
Topics covered: National energy policy generally, including energy pricing, transmission, and conservation; interstate commerce; communications; securities and exchanges; health care; biomedical research; railroads and railroad labor; and consumer affairs and protection.

Subcommittees:
Commerce, Consumer Protection, and Competitiveness/(202) 226-3160
Energy and Power/(202) 226-2500
Health and the Environment/(202) 225-4952

Oversight and Investigations/(202) 225-4441
Telecommunications and Finance/(202) 226-2424
Transportation and Hazardous Materials/(202) 225-9304

* House Committee on Foreign Affairs
2170 Rayburn House Office Building
Washington, DC 20515 (202) 225-5021
Topics covered: foreign relations; international trade and economic policy; Food For Peace; international commodity agreements.

Subcommittees:
Africa/(202) 226-7807
Arms Control, International Security, and Science/(202) 225-8926
Asian and Pacific Affairs/(202) 226-7801
Europe and the Middle East/(202) 225-3345
Human Rights and International Organizations/(202) 226-7825
International Economic Policy and Trade/(202) 226-7820
International Operations/(202) 225-3424
Western Hemisphere Affairs/(202) 226-7812

* House Committee on Government Operations
2157 Rayburn House Office Building
Washington, DC 20515 (202) 225-5051
Topics covered: Executive branch reorganization, intergovernmental relations, and revenue sharing.

Subcommittees:
Commerce, Consumer, and Monetary Affairs/(202) 225-4407
Employment and Housing/(202) 225-6751
Environment, Energy, and Natural Resources/(202) 225-6427
Government Activities and Transportation/(202) 225-7920
Government Information, Justice, and Agriculture/(202) 225-3741
Human Resources and Intergovernmental Relations/(202) 225-2548
Legislation and National Security/(202) 225-5147

* House Committee on House Administration
H-326 Capitol Building
Washington, DC 20515 (202) 225-2061
Topics covered: House administration and management; Federal election legislation; Library of Congress; and the Smithsonian Institution.

Subcommittees:
Accounts/(202) 226-7540
Elections/(202) 226-7616
Libraries and Memorials/(202) 226-2307
Office Systems/(202) 225-1608
Personnel and Police/(202) 226-7641
Procurement and Printing/(202) 225-4568
Task Force on Legislative Service Organizations/(202) 225-2061

* House Committee on Interior and Insular Affairs
1324 Longworth House Office Building
Washington, DC 20515
Topics covered: public lands; national parks and military cemeteries; irrigation; reclamation; U.S. territories and possessions; Indian affair; and regulation of domestic nuclear energy industry.

Subcommittees:
Energy and the Environment/(202) 225-8331
General Oversight and Investigations/(202) 226-4085
Insular and International Affairs/(202) 225-9297
Mining and Natural Resources/(202) 226-7761
National Parks and Public Lands/(202) 226-7736
Water, Power, and Offshore Energy Resources/(202) 225-6042
Indian Affairs Office/(202) 226-7393

* House Committee on the Judiciary
2137 Rayburn House Office Building
Washington, DC 20515 (202) 225-3951
Topics covered: Federal courts; constitutional amendments; immigration and naturalization; Presidential succession; antitrust and monopolies; impeachment resolutions; and patents, trademarks, and copyrights.

Subcommittees:
Administrative Law and Governmental Relations/(202) 225-5741
Civil and Constitutional Rights/(202) 226-7680
Courts, Intellectual Property, and the Administration of Justice/(202) 225-3926
Crime/(202) 225-1695
Criminal Justice/(202) 226-2406
Economic and Commercial Law/(202) 225-2825
Immigration, Refugees, and International Law/(202) 225-5727

Information from Lawmakers

* House Committee on the Merchant Marine and Fisheries
1334 Longworth House Office Building
Washington, DC 20515   (202) 225-4047
Topics covered: regulation and protection of fisheries and wildlife; Coast Guard; merchant marine; and the Panama Canal.

Subcommittees:
Coast Guard and Navigation/(202) 226-3587
Fisheries and Wildlife Conservation and the Environment/(202) 226-3533
Merchant Marine/(202) 226-3500
Oceanography/(202) 226-3504
Oversight and Investigations/(202) 226-3508
Panama Canal and Outer Continental Shelf/(202) 226-3514

* House Committee on the Post Office and Civil Service
309 Cannon House Office Building
Washington, DC 20515   (202) 225-4054
Topics covered: Postal Service; civil service; and Federal statistics.

Subcommittees:
Census and Population/(202) 226-7523
Civil Service/(202) 225-4025
Compensation and Employee Benefits/(202) 226-7546
Human Resources/(202) 225-2821
Investigations/(202) 225-6295
Postal Operations and Services/(202) 225-9124
Postal Personnel and Modernization/(202) 226-7520

* House Committee on Public Works and Transportation
2165 Rayburn House Office Building
Washington, DC 20515   (202) 225-4472
Topics covered: public buildings and roads; bridges and dams; flood control; rivers and harbors; watershed development; mass transit; surface transportation excluding railroads; and civil aviation.

Subcommittees:
Aviation/(202) 225-9161
Economic Development/(202) 225-6151
Investigations and Oversight/(202) 225-3274
Public Buildings and Grounds/(202) 225-9961
Surface Transportation/(202) 225-9989
Water Resources/(202) 225-0060

* House Committee on Rules
H-312 Capitol Building
Washington, DC 20515   (202) 225-9486
Topics covered: resolutions governing the disposition of business on the House floor; rules of the House (except for the House Code of Official Conduct); and waivers relating to legislative deadlines imposed by the Congressional Budget Act.

Subcommittees:
Rules of the House/(202) 225-9091
The Legislative Process/(202) 225-1037

* House Committee on Science, Space, and Technology
2321 Rayburn House Office Building
Washington, DC 20515   (202) 225-6371; FAX 225-8280
Topics covered: astronautical research and development; energy research and development; space; and scientific research and development.

Subcommittees:
Energy Research and Development/(202) 225-2884
Investigations and Oversight/(202) 225-2891
International Scientific Cooperation/(202) 226-3636
Natural Resources, Agriculture Research and Environment/(202) 226-6980
Science, Research, and Technology/(202) 225-1060
Space Science and Applications/(202) 225-7858
Transportation, Aviation, and Materials/(202) 225-8105

* House Committee on Small Business
2361 Rayburn House Office Building
Washington, DC 20515   (202) 225-5821
Topics covered: measures related to small business generally, and to the Small Business Administration.

Subcommittees:
Antitrust, Impact of Deregulation and Privatization/(202) 225-6026
Environment and Labor/(202) 225-7673

Exports, Tax Policy, and Special Problems/(202) 225-8944
Procurement, Tourism, and Rural Development/(202) 225-9368
Regulation, Business Opportunity, and Energy/(202) 225-7797
SBA, The General Economy, and Minority Enterprise Development/(202) 225-5821

* House Committee on Standards of Official Conduct
HT-2, Capitol Building
Washington, DC 20515   (202) 225-7103
Topics covered: enforcement of Code of Official Conduct. The Committee has no subcommittees.

* House Committee on Veterans' Affairs
335 Cannon House Office Building
Washington, DC 20515   (202) 225-3527
Topics covered: veterans' affairs, including pensions, medical care, life insurance, education, and rehabilitation.

Subcommittees:
Hospitals and Health Care/(202) 225-9154
Compensation, Pension, and Insurance/(202) 225-3569
Oversight and Investigations/(202) 225-3541
Education, Training and Employment/(202) 225-9166
Housing and Memorial Affairs/(202) 225-9164

* House Committee on Ways and Means
1102 Longworth House Office Building
Washington, DC 20515   (202) 225-3625
Topics covered: taxation, social security, tariffs, and health care programs financed through payroll taxes.

Subcommittees:
Health/(202) 225-7785
Human Resources/(202) 225-1025
Oversight/(202) 225-5522
Select Revenue Measures/(202) 225-6649
Social Security/(202) 225-3943
Trade/(202) 225-3943

House Investigative Committees and Think Tanks

Many of these House committees conduct hearings and issue reports and recommendations. The Committee on Intelligence, which oversees the Central Intelligence Agency (CIA) and other national security operations, has both investigative and legislative authority. Several of these select committees, such as the Committee on Aging and the Committee on Children, Youth, and Family, will most likely continue their work well into the 1990s. The various political party organizations, such as the Democratic Study Group, issue numerous policy papers on such broad issues as health care, education, and defense. Don't overlook these committees; the staff experts are very knowledgeable.

Permanent Select Committee on Intelligence
Room H-405, The Capitol Building, Washington, DC 20515; (202) 225-4121.
Subcommittees: Legislation/(202) 225-7311;
Oversight and Evaluation/(202) 225-5658; Program and Budget Authorization/(202) 225-7690

Select Committee on Aging
Room H1-712, House Office Building Annex I, 300 New Jersey St., SE, Washington, DC 20515; (202) 226-3375.

Select Committee on Narcotics and Abuse and Control
Room H2-234, House Office Building Annex 2, Second and D Streets, SW, Washington, DC 20515; (202) 226-3040.

Select Committee on Children, Youth, and Families
H2-385 House Office Building Annex 2, Washington, DC 20515; (202) 226-7660.

Select Committee on Hunger
Room H2-507 House Office Building Annex 2, Second and D Sts., SW, Washington, DC 20515; (202) 226-5470.

Federal Government Service Task Force
Room H2-301, House Office Building Annex 2, Washington, DC 20515; (202) 226-2494.

Democratic Congressional Campaign Committee
430 South Capitol St., SE, Washington, DC 20003; (202) 863-1500.

Democratic Steering and Policy Committee
Room H-324, The Capitol Building, Washington, DC 20515; (202) 225-8549.

Democratic Study Group
Room 1422, Longworth House Office Building, Washington, DC 20515; (202) 225-5858.

National Republican Congressional Committee
320 First St., SE, Washington, DC 20003; (202) 479-7000.

Republican Policy Committee
Room 1620 Longworth House Office Building, Washington, DC 20515; (202) 225-6168.

Joint Committees of the U.S. Congress

Congress uses joint committees for study and administrative purposes. Usually joint committees study broad and complex areas of interest to the entire Congress. They are usually permanent bodies composed of an equal number of House and Senate members. Members of these committees are appointed under the provisions of the measure establishing them.

Joint Committee on the Library of Congress
Room H1-103, House Annex I, Washington, DC 20510; (202) 226-7633.

Joint Committee on Printing
Room SH-818, U.S. Hart Senate Office Building, Washington, DC 20510-6650; (202) 224-5241; FAX: 224-1176. Arm of the Committee: Congressional Record Index Office; U.S. Government Printing Office, Room C-738, North Capitol and H Sts., Washington, DC 20401/(202) 275-9009.

Joint Committee on Taxation
Room 1015 Longworth House Office Building, Washington, DC 20515-6453; (202) 225-3621.

Joint Economic Committee
Room SD-G01 Dirksen Senate Office Building, Washington, DC 20510; (202) 224-5171. Subcommittees:
International Economic Policy; National Security Economics; Economic Growth, Trade, and Taxes; Fiscal and Monetary Policy; Economic Goals and Intergovernmental Policy; Economic Resources and Competitiveness; and Investment, Jobs, and Prices Education and Health.

Congressional Budget Office
2nd and D Streets, SW, Washington, DC 20515; (202) 226-2621. This nonpartisan think tank works closely with the House and Senate Budget Committees and helps lawmakers analyze both the fiscal and budgetary consequences of legislation and the interaction between the federal budget and the nation's economy. CBO maintains current tabs of spending actions, prepares cost estimates for bills, provides funding alternatives for bills, reports annual projections for new budget activities, and issues advisory reports that estimate whether the projected deficit exceeds that allowed by law.

Special Interest Congressional Organizations

Congressional Member organizations (CMOs)--commonly known as informal groups, caucuses, coalitions, or ad hoc task forces--are voluntary associations of Members of Congress created to play a role in the policy process. Unlike the formal leadership and party organizations, these groups operate without direct recognition in the chamber rules or line item appropriations. At least 114 congressional Member organizations are currently operating. Listed below are some of the groups which Senators and Congressmen have formed to exercise a stronger voice about certain regional, ethnic, industrial, or other concerns related to their state or congressional district. Some caucuses have a primary mission to disseminate information, while others serve as an informal in-house lobby on various policies. Listed are groups which may be of particular interest to the public as all caucuses produce reports, monitor legislation, and can serve as useful resources.

Adoption, Congressional Coalition on
Room SH-531 Hart Bldg., Washington, DC 20510; (202) 224-2841

Afghanistan, Congressional Task Force on
SH-531 Hart Bldg., Washington, DC 20510; (202) 224-2841

Agricultural Caucus
Northeast-1127 Longworth Bldg., Washington, DC 20515; (202) 225-3665

Agricultural Forum
Congressional-1226 Longworth Bldg., Washington, DC 20510; (202) 225-6605

Air and Space Caucus
Senate-SH-313 Hart Bldg., Washington, DC 20510; (202) 224-6504

Alcohol Fuels Caucus
Congressional-SH-317 Hart Bldg., Washington, DC 20510; (202) 224-2321

Anti-Terrorism Caucus
Senate-SH-520 Hart Bldg., Washington, DC 20510; (202) 224-6542

Arms Control and Foreign Policy Caucus
H2-501 House Office Bldg., Annex 2, Washington, DC 20515; (202) 225-3440

Arts Caucus
Congressional-H2-345 House Office Bldg. Annex 2, Washington, DC 20515; (202) 226-2456

Arts, Concerned Senators for the
SR-140 Senate Russell Bldg., Washington, DC 20510; (202) 224-2315

Automotive Caucus
Congressional-2366 Rayburn Bldg., Washington, DC 20515; (202) 225-2806

Aviation Forum
Congressional-1212 Longworth Bldg., Washington, DC 20515; (202) 225-6216

Balanced Budget, Congressional Leaders United For a
1034 Longworth Bldg., Washington, DC 20515; (202) 225-6611

Baltic States and Ukraine, Ad Hoc Congressional Committee on the
2442 Rayburn Bldg., Washington, DC 20515; (202) 225-6276

Bearing Caucus
Congressional-119 Cannon Bldg., Washington, DC 20515; (202) 225-4476

Beef Caucus
House-118 Cannon Bldg., Washington, DC 20515; (202) 225-6730

Black Caucus
Congressional-H2-344 House Office Bldg. Annex 2, Washington, DC 20515; (202) 226-7790

Border Caucus
Congressional-416 Cannon Bldg., Washington, DC 20515; (202) 225-4831

California Democratic Congressional Delegation
503 House Office Bldg. Annex 1, Washington, DC 20515; (202) 225-6605

Children's Caucus
Senate-SR-444 Russell Bldg., Washington, DC 20510; (202) 224-5630

China Trade Caucus
U.S. Senate-SR-421 Russell Bldg., Washington, DC 20510; (202) 224-2742

Coal Caucus
Senate-SR-173A Russell Bldg., Washington, DC 20510; (202) 224-1160

Corn Caucus, Congressional-SH-331 Hart Bldg., Washington, DC 20510; (202) 224-2854

Crime Caucus
Congressional-SH-303 Hart Bldg., Washington, DC 20510; (202) 224-4254

Drug Enforcement Caucus
Senate-SH-328 Hart Bldg., Washington, DC 20510; (202) 224-4521

Education Study Group, House;Senate International
SR-444 Russell Bldg., Washington, DC 20510; (202) 224-2823

Environmental and Energy Study Conference
H2-515 House Office Bldg. Annex 2, Washington, DC 20515; (202) 226-3300

Ethiopian Jewry, Congressional Caucus for
1536 Longworth Bldg., Washington, DC 20515; (202) 225-2361

Family, Senate Caucus on the
SH-328 Hart Bldg., Washington, DC 20510; (202) 224-4521

Information from Lawmakers

Fire Services Caucus
1233 Longworth Bldg., Washington, DC 20515; (202) 225-2011

Footwear Caucus
House-221 Cannon Bldg., Washington, DC 20515; (202) 225-8273

Forestry 2000 Task Force
431 Cannon Bldg., Washington, DC 20515; (202) 225-5831

Future, Clearinghouse on the, Congressional
H2-555 House Office Bldg., Annex 2, Washington, DC 20515; (202) 226-3434

Hispanic Caucus, Congressional
H2-557 House Office Bldg. Annex 2, Washington, DC 20510;226-3430

Human Rights Caucus, Congressional
H2-552 House Office Bldg., Annex 2, Washington, DC 20515

Human Rights Monitors, Congressional Friends of
2448 Rayburn Bldg., Washington, DC 20515; (202) 225-6465

Insurance Caucus, House
120 Cannon Bldg., Washington, DC 20515; (202) 225-2276

Ireland, Friends of
2229 Rayburn Bldg, Washington, DC 20515; (202) 225-3215

Maritime Caucus
Congressional-H2-531 House Office Bldg. Annex 2, Washington, DC 20515; (202) 226-3500

Military Reform Caucus
307 Cannon Bldg., Washington, DC 20515; (202) 225-5161

Mining Caucus, Congressional
438 Cannon Bldg., Washington, DC 20515; (202) 225-4404

National Security Caucus
SH-328 Hart Bldg., Washington, DC 20515; (202) 484-1677

New York State Congressional Delegation
2108 Rayburn Bldg., Washington, DC 20515; (202) 225-4916

Northeast-Midwest Congressional Coalition
H2-530 House Office Bldg. Annex 2, Washington, DC 20515; (202) 226-3920

Olympic Caucus
1724 Longworth Bldg., Washington, DC 20515; (202) 225-4761

Pennsylvania Congressional Delegation
2186 Rayburn Bldg., Washington, DC 20515

Population and Development, Congressional Coalition
1019 Longworth Bldg., Washington, DC 20515; (202) 225-3571

Populist Caucus, Congressional
328 Cannon Bldg., Washington, DC 20515; (202) 225-5905

Pro-Life Action Task Force for Women, Children, and the Unborn
SH-531 Hart Bldg., Washington, DC 20510; (202) 224-2841

Pro-Life Caucus
2440 Rayburn Bldg., Washington, DC 20515; (202) 225-3765

Rail Caucus, Senate
SR-154 Russell Bldg., Washington, 20510; (202) 224-3244

Rural Caucus, Congressional
2134 Rayburn Bldg., Washington, DC 20515; (202) 225-2876

Rural Health Caucus, Senate
SH-511 Hart Bldg., Washington, DC 20510; (202) 224-2551

Science and Technology, Congressional Caucus for
1717 Longworth Bldg., Washington, DC 20515; (202) 225-5425

Social Security Caucus, Congressional
2407 Rayburn Bldg., Washington, DC 20515; (202) 225-5961

Southern Africa, Congressional Ad Hoc Monitoring Group on
2232 Rayburn Bldg., Washington, DC 20515; (202) 225-3335

Soybean Caucus, Congressional
SH-506 Hart Bldg., Washington, DC 20510; (202) 224-5641

Soviet Jews, Congressional Coalition of
2365 Rayburn Bldg., Washington, DC 20515; (202) 225-7023

Space, Coalition for Peaceful Uses of
2188 Rayburn Bldg., Washington, DC 20515; (202) 225-6161

Space Caucus, Congressional
2188 Rayburn Bldg., Washington, DC 20515; (202) 225-6161

Steel Caucus, Congressional
H2-556 House Office Bldg. Annex 2, Washington, DC 20515; (202) 225-8792

Sunbelt Caucus, Congressional
H2-561 House Office Bldg. Annex 2, Washington, DC 20515; (202) 226-2374

Tennessee Valley Congressional Caucus
125 Cannon Bldg., Washington, DC 20515; (202) 225-6831

Territorial Caucus, Congressional
1130 Longworth Bldg., Washington, DC 20515; (202) 225-1188

Textile Caucus, Congressional
H2-368 House Office Bldg. Annex 2, Washington, DC 20515; (202) 226-3070

Third World Debt Caucus
330 Cannon Bldg., Washington, DC 20515; (202) 225-3661

Travel and Tourism Caucus, Congressional
H2-246 House Office Bldg. Annex 2, Washington, DC 20515; (202) 225-3935

Trucking Caucus, Senate
SD-105 Dirksen Bldg., Washington, DC 20510; (202) 224-4822

Vietnam Era Veterans in Congress
328 Cannon Bldg., Washington, DC 20515; (202) 225-5903

Western State Coalition, Senate
SR-328 Hart Bldg., Washington, DC 20510; (202) 224-4521

Wine Caucus, Senate
SH-720 Hart Bldg., Washington, DC 20510; (202) 224-3841

Women's Issues, Congressional Caucus for
2471 Rayburn Bldg., Washington, DC 20515; (202) 225-6740

For the latest information about the formation of new congressional caucuses or your Member of Congress by calling the Capitol Hill Switchboard Operator at (202) 224-3121.

Legislative Branch Sources

In addition to the powerful information sources of congressional committees and think tanks, the office of your U.S. Senators and Representatives can be very helpful. In this section you'll also find out where to find financial information on federal campaign finance, television coverage of Congress, congressional salaries, and even how to get a flag that was raised over the U.S. Capitol.

* Bicentennial Celebration and Free Publications

The Office of the Historian
House of Representatives
138 Cannon Building
Washington, DC 20515-6701   (202) 225-1153

The Office of the Historian acts as a clearinghouse for historical information on the House of Representatives, for the Members, the public, and the press. The Office periodically publishes a newsletter, *History in the House*, and books and other reference information. The following publications are available free of charge from the Office:

A Guide to Research Collections of Former Members of the U.S. House of Representatives 1789-1987
Black Americans in Congress
Women in Congress
Origins of the U.S. House of Representatives: A Documentary Record
A Brief Architectural History of the U.S. Capitol

* Bills and Laws: Document Rooms

House Document Room
The Capitol, Room H-226
Washington, DC 20515   (202) 225-3456
Senate Document Room
Senate Hart Office Bldg., Room B-04
Washington, DC 20510   (202) 224-7860

Free copies of all bills introduced in the House and Senate are available. Legislation approved by committees and also passed by the full House and/or Senate along with committee reports are available free of charge. To request a bill, you must send a self-addressed mailing label and include the bill number or report number. No more than six requests may be presented at a time. Requests for Senate documents may be made to either of your Senators, and your Representative can get copies of House bills and reports. The Document Rooms maintain current files of legislation including public laws (slip laws). Periodically public laws on a variety of subject areas are compiled and are available for $157 per session from the Government Printing Office.

* Biographical Directory of the U.S. Congress 1774-1989

Superintendent of Documents
Government Printing Office
Washington, DC 20402   (202) 783-3238

The Biographical Directory of the U.S. Congress 1774-1989, contains authoritative biographies of the more than 11,000 men and women who have served in the U.S. Congress from 1789 to 1989, and in the Continental Congress between 1774 and 1789. Many features include a listing of all chairmen of standing committees, all major formal leadership positions, bibliographic citations, and major revisions of political party affiliations reflecting the latest scholarship. You'll also find complete rosters of State congressional delegations for the First through 100th Congresses. This bicentennial edition is the most comprehensive *Biographical Directory of the United States Congress* ever issued. The latest edition published at the beginning of the 101st Congress is available through the Government Printing Office for $82.

* Calendar of the House of Representatives and History of Legislation

Superintendent of Documents
Government Printing Office
Washington, DC 20402   (202) 783-3238
House Document Room
The Capitol, Room H-226
Washington, DC 20515   (202) 225-3456

This calendar contains a list of bills in conference, a list of bills through conference, the *Union Calendar*, the *House Calendar*, a history of actions on each bill of the current session, a subject index of active legislation, and more. It is a weekly (when Congress is in session) publication available on subscription for $159 a year. Free copies can be picked up at the House Document Room.

* Campaign Finance Information

Press Office
Federal Election Commission
999 E Street, NW
Washington, DC 20463   (202) 376-3155

Staff of the Press Office are the FEC's official media spokespersons. In addition to publicizing FEC actions and releasing statistics on campaign finance, they respond to all questions from representatives of the print and broadcast media.

* Campaign Finance Records

Public Records Office
Federal Election Commission
999 E Street, NW
Washington, DC 20463   (202) 376-3140

Commission disclosure of campaign finance activity is based on the reports submitted by political committees. These reports, available from the Public Records Office within 48 hours of receipt as required by law, focus on the flow of money in and out of campaigns and the sources of campaign support.

* Compilation of All Legislation

Congressional Research Service
Bill Digest Section
Library of Congress
Washington, DC 20540   (202) 707-6996

The *Digest Public General Bills and Resolutions* provides summaries of public bills and resolutions and their current status in order of introduction in Congress. The *Digest* includes subject, author, and title. Subscription service consists of cumulative issues for each session of each Congress (two sessions per Congress). Prices per issue vary but average around $40. Subscription information is available from the Superintendent of Documents, Government Printing Office, Washington, D.C. 20402; (202) 783-3238.

* Congress and the Nation

Clerk of the House
House of Representatives
The Capitol
Washington, DC 20515   (202) 225-7000

Congress and the Nation is a summary of material in the *Congressional Quarterly Almanac*. *Volume I* covers the years 1945-1964; thereafter, it is published every four years.

* Congressional Directory

Superintendent of Documents
Government Printing Office
Washington, DC 20402   (202) 783-3238

The *Congressional Directory* has been the official handbook for the Congress since 1821 and is also widely used by Federal agency officials and the general public. Its contents include lists of addresses, rooms, and phone numbers of Members, biographical sketches of Members, Capitol officers and officials, committees, departments, and information on diplomatic offices and statistics. It also includes lists of members of the press admitted to the House and Senate galleries. The *1989-1990 Official Congressional Directory of the 101st Congress* is available for $15 in paperback, $20 in hardback, and $25 for a hardback copy with a thumb index.

* Congressional Documents, Reports, and Hearings

Law Library
Library of Congress
Washington, DC 20540   (202) 707-5079

All Senate and House documents, reports, hearings since 1970, and all bills back to the First Congress are available. Material can be obtained on microfilm.

* Congressional Leaders and Presiding Officers

Ceremonial Office of the Vice President

Information from Lawmakers

Old Executive Office Bldg, Room 272
Washington, DC 20006   (202) 456-6605

Speaker's Office
Room H-204, The Capitol
Washington, DC 20510   (202) 225-8040

Senate Majority Leader
Room S-221, The Capitol
Washington, DC 20510   (202) 224-5556

The Vice President of the United States is the Presiding Officer of the Senate, and in his absence the duties are taken over by a President pro tempore, elected by that body, or someone designated by him. The Presiding Officer of the House of Representatives, the Speaker, is elected by the House; he may designate any Member of the House to act in his absence. The Senate Majority Leader is elected at the beginning of each new Congress by a majority vote of the Senators in the political party which controls the Senate. In cooperation with their party organizations, leaders are responsible for the design and achievement of a legislative program involving legislation, expediting noncontroversial measures, and keeping Members informed regarding proposed action on pending business. The Majority Leader serves as an ex officio member of this party's policy making and organizational bodies and is aided by an assistant floor leader (whip) and a party secretary.

* Congressional Record:
House and Senate Floor Debate

The Superintendent of Documents
Government Printing Office
Washington, DC 20402   (202) 275-3030

Proceedings of Congress are published in the *Congressional Record*, which is issued when Congress is in session. Publication of the *Record* began in March of 1873; it was the first record of debate officially reported, printed, and published directly by the Federal Government. The *Daily Digest of the Congressional Record*, printed in the back of each issue of the *Record*, summarizes the proceedings of that day in each House, and before each of their committees and subcommittees, respectively. The *Digest* also presents the legislative program for each day and, at the end of the week, gives the program for the following week. The subscription price is $225 per year. For information on the Senate portion of the *Congressional Record*, call (202) 224-2658; for the House portion, call (202) 224-5848; for information on committee activities, call Senate (202) 224-2120; House (202) 225-4470.

* Congressional Record Index

House Documents Room
The Capitol, Room H-226
Washington, DC 20515   (202) 225-3456

About once every two weeks, the *Congressional Record Index* is distributed listing *Congressional Record* matters by subject, member, bill number, bill title and every other sort of cross-reference combination. For instance, you can look up a member's name and find everything he or she introduced, made remarks on, submitted, reported, and gave a speech about. You can also look up a subject and find all related articles, editorials, bills, letters, tables, and press releases included during the previous two weeks in the *Congressional Record*.

* Congressional Telephone Directories

The Superintendent of Documents
Government Printing Office
Washington, DC 20402   (202) 275-3030

Telephone directories for the U.S. Senate and the House of Representatives are available for sale. Abbreviated pamphlets providing Members and committees telephone numbers and
addresses are available from the Secretary of the Senate and the Clerk of the House.

* Daily Congressional Schedule

Published weekdays in the *Washington Post* newspaper, the *Today in Congress* column gives a daily rundown on times and subjects of all House and Senate committee hearings and meetings and indicates which are open to the public.

* Election Assistance

Federal Election Commission
Information Services
999 E Street, NW
Washington, DC 20463   (202) 376-3120

In an effort to promote voluntary compliance with the law, this office provides technical assistance to candidates and committees and others involved in elections. Staff will research and answer questions on the Federal Election Campaign Act and FEC regulations, procedures, and advisory opinions; direct workshops on the law; and publish a wide range of materials.

* Federal Election Commission Publications

Federal Election Commission
Information Services
999 E Street, NW   (800) 424-9530
Washington, DC 20463   (202) 376-3120

The following publications are available free of charge from the FEC:

Federal Election Campaign Laws. A complete compilation of Federal election campaign laws.
FEC Regulations. FEC regulations appear in Title 11 of the Code of Federal Regulations, including subject indexes.
FEC Record. This monthly newsletter is the primary source of information on FEC activity, covering reporting, advisory opinions, litigation, legislation, statistics, regulations compliance, and more.
FEC Annual Report.
Supporting Federal Candidates: A Guide for Citizens. For the general public, this booklet discusses how citizens can support Federal candidates through contributions, volunteer work, and independent expenditures.
The First 10 Years. Graphs and text describe the FEC's work during its first decade, including a brief history of campaign finance legislation and an overview of FEC operations.
Campaign Guides. Four separate guides explain how the law affects candidates, parties, corporations/unions, and nonconnected PACs. Election law requirements are explained and illustrated with examples of completed FEC forms.
The FEC and the Federal Campaign Finance Law. Gives a brief overview of the major provisions of the Federal Election Campaign Act and the FEC's role in administering it.
Public Funding of Presidential Elections. For the general public, this brochure gives a brief history of Presidential public funding and describes how the process works.
Using FEC Campaign Finance Information. Explains how to gather information about the financial activity of Federal political committees. It describes FEC's computer indexes and ways to use them.

* Federal Campaign Finance Law Complaints

Federal Election Commission
999 E Street, NW
Washington, DC 20463   (202) 376-5140

If you believe a violation of the Federal campaign finance law has taken place, you may file a complaint with the Federal Election Commission. Send the Commission a letter explaining why you believe the law may have been violated, describe the specific facts and circumstances, and name the individuals or organizations responsible. The letter must be sworn to, signed, and notarized. Complaints of alleged violations receive case numbers and are called MURs, Matters Under Review.

* Federal Elections Clearinghouse

Federal Election Commission
999 E Street, NW
Washington, DC 20463   (202) 376-5670

The Election Clearinghouse assists election officials and the general public by responding to inquiries concerning the electoral process, publishing research, and conducting workshops on all matters related to Federal election administration.

* Federal Elections Library

Federal Election Commission Library
999 E Street, NW
Room 801
Washington, DC 20463   (202) 376-5312

The FEC Library's collection includes basic legal research tools and materials dealing with political campaign finance, corporate and labor political activity, and campaign finance reform. The Library staff prepares indexes to Advisory Opinions and Matters Under Review (MURs), as well as a *Campaign Finance and Federal Election Law Bibliography*, which are available for purchase from the FEC's Public Records Office.

* Financial Disclosure Database
on Federal Candidates

Federal Election Commission
Data Systems Development Division
999 E Street, NW
Washington, DC 20463   (202) 376-3140

The FEC maintains a computer database of information from all reports filed by political committees, individuals, and other entities since 1972. The data is sorted into indexes which permit a detailed analysis of campaign finance activity and, additionally, provide a tool for monitoring contribution limitations. The data can be searched by specific candidate or contributor. By contacting this office, individuals can have searches done on twenty names or less free of charge. For searches of more than 20 names, cost varies depending on computer time needed.

* GAO Congressional Staff Assignments
Congressional Relations
General Accounting Office
441 G St., NW, Room 7025
Washington, DC 20548   (202) 275-5456
Each year GAO assigns between 75 to 125 staff members directly to Congressional committees to help carry out their responsibilities or to assist them in using the results of GAO studies. In addition, GAO provides staff assistance to committees having jurisdiction over revenues, appropriations, and expenditures, and often to other committees as well. The agency does not, however, assign staff to individual members of Congress.

* General Accounting Office Bibliographic Database
GAO/IHSF
P.O. Box 6015
Gaithersburg, MD 20877   (202) 275-5042
The GAO maintains a database which provides bibliographic information on GAO documents and reports. The studies cover a vast array of subjects, as the agency must produce a report on any topic Congress assigns. Reports have ranged from financial audits of government agencies to policy studies of health-related programs. Searches are generally conducted by subject area and specific time period. Searches and printouts are available free of charge by calling (202) 275-6241. GAO will also mail you up to five copies of any report listed, without charge. Each copy requested beyond that is $2. Contact the office above for information regarding the contents of the reports.

* History of the Senate
Senate Historical Office
Secretary of the Senate
The Capitol, Room SH 201
Washington, DC 20510   (202) 224-6900
The Senate Historical Office collects and disseminates information on Senate history and Senate members, including photographs, unpublished documents, and oral history. A free newsletter, *Senate History*, is available, as well as a series of addresses to the Senate on subjects related to its history and traditions, including a list of citations with dates, subjects, and page numbers.

* House Committees Roster
Clerk of the House
House of Representatives
The Capitol
Washington, DC 20515   (202) 225-7000
This listing contains all official and unofficial House committees. The members of each committee are included.

* House Leadership and Ceremonial Posts
Office of the House Majority Leader
Room H-114, The Capitol
Washington, DC 20515   (202) 225-5604
Office of the House Republican Leader
Room H-232, The Capitol
Washington, DC 20515   (202) 225-0600
The leadership of the House of Representatives is elected at the beginning of each Congress. Under the tradition of the two party system in the United States, the leader of the party with the largest number of Members becomes the Majority Leader. The Minority Leader is invariably the Member nominated by the minority party for the Senate.

Sergeant at Arms of the House
Room H-124, The Capitol
Washington, DC 20515   (202) 225-2456
This office enforces the rules of the house and maintains decorum during sessions of the House. The Sergeant at Arms also is in charge of the Mace, the symbol of legislative power and authority. Maintaining the general security of the House buildings and the Capitol is his major responsibility. Another major responsibility is management of the House bank which disburses Members' salaries and travel expenses.

Clerk of the House
Room H-105, The Capitol
Washington, DC 20515   (202) 225-7000
The Clerk is the chief legislative, administrative, and budgetary officer of the U.S. House of Representatives. The Clerk is responsible for directing legislative activities of the House, such as keeping the Journal, taking all votes, certifying passage of bills, and processing all legislation. The Clerk also prepares the budget for the House, disburses funds, serves as the contracting officer of the House, and issues a report available to the public on salaries and expenses. In addition, the Clerk is the purchaser and provider of all furnishings, office equipment, and office supplies.

Doorkeeper of the House
Room H-154, The Capitol
Washington, DC 20515   (202) 225-3505
The Doorkeeper is responsible for physical arrangements for joint sessions and joint meetings of the Congress, announcements of messages from the President and the Senate, announcement of the arrival of the President when he addresses Congress in person, and escorting dignitaries visiting the Capitol.

Chaplain of the House
Room HB-25, The Capitol
Washington, DC 20515   (202) 225-2509
The Chaplain is responsible for the opening prayer at each session of the House, and occasionally invites other clergy to serve as guest chaplains. The Chaplain's Office also coordinates use of the Prayer Room and makes arrangements for pastoral services for Members and staff.

* House of Representatives Research and Library
U.S. House of Representatives and Committees Library
Cannon House Office Bldg., Room B 18
Washington, DC 20515   (202) 225-0462
This library is the official depository of House documents, reports, bills, and more. Its primary function is to serve House members and their staffs. It is open to the public, but no photocopying is permitted.

* House Telephone Directory
Superintendent of Documents
Government Printing Office
Washington, DC 20402   (202) 275-3030
The Committee on House Administration
The Capitol, Room H-326
Washington, DC 20515   (202) 225-2061
The *House Telephone Directory* is produced yearly by the Committee on House Administration. It provides a listing for representatives, a listing for House committees, an alphabetical staff listing, a listing of staffs by representatives, a listing of staffs by committee, listings for senators and Senate committees, a listing for executive branch leaders, a listing for government agencies, and more. It is available for $14.00 from the Superintendent of Documents.

* How Our Laws Are Made
Superintendent of Documents
Government Printing Office
Washington, DC 20402   (202) 275-3030
The booklet, *How Our Laws Are Made*, is prepared by the House of Representatives and provides a plain language explanation of how a legislative idea travels the complex passageways of the federal lawmaking process to become a statute. It is available for $2.50 from the Superintendent of Documents.

* Legislative Archives
National Archives and Records Administration
8th St. & Pennsylvania Ave., NW, Room 307
Washington, DC 20408   (202) 523-4185
The Legislative Archives Center is responsible for the appraisal, preservation, arrangement, description, reference service, and outreach activities associated with all records of the U.S. Senate, House of Representatives, congressional committees, and agencies. The Center includes the Legislative Reference Branch, which provides reference services to Congress and the public pertaining to congressional records, and the Legislative Projects Branch, which has just completed writing two guides to the congressional records.

* Legislative Branch Audit Site
Legislative Branch Audit Site
Accounting and Financial Management Division
General Accounting Office
2nd & D Sts., SW
Washington, DC 20515   (202) 226-2480
This office assists Congress by doing 15 regular annual financial audits of such units as the House Recording Studio and the Senate Restaurant. On a less formal basis, the staff also offers advice and assistance on administrative matters. For free copies (up to five) of Audit Site reports, contact: Information Handling and Support Facilities, General Accounting Office, P.O. Box 6015, Gaithersburg, MD 20877; (202) 275-6241.

* Legislative Histories and Research
Law Library
Library of Congress, LM240
Washington, DC 20540   (202) 707-5065
The Law Library compiles legislative histories which include versions of new public statutes from the time of introduction, through congressional hearings, House and Senate floor debate, vote tallies, and votes.

Information from Lawmakers

* Live TV Coverage of House and Senate Chambers

Cable Satellite Public Affairs Network (C-SPAN)
400 North Capitol St., NW, Suite 650
Washington, DC 20001   (202) 737-3220

C-SPAN is a basic cable service specializing for more than a decade in the coverage of Congress. It shows lawmaking in the raw on Capitol Hill. Created to provide live gavel-to-gavel coverage of the U.S. House of Representatives C-SPAN II began in 1986 to cablecast the live sessions off the U.S. Senate, in their entirety. In addition, C-SPAN offers a front row seat to other public events from the nation's capitol and across the country. Events are aired without commentary or analysis. Each morning at 8 and each evening at 6:30, the network presents "Viewer Call-in" where viewer's questions about major news events are discussed. To receive C-SPAN call your local cable company.

* Monthly Checklist of State Publications

Exchange and Gift Division
State Documents Section
Library of Congress
Washington, DC 20540   (202) 707-9468

The *Monthly Checklist of State Publications* lists documents and publications received in the Library of Congress that are issued by the administrative, judicial, and legislative branches and state university systems of the states and territories. The subscription price is $32.00 per year and can be purchased from the Superintendent of Documents, Government Printing Office, Washington, D.C. 20402; (202) 783-3238.

* New Federal Laws

Office of the Federal Register
National Archives and Records Administration
8th St. & Pennsylvania Ave., NW, Room 8401
Washington, DC 20408   (202) 523-5230

This office receives all the laws enacted by Congress for publication in the Federal Register and can provide information regarding these laws. They also publish *United States at Large*, a compilation of laws enacted during a particular year.

* New Laws: Free Copies of these Statutes

House Documents Room
The Capitol, Room H-226
Washington, DC 20515   (202) 225-3456

The 101st Congress has passed only 149 laws to date. For a complete listing of the new laws passed by the 101th Congress, contact the House Documents Room and ask for a House Calendar which will list the new laws and their bill numbers.

* Online Access to FEC Financial Database

Federal Election Commission
Press Office
999 E Street, NW   (800) 424-9530
Washington, DC 20463   (202) 376-3155

The FEC offers an online computer information system designed for owners of personal computers. The system furnishes campaign finance information in formatted computer indexes and in raw data form. For a specific candidate or committee, the system provides the following information for election cycles beginning in 1985: total receipts and expenditures; total cash on hand; and total debts owed. Contact this office for more information on accessing this information.

* Photographs of Every Member of Congress

The Superintendent of Documents
Government Printing Office
Washington, DC 20402   (202) 275-3030

The *Congressional Pictorial Directory* contains photographs of the President, Vice President, members of the Senate and House, Officers of the Senate and House, Officials of the Capitol, and a list of the Senate delegations and an alphabetical list of senators and representatives. The paperback edition is $4.24, and the hardback copy is $14.00.

* Presidential Political Appointments: The "Plum" Book

Senate Government Affairs Committee
Dirksen Office Building, Room S-340
Washington, DC 20510   (202) 224-3791
Superintendent of Documents
Government Printing Office
Washington, DC 20402   (202) 275-3030

U.S. Policy and Supporting Positions, more commonly known as the *Plum Book*, lists some 3,000 political appointment jobs and describes the type of appointment, tenure, grade, and salary. It is available for sale at the Superintendent of Documents for $14 per copy.

* Public Laws Tape Recording

Office of the Federal Register
National Archives and Records Administration
8th St. & Pennsylvania Ave., NW, Room 8401
Washington, DC 20408   (202) 523-6641

This recording lists the most recent laws which have come to the office for publication in the *Federal Register*.

* Published Congressional Hearings

Documents Clerk
Relevant House and Senate Committee   (202) 224-3121
Superintendent of Documents
Government Printing Office
Washington, DC 20402   (202) 783-3238

House and Senate committees and subcommittees conduct hundreds of informational and investigative hearings practically every week of the year. All of these congressional hearings are published and often available free of charge from the documents clerk of the committee or subcommittee which held the hearings. Many of the hearings also are sold by the Superintendent of Documents.

* Radio Coverage of Committee Hearings and International Events

C-SPAN Audio Networks
400 North Capitol St., NW, Suite 650
Washington, DC 20001   (202) 737-3220

The C-SPAN Audio Networks were created to provide audio coverage of congressional committee hearings and other public affairs events. They are intended to supplement the round-the-clock floor coverage of the House and Senate provided by the C-SPAN and C-SPAN II cable television networks. In addition, the Audio Networks air international public affairs events through retransmissions of foreign English-language shortwave radio programming. C-SPAN Audio I combines the Washington, D.C., and international programming. Future audio programming will provide historical perspective through programming of public events from the past, drawn from the National Archives and other Sources. C-SPAN Audio 2 provides 24-hour retransmissions of the BBC World Service.

* Raise a Flag Over the Capitol

c/o The Capitol
Washington, DC 20515   (202) 224-3121

You can arrange to purchase flags that have been flown over the Capitol by getting in touch with your U.S. Senator or Representative. A certificate signed by the Architect of the Capitol accompanies each flag. Flags are available for purchase in sizes of 3'x5' or 5'x8' in fabrics of cotton and nylon.

* Salaries and Expenses of House of Representatives

Members and Employees
House Document Room
H-226 Capitol Bldg.
Washington, DC 20515   (202) 225-3456

The *Report of the Clerk of the House* includes the salaries of House members' staffs, committee staffs, and House officers and employees. This quarterly report includes a listing of House expenditures.

* Salaries and Expenses of U.S. Senators and Their Staff

Senate Document Room
B-04 Senate Hart Office Building
Washington, DC 20510   (202) 224-7860

The biannual *Report of the Secretary of the* Senate lists expenditures and details the salaries of senators' staff, members, committee staff members, and officers and employees of the Senate.

* Senate Committees Roster

Office of the Secretary of the Senate
The Capitol, Room S-221
Washington, DC 20510   (202) 224-2115

A listing is available of official Senate committees. These include the members of each committee. Also available is the *Unofficial List of Senators*, which gives the names of all Senators, their states, their party affiliations, and the year they are up for reelection.

* Senate Leadership or Ceremonial Posts

Senate Minority Leader
Room S-230, The Capitol
Washington, DC 20510   (202) 224-3135

The Minority Leader is elected at the beginning of each new Congress by the Senators in the political party which does not have a working majority in the Senate. This leader works closely with its party organizations and currently with the White House in terms of getting the President's legislative program enacted.

Secretary of the Senate

Room S-208, The Capitol
Washington, DC 20510   (202) 224-2115

The Secretary is the custodian of the seal of the Senate, and handles the payroll for the Senators, officers, committee staff, and employees, and issues a report disclosing such salaries and expenses. The Secretary's executive duties include certification of extracts from the Journal of the Senate; the attestation of bills and joint, concurrent, and Senate resolutions; in impeachment trials, issuance, under the authority of the Presiding Officer, of all orders, mandates, writs, and precepts, authorized by the Senate; and certification of the President of the United States of the advice and consent of the Senate to ratification of treaties and the names of persons confirmed or rejected upon the nomination of the President.

Sergeant at Arms of the Senate

Room S-321, The Capitol
Washington, DC 20510   (202) 224-2341; FAX: 224-7690

The Senate elects the Sergeant at Arms who serves as its Executive Officer. As law enforcement officer, the Sergeant of Arms has statutory power to make arrests; to locate absentee Senators for a quorum; and to enforce Senate rules and regulations. As Protocol Officer, he is responsible for many aspects of ceremonial functions, including the Presidential inauguration; funeral arrangements of Senators who die in office; escorting the President when he addresses a Joint Session of Congress or attends any function in the Senate; and escorting heads of state when they visit the Senate.

Chaplain of the Senate

Room SH-204, Hart Senate Office Bldg.
Washington, DC 20510   (202) 224-2510

The Chaplain of the Senate serves as pastor to the Senators and their families. He opens the sessions of the Senate each day with a prayer. His office is a resource center for information concerning the Bible, various religious denominations, and the subject of religion in general.

* Senate Research and Library

Senate Library
The Capitol, Suite S-332
Washington, DC 20510   (202) 224-7106

The Senate Library is the official depository of senate documents. Its primary function is service to Senate members and their staffs. To use the library a researcher must have a letter of introduction from a Senator.

* State Access to Financial Disclosure Database

Federal Election Commission
Public Records Office
999 E Street, NW
Washington, DC 20463   (202) 376-3140

Under the State Access Program, individuals and organizations in 15 states now have immediate online access to several standard FEC computer indexes which provide descriptive information on all registered political committees, the total receipts and disbursements of committees, and a listing of all PAC contributions to federal candidates. Participating states with operational terminals within their State Election Offices include: Arizona, Colorado, Connecticut, Georgia, Illinois, Iowa, Massachusetts, Michigan, New Jersey, New Mexico, Ohio, Tennessee, Vermont, Washington, and Wisconsin.

* State Election Finance Records

Federal Election Commission
Public Records Office
999 E Street, NW   (800) 424-9530
Washington, DC 20463   (202) 376-3155

Researchers can obtain campaign finance reports from the records office in each state. Contact this FEC office to order a list of the names, addresses, and phone numbers of national and state disclosure offices.

* Treaties and Nominations

Senate Document Room
Hart Building, Room B-04
Washington, DC 20510   (202) 225-6827

For information on and copies of treaties submitted to the Senate for ratification, contact the Senate Document Room or your Senators.

* U.S. Senate Manual

Superintendent of Documents
Government Printing Office
Washington, DC 20402   (202) 275-3030

Senate Committee on Rules and Administration
Russell Senate Office Building, Room 305
Washington, DC 20510   (202) 224-6352

The biennial *Senate Manual* includes *Jefferson's Manual*, standing rules, orders, and laws and resolutions affecting the business of the U.S. Senate. A list of senators and members of the Executive Branch is also provided. It is published every two years with each new Congress, and sells for $24 from the Superintendent of Documents.

* World's Largest Law Library

Law Library
Library of Congress
Washington, DC 20540   (202) 707-5073

As the world's largest and most comprehensive library of foreign, international, and comparative law, the Law Library provides information for all known legal systems including common law, civil law, Roman law, canon law, Chinese law, Jewish and Islamic law, and ancient and medieval law. Specialists with knowledge of more than fifty languages provide reference and research service in all known legal systems. U.S. legislative documents housed here include the *Congressional Record* (and its predecessors), the serial set, a nearly complete set of bills and resolutions, current documents, committee prints, reports, hearings, etc. plus a complete set of U.S. Supreme Court records and briefs and collections of U.S. Court of Appeals records and briefs. The law library has five major divisions:

American-British Law

United States, Australia, Canada, Great Britain, India, New Zealand, Pakistan, certain other countries of the British Commonwealth and their dependent territories, and Eire: (202) 707-5077.

European Law

Nations of Europe and their possessions, except Spain and Portugal: (202) 707-5088.

Hispanic Law

Spain and Portugal, Latin America, Puerto Rico, the Philippines, and Spanish- and Portuguese-language states of Africa: (202) 707-5070.

Far Eastern Law

Nations of East and Southeast Asia including China, Indonesia, Japan, Korea, Thailand, and former British and French possessions in the area: (202) 707-5085.

Near Eastern and African Law

Middle Eastern countries, including the Arab states, Turkey, Iran, and Afghanistan, and all African countries, except Spanish- and Portuguese-language states and possessions: (202) 707-5073.

Information from Lawmakers

Tracking State Legislation

* See also Information Starting Places; State Information Starting Places Chapter
* See also Current Events and Homework Chapter

Bill Status Information

Most state legislatures maintain an office responsible for providing bill status information to the public. In Ohio, for example, a bank of telephone reference experts answer questions about current or past legislation on any given subject. The researchers rely on their own files and also have access to a computerized database updated by the Senate Clerk's office. Usually these offices can search their databases or indexes in several ways, by keyword or phrase, by specific subject, or by state senator or representative.

About half of the legislatures can send you this information in the form of a computer printout free of charge. In those states which do not operate a central bill status office, it is necessary to contact the Clerk of the House for information on bills pending before the House and similarly a call to the Secretary or Clerk of the Senate for updates on legislation pending before that body. Many legislatures have toll-free numbers which can be accessed only if you are calling from inside the state. Most of the State House hotlines operate just during the regular session of the legislature and, as you might expect, some of the "800" numbers change from one session to the next.

Your initial call to the bill status office will lead you to the appropriate committees, and if no action has been taken on a particular bill, this legislative information office can provide you with the sponsor of the legislation whom you can call directly for more details.

Copies of Bill and Other Legislative Documents

In most states, the legislative information office can send you copies of bills. Indiana is the only state that charges $.10 per page if the bill is more than 10 pages long. All states print the bills at the time of introduction. Over half reprint the amended legislation after committee action, and about two-thirds of all chambers print the legislation after the floor vote. Unlike the U.S. Congress, legislative documentation is skimpy when it comes to committee hearings as well as floor debate. Only about a third of all legislative bodies   tape all committee sessions. You can make arrangements with the Clerk's office to listen to the tapes, and some states, like the Minnesota House, sell audio tapes of committee meetings and floor debates for $12.50 per copy.

Advanced Strategy for Monitoring One or All 50 State Legislatures

Coverage of a state legislature can be substantially enhanced in a number of ways; some are inexpensive and others can be costly:

* Clipping Service:
Newspapers, especially those published in the state capitol, can prove to be a cost effective way of staying informed provided the issues of concern with are controversial or of major significance to capture attention by the local media.

* Local Chamber of Commerce:
This organization may offer information about certain issues it is following on behalf of the business community.

* Stringers:
Often expensive, but there may be no substitute for hiring someone who is in frequent contact with legislators and is a familiar face in the document rooms and statehouse corridors.

* Governor's Legislative Liaison Office:
On major legislative initiatives and politically "hot" issues, try telephoning this office.

* National Conference of State Legislators (NCSL):
Although this organization serves legislators, the staff will respond to requests from the public. The Conference maintains a list of reports and studies by investigative committees in all 50 states. Access to its in-house database may be possible in the future. This national organization of state legislators and legislative staff whose aims are to improve the quality and effectiveness of state legislators, to ensure states a strong, cohesive voice in the federal decision-making process and to foster interstate communication and cooperation. Contact either of the two offices at 1050 17th Street, Suite 2100, Denver, CO 80265; (303) 623-7800; or 444 North Capitol St., NW, Suite 500, Washington, D.C. 20001; (202) 624-5400.

* Council of State Governments/State Information Center:
This arm of the Council of State Governments publishes several useful directories, including *The Book of States*, *State Administration Officials Classified By Function*, and *State Legislative Leadership Committees and Staff*. Its database may soon be available to the public. Contact: State Information Center, Council of State Governments, P.O. Box 11910, Iron Works Pike, Lexington, KY 40578; (606) 252-2291.

* Commerce Clearing House (CCH):
CCH offers the "State Legislative Reporting Service" as well as the Electronic Legislative Search System. The Reporting Service allows you to select only those legislatures you are interested in, whereas the online search system tracks all current legislation in all 50 states. Contact: CCH, 4025 West Peterson Avenue, Chicago, IL 60646; (312) 583-8500.

* Information for Public Affairs:
This private firm offers online access to its database containing the status of legislation pending before the current session of all 50 state legislatures.   Contact: PAI, 1900 14th St., Sacramento, CA 95814; (916)444-0840.

* Other Private Legislative Reporting Services:

Legi-Tech Corporation and other firms specialize in tracking one or two statehouses. About half of the legislatures are covered by such information brokers.

Reports And Resources Available From State Legislatures

A trend among state legislatures is the creation of special investigative committees which have responsibility for oversight and often the power to subpoena. These watchdogs usually have permanent full-time staff and produce reports throughout the year. Frequent contact with these committees is necessary to stay informed about their activities.

Here is a sampling of reports issued by the Virginia Joint Legislative Audits and Review Committee:

Outpatient Care in Virginia
Medical Assistance Programs in Virginia: An Overview
Homes for Adults in Virginia
Social Services (including day care) in Virginia
Vehicle Cost Responsibility in Virginia
Highway Construction, Maintenance, and Transit Needs
The Occupational and Professional Regulatory System
Consolidation of Office Space in Northern Virginia
Special Report: Use of State-Owned Aircraft
Towns in Virginia
Virginia's Correctional System: Population Forecasting

Even those legislatures that compress their work into sixty or ninety day sessions are active year-round. Information about hearings, meetings, and reports produced throughout the Interim can be provided by each state house legislative information office.

State Legislatures:
Bill Status Information Offices

You will find more than 50 information offices listed here because some state houses do not have one centralized legislature reference office.

Alabama

Senate Bill Status, New State House, Montgomery, AL 36130; (205) 261-7826. This office can respond to questions about all Senate bills and refer you to the appropriate committee, document room, etc.

House Bill Status, New State House, Montgomery, AL 36130; (205) 261-7630. This office can provide information on all bills pending before the House of Representatives and can refer you to the appropriate committees, document rooms, etc.

Alaska

Legislative Information, P.O. Box Y, Juneau, AK 99811; (907) 465-4648. This office can provide information on the status of House and Senate bills. It can do subject searches by accessing a database but at this time Legislative Information cannot provide computer printouts. Copies of bills will be sent out by this office.

Arizona

Information Desk, House of Representatives, State House, 1700 West Washington Street, Phoenix, AZ 85007; (602) 542-4221. This Information Desk is the best starting point to learn the status of all bills pending before the House of Representatives. This office will refer you to the appropriate committees, document room, etc.

Senate Information Desk, State House, 1700 West Washington Street, Phoenix, AZ 85007; (602) 542-3559. This Information Desk maintains current information on all bills pending before the Arizona Senate. This office will refer you to the appropriate committees, document rooms, etc.

Arkansas

Office of Legislative Counsel, State Capitol Building, Room 315, Little Rock, AR 72201; (501) 612-1937. This office can provide status information on all legislation pending before the House of Representatives and the Senate. It also has scheduling information and can you refer you to the appropriate committees, document rooms, etc.

California

Office of the Chief Clerk, State Assembly, State Capitol, Room 3196, Sacramento, CA 95814; (916) 445-3614. This office can respond to questions regarding legislation pending before the State Assembly and Assembly committees. This office can refer you to the appropriate offices in the State Capitol such as the document rooms.

Secretary of the Senate, State Capitol, Sacramento, CA 95814; (916) 445-4251. This office can provide information about bills pending before the Senate and the Senate committees. The Secretary of the Senate also will refer you to appropriate offices in the State Capitol such as where to obtain copies of Senate bills.

Colorado

Legislative Information Center, State Capitol Building, Room 0101, 200 E. Colfax Ave., Denver, CO 80203; (303) 866-3055. This office can provide information on the status of both House and Senate bills. The Legislative Information Center also can send you copies of bills as well as mail out status sheets which target on bills pertaining to a specific subject.

Connecticut

Bill Information Room, Law & Legislative Reference Dept., State Library, 231 Capitol Avenue, Hartford, CT 06106; (203) 566-5736. This office can provide information about both House and Senate bills and send you copies of bills. Besides doing a key word or subject search, this office can mail you a printout of all legislation pertaining to one topic.

Delaware

Division of Research, Legislative Counsel, Legislative Hall, Dover, DE 19901; (302) 736-4114; (800) 282-8545. This office can provide status information on both House and Senate bills and send you copies of bills. It can access a legislative computerized database and do searches for free. The toll-free number operates year-round.

Florida

Legislative Information Division, Capitol Building, Room 826, Tallahassee, FL 32399-1400; (904) 488-4371; (800) 342-1827. This office can provide status information on all House and Senate bills. It can send you single copies of up to 10 bills and mail out printouts of all House and Senate bills pertaining to a specific subject.

Georgia

Clerk of the House, Third Floor Post Office, State Capitol, Atlanta, GA 30334; (404) 656-5015; (800) 282-5803. This office can provide up-to-date information on all House bills and send you copies of House bills. The Clerk of the House also will search its database to tell you all legislation that has been introduced on a specific topic.

Secretary of the Senate, State Capitol, Room 353, Atlanta, GA 30334; (404) 656-5040; (800) 282-5803. This office can respond to questions about all bills pending before the Georgia Senate. The Secretary of the Senate can send you copies of Senate bills and search its database for legislation pertaining to a specific subject.

Hawaii

Clerk of the House, State Capitol of Hawaii, Honolulu, HI 96813; (808) 548-7843. This office can respond to questions about bills pending before the House and refer you to the appropriate offices in the State Capitol such as the document room.

Clerk of the Senate, State Capitol of Hawaii, Honolulu, HI 96813; (808) 548-4671. This office can provide status information on all legislation pending before the Hawaii Senate. It can refer you to the appropriate offices in the State Capitol such as the document room.

Idaho

Legislative Information Center, State House Room 301, Boise, ID 83720; (208) 334-2000. This office can give you information on the status of all House and Senate bills. It also can send you copies of bills as well as a printout of all legislation pertaining to a specific topic.

Information from Lawmakers

Illinois

Clerk of the House, State Capitol Building, Room 424, Springfield, IL 62706; (217) 782-6010; (800) 252-6300. This office can respond to questions about both House and Senate bills. It can provide you with copies of bills. The Clerk's office is able to send you printouts, for example, a list of all bills sponsored by one legislator.

Indiana

Legislative Information, Legislative Services Agency, 302 State House, Indianapolis, IN 46204; (317) 232-9856. Ms. Sue Page can give you bill status information and do searches by key word, subject or legislator. Legislative Information can send you copies of bills but charge $.10 per page.

Iowa

Legislative Public Information Office, State Capitol, Room 16, Des Moines, IA 50319; (515) 281-5129. This office can provide information on all House and Senate bills and send you copies of bills. It can access a computerized database and mail you a printout of all legislation pertaining to a specific subject.

Kansas

Legislative Reference, State Library, State Capitol Third Floor, Topeka, KS 66612; (913) 296-2149; (800) 432-3924. This office can tell you the status of all current House and Senate legislation as well as provide bill histories. Legislative Reference can send you copies of bills and voting records.

Kentucky

Bill Status, State Capitol, Room 80, Frankfort, KY 40601; (502) 564-8100; (800) 633-4171. This office can provide information on House and Senate bills pending before the legislature. It can also send you copies of bills.

Louisiana

Legislative Research Library, House of Representatives, P.O. Box 94012, Baton Rouge, LA 70804-9012; (504) 342-2431; (800) 272-8186. During the session call toll-free PULS Line (if out-of-state, (504) 342-2425) for bill status information and send you copies of House and Senate bills. When the legislature is not in session contact the Legislative Research Library.

Maine

Legislative Information Office, State House, Room 314, Station 100, Augusta, ME 04333; (207) 289-1692. This office can respond to questions about House and Senate bills and do key word or subject searches of its database.

Maryland

Legislative Information Desk, Dept. of Legislative Reference, 90 State Circle, Annapolis, MD 21401; (301) 841-3886; (800) 492-7122. This office can provide status information on all House and Senate bills and send you copies of bills. It also can provide you with a printout of all bills which pertain to a specific subject area.

Massachusetts

Citizen Information Service, 1 Ashburton Place, 16th Floor, Boston, MA 02018; (617) 727-7030. This office can provide bill status information and supply copies of bills but you must know the bill number. To obtain bill numbers and other information contact the Clerk of the House which is listed below.

Clerk of the House, House of Representatives, State House, Boston, MA 02133; (617) 722-2356. This office can respond to questions about House and Senate bills and will refer you to the document room and other appropriate offices within the State House.

Michigan

Clerk of the House, State Capitol, Lansing, MI 48909; (517) 373-0135. This office can provide information on the status of House bills and can do searches of its database to identify legislation which pertains to a specific subject. It will refer you to the House document room for copies of bills.

Secretary of the Senate, P.O. Box 30036, Lansing, MI 48933; (517) 373-2400. This office can provide Senate bill status information and also can send you copies of bills.

Minnesota

House Index Office, State Capitol Building, Room 210, St Paul, MN 55155; (612) 296-6646. This office can tell you the status of all House bills but will refer you to the Chief Clerk's office for copies of all House bills. It can search its database to identify all bills that pertain to a specific subject.

Senate Index Office, State Capitol Building, Room 231, St Paul, MN 55155, 612-296-2887-- This office can provide bill status information on all Senate legislation and will refer you to the Secretary of the Senate if you want to obtain copies of bills. It can search its database and identify all bills pertaining to a specific subject.

Mississippi

House Docket Room, PO Box 1018, New Capitol Room 305, Jackson, MS 39215; (601) 359-3358. This office can tell you the status of all House bills and send you copies of proposed laws pending before the House.

Senate Docket Room, PO Box 1018, New Capitol Room 308, Jackson, MS 39215; (601) 359-3229. This office can respond to questions about bills pending before the Mississippi Senate and send you copies of Senate bills.

Missouri

House Information Bill Status, State Capitol, Room 307B, Jefferson City, MO 65101; (314) 751-3659. This office can provide information on bills pending before the House and will refer you to the appropriate offices within the State Capitol such as the document room.

Senate Research, State Capitol Room B-9, Jefferson City, MO 65101; (314) 751-4666. This office can respond to questions about bills pending before the Senate and will refer you to the appropriate offices such as the document room.

Montana

Legislative Counsel, State Capitol, Room 138, Helena, MT 59620; (406) 444-3064, (800) 333-3408. The in-state toll-free number may change in subsequent sessions of the Montana legislature. The Legislative Counsel office can respond to inquiries year-round and send you copies of bills.

Nebraska

Hotline, Office of the Clerk, State Capitol, Room 2018, Lincoln, NE 68509; (402) 471-2709; (800) 742-7456. This office operates an in-state hotline during the session that can provide information on all bills pending before this unicameral legislature. The Clerk can respond to questions year-round.

Nevada

Chief Clerk of the Assembly, Legislative Building, Room 124, 401 S. Carson St., Carson City, NV 89710; (702) 885-5739. This office can provide information about the status of bills pending before the Assembly. The Chief Clerk will refer you to the appropriate offices in the State Capitol such as the documents room or the Clerk of the Senate.

New Hampshire

State Library Government, Information Bureau, 20 Park Street, Concord, NJ 03301; (603) 271-2239. This office can respond to questions about House and Senate bills pending before the legislature. It can send you copies of bills and search its database for bills pertaining to specific subject areas.

New Jersey

Office of Legislative, Services - Bill Room, Statehouse Annex CN068, Trenton, NJ 08625; (609) 292-6395; (800) 792-8630. This office can provide information about House and Senate legislation and send you copies of bills. It will refer you to other offices within the State House if necessary.

New Mexico

Legislative Counsel, State Capitol, Room 334, Sante Fe, NM 87503; (505) 984-9600. This office can provide bill status information on House and Senate legislation. It will refer you to the appropriate offices within the State Capitol such as the document room.

New York

Public Information Office, Room 102 Concourse, Empire State Plaza, Albany, NY 12248; (518) 455-4218; (800) 342-9860. This office can provide information on the status of House and Senate bills and send you copies of bills. It may refer you to your local library if you want a search done to identify all bills which pertain to a specific subject.

North Carolina

Clerk of the House, State Legislative Building, Room 2320, Raleigh, NC 27611; (919) 733-7760. This office can provide information about House and Senate bills and will refer you to the appropriate offices within the State Capitol such as where to obtain copies of bills.

North Dakota

Legislative Counsel Library, State Capitol, Bismarck, ND 58505; (701) 224-2916. This office can provide information about House and Senate bills year-round and will refer you to appropriate offices in the State Capitol. The legislature maintains an in-state toll-free number during the biannual session.

Ohio

Legislative Information, State House, Columbus, OH 43266-0604; (614) 466-8842; (800) 282-0253. This office can provide information on the status of House and Senate legislation and do subject searches. This telephone bank of researchers will route your requests (i.e., copies of bills). In-state toll-free access is available throughout the year.

Oklahoma

Chief Clerk, House of Representatives, State Capitol Bldg., Oklahoma City, OK 73105; (405) 521-2711. This office can respond to questions about bills pending before the House and Senate. It will refer you to the appropriate offices within the State Capitol.

Oregon

Legislative Library, State Capitol S-427, Salem, OR 97310; (503) 378-8871. This office can provide information on House and Senate bills year-round. During the biannual session the legislature offers an in-state toll-free number for bill information.

Pennsylvania

Legislative Reference Bureau, History Room, Main Capitol Building, Room 648, Harrisburg, PA 17120-0033; (717) 787-2342. This office can provide information on House and Senate bills be consulting its card index and computerized database. It will refer you to the appropriate offices, for example, where to obtain copies of bills.

Rhode Island

State Library, State House Room 208, Providence, RI 02903; (401) 277-2473. This office can provide you with information on the status of House and Senate bills and send you copies of bills. It will refer you to the appropriate legislators or committees.

South Carolina

Legislative Information Systems, Room 112, Blatt Building, 1105 Pendleton St., Columbia, SC 29201; (803) 734-2923. This office can respond to inquiries about House and Senate bills and will refer you to the appropriate offices such as where to obtain copies of bills. It can do subject searches but is unable to send out a printout.

South Dakota

Public Information Clerk, Legislative Research Counsel, State Capitol Building, 500 East Capitol, Pierre, SD 57501; (605) 773-4498. Ms. Patsy Summerside can provide information on the status of House and Senate bills. She can access a computerized database and do a search to identify legislation which pertains to a specific subject.

Tennessee

Office of Legislative Services, State Capitol, Room G-20, War Memorial Bldg, Nashville, TN 37219; (615) 741-3511. This office can provide information on House and Senate bills and will send you copies of bills. It can identify all legislation pending on specific subjects.

Texas

Legislative Reference Library, PO Box 12488, Capitol Station, Austin, TX 78711; 512) 463-1252. This office can provide information on the status of all House and Senate bills. It can search its database to identify all legislation which pertains to a specific subject. It will refer you to the appropriate offices such as the document room.

Utah

Legislative Research and General Counsel, 436 State Capitol, Salt Lake City, UT 84114; (801) 538-1032. This office can respond to questions about House and Senate bills. It will refer you to the appropriate offices within the State Capitol.

Vermont

Clerk of the House, Attn: Cathleen Cameron, State House, Montpelier, VT 05602; (802) 828-2247. Ms. Cameron can provide you with information on legislation pending before the House and do subject searches by accessing a computerized database. She will refer you to the appropriate offices in the State House.

Clerk of the Senate, State House, Montpelier, VT 05602; (802) 828-2241. This office can respond to questions about legislation pending before the Senate and will refer you to the appropriate legislators, committees, document rooms, etc.

Virginia

Legislative Information, House of Delegates, P.O. Box 406, Richmond, VA 23203; (804) 786-6530. This office can provide information on House and Senate bills and can send you copies of bills. It can consult a printed index which is updated daily to identify bills which pertain to a specific subject.

Washington

House Workroom, Legislative Building, Third Floor Capitol Campus, Olympia, WA 98504; (206) 786-7780; (800) 562-6000. This office can provide information on the status of bills pending before the House. It can also provide copies of bills. The toll-free number (out of state should call 206-786-7763) is in operation only during the session.

Senate Workroom, Legislative Building AS32, Third Floor Capitol Campus, Olympia, WA 98504; (206) 786-7592; (800) 562-6000. This office can provide information on bills pending before the Senate and can supply you with copies of bills. An in-state toll-free number (out of state call 206-786-7763) provides both House and Senate bill information but only during the session.

West Virginia

Clerk of the House, House of Delegates, State Capitol, Charleston, WV 25305; (304) 340-3200. This office can respond to questions about legislation pending before the House of Delegates and House committees. It will refer you to the appropriate offices in the State Capitol such as where to obtain legislative documents.

Clerk of the Senate, State Capitol, Charleston, WV 25305; (304) 357-7800. This office can provide information on the status of bills pending before the Senate. It will refer you to the appropriate offices in the State Capitol.

Wisconsin

Legislative Reference Bureau, 201 North State Capitol, Madison, WI 53702; (608) 266-0341; (800) 362-9696. The legislature operates a Legislative Hotline during the session (if calling from outside the state, dial 608-266-9960). The Legislative Reference Bureau can respond to questions year-round will refer you to the document room, etc.

Wyoming

Legislative Service Office, State Capitol Building, Room 213, Cheyenne, WY 82002; (307) 777-7881. When the Wyoming legislature is not in session it is necessary to contact this office. During the session, bill status questions are best directed to the two offices noted below.

Senate Information Clerk, State Capitol Building, Cheyenne, WY 82002; (307) 777-6185; (307) 777-7711. This office can respond to questions about the status of bill pendings before the Senate. It will refer you to the Bill Room to obtain copies of bills.

House Information Clerk, State Capitol Building, Cheyenne, WY 82002; (307) 777-7765; (307) 777-7852. This office can provide current information on legislation pending before the House. It will refer you to the proper offices in the State Capitol, for instance, the Bill Room.

Library of Congress

The Library of Congress is the world's largest library, but there are more than dusty old books stored here. The more than 20 million books in 470 languages that it holds represent less than a fourth of the holdings of the Library. There are three million books in the science and technology field. There are also massive collections of manuscripts, maps, music, prints and photographs, and film. In 1800 the Library was founded simply to help Congress make the laws. But now the Library is much more. For instance, more than a million handicapped readers borrow materials in braille and recorded forms each year. And the Library also registers copyright for books, music, films, computer programs, and other works. In celebration of the arts, the Library holds concerts by the Juilliard String Quartet, poetry readings, folk music and dance performances, and showings of classic films. More than 900 specialists provide extensive research and analysis for Congress, much of which is available to you through your Congressman's office. The Library is a major world center for scholarly research with specialists in its 22 reading rooms and in other areas ready to provide information on just about any subject you can name. And much of this information is available to you from exhaustive databases both in printed form and on magnetic tape.

* Books Published Since 1454
Catalog Management and Publications Division
LA 2004
Library of Congress
Washington, DC 20540   (202) 707-5965

The *National Union Catalog* lists the world's books published since 1454 and held in approximately 1,100 North American libraries and other union catalogs that record the location of books in Slavic, Hebraic, Japanese, and Chinese languages (if Romanized). The catalog is produced on microfiche, and many libraries have it.

* Center for the Book: Reading Project
Center for the Book
Library of Congress
Washington, DC 20540   (202) 707-5221

A partnership between the federal government and private industry, the Center for the Book works closely with other organizations to explore important issues dealing with books and educational communities. The Center encourages reading and research about books and reading and serves as a catalyst by bringing together authors, publishers, librarians, booksellers, educators, scholars, and readers to discuss common concerns. Four primary concerns are: television and the printed word, reading development, international role of the book, and publishing. The center is funded by tax-deductible contributions.

* Central Intelligence Agency Declassified Reports
Photoduplication Service
Library of Congress
Washington, DC 20540   (202) 707-5650

The Library of Congress distributes CIA reports that have been released to the public. These reports detail foreign government structures, trade news, economic conditions, and industrial development. Orders must be prepaid or charged to a standing account at the Library of Congress. For $13 the Photoduplication Service can also provide you with a list of CIA reports available. Reports can be purchased on microfilm for $24 per reel.

* Children's Literature Center
Children's Literature Center
National Programs
Library of Congress
Washington, DC 20540   (202) 707-5535

The Center prepares lists and scholarly bibliographies and provides other reference services for individuals who serve children, including scholars, writers, teachers, librarians, and illustrators. The center also has many publishers' catalogs that list titles to be published in the upcoming year, a wide range of periodicals about children's literature, and lists from rare and used book sellers. *Books for Children*, a guide to reference sources for children's literature published annually for $1 per issue, is available from the Superintendent of Documents, Government Printing Office, Washington, D.C. 20402; (202) 783-3238.

* Computer-Generated Bibliographies
Customer Services Section
Cataloging Distribution Service
Library of Congress
Washington, DC 20541   (202) 707-6100

Readers who cannot do their own research in the Library of Congress can request a search of its catalog databases on a fee basis. Through this service, a bibliographic listing can be produced by accessing any data found on a catalog record. The listing can be produced on magnetic tape or in printed form.

* Congressional Documents, Reports, and Hearings
Law Library
Library of Congress
Washington, DC 20540   (202) 707-5079

All Senate and House documents, reports, hearings since 1970, and all bills back to the First Congress are available. Material can be obtained on microfilm.

* Congressional Research Service Reports
Contact your Member of Congress   (202) 224-3121
Refer to Current Events Reports and Homework Chapter
for complete listing of these reports and issue briefs.

The Congressional Research Service at the Library of Congress prepares hundreds of non-partisan background *Reports* each year on current issues large and small, domestic and foreign, social and political. CRS also publishes hundreds of major *Issue Briefs* each year designed to keep members of Congress informed on timely issues. Written in simple and direct language, these briefs provide background information and are updated daily. Free printed copies can be obtained from your Congressman's office. *Audio Briefs* are audio cassette programs produced on topics of Congressional interest, including specially produced programs on issues before Congress featuring CRS experts and nationally recognized experts. CRS products are listed in the *Guide to CRS Products*, published quarterly and in monthly cumulative supplements entitled *Update to the Guide to CRS Products*. Copies of these publications are available from your Congressman. The following are lists of *Issue Briefs* and *Audio Briefs* current in the summer, 1989.

* Copernicus to Star Wars
Science and Technology Division
Library of Congress
Washington, DC 20540   (202) 707-5639

The Science and Technology collection contains more than 3 million scientific and technical books and pamphlets and 3 million technical reports, including those issued by the Department of Energy, NASA, the Department of Defense, and other government agencies. The collections, which are particularly strong in aeronautical materials, contain first editions of Copernicus and Newton and the personal papers of the Wright Brothers and Alexander Graham Bell. Computer terminals provide principal access to the collections. Special scientific finding aids, such as abstracting and indexing journals, are part of the division's reference collection. This Division also prepares an informal series of reference guides called *Tracer Bullets*, which are available free upon request. More extensive bibliographies are published from time to time.

* Copyright Entries Catalogs
Superintendent of Documents
Government Printing Office
Washington, DC 20402   (202) 783-3238

The following copyright catalogs, which list materials registered only during the period covered by each issue, are available on microfiche only and are sold as individual subscriptions:
Part 1: Nondramatic Literary Works (quarterly) $11.00 per year.
Part 2: Serials and Periodicals (semi-annually) $5.00 per year.

Part 3: Performing Arts (quarterly) $11.00 per year.
Part 4: Motion Pictures and Filmstrips (semi-annually) $5 per year.
Part 5: Visual Arts (excluding maps) (semi-annually) $5 per year.
Part 6: Maps (semi-annually) $5 per year.
Part 7: Sound Recordings (semi-annually) $7.50 per year.
Part 8: Renewals (semi-annually) $5.00 per year.
Information on copyrights from 1978 to the present is available online through terminals located in the Copyright Office, and records on all copyrights back to the 1800s are kept in the Copyright Card Catalog Office, Room 459; (202) 707-5063.

* Copyright Examining Practices
Copyright Office
Certifications and Documents
Library of Congress
Washington, DC 20559 (202) 707-6800
The *Compendium II of Copyright Office Practices* is intended as a general guide for those with special interest in copyright examining practices which concern the registration of applications for copyright under the 1976 Copyright Act. It is available for $51 from the Government Printing Office, Washington, D.C. 20402; (202) 783-3238.

* Copyright Office
Copyright Office
Library of Congress
Washington, DC 20559 (202) 707-6540
The Library of Congress Copyright Office grants exclusive rights to reproduce or prepare derivative works on the copyrighted work in copies or on phonorecords and to distribute them to the public by sale, rental, lease, or loan. Copyrightable works include books, periodicals, and other literary works; musical compositions, song lyrics, dramas, and dramatico-musical compositions; pantomimes and choreographic works; pictoral, graphic, and sculptural works; motion pictures and other audiovisual works; and sound recordings. The Library provides information on copyright registration procedures and copyright card catalogs covering more than 16 million works that have been registered since 1870.

* Copyright Research Service
Copyright Office
Reference and Bibliographic Section
Library of Congress
Washington, DC 20559 (202) 707-6850
For a fee of $10 per hour or part thereof, the Copyright Office will research the copyright you need and send you the information by mail. Requests must be in writing, and you must specify exact details you require.

* Domestic and Foreign Periodicals Division
Serial and Government Publication Division
Library of Congress, LM 133
Washington, DC 20540 (202) 707-5647
The Library of Congress has an extensive collection of both domestic and foreign periodicals, government serials, microfilms, and newspapers.

* Folklife Center
American Folklife Center
Library of Congress
Washington, DC 20540 (202) 707-6590
This Center collects and maintains archives, conducts scholarly research, and coordinates the development of field projects, performances, exhibitions, festivals, workshops, publications, and audiovisual programs on American folklife. *Folk Life Center News* is a free quarterly newsletter on folklife activities and programs. The Center maintains and administers an extensive collection of folk music, folk culture, ethnomusicology, and grass-roots oral history--both American and international--in published and unpublished forms. The Archive houses more than 30,000 hours of folk-related recordings, manuscripts, and raw materials. The Archive Reading Room contains more than 4,000 books and periodicals, plus unpublished theses, and dissertations, field notes, and many textual and some musical transcriptions and recordings. A free listing of the Archive's publications is available.

* Free LOC Catalog Cards
Cataloging Distribution Service
Library of Congress
Washington, DC 20541 (202) 707-6100
Individuals or organizations wishing to establish libraries may receive Library of Congress catalog cards free by establishing an account with the above office.

* Geography and Maps Division
Geography and Map Division

Library of Congress
Washington, DC 20540 (202) 707-6277
The Library's cartographic collections, which include 4 million maps, nearly 51,000 atlases, 500 globes, and some 8,000 reference books, are the largest and most comprehensive in the world. The collections include atlases published over the last five centuries covering individual continents, countries, states, counties, and cities as well as the world. Official topographic, geologic, soil, mineral, and resource maps and nautical and aeronautical charts are also available for most countries. There are also complete LANDSAT microimage data sets of images produced by several satellites revolving around the Earth. Subscription information on the microfiche data sets is available from EOSAT, 4300 Forbes Blvd., Lanham, MD 20706; (800) 344-9933.

* High School and Intercollegiate Debate Topics
Your Member of Congress (202) 224-3121
A series of free reports are prepared by the Congressional Research Service of the Library of Congress that contain pertinent excerpts, bibliographic references, and other materials related to debate topics for that year. For high school debate teams, the topics are selected by the National University Extension Service Association, and for college, the topics are selected by the American Speech Association.

* Historical Sound Recordings Division
Motion Picture, Broadcasting,
and Recorded Sound Division
Library of Congress
Washington, DC 20540 (202) 707-5840
The sound recording collection reflects the entire spectrum of history of sound from wax cylinders to quadraphonic discs and includes such diverse media as wire recordings, aluminum discs, zinc discs, acetate-covered glass discs, rubber compound discs, and translucent plastic discs. The division has also recently made all of its materials recorded prior to 1909 available on 8-inch compressed audio discs for individual users in the Recorded Sound Reading Room using a micro computer. Included are the Berliner collection, from the company which invented and introduced disc recording, radio news commentaries from 1944 to 1946, eyewitness descriptions of marine combat and House of Representatives debates. For purchase by researchers, the Division's laboratory is prepared to make taped copies of recordings in good physical condition, when not restricted by copyright, performance rights, or provisions of gift or transfer. The requester is responsible for any necessary search--by mail or in person--of Copyright Office records to determine the copyright status of specific recordings. The Division also offers copies of some of its holdings for sale in disc form. These include a number of LP records of folk music, poetry, and other literature.

* Humanities Library
National Endowment for the Humanities
1100 Pennsylvania Ave., NW, Room 217
Washington, DC 20506 (202) 786-0245
This library focuses on the needs and interests of NEH and has materials on a variety of humanities-related subjects. Individuals may use this library by appointment only.

* Information On Demand
General Reading Rooms Division
Library of Congress, LJ 144
Washington, DC 20540 (202) 707-5543
If you need information that is contained in the material in the Library of Congress collections, the reference staff will find it for you and relay it over the phone. If the information you require is too extensive, however, the reference staff will refer you to private researchers who work on a fee basis.

* Last Resort Interlibrary Loan
Loan Division
Library of Congress
Washington, DC 20540 (202) 707-5444
The Loan Division will loan materials to other libraries when they have exhausted other means of locating the material. If you are having trouble finding material, first contact your local library.

* Law Library on All Legal Systems
Law Library
Library of Congress
Washington, DC 20540 (202) 707-5073
As the world's largest and most comprehensive library of foreign, international, and comparative law, the Law Library provides information for all known legal systems including common law, civil law, Roman law, canon law, Chinese law, Jewish and Islamic law, and ancient and medieval law. Specialists with knowledge of more than fifty languages provide reference and research service in all known legal systems. U.S. legislative documents housed here include the *Congressional Record* (and its predecessors), the serial set, a nearly complete set

of bills and resolutions, current documents, committee prints, reports, hearings, etc. plus a complete set of U.S. Supreme Court records and briefs and collections of U.S. Court of Appeals records and briefs. The law library has five major divisions:

American-British Law: United States, Australia, Canada, Great Britain, India, New Zealand, Pakistan, certain other countries of the British Commonwealth and their dependent territories, and Eire: (202) 707-5077.

European Law: Nations of Europe and their possessions, except Spain and Portugal: (202) 707-5088.

Hispanic Law: Spain and Portugal, Latin America, Puerto Rico, the Philippines, and Spanish- and Portuguese-language states of Africa: (202) 707-5070.

Far Eastern Law: Nations of East and Southeast Asia including China, Indonesia, Japan, Korea, Thailand, and former British and French possessions in the area: (202) 707-5085.

Near Eastern and African Law: Middle Eastern countries, including the Arab states, Turkey, Iran, and Afghanistan, and all African countries, except Spanish- and Portuguese-language states and possessions: (202) 707-5073.

* Legislative Histories and Research

Law Library
Library of Congress, LM240
Washington, DC 20540   (202) 707-5065

The Law Library compiles legislative histories which include versions of new public statutes from the time of introduction, through congressional hearings, House and Senate floor debate, vote tallies, and votes.

* Library of Congress Color Slides

Photoduplication Service
Library of Congress
Washington, DC 20540   (202) 707-5650

Color slides of the Library's buildings and items from its collections are available at $5 per slide. Slides can also be made from a bound volume for $7.

* Library of Congress Free Catalog

Central Services Division
Library of Congress
Washington, DC 20540   (202) 707-5590

The free annual catalog, *Publications in Print*, offers a comprehensive listing of the materials published by or in cooperation with the Library of Congress. Publications may be in print, recorded, or video formats. As new LC publications are issued, they are announced in the weekly *Library of Congress Information Bulletin*, and in the *Monthly Catalog of United States Government Publications* available from the Superintendent of Documents, Government Printing Office, Washington, D.C. 20402; (202) 783-3238.

* Library of Congress Guide

Sales Office
Library of Congress
Washington, DC 20540   (202) 707-5111

Written for both the researcher and the casual visitor, this colorful guide explores the Library's history, architecture, exhibits, holdings, and services. It is available for $5.95 at the Library's Information Counter, or by mail for $5.95 plus $3.50 shipping and handling from the above address.

* Library of Congress Tours

Visitor Services Office
Library of Congress
Washington, DC 20540   (202) 707-5458

The Visitor Services Office shows a film tour of the Library every half hour. Actual tours of the Library are conducted at 10:00 a.m., 1:00 p.m., and 3:00 p.m., weekdays. The tours highlight the art and architecture of the Thomas Jefferson Building, and provide an overview of the Library activities. Tour reservations for groups over 10 must be made in advance.

* Library Services for Blind and Physically

Handicapped Readers Reference Section
National Library Service for the Blind and
Physically Handicapped
Library of Congress
Washington, DC 20542   (202) 707-9287
OR: Your local library

The National Library Service (NLS) maintains a large collection of books, magazines, journals, and music materials in braille, large type, and recorded formats for individuals who cannot read or use standard printed materials

because of temporary or permanent visual loss or physical limitations. Reading materials and necessary playback equipment for books on record and cassette are distributed through a national network of cooperating libraries. Books in the collection are selected on the basis of their appeal to a wide range of interests. Bestsellers, biographies, fiction, and how-to books are in great demand.

* Main Reading Room

Main Reading Room
Library of Congress
Washington, DC 20540   (202) 707-5521

Located on the first floor of the Thomas Jefferson Building, the main reading room contains material on American history, economics, fiction, language and literature, political science, government documents, and sociology. A reference collection for these materials is also housed there. These reading rooms are not equipped to answer reference questions over the telephone, but will provide information on their collections, hours of operation, and the like.

Social Science/(202) 707-5538
Microform/(202) 707-5471
Local History and Genealogy/(202) 707-5537
Newspapers and Current Periodicals/(202) 707-5690
Science/(202) 707-5639
Law Library/(202) 707-5079
Performing Arts/(202) 707-5507
Performing Arts Library at the Kennedy
  Center/(202) 707-6245
Motion Picture, Broadcasting, and Recorded Sound/(202) 707-5840
Archive of Folk Culture/(202) 707-6590
Prints and Photographs/(202) 707-6394
Manuscripts/(202) 707-5383
Rare Book and Special Collections/(202) 707-5434
Geography and Map/(202) 707-6277
Hispanic/(202) 707-5400
European/(202) 707-5415
Asian/(202) 707-5420
African and Middle Eastern Division/(202) 707-5528

* Manuscripts Division

Manuscript Division
Special Collections, LM 102
Library of Congress
Washington, DC 20540   (202) 707-5387

More than 40 million pieces of manuscript material are housed in the Manuscript Division, including the letters, diaries, speech drafts (including the copy of the Gettysburg Address), scrapbooks, telegrams, and so forth of influential people. For instance, the Library owns the papers of 23 of the presidents from George Washington to Calvin Coolidge, as well as materials of Clara Barton, Sigmund Freud, and Benjamin Franklin. The Manuscript is open to persons engaged in serious research who present proper identification. Hours of operation are 8:30 a.m. to 5:00 p.m., Monday through Saturday (except national holidays).

* Motion Picture and Broadcasting Division

Motion Picture, Broadcasting, and Recorded
Sound Division, LM 336
Library of Congress
Washington, DC 20540   (202) 287-5840

The Library's film and television collections contain more than 100,000 titles, and more than 1,000 titles are added each month through copyright deposit, purchase, gift, or exchange. Items selected from copyright deposits include feature films and short works of all sorts, fiction and documentary, exemplifying the range of current film and video production. The collections also include some 90,000 stills. The film and television collections are maintained for research purposes. Limited viewing and listening facilities for individual users are provided in the reading rooms.

* Newspapers and Periodicals From Around the World

Library of Congress
Washington, DC 20540   (202) 707-5650

Hundreds of different newspapers and periodicals from all fifty states and countries around the world are available on microfilm for $24 for domestic and $27 for foreign publications. Subscriptions are available or single issues can be ordered. Orders must be prepaid or charged to a standing account at the Library of Congress.

* Performing Arts Reading Room

Performing Arts Reading Room
Room LM113
Library of Congress
Washington, DC 20540   (202) 707-5504

The Performing Arts Reading Room houses the Library of Congress's non-book collections in the performing arts area: music, dance, sound recordings, motion pictures, and television. The collection includes more than 4,000,000 pieces of music and manuscripts, some 300,000 books and pamphlets, and about 350,000 sound recordings reflecting the development of music in Western civilization from earliest times to the present. Reference services are available. Adjacent to the reading room is the Recorded Sound Reference Center for users primarily interested in sound recordings and radio materials. Listening facilities are available in the reading room, but their use is limited of those doing research of a specific nature leading to publication or production. Musicians who wish to play music drawn from the Library's collection may use the piano available in an adjacent sound proof room.

* Preservation: Newspapers to Motion Pictures

National Preservation Program Office
Library of Congress, LMG 21
Washington, DC 20540 (202) 707-1840

The Preservation Office is involved in a constant race against time to preserve its millions of items from disintegration. Newspapers are immediately microfilmed, motion pictures are rushed to refrigerated vaults, manuscripts are put in fumigating vaults, and maps are encased in polyester envelopes. But the main problem for preservationists is acid and its affect on paper. Recently the Library's chemists developed a technique whereby wood pulp books are placed in huge vacuum tanks which are flooded with diethyl zinc gas, thus deacidifying them for another hundred years. Research continues on longstanding preservation problems. A series of leaflets on various preservation and conservation topics is available from the office.

* Prints and Photographs Division

Prints and Photographs Division
Library of Congress, LM 337
Washington, DC 20540 (202) 707-6394

More than 10 million items in the Library of Congress chronicle American life and society from its earliest days to the present through its prints and photographs. Items include architectural plans, posters, cartoons, drawings, and advertising labels. Reference librarians will assist those doing their own research, and they can furnish names of freelance picture researchers for individuals who cannot get to the Library.

* Private Library Space for Researchers

Research Facilities Section
General Reading Rooms
Library of Congress
Washington, DC 20540 (202) 707-5211

For increased convenience, full-time scholars and researchers may apply for study desks in semi-private areas within the Library of Congress.

* Public Bills, Resolutions and Laws

Congressional Research Service
Bill Digest Section
Library of Congress
Washington, DC 20540 (202) 707-6996

The *Digest Public General Bills and Resolutions* provides summaries of public bills and resolutions and their current status in order of introduction in Congress. The *Digest* includes subject, author, and title. Subscription service consists of cumulative issues for each session of each Congress (two sessions per Congress). Prices per issue vary but average around $40. Subscription information is available from the Superintendent of Documents, Government Printing Office, Washington, D.C. 20402; (202) 783-3238.

* Publishers' ISBN Catalog Numbers

Cataloging-in-Publication
Library of Congress
Washington, DC 20540 (202) 707-6372

Through a program in cooperation with American publishers to print cataloging information in current books, Library of Congress card catalog numbers are assigned by the Cataloging-in-Publication Office prior to publication.

* Rare Books Division

Rare Book and Special Collections Division
Library of Congress, LJ 256
Washington, DC 20540 (202) 707-5434

The Rare Books Division contains about 300,000 volumes and 200,000 pamphlets, broadsides, theater playbills, title pages, manuscripts, posters, and photographs. The collection includes documents of the first fourteen congresses of the United States, the personal libraries of Thomas Jefferson and Harry Houdini, incunabula; miniature books and dime novels, and the Russian Imperial collection. The division has its own central card catalog plus special card files that describe individual collections or special aspects of books from many collections.

* Reproduce Library of Congress Materials

Photoduplication Service
Library of Congress, G1011
Washington, DC 20540 (202) 707-5640

Photostats, microfilms, and other photocopies of manuscripts, prints, photographs, maps, and book materials not subject to copyright and other restrictions are available for a fee. In general, there is, however, a four-to-six-week turnaround time for this service. Order forms for photo reproduction and price schedules for this and other copying services are available.

* Science and Technology Resources

General Reading Rooms
Library of Congress
Washington, DC 20540 (202) 707-5522

The *Science, Technology, and Social Science Database* is a computerized directory of more than 14,000 organizations or individuals who will provide information to the general public on topics primarily in science, technology, and the social sciences. Citations generally contain the name of the organization or person, mailing address, telephone number, areas of interest, special collections, publications, and special services.

* Science Information Tracer Bullets

Science and Technology Division
Reference Section
Library of Congress
Washington, DC 20540 (202) 707-5580

Informal series of reference guides are issued free from the Science and Technology Division under the general title, *LC Science Tracer Bullet*. These guides are designed to help readers locate published material on subjects about which they have only general knowledge. New titles in the series are announced in the weekly Library of Congress *Information Bulletin* that is distributed to many libraries. The following is a list of *Tracer Bullets* currently available:

TB No.Title
80-1 *Green Revolution*
80-3 *Automotive Electronics*
80-4 *Aging*
80-5 *Low-Level Ionizing Radiation: Health Effects*
80-6 *Lasers and Their Applications*
80-7 *Solar Energy*
80-8 *Electric & Hybrid Vehicles*
80-9 *Terminal Care*
80-10 *Infrared Applications*
80-11 *Drug Research on Human Subjects*
80-12 *Ocean Thermal Energy*
80-14 *Automotive Maintenance & Repair*
80-15 *The History of Psychology II*
80-16 *Synthetic Fuels*
80-18 *Health Foods*
80-19 *Industrial Robots*
81-2 *Medicinal Plants*
81-3 *Alcoholism*
81-5 *Wind Power*
81-6 *Pets and Pet Care*
81-9 *Cable Television (Cable TV)*
81-10 *Manned Space Flight*
81-11 *Mariculture*
81-13 *Wood As Fuel*
81-14 *Volcanoes*
81-15 *History of American Agriculture*
81-17 *Epilepsy*
82-1 *Food Additives*
82-2 *Gardening*
82-3 *Earth Sheltered Buildings*
82-4 *Extraterrestrial Life*
82-5 *Jet Engines and Jet Aircraft*
82-6 *Biological Control of Insects*
82-8 *Chemical and Biological Warfare (CBW)*
82-9 *Sickle Cell Anemia*
83-1 *Biofeedback*
83-2 *Power Metallurgy*
83-3 *Hazardous Wastes (Non-nuclear)*
83-4 *Science Policy*
83-5 *Plant Exploration & Introduction*
83-6 *Mental Retardation*
83-7 *Quarks*
83-8 *Women in the Sciences*
83-9 *Geothermal Energy*
83-10 *High Technology*
84-1 *Aquaculture*
84-2 *Edible Wild Plants*
84-3 *Japanese Science & Technology*
84-4 *Sharks*
84-5 *Scientific & Technical Libraries: Administration & Management*
84-7 *Biotechnology*
85-1 *Herbs and Herb Gardening*
85-2 *Landscape Gardening*
85-3 *Endangered Species (Animals)*

Books and Libraries

* Selling to the Library of Congress

Procurement and Supply Division
Library of Congress
1701 Brightseat Rd.
Landover, MD 20785   (202) 707-0419

Those interested in doing business with the Library of Congress can request the pamphlet, *How and What We Purchase* from the above office.

* Social Science Resource Center

General Reading Rooms
Library of Congress
Washington, DC 20540   (202) 707-5522

The *Science, Technology, and Social Science Database* is a computerized directory of more than 14,000 organizations or individuals who will provide information to the general public on topics primarily in science, technology, and the social sciences. Citations generally contain the name of the organization or person, mailing address, telephone number, areas of interest, special collections, publications, and special services.

* Sound Recordings of Poetry and Other Literature

Motion Picture, Broadcasting,
and Recorded Sound Division
Library of Congress
Washington, DC 20540   (202) 707-5840

The Library of Congress offers copies of some of its poetry and literature holdings for sale in disc form. Contact this office for information on what's available, along with prices.

* State Government and University Publications List

Exchange and Gift Division
State Documents Section
Library of Congress
Washington, DC 20540   (202) 707-9468

The *Monthly Checklist of State Publications* lists documents and publications received in the Library of Congress that are issued by the administrative, judicial, and legislative branches and state university systems of the states and territories. The subscription price is $32.00 per year and can be purchased from the Superintendent of Documents, Government Printing Office, Washington, DC 20402, (202) 783-3238.

* Surplus Books Giveaway

Exchange and Gift Division
Library of Congress
Washington, DC 20540   (202) 707-9511

Tens of thousands of surplus books in a wide variety of subjects are available to government agencies, private citizens, and non-profit organizations. The books come from a wide variety of sources including extras from the Copyright Division, books that are not acquired by not selected for the Library's collections, and from private gifts. Government agencies can select from the books available first at no charge. The general public (referred to as book dealers by the Library) can select from books next. They must bid on books by the lot, and the minimum bid is $25. Everything left over is available to non-profit organizations free of charge.

* Telephone Reference Service

Library of Congress
Washington, DC 20540   (202) 707-5522

This service provides information to callers about the collections within the Library of Congress and how they can be used. In planning your research, remember that the Library of Congress is the library of last resort--all other inter-library loan avenues must be exhausted before you may borrow a book from the Library of Congress. Always begin your research with your local library.

Federal Libraries

* African Art

Smithsonian Institution
950 Independence Ave., SW
Washington, DC 20560 (202) 357-4875

The Library maintains a collection of 15,000 books and 280 periodical titles on traditional and contemporary arts of Africa, including sculptural and decorative arts, ethnography, anthropology, craft, architecture, archeology, history, oral tradition and folklore, and African retentions in the New World. The Library is open to the public by appointment.

* Agriculture, U.S. Department of

10301 Baltimore Blvd.
Beltsville, MD 20700 (301) 344-3755

NAL provides comprehensive information services for the food and agricultural sciences through a variety of sources, which include bibliographies, personal reference services, loans, photocopies, and online data files. Services are provided to agricultural colleges, research institutions, government agencies, agricultural associations, industry, individual scientists, and the general public. NAL cooperates with the Library of Congress and the National Library of Medicine to provide access to publications worldwide in the agricultural, chemical, and biological sciences. NAL houses one of the largest collections in the free world on agricultural subjects--1.6 million volumes--including biology, chemistry, nutrition, forestry, soil sciences, and much more.

* Air Force, Department of the

Resource Library
SAF/PAR (202) 697-1128
Washington, D.C. 20330-1000 (202) 697-4100

Not open to the public but they do accept mail requests. They have general information about the air force, as well as biographies. Mail requests to :

* Air Force, Department of the

History Library
USAF/CHO
Building 5681
Bolling Air Force Base
Washington, D.C. 20330 (202) 767-0412

Library is open to the public 8:00 a.m. to 4:30 p.m. Collection includes history of Air Force, history of aircraft, and biographies dating back to WWI.

* Air Force, Department of the

Historical Resource Center
USAFHRC/RF
Maxwell A.F.B., AL 36112-6678 (205) 293-5342

Open 8:00 a.m. to 4:30 p.m. This is a repository of all Air Force historical documents. It contains 550,000 documents and 60 million pages of information.

* American History Branch

National Museum of American History
Smithsonian Institute
Room 5016
12th & Constitution Ave., NW
Washington, DC 20560 (202) 357-2414

The Library houses a collection of 165,000 volumes of book and bound journals on engineering, transportation, military history, science, applied science, decorative arts, and domestic and community life in addition to American history and the history of science and technology. They have special collections of trade literature and materials about world fairs. The Library is open to the public by appointment.

* Architect of the Capitol

U.S. Capitol Bldg.
House Terrace Level, #3
Washington, DC 20515 (202) 225-1222

This small reference library is for researchers only. It is open 9 a.m. - 4:30 p.m., Monday through Friday, and one must secure a visitor's pass to enter.

* Arms Control and Disarmament Agency, U.S.

320 21st St., NW, Room 5840
Washington, DC 20451 (202) 647-5969

As a complement to the much larger State Department Library, the ACDA Library maintains a current collection of books, periodicals, documents, and reference materials relevant to arms control and disarmament issues. The library also includes an information retrieval system and inter-library loan services. Individuals wishing to use the library must call and make an appointment.

* Arts and Museum Management Library

National Endowment for the Arts
1100 Pennsylvania Ave., NW
Washington, DC 20506 (202) 682-5485

This library focuses on the needs and interests of NEA and has materials on the arts and arts management. Individuals may use this library by appointment only.

* Binational Libraries and Cultural Centers Worldwide

Library Programs Division
Bureau of Educational and Cultural Affairs
United States Information Agency
301 Fourth St., SW, Room 314
Washington, DC 20547 (202) 485-2915

USIA maintains or supports 156 libraries and reading rooms in 95 countries, as well as library programs at 111 binational centers in 24 countries. Collections focus on fostering foreign understanding of U.S. people, history, and culture. A bi-weekly bibliography, listing 80-100 titles on international relations and developments in the U.S., is one of many library services provided for the overseas posts, including reference and research assistance.

* Commerce, U.S. Department of

1400 and Constitution Ave. NW, Room 7046
Washington, DC 20230 (202) 377-5511

This collection includes business directories, periodicals, and newspapers.

* Comptroller of Currency, Office of the

U.S. Department of the Treasury
490 L'Enfant Plaza East, SW
Washington, DC 20219 (202) 447-1843

* Congressional Budget Office

Third and D Sts., SW
Room 472
Washington, DC 20515 (202) 226-2635

Open 9 a.m. to 5:30 p.m., Monday through Friday, this library contains information on economics and studies on the budget process.

* Consumer Product Safety Commission

5401 Westbard Ave., NW, Room 546
Washington, DC 20207 (301) 492-6544

The CPSC library's collection includes reference materials on engineering, economics, and health sciences, which CPSC staff and other researchers may use for background on product safety issues. The library does not include CPSC documents and publications.

* Council on Environmental Quality Library

Executive Office of the President
722 Jackson Pl., NW
Washington, DC 20503 (202) 395-5750

This small library contains environmental publications for researchers. Call ahead for an appointment.

* Court of Appeals for the Federal Circuit and U.S. Claims Court, U.S.

Library
717 Madison Place, NW
Washington, DC 20439 (202) 633-5871

This joint library is accessible only to members of the Bar and those involved in cases within the courts.

* Customs Services, U.S.

U.S. Department of Treasury
1301 Constitution Ave., NW
Washington, DC 20229   (202) 566-5406

* Defense, U.S. Department of
Pentagon Library
Room 1A518
Pentagon
Washington, DC 20310   (202) 697-4301
This library is not open to the public, inquiries will be directed to another appropriate library.

* Doris and Henry Dreyfuss Study Center
Cooper-Hewitt Museum
Smithsonian Institution's National Museum of Design
2 East 91st St.
New York, NY 10128   (212) 860-6887
The Study Center and Library serve as a resource for scholars, researchers, designers, and students for the study of design. This library contains fifty thousand volumes, with specialized holdings in decorative arts, textiles, and needlework, wallcoverings, architecture, pattern and ornament, landscape design, industrial design, interior design, theater design, and graphic design. Researchers are asked to call or write in advance. Photographs may be ordered through the museum's Photographic Services Department.

* Education, U.S. Department of
555 New Jersey Ave., NW, MS-1139
Washington, DC 20208   (202) 357-6884
Collection focuses on education and related social sciences information.

* Energy, U.S. Department of
1000 Independence Ave., SW
Room GA138
Washington, DC 20585   (202) 586-9534
This energy library is available to Department of Energy employees, government employees from other agencies, members of the armed forces if in uniform, and for those escorted by a Department of Energy employee.

* Environmental Protection Agency
401 M St., SW, Room 2904   Reference Desk (202) 282-5921
Washington, DC 20460   Main Desk (202) 382-5922
The library's collection focuses on environmental issues.

* Federal Aviation Administration
800 Independence Ave., SW
Washington, DC 20591   (202) 267-3115
Open to the public 9 a.m. to 4 p.m. Collection focuses on commercial and general aviation. Historical aviation information is located at Smithsonian's Air and Space Museum.

* Federal Communications Commission
1919 M St., NW, Suite 639
Washington, DC 20554   (202) 632-7100
The FCC Library is a collection of various types of legal and technical information. The legal collection includes federal and statutory case histories, indexes, reference works, treatises, and looseleaf services. The technical collection covers telecommunications and related subjects. The library also includes a special collection of cross-indexed legislative histories dating back to the early beginnings of communications law, along with a special collection of trade journals, and law and literature reviews.

* Federal Deposit Insurance Corporation (FDIC)
550 17th St., NW, Room 4060
Washington, DC 20429   (202) 898-3631
The FDIC library collection focuses on banking law, with emphasis on bank regulation and supervision, state codes, deposit insurance, international banking, bankruptcy, and consumer affairs. The library is open to the public Tuesdays through Thursdays. Call at least one day in advance to make an appointment to visit.

* Federal Emergency Management Agency
500 C St., SW, Room 123
Washington, DC 20472   (202) 646-3768 or 3769
The library's collection focuses on emergency management topics.

* Federal Energy Regulatory Commission
Reference Room and Information Center
U.S. Department of Energy
825 N. Capitol St.
Room 2200
Washington, DC 20426   (202) 357-8118
This reference center maintains the file of the applications for the Commission. The public is invited to use the facility from 8:30 a.m. - 5:00 p.m., Monday through Friday.

* Federal Reserve Board Research
Room BC241
20th St. & Constitution Ave., NW
Washington, DC 20551   (202) 452-3333
The Federal Reserve System research library contains material on banking, finance, economics, and other areas related to the Federal Reserve System.

* Federal Reserve System Banking Law
Room B1066
20th St. & Constitution Ave., NW
Washington, DC 20551   (202) 452-3284
For information on specific banking laws, contact the Federal Reserve System Banking Law Library.

* Federal Trade Commission (FTC)
6th & Pennsylvania Ave., NW
Room 630
Washington, DC 20580   (202) 326-2395
Contact the FTC's library to use the 120,000 volumes on legal, economic, and business subjects, 1,500 periodicals, interlibrary loans, and photocopy facilities.

* General Accounting Office
441 G St., NW, Room 7016
Washington, DC 20548   (202) 275-5180
This library provides information of GAO interest and has access to databases, government documents, dissertations, research in progress, and organizations. *Library Focus*, published monthly, lists the latest books acquired.

* General Accounting Office Law Library
441 G St., NW, Room 7056
Washington, DC 20548   (202) 275-2585
This library's references include the Legislative History Collection, which documents the creation of public documents and bills. The collection can be read in the library on weekdays between 8 a.m. and 4:45 p.m. A picture ID is required.

* General Services Administration
18th and F Sts., NW, Room 1033
Washington, DC 20405   (202) 535-7788
Collection includes the Federal Acquisition Institute library.

* Health and Human Services, U.S. Department of
Information Center
P.O. Box 1133
Washington, DC 20013   (301) 565-4167 in MD (800) 336-4797
This center should be the initial phone call because it can direct you to more specialized clearinghouses as well as health organizations and foundations. The Information Center, through its resource files and database (DIRLINE), responds to questions regarding health concerns and can send publications, bibliographies, and other material. A library focusing on health topics is open to the public, and the Center also produces many different directories, and resource guides, which are available for a minimal cost. A publications catalog is free of charge.

* House of Representatives Research and Library
Cannon House Office Bldg., Room B-18
Washington, DC 20515   (202) 225-0462
This library is the official depository of House documents, reports, bills, and more. Its primary function is to serve House members and their staffs. It is open to the public, but no photocopying is permitted. The hours are 9 a.m. to 5:30 p.m. Monday through Friday.

* Housing and Urban Development, U.S. Department of
Library
451 7th St., SW
Room 8141

Washington, DC 20410   (202) 755-6370

This library contains a wealth of information on financing, home building, mortgages, and other HUD related topics. Also included are archival documents of old housing agencies. Hours are 8:45 a.m. - 5:15 p.m., Monday through Friday. The Program Information Center at the Library is a source of information on HUD programs. The number is (202) 755-6420.

* Information Agency (USIA), U.S.

Programs Division
Bureau of Educational and Cultural Affairs
301 Fourth St., SW, Room 314
Washington, DC 20547   (202) 485-2915

USIA maintains or supports 156 libraries and reading rooms in 95 countries, as well as library programs at 111 binational centers in 24 countries. Collections focus on fostering foreign understanding of U.S. people, history, and culture. A bi-weekly bibliography, listing 80-100 titles on international relations and developments in the U.S., is one of many library services provided for the overseas posts, including reference and research assistance.

* Information Agency, U.S.

301 Fourth St., SW, Room 135
Washington, DC 20547   (202) 485-8947

The Washington library of USIA houses a varied collection, including a Russian language section. Access is restricted: permission to use the library can be obtained through the Office of Congressional and Public Liaison, address above, Room 602, (202) 485-2355.

* Interior, U.S. Department of the

Natural Resources Library
18th and C Sts., NW
Washington, DC 20240   (202) 343-5815

Information is provided on such topics as Native American Indians, mining and minerals, land reclamation and management, fish and wildlife, water resources, parks and outdoor recreation, and the preservation of scenic and historic sites. The library is open from 7:45 a.m. - 5:00 p.m., Monday through Friday.

* Interior, U.S. Department of the

Earth Science Library
U.S. Geological Survey
National Center, MS 950
4th Floor
Reston, VA 22092   (703) 648-4302

This library contains valuable publications on subjects related to the Geological Survey; however geology, including ground water and water resources, is the primary topic. The hours are 7:30 a.m. -4:15 p.m., Monday through Friday.

* International Development Cooperation Agency, U.S.

1601 North Kent Street
Room 105
Arlington, VA

Agency for International Development
Development Information Center (Mailing Address)
Room 105 SA18
Washington, D.C. 20528-1801   (703) 875-4818

The reference desk is open between 10:00 a.m. and 4:00 p.m. They maintain a database listing all of AID materials. It includes 150 journals of country development, strategy statements.

* International Trade Commission, U.S.

International Trade Library
Office of Data Systems
500 E St., SW, Room 300
Washington, DC 20436   (202) 252-1630

As one of the most extensive libraries on international trade in the United States, the ITC's main library maintains a 100,000-volumes and subscribes to about 2,400 periodicals. Publications on international trade and U.S. tariff commercial policy are housed along with many business and technical journals. An audiovisual room enables visitors to listen to audio tapes and to view video tapes relating to international trade. A rare-book room is also maintained, and the library staff has begun to establish special collection areas for use with ongoing ITC projects. THe library is open to the public from 8 a.m. to 5:15 p.m.

* International Trade Commission Law Library

500 E St., SW, Room 614
Washington, DC 20436   (202) 252-1287

The Law Library, a resource of the ITC's Office of the General Counsel, contains more than 10,000 volumes, participates in an exchange program with

other libraries, and maintains a comprehensive file on documents on legislation affecting U.S. trade. It is open to the public for research.

* Interstate Commerce Commission

12th St. and Constitution Ave., NW, Room 3392
Washington, DC 20423   (202) 275-7328

The Interstate Commerce Commission's library is open to the public, and its collection focuses on transportation and transportation law. You must sign in with the building guard before going up to the library.

* John F. Kennedy Center for the Performing Arts

Performing Arts Library
2700 F St., NW
Washington, DC 20566   (202) 872-0466

The Performing Arts Library is a joint project of the Library of Congress and the Kennedy Center, and offers information and reference assistance on dance, theater, opera, music, film, and broadcasting.

* Justice, U.S. Department of

U.S. Parole Commission
Public Reading Room
U.S. Department of Justice
5550 Friendship Blvd.
1 N. Park Bldg.
Bethesda, MD 20015   (301) 492-5990

Federal Bureau of Investigation
Public Reading Room
U.S. Department of Justice
9th St. & Pennsylvania Ave., NW
Washington, DC 20535   (202) 324-3691

* Labor, U.S. Department of

200 Constitution Ave., NW, Room N2439
Washington, DC 20210   (202) 523-6992

Collection includes information on trade unions, labor movements, women issues, and legal and regulatory topics related to labor.

* Land Management Library, Bureau of

U.S. Department of the Interior
SC 324A
Denver Federal Center
P.O. Box 25007
Denver, CO 80225   (303) 236-6649

A vast collection of information on issues concerning land management is available to the public through this library. The following topics are included: cadestral engineering; forest resources management; land reserve studies; legislation and public land laws; range management; watershed management; mineral, oil and gas leasing; oil shale; and conservation and use of public lands.

* Library of Congress

Washington, DC 20540   (202) 707-6372

The Library of Congress is the world's largest library, but there are more than dusty old books stored here. The more than 20 million books in 470 languages that it holds represent less than a fourth of the holdings of the Library. There are also massive collections of manuscripts, maps, music, prints and photographs, and film. In 1800 the Library was founded simply to help Congress make the laws. But now the Library is much more. For instance, more than a million handicapped readers borrow materials in braille and recorded forms each year. And the Library also registers copyright for books, music, films, computer programs, and other works. In celebration of the arts, the Library holds concerts by the Juilliard String Quartet, poetry readings, folk music and dance performances, and showings of classic films. More than 900 specialists provide extensive research and analysis for Congress, much of which is available to you through your Congressman's office. The Library is a major world center for scholarly research with specialists in its 22 reading rooms and in other areas ready to provide information on just about any subject you can name. And much of this information is available to you from exhaustive databases both in printed form and on magnetic tape.

* Library of Congress International Law Library

Washington, DC 20540   (202) 707-5073

As the world's largest and most comprehensive library of foreign, international, and comparative law, the Law Library provides information for all known legal systems including common law, civil law, Roman law, canon law, Chinese law, Jewish and Islamic law, and ancient and medieval law. Specialists with knowledge of more than fifty languages provide reference and research service in all known legal systems. U.S. legislative documents housed here include the *Congressional Record* (and its predecessors), the serial set, a nearly complete set of bills and resolutions, current documents, committee prints, reports, hearings, etc. plus a complete set of U.S. Supreme Court records and briefs and collections of U.S. Court of Appeals records and briefs. The law library has five major divisions:

American-British Law
United States, Australia, Canada, Great Britain, India, New Zealand, Pakistan, certain other countries of the British Commonwealth and their dependent territories, and Eire: (202) 707-5077.

European Law
Nations of Europe and their possessions, except Spain and Portugal: (202) 707-5088.

Hispanic Law
Spain and Portugal, Latin America, Puerto Rico, the Philippines, and Spanish- and Portuguese-language states of Africa: (202) 707-5070.

Far Eastern Law
Nations of East and Southeast Asia (including China, Indonesia, Japan, Korea, Thailand, and former British and French possessions in the area: 9202) 707-5085.

Near Eastern and African Law
Middle Eastern countries, including the Arab states, Turkey, Iran, and Afghanistan, and all African countries, except Spanish- and Portuguese-language states and possessions: (202) 707-5073.

* Library of Congress: Services for Readers with Vision Impairment and Handicaps
Library Services for Blind and Physically Handicapped
Readers Reference Section
National Library Service for the Blind and
Physically Handicapped
Washington, DC 20540   (202) 707-9287

or: Your local library
The National Library Service (NLS) maintains a large collection of books, magazines, journals, and music materials in braille, large type, and recorded formats for individuals who cannot read or use standard printed materials because of temporary or permanent visual loss or physical limitations. Reading materials and necessary playback equipment for books on record and cassette are distributed through a national network of cooperating libraries. Books in the collection are selected on the basis of their appeal to a wide range of interests. Bestsellers, biographies, fiction, and how-to books are in great demand.

* Library of Congress Law Library
Legislative Histories and Research
LM 240
Washington, DC 20540   (202) 707-5065
This section of the library provides information on legislative history.

* Merit Systems Protection
1120 Vermont Ave., NW, Room 828
Washington, DC 20419   (202) 653-7133
The Library's collection specializes in legal aspects of personnel issues. A reference librarian on staff can direct you to appropriate resources. The library is open to the public, but you should call for an appointment.

* Minerals Management Service
Resource Center
Congressional Liaison Office
U.S. Department of the Interior
18th and C Sts., NW
Room 4241
Washington, DC 20240   (202) 343-3502
This small reference center contains documents including offshore minerals management statistics from the Service. Hours are 8 a.m. - 4 p.m., Monday through Friday. Please call ahead for an appointment.

* Mines, Bureau of
U.S. Department of the Interior
2401 E St., NW
Room 127
Washington, DC 20241   (202) 634-1116
Topics relating to the minerals industry are contained in this library, such as state and county mineral data, mineral supply and demand analyses, congressional reports pertaining to minerals, oil and gas reports, and market studies. The hours are 7:45 a.m. - 4:15 p.m., Monday through Friday.

* National Aeronautics and Space Administration
600 Independence Ave., SW
Washington, DC 20546   (202) 453-8545
The library focuses on aeronautics and space information.

* National Air and Space Museum Branch
National Air and Space Museum
7th & Independence Ave., SW
Room 3100
Washington, DC 20590   (202) 357-3133
This library houses more than 30,000 books, 4,700 periodical titles, 6,000,000 technical reports, and is enriched by a documentary archival collection which includes 900,000 photographs, drawings, and other documents. The scope of the collection covers history of aviation and space, flight technology, aerospace industry, biography, lighter-than-air technology and history, rocketry, earth and planetary sciences, and astronomy. The Library is open to the public by appointment.

* National Credit Union Administration
1176 G St., NW
Washington, DC 20456   (202) 682-9630
The NCUA Law Library is open to the public. A part-time librarian is on duty to offer assistance. You must call for an appointment.

* National Endowment for the Arts
1100 Pennsylvania Ave., NW
Washington, DC 20506   (202) 682-5485
This library focuses on the needs and interests of NEA and has materials on the arts and arts management. Individuals may use this library by appointment only.

* National Endowment for the Humanities
1100 Pennsylvania Ave., NW, Room 217
Washington, DC 20506   (202) 786-0245
This library focuses on the needs and interests of NEG and has materials on a variety of humanities--related subjects. Individuals may use this library by appointment only.

* National Energy Information Center
Public Reading Room
U.S. Department of Energy
1000 Independence Ave., SW
Room 1F048
Washington, DC 20585   (202) 586-8800
This reading room contains research materials pertaining to the energy industry. Hours are 8 a.m. - 5 p.m., Monday through Friday. A picture ID is required.

* National Gallery of Art
Constitution & 6th St., NW
Washington, DC 20565   (202) 842-6511
The Gallery's library has over 150,000 volumes with a specialty in Renaissance and Baroque art. The collection covers the period from Post-Byzantine to the present, focusing on the history and criticism of art. The stacks themselves are closed; however, the library is open to the public, but you should call for the hours to make an appointment.

* National Labor Relations Board
1717 Pennsylvania Ave., NW, Room 900
Washington, DC 20570   (202) 254-9055
The Board's library collection focuses on labor law and labor relations. The library is open to the public and no appointment is necessary.

* National Mediation Board Reading Room
1425 K Street, NW
Washington, D.C. 20570   (202) 523-5996
Mediation files are available for inspection by appointment.

* National Science Foundation
1800 G Street, NW
Room 245
Washington, D.C. 20550   (202) 357-7811
The library is open to the public between 7:30 a.m. to 5:00 p.m. Specialty is science policy, technological innovation, research and development management, science and engineering education.

* National Technical Institute for the Deaf (NTID)

NTIC Resource Center
One Lomb Memorial Dr.
Rochester, NY 14623   (716) 475-6824

* National Zoological Park Branch

Education/Administration Building
3000 Connecticut Ave., NW
Washington, DC 20008   (202) 673-4771

This library houses a collection of 3,500 books and 350 periodical titles on animal behavior, animal nutrition, capture and care of animals in captivity, conservation and endangered species, horticulture, pathology, veterinary medicine, and zoology. THe library is open to the public by appointment.

* Natural History

Smithsonian Institute
10th & Constitution Ave., NW
Washington, DC 20560   (202) 357-4696

This library houses 330,000 books and bound journals and receives 1,963 journal subscriptions. The library consists of a main location and several subject-based locations. Topics covered include biology, geology, paleontology, ecology, anthropology, botany, entomology, and mineral sciences. Call to make an appointment of for information on the location of the subject-based libraries.

* Navy, Department of the

Building 44
Washington Navy Yard
Washington, D.C. 20374-0571   (202) 433-4131

Open 9:00 a.m. to 4:00 p.m. The library contains historical information dating back to the 18th century. They have historical documents and abstracts. They loan books through the interlibrary loan system.

* Nuclear Regulatory Commission

Washington, D.C. 20555   (202) 492-8501

The library is open to the public between 8:00 a.m. to 4:00 p.m.

* Office of Technology Assessment

600 Pennsylvania Ave., SE
Third Fl., Room 304
Washington, DC 20510-8025   (202) 228-6150

This library contains periodicals, books, and archives of the Office of Technology Assessment. One must call ahead for an appointment. Hours are 8:30 a.m. - 5:30 p.m., Monday through Friday.

* Occupational Safety and Health Review Commission

1825 K Street, NW
Room 400
Washington, D.C. 20006   (202) 634-7933

The collection focuses on federal laws.

* Office of Personnel Management

1900 E Street, NW
Room 5L45
Washington, D.C. 20415   (202) 632-7640

The library is open to the public between 8:30 a.m. to 4:30 p.m. The specialty of the library is personnel management

* Peace Corps

1900 K Street, NW
Room 5353
Washington, D.C. 20526   (202) 254-3307

The library is open to the public between 8:30 a.m. to 4:30 p.m. The specialty of the library is the countries the Peace Corps serves and Peace Corps services, volunteerism, and languages.

* Pennsylvania Avenue Development Corporation

1331 Pennsylvania Ave, NW
Suite 1220 N
Washington, D.C. 20005   (202) 724-9091

Their central files contain records of the Corporation and are open to the public by appointment.

* Postal Service, U.S.

475 L'Enfant Plaza, SW, Room 11800

Washington, DC 20260-1641   (202) 268-2904

Along with a working collection of materials in law, the social sciences, and technology, the Postal Library contains a unique collection of postal materials, legislative files from the 71st Congress to date, reports, pamphlets, clippings, photographs, general postal histories, periodicals of the national postal employee organizations, Universal Postal Union studies, and Postal laws and regulations handbooks and manuals. The library is open to the public weekdays from 9 a.m. to 4 p.m. Reading Rooms are located on the 11th Floor North.

* Presidential Libraries

National Archives and Records Administration
8th St. & Pennsylvania Ave., NW, Room 104
Washington, DC 20408   (202) 523-3212

Through the Presidential Libraries, which are located on sites selected by the presidents and built with private funds, the National Archives preserves and makes available for use the Presidential records and personal papers that document the actions of a particular president's administration. In addition to providing reference services on Presidential documents, each library prepares documentary and descriptive publications and operates a museum to exhibit documents, historic objects, and other memorabilia of interest to the public. Each library provides research grants to scholars and graduate students for the encouragement of research in Presidential libraries' holdings and of publication or works based on such research. Public programs of the libraries include conferences, lectures, films, tours, commemorative events, and seminars. For further information, contact the President library of your choice.

Herbert Hoover Library, West Branch, IA 52358; (319) 643-5301
Franklin D. Roosevelt Library, Hyde Park, NY 12358; (914) 229-8114
Harry S. Truman Library, Independence, MO 64050; (816) 374-6719
Dwight D. Eisenhower Library, Abilene, KS, 67410; (913) 263-4751
John F. Kennedy Library, Boston, MA 02125; (617) 929-4500
Lyndon B. Johnson Library, Austin, TX 78705; (512) 482-5137
Gerald R. Ford Library, Ann Arbor, MI 48109; (313) 668-2218
Gerald R. Ford Museum, Grand Rapids, MI 49504; (161) 456-2675
Nixon Presidential Materials Staff, Washington, DC 20408; (703) 756-6498
Jimmy Carter Library, Atlanta, GA 30307; (404) 331-3942

* Reclamation, Bureau of

Water Resources Library
U.S. Department of the Interior
P.O. Box 25007, D79231
Denver Federal Center
Denver, CO 80225-000   (303) 236-6963

The key topics covered at this library include hydrology engineering, groundwater management, dam safety, soil mechanics, and business related issues. Materials can be checked out only through the inter-library loan system.

* Securities and Exchange Commission

450 5th St., NW
Washington, DC 20549   (202) 272-2618

The SEC Library contains resource material on Federal Securities Laws, accounting, economics, and other general financial information. It also houses all SEC published materials. The library is open to the public from 9:00 a.m. to 5:30 p.m., Monday through Friday.

* Senate Research and Library

The Capitol, Suite S-332
Washington, DC 20510

The Senate Library is the official depository of senate documents. Its primary function is service to Senate members and their staffs. To use the library a researcher must have a letter of introduction from a Senator.

* Small Business Administration

1441 L St., NW, Room 218
Washington, DC 20416   (202) 653-6914

To review reference material pertaining to small business, contact the SBA's library. The library is open to the public for reference use only.

* Smithsonian Astrophysical Observatory

Smithsonian Institute
Perkin Building
Center for Astrophysics
60 Garden St.
Cambridge, MA 02138   (617) 495-7264

The collection of 50,000 books and 600 current journal titles are owned jointly by SAO and Harvard College Observatory. Subjects covered include all aspects of astronomy and astrophysics, related fields of physics, mathematics, engineering, and computer science. The library is open to the public by appointment.

Books and Libraries

* Smithsonian Museum Support Center
Smithsonian Institution
42210 Silver Hill Rd.
Suitland, MD 20746   (202) 287-3666
This library provides information about conservational of materials and museum objects, conservation science, which includes archaeometry, the study of museum environments, and the analysis of materials by such means as x-ray, diffraction, and gas chromatography. This library is open to the public by appointment.

* Smithsonian Institution Libraries
10th St. & Constitution Ave., NW
Washington, DC 20560   (202) 357-2139
The libraries of the Smithsonian Institution include approximately 950,000 volumes, with strengths in natural history, museology, history of science, and the humanities. Inquiries on special subjects or special collections should be addressed to the appropriate branch library or to the Central Reference and Loan.

* State, U.S. Department of
2201 C St., NW, Room 3239
Washington, DC 20520   (202) 647-1099
The library, whose collection specializes in the area of foreign affairs, is open to the public only if the information you are looking for cannot be found elsewhere in the Washington area. You must, however, call for an appointment.

* Supreme Court of the United States
Library
1 First St., NE
Washington, DC 20543   (202) 479-3037
Supreme Court records and briefs are available to the public for reproduction. However, only government attorneys and members of the Bar are permitted to use the general collection.

* Tennessee Valley Authority (TVA)
Technical Library Services

400 W. Summit Hill Dr., E2 B7
Knoxville, TN 37902   (615) 632-3464
The TVA library facilities are open to the public, while its specialty libraries cater to various organizations within TVA. Cataloged books, current technical journals, and reports relating to ongoing research in each division are available.

* Transportation, U.S. Department of
400 7th St., SW
M49.33
Room 2200
Washington, DC 20590   (202) 366-0746
Collection covers all modes of transportation except aviation. The library is open 9 a.m. - 4 p.m. with limited staff.

* Treasury, U.S. Department of
1500 Pennsylvania Ave., NW, Room 5310
Washington, DC 20220   (202) 566-2777
By appointment only. The collection includes law, economics, and finance information.

* U.S. Trade Representative, Office of the
Public Documents Room
Executive Office of the President
600 17th St., NW
Washington, DC 20506   (202) 395-6186
You must schedule an appointment to visit this documents area, open 10 to 12 a.m. and 1 to 4 p.m, Monday through Friday.

* Veterans Affairs, U.S. Department of
Central Office Library
810 Vermont Ave., NW, Room 976   (202) 233-2430
Washington, DC 20420   Circulation desk (202) 233-3085
Library resources include circulation collections of books, journals, and audiovisuals.

Government Printing Office

The U.S. Government Printing Office (GPO) along with the National Technical Information Service (NTIS) are Uncle Sam's primary publishers. The Superintendent of Documents at GPO is the official sales agent for many government publications. Approximately 21,000 titles are for sale in a wide variety of subject areas, including business and industry, children and families, careers, and energy. There are how-to guides, government manuals, and in-depth studies on nearly every subject imaginable. GPO publishes many different types of listings of their publications, from the popular *U.S. Government Books*, which lists selected popular recent releases, to the exhaustive *Publications Reference File*, which lists *all* GPO titles. GPO also provides access to their publications through a nationwide system of 1400 libraries and through 24 bookstores located across the country. Online connection through DIALOG is also possible.

* 320 Subject Bibliographies

Subject Bibliography Index
Superintendent of Documents
Government Printing Office
Washington, DC 20402 (202) 783-3238

More than 320 subject bibliographies listing books, periodicals, and subscriptions published by government agencies are available free from GPO. Topics range from accidents to zoning, and touch on most facets of human life. A complete listing of these subject bibliographies, called the *Subject Bibliography Index*, is available free upon request.

* Bestsellers from Uncle Sam

U.S. Government Books
Free Catalog
P.E. Box 37000
Washington, DC 20013-7000

GPO has a catalog of new and popular books sold by the government about agriculture, energy, children, space, health, history, business, vacations, and much more. Find out what government books are all about by ordering this free catalog.

* Bookstores Around the Country

Superintendent of Documents
U.S. Government Printing Office
Bookstore Branch Chief
Stop: SSFB
Washington, DC 20402 (202) 783-3293

GPO operates 24 bookstores that display and sell the most popular of the more than 21,000 titles for sale by the government. If the bookstore does not stock the book you are looking for, they will order it and have it sent to you. Bookstores accept VISA, MasterCard, and Superintendent of Documents deposit account orders. All stores are open Monday through Friday, except the one Kansas City. The following is a listing of the bookstores:

Alabama
O"Neill Building, 2021 Third Ave., North Birmingham, AL 35203; (205) 731-1056

California
ARCO Plaza, C-Level, 505 South Flower St., Los Angeles, CA 90071; (213) 894-5841
Room 1023, Federal Building, 450 Golden Gate Ave., San Francisco, CA 94102; (415) 556-0643

Colorado
Room 117, Federal Building, 1961 Stout St., Denver, CO 80294; (303) 844-3964
World Savings Building, 720 North Main St., Pueblo, CO 81003; (719) 544-3142

District of Columbia
U.S. Government Printing Office, 710 N. Capitol St., NW, Washington, DC 20401
1510 H St. NW, Washington, DC 20005; (202) 653-5075

Florida
Room 158, Federal Building, 400 W. Bay St., Jacksonville, FL 32202; (904) 791-3801

Georgia
Room 100, Federal Building, 275 Peachtree St. NW, P.O. Box 56445, Atlanta, GA 30343; (404) 331-6947

Illinois

Room 1365, Federal Building, 219 S. Dearborn St., Chicago, IL 60604; (312) 353-5133

Maryland
Warehouse Sales Outlet, 8660 Cherry Lane, Laurel, MD 20707; (301) 953-7974; 792-0262

Massachusetts
Thomas P. O'Neill Building, 10 Causeway St., Room 179, Boston, MA 02222; (617) 565-6680

Michigan
Suite 160, Federal Building, 477 Michigan Ave., Detroit, MI 48226; (313) 226-7816

Missouri
120 Bannister Mall, 5600 E. Bannister Rd., Kansas City, MO 64137; (816) 765-2256

New York
Room 110, 26 Federal Plaza, New York, NY 10278; (212) 264-3825

Ohio
Room 1653, Federal Building, 1240 E. 9th St., Cleveland, OH 44199; (216) 522-4922
Room 207, Federal Building, 200 N. High St., Columbus, OH 43215; (614) 469-6956

Oregon
1305 S.W. First Ave., Portland, OR 97201-5801; (503) 221-6217

Pennsylvania
Robert Morris Building, 100 N. 17th St., Philadelphia, PA 19103; (215) 597-0677
Room 118, Federal Building, 1000 Liberty Ave., Pittsburgh, PA 15222; (412) 644-2721

Texas
Room 1C46, Federal Building, 1100 Commerce St., Dallas, TX 75242; (214) 767-0076
Texas Crude Building, 801 Travis St., Suite 120, Houston, TX 77002; (713) 653-3100

Washington
Room 194, Federal Building, 915 Second Ave., Seattle, WA 98174; (206) 442-4270

Wisconsin
Room 190, Federal Building, 517 E. Wisconsin Ave., Milwaukee, WI 53202; (414) 291-1304

* Catalog of Federal Domestic Assistance

Superintendent of Documents
U.S. Government Printing Office
Washington, DC 20402 (202) 783-3238

The *Catalog of Federal Domestic Assistance* is government-wide summary of financial and non-financial Federal programs, projects, services, and activities that provide assistance or benefits to the American public administered by departments and establishments of the Federal government. It describes the type of assistance available and the eligibility requirements for the particular assistance being sought, with guidance on how to apply. Also intended to improve coordination and communication between the federal government and state and local governments. Annual subscriptions, which consist of a basic manual and supplementary material for an indeterminate period, are $38.00.

Books and Libraries

* Congressional Record and Calendars
Superintendent of Documents
Congressional Information Specialist
Stop: SSOI
Washington, DC 20402 (202) 275-3030
GPO publishes major Congressional publications, including the *Congressional Record*, House and Senate *Calendars*, all bills and laws, and related information. All of this information is available by subscription.

* Data Tapes of Government Publications
Superintendent of Documents
U.S. Government Printing Office
P.O. Box 37082
Washington, DC 20013-7082(202) 275-3328
Government publications produced in electronic format are now available in magnetic tape form. Tapes may be purchased on an individual tape basis or by subscription. Individual publications on tape include the *Budget of the United States*, the *Congressional Directory*, and the *Government Manual*. Some of the subscriptions available are the *Congressional Record*, *Federal Register*, and *Daily Bills*.

* Deposit Accounts for Government Publications
Superintendent of Documents
Stop: SSOP
Washington, DC 20402 (202) 783-3238
Deposit accounts are a convenient way to order materials from GPO. A minimum of $50 is required to open the account, and monthly statements are issued. Telephone orders are accepted for any account containing sufficient funds, and order forms are provided for mail orders.

* Discounts on Government Books
Superintendent of Documents
U.S. Government Printing Office
Washington, DC 20402 (202) 783-2328
Designated bookdealers and educational institution bookstores receive a 25 percent discount on publications and subscriptions whether single copies or in bulk. Any customers ordering 100 or more copies of a publication to be delivered to the same address may also receive the discount.

* Federal Depository Libraries
Superintendent of Documents
Library Marketer
Stop: SM
Washington, DC 20402 (202) 275-3635
A national system of nearly 1400 public, academic, and law libraries maintains collections of most government publications. The libraries are located in nearly every state. Their staffs will help you with research questions and can provide information on price and order numbers if you wish to purchase copies. If your library does not have the publication you need, they will borrow it for you. To determine which library serves you, contact your public library or the above.

* Federal Register
Superintendent of Documents
U.S. Government Printing Office
Washington, DC 20402 (202) 783-3238
The *Federal Register*, with daily issues Monday through Friday, except on a legal holidays, announces to the public regulations and legal notices issued by Federal agencies. These include Presidential proclamations and Executive orders and Federal agency documents having general applicability and legal effect, documents required to be published by Act of Congress and other Federal agency documents of public interest. Subscribers to this service will automatically receive copies of the *Federal Register Index* and the *Code of Federal Regulations*, and *LSA List of CFR Sections Affected*, at no additional cost. Subscriptions are $340.00 per year; or $170.00 for six months; or $1.50 for single copies.

* Government Periodicals and Subscription Services
Superintendent of Documents
U.S. Government Printing Office
Washington, DC 20402 (202) 783-3238
Better known as PL 36, *Government Periodicals and Subscription Services* lists all materials available on a subscription basis complete with ordering information and order forms. Single copies of this publication are available.

* Government Publications: Complete Listing
Superintendent of Documents

U.S. Government Printing Office
Washington, DC 20402 (202) 783-3238
A complete master file of GPO publications, entitled *Sales Publications Reference File* (PRF), is available by subscription on microfiche and magnetic tape from GPO. It is also available to subscribers of the DIALOG Information Retrieval System. Users of the system can perform on-line searches of GPO's sales inventory to determine if the publication is for sale, if the item is in stock, and its stock number and current price. DIALOG users can order documents via DIALORDER, a feature of DIALOG.

* Government Publications Ordering Information
Superintendent of Documents
U. S. Government Printing Office
Washington, DC 20402 (202) 783-3238
Orders for government books, pamphlets, posters, and periodicals can be placed by calling the above telephone number between 7:30 a.m. and 4:00 p.m., eastern time. This number may also be used to obtain catalogs of publications plus information on prices, stock numbers, and availability of sales publications. Orders may be charged to MasterCard, VISA, or prepaid Superintendent of Documents deposit accounts.

* Information on GPO Publications
Superintendent of Documents
Research and Analysis Section
Stop: SSOP
Washington, DC 20402 (202) 783-3238
Call or write at the above address for general information on materials available from GPO or for bibliographies, catalogs, or current brochures. For more extensive information on government published information, contact the nearest Federal Depository Library, which maintains copies of all GPO-published materials. To find the library nearest you, contact your local library.

* International Orders
Superintendent of Documents
U. S. Government Printing Office
Washington, DC 20402 (202) 783-3238
Orders for delivery outside the U.S. are subject to a 25% surcharge to provide for the special handling required by international mailing regulations. Orders are mailed surface mail unless airmail is requested (at an additional cost). Payment must accompany every order in U.S. dollars and be in the form of a check drawn on a bank located in the U.S. or Canada, a UNESCO coupon, or an International Postal Money Order made payable to the Superintendent of Documents.

* Mailing Lists
Superintendent of Documents
Mail List User Program
P.O. Box 1908
Washington, DC 20013 (202) 275-9051
Individuals interested in direct mail promotions to subscribers of government periodicals can obtain paid subscriber lists for approximately 70 different government periodicals from GPO. The lists are available on a one-time use basis only.

* Maps, Posters, Charts, Pictures, and Decals
Superintendent of Documents
Research and Analysis Section
Stop: SSOP
Washington, DC 20402 (202) 783-3238
A wide variety of posters, maps, and decals are sold by GPO, including facsimiles of the *Declaration of Independence*, the *Constitution*, NASA posters, and a wide variety of depictions of nature. For a complete price listing, contact the above address.

* New Government Titles
Superintendent of Documents
U.S. Government Printing Office
Washington, DC 20402-9325
The *New Books* catalog is a sampling of new releases from GPO. It is organized by subject area such as agriculture, education, computers, and transportation. These bimonthly listings are available free on a subscription basis. Contact the above address or your nearest U.S. Government bookstore.

* Printing Contracts from GPO
U.S. Government Printing Office
Procurement and Supply Division
Stop: PPS
Washington, DC 20401 (202) 275-3774
GPO awards approximately 46,000 printing contracts to commercial printers each year. To get in on the action, ask for the GPO bidders's information packet,

which contains everything necessary to get started.

* Priority Publication Announcements
U.S. Government Printing Office
Office of Marketing
Stop: SM
Washington, DC 20401   (202) 783-3238

If you are interested in staying up to date in a certain subject, you can request that notification be sent to you when the government publishes something new in your area of interest. GPO maintains lists of materials--called *Priority Announcements*--for nearly 100 subject areas.

* Selling Ink to GPO
U.S. Government Printing Office
General Procurement Division
Washington, DC 20401   (202) 275-2470

If you are a commercial contractor interested in selling ink to GPO, write or call for the brochure, *How to Sell Ink to GPO*, which is designed to provide the necessary information.

* Selling Paper to GPO
U.S. Government Printing Office

Paper Procurement Section
Stop, MMG
Washington, DC 20401   (202) 275-2022

Information is available on procedures for selling paper to GPO.

* Standing Orders: Government Publications
Standing Order Specialist
Publication Order Branch
Stop SSOP
U.S. Government Printing Office
Washington, DC 20402   (202) 275-3082

For your convenience, GPO has instituted a standing order service for many recurring publications. This allows you to place an order once and automatically receive all subsequent editions or issuances in the same series. For complete information and the necessary authorization form, contact the above office.

* Tours of Government Printing Office
U. S. Government Printing Office
Office of Public Affairs
Stop: PA
Washington, DC 20401   (202) 275-3541

For a tour of the world's largest printing plant, contact the above office.

Federal Government Databases

Much of the data found in the thousands of federal databases are not available anywhere else, which makes them unique and invaluable sources of information for research on almost any topic. And because the government agencies do not make an effort to solicit public access, in many instances the existence of government databases is known to only a few specialists. In those cases where commercial vendors are selling government data, you will discover that you can get the data directly from the federal or state agency for much less money. Searches and printouts of many of these databases can be arranged, and often a tape or diskette of a file can be purchased. There are literally tens of thousands of databases generated by federal agencies. Here is just a sampling of what is available. If you are looking for databases other than those listed below, refer to the Information Starting Places Chapter or review Information USA's reference books, the *Federal Database Finder* and the *State Data and Database Finder*.

For a listing of those databases which can be accessed exclusively on-line see the next section titled Government Electronic Bulletin Boards.

* Abandoned Land Mines
Doug J. Godesky
National Inventory Update Committee
U.S. Department of the Interior
1100 L St., NW Suite 5400
Washington, DC 20240 (202) 343-6900
This system provides an inventory of all abandoned mined lands in the United States so that land reclamation may be complete and systematic. For each abandoned mine problem area the following information is provided: location, general features, cost of reclamation and financing to date. The database can be searched by individual states or problem areas. Searches are available upon request and there is no charge.

* Adopt-A-Horse Data System
Charles Boyer
Bureau of Land Management
Denver Federal Center, Building 50
U.S. Department of the Interior
PO Box 25047
Denver, CO 80225 (303) 236-0157
This database supports the Wild Horse and Burro Program. It maintains a listing of several thousand individuals who have applied to adopt wild horses or burros. The listing includes names, addresses, and telephone numbers of each applicant; the species, number and sex of the animals. It also maintains a listing of adopters, their adopters, their addresses, and telephone numbers, and the individual identification numbers for animals obtained and the agency offices approving the adoptions. The data are updated when adopted animals die or are reassigned to other adopters and when titles of ownership are transferred to the adopters. Searches are provided upon request for a fee. Hardcopy reports are produced showing applicants or adopters, mailing addresses and related information as requested.

* Adverse Drug Reaction Reporting System
Gerald Deighton
FOI Staff HFI-35
U.S. FDA
5600 Fishers Lane
Rockville, MD 20857 (301) 443-6310
This office maintains data files from 1969 to present consisting of adverse reactions to marketed drugs and biologics as reported by manufacturers, hospitals, physicians, and contracted collection efforts for the Division of Epidemiology and Surveillance (DES). For more information contact Michael W. Dreis at (301) 443-4580.

* AGRICultural OnLine Access (AGRICOLA)
Technical Services Division
National Agricultural Library
U.S. Department of Agriculture
Beltsville, MD 20705 (301) 344-3834
AGRICOLA is a bibliographic database consisting of records for literature citations of journal articles, monographs, these, patents, software, audiovisual materials and technical reports relating to all aspects of agriculture. It is one of the largest collections of agricultural literature in the world with over 1.8 million volumes. AGRICOLA has been available in magnetic tape form since 1970. It currently has over 2.5 million records. AGRICOLA has many access points,

searching approaches include: personal and corporate authors, subject category codes, date of journal issues, journal titles or journal title abbreviations, languages of text, source codes, subject heading, indexing terms. Online access is offered by the following commercial vendors: DIALOG, BRS Information Technologies. Magnetic tapes for both the current and retrospective files may be purchased from NTIS.

* Agriculture Research Results Database
Jim Hall
Agricultural Research Service, U.S.DA
Room 404, Building 005
Beltsville, MD 20705 (301) 344-4045
This database contains over 1500 one-page narratives of recent research discoveries that are ready for distribution to farms, ranches, and rural communities. The subject matter covers animal and plant production, protection, and agricultural economics. Database reports are available 9 to 18 months before information becomes available through literature publications. The research work included is that which is supported by U.S. Department of Economic Research Service. Free searches and printouts are available through most state extension services, U.S. Department of Agriculture and through Land Grant Universities on a limited basis. Online searching can also be done on the ITT Dailcom system.

* Aircraft Registration Master File
Federal Aviation Administration
Data Services Division, AC-340
Department of Transportation
PO Box 25082
Oklahoma City, OK 73125
The file contains a listing of all civil aircraft registered in the United States. Information given includes data on the aircraft, the engine, the registrant, the base airport, the airworthiness, operation, use, and avionics equipment capability of the aircraft. Printouts are available at 25 cents per page from FAA, Flight Standards Technical Division, Aircraft Registration Branch, P.O. Box 25082, Oklahoma City, Oklahoma 73125 (Attn. AAC 250). To obtain copy on magnetic tape, send a written request to the Data Services Division, listed above.

* Air Industry Data Base System
Office of the Secretary, TAD-25
U.S. Department of Transportation
400 7th St., SW
Washington, DC 20590 (202) 366-4000
The data, available in machine readable form, provide a record for each month for each flight segment of every commercially scheduled airline flight. They describe the originating and destination terminals, detail the aircraft configuration, and report upon utilization of the aircraft. Machine readable reports on activities between city pairs by frequency of flight, load factors, and number of people traveling are generated. Airborne and ground delay time reports are also produced. Contact the office listed above.

* Annual Petroleum Supply Reporting System
National Energy Information Center
U.S. Department of Energy
Room 1F-048

Washington, DC 20585   (202) 586-8800

This system assembles statistical data on an annual basis on liquid hydrocarbon products. It provides data measuring current and sustainable capacity of the significant facilities at all refineries located in the United States, and U.S. Territories. Data are collected on type of plant, storage capacity by product, type of refining facility and capacity. Historical data are available from 1970 to present in automated form.

* Annual Survey of Occupational Injuries and Illnesses

Kathy Shirley
Information Services
U.S. Department of Labor
Bureau of Labor Statistics
441 G St., NW
Washington, DC 20212   (202) 272-3470

This system provides information about the incidence of job-related fatalities and job-related non-fatal injuries and illnesses among employees in the private and public sector. The system provides the Occupational Safety and Health Administration and similar state agencies information to effectively set standards, guide enforcement and consulting activities, and establish educational and training programs. Data are tabulated at the 4-digit Standard Industrial Classification (SIC) level in manufacturing, and 3-digit level in construction, and other non-manufacturing industries. Data are from about 280,000 establishments representing 5 million workplaces. Customized data files, tapes, diskettes or printouts are available on a cost recovery basis.

* Area Resource File System (ARFS) Health Services County Comparison

Mary Morris
Office of Data Analysis and Management
U.S. Department of Health and Human Services
Public Health Service
Health Resources & Services Administration
5600 Fishers La.
Rockville, MD 20857   (301) 443-6920

This system includes 104 separate state reports. Each report contains health resources, trends and socio-demographic information for each state and its counties. Each state report contains two volumes: Selected Geographic Resources and Geographic Trends in Resources. The first volume includes summary material on key measures related to health care resources and delivery for the state and its counties and contains a ranking profile of how each state and county compare on over 30 measures. The trends volume contains time-series tables for health professions supply, population, vital statistics and health facilities. Also included is a detailed profile of physicians by specialty. All 104 separate state reports, diskettes and tapes are for sale from NTIS.

* Bilingual Education Management Information System (BEMIS)

William Wooten
Office of Bilingual Education and Minority Languages Affairs
U.S. Department of Education
400 Maryland Ave., NW
Washington, DC 2020   (202) 732-5063

The system contains information about English education programs for students who do not speak fluent English. Retrievable information includes the name and addresses of the grantees, the period of the grant, the amount of the grant, the native languages of the students served, the number of students in the program, the grade levels of the students, and the school and districts that participate in the program. Searches can be done in a variety of ways. Tapes are not available, but printouts can be ordered. Simple requests are free of charge but the office will charge on a cost recovery basis for more extensive searches.

* BIOETHICSLINE

Joy Kahn
Center for Bioethics Library
Kennedy Institute of Ethics
Georgetown University
Washington, DC 20007   (202) 687-6771

BIOETHICSLINE contains bibliographic citations and abstracts of literature related to moral or ethical public policies issues in medicine, medical research and health care. Journal articles, court cases, laws, government documents and books addressing the legal, medical, philosophical and social- science aspect of bioethics are cited. Topics include professional/patient relationships, allocation of health-care resources, contraception, abortion, reproductive technologies, genetics, human experimentation, animal laboratory research, death and dying, and the prolongation of life. The database can be searched for keyword, author, title and time period. The system was started in 1973 and currently contains 26,000 records. It is updated bimonthly. Searches and printouts are available free of charge from the Bioethics Library. BIOEHTICSLINE is accessible free of charge or the National Library of Medicine's MEDLARS System for which there is a nominal fee.

* Bird Banding Database

John Tautin
Bird Banding Laboratory
U.S. Fish and Wildlife Service
Laurel, MD 20708   (301) 498-0423

This database contains information about game and non- game birds banded and/or recovered since the Banding Program began in 1921. Records exist on all birds banded in North America as well as their recovery from all over the world. The database is international in scope, as birds have been recovered by participants in countries such as Russia, Brazil and India. The database is used to produce quarterly reports to the person who bands the bird and certificates of appreciation to band reporters. It is also used for extensive data analysis of migratory bird populations. The database contains 2.6 million banding records. Searches and printouts are available. Depending upon the nature of your request, you may or may not be charged a fee. There is no determined fee schedule.

* Boating Accident Report (BAR)

Policy Planning and Evaluation Staff (G-BP)
Department of Transportation
2100 Second St., SW
Washington, DC 20593   (202) 267-2229

The system, updated monthly, provides annual statistical summaries on motorboat accidents. The principal data elements are case number, date, state, county, cause, facilities, injuries, operator age, vessel types, time, and environmental conditions. Thirty-two annual reports are generated by this system. One of them is the *Coast Guard Boating Statistics*, which is available upon request. Other data for internal use only.

* Bureau of Labor Statistics Electronic News Releases Service

Kathryn Hoyle
Office of Publications
Bureau of Labor Statistics
441 G St., NW
Washington, DC 20212   (202) 523-1913

BLS Electronic News Service provides direct dial-in access to subscribers of Boeing Computer Services, interested in the Bureau's economic indicators. The BLS releases, available online as soon as the data are officially released to the public include: producer price indexes; employment situation; state and metropolitan area employment and unemployment; consumer price index; real earnings; productivity and costs; and the employment cost index. The service is updated continually. Cost of the Electronic News Releases, which can be transmitted over telephone lines to computer terminals and other remote-access devices, varies. For contract information call Ronald S. Mizerak at Boeing.

* Cardiac Pacemaker Registry (CPR)

Gerald Deighton
FOI Staff HFI-35
U.S. FDA
5600 Fishers Lane
Rockville, MD 20857   (301) 443-6310

Contains data on all pacemakers and leads paid for under Medicare since April of 1985. Some information cannot be released. For more information contact Mac Chapin at (301) 427-8086.

* Catalog of Information on Water Data

Mary Bell Peters
National Water Data Exchange (NAWDEX)
U.S. Geological Survey, U.S. Department of Interior
421 National Center
Reston, VA 22090   (703) 648-5663

This computer file contains over 400,000 entries on streams, lakes, reservoirs, estuaries, and ground water. It contains sources, measurement locations, parameter types, frequency of measurement, and periods of record for data-acquisition programs of Federal/non-Federal agencies and organizations. It also contains water-data collection techniques for surface water, ground water, sediment, biological sediment, soil water, drainage basin characteristics, snow and ice and hydrometeoroloc hydrometeorological observations. Computer printouts, maps, catalogs, referrals and publications are available.

* Census Bureau Transportation Statistics

Bureau of the Census
Data Users Services Division
Customer Services
Washington, DC 20233   (202) 763-4100

The following two data files are available representing survey results taken at 5 year intervals by the Census of Transportation: The Trucking Inventory and Use Survey; and the Commodity Transportation Survey. These surveys present benchmark data on the physical and operational characteristics of our national trucking resources and aggregate statistics on commodity movements by various modes. A machines readable tape is available for each survey. Printed reports and microfiche reports are also generated.

* Climate Assessment Database (CADB)

Vernon Patterson
NOAA, National Meteorological Center W353
WWB, Room 201
Washington, DC 20233   (301) 763-8071

Designed for easy public access, this system provides users with information about short-term climate conditions in the United States and throughout the world. Anyone with a compatible terminal (most home computers are) and telephone linkup can obtain a password and dial directly into the system. Users can then select from a menu of 50 data files summarizing meteorological data on a weekly, monthly and seasonal basis. Examples of data include: temperature, precipitation, weather indexes, heating and cooling days, energy conditions, and assessment of climate on crops. The system contains global surface data collected from 6,000 stations worldwide. Data are contributed from 8,000 stations worldwide. The system is updated continually. For the price of a phone call, anyone with compatible equipment can use the system. Contact Mr. Patterson's office at NOAA to find out if your terminal and telephone linkup are compatible. His office will give you an eight-letter password and the telephone number you can use to enter the system. The users fee ranges from $48-$600.

* Coal Consumption-Manufacturing Plants

Bruce Quaid, Survey Manager
Coal Division - Data Systems Branch
Energy Information Administration
Washington, DC 20585   (202) 586-3544

This information system provides a quarterly census of coal consumption by U.S. manufacturing plants. The data are derived from coal receipts, consumption and stocks. Contact NTIS to purchase tapes or diskettes.

* Coal Distribution

Bruce Quaid, Survey Manager
Coal Division - Data Systems Branch
Energy Information Administration
Washington, DC 20585   (202) 586-3544

The information system covers 99.5 percent of the U.S. coal production and distribution. Data are collected on coal production and purchases, stocks and distribution, including district or origin, method of transportation, and destination by: consumer category and census region and state. Data are collected quarterly, and the system contains over 20,000 records. Contact NTIS to purchase tapes or diskettes.

* Codes for Named Populated Places, Primary
Country Divisions and Other Locations
Entities of the U.S.
U.S. Department of Commerce
National Technical Information Service
Springfield, VA 22161   (703) 487-4807

This ninth update of the Federal Information Processing Standard (FIPS) 55 data file provides a two-character State code and five-character numeric place code to uniquely identify each listed entity. Areas of the United States covered are the fifty states, the District of Columbia, and all outlying territories with significant self-administration. An exhaustive list is carried of incorporated places, census designated places (CDP's), primary county divisions (such as townships, New England towns, and census county divisions), recognized Indian reservations and Alaska Native villages, and counties. The listing also includes unincorporated places, military bases, National parks, airports, and ground transportation points. A two-character class code distinguishes over seventy entity types. Each entity is identified by the county or counties in which it is located. Zip codes are provided for all Post Offices. Available in: 9 track 1600 or 6250 BPI, order number PB87-1424326/HAL at a cost of $525.

* Commuter Air Carrier Statistics: Online O & D and Flight & Traffic Statistics

Richard S. Strite
Department of Transportation
Research and Special Programs Administration
Washington, DC 20590   (202) 366-9058

Online O&D (origination and destination) contains the number of passengers and amount of mail and cargo transported by commuter air carriers between city pairs in scheduled services. Flight and Traffic Statistics provide data on the number of aircraft hours, miles, departures, revenue passenger-miles, available seat-miles, revenue ton-miles and available ton-miles transported by commuter air carriers in scheduled service. The disclosure of data on the file is restricted for a period of 12 months after the close of the year to which the data relate from 1971 to the present. Customized reports are available from these files upon written request. Data tapes are available for a fee.

* Continuing Survey of Food Intakes by Individuals (CSFII)

Gerald Deighton
FOI Staff HFI-35
U.S. FDA
5600 Fishers Lane
Rockville, MD 20857   (301) 443-6310

Annual nationwide food consumption survey of men and women 19-50 and children 1-5 conducted by U.S.DA. Survey began in 1985. Provides data on food and nutrient intakes (up to six non- consecutive days) and vitamin/mineral supplement use. Contains companion food composition data. For more information contact Youngmee K. Park at (202) 485-0089.

* Contractor Accident Injury/Employment System

Richard Smith, Chief
Manager Safety and Health Technology Center
U.S. Department of Labor
Division of Mining Information Systems
PO Box 25367, DFC, Federal Building
Denver, CO 80025-0367   (303) 236-2713

This system collects, edits, updates, stores and reports information pertaining to contractor identification, employment, accidents, injuries and fatalities chargeable to mine, coal metal/non-metal contractors. The information published from this system, including incidence rates and other statistical data, i.e., coal production in tons, is used by many mine industry related organizations, as well as by government personnel. The system is used to store and report contractor identification, address, accident, injury and illness information and statistics computed from these data. Individualized search requests are accepted. Searches are free as long as the information can be extracted easily and is reasonable quantity. Current data is kept for two years. Large projects are accepted and charged a fee under Freedom of Information Act. Data files are also available to purchase for complex projects.

* Countries, Dependencies, and Areas of Special Sovereignty

U.S. Department of Commerce
National Technical Information Service
Springfield, VA 22161   (703) 487-4807

The file contains data from Table 1 of Federal Information Processing Standard Publication (FIPS PUB) 10-3 *Countries, Dependencies, Areas of Special Sovereignty, and Their Principal Administrative Divisions*, including its change notices 1 and 2. The file includes the names and alphabetic two-character codes of each basic entity. In addition, it includes the name and four-character code of each principal division for those basic entities whose divisions are included in FIPS-PUB 10- 3. Records are sequenced in alphabetic order by basic entity. A typical entry consists of the country (basic entity) code and name and, if the basic entity is subdivided, the principal division codes and names. It is available in 9 track 1600 or 6250 BPI, order number PB85-222859/HAL, at a cost of $210.

* Defense Technical Information Center Collection (DTIC Online, DROLS)

National Technical Information Service (NTIS)
5285 Port Royal Rd.
Springfield, VA 22161   (703) 487-4600

DTIC maintains data banks with information about planned, ongoing, and completed DOD-related research and development activities. The collection is multi-disciplinary in scope and spans all fields of science and technology, covering topics such as: aeronautics, missile technology, navigation, space and technology, nuclear science, biology, chemistry, environmental science, oceanography, computer science, and human factors engineering. The four principle data banks are: the Technical Reports (TR) Program which contains bibliographic information on classified/unclassified reports generated by federally sponsored research; the Research and Technology Work Unit Information System (WUIS) containing information about current research being performed; the Research and Development Planning (R&DPP) database, consisting of information about proposed projects; and the Independent Research & Development (IR&D) data bank with information contractors have supplied DOD regarding their independent research efforts. The DTIC collection currently contains two million documents and is updated continually. Universities, U.S. government agencies and associated contractors, subcontractors, and grantees are eligible for most DTIC services. In addition, research and development organization without current contracts may become eligible for service by obtaining a military service authorization under the defense potential contractors programs. If you are registered user for DTIC services, you can obtain direct online access to the DTIC system, have searches and printouts done free of charge, and purchase DTIC documents for a minimal fee - generally $1.50 to $3.00. If you are not DTIC-eligible, you can contact the National Technical Information Service (NTIS) to obtain a limited search of DTIC's Technical Reports Program database. NTIS charges for its services.

* Dental Research Projects

Deane Hill

Grants: Ron Ruben or Carla Flora
National Institute of Dental Research (NIDR)
Research Data and Management Information Section
5333 Westbard Ave., Room 539
Bethesda, MD 20814   (301) 496-7843

NIDR maintains a data bank of information about nationwide research activities in all areas of dental health. The data set is called Dental Proj. The research projects range from very basic to very applied, and most of the listings are NIDR-supported grants, contracts, or in-house projects. Retrievable data include: project title and number; name and address of the principle investigator; grant or contract specialists; project funding plus dates of commencement and completion; and a brief description of the project. Limited information is also available on worldwide dental research activities. Records go back to 1972. The contracts file, which is updated monthly, currently contains 100 active reports. The grants file presently holds 3,600 records and is updated daily. Searches and printouts are available free of charge and only from NIDR. Data will be available online through the National Library of Medicine in the future.

* Dictionary of Occupational Titles, 4th Edition, and 1986 DOT Supplement

U.S. Department of Commerce
National Technical Information Service
Springfield, VA 22161   (703) 487-4807

This is the master file for the fourth edition of the Dictionary of Occupational Titles. it is comprehensive compilation of 12,099 coded (9-digits) job definitions classified in nine defined major categories, 82 defined 2 digit divisions, and 559 defined 3 digit groups. More than 28,800 job titles are in the file. Also included are master titles and definitions, term titles and definitions, glossary terms and 220 industry designation definitions. Available in: 9 track, 1600 or 6250 BPI, order number PB87-194528/HAL, at a cost of $210.

* Diet and Health Surveys

Gerald Deighton
FOI Staff HFI-35
U.S. FDA
5600 Fishers Lane
Rockville, MD 20857   (301) 443-6310

Analysis of national consumer attitudes towards diet and health, updated every two years since 1982. For more information contact Alan S. Levy at (202) 245-1457.

* Driver License Administration Requirements and Fees

Highway Statistics Division
Federal Highway Administration
Department of Transportation
400 7th St., SW
Washington, DC 20590   (202) 366-0180

Data cover the administrative requirements and qualifications necessary to obtain drivers' licenses in the 50 states and D.C. and Canada. Contains narrative summary and 10 detailed tables showing data by state, including requirements for regular licenses and classified licenses; training; examination and renewal; license reciprocity; fees; and suspension, revocation, and reinstatement provisions. Data is updated biennially. Contact the office listed above.

* Drug Quality Reporting System (DQRS)

Gerald Deighton
FOI Staff HFI-35
U.S. FDA
5600 Fishers Lane
Rockville, MD 20857   (301) 443-6310

Nation's pharmacists reporting on the quality of drugs, both RX and OTC, in the U.S. marketplace. (Replaced the former Drug Product Problem Reporting System.) Years covered are 1971 to present. For more information contact George R. Bolger at (301) 443-6044.

* Duck Breeding Ground Survey Database

Byron K. Williams, Acting Chief
Office of Migratory Bird Management
U.S. Department of the Interior
Fish and Wildlife Service
Washington, DC 20240   (703) 358-1714

This survey provides data tables for use in estimating the size of waterfowl populations. It uses a master file of aerial survey data collected each year in July. It provides an index to the number of broods produced and the number of adult birds that are still on nesting territories. Data on age class and number of young per brood are recorded to determine progress and success of the nesting season. Information from this survey is most reliable for the most abundant and widely distributed species such as the mallard; it is less so for species of low abundance or for those species whose nesting is partly outside the survey area. Information is public and questions will be answered for members of the general public. Search requests are accepted through state agencies and University Land Grant Programs.

* Earth Science Data Director

C. R. Baskin
ESDD Project Manager
U.S. Geological Survey
801 National Center
Reston, VA 22092   (703) 648-7112

ESDD is designed to identify earth science and natural resource databases maintained by government agencies, academic institutions, and private sector entities. Users can locate indices, systems, files, documents, maps and other data sets. Databases referenced include those storing information on geologic, hydrologic, cartographic, biologic and conservation sciences. A computer terminal equipped with a modem can access ESDD with no on-line access charge. Menus, cross-referencing, and powerful search features make using the database easy. It is available on CD from OCLC (614-764-6000) in combination with GEOINDEX and U.S.GS LIBRARY. Contact Mr. Baskin to arrange on-line use.

* Earth Science Information Center

Earth Science Information Center (ESIC)
U.S. Geological Survey
507 National Center, Room 1-C-402
Reston, VA 22092   (800) USA-MAPS or (703) 648-6045
or
Contact the ESIC nearest you. There are
approximately 58 state affiliates. Consult
your telephone book under U.S. Govt., Department
of the Interior, U.S.GS.

The Earth Science Information Office operates a nationwide information and sales service for earth science research, maps, products and publications from both governmental and private sources. This network of ESICs (formerly known as National Cartographic Information Centers) provide information about geologic, hydrologic, topographic and land-use maps and publications; aerial, satellite and radar images and related products; cartographic data in digital form (see GeoData entry); and geodetic data. Some of the information dates back to 1700, and the Center has access to EROS Center databases of aerial/space imagery. ESIC staff will search these vast computerized records of cartographic data at your request. Several of the individual U.S.GS databases are described in this section. Most of ESIC's research services are free, and many materials are available for order through ESIC. For others, you will be referred to the proper source.

* Economic and Industry Employment Projections

Howard Iullerton
Office of Economic Growth Projections
U.S. Department of Labor Statistics
441 G St., NW
Washington, DC 20212   (202) 272-5328

The purpose of this system is to provide current and projected information in labor market trends. Information is divided by geographic location, industry and occupation and is intended for use in career guidance, educational planning and training programs. This system contains data on national employment, and projections on about 700 occupations in industries. Data are available for 1982 and projected to 1995. Bureau of Labor Statistics provides a number of services upon request for users of statistical data. These include release of certain categories of unpublished data; development of special surveys and tabulations; duplication of machine-readable data files on either diskettes or magnetic tapes; and sales of statistical software programs. Customized data files are available on a cost recovery basis.

* Economic and Social Data System (ESDS)

Maury Brown
Center for Development Information and Evaluation
U.S. Agency for International Development (AID)
Room 209, SA-1B
Washington, DC 20523   (703) 875-4810

ESDS is a statistical database consisting of development-related information about each country. The data are in a time series format, and collected from government agencies and organization conditions, demography, poverty indicators, labor force, social characteristics; and the population's education, nutrition, health, and food. The general public can obtain standardized reports, prepared from ESDS database searches, for a minimal fee from AID-Document Information and Handling Faculty (DIHF). Contact DIHF to obtain a free listing of available reports. Free specialized searches for AID contractors and federal, state, local and foreign government agencies. Non-AID users should contact the AID library to arrange a search.

* Economic Development Administration Socioeconomic

Government Databases and Bulletin Boards

Data System

U.S. Department of Commerce
Economic Development Administration
Herbert C. Hoover Bldg, Room 7116
Washington, DC 20230   (202) 377-3621

This system identifies socioeconomic characteristics of areas in which the Economic Development Administration (EDA) has approved projects. It includes data for all counties in the U.S. as well as for cities with population over 25,000. Data files are formatted to permit custom retrieval of specified data elements. Data files available through the system include Census Data Files, County Merge, County Business Patterns Files, Income Files, Bureau of Labor Statistics data and population and income figures. Arrangements can be made for individualized searches by EDA.

* Economic Impact Forecast System (EIFS)

Department of Urban and Regional Planning
ETIS Support Center
1003 West Nevada St.
Urbana, IL 61801   (217) 333-1369

EIFS is an information source and analytical tool that allows planners to predict the impact of proposed changes in an activity on the economy of affected areas. The system, which has statistics for every county in the U.S., can gather this information into any size multi-county region to analyze potential impacts. The database contains selected Department of Commerce statistics of social and economic characteristics in all U.S. counties and a variety of other types of information, including the Census of Population, Housing, and Manufacturers, the Bureau of Economic Analysis estimates, and County Business Patterns reports. EIFS contains records on all 3,200 counties in the country. Direct access via a remote terminal is available to ETIS subscribers for $200.00 a year plus $90.00 per hour of computer connect time. Anyone can become an ETIS subscriber and thereby also obtain direct access to other databases maintained by ETIS. ETIS will conduct searches for nonsubscribers. A cost recovery fee, based on $90.00 per hour computer time, plus $25.00 staff time is charged. The average search generally takes 10 minutes.

* Electronic Catalog System

Satellite Data Services Division
Princeton Executive Center
5627 Allentown Rd.
Camp Springs, MD 20746   (301) 763-8399

The Electronic Catalog System is a computerized locator system for digital data transmitted by polar orbit satellite and archived by NOAA. Data can be retrieved by time period, type of satellite, a particular sensor in a satellite, type of coverage, and geographical area. The system, formerly called the Spinner Program, was started in 1979, and currently contains 103,000 records. Nearly 800 records are added weekly. Searches and printouts (listing of digital data) are provided for a fee. Actual digital tapes must be purchased from NOAA.

* Electronic Dissemination Information System (EDI)

James Hawley
National Agriculture Statistical Service
U.S. Department of Agriculture
Administration Building, Room 441W
Washington, DC 20250   (301) 982-6877

Information includes situation and outlook summaries and reports from ER's as well as market reports, crop and livestock statistics, foreign agricultural trade loads, export sales reports and other timely information from AMS, NASS, FAS and other USDA agencies.

* Employment Cost Index System

Albert Schwank
Information Services
U.S. Department of Labor
Bureau of Labor Statistics
441 G St., NW, Room 2028
Washington, DC 20212   (202) 523-1165

The purpose of this system is to produce indexes and rates of change in wage rates and total employee compensation by major industry and occupation groups. The system converts wage and benefit data to a cents-per-hour worked basis and inputs for non-response before generating the indexes and percent changes. Data are collected quarterly from approximately 2,000 occupational employment composition of the private non-farm economy. The major exclusions are self-employed, unpaid family workers and private household employees. The Bureau of Labor Statistics provides a number of services upon request for users of statistical data. These include release of certain categories of unpublished data; development of special surveys and tabulations; duplication of machine-readable data files on either diskettes or magnetic tapes; and sale of statistical software programs. Customized data files are available on a cost recovery basis.

* Employment Hours and Earnings

Albert Schwank
Information Services
U.S. Department of Labor
441 G St., NW
Washington, DC 20212   (202) 523-1165

This program provides current employment, hours, and earnings by industry for the nonagricultural sector of the economy. Data provided are fundamental inputs into the economic decision process at all levels of government, private enterprise and organized labor. It includes a sample of 210,000 nonagricultural establishments, monthly information on employment, wages received and the number of paid hours. Bureau of Labor Statistics provides a number of services upon request for users of statistical data. These include release of certain categories of unpublished data; development of special surveys and tabulations; duplication of machine-readable data files on either diskettes or magnetic tapes; and sales of statistical software programs. Customized data files are available on a cost-of-service basis.

* Establishment Registration (RGN)

Gerald Deighton
FOI Staff HFI-35
U.S. FDA
5600 Fishers Lane
Rockville, MD 20857   (301) 443-6310

Information gathered on these firms includes firm name, address, type of activity, owner/operator name and address, official correspondent name and address, and phone number and other business trading names. Years covered are 1977 to present, and updates are daily. For more information contact Ann C. Tornese at (301) 427-7190.

* Export Grain Information System (EGIS)

U.S.DA, FGIS
Resources Management Division
Room 1642-South
PO Box 96454
Washington, DC 20090-96454   (202) 382-1741

The Export Grain Information System (EGIS) documents U.S. grain exports which were inspected and/or weighed under provisions of the U.S. Grain Standards Act. The database includes information about the quantity and quality of exported grain lots. The system documents information for wheat, corn, soybeans, sorghum, barley, rye, oats, flaxseed, sunflower seeds, and triticale. The database contains information from January 1983, to present, and is updated weekly.

* Fatal Accident Reporting System (FARS)

National Center for Statistics and Analysis
U.S. Department of Transportation
Fatal Accident Reporting System
NRD-32
Washington, DC 20590   (202) 366-4844

FARS is a census of data on all fatal traffic accidents within the 50 states, the District of Columbia and Puerto Rico. To be included in the system the accident must involve a motor vehicle traveling on a traffic way customarily open to the public and result in the death of a person (occupant of a vehicle or non-motorist) within 30 days of the accident. The FARS file contains descriptions, in a standard format, or each fatal accident reported. Each accident has upwards of 90 different coded data elements that characterize the accident, the vehicles and the people involved. Specific data elements may be modified slightly each year to conform to changing user needs, vehicle characteristics and highway safety emphasis areas. Printouts are available at no charge and response time is normally within two weeks. Data are also available on computer tape.

* FDA Import Alert Retrieval System (FIARS)

Gerald Deighton
FOI Staff HFI-35
U.S. FDA
5600 Fishers Lane
Rockville, MD 20857   (301) 443-6310

Contains current information on import alerts and import bulletins (approximately 220) accessible through "keyword" or "text" search. For more information contact John Browne at (301) 443-6553.

* Federal Bureau of Investigation (FBI)

Director of the FBI
Freedom of Information Act Request
10th and Pennsylvania Ave., NW
Washington, DC 20535   (202) 324-5520

The FBI will search their central records system if you write a Freedom of Information Act (FDIA) Request letter describing in as much detail as possible the information you are seeking. Even before the FDIA was enacted the

Research Unit, Office of Congressional Public Affairs provided information in response to requests from the public. They would find the information requested, analyze it, and paraphrase the information. The office has published a 33 page booklet titled *Conducting Research in FBI Records*, which explains what type of information is available and how to use it. The booklet is available from the Research Unit, FBI Office of Congressional and Public Affairs, 10th and Pennsylvania Ave., NW, Room 7350, Washington, D.C. 20535; (202)324-5611.

* Federal Legal Information Through Electronics (FLITE)

Judge Advocate General's Department
United States Air Force
HQ U.S.AF/JAS
Denver, CO 80279-5000   (303) 370-7531

FLITE is an automated legal research system. In addition to its own search system, FLITE has online access to other systems including: JURIS, LEXIS, WESTLAW, DIALOG, LEGI-SLATE and REG-ULATE. These combined resources include federal, State, and military court decisions, administrative agency decisions, statutes, pending regulations, law review articles and many related but non-legal databases of interest to attorneys. FLITE does not render legal opinions. It is available free to Department of Defense and selected federal agencies. Other federal agencies are charged $50.00 per database searched. FLITE is available only for problems related to government business. It is not restricted to attorneys. Your Member of Congress may be able to get FLITE search done for you.

* Federal Procurement Data Center (FPDC)

Liz Smith or Deborah Thompson
Federal Procurement Data Center
General Services Administration
4040 North Fairfax Dr., Suite 900
Arlington, VA 22203   (703) 235-1326

FPDC stores information about federal procurement actions, from 1979 to present, that totaled $25,000 or more. The system will eventually contain 45 data elements, including: purchasing or contracting office; date of award; principal place of performance; dollars obligated; principal product or service; business and labor requirements; type of procurement action; methods of contracting; socioeconomic data; name and address of contractor; and foreign trade data. Examples of federal buying range from research and development to supplies and equipment and services. The database was started in 1979 and contains two million records. Approximately 400,000 contract actions are added yearly. Searches and printouts are available on a cost recovery basis. Requests should be made in writing. If a search on a contractor is requested, the DUNS number will be helpful.

* Financial Disclosure Database on Federal Candidates

Kent Cooper, Public Records Office
Federal Election Commission
999 E St., NW
Washington, DC 20463   (202) 376-3120 or (800) 424-9530

The Financial Disclosure database has both financial and reference information on every candidate for federal office since 1977 and on contributing Political Action Committees and political parties. The system can be searched by specific candidate or contributor, and retrievable data include exact dollar amounts and contact information. The database was started in 1977 and contains nearly 3 1/2 million records. It is updated daily. Searches and printouts amounting to 20 records or less are available free of charge. A nominal fee is charged for each record.

* Financial Markets

Patrick Decker
Financial Markets
International Section
Federal Reserve System
Washington DC 20551   (202) 452-3314

This computer tape contains data on foreign exchange rates and foreign time deposit rates. Data only available on computer tape. Floppy diskettes and printouts not available.

* FIPS State/County Code Tape

U.S. Department of Commerce
National Technical Information Service
Springfield, VA 22161   (703) 487-4807

This tape contains two files: FIPS PUB 5-1 (incl. change notices 1-4) Standard Abbreviations and Codes for States and Outlying Areas of the U.S. and FIPS PUB 6-3 (incl. change notices 1-4), Counties and County Equivalents of the STates of the United States and the District of Columbia. Records in File 1 are sequenced in alphabetic order of the states (incl. D.C.), followed by the major outlying areas. Records in File 2 are sequenced in alphabetic order of county name, within each state and outlying area. Progression of the numeric county

code is consistent with alphabetic order of the counties within each state. Available in: 9 track 1600 or 6250 BPI, order number PB85-152288/HAL, at a cost of $210.

* Firm Profile File (MPQA)

Gerald Deighton
FOI Staff HFI-35
U.S. FDA
5600 Fishers Lane
Rockville, MD 20857   (301) 443-6310

Current compliance status for all drug and medical device manufacturers and repackers for each profile class (manufacturing process) and date of last GMP inspection of each process. For more information contact Anna M. Colandreo at (301) 443-3590.

* Fish and Wildlife Reference Service (FWRS) Database

Department of the Interior
Fish and Wildlife Service
Washington, DC 20240   (202) 343-4717

FWRS operates a bibliographic database containing indexed fish and wildlife-related documents from the following sources: the Federal Aid in Fish and Wildlife Restoration Program; the Adronomous Fish Conservation Program; the Endangered Species Grants program; work done at the Cooperative Fishery and Wildlife Agencies. Documents are selected for their research value to biologists in more than one state. Indexed materials include reports, published papers, technical publications, theses, and special materials such as endangered species recovery plans. Subject coverage includes birds, botany, fish management, hunting and fishing, water resources, pesticides, land use, habitat management and many other topics. The database has over 15,000 records, some dating back to 1945, and is updated continually. Bibliographic searches and documents can be obtained from FWRS. Individuals working on projects funded by FWRS contributors and full-time employees of state fish and wildlife agencies are eligible for "cooperator" status. Free literature searches are performed for "cooperators" and they are not charged for photocopying and microfiche services unless the cost exceeds $10.00. All others termed "clients" are charged a flat fee of $30.00 for a new literature search.

* Foreign Buyer

Foreign Agricultural Service
U.S. Department of Agriculture
Agricultural Information and Marketing Services (AIMS)
Room 4951 - South
Washington, DC 20250-1000

AIMS maintains a database of approximately 13,000 foreign firms from over 70 countries. American firms can obtain lists and match their products with prospective buyers. Foreign buyer lists provide company name, contact, address, telephone, telex, cable, and/or facsimile number. The lists can be formatted to provide foreign buyers by product for the entire world; or foreign buyers by country for all products.

* Foreign Geographic Names

Chief, Geographic Names Branch (GNB)
Defense Mapping Agency
Hydro-Graphic Topal-Graphic Center
Washington, DC 20315   (202) 227-3880

This database manages information about all standardized foreign geographic names approved by GNB. The system is searchable by foreign country and its subdivisions such as listing of a particular country's rivers, populated places, or valleys. Retrievable data include proper name and spelling, longitude/latitude, and type of feature (i.e., city, mountain, administrative area, etc). In the near future, records will exist on all foreign countries. Searches and printouts are expected to be available on a cost recovery basis.

* Foreign Importer Listings Database

Foreign Agricultural Service
U.S. Department of Agriculture
Agricultural Information Marketing Service
4951-South Bldg
Washington, DC 20250   (202) 447-7103

The system includes names, addresses, and telex numbers of firms currently dealing in food and agricultural products in specific countries and of companies which have requested U.S. products in specific countries and of companies who have requested U.S. products during the past three years. Listings are available for all foreign countries for a single product or all importers of all agricultural products in a single country. There is a fee for each listing.

* Foreign Products Estimates

Ed Cissel
U.S. Department of Agriculture

Government Databases and Bulletin Boards

Foreign Agriculture Service
Foreign Production Estimates Division
6503 South Building
Washington, DC 20250 (202) 382-8888

Various commodity databases are available that contain total production figures on foreign raw commodities. Commodities included in these files are grains, rice, dairy, poultry, livestock, oilseeds, cotton, coffee, sugar and tobacco. The Foreign Production Estimates Division can search the database by country or commodity. Each commodity has an expert available to assist with searches. There is no charge for such searches.

* Foreign Trade Statistics

Dick Preuss
U.S. Department of Commerce
Bureau of the Census
Foreign Trade Division
Washington, DC 20233 (202) 763-7754

This statistics system involves the compilation and distribution of a large body of data relating to the imports and exports of the U.S. It is designed to meet the needs of a variety of users. Non-government users in industry, finance, research institutions, transportation and other fields use the data as a statistical base to appraise the general trade situation and outlook, market analysis and market penetration studies; product and market development and for measuring the impact of competition. Special searches and tabulations are furnished at a cost which is determined on the basis of the quantity of data requested, complexity of data specification and costs for personnel and equipment.

* Foreign Traders Index (FTI)

Your U.S. District Office of the
International Trade Administration
or
Information Management Division
U.S. Department of Commerce
IRA/U.S. & FCS/EPS
Room 1322
Washington, DC 20230 (202) 377-8246

The Foreign Traders Index is a list-building file describing foreign firms, their long-term interests and the types of activities they engage in. The database can be searched according to agents, sellers, distributors, users, companies, geographic location, date and number of employees. As of March 1989, the system contains 56,000 records, the majority added within the last few years. Charges include a set-up and per name fee.

* General Accounting Office Bibliographic Database (GAO)

GAO/IHSF
PO Box 6015
Gaithersburg, MD 20877 (202) 275-6241

GAO Bibliographic Database contains citations for every GAO document produced since 1976, and references for some GAO reports produced in the preceding four years. GAO studies cover a vast array of subjects, as the agency must produce a report on any topic Congress assigns. Reports have ranged from financial audits of government agencies to policy studies of health-related programs. Other topics have included environmental issues, social security, foreign relations, commerce, quotas for imported tuna and organized crime. Searches are generally conducted by subject area and specific time period. The system currently holds citations for 40,000 documents, some dating back to 1972. It is updated daily. Searches and printouts are available free of charge. GAO will also mail you up to five copies of any report listed; this service is also free.

* Geographic Information Retrieval and Analysis System (GIRAS)

U.S. Geological Survey
Earth Science Information Center (ESIC)
507 National Center, Room 1-C-402
Reston, VA 22092 (703) 648-6045 (800) USA-MAPS

The U.S. Geological Survey produces land use and land cover maps and associated overlays for the United States. These maps have been digitized, edited and incorporated into a digital database. The data is available to the public in both graphic and digital form and statistics derived from the data are published. Users are able to search for either locations or attributes. To obtain information from this database, contact ESIC.

* Geographic Names Information System (GNIS)

Roger Payne
Manager, GNIS
U.S. Geological Survey
523 National Center
Reston, VA 22092 (703) 648-4544

GNIS is an automated data system developed by U.S.GS to standardize and disseminate information on geographic names. Primary information is provided for all know places, features, and areas in the U.S. identified by a proper name. The system is composed of 3 data bases: National Geographic Names Data Base (NGN), U.S.GS Topographic Map Names Data Base, and Generic Data Base. The Generic Data Base defines the terms used by U.S.GS for 63 broad categories of feature types found in the NGN Data Base (i.e., "stream" is used for rivers, creeks, brooks, etc.). It also contains annotated bibliographic listings of sources used to create the NGN Data Base. NGN and U.S.GS Topographic Map Names Data Base are described in separate entries in this section. Printouts and searches from GNIS are available on a cost recovery basis.

* GEOINDEX

Geologic Division
U.S. Geological Survey
907 National Center
Reston, VA 22092 (703) 648-4388

GEOINDEX consists of bibliographic and location data for all published geologic maps of the U.S. and its territories. Indexed are individual maps; maps in books, journals and guidebooks; USGS Open-File Reports; and maps published by states, universities, societies, and commercial publishers. Maps now out of print are included. Fields include author, date, title, publisher, series, scale, county or region, latitude and longitude extremes and centers, area, and notes. GEOINDEX is available commercially on CDROM from OCLC, Inc.

* Geologic Names of the United States (GEONAMES)

Geologic Division
U.S. Geologic Survey
907 National Center
Reston, VA 22092 (703) 648-4388

GEONAMES is an annotated index of the formal geologic nomenclature of the United States and its territories. Data reflects distribution, geologic age, U.S.GS usage, lithology, thickness, type locality, and a reference to the naming paper. Printouts are not available. Diskettes containing data for 2 or more adjacent states are available from U.S.GS Open-File and Publications, Box 25425 Federal Center, Denver, Colorado 80225 (303) 236-7476. Magnetic tapes can be obtained from NTIS.

* Guaranteed Student Loan Information System

Pat Bridges
Guaranteed Student Loan Branch
Office of Post Secondary Education
U.S. Department of Education
400 Maryland Ave., SW
Washington, DC 20202 (202) 732-4242

This database contains information on the amount of money the U.S. government paid to private guarantee agencies for defaulted student loans. Statistical records are kept on the number of loans made under this program, the number of loans each guarantee agency has guaranteed, the banks participating in the program and the number of defaulted student loans each year. Information on individuals is not available to the public. However, inquiries by borrowers about their loans will be honored. Printouts are free for simple requests. Customized computer tapes are available for about $140.00.

* Hazardous Material Shipper Census/Identification

Bureau of Motor Carrier Safety, HMC-10
Federal Highway Administration
Department of Transportation
400 7th St., SW
Washington, DC 20590 (202) 366-2519

This on-line system, updated daily, contains data, such as name, address, and types of hazardous materials shipped on approximately 21,000 shippers of hazardous materials. Data is for internal use and will be made available to the public as authorized by the Administration.

* Hazardous Materials Incident Reporting System

U.S. Department of Transportation
Research and Special Programs Administration
Information Systems Branch
DHM-63, Room 8112
400 7th St., SW
Washington, DC (202) 366-4555

This database provides a statistical compilation of all accidents and incidents involving hazardous materials. The system contains information on each reported incident and consists of data elements such as: the date of the accident, location, shipper, carrier, commodity involved and other detailed information concerning the packaging and nature of the incident. Customized searches are available upon request. There is a $30.00 minimum charge.

* Highway Statistics System

Federal Highway Administration

Highway Statistics Division
Department of Transportation
400 7th St., SW
Washington, DC 20590 (202) 366-0180

State data includes numbers and characteristics of registered vehicles, drivers' licenses, motor fuel consumed, tax and other highway related revenue, highway bonding, toll financing, roadway extent and characteristics, expenditures by type of governmental highway activity and highway travel. National summary includes highway statistics, national truck characteristics report, drivers' licenses, highway taxes and fees, road user and property fees, and special hardcopy reports as required. Data are primarily byproducts of state and local planning, accounting, and administrative data files and are updated on an ongoing basis. Contact the Highway Statistics Division, listed above.

* Industrial Chemical Residues

Gerald Deighton
FOI Staff HFI-35
U.S. FDA
5600 Fishers Lane
Rockville, MD 20857 (301) 443-6310

Analytical properties of industrial chemical residues, updated annually. For more information, contact Marion O. Clower, Jr., at (202) 245-3138.

* Industrial Directory

Lynda DiNenna
Bureau of the Census, FB-3, Room 2585
U.S. Department of Commerce
Washington, DC 20233 (202) 763-7078

This system is a collection of business firms and the addresses of their offices and plants. It is compiled, maintained and used by the Bureau of the Census on a continuous basis. It contains basic economic information on five and a half million businesses. The following information is maintained for each company: primary name, secondary name, mailing address, actual address, standard industrial classification code, enterprise code, legal form of organization, employer identification number and directory identification number. Reimbursable projects are performed by the Bureau for requesting agencies or organizations.

* Information on Nuclear Sites

Argone National Laboratory
Environmental Impact Studies Division
9700 S. Cass Ave.
Argonne, IL 60493

System to support efforts of the Nuclear Regulatory Commission (NRC) to develop site evaluation guidelines, to establish a general base of information for use by the NRC in other regulatory activities.

* INFOTERRA

U.S. National Focal Point for INFOTERRA
PM 211-A
U.S. Environmental Protection Agency
Washington, DC 20460 (202) 382-5917

INFOTERRA is an information referral service for sources of environmental information. The database contains government agencies, public and private organizations, universities, individuals, etc. from the U.S. and 134 countries worldwide. All those listed have agreed to answer questions and supply information regarding their particular area(s) of expertise. Sources are provided for 26 categories ranging from air to waste. The database can be searched by more than 1,000 different subject terms and retrievable information includes: description of source, contact information, source's output and the availability of materials, the regional area served, and the organization's sponsorship, activities and working language. INFOTERRA contains 10,000 records of which 1,400 refer to United States resources. It is updated every two years. Searches and printouts are available free of charge.

* Inlife

Gerald Deighton
FOI Staff HFI-35
U.S. FDA
5600 Fishers Lane
Rockville, MD 20857 (301) 443-6310

Data captured on an experimental animal during its lifetime, including weight, raw data for food or water consumption calculations, observations and animal removal data. The database covers 1986 to present and is updated daily. For more information contact Ron Barsh at (703) 790-4257.

* Integrated Technical Information System (ITIS)

Office of Science and Technical Information
U.S. Department of Energy
PO Box 62

Oak Ridge, TN 37831 (615) 576-1272

The Integrated Technical Information System (ITIS), an online system developed by the DOE OFfice of Scientific and Technical Information, provides access to DOE databases and electronic mail service among DOE and contractor offices. Databases available on ITIS include the most recent 12 months of the Energy Data Base, reports Holding File, DOE Research in Progress, National Energy Software, etc. ITIS, which was established when DOE/RECON was discontinued in 1986, is available only to DOE and contractor employees.

* International Demographic Database (IDB)

Peter Johnson
Center for International Research
Scuderi Building, Room 614
U.S. Bureau of Census
Washington, DC 20233 (301) 763-4811

The International Demographic Center is developing its International Database which will contain demographic, social, and economic data about every country in the world. Presently, IDB focuses on developing nations, but data on other countries are being added continually. For each country logged, IDB contains 93 different subject tables. Variable stores include the following: an urban/rural breakdown, population by age and sex, birth and death rates, marital status, household size, labor force information, education data, and growth rates. Eventually, IDB will contain the World Population Database. Selected World Bank Data, United Nations material, and a bibliographic file may be added. Online access to the file is available to federal agencies and others may purchase magnetic tapes. Individual searches are available on a limited basis.

* International Marketing Profiles

Foreign Agricultural Service
U.S. Department of Agriculture
Agricultural Information and Marketing Service
Room 4951, South Building
14th Street & Independence Ave., SW
Washington, DC 20250 (202) 475-3422

This database presents statistical information on agricultural trade activity using two profiles: Product Marketing Profiles which examine market performance of specific agricultural products and Country Marketing Profiles which examine the agricultural trade activity in particular countries. Each profile includes an export brief, a list of exporter services, foreign importer mailing list information and a fact sheet summarizing Foreign Agricultural Service responsibility and key contact. There is a $15.00 fee for each profile.

* International Prices Program

Information Services
U.S. Department of Labor
Bureau of Labor Statistics
441 G St., NW
Washington, DC 20212 (202) 523-1221

The purpose of this system is to provide measures of price changes for U.S. exports and imports and to analyze these price trends in world markets. The fundamental data in the system are price indexes for over 5,000 detailed commodities sold in the primary markets in the U.S. Price data are collected monthly from producers for more than 50,000 items covering more than 5,000 commodities. Data tapes and diskettes are available for all published producer price indexes.

* International Trade

U.S. Department of Commerce
International Trade Administration
Office of Trade and Investment Analysis System
14th and Pennsylvania Ave., NW, Room 2202
Washington, DC 20230 (202) 377-2568

This system contains comprehensive information on direct foreign investment transactions in the United States from 1974 to present. The information is for completed transactions only, and it covers manufacturing and all other sectors including real estate. There are data on U.S. enterprises, foreign investors and the terms of the transactions. This information is available on magnetic tape. The typical cost is less than $50.00.

* Inter-University Consortium for Political and Social Research (ICPSR)

ICPSR
PO Box 1248
Ann Arbor, MI 48106 (313) 764-2570

This membership-based organization comprised of over 300 colleges and universities receives, processes and distributes machine readable data on social phenomena occurring in over 130 countries. Surveys of mass and elite attitudes, census records, election returns, international interactions, and legislative records are maintained and easily searched. The contents of the archive extends across economic, sociological, historical, organizational, psychological and political concerns. The largest data collections are U.S. election data (including county and state level variables from 1790 through 1986). Direct access to ICPSR resources are available through CDNet for member schools.

* Jail Contracting Management System

U.S. Marshals Service
600 Army Navy Drive
Arlington, VA 22202   (703) 307-9390

This system monitors performance of approximately 800 contracts with local jails, as well as the financial aspects of these contracts. It contains such information as costs and obligation, population trends and jail inspection data. It produces hardcopy reports on an as-required basis on jail and cost information on as well as allowing interactive file/record query.

* Labor Statistics (LABSTAT)

Connie DiCesare, Chief
Division of Information Services
U.S. Department of Labor
Bureau of Labor Statistics
441 G St., NW
Washington, DC 20212   (202) 523-1090

LABSTAT is the overall system for storing, retrieving and manipulating BLS data. The database contains historic time series data which are generally aggregated at the macro level. The system is the repository for data collected from 20 different broad surveys providing data on the labor force, Consumer Price Index, Producer Price Index, Occupational Safety and Health, productivity data for industry and government, international labor comparisons, unemployment data, and more. Information is retrievable by numerous categories. LABSTAT contains 140,000 historical time series records and two million variable records with time series data. The system is updated 20 times a month. Each BLS division is responsible for data retrieval in its subject area, so contact the appropriate office for the data you need. Some offices may not be familiar with the term LABSTAT; therefore, it's best to simply request the information you need. The office will then try to assist you by consulting its data files, which are actually part of LABSTAT. Depending on the office and your request, you may or may not be charged a fee. To order data tapes, contact the Division of Planning and Financial Management, Room 1077, Bureau of Labor Statistics, Department of Labor, 441 G Street, NW, Washington, DC 20212.

* Low Acid Canned Foods (LACF)

Gerald Deighton
FOI Staff HFI-35
U.S. FDA
5600 Fishers Lane
Rockville, MD 20857   (301) 443-6310

The file, updated monthly, contains all low acid canned products and processes registered for use in the U.S. by domestic and foreign firms. Process data is not available to the public. For more information contact Sharon Schoen at (202) 245-1420.

* Mental Health Research Grants Application System

National Institute of Mental Health
National Institute of Health
Parklawn Building, Room 15-81
5600 Fishers La.
Rockville, MD 20857   (301) 443-3104

This management information system provides data for use in research grant analysis, planning, and administration. It covers all National Institute of Mental Health (NIMH) research grant applications. The file consists of all administrative facts about applications including title, investigator, budget, project dates, sponsoring institution, location, review actions, and funding. A yearly sourcebook is produced. Searches and printouts for specific grant information can be arranged.

* Merchant Vessels of the United States

Information and Analysis Staff (G-MA)
Department of Transportation
2100 Second Street, SW
Washington, DC 20593   (202) 267-2229

This database is an annual listing of all American merchant vessels and yachts registered, including vessels lost, abandoned, transferred to aliens, or removed from registration. The file contains foreword, glossary, listings, and indexes. For registered vessels, listing shows official number, call letters, rig, name, tonnage, dimensions, hull type, when and where built, horsepower, service, owner, and home port. For vessels removed or subject to removal, listings show official number, rig, name of vessel, gross tons, and disposition. A monthly supplement (published 1867-present) presenting data on new registrations and changes is also issued. Contact the office listed above for data on microform or paper.

* Metals and Ceramics Information Center

(MCIC)

General Information, Technical Inquiries
Batelle - Columbus Laboratories
505 King Ave.
Columbus, OH 43201-6376   (614) 424-5000 or (614) 424-6376

MCIC, a DOD-sponsored Information Center, maintains a bibliographic database for worldwide literature pertaining to metals and ceramics technologies. Major emphasis is placed on structural alloys, and retrievable information includes citations, abstracts, and analyses of technical documents from government reports and worldwide open literature. The scope includes selected metals, ceramics, and composite materials of interest to DOD and its contracts and material suppliers. Information cited on all three types of materials covers coatings, environmental effects, physical properties, materials applications, test methods, sources/suppliers, specifications, design characteristics, and various strength steels, and superalloys. Ceramics covered include borides, carbides, carbon/graphite, nitrides, oxides, sulfides, silicides, selected glass, and glass ceramics. MCIC maintains both a computerized and manual database. The computerized portion was started in 1975 and has access to more than 130,000 records. It is updated daily. MCIS will do searches for all sectors of government and industry. Simple searches are done free of charge, while more complex requests are assessed at a cost recovery fee. DOD agencies and contractors can get direct access to the database through the Defense Technical Information Center's DTIC online system (DROLS) which is described earlier in this section.

* Mineral Resources Data Systems

Donald F. Huber
U.S. Department of the Interior
Branch of Resource Analysis
345 Middlefield Rd., Mail Stop 984
Menlo Park, CA 94025   (415) 329-5358

This system serves as a storage and retrieval facility for mineral commodity data, data resulting from the two degree sheet studies, data contributed by other organizations under various types of contracts, and other sources. This system makes it possible on a short notice to search out and synthesize great quantities of diverse data on mineral resources and on individual deposits. Data are available in five versions to public users. Where interest is in less than 10 or less data items, tables or listing can be provided for the desired geographical areas or commodities. Printouts of full or practical versions are available. Computer generated maps can also be made. For large data set requests, the data are provided in tape and diskette form.

* Monthly Motor Gasoline Reported by States

Federal Highway Administration
U.S. Department of Transportation
400 7th St., SW
Washington, DC 20590   (202) 366-0180

This database stores monthly data from taxation reports on gasoline (including gasohol) consumption by state. Data are current to 2-4 months preceding issue date, as state reports become available. Contents include daily average consumption, monthly gasoline consumption for last 4 months and cumulative for the calendar year, monthly and cumulative gasohol consumption, and 12-month moving total of gasoline sales. Contact the office listed above for data available on magnetic tape.

* Monthly Petroleum Supply Reporting System

National Energy Information Center
U.S. Department of Energy
Room 1F, O48
Washington, DC 20585   (202) 586-8800

This system assembles statistical data collected monthly on liquid hydrocarbon products. Information includes production, stock, imports, exports, shipping movements and refinery input. The system provides a comprehensive collection of data on supply and disposition of crude oil and refined products in the United States and its territories. Tapes may be purchased from the National Technical Information Service (NTIS).

* Motor Carrier Census Identification

Federal Highway Administration
Bureau of Motor Carrier Safety, HMC-12
Department of Transportation
400 7th St., SW
Washington, DC 20590   (202) 366-2519

This on-line system, updated daily, contains data, such as name, address, type and area of operation, commodities (including hazardous materials transported), compliance ratings, numbers of vehicles and drivers used, mileage operated, and audit dates for approximately 190,000 interstate motor carriers subject to BMCS jurisdiction. Contact the office listed above concerning availability of data.

* Mourning Dove Database

David Dolton
Office of Migratory Bird Management

U.S. Department of Interior
Fish and Wildlife Service
Patuxent Wildlife Research Center
Laurel, MD 20708 (301) 498-0306

This database contains records from the results of the Annual Call-Count Survey, which are collected according to various ecological strata. The records are used to produce a meaningful index of the size of the mourning dove breeding population and to set annual mourning dove hunting regulations. It is updated annually. Searches and printouts are available. Depending upon the nature of your request, you may or may not be charged a fee. Some information in the database is restricted under the Privacy Act. A States report is produced each year.

* MSA: Metropolitan Statistical Areas Data Tape

U.S. Department of Commerce
National Technical Information Service
Springfield, VA 22161 (703) 487-4807

A total of 257 MSAs are recognized. In addition, there are 23 CMSAs, consisting of 78 PMSAs. This tape contains computer files documenting titles, components and Federal Information Processing Standards (FIPS) codes for Metropolitan Statistical Areas and related statistical areas. It includes two computer files to convert titles, components, and FIPS codes from SMSA to MSA definitions. Available in 9 track 1600 or 6250 BPI, order number PB85-161115/HAL at a cost of $210.

* Munitions Control Database System

James DePalma
Office of Munitions Control
Bureau of Politico-Military Affairs
U.S. Department of State
Washington, DC 20520 (703) 875-6650

The system is designed to record licenses issued authorizing the export of U.S. munitions, list equipment to foreign countries and international organizations, and record the exports against said licenses. Information in the system pertaining to equipment authorized for export includes applicant/licensee, license number, date issued/shipped, quantity, and commodity value. Requests for information contained in the database must be made through the Freedom of Information Act Office. The cost of obtaining the information is charged according to a fee schedule of: professional time at $12.00 per hour, clerical time at $7.00 and a cost for reproduction of documents.

* NASA Scientific and Technical Information (NASA STI or NASA/RECON)

NASA STI Facility
Attn: Registration Services
P.O. Box 8757
BWI Airport
Baltimore, MD 21240 (202) 621-0140 or (301) 859-5300

NASA STI Database provides bibliographic information for worldwide literature in aeronautics, space, and the vast array of topics of interest to NASA via NASA/RECON. The broad-based system contains more than 100 different categories ranging from aerodynamics to urban technology. Many of the reports, journals, books and conference papers cited are highly technical. NASA's wide interests in science include the environment and properties of the earth, moon, and planets; the sun and its relationship to the earth and the rest of the solar system; the space environment; the physical nature of the universe; and the search for extraterrestrial life. In technology, NASA's interests include spacecraft and launch vehicles; aircraft; propulsion; auxiliary power; human factors; electronics; and structures and materials. In applications, NASA's interests include astronomical, geophysical, meteorological and communications systems, as well as emphasis on earth resources, air and water pollution, and urban transportation. The system was started in 1968 and currently has approximately 2.7 million records. NASA offers different levels of service depending on your needs.

* National Accident Sampling System

Grace Hazzard
National Center for Statistics and Analysis (NRD-32)
National Highway Traffic Safety Administration (NHTSA)
400 Seventh St., SW
Washington, DC 20590 (202) 366-4820

This system provides detailed information on all police-reported traffic accidents since 1979. It contains data on more than 10,000 accidents per year in communities ranging from the most rural to the most urban in the nation. Data include: victim's age, sex, height, weight, admission and discharge dates, specific injuries and cause of death of fatally injured victims. This information is coded to provide general statistics while protecting the identity and privacy of the individuals involved. Data are available in report form or magnetic tape.

* National Agricultural Pest Information Services (NAPIS)

Dave Talpas
PPQ/APIS
U.S. Department of Agriculture
Federal Building, Room 640
Hyattsville, MD 20782 (301) 436-8247

This database contains information about insects, weeds, plant diseases and nematodes. Each state collects data and transmits it to the U.S. Department of Agriculture's National Plant Pest Quarantine Office (PPQ) in Maryland. Data from each state include: observation date, State, county, crop, crop growth stage, pest, pest life stage, abundance or incidence, damage or severity and detection method. Searches and printouts are generally available for free.

* National Asset Seizure and Forfeiture System

Office of Legal Counsel
U.S. Marshal Service
600 Army Navy Dr.
Arlington, VA 22202-4210 (202) 307-9000

The system maintains a complete inventory of property seized by the government and placed in the custody of the U.S. Marshals Service. The system will also maintain a complete record of all funds expended to maintain and dispose of the property. Output includes inventory listings, summary reports on inventory items by category and financial reports. To obtain a printout, send a written Freedom of Information request to the above office.

* National Crime Information Center

National Crime Information Center
Technical Services Division
Federal Bureau of Investigation
10th & Pennsylvania Ave., NW
Washington, DC 20535 (202) 324-2606

NCSI provides information on-line to criminal justice agencies concerning wanted persons, missing persons, stolen property, and computerized criminal histories. Input and retrieval are performed via federal, state and local computer/terminal interface with a central FBI computer. Retrievable data includes information on criminal careers and permits authorities to track criminals through the criminal justice system. The system contains more than nine million records and updates are performed on a 24-hour day online basis. Searches and printouts are free and restricted to criminal justice agencies.

* National Diabetes Information Clearinghouse (NDIC)

National Diabetes Information Clearinghouse
Box NDIC
Bethesda, MD 20852 (301) 468-2162

This online database contains citations and abstracts of diabetic patient education materials including books, audiovisuals, teaching manuals and journal articles. Basic information about diabetes, its complications, and information about programs designed for diabetics and health professionals is also stored. The database is patient oriented and does not include highly technical, clinical or research materials. The system, which is updated monthly, became operational in 1985 and contains 6,000 records. NDIC will do searches and provide a bibliographic printout (with abstracts and acquisition source free of charge). It is also available commercially through CHID (Combined Health Database).

* National Financial Summary

Linda Farmer
U.S. Department of Agriculture
Economic Research Service
1301 New York Ave., NW
Washington, DC 20005-4788 (202) 786-1804

This database includes farm income, cash receipts by components, production expenses, capital expenditures, off-farm income, non-money and farm-related income components. It also includes U.S. balance sheet data, 1944-87, and related data on assets and debt. Data disk is available in Lotus for $45. For ordering information, call (800) 999-6779. Stock number 88010.

* National Referral Center
Library of Congress

Resources Analysis Section
General Reading Rooms Division
Library of Congress
Washington, DC 20540 (202) 707-2905

The database of Library of Congress's defunct National Referral Center still exists. This data bank consists of a directory listing more than 12,000 organizations or individuals qualified and willing to provide information on topics primarily in science, technology, and social sciences to the general public. A typical citation contains the name of the resource, mailing address, telephone number, areas of interest, special collections, databases, publications, and special services. Organizations can be located by name or subject. To obtain a listing of sources for your area of interest or a particular industry contact the General Reading Room and if you have difficulties contact your U.S. Representative or

Senator.

* National Resources Inventory (NRI)

U.S. Department of Agriculture
Resources Inventory Division
Soil Conservation Service
PO Box 2890
Washington, DC 20013 (202) 447-6267

This database contains basic information on the U.S. natural resources, such as land use, soil, water and wind erosion, land cover, conservation practices, and treatment needs. These data are collected on sample sites on private lands that were selected using a systematic randomized sampling procedure. The data are site specific, but the data are considered reliable aggregated to the state and national level. The file is updated on a periodic basis and contains approximately 350,000 megabytes. Magnetic tapes are available that can be searched by: kind of soil, by state, by land use, etc. Tapes normally cost less than $100.00. Hard copy is also available upon request.

* National Standard Reference Data System (NSRDS)

Joan Sauerwein
A 320 Physics Building
National Institute of Standards & Technology
Gaithersburg, MD 20899 (301) 975-2208

Each NSRDS Data Center maintains databases of evaluated physical and chemical properties of substances. The system supports NBS' responsibility to promote numerical data in the physical sciences. The evaluations are carried out through a national network of 22 NSRDS Centers and special projects conducted by universities, government laboratories and industry. Each center is responsible for a well-defined technical scope and for compiling a comprehensive indexed bibliographic file with analyses of the world literature within its scope. The Centers assess the accuracy of the data reported in the literature, prepare compilations, and recommend best values. The resulting bibliographic and numeric physical, chemical, and property databases are then made available through publications, magnetic tapes, and online systems. The Center's activities are aggregated into three application-oriented program areas: 1) Energy and Environmental Data, which includes data from fields such as chemical kinetics, spectroscopy, and radiation physics and chemistry which have application to energy-related R&D and environmental modeling; 2) Industrial Process Data, which covers primarily thermodynamic and transport properties of substances important to the chemical and related industries; and 3) Materials Properties Data, which includes structural, electrical, optical, and mechanical properties of solid materials of broad interest.

* National Victim Resource Center (NVA C)

Stephanie L. Greenhouse
Office of Justice Assistance, Research and Statistics
U.S. Department of Justice
Box 6000 AIQ
Rockville, MD 20850 (301) 251-5525 or (301) 251-5519

This system is a computerized national program database containing description of all types of victim assistance programs throughout the country. A legislative database has been developed to track pending and enacted legislation on victim assistance and compensation programs. It also collects and makes literature available (i.e., books, articles, reports and audiovisual materials). This system has access to more than 7,000 victim related books and articles. Information specialists can help you with the federally sponsored victim related research studies, national victimization statistics and information on State victims compensation programs.

* Nationwide Examination of X-Ray Trends (NEXT)

Fred Rueter
National Center for Devices and Radiology Health
DIGP HF2
5600 Fishers La.
Rockville, MD 20857 (301) 443-3446

NEXT contains statistical data and exposure/dose information about diagnostic medical and dental x-rays taken nationwide. Tabulations can be done according to hospitals, private facilities, geographical areas, x-ray techniques, and body organs. Started in 1973, NEXT currently holds 60,000 records. It is updated continuously. Searches and printouts are available free of charge.

* New NEXT (NX2)

Gerald Deighton
FOI Staff HFI-35
U.S. FDA
5600 Fishers Lane
Rockville, MD 20857 (301) 443-6310

The new NEXT (Nationwide Experience in X-ray Trends) system is designed to collect data gathered in states on the performance of X-ray equipment used in radiographic exams measuring exposure values in real life situations. The database is updated annually and covers the years 1984 to present. For more information contact Fred Rueter at (301) 443-3446.

* NHTSA Auto-Safety Hotline

National Highway Traffic Safety Administration
Auto-Safety Hotline
U.S. Department of Transportation
400 Seventh St., SW
Washington, DC 20590 (202) 336-0123 or (800) 424-9393

NHTSA maintains a database of safety information about automobiles manufactured in the past 10 years. The system can be searched by car make, model, year, or equipment. Retrievable information includes: crash test results; repairability and damage statistics; safety recall information; insurance and accident costs; consumer complaints filed about a car; used-car information; and tire treadwear and skid resistance. The database was started in 1972 and is updated daily. Searches and printouts are available free of charge. Unless your request is complex, you can get the data you need quickly by calling the Hotline. An operator will conduct a search while you are still on the phone and a printout will be mailed within 24 hours. NHTSA encourages individuals to call the Hotline whenever they want to register a safety complaint about the automobile. Often NHTSA will investigate the complaint and if necessary contact the manufacturer on the owner's behalf.

* NIOSHTIC

Bill Bennett
Information Acquisition Data Systems
National Institute of Occupational Safety & Health
4676 Columbia Pkwy.
Cincinnati, OH 45226 (513) 533-8317

NIOSHTIC contains bibliographic citations and abstracts of occupational safety and health materials. Input is gathered from U.S. and foreign literature, the personnel files of several distinguished researchers in the field. The system currently contains more than 150,000 records and is increasing by 500 a month. This database dates back to 1860. Currently searches and printouts are available free of charge. This database is available commercially from Dialog, Pergamon and Orbit.

* National Rehabilitation Information Center

National Rehabilitation Information Center
National Institute on Disabled and Rehabilitation Research
Macro Systems, Inc.
8455 Colesville Rd., Suite 935
Silver Spring, MD 20910 (800) 34-NARIC

Updated continually, this bibliographic database contains abstracts of materials on all aspects of disability and rehabilitation. Appropriate research and proceedings reports, books, journals and audiovisual materials are referenced. Examples of subject areas covered include accessibility, behavior modification, deinstitutionalization, funding, statistics, and workers' compensation. The database contains more than 21,000 items, some dating back to the 1950s. The Center will search its own database and several other commercially available databases. The basic charge is $10 for the first 100 citations, and $5.00 for the next 100. No one will be denied access to these resources because of inability to pay. This database is available commercially on BRS.

* Non-Residential Building Energy Consumption Surveys

Julia Oliver
Office of Energy Markets and End Use
End Use Division
U.S. Department of Energy
1000 Independence Ave., SW
Washington, DC 20585 (202) 586-5744

This system is used to determine the energy consuming characteristics of a national scientific sample of non-residential buildings. The information is used for such projects as assessing the possibilities for financial incentives for the installation of energy conservation measures. Data include square footage, type of business, and maintained temperature. Energy consumption and expenditure figures are gathered from fuel suppliers of the sampled buildings. Contact Ms. Oliver or the National Energy Information Center (202) 586-8800 to have specific information retrieved from the database. To purchase the complete tape, contact NTIS (703) 487-4650.

* Official Establishment Inventory

Gerald Deighton
FOI Staff HFI-35
U.S. FDA
5600 Fishers Lane
Rockville, MD 20857 (301) 443-6310

Current inventory, updated monthly, of establishments or individuals whose activities fall under jurisdiction of FDA. Includes name, address, establishment types, industries' date of last inspection, classification, date of last violative inspection, and so on. For more information, contact K. Sterk Larson at (301)

443-3630.

* Operator Sailing Schedules

James E. Saari, FOI Officer
Office of Information Resources Management
Maritime Administration
Department of Transportation
400 7th St., SW
Washington, DC 20590   (202) 366-5807

This system collects advertised sailing schedules of time service operator's vessels. Requests for access to this database, developed for use by the Maritime Administration, may be subject to Privacy Act regulations.

* The Opportunity Bank

Overseas Private Investment Corporation
Opportunities Bank
1615 M St., NW
Washington, DC 20527   (800) 424-OPJC or (202) 457-7010

This database contains information on U.S. companies with interest in possible joint venture investment opportunities in developing countries as well as information about foreign companies and individuals interested in locating American joint venture projects. There is no fee to be included into the database. Access to the system costs $50 for information on 10 or fewer leads that meet your requirements. Currently, the Opportunity Bank contains more than 1000 investment project profiles on a broad cross-section of potential joint venture enterprises in more than 75 countries in the developing world. The company file contains more than 4000 potential investors.

* Personal Census Records Service System

Census History Staff
U.S. Bureau of the Census
Washington, DC 20233   (301) 763-7936

A personal search of census records is available upon proof of authorized representation--parent, spouse, sibling (a named individual or authorized representative heir with proof of death). A staff of employees provide personal data from census records for those individuals who lack documents of birth or citizenship. Extracts of these records are accepted as evidence of age, place of birth, social security benefits, passports and other purposes. The data files contain complete historical census reports since 1920. Personal search requests cost $15.00.

* Petroleum Marketing Monthly

National Energy Information Center
U.S. Department of Energy
1000 Independence Ave., SW, Room 1-F 048
Washington, DC 20585   (202) 586-8800

This system, corresponding to the hard-copy publication with the same title, is a collection of information on petroleum products, including the following: propane, gasoline, kerosene, distillates, aviation fuels, and residual fuel oils. Summaries have been developed to provide petroleum product information, such as distribution, sales volume, and selling prices per state. Some summaries contain the anticipated supply for individual states for the following month. Computer tapes are available from NTIS.

* Physicians Data Query Cancer Information System (PDQ)

International Cancer Information Center
National Cancer Institute
Department of Health and Human Services
International Cancer Research Program
R.A. Bloch Building
9030 Old Georgetown Rd.
Bethesda, MD 20892   (301) 496-3096

Files are hierarchial and must be obtained together. Files are menu driven. A version of PDQ has been developed which uses a MUMPS-based retrieval system which can run on either mini or micro computers. Data on 87 treatments, 12,000 physicians, 1,500 organizations, 1,000 protocols are included in these files. Each file updated monthly. Data are updated monthly. However, addition of chemotherapeutic agents, dose modification and AIDS treatment information limits comparability of current and historical data.

* PIERS

James E. Saari, FOI Officer
Office of Information Resources Management
Maritime Administration
Department of Transportation
400 7th St., SW
Washington, DC 20590   (202) 366-5807

This database stores, sorts and, retrieves statistical data on U.S. imports and exports. Requests for access to this database, developed for use by the Maritime Administration, may be subject to Privacy Act regulations.

* PLASTEC Automated Bibliographic Services

Suseela Chandresekar
Plastics Technical Evaluation Center (PLASTEC)
U.S. Army Armament Research Development Center
Dover, NJ 07801   (201) 724-2778

PLASTEC, a DOD-sponsored information and analysis center, maintains a bibliographic database with abstracts for worldwide technical literature related to plastics, adhesives, and organic matrix composites. References cover all plastic-related technology from applied research through fabrication, with emphasis on properties and performance. Subject areas include structural, electrical, electronic, and packaging applications. Databases containing millions of citations, abstracts, or research summaries can be searched. It is updated every two months, and approximately 3,000 new citations are added yearly. In addition to its own bibliographic database, online access to PLASTEC is available only to government agencies, contractors, and the defense community through OTIC, NASA STI, Dialog and SOC. The center maintains a staff of materials specialists who provide a wide range of services.

* Procurement Automated Source System

Your local SBA Office or
Glen Harwood
Procurement Automated Source System
U.S. Small Business Administration
1441 L St., NW, Room 627
Washington, DC 20416   (202) 653-6586

PASS is a centralized inventory and referral system of small businesses interested in being prime contractors for federal agencies or subcontractor for companies. More than 26,000 minority owned, 27,000 female owned and over 40,000 veteran owned businesses nationwide are listed in the fields of research and development, manufacturing, construction, and services. PASS uses a keyword system which identifies the capabilities of the company. The system can be searched for firms by geographic location, type of ownership, labor surplus area, zip code, minority type, and over 3,000 keywords. PASS, started in October 1978, currently holds reports about 130,000 firms and increases by 200 firms monthly. There are 300 direct access users. Anyone seeking to purchase a product or service from a small business can contact SBA to have a search run. Searches and printouts are provided free of charge. Firms wanting to be listed (no charge) should contact the SBA regional PASS specialist. Federal agencies and prime contractors have online direct access to PASS.

* Profile: National Automated Minority Business Source List Service

James L. Thomas
Information Clearinghouse
Minority Business Development Agency, Room 6708
U.S. Department of Commerce
Washington, DC 20230   (202) 377-2414

This system serves as a minority business locator system established for government purchasing agents. The database contains information about more than 27,000 minority- owned businesses nationwide. It can be searched by specific minority ownership (i.e., black, veteran, etc.), type of firm, size, geographic location and product or service supplied. Retrievable data include contact information and a short profile of the firm describing its capabilities, services, gross sales, and more. It is updated continually. Access is limited.

* Project Share

Ms. Joseph, Project Manager
Project Share
P.O. Box 2309
Rockville, MD 20852   (301) 231-9539 or (800) 537-3784

This database has bibliographic citations and abstracts of literature about improving the delivery and management of human services. Topics include long-term care, substance abuse, transportation, cost effectiveness, vocational rehabilitation, juvenile delinquency, health insurance, grants, fundings and group homes. Cited materials are geared toward managers, supervisors and policy-makers. The database contains 15,000 records on current literature and is updated frequently. Most searches, with printouts, cost $45.00. Several standard searches are available for $10 each.

* Railroad Accident/Incident Reporting System (RAIRS)

Bruce George
Office of Safety RRS-21
Federal Railroad Administration
U.S. Department of Transportation
400 Seventh St., SW
Washington, DC 20590   (202) 366-0533

RAIRS presents historical data on rail-highway crossing accidents/incidents for 1979 through 1988. It combines information from the rail-highway crossing

885

accident/incident file with data in the National Rail-Highway Crossing Inventory and highlights relationships between certain grade-crossing characteristics and accident frequencies. It also gives the physical and operational statistics for all public, at-grade rail-highway crossings, described in the National Inventory of May 1985. The principal data elements includes railroad codes, casualty information, damage costs, location of the accident, train speed, weather, and other grade crossing information. Reports containing detailed tables are available. These statistics are published in various reports by the Federal Railroad Administration and can be obtained by contacting the above office or any of the public information offices located in the FRA regional and division offices around the country.

* Rare-Earth Information Center (RIC)

Jennings Capellan
Rare-Earth Information Center
Energy and Minerals Resources Institute
Iowa State University
Ames, IA 50011 (515) 294-2272

RIC is a bibliographic database of worldwide literature concerning the physical and application aspects of rare-earth. RIC's main emphasis is the physical metallurgy and solid state physics of rare-earth metals and their alloys. Citations of journal articles on ceramics, technology, geochemistry, and toxicity of the elements and their compounds are also provided. RIC can be searched by author, title, time period and subject. The system currently stores 40,000 references, some dating back to 1966. RIC is updated by 3,000 references annually. Searches and printouts are available for a minimum fee of $5.00 which entitles you to up to 25 citations. Twenty-five dollars is assessed for each additional increment of 25 citations, and $2.00 per citation over 25. Fees are waived under special circumstances.

* Recall Monitoring (REC)

Gerald Deighton
FOI Staff HFI-35
U.S. FDA
5600 Fishers Lane
Rockville, MD 20857 (301) 443-6310

This system tracks product recalls from their initial classification as potential recalls through the completion of any necessary product recall and verification by FDA field personnel. Years covered are 1972-1988. For more information, contact James Merritt at (301) 427-8100.

* Red Meats and Poultry Supply and Use

Richard Stillman
Mark Weimar
U.S. Department of Agriculture
Economic Research Service
1301 New York Ave., NW
Washington, DC 20005-4788 (202) 786-1714

Contains supply and use data for beef, pork, veal, lamb, and all red meats, broilers, other chicken, turkey, all poultry, and all red meats and poultry. Quarterly and annual data are included for 1960-87. A data disk in Lotus is available for $25. For ordering information, call (800) 999-6779. Stock number 89008.

* Registry of Toxic Effects of Chemical Substances (RTECS)

Doris Sweet
Information Retrieval and Analyses Section
National Institute for Occupational Safety and Health (NIOSH)
4676 Columbia Pkwy.
Cincinnati, OH 45226 (513) 533-8317

RTECS stores data about 98,000 individual chemicals that have been studied for toxicity. The following information can be retrieved for each chemical: main name, 8+9 collective index name, synonym, molecular weight, and toxicity data. NIOSH will run one or two chemicals and provide printouts at no charge. For more detailed searches for which there is a fee, contact the National Library of Medicine or EPA Chemical Information System.

* Regulated Persons Index Master List

Joseph C. Polking
Secretary
Federal Maritime Commission (FMC)
Department of Transportation
Washington, DC 20573

This is an alphabetized listing of entities subject to FMC regulation, including vessel operating common carriers, non-vessel operating common carriers, marine terminal operators and licensed freight forwarders. This database is available at a modest charge in either hard copy or floppy format. Other files available from this office include Regulated Persons Index--a listing of vessel operating common carriers; and Regulated Persons Index--a listing of non vessel operating common

carriers and a Listing of Licensed Freight Forwarders.

* Reliability Analysis Center (RAC)

Gina Nash
Reliability Analysis Center
PO 4700
Rome, NY 13440-8200 (315) 330-4151

RAC maintains six databases with bibliographic and technical information pertaining to the reliability characteristics of components and systems. The databases are the following: VLSI, on very large scale circuits; IC, on integrated circuits; Hybrid Circuits; Non-Electronic Devices; and Failures Related to Static Electricity (FRSC). Non-operating reliability database equipment is not operational. The scope includes reliability and failure mode/mechanism information that is generated during all phases of component fabrication, testing, equipment assembly, and operation. Information and data on research and development studies, process control, quality analysis practices, screening and burn-in, qualification and environmental testing, failure analysis, reliability protection methods, reliability demonstrations, and field testing and mission deployment are incorporated in the databases. The IC database covers 10,000 devices and has records on 50,000 test results; VLSI covers 300 devices; Hybrid 1,000 devices; FRSE 5,000 devices; and Non- Electric 2,000. Searches and printouts are available on a cost recovery basis. Generally, a bibliographic search runs about $125 to $150.00.

* Residential Energy Consumption Survey

Wendel Thompson, Survey Manager
Energy Information Administration
U.S. Department of Energy
1000 Independence Ave., SW
Washington, DC 20585 (202) 586-1119

This survey provides information on household energy consumption patterns for use in developing effective conservation plans. It aids in monitoring conservation goals, and serves as input for modeling efforts designed to measure the economic impact of proposed energy policies. Households provide such information as energy consumed, house income data, type of heating equipment, area heated, and house characteristics. Tapes are available through National Technical Information Service (NTIS) for $140. The hard copy of the 1987 edition of the survey costs approximately $10.00

* Resource Allocation and Mine Costing Model

National Energy Information Center
U.S. Department of Energy
1000 Independence Ave., SW, Room 1F-048
Washington, DC 20585 (202) 252-8800

The model is designed to develop coal supply curves. Thirty coal type categories, defined by BTU and sulfur content ranges, are considered. The potential annual production and minimum acceptance price of each mine category are calculated, and the production is ordered by price to produce the supply curve. Prices are based on the cost of five surface mine types and four underground mine types, and adjusted for regional factors. The model data originate back to 1974 and the file program is currently being updated. Searches and printouts are available from NTIS.

* Rural Electrification Administration Database (REA)

Gleen Sperle
Statistics and Data Processing Division
Rural Electrification Administration
U.S. Department of Agriculture
14th St. and Independence Ave., SW
Washington, DC 20250 (202) 382-8943

REA contains financial and statistical information about the operations of approximately 2,150 REA electric borrowers individually and as a group. The borrowers are commercial companies and cooperatives providing electric and telephone service in rural areas throughout the U.S. The following information can be retrieved about each borrower: outstanding loans; REA debit service repayments; balance sheet items; revenue and expense items; operations statements, and sales statistics. REA maintains a variety of files containing information, ranging from loan statistics to accounting data. The REA database stores records on about 2,160 borrowers, 43,000 rural revolving accounts and 603,000 bank accounts. Searches, printouts and tapes are available on a cost recovery basis. Hard copy reports are also available. To arrange for searches or tapes contact the Public Information Office, REA, Department of Agriculture, Washington, D.C. 20250; (202) 382-1255.

* Safety Recommendation Information System (SRIS)

J. Richard Vanwoerkom
National Transportation Safety Board (NTSB)
800 Independence Ave., SW
Washington, DC 20594 (202) 382-6817

This interactive online database contains information about all federal safety recommendations issued by NTSB regarding transportation. The system consists of 10-20 categories for each of the following modes of transportation: aircraft, marine, pipeline, highway and railroad. Special studies and evaluations of federal transportation measures and practices are also stored. SRIS can be searched by such keywords as type of operation, vehicle or accident; human and casual factors; and type of recommendation. The system was started in 1976 with information back to 1967 and contains 7800 safety recommendations. It is updated monthly or more often. Searches and printouts are available free of charge.

* Small Business Administration: 8.9 Million Company Database

Bruce Phillips
Director of Database Branch
Office of Advocacy
U.S. Small Business Administration
1441 L St., NW
Washington, DC 20146 (202) 634-7600

The SBA is under a congressional directive to maintain information on all businesses in the country. The result is a database that is the largest government source of company information outside the IRS. The data are derived from the Dun and Bradstreet Corporation, the Yellow Pages, and other sources. It contains names, addresses, and some financial information on all of these companies, as well as statistical data compiled over the years which can identify business growth areas and opportunities. Off-the-shelf reports, customized printouts, and data tapes are all available from SSSI (Scientific Social Systems, Inc.).

* Snow Survey Centralized Forecasting System (CFS)

Tommy A. George
Director, Resources Inventory Division
Soil Conservation Service
P.O. Box 2890
Washington, DC 20013 (202) 447-6267

CFS is an automated information system related to water supply forecasting such as streamflow, precipitation, snow depth and snow water equivalent, and reservoir data. These data are available for the current water year (September 30 through October 1) and for historical water years. Numerous routines and interactive programs for manipulating water supply data are included in utility programs within CFS. CFS also provides access to hydrologic data and interpretative products for a wide variety of governmental agencies and the general public. The system can be accessed by most computers, and it is menu driven for ease of use. These data reside in an automated database consisting of monthly data for 1,700 snow courses, 600 stream gauges, 300 reservoirs, and 1,200 precipitation stations, as well as daily data from 550 SNOTEL sites and 2,000 climatological stations.

* Soils Information Retrieval System

U.S. Army Corps of Engineers
ETIS Support Center
1003 West Nevada St.
Urbana, IL 61801 (312) 333-1369

SOILS provides interaction data retrieval of soils series data. The data is compiled from the U.S. Department of Agriculture's Soil Conservation Services (SCS) reports on the characteristics and interpretive properties of all soils in the United States. Examples of soil information include use restrictions, potential habitat, description of soil, and much more. Information is organized only by soil series. The database and be accessed directly by remote terminal, and SIRS currently contains 16,000 soil series and over 175,000 soil mapping units in the U.S.. Approximately 4,000 charges are made monthly to the data. Direct access is available to ETIS subscribers for $200 a year, plus $90.00 per hour of connect time. Anyone can become an ETIS subscriber and, thereby, also gain access to three other databases maintained by ETIS. ETIS will conduct searches for non-subscribers. A cost recovery fee, based on $90.00 and staff time, is charged. The average search generally takes 10 minutes. ETIS and SOILS subscriptions and assistance are available from ETIS of the University of Illinois, Department of Urban and Regional Planning. SOILS is a cooperative venture between ETIS, the Department of Urban and Regional Planning at the University of Illinois in Urbana-Champaign, the U.S. Army Construction Engineering Laboratory (U.S.A-CERL) and the U.S. Department of Agriculture, Soil Conservation Services (U.S.DA-SCS). U.S.A-CERL obtains updated data tapes from the Statistical Laboratory at Iowa State University in Ames, IA.

* Standard Industrial Classification (SIC)

U.S. Department of Commerce
National Technical Information Service
Springfield, VA 22161 (703) 487-4807

The Standard Industrial Classification (SIC) is the statistical classification standard underlying all establishment-based Federal economic statistics classified by industry. The SIC is used to promote the comparability of establishment data describing various facets of the U.S. economy. The classification covers the entire field of economic activities and defines industries in accordance with the composition and structure of the economy. Available in: 9 track 1600 or 6250 BPI, order number PB87-100020/HAL, at a cost of $210.

* Standard Industrial Classification (SIC) Manual (for Microcomputers)

U.S. Department of Commerce
National Technical Information Service
Springfield, VA 22161 (703) 487-4807

The Standard Industrial Classification (SIC) is the statistical classification standard underlying all establishment-based Federal economic statistics classified by industry. The SIC is used to promote the comparability of establishment data describing various facets of the U.S. economy. The classification covers the entire field of economic activities and defines industries in accordance with the composition and structure of the economy. It is available in 5 1/4 inch diskette, IBM-PC compatible, order number PB87-199568/HAL at a cost of $275; 5 1/4 inch diskette, AT-compatible (1.2 Mb), order number PB87- 199576/HAL, at a cost of $175; 3 1/2 inch diskette, Apple MacIntosh, order number PB87-199584/HAL, at a cost of $425.

* Standard Occupational Classification

U.S. Department of Commerce
National Technical Information Service
Springfield, VA 22161 (703) 487-4807

The SOC provides a statistical classification system for occupations that should make statistics compiled by different agencies much more comparable, as the Standard Industrial Classification does for industries. The system includes all occupations in which work is performed for pay or profit including family members in family-operated businesses. Available in: 9 track 1600 or 6250 BPI, order number PB81-162513/HAL, at a cost of $210.

* State Alcoholism and Drug Abuse Profile (SADAP)

David S. Sanchez, Computer Systems Analyst
Division of Biometry and Epidemiology
NIAAA, Public Health Service
Department of Health and Human Services
Room 14C-26, Parklawn Building
5600 Fishers La.
Rockville, MD 20857 (301) 443-4897

A numeric (aggregate) file containing data voluntarily submitted by the 50 states, Puerto Rico, and the Virgin Islands during state fiscal year 1985 on their alcoholism and drug abuse treatment, research, and prevention programs. There are 100 variables for 52 observations. Coverage of the file is nationwide, and individual states are identified. Data pertain to fiscal year 1985. This file may be purchased from the Alcohol Epidemiologic Data System, CSR, Inc., Suite 600, 1400 Eye St., NW, Washington, D.C. 20005; (202) 847-7600 or National Institute on Alcohol Abuse and Alcoholism at a price to be determined.

* State and Area CPS and Research Database

Local Area Unemployment Statistics
U.S. Department of Labor
Bureau of Labor Statistics (BLS)
441 G St., NW, Room 2083
Washington, DC 20212 (202) 523-1002

This system is designed to provide current population survey (CPS) benchmarked for local area unemployment statistics (LAU.S.) estimates and to support publication of detailed labor force data by state and area, and also to support research in methods for estimating state and area unemployment. The system provides information on state and area employment and unemployment, including CPS data by demographic, social, economic characteristics, and unemployment insurance (UI) based data for research analysis. BLS provides a number of services including: the release of certain categories of unpublished data, development of special surveys and tabulations; customized data files are available on a cost recovery basis. Diskettes or magnetic tapes, as well as statistical software programs, can be purchased from the Division of Planning and Financial Management, Room 1077 BLS, Department of Labor, 441 G Street, NW, Washington, D.C. 20212.

* State Data on Pesticide Residues in Foods (FOODC ONTAM)

Gerald Deighton
FOI Staff HFI-35
U.S. FDA
5600 Fishers Lane
Rockville, MD 20857 (301) 443-6310

A national system to compile and summarize existing data on state analysis of food samples for pesticide and industrial chemical residues. Currently includes about 15,000 sample results from the states of California, Florida, Massachusetts, New York, Virginia, and Wisconsin. Years covered are 1986-1988. For more information, contact Heinz G. Wilms at (301) 443-3360.

Government Databases and Bulletin Boards

* State Financial Summary

Linda Farmer
U.S. Department of Agriculture
Economic Research Service
1301 New York Ave., NW
Washington, DC 20005-4788   (202) 786-1804

This summary includes state-level farm income and balance sheet accounts for 1982-87. It also includes cash receipts by commodity, government payments, and related data. Data disk available in Lotus for $85. For ordering information, call (800) 999-6779. Stock number 88012.

* Tanker Database

James E. Saari, FOI Officer
Office of Information Resources Management
Maritime Administration
Department of Transportation
400 7th St., SW
Washington, DC 20590   (202) 366-5807

Information is provided on physical, financial, and employment characteristics of privately-owned U.S. flag tanker fleet. Requests for access to this database, developed for use by the Maritime Administration, may be subject to Privacy Act regulations.

* Tax Exempt and Non-Profit Organizations

Exempt Organizations Support and Services
Internal Revenue Service
U.S. Department of Treasury
Washington, DC 20224   (202) 535-9578

This IRS file contains the names, addresses, and other pertinent information on over 900,000 U.S. tax exempt organizations. Organizations can be selected by asset size, income, type of organization, and more. Printouts are available for a cost of $100 plus 1.2 cents per name. This database corresponds to the annual publication (#78) available from GPO for $150.

* Tides: Hourly Heights

Tidal Datums Section (N/OMA123)
National Ocean Service
U.S. Department of Commerce
6001 Executive Blvd.
Room 609, WSC-1
Rockville, MD 20852   (301) 443-8467

Tidal hourly heights are the records of the height of the water level (in feet) for each hour of each day at tide observation stations. All heights are referenced to a datum. All tide data are processed in monthly increments and added to the station data file. Users of this data include federal, state, and local agencies, waterborne commerce, port authorities, marinas, coastal industries, engineering, surveying, construction firms, law firms, academia and foreign governments. The records for stations in the National Tide Observation Network (NTON) are available on hard copy and on tape with costs determined by format and amount of information ordered.

* Trade Lead Service

Foreign Agricultural Service
Agricultural Information Marketing Service
U.S. Department of Agriculture
South Building, Room 4951
Washington, DC 20250   (202) 447-7103

This file provides timely sales leads from overseas firms seeking to purchase or represent U.S. agricultural products. Trade leads can be received several ways. Commercial electronic dissemination whereby trade leads are produced daily and available the same day to American exporters through a number of commercial vendors. Export briefs is a weekly bulletin which includes all processed trade leads. There is a charge for the commercial electronic dissemination process. To subscribe to the direct mail or export briefs, call the number above. The information is published three times a year in the Journal of Commerce.

* Trade Opportunities Program (TOP)

U.S. Department of Commerce
The Economic Bulletin Board
Office of Business Analysis
Washington, DC 20230   (202) 377-3870
or
Information Management Division
U.S. Department of Commerce
ITA/U.S. & FCS/EPS
Room 1322
Washington, DC 20230   (202) 377-8246

TOP provides subscribers with up-to-date information about short-term and immediate trade opportunities with foreign agents (government and companies). The system can be searched by country of interest, type of opportunity, notice of listing, and agent or distributor. Collected information is immediately passed to subscribers. Approximately 50 to 100 reports are added daily and rolled over. Data are archived. Only TOP subscribers are eligible for services which cost $25 (one-time fee) to establish an account, and then $37.50 for the first 50 leads you receive. Bulletin and computer tapes can also be purchased.

* Urban Mass Transportation Research Information System (UMTRIS)

Suzanne D. Crowther
UMTRIS - U.S. Department of Transportation
Transportation Research Board
2101 Constitution Ave., NW, Room GR322
Washington, DC 20418   (202) 334-3251

This system provides transportation administrators, researchers, planners, designers, engineers, economists, operators, and government agencies rapid access to information about ongoing and completed transit and transit-related activities. Approximately 19,000 citations are available and 2,500 more are added to the file annually. UMTRIS is one of the active subfiles of the Transportation Research Information Services database which coordinates more than 200,000 citations on modes such as highways, railroads, maritime, and aviation. Fee for literature searches is done on case by case basis. UMTRIS also is available commercially through Dialog. An electronic bulletin board is being considered.

* U.S. Department of Education Investigative Case Tracking System

Leslie Weisman
Office of the Inspector General
U.S. Department of Education
400 Maryland Ave., SW
Washington, DC 20202-1510   (202) 732-4787

The system contains data on criminal cases and criminal allegations involving all federal education programs. Many of the investigations pertain to possible abuses in the government's student loan and college aid programs. Records are kept of allegations, criminal cases, and their outcomes. Statistics on the number of ongoing investigations, the number of indictments and other relevant information are maintained. The information dates back to 1980 and is updated daily. Semi-annual reports containing statistical information are available free of charge. Staff will share other statistical data but will not release information about specific cases.

* U.S. Foreign Trade Forecast

James E. Saari, FOI Officer
Office of Information Resources Management
Maritime Administration
Department of Transportation
400 7th St., SW
Washington, DC 20590   (202) 366-5807

Forecasting data is included on foreign and domestic trade for general cargo, dry bulk, and tanker fleet. Requests for access to this database, developed for use by the Maritime Administration, may be subject to Privacy Act regulations.

* World Agricultural Supply and Demand Estimates (WASDE)

Roger Smith and Raymond Bridge
World Agricultural Outlook Board (WAOB)
U.S. Department of Agriculture
Washington, DC 20250   (202) 447-5447

The WASDE report is reported into USDA's Electronic Dissemination of Information System during the second week of each month (see EDI separate entry). It reports global supply/demand short-term commodity forecasts and two years of historical data covering the United States and abroad. At 12:00 noon, the second work day of each week, WAOB inputs the International Weather and Crop (IWC) Summary into EDI. The IWC report is a joint report of the National Oceanic and Atmospheric Administration (NOAA) and the USDA which assesses the impact of recent meteorological events on domestic and foreign agriculture.

* World Data Bank II

Central Intelligence Agency
Washington, DC 20505
Available from:
National Technical Information Service
5285 Port Royal Rd.
Springfield, VA 22161   (703) 487-4807

This machine readable data file includes the following: a file set of geographic reference files, each file containing digital representation of a portion of the world. Five geographic areas of coverage include N. America, S. America, Europe, Africa, and Asia. Three files exist for each portion of the world represented containing data for coastlines, islands, and lakes; rivers and international boundaries. Order number PB-271869.

* World Population

Peter Johnson
Center for International Research, Room 407
U.S. Census Bureau
Washington, DC 20233   (301) 763-4811

The system contains population data for the overall world, its regions (i.e., Latin America, Asia) and 200 individual countries. Population statistics include the following: total population, estimated projections, growth rate, migratory rate, and crude (number per 1,000) birth and death rates. Data are collected from a survey conducted every two years. The latest statistics were added in March 1983, and the time span covered is 1950 to 1990 (projections). Tapes can be purchased for $175. Online access is intended only for federal employees.

Electronic Bulletin Boards

If you need quick information on microcomputers, highway construction, or even national weather trends, electronic bulletin boards may have the answers. Electronic bulletin boards can offer you low-cost, online access to unique information and resources not normally available through commercial database vendors. And what is more important, the information on electronic bulletin boards is often updated daily, providing you with the newest information not yet available in larger, conventional databases. Another advantage to electronic bulletin boards is their relative easy access. Where accessing conventional online databases may require special knowledge of computer languages, bulletin boards are frequently driven by simple, user-friendly menus.

One of the nicer features of these bulletin boards which most online databases lack is that they often allow dialogue to take place between the user and the system operator (sysop), and even between different users. The Air Force's Small Computer Technical Center, for example, allows you to leave a message on the bulletin board outlining, say, a computer software problem you are having, and if the system operator or one of the other users can help, they can leave you a message, sometimes on the same day. While some bulletin boards require a subscription fee, many do not, which means you pay only for any long distance telephone charges.

Listed below are a sampling of the principal bulletin boards available. Additional online systems are identified in the preceding section on federal government databases.

* Agricultural Library Forum (ALF)
National Agricultural Library (NAL)
U.S. Department of Agriculture   Data: 301-344-8510
10301 Baltimore Blvd.   Data: 301-344-8511
Beltsville, MD 20705   Voice: 301-344-1204
ALF provides a convenient, low-cost tool for electronically accessing information about NAL products and services and for exchanging agricultural information and resources. ALF supports three types of communications: NAL bulletins, messaging and conferencing between users, and file transfers. 24 hours/day; 7 days/week.

* Automated Data Service
U.S. Naval Observatory
Time Services Department
Department of the Navy
34th & Massachusetts Ave., NW   Data: 202-653-1079
Washington, D.C. 20392-5100   Voice: 202-653-1522
ADS is designed to provide a means for the exchange of information among members of the precise time community. The data available on ADS provide measurements of the offsets of various systems of precise time transfer from the U.S. Naval Observatory Master Clock and information about the operational status of these systems.

* BXR Information Corner
Internal Revenue Service
U.S. Department of the Treasury
Systems Services Branch   Data: 703-756-6109
Washington, D.C. 20224   Voice: 703-756-6280
The main message base for this bulletin board concerns technical computer-related topics such as hardware, software, graphics, word-processing and computer security. There are 11 areas for users to discuss ways to enhance productivity. 24 hours/day, 7 days/week. Sysop: Marianne Crockford.

* Climate Analysis Center Bulletin Board
U.S. Department of Commerce
National Weather Service
5200 Auth Road, Room 805   Data: Fee-based, call for details
Washington, D.C. 20233   Voice: 301-763-4670
This bulletin board provides weekly and monthly summaries of temperatures, precipitation, and other climatic conditions, primarily for agricultural and energy applications. Sysop: Vernon Patterson.

* Detroit-Area Office of the Office of Personnel Management Bulletin Board Service
Detroit Area Office
Office of Personnel Management
477 Michigan Ave., Room 565   Data: 313-226-4423
Detroit, MI 48226   Voice: 313-226-7520
Federal job information for the 14 states in the Chicago region is available via this board. Listings include some qualifications and pay scale information, job applications, opportunities for college graduates, and other specialized topics. The board is used by libraries, college placement offices and other schools as well as by individuals. 24 hours/day; 7 days/week. Sysop: Dave Nason.

* Eximbank Bulletin Board Service
Export-Import Bank of the United States
811 Vermont Ave., NW   Data: 202-566-4699
Washington, D.C. 20571   Voice: 202-566-4490
The bulletin board offers descriptions of some of the bank's lending programs and the Foreign Credit Insurance Association's policies. It includes application forms, press releases, seminar schedules, a referral list of banks in the EIB programs and a EIB staff directory.

* Fannie Mae Information Service
Federal National Mortgage Association (Fannie Mae)
3900 Wisconsin Ave., NW
Washington, D.C. 20016-2899   800-752-6440 (fee-based)
The quasi-government agency Fannie Mae utilizes MORNET electronic bulletin boards to broadcast information and provide a message exchange network to meet the needs of the mortgage industry. Topics include pricing, regional office contact lists, news, analysis, legislative reports, debt information and updates to Fannie Mae guides. 7 days/week; 24 hours/day.

* FCC Public Access Link (PAL Online)
Federal Communications Commission (FCC)
1919 M. St., NW
Washington, D.C. 20554   202-632-7581
Manufacturers and importers who submit applications for equipment approval by the FCC can track the status of their applications with this bulletin board. Confidentially assigned code numbers limit access of each user to information on its own application. Limited Access.

* FEBBS (Federal Highway Administration Remote Bulletin Board System)
Federal Highway Administration
U.S. Department of Transportation
400 7th St., SW   Data: 202-366-3764
Washington, DC 20590   Voice: 202-366-9022
FEBBS provides information on FHWA topics including traffic, highways, construction, paving and other related subjects. 24 hours/day; 7 days/week. Sysop: Carl Shea.

* Federal Deposit Insurance Corporation Electronic Bulletin Board
Federal Deposit Insurance Corporation (FDIC)   Data: 202-371-9578
Washington, D.C. 20429   Voice: 202-898-8966
The FDIC Bulletin Board was established to provide a means for FDIC

personnel to practice transferring files. The Board can be accessed by the general public and does not contain bank information. 24 hours/day; 7 days/week. Sysop: Richard Campbell.

* Federal Energy Regulatory Commission Issuance Posting System(CIPS)

Federal Energy Regulatory Commission   Data: 202-357-8997
Washington, D.C. 20426   Voice: 202-357-5570

CIPS provides the full text of the FERC daily issuances, press releases, the Commission agenda, and a daily listing of all filings made to the Commission. 23 hours/day (down 8 AM - 9 AM) Monday - Friday. Sysop: Sid Barinder.

* FE TELENEWS

Office of Fossil Energy
U.S. Department of Energy   Data: 202-586-6496
Washington, D.C. 20585   Voice: 202-586-6503

FE TELENEWS is a free online service for coal, oil, gas and petroleum reserves information, including news announcements, congressional testimony, fact sheets, speeches, federal research and development programs facts. A free user guide is available from TELENEWS Staff, FE-10, Room 4G-085 at the above address. 24 hours/day, 7 days/week.

* Hay Locator Bulletin Board

Rick Westerman
Operations Manager AG Communication Network
Purdue University Cooperative Extension Service
Smith Hall, Room 105
West Lafayette, IN 47907   317-494-8333

This up-to-date, computerized listing of hay and straw for buyers and sellers across the nation can be searched by hay types, location, sellers, and buyers. Available free with 500, 1200, or 2400 baud connection. The system operates on a single user dial-up computer that provides access to the information and some of the programs available in the Indiana FACTS network. Extension newsletters, news stories from Purdue's Agricultural Communications Service and other sources are put on the system daily in preassigned groupings called "topics." Users can search for items of interest and then globally or selectively display items on their terminal screen or to a printing terminal. Subject areas include agricultural, agribusiness and home management. Intended users are any private citizens normally served by the extension. Users pay only for the phone call.

* Information Resource Management Electronic Bulletin Board

Information Resources Management Office
General Accounting Office   Data: 202-275-1050
Washington, D.C.   Voice: 202-275-5327

This is a newsletter and message center bulletin board directed toward users of various information management programs, including word processing, spreadsheets, databases and communications. 24 hours/day, 7 days/week. Sysop: Sheryl Gee.

* Information Resources Service Center

Information Resources Services Office   Data: 202-535-7661 (1200 baud)
General Services Administration   Data: 202-786-9014 (2400 baud)
Washington, D.C. 20405   Voice: 202-566-1683

Nationwide users can access information on contracts awarded by General Services Administration --Information Resources Management Service by accessing this bulletin board. 24 hours/day, 7 days/week. Sysop: Chuck Massey.

* Information Systems Engineering Bulletin Board Systems (ISE BBs)

National Institute of Standards and Technology   Data: 301-948-2048
A257 Technology Building   Data: 301-948-2059
Gaithersburg, MD 20899   Voice: 301-975-3272

The ISE BBS provides access to information on NIST National Computer Systems Laboratory and ISE program activities; summaries of standards reports; publications lists; and a listing of other bulletin board systems. Users can leave messages for each other and questions for the sysop. 24 hours/day, 7 days/week.

* National Aeronautics and Space Administration (NASA) Bulletin Board System

National Aeronautics and Space Administration
Information Technology Center   Data: 202-453-9008
Washington, D.C. 20546   Voice: 202-453-9009

NASA's wildcat bulletin board system was established to provide an information service for messaging and filing, to be used by both NASA employees and the general public. 24 hours/day, 7 days/week. Sysop: Nader Ghabadi, John Walker.

* Naval Aviation News Computer Information (NANci)

Department of the Navy
The Pentagon   Data: 202-475-1173
Washington, D.C. 20350   Voice: 202-433-4407

NANci provides a source of aviation news and historical facts for naval buffs. Messaging is available. Access is sometimes limited during working hours. 24 hours/day, 7 days/week. Sysop: Commander John A. Norton.

* Navy Regional Data Automation Center Remote Bulletin Board System (NARDAC RBBS)

Navy Regional Data Automation Center   804-445-1121
Department of the Navy, VA 23511-6497   Voice: 804-445-4157, (804) 445-1627

NARDAC RBBS is designed to promote the dissemination and exchange of microcomputer-based public domain software for the Department of the Navy. Included are Navy applications, database management systems, word processing, communications, electronic spreadsheets, barcoding and system utilities. The latest information on the microcomputer contracts and conferences can be accessed.

* NOAA FIDO (National Oceanic and Atmospheric Administration)

Information Technology Center
National Oceanic and Atmospheric Administration
U.S. Department of Commerce   Data: 301-770-0069
Washington, D.C. 20230   Voice: 301-443-8225

Designed for non-technical purposes, NOAA FIDO provides for the exchange of information about office automation. NOAA employees and other users interested in PC's usually discuss ways to get the most out of their machines. The public will find NOAA FIDO helpful in that scientists use the board and will often answer questions. 24 hours/day, 7 days/week. Sysop: Tom Murphy.

* Office Automation Bulletin Board (OMSD Bulletin Board)

Bureau of the Census
U.S. Department of Commerce   Data: 301-763-4576
Washington, D.C. 20233   Voice: 301-763-4950

This system was designed to provide for an exchange of information between Bureau employees and other users of office automation. Members share ideas and experience about word processing, graphics, electronics and other utilities. 24 hours/day; 7 days/week. Sysop: Nevins Frankel.

* Office of Program Planning and Evaluation Bulletin Board

Office of Program Planning and Evaluation
U.S. Department of Commerce   Data: 202-377-1423
Washington, D.C. 20230   Voice: 202-377-2949

Designed as an internal communications mechanism for Commerce Department budget and planning officers, bulletins contain information on schedules, staff assignments, and related information. It is also used to transmit documents and spreadsheets to and from Bureaus outside the H.C. Hoover Building. The board is open and users may leave messages requesting help in identifying appropriate contact persons for Commerce Department matters. 24 hours/day; 7 days/week. Sysop: Patricia Spencer.

* OPEnet

U.S. Department of Education
Office of Postsecondary Education
OPEnet Coordinator
c/o Dialcom Services
6120 Executive Blvd., Suite 150
Rockville, MD 20852   301-770-4280

The Office of Postsecondary Education network provides information exchange with financial aid services and administrators, institutions, and the U.S. Department of Education. Included are regulations, notices of proposed rulemaking, news bulletins, calendars, workshop and meeting notices, press releases, and messaging. Subscription required.

* Personnel

Bureau of the Census
U.S. Department of Commerce   Data: 301-763-4574
Washington, D.C. 20233   Voice: 301-763-7448

This service lists Bureau vacancies and describes the positions giving pay plan and other information. Users may leave a message with their name and phone number. 24 hours/day; 7 days/week. Sysop: Nevins Frankel.

Government Databases and Bulletin Boards

* Remote Bulletin Board System

U.S. Department of Energy-Germantown   Data: 301-353-4892
Washington, D.C. 20545   Voice: 301-353-2500

DOE RBBS offers information and public domain utility software for microcomputer users. RBBS allows users to look at bulletins and listings, download information, and post or read messages. 8:30 am to 5:00 pm, Monday-Friday.

* Science Resources Studies Electronic Bulletin Board System

National Science Foundation
Division of Science Resources Studies   Data: 202-634-1764
Washington, D.C. 20550   Voice: 202-634-4250 (SRS Technical Service)

The SRS Electronic Bulletin Board provides up-to-date statistical data and other information on financial and human resources related to science, engineering and technology. The board contains brief narrative reports on current studies and announcements. 24 hours/day, 7 days/week. Sysop: Jean Deans.

* Small Computer Technical Center

Department of the Air Force   Data: 618-256-6510
Scott Air Force Base, IL 62225   Voice: 618-256-4206

This board provides an information exchange network for users of small computers. Discussions usually focus on how to enhance the productivity of computer hardware and software. There is no military information exchanged on the board. 24 hours/day; 7 days/week.

* The Economic Bulletin Board

U.S. Department of Commerce
Office of Business Analysis and Economic Affairs   Data: 202-377-3870
Washington, D.C. 20230   Voice: 202-377-1986

Users may tap in to the latest releases from the Bureau of Economic Analysis, Bureau of the Census, Bureau of Labor Statistics and other federal agencies. Included are GNP, CPI, employment, income, foreign trade data, studies and reports, listings of publications and data bases. Subscriptions and a limited free try-out service are both available. 24 hours/day.

* United States Information Agency Bulletin Service (USIA BBS)

U.S. Information Agency   Data: 202-376-2901
Washington, D.C. 20547   Voice: 202-376-7778

This is a specialized bulletin board service established to facilitate message traffic between USIA and its overseas posts, contractors and clients, and also for the exchange of information between broadcasters. The service is open to USIA employees, clients and contractors; the media; and other BBS operators. Sysop: Pat Pasco.

* Veterans Administration Foreclosed Property Listing Remote Bulletin Board

Veterans Administration
Washington, D.C. 20420

Regional Veterans Administration offices provide online listings of local property foreclosures via remote bulletin board systems. The participating regional offices are listed below. Except where specified, the bulletin boards operate evenings and weekends. The following number for each office is the remote computer bulletin board for property listings. LGO = Loan Guaranty Officer; PMC = Property Management Chief.

Montgomery, AL
Voice: 204-832-7193
Data: 205-832-7202

Anchorage, AK
Voice: 907-271-4562
Data: 907-271-2249

Phoenix, AZ
Voice: 602-241-2748
Data: 602-241-2371

N. Little Rock, AR
Voice: 501-370-3758
Data: 501-370-3881

Denver, CO
Voice: 303-980-2847
Data: 303-980-2984

Hartford, CT
Voice: 203-244-2897
Data: 203-240-3021

St. Louis, MO
Voice: 314-425-5144
Data: 314-539-3145

Fort Harrison, MT
Voice: 406-442-6410
Data: 406-442-7024

Waco, TX
Voice: 817-757-6869
Data: 817-757-6308

Salt Lake City, UT
Voice: 801-588-598
Data: 801-524-3550

Manchester, NH
Voice: 603-666-7656
Data: 603-240-3021

Newark, NJ
Voice: 201-645-3607
Data: 201-645-3953

Los Angeles, CA
Voice: 213-209-7838
Data: 213-209-7920

Washington, D.C.
Voice: 202-275-0611
Data: 202-275-5622

St. Petersburg, FL
Voice: 813-893-3404
Data: 813-822-3821

Atlanta, GA
Voice: 404-881-3474
Data: 404-347-7768

Boise, ID
Voice: 208-334-1910
Data: 208-334-9696

Chicago, IL
Voice: 312-353-4068
Data: 312-353-2382

Louisville, KY
Voice: 502-582-5866
Data: 502-582-5134

New Orleans, LA
Voice: 504-589-6459
Data: 504-589-3871

Togue, ME
Voice: 207-623-5434
Data: 207-240-3021

Baltimore, MD
Voice: 301-962-4467
Data: 301-962-7876

Boston, MA
Voice: 617-223-3052
Data: 203-240-3021

San Francisco, CA
Voice: 415-974-0204
Data: 415-974-9510

Lincoln, NE
Voice: 402-471-5031
Data: 402-471-5034

Indianapolis, IN
Voice: 317-269-7827
Data: 317-269-7527

Des Moines, IA
Voice: 515-284-4657
Data: 515-284-4869

Wichita, KS
Voice: 316-269-6311
Data: 316-269-6739

Winston-Salem, NC
Voice: 919-761-3494
Data: 919-761-3585

Cleveland, OH
Voice: 216-522-3583
Data: 216-522-7664

Muskogee, OK
Voice: 918-687-2161
Data: 918-687-2556

Detroit, MI
Voice: 313-226-7561
Data: 313-226-4227

St. Paul, MN
Voice: 612-725-4054
Data: 612-725-3050

Jackson, MS
Voice: 601-965-4826
Data: 601-965-4825

Houston, TX
Voice: 713-660-4154
Data: 713-660-4140

Albuquerque, NM
Voice: 505-766-2214
Data: 505-766-8335

Buffalo, NY
Voice: 716-846-5295
Data: 716-846-4702

New York, NY
Voice: 212-620-6424
Data: 203-240-3021

Portland, OR
Voice: 503-221-2481
Data: 503-221-6884

Philadelphia, PA
Voice: 215-951-5509
Data: 215-951-5514

Pittsburgh, PA
Voice: 412-644-6979
Data: 412-644-4755

Columbia, SC
Voice: 803-765-5154
Data: 803-765-5407

Nashville, TN
Voice: 615-251-5241
Data: 615-736-2100

San Juan, PR
Voice: 809-766-5216
Data: 809-766-3000

Huntington, WV
Voice: 304-529-5047
Data: 304-529-5434

Honolulu, HI
Voice: 808-546-2160
Data: 808-541-1476

Odds and Ends

Every chapter is filled with all sorts of free publications, posters, and gift ideas. Some special souvenirs and freebies are grouped here along with an assortment of other odds and ends ranging from pet advice to beekeeping.

* 50th Wedding Anniversary Card Signed By the President

Presidential Correspondence
Old Executive Office Building
Room 94
Washington, DC 20500   (202) 456-7639

50th wedding anniversary cards and 80th birthday cards signed by the President are available to the public. The requests must be written and should be received at least one month before the event. Photographs are also available through a written request. Contact the office above.

* 80th Birthday Card Signed by the President

Presidential Correspondence
Old Executive Office Building
Room 94
Washington, DC 20500   (202) 456-7639

Birthday cards signed by the President are available to the public. The requests must be written and should be received at least one month before the event. Photographs are also available through a written request. Contact the office above.

* Aerial Photographs

Customer User Services
Earth Resources Observation System Data Center (EROS)
U.S. Geological Survey
Sioux Falls, SD 57198   (605) 594-6511

Aerial photographs are available from this center for most geographical regions of the country. Prices range from $6 to $65, depending on whether they are black and white or color photographs. Contact this office for ordering information.

* American Flags

c/o The Capitol
Washington, DC 20515   (202) 224-3121

You can arrange to purchase flags that have been flown over the Capitol by getting in touch with your U.S. Senator or Representative. A certificate signed by the Architect of the Capitol accompanies each flag. Flags are available for purchase in sizes of 3 x 5 or 5 x 8 in fabrics of cotton and nylon.

* Animal Poison Control Hotline

National Animal Poison Control Center   (217) 333-3611

The National Animal Poison Control Center, at The University of Illinois, provides 24-hour consultation in diagnosis and treatment of suspected or actual animal poisonings or chemical contaminations. Its emergency response team will rapidly investigate such incidents in North America, and perform laboratory analysis of feeds, animal specimens, and environmental materials for toxicants and chemical contaminants.

* Bees and Beekeeping

Honeybee Breeding Genetics
and Physiology Research Lab
U.S. Department of Agriculture
ARS, 1157 Ben Hur Rd.
Baton Rouge, LA 70820   (504) 766-6064

Scientists are currently at work trying to protect the beekeeping industry and the public from the advent of the Africanized bees that are due to arrive in mid 1990. Research projects include use of a toxic substance that will attract bees and kill them, a repellent that will keep these aggressive bees from stinging, and ways of protecting commercial queen bee farms from invasion of Africanized bees.

* Bugs and Other Household Pests

Executive Officer
U.S. Department of Agriculture
SEA, Room 33A
Administration Building
Washington, DC 20250   (202) 447-3304
OR local County Cooperative Extension Service

Free technical advice is available to aid in controlling cockroaches and other critters. To identify an insect, the local county cooperative extension service often will ask you to send a representative sample in order to suggest the best way to rid your home of this menace.

* Cheese Making

Dairy Laboratory
Department of Agriculture, AR-NER
Eastern Regional Center
600 East Mermaid Lane
Philadelphia, PA 19118   (215) 233-6462

The Dairy Lab has accumulated information on the process of making cheese at home and can share their expertise with you.

* Christmas Trees

Division of Forestry
Bureau of Land Management
U.S. Department of the Interior
Washington, DC 20240   (202) 653-8864

The BLM officials issue permits to cut Christmas trees for a nominal fee on Bureau of Land Management-administered lands in the 11 Western states and Alaska. Free-use permits are available from the Bureau to non-profit organizations for timber and trees to be used exclusively by that organization. This excludes the resale of any free timber or trees by those organizations.

* Comet Haley Atlas

Superintendent of Documents
Government Printing Office
Washington, DC 20402   (202) 783-3238

Census statistics publications are listed in this bibliography. One may send for the Railroad Maps of North America, featuring 5,000 maps and surveys. Weather and political atlases are listed, as well as an atlas to the Comet Haley. Free.

* Dial the Exact Time: The Master Clock

Atomic Clock
Naval Observatory
24th and Massachusetts Ave.
Washington, DC 20392-5100   (202) 653-1541

The Observatory's Master Clock is the source for all standard time in the United States. For the correct time, call the number above, or dial 1-900-410-TIME if you are outside of the D.C. area.

* Family Counseling

Family Branch
U.S. Department of Agriculture
10301 Baltimore Blvd.
Beltsville, MD 20705   (301) 344-3719

This center answers questions about families throughout the lifecycle, from marital relationships and childbearing families to empty nest families and retirement, and deals with matters concerning social environment and family economics education.

* First Lady's Daily Schedule

Office of the First Lady
The White House
Attention: Scheduling Office
Washington, DC 20500   (202) 456-7910

Call (202) 456-6269 to hear a recorded message of the daily schedule of the First Lady. For more information write to the office above.

* Free County Educational Programs

Executive Officer
County Cooperative Extension Service
U.S. Department of Agriculture
Room 340A Administration Building
Washington, DC 20250   (202) 447-4111

The USDA operates an extension program in 3,165 counties located in all of the 50 states and the U.S. territories. Federal, state, and local governments share in financing and conducting cooperative extension educational programs to help farmers, processors, handlers, farm families, communities, and consumers apply the results of food and agricultural research. The Extension Service helps people develop marketable job skills, make informed career decisions, and expand available opportunities. It offers guidance to families such as ways to manage finances and make sound financial decisions; confront and deal with such problems as alcohol and drug abuse, teenage pregnancy, and unemployment; and develop strategies for retirement. The extension offers up-to-date information about the relationship of dietary practices to lifestyle factors. Another major area is revitalizing rural America: programs emphasize how to increase competitiveness and efficiency of rural programs, explore methods to diversify local economies and attract new business, adjust to impact of change, develop ways to finance and deliver services, and train leaders to make sound policy decisions for rural communities. It works with consumers, producers and local government to learn more about the importance of high-quality ground water and the conservation of water resources. Emphasis is also put on the effects of agricultural chemicals and contaminants on water quality. The extension is helping expand youth outreach resources to meet the needs of youth, develop programs for the most susceptible youth populations, provide leadership and job skills, and increase training of professionals and volunteers to work in communities to prevent and treat problems.

* Free Firewood

Contact your nearest forest ranger

Where supply exceeds demand, free firewood is available from public lands. Just contact your nearest forest ranger.

* Free Manure

College Park Holsteins
University of Maryland Dairy Barns
College Park, MD 20742   (301) 454-5918

Many Extension Service offices offer free manure for gardeners. In the Washington, DC, area, manure is available by the barrel or truckload at the above address.

* Genealogy: Plant a Family Tree

Communications Office
U.S. Postal Service
475 L'Enfant Plaza, SW, Room 5300
Washington, DC 20260-3121   (202) 268-2143

The Postal Service launched a "Plant a Family Tree" program to encourage the nation's children to discover their family's genealogy by writing to their grandparents and by filing in a "family tree" made available through post offices.

* Geologic Publications: Caves to Volcanoes

U.S. Geological Survey
Book and Report Sales
Box 25425
Denver, CO 80225   (303) 236-7476

This is a listing of some of the general interest publications available through the U.S. Geological Survey. They are free unless otherwise indicated.

The Antarctic and its Geology
Eruptions of Hawaiian Volcanoes: Past, Present and Future ($4.00)
Eruptions of Mount St. Helens: Past, Present, and Future ($2.75)
Geologic History of Cape Cod, Massachusetts
Geology of Caves
The Great Ice Age
The Interior of the Earth
Landforms of the United States
Marine Geology: Research Beneath the Sea
Our Changing Continent
Permafrost
The San Andreas Fault
Volcanoes
Geysers
Gold
Natural Steam for Power
Glaciers: A Water Resource
Elevations and Distances in the United States
Geologic Maps: Portraits of the Earth
Building Stones of Our Nation's Capital
Steps to the Moon
Tree Rings: Timekeepers of the Past
The Naming (and Misnaming) of America

* Gold Prospecting

Publications Department
Bureau of Mines
U.S. Department of the Interior
18th and C Sts., NW, Room 2647
Washington, DC 20240   (202) 343-5520

The publications department of the Bureau of Mines distributes the free booklet, *How To Mine and Prospect for Gold.*

* Greeting Cards and Gift Items

Jefferson Gift Shop
Library of Congress
Washington, DC 20540   (202) 707-5111

Many gift items, including greeting cards, notepaper, bookplates, posters, recordings, T shirts, are available from the gift shop, which is open 9 a.m. to 5 p.m., Monday through Saturday.

* Medals of the United States Mint

Customer Service Center
U.S. Mint
Department of the Treasury
10001 Aerospace Dr.
Lanham, MD 20706   (301) 436-7400

You can purchase many different types of medals that honor famous people from the U.S. Mint. Medals of all of the U.S. Presidents are available in 3" and 1 5/16" sizes. The Secretaries of the Treasury are featured in a 3" medal series, as well as the Directors of the Mint. Various medals has been issued that commemorate veterans, and famous army and navy heroes. Others include aviation heroes, leaders and statesmen, those who contributed to the arts and culture, doctors, and Chief Justices of the Supreme Court. Checks or Visa and MasterCard payments are accepted.

* Moon and Planets Maps

Distribution Branch
U.S. Geological Survey
Building 810
Denver Federal Center, Box 25286
Denver, CO 80225   (800) USA-MAPS

The USGS established an astrogeology program on behalf of NASA to support lunar and planetary exploration. Many maps of the Moon, Mars, Venus, and Mercury are available.

* National Atlas Updates

Distribution Branch
U.S. Geological Survey
Building 810
Denver Federal Center, Box 25286
Denver, CO 80225   (800) USA-MAPS

The *National Atlas of the United States* (1970) contains 765 maps and charts on 335 pages. Out of print and no longer for sale, it can still be found in most libraries. However, separate sheets of selected reference maps and thematic maps from the *Atlas* are available from the USGS. Some of the sheets have been updated. Some updated thematic maps include potential natural vegetation (1985), monthly average temperature (1986) monthly minimum temperature (1986), monthly maximum temperature (1986), networks of ecological research (1983), and territorial growth (1986).

* Nation's Capitol: History, Books, Tapes

U.S. Capitol Historical Society
200 Maryland Ave., NE
Washington, DC 20002   (202) 543-8919

A non-profit educational organization chartered by Congress, this historical society puts out many publications, including *We the People* and *Washington Past and Present*. The society also sells VHS video cassette tapes, such as *City Out of Wilderness*, which tells the story of Washington, D.C., and the Capitol. It sells for $35, which including postage, or $30 in the Capitol. *Place of Resounding Deeds*, a thirty minute video tour of the Capitol, sells for $29.95 with postage, or $25 in the Capitol. The society has a sales desk in the rotunda with miscellaneous items such as postcards and various books for the public. Symposiums are held annually and are published for the public. Speakers from the Society are available provided advance notice is given.

* Pet Food and Medications

Center for Veterinary Medicine
Division of Animal Feeds
Food and Drug Administration
5600 Fishers Lane
HFV 220, Room 7B45
Rockville, MD 20857   (301) 443-5363

The Food and Drug Administration is responsible for ensuring that animal drugs,

Odds and Ends

devices, and medicated feeds are safe and effective and that food from treated animals is safe to eat. They also make sure the animal and pet foods are safe and properly labeled. Flyers and memos are available for the general public and professionals regarding veterinary medicine. The *FDA Veterinarian*, a bimonthly publication, outlines the latest developments in the field of veterinary medicine, and is available for $5 per year from Superintendent of Documents, Government Printing Office, Washington, DC 20402, (202) 783-3238.

* Pet Problems and Sickness

> Executive Officer
> U.S. Department of Agriculture
> SEA, Room 33A
> Administration Building
> Washington, DC 20250   (202) 447-3304
>   OR local County Cooperative Extension Service

Free technical advice is available to aid in diagnosing sick pets. Your local county cooperative extension service often will analyze your pet's stool and offer guidance over the telephone.

* Pets and Animal Health

> Public Awareness, LPAS
> APHIS
> U.S. Department of Agriculture
> Federal Building, Room 700
> 6505 Belcrest Road
> Hyattsville, MD 20782   (301) 436-7799

Pets--They Need Proper Care to Travel by Air is one of the publications available free. Many other fact sheets are published by APHIS such as housing and caging, training guides and manuals for animal care personnel.

* Presidential Homes and Washington Buildings

> Bureau of Engraving and Printing
> U.S. Department of the Treasury
> 14th and C Sts., SW, Room 602-11A
> Washington, DC 20228   (202) 447-0193

Vignettes of famous Washington buildings and presidential homes are available in the 6" x 8" size for $4.00. The Great Seal of the U.S. and the Department of Treasury Seal, lithographed in color, are also available.

* Presidential Portraits

> Bureau of Engraving and Printing
> U.S. Department of the Treasury
> 14th and C Sts., SW, Room 602-11A
> Washington, DC 20228   (202) 447-0193

Small presidential portraits (6" x 8") and larger presidential portraits (9" x 12") are available from the Bureau of Engraving and Printing for $4.00 and $4.50, respectively. Prices are slightly less at the facility store. There are also 6" x 8" portraits of the Chief Justices of the Supreme Court, available for $4.00.

* President's Schedule

> Office of Presidential Scheduling
> The White House
> 1600 Pennsylvania Ave., NW
> Washington, DC 20500   (202) 456-7560

Contact this office for information on the President's daily schedule, or call (202) 456-2343 to hear a recorded message.

* Public Debt Donations

> Office of the Commissioner
> Bureau of the Public Debt
> U.S. Department of the Treasury
> 999 E St., NW
> Washington, DC 20239   (202) 376-4300

Since the U.S. Government maintains a public debt of more than $1.9 trillion dollars, and is currently paying $176 billion in interest to pay off this debt, they are asking for donations from the general public to pay off the debt. The Treasury has an account into which money received as gifts is deposited. The money is used to pay at maturity, or to redeem or buy before maturity, an obligation of the Government included in the public debt. Donations can be sent to: Bureau of the Public Debt, Department G, Washington, DC 20239-0601.

* Rock Collecting

> U.S. Geological Survey
> Book and Report Sales
> Box 25425
> Denver, CO 80225   (303) 236-7476

Collecting Rocks is a free booklet available from the USGS for those youngsters and adults interested in pursuing this hobby and learning more about geology.

* Sick Plants

> Executive Officer
> U.S. Department of Agriculture
> SEA, Room 33A
> Administration Building
> Washington, DC 20250   (202) 447-3304
> OR local County Cooperative Extension Service

Free technical advice is available to aid in diagnosing and curing diseases of indoor and outdoor plants by contacting your local county cooperative extension service.

* Space Photographs

> Customer Services
> Earth Resources Observation System Data Center (EROS)
> U.S. Geological Survey
> Sioux Falls, SD 57198   (605) 594-6511

The EROS Data Center maintains photographs from many of the space missions, including those of the space shuttle, Apollo, and Gemini. Contact the center directly for information concerning specific topics.

* Stamp Collecting

> Stamp Division
> U.S. Postal Service
> 475 L'Enfant Plaza West, SW
> Washington, DC 20260   (202) 245-5778

Anyone interested in phitalely, the collecting and study of stamps, can receive a free booklet called *Introduction to Stamp Collecting*.

* Tell the President!

> The President of the United States
> White House
> 1600 Pennsylvania Avenue, NW
> Washington, DC 20500   (202) 456-7639

White House operators will take messages for the president. You can also write to the Commander-in-Chief and share your views about current issues.

* Wild Burros and Horses for Adoption

> Office of Public Information
> Bureau of Land Management
> U.S. Department of the Interior
> 18th and C Sts., NW
> Washington, DC 20240-0001   (202) 343-5717

Wild burros and horses that roam on public lands are put up for adoption after a short time to decrease their numbers. If you are interested in adopting one of these animals, you should contact a local BLM adoption center, and there is a fee of $125 per horse and $75 per burro. You must also transport the animals home and provide for their future upkeep. The booklet, *So You'd Like to Adopt A Wild Horse Or Burro?*, answers many of the questions you might have when handling this responsibility. Contact the office above for the adoption centers near you.

* Wine: Home Production

> National Agriculture Library
> U.S. Department of Agriculture
> Beltsville, MD 20705   (301) 344-3755

The U.S. Department of Agriculture has accumulated documentation and can share information to assist you in making wine at home.

* Woodsy Owl: Toys for Tots

> U.S. Department of Agriculture
> Forest Service, P.O. Box 96090
> Washington, DC 20090-6090   (202) 475-3785

To increase children's awareness of our delicate environment, the Forest Service's Woodsy Owl campaign has a variety of materials available, including coloring sheets, detective sheets, song sheets, patches, and stickers.

Current Events and Homework

Whether you are struggling with a school term paper or are eager to impress your boss by obtaining the latest statistics and analysis of practically any subject, help is right at hand. Few people, even those of us living in Washington, D.C., are aware of all the studies generated around the clock by a division of the Library of Congress. Approximately 500 PhDs working at the Congressional Research Service (CRS) grind out these reports on almost any topic imaginable and these studies are made available to all 525 Members of Congress.

Your U.S. Representative and Senators have instantaneous access to over 10,000 reports on current events through a computerized on-line network. And a phone call or letter to one of your legislators is all it takes for you to tap into this rich information resource. To get copies of these report you must go through the office of their U.S. Representative or Senator. There is no charge for these concise reports which are unquestionably the "best information value" because the material contained in these studies are the highlights from materials prepared by other experts in federal government agencies as well as the private sector. Researchers, students of all ages, marketing reps, entrepreneurs, and ordinary citizens should take advantage of this information gold mine.

The Reason Why These Reports Are Constantly Updated

If a congressional committee plans an investigation, for example, on the home health care situation, the CRS specialists will complete a background study and their findings will be available to anyone in the public domain. If a lawmaker is concerned about the situation in Poland, these experts will prepare a complete analysis of the situation and when warranted, they will keep it up-to-date every day as events change. If a Congressman is going to address an industry group on a subject like "Captive Off-Shore Insurance Companies", most likely his staff is going to rely on the information generated by CRS. They can tap into this database and out will spew a 10 to 30 page report written by an expert who spends much of his or her career studying this subject.

CRS Reports Are Easy To Understand . . . They're Written For Congressmen

Although these studies are prepared by PhDs you do not have to worry about being able to understand them. These reports summarize historical context as well as fast breaking developments and are presented in layman's language. Also the CRS adheres to its non-partisan mission to serve all Members of Congress. One rationale for getting CRS studies is actually to see what material legislators and their staff are using for background whether it be for speeches or policy decision making. In additional to covering most any business or student subject area these reports are an easy way to stay current on complex world events and issues of peripheral concern.

How To Get A Report

Getting your hands on a half a dozen reports can be easy. Just remember you cannot get studies directly from CRS but only by contacting a Member's Washington or district office. Sometimes problems arise if you don't have the proper title or publication number. If you don't receive copies in a week or two, a follow up phone call is necessary. Keep in mind that helping constituents in this way is a welcome task, especially when a legislator's reelection is close at hand. If you find one office uncooperative try another. Remember we each have two Senators and one Representative. You can contact all legislators in Washington, D.C. by calling the Capitol Hill Switchboard at (202) 224-3121.

Sample Entry

It is next to impossible to get the *CRS Index to Reports and Issues Briefs* which is why we've reproduced it here. In addition to reports, this list includes Issue Briefs, which are summaries of CRS reports. At the end of the chapter you will find two other CRS products, Info Packs and Audio Briefs.

To make sure you understand the way these reports are listed, we have dissected one entry here.

* Polygraph Testing: Employee and Employer Rights: Issue Brief, Gail McCallion IB87126

    Polygraph Testing: Employee and Employer Rights = Title
    Issue Brief = Issue Brief (rather than a full length CRS report)
    Gail McCallion = Congressional Research Service Author
    IB87126 = Report Number

Although these reports are available through your U.S. Representative or Senator, you may be able to contact the author of the report directly at: Congressional Research Service, Library of Congress, Washington, DC 20540, (202)

707-5700. Also, after reading the reports or issue briefs, you may want to follow up and check with the CRS specialist to track down any of his or her articles which have been published in trade publications. Since the Congressional Research Service is only in the habit of responding to requests from Congress, it is especially important to treat CRS experts with respect.

These thousand of so reports are grouped under several hundred subject categories. It may require you're browsing through this chapter to find the category heading of interest. You'll notice that certain categories are cross-referenced, for example, under "Labor--Earnings and Benefits" is "see Labor -- Policies and Legislation; Family leave, see Families." If you are unable to find a particular category or have no luck locating a report on a given subject, ask your Member of Congress to send you the most recent CRS list of reports for that particular issue. Of course, new reports are added to the CRS immense portfolio every day to reflect the developments both at home and abroad.

Current Events and Homework

ABM Treaty
* Arms Control: Issues for Congress, Issue Brief, Stanley R. Sloan IB87002
* The New Interpretation of the ABM Treaty--Salient Issues, Charles R. Cellner, 87-164 S

Abortion
* see Birth Control--Abortion

Acid Rain
* see Air Pollution--Acid Rain Action
* Action and Its Volunteer Programs, Evelyn Howard, etc., 87-716 EPW

Adult Education
* see Occupational Training--Adult and Vocational Education

Aeronautics
* see also Airline Industry, Aviation Safety and Security, Transportation
* Commercial High Speed Aircraft Opportunities and Issues, Richard E. Rowberg, etc., 89-163 SPR
* The National Aero-Space Plan Program: A Brief History, John D. Moteff, 88-146 SPR

Aeronautics--Airline Industry
* Aircraft Manufacturing: Changing Conditions and Federal Policies, John W. Fischer, 86-76 E
* Airline Industry Expense Components: 1978-1987; An Examination and Analysis of Trends, John W. Fisher, etc., 88-502 E
* Airline Mergers and Labor Protective Provisions: Issue Brief, Linda LeGrande, IB87179
* Airlines under Deregulation at Mid-Decade: Trends and Policy Implications, John W. Fischer, 86-67 E
* Airport and Airway Program Reauthorization: Archived Issue Brief, John W. Fischer, IB87051
* The Airport Improvement Program: Selected Economic, and Legislative Issues, J.F. Hornbeck, 88-683 E
* Civilian and Military Pilots: The Labor Market Relationship, John W. Fischer, etc., 86-28 E
* The Demand for General Aviation Aircraft: Background, Analysis and Outlook, John W. Fischer, etc., 85-1108 E
* Employee Participation in National Mediation Board, Determination of Single Carrier Status, Vincent E. Treacy, 88-433 A
* Employee Protection Legislation: A Comparison of H .R. 1101, H.R. 2828, and H.R. 3332, Mark Jickling, 88-426 E
* Labor Problems at Eastern Air Lines: Issue Brief, Linda LeGrande, IB88052
* The Proposed Airline Passenger Protection Act of 1987: Analysis of the Bankruptcy Transportation Plans With Regard to the Taking Issue, Douglas Reid Weimer, 87-984 A

Aeronautics -- Aviation Safety and Security
* Air Traffic Controllers: Labor Relations Since the Demise of PATCO, Gail McCallion, 87-786 E
* Airlines: Safety and Service Issues; Info Pack, IP386A
* Aviation and the 101st Congress: Safety and Policy Issues; Issue Brief, J. Glen Moore, IB89045
* Aviation Safety and the 100th Congress: Bills, Hearings and a Summary of Major Action, J. Glen Moore, 89-18 SPR
* Aviation Safety, Capacity, and Service; Issue Brief, J. Glen Moore, IB87233
* Aviation Safety: Maintaining Safety in a Deregulated Industry Environment, J. Glen Moore, IB87032
* Aviation Safety: Major Congressional Actions; Archived Issue Brief, J. Glen Moore, IB89018
* Aviation Safety: Policy and Oversight, J. Glen Moore, etc., 86-69 SPR
* Aviation Safety: System Fundamentals and Congressional Actions; Issue Brief, J. Glen Moore, IB88008
* Chronology of Hearings on Aviation Safety and Matters of Related Interest in the 99th Congress, J. Glen Moore, 87-49 SPR
* FAA Proposed Rule to Expand the Use of More C Altitude-Reporting Transponders in the United States, J. Glen Moore, 88-302 SPR
* United States Civil Aviation Security, M. Suzanne Cavanagh, 87-931 GOV

AFDC
* see Public Welfare--AFDC

Affirmative Action Programs
* see Equal Employment Opportunity

Afghanistan
* Afghanistan After Five Years: Status of the Conflict, the Afghan Resistance and the U.S. Role, Richard Cronin, 85-20 F
* Afghanistan After the Soviet Withdrawal: Contenders for Power, Richard P. Cronin, 89-146 F
* Afghanistan Peace Talks: An Annotated Chronology and Analysis for the United Nations-Sponsored Negotiations, Richard P. Cronin, 88-149 F
* Afghanistan: Selected References, Sherry B.Shapiro, 88-308 L
* Afghanistan: Status, U.S. Role, and Implications of a Soviet Withdrawal; Archived Issue Brief, Richard P. Cronin, etc., IB88049
* Television Network Evening News Coverage of Afghanistan: A Perspective After Eight Years of War, Denis Steven Rutkus, 88-319 GOV

Africa
* see Economic Conditions, Individual Countries, Foreign Policy and Assistance Programs
* AIDS in Africa: Background/Issues for U.S. Policy, Raymond W. Copson, 87-768 F
* Angola: Conflict Assessment and U.S.Policy Options, Raymond W. Copson, 86-189 F
* Angola: Issues for the United States; Archived Issue Brief, Raymond Copson, etc., IB81063
* Angola/Namibia Negotiations; Issue Brief, Brenda M. Branaman, IB87047
* Angola/Namibia Peace Prospects: Background, Current Problems and Chronology, Raymond W. Copson, 88-559 F
* The Effectiveness of Food Aid: Implications of Changes in Farm, Food, Aid and Trade Legislation; Proceedings of a CRS Workshop Held on April 25, 1988, Charles E Hanrahan, 88-493 ENR
* Food Production and Food Policy in Sub-Saharan Africa: A 20 Country Survey, Charles Hanrahan, etc., 85-150 ENR
* Mozambique: Conflict Assessment/U.S. Policy, Raymond W. Copson, 85-150 ENR
* Namibia Chronology: February 1986 Through April 1987, Raymond W. Copson, etc., 87-353 F
* Namibia: United Nations Negotiations for Independence/U.S. Interests; Archived Issue Brief, Brenda Branaman, IB9073
* North African Petroleum, Joseph Riva 84-216 SPR
* Population Growth and Natural Resource Deterioration in Drought-Stricken Africa, Susan Abbasi, 85-1149 ENR
* South Africa: African National Congress, Brenda Branaman, 86-186 F
* South Africa: Opposition on the Right, Brenda Branaman, 88-628 F
* South Africa: President's Report on Progress Toward Ending Apartheid, Raymond W. Copson, 88-628 F
* South Africa: Recent Developments; Issue Brief, Brenda Branaman, etc., IB85213
* South Africa: The Current Situation; Info Pack, IP340S
* South Africa: The United Democratic Front, Brenda M. Branaman, 86-758 F
* Southern Africa: U.S. Regional Policy at a Crossroads?, Raymond Copson, 85-201 F
* Sudan: U.S. Foreign Assistance Facts: Issue Brief, Ellen Laipson, etc., IB85065
* Tunisia After Bourguiba: Issues for U.S. Policy, Ellen B. Laipson, 88-31 F
* The United States and Southern Africa: A Review of United Nations Resolutions and United States Voting Patterns, 1946-October 1985, Frankie King, 86-21 F
* U.S. Foreign Assistance to the Middle East and North Africa: Fiscal years 1988, 1989, and 1990, Clyde R.Mark, 89-192 F

Africa - Economic Conditions
* African Debt: The Official Donor Response and Potential Alternative Strategies, Alan K. Yu, IB5014

Credit Act of 1987, Jean M. Rawson, 88-210 ENR
* FmHA Losses and the Federal Budget, Ralph Chite, 89-34 ENR
* History and Operation of the Commodity Credit Corporation, Plus a Compilation of Data, Jasper Womach, etc., 86-151 ENR
* Implementation of the Agricultural Credit Act of 1987; Issue Brief, Ralph Chite, etc., IB88089
* Overview of the Number of Farms Going Out of Business, Jean M. Rawson, 88-228 ENR
* A Review of Farmers Home Administration's New Policy for Delinquent Farm Borrowers, Ralph Chite, 88-715 ENR
* Tax Issues Affecting Family Agriculture: Archived Issue Brief, Jack Taylor, etc., IB88054
* Wheat Price Supports: From Country Loan Rate to Class Loan Rate?, Carl Ek, 88-269 ENR

Agriculture and Food

* Agricultural Export Programs: Current Issues, IB89107
* Agricultural Issues in the 101st Congress, IB89030
* Agricultural Trade, IB88011
* Agriculture and the Budget, IB87032
* Agriculture and the Environment, IB89086
* Agriculture, Drought, and the Federal Response, IB89089
* Agriculture in the GATT: After the Midterm Review, IB89027
* Dairy Issues, IB89063
* Farmers Home Administration: Farm Credit Policies and Issues, IB87215
* Food Labeling, IB80055
* Foreign Food Aid: Reauthorization Issues, IB89097
* Implementation of the Agricultural Credit Act of 1987, IB88089
* Soil and Water Conservation Issues in the 101st Congress, IB89080
* Sugar Policy Issues, IB88091

Agriculture -- Foreign Trade

* Agricultural Exports: Does Administration Effort Match Potential? Summary of Hearings Held February 5, 10, 18, 24, March 18, 25, May 19, and 20, 1987, Susan B. Epstein,. etc., 87-794 ENR
* Agricultural Exports: Overview and Selected Data, Donna U. Vogt, 88-403 ENR
* Agricultural Imports: What, from Whom, Why, How Much?, Jasper Womach, 88-361 ENR
* Agricultural Trade: Issue Brief, Donna U. Vogt, IB88011
* Agricultural Trade Legislation in the 100th Congress: A Comparison of Selected Provisions of H.R. 3 and S. 1420, Charles E. Hanrahan, etc., 87-677 ENR
* Agricultural Trade: The United States and Selected, Developed and Developing Countries, Susan B. Epstein, etc., 87-198 ENR
* Agriculture in the GATT:: After the Midterm Review, Issue Brief, Charles E. Hanrahan, IB89027
* Agriculture in the GATT: Toward the Next Round of Multilateral Trade Negotiations, Charles Hanrahan, etc., 86-98 ENR
* Agriculture in the U.S.-Canada Free Trade Agreement, Charles E. Hanrahan, etc., 88-363 ENR
* Cargo Preference and Agriculture: Background and Current Issues, Carl Ek, 87-134 ENR
* The "Citrus-Pasta Dispute" Between the United States and the European Community, Donna U. Vogt, 87-911 ENR
* The Common Agricultural Policy of the European Community and Implications for U.S. Agricultural Trade, Donna U. Vogt, etc., 86-111 ENR
* Cotton Trade: The United States and Foreign Competition, Susan B. Epstein, 87-557 ENR
* The Effectiveness of Food Aid: Implications of Changes in Farm, Food Aid, and Trade Legislation; Proceedings of a CRS Workshop Held on April 25, 1988, Charles E. Hanrahan, 88-493 ENR
* Export of Pesticides, James V. Aidala, 89-73 ENR
* Exports of High-Valued Agricultural Products: Trends and Issues, Susan B. Epstein, etc., 87-636 ENR
* Grain Quality Issues: A Status Report, Carl W. Ek, 88-323 ENR
* Import Restrictions on Meat-History and Current Issues, Jean Rawson, 85-956 ENR
* International Coffee Agreement, Donna Vogt, 84-224 ENR
* Kangaroo Management Controversy, Malcolm M. Simmons, 88-468 ENR
* Latin American Debt and U.S. Agricultural Exports: Assessment of a Proposed Approach, Charles E. Hanrahan, 87-402 ENR
* Proceedings of the CRS Workshop on Canada-U.S. Free-Trade Agreement: How Will It Affect the United States?, Arlene Wilson, 88-356 E
* Proposed European Community Consumption Tax on Vegetable Oils: A Status Report, Donna Vogt, 87-407 ENR
* Restricting Lamb Imports: A Policy Issue, Jasper Womach, 87-642 ENR
* Selected Data on U.S. Agricultural High-Valued Product Exports, Susan B. Epstein, 87-471 ENR
* Soviet Agriculture: U.S.-U.S.S.R Grain Sales and Prospects for Expanded Agricultural Trade; Archived, Issue Brief, John Hardt, IB86019

* Tensions in United States-European Community Agricultural Trade, Donna Vogt, etc., 86-112 ENR
* U.S. Agricultural trade Opportunities with Pacific, Rim Nations, Robert Goldstein, 88-755 ENR
* The U.S.-Canada Pork Dispute, Susan Epstein, 89-311 ENR
* U.S.-European Community Trade Dispute Over Meat Containing Growth Hormones, Donna Vogt, 89-6 ENR
* U.S. Farm Trade: Selected References, 1985-1985, Rebecca Mazur, 87-5 L
* U.S. Japanese Agricultural Trade Relations: Select ed Information, Donna U. Vogt, 88-159 ENR
* Why U.S. Agricultural Exports Have Declines in the, 1980s, Charles Hanrahan, 84-223 ENR
* Will the Export Enhancement Program Survive?, Susan B. Epstein, 89-139 ENR

Agriculture -- Livestock

* Antibiotics: Health Implications of Use in Animal Feed; Archived Issue Brief, Sarah Taylor, IB85076
* Bovine Growth Hormone (Somatotropin) Agricultural and Regularly Issues, Geoffrey S. Becker, etc., 86-1020 ENR
* The Cattle Industry and Federal Programs that Affect It. A Compilation and Analysis, Jack Taylor, etc., 86-160 E
* Federal Grazing Fees on Lands Administered by the Bureau of Land Management and the Forest Service; A History of Legislation and Administrative Policies, Adela Backiel, etc., 85-592 ENR
* Haying and Grazing on Set-Aside Crop Acreage, Carl W. Ek, 89-9 ENR
* Rangeland Condition: Attempts to Chart Its Progress, Bruce Beard, 84-757 ENR

Agriculture -- Policies and Legislation

* After the Drought: The Next Farm Bill; Audio Brief, Jasper Womach, AB50183
* Agricultural Domestic and Trade Policy: Economic Conditions and Legislative Issues, Jasper Womach, etc., 88-277 ENR
* Agricultural Issues in the 101st Congress: Issue Brief, Geoffrey Becker, IB89030
* Agriculture and the Budget: Issue Brief, Geoffrey Becker, IB87032
* Agriculture and the Gramm-Rudman-Hollings Deficit Control Act, Geoffrey Becker, 86-547 ENR
* Agriculture: The 1985 Farm Bill and After; Info Pack, IP295A
* The Cattle Industry and Federal Programs that Affect It: A Compilation and Analysis, Jack Taylor, etc., 86-160 E
* Decoupling Farm Programs, Carl Ek, 88-604 ENR
* Farm Commodity Promotion Programs, Geoffrey S. Becker, 89-313 ENR
* Farm Problems: Agricultural Legislation in the 100th Congress; Archived Issue Brief, Penelope Cate, IB87006
* Farm Support Programs: Their Purpose and Evolution, Geoffrey S. Becker, 88-160 ENR
* The Farmer-Owned Reserve Program, Carl W. Ek, 88-534 ENR
* Federal Farm marketing Programs, Geoffrey Becker, etc., 86-93 ENR
* Federal Poultry Inspection; A Briefing, Geoffrey S. Becker, 87-432 ENR
* Food for Peace, 1954-1986: Major Changes in Legislation, Susan B. Epstein, 87-409 ENR
* Foreign Food Aid Programs: Effectiveness Issues; Archived Issue Brief, Charles E. Hanrahan, IB88057
* Fundamentals of Domestic Farm Programs, Geoffrey S. Becker, 89-151 ENR
* The Heifer Tax: Uniform Capitalization and Farmers, Gregg A. Esenwein, 88-462 E
* Mandatory Programs for Wheat and Feed Grains: A Pr o/Con Discussion, Carl Ek, 85-833 ENR
* Migrant and Seasonal Farmworkers: Characteristics and Related Federal Laws, Sharon House, 83-174 EPW
* New Crops and New Farm Products: A Briefing, Jean M. Rawson, 88-771 ENR
* Organized Farming: Legislative Proposals: Archived Issue Brief, Jeffrey Zinn, IB83186
* The Payment-In-Kind (PIK) Program: Archived Issue Brief, Mark McMinimy, IB83021
* The Payment Limitation: Background and Current Issues, Carl W. Ek, 87-12 ENR
* Rural Policy in an Era of Change and Diversity, Sandra S. Osbourn, 88-482 GOV
* Small Farms--current Issues and Alternative Policies, Jeffrey Zinn, 86-23 ENR
* Sunflowers: Background and Current Issues, Carl W. Ek, 87-898 ENR
* Tax Effects of Title V of the Family Farm Act (H.R . 1425, 100th Congress), Marie B. Morris, 87-582 A
* The Tobacco Price Support Program: Arguments for a nd Against, Jasper Womach, 85-66 ENR
* The Tobacco Price Support Program: Policy issues; Archived

Current Events and Homework

* CFC Phase-Out Bills in the 101st Congress: Comparison of Provisions, David E. Gushee 89-314 ENR
* Clean Air Act Issues: Ozone Nonattainment; Issue Brief, Mira Courpas IB89046
* Greenhouse Effect and Ozone Depletion; Info Pack, , IP405G
* Ozone and Carbon Monoxide Nonattainment: An Analysis of Title I of S. 1894, Mira Courpas 88-316 ENR
* Ozone and Carbon Monoxide Nonattainment: An Analysis of Title I of the Proposed Clean Air Standards Attainment Act David E. Gushee 87-751 S
* Ozone and Carbon Monoxide Nonattainment: Comparison of the Major House and Senate Bills and the EPA Proposed Policy Mira Courpas, etc. 88-141 ENR
* Ozone and Plants: A Status Report, Jeffrey A. Zinn, etc. 87-496 ENR
* Ozone/Carbon Monoxide Nonattainment: Is It What It Seems to Be?, David E. Gushee 88-148 S
* The Stratospheric Ozone Layer: Regulatory Issues; Issue Brief, David Gushee IB89021
* The Unpredictable Atmosphere: Selected References, Karen L. Alderson, etc. 89-43 L

Airline Industry
* see Aeronautics--Airline Industry, ,

Airplane Crashes
* see Aeronautics--Aviation Safety and Security, ,

Airports
* see Aeronautics--Airline Industry, Aeronautics--Aviation Safety and Security,

Alar
* see Pesticides, ,

Alaska National Interest Lands Conservation Act
* see Arctic National Wildlife Refuge

Alcoholism
* see Drug Abuse--Alcoholism

All-Terrain Vehicles
* see Recreation

Alternative Energy Sources
* see Power Resources-Alternative Energy Sources

Alzheimer's Disease
*see Medicine,

American Samoa
* Territorial Political Development: An Analysis of Puerto Rico, Northern Mariana Islands, Guam, Virgi, Island American Samoa and Micronesian Compacts Bette A. Taylor 88-657 GOV

American Telephone and Telegraph Company
* see, Telecommunication-Telephone Industry, ,
* American Telephone and Telegraph Co. Flow-Through of State Gross Receipts Taxes, Angela Gilroy 87-43 E
* The American Telephone and Telegraph Company Divestiture: Background, Provisions, and Restructuring, Angela A. Gilroy 84-58 E
* Telephone Industry Deregulation: Selected References, Robert Howe 88-751 L
* Telephone Industry Issues; Info Pack, , IB2571

Amtrak
* see Transportation--Railroads, ,
* Amtrak: An Overview, Stephen J. Thompson 88-687 E
* AMTRAK and the Future of Intercity Rail Passenger Service: Issue Brief, Stephen J. Thompson IB88041
* Federal Assistance to Amtrak, Lenore Sek 86-77 E

Angola
* Angola: Conflict Assessment and U.S. Policy Options, Raymond W. Copson 86-189 F
* The Angola Food Emergency: Extend of the Problem and Current U.S. Emergency Assistance Policy, Alan K. Yu 89-14 F
* Angola: Issues for the United States; Archived Issue Brief, Raymond W. Copson, etc. IB81063
* Angola/Namibia Negotiations: Issue Brief, Brenda M. Branaman IB89047
* Angola/Namibia Peace Prospects: Background, Current Problems, and Chronology, Raymond W. Copson 88-559 F
* Southern Africa: U.S. Regional Policy at a Crossroads?, Raymond

W. Copson 85-201 F

Animal Rights
* see Agriculture, Research and Development and Wildlife,

Animal Use in Research
* see Research and Development

Anorexia
* see Medicine

Antarctica
* see Polar Regions

Anti-Drug Abuse Act
* Anti-Drug Abuse Act of 1988 (H.R. 5210, 100th Congress): Highlights of Enacted Bill, Harry Hogan, etc. 88-707 GOV
* Drug Control: Highlights of P.L. 99-570, Anti-Drug, Abuse Act of 1986 (Drug-Related Provisions Only), Harry Hogan, etc. 86-968 GOV
* Narcotics Control Assisance for State and Local Governments: The Anti-drug Abuse Act of 1988, Willian Woldman 89-181 GOV
* State and Local Assistance for Narcotics Control:, The Anti-Drug Abuse Act of 1986, William F. Woldman 87-75 GOV

Antisatellite Weapons
* see Weapons Systems--Space Weapons

Antitrust law
* see also Corporations--Mergers, ,
* The American Telephone and Telegraph Company Divestiture: Background, Provisions, and Restructuring, Angela Gilroy 84-58 E
* Commercial Banking Competition and Regulation: Public Policy Considerations, William Jackson 85-104 E
* Corporate Mergers: A Look at the Record, Kevin F. Winch, etc. 87-612 E
* Corporate Mergers and Acquisitions: Selected References, 1986-1989, Robert S. Kirk 89-114 L
* Economic Concentration in the United States, 1975- 1986: A Selected Bibliography, Edward Knight, etc. 86-82 E
* The Impact of U.S. Antitrust Law on Joint Activity, by Corporations: Some Background, Janice E. Rubin 89-291 A
* Insurance Industry Regulation and Supervision: A Reexamination of the McDarran-Ferguson Act of 1945;, Archived Issue Brief David Whiteman IB86149
* Joint Research and Development Ventures; Antitrust, Considerations: Archived Issue Brief, Wendy Schacht IB83178
* Merger Guidelines--A Case Study of the LTV and Republic Steel Corporations, Gwenell L. Bass 84-133 E
* Merger Tactics and Public Policy, Carolyn Brancato 82-13 E
* Mergers and Their Impact on Today's Economy: A Survey, Julius Allen 82-118 E
* New Directions in Antitrust Law? Current Proposals, for Reform, With Emphasis on Proposals Concerning, Mergers and Monetary Damage Awards Janice E. Rubin 86-1014 A
* Resale Price Maintenance: Does It Help or Harm Consumers? Issue Brief, Bruce K. Mulock IB88103
* Resale Price Maintenance: Recent Supreme Court Decisions (Monsanto Corp. v. Spray-Rite Service Corp; Business Electronics Corp v. Sharp Electronics) Janice E. Rubin 88-639 A

Anzus
* Australia, New Zealand, and the Pacific Islands; Issues for U.S. Policy; Issue Brief, Robert G. Sutter IB86158

Apartheid
* see South Africa

Appropriations
* see Public Finance

Aquaculture
* see Fisheries

Aquino, Corazon
* Phillippines under Aquino; Issue Brief, Larry A. Niksch IB86104

Arctic National Wildlife Refuge
* see also Energy
* Applicability of Alaska State Laws to Oil and Gas Development in the Arctic National Wildlife Refuge, Pamela Baldwin 88-420 A
* The Arctic National Wildlife Refuge: Major Oil Development or Wilderness?, Congressional Research Service 88-161 ENR
* The Arctic National Wildlife Refuge: Oil, Gas, and, Wildlife;

Current Events and Homework

Archived Issue Brief, Lynne Corn, etc. IB87026
* Arctic Resources Controversy: A Comparison of H.R . 3601 and S. 2214, Environment and Natural Resources Policy Division 88-380 ENR
* Arctic Resources Controversy: an Overview; Archived Issue Brief, M. Lynne Corn, etc. IB87228
* Arctic Resources Controversy: Issue Brief, M. Lynne Corn, etc. IB89058
* Environmental Effects of Energy Development in the, Arctic national Wildlife Refuge: A Critique of the Final Legislative Environment Impact Statement M. Lynne Corn, etc. 87-490 ENR
* Oil Companies and the Development of the Arctic National Wildlife Refuge, John J. Schanz 88-106 S
* The Outlook for U.S. Energy Supplies and the Arctic National Wildlife Refuge Decision, John J. Schanz 88-73 S

Argentina
* Debt Rescheduling: The Argentine Case, 1982-1988, Glennon J. Harrison 88-505 E

Arias Plan
* Central American Compliance with the August 5, 1987 Peace Agreement as of November 5, 1987, Nina M. Serafino 87-916 F
* Central American Peace Process: Selected References, Robert S. Kirk 88-389 L
* The Central American Peace Prospects: U.S. Interests and Response; Issue Brief, Nina M. Serafino IB87200
* Costa Rica: Country Background Report, Nina M. Serafino 88-577 F

Arms Control
* see Negotiations and Treaties, U.S. Policies, INF,, Nuclear Energy-Nuclear Exports and Non-Proliferation, and National Defense and Security,
* Arms and Arms Control: An Alphabetical Microthesaurus of Terms Selected from the Legislative Indexing Vocabulary Shirley Loo 87-961 L
* Arms Control and Intelligence: Bibliography-in-Brief, 1979-1987, Terri Lehto, etc. 87-499 S
* Arms Control and Strategic Weapons in the 99th Congress, Robert C. Gray 87-892 F
* Arms Control: Issues for Congress; Issue Brief, Stanley R. Sloan IB87002
* ASATs: Antisatellite Weapons Systems; Issue Brief, Marcia Smith IB85176
* China's Nuclear Weapons and Arms Control Policies:, Implications for the United States, Robert G. Sutter 88-374 F
* Defense Spending: An Introduction to Arms Control,, Burden Sharing, and Other Key Questions; Issue Brief Alice C. Maroni IB88043
* The Implications for Strategic Arms Control of Nuclear Armed Sea Launched Cruise Missiles, Alva Bowen, etc. 86-25 F
* NATO Nuclear Modernization and Arms Control: Issue, Brief, Stanley R. Sloan IB89049

Arms Control -- Negotiations and Treaties
* see INF
* Arms Control: Negotiations to Limit Defense and Space Weapons; Issue Brief, Steven Hildreth IB86073
* Arms Control: Negotiations to Reduce Strategic Offensive Nuclear Weapons; Issue Brief, Steven A. Hildreth, etc. IB88088
* Arms Control: Overview of the Geneva Talks; Archived Issued Brief, Steven Hildreth IB85157
* Assessing the INF Treaty, by Foreign Affairs and National Defense Division, 88-211 F
* British and French Strategic Nuclear Force Modernization: Issues for Western Security and Arms Contr ol Charlotte Phillips, etc. 89-140 F
* Chemical Weapons: A Summary of Proliferation and Arms Control Activities Issue Brief, Steven R. Bowman IB89042
* The Conference on Disarmament in Europe (CDE): Archived Issue Brief, Charlotte Preece, etc. IB84060
* Conventional Arms Control in Europe: Prospects for Accord; Issue Brief, Stanley Sloan IB86064
* East-West Conventional Force Reduction Negotiations: Bibliography-in-Brief, 1980-1987, Valentin Leskovsek 87-313 L
* The Effect of a Comprehensive Test Ban on the Strategic Defense Initiative, Cosmo DiMaggio 85-972 SPR
* The Geneva Negotiations on Space and Nuclear Arms: Soviet Positions and Perspectives, Jeanette Voas 86-512 S
* Implications for NATO Strategy of a Zero-Outcome Internmediate-Range Nuclear Missile Accord, Stanley R. Sloan 87-614 F
* Monitoring Nuclear Test Bans, David W. Cheney 86-155 SPR
* The Moscow Summit at First Glance: Audio Brief, Stuart Goldman, etc. AB50168
* The New Interpretation of the ABM Treaty-Salient Issues,

Charles R. Gellner 87-164 S
* Nuclear Arms Control: Disposal of Nuclear Warheads; Issue Brief, Warren H. Donnely IB88024
* Nuclear Arms Control: The Geneva Talks; Info Pack, IP34IN
* The President's Report onSoviet Noncompliance With Arms Control Agreements: A Discussion of the Char ges Jeanette Voas 84-160 F
* The Resumption of U.S.-Soviet Nuclear Arms Control Talks: The Soviet Point of View, Jeanette Voas 85-605 S
* SALT II Treaty: U.S. and Soviet Interim Observance of Its Terms: Archived Issue Brief, Charles Gellner 87-646 S
* Soviet Compliance Behavior: The Record of the SALT I and II Agreements on Offensive Arms, Charles Gellner 86-541 S
* Soviet SALT II Compliance Behaior: The SS-25 and Encryption of Telemetry, Jeanette Voas 86-734 S
* START: A Current Assessment of U.S. and Soviet Positions, Steven A. Hildreth, etc. 88-400 F
* Statements by Mikhail Gorbachev Relating to Arms Control, July 1, 1986-June 30, 1987, Terri Lehto, etc. 87-646 S
* The Strategic Arms Reduction Talks: Questions of Concern to the 101st Congress, Amy F. Woolf 89-330 F
* The Threshold Test Ban and Peaceful Nuclear Explosion Treaties: Background Information and Senate Ra tification Issues Steven A. Hildreth, etc. 87-34 F
* Verificationa nd Compliance: Soviet Compliance With Arms Control Agreements; Issue Brief, Stuart Goldman, etc. 87-316 F

Arms Control -- U.S. Policies
* The Bush Administration's Proposal for ICBM Modernization, SDI, and the B-2 Bomber, Jonathan Medalia 89-281 F
* Nuclear Risk Reduction Centers: Archived Issue Brief, Steven A. Hildreth IB86142
* Statements by President Reagan Relating to Arms Control, April 1, 1986-January 31, 1987, Terri Lehto 87-116 S
* Statements by President REagan Relating to Arms Control, February 1, 1987-May 31, 1987, Terri Lehto 87-525 S
* Statements by President Reagan Relating to Arms Control: February 2, 1985-December 31, 1985, Jeanette Voas 86-549 F
* Statements by President Reagan Relating to Arms Control: January 1, 1986-March 31, 1986, Jeanette Voas 86-663 S
* Statements by President Reagan Relating to Arms Control: June 1, 1987-December 31, 1987, Terri Lehto 88-69 S
* Statements by President Reagan Relating to the INF Treaty, June 1, 1987-December 31, 1987, Terri Lehto 88-60 S

Arms Sales
* see Military Assistance,

Arms Shipments to Iran
* see Iran

Arms Transfers
* see Military Assistance

Arts and Humanities
* Arts and Humanities: FY88-FY89 Funding Issues; Archived Issue Brief, Robert Lyke IB82026
* Federal Aassistance to Libraries: Background Information and Issues Related to Current Programs, Wayne Riddle 87-647 EPW
* Federal Assistance to Libraries: Current Programs and Issues, Wayne Clifton Riddle 89-197 EPW
* Fundraising Techniques for Groups: Bibliography-in-Brief, 1968-1987, Robert S. Kirk 87-380 L
* Resale Royalties for Visual Artists: Background Information and Analysis, Julius W. Allen 88-416 E

Asbestos
* see Air Pollution--Indoor Air Pollution

Asean
* The Association of Southeast Asian Nations (ASEAN): Economic Development Prospects and the Role for the United States Larry Niksch 84-171 F
* Economic Changes in the Asian Pacific Rim: Policy Prospectus., Congressional Research Service 86-923 S

Asia
* see Economic Conditions, Foreign Relations, Foreign Trade, National Defense, Nuclear Energy Politics, and Government,
* Comparison of the Achievement of American Elementary and Secondary Pupils With Those Abroad--The Ex minations Sponsored by the International Assoc Wayne Riddle 86-683 EPW
* The Indian Community in the United States, Margaret Siciliano 84-792 F
* Japanese Science and Technology: Some Recent Efforts to Improe U.S. Monitoring, Nancy R. Miller 86-195 SPR
* Space Activities of the United States, Soviet Union and Other

Launching Countries/organizations; 195 7-1988 Marcia S. Smith 89-183 SPR
* Space Commercialization in China and Japan, Marcia S. Smith 88-519 SPR
* U.S.-Taiwan Economic Relations: Views of Some Members of the Taiwan Economic Elite, Arlene Wilson 89-21 E

Asia -- Economic Conditions
* The Association of Southeast Asian Nations (ASEAN):, Economic Development Prospects and the Role of the United States Larry Niksch 84-171 F
* Economic Changes in the Asian Pacific Rim: Policy Prospectus, Congressional Research Service 86-923 S
* Hong Kong-U.S. Economic Relations: Some Views from Hong Kong's Economic Elite, Kerry Dumbaugh 89-23 F
* Japan's High Prices: Some Causes and Their Relationship toTrade Policy, Dick K. Nanto 88-243 E
* The Petroleum Endowment of the People's Republic of China, Joseph P. Riva, Jr. 86-102 SPR
* Singapore-U.S. Economic Relations: Some Views from Singapore's Economic Elite, Richard P. Cronin 89-49 F
* The Stock Market in Japan: An Overview and Analysis, Arturo Wiener, etc. 89-306 E
* U.S. Banks and the People's Republic of China, Walter W. Eubanks. 84-840 E
* U.S.-South Korean Economic Relations: Views of Some Members of the Korean Economic Elite, William Cooper 88-656 E

Asia -- Foreign Relations
* Afghanistan Peace Talks: An Annotated Chronology and Analysis of the United Station-Sponsored Negotiations Richard P. Cronin 88-149 F
* Cambodia: U.S. Foreign Assistance Facts; Archived Issue Brief, Robert Sutter IB85153
* The Cambodian Crisis: Problems of a Settlement and Policy Dilemmas for the United States; Issue Brie f Robert G. Sutter I89020
* China-India Border Friction: Background Information and Possible Implications, Robert G. Sutter, etc. 87-514 F
* China-U.S Relations: Issues for Congress; Issue Brief, kerry Dumbaugh IB84135
* Chinese Foreign Policy in Asia and the Sino-Soviet Summit: Background, Prospects and Implications fo r U.S. Policy Robert G. Sutter 89-298 F
* Japan-U.S. Relations in the 1990s, Larry Niksch 89-264 F
* Japan-U.S. Relations; Issue Brief, Robert Sutter IB81026
* Korea and congress, 1950-1990, Kerry Dumbaugh 85-171 F
* Korea and Congress, 1950-1990, Kerry Dumbaugh 85-171 F
* The Missing-In-Aaction (MIAs) and Vietnam-U.S. Relations: Issues for the United States, Robert Sutter 87-655 F
* Pakistan After Zia: Implications for Pakistan and U.S. Interests; Archived Issue Brief, Richard Cronin IB88096
* Pakistan's Request for the U.S. AWACS: Archived Issue Brief, Kerry Dumbaugh IB87188
* Philippines: U.S. Foreign Assistance Facts; Issue Brief, Larry Niksch IB85077
* POWS's and MIAs in Indochina and Korea: Satus and Accounting Issues, Robert L. Goldich IB88061
* Prisoner of War/Missing in Action in SE Asia: Info Pack, IP127P
* The Rajiv Gandhi Visit: Issues in U.S.-India Relations, Richard Cronin 85-838 F
* Sino-Soviet Relations: Recent Improvements and Implications for the United states; Issue Brief, Robert Sutter IB86138
* South Asia: Current Developments and Issues for U. S. Policy; Report on a Trip to Pakistan and India April 8-30, 1986 Richard P. Cronin 86-741 F
* South Korea and the United States: The Chaning Relationship, larry Niksch 87-522 F
* Sri Lanka's Gamble for Ethnic Peace; Archived Issue Brief, Stanley J. Heginbothan IB87183
* Taiwan: Recent Developments and Their Implications for the United states; Issue Brief, Robert Sutter IB87092
* The United States, Pakistan and the Soviet Threat to Southern Asia: Options for Congress, richard Cronin 85-152 F
* United States Policy Toward Vietnam: A Summary Review of Its History, Larry Niksch, etc. 85-16 F
* U.S. -Japan Agreement for Nuclea rcooperations: Monitoring Its Implementation; Issue Brief, Warren H. Donnelly IB88095
* Vietnam in Transaition: Implications for U.S. Policy, Robert G. Sutter 89-177 F

Asia -- Foreign Trade
* European Community-Japan Trade Relations: A Europe an Perspective, Dick E. Nanto 86-166 E
* Exchange Rate Management in Taiwan, South Korea and Hong Kong, Arlene Wilson 87-401 E
* Japan Briefing Book., Congressional Research Service 87-323 E

* The Japan Development Bank, Dick Nanto 83-563 E
* Japan: Increasing Investment in the United States, James Jackson 87-747 E
* Japan-South Korea Economic RElations: South Korea' s Approach to the "Japan Problem", Dick M. Nanto 87-953 E
* Japan-United States Economic Relations: Views of Japan's Economic Decisionmakers, Dick Nanto 86-52 E
* Japan-U.S. Economic Relations: Bibliography-in-Brief, 1986-1987, Robert S. Kirk 87-45 L
* Japan-U.S. Trade and Economic Relations; Info Pack, , IP201J
* Japan-U.S. Trade Relations; Archived issue Brief, Raymond J. Ahearn IB81011
* Japan's Automobile Industry and Barriers to Purchases of U.S. Cars, Dick Nanto, etc. 87-793 E
* Japan's Financial Liberalization: Effects on the United states, James K. Jackson 89-102 E
* Japan's Response to the 1988 Omnibus Trade Bill, Dick Nanto 89-133 E
* JETRO: The Japan External Trade Organization, R. Kevin Flaherty 85-1112 E
* Market Access in Japan: The U.S. Experience, Raymond J. Ahearn 85-37 E
* The MOSS Talks: Success or Failure?, Patricia A. Wertman 85-1129 E
* Sino-Japanese Economic Relations in the Post-Mao Decade, Dick N. Nanto, etc. 86-170 E
* South Korea and Taiwan: Expanding Trade Ties With the United States; Issue Brief, William Cooper IB86151
* Steel Imports of Hot Rolled Sheet from Korea in the Absence of Import Restraint: Hypothetical Efects, on West Coast Steel Producers David J. Cantor 88-678 E
* Taiwan-U.S. Free Trade Area: Economic Effects and Related Issues, William Cooper 89-96 E
* U.S. Aricultural trade Opportunities With Pacfic Rim Nations, Robert Goldstein 88-755 ENr
* U.S. Trade Policy Towards Japan: Where Do We Go from Here?, William Cooper 89-307 E
* U.S. Wood Exports to the Pacific Rim, Ross W. Gorte 88-548 ENR

Asia -- National Defense
* Afghanistan After Five years: Status of the Conflict, the Afghan Resistance and the U.S. Role, Richard Cronin 85-20 F
* Afghanistan After the Soviet Withdrawal: Contenders for Power, Richard Cronin 89-146 F
* Afghanistan: Selected References, Sherry B. Shapiro 88-308 L
* Afghanistan: Status, U.S. Role and Implications of a Soviet Withdrawal; Archived Issue Brief, Richard Cronin, etc. IB88049
* Chinese Arms Sales to the Persian Gulf: A Fact Sheet, Robert Sutter 88-286 F
* FSX Fighter Agreement With Japan: Issue Brief, Richard F. Grimmett IB89060
* FSX Technology: Irs Relative Utility to the United States and Japanese Aerospace Industries, John D. Moteff 89-237 SPR
* Insurgency and Counterinsurgency in the Philippines, Larry Niksch 85-1038 F
* Japan's Military Buildup: Goals and Accomplishments, Gary Reynolds 89-68 F
* The NATO Allies, Japan, and the Persian Gulf, Paul Gallis
* Pakistan's Nuclear Programs: U.S. Foreign Policy Considerations; Issue Brief, Richard Cronin IB87227
* Philippine Bases: U.S. Redeployment Options, Alva Bowen 86-44 F
* Television Network Evening News Coverage of Afghanistan: A Perspective After Eight years of War, Denis Steven Rutkus 88-319 GOV
* Thai-U.S. Economic Relations: Some Views of Thailand's Economic Elite, Raymond Ahearn 89-60 F
* U.S.-Soviet Military Balance, Book VI Far East, Middle East Assessments, John Collins, etc. 80-166 S

Asia -- Nuclear Energy
* China's Nuclear Weapons and Arms Control Policies:, Implications for the United States, Robert G. Suter 88-374 F
* Implementation of the U.S.-Chinese Agreement for Nuclear Cooperation: Archived Issue Brief, Warren Donnelly IB86050
* India and Nuclear Weapons: Issue Brief, Warren Donnelly IB86125
* Pakistan and Nuclear Weapons: Issue Brief, Warren Donnelly IB86110
* Plutonium: Department of Energy Approval of Plutonium Shipment from France to Japan: Archived Issue Brief Warren Donnelly IB84116
* Plutonium Economics and Japan's Nuclear Fuel Cycle Policies, Robert Civiak 88-235 SPR
* The U.S.-China Agreement for Nuclear Cooperation: Congressional Review; Archived Issue Brief, Mark Martel, etc. IB85203

Current Events and Homework

Asia -- Politics and Government
* China's Future; Archived Issue Brief, Kerry Dombaugh IB85108
* China's Prospects for Continuing Reform: The 13th Party Congress and After, Kerry Dumbaugh 88-638 F
* Chinese Leadership Changes: Implications for the United States, Charles Steffens 86-131 F
* Chinese Leadership Stability and Policy Reform: A Report on a Visit to China April 1987, Robert G. Sutter 87-361 F
* Crisis in the Indian Punjab: Evolution, Issues, Competing Positions and Prospects, Richard Cronin 84-152 F
* The Gandhi Assassination: Implications for India and U.S. - Indian Relations, Richard Cronin 84-790 F
* India's Punjab Crisis: Issues, Prospects and Implications, Richard Cronin 87-850 F
* India's Sikhs and the Crisis in Punjab State: Summary Brief Points, Richard Cronin 87-509 F
* Korean Political Tensions: Implications for the United States; Issue Brief, Robert Sutter IB86071
* Philippines under Aquino; Issue Brief, Larry Niksch IB86104
* Tibet: Disputed Facts About the Situation in Tibet, Kerry B. Dumbaugh 88-40 F

Aspartame
* see Food

Association of South East Asian Nations
* see Asean

Astronautics
* see Weapons Systems-- Space Weapons
* Astronautics and Space: An Alphabetical Microthesaurus of Terms Selected from the Legislative Indexi ng Vocabulary Shirley Loo 88-397 L
* Civilian Space Policy under the Reagon Administration: Potential Impact of the January 1988 Directiv e Patricia E. Humphlette 88-237 SPR
* Commercial High speed Aircraft Opportunities and Issues and Issues, Richard Rowberg, etc. 89-163 SPR
* Commercial Space Activities in Europe, Patricia E. Humphlette 88-531 SPR
* Commonly Used Acronyms and Program Names in the Space Program, Marcia Smith 87-256 SPR
* The Future of the Land Remote Sensing Satellite System, Karl A. Rohrer, etc. 89-242 SPR
* Legal and Constitutional Issues Involved in Mediasat Acativities, Rita Ann reimer 87-684 A
* Mediasat: The Use of Remote-Sensing Satellites by News Agencies, Patricia E. Humphlett 87-70 SPR
* The National Aero-Space Plane Program: A Brief History, John Moteff 88-146 SPR
* New Soviet Space Launch Vehicles, Marcia Smith 87-462 SPR
* Radioisotope Thermal Geneerators (RTGs) as Spacecraft Power Sources, Marcia S. Smith 88-111 SPR
* Soviet Space Commercialization Activities, Marcia S. Smith 88-473 SPR
* Space Activities of the United States, Soviet Union and Other Launching Countries/Organizations: 195 7-1988 Marcia S. Smith 89-183 SPR
* Space Commercialization in China and Japan, Marcia S. Smith 88-519 SPR
* Space Facilities: The ISF/CDSF Space Station Controversy: Issue Brief, Marcia S. Smith IB88053
* Space Issue: Info Pack, , IP371S
* Space Issues: Selected References, 1986-1988, B.F. Mangan 88-565 L
* Space Launch Options:, Issue Brief, Patricia Humphlette, etc. IB87018
* Space Policy: Issue Brief, Patricia Humphlette, etc. IB87018
* Space Stations:, Issue Brief, Marcia Smith IB85209
* The UFO Enigma, George Havas, etc. 83-205 SPR
* United States Law Applicable in Outer Space, Daniel Hill Zafren 86-881 A
* U.S. Military Satellites and Survivability, Arthur Manfredi 86-581 SPR
* U.S. Space Commercialization Activities, Patricia E. Humphlette 88-518 SPR

Astronomy
* see Astronautics

AT&T Divestiture
* see American Telephone and Telegraph Company

Atomic Energy
* see Nuclear Energy

Atomic Weapons
* see Weapons Systems-- Nuclear Weapons

Australia
* Australia, New Zealand, and the Pacific Islands; Issues for U.S. Policy; Issue Brief, Robert G. Sutter IB86158
* Australia-U.S. Relations:, A Briefing Paper, Robert G. Sutter 87-383 F
* Kangaroo Management Controversy, Malcolm M. Simmons 88-468 ENR

Authorization
* see Public Finance

Automobile Industry
* see Industry-Automobile Industry

Aviation Safety
* see Aeronautics--Aviation Safety and Security

B-1 Bomber
* B-1B Strategic Bomber: Issue Brief, Dagnija Sterste-Perkins IB87157

Baker Plan
* see International Finance-Foreign Loans
* The "Baker Plan": A Remedy for the International Debt Crisis?: Issue Brief, Patricia Wertman IB86106
* The Mexican Debt Accords and Their Financial Implications: An Overview, Patricia A. Wertman 86-179 E

Balanced Budget and Emergency Deficit Control Act
* see Gramm-Rudman-Hollings Act

Balanced Budgets
* see Gramm-Rudman-Hollings Act, Public Finance-Deficits,

Bank Failures
* see Money and Banking-Failures and Deposit Insurance,

Banking
* see Money and Banking

Bankruptcy
* see Credit

Base Rights Countries
* see National Defense-Military Bases

Beach Closings
* see Coastal Areas

Belize
* Belize: Country Background Report, Mark P. Sullivan 88-568 F

Bicentennial of the Congress
* see Congress,

Bicentennial of the Constitution
* see Constitution (U.S.)

Biennial Budgeting
* see Public Finance-Budget Process

Bilingual Education
* see Elementary and Secondary Education--Policies and Legislation,

Biotechnology
* see Genetics, Research and Development, ,

Birth Control
* see Abortion
* Advertising Condoms: Legal and Constitutional Consideration, Rita Ann Reimer 87-325 A
* Family Planning: Title X of the Public Health Service Act: Issue Brief, Edward Kiebe IB88005
* International Population and Family Planning Programs: Issues for Congress; Archived Issue Brief, Vita Bite IV85187
* Legal Analysis of the Department of Health and Human Services' Proposed Regulations to Amend Current, Regulations Governing the Use of Federal Funds Karen J. Lewis 87-840 EPW

* Teenage Sexual Activity and Childbearing: An Analysis of the Relationships of Behavior to Family and, Personal Background Jeanne E. Griffith 87-637 EPW

Birth Control -- Abortion
* Abortion: An Historical Perspective; Selected References, 1973-1988, Charles P. Dove 88-706
* Abortion in World Religions, Charles H. Whittier 88-357 GOV
* Abortion: Info Pack, , IP001A
* Abortion: Judicial and Legislative Control: Archived Issue Brief, Charles Dale, etc. IB74019
* Abortion: Judicial Control: Issue Brief, , IB88006
* Abortion: Legislative Control: Issue Brief, Thomas P. Carr IB 88007
* Fetal Research: A Survey of State Law, Mildred Washington 88-198 A
* Legal Analysis of Constitutional Issues Raised by the So-Called "Kemp-Hatch" Amendment Restricting F ederal Funding of Abortion Counseling and Referral Charles Dale 85-1142 A
* Legal Analysis of H.R. 1729, the "President's Pro-life Bill of 1987",, Charles V.Dale 87-682 A
* The Moral Arguments in the Controversy Over Abortion, With Reference to "Human Life Amendment" Resol utins Charles H. Whittier 86-802 GOV
* Webster v Reproductive Health Services: Another Look at the Abortion Issue, Karen Lewis 89-245 A

Black Lung
* see Worker's Compensation

Blacks
* see Civil Liberties and Rights-Discrimination and Integration, Equal Employment Opportunity,
* Black Members of the United States Congress 1789-1987, Mildred L. Amer 87-253 GOV
* Black Population in the 99th Congress Districts, David Huckabee 85-764 GOV
* Blacks and Tax Reform, 1985-1986; An Aassessment of Possible Impacts on Blacks of Selected Proposals, by the President and Provisions of the Tax Reform William Ellis, etc. 86-117 GOV
* Comparative Quality of Rental Housing Obtained by Whites, Grace Milgram 87-626 E
* Economic Growth and Changing Labor Markets: Those Left Behind; Adult Black Workers: The Progress of Some Linda LeGrande 84-228 E
* Martin Luther King: Selected References, 1978-1989, Jean Bowers 88-769 L
* Speech Material: Martin Luther King's Birthday; Info Pack, IP372M
* The U.S. Black Population, by Census Division, State and Congressional District, Jennifer D. Williams 86-711 GOV
* The Voting Rights Act of 1965 as Amended, Paul Downing 84-203 GOV

Block Grants
* see State and Local Government--Block Grants

Board of Governors of the Federal Reserve System (U.S.)
* see Money and Banking-Monetary Policy,
* Budget Deficits and Monetary Policy, Carol Leisenring 81-128 E
* The Federal Reserve Discount Rate: Its Significance in Monetary Policy, G. Thomas Woodward 87-17 E
* Federal Reserve System; Info Pack, , IP105F
* Membership of the Board of Governors of the Federal Reserve System, December 1913-October 1986, Roger S. White, etc. 86-985 E
* The Targeting of Monetary Policy: Money Supply Growth or Interest Rates?, Gail E. Makinen 86-596 E

Boland Amendment
* see Foreign Relations, Iran-contra Affair
* The Boland Amendments: A Chronology of Congressional Action, Joseph Maheady 87-833 A
* Contra Aid: Analysis of Whether the National Security Counsil and the NSC Staff are an Agency or Ent ity Involved in Intelligence Activities Larry Eig 87-566 A

Bolivia
* Narcotics Control and the Use of U.S. Military Personnel: Operations in Bolivia and Issues for Congr ess Raphael Perl 86-800 F

Bottle Bills
* see Solid Wastes

Bradley Plan

* see International Finance-Foreign Loans

Brazil
* Brazilian Petroleum Status, Joseph P. Riva, Jr. 89-328 SPR
* Natural Resources Conservation and Development in Brazil: An Overview and Related Issues, Russell Hawkins 84-802 ENR

Brunei
* The Association of Southeast Asian Nations (ASEAN) : Economic Development Prospects and the Role of t he United States Larry Niksch 84-171 F

Budget and Government Spending
* see Defense Economics, Economic Policy, Local Finance, Procurement, Public Finance, State and Local Government--Intergovernmental fiscal relations,

Budget Deficits
* see Gramm-Rudman-Hollings Act, Public Finance-Deficits,
* Agriculture and the Budget, , IB87032
* Budget Action for FY 1990 During 1989, , IB89090
* Budget Background for FY 1990, , IB89072
* Congressional Budget Process Reform: 101st Congress, IB89022
* The Debt Limit, , IB87127
* Deficit Reduction: Spending and Revenue Options, , IB89003
* The Federal Budget for Fiscal Year 1989, , IB84233
* The Federal Debt: Who Bears Its Burdens, , IB84233
* Sequestration Actions for FY 90 Under the Gramm-Rudman-Hollings Act, IB89017

Budget Process
* see Public Finance--Budget Process

Burden Sharing (National Defense)
* see Defense Economics

Bush, George
* The Forty-First President: George Bush, Selected References, 1972-1988, George Walser 88-699 L

Business, Industry, and Consumer Affairs
* Automobile Insurance Crisis, , IB89013
* CFTC Reauthorization and the Futures Trading "Sting", IB89051
* Corporate Mergers, , IB87171
* Industrial Innovation: Debate Over Government Policy, IB84004
* Legal Issues of Insider Trading in Securities, , IB87052
* Leveraged Buyouts, , IB89036
* Products Liability: A Legal Overview, , IB77021
* Resale Price Maintenance: Does It Help or Harm Consumers?, IB88103
* U.S. Postal Service, , IB88084
* The U.S. Postal Service: Its Treatment in the Federal Budget, IB88035
* The U.S. Uranium Industry: Changing Prospects and the Federal Role, IB89079

Business and Society
* see Regulation and Deregulation and Corporations, ,
* Cable Television Franchises; Do Franchising Authorities Have Any Recourse If the Franchisee Raises Subscription Rates? Janice E. Rubin 87-448 A
* The Community Reinvestment Act: Its Role in Local Economic Development, J.F. Hornbeck 88-732 E
* Community Reinvestment Act: Legal Analysis, M. Maureen Murphy 89-135 A
* Confidentiality and Secrecy Orders in Civil Cases, Kenneth R. Thomas 89-225 A
* Corporate Governance in America: The Board and Business Leadership; Corporate Boards; Interaction an d Functional Relationship with Consitutuent Groups Kevin Winch 82-197 E
* Financing Business and Economic Development: Three Private-Sector Initiatives J.F. Hornbeck 88-598 A
* Foreign Corrupt Practices Act Amendments of 1988, Michael V. Seitzinger 88-589 A

Business and Society-- Regulation and Deregulation
* see Corporations-Securities Industry, Money and Banking--Law and Regulation,
* Airlines under Deregulation at Mid-Decade: Trends and Policy Implications, John Fischer 86-67 E
* Broadcast Regulation in the 100th Congress: A Legislative Overview, Bernevia M. McCalip 89-88 E
* Changing Regulation of Surface Transportation: Development and Implications of Current Policies, Kenneth R. DeJarnette 86-64 E
* Cost-Benefit Analysis in Federal Regulation: A Review and

Current Events and Homework

Analysis of Developments, 1978-1984, Julius W. Allen 84-74 E
* Costs and Benefits of Federal Regulation: An Overview, Julius
Allen 78-152 E
* Depository Financial Institutions: Alternative Regulatory
Approaches, F. Jean Wells 86-174 E
* Depository Financial Institutions: Regulatory Restructuring,
F. Jean Wells 84-139 E
* Electric Utilities: Deregulation, Diversification, Acid Rain,
Tall Stack Regulation, and Electric De mand Issues, Archived
Issue Brief Donald Dulchinos, etc. IB85134
* Estimating the Costs of Federal Regulation: Review, of Problems
and Accomplishments to Date, Julius Allen 78-205 E
* Federal Regulation-Issues Before the 100th Congress: Archived
Issue Brief, Rogelio Garcia IB86163
* Financial Deregulation: A Status Report, F. Jean Wells 87-800 E
* Financial Deregulation in the United States: An Introduction,
F. Jean Wells 85-41 E
* Financial Deregulation: Relaxing Ceilings on Deposit Interest
Rates, 1978-1980, William Jackson 81-176 E
* Legislative Aapproaches to Risk Decision Making, Claudia
Copeland 87-945 ENR
* Prohibiting Television Advertising of Alcoholic Beverages: A
Constitutional Analysis, Rita Ann Riemer 88-22 A
* The Report of the Vice President's Task Group on Regulation of
Financial Services: A Brief Summary a nd Evaluation F. Jean Wells
85-693 E
* Shippers by Truck and Rail: Deregulation Effects and Prospects,
Kenneth R. DeJarnette 86-66 E
* Surface Transport Carriers: Deregulation Effects and
Prospects, Lenore Sek, etc. 86-65 E
* Telephone Industry Deregulation: Selected References,
1984-1988, Robert Howe 88-751 L
* Telephone Industry Issues: Info Pack, , IP257T
* Wage and Employment Effects of Transport Deregulation: Pending
Policy Issues, Richard S. Belous 86-68 E

Business Cycles
* see Economic Conditions--Business Cycles, ,

Business Electronics Corp. V. Sharp Electronics Co
* Resale Price Maintenance: Recent Supreme Court Decisions
(Monsanto Co v. Spray-Rite Service Co);, Janice E. Rubin 88-639 A

Business Ethics
* see Business and Society, Corporations--Securities Industry,

Business Failures
* see Credit--Bankruptcy, ,

Business, Industry and Consumer Affairs
* see Antitrust Law, Business and Society, Computers, Consumers,
Corporations, Credit, Industrial Technology, Industry,
Insurance, International Corp,,

Buy American Act
* "Buy American" Regulations: Effects on Surface Transportation,
John W. Fischer 86-78 E
* Protectionist Legislation in 1985, Raymond J. Ahearn, etc.
86-632 E

Cable Television
* see Telecommunication-Television, ,

Cambodia
* Cambodia: U.S. Foreign Assistance Facts: Archived Issue Brief,
Robert Sutter IB85153
* The Cambodian Crisis: Problems of a Settlement and Policy
Dilemmas for the United States: Issue Brie f Robert G. Sutter
IB89020

Campaign Financing
* see Politics and Elections--Campaign Funds

Campaign Funds
* see Congress--Apportionment and Elections, Politics and
Elections--Campign Funds,

Canada
* Agriculture in the U.S.-Canada Free Trade Agreement, Charles E.
Hanrahan, etc. 88-363 ENR
* Automotive Products Trade with Canada and the U.S. Canada Free
Trade Area Agreement, Vladimir N. Pregelj 88-122 E
* The Canada-U.S. Free Trade Agreement: A Selected Bibliography,
1985-1988, Felix Chin 88-388 L
* Canada-U.S. Free Trade Agreement: Issue Brief, Arlene Wilson

IB87173
* Canada-U.S. Free Trade Area Agreement: Info Pack, , IP395C
* Canada-U.S. Free Trade Negotiations; Archived issue Brief,
Raymond J. Ahearn IB85215
* Canada's Progress on Acid Rain Control: Shifting Gears or
Stalled in Neutral?, Mira Couras, etc. 88-353 ENR
* Canadian Electricity: The U.S. Market and the Free Trade
Agreement, Amy Abel 88-427 ENR
* The Canadian Free Trade Agreement and the Textile and Apparel
Industries, Edward Rappaport 87-979 E
* Canadian Nuclear-Powered Attack Sumbarine Program: Issues for
Congress: Archived Issue Brief, Ronald O'Rourke IB88083
* Dispute Settlement Provisions in the United States-Canada Free
Trade Agreement, Jeanne Jagelski, etc. 88-603 A
* The Effect of the Canada-U.S. Free Trade Agreement on U. S.
Industries, Economics Division 88-506 E
* Exempting Forest Products Shipments from the Jones Act
Requirements, Ross W. Gorte 87-887 ENR
* Proceedings of the CRS Workshop on Canada-U.S. Free Trade
Agreement: How Will It Affect the United S tates? Arlene Wilson
88-356 E
* Selected Nonferrous Mineral Subsidies and the U.S. -Canada Free
Trade Agreement, Marc Humphries 88-774 ENR
* Steel Imports from Canada and the President's Steel Program:
Archived Issue Brief, David J. Cantor IB87197
* U.S.-Canada Free Trade Agreement: International Implications,
Raymond J. Ahearn, etc. 88-249 F
* U.S.-Canada Free-Trade Agreement: States Affected by Major
Provisions, Leonore Sek 88-347 E
* The U.S.-Canada Pork Dispute, Susan Epstein 89-311 ENR
* U.S.-Canada Trade: An Overview, Leonore Sek 88-331 E
* U.S. Jewelry Manufacturing, International Competitiveness and
H.R. 3, Bernard A. Gelb 87-875 E

Canada-U.S. Free Trade Agreement
* see Canada

Capital Gains Taxation
* see Taxation-Personal Income Tax, ,

Capital Investments
* see Corporations, ,

Capital Punishment
* see Crimes and Offenses, ,

Caribbean Area
* Belize: Country Background Report, Mark P. Sullivan 88-568 F
* Caribbean Apparel Exports: Greater Access to the U.S. Market,
Edward Rappaport 88-128 E
* Caribbean Area: Bibliography-in-Brief, 1980-1988, Robert S.
Kirk 88-152 L
* Caribbean Basin Initiative: Info Pack, , IP190C
* U.S. Bilateral Economic and Military Assistance to latin
American and the Caribbean: Fiscal Years 1 946-1987 K. Larry
Storrs 87-694 F
Carl D. Perkins Vocational Education Act
* see Occupational Training--Adult and Vocational Education,
* Carl D. Perkins Vocational Education Act: Issues for
Reauthorization; Issue Brief, Paul M. Irwin, etc. IB89069
* The Carl D. Perkins Vocational Education Act (P.L., 98-524):
Summary and Compensation With Selected P rovisions of the
Vocational Education Act, of 1963 Paul Irwin 85-697 EPW
* Federal Policy for Vocational Education: Selected References,
Peter Giodano 88-747 L
* Federal Vocational Education Legislation: Recurring Issues
During the last Quarter Century, Richard N. Apling, etc. 88-704
EPW

Catastrophic Health Insurance
* see Health Insurance

Census
* see Population

Census of Population and Housing (1990)
* Adjusting the 1990 Census: Background and a Pro-Con Analysis,
Alexander Lurie 88-305 GOV
* The Census Bureau's Plans for Using Computerized Maps in 1990:
Fact Sheet, Daniel Melnick 87-206 GOV
* Census Questions and OMB's Review of the Census Bureau
Proposal: A Summary and Brief Analysis, Daniel Melnick, etc.
88-42 GOV
* Counting Undocumented Aliens in the Decennial Census, Thomas M.
Durbin 88-438 A

* House Apportionment Following the 1990 Census: Preliminary Projections, David C. Huckabee 88-567 GOV
* Proposed Exclusion of Illegal Aliens from the Population Used to Apportion the House of Representati ves: A Methodological and Policy Analysis Jennifer D. Williams, etc. 88-418 GOV
* Statistical Adjustment of the Decennial Census: A Constitutional Analysis of Statutory Proposals, Thomas Durbin 87-947 A
* Steps in Conducting the 1990 Census, Daniel Melnick 87-205 GOV
* The 1990 Decennial Census and the Counting of Illegal Aliens, Thomas M. Durbin 88-62 A

Central America
* see Latin America, Foreign Policy and Assistance Programs,
* Belize: Country Background Report, Mark P. Sullivan 88-568 F
* Central America and U.S. Foreign Assistance: Issues for Congress; Issue Brief, Jonathan Sanford IB84075
* Central America: U.S. Relations Wtih Costa Rica, Guatemala, and Honduras; Info Pack, IP352C
* Central American Compliance With the August 5, 1987 Peace Agreement as of November 5, 1987, Nina M. Serafino 87-916 F
* Central American Peace process: Selected References, Robert S. Kirk 88-389 L
* The Central American Peace Prospects: U.S. Interests and Response; Issue Brief, Nina M. Serafino IB87200
* Contra Aid, FY82-FY88: Summary and Chronology of Major Congressional Action on Key Legislation Conce rning U.S. Aid to the Anti-Sandinista Guerillas Nina M. Serafino 88-563 F
* Costa Rica: Country Background Report, Nina M. Serafino 88-577 F
* El Salvador: Info Pack, , IP121E
* El Salvador: U.S.Foreign Assistance Facts: Issue Brief, K. Larry Storrs, etc. IB85113
*. Guatemala: Country Background Report, Maureen Taft-Morales 88-586 F
* Guatemala: U.S. Foreign Assistance Facts; Archived Issue Brief, Jonathan Sanford IB85100
* Honduras: U.S. Foreign Assistance Facts: Archived Issue Brief, Robert E. Sanchez IB85080
* Honduras: U.S. Military Activities; Issue Brief, James Wootten IB84134
* International Commission on Central America: Initial Views; Audio Brief, Larry Storrs AB50176
* Kissinger Commission Implmentation: Action by the Congress Through 1986 on the Recommendations of th e National Bipartisan Commission on Central Amer. K. Larry Stors 87-291 F
* Major Trends in U.S. Foreign Assistance to Central America: 1978-1986, Jonathan Sanford 86-88 F
* Nicaragua: Conditions and Issues for U.S. Policy: Issue Brief, Nina Serafino IB82115
* Nicaragua: Info Pack, , IP073N
* A Summary and Analysis of the Report of the National Bipartisan "Kissinger" Commission on Central Am erica, January 1984 Richard Cronin, etc. 84-39 F
* U.S. Assistance to Nicaragua Guerillas: Issues for, the Congress; Archived Issue Brief, Nina Serafino IB84139
* U.S. Foreign Aid to Central America; 1986-1988, Jonathan E. Sanford 87-465 F

Central American Peace Prospects
* see Arias Plan, Central America, ,

Chastain V. Sundquist
* Summary and Analysis of Chastain V. Sundquist, Recent Court of Appeals Decision Concerning Applicati on of the Oficial Immunity Doctrine to Congress Jay R. Shampansky 88-120 A

Chemical Warfare
* see Weapons Systems--Chemical Warfare, ,

Chemicals
* see Solid Wastes, ,
* After Regulation of Industrial Hazardous Waste: What Role for Incineration?, Barbara B. Black, etc. 89-57 S
* CFC Phase-Out Bills in the 101st Congress: Comparison of Provisions, David E. Gushee 89-314 ENR
* Chemicals in the Environment: Audio Brief, James Aidala AB50152
* Chemicals in the Environment: Selected References on Managing Environmental Risks, Rebecca Mazur 87-26 L
* Degradable Plastics; Issue Brief, Martin R. Lee IB88067
* Environmental Impairment Liability Insurance: Overview of Availability Issues, Rawle O. King 89-269 E
* Hazardous Chemical Facilities and Community Right to-Know: Current Issues; Archived Issue Brief, James Aidala IB86069
* Hazardous Materials Transportation: Laws, Regulations, and Policy; Archived Issue Brief, Paul Rothberg IB76026

* Hazardous Waste and the Superfund Program: Info Pack, IP094H
* Hazardous Waste Fact Book, James E. McCarthy, etc. 87-56 ENR
* Hazardous Waste Management: RCRA Oversight in the 100th Congress; Issue Brief, James McCarthy IB87087
* Liability of Superfund "Response Action Contractors" and EPA for Injury from Contractor-Conducted Cl eanups Robert Meltz 89-292 A
* The Superfund Amendments and Reauthorization Act of 1986: Archived Issue Brief, Mark Anthony Reisch IB87080
* The Toxic Substances Control Act: Implementation Issues; Archived Issue Brief, Jim Aidala IB83190
* U.S. Chemicals Manufacturing: Status, Issues, and Prospects, Bernard A. Gelb 88-387 E
* Waste in the Marine Environment: Selected References, Ted Burch 89-263 L

Child Abandonment
* see Families--Domestic Relations, ,

Child Abuse
* see Families--Child Welfare, ,

Child Pornography
* see Civil Liberties and Rights--Pronography and Obscenity,

Child Support
* see Families--Domestic Relations, ,

Child Welfare
* see Families--Child Welfare, ,

Children
* see Families, ,

China
* see Hong Kong, Taiwan, ,
* China-India Border Friction: Background Information and Possible Implications, Robert G. Sutter, etc. 87-514 F
* China-U.S. Relations: Issues for Congress; Issue Brief, Kerry Dumbaugh IB85108
* China's Nuclear Weapons and Arms Control Policies: Implications for the United States, Robert G. Sutter 88-374 F
* China's Prospects for Continuing Reform: The 13th Party Congress and After, Kerry Dumbaugh 88-638 F
* Chinese Arms Sales to the Persian Gulf: A Fact Sheet, Robert Sutter 88-286 F
* Chinese Foreign Policy in Asia and the Sino-Soviet Summit: Background, Prospects and Implications fo r U.S. Policy Robert G. Sutter 89-298 F
* Chinese Leadership Changes: Implications for the United States, Charles F. Steffens 86-131 F
* Chinese Leadership Stability and Policy Reform: A Report on a Visit to China, April 1987, Robert G. Sutter 87-361 F
* Economic Changes in the Asian Pacific Rim: Policy Prospectus., Prepared by Congressional Research Service 86-923 S
* Gorbachev's Reform Strategy: Comparisons With Hungarian and Chinese Experience, Francis T. Miko, etc. 87-813 F
* Implementation of the U.S.-Chinese Agreement for Nuclear Cooperation; Archived Issue Brief, Warren Donnelly IB86050
* The Petroleum Endowment of the People's Republic of China, Joseph P. Riva 86-102 SPR
* Sino-Japanese Economic Relations in the Post-Mao Decade., Dick N. Nanto, etc. 86-170 E
* Sino-Soviet Relations: Recent Improvements and Implications for the United States; Issue Brief, Robert G. Sutter IB86138
* Space Commercialization in China and Japan, Marcia S. Smith 88-519 SPR
* U.S. Agricultural Trade Opportunities With Pacific Rim Nations, Robert M. Goldstein 88-755 ENR
* U.S. Arms Sales to China, Kerry Dumbaugh, etc. 85-138 F
* U.S. Banks and the People's Republic of China, Walter W. Eubanks 84-840 E
* The U.S.-China Agreement for Nuclear Cooperation: Congressional Review; Archived Issue Brief, Mark Martel, etc. IB85203

Chlorofluorocarbons
* see Air Pollution--Ozone, Chemicals, ,

City of Richmond V. J.A. Croson Co.
* Minority Business Set-Asides and the Constitution: A Legal Analysis of the U.S. Supreme Court Rulin g in City of Richmond V. J.A. Croson Co. Charles V. Dale 89-124 A

Civil Defense

Current Events and Homework

* see Disasters, National Defense, ,

Civil Liberties and Rights
* see Discrimination and Integration, Pornography and Obscenity,
* Civil RICO and Protest Activity, Lou Fields 89-320 A
* Constitutional and Statutory Issues Relating to the Use of Behavior Modification on Children in Inst itutions Nancy L. Jones 86-100 A
* The Constitutional Rights of Mental Patients, Charles Dale 85-585 A
* The Constitutionality of Excessive Corporal Punishment in the Public Schools, David M. Ackerman, etc. 88-413 A
* Court Cases Involving governmental Assistance to the Facilities of Sectarian Institutions and the Es tablishment Clause David M. Ackerman 88-372 A
* Emigration and Human Rights in the U.S.S.R.: Is There a New Approach? Archived Issue Brief, John P. Hardt IB88019
* Emigration: Soviet Compliance With the Helsinki Accords; Archived Issue Brief, John Hardt, etc. IB82080
* Employee Access to Personnel Records and Information: Rights under Federal and State Law, Kirk D. Nemer 89-335 A
* Extension of the Civil Rights Commission: Archived Issue Brief, Paul Downing IB87166
* Fair Housing Act Amendments: Archived Issue Brief, Paul Downing IB87116
* Federal Authority to Prohibit Prerecorded Commercial Telephone Calls:, A Constitutional Analysis, Rita Ann Reimer 87-10 A
* Human Rights in U.S. Foreign Relations: Six Key Questions in the Continuing Policy Deate, Vita Bite 81-257 F
* The Interception of Communications: A Legal Overview of Bugs and Taps, Charles Doyle 88-105 A
* The Judicial and Legislative Treatment of Pregnancy: A Review of Developments from Unprotected Statu s to Anti-Discrimination-Equal Treatment Charles Dale, etc. 87-277 A
* Overview of Recent Judicial Decisions on the Constitutional Right of Mental Patients to Refuse Treat ment Nancy Jones 85-548 A
* Polygraph Testing: Employee and Employer Rights; Issue Brief, Gail McCallion IB87126
* Polygraph Testing of Employees in Private Industry, Britt Liddicoat 85-929 A
* "Public Figures" and the Intentional Infliction of Emotional Distress: Hustler Magazine v. Falwell, Rita Ann Reimer 88-177 A
* Selected Federal Victim Compensation Systems, Gloria E. Moreno 88-573 EPW
* Some Constitutional Questions Regarding the Federal Income Tax Laws, Howard Zaritsky, etc. 84-168 A
* States Designating English as the Official State Language, Mark Gurevitz 89-268 A

Civil Liberties and Rights -- Discrimination and Integration
* see Blacks, Equal Employment Opportunity, Minorities, Women--Policies and Legislation,
* Acquired Immune Deficiency Syndrome (AIDS): A Brief Overview of the Major Legal Issues, Nancy Lee Jones 87-236 A
* AIDS and Discrimination: Legal Limits on Insurance Underwriting Practices, Kirk D. Nemer 88-381 A
* AIDS in the Workplace: Employee V. Employer Interest, Gail McCallion 87-510 E
* American Public Opinion on AIDS: A CRS Major Issue Before the 101st Congress, Rosita M. Thomas 89-85 GOV
* Blood Testing for Antibodies to the AIDS Virus: The Leal Issues, Charles Dale, etc. 87-738 A
* Civil Rights Legislation: Response to Grove City College V. Bell: Archived Issue Brief, Bob Lyke IB87123
* Civil Rights Protection in the United States; Brief Summaries of Constitutional Amendments and of Ma jor Laws and Executive Orders Paul M. Downing 88-341 GOV
* Civil Rights Restoration Aact: Bibliography-in-Brief, 1984-1988, Charles Dov 88-332 L
* The Civil Rights Restoration Act of 1987: Legal Analysis of P.L. 100-259, Karen J. Lewis, etc. 88-171 A
* Comparative Quality of Rental Housing Obtained by Whites, Blacks and Hispanics, Grace Milgram 87-626 E
* Federal Policies and Program Relating to Sex Discrimination and Sex Equity in Education, 1963-1985, Bob Lyke, etc. 85-116 EPW
* Homosexual Rights: Legal Analysis of H.R. 709/S 464, the "Civil Rights Amendments Act of 1987", Charles V. Dale 87-593 A
* Legal Implications of the Contagious Disease or Infections Amendment to the Civil Rights Restoration, Act, S. 557 Nancy Lee Jones 88-214 A
* An Overview of Legal Developments in Homosexual Rights, Charles Dale 85-717 A
* The Potential liability of Insurance Companies and Self-Insured Businesses for Unauthorized Disclosu re of Medical Information

Provided in Connection Kirk D. Nemer 88-509 A
* Prohibiting Discrimination on the Basis of Affectional or Sexual Orientation: Arguments for and Agai nst Proposed Legislation Mark A. Eddy 87-825 GOV
* Prohibiting Discrimination on the Basis of Sexual Orientation: Arguments for and Against Proposed Legislation Mark Eddy 89-222 GOV
* School Board of Nassau County V. Arline: A Person With the Contagious Disease of Tuberculosis May be Covered under Section 504 of the Rehabilitation Ac Nancy Lee Jones 87-238 A
* Segregation, and Discrimination in Housing: A Review of Selected Studies and Legislation, Paul M. Downing, etc. 89-317 GOV
* Sex Discrimination and the United States Supreme Court: Developments in the Law, Karen J. Lewis 88-542 A
* Supreme Court Decisions Interpreting Section 504 of the Rehabilitation Act of 1973, Nancy Jones 85-926 A
* The Voting Rights Act of 1965 as Amended, Paul Downing 84-203 GOV

Civil Liberties and Rights -- Pornography and Obscenity Child
*Pornography: Legal Consideration: Archived Issue Brief Rita Reimer IB83148
* FCC Regulation of Indecent Radio and Television Broadcasting, Rita Ann Reimer 88-291 A
* Federal Obscenity and Child Pornography Law, Henry Cohen 89-255 A
* Obscenity: A Legal Primer, Rita Ann Reimer 87-665 A
* Regulating Record Lyrics: A Constitutional Analysis, Rita Reimer 87-632 A
* Regulation of Sexually Explicit Commercial Telephone Conversation ("dial-a-Porn"): Legal and Constitu tional Analysis Rita Ann Reimer 88-10 A

Civil Rights
* see Blacks, Civil Liberties and Rights, Criminal Procedures, Equal Employment Opportunity, Indians, Minorities, Religion, Women,

Civil Rights and Liberties
* Abortion: Judicial Control, , IB88006
* Abortion: Legislative Control, , IB88007
* Equal Rights for Women, , IB83077
* Parental Leave: Legislation in the 101st Congress, , IB86132
* The School Prayer Controversy: Pro-Con Arguments, , IB84081
* Selected Women's Issues in the 101st Congress, , IB89104
* Supreme Court: Church-State Cases, October 1988 Term, IB88105

Civil Rights Restoration Act
* Civil Rights Legislation: Response to Grove City College V.Bell; Archived Issue Brief, Bob Lyke IB87123
* Civil Rights Restoration Act: Bibliography-in-Brief, 1984-1988, Charles Dove 88-332 L
* The Civil Rights Restoration Act of 1987: Legal Analysis of P.L. 100-259, Karen J. Lewis, etc. 88-171 A

Civil Service
* see Government Employees, ,

Civil Service Retirement System
* see Pensions-Civil Service, ,

Classified Information Procedures Act
* Classified Information Procedures Act (CIPA): An Overview, Larry M. Eig 89-172 A

Clayton Act
* see Antitrust Law, ,

Clean Air Act
* Acid Rain Bills in the 100th Congress: Comparison of the Major Provisions of H.R. 1666, H.R. 4331, S . 316, S. 1894, and the Cuomo-Celeste Proposal Larry Parker, etc. 88-490 ENR
* Acid Rain Control and Clean Coal Technology: An Analysis of Title II of S.1894, Larry Parker 88-266 ENR
* Acid Rain in the 100th Congress: Comparison of the Major Provisions of S. 95, S. 300, S. 316, S. 321 , S. 1123, H.R. 1664, and H.R. 1679 Larry B. Parker 87-82 ENR
* Air Quality: Issue Brief, John E. Blodgett IB87124
* Ambient Air Quality Standards: An Analysis of Title IV of S. 1896, John Blodgett 88-271 ENR
* Clean Air Act: An Overview; Archived Issue Brief, Maria Grimes IB86067
* Clean Air Act: Gasoline Vapor Recovery; Archived Issue Brief,

David Gushee IB87029
* The Clean Air Act in the Courts: Significant Cases from 1980 to 1988, Robert Meltz, etc. 88-460 A
* Clean Air Act Issues: Ozone Nonattainment; Issue Brief, Mira Courpas 89064
* Clean Air Act Provisions to Protect National Parklands, Maria Grimes 85-1013 ENR
* The Clean Air Standards Attainment Act: An Analysis of Welfare Benefits from S. 1894, Larry B. Parker 88-298 ENR
* Emission Controls on Motor Vehicles and Fuels: An Analysis of Title II of S. 1894, David Gushee 88-297 S
* Environmental Protection Legislation in the 101st Congress; Issue Brief, Environmental and Natural Resources Section IB89033
* Hazardous Air Pollutants: A Review of the Statutory Requirements and Their Implementation; Archived Issue Brief Maria Grimes IB85185
* Hazardous Air Pollutants: An Analysis of Title V of S. 1894, James McCarthy 88-402 ENR
* Health Benefits of Air Pollution Control: A Discussion, John Blodgett 89-161 ENR
* Municipal Waste Incineration: An Analysis of Section 306 of S. 1894, James E. McCarthy 88-402 ENR
* Ozone and Carbon Monozide Nonattainment: Comparison of the Major House and Senate bills and the EPA Proposed Policy Mira Courpas, etc. 88-141 ENR
* Protecting Visibility under the Clean Air Act, Joan Hartmann, etc. 85-736 ENR
* The Role of Transportation Controls in Urban Air Quality, David E. Gushee, etc. 88-101 S
* Summary Discussion of S. 1894: The Proposed Clean Air Standards Attainment Act, Congressional Research Service 88-378 ENR

Clean Coal Technology Program
* see Fossil Fuels--Coal

Clean Water Act
* Chronology: EPA Regulation of Stormwater Discharge, Claudia Copeland 88-495 ENR
* Clean Water Act Activities: Post-Public Law 100-4, Claudia Copeland 88-768 ENR
* Clean Water: EPA Municipal Construction Grants Program; Archived Issue Brief, Claudia Copeland, IB83013
* Clean Water: Section 404 Dredge and Fill Permit Program; Archived Issue Brief, Charles Copeland, IB83011
* Environmental Protection Legislation in the 101st Congress; Issue Brief, Environmental and Natural Resources Policy Div. IB89033
* Municipal Compliance With the Clean Water Act: Is the Glass Half Full or Half Empty, Charles Copeland, 88-421 ENR
* Nonpoint Source Provisions of the Clean Water Act Amendments of 1987, John Blodgett, 87-154 ENR
* Water Quality: Addressing the Nonpoint Pollution Problem; Archived Mini Brief, Claudia Copeland, MB83030
* Water Quality: Implementing the Clean Water Act: Archived Issue Brief, Claudia Copeland, IB83030
* Water Quality: 1987 Clean Water Act Amendments: Archived Issue Brief, Claudia Copeland, IB87049
* Wetlands Protection: Issues in the 101st Congress:, Issue Brief, Jeffrey A. Zinn, etc., IB89076

Coal
* see Fossil Fuels--Coal

Coal Gasification
* see Fossil Fuels--Coal

Coastal Areas
* see Water Pollution--Oil Spills
* Coastal Resource Issues: Archived Issue Brief, Jeffrey A. Zinn, IB87144
* Comparison of United States and United Kingdom Offshore Oil and Gas Leasing and Development Systems, Malcolm M. Simmons, 86-1011 ENR
* Compliance Provisions for Resource Conservation: A, Status Report, Jeffrey Zinn, 88-662 ENR
* Declining Bonus Values in Outer Continental Shelf Oil and Gas Lease Sales, Malcolm Simmons, 85-871 ENR
* Infectious Waste and Beach Closing, Martin R. Lee, 88-596 ENR
* Legislation Which Protects Offshore and Coastal Environments, Malcolm Simmons, 86-593 ENR
* Managing Coastal Development Through the Coastal Zone Management and Flood Insurance Programs: Experience to Date and the Views from Selected States, Gary Kamimura, etc., 88-354 ENR
* Outer Continental Shelf Leasing and Development: Issue Brief, Malcolm M. Simmons, etc. IB89028
* Preventing Beach Closings: Legislative Options; Issue Brief, Martin R. Lee, IB88102

* Waste in the Marine Environment: Info Pack IP407W
* Waste in the Marine Environment: Selected References, Ted Burch, 89-263 L
* Wetlands Issues: Info Pack IP423W
* Wetlands Protection: Issues in the 101st Congress; Issue Brief, Jeffrey A. Zinn, etc., IB89076

Cobra
* see Public Finance-Budget Programs

Cocaine
* see Drug Abuse

Columbus Day
* Speech Material; Columbus Day; Info Pack IP380C

Commodities
* see Agriculture and Minerals and Materials

Commodity Credit Corporation
* The Farmer-Owned Reserve program, Carl W. Ek, 88-534 ENR
* Fundamentals of Domestic Farm programs, Geoffrey S. Becker, 89-151 ENR
* History and Operation of the Commodity Credit Corporation, Plus a Compilation of Data, Jasper Womach, etc., 86-151 ENR

Common Agricultural Policy
* see European Economic Community
* The Common Agricultural Policy of the European Community and Implications for U.S. Agricultural Trade, Donna U. Vogt, etc., 86-111 ENR
* An Explanation of the European Community's Sugar Regime and Comparison to the U.S. Sugar Program, Jasper Womach, etc. 85-77 ENR
* Proposed European Community Consumption Tax on Vegetable Oils: A Status Report, Donna U. Vogt, 87-407 ENR
* Tensions in United States-European Community Agricultural Trade, Donna U. Vogt, etc., 86-112 ENR

Communications
* see Postal Service, Press, Public Opinion, Telecommunication,

Communist Countries
* see China, Cuba, Eastern Europe, U.S.S.R.
* High Definition Television, IB89088
* Telephone Industry Residential Subscriber Line Charges and the Lifeline Option, IB85152
* U.S. Postal Service, IB88084
* The U.S. Postal Service: Its Treatment in the Federal Budget, IB88035

Community Reinvestment Act
* The Community Reinvestment Act: Its Role in Local Economic Development, J.F. Hornbeck, 88-732 E
* Community Reinvestment Act: Legal Analysis, M. Maureen Murphy, 89-135 A

Comparable Worth (Wages)
* see Equal Employment Opportunity

Competition in Contracting Act
* The Competition in Contracting Act: Its Application to the Department of Defense, Andrew Mayer 85-115 F
* Competition in Federal Public--The New Look: Changes and Implementation; the Competition in Contracting Act Title VII of Public Law 98-369, Robert G. Lauck, 85-82 A

Competitive Equality Banking Act
* The Competitive Equality Banking Act of 1987 (P.L. 100-86); Archived Issue Brief, Walter W. Eubanks, etc., IB87187
* Financial Industry Restructuring: Developments in the 100th Congress; Archived Issue Brief, F. Jean Wells, IB87194

Competitiveness
* see Foreign Trade-Competitiveness

Comprehensive Environmental Response, Compensation and Liability Act
*see Superfund

Computer Security
* see Computers

Current Events and Homework

Computers

* Automation and Computers: An Alphabetical Microthesaurus of Terms Selected from the Legislative Indexing Vocabulary, Shirley Loo, 86-861 L
* Automation and Small Business: Technological Development and the Competitiveness of U.S. Industry, Wendy H. Schacht, etc. 88-300 SPR
* Computer Crimes and Security: Bibliography-in-Brief 1985-1988, Karen Alderson, 88-654 L
* Computer Security Issues: the Computer Security Act of 1987: Archived Issue Brief, Glenn J. McLoughlin, IB87164
* Computer Viruses: Technical Overview and Policy Considerations, Robert Helfant, etc. 88-556 SPR
* Computers in Elementary and Secondary Schools: An Analysis of Recent Congressional Action, James B. Stedman, 88-419 EPW
* Information Policy and Technology Issues: Public Laws of the 95th Through 100th Congresses, Robert Lee Chartrand, 89-185 SPR
* Information Technology for emergency Operations: Audio Brief, AB50117
* Information Technology in Our Time: Selected References, Robert Chartrand, 88-733 SPR
* the Legislator as User of Information Technology, Robert Chartrand, etc. 87-983 S
* Semiconductor Devices: The Changing Competitiveness of U.S. Merchant Producers, 1977-1987, Gary Guenther, 88-191 E
* Semiconductor Manufacturing Technology Proposal: SEMATECH; Issue Brief, Glenn J. McLoughlin, IB87212
* Semiconductors: Issues Confronting the Industry: Bibliography-in-Brief, 1985-1988, Karen Alderson, 88-445 L
* Supercomputers and Artificial Intelligence: Federal Initiatives; Archived Issue Brief, Nancy Miller, IB85105
* Telecommunications and Information-Systems Standardization-Is America Ready?, David Hack 87-458 SPR
* The U.S. Semiconductor Industry and the SEMATECH Proposal, Glenn J. McLoughlin, etc., 87-354 SPR

Conference on Security and Cooperation in Europe

* Conference on Security and Cooperation in Europe (CSCE): The Vienna Meeting; Issue Brief, Francis T. Miko, IB87220
* Emigration: Soviet Compliance With the Helsinki Accords: Archived Issue Brief, John Hardt, etc., IB82080

Congress

* see Apportionment and Elections, Budget Process, Executive Relations, Foreign Relations, Legislative, Procedure and Operations, Members, Military Policies,
* Bicentennial of the Congress; Selected References, 1970-1989, George Walser, 89-90 L
* Bicentennial of the U.S. Congress: Info Pack, IB411C
* Characteristics of Congress: Audio Brief, AB50129
* Congress: A Selected Annotated Bibliography, Mary Cook, etc. 85-49 GOV
* Congress and Congressional Operations: An Alphabetical Microthesaurus of Terms Selected from the Legislative Indexing Vocabulary, Shirley Loo, 88-595 L
* Congress: Info Pack, IP022C
* Congress: Issues for the 101st Congress; Info Pack, Congressional Reference Division, IP410C
* Congressional Gold Medals, Stephen Stathis 84-117 GOV
* The Congressional Scene: Selected Publications Covering the Congress, Pamela M. Dragovich 89-113 C
* Selected Bicentennial Celebrations Commemorating the 100th Anniversaries of the U.S. Constitution an d of the U.S. Congress Roger H. Davidson, etc. 86-171 S
* U.S. Government: Info Pack, , IP162U
* Washington, DC and the U.S. Capitol Building: Info Pack, IP132W

Congress -- Apportionment and Elections

* Apportioning Seats in the House of Representatives : The Method of Equal Proportions, David C. Huckabee, 88-143 GOV
* The Authority of the Senate to Refuse to Seat Certified Members-Elect, Thomas Durbin, 85-609 A
* Black Population in 99th Congress Districts, David Huckabee 85-764 GOV
* Campaign Activities by Congressional Employees, Jack Maskell 82-165 A
* Campaign Activities by Congressional Staff: Audio Brief, AB50118
* Congressional Districts of the 100th Congress: Rankings by 1980 Population, Land Area, and Population Density, David Huckabee, 87-370 GOV
* Counting Undocumented Aliens in the Decennial Census, Thomas Durbin, 88-438 A
* Hispanic Population in 99th Congress Districts, David Huckabee, 85-763 GOV
* House Apportionment Following the 1990 Census: Preliminary

Projections, David Huckabee, 88-567 GOV
* Procedure for House Contested Election Cases, Thomas Durbin, 84-859 A
* Proposed Exclusion of Illegal Aliens from the Population Used to Apportion the House of Representatives: A Methodological and Policy Analysis Jennifer D. Williams, etc. 88-418 GOV
* Reelection Rates of House Incumbents: 1790-1988, David Huckabee 89-173 GOV
* Remedies Available to the House of Representatives After an Investigation of a Contested Election Case, Thomas Durbin, 85-658 A
* Special Elections and Membership Changes in the 100th Congress, Thomas H. Neale, 89-95 GOV
* 99th Congress Districts Classified by the Proportion of Population Over Age 65 (Ranking All District, by Their Total Population Over 65, etc.), David Huckabee 85-910 GOV

Congress -- Budget Process

* see Public Finance--Budget Process
* Biennial Budgeting: Background and Congressional Options, James V. Saturno 89-295 GOV
* Budget Making and the Legislative Process: Audio Brief, Robert Keith, etc. AB50164
* Budget Process; Info Pack IP012B
* Budget Process Legislation Introduced in the Senate During the 100th Congress; Comparison of Selected Measures, Edward Davis, etc., 87-611 GOV
* Budget Process Reform Legislation Introduced in the 101st Congress: Selected Listing, James Saturno, 89-304 GOV
* Changes in the Congressional Budget Process Made by the 1985 Balanced Budget Act (P.L. 99-177), Robert Keith, 86-713 GOV
* Congress and a Balanced Budget Amendment to the U.S. Constitution, James Saturno 89-4 GOV
* Congressional Approaches to Biennial Budgeting, Michael D. Margeson, etc. 87-653 GOV
* Congressional Approaches to Regulating Continuing Resolutions: Measures Introduced in the 100th Congress, James Saturno, 88-359 GOV
* Congressional Budget Process Reform; Archived Issue Brief, Edward Davis IB89022
* Continuing Appropriations for Fiscal Year 1988; Conference Initiatives in P.L. 100-202, James Saturno, 88-263 GOV
* The Effects of a Two-Year Defense Budget Authorization, Alice Maroni, 85-940 F
* The Federal Budget Process: Selected References, Robert Howe 88-436 L
* An Introduction to the Spending and Budget Process in Congress, Stanley Bach 86-20 GOV
* Legal Analysis of Proposal to Repeal Deferral Authority under the Impoundment Control Act, Richard Ehlke 86-1024 A
* Legislation, Appropriations, and Budgets: The Development of Spending Decision-Making in Congress, Allen Schick, 84-106 GOV
* Legislative Branch: Budget Authority, FY 1962-FY 1988, Paul Dwyer, 88-290 GOV
* Manual on the Federal Budget Process, Allen Schick, etc. 87-286 GOV
* Omnibus Budget Reconciliation Act of 1987; A Summary of Congressional Action on P.L. 100-203, James Saturno, 88-296 GOV
* The Power of the Purse in Foreign Policy; Process and Problems in Congressional Funding, Ellen Collier 85-182 F
* Presidential Impoundment Authority After City of New Haven V. United States, Richard Ehlke, etc., 87-173 A
* Proposed and Actual Budget Totals for the Fiscal Years 1980 Through 1988, Philip D. Winters 88-544 E
* Reconciliation for Fiscal year 1987: A Summary of Congressional Action, James Saturno 87-772 GOV
* Regular Appropriations Enacted Separately and in Continuing Appropriations, Fiscal Years 1977-1987, Sandy Streeter 87-826 GOV
* Selected Tables on the Federal Budget Regarding Chronologies of Certain Actions, Aggregate Budget Levels, and Other Information James Saturno, etc. 87-710 GOV
* Senate Consideration of Regular Appropriations Bill Is under Waivers of Section 303(A) of the 1974 Budget Act Robert Keith 89-37 GOV
* Sequestration of Budgetary Resources for Fiscal Year 1986 under the 1985 Balanced Budget Act, Robert Keith 86-872 GOV
* Summary and Analysis of the Ramifications of Bowsher v. Synar, the Gramm-Rudman-Hollings Deficit Reduction Act Case Morton Rosenbert, etc. 86-788 A
* U.S. House of Representatives and Senate: Budget Authority FY 1962-FY 1988, Paul Dwyer 88-260 GOV
* Waivers of the Congressional Budget Act Granted or Rejected in the Senate During 1986, Edward Davis, etc. 87-78 GOV
* Waivers of the 1974 Budget Act Considered in the Senate During the 100th Congress, Robert Keith 89-76 GOV

Congress--Executive Relations
* see Congress--Foreign Relations, Congress--Oversight,
* Cabinet and Other High Level Nominations that Failed to Be Confirmed, 1789-1989, Rogello Garcia, 89-253 GOV
* Congressional Access to Information from the Executive: A Legal Analysis, Richard Ehlke 86-50 A
* Congressional Control of Agency Decision and Decisionmakers: The Unitary Executive Theory and Separation of Powers, Morton Rosenberg, 87-838 A
* Congressional Control of Executive Actions: Alternatives to the Legislative Veto, Frederick Kaiser, 83-227 GOV
* Congressional Liaison Offices of Selected Federal Agencies, Barbara J. Hilson 88-58 C
* Inspectors General: Resources for Oversight: Audio Brief, AB50109
* Intelligence Reform: Recent History and Proposals, Alfred B. Prados, 88-562 F
* Intelligence Reform: Recent History and Proposals, Alfred B. Prados 88-562 F
* Item Veto: Selected Issues; Archived Issue Brief, Gary Galemore IB84055
* The Possible Interaction Between the Impeachment Process and the Double Jeopardy Clause, Elizabeth B. Bazan 89-112 A
* Presidential Vetoes and Ronald Reagan's Use of the Process in the Second Term: Issue Brief, Gary Galemore IB85093
* Resolutions of Inquiry in the House of Representatives: A Brief Description, Richard S. Beth 87-365 GOV

Congress -- Foreign Relations
* see Presidents(U.S.)--Foreign Relations
* Congress and Foreign Policy: Selected References, Sherry B. Shapiro 89-318 L
* Congress and the President in U.S. Foreign Policymaking: A Selected, Annotated Bibliography, Sherry B. Shapiro, 89-318 L
* Examples of Treaties Not Ratified Due to Senate Reservations and/or Amendments, David M. Ackerman, 87-977 A
* Foreign Policy Roles of the President and Congress, Ellen C. Collier, 86-163 F
* The Growing Role of Congress in Soviet Diplomacy and Negotiations, Joseph G. Whelan 88-714 S
* Korea and Congress, 1950-1990, Kery Dumbaugh, 85-171 F
* The Power of the Purse in Foreign Policy: Process and Problems in Congressional Funding, Ellen Collier 85-182 F
* The Role of Congress in Soviet Diplomacy and Negotiations: Audio Brief, Joseph Whelan AB50175
* The Senate's Amended Rule for Considering Treaties, Stanley Bach 87-876 GOV
* The U.N. Congress: Legislation Affecting Participation and Contributions (98th, 99th, and 100th Congresses), Vita Bite, etc., 89-223 F
* U.S. Senate Rejection of Treaties: A Brief Survey of Past Instances, Ellen Collier, 87-305 F
* U.S.-Soviet Relations: Audio Brief, John Hardt, etc. AB50178

Congress -- Legislative Procedure and Operations
* Abolition of the House Internal Security Committee, Paul Rundquist 88-203 GOV
* The Amending Process in the House of Representatives, Stanley Bach, 87-778 GOV
* The Amending Process in the Senate, Stanley Bach 83-230 GOV
* Arranging the Legislative Agenda of the House of Representatives: The Impact of Legislative Rules and Practices, Stanley Bach, 86-110 GOV
* A Brief Overview of Floor Procedure in the House of Representatives, Stanley Bach, 89-59 S
* Caucuses and Legislative Service Organizations of the 101st Congress: An Information Directory, Sula P. Richardson, 89-277 GOV
* Chairmen of House Standing Committes Who Relinquished Original Chairmanship in Order to Chair a Different House Standing Committee, Carol Hardy 88-393 GOV
* Commissions and board to Which House Party Leaders Appoint Representatives, as of March 28, 1988, Carol Hardy, 88-276 GOV
* Commissions and Boards to Which Senate Senate Leaders Appoint Senators, as of September 22, 1988, Carol Hardy 88-698 GOV
* Committee of the Whole: An Introduction, Ilona Nickels 85-943 GOV
* Conducting Committee Hearings: A Guide for Preparation and Procedure, Richard Sachs 82-211 GOV
* Congress' Contempt Power, Jay Shampansky 86-83 A
* Congressional Adjournment Dates, Targeted and Actual: 95th Through 100th Congress, First Session (1977-1987), Ilona B. Nickels 88-92 GOV
* Congressional Committee Staff and Fundings: Archived Issue Brief, Carol Hardy IB82006
* The Congressional Record, Mildred Amer. 86-152 GOV
* Expedited Procedure: A Definition and Brief Discussion, Ilona

Nickels 85-945 GOV
* Guiding a Bill Through the Legislative Process: Considerations for Legislative Staff, Ilona B. Nickels 87-288 GOV
* House and Senate Rules of Procedure: A Brief Comparison, Ilona Nickels 86-822 GOV
* How to Follow Current Federal Legislation and Regulations, Carol D. Davis 89-115 C
* Immunity for Witnesses Testifying Before Congressional Committees, Jay R. Shampansky 86-1026 A
* Indicators of House of Representatives Workload and Activity, Roger H. Davidson, etc. 87-492 S
* Indicators of Senate Activity and Workload, Roger Davidson, etc. 85-133 S
* An Introduction to Conference Committee and Related Procedures, Stanley Bach 84-215 GOV
* An Introduction to the Legislative Process on the House Floor, Stanley Bach 86-96 GOV
* An Introductory Guide to the Congressional Standing Committee System, Judy Schneider, etc., 87-211
* Joint Sessions and Joint Meetings of Congress, April 6, 1789-March 20, 1987, Clay H. Wellborn, 87-244 GOV
* Legislative Procedure: An Introduction; Info Pack, IP247L
* Legislative Vetoes Enacted After Chadha, Louis Fisher, etc. 87-389 GOV
* The Motion to Recommit in the House: The Minority's Motion, Ilona Nickels, 88-581 GOV
* Overview of Senate Action on Presidential Appointments During 100th Congress, Rogelio Garcia, 88-78 GOV
* Parliamentary Reference Sources: An Introductory Guide, Ilona Nickels, 86-175 GOV
* Points of Order and Appeals in the Senate, Stanley Bach, 89-69 S
* Private Bills: Selected Statistics, 1975-1986, With Special Reference to Private Immigration Bills, Richard S. Beth, 87-650 GOV
* Private Immigration Measures in the House of Representatives: Contemporary Procedure and Its Historical Development, Richard S. Beth, 87-408 GOV
* Resolving Legislative Differences in Congress: Conference Committees and Amendments Between the Houses, Stanley Bach, 84-214 GOV
* Senate Floor Managers: Functions and Duties, Richard S. Beth 87-328 GOV
* Senate Legislative Floor Procedures: Audio Brief,, AB50143
* Senate Procedure, Rules, and Organizations: Proposals for Change in the 100th Congress; Archived Issue Brief, Ilona B. Nickels, IB87120
* Senate Procedure, Rules, and Organization: Proposals for Change in the 101st Congress; Issue Brief, Ilona B. Nickels IB89074
* Senate Rules and Practices on Committee, Subcommittee, and Chairmanship Assignment Limitations, as of October 31, 1988, Judy Schneider 88-695 GOV
* Some Devices for Post-Closure Delay in the Senate, Stanley Bach 88-592 GOV
* Sources of Legislative History as Aids to Statutory Construction, George Costello 86-842 A
* Special Rules Proposing to Limit Floor Amendments, 1981, 1987, Stanley Bach 88-307 GOV
* The State of the Senate: Conditions, Proposals, and Prospects for Change, Stanley Bach 88-136 GOV
* Suspension of the Rules in the House of Representatives, Stanley Bach 86-103 GOV
* Voting by Proxy in Congressional Committees, Richard Sachs 83-81 GOV

Congress -- Members
* Black Members of the United States Congress, 1789-1987, Mildred L. Amer 87-253 GOV
* A Brief History of Congressional Action Restricting Members' Outside Earned Income, Mildred Amer 87-416 GOV
* A Brief History of Congressional Pay Legislation, Paul E. Dwyer, etc. 87-685 GOV
* Colleges and Universities Attended by Representatives of the 100th Congress, Mildred Amer 87-348 GOV
* Colleges and Universities Attended by Representatives of the 101st Congress, Mildred Amer 89-149 GOV
* Colleges and Universities Attended by Senators of the 100th Congress, Mildred Amer 87-349 GOV
* Colleges and Universities Attended by Senators of the 101st Congress, Mildred L. Amer 89-121 GOV
* Commission on Executive, Legislative, and Judicial, Salaries: An Historical Overview, Sharon S. Gressle 89-38 GOV
* Comparison of the Civil Service Retirement System for Members of Congress and Executive Branch Employees Carolyn Merck 85-681 EPW
* Congressional Pay, Selected Wages and Pensions, and Social Security: Compared to CPI, 1969-1989, Frederick H. Pauls, etc. 89-63 GOV

Current Events and Homework

* Congressional Votes on Outside Earned Income and Honoraria, 1974-1987, Mildred Amer 87-982 GOV
* The Constitutional Amendment to Regulate Congressional Salary Increases: A Slumbering Proposal's New, Popularity David Huckabee 86-889 GOV
* The Duties of a Member of Congress, Ilona B. Nickels 86-666 GOV
* Educational Degrees Attained by Members of Congress, 94th Through 101st Congresses, Mildred Amer 89-92 GOV
* The Ethics of a Private Law Practice by Members and, Employees of Congress, Jack Maskell 85-663 A
* Federal Employees' Retirement System Handbook for Members of Congress: Benefits under the Federal Employees' Retirement System Educational and Public Welfare Division 87-189 EPW
* Federal Executive, Legislative, and Judicial Compensation: The Situation and Choices for the 101st Congress James P. McGrath 89-70 GOV
* Federal Tax Law Peculiarly Applicable to Members of Congress, Robert B. Burdette 87-482 A
* Freshmen Members of Congress: 88th-100th Congresses (Number and Percentage for House, Senate, and Combined) Mildred L. Amer 88-328 GOV
* History of the Salary of the Clerk of the House of, Representatives: May 1, 1956-January 1, 1988, Paul Dwyer 87-973 GOV
* Honoraria and Outside Earned Income: Summary of Current Restrictions in the Legislative and Executive Branches Jack Maskell 89-29 A
* House Discipline of Members After Conviction But Before Final Appeal, Jack Maskell 88-197 A
* Independent Investigations of Allegations of Wrongdoing by members of Congress, Jack Maskell 88-488 A
* Ineligibility of a Member of Congress for a Civil Office in the Federal Government Which Was Created , or for Which the Salary was Increased Jack Maskell 87-579 A
* Members of Congress Who Have Served in Both the House and the Senate, 1789-1989, Mildred Amer 89-45 GOV
* Members of the U.S. Congress Who Have Served Thirty Years or More, Mildred Amer 87-130 GOV
* Membership of the 101st Congress: A Profile, Mildred Amer 89-168 GOV
* Organizations that Rate Members of Congress on Their Voting Records, Peggy Garvin 89-116 C
* Partisan Divisions in Congress, 1927-1987, Kevin Coleman 87-214 GOV
* Qualifications and Eligibility of Members of Congress, Thomas Durbin 84-188 A
* Retirement for Members of Congress, Carolyn L. Merck 89-110 EPW
* Salaries and Allowances: Congress, Archived Issue Brief, Paul Dwyer IB80206
* Salaries of Members of Congress: Issue Brief, Paul Dwyer IB86017
* Salaries of members of Congress: Congressional Votes, 1967-1989, Paul Dwyer 89-153 GOV
* Security Clearances for members of Congress and the Judiciary, Frederick M. Kaiser 87-704 GOV
* Selected listing of Education-Related memorials to, Former or Current members of Congress, Christine Tebben, etc. 88-626 EPW
* The Senate Chaplaincy, Charles H. Whittier 86-916 GOV
* Some Federal Tax Implications of Replacing the Current Limitation on a Senator's Acceptance of Honoraria With an Outright Prohibition Against Accept Robert B. Burdette 88-599 A
* Speaker of the House (Former); Office Allowances, Staff Assistance, and Franking Privilege, Paul Dwyer 88-304 GOV
* The Speaker of the House: His Powers and Duties, Ilona B. Nickels 87-64 GOV
* Statistical Summary of Congressional Roll Call and, Other Recorded Votes: First Through Ninety-Ninth Congresses (1789-1986) Sula Richardson, etc. 87-126 GOV
* Summary and Analysis of Chastain v. Sundquist, Recent Court of Appeals Decision Concerning Application of the Official Immunity Doctrine to Members of Jay R. Shampansky 88-120 A
* Voting Records of members of Congress: A Constituent's Self-Help Guide to Their Compilation, Rozanne M. Barry, etc. 88-139 C
* Women in the United States Congress, Mildred L. Amer 89-332 GOV

Congress -- Military Policy
* Congress and the Strategic Defense Initiative: A Detailed Overview of legislative Action, 1984-1987, Robert J. Crawford, etc. 87-749 F
* Congressional Procedure for Considering Legislation Opposing Arms Sales, Richard Grimmett 86-63 F
* Military Base Closures: A Side by Side Comparison of Current Legislation, Andrew C. Mayer 88-472 F
* Military Base Closures: Congress and the Executive, Branch, Andrew Mayer 85-212 F
* Military Base Closures: Issue Brief, Andrew Mayer IB89026
* Sectional Analysis of the "War Powers Resolution" (WPR) as It

Would Be Amended by the "War Powers Re solution Amendments of 1988"(S.J. Res. 323, 100th Raymond J. Celada 88-441 A
* U.S. Defense Planning: A Critique, John Collins, etc. 82-167 S
* The War Powers Resolution: Fifteen years of Experience, Ellen C. Collier 88-529 F
* War Powers Resolution: Info Pack, IB131W
* War Powers Resolution: Presidential Compliances: Issue Brief, Ellen Collier IB81050
* War Powers Resolution: The Controversial Act's Search for a Successful Litigation Posture, Raymond J. Celada 88-64 A
* The War Powers Resolution (WPR): Some Implications, of S.J. Res. 323 "War Powers Resolution Amendment s of 1988" Raymond J. Celada 88-464 A
* War Powers: Selected References, Sherry B. Shapiro 89-305 L
* War Powers Resolution: Info Pack, IP131W
* War Powers Resolution: Presidential Compliance: Issue Brief, Ellen Collier IB81050
* War Powers Resolution: The Controversial Act's Search for a Successful Litigation Posture, Raymond J. Celada 88-64 A
* The War Powers Resolution (WPR): Some Implications, of S.J. Res. 323, "War Powers Resolution Amendments of 1988" Raymond J. Celada 88-464 A
* War Powers: Selected References, Sherry B. Shapiro 89-305 L

Congress--Offices
* Campaign Activities by Congressional Employees, Jack Maskell 82-165 A
* Conducting Legislative Research in a Congressional, office, Clay H. Wellborn 89-331 GOV
* Congressional Office Operations: Info Pack, IP151C
* Constitutionality of Franking Statute Upheld by U. S. District Court in Common Cause v. Bolger, Elizabeth Yadlosky 82-155 S
* Grants Work in a Congressional Office, Rhoda Newman 82-22 C
* Internships and Fellowships: Info Pack, IP0631
* Legislative Research: A Guide to Conducting Legislative Research in a Congressional Office; Info Pack, IP321L
* The Legislator as User of Information Technology, Robert Lee Chartrand, etc. 87-983 S
* Pages of the United States Congress, , 84-73 GOV
* Post Employment Restricting on Employees and Members of the House of Representatives, Jack Maskell 87-573 A

Congress--Oversight
* see Congress--Executive Relations,
* Conducting Oversight: Legal, Procedural, and Practical Aspects; Audio Brief, Walter Oleszek AB50156
* Congress and Intelligence Policy: Selected References, Sherry Shapiro 88-36 L
* Effective Oversight: Planning for the Future; Audio Brief, Walter Oleszek AB50155
* Executive Perspectives on Oversight: Audio Brief, AB50116
* Former Members View Oversight: Audio Brief, AB50111
* A Member's Reflections on Oversight: Audio Brief, AB50112
* Outside Perspectives on Oversight: Audio Brief, Walter Oleszek AB50157
* Oversight Authority and Major Procedures: Audio Brief, AB50114
* Oversight in Action: Audio Brief, AB50110
* The Role of the Media in Oversight: Audio Brief, AB50113

Congress and Foreign Policy
* see Congress--Foreign Relations,

Congressional Budget and Impoundment Control Act
* see Congress-Budget Process,
* Changes in the Congressional Budget Process Made by the 1985 Balanced Budget Act (P.L. 99-177), Robert Keith 86-713 GOV
* Legal Analysis of Proposal to Repeal Deferral Authority under, the Impoundment Control Act, Richard Ehlke 86-1024 A
* Manual on the Federal budget Process, Allen Schick, etc. 87-286 GOV
* Rescissions by the President Since 1974: Background and Proposals for Change, Virginia A. McMurty 89-271 GOV
* Waivers of the Congressional Budget Act Granted or, Rejected in the Senate During 1986, Edward Davis, etc. 87-78 GOV

Congressional Budget Process
* see Congress-Budget Process

Congressional Caucuses
* see Congress-Budget Process

Congressional Districts
* see Congress-Apportionment and Elections

Congressional Elections
* see Congress-Apportionment and Elections

Congressional Ethics
* see Political Ethics

Congressional Oversight
* see Congress-Oversight

Congressional Pay
* see Congress--Members

Congressional-Presidential Relations
* see Congress-Executive Relations, Congress-Foreign, Relations, Congress-Military Policy, Presidents(U .S.)-Foreign Relations, War Powers Resolution,

Congressional Research Service
* The Congressional Research Service, Evelyn Howard, etc. 88-246 PGM

Congressional Veto
* see Congress-Executive Relations

Conrail
* see Transportation--Railroads

Constitution (U.S.)
* Civil Rights Legislation: Response to Grove City College v. Bell; Archived Issue Brief, Bob Lyke IB87123
* Congress and a Balanced Budget Amendment to the U. S. Constitution, James Saturno 89-4 GOV
* Congressional Control of Agency Decision and Decisionmakers: The Unitary Executive Theory and Separation of Powers Morton Rosenberg 897-383 A
* Constitution of the United States: Its History, Development and Amending Process; Info Pack, IP339C
* The Constitutional Amendment to Regulate Congressional Salary Increases: A Slumbering Proposal's New, Popularity David C. Huckabee 86-889 GOV
* Constitutional Amendments to Balance the Budget and Limit Federal Spending in the 100th Congress: A Table of Features Thomas J. Nicola 87-445 A
* Constitutional Conventions: Political and Legal Questions: Issue Brief, David Huckabee, etc. IB80062
* The Constitutionality of Excessive Corporal Punishment in the Public Schools, David M. Ackerman, etc. 88-413 A
* Impeachment: An Overview of Constitutional Provisions, Procedure and Practice, Elizabeth B. Bazan 88-637 A
* Ineligibility of a Member of Congress for a Civil Office in the Federal Government Which Was Created , or for Which the Salary Was Increased Jack Maskell 87-579 A
* A Legal Analysis of the Fourteenth Amendment's Equal Protection Clause and the Proposed Equal Rights, Amendment Karen Lewis 85-662 A
* Morrison V. Olson: Constitutionality of the Independent Counsel Law, Jack H. Maskell 88-469 A
* Presidential Signing Statements--Use in Statutory Construction, George A. costello 87-894 A
* Proposed Amendments to the Constitution of the United States of America Introduced in Congress from the 91st Congress, 1st Session, Through the 98th Richard David 85-36 GOV
* Selected Bicentennial Celebration Commemorating the 200th Anniversaries of the U.S. Constitution and, of the U.S. Congress Roger H. Davidson, etc. 86-171 S.
* The Separation of Powers Doctrine: An Overview of Its Rationale and Application, Jay Shampansky, 86-1027 A

Constitutional Conventions
* see Constitution (U.S.)

Consumer Credit
* see Credit

Consumer Price Index
* see Economic Conditions--Inflation

Consumers
* Accepting or Rejecting an Executory Contract Governing Intellectual Property in Bankruptcy: Legal Analysis of H.R. 4657 Robin Jeweler, etc. 88-557 A
* All-Terrain Vehicles: The December 1987 Consent Agreement and Related Developments, Migdon Segal 88-275 SPR
* Cigarettes and Other Tobacco products: Should Congress Ban All Advertising and Promotion? Archived Issue Brief Bruce Mulock

IB86105
* The Cost of Our Food, Geoffrey S. Becker 88-761 ENR
* Digital Audio Recorder Act of 1987--Analysis of H. R. 1384 and S. 506 With Policy Alternatives, David Hack 87-698 SPR
* Fast Food Restaurant Labeling, Donna V. Porter 87-736 SPR
* Income and Expenditures of Selected Consumer Groups, 1973-1985, Marc E. Smyrl 88-318 S
* Oil Overcharge Restitution: Background and Data, Bernard A. Gelb 88-287 E
* Products Liability: A Legal Overview: Issue Brief, Henry Cohen IB77021
* Products Liability Reform: Analysis of H.R. 1115, 100th Congress, as Reported by Subcommittees, Henry Cohen 88-53 A
* Products Liability: Some Legal Issues, Henry Cohen 88-677 A
* The Proposed Airline Passenger Protection Act of 1987: Analysis of the Bankruptcy Transportation Plans With Regard to the Taking Issue Douglas Reid Weimer 87-984 A
* The Tort Reform Debate: Pros, Cons, Federal Proposals, State Statutes, Henry Cohen 86-579 A
* Tort Reform: State Statutory Caps on Damages, Henry Cohen, etc. 87-835 A

Consumption Taxes
* see Taxation--Consumption Taxes

Contadora Group
* see Central America, Latin America

Contested Congressional Elections
* see Politics and Elections-Election law

Continental Shelf
* see Coastal Areas

Contra Aid and the Reagan Doctrine
* see Contras

Contras
* see Foreign Policy and Assistance Programs
* Arms Shipments to Iran: Archived Issue Brief, Richard M. Preece IB87022
* Central American Peace process: Selected References, Robert Kirk 88-389 L
* Chart of Unclassified Legislative Restrictions Regarding Support for Military or Paramilitary Operations in Nicaragua, 1982-1986, Larry Eig, 87-222 A
* Compilation of Selected Laws Relating to the National Security Council Arms, Transfers, Intelligence, Activities, Aid to the Contras and Appropriation American Law Division 86-1028 A
* Contra Aid, FY82-FY88: Summary and Chronology of Major Congressional Action on Key Legislation Concerning U.S. Aid to the Anti-Sandinista Guerrillas Nina M. Serafino 88-563 F
* Iran Arms and Contra Funds: Selected Chronology of Events, 1979-1987, Richard M. Preece, etc. 86-190 F
* Iran Arms Sales and Contra funds: Summaries of Key Legislative Provisions, Clyde R. Mark, etc. 87-13 F
* Kissinger Commission Implementation: Action by the Congress Through 1986 on the Recommendations of the National Bipartisan Commission on Central Ameri K. Larry Storrs]7-291 F
* Nicaragua: Bibliography-in-Brief, 1986-1987, Valentin Leskovsek 87-382 L
* The Nicaraguan Resistance ("Contras"): Background and Major Concerns of Congress, Veronica R. Clifford 87-943 F
* Nicaragua's "Civic" Opposition: Players, Problems and Prospects, Nina Serafino 87-735 F
* U.S. Assistance to Nicaraguan Guerrillas; Issues for the Congress; Archived Issue Brief, Nina Serafino IB84139

Conventional Force Reduction Talks
* see Arms Control--Negotiations and Treaties

Conventional Weapons
* see Weapons Systems--Non-nuclear Weapons, Weapons Systems-Weapons Facts,

Copyright
* see Patents and Inventions

Corporate Takeovers
* see Corporations-Mergers

Corporation for Public Broadcasting
* see Telecommunication

Current Events and Homework

Corporation Taxes
* see Taxation-Corporation Taxes

Corporations
* see Mergers, Securities Industry, International Corporations, Taxation--Corporation Taxes, Business,, Industry, and Consumer Affairs,
* The American Telephone and Telegraph Company Divestiture: Background, Provisions, and Restructuring, Angela A. Gilroy 84-58 E
* Assessing Structural Tax Revision With Macroeconomic Models: The Treasury Tax Proposals and the Allocation of Investment Jane G. Gravelle 85-645 E
* Capital Sources for U.S.Corporations With particular Reference to Public Policy Issues, Julius W. Allen 86-165 E
* The Corporate Bond Rating Process: An Assessment of Its Accuracy and Usefulness, Gary W. Shorter 87-96 E
* Corporate Debt: A Profile of major Indicators, Carolyn Brancato, etc. 86-94 E
* Corporate Debt Financing: An Annotated Bibliography, Kevin F. Winch, etc. 86-656 E
* Corporate Governance in America: The Board and Business leadership; Annotations of Reports in the Series, Kevin F. Winch 83-644 E
* Corporate Governance In America: The Board and Business Leadership: Corporate Boards: Analysis of Characteristics and Trends, Edward Knight 82-198 E
* Corporate Governance in America: The Board and Business Leadership; Corporate Boards: Interaction and Functional Relationship with Constituent Groups, Kevin Winch 82-197 E
* An Economic Analysis of the Effects of the Finance, Committee Staff Proposal to Revise Subchapter C of Internal Revenue Code on Incentives for Corporations, Donald W. Kiefer 85-1016 E
* Insurance for Directors and Officers: The 1987 Market, Sylvia Morrison 87-545 E
* Japanese Management Practices and Their Implications for U.S. Policy, Dick Nanto 82-114 E
* Patterns in the Financing of U.S. Industry: Gross proceeds of New Security Offerings, Kevin F. Winch 88-616 E
* Public Utilities Holding Company Act of 1935: Is This the Time for Reform: Issue Brief, Amy Abel IB89052

Corporations -- Mergers
* Airline Mergers and Labor Protective Provisions: Issue Brief, Linda LeGrande IB87179
* Corporate Mergers: A Look at the Record, Kevin F. Winch, etc. 87-612 E
* Corporate Mergers: A Snapshot View, Kevin F. Winch, etc. 87-612 E
* Corporate Mergers: An Overview of Major Issues, Carolyn Kay Brancato 87-250 E
* Corporate Mergers and Acquisitions: Selected References, 1986-1989, Robert Kirk 89-114 L
* Corporate Mergers: Issue Brief, Gary Shorter IB87171
* Corporate Ownership of Banks and Savings Institutions, and Interstate Banking: Selected Listings, F. Jean Wells 84-105 E
* Corporate Takeovers: A Survey of Recent Developments and Issues, Julius W. Allen 87-726 E
* Corporate Takeovers: Alternatives for Merger Finance, Kevin F. Winch, etc. 87-254 E
* Employee Protection Legislation: A Comparison of H .R. 1101, H.R. 2828 and H.R. 3332, Mark Jickling 88-426 E
* Foreign Mergers and Acquisitions: Non-U.S. Companies Acquiring U.S. Companies, Kevin F. Winch, etc. 87-711 E
* Greenmail and the market for Corporate Control: Impact on Shareholders, Issues of Fairness and Recent Developments Carolyn Brancato 85-181 E
* Greenmail: Corporate Management vs. Corporate Raiders vs. Corporate Shareholders; Archived Issue Brief Kevin Winch IB87064
* Hostile Corporate Takeovers: Investment Adviser Fees, Kevin Winch 87-217 E
* Impact of Mergers and Related Phenomena on Shareholders, Julius W. Allen 84-199 E
* Insider Trading and Greenmail Payments, Michael V. Seitzinger 87-567
* Legal Analysis of Shareholder Voting Rights During, a Corporate Restructuring, Michael V. Seitzinger 89-123 A
* Leveraged Buyouts and the Pot of Gold: Trends, Public Policy, and Case Studies, Carolyn Kay Brancato, etc. 88-156 E
* Leveraged Buyouts; Info Pack, , IP414L
* Leveraged Buyouts: Issue Brief, Gary W. Shorter, etc. IB89036
* Leveraged Buyouts: Recent Trends, Gary Shorter 89-101 E
* Leveraged Buyouts: Selected References, 1987-1989, Robert Howe 89-156 L
* Merger Activity and Leveraged Buyouts: Sound Corporate Restructuring or Wall Street Alchemy?, Carolyn Kay Brancato, etc. 84-643 E

* Merger and Acquisition Activity: The Level of Hostile Mergers, Carolyn Kay Brancato, etc. 87-507 E
* Merger Credit: Should It Be Regulated? A Preliminary Review, Kevin F. Winch 84-69 E
* Merger Guidelines--A Case Study of the LTV and Republic Steel Corporations, Gwenell L. Bass 84-133 E
* Merger Legislation in the 100th Congress, Mark Jickling 88-453 E
* Merger Tactics and Public Policy, Carolyn Brancato 82-13 E
* Mergers and Acquisitions: A Glossary of Terms, Mark Jickling, etc. 89-128 E
* Mergers and Acquisitions: The Impact on labor, Gail McCallion 87-705 E
* Mergers and Their Impact on Today's Economy: A Survey, Julius Allen 82-118 E
* New Directions in Antitrust Law? Current Proposals, for Reform, With Emphasis on Proposals Concerning, Mergers and Monetary Damage Awards Janice E. Rubin 86-1014 A
* The Role of Secured Bank Credit in Corporate Acquisitions, Kevin Winch 81-186 E
* Securities law: Background and Recent Developments, in Tender Offers and in Insider Trading, Michael V. Seitzinger 88-239 A
* Takeover bids and Highly Confident Letters, Carolyn Kay Brancato 87-724 A
* Tax Aspects of leveraged Buyouts, Jane G. Gravelle 89-142 S
* Tender Offer Laws and Regulations, Michael V. Seitzinger 87-15 A
* Tender Offer Reform Legislation: A Comparison of S. 1323 and H.R. 2172, Gary Shorter 87-963 E
* The United States Bankruptcy Code: A Sectional Analysis of Provisions Governing Liquidation and Reorganization Robin Jeweler 89-122 A

Corporations--Securities Industry
* Arbitration under Section 10(B) of the Securities Exchange Act of 1934, Michael V. Seitzinger 87-881 A
* Capital Market Changes in the United Kingdom, Japan, West Germany, and Singapore: A Brief Survey, Julius W. Allen 88-49 E
* CFTC and SEC: A Comparison of Regulatory Authorities, Mark Jickling 89-199 E
* CFTC Reauthorization and the Futures Trading "Sting": Issue Brief, Mark Jickling, etc. IB89051
* Constitutional Considerations Implicated by a Hypothetical Proposal to Tax the Investment Income of a Tax-Exempt Entity Affiliated With a State or Local, Robert B. Burdette 88-551 A
* Discount Brokerage of Securities: A Status Report, Kevin Winch 84-32 E
* The Dow Jones Industrial Average, Gary Shorter 86-775 E
* Federal Home Loan Mortgage Corporation Preferred Stock Ownership: Lift the Restrictions?: Archived Issue Brief, Barbara L. Miles IB88076
* Financial Markets: A New Framework of Issues, Walter W. Eubanks 88-485 E
* The Glass-Steagall Act: Bibliography-in-Brief, 1981-1988, Felix Chin 88-98 L
* Government Securities Market: Disturbances and Regulation, William Jackson 87-165 E
* Growing Internationalization of Stock Markets: Implications for Financial Regulation: Archived Issue, Brief Edward Knight IB88037
* Insider Trading-Carpenter v. United States, Michael V. Seitzinger 87-946 A
* Institutional Investors and Their Role in Equity Financing and Corporate Governance, Julius W. Allen 88-163 E
* The Internationalization of Securities Trading Markets, Julius Allen 86-14 E
* Issues in the Regulation of Futures and Options Trading, Julius Allen 83-108 E
* Junk Bonds: 1988 Status Report, Kevin F. Winch 89-22 E
* Legal Analysis of the Government Securities Act of, 1986 and Its Application to Broker/Dealers Convinced of Insider Trading Violations Michael V. Seitzinger 87-280 A
* Legal Analysis of What Constitutes Reliance under SEC Rule 10B-5, Michael V. Seitzinger 87-279 A
* Legal Analysis of Whether a Corporation Must Disclose in Public Filings With the Securities and Exchange Commission the Facts of Its Being Investigate Michael V. Seitzinger 88-334 A
* Legal Issues of Insider Trading in Securities: Issue Brief, Michael V. Seitzinger IB87052
* Margin Credit for Securities: Some Recent Proposals, Kevin Winch 85-2070 E
* Margin Use in Securities and Futures Markets: A Glossary of Terms, Kevin Winch 88-47 E
* Margin Use in Securities and Futures Market: An Annotated Bibliography, Kevin Winch, etc. 88-50 E
* Merchant Banking: Opportunities or Problems for U. S. Banks?, Walter Eubanks, etc. 87-351 E
* Money Market Mutual Funds, William Jackson 83-232 E

Chronology of press Reports, David P. fite, etc. 89-218 F
* The Defense Procurement Bribery and Fraud Investigation:
Profiles of Persons and Companies, Mentioned In Press Reports
David Fite 88-528 F
* The Defense Procurement Improvement Act of 1985, Andrew Mayer
86-115 F
* Defense Procurement Investigation: Issue Brief, Gary J.
Pagliano IB88081
* Defense Procurement Managers and Weapons Acquisition Reform,
David Lockwood 86-13 F
* Defense Procurement Reform:: Issue Brief, David E. Lockwood
IB89015
* Defense Procurement Reform: 1988 Procurement Reform: 1988
Procurement Reform Provisions Included in Four Major Statutes
Enacted in 1988 Andrew C. Mayer 89-261 F
* Defense Procurement: The Fraud and Bribery Investigation: Info
Pack, IP404D
* LHX and Army Aviation Modernization: Issues for Congress: Issue
Brief, Steven R. Bowman IB88086
* Military Alcoholic Beverage Procurement: Issues and
Legislation, David F. Burreli 88-411 F
* Military Procurement Procedures of Foreign Governments:
Centralization of the Procurement Function, Andrew Mayer 84-229 F
* The Packard Commission Report and Defense Acquisition
Organization, David Lockwood 86-717 F
* Post Employment "Revolving Door" Restrictions on Department of
Defense Personnel, Jack Maskell 88-478 A
* Selected Defense Procurement Acquisition Profiles: A Data Base,
Alice C. Maroni, etc. 88-234 F
* Statutes and Regulations of Potential Relevance to Allegations
of Defense Procurement Fraud, Jack H. Maskell, etc. 88-457 A
* Under Secretary of Defense for Acquisition: Role and
Responsibilities; Archived Issue Brief, David E. Lockwood
IB88016
* U.S. Defense Acquisition Reform: Major Congressional
Initiatives; Archived Issue Brief, David Lockwood IB85103
* U.S. Weapons Procurement: Should a Civilian Agency Be in
Charge?, David Lockwood 84-61 F

Defense Policy
* see National Defense

Defense Procurement
* see Defense Economics--Procurement

Defense Spending
* see Defense Economics

Deficit Reduction
* see Public Finance--Deficits

Deflation
* see Economic Conditions--Business Cycles, Economic,
Conditions--Inflation,

Deforestation
* see Forests and Forestry

Democratic National Convention (1988:Atlanta, GA.)
* A Summary of National and State Party Laws Concerning the
Election of Delegates to the 1988 Democratic and Republican
National Conventions Kevin Coleman 88-102 GOV

Deposit Insurance
* see Money and Banking--Failures and Deposit Insurance,

Depression (Business Cycles)
* see Economic Conditions--Business Cycles

Deregulation
* see Business and Society--Regulation and Deregulation, Money
and Banking--Law and Regulation,

Desegregation in Education
* see Elementary and Secondary, Education--Policies and
Legislation, Higher Education--Integration,

Decertification
* see International Environmental Affairs

Developing Countries
* see Economic Conditions
* Child Health in the Third World: U.S. and International
Initiatives: Archived issue Brief, Lois McHugh IB85189
* Environmental Protection in Developing Countries: Selected

References, 1983-1987, Rebbecca Mazur 87-488 L
* International Environment: Overview of Major Issues: Issue
Brief, Mary Tiemann, etc. IB89-57
* Missile Proliferation: Survey of Emerging Missile Forces,
Foreign Affairs and National Defense Division 88-642 F
* Tropical Deforestation: International Implications: Issue
Brief, Susan Fletcher IB89010
* Tropical Forests: Bibliography-in-Brief, 1985-1988, Adrienne
C. Boniface 88-274 L

Developing Countries-- Economic Conditions
* The "Banker Plan": A Remedy for the International Debt Crisis?:
Issue Brief, Patricia Wertman IB86106
* The Citicorp Initiative: A Brave New World for the Third World
Debt Problem, Patricia Wertman 87-750 E
* Debt-for-Nature Swaps in Developing Countries: An Overview of
Recent Conservation Efforts, Betsy Cody 88-647 ENR
* Debt Service Indicators of the Seventeen Most Highly Indebted
Developing Countries, 1978-1986, Patricia Wertman, etc. 88-452 E
* The Effectiveness of Food Aid: Implications of Changes in Farm,
Food Aid, and Trade Legislation: Proceedings of a CRS Workshop
Held on April 25, 1988 Charles E. Hanrahan 88-493 ENR
* Environment and International Economic Development : The Role
of Cost-Benefit Analysis, John L. Moore, etc. 87-774 ENR
* Finance and Adjustment: The international Debt Crisis,
1982-1984, Patricia Wertman 84-162 E
* Foreign Food Aid Programs: Effectiveness Issues; Archived Issue
Brief, Charles Hanrahan IB88057
* An International Debt Management Authority: A Brief Overview,
Patricia Wertman 89-208 E
* An International Debt Management Authority: Could It Spell
R-E-L-I-E-F?, Economics Division 88-607 E
* The International Debt Problem: Congressional Proposals:
Archived issue Brief, Patricia Wertman IB86124
* International Fund for Agricultural Development, Susan Epstein
87-4 ENR
* International Monetary Fund: Bibliography-in-Brief,
1983-1987, Robert S. Kirk 87-47L
* Latin American Debt and U.S. Agricultural Exports: Assessment
of a Proposed Approach, Charles E. Hanrahan 87-402 ENR
* A Survey of U.S. International Economic Policy and Problems,
Alfred Reifman 88-666 S
* Trade of the Seventeen Highly Indebted Countries: A Brief
Overview, Patricia Wertman, etc. 88-521 E
* U.S. Agricultural Trade Opportunities With Pacific Rim Nations,
Robert M. Goldstein 88-755 ENR
* U.S. Bank Exposure in the Seventeen Highly Indebted Countries:
1982-1987, Patricia Wertman, etc. 88-522 E
* Developing Countries' Debts see International Finance --
Foreign Loans,

Developmental Disabilities
* see Handicapped

Digital Audio Recorder Act
* Digital Audio Recorder Act of 1987-- Analysis of H.R. 184 and S.
506 With Policy Alternatives, David Hack 87-698 SPR

Disability Insurance
* see Social Security

Disarmament
* see Arms Control--Negotiations and Treaties

Disasters
* see Agriculture, Earth Sciences, Food Relief, National Defense,
Nuclear Energy, Water Resources, Weapons Systems,
* The Chernobyl Accident: Implications for DOE's Production
Reactors: Archived issue Brief, Robert L. Civiak IB86092
* Civil Defense and the Effects of Nuclear War: Info Pack, IP174C
* Civil Defense: Archived issue Brief, Gary Reynolds, etc.
IB8428
* Civil Liability for Transboundary Damage from a Nuclear,
Accident: The Joint International Protocol, Barbara B. Black,
etc. IB89023
* Ethiopia: U.S. Foreign Assistance Facts: Archived Issue Brief,
Raymond Copson, etc. IB85014
* The Evolving National Flood Insurance program, Malcolm M.
Simmons 88-641 ENR
* Federal Disaster Relief Legislation and Administration: A
Summary, Clark F. Norton 88-386 GOV
* International Notification and Assistance for Nuclear
Accidents: Congressional Action on Two Conventions; Archived
Issue Brief Warren H. Donnelly IB87082
* Managing Coastal Development Through the Coastal Zone
Management and Flood Insurance Programs: Experience to Date and

the Views from Selected States Gary Kamimura, etc. 88-354 ENR
* Monitoring and Forecasting Drought and Famine, Charles Hanrahan, etc. 85-1059 ENR
* Nuclear Winter: Bibliography-in-brief, B.F. Mangan 88-325 L
* Population Growth and Natural Resource Deterioration in Drought-Stricken Africa, Susan Abbasi 85-1149 ENR

Discount Brokers
* see Corporation-Securities Industry

Discrimination
* see Blacks, Civil Liberties and Rights-- Discrimination and Integration, Equal Employment Opportunity, Minorities, Women--Policies and Legislation,

Discrimination in Employment
* see Equal Employment Opportunity

District of Columbia
* D.C. Statehood: A Brief Background Report, Bette A. Taylor 87-609 GOV
* Washington, D.C. and the U.S. Capitol Building: Info Pack, IB132W

Dollar Value
* see International Finance--Foreign Exchange Rates

Draft
* see Military Personnel

Dropouts
* see Elementary and Secondary Education

Drought
* see Agriculture--Drought

Drug Abuse
* see Alcoholism, Drug Testing, Policies and Legislation, and Crime and Justice,
* Confronting Students Concerning Suspected Drug Use : Potential Liability of Educators, M. Maureen Murphy 86-952 A
* Drug Abuse in America: Info Pack, IB039D
* Drug Abuse: Selected References, 1986-1988, Elizabeth S. Lane 88-625 L

Drug Abuse -- Alcoholism
* Advertising of Alcoholic Beverages in the Broadcast Media: Archived issue Brief, Bruce K. Mulock IB85097
* Drug and Alcohol Abuse: Prevention, Treatment, and Education, Edward Klebe 86-1052 EPW
* Drunk Driving and Raising the Drinking Age: Info Pack, IP186D
* Drunk Driving: Bibliography-in-Brief, 1983-1988, Edith Suterlin 88-655 L
* Drunk Driving; Issue Brief, Migdon Segal IB83157
* Legal Analysis of Questions Regarding the national, Minimum Drinking Age, Douglas Weimer 85-772 A
* Prohibiting Television Advertising of Alcoholic Beverages: A Constitutional Analysis, Rita Ann Reimer 88-22 A
* Traynor v. Turnage: The Exclusion of Alcoholics from Certain Veterans' Educational Benefits Does no t Violate Section 504 of the Rehabilitation Act of Nancy Lee Jones 88-358 A

Drug Abuse-- Drug Testing
* Constitutional Analysis of Proposals to Establish a Mandatory Public Employee Drug Testing Program, Charles V. Dale 88-293 A
* Drug Free Workplace Initiatives: Federal Legislation Affecting the Private Sector, Gail McCallion 88-508 E
* Drug Testing and Urinalysis in the Workplace: Legal Aspects, M. Maureen Murphy, etc. 86-996 A
* Drug Testing for Illegal Substances, Blanchard Randall IV 87-36 SPR
* Drug Testing in the Workplace: An Overview of Employee and Employer Interests: Issue Brief, Gail McCallion IB87139
* Drug Testing in the Workplace: Federal programs; Issue Brief, Sharon S. Gressle IB87174
* Drug Testing: Selected References, 1986-1987, Rebecca Mazur 88-33 L
* Drug Testing: The Experience of the Transportation Industry, Gail McCallion 89-26 E
* Drug Testing: The Response to Drugs in the Workplace; Info Pack, IB350D
* Legal Analysis of Recent Appropriation Riders to Insure a "Drug-Free Workplace", Charles V. Dale 88-450 A

Drug Abuse-- Policies and Legislation

* Alcohol, Drug Abuse, and Mental Health Block Grant, and Related Programs: Issue Brief, Edward Klebe IB88009
* Anti-Drug Abuse Act of 1988 (H.R. 5210, 100th Congress): Highlights of Enacted Bill, Harry Hogan, etc. 88-707 GOV
* Anti-Drug Abuse Act of 1988 (P.L. 100-690): Summary of Major Provisions, Harry Hogan, etc. 89-288 GOV
* The Defense Department's Drug Law Enforcement and Narcotics Interdiction Responsibilities: A Comparison of House and Senate Amendments in the Defense Roy Surrett 88-406 F
* Drug Abuse: Treatment, Prevention and Education; Info Pack, IP400D
* Drug and Alcohol Abuse: Prevention and Treatment: Selected References, 1985-1988, Edith Sutterlin 88-622 L
* Drug and Alcohol Abuse: Prevention, Treatment, an d Education, Edward Klebe 86-1052 EPW
* Drug Control at the Federal Level: Coordination an d Direction, Harry Hogan 87-780 GOV
* Drug Control: Federal Efforts to Reduce the Supply ; Info Pack, IP334 D
* Drug Control: Highlights of P.L. 99-570, Anti Drug, Abuse Act of 1986 (Drug Related provisions Only), Harry Hogan, etc. 86-968 GOV
* Drug Control: International Policy and Options: Is sue Brief, Raphel F. Perl IB88093
* Drug Control: Issue Brief, Harry Hogan IB87013
* Drug Legalization: Bibliography-in-Brief, Elizabeth S. Lane 88-432 L
* Drug Legalization: pro and Con, Harry Hogan 88-500 GOV
* Drugs of Abuse: The Legalization Debate; Info Pack, , IP401D
* Federal Laws Relating to the Control of Narcotics and Other Dangerous Drugs, Enacted 1961-1985: Brie f Summaries Harry Hogan 86-12 GOV
* Heroin: legalization for Medical use, Blanchard Randall 88-86 SPR
* International Narcotics Control and Foreign Assistance Certification: Requirements, Procedures, Timetables and Guidelines Raphael F. Perl 88-175 F
* International Narcotics Control: The President's March 1, 1988 Certification for Foreign Assistance Eligibility and Options for Congressional Action; Raphael F. Perl 88-175 F
* The International narcotics Trade: An Overview of Its Dimensions, Production, sources, and Organizations William Roy Surrett 88-643 F
* Narcotic and Illicit Drug Trafficking: Selected References, 1986-1988, Edith Sutterlin 88-579
* Narcotics Control and the Use of U.S. Military Personnel: Operations in Bolivia and Issues for Congress Raphael Perl 86-800 F
* Narcotics Control Assistance for State and Local Governments: The Anti-Drug Abuse Act of 1988, William Woldman 89-181 GOV
* Narcotics Interdiction and the Use of the Military : Bibliography-in-Brief, 1982, 1988, Sherry B. Shapiro 88-408 L
* Omnibus Drug Initiative Act of 1988: Summary of Major Provisions (H.R. 5210, 100th Congress, as Pass d by the House) Harry Hogan 88-640 GOV
* The Role of the U.S. Military in Narcotics Interdiction: Audio Brief, Raphael Perl AB50171
* State and Local Assistance for Narcotics Control: The Anti-Drug Abuse Act of 1986, William Woldman 87-75 GOV
* U.S. Sanctions and the State of the Panamanian Economy, Mark P. Sullivan 88-578 F

Drug Abuse Control
* see Drug Abuse--Policies and Legislation

Drug Abuser Rehabilitation
* see Drub Abuse--Policies and Legislation

Drug Legalization
* see Drug Abuse--Policies and Legislation

Drug Testing
* see Drug Abuse--Drug Testing

Drugs
* see Genetics
* Biotechnology: Bibliography-in-brief, 1985-1988, B.F. Mangan 88-566 L
* Drug Approval: Access to Experimental Drugs for Severely Ill Patients; Issue Brief, Blanchard Randall, etc. IB89016
* "The Applicability of the Export Proviso of the Federal Food, Drug and Cosmetic Act to "New Drugs", Cathy Gilmore 85-848 A

Drunk Driving
* see Drug Abuse--Alcoholism

Dumping (Foreign Trade)
* see Foreign Trade--Trade Policy

Earth Sciences
* see Disasters
* Agriculture and the Environment: Issue Brief, Geoffrey Becker, etc. IB89086
* Carbon Dioxide, the Greenhouse Effect, and Climate; A Primer, John Justus 84-594 SPR
* CFC Phase-Out Bills in the 101st Congress; Comparison of Provisions, David E. Gushee 89-314 ENR
* The Drought of 1988: Bibliography-in-Brief, Ted L. Burch 88-553 L
* Ethanol Fuel and Global Warming, Migdon Segal 89-164 SPR
* The Federal Cave Resources Protection Act: A Review of a Proposed Bill, George Siehl 85-875 ENR
* The Future of the Land Remote Sensing Satellite System, Karl A. Rohrer, etc. 89-242 SPR
* Global Climate Change: Audio Brief, David Gushee, etc. AB50189
* Global Climate change: Issue Brief, Robert E. Morrison IB89005
* Global Climate Changes and the Green House Effect: Congressional Activity and Options; Archived Issue, Brief David E. Gushee IB88077
* The Global Environment: Audio Brief, AB50063
* Greenhouse Effect and Ozone Depletion: Info Pack, IP405G
* International Environment: Overview of Major Issues; Issue Brief, Mary Tiemann, etc. IB89057
* Monitoring and Forecasting Drought and Famine, Charles Hanrahan, etc. 85-1059 ENR
* The National Climate Program: Background and Implementation, John R. Justus, etc. 88-289 SPR
* Nuclear Winter: Bibliography-in-Brief, B.F. Mangan 88-325 L
* Potential Improvements in the National Weather Service Through New Technology, Robert Morrison, etc. 85-69 SPR
* The Unpredictable Atmosphere: Selected References, Karen L. Alderson, etc. 89-43 L

East-West Trade
* see Foreign Trade-East-West

Eastern Air Lines, Inc.
* Labor Problems at Eastern Air Lines: Issue Brief, Linda LeGrande IB88052

Eastern Europe
* see Economic Conditions, Foreign Relations, Foreign Trade, National Defense, Politics and Government Foreign Policy and Assistance Programs,
* The Chernobyl Accident: Health and Agricultural Effects; Archived Issue Brief, Christopher H. Dodge IB86122
* The Chernobyl Nuclear Accident: Causes, Initial Effects, and Congressional Response; Archived Issue Brief Warren Donnelly, etc. IB86077
* The Chernobyl Nuclear Accident: Long-term Political, Economic, and Foreign Policy Implications; Archived Issue Brief Jean Boone, etc. IB86063
* Mineral Development in Yugoslavia, Marc Humphries 88-688 ENR
* Soviet Space Commercialization Activities, Marcia S. Smith 88-473 SPR
* Space Activities of the United States, Soviet Union and Other Launching Countries/Organizations: 195 7-1988 Marcia S. Smith 89-183 SPR

Eastern Europe -- Economic Conditions
* Gorbachev's Reform: The Consumer Goods and Services Sector, F. Mike Miles 87-763 F
* Oil Price Behavior: Implications for the Soviet Union; Report of the CRS Workshop, June 26, 1986, John P. Hardt, etc. 86-886 S
* Poland's Economic Recovery: U.S. Policy Interests; Archived Issue Brief, John Hardt, etc. IB86070
* Poland's Renewal and U.S. Options: A Policy Reconnaissance, Update, John P. Hardt, etc. 87-889 S
* Soviet Oil Prospects, Joseph Riva 81-91 SPR

Eastern Europe--Foreign Relations
* Andropov and Reagan as Negotiators: Contexts and Styles in Contrast, Joseph Whelan 83-141 S
* Arms Control: Overview of the Geneva Talks; Archived Issue Brief, Steven Hildreth IB85157
* Emigration and Human Rights in the U.S.S.R.: Is There a New Approach? Archived Issue Brief, John P. Hardt IB88019
* Emigration: Soviet Compliance With the Helsinki Accords: Archived Issue Brief, John Hardt, etc. IB82080
* The Moscow Summit at First Glance: Audio Brief, Stuart Goldman, etc. AB50168

* The Role of Congress in Soviet Diplomacy and Negotiations: Audio Brief, Joseph Whelan AB50175
* Sino-Soviet Relations: Recent Improvements and Implications for the United States; Issue Brief, Robert G. Sutter IB86138
* Soviet-American Relations in 1977: A Chronological Summary and Brief Analysis, William Cooper 79-60 S
* Soviet and American Negotiating Characteristics, Joseph G. Whelan 89-191 S
* Soviet Diplomacy and Negotiating Behavior, 1979-1988: Implications for U.S. Diplomacy in the Soviet- American Future Joseph G. Whelan 88-674 F
* Soviet Foreign Policy under Gorbachev: Determinants, Developments, Prospects, and Implications, Francis T. Miko 87-39 F
* Soviet Policy in Nordic Europe: New Focus on the Forgotten Flank?, Francis Miko 85-33 F
* Soviet Policy Toward Iran and the Strategic Balance in Southwest Asia, Stuart D. Goldman 87-592 F
* Soviet-U.S. Relations: The Lessons of Past Summit Meetings?, Francis Miko, etc. 85-1037 G
* Soviet-U.S. Summit Meetings Since the 1950s: Selected References, Sherry Shapiro 87-912 L
* Thirty Years of U.S. Soviet Summit Meetings; a Capsule Summary, Stuart Goldman 85-1055 F
* U.S.-Soviet Relations in a Period of Summitry: Archived Issue Brief, Stuart Goldman IB83066
* U.S.-Soviet Relations: Info Pack, IP233U
* U.S.-Soviet Relations: Selected References, 1986-1988, Elizabeth S. Lane 88-155 L

Eastern Europe -- Foreign Trade
* see Foreign Trade-East-West
* Most Favored National Policy Toward Communist Countries: Archived issue Brief, Vladimir N. Pregelj IB74139
* Potential Economic Effects of Granting Most Favored Nation Treatment to the Soviet Union, George D. Holliday 85-886 E
* Soviet Agriculture: U.S.-U.S.S.R. Grain Sales and Prospects for Expanded Agricultural Trade: Archive d Issue Brief John Hardt IB86019
* U.S. Export Control Policy and Competitiveness: Proceedings of the CRS Symposium, John P. Hardt, etc. 87-388 S
* U.S.-Soviet Commercial Relations in a Period of Negotiation: Archived Issue Brief, John P. Hardt IB88065
* U.S. Trade Relations With the Soviet Union Since World War II: A Chronology, Vladimir N. Pregelz 89-241 E
* U.S.-U.S.S.R. Commercial Relations: Issues in East -West Trade: Archived Issue Brief, John Hardt, etc. IB86020

Eastern Europe -- National Defense
* Arms Control: Negotiations to Limit Defense and Space Weapons; Issue Brief, Steven Hildreth IB86073
* Arms Control: Negotiations to Reduce INF Weapons: Archived Issue Brief, Paul Gallis IB86054
* The Conference on Disarmament in Europe (CDE): Archived Issue Brief, Charlotte Preece, etc. IB84060
* Conference on Security and Cooperation in Europe (CSCE): The Vienna Meeting: Issue Brief, Francis T. Miko IB87220
* Confidence Building Measures and Force Constraints for Stabilizing East-West Military Relations in E urope Stanley R. Sloan, etc. 88-591 F
* Conventional Arms Control and Military Stability in Europe, Stanley R. Sloan, etc. 87-831 F
* Conventional Arms Control in Europe: Prospects for Accord; Issue Brief, Stanley Sloan 86064
* East West Conventional Force Reduction negotiations: Bibliography-in-Brief, 1980-1987, Valentin Leskovsek 87-313 L
* Essentials of Net Assessment: An Objective Means of Comparing Military Capabilities, John Collins, etc. 80-168 S
* Estimates of Soviet Defense Expenditures: Methodological Issues and Policy Implications, Robert Foelber, etc. 85-131 F
* Monitoring Nuclear Test Bans, David W. Cheney 86-155 SPR
* SALT II Treaty: U.S. and Soviet Interim Observance of Its Terms: Archived Issue Brief, Charles Gellner IB80018
* Strategic Nuclear Forces: Potential U.S./Soviet Trends With or Without SALT: 1985-2000, Jonathan Medalia, etc. 86-135 F
* United States/Soviet Military Balance: Archived Issue Brief, John Collins, etc. IB78029
* U.S. Soviet Military Balance. Book I. Organization, Budgets, Manpower, Technology, John Collins, etc. 80-161 S
* U.S.-Soviet Military Balance. Book II. Strategic Nuclear Trends, John Collins, etc. 80-162 S
* U.S.-Soviet Military Balance. Book III. General Purpose Force Trends, John Collins, etc. 80-163 S
* U.S.-Soviet Military Balance. Book IV. Airlift and Sealift, John Collins, etc. 80-164 S
* U.S. Soviet Military Balance Book V. NATO and the Warsaw Pact, John Collins, etc. 80-165 S
* U.S.-Soviet Military Balance. Book VI. Far East, Middle East

Current Events and Homework

Jane Bolle, etc. AB50180
* Are Mandatory Wage and Price Controls Needed to Combat Current Inflation?, Edward Knight 80-64 E
* Budget Deficits and Monetary Policy, Carol Leisenring 81-128 E
* The Dollar and the Trade Deficit: What's to be Done?, Craig Elwell, etc. 88-430 E
* Economic Growth and Inflation, Brian Cashell 88-742 E
* Economic Policy: Selected Issues of Interest to the 101st Congress, Edward Knight 89-209 E
* Economic Policymaking in, U.S. Government: Proceedings of a Congressional Symposium, April 26, 1988, Congressional Research Service 88-461 E
* Economic Policymaking Problems. part One: Institutions and Processes, Leon M. Cole, etc. 89-299 E
* Economic Policymaking Problems: Part Two: Theories and Forecasts, Leon M. Cole, etc. 89-300 E
* The Economy's Performance Since 1981: A Comparative Analysis, Edward Knight 88-336 E
* Effectiveness of mandatory Wage and Price Controls, During the Nixon Administration, a Selected Annotated Bibliography Edward Knight, etc. 80-91 E
* The Employment Act of 1946, as Amended, and the Opportunity for Economic Planning: The Federal Government's Response Dennis Roth 82-21 E
* Federal Reserve System Special Anti-Inflation programs Announced March 14, 1980: A Brief Description, Roger White 80-73 E
* Prospects for an Economic Downturn, G. Thomas Woodward 89-105 E
* The Reagan Economic Strategy: Implications for Small Business, Edward Knight 81-232 E
* The Reagan Strategy for Economic Revitalization: The Results Thus Far, Edward Knight 83-218 E
* Recession in the United States: Economic Effects and Policy Implications, Economics Division 80-134 E
* The Slowdown in the Current Economic Expansion: Recession or Soft Landing?, Gail Makinen 88-718 E
* A Survey of U.S. International Economic Policy and Problems, Alfred Reifman 88-666 S
* U.S. Economic Policy in an International Context: Deficits, Taxes, and Monetary Policy, Jane G. Gravelle, etc. 84-12 E
* U.S. Economic Policy in an International Context: U.S. Wages and Unit labor Costs in a World Economy, Richard S. Belous 84-172 E

Economic Recovery
* see Economic Conditions--Business Cycles

Economic Statistics
* see Economic Conditions

Education
* see Elementary and Secondary Education, Federal Aid to Education, Higher Education, Occupational Training,
* Adult Literacy Issues, Programs, and Options, IB85167
* Carl D. Perkins Vocational Education Act: Issues for Reauthorization, IB89069
* Early Childhood Education and Development: Federal Policy Issues, IB88048
* Education: Federal Concerns, IB87151
* Education Funding Issues for FY 90, IB89039
* Guaranteed Student Loans: Defaults, IB88050
* Saving for College, , IB89078
* Science, Engineering, and Mathematics Precollege and College Education, IB88068
* Teachers: Issues for the 101st Congress, IB89098

Education Consolidation and Improvement Act
* Education Block Grant Reauthorization: Selected Options, Paul M. Irwin 87-494 EPW
* Education for Disadvantaged Children: Reauthorization Issues: Archived Issue Brief, Wayne Riddle IB87070
* Vouchers for the Education of Disadvantaged Children: Analysis of the Reagan Administration Proposal, Wayne Riddle 85-1022 EPW

Education for all Handicapped Children Act
* Constitutional and Statutory Issues Relating to the Use of Behavior Modification on Children in Institutions Nancy L. Jones 86-1000 A
* P.L. 94-142, the Education for All Handicapped Children Act: Its Development, Implementation, and Current Issues Charlotte Fraas 86-552 EPW
* The "Stay Put" Provision of the Education for All Handicapped Children Act: Honig, California Superintendent of Public Instruction v. Doe Et Al Meredith A. Yancey 88-494 A

Education Funding

* see Federal Aid to Education, Higher Education--Student Aid,

Education of Handicapped Children
* see Handicapped--Children

Education of the Handicapped Act
* Education of the Handicapped Act Discretionary Programs: Background and Current Issues, Margot A. Schenet 89-67 EPW
* Summary of the Education of the Handicapped Act Amendments of 1986, P.L. 99-457, Charlotte Jones Fraas 86-926 EPW

Education Savings Bond Program
* Saving for College With Education Savings Bonds, Gerald Mayer 89-207 E

Educational Reform
* see Elementary and Secondary Education, Higher Education,

Egypt
* Egypt: U.S. Foreign Assistance Facts: Archived Issue Brief, Ellen B. Laipson IB85060

El Savador
* Central American Peace Proces: Selected References, Robert Kirk 88-389 L
* El Salvador Aid: Congressional Action, 1981-1986 on President Reagan's Request for Economic and Military Assistance for El Salvador K. Larry Storrs 87-230 F
El Salvador: Bibliography-in-Brief, 1986-1989, Robert S. Kirk 89-204 L
* El Salvador: Info Pack, , IP121E
* El Salvador: U.S. Foreign Assistance Facts; Issue Brief, K. Larry Storrs, etc. IB85113
* El Salvador, 1982-1984: A Chronology of a Period of Transition Resulting from the 1982 and 1984 elections K. Larry Storrs 87-656 F
* A Summary and Analysis of the Report of the National Bipartisan "Kissinger" Commission on Central American, January 1984 Richard Cronin, etc. 84-39 F

Elderly
* see Old Age

Election law
* see Congress-Apportionment and Elections, Politics, and Elections--Election Law,

Elections
* see Congress, Politics and Elections, Presidents (U.S.),
* Campaign Financing, IB87020
* The Fairness Doctrine and the Equal Opportunities Doctrine, IB82087
 * Federal Elections Commission, , IB81104

Electoral College
* see Politics and Elections--Election Law

Electronic Funds Transfers
* see Money and Banking--Financial Institutions

Elementary and Secondary Education
* see Policies and Legislation, Prayer and Religion Federal Aid to Education--Elementary and Secondary,
* Adult Illiteracy: Selected References, Peter Giordano 89-249 L
* Adult Literacy Issues, Programs, and Options; Issue Brief, Paul Irwin IB85167
* AIDS and the Public Schools: Legal Issues Involved in the Education of Children, Nancy Lee Jones 88-329 A
* Comparative Education: Statistics on Education in the United States and Selected Foreign Nations, Kenneth Redd 88-764 EPW
* Comparison of the Achievement of American Elementary and Secondary Pupils With Those Abroad--The Examinations Sponsored by the Inter. Assoc. for Eval o Wayne Riddle 86-683 EPW
* Computers in Elementary and Secondary Schools: An Analysis of Recent Congressional Action, James Stedman 88-419 EPW
* Confronting Students Concerning Suspected Drug Use: Potential Liability of Educators, M. Maureen Murphy 86-952 A
* Constitutional Rights of High School Students: A Select Overview, Rita Ann Reimer 88-224 A
* The Constitutionality of Excessive Corporal Punishment in the Public Schools, David M. Ackerman, etc. 88-413 A
* Dropping Out: The Educational Vulnerability of at-Risk Youth, Congressional Research Service 88-417 EPW
* Early Childhood Education and Development: Federal, Policy Issues; Issue Brief, Wayne Riddle IB88048

* Economic Benefits of Education, Linda LeGrande 88-753 E
* Education: An Alphabetical Microthesaurus of Terms, Selected from the legislative Indexing Vocabulary, Shirley Loo 89-54 L
* The Education of the Handicapped: Selected References, 1984-1987, Marsha K. Cerny 87-529 L
* The Educational Attainment of Select Groups of "at Risk" children and Youth, James Stedman 87-290 EPW
* A Guide to Print and Non-Print Teaching Aids, Winfield Swanson, etc. 83-184 C
* High School Dropouts: Archived Issue Brief, Robert F. Lyke IB87167
* High School Dropouts: Bibliography-in-Brief, 1986-1988, Peter Giordano 88-580 L
* Leadership in Educational Administration Development Program: A Summary of Provision, James B. Stedman 87-204 EPW
* Public School Choice: Recent Developments and Analysis of Issues, Wayne Riddle, etc. 89-219 EPW
* State Funding for Education Reform, K. Forbis Jordan 86-735 S
* Teacher Supply and Demand, Forbis Jordan 85-994 EPW
* Teachers: Issues for the 101st Congress: Issue Brief, James Stedman IB89098
* Elementary and Secondary Education -- Policies and Legislation Adult Education Act Reauthorization: Selected Options Paul M. Irwin 87-57 EPW
* Background Information on Equal Access Statute, David Ackerman 84-842 A
* Bilingual Education: Recent Evaluations of Local School District Programs and Related Research on Second-language Learning Rick Holland 86-611 EPW
* Chapter 1 Concentration Grants: An Analysis of the, Concept, and Its Embodiment in Federal Elementary, and Secondary Education legislation Wayne Riddle 88-670 EPW
* A Comparison of the Education Provisions in the Omnibus Trade Bill, H.R. 3, as Passed by the House b y the Senate Paul M. Irwin, etc. 87-634 EPW
* The Concept of "Secular Humanism" in the Context of Elementary and Secondary Education: Discussion o f the Variety of Meanings, and References in Feder Wayne Riddle 86-545 EPW
* Dwight D. Eisenhower Mathematics and Science Education Act: An Analysis of Recent Legislative Action, and Program Evaluations James Stedman 89-24 EPW
* Education: Federal Concerns; Issue Brief, Angela Evans IB87151
* Education for Disadvantaged Children: Major Themes in the 1988 Reauthorization of Chapter 1, Wayne Riddle 89-7 EPW
* Education: Issues of Quality and Reform: Info Pack, IP256 E
* Education Legislation in the 100th Congress: A Brief Summary; Archived Issue Brief, Wava Gregory IB87134
* Education of the Handicapped Act Discretionary Programs: Background and Current Issues, Margot A. Schenet 89-67 EPW
* Education Proposals in Trade Competitiveness Legislation: Archived Issue Brief, K. Forbis Jordan, etc. IB87108
* Education provisions of the Trade Act of 1988, P.L . 100-418, Paul Irwin, etc. 88-750 EPW
* Education Reform Reports: Content and Impact, James Stedman, etc. 86-56 EPW
* Elementary and Secondary Education: A Summary of the Augustus F. Hawkings-Robert Tl Stafford Element ary and Secondary School Improvement Amendments of Education and Public Welfare Division 88-458 EPW
* Employer Education Assistance: A Brief Discussion of Current Legislation and Issues, Bob Lyle 88-202 EPW
* The Federal Agency for Education: History and Background Information, Angela Evans 81-93 EPW
* Federal Education Policies and Programs: Selected References, 1981-1988, Peter Giordano 89-12 L
* Federal Education Programs Serving Limited English, Proficient Students, RubyAnn M. Esquibel 89-285 EPW
* Federal Policies and Programs Relating to Sex Discrimination and Sex Equity in Eduation, 1963-1985, Bob Lyke, etc. 85-116 EPW
* Head Start Issues in FY 1986: Funding, Adminstration, and Recent Evaluation, Sharon Stephan 86-554 EPW
* The Impact Aid Program under Section 3 of Public Law 81-874: Financial Assistance for Local Educatio n Agencies in Areas Affected by Federal Activities Richard N. Apling 88-440 EPW
* The Impact Aid Programs (P.L. 81-874 and P.L. 81-815): Modification Resulting from the Augustus F. H awkins-Robert T. Stafford Elementary and Secondary Richard N. Apling 88-399 EPW
* Legal Implications for Federal Civil Rights Enforcement of Judge Pratt's Recent Order Dismissing the, Action in Adam v. Bennett Charles V. Dale 88-85 A
* National Teachers' Examination: Background and Issues, Forbis Jordan 85-732 EPW
* Provisions of the Tax Reform Act of 1986 Pertaining to Education, Robert Lyke 87-67 EPW
* Section 2 of P.L. 81-874, Federal Impact Aid to Local School District: Background, Funding History, and Recent Regulation Richard N. Apling 88-220 EPW
* The "Stay Put" Provisions of the Education for All Handicapped

Children Act: Honig, California Super intendent of Public Instruction V. Doe Et Al Meredith A. Yancey 88-494 A
* Summary and Analysis of the Education Amendments of 1984, P.L. 98-511, Angela Giordano-Evans, etc. 84-769 EPW
* Summary of Adult Eduation Act, as Amended by the Education Amendments of 1984 (P.L. 98-511), Paul Irwin 84-829 EPW
* Summary of the Education of the Handicapped Act Amendments of 1986, P.L. 99-457, Charlotte Jones Fraas 86-926 EPW

Elementary and Secondary Education -- Prayer and Religion
* Prayer and Religion in the Public Schools: What Is and Not, Permitted David M. Ackerman 89-25 A
* Prayer and Religion in U.S. Public Schools: Bibliography-in-Brief, 1983-1988, Edith Sutterlin 88-663 L
* Religion in the Public Schools: Judicial Decisions, David M. Ackerman 88-770 A
* Relgion in the Public Schools: Pluralism and Teaching About Religions, Charles H. Whittier 89-104 GOV
* The School Prayer Controversy: Pro-Con Arguments; Issue Brief, Charles Whittier IB84081
* School Prayer: The Congressional Response, 1962-1988, David Ackerman 88-676 A

Embassies and Diplomatic Corps
* see Foreign Relations

Emigration
* see Immigration

Employee Retirement Income Security Act
* Private Pension Plan Standards: A Summary of the Employment Retirement Income Security Act of 1974 (ERISA) as Amended Ray Schmitt 88-681 EPW
* Retirement Income: Bibliography-in-Brief, 1986-1987, Edith Sutterlin 88-28 L
* Women's Pension Equity: A Summary of the Retirement Equity Act of 1984, Ray Schmitt 84-217 EPW

Employment Discrimination
* see Equal Employment Opportunity

Endangered Species Act
* Consideration of Economic Factors under the Endangered Species Act, Pamela Baldwin 89-274 A
* Endangered Species Act: Reauthorization and Funding: Issue Brief, M. Lynn Cron IB87089
* Endangered Species, Bibliography-in-Brief, 1986-1987, Adrienne C. Grenfell 87-459 L
* Kangaroo Management Controversy, Malcolm M. Simmons 88-468 ENR
* Spotted Owls and the Timber Industry; Issue Brief, M. Lynne Corn IB89077

Energy
* see Fossil Fuels, Nuclear Energy, Power Resources
* Alcohol Fuels, IB74087
* Arctic Resources Controversy, IB89058
* Civil Liability for Transboundary Damage from a Nuclear Accident: the Joint International protocol, IB89023
* Coal Slurry Pipeline Issues, IB89105
* DOE's Clean Coal Technology Program: Goals and Fun ding, IB88071
* Domestic Natural Gas Production, , IB89009
* Domestic Oil Production Under Conditions of Contin ued Low Drilling Activity, IB87068
* Energy Conservation: Technical Efficiency and Prog ram Effectiveness, IB85130
* Energy Security, IB89006
* Nuclear Energy Policy, IB88090
* Nuclear Power Plant Safety and Regulation, IB86130
* Nuclear Power: Technology Overview, Statistics, and Projections, IB81070
* Nuclear Weapons Production Compelx: Modernization and Cleanup, IB89062
* Oil Storage Tanks: Construction and Testing Issues, Since the Ashland Oil Spill, IB88015
* Outer Continental Shelf Leasing and Development, IB89028
* Public Utilities Holding Company Act of 1935: Is This the Time for Reform?, IB89052
* Reneweable Energy: Federal programs, IB87050
* The Strategic Petroleum Reserve, IB87050
* U.S. -Japan Agreement for Nuclear Cooperation: Monitoring Its Implementation, IB88095

Energy Conservation

* see Power Resources--Energy Conservation

Energy Development on Public Lands
* see Public Lands

Energy Policy
* see power Resources--Energy Policy

Energy Security
* see Fossil Fuels-Petroleum

England
* see Great Britain

English As the Official U.s. Language
* see Minorities

Enterprise Zones
* see Urban Affairs

Entitlement Programs
* see Pensions, Public Welfare, Social Security

Environmental Law -- Waste Quality
* Oil Pollution Liability and Compensation, Martin R. Lee 88-611 ENR

Environment
* Antarctica: Environemntal Protection Issues: Summary of a CRS Research Workshop, Susan R. Fletcher 89-272 ENR
* Directory of Environmental and Conservation Organizations in the Washington, D.C. Metropolitan Area, Mira Courpas 89-99 ENR
* International Environment: Overview of Major Issues: Issue Brief, Mary Tiemann, etc. IB89057
* Nuclear Weapons Production Complex: Modernization and Cleanup; Issue Brief, David W. Cheney, etc. IB89062
* Environmental Economics The Clean Air Standards Attainment Act: An Analysi s of Welfare Benefits from S. 1894 Larry B. Parker 88-298 ENR
* Controlling Carbon Dioxide Emissions, Amy Abel, etc. 89-157 ENR
* Environmental Factors in Benefit-Cost Analyses of Development Activities, Ross Gorte 86-702 ENR
* Ozone and Carbon Monoxide Nonattainment: An Analysis of Title I of S. 1894, Mira Courpaas 88-316 ENR

Environmental Health
* see Air Pollution--Indoor Air Pollution, Chemicals , Occupational Health and Safety,
* Agent Orange: Veterans' Complaints and Studies of Health Effect; Archived Issue Brief, Sam Merrill, etc. IB83043
* Asbestos in Buildings: Current Issues; Issue Brief, Claudia Copeland IB86084
* Brief Summary of Several Federal Statutes Which Arguably Provide the Federal Government the Authroit y to Control the Disposal of Infectious Hospital Cathy Gilmore 87-658 A
* The Chernobyl Accident: Health and Agricultrual Effects; Archived Issue Brief, Christopher H. Dodge IB86122
* The Clean Air Standards Attainment Act: An Analysis of Welfare Benefits from S. 1894, Larry Parker 88-298 ENR
* Hazardous Chemical Facilities and Community Right-to-Know: Current Issues; Archived Issue Brief, James Aidala IB86069
* Health Benefits of Air Pollution Control: A Discussion, John Blodgett 89-161 ENR
* Risk Assessment in Health and Environmental Regulation; Archived Issue Brief, David Cheney IB84124
* Summary Discussion of S. 1894: The Proposed Clean Air Standards Attainment Act, Congressional Research Service 88-378 ENR
* Toxic Chemicals: Environmental and Health Issues; Audio Brief, AB50104
* The Toxic Substances Control Act: Implementation Issues; Archived Issue Brief, Jim Aidala IB83190
* Underground Storage of Natural Gas, James E. Mielke, etc. 88-187 SPR

Environmental Law
* see Air Quality, Hazardous Substances, Water Quality,
* Antarctica: Environmental Protection Issues; Summary of a CRS Research Workshop, Susan R. Fletcher 89-272 ENR
* Beverage Container Deposit Laws in the States, Mark Gurevitz 89-334 A
* CFC Phase-Out Bills in the 101st Congress: Comparison of Provisions, David E. Gushee 89-314 ENR
* The Clean Air Act in the Courts: Significant Cases from 1980 to 1988, Robert Meltz, etc. 88-460 A

* Environmental Block Grants: A Discussion of Current Issues, Claudia Copeland 86-561 ENR
* Environmental Impairment Liability Insurance: Overview of Availability Issues, Rawle O. King 89-269 E
* Environmental Protection Agency: FY 90 Funding: Issue Brief, Martin R. Lee IB88062
* The Environmental Protection Agency's Proposed Strategy for Post-1987 Nonattainment Areas, Mira Courpas 87-980 ENR
* Environmental Protection: An Alphabetical Microthesaurus of Terms Selected from the Legislative Indexing Vocabulary Shirley Loo 87-792 L
* Environmental Protection Legislation in the 100th Congress: Archived Issue Brief, Environment and Natural Resources Policy Division IB87065
* Environmental Protection Legislation in the 101st Congress; Issue Brief, Environmental and Natural Resources Policy Division IB89033
* Environmental Protection Legislation: Reference Guide, Eugene H. Buck 87-519 ENR
* Export of Pesticides, James Aidala 89-73 ENR
* International Environmental: Overview of Major Issues: Issues Brief, Mary Tiemann, etc. IB89057
* Licensing and Special Use Permit Requirements for Hydroelectric Dam Projects under the Federal Power, Act and the Federal land Policy and Management Ac Robin Jeweler 88-459 A
* Outdoor Advertising Control Along Federal-Aid Highways, Malcolm Simmons 86-605 ENR
* RCRA Authorization: Audio Brief, Jim McCarthy, etc. AB50179
* Summaries of Federal Environmental Laws Administered by EPA, Environment and Natural Resources Policy Division 87-226 ENR
* Wetlands Protection: Issues in the 101st Congress: Issue Brief, Jeffrey A. Zinn, etc. IB89076

Environmental Law -- Air Quality
* Acid Rain Bills in the 100th Congress; Comparison of the Major Provisions of H.R. 2666, H.R. 4331, S., 316, 1894, and the Cuomo-Celeste Proposal Larry Parker, etc. 88-490 ENR
* Acid Rain Control and Clean Coal Technology: An Analysis of Title II of S. 1894, Larry Parker 88-266 ENR
* Acid Rain Control: What Is a 10 Million Ton S02 Reduction?, Larry B. Parker, etc. 89-243 ENR
* Acid Rain Legislation and the Domestic Aluminum Industry, Marc Humphries, etc. 89-327 ENR
* Ambient Air Quality Standards: An Analysis of Title IV of S. 1896, John E. Blodgett 88-271 ENR
* Asbestos in Public Buildings: Comparison of Two Bills, Claudia Copeland 88-368 ENR
* Availability of Trained Persons To Implement the Asbestos Hazard Emergency Response Act, Claudia Copeland 88-259 ENR
* The Clean Air Act in the Courts: Significant Cases from 1980 to 1988, Robert Meltz, etc. 88-460 A
* Comparison of Bills To Amend the Asbestos Hazard Emergency Response Act, Claudia Copeland 88-262 ENR
* Emission Controls on Motor Vehicles and Fuels: An Analysis of Title II of S. 1894, David E. Gushee 88-297 S
* Glossary of Air Quality Terms, Mira Courpas 89-247 ENR
* Hazardous Air Pollutants: An Analysis of Title V of S. 1894, James E. McCarthy 88-265 ENR
* Health Benefits of Air Pollution Control: A Discussion, John Blodgett 89-161 ENR
* House Acid Rain Bills in the 100th Congress: Comparison of the Major Provision of H.R. 1664, H.R. 16 79, H.R. 2497/H.R. 2498, H.R. 2666, H.R. 3632, H.R Larry Parker, etc. 88-226 ENR
* House Acid Rain Bills in the 101st Congress: Comparison of the Major Provisions of H.R. 144 and H.R., 1470 Larry Parker, etc. 89-226 ENR
* Ozone and Carbon Monoxide Nonattainment: An Anlysis of Title I of S. 1894, Mira Courpas 88-316 ENR
* The Stratospheric Ozone Layer: Regulatory Issues; Issue Brief, David Gushee IB89021
* Summary Discussion of S. 1894: The Proposed Clean Air Standards Attainment Act, Congressional Research Service 88-378 ENR

Environmental Law -- Hazardous Substances
* Chemicals in the Environment: Audio Brief, James Aidala AB50152
* Chemicals in the Environment: Selected References on Managing Environmental Risks, Rebecca Mazur 87-26 L
* Incinerating Municipal Solid Waste: A Health Benefit Analysis of Controlling Emissions, Environmental and Natural Resources Policy Div. 89-260 ENR
* Liability of Superfund "Response Action Contractors" and EPA for Injury from Contractor-Conducted Cl eanups Robert Meltz 89-292 A
* Municipal Waste Incineration: An Analysis of Section 3016 of S. 1984, James McCarthy 88-402 ENR
* The Toxic Substances Control Act: Implementation Issues; Archvied issue Brief, Jim Aidala IB83190

Current Events and Homework

* Waste Management: Issue Brief, James E. McCarthy IB89007

Environmental Law -- Water Quality
* After the Exxon Valdez Spill: Oil Pollution Liability and Compensation Legislation, Martin R. Lee 89-266 ENR
* The Alaskan Oil Spill and Gasoline Prices, Lawrence C. Kumins 89-250 ENR
* Chonrology: EPA Regulation of Stormwater Discharge, Claudia Copeland 88-495 ENR
* Clean Water Act Activities: Post Public Law 100-4, Claudia Copeland 88-768 ENR
* Clean Water Act Citizen Suits Held Limited to Ongoing Violations: Gwaltney of Smithfield v. Chesapea e Bay Foundation George A. Costello 88-46 A
* The Exxon Valdez Oil Spill: Issue Brief, Martin R. Lee, etc. IB89075
* Groundwater Quality: Current Federal Programs and Recent Congressional Activities, Jeffrey Zinn, etc. 89-195 ENR
* Groundwater Quality Protection: Issues in the 1201 Congress: Issue Brief, Mary Tiemann IB89081
* Infectious Waste and Beach Closings, Martin R. Lee 88-596 ENR
* Municipal Compliance With the Clean Water Act: Is the Glass Half Full or Half Empty?, Claudia Copeland 88-421 ENR
* Oil Pollution Liability and Compensation Legislation After the Exxon Valdez Oil Spill: Issue Brief, Martin R. Lee IB89082
* Preventing Beach Closings: Legislative Options; Issue Brief, Martin R. Lee IB88102
* A Review of Oil Pollution Prevention Regulations After the Monongahela River Spill, Martin R. Lee 88-448 ENR
* Waste in the Marine Environment: Selected References, Ted Burch 89-263 L

Environmental Protection
* see Air Pollution, Chemicals, Environmental Economics, Environmental Health, Environmental law, Solid Wastes, Water Pollution,
* Acid Rain, Air Pollution, and Forest Decline, IB86031
* Acid Rain: Issues in the 101st Congress, IB87045
* Agriculture and the Environment, IB89086
* Air Quality, IB87124
* Asbestos in Buildings: Current Issues, , IB86084
* Clean Air Act Issues: Motor Vehicle Emission Standards and Alternative Fuels, IB86140
* Clean Air Act Issues: Ozone Nonattainment, , IB89064
* Degradable Plastics, , IB88067
* Environmental Protection Agency: FY 90 Funding, IB89032
* Environmental Protection Legislation in the 101st Congress, IB89033
* The Exxon Valdez Oil Spill, , IB89033
* Global Climate Change, , IB89005
* Groundwater Quality Protection: Issues in the 101st Congress, IB89081
* Hazardous Air Pollutants: Proposals for Revising Section 112 of the Clean Air Act, IB87087
* Hazardous Waste Management: RCRA Oversight in the 101st Congress, IB87087
* Indoor Air Pollution, IB88092
* International Environment: Overview of Major Issues, IB89057
* Oil Pollution Liability and Compensation Legislation After the Exxon Valdez Oil Spill, IB89082
* Oil Storage Tanks: Construction and Testing Issues, Since the Ashland Oil Spill, IB88015
* Preventing Beach Closings: Legislative Options, IB88102
* Solid Waste Management, IB87176
* Stratospheric Ozone Depletion: Regulatory Issues, IB89021
* Tropical Deforestation: International Implications, IB89010
* Waste Management, IB89007
* Water Quality: Implementing the Clean Water Act, IB89102

Equal Access to Justice Act
* see Law

Equal Employment Opportunity
* Affirmative Action in the Employment of Persons With Handicaps under Federal Contracts: Section 503 of the Rehabilitation Act mary F. Smith 88-701 EPW
* Affirmative Action Revisited: A Review of Recent Supreme Court Actions, Charles V. Dale 87-442 A
* Age Discrimination in Employment Act: Recent Enforcement Actions by the Equal Employment Opportunity, Commission Charles V. Dale 87-783 A
* Age Discrimination in Employment: Current Legal Developments, Patricia A. Prochaska 87-681 A
* The Americans With Disabilities Act (ADA): Legal Analysis of Proposed Legislation Prohibiting Discrimination on the Basis of Handicap Nancy Lee Jones 88-621 A
* Comparable Worth/Pay Equity in the Federal Government: Issue Brief, Linda Le Grande IB85116
* Comparative Analysis of Title VII of the 1964 Civil Rights Act, the Age Discrimination in Employment Act, and The Rehabilitation Act of 1973 Charles V. Dale 89-240 A
* The Economic Equity Act of 1987: Archived issue Brief, Leslie Gladstone IB87221
* Elimination of the Professional and Administrative, Career Examination (PACE) and Proposed Alternative Selection procedures Paul Downing 89-315 GOV
* Federal Policies and Programs Relating to Sex Discrimination and Sex Equity in Education, 1963-1985, Bob Lyke, etc. 85-116 EPW
* Legal Implications of the Contagious Disease or Infections Amendment of the Civil Rights Restoration Act, S. 557, Nancy Lee Jones 88-214 A
* The Results of Affirmative Action under Executive Order 11146: Summaries of Recent Studies, Paul M. Downing 86-672 GOV
* Survey of state Statutes Concerning Employment Discrimination of Handicapped Persons, M. Ann Wolfe 87-561 A

Equal Rights Amendment (Proposed)
* see Women

ERISA
* see Employee Retirement Income Security Act

Espionage
* see Intelligence Activities, Internal Security

Estonia
* Estonia: Background Information, Larry Silverman 83-64 F

Ethanol
* see Power Resources--Alternative Energy Sources

Ethics in Government Act
* see Government Employees-Ethics Political Ethics
* Conflicts of Interest: The Department of Defense and the Revolving Door Problem, Andrew C. mayer 86-188 F
* Legislative History and Purposes of Enactment of the Independent Counsel (Special Prosecutor)Provisi ons of the Ethics in Government ACt of 1978 Jack Maskell 87-192 A
* Overview of the Independent Counsel Provisions of the Ethics in Government Act, Jack Maskell 88-631 A
* Summary of Constitutional Issues Raised in Challenges to the Independent Counsel Provisions of Feder al Law Jack Maskell 87-483 A

Ethiopia
* Ethiopia: U.S. Foreign Assistance Facts: Archived Issue Brief, Raymond Copson, etc. IB85014
* World Bank Activities in Ethiopia, Jonathan E. Sanford 87-857 F

European Ecomoic Community
* The "Citrus-Pasta Dispute" Between the United States and the European Community, Donna U. Vogt 7-911 ENR
* The Common Agricultural Policy of the European Community and Implications for U.S Agricultural Trade, Donna U. Vogt, etc. 86-111 ENR
* The Europe 1992 Plan: Science and Technology Issue, Science Policy Research Division 89-178 SPR
* European Community: Issues Raised by 1992 Integration, Congressional Research Service 89-323 E
* The European Community: Its Structure and Development, Martin E. Elling 88-620 F
* European Community-Japan Trade Relations: A European Perspective, Dick Nanto 86-166 E
* European Community: The 1991 Plan: Info Pack, IP408E
* The European Community: 1992 and Reciprocity, Glennon J. Harrison 89-227 E
* European Community: 1992 Plan for Economic Integration: Issue Brief, Glennon Harrison IB89043
* The European Community's 1992 Plan: An Overview of the Proposed "Single Market", Glennon J. Harrison 88-623 E
* The European Community's 1992 Plan: Bibliography-in-Brief, 1986-1988, Robert Howe 88-754 L
* The European Community's 1992 Plan: Effects on American Direct Investment, James K. Jackson 89-339 E
* An Explanation of the European Community's Sugar Regime and Comparison to the U.S. Sugar Program, Jasper Womach, etc. 85-77 ENr
* Tensions in the United States-European Community Agricultural Trade, Donna Vogt, etc. 86-112 ENR
* U.S. Commercial Relations With the European Community, George D. Holliday 85-32 E
* U.S.-European Community Trade Dispute Over Meat Containing Growth Hormones, Donna Vogt 89-6 ENR

Exchange Rates
* see International Finance-Foreign Exchange Rates

Excise Taxes
* see Taxation-Consumption Taxes

Executive Organization
* see Presidential Appointements
* Administering Public Functions at the Martin of Government: The Case of Federal Corporations, Ronald Moe 83-236 GOV
* Amendments to the Prompt Payment Act of 1982: Action in the 100th Congress, Thomas Youth 87-558 GOV
* Analysis of the Office of Science and Technology Policy, Genevieve J. Knezo 88-205 SPR
* Awards of Attorneys' Fees by Federal Courts and Federal Agencies, Henry Cohen 89-205 A
* The Central Intelligence Agency: Organizational History, Mark Lowenthal 78-168 F
* Commission on Executive, Legislative, and Judicial, Salaries: An Historical Overview, Sharon S. Gressle 88-667 GOV
* Extension of the Civil Rights Commission: Archived, Issue Brief, Paul Downing IB87166
* The Federal Agency for Education: History and Back ground Inforamtion, Angela Evans 81-93 EPW
* The Federal Executive Establishment: Evolution and rends, Ronald Moe 79-255 GOV
* A Gudie to Using the Federal Register and the Code, of Federal Regulations, Rita Reimer 86-57 A
* How to Follow Current Federal Legislation and Regulation, Carol D. Davis 89-115 C
* Intelligence Reform: Recent History and Proposals, Alfred B. Prados 88-562 F
* The Iran/Contra Affair: Implications for the National Security Adviser and the NSC Staff; Archvied I ssue Brief Joel M. Woldman IB87107
* National Economic Commission: Equitable Deficit Reduction; Archvied Issue Brief, Barry Molefsky IB88032
* The National Security Council: Organizational History, Mark Lowenthal 78-104 F
* Office of Inspector General in the Central intelligence Agency: Development and Proposals, Frederick M. Kaiser 89-129 GOV
* OMB and Agency Rulemakings: A Description of the Regulatory Review Process under Executive Orders 12 498 and 12291 Morton Rosenberg 85-728 A
* Planning, Managing, and Funding DoD's Technology Base Programs, Michael E. Davey 89-319 SPR
* Presidential Commissions: Their Purpose and Impact, Stephanie Smith 87-668 GOV
* The President's Cabinet, Ronald Moe 86-982 GOV
* Privatization of the National Technical Information Service, Jane Bortnick, etc. 87-492 SPR
* Social Security: The Independent Agency Question: Issue Brief, David Koitz IB86120
* U.S. Government: Info Pack, , IP162U
* What Would It Mean to Make the Social Security Administration an Independent Entity, David Koitz 89-309 EPW

Executive Organization--Presidential Appointments
* Cabinet and Other High Level Nominations that Failed to Be Confirmed, 1789-1989, Rogelio Garcia 89-253 GOV
* The Forest Service Budget: Trust Funds and Special Accounts, Ross W. Gorte, etc. 89-75 ENR
* Overview of Senate Action on Presidential Appointments During 100th Congress, Rogelio W. Gorte 88-78 GOV
* Presidential Nominations and Appointments to Full- time Position in Executive and Legislative Branche s, 1987-1988 Rogelio Garcia 89-55 GOV
* Presidential Nominations to Full-Time Positions on, Regulatory Boards and Commission, 1987-1988, Rogelio Garcia 89-64 GOV
* Women Nominated and Appointed to Full-Time Civilian Positions by President Reagan, Rogelia Garcia 89-236 GOV

Export Administration Act
* *Export Control Reform in the 100th Congress: A Comparison of Selected Provisions of H.R. 3 and S. 14 09 Glennon Harrison 87-529 E*
* *Export Controls: Issue Brief, George Holliday, etc. IB87122*
* *U.S. Export Control Policy and Competitiveness: Proceedings of the CRS Symposium, John P. Hardt, etc. 87-388 S*

Export Controls
* see Foreign Trade-East-West

Export-Import Bank of the United States
* Export-Import Bank Financial Issues: Archived Issue Brief, James Jackson IB88013

* Export-Import Bank: Financing Problems and Issues, James Jackson 88-61 E

Exports
* see Agriculture--Foreign Trade, Foreign Trade-Imports and Exports,

Fair Housing Act
* Fair Housing Act Amendments: Archived Issue Brief, Paul Downing IB87116
* Fair Housing Amendments Prohibiting Discrimination Against Families With children Except in Housing for Older Persons, Henry Cohen 89-111 A
* Segregation and Discrimination in Housing: A Review of Selected Studies and Legislation, Paul Downing, etc. 89-317 GOV

Fair Labor Standards Act
* The Fair labor Standards Act Amendments of 1977(P. L. 95-151): Discussion With Historical Background, William Whittaker, etc. 78-171 E
* Fair Labor Standards Act: Treatment of State and Local Government: Archived Issue Brief, Dennis M. Roth, etc. IB85195
* The Federal Minimum Wage: Consideration in the 100th Congress; Archived Issue Brief, William G. Whittaker IB87063
* Minimum Wage Issues: Info Pack IP249M
* Minimum Wage: Selected References, 1978-1987, Felix Chin 87-162 L
* Mimimum Wage Standards under the Fair Labor Standards Act: Background Analysis and Recent Legislative Interest, William G. Whittaker 87-111 E
* Sheltered Workshops for Persons With Handicaps: Background Information and Recent Legislative Change s Mary F. Smith 87-362 EPW

Fairness Doctrine
* see Politics and Elections--Election law, Telecommunication

Families
* see Child Welfare, Day Care, Domestic Relations
* Analysis of Legal and Constitutional Issues Involved in Surrogae Motherwood Rita Reimer 88-240 A
* Assistance to Families: A Chart Comparing Some Existing Tax Provisions and Pending Proposals Marie B. Morris 89-279 A
* Child Nutrition Program Information and Data Jean Yavis Jones 88-248 EPW
* Children, Families, and Domestic Relations: An Alphabetical Microthesaurus of Terms Selcted from the Legislative Indexing Vocabulary Shirley Loo 87-967 L
* The Earned Income Tax Credit Carmen Solomon 86-1031 EPW
* Elder Abuse: Bibliography-in-Brief, 1980-1988 Edith Sutterlin, etc. 88-221 L
* Fair Housing Amendments Prohibiting Discrimination Against Families With Children Except in Housing for Older Persons Henry Cohen 89-111 A
* Family Leave: Bibliography-in-Brief, 1985-1988 Edith Sutterlin 89-107 L
* The Judicial and Legislative Treatment of Pregnancy: A Review of Developments from Unprotected Status to Anti-Discrimination-Equal Treatment and Speci Charles Dale, etc. 87-277 A
* Maternity and Parental Leave Policies: A Comparative Analysis Leslie Gladstone, etc. 85-148 GOV
* Military Benefits for Former Spouses: Legislation and Policy Issues David Burreli 89-187 F
* Parental leave: Info Pack IP367P
* Parental Leave: Legislation in the 100th Congress; Issue Brief Leslie Gladstone IB86132
* Surrogate Mothers: Bibliography-in-Brief, 1985-1988 Edith Sutterlin 88-268 L
* Teenage Pregnancy: Selected Reference, 1986-1988 Peter Giordano 89-119 L

Families -- Child Welfare
* Cash Welfare Funds and Homeless Families With Children Carmen D. Solomon 88-394 EPW
* Child Abuse and Neglect: Data and Federal Programs Dale Robinson 89-127 EPW
* Child Abuse and Neglect in the United States: Legislative Issues: Selected References, 1985-1988 Edith Sutterlin 89-13 L
* Child Abuse: Info Pack IP019C
* Child Health in the Third World: U.S. and International Initiatives: Archived Issue Brief Lois McHugh IB85189
* Child Nutrition: Issues in the 101st Congress; Issue Brief Jean Yavis Jones IB89-48
* Child Pornography: Legal Considerations; Archived Issue Brief Rita Reimer IB83148

* Adult Literacy Issues, Programs, and Options; Issue Brief Paul Irwin IB85167
* Analysis of the Constitutionality of the Administration's Chapter 1 Voucher Proposal under the Establishment of Relegion Clause of the First Amendment David Ackerman 85-1143 A
* Block Grant Funding for Federal Education programs : Background and Pro and Con Discussions K. Forbis Jordan 86-992 S
* Carl D. Perkins Vocational Education Act: Issues for Reauthorization; Issue Brief Paul Irwin, etc. IB890069
* A Comparison of the Education Provisions in the Omnibus Trade Bill, H.R. 3, as Passed by the House and by the Senate Paul Irwin, etc. 87-634 EPW
* Department of Education programs for Science and Mathematics Education: Background, Status, Issues, and Options K. Forbis Jordan 86-739 S
* Education Block Grant Reauthorization: Selected Options Paul Irwin 87-494 EPW
* Education: Federal Concerns: Issue Brief Angela Evans IB87151
* Education Funding Issues for FY 89; Archived Issue Brief, Angela Evans IB88036
* Education Funding Issues for FY 90: Issue Brief, Angela Evans IB89-39
* Education: Funding Issues; Info Pack   IP199E
* Education Legislation in the 100th Congress: A Brief Summary: Archived Issue Brief Wava Gregory IB87134
* Education of the Handicapped Act Discretionary Programs; Background and Current Issues Margaret A. Schenet 89-67 EPW
* Education Provisions of the Trade Act of 1988, P.L . 100-418, Paul Irwin, etc. 88-750 EPW
* Federal Assistance to Libraries Current Program and Issues, Wayne Clifton Riddle 89-197 EPW
* Federal Eduation Policies and Programs; Selected References, 1987-1988 Peter Giordano 89-12 L
* Federal Education Programs Serving Limited English Proficient Students, Ruby Ann M. Esquibel 89-285 EPW
* Federal Impact Aid and State School Finance Equalization Programs, K. Forbis Jordan 87-589 S
* Federal Programs Affecting Children,   Sharon House, etc. 87-306 EPW
* Federal Vocational Eduation Legislation: Recurring Issues During the last Quarter Century Richard Apling, etc. 88-704 EPW
* Gramm-Rudman-Hollings and Department of Education Programs, Angela Evans 86-544 EPW
* State Allotments for Education programs under H.R. 3, the Omnibus Trade Bill of 1987, as Passed by t he House and the Senate Paul M. Irwin, etc. 87-683 EPW
* State Funding for Education Reform, K. Forbis Jordan 86-735 S
* Summary and Analysis of the Education Amendments of 1984, P.L. 98-511 Angela Giordano-Evans, etc. 84-769 EPW
* Summary of the Adult Education Act, as Amended by the Education Amendments of 1984 (P.L. 98-522) Paul Irwin 84-829 EPW
* Teacher Training and Improvement, FY88 Budget Proposal; Archived Issue Brief K. Forbis Jordan IB86047
* U.S. Department of Education: Major Program Trends, Fiscal Years 1980-1990 Education and Public Welfare Division 89-144 EPW
* Vocational Education and Proposals for Trade Competitiveness, Paul M. Irwin 87-340 EPW
* Vouchers for the Education of Disadvantaged Children; Analysis of the Reagan Administration Proposal Wayne Riddle 85-1022 EPW

Federal Aid to Education -- Elementary and Secondary
* Chapter 1 Concentration Grants: An Analysis of the Concept, and Its Embodiment in Federal Elementary and Secondary Education Legislation Wayne Riddle 88-670 EPW
* Computers in Elementary and Secondary Schools: An Analysis of Recent Congressional Aaction James Stedman 88-419 EPW
* Dwight D. Eisenhower Mathematics and Science Education Act: An Analysis of Recent Legislative Action and Program Evaluations James Stedman 89-24 EPW
* Education for Disadvantaged Children: Major Themes in the 1988 Reauthorization of Chapter 1 Wayne C. Riddle 89-7 EPW
* Education for Disadvantaged Children: Reauthorization Issues; Archived Issue Brief Wayne Riddle IB87070
* Elementary and Secondary Education; A Summary of the Augustus F. Hawkins-Robert T. Stafford Elementary and Secondary School Improvement Amendments of Education and Public Welfare Division 88-458 EPW
* Federal Aid to Elementary and Secondary Education : A Side-by-Side Comparison of Current Law with H. R. 5, as Passed by the House of Representatives Eduation and Public Welfare Division 88-42 EPW
* Federal Assistance for Elementary and Secondary Education; Background Information on Selected Programs Likely to Be Considered for Reauthorization by Educationand Public Welfare Division. Education 87-330 EPW
* Federal Elementary and Secondary Education programs: Reauthorization Issies: Archived Issue Brief K. Forbis Jordan IB87055

* The Impact Aid Program under Section 3 of the Public Law 81-874: Financial Assistance for Local Eduation Agencies in Areas Affected by Federal Activities Richard Apling 88-440 EPW
* The Impact Aid Programs (P.L. 81-874 and P.L. 81-8 15): Modification Resulting from the Augustus F. Hawkins-Robert T. Stafford Elementary and Secondary Richard N. Apling 88-399 EPW
* Public School Choice: Recent Developments and Analysis of Issues Wayne Riddle, etc. 89-219 EPW
* School Assistance for Federally Affected Areas(Impact Aid): Background and Reauthorization Options f or P.L. 81-874 K. Forbis Jordan 87-606 S
* Section 2 of P.L. 81-874, Federal Impact Aid to Local School Districts: Background, Funding History , and Recent Regulations Richard Apling 88-220 EPW
* Summary of the Education of the Handicapped Act Amendments of 1986, P.L. 99-457 Charlotte Jones Fraas 86-926 EPW

Federal Aid to Education -- Higher Education
* Appropriations Enacted for Specific Colleges and Universities by the 96th Through 100th Congress Susan H. Boren 89-82 EPW
* Civil Rights Legislation: Response to Grove City College v. Belt; Archived Issue Brief Bob Lyke IB87123
* Guides to Financial Aid for Stdents: A Checklist, Peter Giordano 89-98 L
* The Higher Education Amendments of 1986 (P.L. 99-498): A Summary of Provisions Education and Public Welfare Division 87-187 EPW
* Revenue Sources for Higher Education Institutions, K. Forbis Jordan 86-956 S
* Saving for College With Education Savings Bonds,   Gerald Mayer 89-207 E
* Student Financial Aid: Authorizations of Appropriations, Budget Requests, Enacted Appropriations and Outlays for Federal Student Financial Aid Program Susan H. Boren 89-184 EPW

Federal Aid to Housing
* see Housing--Assistance

Federal Budget
* see Public Finance

Federal Deposit Insurance Corporation
* see Money and Banking--Failures and Deposit Insurance
* Bank Bailouts: Open-Bank Assistance by the Federal Deposit Insurance Corporation William Jackson 86-1041 E
* Depository Financial Institution Failures: The 1980s Experience Pauline H. Smale 88-549 E
* The Economics of Deposit Insurance   G. Thomas Woodward 89-32 E
* Federal Deposit Insurance Funds: An Overview of FDIC and FLIC Finances William Jackson 87-2 E
* Federal Deposit Insurance Funds and Regulatory Agencies: Merger and Consolidation Issues F. Jean Wells 88-279 E
* The Federal Deposit Insurance Funds: Their Financial Condition and Public Policy Proposals in the 100th Congress; Archived Issue Brief F. Jean Wells IB88082
* Financial Institutions: Problems and Restructuring: A CRS Compilation Walter Eubanks. 87-586 E

Federal Election Campaign Act
* see Politics and Elections--Campaign Funds

Federal Employees
* see Government Employees

Federal Employees' Retirement System
* see Pensions--Civil Service
* Federal Employees Retirement System Handbook for Members of Congress; Benefits under the Federal Employees Retirement System Education and Public Welfare Division 87-189 EPW
* A Retirement Plan for Federal Workers Covered by Social Security: An Analysis of the Federal Employe es Retirement System (P.L. 99-335) Education and Public Welfare Division. Civil Service, 86-137 EPW

Federal Food, Drug, and Cosmetic Act
* The Applicability of the Export Proviso of the Federal Food, Drug and Cosmetic Act to "New Drugs" Cathy Gilmore 85-848 A

Federal Home Loan Morgage Corporation
* Federal Home Loan Morgage Corporation Preferred Stock Ownership: Lift the Restrictions?: Archived Issue Brief Barbara L. Miles IB88076

Federal Insecticide, Fungicide, and Rodenticide Act
*see Pesticides

and Vegetables, James V. Aidala 89-166 ENR
* Fast Food Restaurant Labeling, Donna V. Porter 87-736 SPR
* Federal Poultry Insepction: A Brief, Geoffrey S. Becker 87-432 ENR
* Food Labeling: Issue Brief, Donna V. Porter IB80055
* Food Safety Policy: Selected Scientific and Regulartory Issues; Archived Issue Brief, Sarah Taylor, etc. IB83158
* Import Restirctions on Meat-History and Current Issues, Jean Rawson 85-956 ENR
* Labeling of Tropical Oils: Legislation, Health and, Trade Issues, Donna Porter, etc. 87-910 SPR
* Mandatory Fedreal Seafood Inspection: An Overview, Geoffrey Becker 83-198 ENR
* Pesticide Monitoring Program: Developing New Methods to Detect Pesticide Residues in Food, Sara Taylor 87-413 SPR

Food Relief
* see Domestic, Foreign,
* Child Nutrition program Information and Data, Jean Yavis Jones 88-248 EPW
* Selected Reports Available on Food and Agricultural Topics, Environment and Natural Resources Policy Div. 89-244 ENR

Food Relief--Domestic
* AFDC, Food Stamps, and Work: History, Rules and Research, Emmett Carson, Etc. 87-599 EPW
* Child Nutrition: Issues in the 101st Congress; Issue Brief, Jean Yavis Jones IB89-48
* Chronology and Brief Description of Fedral Food Assistance Legislation, 1935-1987, Jean Yavis Jones 88-100 EPW
* Commodity Donations for Domestic Food Programs: Issue Brief, Jean Yavis Jones IB89070
* Domestic Food Assistance: Overview of Programs, Issues and Legislation: Archived Issue Brief, Jean Yavis Jones, etc. IB88059
* Expected Impact of the Drought on Food Prices and Federal Food Aid, Geoffrey S. Becker, etc. 88-633 ENR
* Federal Faassistance programs and a Brief Bibliography on Hunger in the United States, Virginia MacEwen, etc. 86-719 L
* Food Stamps in the United States: Bibliography-in-Brief, 1986-1988, Edith Sutterlin 88-424 L
* Food Stamps: 1986 Issues; Archived Issue Brief, Joe Richardson IB86038
* Food Stamps: 1987 Issues; Archvied Issue Brief, Joe Richardson IB88045
* How the Food Stamp Program Works: 11th Edition, Joe Richardson 89-196 EPW
* Hunger in Brief: Reports and Proposals for Expanded Federal Efforts, Donna V. Porter, etc. 86-703 SPR
* Special Supplemental Food Program for Women, Infants, and Children (WIC): Description, History and D ata Jean Yavis Jones 86-794 EPW
* Summary of Reports Concerning Hunger in American, 1983-1986, Donna V. Porter, etc. 86-791 SPR
* Temporary Emergency Food Assistance Program (TEFAP): 1987Issues; Archived Issue Brief, Jean Jones IB87090
* USDA's Commodity Inventory: Food for the Hungry?, Geoffrey S. Becker 87-880 ENR
* USDA's "Section 32" Fund, Geoffrey S. Becker 88-532 ENR

Food Relief--Foreign
* The Angola Food Emergency: Extent of the Problem and Current U.S. Emergency Assistance Policy, Alan K. Yu 89-14 F
* Cargo Preference and Agriculture: Background and Current Issues, Carl Ek 87-134 ENR
* The Effectiveness of Food Aid: Implications of Changes in Farm, Food Aid, and Trade Legislation; Proceedings of a CRS Workshop Held on April 25, 1988 Charles E. Hanrahan 88-493 ENR
* Ethiopia: U.S. Foreign Assistance Facts: Archived Issue Brief, Raymond Copson, etc. IB85014
* Food for Peace, 1954-1986: Major Changes in Legislation, Susan B. Epstein 87-490 ENR
* Food Production and Food Policy in Subsaharan Africa: A 20 Country Survey, Charles Hanrahan, etc. 85-150 ENR
* Foreign Food Aid: Current Policy Issues, Charles E. Hanrahan, etc. 87-923 ENR
* Foreign Food Aid Programs: Effectiveness Issues: Archvied Issue Brief, Charles E. Hanrahan IB88057
* International Fund for Agricultural Development, Susan Epstein 87-4 ENR
* Monitoring and Forecasting Drought and Famine, Charles E. Hanrahan, etc. 85-1059 ENR
* U.S. Bilateral and Multilateral Food Assistance Programs, Susan Epstein 85-114 ENR

Food Safety
* see Food--Labeling and Safety,

Food Security Act
* see also Agriculture,
* Cargo Preference and Agriculture: Background and Current Issues, Carl Ek 87-134 ENr
* Compliance Provisions for Resource Conservation: A Status Report, Jeffrey Zinn 88-662 ENR
* The Conservation Reserve: A Status Report, Jeffrey Zinn 88-716 ENR
* Dairy Issues: Issue Brief, Jasper Womach IB89063
* The Effectivness of Food Aid: Implications of Changes in Farm, Food Aid, and Trade Legislation: Proceedings of a CRS Workshop Held on April 25, 1988 Charles E. Hanrahan 88-493 ENR
* Soil and Water Conservation Issues in the 101st Congress: Issue Brief, Jeffrey Zinn IB89080
* The 1990 Farm Bill: Issues Likely to Shape the Policy Debate, Jasper Womach 88-700 ENR

Food Stamp Plan
* see Food Relief--Domestic,

Foreign Aid
* see Africa, Asia, Latin America, Middle East, Foreign Investments, Foreign Trade, Military Assistance,
* Child Health in the Third World: U.S. and International Initiatives; Archived Issue Brief, Lois McHugh IB85189
* Current Issues With the "Base-Rights" Countries and Their Implications, Richard Grimmett 88-726 F
* Defense and Foreign Aid Budget Analysis and the Use of Constant Dollars, Alice C. Maroni, etc. 86-154 F
* Department of Defense Humanitarian Aid, Carol R. Kuntz, etc. 87-808 F
* Development Assistance Policy: A Historical Overview, Theodore W. Galdi 88-285 F
* The Effectiveness of Food Aid: Implications of Changes in Farm, Food Aid, and Trade Legislation; Pro eedings of a CRS Workshop Held on April 25, 1988 Charles E. Hanrahan 88-493 ENR
* The Foreign Affiars Funding Debate in 1987, Larry Q. Nowels 89-154 F
* Foreign Aid--A Policy Overview: Archived Issue Brief, Gary J. Pagiliano, etc. IB87016
* Foreign Aid: Info Pack, IP044F
* Foreign Assistance and Defense Transactions and Their Direct Effect on the U.S. Balance of Payments:, Summary of Statistical Data, 1960-1987 Vladimir N. Pregelj 88-545 E
* Foreign Assistance Budget and Policy Issues for FY 89: Archived Issue Brief, Larry Q. Nowels IB88056
* International Narcotics Control and Foreign Assistance Certification: Requriements, Procedures, Time tables and Guidelines Raphael F. Perl 88-130 F
* International Population and Family Planning Programs: Issues for Congress; Archived Issue Brief, Vita Bite IB85187
* An Overview of the Economic Support Fund, Larry Q. Nowels 88-284 F
* An Overview of U.S. Foreign Aid Programs, Stanley J. Heginbotham, etc. 88-283 F
* Population Programs of AID: Background of Legislation--99th Congress, Vita Blue 86-109 F
* The Power of the Purse in Foreign Policy: Process and Problems in Congressional Funding, Ellen Colier 85-182 F
* Reforming the Foreign Assistance Programs: Audio Brief, Larry Nowels AB50185
* The World Bank: Eighteen Questions and Answers, Jonathan E. Sanford 86-769 F

Foreign Aid-- Africa
* African Debt: The Official Donor Response and Potential Alternative Strategies, Alan K. Yu 89-228 F
* The Angola Food Emergency: Extent of the Problem and Current U.S. Emergency Assistance Policy, Alan K. Yu 89-14 F
* Angola: Issues for the United States; Archived Issue Brief, Raymond Copson, etc. IB81063
* Ethiopia: U.S. Foreign Assistance Facts; Archived Issue Brief, Raymond Copson, etc. IB85014
* Mozambique: U.S. Foreign Assitance Facts; Issue Brief, Ellen Laipson, etc. IB85065
* U.S. Foreign Assistance to the Middle East and north Africa: Fiscal Years 1988, 1989, and 1990, Clyde R. Mark 89-192 F
* The 99th Congress adn the African Economic Crisis, Carol Lancaster 87-914 F

Foreign Aid -- Asia
* Cambodia: U.S. Foreign Aassistance Facts; Archived, Issue Brief, Robert Sutter IB85153
* Pakistan: U.S. Foreign Assistance Facts; Archived, Issue Brief, Richard P. Cronin IB85112
* Philippines: U.S. Foreign Assistance Facts; Issue Brief, Larry Niksch IB85077

Foreign Aid -- Europe
* see also Contras,
* Belize: Country Background Report, Mark P. Sullivan 88-568 F
* Caribbean Basin Initiative: Info Pack, IB190C
* Central America and U.S. Foreign Assistance: Issues for Congress; Issue Brief, Jonathan Sanford IB84075
* Compilation of Selected laws Relating to the National Security Council, Arms Transfers, Intelligence, Activities, Aid to the Contras, and Appropriation American law Division 86-1028
* El Salvador Aid: Congressional Action, 1981-1986, on President Reagan's Requests for Economic and Military Assistance for El Salvador Larry K. Storrs 87-230 F
* El Salvador: U.S. Foreign Assistance Facts; Issue Brief, K. Larry Storrs, etc. IB85113
* Guatemala: U.S. Foreign Assistance Facts; Archived, Issue Brief, Jonathan Sanford IB85100
* Honduras: U.S. Foreign Assistance Facts; Archived Issue Brief, Robert Sanchez IB85080
* International Commission on Central America: Initial Views; Audio Brief, Larry Storrs AB50176
* Lend-Lease: An Historic Overview and Repayment Issues, Patricia Wertman 85-844 E
* Major Trends in U.S. Foreign Assistance to Central, America: 1978-1986, Jonathan Sanford 86-88 F
* U.S. Bilateral Economic and Military Assistance to, Latin America and the Carribean: Fiscal Years 194 6 to 1987 K. Larry Storrs 87-694 F
* U.S. Foreign Aid to Central America: 1986-1988, Jonathan Sanford 87-465 F
* U.S. Mexico Economic Relations: An Overview, Lenore Sek 87-485 E

Foreign Aid -- Middle East
* Egypt: U.S. Foreign Assistance Facts: Archived Issue Brief, Ellen B. Laipson IB85060
* Israel: U.S. Foreign Assistance Facts: Issue Brief, Clyde Mark IB85066
* Jordan: U.S. Foreign Assistance Facts; Archived Issue Brief, Richard Preece IB85120
* U.S. Foreign Assistance to the Middle East and North Africa: Fiscal years 1988, 1989, and 1990, Clyde R. Mark 89-192 F

Foreign Competition
* see Foreign Trade--Competitiveness,

Foreign Debt
* see International Finance--Foreign Loans,

Foreign Exchange Rates
* see International Finance--Foreign Exchange Rate,

Foreign Investments
* see also Foreign Aid, Foreign Trade,
* American Direct Investment Abroad: Effects on Trade, Jobs, and the Balance of Payments, James K. Jackson 88-546 E
* American Direct Investments Abroad: How Much Are They Worth?, James K. Jackson 88-507 E
* The Citicorp Initiative: A Brave New World for the, Third World Debt Problem, Patricia A. Wertman 87-750 E
* European Community: Issues Raised by 1992 Integration, Congressional Research Service 89-323 E
* Foreign Direct Investments in the United States: Data Collection, Disclosure, and Effects, James K. Jackson 88-79 E
* Foreign Direct Investment in the United States: Issue Brief, James Jackson 87226
* The Foreign Investment Conundrum, James K. Jackson 89-58 E
* Foreign Investment in the United States: Major Federal Restrictions, Michael V. Seitzinger 88-164 A
* Foreign Investments in the United States: Selected, References, 1985-1989, Robert Howe 89-316 L
* Foreign Investments in the United States; Trends and Impact, William Cooper 85-932 E
* Foreign Investments in the U.S.; Info Pack, IP398F
* Foreign Mergers and Acquisitions: Non-U.S. Companies Acquiring U.S. Companies, Kevin F. Winch, etc. 87-711 E
* Foreign Ownership of U.S. Assets: Past, Present, and Prospects, James K. Jackson, etc. 88-295 E
* Japan: Increasing Investment in the United States, James Jackson 89-102 E
* Japan's Financial Liberalization: Effects on the United States, James Jackson 89-102 E
* Major Federal Tax Provisions that Directly Affect International Trade and Investment, David Brumbaugh 86-764 E
* Mineral Development in Uugoslavia, Marc Humphries 88-688 ENR
* Offshore Manufacturing by U.S. Corporations; Selected

Bibliography, With Introductory Readings, Robert S. Kirk 86-834 L
* Registering Foreign Investment: Proposed Legislation; Issue Brief, James Jackson IB89-92
* State Regulation of the Purchase of Real Property by Foreign Citizens, Michael V. Seitziner 88-451 A
* A Survey of U.S. International Economic Policy and Problems, Alfred Reifman 88-666 S
* Tariff Items 807.00 and 806.30 and the Mexican Maquiladoras, Patricia Wertman 87-500 E
* Tax Reform and Foreign Investment by U.S. Firms, David Brumbaugh 87-89 E
* Taxation of Overseas Investment Subpart F and the Tax Reform Act of 1986, David Brumbaugh 87-167 E
* The United States as a Debtor Nation and International Capital Flows: Bibliography-in-Brief, 1984=19 87 Robert S. Kirk 88-11 L
* U.S. Foreign Direct Investment Policy: Response to, Foreign Government Barriers and Distortions, Raymond Ahearn 82-20 E
* U.S.-Mexico Economic Relations: An Overview, Lenore Sek 87-485 E

Foreign Loans
* see International Finance--Foreign Loans,

Foreign Policy and Assistance Programs
* see Arms Control, Foreign Aid, Foreign Relations, Intelligence Activities, International Agencies, I nternational Law, Military Assistance,,
* AIDS: International Problems and Issues, IB87214
* Angola/Namibia Negotiations, IB89047
* Australia, New Zealand, and the Pacific Islands: I ssues for U.S. Policy, IB86158
* Cambodian Crisis: Problems of a Settlement and Pol icy Dilemmas for the United States, IB89020
* Central America and U.S. Foreign Assistance: Issue s for Congress, IB84075
* Central American Peace Prospects: U.S. Interests a nd Response, IB87200
* China in Crisis: Public Dissent and the Power Stru ggle, IB89100
* China-U.S. Relations: Issues for Congress, IB84135
* Drug Control: International Policy and Options, IB88093
* El Salvador: U.S. Foreign Assistance Facts, IB85113
* Foreign Aid: Budget, Policy, and Reform, IB89014
* Foreign Food Aid: Reauthorization Issues, IB89097
* Greece and Turkey: U.S. Foreign Assistance Facts, IB86065
* Honduras: U.S. Military Activities, IB84134
* Implementation of the U.S.-Chinese Agreement for N uclear Cooperation, IB86050
* India and Nuclear Weapons, IB86125
* Iran-Iraw War, IB88060
* Israel and Nuclear Weapons, IB87079
* Israel: U.S. Foreign Assistance Facts, IB85066
* Israeli-Am,erican Relations, IB82008
* Japan-U.S. Relations, IB81026
* Korean Political Tensions: Implications for the United States, IB86071
* Lebanon: The Remaining U.S. Hostages, IB85183
* Mexico-U.S. RElations: Issues for Congress, IB86111
* Middle East Peace Proposals, IB82127
* Nicaragua: Conditions and Issues for U.S. Policy, IB82115
* Northern Ireland and the Republic of Ireland: U.S., Foreign Assistance Facts, IB87069
* Nuclear Arms Control: Disposal of Nuclear Warheads, IB88024
* Pakistan and Nuclear Weapons, IB86110
* Pakistan's Nuclear Program: U.S. Foreign Policy Considerations, IB87227
* Palestine and the Palestinians, IB76048
* Panama: U.S. Policy After the May 1989 Elections, IB89106
* Panama's Political Crisis: Prospects and U.S. Policy Concerns, IB87230
* Philippines Under Aquino, IB86104
* Philippines: U.S. Foreign Assistance Facts, IB85077
* POWs and MIAs in Indochina and Korea: Status and Accounting Issues, IB88061
* Sino-Soviet Relations: Recent Improvements and Implications for the United States, IB86138
* South Africa: Recent Developments, IB85213
* South Africa, Nuclear Weapons, and the IAEA, IB87199
* South Africa: U.S. Policy After Sanctions, IB87128
* Southern Africa: U.S. Foreign Assistance, IB87152
* Soviet Perestroika: Political and Conomic Change Under Gorbachev, IB89038
* Sudan: Foreign Assistance Facts, IB85065
* Taiwan: Recent Developments and their Implications, for the United States, IB87092
* U.N. System Funding: Congressional Issues, IB86116
* U.S.-Japan Agreement for Nuclear Cooperation: Monitoring Its Implementation, IB88095

* U.S.-Soviet Relations, IB89008
* Vietnam-U.S. Relations: The Missing-in-Action (MIA) and the Problem of Cambodia, IB87210

Foreign Relations

* see Africa, Asia, Eastern Europe, Latin America, Middle East, Pacific Area, Reagan Doctrine, Western, Europe, Iran-Contra Affair, Terrorism,
* America in Economic Decline?, Alfred Reifman 89-182 S
* Anti-Terrorism Policy: A Pro-Con Discussion of Retaliation and Deterrence Options, James Wooten, etc. 85-832 F
* Case Studies of Counter-Insurgencies, Larry Niksch 85-60 F
* Chart of Diplomatic and Consular Immunities, Larry Eig 88-183 A
* Congress and Foreign Policy: Selected References, Sherry Shapiro 89-318 L
* Congress and the President in U.S. Foreign Policymaking: A Selected Annotated Bibliography, Sherry B. Shapiro 86-183 L
* Diplomacy and the U.S. Foreign Service: A Glossary, of Basic Terms, Joel M. Woldman 86-159 F
* Diplomatic Security: The Marine Security Guard Program at U.S. Missions Abroad, Joel Woldman 87-602 F
* Embassy Demonstrations in the District of Columbia : An Overview of Boos v. Barry, Larry Eig 88-343 A
* Examples of Treaties Not Ratified Due to Senate Reservations and/or Amendments, David M. Ackerman 87-977 A
* Foreign Policy and International Relations: An Alphabetical Microthesaurus of Terms Selected from th e Legislative Indexing Vocabulary Shirley Loo 86-725 L
* Foreign Policy: Info Pack, IP297F
* Foreign Policy Roles of the President and Congress, Ellen C. Collier 86-163 F
* Human Rights in the U.S. Foreign Relations: Six Key Questions in the Continuing Policy Debate, Vita Blue 81-257 F
* The National Endowment for Democracy: Archived Issue Brief, Joel Woldman IB83107
* The Power of the Purse in Foreign Policy: Process and Problems in Congressional funding, Ellen Collier 85-182 F
* President and Foreign Policy: Selected References, Sherry Shapiro 88-219 L
* Privatization in the Conduct of U.S. Foreign Policy: A Survey of Past and Current Practice, Ellen Collier 88-327 F
* The Rise and Fall of Nations: Is America In Decline? a Bibliography of Points of View, Robert S. Kirk 89-214 L
* Sectional Analysis of the "War Powers Resolution" (WPR) as It Would Be Amended by the "War Powers Am endment of 1988" (S.J. Res. 323, 100th Congress, 2 Raymond J. Celada 88-441 A
* The Security of U.S. Embassies and Other Overseas Civilian Installations, Joel Woldman 85-11 F
* Soviet and American Negotiating Characteristics, Joseph G. Whelan 89-191 S
* Terrorism: U.S. Policy Options; Issue Breif, James Wooten IB81141
* The United States Institute of Peace, Joel Woldman 86-15 F
* U.S. Canada Free Trade Agreement: International Implications, Raymond J. Ahearn, etc. 88-249 F
* U.S. Presidential National Security Advisers: Changing Roles and Relationships, Joel Woldman 87-334 F
* U.S. Senate Rejection of Treaties: A Brief Survey of Past Instances, Ellen Collier 87-305 F
* War Powers Resolution: Info Pack, IP131 W
* War Powers Resolution: Presidential Compliance; Issue Brief, Ellen Collier IB81050
* War Powers Resolution: The Controversial Act's Search for a Successful Litigation Posture, Raymond J. Celada 88-64 A
* The War Powers Resolution (WPR): Some Implications, of S.J. Res. 323, "War Powers Resolution Amendmen ts of 1988" Raymond J. Celada 88-464 A

Foreign Relations--Africa

* Angola: Conflict Assessment and U.S. Policy Options, Raymond Copson 86-189 F
* Angola: Issues for the United States; Archived Issue Brief, Raymond Copson, etc. IB81063
* Angola/Namibia Peace Prospects: Background, Current Problems, and Chronology, Raymond W. Copson 88-559 F
* Mozambique: Conflict Assessments/U.S. Policy, Raymond Copson 88-516 F
* Sanctions Against South Africa: Impact on the United States; Issue Brief, William Cooper IB87198
* South Africa: International Sactions; Archived Issue Brief, Jeanne Affelder, etc. IB86157
* South Africa: Legislation of the 99th Congress, Brenda Branaman 85-799 F
* South Africa: President's Report on Progress Toward Ending Apartheid, Raymond Copson 87-829 F
* South Africa: Recent Developements; Issue Brief, Brenda Branaman, etc. IB85213
* South Africa: Selected References, Sherry Shapiro 88-435 L

* South Africa: U.S. Policy After Sanctions; Issue Brief, Brenda Branaman IB87128
* Southern Africa: U.S. Regional Policy at a Crossroads?, Raymond Copson 85-201 F
* The United States and Southern Africa: A Review of, United Nations REsolutions and United States Voting Patterns, 1946-October 1985 Frankie King 86-21 F

Foreign Relations--Asia

* Afghanistan After Five Years: Status of the Conflict, the Afghan Resistance and the U.S. Role, Richard Cronin 85-20 F
* Afghanistan After the Soviet Withdrawal: Contenders for Power, Richard Cronin 89-146 F
* Afghanistan Peace Talks: An Annotated Chronology and Analysis of the United Nations-Sponsored Negotiations Richard Cronin 88-149 F
* Cambodia: U.S. Foreign Assistance Fact: Archived Issue Brief, Robert Sutter IB85153
* The Cambodia Crisis: Problems of a Settlement and Policy Dilemmas for the United States: Issue Brief, Robert Sutter IB89020
* China-U.S. Relations: Issues for Congress; Issue Brief, Kerry Dumbaugh IB84135
* China's Future: Archived Issue Brief, Kerry Dumbaugh IB85108
* China's Nuclear Weapons and Arms Control Policies;, Implications for the United States, Robert. G. Sutter 88-374 F
* Chinese Foreign Policy in Asia and the Sino-Soviet, Summit: Background, Prospects and Implications fo r U.S. Policy Robert G. Sutter 89-298 F
* Chinese Leadership Changes: Implications for the United States, Charles F. Steffens 86-131 F
* FSX Fighter Agreement With Japan: Issue Brief, Richard F. Grimmett IB89060
* The Gandhi Assassination: Implications for India and U.S. Indian Relations, Richard Cronin 84-790 F
* Hong Kong-U.S. Economic Relations: Some Views from, Hong Kong's Economic Elite, Kerry Dumbaugh 89-23 F
* Japan-U.S. Relations in the 1990s, Larry Niksch 89-264 F
* Japan-U.S. Relations: Issue Brief, Robert Sutter IB81026
* Korea and Congress, 1950-1990, Kerry Dumbaugh 85-171 F
* Korean Political Tensions: Implications for the United States; Issue Brief, Robert Sutter IB86071
* The Missing-In-Action (MIAs) and Vietnam-U.S. Relations: Issues for the United States, Robert Sutter 87-655 F
* Pakistan After Zia: Implications for Pakistan and U.S. Interest; Archived Issue Brief, Richard P. Cronin IB88096
* The Rajiv Gandhi Visit: Issues in the U.S. -India Relations, Richard Cronin 85-838 F
* Singapore-U.S. Economic Relations: Some views from, Singapore's Economic Elite, Richard Cronin 89-49 F
* South Korea and the United States: The Changing Relationship, Larry Niksch 87-522 F
* Sri Lanka's Gamble for Ethnic Peace: Archived Issue Brief, Stanley J. Heginbotham IB87183
* Taiwan: Recent Developments and Their Implications, for the United States Issue Brief, Robert G. Sutter IB87092
* Thai-U.S. Economic Relations: Some Views of Thailand's Economic Elite, Raymond J. Ahearn 89-60 F
* The United States, Pakistan the Soviet Threat to Southern Asia: Options for Congress, Richard Cronin 85-152 F
* United States Policy Toward Vietnam: A Summary Review of Its History, Larry Niksch, etc. 85-16 F
* The U.S. China Agreement for Nuclear Cooperation: Congressional Review; Archived Issue Brief, Mark Martel, etc. IB85203
* U.S.-Japan Agreement for Nuclear Cooperation: Monitoring Its Implementation; Issue Brief, Warren H. Donnelly IB85203
* Vietnam in Transition: Implications for U.S. Policy, Robert G. Sutter 89-177 F
* Vietnam-U.S. Relations: The Missing-in-Action (MIAs) and the Impasse Over Cambodia: Issue Brief, Robert G. Sutter IB87210
* Visit to South Korea and Taiwan, September 11-24, 1988 Trip Report, Larry Niksch 88-740 F

Foreign Relations--Eastern Europe

* Andropov and Reagan as Negotiators: Contexts and Styles in Contrast, Joseph Whelan 83-141 S
* Arms Control: Negotiations to Reduce INF Weapons; Archived Issue Brief, Paul Gallis IB856054
* Continuity and Change in Soviet Diplomacy and Negotiations under Gorbachev, Joseph G. Whelan 89-39 F
* Embassy Construction Controversies: Moscow and Washington; Issue Brief, Joel Woldman IB87232
* Gorbachev Reform Program After the 1988 Party Conference; Summary of a Roundtable Workshop, Francis T. Miko 89-130 F
* The Gorbachev Speech to the United Nations, New York, Dec. 7, 1988, Foreign Affairs and National Defense Division 88-776 F
* The Growing Role of Congress in the Soviet Diplomacy and Negotiations, Joseph G. Whelan 88-714 S

Currents Events and Homework

* Implications for U.S. Diplomacy in the U.S. Soviet Future:
Audio Brief, Joseph Whelan AB50173
* The Moscow Summit at First Glance: Audio Brief, Stuart Goldman,
etc. AB50168
* Nuclear Risk Reduction Centers; Archvied Issue Brief, Steven
Hildreth IB86142
* The Resumption of U.S.-Soviet Nuclear Arms Control, Talks: The
Soviet Point of View, Jeanette Voas 85-605 S
* The Role of Congress in Soviet Diplomacy and Negotiations:
Audio Brief, Joseph Whelan AB50173
* Soviet-American Relations in 1977: A Chronological, Summary and
Brief Analysis, William Cooper 79-60 S
* Soviet Diplomacy and Negotiating Behavior, 1979-1988:
Implications for U.S. Diplomacy in the Soviet- American Future
Joseph G. Whelan 88-674 F
* Soviet-U.S. Relations: A Briefing Book, Congressional Research
Service 89-342 F
* Soviet-U.S. Relations: The Lessons of Past Summit Meetings,
Francis T. Miko, etc. 85-1037 F
* Soviet-U.S. Summit Meetings Since the 1950s: Selected
References, Sherry Shapiro 87-912 L
* Thirty Years of U.S.=Soviet Summit Meetings; A Capsule Summary,
Stuart Goldman 85-1055 F
* U.S.-Soviet Relations in a Period of Summitry: Archived Issue
Brief, Stuart Goldman IB83066
* U.S.-Soviet Relations in the Gorbachev Era: Selected
References, Robert S. Kirk 89-51 L
* U.S.-Soviet Relations: Info Pack, IP233U
* U.S.-Soviet Relations: Selected References, 1986-1988,
Elizabeth S. Lane 88-155 L
* The 1987 Reagan-Gorbachev Summit Agenda, Francis T. Miko
87-925 F

Foreign Relations -- Latin America
* Arms Shipments to Iran: Archvied Issue Brief, Richard M. Preece
IB87022
* Belize: Country Background Report, Mark P. Sullivan 88-568 F
* The Boland Amendments: A Chronology of Congressional Action,
Joseph Maheady 87-833 A
* Central America, Selected References, 1985-1988, Valentin
Leskovsek 89-28 L
* Central America: U.S. Relations With Costa Rica, Guatemala, and
Honduras: Info Pack, IP352C
* Central American Compliance With the Augsut 5, 1987 Peace
Agreement as of November 5, 1987, Nina M. Serafino 87-916 F
* The Central American Peace Prospects: U.S. Interests and
Response: Issue Brief, Nina M. Serafino IB87200
* Chart of Unclassified Legislative Restrictions Regarding
Support for Military or Paramilitary Operat ions in Nicaragua,
1982-1986 Larry Eig 87-222 A
* Compilation of Selected Laws Relating to the National Security
Council, Arms Tranfers, Intelligence Activities, Aid to the
Contras, and Appropriations American Law Division 86-1028 A
* Congress and U.S. Policy Toward Nicaragua in 1987, Linda
Robinson 89-158 F
* Contra Aid: Analysis of Whether the National Security Council
(NSC) and the NSC Staff are an "agency, or Entity Involved in
Intelligence Activities" co Larry E. Eig 87-566 A
* Contra Aid, FT82-FY88: Summary and Chronology of Major
Congressional Action on Key Legislation Concerning U.S. Aid to
the Anti-Sandinista Guerrillas Nina M. Serafino 88-563 F
* Costa Rica: Country Background Report, Nina M. Serafino 88-577
F
* El Salvador Aid: Congressional Action, 1981-1986, on President
Reagan's Requests for Economic and Military Assistance for El
Salvador K. Larry Storrs 87-230 F
* El Salvador: Bibliography-in-Brief, 1986-1989, Robert S. Kirk
89-204 L
* El Salvador: Info Pack, IP121E
* El Salvador: U.S. Foreign Assistance Facts: Issue Brief, K.
Larry Storrs, etc. IB85113
* Grenada: Issues Concerning the Use of U.S. Forces;, Archived
Issue Brief, Janice Hanover IB83170
* Guatemala: Country Background Report, Maureen Taft-Morales
88-586 F
* Iran Arms Sales and Contra Funds: Summaries of Key, Legislative
provisions, Clyde R. Mark, etc. 87-13 F
* Kissinger Commission Implementation: Action by the, Congress
Through 1986 on the Recommendations of the National bipartisan
Commission on Central Ameri K. Larry Storrs 87-291 F
* Mexico-U.S. Relations: Issues for Congress; Issue Brief, K.
Larry Storrs, etc. IB86111
* The Monroe Doctrine and U.S. Policy Options for the Western
Hemisphere, Raphael Perl 84-225 F
* Narcotics Control and the Use of U.S. Military Personnel:
Operations in Boliva and Issues for Congress Raphael Perl 86-800
F
* Nicaragua: An Overview of US. Policy, 1979-1986, Mark P.

Sullivan 87-855 F
* Nicaragua: Bibliography-in-Brief, 1986-1987, Valentin
Leskovsek 87-382 L
* Nicaragua: Conditions and Issues for U.S. Policy: Issue Brief,
Nina Serafino IB82115
* Nicaragua v. United States: the International Court of Justic
Decision, David Hill Zafren 86-748 A
* Panama: Trade, Finance, and Proposed Economic Sanctions,
Glennon J. Harrison 88-188 E
* Panama's Political Crisis: Prospects and U.S. Policy Concerns:
Issue Brief, Mark P. Sullivan IB87230
* A Summary and Analysis of the Report of the national Bipartisan
"Kissinger" Commission on Centrla Am erica, January 1984 Richard
Cronin, etc. 84-39 F
* The United States and Cuba During the Reagan Administration,
Margaret Siliciano, etc. 85-988 F
* The United States and Cuba During the Reagan Administration,
Judith Levenfeld, etc. 85-989 F
* U.S. Assistance to Nicaraguan Guerillas: Issues for the
Congress; Archvied Issue Brief, Nina Serafino IB84139
* U.S. Sanctions and the State of the Panamanian Economy, Mark
Sullivan 88-578 F

Foreign Relations -- Middle East
* Arms Shipments to Iran: Archvied Issue Brief, Richard M. Preece
IB87022
* Compilation of Selected Laws Relating to the National Security
Council, Arms Transfers, Intelligence, Activities, Aid to the
Contras, and Appropriation American Law Division 86-1028 A
* Congress and the Iran-Contra Affair, Joel M. Woldman 88-765 F
* Insuring U.S.Interests in the Persian Gulf: Summary and
Proceedings of the Workshop Held on October 6, 1987 Congressional
Research Service, Gary Pagliano 88-725 F
* Iran Arms and Contra Funds: Selected Chronology of Events,
1979-1987, Richard Preece, etc. 86-190 F
* Iran Arms Sales adn Contra Funds: Summaries of Key, Legislative
Provisions, Clyde R. Mark, etc. 87-13 F
* The Iran/Contra Affair: Implications for the National Security
Adviser and the NSC Staff; Archived I ssue Brief Joel Woldman
IB87107
* Iran-Contra Affair: Organization Profiles, Heather B. Longton
87-625 F
* Iran-Contra Affair: Status of the Recommendations Contained in
the Joint Report of the House and Sen ate Selecte Committees Clyde
R. Mark 88-324 F
* Iran-Iraq War: Issue Brief, Richard Preece IB88060
* Israeli-American Relations: Issue Brief, Ellen B. Laipson
IB82008
* Israeli-Palestinian Conflict: Bibliography-in-Brief,
1982-1988, Robert Kirk 88-251 L
* Israel's Interest in Nuclear Power: Implications for U.S.
Non-Proliferation Policy: Archived Issue Brief Mark Martel, etc.
IB85166
* Israel's Participation in the International Atomic, energy
Agency and the 32nd IAEA General Conference: Archived Issue Brief
Warren Donnelly IB88072
* Issues in the Middle East: Audio Brief, Clyde Mark, etc.
AB50177
* Laws Implicated by Shipments of Military Materials, to Iran,
Raymond J. Celada 86-1005 A
* Lebanon: The Remaining U.S Hostages; Issue Brief, Clyde Mark
IB85183
* Libya: U.S. Relations: Archived Issue Brief, Raymond Copson,
etc. IB86040
* Middle East Peace Proposals: Issue Brief, Clyde Mark IB82127
* Palestine Liberation Organization Offices in the United States,
Clyde Mark IB87207
* Persian Gulf: Iran Air Flight 655: Archvied Issue Brief, Ellen
Laipson IB88080
* Persian Gulf: Selected References, Sherry Shapiro 88-533 L
* Persian Gulf: U.S. Military Operations; Archived Issue Brief,
Ronald O'Rourke IB87145
* Saudi Arabia: U.S. Missile Sale, 1986; Archived Issue Brief,
Clyde Mark IB86068
* Soviet Policy Toward Iran and the Stragetic Balance in
Southwest Asia, Stuard Goldman 87-592 F
* United States Interests in Lebanon, John Creed 85-873 F
* United States-Iraqi Relations, Richard Preece 86-142 F
* U.S. Policy Toward Iran: 1979-1986, Richard M. Preece 87-974 F

Foreign Relations -- Pacific Area
* Australia, New Zealand, and the Pacific Islands: Issues for
U.S. Policy; Issue Brief, Robert G. Sutter IB86158
* Oceania and the United States: A Primer, Robert Sutter 85-218 F
* Palau's Evolving Relationship With the United States:
Introduction and Chronology of Developments, Luella S.
Christopher 88-442 F

Foreign Relations-- Reagan Doctrine

* Angola: Issues for the United States; Archived Issue Brief, Raymond Copson, etc. IB81063
* Cambodia: U.S. Foreign Assistance Facts; Archived Issue Brief, Robert Sutter IB85153
* Mozambique: U.S. Foreign Assistance Facts; Archived Issue Brief, Raymond Copson IB85114
* Reagan Doctrine: Selected References, 1979-1988, Sherry Shapiro 88-395 L
* The Reagan Doctrine: U.S. Assistance to Anti-Marxist Guerrillas; Archived Issue Brief, Raymond W. Copson IB87005

Foreign Relations-- Western Europe

* European Community: Issues Raised by 1992 Integration,, Congressional Research Service 89-323 E
* The European Community: Its structure and Development, Martin E. Elling 88-620 F
* Greek-Turkish Relations: Beginning of a New Era?, Ellen Laipson 88-724 F
* The INF Treaty and Its Politcal-Military Implications for Western Europe, Hugh DeSantis 88-57 F
* The Netherlands Elections and the Cruise Missile Issue: Implications for the United States and for NATO Paul Gallis 86-27 F
* Soviet Policy in Nordic Europe: New focus on the Forgotten Flank?, Francis Miko 85-33 F
* The Strategic Defense Initiative and United States, Alliance Strategy, Paul Gallis, etc. 85-48 F
* United States Military Installations in Spain, Richard Grimmett 84-149 F
* The U.S. Commitment to Europe's Defense: A Review of Cost Issues and Estimates, Alice Maroni, etc. 85-211 F

Foreign Service (U.S. State Dept.)

* see Foreign Relations,

Foreign Trade

* see Competitiveness, East-West, Imports and Exports, Sanctions, Trade Agreements and Negotiations, Trade Policy, Agriculture-Foreign Trade, Foreign Aid,
* America in Economic Decline?, Alfred Reifman 89-182 S
* American Direct Investment Abroad: Effects on Trade, Jobs, and the Balance of Payments, James K. Jackson 88-546 E
* American Direct Investments Abroad: How Much are They Worth?, James K. Jackson 88-507 E
* Chronology of Important Events in International Economics, George Holliday 85-512 E
* The European Community: 1992 and Reciprocity, Glennon J. Harrison 89-227 E
* Foreign Assistance and Defense Transactions and Their Direct Effect on the U.S. Balance of Payments:, Summary of Statistical Data, 1960-1987 Vladimir N. Pregelj 88-545 E
* Selected Reports Available on Food and Agricultural Topics, Environment and Natural Resources Policy Division 89-244 ENR
* Trade and International Finance: An Alphabetical Microthearus of Terms Selected from the Legislative Indexing Vocabulary Shirley Loo 87-369 L
* The United States as a Debtor Nation and International Capital flows: Bibliography-in-Brief, 1984-19 87 Robert Kirk 88-11 L
* Will the Export Enhancement Program Survive?, Susan B. Epstein 89-139 ENR

Foreign Trade -- Competitiveness

* The American Response to Foreign Competition: Audio Brief, Mary Jane Bolle, etc. AB50180
* Automation and Small Business: Technological Development and the Competitiveness of U.S. Industry, Wendy Schacht, etc. 88-300 SPR
* Balancing the National Interest: U.S. National Security Export Controls and Global Economic Competit ion: A Summary of the National Academy of Sciences John P. Hardt, etc. 87-119 S
* Commercialization of Technology and Issues in the Competitiveness of Selected U.S. Industries: Semic onductors, Biotechnology, and Superconductors Lennard G. Kruger, etc. 88-486 SPR
* A Comparison of the Education Provisions in the Omnibus Trade Bill, H.R. 3, as Passed by the House a nd by the Senate Paul Irwin, etc. 87-634 EPW
* Competitiveness: Current Issues and Proposals; Info Pack, IP368C
* Cooperative R&D: Federal Efforts to Promote Industrial Competitiveness: Issue Brief, Wendy Schacht IB89056
* Corporate Tax Reform and International Competitiveness, Jane Gravelle 86-42 E
* Education Proposals in Trade Competitiveness Legislation: Archived Issue Brief, K. Forbis Jordan, etc. IB87108
* Education Provisions of the Trade Act of 1988, P.L . 100-418,

Paul Irwin, etc. 88-750 EPW
* The Export Enhancement Program One Year later, Susan Epstein 86-695 ENR
* Foreign Trade and U.S. Employment: Bibliography-in -Brief, 1983-1987, Robert Kirk 87-344 L
* High-Technology Trade: Bibliography-in-Brief, 1985-1988, Robert Kirk 88-572 L
* International Competitiveness and the Tax Reform Act of 1986, Jane Gravelle 87-428 E
* Japan's Steel Industry: Positioning for Survival, James K. Jackson 88-346 E
* Machine Tools: Imports and the U.S. Industry, Economy and Defense Industrial Base, Gary Guenther 86-762 E
* Major Federal Tax Provisions that Directly Affect International Trade and Investment, David Brumbaugh 86-764 E
* The Omnibus Trade and Competitiveness Act of 1988 (P.L. 100-418); An Analysis of the Major Trade Provisions Economics Division 88-390 E
* The Omnibus Trade and Competitiveness Act: Technology Development Provisions, Wendy Schacht 89-93 SPR
* Research and Development Funding: FY 1990: Issue Brief, Science Policy Research Division IB89040
* Research and Development Funding: FY 89: Archived Issue Brief, Michael Davey IB88040
* Science, Technology, and the International Competitiveness of American Industry: Selected References , 1985-1988 B. F. Mangan 88-587 L
* Semiconductor Devices: The Changing Competitiveness of U.S. Merchant Producers, 1977-87, Gary Guenther 88-191 E
* Semiconductor Manufacturing Technology Proposal: SEMATECH: Issue Brief, Glenn J. McLoughlin IB87212
* Semiconductors: Issues Confronting the Industry: Bibliography-in-Brief, 1985-1988, Karen Alderman 88-445 L
* State Allotments for Education programs under H.R., 3, the Omnibus Trade Bill of 1987, as Passed by t he house and The Senate Paul Irwin, etc. 87-683 EPW
* Steel Imports of Hot Rolled Sheet from Korea in the Absence of Import Restraints: Hypothetical Effec ts on West Coast Steel Producers David J. Cantor 88-678 E
* Taxation of U.S. Investment Abroad: Archvied Issue, Brief, David Brumbaugh IB87060
* Technological Advancement and the Competitiveness of Selected U.S. Industries: Issues for Consderati on Wendy Schacht, etc. 87-345 SPR
* Technological Advancement and U.S. Industrial Competitiveness, Wendy Schacht IB87053
* Trade, Technology, and Competitiveness: Issue Brief, Wendy Schacht IB87053
* U.S. Economic Policy in an International Context: U.S. Wages and Unit Labor Costs in a World Economy, Richard Belous 84-172 E
* U.S. Export Control Policy and Competitiveness: Proceedings of the CRS Symposium, John P. Hardt, etc. 87-388 S
* U.S. Jewelry Manufacturing, International Competitiveness, and H.R. 3, Bernard Gelb 87-875 E
* The U.S. Semiconductor Industry and the SEMATECH Proposal, Gelnn McLoughlin, etc. 87-354 SPR
* Vocational Education and Proposals for Trade Competitiveness, Paul Irwin 87-340 EPW
* Wage Rates and Exchange Rates, Linda LeGrande 88-252 E

Foreign Trade -- East-West

* Balancing the National Interest: U.S. National Security Export Controls, and Global Economic Competition: A Summary of the National Academy of Science John P. Hardt, etc. 87-119 S
* A Congressional Guide for Economic Negotiations With the Soviet Union, John P. Hardt, etc. 88-19 S
* Export Control Reform in the 100th Congress: A Comparison of Selected Provisions of H.R. 3 and S. 14 09 Glennon Harrison 87-529 E
* Export Controls: Issue Brief, George Holliday, etc. IB87122
* Hong Kong-U.S. Economic Relations: Some Views from, Hong Kong's Economic Elite, Kerry Dumbaugh 89-23 F
* Most-Favored-Nation Policy Toward Communist Countries: Archived Issue Brief, Vladimir N. Pregelj IB74139
* Potential Economic Effects of Granting Most-Favored-National Treatment to the Soviet Union, George Holliday 85-886 E
* Singapore-U.S. Economic Relations: Some Views from, Singapore's Economic Elite, Richard Cronin 89-49 F
* Thai-U.S. Economic Relations: Some Views of Thailand's Economic Elite, Raymond Ahearn 89-60 F
* The Toshiba/Kongsberg Case: Proposals to Expand U. S. Penalties for Illegal Exports of High Technology goods Glennon Harrison 87-988 F
* Toshiba-Kongsberg Technology Diversion: Issues for, Congress; Archived Issue Brief, Raymond Ahearn, etc. IB87184
* U.S. Export Control Policy and Competitiveness: Proceedings of the CRS Symposium, John P. Hardt, etc. 87-388 S
* U.S. Soviet Commercial Relations in a Period of Negotiation:

Currents Events and Homework

Archived Issue Brief, John Hardt IB88065
* U.S. Soviet Relations in the Gorbachev Era: Selected
References, Robert Kirk 89-51 L
* U.S. Taiwan Economic Relations: Views of Some Members of the
Taiwan Economic Elite, Alren Wilson 89-21 E
* U.S. Trade Relations With the Soviet Union Since World War II: A
Chronology, Vladimir N. Pregelj 89-241 E
* U.S.-U.S.S.R. Commercial Relations: Issues in East -West Trade:
Archived Issue Brief, John Hardt, etc. IB86020

Foreign Trade -- Imports and Exports
* Agricultural Exports: Overview and Selected Data, Donna Vogt
88-403 ENR
* Agricultural Imports: What, from Whom, Why, How Much, Jasper
Womach 88-361 ENR
* Agriculture in the GATT: After the Midterm Review; Issue Brief,
Charles Hanrahan IB89027
* Alaskan Oil Exports; Archvied Issue Brief, Gary Pagliano
IB84085
* America's Steel Industry: Modernizing to Compete, David Cantor
84-786 E
* Brazil: Selected Foreign Trade Data, Rawle O. King 88-320 E
* Caribbean Apparel Exports: Greater Access to the U S. Market,
Edward B. Rappaport 88-128 E
* Cotton Trade: The United States and Foreign Competition, Susan
Epstein 87-557 ENR
* Customs Ruling on Multipurpose Vehicles: Archived Issue Brief,
Gwenell Bass IB89053
* Digital Audio Recorder Act of 1987-- Analysis of H .R. 1384 and
S. 506 With Policy Alternatives, David Hack 87-698 SPR
* Disposition of Import Relief Cases under Section 201 of the
Trade Act of 1974 Since 1981: A Survey, Vladimir Pregelj 88-207 E
* The Dollar and the Trade Deficit: An Updated on Recent Trends,
Forecasts;, and Policy Options, Craig K. Elwell 88-693 E
* The Dollar and the Trade Deficit: What's to be Done?, Craig
Elwell, etc. 88-430 E
* The Dollar, the Trade Deficit, and the Economy, G. Thomas
Woodward 88-722 E
* The Dollar, the trade Deficit, and the U.S. Economy: Audio
Brief, William Cooper, etc. AB50174
* Drawback of Sugar Duties and Fees: Lengthening the Time
Allowance, Jasper Womach 87-742 ENR
* Employment and Output Effects of the Extension of Japan's
Voluntary Automobile Export Restraints on the U.S. Automobile and
Steel Industries Gwenell Bass 85-710 E
* Foreign Sourcing by the U.S. Automobile Industry, Kevin
Flaherty 85-1052 E
* Foreign-Trade Zones and the U.S. Automobile Industry, Gwenell
L. Bass, etc 88-659 E
* The "Gephardt Amendment": A Comparison to "Super 301" in the
Senate Trade Bill, Lenore Sek 88-206 E
* The Gray Market for Imported Automobiles, R. Kevin Flaherty
85-651 E
* Implementation of the President's Steel Program: Implications
for Output and Employment of the Steel and Steel-Related
Industries David J. Cantor 86-518 E
* Import Penetration During the Eighties: Analtomy of the Data,
Bernard A. Gelb 86-876 E
* Japan's automobile Industry and Barriers to Purchases of U.S.
Cars, Dick K. Nanto, etc. 87-793 E
* Kangaroo Management Controversy, Malcolm M. Simmons 88-468 ENR
* Machine Tools: Imports and the U.S. Industry, Economy and
Defense Industrial Base, Gale Guenther 86-762 E
* Manufactured Exports and Regional Economic Growth in the United
States, 19877 to 1983: A Preliminary, Assessment Gary Guenther
86-855 E
* Market Access in Japan: The U.S. Experience, Raymond Ahearn
85-37 E
* Offshore Manufacturing by U.S. Corporations: Selected
Bibliography, With Introductory Readings, Robert Kirk 86-834 L
* The "Oil Import Bill" Of the United States, 1945-1987: A
Historical Record of U.S Merchandise Trade and Petroleum With
Related Balances Dario Scuka 88-107 E
* Oil Import Fees (Taxes) for Deficit Reduction: Revenue and
Economic Effects: Issue Brief, Salvatore Lazzari IB87189
* Oil Import Tax: Some General Economic Effects, Bernard Gelb
87-259 E
* Oil Import Taxes: An Economic Analysis of S. 694, the Economic
Security Act of 1987, Salvatore Lazzari 87-779 E
* Oil Import Taxes: Revenue and Economic Effects, Bernard Gelb,
etc. 86-572 E
* Oil Imports from OPEC: Recent and Projected Trends, Bernard
Gelb 88-558 E
* Petroleum in the United States: Selected Data Focused on the Oil
Import Tax Issue, Bernard Gelb 86-1054 E
* Selected Data on U.S. Agricultural High-Valued Product Exports,
Susan Epstein 87-471 ENR
* South Korea and Taiwan: Expanding Trade Ties With the United

States; Issue Brief, William Cooper IB86151
* Status of the U.S. commercial Fishing Industry: Summary of
Information, Eugene Buck 88-444 ENR
* Steel Imports: Are the VRA Countries Filling Their, Quota,
David J. Cantor 89-81 E
* Steel Imports: Arguments for and Against Extension, of the
President's Steel Program: Issue Brief, David J. Cantor IB88109
* Steel Prices and Import Restraints, David Cantor 88-204 E
* Sugar Policy: Current Issues; Issue Brief, Jasper Womach
IB88091
* Summary of Information About Foreign Trade by States Available
from Federal and Non-Federal Sources, Dario Scuka 84-588 E
* Tariff Items 807.00 and 806.30 and the Mexican Maquiladoras,
Patricia Wertman 87-500 E
* "The Applicability of the Export Proviso of the Federal Food,
Drug and Cosmetic Act to "New Drugs"", Cathy Gilmore 85-848 A
* Trade and Current Account Balances: Statistics: Archived Issue
Brief, Glennon J. Harrison IB87112
* Trade Deficits and the Dollar: Bibliography-in-Brief,
1984-1987, Robert Kirk 87-888 L
* Trade in Telecommunications Products and Services:,
Legislation in the 100th Congress, Glennon Harrison 87-844 E
* Trade Issues and Trade Deficits: Background, Statistics, adn
Proposed Legislation; Info Pack, IP263T
* Trade of the Seventeen Highly Indebted Countries: A Brief
Overview, Patricia Wertman, etc. 88-521 E
* United States Merchandise Trade and Balances With Major Trading
Partners, 1985, Dario Scuka 88-81 E
* United States Merchandise Trade and Trade Balances, With W.
Germany, 1960-1987, Dario Scuka 88-117 E
* United States Merchandise Trade and Trade Balances , 1945-1987,
Dario Scuka 88-104 E
* U.S. Automobile Industry: Issues and Statistics, Gwenell L.
Bass 85-792 E
* U.S. Commercial Relations With the European Community, George
D. Holliday 85-32 E
* U.S. Economic Policy in an International Context: The U.S.
Automobile Industry in International Comp etition: Voluntary
Export Restraints and Domestic Dick K. Nanto 85-34 E
* U.S. Exports of Solid Wood Products, Ross Gorte 87-208 ENR
* U.S. Jewelry Manufactuing International Competitiveness and
H.R. 3, Bernard A. Gelb 87-875 E
* U.S. Trade and Payments Balances: What Do They Mean ?, Arlene
Wilson 85-26 E
* The U.S. Trade Deficit: Causes, Consequences and Cures, Craig
Elwell, etc. 86-116 E
* U.S. Wood Exports to the Pacific Rim, Ross Gorte 88-548 ENR

Foreign Trade -- Sanctions
* Ban on Imports from Iran: Economic Effect on the United States,
Bernard A. Gelb 88-6 E
* Panama: Trade, Finanace, and Proposed Economic Sanctions,
Glennon Harrison 88-188 E
* The Reagan Administration Sanctions Against South Africa: Their
Potential Economic Impact, William Cooper 85-955 E
* Restrictions on U.S. Trade With Cuba: A Chronology, of Major
Actions and Present Status, Vladimir N. Pregelj 86-909 E
* Sanctions Against South Africa: Activities of the 99th
Congress, Brenda Branaman 87-200 F
* Sanctions Against South Africa: Impact on the United States:
Issue Brief, William Cooper IB87198
* Seizure of Foreign Vessels in United States Ports, Daniel Hill
Zafren 87-760 A
* South Africa: International Sanctions; Archived Issue Brief,
Jeanne S. Affelder, etc. IB86157
* South Africa: Legislation of the 99th Congress, Brenda
Branaman 85-799 F
* South Africa-U.S. Economic ties: Emerging Issues; Archvied
Issue Brief, William Cooper IB85117
* South Africa: U.S. Policy After Sanctions; Issue Brief, Brenda
Branaman IB87128
* Southern Africa: U.S. Foreign Assistance; Issue Brief, Raymond
W. Copson IB87152
* Tax Sanctions and U.S. Investment in South Africa, David
Brumbaugh 88-112 E
* U.S. Economic Sanctions Imposd Against Specific Foreign
Countries 1979 to the Present, Theodor W. Galdi, etc. 88-612 F
* U.S.-European Community Trade Dispute Over Meat Containing
Growth Hormones, Donna Vogt 89-6 ENR
* U.S. Foreign Trade Sanctions Imposed for Foreign Policy Reasons
in Force as of April 10, 1988, Vladimir Pregelj 88-301 E
* U.S. Sanctions and the State of the Panamanian Economy, Mark
Sullivan 88-578 F
* The U.S. Trade Embargo Against Nicaragua After Two -and-a-Half
Years, Glennon J. Harrison 87-870 E

Foreign Trade -- Trade Agreements and Negotiations

* Agriculture in the U.S.-Canada Free Trade Agreement, Charles Hanrahan, etc. 88-363 ENR
* Automotive Products Trade With Canada and the U.S. -Canada Free Trade Area Agreement, Vladimir Pregelj 88-122 E
* The Canada-U.S. Free Trade Agreement: A Selected Bibliography, 1985-1988, Felix Chin 88-388 L
* Canada-U.S. Free Trade Agreement; Issue Brief, Arlene Wilson IB87173
* Canada-U.S. Free Trade Area Agreement: Info Pack, IP395C
* Canada-U.S. Free Trade Negotiations: Archvied Issue Brief, Raymond Ahearn IB85215
* Canadian Electricity: The U.S. Market and the Free, Trade Agreement, Amy Abel 88-427 ENR
* The Canadian Free Trade Agreement and the Textile and Apparel Industries, Edward Rappaport 87-979 E
* A Congressional Guide for Economic Negotiations With the Soviet Union, John P. Hardt, etc. 88-19 S
* Dispute Settlement and the General Agreement on tariffs and Trade, Raymond Ahearn 85-680 E
* The Effect of the Canada-U.S. Free Trade Agreement, on U.S. Industries, Economics Division 88-506 E
* The Europe 1992 Plan: Science and Technology Issues, Science and Policy Research Division 89-178 SPR
* European Community: Issues Raised by 1992 Integration,, Congressional Research Service 89-323 E
* European Community: The 1992 Plan; Info Pack, IP408E
* The European Community: 1992 and Reciprocity, Glennon Harrison 89-227 E
* European Community: 1992 Plan for Economic Integration; Issue Brief, Glennon Harrison IB89043
* The European Community's 1992 Plan: An Overview of the Proposed "Single Market", Glennon Harrison 88-623 E
* The European Community's 1992 Plan: Bibliography-in-Brief, 1986-1988, Robert Howe 88-754 L
* Japan's Response to the 1988 Omnibus Trade Bill, Dick Nanto 89-133
* The MOSS Talks: Success or Failure?, Patricia Wertman 85-1129 E
* Negotiating Authority for the Uruguay Round of Multilateral Trade Negotiations, Jeanne Jagelski 87-103 A
* Proceedings of the CRS Workshop on Canada-U.S. Free-Trade Agreement: How Will It Affect the United States? Arlene Wilson 88-356 E
* Selected Nonferrous Mineral Subsidies and the U.S. -Canada Free Trade Agreement, Marc Humphries 88-774 ENR
* The Smoot-Hawley Tariff Act of 1930: Its Effects on U.S. Trade and Its Role in the Great Depression of 1929-1933 George Holliday, etc. 87-993 E
* Taiwan-U.S. Free Trade Area: Economic Effects and Related Issues, William Cooper 89-96 E
* Trade Negotiations: The Uruguay Round; Issue Brief, Lenore Sek IB86147
* U.S.-Canada Free Trade Agreement: International Implications, Raymond Ahearn, etc. 88-249 F
* U.S.-Canada Free Trade Agreement: States Affected by Major Provisions, Lenore Sek 88-347 E
* U.S.-Canada Trade: An Overview, Lenore Sek 88-331 E

Foreign Trade -- Trade Policy

* Agricultural Trade Legislation in the 100th Congress: A Comparison of Selected Provisions of H.R. 3 and S. 1420 Charles Hanrahan, etc. 87-677 ENR
* Auctioning Import Quotas, Lenore Sek 87-669 E
* Background Information on Casein, Geoffrey S. Becker 87-505 ENR
* "Buy America" Regulations: Effects on Surface Transportation, John Fischer 86-78 E
* A Comparison of the Education Provisions in the Omnibus Trade Bill, H.R. 3, as Passed by the House and by the Senate Paul Irwin, etc. 87-634 EPW
* Customs Service User Fees, Frederick M. Kaiser 87-676 GOV
* Dispute Settlement Provisions in the United States -Canada Free Trade Agreement, Jeanne Jagelski, etc. 88-603 A
* Exports Credits: Proposals to Combat the Use by Foreign Governments of Mixed Credits, George Holliday 85-1061 E
* Export-Import Bank Financial Issues; Archived Issue Brief, James Jackson IB88013
* Export-Import Bank: Financing Problems and Issues, James K. Jackson 88-61 E
* Exports of High Valued Agricultural Products: Trends and Issues, Susan Epstein, etc. 87-636 ENR
* Foreign Trade and U.S. Employment: Bibliography in Brief, 1983-1987, Robert Kirk 87-344 L
* Free Trade and Protection: Selected Bibliography, 1983-1987, With Introductory Readings, Robert Kirk 87-734 L
* Free Trade Versus Protectionism: An Analysis of the Issue, Raymond Ahearn 78-32 E
* The "Gephardt Amendment": A Comparison to "Super 301" in the Senate Trade Bill, Lenore Sek 88-206 E

* Import Relief: A Brief Historical Survey of Presential Discretion in Provising a Remedy in Escape Clause/Import Relief Investigations Vladimir N. Pregelj 87-542 E
* Japan Briefing Book., Congressional Research Service 87-323 E
* Japan-South Korea Economic Relations: South Korea' s Approach to the "Japan Problem", Dick Nanto 87-953 E
* Japan-United States Economic Relations: Views of Japan's Economic Decisionmakers, Dick Nanto 86-52 E
* Japan-U.S. Economic Relations; Bibliography-in-Brief 1986-1987, Robert Kirk 87-45 L
* Japan-U.S. Economic Relations: Cooperation or Confrontation? Issue Brief, William Cooper IB87158
* Japan-U.S. Relations: Issue Brief, Robert Sutter IB81026
* Japan-U.S. Trade: An Overview, William Cooper 88-127 E
* Japan-U.S. Trade and Economic Relations: Info Pack, IP201J
* Japan-U.S. Trade Relations: Archived Issue Brief, Raymond Ahearn IB81011
* Japan's High Prices: Some Causes and Their Relationship to Trade Policy, Dick K. Nanto 88-243 E
* Most-Favored-Nation Treatment of Foreign Trading Partners by the United States: A Summary, Vladimir Pregelj 87-211 E
* Negotiating Authority for the Uruguay Round of Multilateral Trade Negotiations, Jeanne Jagelski 87-103 A
* The Omnibus Trade and Competitiveness Act of 1988(P.L. 100-418): An Analysis of the Major Trade Prov isions Economics Division 88-390 E
* The President's Steel Program: Background and Implementation, David J. Cantor 86-658 E
* Proceedings of the CRS Symposium on U.S. Trade: Policy Issues Confronting the 100th Congress, William Cooper 87-267 E
* Protectionist Legislation in 1985, Raymond Ahearn, etc. 86-632 E
* Protectionist Policies of Major U.S. Trading Partners, Raymond J. Ahearn 86-655 E
* Restricting Lamb Imports: A Policy Issue, Jasper Womach 87-642 ENR
* Steel Imports from Canada and the President's Steel Program: Archived Issue Brief, David Cantor IB87197
* Steel Imports: Is the President's Steel Program Working?; Archived Issue Brief, David J. Cantor IB86141
* A Survey of U.S. International Economic Policy and Problems, Alfred Reifman 88-666 S
* Telecommunications Trade: market Access Legislation; Archvied Issue Brief, Raymond Ahearn, etc. IB85206
* Textile and Apparel Trade Protection: Issue Brief, Edward B. Rappaport IB87109
* Textile Trade Controls: A Comparison of Bills in the 99th Congress, Edward Rappaport 87-607 E
* Trade: Issue Brief, Arlene Wilson, etc. IB87003
* Trade Remedies Available to the United States under International Agreements and Corresponding Domestic Laws Vladimir N. Pregelj 85-1008 E
* Trade Remedy Reform, Raymond J. Ahearn 87-117 E
* Trade, Technology, and Competitiveness: Issue Brief, Wendy Schacht IB87053
* Unfair Foreign Trade Practices: Section 301 of the, Foreign Trade Act of 1974: Archived Issue Brief, Lenore Sek IB88051
* Unfair Foreign Trade Practices: Section 301 of the, Trade Act of 1974, Lenore Sek 87-960 E
* United States-Mexican Trade Relations: Present Problems, Future Prospects, Patricia Wertman 85-139 E
* U.S. Agricultural Trade Opportunities With Pacific, Rim Nations, Robert M. Goldstein 88-755 ENR
* The U.S.-Canada Pork Dispute, Susan Epstein 89-311 ENR
* U.S. Export Development Assistance for Manufactured Goods: Alternative Approaches, William Cooper 86-47 E
* U.S. Intellectural Property Rights and Trade, Lenore Sek 86-383 E
* U.S.-Japanese Agricultural Trade Relations: Selected Information, Donna Vogt 88-159 ENR
* U.S.-South Korean Economic Relations: Views of Some Members of the Korean Economic Elite, William H. Cooper 88-656 E
* U.S. Trade Policy Towards Japan: Where Do We Go from Here?, William Cooper 89-307 E
* Vocational Education and Proposals for Trade Competitiveness, Paul Irwin 87-340 EPW

Forests and Forestry

* Acid Rain, Air Pollution, and Forest Decline: Issue Brief, Adela Backlei IB86031
* Air Pollution-Induced Stress to Forest Ecosystems- An Overview of Forest Damage, Adela Backlei, etc. 86-560 ENR
* The Alaska National Interest Lands Conservation Act: Legislative History of the Tongass Timber Provi sions Adela Backlei, etc. 87-434 ENR
* Arctic Resources Controversy: Issue Brief, M. Lynne Corn, etc. IB89058
* Debt-for-Nature Swaps in Developing countries: An Overview of

Currents Events and Homework

Recent Conservation Efforts, Betsy Cody 88-647 ENR
* Dominant Use Management in the National Forest system, Ross Gorte 86-714 ENR
* Exempting Forest Products Shipments from the Jones Act Requirements, Ross W. Gorte 87-887 ENR
* Federal land Management Transfers Proposed Between, Bureau of Land Management and Forest Service: Arc hived Issue Brief Ross Gorte, etc. IB85101
* Federal Timber Sales, John Beuter 85-96 ENR
* The Forest Service Budget: Trust Funds and Special, Accounts, Ross Gorte, etc. 89-75 ENR
* Forest Service Land and Resource Planning: A Chronology of Laws, Adela Backlei 86-986 ENR
* The Forest Service's 1980 RPA Program: Comparison With Accomplishments, Ross Gorte 86-902 ENR
* Future U.S. Forestry Issues, Ross W. Gorte 87-854 ENR
* History of Release Language in Wilderness Legislation, 1979-1984, Ross Gorte 87-559 ENR
* International Environement: Overview of Major Issues; Issue Brief, Mary Tiemann, etc. IB89057
* The Major Federal Land Management Agencies: Management of Our Nation's Lands and Resources, Adela Backlei, etc. 87-22 ENR
* Modifying BLM Timber Contracts: An Anlysis of a Recept Proposal, Ross Gorte 87-757 ENR
* National Forest Receipts: Sources and Dispositions, Ross Gorte 89-284 ENR
* Natural Resources Conservation and Developments in, Brazil: An Overview and Related Issues, Russell Hawkins 84-802 ENR
* An Overview of Federal Tax Policies Encouraging Do nations of Conservation Easements to Preserve Natural Areas Richard Dunford 84-48 ENR
* Ozone and Plants: A Status Report, Jeffrey A. Zinn, etc. 87-496 ENR
* Policy Analysis of the Proposed Revision of the Forest Service Administrative Appeals Regulations: Public Input, Timing, and Delays Ross W. Gore 88-483 ENR
* The Renewable Resources Extension Act, Adela Backlei 86-821 ENR
* Special Management Areas in the National Forest System, Ross Gorete 88-571 ENR
* Spotted Owls and the Timber Industry: Issue Brief, M. Lynne Corn IB89077
* Summary of Recent Reports on Forest Service Timber Sale Costs and Revenues, Ross Gorte 84-799 ENR
* Tongass National forest Issues: Issue Brief, Adela Backeil IB89055
* Tropical Deforestation; Info Pack, IP416T
* Tropical Deforestation: International Implications ; Issue Brief, Susan R. Fletcher IB89010
* Tropical Deforestation: The International Tropical, Timber Agreement, Ross Gorte 87-795 ENR
* Tropical Forests: Bibliography-in-Brief, 1985-1988, Adrienne C. Boniface 88-274 L
* U.S. Exports of Solid Wood Products, Ross Gorte 87-208 ENR
* U.S. Wood Exports to the Pacifc Rim, Ross Gorte 88-548 ENR
* Wilderness: Additions to the National Wilderness Preservation System; Archvied Issue Brief, Ross Gorte IB83151
* Wilderness Areas and Federal Water rights, Pamela Baldwin 89-11 A
* Wilderness: Overview and Statistics, Ross G. Gorte 88-16 ENR

Fossil Fuels

* see Coal, Gasoline, Natural Gas, Petroleum, and Energy,
* Controlling Carbon Dioxide Emissions, Amy Abel, etc. 89-157 ENR
* Energy Impacts: Archived Issue Brief, Duane Thompson, etc. IB87021
* Public Utilities Holding Company Act of 1935: Is This the Time for reform: Issue Brief, Amy Abel IB89052
* Royalty Rates for Coal, Oil and Gas Production on Federally Administered Lands, Adela Backiel, etc. 83-595 S

Fossil Fuels -- Coals

* The Abandoned Mine Land Reclamation Program: Too Little, Too Late, to Complete, Duane Thompson 86-730 ENR
* Acid Rain Control and Clean Coal Technology: An Analysis of Title II of S. 1894, Larry Parker 88-266 ENR
* Acid Rain Control: What Is a 10 Million Ton S02 Reduction?, Larry B. Parker, etc. 89-243 ENR
* Acid Rain, DOEs Clean Coal Technology Program, and, the Lewis-Davis Report: Squaring a Circle?, Larry B. Parker 87-60 ENR
* Coal Slurry Pipelines: Archived Issue Brief, Robert Bamberger IB83008
* Department of Energy's Clean Coal technology Program: Demonstrating Better Ways to Use American's Black Gold; Archived Issue Brief Paul F. Rothberg IB87093
* DOE's Clean Coal Technology Program: Demonstrating, Better Ways to Use America's Black Gold, Paul Rothberg 87-393 SPR

* DOE's Clean Coal Technology Program: Goals and Funding; Issue Brief, Larry Parker IB88071
* House Acid Rain Bills in the 101st Congress: Comparison of the Major Provisions of H.R. 144 and H.R., 1470 Larry Parker, etc. 89-226 ENR
* Royalties on Federal Coal: Issues in the Treatment, of Royalty Payments and Externally-Realted Taxes, Salvatore Lazzari, etc. 88-250 E

Fossil Fuels -- Gasoline

* The Alaskan Oil Spill and Gasoline Prices, Lawrence C. Kumins 89-250 ENR
* Automobile Fuel Economy Standards: Another Roll Back? Archived Issue Brief, Robert Bamberger IB88046
* Clean Air Act: Gasoline Vapor Recovery; Archived Issue Brief, David E. Gushee IB87029
* Emissions Impact of Oxygenated (Alcohol/Gasoline) Fuels, David Gushee 87-436 S
* Gasoline Excise Tax: Economic Impacts of an Increase; Issue Brief, Bernard A. Gelb, etc. IB87078
* Gasoline: Lead Phasedown: Archived Mini Brief, Robert Bamberger IB83220
* Oil Price Implications: Reshuffling Energy Policy? : Archived Issue Brief, Robert Bamberger, etc. IB86146

Fossil Fuels -- Natural Gas

* Domestic Natural Gas production: Issue Brief, Joseph Riva IB89009
* The Enigma of Natural Gas, Joseph P. Riva 88-561 SPR
* Natural Gas: Background, Perspectives, and Issues:, Archived Issue Brief, Larry Kumins, etc. IB86011
* Natural Gas Pipelines: Federal Policy Issues in Contract Carriage, Donald Dulchinos 86-74 S
* Natural Gas Policy: Archived Issue Brief, Lawrence Kumin IB81020
* Underground Storage of Natural Gas, James E. Mielke, etc. 88-187 SPR

Fossil Fuels -- Petroleum

* After the Exxon Valdez Spill: Oil Pollution Liability and Compensation Legislation, Martin R. Lee 89-266 ENR
* Alaskan Oil Exports: Archived Issue Brief, Gary Pagliano IB84085
* Applicability of Alaska State Laws to Oil and Gas Development in the Arctic National Wildlife Refuge, Pamela Baldwin 88-420 A
* Arctic National Wildlife Refuge: Bibliography-in-Brief, Adrienne C. Grenfell 88-30 L
* The Arctic Natinal Wildlife Refuge: Major Oil Development or Wilderness?, Congressional Research Service 88-161 ENR
* The Arctic National Wildlife Refuge: Oil, Gas, and, Wildlife: Archived Issue Brief, Lynne Corn, etc. IB87026
* Arctic Resources Controversy: A Comparison of H.R., 3601 and S. 2214, Environment and Natural Resources Policy Division 88-380 ENR
* Arctic Resources Controversy: Issue Brief, M. Lynne Corn, etc. IB89058
* Aspects of the Mobilization of the Petroleum Industry in World War II and the Korean War, Robert Bamberger 84-773 ENR
* Brazilian Petroleum Status, Joseph P. Riva 89-328 SPR
* Comparison of United States and United Kingdom Offshore Oil and Gas Leasing and Development Systems, Malcolm M. Simmons 86-1011 ENR
* Declining Bonus Values in Outer Continental Shelf, Oil and Gas Lease Sales, Malcolm Simmons 85-871 ENR
* Disruption of Oil Supply from the Persian Gulf: Near-Term U.S. Vulnerability (Winter 1987/88), Clyde R. Mark, etc. 87-863 ENR
* Domestic Oil Production under Conditions of Continued Low Drilling Activity: Issue Brief, Joseph R. Riva, jr. IB87068
* Energy Security: Issue Brief, Carl E. Behrens IB89006
* Energy Tax Options to Increase Federal Revenue, Salvatore Lazzari 87-539 E
* Enhanced Oil Recovery Methods, Joseph Riva 87-827 SPR
* Environmental Effects of Energy Development in the, Arctic National Wildlife Refuge: A Critique of the Final Legislative Environmental Impact Statement M. Lynne Corn, etc. 87-490 ENR
* The Exxon Valdez Oil Spill: Issue Brief, Martin R. Lee, etc. IB89075
* Federal Regulation of Used Oil, Mark Reisch 86-747 ENR
* The Financial Impact of Oil Price Behavior on International Development and Trade: Transational Oil Companies and Persian Gulf Oil Exporters; Report Clyde R. Mark, etc. 86-903 F
* A History of Federal Energy Tax Policy: Conventional as Compared to Renewable and Nonconventional Energy Resources Salvatore Lazzari 88-455 E
* Mexican Petroleum, Joseph Riva 83-178 SPR
* The NATO Allies, Japan, and the Persian Gulf, Paul Gallis 84-184 F

* North African Petroleum, Joseph Riva 84-216 SPR
* Northwest European Region Petroleum (Including the, North Sea), Joseph Riva 85-187 SPR
* Oil Companies and the Acquisition of Federal Petroleum Leases, John J. Schanz 88-213 S
* Oil Companies and the Development of the Arctic National Wildlife Refuge, John J. Schanz 88-106 S
* Oil from the Persian Gulf: Production, Disposition , and Transportation; Archived Issue Brief, Robert Bamberger, etc. IB88063
* The "Oil Import Bill" of the United States, 1945-1987: A Historical Record of U.S. Merchandise Trade, and Petroleum With Related Blances Dario Scuka 88-107 E
* Oil Import Fees (Taxes) for Deficit Reduction: Revenue and Economic Effects; Issue Brief, Salvatore Lazzari IB87189
* Oil Import Tax: Some General Economic Effects, Bernard Gelb 87-259 E
* Oil Import Taxes: An Economic Analysis of S. 694, the Economic Security Act of 1987, Salvatore Lazzari 87-779 E
* Oil Imports from OPEC: Recent and Project Trends, Bernard Gelb 88-558 E
* Oil Overcharge Restitution: Background and Data, Bernard Gelb 88-287 E
* Oil Pollution Liability and Compensation Legislation After the Exxon Valdez Oil Spill: Issue Brief, Martin R Lee IB89082
* Oil Price Behavior: Implications for the Soviet Union: Report of the CRS Workshop, June 26, 1986, John P. Hardt, etc. 86-886 S
* Oil Price Decreases: Illustrative Effects on U.S. Oil Use, Production, and Imports, Bernard Gelb 86-599 E
* Oil Price Implications: Reshuffling Energy Policy: ? Archived Issue Brief, Robert Bamberger, etc. IB86146
* Oil Prospect Profitability in the United States: Estimated Expectation in 1972, 1981, 1985, and 1986, Bernard Gelb, etc. 87-38 E
* Oil Royalty Trusts, Carolyn K. Brancato 84-575 E
* Oil Storage Tanks: Construction and Testing Issues, Since the Ashland Oil Spill: Issue Brief, Fred J. Sissine IB88015
* Onshore Oil and Gas Resources on Federal Lands: Evaluating the Current Leasing System: Archived Issu e Brief Adela Backiel, etc. IB87077
* Outer Continental Shelf Leasing and Development: Issue Brief, Malcolm M. Simmons, etc. IB89028
* The Outlook for U.S. energy Supplies and the Arctic National Wildlife Refuge Decision, John Schanz 88-73 S
* An Overview of Soviet Oil and Gas in the World Arena, John P. Hardt, etc. 88-157 S
* The Petroleum Endowment of the People's Repulbic of China, Joseph P. Riva 86-102 SPR
* Petroleum in the United States: Selected Data Focused on the Oil Import Tax Issue, Bernard Gelb 86-1054 E
* Proceedings of the CRS Workshop on Canada-U.S. Free-Trade Agreement: How Will It Affect the United States? Arlene Wilson 88-356 E
* A Review of Oil Pollution Prevention Regulations After the Monongahela River Spill, Martin R. Lee 88-448 ENR
* Soviet Oil Prospects, Joseph Riva 81-91 SPR
* The Strategic Petroleum Reserve: Issue Brief, Robert Bamberger IB87050
* The World's Conventional Oil Production Capability Projected into the Future by Country, Joseph P. Riva, Jr. 87-414 SPR

Foundations
* see Arts and Humanities,

France
* British and French Strategic Nuclear Force Modernization: Issues for Western Security and Arms Contr ol Charlotte Philips Preece, etc. 89-140 F
* The Clandestine Trade in Heavy Water: A Chronology, Barbara B. Black, etc. 89-66 ENR
* Franco-German Security Cooperation: Implications for the NATO Alliance, Paul Gallis 89-16 F

Franking Privilege
* see Postal Service,

Freedom of Information Act
* see also Government Information,
* Freedom of Information Act/Privacy Act: A Guide to, Their Use; Info Pack, IP047F

FSLIC
* see Federal Savings and Loan Insurance Coporation,, Money and Banking--Failures and Deposit Insurance,

FSC (Fighter)

* see Weapons Systems--Non-Nuclear Weapons),

Gandhi, Indira
* The Gandhi Assassination: Implications for India a nd U.S.-Indian Relations, Richard Cronin 84-790 F

Gandhi, Rajiv
* The Rajiv Gandhi Visit: Issues in U.S.-India Relat ions, Richard Cronin 85-383 F

Gasohol
* see Power Resources--Alternative Energy Sources,

Gasoline
* see Fossil Fuels--Gasoline,

Gasoline Tax
* see Taxation--Consumption Taxes,

Gatt
* see General Agreement on Tariffs and Trade,

Gay Rights
* see Civil Liberties and Rights--Discrimination and, Integration,

Gaza Strip
* Israeli-Palestinian Conflict: Bibliography-in-Brief, 1982-1988, Robert Kirk 88-251 L
* Israeli-Palestinian Conflict: Info Pack,   IP397I
* Palestinian Disturbances in the Gaza Strip and West Bank: Policy Issues and Chronology, Ellen Laipson 88-114 F

Gene Therapy
* see Genetics,

General Agreement on Tariffs and Trade
* see also Foreign Trade--Trade Agreements and Negotiations,
* Agricultural Trade: Issue Brief, Donna Vogt IB88011
* Agriculture in the GATT: After the Midtern Review; Issue Brief, Charles Hanrahan IB89027
* Agriculture in the GATT: Toward the Next Round of Multilateral Trade Negotiations, Charles Hanrahan, etc. 86-98 ENR
* Auctioning Import quotaas, Lenore Sek 87-669 E
* Decoupling Farm Programs, Carl W. Ek 88-604 ENR
* Dispute Settlement and the General Agreement on Tariffs and Trade, Raymond Ahearn 85-680 E
* Negotiating Authority for the Uruguay Round of Multilateral Trade Negotiations, Jeanne Jagelski 87-103 A
* Textile Trade Controls: A Comparison of Bills in the 99th and 100th Congresses, Edward Rappaport 87-607 E
* Trade Negotiations: The Uruguay Round: Issue Brief, Lenore Sek IB86147
* Trade Remedies Available to the United States under International Agreements and Corresponding Domestic Laws Vladimir N. Pregelj 85-1008 E
* U.S. Agricultural Trade Opportunities With Pacific, Rim Nations, Robert M. Goldstein 88-755 ENR
* U.S.-Canada Free Trade Agreement: International Implications, Raymond J. Ahearn, etc. 88-249 F

General Interest
* see History (U.S.) and References Sources,
* Additions to the Major Issues File,   IB89001
* Archived Issue Brief List,   IB89000
* CRS Television Program Schedule Channel 6 Congressional Cable System, IB83145

Genetics
* see also Research and Development,
* Agricultural Research: Issues for the 1980s, Christine Matthews Rose 87-430 SPR
* Bovine Growth Hormone(Somatotropin): Agricultural and Regulatory Issues, Geoffrey S. Becker, etc. 86-1020 ENR
* Commercialization of Technology and Issues in the Competitiveness of Selected U.S. Industries; Semic onductors, Biotechnology, and Superconductors Lennard G. Kruger, etc. 88-486 SPR
* Federal Regulation of Biotechnology: Issue Brief, Judith Johnson;, etc. IB89068
* Human Gene Therapy: Archived Issue Brief, Judith Johnson IB84119
* Human Gene Therapy: Issue Brief, Judith Johnson IB87040
* Patenting Life: Issue Brief, Sarah Taylor IB87222
* Proposal to Map and Sequence the Human Genome: Issue Brief,

Currents Events and Homework

Irene Stith-Coleman IB88012

Genocide
* see International Law--Human Rights,

Genocide Convention
* Genocide Convention; Archvied Issue Brief, Vita Blue IB74129

Gephardt Amendment
* see Foreign Trade--Trade Policy,

Germany
* see Eastern Europe, West Germany,

Glasnost
* see U.S.S.R. -- Politics and Government,

Glass-Steagall Act
* see also Corporations--Securities Industry, Money and
Banking--Law and Regulation,
* Bank Service Diversification: A Comparative Summary of Major
Financial Reform Measures Facing the Co ngress William Jackson,
etc. 88-84 E
* Bank Soundness in Light of the Tax Reform Act of 1986 and
Possible Glass-Steagall Act Repeal, Walter W. Eubanks 88-118 E
* Banker-Broker Competition and the Glass-Steagall Act: The
Mutual Funds Example, William Jackson 87-921 E
* Banks and Thrift Institutions: Restructuring and Solvency
Issues, F. Jean Wells 88-749 E
* The Glass-Steagall Act: A Legal Overview, Henry Cohen 82-189 A
* The Glass-Steagall Act: Bibliography-in-Brief, 1981-1988,
Felix Chin 88-98 L
* Glass-Steagall Act: Issue Brief, William Jackson IB87061
* Glass-Steagall Act: The Legal Landscape of Financial
Restructuring, M. Maureen Murphy 88-335 A
* The Separation of Banking and Commerce, William Jackson 87-352
E

Global Climatic Changes
* see Earth Sciences,

Gorbachev, M.S.
* Continuity and Change in Soviet Diplomacy and Negotiations
under Gorbachev, Joseph G.Whelan 89-39 F
* Gorbachev Reform Program After the 1988 Party Conference:
Summary of a Roundtable Workshop, Francis T. Miko 89-130 F
* The Gorbachev Speech to the United Nations, New York, Dec. 7,
1988, Foreign Affairs and National Defense Division 88-776 F
* Gorbachev's Reform Strategy: Comparisons With the Hungarian and
Chinese Experience, Francis T. Miko, etc. 87-813 F
* Gorbachev's Reform: The Consumer Goods and Services Secotr, F.
Mike Miles 87-763 F
* Soviet Foreign Policy under Gorbachev: Determinants,
developments, Prospects, and Implications, Francis T. Miko 87-39
F
* Soviet "Restructuring" under Gorbachev: A Chronology, January
1985-June 1987, F. Mike Miles 87-551 F
* Statements by Mikhail Gorbachev Relating to Arms Control, July
1, 1986-June 30, 1987, Terri Lehto, etc. 87-646 S

Government and Politics
* see Congress, Constitution(U.S.), Executive Organization,
Government Employees, Government Information, History(U.S.),
Political Ethics, Politics and,

Government Contracts
* see Defense Economics--Procurement, Procurement, Ethics, Pay
and Benefits, Political Activities, Military personnel, Military
Personnel-Pensions, Pens,

Government Employees
* see Ethics, Pay and Benefits, Political Activities , Military
Personnel, Military Personnel-Pensions, Pensions-Civil Service,

* Brief Summary of Statutory and Regulatory Procedural Rights of
Federal Employees in the Event of an Agency Disciplinary
Proceeding Michael V. Seitzinger 86-962 A
* Career Guidance and Federal Job Information: Info Pack, IP016C
* Constitutional Analysis of Proposals to Establish a Mandatory
Public Employee Drug Testing program, Charles V. Dale 88-293 A
* Displaced Employee Assistance: Federal Civilian Programs,
Sharon Gressle 86-976 A
* Drug Testing in the Workplace: Federal Programs; Issue Brief,
Sharon Gressle IB87174
* Elimination of the Professional and Administrative, Career

Examination (PACE) and Proposed Alternative Selection Procedures
Paul M. Downing 89-315 GOV
* Internships and Fellowships: Info Pack,   IP063I
* Legal Analysis of S. 541, 100th Congress, a Bill to Provide that
Certain Postal Service Employees Have Procedural and Appeal
Rights in the Event of Ad Michael Seitzinger 87-433 A
* President Reagan's Productivity Improvement Program: Deja Vu,
fresh Start to an Old Story, or Lasting Reform? Peter Benda, etc.
86-89 S
* The Priority Placement Program (PPP) in the Department of
Defense, James McGrath 86-977 GOV
* Public Employment in the United States: A Compilation of
Statistical Trends, 1950-1983, Barbara Schwemie, etc. 84-91 GOV
* Security Clearances for Congressional and Judicial, Employees,
Frederick M. Kaiser 87-809 GOV
* The Senior Executive Service (SES): Morale and Staffing
Problems--A Brief Overview, James McGrath 87-315 GOV

Government Employees -- Ethics
* The Acceptance of Gifts by Employees in the Executive Branch,
Jack Maskell 85-1089 A
* The Appearance of Impropriety as a Standard for Disciplining
Federal Employees, Jack Maskell 85-687 A
* Conflicts of Interest: The Department of Defense and the
Revolving Door Problem, Andrew Mayer 86-188 F
* Constitutional Analysis of "Revolving Door" Proposal Regarding
Expansion of Post-Employment Conflicts of Interest Law for
Federal Officials Jack Maskell 88-590 A
* The Defense Procurement Bribery and Fraud Investigation:
Profiles of Persons and Companies Mentioned, in Press Reports
David P. Fite 88-528 F
* Defense Procurement Investigation: Issue Brief, Gary J.
Pagliano IB88081
* Defense Procurement: The Fraud and Bribery Investigation: Info
Pack, IP404D
* Overview of Ethics and Conflict of Interest provisions
Applicable to Executive Branch Employees, Jack Maskell 85-667 A
* Overview of Whistleblower Protections in Federal Law, Jack
Maskell 86-1018 A
* Post Employment "revolving Door" restrictions on Department of
Defense Personnel, Jack Maskell 88-478 A
* Regulations on the Receipt of Gifts by Spouses of Government
Employees, Jack Maskell 85-689 A

Government Employees -- Pay and Benefits
* Benefit and Pay Increases in Selected Federal Programs, Carolyn
L. Merck 88-696 EPW
* Benefits to Individuals Based on Previous Employment:
Interactions and Offsets in Selected Programs, Carolyn Merck
85-869 EPW
* Civil Service Retirement: Bibliography-in-Brief, 1985-1988,
Edith Sutterlin 88-538 L
* Commission on Executive, Legislative, and Judicial, Salaries:
An Historical Overview, Sharon S. Gressle 89-38 GOV
* Comparable Worth/Pay Equity in the Federal Government: Issue
Brief, Linda LeGrande IB85116
* Comparison of Retirement Systems for Executive Branch
Employees, Members of Congress and Active Duty, Military
Personnel Carolyn Merck, etc. 85-685 EPW
* Congressional Pay, Selected Wages and Pensions, and Social
Security: Compared to CPI, 1969-1989, Frederick H. Pauls, etc.
89-63 GOV
* Constitutionality of Delegating Pay-Setting Authority in the
Federal Salary Act, Thomas Nicola 87-137 A
* Fair Labor Standards Act: Treatment of State and Local
Government; Archvied Issue Brief, Dennis Roth, etc. IB85195
* Federal Civil Service Retirement for People With Military
Service and Social Security: "Catch 62", Carolyn Merck 84-680 EPW
* Federal Employees Health Benefits Program: Issues and problems;
Archived Issue Brief, Janet Lundy IB83134
* Federal Executive, Legislative, and Judicial Compensation: The
Situation and Choices for the 101st C ongress James McGrath 89-70
GOV
* Fiduciary Responsibility Requirements of the Pension and
Retirement Plans for State Employees, Joyce A. Thorpe, etc.
88-614 A
* Honoriaria and Outside Earned Income: Summary of Current
Restrictions in the Legislation and Executive Branches Jack
Maskell 89-29 A
* Medicare Coverage of Employees of State and Local Governments,
David Koitz 88-369 EPW
* Pay Reform for Federal White-Collar Employees: A Conceptual
Analysis and Comparison of Two Legislative Proposals Barbara L.
Schwemie 87-828 GOV
* Provisions of the Balanced Budget and Emergency Deficit Control
act of 1985 Affecting Pay and Benefits for Federal Workers and
Retirees Carolyn Merck 86-502 EPW
* Provisions of the Tax Reform Act of 1986 Affecting, Federal

Workers and Retirees, Carolyn Merck 86-928 EPW
* Retirement Systems for Federal Employees; Info Pack, IP205R
* Salaries and Allowances: The Executive Branch; Issue Brief, Sharon Gressle IB81263
* Social Security and Medicare Coverage of Employees, of State and Local Governments, David Koitz, etc. 87-132 EPW
* Treatment of Former Spouses under Various Federal Retirement Systems, Marie B. Morris 88-512 A

Government Employees -- Political Activities
* A Compilation of State Laws Governing Political Activity of Public Employees, Jack Maskell, etc. 87-904 A
* Hatch Act Amendments: Political Activity and the Civil Service; Issue Brief, Barbara L. Schwemie IB87153
* Hatch Act: Bibliography-in-Brief, 1976-1987, Rebecca Mazur 88-94 L
* The Hatch Act: Existing Statute Compared With House and Senate Proposals, Barbara L. Schwemie 89-282 GOV
* Hatch Act; Info Pack, IP298H
* Legal and Constitutional Framework of "Hatch Act" Restrictions on Political Activities of Federal Employees Jack Maskell 89-280 A
* State Statutory Provisions Regarding Political Activities by Public Employees, Jack Maskell 87-841 A

Government Information
* Classified Information Procedure Act (CIPA): An Overview, Larry Eig 89-172 A
* Confidentiality and Secrecy Orders in Civil Cases, Kenneth R. Thomas 89-225 A
* Congressional Access to Information from the Executive: A, Legal Analysis, Richard Ehlke 86-50 A
* Form Letters: Tell Your Constiuents Where to Get Government Publications; Info Pack, IP222F
* Freedom of Information Act/Privacy Act: a Guide to, Their Use; Info Pack, IP047F
* Government Publications--How, What, When, Where, and Why: Info Pack, IP264G
* Information Policy and Technology Issues: Public Laws of the 95th Through 100th Congresses, Robert Lee Chartrand 89-185 SPR
* Paperwork Management in the Federal Government, Stephanie Smmith 89-189 GOV
* Privatization of the National Technical Information Service, Jane Bortnick, etc. 87-491 SPR
* Protecting Classified Information: A Compilation and Index of Major Findings and Recommendations, 1905-1987 Frederick M. Kaiser, etc. 87-293 GOV
* Security Clearances for Congressional and Judicial, Employees, Frederick M. Kaiser 87-809 GOV
* Security Clearances for Members of Congress and the Judiciary, Frederick M. Kaiser 87-704 GOV
* Sources of State Juror Lists, Paul L. Morgan 89-337 A
* Where to Get Publications from the Executive and Independent Agencies: A Directory of Sources for Official Documents Deborah C. Brudno, etc. 89-167 C

Government and Politics
* Congressional Committee Staff and Funding, IB82006
* Constitutional Conventions: Political and Legal Questions, IB80062
* Hatch Act Amendments: Political Activity and the Civil Service, IB87153
* Presidential Nominating Process: Proposed Reforms, IB86117
* Presidential Nominating Process: Proposed Reforms, IB86117
* Puerto Rico: Political Status Options, IB89065
* Retirement for Federal Employees: FY 90 Budget Issues, IB89034
* Salaries and Allowances: The Executive Branch, IB81263
* Salaries for Members of Congress, IB86017
* Senate Procedure, Rules, and Organization: Proposals for Change in the 101st Congress, IB89074

Government Procurement
* see Defense Economics--Procurement, Procurement,

Government Regulation
* see Business and Society-Regulation and Deregulati on, Money and Banking--Law and Regulation,

Government Securities Act
* Legal Analysis of the Government Securities Act of, 1986 and Its Application to Broker/Dealers Convic ted of Insider Trading Violation Michael V. Seitzinger 87-280 A

Government Spending
* see Public Finance,

Gramm-Rudman-Hollings Act
* see also Public Finance-Deficits,
* Agriculture and the Gramm-Rudman-Hollings Deficit Control Act, Geoffrey Becker 86-547 ENR
* Budget Cuts: Updated Projections and Gramm-Rudman- Hollings; Archvied Issue Brief, William Cox IB86072
* Budget Sequestration Procedures for Fiscal year 1987: Summary of Congressional Action, Robert Keith 86-1049 GOV
* Debt-Limit Increase and 1985 Balanced Budget Act Reaffirmation: Summary of Public Law 100-199(H.J. Re s. 324) Edward Davis, etc. 87-865 GOV
* Debt-Limit Increases for Fiscal Year 1987: Summary, of Congressional Action in 1986 (Including Propos ed Modifications to the 1985 Balanced Budget Act) Robert A. Keith, etc. 86-974 GOV
* Deficit Reduction in 1988: Archived Issue Brief, William Cox IB87023
* Economic Forecasts and Gramm-Rudman-Hollings, Brian Cashell 87-934 E
* Explanation of the Balanced Budget and Emergency D eficit Control Act of 1985-P.L. 99-177 (the Gramm- Rudman-Hollings Act) Allen Schick 85-1130 GOV
* The Federal Budget for Fiscal year 1988: Archived Issue Brief, Philip D. Winters IB87057
* The Federal Budget For Fiscal Year 1989: Issue Brief, Philip Winters IB88064
* The Federal Budget Process: Selected References, Robert Howe 88-436 L
* The Forest Service Budget: Trust Funds and Special, Accounts, Ross Gorte, etc, 89-75 ENR
* Gramm-Rudman-Hollings and Department of Education Programs, Angela Evans 86-544 EPW
* Gramm-Rudman-Hollings Budget Adjustments: Sensitivity to Economic Assumptions; Archived Issue Brief, Barry Molefsky, etc. IB85217
* The Gramm-Rudman-Hollings Deficit Reduction Plan: The Target of a Balanced Budget and the risk of Re cession Craig Elwell 86-534 E
* The Gramm-Rudman-Hollings Deficit Reduction Process (P.L. 99-177) and the Department of Defense: A S ummary Review Alice Maroni, etc. 86-7 F
* The Gramm-Rudman-Hollings Deficit Reduction Process: The Defense Aspects of the initial Sequestratio n Report for Fiscal year 1987 Alice Maroni, etc. 86-875 F
* Gramm-Rudman-Hollings: Potential Economic Effects of meeting Deficit Targets; Archived Issue Brief, Brian W. Cashell IB87059
* The Gramm-Rudman-Hollings Sequestration process fo r FY 1986: A Summary of DoD Elements in the OMB/CB O and GAO Sequestration Reports: Policy Alert Alice Maroni, etc. 86-16 F
* The Gramm-Rudman-Hollings Targets: How Might They Affect the Economy, Gail Makinen, etc. 86-1036 E
* Health Programs and the Gramm-Rudman-Hollings Legi slation: The 1986 Sequestration and the President' s FY 87 Budget Proposal James Reuter 86-648 EPW
* Implications of Uncertainty in Economic Forecastin g under Gramm-Rudman-Hollings: Options for Congres ional Response David Grinnell 86-829 S
* Manual on the Federal Budget Process, Allen Schick, etc. 87-286 GOV
* Provisions of the Balanced Budget and Emergency De ficit Control Act of 1985 Affecting Pay and Benefi ts for Federal Workers and Retirees Carolyn Merck 86-502 EPW
* Selected Federal Research and Development Agencies, and Programs and the Gramm-Rudman-Hollings Defici t Reduction Act: An Analysis of the Impact on Thei Michael E. Davey 86-37 SPR
* Sequestration Actions for Fiscal Year 1988 under t he Gramm-Rudman-Hollings Act: Archived Issue Brief, Robert Keith IB87224
* Sequestration Actions for FY 89 under the Gramm-Ru dman-Hollings Act: Archived Issue Brief, Robert Keith IB88078
* Sequestration Actions for FY 90 under the Gramm-Ru dman-Hollings Act: Issue Brief, Robert Keith IB89-71
* Sequestration of Budgetary Resources for Fiscal Ye ar 1986 under the 1985 Balanced Budget Act, Robert A. Keith 86-872 GOV
* Summary and Analysis of the Ramifications of Bowsh er v. Synar, the Gramm-Rudman-Hollings Deficit Red uction Act Case Morton Rosenberg, etc. 86-788 A
* Wastewater Treatment Programs; Impact of Gramm-Rud man-Hollings Act and Prospects for Federal Funding (With Appendix); Archived Issue Brief Claudia Copeland IB86018

Grants
* see Reference Sources--Grants,

Great Britain
* British and French Strategic Nuclear Force Moderni zation: Issues for Western Security and Arms Control Charlotte Phillips Preece, etc. 89-140 F
* The British Experience With Indexed Bonds, G. Thomas Woodward

87-926 E
* Comparison of United States and United Kingdom Off shore Oil and Gas Leasing and Development Systems, Malcolm M. Simmons 86-1011 ENR
* U.S. Civilian and Defense Research and Development, Funding: Some Trends and Comparisons With Selecte d Industrialized Nations William Boesman, etc. 84-195 SPR

Greece
* Current Issues With the "Base-Rights" Countries an d Their Implications, Richard F. Grimmett 88-726 F
* Greece and Turkey: U.S. Foreign Assistance Fact: I ssue Brief, Ellen B. Laipson IB86065
* Greek-Turkish Relations: Beginning of a New Era?, Ellen Laipson 88-724 F
* The Seven-Ten Ratio in Military Aid to Greece and Turkey: A Congressional Tradition, Ellen Laipson 85-79 F
* United States Military Installations in Greece, Richard Grimmett 84-24 F

Greenhouse Effect
* see Earth Sciences,

Grenada
* Grenada: Issues Concerning the Use of U.S. Forces;, Archived Issue Brief, Janice Hanover IB83170

Ground Wave Emergency Network (GWEN)
* The Ground Wave Emergency Network, Gary K. Reynolds 89-206 F

Groundwater Contamination
* see Water Pollution--Groundwater,

Grove City College v. Bell
* Civil Rights Legislation: Response to Grove City C ollege v. Bell; Archived Issue Brief, Bob Lyke IB87123

Guam
* Territorial Political Development: An Analysis of Puerto Rico, Northern Mariana Islands, Guam, Virgi n Islands, and American Samoa, and the Micronesian Bette A. Taylor 88-657 GOV

Guatemala
* Central America: U.S. RElations With Costa Rica, G uatemala, and Honduras: Info Pack, IP352C
* Central American peace Process: Selected Reference s, Robert Kirk 88-389 L
* Guatemala: Country Background Report, Maureen Taft-Morales 88-586 F
* Guatemala: U.S. Foreign Assistance Facts; Archived, Issue Brief, Jonathan Sanford IB85100

Gulf Cooperation Council
* The Gulf Cooperation Council, Richard Preece 85-516 F

Gun Control
* see Crimes and Offenses--Gun Control,

Gun Control Act
* Gun Control Act of 1968, as Amended: Digest of Maj or Provisions, P.L. 90-618, 90th Congress, H.R. 17 735, October 22, 1968 Harry Hogan 85-166 GOV

Haiti
* Haiti: Political Developments and U.S.Policy Concerns: Archived Issue Brief, Maureen Taft-Morales IB88104

Handicapped
* see Children, Employment, Rehabilitation Act, Social Services,

* Accessiblity for the Handicapped in Federally Funded Buildings: The law and Its Implementation, Mary Smith 85-613 EPW
* Architectural Barriers and the physically Handicapped: Selected References, 1974-1988, Charles Dove 89-108 L
* Bibliography of Selected law Review Articles Concerning Handicapped Persons, M. Ann Wolfe 87-968 A
* Community-Based Services for Individuals With Severe Disabilities: Summary and Analysis of S. 1673 a nd H.R. 3454 Mary F. Smith 88-212 EPW
* Comparative Analysis of Title VII of the 1964 Civil Rights Act, the Age Discrimination in Employment, Act, and the Rehabilitation Act of 1973 Charles V. Dale 89-240 A
* Developmental Disabilities Programs; FY 1989 Budget Information, Mary F. Smith 88-181 EPW
* Developmental Disabilities Programs; Statutory Authority and

Program Operations, Mary F. Smith 88-52 EPW
* Digest of Data on Persons With Disabilities, 84-115 EPW
* Housing for the Elderly and Handicapped: Section 202; Issue Brief, Susan M. Vanhorenbeck IB84038
* Medicaid Services for persons With Mental Retardation or Related Conditions, Mary F. Smith 88-759
* Regulations Promulgated Pursuant to Section 504 of, the Rehabilitation Act of 1973: A Brief History a nd Present Status Nancy Jones, etc. 86-53 A
* Remedies and Standing to Sue under S. 933, the "Americans With Disabilities Act of 1989", Charles V. Dale 89-336 A
* School Board of Nassau County v. Arline: A Person With the Contagious Disease of Tuberculosis May Be, Covered under Section 504 of the Rehabilitation Nancy Lee Jones 87-238 A
* Section 504 of the Rehabilitation Act: Statutory Provisions, Legislative History, and Regulatory Req uirement Mary F. Smith 89-48 EPW
* Selected Legislation Affecting Persons With Handicaps: 100th Congress, Mary F. Smith 89-106 EPW
* Social Security: Re-Examining Eligibility for Disability Benefits; Archived Issue Brief, David Koitz IB82078
* Social Security: The 5-Month Waiting Period for Disability Insurance Benefits, David Koitz 79-239 EPW
* Supreme Court Decisions Interpreting Section 504 of the Rehabilitation Act of 1973, Nancy Jones 85-926 A
* Tax Code Provisions of Interest to the Disabled and Handicapped, Louis Alan Talley 87-721 E
* Telephone Access for the Hearing Impaired: Federal, Actions to Increase Availability, Angele A. Gilroy 86-917 E
* Transportation for Elderly and Handicapped People: Programs, Regulations, and Issues, Lenore Sek 85-699 E

Handicapped -- Children
* Constitutional and Statutory Issues Relating to the Use of Behavior Modification on Children in Institutions Nancy Jones 86-1000 A
* Education of the Handicapped Act Discretionary Programs: Background and Current Issues, Margot A. Schenet 89-67 EPW
* The Education of the Handicapped: Selected References, 1984-1987, Marsha Cerny 87-520 L
* P.L. 94-142, the Education for All Handicapped Children: Background, Issues, and Federal Policy Opti ons Charlotte Fraas 86-55 EPW
* Preschool Programs for the Education of Handicapped Children: Background, Issues, and Federal Policy, Options Charlotte Fraas 86-55 EPW
* The "Stay Put" Provision of the Education for All Handicapped Children Act: Honig, California Superi ntendent of Public Instruction v. Doe Et Al Meredith A. Yancey 88-494 A
* Summary of the Educationof the Handicapped Act Amendments of 1986, P.L. 99-457,, Charlotte Jones Fraas 86-926 EPW
* Vouchers for the Education of Disadvantaged Children: Analysis of the Reagan Administration Proposal, Wayne Riddle 85-1022 EPW

Handicapped - Employment
* Affirmative Action in the Employment of Persons With Handicaps under Federal Contracts: Section 503 of the Rehabilitation Act Mary F. Smith 88-701 EPW
* The Americans With Disabilities Act (ADA): Legal Analysis of Proposed Legislation Prohibiting Discri mination on the Basis of Handicap Nancy Lee Jones 88-621 A
* Employment of Persons With Handicaps under the Javits-Wagner-O'Day Act: Summary of the Special Procurement Program and Current Issues Mary F. Smith 88-610 EPW
* Randolph-Sheppard Act: the Blind Vendors Program, Mary F. Smith 85-603 EPW
* Sheltered Workshops for Persons With Handicaps: Background Information and Recent Legislative Change, Mary F. Smith 87-362 EPW
* Survey of State Statutes Concerning Employment Discrimination of Handicapped Persons, M. Ann Wolfe 87-561 A
* Vocational Rehabilitation and Related Programs for, Persons With Handicaps: FY 1990 Budget Request, Mary F. Smith 89-176 EPW
* Work Disincentives and Disability Insurance, David Koitz 80-160 EPW
* Work Incentives for Disabled Supplemental Security Income (SSI) Recipients: Section 1619 of the Soc ial Security Act Carmen D. Solomon 87-427 EPW

Hatch Act
* see also Government Employees--Political Activitie,
* A Compilation of State Laws Governing Political Activity of Public Employees, Jack Maskell, etc. 87-904 A
* Hatch Act Amendments: Political Activity and the Civil Service: Issue Brief, Barbara Schwemle IB87153
* Hatch Act: Bibliography-in-brief, 1976-1987, Rebecca Mazur 88-94 L

Currents Events and Homework

* National Mean Scores of the Scholastic Aptitude Test and the American College Test, Steven R. Aleman 89-97 EPW
* The National Sea Grant College Program: Issue Brief, Robert Morrison IB87163
* The National Sea Grant Program: Comparisons With Land Grant, Robert Morrison, etc. 85-1148 SPR
* Revenue Sources for Higher Education Institutions, K. Forbis Jordan 86-956 S
* Speech Material: Graduation; Info Pack, IB379G
* Study Abroad: Bibliography-in-Brief, Peter Giordano 88-627 L

Higher Education -- Integration
* Civil Rights Legislation: Response to Grove City College v. Bell; Archived Issue Brief, Bob Lyke IB87123
* Civil Rights Restoration Act: Bibliography-in-Brief, 1984-1988, Charles Dove 88-332 L
* The Civil Rights Restoration Act of 1987: Legal Analysis of P.L. 100-259, Karen J. Lewis, etc. 88-171 A
* Federal Policies and Programs Relating to Sex Discrimination and Sex Equity in Education, 1963-1985, Bob Lyke, etc. 85-116 EPW

Higher Education-- Student Aid
* The College Assistance Migrant Program and the Migrant High School Equivalency Program, Robert Lyke 86-749 EPW
* College Costs: Analysis of Trends in Costs and sou rces of Support, Margot A. Schenet 88-694 EPW
* College Costs and Student Financial Aid: Selected References, Peter Giordano 89-117 L
* Employer Education Assistance: A Brief Discussion of Current Legislation and Issues, Bob Lyke 88-202 EPW
* Employer Education Assistance: A Profile of Recipi ents, Their Educational Pursuits, and Employers, Steven R. Aleman 89-33 EPW
* Employer Education Assistance: Current Tax Status, and Issues, Bob Lyke 89-148 EPW
* Financial Aid for Students; Info Pack, IP042F
* Financing Postsecondary Education Attendance: Curr ent Issues Involving Access and Choice, James B. Stedman 88-315 EPW
* Guaranteed Student Loan (GSL) Deferments: A Pro/Co n Analysis, Charlotte Jones Fraas 87-118 EPW
* The Guaranteed Student Loan Program: Current Statu s and Issues, Charlotte Fraas 88-727 EPW
* Guaranteed Student Loans: Defaults; Issue Brief, Charlotte Fraas IB88050
* Guides to Financial Aid for Students: A Checklist, Peter Giordano 89-98 L
* The Higher Education Amendments of 1986(P.L. 99-49 8): A Summary of Provisions, Education and Public Welfare Division 87-187 EPW
* Internships and Fellowships; Info Pack, IP063I
* National Service: Selected References, Peter Giordano 89-165 L
* The New GI bill: Recruiting and Retention, David Burrelli 87-652 F
* Proprietary Vocational Schools: Bibliography-in-Br ief, Peter Giordano 88-515 E
* Saving for College: Issue Brief, Robert Lyke IB89078
* Saving for College With Education Savings Bonds, Gerald Mayer 89-207 E
* Student Financial Aid: Authorization of Appropriat ions, Budget Requests, Enacted Appropriations and Outlays for Federal Student Financial Aid Program Susan H. Boren 89-184 EPW
* Student Loans--An Income Contigent Approach Propos ed by the Reagan Administration for National Direct Student Loans Wayne Riddle 86-669 EPW

Higher Education Act
* see Federal Aid to Education--Higher Education, Hi gher Education,

Highway Beautification Act
* Outdoor Advertising Control Along Federal-Aid Highways, Malcolm Simmons 86-605 ENR

Highway Safety
* see Highways--Safety Measures,

Highway Trust Fund
* Federal Excise Taxes on Gasoline and the Highway Trust Fund--a Short History, Louis Alan Talley 89-174 E

Highway
* see Safety Measures, Infrastructure, Transportation,
* The "Bridge Crisis": An Economic Development Perspective; Issue Brief, J.F. Hornbeck IB88085
* Federal Excise Taxes on Gasoline and the Highway Trust Fund-A Short History, Louis Alan Talley 89-174 E
* Outdoor Advertising Control Along Federal-Aid High ways,

Malcolm Simmons 86-605 ENR

Highways--Safety Measures
* Automobile Crash Protection: Issue Brief, Migdon Segal IB83085
* Drunk Driving and Raising the Drinking Age: Info P ack, IP186D
* Drunk Driving: Bibliography-in-Brief, 1983-1988, Edith Sutterlin 88-665 L
* Drunk Driving: Issue Brief, Migdon Segal IB83157
* Legal Analysis of Questions Regarding the National, Minimum Drinking Age, Douglas Weimer 85-772 A
* Motor Vehicle Safety: Policy Trends and Prospects, Migdon Segal 85-184 SPR
* Motor Vehicle Safety: Research and Development, Migdon Segal 85-184 SPR
* Roadway Safety Issues: The Federal program, Cosmo DiMaggio 85-62 E
* Roadway Safety: National Trends and Policies, Cosmo DiMaggio 86-71 SPR
* Three-Wheel All-Terrain Vehicles: Safety problems, Migdon Segal 85-749 SPR
* Truck Safety: Issue Brief, Migdon R. Segal IB88022
* The 55-MPH National Speed Limit: Issue Brief, Migdon Segal IB86153

Hispanic Americans
* see Minorities,

History (U.S.)
* Bicentennial of the Congress: Selected References, 1970-1989, George Walser 89-90 L
* Bicentennial of the U.S. Congress; Info Pack, IP411C
* Cabinet and Other High Level Nominations that Failed to Be Confirmed, 1789-1989, Rogelio Garcia 89-253 GOV
* Congressional Gold Medals, Stephan Stathis 84-117 GOV
* Constitution of the United States: Its History, Development and Amending Process; Info Pack, IP339C
* Federal Holiday Legislation, Stephan Stathis 86-759 GOV
* Federalism: Key Episodes in the History of the American Federal System, Sandra Osborn 82-139 GOV
* The Flag: Info Pack, IP365F
* Foreign Ownership Of U.S. Assets: Past, Present, and Prospects, James K. Jackson, etc. 88-295E
* Historic Preservation Program: Structure, History, and Congressional Policies, Malcolm Simmons 87-302 ENR
* Inauguration of the President: Info Pack, IP316I
* Individuals Arrested on Charges of Espionage Against the United States Government: 1966-1989, Suzanne Cavanaugh 89-324 GOV
* Major Acts of Congress and Treaties Approved by the Senate, 1789-1980, Christopher Deli, etc. 82-156 GOV
* Manassas National Battlefield Park: The Battle Continues, John O. Spengler, etc. 88-514 ENR
* Martin Luther King: Selected References, 1978-1989, Jean Bowers 88-769 L
* Members of Congress Who Have Served in Both the House and the Senate, 1789-1989, Mildred L. Amer 89-45 GOV
* The Presidency of the United States: Info Pack, IP409P
* Reelection Rates of House Incumbents: 1790-1988, David C.Huckabee 89-173 GOV
* Rural Policy in an Era of Change and Diversity, Sandra S. Osborn 88-482 GOV
* Rural Policy in the United States: A History, Sandra S. Osborn 88-487 GOV
* Selected Bicentennial Celebrations Commemorating the 200th Anniversaries of the U.S. Constitution an d of the U.S. Congress Roger Davidson, etc. 86-171 * Speech Material: Abraham Lincoln's and George Washington's Birthdays; Info Pack, IP373A
* Speech Material: Columbus Day; Info Pack, IP380C
* Speech Material: Fourth of July; Info Pack, IP377F
* Speech Material: Martin Luther King's Birthday; Info Pack, IP372M
* Speech Material: Thanksgiving Day; Info Pack, IP381T
* Vice Presidents of the United States, 1789-1981: Brief Biographical Notes, Christopher Deli 81-23 GOV
* The Virgin Islands of the United States: A Descriptive and Historical Profile, Bette Taylor 88-429 GOV
* Women in the United States Congress, Mildred Amer 89-332 GOV

H.K. Porter, Co, Inc. v. Dade Co, Florida
* United States Supreme Court Actions Regarding Mino rity Business Set-Asides After City of Richmond v. J.A. Croson Co. Charles V. Dale 89-202 A

Holidays
* see Reference Sources--Speechwriting,

Homeless

* see Public Welfare--Homeless,

Honduras
* Central America: U.S. Relations With Costa Rica, G atemala, and Honduras: Info Pack, IP352C
* Central American Peace Process: Selected Reference s, Robert Kirk 88-389 L
* Honduras: U.S. Foreign Assistance Facts, Archived Issue Brief, Robert Sanchez IB85080
* Honduras: U.S. Military Activities: Issue Brief, James Wooten IB84134

Hong Kong
* Exchange Rate Management in Taiwan, South Korea an, Hong Kong, Arlene Wilson 87-41 E
* U.S. Agricultural Trade Opportunities With Pacific, Rim Nations, Robert Goldstein 88-755 ENR

Hormones in Meat
* see Agriculture--Foreign Trade, Agriculture--Lives ock,

Hospitals
* see Health Facilities,

House of Representatives
* see Congress,

Housing
* see Assistance, Finance,
* Abstracts of Recommendations of Certain Organizat ions on National Housing Policy, Economics Division 88-23 E
* Affordability of Moderate Income Housing in the 19 80s: Bibliography-in-Brief, 1984-1988, Robert Howe 88-669 L
* Bank Diversification: Into Real Estate, William Jackson 88-648 E
* Border State "Colonias": Background and Options fo r Federal Assistance, Claudia Copeland, etc. 87-906 ENR
* Comparative Quality of Rental Housing Obtained by Whites, Blacks, and Hispanics, Grace Milgram 87-626 E
* Comparison of the Departments of Energy and health, and Human Services Weatherization Assistance Prog rams Mary Smith, etc. 89-229 EPW
* Existing Housing Resources v. Need, Grace Milgram, etc. 87-81 E
* Expanding Housing Opportunities Through Residentia l Conversions and Homesharing, Nancy Saltojanes 84-70 S
* Fair Housing Act Amendments: Archived Issue Brief, Paul Downing IB87116
* Fair Housing Amendments Prohibiting Discrimination, Against Families With Children Except in Housing for Older Persons Henry Cohen 89-111 A
* Homeless Housing: HUD's Shelter Programs; Archived, Issue Brief, Susan Vanhorenbeck IB87098
* Housing Alternatives: Archived Issue Brief, Morton J. Schussheim IB87024
* Housing and Housing Finance: An Alphabetical Micro thesaurus of Terms Selcted from the Legislative In dexing Vocabulary Shirley Loo 86-1033 L
* Housing Conditions of Hispanic Americans, Susan M. Vanhorenbeck 85-952 E
* Housing in Rural Areas, Nancy Saltojanes 85-61 S
* Housing Policy and Implications for current Progra ms: Info Pack, Ip417H
* Housing Policy: Homeownership Affordability: Issue, Brief, Barbara Miles IB88108
* Major Repairs of Non-Routine Maintenance: Defining, Davis-Bacon Coverage under the Comprehensive Impr ovement Assistance Program William G. Whittaker 85-887 E
* Manufactured Housing: Trends and Prospects, Marc E. Smyrl 88-303 S
* Restrictive Rental Practices and Families With Chi ldren, Susan Vanhorenbeck 86-746 E
* Segregation and Discrimination in Housing: A Revie w of Selected Studies and Legislation, Paul Downing, etc. 89-317 GOV
* Summaries of Papers on U.S. Housing Policy Prepare for the Center for Real Estate Development, the Ma ssachusetts Institute of Technology Morton J. Schussheim 88-222 S
* The Tax Reform Act of 1986 and Owners of Rental Ho using, Richard Bourdon 86-919 E
* The Theory of Rent Control, Barbara Miles 78-109 E
* Homelessness: Issues and Legislation in the 101st Congress, IB88070
* Housing and Community Development, IB89004
* Housing for the Elderly and Handicapped: Section 2 02, IB84038
* Housing Policy: Homeownership Affordability, IB88108
* Housing Policy: Low- and Moderate- Income, IB88106
* Mortgage Revenue Bonds for First-Time HomeBuyers: Should the

Program be Continued Beyond 1989?, IB87181

Housing -- Assistance
* The Assisted Housing Stock: Potential Losses from Prepayment and "Opt-Outs", Grace Milgram 87-879 E
* Congregate Housing: The Federal Programs and Examp les of State Programs, Susan Vanhorenbeck 86-918 E
* Federal Housing programs Affecting Elderly People, Susan Vanhorenbeck 88-576 E
* Home Buyer Assistance; Tax Deferred Savings for Do wnpayments, Richard Bourdon 88-576 E
* Housing: Access and Affordability: Audio Brief, Mort Schussheim AB50172
* The Housing and Community Development Act of 1987 and the Steward B. McKinney Homeless Assistance Ac t: Summary and Analysis Barbara Miles 88-481 E
* Housing and Community Development: Audio Brief, Morton Schussheim, etc. AB50184
* Housing and Community Development; Issue Brief, Morton J. Schussheim IB89004
* Housing Assistance: A Brief History and Descriptio n of Current HUD Programs, Grace Milgram 88-712 E
* Housing for the Elderly and Handicapped: Section 1 01; Issue Brief, Susan Vanhorenbeck IB84038
* Housing Low-Income Persons through Use of Existing, Housing Stock, Susan Vanhorenbeck 88-584 E
* Housing Policy- and Moderate-Income Assistance; Is sue Brief, Grace Milgram IB88106
* Housing Programs: Issues in-and Moderate-Income Ho using Assistance; Archived Issue Brief, Grace Milgram IB87101
* Housing the Low-Income Family With Children, Morton J. Schussheim 87-518 S
* Rent Control and the Potential Denial of Federal Housing Assistance, Richard Bourdon 88-431 E
* Rural Housing Programas of the Farmers Home Administration: Brief Descriptions and Budget Data, B. Ellington Foote 87-171 E
* Tax Subsidies to Housing, 1953-83, Jane Gravelle 82-178 E
* Trends in Funding and Numbers of Households in HUD-Assisted Housing, Fiscal Years 1975-1989, Grace Milgram 89-200 E
* Urban Housing Assistance Programs in the United States, Grace Milgram 89-137 E

Housing -- Finance
* The Decision to Refinance a High-Rate Mortgage, E. Richard Bourdon 86-85 E
* Federal and Related Agencies Supporting Home Mortgage Markets, William Jackson, etc. 88-360 E
* Federal Home Loan Mortgage Corporation Preferred Stock Ownership: Lift the Restrictions?: Archived I ssue Brief Barbara Miles IB88076
* The Federal Housing Administration: Limits on Insurance Commitments, B. Ellington Foote 88-366 E
* Federal Housing Administration: Raising the Mortgage Limit, B. Ellington Foote 89-252 E
* FHA's Morgage Insurance Premium Refund Programs, Barbara L. Miles 87-709 E
* Financial Markets: A New Framework of Issues, Walter W. Eubanks 88-485 E
* The Financing of Rental Housing, Keith P. Rasey 86-1045 S
* Home Equity Loans: Bibliography-in-Brief, 1984-1988, Felix Chin 88-511 L
* Home Equity Loans under the New Tax Reform Act: Possible Benefits and Potential Dangers, Richard Bourdon 87-692 E
* The Home Mortgage Interest Deduction for Boats Used as Second Homes, Richard Bourdon 87-366 E
* The Home Mortgage Interest Deduction: Recent Changes in the Tax Laws, Richard Bourdon 88-126 E
* Housing Finance: Development and Evolution in Mortgage Markets, Barbara Miles 83-44 E
* Housing Progrmas of VA and FHA: A Comparison, B. Ellington Foote 88-504 E
* A Housing Trust Fund: Some Potential Sources, Barbara L. Miles, etc 88-234 E
* Income Tax Treatment of Rental Housing and Real Estate Investment AFter the Tax Reform Act of 1986, Jack Taylor 87-603 E
* Mortgage Commitments and Interest Rate "Lock-Ins":, What is the Problem?, Barbara Miles 87-873 E
* Mortgage Revenue Bonds for First-Time Home Buyers:, Should the Program Be Continued Beyond 1988? Issue Brief Richard Bourdon IB87181
* Recent Developments in the Real Estate Settlement Procedures Act, Richard Bourdon 88-730 E
* REMIC (Real Estate Mortgage Investment Conduit): The New Security for Financing Real Estate, Barbara Miles 87-73 E
* Tax Policy and Rental Housing: An Economic Analysis, Jane Gravelle 87-536 E
* Veterans Administration Guaranteed Housing Loans:Raising the Funding Fee; Archived Issue Brief, Ellington Foote IB87146

Currents Events and Homework

* Veterans Adminsitration Guaranteed Housing Loans: The Rising Cost of VA Mortgages, B. Ellington Foote 87-453 E

Housing and Community Development Act
* The Housing and Community Development Act of 1987 and the Stewart B. McKinney Homeless Assistance Act: Summary and Analysis Barbara Miles 88-481 E

Housing for the Aged
* see Old Age--Housing,

Housing Subsidies
* see Housing--Assistance,

Housing Trust Fund
* A Housing Trust Fund: Some Potential Sources, Barbara L. Miles, etc. 88-134 E

Human Rights
* see International Law-- Human Rights,

Hungary
* Gorbachev's Reform Strategy: Comparisons With the Hungarian and Chinese Experience, Francis T. Miko, etc. 87-813 F

Hunger
* see Food Relief, Public Welfare,

Hydropower
* see Water Resources,

Illegal Aliens
* see Immigration,

Illiteracy
* see Elementary and Secondary Education,

Immigration
* Alien Eligibility Requirements for Major Federal A ssistance Programs, Joyce Vialet 86-49 EPW
* A Brief History of U.S. Immigration Policy, Joyce Vialet 88-713 EPW
* Comparison of Legal Immigration Legislation in the, 101st Congress, S. 358, H.R. 672, and S. 448, Wit h Existing Law Joyce C. Vialet 89-190 EPW
* Counting Undocumented Aliens in the Decennial Cens us, Thomas C. Durbin 88-438 A
* El Salvador: Bibliography-in-Brief, 1986-1989, Robert S. Kirk 89-204 L
* Emigration: Soviet Compliance With the Helsinki Ac cords; Archived Issue Brief, John Hardt, etc. 85-599 EPW
* Extended Voluntary Departure and Other Grants of B lanket Relief from Deportation, Sharon Stephen 85-599 EPW
* The Immigration and Nationality Act--Questions and, Answers, Joyce Vialet 87-917 EPW
* Immigration and Refugee Policy: Info Pack, IP164I
* Immigration and Related Legislation Enacted in the, 100th Congress, 1987-1988, Joyce Vialet 88-766 EPW
* Immigration: Issues and Legislation in the 100th C ongress; Archived Issue Brief, Joyce Vialet IB87014
* Immigration: Numberical Limits and the Preference System; Issue Brief, Joyce Vialet IB88018
* Immigration: Status of Undocumented Salvadorans an d Nicaraguans: Issue Brief, Ruth Ellen Wasem IB87205
* Legal Immigration and Immigrants in the U.S.; Sele cted References, Peter Giordano 89-297 L
* Mexico-U.S. Relations: Issues for Congress; Issue Brief, K. Larry Storrs, etc. IB86111
* Numerical Limits and the preference System for Imm igrants in the Simpson-Mazzoli Bills, 97th and 98t h Congress; Summary and Debate Joyce Vialet 87-958 EPW
* Overview of Deportation Procedures, Larry Eig 88-743 A
* Private Bills: Selected Statistics, 1975-1986, Wit h Special Refernce to Private Immigration Bills, Richard Beth 87-650 GOV
* Private Immigration Measures in the House of Repre sentatives: Contemporary Procedure and Its Histori cal Development Richard Beth 87-408 GOV
* Proposed Exclusion of Illegal Aliens from the Popu lation Used to Apprtion the House of Representativ es: A Methodological and Policy Analysis Jennifer D. Williams, etc. 88-418 GOV
* Refugee Admissions and Resettlement Policy: Issue Brief, Joyce Vialet IB89025
* Social Security: Alien Beneficiaries; Archived Iss ue Brief, David Koitz IB82001
* "Sponsored Aliens" and Refugees: Immigrant Status and

Eligibility for Selected Benefits and Services, Ruth Ellen Wasem 88-334 EPW
* The 1990 Decennial Census and the Counting of Ille gal Aliens, thomas Durbin 88-62 A
* Immigration: Numerical Limits and the Preference S ystem, IB88018
* Immigration Status of Salvadorans and Nicaraguans, IB87205
* Refugee Admissions and Resettlement Policy, IB89025

Import Quotas
* see Foreign Trade--Imports and Exports,

Incineration of Wastes
* see Solid Wastes,

Income
* see Economic Conditions--Income, Labor--Earnings and Benefits,

Income Distribution
* see Economic Conditions--Income, Labor--Earnings a nd Benefits,

Income Maintenance Programs
* see Food Relief--Domestic, Pensions, Public Welfar e, Social Security, Workers' Compensation,
* Health Benefit Plans and the Impact of Section 89, IB89083
* Health Benefits for Retirees: An Uncertain Future, IB88004
* Individual Retirement Account Issues and Savings Account proposals, IB89085
* Pension Asset Reversions: Whose Money Is it?, IB89091
* Railroad Retirement and Unemployment: Recent Issues, IB84068
* Refundable Tax Credits To Aid Working Poor Families, IB86120
* Social Security: The Independent Agency Question, IB86120
* Welfare, IB87007

Income Tax
* see Taxation--Corporation Taxes, Taxation--Personal Income Tax,

Indexing (Economic Policy)
* see Economic Conditions--Inflation, Public Welfare , Social Security, Taxation,

India
* China-India Border Friction: Background Information and Possible Implications, Robert Sutter, tec. 87-514 F
* Crisis in the Indian Punjab: Evolution, Issues, Competing Positions and Prospects, Richard Cronin 84-152 F
* The Gandhi Assassination: Implicatoins for India and U.S.-Indian Relations, Richard Cronin 84-790 F
* India and Nuclear Weapons: Issue Brief, Warren Donnelly IB86125
* The Indian Community in the United States, Margaret Siciliano 84-792 F
* India's Punjab Crisis: Issues, Prospects and Implications, Richard Cronin 87-850 F
* India's Sikhs and the Crisis in Punjab State: Summary Briefing Points, Richard P. Cronin 87-509 F
* The Rajiv Gandhi Visit: Issues in U.S.-India Relations, Richard Cronin 85-838 F
* South Asia: Current Developments and Issues for U. S. Policy: Report on a Trip to Pakistan and India,, April 8-30, 1986 Richard P. Cronin 86-741 F

Indians
* American Indian Budget Issues: 101st Congress; Issue Brief, Roger Walke IB89046

* American Indian Policy: Background, nature, History, Current Issues, Future Trends, Richard Jones 87-227 GOV
* American Indian Policy: Selected Budget Issues in the 100th Congress; Archvied Issue Brief, Roger Walke IB87103
* American Indian Religious Freedom: The Legal Landscape, M. Maureen Murphy 88-370 A
* The Catawba Indian Tribe's Land Claim: A Legal Analysis, M. Maureen Murphy 89-293 A
* Gambling on Indian Reservations, M. Maureen Murphy 85-743 A
* Gambling on Indian Reservations: Archvied Issue Brief, Roger Walke IB86087
* Indian Affairs Legislation Enacted or Considered by the 98th Congress, Richard Jones 85-90 GOV
* Indian and Indian-Interest Organziations, Richard Jones, etc. 84-131 GOV
* Indian Tribal Government Zoning Authority, M. Maureen Murphy 88-744 A

946

* Indians: Land Claims by Eastern Tribes; Archived Issue Brief, Richard Jones IB77040
* Native Americans: Nutrition and Diet-Related Diseases, Donna Porter 87-246 SPR
* Navajo-Hopi Relocation: Issue Brief, Roger Walke IB86021
* Taxation Within Indian Lands: The Legal Framework, M. Maureen Murphy 87-249 A
* Territorial Extent of Indian Tribal Civil Jurisdiction: Diestablishment of Reservation Status, M. Maureen Murphy 87-976 A

Individual Retirement Accounts
* see Pensions,

Indonesia
* The Association of Southeast Asian Nations (ASEAN) : Economic Development Prospects and the Role of the United States Larry Niksch 84-171 F
* Economic Changes in the Asian Pacific Rim: Policy Prospectus, Congressional Research Service 86-923 S
* U. S. Agricultural Trade Opportunities With Pacific Rim Nations, Robert M. Goldstein 88-755 ENR

Indoor Air Pollution
* see Air Pollution--Indoor Air Pollution,

Industrial Competitiveness
* see Foreign Trade--Competitiveness, Industry,

Industrial Policy
* see Foreign Trade--Competitiveness, Industry,

Industrial Technology
* America's Steel Industry: Modernizing to Compete, David J. Cantor 84-786 E
* Automation and Small Business: Technological Devel opment and the Competitiveness of U.S. Industry, Wendy Schacht, etc. 88-300 SPR
* Clean Air Act: Gasoline Vapor Recovery; Archived I ssue Brief, David E. Gushee IB87029
* Commercialization of Technology and Issues in the Competitiveness of Selected U.S. Industries; Semic onductors, Biotechnology, and Superconductors Lennard G. Kruger, etc. 88-486 SPR
* Controlling Carbon Dioxide Emissions, Amy Abel, etc. 89-157 ENR
* Direct Federal Support for Technological Innovatio n: Issues and Options, Christopher Hill, etc. 84-118 S
* The Effect, of the Tax Reform Act of 1986 on Techn ological Innovation, Jane Gravelle 87-124 E
* Enhanced Oil REcovery Methods, Joseph Riva 87-827 SPR
* Industrial Innovation:, The Debate Over Government, Policy: Issue Brief, Wendy Schacht IB84004
* Japanese Science and Technology: Some Recent Effor ts to Improve U.S. monitoring, Nancy Miller 86-195 SPR
* Science and Technology: Federal Policy and Economi c Impact: Bibliography-in-Brief, 1983-1986, Virginia MacEwen 87-79 L
* Science, Technology, and the International Competi tivness of American Industry: Selected References,, 1985-1988 B.F. Mangan 88-587 L
* Semiconductor Manufacturing Technology Proposal: S EMATECH; Issue Brief, Glenn J. McLoughlin IB87212
* Social Science Approaches to Innovation and Produc tivity, Christine Matthews Rose 86-710 SPR
* Stevenson-Wydler Technology Innovation Act: A Fede ral Effort to Promote Industrial Innovation: Archi ved Issue Brief Wendy Schacht IB85082
* Superconductivity: Bibliography-in-Brief, 1980-198 8, B.F. Mangan 88-632 L
* Technological Advancement and the Competitivness o f Selected U.S. Industries: Issues for Considerati on Wendy Schacht, etc. 87-345 SPR
* The Toshiba/Kongsberg Case: Proposals to Expand U. S. Penalties for Illegal Exports of High Technolog y Goods Glennon Harrison 87-988 E
* Toshiba-Kongsberg Technology Diversion: Issues for, Congress; Archived Issues Brief, Raymond Ahearn, etc. IB87184
* Trade, Technology, and Competitivness: Issue Brief, Wendy Schacht IB87053
* The U.S. Semiconductor Industry and the SEMATECH P roposal, Glenn J. McLoughlin, etc. 87-354 SPR
* U.S. Space Commercialization Activities, Patricia Humphlett 88-518 SPR

Industry

* see Automobile Industry, High Technology Industrie s, Steel Industry, Textile Industry, Business and Society, Computers, Corporations, Foreign Trade,
* The American Response to Foreign Competition; Audi o Brief, Mary Jane Bolle, etc. AB50180
* Concentration in the U.S Daily Newspaper Industry:, Trends and Issues, R. Kevin Flaherty 84-727 E
* Cooperative R&D: Federal Efforts to Promote Indust rial Competitiveness; Issue Brief, Wendy H. Schacht IB89056
* The Effect of the Canada-U.S. Free Trade Agreement, on U.S. Industries, Economics Division 88-506 E
* Equity, Excellence, adn the Distribution of Federa l REsearch and Devleopment Funds, William C. Boesman, etc. 88-422 SPR
* Impact of the Business Cycle on Productivity Growt h in the U.S. Economy, Mary Jane Bolle 82-172 E
* The Impact of U.S. Antitrust Law on Joint Activity, by Corporations: Some Background, Janice E. Rubin 89-291 A
* Japanese Management Practices and Their Implicatio ns for U.S. Policy, Dick Nanto 82-114 E
* Limiting the Growth of Tax-Exempt Industrial Devel opment Bonds: An Economic Evaluation, Dennis Zimmerman 84-37 E
* Machine Tools: Improts and the U.S. Industry, Econ omy, and Defense Industrial Base, Gary Guenther 86-762 E
* The Research and Development Tax Credit: A Compari son of the Arguments for and Against, Office of Senior Specialists 88-333 S
* A Secondary Market for Industrial Mortgages: A New, Method for Financing Industrial Development, Edward Knight 84-111 E
* Service Sector Productivity in the United States: A Survey, Julius Allen 88-717 E
* Technological Advancement and U.S. Industrial Comp etitiveness, Wendy Schacht 88-689 SPR
* U.S. Chemicals Manufacturing: Status, Issues, and Prospects, Bernard Gelb 88-387 E
* U.S.Jewelry Manufacturing, International Competiti veness, and H.R. 3, Bernard Gelb 87-875 E
* Wage Rates and Exchange Rates, Linda LeGrande 88-252 E

Industry -- Automobile Industry
* Automobile Fleet Incentives or Split-Pricing Practices, Gwenell L. Bass 85-714 E
* Automobile Fuel Economy Standards: Another roll Back? Archived Issue Brief, Robert Bamberger IB88046
* Customs Ruling on Multipurpose Vehicles; Archived Issue Brief, Gwenell Bass IB89053
* Employment and Output Effects of the Extension of Japan's Voluntary Autombile Export Restraints on t e U.S. Automobile and Steel Industries Gwenell Bass 85-710 E
* Foreign Sourcing by the U.S. Automobile Industry, Kevin Flaherty 85-1052 E
* Foreign Trade Zones and the U.S. Automobile Industry, Gwenell Bass, etc. 88-659 E
* The Gray Market for Imported Automobiles, R. Kevin Flaherty 85-651 E
* Japan's Automobile Industry and Barriers to Purchases of U.S. Cars, Dick Nanto, etc. 87-793 E
* Transport Manufacturing: A Review and Appraisal of, Federal Assistance Policies, Gwenell Bass 86-75 E
* U.S. Automobile Industry: Issues and Statistics, Gwenell Bass 85-792 E
* U.S. Economic Policy in an International Context: The U.S. Automobile Industry in International Comp etition: Voluntary Export Restraints and Domestic Dick K. Nanto 85-34 E

Industry -- High Technology Industries
* Commercialization of Technology and Issues inthe Competitivness of Selected U.S. Industries: Semicon ductors, Biotechnology, and Superconductors Lennard G. Kurger, etc. 88-486 SPR
* High-Technology Trade: Bibliography-in-Brief, 1985-1988, Robert Kirk 88-572 L
* Semiconductor Devices: The Changing Competitiveness of U.S. Merchant Producers, 1977-87, Gary Guenther 88-191 E
* Semiconductors: Issues Confronting the Industry: B ibliography-in-Brief, 1985-1988, Karen Alderson 88-445 L

Industry -- Steel Industry
* America's Steel Industry: Modernizing to Compete, David Cantor 84-786 E
* Compensation in U.S. and Foreign Steel Industries, Linda LeGrande 88-314 E
* Employment and Output Effects of the Extension of Japan's Voluntary Automobile Export Restraints on the US. Automobile and Steel Industries Gwenell Bass 85-710 E
* An Evaluation of the Reconstruction Finance Corporation With Implications for Current Capital Needs of the Steel Industry

James Bickley 80-43 E
* Federal Taxes, the Steel Industry, and Net Operating Loss
Carryforwards, David Brumbaugh 88-5 E
* Hypothetical Effects of Lower Interest Rates on the Costs of
Production of the Integrated Steel Indu stry David Cantor 85-738
E
* Implementation of the President's Steel Program: Implications
for Output and Employment of the Steel, and Steel-Related
Industries David Cantor 86-518 * The Influence of Labor Costs on
the Total Cost of Steel Production in Integrated Steel Mills:
Effect s of Hypothetical Labor Cost Reductions David Cantor
85-912 E
* Japan's Steel Industry: Positioning for Survival, James
Jackson 88-346 E
* Merger Guidelines--a Case Study of the LTV and Republic Steel
Corporations, Gwenell Bass 84-133 E
* New Technology for the U.S. Steel Industry: A Great Leap
Forward?, Lennard Kruger 86-636 SPR
* The President's Steel Program: Background and Implementation,
David J. Cantor 86-658 E
* Steel Imports: Arguments for and Against Extension, of the
President's Program: Issue Brief, David Cantor IB88109
* Steel Imports from Canada and the President's Steel Program:
Archived Issue Brief, David Cantor IB87197
* Steel Imports: Is the President's Steel Program Working?
Archived Issue Brief, David Cantor IB86141
* Steel Imports of Hot Rolled Sheet from Korea in the Absence of
Import Restraints: Hypothetical Effec ts on West Coast Steel
Producer David Cantor 88-678 E
* The Steel Industry's Impact on the Economy in 1988, David
Cantor 88-664 E
* Steel Manufacturing in the United States: Can a Smaller
Industry Be Profitable?, David Cantor 87-649 E
* Steel Markets in the United States: Where Have All, the Buyers
Gone?, David Cantor 87-474 E
* Steel Prices and Import Restraints, David Cantor 88-204 E
* Steel Prices in 1987 and 1988: How Have the Small Buyers Fared?,
David Cantor 89-230 E
* The U.S. Steel Industry: Factors Influencing Gains, in Industry
Productivity, David Cantor 87-498 E

Industry -- Textile Industry
* The Canadian Free Trade Agreement and the Textile and Apparel
Industries, Edward Rappaport 87-979 E
* Compensation in the Textile and Apparel Industries :
International and Domestic Comparisons, Dennis Roth, etc. 85-671
E
* Textile and Apparel Trade Protection: Issue Brief, Edward B.
Rappaport IB87109
* Textile Trade Controls: A Comparison of Bills in t he 99th and
100th Congress, Edward Rappaport 87-607 E

INF
* see Arms Control, Weapons Systems--Nuclear Weapons,
* Arms Control: Negotiations to Reduce INF Weapons: rchived Issue
Brief, Paul Gallis IB86054
* Arms Control: Ratification of the INF Treaty; Arch ived Issue
Brief, Paul Gallis IB88003
* Assessing the INF Treaty, Foreign Affairs and National Defense
Division 88-211 F
* Chemical Weapons Disarmament Talks: Archived Issue, Brief,
Steven R. Bowman IB87047
* Implications for NATO Strategy of a Zero-Outcome I
ntermediate-Range Nuclear Missile Accord, Stanley Sloan 87-614
* INF and the INF Treaty: Bibliography-in-Brief, 198 3-1988,
Valentin Leskovsek 88-454 L
* The INF Treaty and Its Political-Military Implicat ions for
Western Europe, Hugh DeSantis 88-57 F
* INF Treaty: Environmental Issues; Archived Issue B rief, Mary
E. Tiemann IB88023
* INF Treaty: Info Pack, IP392I
* Intermediate-Range Nuclear Forces Treaty: Timetabl e of
Elimination and Verification Provisions and G lossary of Key
Terms Joseph M. Freeman 88-153 * Nuclear Arms Control: Disposal
of Nuclear Warheads ; Issue Brief, Warren Donnelly IB88024
* Statements by Presiden Reagan Relating to the INF Treaty, June
1, 1987-December 31, 1987, Teri Lehto 88-60 S

Inflation
* see Economic Conditions-Inflation,

Information and Privacy
* see Civil Liberties and Rights, Computers,

Infrastructure
* see Highways, Marine Transportation, Procurement, Regional
Development, Solid Wastes, Transportation , Urban Affairs, Water

Resources,
* The American Infrastructure: Selected References, 1985-1988,
Robert Howe 89-41 L
* The "Bridge Crisis": An Economic Development Perspective: Issue
Brief, J.F Hornbeck IB88085
* The FY 1989 Federal Budget for Public Works Infrastructure,
Claudia Copeland 88-176 ENR
* Infrastructure: A Brief Overview from the National, Level,
William Ellis, etc. 87-30 S
* The Nation's Water Supply: An Overview of Conditions and
Prospects, 86-893 ENR
* Rural Community Development: Selected References, Rebecca
Mazur 88-17 L
* Transportation Infrastructure and Economic Development,
J.F.Hornbeck 89-109 E

INS v. Chadha
* see Congress--Executive Relations,

Insider Trading
* see Corporations--Securities Industry,

Institute for Scientific and Technological Cooperation
*Institute for Scientific and Technological Coopera tion:
Archived Issue Brief Genevieve Knezo IB79033

Insurance
* see Liability Issues, Health Insurance,
* AIDS and Discrimination: Legal Limits on Insurance,
Underwriting Practices, Kirk Nemer 88-381 A
* Automobile Insurance Controversy, Rawle King 88-731 E
* Automobile Insurance Crisis: Issue Brief, Rawle King IB89013
* Captive Off-Shore Insurance Companies, David Whiteman 84-507 E
* The Evolving National Flood Insurance Program, Malcolm M.
Simmons 88-641 ENR
* Federal Crop Insurance: Background and Current Issues, Ralph
Chite 88-739 ENR
* FHA's Mortgage Insurance Premium Refund Programs, Barbara
Miles 87-709 E
* Fraternal Association Insurance as a Source of Life and Health
Coverage, David Whiteman 87-784 E
* How Life Insurance Policies Generate Investment Income, Jack
Taylor 88-326 E
* Insurance: An Alphabetical Microthesaurus of Terms, Selected
from the Legislative Indexing Vocabulary, Shirley Loo 88-582 L
* Insurance Industry Regulation and Supervision: A Reexamination
of the McDarran-Ferguson Act of 1945;, Archived Issue Brief David
Whiteman IB86149
* Insurance Underwriting and the Insurance Rate Classification
Proces, David Whiteman 84-550 E
* Managing Coastal Development Through the Coastal Zone
Management and Flood Insurance Programs: Experience to Date and
the Views from Selected States Gary Kamimura, etc. 88-354 ENR
* The "Pooling" Process in Insurance and Reinsurance, David
Whiteman 84-540 E
* Property-Casualty Insurance market Operation, David Whiteman
85-629 E
* Single-Premium Life Insurance Market Operation, Jack Taylor
IB88074
* A Summary of the Provisions of the Tax Reform of 1986 Affecting
the Treatment of Insurance Companies, and Products Robert
Burdette 87-696 A

Insurance -- Liability Issues
* Commercial Insurance and Liability Problems: Legislative
Proposals in the 99th Congress, Kevin Flaherty 86-731 E

* Environmental Impairment Liability Insurance: Overview of
Availability Issues, Rawle King 89-269 E
* Federal Tort Claims Act: Current Legislative and Judicial
Issues, Henry Cohen 88-168 A
* Insurance for Directors and Officers: The 1987 Market, Sylvia
Morrison 87-545 E
* Liability Insurance and Tort Liability Reform: Legislative
Proposals in the 99th Congress, Edward Rappaport, etc. 87-97 E
* Liability Insurance and Tort Reform: Archive Issue, Brief,
Henry Cohen, etc. IB87015
* Liability Insurance Availability and Affordability Problems as
a Function of Property-Casualty Insur ance Market Fluctuations
David Whiteman 85-826 E
* The Liability Insurance Controversy: Archived Issue Brief,
David Whiteman IB86154
* Liability Insurance: Selected References, 1986-1988, Felix
Chin 88-163 L
* Liability Insurance: The Allocation of Investment Income by
Line of Insurance, David Cantor 86-858 E
* Nuclear Liability Legislation: price-Anderson Act Renewal

Issues: Archived Issue Brief, Mark Holt IB88034
* Products Liability: A Legal Overview: Issue Brief, Henry Cohen IB77021
* Products Liability Reform: Analysis of H.R. 1115, 100th Congress, as Reported by Subcommittee, Henry Cohen 88-53 A
* Recent Judicial Expansions of Products Liability and Other Tort Law, Henry Cohen 86-847 A
* State Initiatives Regarding Commercial Liability Insurance: 1986 Efforts to Address the Shortage of Coverage and Its High Price Sylvia Morrison 86-971 E
* Tort Injury Compensation Reform: Various Approaches, Henry Cohen 87-666 A
* The Tort Reform Debate: Pros, Cons, Federal Proposals, State Statutes, Henry Cohen 86-579 A
* Tort Reform: State Statutory Caps on Damages, Henry Cohen, etc. 87-835 A

Integration
* see Blacks, Civil Liberties and Rights--Discrimina tion and Integration, Equal Employment Opportunity , Higher Education--Integration, Housing,

Intelligence Activities
* Arms Control and Intelligence: Bibliography-in-Bri ef, 1979-1987, Teri Lehto, etc. 87-499 S
* The Central Intelligence Agency: Organizational History, Mark Lowenthal 78-168 F
* Congress and Intelligence Policy: Selected References, Sherry Shapiro 88-36 L
* Contra Aid: Analysis of Whether the National Security Council (NSC) and the NSC Staff Are an "agency, or Entity Involved in Intelligence Activities" Co Larry E. Eig 87-566 A
* Covert Actions: Congressional Oversight: Archvied Issue Brief, Richard F. Grimmett IB87208
* Individuals Arrested on Charges of Espionage Against the United States Government: 1966-1989, Suzanne Cavanagh 89-324 GOV
* Intelligence Reform Issues: Issue Brief, Alfred B. Prados IB88029
* Intelligence Reform: Recent History and Proposals, Alfred Prados 88-562 F
* Office of Inspector General in the Central Intelligence Agency: Development and Proposals, Frederick M. Kaiser 89-129 GOV
* Special Access Programs, Confidential Funding, and the Defense Budget: Bibliography-in-Brief, Sherry Shapiro 87-802 L
* U.S. Defense Planning: A Critique, John Collins, etc. 82-167 S

Interest Rates
* see Money and Banking--Interest Rates,

Intergovernmental Fiscal Relations
* see State and Local Government--Intergovernmental Fiscal Relations,

Internal Security
* Abolition of the House Internal Security Committee, Paul Rundquist 88-203 GOV
* Classified Information Procedures Act (CIPA): An Overview, Larry Eig 89-172 A
* Contra Aid: Analysis of Whether the National Security Council (NSC) and the NSC Staff Are an "agency, or Entity Involved in Intelligence Activities" Co Larry E. Eig 87-566 A
* Individuals Arrested on Charges of Espionage Against the United States Government: 1966-1989, Suzanne Cavanagh 89-324 GOV
* Protecting Classified Information: A Compilationa and Index of Major Findings and Recommendations, 1 905-1987 Frederick M. Kaiser, etc. 87-293 GOV
* Scientific Communication and National Secuirty: Bibliography-in-Brief, 1982-1987, Virginia MacEwen, etc. 87-110 L
* Security Clearances for Congressional dn judicial Employees, Frederick Kaiser 87-809 GOV
* Security Clearances for Members of Congress and the Judiciary, Frederick M. Kaiser 87-704 GOV

International Agencies
* Access to World Bank Information, Jonathan E. Sanford 89-89 F
* Answers to Nine Questions on the United Nations, Lois McHugh 84-31 F
* International Atomic energy Agency: Bibliography-in-Brief, Bonnie F. Mangan 89-259 L
* International Fund for Agricultural Development, Susan Epstein 87-4 ENR
* International Labor Organizations: Issues of U.S. Membership: Archvied Issue Brief, Lois McHugh IB77073
* Interntional Monetary Fund and World Bank: Info Pack, IP2451
* International Monetary Fund: Bibliography-in-Brief ,

1983-1987, Robert Kirk 87-47 L
* Israel's Participation in the International Atomic, Energy Agency and the 32nd IAEA General Conferenc e: Archived Issue Brief Warren Donnelly I88072
* Presidential Remarks About the International Atomic Energy Agency: Selected Excerpts, Barbara Black 89-27 ENR
* The Soviet Union and the United Nations: Congressional issues; Archived Issue Brief, Vita Blue IB88069
* The U.N. and Congress: Legislation Affecting Participation and Contributions (98th, 99th, and 100th Congress) Vita Blue, etc. 89-223 F
* U.N. Funding: Congressional Issues; Issue Brief, Vita Blue IB86116
* UNESCO-U.S. Withdrawal in Persepctive: Archived Issue Brief, Lois McHugh IB84086
* United Nations Reform: Issues for Congress, Marjorie Ann Browne 88-593 F
* United Nations Role in the Iran-Iraq War: Issues and Options, Lois B. McHugh, etc. 88-463 F
* The United States and Southern Africa: A Review of United Nations Resoltuions and United States Voti ng Patterns, 1946-October 1985 Frankie King 86-21 * United States Contributions to UNICEF, Lois McHugh 88-154 F
* U.S. Bilateral and Multilateral Food Assistance Programs, Susan Epstein 85-114 ENR
* U.S. Withdrawal from the International Labor Organization: Successful Precedent for UNESCO?, Lois McHugh 84-202 F
* The World Bank: Eighteen Questions and Answers, Jonathan E. Sanford 86-769 F
* World Health Organization: Effects of Reduced U.S., Contributions, Lois McHugh 87-108 F

International Atomic Energy Agency
* Implementation of the U.S.-Chinese Agreement for Nuclear Cooperation: Archived Issue Brief, Warren Donnelly IB86050
* International Atomic Energy Agency: Bibliography-in-Brief, Bonnie Mangan 89-259 L
* Israel's Participation in the International Atomic, Energy Agency and the 32nd IAEA General Conferenc e: Archived Issue Brief Warren H. Donnelly IB88072
* Presidential Remarks About the International Atomic Energy Agency: Selected Excerpts, Barbara Black 89-27 ENR

International Brotherhood of Teamsters, Chauffeurs, Warehousemen and Helpers of America,
* The International Brotherhood of Teamsters; an Historical and Bibliographical Review, William Whittaker 77-71 E

International Coffee Agreement
* International Coffee Agreement, Donna Vogt 84-224 ENR

International Commission on Central American Recovery and Development,
* International Commission on Central America: Initi al Views; Audio Brief, Larry Storrs AB50176

International Competitiveness
* see Foreign Trade--Competitiveness,

International Corporations
* The European Community's 1992 Plan: Effects on Ame rican Direct Investment, James K. Jackson 89-339 E
* The Financial Impact of Oil Price Behavior on International Development and Trade: Transnational Oil, Companies and Persian Gulf Exporters; Report of Clyde R. Mark, etc. 86-903 F
* Foreign Corrupt Practices Act Amendments of 1988, Michael V. Seitzinger 88-589 A
* Foreign Mergers and Acquisitions: Non-U.S. Companies Acquiring U.S. Companies, Kevin F. Winch, etc. 87-711 E
* Major Federal Tax provisions that Directly Affect International Trade and Investment, David Brumbaugh 86-764 E
* Offshore Manufacturing by U.S Corporations: Selected Bibliography, With Introductory Readings, Robert Kirk 86-834 L
* Taxation of Foreign-Source Income: A Survey: a Brief Overview of Concepts, Provisions, and Issues in, the Federal Taxation of Foreign-Source Income David L. Brumbaugh 83-636 E
* Taxation of Foreign-Source-Income: A Survey: the U .S. Foreign Tax Credits: Provisions, Effects and I ssues David Brumbaugh 83-222 E

International Debt Crisis
* see International Finance--Foreign Loans,

International Economic Relations
* see Foreign Aid, Foreign Investment, Foreign Trade,

Currents Events and Homework

International Environmental Affairs
* Agriculture and the Environment: Issue Brief, Geoffrey Becker, etc. IB89086
* Anarctica: Environmental Protection Issues: Summary of a CRS Research Workshop, Susan Fletcher 89-272 ENR
* Canada's Progress on Acid Rain Control: Shifting Gears or Stalled in Neutral?, Mira Courpas, etc. 89-272 ENR
* CFC Phase-Out Bills in the 101st Congress: Comparison of Provisions, David Gushee 89-314 ENR
* Debt-for-Nature Swaps in Developing Countries: An Overview of Recent Conservation Efforts, Betsy Cody 88-647 ENR
* Desertification: Overview of a Global Environmental Problem, Susan Abbasi 84-599 ENR
* Environment and International Economic Development : The Role of Cost-Benefit Analysis, John Moore, etc. 87-774 ENR
* Environmental Protection in Developing Countries: Selected References, 1983-1987, Rebecca Mazur 87-488
* Export of Pesticides, James V. Aidala 89-73 ENR
* Global Climate Changes and the Green House Effect:, Congressional Activity and Options: Archived Issu e Brief David Gushee IB88077
* The Global Environment: Audio Brief, AB50063
* International Environment: Overview of Major Issues: Issue Brief, Mary Tiemann, etc. IB89057
* The Stratospheric Ozone Layer: Regulatory Issues: Issue Brief, David Gushee IB89021
* Tropical Deforestation: Info Pack, IP416T
* Tropical Deforestation: International Implications : Issue Brief, Susan Fletcher IB89010
* Tropical Deforestation: The International Tropical, Timber Agreement, Ross W. Gorte 87-795 ENR
* The Unpredictable Atmosphere: Selected REferences, Karen Alderson, etc. 89-43 L
* Waste in the Marine Environment: Selected References, Ted Burch 89-263 L
* Whale Conservation, Eugene H. Buck, etc. 88-391 ENR

International Finance
* see Foreign Exchange Rates, Foreign Loans, Multila teral Development Banks,
* The British Experience With Indexed Bonds, G. Thomas Woodward 87-926 E
* Capital Market Changes in the United Kingdom, Japan, West Germany, and Singapore: A Brief Survey, Julius W. Allen 88-49 E
* Chronology of Important Events in International Economics, George Holliday 85-512 E
* Doemstic and International Monetary=Fiscal Policy Coordiantion, Thomas F. Dernburg 84-145 E
* The Financial Impact of Oil Price Behavior on International Development and Trade: Transnational Oil, Companies and Persian Gulf Oil Exporters: Clyde R. Mark, etc. 86-903 F
* Financial markets: A New Framework of Issues, Walter Eubanks 88-485 E
* Growing Internationalization of Stock Markets: Implications for Financial Regulation: Archived Issue, Brief Edward Knight IB88037
* International Banking Facilities and the Eurocurrency market, William Jackson, etc. 82-27 E
* The Internationalization of Securities Trading Markets, Julius W. Allen 86-14 E
* Is Faster Growth in Germany and Japan the Key to Faster U.S. Growth?, Gail E. Makinen 86-836 E
* Japan's Financial Liberalization: Effects on the United States, James K. Jackson 89-102 E
* Merchant Banking: Opportunities or Problems for U.S. Banks?, Walter Eubanks, etc. 87-351

* Progress Against Poverty in the United States (1959 to 1987), Thomas Gabe 89-211 EPW
* The Role of Gold in the International Monetary System, Arlene Wilson 80-47 E
* A Survey of U.S. International Economic Policy and Problems, Alfred Reifman 88-666 S
* Trade and Current Account Balances: Statistics: Archived Issue Brief, Glennon J. Harrison IB87112
* Trade and International Finance: An Alphabetical Microthesaurus of Terms Selected from the legislati ve Indexing Vocabulary Shirley Loo 87-369 L

International Finance -- Foreign Exchange Rates
* Deficit Reduction and the Foreign Exchange Value o f the Dollar, Brian W. Cashell, etc. 87-990 E
* The Dollar and the Trade Deficit: What's to Be Done?, Craig Elwell, etc. 88-430 E
* Domestic and International Monetary-Fiscal Policy Coordination, Thomas F. Dernburg 84-145 E

* Exchange Rate Management in Taiwan, South Korea and Hong Kong, Arlene Wilson 87-401 E
* Exchange Rates: The Dollar in International Markets: Archived Issue Brief, Arlene Wilson IB78033
* A Falling Dollar and Domestic Inflation, Craig K. Elwell 86-127 E
* Foreign Exchange Intervention, Arlene Wilson 86-915 E
* How Much Has the International Exchange Value of the Dollar Declined?, Gail Makinen 87-429 E
* Next Steps in International Monetary Reform: Exchange Rate Targeting?, Alfred Reifman 88-1 S
* Special Drawing Rights in the International Monetary System: Their Nature, evolution, and Future Rol e Craig Elwell 88-348 E
* Trade Deficits and the Dollar: Bibliography-in-Brief, 1984-1987, Robert S. Kirk 87-88 L
* Trade: Issue Brief, Arlene Wilson, etc. IB87003
* Wage Rates and Exchange Rates, Linda LeGrande 88-252 E

International Finance -- Foreign Loans
* African Debt: The Offical Donor Response and Poten tial Alternative Strategies, Alan K. Yu 89-228 F
* The "Baker Plan": A Remedy for the International Debt Crisis?: Issue Brief, Patricia Wertman IB86106
* Bank Lending to the Third World: Risk Considerations, William Jackson 88-525 E
* The Citiccorp Initiative: A Brave New World for the Third World Debt Problem, Patricia Wertman 87-750 E
* Debt-for-Nature Swaps in Developing Countries: An Overivew of Recent Conservation Efforts, Betsy Cody 88-647 ENR
* Debt Rescheduling Agreements in Latin America, 1980-86, Glennon Harrison 87-360 E
* Debt Rescheduling: The Argentine Case, 1982-1988, Glennon Harrison 88-505 E
* Debt Service Indicators of the Seventeen Most Highly Indebted Developing Countries, 1978-1986, Patricia Wertman, etc.
* Finance and Adjustment: The International Debt Crisis, 1982-84, Patricia Wertman 84-162 E
* The Growing U.S. External Debt: Nature and Implications, Craig Elwell 87-798 E
* An International Debt Management Authority: Could It Spell R-E-L-I-E-F?, Economics Division 88-607 E
* The International Debt problem: Congressional Proposals: Archived Issue Brief, Patricia Wertman IB86124
* The International Debt Problem: Impact and Response, Glennon Harrison, etc. 88-76 E
* The International Debt Problem: Options for Solution, Patricia Wertman 86-922 E
* International Debt Problems: Background, Statistics, Proposed Solutions: Info Pack, IP234I
* International Lending Patterns of U.S. Banks: Financial and Regulatory Trends, William Jackson 85-124 E
* Latin American Debt and U.S. Agricultural Exports:, Assessment of a Proposed Approach, Charles E. Hanrahan 87-304 ENR
* Latin American Debt Crisis: Selected References, 1986-1989, Robert Howe 89-301 L
* The Mexican Debt Accords and Their Financial Implications: An Overview, Patricia Wertman 86-179 E
* The Mexican Debt Swap: The Advent of Debt Relief?, Patricia Wertman 88-145 E
* Poland's Economic Recovery: U.S. Policy Interests:, Archived Issue Brief, John Hardt, etc. IB86070
* Rescheduling International Debt, Glennon Harrison 89-126 E
* The South Africa Financial Crisis: The Role of U.S . Banks, Walter Eubanks 86-550 E
* Trade of the Seventeen Highly Indebted Countries: A Brief Overview, Patricia Wertman, etc. 88-521 E
* U.S. Bank Exposure in the Seventeen Highly Indebted Countries: 1982-1987, Patricia Wertman, etc. 88-522 E
* U.S. Banks and the People's Republic of China, Walter Eubanks 84-840 E
* U.S. Tax Treatment of Bad Foreign Loans, David L. Brumbaugh 89-302 E
* Worldwide Bank Exposure in the Seventeen Highly Indebted Countries, 1982-1987, Patricia Wertman 88-527 E

International Finance -- Multilateral Development
* Banks,
* Access to World Bank Information, Jonathan E. Sanford 89-89 F
* International Monetary Fund and World Bank: Info Pack, IP2245I
* Internationalmonetary Fund: Bibliography-in-Brief,, 1983-1987, Robert Kirk 87-47 L
* Multilateral Development Banks: Issues for the 101st Congress; Archived Issue Breif, Jonathan E. Sanford IB87218
* World Bank Activities in Ethiopia, Jonathan E. Sanford 87-857 F
* The World Bank: Eighteen Questions and Answers, Jonathan E. Sanford 86-769 F

950

Currents Events and Homework

* Japan-South Korea Economic Relations: South Korea's Appraoch to the "Japan Problem", Dick Nanto 87-953 E
* Japan-United States Economic Relations: Views of Japan's Economic Decisionmakers, Dick Nanto 86-52 E
* Japan-U.S. Economic Relations: Bibliography-in-Brief, 1986-1987, Robert Kirk 87-45 L
* Japan-Us. Relations in the 1990s, Larry Niksch 89-264 F
* Japan-U.S. Relations: Issue Brief, Robert Sutter IB81026
* Japan-U.S. Trade: An Overview, William H. Cooper 88-127 E
* Japan-U.S. Trade and Economic Relations: Info Pack, IP201J
* Japan-U.S. Trade Relations: Archived Issue Brief, Raymond Ahearn IB81011
* Japanese Management practices and Their Implications for U.S. Policy, Dick Nanto 82-114 E
* Japanese Science and Technology: Some Recent Efforts to Improve U.S. Monitoring, Nancy Miller 86-195 SPR
* Japanese Technical Information: Opportunities to Improve U.S. Access, Christopher Hill 87-818 S
* Japan's Automobile Industry and Barriers to Purchases of U.S. Cars, Dick Nanto, etc. 87-793 E
* Japan's Financial Liberalization: Effects on the United States, James Jackson 89-102 E
* Japan's Military Buildup: Goals and Accomplishments, Gary Reynolds 89-68 F
* JETRO: The Japan External Trade Organiztion, R. Kevin Flaherty 85-1112 E
* Market Access in Japan: The U.S. Experience, Raymond Ahearn 85-37 E
* The MOSS Talks: Success or Failure?, Patricia Wertman 85-1129 E
* The NATO Allies, Japan, and the Persian Gulf, Paul Gallis 84-184 F
* Plutonium Economics and Japan's Nuclear Fuel Cycle Policies, Robert Civiak 88-235 SPR
* Sino-Japanese Economic Relations in the Post Mao Decade., Dick Nanto, etc. 86-170 E
* Space Commercialization in China and Japan, Marcia S. Smith 88-519 SPR
* The Stock Market in Japan: An Overivew and Analysis, Arturo Wiener, etc. 89-306 E
* United States Merchandise Trade and Trade Balances With Japan, 1960-1987, Dario Scuka 88-81 E
* U.S. Agricultural Trade Opportunities With Pacific Rim Nations, Robert Goldstein 88-755 ENR
* U.S. Civilian and Defense Research and Development Funding: Some Trends and Comparisons With Selecte d Industrialized Nations William Boesman, etc. 84-195 SPR
* U.S. Japanese Agricultural Trade Relations: Selected Information, Donna Vogt 88-159 ENR

Job Retraining
* see Occupational Training,

Job Training Partnership Act
* Job Training: FY 88 Budget and Legislative Issues: Archvied Issue Brief, Karen Spar IB87039

Jordan
* Jordan: U.S. Foreign Assistance Facts: Archived Issue Brief, Richard Preece IB85120

Judiciary
* see also Supreme Court,
* An Analysis of S.J. Res. 113, a Proposed Constitutional Amendment Relating to the Removal of Federal, Judges Elizabeth Bazan 87-764 A
* Commission on Executive, Legislative, and Judicial Salaries: An Historical Overview, Sharon Gresle 88-667 GOV
* Confidentiality and Secrecy Orders in Civil Cases, Kenneth Thompson 89-225 A
* Election of Federal Judges, Paul Morgan 88-179 A
* Establishing Federal Judicial Districts, Paul Morgan 88-344 A
* Federal, Executive, Legislative and Judicial Compensation: The Situation and Choices for the 101st C ongress James McGrath 89-70 GOV
* President Reagan's Judcial Nominations During the 100th Congress: A Statistical OVerview and Listing, of Nominees and Dates of Confirmation or other Denis Stevens Rutkus 89-50 GOV
* Salaries and Allwoances: The Judiciary: Issue Brief, Sharon Gressle IB81264
* Sources of Legislative History as Aids to Statutory Construction, George A. Costello 89-86 A
* Sources of State Juror Lists, Paul Morgan 89-337 A
* United States Sentencing Commission: Preliminary Analysis, Charles Doyle 89-308 A
* U.S. Government: Info Pack, IP162U

Judiciary -- Supreme Court
* The Speed With Which action Has Been Taken on Supreme Court Nominations in the Last 25 Years, Denis Steven Rutkus 87-576 A
* Supreme Court: Bibliography-in-Brief, 1970-1988, Charles P. Dove 88-192 L
* Supreme Court: Church-State Cases, October 1984 Term; Archived Issue Brief, David Ackerman IB84229
* Supreme Court: Church-State Cases, October 1984 Term; Archived Issue Brief, David Ackerman IB85207
* Supreme Court: Church-State Cases, October 1986 Term; Archived Issue Brief, David Ackerman IB86129
* Supreme Court Church-State Cases, October 1987 Term; Archived Brief, David Ackerman IB87217
* Supreme Court: Church-State Cases, October 1988 Term; Issue Brief, David Ackerman IB88105

Junk Bonds
* see Corporations-Securities Industry,

Juvenile Delinquency
* see Crimes and Offenses,

King, Martin Luther
* Martin Luther King: Selected References, 1978-1989, Jean Bowers 88-769 L
* Speech Material: Martin Luther King's Birthday; Info Pack., IP372M

Kissinger Commission
* Kissinger Commission Implementation: Action by the, Congress Through 1986 on the Recommendations of the National Bipartisan Commission on Central Ameri K. Larry Storrs 87-291 F
* A Summary and Analysis of the Report of the National Bipartisan "Kissinger" Commission on Central Am erica, January 1984, Richard Cronin, etc. 84-39 F

Korea
* U.S. Agricultural Trade Opportunities With Pacific, Rim Nations, Robert M. Goldstein 88-755 ENR

Labor
* see, Earnings and Benefits, Minimum Wages, Policies and Legislation, Productivity, Unemployment, Unions,
* Career Guidance and Federal Job Information: Info Pack, IP016C
* Civilian and Military Pilots: The Labor Market Relationship, John W. Fischer, etc. 86-28 E
* Counting Migrant and Seasonal Farmworkers: A Persistent Data Void, Dennis M. Roth 85-797 E
* A Demographic Portrait of Older Workers, Gail McCallion 88-636 E
* Early Retirement Incentive Plans under the Age Discrimination in Employment Act of 1967, as Amended., Kathleen S. Swendiman 88-608 A
* Economic Conditions: Archived Issue Brief, Gail Makinen IB87004
* Economic Policy: Selected Issues of Interest to the 101st Congress, Edward Knight 89-209 E
* Education and Job Growth, Linda LeGrande 88-476 E
* Employment Abroad: Info Pack, IP065E
* Employment and Labor: An Alphabetical Microthesaurus of Terms Selected from the Legislative Indexing Vocabulary Shirley Loo 88-748 L
* Employment and Unemployment: Some International Comparisons, Gail McCallion 88-673 E
* Employment Status of the States: Data and Trends: Archived Issue Brief, Linda LeGrande IB82098
* Employment Trends in the 1980s from a National Industrial, and Geographic Perspective, Linda LeGrande, ect. 86-130 E
* Employment Trends Through the 1990s: Selected References, 1986-1989, Robert Howe 89-203 L
* Farmer Transition Programs, Rebecca Mazur 88-364 L
* Hours of Work: Historical Trends and Recent Policy, Initiative, William G. Whittaker 86-61 E
* The Impact of Defense Spending on Employment, Carolyn Brancato, etc. 82-182 E
* The Influence of Labor Costs on the Total Cost of Steel Production in Integrated Steel Mills: Effect s of Hypothetical Labor Cost Reductions David J. Cantor 85-912 E
* Internships and Fellowships: Info Pack, IP063I
* Older Workers: the Transition to Retirement, Gail McCallion 89-286 E
* Polygraph Testing of Employees in Private Industry, Britt Liddicoat 85-929 A
* Service Sector Productivity in the United States: A Survey, Julius W. Allen 88-717 E
* Airline Mergers and labor Protective Provisions, IB87179
* Comparable Worth/Pay Equity in the Federal Governm ent,

etc. 86-89 S
* Productivity and U.S. Living Standards: Issue Brief, William A. Cox IB88107
* Social Science Approaches to Innovation and Productiviy, Christine Matthews 86-710 SPR
* The U.S. Steel Industry: Factors Influencing Gains in Industry Productivity, David J. Cantor 87-498 E

Labor -- Unemployment

* American Direct Investment Abroad: Effects on Trade, Jobs, and the Balance of Payments, James K. Jackson 88-546 E
* Declining Unemployment: some Observations, Dennis M. Roth 87-679 E
* Economic Growth and Changing Labor Markets: Those Left Behind; Adult Black Workers: the Progress of Some Linda LeGrande 84-228 E
* Economic Growth and Changing Labor Markets: Those Left Behind; Women Workers (Un)changed Position, Linda LeGrande 84-112 E
* Foreign Trade and U.S. Employement: Bibliography-in-Brief, 1983-1987, Robert S. Kirk 87-344 L
* Is the Service Sector Recession-Proof?, Linda LeGrande 88-132 E
* The Labor Market of the 1980s: Unemployment Omens in a Growing Economy; Archived Issue Brief, Dennis M. Roth IB87110
* Manufacturing Job Trends by Geographic Area, Linda LeGrande 88-55 E
* Mergers and Acquisitions: The Impact on Labor, Gail McCallion 87-705 E
* The Phillips Curve vs. the Natural Rate of Unemployment: Their Potential as Policymaking Guides in Our Modern Economy Charles V. Ciccone 86-896 E
* Plant Closing Legislation: Economic Dislocation and Worker Adjustment Assistance Act; Issue Brief, Mary Jane Bolle IB87160
* Plant Closings: Selected References, 1984-1988, Felix Chin 88-615 L
* The Relationship Between "Right-to-Work" Laws and Unemployment, Richard S. Belous 84-632 E
* States/Counties of the Lower Mississippi River Valley: Statistics on Per Capita Personal Income and Unemployment Rates Jan E. Christopher 88-254 E
* Targeted Jobs Tax Credit: Action in the 100th Congress; Issue Brief, Linda LeGrande IB87142
* The Targeted Jobs Tax Credit, 1978-1987, Linda LeGrande 87-616 E
* Unemployment: Why and How It Is Falling, Linda LeGrande 89-78 E

Labor -- Unions

* Air Traffic Controllers: Labor Relation Since the Demise of PATCO, Gail McCallion 87-786 E
* Airline Mergers and Labor Protective Provisions: Issue Brief, Linda LeGrande IB87179
* Collective-Gargaining Trends: the 1980s and Beyond, Gail McCallion 88-208 E
* Construction Industry collective Bargaining: Prehire Agreements and Double Breasting; Issue Brief, Gail McCallion IB85177
* The International Brotherhood of Teamsters; an Historical and Bibliographical Review, William Whittaker 77-71 E
* Labor Problems at Eastern Air Lines: Issue Brief, Linda LeGrande IB88052
* Strike Activity: Recent Trends, Gail McCallion 88-446 E
* Use of Compulsory Union Dues for Political and ideological Purposes: An Analysis of Supreme Court Decisions and Federal Legislation Re Such Use Thomas M. Durbin 86-1056 A
* Use of Compulsory Union Dues for Political and Other ideological Purposes, Thomas M. Durbin 88-737 A

Land Use

* Compensation for Regulatory "Takings": First English Evangelical Lutheran Church of Glendale v. County of Los Angeles Joseph Maheady 87-623 A
* Compliance Provisions for Resource Conservation: A, Status Report, Jeffery Zinn 88-662 ENR
* Consideration of Economic Factors under the Endangered Species Act, Pamela Baldwin 89-274 A
* The Federal Power of Eminent Domain: A Summary of Principles, Robert Meltz 85-206 A
* Haying and Grazing on Set-Aside Crop Acreage, Carl W. Ek 89-9 ENR
* Indian Tribal Government Zoning Authority, M. Maureen Murphy 88-744 A
* Land and Water Conservation Fund: Information and Status, George H. Siehl 89-159 ENR
* Manassas National Battlefield Park: The Battle Continues, John O. Spengler, etc. 88-514 ENR
* Revisiting the Law of Regulatory Takings: the Supreme Court's Decisions in Keystone, Nollan, and First English Robert Meltz 87-959 A
* Taking Decisions of the Supreme Court: A Compilation of Holding

on Selected Issues, Robert Meltz 87-737 A
* Wetlands Protection: Issue in the 101st Congress; Issue Brief, Jeffery A. Zinn, etc. IB89076

Latin America

* See, Economic Conditions, Foreign Aid, Foreign Relations, Foreign Trade, National Defense, Politics and Government, see also, Central American,
* Caribbean Area: Bilbliography-in-Brief, 1980-1988, Robert S. Kirk 88-152 L
* International Commission on Central America: Initial Views; Audio Brief, Larry Storrs AB50176
* Natural Resources Conservation and Development in Brazil: An Overview and Related Issue, Russell Hawkins 84-802 ENR

Latin America -- Economic Conditions

* Brazilian Petroleum Status, Joseph P. Riva, Jr. 89-328 SPR
* Debt Rescheduling Agreements in Latin America, 1980-86, Glennon J. Harrison 87-360 E
* Debt Rescheduling: the Argentine Case, 1982-1988, Glennon J. Harrison 88-505 E
* Debt Service Indicators of the Seventeen Most Highly Indebted Developing Countries, 1978-1986, Patricia A. Wertman, etc. 88-452 E
* Latin American Debt Crisis: Selected References, 1986-1989, Robert Howe 89-301 L
* The Mexican Debt Accords and Their Financial Implications: An Overview, Patricia A. Wertman 86-179 E
* The Mexican Debt Swap: The Advent of Debt Relief?, Patricia A. Wertman 88-145 E
* Mexican Petroleum, Joseph Riva 83-178 SPR
* Trade of the Seventeen Highly Indebted Countries: A Brief Overview, Patricia A. Wertman, etc. 88-521 E
* U.S. Bank Exposure in the Seventeen Highly Indebted countries: 1982-1987, Patricia A. Wertman, etc. 88-522 E
* U.S.-Mexico Economic Relations: An Overview, Lenore Sek 87-485 E
* Worldwide Bank Exposure in the Seventeen Highly Indebted Countries, 1982-1987, Patricia A. Wertman, etc. 88-527 E

Latin America -- Foreign Aid

* Caribbean Basin Initiative: Info Pack, IP190C
* Central America and U.S. Foreign Assistance: Issues for Congress; Issue Brief, Jonathan Sanford IB84075
* El Salvador Aid: congressional Action, 1981-1986, on President Reagan's Requests for Economic and Military Assistance for El Salvador K. Larry Storrs 87-230 F
* El Salvador: U.S. Foreign Assistance Facts; Issue Brief, K. Larry Storrs, etc. IB85113
* Guatemala: U.S. Foreign Assistance Facts; Archived Issue Brief, Jonathan Sanford IB85100
* Honduras: U.S. Foreign Assistance Facts; Archived Issue Brief, Robert E. Sanchez IB85080
* Major Trends in U.S. Foreign Assistance to Central America: 1978-1986, Jonathan Sanford 86-88 F
* U.S. Assistance to Nicaraguan Guerillas: Issues for the Congress: Archived Issue Brief, Nina Serafino IB84139
* U.S. Bilateral Economic and Military Assistance to, Latin America and the Caribbean: Fiscal Year 1946, to 1987 K. Larry Storrs 87-694 F
* U.S. Foreign Aid to Central America; 1986-1988, Jonathan E. Sanford 87-465 F

Latin America -- Foreign Relations

* The Boland Amendments: A Chronology of Congressional Action, Joseph Maheady 87-833 A
* The Central American Peace Prospects: U.S. Interests and Response; Issue Brief, Nina M. Serafino IP352C
* The Central American Peace Prospects: U.S. Interests and Response; Issue Brief, Nina M. Serafino IB87200
* Congress and U.S. Policy Toward Nicaragua in 1987, Linda Robinson 89-158 F
* Contra Aid: Analysis of Whether the National Security Council(NSC) and the NSC Staff Are an "Agency or Entity Involved in Intelligence Activities" Cov Larry E. Eig 87-566 A
* Kissinger Commission Implementation: Action by the Congress Through 1986 on the Recommendation of the, National Bipartisan Commission on Central America K. Larry Storrs 87-291 F
* Legislative Histories of Statutory Restrictions on Funding for Covert Assistance for Military or Paramilitary Operations in Nicaragua, FY 1983-FY 1986 Larry M. Eig 87-538 A
* Mexico-U.S. Relations: Issues for Congress; Issue Brief, K. Larry Storrs, etc. IB86111
* Narcotics Control and the Use of U.S. Military Personnel: Operations in Bolivia and Issues for Congress Raphael Perl 86-800 F
* Nicaragua: An Overview of U.S. Policy, 1979-1986, Mark P.

Sullivan 87-855 F
* Nicaragua: Conditions and Issues for U.S. Policy: Issue Brief, Nina Serafino IB82115
* Nicaragua v. United States: The International Court of Justice Decision, Daniel Hill Zafren 86-748 A
* The Nicaraguan Resistance ("Contras"): Background and Major Concerns of Congress, Veronica R. Clifford 87-943 F
* Panama: Trade, Finance, and Proposed Economic Sanctions, Glennon J. Harrison 88-188 E
* Panama's Political Crisis: Prospects and U.S. Policy Concerns: Issue Brief, Mark P. Sullivan IB87230
* A Summary and Analysis of the Report of the National Bipartisan "Kissinger" Commission on Central America, January 1984 Richard Cronin, etc. 84-39 F
* The United States and Cuba During the Carter Administration, Margaret Siliciano, etc. 85-988 F
* The United States and Cuba During the Reagan Administration, Judith Levenfeld, etc. 85-989 F
* U.S. Sanctions and the State of the Panamanian Economy, Mark P. Sullivan 88-578 F

Latin America -- Foreign Trade
* Brazil: Selected Foreign Trade Data, Rawle O. King 88-320 E
* Restrictions on U.S. Trade With Cuba: A Chronology of Major Actions and Present Status, Aladimir N. Preglj 86-909 E
* Seizure of Foreign Vessels in United States Ports, Daniel Hill Zafren 87-760 A
* Tariff Items 807.00 and 806.30 and the Mexican Maquiladoras, Patricia Wertman 87-500 E
* United States-Mexican Trade Relations: Present Problems, Future Prospects, Patricia Wertman 85-139 E
* The U.S. Trade Embargo Against Nicaragua After Two-and-a-Half Years, Glennon J. Harrison 87-870 E

Latin America -- National Defense
* Arms Shipments to Iran: Archived Issue Brief, Richard M. Preece IB87022
* Chart of Unclassified Legislative Restrictions Regarding Support for Military or Paramilitary Operations in Nicaragua, 1982-1986 Larry Eig 87-222 A
* Contra Aid FY82-FY88: Summary and Chronology of Major Congressional Action on Key Legislation Concerning U.S. Aid to the Anti-Sandinista Guerrillas Nina M. Serafino 88-563 F
* Grenada: Issues Concerning the Use of U.S. Forces;, Archived Issue Brief, Janice Hanover IB83170
* Iran Arms and Contra Funds: Selected Chronology of Events, 1979-1987, Richard M. Preece, etc. 86-190 F
* Iran Arms Sales and Conra Funds: Summaries of Key Legislative Provisions, Clyde R. Mark, etc. 87-13 F

Latin America -- Politics and Government
* Belize: Country Background Report, Mark P. Sullivan 88-568 F
* Costa Rica: Country Background Report, Nina M. Serafino 88-577 F
* El Salvador: Bibliography-in-Brief, 1986-1989 Robert S. Kirk 89-204 L
* El Salvador: Info Pack, IP121E
* El Salvador, 1982-1984: A Chronology of a Period of Transition Resulting from the 1982 and 1984 Elections K. Larry Storrs 87-656 F
* Guatemala: Country Background Report, Maureen Taft-Morales 88-586 F
* Haiti: Political Developments and U.S. Policy Concerns: Archived Issue Brief, Maureen Taft-Morales IB88104
* Mexico: Problems and Prospects; Info Pack, IP358M
* Nicaragua: Bibliography-in-Brief, 1986-1987, Valentin Leskovsek 87-382 L
* Nicaragua: Info Pack, IP073N
* Nicaragua's "Civic" Opposition: Players, Problems and Prospects, Nina M. Serafino 87-735 F
* Puerto Rico: Political Status Options; Issue Brief, Bette A. Taylor IB89065

Latvia
* Latvia: Background Information, Allan Nanes, etc. 83-154 F

Law
* Awards of Attorney's Fees Against the United States: The Equal Access to Justice Act, as Interpreted, by the Supreme Court in Pierce v. Underwood Henry Cohen 88-570 A
* Awards of Attorney's Fees by Federal Courts and Federal Agencies, Henry Cohen 87-100 A
* The Constitutionality of Federal Tort Reform, Henry Cohen 86-941 A
* The Ethics of a Private Law Practice by Members and Employees of Congress, Jack Maskell 85-663 A
* Federal Statutory Research, Rita Reimer 85-219 A

* Federal Tort Claims Act: Current Legislative and Judicial Issues, Henry Cohen 88-168 A
* Subsequent Legislative History as an Aid to Statutory Construction: Recent Supreme Court Usages, George Costello 85-1081 A
* Tort Injury Compensation Reform: Various Approaches, Henry Cohen 87-666 A
* The Tort Reform Debate: Pros, Cons, Federal Proposals, State Statutes, Henry Cohen 86-579 A
* Tort Reform: State Statutory Caps on Damages, Henry Cohen, etc. 87-835 A
* Use of the Military to Enforce Civilian Law: Posse Comitatus Act and Other Considerations, Charles Doyle 88-583 A
* Waiver of Eleventh Amendment Immunity from Suit: State Survey, Kirk D. Nemer 88-465 A

Law, Crime, and Justice
* see, Crimes and Offenses, Criminal Procedure, Drug, Abuse, Internal Security, Judiciary, Law, Police, Prisons,
* Crime Control: Federal Initiatives, IB86042
* Drug Control, IB87013
* Drug Testing in the Workplace: An Overview of Empl oyee and Employer Interests, IB87139
* Gun Control, IB89093
* Legal Issues of Insider Trading in Securities, IB87052
* Prison Conditions: Congressional Response, IB81171
* Supreme Court: Church-State Cases, October 1988 Te rm, IB88105

Lebanon
* Lebanon: The Remaining U.S. Hostages; a Chronology , 1984-1987, Clyde R. Mark 88-499 F
* Lebanon: The Remaining U.S. Hostages; Issue Brief, Clyde Mark IB85183
* United States Interests in Lebanon, John Creed 85-873 F

Legislative Procedure
* see, Congress-Legislative Procedure and Operations,

Legislative Veto
* see, Congress--Executive Relations,

Lend-Lease Settlement Agreement
* Lend-Lease: An Historic Overview and Repayment Issues, Patricia Wertman 85-844 E

Leveraged Buyouts
* see, Corporations--Mergers,
Liability Insurance Crisis
* see, Insurance--Liability Issues,

Libraries
* see, Arts and Humanities,

Libya
* Libya: U.S. Relations; Archived Issue Brief, Raymond Copson, etc. IB86040
* Libya's Nuclear Energy Situation: Archived Issue Brief, Mark Martel, etc. IB85079

Lifeline Telephone Service Act
* see, Telecommunication--Telephone Industry,

Lincoln, Abraham
* Speech Material: Abraham Lincoln's and George Washington's Birthdays; Info Pack, IP373A

Literacy
* see, Elementary and Secondary Education,

Lithuania
* Lithuania: Background Information, Dorothy Fontana 83-53 F

Lobbying
* see, Politics and Elections--Practical Politics,

Local Finance
* the ABCs of Public Venture Captial Investment, Jan E. Christopher 88-757 E
* American Telephone and Telegraph Co. Flow-Through of State Gross Receipts Taxes, Angele Gilroy 87-43 E
* Comments Concerning the Supreme Court's Decision in South Carolina v. Baker, Robert B. Burdette 88-443 A
* Compilation of State Laws Pertaining to the Exemptions from State Sales Teaxes for Federal Purchases, Mark Gurevitz 89-232 A

* Crowding Out? Federal, State and Local Government Borrowing and the Debt Economy, William Jackson 87-274 E
* Federal Budget and Tax Policy and the State-Local Sector: Retrenchments in the 1980s, Lillian Rymarowicz, etc. 88-600 E
* Federal Income Tax Deduction for State and Local Taxes: A Brief History of the Law, Thomas Ripy 85-853 A
* Limiting the Growth of Tax-Exempt Industrial Development Bonds: An Economic Evaluation, Dennis Zimmerman 84-37 E
* Lotteries: Bibliography-in-Brief, 1974-1987, Marsha Cerny 87-392 L
* The Payments in Lieu of Taxes Program: Background and Current Status, Stacey M. Kean 87-321 E
* Selective Local Government Excise Taxes on Hotel, Motel, and Other Transient Lodging as of July 1, 1986 Lillian Rymarowicz 86-793 E
* State Taxation of Nonresidents' Retirement Income, Robert B. Burdette 89-224 A
* Tax-Exempt Bond-Financed Takeover of Investor-Owned Utilities: An Issue of Privatization and Competition Dennis Zimmerman 88-174 E
* Tax-Exempt Bond Provisions of the Technical and Miscellaneous Revenue Act of 1988, Dennis Zimmerman 88-741 E
* Tax-Exempt Bonds: A Summary of Changes Made by the Tax Reform Act of 1986, Robert B. Burdette 87-9 A
* Tax-Exempt Bonds and Twenty Years of Tax Reform: Controlling Public Subsidy of Private Activities, Dennis Zimmerman 87-922 E
* Tax Reform: Its Potential Effect on the State and Local Sector, Dennis Zimmerman 87-233 E
* Taxation Within Indian Lands: The Legal Framework, M. Maureen Murphy 87-249 A

Long-Term Care
* see, Old Age-Health Issues,

LTV Corporation
* Legal Analysis of LTV Corporation's Unilateral Termination of Retirees' Health and Life Insurance Benefits on the Date of Filing in Bankruptcy Vincent E. Treacy 86-845 A

Luxury Tax
* see, Taxation-Consumption Taxes,

M-X Missile
* see, Weapons Systems--Nuclear Weapons,
* Strategic Forced: MX ICBM (Weapons Facts); Archived Issue Brief, Jonathan Medalia, etc. IB84046

Magnuson Fishery Conservation and Management Act
* Fisheries Conservation and Management: The Magnuson Act in the 100th Congress, Eugene H. Buck 89-65 ENR

Malaysia
* The Association of Southeast Asian Nations (ASEAN) : Economic Development Prospects and the Role of the United States Larry Niksch 84-171 F
* Economic Changes in the Asian Pacific Rim: Policy Prospectus., Congressional Research Service 86-923 S
* U.S. Agricultural Trade Opportunities With Pacific Rim Nations, Robert M. Goldstein 88-755 ENR

Manassas National Battlefield Park
* Manassas National Battlefield Park: The Battle Continues, John O. Spengler, etc. 88-514 ENR

Mandela, Nelson
* South Africa: African National Congress Brenda Branaman 86-186 F

Manpower Training Programs
* see, Occupational Training,

Marine Mammal Protection Act
* see, Fisheries,

Marine Transportation
* see, Infrastructure,
* After the Exxon Valdez Spill: Oil Pollution Liability and Compensation Legislation, Martin R. Lee 89-266 ENR
* Cargo Preference and Agriculture: Background and Current Issues, Carl Ek. 87-134 ENR
* The Exxon Valdez Oil Spill: Issue Brief, Martin R. Lee, etc. IB89075
* Oil Pollution Liability and Compensation Legislation After the Exxon Valdez Oil Spill: Issue Brief, Martin R. Lee IB89082
* Seizure of Foreign Vessels in United States Ports, Daniel Hill Zafren 87-760 A
* U.S. Merchant Shipping: Federal Assistance and Policy Issues, Lenore Sek 86-79 E

Marshall Islands
* Territorial Political Development: An Analysis of Puerto Rico, Northern Mariana Islands, Guam, Virgin Islands, and American Samoa, and the Micronesian Bette A. Taylor 88-657 GOV

MBFR
* see, Mutual Balanced Force Reduction Talks,

Meat
* see, Agriculture--Livestock Food,

Medicaid
* see, Medicare and Medicaid--Medicaid,

Medical Economics
* AIDS: Acquired Immune Deficiency Syndrome; Selected References, B.F. Mangan 89-333 L
* Health Care Cost Containment: Bibliography-in-Brief, 1986-1988, Charles P. Dove 88-376 L
* Health Care Costs: Info Pack, IP223H
* Health Care Expenditures and Prices: Issue Brief, James Reuter IB77066
* Health Care Financing and Health Insurance: A Glossary of Terms, Education and Public Welfare Division. Health Sect 88-539 EPW
* Health Care: Issue Brief, Janet Kline IB87009
* Health Insurance and the Uninsured: Background Data and Analysis, Education and Public Welfare Division. Health Insu 88-537 EPW
* Medicare: Geographic Variations in Payments for Physician Services, James A. Reuter 88-775 EPW
* Medicare: Prospective Payments for Inpatient Hospital Services; Issue Brief, Julian Pettingill, etc. IB87180
* Medicare: Recalculating Payment Rates under the Prospective Payment System, Mark Merlis 87-574 EPW
* Medicare Reimbursement: Selected References, 1986-1988, Peter Giordano 88-679 L
* Medicare's Prospective Payment System: An Analysis of the Financial Risk of Outlier Cases, Congressional Research Service 87-877 EPW
* Medicare's Prospective Payment System: The 98th and 99th Congresses, Joseph Cislowski, etc. 87-862 EPW
* A Prospective Payment System for Hospital-Based Physician Services under Medicare; a Report Prepared, for the Subcommittee on Health, Committee on Ways Education and Public Welfare Division 87-715 EPW
* Public Health and the Congress: Selected References, Karen Alderson, etc. 89-147 L
* Rural Hospitals under Medicare's Prospective Payment System and the Omnibus Budget Reconciliation Ac t of 1986 (P.L.99-509) Joseph A. Cislowski, etc. 87-816 EPW

Medical Personnel
* Health Professions Education and Nurse Training Programs: Titles VI and VIII; Issue Brief, Edward Klebe IB88055
* Medicare Payments to Hospitals and Physicians: Info Pack., IP317M
* Medicare: Physicians Payments, James Reuter 88-658 EPW
* Nurses: Supply and Demand; Bibliography-in-Brief, 1981-1988, Edith Sutterlin 88-729 L

Medicare
* see, Medicare and Medicaid--Medicare,

Medicare and Medicaid
* Following the general materials listed below; this, subject heading is subdivided as follows: Medicaid, Medicare,
* Medicare and Medicaid: Bibliography-in-Brief, 1986-1988, Edith Sutterlin 88-560 L
* Medicare, Medicaid, and Maternal and Child Health Programs: An Overview of Major Legislation Enacted, from 1980 Through 1986 Janet Kline, etc. 87-296 EPW
* Medicare-Medicaid: Info Pack, IP067M

Medicare and Medicaid -- Medicaid
* Health Care for Children: Federal Programs and Policies, Joseph A. Cislowski 88-217 EPW
* Medicaid Eligibility for the Elderly in Need of Long Term Care, Edward Neuschler, etc. 87-986 EPW
* Medicaid: FY90 Budget; Issue Brief, Mark Merlis IB89031
* Medicaid Services for Persons With Mental Retardation or Related Conditions, Mary F. Smith 88-759

* Medicaid: Spousal Impoverishment, Jennifer O'Sullivan 87-648 EPW
* Medicaid "2176" Waivers for Home and Community-Based Care, Caral O'Shaughnessy, etc. 85-817 GOV

Medicare and Medicaid -- Medicare
* Catastrophic Health Insurance: Bibliography-in-Brief, 1986-1988, Marsha Cerny, etc. 88-401 L
* Catastrophic Health Insurance: Comparison of the Major Provision of the "Medicare Catastrophic Protection Act of 1987" (H.R. 2470 as Passed by the Hou Jennifer O'Sullivan, etc. 87-948 EPW
* Catastrophic Health Insurance: Medicare; Issue Brief, Jennifer O'Sullivan IB87106
* Financing Catastrophic Health Care: Possible Effects on Marginal and Average Income Tax Rates, Gregg A. Esenwein 89-132 E
* Growth in the Volume of Medicare Physician Services: A Framework for Analysis, Gene Falk 88-466 EPW
* Hospital Capital cost Reimbursement under Medicare, Joseph Cislowski, etc. 86-598 EPW
* Long-Term Care Legislation: Summary of Selected Bills, Carol O'Shaughnessy, etc. 89-238 EPW
* Medicare: Arguments for and Against Continuing Coverage for Disability Insurance Recipients Who Retu rn to Work David Koitz 87-837 EPW
* Medicare: Arguments for and Against the Medicare 24-Month Waiting Period for the Disabled, David Koitz 87-484 EPW
* Medicare Catastrophic Coverage Act of 1988 (P.L. 100-360), Jennifer O'Sullivan 89-155 EPW
* Medicare Coverage of Employees of State and Local Governments, David Koitz 88-369 EPW
* Medicare: FY90 Budget; Issue Brief, James A. Reuter, etc. IB89029
* Medicare: Geographic Variations in Payments for Physician Services, James A. Reuter 88-775 EPW
* Medicare: Its Use, Funding, and Economic Dimensions, David Koitz, etc. 89-134 EPW
* Medicare Part B: The Supplementary Medical Insurance Program, James Reuter, etc. 86-153 EPW
* Medicare Payments to Hospitals and Physicians: Info Pack, IP317M
* Medicare: Physician Payments, James Reuter 88-658 EPW
* Medicare: Prospective Payments for Inpatient Hospital Services; Issue Brief, Julian Pettingill , etc. IB87180
* Medicare: Recalculatiing Payment Rates under the Prospective Payment System, Mark Merlis 87-574 EPW
* Medicare Reimbursement: Selected References, 1986-1988, Peter Giordano 88-679 L
* Medicare: Risk Contracts With Health Maintenance Organizations and Competitive Medical Plans, Mark Merlis 88-138 EPW
* Medicare's Prospective Payments System: An Analysis of the Financial Risk of Outlier Cases, Congressional Research Service 87-877 EPW
* Medicare's Prospective Payment System: The 98th and 99th Congresses, Joseph Cislowski, etc. 87-862 EPW
* The Peer Review Organization Program, Joseph Cislowski 87-860 EPW
* Premium Effect of Proposed Medicare Catastrophic Legislation on Federal Annuitants, Janet P. Lundy 87-801 EPW
* A Prospective Payment System for Hospital-Based Physician Services under Medicare; a Report Prepared, for the Subcommittee on Health, Committee on Ways Education and Public Welfare Division 87-715 EPW
* Rural Hospitals under Medicare's Prospective Payment System and the Omnibus Budget Reconciliation Ac t of 1986 (P.L. 99-509) Joseph A. Cislowski, etc. 87-816 EPW
* Social Security Medicare Coverage of Employees of State and Local Governments, David Koitz, etc. 87-132 EPW
* Social Security and Medicare: How Are They Treated, in Determining the National Debt?, David Koitz 85-1132 EPW

Medicare Catastrophic Coverage Act
* Medicare Catastrophic Coverage Act of 1988 (P.L. 100-360), Jennifer O'Sullivan 89-155 EPW

Medicine
* see, Aids, Ethical Issues, Genetics, Public Health,
* Alzheimer's Disease: Bibliography-in-Brief, 1982-1987, B.F. Mangan 88-312 L
* Alzheimer's Disease: Issue Brief, Samuel Merrill IB83128
* Biotechnology: Bibliography-in-Brief, 1985-1988, B.F. Mangan 88-566 L
* Brief Summary of Several Federal Statues Which Arguably Provide the Federal Government the Authority, to Control the Disposal of Infectious Hospital Wa Cathy Gilmore 87-658 A
* Eating Disorders: Anorexia Nervosa and Bulimia, Bernice S. Reyes, etc. 87-630 SPR

* Organ Transplantation in the United States: Analysis of Selected Ethical Issues, Marilyn Littlejohn 89-103 SPR
* Osteoporosis: An Overview of Recent Developments, Bernice S. Reyes, etc. 87-843 SPR
* Vaccine Injury Compensation; Archived Issue Brief, Pamela W. Smith IB87046

Medicine -- Aids
* Acquired Immune Deficiency Syndrome (AIDS): A Brief Overview of the Major Legal Issues, Nancy Lee Jones 87-236 A
* Acquired Immune Deficiency Syndrome and Military Manpower Policy: Issue Brief, David F. Burrelli IB87202
* Acquired Immunodeficiency Syndrome (AIDS): Health Care Financing and Services; Issue Brief, Mark Merlis IB87219
* Advertising Condoms: Legal and Constitutional Considerations, Rita Ann Reimer 87-325 A
* AIDS--Health Care Costs: Bibliography-in-Brief, 1985-1986, Bonnie Mangan 87-32 L
* AIDS: Acquired Immune Deficiency Syndrome; Info Pack, IP261A
* AIDS: Acquired Immune Deficiency Syndrome: Selected References, B.F. Mangan 89-333 L
* AIDS: An Overview of Issues: Issue Brief, Pamela Smith, etc. IB87150
* AIDS and Discrimination: Legal Limits on Insurance Underwriting Practices, Kirk D. Nemer 88-381 A
* AIDS and the Public Schools: Legal Issues Involved in the Education of Children, Nancy Lee Jones 88-329 A
* AIDS: Audio Brief, Mark Merlis, etc. AB50186
* AIDS in Africa: Background/Issues for U.S. Policy, Raymond W. Copson 87-768 F
* AIDS in the Workplace: Employee Vs Employer Interest, Gail McCallion 87-510 E
* AIDS: International Problems and Issues; Issue Brief, Lois B. McHugh IB87214
* AIDS Prevention: State Law Regulating Hypodermic Devices Which Could Affect Needle Exchange Programs, M. Ann Wolfe 89-234 A
* American Public Opinion on AIDS: A CRS Major issue Before the 101st Congress, Rosita M. Thomas 89-85 GOV
* Blood: Collection, Testing, and Processing, Irene Stith-Coleman 87-641 SPR
* Blood Testing for Antibodies to the AIDS Virus: The Legal Issues, Charles Dale, etc. 87-738 A
* Federal Funding for AIDS Research and Prevention: Issue Brief, Judith A. Johnson IB87028
* Fifty State Survey of States Statutes Concerning Veneral Disease as It May Relate to AIDS, M. Ann Wolfe 87-240 A
* The Potential Liability of Insurance Companies and, Self-Insured Businesses for Unauthorized Disclosure of Medical Information Provided in Connection W Kirk D. Nemer 88-509 A
* Summary of State Statutes Which Specifically Mention Acquired Immune Deficiency Syndrome, M. Ann Wolfe 87-239 A

Medicine -- Ethical Issues
* Animal Use in Biomedical Research: Info Pack, IP360A
* Animal Use in Research: Bibliography-in-Brief, 1985-87, Adrienne C. Grenfell 88-72 L
* Biomedical Ethics and Congress: History and Current Legislative Activity; Issue Brief, Irene Stith-Coleman IB86078
* Biomedial Ethics: Audio Brief, Science Policy Research Division AB50004
* Biomedical Research: Use of Animals; Issue Brief, Blanchard Randall IB83161
* Fetal Research: A Survey of State Law, Mildred Washington 88-198 A
* Human Fetal Research and Tissue Transportation: Issue Brief, Irene Stith-Coleman IB88100

Members of Congress
* see, Congress--Members,

Mental Health
* Community-Based Services for Individuals With Severe Disabilities: Summary and Analysis of S. 1673 and H.R. 3454 Mary F. Smith 88-212 EPW
* Constitutional and Statutory Issues Relating to the Use of Behavior Modification on Children in Institutions Nancy L. Jones 86-1000 A
* The Constitutional Rights of Mental Patients, Charles Dale 85-585 A
* Eating Disorders: Anorexia Nervosa and Bulimia, Bernice S. Reyes, etc. 87-630 SPR
* Homelessness and Commitment: The Cases of Joyce Brown (a/K/a Billie Boggs), Kirk D. Nemer 88-186 A
* Overview of Recent Judicial Decisions on the Constitutional Right of Mental Patients to Refuse Treat ment Nancy Jones 85-548 A
* Teenage Suicide: Bibliography-in-Brief, 1982-1988, Peter Giordano, etc. 88-652 L

* Youth Suicide: Sudden Adolescent Death, Edith Fairman Cooper
88-428 SPR

Mentally Retarded
* see, Handicapped,

Mergers
* see, Corporations--Mergers,

Methanol
* see, Power Resources--Alternative Energy Sources,

Mexico
* The Mexican Debt Accords and Their Financial Implications: an
Overview, Patricia A. Wertman 86-179 E
* Mexican Petroleum, Joseph Riva 83-178 SPR
* Mexico: Problems and Prospects; Info Pack, IP358M
* Mexico-U.S. Relations: Issues for Congress; Issue Brief, K.
Larry Storrs, etc. IB86111
* Tariff Items 807.00 and 806.30 and the Mexican Maquiladoras,
Patricia Wertman 87-500 E
* United States-Mexican Trade Relations: Present Problems,
Future Prospects, Patricia Wertman 85-139 E
* U.S.-Mexico Economic Relations: An Overview, Lenore Sek 87-485
E
Mias
* see, Military Personnel,

Microthesauri
* see, Reference Source--Microthesauri,

Middle East
* see, Arab-Israeli Conflict, Arms Sales and Foreign, Assistance,
Iran-Iraq War, Petroleum, U.S. Concerns, Iran-Contra Affair,
Persian Gulf,
* The Gulf Cooperation Council, Richard Preece 85-516 F
* The Holy See and Recognition of Israel, Charles J. Whittier
86-833 GOV
* The Israeli Economy: Archived Issue Brief, Clyde Mark IB84138
* Israel's Participation in the International Atomic, Energy
Agency and the 32nd IAEA General Conference: Archived Issue Brief
Warren H. Donnelly IB88072
* Libya's Nuclear Energy Situation: Archived Issue Brief, Mark
Martel, etc. IB85079
* Soviet Policy Toward Iran and the Strategic Balance in
Southwest Asia, Stuart D. Goldman 87-592 F

Middle East -- Arab-Israeli Conflict
* Israeli-Palestinian Conflict: Bibliography-in-Brief,
1982-1988, Robert S. Kirk 88-251 L
* Israeli-Palestinian Conflict: Info Pack, IP397I
* Middle East Military Balance, Clyde Mark 85-591 F
* Middle East Peace Proposals: Issue Brief, Clyde Mark IB82127
* Palestine and the Palestinians: Issue Brief, Clyde Mark
IB76048
* Palestinian Disturbances in the Gaza Strip and West Bank:
Policy Issues and Chronology, Ellen Laipson 88-114 F

Middle East -- Arms Sales and Foreign Assistance
* Arms Shipments to Iran: Archived Issue Brief, Richard M. Preece
IB87022
* Arms Transfers to Iran Since 1979: Reports from the Media,
Jonathan Medalia 86-187 F
* Background on Delivery of AWACS Aircraft to Saudi Arabia,
Richard F. Grimmett 86-744 F
* Egypt: U.S. Foreign Assistance Facts; Archived Issue Brief,
Ellen B. Laipson IB85060
* Iran Arms Sales and Contra Funds: Summaries of Key Legislative
Provisions, Clyde R. Mark, etc. 87-13 F
* Israel: U.S. Foreign Assistance Facts; Issue Brief, Clyde Mark
IB85066
* Jordan: U.S. Foreign Assistance Facts; Archived Issue Brief,
Richard Preece IB85120
* Laws Implicated by Shipments of Military Materials to Iran,
Raymond C. Celada 86-1005 A
* Saudi Arabia Arms Sales, 1987: Archived Issue Brief, Clyde R.
Mark, etc. IB87209
* Saudi Arabia: U.S. Missile Sale, 1986: Archived Issue Brief,
Clyde Mark IB86068
* U.S. Foreign Assistance to the Middle East and North Africa:
Fiscal Years 1988, 1989, and 1990, Clyde R. Mark 89-192 F

Middle East -- Iran-Iraq War
* Iran-Iraq War: Issue Brief, Richard M. Preece IB88060
* The NATO Allies, Japan, and the Persian Gulf, Paul Gallis
84-184 F

* Persian Gulf and the War Powers Debate: Issue Summary and Review
of Events; Archived Issue Brief, Clyde R. Mark IB87207
* Persian Gulf: Iran Air Flight 655: Archived Issue Brief, Ellen
Laipson IB88080
* Persian Gulf: Overview of Issue; Archived Issue Brief, Ellen B.
Laipson IB87229
* Persian Gulf: Selected References, Sherry B. Shapiro 88-533 L
* United Nations Role in the Iran-Iraq War: Issues and Options,
Lois B. McHugh, etc. 88-463 F

Middle East -- Petroleum
* Energy Security: Issue Brief, Carl E. Behrens IB89006
* The Financial Impact of Oil price Behavior on International
Development and Trade: Transnational Oil Companies and Persian
Gulf Oil Exporters; Report o Clyde R. Mark, etc. 86-903 F
* Oil from the Persian Gulf: Production, Disposition , and
Transportation; Archived issue Brief, Robert Bamberger, etc.
IB88063
* Oil Imports from OPEC: Recent and Projected Trends, Bernard A.
Gelb 88-558 E
* The World's Conventional Oil Production Capability Projected
into the Future by Country, Joseph P. Riva, Jr. 87-414 SPR

Middle East -- U.S. Concerns
* Ban on Imports from Iran: Economic Effect on the United States,
Bernard A. Gelb 88-6 E
* Disruption of Oil Supply from the Persian Gulf: Near-Term U.S.
Vulnerability (Winter 1987/88), Clyde R. Mark, etc. 87-863 ENR
* Insuring U.S. Interests in the Persian Gulf: Summary and
Proceedings of the Workshop Held on October, 6, 1987 by the
Congressional Research Service Gary J. Pagliano 88-725 F
* Israeli-American Relations: Issue Brief, Ellen B. Laipson
IB82008
* Israel's Interest in Nuclear Power: Implications for U.S.
Non-Proliferation Policy; Archived Issue Brief Mark Martel, etc.
IB85166
* Issues in the Middle East: Audio Brief, Clyde Mark, etc.
AB50177
* Lebanon: The Remaining U.S. Hostages; a Chronology , 1984-1987,
Clyde R. Mark 88-499 F
* Lebanon: The Remaining U.S. Hostages; Issue Brief, Clyde Mark
IB85183
* Libya: U.S. Relations; Archived Issue Brief, Raymond Copson,
etc. IB86040
* Palestine Liberation Organization Offices in the United States,
Clyde R. Mark 88-484 F
* Persian Gulf: U.S. Military Operations; Archived Issue Brief,
Ronald O'Rourke IB87145
* United States Interests in Lebanon, John Creed 85-873 F
* United States-Iraqi Relations, Richard M. Preece 86-142 F
* U.S. Policy Toward Iran: 1979-1986, Richard M. Preece 87-974 F
* U.S., Soviet, and Western European Naval Forces in the Persian
Gulf Region, Robert J. Ciarrocchi 87-956 F
* U.S.-Soviet Military Balance. Book VI. Far East, Middle East
Assessments, John Collins, etc. 80-166 S

Midgetman (Missile)
* "Midgetman" Small ICBM (Weapon Acts): Archived Issue Brief,
Jonathan Medalia, etc. IB84044

Migrant Labor
* see, Labor,

Military Assistance
* see, Africa, Asia, Latin America, Middle East,
* Arms Sales: U.S. Policy: Info Pack, IP214A
* Congressional Procedure for Considering Legislation Opposing
Arms Sales, Richard Grimmett 86-63 F
* Current Issues With the "Base-Rights" Countries and Their
Implications, Richard F. Grimmett 88-726 F
* Defense Articles and Services Supplied to Foreign Recipients:
Legislative Restrictions on Their Use, Richard Grimmett 86-18 F
* Department of Defense Humanitarian Aid, Carol R. Kuntz, etc.
87-808 F
* Leases of Defense Articles: Legislative Provisions and
Restrictions, Richard F. Grimmett 87-396 F
* Lend-Lease: An Historic Overview and Repayment Issues, Patricia
Wertman 85-844 E
* Missle Proliferation: Survey of Emerging Missile Forces,
Foreign Affairs and National Defense Division 88-642 F
* An Overview of United States Military Assistance Programs,
Richard F. Grimmett 88-282 F
* Pros and Cons of Military Intervention: Audio Brief, Foreign
Affairs and National Defense Division AB50033
* The Seven-Ten Ratio in Military Aid to Greece and Turkey: A
Congressional Tradition, Ellen Laipson 85-79 F
* Trends in Conventional Arms Transfers to the Third, World by

Major Supplier, 1980-1987, Richard F. Grimmett 88-352 F

Military Assistance -- Africa
* Angloa: Issues for the United States; Archived Issue Brief, Raymond Copson, etc. IB81063
* Mozambique: U.S. Foreign Assistance Facts; Archived Issue Brief, Raymond Copson IB85114
* Sudan: U.S. Foreign Assistance Facts; Issue Brief, Ellen Laipson, etc. IB85065
* U.S. Foreign Assistance to the Middle East and North Africa: Fiscal Years 1988, 1989, and 1990, Clyde R. Mark 89-192 F

Military Assistance -- Asia
* Cambodia: U.S. Foreign Assistance Facts; Archived Issue Brief, Robert Sutter IB85153
* Chinese Arms Sales to the Persian Gulf: A Fact Sheet, Robert G. Sutter 88-286 F
* Pakistan: U.S. Foreign Assistance Facts; Archived Issue Brief, Richard P. Cronin IB85112
* Pakistan's Request for the U.S. AWACS: Archived Issue Brief, Kerry B. Dumbaugh IB87188
* Philippines: U.S. Foreign Assistance Facts; Issue Brief, Larry Niksch IB85077
* U.S. Arms Sales to China, Kerry Dumbaugh, etc. 85-138 F

Military Assistance -- Latin America
* Central America and U.S. Foreign Assistance: Issues for Congress; Issue Brief, Jonathan Sanford IB84075
* Central America: U.S. Relations With Costa Rica, Guatemala, and Honduras; Info Pack, IP352C
* Chart of Unclassified Legislative Restrictions Regarding Support for Military or Paramilitary Operations in Nicaragua, 1982-1986 Larry Eig 87-222 A
* Compilation of Selected Laws Relating to the National Security Council, Arms Tranfers, Intelligence Activities, Aid to the Contras, and Appropriations American Law Division 86-1028 A
* El Salvador Aid: Congressional Action, 1981-1986, on President Reagan's Requests for Economic and Military Assistance for El Salvador K. Larry Storrs 87-230 F
* El Salvador: U.S. Foreign Assistance Facts; Issue Brief, K. Larry Storrs, etc. IB85113
* Guatemala: Country Background Report, Maureen Taft-Morales 88-586 F
* Guatemala: U.S. Foreign Assistance Facts; Archived, Issue Brief, Jonathan Sanford IB85100
* Honduras: U.S. Foreign Assistance Facts; Archived Issue Brief, Robert E. Sanchez IB85080
* Legislative Histories of Statutory Restrictions on, Funding for Covert Assistance for Military or Paramilitary Operations in Nicaragua, FY 1983-1986 Larry M. Eig 87-538 A
* The Reagan Doctrine: U.S. Assistance to Anti-Marxist Guerrillas; Archived Issue Brief, Raymond W. Copson IB87005
* U.S. Bilateral Economic and Military Assistance to, Latin America and the Caribbean: Fiscal Years 194 6 to 1987 K. Larry Storrs 87-694 F

Military Assistance -- Middle East
* Arms Shipments to Iran: Archived Issue Brief, Richard M. Preece IB87022
* Arms Transfers to Iran Since 1979: Reports from the Media, Jonathan Medalia 86-187 F
* Background on Delivery of AWACS Aircraft to Saudi Arabia, Richard F. Grimmett 86-744 F
* Egypt: U.S. Foreign Assistance Facts; Archived Issue Brief, Ellen B. Laipson IB85060
* Iran Arms and Contra Funds: Selected Chronology of Events, 1979-1987, Richard M. Preece, etc. 86-190 F
* Israel: U.S. Foreign Assistance Facts; Issue Brief, Clyde Mark IB85066
* Jordan: U.S. Foreign Assistance Facts; Archived Issue Brief, Richard Preece IB85120
* Laws Implicated by Shipments of Military Material to Iran, Raymond J. Celada 86-1005 A
* Saudi Arabia Arms Sales, 1987: Archived Issue Brief, Clyde R. Mark, etc. IB87209
* Saudi Arabia: U.S. Missile Sale, 1986; Archived Issue Brief, Clyde Mark IB86068
* U.S. Foreign Assistance to the Middle East and North Africa: Fiscal Years 1988, 1989, and 1990, Clyde R. Mark 89-192 F

Military Bases
* see, National Defense--Military Bases,

Military Pensions
* see, Military Personnel--Pensions,

Military Personnel
* see, Pensions,
* Acquired Immune Deficiency Syndrome and Military Manpower Policy: Issue Brief, David F. Burrelli IB87202
* Civilian and Military Pilots: The Labor Market Relationship, John W. Fischer, etc. 86-28 E
* Military Manpower and Compensation: FY88 Budget Issues; Archived Issue Brief, Robert L. Goldich IB87081
* Military Manpower and Compensation: FY89 Budget Issues; Issue Brief, Robert L. Goldich IB88025
* Military Manpower and Compensation: FY90 Budget Issues; Issue Brief, Robert L. Goldich IB89024
* Military Medical Care Services: Questions and Answers; Issue Brief, David F. Burrelli IB87155
* Military Personnel Overseas Allowances: Issues and Legislation, David F. Burrelli 89-216 F
* Military Recruiting: Controversy Over the Use of Educational Credentials, David F. Burrelli 88-474 F
* National Guard Overseas Training Missions: An Issue for U.S. Military Manpower Policy, David F. Burrelli 86-181 F
* National Services: Info Pack, IP418N
* National Service: Selected References, Peter Giordano 89-165 L
* The New GI Bill: Recruiting and Retention, David F. Burrelli 87-652 F
* POWs and MIAs in Indochina and Korea: Status and Accounting Issues, Robert L. Goldich IB88061
* Prisoner of War/Missing in Action in SE Asia: Info, Pack, IP127P
* Special Operations Forces: Issues for Congress, James Wootten 84-227 F
* Standby Draft Registration: Archived Issue Brief, David Burrelli IB82101
* State Income Taxation of Military Personnel and United States Citizens Residing Outside of the United States Joyce Thorpe, etc. 87-706 A
* Vietnam-U.S. Relations: The Missing-in-Action (MIAs) and the Impasse Over Cambodia; Issue Brief, Robert G. Sutter IB87210
* Women in the Armed Forces (With Appendix): Archived Issue Brief, Ellen Collier IB79045

Military Personnel -- Persons
* Benefits for Former Military Spouses: Info Pack, IP313B
* COLAs for Military Retirees: Summary of Congressional and Executive Branch Action Since 1982, Robert L. Goldich 89-3 F
* Comparison of Retirement Systems for Executive Branch Employees, Members of Congress and Active Duty, Military Personnel Carolyn Merck, etc. 85-685 EPW
* Congressional Pay, Selected Wages and Pension, and, Social Security: Compared to CPI, 1969-1989, Frederick H. Pauls, etc. 89-63 GOV
* Military Benefits for Former Spouses: Legislation and Policy Issues, David F. Burrelli 89-63 GOV
* Military Retirement: Major Legislative Issues; Issue Brief, Robert Goldich IB85159
* The Military Retirement Reform Act of 1986: Issues, and Implications, Robert L Goldich 87-702 F
* The Military Survivor Benefit Plan: A Description of Its Provisions, David F. Burrelli 89-186 F
* Treatment of former Spouses under Various Federal Retirement Systems, Marie B. Morris 88-512 A

Military Retirement
* see, Military Personnel--Pensions,

Milliken v. Michigan Road Builders Assn.
* United States Supreme Court Actions Regarding Minority Business Set-Asides After City of Richard v. J.A. Croson Co Charles V. Dale 89-202 A

Minerals and Materials
* see, National Defense--Strategic Stockpiles,
* Acid Rain Legislation and the Domestic Aluminum Industry, Marc Humphries, etc. 89-327 ENR
* Antarctic Mineral Resources Regime: Diplomacy and Development; Issue Brief, James E. Mielke, etc. IB88101
* Antarctica: Environmental Protection Issues: Summary of a CRS Research Workshop, Susan R. Fletcher 89-272 ENR
* Asbestos in Buildings: Activity in the 100th Congress, Claudia Copeland 89-267 ENR
* Asbestos in Buildings: Current Issues; Issue Brief, Claudia Copeland IB86084
* Economic Conditions of the U.S. Tungsten Industry, Bernard A. Gelb 86-964 E
* Hard Minerals in the U.S. Exclusive Economic Zone:, Resource Assessments and Expectations. Part I--Sand and Gravel, Placers, and Phosphorite James E. Mielke 87-885 SPR
* Hard Minerals in the U.S. Exclusive Zone: Resource, Assessments

and Expectations. Part II--Ferromanganese Modules,
Cobalt-Manganese Crusts, and Polymet James E. Mielke 87-975 SPR
* International Mineral Market Control and Stabilization:
Historical Perspectives, John Schanz, etc. 86-601 S
* Materials Availability: A Cause for Concern?, Lennard Kruger,
etc. 83-171 SPR
* Mineral Development in Yugoslavia, Marc Humphries 88-688 ENR
* National Forest Receipts: Sources and Dispositions, Ross W.
Gorte 89-284 ENR
* The Rural Abandoned Mine Program: A Brief Background, Duane A.
Thompson 87-105 ENR
* Selected Nonferrous Mineral Subsidies and the U.S. -Canada Free
Trade Agreement, Marck Humphries 88-774 ENR
* Strategic and Critical Materials Policy: Research and
Development: Archived Issue Brief, Lennard Kruger IB74094
* The Subsidization of Non-Fuel Mineral Production at Home and
Abroad, John J. Schanz, Jr. 87-62 S
* The U.S. Uranium Industry: Changing Prospects and the Federal
Role; Issue Brief, Barbara B. Black IB89079

Minimum Wages
* see, Labor--Minimum Wages,

Minorities
* see, Blacks, Civil Liberties and Rights--Discrimination and
Intergration, Equal Employment Opportuni ty, Indians, Women,
* Armenian Population by State, 1980, Jennifer D. Williams
86-853 GOV
* Bilingual Education: Recent Evaluations of Local School
Districts Programs and Related Research on Second-Language
Learning Rick Holland 86-611 EPW
* Comparative Quality of Rental Housing Obtained by Whites,
Blacks, and Hispanics, Grace Milgram 87-626 E
* Czechoslovak Population by State, 1980, Jennifer D. Williams
86-837 GOV
* Federal Education Programs Serving Limited English, Proficient
Students, RubyAnn M. Esquibel 89-285 EPW
* Federal Programs for Minority and Women-Owned Businesses, Mark
Eddy 89-278 GOV
* Financing Postsecondary Education Attendence: Current Issues
Involving Access and Choice, James B. Stedman 88-315 EPW
* Greek Population by State and Congressional District, Jennifer
Williams 85-827 GOV
* Hispanic Children in Poverty, Vee Burke, etc. 85-170 EPW
* Hispanic Population in 99th Congress Districts, David Huckabee
85-763 GOV
* Housing Conditions of Hispanic Americans, Susan M.
Vanhorenbeck 85-952 E
* The Indian Community in the United States, Margaret Siciliano
84-792 F
* Issue in the 100th Congress of Special Interest to, Hispanics:
An Overview of Major Issues Identified, by the Congressional
Hispanic Caucus Jennifer D. Williams 87-755 GOV
* Lithuanian Population by State, 1980, Jennifer Williams 87-71
GOV
* Minority Business Set-Asides and the Constitution:, A Legal
Analysis of the U.S. Supreme Court Ruling, in City of Richmond v.
J.A. Croson Co Charles V. Dale 89-124 A
* Minority Ownership of Broadcast Facilities: A Summary of
Federal Communications Commission's Policie s and Rules Bernevia
M. McCalip 87-273 E
* Selected Demographic Characteristics of the U.S. Hispanic
Population and of Hispanic Subgroups, Jennifer Williams 86-536
GOV
* States Designating English as the Official State Language, Mark
Gurevitz 89-268 A
* Turkish Population by State, Jennifer Williams 85-1067 GOV
* United States Supreme Court Actions Regarding Minority Business
Set-Asides After City of Richmond v., J.A. Croson, Co Charles V.
Dale 89-202 A
* The U.S. Asian Population, by Census Division, State, and
Congressional District, Jennifer D. Williams 86-771 GOV
* The U.S. Filipino Population, by Congressional District,
Jennifer D. Williams 86-760 GOV
* The U.S. Hispanic Population Living in Counties Located Within
100, 150, and 200 Miles of the Mexica n Border Jennifer D.
Williams 87-146 GOV

Minority Business Set Asides
* see, Minorities,

Minority Issues
* American Indian budget Issues: 101st Congress, IB89046
* Navajo-Hopi Relocation, IB86021
* Selected Women's Issues in the 101st Congress, IB89104

Miranda Decision

* see, Criminal Procedure,

Missing in Action
* see, Military Personnel,

Mississippi Power & Light Co. v. Mississippi Ex Re
* State Versus Federal Ratemaking Authority: Mississippi Power &
Light Co. v. Mississippi Ex Rel. Moor e Robin Jeweler 88-651 A

Mississippi River
* Legal Issues Related to Diversion of Water from Lake Michigan to
the Mississippi River, Pamela Baldwin 88-585 A

Monetary Policy
* see, Money and Banking--Monetary Policy,

Money and Banking
* see, Failures and Deposit Insurance, Financial Institutions,
Interest Rates, Law and Regulation, Mon etary Policy,
* Capital Sources for U.S. Corporations With Particular Reference
to Public Issues, Julius W. Allen 86-165 E
* The Citicorp Initiative: A Brave New World for the Third World
Debt Problem, Patricia A. Wertman 87-750 E
* Common Legal Questions and Answers Concerning Currency, Legal
Tener and Money, 83-150 A
* Debit Cards: Background and Public Policy Issues, Pauline H.
Smale 84-120 E
* Farmer Mac and the Agricultural Secondary Market, Ralph Chite
89-246 ENR
* Foreign Ownership of U.S. Assets: Past, Present, and Prospects,
James K. Jackson, etc. 88-295 E
* Gold Use, Production, and Trade: A Profile, Bernard A. Gelb
88-613 E
* Individual Retirement Accounts and Financial Savings: New
Evidence, William Jackson 86-125 E
* Money and Banking: An Alphabetical Microthesarus of Terms
Selected from the Legislative Indexing Vocabulary Shirley Loo
88-530 L
* Money and Near-Monies: A Primer, John B. Henderson 83-125 E
* A New U.S. Dollar Coin, Pauline Smale 88-75 E
* Redesign of the U.S. Currency, Pauline Smale 87-301 E
* The Role of Gold in the International Monetary System, Arlene
Wilson 80-47 E
* Tax-Favored Savings: All Savers Certificates and Individual
Retirement Accounts, William Jackson 85-168 E
* U.S. Tax Treatment of Bad Foreign Loans, David L. Brumbaugh
89-302 E

Money and Banking -- Failures and Deposit Insurance
* Bank Bailouts: Open-Bank Assistance by the Federal, Deposit
Insurance Corporation, William Jackson 86-1041 E
* Bank Failures: Recent trends and Policy Options; Issue Brief,
Pauline Smale IB86148
* Banks and Thrift Institutions: Restructuring and Solvency
Issues, F. Jean Wells 88-749 E
* Banks and Thrifts: Restructuring and Solvency; Issue Brief, F.
Jean Wells IB89002
* Banks, Savings and Loan Associations, and Their Federal Deposit
Insurance Funds: A Financial Analysi s William Jackson 83-82 E
* Depository Financial Institution Failures: The 1980s
Experience, Pauline H. Smale 88-549 E
* The Economics of Deposit Insurance, G. Thomas Woodward 89-32 E
* Federal Deposit Insurance Coverage of Public Funds, F. Jean
Wells 87-517 E
* Federal Deposit Insurance Funds: An Overview of FDIC and FSLIC
Finances, William Jackson 87-2 E
* Federal Deposit Insurance Funds and Regulatory Agencies: Merger
and Consolidation Issues, F. Jean Wells 88-279 E
* The Federal Deposit Insurance Funds: Their Financial Condition
and Public Policy Proposals in the 10 0th Congress; Archived
Issue Brief F. Jean Wells IB88082
* The Federal Deposit Insurance Mechanism: Recent Economic
Literature, F. Jean Wells 85-65 E
* The Federal Regulation of Depository Institutions:, A Brief
Overview, Maureen Murphy 87-511 E
* Federal Regulation of the Savings and Loan Industry: Legal
Framework, Michael V. Seitzinger 88-734 A
* Federal Savings and Loan Insurance Corporation: Current
Estimates of Future Costs of Resolving "problem-Institution"
Cases F. Jean Wells 88-520 E
* Federal Savings and Loan Insurance Corporation
Recapitalization Act of 1986: A Brief Explanation and, Analysis
F. Jean Wells 86-728 E
* Federal Savings and Loan Insurance Corporation:
Recapitalization and Alternatives; Archived Issue Br ief F. Jean
Wells IB87027

* Federal Savings and Loan Insurance Corporation: Studies for the 101st Congress, F. Jean Wells 88-672 E
* Financial Crises of the 1970s and 1980s: Causes, Developments, and Government Responses, William Jackson, etc. 89-290 E
* The FSLIC Issue: A Status Report, F. Jean Wells 89-77 E
* FSLIC Policy Options, F. Jean Wells 89-56 E
* FSLIC, the Budget, and the Economy, G. Thomas Woodward 89-17 E
* Public Rescue of Private Liabilities: The Continental Illinois Case, William Jackson 85-172 E
* Restructuring the Savings and Loan Industry: Bibli ography-in-Brief, 1986-1989, Robert Howe 89-162 L
* S&L Problems and FSLIC; Info Pack, IP415S

Money and Banking -- Financial Institutions
* Automated Teller Machine (ATM) Security: State and, Federal Legislation, LaVonne M. Grabiak, etc. 87-375 A
* Bank Diversification: Into Real Estate?, William Jackson 88-648 E
* Bank Holding Companies, William Jackson 84-76 E
* The Bank Holding Company Act: Background, Summary, and Analysis, William Jackson, etc. 86-26 A
* Bank and Securities: An Overview of Their Workforces, Linda LeGrande 88-35 E
* Banking Fees and Service Charges, Pauline H. Smale 86-39 E
* Banks, Savings and Loan Associations, and Their Federal Deposit Insurance Funds: A Financial Analysis William Jackson 83-82 E
* The Conservation Reserve: A Status Report, Jeffrey Zinn 88-716 ENR
* Corporate Ownership of Banks and Savings Institutions, and Interstate Banking: Selected Listings, F. Jean Wells 84-105 E
* Deregulation or Re-Regulation of Financial Services? Activities of the Depository Institutions Deregulation Committee, 1980-82 William Jackson 83-87 E
* Electronic Fund Transfers: Regulation of Paperless -Entry Transactions, Including Automatic Payroll Deposits M. Maureen Murphy 89-62 A
* Financial Institutions: Problems and Prospects; Info Pack, IP291F
* Foreign Banking in the U.S.: Issue Brief, William Jackson IB87104
* International Banking Facilities and the Eurocurrency Market, William Jackson, etc. 82-27 E
* International Lending Patterns of U.S. Banks: Financial and Regulatory Trends, William Jackson 85-124 E
* Merchant Banking: Opportunities of Problems in U.S . Banks?, Walter Eubanks, etc. 87-351 E
* P.L. 97-320, Garn-St. Germain Depository Institutions Act of 1982: A Brief Explanation, F. Jean Wells 82-177 E
* Proposed Federal Taxation of Credit Unions: A Pro/Con Analysis, James M. Bickley 86-84 E
* Should Credit Unions Be Taxed: Issue Brief, James M. Bickley IB89066
* U.S. Bank Exposure in the Seventeen Highly Indebted Countries: 1982-1987, Patricia A. Wertman, etc. 88-522 E
* U.S. Banks and the People's Republic of China, Walter W. Eubanks 84-840 E

Money and Banking -- Interest Rates
* Capital, Credit, and Crowding Out: Cycles and Trends in Flows of Funds Over Three Decades, William Jackson 82-142 E
* Crowding Out? Federal, State and Local Government Borrowing and the Debt Economy, William Jackson 87-274 E
* Do Deficits Influence the Level of Interest Rates?, G. Thomas Woodward 85-14 E
* An Economic Analysis and Brief Legislative Overview of Usury Ceilings, William Anderson 81-172 E
* Financial Deregulation: Relaxing Ceilings on Deposit Interest Rates, 1978-1980, William Jackson 81-176 E
* Government Actions that Affect Interest Rates: Mechanisms and Macroeconomic Repercussions, Craig Elwell 82-128 E
* High Interest Rates: Causes, Consequences, and Issues, Thomas F. Dernburg 84-53 E
* Hypothetical Effects of Lower Interest Rates on the Costs of Production of the Integrated Steel Industry David J. Cantor 85-738 E
* Interests Rates on Consumer and Commerical Loans: Why the Difference?, Helen J. Scott 85-818 E
* A National Interest Rate Ceiling for the U.S. Economy?, Jonathan Henderson, etc. 82-57 E
* Rising Interest Rates and the Economic Expansions:, Can They Co-Exist?, Craig K. Elwell 84-818 E
* Saving and Rate of Return Incentives: Estimates of, the Interest Elasticity of Personal Saving, William Jackson 81-198 E

Money and Banking -- Law and Regulation
* see, Glass-Steagail Act,
* Bank Service Diversification: A Comparative Summary of Major

Financial Reform Measures Facing the Co ngress William Jackson, etc. 88-84 E
* Bank Soundness in Light of the Tax Reform Act of 1986 and Possible Glass-Stegall Act Repeal, Walter W. Eubanks 88-118 E
* Bank-Broker Competition and the Glass-Stegall Act:, The Mutual Funds Example, William Jackson 87-921 E
* Banking Acts: Major Federal Legislation Since the American Revon Necessary? Issue Brief, Mary Jane Bolle IB86150

Money and Banking --, Monetary Policy
* Budget Deficits and Monetary Policy, Carol Leisenring 81-128 E
* Domestic and International Monetary-Fiscal Policy Coordination, Thomas F. Dernburg 84-145 E
* The Federal Reserve Discount Rate: Its Significanc e in Monetary Policy, G. Thomas Woodward 87-17 E
* Federal Reserve System: Info Pack, IP105F
* Membership of the Board of Governors of the Federa l Reserve System, December 1913-October 1986, Roger S. White, etc. 86-985 E
* Monetarist and Keynesian Worlds--What's the Differ ence?, Helen J. Scott 84-181 E
* Monetary Policy: Basic Principles, Current Conditi ons, and Prospects, G. Thomas Woodward 88-255 E
* Monetary Policy: Current Policy and Conditional; A rchived Issue Brief, G. Thomas Woodward IB87113
* The Targeting of Monetary Policy: Money Supply Gro wth or Interest Rates?, Gail E. Makinen 86-596 E
* Targets for Monetary Policy, G. Thomas Woodward 88-256 E
* U.S. Economic Policy in an International Context: Deficits, Taxes, and Monetary Policy, Jane G. Gravelle, etc. 84-125 E
* U.S. Monetary Policy, the Economy and the Foreign Exchange Value of the Dollar, 1960-1986, Helen J. Scott 86-109 E

Monroe Doctrine
* The Monroe Doctrine and U.S. Policy Options for the Western Hemisphere, Raphael Perl 84-225 F

Mortgages
* see Housing--Finance,

Most Favored Nation Trade Policies
* see, Foreign Trade--East-West, Foreign Trade--Trad e Policy,

Mozambique
* Mozambique: Conflict Assessment/U.S. Policy, Raymond W. Copson 88-516 F
* Mozambique: U.S. Foreign Assistance Facts; Achived, Issue Brief, Raymond Copson IB85114
* Southern Africa: U.S. Regional Policy at a Crossro ads?, Raymond Copson 85-201 F

Multilateral Development Banks
* see, International Finance--Multilateral Developme nt Banks,

Multinational Corporations
* see, International Corporations,

Mutual Balanced Force Reduction Talks
* Conventional Arms Control in Europe: Prospects for, Accord: Issue Brief, Stanley Sloan IB86064
* East-West Conventional Force Reduction Negotiation s: Bibliography-in-Brief, 1980-1987, Valentin Leskovsek 87-313 L

Namibia
* Angola/Namibia Negotiations: Issue Brief, Brenda M. Branaman IB89047
* Angola/Namibia Peace Prospects: Background, Curren t Problems, and Chronology, Raymond W. Copson 88-559 F
* Namibia Chronology: February 1986 Through April 19 87, Raymond W. Copson, etc. 87-353 F
* Namibia: United Nations Negotiations for Independe nce/U.S. Interests; Archived Issue Brief, Brenda Branaman IB79073
* Southern Africa: U.S. Regional Policy at a Crossro ads?, Raymond Copson 85-201 F
* The United States and Southern Africa: A Review of, United Nations Resolutions and United States Voti ng Patterns, 1946-October 1985 Frankie King 86-21 F

Narcotics
* see, Drug Abuse, Drugs,

National Ambient Air Quality Standards (NAAQS)
* Ozone and Carbon Monoxide Nonattainment: An Analys is of Title I of S. 1894, Mira Courpas 88-316 ENR
* Ozone and Carbon Monoxide Nonattainment: An Analysis of Title I of the Proposed Clean Air Standards Attainment Act David E.

Gushee 87-751 S
* Ozone/Carbon Monoxide Nonattainment: Is It What It, Seems to Be?, David E. Gushee 88-148 S

National Credit Union Share Insurance Fund
* see, Money and Banking--Failures and Deposit Insurance,
* Depository Financial Institution Failures: The 1980s Experience, Pauline H. Smale 88-549 E
* Federal Deposit Insurance Funds and Regulatory Agencies: Merger and Consolidation Issues, F. Jean Wells 88-279 E
* The Federal Deposit Insurance Funds: Their Financial Condition and Public Policy Proposals in the 100th Congress; Archived Issue Brief F. Jean Wells IB88082

National Debt
* see, Public Finance--Deficits,

National Defense
* see, Military Balance, Military Bases, Strategic S tockpiles, Arms Control, Defense Economics, Intern al Security, Military Assistance, Military Personn,
* Arms and Arms Control: An Alphabetical Microthesar us of Terms Selected from the Legislative Indexing, Vocabulary Shirley Loo 87-961 L
* The Bush Administration's Proposal for ICBM Modern ization, SDI, and the B-2 Bomber, Jonathan Medalia 89-281 F
* Case Studies of Counter-Insurgencies, Larry Niksch 85-60 F
* Chemical-Biological Warfare: Bibliography-in-Brief, 1985-1988, Valentin Leskovsek 88-605 L
* The Clandestine Trade in Heavy Water: A Chronology, Barbara B. Black, etc. 89-66 ENR
* Classified Information Procedures Act (CIPA): An O verview, Larry M. Eig 89-172 A
* The Defense Department's Drug Law Enforcement and Narcotics Interdiction Responsibilities: A Compari son of House and Senate Amendments in the Defense Roy Surrett 88-406 F
* Defense-Related Independent Research and Developme nt in Industry, Joan Winston 85-205 S
* The Defense Spending Dilemma: Audio Brief, Daniel Lockwood, etc. AB50181
* Defense Technology and Industrial Base: Bibliograp hy-in-Brief, Karen L. Alderson 89-145 L
* Department of Defense Organization: Current Legisl ative Issues; Archived Issue Brief, Robert Goldich IB86036
* FSX Fighter Agreement With Japan: Issue Brief, Richard F. Grimmett IB89060
* FSX Technology: Its Relative Utility to the United, States and Japanese Aerospace Industries, John D. Moteff 89-237 SPR
* The Ground Wave Emergency Network, Gary K. Reynolds 89-206 F
* Honduras: U.S. Military Activities; Issue Brief, James Wootten IB84134
* Insurgency and Counterinsurgency in the Philippine s, Larry Niksch 85-1038 F
* Managing Defense Department Technology Base Progra ms, Michael E. Davey 88-310 SPR
* Military Research and Development: Implications fo r Civilian Science and the Economy; Bibliography-i n-Brief, 1982-1986 Virginia MacEwen 87-59 L
* Military Strategy: Bibliography-in-Brief, 1983-198 6, Valentin Leskovsek 87-40 L
* Narcotics Interdiction and the Use of the Military : Bibliography-in-Brief, 1982-1988, Sherry B. Shapiro 88-408 L
* National Defense and Military Operations: An Alpha betical Microthesaurus of Terms Selected from the Legislative Indexing Vocabulary Shirley Loo 88-77 L
* The National Security Council: Organizational Hist ory, Mark Lowenthal 78-104 F
* NATO at 40: Bibliography Resources, Sherry B. Shapiro 89-175 L
* NATO Burdensharing: An Analysis of Major Legislati on in the 100th Congress, Christopher C. Bolkcom 88-772 F
* Nuclear Escalation, Strategic Anti-Submarine Warfa re, and the Navy's Forward Maritime Strategy, Ronald O'Rourke 87-138 F
* Planning Managing, and Funding DOD's Technology Ba se Programs, Michael E. Davey 89-319 SPR
* Pros and Cons of Military Intervention: Audio Brie f, Foreign Affairs and National Defense Division AB50033
* Review of U.S. Research and Development Programs i n Ballistic Missile Defense, John D. Moteff 89-150 SPR
* The Rise and Fall of Nations: Is America in Declin e?; a Bibliography of Points of View, Robert S. Kirk 89-214 L
* The Role of the U.S. Military in Narcotics Interdi ction: Audio Brief, Raphael Perl AB50171
* Science and Engineering Education: The Role of the, Department of Defense, Christine M. Matthews 89-256 SPR
* Sectional Analysis of the "War Powers Resolution" (WPR) as It Would Be Amended by the "War Powers Re solution Amendments of 1988" (S.J. Res. 323, 100th Raymond J. Celada 88-441 A

* The Strategic Defense Initiative: Program Descript ion and Major Issues, John D. Moteff 88-721 SPR
* Strategic Policy at a Crossroads: Critical Choices, and Policy Dilemmas Facing the United States Toda y Amy F. Woolf, etc. 89-210 F
* U.S. Defense Planning: A Critique, John Collins, etc. 82-167 S
* Use of the Military to Enforce Civilian Law: Posse, Comitatus Act and Other Considerations, Charles Doyle 88-583 A
* War Powers Resolutions: Presidential Compliance; I ssue Brief, Ellen Collier IB81050
* War Powers Resolution: The Controversial Act's Sea rch For a Successful Litigation Posture, Raymond J. Celada 88-64 A

National Defense -- Military Balance
* Allied Burdensharing: Audio Brief, Paul Gallis, etc. AB50182
* Balance of Power; Selected References, 1985-1989, Valentin Leskovsek 89-325 L
* Burdensharing: Selected References, 1979-1988, Sherry B. Shapiro 88-423 L
* Conference on Security and Cooperation in Europe (CSCE): The Vienna Meeting; Issue Brief, Francis T. Miko IB87220
* Confidence Building Measures and Force Contraints for Stabilizing East-West Military Relations in Eu rope Stanley R. Sloan, etc. 88-591 F
* Conventional Arms Control in Europe: Prospects for, Accord: Issue Brief, Stanley Sloan IB86064
* Defense Capability: Issue for Congress; Archived Issue Brief, Robert E. Foelber IB87012
* Defense Spending: an Introduction to Arms Control, Burden Sharing, and Other Key Questions; Issue Br ief Alice C. Maroni IB88043
* Essentials of Net Assessment: An Objective Means of Comparing Military Capabilities, John Collins, etc. 80-168 S
* Estimates of Soviet Defense Expenditures: Methodological Issues and Policy Implications, Robert Foelber, etc. 85-131 F
* Japan's Military Buildup: Goals and Accomplishments, Gary K. Reynolds 89-68 F
* Middle East Military Balance, Clyde Mark 85-591 F
* Military Balance: Info Pack, IP069M
* The NATO Allies, Japan, and the Persian Gulf, Paul Gallis 84-184 F
* NATO Conventional Force Structure and Doctrine: Possible Defensive Changes After an INF Treaty, Robert L. Goldich 88-169 F
* Soviet Policy in Nordic Europe: New Focus on the Forgotten Flank?, Francis Miko 85-33 F
* Soviet Policy Toward Iran and the Strategic Balance in Southwest Asia, Stuart D. Goldman 87-592 F
* Toshiba-Kongsberg Technology Diversion: Issues for, Congress; Archived Issue Brief, Raymond Ahearn, etc. IB87184
* United States and Soviet Special Operations, John M. Collins 87-398 S
* United States/Soviet Military Balance: Archived Issue Brief, John Collins, etc. IB78029
* The U.S. Commitment to Europe's Defense: A Review of Cost Issues and Estimates, Alice Maroni, etc. 85-211 F
* U.S., Soviet, and Western European Naval Forces in, the Persian Gulf Region, Robert J. Ciarrocchi 87-956 F
* U.S.-Soviet Military Balance. Book I. Organization , Budgets, Manpower, Technology, John Collins, etc. 80-161 S
* U.S.-Soviet Military Balance. Book II. Strategic N uclear Trends, John Collins, etc. 80-162 S
* U.S.-Soviet Military Balance. Book III. General Purpose Force Trends, John Collins, etc. 80-163 S
* U.S.-Soviet Military Balance. Book IV. Airlift and, Sealift, John Collins, etc. 80-164 S
* U.S.-Soviet Military Balance. Book V. NATO and the, Warsaw Pact, John Collins, etc. 80-165 S
* U.S.-Soviet Military Balance. Book VI. Far East, Middle East Assessments, John Collins, etc. 80-166 S
* U.S./Soviet Military Balance: Statistical Trends, 1970-1979 (End of Year Figures), John M. Collins, etc. 87-839 S
* U.S./Soviet Military Balance: Statistical Trends, 1980-1987 (as of January 1, 1988), John M. Collins, etc. 88-425 F
* US-Soviet Military Balance, 1980-1985, John Collins 85-89 S

National Defense -- Military Bases
* Current Issues With the "Base-Rights" Countries and Their Implications, Richard F. Grimmett 88-726 F
* Military Base Closures: A Side by Side Comparison of Current Legislation, Andrew C. Mayer 88-472 F
* Military Base Closures: Congress and the Executive, Branch, Andrew Mayer 85-212 F
* Military Base Closures: Issue Brief, Andrew Mayer IB89026
* The Navy's Strategic Homeporting Program: Issue for Congress; Archived Issue Brief, Ronald O'Rourke IB85193
* Philippine Bases: U.S. Redeployment Options, Alva Bowen 86-44 F
* United States Military Installations in Greece, Richard

Grimmett 84-24 F
* United States Military Installations in Italy, Richard
Grimmett 84-12 F
* United States, Military Installations in Portugal, Richard
Grimmett 86-6 F
* United States Military Installations in Spain, Richard
Grimmett 84-149 F
* United States Military Installations in Turkey, Richard
Grimmett 84-221 F
* U.S.-Spanish Bases Agreement: Issue Brief, Richard F. Grimmett
IB88010

National Defense and Security
* A-12 Advanced Tactical Aircraft (ATA) Program Weap ons Facts,
IB87115
* Acquired Immune Deficiency Syndrome and Military M anpower
Policy, IB87202
* Advanced Tactical Fighter (ATF) Aircraft (Weapons Facts),
IB87111
* Argentina, Brazil, and Nuclear Proliferation, IB89103
* Arms Control: Issues for Congress, IB87002
* Arms Control: Negotiations to Limit Defense and Sp ace Weapons,
IB86073
* Arms Copntrol: Negotiations to Reduce Strategic Of fensive
Nuclear Weapons, IB88088
* ASATs: Antisatellite Weapon Systems, IB85176
* AV-8B V/STOL Aircraft (Weapons Facts), IB88044
* B-1B Strategic Bomber, IB87157
* B-2 Advanced Technology Bomber, IB87216
* Chemical Weapons: A Summary of Proliferation and A rms Control
ACtivities, IB89042
* Conference on Security and Cooperation in Europe (CSCE): After
the Vienna Meeting, IB87220
* Conventional Arms Control in Europe: Prospects for, Accord,
IB86064
* Defense Budget for FY 1990: Congressional Action, IB89054
* Defense Procurement: Investigation into Alleged Ab uses,
IB88081
* Defense Procurement Reform, IB89015
* Defense Spending: An Introduction to Arms Control,
Burdensharing, and Other Key Questions, IB88043
* Defense Spending Priorities, IB87231
* Embassy Construction Controversies: Moscow and Was hington,
IB87232
* F-14D Fighter Aircraft (Weapons Facts), IB89101
* FSX Fighter Agreement With Japan, IB89060
* Funding for Selected Defense Programs: FY 1990 Aut horization
and Appropriation, IB89087
* The FY 1990 Budget Debate: How Much for Defense?, IB89073
* Intelligence Reform Issues, IB88029
* LHX and Army Aviation Modernization: Issues for Co ngress,
IB88086
* Military Base Closures, IB89026
* Military Manpower and Compensation: FY 90 Budget I ssues,
IB89024
* Military Medical Care Services: Questions and Answ ers,
IB87155
* Military Retirement: Major Legislative Issues, IB85159
* MX, "Midgetman," and Minuteman Missile Programs, IB77080
* NATO Nuclear Modernization and Arms Control, IB89049
* Nuclear Arms Control: Disposal of Nuclear Warheads, IB88024
* Nuclear Nonproliferation Policy in the 101st Congr ess,
IB89084
* Nuclear Weapons Production Complex: Moderniation a nd Cleanup,
IB89062
* Seawolf or SSN-21 Nuclear-Powered Attack Submarine, IB85169
* Special Access Programs and the Defense Budget: Un derstanding
the "Black Budget", IB87201
* The Strategic Defense Initiative: Issues for Congr ess,
IB88033
* Strategic Defense Initiative (SDI): Mission Object ives for
Directing the Program, IB88028
* Terrorism: U.S. Policy Options, IB81141
* Terrorist Incidents Involving U.S. Citizens or Pro perty
1981-1989: A Chronology, IB86096
* Trident Program, IB73001
* U.S.-Spanish Bases Agreement, IB88010
* V-22 Osprey Tilt Rotor Aircraft (Weapons Facts), IB86103
* Verification and Compliance: Soviet Compliance Wit h Arms
Control Agreements, IB84131
* War Powers Resolution: Presidential Compliance, IB81050

National Defense -- Strategic Stockpiles
* Aspects of the Mobilization of the Petroleum Indus try in World
War II and the Korean War, Robert Bamberger 84-773 ENR
* Defense Petroleum Reserve: Organizational Options for Meeting
DOD's Emergency Fuel Supply Requiremen ts David Lockwood 84-201 F
* National Defense Stockpile Policy--The Congression al Debate,

Alfred R. Greenwood 86-863 ENR
* Nuclear Weapons Material Production: Options for M eeting
Tritium and Plutonium Needs; Archived Issue, Brief David W.
Cheney, etc. IB88099
* The Reagan Administration Proposes Dramatic Change s to
National Defense Stockpile Goals, Alfred Greenwood 86-578 ENR
* Strategic and Critical Materials Policy: Research and
Development: Archived Issue Brief, Lennard Kruger IB74094

National Defense Student Loan Program
* see, Higher Education--Student Aid,

National Economic Commission (U.S.)
* Deficit Reduction: The National Economic Commissio n Options
Model, Barry Molefsky, etc. 88-606 E
* National Economic Commission: Equitable Deficit Re duction;
Archived Issue Brief, Barry Molefsky IB88032

National Flood Insurance Program
* see, Water Resources,

National Priorities
* Congress: Issue for the 101st Congress; Info Pack,
Congressional Reference Division IP410C
* CRS Major Issues for the 101st Congress, First Session,
Congressional Research Service 89-2 S
* Economic Policymaking the U.S. Government: Proceedings of a
Congressional Symposium, April 26, 1988, Congressional, Research
Service 88-461 E
* Economic Policymaking Problems. Part One: Institutions and
Processes, Leon M. Cole, etc. 89-299 E
* Economic Policymaking Problems. Part Two: Theories, and
Forecasts, Leon M. Cole, etc. 89-300 E
* Federalism is the United States: Toward the Third Century; an
Overview of Trends and Issues, Sandra S. Osbourn 89-262 GOV
* Rural Policy in the United States: A History, Sandra S. Osbourn
88-487 GOV

National Science Foundation (U.S.)
* Federal Support of Basic Research and the Establishment of the
National Science Foundation and Other, Research Agencies William
C. Boesman 88-456 SPR

National Security Council (U.S.)
* Compilation of Selected Laws Relating to the National Security
Council, Arms Transfers, Intelligence, Activities, Aid to the
Contras, and Appropriation American Law Division 86-1028 A
* Contra Aid: Analysis of Whether the National Security Council
(NSC) and the NSC Staff Are an "agency, or Entity Involved in
Intelligence Activities" Co Larry E. Eig 87-566 A
* The National Security Council: Organizational History, Mark
Lowenthal 78-104 F
* U.S. Presidential National Security Advisers: Changing Roles
and Relationships, Joel M. Woldman 87-334 F

National Service
* see, Public Welfare,

National Wilderness Preservation System
* Wilderness Areas and Federal Water Rights, Pamela Baldwin
89-11 A

NATO
* see, North Atlantic Treaty Organization,

Natural Disasters
* see, Disasters,

Natural Gas
* see, Fossil Fuel--Natural Gas,

Natural Resources
* see, Coastal Area, Fisheries, Forests and Forestr y, Fossil
Fuels, Land Use, Minerals and Materials, Oceanography, Public
Lands, Water Resources,
* Agricultural Resource Conservation Issues: Archive d Issue
Brief, Jeffrey A. Zinn IB87132
* Agriculture and the Environment: Issue Brief, Geoffrey Becker,
etc. IB89086
* Antarctic Mineral Resources Regime: Diplomacy and Development;
Issue Brief, James E. Mielke, etc. IB88101
* Antarctica: Environmental Protection Issues; Summa ry of a CRS
Research Workshop, Susan R. Fletcher 89-272 ENR
* Arctic Resources Controversy: Issue Brief, M. Lynne Corn, etc.
IB89058

* Coastal Resource Issues: Archived Issue Brief, Jeffrey A. Zinn IB87144
* Compliance Provisions for Resource Conservation: A Status Report, Jeffrey Zinn 88-662 ENR
* The Conservation Reserve: A Status Report, Jeffrey Zinn 88-716 ENR
* Consideration of Economic Factors under the Endangered Species Act, Pamela Baldwin 89-274 A
* Debt-for-Nature Swaps in Developing Countries: An Overview of Recent Conservation Efforts, Betsy Cody 88-647 ENR
* Environmental Protection in Developing Countries: Selected References, 1983-1987, Rebecca Mazur 87-488 L
* Federal Agency Programs in Living Aquatic Resources and Aquatic Habitat Protection, Eugene H. Buck 89-53 ENR
* The Major Federal Land Management Agencies: Management of Our Nation's Lands and Resources, Adela Backiel, etc. 87-22 ENR
* Managing Coastal Development Through the Coastal Zone Management and Flood Insurance Programs: Experience to Date and the Views from Selected States, Gary Kamimura, etc. 88-354 ENR
* Natural Resources Conservation and Development in Brazil: An Overview and Related Issues, Russell Hawkins 84-802 ENR
* Policy Analysis of the Proposed Revision of the Forest Service Administrative Appeals Regulations: Public Input, Timing, and Delays, Ross W. Gorte 88-483 ENR
* Population Growth and Natural Resource Deterioration in Drought-Stricken Africa, Susan Abbasi 85-1149 ENR
* Selected Reports Available on Food and Agricultural Topics, Environment and Natural Resources Policy Division 89-244 ENR
* Soil and Water Conservation Issues in the 101st Congress: Issue Brief, Jeffrey A. Zinn IB89080
* Spotted Owls and the Timber Industry: Issue Brief, M. Lynne Corn IB89077
* The Subsidization of Natural Resources in the United States, Environment and Natural Resources Policy Division 86-588 S
* Tongass National Forest Issues Brief, Adela Backiel IB89055
* Westlands Issues: Info Pack, IP423W
* Westlands Protection: Issues in the 101st Congress; Issue Brief, Jeffrey A. Zinn, etc. IB89076
* Antarctic Mineral Resources Regime: Diplomacy and Development, IB88101
* Arctic Resources Controversy, IB89058
* Coastal Barrier Protection Issues in the 101st Congress, IB89095
* Endangered Species Act: Reauthorization and Funding, IB87089
* Fisheries Issues in the 101st Congress: Commercial, Recreational, and Aquaculture, IB89041
* Outer Continental Shelf Leasing and Development, IB89028
* Soil and Water Conservation Issues in the 101st Congress, IB89080
* Spotted Owls and the Timber Industry, IB87088
* Tongass National Forest Issues, IB89055
* Tropical Deforestation: International Implications, IB89010
* Water Resources Development Act: Implementing the Omnibus Project Reforms, IB87088
* Wetlands Protection: Issues in the 101st Congress, IB89076

Naval Petroleum Reserves
* see, National Defense--Strategic Stockpiles,

Netherlands
* The Netherlands Elections and the Cruise Missile Issue: Implications for the United States and for NATO, Paul Gallis 86-27 F

New Zealand
* Australia, New Zealand, and the Pacific Islands: Issue for U.S. Policy; Issue Brief, Robert G. Sutter IB86158

Newspaper Preservation Act
* The Newspaper Preservation Act (15 U.S.C.[Sections] 1801-1804), Janice E. Rubin 89-239 A

Nicaragua
* The Boland Amendments: A Chronology of Congressional Action, Joseph Maheady 87-833 A
* Central American Peace Process: Selected References, Robert Kirk 88-389 L
* Chart of Unclassified Legislative Restrictions Regarding Support for Military or Paramilitary Operations in Nicaragua, 1982-1986, Larry Eig. 87-222 A
* Compilation of Selected Laws Relating to the National Security Council, Arms Transfers, Intelligence, Activities, Aid to the Contras, and Appropriation, American Law Division 86-1028 A
* Congress and U.S. Policy Toward Nicaragua in 1987, Linda Robinson 89-158 F
* Contra Aid: Analysis of Whether the National Security Council (NSC) and the NSC Staff Are an "agency, or Entity Involved in Intelligence Activities" Co., Larry E. Eig 87-566 A
* Contra Aid, FY82-FY88: Summary and Chronology of Major Congressional Action on Key Legislation Concerning U.S. Aid to the Anti-Sandinista Guerrillas, Nina M. Serafino 88-563 F
* Iran Arms and Contra Funds: Selected Chronology of Events, 1979-1987, Richard D. Shuey, etc. 86-190 F
* The Iran/Contra Affair: Implications for the National Security Adviser and the NSC Staff; Archived Issue Brief, Joel M. Woldman IB87107
* Legislative Histories of Statutory Restrictions on Funding for Covert Assistance for Military or Paramilitary Operations in Nicaragua, FY 1983-FY 1986, Larry M. Eig 87-538 A
* Nicaragua: An Overview of U.S. Policy, 1979-1986, Mark P. Sullivan 87-855 F
* Nicaragua: Bibliography-in-Brief, 1986-1987, Valentin Leskovsek 87-382 L
* Nicaragua: Conditions and Issues for U.S. Policy; Issue Brief, Nina Serafino IB82115
* Nicaragua: Info Pack, IP073N
* Nicaragua v. United States: The International Court of Justice Decision, Daniel Hill Zafren 86-748 A
* The Nicaraguan Resistance ("Contras"): Background and Major Concerns of Congress, Veronica R. Clifford 87-943 F
* Nicaragua's "Civic" Opposition: Players, Problems and Prospects, Nina M. Serafino 87-735 F
* A Summary and Analysis of the Report of the National Bipartisan "Kissinger" Commission on Central America, January 1984, Richard Cronin, etc. 84-39 F
* U.S. Assistance to Nicaraguan Guerrillas: Issues for the Congress; Archived Issue Brief, Nina Serafino IB84139
* The U.S. Trade Embargo Against Nicaragua After Two-and-a-Half Years, Glennon J. Harrison 87-870 E

Nobel Prizes
* The Nobel-Prize Awards in Science as a Measure of National Strength in Science, Christopher T. Hill, etc. 86-727 S

North Atlantic Treaty Organization
* Burdensharing: Selected References, 1979-1988, Sherry B. Shapiro 88-423 L
* Confidence Building Measures and Force Constraints for Stabilizing East-West Military Relations in Europe, Stanley R. Sloan, etc. 88-591 F
* Defense Burdensharing: U.S. Relations With NATO Allies and Japan, Stanley R. Sloan 88-449 F
* Franco-German Security Cooperation: Implications for the NATO Alliance, Paul E. Gallis 89-16 F
* Implications for NATO Stratress: A Brief Constitutional Analysis, Rita Ann Reimer 87-422 A
* Television Network Evening News Coverage of Afghanistan: A Perspective After Eight Years of War, Denis Stevens Rutkus 88-319 GOV

Northern Ireland
* Northern Ireland and the Republic of Ireland: U.S. Foreign Assistance Facts; Issue Brief. Bert H. Cooper, Jr. IB87069
* Northern Ireland: The Anglo-Irish Agreement and Its Implications for Congress: Policy Alert. Allan Nanes 85-1107 F

Northern Mariana Islands
* Territorial Political Development: An Analysis of Puerto Rico, Northern Mariana Islands, Guam, Virgin Islands, and American Samoa, and the Micronesian, Bette A. Taylor 88-657 GOV

Nuclear Energy
* see, Accidents and Safety, Nuclear Exports and Non-Proliferation Power Production, Arms Control, Disasters, Solid Wastes--Radioactive Wastes, Weapons S
* Controlling Carbon Dioxide Emissions. Amy Abel, etc. 89-157 ENR
* International Atomic Energy Agency: Bibliography-in-Brief. Bonnie F. Mangan 89-259 L
* Nuclear Energy: An Alphabetical Microthesaurus of Terms Selected from the Legislative, Indexing Vocabulary, Shirley Loo 87-962 L
* Nuclear Energy Policy: Issue Brief. Mark Holt, etc. IB88090
* Nuclear Energy Policy: Selected References, 1985-1988. Karen L. Alderson 88-763 L
* Nuclear Weapons Production Complex: Modernization and Cleanup; Issue Brief. David W. Cheney, etc. IB89062
* Nuclear Winter: Bibliography-in-Brief. B.F. Mangan 88-325 L
* Presidential Remarks About the International Atomic Energy Agency: Selected Excerpts. Barbara Black 89-27 ENR
* Superconducting Super Collider: Issue Brief. William C. Boesman IB87096
* Superconducting Super Collider: Issues; Info Pack. IP384S
* Superconducting Super Collider: Bibliography-in-Brief. Bonnie F.

Mangan 88-45 L
* The U.S. Uranium Industry: Changing Prospects and the Federal Role; Issue Brief. Barbara B. Black IB89079

Nuclear Energy -- Accidents and Safety

* The Chernobyl Accident: Health and Agricultural Effects; Archived Issue Brief. Christopher H. Dodge IB86122* The Chernobyl Accident: Implications for DOE's Production Reactors; Archived Issue Brief. Robert L. Civiak IB86092
* The Chernobyl Nuclear Accident: Causes, Initial Effects, and Congressional Response; Archived Issue Brief, Warren Donnelly, etc. IB86077
* The Chernobyl Nuclear Accident: Long-Term Political, Economic, and Foreign Policy Implications; Archived Issue Brief, Jean Boone, etc. IB86083
* Civil Liability for Transboundary Damage from a Nuclear Accident: The Joint International Protocol. Barbara B. Black, etc. IB89023
* International Notifications and Assistance for Nuclear Accidents: Congressional Action on Two Conventions; Archived Issue Brief, Warren H. Donnelly IB87082
* Nuclear Powerplant Safety and Regulation: Issue Brief. Robert L. Civiak, etc. IB86130
* Nuclear Powerplants: Emergency Planning; Archived Issue Brief. Cosmo DiMaggio IB86127

Nuclear Energy -- Nuclear Exports and Non-Proliferation

* China's Nuclear Weapons and Arms Control Policies: Implications for the United States. Robert G. Sutter 88-374 F
* The Clandestine Trade in Heavy Water: A Chronology. Barbara B. Black, etc. 89-66 ENR
* Implementation of the U.S.-Chinese Agreement for Nuclear Cooperation: Archived Issue Brief. Warren Donnelly IB86050
* India and Nuclear Weapons: Issue Brief. Warren Donnelly IB86125
* Israel and Nuclear Weapons: Issue Brief. Warren H. Donnelly IB87079
* Israel's Interests in Nuclear Power: Implications for U.S. Non-Proliferation Policy; Archived Issue Brief, Mark Martel, etc. IB85166
* Israel's Participation in the International Atomic Energy Agency and the 32nd IAEA General Conference: Archived Issue Brief, Warren H. Donnelly IB88072
* Libya's Nuclear Energy Situation: Archived Issue Brief, Mark Martel, etc. IB85079
* Nuclear Arms Control: Disposal of Nuclear Warheads; Issue Brief, Warren H. Donnelly IB88024
* Nuclear Material from Dismantled Warheads: What to Do With It and How to Verify Its Disposal: A Preliminary Analysis, Warren H. Donnelly 87-437 S
* Nuclear Nonproliferation Policy in the 101st Congress: Issue Brief, Warren H. Donnelly IB89084
* Nuclear Nonproliferation: Selected References, 1985-1988, B.F. Mangan 88-682 L
* Nuclear Terrorism: Implementation of Title VI of the Omnibus Diplomatic Security and Antiterrorism Act of 1986; Archived Issue Brief, Warren H. Donnelly IB87213
* Nuclear Waste Management: Selected References, 1985-1988, Karen L. Alderson 89-118 L
* Pakistan and Nuclear Weapons: Issue Brief, Warren Donnelly IB86110
* Pakistan's Nuclear Program: U.S. Foreign Policy Considerations; Issue Brief, Richard P. Cronin IB87227
* Plutonium: Department of Energy Approval of Plutonium Shipment from France to Japan; Archived Issue Brief, Warren H. Donnelly IB84116
* South Africa, Nuclear Weapons and the IAEA: Issue Brief, Warren H. Donnelly IB87199
* Uranium Hexafluoride Imports from South Africa: Archived Issue Brief, Barbara B. Black, etc. IB88066
* The U.S.-China Agreement for Nuclear Cooperation: Congressional Review; Archived Issue Brief, Mark Martel, etc. IB85203
* U.S.-Japan Agreement for Nuclear Cooperation: Monitoring Its Implementation; Issue Brief, Warren H. Donnelly IB88095
* U.S.-Japanese Nuclear Cooperations: Revision of the Bilateral Agreement; Archived Issue Brief, Warren H. Donnelly IB87159

Nuclear Energy -- Power Production

* Cost Accounting, Pricing, and Cost Recovery in DOE's Uranium Enrichment Program, Robert Civiak 85-1041 SPR
* Economic Analysis of the Tax Treatment of Nuclear Power Plant Decommissioning Costs, Donald W. Kiefer 84-28 E
* Economics of Plutonium Use in Light Water Reactions, Robert Civiak 85-780 SPR
* Federal and State Regulation of Nuclear and Non-Nuclear Electric

Utilities and of Nuclear Materials, Michael V. Seitzinger 87-221 A
* Nuclear Energy: Enrichment and Reprocessing of Nuclear Fuels: Archived Issue Brief, Robert Civiak IB77126
* Nuclear Energy: Safety and Waste Issues. Info Pack IP074N
* Nuclear Energy: Uranium Enrichment; Archived Issue Brief, Robert Civiak IB84008
* Nuclear Fusion Power: Archived Issue Brief, Robert Civiak, etc. IB76047
* Nuclear Liability Legislation: Price-Anderson Renewal Issues; Archived Issue Brief, Mark Holt IB88034
* Nuclear Material from Dismantled Warheads: What to Do With It and How to Verify Its Disposal: A Preliminary Analysis, Warren H. Donnelly 87-437 S
* Nuclear Material Transportation: Safety Concerns, Governmental Regulations and Activities, and Options to Improve Federal Programs, Paul Rothberg 84-45 SPR
* Nuclear Power: Technology Overview, Statistics and Projections; Issue Brief, Mark Holt IB81070* Nuclear Powerplant Safety and Regulation: Issue Brief, Robert L. Civiak, etc. IB86130
* The Nuclear Regulatory Commission: Organization History, Robert Civiak 81-147 SPR
* Nuclear Weapons Material Production: Options for Meeting Tritium and Plutonium Needs; Archived Issue Brief, David W. Cheney, etc. IB88099
* Plutonium Economics and Japan's Nuclear Fuel Cycle Policies, Robert Civiak 88-235 SPR
* Uranium Enrichment: Projected Earnings of the Proposed U.S. Enrichment Corporation, Robert L. Civiak 88-232 SPR
* The U.S. Uranium Industry: What Assistance Does It Need? Barbara B. Black, etc. 88-760 ENR

Nuclear Exports

* see, Nuclear Energy--Nuclear Exports and Non-Proliferation

Nuclear Non-Proliferation

* see, Nuclear Energy--Nuclear Exports and Non-Proliferation

Nuclear Power

* see, Nuclear Energy--Power Production

Nuclear Power Plant Accidents

* see, Nuclear Energy--Accidents and Safety

Nuclear Waste

* see, Solid Wastes--Radioactive Wastes

Nuclear Weapons

* see, Arms Control, Nuclear Energy--Nuclear Exports and Non-Proliferation, Weapons Systems--Nuclear Weapons Nuclear Winter
* see, Disasters

Nursing Homes

* see, Health Facilities

Nutrition

* see, Food, Food Relief

Occupational Health and Safety

* AIDS in the Workplace: Employee Vs Employer Interest, Gail McCallion 87-510 E
* Black Lung Programs: 1987 Issues and Action, Gloria E. Moreno, etc. 88-68 EPW
* High Risk Occupational Disease Notification and Prevention Act of 1987: Side-by-Side Comparison of H.R. 162 and S. 79, Mary Jane Bolle 88-43 E
* Occupational Disease Notification Proposals: Is Legislation Necessary? Issue Brief, Mary Jane Bolle IB86150
* OSHA Safety Inspection Targeting: Causes and Effects, Mary Jane Bolle 88-194 E
* Tort Liability of the Federal Government and Its Contractors to Veterans Exposed to Atomic Radiation, Henry Cohen 86-979 A
* Video Display Terminals (VDT's): Health, Safety, and Labor-Management Issues, Christopher H. Dodge, etc. 87-314 SPR

Occupational Training

* see, Adult and Vocational Education
* A Comparison of the Education Provisions in the Omnibus Trade Bill, H.R. 3, as Passed by the House and by the Senate, Paul M. Irwin, etc. 87-634 EPW
* Education and Job Growth, Linda LeGrande 88-476 E
* Education Proposals in Trade Competitiveness Legislation: Archived Issue Brief, K. Forbis Jordan, etc. IB87108
* Education Provisions of the Trade Act of 1988, P.L. 100-418, Paul M. Irwin, etc. 88-750 EPW

84-19 EPW
* Federal Housing Programs Affecting Elderly People, Susan Vanhorenbeck 88-576 E
* Housing for the Elderly and Handicapped: Section 202; Issue Brief, Susan M. Vanhorenbeck IB84038

Older American Act

* Older Americans Act Amendments of 1987: P.L. 100-175; A Summary of Provisions, Carol O'Shaughnessy 88-233 EPW
* Older Americans Act: Participants in Supportive and Nutrition Services, Carol O'Shaughnessy 86-867 EPW
* Older Americans Act Programs: Brief Summary and Funding Levels, Carol O'Shaughnessy 88-685 EPW

Omnibus Budget Reconciliation Act

* The Estate Freeze Controversy, Salvatore Lazzari 89-125 E

Omnibus Taxpayer Bill of Rights

* The Omnibus Taxpayer Bill of Rights, Marie B. Morris, etc. 89-136 A

Omnibus Trade and Competitiveness Act

* Education Provisions of the Trade Act of 1988, P.L. 100-418, Paul M. Irwin, etc. 88-750 EPW
* Japan's Response to the 1988 Omnibus Trade Bill, Dick K. Nanto 89-133 E
* The Omnibus Trade and Competitiveness Act. Technology Development Provisions, Wendy H. Schacht 89-93 SPR

Opec Countries

* see, Middle East

Osha

* see, Occupational Health and Safety

Ozone

* see, Air Pollution-Ozone

Ozone Layer (Upper Atmosphere)

* see, Earth Sciences

Pacific Area

* see, Names of Individual Countries
* Australia, New Zealand, and the Pacific Islands: Issue for U.S. Policy; Issue Brief, Robert G. Sutter IB86158
* Australia-U.S. Relations: A Briefing Paper, Robert G. Sutter 87-858 F
* Economic Changes in the Asian Pacific Rim: Policy Prospectus, Congressional Research Service 86-923 S
* Kangaroo Management Controversy, Malcolm M. Simmons 88-468 ENR
* Oceania and the United States: A Primer, Robert Sutter 85-218 F
* Palau's Evolving Relationship With the United States: Introduction and Chronology of Development, Luella S. Christopher 88-442 F
* Territorial Political Development: An Analysis of Puerto Rico, Northern Mariana Islands, Guam, Virgin Islands, and America Samoa, and the Micronesian, Bette A. Taylor 88-657 GOV
* U.S. Wood Exports to the Pacific Rim, Ross W. Gorte 88-548 ENR

Pakistan

* Pakistan After Zia: Implications for Pakistan and U.S. Interests; Archived Issue Brief, Richard P. Cronin IB88096
* Pakistan and Nuclear Weapons: Issue Brief, Warren Donnelly IB86110
* Pakistan: U.S. Foreign Assistance Facts; Archived Issue Brief, Richard P. Cronin IB85112
* Pakistan's Nuclear Program: U.S. Foreign Policy Considerations; Issue Brief, Richard P. Cronin IB87227
* Pakistan's Request for the U.S. AWACS: Archived Issue Brief, Kerry B. Dumbaugh IB87227
* South Asia: Current Developments and Issues for U. S. Policy; Report on a Trip to Pakistan and India, April 8-30, 1986, Richard P. Cronin 86-741 F
* The United States, Pakistan and the Soviet Threat to Southern Asia: Options for Congress, Richard Cronin 85-152 F

Palau Islands

* Palau's Evolving Relationship With the United States: Introduction and Chronology of Developments, Luella S. Christopher 88-442 F
* Territorial Political Development: An Analysis of Puerto Rico, Northern Mariana Islands, Guam, Virgin Islands, and American Samoa, etc., Bette Taylor 88-657 GOV

Palestine

* Israeli-Palestinian Conflict: Bibliography-in-Brief, 1982-1988, Robert Kirk 88-251 L
* Israeli-Palestinian Conflict: Info Pack IP397I
* Middle East Peace proposals: Issue Brief, Clyde Mark IB82127
* Palestine and the Palestinian: Issue Brief, Clyde Mark IB76048
* Palestinian Disturbances in the Gaza Strip and West Bank: Policy Issues and Chronology, Ellen Laipson 88-114 F

Palestine Liberation Organization

* see Middle East-Arab-Israeli Conflict

Palestinians

* see Middle East-Arab-Israeli Conflict

Panama

* Panama: Trade, Finance, and Proposed Economic Sanctions, Glennon J. Harrison 88-188 E
* Panama's Political Crisis: Prospects and U.S. Policy Concerns: Issue Brief, Mark Sullivan IB87230
* U.S. Sanctions and the State of the Panamanian Economy, Mark Sullivan 88-578 F

Parental Kidnapping

* see Families--Domestic Relations

Parental Kidnapping Prevention Act

* The Parental Kidnapping Prevention Act of 1980: Background, Analysis and Subsequent Development, Rita Ann Reimer 88-294 A
* Thompson v. Thompson: Federal Courts Are Not Authorized to Resolve State Custody Disputes Arising under the Parental Kidnapping Prevention Act, Rita Ann Reimer 88-63 A

Parental Leave

* see Families

Parks

* Arctic National Wildlife Refuge: Bibliography-in-Brief, Adrienne Grenfell 88-30 L
* The Arctic National Wildlife Refuge: Oil, Gas, and Wildlife: Archived Issue Brief, Lynne Corn, etc. IB87026
* Arctic Resources Controversy: Issue Brief, M. Lynne Corn, etc. IB89058
* Clean Air Act Provisions to Protect National Parklands, Maria Grimes 85-1013 ENR* A Comparison of Provisions of Bills Introduced in the 99th Congress to Create A Columbia Gorge National Scenic Area, M. Lynne Corn 86-629 ENR
* Establishment of New National Park System Units: A Brief Review, George Siehl 87-699 ENR
* The Federal Cave Resources Protection Act: A Review of a Proposed Bill, George Siehl 85-875 ENR
* Impact of Air Pollution on National Park Units: A Summary of Hearings Held by the House Subcommittee on National Parks and Recreation, May 20, 21, 1985, George Siehl, etc. 85-933 ENR
* Issues Surrounding the Greater Yellowstone Ecosystem: A Brief Review, M. Lynne Corn, etc. 85-1146 ENR
* Land and Water Conservation Fund: Information and Status, George Siehl 89-159 ENR
* The Major Federal Land Management Agencies: Management of Our Nation's Lands and Resources, Adela Backiel, etc. 87-22 ENR
* Manassas National Battlefield Park: The Battle Continues, John O. Spengler, etc. 88-514 ENR
* National Park Entrance and Recreation User Fees: Archived Issue Brief, George Siehl IB87121
* National Park Issues in the 100th Congress, George Siehl 87-179 ENR
* National Recreation Areas, George Siehl 88-644 ENR
* An Overview of National Park Issues in the 100th Congress: Archived Issue Brief, George Siehl IB87072
* The Sawtooth National Recreation Area: Potential National Park, Ross W. Gorte 87-951 ENR
* Scenic Byways: Issues and Action, John Spengler, etc. 88-479 ENR
* Trails Programs in Federal Agencies: A Data Compilation, George Siehl 89-8 ENR

Patents and Inventions

* Accepting or Rejecting an Executory Contract Governing Intellectual Property in Bankruptcy: Legal Analysis of H.R. 4657, Robin Jeweler, etc. 88-557 A
* Copyright--Application Procedures: Info Pack IP215C
* Copyright Law: Legalizing Home Taping of Audio and Video Recordings: Archived Issue Brief, Paul Wallace IB2075
* Digital Audio Recorder Act of 1987-- Analysis of H.R. 1384 and S. 506 With Policy Alternatives, David Hack 87-698 SPR
* Legal Analysis of a Memorandum of Understanding Between the United States and the Federal Republic of Germany Concerning

Current Events and Homework

Patent Rights Resulting from, Michael V. Seitzinger 87-281 A
* Patenting Life: Issue Brief, Sarah Taylor IB87222
* Resale Royalties for Visual Artists: Background Information and Analysis, Julius Allen 88-416 E
* U.S. Intellectual Property Rights and Trade, Lenore Sek 86-383 E
* Videocassette Recorders: Legal Analysis of Home Use, Douglas Reid Weimer 89-30 A

Payment-in-Kind Program
* see Agriculture--Policies and Legislation

Peaceful Nuclear Explosions Treat
* The Threshold Test Ban and Peaceful Nuclear Explosion Treaties: Background Information and Senate Ratification Issues, Steven A. Hildreth, etc. 87-34 F

Pensions
* see also Civil Service, Social Security
* Benefit and Pay Increases in Selected Federal Programs, Carolyn L. Merck 88-696 EPW
* Constitutional Considerations Implicated by a Hypothetical Proposal to Tax the Investment Income of a Tax-Exempt Entity Affiliated with a State or Local, Robert B. Burdette 88-551 A
* Early Retirement Incentive Plans under the Age Discrimination in Employment Act of 1967, as Amended, Kathleen S. Swendiman 88-608 A
* Effects of Stock Market Downturn on Pensions, Ray Schmitt 88-15 EPW
* Four Questions About National Retirement Income Security, Rich Hobbie, etc. 88-242 EPW
* The Indexation of Federal Programs, Royal Ship 82-103 S
* Individual Retirement Account Issues and Savings Accounts Proposals: Issue Brief, James Storey IB89085
* Individual Retirement Accounts and Financial Savings: New Evidence, William Jackson 86-125 E
* Individual Retirement Accounts (IRAs) After the Tax Reform Act of 1986, Gregg A. Esenwein 87-712 E
* Individual Retirement Accounts: Issues After Enactment of the 1986 Tax Reform: Archived Issue Brief, James Storey, etc. IB87225
* Legal Analysis of LTV Corporation's Unilateral Termination of Retiree's Health and Life Insurance Benefits on the Date of Filing in Bankruptcy, Vincent Treacy 86-845 A
* Legal Authority of Bankrupt Employer Unilaterally to Terminate Retirees Benefits under a Collective Bargaining Agreement, Vincent Treacy 86-826 A
* Meeting the Pension Obligation: Underfunding and Overfunding Issues: Archived Issue Brief, Ray Schmitt IB87170
* Minimum Universal Pension System, Ray Schmitt 87-197 EPW
* New Vesting Requirements for Private Pension Plans, Ray Schmitt 88-166 EPW* Paying for the Baby Boom's Retirement, Congressional Research Service 87-905 EPW
* Pension Asset Reversions: Whose Money Is It? Issue Brief, Raymond Schmitt, etc. IB89091
* Pension Portability: What Does It Mean? How Does It Work? What Does It Accomplish? Ray Schmitt 88-498 EPW
* Private Pension Plan Standards: A Summary of the Employment Retirement Income Security Act of 1974 (ERISA) as Amended, Ray Schmitt 88-681 EPW
* Railroad Retirement and Employment: Recent Issues: Issue Brief, Dennis Snook, etc. IB84068
* Retirement Benefits Security Act of 1987: Legal Analysis of S. 548, 100th Congress, Vincent Treacy 87-294 A
* Retirement for Members of Congress, Carolyn L. Merck 89-110 EPW
* Retirement Income: Bibliography-in-Brief, 1986-1987, Edith Sutterlin 88-28 L
* Salary Reduction Retirement Plans: How They Work After the 1986 Tax Reform, James Storey 88-226 EPW
* Section 89 Nondiscrimination Rules for Employee Benefits, Ray Schmitt, etc. 88-470 EPW
* State Taxation of Nonresidents' Retirement Income, Robert Burdette 89-224 A
* States that Will Award Spouses a Share of Retirement Benefits at the Time of Divorce, Marie Morris, etc. 87-782 A
* Tax-Favored Savings: All Savers Certificates and Individual Retirement Accounts, William Jackson 85-168 E
* Women's Pension Equity: A Summary of the Retirement Equity Act of 1984, Ray Schmitt 84-217 EPW
* Working AFter Normal Retirement Age: Pension Accruals for Post-65 Service, Ray Schmitt 88-618 EPW
* Young v. Old? Intergenerational Economic Equity: Bibliography-in-Brief, 10978-1987, Saundra Shirley-Reynolds 87-467 L

Pensions -- Civil Service
* Benefits to Individuals Based on Previous Employment:

Interactions and Offsets in Selected Programs, Carolyn Merck 85-869 EPW
* Civil Service Retirement: Bibliography-in-Brief, 1985-1988, Edith Sutterlin 88-538 L
* Civil Service Retirement: Withdrawal of Contributions ("Lump-Sum Payments") and Taxation of Benefits, Carolyn L. Merck 87-99 EPW
* Comparison of Retirement Systems for Executive Branch Employees, Members of Congress and Active Duty Military Personnel, Carolyn Merck, etc. 85-685 EPW
* Comparison of the Civil Service Retirement System for Members of Congress and Executive Branch Employees, Carolyn Merck 85-681 EPW
* Criteria and Precedents for Providing Federal Civil Service Retirement Credit for Non-Federal Employment, Carolyn Merck 88-317 EPW
* Federal Civil Service Retirement for People With Military Service and Social Security: "Catch 62", Carolyn Merck 84-680 EPW
* Federal Employees Retirement System Handbook for Members of Congress: Benefits under the Federal Employees' Retirement System, Education and Public Welfare Division 87-189 EPW
* Fiduciary Responsibility Requirements of the Pension and Retirement Plans for State Employees, Joyce Thorpe, etc. 88-614 A
* Financing the Civil Service Retirement System: Payments Into and Out of the Trust Fund, Carolyn Merck 86-664 EPW
* Post-Retirement Maintenance of Real Benefit Level, Civil Service Retirement Team 85-750 EPW
* Premium Effect of Proposed Medicare Catastrophic Legislation on Federal Annuitants, Janet Lundy 87-801 EPW
* Provisions of the Balanced Budget and Emergency Deficit Control Act of 1985 Affecting Pay and Benefits for Federal Workers and Retirees, Carolyn Merck 86-502 EPW
* Provisions of the Tax Reform Act of 1986 Affecting Federal Workers and Retirees, Carolyn Merck 86-928 EPW
* Retirement for Federal Employees: FY 90 Budget Issues: Issue Brief, Carolyn Merck IB89034
* A Retirement Plan for Federal Workers Covered by Social Security: An Analysis of the Federal Employees Retirement System (P.L. 99-335), Education and Public Welfare Division 86-137 EPW
* Retirement Systems for Federal Employees: Info Pack IP205R
* Social Security: The Offset of Social Security Spousal Benefits for Government Pensions, Nancy Miller, etc. 86-43 EPW
* State Taxation of Federal Retirement Income: Davis v. Michigan Department of Treasury, Marie B. Morris 89-233 A
* States Affected by the Supreme Court Ruling on Tax Discrimination Against Federal Retirees, Mark Gurevitz, etc. 89-275 A
* Summary and Analysis of the Civil Service Retirement Spouse Equity Act, as Amended, Rita Ann Reimer 87-781 A
* Treatment of Former Spouses under Various Federal Retirement Systems, Marie Morris 88-512 A

Perestroika
* see U.S.S.R. -- Politics and Government

Persian Gulf
* see also National Defense and Security* Chinese Arms Sales to the Persian Gulf: A Fact Sheet, Robert Sutter 88-286 F
* Disruption of Oil Supply from the Persian Gulf: Near-Term U.S. Vulnerability (Winter 1987/88), Clyde Mark, etc. 87-863 ENR
* Insuring U.S.Interests in the Persian Gulf: Summary and Proceedings of the Workshop Held on October 6, 1987 by the Congressional Research Service, Gary J. Pagliano 88-725 F
* The NATO Allies, Japan, and the Persian Gulf, Paul Gallis 84-184 F
* Oil from the Persian Gulf: Production, Disposition, and Transportation: Archived Issue Brief, Robert Bamberger, etc. IB88063
* Persian Gulf and the War Powers Debate: Issue Summary and Review of Events: Archived Issue Brief, Clyde Mark IB87207
* Persian Gulf: Iran Air Flight 655: Archived Issue Brief, Ellen Laipson IB88080
* Persian Gulf: Overview of Issues: Archived Issue Brief, Ellen Laipson IB87220
* Persian Gulf: Selected References, Sherry Shapiro 88-533 L
* Persian Gulf: U.S. Military Operations: Archived Issue Brief, Ronald O'Rourke IB87145
* The Persian Gulf, 1987: A Chronology of Events, Clyde Mark 88-129 F
* United Nations Role in the Iran-Iraq War: Issues and Options, Lois McHugh, etc. 88-463 F
* U.S., Soviet, and Western European Naval Forces in the Persian Gulf Region, Robert J. Ciarrocchi 87-956 F

Pesticides
* Agent Orange: Veterans' Complaints and Studies of Health Effects: Archived Issue Brief, Sam Merrill, etc. IB83043

87-80 A
* Foreign Participation in Federal Elections: A Legal Analysis, Thomas Durbin 87-554 A
* House Campaign Expenditures: 1980-1986, David C. Huckabee, etc. 87-451 GOV
* Legal Analysis of Specialized Multicandidate PACs and Private Tax-Exempt Foundations of Potential Federal Office Candidates, Thomas Durbin 86-844 A
* Limits on Lobbying and Political Activity by Tax-Exempt Organizations: Historical Background and Continuing Issues, Marie Morris 87-821 A
* Political Action Committee Contributions Received by House Candidates: 1980-1986, David Huckabee, etc. 87-550 GOV
* Political Action Committees (PACs): Info Pack IP296P
* The Presidential Election Campaign Fund and Tax Checkoff, Joseph Cantor 85-180 GOV
* Prohibiting All PAC Contributions to Federal Office Candidates: A Constitutional Analysis, Thomas Durbin 87-549 A
* Senate Campaign Expenditures, Receipts and Sources of Funds: 1980-1988, David Huckabee, etc. 89-287 GOV
* "Soft Money" in Federal Elections: A Legal Analysis, Thomas Durbin 88-492 A
* Use of Compulsory Union Dues for Political and Ideological Purposes: An Analysis of Supreme Court Decisions and Federal Legislation Re Such Use, Thomas Durbin 86-1056 A
* Whether or Not Senatorial Public Financing Proposals Impose Unconstitutional Monetary Sanctions, Thomas Durbin 87-660 A
* Whether Senatorial Public Financing Proposals Violate the Constitutional Rights of Contributors, Thomas Durbin 87-459 A

Politics and Elections -- Election Law
* The American Electoral College: Origins, Development, Proposals for Reform or Abolition, Thomas Neale 79-72 GOV
* Campaign Financing/Public Financing: Archived Issue Brief, Thomas Durbin IB73017
* Constitutionality of Legislation Providing for Mail Registration and Election Day Registration for Federal Elections, Thomas Durbin 87-247 A
* The Eighteen Years Old Vote: the Twenty-Sixth Amendment and Subsequent Voting Rates of Newly Enfranchised Age Groups, Thomas Neale 83-103 GOV
* Electoral College: Bibliography-in-Brief, 1958-1988, George Walser 88-680L
* Electoral College: Info Pack IP031E
* The Electoral College Method of Electing the President and Vice President and Proposals for Reform, Thomas Durbin 88-555 A
* Extending the Fairness Doctrine to the Print Media, Thomas Durbin 87-584 A
* The Fairness Doctrine: Selected References, 1979-1987, Rebecca Mazur 88-24 L
* Hatch Act: Info Pack IP298H
* A Legal Analysis of the Equal Time Rule After the FCC's Abolition of the Fairness Doctrine, Thomas Durbin 87-754 A
* Legal and Constitutional Framework of "Hatch Act" Restrictions on Political Activities of Federal Employees, Jack Maskell 89-280 A
* Making the General Election Day a Holiday or Changing the General Election Day to Sunday, Thomas M. Durbin 87-596 A
* Proposals to Reform Our Presidential Electoral System: A Survey of the Historical Background and Development of the Electoral College, A Compilation, Thomas Durbin 84-150 A
* Remedies Available to the House of Representatives After an Investigation of a Contested Election Case, Thomas Durbin 85-658 A
* Special Elections and Membership Changes in the 100th Congress, Thomas Neale 89-95 GOV
* State Statutory Provisions Regarding the Political Activities by Public Employees, Jack Maskell 87-841 A
* A Summary of National and State Party Laws Concerning the Election of Delegates to the 1988 Democratic and Republican National Conventions, Kevin Coleman 88-102 GOV
* Use of Compulsory Union Dues for Political and Other Ideological Purposes, Thomas Durbin 88-737 A
* Voter Registration and Turnout: 1948-1988, Royce Crocker 89-179 GOV
* The Voting Rights Act of 1965 as Amended, Paul Downing 84-203 GOV

Politics and Elections -- Practical Politics
* Brief Histories of Major and Minor Political Parties in the United States--A Compilation of Extracts 1789-1979 Frederick Paula, etc. 80-169 GOV* Changes in the Presidential Nomination Process: Looking to 1988: Issue Brief, Kevin Coleman IB86117
* The Fairness Doctrine and the Equal Opportunities Doctrine: Issue Brief, Thomas Durbin 82087
* Final Delegate Totals and Dates for Presidential Primaries and Caucuses, 1988, Kevin J. Coleman 89-180 GOV
* A Guide to the Presidential Election Process, Joseph Cantor, etc.

88-629 GOV
* Interest Groups and Lobbying: Selected References, 1987-1989, Jean Bowers 89-257 L
* Lobbying: Info Pack IP066L
* Negative Campaigning in National Politics: An Overview, Thomas Neale 87-868 GOV
* The New Religious Right: Background, Current Agenda, Future Prospects, Charles Whittier 87-615 GOV
* Reelection Rates of House Incumbents: 1790-1988, David Huckabee 89-173 GOV
* Speechwriting and Delivery: Info Pack IP139S
* Speechwriting in Perspective: A Brief Guide to Effective and Persuasive Communication, Charles Whittier 86-1034 GOV
* The 1984 Presidential Election: The Platforms Presented by the Democratic Party (Mondale/Ferraro) and the Republican Party (Reagan/Bush), Kevin Coleman 84-182 GOV

Polygraph Testing of Employees
* see Labor

Poor
* see Public Welfare

Population
* Adjusting the 1990 Census: Background and a Pro-Con Analysis, Alexander Luri 88-305 GOV
* The Census Bureau's Plans for Using Computerized Maps in 1990: Fact Sheet, Daniel Melnick 87-206 GOV
* Census Questions and OMB's Review of the Census Bureau Proposal: A Summary and Brief Analysis, Daniel Melnick, etc. 88-42 GOV
* Counting Undocumented Aliens in the Decennial Census, Thomas Durbin 88-438 A
* House Apportionment Following the 1990 Census: Preliminary Projections, David Huckabee 88-567 GOV
* International Population and Family Planning Programs: Issues for Congress: Archived Issue Brief, Vita Blue IB85187
* Population Growth and Natural Resource Deterioration in Drought-Stricken Africa, Susan Abbasi 85-1149 ENR
* Population Programs of AID: Background of Legislation--99th Congress, Vita Blue 86-1009 F
* Proposed Exclusion of Illegal Aliens from the Population Used to Apportion the House of Representatives: A Methodological and Policy Analysis, Jennifer D. Williams, etc. 88-418 GOV
* Statistical Adjustment of the Decennial Census: Constitutional Analysis of Statutory Proposals, Thomas Durbin 87-947 A
* Steps in Conducting the 1990 Census, Daniel Melnick 87-205 GOV
* The U.S. White Population, by Census Division, State, and Congressional District, Jennifer Williams 86-860 GOV
* The 1990 Decennial Census and the Counting of Illegal Aliens, Thomas Durbin 88-62 A
* 99th Congress Districts Classified by the Proportion of Population Over Age 65 (Ranking all Districts by Their Total Population over 65 and Percent over), David Huckabee 89-910 GOV

Pornography and Obscenity
* see Civil Liberties and Rights--Pornography and Obscenity

Portugal
* Current Issues With the "Base-Rights" Countries and Their Implications, Richard Grimmett 88-726 F
* United States Military Installations in Portugal, Richard Grimmett 86-6 F

Posse Comitatus Act
* Use of the Military to Enforce Civilian Law: Posse Comitatus Act and Other Considerations, Charles Doyle 88-583 A

Postal Service
* Commemorative Postage Stamps: History, Selection, Criteria, and Revenue Raising Potential, Bernevia M. McCalip 88-575 E
* Constitutionality of Franking Statute Upheld by U.S. District Court in Common Cause v. Bolger, Elizabeth Yadlosky 82-155 S
* Legal Analysis of S. 541, 100th Congress, a Bill to Provide that Certain Postal Service Employees Have Procedural and Appeal Rights in the Event of Ad, Michael Seitzinger 87-433 A
* Postal Workers Negotiations: The 1987 Contract, Gail McCallion 87-851 E
* The U.S. Postal Service: A Public or Private Enterprise?: Issue Brief, Bernevia M. McCalip IB88084
* The Postal Service: Its Treatment in the Federal Budget: Issue Brief, Bernevia McCalip IB88035* The U.S. Postal Service Monopoly: Should It Be Repealed? : Archived Issue Brief, Bernevia McCalip IB85182

Power Resources
* see Alternative Energy Sources, Electric Power, Energy Conservation, Energy Policy, Fossil Fuels, and Nuclear Energy
* Controlling Carbon Dioxide Emissions, Amy Abel, etc. 89-157 ENR
* The Europe 1992 Plan: Science and Technology Issues, Science Policy Research Division 89-178 SPR

Power Resources -- Alternative Energy Sources
* Alcohol Fuels: Bibliography-in-Brief, Karen Alderson 88-415 L
* Alcohol Fuels: Issue Brief, Migdon Segal IB74087
* Alcohol Fuels Tax Incentives: Current Law and Proposed Option to Expand Current Law, Salvatore Lazzari 89-343 E
* Alternative Fuels for Motor Vehicles: Some Environmental Issues, David Gushee 88-624 S
* Analysis of Possible Effects of H.R. 2031, Legislation Mandating Use of Ethanol and Methanol in Gasoline, Congressional Research Service 88-71 SPR
* Analysis of Possible Effects of H.R. 2052, Legislation Mandating Use of Ethanol in Gasoline, Migdon Segal, etc. 87-819 SPR
* Ethanol Fuel and Global Warming, Migdon Segal 89-164 SPR
* Handbook of Alternative Energy Technology Development and Policy, Science Policy Research Division 83-43 SPR
* Renewable Energy: Federal Program: Issue Brief, Fred Sissine IB87140
* Renewable Energy Technology: A Review of Legislation, Research, and Trade, Fred Sissine, etc. 87-318 SPR
* Utility Fuel Options: Using Excess Corn Supplies, Duane A. Thompson 87-541 ENR
* Wind Energy: Archived Issue Brief, Fred Sissine IB80091
* Wind Energy Development and Utility Capacity Credits: A Review of Research, Implementation and Policy Issues under the Public Utility Regulatory Act, Fred Sissine 84-101 SPR

Power Resources
* Accelerated Depreciation, the Investment Tax Credit, and Their Required Ratemaking Treatment in the Public Utility Industry: A Background Report, Donald W. Kiefer 87-312 S
* Acid Rain Legislation and Midwest Industry: A Mountain or a Mole Hill? Larry Parker, etc. 85-1152 ENR
* The Bonneville Power Administration: To Sell or Not to Sell, Alvin Kaufman, etc. 86-176 E
* Canadian Electricity: The U.S. Market and the Free Trade Agreement, Amy Abel 88-427 ENR
* The Effect of Alternative Depreciation Systems on Marginal Effective Tax Rates on Public Utility Property, Donald Keifer 86-506 E
* Electric Rate Effects of Cogeneration and Wheeling : Should PURPA Be Amended? Archived Issue Brief, Sylvia Morrison IB87119
* Electric Utilities: Deregulation, Diversification, Acid Rain, Tall Stack Regulation, and Electric Demand Issues: Archived Issue Brief, Donald Dulchinos, etc. IB85134
* Electric Utility Regulation in the Brave New World, Alvin Kaufman 88-135 ENR
* Federal and State Regulation of Nuclear and Non-Nuclear Electric Utilities and of Nuclear Materials, Michael Seitzinger 87-221 A
* Federal Hydropower: Repaying the Debt: Archived Issue Brief, John Moore IB85125
* Federal Hydropower: The Administration's Proposal to Sell Government Assets: Archived Issue Brief, John Moore IB86057
* The Federal Power Marketing Administrations: To Privatize or Not to Privatize, Alvin Kaufman, etc. 86-90 S
* Licensing and Special Use Permit Requirements for Hydroelectric Dam Projects under the Federal Power Act and the Federal Land Policy and Mnagement Act, Robin Jeweler 88-459 A
* Public Utilities Holding Company Act of 1935: Is This the Time for Reform: Issue Brief, Amy Abel IB89052
* PURPA: Should It Be Amended to Facilitate the Sale of Bulk Power by Bid?: Archived Issue Brief, Sylvia Morrison IB88014
* Rural Electric Cooperative Defaults: Origins, Current Status, and Legislative Implications, Sylvia Morrison 88-665 S
* State Versus Federal Ratemaking Authority: Mississippi Power & Light Co. v. Mississippi Ex Rel. Moore, Robin Jeweler 88-651 A
* Superconductivity: An Overview: Issue Brief, Richard Rowberg, etc. IB87191
* Superconductivity: Bibliography-in-Brief, 1980-1988, B.F. Mangan 88-632 L
* Superconductors: Info Pack IB390S
* The Tax Reform Act of 1986: The Effects on Public Utilities, Donald Kiefer 84-211 E
* The United States Bankruptcy Code: Legal Implications of an Investor-Owned Utility Reorganization under Chapter, Robin Jeweler 88-140 A
* Wheeling in the Electric Utility Industry, Environment and Natural Resources Policy Division 87-289 ENR

Power Resources -- Energy Conservation
* Comparison of the Departments of Energy and Health and Human Services Weatherization Assistance Programs, Mary Smith, etc. 89-229 EPW* DOE Energy Conservation Budget Trends: A Review With Comparisons to Other DOE Programs, Fred Sissine 87-486 SPR
* Energy Conservation: Prospects for Cogeneration Technology: Archived Issue Brief, Fred Sissine IB83068
* Energy Conservation: Technical Efficiency and Program Effectiveness: Archived Issue Brief, Fred Sissine IB85130

Power Resources -- Energy Policy
* Energy Excise Taxes for Deficit Reduction: Archived Issue Brief, Salvatore Lazzari IB87172
* Energy Impacts: Archived Issue Brief, Duane Thompson, etc. IB87021
* Energy Security: Issue Brief, Carl Behrens IB89006
* A History of Federal Energy Tax Policy: Conventional as Compared to Renewable and Nonconventional Energy Resources, Salvatore Lazzari 88-455 E

Practical Politics
* see Congress--Apportionment and Elections, Politics and Elections--Practical Politics

Prayer in the Public Schools
* see Elementary and Secondary Education--Prayer and Religion

Presidential Appointments
* see Executive Organization--Presidential Appointments, Presidents (U.S.)

Presidential-Congressional Relations
* see Congress--Executive Relations, Congress--Foreign Relations, Congress--Military Policy, Presidents (U.S.)--Foreign Relations, War Powers Resolution

Presidents (U.S.)
* see also Foreign Relations
* Federal Benefits to Former Presidents and Their Widows, Stephanie Smith 85-173 GOV
* Federal Expenditures for Former Presidents: Archived Issue Brief, Stephanie Smith IB85129
* The Forty-First President: George Bush, Selected References, 1972-1988, George Walser 88-699 L
* Inauguration of the President: Info Pack IP316I
* The Presidency of the United States: Info Pack IP409P
* The Presidency: Selected References, 1985-1988, Elizabeth Lane 89-84 L
* Presidential Commissions: Their Purpose and Impact, Stephanie Smith 87-668 GOV
* Presidential Emergency Powers Over Domestic Affairs: Executive Order No. 211490 and P.R.M. No. 32: Archived Issue Brief, Raymond Nattern IB80087
* Presidential Remarks About the International Atomic Energy Agency: Selected Excerpts, Barbara Black 89-27 ENR
* Presidential Signing Statements--Use in Statutory Construction, George Costello 87-894 A
* Presidential Succession: A Short History, Ronald Moe 78-244 GOV
* Presidential Tenure: A History and Analysis of the President's Term of Office, Stephen Stathis 81-129 GOV
* Presidential Transition: Selected References, 1960-1988, George Walser 88-691 L
* Presidential Vetoes and Ronald Reagan's Use of the Process in the Second Term: Issue Brief, Gary Galemore IB85093
* Presidential Vetos and Ronald Reagan's Use of the Process in His First Term: Archived Issue Brief, Gary Galemore IB81174
* Recess Appointment: Legal Overview, Richard C. Ehlke 87-832 A
* Salary of the President of the United States Compared with that of Other High-Level Government Officials, Sharon Gressle 89-35 GOV
* U.S. Presidents: An Alphabetical Microthesaurus of Terms Selected from the Legislative Indexing Vocabulary , Shirley Loo 89-131 L
* Vetoes During President Reagan's First Term, 1981-1984, Gary Galemore 86-681 GOV
* Vice Presidents of the United States, 1789-1981: Brief Bibliographical Notes, Christopher Dell 81-23 GOV

Presidents (U.S.) -- Foreign Relations
* Andropov and Reagan as Negotiators: Context and Styles in Contrast, Joseph Whelan 83-141 S
* Central American Peace Process: Selected References, Robert Kirk 88-389 L
* Congress and the President in U.S. Foreign Policymaking: A

Current Events and Homework

Selected, Annotated Bibliography, Sherry Shapiro 86-183 L
* Foreign Policy Roles of the President and Congress, Ellen C. Collier 86-163 F
* The Iran/Contra Affair: Implications for the National Security Adviser and the NSC Staff: Archived Issue Brief, Joel Woldman IB87107
* President and Foreign Policy: Selected References, Sherry Shapiro 88-219 L
* Sectional Analysis of the "War Powers Resolution" (WPR) as It Would Be Amended by the "War Powers Resolution Amendments of 1988" (S.J. Res. 323, 100th), Raymond J. Celada 88-441 A
* Statements by President Reagan Relating to Arms Control, April 1, 1986-January 31, 1987, Teri Lehto 87-116 S* Statements by President Reagan Relating to Arms Control, February 1, 1987-May 31, 1987, Teri Lehto 87-525 S
* Statements by President Reagan Relating to Arms Control: February 2, 1985-December 31, 1985, Jeanette Voas 86-549 F
* Statements by President Reagan Relating to Arms Control, January 1, 1984-March 31, 1984, Lynn Rusten 84-616 F
* Statements by President Reagan Relating to Arms Control: January 1, 1986-March 31, 1986, Jeanette Voas 86-663 S
* Statements by President Reagan Relating to Arms Control: June 1, 1987-December 31, 1987, Teri Lehto 88-69 S
* Statements by President Reagan Relating to the INF Treaty, June 1, 1987-December 31, 1987, Teri Lehto 88-60 S
* U.S. Presidential National Security Advisers: Changing Roles and Relationships, Joel Woldman 87-334 F
* The War Powers Resolution: Fifteen Years of Experience, Ellen Collier 88-529 F
* War Powers Resolution: Info Pack   IP131W
* War Powers Resolution: Presidential Compliance: Issue Brief, Ellen Collier IB81050
* War Powers Resolution: The Controversial Act's Search for a Successful Litigation Posture, Raymond J. Celada 88-64 A
* The War Powers Resolution (WPR): Some Implications of S.J. Res. 323, "War Powers Resolution Amendments of 1988", Raymond J. Celada 88-464 A
* War Powers: Selected References, Sherry Shapiro 89-305 L

Press
* Concentration in the U.S. Daily Newspaper Industry: Trends and Issues, R. Kevin Flaherty 84-727 E
* Confidentiality and Secrecy Orders in Civil Cases, Kenneth Thomas 89-225 A
* Extending the Fairness Doctrine to the Print Media, Thomas Durbin 87-584 A
* High School Student Press Rights: Hazelwood School District v. Kuhlmeier, Rita Ann Reimer 88-167 A
* Mediasat: The Use of Remote Sensing Satellites by News Agencies, Patricia E. Humphlett 87-70 SPR
* The Newspaper Preservation Act (15 U.S.C. (Sections) 1801-1804), Janice E. Rubin 89-239 A
* "Public Figures" and the Intentional Infliction of Emotional Distress: Hustler Magazine v. Falwell, Rita Ann Reimer 88-177 A
* Research Journal Prices--Trends and Problems, Richard Rowberg 88-264 SPR
* Taxation of the Press: A Brief Constitutional Analysis, Rita Ann Reimer 87-422 A
* Television Network Evening News Coverage of Afghanistan: A Perspective After Eight Years of War, Denis Stevens Rutkus 88-319 GOV

Price-Anderson Insurance and Indemnity Act
* see also Nuclear Energy--Accidents and Safety,
* Nuclear Liability Legislation: Price-Anderson Act Renewal Issues: Archived Issue Brief, Mark Holt IB88034

Prisoners of War in Southeast Asia
* see Military Personnel,

Prisons
* Prison Conditions: The Congressional Response-Issue Brief, William Woldman IB81171
* Prison Reform: Federal Role: Archived Issue Brief, Barbara McClure IB75077
* Social Security Benefits for Prisoners: Archived Issue Brief, David Koitz IB81163

Privacy
* see Civil Liberties and Rights,

Privatization
* see Public Finance--Privatization,

Procurement
* see also Defense Economics--Procurement, Infrastructure,

* Administrative Discretion to Set Aside the Eight-Hour Provisions of the Walsh-Healey Public Contracts Act (1936) and the Contract Work Hours Standards, William G. Whittaker 83-500 E
* Amendments to the Prompt Payment Act of 1982: Action in the 100th Congress, Thomas Youth 87-558 GOV
* Asbestos in Buildings: Activity in the 100th Congress, Claudia Copeland 89-267 ENR
* Avoiding Urban/Rural Wage Inequities in Determination of Prevailing Wage Rates under the Davis-Bacon Act, William Whittaker 85-631 E* Business: Doing Business with the Federal Government: Info Pack, IP30B
* Competition in Federal Public Contracting--the New Look: Changes and Implementation: the Competition Contracting Act Title VII of Public Law 98-369, Robert G. Lauck 85-82 A
* Compilation of State Laws Pertaining to the Exemptions from State Sales Taxes for Federal Purchases, Mark Gurevitz 89-232 A
* The Davis Bacon Act: A Review of the Literature, William Whittaker 84-137 E
* The Davis-Bacon Act and Federal Contract Construction Wage Policy: Background Analysis and Recent Legislative Interest, William Whittaker 87-563 E
* Federal Civilian Procurement Reform Initiatives: Archived Issue Brief, Stephanie Smith IB86126
* Federal Programs for Minority and Women-Owned Businesses, Mark Eddy 89-278 GOV
* Liability of Superfund "Response Action Contractors" and EPA for Injury from Contractor-Conducted Cleanups, Robert Meltz 89-292 A
* The McNamara-O'Hara Service Contract Act: Discretionary Authority of the Secretary of Labor under Section 4(B) and the Mandatory Wage Rate Determination, William G. Whittaker 86-533 E
* Minority Business Set-Asides and the Constitution: A Legal Analysis of the U.S. Supreme Court Ruling in City of Richmond v. J.A. Croson Co., Charles V. Dale 89-124 A
* Productivity in Public Works Construction--Options for Improvement, Russell Vakharia 88-97 SPR
* The Service Contract Act of 1965, Robert Lauck 86-779 A
* United States Supreme Court Actions Regarding Minority Business Set-Asides After City of Richmond v. J.A. Croson, Charles V. Dale 89-202 A

Productivity
* see Labor-Productivity,

Products Liability
* see Consumers, Insurance--Liability Issues,

Professional and Administrative Career Examination
* Elimination of the Professional and Administrative Career Examination (PACE) and Proposed Alternative Selection Procedures, Paul Downing 89-315 GOV

Program Trading
* see Corporations--Securities Industry,

Protectionism
* see Foreign Trade--Imports and Exports, Foreign Trade--Trade Policy,

Public Administration
* Privatization from a Public Management Perspective, Ronald Moe 89-160

Public Broadcasting
* see Telecommunications,

Public Finance
* see Budget Process, Budget Programs, Credit Programs, Deficits, Fiscal Policy, Privatization, Congress-Budget Process, Local Finance,
* Budget Background for FY 1990: Issue Brief, Philip D. Winters IB89072
* Budget for Fiscal Year 1989: Info Pack, IP394B
* Budget for Fiscal Year 1990: Info Pack, IP413B
* The Capital Gains Response to a Tax Rate Change: Is It Overestimated?, Donald Kiefer 88-216 S
* Economic Policymaking Problems, Part One: Institutions and Processes, Leon M. Cole, etc. 89-299 E
* Economic Policymaking Problems: Part Two: Theories and Forecasts, Leon M. Cole, etc. 89-300 E
* The Effect of Federal Tax and Budget Policies in the 1980s on the State-Local Sector, Lillian Rymarowicz, etc. 86-2 E
* Federal Budget and Tax Policy and the State-Local Sector: Retrenchment in the 1980s, Lillian Rymarowicz, etc. 88-600 E
* The Federal Budget for Fiscal Year 1988: Archived Issue Brief,

Philip Winters IB87057
* The Federal Budget for Fiscal Year 1989: Issue Brief, Philip Winters IB88064
* Financial Crises of the 1970s and 1980s: Causes, Developments, and Government Responses, William Jackson, etc. 89-290 E
* Government Securities Market: Disturbances and Regulation, William Jackson 87-165 E
* A National Lottery: Overview and Economic Analysis, Gregg A. Esenwein, etc. 87-811 E
* Proposed and Actual Budget Totals for the Fiscal Years 1980 Through 1988, Philip D. Winters 88-544 E
* Should the Treasury Issue Indexed Bonds?, G. Thomas Woodward 88-4 E
* Summary and Legislative History of Public Law 98-473: Continuing Appropriations for Fiscal Year 1985, (H.J. Res. 648), Edward Davis, etc. 85-12 GOV* U.S. Savings Bonds; Benefits and Costs of Variable Rates, James M. Bickley 86-924 E

Public Finance--Budget Process
* Biennial Budgeting: Background and Congressional Options, James V. Saturno 89-295 GOV
* Budget Making and the Legislative Process: Audio Brief, Robert Keith, etc. AB50164
* Budget Process: Info Pack, IP012B
* Budget Process Legislation Introduced in the Senate During the 100th Congress: Comparison of Selected Measures, Edward Davis, etc. 87-611 GOV
* Budget Process Reform Legislation Introduced in the 101st Congress: Selected Listing, James V. Saturno 89-304 GOV
* Budget Sequestration Procedures for Fiscal Year 1987: Summary of Congressional Action, Robert Keith 86-1049 GOV
* Changes in the Congressional Budget Process made by the 1985 Balanced Budget Act (P.L. 99-177), Robert Keith 86-713 GOV
* Congressional Approaches to Biennial Budgeting, Michael D. Margeson, etc. 87-653 GOV
* Congressional Approaches to Regulating Continuing Resolutions: Measures Introduced in the 100th Congress, James Saturno 88-350 GOV
* Congressional Budget Process Reform: Archived Issue Brief, Edward Davis IB87196
* The Effects of a Two-Year Defense Budget Authorization, Alice Maroni 85-940 F
* The Federal Budget Process: Selected References, Robert Howe 88-436 L
* An Introduction to the Spending and Budget Process in Congress, Stanley Bach 86-20 GOV
* Item Veto Bills Introduced in the House of Representatives During the 100th Congress, Gary Galemore 87-468 GOV
* Legal Analysis of Proposal to Repeal Deferral Authority under the Impoundment Control Act, Richard Ehlke 86-1024 A
* Legal Analysis of the Government Securities Act of 1986 and Its Application to Broker/Dealers Convicted of Insider Trading Violations Michael V. Seitzinger 87-280 A
* Legislation, Appropriations, and Budgets: The Development of Spending Decision-Making in Congress, Allen Schick 84-106 GOV
* Legislative Branch: Budget Authority, FY 1962-FY 1988, Paul Dwyer 88-290 GOV
* Manual on the Federal Budget Process, Allen Schick, etc. 87-286 GOV
* Omnibus Budget Reconciliation Act of 1987: A Summary of Congressional Action on P.L. 100-203, James Saturno 88-296 GOV
* The Power of the Purse in Foreign Policy: Process and Problems in Congressional Funding, Ellen Collier 85-182 F
* Presidential Impoundment Authority After City of New Haven v. United States, Richard Ehlke, etc. 87-173 A
* The President's Budget Submission: Format, Deadlines, and Transition Years, Virginia A. McMurtry, etc. 88-661 GOV
* Reconciliation for Fiscal Year 1987: A Summary of Congressional Action, James Saturno 87-772 GOV
* Regular Appropriations Enacted Separately and in Continuing Appropriations, Fiscal Years 1977-1987, Sandy Streeter 87-826 GOV
* Rescissions by the President Since 1974: Background and Proposals for Change, Virginia A. McMurtry 89-271 GOV
* Selected Tables on the Federal Budget Regarding Chronologies of Certain Actions, Aggregate Budget Levels, and Other Information, James Saturno, etc. 87-710 GOV
* Senate Consideration of Regular Appropriations Bills under Waivers of Section 303(A) of the 1974 Budget Act, Robert Keith 89-37 GOV
* Sequestration Actions for FY 90 under the Gramm-Rudman-Hollings Act: Issue Brief, Robert Keith IB89071
* Sequestration of Budgetary Resources for Fiscal Year 1986 under the 1985 Balanced Budget Act, Robert A. Keith 86-872 GOV
* Summary and Analysis of the Ramifications of Bowsher v. Synar, the Gramm-Rudman-Hollings Deficit Reduction Act Case, Morton Rosenberg, etc. 86-788 A
* Waivers of the 1974 Budget Act Considered in the Senate During the 100th Congress, Robert Keith 89-76 GOV

Public Finance--Budget Programs
* Adult Education Act Reauthorization: Selected Options, Paul Irwin 87-57 EPW
* Agriculture and the Budget: Issue Brief, Geoffrey Becker IB87032
* Airport and Airway Program Reauthorization; Archived Issue Brief, John Fischer IB87051
* Arts and Humanities: FY88-FY89 Funding Issues; Archived Issue Brief, Robert Lyke IB82026
* Defense and Foreign Aid Budget Analysis and the Use of Constant Dollars, Alice C. Maroni, etc. 86-154 F
* Developmental Disabilities Programs: FY 1989 Budget Information, Mary F. Smith 88-181 EPW* Education for Disadvantaged Children: Reauthorization Issues: Archived Issue Brief, Wayne Riddle IB87070
* Education Funding Issues for FY 89: Archived Issue Brief, Angela Evans IB88036
* Education Legislation in the 100th Congress: A Brief Summary; Archived Issue Brief, Wava Gregory IB87134
* Entitlements and Other Mandatory Spending Accounts in the Federal Budget, Gene Falk 87-920 EPW
* Environmental Protection Agency: FY 90 Funding: Issue Brief, Martin R. Lee IB89032
* The Environmental Protection Agency's FY89 Budget; Archived Issue Brief, Martin R. Lee IB88062
* Federal Aid to Domestic Transportation: A Brief History from the 1800s to the 1980s, Nancy Heiser 88-574 E
* Federal Budget Policies and the State-Local Sector; 1980-1986, Lillian Rymarowicz, etc. 87-234 E
* Federal Programs Affecting Children, Sharon House, etc. 87-306 EPW
* Federal Spending Proposed in the Fiscal Year 1989 Budget for Selected Major Income Maintenance Programs, Vee Burke 88-227 EPW
* The Forest Service Budget: Trust Funds and Special Accounts, Ross W. Gorte, etc. 89-75 ENR
* The FY 1989 Federal Budget for Public Works Infrastructure, Claudia Copeland 88-176 ENR
* The Gramm-Rudman-Hollings Deficit Reduction Process: The Defense Aspects of the Initial Sequestration Report for FY 1987, Alice Maroni;, etc. 86-875 F
* A Guide to Trust Funds, Special Accounts, and Foundations in the Fish and Wildlife Service Budget, M. Lynne Corn 86-722 ENR
* Health Programs and the Gramm-Rudman-Hollings Legislation: The 1986 Sequestrations and the President's FY 87 Budget Proposal, James Reuter 86-648 EPW
* Health Programs Appropriations: FY 1980-FT 1989, Edward Klebe 89-79 EPW
* Job Training: FT 88 Budget and Legislative Issues:, Archived Issue Brief, Karen Spar IB87039
* Land and Water Conservation Fund: Information and Status, George Siehl 89-159 ENR
* Mllitary Manpower and Compensation: FY 88 Budget Issues: Archived Issue Brief, Robert L. Goldich IB87081
* National Forest Receipts: Sources and Dispositions, Ross W. Gorte 89-284 ENR
* The National Marine Fisheries Service Budget: A Guide to Special Accounts, Eugene Buck, etc. 86-894 ENR
* An Overview of National Park Issues in the 100th Congress: Archived Issue Brief, George H. Siehl IB87072
* Repayment of Corps of Engineers Construction Costs, Malcolm M. Simmons 87-262 ENR
* Research and Development Funding: FY 86 and FY 87: Issue Brief, Science Policy Research Div, Genevieve Knezo IB86062
* Research and Development Funding: FY 88: Archived Issue Brief, Research and Development Team, Science Policy Res IB87083
* Research and Development Funding: FY 89: Archived Issue Brief, Michael E. Davey IB88040
* Rural Areas and Clean Water: Impacts of the Water Quality Act of 1987, Claudia Copeland 87-257 ENR
* Selected Federal Research and Development Agencies and Programs and the Gramm-Rudman-Hollings Deficit Reduction Act: An Analysis of the Impact on FY 8, Michael E. Davey, etc. 86-37 SPR
* Social Security: The Effect of National Debt Limitations in 1985, David Koitz 85-1118 EPW
* The Superfund Amendments and Reauthorization Act of 1986: Archived Issue Brief, Mark E. Anthony Reisch IB87080
* U.S. Department of Education: Major Program Trends, Fiscal Years 1980-1990, Education and Public Welfare Division 89-144 EPW
* The U.S. Postal Service: Its Treatment in the Federal Budget; Issue Brief, Bernevia M. McCalip IB88035
* Veterans Programs: FY 89 Budget; Archived Issue Brief, Anne C. Steward IB88047
* Waste Management: Issue Brief, James McCarthy IB89007
* Wastewater Treatment Programs; Impact of Gramm-Rudman-Hollings Act and Prospects for Federal Funding

Current Events and Homework

(With Appendix); Archived Issue Brief, Claudia Copeland IB86018
* 1989 Budget Perspectives: Federal Spending for the Human Resource Programs: Tables and Figures Portraying the President's 1989 Budget Plan in the Cont., Gene Falk 88-351 EPW
* 1990 Budget Perspective: Federal Spending for the Human Resource Programs, 1965-1988, Gene Falk, etc. 89-87 EPW

Public Finance-- Credit Programs
* Credit Reform: Chiles-Comenici Proposal Contrasted With Reagan Proposal, James Bickley 87-939 E
* Credit Reform Proposal of the Reagan Administration: Analysis and Policy Issues, James Bickley 87-456 E
* Debt Collection by the United States Government: Existing Legal Options, Henry Cohen 88-412 A
* An Evaluation of the Reconstruction Finance Corporation With Implications for Current Capital Needs of the Steel Industry, James Bickley 80-43 E* Federal Credit Policies and Credit Allocation by Economic Objectives, James Bickley 86-3
* Transport Manufacturing: A Review and Appraisal of Federal Assistance Policies, Gwenell L. Bass 86-75 E

Public Finance--Deficits
* see also Budget and Government Spending,
* Agriculture and the Gramm-Rudman-Hollings Deficit Control Act, Geoffrey Becker 86-547 ENR
* Budget Action for FY 1990 During 1989: Issue Brief, Philip D. Winters IB89090
* Budget Action in the 100th Congress, 1st Session (1987): Archived Issue Brief, William Cox IB88030
* Budget Cuts: Updated Projections and Gramm-Rudman-Hollings; Archived Issue Brief, William Cox IB86072
* Budget Deficits and Monetary Policy, Carol Leisenring 81-128 E
* Congress and a Balanced Budget Amendment to the U. S. Constitution, James Saturno 89-4 GOV
* Constitutional Amendments to Balance the Budget and Limit Federal Spending in the 100th Congress: A Table of Features, Thomas Nicola 87-445 A
* Crowding Out? Federal, State and Local Government Borrowing and the Debt Economy, William Jackson 87-274 E
* The Debt Limit in 1987: Issue Brief, Philip Winters IB87127
* Debt-Limit Increase and 1985 Balanced Budget Act Reaffirmation: Summary of Public Law 100-119 (H.J. Res. 324), Edward Davis, etc. 87-865 GOV
* Debt-Limit Increases for FY 1987: Summary of Congressional Action in 1986 (Including Proposed Modifications to the 1985 Balanced Budget Act), Robert Keith, etc. 86-974 GOV
* Deficit Reduction and Economic Growth, Brian W. Cashell 89-349 E
* Deficit Reduction in 1988: Archived Issue Brief, William A. Cox IB87023
* Deficit Reduction Issues: Info Pack, IP274D
* Deficit Reduction: Spending and Revenue Options: Issue Brief, Donald W. Kiefer IB89003
* Deficit Reduction: The National Economic Commission Options Model, Barry Molefsky, etc. 88-606 E
* Deficit Targets, National Savings, and Social Security, Jane Gravelle 88-513 S
* Do Deficits Influence the Level of Interest Rates?, G. Thomas Woodward 85-14 E
* Energy Excise Taxes for Deficit Reduction: Archived Issue Brief, Salvatore Lazzari IB87172
* Explanation of the Balanced Budget and Emergency Deficit Control Act of 1985--Public Law 99-177 (the Gramm-Rudman-Hollings Act), Allen Schick 85-1130 GOV
* Federal Debt and Interest Measures Used in the Federal Budget, Philip D. Winters 83-158 E
* The Federal Debt: Who Bears Its Burdens? Issue Brief, William Cox IB84233
* Gramm-Rudman-Hollings and Department of Education Programs, Angela Evans 86-544 EPW
* Gramm-Rudman-Hollings Budget Adjustments: Sensitivity to Economic Assumptions; Archived Issue Brief, Barry Molefsky, etc. IB85217
* The Gramm-Rudman-Hollings Deficit Reduction Plan: The Target of a Balanced Budget and the Risk of Recession Review, Craig K. Elwell 86-534 E
* The Gramm-Rudman-Hollings Deficit Reduction Process (P.L. 99-177) and the Department of Defense: A Summary Review, Alice Maroni, etc. 86-7 F
* Gramm-Rudman-Hollings: Potential Economic Effects of Meeting Deficit Targets: Archived Issue Brief, Brian W. Cashell IB87059
* The Gramm-Rudman-Hollings Sequestration Process for FY 1986: A Summary of DOD Elements in the OMB/CB O and GAO Sequestration Reports; Policy Alert, Alice Maroni, etc. 86-16 F
* The Gramm-Rudman-Hollings Targets: How Might They Affect the Economy, Gail Makinen, etc. 86-1036 E
* House and Senate Action on Legislation Increasing the Debt Limit

for Fiscal Year 1987 (H.J. Res. 668 and H.R. 5395) (Including Modifications to the 1985), Robert A. Keith, etc. 86-871 GOV
* How the Government Borrows: A Primer, Thomas Woodward 85-762 E
* Implications of Uncertainty in Economic Forecasting under Gramm-Rudman-Hollings: Options for Congressional Response, David Grinnell 86-829 S
* Is the National Debt a Burden on Future Generation ?, Gail Makinen 86-682 E
* Major Revenue Raising Options: An Overview, Gregg A. Esenwein 88-756 E
* Management of the Federal Loan Portfolio: Recent Developments in Debt Collection and Sale of Loan As Sets, Virginia A. McMurtry 87-140 GOV
* National Economic Commission: Equitable Deficit Reduction: Archived Issue Brief, Barry Molefsky IB88032* A Proposal for Raising Revenue by Reducing Capital Gains Taxes, Jane G. Gravelle 87-562 E
* Reducing the Deficit With Energy Taxes, Craig K. Elwell 86-653 E
* Revenue-Raising Options: Archived Issue Brief, Gregg A. Esenwein IB87169
* Rural Electric Cooperative Defaults: Origins, Current Status, and Legislative Implications, Sylvia Morrison 88-665 E
* Sequestration Actions for Fiscal Year 1988 under the Gramm-Rudman-Hollings Act: Archived Issue Brief, Robert Keith IB88078
* Social Security and Medicare: How Are They in Determining the National Debt?, David Koitz 85-1132 EPW
* Social Security: Issues in Taxing Benefits under Current Law and under Proposals to Tax a Greater Share of Benefits, Geoffrey Kollmann 89-40 EPW
* Social Security: Its Impact on the Federal Budget Deficit, David Koitz 88-218 EPW
* Value-Added Tax for Deficit Reduction: Issue Brief, James Bickley IB87097
* What Large Deficits Will Do If They Continue (and What Will Happen If They are Reduced), G. Thomas Woodward 85-102 E

Public Finance--Fiscal Policy
* Capital, Credit, and Crowding Out: Cycles and Trends in Flows of Funds Over Three Decades, William Jackson 82-142 E
* Domestic and International Monetary-Fiscal Policy Coordination, Thomas F. Dernburg 84-145 E
* Government Actions that Affect Interest Rates: Mechanisms and Macroeconomic Repercussions, Craig Elwell 82-128 E
* Monetarist and Keneysian Worlds-What's the Difference?, Helen J. Scott 84-181 E
* Prospects for an Economic Downturn, G. Thomas Woodward 89-105 E
* Tax Policy and Spillover Effects: The Use of Tax Provisions to Induce Socially Desirable Activities, Jane Gravelle 80-186 E
* Tax Policy Prospects in the Bush Administration: Issue Brief, Salvatore Lazzari IB89019
* U.S. Economic Policy in an International Context: Deficits, Taxes, and Monetary Policy, Jane Gravelle, etc. 84-125 E

Public Finance--Privatization
* The Bonneville Power Administration: To Sell or Not to Sell, Alvin Kaufman, etc. 86-176 E
* Conrail: An Analysis of the Federal Assistance Policy and Proposed Sale, Kenneth R. DeJarnette 86-51 E
* Customs Service User Fees, Frederick M. Kaiser 87-676 GOV
* Federal Hydropower: The Administration's Proposal to Sell Government Assets; Archived Issue Brief, John Moore IB86057
* The Federal Power Marketing Administrations: To Privatize or Not to Privatize, Alvin Kaufman, etc. 86-90 S
* Privatization from a Public Management Perspective, Ronald C. Moe 89-160 GOV
* Privatization of the National Technical Information Service, Jane Bortnick, etc. 87-491 SPR
* Tax-Exempt Bond-Financed Takeover of Investor-Owned Utilities: An Issue of Privatization and Competition, Dennis Zimmerman 88-174 E
* The U.S. Postal Service: A Public or Private Enterprise? Issue Brief, Bernevia M. McCalip IB88084

Public Health
* Antibiotics: Health Implications of Use in Animal Feed; Archived Issue Brief, Sarah Taylor IB85076
* Blood: Collection, Testing, and Processing, Irene Stich-Coleman 87-641 SPR
* Child Health in the Third World: U.S. and International Initiatives; Archived Issue Brief, Lois McHugh IB85189
* Cigarettes and Other Tobacco Products; Should Congress Bank All Advertising and Promotion?, Bruce K. Mulock 87-23 E
* Cigarettes and Other Tobacco Products: Should Congress Ban All

Advertising and Promotion? Archived Issue Brief, Bruce Mulock IB86105
* Demographic and Social Patterns of Infant Mortality, Jeanne Griffith 86-133 EPW
* The Elderly and the Health Care Dilemma: Is an Ounce of Prevention Worth a Pound of Cure?, Science Policy Research Division-Life Sciences Sec 85-968 SPR
* Fluoride in Drinking Water: Should the National Standard Be Made Less Stringent? Archived Issue Brief, Donald Feliciano IB86014
* Health Benefits of Air Pollution Control: A Discussion, John Blodgett 89-161 ENR
* Health Care for Children: Federal Programs and Policies, Joseph A. Cislowski 88-217 EPW
* Health Care: Issue Brief, Janet Kline IB87009
* Health Programs and the Gramm-Rudman-Hollings Legislation: The 1986 Sequestration and the President's FY 87 Budget Proposal, James Reuter 86-648 EPW* Health Programs Appropriations: FY 1980-FY 1989, Edward Klebe 89-79 EPW
* Health Promotion and Disease Prevention for the Elderly, James Reuter, etc. 86-40 EPW
* Native Americans: Nutrition and Diet-Related Diseases, Donna V. Porter 87-246 SPR
* The Proposed Prohibition on Advertising Tobacco Products: A Constitutional Analysis, Rita Ann Reimer 87-3 A
* Public Health Policy and the Congress: Selected References, Karen Alderson, etc. 89-147 L
* Right of Minors to Consent to Medical Care, Rita Ann Reimer 86-939 A
* Smokeless Tobacco: Health Concerns Spark Advertising and Labeling Controversy, Bruce K. Mulock 86-519 E
* Smokeless Tobacco: Snuff and Chewing Tobacco; Bibliography-in-Brief, 1983-1987, Edith Sutterlin 88-115 L
* Smoking and Tobacco Issues: Info Pack, IP356S
* Survey of the Fifty States and the District of Columbia Statutes Generally Concerning the Quarantine and Isolation of Persons Having A Contagious or, M. Ann Wolfe 87-765 A
* World Health Organization: Effects Reduced U.S. Contributions, Lois B. McHugh 87-108 F

Public Lands
* see also Forests and Forestry, Parks,
* The Catawba Indian Tribe's Land Claim: A Legal Analysis, M. Maureen Murphy 89-293 A
* Dominant Use Management in the National Forest System, Ross Gorte 86-714 ENR
* Federal Grazing Fees on Lands Administered by the Bureau of Land Management and the Forest Service: A History of Legislation and Administration Policy, Adela Backiel, etc. 85-592 ENR
* Federal Land Management Transfers Proposed Between Bureau of Land Management and Forest Service: Archived Issue Brief, Ross Gorte, etc. IB85101
* The Federal Power of Eminent Domain: A Primer, Robert Meltz 85-1086 A
* Forest Service Land and Resource Planning: A Chronology of Laws, Adela Backiel 86-986 ENR
* History of Release Language in Wilderness Legislation, 1979-1984, Ross Gorte 87-559 ENR
* Licensing and Special Use Permit Requirements for Hydroelectric Dam Projects under the Federal Power Act and the Federal Land Policy and Management Act, Robin Jeweler 88-459 A
* The Major Federal Land Management Agencies: Management of Our Nation's Lands and Resources, Adela Backiel, etc. 87-22 ENR
* National Recreation Areas, George Siehl 88-644 ENR
* Oil Companies and the Acquisition of Federal Petroleum Leases, John J. Schanz 88-213 S
* Onshore Oil and Gas Resources on Federal Lands: Evaluating the Current Leasing System: Archived Issue Brief, Adela Backiel, etc. IB87077
* Public Access Across Private Lands to Federal Lands, Adela Backiel, etc. 86-650 A
* Public Land Management: Issues in the Bureau of Land Management; Archived Issue Brief, Adela Backiel, etc. IB87076
* Rangeland Condition: Attempts to Chart Its Progress, Bruce Beard 84-757 ENR
* Royalty Rates for Coal, Oil and Gas Production on Federally Administered Lands, Adela Backiel, etc. 83-595 S
* Summary of Recent Reports on Forest Service Timber, Sale Costs and Revenues, Ross Gorte 84-799 ENR
* Wilderness Areas and Federal Water Rights, Pamela Baldwin 89-11 A

Public Opinion
* American Public Opinion on AIDS: A CRS Major Issue Before the 101st Congress, Rosita M. Thomas 89-85 GOV
* A Guide to the Survey Polls File on SCORPIO, Office of Automated Information Services. Informat 86-138 AU
* Hong Kong-U.S. Economic Relations: Some Views from Hong Kong's Economic Elite, Kerry Dumbaugh 89-23 F

* Public Opinion and Tax Reform: What Do the Polls Mean?, Wayne M. Morrison 85-878 E

Public Utility Regulatory Policies Act
* Electric Rate Effects of Cogeneration and Wheeling : Should PURPA Be Amended?; Archived Issue Brief, Sylvia Morrison IB87119
* PURPA: Should It be Amended to Facilitate the Sale of Bulk Power by Bid? Archived Issue Brief, Sylvia Morrison IB88014
* Wind Energy Development and Utility Capacity Credits: A Review of Research, Implementation and Policy Issues under the Public Utility Regulatory Policy, Fred Sissine 84-101 SPR

Public Welfare
see also AFDC, Homeless, Income Maintenance or Social Services, * ACTION and Its Volunteer Program, Evelyn Howard, etc. 87-716 EPW
* Alien Eligibility Requirements for Major Federal Assistance Programs, Joyce Vialet 86-49 EPW
* Cash and Noncash Benefits for Persons With Limited Income: Eligibility Rules, Recipient and Expenditure Data, FY 1985-87, Vee Burke 88-526 EPW
* Community Services Block Grants: FY 89 Budget Issues, Karen Spar 88-193 EPW
* Community Services Block Grants: History, Funding, Program Data, Karen Spar, etc. 87-739 EPW
* Comparison of the Departments of Energy and Health and Human Services Weatherization Assistance Programs, Mary Smith, etc. 89-229 EPW
* Federal Programs Affecting Children, Sharon House, etc. 87-306 EPW
* Federal Spending Proposed in the Fiscal Year 1989 Budget for Selected Major Income Maintenance Programs, Vee Burke 88-227 EPW
* Head Start Issues in FY 1986: Funding, Administration, and Recent Evaluations, Sharon Stephan 86-554 EPW
* Hispanic Children in Poverty, Vee Burke, etc. 85-170 EPW
* Housing the Low-Income Family With Children, Morton J. Schussheim 87-518 S
* Income Support Programs: Changes in Spending, Distribution and Impact on Poverty of Government Benefit Programs, Gene Falk 86-141 EPW
* The Indexation of Federal Programs, Royal Shipp 82-103 S
* Inventory of Federally Indexed Programs, Vee Burke 81-168 EPW
* National Service: Info Pack, IP418N
* National Service: Issues and Proposals in the 101st Congress; Issue Brief, Karen Spar IB89071
* National Service Proposals: The Implications for Federal Student Aid, Steven Aleman, etc. 89-254 EPW
* National Service: Selected References, Peter Giordano 89-165 L
* Progress Against Poverty in the United States (1959 to 1987), Thomas Gabe 89-211 EPW
* Public Welfare: An Alphabetical Microthesaurus of Terms Selected from the Legislative Indexing Vocabulary, Shirley Loo 87-390 L
* Social Security Benefits, Cash Relief, and Food Aid: A Short History, Vee Burke 86-45 EPW
* The Social Services Block Grant Program: History, Description, and Current Trends, Evelyn Howard 86-145 EPW
* Solicitation of Charitable Contributions: A Survey of State Statutes, John Luckey, etc. 87-950 A
* Welfare and Poverty: Info Pack, IP098W
* Welfare: Issue Brief, Vee Burke IB87007
* Welfare Reform: Archived Issue Brief, Vee Burke IB77069
* Welfare Reform: Bibliography-in-Brief, 1986-1987, Edith Sutterlin 88-25 L
* Welfare Reform: Brief Summaries of Selected Major Proposals, Vee Burke, etc. 88-223 EPW
* Work Disincentives in Income-Tested Programs, Vee Burke 80-158 EPW
* Work Incentives for Disabled Supplemental Security Income (SSI) Recipients: Section 1619 of the Social Security Act, Carmen Solomon 87-427 EPW

Public Welfare -- AFDC
* AFDC, Food Stamps, and Work: History, Rules, and Research, Emmett Carson, etc. 87-599 EPW
* Aid to Families With Dependent Children (AFDC) and Work: Tables Summarizing Treatment of Earnings, Vee Burke 87-74 EPW
* Aid to Families With Dependent Children (AFDC): Need Standards, Payment Standards, and Maximum Benefits for Families With No Countable Income, Carmen Solomon 88-602 EPW
* Aid to Families With Dependent Children (AFDC): Work and Training Issues: Archived Issue Brief, Carmen Solomon IB86094
* Aid to Families With Dependent Children (AFDC), Work Programs, and Child Support: A Comparison of H. R. 3100/S. 1655 With Current Policy, Carmen Solomon 87-907 EPW
* Analysis of Federal-State Cost-Sharing in the Aid to Families With Dependent Children Program, Education and Public Welfare

Division 82-62 EPW
* Child Support: Bibliography-in-Brief, 1984-1988, Edith Sutterlin 88-510 L
* The Family Support Act of 1988: How It Changes the Aid to Families With Dependent Children (AFDC) and Child Support Enforcement Programs, Carmen D. Solomon 88-702 EPW
* State Use of the Aid to Families With Dependent Children-Unemployed Parent (AFDC-UP) Program: An Overview, Celinda M. Franco, etc. 87-969 EPW
* Statistical and Program Data on Single-Parent Families With Children, Carmen Solomon 86-723 EPW

Public Welfare--Homeless
* Cash Welfare Funds and Homeless Families With Children, Carmen Solomon 88-394 EPW* Constitutional Analysis of Proposed Regulations Issued by the Department of Housing and Urban Development Regarding the Participation of Religious Or, David M. Ackerman 87-444 A
* Homeless Housing: HUD's Shelter Programs; Archived Issue Brief, Susan Vanhorenbeck IB87098
* Homeless in America: Info Pack, IP314H
* The Homeless: Overview of the Problem and the Federal Response, Susan Schillmoeller, etc. 87-927 EPW
* Homelessness and Commitment: The Cases of Joyce Brown (AKA Billie Boggs), Kirk D. Nemer 88-186 A
* Homelessness in the U.S.: Bibliography-in-Brief, 1986-1988, Edith Sutterlin 88-396 L
* Homelessness: Issues and legislation in 1988: Issue Brief, Ruth Ellen Wasem IB88070
* The Homelessness Problem: Background and Legislation: Archived Issue Brief, David Koitz IB87143
* The Housing and Community Development Act of 1987 and the Stewart B. McKinney Homeless Assistance Act Summary and Analysis, Barbara Miles 88-481 E
* Programs Benefiting the Homeless: FY 87-FY89 Appropriations Trends, Ruth Ellen Wasem 89-20 EPW

Public Works
* see Infrastructure, Procurement,

Puerto Rico
* Puerto Rico: Political Status Options: Issue Brief, Bette Taylor IB89065
* Territorial Political Development: An Analysis of Puerto Rico, Northern Mariana Islands, Guam, Virgin Islands, and American Samoa, and the Micronesian, Bette A. Taylor 88-657 GOV

Punjab
* India's Punjab Crisis: Issues, Prospects, and Implications, Richard P. Cronin 87-850 F
* India's Sikhs and the Crisis in Punjab State: Summary Briefing Points, Richard Cronin 87-509 F

Purpa
* see Public Utility Regulatory Policies Act,

Radioactive Wastes
* see Solid Wastes--Radioactive Wastes,

Radon
* see Air Pollution--Indoor Air Pollution,

Railroads
* see Transportation--Railroads,

Rangeland
* see Agriculture-Livestock,

Reagan Doctrine
* see Foreign Relations--Reagan Doctrine,

Reagan, Ronald
* Andropov and Reagan as Negotiators: Contexts and Styles in Contrast, Joseph Whelan 83-141 S
* Presidential Vetoes and Ronald Reagan's Use of the Process in the Second Term: Issue Brief, Gary Galemore IB85093
* Statements by President Reagan Relating to Arms Control April 1, 1986-January 31, 1987, Teri Lehto 87-116 S
* Statements by President Reagan Relating to Arms Control; February 2, 1985-December 31, 1985, Jeanette Voas 86-549 F
* Statements by President Reagan Relating to Arms Control, January 1, 1984-March 31, 1984, Lynne Rusten 84-616 F
* Statements by President Reagan Relating to Arms Control, January 1, 1986-March 31, 1986, Jeanette Voas 86-663 S
* Statements by President Reagan Relating to Arms Control: June 1,

1987-December 31, 1987, Teri Lehto 88-60 S
* Statements by President Reagan Relating to the INF Treaty, June 1, 1987-December 31, 1987, Teri Lehto 88-60 S
* Vetoes During President Reagan's First Term, 1981-1984, Gary Galemore 86-681 GOV

Real Estate Settlement Procedures Act
* Recent Developments in the Real Estate Settlement Procedures Act, Richard Bourdon 88-730 E

Recession
* see Economic Conditions--Business Cycles,

Recombinant DNA
* see Genetics,

Recreation
* All-Terrain Vehicles: The December 1987 Consent Agreement and Related Developments, Migdon Segal 88-275 SPR
* Land and Water Conservation Fund: Information and Status, George H. Siehl 89-159 ENR
* National Forest Receipts: Sources and Disposition, Ross W. Gorte 89-284 ENR
* National Recreation Areas, George Siehl 88-644 ENR
* Outdoor Recreation: A Comparison of Two Federal Commissions, George Siehl 87-61 ENR
* Outdoor Recreation: A New Commission Is Created: Archived Issue Brief, George Siehl IB83223
* Scenic Byways: Issues and Action, John Spengler, etc. 88-479 ENR
* Special Management Areas in the National Forest System, Ross Gorte 88-571 ENR
* Trails Programs in Federal Agencies: A Data Compilation, George Siehl 89-8 ENR

Reference Sources
* see Directories, Microthesauri, Scorpio, Speechwriting,
* Conducting Legislative Research in a Congressional Office, Clay H. Wellborn 89-331 GOV
* Form Letters: Tell Your Constituents Where to Get Government Publications; Info Pack, IP222F
* Government Publications--How, What, When, Where, and Why: Info Pack, IP264G
* A Guide to Print and Non-Print Teaching Aids, Winfield Swanson, etc. 83-184 C
* How to Find Information About Your Subject: A Guide to Reference Materials in Local Libraries, Merete Gerli 88-299 C
* How to Follow Current Legislation and Regulations:, Info Pack, IP122H
* Legislative Research: A Guide to Conducting Legislative Research in a Congressional Office: Info Pack, IP32IL

Reference Sources -- Directories
* Congressional Liaison Offices of Selected Federal Agencies, Barbara Hillson 88-58C
* The Congressional Scene: Selected Publications Covering the Congress, Pamela Dragovich 89-113 C
* Directory of Environmental and Conservation Organizations in the Washington, D.C. Metropolitan Area, Mira Courpas 89-99 ENR
* Hotlines and Other Useful Government Telephone Numbers: Info Pack, IP106H
* Indian and Indian-Interest Organizations, Richard Jones, etc. 84-131 GOV
* Internships and Fellowships: Congressional, Federal and Other Work Experience Opportunities, Betsy Reifsnyder 87-237 C
* Organizations that Rate Members of Congress on Their Voting Records, Peggy Garvin 89-116 C
* Pictures of Government Officials, Treva Turner 88-59 C
* Where to Get Publications from the Executive and Independent Agencies: A Directory of Sources for Official Documents, Deborah C. Brudno, etc. 89-167 C

Reference Sources -- Grants
* Fundraising Techniques for Groups: Bibliography-in-Brief, 1968-1987, Robert Kirk 87-380 L
* Grants and Foundation Support: Info Pack, IP050G
* Grants and Foundation Support: Selected Sources of Information, Betsy Reifsnyder 87-970 C
* Writing the Grant Proposal, Lee Decker 85-8C

Reference Sources -- Microthesauri
* Aging and the Elderly: An Alphabetical Microthesaurus of Terms Selected from the Legislative Indexing Vocabulary, Shirley Loo 88-752 L
* Agriculture and Food: An Alphabetical Microthesaurus of Terms Selected from the Legislative Indexing, Vocabulary, Shirley Loo

84-820 L

* Arms and Arms Control: An Alphabetical Microthesaurus of Terms Selected from the Legislative Indexing Vocabulary, Shirley Loo 87-961 L
* Astronautics and Space: An Alphabetical Microthesaurus of Terms Selected from the Legislative Indexing Vocabulary, Shirley Loo 88-397 L
* Automation and Computers: An Alphabetical Microthesaurus of Terms Selected from the Legislative Indexing Vocabulary, Shirley Loo 86-861 L
* Children, Families and Domestic Relations: An Alphabetical Microthesaurus of Terms Selected from the Legislative Indexing Vocabulary, Shirley Loo 87-967 L
* Congress and Congressional Operation: An Alphabetical Microthesaurus of Terms Selected from the Legislative Indexing Vocabulary, Shirley Loo 88-595 L* Crime and Criminal Justice: An Alphabetical Microthesaurus of Terms Selected from the Legislative Indexing Vocabulary, Shirley Loo 88-437 L
* Education: An Alphabetical Microthesaurus of Terms Selected from the Legislative Indexing Vocabulary, Shirley Loo 88-748 L
* Employment and Labor: An Alphabetical Microthesaurus of Terms Selected from the Legislative Indexing Vocabulary, Shirley Loo 88-748 L
* Environmental Protection: An Alphabetical Microthesaurus of Terms Selected from the Legislative Indexing Vocabulary, Shirley Loo 87-792 L
* Foreign Policy and International Relations: An Alphabetical Microthesaurus of Terms Selected from the Legislative Indexing Vocabulary, Shirley Loo 86-725 L
* Housing and Housing Finance: An Alphabetical Microthesaurus of Terms Selected from the Legislative Indexing Vocabulary, Shirley Loo 86-1033 L
* Insurance: An Alphabetical Microthesaurus of Terms Selected from the legislative Indexing Vocabulary, Shirley Loo 88-582 L
* Money and Banking: An Alphabetical Microthesaurus of Terms Selected from the Legislative Indexing Vocabulary, Shirley Loo 88-530 L
* National Defense and Military Operations: An Alphabetical Microthesaurus of Terms Selected from the Legislative Indexing Vocabulary, Shirley Loo 88-77 L
* Nuclear Energy: An Alphabetical Microthesaurus of Terms Selected from the Legislative Indexing Vocabulary, Shirley Loo 87-962 L
* Political Campaigns and Elections: An Alphabetical Microthesaurus of Terms Selected from the Legislative Indexing Vocabulary, Shirley Loo 88-671 L
* Public Welfare: An Alphabetical Microthesaurus of Terms Selected from the Legislative Indexing Vocabulary, Shirley Loo 87-390 L
* Taxes and Taxation: An Alphabetical Microthesaurus of Terms Selected from the Legislative Indexing Vocabulary, Shirley Loo 85-819 L
* Trade and International Finance: An Alphabetical Microthesaurus of Terms Selected from the Legislative Indexing Vocabulary, Shirley Loo 87-369 L
* Transportation: An Alphabetical Microthesaurus of Terms Selected from the Legislative Indexing Vocabulary, Shirley Loo 88-524 L
* U.S. Presidents: An Alphabetical Microthesaurus of Terms Selected from the Legislative Indexing Vocabulary, Shirley Loo 89-131 L
* Water and Water Resources Development: An Alphabetical Microthesaurus of Terms Selected form the Legislative Indexing Vocabulary, Shirley Loo 85-1114 L
* Women: An Alphabetical Microthesaurus of Terms Selected from the Legislative Indexing Vocabulary, Shirley Loo 88-710 L

Reference Sources -- Scorpio

* A Guide to the Survey Polls File on SCORPIO, Office of Automated Information Services 86-138 AU
* SCORPIO Reference Manual, Congressional Research Service Automation Office 89-1 AU

Reference Sources -- Speechwriting

* Public Speaking: Bibliography-in-Brief, 1983-1987, Adrienne C. Grenfell 87-790 L
* Speech Material: Abraham Lincoln's and George Washington's Birthdays: Info Pack, IP373A
* Speech Material: Columbus Day; Info Pack, IP380C
* Speech Material: Fourth of July; Info Pack, IP377F
* Speech Material: Graduation; Info Pack, IP379G
* Speech Material: Martin Luther King's Birthday; Info Pack, IP372M
* Speech Material: Thanksgiving Day; Info Pack, IP381T
* Speech Material: Veterans Day; Info Pack, IP378V
* Speechwriting and Delivery: Info Pack, IP139S
* Speechwriting in Perspective: A Brief Guide to Effective and

Persuasive Communication, Charles H. Whittier 86-1034 GOV

Refugees
* see Immigration,

Regional Development

* see also Infrastructure,
* The ABCs of Public Venture Capital Investment, Jan E. Christopher 88-757 E
* The "Bridge Crisis": An Economic Development Perspective; Issue Brief, J.F. Hornbeck IB88085
* The Community Reinvestment Act: Its Role in Local Economic Development, J.F. Hornbeck 88-732 E
* Community Reinvestment Act: Legal Analysis, M. Maureen Murphy 89-135 A* Earnings as a Measure of Regional Economic Performance, Linda LeGrande, etc. 87-377 E
* Economic Development: A Listing of Federal Programs, Jan E. Christopher 88-536 E
* The Economic Health of the Lower Mississippi River Valley, Jan Christopher 88-253 E
* Economic Policy: Selected Issues of Interest of the 101st Congress, Edward Knight 88-703 E
* Economic Redevelopment in the Cities, Jan E. Christopher 88-703 E
* Federal Enterprise Zone: The Prospect for Economic Development: Issue Brief, J.F. Hornbeck IB89050
* Financing Business and Economic Development: Three Private-Sector Initiatives, J. F. Hornbeck 88-598 E
* Infrastructure: A Brief Overview from the National Level, William W. Ellis, etc. 87-30 S
* Manufactured Exports and Regional Economic Growth in the United States, 1977 to 1983: A Preliminary Assessment, Gary L. Guenther 86-855 E
* Regional Economic Development Programs of the Federal Government, Jan E. Christopher 88-309 E
* Rural Community Development: Selected References, Rebecca Mazur 88-17 L
* Rural Policy in an Era of Change and Diversity, Sandra Osborne 88-482 GOV
* Rural Policy in the United States: A History, Sandra S. Osborne 88-487 GOV
* Selected Options for Federal Support of State and Local Technology Development Programs, Wendy H. Schacht 87-201 SPR
* State and Local Equity Capital Funds: Selected Case Studies, Jan E. Christopher 88-758 E
* States/Counties of the Lower Mississippi River Valley: Statistics on Per Capita Personal Income and Unemployment Rates, Jan Christopher 88-254 E
* Transportation Infrastructure and Economic Development, J.F. Hornbeck 89-109 E

Regulatory Reform
* see Business and Society-Regulation and Deregulation,

Rehabilitation Act

* see also Handicapped,
* Affirmative Action in the Employment of Persons With Handicaps under Federal Contracts: Section 503 of the Rehabilitation Act, Mary Smith 88-701 EPW
* Regulations Promulgated Pursuant to Section 404 of the Rehabilitation Act of 1973: A Brief History and Present Status, Nancy Jones, etc. 86-53 A
* School Board of Nassau County v. Arline: A Person With the Contagious Disease of Tuberculosis May be Covered under Section 504 of the Rehabilitation Act, Nancy Lee Jones 87-238 A
* Section 504 of the Rehabilitation Act: Statutory Provisions, Legislative History, and Regulatory Requirements, Mary F. Smith 89-48 EPW
* Supreme Court Decisions Interpreting Section 504 of the Rehabilitation Act of 1973, Nancy Jones 85-926 A

Religion

* Abortion in World Religions, Charles H. Whittier 88-357 GOV
* American Indian Religious Freedom: The Legal Landscape, M. Maureen Murphy 88-370 A
* Background Information on Equal Access Statute, David Ackerman 84-842 A
* Catholic Social Teaching and the U.S. Economy: The Pastoral Letter of the American Catholic Bishops, Charles Whittier 87-104 GOV
* Church-State and Nondiscrimination Aspects of H.R. 36670, the "Act for Better Child Care Services of 1988", as Approved by the House Subcommittee on, David M. Ackerman 88-497 A
* The Concept of "Secular Humanism" in the Context of Elementary and Secondary Education: Discussion of the Variety of Meanings, and References in Feder, Wayne Riddle 86-545 EPW
* Court Cases Involving Governmental Assistance to the Facilities of

Sectarian Institutions and the Establishment Clause, David Ackerman 88-372 A
* Creationism in the Public Schools: Summary and Analysis of Edwards v. Aguillard, David Ackerman 89-170 A
* Day Care and the Law of Church and State: Constitutional Mandates and Policy Options, David Ackerman 89-170 A
* Exempt Status of Religious Groups, Marie B. Morris 87-846 A
* The Holy See and Recognition of Israel, Charles H. Whittier 86-833 GOV
* India's Sikhs and the Crisis in Punjab State: Summary Briefing Points, Richard P. Cronin 87-509 F
* The Just War in Certain Religious Traditions: Christianity; Judaism; Islam, and Buddhism, Charles A. Whittier 87-915 GOV*
The New Religious Right: Background, Current Agenda, Future Prospects, Charles Whittier 87-615 GOV
* Prayer and Religion in the Public Schools: What Is, and Is Not, Permitted, David Ackerman 89-25 A
* Prayer and Religion in U.S. Public Schools: Bibliography-in-Brief, 1983-1988, Edith Sutterlin 88-663 L
* Religion and Public Policy: Background and Issues in the 80's, Charles Whittier 84-104 GOV
* Religion in the Public Schools: Judicial Decisions, David Ackerman 88-770 A
* Religion in the Public Schools: Pluralism and Teaching About Religions, Charles Whittier 89-104 GOV
* The School Prayer Controversy: Pro-Con Arguments; Issue Brief, Charles Whittier IB84081
* School Prayer: The Congressional Response, 1962-1988, David Ackerman 88-676 A
* Science and Religion: Conflict and Accommodations in the Darwinian Controversy, Charles Whittier 87-395 GOV
* The Senate Chaplaincy, Charles Whittier 86-916 GOV
* Silent Prayer and Mediation in World Religions, Charles Whittier 88-18 GOV
* Supreme Court: Church-State Cases, October 1984 Term; Archived Issue Brief, David Ackerman IB84229
* Supreme Court: Church-State Cases: October 1985 Term; Archived Issue brief, David Ackerman IB85207
* Supreme Court: Church-State Cases, October 1986 Term; Archived Issue Brief, David Ackerman IB86129
* Supreme Court: Church-State Cases, October 1987 Term; Archived Brief, David Ackerman IB88105

Republican National Convention (1988: New Orleans)

* A Summary of National and State Party Laws Concerning the Election of Delegates to the 1988 Democratic and Republican National Conventions, Kevin Coleman 88-102 GOV

Research and Development

* see also Funding and Genetics,
* Agricultural Research: Issues for the 1980s, Christine Matthews Rose 87-430 SPR
* Allocation of Research and Development Costs and the U.S. Foreign Tax Credit, David Brumbaugh 89-220 E
* Analysis of the Office of Science and Technology Policy, Genevieve J. Knezo 88-205 SPR
* Animal Use in Biomedical Research; Info Pack, IP360A
* Animal Use in Research: Bibliography-in-Brief, 1985-87, Adrienne C. Grenfell 88-72 L
* Biomedical Ethics and Congress: History and Current Legislative Activity; Issue Brief, Irene Stith-Coleman IB86078
* Biomedical Research: Use of Animals; Issue Brief, Blanchard Randall IB83161
* Brief Summaries of Federal Animal Protection Statutes, Henry Cohen 88-541 A
* Commercialization of Technology and Issues in the Competitiveness of Selected U.S. Industries: Semiconductors, Biotechnology, and Superconductors Leonard G. Kruger, etc. 88-486 SPR
* Cooperative R&D: Federal Efforts to Promote Industrial Competitiveness: Issue Brief, Wendy Schacht IB89056
* Defense-Related Independent Research and Development in Industry, Joan Winston 85-205 S
* Defense Technology and Industrial Base: Bibliography-in-Brief, Karen Alderson 89-145 L
* Economic Policy: Selected Issues of Interest to the 101st Congress, Edward Knight 89-209 E
* The Impact of U.S. Antitrust Law on Joint Activity by Corporations: Some Background, Janice E. Rubin 89-291 A
* Industrial Innovation: The Debate Over Government Policy: Issue Brief, Wendy Schacht IB84004
* Japanese Science and Technology: Some Recent Efforts to Improve U.S. Monitoring, Nancy R. Miller 86-195 SPR
* Japanese Technical Information: Opportunities to Improve U.S. Access, Christopher T. Hill 87-818 S
* Joint Research and Development Ventures: Antitrust,

Considerations; Archived Issue Brief, Wendy Schacht IB83178
* Managing Defense Department Technology Base Programs, Michael Davey 88-310 SPR
* Military Research and Development: Implications for Civilian Science and the Economy; Bibliography-in-Brief, 1982-1986, Virginia MacEwen 87-59 L
* Planning, Managing, and Funding DOD's Technology Base, Michael Davey 89-319 SPR
* Productivity and U.S. Living Standards; Issue Brief, William A. Cox IB88107
* Research Journal Prices-Trends and Problems, Richard Rowberg 88-264 SPR
* Review of U.S. Research and Development Programs in Ballistic Missile Defense, John D. Moteff 89-150 SPR
* Science and Technology: Federal Policy and Economic Impact: Bibliography-in-Brief, 1983-1986, Virginia MacEwen 87-79 L*
Science and Technology Policies and Practices in Industrialized Countries Other Than the U.S.: Bibliography-in-Brief, Karen L. Alderson 89-46 L
* Scientific Communication and National Security: Bibliography-in-Brief, 1982-1987, Virginia MacEwen, etc. 87-110 L
* Small Business Innovation Development Act: H.R. 4260 Amendments to P.L. 97-219; Archived Issue Brief, Wendy Schacht IB86118
* Technological Advancement and U.S. Industrial Competitiveness, Wendy Schacht 88-689 SPR
* Technology Transfer: Utilization of Federally Funded Research and Development; Issue Brief, Wendy Schacht IB85031
* World Inventory of "Big Science" Research Instruments and Facilities, William C. Boesman 88-38 SPR

Research and Development -- Funding

* Direct Federal Support for Technological Innovation: Issues and Options, Christopher Hill, etc. 84-118 S
* Equity, Excellence, and the Distribution of Federal Research and Development Funds, William C. Boesman, etc. 88-422 SPR
* The Federal Contribution to Basic Research: Background Material for 1987 Hearings, Michael Davey, etc. 87-633 SPR
* Federal Support of Basic Research and the Establishment of the National Science Foundation and Other Research Agencies, William C. Boesman 88-456 SPR
* The "Grace" Report on R&D (The President's Private Sector Survey on Cost Control in the Federal Government: Task Force Report on Research and Develop), William Boesman 84-65 SPR
* Research and Development Funding: FY 1990; Issue Brief, Science Policy Research Division IB89040
* Research and Development Funding: FY 86 and FY 87: Issue Brief, Science Policy Research Division. Genevieve Knezo IB86062
* Research and Development Funding: FY 88; Archived Issue Brief, Research and Development Team. Michael Davey IB87083
* Research and Development Funding: FY 89; Archived Issue Brief, Michael Davey IB88040
* The Research and Development Tax Credit: A Comparison of the Arguments For and Against, Office of Senior Specialists 88-333 S
* Science and Technology Policy and Funding: Reagan Administration; Archived Issue Brief, Genevieve Knezo IB82108
* Selected Federal Research and Development Agencies, and Programs and the Gramm-Rudman-Hollings Deficit Reduction Act: An Analysis of the Impact on Them, Michael Davey 86-37 SPR
* The Tax Credit for Research and Development: An Analysis, Jane G. Gravelle 85-6 E
* U.S. Civilian and Defense Research and Development Funding: Some Trends and Comparisons With Selected Industrialized Nations, William Boesman, etc. 84-195 SPR

Resource Conservation and Recovery Act

* see also Solid Waste,
* Environmental Impairment Liability Insurance: Overview of Availability Issues, Rawle O. King 89-269 E
* Environmental Protection Legislation in the 101st Congress; Issue Brief, Environmental and Natural Resources Policy Div. IB89033
* Hazardous Waste Fact Book, James E. McCarthy, etc. 87-56 ENR
* Hazardous Waste Management: RCRA Oversight in the 100th Congress; Issue Brief, James E. McCarthy IB87087
* Preventing Beach Closings: Legislative Options; Issue Brief, Martin R. Lee IB88102
* RCRA Authorization: Audio Brief, Jim McCarthy, etc. AB50179
* Waste Management: Issue Brief, James McCarthy IB89007

Retirement

* see Military Personnel--Pensions, Old Age, Pensions, Social Security,

Retirement Equity Act

* Women's Pension Equity: A Summary of the Retirement Equity Act of 1984, Ray Schmitt 84-217 EPW

Revolving Door (Post Federal Employment Ethics)
* see Political Ethics,

Rico
* see Crimes and Offenses,

Right to Die
* see Medicine,

Safe Drinking Water Act
* see also Water Pollution,
* Safe Drinking Water; Archived Issue Brief, Mary E. Tiemann IB86080

Sales Tax
* see Taxation--Consumption Taxes,

Salt Talks
* see Strategic Arms Limitation Talks,

Sanctions
* see Foreign Trade-Sanctions,

SAT Tests
* see Higher Education,

Saudi Arabia
* Background on Delivery of AWACS Aircraft to Saudi Arabia, Richard F. Grimmett 86-744 F
* Saudi Arabia: U.S. Missile Sale, 1986; Archived Issue Brief, Clyde Mark., IB86068

Savings
* see Economic Conditions

Savings and Loan Institutions
* see Money and Banking--Failures and Deposit Insurance, Money and Banking--Financial Institutions

School Integration
* see Elementary and Secondary Education--Policies and Legislation, Higher Education--Integration

School Lunch Program
* see Food Relief--Domestic

School Prayer
* see Elementary and Secondary Education--Prayer and Religion

Schools
* see Elementary and Secondary Education, Federal Aid to Education, Higher Education

Science and Technology
* see Astronautics, Chemicals, Computers, Earth Sciences, Genetics, Industrial Technology, Medicine, Minerals and Materials, Oceanography, Patents and Inventions, Research and Development, Science Manpower, Science Policy, Standards, Technology and Civilization, Telecommunication
* Biomedical Ethics and Congress: History and Current Legislative Activity, IB86078
* Biomedical Research: Use of Animals, IB83161
* Drug Approval: Access to Experimental Drugs For Severely Ill Patients, IB89016
* Federal Regulation of Biotechnology, IB89068
* Global Climate Change, IB89005
* Human Fetal Research and Tissue Transplantation, IB88100
* Human Gene Therapy, IB87040
* National Oceans Policy Commission Proposal, IB87203
* National Sea Grant College Program, IB87163
* Patenting Life, IB87222
* Proposal to Map and Sequence the Human Genome, IB88012
* Research and Development Funding: FY 1990, IB89040
* Science, Engineering, and Mathematics Precollege and College Education, IB88068
* Semiconductor Manufacturing Technology Proposal: SEMATECH, IB87212
* Space Facilities: The ISF/CDSF/Space Station Controversy, IB88053
* Space Launch Options, IB86121
* Space Policy, IB87018
* Space Stations, IB85209

* Superconducting Super Collider, IB87096
* Superconductivity: An Overview, IB87191
* Technology Transfer: Utilization of Federally Funded Research and Development, IB85031

Science Manpower
* Department of Education Programs for Science and Mathematics Education: Background, Status, Issues, and Options, K. Forbis Jordan., 86-739 S
* Dwight D. Eisenhower Mathematics and Science Education Act: An Analysis of Recent Legislative Action and Program Evaluations, James B. Stedman. 89-24 EPW
* The Nobel-Prize Awards in Science as a Measure of National Strength in Science, Christopher T. Hill and Joan D. Winston., 86-727 S
* Science and Engineering Education: The Role of the Department of Defense, Christine M. Matthews. 89-256 SPR
Science, Engineering, and Mathematics Precollege and College Education: Issue Brief, Christine Matthews Rose., IB88068

Science Policy
* Analysis of the Office of Science and Technology Policy, Genevieve J. Knezo. 88-205 SPR
* Establishing a Department of Science and Technology: An Analysis of the, Proposal of the President's Commission on Industrial Competitiveness, Michael Davey, Christopher Hill and Wendy Schacht., 85-122 SPR
* The Federal Contribution to Basic Research: Background Material for 1987 Hearings, Michael E. Davey and Genevieve Knezo., 87-633 SPR
* Federal Support of Basic Research and the Establishment of the National Science Foundation and Other Research Agencies, William C. Boesman. 88-456 SPR
* Information Policy and Technology Issues: Public Laws of the 95th Through 100th Congresses, Robert Lee Chartrand. 89-185 SPR
* Institute for Scientific and Technological Cooperation: Archived Issue Brief, Genevieve Knezo. IB79033
* The Nobel-Prize Awards in Science as a Measure of National Strength in Science, Christopher T. Hill and Joan D. Winston., 86-727 S
* Public Health Policy and the Congress: Selected References, Karen Alderson, Charles Dove, Peter Giordano, Bonnie Mangan and Edith Sutterlin, 89-147 L
* Science and Engineering Education: The Role of the Department of Defense, Christine M. Matthews. 89-256 SPR
* Science and Technology Policies and Practices in Industrialized Countries Other Than the U.S.: Bibliography-in-Brief, Karen L. Alderson., 89-46 L
* Science and Technology Policy and Funding: Reagan Administration; Archived Issue Brief, Genevieve Knezo. IB82108

Scorpio
* see Reference Sources--Scorpio

SDI
* see Strategic Defense Initiative

Secondary Market for Industrial Mortgages
* see Industry

Securities Exchange Act
* see also Corporations--Securities Industry
* Arbitration under Section 10 (B) of the Securities Exchange Act of 1934, Michael V. Seitzinger., 87-881 A
* Insider Trading and Greenmail Payments, Michael V. Seitzinger. 87-567 A
* Legal Analysis of What Constitutes Reliance under SEC Rule 10b-5, Michael V. Seitzinger. 87-279 A
* Securities Law: Analysis of Cases Concerning Insider Trading under Section 10 (B) of the Securities Exchange Act of 1934, Michael V. Seitzinger. 87-480 A
* The Stock Market "Crash" of 1987: The Early Response of Regulators, Kevin F. Winch. 87-989 E
* Tender Offer Laws and Regulations, Michael V. Seitzinger., 87-15 A

Securities Industry
* see Corporations--Securities Industry

Securities Investor Protection Corporation
* Securities Investor Protection Corporation (SIPC): Customer Indemnification When a Securities Firm Fails, Kevin Winch., 82-125 E

Current Events and Homework

Sematech
* see Computers

Semiconductors
* see Computers

Senate
* see Congress

Sentencing Reform Act
* see also Criminal Procedure
* United States Sentencing Commission Guidelines: Preliminary Legal Analysis, Charles Doyle. 88-13 A

Sex Discrimination
* see Women

Sherman Act
* see Antitrust Law

Shipping
* see Marine Transportation, Transportation

Singapore
* The Association of Southeast Asian Nations (ASEAN): Economic Development Prospects and the Role of the United States, Larry Niksch. 84-171 F
* Singapore-U.S. Economic Relations: Some Views from Singapore's Economic Elite, Richard P. Cronin. 89-49 F
* U.S. Agricultural Trade Opportunities With Pacific Rim Nations, Robert M. Goldstein. 88-755 ENR

Small Business
* The ABCs of Public Venture Capital Investment, Jan E. Christopher. 88-757 E
* Automation and Small Business: Technological Development and the Competitiveness of U.S. Industry, Wendy H. Schacht and Glenn J. McLoughlin. 88-300 SPR
* Business: Doing Business With the Federal Government; Info Pack., IP305B
* Cable Television Franchises: Do Franchising Authorities Have Any Recourse If the Franchisee Raises Subscription Rates?, Janice E. Rubin. 87-448 A
* Economic Effects of a VAT on Small Business, James M. Bickley. 88-288 E
* Federal Programs for Minority and Women-Owned Businesses, Mark Eddy. 89-278 GOV
* Financing Business and Economic Development: Three Private-Sector Initiatives, J. F. Hombeck. 88-598 E
* Minority Business Set-Asides and the Constitution: A Legal Analysis of the U.S. Supreme Court Ruling in City of Richmond v. J.A. Croson Co, Charles V. Dale. 89-124A
* Minority Ownership of Broadcast Facilities: A Summary of Federal Communications Commission's Policies and Rules, Bernevia M. McCalip. 87-273 E
* The Reagan Economic Strategy: Implications for Small Business, Edward Knight. 81-232E
* Small Business Assistance Programs Sources of Information: Info Pack., IP422S
* Small Business Innovation Development Act: H.R. 4260 Amendments to P.L. 97-219; Archived Issue Brief, Wendy H. Schacht., IB86118
* State and Local Equity Capital Funds: Selected Case Studies, Jan E. Christopher. 88-758E
* United States Supreme Court Actions Regarding Minority Business Set-Asides After City of Richmond v. J.A. Croson Co, Charles V. Dale. 89-202A

Smoking
* see Public Health

Smoot-Hawley Tariff Act
* The Smoot-Hawley Tariff Act of 1930: Its Effects on U.S. Trade and Its Role in the Great Depression of 1929-1933, George Holliday and Gail Makinen. 87-993 E

Social Security
* see Benefits, Finance, Income Maintenance
* Changing Progressivity of the Federal Individual Income Tax and Social Security Tax, Donald W. Kiefer., 87-723 E
* A Consumer Price Index for the Elderly: Would It Make Any Difference? Brian W. Cashell., 87-552 E
* Deficit Targets, National Savings, and Social Security, Jane G. Gravelle., 88-513 S

* How Long Does It Take for New Retirees to Recover the Value of Their Social Security Taxes?, Geoffrey Kollman, etc., 88-384 EPW
* Income Support Programs: Changing in Spending, Distribution, and Impact on Poverty of Government Benefit Programs, Gene Galk., 86-141 EPW.
* The Indexation of Federal Programs, Royal Shipp, 82-103 S.
* Major Decisions in the House and Senate Chambers on Social Security: 1935-1985, Carmen D. Solomon, 86-193 EPW
* The Social Security Amendments of 1983:, Archived Issue Brief, Geoffrey Kollman. IB83070
* Social Security: An Overview of President Reagan's 1981 Proposals:, Archived Issue Brief, David Koitz, etc. IB81036.
* Social Security and Medicare Coverage of Employees of State and Local Government, David Koitz, etc. 87-132 EPW.
* Social Security and Medicare: How Are They Treated in Determining the National Debt? David Koitz, 85-1132 EPW
* Social Security: How Is It Treated in Determining the Federal Budget? David Koitz, 87-978 EPW
* Social Security: National Committee to Preserve Social Security and Medicare; Info Pack., IP345S
* The Social Security Notch, David Koitz, etc. 83-565 EPW
* The Social Security Number:, Its Historical Development and Legal Restrictions on Its Use, Joseph Maheady, etc. 85-655 A
* Social Security:, The Earnings Test, Geoffrey Kollman, 88-89 EPW.
* Social Security:, The Effect of National Debt Limitations in 1985, David Koitz, 85-1118 EPW.
* Social Security:, The Independent Agency Questions; Issue Brief, David Koitz, IB86120.
* What Would It Mean to Make the Social Security Administration an Independent Entity? David Koitz, 89-309 EPW
* Work Disincentives and Disability Insurance, David Koitz, 80-160 EPW.

Social Security--Benefits
* An Analysis of a Proposal to Authorize "Super IRA's" as an Alternative to Social Security Benefits, David Koitz, 87-14 EPW.
* The Automatic Benefit Increase in Social Security, David Koitz, etc. 83-22 EPW.
* Social Security: Alien Beneficiaries; Archived Issue Brief, David Koitz, IB82001.
* Social Security and Tax-Free Fringe Benefits: Background and Issues, Geoffrey Kollman, 85-124 EPW.
* Social Security Benefits, Cash Relief, and Food Aid: A Short History, Vee Burke, 86-45 EPW.
* Social Security Benefits for Prisoners: Archived Issue Brief, David Koitz, IB81163.
* Social Security: Current Issues, Benefits and Financing; Info Pack, IP153S.
* Social Security:, Illustrations of Current Benefit Levels for Persons Born from 1895 to 1935, Geoffrey Kollman, etc. 88-248 EPW.
* Social Security:, Issues in Taxing Benefits under Current Law and under Proposals to Tax a Greater Share of Benefits, Geoffrey Kollman, 89-40 EPW.
* The Social Security Notch, David Koitz, etc. 83-565 EPW.
* The Social Security "Notch": Info Pack, IP266S
* Social Security: Re-Examining Eligibility for Disability Benefits: Archived Issue Brief, David Koitz, IB82078.
* Social Security: Technical Comparison of Various "Notch" Bills Introduced in the 100th Congress, David Koitz., 88-257 EPW
* Social Security: The Cost-of-Living Adjustment (COLA) in January 1989, David Koitz and Geoffrey Kollmann. 88-675 EPW
* Social Security: The Offset of Social Security Spousal Benefits for Government Pensions, Nancy Miller and Geoffrey Kollman. 86-43 EPW
* Social Security: The Relationship of Taxes and Benefits for Future Retirees, Geoffrey Kollmann., 87-203 EPW
* Social Security: The Windfall Benefit Provision; Archived Issue Brief, Geoffrey Kollmann. IB87211
* Social Security: The 5-Month Waiting Period for Disability Insurance Benefits, David Koitz. 79-239 EPW
* Summary of Major Changes in the Social Security Cash Benefits Program: 1935-1987, Geoffrey Kollmann. 88-137 EPW
* Taxing Social Security Benefits: Background and Programmatic Issues, Geoffrey Kollman., 83-152 EPW
* Treatment of Former Spouses under Various Federal Retirement Systems, Marie B. Morris., 88-512 A
* Various Effects of Raising the Normal Retirement Age for Social Security Benefits, David Koitz., 84-677 EPW

Social Security -- Finance
* Paying for the Baby Boom's Retirement, Congressional Research Service. 87-905 EPW
* Social Security Financing: Bibliography-in-Brief, 1985-1988, Charles P. Dove., 88-434 L
* Social Security: Its Funding Outlook and Significance for Government Finance, David Koitz., 86-674 EPW

* Social Security: Its Impact on the Federal Budget Deficit, David Koitz., 88-218 EPW
* The Social Security Surplus: A Discussion of Some of the Issues, David S. Koitz. 88-709 EPW
* Social Security: The Effect of the Baby Boom, Geoffrey Kollmann., 87-981 EPW

Social Services
* see Families, Federal Aid to Education, Food Relief, Handicapped, Housing, Medicare and Medicaid, Occupational Training, Old Age, Pensions, Public Welfare, Veterans
* Alcohol, Drug Abuse, and Mental Health Block Grant, and Related Programs, IB88009
* Child Day Care, IB89011
* Child Nutrition: Issues in the 101st Congress, IB89048
* Commodity Donations for Domestic Food Programs, IB89070
* Economic Status of the Elderly, IB87095
* Family Planning: Title X of the Public Health Service Act, IB88005
* Homelessness: Issues and Legislation in the 101st Congress, IB88070
* Long-Term Care for the Elderly, IB88098
* National Service: Issues and Proposals in the 101st Congress, IB89071
* Teenage Pregnancy: Issues and Legislation, IB86128

Solid Wastes
* see also Infrastructure, Superfund
* After Regulation of Industrial Hazardous Waste: What Role for Incineration?, Barbara B. Black and David E. Gushee., 89-57 S
* Beverage Container Deposit Laws in the States, Mark Gurevitz., 89-334 A
* Degradable Plastics: Issue Brief, Martin R. Lee. Updated regularly., IB88067
* Environmental Impairment Liability Insurance: Overview of Availability Issues, Rawle O. King., 89-269 E
* Federal Regulation of Used Oil, Mark Reisch. .86-747 ENR
* Hazardous Waste and the Superfund Program: Info Pack. IP094H
* Hazardous Waste Fact Book, James E. McCarthy and Mark E. Anthony Reisch. 87-56 ENR
* Hazardous Waste Management: RCRA Oversight in the 100th Congress; Issue Brief, James E. McCarthy. IB87087
* Hazardous Wastes: Selected References, 1986-1987, Adrienne C. Grenfell. 87-874 L
* Incinerating Municipal Solid Waste: A Health Benefit Analysis of Controlling Emissions, Environmental and Natural Resources Policy Division. 89-260 ENR
* International Environment: Overview of Major Issues; Issue Brief, Mary Tiemann and Susan R. Fletcher. IB89057
* Liability of Superfund "Response Action Contractors" and EPA for Injury from Contractor-Conducted Cleanups, Robert Meltz., 89-292 A
* Marine Plastics Pollution Control Legislation, Martin R.Lee. 88-377 ENR
* Municipal Waste Incineration: An Analysis of Section 306 of S. 1894, James E. McCarthy. 88-402 ENR
* Preventing Beach Closings: Legislative Options; Issue Brief, Martin R. Lee. IB88102
* RCRA Authorization: Audio Brief, Jim McCarthy, etc. AB50179.
* Solid Waste Management: Info Pack IP396S.
* Solid Waste Management: Issue Brief, Renee E. Pannebaker, etc. IB87176.
* Solid Waste Management: Selected References, Rebecca Mazur, 89-273 L.
* The Superfund Amendments and Reauthorization Act of 1986: Archived Issue Brief, Mark E. Anthony Reisch, IB87080.
* Toxic Waste Incineration at Sea: Archived Issue Brief, Martin lee IB85131.
* Waste in the Marine Environment; Info Pack, IP407W
* Waste in the Marine Environment: Selected References, Ted L. Burch, 89-263 L
* Waste Management: Issue Brief, James E. McCarthy, IB89007.

Solid Wastes -- Radioactive Wastes
* The Administration's Proposed Hazardous Materials Transportation Safety Bill: Selected Comments and Analysis, Paul Rothberg, 87-693 A.
* Hazardous Materials Transportation: Laws, Regulations, and Policy: Archived Issue Brief, Paul Rothberg, IB76026.
* Legal Analysis of Whether a State Can Exclude Low-Level Radioactive Waste Generated Outside the State from Disposal Within the State, Michael V. Seitzinger, 86-957 A.
* Nuclear Material from Dismantled Warheads: What to Do With It and How to Verify Its Disposal: A Preliminary Analysis, Warren H. Donnelly, 87-437 S.
* Nuclear Waste Disposal: Archived Issue Brief, Carl E. Behrens, IB87178.

* Nuclear Waste: Low-Level Disposal Facilities; Archived Issue Brief, Carl Behrens, IB85214.
* Nuclear Waste Management: Selected References, 1985-1988, Karen L. Alderson, 89-118 L.

South Africa
* Angola/Namibia Peace Prospects: Background, Current Problems, and Chronology, Raymond W. Copson, 88-559 F.
* The Reagan Administration Sanctions Against South Africa: Their Potential Economic Impact, William H. Cooper, 85-955 E.
* Sanctions Against South Africa: Activities of the 99th Congress, Brenda M. Branaman, 87-200 F.
* Sanctions Against South Africa: Impact on the United States; Issue Brief, William Cooper, IB87198.
* South Africa: African National Congress, Brenda Branaman, 86-186 F
* The South Africa Financial Crisis: The Role of U.S. Banks, Walter Eubanks, 86-550 E.
* South Africa: International Sanctions; Archived Issue Brief, Jeanne S. Affelder, etc. IB86157.
* South Africa: Legislation of the 99th Congress, Brenda Branaman, 85-799 F.
* South Africa, Nuclear Weapons and the IAEA: Issue Brief, Warren H. Donnelly, IB87199.
* South Africa: Opposition on the Right, Brenda Branaman, 88-628 F.
* South Africa: President's Report on Progress Toward Ending Apartheid, Raymond W. Copson, 87-829 F.
* South Africa: Recent Developments: Issue Brief, Brenda Branaman, etc. IB85213.
* South Africa: Selected References, Sherry Shapiro, 88-435 L.
* South Africa: The Current Situation; Info Pack, IP340 S.
* South Africa: The United Democratic Front, Brenda M. Branaman, 86-758 F.
* South Africa-U.S. Economic Ties: Emerging Issues; Archived Issue Brief, William H. Cooper, IB87128.
* South Africa: U.S. Policy After Sanctions; Issue Brief, Brenda M. Branaman, IB87128
* Southern Africa: U.S. Regional Policy at a Crossroads, Raymond Copson, 85-201 F.
* The United States and Southern Africa: A Review of United Nations Resolutions and United States Voting Patterns, 1946-October 1985, Frankie King, 86-21.
The 99th Congress and South Africa Sanctions, Robert Shepard. 87-942 F

South Korea
* Exchange Rate Management in Taiwan, South Korea and Hong Kong, Arlene Wilson. 87-401E
* Japan-South Korea Economic Relations: South Korea's Approach to the "Japan Problem", Dick M. Nanto. 87-953 E
* Korea and Congress, 1950-1990, Kerry Dumbaugh. 85-171 F
* Korean Political Tensions: Implications for the United States; Issue Brief, Robert Sutter. IB86071
* South Korea and Taiwan: Expanding Trade Ties With the United States; Issue Brief, William H. Cooper., IB86151
* South Korea and the United States: The Changing Relationship, Larry A. Niksch. 87-522 F
* Visit to South Korea and Taiwan, Larry A. Niksch. 88-740 F

South West Africa People's Organization
* Angola/Namibia Peace Prospects: Background, Current Problems, and Chronology, Raymond W. Copson. 88-559 F
* Namibia Chronology: February 1986 Through April 1987, Raymond W. Copson and Lynn Thomas., 87-353 F

Soviet Union
* see U.S.S.R

Space Policy
* see Astronautics

Space Shuttle
* see Astronautics

Space Weapons
* see Weapons Systems--Space Weapons

Spain
* Current Issues With the "Base-Rights" Countries and Their Implications, Richard F. Grimmett., 88-726 F
* United States Military Installations in Spain, Richard Grimmett., 84-149 F
* U.S.-Spanish Bases Agreement: Issue Brief, Richard F. Grimmett. IB88010

Current Events and Homework

Spanish Americans (U.S.)
* see Minorities

Speechwriting
* see Reference Sources--Speechwriting

Spetsnaz
* United States and Soviet Special Operations, John M. Collins., 87-398 S

Sports
* see Recreation

Staggers Rail Act
* see also Transportation--Railroads
* The Rail Captive Shipper Question, Kenneth R. DeJarnette., 88-649 E
* Railroad Economic Regulation: Issue Brief, Stephen J. Thompson and Rick Holland. IB85017
* Summary of the Staggers Rail Act of 1980, Stephen J.Thompson. 85-9 E

Standards
* Daylight Saving Time: Archived Issue Brief, David Hack. IB77020.
* Telecommunications and Information-Systems Standardization--Is America Ready?, David Hack. 87-458 SPR

Star Wars Weapons
* see Weapons Systems--Space Weapons

Start Talks
* see Strategic Arms Reduction Talks

State and Local Government
* see Block Grants, Intergovernmental Fiscal Relations, State Governments

State and Local Government -- Block Grants
* Alcohol, Drug Abuse, and Mental Health Block Grant and Related Programs: Issue Brief, Edward Klebe., IB88009
* Block Grant Funding for Federal Education Programs: Background and Pro and Con Discussion, K. Forbis Jordan., 86-992 S
* Block Grants: Inventory and Funding History, Sandra S. Osbourne. 87-845 GOV
* Community Health Centers and the Primary Care Block Grant, John Gray. 86-899 EPW
* Community Services Block Grants: FY89 Budget Issues, Karen Spar., 88-193 EPW
* Community Services Block Grants: History, Funding, Program Data, Karen Spar and Kimberly T. Henderson. 87-739 EPW
* Education Block Grant Reauthorization: Selected Options, Paul M. Irwin. 87-494 EPW
* Environmental Block Grants: A Discussion of Current Issues, Claudia Copeland. 86-561 ENR
* The Social Services Block Grant Program: History, Description, and Current Trends, Evelyn Howard. 86-145 EPW

State and Local Government -- Intergovernmental Fiscal Relations
* Constitutional Considerations Implicated, a Hypothetical Proposal to Tax the Investment Income of a Tax-Exempt Entity Affiliated With a State or Local Government, Robert B. Burdette., 88-551 A
* Economic Development: A Listing of Federal Programs, Jan E. Christopher. 88-536 E
* Economic Development and Community Revitalization Programs: Sources of Information; Info Pack., IP412E
* The Effect of Federal Tax and Budget Policies in the 1980s on the State-Local Sector, Lillian Rymarowicz and Dennis Zimmerman., 86-2 E
* Federal Budget and Tax Policy and the State-Local Sector: Retrenchment in the 1980s, Lillian Rymarowicz and Dennis Zimmerman., 88-600 E
* Federal Budget Policies and the State-Local Sector: 1980-1986, Lillian Rymarowicz and Dennis Zimmerman., 87-234 E
* Federal Tax Payments, State Residents and Federal Expenditures in Individual States, Fiscal Year 1986, Lillian Rymarowicz., 88-398 E
* Federal Tax Payments, State Residents and Federal Expenditures in Individual States, Fiscal Year 1987, Lillian Rymarowicz., 88-409 E
* Federalism in the United States: Toward the Third Century; an Overview of Trends and Issues, Sandra S. Osbourn. 89-262 GOV
* Grants Work in a Congressional Office, Rhoda Newman., 82-22 C
* Medicare, Medicaid, and Maternal and Child Health Programs: An Overview of Major Legislation Enacted from 1980 Through 1986,

Janet Kline, Jennifer O'Sullivan and Joseph A. Cislowski. 87-296 EPW
* The Payments in Lieu of Taxes Program: Background and Current Status, Stacey M. Kean. 87-321 E
* Regional Economic Development Programs of the Federal Government, Jan E. Christopher., 88-309 E
* Targeted Fiscal Assistance, Stacey M. Kean. 87-347 E
* Tax Reform: Its Potential Effect on the State and Local Sector, Dennis Zimmerman. 87-233 E

State and Local Government-- State Governments
* The Governors and Lieutenant Governors of the States and Other Jurisdictions, Isabelle Malloy., 89-270 C
* Partisan Divisions in State Legislatures; Combined Upper and Lower House Totals, 1927-1987, Kevin Coleman. 87-213 GOV
* Summary of State Statutes Which Specifically Mention Acquired Immune Deficiency Syndrome, M. Ann Wolfe. 87-239 A
* Waiver of Eleventh Amendment Immunity from Suit: State Survey, Kirk D. Nemer. 88-465 A

Steel Industry
* see Industry--Steel Industry

Stevenson-Wydler Technology Innovation Act
* Direct Federal Support for Technological Innovation: Issues, and Options, Christopher Hill and Wendy Schacht. 84-118 S
* Stevenson-Wydler Technology Innovation Act: A Federal Effort to Promote Industrial Innovation; Archived Issue Brief, Wendy Schacht. 1B85082

Stewart B. McKinney Homeless Assistance Act
* Homelessness in the U.S.: Bibliography-in-Brief, 1986-1988, Edith Sutterlin, 88-396 L
* The Housing and Community Development Act of 1987 and the Steward B. McKinney Homeless Assistance Act: Summary and Analysis, Barbara Miles, 88-481 E
* Programs Benefiting the Homeless: FY87-FY89 Appropriations Trends, Ruth Ellen Wasem, 89-20 EPW.

Stock Market
* see Corporations--Securities Industry

Stock Market Crash
* see Corporations--Securities Industry

Strategic Arms Limitation Talks
* see also Arms Control
* Arms Control: Issues for Congress; Issue Brief, Stanley R. Sloan, IB87002.
* SALT II Treaty: U.S. and Soviet Interim Observance of Its Terms: Archived Issue Brief, Charles Gellner, IB80018.
* Soviet Compliance Behavior: The Record of the SALT I and II Agreements on Offensive Arms, Charles Gellner., 86-541 S
* Soviet SALT II Compliance Behavior: The SS-25 and Encryption of Telemetry, Jeanette Voas. 86-734 S
* Verification and Compliance: Soviet Compliance With Arms Control Agreements; Issue Brief, Stuart Goldman., IB84131

Strategic Arms Reduction Talks
* see also Arms Control
* Arms Control: Negotiations to Reduce Strategic Offensive Nuclear Weapons; Issue Brief, Steven A. Hildreth and Amy F. Woolf. IB88088
* START: A Current Assessment of U.S. and Soviet Positions, Steven A. Hildreth, Al Tinajero and Amy Woolf. 88-400 F
* The Strategic Arms Reduction Talks: Questions of Concern to the 101st Congress, Amy F. Woolf. 89-330 F

Strategic Defense Initiative
* Arms Control and Strategic Weapons in the 99th Congress, Robert C. Gray., 87-892 F
* Arms Control: Issues for Congress; Issue Brief, Stanley R.Sloan. IB87002
* Arms Control: Negotiations to Limit Defense and Space Weapons; Issue Brief, Steven Hildreth. IB86073
* Arms Control: Overview of the Geneva Talks; Archived Issue Brief, Steven Hildreth. IB85157
* Congress and the Strategic Defense Initiative: A Detailed Overview of Legislative Action, 1984-1987, Robert J. Crawford and Steven A. Hildreth. 87-749 F
* Directed Energy Weapons Research: Status and Outlook, Cosmo DiMaggio. 85-183 SPR
* The Effect of a Comprehensive Test Ban on the Strategic Defense Initiative, Cosmo DiMaggio. 85-972 SPR

Spanish Americans / Taxation

* Ethical and Religious Aspects of SDI: Pro and Con, Charles H. Whittier., 87-535 GOV
* The Geneva Negotiations on Space and Nuclear Arms: Soviet Positions and Perspectives, Jeanette Voas. 86-512 S
* Legal Analysis of a Memorandum of Understanding Between the United States and the Federal Republic of Germany Concerning Patent Rights Resulting from Strategic Defense Initiative Research, Michael V. Seitzinger. 87-281 A
* The New Interpretation of the ABM Treaty--Salient Issues, Charles R. Gellner., 87-164 S
* Potential Offensive Capabilities of SDI Space Weapons, Cosmo DiMaggio., 87-807 SPR
* The Strategic Defense Initiative: A Model for Estimating Launch Costs, Cosmo DiMaggio and Robert L. Civiak. 87-475 SPR
* The Strategic Defense Initiative and United States Alliance Strategy, Paul Gallis, Mark Lowenthal and Marcia Smith. 85-48 F
* Strategic Defense Initiative: Info Pack., IP346S
* The Strategic Defense Initiative: Is the Software Feasible? Audio Brief., AB50141
* The Strategic Defense Initiative: Issues for Congress; Issue Brief, Steven Hildreth., IB85170
* The Strategic Defense Initiative: Issues for Phase I Deployment; Issue Brief, Steven A. Hildreth, IB88033
* The Strategic Defense Initiative : Program Description and Major Issues, Cosmo DiMaggio, Arthur Manfredi, and Steven Hildreth, 86-8 SPR
* Strategic Defense Initiative (SDI): Mission Objectives for Directing the Program; Issue Brief, Cosmo DiMaggio and Jack Moteff, IB88028.
* Strategic Defense Initiative: Selected References, 1986-1988, Valentin Leskovsek, 88-184 L.

Strategic Defense Stockpiles
* see National Defense--Strategic Stockpiles

Strategic Petroleum Reserve Program
* Defense Petroleum Reserve: Organizational Options for Meeting DOD's Emergency Fuel Supply Requirements, David Lockwood, 84-201 F.
* The Strategic Petroleum Reserve: Issue Brief, Robert Bamberger, IB87050.

Stratospheric Ozone Layer
* see Earth Sciences

Student Aid
* see Higher Education-Student Aid

Student Loans
* see Higher Education--Student Aid

Sudan
* Sudan: U.S. Foreign Assistance Facts; Issue Brief, Ellen Laipson and Raymond Copson, IB85065

Sugar Industry
* see Agriculture--Sugar Industry

Summit Meetings (U.S.-U.S.S.R.)
* see U.S.S.R.--Foreign Relations

Superconducting Super Collider
* see Nuclear Energy

Superconductivity
* see Power Resources--Electric Power

Superconductors
* see Power Resources--Electric Power

Superfund
* see also Solid Wastes
* Chemicals in the Environment: Audio Brief, James Aidala. AB50152
* Environmental Impairment Liability Insurance: Overview of Availability Issues, Rawle O. King. 89-269 E
* Environmental Protection Legislation in the 101st Congress; Issue Brief, Environmental and Natural Resources Policy Division. Environmental Protection Section. IB89033
* Hazardous Waste Fact Book, James E. McCarthy and Mark E. Anthony Reisch. 87-56 ENR
* Indoor Air Pollution: Issue Brief, Mira Courpas, Christopher H. Dodge and Fred J. Sissine. IB88092
* Liability of Superfund "Response Action Contractors" and EPA for Injury from Contractor-Conducted Cleanups, Robert Meltz.,

89-292 A
* The Superfund Amendments and Reauthorization Act of 1986: Archived Issue Brief, Mark E. Anthony Reisch. IB87080
* Waste Management: Issue Brief, James E. McCarthy. IB89007

Supplemental Security Income Program
* see Public Welfare

Support of Dependents
* see Families

Supreme Court
* see Judiciary--Supreme Court

Surrogate Motherhood
* see Families

Synthetic Fuels
* see Fossil Fuels--Coal

Taiwan
* Exchange Rate Management in Taiwan, South Korea and Hong Kong, Arlene Wilson. 87-401 E
* South Korea and Taiwan: Expanding Trade Ties With the United States; Issue Brief, William H. Cooper., IB86151
* Taiwan: Recent Developments and Their Implications for the United States; Issue Brief, Robert G. Sutter. IB87092
* U.S. Agricultural Trade Opportunities With Pacific Rim Nations, Robert M. Goldstein. 88-755 ENR
* U.S.-Taiwan Economic Relations: Views of Some Members of the Taiwan Economic Elite, Arlene Wilson. 89-21 E
* Visit to South Korea and Taiwan, Trip Report, Larry A. Niksch. 88-740 F

Tariffs
* see Foreign Trade--Imports and Exports, Foreign Trade--Trade Agreements and Negotiations, Foreign Trade--Trade Policy

Tax Reform
* see Taxation--Tax Reform

Tax Reform Act of 1986
* The Heifer Tax: Uniform Capitalization and Farmers, Gregg A. Esenwein. 88-462 E
* The Home Office Deduction under the Tax Reform Act of 1986, John Luckey. 86-973 A

Taxation
* see Consumption Taxes, Corporation Taxes, Personal Income Tax, Tax Reform, Local Finance
* Alcohol Fuels Tax Incentives: Current Law and Proposed Options to Expand Current Law, Salvatore Lazzari. 89-343 E
* The Anti-Injunction Act: A Brief Legislative and Judicial History of Section 7421 of the Internal Revenue Code of 1986, John R. Luckey. 87-597 A
* Constitutional Considerations Implicated, a Hypothetical Proposal to Tax the Investment Income of a Tax-Exempt Entity Affiliated With a State or Local Government, Robert B. Burdette., 88-551 A
* The Effect of Federal Tax and Budget Policies in the 1980s on the State-Local Sector, Lillian Rymarowicz and Dennis Zimmerman., 86-2 E
* Employee Stock Ownership Plans: An Overview, Gerald Mayer. 89-80 E
* Employee Stock Ownership Plans: Minimum Requirements to Qualify for Tax Advantages, Gerald Mayer., 89-36 E
* Exempt Status of Religious Groups, Marie B. Morris. 87-846 A
* Federal Budget and Tax Policy and the State-Local Sector: Retrenchment in the 1980s, Lillian Rymarowicz and Dennis Zimmerman., 88-600 E
* Federal Tax Payments, State Residents and Federal Expenditures in Individual States, Fiscal Year 1986, Lillian Rymarowicz., 88-398 E
* Federal Tax Payments State Residents and Federal Expenditures in Individual States, Fiscal Year 1987, Lillian Rymarowicz., 88-409 E
* A Financial Transactions Tax? The Proposed Federal Par User's Fee, William Jackson and Jack Taylor., 88-103 E
* The Gramm-Rudman-Hollings Targets: How Might They Affect the Economy, Gail Makinen and Brian Cashell. 86-1036 E
* The Heifer Tax: Uniform Capitalization and Farmers, Gregg A. Esenwein., 88-462 E
* Limits on Lobbying and Political Activity, Tax-Exempt Organizations: Historical Background and Continuing Issues, Marie B. Morris. 88-821 A
* Major Revenue Raising Options: An Overview, Gregg A. Esenwein. 88-756 E

Current Events and Homework

* Overview of Internal Revenue Code Changes Affecting Tax-Exempt Organizations in Years 1986-1988, Marie B. Morris., 88-738 A
* A Proposal for Raising Revenue Reducing Capital Gains Taxes?, Jane G. Gravelle. 87-562 E
* Proposed Federal Taxation of Credit Unions: A Pro/Con Analysis, James M. Bickley. 86-84E
* Revenue-Raising Options: Archived Issue Brief, Gregg A. Esenwein. IB87169
* Should Credit Unions Be Taxed: Issue Brief, James M. Bickley. IB89066
* Significant Federal Tax Acts: 1954-1986, Louis Alan Talley. 87-727 E
* Significant Federal Tax Legislation, 1960-1969, Louis Talley. 79-232 E
* Significant Federal Tax Legislation, 1970-1978, Louis Talley. 79-207 E
* Some Constitutional Questions Regarding the Federal Income Tax Laws, Howard Zaritsky and John R. Luckey., 84-168 A
* A Stock Transfer Tax: Preliminary Economic Analysis, Donald W. Kiefer., 87-278 S
* The Targeted Jobs Tax Credit, 1978-1987, Linda LeGrande. 87-616 E
* Tax Effects of Title V of the Family Farm Act (H.R. 1425, 100th Congress), Marie B., Morris. 87-582 A
* Tax-Exempt Bonds: A Summary of Changes Made, the Tax Reform Act of 1986, Robert B. Burdette. 87-9 A
* Tax Issues Affecting Family Agriculture: Archived Issue Brief, Jack Taylor and Gregg A. Esenwein. IB88054
* Tax Policy and Spillover Effects: The Use of Tax Provisions to Induce Socially Desirable Activities, Jane Gravelle., 80-186 E
* Tax Subsidies to Housing, 1953-83, Jane Gravelle. 82-178 E
* Taxation Within Indian Lands: The Legal Framework, M. Maureen Murphy., 87-249 A
* Taxes and Taxation: An Alphabetical Microthesaurus of Terms Selected from the Legislative Indexing Vocabulary, Shirley Loo. 85-819 L
* The Underground Economy: Selected References, Barry Molefsky. 84-738 E
* U.S. Economic Policy in an International Context: The U.S. Tax Structure: Its Level, Composition and Progressivity Compared to Seven Other Nations, Donald W. Kiefer and Gregg A. Esenwein. 84-233 E
* U.S. Tax Treatment of Bad Foreign Loans, David L. Brumbaugh. 89-302 E
* Gasoline Excise Tax: Economic Impacts of an Increase, IB87078
* Oil Import Fees (Taxes) For Deficit Reduction: Revenue and Economic Effects, IB87189
* Should Credit Unions Be Taxed, IB89066
* Tax Policy Prospects in the Bush Administration, IB89019
* Taxation of Capital Gains, IB89108
* A Value-Added Tax contrasted with a National Sales Tax, IB87156
* Value-Added Tax for Deficit Reduction, IB87097

Taxation -- Consumption Taxes
* Broad-Based Federal Consumption Taxation: A Value-Added Tax Contrasted With a National Sales Tax, James M. Bickley., 87-787 E
* Economic Effects of a VAT on Small Business, James M. Bickley. 88-288 E
* Effects of a Value Added Tax on Capital Formation, Jane G. Gravelle., 88-697 S
* Federal Excise Taxes on Alcoholic Beverages: A Summary of Present Law and a Brief History, Thomas B. Ripy. 89-72 A
* Federal Excise Taxes on Gasoline and the Highway Trust Fund--A Short History, Louis Alan Talley., 89-174 E
* Gasoline Excise Tax: Economic Impacts of an Increase; Issue Brief, Bernard A. Gelb and Salvatore Lazzari. IB87078
* History and Economics of U.S. Excise Taxation of Luxury Goods, Louis Alan Talley, Jack Taylor and Dennis Zimmerman., 87-515 E
* A History of Federal Energy Tax Policy: Conventional as Compared to Renewable and Nonconventional Energy Resources, Salvatore Lazzari. 88-455 E
* National Sales Tax: Selected Policy Issues, James M. Bickley. 84-141 E
* Oil Import Fees (Taxes) for Deficit Reduction: Revenue and Economic Effects; Issue Brief, Salvatore Lazzari. IB87189
* Oil Import Taxes: Revenue and Economic Effects, Bernard A. Gelb and Salvatore Lazzari. 86-572 E
* Reducing the Deficit With Energy Taxes, Craig K. Elwell. 86-653 E
* Telephone Excise Tax: Archived Issue Brief, Louis Alan Talley. IB87185
* A Value-Added Tax Contrasted With a National Sales Tax: Issue Brief, James M. Bickley. IB87156
* Value-Added Tax for Deficit Reduction: Issue Brief, James M. Bickley., IB87097
* Value Added Tax: Tax Bases and Revenue Yields, James M.

Bickley. 89-52 E

Taxation -- Corporation Taxes
* Accelerated Depreciation, the Investment Tax Credit, and Their Required Rate-making Treatment in the Public Utility Industry: A Background Report, Donald W. Kiefer. 87-312 S
* Allocation of Research and Development Costs and the U.S. Foreign Tax Credit, David L. Brumbaugh. 89-220 E
* Assessing Structural Tax Revision With Macroeconomic Models: The Treasury Tax Proposals and the Allocation of Investment, Jane G. Gravelle. 85-645 E
* Business Taxes and Inflation Following the Tax Reform Act of 1986, David L. Brumbaugh. 88-719 E
* Captive Off-Shore Insurance Companies, David Whiteman., 84-507 E
* Comparative Corporate Tax Burdens in the United States and Japan and Implications for Relative Economic Growth, Jane Gravelle. 83-177 E
* The Corporate Income Tax and the U.S. Economy, David L. Brumbaugh and Jane G. Gravelle. 84-143 E
* The Corporate Minimum Tax: Rationale, Effects, and Issues, David L. Brumbaugh. 89-213 E
* An Economic Analysis of the Effects of the Finance Committee Staff Proposal to Revise Subchapter C of the Internal Revenue Code on Incentives for Corporate Reorganization, Donald W. Kiefer. 85-1016 E
* Economic Analysis of the Tax Treatment of Nuclear Power Plant Decommissioning Costs, Donald W. Kiefer. 84-28 E
* The Effect of Alternative Depreciation Systems on Marginal Effective Tax Rates on Public Utility Property, Donald W. Kiefer. 86-506 E
* Energy Tax Options to Increase Federal Revenue, Salvatore Lazzari. 87-539 E
* Federal Income Taxation of Corporate Farms, Jack Taylor. 87-940 E
* Federal Taxes, the Steel Industry, and Net Operating Loss Carryforwards, David L. Brumbaugh. 88-5 E
* History and Continuing Issues on Unrelated Trade or Business Income Tax: Sections 511-513 of the Internal Revenue Code, Thomas B. Ripy, Marie B. Morris and Carmen Pomares., 87-248 A
* How Are Windfall Profit Tax Revenues Used?, Bernard A. Gelb. 84-651 E
* Leveraged Buyouts: Selected References, 1987-1989, Robert Howe. 89-156 L * Major Federal Tax Provisions that Directly Affect International Trade and Investment, David L. Brumbaugh., 86-764 E
* Merger Activity and Leveraged Buyouts: Sound Corporate Restructuring or Wall Street Alchemy?, Carolyn Kay Brancato and Kevin F. Winch. 84-643 E
* Oil Import Tax: Some General Economic Effects, Bernard A. Gelb. 87-259 E
* Oil Royalty Trusts, Carolyn Kay Brancato. 84-575 E
* The Possessions Tax Credit (IRC Section 936): Background and Issues, David L. Brumbaugh. 88-200 E
* The Research and Development Tax Credit: A Comparison of the Arguments for and Against, Office of Senior Specialists. 88-333 S
* Royalties on Federal Coal: Issues in the Treatment of Royalty Payments and Externality-Related Taxes, Salvatore Lazzari, Duane Thompson and Dennis Zimmerman., 88-250 E.
* Tax Aspects of Leveraged Buyouts, Jane G. Gravelle. 89-142 S
* The Tax Credit for Research and Development: An Analysis, Jane G. Gravelle. 85-6E
* Tax Sanctions and U.S. Investment in South Africa, David L. Brumbaugh., 88-112 E
* Taxation of Foreign-Source Income: A Survey; A Brief Overview of Concepts, Provisions, and Issues in the Federal Taxation of Foreign-Source Income, David L. Brumbaugh., 83-636 E
* Taxation of Foreign-Source Income: A Survey; The U.S. Foreign Tax Credit: Provisions, Effects and Issues, David L. Brumbaugh., 83-222 E
* Taxation of Overseas Investment: Subpart F and the Tax Reform Act of 1986, David L. Brumbaugh. 87-167 E
* Taxation of the Press: A Brief Constitutional Analysis, Rita Ann Reimer., 87-422 A
* Taxation of U.S. Investment Abroad: Archived Issue Brief, David L. Brumbaugh. IB87060
* Taxes in Public Utility Rates: Phantom Taxes or Real Tax Benefits?, Donald W. Kiefer. 84-21 1 E
* Why Some Corporations Don't Pay Taxes, David L. Brumbaugh and Wayne M. Morrison. 85-75 E
* Wind Energy Development and Utility Capacity Credits: A Review of Research, Implementation and Policy Issues under the Public Utility Regulatory Policies Act, Fred Sissine. 84-101 SPR

Taxation -- Personal Income Tax
* Assistance to Families: A Chart Comparing Some Existing Tax Provisions and Pending Proposals, Marie B. Morris. 89-279 A

Taxation -- Tax Reform

Morris. 87-440 A

Teachers
* see Elementary and Secondary Education

Technological Innovation
* see Research and Development

Technology and Civilization
* Balancing the National Interest: U.S. National Security Export Controls and Global Economic Competition: A Summary of the National Academy of Sciences Study, John P. Hardt and Jean F. Boone. 87-119S
* Controlling Carbon Dioxide Emissions, Amy Abel, Mark E. Holt and Larry B. Parker. 89-157 ENR
* Direct Federal Support for Technological Innovation: Issues and Options, Christopher Hill and Wendy Schacht. 84-118 S
* The Europe 1992 Plan: Science and Technology Issues, Science Policy Research Division. 89-178 SPR
* European Community: Issues Raised by 1992 Integration, Congressional Research Service. .89-323 E
* Export Controls: Issue Brief, George Holliday and Glennon J. Harrison. IB87122
* High-Technology Trade: Bibliography-in-Brief, 1985-1988, Robert S. Kirk. 88-572L
* Institute for Scientific and Technological Cooperation: Archived Issue Brief, Genevieve Knezo. IB79033
* Japanese Technical Information: Opportunities to Improve U.S. Access, Christopher T. Hill. 87-818 S
* New Crops and New Farm Products: A Briefing, Jean M.Rawson. 88-771 ENR
* The Omnibus Trade and Competitiveness Act: Technology Development Provisions, Wendy H. Schacht, 89-93 SPR
* Proceedings of the CRS Symposium on U.S. Trade; Policy Issues Confronting the 10th Congress, William Cooper, 87-267 E.
* Risk Assessment in Health and Environmental Regulation; Archived Issue Brief, David Cheney IB84124.
* Science and Technology: Federal Policy and Economic Impact: Bibliography-in-Brief, 1983-1986, Virginia MacEwen, 87-79 L
* Stevenson-Wydler Technology Innovation Act: A Federal Effort to Promote Industrial Innovation: Archived Issue Brief, Wendy Schacht, IB85082.
* Technology Transfer: Utilization of Federally Funded Research and Development; Issue Brief, Wendy Schacht. IB85031
* U.S. Export Control Policy and Competitiveness; Proceedings of the CRS Symposium, John P. Hardt, and Jean F. Boone, 87-388 S.

Technology Transfer
* see Technology and Civilization

Teenage Pregnancy
* see Families

Teenage Suicide
* see Families

Telecommunication
* see Telephone Industry, Television, Communications
* Advertising of Alcoholic Beverages in the Broadcast Media: Archived Issue Brief, Bruce K. Mulock, IB85097
* Constitutional Issues Relevant to Consideration of FCC Policy on Minority "Preferences" or "Merits" in Broadcast Licensing Proceedings, Charles V. Dale, 87-8 A.
* Copyright Law: Legalizing Home Taping of Audio and Video Recordings: Archived Issue Brief, Paul Wallace, IB82075.
* Extending the Fairness Doctrine to the Print Media, Thomas M. Durbin, 87-584 A.
* The Fairness Doctrine and the Equal Opportunities Doctrine; Issue Brief, Thomas Durbin IB82087.
* FCC Regulation of Indecent Radio and Television Broadcasting, Rita Ann Reimer, 88-291 A
* The Ground Wave Emergency Network, Gary K. Reynolds, 89-206 F.
* Information Policy and Technology Issues: Public Laws of the 95th Through 100th Congresses, Robert Lee Chartrand. 89-185 SPR.
* Information Technology in Our Time: Selected References, Robert L. Chartrand, 88-733 SPR.
* Information Technology Utilization in Emergency Management, Robert Chartrand, and Trudie Punaro, 85-74 S.
* The Interception of Communications: A Legal Overview of Bugs and Taps, Charles Doyle, 88-105 A.
* A Legal Analysis of the FCC's Abolition of the Fairness Doctrine, Thomas M. Durbin, 87-754 A.
* Media Entertainment Sex and Violence: Impact on Society, Especially Children, Edith Fairman Cooper, 86-925 SPR.
* Mediasat:The Use of Remote Sensing Satellites by News Agencies,

Patricia E. Humphlett, 87-70 SPR.
* Minority Ownership of Broadcast Facilities: A Summary of Federal Communications Commission's Policies and Rules, Bernevia McCalip, 87-273 E.
* Multiple Ownership of Radio and Television Stations; History, Background and Recent Rule Changes, Bernevia McCalip, 85-153 E.
* Space Commercialization in China and Japan, Marcia S. Smith, 88-519 SPR.
* Telecommunications and Information Systems Standardization--Is America Ready?, David Hack, 87-458 SPR.
* Telecommunications Trade: Market Access Legislation; Archived Issue Brief, Raymond Ahearn and Donald Dulchinos, IB85206
* Trade in Telecommunications Products and Services; Legislation in the 100th Congress, Glennon J. Harrison, 87-844 E.
* U.S. Space Commercialization Activities, Patricia E. Humphlett, 88-518 SPR.
* Videocassette Recorder: Legal Analysis of Home Use, Douglas Reid Weimer, 89-30 A.

Telecommunication -- Telephone Industry
* Access Charges for Enhanced Service Providers: FCC Proposal to Eliminate Exemption Provides Controversy: Archived Issue Brief, Brucke K. Mulock, IB87223.
* American Telephone and Telegraph Co. Flow-Through of State Gross Receipts Taxes, Angela Gilroy, 87-43 E.
* The American Telephone and Telegraph Company Divestiture: Background, Provisions, and Restructuring, Angela A. Gilroy, 84-58 E.
* Federal Authority to Prohibit Prerecorded Commercial Telephone Calls: A Constitutional Analysis, Rita Ann Reimer, 87-10 A.
* Lifeline Telephone Service: Federal Activity and Controversies, Angela Gilroy, 88-90 E.
* Telephone Access for the Hearing Impaired: Federal Actions to Increase Availability, Angela A. Gilroy. 86-917 E.
* Telephone Excise Tax: Archived Issue Brief, Louis Alan Talley. IB87185
* Telephone Industry Deregulation: Selected References, 1984-1988, Robert Howe. 88-751 L
* Telephone Industry Issues: Info Pack., IP257T
* Telephone Industry Residential Subscriber Line Charges and the Lifeline Options; Issue Brief, Angela A. Gilroy. IB85152

Telecommunication -- Television
* Broadcast Regulation in the 100th Congress: A Legislative Overview, Bernevia M. McCalip, 89-88E
* Cable Television Franchises: Do Franchising Authorities Have Any Recourse If the Franchisee Raises Subscription Rates?, Janice E. Rubin., 87-448 A
* Cable Television: Selected References, 1986-1989, Felix Chin. 89-212 L
* Cable TV: Info Pack., IP104C
* Commercial Television: Should Children's Television Be Regulated?, Bernevia M. McCalip. 84-663 E
* High-Definition Television (HDTV) in the United States--What Does an "Even Playing-Field" Look Like? (With Policy Options), David B. Hack. 88-365 SPR
* High-Definition Television: Issue Brief, David Hack. IB89088
* The Home Dish Market: H.R. 2848 (100th Congress) and the Copyright Liability of Satellite Carriers, Angela A. Gilroy. 88-728 E
* The Scrambling of Cable Satellite Programming and the Backyard Satellite Dish Market: Archived Issue Brief, Angela A. Gilroy., IB86123
* The Scrambling of Satellite Signals and the Backyard Satellite Dish Market: Background, Controversies and Congressional Activity, Angela A. Gilroy. 86-120 E
* Television Network Evening News Coverage of Afghanistan: A Perspective After Eight Years of War, Denis Steven Rutkus. 88-319 GOV
* Videocassette Recorders: Legal Analysis of Home Use, Douglas Reid Weimer., 89-30 A

Telephone Industry
* see Telecommunication --Telephone Industry

Television
* see Telecommunication --Television

Temporary Emergency Food Assistance Program
* Temporary Emergency Food Assistance Program (TEFAP): 1987 Issues; Archived Issue Brief, Jean Jones. IB87090

Tender Offers
* see Corporations --Mergers

Territories

* The Governors and Lieutenant Governors of the States and Other Jurisdictions, Isabelle Malloy. .89-270 C
* Palau's Evolving Relationship With the United States: Introduction and Chronology of Developments, Luella S. Christopher. 88-442 F
* The Possessions Tax Credit (IRC Section 936): Background and Issues, David L. Brumbaugh. 88-200 E
* Puerto Rico: Political Status; Info Pack., IP419P
* Puerto Rico: Political Status Options; Issue Brief, Bette A. Taylor. IB89065
* Territorial Political Development: An Analysis of Puerto Rico, Northern Mariana Islands, Guam, Virgin Islands, and American Samoa, and the Micronesian Compacts of Free Association, Bette A. Taylor., 88-657 GOV
* The Virgin Islands of the United States: A Descriptive and Historical Profile, Bette A. Taylor. .88-429 GOV

Terrorism

* The Anti-Terrorism Act of 1987: Constitutional and Statutory Issues Which May Be Raised in Relation to Its Interpretation and Enforcement, Kenneth R. Thomas. 88-382 A
* Anti-Terrorism Policy: A Pro-Con Discussion of Retaliation and Deterrence Options, James Wootten and Raphael Perl. 85-832 F
* The Changing Nature of International Terrorism, Allan Nanes. 85-625 F
* Combatting International Terrorism: Audio Brief, James P. Wootten. AB50151
* Combatting State-Supported Terrorism: Differing U.S. and West European Perspectives, Paul E. Gallis and James P. Wootten., 88-313 F
* Lebanon: The Remaining U.S. Hostages; a Chronology, 1984-1987, Clyde R. Mark. 88-499 F
* Lebanon: The Remaining U.S. Hostages; Issue Brief, Clyde Mark., IB85183
* Nuclear Terrorism: Implementation of Title VI of the Omnibus Diplomatic Security and Antiterrorism Act of 1986; Archived Issue Brief, Warren H. Donnelly. IB87213
* The Security of U.S. Embassies and Other Overseas Civilian Installations, Joel Woldman. 85-11 F
* Statutes Authorizing Sanctions Against Countries Supporting International Terrorism, Jeanne Jagelski. 87-327
* A Terrorism Chronology: 1981-1986: Incidents Involving U.S. Citizens or Property, Richard Dulaney. 86-531 F
* Terrorism: Info Pack., IP299T
* Terrorism: U.S. Policy Options; Issue Brief, James Wootten., IB81141
* Terrorist Incidents Involving U.S. Citizens or Property 1981-1986: A Chronology; Issue Brief, James P. Wootten. IB86096
* The 99th Congress and the Response to International Terrorism, Richard W. Boyd and Martha Crenshaw. 87-893 F

Textile Industry

* see Industry--Textile Industry

Thailand

* The Association of Southeast Asian Nations (ASEAN): Economic Development Prospects and the Role of the United States, Larry Niksch. 84-171 F
* Economic Changes in the Asian Pacific Rim: Policy Prospectus. Prepared by the Congressional Research Service., 86-923 S
* Thai-U.S. Economic Relations: Some Views of Thailand's Economic Elite, Raymond J. Ahearn. 89-60 F

Third World

* see Developing Countries

Tibet

* Tibet: Disputed Facts About the Situation in Tibet, Kerry B.Dumbaugh. 88-40F

Tobacco Industry

* see Agriculture--Policies and Legislation

Tokyo Stock Exchange

* The Stock Market in Japan: An Overview and Analysis, Arturo Wiener and Edward Knight. 89-306 E

Torts

* see Law

Toshiba/Kongsberg Illegal Exports Affair

* see Foreign Trade--East-West

Toxic Substances

* see Chemicals, Pesticides, Solid Wastes

Toxic Substances Control Act

* Environmental Protection Legislation in the 101st Congress; Issue Brief, Environmental and Natural Resources Policy Division. Environmental Protection Section. IB89033
* The Toxic Substances Control Act: Implementation Issues; Archived Issue Brief, Jim Aidala. IB83190

Toxic Wastes

* see Solid Wastes, Superfund

Trade

* see Agriculture--Foreign Trade, Foreign Trade, International Finance

Trade Act

* see Foreign Trade--Trade Policy

Trade Deficit

* see Foreign Trade--Imports and Exports, Foreign Trade--Trade Policy

Trade and International Finance

* The "Baker Plan": A Remedy for the International Debt Crisis, IB86106
* Canada-U.S. Free Trade Agreement, IB87173
* CBI II: Expanding the Caribbean Basin Economic Recovery Act, IB89096
* Cooperative R&D: Federal Efforts to Promote Industrial Competitiveness, IB89056
* European Community: 1992 Plan for Economic Integration, IB89043
* Export Controls, IB87122
* Export-Import Bank Financial Issues, IB88013
* Foreign Direct Investment in the United States, IB87226
* Japan-U.S. Economic Relations: Cooperation or Confrontation?, IB87158
* Multilateral Development Banks: Issues for the 101st Congress, IB87218
* Registering Foreign Investment: Proposed Legislation, IB89092
* Sanctions Against South Africa: Impact on the United States, IB87198
* South Korea and Taiwan: Expanding Trade Ties with the United States, IB86151
* Steel Imports: Arguments For and Against Extension of the President's Steel Program, IB88109
* Trade, IB87003
* Trade Negotiations: The Uruguay Round, IB86147
* Trade, Technology, and Competitiveness, IB87053
* U.S.-Soviet Commercial Relations, IB89110

Trade Legislation

* see Foreign Trade--Trade Policy

Trade Negotiations

* see Foreign Trade--Trade Agreements and Negotiations

Transportation

* see Railroads, Aeronautics, Highways, Infrastructure, Marine Transportation
* The Administration's Proposed Hazardous Materials Transportation Safety Bill: Selected Comments and Analysis, Paul F. Rothberg., 87-693 SPR
* Air Pollution: Are Current Standards for Trucks Sufficient?; Issue Brief, David E. Gushee. IB86140
* Alternative Fuels for Motor Vehicles: Some Environmental Issues, David E. Gushee. 88-624S
* "Buy American" Regulations: Effects on Surface Transportation, John W. Fischer. 86-78E
* Changing Regulation of Surface Transportation: Development and Implications of Current Policies, Kenneth R. DeJarnette., 86-64 E
* Federal Aid to Domestic Transportation: A Brief History from the 1800s to the 1980s, Nancy Heiser. 88-574 E
* Hazardous Materials Transportation: Laws, Regulations, and Policy; Archived Issue Brief, Paul Rothberg. IB76026
* Shippers by Truck and Rail: Deregulation Effects and Prospects, Kenneth R. DeJarnette. 86-66E
* Surface Transport Carriers: Deregulation Effects and Prospects, Lenore Sek and Stephen J. Thompson. 86-65 E
* Transport Manufacturing: A Review and Appraisal of Federal Assistance Policies, Gwenell L. Bass. 86-75 E
* Transportation: An Alphabetical Microthesaurus of Terms Selected from the Legislative Indexing Vocabulary, Shirley Loo., 88-524 L
* Transportation for Elderly and Handicapped People: Programs, Regulations, and Issues, Lenore M. Sek. 85-699 E

Current Events and Homework

* Transportation in the United States: Perspectives on Federal Policies, Congressional Research Service., 89-100 E
* Trucking Economic Regulation: Issue Brief, Stephen J. Thompson. IB76019
* Wage and Employment Effects of Transport Deregulation: Pending Policy Issues, Richard S. Belous. 86-68 E
* Airline Mergers and Labor Protective Provisions, IB87179
* Amtrak: Can It Save $100 Million a Year on Workers' Compensation and Employee Retirement?, IB88041
* Automobile Crash Protection, IB83085
* Aviation and the 101st Congress: Safety and Policy Issues, IB89045
* The Bridge "Crisis": An Economic Development Perspective, IB88085
* Drunk Driving, IB83157
* Railroad Economic Issues in the 101st Congress, IB85017
* Speed Limits for Motor Vehicles, IB86153
* Truck and Bus Safety, IB88022
* Trucking Economic Issues in the 101st Congress, IB76019

Transportation -- Railroads
* Amtrak: An Overview, Stephen J. Thompson. 88-687 E
* AMTRAK and the Future of Intercity Rail Passenger Service: Issue Brief, Stephen J. Thompson., IB88041
* Conrail: An Analysis of the Federal Assistance Policy and Proposed Sale, Kenneth R. DeJarnette., 86-51 E
* Federal Assistance to AMTRAK, Lenore Sek., 86-77 E
* High Speed Ground Transportation (HSGT): Prospects and Public Policy., Stephen J. Thompson., 89-221 E
* High Speed Passenger Trains: Foreign Experience and U.S. Prospects, John Fischer and Lenore Sek., 82-157 E
* Labor Protection in Railroad Industry: Issue Brief, Linda LeGrande. IB87204
* The Rail Captive Shipper Question, Kenneth R. DeJarnette., 88-649 E
* Railroad Economic Regulation: Issue Brief, Stephen J. Thompson and Rick Holland. IB85017
* Railroad Economic Trends, Stephen J. Thompson. 87-521 E
* Railroad Retirement and Employment: Recent Issues; Issue Brief, Dennis Snook, Richard Hobbie and Emmett Carson. IB84068
* Railroad Safety: Selected Options That Might Promote Safety; Archived Issue Brief, Paul F. Rothberg. IB87138
* Summary of the Staggers Rail Act of 1980, Stephen J.Thompson. 85-9 E

Treaties
* see Arms Control--Negotiations and Treaties, Congress, Foreign Relations, Foreign Trade--Trade Agreements and Negotiation, International Law

Treaty on the Non-Proliferation of Nuclear Weapons
* Nuclear Non-proliferation: Selected References, 1985-1988, B. F. Mangan., 88-682 L
* South Africa, Nuclear Weapons and the IAEA: Issue Brief, Warren H. Donnelly., IB87199

Trucking
* see Transportation

Trust Territory of the Pacific Islands
* Territorial Political Development: An Analysis of Puerto Rico, Northern Mariana Islands, Guam, Virgin Islands, and American Samoa, and the Micronesian Compacts of Free Association, Bette A. Taylor., 88-657 GOV

Tuition Tax Credits
* see Elementary and Secondary Education--Policies and Legislation

Tunisia
* Tunisia After Bourguiba: Issues for U.S. Policy, Ellen B. Laipson. 88-31 F

Turkey
* Current Issues With the "Base-Rights" Countries and Their Implications, Richard F. Grimmett. 88-726 F
* Greece and Turkey: U.S. Foreign Assistance Facts; Issue Brief, Ellen B. Laipson. IB86065
* Greek-Turkish Relations: Beginning of a New Era?, Ellen Laipson., 88-724 F
* The Seven-Ten Ratio in Military Aid to Greece and Turkey: A Congressional Tradition, Ellen Laipson., 85-79 F
* United States Military Installations in Turkey, Richard Grimmett., 84-221 F

UFOS
* see Astronautics,

Unemployment,
* see Labor--Unemployment

Unemployment Compensation
see Workers' Compensation

UNESCO
* UNESCO-U.S. Withdrawal in Perspective: Archived Issue Brief, Lois McHugh. IB84086
* U.S. Withdrawal from the International Labor Organization: Successful Precedent for UNESCO?, Lois McHugh. 84-202 F

UNICEF
* United States Contributions to UNICEF, Lois McHugh. 88-154 F

Uniformed Services Former Spouses Protection Act
* Military Benefits for Former Spouses: Legislation and Policy Issues, David F. Burrelli. 89-187 F

UNITA
* Angola: Conflict Assessment and U.S. Policy Options, Raymond W. Copson., 86-189 F
* Angola: Issues for the United States; Archived Issue Brief, Raymond Copson and Robert Shepard. IB81063
* Angola/Namibia Peace Prospects: Background, Current Problems, and Chronology, Raymond W. Copson. 88-559 F

United Nations
* Answers to Nine Questions on the United Nations, Lois McHugh. 84-31 F
* Namibia: United Nations Negotiations for Independence/U.S. Interests; Archived Issue Brief, Brenda Branaman. IB79073
* Palestine Liberation Organization Offices in the United States, Clyde R. Mark. 88-484 F
* U. N. Funding: Congressional Issues; Issue Brief, Vita Bite. IB86116
* United Nations Reform: Issues for Congress, Marjorie Ann Browne. 88-593 F
* United Nations Role in the Iran-Iraq War: Issues and Options, Lois B. McHugh and Gary J. Pagliano., 88-463 F
* The United States and Southern Africa: A Review of United Nations Resolutions and United States Voting Patterns, 1946-October 1985, Frankie King., 86-21 F

United Nations Conference on the Law of the Sea
* The Law of the Sea Conference: A U.S. Perspective; Archived Issue Brief, Marjorie Browne. IB881153

United States Postal Service
* see Postal Service

United States Sentencing Commission
* United States Sentencing Commission: Preliminary Analysis, Charles Doyle. 89-308 A

Uranium
* see Nuclear Energy

Urban Affairs
* see also Infrastructure
* The ABCs of Public Venture Capital Investment, Jan E. Christopher. 88-757 E
* Border State "Colonias": Background and Options for Federal Assistance, Claudia Copeland and Mira Courpas. 87-906 ENR
* Economic Development and Community Revitalization Programs: Sources of Information; Info Pack. IP412E
* Economic Redevelopment in the Cities, Jan E. Christopher., 88-703 E
* Enterprise Zone and Alternative Area Redevelopment Legislation: Archived Issue Brief, Dennis M. Roth and Jan E. Christopher., IB85135
* Federal Enterprise Zone: The Prospect for Economic Development; Issue Brief, J. F. Hombeck. IB89050
* Municipal Compliance With the Clean Water Act: Is the Glass Half Full or Half Empty?, Claudia Copeland. 88-421 ENR
* Transportation Infrastructure and Economic Development, J. F. Hombeck. 89-109 E

Urban and Regional Development
* see Infrastructure, Land Use, Regional Development, Urban Affairs
* Federal Enterprise Zones: The Prospect for Economic Development, IB89050

Urban Transit
* see Transportation

Uruguay Round of Multilateral Trade Negotiations
* see also Foreign Trade--Trade Agreements and Negotiations
* Agriculture in the GATT: After the Midterm Review; Issue Brief, Charles E. Hanrahan. IB89027
* Negotiating Authority for the Uruguay Round of Multilateral Trade Negotiations, Jeanne Jagelski. 87-103 A
* Trade Negotiations: The Uruguay Round; Issue Brief, Lenore Sek., IB86147

U.S. Air Force
* see National Defense

U.S. Army
* see National Defense

U.S. Bureau of the Census
* see Population

U.S. Central Intelligence Agency
* see Intelligence Activities

U.S. Central Intelligence Agency, Office of Inspector General
* Office of Inspector General in the Central Intelligence Agency: Development and Proposals, Frederick M. Kaiser. 89-129 GOV

U.S. Commission on Executive, Legislative, and Judicial Salaries
* Commission on Executive, Legislative, and Judicial Salaries: An Historical Overview, Sharon S. Gressle. 89-38 GOV

U.S. Commodity Futures Trading Commission
* CFTC and SEC: A Comparison of Regulatory Authorities, Mark Jickling., 89-199 E
* CFTC Reauthorization and the Futures Trading "Sting": Issue Brief, Mark Jickling and Kevin F. Winch. IB89051

U.S. Congress, House, Committee on Internal Security
* Abolition of the House Internal Security Committee, Paul Rundquist., 88-203 GOV

U.S. Congress. House. Committee on Un-American Activities
* Abolition of the House Internal Security Committee, Paul Rundquist., 88-203 GOV

U.S. Dept. of Agriculture
* see Agriculture

U.S. Dept. of Defense
* see National Defense

U.S. Dept. of Education
* see Elementary and Secondary Education, Federal Aid to Education, Higher Education

U.S. Dept. of Energy
* see Fossil Fuels, Nuclear Energy, Power Resources

U.S. Environmental Protection Agency
* see also Environmental Law
* Apple Alarm: Public Concern About Pesticide Residues in Fruits and Vegetables, James V. Aidala. 89-166 ENR

U.S. Farmers Home Administration
* Farm Income and Debt: Bibliography-in-Brief, 1988, Rebecca Mazur. 88-480 L
* Farmers Home Administration: Farm Credit Policies and Issues; Issue Brief, Ralph Chite. IB87215
* FmHA Losses and the Federal Budget, Ralph Chite. 89-34 ENR
* Implementation of the Agricultural Credit Act of 1987: Issue Brief,

Ralph Chite and Remy Jurenas. IB88089
* A Review of Farmers Home Administration's New Policy for Delinquent Farm Borrowers, Ralph Chite. 88-715 ENR

U.S. Federal Aviation Administration
* Aviation Safety and the 100th Congress: Bills, Hearings and a Summary of Major Action, J. Glen Moore. 89-18 SPR
* Aviation Safety, Capacity, and Service: Issue Brief, Glen Moore. IB87233
* Aviation Safety: Major Congressional Actions; Archived Issue Brief, J. Glen Moore. IB89018
* FAA Proposed Rule to Expand the Use of More C Altitude-Reporting Transponders in the United States, J. Glen Moore., 88-302 SPR

U.S. Federal Election Commission
* see Politics and Elections--Campaign Funds

U.S. Federal Emergency Management Agency
* see Disasters

U.S. Federal Housing Administration
* see Housing--Finance

U.S Forest Service
* see Forests and Forestry

U.S. National Aeronautics and Space Administration
* see also Aeronautics, Astronautics
* Civilian Space Policy under the Reagan Administration: Potential Impact of the January 1988 Directive, Patricia E. Humphlett. 88-237 SPR
* Commercial High Speed Aircraft Opportunities and Issues, Richard E. Rowberg, Kathleen Hancock and Christopher T. Hill., 89-163 SPR
* Space Facilities: The ISF/CDSF Space Station Controversy; Issue Brief, Marcia S. Smith. IB88053
* Space Issues: Info Pack., IP371S
* Space Issues: Selected References, 1986-1988, B. F.Mangan. 88-565 L

U.S. National Mediation Board
* Employee Participation in National Mediation Board Determination of Single Carrier Status, Vincent E. Treacy. 88-433 A

U.S. National Park Service
* see Parks,

U.S. Nuclear Regulatory Commission
* see Nuclear Energy

U.S. Postal Service
* see Postal Service

U.S. Securities and Exchange Commission
* CFTC and SEC: A Comparison of Regulatory Authorities, Mark Jickling., 89-199 E

U.S. Selective Service System. National Service System
* see Military Personnel

U.S. Special Operations Forces
* United States and Soviet Special Operations, John M. Collins. 87-398 S

U.S. Strategic Petroleum Reserve
* see National Defense--Strategic Stockpiles

U.S. Supreme Court
* see Judiciary--Supreme Court

U.S. Veterans Administration
* see Veterans
* Traynor v. Turnage: The Exclusion of Alcoholics from Certain Veterans' Educational Benefits Does Not Violate Section 504 of the Rehabilitation Act of 1973, Nancy Lee Jones. 88-358 A

U.S. as a Debtor Nation
* see Foreign Investments, International Finance

Brief, James Wootten. IB84099
* Canadian Nuclear-Powered Attack Submarine Program: Issues for Congress; Archived Issue Brief, Ronald O'Rourke. IB88083
* Conventional Arms Control and Military Stability in Europe, Stanley R. Sloan, Steven R. Bowman, Paul E. Gallis and Stuart D. Goldman. 87-831 F
* The Cost of a U.S. Navy Aircraft Carrier Battlegroup, Ronald O'Rourke. 87-532 F
* East-West Conventional Force Reduction Negotiations: Bibliography-in-Brief, 1980-1987, Valentin Leskovsek. 87-313 L
* FSX Fighter Agreement With Japan: Issue Brief, Richard F. Grimmett. IB89060
* FSX Fighter Program: Info Pack., IP420F
* FSX Technology: Its Relative Utility to the United States and Japanese Aerospace Industries, John D. Moteff. 89-237 SPR
* LHX and Army Aviation Modernization: Issues for Congress; Issue Brief, Steven R. Bowman. IB88086
* LHX Helicopter Program (Weapons Facts): Archived Issue Brief, Steve Bowman., IB86095
* Nuclear Escalation, Strategic Anti-Submarine Warfare, and the Navy's Forward Maritime Strategy, Ronald O'Rourke. 87-138 F
* Soviet Tank Improvements vs. U.S. Army Antitank Weapons: Addressing the Imbalance, Floyd Mike Miles. 89-71 F
* Stinger Air Defense Missiles: Characteristics and Distribution, Steven R. Bowman. 87-824 F
* V-22 Osprey Tilt-Rotor Aircraft (Weapons Facts): Issue Brief, Bert H. Cooper. IB86103

Weapons Systems-- Nuclear Weapons
* see INF, Nuclear Energy--Nuclear Exports and Non-Proliferation
* An Accidental Launch Protection System (ALPS): Requirements and Proposed Concepts; Archived Issue Brief, Amy F. Woolf. IB88079
* British and French Strategic Nuclear Force Modernization: Issues for Western Security and Arms Control, Charlotte Phillips Preece and Joseph M. Freeman., 89-140 F
* The Bush Administration's Proposal for ICBM Modernization, SDI, and the B-2 Bomber, Jonathan Medalia. 89-281 F
* The Chernobyl Accident: Implications for DOE's Production Reactors; Archived Issue Brief, Robert L. Civiak. IB86092
* China's Nuclear Weapons and Arms Control Policies: Implications for the United States, Robert G. Sutter. 88-374 F
* Civil Defense and the Effects of Nuclear War: Info Pack. IP174C
* Civil Defense: Archived Issue Brief, Gary Reynolds and Dagnija Sterste-Perkins., IB84128
* Estimating Funding for Strategic Forces; a Review of the Problems, Alice Maroni. 84-652 F
* The Geneva Negotiations on Space and Nuclear Arms: Soviet Positions and Perspectives, Jeanette Voas., 86-512 S
* Implications for NATO Strategy of a Zero-Outcome Intermediate-Range Nuclear Missile Accord, Stanley R. Sloan. 87-614 F
* The Implications for Strategic Arms Control of Nuclear Armed Sea Launched Cruise Missiles, Alva Bowen, Stanley Sloan and Ronald O'Rourke. 86-25 F
* Israel and Nuclear Weapons: Issue Brief, Warren H. Donnelly. IB87079
* "Midgetman" Small ICBM: Issues Facing Congress in 1986, Jonathan Medalia., 86-58 F
* "Midgetman" Small ICBM (Weapon Acts): Archived Issue Brief, Jonathan Medalia and Alice Maroni. IB84044
* MX, "Midgetman," and Minuteman Missile Programs: Issue Brief, Jonathan Medalia. IB77080
* NATO Nuclear Modernization and Arms Control: Issue Brief, Stanley R. Sloan. 1B89049
* The Netherlands Elections and the Cruise Missile Issue: Implications for the United States and for NATO, Paul Gallis., 86-27 F
* Nuclear Escalation, Strategic Anti-Submarine Warfare, and the Navy's Forward Maritime Strategy, Ronald O'Rourke., 87-138 F
* Nuclear Explosions in Space: The Threat of EMP (Electromagnetic Pulse); Archived Mini Brief, Robert Civiak. MB82221
* Nuclear Material from Dismantled Warheads: What to Do With It and How to Verify Its Disposal: A Preliminary Analysis, Warren H. Donnelly. 87-437 S
* Nuclear Nonproliferation: Selected References, 1985-1988, B. F. Mangan. 88-682 L
* Nuclear Risk Reduction Centers: Archived Issue Brief, Steven A. Hildreth., IB86142
* Nuclear Weapons Production Complex: Modernization and Cleanup; Issue Brief, David W. Cheney and Mark Holt., IB89062
* Nuclear Weapons Use: International Law and the United States Position, Ellen Collier., 84-109 F
* Nuclear Winter: Bibliography-in-Brief, B. F. Mangan. 88-325 L
* Seawolf or SSN-21 Nuclear-Powered Attack Submarine: Issue Brief, Ronald O'Rourke. IB85169
* Strategic Forces: MX ICBM (Weapons Facts); Archived Issue

Brief, Jonathan Medalia and Alice Maroni. IB84046
* Strategic Nuclear Forces: Potential U.S./Soviet Trends With or Without SALT: 1985-2000, Jonathan Medalia, A1 Tinajero and Paul Zinsmeister. 86-135F
* Tort Liability of the Federal Government and Its Contractors to Veterans Exposed to Atomic Radiation, Henry Cohen. 86-979 A
* Trident II Missile (Weapons Facts); Archived Issue Brief, Jonathan Medalia and Alice Maroni. IB84045
* Trident Program: Issue Brief, Jonathan Medalia. IB73001

Weapons Systems -- Space Weapons
* Arms Control: Negotiations to Limit Defense and Space Weapons; Issue Brief, Steven Hildreth., IB86073
* Arms Control: Overview of the Geneva Talks; Archived Issue Brief, Steven Hildreth. IB85157
* SATs: Antisatellite Weapons Systems; Issue Brief, Marcia Smith., IB85176
* Congress and the Strategic Defense Initiative: A Detailed Overview of Legislative Action, 1984-1987, Robert J. Crawford and Steven A. Hildreth. 87-749F
* Directed Energy Weapons Research: Status and Outlook, Cosmo DiMaggio. 85-183 SPR
* The Effect of a Comprehensive Test Ban on the Strategic Defense Initiative, Cosmo DiMaggio. 85-972 SPR
* Ethical and Religious Aspects of SDI: Pro and Con, Charles H. Whittier. 87-535 GOV
* Legal Analysis of a Memorandum of Understanding Between the United States and the Federal Republic of Germany Concerning Patent Rights Resulting from Strategic Defense Initiative Research, Michael V. Seitzinger., 87-281 A
* Potential Offensive Capabilities of SDI Space Weapons, Cosmo DiMaggio. 87-807 SPR
* Project Defender., Prepared, the Office of Senior Specialists. 87-689 S
* The Strategic Defense Initiative: A Model for Estimating Launch Costs, Cosmo DiMaggio and Robert L. Civiak. 87-475 SPR
* The Strategic Defense Initiative and United States Alliance Strategy, Paul Gallis, Mark Lowenthal and Marcia Smith. 85-48 F
* Strategic Defense Initiative: Info Pack., IP346S
* The Strategic Defense Initiative: Is the Software Feasible? Audio Brief., AB50141
* The Strategic Defense Initiative: Issues for Congress; Issue Brief, Steven Hildreth. IB85170
* The Strategic Defense Initiative: Issues for Phase I Deployment; Issue Brief, Steven A. Hildreth. IB88033
* The Strategic Defense Initiative: Program Description and Major Issues, Cosmo DiMaggio, Arthur Manfredi and Steven Hildreth. 86-8 SPR
* Strategic Defense Initiative (SDI): Mission Objectives for Directing the Program; Issue Brief, Cosmo DiMaggio and Jack Moteff. IB88028
* Strategic Defense Initiative: Selected References, 1986-1988, Valentin Leskovsek. 88-184L
* U.S. Military Satellites and Survivability, Arthur Manfredi. 86-581 SPR

Weapons Systems -- Weapons Facts
* A-12 Advanced Tactical Aircraft (ATA) Program (Weapons Facts): Issue Brief, Bert H. Cooper. IB87115
* Advanced Tactical Fighter (ATF) Aircraft (Weapons Facts): Issue Brief, Bert H. Cooper. IB87111
* Advanced Technology Bomber: Issue Brief, Dagnija Sterste-Perkins., IB87216
* Aircraft Carriers (Weapons Facts): Archived Issue Brief, Ronald O'Rourke. IB87043
* AMRAAM Air-to-Air Missile (Weapons Facts); Archived Issue Brief, Bert H. Cooper. IB86041
* Army Forward Area Air Defense System: Weapons Facts: Archived Issue Brief, Steven R. Bowman. IB87136
* Army Issues: Bradley Fighting Vehicle (Weapons Facts): Archived Issue Brief, Steven Bowman. IB86061
* ASATs: Antisatellite Weapons Systems; Issue Brief, Marcia Smith. IB85176
* Attack Submarines and Aircraft Carrier Battlegroups: A New Mix for the U.S. Navy?, Ronald O'Rourke. 88-635 F
* AV-8B V/STOL Aircraft (Weapons Facts); Issue Brief, Bert H. Cooper. IB88044
* LHX Helicopter Program (Weapons Facts): Archived Issue Brief, Steve Bowman., IB86095
* "Midgetman" Small ICBM (Weapon Acts): Archived Issue Brief, Jonathan Medalia and Alice Maroni. IB84044
* MX, "Midgetman," and Minuteman Missile Programs: Issue Brief, Jonathan Medalia. IB77080
* Seawolf or SSN-21 Nuclear-Powered Attack Submarine: Issue Brief, Ronald O'Rourke. IB85169
* Stinger Air Defense Missiles: Characteristics and Distribution, Steven R. Bowman. 87-824F

Current Events and Homework

* The Strategic Defense Initiative: Issues for Congress; Issue Brief, Steven Hildreth. IB85170
* Strategic Forced: MX ICBM (Weapons Facts); Archived Issue Brief, Jonathan Medalia and Alice Maroni. IB84046
* Trident II Missile (Weapons Facts); Archived Issue Brief, Jonathan Medalia and Alice Maroni. IB84045
* Trident Program: Issue Brief, Jonathan Medalia. IB73001
* V-22 Osprey Tilt-Rotor Aircraft (Weapons Facts): Issue Brief, Bert H. Cooper. 86103

Weather
* see Earth Sciences

Weatherization Assistance
* see Power Resources-- Energy, Conversation

Welfare
* see Public Welfare

West Bank
* Israeli-Palestinian Conflict: Bibliography-in-Brief, 1982-1988, Robert S. Kirk. 88-251 L
* Israeli-Palestinian Conflict: Info Pack. IP397I
* Palestinian Disturbances in the Gaza Strip and West Bank: Policy Issues and Chronology, Ellen Laipson. 88-114 F

West Germany
* Franco-German Security Cooperation: Implications for the NATO Alliance, Paul E. Gallis. 89-16F
* Is Faster Growth in Germany and Japan the Key to Faster U.S. Growth?, Gail E. Makinen. 86-836E
* Legal Analysis of a Memorandum of Understanding Between the United States and the Federal Republic of Germany Concerning Patent Rights Resulting from Strategic Defense Initiative Research, Michael V. Seitzinger. 87-281 A
* United States Merchandise Trade and Trade Balances With W. Germany, 1960-1987, Dario Scuka. 88-117 E

Western Europe
* see National Defense, European Economic Community
* The "Citrus-Pasta Dispute" Between the United States and the European Community, Donna U. Vogt. 33 p.87-911 ENR
* Commercial Space Activities in Europe, Patricia E. Humphlett. 88-531 SPR
* The Common Agricultural Policy of the European Community and Implications for U.S. Agricultural Trade, Donna U. Vogt, Jasper Womach and Rebecca Mazur. 86-111 ENR
* Cyprus: Turkish Cypriot "Statehood" and Prospects for Settlement: Archived Issue Brief, Ellen B. Laipson. 1B84062
* Employment and Unemployment: Some International Comparisons, Gail McCallion. 88-673 E
* European Community: Issues Raised, 1992 Integration, Congressional Research Service., 89-323 E
* The European Community: Its Structure and Development, Martin E. Elling. 88-620 F
* European Community-Japan Trade Relations: A European Perspective, Dick K. Nanto. 86-166 E
* European Community: The 1992 Plan; Info Pack. IP408E
* European Community: 1992 Plan for Economic Integration; Issue Brief, Glennon J. Harrison. IB89043
* The European Community's 1992 Plan: Bibliography-in-Brief, 1986-1988, Robert Howe. 88-754 L
* The European Community's 1992 Plan: Effects on American Direct Investment, James K. Jackson. 89-339 E
* An Explanation of the European Community's Sugar Regime and Comparison to the U.S. Sugar Program, Jasper Womach and Donna Vogt. 85-77 ENR
* Greece and Turkey: U.S. Foreign Assistance Facts; Issue Brief, Ellen B. Laipson. IB86065
* Greek-Turkish Relations: Beginning of a New Era?, Ellen Laipson. 88-724 F
* The Holy See and Recognition of Israel, Charles H. Whittier. 86-833 GOV * Northern Ireland and the Republic of Ireland: U.S. Foreign Assistance Facts; Issue Brief, Bert H. Cooper, Jr. IB87069
* Northern Ireland: The Anglo-Irish Agreement and Its Implications for Congress: Policy Alert, Allan Nanes. 85-1107 F
* Northwest European Region Petroleum (Including the North Sea), Joseph Riva. 85-187 SPR
* Plutonium: Department of Energy Approval of Plutonium Shipment from France to Japan; Archived Issue Brief, Warren H. Donnelly. IB84116
* Proposed European Community Consumption Tax on Vegetable Oils: A Status Report, Donna U. Vogt.87-407 ENR
* Space Activities of the United States, Soviet Union and Other Launching Countries/Organizations: 1957-1988, Marcia S. Smith. 89-183 SPR

* Tensions in United States-European Community Agricultural Trade, Donna U. Vogt and Jasper Womach. 86-112 ENR
* United States Merchandise Trade and Trade Balances With W. Germany, 1960-1987, Dario Scuka. 88-117 E
* U.S. Commercial Relations With the European Community, George D. Holliday. 85-32 E

Western Europe -- National Defense
* British and French Strategic Nuclear Force Modernization: Issues for Western Security and Arms Control, Charlotte Phillips Preece and Joseph M. Freeman. 89-140 F
* The Conference on Disarmament in Europe (CDE): Archived Issue Brief, Charlotte Preece and Steven Bowman. IB84060
* Conference on Security and Cooperation in Europe (CSCE): The Vienna Meeting; Issue Brief, Francis T. Miko. IB87220
* Confidence Building Measures and Force Constraints for Stabilizing East-West Military Relations in Europe, Stanley R. Sloan and Mikaela Sawtelle., 88-591 F
* Conventional Arms Control and Military Stability in Europe, Stanley R. Sloan, Steven R. Bowman, Paul E. Gallis and Stuart D. Goldman. 87-831 F
* Defense Burden Sharing: The United States, NATO and Japan; Info Pack., IP399D
* Franco-German Security Cooperation: Implications for the NATO Alliance, Paul E. Gallis. 89-16F
* Implications for NATO Strategy of a Zero-Outcome Intermediate-Range Nuclear Missile Accord, Stanley R.Sloan. 87-614 F
* The NATO Allies, Japan, and the Persian Gulf, Paul Gallis. 84-184 F
* NATO at 40: Bibliographic Resources, Sherry B. Shapiro. 89-175 L
* NATO Burdensharing: An Analysis of Major Legislation in the 100th Congress, Christopher C. Bolkcom. 88-772 F
* NATO Conventional Force Structure and Doctrine: Possible Defensive Changes After an INF Treaty, Robert L. Goldich. 88-169 F
* NATO Nuclear Modernization and Arms Control: Issue Brief, Stanley R. Sloan. IB89049
* The Netherlands Elections and the Cruise Missile Issue: Implications for the United States and for NATO, Paul Gallis. 86-27 F
* The Seven-Ten Ratio in Military Aid to Greece and Turkey: A Congressional Tradition, Ellen Laipson. 85-79 F
* The Strategic Defense Initiative and United States Alliance Strategy, Paul Gallis, Mark Lowenthal and Marcia Smith. 85-48 F
* United States Military Installations in Greece, Richard Grimmett. 84-24 F
* United States Military Installations in Italy, Richard Grimmett. 84-12 F
* United States Military Installations in Portugal, Richard Grimmett. 86-6 F
* United States Military Installations in Spain, Richard Grimmett. 84-149 F
* United States Military Installations in Turkey, Richard Grimmett. 84-221 F
* The U.S. Commitment to Europe's Defense: A Review of Cost Issues and Estimates, Alice Maroni and John Ulrich. 85-211 F

Wetlands
* see Coastal Areas

Wilderness Areas
* see Forests and Forestry

Wildlife
* Applicability of Alaska State Laws to Oil and Gas Development in the Arctic National Wildlife Refuge, Pamela Baldwin, 88-420 A
* Arctic National Wildlife Refuge: Bibliography-in-Brief, Adrienne C. Grenfell. 88-30L
* The Arctic National Wildlife Refuge: Major Oil Development or Wilderness?, Congressional Research Service. Edited by John E. Blodgett and John L. Moore, Environment and Natural Resources Policy Division., 88-161 ENR
* The Arctic National Wildlife Refuge: Oil, Gas, and Wildlife; Archived Issue Brief, Lynne Corn and John Schanz. IB87026
* Arctic Resources Controversy: A Comparison of H.R. 3601 and S. 2214, Environment and Natural Resources Policy Division., 88-380 ENR
* Arctic Resources Controversy; an Overview; Archived Issue Brief, M. Lynne Corn, John E. Blodgett and Pamela Baldwin. IB87228
* Arctic Resources Controversy: Issue Brief, M. Lynne Corn, Claudia Copeland and Pamela Baldwin. IB89058
* Brief Summaries of Federal Animal Protection Statutes, Henry Cohen. 88-541 A
* Consideration of Economic Factors under the Endangered Species Act, Pamela Baldwin. 89-274 A

* Debt-for-Nature Swaps in Developing Countries: An Overview of Recent Conservation Efforts, Betsy Cody. 88-647 ENR
* Endangered Species Act: Reauthorization and Funding; Issue Brief, M. Lynne Corn. IB87089
* Endangered Species, Bibliography-in-Brief, 1986-1987, Adrienne C. Grenfell. 87-450 L
* Endangered Species: Info Pack., IP192E
* Environmental Effects of Energy Development in the Arctic National Wildlife Refuge: A Critique of the Final Legislative Environmental Impact Statement, M. Lynne Corn, John Blodgett, Eugene H. Buck, Claudia Copeland and Mark R. Dillenbeck. 87-490 ENR
* The Exxon Valdez Oil Spill: Issue Brief, Martin R. Lee and Robert Bamberger. IB89075
* A Guide to Trust Funds, Special Accounts, and Foundations in the Fish and Wildlife Service Budget, M. Lynne Corn., 86-722 ENR
* Kangaroo Management Controversy, Malcolm M. Simmons. 88-468 ENR
* The Major Federal Land Management Agencies: Management of Our Nation's Lands and Resources, Adela Backiel, M. Lynne Corn, Ross Gorte, George Siehl and Pamela Baldwin. 87-22 ENR
* Marine Mammal Protection Act Reauthorization: Population--Too Large or Too Small? Issue Brief, Eugene H. Buck. IB88038
* North Pacific Fur Seals: Issues and Options, Eugene Buck., 85-654 ENR
* Oil Companies and the Development of the Arctic National Wildlife Refuge, John J. Schanz. 88-106 S
* The Outlook for U.S. Energy Supplies and the Arctic National Wildlife Refuge Decision, John J. Schanz. 88-73 S
* An Overview of Federal Tax Policies Encouraging Donations of Conservation Easements to Preserve Natural Areas, Richard Dunford. 84-48 ENR
* Predator Control and Compound 1080: Archived Mini Brief, Jim Aidala. MB82241
* Protecting Endangered and Threatened Sea Turtles, Eugene H. Buck. 87-540 ENR
* Special Management Areas in the National Forest System, Ross W. Gorte., 88-571 ENR
* Spotted Owls and the Timber Industry: Issue Brief, M. Lynne Corn. IB89077
* Wetlands Protection: Issues in the 101st Congress; Issue Brief, Jeffrey A. Zinn, M. Lynne Corn and Claudia L. Copeland. IB89076
* Whale Conservation, Eugene H. Buck and Jennifer A. Heck. 88-391 ENR
* Wild Horses and Burros: Federal Management Issues; Archived Issue Brief, Adela Backiel and Alison Holt. IB85138
* Wilderness: Overview and Statistics, Ross W. Gorte. 88-16 ENR

Windfall Profits Tax
* see Taxation--Corporation Taxes

Women
* see also Policies and Legislation, Civil Liberties and Rights--Discrimination and Integration, Equal Employment Opportunity, Pensions
* Economic Growth and Changing Labor Markets: Those Left Behind; Women Workers (Un)changed Position, Linda LeGrande. 84-112 E
* Surrogate Mothers: Bibliography-in-Brief 1985-1988, Edith Sutterlin. 88-268 L
* Women: An Alphabetical Microthesaurus of Terms Selected from the Legislative Indexing Vocabulary, Shirley Loo. 88-710L
* Women in the Armed Forces (With Appendix): Archived Issue Brief, Ellen Collier. IB79045
* Women in the United States Congress, Mildred L. Amer. 89-332 GOV
* Women Nominated and Appointed to Full-Time Civilian Positions, President Reagan, Rogelio Garcia. 89-236 GOV
* Women's Pension Equity: A Summary of the Retirement Equity Act of 1984, Ray Schmitt. 84-217 EPW

Women--Policies and Legislation
* Comparable Worth/Pay Equity in the Federal Government: Issue Brief, Linda LeGrande. IB85116
* Displaced Homemakers: Issue Brief, Leslie Gladstone. IB84132
* The Economic Equity Act of 1987: Archived Issue Brief, Leslie Gladstone. IB87221
* Equal Rights for Women: Issue Brief, Leslie Gladstone..IB83077
* Federal Councils on the Status of Women, Established Executive Order: Summary and Analysis, Leslie Gladstone. 85-1121 GOV
* Federal Policies and Programs Relating to Sex Discrimination and Sex Equity in Education, 1963-1985, Bob Lyke and Rick Holland. 85-116 EPW
* Federal Programs for Minority and Women-Owned Businesses, Mark Eddy. 89-278 GOV
* A Legal Analysis of the Fourteenth Amendment's Equal Protection Clause and the Proposed Equal Rights Amendment,

Karen Lewis. 85-662A
* Maternity and Parental Leave Policies: A Comparative Analysis, Leslie Gladstone, Jennifer Williams and Richard S.Belous., 85-148 GOV
* Parental Leave: Info Pack., IP367P
* The Proposed Equal Rights Amendment, Leslie Gladstone. 85-154 G0V
* Selected Women's Issues in the 100th Congress: Archived Issue Brief, Leslie W. Gladstone. IB87133
* Selected Women's Issues Legislation Enacted Between 1832-1986, Leslie Gladstone. 88-621 GOV
* Sex Discrimination and the United States Supreme Court: Developments in the Law, Karen J. Lewis. 88-542 A

Workers' Compensation
* Black Lung Programs: 1987 Issues and Action, Gloria E. Moreno and Joe Richardson. 88-68 EPW
* Federal Black Lung Disability Benefits Program, Barbara McClure., 81-239 EPW
* How the Unemployment Compensation System Works, Celinda M. Franco. 89-326EPW
* Railroad Retirement and Employment: Recent Issues; Issue Brief, Dennis Snook, Richard Hobbie and Emmett Carson. IB84068
* Selected Federal Victim Compensation Systems, Gloria E.Moreno. 88-573 EPW
* Summary and Legislative History of P.L. 97-1 19, "Black Lung Benefits Revenue Act of 1981", Barbara McClure. 88-59 EPW
* Unemployment Compensation: Problems and Issues, Education and Public Welfare Division. Unemployment Compensation Team. 88-597 EPW
* Unemployment Insurance: Changes Made by the 98th Congress, Emmett Carson. 85-230 EPW
* Work Disincentives in the Unemployment Insurance (UI) System, Richard Hobbie. 80-159 EPW

World Bank
* International Monetary Fund and World Bank: Info Pack. IP245I
* Multilateral Development Banks: Issues for the 101st Congress; Archived Issue Brief, Jonathan E. Sanford, IB87218
* World Bank Activities in Ethiopia, Jonathan Sanford, 87-857 F.
* The World Bank: Eighteen Questions and Answers, Jonathan E. Sanford, 86-769 F

World Health Organization
* World Health Organization: Effects of Reduced U.S. Contributions, Lois McHugh, 87-108 F

Yellowstone National Park
* Issues Surrounding the Greater Yellowstone Ecosystem: A Brief Review, M. Lynne Corn, Ross W. Gorte and George Siehl, 85-1146 ENR

Youth Employment
* see Labor

Yugoslavia
* Mineral Development in Yugoslavia, Marc Humphries, 88-688 ENR

Zimbabwe
* The United States and Southern Africa: A Review of the United Nations Resolutions and United States Voting Patterns, 1946-October 1985, Frankie King,

Audio Brief List

Acid Rain; Scientific Progress and Outlook: Audio Brief, AB50128
After the Drought: The Next Farm Bill; Audio Brief, AB50183
AIDS: Audio Brief, AB50186
Allied Burdensharing: Audio Brief, AB50182
The American Response to Foreign Competition: Audio Brief, AB50180
Biomedical Ethics: Audio Brief, AB50004
Budget Making and the Legislative Process: Audio Brief, AB50164
Campaign Activities By Congressional Staff: Audio Brief, AB50164
Characteristics of Congress: Audio Brief, AB50129
Chemicals in the Environment: Audio Brief, AB50152
Combatting International Terrorism: Audio Brief, AB50151
Conducting Oversight: Legal, Procedural, and Practical Aspects; Audio Brief, AB50156
The Defense Spending Dilemma: Audio Brief, AB50181
The Dollar, the Trade Deficit, and the U.S. Economy: Audio Brief, AB50174
Effective Oversight: Planning for the Future; Audio Brief, AB50155
Executive Perspectives on Oversight: Audio Brief, AB50116

Current Events and Homework

Financing Long-Term Care for the Elderly: Audio Brief, AB50187
Former Members View Oversight: Audio Brief, AB50111
Global Climate Change: Audio Brief, AB50189
The Global Environment: Audio Brief, AB50063
Housing: Access and Affordability: Audio Brief, AB50172
Housing and Community Development: Audio Brief, Ab50184
Implications for U.S. Diplomacy in the U.S.-Soviet Future: Audio Brief, AB50173
Increasing Access to Health Insurance: Audio Brief, AB50166
Indoor Air Pollution: Audio Brief, AB50188
Information Technology for Emergency Operations: Audio Brief, AB50117
Inspectors General: Resources for Oversight; Audio Brief, AB50109
International Commission on Central America: Initial Views; Audio Brief, AB50176
Issues in the Middle East: Audio Brief, AB50177
A Member's Reflections on Oversight: Audio Brief, AB50112
The Moscow Summit at First Glance: Audio Brief, AB50168
Outside Perspectives on Oversight: Audio Brief, AB50157
Oversight Authority and Major Procedures: Audio Brief, AB50114
Oversight in Action: Audio Brief, AB50110
Oversight Powers and Constraints: Audio Brief, AB50115
Pros and Cons of Military Intervention: Audio Brief, AB50033
RCRA Authorization: Audio Brief, AB50179
Reforming the Foreign Assistance Program: Audio Brief, AB50185
The Role of Congress in Soviet Diplomacy and Negotiations: Audio Brief, AB50175
The Role of the Media in Oversight: Audio Brief, AB50113
The Role of the U.S. Military in Narcotics Interdiction: Audio Brief, AB50171
Senate Legislative Floor Procedures: Audio Brief, AB50143
Soviet Diplomacy under Gorbachev: Continuity and Change; Audio Brief, AB50190
The Strategic Defense Initiative: Is the Software Feasible?; Audio Brief, AB50141
Strategic Policy Issues: The Bush Administration's ICBM Modernization Program; Audio Brief, AB50191
Toxic Chemicals: Environmental and Health Issues; Audio Brief, AB50104
U.S.-Soviet Relations: Audio Brief, AB50178

Info Pack Listing

Abortion: Info Pack, IP001A
Acid Rain: Info Pack, IP134A
Affirmative Action: Info Pack, IP424A
Aged: Info Pack, IP003A
Agriculture: Drought of 1988; Info Pack, IP403A
Agriculture: The Farm Financial Situation; Info Pack, IP323A
Agriculture: The 1985 Farm Bill and After; Info Pack, IP295A
AIDS: Acquired Immune Deficiency Syndrome; Info Pack, IP261A
Air Pollution-Clean Air Act: Info Pack, IP008A
Airlines: Safety and Service Issues: Info Pack, IP386A
Animal Use in Biomedical Research: Info Pack, IP360A
Arms Sales: U.S. Policy: Info Pack, IP214A
Benefits for Former Military Spouses: Info Pack, IP313B
Bicentennial of the U.S. Congress: Info Pack, IP411C
Budget for Fiscal Year 1989: Info Pack, IP394B
Budget for Fiscal Year 1990; Info Pack, IP413B
Budget Process: Info Pack, IP012B
Business: Doing Business With the Federal Government; Info Pack, IP305B
Cable TV: Info Pack, IP104C
Campaign Finance: Info Pack, IP014C
Canada-U.S. Free Trade Area Agreement; Info Pack, IP395C
Capital Punishment: Info Pack, IP015C
Career Guidance and Federal Job Information: Info Pack, IP016C
Catastrophic Health Insurance: Info Pack, IP370C
Central America: U.S. Relations With Costa Rica, Guatemala, and Honduras; Info Pack, IP352C
Child Abuse: Info Pack, IP019C
Child Day Care: Info Pack, IP306C
Child Support: Issues and Legislation; Info Pack, IP286C
Civil Defense and the Effects of Nuclear War; Info Pack, IP174C
Competitiveness: Current Issues and Proposals; Info Pack, IP368C
Congress: Info Pack, IP022C
Congress: Issues for the 101st Congress; Info Pack, IP410C
Congressional Office Operations: Info Pack, IP151C
Constitution of the United States: Its History, Development, and Amending Process; Info Pack, IP339C
Copyright-Applications Procedures: Info Pack, IP215C
Defense Burden Sharing: The United States, NATO and Japan; Info Pack, IP399D
Defense Procurement: The Fraud and Bribery Investigation; Info Pack, IP404D
Defense Spending: Info Pack, IP028D
Deficit Reduction Issues: Info Pack, IP274D
Drug Abuse in America: Info Pack, IP303D
Drug Abuse: Treatment, Prevention and Education: Info Pack, IP400D
Drug Control: Federal Efforts to Reduce the Supply; Info Pack, IP334D
Drug Testing: The Response to Drugs in the Workplace; Info Pack, IP350D
Drugs of Abuse: The Legalization Debate; Info Pack, IP401D
Drunk Driving and Raising the Drinking Age: Info Pack, IP186D
Economic Development and Community Revitalization Programs; Sources of Information; Info Pack, IP412E
Economy: Background and Prospects; Info Pack, IP393E
Education: Funding Issues: Info Pack, IP199E
Education: Issues of Quality and Reform; Info Pack IP256E
El Salvador: Info Pack, IP121E
Electoral College: Info Pack, IP031E
Employment Abroad: Info Pack, IP065E
Endangered Species: Info Pack, IP192E
European Community: The 1992 Plan; Info Pack, IP408E
Federal Reserve System: Info Pack, IP105F
Financial Aid for Students; Info Pack, IP042F
Financial Institutions: Problems and Prospects: Info Pack, IP291F
The Flag: Info Pack, IP365F
Foreign Aid: Info Pack, IP044F
Foreign Investments in the U.S.: Info Pack, IP398F
Foreign Policy: Info Pack, IP297F
Form Letters: Tell Your Constituents Where to Get Government Publications; Info Pack, IP222F
Freedom of Information Act/Privacy Act: A Guide to Their Use; Info Pack, IP047F
FSX Fighter Program: Info Pack, IP420F
Government Publications--How, What, When, Where, and Why: Info Pack, IP264G
Grants and Foundation Support: Info Pack, IP050G
Greenhouse Effect and Ozone Depletion: Info Pack, IP405G
Gun Control: Info Pack, IP051G
Hatch Act: Info Pack, IP298H
Hazardous Waste and the Superfund Program; Info Pack, IP094H
Health Care Access: Federal Policy Issues: Info Pack, IP421H
Health Care Costs: Info Pack, IP223H
Health Insurance: Employer Benefits Required under COBRA and Pending Proposals: Info Pack, IP389H
Health Insurance: Info Pack, IP072H
Health: Long-Term Care: Info Pack, IP402H
Homeless in America: Info Pack, IP314H
Hotlines and Other Useful Government Telephone Numbers: Info Pack, IP106H
Housing Policy and Implications for Current Programs; Info Pack, IP417H
How to Follow Current Federal Legislation and Regulations: Info Pack, IP122H
Immigration and Refugee Policy: Info Pack, IP164I
INF Treaty: Info Pack, IP392I
International Debt Problems: Background, Statistics, Proposed Solutions; Info Pack, IP234I
International Monetary Fund and World Bank: Info Pack, IP245I
Internships and Fellowships: Info Pack, IP063I
Israeli-Palestinian Conflict: Info Pack, IP397I
Japan-U.S. Trade and Economic Relations: Info Pack, IP201J
Jobs: The Employment Situation and Job training Programs: Info Pack, IP246J
Legislative Procedure: An Introduction; Info Pack, IP247L
Legislative Research: A Guide to Conducting Legislative Research in a Congressional Office; Info Pack, IP321L
Leveraged Buyouts: Info Pack, IP414L
Lobbying: Info Pack, IP067M
Medicare-Medicaid: Info Pack, IP067M
Medicare Payments to Hospitals and Physicians: Info Pack, IP371M
Mexico: Problems and Prospects: Info Pack, IP358M
Military Balance: Info Pack, IP069M
Minimum Wage Issues: Info Pack, IP249M
National Service: Info Pack, IP418N
NATO: Conventional Arms Control and Related Political Issues: Info Pack, IP425N
Nicaragua: Info Pack, IP073N
Nuclear Arms Control: The Geneva Talks: Info Pack, IP341N
Nuclear Energy: Safety and Waste Issues; Info Pack, IP074N
Oil Spills: Info Pack, IP42660
Parental Leave: Info Pack, IP367P
Political Action Committees (PACs): Info Pack, IP196P
The Presidency of the United States; Info Pack, IP409P
Prisoner of War/Missing in Action in SE Asia; Info Pack, IP127P
Puerto Rico: Political Status: Info Pack, IP419P
Radon: An Overview of Health and Environmental Issues; Info Pack, IP363R
Retirement Systems for Federal Employees: Info Pack, IP205R
S&L Problems and FSLIC: Info Pack, IP415S
Small Business Assistance Programs Sources of Information: Info Pack, IP422S
Smoking and Tobacco Issues; Info Pack, IP356S

Social Security: Current Issues, Benefits and Financing: Info Pack, IP153S

Social Security: National Committee to Preserve Social Security and Medicare; Info Pack, Ip345S

The Social Security "Notch": Info Pack, IP266S

Solid Waste Management: Info Pack, IP396S

South Africa: The Current Situation: Info Pack, IP340S

Space Issues: Info Pack, IP371S

Speech Material: Captive Nations Week: Info Pack, IP375C

Speech Material: Labor Day; Info Pack, IP374L

Speechwriting and Delivery: Info Pack, IP139S

Strategic Defense Initiative: Info Pack, IP346S

Superconducting Super Collider: Issues; Info Pack, IP384S

Superconductors: Info Pack, IP390S

Telephone Industry Issues: Info Pack, IP257T

Terrorism: Info Pack, IP299T

Trade Issues and Trade Deficits: Background, Statistics, and proposed Legislation: Info Pack, IP263T

Tropical Deforestation: Info Pack, IP416T

U.S. Government: Info Pack, IP162U

U.S.-Soviet Relations: Info Pack, IP233U

War Powers Resolution: Info Pack, IP131W

Washington, D.C. and the U.S. Capitol Building: Info Pack, IP132W

Waste in the Marine Environment: Info Pack, IP407W

Water Resources: Quality and Quantity: Info Pack, IP369W

Welfare and Poverty: Info Pack, IP098W

Wetlands Issues: Info Pack, IP423W

8,000 Free Experts

You may have heard of the "seven-phone call rule" for tracking down an expert who will help you for free. Well, now you can throw that phrase out the window. With this handy list of 8,000 government experts you are likely to find the right subject specialist in only ONE phone call.

Do you have a new idea to revolutionize the crayon market? Linda Linkins at the U.S. International Trade Commission has spent her career analyzing this market. Want to know the latest therapy for cross-eye? Contact the expert here at the National Eye Institute. You'll find six bureaucrats listed in this chapter who monitor Czechoslovakia. There are professionals specializing in Care Labeling, Cash Discounts, Chickenpox, and even Canoes. These examples reflect just a tiny sample of the names and phone numbers of experts under the letter "C". So you can imagine what else you'll find. Remember each of these professionals has devoted his or her life work to studying a specific area and will share their knowledge without charging a penny **just as long as you treat them right.** (Refer to the Information Is Power Chapter, specifically "Finding Mr. Potato" and "Case Study: Jelly Beans", for guidance on how to deal with bureaucrats.)

The abbreviations for the federal agency which precede an expert's telephone number are spelled out below. If you have trouble with a telephone number, afterall numbers change all the time, simply contact the agency directly.

ACYF = Administration for Children, Youth, and Family, HHS, 330 C St., SW, Room 2024, Washington, DC 20201

ADAMHA = Alcohol, Drug Abuse, & Mental Health Administration, HHS, 5600 Fishers Lane, Room 12-105, Rockville, MD 20857

AGRI = National Agricultural Statistics Service, U.S. Department of Agriculture, 14th and Independence Ave., SW, Washington, DC 20250; (202) 447-2122

AID = Agency for International Development, 320 21st Street, NW, Washington, DC 20523

AU = American University, 4400 Massachusetts Ave., NW, Washington, DC 20016

BEIB = Biomedical Engineering and Instrumentation Branch, NIH, 9000 Rockville Pike, Bldg. 13, Room 3W13, Bethesda, MD 20892

BHCDA = Bureau of Health Care Delivery and Assistance, HHS, 5600 Fishers Lane, Room 7-05, Rockville, MD 20857

BJS = Bureau of Justice Statistics, U.S. Department of Justice, 633 Indiana Ave., NW, Washington, DC 20531

CC = Clinical Center, NIH, 9000 Rockville Pike Bldg. 10, Room 2C128, Bethesda, MD 20892

CDC = Centers for Disease Control, HHS, 1600 Clifton Rd., NE, Atlanta, GA 30333

CDCW = Centers for Disease Control Washington, 200 Independence Ave., SW, Room 714B, Washington, DC 20201

CENSUS = Data Users Service Division, Customer Service, Bureau of Census, U.S. Department of Commerce, Washington, DC 20233; (301) 763-4100

COMMERCE = Industry Experts, Public Affairs, International Trade Administration, Washington, DC 20230; (202) 377-3808

COMM FUTURES = Central Region Market Surveillance Branch, Commodity Futures Trading Commission, 233 South Wacker Dr., Suite 4600, Chicago, IL 60606; (312) 353-9000

CNTY AID = Agency for International Development,, 320 21st St., NW, Washington, DC 20523

CNTY COMMERCE = Country Officers, International Trade Administration, U.S. Department of Commerce, Washington, DC 20230

CNTY MINES = Bureau of Mines, U.S. Department of Interior, Columbia Plaza, Washington, DC 20241

CNTY STATE = Department of State, 2201 C St., NW, Washington, DC 20520

CON PROD SAFE = Consumer Product Safety Commission, 5401 Westbard Ave., Bethesda, MD 20207

CUSTOMS = U.S. Customs, Department of Justice, 1301 Constitution Ave., NW, Washington, DC 20229

DAS = Division of Administrative Services, National Institutes of Health, NIH Building 1, Room 160, 9000 Rockville Pike, Bethesda, MD 20892

DC = District of Columbia

DCRT = Division of Computer Research and Technology, NIH, 9000 Rockville Pike, Bldg. 12, Room 3033, Bethesda, MD 20892

DEO = Division of Equal Opportunity, NIH, 9000 Rockville Pike, Bldg. 31, Room 2B40, Bethesda, MD 20892

DMCH = Division of Maternal and Child Health, HHS, 5600 Fishers Lane, Room 9-31, Rockville, MD 20857

DN = Division of Nursing, HHS, 5600 Fishers Lane, Room 5C-26, Rockville, MD 20857

DPCS = Division of Primary Care Services, HHS, 5600 Fishers Lane, Room 7A-55, Rockville, MD 20857

DPM = Division of Personnel Management, NIH, 9000 Rockville Pike, Bldg. 1, Room B1-60, Bethesda, MD 20892

DRG = Division of Research Grants, NIH, 4333 Westbard Ave., Room 450, Bethesda, MD 20892

DRR = Division of Research Resources, NIH, 9000 Rockville Pike, Bldg. 31, Room 5B03, Bethesda, MD 20892

DRS = Division of Research Services, NIH, 9000 Rockville Pike, Bldg. 12, Room 4007, Bethesda, MD 20892

ECONOMICS = Bureau of Economic Analysis, U.S. Department of Commerce, Washington, DC 20230

EPA = Environmental Protection Agency, 401 M St., SW, Washington, DC 20460

FAES = Foundation for Advanced Education in the Sciences, 1 Cloister Court, Suite 230, Bethesda, MD 20814-1460

FCC = Federal Communications Commission, 1919 M St., NW, Washington, DC 20554

FED TRADE COM = Federal Trade Commission (FTC), 6th St. and Pennsylvania Ave., NW, Washington, DC 20580

FIC = Fogarty International Center, NIH, 9000 Rockville Pike, Bldg. 38, Room 605A, Bethesda, MD 20892

GSA = General Services Administration, 18th and F Sts., NW, Washington, DC 20405

HRSA = Health Resources and Services Administration, HHS, 5600 Fishers Lane, Room 14-05, Rockville, MD 20857

HU = Howard University, 2400 6th St., NW, Washington, DC 20059

ITC = Office of Industries, U.S. International Trade Commission, 500 E St., SW, Washington, DC 20436

JUSTICE = National Institute of Justice, U.S. Department of Justice, 633 Indiana Ave., NW, Washington, DC 20531

LABOR = Bureau of Labor Statistics, U.S. Department of Labor, 441 G St., NW, Room 2822, Washington, DC 20212

MAPB = Medical Arts and Photography Branch, 9000 Rockville Pike, Bldg. 10, Room B2L326, Bethesda, MD 20892

MD = Maryland

MINES = Division of Mineral Commodities, Bureau of Mines, U.S. Department of Interior, Columbia Plaza, Washington, DC 20241

NASA = National Aeronautical and Space Administration, Washington, DC 20546

NCALI = National Clearinghouse for Alcohol Information, HHS, P.O. Box 2345, Rockville, MD 20852

NCDB = National Center for Drugs and Biologics, NIH, 9000 Rockville Pike, Bldg. 29, Room 130, Bethesda, MD 20892

NCDRH = National Center for Devices and Radiological Health, HHS, 5600 Fishers Lane, Rockville, MD 20857

NCEMCH = National Center for Education in Maternal and Child Health, 38th and R St., NW, Washington, DC 20057

NCHS = National Center for Health Statistics, HHS, 3700 East-West Hwy., Hyattsville, MD 20787

NCI = National Cancer Institute, NIH, 9000 Rockville Pike, Bldg. 31, Room 11A48, Bethesda, MD 20892

NCNR = National Center for Nursing Research, NIH, 9000 Rockville Pike, Bldg. 31, Room 5B03, Bethesda, MD 20892

NEI = National Eye Institute, NIH, 9000 Rockville Pike, Bldg. 31, Room 6A03B, Bethesda, MD 20892

NHLBI = National Heart, Lung, and Blood Institute, NIH, 9000 Rockville Pike, Bldg. 31, Room 5A52, Bethesda, MD 20892

NIA = National Institute on Aging, NIH, 9000 Rockville Pike, Bldg. 31, Room 2C02, Bethesda, MD 20892

NIAID = National Institute of Allergy and Infectious Diseases,NIH, 9000 Rockville Pike, Bldg. 31, Room 7A03C, Bethesda, MD 20892

NIAMS = National Institute of Arthritis and Musculoskeletal and Skin Diseases, 9000 Rockville Pike, Bldg. 31, Room 4C32, Bethesda, MD 20892

NICHD = National Institute of Child Health and Human Development, NIH, 9000 Rockville Pike, Bldg. 31, Room 2A03, Bethesda, MD 20892

NIDDK = National Institute of Diabetes and Digestive and Kidney Diseases, NIH, 9000 Rockville Pike, Bldg. 31, Room 9A52, Bethesda, MD 20892

NIDA = National Institute on Drug Abuse, HHS, 5600 Fishers Lane, Room 10-05, Rockville, MD 20857

NIDR = National Institute of Dental Research, NIH, 9000 Rockville Pike, Bldg. 31, Room 2C39, Bethesda, MD 20892

NIEHS = National Institute of Environmental Health Sciences, NIH, P.O. Box 12233, Research Triangle Park, NC 27709

NIGMS = National Institute of General Medical Sciences, NIH, 5333 Westbard Ave., Room 926, Bethesda, MD 20892

NIH = National Institutes of Health, 9000 Rockville Pike, Bldg. 1, Room 126, Bethesda, MD 20892

NIMH = National Institute of Mental Health, NIH, 5600 Fishers Lane, Room 17-99, Rockville, MD 20857

NINCDS = National Institute of Neurological and Communicative Disorders and Stroke, 9000 Rockville Pike, Bldg. 31, Room 8A52A, Bethesda, MD 20892

NIOSH = National Institute for Occupational Safety and Health, 1600 Clifton Rd., NE, Room 3007, Atlanta, GA 30333

NLM = National Library of Medicine, 9000 Rockville Pike, Bldg. 38, Room 2510, Bethesda, MD 20892

NTP = National Toxicology Program, P.O. Box 12233, Research Triangle Park, NC 27709

OASH = Office of the Assistant Secretary for Health, HHS, 200 Independence Ave., SW, Room 716G, Washington, DC 20201

OB = Office of Biologics, NIH, 9000 Rockville Pike, Bldg. 29, Room 122A, Bethesda, MD 20892

OC = Office of Communications, NIH, 9000 Rockville Pike, Bldg. 1, Room 344, Bethesda, MD 20892

OD = Office of the Director, NIH, 9000 Rockville Pike, Bldg. 1, Room 126, Bethesda, MD 20892

OERT = Office of Extramural Research and Training, NIH, P.O. Box 12233, Research Triangle Park, NC 27709

OHDS = Office of Human Development Services, HHS, 200 Independence Ave., SW, Room 309F, Washington, DC 20201

OPRR = Office for Protection from Research Risks, NIH, 9000 Rockville Pike, Bldg. 31, Room 5B59, Bethesda, MD 20892

ORS = Office of Research Services, NIH, 9000 Rockville Pike, Bldg. 1, Room 160, Bethesda, MD 20892

PHS = Public Health Service, HHS, 200 Independence Ave., SW, Room 716G, Washington, DC 20201

U MD = University of Maryland, University of Maryland-College Park, College Park, MD 20742

US TRADE REP = Office of the U.S. Trade Representative, 600 17th St., NW, Washington, DC 20506

U VA = University of Virginia, Charlottesville, VA 22903

VA = Virginia

VIC = Visitor Information Center, NIH, 9000 Rockville Pike, Bldg. 10, Room B1C218, Bethesda, MD 20892

VRB = Veterinary Resources Branch, NIH, 9000 Rockville Pike, Bldg. 14, Room 102, Bethesda, MD 20892

A

ABS resins....Taylor, Ed   USITC   202-252-1362
ACTH, Excessive Secretion....Staff   NHLBI   301-496-4236
ADP Support, Aerospace....Westover, Harlan   Commerce   202-377-3068
AIDS....Staff   PHS   800-843-9388
AIDS....Staff   NIAID   301-496-5717
AIDS....Staff   NCI   301-496-5583
AIDS....Staff   NIAID   301-496-5717
AIDS....Staff   NCI   301-496-5583
AIDS (Pediatric)....Staff   NICHD   301-496-5133
AIDS - PHS....Staff   PHS   800-843-9388
AIDS, Neurological Symptoms or Effects of....Staff   NINCDS   301-496-5751
AIDS-Control of Symptoms....Staff   NCNR   301-496-0526
AM Intercity Relays -FCC....staff   FCC   202-634-6307
AM Radio Advertising....Staff   FCC   202-632-7551
AM Radio Assignment & Transfer Applications....Staff   FCC   202-254-9470
AM Radio Construction Permit Applications....Staff   FCC   202-254-9570
AM Radio Radio Programming....Staff   FCC   202-632-7048
AM Radio Station--New....Staff   FCC   202-254-9570
AM Radio Stations....Staff   FCC   202-632-7010
AM Remote Pickups....Staff   FCC   202-634-6307
ARC (AIDS-Related Complex)....Staff   NIAID   301-496-5717
ASEAN....Linda Droker   Cnty Commerce   202-377-3875
Abaca....Cook, Lee   USITC   202-252-1471
Abortion....Staff   NCHS   301-436-8500
Abortion....Staff   CDC   404-329-3535
Abrasion (Corneal)....Staff   NEI   301-496-5248
Abrasive....White, Linda A.   USITC   202-252-1427
Abrasive Products....Presbury, Graylin   Commerce   202-377-5157
Abrasives....Bunin, J.   Customs   212-466-5796
Abrasives, Manmade....Austin, Gordon   Mines   202-634-1206
Abrasives, Natural...Austin, Gordon   Mines   202-634-1206
Access Charge Rules and Policies....Staff   FCC   202-632-9342
Access Charge Tariff....Staff   FCC   202-632-6387
Accident Prevention and the Elderly....Staff   NIA   301-496-1752
Accident Statistics....Staff   NCHS   301-496-8500
Accident Statistics....Staff   CDC   404-329-3534
Accidental releases....William J. Rhodes   EPA   919-541-2853
Accounting....McAdam, Milton B.   Commerce   202-377-0346
Accreditation (Health Professions)....Staff   HRSA/BHPr   301-443-6853
Accreditation (Nurse Training)....Staff   HRSA/BHPr   301-443-5786
Acetal resins....Taylor, Ed   USITC   202-252-1362
Acetates....Michels, David   USITC   202-252-1352
Acetic acid....Michels, David   USITC   202-252-1352
Acetone....Michels, David   USITC   202-252-1352
Acetoricinoleic acid ester....Johnson, Larry   USITC   202-252-1351
Achondroplasia....Staff   NICHD   301-496-5133
Acid deposition....Mike Barnes   EPA   919-541-2184
Acid rain....Michael A. Maxwell   EPA   919-541-3091
Acid rain - biological...John G. Eaton   EPA   218-720-5557
Acid rain effects....Robert T. Lackey   EPA   503-757-4634
Acid, oleic....Randall, Rob   USITC   202-252-1366
Acid, stearic....Randall, Rob   USITC   202-252-1366
Acidosis....Staff   NICHD   301-496-5133
Acids, inorganic....Trainor, Cynthia   USITC   202-252-1354
Acne....Staff   NIAMS   301-496-8188
Acne (Cystic)....Staff   NCI   301-496-5583
Acne (Cystic)....Staff   NIAMS   301-496-8188
Acoustic Neuroma....Staff   NINCDS   301-496-5751
Acoustics/Measurements....Harlan Holmes   NASA   804-865-3483
Acquired Immune Deficiency Syndrome (AIDS)....Staff   NIAID   301-496-5717
Acquired Immune Deficiency Syndrome (AIDS)....Staff   NCI   301-496-5583
Acquired Immune Deficiency Syndrome (AIDS)....Staff   PHS   301-843-9388
Acromegaly....Staff   NIDDK   301-496-3583
Acrylates....Michels, David   USITC   202-252-1352
Acrylic resins....Taylor, Ed   USITC   202-252-1362
Acrylonitrile....Michels, David   USITC   202-252-1352
Activated carbon....Randall, Bob   USITC   202-252-1366
Activated carbon adsorption....Richard Miltner   EPA   513-569-7403
Acupuncture....Staff   NINCDS   301-496-5751
Acute Hemorrhagic Conjunctivitis....Staff   NEI   301-496-5248

Acute Leukemia....Staff   NCI   301-496-5583
Acyclic plasticzers....Johnson, Larry   USITC   202-252-1351
Adaptation and Functioning in Chronic Illness....Staff   NCNR   301-496-0526
Adding Machines....Fletcher, William   USITC   202-252-1407
Addison's Disease....Staff   NIDDK   301-496-3583
Adenoma of the Thyroid....Staff   NIDDK   301-496-3583
Adherence to Therapeutic Regimens....Staff   NCNR   301-496-0526
Adhesives....Randall, Rob   USITC   202-252-1366
Adhesives/Sealants....Prat, Raimundo   Commerce   202-377-0128
Adipic acid esters...Johnson, Larry   USITC   202-252-1351
Adjudication...Bernard Auchter   Justice   202-724-7684
Adjudication...Jay Merrill   Justice   202-724-2959
Adjudication...Richard Rau   Justice   202-724-2951
Adjudication...Lauresa Stillwell   Justice   202-724-2962
Adjudication...Fred Heinzelmann   Justice   202-724-2949
Adjudication...Cheryl Martorana   Justice   202-724-2965
Adjudication...John Spevacek   Justice   202-272-6010
Adjudication...Martin Lively   Justice   202-724-2966
Adjudication...Patrick Langan   Justice Stat   202-724-7774
Adjudication...Carla Gaskins   Justice Stat   202-724-7774
Admission (Health Professions Schools)....Staff   BHPr   301-443-2060
Admission Procedures (Patient)....Staff   CC   301-496-4891
Adolescence....Staff   NIMH   301-443-4515
Adolescence....Staff   NICHD   301-496-5133
Adolescent Pregnancy....Staff   NICHD   301-496-5133
Adoption....Staff   OHDS/ACYF   301-426-2822
Adrenal Gland....Staff   NIDDK   301-496-3583
Adrenoleukodystrophy....Staff   NINCDS   301-496-5751
Advanced ATC/Aircraft Interaction....Bill Howell   NASA   804-865-2224
Advanced Adaptive Wall Wind Tunnel Instrumentation....George Lee   NASA   415-694-5861
Advanced Aircraft Systems....Samuel Dollyhigh   NASA   804-865-3294
Advanced Composite Mechanics....Christos Chamis   NASA   216-433-3252
Advanced Composite Structures, Computational Struc....James Starnes   NASA   804-865-2552
Advanced Computer Graphics....John Hogge   NASA   804-865-3547
Advanced Control Display Technology....Jack Hatfield   NASA   804-865-3777
Advanced Controls, Guidance, and Flight Computer....Wayne Bryant   NASA   804-865-3535
Advanced Development (Life Sciences)....Roger Arno   NASA   415-694-6640
Advanced Digital Flight Control....Kevin Peterson   NASA   805-258-3189
Advanced Electronics Systems....Glenn Taylor   NASA   804-865-3541
Advanced Instrumentation...Joseph Marvin   NASA   415-694-5390
Advanced Light Alloy and Metal Matrix Composites....Barry Lisagor   NASA   804-865-2036
Advanced Materials....Sorrell, Charles   Mines   202-634-4773
Advanced Military A/C and Missiles....Wallace Sawyer   NASA   804-865-2658
Advanced Programs (Engineering)....Robert Reid   NASA   713-483-6606
Advanced Studies....Staff   FIC   301-496-2516
Advanced Test Techniques....Robert Kilgore   NASA   804-865-3713
Advanced Training (Registered Nurse)....Staff   BHPr   301-443-5786
Advanced Turboprops Noise Reduction....William Henderson   NASA   804-865-2676
Advertising....Umstead, Dwight   Commerce   202-377-3050
Advertising & Labeling...Judith Wilkenfeld   Fed Trade Com   202-326-3150
Advertising Allowances, Evaluation....Staff   Fed Trade Com   202-326-3300
Advertising Substantiation, Advertising Practices....Staff   Fed Trade Com   202-326-3076
Advertising by Professions....Matthew Daynard   Fed Trade Com   202-326-3291
Advertising, Credit Practices....Staff   Fed Trade Com   202-326-3175
Adynamia....Staff   NINCDS   301-496-5751
Aerial Cable....Staff   FCC   202-634-1800
Aero-space Plane Propulsion and Airframe Structura....Donald Rummler   NASA   804-865-3451
Aeroacoustics....S. Paul Pao   NASA   804-865-2645
Aerodynamics and Handling Qualities (Gen. Aviation....Joseph Johnson   NASA   804-865-2184
Aeronautics....Don Ehrreich   NASA   415-694-5067
Aerosol chemistry....William E. Wilson   EPA   919-541-2551

Aerosols & inhalation toxicology....Judith Graham EPA
919-541-4159
Aerospace Applications of High-Temperature Superco....Denis
Conolly NASA 216-433-3503
Aerospace Financing Issues....Zakour, Charlotte Commerce
202-377-8228
Aerospace Industry Analysis....Kingsbury, Gene Commerce
202-377-0678
Aerospace Industry Data....Kingsburg, Gene Commerce
202-377-0678
Aerospace Information and Analysis....Kingsbury, Gene Commerce
202-377-0678
Aerospace Market Development....Bowie, David C. Commerce
202-377-8228
Aerospace Market Promo.....Sarsfield, Claudette Commerce
202-377-2835
Aerospace Market Promo.....White, John Commerce 202-377-2835
Aerospace Marketing Support....Driscoll, George Commerce
202-377-8228
Aerospace Policy and Analysis....Bath, Sally M. Commerce
202-377-8228
Aerospace Trade Policy Issues....Bath, Sally Commerce
202-377-8228
Aerospace Trade Promo.....White, John C. Commerce
202-377-3353
Aerospace, Space Market Support....Bowie, David C. Commerce
202-377-8228
Aerospace, Space Programs....Bowie, David C. Commerce
202-377-8228
Aerothermal Materials and Structures....Howard Goldstein NASA
415-694-6103
Aerothermodynamics....George Deiwert NASA 415-694-6198
Afghanistan....Stan Bilinski Cnty Commerce 202-377-2954
Afghanistan (Kabul)...James Bruno Cnty State 202-647-9552
Afghanistan (Kabul)...Steven Ghitelman Cnty State 202-647-9552
Afghanistan (Kabul)...Desiree Milliken Cnty AID 202-647-9552
Afghanistan/Minerals....David Yen Cnty Mines 202-634-9799
Africa/trade matters....Staff US Trade Rep 202-395-6135
Agammaglobulinemia....Staff NIAID 301-496-5717
Agar agar....Jonnard, Aimison USITC 202-252-1350
Age Search....Census History Staff Census 301-763-7936
Age, States....Staff Census 301-763-7950
Age, U.S.....Staff Census 301-763-7950
Ageism....Staff NIA 301-496-1752
Agglomerating machinery....Green, William USITC 202-252-1405
Aging....Staff NIA 301-496-1752
Aging (Mental Health)....Staff NIMH 301-443-4515
Aging Population....Golstein, Arnold Census 301-763-7883
Aging Related Research....Staff NCNR 301-496-0526
Aging-Related Maculopathy....Staff NEI 301-496-5248
Agribusiness, Major Proj.....Bell, Richard Commerce 202-377-4146
Agricultural Chemicals....Maxey, Francis P. Commerce
202-377-0128
Agricultural History, Economics....Bowers, Douglas Agri
202-786-1896
Agricultural Labor, Economics....Coltrane, Robert Agri
202-786-1932
Agricultural Machinery....Weining, Mary Commerce 202-377-4708
Agricultural Machinery, Trade Promo.....Weining, Mary Commerce
202-377-4708
Agricultural implement....O'Connell, W. Customs 212-466-5668
Agricultural machinery....Lippa, Alison USITC 202-252-1398
Agriculture Division....Pautler, Charles Census 301-763-8555
Agriculture and Commodities/trade matters....Staff US Trade Rep
202-395-6127
Agriculture, Community Linkages, Economics....Hines, Fred Agri
202-786-1525
Agriculture, Crop Statistics....Jahnke, Donald Census 301-763-8567
Agriculture, Farm Economics....Liefer, James A. Census
301-763-8566
Agriculture, General Information....Prout, Brenda Census
301-763-1113
Agriculture, Guam....Hoover, Kent Census 301-763-8564
Agriculture, Livestock Statistics....Monroe, Thomas Census
301-763-8569
Agriculture, No. Marianas....Hoover, Kent Census 301-763-8564
Agriculture, Puerto Rico....Hoover, Kent Census 301-763-8564
Agriculture, State - Alabama, Montgomery....Dantzler, M. L. Agri
205-832-7263
Agriculture, State - Alaska, Palmer....Brown, D.A. Agri
907-745-4272
Agriculture, State - Arizona, Phoenix....Bloyd, B. L. Agri
602-241-2573
Agriculture, State - Arkansas, Little Rock....Von Steen, D. H. Agri
501-378-5145
Agriculture, State - California, Sacramento....Tippett, H. J. Agri
916-551-1533
Agriculture, State - Colorado, Denver....Hudson, C. A. Agri

303-964-0250
Agriculture, State - Connecticut....Hammond, C. W. Agri
603-224-9639
Agriculture, State - Florida, Orlando....Freie, R. L. Agri
305-648-6013
Agriculture, State - Georgia, Athens....Snipes, L. E. Agri
404-546-2236
Agriculture, State - Hawaii, Honolulu....Davis, Jr., A.R. Agri
808-548-7155
Agriculture, State - Idaho, Boise....Max, R. C. Agri 208-334-1507
Agriculture, State - Illinois, Springfield....Barrett, F. S. Agri
217-492-4295
Agriculture, State - Indiana, West Lafayette....Gann, R. W. Agri
317-494-8371
Agriculture, State - Iowa, Des Moines....Skow, D. M. Agri
515-284-4340
Agriculture, State - Kansas, Topeka....Johnson, M. E. Agri
913-295-2600
Agriculture, State - Kentucky, Louisville....Williamson, D. D. Agri
502-582-5293
Agriculture, State - Louisiana, Alexandria....Nelson, B. A. Agri
318-473-7971
Agriculture, State - Maine....Hammond, C. W. Agri 603-224-9639
Agriculture, State - Massachusetts....Hammond, C. W. Agri
603-224-9639
Agriculture, State - Michigan, Lansing....Fedewa, D. J. Agri
517-377-1831
Agriculture, State - Minnesota, St. Paul....Rock, C. G. Agri
612-296-2230
Agriculture, State - Mississippi, Jackson....Knight, G. R. Agri
601-965-4575
Agriculture, State - Missouri, Columbia....Bay, D. M. Agri
314-875-5233
Agriculture, State - Montana, Helena....Pratt, L. H. Agri
406-449-5303
Agriculture, State - Nebraska, Lincoln....Aschwege, J. L. Agri
402-471-5541
Agriculture, State - Nevada, Reno....Lies, C. R. Agri 702-784-5584
Agriculture, State - New Hampshire, Concord....Hammond, C. W.
Agri 603-224-9639
Agriculture, State - New Jersey, Trenton....Gibson, J. R. Agri
609-292-6385
Agriculture, State - New Mexico, Las Cruces....Gerhardt, D. G.
Agri 505-523-6168
Agriculture, State - New York, Albany....Suter, G. W. Agri
518-457-5570
Agriculture, State - North Carolina, Raleigh....Olson, J. L. Agri
919-856-4394
Agriculture, State - North Dakota, Fargo....Carver, R. F. Agri
701-237-5771
Agriculture, State - Ohio, Columbus....Carter, H. S. Agri
614-469-5590
Agriculture, State - Oklahoma, Oklahoma City....Bellinghausen, R. P.
Agri 405-525-9226
Agriculture, State - Oregon, Portland....Williamson, P. M. Agri
503-221-2131
Agriculture, State - Pennsylvania, Harrisburg....Evans, W. C. Agri
717-787-3904
Agriculture, State - Rhode Island....Hammond, C. W. Agri
603-224-9639
Agriculture, State - South Carolina, Columbia....Power, H. J. Agri
803-765-5333
Agriculture, State - South Dakota, Sioux Falls....Ranek, J. C. Agri
605-336-2980
Agriculture, State - Tennessee, Nashville....Brantner, C. R. Agri
615-736-5136
Agriculture, State - Texas, Austin....Findley, D. S. Agri
512-482-5581
Agriculture, State - Utah, Salt Lake City....Gneiting, D. J. Agri
301-524-5003
Agriculture, State - Vermont....Hammond, C. W. Agri
603-224-9639
Agriculture, State - Virginia, Richmond....Dunkerley, C. A. Agri
804-786-3500
Agriculture, State - Washington, Olympia....Hasslen, D. A. Agri
206-586-8919
Agriculture, State - West Virginia, Charleston....Brueggen, J. J.
Agri 304-348-2217
Agriculture, State - Wisconsin, Madison....Spencer, C. D. Agri
608-264-5317
Agriculture, State - Wyoming, Cheyenne....Hundley, S. J. Agri
307-772-2181
Agriculture, State-Maryland, Annapolis (Delaware)....West, M. B.
Agri 301-841-5740
Agriculture, Virgin Islands....Hoover, Kent Census 301-763-8564
Air & energy environmental assessment & control....Frank T.
Princiotta EPA 919-541-2821
Air Compressors, Gas....McDonald, Edward Commerce

202-377-0680
Air Conditioning Equipment....Shaw, Eugene
    Commerce 202-377-3494
Air Gas Compressors, Trade Promo.....Zanetakos, George
    Commerce 202-377-0552
Air Pollution....Staff EPA 301-382-7645
Air Pollution....Staff EPA 301-382-5575
Air Pollution Control Equipment....Jonkers, Loretta Commerce
    202-377-0564
Air Traffic Control (Market Support)....Driscoll, George
    Commerce 202-377-8228
Air Treatment Devices....Staff OD/ORS 301-496-2960
Air conditioners....Mata, Ruben USITC 202-252-1403
Air monitoring....Thomas Hartledge EPA 919-541-3008
Air monitoring....Barry Martin EPA 919-541-4386
Air pollutants, toxicologic & carcinogenic effects....Charalingayya
    Hiremath EPA 202-382-5898
Air pollution effects on vegetation....Christian P. Andersen EPA
    503-757-4605
Air pollution effects on vegetation....William E. Hogsett, III EPA
    503-757-4632
Air pollution effects on vegetation....David T. Tingey EPA
    503-757-4621
Air pollution effects on vegetation....James A. Weber EPA
    503-757-4503
Air quality data....Thomas McMullen EPA 919-541-4150
Air toxics control....Wade H. Ponder EPA 919-541-2818
Airborne Detection of Wind Shear Research....Roland Bowles
    NASA 804-865-3621
Airborne Science....Phil Russell NASA 415-694-5404
Aircraft....Andersen, Peder USITC 202-252-1388
Aircraft Aeroelasticity....Rodney Ricketts NASA 804-865-2960
Aircraft Automation....Lee Duke NASA 805-258-3802
Aircraft Auxiliary Equipment, Market Support....Driscoll, George
    Commerce 202-377-8228
Aircraft Conceptual Design....Thomas Galloway NASA
    415-694-6181
Aircraft Engines, Market Support....Driscoll, George Commerce
    202-377-8228
Aircraft Engines, Trade Promo.....White, John C. Commerce
    202-377-3353
Aircraft Engines, Trade Promo....Grafeld, George Commerce
    202-377-3353
Aircraft Equipment, Trade Promo.....Grafeld, George Commerce
    202-377-3353
Aircraft Icing....John Reinmann NASA 216-433-3900
Aircraft Parts, Market Support....Driscoll, George Commerce
    202-377-8228
Aircraft Parts, Trade Promo/Aux Equipment....White, John C.
    Commerce 202-377-3353
Aircraft Propulsion Systems Analysis....Daniel Mikkelson NASA
    216-433-5637
Aircraft Safety and Crash Survivability....John Tanner NASA
    804-865-2796
Aircraft power Transfer Technology....John Coy NASA
    216-433-3915
Aircrafts....Dicerbo, M. Customs 212-466-5672
Airfoil Aerodynamics....William Harvey NASA 804-865-2631
Airlines....Miller, Randall E. Commerce 202-377-5071
Airport Equipment, Market Support....Driscoll, George Commerce
    202-377-8228
Airport Equipment, Trade Promo.....White, John C. Commerce
    202-377-3353
Airports, Ports, Harbors, Major Projects....Piggot, Deborne
    Commerce 202-377-3352
Albania....John A. Cloud, Jr. Cnty State 202-647-3298
Albania....Diana M. Montgomery Cnty State 202-647-3052
Albania....William Warren Cnty AID 202-647-1457
Albania....Vacant Cnty Commerce 202-377-2645
Albania\Minerals....Walter Steblez Cnty Mines 202-632-5047
Albinism (Eyes)....Staff NEI 301-496-5248
Albright's Syndrome....Staff NIAMS 301-496-8188
Albums (autograph, photograph)....Stahmer, Carsten USITC
    202-252-1321
Alcohol....Staff ADAMHA 301-443-4883
Alcohol....Staff NCALI 301-468-2600
Alcohol (and Cancer)....Staff NCI 301-496-5583
Alcohol and Aging....Staff NIA 301-496-1752
Alcohol and Aging....Staff NCALI 301-468-2600
Alcohol and Aging....Staff ADAMHA 301-443-4883
Alcohol, oleyl....Randall, Rob USITC 202-252-1366
Alcoholism....Staff ADAMHA 301-443-4883
Alcoholism....Staff NCALI 301-468-2600
Alcohols....Michels, David USITC 202-252-1352
Alcohols, polyhydric, fatty acids....Land, Eric USITC 202-252-1349
Aldehydes....Michels, David USITC 202-252-1352
Aldosteronism....Staff NHLBI 301-496-4236
Alexander's Syndrome....Staff NINCDS 301-496-5751

Algae....R.L. Steele EPA 401-782-3000
Algeria....Jeffrey Johnson Cnty Commerce 202-377-4652
Algeria (Algiers)....Kathleen Fitzpatrick Cnty State 202-647-4680
Algeria (Algiers)....Richard Delaney Cnty AID 202-647-9001
Algeria/Minerals....Bernadette Michalski Cnty Mines 202-632-5065
Alien Restricted Permits....Staff FCC 202-632-7240
Alkaloids....Nesbitt, Elizabeth USITC 202-252-1355
Alkaptonuria....Staff NHLBI 301-496-4236
Alkylating Agents....Staff NCI 301-496-5583
Allergies....Staff NIAID 301-496-5717
Allergies (Eyes)....Staff NEI 301-496-5248
Allied Health Manpower....Staff HRSA/BHPr 301-443-6853
Allied Health Professions....Staff HRSA/BHPr 301-443-5794
Allied Health Workers....Staff HRSA/BHPr 301-443-5794
Alloying Metals and Vapor Crystal Growth Evaluatio....J. Lindsay
    NASA 205-544-1301
Almonds....Burket, Stephen USITC 202-252-1318
Alopecia....Staff NIAMS 301-496-8188
Alpaca....Freund, Kimberlie USITC 202-252-1456
Alpers Syndrome....Staff NINCDS 301-496-5751
Alpha-1-antitrypsin Deficiency....Staff NIDDK 301-496-3583
Alpha-1-antitrypsin Deficiency....Staff NHLBI 301-496-4236
Alternate energy....Foreso, Cynthia USITC 202-252-1348
Alum. Forgings, Electro....Cammarota, David Commerce
    202-377-0575
Alum. Sheet, Plate/Foil....Cammarota, David Commerce
    202-377-0575
Aluminum....McNay, Deborah USITC 202-252-1425
Aluminum....Plunkert, Patricia Mines 202-634-1080
Aluminum....Fitzgerald, J. Customs 212-466-5492
Aluminum Extrud. Alum Rolling....Cammarota, David Commerce
    202-377-0575
Aluminum Futures....Helen Cadden Comm Futures 212-668-2081
Aluminum compounds....Greenblatt, Jack USITC 202-252-1352
Alveolar Bone (Regeneration/Resorption)....Staff NIDR
    301-496-4261
Alveolar Microlithiasis....Staff NHLBI 301-496-4236
Alveolar Proteinosis....Staff NHLBI 301-496-4236
Alzheimer's Disease....Staff NIA 301-496-1752
Alzheimer's Disease....Staff NINCDS 301-496-5751
Alzheimer's Disease....Staff NIMH 301-443-4513
Alzheimer's Disease....Staff NCNR 301-496-0526
Amateur Licenses....Staff FCC 717-337-1212
Amaurotic Idiocy....Staff NINCDS 301-496-5751
Ambergris....Land, Eric USITC 202-252-1349
Amblyopia....Staff NEI 301-496-5248
Ambulance & Rescue Squads....Staff FCC 717-337-1212
Amebiasis....Staff NIAID 301-496-5717
American Nurses' Association....Staff 816-474-5720
American fisheries products....Corey, Roger USITC 202-252-1327
Amides....Michels, David USITC 202-252-1352
Amides, fatty acids of....Land, Eric USITC 202-252-1349
Amines....Michels, David USITC 202-252-1352
Amines, fatty acids of....Land, Eric USITC 202-252-1349
Amino Acid Disorders....Staff NICHD 301-496-5133
Amino acids....Michels, David USITC 202-252-1352
Ammonia....Trainor, Cynthia USITC 202-252-1354
Ammonia....Russell J. Erickson EPA 218-720-5534
Ammonia/nitrite toxicity to aquatic organisms....Rosemarie C. Russo
    EPA 404-546-3134
Ammonium nitrate, fuel-sensitized....Johnson, Larry USITC
    202-252-1351
Ammonium nitrate, non-explosive or non-fertilizer....Greenblatt,
    Jack USITC 202-252-1353
Ammonium phosphate....Greenblatt, Jack USITC 202-252-1353
Ammonium sulfate....Greenblatt, Jack USITC 202-252-1353
Ammunition....Robinson, Hazel USITC 202-252-1355
Ammunitions Ex. Small Arms Nec, Trade Promo.....Cummings,
    Charles Commerce 202-377-5361
Amniocentesis....Staff NICHD 301-496-5133
Amonium nitrate, fertilizer....Trainor, Cynthia USITC
    202-252-1354
Amyloid Polyneuropathy....Staff NIADDK 301-496-8188
Amyloidosis....Staff NIADDK 301-496-3583
Amyloidosis....Staff NAIMS 301-496-8188
Amyloidosis....Staff NEI 301-496-5248
Amyotonia Congenita....Staff NINCDS 301-496-5751
Amyotrophic Lateral Sclerosis....Staff NIDDK 301-496-5924
Analgesic-Associated Nephropathy....Staff NIDDK 301-496-3583
Analgesics....Nesbitt, Elizabeth USITC 202-252-1355
Analytical Chemistry....Staff NIGMS 301-496-7301
Analytical Instrument (Trade Promo)....Gwaltney, G.P. Commerce
    202-377-3090
Analytical Instruments....Donnelly, Margaret Commerce
    202-377-5466
Analytical chemistry....Ronald K. Mitchum EPA 702-798-2103
Analytical chemistry....Jimmie D. Petty EPA 702-798-2383
Analytical chemistry....Fred Pfeffer EPA 405-332-2305

Analytical chemistry....Bert Bledsoe   EPA 405-332-2324
Analytical chemistry....James C. Moore   EPA 904-932-5311
Analytical chemistry....Leonard H. Mueller   EPA 904-932-5311
Analytical environmental chemistry....Eugene P. Meier   EPA
   702-798-2237
Analytical methods development....Nancy Wilson   EPA
   919-541-4723
Anaplasis....Staff   NCI 301-496-5583
Andalusite....Lukes, James   USITC 202-252-1426
Andorra....Mary Daly   Cnty State 202-647-1412
Andorra....James Swigert   Cnty State 202-647-1412
Andorra....J. Michael Lekson   Cnty AID 202-647-2633
Anemia....Staff   NIDDK 301-496-3583
Anemia (Hemolytic and Aplastic)....Staff   NCI 301-496-5583
Anemia (Hemolytic and Aplastic)....Staff   NHLBI 301-496-4236
Anemia (Hemolytic and Aplastic)....Staff   NIAID 301-496-5717
Anencephaly....Staff   NINCDS 301-496-5751
Anesthesiology....Staff   NIGMS 301-496-7301
Anesthesiology (Dental)....Staff   NIDR 301-496-4261
Anesthesiology (Pain Therapy)....Staff   CC 301-496-5666
Anesthetist (Nurse)....Staff   HRSA/BHPr 301-443-2134
Aneurysm....Staff   NHLBI 301-496-4236
Aneurysm (Brain or Cerebral)....Staff   NINCDS 301-496-5751
Angina Pectoris....Staff   NHLBI 301-496-4236
Angioedema....Staff   NIAID 301-496-5717
Angiography....Staff   NHLBI 301-496-4235
Angiography....Staff   NHLBI 301-496-4236
Angles, shapes, and sections (steel)....Paulson, Mark   USITC
   202-252-1432
Angola....John Crown   Cnty Commerce 202-377-0357
Angola (Luanda)....Michael McKinley   Cnty State 202-647-9429
Angola (Luanda)....Gerard M. Galluci   Cnty AID 202-647-9429
Angola (Luanda)....Cheryl Anderson   Cnty AID 202-647-4230
Angola/Minerals....Hendrik van Oss   Cnty Mines 202-632-5065
Angora....Freund, Kimberlie   USITC 202-252-1456
Anguilla (The Valley)....Avon Williams   Cnty State 202-647-2621
Aniline Dyes (and Cancer)....Staff   NCI 301-496-5583
Animal (Caging, Housing, Watering)....Staff   DRR 301-496-5175
Animal Bedding....Staff   OD/DAS 301-496-1160
Animal Care Technician Training....Staff   DRS 301-496-2527
Animal Colonies and Models (Special)....Staff   DRR 301-496-5175
Animal Facilities....Staff   DRS/VRB 301-496-2527
Animal Feed....Janis, William V.   Commerce 202-377-2250
Animal Food....Staff   OD/DAS 301-496-1160
Animal Genetics....Staff   DRS/VRB 301-496-4481
Animal Health....Staff   DRS/VRB 301-496-4463
Animal Holding (Rodent and Rabbit)....Staff   DRS/VRB
   301-496-4481
Animal Husbandry....Staff   DRS/VRB 301-496-2527
Animal Models for Aging Research....Staff   NIA 301-496-1752
Animal Nutrition....Staff   DRS/VRB 301-496-4481
Animal Research....Staff   DRR 301-496-5545
Animal Research....Staff   OD/DC 301-496-8740
Animal Research (Intramural)....Staff   DRS/VRB 301-496-5795
Animal Research (Intramural)....Staff   OD/DC 301-496-8740
Animal Resources Program....Staff   DRR 301-496-5175
Animal Sanitation....Staff   ID/ORS 301-496-2960
Animal Welfare....Staff   DRR 301-496-5545
Animal Welfare....Staff   OD/DC 301-496-2535
Animal Welfare Policy....Staff   OPRR 301-496-7163
Animal feeds....Pierre-Benoist, John   USITC 202-252-1320
Animal feeds....Conte, R.   Customs 212-466-5881
Animal oil, fats, greases....Reeder, John   USITC 202-252-1319
Animals, live....Ludwick, David   USITC 202-252-1329
Animals, live....Persky, H.   Customs 212-466-5881
Animals: Guide for the Care and Use of Lab Animals....Staff   DRR
   301-496-5545
Aniridia....Staff   NEI 301-496-5248
Ankylosing Spondylitis....Staff   NIAMS 301-496-8188
Anorexia Nervosa....Staff   NICHD 301-496-5133
Anorexia Nervosa....Staff   NIMH 301-496-4515
Anosmia....Staff   NINCDS 301-496-5751
Anoxia....Staff   NHLBI 301-496-4236
Antenatal Diagnosis....Staff   NICHD 301-496-5133
Antenna Structures & Towers....Staff   FCc 202-634-7521
Anthracite....Foreso, Cynthia   USITC 202-252-1348
Anthrax....Staff   NIAID 301-496-5717
Anti-infective agents....Nesbitt, Elizabeth   USITC 202-252-1355
Anti-inflammatory agents....Nesbitt, Elizabeth   USITC 202-252-1355
Antialphatrypsin....Staff   NIDDK 301-496-3583
Anticoagulant Drugs....Staff   NHLBI 301-496-4236
Anticoagulants (Native)....Staff   NIDDK 301-496-3583
Anticonvulsants....Nesbitt, Elizabeth   USITC 202-252-1355
Antidiuretic Hormone....Staff   NIDDK 301-496-3583
Antidiuretic Hormone....Staff   NHLBI 301-496-4236
Antigua and Barbuda (St. John's)....Avon Williams   Cnty State
   202-647-2621
Antigua and Barbuda (St. John's)....John Foarde   Cnty AID

   202-647-7851
Antihistamines....Nesbitt, Elizabeth   USITC 202-252-1355
Antimetabolites....Staff   NCI 301-496-5583
Antimony....Wagner, Lorie   USITC 202-252-1439
Antimony....Llewellyn, Thomas   Mines 202-634-1084
Antimony compounds....Greenblatt, Jack   USITC 202-252-1353
Antipyretics....Nesbitt, Elizabeth   USITC 202-252-1355
Antiques....Spalding, Josephine   USITC 202-252-1498
Antiques....Mushinske, L.   Customs 212-466-5739
Antisocial Behavior....Staff   NIMH 301-496-4515
Antitrust, Insurance....Michael Antalics   Fed Trade Com
   202-326-2682
Antiviral Substances....Staff   NIAID 301-496-5717
Aorta....Staff   NHLBI 301-496-4236
Aortic Insufficiency/Stenosis....Staff   NHLBI 301-496-4236
Aortic Valve....Staff   NHLBI 301-496-4236
Aortitis....Staff   NHLBI 301-496-4236
Apes and Monkeys (Medical Research)....Staff   DRR 301-496-5545
Aphakia....Staff   NEI 301-496-5248
Aphasia....Staff   NINCDS 301-496-5751
Aphthous Stomatitis-Recurrent....Staff   NIDR 301-496-4261
Aplastic Anemia....Staff   NHLBI 301-496-4236
Apparel....Dulka, William   Commerce 202-377-4058
Appliance Labeling....Ronald Rowe   Fed Trade Com 202-326-2610
Appliances Labeling....James Mills   Fed Trade Com 202-326-3035
Appliances, Household....Harris, John M.   Commerce 202-377-1178
Appliances, Household, Export Promo.....Johnson, Charles E.
   Commerce 202-377-3422
Applied Computational Fluid Dynamics....Terry Holst   NASA
   415-694-6032
Apportionment....Speaker, Robert   Census 301-763-7962
Apraxia....Staff   NINCDS 301-496-5751
Aquatic biology....Cornelius Weber   EPA 513-527-8350
Aquatic biology....Donald L. Brockway   EPA 404-546-3422
Aquatic ecology....Frank G. Wilkes   EPA 904-932-5311
Aquatic ecology....Foster L. Mayer   EPA 904-932-5311
Aquatic ecology....James R. Clark   EPA 904-932-5311
Aquatic ecology....David Flemer   EPA 904-932-5311
Aquatic ecology....Rodney Parrish   EPA 904-932-5311
Aquatic toxicology....Alan V. Nebeker   EPA 503-757-4875
Aquatic toxicology....arry Goodman   EPA 904-932-5311
Aquatic toxicology and water quality criteria....G.A. Chapman   EPA
   401-782-3000
Aquatic/terrestrial ecology....Robert T. Lackey   EPA 503-757-4634
Aquifer restoration....James F. McNabb   EPA 405-332-2251
Arachnoiditis....Staff   NINCDS 301-496-5751
Aran Duchenne Spinal Muscular Dystrophy....Staff   NINCDS
   301-496-5751
Area Health Education Centers....Staff   HRSA/BHPr 301-443-6190
Area Measurement....Durland, Robert   Census 301-763-7214
Argentina....Mark Siegelman   Cnty Commerce 202-377-1548
Argentina (Buenos Aires)....John P. Caulfield   Cnty State
   202-647-2401
Argentina (Buenos Aires)....Donald Harrington   Cnty AID
   202-647-9166
Argentina (Buenos Aires)....Marvin Schwartz   Cnty AID
   202-647-4376
Argentina/Minerals....Pablo Velasco   Cnty Mines 202-632-5060
Arms....Robinson, Hazel   USITC 202-252-1496
Arnold-Chiari Malformations....Staff   NINCDS 301-496-5751
Aromatic Substances....Joseph, S.   Customs 212-466-5678
Arrhythmias....Staff   NHLBI 301-496-4236
Arsenic....Kollins, Susan   USITC 202-252-1441
Arsenic....Loebenstein, Roger   Mines 202-634-1058
Arsenic compounds....Greenblatt, Jack   USITC 202-252-1353
Art, works of....Spalding, Josephine   USITC 202-252-1498
Arteriosclerosis....Staff   NHLBI 301-496-4236
Arteriosclerosis (Cerebral)....Staff   NINCDS 301-496-5751
Arteritis (eyes)....Staff   NEI 301-496-5248
Arthritis....Staff   NIAMS 301-496-8188
Arthritis....Staff   NIA 301-496-1752
Arthritis....Staff   NCNR 301-496-0526
Arthritis Information Clearinghouse....Staff   NIAMS 301-468-3235
Arthrogryposis Multiplex Congenita....Staff   NIAMS 301-496-8188
Artifical Intelligence....Robert Savely   NASA 713-483-8105
Artificial Blood Vessels....Staff   NHLBI 301-496-4236
Artificial Heart....Staff   NHLBI 301-496-4236
Artificial Heart Valve....Staff   NHLBI 301-496-4236
Artificial Insemination....Staff   NICHD 301-496-5133
Artificial Intelligence....Staff   NLM 301-496-9300
Artificial Intelligence (Engineering)....Kathleen Healey   NASA
   713-483-4776
Artificial Joints....Staff   NIAMS 301-496-8188
Artificial Lung....Staff   NHLBI 301-496-4236
Artificial Skin....Staff   NIGMS 301-496-7301
Artificial flowers....Spalding, Josephine   USITC 202-252-1491
Artificial flowers of man-made fibers....Cook, Lee   USITC
   202-252-1471

Artificial flowers, foliage, of rubber/plastics....Truskett, Brooks
 USITC 202-252-1364
Artificial mixtures of fatty substances....Randall, Rob USITC
 202-252-1366
Aruba...Avon Williams Cnty State 202-647-2621
Aruba/Minerals...Ivette Torres Cnty Mines 202-632-9352
Asbestos....White, Linda USITC 202-252-1427
Asbestos....Virta, Robert Mines 202-634-1206
Asbestos....Michael Beard EPA 919-541-2623
Asbestos & toxics control....Roger Wilmoth EPA 513-569-7509
Asbestos (and Cancer)....Staff NCI 301-496-5583
Asbestos Prod....Pitcher, Charles Commerce 202-377-0132
Asbestos-fiber data....Philip M. Cook EPA 218-720-5553
Asbestosis....Staff NHLBI 301-496-4236
Asbestosis....Staff CDC/NIOSH 404-329-3534
Asia/trade matters....Staff US Trade Rep 202-395-3900
Asparagus....McCarty, Tim USITC 202-252-1324
Aspartame, Neurological Effects of....Staff NINCDS 301-496-5751
Asperger's Syndrome....Staff NINCDS 301-496-5751
Aspergillosis....Staff NIAID 301-496-5717
Asphalt....White, Linda USITC 202-252-1427
Asphalt, Natural...Johnson, Wilton Mines 202-634-1184
Asphyxia....Staff NINCDS 301-496-5751
Aspirin Allergy....Staff NIAID 301-496-5717
Aspirin-Myocardial Infarction Study (AMIS)....Staff NHLBI
 301-496-4236
Assembly Equipment....Abrahams, Edward Commerce
 202-377-0312
Associate Degree (Nursing Schools)....Staff HRSA/BHPr
 301-443-5786
Association of Southeast Asian Nations (ASEAN)....Karl Schwartz
 Cnty AID 202-647-9240
Asteroid Dynamics....James Williams NASA 818-354-6466
Asthma....Staff NIAID 301-496-5717
Asthma....Staff NHLBI 301-496-4236
Astigmatism....Staff NEI 301-496-5248
Astrophysics....Robert Preston NASA 818-354-6895
Asymmetric Septal Hypertrophy (ASH)....Staff NHLBI
 301-496-4236
Ataxia....Staff NINCDS 301-496-5751
Ataxia Telangiectasia....Staff NCI 301-496-5583
Ataxia Telangiectasia....Staff NINCDS 301-496-5751
Atelectasis....Staff NHLBI 301-496-4236
Atherosclerosis....Staff NINCDS 301-496-4231
Atherosclerosis....Staff NHLBI 301-496-4236
Atherosclerosis (Cerebral)....Staff NINCDS 301-496-5751
Atherosclerosis (Effect on Vision)....Staff NEI 301-496-5248
Athetosis....Staff NINCDS 301-496-5751
Athletic equipment....Robinson, Hazel USITC 202-252-1496
Atmospheric Chemistry....Michael Prather NASA 212-678-5625
Atmospheric Dynamics...Michael Allison NASA 212-678-5554
Atmospheric processes....Jack H. Shreffler EPA 919-541-2194
Atmospheric studies....Gary J. Foley EPA 919-541-2601
Atopic Dermatitis....Staff NIAID 301-496-5717
Atrial Fibrillation....Staff NHLBI 301-496-4236
Atrophy....Staff NINCDS 301-496-5751
Auctions....Staff FCC 202-632-7521
Audio Visual Equipment, Export Promo.....Beckham, Reginald
 Commerce 202-377-5478
Audio Visual Services....Siegmund, John Commerce 202-377-4781
Audio components....Baker, Scott USITC 202-252-1386
Audiology (Clinical Center patients)....Staff CC 301-496-5368
Audiovisual Films - GSA/National Audio Visual Ctr....Staff
 301-763-1896
Audiovisual Material (For Health Prof. Education)....Staff NLM
 301-496-6095
Audiovisual Materials (Nursing)....Staff HRSA/BHPr 301-443-5786
Australia....Travis Lyday Cnty Mines 202-632-1272
Australia....Gary Bouck/Tony Costanao Cnty Commerce
 202-377-3647
Australia (Canberra)....Jeffrey Buczacki Cnty State 202-647-9691
Australia (Canberra)....Frank Tatu Cnty AID 202-647-9690
Austria....Philip Combs Cnty Commerce 202-377-2920
Austria (Vienna)....William Millan Cnty State 202-647-1484
Austria (Vienna)....Robert M. Beecroft Cnty AID 202-647-2005
Austria/Minerals....George Rabchevsky Cnty Mines 202-632-5053
Autism....Staff NINCDS 301-496-5751
Autism....Staff NICHD 301-443-4515
Autism....Staff NIMH 301-443-4515
Auto Ind. Affairs Parts....Jerschkowsky, Oleg Commerce
 202-377-1514
Auto Ind. Affairs Parts/Suppliers....Semb, Deborah Commerce
 202-377-1418
Auto Ind. Affairs Parts/Suppliers....Jones, Heather Commerce
 202-377-1418
Auto Ind. Affairs Parts/Suppliers....Allison, Loretta M. Commerce
 202-377-4019
Auto Ind. Affairs Parts/Suppliers....Reck, Robert O. Commerce

 202-377-1419
Auto Industry Affairs....Warner, Albert T. Commerce 202-377-0669
Autoimmune Disease....Staff NIAID 301-496-5717
Autoimmune Disease....Staff NIAMS 301-496-8188
Automated Construction of Large Space Structures....Al Meintel
 NASA 804-865-2489
Automatic Teller Machine Theft....Carol Kaplan Justice Stat
 202-724-7759
Automation (Laboratory Apparatus and Processes)....Staff
 DRS/BEIB 301-496-4426
Automibiles....Kavalauskas, Juanita USITC 202-252-1402
Automobile....Desoucey, R. Customs 212-466-5667
Automobile Dealers....Kostecka, Andrew Commerce 202-377-0342
Automobile Emergency....Staff FCC 727-337-1212
Autonomic drugs....Nesbitt, Elizabeth USITC 202-252-1355
Aviation & Marine Development Stations....Staff FCC
 717-337-1431
Aviation Licenses....Staff FCC 717-337-1212
Aviation Rules & Hearings....Staff FCC 202-632-7175
Aviation and Helicopter Services....Miller, Randall Commerce
 202-377-5071
Avionics Marketing....Driscoll, George Commerce 202-377-8228
Avionics Systems (Engineering)....Edward Chevers NASA
 713-483-8225
Azides....Johnson, Larry USITC 202-252-1351

B

BCG (Bacillus Calmette-Guerin)....Staff NCI 301-496-5583
Baby carriages, strollers, and parts....Seastrum, Carl USITC
 202-252-1493
Baccalaureate Nursing Schools....Staff HRSA/BHPr 301-443-2134
Back Problems....Staff NINCDS 301-496-5751
Back Problems....Staff NIAMS 301-496-8188
Bacterial Meningitis....Staff NIAID 301-496-5717
Bacterial Meningitis....Staff NINCDS 301-496-5751
Bacteriologic Media....Staff OD/ORS 301-496-6107
Bacteriology....Staff NIAID 301-496-5717
Bacteriology....Gerard Stelma EPA 513-569-7384
Bags....Gorman, K Customs 212-466-5893
Bags or sacks....Cook, Lee USITC 202-252-1471
Bahamas....Mark Tadeu Cnty Commerce 202-377-2527
Bahamas (Nassau)....Nancy Lees Cnty State 202-647-2621
Bahamas (Nassau)....Michael Kirby Cnty AID 202-647-7385
Bahamas/Minerals....Ivette Torres Cnty Mines 202-632-9352
Bahrain....Claude Clement Cnty Commerce 202-377-5545
Bahrain (Manama)....Jane McVerry Cnty State 202-647-6572
Bahrain (Manama)....Kathleen Allegrone Cnty AID 202-647-2329
Bahrain/Minerals....Bernadette Michalski Cnty Mines 202-632-5065
Bail....Herbert Koppel Justice Stat 202-724-7770
Bail (Federal)....Carol Kaplan Justice Stat 202-724-7759
Bail/Pretrial Release....Richard Rau Justice 202-724-2951
Bail/Pretrial Release....John Spevacek Justice 202-272-6010
Bail/Pretrial Release....Bruce Johnson Justice 202-272-6010
Bail/Pretrial Release....Lauresa Stillwell Justice 202-724-2962
Bail/Pretrial Release....Cheryl Martorana Justice 202-724-2965
Bait & Switch, Marketing Practices.... Fed Trade Com
 202-326-3128
Bakery Products....Janis, William V. Commerce 202-377-2250
Ball Bearings....Fletcher, William E. Commerce 202-377-0309
Balls....Tomenga, Y. Customs 212-466-5540
Balls, sports and play....Robinson, Hazel USITC 202-252-1496
Baltic States....John W. Zerolis Cnty State 202-647-1070
Baltic States....Terry R. Snell Cnty AID 202-647-4138
Baltimore Longitudinal Study of Aging....Staff NIA 301-496-1752
Baltimore Longitudinal Study of Aging....Staff NIA 301-550-1707
Bamboo....Westcot, Thomas USITC 202-252-1325
Bandages....Brownchweig, G. Customs 212-466-5744
Bandages, impregnated w/ medicinals....Randall, Rob USITC
 202-252-1366
Bangladesh....Polly Holcombe Cnty Commerce 202-377-2954
Bangladesh (Dhaka)....Siria Lopez Cnty State 202-647-9552
Bangladesh (Dhaka)....Alexander Shapleigh Cnty AID
 202-647-4516
Bangladesh/Minerals....David Doan Cnty Mines 202-634-1272
Barbados....Robert Dormitzer Cnty Commerce 202-377-2527
Barbados (Bridgetown)....John Foarde Cnty AID 202-647-8451
Barbados (Bridgetown)....Peter Kolar Cnty AID 202-647-3447
Barbados/Minerals....Ivette Torres Cnty Mines 202-632-9352
Barbasco....Wanser, Stephen USITC 202-252-1363
Barbiturates....Nesbitt, Elizabeth USITC 202-252-1355
Barite....Johnson, Larry USITC 202-252-1351
Barium....Wagner, Lorie USITC 202-252-1439
Barium....Ampian, Sarkis G. Mines 202-634-1180
Barium carbonate....Johnson, Larry USITC 202-252-1351

Barium compounds....Greenblatt, Jack USITC 202-252-1353
Barium pigments...Johnson, Larry USITC 202-252-1351
Barium sulfate...Johnson, Larry USITC 202-252-1351
Barlow's Syndrome (Mitral Valve Prolapse)....Staff NHLBI 301-496-4236
Barlow's Syndrome (Mitral Valve Prolapse)....Staff NHLBI 301-496-4236
Barrettes....Linkins, Linda USITC 202-252-1499
Bars (steel)....Fulcher, Nancy USITC 202-252-1434
Bartter's Syndrome....Staff NHLBI 301-496-4236
Basal Cell....Staff NCI 301-496-5583
Basic Research....Staff NIGMS 301-496-7301
Basic Shapes and Forms....Ilardi, P. Customs 212-466-5476
Basketwork, wickerwork, related products....Westcot, Thomas USITC 202-252-1325
Bathing caps....Worrell, Jackie USITC 202-252-1466
Batten's Disease....Staff NINCDS 301-496-5751
Battered Spouses....Staff NIMH 301-443-4515
Battered Spouses....Staff Hot-Line 301-654-1881
Batteries....Hagey, Michael USITC 202-252-1392
Batteries....Streeter, Jonathan Commerce 202-377-2132
Batteries....Miller, J. Customs 212-466-5689
Batteries, Storage....Larrabee, David Commerce 202-377-0575
Bauxite....Cammarota, David Commerce 202-377-0575
Bauxite....Baumgardner, Luke Mines 202-634-1081
Bauxite (for metal)....McNay, Deborah USITC 202-252-1425
Bauxite calcined....White, Linda USITC 202-252-1427
Bay rum or bay water....Land, Eric USITC 202-252-1349
Beads....Witherspoon, Ricardo USITC 202-252-1489
Beads, articles of....Witherspoon, Ricardo USITC 202-252-1489
Beans, ex oilseed....McCarty, Tim USITC 202-252-1324
Bearings....Riedl, K. Customs 212-466-5493
Bearings, ball and roller....Murphy, Mary USITC 202-252-1401
Bed Wetting....Staff NIMH 301-443-4515
Bedding....Ellis, Kevin Commerce 202-377-1140
Bedding....Eyskens, R. Customs 212-466-5854
Bedsonia....Staff NICHD 301-496-5133
Bedsonia....Staff NIDDK 301-496-3583
Bedspreads....Borsari, Marilyn USITC 202-252-1465
Beef....Ludwick, David USITC 202-252-1329
Beer....Lipovsky, William USITC 202-252-1331
Beer....Maria, J. Customs 212-466-5730
Behavioral toxicology....Robert A. Drummond EPA 218-720-5733
Behavioral toxicology and pharmacology....Robert C. MacPhail EPA 919-541-2671
Behaviorial and Social Sciences....Staff NICHD 301-496-6832
Behcet's Disease (Eyes)....Staff NEI 301-496-5248
Behcet's Disease (Systemic)....Staff NIDR 301-496-4261
Behcet's Disease (Systemic)....Staff NIAMS 301-496-8188
Belgium....Boyce Fitzpatrick Cnty Commerce 202-377-5401
Belgium (Brussels)....Elenore Raven-Hamilton Cnty State 202-647-6664
Belgium (Brussels)....Yvette Wong Cnty State 202-647-6664
Belgium (Brussels)....James G. Huff Cnty AID 202-647-6046
Belgium (Brussels)....Richard A. Christenson Cnty AID 202-647-4484
Belgium/Minerals....George Rabchevsky Cnty Mines 202-632-5053
Belize....Kristen Baumgart Cnty Commerce 202-377-2527
Belize (Belize City)....Bruce Knotts Cnty State 202-647-3681
Belize (Belize City)....Edward Campbell Cnty AID 202-647-4105
Belize (Belize City)....William Schofield Cnty AID 202-647-2152
Belize/Minerals....Ivette Torres Cnty Mines 202-632-9352
Bell's Palsy....Staff NINCDS 301-496-5751
Belting and Hose....Prat, Raimundo Commerce 202-377-0128
Belting and Hose....Prat, Raimundo Commerce 202-377-0128
Belting of rubber or plastics (for machinery)....Truskett, Brooks USITC 202-252-1363
Belting, industrial....Cook, Lee USITC 202-252-1471
Belts....Persky, H. Customs 212-466-5881
Belts, Machine....Barth, G. Customs 212-466-5884
Belts, apparel: Leather....Worrell, Jackie USITC 202-252-1466
Belts, apparel: Other mens and boys....Shetty, Sundar USITC 202-252-1457
Belts, apparel: Other womens and girls....MacKnight, Peggy USITC 202-252-1468
Benign Congenital Hypotonia....Staff NINCDS 301-496-5751
Benign Mucosal Pemphigoid....Staff NCI 301-496-5583
Benign Mucosal Pemphigoid....Staff NIAMS 301-496-8188
Benign Prostatic Hyperplasia....Staff NIDDK 301-496-3583
Benin....Reginald Biddle Cnty Commerce 202-377-4388
Benin....Theresa Queenan Peace Corps 202-254-7036
Benin (Cotonou)....Frederick Kaplan Cnty State 202-647-3391
Benin (Cotonou)....John A. Hedges Cnty AID 202-647-6980
Benin (Cotonou)....Mable S. Meares Cnty AID 202-647-6154
Benin/Minerals....Hendrik van Oss Cnty Mines 202-632-5065
Bensenoid intermediates, miscellaneous....Matusik, Ed USITC 202-252-1356
Benthic toxicity testing....R.C. Swartz EPA 401-782-3000

Bentonite....Lukes, James USITC 202-252-1426
Benzene....Raftery, Jim USITC 202-252-1365
Benzenoid Compound....Winters, W. Customs 212-466-5747
Benzenoid paints...Johnson, Larry USITC 202-252-1351
Benzenoid plasticizers...Johnson, Larry USITC 202-252-1351
Benzenoid plastics....Taylor, Ed USITC 202-252-1362
Benzenoid varnishes...Johnson, Larry USITC 202-252-1351
Benzo(a)pyrene....Staff NCI 301-496-5583
Benzoic acid....Matusik, Ed USITC 202-252-1356
Berger's Disease....Staff NIDDK 301-496-3583
Beriberi (Neurological)....Staff NINCDS 301-496-5751
Beriberi (Nutritional)....Staff NIDDK 301-496-3583
Bermuda....Mack Tadeu Cnty Commerce 202-377-2527
Bermuda (Hamilton)....Charles Peacock Cnty State 202-647-8027
Bermuda (Hamilton)....James C. Whitlock, Jr. Cnty AID 202-647-2622
Bermuda (Hamilton)....Richard A. Christenson Cnty AID 202-647-4484
Bermuda/Minerals....Ivette Torres Cnty Mines 202-632-9352
Berylium....Stonfer, David Commerce 202-377-0575
Beryllium....Kollins, Susan USITC 202-252-1441
Beryllium....Kramer, Deborah A. Mines 202-634-1083
Beryllium compounds....Greenblatt, Jack USITC 202-252-1353
Beta-thalassemia (Cooley's Anemia)....Staff NHLBI 301-496-4236
Betatron....Staff NCI 301-496-5583
Beverages....Lipvosky, William USITC 202-252-1331
Beverages....Kenney, Cornelius Commerce 202-377-2428
Bhutan....John Lister Cnty State 202-647-2141
Bhutan....Scott Delisi Cnty AID 202-647-5466
Bhutan....Sean Gallagher Cnty Commerce 202-377-2954
Bhutan/Minerals....David Doan Cnty Mines 202-634-1272
Bicycles....Vanderwolf, John Commerce 202-377-0348
Bicycles....Tomenga, Y. Customs 212-466-5540
Bicycles and parts....Seastrum, Carl USITC 202-252-1493
Bilateral Agreements....Staff FIC 301-496-5903
Biliary Cirrhosis....Staff NIDDK 301-496-3583
Bilirubinemia....Staff NICHD 301-496-5133
Billfolds....Seastrum, Carl USITC 202-252-1493
Billiard cloth....Cook, Lee USITC 202-252-1471
Billing....Staff Fed Trade Com 202-326-3175
Binocular Vision....Staff NEI 301-496-5248
Binswanger's Disease....Staff NINCDS 301-496-5751
Bio-Technology, Dairy, Economics....Fallert, Richard Agri 202-786-1820
Bio-Technology, Economics....Schaub, John Agri 202-786-1469
Bio-related Chemistry....Staff NIGMS 301-496-7301
Bioaccumulation....J.L. Lake EPA 401-782-3000
Bioaccumulation....N.I. Rubinstein EPA 401-782-3000
Bioaccumulation processes....H. Lee III EPA 401-782-3000
Bioavailability....Philip M. Cook EPA 218-720-5553
Bioavailability....H. Lee III EPA 401-782-3000
Biochemical and inhalation toxicology....Fred J. Miller EPA 919-541-2655
Biochemistry....William J. Dunlap EPA 405-332-2314
Biochemistry....John E. Rogers EPA 404-546-3103
Biochemistry....Peter Chapman EPA 904-932-5311
Biochemistry....Wilhelm Peter Schoor EPA 904-932-5311
Biochemistry....G.E. Zaroogian EPA 401-782-3000
Biochemistry Instrumentation....Staff DRR 301-496-5545
Biodegradation....Parmely H. Pritchard EPA 904-932-5311
Biodegradation....Peter Chapman EPA 904-932-5311
Biodegradation....Richard W. Eaton EPA 904-932-5311
Biodynamics....Barbara Woolford NASA 713-483-3701
Bioeffects of radiofrequency radiation....Joe A. Elder EPA 919-541-2339
Biofeedback....Staff NIMH 301-443-4515
Biofeedback....Staff NHLBI 301-496-4236
Biohazard Control....Staff OD/ORS 301-496-2960
Biohazard Identification....Staff OD/ORS 301-496-2960
Biohazards (Cancer Research)....Staff NCI 301-496-5583
Biological Materials Preparation Centers....Staff DRR 301-496-5545
Biological Processing in Weightlessness....Clarence Sams NASA 713-483-7160
Biological analyses....Robert Smith EPA 405-332-2248
Biological effects....R.L. Steele EPA 401-782-3000
Biological oceanography....G.G. Pesch EPA 401-782-3000
Biological testing....Llewellyn R. Williams EPA 702-798-2138
Biology....Dorothy Peteet NASA 212-678-5587
Biomagnification....D.R. Young EPA 401-782-3000
Biomarkers....S. Baksi EPA 401-782-3000
Biomarkers....E.H. Jackim EPA 401-782-3000
Biomarkers....A.R. Malcolm EPA 401-782-3000
Biomathematical models....Richard Hertzberg EPA 513-569-7582
Biomedical Communications....Staff NLM 301-496-6308
Biomedical Computer Centers....Staff DRR 301-496-5411
Biomedical Engineering....Staff NIGMS 301-496-7301
Biomedical Engineering....Staff DRS/BEIB 301-496-4741

Bulgaria (Sofia)....Ben F. Fairfax   Cnty AID   202-647-1739
Bulgaria/Minerals....Walter Steblez   Cnty Mines   202-632-5047
Bulimia....Staff   NIMH   301-443-4513
Bulimia....Staff   NICHD   301-496-5133
Bullous Pemphigoid....Staff   NIAMS   301-496-8188
Bullous Pemphigoid....Staff   NCI   301-496-5583
Bunker "C" fuel oil....Foreso, Cynthia   USITC   202-252-1348
Burglary....Lois Mock   Justice   202-724-7684
Burkina Faso....Vacant   Cnty Commerce   202-377-4564
Burkina Faso (Ouagadougou)....Frankie Calhoun   Cnty State   202-647-2865
Burkina Faso (Ouagadougou)....Deborah Odell   Cnty AID   202-647-2865
Burkina Faso (Ouagadougou)....Ronnie G. Daniel   Cnty AID   202-647-6039
Burkina Faso/Minerals....Hendrik van Oss   Cnty Mines   202-632-5065
Burkitt's Lymphoma....Staff   NCI   301-496-5583
Burma....Kyaw Win   Cnty Commerce   202-377-5334
Burma (Rangoon)....Thomas Reich   Cnty State   202-647-7108
Burma (Rangoon)....Kathryn (Dee) Robinson   Cnty AID   202-647-7108
Burma (Rangoon)....Michael Feldstein   Cnty AID   202-647-9137
Burma/Minerals....David Doan   Cnty Mines   202-634-1272
Burn Research....Staff   NIGMS   301-496-7301
Bursitis....Staff   NIAMS   301-496-8188
Burundi....John Crown   Cnty Commerce   202-377-0357
Burundi....Tom Elam   Peace Corps   202-254-8694
Burundi (Bujumbura)....Kevin Brown   Cnty State   202-647-3139
Burundi (Bujumbura)....Judith B. Cefkin   Cnty AID   202-647-3138
Burundi (Bujumbura)....Harold Marwitz   Cnty AID   202-647-9762
Burundi/Minerals....Lloyd Antonides   Cnty Mines   202-632-5065
Buses....Kavalauskas, Juanita   USITC   202-252-1402
Business & Industry, Economics....Bluestone, Herman   Agri   202-786-1547
Business Division....Hamilton, Howard   Census   301-763-7564
Business Forms....Bratland, Rose Marie   Commerce   202-377-0380
Business Licenses....Staff   FCC   717-337-1212
Business Radio....Staff   FCC   717-337-1212
Business Statistics, Business Owners' Characterist....Allen, Peggy   Census   301-763-5779
Business Statistics, Minority Businesses....McCutcheon, Donna   Census   301-763-5517
Business Statistics, Retail Trade, Adv Mthly Sales....Piencykoski, Ronald   Census   301-763-5294
Business Statistics, Retail Trade, Annual Sales....Piencykoski, Ronald   Census   301-763-5294
Business Statistics, Retail Trade, Census....Wallace, Mark   Census   301-763-7038
Business Statistics, Retail Trade, Mo. Inventories....Piencykoski   Ronald   Census   301-763-5294
Business Statistics, Retail Trade, Mthly Trade Rpt....True, Irving   Census   301-763-7128
Business Statistics, Service Industries, Census....Marcus, Sidney   Census   301-763-5930
Business Statistics, Svc Ind, Curr Select Svc Rept....Zabelsky, Thomas   Census   301-763-5528
Business Statistics, Wholesale Trade, Census....Trimble, John   Census   301-763-5281
Business Statistics, Wholesale Trade, Current Sale....Roberts, Shirley   Census   301-763-3916
Business Statistics, Wholesale Trade, Inventories....Roberts, Shirley   Census   301-763-3916
Business Statistics, Women-Owned Businesses....McCutcheon, Donna   Census   301-763-5517
Butadiene....Raftery, Jim   USITC   202-252-1365
Butane....Land, Eric   USITC   202-252-1349
Butter....Warren, J Fred   USITC   202-252-1311
Buttons....Rodriguez, Laura   USITC   202-252-1486
Buttons....Rauch, T.   Customs   212-466-5892
Butyl alcohol....Michels, David   USITC   202-252-1352
Butyl benzyl phthalate....Johnson, Larry   USITC   202-252-1351
Butyl oleate....Johnson, Larry   USITC   202-252-1351
Butyl rubber....Taylor, Ed   USITC   202-252-1362
Butyl stearate....Johnson, Larry   USITC   202-252-1351
Butylene....Raftery, Jim   USITC   202-252-1365
Byssinosis (Brown Lung Disease)....Staff   NHLBI   301-496-4236

C

CAD/CAM....McGibbon, Paatrick   Commerce   202-377-0315
CAD/CAM, Trade Promo.....Manzolillo, Frank   Commerce   202-377-2991
CEA (Carcinoembryonic Antigen)....Staff   NCI   301-496-5583
CSCE....Michael Klosson   Cnty AID   202-647-8050

CSCE....Peter R. Keller   Cnty AID   202-647-7558
Cable Access Policy....Staff   FCC   202-632-7265
Cable Broadcasting....Siegmund, John   Commerce   202-377-4781
Cable Ocean Systems....Staff   FCC   202-632-7265
Cable Pole Attachments....Staff   FCC   202-632-4890
Cable Telephone....Staff   FCC   202-634-1830
Cable Television Complaints....Staff   FCC   202-632-7048
Cable Television Cross Owner5ship....Staff   FCC   202-634-1830
Cable Televison Franchising....Staff   FCC   202-632-7076
Cablegrams....Staff   FCC   202-632-7265
Cadmium....Wagner, Lorie   USITC   202-252-1439
Cadmium....Llewellyn, Thomas   Mines   202-634-1084
Caffeine and its compounds....Nesbitt, Elizabeth   USITC   202-252-1355
Calcium....Wagner, Lorie   USITC   202-252-1439
Calcium....Morse, David   Mines   202-634-1194
Calcium Carbonate....Tepordei, Valentin V.   Mines   202-634-1185
Calcium Comps....Morse, David   Mines   202-634-1190
Calcium carbonate....Johnson, Larry   USITC   202-252-1351
Calcium compounds....Greenblatt, Jack   USITC   202-252-1353
Calcium pigments....Johnson, Larry   USITC   202-252-1351
Calcium sulfate....Johnson, Larry   USITC   202-252-1351
Calculators....Baker, Scott   USITC   202-252-1386
Calculus....Staff   NIDR   301-496-4261
Calendaring machines....Slingerland, David   USITC   202-252-1400
Call Sign Block Allocation....Staff   FCC   202-653-8126
Call Signs Allocation....Staff   FCC   202-634-1923
Cambodia....JeNelle Matheson   Cnty Commerce   202-377-2462
Cambodia (Phom Penh)....Harvey Somers   Cnty State   202-647-3133
Cambodia (Phom Penh)....Terry Breese   Cnty AID   202-647-3132
Cambodia/Minerals....David Doan   Cnty Mines   202-634-1272
Cameos....Witherspoon, Ricardo   USITC   202-252-1489
Cameras....Kieper, B.   Customs   212-466-5685
Cameras (except television)....Bishop, Kate   USITC   202-252-1494
Cameroon....Ian Davis   Cnty Commerce   202-377-0357
Cameroon....Djodi Deutsch   Peace Corps   202-254-8397
Cameroon (Yaounde)....Susan Zelle   Cnty State   202-647-4965
Cameroon (Yaounde)....T. Dennis Reece   Cnty AID   202-647-7468
Cameroon (Yaounde)....Abbe Fessenden   Cnty AID   202-647-7986
Cameroon/Minerals....Thomas Dolley   Cnty Mines   202-632-5065
Camphor....Randall, Rob   USITC   202-252-1366
Campus Radio Stations....Staff   FCC   202-653-6288
Canada....William Cavitt/Kenneth Fernandez/Stephen Jacobs   Cnty Commerce   202-377-3643
Canada (Ottawa)....Gil Donahue   Cnty State   202-647-1097
Canada (Ottawa)....Sam Fromowitz   Cnty AID   202-647-3135
Canada (Ottawa)....Wilson A. Riley, Jr.   Cnty AID   202-647-3138
Canada (Ottawa)....Larry G. Butcher   Cnty AID   202-647-1097
Canada (Ottawa)....George T. Boutin   Cnty AID   202-647-1096
Canada/Minerals....Alfredo Gurmendi   Cnty Mines   202-632-9352
Canada/trade matters....Staff   US Trade Rep   202-395-5663
Canavan's Disease....Staff   NINCDS   301-496-5751
Cancer (Reproductive Tract)....Staff   NCI   301-496-5583
Cancer (Reproductive Tract)....Staff   NICHD   301-496-5133
Cancer Control Program....Staff   NCI   301-496-5583
Cancer Research....Staff   NCNR   301-496-0526
Cancer and Aging....Staff   NCI   301-496-5583
Cancer and Aging....Staff   NIA   301-496-1752
Cancer assessments....Debdas Mukerjee   EPA   513-569-7572
Candida....Staff   NIAID   301-496-5717
Candida....Staff   NIDR   301-496-4261
Candidiasis....Staff   NIAID   301-496-5717
Candidiasis....Staff   NIDR   301-496-4261
Candles....Spalding, Josephine   USITC   202-252-1498
Candles....Brownchweig, G.   Customs   212-466-5744
Canes....Linkins, Linda   USITC   202-252-1499
Canker Sores....Staff   NIDR   301-496-4261
Canoes....Lahey, Kathleen   USITC   202-252-1409
Capacitors....Sherman, Thomas   USITC   202-252-1389
Capacitors....Joseph, I.   Customs   212-466-5673
Cape Verde....Philip Michelini   Cnty Commerce   202-377-4388
Cape Verde....Theresa Queenan   Peace Corps   202-254-7036
Cape Verde (Praia)....Bisa Williams-Manigault   Cnty State   202-647-3395
Cape Verde (Praia)....Thomas Burke   Cnty AID   202-647-8436
Cape Verde (Praia)....Louise H. Werlin   Cnty AID   202-647-8125
Cape Verde Islands/Minerals....Hendrik van Oss   Cnty Mines   202-632-5065
Capital Goods DAS Acting....Hart, Williams   Commerce   202-377-5023
Capital Punishment....Lawrence Greenfeld   Justice Stat   202-724-7755
Capitation Grants for Health Professions Schools....Staff   HRSA/BHPr   301-443-5794
Capitation Grants for Nurse Training....Staff   HRSA/BHPr   301-443-5786
Caprolactam monomer....Matusik, Ed   USITC   202-252-1356

Experts

Caps....Worrell, Jackie   USITC   202-252-1466
Carbon....Johnson, Larry   USITC   202-252-1351
Carbon Black....Prat, Raimundo   Commerce   202-377-0128
Carbon Cycle....Inez Fung   NASA   212-678-5590
Carbon and graphite electrodes....White, Linda   USITC   202-252-1427
Carbon black...Johnson, Larry   USITC   202-252-1351
Carbon monoxide....James Raub   EPA   919-541-4157
Carbon tetrachloride....Michels, David   USITC   202-252-1352
Carbon, activated....Randall, Rob   USITC   202-252-1366
Carboxylic acids....Michels, David   USITC   202-252-1352
Carboxymethyl cellulose salts (surface active)....Land, Eric   USITC   202-252-1349
Carcalon (Krebiozen)....Staff   NCI   301-496-5583
Carcin and Neo-Carcin....Staff   NCI   301-496-5583
Carcinogen....Staff   NCI   301-496-5583
Carcinogen Risk Assessment Endeavor....Rita Schoeny   EPA   513-569-7544
Carcinogenicity....Rodney Johnson   EPA   218-720-5731
Carcinoma....Staff   NCI   301-496-5583
Card cases....Seastrum, Carl   USITC   202-252-1493
Cardiac Disease....Staff   NHLBI   301-496-4236
Cardiac Pacemakers....Staff   NHLBI   301-496-4236
Cardiomegaly....Staff   NHLBI   301-496-4236
Cardiomyopathy (Hypertrophic, Dilated)....Staff   NHLBI   301-496-4236
Cardiopulmonary Resuscitation (CPR)....Staff   NHLBI   301-496-4236
Cardiovascular Disease....Staff   NHLBI   301-496-4236
Cardiovascular drugs....Nesbitt, Elizabeth   USITC   202-252-1355
Carditis....Staff   NHLBI   301-496-4236
Care (Mothers, Infants, Children)....Staff   HRSA/BHCDA/DMCH   301-443-2170
Care Labeling of Text. Wearing Apparel....Steve Ecklund   Fed Trade Com   202-326-3034
Care Labeling, Automotive....Steve Ecklund   Fed Trade Com   202-326-3034
Career Criminals....Patrick Langan   Justice Stat   202-724-7774
Career Criminals....Lawrence Greenfeld   Justice Stat   202-724-7755
Careers in Nursing....Staff   DRR   301-443-5786
Caribbean....Staff   US Trade Rep   202-395-6135
Caribbean Primate Research Center....Staff   DRR   301-496-5545
Caries....Staff   NIDR   301-496-4261
Carpal Tunnel Syndrome....Staff   NINCDS   301-496-5751
Carpal Tunnel Syndrome....Staff   NIAMS   301-496-8188
Carpets....Borsari, Marilyn   USITC   202-252-1465
Carrier Equipment....Staff   FCC   202-634-1800
Carrots....McCarty, Tim   USITC   202-252-1324
Casein....Randall, Rob   USITC   202-252-1366
Cases....Gorman, K.   Customs   212-466-5893
Cash Discounts....Staff   Fed Trade Com   202-326-3175
Cash registers....Fletcher, William   USITC   202-252-1407
Castile soap....Land, Eric   USITC   202-252-1349
Casting machines....Greene, William   USITC   202-252-1405
Cat Cry Syndrome (Cri Du Chat)....Staff   NICHD   301-496-5133
Cat Scratch Fever....Staff   NIAID   301-496-5717
Catalytic reduction....James H. Abbott   EPA   919-541-3443
Cataplexy....Staff   NINCDS   301-496-5751
Cataract....Staff   NEI   301-496-5248
Catfish, Statistics....Sitzman, Ron   Agri   202-447-3244
Catheterization (Cardiac or Heart)....Staff   NHLBI   301-496-4236
Cattle....Ludwick, David   USITC   202-252-1329
Cattle, Economics....Gustafson, Ron   Agri   202-786-1830
Cattle, Feeder, Futures With Options....Carl Schmiedeskamp   Comm Futures   312-353-9014
Cattle, Live, Futures With Options....Carl Schmiedeskamp   Comm Futures   312-353-9014
Cattle, Statistics....Noyes, Steve   Agri   202-447-3040
Cattle, World, Economics....Bailey, Linda   Agri   202-786-1691
Caulking compounds....Johnson, Larry   USITC   202-252-1351
Caulks....Johnson, Larry   USITC   202-252-1351
Caustic potash....Greenblatt, Jack   USITC   202-252-1353
Caustic soda....Greenblatt, Jack   USITC   202-252-1353
Cayman Islands....Dale Shaffer   Cnty State   202-647-2620
Caymans....Mack Tadeu   Cnty Commerce   202-377-2527
Cedar leaf....Land, Eric   USITC   202-252-1349
Celiac Disease....Staff   NIDDK   301-496-3583
Celiac Disease....Staff   NCI   301-496-5583
Celiac Disease....Staff   NIAID   301-496-5717
Cell Aging....Staff   NIA   301-496-1752
Cell Bank....Staff   NIGMS   301-496-7301
Cell Biology....Staff   NIGMS   301-496-7301
Cellular Function....Staff   NIGMS   301-496-7301
Cellular Mobile Radio....Staff   FCC   202-653-6400
Cellular Phone Investment, Automotive...Jay Bratt   Fed Trade Com   202-326-3321
Cellular Structure....Staff   NIGMS   301-496-7301
Cement....Pitcher, Charles   Commerce   202-177-0132

Cement....Johnson, Wilton   Mines   202-634-1184
Cement Plants, Major Proj.....White, Barbara   Commerce   202-377-4160
Cement, hydraulic....White, Linda   USITC   202-252-1427
Cements of rubber, vinyl, etc.....Randall, Rob   USITC   202-252-1388
Cements, dental....Randall, Rob   USITC   202-252-1366
Census Geographic Concepts....Staff   Census   301-763-5720
Census Tracts, Address Allocations....Swapshur, Ernie   Census   301-763-5720
Census Tracts, Boundaries....Miller, Cathy   Census   301-763-3827
Census Tracts, Codes....Miller, Cathy · Census   301-763-5720
Census Tracts, Delineation....Miller, Cathy   Census   301-763-3827
Census of Retail Trade, Guam....Larson, OdellBostrom, Carl   Census   301-763-8226
Census of Retail Trade, Guam....Hoover, Kent   Census   301-763-8564
Census of Retail Trade, Puerto Rico....Larson, Odell   Census   301-763-8226
Census of Retail Trade, Puerto Rico....Hoover, Kent   Census   301-763-8564
Census of Retail Trade, Virgin Islands....Larson, Odell   Census   301-763-8226
Census of Retail Trade, Virgin Islands....Hoover, Kent   Census   301-763-8564
Census of Selected Service Industries, Guam....Larson, Odell   Census   301-763-8226
Census of Selected Service Industries, Guam....Hoover, Kent   Census   301-763-8564
Census of Selected Service Industries, Puerto Rico....Larson, Odell   Census   301-763-8226
Census of Selected Service Industries, Puerto Rico....Hoover, Kent   Census   301-763-8564
Census of Selected Service Industries, Virgin Isl....Larson, Odell   Census   301-763-8226
Census of Selected Service Industries, Virgin Isl....Hoover, Kent   Census   301-763-8564
Census of Wholesale Trade, Guam....Larson, Odell   Census   301-763-8226
Census of Wholesale Trade, Guam....Hoover, Kent   Census   301-763-8564
Census of Wholesale Trade, Puerto Rico....Larson, Odell   Census   301-763-8226
Census of Wholesale Trade, Puerto Rico....Hoover, Kent   Census   301-763-8564
Census of Wholesale Trade, Virgin Islands....Larson, Odell   Census   301-763-8226
Census of Wholesale Trade, Virgin Islands....Hoover, Kent   Census   301-763-8564
Centenarians....Staff   NIA   301-496-1752
Center for Economic Studies....McGuckin, III, Robert   Census   301-763-2337
Centers for Disease Control....Staff   CDC   404-329-3291
Centers for Disease Control....Staff   CDC   404-329-3291
Centers of Population....Hirschfield, Don   Census   301-763-5962
Central Africa Republic....Ian Davis   Cnty Commerce   202-377-0357
Central African Republic....Tom Elam   Peace Corps   202-254-8694
Central African Republic (Bangui)....Kevin Brown   Cnty State   202-647-3139
Central African Republic (Bangui)....Judith B. Cefkin   Cnty AID   202-647-3138
Central African Republic (Bangui)....Abbe Fessenden   Cnty AID   202-647-7986
Central African Republic/Minerals....Thomas Dolley   Cnty Mines   202-632-5065
Central America (ROCAP)...John Lovaas   Cnty AID   202-647-6181

Central Core Disease....Staff   NINCDS   301-496-9156
Central Core Disease....Staff   NINCDS   301-496-5751
Central Storeroom....Staff   OD/DAS   301-496-9156
Centrifuges....Slingerland, David   USITC   202-252-1400
Ceramic construction articles....Lukes, James   USITC   202-252-1426
Ceramic table, kitchen articles....McNay, Deborah   USITC   202-252-1425
Ceramics....Shea, Moira   Commerce   202-377-0128
Ceramics....Kalkines, G.   Customs   212-466-5794
Ceramics (Advanced)....Kamenicky, Vincent   Commerce   202-377-0128
Ceramics and Ceramic-matrix Composites....Stanley Levine   NASA   216-433-3276
Cereal breakfast foods...James, Antoinette   USITC   202-252-1313
Cereal grains....Pierre-Benoist, John   USITC   202-252-1320
Cereals....Janis, William V.   Commerce   202-377-2250
Cerebellar Arteriosclerosis....Staff   NINCDS   301-496-5751
Cerebellar Ataxia....Staff   NINCDS   301-496-5751
Cerebellar Ataxia....Staff   NINCDS   301-496-5751
Cerebellar Lesions....Staff   NINCDS   301-496-5751

Computers in Medical Research....Staff DRR 301-496-5545
Computers, Office of Business Equipment....McPhee, John E. Commerce 202-377-0572
Computers, Trade Promo.....Fogg, Judy A. Commerce 202-377-4936
Computers, Trade Promo.....Swann, Vera A. Commerce 202-377-0396
Computing Device Emission Standards....Staff FCC 202-653-6288
Con. tech. for simlt. removal of NOx & SOx....G. Blair Martin EPA 919-541-7504
Concepts for Advanced Space Structures of large....Martin Mikulas NASA 804-865-2551
Concrete and products....White, Linda USITC 202-252-1427
Condensate, lease....Foreso, Cynthia USITC 202-252-1348
Conductors....Cutchin, John USITC 202-252-1396
Conduit....Cutchin, John USITC 202-252-1396
Conduits....Miller, J. Customs 212-466-5680
Confectionery....Gallagher, Joan USITC 202-252-1317
Confectionery Products....Kenney, Cornelius Commerce 202-377-2428
Conference on Security & Cooperation in Europe....Richard Boucher Cnty State 202-647-8050
Confidentality of Data....Carol Kaplan Justice Stat 202-724-7759
Configuration Management....H. Thrower NASA 205-544-2375
Congenital Abnormalities....Staff NICHD 301-496-5133
Congenital Abnormalities....Staff NINCDS 301-496-5751
Congenital Abnormalities....Staff NEI 301-496-5248
Congenital Heart Disease....Staff NHLBI 301-496-4236
Congenital Infections....Staff NIAID 301-496-5717
Congestive Heart Failure....Staff NHLBI 301-496-4236
Congo....Ian Davis Cnty Commerce 202-377-0357
Congo (Brazzaville)....Earl Irving Cnty State 202-647-4965
Congo (Brazzaville)....Ned McMahon Cnty AID 202-647-1637
Congo (Brazzaville)....Mary Ann Riegelman Cnty AID 202-647-7984
Congo/Minerals....Thomas Dolley Cnty Mines 202-632-5065
Congressional Districts, Address Allocations....Swapshur, Ernie Census 301-763-5692
Congressional Districts, Boundaries....Shaw, Kevin Census 301-763-4667
Congressional Districts, Component Areas....Shaw, Kevin Census 301-763-4667
Congressional Liaison/Congressional Relations....Staff Fed Trade Com 202-326-2186
Conjunctivitis....Staff NEI 301-496-5248
Connective Tissue Diseases....Staff NIAMS 301-496-8188
Constipation....Staff NIDDK 301-496-3583
Constipation and Aging....Staff NIA 301-496-1752
Construction Grants for Health Professions Schools....Staff HRSA/BHPr 301-443-5786
Construction Machinery....Heimowitz, L. Commerce 202-377-0558
Construction Machinery, Trade Promo.....Heinowitz, Leonard Commerce 202-377-0558
Construction Statistics Division....Gross, Leonora M. Census 301-763-7163
Construction Statistics, Census/Industry Surveys....dRappaport, Barry A. Census 301-763-5435
Construction Statistics, Contractors....Visnansky, Andrew Census 301-763-7546
Construction Statistics, Current Programs....Mittendorf, William Census 301-763-7165
Construction Statistics, New Residential, Charact....Berman, Steve Census 301-763-7842
Construction Statistics, New Residential, Sales....Berman, Steve Census 301-763-7842
Construction Statistics, Residental Alterations....Roff, George Census 301-763-5705
Construction Statistics, Special Trades....Visnansky, Andrew Census 301-763-7546
Construction Statistics, Vacancy Data....Harple, Jr., Paul R. Census 301-763-2880
Construction Stats, Constr Authorzd by Bldg Permit....Hoyle, Linda Census 301-763-7244
Construction Stats, New Residential, House Complet....Rolark, Stanley Census 301-763-5731
Construction Stats, New Residential, Housing Start....Fondelier, David Census 301-763-5731
Construction Stats, New Residential, In Select MSA....Jacobson, Dale Census 301-763-7842
Construction Stats, New Residential, Price Index....Berman, Steve Census 301-763-7842
Construction Stats, Residential Repairs....Roff, George Census 301-763-5705
Construction Stats, Value New Constr Put in Place....Meyer, Allan Census 301-763-5717
Construction paper....Rhodes, Richard USITC 202-252-1322
Construction, Domestic....MacAuley, Patrick Commerce 202-377-0132
Construction, Nonresidential, Domestic....MacAuley, Patrick Commerce 202-377-0132
Consumer Auto Complaints (not GM), Mktg Practices....Staff Fed Trade Com 202-326-3128
Consumer Electronics....Streeter, Jonathan Commerce 202-377-2132
Consumer Electronics, Export Promo.....Kimmel, Edward K. Commerce 202-377-3640
Consumer Expenditure Survey....Hoff, Gail Census 301-763-2764
Consumer Goods....Boyd, John H. Commerce 202-377-0337
Consumer Leasing Act....Staff Fed Trade Com 202-326-3175
Contact Lenses....Staff NEI 301-496-5248
Container....Hantman, S. Customs 212-466-5678
Containers (of wood)....Westcott, Thomas USITC 202-252-1325
Containers and Packaging....Copperthite, Kim Commerce 202-377-0595
Containers, of base metal....Fulcher, Nancy USITC 202-252-1434
Containment technology-permeable treatment....Jonathan Herrmann EPA 513-569-7839
Containment technology-plume management....Naomi Barkley EPA 513-569-7854
Contaminant transport and fate....D.J. Baumgartner EPA 401-782-3000
Contaminant transport modeling....Carl G. Enfield EPA 405-332-2210
Contaminant transport modeling....Jong Cho EPA 405-332-2271
Contaminant transport modeling....Wayne Downs EPA 405-332-2272
Contaminant transport modeling....Steve Schmelling EPA 405-332-2315
Contaminant transport modeling....Thomas Short EPA 405-332-2234
Contaminant transport modeling...James Weaver EPA 405-332-2420
Continuing Guarantees....Bret Smart Fed Trade Com 213-209-7890
Continuous Ambulatory Peritoneal Dialysis (CAPD)....Staff NIDDK 301-496-3583
Contraception....Staff NICHD 301-496-5133
Contraceptives....Staff NICHD 301-496-5133
Contract Machining....McGibbon, Patrick Commerce 202-377-0314
Control Algorithm for Wind Tunnel Support Systems....Staff NASA 415-694-5850
Control Devices (non-licenses)....Staff FCC 202-653-6288
Control Mechanisms....V. R. Neiland NASA 205-544-7143
Control technology....Robert R. Swank, Jr. EPA 404-546-3128
Controls for Vehicles....N. D. Hendix NASA 205-544-1451
Convection and Clouds....Anthony Del Genio NASA 212-678-5588
Conventional Fossil Fuel Power (Major Projects)....Gaines, William Commerce 202-377-4332
Converters....Greene, William USITC 202-252-1405
Conveyors/Conveying Equipment, Trade Promo.....Wiening, Mary Commerce 202-377-4708
Cook Islands....Ann M. Cambara Cnty State 202-647-3546
Cook Islands....Carla Joyner Peace Corps 202-254-3227
Cook Islands (Rarotonga)....Robert A. Millspaugh Cnty AID 202-647-3546
Cook Islands (Rarotonga)....Chris Brown Cnty AID 202-647-9137
Cooley's Anemia....Staff NHLBI 301-496-4236
Cooling Off Rule, Cigarettes....Joyce Plyler Fed Trade Com 202-326-3021
Copper....Kollins, Susan USITC 202-252-1441
Copper....Stonfer, David Commerce 202-377-0575
Copper....Jolly, Janice L. Mines 202-634-1053
Copper....Edelstein, Dan Mines 202-634-1053
Copper Futures....Helen Cadden Comm Futures 212-668-2081
Copper Mills/Brass....Stonfer, David Commerce 202-377-0575
Copper Wire Mills....Stonfer, David Commerce 202-377-0575
Copper compounds....Greenblatt, Jack USITC 202-252-1353
Copra and coconut oil....Reeder, John USITC 202-252-1319
Cor Pulmonale....Staff NHLBI 301-496-4236
Cordage....Edert, R. Customs 212-466-5885
Cordage machines....Greene, William USITC 202-252-1405
Cordless Telephone....Staff FCC 202-653-6288
Cork and cork products....Westcot, Thomas USITC 202-252-1325
Corn Futures With Options....Judy Sepsey Comm Futures 312-353-9025
Corn Grains, Economics....Hull, Dave Agri 202-786-1840
Corn Grains, Statistics....Van Lahr, Charles Agri 202-447-7369
Corn Grains, World, Economics....Riley, Peter Agri 202-786-1692
Corn Products....Janis, William V. Commerce 202-377-2250
Corn, field....Pierre-Benoist, John USITC 202-252-1320
Corneal Disorders....Staff NEI 301-496-5248
Corneal Transplantation....Staff NEI 301-496-5248
Cornelia deLange Syndrome....Staff NICHD 301-496-5133
Coronary Angioplasty....Staff NHLBI 301-496-4236
Coronary Artery Surgery Study (CASS)....Staff NHLBI

301-496-4236
Coronary Bypass....Staff NHLBI 301-496-4236
Coronary Disease....Staff NHLBI 301-496-4236
Corrections....Anne Schmidt Justice 202-724-2959
Corrections....Thomas F. Albrecht Justice 202-272-6040
Corrections....Voncile Gowdy Justice 202-724-2951
Corrections...Bruce Johnson Justice 202-272-6010
Corrections...Jay Merrill Justice 202-724-2959
Corrections....Fred Heinzelmann Justice 202-724-2949
Corrections....Christopher Innes Justice Stat 202-724-6100
Corrections....Allan Beck Justice Stat 202-724-7755
Corrections....Lawrence Greenfeld Justice Stat 202-724-7755
Corrections....Stephanie Minor-Harper Justice Stat 202-724-7755
Corrections....Phyllis Jo Baunach Justice Stat 202-724-7755
Corrections - Community....Phyllis Jo Baunach Justice Stat
    202-724-7755
Corrections - Geneal...Lawrence Greenfeld Justice Stat
    202-724-7755
Corrections - General....Phyllis Jo Baunach Justice Stat
    202-724-7755
Corrections - General....Stephanie Minor-Harper Justice Stat
    202-724-7755
Corrections - General...Allan Beck Justice Stat 202-724-7755
Corrections - General....James Stephan Justice Stat 202-724-6100
Corrections - General....Christopher Innes Justice Stat
    202-724-6100
Corrections - General....Susan Kline Justice Stat 202-724-6100
Corrections - General....Angela Lane Justice Stat 202-724-6100
Corrections - State....Bernard Shipley Justice Stat 202-724-7770
Corrections Alternatives....Bruce Johnson Justice
    202-272-6010
Corrections Alternatives....Edwin Zedlewski Justice
    202-724-2953
Corrosion....Marvin Gardels EPA 513-569-7217
Corundum-Emery....Austin, Gordon Mines 202-634-1206
Cosmetic Allergy....Staff FDA 301-245-1061
Cosmetic creams....Land, Eric USITC 202-252-1349
Cosmetics....McIntyre, Leo R. Commerce 202-377-0128
Cosmetics, perfumery, toilet preparations....Land, Eric USITC
    202-252-1349
Cosmic Ray Research....T. Parnell NASA 205-544-7690
Cosmic Rays....J. F. Ormes NASA 301-286-5705
Cost of Crime - General....Sue Lindgren Justice Stat 202-724-7759
Cost of Crime - General....Michael Rand Justice Stat
    202-724-7774
Cost of Crime - To Government....Sue Lindgren Justice Stat
    202-724-7759
Cost of Crime - To Victims....Patsy Klaus Justice Stat
    202-724-7774
Cost of Nursing Care....Staff NCNR 301-496-0526
Costa Rica....Brigit Helms Cnty Commerce 202-377-2527
Costa Rica (San Jose)....Brian Dickson Cnty State 202-647-4980
Costa Rica (San Jose)....Frances Jones Cnty AID 202-647-3385
Costa Rica (San Jose)....Donald Enos Cnty AID 202-647-5101
Costa Rica/Minerals....Ivette Torres Cnty Mines 202-632-9352
Costimes....Persky, H. Customs 212-466-5881
Costochondritis....Staff NIAMS 301-496-8188
Cote d'Ivoire (Abidjan)....Leslie A. Bassett Cnty State
    202-647-3066
Cotton....Enfield, Mary USITC 202-252-1455
Cotton Futures....Linda Chalet Comm Futures 212-668-2080
Cotton Seed Oil....Janis, William V. Commerce 202-377-2250
Cotton, Economics....Skinner, Robert Agri 202-786-1840
Cotton, Statistics....Edwards, Radley Agri 202-447-5944
Cotton, World, Economics....Whitton, Carolyn Agri 202-786-1691
Cottonseed and cottonseed oil....Reeder, John USITC
    202-252-1319
Council of Europe....Mark A. Tokola Cnty State 202-647-1708
Council of Europe....Judith M. Heimann Cnty AID 202-647-4418
Counterfeit Goods, Marketing Practices....Staff Fed Trade Com
    202-326-3128
County Business Patterns....Stoetzel, Faran E. Census
    301-763-5430
Coupons, Marketing Practices....Staff Fed Trade Com
    202-326-3128
Court Appeals....Carla Gaskins Justice Stat 202-724-7774
Court Appeals....Patrick Langan Justice Stat 202-724-7774
Court Appeals....Sue Lindgren Justice Stat 202-724-7759
Court Case Processing Time....Carla Gaskins Justice Stat
    202-724-7774
Court Case Processing Time - Federal....Carol Kaplan Justice Stat
    202-724-7759
Court Caseload....Carla Gaskins Justice Stat 202-724-7774
Court Caseload....Patrick Langan Justice Stat 202-724-7774
Court Delay....Bernard Auchter Justice 202-724-7684
Court Delay...Richard Rau Justice 202-724-2951
Court Delay...Jay Merrill Justice 202-724-2959
Court Delay....Cheryl Martorana Justice 202-724-2965

Court Delay....Joel Garner Justice 202-724-7635
Court Organization....Carla Gaskins Justice Stat 202-724-7774
Court Organization....Patrick Langan Justice Stat 202-724-7774
Courts....Patrick Langan Justice Stat 202-724-7774
Courts....Carla Gaskins Justice Stat 202-724-7774
Cranes....Greene, William USITC 202-252-1405
Cranial Abnormalities....Staff NIDR 301-496-4261
Craniofacial Malformations....Staff NIDR 301-496-4261
Crayons....Linkins, Linda USITC 202-252-1499
Creams, cosmetic....Land, Eric USITC 202-252-1349
Credit Cards....Staff Fed Trade Com 202-326-3175
Credit Practices Rules....Staff Fed Trade Com 202-326-3175
Cretinism....Staff NIDDK 301-496-3583
Creutzfeldt-Jakob Disease....Staff NINCDS 301-496-5751
Crew Station Technology...Jack Hatfield NASA 804-865-3917
Crew and Thermal Systems (Engineering....Chin Lin NASA
    713-483-9126
Cri Du Chat (Cat Cry Syndrome)....Staff NICHD 301-496-5133
Crib Death (SIDS)....Staff NICHD 301-496-5133
Crigler-Najar Syndrome....Staff NIDDK 301-496-3583
Crime Analysis....William Saulsbury Justice 202-724-7685
Crime Analysis....Lawrence Bennett Justice 202-724-2956
Crime Incidence, Rates, and Trends....Anita Timrots Justice Stat
    202-724-7774
Crime Incidence, Rates, and Trends....Patsy Klaus Justice Stat
    202-724-7774
Crime Incidence, Rates, and Trends....Bruce Taylor Justice Stat
    202-724-7774
Crime Measurement Methods....Richard Dodge Justice Stat
    202-724-6100
Crime Measurement Methods....Bruce Taylor Justice Stat
    202-724-7774
Crime Measurement Methods....Michael Rand Justice Stat
    202-724-7774
Crime Prevention....Lois Mock Justice 202-724-7684
Crime Prevention....Richard Titus Justice 202-724-7684
Crime Prevention....Carol Dorsey Justice 202-272-6001
Crime Prevention....Lawrence Bennett Justice 202-724-2956
Crime Prevention....Fred Heinzelmann Justice 202-724-2949
Crime Prevention Measures....Catherine Whitaker Justice Stat
    202-724-7755
Crime Seasonality....Richard Dodge Justice Stat 202-724-6100
Crime Severity....Patsy Klaus Justice Stat 202-724-7774
Crime Surveys, General Information....McGinn, Larry Census
    301-763-1735
Crime Surveys, Victimization....McGinn, Larry Census
    301-763-1735
Crime Types: Homicide....Marianne Zawitz Justice Stat
    202-724-6100
Crime Types: Homicide....Paul White Justice Stat 202-724-7770
Crime Types: Federal, Bank Robbery, Computer....Carol Kaplan
    Justice Stat 202-724-7759
Crime Types: Rape, Robbery, Assault, Theft....Patsy Klaus Justice
    Stat 202-724-7774
Crime Types: Rape, Robbery, Assault, Theft....Michael Rand
    Justice Stat 202-724-7774
Crime Types: Rape, Robbery, Assault, Theft....Caroline Harlow
    Justice Stat 202-724-7755
Crime and the Elderly....Staff NIA 301-496-1752
Crime, Ethnicity & Social Policy....Winifred Reed Justice
    202-724-7635
Crime, Incidence, Rates, and Trends....Michael Rand Justice Stat
    202-724-7774
Crime, Location of....Richard Dodge Justice Stat 202-724-6100
Criminal Defendants....Carla Gaskins Justice Stat 202-724-7774
Criminal Defendants....Patrick Langan Justice Stat
    202-724-7774
Criminal Defendants - Federal....Carol Kaplan Justice Stat
    202-724-7759
Criminal History Data Quality....Carol Kaplan Justice Stat
    202-724-7759
Criminal Justice Agencies....Sue Lindgren Justice Stat
    202-724-7759
Criminal Justice Expenditure and Employment....Sue Lindgren
    Justice Stat 202-724-7759
Criminal Justice Systems...Joseph Kochanski Justice
    202-724-2692
Criteria air pollutants....Lester Grant EPA 919-541-4173
Critical Care Medicine Department....Staff CC 301-496-9565
Crohn's Disease....Staff NIDDK 301-496-3583
Cross-Eye....Staff NEI 301-496-5248
Crude cresylic acid....Foreso, Cynthia USITC 202-252-1348
Crude petroleum....Foreso, Cynthia USITC 202-252-1348
Crushing machines....Greene, William USITC 202-252-1405
Crustacean culture....Geraldine Cripe EPA 904-932-5311
Cryogenic Physics....E. Urban NASA 205-544-7721
Cryolite....White, Linda USITC 202-252-1427
Cryosurgery (Eyes)....Staff NEI 301-496-5248

Cryosurgery (Eyes)....Staff NCI 301-496-5583
Cryptococcosis....Staff NIAID 301-496-5717
Cryptosporidiosis....Staff NIAID 301-496-5717
Crystal Growth in Fluid Field and Particle Dynamic...J. Lindsay NASA 205-544-1301
Cuba....Ted Johnson Cnty Commerce 202-377-2527
Cuba (Havana)....James Pettit Cnty State 202-647-9272
Cuba (Havana)....David Nolan Cnty State 202-647-9272
Cuba (Havana)....Daniel Russell Cnty State 202-647-9273
Cuba (Havana)....John P. Modderno Cnty AID 202-647-1476
Cuba (Havana)....John A. Ritchie Cnty AID 202-647-1503
Cuba (Havana)....Catherine Barry Cnty AID 202-647-1658
Cuba (Havana)....David D. Nelson Cnty AID 202-647-1476
Cuba/Minerals....Ivette Torres Cnty Mines 202-632-9352
Cucumbers....McCarty, Tim USITC 202-252-1324
Culm....Foreso, Cynthia USITC 202-252-1348
Cuprous oxide...Johnson, Larry USITC 202-252-1351
Currencies Futures With Options....David Bice Comm Futures 312-353-9018
Current Population Surveys....Creighton, Kathleen Census 301-763-2773
Curtains....Borsari, Marilyn USITC 202-252-1465
Cushing's Syndrome....Staff NIDDK 301-496-3583
Cushing's Syndrome....Staff NINCDS 301-496-5751
Cushions....Linkins, Linda USITC 202-252-1499
Cut flowers....Burket, Stephen USITC 202-252-1318
Cutis Laxa....Staff NHLBI 301-496-4236
Cutlery....Laney-Cummings, Karen USITC 202-252-1431
Cutlery....Correa, Judith Commerce 202-377-0311
Cutlery....Preston, J. Customs 212-466-5488
Cutting machines textile....Greene, William USITC 202-252-1405
Cyclic Idiopathic Edema....Staff NHLBI 301-496-4236
Cyclitis....Staff NEI 301-496-5248
Cyprus....Ann Corro Cnty Commerce 202-377-3945
Cyprus (Nicosia)....Richard V. Fisher Cnty State 202-647-6113
Cyprus (Nicosia)....William J. Kushlis Cnty AID 202-647-1429
Cyprus (Nicosia)....Christine Adamczyk Cnty AID 202-647-9114
Cyprus (Nicosia)....Milford N. Reed Cnty AID 202-647-8226
Cyprus/Minerals....Lloyd Antonides Cnty Mines 202-632-5065
Cystic Acne....Staff NCI 301-496-5583
Cystic Acne....Staff NIAMS 301-496-8188
Cystic Fibrosis (Pancreas)....Staff NIDDK 301-496-3583
Cystinosis....Staff NICHD 301-496-5133
Cystinuria....Staff NIDDK 301-496-3583
Cystitis....Staff NIDDK 301-496-3583
Cytology....Staff NCI 301-496-5583
Cytomegalic Inclusion Disease....Staff NINCDS 301-496-5751
Cytomegalovirus (Congenital)....Staff NHLBI 301-496-4236
Cytomegalovirus (Congenital)....Staff NICHD 301-496-5133
Cytomegalovirus (Congenital)....Staff NIAID 301-496-5717
Czechoslovakia....Vacant Cnty Commerce 202-377-2645
Czechoslovakia (Prague)....Daniel B. Smith Cnty State 202-647-3187
Czechoslovakia (Prague)...Laurie Tracy Cnty State 202-647-3052
Czechoslovakia (Prague)....John J. Boris Cnty AID 202-647-1457
Czechoslovakia (Prague)....Barbara K. Griffiths Cnty AID 202-647-3191
Czechoslovakia/Minerals....John Panulas Cnty Mines 202-634-1277

D

D'Jibouti....James Robb Cnty Commerce 202-377-4564
DES (Diethylstilbestrol)....Staff NCI 301-496-5583
DES (Diethylstilbestrol)....Staff NICHD 301-496-5133
DES (Diethylstilbestrol)....Staff FDA 301-443-3170
DMSO (Dimethylsulfoxide)....Staff NCI 301-496-5583
DMSO (Dimethylsulfoxide)....Staff FDA/NCDB 301-443-1016
DNA....Staff NCI 301-496-5583
DNA....Staff NIGMS 301-496-7301
DNA Activities....Staff 301-770-0131
DWI....Fred Heinzelmann Justice 202-724-2949
DWI....Bernard Gropper Justice 202-724-7631
DWI....Lois Mock Justice 202-724-7684
DWI....Lauresa Stillwell Justice 202-724-2962
Dairy Products....Janis, William V. Commerce 202-377-2250
Dairy Products....Brady, T. Customs 212-466-5790
Dairy Products, Economics....Miller, Jim Agri 202-786-1830
Dairy Products, Economics....Short, Sara Agri 202-786-1830
Dairy Products, Statistics....Buckner, Dan Agri 202-447-4448
Dairy products....Warren, J Fred USITC 202-252-1311
Dance Studios, Credit....Wallace Witkowski Fed Trade Com 202-326-3015
Dandy-Walker Syndrome....Staff NINCDS 301-496-5751
Darier's Disease....Staff NIAMS 301-496-8188

Data Base Machines....Regina Brown NASA 301-286-6595
Data Base Services....Inoussa, Mary Commerce 202-377-1114
Data Base Services....Inoussa, Mary C. Commerce 202-377-5820
Data Base Services, Electronic....Inoussa, Mary Commerce 202-377-5820
Data Flow Technology....Sol Broder NASA 301-286-7088
Data Processing Services....Atkins, Robert G. Commerce 202-377-1114
Data Processing Services....Atkins, Robert G. Commerce 202-377-4781
Data processing machines....Fletcher, William USITC 202-252-1407
Deafness....Staff NINCDS 301-496-5751
Death and Dying....Staff NIMH 301-443-4515
Death and Dying....Staff NIA 301-443-1752
Debit Cards....Staff Fed Trade Com 202-326-3175
Decalcomanias (decals)....Stahmer, Carsten USITC 202-252-1321
Decennial Census, 1980 Counts f/Current Boundaries....Miller, Joel Census 301-763-1996
Decennial Census, Content & Tabula, Program Design....Berman, Patricia Census 301-763-7094
Decennial Census, Content, General....Paez, Al Census 301-763-5987
Decennial Census, Content, General....Lichtman-Panzer, Paulette Census 301-763-5270
Decennial Census, Count Questions, 1980 Census....Elam, Edgar Census 301-763-2685
Decennial Census, Housing Data....Downs, Bill Census 301-763-8553
Decennial Census, Population Data....Cowan, Rosemarie Census 301-763-7947
Decennial Census, Publications, General....Landman, Cheryl Census 301-763-3938
Decennial Census, Publications, General....Porter, Gloria Census 301-763-4908
Decennial Census, Tabulations, General....Landman, Cheryl Census 301-763-3938
Decennial Census, Tabulations, General....Porter, Gloria Census 301-763-4908
Decennial Operations Division...Jackson, Arnold A. Census 301-763-2682
Decennial Planning Division...Miskura, Susan M. Census 301-763-7670
Decision support/expert systems....Thomas O. Barnwell, Jr. EPA 404-546-3210
Decontamination....Staff OD/ORS 301-496-2960
Decontamination (Radioactive Spills)....Staff OD/ORS 301-496-2254
Decubitus Ulcers....Staff NIA 301-496-1752
Defender Services....Richard Rau Justice 202-724-2951
Defender Services....Martin Lively Justice 202-724-2965
Degenerative Basal Ganglia Disease....Staff NIA 301-496-5751
Degenerative Joint Disease....Staff NIAMS 301-496-8188
Deglutition....Staff NIDR 301-496-4261
Dejerine-Sottas Disease....Staff NINCDS 301-496-5751
Delivery of Nursing Care....Staff NCNR 301-496-0526
Dementia....Staff NINCDS 301-496-5751
Demographic Studies, Center for....Wetzel, James R. Census 301-763-7720
Demographic Surveys Division....Walsh, Thomas C. Census 301-763-2776
Demography....Staff NICHD 301-496-5133
Demography of Aging....Staff NIA 301-496-1752
Demyelinating Diseases....Staff NINCDS 301-496-5751
Dengue....Staff NIAID 301-496-5717
Denmark....Maryanne Lyons Cnty Commerce 202-377-3254
Denmark (Copenhagen)....Kenneth Kolb Cnty State 202-647-5669
Denmark (Copenhagen)....R. Ross Rodgers Cnty AID 202-647-1774
Denmark (Copenhagen)....Richard A. Christenson Cnty AID 202-647-4484
Denmark/Minerals....Donald Buck Cnty Mines 202-632-5052
Dental Assistants (Education)....Staff HRSA/BHPr 301-443-6837
Dental Care Programs (Aged, Handicapped, Prepaid)....Staff 301-443-6853
Dental Diseases/Disorders....Staff NIDR 301-496-4261
Dental Restorative Materials....Staff NIDR 301-496-4261
Dental cements....Randall, Rob USITC 202-252-1366
Dentists, Health Care Staff....Staff Fed Trade Com 202-326-2756
Dentobacterial Plaque Infection....Staff NIDR 301-496-4261
Dentures....Staff NIDR 301-496-4261
Depreciation Rules....Staff FCC 202-632-7500
Depression....Staff NIMH 301-443-4515
Depression and Aging....Staff NIMH 301-443-1185
Depression and Aging....Staff NIA 301-496-1752
Depth Perception....Staff NEI 301-496-5248
Dermatitis Herpetiformis....Staff NCI 301-496-5583
Dermatological agents....Nesbitt, Elizabeth USITC 202-252-1355
Dermatology....Staff NIAMS 301-496-8188

Dermatology....Staff NCI 301-496-5583
Dermatomyositis....Staff NIAMS 301-496-8188
Dermatomyositis....Staff NINCDS 301-496-5751
Dermographism....Staff NIAID 301-496-5717
Design (Engineering)....Staff DRS/BEIB 301-496-4426
Detergents....Land, Eric USITC 202-252-1349
Detergents....McIntyre, Leo R. Commerce 202-377-0128
Deterrence and Incapacitation Studies....Joel Garner Justice 202-724-7635
Developmental Disorders....Staff NINCDS 301-496-5751
Developmental biochemistry....M. Kate Smith EPA 513-569-7577
Devic's Syndrome....Staff NINCDS 301-496-5751
Dextrans/Dextranase....Staff NIDR 301-496-4261
Dextrine....Randall, Rob USITC 202-252-1366
Di(2-ethylhexyl) adipate...Johnson, Larry USITC 202-252-1351
Di(2-ethylhexyl) phthalate...Johnson, Larry USITC 202-252-1351
Diabetes....Staff NCNR 301-496-0526
Diabetes (And Arteriosclerosis)....Staff NHLBI 301-496-4236
Diabetes (Juvenile)....Staff NIDDK 301-496-3583
Diabetes Clearinghouse....Staff NIDDK 301-468-2162
Diabetes Insipidus....Staff NIDDK 301-496-3583
Diabetes Mellitus....Staff NIDDK 301-496-3583
Diabetes and Aging (Type 1 and Type 2)....Staff NIDDK 301-496-3583
Diabetes and Aging (Type 1 and Type 2)....Staff NIA 301-496-1752
Diabetes and Pregnancy....Staff NICHD 301-496-5133
Diabetes with Insulin Allergy or Resistance....Staff NIAID 301-496-5717
Diabetes with Insulin Allergy or Resistance....Staff NIDDK 301-496-3583
Diabetic Neuropathy....Staff NINCDS 301-496-5751
Diabetic Retinopathy....Staff NEI 301-496-5248
Diagnostic Laboratories for Animal Disease....Staff DRR 301-496-5175
Diagnostic Radiology....Staff CC 301-496-7700
Dial-a-Porn Complaints....Staff FCC 202-632-7553
Dialysis, Kidney....Staff NIDDK 301-496-3583
Diamond....Austin, Gordon Mines 202-634-1206
Diamonds....White, Linda USITC 202-252-1427
Diarrheal Illnesses....Staff NIDDK 301-496-3583
Diarrheal Illnesses....Staff NIAID 301-496-5717
Diathermy Approval....Staff FCC 301-725-1585
Diatomite....White, Linda USITC 202-252-1427
Diatomite....Meisinger, Arthur C. Mines 202-634-1184
Diego Garcia....Wlater Manger Cnty State 202-647-8913
Diego Garcia....Robert Snyder Cnty AID 202-647-3040
Diethylstilbestrol (DES)....Staff NCI 301-496-5583
Diethylstilbestrol (DES)....Staff FDA 301-443-3170
Diethylstilbestrol (DES)....Staff NICHD 301-496-5133
Diffuse Sclerosis....Staff NINCDS 301-496-5751
Digestive Diseases....Staff NIDDK 301-496-3583
Digestive Diseases Clearinghouse....Staff NIDDK 301-468-6344
Digestive/Nutrition Research....Staff NCNR 301-496-0526
Digital Data Acquisition....Robert Krieger NASA 804-865-2031
Digital Electronic Message Service....Staff FCC 202-634-1706
Digital Terminations Systems....Staff FCC 202-634-1706
Dijibouti Republic of (Dijibouti)....Virginia Szymanski Cnty AID 202-647-3355
Dijibouti, Republic of (Dijibouti)...John Bernsten Cnty State 202-647-8852
Dilsobutylene....Raftery, Jim USITC 202-252-1365
Dilsodecyl phthalate...Johnson, Larry USITC 202-252-1351
Dinnerware of ceramic....McNay, Deborah USITC 202-252-1425
Dioxin....Robert Harless EPA 919-541-2248
Diphtheria....Staff NIAID 301-496-5717
Diploma Schools of Nursing....Staff HRSA/BHPr 301-443-2134
Direct Broadcasting Satellites....Staff FCC 202-632-9356
Direct Distance Dialing....Staff FCC 202-632-5550
Disability....McNeil, Jack Census 301-763-8578
Discoid Lupus Erythematosus....Staff NIAMS 301-496-8188
Disease Prevention....Staff NCNR 301-496-0526
Disinfection....Staff OD/ORS 301-496-2960
Disinfection byproducts & organics control....Alan Stevens EPA 513-569-7342
Disposable Apparel....Persky, H. Customs 212-466-5881
Disposal (Anim. Waste, Dead Anim., Infect. Mater.)....Staff OD/ORS 301-496-2960
Dispute Resolution....Bernard Auchter Justice 202-724-7684
Dispute Resolution....John Thomas Justice 202-272-6004
Dispute Resolution....Richard Rau Justice 202-724-2951
Dispute Resolution....Martin Lively Justice 202-724-2966
Dissolved oxygen....D.C. Miller EPA 401-782-3000
Distillate fuel oil....Foreso, Cynthia USITC 202-252-1348
Distilled Spriits....Maria, J. Customs 212-466-5730
Distilled Water....Staff OD/ORS 301-496-2960
Diuretics....Staff NHLBI 301-496-4236
Diverticulitis....Staff NIDDK 301-496-3583

Dizziness....Staff NINCDS 301-496-5751
Djibouti Republic of (Djibouti)....Richard H. Eney Cnty AID 202-647-8145
Djibouti/Minerals....Lloyd Antonides Cnty Mines 202-634-5065
Doll carriages, stroller, and parts....Seastrum, Carl USITC 202-252-1493
Dollar, U.S. Index....Heidilynne Schultheiss Comm Futures 212-668-2082
Dolls....Langer, Eric USITC 202-252-1497
Dolomite, dead burned....DeSapio, Vincent USITC 202-252-1435
Domestic Satellite Licenses....Staff FCC 202-634-1624
Domestic Violence....Patsy Klaus Justice Stat 202-724-7774
Domestic Violence....Michael Rand Justice Stat 202-724-7774
Domestic Violence....Patrick Langan Justice Stat 202-724-7774
Dominica....Robert Dormitzer Cnty Commerce 202-377-2527
Dominica (Roseau)....Vonda Delawie Cnty State 202-647-2621
Dominica (Roseau)....John Foarde Cnty AID 202-647-8451
Dominican Republic....Kirsten Baumgart Cnty Commerce 202-377-2527
Dominican Republic (Santo-Domingo)....Phillip Carter Cnty State 202-647-4195
Dominican Republic (Santo Domingo)....David F. Rogus Cnty AID 202-647-2130
Dominican Republic (Santo Domingo)....Peter Kolar Cnty AID 202-647-3447
Dominican Republic/Minerals....Ivette Torres Cnty Mines 202-632-9352
Door to Door Sales...Joyce Plyler Fed Trade Com 202-326-3021
Dose-response....James McKim EPA 218-720-5567
Down Filled Garments....Bret Smart Fed Trade Com 213-209-7890
Down Filled Products....Constance Vecellio Fed Trade Com 202-326-2966
Down Syndrome....Staff NICHD 301-496-5133
Down apparel....Worrell, Jackie USITC 202-252-1466
Drag Reduction....Bruce Holmes NASA 804-865-3274
Draperies....Borsari, Marilyn USITC 202-252-1465
Drawing instruments....Moller, Ruben USITC 202-252-1496
Drawings....Mushinske, L. Customs 212-466-5739
Dredging....N.I. Rubinstein EPA 401-782-3000
Dresses....Bryant, Judith USITC 202-252-1464
Dressing machines (textile)....Greene, William USITC 202-252-1405
Drilling Mus/Soft Compounds....Greer, Damon Commerce 202-377-0564
Drink-preparing machines....Jackson, Georgia USITC 202-252-1399
Drinking and Cancer....Staff NCI 301-496-5583
Drinking water disinfectants....Annette Gatchett EPA 513-569-7813
Drinking water field evaluations....Benjamin Lykins EPA 513-569-7560
Drinking water inorganics control....Thomas Sorg EPA 513-569-7370
Drinking water microbiological treatment....Gary Logsdon EPA 513-569-7345
Drinking water treatment....Robert Clark EPA 513-569-7201
Drug Allergy....Staff NIAID 301-496-5717
Drug Hemolytic Anemia....Staff NIDDK 301-496-3583
Drug Prevention Education....Carol Dorsey Justice 202-272-6001
Drug Prevention Education....Bernard Gropper Justice 202-724-7631
Drug Purpura....Staff NIDDK 301-496-3583
Drug Resistance....Staff NIAID 301-496-5717
Drug Testing...John Spevacek Justice 202-272-6010
Drugs....McIntyre, Leo R. Commerce 202-377-0128
Drugs....Reilly, N. Customs 212-466-5770
Drugs (Cancer)....Staff NCI 301-496-5583
Drugs (Cardiac)....Staff NHLBI 301-496-4236
Drugs (Eyes)....Staff NEI 301-496-5248
Drugs (Ototoxic)....Staff NIEHS 919-541-3345
Drugs (Use and Abuse)....Staff NIDA 301-443-6500
Drugs - General....Sue Lindgren Justice Stat 202-724-7759
Drugs and Aging....Staff NIA 301-496-1752
Drugs and Prisoners....Phyllis Jo Baunach Justice Stat 202-724-7755
Drugs and Prisoners....James Stephan Justice Stat 202-724-7755
Drugs, Alcohol and Crime....Bernard Gropper Justice 202-724-7631
Drugs, natural....Nesbitt, Elizabeth USITC 202-252-1355
Drugs, synthetic....Nesbitt, Elizabeth USITC 202-252-1355
Drunk Driving....Marianne Zawitz Justice Stat 202-724-6100
Dry Cleaning Machinery....Brodbeck, A. Customs 212-466-5490
Dry Eyes....Staff NEI 301-496-5248
Dry-cleaning machines....Jackson, Georgia USITC 202-252-1399
Drying machines....Jackson, Georgia USITC 202-252-1399
Duchenne Muscular Dystrophy....Staff NINCDS 301-496-5751
Dumpsite designation....H.A. Walker EPA 401-782-3000
Dupuytren's Contracture....Staff NIAMS 301-496-8188
Dupuytren's Contracture....Staff NINCDS 301-496-5751
Durable Goods....Gordon, Gerald F. Commerce 202-377-1176

Dust Inhalation Diseases (Pneumonconioses)....Staff NHLBI 301-496-4236

Dust Inhalation Diseases (Pneumonconioses)....Staff FDA 301-443-3170

Dust Inhalation Diseases (Pneumonconioses)....Staff CDCW/NIOSH 301-329-3534

Dwarfism....Staff NICHD 301-496-5133

Dye chemistry....George L. Baughman EPA 404-546-3103

Dyeing machines....Greene, William USITC 202-252-1405

Dyeing/Tanning Products....Brownchweig, G Customs 212-466-5744

Dyes....Wanser, Stephen USITC 202-252-1363

Dynamite...Johnson, Larry USITC 202-252-1351

Dysautonomia....Staff NINCDS 301-496-5751

Dysentary....Staff NIAID 301-496-5717

Dyskinesia....Staff NINCDS 301-496-5751

Dyslexia....Staff NICHD 301-496-5133

Dyslexia....Staff NINCDS 301-496-5751

Dyslexia....Staff NIMH 301-443-4513

Dystonia....Staff NINCDS 301-496-5751

Dystonia Musculorum Deformans (Torsion Dystonia)....Staff NINCDS 301-496-5751

E

E. Carribean....Robert Dormitzer Cnty Commerce 202-377-2527

ECG....Staff NHLBI 301-496-4236

EKG....Staff NHLBI 301-496-4236

Ear Infection....Staff NINCDS 301-496-5751

Earth Radiation Budget Experiment....Bruce Barkstrom NASA 804-865-2977

Earth-moving machines....Shapiro, Lena USITC 202-252-1408

Earthenware....Corea, Judy Commerce 202-377-0311

Earthenware, articles of....McNay, Deborah USITC 202-252-1425

Echocardiography....Staff NHLBI 301-496-4236

Ecological Life Support Studies....Donald Henninger NASA 713-483-5034

Ecological effects...Jerry N. Jones EPA 405-332-2303

Ecological effects....R. Douglas Kreis EPA 405-332-2303

Ecological effects....William Sanville EPA 218-720-5723

Ecological effects....John Arthur EPA 218-720-5565

Ecological modeling....Daniel H. McKenzie EPA 503-753-4666

Ecological risk assessment....A.D. Beck EPA 401-782-3000

Ecological studies....Jay Messer EPA 919-541-0150

Ecological toxicity...J.H. Gentile EPA 401-782-3000

Ecology...John E. Rogers EPA 404-546-3103

Ecology...Lawrence A. Burns EPA 404-546-3511

Ecology....Ray R. Lassiter EPA 404-546-3208

Ecology....Donald L. Phillips EPA 503-757-4355

Ecology...Jeffry Lee EPA 503-753-4666

Ecology....Harold V. Kibby EPA 503-757-4625

Ecologyical risk assessment....M. Craig Barber EPA 404-546-3147

Econ Growth/Empl Proj, Occupatl Outlook Qrtly....Fountain, Melvin Labor 202-272-5298

Econ Growth/Empl Projs, Associate Commissioner....Kutscher, Ronald Labor 202-272-5381

Econ Growth/Empl Projs, Data Diskettes....Personick, Valerie Labor 202-272-5327

Econ Growth/Empl Projs, Economic Growth Projection....Bowman, Charles Labor 202-272-5383

Econ Growth/Empl Projs, Employment Requirements....Horowitz, Karen Labor 202-272-5221

Econ Growth/Empl Projs, Ind-Occpl Empl Matrix....Turner, Delores Labor 202-272-5283

Econ Growth/Empl Projs, Ind-Occpl Matrix Data Tape....Turner, Delores Labor 202-272-5283

Econ Growth/Empl Projs, Industry Data Tapes....Franklin, James Labor 202-272-5240

Econ Growth/Empl Projs, Input-Output Data Tapes....Franklin, James Labor 202-272-5240

Econ Growth/Empl Projs, Labor Force Projections....Fullerton, Howard Labor 202-272-5328

Econ Growth/Empl Projs, Occcupatl Outlook Handbook....Pilot, Michael Labor 202-272-5282

Econ Growth/Empl Projs, Occupatl Projections....Rosenthal, Neal Labor 202-272-5382

Econ Grwoth/Empl Projs, Industry Projections....Bowman, Charles Labor 202-272-5383

Economic Census Staff....Mesenbourg, Thomas Census 301-763-7356

Economic Commission for Europe (ECE)....Robert A. Windsor Cnty State 202-647-2820

Economic Programming Division....Cohen, Barry M. Census 301-763-2912

Economic Surveys Division....Richardson, W. Joel Census 301-763-7735

Economizers....Lippa, Alison USITC 202-252-1398

Ecosystem Science and Technology....Jim Lawless NASA 415-694-5900

Ecosystem modeling....Doug Endicott EPA 313-675-2245

Ecosystem modeling waste load allocation....William L. Richardson EPA 313-675-2245

Ecosystem-chemical effects....Russel Kreis EPA 313-675-2245

Ectopic Hormones....Staff NIDDK 301-496-3583

Ecuador....Herbert Lindow Cnty Commerce 202-377-4303

Ecuador (Quito)...Milton Drucker Cnty State 202-647-3338

Ecuador (Quito)....Gerald McCulloch Cnty AID 202-647-5864

Ecuador (Quito)....Marvin Schwartz Cnty AID 202-647-4358

Ecuador/Minerals....Alfredo Gurmendi Cnty Mines 202-632-9352

Eczema....Staff NIAID 301-496-5717

Edema....Staff NHLBI 301-496-4236

Edge Tools Ex. Mach. TI/Saws....Shaw, Eugene Commerce 202-377-3494

Edible Preparations....Hopard, S. Customs 212-466-5760

Edible gelatin...Jonnard, Aimison USITC 202-252-1350

Edible preparations....James, Antoinette USITC 202-252-1313

Education....Siegel, Paul Census 301-763-1154

Education (Nursing)....Staff HRSA/BHPr/DN 301-443-2134

Education Facilities, Major Proj.....White, Barbara Commerce 202-377-4160

Educational Television....Staff FCC 202-632-6908

Educational Television....Staff FCC 202-632-6357

Educational/Training....Francis, Simon Commerce 202-377-0350

Effects assessment....Russel Kreis EPA 313-675-2245

Eggs....Newman, Douglas USITC 202-252-1328

Eggs, Economics....Christensen, Lee Agri 202-786-1830

Eggs, Statistics....Drain, Al Agri 202-447-6147

Eggs, World, Economics....Bailey, Linda Agri 202-786-1691

Egypt...Jeffrey Johnson Cnty Commerce 202-377-4652

Egypt Arab Republic of (Cairo)....David Greenlee Cnty AID 202-647-2802

Egypt Arab Republic of (Cairo)....John Jacob Norris Cnty AID 202-647-2802

Egypt Arab Republic of (Cairo)....Brent Hartley Cnty AID 202-647-1169

Egypt Arab Republic of (Cairo)....Richard Handler Cnty AID 202-647-9114

Egypt, Arab Republic of (Cairo)....Mary T. Curtin Cnty State 202-647-1228

Egypt, Arab Republic of (Cairo)....Paul E. Simons Cnty State 202-647-1228

Egypt, Arab Republic of (Cairo)....Gerald M. Feierstein Cnty State 202-647-2802

Egypt, Arab Republic of (Cairo)....Steven Savage Cnty AID 202-647-1169

Egypt/Minerals....Thomas Dolley Cnty Mines 202-632-5065

Ehlers-Danlos Syndrome....Staff NIAMS 301-496-8188

Eisenmenger's Syndrome....Staff NHLBI 301-496-4236

El Salvador....Brigit Helms Cnty Commerce 202-377-2527

El Salvador (San Salvador)....Patricia Butenis Cnty State 202-647-3681

El Salvador (San Salvador)....Kevin Witaker Cnty State 202-647-3681

El Salvador (San Salvador)....H. Carl Gettinger Cnty AID 202-647-5034

El Salvador (San Salvador)....Richard Nelson Cnty AID 202-647-9551

El Salvador/Minerals....Ivette Torres Cnty Mines 202-632-9352

Elastic fabrics....Enfield, Mary E USITC 202-252-1455

Elastomers....Taylor, Ed USITC 202-252-1362

Elderly Victims....Patsy Klaus Justice Stat 202-724-7774

Elderly Victims....Catherine Whitaker Justice Stat 202-724-7755

Elec. Equipment, Trade Promo.....Brades, Jay Commerce 202-377-0560

Elec. Power Gen.....Climer, David Commerce 202-377-0681

Electric Lighting....Kalkines, G. Customs 212-466-5794

Electric Propulsion....Larry Diehl NASA 216-433-2438

Electric, Motors & Engines....Joseph, I. Customs 212-466-5673

Electrical Articles....Miller, J. Customs 212-466-5680

Electrical Engineering....William King Con Product Safe 202-492-6508

Electrical Power Plants, Major Proj.....Gaines, William Commerce 202-377-4332

Electrical System....D. Wekks NASA 205-544-3309

Electrical Test and Measuring....Donnelly, Margaret T. Commerce 202-377-5466

Electrical and Powered Equipment Hazards....Carl Blechschmidt Con Product Safe 202-492-6554

Electricity....Sugg, William Commerce 202-377-1466

Electro-mechanical Sensors and Structural Dynamics....Harlan Holmes NASA 804-865-3483

ElectroOptical Instruments....Donnelly, Margaret T. Commerce

Encephalitis....Staff NINCDS 301-496-5751
Endocarditis....Staff NHLBI 301-496-4236
Endocardium....Staff NHLBI 301-496-4236
Endocrine Gland....Staff NICHD 301-496-5133
Endocrinologic Muscle Disease....Staff NINCDS 301-496-5751
Endocrinology....Staff NIDDK 301-496-3583
Endocrinology (Sexual Development)....Staff NICHD 301-496-5133
Endocrinology of Aging....Staff NIA 301-496-1752
Endodontics....Staff NIDR 301-496-4261
Endometriosis....Staff NICHD 301-496-5133
Energy Equipment, Renewable....Garden, Les Commerce
  202-377-0556
Energy, Advertising....Michael Dershowitz Fed Trade Com
  202-326-3158
Energy, Commodities....Yancik, Joseph J. Commerce 202-377-1466
Energy, Economics....Gill, Mohinder Agri 202-786-1456
Energy, Mining, Metals....Goodwin, Michael A. Commerce
  202-377-3867
Energy, Renewable....Rasmussen, John Commerce 202-377-1466
Energy, World, Economics....Taylor, Richard Agri 202-786-1708
Energy-Related Matters...James Mills Fed Trade Com
  202-326-3035
Engineering (Biomedical)....Staff DRS/BEIB 301-496-4426
Engineering (Biomedical)....Staff DCRT 301-496-1111
Engineering (Biomedical)....Staff NIGMS 301-496-7301
Engineering Services, Trade Promo.....Ruan, Robert Commerce
  202-377-0359
Engineering Surveys--Field Strength....Staff FCC 202-632-7080
Engineering resins....Taylor, Ed USITC 202-252-1362
Engines...Joseph, I. Customs 212-466-5673
Engines, Non-Electric....Cummings, Charles Commerce
  202-377-5361
Engines: aircraft....Anderson, Peder USITC 202-252-1388
Engines: other engines....Hagey, Michael USITC 202-252-1392
Environmental engineering....R.W. Latimer EPA 401-782-3000
Enterprise Statistics....Monaco, Johnny Census 301-763-1758
Entertainment Industries....Siegmund, John Commerce
  202-377-4781
Entry Fluid Physics....Kenneth Sutton NASA 804-865-3031
Environmental Carcinogens....Staff NCI 301-496-5583
Environmental Control....Staff OD/ORS 301-496-3537
Environmental Health....Staff NIEHS 919-541-3345
Environmental Law....Staff FCC 202-632-6990
Environmental Mutagenesis....Staff NIEHS 919-541-3345
Environmental Requirements for Laboratory Animals....Staff OD
  919-541-3345
Environmental Safety....Staff OD/ORS 301-496-3537
Environmental Security....Richard Titus Justice 202-724-7684
Environmental Teratology....Staff NIEHS 919-541-3345
Environmental Testing....R. Stevens NASA 205-544-1336
Environmental and analytical chemistry....R.J. Pruell EPA
  401-782-3000
Environmental biology....J. Gareth Pearson EPA 702-798-2203
Environmental chemistry....Richard L. Garnas EPA 702-798-2564
Environmental chemistry....Douglas W. Kuehl EPA 218-720-5558
Environmental chemistry....J.L. Lake EPA 401-782-3000
Environmental chemistry....D.R. Young EPA 401-782-3000
Environmental criteria....D.C. Miller EPA 401-782-3000
Environmental engineering....Pong N. Lem EPA 702-798-2522
Environmental legislation....Michael Berry EPA 919-541-4172
Environmental monitoring....Robert N. Snelling EPA 702-798-2525
Environmental photochemistry....Richard G. Zepp EPA
  404-546-3428
Environmental science....Donald T. Wruble EPA 702-798-2530
Environmental toxicology....Lawrence W. Reiter EPA 919-541-2281
Enzymes....Nesbitt, Elizabeth USITC 202-252-1355
Eosinophilic Granuloma of the Lung....Staff NHLBI 301-496-4236
Eosinophilic Syndrome....Staff NIAID 301-496-5717
Epidemiology....Richard B. Everson EPA 919-541-1963
Epidemiology & pulmonary effects....Dennis Kotchmar EPA
  919-541-4158
Epidemiology of Aging....Staff NIA 301-496-1752
Epidermodysplasis Verruciformis....Staff NCI 301-496-5583
Epidermolysis Bullosa....Staff NIAMS 301-496-8188
Epikeratophakia....Staff NEI 301-496-5248
Epilepsy....Staff NINCDS 301-496-5751
Epistaxis (Nosebleed)....Staff NHLBI 301-496-4236
Epoxides....Michels, David USITC 202-252-1352
Epoxidized ester....Johnson, Larry USITC 202-252-1351
Epoxidized linseed oils....Johnson, Larry USITC 202-252-1351
Epoxidized soya oils....Johnson, Larry USITC 202-252-1351
Epoxy resins....Taylor, Ed USITC 202-252-1362
Epstein-Barr Syndrome....Staff NIAID 301-496-5717
Epstein-Barr Virus....Staff NIAID 301-496-5717
Equal Credit Oppor. Act, Credit Practices (Energy)....Staff Fed
  Trade Com 202-326-3175
Equal Credit Opportunity Acts....Staff Fed Trade Com
  202-326-3175

Equal Employment Opportunity....Staff OD/DEO 301-496-6301
Equatorial Guinea....John Crown Cnty Commerce 202-377-0357
Equatorial Guinea....Djodi Deutsch Peace Corps 202-254-8397
Equatorial Guinea (Malabo)....Earl Irving Cnty State 202-647-4965
Equatorial Guinea (Malabo)....T. Dennis Reece Cnty AID
  202-647-7468
Equatorial Guinea (Malabo)....Abbe Fessenden Cnty AID
  202-647-7986
Equatorial Guinea/Minerals....Thomas Dolley Cnty Mines
  202-632-5065
Equipment Measurement Authorization....Staff FCC 301-725-1585
Equipment Standards....Lester Shubin Justice 202-272-6007
Equipment, General....Walmsley, William A. Commerce
  202-377-5455
Equivalent methods....Frank McElroy EPA 919-541-2622
Erythema Elevatum Diutinum....Staff NCI 301-496-5583
Erythema Nodosum....Staff NIAID 301-496-5717
Erythrocytes (Red Blood Cells)....Staff NHLBI 301-496-4236
Erythrocytes (Red Blood Cells)....Staff FDA/NCDB 301-496-3556
Esophagus, Carcinoma....Staff NCI 301-496-5583
Esotropia....Staff NEI 301-496-5248
Essential Hypertension....Staff NHLBI 301-496-4236
Essential oils....Land, Eric USITC 202-252-1349
Esters, fatty-acid, of polyhydric alcohols....Land, Eric USITC
  202-252-1349
Estonia....John W. Zerolis Cnty State 202-647-1070
Estonia....Terry R. Snell Cnty AID 202-647-4138
Estrogen Replacement Therapy....Staff NICHD 301-496-5133
Estrogen Replacement Therapy....Staff NCI 301-496-5583
Estrogen Replacement Therapy....Staff FDA 301-443-3170
Estrogen Replacement Therapy....Staff NIAMS 301-496-8188
Estrogen Replacement Therapy....Staff NIA 301-496-1752
Estrogen Therapy....Staff NIA 301-496-1752
Ethane....Land, Eric USITC 202-252-1349
Ethane....Land, Eric USITC 202-252-1349
Ethanolamines....Michels, David USITC 202-252-1352
Ethers....Michels, David USITC 202-252-1352
Ethers, fatty-acid, of polyhydric alcohols....Land, Eric USITC
  202-252-1349
Ethical Decisions Related to Patient Care....Staff NCNR
  301-496-0526
Ethics in Government Act, Energy....Chris White Fed Trade Com
  202-326-2476
Ethiopia....James Robb Cnty Commerce 202-377-4564
Ethiopia (Addis Ababa)....John Berntsen Cnty State 202-647-8852
Ethiopia (Addis Ababa)....Virginia Szymanski Cnty AID
  202-647-3355
Ethiopia (Addis Ababa)....Richard H. Eney Cnty AID
  202-647-8145
Ethiopia/Minerals....Lloyd Antonides Cnty Mines 202-632-5065
Ethnic Statistics, Ethnic Populations....Sweet, Nancy Census
  301-763-7571
Ethnic Statistics, Spanish Population....Cresce, Arthur Census
  301-763-5219
Ethnic Statistics, Spanish Population....DeNavas, Carmen Census
  301-763-5219
Ethyl alcohol (ethanol) for nonbeverage use....Michels, David
  USITC 202-252-1352
Ethylene....Raftery, Jim USITC 202-252-1365
Ethylene dibromide....Michels, David USITC 202-252-1352
Ethylene glycol....Michels, David USITC 202-252-1352
Ethylene oxide....Michels, David USITC 202-252-1352
Ethylene-propylene rubber....Taylor, Ed USITC 202-252-1362
Euro-Diff Contracts....David Bice Comm Futures 312-353-9018
Eurodollars Futures With Options....David Rosenfeld Comm
  Futures 312-353-9026
Europe/trade matters....Staff US Trade Rep 202-395-4620
European Atomic Energy Commission (Euratom)....Judith M.
  Heimann Cnty AID 202-647-4418
European Coal and Steel Community (ECSC)....Lynne F. Lambert
  Cnty AID 202-647-1708
European Communities....Patrick Garland Cnty State 202-647-6519
European Communities....Lynne F. Lambert Cnty AID
  202-647-1708
European Community....Charles Ludolph Cnty Commerce
  202-377-5276
European Economic Community (EEC)....Lynne F. Lambert Cnty
  AID 202-647-1708
European Economic Community (EEC)....K. Patrick Garland Cnty
  State 202-647-1708
European Free Trade Association (EFTA)....Brendan A. Hanniffy
  Cnty AID 202-647-8263
European Programs....Christine Adamczyk Cnty AID 202-647-9114
European Space Agency (ESA)....Sherwood McGinnis Cnty AID
  202-647-7558
Eutrophication....William L. Richardson EPA 313-675-2245
Eutrophication....J.C. Prager EPA 401-782-3000
Ewing's Sarcoma....Staff NCI 301-496-5583

Ex Parte Rules....Staff FCC 202-632-6990
Exclusionary Rule....Martin Lively Justice 202-724-2965
Exclusionary Rule....William Saulsbury Justice 202-724-7685
Exercise and Aging....Staff NIA 301-496-1752
Exercise and the Heart....Staff NHLBI 301-496-4236
Exotropia....Staff NEI 301-496-5248
Experimental Aerodynamics....Vic Corsiglia NASA 415-694-6677
Experimental Allergic Encephalomyelitis (EAE)....Staff NINCDS 301-496-5751
Experimental Development Stations....Staff FCC 202-653-6288
Experimental Fluid Mechanics....Brent Miller NASA 216-433-5815
Experimentational Instrumentation Branch....Jack Bufton NASA 301-286-8591
Expert Systems....Bill Campbell NASA 301-286-8785
Expert Systems & Software Engineering....Doly Perkins NASA 301-286-6887
Explosives...Johnson, Larry USITC 202-252-1351
Explosives....Maxey, Francis P. Commerce 202-377-0128
Explosives....Contrell, Raymond Mines 202-634-1687
Explosives....Preston, J. Customs 212-466-5488
Export (Webb-Pomerene Act)....Edward Glynn Fed Trade Com 202-326-2948
Export Examination (Animal)....Staff DRS/VRB 301-496-4463
Export Trading Companies....Stiner, John Commerce 202-377-5131
Exposure and risk assessment modeling....Robert B. Ambrose, Jr. EPA 404-546-3130
Exposure assessment....Gerald G. Akland EPA 919-541-2346
Exposure assessment....William Nelson EPA 919-541-3184
Exposure assessment....Charles H. Nauman EPA 702-798-2258
Exposure assessment....E.H. Dettmann EPA 401-782-3000
Exposure assessment....J.F. Paul EPA 401-782-3000
Exposure-effects modeling....Lawrence A. Burns EPA 404-546-3511
Exposure-effects modeling....Ray R. Lassiter EPA 404-546-3208
Extramural Associates Program....Staff OERT 301-496-9728
Extrapyramidal Disorders....Staff NINCDS 301-496-5751
Eye (Radiation and Ultra Violet Effect)....Staff FDA/NCDRH 301-443-4690
Eye (Statistics)....Staff NCHS 301-436-8500
Eye Banks....Staff NEI 301-496-5248
Eye Care....Staff NEI 301-496-5248
Eye Diseases....Staff NEI 301-496-5248
Eye Exercises....Staff NEI 301-496-5248
Eye Strain....Staff NEI 301-496-5248
Eye glasses....Johnson, Christopher USITC 202-252-1488
Eyeglasses....Staff NEI 301-496-5248
Eyeglasses....Ruth Fitzpatrick Fed Trade Com 202-326-3277
Eyeglasses, Service Industry Practices....Staff Fed Trade Com 202-326-3303
Eyewitnesses....Anne Schmidt Justice 202-724-2959

F

FAES (Foundation for Adv. Educa. in the Sciences)....Staff 301-496-7976
FM Radio Advertising....Staff FCC 202-632-7551
FM Radio Intercity Relays....Staff FCC 202-634-6307
FM Radio Remote Pickup....Staff FCC 202-634-6307
FM Radio Stations....Staff FCC 202-632-6908
FM Radio Stations--New....Staff FCC 202-632-6908
FM Translators/Boosters....Staff FCC 202-634-6307
Fabric folding machines....Greene, William USITC 202-252-1405
Fabricated Metal Construction Materials....Williams, Frankin Commerce 202-377-0132
Fabrics, tufted: woven glass....Butler, R Larry USITC 202-252-1470
Fabrics, tufted: woven jute....Cook, Lee USITC 202-252-1471
Fabrics, tufted: woven cotton....Williams, Joe USITC 202-252-1459
Fabrics: Tufted....Enfield, Mary E USITC 202-252-1455
Fabrics: billiard cloth....Cook, Lee USITC 202-252-1471
Fabrics: bolting cloth....Cook, Lee USITC 202-252-1471
Fabrics: coated....Cook, Lee USITC 202-252-1471
Fabrics: elastic....Enfield, Mary E USITC 202-252-1455
Fabrics: impression....Enfield, Mary E USITC 202-252-1455
Fabrics: knit....Enfield, Mary E USITC 202-252-1455
Fabrics: narrow....Enfield, Mary E USITC 202-252-1455
Fabrics: nonwoven....Cook, Lee USITC 202-252-1471
Fabrics: oil cloths....Cook, Lee USITC 202-252-1471
Fabrics: ornamented....Enfield, Mary E USITC 202-252-1455
Fabrics: pile....Enfield, Mary E USITC 202-252-1455
Fabrics: tapestry, woven....Cook, Lee USITC 202-252-1471
Fabrics: tire....Cook, Lee USITC 202-252-1471
Fabrics: tracing cloth....Cook, Lee USITC 202-252-1471
Fabry's Disease....Staff NINCDS 301-496-5751
Fabry's Disease....Staff NICHD 301-496-5133
Facial Neuralgia (Tic Douloureux)....Staff NINCDS 301-496-5751
Facsimile (FAX)--Wire....Staff FCC 202-634-1800

Fainting (Syncope)....Staff NHLBI 301-496-4236
Fair Credit Billing Act....Staff Fed Trade Com 202-326-3175
Fair Credit Reporting Act....Staff Fed Trade Com 202-326-3175
Fair Debit Collection Practices Act....Staff Fed Trade Com 202-326-3175
Fair Packaging & Labeling....Steve Ecklund Fed Trade Com 202-326-3034
Familial Dysautonomia (Riley-Day Syndrome)....Staff NINCDS 301-496-5751
Familial Hypertension....Staff NHLBI 301-496-4236
Familial Periodic Paralysis....Staff NINCDS 301-496-5751
Families....Staff Census 301-763-7987
Family Medicine Training....Staff HRSA/BHPr 301-443-6837
Family Nursing Practitioner....Staff HRSA/BHPr 301-443-6333
Family Planning....Staff NCNR 301-496-0526
Family Planning....Staff NCNR 301-496-0526
Family Planning (Research)....Staff NICHD 301-496-5133
Family Size....Staff NICHD 301-496-5133
Family Violence....Carol Dorsey Justice 202-272-6001
Family Violence....Joel Garner Justice 202-724-7635
Family Violence....John Thomas Justice 202-272-6004
Family Violence....Richard Titus Justice 202-724-7684
Family Violence....Lois Mock Justice 202-724-7684
Family and Aging....Staff NIA 301-496-1752
Fanconi's Anemia....Staff NHLBI 301-496-4236
Fans....Mata, Ruben USITC 202-252-1403
Far Infrared Sensor Technology....Ira Nolt NASA 804-865-3761
Farm Finances, Agri Finances, Labor, Economics....Coltrane, Robert Agri 202-786-1932
Farm Finances/Agri Fin, Prod Costs, Crops, Econ....McElroy, Bob Agri 202-786-1801
Farm Finances/Agri Fin, Prod Costs, Dairy, Econ....Betts, Carolyn Agri 202-786-1823
Farm Finances/Agri Fin, Prod Costs, Lvstock, Econ....Bowe, Russell Agri 202-786-1821
Farm Finances/Agri Finances, Agri Finances, Econ....Johnson, Jim Agri 202-786-1800
Farm Finances/Agri Finances, Agri Finances, Econ....Ericksen, Ken Agri 202-786-1798
Farm Finances/Agri Finances, Cash Receipts, Econ....Strickland, Roger Agri 202-786-1804
Farm Finances/Agri Finances, Cash Receipts, Econ....Dixon, Connie Agri 202-786-1804
Farm Finances/Agri Finances, Farm Costs, Economics....Morehart, Mitch Agri 202-786-1801
Farm Finances/Agri Finances, Farm Costs, Economics....Banker, David Agri 202-786-1800
Farm Finances/Agri Finances, Farm Credit, Economic....Stam, Jerry Agri 202-786-1885
Farm Finances/Agri Finances, Farm Credit, Economic....Ryan, Jim Agri 202-786-1798
Farm Finances/Agri Finances, Farm Income, Economic....Lucier, Gary Agri 202-786-1807
Farm Finances/Agri Finances, Farm Income, Economic....Strickland, Roger Agri 202-786-1804
Farm Finances/Agri Finances, Farm Returns, Econ....Morehart, Mitch Agri 202-786-1801
Farm Finances/Agri Finances, Farm Returns, Econ....Banker, David Agri 202-796-1800
Farm Finances/Agri Finances, Farm Subsidies, Econ....Chattin, Barbara Agri 202-786-1790
Farm Finances/Agri Finances, Indexes, Economics....Rude, Leroy Agri 202-786-1790
Farm Finances/Agri Finances, Indexes, Paid, Stats....Kleweno, Doug Agri 202-447-4214
Farm Finances/Agri Finances, Indexes, Recd, Stats....Buche, John Agri 202-447-5446
Farm Finances/Agri Finances, Indexes, Statistics....Thorpe, Fred Agri 202-447-3570
Farm Finances/Agri Finances, Labor, Statistics....Placke, Tim Agri 202-475-3228
Farm Finances/Agri Finances, Parity, Economics....Rude, Leroy Agri 202-786-1790
Farm Finances/Agri Finances, Parity, Paid, Stats....Kleweno, Doug Agri 202-447-4214
Farm Finances/Agri Finances, Parity, Recd, Stats....Buche, John Agri 202-447-5446
Farm Finances/Agri Finances, Parity, Statistics....Thorpe, Fred Agri 202-447-3570
Farm Finances/Agri Finances, Prices, Economics....Rude, Leroy Agri 202-786-1790
Farm Finances/Agri Finances, Prices, Paid, Stats....Kleweno, Doug Agri 202-447-4214
Farm Finances/Agri Finances, Prices, Recd, Stats....Buche, John Agri 202-447-5446
Farm Finances/Agri Finances, Prices, Statistics....Thorpe, Fred Agri 202-447-3570
Farm Finances/Agri Finances, Prod Costs Economics....Jagger, Craig

Agri 202-786-1804
Farm Finances/Agri Finances, Prod Costs, Statistic....Kleweno, Doug Agri 202-447-4214
Farm Finances/Agri Finances, Wages, Eonomics....Coltrane, Robert Agri 202-786-1932
Farm Finances/Agri Finanges, Wages, Statistics....Placke, Tim Agri 202-475-3228
Farm Household Income, Economics....Ahearn, Mary Agri 202-786-1807
Farm Machinery....Lien, John A. Commerce 202-377-0679
Farm Machinery, Economics....Daberkow, Stan Agri 202-786-1456
Farm Machinery, Trade Promo.....Wiening, Mary Commerce 202-377-4708
Farm Population, Census....DeAre, Diana Census 301-763-3850
Farm Population, Current Surveys....DeAre, Diana Census 301-763-3850
Farms & Land, Corporate, Economics....Reimund, Donn Agri 202-786-1523
Farms & Land, Family Farms, Economics....Reimund, Donn Agri 202-786-1523
Farms & Land, Farm Numbers, Statistics....Dillard, Dave Agri 202-475-3230
Farms & Land, Farm Productivity, Economics....Conway, Roger Agri 202-786-1459
Farms & Land, Farm Real Estate, Economics....Heneberry, William Agri 202-786-1428
Farms & Land, Foreign Land Ownership, Economics....DeBraal, Peter Agri 202-786-1425
Farms & Land, Land Use Planning, Economics....Anderson, William Agri 202-786-1424
Farms & Land, Land Use Planning, Economics....Hexem, Roger Agri 202-786-1420
Farsightedness....Staff NEI 301-496-5248
Fasteners, nails, hooks, etc.....Fitzgerald, J. Customs 212-466-5492
Fate and treatability of toxics....Richard Dobbs EPA 513-569-7649
Fate constant database....Heinz P. Kolig EPA 404-546-3770
Fate of organic pollutants....Eric J. Weber EPA 404-546-3198
Fatigue and Fracture of Metals and Composites....Charles Harris NASA 804-865-3013
Fatigue and Fracture of Metals and Composites....Charles Harris NASA 804-865-3013
Fats and Oils....Janis, William V. Commerce 202-377-2250
Fats, oils and greases, coconut, palm, wool, other....Land, Eric USITC 202-252-1349
Fatty Substances....Joseph, S. Customs 212-466-5768
Fatty acids....Randall, Rob USITC 202-252-1366
Fatty alcohols of animal or vegetable origin....Randall, Rob USITC 202-252-1366
Fatty ethers of animal or vegetable origin....Randall, Rob USITC 202-252-1366
Fatty substances derived from animal, marine, veg....Randall, Rob USITC 202-252-1366
Fatty-acid amines....Land, Eric USITC 202-252-1349
Fatty-acid esters of polyhydric alcohols....Land, Eric USITC 202-252-1349
Fatty-acid quaternary ammonium salts (surface act)....Land, Eric USITC 202-252-1349
Fault-Tolerant Systems....Charles Meissner NASA 804-865-3681
Fear of Crime....William Saulsbury Justice 202-724-7685
Fear of Crime....Lawrence Bennett Justice 202-724-2956
Fear of Crime....Lois Mock Justice 202-724-7684
Fear of Crime....Richard Titus Justice 202-724-7684
Fear of Crime....Sue Lindgren Justice Stat 202-724-7759
Fear of Crime....Patsy Klaus Justice Stat 202-724-7774
Fear of Crime....Michael Rand Justice Stat 202-724-7774
Feather products....Spalding, Josephine USITC 202-252-1498
Feathers....Steller, Rose USITC 202-252-1323
Feathers....Persky, H. Customs 212-466-5881
Febrile Convulsions....Staff NINCDS 301-496-5751
Federal Justice....Carol Kaplan Justice Stat 202-724-7759
Federal State Relations....Bruce Freedman Fed Trade Com 202-326-2464
Federated States of Micronesia...James D. Berg Cnty State 202-647-0108
Feed Grains, Economics....Hull, Dave Agri 202-786-1840
Feed Grains, Statistics....Van Lahr, Charles Agri 202-447-7369
Feed Grains, World, Economics....Riley, Peter Agri 202-786-1692
Feeding Impairments....Staff NIDR 301-496-4261
Feeds, animal....Pierre-Benoist, John USITC 202-252-1320
Feldspar....White, Linda USITC 202-252-1427
Feldspar....Potter, Michael J. Mines 202-634-1180
Female Offenders....Anne Schmidt Justice 202-724-2959
Female Offenders....Phyllis Jo Baunach Justice Stat 202-724-7755
Female Offenders....Stephanie Minor-Harper Justice Stat 202-724-7755
Female Offenders - Federal....Carol Kaplan Justice Stat 202-724-7759
Female Victims....Patsy Klaus Justice Stat 202-724-7774

Fencing, Metal....Williams, Franklin Commerce 202-377-0132
Ferments....Nesbitt, Elizabeth USITC 202-252-1355
Ferricyanide blue...Johnson, Larry USITC 202-252-1351
Ferroalloys....Neuharth, Clark Mines 202-634-1753
Ferroalloys Products....Bell, Charles Commerce 202-377-0609
Ferrous Scrap....Sharkey, Robert Commerce 202-377-0606
Fertility....Staff NICHD 301-496-5133
Fertility Births, No. Geographic Concepts/Products....O'Connell, Martin/Bachu, Amara Census 301-763-5303
Fertility Births, No. Geographic Concepts/Products....Bachu, Amaru Census 301-763-5303
Fertilizer, Economics....Andrilenas, Paul Agri 202-786-1456
Fertilizers....Trainor, Cynthia USITC 202-252-1354
Fertilizers....Maxey, Francis P. Commerce 202-377-0128
Fertilizers....Brownchweig, G. Customs 212-466-5744
Fetal Monitoring....Staff NICHD 301-496-5133
Fetus....Staff NICHD 301-496-5133
Fever....Staff NIAID 301-496-5717
Fever Blisters....Staff NIDR 301-496-4261
Fiber Optic Sensors for Structural Dynamics....Robert Rogowski NASA 804-865-3036
Fibers....Edert, R. Customs 212-466-5885
Fibers, Economics....Lawler, John Agri 202-786-1840
Fibers: Alpaca....Freund, Kimberlie USITC 202-252-1456
Fibers: abaca....Cook, Lee USITC 202-252-1471
Fibers: camel hair....Freund, Kimberlie USITC 202-252-1456
Fibers: cashmere....Freund, Kimberlie USITC 202-252-1456
Fibers: cotton....Enfield, Mary E USITC 202-252-1455
Fibers: flax....Cook, Lee USITC 202-252-1471
Fibers: jute....Cook, Lee USITC 202-252-1471
Fibers: angora....Freund, Kimberlie USITC 202-252-1456
Fibrillation....Staff NHBLI 301-496-4236
Fibrin....Randall, Rob USITC 202-252-1366
Fibrinolysis....Staff NHBLI 301-496-4236
Fibromuscular Hyperplasia....Staff NHBLI 301-496-4236
Fibrositis....Staff NIAMS 301-496-8188
Fibrotic Lung Diseases....Staff NHLBI 301-496-4236
Field Disturbance....Staff FCC 202-653-6285
Field applicability....Steven F. Hedtke EPA 218-720-2492
Field sampling methods....Charles N. Smith EPA 404-546-3175
Fields and particles....Keith Ogilvie NASA 301-286-5904
Fiji...Carla Joyner Peace Corps 202-254-3227
Fiji (Suva)....Ann M. Cambara Cnty State 202-647-3546
Fiji (Suva)....Robert A. Benziger Cnty AID 202-647-3546
Fiji (Suva)....Michael Feldstein Cnty AID 202-647-9137
Fiji/Minerals....Travis Lyday Cnty Mines 202-634-1272
Filariasis....Staff NIAID 301-496-5717
Filberts....Burket, Stephen USITC 202-252-1318
Film....Brownchweig, G Customs 212-466-5744
Film (photographic)....Bishop, Kate USITC 202-252-1494
Film, plastics....Truskett, Brooks USITC 202-252-1364
Filtering/Purifying Apparatus....Rocks, M. Customs 212-466-5669
Filters/Purifying Equipment....Jonkers, Loretta Commerce 202-377-0564
Finance and Management Ind.....Candilis, Wray O. Commerce 202-377-0339
Financial Markets, Economics....Sullivan, Pat Agri 202-786-1290
Finland....Maryanne Lyons Cnty Commerce 202-377-3254
Finland (Helsinki)....George Boutin Cnty State 202-647-5669
Finland (Helsinki)....Richard A. Christenson Cnty AID 202-647-0624
Finland/Minerals....Harold Newman Cnty Mines 202-634-1276
Fire....Staff FCC 717-337-1212
Fire and Thermal Burn....James Hoebel Con Product Safe 202-492-6554
Firearms....Robinson, Hazel USITC 202-252-1496
Firearms....Preston, J. Customs 212-466-5488
Firewood....Ruggles, Frederick USITC 202-252-1326
Fireworks....Spalding, Josephine USITC 202-252-1498
First aid kits....Randall, Rob USITC 202-252-1366
Fish....Corey, Roger USITC 202-252-1327
Fish....Brady, T. Customs 212-466-5790
Fish Nets and Fish Nettings....Barth, G. Customs 212-466-5884
Fish and fish food taxonomy....Richard E. Siefert EPA 218-720-5552
Fish culture....Douglas P. Middaugh EPA 904-932-5311
Fish nets and netting....Cook, Lee USITC 202-252-1471
Fish oils....Reeder, John USITC 202-252-1319
Fish toxicology....Donald L. Brockway EPA 404-546-3422
Fisheries, Major Proj.....Bell, Richard Commerce 202-377-2460
Fishing tackle....Robinson, Hazel USITC 202-252-1496
Fixtures....Mearman, John Commerce 202-377-0315
Flags....Cook, Lee USITC 202-252-1471
Flammable Fabric Issues, Consum. Prod. Saf. Comm.....Staff Fed Trade Com 202-634-7700
Flares....Spalding, Josephine USITC 202-252-1498
Flashlights....Hagey, Michael USITC 202-252-1392
Flat Goods....Gorman, K. Customs 212-466-5893

Experts

Flat glass and products....Bedore, James USITC 202-252-1424
Flat goods....Seastrum, Carl USITC 202-252-1493
Flavoring Extract...Joseph, S. Customs 212-466-5768
Flavoring Extracts....McIntyre, Leo R. Commerce 202-377-0128
Flaxseed and linseed oil....Reeder, John USITC 202-252-1319
Flexible Mftg. Systems....McGibbon, Patrick Commerce 202-377-0314
Flexible Mftg. Systems, Trade Promo.....Manzolillo, Franc Commerce 202-377-2991
Flight Dynamics....Don Berry NASA 805-258-3140
Flight Dynamics....Frank McGarry NASA 301-286-6846
Flight Dynamics....Joseph Johnson NASA 804-865-2184
Flight Dynamics and Control...Jarrell Elliott NASA 804-865-3291
Flight Dynamics and Controls....Vic Lebacqz NASA
Flight Experiments and Shuttle Payloads....Roger Breckenridge NASA 804-865-4834
Flight Management Technology Advanced Crew Interfa....Sam Morello NASA 804-865-3621
Flight Research Measurement Techniques....Bruch Holmes NASA 804-865-3274
Flight Systems....Jim Phelphs NASA 805-258-3117
Flight Test Measurement and Instrumentation....Rodney Boge NASA 805-258-3158
Flight simulating machines....Andersen, Peder USITC 202-252-1388
Floaters....Staff NEI 301-496-5248
Floating structures....Kavalauskas, Juanita USITC 202-252-1402
Floor Coverings....Eyskens, R. Customs 212-466-5854
Floor Coverings, Hard Surfaces....Rubenstein, Nathan Commerce 202-377-0132
Floor coverings, non-textile....Rodriguez, Laura USITC 202-252-1499
Floor coverings, textile....Borsari, Marilyn USITC 202-252-1465
Flooring (wood)....Vacant USITC 202-252-1326
Floppy Baby (Nemaline Myopathy)....Staff NINCDS 301-496-5751
Floral waters....Land, Eric USITC 202-252-1349
Flour....Janis, William V. Commerce 202-377-2250
Flour (grain)....Pierre-Benoist, John USITC 202-252-1320
Flower and foliage: artificial, other....Spalding, Josephine USITC 202-252-1498
Flower and foliage: preserved, other....Spalding, Josephine USITC 202-252-1498
Flowers....Janis, William V. Commerce 202-377-2250
Flowers and foilage: artificial and plastics....Truskett, Brooks USITC 202-252-1364
Flowers and foliage: preserved, plastics....Truskett, Brooks USITC 202-252-1364
Flowers, artificial....Rauch, T. Customs 212-466-5892
Flue gas cleaning technologies....J. David Mobley EPA 919-541-2612
Fluid Dynamics....F. Leslie NASA 205-544-1633
Fluid Mechanics and Physics....Robert Meyers NASA 805-258-3707
Fluid Power....McDonald, Edward Commerce 202-377-0680
Fluorescein Angiography....Staff NEI 301-496-5248
Fluoridation....Staff CDC 404-329-3534
Fluoridation....Staff NIDR 301-496-4261
Fluoride Research....Staff NIDR 301-496-4261
Fluorocarbons....Michels, David USITC 202-252-1352
Fluorspar....DeSapio, Vincent USITC 202-252-1435
Fluorspar....Manion, James J. Commerce 202-377-5157
Fluorspar....Morse, David Mines 202-634-1190
Fluxes....White, Linda USITC 202-252-1427
Fogarty Publications....Staff FIC 301-496-2075
Fogarty Scholars....Staff FIC 301-496-4161
Foil, metal: aluminum....McNay, Deborah USITC 202-252-1425
Foil, metal: other....Kollins, Susan USITC 202-252-1441
Food & Drug, Advertising Practices....Staff Fed Trade Com 202-326-3076
Food Additives....Staff FDA 301-472-4750
Food Grains, Economics....Schienbein, Allen Agri 202-786-1840
Food Grains, Statistics....Siegenthaler, Vaughn Agri 202-447-8068
Food Grains, World, Economics....Schwartz, Sara Agri 202-786-1693
Food Labeling....Staff FDA 301-472-4750
Food Products Machinery....Axelrod, Irvin Commerce 202-377-0310
Food Retailing....Kenney, Cornelius Commerce 202-377-2428
Food, Agriculture Policy, Economics....Leaderer, Tom Agri 202-786-1780
Food, Agriculture Policy, Economics....Pollack, Susan Agri 202-786-1780
Food, Agriculture Policy, World, Economics....Sharples, Jerry Agri 202-786-1636
Food, CPI, Economics....Parlett, Ralph Agri 202-786-1870
Food, CPI, Economics....Dunham, Denis Agri 202-786-1870
Food, Food & Nutrition Policy, Economics....Smallwood, Dave Agri 202-786-1864
Food, Food Assistance Research, Economics....Smallwood, Dave Agri 202-786-1864
Food, Food Away From Home, Economics....Linstrom, Harold Agri 202-786-1864
Food, Food Consumption, Economics....Putnam, Judy Agri 202-786-1866
Food, Food Demand, Economics....Haidacher, Richard Agri 202-786-1862
Food, Food Demand, World, Economics....Korb, Peni Agri 202-786-1688
Food, Food Expenditures, Economics....Haidacher, Richard Agri 202-786-1862
Food, Food Expenditures, World, Economics....Korb, Penni Agri 202-786-1688
Food, Food Manufacturing, Economics....Handy, Charles Agri 202-786-1862
Food, Food Policy, Economics....Leaderer, Tom Agri 202-786-1780
Food, Food Policy, Economics....Pollack, Susan Agri 202-786-1780
Food, Food Policy, World, Economics....Sharples, Jerry Agri 202-786-1636
Food, Food Prices, Economics....Parlett, Ralph Agri 202-786-1870
Food, Food Prices, Economics....Dunham, Denis Agri 202-786-1870
Food, Food Quality, Economics....Roberts, Tanya Agri 202-786-1787
Food, Food Retailing, Economics....Handy, Charles Agri 202-786-1862
Food, Food Safety, Economics....Roberts, Tanya Agri 202-786-1787
Food, Food Wholesaling, Economics....Epps, Walter Agri 202-786-1866
Food, Marketing Margins, Economics....Dunham, Denis Agri 202-786-1870
Food, Marketing Margins, Economics....Elitzak, Howard Agri 202-786-1870
Food, Marketing Margins, Economics....Handy, Charles Agri 202-786-1862
Food, Marketing Statistics, Economics....Dunham, Denis Agri 202-786-1870
Food, Marketing Statistics, Economics....Elitzak, Howard Agri 202-786-1870
Food, Marketing Statistics, Economics....Handy, Charles Agri 202-786-1862
Food, Meat Demand, Economics....Ginzel, John Agri 202-786-1823
Food, Meat Demand, Economics....Gustafson, Ron Agri 202-786-1830
Food, Meat Demand, Economics....Hahn, Bill Agri 202-786-1830
Food, Meat Price Spreads, Economics....Duewer, Larry Agri 202-786-1821
Food, Meat Price Spreads, Economics....Nelson, Ken Agri 202-786-1820
Food-preparing machines....Jackson, Georgia USITC 202-252-1399
Footwear....Burns, Gail USITC 202-252-1469
Footwear....Byron, James Commerce 202-377-4034
Footwear....Sheridan J. Customs 212-466-5889
Footwear....Francke, E. Customs 212-466-5890
Footwear, parts & accessories....Sheridan, J. Customs 212-466-5889
Forecasting Prison Populations....Bernard Shipley Justice Stat 202-724-7770
Foreign Geography....Durland, Robert Census 301-763-1779
Foreign Owned U.S. Firms....McDonald, Jerry Census 301-763-5182
Foreign Scientists Assistance....Staff FIC 301-472-6166
Foreign Trade Data Services....Davis, Minnie M. Census 301-763-7754
Foreign Trade Data Services....Staff Census 301-763-5140
Foreign Trade Division....Adams, Don L. Census 301-763-5342
Forensics and Technology....Joseph Kochanski Justice 202-724-2962
Forest Products....Butts, Donald W. Commerce 202-377-0375
Forest Products....Staff FCC 717-337-1212
Forest Products, Domestic Construction....Kristensen, Chris Commerce 202-377-0384
Forest Products, Trade Policy....Smith, Mary Anne Commerce 202-377-0132
Forest ecological systems....Darcy Campbell EPA 919-541-4477
Forest ecology....Roger Blair EPA 503-757-4662
Forfeiture....Marianne Zawitz Justice Stat 202-724-6100
Forfeiture of Assets....John Spevacek Justice 202-272-6010
Forged-steel grinding balls....Murphy, Mary USITC 202-252-1401
Forgings Semifinished Steel....Bell, Charles Commerce 202-377-0609
Fork-lift trucks....Murphy, Mary USITC 202-252-1401
Formaldehyde....Michels, David USITC 202-252-1352
Fort Detrick....Staff NCI 301-496-5583
Fossil Fuel Power Generation, Major Proj.....Gaines, William S. Commerce 202-377-4332
Foundry Equipment....Comer, Barbara Commerce 202-377-0316
Foundry Industry....Bell, Charles Commerce 202-377-0609
Foundry products....Paulson, Mark USITC 202-252-1432

Fracture Healing....Staff NIAMS 301-496-8188
Fractured....Steve Schmelling EPA 405-332-2315
France....Maria Aronson Cnty Commerce 202-377-8008
France (Paris)....Deborah Graze Cnty State 202-647-2633
France (Paris)...Josef Ruth Cnty State 202-647-2633
France (Paris)....Brian D. Curran Cnty AID 202-647-2633
France (Paris)....Karen Milliken Cnty AID 202-647-3746
France/Minerals....Donald Buck Cnty Mines 202-632-5052
Franchise Rule, Business Opportunities
Fraud....(Non-Investment)/Marketing Practices Fed Trade Com
  202-326-3128
Franchising....Kostecka, Andrew Commerce 202-377-0342
Franchising....Staff FCC 202-254-3407
Freedom of Information....Staff OD/DC 301-496-5633
French Antilles....Avon Williams Cnty State 202-647-2621
French Antilles....David F. Rogus Cnty AID 202-647-2130
French Guiana....Avon Williams Cnty State 202-647-2621
French Guiana....Mack Tadeu Cnty Commerce 202-377-2527
French Guinea/Minerals....Alfredo Gurmendi Cnty Mines
  202-632-9352
French Polynesia....Ann M. Cambara Cnty State 202-647-4965
French Polynesia (Papeete)....Robert A. Benziger Cnty AID
  202-647-3546
Freon (chlorofluorocarbons)....Michels, David USITC
  202-252-1352
Frequencies Allocations, Government....Staff FCC 202-653-8147
Frequencies Allocations, International....Staff FCC 202-653-8126
Frequencies Allocations, Non-Government....Staff FCC
  202-653-8108
Frequency Standards Research....Lute Maleki NASA 818-354-3688
Friedreich's Ataxia....Staff NINCDS 301-496-5751
Frohlich's Syndrome....Staff NINCDS 301-496-5751
Fructose....Randall, Rob USITC 202-252-1355
Fruit, edible, ex citrus....Macomber, Alvin USITC 202-252-1315
Fruits....Hopard, S. Customs 212-466-5760
Fruits, Canned....Hodgen, Donald A. Commerce 202-377-3346
Fruits, Economics....Huang, Ben Agri 202-786-1767
Fruits, Economics....Buxton, Boyd Agri 202-786-1767
Fruits, Statistics....Johnson, Doyle Agri 202-447-5412
Fuchs' Dystrophy....Staff NEI 301-496-5248
Fuel Saving Devices....Michael Dershowitz Fed Trade Com
  202-326-3158
Fuel oil (nos. 1, 2, 3, 4, 5, 6)....Foreso, Cynthia USITC
  202-252-1348
Fuel oil, bunker "C"....Foreso, Cynthia USITC 202-252-1348
Fuel oil, navy special....Foreso, Cynthia USITC 202-252-1348
Fuel, jet....Foreso, Cynthia USITC 202-252-1348
Fugitive dust control....Paul dePercin EPA 513-569-7797
Full-Scale Reynolds Number Test Technique....Lawrence putnam
  NASA 804-865-2601
Fulminates...Johnson, Larry USITC 202-252-1351
Fumes (Hazardous)....Staff OD/ORS 301-496-2960
Funeral Rule Review....Raouf Abdullah Fed Trade Com
  202-326-3024
Funeral Rule, Energy....Carol Jennings Fed Trade Com
  202-326-3010
Fungal Diseases (Eyes)....Staff NEI 301-496-5248
Fungal Infections....Staff NIAID 301-496-5717
Fur Goods....Enright, Joe Commerce 202-377-3459
Fur and furlike apparel....Worrel, Jackie USITC 202-252-1466
Furfural....Michels, David USITC 202-252-1352
Furnace black...Johnson, Larry USITC 202-252-1351
Furnaces....Mata, Ruben USITC 202-252-1403
Furnaces....Riedl, K. Customs 212-466-5493
Furnishings & Related Articles....Eyskens, R. Customs
  212-466-5854
Furniture....Linkins, Linda USITC 202-252-1499
Furniture....Ellis, Kevin Commerce 202-377-1140
Furniture....Mishinske, L. Customs 212-466-5739
Furniture Guides....Wally Witkowski Fed Trade Com 202-326-3015
Furskins....Steller, Rose USITC 202-252-1323
Fused Alumina, Abrasive....Austin, Gordon Mines 202-634-1206
Fuses: Blasting....Spalding, Josephine USITC 202-252-1498
Fuses: electrical....Vacant USITC 202-252-1391
Fusion energy....Greenblatt, Jack USITC 202-252-1353
Futures Markets, Economics....Heifner, Richard Agri 202-786-1868
Futures Markets, Livestock, Economics....Ginzel, John Agri
  202-786-1830

G

GPD Deficiency....Staff NHLBI 301-496-4236
GBF/DIME System....Staff Census 301-763-4664
GM Auto Complaints, Enforcement....Staff Fed Trade Com
  202-326-3027
Gabon....Ian Davis Cnty Commerce 202-377-0357

Gabon....Djodi Deutsch Peace Corps 202-254-8397
Gabon (Libreville)....Susan Zelle Cnty State 202-647-4965
Gabon (Libreville)....T. Dennis Reece Cnty AID 202-647-7468
Gabon (Libreville)....Abbe Fessenden Cnty AID 202-647-7986
Gabon/Minerals....Hendrik van Oss Cnty Mines 202-632-5065
Galactorrhea....Staff NIDDK 301-496-3583
Galactosemia....Staff NIDDK 301-496-3583
Galactosemia....Staff NICHD 301-496-5133
Galactosemia....Staff NINCDS 301-496-5751
Gallbladder....Staff NIDDK 301-496-3583
Gallium....Wagner, Lorie USITC 202-252-1439
Gallium....Cammarota, David Commerce 202-377-0575
Gallium....Kramer, Deborah A. Mines 202-634-1083
Gallstones....Staff NIDDK 301-496-3583
Gambia....Philip Michelini Cnty Commerce 202-377-4388
Gambia The (Banjul)....Jean G. Soso Cnty AID 202-647-2865
Gambia The (Banjul)....Yvonne Y. John Cnty AID 202-647-6049
Gambia, The (Banjul)....Stephen Kelly Cnty State 202-647-2865
Gambia/Minerals....Hendrik van Oss Cnty Mines 202-632-5065
Game animals....Ludwick, David USITC 202-252-1329
Games....Robinson, Hazel USITC 202-252-1496
Games....McKenna, T. Customs 212-466-5475
Games and Childrens' Vehicles....Hughes, Patrick Commerce
  202-377-5479
Games of Chance, Energy...John Mendenhall Fed Trade Com
  216-942-4210
Gamma Ray Astronomy....G. Fishman NASA 205-544-7691
Gamma spectrometry....Daryl L.Thome EPA 702-798-2158
Garage Door Openers--Licenses....Staff FCC 717-337-1212
Garage Door Openers--Not Licensed....Staff FCC 202-653-6288
Garments, body support....Davis, H. Customs 212-466-5880
Garnet....Austin, Gordon Mines 202-634-1206
Garters and suspenders....MacKnight, Peggy USITC 202-252-1468
Gas....Perry, Douglas Commerce 202-377-1466
Gas generators....Fravel, Dennis USITC 202-252-1404
Gas kinetics....Joseph J. Bufalini EPA 919-541-2422
Gas oil....Foreso, Cynthia USITC 202-252-1348
Gas, Gems, & Oil....Dave Fix Fed Trade Com 202-326-3298
Gas, Natural....Perry, Douglas Commerce 202-377-1466
Gas-operated metalworking appliances....Fravel, Dennis USITC
  202-252-1404
Gasketing Materials....Fletcher, William E. Commerce
  202-377-0309
Gaskets/Gasketing Materials....Fletcher, William E. Commerce
  202-377-0309
Gasoline....Foreso, Cynthia USITC 202-252-1348
Gasoline Futures....Anthony Criso Comm Futures 212-668-2080
Gastric Hypersecretion....Staff NIDDK 301-496-3583
Gastrinoma....Staff NIDDK 301-496-3583
Gastrointestinal Disorders....Staff NIDDK 301-496-3583
Gastrointestinal Tract Diseases....Staff NIDDK 301-496-3583
Gaucher's Disease....Staff NINCDS 301-496-5751
Gauze, impregnated with medicinals....Randall, Rob USITC
  202-252-1366
Gears....Riedl, K. Customs 212-466-5493
Gelatin, articles of....Spalding, Josephine USITC 202-252-1498
Gelatin, edible....Jonnard, Aimison USITC 202-252-1350
Gelatin, inedible....Jonnard, Aimison USITC 202-252-1350
Gelatin, photographic....Jonnard, Aimison USITC 202-252-1350
Gelatine....Brownchweig, G. Customs 212-466-5744
Gems....White, Linda USITC 202-252-1427
Gemstone Investments, Energy....Dave Fix Fed Trade Com
  202-326-3298
Gemstones....Austin, Gordon Mines 202-634-1206
Gemstones, imitation....Witherspoon, Ricardo USITC
  202-252-1489
GenBank (Genetic Sequence Data Bank)....Staff NIGMS
  301-496-7301
General Agreement on Trade and Tariffs (GATT)....Staff US Trade
  Rep 202-395-6843
General Aviation Aircraft (Industry Analysis)....Kingsbury, Gene
  Commerce 202-377-0677
General Clinical Research Centers Program....Staff DRR
  301-496-6595
General Information, Credit....Staff Fed Trade Com
  202-326-3175
General Mobile Licenses....Staff FCC 717-337-1212
General Mobile Radio Service....Staff FCC 717-337-1212
Generator Sets....Climer, David Commerce 202-377-0681
Generator Sets, Major Proj/Turbines....Gaines, William S.
  Commerce 202-377-4332
Generators....Cutchin, John USITC 202-252-1396
Generators....Climer, David Commerce 202-377-0681
Genetic Pancrea. Involv.not due to Cystic Fibrosis....Staff NIDDK
  301-496-3583
Genetic toxicology....G.G. Pesch EPA 401-782-3000
Genetic toxicology....Michael D. Waters EPA 919-541-2537
Genetic toxicology of complex mixtures....Joellen Lewtas EPA

919-541-3849

Genetics....Staff NINCDS 301-496-5751
Genetics....Staff NIGMS 301-496-7301
Genetics....Staff NIDR 301-496-4261
Genetics....Staff NICHD 301-496-5133
Genetics (Animal Monitoring)....Staff DRS/VRB 301-496-9188
Genetics of Aging....Staff NIA 301-496-1752
Genital Herpes....Staff NIAID 301-496-5717
Genital Warts....Staff NIAID 301-496-5717
Geochemistry....Robert Puls EPA 405-332-2262
Geodynamics...Jean Dickey NASA 818-354-3235
Geographical information systems....Thomas H. Mace EPA
    702-798-2262
Geography/cartography....James M. Omernik EPA 503-753-4666
Geology Geophysics...J. Heirtzler NASA 301-286-5213
Geriatric Medicine....Staff NIA 301-496-1752
Geriatric Psychiatry....Staff NIMH 301-443-4515
Geriatric Psychiatry....Staff NIA 301-496-1752
Geriatrics....Staff NIA 301-496-1752
German Democratic Republic (Berlin)....Charles Skinner Cnty
    State 202-647-2005
German Measles (Rubella)....Staff NIAID 301-496-5717
Germanium....Wagner, Lorie USITC 202-252-1439
Germanium....Cammarota, David Commerce 202-377-0575
Germanium....Llewellyn, Thomas Mines 202-634-1084
Germany Democratic Republic (Berlin)....James B. Lane Cnty AID
    202-647-2721
Germany, East....Vacant Cnty Commerce 202-377-2654
Germany, East/Minerals....George Rabchevsky Cnty Mines
    202-632-5053
Germany, Federal Republic of (Bonn)....Timothy Savage Cnty State
    202-647-2155
Germany, Federal Republic of (Bonn)....Ken Pitterle Cnty State
    202-647-2005
Germany, Federal Republic of (Bonn)....Larry Nelsen Cnty State
    202-647-2155
Germany, Federal Republic of (Bonn)....Timothy Tulenko Cnty
    State 202-647-2155
Germany, Federal Republic of (Bonn)....William R. Salisbury Cnty
    AID 202-647-7205
Germany, Federal Republic of (Bonn)....Robert M. Beecroft Cnty
    AID 202-647-2155
Germany, Federal Republic of (Bonn)....Carol L. Van Voorst Cnty
    AID 202-647-1092
Germany, Federal Republic of (Bonn)....E. Wayne Merry Cnty
    AID 202-647-2310
Germany, West....Velizar Stanoyevitch Cnty Commerce
    202-377-2434
Germany, West/Minerals....George Rabchevsky Cnty Mines
    202-632-5053
Germfree Rodents....Staff DRS/VRB 301-496-3601
Gerontology....Staff NIA 301-496-1752
Gerson Method....Staff NCI 301-496-5583
Gestation....Staff NICHD 301-496-5133
Ghana....Reginald Biddle Cnty Commerce 202-377-4388
Ghana...Anna West Peace Corps 202-254-5644
Ghana (Accra)....Frederick Kaplan Cnty State 202-647-3391
Ghana (Accra)....Thomas J. Burke Cnty AID 202-647-8436
Ghana (Accra)....Rudolph Thomas Cnty AID 202-647-7985
Ghana/Minerals....Hendrik van Oss Cnty Mines 202-632-5065
Giardiasis....Staff NIAID 301-496-5717
Gibraltar....Howard Perlow Cnty State 202-647-8027
Gibraltar...James B. Whitlock Cnty AID 202-647-2622
Gibraltar...Richard A. Christenson Cnty AID 202-647-4484
Gigantism....Staff NIDDK 301-496-3583
Gilbert's Syndrome....Staff NIDDK 301-496-3583
Gilles de la Tourette's Disease....Staff NINCDS 301-496-5751
Gingival Diseases....Staff NIDR 301-496-4261
Girls' & Infant's Apparel....Kirschner, B. Customs 212-466-5865
Glace fruit and vegetable substances....Macomber, Alvin USITC
    202-252-1315
Glands....Staff NIDDK 301-496-3583
Glass....Bedore, James USITC 202-252-1424
Glass....Bunin, J. Customs 212-466-5796
Glass articles, nspf....Bedore, James USITC 202-252-1424
Glass fiber....Bedore, James USITC 202-252-1424
Glass yarn....Butler, R Larry USITC 202-252-1471
Glass, Flat....Williams, Franklin Commerce 202-377-0132
Glassblowing....Staff DRS/BEIB 301-496-5195
Glassware....McNay, Deborah USITC 202-252-1425
Glassware....Corea, Judy Commerce 202-377-0311
Glassware (Issue and Washing)....Staff OD/ORS 301-496-4595
Glassworking machines....Lippa, Alison USITC 202-252-1398
Glaucoma....Staff NEI 301-496-5248
Glazing compounds...Johnson, Larry USITC 202-252-1351
Gliomas....Staff NINCDS 301-496-5751
Global Cloud Properties....William Rossow NASA 212-678-5567
Global Modeling and Simulation....Marvin Geller NASA

301-286-5002

Global change issues....Steve Bromberg EPA 919-541-2919
Global climate change....Michael A. Maxwell EPA 919-541-3091
Global climate change....Richard G. Zepp EPA 404-546-3428
Global climate change....Peter A. Beedlow EPA 503-757-4791
Globoid Cell Leukodystrophy....Staff NINCDS 301-496-5751
Glomerulonephritis....Staff NIDDK 301-496-3583
Gloves....Worrell, Jackie USITC 202-252-1466
Gloves (Work)....Enright, Joe Commerce 202-377-3459
Gloves, dress & work....Davis, H. Customs 212-466-5880
Glucose Intolerance....Staff NIDDK 301-496-3583
Glue....Brownchweig, G. Customs 212-466-5744
Glue size...Jonnard, Aimison USITC 202-252-1350
Glue, articles of....Spalding, Josephine USITC 202-252-1498
Glue, of animal or vegetable origina....Jonnard, Aimison USITC
    202-252-1350
Glue, vegetable...Jonnard, Aimison USITC 202-252-1350
Glycerine....Michels, David USITC 202-252-1352
Glycogen Storage Disease....Staff NIDDK 301-496-3583
Glycogen Storage Disease....Staff NICHD 301-496-5133
Glycols....Michels, David USITC 202-252-1352
Goiter....Staff NIDDK 301-496-3583
Gold....Kollins, Susan USITC 202-252-1441
Gold....Lucus, John M. Mines 202-634-1070
Gold Futures....Rick Sanborn Comm Futures 212-668-2079
Gold compounds....Greenblatt, Jack USITC 202-252-1353
Golf equipment....Robinson, Hazel USITC 202-252-1496
Gonads....Staff NICHD 301-496-5133
Gonorrhea....Staff NIAID 301-496-5717
Goodpasture's Syndrome....Staff NHLBI 301-496-4236
Goodpasture's Syndrome....Staff NIDDK 301-496-3583
Gorgas Memorial Institute....Staff FIC 301-496-1415
Gout....Staff NIAMS 301-496-8188
Governments Division....Coleman, John R. Census 301-763-7366
Governments, Criminal Justice Statistics....Cull, Diana Census
    301-763-7789
Governments, Eastern States Government Sector....Speight,
    Genevieve Census 301-763-7783
Governments, Employment....Stevens, Alan Census 301-763-5086
Governments, Federal Expenditure Data....Kellerman, David
    Census 301-763-5276
Governments, Finance....Wulf, Henry Census 301-763-7664
Governments, Governmental Organization....Cull, Diana Census
    301-763-7789
Governments, Revenue Sharing....Hogan, James Census
    301-763-5120
Governments, Special Projects....Cull, Diana Census 301-763-7789
Governments, Taxation....Keffer, Gerard Census 301-763-5356
Governments, Western States Government Sector....Harris, Ulvey
    Census 301-763-5344
Grain....Conte, R. Customs 212-466-5759
Grain products, milled....Pierre-Benoist, John USITC 202-252-1320
Grains....Pierre-Benoist, John USITC 202-252-1320
Granite....White, Linda USITC 202-252-1427
Granular activated carbon....J Keith Carswell EPA 513-569-7389
Granulocytopenia....Staff NIDDK 301-496-3583
Granulomatous Diseases....Staff NIAID 301-496-5717
Grape Cure....Staff NCI 301-496-5583
Grapefruit oil (essential oil)....Land, Eric USITC 202-252-1349
Graphite....White, Linda USITC 202-252-1427
Graphite....Taylor, Harold A. Mines 202-634-1180
Grave's Disease....Staff NEI 301-496-5248
Gravel....Tepordei, Valentin V. Mines 202-634-1185
Gravitational Wave Studies....John Armstrong NASA 818-354-3151
Grease, lubricating....Foreso, Cynthia USITC 202-252-1348
Great Lakes....William L. Richardson EPA 313-675-2245
Greece....Ann Corro Cnty Commerce 202-377-3945
Greece (Athens)....James F. Jeffrey Cnty State 202-647-6113
Greece (Athens)....Alexander Karagiannis Cnty State 202-647-6113
Greece (Athens)....David T. Jones Cnty AID 202-647-1563
Greece (Athens)....David D. Pearce Cnty AID 202-647-7576
Greece/Minerals....John Panulas Cnty Mines 202-634-1277
Greenhouse Effect....James Hansen NASA 212-678-5619
Greenland....Kenneth Kolb Cnty State 202-647-5669
Greenland....R. Ross Rodger Cnty AID 202-647-1774
Greenland....Richard A. Christenson Cnty AID 202-647-4484
Greenland/Minerals....Donald Buck Cnty Mines 202-632-5052
Greensand....Searls, James P. Mines 202-634-1190
Greeting Cards....Bratland, Rose Marie Commerce 202-377-0380
Grenada....Robert Dormitzer Cnty Commerce 202-377-2527
Grenada (St. George's)....Vonda Delawie Cnty State 202-647-2621
Grenada (St. George)....Walter Andrusyszyn Cnty AID
    202-647-4195
Grenada (St. George)....Ingrid Peters Cnty AID 202-647-3447
Grid Generation and Numerical Techniques....Robert Smith NASA
    804-865-3978
Grinding machines....Greene, William USITC 202-252-1405
Ground fish....Corey, Roger USITC 202-252-1327

Ground-water modeling....Joseph J. D'Lugosz EPA 702-798-2598
Ground-water monitoring....Eugene P. Meier EPA 702-798-2237
Ground-water monitoring....Lowell Leach EPA 405-332-2333
Growth Hormone Deficiency....Staff NIDDK 301-496-3583
Growth Hormone Deficiency....Staff NCI 301-496-5583
Growth and Development....Staff NICHD 301-496-5133
Guadaloupe/Minerals....Ivette Torres Cnty Mines 202-632-9352
Guadeloupe....Mack Tadeu Cnty Commerce 202-377-2527
Guadeloupe (Basse-Terre)....Avon Williams Cnty State
    202-647-2621
Guadeloupe (Basse-Terre)....David F. Rogus Cnty AID
    202-647-2130
Guarantees (Consumer Inquiries), Mktg Practices....Staff Fed Trade
    Com 202-326-3128
Guatemala....Ted Johnson Cnty Commerce 202-377-2527
Guatemala (Guatamala City)....Richard Dotson Cnty State
    202-647-3681
Guatemala (Guatamala)....James C. Cason Cnty AID 202-647-8276
Guatemala (Guatamala)....Carl Dutto Cnty AID 202-647-5101
Guatemala/Minerals....Ivette Torres Cnty Mines 202-632-9352
Guide & Navigation Automation (Aeronautics)....Dallas Denery
    NASA 415-694-5427
Guide for the Care and Use of Laboratory Animals....Staff NCI
    301-496-5545
Guillain-Barre Syndrome (Polyneuritis)....Staff NINCDS
    301-496-5751
Guinea....Philip Michelini Cnty Commerce 202-377-4388
Guinea....R. J. Benn Peace Corps 202-254-3185
Guinea (Conakry)....Leslie A. Bassett Cnty State 202-647-3066
Guinea (Conakry)....John A. Hedges Cnty AID 202-647-6980
Guinea (Conakry)....Mable S. Meares Cnty AID 202-647-6154
Guinea Bissau....Theresa Queenan Peace Corps 202-254-7036
Guinea-Bissau....Philip Michelini Cnty Commerce 202-377-4388
Guinea-Bissau (Bissau)....Leslie A. Bassett Cnty State 202-647-3066
Guinea-Bissau (Bissau)....Thomas J. Burke Cnty AID 202-647-8436
Guinea-Bissau (Bissau)....Mable S. Meares Cnty AID 202-647-6154
Guinea-Bissau/Minerals....Hendrik van Oss Cnty Mines
    202-632-5065
Guinea/Minerals....Hendrik van Oss Cnty Mines 202-632-5065
Gulf Cooperation Council (GCC)....John Riddle Cnty State
    202-647-7550
Gulf Cooperation Council (GCC)....Janet Sanderson Cnty AID
    202-647-1794
Gum Chemicals....Shea, Moira Commerce 202-377-0128
Gum Disease....Staff NIDR 301-496-4261
Gums and resins....Reeder, John USITC 202-252-1319
Gun and Wood Chemicals....McIntyre, Leo R. Commerce
    202-377-0128
Gun cotton....Johnson, Larry USITC 202-252-1351
Gunpowder....Johnson, Larry USITC 202-252-1351
Guns and Ammunition....Vanderwolf, John Commerce
    202-377-0348
Gut, articles of....Spalding, Josephine USITC 202-252-1498
Gut; catgut, whip gut, oriental gut, and wormgut....Ludwick, David
    USITC 202-252-1329
Guyana....Robert Dormitzer Cnty Commerce 202-377-2527
Guyana (Georgetown)....John Schlosser Cnty State 202-647-4195
Guyana (Georgetown)....Jim McHugh Cnty AID 202-647-6386
Guyana (Georgetown)....Edward Campbell Cnty AID 202-647-3447
Guyana/Minerals....Alfredo Gurmendi Cnty Mines 202-632-9352
Gynecology....Staff NICHD 301-496-5133
Gynecomastia....Staff NICHD 301-496-5133
Gypsum....White, Linda USITC 202-252-1427
Gypsum....Davis, Lawrence L. Mines 202-634-1206
Gypsum board....Vacant USITC 202-252-1326
Gyrate Atrophy....Staff NEI 301-496-5248

H

HIV Infection....Staff NIAID 301-496-5717
HIV Infection....Staff NCI 301-496-5583
Habeas Corpus....Carol Kaplan Justice Stat 202-724-7759
Hafnium....DeSapio, Vincent USITC 202-252-1435
Hafnium....Hedrick, James Mines 202-634-1058
Hailey's Disease....Staff NIDDK 301-496-3583
Hair....Steller, Rose USITC 202-252-1323
Hair Loss....Staff NIAMS 301-496-8188
Hair Spray....Staff FDA 301-245-1061
Hair curlers, nonelectric....Linkins, Linda USITC 202-252-1499
Hair ornaments....Linkins, Linda USITC 202-252-1499
Hair, articles of....Spalding, Josephine USITC 202-252-1498
Haiti....Mack Tadeu Cnty Commerce 202-377-2527
Haiti (Port-au-Prince)....Robert Holley Cnty State 202-647-2280
Haiti (Port-au-Prince)....Mike Shelton Cnty AID 202-647-3449
Haiti (Port-au-Prince)....James Manley Cnty AID 202-647-2116
Haiti/Minerals....Ivette Torres Cnty Mines 202-632-9352

Hallervorden-Spatz Disease....Staff NINCDS 301-496-5751
Halogen Occulation Experiment....Edward Sullivan NASA
    804-865-4784
Halogenated hydrocarbons....Michels, David USITC 202-252-1352
Hand Tools....Shaw, Eugene Commerce 202-377-3494
Hand Tools, Power....Abrahams, Edward Commerce 202-377-0312
Hand tools with self-contained motor....Cutchin, John USITC
    202-252-1396
Hand tools: household....Brandon, James USITC 202-252-1433
Hand tools: other....Brandon, James USITC 202-252-1433
Handbags....Seastrum, Carl USITC 202-252-1493
Handbags....Enright, Joseph Commerce 202-377-3459
Handbags....Gorman, K. Customs 212-466-5893
Handicapped, Clearinghouse for....Staff 301-245-1961
Handkerchiefs....Shetty, Sundar USITC 202-252-1457
Handkerchiefs....Persky, H. Customs 212-466-5881
Handwork yarns: cotton....Enfield, Mary E USITC 202-252-1455
Handwork yarns: manmade fibers....Butler, R Larry USITC
    202-252-1470
Handwork yarns: wool....Freund, Kimberlie USITC 202-252-1456
Hangings, wall hangings....Eyskens, R. Customs 212-466-5854
Hansen's Disease....Staff NIAID 301-496-5717
Harada's Disease....Staff NEI 301-496-5248
Harbors, Major Proj.....Piggot, Deborne Commerce 202-377-3352
Hardboard....Vacant USITC 202-252-1326
Hardening of the Arteries....Staff NHLBI 301-496-4236
Hardware, Export Promo....Johnson, Charles E. Commerce
    202-377-3422
Harrassing Telephone Calls....Staff FCC 202-632-7553
Hart Scott Rodino Inquiries, Premerger Staff....Staff Fed Trade
    Com 202-326-3100
Hashimoto's Disease....Staff NIDDK 301-496-3583
Hats....Worrell, Jackie USITC 202-252-1466
Hay, Economics....Hull, David Agri 202-786-1840
Hay, Statistics....Ransom, Darwin Agri 202-447-7621
Hazard assessment....William W. Sutton EPA 404-546-3422
Hazard assessment....J.F. Paul EPA 401-782-3000
Hazard assessment and biological effects....W.G. Nelson EPA
    401-782-3000
Hazardous Substances Information....Staff NLM 301-496-1131
Hazardous waste alternative technologies....Clyde Dial EPA
    513-569-7601
Hazardous waste incineration....Robert E. Hall EPA 919-541-2477
Hazardous waste management....Lee A. Mulkey EPA 404-546-3546
Hazardous waste management....E Timothy Oppelt EPA
    513-569-7418
Hazardous waste treatment....Benjamin Blaney EPA 513-569-7519
Hazardous wastes biological processes....John Matthews EPA
    405-332-2233
Head Injury....Staff NINCDS 301-496-5751
Headache....Staff NINCDS 301-496-5751
Headwear....Worrell, Jackie USITC 202-252-1466
Headwear....Eyskens, R. Customs 212-466-5854
Health....Francis, Simon Commerce 202-377-0350
Health & Safety Risk Disclosures, Mktg Practices....Staff Fed Trade
    Com 202-326-3128
Health Benefits (Employee)....Staff 301-
Health Insurance & Medicare, Health Care Staff....Staff Fed Trade
    Com 202-326-2756
Health Manpower Education....Staff HRSA/BHPr 301-443-2060
Health Professionals....Staff HRSA/BHPr 301-443-2060
Health Promotion....Staff NCNR 301-496-0526
Health Seeking Behaviors....Staff NCNR 301-496-0526
Health Spas....Walter Gross Fed Trade Com 202-326-3319
Health Surveys....Mangold, Robert Census 301-763-5508
Health physics....Norman R. Sunderland EPA 702-798-2331
Health physics....Daryl L. Thome EPA 702-798-2158
Health services industry....Jonnard, Aimison USITC 202-252-0345
Hearing Aids, Marketing Practices....Staff Fed Trade Com
    202-326-3128
Hearing Disorders....Staff NINCDS 301-496-5751
Hearing Loss and Aging....Staff NINCDS 301-496-5751
Hearing Loss and Aging....Staff NIA 301-496-1752
Hearing Loss and Aging....Staff CC 301-496-5368
Heart Attacks....Staff NHLBI 301-496-4236
Heart Block....Staff NHLBI 301-496-4236
Heart Disease....Staff NHLBI 301-496-4236
Heart Pacemaker....Staff NHLBI 301-496-4236
Heart Transplantation....Staff NHLBI 301-496-4236
Heart Valves....Staff NHLBI 301-496-4236
Heart-Lung Machines....Staff NHLBI 301-496-4236
Heat Stroke and Aging....Staff NIA 301-496-1752
Heat Treating Equipment....Vacant Commerce 202-377-0316
Heat process equipment....Slingerland, David USITC 202-252-1400
Heat-insulating articles....DeSapio, Vincent USITC 202-252-1435
Heating Equipment Ex. Furnaces....Shaw, Eugene Commerce
    202-377-3494
Heating Equipment, Warm Air....Shaw, Eugene Commerce

202-377-3494
Heating Oil Futures....Staff Comm Futures 212-668-2080
Heavy Equipment....Lien, John Commerce 202-377-0679
Heavy Industrial Machinery....Horowitz, A. Customs 212-466-5494
Heavy Metals (Cadmium, Zinc, Mercury)....Staff NIEHS
919-541-3345
Heavy Rain Effects....R. Earl Dunham NASA 804-865-3611
Heavy metals....Robert Elias EPA 919-541-4167
Helicopter Acoustics, Propeller Noise, Laminar Flo....David
Chestnutt NASA 804-865-3841
Helicopter Services....Miller, Randall Commerce 202-377-5071
Helicopters, Market Support....Driscoll, George Commerce
202-377-8228
Heliotropin....Land, Eric USITC 202-252-1349
Helium....Leachman, William Mines 806-376-2062
Hemiplegia....Staff NINCDS 301-496-5751
Hemodialysis....Staff NIDDK 301-496-3583
Hemoglobin Genetics....Staff NIDDK 301-496-3583
Hemoglobinopathies....Staff NIDDK 301-496-3583
Hemolytic Anemia....Staff NIDDK 301-496-3583
Hemolytic Anemia....Staff NIAID 301-496-5717
Hemolytic Disease (Newborn)....Staff NICHD 301-496-5133
Hemolytic Disease (Newborn)....Staff NHLBI 301-496-4236
Hemophilia....Staff NHLBI 301-496-4236
Hemophilus Influenzae....Staff NIAID 301-496-5717
Hemorrhagic Diseasess....Staff NIDDK 301-496-3583
Hemorrhagic Diseasess....Staff NHLBI 301-496-4236
Hemorrhoids....Staff NHLBI 301-496-4236
Hemosiderosis....Staff NHLBI 301-496-4236
Hepatitis....Staff NIAID 301-496-5717
Hepatitis....Staff NIDDK 301-496-3583
Hepatitis (Treatment of Acute or Chronic)....Staff NIDDK
301-496-3583
Hepatitis (Treatment of Acute or Chronic)....Staff NIAID
301-496-5717
Hereditary Cerebellar Ataxia....Staff NINCDS 301-496-5751
Hereditary Emphysema....Staff NHLBI 301-496-4236
Hereditary Movement Disorders....Staff NINCDS 301-496-5751
Hereditary Nervous System Tumors....Staff NINCDS 301-496-5751
Heredity and Cancer....Staff NCI 301-496-5583
Heritable Disorders of Connective Tissue....Staff NHLBI
301-496-4236
Heritable Disorders of Connective Tissue....Staff NIAMS
301-496-8188
Hernias (Abdominal, Bladder)....Staff NIDDK 301-496-3583
Herniated Disc....Staff NIAMS 301-496-8188
Herpes (Nervous System Involvement)....Staff NINCDS
301-496-5751
Herpes Simplex (Eye Effects)....Staff NEI 301-496-5248
Herpes Simplex Virus (Oral Lesions)....Staff NIDR 301-496-4261
Herpes Simplex Virus (Type II)....Staff NIAID 301-496-5717
Herpes Zoster (Shingles)....Staff NINCDS 301-496-5751
Herpes Zoster-Varicella Infections....Staff NIAID 301-496-5717
Hiatal Hernia....Staff NIDDK 301-496-3583
Hiccups....Staff NHLBI 301-496-4236
Hide cuttings....Trainor, Cynthia USITC 202-252-1354
Hides....Steller, Rose USITC 202-252-1323
High Blood Pressure....Staff NHLBI 301-496-4236
High Blood Pressure....Staff NIA 301-496-1752
High Blood Pressure....Staff NHLBI/IC 301-951-3260
High Energy Gamma Rays....C. E. Fichtel NASA 301-286-6281
High Performance Aircraft Propulsion Technology....Peter Batterton
NASA 216-433-3912
High Reynolds Number Research and Config. Aerodyna....Lawrence
Putnam NASA 804-865-2045
High Speed Computer Architectures (Aerophysics)....Kenneth
Stevens NASA 415-694-5949
High Tech Trade, U.S. Competitiveness....Hatter, Victoria L.
Commerce 202-377-3913
High Temperature-Structural and Thermal Protection....Bland Stein
NASA 804-865-2125
High Voltage Electron Microscopy....Staff DRR 301-496-5545
High-Performance Polymer Concepts, Tough Composite....Terry
Clair NASA 804-865-4194
High-Speed Aerodynamics....Robert Jones NASA 804-865-3783
High-density Lipoproteins (HDL)....Staff NHLBI 301-496-4236
Hirsutism....Staff NIAMS 301-496-8188
Histiocytosis....Staff NCI 301-496-5583
Histiocytosis....Staff NHLBI 301-496-4236
Histological responses....G.R. Gardner EPA 401-782-3000
Histological responses....R.J. Haebler EPA 401-782-3000
Histoplasmosis....Staff NIAID 301-496-5717
Histoplasmosis (Eye)....Staff NEI 301-496-5248
Historical Medical Prints and Photographs....Staff NLM
301-496-5961
History of Medicine....Staff NLM 301-496-5405
Histotechnology - fish....Rodney Johnson EPA 218-720-5731
Hives....Staff NIAID 301-496-5717

Hobby Protection Act....Robert Easton Fed Trade Com
202-326-3029
Hodgkin's Disease....Staff NCI 301-496-5583
Hogs....Ludwick, David USITC 202-252-1329
Hogs, Economics....Southard, Leland Agri 202-786-1830
Hogs, Live, Futures With Options....Jon Prentice Comm Futures
312-353-9026
Hogs, Statistics....Wiyatt, Steve Agri 202-447-3106
Hoists, Trade Promo.....Wiening, Mary Commerce 202-377-4708
Hoists/Overhead Cranes....Lien, John A. Commerce 202-377-0679
Holder-in-Due-Course Rule, Credit Practices....Staff Fed Trade
Com 202-326-3175
Holder-in-Due-Course, Credit....Staff Fed Trade Com
202-326-3175
Home Appliance Rule....James Mills Fed Trade Com 202-326-3035
Home Care, Nursing Home Care, Hospital Care....Staff NCNR
301-496-0526
Home Improvement Products, Mktg Practices....Staff Fed Trade
Com 202-326-3035
Home funishings....Borsari, Marilyn USITC 202-252-1465
Home, Energy...Michael Dershowitz Fed Trade Com
202-326-3158
Homocystinuria....Staff NICHD 301-496-5133
Homocystinuria....Staff NHLBI 301-496-4236
Honduras....Brigit Helms Cnty Commerce 202-377-2527
Honduras (Tegucigalpa)....Christopher Sandrolini Cnty State
202-647-4980
Honduras (Tegucigalpa)....Steve Wesche Cnty AID 202-647-4980
Honduras (Tegucigalpa)....Emily Leonard Cnty AID 202-647-5101
Honduras/Minerals....Ivette Torres Cnty Mines 202-632-9352
Hong Kong...John Adams Cnty State 202-647-6801
Hong Kong....David Shear Cnty AID 202-647-1004
Hong Kong....Peter Chase Cnty AID 202-647-1322
Hong Kong....JeNelle Matheson Cnty Commerce 202-377-2462
Hong Kong/Minerals....Edmond Chin Cnty Mines 202-634-1272
Hoof, articles of....Spalding, Josephine USITC 202-252-1498
Hoofs, crude....Ludwick, David USITC 202-252-1329
Hooks and eyes....Linkins, Linda USITC 202-252-1486
Hormone Distribution....Staff NIDDK 301-496-3583
Hormones....Nesbitt, Elizabeth USITC 202-252-1355
Hormones....Staff NIDDK 301-496-3583
Hormones (Sex)....Staff NICHD 301-496-5133
Hormones and Cancer....Staff NCI 301-496-5583
Horn, articles of....Spalding, Josephine USITC 202-252-1498
Horn, crude....Ludwick, David USITC 202-252-1329
Horse Racing Programming and Advertising....Staff FCC
202-632-7048
Horses....Ludwick, David USITC 202-252-1329
Horticultural machinery....Lippa, Alison USITC 202-252-1398
Hose and Belting....Prat, Raimundo Commerce 202-377-0128
Hose, industrial....Cook, Lee USITC 202-252-1471
Hose, of rubber or plastics....Truskett, Brooks USITC
202-252-1354
Hosiery....Bryant, Judith USITC 202-252-1464
Hosiery....Persky, H. Customs 212-466-5881
Hospice Care....Staff NIA 301-496-1752
Hospital Administrators....Staff HRSA/BHPr 301-443-2134
Hospital Infections....Staff NIAID 301-496-5717
Hospital-Based Schools of Nursing....Staff HRSA/BHPr
301-443-2134
Hotel, Export Promo and Restaurants....Kimmel, Edward K.
Commerce 202-377-3640
Hotels and Motels....Sousane, J. Richard Commerce 202-377-4581
Household Articles, plastics....Rauch, T. Customs 212-466-5892
Household Furniture....Ellis, Kevin Commerce 202-377-1140
Household Wealth....Lamas, Enrique Census 301-763-8578
Household, Structural Products Hazards....James Hoebel Con
Product Safe 202-492-6554
Households....Staff Census 301-763-7987
Households Touched by Crime....Michael Rand Justice Stat
202-724-7774
Housewares, Export Promo.....Johnson, Charles E. Commerce
202-377-3422
Housing Construction....Mathieu, Renee Commerce 202-377-0132
Housing Division....Acting Chief Census 301-763-8550
Housing and Urban Development. Major Proj.....White, Barbara
Commerce 202-377-4160
Housing, American Housing Survey....Montfort, Edward Census
301-763-8551
Housing, Components of Inventory Change Survey....Maynard, Jane
Census 301-763-8551
Housing, Decennial Census....Downs, Bill Census 301-763-8553
Housing, Information....Downs, Bill Census 301-763-8553
Housing, Market Absorption....Smoler, Anne Census 301-763-8552
Housing, Residential Finance....Fronczek, Peter Census
301-763-8552
Hubble Space Telescope System Design...J. Laux NASA
205-544-2418

Hubble Space Telescope System Requirements....J. Loose   NASA 205-544-2422
Human Development....Staff   NICHD   301-443-5133
Human Factors....Mike Shafto   NASA   415-694-6170
Human Factors....Kelli Willshire   NASA   804-865-4834
Human Genetic Mutant Cell Repository....Staff   NIGMS 301-496-7301
Human Papilloma Virus (HPV)....Staff   NCI   301-496-5583
Human Papilloma Virus (HPV)....Staff   NIAID   301-496-5717
Human inhalation toxicology....John J. O'Neil   EPA   919-541-6203
Hungary....Karen Ware   Cnty Commerce   202-377-2645
Hungary....Charles Howell   Peace Corps   202-254-3040
Hungary (Budapest)....Jeanne L. Schulz   Cnty State   202-647-3187
Hungary (Budapest)....Laurie Tracy   Cnty State   202-647-3052
Hungary (Budapest)....Terry R. Snell   Cnty AID   202-647-4138
Hungary (Budapest)....Barbara J. Griffiths   Cnty AID   202-647-3191
Hungary/Minerals....Walter Steblez   Cnty Mines   202-632-5047
Hunt's Disease....Staff   NINCDS   301-496-5751
Hunter's Syndrome....Staff   NIDDK   301-496-3583
Huntington's Disease....Staff   NINCDS   301-496-5751
Hurler's Syndrome....Staff   NICHD   301-496-5133
Hurler's Syndrome....Staff   NIDDK   301-496-3583
Hyaline Membrane Disease....Staff   NICHD   301-496-5133
Hyaline Membrane Disease....Staff   NHLBI   301-496-4236
Hydro Power Plants, Major Proj.....Mazur, Janice   Commerce 202-377-4333
Hydrocarbons....Raftery, Jim   USITC   202-252-1365
Hydrocarbons & ozone....Beverly Tilton   EPA   919-541-4161
Hydrocephalus....Staff   NINCDS   301-496-5751
Hydrocephalus....Staff   NICHD   301-496-5133
Hydrochloric acid....Trainor, Cynthia   USITC   202-252-1354
Hydrodynamics....Steve C. McCutcheon   EPA   404-546-3301
Hydrofluoric acid....Trainor, Cynthia   USITC   202-252-1354
Hydrogeology...Joseph J. D'Lugosz   EPA   702-798-2598
Hydrogeology....Don Draper   EPA   405-332-2202
Hydrogeology....Randall Ross   EPA   405-332-2313
Hydrogeology....Jerry Thornhill   EPA   405-332-2310
Hydrology....Dom DiGiulio   EPA   405-332-2271
Hydrology....Parker J.Wigington   EPA   503-757-4640
Hydrology/Water Resources....R. Gurney   NASA   301-286-5480
Hydrolysis/redox reactions in water....N. Lee Wolfe   EPA 404-546-3429
Hygienists (Education)....Staff   HRSA/BHPr   301-443-6837
Hyperactivity....Staff   NIMH   301-443-4515
Hyperactivity....Staff   NICHD   301-496-5133
Hyperbaric Chamber - U MD Shock Trauma Center....Staff 301-528-6294
Hyperbaric Oxygenation....Staff   NHLBI   301-496-4236
Hyperbilirubinemia....Staff   NICHD   301-496-5133
Hyperbilirubinemia....Staff   NIDDK   301-496-3583
Hypercalcemia....Staff   NIDDK   301-496-3583
Hypercalciuria....Staff   NIDDK   301-496-3583
Hypercholesterolemia....Staff   NHLBI   301-496-4236
Hypercube....David Rogstad   NASA   818-354-3573
Hyperglycemia....Staff   NIDDK   301-496-3583
Hyperkinesis....Staff   NIMH   301-443-4515
Hyperlipidemia....Staff   NHLBI   301-496-4236
Hyperlipoproteinemia....Staff   NHLBI   301-496-5343
Hyperparathyroidism....Staff   NIDDK   301-496-3583
Hyperpyrexia (heat stroke/heat exhaustion)....Staff   NIA 301-496-1752
Hypersensitivity Pneumonitis....Staff   NIAID   301-496-5717
Hypersonic Propulsion Research....Griffin Anderson   NASA 804-865-3772
Hypersonic Propulsion Technology....Robert Coltrin   NASA 216-433-2181
Hypersonics....Terry Holst   NASA   415-694-6032
Hypertension....Staff   NHLBI/IC   301-951-3260
Hypertension....Staff   NCNR   301-496-0526
Hyperthermia....Staff   NCI   301-496-5583
Hyperthyroidism....Staff   NIDDK   301-496-3583
Hypertriglyceridemia....Staff   NHLBI   301-496-4236
Hyperuricemia....Staff   NIDDK   301-496-3583
Hyperventilation....Staff   NHLBI   301-496-4236
Hypnotics....Nesbitt, Elizabeth   USITC   202-252-1355
Hypobetalipoproteinemia....Staff   NHLBI   301-496-4236
Hypocomplementemic Glomerulonephritis....Staff   NIAID 301-496-5717
Hypoglycemia....Staff   NHLBI   301-496-4236
Hypoglycemia....Staff   NIDDK   301-496-3583
Hypogonadism....Staff   NIDDK   301-496-3583
Hypogonadism....Staff   NICHD   301-496-5133
Hypokalemia....Staff   NHLBI   301-496-4236
Hypokalemic Periodic Paralysis....Staff   NINCDS   301-496-5751
Hypolipoproteinemia....Staff   NIDDK   301-496-4236
Hypoparathyroidism....Staff   NIDDK   301-496-3583
Hypopituitarism....Staff   NIDDK   301-496-3583
Hypotension....Staff   NHLBI   301-496-4236

Hypothalamus....Staff   NIDDK   301-496-3583
Hypothalamus....Staff   NICHD   301-496-5133
Hypothermia (Accidental)....Staff   NIA   301-496-1752
Hypothyroidism, Goitrous....Staff   NIA   301-496-3583
Hypotonia....Staff   NINCDS   301-496-5751
Hypoventilation....Staff   NHLBI   301-496-4236
Hypoxia....Staff   NHLBI   301-496-4236
Hypsarrhythmia....Staff   NINCDS   301-496-5751

I

IGE....Staff   NIAID   301-496-5717
Iceland....Maryanne Lyons   Cnty Commerce   202-377-3254
Iceland (Rehkjavik)....R. Ross Rodgers   Cnty AID   202-647-1774
Iceland (Rehkjavik)....Richard A. Christenson   Cnty AID 202-647-4484
Iceland (Reykjavik)....Kenneth Longmyer   Cnty State   202-647-9980
Iceland Disease....Staff   NINCDS   301-496-5751
Iceland/Minerals....Harold Newman   Cnty Mines   202-634-1276
Ichthyology....William P. Davis   EPA   904-932-5311
Ichthyosis....Staff   NIAMS   301-496-8188
Idiopathic Hypertrophic Subaortic Stenosis (IHSS)....Staff   NHLBI 301-496-4236
Idiopathic Inflammatory Myopathy....Staff   NINCDS   301-496-5751
Idiopathic Osteoporosis....Staff   NIAMS   301-496-8188
Idiopathic Thrombocytopenic Purpura (ITP)....Staff   NHLBI 301-496-4236
Idiopathic Thrombocytopenic Purpura (ITP)....Staff   NIDDK 301-496-3581
Ignition equipment....Hagey, Michael   USITC   202-252-1392
Ileitis....Staff   NIDDK   301-496-3583
Image Processing....Staff   DCRT   301-496-2250
Image Processing....Staff   DCRT   301-496-7963
Image Processing Applications and Development....Ray Wall   NASA   818-354-5016
Imaging Systems....Robert Lockhard   NASA   818-354-6350
Immiscible flow....Dennis Miller   EPA   405-332-2263
Immune Deficiency Diseases....Staff   NCI   301-496-5583
Immune Deficiency Diseases....Staff   NIAID   301-496-5717
Immune Serums (Animal)....Staff   DRS/VRB   301-496-9416
Immunity, Disorders....Staff   NCI   301-496-5583
Immunity, Disorders....Staff   NIAID   301-496-5717
Immunizations (Foreign)....Staff   CDC   404-329-3534
Immunology....Staff   NIAID   301-496-5717
Immunology....Bennett Smith   EPA   513-569-7543
Immunology (Cancer)....Staff   NCI   301-496-5583
Immunotherapy (Cancer)....Staff   NCI   301-496-5583
Implantable Defibrillator....Staff   NHLBI   301-496-4236
Implants, Lens....Staff   NEI   301-496-5248
Impotence....Staff   NIMH   301-443-4515
Impotence....Staff   NHLBI   301-496-3583
In Vitro Fertilization....Staff   NICHD   301-496-5133
In-Space Technology Experiments....Jack Salzman   NASA 216-433-2868
Inappropriate Antidiuretic Hormone Syndrome....Staff   NHLBI 301-496-4236
Inborn Errors of Metabolism....Staff   NICHD   301-496-5133
Inborn Errors of Metabolism....Staff   NINCDS   301-496-5751
Inborn Errors of Metabolism....Staff   NHLBI   301-496-4236
Inborn Errors of Metabolism....Staff   NICHD   301-496-5133
Inborn Heart Defects....Staff   NHLBI   301-496-4236
Incapacitation....Patick Langan   Justice Stat   202-724-7774
Incapacitation....Lawrence Greenfeld   Justice Stat   202-724-7755
Incidental Radiation Devices....Staff   FCC   202-653-6288
Income Statistics....Staff   Census   301-763-8576
Income Surveys....Bowie, Chester   Census   301-763-2764
Incontinence....Staff   NIA   301-496-1752
India....Richard Harding/Polly Holcombe/Sean Gallagher   Cnty Commerce   202-377-2954
India (New Delhi)....Thomas C. Krajeski   Cnty State   202-647-2351
India (New Delhi)....John Lister   Cnty State   202-647-2141
India (New Delhi)....Louis B. Warren   Cnty State   202-647-1450
India (New Delhi)....Frances Culpepper   Cnty AID   202-647-1289
India (New Delhi)....Reynold A. Riemer   Cnty AID   202-647-5699
India (New Delhi)....William Sugrue   Cnty AID   202-647-4516
India/Minerals....David Doan   Cnty Mines   202-634-1272
Indigent Defense....Carla Gaskins   Justice Stat   202-647-7774
Indium....Wagner, Lorie   USITC   202-252-1439
Indium....Jasinski, Stephen M.   Mines   202-634-1063
Indonesia....Don Ryan/Linda Droker   Cnty Commerce 202-377-3875
Indonesia (Jakarata)....Donald Camp   Cnty State   202-647-3277
Indonesia (Jakarata)....Charles Morris   Cnty AID   202-647-3733
Indonesia (Jakarta)....Christopher Brown   Cnty AID   202-647-6362
Indonesia/Minerals....John Wu   Cnty Mines   202-634-1272
Indoor air pollution....Norman Childs   EPA   919-541-2229

Indoor air pollution....Harriet Ammann EPA 919-541-4930
Indoor air quality....Everett L. Plyler EPA 919-541-2918
Induced Movement Disorders....Staff NINCDS 301-496-5751
Indus. Mach. Nec.,General, Exc. 35691....Shaw, Eugene Commerce 202-377-3494
Indus. Refrig. Equipment....Shaw, Eugene Commerce 202-377-3494
Industrial Chemicals (Effects on Human Health)....Staff NIEHS 919-541-3345
Industrial Chemicals and Cancer....Staff NCI 301-496-5583
Industrial Controls....Whitley, Richard A. Commerce 202-377-0682
Industrial Drives/Gears....Fletcher, William E. Commerce 202-377-0309
Industrial Gases....Donahue, Kevin Commerce 202-377-0128
Industrial Heating Equipment....Staff FCC 202-653-6288
Industrial Hygiene....Staff OD/ORS 301-496-2960
Industrial Machinery, General....Donahoe, William Commerce 202-377-5455
Industrial Organic Chemicals....Kamenicky, Vincent Commerce 202-377-0128
Industrial Process Controls....Donnelly, Margaret T. Commerce 202-377-5466
Industrial Robots....Mearman, John Commerce 202-377-0315
Industrial Robots, Trade Promo.....Manzolillo, Franc Commerce 202-377-2991
Industrial Sewing Machines....Holley, Tyrena Commerce 202-377-3509
Industrial Structure....Davis, Lester A. Commerce 202-477-4924
Industrial Trucks....Wiening, Mary Commerce 202-377-4608
Industrial Trucks, Trade Promo.....Wiening, Mary Commerce 202-377-4608
Industrial ceramics....Lukes, James USITC 202-252-1426
Industrial diamonds....White, Linda USITC 202-252-1426
Industrial licenses....Staff FCC 717-337-1212
Industrial sources....Robert R. Swank, Jr. EPA 404-546-3128
Industrial wastewater treatment....Alden Christianson EPA 513-569-7406
Industrial wastewater treatment....Kenneth Dostal EPA 513-569-7503
Industrial, Scientific, & Medical Equipment....Staff FCC 202-653-6288
Industry Classification....Monk, Jr., C. Harvey Census 301-763-1935
Industry Division....Worden, Gaylord E. Census 301-763-5850
Industry Machinery, Nec, Special....Holley, Tyrena Commerce 202-377-3709
Industry Machinery, Special....Smith, Edward G. Commerce 202-377-0302
Industry Statistics....Priebe, John Census 301-763-8575
Industry Statistics....Masumura, Wilfred Census 301-763-8575
Industry and Services/trade matters....Staff US Trade Rep 202-395-7320
Inedible gelatin....Jonnard, Aimison USITC 202-252-1350
Infant Mortality....Staff NICHD 301-496-5133
Infant Mortality....Staff NCHS 301-436-8500
Infant Mortality....Staff CDC 404-329-3534
Infant Nutrition....Staff NICHD 301-496-5133
Infantile Muscular Atrophy....Staff NINCDS 301-496-5751
Infantile Spinal Muscular Atrophy....Staff NINCDS 301-496-5751
Infants (Care)....Staff HRSA 301-443-2086
Infants' acessories or apparel....MacKnight, Peggy USITC 202-252-1468
Infections, Pyogenic, Recurrent....Staff NIAID 301-496-5717
Infectious Arthritis....Staff NIAMS 301-496-8188
Infectious Eye Disease....Staff NEI 301-496-5248
Infectious Materials (Disposal)....Staff OD/ORS 301-496-2960
Infectious Mononucleosis....Staff NIAID 301-496-5717
Infertility....Staff NICHD 301-496-5133
Inflammatory Bowel Disease....Staff NIDDK 301-496-3583
Inflammatory Bowel Disease....Staff NIAID 301-496-5717
Inflatable Articles....McKenna, T. Customs 212-466-5475
Influenza....Staff NIAID 301-496-5717
Information Industries....Crupe, Friedrich R. Commerce 202-377-4781
Information Services....Inoussa, Mary C. Commerce 202-377-5820
Information Systems....Robert Tausworthe NASA 818-354-2773
Information Theory and Coding....Laif Swanson NASA 818-354-2757
Infraared Astronomy....Michael Hauser NASA 301-286-8701
Infraction Reports--International....Staff FCC 202-653-8138
Infrared Astronomy....C. Telesco NASA 205-544-7723
Infrared Astronomy and Astrophysics....David Black NASA 415-694-4912
Infrared Spectroscopy & Molecular Structures....John Hillman NASA 301-286-7974
Infrared and Analytical Instrument Systems....John Wellman NASA 818-354-7696
Ingot molds....Greene, William USITC 202-252-1405
Inherited Blood Abnormalities....Staff NHLBI 301-496-4236
Inherited Blood Abnormalities....Staff NIDDK 301-496-3583

Inherited Metabolic Disorders....Staff NIDDK 301-496-3583
Inherited Neurologic Abnormalities....Staff NINCDS 301-496-5751
Injunctions....Staff FCC 202-632-7112
Injuries (Eye)....Staff NEI 301-496-5248
Ink powders....Johnson, Larry USITC 202-252-1351
Inks....Johnson, Larry USITC 202-252-1351
Inorganic Chemicals....Donahue, Kevin Commerce 202-377-0128
Inorganic Pigments....Donahue, Kevin Commerce 202-377-0128
Inorganic acids....Trainor, Cynthia USITC 202-252-1354
Inorganic analysis....Nicholas T. Loux EPA 404-546-3174
Inorganic analytical chemistry....Don Clark EPA 405-332-2311
Inorganic compounds and mixtures....Greenblatt, Jack USITC 202-252-1353
Inorganic methods....Larry Lobring EPA 513-569-7372
Inorganic/organic Compounds....Dimaria, J. Customs 212-466-5769
Inorganics analysis....Warren Loseke EPA 919-541-2173
Insanity Defense....Bernard Auchter Justice 202-724-7684
Insanity Defense....Phyllis Jo Bauanch Justice Stat 202-724-7755
Insect Stings Allergy....Staff NIAID 301-496-5717
Insomnia....Staff NIMH 301-443-4515
Institutional Computing and Mission Operations....Kris Blom NASA 818-354-0119
Institutional Population....Smith, Denise Census 301-763-7883
Instrument (Fabrication, Maintenance and Repair)....Staff DRS/BEIB 301-496-4131
Instrument Development....Staff DRS/BEIB 301-496-4741
Instrument Fabrication (Electronic)....Staff DRS/BEIB 301-496-4131
Instrument Rental....Staff DRS/BEIB 301-496-9748
Instrumentation and Controls Technology....Norman Wengler NASA 216-433-3730
Instruments: controlling....Moller, Ruben USITC 202-252-1495
Instruments: dental...Johnson, Christopher USITC 202-252-1488
Instruments: drawing....Moller, Ruben USITC 202-252-1495
Instruments: mathematical calculating....Moller, Ruben USITC 202-252-1495
Instruments: measuring....Moller, Ruben USITC 202-252-1495
Instruments: measuring or checking....Moller, Ruben USITC 202-252-1495
Instruments: medical....Johnson, Christopher USITC 202-252-1488
Instruments: meteorological....Moller, Ruben USITC 202-252-1495
Instruments: musical....Witherspoon, Ricardo USITC 202-252-1489
Instruments: navigational....Moller, Ruben USITC 202-252-1495
Instruments: surgical....Johnson, Christopher USITC 202-252-1488
Instruments: surveying....Moller, Ruben USITC 202-252-1495
Instruments: testing....Moller, Ruben USITC 202-252-1495
Insulation....Williams, Franklin Commerce 202-377-0132
Insulation....Kent Howerton Fed Trade Com 202-326-3013
Insulation (R-Value)....Kent Howerton Fed Trade Com 202-326-3013
Insulation, Advertising....Kent Howerton Fed Trade Com 202-326-3013
Insulators, ceramic....Lukes, James USITC 202-252-1426
Insulinomas....Staff NIDDK 301-496-3583
Insurance....Fenwick, Thomas R. Commerce 202-377-0347
Integrated Data Processing, Transmission of....Staff FCC 202-632-5550
Integrated Fluid-Thermal Structural Analysis Techn....Allan Wieting NASA 804-865-3423
Integrated Multidisciplinary Analysis Capability....Robert Tolson NASA 804-865-2887
Integrated Test Systems and Aircraft Simulation....Dale Mackall NASA 805-258-3408
Intellectual Development....Staff NICHD 301-496-5133
Intellectual Property Rights, Services....Siegmund, John E. Commerce 202-377-4781
Intelligent Cockpit Aids Research....Kathy Abbott NASA 804-865-3621
Intelligent Systems Technology (Aerophysics)....Donald Mckellar NASA 415-694-4162
Interception of Radio Communications....Staff FCC 202-632-6990
Interconnection of Telephone Equipment....Staff FCC 202-634-1800
Interferon....Staff NIAID 301-496-5717
Interferon....Staff NCI 301-496-5583
Interior Noise Control, Acoustic Response and Soni....Clemans Powell NASA 804-865-3561
Interlocking Directors....Staff FCC 202-632-4887
Internal Combustion Engines, Nec, Trade Promo.....Cummings, Charles Commerce 202-377-5361
International Allocation Treatries, Agreements....Staff FCC 202-653-8144
International Antitrust....Edward Glynn Fed Trade Com

202-326-2948
International Commodities....Siesseger, Fred   Commerce
202-377-5124
International Crime Data....Carol Kalish   Justice Stat
202-724-6100
International Major Projects Actg.....Engelson, Leo   Commerce
202-377-2732
International Statistical Programs Center....Bartram, Robert O.
Census   301-763-2832
International Statistics, Africa....Way, Peter   Census   301-763-4086
International Statistics, Asia....Adlakha, Arjun   Census   301-763-4221
International Statistics, Caribbean....Way, Peter   Census
301-763-4086
International Statistics, China, People's Republic....Banister, Judith
Census   301-763-4012
International Statistics, Europe....Adlakha, Arjun   Census
301-763-4221
International Statistics, International Data Base....Johnson, Peter
Census   301-763-4811
International Statistics, Latin America....Way, Peter   Census
301-763-4086
International Statistics, North America...Adlakha, Arjun   Census
301-763-4221
International Statistics, Oceania...Adlakha, Arjun   Census
301-763-4221
International Statistics, Soviet Union....Sagers, Matthew   Census
301-763-4022
International Statistics, Women in Development...Jamison, Ellen
Census   301-763-4221
Interstellar Medium....Theodore Gull   NASA   301-286-8701
Interstitial Cystitis....Staff   NIDDK   301-496-2583
Interstitial Lung Diseases....Staff   NHLBI   301-496-4236
Interstitial Nephritis....Staff   NIDDK   301-496-3583
Interstitial Nephritis....Staff   NIDDK   301-496-3583
Intestinal Malabsorption Syndrome....Staff   NIDDK   301-496-3583
Intl Research, Center for....Torrey, Barbara Boyle   Census
301-763-2870
Intl, Bal of Payments, Current Acct Estimates....Kealy, Walter G.
Economic   202-523-0625
Intl, Bal of Payments, Special Studies....Kreuger, Russell C.
Economic   202-523-0628
Intl, Balance of Payments....Bach, Christopher L.   Economic
202-523-0620
Intl, Balance of Payments, Current Acct Analysis....DiLullo, Anthony
J.   Economic   202-523-0621
Intl, Cap Expend-Majority Owned For Affil US Co's....Herr, Ellen
M.   Economic   202-523-0661
Intl, Foreign Direct Inv-US, Analysis....Howenstine, Ned G.
Economic   202-523-0650
Intl, Foreign Direct Inv-US, Annl Bal of Pay Data....Fouch, Gregroy
G.   Economic   202-523-0547
Intl, Foreign Direct Inv-US, Annual Surveys....Bomkamp, James L.
Economic   202-523-0559
Intl, Foreign Direct Inv-US, Benchmark Surveys....Bomkamp, James
L.   Economic   202-523-0559
Intl, Foreign Direct Inv-US, Qtly Bal of Pay Data....Fouch, Gregory
G.   Economic   202-523-0547
Intl, Foreign Military Sales....McCormick, William O.   Economic
202-523-0619
Intl, Government Capital....Kerber, Eugene S.   Economic
202-523-0614
Intl, Government Grants....Kerber, Eugene S.   Economic
202-523-0614
Intl, Intl Transportation....Font, Rafael I.   Economic   202-523-0611
Intl, Intl Travel....Bolyard, Joan E.   Economic   202-523-0609
Intl, Merchandise Trade....Murad, Howard   Economic   202-523-0668
Intl, Multinational Corps, Analysis of Activities....Belli, R. David
Economic   202-523-0657
Intl, Private Capital Transactions....Scholl, Russell B.   Economic
202-523-0603
Intl, US Dir Inv Abroad, Analysis....Belli, R. David   Economic
202-523-0657
Intl, US Direct Inv Abroad, Annl Bal of Pay Data....Kazlow, Ralph
Economic   202-523-0661
Intl, US Direct Inv Abroad, Annual Survey....Walker, Patricia C.
Economic   202-523-0661
Intl, US Direct Inv Abroad, Benchmark Survey....Walker, Patricia C.
Economic   202-523-0661
Intl, US Direct Inv Abroad, Qtly Bal of Pay Data....Walker, Patricia
C.   Economic   202-523-0661
Intl,US Svcs Transac w/Unaf Foreignrs Benchmk Surv....Bogumill,
John   Economic   202-523-0637
Intracranial Aneurysm....Staff   NINCDS   301-496-5751
Intraocular Lenses....Staff   NEI   301-496-5248
Intrauterine Growth Retardation....Staff   NICHD   301-496-5133
Intrusion Alarms....Staff   FCC   202-653-6288
Invention Promotion, Mktg Practices (Insurance)....Staff   Fed Trade
Com   202-326-3128

Invertebrate taxonomy/toxicology....Gerald S. Schuytema   EPA
503-757-4764
Invertebrates....Richard L. Anderson   EPA   218-720-5616
Investment Management....Fenwick, Thomas R.   Commerce
202-377-0347
Iodine....Trainor, Cynthia   USITC   202-252-1354
Iodine....Lyday, Phillis A.   Mines   202-634-1177
Ion chromatography....James Mulik   EPA   919-541-3067
Ionosphere....Staff   FCC   202-653-8166
Iran....Claude Clement   Cnty Commerce   202-377-5545
Iran (Tehran)....Charles Dunne   Cnty State   202-647-6111
Iran (Tehran)....Peter J. Lydon   Cnty AID   202-647-5449
Iran (Tehran)....Donald A. Roberts   Cnty AID   202-647-5449
Iran/Minerals....Lloyd Antonides   Cnty Mines   202-632-5065
Iraq....Thomas Sams   Cnty Commerce   202-377-5767
Iraq (Baghdad)....Phillip Remler   Cnty State   202-647-5692
Iraq (Baghdad)....W. Gregory Berry   Cnty AID   202-647-5692
Iraq/Minerals....George Morgan   Cnty Mines   202-632-5065
Ireland....Brenda Hogan   Cnty Commerce   202-377-4104
Ireland (Dublin)....Kenneth Longmyer   Cnty State   202-647-9980
Ireland (Dublin)....Sarah R. Horsey   Cnty AID   202-647-1194
Ireland (Dublin)....Richard A. Christenson   Cnty AID   202-647-4484
Ireland (Dublin)....Christine Adamczyk   Cnty AID   202-647-9114
Ireland, Northern....Kenneth Longmyer   Cnty State   202-647-9980
Ireland/Minerals....Harold Newman   Cnty Mines   202-634-1276
Iridocyclitis....Staff   NEI   301-496-5248
Iritis....Staff   NEI   301-496-5248
Iron....Peters, Anthony   Mines   202-634-1022
Iron Deficiency Anemia....Staff   NIDDK   301-496-3583
Iron Ore....Kuck, Peter H.   Mines   202-634-1023
Iron Oxide Pigments....Mickelsen, Donald P.   Mines   202-634-1023
Iron Scrap....Brown, Raymond E.   Mines   202-634-1752
Iron Slag....Owens, Judith   Mines   202-634-1024
Iron blues....Johnson, Larry   USITC   202-252-1351
Iron compounds....Greenblatt, Jack   USITC   202-252-1353
Iron ore....Boszormenyl, Laszio   USITC   202-252-1437
Irrigation Equipment....Greer, Damon   Commerce   202-377-0564
Irrigation, Economics....Hostetler, John   Agri   202-786-1410
Irrigation, Major Proj.....Bell, Richard   Commerce   202-377-2460
Irritable Bowel Syndrome....Staff   NIDDK   301-496-3583
Isador....Staff   NCI   301-496-5583
Ischemia....Staff   NHLBI   301-496-4236
Ischemic Heart Disease....Staff   NHLBI   301-496-4236
Isinglass....Jonnard, Aimison   USITC   202-252-1350
Islet Cell Hyperplasia....Staff   NIDDK   301-496-3583
Islet Cell Transplants....Staff   NIDDK   301-496-3583
Isobutane....Raftery, Jim   USITC   202-252-1365
Isobutylene....Raftery, Jim   USITC   202-252-1365
Isolated IGA Deficiency....Staff   NCI   301-496-5583
Isoprene....Raftery, Jim   USITC   202-252-1365
Isopropyl myristate....Johnson, Larry   USITC   202-252-1351
Isotopes....Staff   NCI   301-496-5583
Israel....Cherie Loustaunau/Doris Nelmes   Cnty Commerce
202-377-4652
Israel (Tel Aviv)....Stephen Noble   Cnty State   202-647-3672
Israel (Tel Aviv)....Dale Dean   Cnty State   202-647-3672
Israel (Tel Aviv)....Andrea Richhart   Cnty State   202-647-3672
Israel (Tel Aviv)....Margaret Scobey   Cnty State   202-647-3672
Israel (Tel Aviv)....Ryan Crocker   Cnty AID   202-647-3672
Israel (Tel Aviv)....Barbara Bodine   Cnty AID   202-647-3672
Israel (Tel Aviv)....Keith Loken   Cnty AID   202-647-3672
Israel (Tel Aviv)....David Satterfield   Cnty AID   202-647-3672
Israel (Tel Aviv)....Timothy Hauser   Cnty AID   202-647-3672
Israel (Tel Aviv)....Phillip-Michael Gary   Cnty AID   202-647-7367
Israel/Minerals....Bernadette Michalski   Cnty Mines   202-632-5065
Italy....Noel Negretti   Cnty Commerce   202-377-2177
Italy (Naples)....Marx Sterne   Cnty AID   202-647-9001
Italy (Rome)....Raymond Snider   Cnty State   202-647-2453
Italy (Rome)....D. Thomas Longo   Cnty AID   202-647-2453
Italy (Rome)....Karen Milliken   Cnty AID   202-647-3746
Italy (Rome)....William G. Perett   Cnty AID   202-647-8210
Italy/Minerals....John Panulas   Cnty Mines   202-634-1277
Ivory....Persky, H.   Customs   212-466-5881
Ivory Coast....Philip Michelini   Cnty Commerce   202-377-4388
Ivory Coast....R. J. Benn   Peace Corps   202-254-3185
Ivory Coast (Abidjan)....John A. Hedges   Cnty AID   202-647-6980
Ivory Coast (Abidjan)....Rudolph Thomas   Cnty AID   202-647-7985
Ivory Coast/Minerals....Hendrik van Oss   Cnty Mines   202-632-5065
Ivory, articles of....Spalding, Josephine   USITC   202-252-1498
Ivory, tusks....Ludwick, David   USITC   202-252-1329

J

Jackets: mens and boys....Shetty, Sundar   USITC   202-252-1457
Jackets: womens and girls....MacKnight, Peggy   USITC
202-252-1468

Jails, Inmates, and Crowding....Phyllis Jo Baunach   Justice Stat
    202-724-7755
Jails, Inmates, and Crowding....James Stephan   Justice Stat
    202-724-6100
Jails, Inmates, and Crowding....Lawrence Greenfeld   Justice Stat
    202-724-7755
Jails, Inmates, and Crowding....Stephanie Minor-Harper   Justice
    Stat 202-724-7755
Jamaica....Kristen Baumgart   Cnty Commerce 202-377-2527
Jamaica (Kingston)....Dale Shaffer   Cnty State 202-647-2620
Jamaica (Kingston)....Robert J. Blohm   Cnty AID 202-647-2621
Jamaica (Kingston)....Paul Wenger   Cnty AID 202-647-2116
Jamaica/Minerals....Ivette Torres   Cnty Mines 202-632-9352
Jams and Jellies....Hodgen, Donald A.   Commerce 202-377-3346
Jams, jellies, and marmalades....Macomber, Alvin   USITC
    202-252-1315
Japan....Ed Leslie   Cnty Commerce 202-377-4527
Japan (Tokyo)....Timothy Betts   Cnty State 202-647-2912
Japan (Tokyo)....Kenneth Chern   Cnty State 202-647-3152
Japan (Tokyo)....Edward Kloth   Cnty State 202-647-3152
Japan (Tokyo)....David Olive   Cnty State 202-647-3152
Japan (Tokyo)....James Pierce   Cnty State 202-647-2912
Japan (Tokyo)....William G. Corbett   Cnty AID 202-647-2912
Japan (Tokyo)....John G. Scott   Cnty AID 202-647-2912
Japan (Tokyo)....Robert Reis   Cnty AID 202-647-3152
Japan (Tokyo)....Brian Mohler   Cnty AID 202-647-3152
Japan/Minerals....John Wu   Cnty Mines 202-634-1272
Japan/trade matters....Staff   US Trade Rep 202-395-3900
Jet fuel....Foreso, Cynthia   USITC 202-252-1348
Jewelery....Piropato, L.   Customs 212-466-5895
Jewelery, Export Promo.....Beckham, Reginald   Commerce
    202-377-5478
Jewelry....Witherspoon, Richardo   USITC 202-252-1489
Jewelry, Costume....Harris, John M.   Commerce 202-377-1178
Jewelry, Diamonds, Silver Flat., Hollow., Watches....Susanne
    Patch   Fed Trade Com 202-326-2981
Jewelry. Precious Metal....Harris, John M.   Commerce
    202-377-1178
Jordan....Thomas Sams   Cnty Commerce 202-377-5767
Jordan (Amman)....George Malleck   Cnty State 202-647-1022
Jordan (Amman)....Jeff Irwin   Cnty State 202-647-1058
Jordan (Amman)....Thomas Dowling   Cnty AID 202-647-4453
Jordan (Amman)....James Bever   Cnty AID 202-647-9000
Jordan (Amman)....Jay Bruns   Cnty AID 202-647-2481
Jordan/Minerals....Thomas Dolley   Cnty Mines 202-632-5065
Joseph's Disease....Staff   NINCDS 301-496-5751
Journey to Work....Boertlein, Ceilia   Census 301-763-3850
Judges....Carla Gaskins   Justice Stat 202-724-7774
Judges....Patrick Langan   Justice Stat 202-724-7774
Judicial Discovery, Cigarettes....Larry DeMille-Wagman   Fed
    Trade Com 202-326-2448
Judiciary....Carla Gaskins   Justice Stat 202-724-7774
Judiciary....Patick Langan   Justice Stat 202-724-7774
Juices....Maria, J.   Customs 212-466-5895
Juices....Maria, J.   Customs 212-466-5730
Juices, fruit....Dennis, Alfred   USITC 202-252-1316
Juices, vegetable....Dennis, Alfred   USITC 202-252-1316
Jute Products....Ives III, Ralph F.   Commerce 202-377-5124
Juvenile Corrections...Phyllis Jo Banauch   Justice Stat
    202-724-7759
Juvenile Corrections....Susan Kline   Justice Stat 202-724-6100
Juvenile Delinquency....Staff   NIMH 301-443-4515
Juvenile Diabetes....Staff   NIDDK 301-443-3583
Juvenile Rheumatoid Arthritis....Staff   NIAMS 301-496-8188
Juvenile Spin. Musc. Atrophy (Kug.-Wel. Disease)....Staff
    NINCDS 301-496-5751
Juvenile Spin.Muscular Atrophy (Kug.-Wel. Disese....Staff
    NIAMS 301-496-8188
Juveniles - General....Sue Lindgren   Justice Stat 202-724-7759
Juxtaglomerular Hyperplasis (Bartter's Syndrome)....Staff
    NHLBI 301-496-4236

K

Kampuchea....JeNelle Matheson   Cnty Commerce 202-377-2462
Kanner's Syndrome....Staff   NINCDS 301-496-5751
Kaolin....Lukes, James   USITC 202-252-1426
Kaposi's Sarcoma....Staff   NCI 301-496-5583
Kawasaki Disease....Staff   NIAID 301-496-5717
Kawasaki Disease....Staff   CDC 401-329-3534
Kearns-Sayre Syndrome....Staff   NINCDS 301-496-5751
Kenya....James Robb   Cnty Commerce 202-377-4564
Kenya....Bill Ferguson   Peace Corps 202-254-5634
Kenya (Nairobi)....James F. Entwistle   Cnty State 202-647-8913
Kenya (Nairobi)....J. Bradley Swanson   Cnty AID 202-647-3356
Kenya (Nairobi)....Cheryl A. McCarthy   Cnty AID 202-647-9762

Kenya/Minerals....Lloyd Antonides   Cnty Mines 202-632-5065
Keratitis....Staff   NEI 301-496-5248
Keratoconus....Staff   NEI 301-496-5248
Keratomileusis....Staff   NEI 301-496-5248
Keratoplasty....Staff   NEI 301-496-5248
Keratosis Palmaris et Plantaris....Staff   NCI 301-496-5583
Kerosene....Foreso, Cynthia   USITC 202-252-1348
Ketones....Michels, David   USITC 202-252-1352
Key cases....Seastrum, Carl   USITC 202-252-1493
Kidney....Staff   NIDDK 301-496-3583
Kidney Disease (Financial Reimbursement Info.)....Staff
    301-594-7712
Kidney Stones....Staff   NIDDK 301-496-3583
Kidney, Urology Clearinghouse....Staff   NIDDK 301-468-6345
Kinin....Staff   NIAID 301-496-5717
Kiribati (Tarawa)....Ann M. Cambara   Cnty State 202-647-3546
Kiribati....Brian Richmond   Peace Corps 202-254-3231
Kiribati (Gilbert Islands)/Minerals....Travis Lyday   Cnty Mines
    202-634-1272
Kiribati (Tarawa)....Robert A. Benziger   Cnty AID 202-647-3546
Kiribati (Tarawa)....Michael Feldstein   Cnty AID 202-647-9137
Kitchen Cabinets....Wise, Barbara   Commerce 202-377-0375
Kleine-Levin Syndrome....Staff   NINCDS 301-496-5751
Klinefelter's Syndrome....Staff   NCI 301-496-5133
Knitted Fabrics....Edert, R.   Customs 212-466-5885
Knitting machines....Greene, William   USITC 202-252-1405
Knotted Netting....Barth, G.   Customs 212-466-5884
Knowledge Engineering (Aerophysics)....Donald McKellar   NASA
    415-694-4162
Knowledge-Based Systems....M. Freeman   NASA 205-544-5456
Koch Antitoxins....Staff   NCI 301-496-5583
Korea....W. David Straub   Cnty AID 202-647-7717
Korea....James Gagnon   Cnty AID 202-647-7717
Korea....Lee Coldren   Cnty AID 202-647-7717
Korea....Michael Feldstein   Cnty AID 202-647-9137
Korea, North....Lilliana Monk   Cnty Commerce 202-377-3583
Korea, North and South....Mark T. Fitzpatrick   Cnty State
    202-647-7717
Korea, North and South....Roberta L. Chew   Cnty State
    202-647-7717
Korea, North and South....Tony Interlandi   Cnty State
    202-647-7717
Korea, North and South....Lawrence Walker   Cnty State
    202-647-7717
Korea, North/Minerals....Chin Kuo   Cnty Mines 202-632-5066
Korea, South....Karen Chopra/Scott Goddin   Cnty Commerce
    202-377-4957
Korea, South/Minerals....Chin Kuo   Cnty Mines 202-632-5066
Krabbe's Disease....Staff   NINCDS 301-496-5751
Krebiezen (Carcalon)....Staff   NCI 301-496-5583
Kugelberg-Welander Disease (Juv. Spi. Mus. Atoph.)....Staff
    NINCDS 301-496-5751
Kuru....Staff   NINCDS 301-496-5751
Kuwait....Thomas Sams   Cnty Commerce 202-377-5767
Kuwait (Kuwait)....Gordon Gray   Cnty State 202-647-6562
Kuwait (Kuwait)....Janet Sanderson   Cnty AID 202-647-1794
Kuwait/Minerals....Bernadette Michalski   Cnty Mines
    202-632-5065
Kyanite-Mullite....Potter, Michael J.   Mines 202-634-1180

L

LIMB demonstrations....Richard D. Stern   EPA 919-541-2973
LNG Plants, Major Proj.....Thomas, Janet   Commerce 202-377-4146
Labels....Cook, Lee   USITC 202-252-1471
Labor Force....Palumbo, Thomas   Census 301-763-8574
Labor Force....Lester, Gordon   Census 301-763-8574
Laboratory Animals....Staff   DRR 301-496-5545
Laboratory Animals....Staff   DRS/VRB 301-496-2527
Laboratory Glassware....Staff   OD/ORS 301-496-4595
Laboratory Instruments....Donnelly, Margaret T.   Commerce
    202-377-5466
Laboratory Instruments, Trade Promo.....Gwaltney, G.P.
    Commerce 202-377-3090
Laboratory ecosystems....J.D. Yount   EPA 218-720-5752
Laboratory for Oceans....Erik Mollo-Christensen   NASA
    301-286-6171
Labyrinthitis....Staff   NINCDS 301-496-5751
Lace....Enfield, Mary E   USITC 202-252-1455
Lace and Net Fabrics....Edert, R.   Customs 212-466-5885
Lacemaking machines....Greene, William   USITC 202-252-1405
Lacings....Cook, Lee   USITC 202-252-1471
Lacquers....Johnson, Larry   USITC 202-252-1351
Lacrimal Glands....Staff   NEI 301-496-5248

Lactation....Staff NIDDK 301-496-3583
Lactose....Randall, Rob USITC 202-252-1366
Lactose Intolerance....Staff NIDDK 301-496-3583
Laetrile....Staff NCI 301-496-5583
Lake/stream ecology....D. Phillip Larsen EPA 503-756-4666
Lakes....Wanser, Stephen USITC 202-252-1363
Lamb....Ludwick, David USITC 202-252-1329
Laminar Flow Rooms....Staff OD/ORS 301-496-2960
Laminar-Flow Control....Richard Wagner NASA 804-865-2045
Lamp Bulbs....Boderick, Nancy Commerce 202-377-0348
Lamp black....Johnson, Larry USITC 202-252-1351
Lamps (bulbs)....Hagey, Michael USITC 202-252-1392
Land Mobile Common Carrier....Staff FCC 202-653-5560
Land Mobile Frequent Assignment Techniques....Staff FCC 717-337-1411
Land Mobile Operational Review of Radio....Staff FCC 202-632-6497
Land Sales, Marketing Practices....Staff Fed Trade Com 202-326-3128
Land Transportation...Staff FCC 717-337-1212
Land disposal bans....Harlal Choudhury EPA 513-569-7536
Land treatment....H. George Keeler EPA 405-332-2212
Land treatment....Scott Huling EPA 405-332-2313
Landfill design and operation....Robert Landreth EPA 513-569-7836
Landfill permitting/site selection....Lee A. Mulkey EPA 404-546-3546
Landscape ecology....Peter A. Beedlow EPA 503-757-4791
Language....Staff NINCDS 301-496-5751
Language Development....Staff NICHD 301-496-5133
Language, Current: Mother Tongue....Siegel, Paul Census 301-763-1154
Laos....JeNelle Matherson Cnty Commerce 202-377-2462
Laos (Vientiane)....Harvey Somers Cnty State 202-647-3133
Laos (Vientiane)....Terry Breese Cnty AID 202-647-3132
Laos/Minerals....David Doan Cnty Mines 202-634-1272
Large-Scale Turbulence....Vittorio Canuto NASA 212-678-5571
Laser (Cancer Surgery)....Staff NCI 301-496-5583
Laser Angioplasty....Staff NHLBI 301-496-4236
Laser Treatment (Eyes)....Staff NEI 301-496-5248
Lasers, Trade Promo.....Gwaltney, G.P. Commerce 202-377-3090
Lassa Fever....Staff NIAID 301-496-5717
Latin America/trade matters....Staff US Trade Rep 202-395-6135
Latvia....John W. Zerolis Cnty State 202-647-1070
Latvia....Terry R. Snell Cnty AID 202-647-4138
Laundry machines....Jackson, Georgia USITC 202-252-1399
Laurence-Moon-Bardet-Biedl Syndrome....Staff NINCDS 301-496-5751
Law Enforcement, Prosecution & Courts - State....Donald Manson Justice Stat 202-724-7770
Law Suits Litigation....Staff FCC 202-632-7112
Lawn & Garden Equipment....Streeter, Jonathan Commerce 202-377-2132
Lawyers, Licensed Occupation....Staff Fed Trade Com 202-326-2920
Lead....Wagner, Lorie USITC 202-252-1439
Lead....Woodbury, William D. Mines 202-634-1083
Lead Based Paints....Staff CDC 404-329-3534
Lead Encephalopathy....Staff NINCDS 301-496-5751
Lead Poisoning....Staff CDC 404-329-3534
Lead Poisoning....Staff NIEHS 919-541-3345
Lead Products....Larrabee, David Commerce 202-377-0575
Lead compounds....Greenblatt, Jack USITC 202-252-1353
Lead pigments....Johnson, Larry USITC 202-252-1351
Lead-Poisoning Anemia....Staff NHLBI 301-496-4236
Leads....Linkins, Linda USITC 202-252-1499
Learning Center for Interactive Technology....Staff NLM 301-496-6280
Learning Disabilities....Staff NINCDS 301-496-5751
Learning Disabilities....Staff NICHD 301-496-5133
Learning Disabilities....Staff NIMH 301-443-4513
Lease condensate....Foreso, Cynthia USITC 202-252-1348
Leasing Equipment and Vehicles....McAdam, Milton B. Commerce 202-377-0346
Leasing by Consumers, Credit Practices....Staff Fed Trade Com 202-326-3175
Leasing, Credit Practices, Automotive....Staff Fed Trade Com 202-326-3175
Leather....Steller, Rose USITC 202-252-1323
Leather Products....Enright, Joe Commerce 202-377-3459
Leather Tanning....Byron, James E. Commerce 202-377-4034
Leather and Fur Articles....Persky, H. Customs 212-466-5881
Leather apparel....Worrell, Jackie USITC 202-252-1466
Leather footwear parts....Burns, Gail USITC 202-252-1469
Leather/Down Wearing Apparel....Persky, H. Customs 212-466-5881
Lebanon....Thomas Sams Cnty Commerce 202-377-5767
Lebanon (Beirut)....Joseph LeBaron Cnty State 202-647-1030

Lebanon (Beirut)....Jeff Irwin Cnty State 202-647-1058
Lebanon (Beirut)....Philo Dibble Cnty AID 202-647-1018
Lebanon (Beirut)....Jay Bruns Cnty AID 202-647-2481
Lebanon (Beirut)....Marx Sterne Cnty AID 202-647-9001
Lebanon/Minerals....Bernadette Michalski Cnty Mines 202-632-5065
Leber's Disease....Staff NEI 301-496-5248
Left Ventricular Assist Device....Staff NHLBI 301-496-4236
Legal Services....McAdam, Milton B. Commerce 202-377-0346
Legg-Perthes Disease....Staff NIAMS 301-496-8188
Legionella Pneumophila....Staff NIAID 301-496-5717
Legionnaire's Disease....Staff NIAID 301-496-5717
Legislative Information....Staff 301-496-3471
Leigh's Disease (Subacute Necrotizing Encephal.)....Staff NINCDS 301-496-5751
Leishmaniasis....Staff NIAID 301-496-5717
Lemon oil (essential oil)....Land, Eric USITC 202-252-1349
Lens....Staff NEI 301-496-5248
Lens Implants....Staff NEI 301-496-5248
Lenses....Johnson, Christopher USITC 202-252-1488
Leprosy....Staff NIAID 301-496-5717
Lesch-Nyhan Disease....Staff NIAMS 301-496-8188
Lesch-Nyhan Disease....Staff NINCDS 301-496-5751
Lesch-Nyhan Disease....Staff NIMH 301-443-4515
Lesotho....Fred Stokelin Cnty Commerce 202-377-5148
Lesotho....Carrie Wiltshire Peace Corps 202-254-6046
Lesotho (Maseru)....June Perry Cnty State 202-647-8434
Lesotho (Maseru)....Kenneth H. Kolb Cnty AID 202-647-8434
Lesotho (Maseru)....Leonard Pompa Cnty AID 202-647-4287
Lesotho/Minerals....Hendrik van Oss Cnty Mines 202-632-5065
Leukemia....Staff NCI 301-496-5583
Leukocyte and Platelet Isoantibodies....Staff NIDDK 301-496-3583
Leukodystrophy....Staff NINCDS 301-496-5751
Leukoencephalopathy....Staff NINCDS 301-496-5751
Leukoplakia....Staff NIDR 301-496-4261
Levulose....Randall, Rob USITC 202-252-1366
Liberia....Philip Michelini Cnty Commerce 202-377-4388
Liberia....Anna West Peace Corps 202-254-5644
Liberia (Monrovia....Emily B. McPhee Cnty AID 202-647-7988
Liberia (Monrovia)....Ed McMahon Cnty State 202-647-3395
Liberia (Monrovia)....Constance Freeman Cnty AID 202-647-8354
Liberia/Minerals....Hendrik van Oss Cnty Mines 202-632-5065
Librarians Office....Staff DRS 301-496-2447
Libya....Simon Bensimon Cnty Commerce 202-377-5737
Libya (Tripoli)....Sharon Wiener Cnty State 202-647-4674
Libya (Tripoli)....Roger Dankert Cnty AID 202-647-9373
Libya/Minerals....Thomas Dolley Cnty Mines 202-632-5065
Lice....Staff NIAID 301-496-5717
Lichen Planus....Staff NIDR 301-496-4261
Lichen Planus....Staff NIAMS 301-496-8188
Liechtenstein....William Millan Cnty State 202-647-1484
Liechtenstein....Robert M. Beecroft Cnty AID 202-647-2005
Life Cycle....Staff NIA 301-496-1752
Life Expectancy....Staff NIA 301-496-1752
Life Extension....Staff NIA 301-496-1752
Life Review....Staff NIA 301-496-1752
Light Bulb Rule....George O'Brien Fed Trade Com 202-326-2972
Light oil....Foreso, Cynthia USITC 202-252-1348
Lighting Devices....Staff FCC 202-653-6288
Lighting Fixtures, Commercial....Whitley, Richard A. Commerce 202-377-0682
Lighting Fixtures, Residential....Whitley, Richard A. Commerce 202-377-0682
Lighting equipment....Hagey, Michael USITC 202-252-1392
Lightning Fixtures, Outdoor....Whitley, Richard A. Commerce 202-377-0682
Lightning, Severe Storms....Bruce Fisher NASA 804-865-3274
Ligninsulfonic acid and its salts....Land, Eric USITC 202-252-1349
Lignite....Foreso, Cynthia USITC 202-252-1348
Lime....White, Linda USITC 202-252-1427
Lime....Ober, Joyce Mines 202-634-1177
Limestone....White, Linda USITC 202-252-1427
Limnology....M. Robbins Church EPA 503-753-4666
Limnology....Dixon H. Landers EPA 503-757-4695
Limnology/lake restoration....Spencer A. Peterson EPA 503-757-4605
Line of Business....William Long Fed Trade Com 202-326-3353
Linear Accelerator....Staff NCI 301-496-5583
Lipid Research Clinics....Staff NHLBI 301-496-4236
Lipid Storage Diseases....Staff NINCDS 301-496-5751
Lipid Transport Disorders....Staff NHLBI 301-496-4236
Lipidemia....Staff NHLBI 301-496-4236
Lipidosis....Staff NINCDS 301-496-5751
Lipoproteins....Staff NHLBI 301-496-4236
Liquefied natural gas (LNG)....Land, Eric USITC 202-252-1349
Liquefied petroleum gas (LPG)....Land, Eric USITC 202-252-1349
Liquefield refinery gas (LRG)....Land, Eric USITC 202-252-1349

Liquid Propulsion Dynamic Analysis....P. Vallely   NASA
  205-544-1440
Liquid Rocket Propulsion....Carl Aukerman   NASA   216-433-2441
Liquid Waste....Staff   OD/ORS   301-496-2960
Liquid Waste (Radioactive)....Staff   OD/ORS   301-496-2254
Listeriosis....Staff   NIAID   301-496-5717
Lithium....Trainor, Cynthia   USITC   202-252-1354
Lithium....Ober, Joyce A.   Mines   202-634-1177
Lithium compounds....Greenblatt, Jack   USITC   202-252-1353
Lithium stearate....Randall, Rob   USITC   202-252-1366
Lithuania....John W. Zerolis   Cnty State   202-647-1070
Lithuania....Terry R. Snell   Cnty AID   202-647-4138
Liver....Staff   NIDDK   301-496-3583
Living Arrangements....Saluter, Arlene   Census   301-763-7987
Local Government Radio....Staff   FCc   717-337-1212
Local Governments, Economics....Long, Richard   Agri
  202-786-1544
Local Television Transmission....Staff   FCC   202-634-1706
Locks....Hantman, S.   Customs   212-466-5678
Locks and Keys....Staff   OD/DAS/Locksmith   301-496-3507
Loeffler's Syndrome....Staff   NIAID   301-496-5717
Logs, Wood....Hicks, Michael   Commerce   202-377-0375
Logs, rough....Vacant   USITC   202-252-1326
Long Term Offenders....Anne Schmidt   Justice   202-724-2959
Long Term Offenders....Voncile Gowdy   Justice   202-724-2951
Longevity (Statistics)....Staff   NCHS   301-436-8500
Longevity (Statistics)....Staff   NIA   301-496-1752
Longitudinal Surveys....Dopkowski, Ronald   Census   301-763-2767
Longterm Care....Staff   NCNR   301-496-0526
Lotteries....Staff   FCC   202-632-6999
Lou Gehrig's Disease....Staff   NINCDS   301-496-5751
Low Back Pain....Staff   NIAMS   301-496-8188
Low Back Pain....Staff   NINCDS   301-496-5751
Low Birth Weight....Staff   NICHD   301-496-5133
Low Blood Pressure....Staff   NHLBI   301-496-4236
Low Energy Gamma Rays....T. L. Cline   NASA   301-286-8375
Low NOx burners....G. Blair Martin   EPA   919-541-7504
Low Power Television Stations....Staff   FCC   202-632-7426
Low Power Transmitters....Staff   FCC   202-653-6288
Low Thrust Propulsion Fundamentals....David Byers   NASA
  216-433-2447
Low Vision Aids....Staff   NEI   301-496-5248
Low-Density Lipoproteins (LDL)....Staff   NHLBI   301-496-4236
Low-Gravity Science....F. Szofran   NASA   205-544-7777
Low-Speed Aircraft....Bruce Holmes   NASA   804-865-3274
Low-Speed Aircraft, Rotorcraft Structural Dynamics....Robert
  Huston   NASA   804-865-4301
Lowe's Syndrome....Staff   NEI   301-496-5248
Lube fittings....Fravel, Dennis   USITC   202-252-1404
Lubricating grease....Foreso, Cynthia   USITC   202-252-1348
Lubricating oil....Foreso, Cynthia   USITC   202-252-1348
Luggage....Seastrum, Carl   USITC   202-252-1493
Luggage....Enright, Joe   Commerce   202-377-3459
Luggage....Gorman, K.   Customs   212-466-5893
Lumber....Vacant   USITC   202-252-1326
Lumber....Wise, Barbara   Commerce   202-377-0375
Lumber Futures With Options....David Rosenfeld   Comm Futures
  312-353-9026
Lung Cancer....Staff   NCI   301-496-5583
Lung Disease (Asbestosis)....Staff   NIEHS   919-541-3345
Lung Disease (Infectious/Allergenic)....Staff   NIAID   301-496-5717
Lung Disease (Non-infec., Non-aller., Non-tumor.)....Staff
  NHLBI   301-496-4236
Lung Disease (Tumorous/Cancerous)....Staff   NCI   301-496-5583
Lupus Erythematosus....Staff   NIAMS   301-496-8188
Lupus Erythematosus....Staff   NINCDS   301-496-5751
Lupus Erythematosus....Staff   NIAID   301-496-5717
Luxembourg....Boyce Fitzpatrick   Cnty Commerce   202-377-5401
Luxembourg....Yvette Wong   Cnty State   202-647-6664
Luxembourg/Minerals....George Rabchevsky   Cnty Mines
  202-632-5053
Luxemburg (Luxemburg)....James G. Huff   Cnty AID   202-647-6046
Luxemburg (Luxemburg)....Richard A. Christenson   Cnty AID
  202-647-4484
Lyme Arthritis/Lyme Disease....Staff   NIAID   301-496-5717
Lyme Arthritis/Lyme Disease....Staff   NIAMS   301-496-8188
Lymphadenopathy Syndrome (LAD)....Staff   NIAID   301-496-5717
Lymphedema....Staff   NCI   301-496-5583
Lymphoblastic Lymphosarcoma....Staff   NCI   301-496-5583
Lymphoma....Staff   NCI   301-496-5583
Lymphosarcoma....Staff   NCI   301-496-5583

M

MARC (Minority Access to Research Careers)....Staff   NIGMS
  301-496-7301

MBS resins....Taylor, Ed   USITC   202-252-1362
Macao....JeNelle Matherson   Cnty Commerce   202-377-2462
Macaroni and other alimentary pastes....James, Antoinette   USITC
  202-252-1313
Macau....John Adams   Cnty State   202-647-6301
Macau....David Shear   Cnty AID   202-647-1004
Macau....Peter Chase   Cnty AID   202-647-1322
Machine Tool Accessories....McGibbon, Patrick   Commerce
  202-377-0314
Machine Tools....Losche, R.   Customs   212-466-5670
Machines and machinery: adding....Fletcher, William   USITC
  202-252-1407
Machines and machinery: addressing....Fletcher, William   USITC
  202-252-1407
Machines and machinery: agglomerating....Greene, William
  USITC   202-252-1405
Machines rolling (textile)....Greene, William   USITC
  202-252-1405
Machines, spraying: agricultural/horticultural....Fravel,
  Dennis   USITC   202-252-1405
Machines, spraying: other....Slingerland, David   USITC
  202-252-1400
Machines, textile: bleaching....Greene, William   USITC
  202-252-1405
Machines, textile: calendering and rolling....Greene, William
  USITC   202-252-1405
Machines, textile: cleaning....Greene, William   USITC
  202-252-1405
Machines, textile: coating....Greene, William   USITC
  202-252-1405
Machines, textile: drying....Greene, William   USITC
  202-252-1405
Machines, textile: dyeing....Greene, William   USITC
  202-252-1405
Machines, textile: embroidery....Greene, William   USITC
  202-252-1405
Machines, textile: knitting....Greene, William   USITC
  202-252-1405
Machines, textile: lacemaking....Greene, William   USITC
  202-252-1405
Machines, textile: printing....Greene, William   USITC
  202-252-1405
Machines, textile: spinning....Greene, William   USITC
  202-252-1405
Machines, textile: tobacco....Jackson, Georgia   USITC
  202-252-1399
Machines, textile: tools, machine....Travel, Dennis   USITC
  202-252-1404
Machines, textile: vending....Jackson, Georgia   USITC
  202-252-1399
Machines, textile: washing....Greene, William   USITC
  202-252-1405
Machines, textile: weaving....Greene, William   USITC
  202-252-1405
Machines, textile: weighing....Slingerland, David   USITC
  202-252-1400
Machines: agricultural or horticultural....Lippa, Alison   USITC
  202-252-1398
Machines: bookbinding....Slingerland, David   USITC
  202-252-1400
Machines: calculators....Baker, Scott   USITC   202-252-1386
Machines: cash registers....Fletcher, William   USITC
  202-252-1407
Machines: casting machines....Greene, William   USITC
  202-252-1405
Machines: checkwriting....Fletcher, William   USITC   202-252-1407
Machines: cleaning (heat process equipment)....Slingerland, David
  USITC   202-252-1400
Machines: cleaning (textiles)....Greene, William   USITC
  202-252-1405
Machines: coating....Greene, William   USITC   202-252-1405
Machines: converters....Greene, William   USITC   202-252-1405
Machines: cordage....Greene, William   USITC   202-252-1405
Machines: crushing....Greene, William   USITC   202-252-1405
Machines: cutting....Greene, William   USITC   202-252-1405
Machines: data processing....Fletcher, William   USITC
  202-252-1407
Machines: dressing....Greene, William   USITC   202-252-1405
Machines: drink preparing....Jackson, Georgia   USITC
  202-252-1399
Machines: dry cleaning....Jackson, Georgia   USITC   202-252-1399
Machines: drying....Jackson, Georgia   USITC   202-252-1399
Machines: dyeing....Greene, William   USITC   202-252-1405
Machines: earth moving....Shapiro, Lena   USITC   202-252-1408
Machines: embroidery....Greene, William   USITC   202-252-1405
Machines: fabric folding....Greene, William   USITC   202-252-1405
Machines: farm....Lippa, Alison   USITC   202-252-1398
Machines: flight simulators....Anderson, Peder   USITC

202-647-0108
Martinique....Mack Tadeu   Cnty Commerce   202-377-2527
Martinique (Fort-de-France)....Avon Williams   Cnty State
   202-647-2621
Martinique (Fort-de-France)....David F. Rogus   Cnty AID
   202-647-2130
Martinique/Minerals....Ivette Torres   Cnty Mines   202-632-9352
Mass Spectrometers....Staff   DRR   301-496-5545
Mass Spectronomy/Gas Chromatography....George Wood   NASA
   804-865-2466
Mass Spectronomy....Hasso Niemann   NASA   301-286-8706
Mass Transit, Major Proj.....Smith, Jay L.   Commerce
   202-377-4642
Mass spectrometry....Ronald K. Mitchum   EPA   702-798-2103
Mass spectrometry....Stephen Billets   EPA   702-798-2232
Mass spectrometry....John M. McGuire   EPA   404-546-3185
Mastectomy....Staff   NCI   301-496-5583
Mastication....Staff   NIDR   301-496-4261
Matches....Spalding, Josephine   USITC   202-252-1498
Materials, Advanced....Cammarota, David   Commerce   202-377-0575
Mathematical statistics....Daryl L. Thome   EPA   702-798-2158
Mattresses....Linkins, Linda   USITC   202-252-1499
Mattresses....Ellis, Kevin   Commerce   202-377-1140
Mauritana....Vacant   Cnty Commerce   202-377-4564
Mauritania....Mary Lange   Peace Corps   202-254-7004
Mauritania (Nouakchott)....Stephen Kelly   Cnty State
   202-647-2865
Mauritania (Nouakchott)....Jean G. Soso   Cnty AID   202-647-2865
Mauritania (Nouakchott)....Yvonne Y. John   Cnty AID
   202-647-6049
Mauritania/Minerals....Bernadette Michalski   Cnty Mines
   202-632-5065
Mauritius (Port Louis)....Walter Manger   Cnty State   202-647-8913
Mauritius (Port Louis)....Robert Snyder   Cnty AID   202-647-3040
Mauritius (Port Louis)....Stephen Pulaski   Cnty AID   202-647-9763
Mauritius/Minerals....Lloyd Antonides   Cnty Mines   202-632-5065
McArdle's Disease....Staff   NINCDS   301-496-5751
Measles....Staff   NIAID   301-496-5717
Measles....Staff   NINCDS   301-496-5751
Measles-Immunization....Staff   CDC   404-329-3534
Measles-Rubeola....Staff   NIAID   301-496-5717
Measurement and Modeling....F. Leslie   NASA   205-544-1633
Measurements of Air Pollution From Satellites (MAP....Harry
   Reichle   NASA   804-865-2576
Measuring....Donnelly, Margaret T.   Commerce   202-377-5466
Measuring Instruments....Riedl, K.   Customs   212-466-5493
Meat....Brady, T.   Customs   212-466-5790
Meat Packing Plants....Hodgen, Donald A.   Commerce   202-377-3346
Meat, edible....Ludwick, David   USITC   202-252-1329
Meat, inedible....Ludwick, David   USITC   202-252-1329
Meats, Prepared....Hodgen, Donald A.   Commerce   202-377-3346
Mech. Power Transmission Eqmt. Nec.....Fletcher, William E.
   Commerce   202-377-0309
Mechanical Engineering....James Price   Con Product Safe
   202-492-6494
Mechanical and Chemical Systems....Donald Rapp   NASA
   818-354-4931
Mechanisms of toxic action....Steven Bradbury   EPA   218-720-5527
Media (Bacteriologic)....Staff   OD/ORS   301-496-6017
Medical Care for Aged....Staff   NIA   301-496-1752
Medical Equipment....Staff   FCC   202-653-6288
Medical Facilities, Major Proj.....White, Barbara   Commerce
   202-377-4160
Medical Information System (MIS)....Staff   CC   301-496-7946
Medical Instruments....Fuchs, Michael   Commerce   202-377-0550
Medical Instruments....Preston, J.   Customs   212-466-5492
Medical Instruments, Trade Promo.....Keen, George B.   Commerce
   202-377-2010
Medical Photography....Staff   DRS/MAPB   301-496-5995
Medical Scientist Training Program....Staff   NIGMS   301-496-7301
Medical Staff Fellowship Training Program....Staff   CC
   301-496-2427
Medical apparatus....Johnson, Christopher   USITC   202-252-1488
Medicine for the Layman (Lect., Videos, Booklets)....Staff   CC
   301-496-2563
Mediterranean Fever....Staff   NIAID   301-496-5717
Mediterranean/trade matters....Staff   US Trade Rep   202-395-4620
Medlars/Medline....Staff   NLM   301-496-6193
Meige's Syndrome (Facial Dystonia)....Staff   NINCDS
   301-496-5751
Melamine....Michels, David   USITC   202-252-1352
Melamine resins....Taylor, Ed   USITC   202-252-1362
Melanoma....Staff   NCI   301-496-5583
Melanoma....Staff   NEI   301-496-5248
Memory....Staff   NINCDS   301-496-5751
Memory....Staff   NIMH   301-443-4515
Memory Loss....Staff   NIA   301-496-1752
Meniere's Disease....Staff   NINCDS   301-496-5751

Meningitis....Staff   NIAID   301-496-5717
Meningitis....Staff   NINCDS   301-496-5751
Meningocele....Staff   NINCDS   301-496-5751
Meningococcal Meningitis....Staff   NIAID   301-496-5717
Menkes' Disease....Staff   NINCDS   301-496-5751
Menopause....Staff   NIA   301-496-1752
Menstruation....Staff   NICHD   301-496-5133
Menstruation and Menopause....Staff   NCNR   301-496-0526
Mental Health and Aging....Staff   NIMH   301-443-4515
Mental Health and Aging....Staff   NIA   301-496-1752
Mental Retardation....Staff   NICHD   301-496-5133
Menthol....Land, Eric   USITC   202-252-1349
Mercury....DeSapio, Vincent   USITC   202-252-1435
Mercury....Reese, Jr., Robert   Mines   202-634-1206
Mercury Poisoning....Staff   NINCDS   301-496-5751
Mercury compounds....Greenblatt, jack   USITC   202-252-1353
Mercury in Fish....Staff   EPA   301-755-0100
Mercury, Fluorspar....Manion, James J.   Commerce   202-377-5157
Mergers and Acquisitions....Staff   FCC   202-632-4887
Mergers, Premerger Staff....Staff   Fed Trade Com   202-326-3100
Metabolic (Nervous System)....Staff   NINCDS   301-496-5751
Metabolic Disorders....Staff   NIDDK   301-496-3583
Metabolism....Steven Bradbury   EPA   218-720-5527
Metabolism (Inborn Errors)....Staff   NICHD   301-496-5133
Metabolism (Inborn Errors)....Staff   NINCDS   301-496-5751
Metachromatic Leukodystrophy....Staff   NINCDS   301-496-5751
Metal....Reiley, Robert C.   Commerce   202-377-0575
Metal Articles....Shulberg, M.   Customs   212-466-5478
Metal Building Products....Williams, Franklin   Commerce
   202-377-0132
Metal Cookware....Corea, Judy   Commerce   202-377-0311
Metal Cutting Machine Tools....Mearman, John   Commerce
   202-377-0315
Metal Cutting Machine Tools, Trade Promo.....Manzolillo, Franc
   Commerce   202-377-2991
Metal Cutting Tools....Comer, Barbara   Commerce   202-377-0316
Metal Cutting Tools Fr Mach Tools....Vacant   Commerce
   202-377-0316
Metal Foil....Fitzgerald, J.   Customs   212-466-5492
Metal Forming Machine Tools....McGibbon, Patrick   Commerce
   202-377-0314
Metal Forming Machine Tools (Trade Promo)....Manzolillo, Franc
   Commerce   202-377-2991
Metal Household Articles....Hantman, S.   Customs   212-466-5678
Metal Metabolism....Staff   NIDDK   301-496-3583
Metal Powders....Cammarota, David   Commerce   202-377-0575
Metal adsorption/speciation....Nicholas T. Loux   EPA
   404-546-3174
Metal rolling mills....Fravel, Dennis   USITC   202-252-1404
Metal sorption....George W. Bailey   EPA   404-546-3307
Metal working machines....Fravel, Dennis   USITC   202-252-1404
Metal-humic interactions....Leo V. Azarraga   EPA   404-546-3453
Metallic Materials Research....P. Schuerer   NASA   205-544-2566
Metals....Goodwin, Michael A.   Commerce   202-377-3118
Metals....Russell J. Erickson   EPA   218-720-5534
Metals....Fitzgerald, J.   Customs   212-466-5492
Metals Matrix and Intermetallic Matrix Composites....Hugh Gray
   NASA   216-433-3230
Metals speciation....David S. Brown   EPA   404-546-3310
Metals transport....Bert Bledsoe   EPA   405-332-2324
Metals, Minerals and Commodities....Reiley, Robert C.   Commerce
   202-377-0575
Metals, Nonferrous....Reiley, Robert C.   Commerce   202-377-0575
Metals, Secondary....Thompson, Ralph   Commerce   202-377-0606
Metalworking....Mearman, John   Commerce   202-377-0315
Metalworking Equipment Nec.....Mearman, John   Commerce
   202-377-0315
Metastases....Staff   NCI   301-496-5583
Metastic Tumors (Central Nervous System)....Staff   NINCDS
   301-496-5751
Meteorological....Moller, Ruben   USITC   202-252-1495
Meteorological modeling....Francis A. Schiermeier   EPA
   919-541-4542
Metered Service--Message Units....Staff   FCC   202-632-4887
Methacrylates....Michels, David   USITC   202-252-1352
Methane....Land, Eric   USITC   202-252-1349
Methods and quality assurance....Thomas A. Clark   EPA
   513-569-7301
Methods and quality assurance....Gerald McKee   EPA   513-569-7303
Methods and quality assurance....Robert Booth   EPA   513-569-7364
Methods evaluation, standarization....Larry J. Purdue   EPA
   919-541-2665
Methods standardization....Raymond Wesselman   EPA
   513-569-7325
Methyl alcohol (methanol)....Michels, David   USITC   202-252-1352
Methyl ethyl ketone....Michels, David   USITC   202-252-1352
Methyl oleate....Johnson, Larry   USITC   202-252-1351
Metropolitan Areas....Forstall, Richard   Census   301-763-5158

Mexico....Melissa Coyle/Thomas Welch/Brent Fogt/Paul Dacher
Cnty Commerce 202-377-2332
Mexico (Mexico, D.F.)....Don McNally Cnty State 202-647-9292
Mexico (Mexico, D.F.)....James McAnulty Cnty State 202-647-8529
Mexico (Mexico, D.F.)....George B. High Cnty AID 202-647-9894
Mexico (Mexico, D.F.)....James S. Landberg Cnty AID
202-647-9292
Mexico (Mexico, D.F.)....Nancy M. Mason Cnty AID 202-647-1881
Mexico (Mexico, D.F.)....James Reilly Cnty AID 202-647-1865
Mexico (Mexico, D.F.)....Paul Kline Cnty AID 202-647-9364
Mexico (Mexioc D.F.)....Marvin Schwartz Cnty AID 202-647-4358
Mexico/Minerals....Jerome Machamer Cnty Mines 202-632-9352
Mexico/trade matters....Staff US Trade Rep 202-395-5663
Mica....White, Linda USITC 202-252-1427
Mica....Davis, Lawrence L. Mines 202-634-1206
Microbial biotransformation processes....David L. Lewis EPA
404-546-3358
Microbial ecology....Parmely H. Pritchard EPA 904-932-5311
Microbial ecology....Tamar Barkay EPA 904-932-5311
Microbial ecology....Fred J. Genthner EPA 904-932-5311
Microbial ecology/biotechnology....Ramon J. Seidler EPA
503-757-4661
Microbial genetics....Stephen M. Cuskey EPA 904-932-5311
Microbial genetics....Richard W. Eaton EPA 904-932-5311
Microbial kinetic constant measurement....William C. Steen EPA
404-546-3776
Microbial kinetics....John E. Rogers EPA 404-546-3103
Microbial pesticides....Clinton Y. Kawanishi EPA 919-541-7965
Microbiological Monitoring....Staff OD/ORS 301-496-2960
Microbiology...Alfred Dufour EPA 513-569-7218
Microbiology...James F. McNabb EPA 405-332-2416
Microbiology....Charles W. Hendricks EPA 503-757-4640
Microbiology....Bruce Lighthart EPA 503-757-4350
Microcephaly....Staff NINCDS 301-496-5751
Microcosms....Steven F. Hedtke EPA 218-720-2492
Microgravity Materials Science....Thomas Glasgow NASA
216-433-5013
Microgravity Science and Applications....Fred Kohl NASA
216-433-2866
Micronesia....Brian Richmond Peace Corps 202-254-3231
Microorganisms Control....Staff OD/ORS 301-496-2960
Microscopes...Johnson, Christopher USITC 202-252-1488
Microtropia....Staff NEI 301-496-5248
Microvascular Surgery....Staff NINCDS 301-496-5751
Microwave Auxiliary--Common Carrier....Staff FCC 202-634-1706
Microwave Auxiliary--Mass Media....Staff FCC 202-634-6307
Microwave Cable Television Relay Service....Staff fCC
202-254-3420
Microwave Closed Loop....Staff FCC 202-634-1706
Microwave Common Carrier Licenses....Staff FCC 202-634-1706
Microwave Licenses....Staff FCC 202-634-1706
Microwave Monitoring Stations....Staff FCC 202-634-7593
Microwave Multipoint Distribution....Staff FCC 202-634-1706
Microwave Observational Systems....Paul Swanson NASA
818-354-3274
Microwave Ovens....Staff FCC 202-653-6288
Microwave Radio Relay....Staff FCC 202-634-1706
Microwave Sensors and Data Communication Branch....Thomas
Wilheit NASA 301-286-9831
Microwave Television--Pickup....Staff FCC 202-634-1706
Microwave, Protection from Interference....Staff FCC
202-634-7593
Middle Ear Infections....Staff NINCDS 301-496-5751
Migraine (Headache)....Staff NINCDS 301-496-5751
Migration/Geographic Mobility, Current Statistics....Hansen,
Kristin Census 301-763-3850
Migration/Geographic Mobility, Current Statistics....Deare,
Diana Census 301-763-3850
Military Stations....Staff FCC 202-653-8141
Milk....Warren, J Fred USITC 202-252-1311
Milk Intolerance....Staff NIDDK 301-496-3583
Milk, Economics....Miller, Jim Agri 202-786-1830
Milk, Economics....Short, Sara Agri 202-386-1830
Milk, Statistics....Buckner, Dan Agri 202-447-4448
Milk, World, Economics....Bailey, Linda Agri 202-786-1691
Million-Volt Electron Microscope Resources....Staff DRR
301-496-5545
Millnery ornaments....Spalding, Josephine USITC 202-252-1498
Millwork....Auerbach, Mitchel Commerce 202-377-0375
Minamata Disease (Mercury Poisoning)....Staff NINCDS
301-496-5751
Mineral Based Cons. Mats, Asphalt....Pitcher, Charles B.
Commerce 202-377-0132
Mineral Based Cons. Mats., Gypsum....Pitcher, Charles B.
Commerce 202-377-0132
Mineral Based Cons. Mats., Stone....Pitcher, Charles B.
Commerce 202-377-0132
Mineral Based Const. Mats., Clay....Pitcher, Charles B.

Commerce 202-377-0132
Mineral Based Const. Mats., Concrete....Pitcher, Charles B.
Commerce 202-377-0132
Mineral Metabolism....Staff NIDDK 301-496-3583
Mineral oil....Foreso, Cynthia USITC 202-252-1348
Mineral salts....Randall, Rob USITC 202-252-1366
Mineral wool....White, Linda USITC 202-252-1427
Minerals Nec, Nonmetallic....Manson, James J. Commerce
202-377-5157
Minerals Non-metalic....Bunin, J. Customs 212-466-5796
Minerals in the World Economy/Minerals....Charles Kimbell Cnty
Mines 202-634-1713
Minimal Brain Dysfunction....Staff NINCDS 301-496-5751
Minimal Brain Dysfunction....Staff NIMH 301-443-4515
Mining....Shapiro, Lena USITC 202-252-1408
Mining....Staff FCC 717-337-1212
Mining Machinery....McDonald Edward Commerce 202-377-0680
Mining Machinery, Trade Promo.....Zanetakos, George Commerce
202-377-0552
Mining Trends....Tanner, Arnold O. Mines 202-634-1019
Mining machines....Shapiro, Lena USITC 202-252-1408
Minority Access to Research Careers (MARC)....Staff NIGMS
301-496-7301
Minority Aging....Staff NIA 301-496-1752
Minority Biomedical Research Support Program....Staff DRR
301-496-6743
Misc. Textiles....Falcone, A. Customs 212-466-5886
Miscellaneous animal products....Ludwick, David USITC
202-252-1329
Miscellaneous articles of pulp and paper....Rhodes, Richard
USITC 202-252-1322
Miscellaneous benzenoid intermediates....Matusik, Ed USITC
202-252-1356
Miscellaneous fish products....Corey, Roger USITC 202-252-1327
Miscellaneous products.....Spalding, Josephine USITC
202-252-1498
Miscellaneous vegetable products....Pierr-Benoist, John USITC
202-252-1320
Miscellaneous wood products....Westcot, Thomas USITC
202-252-1325
Mitral Valve....Staff NHLBI 301-496-4236
Mixed Connective Tissue Disease....Staff NIAMS 301-496-8188
Mixture toxicity....Steven J. Broderius EPA 218-720-5574
Mixtures (artificial) of fatty substances....Randall, Rob USITC
202-252-1366
Mixtures of inorganic compounds....Greenblatt, Jack USITC
202-252-1353
Mixtures of organic compounds....Michels, David USITC
202-252-1352
Mobile Homes....Mathieu, Renee Commerce 202-377-0132
Mobile Homes, Marketing Practices (Labeling)....Staff Fed Trade
Com 202-326-3128
Mobile Services Licenses....Staff FCC 202-634-6400
Mobile Telephone Services....Staff FCC 202-653-5560
Mobile sources....Frank M. Black EPA 919-541-3039
Mobilization Planning....Staff FCC 202-632-7025
Moccasins....Burns, Gail USITC 202-252-1469
Model Airplanes....Staff FCC 717-337-1212
Model development....John F. Clarke EPA 919-541-3660
Modeling....Dave Walters EPA 405-332-2261
Modeling theory....Doug Endicott EPA 313-675-2245
Models....Langer, Eric USITC 202-252-1497
Models....Wong, A. Customs 212-466-5538
Models (Mathematical)....Staff DRS/BEIB 301-496-5771
Molasses....James, Antoinette USITC 202-252-1313
Molders' boxes, forms, and patterns....Greene, William USITC
202-252-1405
Moldings, wooden....Vacant USITC 202-252-1326
Molecular Biology....Staff NIGMS 301-496-7301
Molecular Calculations....Sheldon Green NASA 212-678-5562
Molecular Genetics....Staff NIGMS 301-496-7301
Molecular genetics....John L. Armstrong EPA 503-757-4760
Molecular spectroscopy....Leo V. Azarraga EPA 404-546-3453
Molecular spectroscopy....Timothy W. Collette EPA 404-546-3525
Molybdenum....Kollins, Susan USITC 202-252-1441
Molybdenum....Cammarota, David Commerce 202-377-0575
Molybdenum....Blossom, John Mines 202-634-1021
Molybdenum compounds....Greenblatt, Jack USITC 202-252-1353
Monaco....Deborah Graze Cnty State 202-647-2633
Monaco....Brian D. Curran Cnty AID 202-647-2633
Mongolia....Mark Wong Cnty State 202-647-9141
Mongolia....David Shear Cnty AID 202-647-1004
Mongolia....Lilliana Monk Cnty Commerce 202-377-3583
Mongolia/Minerals....John Wu Cnty Mines 202-634-1272
Mongolism (Down Syndrome)....Staff NICHD 301-496-5133
Monitoring....M. Richard Scalf EPA 405-332-2308
Monitoring Stations, Protection from Interference....Staff FCC
202-632-7593

National Crime Survey - General....Anita Timrots   Justice Stat
202-724-7774
National Crime Survey - General....Cathy Whitaker   Justice Stat
202-724-7755
National Crime Survey - General....Caroline Harlow   Justice Stat
202-724-7755
National Crime Survey - Redesign....Bruce Taylor   Justice Stat
202-724-7774
National Crime Survey - Redesign....Richard Dodge   Justice Stat
202-724-6100
National Crime Survey - Supplements....Charles Kindermann
Justice Stat 202-724-7774
National Environmental Policy Act....Staff   FCC 202-632-6990
National Estuary Program....A.D. Beck   EPA 401-782-3000
National Health Insurance - Heal. Sec. Act. Coun.....Staff HSAC
301-223-9685
National Health Service Corps....Staff   NHRS/BHCDA
301-443-2900
National High Blood Pressure Education Program....Staff   NHLBI
301-496-0554
National Space Science Data Center....Barry Jacobs   NASA
301-286-5661
National, Auto Output....McCully, Clint   Economic 202-523-0819
National, Business Cycles Indicators....Green, George   Economic
202-523-0701
National, Business Cycles Indicators....Beckman, Barry A.
Economic 202-523-0755
National, Capital Consumption Allowance....Gorman, John A.
Economic 202-523-0803
National, Capital Expend, Gross Priv Fixed Invest....Cartwright,
David W.   Economic 202-523-0791
National, Capital Expenditures, Equipment....Seskin, Eugene, P.
Economic 202-523-0874
National, Capital Expenditures, Plant....Seskin, Eugene P.
Economic 202-523-0874
National, Capital Stock....Musgrave, John C.   Economic
202-523-0837
National, Compos Indx-Bus Cyc Ind, Data....Young, Mary D.
Economic 202-523-0589
National, Compos Indx-Bus Cyc Indicator, Methodol....Beckman,
Barry A.   Economic 202-523-0755
National, Compos Indx-Bus Cyc Indicators, Methodol....Kajutti,
Brian   Economic 202-523-0800
National, Compos Indx-Bus Cycle Indicators, Analy....Beckman,
Barry A.   Economic 202-523-0755
National, Compos Indx-Bus Cycle Indicators, Analy....Kajutti, Brian
Economic 202-523-0800
National, Construction....Cartwright, David   Economic 202-523-0791
National, Corporate Profits....Petrick, Kenneth A.   Economic
202-523-0888
National, Depreciation....Gorman, John A.   Economic 202-523-0803
National, Econometric Models, Development....Hirsch, Albert A.
Economic 202-523-0729
National, Econometric Models, Forecasts....Grimm, Bruce T.
Economic 202-523-0584
National, Econometric Models, National....Green, George R.
Economic 202-523-0701
National, Econometric Models, Structure....Hirsch, Albert A.
Economic 202-523-0729
National, Employee Compensation....Cypert, Pauline M.   Economic
202-523-0832
National, Environmental Studies....Rutledge, Gary L.   Economic
202-523-0687
National, Equipment Expenditures....Seskin, Eugene P.   Economic
202-523-0874
National, Exports, Net....Bernstein, Leo M.   Economic
202-523-0824
National, Farm Output....Smith, George   Economic 202-523-0821
National, Fed Govt, Natl Defense Purchases of Svcs....Galbraith, Karl
D.   Economic 202-523-5027
National, Fed Govt,Natl Defense Purchases of Goods....Galbraith,
Karl D.   Economic 202-523-5027
National, Federal Government, Contributions....Anglin, Hermione A.
Economic 202-523-0885
National, Federal Government, Expenditures....Dobbs, David T.
Economic 202-523-0744
National, Federal Government, Grants-in-Aid....Tolson, Deloris T.
Economic 202-523-0896
National, Federal Government, Receipts....Dobbs, David T.
Economic 202-523-0744
National, Federal Government, Transfers....Anglin, Hermione A.
Economic 202-523-0885
National, Forecasts, National....Grimm, Bruce T.   Economic
202-523-0584
National, Gross National Product by Industry....Peterson, Milo O.
Economic 202-523-0808
National, Gross Natl Product, Current Estimates....Bernstein, Leo M.
Economic 202-523-0824

National, Gross Private Domestic Investment....Cartwright, David W.
Economic 202-523-0791
National, Input-Output....Young, Paula C.   Economic 202-523-0683
National, Input-Output, Annual Tables....Planting, Mark A.
Economic 202-523-0867
National, Input-Output, Computer Tapes....Morton, Arthur A.
Economic 202-523-0686
National, Input-Output, Goods....Young, Paula C.   Economic
202-523-0683
National, Input-Output, Services....Young, Paula C.   Economic
202-523-0683
National, Interest Income....Hook, Mary W.   Economic
202-523-0813
National, Interest Payments....Hook, Mary W.   Economic
202-523-0813
National, Inventories....Baldwin, Steve   Economic 202-572-0784
National, Local Government, Expenditures....Peters, Donald L.
Economic 202-523-0725
National, Local Government, Purchases of Goods....Levin, David J.
Economic 202-523-0725
National, Local Govt, Purchase of Services....Levin, David J.
Economic 202-523-0725
National, Local Govt, Receipts....Levin, David J.   Economic
202-523-0725
National, National Income....Hook, Mary   Economic 202-523-0813
National, National Income, Computer Tapes....Blue, Eunice V.
Economic 202-523-0804
National, National Income, Diskettes....Blue, Eunice V.   Economic
202-523-0804
National, Persl Consumption Expend, Other Goods....Key, Greg
Economic 202-523-0836
National, Persl Consumption Expenditures, Prices....McCully, Clint
Economic 202-523-0836
National, Personal Consumption Expenditures....McCully, Clint
Economic 202-523-0819
National, Personal Consumption Expenditures, Autos....Johnson,
Everette   Economic 202-523-0807
National, Personal Consumption Expenditures, Svcs....Mataloni,
Raymond   Economic 202-523-0829
National, Personal Income....Cypert, Pauline M.   Economic
202-523-0832
National, Personal Income, Disposable....Cypert, Pauline M.
Economic 202-523-0832
National, Pollution Abatement Capital Spending....Rutledge, Gary L.
Economic 202-523-0687
National, Producers' Durable Equipment....Crawford, Jeffrey W.
Economic 202-523-0782
National, Product Accounts, Computer Tapes....Blue, Eunice V.
Economic 202-523-0804
National, Product Accounts, Diskettes....Blue, Eunice V.   Economic
202-523-0804
National, Projections, National....Grimm, Bruce T.   Economic
202-523-0584
National, Projections, National Economy....Green, George R.
Economic 202-523-0701
National, Proprietors Income, Nonfarm....Den Herder, Susan P.
Economic 202-523-0811
National, Rental Income....Hook, Mary W.   Economic 202-523-0813
National, Residential Construction....Cartwright, David   Economic
202-523-0791
National, Saving....Gorman, John   Economic 202-523-0803
National, Seasonal Adjustment Methods....Somer, Morton
Economic 202-523-0505
National, State Government, Expenditures....Peters, Donald L.
Economic 202-523-0725
National, State Government, Purchases of Goods....Levin, David J.
Economic 202-523-0725
National, State Government, Receipts....Peters, Donald L.
Economic 202-523-0725
National, State Govt, Purchase of Services....Levin, David J.
Economic 202-523-0725
National, System of National Accounts, O.E.C.D.....Somer, Morton
Economic 202-523-0505
National, System of Natl Accts, United Nations....Somer, Morton
Economic 202-523-0505
National, Wealth Estimates....Gorman, John A.   Economic
202-523-0803
Natl, Fed Govt, Nondef Pur-Goods, Constant Dollar....Mangan,
Robert   Economic 202-523-5107
Natl, Fed Govt, Nondef Pur-Goods, Current Dollars....Dobbs, David
T.   Economic 202-523-0744
Natl, Fed Govt, Nondef Pur-Svcs, Constant Dollars....Mangan,
Robert   Economic 202-523-5017
Natl, Fed Govt, Nondef Pur-Svcs, Current Dollars....Dobbs, David T.
Economic 202-523-0744
Natl, Price Measures, Fixed-Weight Price Indx, Etc....Herman,
Shelby A.   Economic 202-523-0828
Natural Resource Policy, Economics....Grano, Anthony   Agri

202-786-1401
Natural Resource Policy, Economics....Alt, Klaus Agri
202-786-1401
Natural Resource Policy, World, Economics....Vocke, Gary Agri
202-786-1706
Natural gas....Land, Eric USITC 202-252-1349
Natural gas liquids (NGL)....Land, Eric USITC 202-252-1349
Natural pearls....Witherspoon, Ricardo USITC 202-252-1489
Natural rubber....Taylor, Ed USITC 202-252-1362
Nauru....Stanley R. Ifshin Cnty State 202-647-3546
Nauru....Caryl M. Courtney Cnty AID 202-647-3546
Nauru/Minerals....Travis Lyday Cnty Mines 202-634-1272
Navigation, Air or Water....Staff FCC 202-632-7175
Navigational instruments....Moller, Ruben USITC 202-252-1495
Navigational/Drafting Inst.....Losche, R. Customs 212-466-5670
Navy special fuel oil....Foreso, Cynthia USITC 202-252-1348
Nearsightedness....Staff NEI 301-496-5248
Necties....Shetty, Sundar USITC 202-252-1457
Negative Option Purchasing....Elaine Kolish Fed Trade Com
202-326-3042
Neighborhood Watch....Richard Titus Justice 202-724-7684
Neighborhood Watch....Lois Mock Justice 202-724-7684
Neighborhood Watch....Richard Rau Justice 202-724-2951
Nemaline Myopathy (Floppy Baby)....Staff NINCDS 301-496-5751
Neonatal Adaptation....Staff NICHD 301-496-5133
Neonatal Asphyxia....Staff NINCDS 301-496-5751
Neoplasms (Trophoblastic)....Staff NCI 301-496-5583
Nepal....Sean Gallagher Cnty Commerce 202-377-2954
Nepal....Catherine Bachy Peace Corps 202-254-3118
Nepal (Kathmandu)....Marcia S. Bernicat Cnty State
202-647-1450
Nepal (Kathmandu)....Scott Delisi Cnty AID 202-647-5466
Nepal (Kathmandu)....Carol Scherrer-Palma Cnty AID
202-647-3261
Nepal/Minerals....David Doan Cnty Mines 202-634-1272
Nepheline Syenite....Potter, Michael J. Mines 202-634-1180
Nephritis....Staff NIDDK 301-496-5583
Nephrocalcinosis....Staff NIAMS 301-496-8188
Nephrolithiasis....Staff NIDDK 301-496-3583
Nephrotic Syndrome....Staff NIDDK 301-496-3583
Nerve Damage....Staff NINCDS 301-496-5751
Netherlands....Boyce Fitzpatrick Cnty Commerce 202-377-5401
Netherlands (The Hague)....Elenore Raven-Hamilton Cnty State
202-647-6664
Netherlands (The Hague)....Yvette Wong Cnty State 202-647-6664
Netherlands (The Hague)....James G. Huff Cnty AID 202-647-6064
Netherlands (The Hague)....Richard A. Christenson Cnty AID
202-647-4484
Netherlands Antilles....Robert Dormitzer Cnty Commerce
202-377-2527
Netherlands Antilles (Curacao)....Avon Williams Cnty State
202-647-2621
Netherlands Antilles (Curacao)....Michael Kirby Cnty AID
202-647-7385
Netherlands Antilles/Minerals....Ivette Torres Cnty Mines
202-632-9352
Netherlands/Minerals....Donald Buck Cnty Mines 202-632-5052
Nettings: fish....Cook, Lee USITC 202-252-1471
Nettings: other....Enfield, Mary E USITC 202-252-1455
Neural Stimulation.....Staff NINCDS 301-496-5751
Neural Tube Defects....Staff NINCDS 301-496-5751
Neuralgia....Staff NINCDS 301-496-5751
Neuritis (Peripheral Neuropathy)....Staff NINCDS 301-496-5751
Neuro-Ophthalmology....Staff NEI 301-496-5248
Neuroaxonal Dystrophy....Staff NINCDS 301-496-5751
Neurobehavioral toxicology & teratology...J Michael Davis EPA
919-541-4162
Neuroblastoma....Staff NEI 301-496-5583
Neurofibromatosis (von Recklinghausen's)....Staff NINCDS
301-496-5751
Neurogenic Disability (Mouth and Pharynx)....Staff NIDR
301-496-4261
Neurologic Disease....Staff NINCDS 301-496-5751
Neuromuscular Disease....Staff NINCDS 301-496-5751
Neuromyopathies....Staff NINCDS 301-496-5751
Neuromyositis....Staff NINCDS 301-496-5751
Neuronal Ceroid Lupofuscinoses....Staff NINCDS 301-496-5751
Neuropathies....Staff NINCDS 301-496-5751
Neuropathology....David Weil EPA 919-541-4163
Neuropharmacology....Staff NINCDS 301-496-5751
Neurophysiological toxicology....William K. Boyes EPA
919-541-7538
Neurosciences....Mal Cohen NASA 415-694-6441
Neurosclerosis....Staff NINCDS 301-496-5751
Neurosyphilis....Staff NINCDS 301-496-5751
Neutral Buoyancy....B. Dickson NASA 205-544-1296
New Caledonia....Ann M. Cambara Cnty State 202-647-3546
New Caledonia and Vanatu....Robert A. Benziger Cnty AID

202-647-3546
New Caledonia/Minerals....Travis Lyday Cnty Mines 202-634-1272
New Guinea....Toni Borge Peace Corps 202-254-3231
New Housing Construction & Warran., Mktg Practices....Staff Fed
Trade Com 202-326-3128
New Zealand....Gary Bouch/Tony Costanzo Cnty Commerce
202-377-3647
New Zealand (Wellington)....Robert Hughes Cnty State
202-647-9691
New Zealand (Wellington).... Cnty AID 202-647-9690
New Zealand (Wellington)....Gary Bouch Cnty AID 202-647-9690
New Zealand/Minerals....Travis Lyday Cnty Mines 202-634-1272
Newborn....Staff NINCDS 301-496-5133
News Gathering and Publishing....Staff FCC 717-337-1212
Newspaper....Janis, William V. Commerce 202-377-2250
Newsprint....Stahmer, Carsten USITC 202-252-1321
Nicaragua....Ted Johnson Cnty Commerce 202-377-2527
Nicaragua (Managua)....Robert Witajewski Cnty State
202-647-2205
Nicaragua (Managua)....Norma Harms Cnty AID 202-647-2205
Nicaragua (Managua)....John Lovaas Cnty AID 202-647-6181
Nicaragua/Minerals....Ivette Torres Cnty Mines 202-632-9352
Nickel....Kollins, Susan USITC 202-252-1441
Nickel....Kirk, William Mines 202-634-1025
Nickel Products....Presbury, Graylin Commerce 202-377-0575
Nickel compounds....Greenblatt, Jack USITC 202-252-1353
Niemann-Pick Disease....Staff NINCDS 301-496-5751
Niemann-Pick Disease....Staff NEI 301-496-5248
Niger....Vacant Cnty Commerce 202-377-4564
Niger....Djodi Deutsch Peace Corps 202-254-8397
Niger (Niamey)....Frankie Calhoun Cnty State 202-647-2865
Niger (Niamey)....Stephen G. Brundage Cnty AID 202-647-3006
Niger (Niamey)....Helen Vaitaitis Cnty AID 202-647-8124
Niger/Minerals....Hendrik van Oss Cnty Mines 202-632-5065
Nigeria....Reginald Biddle Cnty Commerce 202-377-4388
Nigeria (Lagos)....Donald Hester Cnty State 202-647-3406
Nigeria (Lagos)....Marshall McCallie Cnty AID 202-647-3066
Nigeria (Lagos)....Rudolph Thomas Cnty AID 202-647-7985
Nigeria/Minerals....Bernadette Michalski Cnty Mines
202-632-5065
Night Blindness....Staff NEI 301-496-5248
Nimbus7/LIMS and SAM II Data Processing, Analysis....Edward
Sullivan NASA 804-865-4784
Nitric acid....Trainor, Cynthia USITC 202-252-1354
Nitrites....Michels, David USITC 202-252-1352
Nitrogen....Contrell, Raymond Mines 202-634-1687
Nitrogenous fertilizers....Trainor, Cynthia USITC
202-252-1354
Nitrosamines....Staff NCI 301-496-5583
Niue....Ann M. Cambara Cnty State 202-647-3546
Niue....Michael Feldstein Cnty AID 202-647-9137
Nobel Prize....Staff NIGMS 301-496-7301
Noise....Staff NINCDS 301-496-5751
Noise (Effects on Human Health)....Staff NIEHS 919-541-3345
Noise Problems....Staff OD/ORS 301-496-2960
Non Woven/Coated/Filled Fabric....Barth, G. Customs
212-466-5884
Non-Electrical Engines & Motor....Riedl, K. Customs
212-466-5493
Non-Hodgkins Malignant Lymphoma....Staff NCI 301-496-5583
Non-benzenoid resins....Taylor, Ed USITC 202-252-1362
Non-electric motors and engines....Hagey, Michael USITC
202-252-1392
Non-intrusive Measurements....Steward Ocheltree NASA
804-865-2791
Nondurable Goods....Bhagat, Nazir Commerce 202-377-0341
Nonenumerated products....Spalding, Josephine USITC
202-252-1498
Nonferrous Foundries....Sugg, William Commerce 202-377-0610
Nonferrous Metals....Reiley, Robert C. Commerce 202-377-0575
Noninfectious Chemical Agents (Eff. on Human Hea.)....Staff
NIEHS 919-541-3345
Nonlinear Acoustics, Elastic Behavior, Electron....John
Cantrell NASA 804-856-3036
Nonmetallic Materials Research....C. McIntosh NASA
205-544-2620
Nonmetallic minerals....Lukes, Jim USITC 202-252-1426
North Atlantic Assembly (NAA)....Edward Nolan Cnty State
202-647-3198
Norwalk Agent....Staff NIAID 301-496-5717
Norway....Richard Christenson Cnty AID 202-647-4484
Norway....James Devlin Cnty Commerce 202-377-4414
Norway (Oslo)....Kenneth Kolb Cnty State 202-647-5669
Norway (Oslo)....R. Ross Rodgers Cnty AID 202-647-1774
Norway/Minerals....Donald Buck Cnty Mines 202-632-5052
Nosebleed (Epistaxis)....Staff NHLBI 301-496-4236
Nuclear (Heart Pacemaker)....Staff NHLBI 301-496-4236
Nuclear Magnetic Resonance Spectrometers....Staff DRR
301-496-5545

Nuclear Medicine Department....Staff CC 301-496-6455
Nuclear Power Plants, Major Proj.....Dollison, Robert Commerce
  202-377-2733
Nuclear energy....Greenblatt, Jack USITC 202-252-1353
Numbering machines....Baker, Scott USITC 202-252-1386
Numerical Contrls. Fr. Mach. Tools....Mearman, John Commerce
  202-377-0315
Numerical analysis, mass transport phenomena....Fred K. Fong
  EPA 404-546-3330
Nurse Practitioners & Midwives, Health Care Staff....Staff Fed
  Trade Com 202-326-2756
Nurse Practitioners, Health Care Staff....Staff Fed Trade Com
  202-326-2756
Nursing Homes....Staff NIA 301-496-1752
Nursing Homes....Matthew Daynard Fed Trade Com 202-326-3291
Nursing Homes and Care....Staff HRSA/DPCS 301-443-2270
Nursing Interventions....Staff NCNR 301-496-0526
Nursing Systems....Staff NCNR 301-496-0526
Nutrient cycling....H.A. Walker EPA 401-782-3000
Nutrition....Staff NICHD 301-496-5133
Nutrition....Staff HRSA/DMCH 301-443-4026
Nutrition....Staff NIDDK 301-496-3583
Nutrition Coordinating Committee....Staff OD 301-496-9281
Nutrition and Aging....Staff NIA 301-496-1752
Nutritional Requirements Related to Devel. Phases....Staff NCNR
  301-496-0526
Nuts....Conte, R. Customs 212-466-5759
Nuts, Bolts, Washers....Reise, Richard Commerce 202-377-3489
Nuts, Economics....Huang, Ben Agri 202-786-1767
Nuts, Economics....Buxton, Boyd Agri 202-786-1767
Nuts, Edible....Janis, William V. Commerce 202-377-2250
Nuts, Statistics....Johnson, Doyle Agri 202-447-5412
Nuts, edible....Burket, Stephen USITC 202-252-1318
Nystagmus....Staff NEI 301-496-5248

O

OECD....James R. Tarrant Cnty AID 202-647-7575
ORganic analytical chemistry....Garmon Smith EPA 405-332-2316
OSHA Stats, Annl Surv Occl Injuries and Illnesses....Taylor,
  Katherine Labor 202-272-3470
OSHA Stats, Assistant Commissioner, Safety & Hlth....Eisenberg,
  William M. Labor 202-272-3467
OSHA Stats, Characteristics Injuries and Illnesses....Anderson,
  John Labor 202-272-3463
OSHA Stats, Chief, Safety & Health Statistics....Newell, Steve
  Labor 202-272-3473
OSHA Stats, Data Diskettes....Taylor, Katherine Labor
  202-272-3470
OSHA Stats, Data Tapes....Taylor, Katherine Labor 202-272-3470
OSHA Stats, Health Studies....Hilaski, Harvey Labor
  202-272-3459
OSHA Stats, Special Projects....Hilaski, Harvey Labor
  202-272-3459
OSHA Stats, Supp Data Sysm-Wkrs Comp Stats....Anderson, John
  Labor 202-272-3463
OSHA Stats, Work Injury Reports Surveys....Vacant Labor
  202-272-3459
OSHA, Industry Estimates....Taylor, Katherine Labor
  202-272-3470
OSHA, Industry Incidence Rates....Taylor, Katherine Labor
  202-272-3470
Oakum....Cook, Lee USITC 202-252-1471
Oats, Futures....Judy Sepsey Comm Futures 312-353-9025
Obesity....Staff NIDDK 301-496-3583
Obesity....Staff NCNR 301-496-0526
Obesity in Children....Staff NICHD 301-496-5133
Observational Science Branch....Dave Clem NASA 804-824-1515
Observational Systems....Kane Casani NASA 818-354-4040
Obstruction Markings--Antenna....Staff FCC 202-632-7521
Occupation Statistics....Priebe, John Census 301-763-8575
Occupation Statistics....Masumura, Wilfred Census 301-763-8575
Occupational Deregulation, Service Industry Prac.....Staff Fed
  Trade Com 202-326-3303
Occupational Diseases....Staff CDC/NIOSH 404-329-3534
Occupational Lung Disease....Staff NHLBI 301-496-4236
Ocean Data Systems....Charles Vermillion NASA 301-286-5111
Ocean disposal....D.J. Baumgartner EPA 401-782-3000
Ocean disposal....J.F. Paul EPA 401-782-3000
Ocean disposal....H.A. Walker EPA 401-782-3000
Oceans and Ice Branch....Nancy Maynar NASA 301-286-4718
Octane Disclosure Rule....Neil Blickman Fed Trade Com
  202-326-3038
Ocular Hypertension....Staff NEI 301-496-5248
Oculocraniosomatic Neuromuscular Disease....Staff NINCDS
  301-496-5751

Odor....Staff NINCDS 301-496-5751
Odoriferous or aromatic substances....Land, Eric USITC
  202-252-1349
Off-Track Betting....Staff FCC 202-632-7048
Off-the-Air Pickup....Staff FCC 202-634-1706
Offender Classification Prediction....Richard Laymon Justice
  202-724-7635
Offender-based Transaction Statistics....Donald Manson Justice
  Stat 202-724-7770
Offender-based Transaction Statistics....Patrick Langan
  Justice Stat 202-724-7774
Offenders....Phyllis Jo Baunach Justice Stat 202-724-7755
Offenders....Lawrence Greenfeld Justice Stat 202-724-7755
Offenders....Stephanie Minor-Harper Justice Stat 202-724-7755
Offenders....James Stephan Justice Stat 202-724-6100
Offenders....Allen Beck Justice Stat 202-724-7755
Offenders....Angela Lane Justice Stat 202-724-6100
Offenders - Federal....Carol Kaplan Justice Stat 202-724-7759
Offenders, Female....Phyllis Jo Baunach Justice Stat
  202-724-7755
Offenders, Female....Stephanie Minor-Harper Justice Stat
  202-724-7755
Offenders, Female - Federal....Carol Kaplan Justice Stat
  202-724-7759
Office copying machines....Baker, Scott USITC 202-252-1386
Office machines, not enumerated....Fletcher, William USITC
  202-252-1407
Office/Textile Machinery....Brodbeck, A. Customs 2120466-5490
Offshore Radio Telecommunications Service....Staff FCC
  202-653-5560
Oil....Perry, Douglas Commerce 202-377-1466
Oil Development & Refining, Maj. Proj.....Thomas, Janet
  Commerce 202-377-4146
Oil Field Machinery....McDonald, Edward Commerce
  202-377-0680
Oil Field Machinery, Trade Promo.....Cummings, Charles
  Commerce 202-377-5361
Oil Shale, Major Proj.....Thomas, Janet Commerce 202-377-4146
Oil, Crude, Futures....Anthony Criso Comm Futures 212-668-2080
Oil, lubricating....Foreso, Cynthia USITC 202-252-1348
Oilcloth....Cook, Lee USITC 202-252-1471
Oils....Maria, J. Customs 212-466-5730
Oils, essential....Land, Eric USITC 202-252-1349
Oilseeds....Reeder, John USITC 202-252-1319
Oilseeds, Economics....Hoskin, Roger Agri 202-786-1840
Oilseeds, Economics....Schaub, Jim Agri 202-786-1840
Oilseeds, Statistics....Hayes, Craig Agri 202-447-9526
Oilseeds, World, Economics....Bickerton, Tom Agri 202-786-1693
Older Women....Staff NIA 301-496-1752
Oleic acid....Randall, Rob USITC 202-252-1366
Oleic acid ester....Johnson, Larry USITC 202-252-1351
Oleyl alcohols....Randall, Rob USITC 202-252-1366
Olivopontocerebellar Atrophy....Staff NINCDS 301-496-5751
Oman....Claude Clement Cnty Commerce 202-377-5545
Oman (Muscat)....Haywood Rankin Cnty State 202-647-6558
Oman (Muscat)....William Pierce Cnty AID 202-647-1334
Oman (Muscat)....Peter Deinken Cnty AID 202-647-9000
Oman/Minerals....Bernadette Michalski Cnty Mines 202-632-5065
Onchocerciasis....Staff NEI 301-496-5248
Oncology....Staff NCI 301-496-5583
One-Way Paging and Signaling....Staff FCC 202-653-5560
Operating Revenues, International Telephone & Tele....Staff FCC
  202-632-7084
Operations & Maintenance....Chittum, J. Marc Commerce
  202-377-0345
Ophthalmia Neonatorum....Staff NEI 301-496-5248
Ophthalmic....Johnson, Christopher USITC 202-252-1488
Ophthalmic Congenital and Genetic Disease....Staff NEI
  301-496-5248
Ophthalmology Research....Staff NEI 301-496-5248
Opitical Equipment....Kiefer, B. Customs 212-466-5685
Oppenheim's Disease (Amyotonia Congenita)....Staff NINCDS
  301-496-5751
Optic Atrophy....Staff NEI 301-496-5248
Optic Neuritis....Staff NEI 301-496-5248
Optical Communication....James Lesh NASA 818-354-2766
Optical Disks....Joseph King NASA 301-286-7355
Optical Fabrication....Staff DRS/BEIB 301-496-5195
Optical Interferometry/Photography....John Hoppe NASA
  804-865-3234
Optical Sciences and Applications....James Breckinridge NASA
  818-354-6785
Optical Storage Data....Thomas Shull NASA 804-865-3917
Optical Systems....E. Reinbolt NASA 205-544-3462
Optical elements....Johnson, Christopher USITC 202-252-1488
Optical goods....Johnson, Christopher USITC 202-252-1488
Optical-Laser Spectroscopy....Reginald Exton NASA
  804-865-2791

Experts

Optics Laboratory...John Osantowski NASA 301-286-6706
Optometry Research...Staff NEI 301-496-5248
Oral Cancer....Staff NIDR 301-496-4261
Oral Contraceptives....Staff NICHD 301-496-5133
Oral Surgery-Intravenous Sedation....Staff NIDR 301-496-4261
Orange oil (essential oil)....Land, Eric USITC 202-252-1349
Orbital Debris....Donald Kessler NASA 713-483-5313
Ores....Fitzgerald, J. Customs 212-466-5492
Organ Donations (Eyes)....Staff NEI 301-496-5248
Organ Transplant (Donor Information)....Staff OD/OC
    301-496-5895
Organic ID...Timothy W. Collette EPA 404-546-3525
Organic ID...John M. McGuire EPA 404-546-3185
Organic acids....Michels, David USITC 202-252-1352
Organic analytical chemistry....Roger Cosby EPA 405-332-2320
Organic chemical analysis...Arthur W. Garrison EPA 404-546-3145
Organic chemicals....Mark Greenberg EPA 919-541-4156
Organic chemistry....Jimmie D. Petty EPA 702-798-2383
Organic methods....Robert Graves EPA 513-569-7315
Organic sorption process....Chad T. Jafvert EPA 404-546-3186
Organics analysis....Joe Bumgarner EPA 919-541-2430
Organics in tissue and water....Douglas W. Kuehl EPA
    218-720-5558
Organization for Economic Cooperation & Develop.....Daniel V.
    Grant Cnty State 202-647-1697
Organized Crime....Lois Mock Justice 202-724-7684
Organo-metallic compounds....Michels, David USITC 202-252-1352
Original Telephone & Telephone Plant Cost....Staff FCC
    202-632-3772
Ornamented fabrics....Enfield, Mary E USITC 202-252-1455
Orotic Aciduria....Staff NIAMS 301-496-8188
Orphan Drugs....Staff NINCDS 301-496-5751
Orthodontics....Staff NIDR 301-496-4261
Orthognathic Surgery....Staff NIDR 301-496-4261
Orthokeratology....Staff NEI 301-496-5248
Orthopedic Implants....Staff NIAMS 301-496-8188
Orthostatic Hypotension....Staff NHLBI 301-496-4236
Orthotics....Staff NIAMS 301-496-8188
Ossein....Jonnard, Aimison USITC 202-252-1350
Osteitis Deformans....Staff NIAMS 301-496-8188
Osteoarthritis....Staff NIAMS 301-496-8188
Osteoarthritis with Age....Staff NIA 301-496-1752
Osteogenesis....Staff NIAMS 301-496-8188
Osteogenesis Imperfecta....Staff NIAMS 301-496-8188
Osteogenic Sarcoma....Staff NCI 301-496-5583
Osteomalacia....Staff NIAMS 301-496-8188
Osteomyelitis....Staff NIAID 301-496-5717
Osteomyelitis....Staff NIAMS 301-496-8188
Osteoporosis....Staff NIAMS 301-496-8188
Osteoporosis with Age....Staff NIA 301-496-1752
Osteoporosis with Age....Staff NIAMS 301-496-8188
Osteosclerosis (Osteopetrosis)....Staff NIAMS 301-496-8188
Ostomy....Staff NIDDK 301-496-3583
Other Investments....Robert Friedman Fed Trade Com
    202-326-3297
Otitis Media....Staff NINCDS 301-496-5751
Otitis Media....Staff NIAID 301-496-5717
Otosclerosis....Staff NINCDS 301-496-5751
Outdoor channels....Steven F. Hedtke EPA 218-720-2492
Outlying Areas....Flaim, Lourdes Census 301-763-2903
Output, Economics....Conway, Roger Agri 202-786-1459
Output, World, Economics....Urban, Francis Agri 202-786-1624
Ovarian Cancer....Staff NCI 301-496-5583
Ovens....Mata, Ruben USITC 202-252-1403
Oviduct....Staff NICHD 301-496-5133
Ovulation....Staff NICHD 301-496-5133
Ovum....Staff NICHD 301-496-5133
Oxygenators (Artificial Lungs)....Staff NHLBI 301-496-4236
Ozone....Basil Dimitriades EPA 919-541-2706
Ozone....James Raub EPA 919-541-4157
Ozone non-attainment....Robert H. Hangebrauck EPA
    919-541-4134
Ozone non-attainment....William J. Rhodes EPA 919-541-2853

P

PKU (Phenylketonuria)....Staff NICHD 301-496-5133
Pacemaker (Cardiac/Heart)....Staff NHLBI 301-496-4236
Pacific Islands....Gary Bouck Cnty Commerce 202-377-3647
Pacific Islands (General)....Ann M. Cambara Cnty State
    202-647-3546
Pacific Islands (General)....Stanley R. Ifshin Cnty State
    202-647-3546
Pacific Islands (General)....Carly M. Courtney Cnty AID
    202-647-3546

Pacific Islands (General)....Michael Feldstein Cnty AID
    202-647-9137
Pacific/trade matters....Staff US Trade Rep 202-395-3900
Packaging Machinery....Axelrod, Irvin Commerce 202-377-0310
Packaging machines....Slingerland, David USITC 202-252-1400
Packing and Containers....Copperwhite, Kim Commerce
    202-377-0608
Paget's Disease of Bone (Osteitis Deformans)....Staff NIAMS
    301-496-8188
Paging--Common Carrier....Staff FCC 202-653-5560
Paging--One Way....Staff FCC 717-337-1212
Pain....Staff NCNR 301-496-0526
Pain....Staff NINCDS 301-496-5751
Pain (Cancer Related)....Staff NCI 301-496-5583
Pain (Oral-Facial)....Staff NIDR 301-496-4261
Pain and the Elderly....Staff NIA 301-496-1752
Paint....Brownchweig, G Customs 212-466-5744
Paint rollers....Linkins, Linda USITC 202-252-1499
Paint sets, artists....Johnson, Larry USITC 202-252-1351
Paints....Johnson, Larry USITC 202-252-1351
Paints/Coatings....Prat, Raimundo Commerce 202-377-0128
Pajamas: mens and boys....Shetty, Sundar USITC 202-252-1457
Pajamas: womens, girls, and infants....MacKnight, Peggy USITC
    202-252-1468
Pakistan....Stan Bilinski Cnty Commerce 202-377-2954
Pakistan....Catherine Bachy Peace Corps 202-254-3118
Pakistan (Islamabad)....Robert Boggs Cnty State 202-647-9823
Pakistan (Islamabad)....Mary Shoemaker Cnty AID 202-647-2441
Pakistan (Islamabad)....Robert Dakan Cnty AID 202-647-3517
Pakistan/Minerals....David Yen Cnty Mines 202-634-9799
Palau (Koror)....James D. Berg Cnty State 202-647-0108
Paleoclimate-Pollen Studies....Dorothy Peteet NASA
    212-678-5587
Palladium Futures....Rick Sanborn Comm Futures 212-668-2079
Palm oil....Reeder, John USITC 202-252-1319
Palmitic acid esters....Johnson, Larry USITC 202-252-1351
Palpitation....Staff NHLBI 301-496-4236
Palsy....Staff NINCDS 301-496-5751
Panama....Brigit Helms Cnty Commerce 202-377-2527
Panama (Panama City)....Peter Secor Cnty State 202-647-4986
Panama (Panama)....Sherman Hinson Cnty AID 202-647-4986
Panama (Panama)....Kenneth R. Audroue Cnty AID 202-647-4985
Panama (Panama)....Carl Dutto Cnty AID 202-647-5101
Panama/Minerals....Ivette Torres Cnty Mines 202-632-9352
Pancreatic Diseases....Staff NIDDK 301-496-3583
Panencephalitis....Staff NINCDS 301-496-5751
Panty hose....Bryant, Judith USITC 202-252-1464
Pap Smear....Staff NCI 301-496-5583
Papa....Toni Borge Peace Corps 202-254-3290
Paper....Rhodes, Richard USITC 202-252-1322
Paper....Butts, Donald Commerce 202-377-0375
Paper Board Mfg.....Butts, Donald W. Commerce 202-377-0382
Paper Industries Machinery...Abrahams, Edward Commerce
    202-377-0312
Paper Packaging and Board....Smith, Leonard S. Commerce
    202-377-0375
Paper Prod., Converted....Stanley, Gary Commerce 202-377-0375
Paper and Board, Basic Mfg....Butts, Donald W. Commerce
    202-377-0382
Paper machines....Slingerland, David USITC 202-252-1400
Paper, products of....Stahmer, Carsten USITC 202-252-1321
Paper/Paper Products....Abromowitz, C. Customs 212-466-5733
Paperboard....Rhodes, Richard USITC 202-252-1322
Paperboard machines....Slingerland, David USITC 202-252-1400
Paperboard, products of....Stahmer, Carsten USITC 202-252-1321
Papermakers' felts....Cook, Lee USITC 202-252-1471
Papermaking materials....Rhodes, Richard USITC 202-252-1322
Paperwork Reduction Act....Chris White Fed Trade Com
    202-326-2476
Papilloma Virus and Cancer....Staff NCI 301-496-5583
Papua New Guinea (Port Moresby)....Stanley R. Ifshin Cnty State
    202-647-3546
Papua New Guinea (Port Moresby)....Carly M. Courtney Cnty AID
    202-647-3546
Papua New Guinea (Port Moresby)....Michael Feldstein Cnty AID
    202-647-9137
Papua New Guinea/Minerals....Travis Lyday Cnty Mines
    202-634-1272
Paraguay....Mark Siegelman Cnty Commerce 202-377-1548
Paraguay (Asuncion)....Mike Shelton Cnty State 202-647-1551
Paraguay (Asuncion)....Stephanie Kinney Cnty AID 202-647-1551
Paraguay (Asuncion)....Maria Mamlouk Cnty AID 202-647-4365
Paraguay/Minerals....Alfredo Gurmendi Cnty Mines 202-632-9352
Paralysis Agitans....Staff NINCDS 301-496-5751
Paralysis, Periodic....Staff NINCDS 301-496-5751
Paramedical Training....Staff HRSA/BHPr 301-443-5794
Paramyotonia Congenita....Staff NINCDS 301-496-5751
Paraplegia....Staff NINCDS 301-496-5751

Parasitic Disease....Staff NIAID 301-496-5717
Parasitology....Staff NIAID 301-496-5717
Parasitology....Walter Jakubowski EPA 513-569-7385
Parathyroid Disorders....Staff NIDDK 301-496-3583
Parchutes....Andersen, Peder USITC 202-252-1388
Parkinson's Disease....Staff NINCDS 301-496-5751
Parkinsonism-Dementia....Staff NINCDS 301-496-5751
Parole and Parolees....Stephanie Minor-Harper Justice Stat
    202-724-7755
Parole and Parolees....Lawrence Greenfeld Justice Stat
    202-724-7755
Paroxysmal Atrial Tachycardia (PAT)....Staff NHLBI
    301-496-4236
Paroxysmal Nocturnal Hemoglobinuria....Staff NHLBI
    301-496-4236
Pars Planitis....Staff NEI 301-496-5248
Particle board....Vacant USITC 202-252-1326
Particles bioassays....Philip M. Cook EPA 218-720-5553
Particulate control....Wade H. Ponder EPA 919-541-2818
Party favors....Langer, Eric USITC 202-252-1491
Passenger autos, trucks, and buses....Kavalauskas, Juanita
    USITC 202-252-1402
Pasta....Janis, William V. Commerce 202-377-2250
Pathogen-Free Mice and Rats....Staff DRS/VRB 301-496-5255
Pathology....John A. Couch EPA 904-932-5311
Pathology....John Fournie EPA 904-932-5311
Patrol Resource Allocation....William Saulsbury Justice
    202-724-7685
Patrol Resource Allocation....George Shollenberger Justice
    202-724-2956
Patrol Resource Allocation...John Lucey Justice 202-272-6004
Paving Materials, Asphalt....Pitcher, Charles Commerce
    202-377-0132
Paving Materials, Concrete....Pitcher, Charles Commerce
    202-377-0132
Pay Cable Television....Staff FCC 202-632-7480
Payloads....M. Slayden NASA 205-544-2391
Peanuts....Burket, Stephen USITC 202-252-1318
Peanuts, Economics....Schaub, Jim Agri 202-786-1840
Peanuts, Statistics....Edwards, Radley Agri 202-447-5944
Peanuts, World, Economics....Surls, Fred Agri 202-786-1693
Pearl essence...Johnson, Larry USITC 202-252-1351
Pearls....Witherspoon, Ricardo USITC 202-252-1489
Peat....Contrell, Raymond Mines 202-634-1687
Peat moss....Trainor, Cynthia USITC 202-252-1354
Pectin...Jonnard, Aimison USITC 202-252-1350
Pectin...Janis, William V. Commerce 202-377-2250
Pectus Excavatum (Funnel Chest)....Staff NHLBI 301-496-4236
Pedodontics....Staff NIDR 301-496-4261
Pelizaeous-Merzbacher Disease....Staff NINCDS 301-496-5751
Pelvic Inflammatory Disease....Staff NIAID 301-496-5717
Pemphigis Vulgaris....Staff NIAMS 301-496-8188
Pemphigis Vulgaris....Staff NCI 301-496-5583
Pemphigoid....Staff NCI 301-496-5583
Pencil....Hantman, S. Customs 212-466-5678
Pencils....Linkins, Linda USITC 202-252-1499
Pencils/Pens, etc.....Harris, John Commerce 202-377-1178
Penicillin....Nesbitt, Elizabeth USITC 202-252-1355
Pens....Linkins, Linda USITC 202-252-1499
Pens....Hantman, S. Customs 212-466-5678
People/China....Jeffrey Lee Cnty Commerce 202-377-3583
Peptic Ulcers....Staff NIDDK 301-496-3583
Perchloroethylene....Michels, David USITC 202-252-1352
Performance audits....William J. Mitchell EPA 919-541-2769
Perfumery, cosmetics, and toilet preps....Land, Eric USITC
    202-252-1349
Periarteritis Nodosa....Staff NHLBI 301-496-4236
Periarteritis Nodosa....Staff NIAID 301-496-5717
Pericardial Tamponade....Staff NHLBI 301-496-4236
Pericarditis....Staff NHLBI 301-496-4236
Pericardium....Staff NHLBI 301-496-4236
Perinatal Biology....Staff NICHD 301-496-5133
Periodic Paralysis....Staff NINCDS 301-496-5751
Periodicals....Bratland, Rose Marie Commerce 202-377-0380
Periodontal Diseases....Staff NIDR 301-496-4261
Peripheral Nerve Tumor....Staff NINCDS 301-496-5751
Peripheral Neuropathy (Neuritis)....Staff NINCDS 301-496-5751
Peripheral Vascular Disease....Staff NHLBI 301-496-4236
Perlite....Meisinger, Arthur C. Mines 202-634-1185
Pernicious Anemia....Staff NIDDK 301-496-3583
Peroneal Muscular Atrophy....Staff NINCDS 301-496-5751
Personal leather goods....Seastrum, Carl USITC 202-252-1493
Personality....Staff NIMH 301-443-4515
Pertussis....Staff NIAID 301-496-5717
Peru....Ann Beard Cnty Commerce 202-377-2521
Peru (Lima)....Edward Vazquez Cnty State 202-647-3360
Peru (Lima)....Heather Hodges Cnty AID 202-647-3360
Peru (Lima)....Maria Mamlouk Cnty AID 202-647-4365

Peru/Minerals....Pablo Velasco Cnty Mines 202-632-5060
Pest Control Devices, Marketing Practices....Staff Fed Trade
    Com 202-326-3128
Pesticide and groundwater leachate modeling....Robert F. Carsel
    EPA 404-546-3476
Pesticide bioassays....Richard E. Siefert EPA 218-720-5552
Pesticide bioassays...Alfred W. Jarvinen EPA 218-720-5561
Pesticide dynamics....Charles N. Smith EPA 404-546-3175
Pesticides....Wanser, Stephen USITC 202-252-1363
Pesticides....Staff NIEHS 919-541-3345
Pesticides....Beverly Comfort EPA 919-541-4165
Pesticides, Economics....Delvo, Herman Agri 202-786-1456
Pet Food...Janis, William V. Commerce 202-377-2250
Pet Toys....Persky, H. Customs 212-466-5881
Pet animals (live)....Ludwick, David USITC 202-252-1329
Petrochem, Cyclic Crudes....Cosslett, Pat Commerce
    202-377-0128
Petrochemicals....Kamenicky, Vincent Commerce 202-377-0128
Petrochemicals Plants, Major Proj.....Haraguchi, Wally Commerce
    202-377-4877
Petroleum....Foreso, Cynthia USITC 202-252-1348
Petroleum....Ronald Rowe Fed Trade Com 202-326-2610
Petroleum....Winters, W. Customs 212-466-5747
Petroleum Offshore Drilling....Staff FCC 717-337-1212
Petroleum, Crude and Refined Products....Perry, Douglas
    Commerce 202-377-1466
Peyronie's Disease....Staff NIDDK 301-496-3583
Phacoemulsification....Staff NEI 301-496-5248
Pharmaceuticals....McIntyre, Leo Commerce 202-377-0128
Pharmacodynamics....James McKim EPA 218-720-5567
Pharmacokinetics....Bruce Peirano EPA 513-569-7540
Pharmacokinetics Research....Nitza Cintron NASA 713-483-7165
Pharmacokinetics of biological systems....Luis A. Suarez EPA
    404-546-2301
Pharmacology Information System (PROPHET)....Staff DRR
    301-496-5411
Pharmacology Research Associate Training Program....Staff
    NIGMS 301-496-7301
Pharmacology/Toxicology....Staff NIGMS 301-496-7301
Pharmacology/Toxicology....Staff NIEHS 919-541-3345
Pharyngeal Disabilities....Staff NIDR 301-496-4261
Pharynx....Staff NIDR 301-496-4261
Phenol....Matusik, Ed USITC 202-252-1356
Phenolic resins....Taylor, Ed USITC 202-252-1362
Phenylketonuria (PKU)....Staff NICHD 301-496-5133
Pheochromocytema....Staff NHLBI 301-496-4236
Philippines....George Paine Cnty Commerce 202-377-3875
Philippines (Manila)....Raymond Richart Cnty State
    202-647-1221
Philippines (Manila)...James Zumwaldt Cnty State 202-647-1222
Philippines (Manila)....John H. Andre, II Cnty State
    202-647-1222
Philippines (Manila)....Geraldeen Chester Cnty State
    202-647-1222
Philippines (Manila)....John Finney Cnty AID 202-647-9270
Philippines (Manila)....Ravik Huso Cnty AID 202-647-1669
Philippines (Manila)....Verne R. Dickey Cnty AID 202-647-1669
Philippines (Manila)....Kevin Kearns Cnty AID 202-647-1221
Philippines (Manila)....Michael Morfit Cnty AID 202-647-9139
Philippines (Manila)....Akim Martinez-Reboyras Cnty AID
    202-647-9139
Philippines/Minerals....Travis Lyday Cnty Mines 202-634-1272
Phlebitis....Staff NHLBI 301-496-4236
Phlebothrombosis....Staff NHLBI 301-496-4236
Phobias....Staff NIMH 301-496-4513
Phonograph records....Bishop, Kathryn USITC 202-252-1494
Phonographic equipment....Kitzmiller, John USITC 202-252-1387
Phonographs....Kitzmiller, John USITC 202-252-1387
Phosphate Rock....Stowasser, William F. Mines 202-634-1189
Phosphatic fertilizers....Trainor, Cynthia USITC 202-252-1354
Phosphoric acid....Trainor, Cynthia USITC 202-252-1354
Phosphoric acid esters....Johnson, Larry USITC 202-252-1351
Phosphorus....Trainor, Cynthia USITC 202-252-1354
Phosphorus compounds....Greenblatt, Jack USITC 202-252-1353
Photochemistry....Basil Dimitriades EPA 919-541-2706
Photocoagulation....Staff NEI 301-496-5248
Photocopy Services....Staff NIH Library/DRS 301-496-2983
Photographic Equipment....Watson, Joyce Commerce 202-377-0574
Photographic film: scrap....Bishop, Kathryn USITC
    202-252-1494
Photographic film: waste....Bishop, Kathryn USITC
    202-252-1494
Photographic gelatin....Jonnard, Aimison USITC 202-252-1350
Photographic supplies....Bishop, Kathryn USITC 202-252-1494
Photographs....Stahmer, Carsten USITC 202-252-1321
Photographs (Historical)....Staff NLM 301-496-5961
Photography....Staff DRS/MAPB 301-496-5995
Photography (Outside Contract)....Staff DRS/MAPB 301-496-4960

Experts

Photovoltaic Space Systems....Dennis Flood NASA 216-433-2303
Phthalic acid esters....Johnson, Larry USITC 202-252-1351
Phthalic anhydride....Matusik, Ed USITC 202-252-1356
Physical Environment. Agents....Staff
    NIEHS 919-541-3345
Physical Therapist....Staff HRSA/BHPr 301-443-5794
Physical analytical chemistry....Stephen Billets EPA 702-798-2232
Physical organic chemistry....Ronald K. Mitchum EPA
    702-798-2103
Physician's Assistant....Staff HRSA/BHPr 301-443-5794
Physicians Radio--Private....Staff FCC 717-337-1212
Physiological response....S. Baksi EPA 401-782-3000
Physiological responses....A.R. Malcolm EPA 401-782-3000
Physiology....Staff NIGMS 301-496-7301
Physiology....Leroy Folmar EPA 904-932-5311
Physiology....Charles L. McKenney EPA 904-932-5311
Physiology & health assessment....Lynn Papa EPA 513-569-7587
Pi-Mesons (Cancer Treatment)....Staff NCI 301-496-5583
Pi-Mesons (Cancer Treatment)....Staff NCI 301-496-5583
Pick's Disease....Staff NINCDS 301-496-5751
Pig iron....Boszormenyi, Laszio USITC 202-252-1437
Pigments....Brownchweig, G. Customs 212-466-5744
Pigments, inorganic...Johnson, Larry USITC 202-252-1351
Pigments, organic....Wanser, Stephen USITC 202-252-1363
Pile Fabrics....Edert, R. Customs 212-466-5885
Pillow blocks....Fravel, Dennis USITC 202-252-1404
Pillowcases....Borsari, Marilyn USITC 202-252-1465
Pillows....Linkins, Linda USITC 202-252-1499
Pilot Workload/Performance Research....Randall Harris NASA
    804-865-3917
Piloted Simulation....Billy Ashworth NASA 804-865-3874
PinWorms....Staff NIAID 301-496-5717
Pinball machines....Robinson, Hazel USITC 202-252-1496
Pinene....Michels, David USITC 202-252-1352
Pink Eye....Staff NEI 301-496-5248
Pins....Robinson, Hazel USITC 202-252-1496
Pipe, of rubber or plastics....Truskett, Brooks USITC
    202-252-1364
Pipes, tobacco...Johnson, Christopher USITC 202-252-1366
Pitch from wood....Randall, Rob USITC 202-252-1366
Pituitary Tumors....Staff NINCDS 301-496-5751
Pituitary Tumors....Staff NIDDK 301-496-3583
Pityriasis Rosea....Staff NIAMS 301-496-8188
Pityriasis Rubra Pilaris....Staff NCI 301-496-5583
Pityriasis Rubra Pilaris....Staff NIAMS 301-496-8188
Place of Birth....Hansen, Kristin Census 301-763-3850
Placenta....Staff NICHD 301-496-5133
Planetary Atmospheres....Michael Mumma NASA 301-286-6994
Planetary Atmospheres....larry Brace NASA 301-286-8575
Planetary Atmospheres and Interplanetary Media....Richard Woo
    NASA 818-354-3945
Planetary Biology....Sherwood Chang NASA 415-694-5733
Planetary Dynamics....Robert Preston NASA 818-354-6895
Planetary Materials Analysis....William Phinney NASA
    713-483-4464
Planetary Radar Astronomy....R. Jurgens NASA 818-354-4974
Planetary and Earth Atmosphere Sciences....Phil Russell NASA
    415-694-5404
Plant ecology....Lawrence Kaputska EPA 503-757-4606
Plant ecology....Paul T. Rygiewicz EPA 503-757-4833
Plant pathology....Raymond G. Wilhour EPA 904-932-5311
Plant physiology....J. Craig McFarlane EPA 503-757-4670
Plants....Conte, R. Customs 212-466-5759
Plants, live....Burket, Stephen USITC 202-252-1318
Plaque (Dental)....Staff NIDR 301-496-4261
Plasma Cell Cancer....Staff NCI 301-496-5583
Plaster products (except wallboard)....White, Linda USITC
    202-252-1427
Plastic & Rubber Articles....Mazzola, J. Customs 212-466-5580
Plastic Construction Products, Most....Williams, Franklin
    Commerce 202-377-0132
Plastic Household....Rauch, T. Customs 212-466-5892
Plastic Materials....Shea, Moira Commerce 202-377-0128
Plastic Products....Prat, Raimundo Commerce 202-377-0128
Plastic Products Machinery....Shaw, Eugene Commerce
    202-377-3494
Plastic wood...Johnson, Larry USITC 202-252-1351
Plastic/Fur Wearing Apparel....Persky, H. Customs 212-466-5881
Plasticizers...Johnson, Larry USITC 202-252-1351
Plastics....Taylor, Ed USITC 202-252-1362
Plastics products....Truskett, Brooks USITC 202-252-1364
Platelet Requests....Staff NHLBI 301-496-4236
Platelet Requests....Staff NCI 301-496-5583
Platelet Requests....Staff CC 301-496-3608
Plateletpheresis Center....Staff CC 301-496-4321
Platinum Futures....Rick Sanborn Comm Futures 212-668-2079
Platinum Group Metals....Loebenstein, J. Roger Mines
    202-634-1058

Platinum compounds....Greenblatt, Jack USITC 202-252-1353
Platinum group metals....Kollins, Susan USITC 202-252-1441
Pleasure boats....Lahey, Kathleen USITC 202-252-1409
Pleurisy....Staff NHLBI 301-496-4236
Plumbing Fittings....Pitcher, Charles Commerce 202-377-0132
Plumbing Fixtures and Fittings....Pitcher, Charles Commerce
    202-377-0132
Plutonium....Greenblatt, Jack USITC 202-252-1353
Plywood....Vacant USITC 202-252-1326
Plywood/Panel Products....Auerbach, Mitchel Commerce
    202-377-0375
Pneumatic Tubes....Staff OD/ORS 301-496-5518
Pneumococcal Infections....Staff NIAID 301-496-5717
Pneumoconioses (Dust Inhalation Disease)....Staff NHLBI
    301-496-4236
Pneumocystis Carinii....Staff NIAID 301-496-5717
Pneumothorax....Staff NHLBI 301-496-4236
Point of Sales Practices, Marketing Practices....Staff Fed
    Trade Com 202-326-3128
Point-to-Point Microwave Common Carrier....Staff FCC
    202-634-1706
Pointing Control Systems....H. Waites NASA 205-544-1441
Poison Control Ctrs.....Staff DC 202-835-4080
Poison Control Ctrs.....Staff MD 301-530-3880
Poison Control Ctrs.....Staff VA 703-379-3700
Poison Ivy....Staff NIAID 301-496-5717
Poison Prevention....Marilyn Wind Con Product Safe
    202-492-6477
Poland....Kate Scanlon Cnty Commerce 202-377-2645
Poland....Charles Howell Peace Corps 202-254-3040
Poland (Warsaw)....Daniel Fried Cnty State 202-647-1070
Poland (Warsaw)....Laurie Tracy Cnty State 202-647-3052
Poland (Warsaw)....Patrick Folan Cnty AID 202-647-6126
Poland (Warsaw)....Barbara Giffiths Cnty AID 202-647-3191
Poland (Warsaw)....Christine Adamczyk Cnty AID 202-647-9114
Poland/Minerals....Walter Stebiez Cnty Mines 202-632-5047
Pole Attachments....Staff FCC 202-632-890
Police....Louis A. Mayo Justice 202-272-6004
Police....George Shollenberger Justice 202-724-2956
Police....William Saulsbury Justice 202-724-7685
Police....Lawrence Bennett Justice 202-724-2956
Police....John Lucey Justice 202-272-6004
Police....John Spevacek Justice 202-272-6010
Police Chief Role....Louis A. Mayo Justice 202-272-6004
Police Management and Administration....Louis A. Mayo Justice
    202-272-6004
Police Management and Administration....William Saulsbury
    Justice 202-724-7685
Police Management and Administration....Lawrence Bennett
    Justice 202-724-2956
Police Management and Administration....Martin Lively Justice
    202-724-2966
Police Statistics....Paul White Justice Stat 202-724-7770
Police Statistics....Donald Manson Justice Stat 202-724-7770
Police Training....John Lucey Justice 202-272-6004
Polioencephalitis....Staff NINCDS 301-496-5751
Poliomyelitis....Staff NIAID 301-496-5717
Polishes under 10 lbs each....Randall, Rob USITC 202-252-1366
Political Broadcasting....Staff FCC 202-632-7586
Political Broadcasts on Television....Staff FCC 202-632-7586
Pollution (Air, Waste, Water)....Staff OD/ORS 301-496-3537
Pollution (Air, Waste, Water)....Staff EPA 301-382-5508
Pollution Control Equipment....Jonkers, Loretta Commerce
    202-377-0564
Pollution ecology....Andrew J. McErlean EPA 904-932-5311
Polyarteritis....Staff NHLBI 301-496-4236
Polycarbonate resins....Taylor, Ed USITC 202-252-1362
Polycystic Kidney Disease....Staff NIDDK 301-496-3583
Polycythemia (Secondary)....Staff NHLBI 301-496-4236
Polycythemia (Vera)....Staff NCI 301-496-5583
Polyester resins....Taylor, Ed USITC 202-252-1362
Polyethylene....Taylor, Ed USITC 202-252-1362
Polyethylene terephthalate (PET) resins....Taylor, Ed USITC
    202-252-1362
Polyhydric alcohol....Michels, David USITC 202-252-1352
Polyhydric alcohols of polysaccharides and rare....Randall, Rob
    USITC 202-252-1366
Polyhydric alcohols, fatty acids of, animal/veg....Land, Eric
    USITC 202-252-1349
Polyisoprene rubber....Taylor, Ed USITC 202-252-1362
Polymers....Taylor, Ed USITC 202-252-1362
Polymers and Polymer-Matrix Compsoites....Raymond Vannucci
    NASA 216-433-3202
Polymyalgia Rheumatica....Staff NIAMS 301-496-8188
Polymyositis....Staff NIAMS 301-496-8188
Polymyositis....Staff NINCDS 301-496-5751
Polyneuritis (Guillain-Barre Syndrome)....Staff NIAMS
    301-496-8188

Labor 202-272-5113

Prices/Living Conds, PPI, Data Diskettes....Rosenberg, Elliott Labor 202-272-5118

Prices/Living Conds, PPI, Electric Machinery....Sinclair, James Labor 202-272-5052

Prices/Living Conds, PPI, Energy....Lavish, Kenneth Labor 202-272-5210

Prices/Living Conds, PPI, Forestry....Wallenstein, David Labor 202-272-5127

Prices/Living Conds, PPI, Leather....Wallenstein, David Labor 202-272-5127

Prices/Living Conds, PPI, Metals....Kazanowski, Edward Labor 202-272-5204

Prices/Living Conds, PPI, Methodology....Rosenberg, Elliott Labor 202-272-5118

Prices/Living Conds, PPI, Recorded Detail....24-Hour Hotline Labor 202-523-1765

Prices/Living Conds, PPI, Revision....Tibbetts, Thomas Labor 202-272-5110

Prices/Living Conds, PPI, Textiles....Wallenstein, David Labor 202-272-5127

Prices/Living Conds, PPI, Transportation Equipment....Sinclair, James Labor 202-272-5052

Prices/Living Conds, Price Research Studies....Zieschang, Kimberly Labor 202-272-5096

Prices/Living Conds, Producer Price Indexes....Tibbetts, Thomas Labor 202-272-5110

Prices/Living Conds, Retail Prices, Fuels, Mthly....Ginsburg, Daniel Labor 202-272-5177

Prices/Living Conds, Retail Prices, Gasoline....Rice, Betty Labor 202-272-5080

Prices/Living Conds, Retail Prices, Utils, Mthly....Ginsburg, Daniel Labor 202-272-5177

Prices/Living Conds, Svc Industry Price Indexes....Weeden, George Labor 202-272-5130

Prices/Living Conds, Transportation Price Indexes....Royce, John Labor 202-272-5131

Pricing Guides (Deceptive), Marketing Practices....Staff Fed Trade Com 202-326-3128

Primary Commodities....Siesseger, Fred Commerce 202-377-5124

Primary Lateral Sclerosis....Staff NINCDS 301-496-5751

Primate Research....Staff DRR 301-496-5545

Primate Research Centers Program....Staff DRR 301-496-5175

Primates....Staff OD/DAS 301-496-9330

Printed Matter....Abromowitz, C. Customs 212-466-5733

Printed matter....Stahmer, Carsten USITC 202-252-1321

Printing....Lofquist, William Commerce 202-377-0379

Printing Trades Machines/Equipment....Kemper, Alexis Commerce 202-377-5956

Printing ink....Johnson, Larry USITC 202-252-1351

Printing machines....Slingerland, David USITC 202-252-1400

Printing machines (textiles)....Greene, William USITC 202-252-1405

Prison Industries....Thomas F. Albrecht Justice 202-272-6040

Prison Industries....Virginia Baldau Justice 202-272-6010

Prisoner Surveys, National Prisoner Statistics....McGinn, Larry Census 301-763-1735

Prisons, Prisoners, and Crowding....Allan Beck Justice Stat 202-724-7755

Prisons, Prisoners, and Crowding....Christopher Innes Justice Stat 202-724-6100

Prisons, Prisoners, and Crowding....Phyllis Jo Baunach Justice Stat 202-724-7755

Prisons, Prisoners, and Crowding....Lawrence Greenfeld Justice Stat 202-724-7755

Prisons, Prisoners, and Crowding....Tom Hester Justice Stat 202-724-7755

Prisons, Prisoners, and Crowding....Stephanie Minor-Harper Justice Stat 202-724-7755

Prisons, Prisoners, and Crowding....James Stephan Justice Stat 202-724-6100

Prisons, Prisoners, and Crowding....Angela Lane Justice Stat 202-724-6100

Prisons/Jails....Anne Schmidt Justice 202-724-2959

Prisons/Jails....Voncile Gowdy Justice 202-724-2951

Prisons/Jails....Jay Merrill Justice 202-724-2959

Privacy Act, Cigarettes....Julia Oas Fed Trade Com 202-326-2483

Privacy and Security of Data....Carol Kaplan Justice Stat 202-724-7759

Private Carriers Communications....Staff FCC 717-337-1212

Private Operational Fixed Services....Staff FCC 717-337-1212

Private Security....George Shollenberger Justice 202-724-2956

Private Security....Marianne Zawitz Justice Stat 202-724-6100

Private Wire Systems--Telephone & Telegraph....Staff FCC 202-634-1800

Privatization....Virginia Baldau Justice 202-272-6010

Privatization....John Thomas Justice 202-272-6004

Privatization....Voncile Gowdy Justice 202-724-2951

Privatization of Corrections....Sue Lindgren Justice Stat 202-724-7759

Probabilistic Structural Mechanics....Christos Chamis NASA 216-433-3252

Probation and Probationers....Stephanie Minor-Harper Justice Stat 202-724-7755

Probation and Probationers....Lawrence Greenfeld Justice Stat 202-724-7755

Probation/Parole....Voncile Gowdy Justice 202-724-2951

Probation/Parole....Anne Schmidt Justice 202-724-2959

Procaine....Staff NIA 301-496-1752

Procelain Electrical Supplies, Part....Whitley, Richard A. Commerce 202-377-0682

Process Control Instruments....Donnelly, Margaret T. Commerce 202-377-5466

Process Control Instruments, Trade Promo.....Gwaltney, G. P. Commerce 202-377-3090

Processing & Special Equipment....Fletcher, William Commerce 202-377-0309

Processing Engineering Research....M.H. Sharpe NASA 205-544-2714

Processing and Joining Methods for Lighter Weight....Barry Lisagor NASA 804-865-2036

Product Reliability, Marketing Practices....Staff Fed Trade Com 202-326-3128

Product Safety Assessment....Frank Brauer Con Product Safe 202-492-6554

Product Standards & Certification....Dean Graybill Fed Trade Com 202-326-3284

Productivity, Economics....Conway, Roger Agri 202-786-1459

Productivity, World, Economics....Urban, Francis Agri 202-786-1624

Productivity/Technology, Associate Commissioner....Mark, Jerome A. Labor 202-523-9294

Products Data....Tinari, Robert Census 301-763-1924

Prodvty/Techlgy, Compensation, Foreign Countries....Capdevielle, Patricia Labor 202-523-9292

Prodvty/Techlgy, Data Diskettes....Fulco, Lawrence J. Labor 202-523-9261

Prodvty/Techlgy, Data Tapes....Harper, Michael Labor 202-523-9261

Prodvty/Techlgy, Earnings, Foreign Countries....Capdevielle, Patricia Labor 202-523-9292

Prodvty/Techlgy, Foreign Countries, Labor Costs....Neef, Arthur Labor 202-523-9291

Prodvty/Techlgy, Foreign Countries, Labor Force....Sorrentino, Constance Labor 202-523-9304

Prodvty/Techlgy, Foreign Countries, Other Econ Ind....Neef, Arthur Labor 202-523-9291

Prodvty/Techlgy, Foreign Countries, Prodvty....Neef, Arthur Labor 202-523-9291

Prodvty/Techlgy, Foreign Countries, Unemployment....Sorrentino, Constance Labor 202-523-9304

Prodvty/Techlgy, Prices, Foreign Countries....Capdevielle, Patricia Labor 202-523-9292

Prodvty/Techlgy, Productivity Research....Dean, Edwin Labor 202-523-6010

Prodvty/Techlgy, Productivity in Government....Fisk, Donald W. Labor 202-523-9156

Prodvty/Techlgy, Prodvty Trends Federal Govt....Ardolini, Charles W. Labor 202-523-9244

Prodvty/Techlgy, Prodvty Trends Selected Industry....Ardolini, Charles W. Labor 202-523-9244

Prodvty/Techlgy, Prodvty and Costs-News Release....Fulco, Lawrence J. Labor 202-523-9261

Prodvty/Technlgy, Technological Trends, Major Ind....Ardolini, Charles W. Labor 202-523-9244

Prodvy/Techlgy, Cost-of-Living Abroad....Capdevielle, Patricia Labor 202-523-9292

Professional Health Services....Richard Kelly Fed Trade Com 202-326-3304

Progeria....Staff NIA 301-496-1752

Progestins and Progesterone....Staff NICHD 301-496-5133

Progestins and Progesterone....Staff HRSA/DMCH 301-443-4026

Progressive Cerebral Degeneration....Staff NINCDS 301-496-5751

Progressive Dementia in Children....Staff NINCDS 301-496-5751

Progressive Infantile spinal Muscular Atrophy....Staff NINCDS 301-496-5751

Progressive Infantile spinal Muscular Atrophy....Staff NINCDS 301-496-5751

Progressive Leukodystrophy....Staff NINCDS 301-496-5751

Progressive Multifocal Leukoencephalopathy....Staff NINCDS 301-496-5751

Progressive Muscular Atrophy....Staff NINCDS 301-496-5751

Progressive Supranuclear Palsy....Staff NINCDS 301-496-5751

Progressive Systemic Sclerosis....Staff NINCDS 301-496-5751

Progressive Systemic Sclerosis....Staff NIAMS 301-496-8188

Projectors (photographic)....Bishop, Kathryn USITC
   202-252-1494
Propagation--Radio Waves....Staff FCC 202-632-7025
Propane....Land, Eric USITC 202-252-1349
Propane Futures....Staff Comm Futures 212-668-2080
Propeller Aerodynamics and Acoustics...John Groeneweg NASA
   216-433-3945
Property Records--Common Carrier....Staff FCC 202-634-1861
Propulsion....Ralph Taeuber NASA 713-483-9002
Propulsion Integration....William Henderson NASA 804-865-2676
Propulsion/Performance....Larry Myers NASA 805-258-3708
Propylene....Raftery, Jim USITC 202-252-1365
Propylene glycol....Michels, David USITC 202-252-1352
Propylene oxide....Michels, David USITC 202-252-1352
Prosecution....Bernard Auchter Justice 202-724-7684
Prosecution...Jay Merrill Justice 202-724-2959
Prosecution....Martin Lively Justice 202-724-2965
Prosecution....Carla Gaskins Justice Stat 202-724-7774
Prosecution....Patrick Langan Justice Stat 202-647-7774
Prospective Payment Systems....Staff NCNR 301-496-0526
Prostaglandins....Staff NICHD 301-496-5133
Prostaglandins....Staff NHLBI 301-496-4236
Prostate/Hyperplasis of the Prostate....Staff NIA 301-496-1752
Prostate/Hyperplasis of the Prostate....Staff NIDDK
   301-496-3583
Prostheses (Heart and Blood Vessel)....Staff NHLBI
   301-496-4236
Prostheses (Orthotics)....Staff NIAMS 301-496-8188
Prosthodontics....Staff NIDR 301-496-4261
Protein Abnormalities with Neurologic Disease....Staff NINCDS
   301-496-5751
Protein Engineering....Staff DCRT 301-496-1100
Protein Supplements....Harrison Shepard Fed Trade Com
   415-995-5220
Prurigo Nodularis....Staff NIAMS 301-496-8188
Pseudogout....Staff NIAMS 301-496-8188
Pseudosenility....Staff NIA 301-496-1752
Pseudotumor Cerebri....Staff NEI 301-496-5248
Pseudotumor Cerebri....Staff NINCDS 301-496-5751
Pseudoxanthoma Elasticum....Staff NHLBI 301-496-4236
Psittacosis....Staff NIAID 301-496-5717
Psoriasis....Staff NIAMS 301-496-8188
Psoriatic Arthritis....Staff NIAMS 301-496-8188
Psychopharmacology....Staff NIMH 301-443-4515
Psychotherapeutic agents....Nesbitt, Elizabeth USITC
   202-252-1355
Psychotic Episodes....Staff NIMH 301-443-4515
Pterygium....Staff NEI 301-496-5248
Ptosis....Staff NEI 301-496-5248
Public Accounting Professionals, Licen. Occupation....Staff
   Fed Trade Com 202-326-2920
Public Cellular Radio....Staff FCC 202-632-6400
Public Defense....Carla Gaskins Justice Stat 202-724-7774
Public Land Mobile Radio Service....Staff FCC 202-653-5560
Public Microwave....Staff FCC 202-634-1706
Public Opinion About Crime....Sue Lindgren Justice Stat
   202-724-7759
Public Opinion About Crime....Marianne Zawitz Justice Stat
   202-724-6100
Public Rural Radio....Staff FCC 202-653-5560
Publishing....Lofquist, William Commerce 202-377-0379
Pulleys....Fravel, Dennis USITC 202-252-1404
Pulmonary Alveolar Proteinosis....Staff NHLBI 301-496-4236
Pulmonary Angiomyomatosis....Staff NHLBI 301-496-4236
Pulmonary Diseases (Infectious/Allergenic)....Staff NIAID
   301-496-5717
Pulmonary Diseases (Non-Inf., Non-All., Non-Tum.)....Staff
   NHLBI 301-496-4236
Pulmonary Diseases (Tumorous/Cancerous)....Staff NCI
   301-496-5583
Pulmonary Edema....Staff NHLBI 301-496-4236
Pulmonary Embolism....Staff NHLBI 301-496-4236
Pulmonary Emphysema....Staff NHLBI 301-496-4236
Pulmonary Fibrosis....Staff NHLBI 301-496-4236
Pulmonary toxicology....Daniel L. Costa EPA 919-541-2531
Pulp Mills, Major Proj.....White, Barbara Commerce
   202-377-4160
Pulp machines....Slingerland, David USITC 202-252-1400
Pulp, articles of....Rhodes, Richard USITC 202-252-1322
Pulpmills....Stanley, Gary Commerce 202-377-0375
Pulpwood....Vacant USITC 202-252-1326
Pumice....White, Linda USITC 202-252-1427
Pumice....Meisinger, Arthur C. Mines 202-634-1185
Pumps....McDonald, Edward Commerce 202-377-0680
Pumps, Pumping Eqpt Valves, Comp (Trade Promo.)....McDonald,
   Edward Commerce 202-377-0680
Pumps, air and vacuum....Mata, Ruben USITC 202-252-1403
Pumps, liquid....Mata, Ruben USITC 202-252-1403

Pure Red Cell Aplasia....Staff NHLBI 301-496-4236
Purpura....Staff NIAMS 301-496-8188
Putty...Johnson, Larry USITC 202-252-1351
Puzzles....Robinson, Hazel USITC 202-252-1496
Puzzles....McKenna, T. Customs 212-466-5475
Pyelonephritis....Staff NIDDK 301-496-3583
Pyorrhea....Staff NIDR 301-496-4261
Pyramid Sales Plans, Marketing Practices....Staff Fed Trade Com
   202-326-3128
Pyrethrum....Wanser, Stephen USITC 202-252-1363
Pyridine....Foreso, Cynthia USITC 202-252-1348
Pyrotechnics....Spalding, Josephine USITC 202-252-1498

Q

QC/PE samples....Harold Clements EPA 513-569-7325
Qatar....Claude Clement Cnty Commerce 202-377-5545
Qatar (Doha)....Jane McVerry Cnty State 202-647-6572
Qatar (Doha)....William Pierce Cnty AID 202-647-1334
Qatar/Minerals....Bernadette Michalski Cnty Mines
   202-632-5065
Quadriplegia....Staff NINCDS 301-496-5751
Quality Control--Common Carrier....Staff FCC 202-634-1800
Quality Engineering....R. Bledsoe NASA 205-544-7406
Quality assurance...John C. Puzak EPA 919-541-0944
Quality assurance....D. Gene Easterly EPA 702-798-2108
Quality assurance....J. Gareth Pearson EPA 702-798-2203
Quality assurance matters....John Winter EPA 513-569-7325
Quality assurance statistics....Raymond C. Rhodes EPA
   919-541-2574
Quarrying Trends....Tanner, Arnold O. Mines 202-634-1019
Quarterly Financial Report....Zarrett, Paul Census
   301-763-2718
Quarterly Financial Report, Accounting....Lee, Ronald Census
   301-763-4270
Quarterly Financial Report, Classification....Hartman, Frank]
   Census 301-763-4274
Quarterly Financial Report, Related Issues....Lee, Ronald
   Census 301-763-4270
Quartz Chrystal....Ober, Joyce A. Mines 202-634-1177
Quartzite....White, Linda USITC 202-252-1427
Quaternary ammonium salts, fatty acids....Land, Eric USITC
   202-252-1349
Quebracho....Wanser, Stephen USITC 202-252-1363
Quill, articles of....Spalding, Josephine USITC 202-252-1498
Quilts....Borari, Marilyn USITC 202-252-1465

R

R-Value Rule....Kent Howerton Fed Trade Com 202-326-3013
Rabies....Staff NIAID 301-496-5717
Race Statistics....Staff Census 301-763-2607
Race Statistics, Spanish Population....Cresce, Arthur Census
   301-763-5219
Race Statistics, Spanish Population....DeNavas, Carmen Census
   301-763-5219
Racing shells....Lahey, Kathleen USITC 202-252-1409
Radar Intrusion Alarms (unlicensed)....Staff Staff
   202-653-6288
Radar Remote Sensing of the Earth....Howard Zebker NASA
   818-354-8780
Radar apparatus....Fletcher, William USITC 202-252-1407
Radial Keratotomy....Staff NEI 301-496-5248
Radiation....Staff NCI 301-496-5583
Radiation (Effect on Eyes)....Staff NEI 301-496-5248
Radiation (Effect on Teeth)....Staff NIDR 301-496-4261
Radiation (Nervous System)....Staff NINCDS 301-496-5751
Radiation (Nonionizing)....Staff OD/ORS 301-496-2960
Radiation (Nonionizing)....Staff NIEHS 919-541-3345
Radiation (X-ray) Effects on Fetus....Staff FDA 301-443-2356
Radiation Hazards....Staff FCC 202-653-8169
Radiation Safety (Radio. Spills, Lab. Surveys)....Staff OD/ORS
   301-496-5774
Radiation Safety Badges....Staff OD/ORS 301-496-2254
Radiation Safety Officer....Staff NIH 301-496-2254
Radiation safety...James G. Payne, Jr. EPA 702-798-2237
Radiation safety....Charles F. Costa EPA 702-798-2305
Radiation, toxicology, & biology....William Ewald EPA
   919-541-4164
Radio Broadcasting Advisory Committee....Staff FCC
   202-632-6485
Radio Broadcasting and TV....Siegmund, Johnrt J. Commerce

202-377-4781

Radio Communications Eqmt.....Pleasants, Arthur Commerce 202-377-2872

Radio Control Devices (non-licensed)....Staff FCC 202-653-6388

Radio Frequency Devices....Staff FCC 202-653-6288

Radio Noise....Staff FCC 202-632-7025

Radio Progagation....Staff FCC 202-632-7025

Radio navigational apparatus....Fletcher, William USITC 202-252-1407

Radio receivers....Vacant USITC 202-252-1387

Radioactive Materials (Shipping & Receiving)....Staff OD/ORS 301-496-2254

Radioactive Transfer....Larry Travis NASA 212-678-5599

Radioactive Waste Disposal at NIH (Solid & Liquid)....Staff OD/ORS 301-496-2254

Radiochemistry....Chung-King Liu EPA 702-798-2136

Radiograms....Staff FCC 202-632-7265

Radiolocation--Industrial....Staff FCC 717-337-1212

Radionuclide Techniques in CV Diagnosis....Staff NHLBI 301-496-4236

Radionuclides....Thomas Sorg EPA 513-569-7370

Radios....Dicerbo, M. Customs 212-466-5672

Radiotelegraph Common Carrier....Staff FCC 202-632-7265

Radiotelegraph Operator License....Staff FCC 202-632-7240

Radiotelephone Common Carrier Services....Staff FCC 202-653-5560

Radiotelephone Equipment....Staff FCC 301-725-1585

Radiotherapy (Cancer)....Staff NCI 301-496-5583

Radium....Staff NCI 301-496-5583

Radon control....Everett L. Plyler EPA 919-541-2918

Radon mitigation....W. Gene Tucker EPA 919-541-2746

Rags....Cook, Lee USITC 202-252-1471

Rail, locomotives....Lahey, Kathleen USITC 202-252-1409

Railroad Equipment, Trade Promo.....Heimowitz, Leonard Commerce 202-377-0558

Railroad Services....Sousane, J. Richard Commerce 202-377-4582

Railroad/Rail Equipment....O'Connell, W. Customs 212-466-5668

Railroads....Staff FCC 717-337-1212

Railway rolling stock....Lahey, Kathleen USITC 202-252-1409

Rainwear....Shetty, Sundar USITC 202-252-1457

Ramsey Hunt Syndrome....Staff NINCDS 301-496-5751

Rape....Staff NIMH 301-443-4513

Rare Disorders (Nuerological)....Staff NINCDS 301-496-5751

Rare Disorders (Nuerological)....Staff NINCDS 301-496-5751

Rare Earths....Hedrick, James B. Mines 202-634-1058

Rare saccharides....Randall, Rob USITC 202-252-1366

Rare-earth compounds....Greenblatt, Jack USITC 202-252-1353

Rare-earth metals....DeSapio, Vincent USITC 202-252-1435

Rate Base (International, Telegraph & Telephone)....Staff FCC 202-632-3772

Rate Level (International, Telegraph & Telephone)....Staff FCC 202-632-5550

Rate Structure (International, Telegraph & Telepho....Staff FCC 202-632-3772

Rate of Return (International, Telegraph & Telepho....Staff FCC 202-632-3772

Rattan....Westcot, Thomas USITC 202-252-1325

Raynaud's Disease....Staff NHLBI 301-496-4236

Raynaud's Disease....Staff NIAMS 301-496-8188

Reading Development....Staff NINCDS 301-496-5751

Reading Development....Staff NICHD 301-496-5133

Reading Disorders....Staff NICHD 301-496-5133

Reading Disorders....Staff NINCDS 301-496-5751

Reading Disorders....Staff Dept. of Education 202-245-8707

Real Estate....Jacques Feuillan Fed Trade Com 202-326-2739

Real Estate Brokerage....Paul Roark Fed Trade Com 213-793-7870

Real Estate Brokers...Jacques Feuillan Fed Trade Com 202-326-2739

Reapportionment....Turner, Marshall Census 301-763-4686

Recidivism...Alan Beck Justice Stat 202-724-7755

Recidivism....Lawrence Greenfeld Justice Stat 202-724-7755

Recidivism....Bernard Shipley Justice Stat 202-724-7770

Recidivism and Criminal Career Studies....Richard A. Linster Justice 202-724-7631

Recombinant DNA....Staff NIAID 301-496-5717

Recombinant DNA....Staff NCI 301-496-5583

Recombinant DNA....Staff NIGMS 301-496-7301

Recombinant DNA (Policy Guidelines)....Staff Dir., Of. of Re. DNA Act. 301-770-0131

Recombinant DNA Activities....Staff 301-770-0131

Recombinant DNA Activity....Staff OD 301-770-0131

Reconstituted crude petroleum....Foreso, Cynthia USITC 202-252-1348

Recording media....Bishop, Kathryn USITC 202-252-1494

Recordkeeping Requirements Under OSHA....Whitmore, Robert Labor 202-272-3462

Recreational Equipment, Export Promo.....Cox, Thomas Commerce 202-377-5852

Rectifiers....Joseph, I. Customs 212-466-5673

Recurrent Fever....Staff NIAID 301-496-5717

Recurrent Pyogenic Infections....Staff NIAID 301-496-5717

Red Blood Cells (Erythrocytes)....Staff FDA/NCDB 301-496-3556

Red Blood Cells (Erythrocytes)....Staff NHLBI 301-496-4236

Redistricting....Talbert, Cathy Census 301-763-3856

Reduction of Carrier Service....Staff FCC 202-632-7553

Reeling machines....Greene, William USITC 202-252-1405

Reflex Sympathetic Dystrophy Syndrome....Staff NIAMS 301-496-8188

Reflux Nephropathy....Staff NIDDK 301-496-3583

Refractive Errors....Staff NEI 301-496-5248

Refractories....DeSapio, Vincent USITC 202-252-1435

Refractory Anemia....Staff NHLBI 301-496-4236

Refractory Products....Raymond, Jon Commerce 202-377-0610

Refrig. Equipment, Commercial....Shaw, Eugene Commerce 202-377-3494

Refrigeration....Rocks, M. Customs 212-466-5669

Refrigeration equipment....Mata, Ruben USITC 202-252-1403

Refsum's Disease....Staff NINCDS 301-496-5751

Regional Enteritis....Staff NIDDK 301-496-3583

Regional, BEA Economic Areas....Trott, Jr., Edward A. Economic 202-523-0973

Regional, Counties, Dividends....Jolley, Charles A. Economic 202-523-0516

Regional, Counties, Employment....Evans, Carol E. Economic 202-523-0945

Regional, Counties, Employment....Hazen, Linnea Economic 202-523-0951

Regional, Counties, Farm Proprietors Employment....Zavrel, James M. Economic 202-523-0932

Regional, Counties, Farm Proprietors Income....Zavrel, James M. Economic 202-523-0932

Regional, Counties, Interest....Jolley, Charles A. Economic 202-523-0516

Regional, Counties, Metholodogy....Bailey, Wallace Economic 202-523-0524

Regional, Counties, Military Employment....Reed, John M. Economic 202-523-0551

Regional, Counties, Military Pay....Reed, John M. Economic 202-523-0551

Regional, Counties, Nonfarm Proprietors Employment....Sensenig, Arthur L. Economic 202-523-0937

Regional, Counties, Nonfarm Proprietors Income....Sensenig, Arthur L. Economic 202-523-0937

Regional, Counties, Personal Income....Hazen, Linnea Economic 202-523-0951

Regional, Counties, Personal Income, Disposable....Brown, Robert L. Economic 202-523-0571

Regional, Counties, Personal Income, State Qtly....Hazen, Linnea Economic 202-523-0951

Regional, Counties, Rental Income....Jolley, Charles A. Economic 202-523-0516

Regional, Counties, Requests for Empl Data....Regional Ecoomic Information System Staff Economic 202-523-0966

Regional, Counties, Requests for Persl Income Data....Regional Economic Information System Staff Economic 202-523-0966

Regional, Counties, Residence Adjustment....Silverman, Albert Economic 202-523-0376

Regional, Counties, Shift-Share Analysis....Levine, Bruce Economic 202-523-0938

Regional, Counties, Transfer Payments....Brown, Robert L. Economic 202-523-0551

Regional, Counties, Wage & Salary Income....Evans, Carol E. Economic 202-523-0945

Regional, Counties, Work Force Data....Levine, Bruce Economic 202-523-0938

Regional, Econometric Modeling, State....Kort, John R. Economic 202-523-0591

Regional, Econometric Models....Beemiller, Richard M. Economic 202-523-0594

Regional, Economic Situation, Current....Friedenberg, Howard L. Economic 202-523-0979

Regional, Gross State Product Esimates....Trott, Jr., Edward A. Economic 202-523-0973

Regional, Input-Output Modeling, Regional....Beemiller, Richard M. Economic 202-523-0594

Regional, Metro Areas, Personal Income, Disposable....Brown, Robert L. Economic 202-523-0571

Regional, Metro Areas, Requests for Empl Data....Regional Economic Information System Staff Economic 202-523-0966

Regional, Metro Areas, Requests for Persl Inc Data....Regional Economic Information System Staff Economic 202-523-0966

Regional, Metropol Areas, Farm Proprietors Empl....Zavrel, James M. Economic 202-523-0932

Regional, Metropol Areas, Farm Proprietors Income....Zavrel, James M. Economic 202-523-0932

Regional, Metropol Areas, Nonfarm Proprietors Empl....Sensenig, Arthur L. Economic 202-523-0937

Regional, Metropol Areas, Nonfarm Proprietors Inc....Sensenig, Arthur L. Economic 202-523-0937

Regional, Metropol Areas, Persnal Inc, State Qtly....Hazen, Linnea Economic 202-523-0951

Regional, Metropolitan Areas, Dividends....Jolley, Charles A. Economic 202-523-0516

Regional, Metropolitan Areas, Employment....Evans, Carol E. Economic 202-523-0945

Regional, Metropolitan Areas, Employment....Hazen, Linnea Economic 202-523-0951

Regional, Metropolitan Areas, Interest....Jolley, Charles A. Economic 202-523-0516

Regional, Metropolitan Areas, Methodology....Bailey, Wallace K. Economic 202-523-0524

Regional, Metropolitan Areas, Military Employment....Reed, John M. Economic 202-523-0551

Regional, Metropolitan Areas, Military Pay....Reed, John M. Economic 202-523-0551

Regional, Metropolitan Areas, Personal Income....Hazen, Linnea Economic 202-523-0951

Regional, Metropolitan Areas, Rental Income....Jolley, Charles A. Economic 202-523-0516

Regional, Metropolitan Areas, Residence Adjustment....Silverman, Albert Economic 202-523-0376

Regional, Metropolitan Areas, Shift-Share Analysis....Levine, Bruce Economic 202-523-0938

Regional, Metropolitan Areas, Wage & Salary Income....Evans, Carol E. Economic 202-523-0945

Regional, Metropolitan Areas, Work Force Data....Levine, Bruce Economic 202-523-0938

Regional, Metropolitan, Transfer Payments....Brown, Robert L. Economic 202-523-0551

Regional, Migration Patterns....Levine, Bruce Economic 202-523-0938

Regional, Personal Income, State Quarterly....Whiston, Isabelle P. Economic 202-523-0911

Regional, Projections, Metropolitan Areas....Johnson, Kenneth P. Economic 202-523-0971

Regional, Projections, States....Johnson, Kenneth P. Economic 202-523-0971

Regional, State, Employment, Farm Proprietor's....Zavrel, James M. Economic 202-523-0932

Regional, States, Employment....Hazen, Linnea Economic 202-523-0951

Regional, States, Employment, Military....Reed, John M. Economic 202-523-0571

Regional, States, Employment, Nonfarm Proprietors'....Sesensig, Arthur L. Economic 202-523-0937

Regional, States, Employment, Requests for Data....Regional Economic Information System Staff Economic 202-523-0966

Regional, States, Employment, Wage and Salary....Evans, Carol E. Economic 202-523-0945

Regional, States, Income, Farm Proprietor....Zavrel, James M. Economic 202-523-0932

Regional, States, Income, Nonfarm Proprietors'....Sensenig, Arthur L. Economic 202-523-0937

Regional, States, Income, Wage and Salary....Evans, Carol E. Economic 202-523-0945

Regional, States, Interest Income....Jolley, Charles A. Economic 202-523-0516

Regional, States, Methodology....Bailey, Wallace K. Economic 202-523-0524

Regional, States, Military Pay....Reed, John M. Economic 202-523-0571

Regional, States, Persnal Income, Request for Data....Hazen, Linnea Economic 202-523-0951

Regional, States, Personal Income....Hazen, Linnea Economic 202-523-0951

Regional, States, Personal Income, Disposable....Brown, Robert L. Economic 202-523-0551

Regional, States, Personal Income, Dividends....Jolley, Charles A. Economic 202-523-0516

Regional, States, Rental Income....Jolley, Charles A. Economic 202-523-0516

Regional, States, Requests for Persnal Income Data....Regional Economic Information Sysem Staff Economic 202-523-0966

Regional, States, Residence Adjustment....Silverman, Albert Economic 202-523-0376

Regional, States, Shift-Share Analysis....Levine, Bruce Economic 202-523-0938

Regional, States, Transfer Payments....Brown, Robert L. Economic 202-523-0551

Regional, States, Work Force Data....Levine, Bruce Economic 202-523-0938

Regional, Work History Sample, Continuous....Levine, Bruce Economic 202-523-0938

Regulators....Hagey, Michael USITC 202-252-1392

Regulatory use of models....James L. Dicke EPA 919-541-5682

Reiter's Syndrome....Staff NIAMS 301-496-8188

Relays....Miller, J. Customs 212-466-5680

Reliability Engineering....F. Safie NASA 205-544-5278

Remission....Staff NCI 301-496-5583

Remote Sensing....Harvey Melfi NASA 301-286-7024

Remote sensing....James G. Payne, Jr. EPA 702-798-2237

Remote sensing....Thomas H. Mace EPA 702-798-2262

Remote sensing....John H. Montanari EPA 703-349-3110

Remote sensing....J.F. Paul EPA 401-782-3000

Renal Disorders in Children....Staff NIDDK 301-496-3583

Renal Glycosuria....Staff NIDDK 301-496-3583

Renal Hypertension....Staff NIDDK 301-496-3583

Renal Tubular Acidosis....Staff NIDDK 301-496-3583

Renal Vascular Disease....Staff NIDDK 301-496-3583

Renovascular Hypertension....Staff NIDDK 301-496-3583

Rental (Scientific)....Staff DRS 301-496-4131

Reporting Crime to Police....Caroline Harlow Justice Stat 202-724-7755

Reproductive Disorders....Staff NICHD 301-496-5133

Reproductive and developmental toxicology....Harold Zenick EPA 202-382-7303

Reproductive physiology....Sally P. Darney EPA 919-541-2782

Reproductive toxicology....Robert J. Kaviock EPA 919-541-2771

Rescue Squads....Staff FCC 717-337-1212

Research & Development....Price, James B. Commerce 202-377-4781

Research (ethical issues)....Staff OD/OPRR 301-496-7005

Research Career Development....Staff DRG 301-496-7441

Research Grants....Staff DRG 301-496-7441

Research Training....Staff DRG 301-496-7441

Research Training....Staff NIGMS 301-496-7301

Research methods development....Robert E. Lee EPA 919-541-2454

Residual fuel oil....Foreso, Cynthia USITC 202-252-1348

Resistors....Sherman, Thomas USITC 202-252-1389

Resistors....Joseph, I. Customs 212-466-5673

Respiratory Diseases (Infectious/Allergenic)....Staff NIAID 301-496-5717

Respiratory Diseases (Non-In., Non-All., Non-Tum.)....Staff NHLBI 301-496-4236

Respiratory Diseases (Tumorous/Cancerous)....Staff NCI 301-496-5583

Respiratory physiology....Timothy R. Gerrity EPA 919-541-6206

Responses to Illness or Disability....Staff NCNR 301-496-0526

Restless Leg Syndrome....Staff NINCDS 301-496-5751

Restricted Radiation Devices....Staff FCC 202-653-6288

Retail Trade....Margulies, Marvin J. Commerce 202-377-5086

Retinal Degeneration....Staff NEI 301-496-5248

Retinal Detachment....Staff NEI 301-496-5248

Retinal Diseases....Staff NEI 301-496-5248

Retinal Vascular Disease....Staff NEI 301-496-5248

Retinitis Pigmentosa....Staff NEI 301-496-5248

Retinoblastoma....Staff NEI 301-496-5248

Retinopathies....Staff NEI 301-496-5248

Retirement....Staff NIA 301-496-1752

Retirement of Telephone Plants....Staff FCC 202-634-1861

Rett's Syndrome....Staff NINCDS 301-496-5751

Reunion....Deborah Graze Cnty State 202-647-2633

Reunion....Brian D. Curran Cnty AID 202-647-2633

Reunion/Minerals....Lloyd Antonides Cnty Mines 202-632-5065

Reye's Syndrome....Staff NINCDS 301-496-5751

Rh Factor....Staff NHLBI 301-496-4236

Rhabdomyosarcoma and Undifferentiated Sarcomas....Staff NCI 301-496-5583

Rhenium....Kollins, Susan USITC 202-252-1441

Rhenium....Blossom, John Mines 202-634-1021

Rheumatic Heart....Staff NHLBI 301-496-4236

Rheumatoid Arthritis....Staff NIAMS 301-496-8188

Rhinitis....Staff NIAID 301-496-5717

Rhodium compounds....Greenblatt, Jack USITC 202-252-1353

Ribbons: inked....Cook, Lee USITC 202-252-1471

Ribbons: other....Enfield, Mary E USITC 202-252-1455

Ribbons: typewriter....Enfield, Mary E USITC 202-252-1455

Rice....Pierre-Benoist, John USITC 202-252-1320

Rice Futures....Judy Sepsey Comm Futures 312-353-9025

Rice Milling....Janis, William V. Commerce 202-377-2250

Rice, Economics....Livezey, Janet Agri 202-786-1840

Rice, Statistics....James, Clif Agri 202-447-2157

Rice, World, Economics....Schwartz, Sara Agri 202-786-1693

Ricinoleic acid esters....Johnson, Larry USITC 202-252-1351

Rickets, Vitamin-D Resistant....Staff NIDDK 301-496-3583

Rickettsial Diseases....Staff NIAID 301-496-5717

Riding crops....Linkins, Linda USITC 202-252-149
Rifles....Robinson, Hazel USITC 202-252-1496
Riley-Day Syndrome....Staff NINCDS 301-496-5751
Ringworm....Staff NIAID 301-496-5717
Risk characterization....J.F. Paul EPA 401-782-3000
River Blindness....Staff NEI 301-496-5248
Roads, Major Proj.....Smith, Jay L. Commerce 202-377-4642
Robots....Mearman, John Commerce 202-377-0315
Robust/Failure Accommodating Control Design Metho....Dlaude
      Keckler NASA 804-865-4591
Rocket-Borne, Small-scale Flight Research....Bruce Holmes NASA
      804-865-3274
Rocky Mountain Spotted Fever....Staff NIAID 301-496-5717
Rods, plastics....Truskett, Brooks USITC 202-252-1364
Roller Bearings....Fletcher, William E. Commerce 202-377-0309
Rolling Mill Machinery....Comer, Patrick Commerce 202-377-0316
Rolling machines, except metal....Slingerland, David USITC
      202-252-1400
Rollings mills, metal....Fravel, Dennis USITC 202-252-1404
Romania....William Winter Cnty Commerce 202-377-2645
Romania (Bucharest)....Frederick A. Becker Cnty State
      202-647-3298
Romania (Bucharest)....Thomas A. Lynch Cnty AID 202-647-3298
Romania (Bucharest)....Ben F. Fairfax Cnty AID 202-647-1739
Romania/Minerals....Donald Buck Cnty Mines 202-632-5052
Roofing, Asphalt....Pitcher, Charles Commerce 202-377-0132
Rope....Cook, Lee USITC 202-252-1471
Rope....Edert, R. Customs 212-466-5885
Rosemary oil (essential oil)....Land, Eric USITC 202-252-1349
Rotary Wing Aeromechanics....William Warmbrodt NASA
      415-694-5642
Rotavirus....Staff NIAID 301-496-5717
Rothmund-Thompson Syndrome....Staff NCI 301-496-5583
Rotor Blade Aerodynamics....I.C. Chang NASA 415-694-6396
Rotorcraft & Power Lift Flight....Bill Snyder NASA 415-694-6570
Rouges....Land, Eric USITC 202-252-1349
Rubber....Prat, Raimundo Commerce 202-377-0128
Rubber Products....Prat, Raimundo Commerce 202-377-0128
Rubber, Synthetic....Cosslett, Pat Commerce 202-377-0128
Rubber, natural....Taylor, Ed USITC 202-252-1362
Rubber, synthetic....Taylor, Ed USITC 202-252-1362
Rubella....Staff NIAID 301-496-5717
Rubeola....Staff NIAID 301-496-5717
Rubidium....Reese, Jr., Robert Mines 202-634-1071
Rugs....Borsari, Marilyn USITC 202-252-1465
Rugs....Barth, G. Customs 212-466-5884
Rulemaking Procedures....Bill Golden Fed Trade Com
      202-326-2494
Rural Aged....Staff NIA 301-496-1752
Rural Aged....Staff NIA 301-496-1752
Rural Income, Economics....Ross, Peggy Agri 202-786-1537
Rural Labor, Economics....McGranahan, David Agri 202-786-1540
Rwanda....John Crown Cnty Commerce 202-377-0357
Rwanda....Tom Elam Peace Corps 202-254-8694
Rwanda (Kigali)....Kevin Brown Cnty State 202-647-3139
Rwanda (Kigali)....Judith B. Cefkin Cnty AID 202-647-3138
Rwanda (Kigali)....Harald R. Marwitz Cnty AID 202-647-9762
Rwanda/Minerals....Lloyd Antonides Cnty Mines 202-632-5065

S

SAN resins....Taylor, Ed USITC 202-252-1362
Saccharin....Land, Eric USITC 202-252-1349
Saddlery & Harness Products....Enright, Joe Commerce
      202-377-3459
Safe Schools....Thomas F. Albrecht Justice 202-272-6040
Safety Equipment, Trade Promo.....Fleming, Howard Commerce
      202-377-5163
Safety, Reliability, and Quality Assurance....Staff NASA
      713-483-4290
Salicin....Randall, Rob USITC 202-252-1366
Saliva....Staff NIDR 301-496-4261
Salivary System Diseases....Staff NIDR 301-496-4261
Salmonella Infections....Staff NIAID 301-496-5717
Salmonellosis and Turtles....Staff CDC 404-329-3534
Salt....Greenblatt, Jack USITC 202-252-1353
Salt....Kostick, Dennis S. Mines 202-634-1177
Salts, inorganic....Greenblatt, Jack USITC 202-252-1353
Salts, organic....Michels, David USITC 202-252-1352
Sampling Methods, Current Programs....Shapiro, Gary Census
      301-763-2674
Sampling Methods, Decennial Census....Griffin, Richard Census
      301-763-4154
San Marino....Raymond Snider Cnty State 202-647-2453
San Marino....Sharon White Cnty State 202-647-2453

San Marino....William G. Perett Cnty AID 202-647-8210
Sand....White, Linda USITC 202-252-1427
Sand....Tepordei, Valentin V. Mines 202-634-1185
Sandals....Burns, Gail USITC 202-252-1469
Sanitation....Staff OD/ORS 301-496-2960
Santavuori Disease....Staff NINCDS 301-496-5751
Sao Tome & Principe....John Crown Cnty Commerce
      202-377-0357
Sao Tome and Principe....Susan Zelle Cnty State 202-647-4965
Sao Tome and Principe....Abbe Fessenden Cnty AID 202-647-7986
Sao Tome and Principe....T. Dennis Reece Cnty AID 202-647-7468
Sao Tome and Principe/Minerals....Thomas Dolley Cnty Mines
      202-632-5065
Saphenous Vein Bypass Grafts....Staff NHLBI 301-496-4236
Saran....Taylor, Ed USITC 202-252-1362
Sarcoidosis....Staff NIAID 301-496-5717
Sarcoidosis....Staff NHLBI 301-496-4236
Sarcoidosis....Staff NEI 301-496-5248
Sarcoma....Staff NCI 301-496-5583
Sarcoma of Bone and Soft Tissue....Staff NCI 301-496-5583
Sardines....Corey, Roger USITC 202-252-1327
Satellite Communications Systems Technology....James Bagwell
      NASA 216-433-3503
Satellite Coordination & Interference....Staff FCC
      202-653-8153
Satellite Rates....Staff FCC 202-632-5550
Satellite Spread Spectrum....Staff FCC 202-653-8163
Satellite Systems....Staff FCC 202-634-1624
Satellite Systems Coordination....Staff FCC 202-653-8153
Satellite, Domestic Facilities....Staff FCC 202-634-1624
Satellite, International Coordination....Staff FCC
      202-653-8144
Satellite, International Facilities....Staff FCC 202-632-7265
Satellite, Maritime....Staff FCC 202-632-7175
Satellites, Communications....Shea, Timothy Commerce
      202-377-4666
Satellites, Marketing....White, John Commerce 202-377-2835
Satin white...Johnson, Larry USITC 202-252-1351
Saudi Arabia....Cynthia Anthony Cnty Commerce 202-377-4652
Saudi Arabia (Riyadh)...John Riddle Cnty State 202-647-7550
Saudi Arabia (Riyadh)....Bruce Strathearn Cnty AID
      202-647-7550
Saudi Arabia/Minerals....Bernadette Michalski Cnty Mines
      202-632-5065
Sausages....Ludwick, David USITC 202-252-1329
Saw Blades....Shaw, Eugene Commerce 202-377-3494
Saws, Hand....Shaw, Eugene Commerce 202-377-3494
Scabies....Staff NIAID 301-496-5717
Scales....Slingerland, David USITC 202-252-1400
Scandium....Hedrick, James B. Mines 202-634-1058
Scarves....Shetty, Sundar USITC 202-252-1457
Scarves....Persky, H. Customs 212-466-5881
Schilder's Disease....Staff NINCDS 301-496-5751
Schistosomiasis....Staff NIAIDS 301-496-5717
Schistosomiasis....Staff NIAID 301-496-5717
Schizophrenia....Staff NIMH 301-443-4515
Scholars-in-Residence....Staff FIC 301-496-4161
School Enrollment....Siegel, Paul Census 301-763-1154
Sciatica....Staff NIAMS 301-496-8188
Scientific Instruments, Trade Promo.....Gwaltney, G. P.
      Commerce 202-377-3090
Scientific Measurement/Control Equipment....Donnelly, Margaret
      Commerce 202-377-5466
Scientific outreach....Robert A. Drummond EPA 218-720-5733
Scleroderma....Staff NIAMS 301-496-8188
Sclerosis....Staff NINCDS 301-496-5751
Sclerosis, Multiple....Staff NINCDS 301-496-5751
Scoliosis....Staff NIAMS 301-496-8188
Scrap cordage....Cook, Lee USITC 202-252-1471
Screening machines....Greene, William USITC 202-252-1405
Screw Machine Products....Reise, Richard Commerce 202-377-3489
Screws....Brandon, James USITC 202-252-1433
Screws, Washers....Reise, Richard Commerce 202-377-3489
Sculpture....Mushinske, L. Customs 212-466-5739
Sea Safety....Staff FCC 202-632-7175
Sealing machinery....Slingerland, David USITC 202-252-1400
Search for Extraterrestrial Intelligence....Bernard Oliver
      NASA 415-694-5166
Seat belts....Cook, Lee USITC 202-252-1471
Sebacic acid esters....Johnson, Larry USITC 202-252-1351
Security Brokers....Fenwick, Thomas R. Commerce 202-377-0347
Security Equipment, Trade Promo.....Fleming, Howard Commerce
      202-377-5163
Security Management....Chitum, J. Marc Commerce 202-377-0345
Sedatives....Nesbitt, Elizabeth USITC 202-252-1355
Sediment criteria....R.C. Swartz EPA 401-782-3000
Sediment transport....Steve C. McCutcheon EPA 404-546-3301
Sediment transport....J.F. Paul EPA 401-782-3000

Seeds, field and garden....Pierre-Benoist, John USITC 202-252-1320
Seeds, oil-bearing....Reeder, John USITC 202-252-1319
Seeds, spice...Lipovsky, William USITC 202-252-1331
Selenium....Kollins, Susan USITC 202-252-1441
Selenium....Edelstein, Daniel Mines 202-634-1053
Selenium compounds....Greenblatt, Jack USITC 202-252-1353
Self Protection, Justifiable Use of Force....Marianne Zawitz Justice Stat 202-724-6100
Semiconductor Detector Technology....William Miller NASA 804-865-3761
Semiconductor Material Growth in Low-G Environment....Harry Benz NASA 804-865-3777
Semiconductor Prod. Equipment & Materials....Haggerty, Peggy Commerce 202-377-3360
Semiconductors....Vacant USITC 202-252-1391
Semiconductors....Rolf, Joan Commerce 202-377-8411
Senegal....Philip Michelini Cnty Commerce 202-377-4388
Senegal...R. J. Benn Peace Corps 202-254-3185
Senegal (Dakar)....Stephen Kelly Cnty State 202-647-2865
Senegal (Dakar)....Jean G. Soso Cnty AID 202-647-2865
Senegal (Dakar)....Helen Vaitaitis Cnty AID 202-647-9207
Senegal/Minerals....Hendrik van Oss Cnty Mines 202-632-5065
Senile Dementia....Staff NIA 301-496-1752
Senile Dementia....Staff NINCDS 301-496-5751
Senile Dementia....Staff NIMH 301-443-1185
Senile Macular Degeneration....Staff NEI 301-496-5248
Sentencing...Jay Merrill Justice 202-724-2959
Sentencing....Bernard Auchter Justice 202-724-7684
Sentencing...Richard Rau Justice 202-724-2951
Sentencing....Cheryl Martorana Justice 202-724-2965
Sentencing...Martin Lively Justice 202-724-2966
Sentencing....Carla Gaskins Justice Stat 202-724-7774
Sentencing....Herbert Koppel Justice Stat 202-724-7770
Sentencing...Phyllis Jo Baunach Justice Stat 202-724-7755
Sentencing - Federal....Carol Kaplan Justice Stat 202-724-7759
Septal Defects....Staff NHLBI 301-496-4236
Seronomy....M. Torr NASA 205-544-7676
Serum Protein Abnormalities....Staff NCI 301-496-5583
Service Industries....Free, Brant W. Commerce 202-377-3575
Services Data Base Development....McMeans, David Commerce 202-377-0351
Services Data Base Development....Atkins, Robert G. Commerce 202-377-4781
Services Industries Curguay Round....Dowling, Jay Commerce 202-377-1134
Services, DAS....Luft, R. David Commerce 202-377-5261
Severe Combined Immunodeficiency....Staff NCI 301-496-5583
Severe Storms....Franco Einaudi NASA 301-286-6786
Sewing and knitting needles....Laney-Cummings, Karen USITC 202-252-1431
Sewing machine needles....Greene, William USITC 202-252-1405
Sewing machines....Greene, William USITC 202-252-1405
Sewing thread: cotton....Enfield, Mary E USITC 202-252-1455
Sewing thread: manmade fibers....Butler, R Larry USITC 202-252-1470
Sewing thread: silk....Freund, Kimberlie USITC 202-252-1456
Sewing thread: wool....Freund, Kimberlie USITC 202-252-1456
Sex Change....Staff NICHD 301-496-5133
Sex Determination....Staff NICHD 301-496-5133
Sex Hormones....Staff NICHD 301-496-5133
Sex and Aging....Staff NIA 301-496-1752
Sex, States....Staff Census 301-763-5072
Sex, U.S.....Staff Census 301-763-5072
Sexual Development....Staff NICHD 301-496-5133
Sexually Transmitted Diseases....Staff NIAID 301-496-5717
Seychelles....James RObb Cnty Commerce 202-377-4564
Seychelles (Victoria)....Frank G. Light Cnty State 202-647-5684
Seychelles (Victoria)....Christopher Murray Cnty AID 202-647-4536
Seychelles (Victoria)....Stephen Pulaski Cnty AID 202-647-9763
Seychelles/Minerals....Lloyd Antonides Cnty Mines 202-632-5065
Sezary Syndrome....Staff NCI 301-496-5583
Shale oil....Foreso, Cynthia USITC 202-252-1348
Shared Instrumentation Grant....Staff DRR 301-496-5545
Shawls....Shetty, Sundar USITC 202-252-1457
Sheep....Ludwick, David USITC 202-252-1329
Sheep, Statistics....Cole, John Agri 202-447-3578
Sheet, plastics....Truskett, Brooks USITC 202-252-1364
Sheets, bed....Borsari, Marilyn USITC 202-252-1465
Shell Fish....Brady, T. Customs 212-466-5790
Shell, articles of....Spalding, Josphine USITC 202-252-1498
Shellac and other lacs....Reeder, John USITC 202-252-1319
Shellac, varnish...Johnson, Larry USITC 201-252-1351
Shellfish....Newman, Douglas USITC 202-252-1328
Shells, freshwater, crude....Ludwick, David USITC 202-252-1329
Shells, marine, crude....Ludwick, David USITC 202-252-1329
Shingles (Herpes Zoster)....Staff NINCDS 301-496-5751

Shingles (Herpes Zoster)....Staff NIAID 301-496-5717
Shingles and shakes (wood)....Westcot, Thomas USITC 202-252-1325
Shingles, Wood....Wise, Barbara Commerce 202-377-0375
Shingles, asphalt....Rhodes, Richard USITC 202-252-1322
Ship Earth Stations....Staff FCC 202-632-7175
Ship Inspections....Staff FCC 202-632-7014
Ship Licensing....Staff FCC 717-337-1212
Shipping, Ocean...Johnson, C. William Commerce 202-377-0512
Shirts: mens and boys....Shetty, Sundar USITC 202-252-1457
Shirts: womens and girls....MacKnight, Peggy USITC 202-252-1468
Shock (Cardiogenic)....Staff NHLBI 301-496-4236
Shock (Hemorrhagic)....Staff NHLBI 301-496-4236
Shock Trauma Center....Staff U MD 301-528-6294
Shoe machinery....Fravel, Dennis USITC 202-252-1404
Shoe parts....Burns, Gail USITC 202-252-1469
Shoes....Burns, Gail USITC 202-252-1469
Shorts: mens and boys....Shetty, Sundar USITC 202-252-1457
Shorts: womens and girls....MacKnight, Peggy USITC 202-252-1468
Shotguns....Robinson, Hazel USITC 202-252-1496
Shrimp....Newman, Douglas USITC 202-252-1328
Shy-Drager Syndrome....Staff NINCDS 301-496-5751
Shy-Drager Syndrome....Staff NIMH 301-443-4515
Sickle Cell Anemia....Staff NHLBI 301-496-4236
Sideroblastic Anemia....Staff NHLBI 301-496-4236
Siding (wood)....Vacant USITC 202-252-1326
Sierra Leone....Philip Michelini Cnty Commerce 202-377-3288
Sierra Leone....Anna Weset Peace Corps 202-254-5644
Sierra Leone (Freetown)....Bisa Williams-Manigault Cnty State 202-647-3395
Sierra Leone (Freetown)....Kathleen Davis Cnty AID 202-647-8354
Sierra Leone (Freetown)....Emily B. McPhie Cnty AID 202-647-7985
Sierra Leone/Minerals....Bernadette Michalski Cnty Mines 202-632-5065
Sight Substitution Systems....Staff NEI 301-496-5248
Silica....White, Linda USITC 202-252-1427
Silicon....Boszormenyi, Laszio USITC 202-252-1437
Silicon....Gambogi, Joseph Mines 202-634-1015
Silicon Carbide Abrasive....Austin, Gordon Mines 202-634-1206
Silicone resins....Taylor, Ed USITC 202-252-1362
Silicones....Michels, David USITC 202-252-1352
Silk....Freund, Kimberlie USITC 202-252-1456
Sillimanite....Lukes, James USITC 202-252-1426
Silver....Kollins, Susan USITC 202-252-1441
Silver....Reese, Jr., Robert G. Mines 202-634-1070
Silver Futures....Helen Cadden Comm Futures 212-668-2081
Silver compounds....Greenblatt, Jack USITC 202-252-1353
Singapore....Don Ryan Cnty Commerce 202-377-3875
Singapore (Singapore)....Sharie Villarosa Cnty State 202-647-3278
Singapore (Singapore)....Lawrence Mondschein Cnty AID 202-647-3276
Singapore (Singapore)....Karl Schwartz Cnty AID 202-647-9240
Singapore/Minerals....Chin Kuo Cnty Mines 202-632-5066
Single Side Band--Standards....Staff FCC 202-653-6288
Sinusitis....Staff NIAID 301-496-5717
Sirups....James, Antoinette USITC 202-252-1313
Sisal Products....Shaw, Clinton R. Commerce 202-377-5124
Site-specific water quality....Anthony R. Carlson EPA 218-720-5523
Sjogren's Syndrome....Staff NIAMS 301-496-8188
Sjogren's Syndrome....Staff NIAID 301-496-5717
Sjogren's Syndrome....Staff NINCDS 301-496-5751
Sjogren's Syndrome....Staff NEI 301-496-5248
Sjogren's Syndrome....Staff NIDR 301-496-4261
Ski equipment....Robinson, Hazel USITC 202-252-1496
Skin Cancer....Staff NCI 301-496-5583
Skin Diseases....Staff NIAMS 301-496-8188
Skin and Aging....Staff NIA 301-496-1752
Skins (animal)....Steller, Rose USITC 202-252-1323
Skirts....MacKnight, Peggy USITC 202-252-1468
Slack....Foreso, Cynthia USITC 202-252-1348
Slacks, mens and boys....Shetty, Sundar USITC 202-252-1457
Slacks, womens and girls....MacKnight, Peggy USITC 202-252-1468
Slate....White, Linda USITC 202-252-1427
Sleep Disturbances....Staff NIMH 301-443-4515
Sleep and Aging....Staff NIA 301-496-1752
Sleep and Aging....Staff NIMH 301-443-1185
Slide fasteners....Rodriguez, Laura USITC 202-252-1486
Slow Viruses....Staff NINCDS 301-496-5751
Sludge disposal & reuse methodology....Randall Bruins EPA 513-569-7539
Sludge effects....D.J. Hansen EPA 401-782-3000

Small Appliances....Hantman, S. Customs 212-466-5678
Small Appliances....Hantman, S. Customs 212-466-5678
Small Cell Carcinoma....Staff NCI 301-496-5583
Smallpox....Staff NIAID 301-496-5717
Smell (Disorders)....Staff NINCDS 301-496-5751
Smoking (Cancer related)....Staff NCI 301-496-5583
Smoking and Health....Staff Off. on Smok. and Health 301-443-1575
Smoking and Heart Disease....Staff NHLBI 301-496-4236
Smoking and Tobacco Use....Staff NCNR 301-496-0526
Snackfood....Janis, William V. Commerce 202-377-2250
Soap, castile....Land, Eric USITC 202-252-1349
Soap, surface-active agents, synthetic detergent....Land, Eric USITC 202-252-1349
Soap, toilet....Land, Eric USITC 202-252-1349
Soaps....McIntyre, Leo R. Commerce 202-377-0128
Soapstone....White, Linda USITC 202-252-1427
Social Stratification....Siegel, Paul Census 301-763-1154
Social Stratification....Siegel, Paul Census 301-763-1154
Social Work Department....Staff CC 301-496-2381
Social and Behavioral Research on Aging....Staff NIA 301-496-1752
Social and Behavioral Sciences....Staff NICHD 301-496-6832
Socks....Bryant, Judith USITC 202-252-1464
Soda ash....Greenblatt, Jack USITC 202-252-1353
Sodium Compounds....Kostick, Dennis S. Mines 202-634-1177
Sodium and pottassium salts of oils, greases, fat....Land, Eric USITC 202-252-1349
Sodium benzoate....Matusik, Ed USITC 202-252-1356
Sodium compounds....Greenblatt, Jack USITC 202-252-1353
Software....Miles, Tim Commerce 202-377-2990
Software....Woods, Clay Commerce 202-377-0571
Software and Data Management....D. Aichele NASA 205-544-3721
Software, Export Promo.....Fogg, Judy Commerce 202-377-4936
Soil Conservation, Economics....Magleby, Richard Agri 202-786-1435
Soil Conservation, Economics....Grano, Anthony Agri 202-786-1401
Soil chemistry....Don Kampbell EPA 405-332-2358
Soil chemistry....George W. Bailey EPA 404-546-3307
Soil invertebrate ecology....Clarence A. Callahan EPA 503-757-4764
Soil science....Frank Beck EPA 405-332-2246
Soil science....Susan Mravik EPA 405-332-2434
Soil science....Joe Williams EPA 405-332-2246
Soils....Dave Walters EPA 405-332-2261
Solar Advertising Guides....Michael Dershowitz Fed Trade Com 202-326-3158
Solar Burns (Eye Effects)....Staff NEI 301-496-5248
Solar Cells/Photovoltaic Devices....Garden, Les Commerce 202-377-0556
Solar Eqmt. Ocean....Garden, Les Commerce 202-377-0556
Solar Equipment, Biomass....Garden, Les Commerce 202-377-0556
Solar Physics....Stuart Jordan NASA 301-286-8811
Solar Physics....J. Davis NASA 205-544-7600
Solar Radiation....Eugene Maier NASA 301-286-4425
Solar System Exploration....Staff NASA 415-694-5765
Solar System Exploration Projects & Technology Dev....Joel Sperams NASA 415-694-5706
Solar Terrestrial Studies....Daniel Baker NASA 301-286-8112
Solar energy....Foreso, Cynthia USITC 202-252-1348
Solid Earth Geophysics....D. Smith NASA 301-286-8555
Solid Waste Disposal....Staff OD/ORS 301-496-3537
Solid Waste Disposal (Radioactive)....Staff OD/ORS 301-496-2254
Solid-State Laser Development....Charles Byvik NASA 804-865-3761
Solomon Islands....Brian Richmond Peace Corps 202-254-3231
Solomon Islands (Honiara)....Stanley R. Ifshin Cnty State 202-647-3546
Solomon Islands (Honiara)....Carly M. Courtney Cnty AID 202-647-3546
Solomon Islands (Honiara)....Michael Feldstein Cnty AID 202-647-9137
Solomon Islands/Minerals....Travis Lyday Cnty Mines 202-634-1272
Somalia....James Robb Cnty Commerce 202-377-4564
Somalia (Mogadishu)....Frank G. Light Cnty State 202-647-5684
Somalia (Mogadishu)....Christopher Murray Cnty AID 202-647-4030
Somalia (Mogadishu)....Deborah Mendelson Cnty AID 202-647-8145
Somalia/Minerals....Lloyd Antonides Cnty Mines 202-632-5065
Sorbitol....Randall, Rob USITC 202-252-1366
Sorption modeling....Steve C. McCutcheon EPA 404-546-3301
Sorting machines....Greene, William USITC 202-252-1405
Sound signaling apparatus....Taylor, Kayla USITC 202-252-1390

Source methods....Rodney Midgett EPA 919-541-2196
Source methods....Joe Knoll EPA 919-541-2952
South Africa....Davis Coale/Emily Solomon Cnty Commerce 202-377-5148
South Africa, Republic of (Pretoria)....Mark Bellamy Cnty State 202-647-8433
South Africa/Minerals....George Morgan Cnty Mines 202-632-5065
South African Republic (Pretoria)....Robert Kott Cnty AID 202-647-3274
South African Republic (Pretoria)....Jonathan Conly Cnty AID 202-647-4230
South Pacific Commission....Stanley R. Ifshin Cnty State 202-647-8433
South Pacific Commission....Robert A. Benziger Cnty AID 202-647-3546
Soviet Studies/Minerals....Vasilii Strishkov Cnty Mines 202-632-5060
Soy Oil Futures With Options....Peter Christensen Comm Futures 312-353-9027
Soy Products....Janis, William V. Commerce 202-377-2250
Soybeans Futures With Options....Peter Christensen Comm Futures 312-353-9027
Soybeans and soybean oil....Reeder, John USITC 202-252-1319
Soybeans, Economics....Hoskin, Roger Agri 202-786-1840
Soybeans, Economics....Schaub, Jim Agri 202-786-1840
Soybeans, Statistics....Hayes, Craig Agri 202-447-9526
Soybeans, World, Economics....Bickerton, Tom Agri 202-786-1693
Soymeal Futures With Options....Peter Christensen Comm Futures 312-353-9027
Space Biology....Emily Holton NASA 415-694-5471
Space Biomedical Research Institute....John Chalres NASA 713-483-7224
Space Commercialization, Equipment....Bowie, David C. Commerce 202-377-8228
Space Commercialization, Services....Crupe, Friedrich R. Commerce 202-377-4781
Space Communications Components....Denis Connolly NASA 216-433-3503
Space Communications Systems Analysis....Edward Miller NASA 216-433-3479
Space Data and Computing Division....Jaylee Mead NASA 301-286-8543
Space Environmental Effecs on Materials....R. Gause NASA 205-544-2508
Space Environmental Interactions....Carolyn Purvis NASA 216-433-2307
Space Human Factors (Space Sciences)....Everett Palmer NASA 415-694-6073
Space Life Support Development....Hatice Cullingford NASA 713-483-8402
Space Mission Models....Thomas Miller NASA 216-433-2867
Space Phsiology....Alan Hargens NASA 415-694-5746
Space Policy Development....Grafeld, George Commerce 202-377-9228
Space Policy Development, Services....Crupe, Frriedrich R. Commerce 202-377-4781
Space Power Mangaement and Distribution Technology....Robert Bercaw NASA 216-433-6112
Space Radiation....Adrei Konradi NASA 713-483-5059
Space Services....Crupe, Friedrich R. Commerce 202-377-4781
Space Shuttle Systems....P. Hoag NASA 205-544-2361
Space Station....Ray Hook NASA 804-865-4469
Space Station Workstations....M. Boyd NASA 205-544-2472
Space Systems Technology....Bernard Garrett NASA 804-865-3667
Space Technology Experiments....Kenneth Sutton NASA 804-856-3031
Space, Commercialization of (Market)....Bowie, David Commerce 202-377-8228
Space, Commercialization of, Services....Crupe, Friedrich R. Commerce 202-377-4781
Spacecraft....Anderson, Peder USITC 202-252-1388
Spacecraft Structural Dynamics, Advanced Flexible....Brantley Hanks NASA 804-865-3054
Spain....Christine Sloop Cnty Commerce 202-377-4508
Spain (Madrid)....Mary Daly Cnty State 202-647-1412
Spain (Madrid)....Mary Daly Cnty State 202-647-1412
Spain (Madrid)....James Swigert Cnty State 202-647-1412
Spain (Madrid)....J. Michael Lekson Cnty AID 202-647-1726
Spain (Madrid)....Christine Adamczyk Cnty AID 202-647-9114
Spain/Minerals....John Panulas Cnty Mines 202-634-1277
Spasmodic Dysphonia....Staff NINCDS 301-496-5751
Spasmodic Torticollis....Staff NINCDS 301-496-5751
Spastic Hemiplegia....Staff NINCDS 301-496-5751
Spastic Paraplegia....Staff NINCDS 301-496-5751
Spastic Quadriplegia....Staff NINCDS 301-496-5751
Spasticity....Staff NINCDS 301-496-5751
Special Population Censuses....Hurn, George Census 301-763-7854

Special Purpose Vehicles....Desoucey, R. Customs 212-466-5667
Special Surveys....Dopkowski, Ronald Census 301-763-2380
Special classification provisions....Rodriguez, Laura USITC 202-252-1486
Spectacles....Johnson, Christopher USITC 202-252-1488
Speech....Staff NIDR 301-496-4261
Speech and Language Disorders....Staff NINCDS 301-496-5751
Speech and Language Disorders....Staff NICHD 301-496-5133
Speed Changers....Fletcher, William E. Commerce 202-377-0309
Speed changers....Fravel, Dennis USITC 202-252-1404
Sphingolipidoses....Staff NINCDS 301-496-5751
Sphingolipidoses Mucopolysaccaridoses & Stor. Dis.....Staff NINCDS 301-496-5751
Spices....Lipovsky, William USITC 202-252-1331
Spices....Conte, R. Customs 212-466-5759
Spielmeyer-Sjogren's Disease....Staff NINCDS 301-496-5751
Spina Bifida....Staff NINCDS 301-496-5751
Spinal Arachnoiditis....Staff NINCDS 301-496-5751
Spinal Cord Lesions....Staff NINCDS 301-496-5751
Spinal Cord Tumors....Staff NINCDS 301-496-5751
Spinal Muscular Atrophy....Staff NINCDS 301-496-5751
Spinning machines....Greene, William USITC 202-252-1405
Spinocerebellar Degeneration....Staff NINCDS 301-496-5751
Split Channel Operations....Staff FCC 202-653-5560
Sponge, articles of....Spalding, Josephine USITC 202-252-1498
Sponges, marine....Ludwick, David USITC 202-252-1329
Sporting Goods and Athletic....Ellis, Kevin Commerce 202-377-1140
Sporting Goods, Export Promo.....Cox, Thomas Commerce 202-377-5852
Sporting goods....Robinson, Hazel USITC 202-252-1496
Sports Blackouts....Staff FCC 202-632-7048
Sports Equipment....Tomenga, Y. Customs 212-466-5540
Sports Medicine....Staff NIAMS 301-496-8188
Spraying machinery: agricultural/horticultural....Lippa, Alison USITC 202-252-1398
Spraying machinery: other....Slingerland, David USITC 202-252-1400
Squamous Cell....Staff NCI 301-496-5583
Sri Lanka....Sean Gallagher Cnty Commerce 202-377-2954
Sri Lanka....Catherine Bachy Peace Corps 202-254-3118
Sri Lanka (Ceylon) (Colombo)....Donald Camp Cnty AID 202-647-2351
Sri Lanka (Ceylon) (Colombo)....Carol Scherrer-Palma Cnty AID 202-647-3261
Sri Lanka (Colombo)....James Joseph Barnes Cnty State 202-647-2351
Sri Lanka/Minerals....David Doan Cnty Mines 202-634-1272
St. Bartholomey....Mack Tadeu Cnty Commerce 202-377-2527
St. Kitts-Nevis....Avon Williams Cnty State 202-647-2621
St. Kitts-Nevis....Robert Dormitzer Cnty Commerce 202-377-2527
St. Lucia....Robert Dortmizer Cnty Commerce 202-377-2527
St. Lucia (Castries)....Vonda Delawie Cnty State 202-647-2621
St. Maarten....Mack Tadeu Cnty Commerce 202-377-2527
St. Vincent Grenadines....Robert Dormitzer Cnty Commerce 202-377-2527
St. Vincent and The Grenadines (Kingstown)....Vonda Delawie Cnty State 202-647-2621
Stained Teeth (Tetracycline)....Staff NIDR 301-496-4261
Stains....Johnson, Larry USITC 202-252-1351
Stall/Spin....H. Paul Stough NASA 804-865-3274
Standard & Poor 500 Index....Robert Fedinets Comm Futures 312-353-9016
Standardization and certification...James Lichtenberg EPA 513-569-7306
Standards and Calibration....Bruce Guenther NASA 301-286-5205
Staphylococcal Infections....Staff NIAID 301-496-5717
Staple, manmade....Butler, R Larry USITC 202-252-1470
Starches....Pierre-Benoist, John USITC 202-252-1320
Starches, chemically treated....Randall, Rob USITC 202-252-1366
Stars, Climate Studies....Richard Sothers NASA 212-678-5605
State & Federal Access Requests, Cigarettes....Betty Worthy Fed Trade Com 202-326-2459
State Governments, Economics....Long, Richard Agri 202-786-1544
State Statistical Programs....Herbert Koppel Justice Stat 202-724-7770
Stationary sources....Kenneth T. Knapp EPA 919-541-3085
Statistical Areas....Staff Census 301-763-3827
Statistical Methods Division....Waite, Preston Jay Census 301-763-2672
Statistical Support Division....Thompson, John Census 301-763-2672
Statistics (Blindness and Visual Disorders)....Staff NEI 301-496-5248
Statistics (Health)....Staff NCHS 301-496-8500
Statistics (Health)....Staff CDC 404-329-3534
Statistics and design....Dave Holland EPA 919-541-3126

Staurolite....Taylor, Harold A. Mines 202-634-1180
Stearic acid....Randall, rob USITC 202-252-1366
Stearic acid esters....Randall, Rob USITC 202-252-1366
Steatite....White, Linda USITC 202-252-1427
Steel....Peters, Anthony Mines 202-634-1022
Steel....Ilardi, P. Customs 212-466-5476
Steel Industry....Thompson, Ralph F. Commerce 202-377-0606
Steel Industry Products....Bell, Charles Commerce 202-377-0608
Steel Markets....Bell, Charles Commerce 202-377-0608
Steel Scrap....Brown, Raymond E. Mines 202-634-1752
Steel Slag....Owens, Judith Mines 202-634-1024
Steel: Ingots, blooms, and billets....Paulson, Mark USITC 202-252-1432
Steel: angles, shapes, and sections....Paulson, Mark USITC 202-252-1432
Steel: bars....Fulcher, Nancy USITC 202-252-1434
Steel: pipe and tube and fittings....Gannon, Norbert USITC 202-252-1430
Steel: plate....Avery, Peter USITC 202-252-1429
Steel: rails....Gannon, Norbert USITC 202-252-1430
Steel: sheet....Avery, Peter USITC 202-252-1429
Steel: strip....Avery, Peter USITC 202-252-1429
Steel: tubes....Laney-Cummings, Karen USITC 202-252-1431
Steel: waste and scrap....Boszormenyi, Laszio USITC 202-252-1437
Steel: wire....Vacant USITC 202-252-1442
Steel: wire rods....Vacant USITC 202-252-1442
Steel: pipes....Laney-Cummings, Karen USITC 202-252-1431
Steele-Richardson Disease....Staff NINCDS 301-496-5751
Stereo apparatus....Baker, Scott USITC 202-252-1386
Sterilization....Staff NICHD 301-496-5133
Steroid Contraceptives....Staff NICHD 301-496-5133
Steroid Hypertension....Staff NHLBI 301-496-4236
Stiff Man Syndrome....Staff NINCDS 301-496-5751
Still's Disease....Staff NIAMS 301-496-8188
Stirling Dynamic Power Systems....Donald Beremand NASA 216-433-6110
Stock Index Futures....Tiffany Hott Comm Futures 212-668-2079
Stomach Cancer....Staff NCI 301-496-5583
Stomatitis....Staff NIDR 301-496-4261
Stone....Bunin, J. Customs 212-466-5796
Stone and products....White, Linda USITC 202-252-1427
Stone, Crushed....Tepordei, Valentin V. Mines 202-634-1185
Stone, Dimension....Taylor, Harold A. Mines 202-634-1180
Stone-processing machines....Greene, William USITC 202-252-1405
Stoneware articles....McNay, Deborah USITC 202-252-1425
Stoneworking machines....Fravel, Dennis USITC 202-252-1404
Stoves....Fitzgerald, J. Customs 212-466-5492
Strabismus....Staff NEI 301-496-5248
Stranger-to-Stranger Crime....Michael Rand Justice Stat 202-724-7774
Stranger-to-Stranger Crime....Anita Timrots Justice Stat 202-724-7774
Stratosphere Chemistry and Dynamics....Robert Hudson NASA 301-286-5485
Stratospheric Aerosol and Gas Experiment (SAGE)....Leonard McMaster NASA 804-865-2065
Stratospheric ozone depletion....William J. Rhodes EPA 919-541-2853
Streptococcal Infections....Staff NIAID 301-496-5717
Streptokinase....Staff NHLBI 301-496-4236
Stress....Staff NIMH 301-496-4513
Stress....Staff NCNR 301-496-0526
Stress (EKG)....Staff NHLBI 301-496-4236
Stress and Aging....Staff NIA 301-496-1752
Stress physiology....Richard D. Phillips EPA 919-541-2772
Stroke....Staff NINCDS 301-496-5751
Stroke (Hypertension)....Staff NHLBI 301-496-4236
Strontium....Wagner, Lorie USITC 202-252-1439
Strontium....Ober, Joyce A. Mines 202-634-1177
Strontium compounds....Greenblatt, Jack USITC 202-252-1353
Strontium pigments....Johnson, Larry USITC 202-252-1351
Structual Analysis and Life Prediction....John Shannon NASA 216-433-3211
Structural Assessment....C. J. Blanca NASA 205-544-7182
Structural Design....P. I. Rodriguez NASA 205-544-7006
Structural Dynamics....Mike Kehoe NASA 805-258-3708
Structural Dynamics....James Kiraly NASA 216-433-6023
Structural Dynamics....W. Holland NASA 205-544-1495
Structural Integrity....John Gyekenyesi NASA 216-433-3210
Structural and Dynamic Testing....N. Fama NASA 205-544-1103
Structure activity....GIlman D. Veith EPA 218-720-5550
Structure-activity relationships (biological)....Susan A. Moore EPA 404-546-3469
Structure-activity relationships (chemical)....Samuel W. Karickhoff EPA 404-546-3149
Structures and Mechanics....Royce Forman NASA 713-483-8926

Structures of base metals....Brandon, James USITC 202-252-1433

Studio Transmitter Links, Common Carrier....Staff FCC
202-634-1706

Studio Transmitter Links, Mass Media....Staff FCC 202-634-6307

Sturge-Weber Syndrome....Staff NINCDS 301-496-5751

Stuttering....Staff NINCDS 301-496-5751

Sty....Staff NEI 301-496-5248

Styrene (monomer)....Matusik, Ed USITC 202-252-1356

Styrene resins....Taylor, Ed USITC 202-252-1362

Subacute Necrotizing Encephalomyelopathy (Leighs')....Staff
NINCDS 301-496-5751

Subacute Sclerosing Panencephalitis....Staff NINCDS
301-496-5751

Subarachnoid Hemorrhage....Staff NINCDS 301-496-5751

Submarine Cable....Staff FCC 202-632-7265

Subscription Televison....Staff FCC 202-632-6357

Subsonic Aerodynamics (Fluid Physics)....Joseph Stickle NASA
804-865-2037

Subsurface abiotic processes....Dermont Bouchard EPA
405-332-2321

Subsurface abiotic processes....Candida West EPA 405-332-2257

Subsurface abiotic processes....Lynn Wood EPA 405-332-2420

Subsurface biorestoration....John Wilson EPA 405-332-2259

Subsurface biotransformations....Steve Hutchins EPA
405-332-2327

Subsurface biotransformations....Guy Sewell EPA 405-332-2232

Sudan....James Robb Cnty Commerce 202-377-4564

Sudan...Djodi Deutsch Peace Corps 202-254-8397

Sudan (Khartoum)...Russell Trowbridge Cnty State 202-647-5684

Sudan (Khartoum)....Eric Madison Cnty AID 202-647-7645

Sudan (Khartoum)....Mary-Rita Zeleke Cnty AID 202-647-3447

Sudan/Minerals....Lloyd Antonides Cnty Mines 202-632-5065

Sudanophilic Leukodystrophy....Staff NINCDS 301-496-5751

Sudden Cardiac Death....Staff NHLBI 301-496-4236

Sudden Infant Death Syndrome....Staff NICHD 301-496-5133

Sugar....James, Antoinette USITC 202-252-1313

Sugar....Maria, J. Customs 212-466-5730

Sugar No. 11 Futures...Anita Schwartz Comm Futures
212-668-2075

Sugar No. 14 Futures...Anita Schwartz Comm Futures
212-668-2075

Sugar, Economics....Barry, Robert Agri 202-786-1769

Sugar, Economics....Angelo, Luigi Agri 202-786-1769

Sugar, Economics....Harvey, David Agri 202-786-1769

Sugar, Statistics....Ransom, Darwin Agri 202-447-7621

Suger Products....Ives III, Ralph F. Commerce 202-377-5124

Suicide....Staff NIMH 301-443-4513

Suits and Life Support (Space Sciences)....Bruce Webbon NASA
415-694-5385

Sulfur....Trainor, Cynthia USITC 202-252-1354

Sulfur....Morse, David E. Mines 202-634-1190

Sulfur dioxide....Greenblatt, Jack USITC 202-252-1353

Sulfuric acid...Trainor, Cynthia USITC 202-252-1354

Sunlight and Skin Cancer....Staff NCI 301-496-5583

Sunshine Act, Cigarettes....Maryanne Kane Fed Trade Com
202-326-2450

Sunspot Cycle....Staff FCC 202-653-8166

Superconductors....Chiarado, Roger Commerce 202-377-0402

Superconductors, Electronics....Marcus, Phil Commerce
202-377-1330

Superfund & solid waste....Christopher DeRosa EPA 513-569-7534

Superfund engineering technology....Ronald Hill EPA
513-569-7861

Supermarket-Related Matters...Joan Greenbaum Fed Trade Com
202-326-2629

Superphosphates....Trainor, Cynthia USITC 202-252-1354

Supp Data System, Workers Comp Statistics....Anderson, John
Labor 202-272-3463

Supplies (Central Storeroom)....Staff OD/DAS 301-496-9156

Surcharges....Staff Fed Trade Com 202-326-3175

Surface impoundments & stabilization....Carlton Wiles EPA
513-569-7795

Surface microlayers....K.T. Perez EPA 401-782-3000

Surface-Active Agents....Joseph, S. Customs 212-466-5768

Surface-active agents....Land, Eric USITC 202-252-1349

Surgery (Cancer)....Staff NCI 301-496-5583

Surgery (Oral)....Staff NIDR 301-496-4261

Surgical Treatment of Heart Disease....Staff NHLBI 301-496-4236

Surgical apparatus....Johnson, Christopher USITC 202-252-1488

Suriname....Robert Dormitzer Cnty Commerce 202-377-2527

Suriname (Paramaribo)...John Schlosser Cnty State 202-647-4195

Suriname (Paramaribo)...Jim McHugh Cnty AID 202-647-6386

Suriname/Minerals....Alfredo Gurmendi Cnty Mines 202-632-9352

Surinmae (Paramaribo)....Edward Campbell Cnty AID
202-647-3447

Survey of Income and Program Participation....Kaspryzk, Daniel
Census 301-763-5784

Suspended solids....Philip M. Cook EPA 218-720-5553

Sutures, surgical....Randall, Rob USITC 202-252-1366

Swaziland....Fred Stokelin Cnty Commerce 202-377-5148

Swaziland....Carrie Wiltshire Peace Corps 202-254-6046

Swaziland (Mbabane)...June Perry Cnty State 202-647-8434

Swaziland (Mbabane)....Nancy J. Newman Cnty AID 202-647-4287

Swaziland (Mbabane)....Kenneth Kolb Cnty AID 202-647-8439

Swaziland/Minerals....Hendrik van Oss Cnty Mines 202-632-5065

Sweat Gland Disorders....Staff NIAMS 301-496-8188

Sweaters: mens and boys....Shetty, Sundar USITC 202-252-1457

Sweaters: womens and girls....MacKnight, Peggy USITC
202-252-1468

Sweden....James Devlin Cnty Commerce 202-377-4414

Sweden (Stockholm)....George Boutin Cnty State 202-647-5669

Sweden (Stockholm)....Richard A. Christenson Cnty AID
202-647-4484

Sweden/Minerals....Harold Newman Cnty Mines 202-634-1276

Sweepstakes, Marketing Practices....Staff Fed Trade Com
202-326-3128

Sweepstakes-Food Stores & Gas Stations....John Mendenhall Fed
Trade Com 216-942-4210

Sweeteners, Economics....Barry, Robert Agri 202-786-1769

Sweeteners, Economics....Angelo, Luigi Agri 202-786-1769

Sweeteners, Economics....Harvey, David Agri 202-786-1769

Sweeteners, Statistics....Ransom, Darwin Agri 202-447-7621

Swimwear....Shea, G. Customs 212-466-5878

Swimwear: mens and boys....Shetty, Sundar USITC 202-252-1457

Swimwear: womens and girls....MacKnight, Peggy USITC
202-252-1468

Swine Flu....Staff NIAID 301-496-5717

Switchboard Apparatus....Whitley, Richard A. Commerce
202-377-0682

Switchgear....Hayes, Albert USITC 202-252-1391

Switzerland....Philip Combs Cnty Commerce 202-377-2920

Switzerland (Bern)....William Millan Cnty State 202-647-1484

Switzerland (Bern)....John L. Nesrig Cnty AID 202-647-2005

Switzerland/Minerals....George Rabchevsky Cnty Mines
202-632-5053

Sydenham's Chorea....Staff NINCDS 301-496-5751

Syncope (Fainting)....Staff NHLBI 301-496-4236

Synovitis....Staff NIAMS 301-496-8188

Synthetic Resin & Rubber....Joseph, S. Customs 212-466-5768

Synthetic detergents....Land, Eric USITC 202-252-1349

Synthetic iron oxides and hydroxides....Johnson, Larry USITC
202-252-1349

Synthetic natural gas (SNG)....Land, Eric USITC 202-252-1349

Synthetic rubber....Taylor, Ed USITC 202-252-1362

Syphilis....Staff NINCDS 301-496-5717

Syria....Thomas Sams Cnty Commerce 202-377-5767

Syria/Minerals....Bernadette Michalski Cnty Mines
202-632-5065

Syrian Arab Republic (Damascus)....William Jordan Cnty State
202-647-1131

Syrian Arab Republic (Damascus)....Jeff Irwin Cnty State
202-647-1058

Syrian Arab Republic (Damascus)....William Burns Cnty AID
202-647-4714

Syrian Arab Republic (Damascus)....Jay Burns Cnty AID
202-647-2481

Syringomyelia....Staff NINCDS 301-496-5751

System Identification/Adaptie Control of Large Fle....Claude
Keckler NASA 804-865-4591

Systemic Lupus Erythematosus....Staff NIAMS 301-496-8188

Systems Development and Simulation....James Lawrence NASA
713-483-1553

Systems Division...J. Redus NASA 205-544-7106

Systems ecology....Mostafa A. Shirazi EPA 503-753-4666

Systems engineering...John M. Moore EPA 702-798-2304

Systolic Hypertension in the Elderly (SHEP)....Staff NHLBI
301-496-4236

Systolic Hypertension in the Elderly (SHEP)....Staff NIA
301-496-1752

T

T-Bills Futures With Options....David Rosenfeld Comm Futures
312-353-9026

T-Bonds Futures With Options....Nancy L. Redheffer Comm
Futures 312-353-9015

T-Cell (Specialized Centers of Research)....Staff NIAID
301-496-5717

T-Notes (5 yr.) Futures....Penny Sympson Comm Futures
312-353-9015

T-Notes (5-10 yr.) Futures With Options....Penny Sympson Comm
Futures 312-353-9015

TELEX, International & Domestic....Staff FCC 202-632-7265

TIGER System Products....Piepenburg, Sheldon   Census
301-763-1580

TSH, Excessive Secretion....Staff   NIDDK   301-496-3583

Tablecloths....Borsari, Marilyn   USITC   202-252-1465

Tachycardia....Staff   NHLBI   301-496-4236

Taiwan....Dan Duvall/Jeff Hardee   Cnty Commerce   202-377-4957

Taiwan Coordination....Daniel Kiang   Cnty State   202-647-7711

Taiwan Coordination....Mark S .Pratt   Cnty AID   202-647-7711

Taiwan Coordination....Bruce Gray   Cnty AID   202-647-7711

Taiwan Coordination....Peter Vaden   Cnty AID   202-647-7711

Taiwan/Minerals....Edmond Chin   Cnty Mines   202-634-1272

Talc....White, Linda   USITC   202-252-1427

Talc....Virta, Robert   Mines   202-634-1206

Tall oil....Randall, Rob   USITC   202-252-1366

Tangier Disease....Staff   NHLBI   301-496-4236

Tangier Disease....Staff   NINCDS   301-496-5751

Tanks....O'Connell, W.   Customs   212-466-5668

Tanning products and agents....Wanser, Stephen   USITC
202-252-1363

Tantalum....DeSapio, Vincent   USITC   202-252-1435

Tantalum....Cunningham, Larry D.   Mines   202-634-1029

Tanzania...James Robb   Cnty Commerce   202-377-4564

Tanzania....Bill Ferguson   Peace Corps   202-254-5634

Tanzania/Minerals....Lloyd Antonides   Cnty Mines   202-632-5065

Tape Players....Dicerbo, M.   Customs   212-466-5672

Tape Players....Dicerbo, M.   Customs   212-466-5672

Tape players and combinations....Sherman, Thomas   USITC
202-252-1389

Tape recordings....Bishop, Kathryn   USITC   202-252-1494

Tapestries....Borsari, Marilyn   USITC   202-252-1465

Tapestries....Eyskens, R.   Customs   212-466-5854

Taping of Telephone Calls....Staff   FCC   202-632-6990

Taps....Mata, Ruben   USITC   202-252-1403

Tar sands oil....Foreso, Cynthia   USITC   202-252-1348

Tar, Nicotine & Carbon Monoxide Test, Cigarettes....Staff   Fed
Trade Com   202-326-3150

Tardive Dyskinesia....Staff   NIMH   301-443-4515

Tarsal Tunnel Syndrome....Staff   NINCDS   301-496-5751

Taste....Staff   NIDR   301-496-4261

Taste and Smell Dysfunction....Staff   NINCDS   301-496-5751

Taxes, Economics....Durst, Ronald   Agri   202-786-1889

Tay-Sach's Disease....Staff   NINCDS   301-496-5751

Tea....Lipovsky, William   USITC   202-252-1331

Tea....Janis, William V.   Commerce   202-377-2250

Tea....Conte, R.   Customs   212-466-5759

Tea, Economics....Gray, Fred   Agri   202-686-1769

Technological Developments and Nursing Care....Staff   NCNR
301-496-0526

Technology....Lester Shubin   Justice   202-272-6007

Technology....Joseph Kochanski   Justice   202-724-2962

Technology Affairs....Shykind, Edwin B.   Commerce   202-377-4694

Technology Assessment Program....Lester Shubin   Justice
202-272-6007

Technology transfer....Nelson A. Thomas   EPA   218-720-5702

Teenage Pregnancy....Staff   NICHD   301-496-5133

Teenage Victims....Catherine Whitaker   Justice Stat   202-724-7755

Teeth....Staff   NIDR   301-496-4261

Telangiectasis (Rendu-Osler-Weber Dis., Syndrome)....Staff
NHLBI   301-496-4236

Telecommunication Devices for the Deaf....Staff   FCC
202-632-6999

Telecommunications....Stechschulte, Roger   Commerce
202-377-4466

Telecommunications....Jim Hart   NASA   415-694-6251

Telecommunications (Network Eqpt)....Henry, John   Commerce
202-377-4466

Telecommunications (TV Broadcast)....Paddock, Richard
Commerce   202-377-4466

Telecommunications Services, Value Added....Atkins, Robert G.
Commerce   202-377-4781

Telecommunications, CPE....Henry, John   Commerce   202-377-4466

Telecommunications, Cellular....Gossack, Linda   Commerce
202-377-4466

Telecommunications, Fiber Optics....McCarthy, James   Commerce
202-377-4466

Telecommunications, Major Projects....Coady, Christine
Commerce   202-377-4466

Telecommunications, Network Equipment....Kellagher, Joseph
Commerce   202-377-4466

Telecommunications, Radio....Liebenow, Jay   Commerce
202-377-4466

Telecommunications, Satellites....Shea, Timothy   Commerce
202-377-4466

Telecommunications, Services....Atkins, Robert G.   Commerce
202-377-4781

Telecommunications, Services....Shetrin, Ivan   Commerce
202-377-4466

Telecommunications, Trade Promo.....Rettig, Theresa E.
Commerce   202-377-4466

Telegraph & Telephone Rates....Staff   FCC   202-632-5550

Telegraph Service....Staff   FCC   202-632-7876

Telegraph and telephone apparatus....Taylor, Kayla   USITC
202-252-1390

Teleoperations....Charles Price   NASA   713-483-1532

Teleopertor/Robotics System Technology...Al Meintel   NASA
804-865-2489

Telephone....Dicerbo, M.   Customs   212-466-5672

Telephone Equipment Interconnection....Staff   FCC   202-634-1800

Telephone Lines....Staff   FCC   202-632-1800

Telephone Marketing....Ruth Fitzpatrick   Fed Trade Com
202-326-3277

Telephone Telegraph Rates....Staff   FCC   202-632-5550

Teleprinter (Telephone, Telegraph)....Staff   FCc   202-634-1800

Telescopes...Johnson, Christopher   USITC   202-252-1488

Teletext Services...Inoussa, Mary   Commerce   202-377-5820

Television Advertising....Staff   FCC   202-632-7551

Television Advertising Intercity Relays....Staff   FCC   202-634-6307

Television Political Broadcasting Fairness....Staff   FCC
202-632-7586

Television Programming....Staff   FCC   202-632-7048

Television Religious Petition....Staff   FCC   202-632-7000

Television Remote Pickups....Staff   FCC   202-634-6307

Television Stations--New....Staff   FCc   202-632-6495

Television Translators....Staff   FCC   202-632-3894

Television equipment....Kitzmiller, John   USITC   202-252-1387

Television programming....Staff   FCC   202-632-7551

Televisions....Dicerbo, M.   Customs   212-466-5672

Tellurium....Edelstein, Daniel   Mines   202-634-1053

Tellurium compounds....Greenblatt, Jack   USITC   202-252-1353

Temporal Arteritis (Eyes)....Staff   NEI   301-496-5248

Temporomandibular Joint Disorders....Staff   NIDR   301-496-4261

Tendonitis....Staff   NIAMS   301-496-8188

Tennis equipment....Robinson, Hazel   USITC   202-252-1496

Tents and tarpaulins....Cook, Lee   USITC   202-252-1471

Terrestrial ecology....Raymond G. Wilhour   EPA   904-932-5311

Terrestrial exposure....David S. Brown   EPA   404-546-3310

Test Division....R. C. Shaw   NASA   205-544-1244

Test Tube Babies....Staff   NICHD   301-496-5133

Testicular Cancer....Staff   NCI   301-496-5583

Tetanus....Staff   NIAID   301-496-5717

Tetraethyl lead....Michels, David   USITC   202-252-1352

Tetralogy of Fallot....Staff   NHLBI   301-496-4236

Tetramer of propylene....Raftery, Jim   USITC   202-252-1365

Tetramethyl lead....Michels, David   USITC   202-252-1352

Tetrapropylene....Raftery, Jim   USITC   202-252-1365

Textile Machinery....Holley, Tyrena   Commerce   202-377-3509

Textile Registration Numbers, Enforcement....Staff   Fed Trade
Com   202-326-3175

Textile Regulations....Steve Ecklund   Fed Trade Com
202-326-3034

Textile calendering and rolling machines....Greene, William
USITC   202-252-1405

Textile finishing agents....Land, Eric   USITC   202-252-1349

Textile machines....Greene, William   USITC   202-252-1405

Textile washing, bleaching, dyeing, machines....Green, William
USITC   202-252-1405

Textile, Wool, & Fur Labeling....Bret Smart   Fed Trade Com
213-209-7890

Textiles....Dulka, William A.   Commerce   202-377-4058

Thailand....Donald Ryan/Linda Droker   Cnty Commerce
202-377-3875

Thailand (Bangkok)...Rebecca Van Doren-Shulkin   Cnty State
202-647-7108

Thailand (Bangkok)...Nancy Boshoven   Cnty State   202-647-7108

Thailand (Bangkok)...Janet Malkemes   Cnty AID   202-647-7474

Thailand (Bangkok)...Nick Mauger   Cnty AID   202-647-7474

Thailand (Bangkok)...Karl Schwartz   Cnty AID   202-647-9240

Thailand/Minerals....David Doan   Cnty Mines   202-634-1272

Thalassemia....Staff   NHLBI   301-496-4236

Thalassemia....Staff   NIDDK   301-496-3583

Thallium....Llewellyn, Thomas   Mines   202-634-1084

Thallium compounds....Greenblatt, Jack   USITC   202-252-1353

The Gambia....R. J. Benn   Peace Corps   202-254-3185

Theoretical Astrophysics....Pat Cassen   NASA   415-694-5547

Theoretical Dynamics and Control Applied Control...Jarrell
Elliott   NASA   804-865-3291

Theoretical and Experimental Aerodynamics Aerolast....John
Edwards   NASA   804-865-4236

Theoretical chemistry....Jeno P. Bercz   EPA   513-569-7480

Theories of Aging....Staff   NIA   301-496-1752

Thermal Analysis: Solid Rocket Motor....K. McCoy   NASA
205-544-7211

Thermal Analysis:Liquid Propulsion Systems....J. Owen   NASA
205-544-7213

Thermal Management for Space Power Conversion Syst....Marvin

Experts

Warshay NASA 216-433-6126

Thermal Measurements....S. Franklin Edwards NASA 804-865-2466

Thermal Protection Systems for Sapce Transportatio....Donald Rummler NASA 804-865-2422

Thermal Protection Systems for Space Trasnprotatio....Martin Mikulas NASA 804-865-2551

Thermal Wave and Diffusion Analysis....William Winfree NASA 804-865-4928

Thermal destruction & combustion....George Huffman EPA 513-569-7881

Thermal destruction & industrial wastewater....Clyde Dempsey EPA 513-569-7504

Thermal destruction of hazardous materials....Donald Oberacker EPA 513-569-7431

Thermal/Environmental Computational Analysis....J. Sims NASA 205-544-7212

Thorium....DeSapio, Vincent USITC 202-252-1435

Thorium....Hedrick, James B. Mines 202-634-1058

Thorium compounds....Greenblatt, Jack USITC 202-252-1353

Thread: cotton....Enfield, Mary E USITC 202-252-1455

Thread: manmade fibers....Butler, R Larry USITC 202-252-1470

Thread: silk....Freund, Kimberlie USITC 202-252-1456

Three-Dimensional Computer Graphics (Aerophysics)....Arsi Vaziri NASA 415-694-4799

Thrombasthenia....Staff NIDDK 301-496-3583

Thrombocytopenia....Staff NIDDK 301-496-3583

Thromboembolism....Staff NHLBI 301-496-4236

Thrombolysis....Staff NHLBI 301-496-4236

Thrombophlebitis....Staff NHLBI 301-496-4236

Thrombosis....Staff NHLBI 301-496-4236

Thyroid (Adenoma of)....Staff NIDDK 301-496-3583

Thyroiditis....Staff NIDDK 301-496-3583

Thyroma....Staff NCI 301-496-5583

Thyrotoxic Periodic Paralysis....Staff NINCDS 301-496-5751

Thyroxine-iodine....Staff NIDDK 301-496-3583

Tic Douloureux (Trigeminal Neuralgia)....Staff NINCDS 301-496-5751

Ticket-issuing machines....Fletcher, William USITC 202-252-1407

Ticks....Staff NIAID 301-496-5717

Tie-line--Telegraph Telephone....Staff FCC 202-632-5550

Ties....Persky, H. Customs 212-466-5881

Tiles, ceramic....Lukes, James USITC 202-252-1426

Timber Products, Tropical....Shaw, Clinton R. Commerce 202-377-5124

Time Served in Prison....Allen Beck Justice Stat 202-724-7755

Time Served in Prison....Christopher Innes Justice Stat 202-724-6100

Time Served in Prison....Lawrence Greenfeld Justice Stat 202-724-7755

Time Served in Prison....Tom Hester Justice Stat 202-724-7755

Time Served in Prison - Federal....Carol Kaplan Justice Stat 202-724-7759

Time switches....Langer, Eric USITC 202-252-1497

Timesharing of Property, Marketing Practices....Staff Fed Trade Com 202-326-3128

Timing apparatus....Langer, Eric USITC 202-252-1497

Tin....DeSapio, Vincent USITC 202-252-1435

Tin....Carlin, Jr., James F. Mines 202-634-1073

Tin Products....Manager, Jon Commerce 202-377-5124

Tin compounds....Greenblatt, Jack USITC 202-252-1353

Tinnitus....Staff NINCDS 301-496-5751

Tires....Prat, Raimundo Commerce 202-377-0128

Tires....Rauch, T. Customs 212-466-5892

Tires and tubes, of rubber of plastics....Raftery, Jim USITC 202-252-1365

Tissue Culture Cells (Freezing and Storage)....Staff OD/ORS 301-496-2960

Tissue Culture Media....Staff OD/ORS 301-496-6017

Tissue Plasminogen Activator (TPA)....Staff NHLBI 301-496-4236

Tissue Typing....Staff NIAID 301-496-5717

Titanium....DeSapio, Vincent USITC 202-252-1435

Titanium....Lynd, Langtry E. Mines 202-634-1073

Titanium compounds....Greenblatt, Jack USITC 202-252-1353

Titanium dioxide....Johnson, Larry USITC 202-252-1351

Titanium pigments....Johnson, Larry USITC 202-252-1351

Tobacco....Conte, R. Customs 212-466-5759

Tobacco Products....Kenney, Cornelius Commerce 202-377-2428

Tobacco and tobacco products....Lipovsky, William USITC 202-252-1331

Tobacco machines....Jackson, Georgia USITC 202-252-1399

Tobacco pipes....Johnson, Christopher USITC 202-252-1488

Tobacco, Economics....Grise, Verner Agri 202-786-1768

Tobacco, Statistics....Ransom, Darwin Agri 202-447-7621

Togo....Reginald Biddle Cnty Commerce 202-377-4388

Togo....Theresa Queenan Peace Corps 202-254-7036

Togo (Lome)....Frederick Kaplan Cnty State 202-647-3391

Togo (Lome)....John A. Hodges Cnty AID 202-647-6980

Togo (Lome)....Mable Meares Cnty AID 202-647-6154

Togo/Minerals....Hendrik van Oss Cnty Mines 202-632-5065

Toilet preps, cosmetics, and perfumery....Land, Eric USITC 202-252-1349

Toilet soaps....Land, Eric USITC 202-252-1349

Tokelau....Ann M. Cambara Cnty State 202-647-3546

Toll Charges....Staff FCc 202-632-5550

Toluene....Raftery, Tim USITC 202-252-1365

Tomatoes....McCarty, Tim USITC 202-252-1324

Toners....Wanser, Stephen USITC 202-252-1363

Tonga....Carla Joyner Peace Corps 202-254-3227

Tonga (Nuku'alofa)....Ann M. Cambara Cnty State 202-647-3546

Tonga (Nuku'alofa)....Robert A. Benziger Cnty AID 202-647-3546

Tonga (Nuku'alofa)....Michael Feldstein Cnty AID 202-647-9137

Tonga/Minerals....Travis Lyday Cnty Mines 202-634-1272

Tongue....Staff NIDR 301-496-4261

Tools....Shulbertg, M. Customs 212-466-5487

Tools/Dies/Jigs/Fixtures....Mearman, J. Commerce 202-377-0315

Topper crude petroleum....Foreso, Cynthia USITC 202-252-1348

Torsion Dystonia (Dystonia Musculorum Deformans)....Staff NINCDS 301-496-5751

Tort Claims....Julia Oas Fed Trade Com 202-326-2483

Torticollis (Wryneck)....Staff NINCDS 301-496-5751

Tourette Syndrome....Staff NINCDS 301-496-5751

Tourette Syndrome....Staff NIMH 301-443-4515

Tourism Services....Sousane, J. Richard Commerce 202-377-4581

Tourism, Major Proj.....White, Barbara Commerce 202-377-4160

Tow, manmade....Butler, R Larry USITC 202-252-1470

Towels....Borsari, Marilyn USITC 202-252-1465

Towels....Eyskens, R. Customs 212-466-5854

Towers--Painting and Lighting of....Staff FCC 202-632-7521

Toxic Shock Syndrome....Staff NIMH 301-496-5717

Toxic Shock Syndrome....Staff NICHD 301-496-5133

Toxic Shock Syndrome....Staff CDC 401-639-3534

Toxic mechanisms....Steven J. Broderius EPA 218-720-5574

Toxic mechanisms....John A. Couch EPA 904-932-5311

Toxicity data bases....Gilman D. Veith EPA 218-720-5550

Toxicity reduction....Donald I. Mount EPA 218-720-5528

Toxicity testing....D.J. Hansen EPA 401-782-3000

Toxicity testing....S.C. Schimmel EPA 401-782-3000

Toxicity testing chemical/microbial pesticides....Richard L. Anderson EPA 218-720-5616

Toxicity testing-field response sediment criteria....Anthony R. Carlson EPA 218-720-5523

Toxicokinetics....Steven Bradbury EPA 218-720-5527

Toxicologic mechanisms....F. Bernard Daniel EPA 513-569-7411

Toxicology....Foster L. Mayer EPA 904-932-5311

Toxicology....James R. Clark EPA 904-932-5311

Toxicology....Geraldine Cripe EPA 904-932-5311

Toxicology....Leroy Folmar EPA 904-932-5311

Toxicology....Douglas P. Middaugh EPA 904-932-5311

Toxicology....Rodney Parrish EPA 904-932-5311

Toxicology Programs/Special. Information Services....Staff NLM 301-496-1131

Toxicology/Pharmacology....Staff NIEHS 919-541-3345

Toxicology/Pharmacology....Staff NIGMS 301-496-7707

Toxocariasis....Staff NEI 301-496-5248

Toxoplasmosis....Staff NIAID 301-496-5717

Toxoplasmosis....Staff NEI 301-496-5248

Toy Animals....McKenna, T. Customs 212-466-5854

Toys....Langer, Eric USITC 202-252-1497

Toys....Corea, Judy Commerce 202-377-0311

Toys....Wong, A. Customs 212-466-5538

Toys and Games (Export Promo)....Beckham, Reginald Commerce 202-377-5478

Toys for pets, christmas deco, figurines, etc.....Truskett, Brooks USITC 202-252-1364

Trace Metals (and CVD)....Staff NHLBI 301-496-4236

Trace level environmental contaminant analysis....Jimmie D. Petty EPA 702-798-2383

Traceability protocols....Darryl J. von Lehmden EPA 919-541-2415

Trachoma....Staff NEI 301-496-5248

Tracking and Communications....Kumar Krishen NASA 713-483--207

Tractors (except truck tractors)....Lippa, Alison USITC 202-252-1398

Trade Promo. Coordinator, CGIC....Morse, Jerome Commerce 202-377-5907

Trade Related Employment....Davis, Lester A. Commerce 202-377-4924

Traffic Safety....Marianne Zawitz Justice Stat 202-724-6100

Trailers and other vehicles not self-propelled....Murphy, Mary USITC 202-252-1401

Trailers, other vehicles not self-propelled....Murphy, Mary USITC 202-252-1401

Transborder Data Flows....Inoussa, Mary C. Commerce 202-377-5820

Transceivers....Kitzmiller, John   USITC   202-252-1387
Transformation (Cell)....Staff   NCI   301-496-5583
Transformation rate constants....William T. Donaldson   EPA
    404-546-3183
Transformers....Cutchin, John   USITC   202-252-1396
Transformers....Whitley, Richard A.   Commerce   202-377-0682
Transfusional Hemosiderosis....Staff   NHLBI   301-496-4236
Transient Ischemic Attacks....Staff   NINCDS   301-496-5751
Transmissions....Riedl, K.   Customs   212-466-5493
Transonic Aerodynamics (Fluid Dynamics)....Percy Bobitt   NASA
    804-865-2961
Transplantation (Cornea)....Staff   NEI   301-496-5248
Transplantation Immunology....Staff   NIAID   301-496-5717
Transplants (He, Valv, Lung, Blo, Vess, Vei, Ar)....Staff   NHLBI
    301-496-4236
Transplants (Liver, Pancreas, Kidney)....Staff   NIDDK
    301-496-3583
Transplants (Organ Procurement)....Staff   HRSA   301-443-7577
Transportation....Staff   OD/Motor Pool   301-496-3426
Transportation (Antitrust)...James Egan   Fed Trade Com
    202-326-2682
Transportation Ind....Alexander, Albert   Commerce   202-377-4581
Transportation Industries....Alexander, Albert   Commerce
    202-377-4581
Transportation Systems....Doug Price   NASA   804-865-4591
Transportation Systems....Delma Freeman   NASA   804-865-3912
Transportation, Commodity Transportation Survey....Crowther,
    Robert   Census   301-763-4364
Transportation, Economics....Hutchinson, T. Q.   Agri
    202-786-1840
Transportation, Truck Inventory....Crowther, Robert   Census
    301-763-4364
Transportation, Truck Use....Campbell, Carmen   Census
    301-763-1744
Transposition of the Great Vessels....Staff   NHLBI   301-496-4236
Transsexuality....Staff   NICHD   301-496-5133
Transverse Myelitis....Staff   NINCDS   301-496-5751
Trauma Research....Staff   NIGMS   301-496-7301
Trauma Research (Cent. Ner. Sys., Head, Spin. Cr.)....Staff
    NINCDS   301-496-5751
Travel & Tourism....Sousane, J. Richard   Commerce   202-377-4582
Travel Fraud, Marketing Practices....Staff   Fed Trade Com
    202-326-3128
Travel Surveys....Cannon, John   Census   301-763-5468
Travel goods....Seastrum, Carl   USITC   202-252-1493
Tremors....Staff   NINCDS   301-496-5751
Trench Mouth....Staff   NIDR   301-496-4261
Tribology....Stephen Pepper   NASA   216-433-6061
Trichinosis....Staff   NIAID   301-496-5717
Trichloroethylene....Michels, David   USITC   202-252-1352
Trichomoniasis....Staff   NIAID   301-496-5717
Tricks....Langer, Eric   USITC   202-252-1497
Tricuspid Valve....Staff   NHLBI   301-496-4236
Tricycles....Seastrum, Carl   USITC   202-252-1493
Trigeminal Neuralgia (Tic Douloureux)....Staff   NINCDS
    301-496-5751
Triglycerides....Staff   NHLBI   301-496-4236
Trimellitic acid esters....Johnson, Larry   USITC   202-252-1351
Trindad and Tobago (Port-of-Spain)....Nancy Lees   Cnty State
    202-647-2621
Trindad and Tobago (Port-of-Spain)....Michael Kirby   Cnty AID
    202-647-7385
Trinidad & Tobago....Robert Dormitzer   Cnty Commerce
    202-377-2527
Trinidad and Tobago/Minerals....Ivette Torres   Cnty Mines
    202-632-9352
Trinitrotoluene....Johnson, Larry   USITC   202-252-1351
Tripoli....Austin, Gordon   Mines   202-634-1206
Tropical Commodities....Ives III, Ralph F.   Commerce
    202-377-5124
Tropical Spastic Paraparesis....Staff   NINCDS   301-496-5751
Troposphere Interference....Staff   FCC   202-653-8141
Troposphere, Interference to Wash, DC Area....Staff   FCC
    301-962-2729
Tropospheric Air Quality Research....James Heoll   NASA
    804-865-4779
Trousers: mens and boys....Shetty, Sundar   USITC   202-252-1457
Trousers: womens and girls....MacKnight, Peggy   USITC
    202-252-1468
Trucking Services....Sousane, J. Richard   Commerce   202-377-4581
Truncus Arteriosus....Staff   NHLBI   301-496-4236
Trust Territory of the Pacific Islands (Saipan)....Robert A.
    Benziger   Cnty AID   202-647-3546
Truth-in-Lending Issues....Staff   Fed Trade Com   202-326-3175
Truth-in-Lending, Annl Percent. Rate, Credit Prac.....Staff   Fed
    Trade Com   202-326-3175
Trypanosomiasis....Staff   NIAID   301-496-5717
Typsinogen Deficiency....Staff   NIDDK   301-496-3583

Tuberculosis....Staff   NIAID   301-496-5717
Tuberculosis....Staff   CDC   404-329-3534
Tuberous Sclerosis....Staff   NINCDS   301-496-5751
Tubes (Pneumatic)....Staff   OD/ORS   301-496-5518
Tubes for pneumatic tires....Raftery, Jim   USITC   202-252-1365
Tubing of rubber of plastics....Truskett, Brooks   USITC
    202-252-1354
Tufted, Fabrics....Edert, R.   Customs   212-466-5885
Tularemia....Staff   NIAID   301-496-5717
Tumor....Staff   NCI   301-496-5583
Tumor Immunology....Staff   NCI   301-496-5583
Tumors (Eye)....Staff   NEI   301-496-5248
Tumors with Endocrine Function....Staff   NIDDK   301-496-3583
Tuna....Corey, Roger   USITC   202-252-1327
Tungsten....Wagner, Lorie   USITC   202-252-1439
Tungsten....Smith, Gerald R.   Mines   202-634-1029
Tungsten Products....Manager, Jon   Commerce   202-377-5124
Tungsten compounds....Greenblatt, Jack   USITC   202-252-1353
Tunisia....Simon Bensimon   Cnty Commerce   202-377-4652
Tunisia....Karen Blyth   Peace Corps   202-254-3196
Tunisia (Tunis)....John Kunstadter   Cnty State   202-647-3614
Tunisia (Tunis)....Rosemary O'Neill   Cnty AID   202-647-3614
Tunisia (Tunis)....Richard Delaney   Cnty AID   202-647-9001
Tunisia/Minerals....Thomas Dolley   Cnty Mines   202-632-5065
Turbine Engine Technology....Clavin Ball   NASA   216-433-3397
Turbines and Turbine Generators Sets....Climer, David   Commerce
    202-377-0681
Turbins, Major Proj.....Gaines, William S.   Commerce
    202-377-4332
Turbulence Physics....John Kim   NASA   415-694-5867
Turbulent Drag Reduction....Dennis Bushness   NASA   804-865-4546

Turkey....Geoffrey Jackson   Cnty Commerce   202-377-3945
Turkey (Ankara)....Carolyn Huggins   Cnty State   202-647-6114
Turkey (Ankara)....Lucy Uncu   Cnty State   202-647-6114
Turkey (Ankara)....Arma J. Karaer   Cnty AID   202-647-1562
Turkey (Ankara)....Angel M. Rabasa   Cnty AID   202-647-4477
Turkey (Ankara)....Christine Adamczyk   Cnty AID   202-647-9114
Turkey/Minerals....Hendrik van Oss   Cnty Mines   202-632-5065
Turkeys, Economics....Weimer, Mark   Agri   202-786-1830
Turkeys, Statistics....Sitzman, Ron   Agri   202-447-3244
Turks & Caicos Islands....Mack Tadeu   Cnty Commerce
    202-377-2527
Turks and Caicos....Nancy Lees   Cnty State   202-647-2621
Turner Syndrome....Staff   NICHD   301-496-5133
Turpentine....Reeder, John   USITC   202-252-1319
Turtles (Salmonellosis)....Staff   CDC   404-329-3534
Tuvalu....Carla Joyner   Peace Corps   202-254-3227
Tuvalu (Funafuti)....Ann M. Cambara   Cnty State   202-647-3546
Tuvalu (Funafuti)....Robert A. Benziger   Cnty AID   202-647-3546
Tuvalu (Funafuti)....Michael Feldstein   Cnty AID   202-647-9137
Twine....Cook, Lee   USITC   202-252-1471
Typewriters....Baker, Scott   USITC   202-252-1386
Typhoid Fever....Staff   NIAID   301-496-5717

U

U.S.S.R./Minerals....Richard Levine   Cnty Mines   202-632-5048
UNAMAP....D. Bruce Turner   EPA   919-541-4564
US Trade/Foreign Agri, Africa, Economics....Kurtzig, Michael
    Agri   202-786-1680
US Trade/Foreign Agri, Agri Development, Economics....Shane,
    Matt   Agri   202-786-1705
US Trade/Foreign Agri, Asia, Economics....Landes, Rip   Agri
    202-786-1610
US Trade/Foreign Agri, China, Economics....Tuan, Francis   Agri
    202-786-1616
US Trade/Foreign Agri, Eastern Europe, Economics....Gray,
    Kenneth   Agri   202-786-1710
US Trade/Foreign Agri, Eastern Europe, Economics....Zeimetz,
    Katherine   Agri   202-786-1710
US Trade/Foreign Agri, Economic Policy, Economic....Chattin,
    Barbara   Agri   202-786-1688
US Trade/Foreign Agri, Economic Policy, Economics....Mageria,
    Steve   Agri   202-786-1630
US Trade/Foreign Agri, Exports, Economics....Stallings, David
    Agri   202-786-1621
US Trade/Foreign Agri, Exports, Programs, Economic....Smith,
    Mark   Agri   202-786-1610
US Trade/Foreign Agri, Exports, Stats, Economics....Warden,
    Thomas   Agri   202-786-1621
US Trade/Foreign Agri, Food Aid, Economics....Nightingale, Ray
    Agri   202-786-1705
US Trade/Foreign Agri, Imports, Economics....Stallings, David
    Agri   202-786-1621
US Trade/Foreign Agri, Imports, Programs, Economic....Smith,

Mark Agri 202-786-1610
US Trade/Foreign Agri, Imports, Stats, Economics....Warden, Thomas Agri 202-786-1621
US Trade/Foreign Agri, Intl. Finance, Economics....Baxter, Tim Agri 202-786-1688
US Trade/Foreign Agri, Latin America, Economics....Link, John Agri 202-786-1688
US Trade/Foreign Agri, Middle East, Economics....Kurtzig, Michael Agri 202-786-1680
US Trade/Foreign Agri, Pacific Rim, Economics....Coyle, William Agri 202-786-1610
US Trade/Foreign Agri, Trade Policy, Economics....Mageria, Steve Agri 202-786-1630
US Trade/Foreign Agri, Trade Policy, Economics....Chattin, Barbara Agri 202-786-1688
US Trade/Foreign Agri, USSR, Economics....Gray, Kenneth Agri 202-786-1710
US Trade/Foreign Agri, USSR, Economics....Zeimetz, Katherine Agri 202-786-1710
US Trade/Foreign Agri, Western Europe, Economics....Newman, Mark Agri 202-786-1720
USSR...Jack Brougher Cnty Commerce 202-377-4655
USSR (Moscow)....Ints Silins Cnty State 202-647-8671
USSR (Moscow)....Steven Pifer Cnty State 202-647-9806
USSR (Moscow)....John Herbst Cnty State 202-647-9370
USSR (Moscow)....Louis D. Sell Cnty AID 202-647-8671
USSR (Moscow)....Bruce D. Burton Cnty AID 202-647-3839
USSR (Moscow)....Thomas R. Maertens Cnty AID 202-647-3071
UV-Optical Astronomy....David Leckrone NASA 301-286-8904
Uganda....James Robb Cnty Commerce 202-377-4564
Uganda (Kampala)....James F. Entwistle Cnty State 202-647-8913
Uganda (Kampala)....J. Bradley Swanson Cnty AID 202-647-3356
Uganda (Kampala)....John Rose Cnty AID 202-647-9762
Uganda/Minerals....Lloyd Antonides Cnty Mines 202-632-5065
Ulcerative Colitis....Staff NIDDK 301-496-3583
Ulcerative Lesions (Oral)....Staff NIDR 301-496-4261
Ulcers....Staff NIDDK 301-496-3583
Ultrasonic Arrays, Signal Processing & Image Analy....Patrick Johnson NASA 804-865-4928
Ultrasonic Progagation and Scattering in Composite....Eric Madaras NASA 804-865-3249
Ultrasonics Equipment....Staff FCC 202-653-8247
Umbrellas....Linkins, Linda USITC 202-252-1499
Umbrellas....Persky, H. Customs 212-466-5881
Unavailability of Advertized Items in Food Stores....Walter Gross Fed Trade Com 202-326-3319
Undercount, Demographic Analysis....Robinson, Gregg Census 301-763-5590
Underground injection....Jerry Thornhill EPA 405-332-2310
Underground injection (UIC)....Don Draper EPA 405-332-2202
Underwear....Bryant, Judith USITC 202-252-1464
Underwear....Davis, H. Customs 212-466-5880
Unemployment....Palumbo, Thomas Census 301-763-8574
Unemployment....Lester, Gordon Census 301-763-8574
Unfinished oils....Foreso, Cynthia USITC 202-252-1348
Uniform Crime Reports - Redesign Implementation....Paul White Justice Stat 202-724-7770
Uniform Crime Reports - Redesign Implementation....Donald Manson Justice Stat 202-724-7770
Uniforms....Persky, H. Customs 212-466-5881
United Arab Emirates....Claude Clement Cnty Commerce 202-377-5545
United Arab Emirates (Abu Dhabi)....haywood Rankin Cnty State 202-647-6558
United Arab Emirates (Abu Dhabi)....Janet Sanderson Cnty AID 202-647-1794
United Arab Emirates/Minerals....Lloyd Antonides Cnty Mines 202-632-5065
United Kingdom....Robert McLaughlin Cnty Commerce 202-377-3748
United Kingdom (London)....Howard Perlow Cnty State 202-647-8027
United Kingdom (London)....James Whittlocker Cnty AID 202-647-2622
United Kingdom (London)....Richard A. Christenson Cnty AID 202-647-4484
United Kingdom/Minerals....Harold Newman Cnty Mines 202-634-1276
United Republic of Tanzania (Dar es Salaam)....Wlater Manger Cnty State 202-647-8913
United Republic of Tanzania (Dar es Salaam)....Robert Snyder Cnty AID 202-647-3040
United Republic of Tanzania (Dar es Salaam)....John Rose Cnty AID 202-647-9762
Universal joints....Fravel, Dennis USITC 202-252-1404
Unordered Merchandise, Enforcement....Staff Fed Trade Com 202-326-3768
Unresectable Chrondosarcoma or Osteogenic Sarcoma....Staff NCI

301-496-5583
Unsaturated....Thomas Short EPA 405-332-2234
Upholstery fabrics....Enfield, Mary E USITC 202-252-1455
Upper Atmospheric Research....Robert Seals NASA 804-865-2576
Uranium...DeSapio, Vincent USITC 202-252-1435
Uranium....Perry, Douglas Commerce 202-377-1466
Uranium compounds....Greenblatt, Jack USITC 202-252-1353
Uranium oxide....Greenblatt, Jack USITC 202-252-1353
Urban/Rural Residence....Staff Census 301-763-7962
Urea....Trainor, Cynthia USITC 202-252-1354
Urea resins....Taylor, Ed USITC 202-252-1362
Uremia....Staff NIDDK 301-496-3583
Uric Acid Kidney Stones....Staff NIDDK 301-496-3583
Urinary Incontinence....Staff NCNR 301-496-0526
Urinary Tract Diseases....Staff NIDDK 301-496-3583
Urinary Tract Infections....Staff NIDDK 301-496-3583
Urinary Tract Tumors....Staff NIDDK 301-496-3583
Urine Volume....Staff NIDDK 301-496-3583
Urokinase....Staff NHLBI 301-496-4236
Urolithiasis....Staff NIDDK 301-496-3583
Urticaria....Staff NIAID 301-496-5717
Uruguay....Brian Hannon Cnty Commerce 202-377-1495
Uruguay (Montevideo)....Mike Shelton Cnty State 202-647-1551
Uruguay (Montevideo)....Stephanie Kinney Cnty AID 202-647-1551
Uruguay (Montevideo)....Maria Mamlouk Cnty AID 202-647-4365
Uruguay/Minerals....Alfredo Gurmendi Cnty Mines 202-632-9352
Used Car Rule....Joyce Plyler Fed Trade Com 202-326-3021
Used Car Rule....Joyce Plyler Fed Trade Com 202-326-3021
Uterus....Staff NICHD 301-496-5133
Uveitis....Staff NEI 301-496-5248

V

VD....Staff NIAID 301-496-5717
VD (Control and Treatment)....Staff CDC 404-329-3534
VLSI Systems and Prototyping....David Howell NASA 301-286-6373
VOC sources....Robert H. Hangebrauck EPA 919-541-4134
Vacancies, NIH Recording....Staff NIH 301-496-1209
Vaccines....Nesbitt, Elizabeth USITC 202-252-1355
Vaccines....Staff FDA/NCDB/OB 301-496-3556
Vaccines....Staff NIAID 301-496-5717
Vacuum cleaners....Jackson, Georgia USITC 202-252-1399
Vaginitis....Staff NIAID 301-496-5717
Valves....Riedl, K. Customs 212-466-5493
Valves (Heart)....Staff NHLBI 301-496-4236
Valves and cocks....Mata, Ruben USITC 202-252-1403
Valves, Pipefittings Ex Brass....Reise, Richard Commerce 202-377-3489
Valvular Heart Disease....Staff NHLBI 301-496-4236
Vanadium...DeSapio, Vincent USITC 202-252-1435
Vanadium....Hilliard, Henry E. Mines 202-634-1015
Vanadium compounds....Greenblatt, Jack USITC 202-252-1353
Vanatu (Port Vila)....Stanley R. Ifshin Cnty State 202-647-3546
Vanillin....Land, Eric USITC 202-252-1349
Vanuatu (Port Vila)....Carly M. Courtney Cnty AID 202-647-3546
Vanuatu (Port Vila)....Michael Feldstein Cnty AID 202-647-9137
Vanuatu/Minerals....Travis Lyday Cnty Mines 202-634-1272
Vapor transport....Don Kampbell EPA 405-332-2358
Vapor transport....Dennis Miller EPA 405-332-2263
Vapor transport....Jong Cho EPA 405-332-2271
Varicella, Congenital....Staff NINCDS 301-496-5751
Varicose Veins....Staff NHLBI 301-496-4236
Varnish....Brownchweig, G. Customs 212-466-5744
Varnishes....Johnson, Larry USITC 202-252-1351
Vascular Collapse....Staff NHLBI 301-496-4236
Vasculitis....Staff NHLBI 301-496-4236
Vasculitis....Staff NIAID 301-496-5717
Vasculitis....Staff NCI 301-496-5583
Vasectomy....Staff NICHD 301-496-5133
Vatican....Sharon White Cnty State 202-647-2453
Vatican....William G. Perett Cnty AID 202-647-8210
Vegetable fibers (except cotton)....Cook, Lee USITC 202-252-1471
Vegetable glue....Jonnard, Aimison USITC 202-252-1350
Vegetables....McCarty, Tim USITC 202-252-1324
Vegetables....Hodgen, Donald A. Commerce 202-377-3346
Vegetables, Economics....Hamm, Shannon Agri 202-786-1767
Vegetables, Economics....Buxton, Boyd Agri 202-786-1767
Vegetables, Economics....Greene, Catherine Agri 202-786-1767
Vegetables, Fresh, Statistics....Brewster, Jim Agri 202-447-7688

Vegetables, Processing, Statistics....Budge, Arvin Agri 202-447-4285

Veiling....Enfield, Mary E USITC 202-252-1455

Vending machines....Jackson, Georgia USITC 202-252-1399

Venereal Disease....Staff NIAID 301-496-5717

Venereal Disease (Control and Treatment)....Staff CDC 404-329-3534

Venezuela....Marie Haugen Cnty Commerce 202-377-1659

Venezuela (Caracas)....Allen Yale Cnty State 202-647-3338

Venezuela (Caracas)....Linda Pfeffle Cnty AID 202-647-3338

Venezuela (Caracas)....Marvin Schwartz Cnty AID 202-647-4358

Venezuela/Minerals....Robert Ensminger Cnty Mines 202-632-5062

Venezuelan Equine Encephalitis....Staff NIAID 301-496-5717

Ventilation....Staff OD/ORS 301-496-2960

Vermiculite....Meisinger, Arthur C. Mines 202-634-1185

Vertigo....Staff NINCDS 301-496-5751

Vests, mens'....Shetty, Sundar USITC 202-252-1457

Veterans Status....Lester, Gordon Census 301-763-8574

Veterinary instruments...Johnson, Christopher USITC 202-252-1488

Vibroacoustics....H. J. Bandgren NASA 205-544-5714

Victim and Witness Assistance Programs....Carol Kaplan Justice Stat 202-724-7759

Victim and Witness Assistance Programs....Marianne Zawitz Justice Stat 202-724-6100

Victims and Victimization....Carol Dorsey Justice 202-272-6001

Victims and Victimization....Richard Titus Justice 202-724-7684

Victims and Victimization....Lois Mock Justice 202-724-7684

Victims and Victimization....Cheryl Martorana Justice 202-724-2965

Victims of Crime....Michael Rand Justice Stat 202-724-7774

Victims of Crime....Patsy Klaus Justice Stat 202-724-7774

Victims of Crime....Bruce Taylor Justice Stat 202-724-7774

Video Transmission--Common Carrier....Staff FCC 202-634-1706

Video games....Robinson, Hazel USITC 202-252-1496

Videotex Services....Siegmund, John Commerce 202-377-4781

Videotex Services....Inoussa, Mary C. Commerce 202-377-5820

Vietnam....Donald Stader Cnty State 202-647-3132

Vietnam....Stephen Johnson Cnty AID 202-647-3132

Vietnam....JeNelle Matheson Cnty Commerce 202-377-3583

Vietnam/Minerals....David Doan Cnty Mines 202-634-1272

Vincent's Infection....Staff NIDR 301-496-4261

Vinyl chloride monomer....Michels, David USITC 202-252-1352

Vinyl resins or plastics....Taylor, Ed USITC 202-252-1362

Violent Crimes....Lois Mock Justice 202-724-7684

Violent Crimes....Helen Erskine Justice 202-724-7631

Violent Criminal Behavior....Helen Erskine Justice 202-724-7631

Virgin Islands (UK)....Mack Tadeu Cnty Commerce 202-377-2527

Virgin Islands (US)....Ted Johnson Cnty Commerce 202-377-2527

Virgin Islands, British....Avon Williams Cnty State 202-647-2621

Virology....Staff NIAID 301-496-5717

Virology....Robert Safferman EPA 513-569-7334

Virus (Cancer Related)....Staff NCI 301-496-5583

Vision Care (Statistics)....Staff NCHS 301-436-8500

Vision and Aging....Staff NEI 301-496-5248

Vision and Aging....Staff NIA 301-496-1752

Visors....Persky, H. Customs 212-466-5881

Visual signaling apparatus....Taylor, Kayla USITC 202-252-1390

Vitamin E (and Cardiovascular Disease)....Staff NHLBI 301-496-4236

Vitamin Supplements and Aging....Staff NIA 301-496-1752

Vitamins....Nesbitt, Elizabeth USITC 202-252-1355

Vitamins C,D,E, (and CVD)....Staff NHLBI 301-496-4236

Vitiligo....Staff NIAMS 301-496-8188

Vitrectomy....Staff NEI 301-496-5248

Vocal Cord Paralysis....Staff NINCDS 301-496-5751

Vocational Schools & Correspondence Schools....Walter Gross Fed Trade Com 202-326-3319

Vogt-Koyanagi Disease....Staff NEI 301-496-5248

Volkswagen...Janice Frankle Fed Trade Com 202-326-3022

Von Recklinghausen's Disease....Staff NINCDS 301-496-5751

Von Willebrand's Disease....Staff NHLBI 301-496-4236

Voting Districts....Davis, Virgeline Census 301-763-3827

Voting and Registration...Jennings, Jerry Census 301-763-4547

W

WARC Frequency Allocations....Staff FCC 202-632-7025

WARC Frequency Coordination....Staff FCC 202-653-8126

WARC Frequency lists, Notification & Registration....Staff FCC 202-653-8126

WARC Interference....Staff FCC 202-653-8126

Wages/Indl Rels, Administrative Pay....Smith, William Labor 202-523-1570

Wages/Indl Rels, Agreements, Coll Barg, Publc File....Ruben, George Labor 202-523-1320

Wages/Indl Rels, Assistant Commissioner....Eisenberg, William M. Labor 202-272-3467

Wages/Indl Rels, Clerical Pay....Smith, William Labor 202-523-1570

Wages/Indl Rels, Collect Barg Agreements Analysis....Ruben, George Labor 202-523-1320

Wages/Indl Rels, Collect Barg Settlements, Major....Weinstein, Harriet Labor 202-523-1308

Wages/Indl Rels, Current Wage Developments....Ruben, George Labor 202-523-1320

Wages/Indl Rels, Empl Benefit Surv, Insurance....Thompson, John Labor 202-523-9241

Wages/Indl Rels, Empl Benefit Surv, Other Benefits....Houff, James Labor 202-523-8791

Wages/Indl Rels, Empl Benefit Surv, Paid Leave....Houff, James Labor 202-523-8791

Wages/Indl Rels, Empl Benefit Surv, Pension Plans....Thompson, John Labor 202-523-9241

Wages/Indl Rels, Employee Assns, Membership....Leroy, Douglas Labor 202-523-1921

Wages/Indl Rels, Employment Cost Index....Nathan, Felicia Labor 202-513-1165

Wages/Indl Rels, Employment Cost Index Data Disks....Nathan, Felicia Labor 202-523-1165

Wages/Indl Rels, Health Studies....Hilaski, Harvey Labor 202-272-3459

Wages/Indl Rels, Hourly Earnings Index....Braden, Brad Labor 202-523-1165

Wages/Indl Rels, Illness Tapes/Disks....Jackson, Ethel Labor 202-272-3460

Wages/Indl Rels, Industry Wage Surveys....Williams, Harry Labor 202-523-1667

Wages/Indl Rels, Injury Tapes/Disks....Jackson, Ethel Labor 202-272-3460

Wages/Indl Rels, Injury/Illness Data....Jackson, Ethel Labor 202-272-3460

Wages/Indl Rels, Professional Pay....Smith, William Labor 202-523-1570

Wages/Indl Rels, Service Contract Act Surveys....Hoffman, Kenneth Labor 202-523-1536

Wages/Indl Rels, Special Projects....Hilaski, Harvey Labor 202-272-3459

Wages/Indl Rels, Technical Pay....Smith, William Labor 202-523-1570

Wages/Indl Rels, Unions, Membership....Leroy, Douglas Labor 202-523-1921

Wages/Indl Rels, Wage Chronologies....Ruben, George Labor 202-523-1320

Wages/Indl Rels, Wages, Local Governments....Field, Charles Labor 202-523-1570

Wages/Indl Rels, Wages, State Governments....Field, Charles Labor 202-523-1570

Wages/Indl Rels, Work Stoppages....Ruben, George Labor 202-523-1320

Wages/Indrl Rels, Area Wage Surveys....Buckley, John Labor 202-523-1763

Wages/Industrial Relations, Associate Commissioner....Stelluto, George Labor 202-523-1382

Wake Vortex Minimization....George Green NASA 804-865-4546

Walkie-Talkies (unlicensed)....Staff FCC 202-653-6288

Walking sticks....Linkins, Linda USITC 202-252-1499

Wall coverings, of rubber or plastics....Truskett, Brooks USITC 202-252-1364

Wallets....Seastrum, Carl USITC 202-252-1493

Wallets, Billfolds, Flatgoods....Enright, Joe Commerce 202-377-3459

Walleye....Staff NEI 301-496-5248

Wallis and Futuna Islands....Ann M. Cambara Cnty State 202-647-3546

Wallpaper....Stahmer, Carsten USITC 202-252-1321

Warranty (General Info/Mktg Practices), Automotive....Staff Fed Trade Com 202-326-3128

Warranty-Related Matters, Marketing Practices....Staff Fed Trade Com 202-326-3128

Warts....Staff NIAID 301-496-5717

Waste Treatment and Disposal....Staff EPA 301-382-4627

Waste and scrap (metals)....Boszormenyi, Laszio USITC 202-252-1437

Waste leaching & pollutant migration....Michael Roulier EPA 513-569-7796

Waste load allocation....J.F. Paul EPA 401-782-3000

Waste minimization....Harry Freeman EPA 513-569-7529

Waste or scrap....Spalding, Josephine USITC 202-252-1498

Waste, textile: cotton....Enfield, Mary E USITC 202-252-1455

Waste, textile: manmade fiber....Butler, R Larry USITC 202-252-1470

Experts

Waste, textile: silk....Freund, Kimberlie USITC 202-252-1456
Waste, textile: wool...Freund, Kimberlie USITC 202-252-1456
Wasteload allocation...H.A. Walker EPA 401-782-3000
Wastepaper....Stanley, Gary Commerce 202-377-0375
Watch Industry Guidelines....Susanne Patch Fed Trade Com
   202-326-2981
Watches....Langer, Eric USITC 202-252-1497
Watches....Harris, John Commerce 202-377-1178
Watches....Piropato, L. Customs 212-466-5895
Water Hardness (and CVD)....Staff NHLBI 301-496-4236
Water Pollution....Staff EPA 301-382-5508
Water Quality, Economics....Lee, Linda Agri 202-786-1444
Water Resource Equipment....Greer, Damon Commerce
   202-377-0564
Water Resources, Economics....Hostetler, John Agri
   202-786-1410
Water Supply....Staff OD/ORS 301-496-3537
Water Treatment Plants, Major Proj.....Healey, Mary Alice
   Commerce 202-377-4643
Water Treatment, Point-of-Use....Greer, Damon Commerce
   202-377-0564
Water and sediment criteria...D.J. Hansen EPA 401-782-3000
Water quality....Llewellyn R. Williams EPA 702-798-2138
Water quality control...D.J. Hansen EPA 401-782-3000
Water quality criteria documents....Charles E. Stephan EPA
   218-720-5510
Water quality modeling....Thomas O. Barnwell, Jr. EPA
   404-546-3210
Water quality modeling....E.H. Dettmann EPA 401-782-3000
Water quality modeling....N.A. Jaworski EPA 401-782-3000
Watersheds....John Arthur EPA 218-720-5565
Wax, articles of....Spalding, Josephine USITC 202-252-1498
Waxes....Randall, Rob USITC 202-252-1366
Waxes....Brownchweig, G. Customs 212-466-5744
Weapons and Crime....Lois Mock Justice 202-724-7684
Weapons and Crime...Richard Rau Justice 202-724-2951
Weapons and Crime....Joel Garner Justice 202-724-7635
Weapons and Crime....Michael Rand Justice Stat 202-724-7774
Weapons and Crime....Bruce Taylor Justice Stat 202-724-7774
Weather, Statistics....James, Clif Agri 202-447-7960
Weaving machines....Greene, William USITC 202-252-1405
Weber-Christian Disease....Staff NIAMS 301-496-8188
Weber-Christian Disease....Staff NIAID 301-496-5717
Wegener's Granulomatosis....Staff NIAMS 301-496-8188
Wegener's Granulomatosis....Staff NIAID 301-496-5717
Weighing Machinery....Hantman, S. Customs 212-466-5678
Weighing machinery....Slingerland, David USITC 202-252-1400
Welding Apparatus....Comer, Barbara Commerce 202-377-0314
Welding apparatus....Mata, Ruben USITC 202-252-1403
Werdnig-Hoffmann Disease....Staff NINCDS 301-496-5751
Werner's Syndrome....Staff NIDDK 301-496-3583
Wernicke's Disease....Staff NINCDS 301-496-5751
Western European Union (WEU)....Edward Nolan Cnty State
   202-647-3198
Western European Union (WEU)....Michael Klosson Cnty AID
   202-647-8050
Western Sahara....Stephen Kelly Cnty State 202-647-2865
Western Sahara....Jean G. Soso Cnty AID 202-647-2865
Western Samoa....Carla Joyner Peace Corps 202-254-3227
Western Samoa (Apia)....Ann M. Cambara Cnty State
   202-647-3546
Western Samoa (Apia)....Michael Feldstein Cnty AID
   202-647-9137
Western Samoa (Apia)....Robert A. Benziger Cnty AID
   202-647-3546
Wet Corn Milling, Dextrive....McIntyre, Leo R. Commerce
   202-377-0128
Wetlands....William Sanville EPA 218-720-5723
Wetlands....Steven F. Hedtke EPA 218-720-2492
Wetlands ecology....Eric P. Preston EPA 503-753-4666
Wetlands ecology....Richard R. Sumner EPA 503-753-4666
Wetlands environment....John H. Montanari EPA 703-349-3110
Whalebone, articles of....Spalding, Josephine USITC
   202-252-1498
Wheat....Pierre-Benoist, John USITC 202-252-1320
Wheat Futures With Options....Judy Sepsey Comm Futures
   312-353-9025
Wheat Grains, Economics....Schienbein, Allen Agri 202-786-1840
Wheat Grains, Statistics....Siegenthaler, Vaughn Agri
   202-447-8068
Wheat Grains, World, Economics....Scwartz, Sara Agri
   202-786-1693
Wheel goods: motorized....Kavalauskas, Jaunita USITC
   202-252-1402
Wheel goods: non-motorized....Seastrum, Carl USITC
   202-252-1493
Whiplash....Staff NINCDS 301-496-5751
Whips....Linkins, Linda USITC 202-252-1499

Whiskey....Lipovsky, William USITC 202-252-1331
White Collar Crime....Bernard Auchter Justice 202-724-7684
White Collar Crime....Carol Kaplan Justice Stat 202-724-7759
Whole effluent toxicity....Donald I. Mount EPA 218-7205528
Wholesale Trade....Umstead, Dwight Commerce 202-377-3050
Whooping Cough....Staff NIAID 301-496-5717
Wigs....Persky, H. Customs 212-466-5881
Wildlife ecology/toxicology....Rciahrd S. Bennett EPA
   503-757-4582
Wildlife ecology/toxicology....Anne Fairbrother EPA
   503-757-4716
Wildlife physiology/toxicology....Bill A. Williams EPA
   503-757-4679
Wilms' Tumor....Staff NCI 301-496-5583
Wilson Disease....Staff NIDDK 301-496-3583
Wilson Disease....Staff NINCDS 301-496-5751
Wind Tunnel Automation....Daniel Petroff NASA 415-694-5850
Wind Tunnel Composites Applications....Daniel Petroff NASA
   415-694-5850
Wind Tunnel Performance Enhancement (Aerophysics)....Daniel
   Petroff NASA 415-694-5850
Wind tunnel....William H. Snyder EPA 919-541-1198
Windmill Components....Garden, Les Commerce 202-377-0556
Wines....Lipovsky, William USITC 202-252-1331
Wire....Boszormenyi, Laszio USITC 202-252-1437
Wire....Fitzgerald, J. Customs 212-466-5492
Wire Cloth....Rubenstein, Nathan Commerce 202-377-0132
Wire Cloth, Industrial....Fletcher, William E. Commerce
   202-377-0309
Wire Facilities....Staff FCc 202-634-1800
Wire Rods....Fitzgerald, J. Customs 212-466-5492
Wire and Wire Products....Thompson, Ralph Commerce
   202-377-0606
Wire or Cable Licenses....Staff FCC 202-634-1800
Wire rods....Vacant USITC 202-252-1442
Wireless Microphones (licensed)....Staff FCC 717-337-1212
Wireless Microphones (non-licensed)....Staff FCC 202-653-6288
Wiretapping....Staff FCC 202-632-6990
Wiring Devices, Current-Carrying....Whitley, Richard A. Commerce
   202-377-0682
Wiring Devices, Noncurrent Carrying....Whitley, Richard A.
   Commerce 202-377-0682
Wiring sets....Hagey, Michael USITC 202-252-1392
Wiskott-Aldrich Syndrome....Staff NCI 301-496-5583
Witnesses....Richard Rau Justice 202-724-2951
Witnesses....Richard Titus Justice 202-724-7684
Witnesses....Cheryl Martorana Justice 202-724-2965
Wolff-Parkinson-White Syndrome (WPW)....Staff NHLBI
   301-496-4236
Wollastonite....Potter, Michael J. Mines 202-634-1180
Women....Smith, Denisehia Census 301-763-7883
Women's Health Issues-Related Research....Staff NCNR
   301-496-0526
Women's Knitted Wearing Appare....Crowley, M. Customs
   212-466-5852
Women's Woven Wearing Apparel....Crowley, E. Customs
   212-466-5866
Wood (densified)....Westcot, Thomas USITC 202-252-1325
Wood Containers....Hicks, Michael Commerce 202-377-0375
Wood Preserving....Hicks, Michael Commerce 202-377-0375
Wood Products....Butts, Donald Commerce 202-377-0375
Wood Products....Garretto, P. Customs 212-466-5779
Wood Products, Misc.....Butts, Donald Commerce 202-377-0375
Wood Working Machinery....McDonald, Edward Commerce
   202-377-0680
Wood products, rough primary....Vacant USITC 202-252-1326
Wood pulp....Rhodes, Richard USITC 202-252-1322
Wood veneers....Vacant USITC 202-252-1326
Woodstove designs....Wade H. Ponder EPA 919-541-2818
Wool....Freund, Kimberlie USITC 202-252-1456
Wool grease, sulfonated or sulfated....Land, Eric USITC
   202-252-1349
Wool, Economics....Lawler, John Agri 202-786-1840
Wool, Statistics....Cole, John Agri 202-447-3578
Work of Art....Mushinske, L. Customs 212-466-5739
Wound Healing (LDBA)....Staff NIDR 301-496-4261
Woven Fabrics....Titelman, A. Customs 212-466-5896
Woven Outerwear, Cold Weather....Raftery, W. Customs
   212-466-5851
Woven Wearing Apparel, Men's....Ryan, M. Customs 212-466-5877

Wryneck (Torticollis)....Staff NINCDS 301-496-5751

X

X-Ray Astronomy....M. Weisskopf NASA 205-544-7740
X-Ray Calibration....C. Reily NASA 205-544-1298
X-Ray Tomography for Stressed Solids....Min Namkung NASA 804-865-3036
X-Rays....E. A. Boldt NASA 301-286-5853
X-ray (Radiation Effects on Fetus)....Staff FDA 301-443-2356
X-ray Technician....Staff HRSA/BHPr 301-443-5794
X-ray apparatus....Johnson, Christopher USITC 202-252-1488
Xanthinuria....Staff NIDDK 301-496-3583
Xanthomatosis....Staff NHLBI 301-496-4236
Xeroderma Pigmentosum....Staff NCI 301-496-5583
Xerophtalmia....Staff NEI 301-496-5248
Xeroradiography....Staff NCI 301-496-5583
Xerostomia (Dry Mouth)....Staff NIDR 301-496-4261
Xylene....Raftery, Jim USITC 202-252-1365
Xylenol...Matusik, Ed USITC 202-252-1356

Y

YAG Laser....Staff NEI 301-496-5248
Yarn: wool....Freund, Kimberlie USITC 202-252-1456
Yarns: cotton....Enfield, Mary E USITC 202-252-1455
Yarns: elastic....Enfield, Mary E USITC 202-252-1455
Yarns: flax....Cook, Lee USITC 202-252-1471
Yarns: glass....Butler, R Larry USITC 202-252-1470
Yarns: jute....Cook, Lee USITC 202-252-1471
Yarns: manmade....Butler, R Larry USITC 202-252-1470
Yarns: metalized....Cook, Lee USITC 202-252-1471
Yarns: paper....Cook, Lee USITC 202-252-1471
Yarns: silk....Freund, Kimberlie USITC 202-252-1456
Yeast....Janis, William V. Commerce 202-377-2250
Yeast Infections....Staff NIAID 301-496-5717
Yellow Fever....Staff NIAID 301-496-5717
Yellow Page Advertising....Staff FCC 202-632-7553
Yellowcake....Greenblatt, Jack USITC 202-252-1353
Yemen....Karen Blyth Peace Corps 202-254-3196
Yemen (Aden)/Minerals....Bernadette Michalski Cnty Mines 202-632-5065
Yemen (Sana)/Minerals....Bernadette Michalski Cnty Mines 202-632-5065
Yemen Arab Republic (Sanaa)....Laurie Johnston Cnty State 202-647-6571
Yemen Arab Republic (Sanaa)....Peter Deinken Cnty AID 202-647-9001
Yemen Arab Republic (Sanaa)....Kathleen Allegrone Cnty AID 202-647-2329
Yemen People's Democratic Republic of....Kathleen Allegrone Cnty AID 202-647-2329
Yemen, North....Cynthia Anthony Cnty Commerce 202-377-4652
Yemen, People's Democratic Republic of....Laurie Johnston Cnty State 202-647-6571
Yemen, South....Cynthia Anthony Cnty Commerce 202-377-4652
Yttrium....Hedrick, James B. Mines 202-634-1058
Yugoslavia....Jeremy Keller Cnty Commerce 202-377-5373
Yugoslavia (Belgrade)...John R. Schmidt Cnty State 202-647-4138
Yugoslavia (Belgrade)....Diana M. Montgomery Cnty State 202-647-3052
Yugoslavia (Belgrade)....Diana M. Montgomery Cnty State 202-647-3052
Yugoslavia (Belgrade)....Razvigor Bazala Cnty AID 202-647-3655
Yugoslavia (Belgrade)....Ben F. Fairfax Cnty AID 202-647-1739
Yugoslavia/Minerals....Walter Steblez Cnty Mines 202-632-5047

Z

ZIP Codes....Quarato, Rose Census 301-763-4667
Zaire....Ian Davis Cnty Commerce 202-377-0357
Zaire....Tom Elam Peace Corps 202-254-8694
Zaire Republic of (Kinshasa)....Mary Ann Riegelman Cnty AID 202-647-9809
Zaire Republic of (Kinshasa)....Ralph Bresler Cnty AID 202-647-1637
Zaire, Republic of (Kinshasa)....Jack Aubert Cnty State 202-647-1707

Zaire/Minerals....George Morgan Cnty Mines 202-632-5065
Zambia....Emily Solomon Cnty Commerce 202-377-5148
Zambia (Lusaka)....Robert Kiser Cnty State 202-647-8434
Zambia (Lusaka)....Robyn Hinson-Jones Cnty AID 202-647-8851
Zambia (Lusaka)....Teresa Ware Cnty AID 202-647-4326
Zambia/Minerals....Lloyd Antonides Cnty Mines 202-632-5065
Zeolites....Virta, Robert Mines 202-634-1206
Zimbabwe....Emily Solomon Cnty Commerce 202-377-5147
Zimbabwe (Harare)....Helen Weinland Cnty State 202-647-8434
Zimbabwe (Harare)....Kenneth H. Kolb Cnty AID 202-647-8434
Zimbabwe (Harare)....Keith Brown Cnty AID 202-647-4287
Zimbabwe/Minerals....Lloyd Antonides Cnty Mines 202-632-5065
Zinc....Wagner, Lorie USITC 202-252-1439
Zinc...Jolly, James H. Mines 202-634-1063
Zinc compounds....Greenblatt, Jack USITC 202-252-1353
Zippers....Rodriguez, Laura USITC 202-252-1486
Zirconium....DeSapio, Vincent USITC 202-252-1435
Zirconium...Hedrick, James Mines 202-634-1058
Zirconium compounds....Greenblatt, Jack USITC 202-252-1353
Zollinger-Ellison Syndrome....Staff NIDDK 301-496-3583
Zoonoses....Staff NIAID 301-496-5717
Zoris....Burns, Gail USITC 202-252-1469

2-Year T-Note Futures....Heidilynne Schultheiss Comm Futures 212-668-2082
30-Day Interest Rates....Penny Sympson Comm Futures 312-353-9015
5-Year T-Note Futures....Heidilynne Schultheiss Comm Futures 212-668-2082

household appliances, 746
housing efficiency, 62
hydroelectric power, 750, 792
industrial processes, 751
industrial use, 698
international assistance, 663, 751
international economic research, 624
international policy, 601, 605, 747
inventions, 171, 546
Lawrence Berkeley Laboratory, 749
legislation, 752
management, 749
markets, 752
municipal waste, 698
National Energy Information Center, 752
national outlook, 704, 756
national policy, 847
nuclear, 763, 767
ocean thermal, 702, 747, 863
ocean, 698, 753, 754, 771
offshore resources, 698, 848
passive solar homes, 63
photovoltaic power, 753, 754
prices, 752, 847
production, 752
regulation, 749, 754, 845
renewable, 754
research and development, 104, 116, 848
residential, 698, 755, 886
resource development, 782
science research grants, 171
seminar grants, 104
Senate committee, 845
small business loans, 521
software, 753
solar thermal, 754, 755
solar, 698, 702, 747, 755, 756, 863
Soviet, 698
state conservation programs, 756
storage, 754
supplies, 752
supply and demand, international, 751
supply disruptions, 761
systems vulnerability, 695, 756
taxation, 845
transmission, 847
transportation, 578, 755
water heating, 551, 756
weatherization, 246, 756
wind power, 702, 746, 747, 754, 863
Energy, U.S. Department of
freedom of information, 753
libraries, 752
Engineering, 708, 724, 751
adhesives, 689
agricultural, 730, 779
air traffic control, 134, 557
apprenticeships, 690
Army Corps of Engineers, 685
automotive, 793
bridge, 565, 582
cadastral, 800
ceramics, 715
chemical, 715, 723, 813
coastal, 264, 567
construction, 685
demographics, 698
education, 698
electrical, 716
electronics, 716
Engineering Laboratory, National, 720
environmental, 781, 784, 787, 795, 817
evaluation, 686
exporting, 610
fire protection, 717
genetic, 783, 786
hydrocarbons, 718
hydrology, 796
information systems, 695, 715, 718
international construction contracts, 601
manufacturing, 723
marine, 568, 807
materials scarcity, 698
mining, 572
noise control, 785
nuclear, 816
oceanographic, 772, 793
procurement contracts, 587
public health, 817
research grants, 116, 166, 171

sanitation, 814
standards, 719
statistical, 725
structural, 725
systems, 692
Engines, jets, 552, 702, 864
Enterprise zones, 63
Entomology 191, 200
Environment, 680, 698, 779, 796
acid drainage in mines, 572, 795, 813
acid rain, 749, 786
acrylonitrile, 815
aerosols, 790
agricultural research, 734
agronomy, 731
air and water protection, 788
aquatic weed control, 805
atmospheric research, 770, 790
bicycle paths, 259, 580, 583, 788
biological sciences, 807
Clean Air Act, 791
cloud seeding, 794
coal leasing, 698
coal mining, 572, 575, 801
Coast Guard, U.S., 567, 667, 784
complaints, 815
congressional study conference, 850
Council on Environmental Quality, 786
database, 881
deep seabed mining, 572, 747, 792
dispute resolution, 780
Earth-space, 772, 788
education programs, 94, 95, 781, 787
education, 95, 787
energy development and use, 749
engineering, 784, 791, 795
fertilizer research, 732
fire protection, 799
fly ash, 572, 791
foreign investment, impact of, 608
geology, 711
global climate changes, 749, 799
Great Lakes, 782
greenhouse effect, 702, 783
hazardous chemicals, 346
hazardous waste sites, 817
health, 114, 224
highways, impact of, 583
human health studies, 785
impact statements, 749, 782, 783
interest groups, 815
international assistance, 670
international policies, 688, 749, 784
international profiles, 668
lake restoration, 793
legal issues, 787, 795, 817
legislation, 785
legislation, state, 207, 856
litigation, 417
Love Canal, 698
low-level radioactive waste, 694, 814
marine assessments, 772, 793
marine protection, 264, 567, 794, 806
Marine Protection, Research and Sanctuaries
Act, 786
marine, 567, 793, 807, 816
medical waste technology, 696, 815
methyl chloride, 815
monitoring methods, 785
mutagens, 385, 785, 814
natural hazards, 44, 814
New England, 782
nuclear energy interest group, 816
nuclear regulation, 845
nuclear waste, 694, 814, 815
ocean dumping, 264, 418, 695, 780
Oceanic and Atmospheric Administration,
National, 772
oceanographic research, 568, 772
oceans, 568, 772
oil spills, 568, 668, 784, 794, 816
organic wastes, 734, 801
oxidant pollution, 790
ozone, 702, 749, 783
ozone depletion, 702, 783
PCBs, 816
pesticides, 733, 734, 801, 817
professionals, 786
radiation, 766, 782, 786, 816
radioactive waste storage, 756, 768

range and wildlife ecology, 799
recycling, 211, 816
Resource Conservation and Recovery Act,
787, 817
RTECS database, 346
Senate committee, 845
Sierra Club, 808
soil, 792
solid waste, 814, 817
speakers, 681
spray finishing, 795
standards, 790
subsurface, 792
Superfund, 81
toxic chemicals, 382, 782
TOXLINE database, 346
TOXNET database, 346
transportation industry, 578
tropical deforestation, 784
TVA programs, 788
U.S. foreign policy, 784
underground storage tanks, 762, 818
water quality, 205, 731, 735, 895
watershed and aquatic habitat, 799
wetlands, 797, 809
wildland fire, 802
wildlife contaminants, 809
Environmental Barriers, 379
Environmental Protection
air pollution control, 234
education programs, 94, 781
fraud hotline, 784
grants, 235, 236
hazardous waste, 219
health research grants, 170
marine research grants, 166
research grants, 102, 166, 167, 171
Senior Employment Program, 246
training grants, 104
water pollution, 234
water quality, 235
Enzyme aspartate aminotransferase, 725
Epidemiology, 133
Epilepsy, 352, 371, 702, 864
Equal employment opportunity, 616
Erosion control, 680, 779, 796, 884
Estrogen and osteoporosis, 355, 377
Estuaries, 793, 876
Ethanol production, 732, 754
Ethics
medical research, 875
Senate committee, 846
Ethiopia, 850
Ethnic
alcoholism, 400
disputes, 210, 419, 422
drug prevention, 400
Ethnomusicology, 187, 861
Europe, 562, 847
European Commission, 596, 695
Exchange rates, 879
Exercise
arthritis, 352
elderly, 352, 376, 377
heart disease, 353
obesity, 358
orthopedic research, 348
President's Council on Physical Fitness, 353
President's physical fitness awards, 354
swimming, 353
walking, 353
Exhaust systems, 791
Expertise, federal laboratories, 691
Explosives, 689, 698
commerce, 552
forensic studies, 550
hotline, 43, 55
identification, 419
storage, 552
tracing, 419
Export-Import Bank, 279, 601, 610
Expropriation, 609
Extraditions, 408
Extraterrestrial life, 702, 705, 864
Eyesight
elderly, 378
free library services, 379
macular degeneration, 378
National Eye Institute, 346, 367
research, 346, 367

F _____

O

Here is a current listing of business books, special reports, periodicals as well as several trade publications that are all available directly from Information USA, Inc.

The Federal Data Base Finder

This unique resource which identifies thousands of government data sources is a bestseller. This book identifies free data bases which your computer can access, for example, news about the latest economic indicators, weather, or crude oil availability. Instead of paying as much as $100 per hour to a commercial vendor, "The Federal Data Base Finder" will show you how to tap the same computerized files free on international demographics, health markets, etc. Also, this directory describes hundreds of tapes that you can load into a large mainframe. The third edition costs $125.00. The book and a 5 1/4" or 3 1/2" diskette copy are available for $325.00.

The Data Informer

This monthly newsletter shows decision makers and researchers how to take advantage of unusual sources of information on markets. companies. demographics and technology. Each 12-page issue also identifies little-known databases. free professional bulletin boards. public documents available from federal. state and local government. reports published by private and non-profit organizations. plus free experts in both the public and private sector. Annual subscription is $128.00 (Back issues available for $10.00 each.)

State Data and Database Finder

This unique reference source identifies thousands of databases and data sources which are hidden within each of the 50 state governments. State offices are fast becoming capable of producing more market. competitive and demographic data than what are available in the federal government. This information tends to be available faster. cheaper and in more detail than what can be obtained from the federal government or private commercial vendors. Cost is $145.00. Book and 5¹/₄" diskette copy available for $345.

Government Giveaways For Entrepreneurs

The second edition of this 630 page book shows over 9.000 sources of money and free expertise that are available to entrepreneurs who want to start or expand their business. It identifies over 300 federal. state and private sources of loans. grants and venture capital. as well as literally thousands of free sources of expertise to help with problems on markets. competition. and technology. The cost if $29.95 plus $4.00 postage and handling (only prepaid or credit card orders accepted on this product).

Also available is Matthew Lesko's 2-hour cassette tape that will continue to motivate you to start or expand your business and get government funds. or contracts to make it grow. Listen your way to success. (Only $16.95)

Government Giveaways For Entrepreneurs Video

A companion to Matthew Lesko's highly acclaimed book. Government Giveaways For Entrepreneurs. This is an exciting new video which walks you through the process of starting or expanding a business. As a bestselling author, Matthew Lesko, a small business owner himself. has appeared on such well-known television shows as Late Night With David Letterman. The Larry King Show. Good Morning America, and Donahue. Now he has put his talents to work in creating this energetic video which shows you some of the hundreds of actual individuals and offices from the federal, state, and local governments mentioned in his book who are out there to help you start your own business. VHS only. Cost is $29.95 plus $4.00 postage and handling (only prepaid or credit orders accepted on this product).

Lesko's Info-Power Sourcebook

For those who truly appreciate the power of information, this book with over 10.000 sources will show you where to get the most up-to-date information on virtually every subject imaginable, from business finance and modern art to extraterrestials, surplus property and even iguana farming. So whether you are a consumer who needs to know the best woodburning stove to buy or a business executive who needs to know the market potential of a product in Peru, this one-of-a-kind sourcebook will help you get the answers you need when you need them. The cost is $33.95 plus $4.00 postage and handling (only prepaid or credit orders accepted on this product).